The New College
LATIN & ENGLISH
Dictionary

SECOND EDITION

JOHN C. TRAUPMAN, Ph.D.

St. Joseph's University, Philadelphia

AMSCO SCHOOL PUBLICATIONS, INC.

315 Hudson Street/New York, N.Y. 10013

THE NEW COLLEGE LATIN & ENGLISH DICTIONARY, SECOND EDITION

When ordering this book, please specify:
either **R 617 P** or LATIN DICTIONARY

ISBN 0-87720-561-2

Published by Amsco School Publications, Inc., by arrangement
with the copyright owners.

The cover shows the Ara Pacis (detail), Rome. Photo Alinari.

Printed in the United States of America

7 8 9 10   04 03

Contents

Elmont High School
White Oak Lane
Scarsdale, New York 10583

Preface to the Second Edition

This totally revised and expanded edition, with over 43,000 entries, includes not only additional authors, such as Martial, Juvenal, Suetonius, Tacitus, and Curtius, but also additional works by standard authors, such as the correspondence and philosophical essays of Cicero and the *Eclogues* and *Georgics* of Vergil. It also provides a much larger range of illustrative phrases, all of which are translated and arranged in alphabetical order. There are separate entries for prefixes and suffixes. As an additional new feature, this edition includes a Guide to Latin Grammar, which provides the following: the declension of nouns (including Greek nouns), pronouns, and adjectives; the irregular comparison of adjectives and adverbs; and the conjugation of verbs. There is also a list of Roman numerals.

The level of usage of Latin words and phrases is faithfully reflected in the level of usage of the English translations, so that, if the Latin word is colloquial, slang, or vulgar, the English translation corresponds. Variant spellings of Latin words are given within the entries. Additional features are provided in the Guide to the Dictionary.

The author wishes to thank Donald Reis, formerly of Bantam Books, under whose direction the first edition of this dictionary was undertaken. A debt of gratitude is due to the late Edwin B. Williams, former general editor of the New College Bantam Dictionary Series, for his guidance in the preparation of the first edition. Special thanks are due to James T. McDonough for proofreading the manuscript of the revised edition and for his many suggestions for improvement in both form and substance. The author gratefully acknowledges the kind support of Beverly Susswein, of Bantam Doubleday Dell, and Lawrence Weisburg, of Amsco School Publications.

A Guide to the Dictionary

The main entry, its inflected forms, spelling variants, and illustrative phrases are set in boldface. Part-of-speech labels are set in italics.

Centered periods within entry words indicate division points at which inflectional elements are to be added, without regard to syllabification, e.g.,

rd·ō -inis = ordō, ordinis

Compound words are generally given in their assimilated forms, e.g., **accurrō** rather than **adcurrō**. Cross-references are provided as guides for those using texts which employ the unassimilated forms, e.g.,

dc- = acc-

sēpiō *see* **saepio**

Spelling variants are indicated in bold type in parentheses after the part-of-speech abbreviation, e.g.,

affīnit·ās -ātis *f* **(adf-)** affinity, connection; relationship by marriage

However, nouns with both Greek and Latin endings are shown in full, e.g.,

troch·us *or* **troch·os -ī** *m* hoop

Tened·os *or* **Tened·us   -ī** *f* Tenedos *(island off the coast of Troy)*

Adjectives of three endings, whether of the first and second or of the third declension, are shown with three endings; adjectives with a single ending are shown in the nominative, followed by the genitive ending, e.g.,

curv·us -a -um *adj* curved

simil·is -is -e *adj* similar

dīlig·ens -entis *adj* careful; diligent

When constructions are provided, cases are not shown with the most common prepositions **ab, ad, ex,** *or* **cum.** For all other prepositions, the case that the preposition governs is shown, e.g.,

stō stāre stetī statum *intr* to stand; *(w.* **ex)** to consist of; *(w. abl or* **in** + *abl)* to depend on; *(w.* **per** + *acc)* to be due to, thanks to

Synonymous meanings are separated by commas; distinct meanings are separated by semicolons. When a grammatical construction applies to several distinct meanings, thus extending beyond semicolons, the distinct meanings are numbered, e.g.,

perfugiō *intr (w.* **ad** *or in* + *acc)* **1** to flee to for refuge; **2** to desert to; **3** to have recourse to

Discriminations between two or more meanings of an entry word are often shown by means of English words in parentheses, coming before or after the English meaning, e.g.,

argūt·us -a -um *adj* bright, smart *(person);* rustling *(leaves);* babbling *(brook);* chirping *(bird, cricket);* pungent *(smell);* expressive *(eyes, gestures)*

aspect·ō -āre -āvī -ātus *tr* **(ads-)** to look at, gaze at; *(of a place)* to face; to obey *(orders)*

However, words in parentheses, but not in italics, coming before or after a meaning are optional additions to the word in the target language, e.g.,

avuncul·us -ī *m* (maternal) uncle

abi·es -etis *f* fir (tree)

Level of usage of Latin words, indicated by the abbreviations *(coll)* for

1

"colloquial," *(sl)* for "slang," and *(vulg)* for "vulgar," is reflected in the level of usage of the English translation of the Latin word, e.g.,

admutil·ō -āre *tr* to clip close; *(coll)* to clip, cheat

ab·eō -īre -īvī *or* **-iī itum** *vi* to go away, depart; **abi in malam rem!** *(sl)* go to hell!

cole·ī -ōrum *mpl (vulg)* balls

Subject labels are given in italics and listed in alphabetical order, e.g.,

concurs·us -ūs *m* a running together, concourse; *(astr)* conjunction; *(gram)* juxtaposition *(of letters); (leg)* joint-right; *(mil)* charge, clash

When an entry word is a proper noun, the proper noun is not repeated in English if the form is the same in Latin and in English; but when the proper noun has two possible endings, the form used in English is provided, e.g.,

Eurīpid·ēs -is *m* Athenian tragic playwright *(480-406 B.C.)*

Eurōp·a -ae *or* **Eurōp·ē -ēs** *f* Europa *(daughter of the Phoenician king Agenor)* ‖ (continent of) Europe

Substantives formed from adjectives are generally listed under the adjectives from which they are derived and are separated by vertical parallel bars, e.g.,

dialectic·us -a -um *adj* logical ‖ *m* logician ‖ *f* logic ‖ *npl* dialectics

Proper nouns derived from adjectives or from common nouns are subsumed, in short entries, under the adjective and common noun respectively, e.g.,

daedal·us -a -um *adj* skillful, artistic; intricately constructed ‖ **Daedal·us -ī** *m* builder of the Labyrinth in Crete

Tarquini·ī -us -um *adj* Tarquinian ‖ *m* Tarquinius Priscus *(fifth king of Rome, c. 616-579 B.C.)* ‖ Tarquinius Superbus *(seventh and last king of Rome, c. 534-510 B.C.)*

cast·or -ōris *m* beaver ‖ **Castor** son *of Tyndareus, twin brother of Pollux*

Vertical parallel bars are used to separate different parts of speech of the entry word, for instance, pronominal adjectives from pronouns, e.g.,

alt·er -era -erum *adj* one *(of two);* a second, the second; the next ‖ *pron* one *(of two),* the one, the other; a second one

Vertical parallel bars are used to separate past participles, when occurring as separate entries, from adjectives and substantives derived from them, e.g.,

impens·us -a -um *pp of* **impendo** ‖ *adj* high, costly, expensive; ‖ *f see* **impensa** ‖ *n* high price

Vertical parallel bars are used to separate nouns in the singular from nouns in the plural when the plural of the nouns carries a special meaning, e.g.,

aed·es *or* **aed·is -is** *f* room; apartment; shrine, temple ‖ *fpl* house, home

Vertical parallel bars are used to separate common nouns from proper nouns, e.g.,

urs·a -ae *f* she-bear ‖ **Ursa Major** *(astr)* Great Bear; **Ursa Minor** *(astr)* Little Bear

Vertical parallel bars are used to separate verb functions. Transitive *(tr),* reflexive *(refl),* passive (with intransitive sense) *(pass),* intransitive *(intr),* and impersonal *(v impers)* functions of verbs with their dependent constructions are clearly differentiated and are presented in the fixed order as listed above, e.g.,

ēmer·gō -gĕre -sī -sus *vt* to raise *(from the water)* ‖ *refl or pass*

2

to rise **ll** *intr* to emerge; to rise *(in power)*

Illustrative phrases are provided at the end of entries in strict alphabetical order. However, when a Latin phrase illustrates a specific meaning, for instance, when the main entry is a prefix suffix, or preposition, the phrase is placed immediately after that meaning and introduced by a colon, e.g.,

-i·cō -āre *vbl suff* **1** used to form verbs from adjectives: **claudicāre** to be lame, to limp; **2** used to form verbs from other verbs: **fodicāre** to stab *(from* **fodĕre)**

For the sake of clarity, optional variants in illustrative phrases are placed in parentheses, e.g.,

vera et falsa *(or* **vera a falsis) dijudicare** to distinguish truth from falsehood

Vowel lengths are not shown on words within an entry except when clarity demands them, e.g.

succīdere [sub + caedere] to cut down (in order to distinguish it from **succĭdere [sub + cadere]** to collapse)

adversā viā up the road

nullā condicione by no means

de industriā on purpose

When a noun may be either masculine or feminine, the abbreviations are written together, but when a noun is generally, say, masculine but only rarely feminine or neuter, the rarer gender is shown in parentheses, e.g.,

serp·ens -entis *mf* serpent

pampin·us -ī *m (f)* vine shoot

sāl salis *m (n)* salt

Past participles are listed as separate entries when difference in form from the first person singular present indica-tive warrants such listing, provided they fall alphabetically more than one word before or after their verb, e.g.,

vīs·us -a -um *pp of* **video**

Similarly, the perfect form of a verb is listed as a separate entry in its alphabetical position, e.g.,

trīvī *perf of* **tero**

On the Latin-English side, the two-fold purpose in marking the quantity of vowels is

1. to indicate accentuation of words
2. to provide the basis for scansion of Classical Latin verse

Thus, all vowels that are long by nature and occur in open syllables are marked, whereas vowels in closed syllables, whether long or short by nature, are not marked, since the syllable in either case is long. However, since a vowel followed by a mute and a liquid can be open or closed, its quantity is marked when it is long.

On the English-Latin side, Latin vowels are marked to distinguish:

1. words otherwise spelled alike: **lēvis** (smooth), **lĕvis** (light)
2. the ablative singular from the nominative singular of nouns of the first declension whenever the distinction is not clear from the context
3. the infinitive of verbs of the second conjugation from the infinitive of verbs of the third conjugation
4. the genitive singular and nominative and accusative plural from the nominative singular of the fourth declension whenever the distinction is not clear from the context

On the English-Latin side, a bold-face dash represents the vocabulary entry, e.g.,

awake *adj* vigil, vigilans; **to be** — vigilare

3

PRONUNCIATION

Vowels

CLASSICAL METHOD	ECCLESIASTICAL METHOD
ă *a* in ago: **compărō**	
ā *a* in father: **imāgō**	
ĕ *e* in pet: **propĕrō**	Generally the same as the
ē *a* in late: **lēnis**	Classical Method. However, in
ĭ *i* in hit: **ĭdem**	practice the different values of the
ī *ee* in keen: **amīcus**	vowels are frequently not rigidly
ŏ *o* in often: **mŏdus**	adhered to.
ō *o* in hope: **nōmen**	
ŭ *u* in put: **ŭt**	
ū *u* in rude: **ūtor**	
ў *ü* in German Hütte: **mўrta**	
ȳ *ü* in German über: **Tȳdeus**	

Diphthongs

CLASSICAL METHOD	ECCLESIASTICAL METHOD
ae *y* in by: **caecus**	ae *a* in late: **caecus**
au *ow* in now: **nauta**	au as in Classical Method
eî *ey* in they: **heî**	ei as in Classical Method
eû *eu* in feud: **Orpheûs**	eu *eu* in Italian neutro: **euge**
oê *oi* in oil: **coêpit**	oe *a* in late: **coepit**
uî *uey* in gluey: **cuî;**	ui same as Classical Method
after **q,** *wee* in week: **qui**	

Consonants

CLASSICAL METHOD	ECCLESIASTICAL METHOD
b English b	b English b
c always *c* in can: **cīvis, cantō, cedō**	c before **e, i, ae,** or **oe** = *ch* in cherry: **celsus, civis, caelum, coepit,** but before other letters, *c* in can: **cantō, actus**
d English d	d English d
f English f	f English f
g always *g* in go: **gallīna, genus, grātus, gula**	g before **e** or **i** = *g* in gentle: **genus, regīna,** but before other letters except **g** and **n** (see under Consonant Groups) = *g* in go: **gallīna, grātus, gula, rogō**
h English h	h English h

4

j *y* in yes: *j*am, *j*ungō	**j** as in Classical Method
k English k, but unaspirated	**k** English k
l English l	**l** English l
m English m, but in verse final **m** before an initial vowel or **h** in the following word was presumably not pronounced	**m** English m
n English n	**n** English n
p English p, but unaspirated	**p** English p
q English q	**q** English q
r trilled r as in the Romance languages	**r** as in Classical Method
s always *s* in sing: mi**s**er, mor**s**	**s** *s* in sing: sal**ū**s, but when standing between two vowels or when final and preceded by a voiced consonant = *z* in dozen: mi**s**er, mor**s**
t English t, but unaspirated	**t** as in Classical Method
u *w* in wine, when unaccented, preceded by q, sometimes by s, and sometimes by g, and followed by a vowel: q**u**i·a, s**u**ā·vis (but s**u**·ō·rum), dis·tin·g**u**ō (but ex·i·g**ŭ**·**u**s)	**u** in Classical Method
v *w* in wine: vīvō	**v** English v
x *x* (= ks) in six: extrā	**x** *x* (as ks) in six: pax; but in words beginning with ex and followed by a vowel, h, or s, = *x* (as gz) in exhaust: exaudī, exhālō, exsolvō
z *dz* in adze: zōna	**z** as in Classical Method

Consonant Groups

CLASSICAL METHOD	ECCLESIASTICAL METHOD
bs *ps* in apse: o**bs**idō, ur**bs**	**bs** bs in obsession: o**bs**idō, but in the final position = **bs** (= bz) in observe: ur**bs**
bt *pt* in captain: o**bt**inēre	**bt** bt in obtain: o**bt**inēre
cc *kk* in bookkeeper: e**cc**e, o**cc**īdō, o**cc**āsum, o**cc**lūdō	**cc** before **e** or **i** = tch in catch: e**cc**e, o**cc**īdō; but before other letters = kk in bookkeeper; o**cc**āsum, o**cc**lūdō
ch *ch* in chaotic: pul**ch**er	**ch** as in Classical Method
gg *gg* in leg guard: a**gg**er	**gg** before **e** or **i** = dj in adjourn: a**gg**er; but before other letters = gg in leg guard: a**gg**rĕgō
gn *gn* in indignant: di**gn**us	**gn** ny in canyon: di**gn**us
gu see consonant **u**	**gu** as in Classical Method

5

ph	*p-h* in top-heavy: *ph*ōca	**ph**	ph in phoenix: *ph*ōca
qu	see consonant **u**	**qu**	as in Classical Method
sc	*sc* in scope: *sc*iō, *sc*ūtum	**sc**	before **e** or **i** = **sh** in **sh**in: a**sc**endō, **sc**iō; but before other letters = sc in scope: *sc*andō, *sc*ūtum
su	see consonant **u**	**su**	as in Classical Method
th	*t* in take: *th*eātrum	**th**	as in Classical Method
ti	*ti* in English patio: nā*tĭ*ō	**ti**	when preceded by **s**, **t**, or **x**, or when followed by a consonant = **ti** in English patio: hos*tĭ*a, admix*tĭ*ō, for*tĭ*ter; but when unaccented, followed by a vowel, and preceded by any letter except **s**, **t**, or **x** = tzy in ritzy: nā*tĭ*ō, pre*tĭ*um

Syllabification

1. Every Latin word has as many syllables as it has vowels or diphthongs: ae·ger, fī·li·us, Bai·ae

2. When a word is divided into syllables:

   a) a single consonant between two vowels goes with the following syllable (h is regarded as a consonant; ch, ph, th, qu, and sometimes gu and su are regarded as single consonants)*; a·ger, ni·hil, a·qua, ci·hor·rē·um

   b) the first consonant of a combination of two or more consonants goes with the preceding vowel: tor·men·tum, mit·tō, mon·strum

   c) a consonant group consisting of a mute (b, c, d, g, p, t) followed by l or r is generally left undivided and goes with the following vowel: pā·trēs, a·cris, du·plex. In Classical poetry this combination is often treated like any other pair of consonants: pāt·rēs, ac·ris, dup·lex

   d) prefixes form separate syllables even if the division is contrary to above rules: ab·est, ob·lā·tus, abs·ti·nē·ō, ab·stō

3. A syllable ending in a vowel or diphthong is called *open;* all others are called *closed*

4. The last syllable of a word is called the *ultima;* the next to last is called the *penult;* the one before the penult is called the *antepenult*

---

* The double consonant x goes with the preceding vowel: dix·it

Quantity of Vowels

1. A vowel is *long* (lēvis) or *short* (lĕvis) according to the length of time required for its pronunciation

2. A vowel is long:

   a) before ns, nf, (and perhaps gn): ingēns, īnfāns, (māgnus)

3. A vowel is short:

   a) before another vowel or h: dĕa, trăhō

   b) generally before nd and nt: amăndus, amănt

4. Diphthongs are long: causa

6

Quantity of Syllables

1. Syllables are distinguished as *long* or *short* according to the length of time required for their pronunciation

2. A syllable is long:

   a) if it contains a long vowel or a diphthong: **vē·nī scrī·bō, caus·ae** (such a syllable is said to be *long by nature*)

   b) if it contains a short vowel followed by **x, z,** or any two consonants except a mute (**b, d, g, p, t, c**) followed by **l** or **r: sax·um, gaz·a, mit·tō, cur·sor** (such a syllable is said to be *long by position*, but the vowel is pronounced *short*)

3. A syllable is short:

   a) if it contains a short vowel followed by a vowel or by a single consonant (**h** is regarded as a consonant; **ch, ph, th, qu,** and sometimes **gu** and **su** are regarded as single consonants): **me·us, ni·hil, ge·rit, a·qua**

   b) if it contains a short vowel followed by a mute (**b, d, g, p, t, c**) plus **l** or **r,** but it is sometimes long in verse: **flă·grans, ba·ră·thrum, ce·lĕ·brō** (such a syllable is said to be *common*)

NOTE: In this dictionary, on the Latin-English side, long vowels are marked except before **x, z,** or two or more consonants unless the two consonants are a mute plus a liquid (e.g., **pātris**). The short penult of the infinitive of verbs of the third conjugation is marked with a breve (e.g., **vincĕre**) to distinguish it from the long penult of the infinitive of verbs of the second conjugation (e.g., **vidēre**). In addition, the short syllable of words is marked to contrast it with the long syllable of otherwise homographs, e.g., **concīdĕre** (to kill) and **concĭdĕre** (to collapse); **ănus** (old woman) and **ānus** (anus, rectum).

Accent

1. Words of two syllables are accented on the first syllable: **om′nēs, tan′gō, ge′rit**

2. Words of more than two syllables are accented on the penult if it is long: **a·mī′cus, re·gun′tur,** and on the antepenult if the penult is short: **fa·mi′lĭ·a, ge′rĭ·tur**

3. These rules apply to words with enclitics appended (**-ce, -dum, -met, -ne, -que, -ve**): **vos′met, lau·dat′ne, de′ă·que** (nominative), **dē·ā′que** (ablative)

4. In the second declension, the contracted genitive and the contracted vocative of nouns in **-ius** and the contracted genitive of those in **-ium** retain the accent of the nominative: **Vir·gī′lī, in·gĕ′nī**

5. Certain words which have lost a final **-e** retain the accent of the complete forms: **il·līc′** for **il·lī′ce, tan·tōn′** for **tan·tō′ne**

6. Certain compounds of **faciō,** in which a feeling for the individuality of the components was preserved, retain the accent of the simple verb: **be·ne·fă′cit**

7

Guide to Latin Grammar

Nouns

FIRST DECLENSION SINGULAR		SECOND DECLENSION SINGULAR		
rosa *f*		**sonus** *m*	**puer** *m*	**ager** *m*
rose		sound	boy	field
NOM	rosa	sonus	puer	ager
GEN	rosae	sonī	puerī	agrī
DAT	rosae	sonō	puerō	agrō
ACC	rosam	sonum	puerum	agrum
ABL	rosā	sonō	puerō	agrō

FIRST DECLENSION PLURAL		SECOND DECLENSION PLURAL		
NOM	rosae	sonī	puerī	agrī
GEN	rosārum	sonōrum	puerōrum	agrōrum
DAT	rosīs	sonīs	puerīs	agrīs
ACC	rosās	sonōs	puerōs	agrōs
ABL	rosīs	sonīs	puerīs	agrīs

SECOND DECLENSION SINGULAR

	vir *m*	**dōnum** *n*	**servos** *m*	**fīlius** *m*	**ingenium** *n*
	man	gift	servant	son	talent
NOM	vir	dōnum	servos	fīlius	ingenium
GEN	virī	dōnī	servī	fīl·iī *or* -ī	ingen·iī *or* -ī
DAT	virō	dōnō	servō	fīliō	ingeniō
ACC	virum	dōnum	servom	fīlium	ingenium
ABL	virō	dōnō	servō	fīliō	ingeniō

SECOND DECLENSION PLURAL

NOM	virī	dōna	servī	fīliī	ingenia
GEN	virōrum	dōnōrum	servōrum	fīliōrum	igeniōrum
DAT	virīs	dōnīs	servīs	fīliīs	ingeniīs
ACC	virōs	dōna	servōs	fīliōs	ingenia
ABL	virīs	dōnīs	servīs	fīliīs	ingeniīs

NOTES (a) The vocative singular of **-us** nouns ends in **-e: amīce**. The vocative singular (and sometimes the genitive singular) of **-ius** nouns ends in **-ī: fīlī, Tiberī**. But the vocative of **deus** is **deus**.

(b) The earlier inflection of masculine nouns of the second declension, down to Caesar and Cicero, followed the pattern of **servos**.

Third Declension Masculine/Feminine Nouns Singular

	rex *m* king	mīles *m* soldier	princeps *m* chief	māter *f* mother
Nom	rex	mīles	princeps	māter
Gen	rēgis	mīlitis	principis	mātris
Dat	rēgī	mīlitī	principī	mātrī
Acc	rēgem	mīlitem	principem	mātrem
Abl	rēge	mīlite	principe	mātre

Third Declension Masculine/Feminine Nouns Plural

Nom	rēgēs	mīlitēs	principēs	mātrēs
Gen	rēgum	mīlitum	principum	mātrum
Dat	rēgibus	mīlitibus	principibus	mātribus
Acc	rēgēs	mīlitēs	principēs	mātrēs
Abl	rēgibus	mīlitibus	principibus	mātribus

Third Declension Masculine/Feminine Nouns Singular

	hostis *m* enemy	custōs *m* guard	vigil *m* fireman	nox *f* night
Nom	hostis	custōs	vigil	nox
Gen	hostis	custōdis	vigilis	noctis
Dat	hostī	custōdī	vigilī	noctī
Acc	host·em *or* -im	custōdem	vigilem	noctem
Abl	host·e *or* -ī	custōde	vigile	nocte

Third Declension Masculine/Feminine Nouns Plural

Nom	hostēs	custōdēs	vigilēs	noctēs
Gen	hostium	custōdum	vigilum	noctium
Dat	hostibus	custōdibus	vigilibus	noctibus
Acc	host·ēs *or* -īs	custōdēs	vigilēs	noctēs
Abl	hostibus	custōdibus	vigilibus	noctibus

Third Declension Neuter Nouns Singular

	nōmen *n* name	caput *n* head	opus *n* work	iter *n* road	mare *n* sea	animal *n* animal	cor *n* heart
Nom	nōmen	caput	opus	iter	mare	animal	cor
Gen	nōminis	capitis	operis	itineris	maris	animālis	cordis
Dat	nōminī	capitī	operī	itinerī	marī	animālī	cordī
Acc	nōmen	caput	opus	iter	mare	animal	cor
Abl	nōmine	capite	opere	itinere	marī	animālī	corde

Third Declension Neuter Nouns Plural

Nom	nōmina	capita	opera	itinera	maria	animālia	corda
Gen	nōminum	capitum	operum	itinerum	marium	animālium	—
Dat	nōminibus	capitibus	operibus	itineribus	maribus	animālibus	cordibus
Acc	nōmina	capita	opera	itinera	maria	animālia	corda
Abl	nōminibus	capitibus	operibus	itineribus	maribus	animālibus	cordibus

Notes (a) Masculine and feminine ĭ-stem nouns, such as **hostis**, regularly end in
-is in the nominative singular, and always have -ium in the genitive
plural. The accusative singular ends in -em *or* -im, and the ablative in
-e *or* -ī, and the accusative plural in -ēs *or* -īs.

(b) A number of monosyllabic nouns with mute stems (like **cor**) lack the
genitive plural.

	FOURTH DECLENSION SINGULAR			FIFTH DECLENSION SINGULAR	
	fructus *m*	**manus** *f*	**genū** *n*	**diēs** *m*	**rēs** *f*
	fruit	hand	knee	day	thing
NOM	fructus	manus	genū	diēs	rēs
GEN	fructūs	manūs	genūs	diēī	rēī
DAT	fructuī	manuī	genū	diēī	rēī
ACC	fructum	manum	genū	diem	rem
ABL	fructū	manū	genū	diē	rē

	FOURTH DECLENSION PLURAL			FIFTH DECLENSION PLURAL	
NOM	fructūs	manūs	genua	diēs	rēs
GEN	fructuum	manuum	genuum	diērum	rērum
DAT	fructibus	manibus	genibus	diēbus	rēbus
ACC	fructūs	manūs	genua	diēs	rēs
ABL	fructibus	manibus	genibus	diēbus	rēbus

NOTE (a) Nouns of the fourth declension are mostly masculine nouns. The following nouns in **-us** are feminine: **acus** needle; **domus** house; **manus** hand; **porticus** colonnade; **tribus** tribe; **īdūs** *(pl)* Ides; also most names of trees, such as **quercus** oak.

(b) All fifth-declension nouns are feminine, except **diēs** *m* "day" and **merīdiēs** *m* "midday, noon." But **diēs** is sometimes feminine in the singular, especially in phrases indicating a fixed time, and regularly when used of time in general, e.g., **constitūtā diē** on the appointed day; **longa diēs** a long time.

Greek Nouns

FIRST DECLENSION

Greek nouns that end in **-ē** are feminine; those that end in **-ās** and **-ēs** are masculine. In the plural, when found, they are declined like regular Latin nouns of the first declension.. In the singular they are declined as follows:

	Aenēās *m*	**Anchīsēs** *m*	**Pēnelopē** *f*	**Persēs** *m*
	Aeneas	Anchises	Penelope	Persian
NOM	Aenēās	Anchīsēs	Pēnelopē	Persēs
GEN	Aenēae	Anchīsae	Pēnelopēs	Persae
DAT	Aenēae	Anchīsae	Pēnelopae	Persae
ACC	Aenē·am *or* -ān	Anchīs·ēn, -am	Pēnelopēn	Pers·ēn *or* -am
ABL	Aenēā	Anchīs·ē *or* -ā	Pēnelopē	Pers·ē *or* -ā
VOC	Aenē·ā *or* -ă	Anchīs·ē *or* -ā *or* -ă	Pēnelopē	Persa *or* -ă

SECOND DECLENSION

Greek nouns of the second declension end in **-os** *or* **-ōs** and are masculine or feminine; those ending in **-on** are neuter. In the plural, when found, they are declined like regular Latin nouns. They are mostly proper names and are declined as follows in the singular:

	Lesbŏs *f*	**Athōs** *m*	**Īlion** *n*	**Panthūs** *m*
	Lesbos	Athos	Ilium	Panthus
NOM	Lesb·ŏs *or* -us	Athōs *or* o	Īli·on *or* -um	Panthūs
GEN	Lesbī	Ath·ō *or* ōnis	Īliī	Panthī

10

			Ī́liō	Panthṓ
DAT	Lesbō	Athō		
ACC	Lesb·on *or* -um	Ath·ōn *or* -um	Ī́li·on *or* -um	Panthū́n
ABL	Lesbō	Athō *or* -ōne	Ī́liō	Panthō
VOC	Lesbō	Athōs	Ī́li·on *or* -um	Panthū́

THIRD DECLENSION SINGULAR

	hērōs *m*	basis *f*	naïs *f*	tigris *mf*	lampas *f*
	hero	base	naiad	tiger	torch
NOM	hērōs	basis	naïs	tigris	lampas
GEN	hērōïs	bas·eōs *or* -idos	naïd·os *or* -is	tigr·is *or* -idis	lampados
DAT	hērōï	basī	naïdī	tigrī	lampadī
ACC	hērōa	bas·in *or* -ida *or* -im	naïda	tigr·in *or* -idem	lampada
ABL	hērōë	basī	naïde	tigr·ī *or* -ide	lampade

THIRD DECLENSION PLURAL

NOM	hērōĕs	basēs	naïdĕs	tigrēs	lampadĕs
GEN	hērōum	bas·eōn *or* -ium	naïdum	tigrium	lampadum
DAT	hērōïbus	basibus	naïdibus	tigribus	lampadibus
ACC	hērōăs	basīs *or* -eīs	naïdăs	tigr·īs *or* -idăs	lampadăs
ABL	hērōïbus	basibus	naïdibus	tigribus	lampadibus

THIRD DECLENSION PROPER NAMES

NOM	Dīdō	Capys	Paris	Orpheûs
GEN	Dīdōnis *or* Dīdūs	Capyos	Paridis	Orph·eī *or* -eōs
DAT	Dīdōnī *or* Dīdō	Capyī	Paridī	Orph·eō *or* -eī
ACC	Dīdō *or* Dīdōnem	Capyn	Parid·em *or* -im *or* -in	Orphe·um *or* -a
ABL	Dīdōne *or* -ō	Capyë	Paridē *or* Parī	Orpheō
VOC	Dīdō *or* Dīdō	Capy	Pari	Orpheû

NOM	Periclēs	Simoïs	Atlās	Selīnūs
GEN	Pericl·īs *or* -ī	Simoënt·is *or* -os	Atlantis	Selīnuntis
DAT	Pericl·ī *or* -ĭ	Simoëntī	Atlantī	Selīnuntī
ACC	Pericl·em *or* -ea *or* -ēn	Simoënta	Atlanta	Selīnuntā
ABL	Pericle	Simoënte	Atlante	Selīnunte
VOC	Pericl·ēs *or* -ē	Simoïs	Atlā	Selīnūs

NOTES (a) The regular Latin forms may be used for most of the above.

(b) Most stems in ĭd- *(nom: -is)*, as **tigris**, often have also the forms of **i**-stems: *gen:* -ĭdis *or* -ĭdos *or* -is; *acc:* -ĭdem *or* -ĭda *or* -im *or* -in; *abl:* -ĭde *or* -ī. However, most feminine proper names have *acc* -idem *or* -ida, *abl:* -ide, — not -im *or* -ī.

(c) Stems in **ant-**, **ent-**, and a few in **unt-** follow the model of **Simoïs**, **-entis**, **Atlās**, **-antis** and **Selīnūs -untis**.

(d) Many Greek names, of the third declension in Latin, pass over into the first declension in the plural, as, **Hyperid·ae -ārum**, etc.

(e) Many names in **-ēs** belonging to the third declension have also genitive in **-ī**, e.g., **Pericl·ēs -is** *or* **-ī**.

(f) Greek names in **-eûs**, like **Orpheûs**, have forms of the second and third declensions.

(g) Greek nouns of the third declension end in **-ĕs** in the nominative plural, as **Phrygĕs** Phrygians, and end in **-ăs** in the accusative plural, as **Phrygăs** Phrygians.

11

Pronouns

Personal Pronouns

ego I   **tu** you   **is** he   **ea** she   **id** it

	1st Pers	*2nd Pers*	*3rd Pers*		
NOM	ego	tū	is	ea	id
GEN	meī	tuī	ejus	ejus	ejus
DAT	mihi *or* mī	tibi	eī	eī	eī
ACC	mē	tē	eum	eam	id
ABL	mē	tē	eō	eā	eō

PLURAL

	1st Pers	*2nd Pers*	*3rd Pers*		
NOM	nōs	vōs	eī *or* iī	eae	ea
GEN	nostrum	vestrum	eōrum	eārum	eōrum
	nostrī	vestrī			
DAT	nōbīs	vōbīs	eīs	eīs	eīs
ACC	nōs	vōs	eōs	eās	ea
ABL	nōbīs	vōbīs	eīs	eīs	eīs

NOTES (a) The forms **nostrum** and **vestrum** are used partitively, e.g.,
ūnusquisque nostrum each one of us; otherwise, the forms **nostrī**
and **vestrī** are used, e.g., **meminit vestrī** he remembered you.
(b) The form **mī** is sometimes used in poetry instead of **mihi**.

Reflexive Pronouns

SINGULAR

	1st Pers	*2nd Pers*	*3rd Pers*
NOM	——	——	——
GEN	meī	tuī	suī
DAT	mihi	tibi	sibi
ACC	mē	tē	sē *or* sēsē
ABL	mē	tē	sē *or* sēse

NOTES (a) The reflexive of the third persons serves for *all genders*. Thus, **suī**
may mean "of himself", "of herself", or "of itself".
(b) All of the reflexive pronouns can serve as reciprocal pronouns, e.g.,
inter se culpant they blame each other (one another).

PLURAL

	1st Pers	*2nd Pers*	*3rd Pers*
NOM	——	——	——
GEN	nostrī	vestrī	suī
DAT	nōbīs	vōbīs	sibi
ACC	nōs	vōs	sē *or* sēsē
ABL	nōbīs	vōbīs	sē *or* sēsē

Demonstrative Pronouns

hīc this (one)   **haec** this (one)   **hōc** this (one)

SINGULAR

	masc	*fem*	*neut*
NOM	hīc	haec	hōc
GEN	hūjus	hūjus	hūjus
DAT	huic	huic	huic
ACC	hunc	hanc	hōc
ABL	hōc	hāc	hōc

PLURAL

	masc	*fem*	*neut*
NOM	hī	hae	haec
GEN	hōrum	hārum	hōrum
DAT	hīs	hīs	hīs
ACC	hōs	hās	haec
ABL	hīs	hīs	hīs

ille that (one)   **illa** that (one)   **illud** that (one)

SINGULAR

	masc	*fem*	*neut*
NOM	ille	illa	illud
GEN	illīus	illīus	illīus
DAT	illī	illī	illī
ACC	illum	illam	illud
ABL	illō	illā	illō

PLURAL

	masc	*fem*	*neut*
NOM	illī	illae	illa
GEN	illōrum	illārum	illōrum
DAT	illīs	illīs	illīs
ACC	illōs	illās	illa
ABL	illīs	illīs	illīs

NOTES (a) **Iste, ista, istud** ("that") is declined like **ille.**

(b) **Ille** and **iste** appear in combination with the demonstrative particle **-c,** shortened from **-ce** (giving the sense "that there") in the following forms:

SINGULAR

	masc	*fem*	*neut*
NOM	illic	illaec	illuc *or* illoc
ACC	illunc	illanc	illuc *or* illoc
ABL	illōc	illāc	illōc

PLURAL

	masc	*fem*	*neut*
NOM	——	——	illaec
ACC	——	——	illaec

13

	masc	*fem*	*neut*
Nom	istic	istaec	istuc *or* istoc
Acc	istunc	istanc	istuc *or* istoc
Abl	istōc	istāc	istōc

PLURAL

	masc	*fem*	*neut*
Nom	——	——	istaec
Acc	——	——	istaec

īdem the same   **eadem** the same   **idem** the same

SINGULAR

	masc	*fem*	*neut*
Nom	īdem	eadem	idem
Gen	ejusdem	ejusdem	ejusdem
Dat	eīdem	eīdem	eīdem
Acc	eundem	eandem	idem
Abl	eōdem	eādem	eōdem

PLURAL

	masc	*fem*	*neut*
Nom	eīdem *or* iīdem	eaedem	eadem
Gen	eōrundem	eārundem	eōrundem
Dat	eīsdem *or* īsdem	eīsdem *or* īsdem	eīsdem *or* īsdem
Acc	eōsdem	eāsdem	eadem
Abl	eīsdem *or* īsdem	eīsdem *or* īsdem	eīsdem *or* īsdem

Intensive Pronouns

ipse -self   **ipsa** -self   **ipsum** -self

SINGULAR

	masc	*fem*	*neut*
Nom	ipse	ipsa	ipsum
Gen	ipsīus	ipsīus	ipsīus
Dat	ipsī	ipsī	ipsī
Acc	ipsum	ipsam	ipsum
Abl	ipsō	ipsā	ipsō

PLURAL

	masc	*fem*	*neut*
Nom	ipsī	ipsae	ipsa
Gen	ipsōrum	ipsārum	ipsōrum
Dat	ipsīs	ipsīs	ipsīs
Acc	ipsōs	ipsās	ipsa
Abl	ipsīs	ipsīs	ipsīs

Relative Pronouns

quī who, that   **quae** who, that   **quod** which, that

SINGULAR

	masc	*fem*	*neut*
NOM	quī	quae	quod
GEN	cūjus	cūjus	cūjus
DAT	cui	cui	cui
ACC	quem	quam	quod
ABL	quō	quā	quō

PLURAL

	masc	*fem*	*neut*
NOM	quī	quae	quae
GEN	quōrum	quārum	quōrum
DAT	quibus	quibus	quibus
ACC	quōs	quās	quae
ABL	quibus	quibus	quibus

NOTE (a) The interrogative adjective **quī, quae, quod** (what? what kind of? which?), is declined throughout like the relative pronoun.

Interrogative Pronouns

quis who?   **quid** what?

	masc & fem	*neut*
NOM	quis	quid
GEN	cūjus	cūjus
DAT	cui	cui
ACC	quem	quid
ABL	quō	quō

NOTES (a) The rare form of the plural follows the declension of the relative pronoun.

(b) **Quī** is sometimes used for **quis** in indirect questions.

(c) **Quis,** when modifying words denoting persons, is sometimes an adjective: **quis homō** = what man? whereas **quī homō** = what sort of man?

(d) The pronoun **quis** and the pronominal adjective **quī** may be strengthened by adding **-nam**, e. g., **quisnam** just who? exactly who?; **quidnam** just what?, exactly what?; **quīnam, quaenam, quodnam** of exactly what kind?

Indefinite Pronouns

aliquis somone **aliqua** someone **aliquid** something

	masc	*fem*	*neut*
NOM	aliquis (aliquī)	aliqua	aliquid (aliquod)
GEN	alicūjus	alicūjus	alicūjus
DAT	alicui	alicui	alicui
ACC	aliquem	aliquam	aliquid (aliquod)
ABL	aliquō	aliquā	aliquō

PLURAL

	masc	*fem*	*neut*
NOM	aliquī	aliquae	aliqua
GEN	aliquōrum	aliquārum	aliquōrum
DAT	aliquibus	aliquibus	aliquibus
ACC	aliquōs	aliquās	aliqua
ABL	aliquibus	aliquibus	aliquibus

NOTES
(a) The indefinite adjective **aliquī** "some" is declined in the same way as the indefinite pronoun **aliquis** "someone" except in the three cases indicated above in parentheses: nominative masculine singular, neuter nominative singular, and neuter accusative singular.
(b) **Quis** is used instead of **aliquis** after **nē, sī, nisi,** and **num,** e.g., **sī quis** "if anyone".

quīdam, quaedam a certain person **quiddam** a certain thing

SINGULAR

	masc	*fem*	*neut*
NOM	quīdam	quaedam	quiddam
GEN	cūjusdam	cūjusdam	cūjusdam
DAT	cuidam	cuidam	cuidam
ACC	quendam	quandam	quiddam
ABL	quōdam	quādam	quōdam

PLURAL

	masc	*fem*	*neut*
NOM	quīdam	quaedam	quaedam
GEN	quōrundam	quārundam	quōrundam
DAT	quibusdam	quibusdam	quibusdam
ACC	quōsdam	quāsdam	quaedam
ABL	quibusdam	quibusdam	quibusdam

NOTES
(a) The corresponding pronomimal adjective differs only in these forms: **quoddam** for **quiddam**.
(b) There are two indefinite relative pronouns: **quīcumque** and **quisquis** "whoever". **Quīcumque** declines only the first part; **quisquis** declines both but has only **quisquis, quidquid,** and **quōquō** in common use.

Adjectives

First and Second Declensions Singular

	masc	fem	neu		masc	fem	neut
	bonus good				**tener** tender		
Nom	bonus	bona	bonum		tener	tenera	tenerum
Gen	bonī	bonae	bonī.		tenerī	tenerae	tenerī
Dat	bonō	bonae	bonố		tenerō	tenerae	tenerō
Acc	bonum	bonam	bonum		tenerum	teneram	tenerum
Abl	bonō	bonā	bonō		tenerō	tenerā	tenerō

First and Second Declensions Plural

	masc	fem	neu		masc	fem	neut
Nom	bonī	bonae	bona		tenerī	tenerae	tenera
Gen	bonōrum	bonārum	bonōrum		tenerōrum	tenerārum	tenerōrum
Dat	bonīs	bonīs	bonīs		tenerīs	tenerīs	tenerīs
Acc	bonōs	bonās	bona		tenerōs	tenerās	tenerā
Abl	bonīs	bonīs	bonīs		tenerīs	tenerīs	tenerīs

First and Second Declensions Singular

sacer sacred

	masc	fem	neut
Nom	sacer	sacra	sacrum
Gen	sacrī	sacrae	sacrī
Dat	sacrō	sacrae	sacrō
Acc	sacrum	sacram	sacrum
Abl	sacrō	sacrā	sacrō

Nine Irregular Adjectives

alter the other .... *see below*
alius another .... *see below*
nullus none .... same as tōtus
neuter neither .... same as uter
sōlus alone .... same as tōtus
tōtus whole .... *see below*
ullus any .... same as tōtus
ūnus one .... same as tōtus
uter which (of two)? ..... *see below*

First and Second Declensions Plural

	masc	fem	neut
Nom	sacrī	sacrae	sacra
Gen	sacrōrum	sacrārum	sacrōrum
Dat	sacrīs	sacrīs	sacrīs
Acc	sacrōs	sacrās	sacra
Abl	sacrīs	sacrīs	sacrīs

First and Second Declension Irregular Adjectives

They are declined in the singular as follows (the plural is regular):

	masc	fem	neut	masc	fem	neut
Nom	alius	alia	aliud	alter	altera	alterum
Gen	alterīus	alterīus	alterīus	alterīus	alterīus	alterīus
	alīus	alīus	alīus			
Dat	aliī	aliī	aliī	alterī	alterī	alterī
Acc	alium	aliam	aliud	alterum	alteram	alterum
Abl	aliō	aliā	aliō	alterō	alterā	alterō

	masc	fem	neut	masc	fem	neut
Nom	uter	utra	utrum	tōtus	tōta	tōtum
Gen	utrīus	utrīus	utrīus	tōtīus	tōtīus	tōtīus
Dat	utrī	utrī	utrī	tōtī	tōtī	tōtī
Acc	utrum	utram	utrum	tōtum	tōtam	tōtum
Abl	utrō	utrā	utrō	tōtō	tōtā	tōtō

THIRD DECLENSION ADJECTIVES OF THREE ENDINGS: SINGULAR

alacer lively

	masc	fem	neut
NOM	alacer	alacris	alacre
GEN	alacris	alacris	alacris
DAT	alacrī	alacrī	alacrī
ACC	alacrem	alacrem	alacre
ABL	alacrī	alacrī	alacrī

THIRD DECLENSION ADJECTIVES OF THREE ENDINGS: PLURAL

	masc	fem	neut
NOM	alacrēs	alacrēs	alacria
GEN	alacrium	alacrium	alacrium
DAT	alacribus	alacribus	alacribus
ACC	alacr·ēs or -īs	alacr·ēs or -īs	alacria
ABL	alacribus	alacribus	alcribus

THIRD DECLENSION ADJECTIVES OF TWO ENDINGS: SINGULAR

fortis brave **fortior** braver

	masc & fem	neut	masc & fem	neut
NOM	fortis	forte	fortior	fortius
GEN	fortis	fortis	fortiōris	fortiōris
DAT	fortī	fortī	fortiōrī	fortiōrī
ACC	fortem	forte	fortiōrem	fortius
ABL	fortī	fortī	fortiō·re or -rī	fortiō·re or -rī

THIRD DECLENSION ADJECTIVES OF TWO ENDINGS: PLURAL

	masc & fem	neut	masc & fem	neut
NOM	fortēs	fortia	fortiōrēs	fortiōra
GEN	fortium	fortium	fortiōrum	fortiōrum
DAT	fortibus	fortibus	fortiōribus	fortiōribus
ACC	fort·ēs or -īs	fortia	fortiōr·ēs or -īs	fortiōra
ABL	fortibus	fortibus	fortiōribus	fortiōribus

THIRD DECLENSION ADJECTIVES OF ONE ENDING: SINGULAR

audax bold **potens** powerful **vetus** old

	masc & fem	neut	masc & fem	neut	masc & fem	neut
NOM	audax	audax	potens	potens	vetus	vetus
GEN	audācis	audācis	potentis	potentis	veteris	veteris
DAT	audācī	audācī	potentī	potentī	veterī	veterī
ACC	audācem	audax	potentem	potens	veterem	vetus
ABL	audācī	audācī	potentī	potentī	vetere	vetere

THIRD DECLENSION ADJECTIVES OF ONE ENDING: PLURAL

	masc & fem	neut	masc & fem	neut	masc & fem	neut
NOM	audācēs	audācia	potentēs	potentia	veterēs	vetera
GEN	audācium	audācium	potentium	potentium	veterum	veterum
DAT	audācibus	audācibus	potentibus	potentibus	veteribus	veteribus
ACC	audāc·ēs -īs	audācia	potentia	potentia	veterēs	vetera
ABL	audācibus	audācibus	potentibus	potentibus	veteribus	veteribus

COMPARISON OF IRREGULAR ADJECTIVES

Positive	Comparative	Superlative
bonus, *good*	melior, *better*	optimus, *best*
exter, *external*	exterior, *outer*	extrēmus, *outermost*
frūgī, *thrifty*	frūgālior, *thriftier*	frūgālissimus, *thriftiest*
magnus, *big*	major, *bigger*	maximus, *biggest*
malus, *bad*	pējor, *worse*	pessimus, *worst*
multus, *bad*	plūs, *more*	plūrimus, *most*
nēquam, *worthless*	nēquior, *worse*	nēquissimus, *worst*
posterus, *following*	posterior, *later*	postrēmus, postumus, *last*
superus, *upper*	superior, *higher*	suprēmus, summus, *highest*
————	dēterior, *worse*	dēterrimus, *worst*
————	inferior, *lower*	infimus, īmus, *lowest*
————	interior, *inner*	intimus, *innermost*
————	ocior, *swifter*	ocissimus, *swiftest*
————	potior, *preferable*	potissimus, *most important*
————	prior, *former*	prīmus, *first*
————	propior, *nearer*	proximus, *nearest*
falsus, *false*	————	falsissimus, *most false*
fīdus, *faithful*	————	fīdissimus, *most faithful*
novus, *new*	(recentior), *more recent*	novissimus, *latest, newest*
sacer, *sacred*	————	sacerrimus, *most sacred*
vetus, *old*	(vetustior), *older*	veterrimus, *oldest*

NOTES (a) For the declension of the comparative degree, see **fortior, fortius** above.

(b) Adjectives in **-er** form the superlative by adding **-rimus** to the nominative of the positive. The comparative is regular. Thus:

ācer, *sharp*	ācrior, *sharper*	ācerrimus, *sharpest*
celer, *swift*	celerior, *swifter*	celerrimus, *swiftest*
miser, *wretched*	miserior, *more w.*	miserrimus, *most w.*

(c) Five adjectives in **-ilis** form the superlative by adding **-limus** to the stem of the positive. The comparison is regular. Thus:

facilis, *easy*	facilior, *easier*	facillimus, *easiest*
difficilis, *difficult*	difficilior, *more d.*	difficillimus *most d.*
similis, *similar*	similior, *more s.*	simillimus, *most s.*
dissimilis, *unlike*	dissimilior, *more u.*	dissimillimus, *most u.*
humilis, *low*	humilior, *lower*	humillimus, *lowest*

Adverbs

Comparison of Irregular Adverbs

bene, *well*	melius, *better*	optimē, *best*
diū, *long*	diūtius, *longer*	diūtissimē, *longest*
magnopere, *greatly*	magis, *more*	maximē, *most*
male, *badly*	pejus, *worse*	pessimē, *worst*
multum, *much*	plūs, *more*	plūrimum, *most*
nēquiter, *worthlessly*	nēquius, *more w.*	nēquissimē, *most w.*
nūper, *recently*	————	nūperrimē, *most r.*
parum, *little*	minus, *less*	minimē, *least*
prope, *near*	propius, *more c.*	proximē, *most c.*
saepe, *often*	saepius, *oftener*	saepissimē, *most o.*
secus, *otherwise*	sētius, *otherwise*	————
————	potius, *rather*	potissimum, *especially*
————	prius, *previously*	prīmum, *first*

19

First Conjugation Verbs

Principal parts: amō   I love
                      amāre   to love
                      amāvī   I loved, I have loved
                      amātus   (having been) loved

Indicative Mood

| | *Active Voice* | | *Passive Voice* | |
| *Singular* | *Plural* | *Singular* | *Plural* | |

PRESENT

amō	amāmus	amor	amāmur
amās	amātis	amā·ris *or* -re	amāminī
amat	amant	amātur	amantur

IMPERFECT

amābam	amābamus	amābar	amābāmur
amābās	amābātis	amābā·ris *or* -re	amābāminī
amābat	amābant	amābātur	amābantur

FUTURE

amābō	amābimus	amābor	amābimur
amābis	amābitis	amābe·ris *or* -re	amābiminī
amābit	amābunt	amābitur	amābuntur

PERFECT

amāvī	amāvimus	amātus sum	amātī sumus
amāvistī	amāvistis	amātus es	amātī estis
amāvit	amāvē·runt *or* -re	amātus est	amātī sunt

PLUPERFECT

amāveram	amāverāmus	amātus eram	amātī erāmus
amāverās	amāverātis	amātus erās	amātī erātis
amāverat	amāverant	amātus erat	amātī erant

FUTURE PERFECT

amāverō	amāverimus	amātus erō	amātī erimus
amāveris	amāveritis	amātus eris	amātī eritis
amāverit	amāverint	amātus erit	amātī erunt

Subjunctive Mood

Active Voice		Passive Voice	
Singular	*Plural*	*Singular*	*Plural*
PRESENT			
amem	amēmus	amer	amēmur
amēs	amētis	amē·ris *or* -re	amēminī
amet	ament	amētur	amentur
IMPERFECT			
amārem	amārēmus	amārer	amārēmur
amārēs	amārētis	amārē·ris *or* -re	amārēminī
amāret	amārent	amārētur	amārentur
PERFECT			
amāverim	amāverīmus	amātus sim	amātī sīmus
amāverīs	amāverītis	amātus sīs	amātī sītis
amāverit	amāverint	amātus sit	amātī sint
PLUPERFECT			
amāvissem	amāvissēmus	amātus essem	amātī essēmus
amāvissēs	amāvissētis	amātus essēs	amātī essētis
amāvisset	amāvissent	amātus esset	amātī essent

Imperative Mood

Active Voice		Passive Voice	
Singular	*Plural*	*Singular*	*Plural*
PRESENT			
amā *(2nd pers)*	amāte *(2nd pers)*	amāre *(2nd pers)*	amāminī *(2nd pers)*
FUTURE			
amātō *(2nd pers)*	amātōte *(2nd pers)*	amātor *(2nd pers)*	———
amātō *(3rd pers)*	amantō *(3rd pers)*	amātor *(3rd pers)*	amantor *(3rd pers)*

Infinitive	**Participle**	**Infinitive**	**Participle**
PRESENT			
amāre	am·ans, -antis	amārī	———
PERFECT			
amāvisse	———	amātus esse	amātus
FUTURE			
amātūrus esse	amātūrus	amātum īrī	amandus *(gerundive)*

	Gerund	**Supine**
GEN	amandī	———
DAT	amandō	———
ACC	amandum	amātum
ABL	amandō	amātū

21

Second Conjugation Verbs

Principal parts: moneō — I advise
monēre — to advise
monuī — I advised, have advised
monitus — (having been) advised

Indicative Mood

Active Voice		*Passive Voice*	
Singular	*Plural*	*Singular*	*Plural*

PRESENT

moneō	monēmus	moneor	monēmur
monēs	monētis	monē·ris *or* -re	monēminī
monet	monent	monētur	monentur

IMPERFECT

monēbam	monēbāmus	monēbar	monēbāmur
monēbās	monēbātis	monēbā·ris *or* -re	monēbāminī
monēbat	monēbant	monēbātur	monēbantur

FUTURE

monēbō	monēbimus	monēbor	monēbimur
monēbis	monēbitis	monēbe·ris *or* -re	monēbiminī
monēbit	monēbunt	monēbitur	monēbuntur

PERFECT

monuī	monuimus	monitus sum	monitī sumus
monuistī	monuistis	monitus es	monitī estis
monuit	monuē·runt *or* -re	monitus est	monitī sunt

PLUPERFECT

monueram	monuerāmus	monitus eram	monitī erāmus
monuerās	monuerātis	monitus erās	monitī erātis
monuerat	monuerant	monitus erat	monitī erant

FUTURE PERFECT

monuerō	monuerimus	monitus erō	monitī erimus
monueris	monueritis	monitus eris	monitī eritis
monuerit	monuerint	monitus erit	monitī erunt

Subjunctive Mood

	Active Voice		Passive Voice	
	Singular	*Plural*	*Singular*	*Plural*

PRESENT

moneam	moneāmus	monear	moneāmur
o	moneātis	moneā·ris *or* -re	moneāminī
moneat	moneant	moneātur	moneantur

IMPERFECT

monērem	monērēmus	monērer	monērēmur
monērēs	monērētis	monērē·ris *or* -re	monērēminī
monēret	monērent	monērētur	monērentur

PERFECT

monuerim	monuerīmus	monitus sim	monitī sīmus
monuerīs	monuerītis	monitus sīs	monitī sītis
monuerit	monuerint	monitus sit	monitī sint

PLUPERFECT

monuissem	monuissēmus	monitus essem	monitī essēmus
monuissēs	monuissētis	monitus essēs	monitī essētis
monuisset	monuissent	monitus esset	monitī essent

Imperative Mood

	Active Voice		Passive Voice	
	Singular	*Plural*	*Singular*	*Plural*

PRESENT

monē *(2nd pers)*   monēte *(2nd pers)*   monēre *(2nd pers)*   monēminī *(2nd pers)*

FUTURE

monētō *(2nd pers)*   monētōte *(2nd pers)*   monētor *(2nd pers)*   ————

monētō *(3rd pers)*   monentō *(3rd pers)*   monētor *(3rd pers)*   monentor *(3rd pers)*

Infinitive	Participle	Infinitive	Participle
PRESENT			
monēre	mon·ens, -entis	monērī	————
PERFECT			
monuisse	————	monitus esse	monitus
FUTURE			
monitūrus esse	monitūrus	monitum īrī	monendus *(gerundive)*

	Gerund	Supine
GEN	monendī	————
DAT	monendō	————
ACC	monendum	monitum
ABL	monendō	monitū

23

Third Conjugation Verbs

Principal parts:	**regō**	I rule
	regĕre	to rule
	rexī	I ruled, have ruled
	rectus	(having been) ruled

Indicative Mood

Active Voice		*Passive Voice*	
Singular	*Plural*	*Singular*	*Plural*

PRESENT

regō	regimus	regor	regimur
regis	regitis	rege·ris *or* -re	regiminī
regit	regunt	regitur	reguntur

IMPERFECT

regēbam	regēbāmus	regēbar	regēbamur
regēbās	regēbātis	regēbā·ris *or* -re	regēbāminī
regēbat	regēbant	regēbātur	regēbantur

FUTURE

regam	regēmus	regar	regēmur
regēs	regētis	regēr·is *or* -re	regēminī
reget	regent	regētur	regentur

PERFECT

rexī	reximus	rectus sum	rectī sumus
rexistī	rexistis	rectus es	rectī estis
rexit	rexē·runt *or* -re	rectus est	rectī sunt

PLUPERFECT

rexeram	rexerāmus	rectus eram	rectī erāmus
rexerās	rexerātis	rectus erās	rectī erātis
rexerat	rexerant	rectus erat	rectī erant

FUTURE PERFECT

rexerō	rexerimus	rectus erō	rectī erimus
rexeris	rexeritis	rectus eris	rectī eritis
rexerit	rexerint	rectus erit	rectī erunt

Subjunctive Mood

Active Voice		Passive Voice	
Singular	*Plural*	*Singular*	*Plural*

PRESENT

regam	regāmus	regar	regāmur
regās	regātis	regā·ris *or* -re	regāminī
regat	regant	regātur	regantur

IMPERFECT ·

regerem	regerēmus	regerer	regerēmur
regerēs	regerētis	regerē·ris *or* -re	regerēminī
regeret	regerent	regerētur	regerentur

PERFECT

rexerim	rexerīmus	rectus sim	rectī sīmus
rexerīs	rexerītis	rectus sīs	rectī sītis
rexerit	rexerint	rectus sit	rectī sint

PLUPERFECT

rexissem	rexissēmus	rectus essem	rectī essēmus
rexissēs	rexissētis	rectus essēs	rectī essētis
rexisset	rexissent	rectus esset	rectī essent

Imperative Mood

Active Voice		Passive Voice	
Singular	*Plural*	*Singular*	*Plural*

PRESENT

rege *(2nd pers)*	regite *(2nd pers)*	regĕre *(2nd pers)*	regiminī *(2nd pers)*

FUTURE

regitō *(2nd pers)*	regitōte *(2nd pers)*	regitor *(2nd pers)*	————
regitō *(3rd pers)*	reguntō *(3rd pers)*	regitor *(3rd pers)*	reguntor *(3rd pers)*

Infinitive	Participle	Infinitive	Participle
PRESENT			
regĕre	reg·ens, -entis	regī	—
PERFECT			
rexisse	—	rectus esse	rectus
FUTURE			
rectūrus esse	rectūrus	rectum īrī	regendus *(gerundive)*

	Gerund	Supine	
GEN	regendī	————	
DAT	regendō	————	
ACC	regendum	rectum	
ABL	regendō	rectū	

Third Conjugation Verbs in -*io*

Principal parts:

capiō	I take	
capĕre	to take	
cēpī	I took, have taken	
captus	(having been) taken	

Indicative Mood

Active Voice		*Passive Voice*	
Singular	*Plural*	*Singular*	*Plural*

PRESENT

capiō	capimus	capior	capimur
capis	capitis	cape·ris *or* -re	capiminī
capit	capiunt	capitur	capiuntur

IMPERFECT

capiēbam	capiēbāmus	capiēbar	capiēbāmur
capiēbās	capiēbātis	capiēbā·ris *or* -re	capiēbāminī
capiēbat	capiēbant	capiēbātur	capiēbāntur

FUTURE

capiam	capiēmus	capiar	capiēmur
capiēs	capiētis	capiē·ris *or* -re	capiēminī
capiet	capient	capiētur	capientur

PERFECT

cēpī	cēpimus	captus sum	captī sumus
cēpistī	cēpistis	captus es	captī estis
cēpit	cēpē·runt *or* -re	captus est	captī sunt

PLUPERFECT

cēperam	cēperāmus	captus eram	captī erāmus
cēperās	cēperātis	captus erās	captī erātis
cēperat	cēperant	captus erat	captī erant

FUTURE PERFECT

cēperō	cēperimus	captus erō	captī erimus
cēperis	cēperitis	captus eris	captī eritis
cēperit	cēperint	captus erit	captī erunt

Subjunctive Mood

Active Voice		Passive Voice	
Singular	*Plural*	*Singular*	*Plural*

PRESENT

capiam	capiāmus	capiar	capiāmur
capiās	capiātis	capiā·ris *or* -re	capiāminī
capiat	capiant	capiātur	capiantur

IMPERFECT

caperem	caperēmus	caperer	caperēmur
caperēs	caperētis	caperē·ris *or* -re	caperēminī
caperet	caperent	caperētur	caperentur

PERFECT

cēperim	cēperīmus	captus sim	captī sīmus
cēperīs	cēperītis	captus sīs	captī sītis
cēperit	cēperint	captus sit	captī sint

PLUPERFECT

cēpissem	cēpissēmus	captus essem	captī essēmus
cēpissēs	cēpissētis	captus essēs	captī essētis
cēpisset	cēpissent	captus esset	captī essent

Imperative Mood

Active Voice		Passive Voice	
Singular	*Plural*	*Singular*	*Plural*

PRESENT

cape *(2nd pers)*·	capite *(2nd pers)*	capĕre *(2nd pers)*	capiminī *(2nd pers)*

FUTURE

capitō *(2nd pers)*	capitōte *(2nd pers)*	capitor *(2nd pers)*	——
capitō *(3rd pers)*	capiuntō *(3rd pers)*	capitor *(3rd pers)*	capiuntor *(3rd pers)*

Infinitive	Participle	Infinitive	Participle
PRESENT			
capĕre	cap·iens, -entis	capī	——
PERFECT			
cēpisse	——	captus esse	captus
FUTURE			
captūrus esse	captūrus	captum īrī	capiendus *(gerundive)*

	Gerund	Supine	
GEN	capiendī	——	
DAT	capiendō	——	
ACC	capiendum	captum	
ABL	capiendō	captū	

27

Fourth Conjugation Verbs

Principal parts: audiō   I hear
audīre   to hear
audīvī   I heard, have heard
audītus   (having been) heard

Indicative Mood

Active Voice		*Passive Voice*	
Singular	*Plural*	*Singular*	*Plural*

PRESENT

audiō	audīmus	audior	audīmur
audīs	audītis	audī·ris *or* -re	audīminī
audit	audiunt	audītur	audiuntur

IMPERFECT

audiēbam	audiēbāmus	audiēbar	audiēbāmur
audiēbās	audiēbātis	audiēbā·ris *or* -re	audiēbāminī
audiēbat	audiēbant	audiēbātur	audiēbantur

FUTURE

audiam	audiēmus	audiar	audiēmur
audiēs	audiētis	audiē·ris *or* -re	audiēminī
audiet	audient	audiētur	audientur

PERFECT

audīvī	audīvimus	audītus sum	audītī sumus
audīvistī	audīvistis	audītus es	audītī estis
audīvit	audīvēr·unt *or* -re	audītus est	audītī sunt

PLUPERFECT

audīveram	audīverāmus	audītus eram	audītī erāmus
audīverās	audīverātis	audītus erās	audītī erātis
audīverat	audīverant	audītus erat	audītī erant

FUTURE PERFECT

audīverō	audīverimus	audītus erō	audītī erimus
audīveris	audīveritis	audītus eris	audītī eritis
audīverit	audīverint	audītus erit	audītī erunt

Subjunctive Mood

Active Voice		Passive Voice	
Singular	*Plural*	*Singular*	*Plural*

PRESENT

audiam	audiāmus	audiar	audiāmur
audiās	audiātis	audiā·ris *or* -re	audiāminī
audiat	audiant	audiatur	audiantur

IMPERFECT

audīrem	audīrēmus	audīrer	audīrēmur
audīrēs	audīrētis	audīrē·ris *or* -re	audīrēminī
audīret	audīrent	audīrētur	audīrentur

PERFECT

audīverim	audīverīmus	audītus sim	audītī sīmus
audīverīs	audīverītis	audītus sīs	audītī sītis
audīverit	audīverint	audītus sit	audītī sint

PLUPERFECT

audīvissem	audīvissēmus	audītus essem	audītī essēmus
audīvissēs	audīvissētis	audītus essēs	audītī essētis
audīvisset	audīvissent	audītus esset	audītī essent

Imperative Mood

Active Voice		Passive Voice	
Singular	*Plural*	*Singular*	*Plural*

PRESENT

audī *(2nd pers)*	audīte *(2nd pers)*	audīre *(2nd pers)*	audīminī *(2nd pers)*

FUTURE

audītō *(2nd pers)*	audītōte *(2nd pers)*	audītor *(2nd pers)*	————
audītō *(3rd pers)*	audiuntō *(3rd pers)*	audītor *(3rd pers)*	audiuntor *(3rd pers)*

Infinitive	Participle	Infinitive	Participle
PRESENT			
audīre	audi·ens, -entis	audīrī	————
PERFECT			
audīvisse	————	audītus esse	audītus
FUTURE			
audītūrus esse	audītūrus	audītum īrī	audiendus *(gerundive)*

	Gerund	**Supine**
GEN	audiendī	————
DAT	audiendō	————
ACC	audiendum	audītum
ABL	audiendō	audītū

Conjugation of *sum*

Principal parts: **sum**   I am
                   esse   to be
                   fuī   I was, have been
                   futūrus   about to be

Indicative Mood

Singular	*Plural*
PRESENT	
sum	sumus
es	estis
est	sunt
IMPERFECT	
eram	erāmus
erās	erātis
erat	erant
FUTURE	
erō	erimus
eris	eritis
erit	erunt
PERFECT	
fuī	fuimus
fuistī	fuistis
fuit	fuē·runt *or* -re
PLUPERFECT	
fueram	fuerāmus
fuerās	fuerātis
fuerat	fuerant
FUTURE PERFECT	
fuerō	fuerimus
fueris	fueritis
fuerit	fuerint

Subjunctive Mood

Singular	*Plural*
PRESENT	
sim	sīmus
sīs	sītis
sit	sint
IMPERFECT	
essem	essēmus
essēs	essētis
esset	essent
PERFECT	
fuerim	fuerīmus
fuerīs	fuerītis
fuerit	fuerint
PLUPERFECT	
fuissem	fuissēmus
fuissēs	fuissētis
fuisset	fuissent

Imperative Mood

Singular	*Plural*
PRESENT	
es *(2nd pers)*	este *(2nd pers)*
FUTURE	
estō *(2nd pers)*	estōte *(2nd pers)*
estō *(3rd pers)*	suntō *(3rd pers)*

Infinitive	**Participle**
PRESENT	
esse	———
PERFECT	
fuisse	———
FUTURE	
futūrus esse	futūrus

Conjugation of *volo, nolo, malo*

Principal parts:

volō I wish	**velle** to wish	**voluī** I wished
nōlō I do not wish	**nolle** to be unwilling	**nōluī** I did not wish
mālō I prefer	**malle** to prefer	**māluī** I preferred, have preferred

Indicative Mood

PRESENT	volō	nōlō	mālō
	vīs	nōn vīs	māvīs
	vult	nōn vult	māvult
	volumus	nōlumus	mālumus
	vultis	nōn vultis	māvultis
	volunt	nōlunt	mālunt
IMPERFECT	volēbam	nōlēbam	mālēbam
FUTURE	volam	nōlam	mālam
PERFECT	voluī	nōluī	māluī
PLUPERFECT	volueram	nōlueram	mālueram
FUTURE PERFECT	voluerō	nōluerō	māluerō

Subjunctive Mood

PRESENT	velim	nōlim	mālim
	velīs	nōlīs	mālīs
	velit	nōlit	mālit
	velīmus	nōlīmus	mālīmus
	velītis	nōlītis	mālitis
	velint	nōlint	mālint
IMPERFECT	vellem	nollem	mallem
PERFECT	voluerim	nōluerim	māluerim
PLUPERFECT	voluissem	nōluissem	māluissem

Imperative Mood

PRESENT nōlī; nōlīte *(2nd pers)*

FUTURE nōlītō; nōlītōte *(2md pers)*
nōlītō; nōluntō *(3rd pers)*

Infinitive

PRESENT	velle	nolle	malle
PERFECT	voluisse	nōluisse	māluisse

Participle

PRESENT	vol·ens, -entis	nōl·ens, -entis	————

31

Conjugation of *eo*

Principal parts: eō — I go
 īre — to go
īvī *or* iī — I went
itum (est) — people went

Indicative Mood

	Singular	*Plural*
PRESENT	eō	īmus
	īs	ītis
	it	eunt
IMPERFECT	ībam	ībāmus
FUTURE	ībō	ībimus
PERFECT	īvī *or* iī	īvimus *or* iimus
PLUPERFECT	īveram *or* ieram	īverāmus *or* ierāmus
FUTURE PERFECT	īverō *or* ierō	īverimus *or* ierimus

Subjunctive Mood

PRESENT	eam	eāmus
IMPERFECT	īrem	īrēmus
PERFECT	īverim *or* ierim	īverīmus *or* ierīmus
PLUPERFECT	īvissem *or* iissem	īvissēmus *or* iissēmus

Imperative Mood

PRESENT	ī *(2nd pers)*	īte *(2nd pers)*
FUTURE	ītō *(2nd pers)*	ītōte *(2nd pers)*
	ītō *(3rd pers)*	euntō *(3rd pers)*

	Infinitive	**Participle**
PRESENT	īre	iens, euntis
PERFECT	īvisse *or* isse	————
FUTURE	itūrus esse	itūrus
		eundum *(gerundive)*

	Gerund	**Supine**
GEN	eundī	————
DAT	eundō	————
ACC	eundum	itum
ABL	eundō	itū

Conjugation of *fio*

Principal parts: **fīō** I am made, become
fierī to be made, become
factus sum I was made, became

Indicative Mood

	Singular	Plural
PRESENT	fīō	fīmus
	fīs	fītis
	fit	fiunt
IMPERFECT	fīēbam	fīēbāmus
FUTURE	fīam	fīēmus
PERFECT	factus sum	factī sumus
PLUPERFECT	factus eram	factī erāmus
FUTURE PERFECT	factus erō	factī erimus

Subjunctive Mood

PRESENT	fīam	fiāmus
IMPERFECT	fierem	fierēmus
PERFECT	factus sim	factī sīmus
PLUPERFECT	factus essem	factī essēmus

Imperative Mood

Singular	Plural
fī	fīte

Infinitive   Participle

	Infinitive	Participle
PRESENT	fierī	———
PERFECT	factus esse	factus
FUTURE	factum īrī	faciendus (*gerundive*)

Roman Numerals

	Cardinal	*Ordinal*	
1	ūnus, ūna, ūnum	prīmus	I
2	duo, duae, duo	secundus	II
3	trēs, tria	tertius	III
4	quattuor	quartus	IV
5	quinque	quintus	V
6	sex	sextus	VI
7	septem	septimus	VII
8	octō	octāvus	VIII
9	novem	nōnus	IX
10	decem	decimus	X
11	undecim	undecimus	XI
12	duodecim	duodecimus	XII
13	tredecim	tertius decimus	XIII
14	quattuordecim	quartus decimus	XIV
15	quindecim	quintus decimus	XV
16	sēdecim	sextus decimus	XVI
17	septendecim	septimus decimus	XVII
18	duodēvīgintī	duodēvīcēsimus	XVIII
19	ūndēvīgintī	ūndēvīcēsimus	XIX
20	vīgintī	vīcēsimus	XX
21	vīgintī ūnus	vīcēsimus prīmus	XXI
	ūnus et vīgintī		
22	vīgintī duo	vīcēsimus secundus	XXII
	duo et vīgintī		
30	trīgintā	trīcēsimus	XXX
40	quadrāgintā	quadrāgēsimus	XL
50	quinquāgintā	quinquāgēsimus	L
60	sexāgintā	sexāgēsimus	LX
70	septuāgintā	septuāgēsimus	LXX
80	octōgintā	octōgēsimus	LXXX
90	nōnāgintā	nōnāgēsimus	XC
100	centum	centēsimus	C
101	centum ūnus	centēsimus prīmus	CI
	centum et ūnus		
200	ducentī, -ae, -a	ducentēsimus	CC
300	trecentī, -ae, -a	trecentēsimus	CCC
400	quadringentī, -ae, -a	quadringentēsimus	CCCC
500	quingentī, -ae, -a	quingentēsimus	D
600	sescentī, -ae, -a	sescentēsimus	DC
700	septingentī, -ae, -a	septingentēsimus	DCC
800	octingentī, -ae, -a	octingentēsimus	DCCC
900	nongentī, -ae, -a	nongentēsimus	DCCCC
1,000	mille	millēsimus	M
2,000	duo mīlia	bis millēsimus	MM
10,000	decem mīlia	deciēs millēsimus	CCIↃ
100,000	centum mīlia	centiēs millēsimus	CCCIↃↃ

NOTES (a) -ensimus and -iens are often written in the numerals instead of -ēsimus and -iēs.
(b) The declension of ūnus, ūna, ūnum is indicated under "Nine Irregular Adjectives," p. 17.

Declension of duo and tres

	masc	*fem*	*neut*			
NOM	duo	duae	duo	trēs	trēs	tria
GEN	duōrum	duārum	duōrum	trium	trium	trium
DAT	duōbus	duābus	duōbus	tribus	tribus	tribus
ACC	duōs, duo	duās	duo	trēs (trīs)	trēs (trīs)	tria
ABL	duōbus	duōbus	duōbus	tribus	tribus	tribus

A

A. *abbr* **Aulus** *(Roman first name, praenomen); (leg)* **Absolvo** I acquit; *(pol)* **Antiquo** I vote "no" *(on the bill)* **-a** *masc suf* indicating occupation or profession, *e.g.:* **agricola** one who tills a field, farmer; **scriba** one who writes, scribe **-ā-** *advl suf* forms adverbs which are also used as prepositions, *e.g.,* **suprā** above

ā *or* **āh** *interj* ah!

ā *or* **ab** *prep (w. abl)* **1** *(of agency)* by, at the hands of: **a Caesare in servitutem redactus** reduced to slavery by Caesar; **2** *(of time)* since, from, after: **a puero** since childhood; **a somno** after a sleep; **3** *(of space)* from, away from: **a castris perfuga** a deserter from the camp; **4** *(named)* after: **oppidum a Latini filiā appellatum** a town named after the daughter of Latinus; **5** on: **a dextro latere** on the right side; **6** in: **a tergo** in the rear; **ab una parte corporis** in one part of the body; **7** *(of cause, motive)* out of, from: **ab singulari amore** out of unparalleled love; **8** *(designating an office):* **ab epistulis** secretary; **a rationibus** accountant; **9** *(in respect to):* **dolere ab stomacho** to have a stomachache (to ache in respect to the stomach); **10** on the side of: **ab senatu stare** to side with the Senate (to stand on the side of the Senate)

ā- *or* **ab- abs-** *pref (before initial* **f** *becomes* **au-:** **auferre** to take away; *before* **p** *becomes* **as-:** **asportare** to take away, carry off) *with the sense of:* **1** from, away, away from: **abducere** to lead away; **2** off: **abscidere** to cut off; **3** at a distance: **abesse** to be at a distance, be absent; **4** completely, thoroughly: **abuti** to use up, exhaust by using; **5** the absence of what the noun implies: **amens** demented; **6** a more remote degree of relationship: **abnepos** great-great-grandson

abactus *pp of* **abigo**

abac·us -ī *m* cupboard; game board; abacus *(calculator);* panel; tray

abaliēn·ō -āre -āvī -ātus *tr* to alienate, estrange; to sell; to separate; **alicujus animum a se abalienare** to turn s.o. else's attention away from oneself

Abantiad·ēs -ae *m* descendant of Abas

Ab·ās -antis *m* king of Argos, father of Acrisius, and grandfather of Perseus

abav·us -ī *m* great-great-grandfather

Abdēr·a -ōrum *npl or* **Abdēr·a -ae** *f* town in S. Thrace, notorious for the alleged stupidity of its people

abdicāti·ō -ōnis *f* abdication, renunciation, resignation

abdĭc·ō -āre -āvī -ātus *tr* to abdicate, renounce, resign; to disinherit **‖** *refl* **se magistratu abdicare** to resign from office

ab·dīcō -dīcĕre -dixī -dictus *tr (in augury)* to disapprove of, forbid

abditē *adv* secretly, privately

abdit·us -a -um *adj* hidden, secret; secluded; abstruse; **abditus a conspectu** hidden from view

ab·dō -dĕre -didī -ditus *tr* to hide; to remove, withdraw; to banish; to plunge *(e.g., a sword)*

abdōm·en -inis *n* abdomen, belly; *(fig)* gluttony, greed

ab·dūcō -dūcĕre -duxī -ductus *tr* to lead away, take away; to withdraw *(troops);* to seduce; to alienate; *(w. ab)* to distinguish from; **animum abducere** to distract attention

ab·eō -īre -iī -itum *intr* to go away, depart; to disappear: **ab oculis** *(or* **e conspectu)** **abire** to disappear from sight; to pass away, die; *(of time)* to pass, elapse; to change, be changed; to retire; **abi in malam rem!** *(sl)* go to hell!

abequit·ō -āre -āvī *intr* to ride off

aberrāti·ō -ōnis *f* wandering; escape, relief

aberr·ō -āre -āvī -ātum *intr* to wander, go astray; to get lost; to make a mistake, go wrong; to do wrong; to digress; *(of a stream)* to overflow; *(w. ab)* **1** to disagree with; **2** to get one's mind off *(e.g., sadness);* **3** to deviate from; **4** to differ from

abesse *inf of* **absum**

abhinc *adv (w. acc or abl of time)* ago; **abhinc annos centum** a hundred years ago

abhorr·eō -ēre -uī *intr* to shrink back; *(w. ab)* **1** to be averse to; **2** to be inconsistent with; **3** to differ from; **4** to be free from

abiegn·us -a -um *adj* (**-gne·us** *or* **-gine·us** *or* **-gni·us**) fir

abi·es -etis *f* fir (tree); ship; spear; writing tablet

ab·igo -igĕre -ēgī -actus *tr* to drive away, get rid of; to banish, expel

abit·us -ūs *m* departure; outlet; end

abjectē *adv* negligently; unworthily

abject·us -a -um *adj* dejected, downhearted; undistinguished; unimportant; despicable; groveling

ab·jiciō -jicĕre -jēcī -jectus *tr* (**abic-**) to throw away, throw down; to push away; to understate; to belittle, slight; to give up; to humble, debase; to cow, reduce to despair; to sell cheaply, sacrifice; to express carelessly *or* perfunctorily; to discard; to cease to wear, take off; to expose

(a child to die); to leave (a corpse) unburied; to turn down *(an offer);* to give up *(practices, intentions, attitudes);* **animam** *(or* **vitam) abjicere** to give up (this) life; **arma abjicere** to throw down one's arms **‖** *refl* to throw oneself down, fall down; **se ad pedes alicujus abjicere** to throw oneself down at s.o.'s feet; **se in herba abjicere** to fall down on the grass
abjūdic·ō -āre -āvī -ātus *tr* to take away *(by judicial decree);* to reject
abjun·gō -gĕre -xī -ctus *tr* to unyoke; to detach **‖** *refl (w.* **ab)** to detach oneself from, give up *(an activity);* **se ab hoc refractariolo dicendi genere abjungere** to depart from this quibbling style of speaking
abjūr·ō -āre -āvī -ātus *tr* to deny under oath
ablātīv·us -a -um *adj & m* ablative
ablāt·us -a -um *pp of* **aufero**
ablēgāti·ō -ōnis *f* sending off; banishment
ablēg·ō -āre -āvī -ātus *tr* to send away; to remove, banish; to dismiss, get rid of
abligū(r)r·iō -īre -īvī *or* **-iī** *tr* to eat up; *(coll)* to gobble up, waste, squander
abloc·ō -āre -āvī -ātus *tr* to lease, rent out
ab·lūdō -lūdĕre *intr* to be unlike; *(w.* **ab)** to differ from, fall short of
ab·luō -luĕre -luī -lūtus *tr* to wash away, cleanse, remove; *(poet)* to bathe, refresh
abneg·ō -āre -āvī -ātus *tr* to refuse, turn down
abnep·ōs -ōtis *m* great-great-grandson
abnept·is -is *f* great-great-granddaughter
abnoct·ō -āre *intr* to spend the night
abnorm·is -is -e *adj* irregular, unorthodox
ab·nuō -nuĕre -nuī *tr* to refuse *(to do s.th.);* to deny *(an assertion, allegation, one's guilt);* to repudiate responsibility for *(a crime);* to reject, refuse *(an offer);* to refuse to grant *(e.g., an interview);* to refuse to submit to *(authority);* to forbid, rule out *(e.g., hope);* to decline *(battle);* to refuse to perform *(a duty, task);* to disown *(children); (w.* **acc &** *inf)* to forbid *(the occurrence of an event);* **non abnuere** to admit, not to deny **‖** *intr* to say "no"; *(w.* **de** + *abl)* to say "no" to; **de societate haud abnuerunt barbari** the barbarians did not say "no" to (the idea of) an alliance
abnūt·ō -āre *intr* to keep saying "no" *(with a nod)*
abol·eō -ēre -ēvī -itus *tr* to abolish, efface; to destroy, obliterate; to banish from the mind, efface the memory of; to allow *(a practice)* to lapse, drop; to prohibit, ban; to put an end to *(an institution);* to rescind *(a law);* **abolere memoriam** *(w. gen)* to blot out the memory of *(s.th. unpleasant);* **abolere reum** *(leg)* to give up prosecuting a defendant

abol·escō -escĕre -ēvī *intr* to decay, vanish, die out; *(of things)* to be forgotten; *(of a memory)* to fade
aboliti·ō -ōnis *f* abolition, rescinding *(of a law, sentence);* amnesty
aboll·a -ae *f* cloak; *(fig)* wearer of a cloak
abōminand·us -a -um *adj* ill-omened; detestable, abominable
abōmin·or -ārī -ātus sum *tr* to loathe, detest; to seek to avert *(e.g., a bad omen, destruction)* by prayer
Aborīgin·ēs -um *mpl* aborigines, original inhabitants, natives
ab·orior -orīrī -ortus sum *intr* to miscarry; to fail; *(of stars, etc.)* to set
aborti·ō -ōnis *f* miscarriage, abortion
abortīv·us -a -um *adj* prematurely born **‖** *n* drug causing abortion
abort·us -ūs *m* miscarriage; **abortum facere** to have *or* to cause a miscarriage
ab·rādō -rādĕre -rāsī -rāsus *tr* to scrape off, shave; *(fig)* to squeeze out, rob
ab·ripiō -ripĕre -ripuī -reptus *tr* to take away by force, kidnap; to seize *(as booty);* to squander; *(of the wind)* to blow, drive *(off course);* to rescue *(from a bad situation);* **abripere mordicus** to bite off **‖** *refl* to hurry away, get away
ab·rōdō -rōdĕre -rōsī -rōsus *tr* to gnaw off
abrogāti·ō -ōnis *f* repeal
abrog·ō -āre -āvī -ātus *tr* to repeal, annul
abroton·um -ī *n* **(hab-)** southernwood *(aromatic medicinal plant)*
ab·rumpō -rumpĕre -rūpī -ruptus *tr* to break off; to tear, sever; to burst apart *(e.g., the clouds);* to rupture *(a body part);* to put an end to, cut short **‖** *refl (w. abl)* to dissociate oneself from
abruptē *adv* abruptly; rashly
abrupti·ō -ōnis *f* breaking off *(of relations);* divorce
abrupt·us -a -um *pp of* **abrumpo ‖** *adj* abrupt, steep **‖** *n* precipice
abs *prep (w. abl, confined almost exclusively to the combination* **abs te)** by, from
abs- *pref see* **ā-, ab-, abs-**
abs·cēdō -cēdĕre -cessī -cessum *intr* **(aps-)** to go away, depart; to vanish; to retire *(from work);* to desist; *(w. dat)* to cease to support; *(of feelings, illness)* to pass; *(of heavenly bodies)* to move farther away; *(mil)* to retreat; **non abscedere a corpore** not to leave the body *(of a deceased person)*
abscessi·ō -ōnis *f* diminution, loss
abscess·us -ūs *m* departure; absence; remoteness
abs·cīdō -cīdĕre -cīdī -cīsus *tr* **(aps-)** to cut off, chop off; to cut short; to destroy *(hope);* to banish *(from the mind)*
ab·scindō -scindĕre -scĭdī -scissus *tr* to tear off, break off; to renounce; to divide

abscīs·us -a -um *pp of* **abscīdo** ‖ *adj* steep, precipitous; concise; abrupt

absconditē *adv* secretly; obscurely; profoundly

abscondit·us -a -um *adj* concealed, secret; abstruse, profound

abscon·dō -děre -dī *or* **-didī -ditus** *tr* to hide; to keep secret, conceal; to lose sight of, leave behind; to shroud (in darkness); *(w.* **in** + *acc)* to plunge *(weapon)* into ‖ *refl & pass* to hide

abs·ens -entis *pres p of* **absum** ‖ *adj* absent; in spite of being absent; non-existent; **praesens absens** whether present or absent

absenti·a -ae *f* (aps-) absence; non-appearance in court

absil·iō -īre -(i)ī *intr* to jump away

absimil·is -is -e *adj (w.* dat*)* unlike

absinth·ium -(i)ī *n* wormwood *(plant yielding bitter extract, used in flavoring wine)*

abs·is -idis *f* (aps-) vault, arch; orbit *(of a star)*

ab·sistō -sistěre -stitī *intr* to stand back, retire, withdraw, depart; to cease

absolūtē *adv* absolutely; perfectly

absolūti·ō -ōnis *f* exhaustiveness, completeness; perfection; acquittal; release *(from an obligation)*

absolūtōri·us -a -um *adj* of acquittal, granting acquittal

absolūt·us -a -um *adj* perfect, complete, unqualified

absol·vō -věre -vī -ūtus *tr* (aps-) to release, set free; to detach; to acquit; to get *(s.o.)* acquitted; *(of single juror)* to vote for the acquittal of; to complete, finish *(task, transaction);* to put the finishing touches to *(an operation);* to pay off, discharge *(an account, debt); (w.* gen *or* abl *of the charge)* to prove *(s.o.)* innocent of; **verbo** *(or* **paucis** *or* **breviter) absolvere** to sum up, put in a nutshell

abson·us -a -um *adj* (aps-) discordant, harsh *(sound);* unpleasant, jarring; *(w.* dat *or* abl*)* inconsistent with

absor·beō -bēre -buī *(or* **-psī) -ptus** *tr* (aps-) to swallow, devour; to absorb; to engross; to engulf

absque *prep* (aps-) *(w.* abl*)* without, apart from, but for: **absque me foret** had it not been for me; **absque unā hāc foret** but for this one thing

abstēmi·us -a -um *adj* abstemious, temperate, sober

abster·geō -gēre -sī -sus *or* **absterg·ō -ěre** *tr* (aps-) to wipe off, wipe dry; to expel, banish; **fletum abstergere** to wipe away tears

absterr·eō -ēre -uī -itus *tr* (aps-) to scare away; to deter

abstin·ens -entis *adj* temperate, fore-bearing; chaste; *(w.* gen *or* abl*)* showing restraint in respect to, not greedy for

abstinenter *adv* with restraint

abstinenti·a -ae *f* restraint, self-control; integrity; *(w.* gen *or* abl*)* **1** restraint in respect to; **2** abstinence from

abs·tineō -tinēre -tinuī -tentus *tr* (aps-) to withold, keep away, hold back; to restrain ‖ *refl (w.* abl *or* ab*)* to refrain from, keep oneself from ‖ *intr* to abstain, refrain; *(w.* gen, abl *or w.* ab, *w.* inf, *w.* quin *or* quominus*)* to refrain from

abst·ō -āre *intr* (aps-) to stand at a distance, stand aloof

abstra·hō -hěre -xī -ctus *tr* (aps-) to pull away, draw away, remove; to detach; to split; to deduct, subtract; to distract, divert; to exclude, except

abstrū·dō -děre -sī -sus *tr* (aps-) to push away; to conceal, suppress ‖ *pass* to be concealed *(by intervening object)*

abstrūs·us -a -um *pp of* **abstrudo** (aps-) ‖ *adj* hidden, concealed, secret; profound, abstruse; reserved *(person);* secluded

abstulī *perf of* **aufero**

absum abesse āfuī āfutūrus *intr* to be away, be absent; be distant; to be missing; to be unsuitable, be inappropriate; to be wanting; *(w.* abl *or* ab*)* to be removed from, keep aloof from, be disinclined to; *(w.* ab*)* **1** to be different from; **2** to be inconsistent with; **3** to be free from; **4** to be unsuitable for, be unfit for; *(w.* dat*)* to be of no help to; **ab hoc consilio abesse** to have no part in this strategy; **a culpa abesse** to be free of guilt; **a periculis abesse** to avoid dangers; **legatos haud procul afuit quin violarent** they came close to outraging the ambassadors; **non multum aberat ab eo quin** he was not far from, he was almost on the point of; **tantum aberat a bello, ut** he was so averse to war, that

absūm·ō -ěre -psī -ptus *tr* to take away, diminish; to consume, use up, waste; to exhaust; to destroy; to spend *(time);* to cause the death of, carry off ‖ *pass (w.* **in** + *acc)* to disappear into

absurdē *adv* (aps-) out of tune; absurdly

absurd·us -a -um *adj* (aps-) out of tune; absurd, illogical, senseless, silly

Absyrt·us -ī *m* brother of Medea and son of Aeëtes, the king of Colchis, brother of Medea

abund·ans -antis *adj* abundant, overflowing; affluent; more than enough; *(of rivers)* in flood; *(w.* gen *or* abl*)* abounding in, rich in

abundanter *adv* abundantly; profusely

abundanti·a -ae *f* abundance; affluence; lavishness; profusion

abundē *adv* abundantly, amply

abūsi·ō -ōnis *f* incorrect use *(of words)*
abusque *prep (w. abl)* all the way from
ab·ūtor -ūtī -ūsus sum *intr (w. abl)* **1** to use up; **2** to misuse, abuse
Abȳd·os *or* **Abȳd·us -ī** *f* town on the Hellespont
ac *conj (usually before consonants)* and, and also, and moreover; *(connecting a more emphatic sentence element)* and in particular, and what is more; *(connecting a sentence element which strengthens or corrects the first element)* and in fact; *(in comparisons)* than, as
Acadēmi·a -ae *f* Academy *(where Plato taught);* Platonic philosophy; Cicero's villa near Puteoli
Acadēmic·us -a -um *adj* Academic ‖ *m* Academic philosopher ‖ *npl* Cicero's treatise on Academic philosophy
acalanth·is -idis *f* goldfinch *(bird)*
acanth·us *or* **acanth·os -ī** *m (bot)* acanthus *(plant on whose leaves the architectural ornament of capitals of Corinthian columns was patterned)*
Acarnāni·a -ae *f* district in N.W. Greece
Acast·us -ī *m* son of Pelias
ac·cēdō -cēdĕre -cessī -cessum *tr* **(adc-)** to come up to, approach ‖ *intr* to approach; *(w.* ad**)** to come up to, approach; *(w. dat or* ad**) 1** to agree with, approve of; **2** to be like, resemble; *(w.* ad *or* in + *acc)* to enter upon, undertake; **accedit ut** *or* **quod** there is the additional fact that
acceler·ō -āre -āvī -ātus *tr* to speed, quicken ‖ *intr* to hurry
accen·dō -dĕre -dī -sus *tr* to light *(a fire, lamp);* to set on fire; to arouse *(emotions);* to aggravate *(conditions);* to work up, incite *(people);* to raise *(prices);* to light up, brighten; **accensa lumina** lamp-lighting time, dusk
accens·eō -ēre -uī -us *tr* to regard; to assign *(as attendant)*
accens·us -a -um *pp of* **accendo** ‖ *adj* on fire
accens·us -ī *m* attendant, orderly ‖ *mpl* rear-echelon troops
accent·us -ūs *m* accent, intonation
accepti·ō -ōnis *f* accepting, receiving
accept·ō -āre -āvī -ātus *tr* to accept, receive *(regularly);* to be given *(a name)*
accept·or -ōris *m* recipient; approver
acceptr·ix -īcis *f* recipient *(female)*
accept·us -a -um *pp of* **accipio** ‖ *adj* welcome, pleasing, acceptable ‖ *n* receipt; credit side *(in account books);* **acceptum facere** *(or* **ferre**) to treat *(a debt)* as paid off; **acceptum fieri** *(w. dat)* to be set down to the credit of; **acceptum referre** *(w. dat)* to set down to the credit side, have *(him, her, etc.)* to thank for
accersō *or* **arcess·ō -ĕre -īvī** *or* **-iī -ītus** *tr* to call, summon; to bring, procure

accessi·ō -ōnis *f* approach; addition, increase; additional payment, bonus; intensification; appendage, accessory; addition to one's resources; **accessionem facere** to make progress, gain ground; **accessio temporis** *(leg)* extra time *(added to possessorship)*
access·us -ūs *m* act of approaching, approach; attack; rising *(of heavenly bodies);* blowing *(of the wind);* going at, tackling *(a task);* right to approach, access; entry, way in, passage; **accessus et recessus aestuum** flow and ebb of the tide
Accher·uns -untis *mf* lower world
ac·cī·dō -cīdĕre -cīdī -cīsus *tr* to cut down; to impair, weaken; to decimate
ac·cīdō -cīdĕre -cīdī *intr* to happen, occur, come to pass; *(w. dat of person affected)* to happen to, befall; *(w. adv)* to turn out; *(w. abl of cause)* to happen as the result of; *(w. dat)* to strike *(s.o. as), e.g.:* **hoc tibi insolentia praeter opinionem accidebat** this struck you as exceptional insolence; *(w.* in + *acc)* **1** to fall upon; **2** to be applicable to; *(w. dat or* ad**)** to fall at *(e.g., s.o.'s feet);* **aures** *(or* **auribus** *or* ad **aures) accidere** *(w. gen)* to reach the ears of; **accidit ut** *(w. subj or* **quod** *w. indic)* it happens that; **si quid mihi acciderit** if anything should happen to me
accin·gō -gĕre -xī -ctus *tr* to gird; to gird up, tuck up *(one's clothing)* ‖ *refl & pass (w. abl)* to arm oneself with, equip oneself with; **accingi** *or* **se accingere** *(w. dat or* ad *or* in + *acc)* to prepare oneself for, to enter upon, to undertake; **ferro accingi** to put on the sword
ac·ciō -cīre -cīvī -cītus *tr* to call, send for, invite; **mortem sibi accire** to commit suicide
ac·cipiō -cipĕre -cēpī -ceptus *tr* to take, receive, accept; to welcome, entertain; to hear, learn, understand; to interpret, explain; to undertake *(a task);* to assume *(a responsibility);* to take *(medicine, food);* to incur *(a wound, loss);* to accept *(a post, office);* to borrow *(money);* to approve of, agree to; to have room for, accommodate; to welcome, entertain; to accept as valid, admit; to learn, hear, be told of; to infer, conclude; *(geol)* to let in *(the sea);* **accipere dareque** to exchange; **actionem accipere** *(leg)* to be granted a hearing; **auribus accipere** to hear, learn by listening; **initium** *(or* **originem** *or* **ortum) accipere** to begin; **finem accipere** to come to an end
accipi·ter -tris *m* hawk
accīs·us -a -um *pp of* **accīdō** ‖ *adj* impaired, ruined; troubled, disordered
accīt·us -ūs *m* summons, call

Acc·ius -(i)ī *m* Roman tragic poet *(170– 85? B.C.)*
acclāmāti·ō -ōnis *f* **(adc-)** shout *(of approval or disapproval)*
acclām·ō -āre -āvī -ātus *tr* to hail, acclaim ‖ *intr* to shout *(in approval); (w. dat)* to shout at
acclār·ō -āre -āvī *tr* **(adc-)** to clarify
acclīnāt·us -a -um *adj* prostrate; sloping; *(w. dat)* **1** leaning on; **2** inclined toward, disposed to
acclīn·ō -āre -āvī -ātus *tr* **(adc-)** *(w. dat or* **in** + *acc)* to lean *or* rest *(s.th.)* against ‖ *refl (w.* **ad***) (fig)* to be inclined toward
acclīv·is -is -e *adj* **(adc-)** sloping upwards, uphill, steep
acclīvit·ās -ātis *f* **(adc-)** slope, ascent
accol·a -ae *m* **(adc-)** neighbor
ac·colō -colěre -coluī -cultus *tr* **(adc-)** to dwell near
accommodātē *adv* **(adc-)** suitably, fittingly; comfortably
accommodāti·ō -ōnis *f* **(adc-)** adjustment; compliance, accommodation
accommodāt·us -a -um *adj* **(adc-)** *(w. dat or* **ad***)* fit for, adapted to, suitable for
accommod·ō -āre -āvī -ātus *tr* **(adc-)** *(w. dat or* **ad***)* to adjust *or* adapt *or* apply *(s.th.)* to ‖ *refl (w.* **ad***)* to apply *or* devote oneself to
accommod·us -a -um *adj* **(adc-)** *(w. dat)* fit for, adapted to, suitable for
accrē·dō -děre -didī -ditum *intr* **(adc-)** *(w. dat)* to believe, put faith in, trust
accr·escō -escěre -ēvī -ētum *intr* **(adc-)** to grow larger, increase; to be added
accrēti·ō -ōnis *f* **(adc-)** increase
accubiti·ō -ōnis *f* **(adc-)** reclining *(at meals)*
accub·ō -āre *intr* to lie nearby; to recline at table; *(w. dat)* to lie near
accūd·ō -ěre *tr* **(adc-)** to coin
ac·cumbō -cumběre -cubuī -cubitum *intr* **(adc-)** to take one's place at table; *(w.* **cum***)* to lie down with
accumulātē *adv* **(adc-)** abundantly
accumulāt·or -ōris *m* **(adc-)** hoarder
accumul·ō -āre -āvī -ātus *tr* **(adc-)** to heap up, accumulate, amass; to load, overwhelm
accūrātē *adv* **(adc-)** carefully, accurately, exactly, meticulously
accūrāti·ō -ōnis *f* **(adc-)** carefulness, accuracy
accūrāt·us -a -um *adj* **(adc-)** careful, accurate, exact; studied
accūr·ō -āre -āvī -ātus *tr* **(adc-)** to take care of, attend to; *(w. subj,* **ut, ne***)* to see to it (that, that not)
ac·currō -currěre -currī *or* **-cucurrī -cursum** *intr* **(adc-)** to run up; *(w.* **ad** *or* **in** + *acc)* to run to

accurs·us -ūs *m* **(adc-)** running, concourse; *(mil)* attack, charge
accūsābil·is -is -e *adj* reprehensible
accūsāti·ō -ōnis *f* accusation; *(leg)* (bill of) indictment
accūsātīv·us -a -um *adj* & *m* accusative
accūsāt·or -ōris *m* accuser, prosecutor; informant
accūsātōriē *adv* like an accuser, prosecutorial
accūsātōri·us -a -um *adj* accuser's, prosecutor's
accūsātr·ix -īcis *f* accuser *(female)*
accūsit·ō -āre -āvī -ātus *tr* to keep on accusing
accūs·ō -āre -āvī -ātus *tr* to accuse; to prosecute; to reproach, blame; *(w. gen of the charge or w.* **de** + *abl)* to accuse of
ac·er -eris *n* maple tree; maple wood
a·cer -cris -cre *adj* sharp, pointed; alert, vigilant; shrewd; energetic, active; excited, eager, enthusiastic; strict, stern, hard; pinched, sharp *(features);* strong *(drink);* fierce, sharp *(bite);* bright, vivid *(color);* strong, pungent *(odor);* strong, bitter *(taste);* wild, savage *(animal);* fierce, relentless *(enemy);* violent *(storm);* biting *(cold);* strong, high *(wind);* swift *(river);* intense *(hunger, pain);* drastic *(remedy);* strong, powerful *(incentive);* serious, critical *(situation); (coll)* huge, terrific; **naribus acer** keen-scented
acer·a -ae *f* incense box
acerbē *adv* bitterly, harshly
acerbit·ās -ātis *f* bitterness, harshness, sharpness, sourness; distress, painful experience; ill-feeling, bitterness; satirical quality *(of writing)*
acerb·ō -āre -āvī -ātus *tr* to embitter; to exacerbate; render *(s.th.)* disagreeable
acerb·us -a -um *adj* bitter, harsh, sour *(flavor, taste);* unripe, green *(fruit);* cruel, hostile, pitiless *(enemy);* harsh *(speech, remark);* untimely, premature *(death);* bitter *(feelings; cold);* rough *(winter);* strict, severe *(person in authority); (in a weakened sense)* troublesome, disagreeable
acern·us -a -um *adj* maple
acerr·a -ae *f* incense box
acersecom·ēs -ae *m* young man
acervātim *adv* in heaps; briefly
acerv·ō -āre -āvī -ātus *tr* to heap *or* pile up
acerv·us -ī *m* heap, pile; multitude; *(in logic)* sorites
acescō acescěre acuī *intr* to turn sour
Acest·ēs -ae *m* king of Sicily
acētābul·um -ī *n* vinegar bottle
acēt·um -ī *n* sour wine, vinegar; *(fig)* sharp tongue
Achaemen·ēs -is *m* first king of Persia, great-grandfather of Cyrus

Achaemenid·ēs -ae *m* follower of Ulysses who was left behind in Sicily

Achaemeni·us -a -um *adj (poet)* Persian; Parthian

Achae·us -a -um *adj & m* Achaean; Greek

Achai·a *or* **Achāï·a -ae** *f* province in N. part of Peloponnesus on Gulf of Corinth; Greece

Achāï·cus -a -um *adj & m* Achaean; Greek

Achāt·ēs -ae *m* companion of Aeneas ‖ river in Sicily

Achelō·is -idis *f* daughter of Acheloüs; a Siren; a water nymph

Achelōi·us -a -um *adj* of the river Acheloüs; of Acheloüs *(the river god);* descended from Acheloüs

Achelō·üs -ī *m* river in N.W. Greece, flowing between Aetolia and Acarnania; god of this river

Acher·ōn -ontis *or* **Acher·uns -untis** *m (f)* Acheron *(river in Hades);* god of this river

Acher·uns -untis *mf* lower world

Acheruntic·us -a -um *adj* of the lower world

Acherūsi·us -a -um *adj* of the river Acheron

Achill·ās -ae *m* Egyptian who murdered Pompey

Achill·ēs -is *or* **-ī** *or* **-eī** *m* Greek warrior, son of Peleus and Thetis

Achillē·us -a -um *adj* of Achilles

Achillīd·ēs -ae *m* son *or* descendant of Achilles

Achīv·us -a -um *adj* Achaean, Greek

Acīdali·a -ae *f* Venus

acid·us -a -um *adj* sour, tart; *(of sound)* harsh, shrill; sharp, keen; pungent; unpleasant, disagreeable

aci·ēs -eī *f* sharpness, sharp edge; keenness of vision; glance; eyesight, eye; pupil *(of the eye);* mental power; battleline, battle array; battlefield, battle; debate

acīnac·ēs -is *m* scimitar

acin·um -ī *n or* **acin·us -ī** *m* berry; grape; seed in berry

acipens·er -eris *or* **acipens·is -is** *m* sturgeon

āc·is -idis *m* son of Faunus, loved by Galatea, changed into a river

acl·ys -ydis *f* small javelin

aconīt·um -ī *n (bot)* wolfsbane; strong poison

ac·or -ōris *m* sour taste, sourness

acqui·escō -escĕre -ēvī -ētum *intr* (adqu-) to become quiet; to rest; to die; *(w. abl, dat, or* in + *abl)* 1 to find rest in; 2 to acquiesce in, be content with; 3 find pleasure in, rejoice in

acquī·rō -rĕre -sīvī -sītus *tr* (adqu-) to acquire, obtain, gain, win

Acrae·us -a -um *adj (title of the gods)* dwelling on the heights, on high

Acrag·ās -antis *m* town on S.W. coast of Sicily *(poetic and Greek for Agrigentum)*

acrātophor·um -ī *n* vessel for holding unmixed wine

acrēdul·a -ae *f* bird *(species unknown)*

ācricul·us -a -um *adj* irritable, peevish

ācrimōni·a -ae *f* sharpness, pungency; irritation; energy

Acrisiōnē·us -a -um *adj* of Acrisius

Acrisiōniad·ēs -ae *m* descendant of Acrisius; Perseus

Acris·ius -(i)ī *m* king of Argos, father of Danaë, grandfather of Perseus

ācriter *adv* sharply, keenly; clearly, in a distinctive manner; closely, attentively; with vigor, with enthusiasm; severely; vehemently; bitterly, hard

ācroām·a -atis *n* entertainment

acroās·is -is *f* public lecture

Acrocerauni·a -ōrum *npl* promontory in Epirus on the Adriatic Sea

Acrocorinth·us -ī *f* citadel of Corinth

act·a -ae *f* seashore; seaside resort; beach party

act·a -ōrum *npl see* **actum**

Actae·ōn -onis *m* grandson of Cadmus, changed into a stag, and devoured by his own dogs

Actae·us -a -um *adj* Attic, Athenian; **Actaea virgo** Athena

Actiac·us -a -um *adj* of Actium; celebrating the victory of Actium

acti·ō -ōnis *f* doing, performance, action, activity; proceedings; act, deed; proposal, measure; delivery *(of orator or actor);* plot, action *(of play);* (leg) suit, right to bring a suit; **gratiarum actio** expression of gratitude; **naturales actiones** physiological functions

actit·ō -āre -āvī -ātus *tr* to do *(repeatedly);* to plead *(cases regularly);* to act *(often)* in *(plays)*

Acti·um -ī *n* promontory in Epirus *(where Octavian defeated Antony and Cleopatra in 31 B.C.)*

actīv·us -a -um *adj* practical *(philosophy);* (gram) active

act·or -ōris *m* doer, performer; agent, manager; actor, player; herdsman; *(leg) (with or without* **causae)** 1 defense counsel; 2 prosecutor; **actor summarum** cashier

Act·or -ōris *m* companion of Aeneas

actuāriol·um -ī *n* small, fast boat

actuāri·us -a -um *adj* swift ‖ *m* stenographer ‖ *f* swift passenger ship *(having both sails and oars)*

act·um -ī *n* act, deed; transaction ‖ *npl* great deeds, exploits, achievements; official records *(of events; of business transacted by the Senate, emperors, etc.);* decrees *(of a magistrate, general, etc.);* **acta diurna** day-by-day record of events;

acta Herculis labors of Hercules; acta
mittere to publish the news
actuōsē *adv* actively, energetically
actuōs·us -a -um *adj* active, energetic
actus *pp of* ago **||** *adj* finished, past
act·us -ūs *m* act, performance; physical
movement; driving *(of cattle or wagon);*
right of way; cow path; wagon track;
path, course *(of sun);* linear land measure *(120 ft.);* sequence *(of numbers);*
drawing *(of breath);* transaction *(of business);* performance *(of a play);* act *(of a
play);* delivery *(of a speech);* **deducere
in actus** to dramatize; **in actu esse** to be
active
actūtum *adv* instantly, immediately
acul·a *or* aquol·a -ae *f* small stream
aculeāt·us -a -um *adj* prickly; *(of insects)*
having a sting; *(fig)* stinging, barbed
acule·us -ī *m* sting, proboscis *(of insects);*
barb *(of arrow);* spike; sharp point; sarcasm; **aculeum emittere** *(fig)* to shoot
one's wad, spend all one's money
acūm·en -inis *n* point, sharpness; sting *(of
insects);* cunning; clever trick; **ingenii
acumen** mental acumen
acuō acuěre acuī acūtus *tr* to sharpen,
make pointed; to whet; to tune *(musical
instruments);* to stir emotionally; to
stimulate; to quicken *(one's pace);* to
accent *(syllable)*
ac·us -ūs *f* needle, pin; hairpin; curling
iron; **ab acia et acu** in great detail; **acu
rem tangere** to hit the nail on the head
acūtē *adv* acutely, sharply, keenly
acūtul·us -a -um *adj* somewhat sharp,
rather subtle
acūt·us -a -um *pp of* acuo **||** *adj* sharp,
pointed; shrill *(sound);* keen *(senses,
mind);* shrewd, intelligent *(person);*
piercing *(cold);* fiercely hot *(sun);* nimble
(movement); pungent *(smell, taste);*
subtle *(distinction)*
ad *prep (w. acc) (of space)* to, towards, at,
near; *(often w.* usque) reaching to, as far
as; for the purpose of, to; according to;
in consequence of; with respect to; compared with; at the house of, with; in the
company of; before *(judge, magistrate);*
(of time) toward, about, until, at, on, by;
(with numbers) about, almost; **ad diem**
on the right day, promptly; **ad extremum** to the very end; **ad manum** on
hand, available; **ad omnia** in all directions; **ad prima** to the highest degree;
ad summam in short; **ad summum** at
most; **ad tempus** on time, in time; **ad
ultimum** utterly; **ad unum** one and all
ad- *pref* 1 at: **adclāmāre** *(or* **acclamare)**
to shout at; 2 toward, aiming at: **adire** to
go toward; 3 bringing things together:
adstringere *(or* **astringere** to tie up; 4
towards a purpose: **adjurare** to swear

to, swear by; 5 of increase or addition:
addere to add; 6 of intensity: **adamare**
to love deeply
adacti·ō -ōnis *f* administering *(an oath)*
adactus *pp of* adigo
adact·us -ūs *m* bringing together; snapping *(of jaws)*
adaequē *adv* equally
adaequ·ō -āre -āvī -ātus *tr* to make level;
to equal, match, come up to the level of;
(fig) to put on the same level; **adaequare
solo** to level to the ground **||** *intr* to be on
the same level, be equal; *(of votes)* to be
equally divided *(for acquittal and for
condemnation);* *(w. dat)* to be level with;
(w. abl) to be on a par with, be equal to
(in some respect)
adamantē·us -a -um *adj* made of steel
adamantin·us -a -um *adj* hard as steel,
adamantine; **saxa adamantina** diamonds
adam·ās -antis *m* adamant; steel; diamond
adambul·ō -āre *intr (w. dat or* ad) to walk
beside
adam·ō -āre -āvī -ātus *tr* to love deeply;
to fall in love with
adaper·iō -īre -uī -tus *tr* to uncover, throw
open; to open up; to disclose to view,
make visible; to open wide *(mouth,
door);* to uncover *(head as sign of respect);* *(med)* to loosen *(bowels)*
adapertil·is -is -e *adj* that can be opened
adapert·us -a -um *adj* open *(door, flower)*
adapt·ō -āre -āvī -ātus *tr* to adapt, modify;
(w. dat) to fit to
adaqu·ō -āre *tr* to water **||** *intr* to fetch
water
adauct·us -ūs *m* growth
adau·geō -gēre -xī -ctus *tr* to increase; to
increase the number of; to exaggerate;
(w. abl) to crown with
adaugesc·ō -ěre *intr* to begin to grow
adbib·ō -ěre -ī *tr* to begin to drink; to
listen attentively to
adbīt·ō -ěre *intr* to approach
adc- = acc-
addec·et -ēre *v impers* it is proper
addens·eō -ēre *or* addens·ō -āre *tr* to
close *(ranks)*
ad·dīcō -dīcěre -dixī -dictus *tr (w. dat)* 1
(leg) to assign *(property)* to; 2 to give
custody of *(debtor)* to *(creditor);* 3 to
sell *(by sale or auction)* to; 4 to award
(prizes, provinces) to; 5 to ascribe to
(author); 6 to condemn, doom to **||** *refl &
pass (w. dat)* to give one's support to **||**
intr (in augury) to be favorable
addict·us -a -um *adj (w. dat)* addicted to,
a slave of; *(w. inf)* bound to *(do s.th.)* **||**
mf person enslaved for debt or theft
ad·discō -discěre -didicī *tr* to learn in
addition
additāment·um -ī *n* addition
ad·dō -děre -didī -ditus *tr* to add; to give

additionally; to add by way of exaggeration; to increase; to quicken *(one's pace);* to impart; to insert; to put *(into a container); (w. dat)* 1 to attach to, fit onto; 2 to serve *(a drink)* to; 3 to give to, confer on, inflict on; 4 to attribute to; 5 to intensify *(feelings);* **manus in vincla addere** to tie one's hands

addoc·eō -ēre -uī *tr* to teach in addition, teach new *(skills, etc.)*

addubit·ō -āre -āvī -ātus *tr* to call into doubt **‖** *intr* to begin to feel doubt; to hesitate

addū·cō -cěre -xī -ctus *tr* to lead up, bring up; to bring with one, bring along; to import; to bring up *(reinforcements);* to lead *(the mind to);* to introduce *(arguments);* to draw together, wrinkle; to induce; to sail *(a ship to);* to bring *(water to a town);* to shut *(door);* to shorten *(rein);* to draw back *(bowstring);* to bend *(bow); (of time, conditions)* to bring on; *(leg)* to prosecute, bring to trial; **(in judicium) adducere** to take to court

adduct·us -a -um *adj* drawn tight, strained; narrow, tight *(place);* strict, serious *(character)*

ad·edō -eděre -ēdī -ēsus *tr* to nibble at; to eat up; to waste; *(of fire)* to scorch; *(of water)* to erode

adempti·ō -ōnis *f* taking away

ad·eō -īre -iī *or* **-īvī -itus** *tr* to approach; to attack; to consult; to visit; to undertake, set about, undergo; to consult *(an oracle)* **‖** *intr* to go up, come up; *(w.* **ad)** 1 to go up to, approach; 2 to enter upon, undertake, set about; 3 to meet *(danger);* **ad rempublicam adire** to go into politics

adeō *adv* to such a degree, so; even, indeed, truly; very, extremely; *(following pronouns and numerals, to give emphasis)* precisely, exactly; quite, just, chiefly; *(at the beginning of sentence)* thus far, to such an extent; *(w.* **ut** + *subj)* to the end that; *(w.* **ne** + *subj)* to the end that…not; *(w.* **dum, donec,** *etc.)* to the point of time when; **adeo non** much less

ad·eps -ipis *mf* fat; corpulence

adepti·ō -ōnis *f* obtaining, acquisition

adeptus *pp of* **adipiscor**

adequit·ō -āre -āvī -ātum *intr* to ride up; *(w. dat or* **ad)** to ride up to, ride towards

adesse *inf of* **adedo** & *of* **adsum**

adēsur·iō -īre -īvī *intr* to be very hungry

adēsus *pp of* **adedo**

ad·haereō -haerēre -haesī -haesum *intr (w. dat, abl,* **ad** *or* **in** + *acc)* 1 to cling to, stick to; 2 to keep close to, hang on to; 3 *(anat)* to be attached to; 4 *(of land)* to be contiguous with, be near; **lateri adhaerere** to stick to *(a person's)* side; **memoriae adhaerere** to stick in one's memory

adhae·rescō -rescěre -sī -sum *intr* to stick; to falter; *(w. dat, abl,* **in** + *abl, or* **ad)** 1 to stick to, cling to; 2 to be devoted to; 3 to correspond to, accord with; 4 *(of weapons)* to become lodged in; 5 to run aground on

adhaesi·ō -ōnis *f* clinging, adhesion

adhaes·us -ūs *m* clinging, adhesion

Adherb·al -is *m* son of Micipsa (king of Numidia), murdered by Jugurtha

adhib·eō -ēre -uī -itus *tr* to stretch out *(hands);* to apply *(remedies, fetters, treatment);* to administer *(medicine);* to call in *(as advisor, witness, expert);* to invite *(as a guest);* to cite *(an authority); (w. abl)* to supply *(s.o.)* with; **animum adhibere** *(w. dat)* to turn one's attention to; **fidem adhibere** *(w. dat)* to lend credence to **‖** *refl* to conduct oneself, behave

adhinn·iō -īre -iī *or* **-īvī -ītus** *tr* to whinny after; to lust after **‖** *intr (w. dat or* **ad** *or* **in** + *acc)* 1 to whinny after; 2 to lust after, crave; 3 to chuckle in delight at

adhortāti·ō -ōnis *f* exhortation, encouragement

adhortāt·or -ōris *m* fan, supporter

adhort·or -ārī -ātus sum *tr* to cheer on, encourage

adhūc *adv* thus far, hitherto; till now; as yet, still; besides, in addition, moreover; to a greater degree, still further; *(w. numerals)* besides; **nihil adhuc** nothing as yet

ad·igō -igěre -ēgī -actus *tr* to drive *(cattle);* to move up *(siege engine);* to assemble *(ships);* to hurl *(weapon);* to inflict *(wound);* to plunge *(weapon)* into; **aliquem jus jurandum adigere** to have s.o. swear allegiance; **provinciam in verba sua et Pompeii jus jurandum adigere** to have the province swear allegiance to himself and Pompey

ad·imō -iměre -ēmī -emptus *tr (w. dat)* to take away from; **alicui vitam (or libertatem) adimere** to deprive s.o. of life *or* liberty

adipātus -a -um *adj* fatty, greasy; gross, bombastic **‖** *n* pastry *(made in fat)*

ad·ipiscor -ipiscī -eptus sum *tr* to get, obtain; to arrive at, reach; to inherit; to win *(victory);* **mortem adipisci** to commit suicide

aditiāl·is -is -e *adj* inaugural

aditi·ō -ōnis *f* a going to

adit·us -ūs *m* doorway, entrance, passage; extent to which a door is opened, opening; approach; arrival; access; entrance; right of entry, admittance; right to hold *(an office);* audience, interview; beginning, commencement; chance, opportunity; hostile approach, attack; chance of attacking, an "opening"; **primus aditus** first encounter *(with a person)*

adjac·eō -ēre -uī *tr* to adjoin ‖ *intr (w. dat or* **ad**) to lie near; to border

adjecti·ō -ōnis *f* addition; annexation

adjectīv·us -a -um *adj* adjectival ‖ *n* adjective

ad·jiciō -jicĕre -jēcī -jectus *tr* to add; to increase; *(w. dat or* **ad**) **1** to hurl *(weapon, insults)* at; **2** to add *(s.th.)* to; **c** to turn *(eyes, attention)* to; *(w.* in + *acc)* to hurl *(weapon)* at

adjūdic·ō -āre -āvī -ātus *tr* to adjudge, award; to ascribe, assign

adjūment·um -ī *n* help, support

adjunct·a -ōrum *npl* attendant circumstances; **ad nomina adjuncta** epithets, nicknames

adjuncti·ō -ōnis *f* joining, union; addition; *(rhet)* repetition

adjun·gō -gĕre -xī -ctus *tr (w. dat)* **1** to yoke *or* harness *(animal)* to; **2** to add *(ingredients);* **3** to ascribe *(qualities)* to; **4** to bestow *(praise, honor)* on; *(w. dat or* **ad**) **1** to add, attach *(s.th.)* to; **2** to apply, direct *(mind, attention, etc.)* to; **uxorem adjungere** to get married ‖ *refl (w. dat)* to join

adjūr·ō -āre -āvī -ātus *tr* to swear to; to swear by ‖ *intr* to swear

adjūtābil·is -is -e *adj* helpful

adjūt·ō -āre -āvī -ātus *tr* to help ‖ *intr (w. dat)* to be of assistance to

adjūt·or -ōris *m* helper, assistant; aide, adjutant, deputy; supporting actor

adjūtōr·ium -(i)ī *n* help, support

adjūtr·ix -īcis *f* helper *(female)*

ad·juvō -juvāre -jūvī -jūtus *tr* to help; to encourage; to keep *(the fire)* going; *(med)* to relieve; *(w.* ad *or* in + *acc)* to contribute to ‖ *v impers* it helps, it is an advantage, it is useful

adl- = all-

admātūr·ō -āre *tr* to bring to maturity, ripen; to speed up, expedite

ad·mētior -mētīrī -mensus sum *tr* to prop, support

Admēt·us -ī *m* king of Pherae in Thessaly, husband of Alcestis

admīgr·ō -āre *intr (w.* **ad**) to move to

adminicul·ō -āre -āvī -ātus *tr* to prop up

adminicul·um -ī *n* prop, support, stake, pole; rudder; aid; assistant

adminis·ter -trī *m* assistant; server, waiter

administr·a -ae *f* assistant, handmaid; waitress

adminstrāti·ō -ōnis *f* handling, administration, management, government; method of dealing with ‖ *fpl* administrative function *or* duties; administrative qualities

adminstrāt·or -ōris *m* administrator, director, manager

administr·ō -āre -āvī -ātus *tr* to administer, direct

admīrābil·is -is -e *adj* admirable, wonderful; strange, surprising; **admirabile est** it is remarkable

admīrābilit·ās -ātis *f* admiration, wonder; wonderfulness

admīrābiliter *adv* admirably; astonishingly

admīrāti·ō -ōnis *f* admiration, wonder; surprise

admīrāt·or -ōris *m* admirer

admīr·or -ārī -ātus sum *tr* to admire, wonder at; to be surprised at

admi·sceō -scēre -scuī -xtus *tr* to mix in, add; to involve, implicate; to join, mingle; *(w. dat,, w.* ad *or* in + *acc or* cum) to add *(s.th.)* to, to mix *or* mix up *(s.th.)* with ‖ *refl* to get involved

admissār·ius -(i)ī *m* stallion; *(fig)* stud

admissi·ō -ōnis *f* audience, interview

admiss·um -ī *n* crime

ad·mittō -mittĕre -mīsī -missus *tr* to let in, admit; to allow; to let loose; to listen to; to put at a gallop; to let *(water, hair)* flow; to allow; to commit *(crime);* **facinus in se admittere** to commit a crime; **ad animum admittere** to consider; **auribus** *(or* **ad aures**) **admittere** to listen to ‖ *intr (in augury)* to be propitious

admixti·ō -ōnis *f* admixture

admixtus *pp of* **admisceo**

admoderātē *adv* appropriately

admodum *adv* to the limit; very, quite, fully; *(w. numbers)* just about; *(w. negatives)* at all; *(in answers)* quite so, yes

admoen·iō -īre -īvī -ītus *tr* to besiege

admol·ior -īrī -ītus sum *tr* to pile up; **manūs admoliri** *(w. dat)* to lay violent hands on ‖ *intr (w.* ut + *subj)* to struggle to

admon·eō -ēre -uī -itus *tr* to admonish, remind, suggest; to warn; *(w. acc or gen)* to recall

admoniti·ō -ōnis *f* admonition, reminder, suggestion

admonit·or -ōris *m* reminder

admonit·um -ī *n* advice, warning

admonit·us -ūs *m* advice; suggestion; warning; command *(given to an animal)*

admordeō admordēre — admorsus *tr* to bite at; *(fig)* to fleece

admōti·ō -ōnis *f* moving, movement

ad·moveō -movēre -mōvī -mōtus *tr* to move up, bring up, bring near; to lead on, conduct; to employ *(fear, flattery); (w. dat or* **ad**) **1** to move *or* bring *(s.th.)* to; **2** to apply *(s.th.)* to; **3** to direct *(attention, etc.)* to; **aurem admovere** to give heed; **calcar** *(or* **stimulum**) **admovere** *(w. dat)* to spur

admūg·iō -īre *intr (w. dat)* to bellow to

admurmurāti·ō -ōnis *f* murmuring

admurmur·ō -āre -āvī -ātum *intr* to murmur *(in approval or disapproval)*

admutil·ō -āre -āvī -ātus *tr* to clip close; *(coll)* to clip, cheat

adn- = ann-

ad·oleō -olēre -oluī -ultus *tr* to honor, worship, sacrifice to; to burn *(ritually);* to cremate; to light *(pyre);* to destroy by fire, burn; **adolere altaria donis** to pile the altar high with gifts; **flammis adolere penatis** *(fig)* to light the hearth; **honores adolere** *(dat)* to make burnt offerings to

adol·eō -ēre *intr* to smell

adolesc·ens -entis *m* young man **ǁ** *f* young lady

adol·escō -escĕre -ēvī **adultum** *intr* (adul-) to grow up; to become mature; to increase; *(of habits, etc.)* to become established

Adōn·is -is *or* -idis *m* son of Cinyras (king of Cyprus), loved by Venus, killed by a wild boar

adoper·iō -īre -uī -tus *tr* to cover up; to close

adopert·us -a -um *adj* covered; veiled; hiding; shut, closed; *(poet)* clothed

adopīn·or -ārī -ātus sum *tr* to suppose, conjecture further

adoptāti·ō -ōnis *f* adoption *(into a family)*

adopti·ō -ōnis *f* adoption *(into a family)*

adoptīv·us -a -um *adj* adoptive

adopt·ō -āre -āvī -ātus *tr* to adopt; to select; to graft *(plants)*

ad·or -ōris *n* spelt *(hardy European type of wheat)*

adōrāti·ō -ōnis *f* adoration, worship

adōre·a -ae *f* reward for valor; praise, glory

adōre·us -a -um *adj* of spelt, of wheat

ad·orior -orīrī -ortus sum *tr* to rise up against, attack; to attempt; to undertake

adorn·ō -āre -āvī -ātus *tr* to adorn; to equip, get ready

adōr·ō -āre -āvī -ātus *tr* to implore, entreat; to ask for; to adore, worship

adp- = app-

adq- = acq-

adr- = arr-

ad·rādō -rādĕre -rāsī -rāsus *tr* to shave close

Adrast·us -ī *m* king of Argos, father-in-law of Tydeus and Polynices

Adri- = Hadri-

adsc- = asc-

adsi- = assi-

adso- = asso-

adsp- = asp-

adst- = ast-

adsu- = assu-

ad·sum -esse -fuī -futūrus *intr* to be present; to appear; *(of conditions)* to exist; *(of time, events)* to be at hand; to be of assistance; *(of an assembly)* to

convene; *(w. dat)* **1** to share in, participate in; **2** to assist, stand by; **3** *(leg)* to serve as attorney for; **4** *(of gods)* to look favorably on; **adesse animo** *(or* **animis)** to pay attention; to cheer up; **adesse illi corporis pulchritudo** he has a handsome physique

adt- = att-

adūlāti·ō -ōnis *f* flattery; fawning, cringing

adūlāt·or -ōris *m* flatterer

adūlātōri·us -a -um *adj* flattering

adulesc·ens -entis *m* (adol-) young man **ǁ** *f* young lady

adulescenti·a -ae *f* (adol-) youth, young people

adulescentul·a -ae *f* girl

adulescentul·us -ī *m* boy

adūl·ō -āre *tr* to fawn on *(like a dog)*

adūl·or -ārī -ātus sum *tr* to fawn on **ǁ** *intr* *(w. dat)* to kowtow to

adult·er -era -erum *adj* adulterous, unchaste; cross-bred *(plants);* debased *(coinage);* **adultera clavis** skeleton key **ǁ** *m* lover, adulterer **ǁ** *f* adulteress

adulterīn·us -a -um *adj* adulterous; counterfeit

adulter·ium -(i)ī *n* adultery; adulteration

adulter·ō -āre -āvī -ātus *tr* to defile, corrupt; to adulterate; to counterfeit; to falsify *(documents)* **ǁ** *intr* to commit adultery

adult·us -a -um *adj* grown, mature, adult

adumbrātim *adv* in outline

adumbrāti·ō -ōnis *f* sketch, outline

adumbrāt·us -a -um *adj* shadowy, sketchy; spurious

adumbr·ō -āre -āvī -ātus *tr* to shade; to obscure *(truth);* to sketch; to counterfeit

aduncit·ās -ātis *f* curvature

adunc·us -a -um *adj* curved, hooked

adurg·eō -ēre *tr* to be in hot pursuit of

ad·ūrō -ūrĕre -ussī -ustus *tr* to scorch, singe; to cause a burning sensation in, to burn; to nip, freeze; to desiccate; *(med)* to cauterize

adusque *prep* all the way to, right up to

adusti·ō -ōnis *f* burning; *(med)* burn; heatstroke

adust·us -a -um *pp of* **aduro** **ǁ** *adj* scorched; **nivibus adustus** frostbitten; **sole adustus** sunburned

advectīci·us -a -um *adj* imported, foreign

advect·iō -ōnis *f* transportation

advect·ō -āre *tr* to import

advect·us -ūs *m* importation

adve·hō -hĕre -xī -ctus *tr* to convey; to ship; to import **ǁ** *pass* to ride; **equo advehi** (ad *or* in + *acc*) to ride to; **navi advehi** (in + *acc*) to sail to

advēl·ō -āre *tr* to veil; to wreathe

adven·a -ae *mf* stranger, foreigner

ad·veniō -venīre -vēnī -ventum *intr* to

arrive; *(of periods of time, events)* to draw near, approach, be imminent; *(w.* **ad** *or* **in** + *acc, or acc of limit of motion)* to arrive at, come to, reach; *(w. dat) (of possession)* to come into the hands of; *(pres participle)* at *or* upon my (your, his, her, etc.)* arrival; **advenientem ilico ad cenam adduxi** immediately upon his arrival I took him to dinner

adventīci·us -a -um *adj* foreign; imported; extraneous; unusual; migratory *(birds);* **cena adventicia** reception; **ex adventicio** from an extraneous source

advent·ō -āre -āvī -ātum *intr* to keep coming closer; to turn up *(at a place); (of tide)* to come in; *(of time, events)* to draw near

advent·or -ōris *m* visitor, guest; customer

advent·us -ūs *m* arrival, approach; visit; (official) visitation

adversāri·us -a -um *adj* **(-vors-)** *(w. dat)* turned towards, opposed to, opposite **‖** *mf* adversary **‖** *npl* journal, notebook, memoranda; assertion *(of opponent)*

adversātr·ix -īcis *f* **(-vors-)** opponent *(female)*

adversi·ō -ōnis *f* directing

advers·ō -āre -āvī -ātus *tr* **(-vors-)** to turn, direct; **animum adversare** to direct attention; *(w.* **ne)** to be careful not to

advers·or -ārī -ātus sum *intr* **(-vors-)** to put up opposition; to be unfavorable; *(w. dat)* **1** to oppose, resist; **2** to be incompatible with; **3** to be inconsistent with

adversum *or* **adversus** *adv* **(-vors-)** in the opposite direction **‖** *prep (w. acc)* facing, opposite, towards; in the direction of; in the opposite direction to, against; to the disadvantage of; *(after verbs expressing hostile intent)* to meet, face; compared with; contrary to; in the eyes of; in criticism of; in reply to, in response to; **adversus clivum** *(or* **collem)** uphill

advers·us -a -um *adj* **(-vors-)** opposite, in front; facing; unfavorable; hostile; *(astr)* diametrically opposite; **adversā viā** up the road; **adverso flumine** upstream; **frontibus adversis** head-on; **res adversae** misfortunes; **ventus adversus** head wind **‖** *n* trouble, adversity, misfortune; the opposite; **in adversum** forwards; *(of several things)* in the opposite direction; **in adversum subire** to go uphill; **per adversum** in the opposite direction

adver·tō -tĕre -tī -sus *tr* **(-vor-)** *(w. dat or* **in** + *acc)* **1** to turn *or* direct *(s.th.)* toward; **2** to steer *(ship)* towards; **animos** *(or* **aures** *or* **oculos) advertere** to attract attention; **animum advertere** *(w. dat or* **ad)** to pay attention to, heed, observe **‖** *intr* to land; *(w.* **in** + *acc)* to punish

advesper·ascit -ascĕre -āvit *v impers* evening approaches

advigil·ō -āre -āvī -ātum *intr* to be vigilant, keep watch; *(w. dat)* to keep watch over, bestow attention on; *(w.* **pro** + *abl)* to watch out for

advocāt·a -ae *f* supporter *(female)*

advocāti·ō -ōnis *f* legal assistance; legal counsel; the bar; period of time allowed to procure legal assistance; delay, adjournment

advocāt·us -ī *m* helper, supporter; *(leg)* attorney

advoc·ō -āre -āvī -ātus *tr* to call; to convoke; to invoke; to invoke the help of; to invite *(to a meal);* to consult; to cite; *(leg)* to adjourn

advol·ō -āre -āvī -ātum *intr* *(w. dat or* **ad)** **1** to fly toward; **2** to rush at; **3** *(mil)* to swoop down on

advol·vō -vĕre -vī -ūtus *tr* *(w. dat or* **ad)** to roll *(s.th.)* to *or* toward **‖** *refl* **se advolvere ad genua** *(or* **genibus)** *(w. gen)* to fall prostrate before

advor- = **adver-**

adyt·um -ī *n* sanctuary; *(fig)* tomb

Aeacidēi·us -a -um *adj* of the descendants of Aeacus; **Aeacideia regna** Aegina

Aeacid·ēs -ae *m* descendant of Aeacus

Aeac·us *or* **Aeac·os -ī** *m* king of Aegina, father of Peleus, Telamon, and Phocus, and judge of the dead

aed·ēs *or* **aed·is -is** *f* room, apartment; shrine, temple **‖** *fpl* house

aedicul·a -ae *f* chapel, shrine; small room, closet; small house **‖** *fpl* small house

aedificāti·ō -ōnis *f* constructing, building; structure, building

aedificātiuncul·a -ae *f* tiny building

aedificāt·or -ōris *m* builder, architect; **aedificator mundi** creator of the world

aedific·ium -(i)ī *n* building, edifice

aedific·ō -āre -āvī -ātus *tr* to build; **locum aedificare** to erect buildings on a site **‖** *intr* to erect a building

aedīlīci·us -a -um *adj* aedile's **‖** *m* ex-aedile

aedīl·is -is *m* **(ēd-)** aedile *(Roman magistrate charged with the supervision of public buildings, markets, grain supply, games, and theatrical productions);* magistrate in Italian and other towns; **aedilis cerealis** aedile in charge of the grain supply

aedīlit·ās -ātis *f* aedileship

aedis *see* **aedes**

aeditu·us *or* **aeditim·us** *or* **aeditum·us -ī** *m* sacristan

Aedu·ī -ōrum *mpl* **(Haed-)** Gallic tribe occupying the territory between the Saône and the Loire

Aeēt·ēs *or* **Aeēt·ās -ae** *m* Aeëtes *(king of Colchis and father of Medea)*

Aeētae·us -a -um *adj* of Aeëtes
Aeēti·as -adis *f* daughter of Aeëtes *(i.e., Medea)*
Aegae·us -a -um *adj* (Aegē·us, Ēgē·us) Aegean **ǁ** *n* Aegean Sea
Aegāt·ēs -um *fpl* Aegatian Islands *(three islands off the W. coast of Sicily)*
ae·ger -gra -grum *adj* sick; *(w. abl of cause or* ex) sick from; diseased; weary, exhausted; depressed; depraved *(character, mind);* labored *(breathing, words);* corrupt *(institutions)* **ǁ** *mf* patient
Aeg·ēus -ēī *m* king of Athens and father of Theseus
Aegīd·ēs -ae *m* son of Aegeus, Theseus
Aegīn·a -ae *f* island off Attica **ǁ** mother of Aeacus
aeg·is -idis *f* shield of Minerva and of Jupiter; aegis, protection
Aegisth·us -ī *m* son of Thyestes and murderer of Agamemnon
aegrē *adv* painfully; with difficulty; reluctantly; hardly, scarcely; aegre ferre *(or* pati) to take (it) hard, resent
aegr·eō -ēre *intr* to be sick
aegresc·ō -ĕre *intr* to become sick; to get worse; to be distressed
aegrimōni·a -ae *f* distress, trouble
aegritūd·ō -inis *f* sickness; sorrow
aegr·or -ōris *m* illness
aegrōtāti·ō -ōnis *f* sickness, disease; sorrow
aegrōt·ō -āre -āvī -ātum *intr* to be sick; animo aegrotare to be mentally ill
aegrōt·us -a -um *adj* sick; love-sick
Aegypti·us -a -um *adj* of Egypt, Egyptian
Aegypt·us -ī *f* Egypt **ǁ** *m* mythical king of Egypt, whose 50 sons married the 50 daughters of his brother Danaüs
aelinon *interj* exclamation of sorrow, said to signify "alas for Linus"
Aemili·us -a -um *adj* name of a Roman clan *(nomen), esp.* Lucius Aemilius Paullus, who defeated Perseus at Pydna in 168 B.C.; Via Aemilia road from Ariminum to Placentia
aemul·a -ae *f* rival *(female);* rival city
aemulāti·ō -ōnis *f* emulation, rivalry
aemulāt·or -ōris *m* rival, imitator
aemulāt·us -ūs *m* emulation, rivalry
aemul·or -ārī -ātus sum *or* aemul·ō -āre *tr* to emulate, rival **ǁ** *intr (w. dat)* to be jealous of
aemul·us -a -um *adj (w. gen or dat)* 1 jealous of, striving after; 2 *(of things)* similar to, comparable to **ǁ** *m* rival
Aenead·ēs -ae *m* descendant of Aeneas; Trojan; Roman; Augustus
Aenē·ās -ae *m* son of Venus and Anchises, and hero of Vergil's epic
Aenē·is -idis *or* -idos *f* the *Aeneid*
aēne·um *or* ahēneum *or* a(h)ē·um -ī *n* bronze vessel, cauldron, pot

aēne·us *or* ahēne·us *or* a(h)ēn·us -a -um *adj* bronze; hard as bronze; bronze-colored
Aenīd·ēs -ae *m* son of Aeneas, Ascanius
aenigm·a -atis *n* enigma, riddle
aēnum *see* aēneum
aēnus *see* aeneus
Aeoli·a -ae *f* realm of Aeolus, king of winds; group of islands near Sicily
Aeoli·ī -ōrum *or* Aeol·ēs -um *mpl* Aeolians *(in N.W. Asia Minor)*
Aeol·is -idis *or* idos *f* Aeolia *(N.W. part of Asia Minor)*
Aeol·us -ī *m* god of winds
aequābil·is -is -e *adj* equal; alike; consistent, uniform; fair, impartial
aequābilit·ās -ātis *f* equality; uniformity; impartiality
aequābiliter *adv* equally; uniformly
aequaev·us -a -um *adj* of the same age, coeval
aequāl·is -is -e *adj* equal; of equal importance; even, level; of the same age; contemporary; symmetrical; affecting all equally, universal, general; *(of conditions, etc.)* comparable; uniform *(in consistency, shape, color, content, style);* homogeneous; *(of natural phenomena)* regular, continuous; *(of weather)* settled; equally balanced *(contest); (w. dat)* level with, on a level with, on a par with; *(w. ad)* equally disposed to **ǁ** *mf* comrade; contemporary
aequālit·ās -ātis *f* equality *(of age, status, merit);* regularity; evenness; smoothness
aequāliter *adv* equally; evenly
aequanimit·ās -ātis *f* calmness, patience; kindness; impartiality
aequāti·ō -ōnis *f* equal distribution
aequē *adv* equally; justly, fairly; aeque...ac *or* atque *or* et just as if; aeque...quam as...as, in the same way as
Aequ·ī -ōrum *mpl* a people of central Italy
aequilibrit·ās -ātis *f* balance
aequilibr·ium -(i)ī *n* horizontal position; equilibrium
aequinoctiāl·is -is -e *adj* equinoctial
aequinoct·ium -(i)ī *n* equinox
aequiperābil·is -is -e *adj (w. dat or* cum) comparable to
aequiper·ō -āre -āvī -ātus *tr* (-par-) to compare; to equal, rival, come up to; *(w. dat, w.* ad *or* cum) to compare *(s.th.)* to **ǁ** *intr (w. dat)* to become equal to, be equal to
aequit·ās -ātis *f* evenness; conformity; symmetry; equity; calmness; animi aequitas equanimity
aequ·ō -āre -āvī -ātus *tr* to make level; to smooth (out); to equalize; to equal, match, rival; to reach as high *(or* as deep) as; to keep pace with; to balance

(scales); (w. dat) to liken to; **gradus aequare** to keep pace; **solo aequare** to raze to the ground; **sortes aequare** to shake up the lots fairly

aequ·or -oris *n* level surface; plain; sea

aequore·us -a -um *adj* of the sea, marine

aequ·us -a -um *adj* level, even, flat, smooth; on a level *(with),* as tall *or* as high *(as);* fair-minded, impartial, just, reasonable; evenly balanced; *(of laws, treaties)* giving equal rights, fair; *(of persons)* on an equal footing, equal *(in strength, etc.);* *(of qualities)* matching, equal, alike; *(of love)* reciprocated; *(of verse)* regular, uniform; *(of movement)* steady, calm; *(of the mind)* calm, resigned; *(of things)* favorable, advantageous; *(w. dat)* **1** inclined towards; **2** sympathetic to, favorable to; **3** content with; **aequā mente** with calmness, patiently; **aequa pars** a half; **aequā parte** on a basis of equality; **aequi facere** to regard as immaterial, regard as a matter of indifference; **aequis manibus** *(of battles)* equally balanced; **aequo animo** with calmness, patiently; **aequo campo** *(mil)* on a level field *(offering advantage to neither side);* **aequo fronte** *(mil)* in a straight line, in line; **aequo Marte** *(of battles)* evenly balanced; **aequo pede** on even terms, on an equal footing; **aequum est** it is right (that); **aequum solo ponere** to raze to the ground; **ex inferiore loco loquitur sive ex aequo sive ex superiore** whether he speaks before the judges on the bench or in the Senate, or from the rostra ‖ *n* level, plain; justice, fairness; **ex aequo** from the same level; *(fig)* equally

ā·ēr -ěris *m* air; atmosphere; sky; weather; mist

aerāment·um -ī *n* bronze utensil

aerāri·us -a -um *adj* copper, bronze; of mines; financial, fiscal ‖ *m* coppersmith; low-class Roman citizen ‖ *f* mine; smelting furnace ‖ *n* treasury; funds contained in the treasury; *(specifically)* public treasury at Rome, kept in the temple of Saturn in the Forum; **aerarium militare** treasury for veterans' benefits; **aerarium sanctius** a special inner treasury; *(in Rome)* the part of the treasury containing a special war reserve

aerāt·us -a -um *adj* copper, bronze; rich

aere·us -a -um *adj* bronze; bronze-armored; bronze-beaked *(ships)*

āēre·us -a -um *adj see* **aērius**

aerif·er -era -erum *adj* carrying (bronze) cymbals

aerip·ēs -edis *adj* bronze-footed

Āěri·us -a -um *adj* aerial, lofty; airy; airborne; **aerium mel** dew

Āěrop·ē -ēs *or* **Āěrop·a -ae** *f* Aërope *(wife*

of Atreus, mother of Agamemnon and Menelaus)

aerūginōs·us -a -um *adj* rusty

aerūg·ō -inis *f* copper rust, verdigris; corroding passion, envy, greed

aerumn·a -ae *f* trouble; distress; task

aerumnābil·is -is -e *adj* distressing

aerumnōs·us -a -um *adj* full of troubles, distressed; causing distress, calamitous

aes aeris *n* copper, bronze; bronze object; armor; statue; utensil; trumpet; money, cash; bronze coin, a copper; inscribed bronze tablet; payment; reward; **aes album** *(or* **candidum)** brass; **aes alienum** debt; **aes et libra** *(leg)* (symbolical) copper coin and scales *(used in transactions over property, emancipation of slaves, etc.);* **aes militare** military pay; **in meo aere sum** I am free of debt

Aeschin·ēs -is *m* famous Athenian orator and opponent of Demosthenes ‖ Milesian orator contemporary of Cicero ‖ follower of Socrates

Aeschyl·us -ī *m* Athenian tragic poet *(525–456 B.C.)*

Aesculāp·ius -(i)ī *m* god of medicine

aesculēt·um -ī *n* (esc-) oak forest

aescule·us -a -um *adj* oak

aescul·us -ī *f* (esc-) Italian oak

Aeserni·a -ae *f* town in Samnium

Aesernīn·us -a -um *adj* of Aesernia

Aes·ōn -onis *m* father of Jason

Aesonid·ēs -ae *m* son of Aeson, Jason

Aesoni·us -a -um *adj* of Aeson, of Jason

Aesōp·us -ī *m* Aesop

aest·ās -ātis *f* summer; summer heat, summer weather

aestif·er -era -erum *adj* sultry; *(of a constellation)* that brings on the hot weather

aestimābil·is -is -e *adj* valuable

aestimāti·ō -ōnis *f* (-tum-) appraisal, assessment; esteem; value; **litis** *(or* **litium) aestimatio** *(leg)* assessment of damages *or* penalty

aestimāt·or -ōris *m* appraiser

aestim·ō -āre -āvī -ātus *tr* (-tum-) to appraise, rate, value, estimate; to esteem highly; to judge; to consider, think; *(w. gen or abl of value)* to consider worth; **litem (lites) aestimare** *(leg)* to assess the damages; **magni** *(or* **parvi) aestimare** to consider *(s.th. or s.o.)* worth much *(or* little)

aestīv·a -ōrum *npl* summer camp; campaign season, campaign; summer pastures

aestīvē *adv* scantily *(clad)*

aestīv·ō -āre -āvī -ātum *intr* to spend the summer

aestīv·us -a -um *adj* summer; **occasus aestivus** northwest; **oriens aestivus** northeast

aestuār·ium -(i)ī *n* estuary, lagoon; marsh; air shaft

aestu·ō -āre -āvī -ātum *intr* to boil, seethe; to burn, glow; to undulate, swell; to be tossed, heave; to waver; to be in heat, be all worked up

aestuōsē *adv* hotly, impetuously

aestuōs·us -a -um *adj* sultry; billowy; raging, seething; passionate; wavering

aest·us -ūs *m* agitation; glow, heat, sultriness; surge, billows; tide

aet·ās -ātis *f* lifetime, age; period of life; generation; passage of time; age group; era; **aetatem agere** to spend one's life; **aetatem exigere** to live out one's life; **id** (*or* **hoc**) **aetatis** at this time of life; **media** (*or* **constans,** *or* **firmata**) **aetas** middle age; **provecta aetas** old age

aetātul·a -ae *f* tender age

aeternit·ās -ātis *f* eternity; immortality; (*of things*) durability; courtesy title of the Emperor

aeternō *adv* forever

aetern·ō -āre *tr* to perpetuate, immortalize

aeternum *adv* forever; constantly

aetern·us -a -um *adj* eternal, everlasting, immortal; imperishable; durable; permanent, enduring a lifetime; (*of events*) remembered for ever; **in aeternum** forever

aeth·ēr -eris *m* upper air (*opp* **āēr**); sky, heaven; upper world (*opp* **Hades**)

aetheri·us -a -um *adj* ethereal, heavenly; of the upper world

Aethiopi·a -ae *f* Ethiopia

Aethi·ops -opis *m* Ethiopian; black man; (*poet*) Egyptian

aethr·a -ae *f* pure air, serene sky; air, sky, heavens

Aethr·a -ae *f* wife of Aegeus and mother of Theseus ‖ daughter of Oceanus and mother of Hyas ‖ wife of Hyperion

Aetn·a -ae *or* **Aetn·ē -ēs** *f* Mt. Etna

Aetnae·us -a -um *adj* of Etna; **fratres Aetnaei** the Cyclopes

Aetōli·a -ae *f* district in N.W. Greece

Aetōlic·us *or* **Aetōli·us -a -um** *adj* Aetolian

Aetōl·us -a -um *adj* of Aetolia, Aetolian; of Diomedes; of Meleager, like those of Meleager; of Tydeus ‖ *mpl* Aetolians

aevit·ās -ātis *f* age, lifetime

aev·um -ī *n or* **aev·us -ī** *m* age, lifetime, life; time, period; generation; eternity; **ad hoc aevi** hitherto; **aevo** (*or* **aevis**) for ages; **aevum agere** (*or* **agitare, degere, exigere**) to spend one's life; **ex ineunte aevo** from one's earliest years; **in** (*or* **per**) (**omne**) **aevum** forever; **primum aevum** early youth

Ā·fer -fra -frum *adj* African; **Afer turbo** S.W. Wind ‖ *m* African ‖ **Publius Terentius Afer** (*i.e.*, Terence, playwright,

d. 159 B.C.) ‖ *mpl* Africans; inhabitants of the Roman province of N. Africa

affābil·is -is -e *adj* (**adf-**) affable; kind

affābilit·ās -ātis *f* (**adf-**) affability

affabrē *adv* (**adf-**) skillfully, ingeniously

affatim *or* **ad fatim** *adv* (**adf-**) sufficiently, enough

affāt·us -ūs *m* (**adf-**) address, discourse

affectāti·ō -ōnis *f* (**adf-**) disposition, state of mind; affectation, conceit

affectāt·or -ōris *m* (**adf-**) (*w. gen*) aspirant to

affectāt·us -a -um *adj* (**adf-**) affected

affecti·ō -ōnis *f* (**adf-**) frame of mind, mood; feeling; attitude, point of view; inclination, partiality; affection

affect·ō -āre -āvī -ātus *tr* (**adf-**) to grasp; to strive after, aim at; to try to win over; to affect; (*w. inf*) to aim to; **iter** (*or* **viam**) **affectare** to set out on a journey; **spem affectare** to cherish a hope

affect·us -a -um *adj* (**adf-**) furnished, provided; gifted; weakened, sick; affected, moved, touched

affect·us -ūs *m* (**adf-**) state, disposition, mood; feeling, emotion; affection

afferō afferre attulī allātus *tr* (**adf-**) to bring; to carry, convey; to report, announce; to introduce; to apply, employ, exert, exercise; to produce, cause, occasion; to impart; to allege; to assign; to contribute; to help; to offer for sale; **auxilium** (*or* **opem**) **afferre** to bring help; **causam afferre** (*w. gen or dat*) to be the cause of; **in judicium causam afferre** to prefer charges; **manus afferre** (*w. dat*) to lay violent hands on, attack

af·ficiō -ficĕre -fēcī -fectus *tr* (**adf-**) to treat, handle, manage; to influence, move; to attack, afflict; to impair; (*w. adv*) to treat (*in a certain way*); (*abl and verb may be rendered by the English verb corresponding to the Latin abl*): **cruce afficere** to crucify; **honoribus afficere** to honor; **supplicio afficere** to punish

af·fīgō -fīgĕre -fixī -fixus *tr* (**adf-**) (*w. dat or* **ad**) to fasten, attach, nail to; to apply (*as a remedy*); **animo affigere** to impress on the mind

af·fingō -fingĕre -finxī -fictus *tr* (**adf-**) to form, fashion besides; to make up, invent; (*w. dat*) **1** to attach, affix, add, join, contribute (*s.th.*) to; **2** to connect with, associate with; **3** to ascribe to, attribute to

affīn·is -is -e *adj* (**adf-**) adjoining, neighboring; related by marriage; (*w. dat or* **ad**) taking part in, privy to, associated with; subject to (*an affliction*) ‖ *mf* neighbor; in-law

affīnit·ās -ātis *f* (**adf-**) affinity, connection; relationship by marriage

affirmātē *adv* (adf-) with solemn assurance, positively

affirmāti·ō -ōnis *f* (adf-) affirmation, assertion, declaration; emphasis

affirm·ō -āre -āvī -ātus *tr* (adf-) to strengthen; to confirm, encourage; to assert

affix·us -a -um *pp of* affigo (adf-) ‖ *adj (w. dat)* 1 *(of guards, attendants)* assigned to; 2 attached to, devoted to; 3 intent on

afflāt·us -ūs *m* (adf-) blast, breeze; breath; inspiration

afflictāti·ō -ōnis *f* affliction

afflict·ō -āre -āvī -ātus *tr* (adf-) to strike repeatedly; *(of storms)* to toss about; to shatter, damage; to trouble, distress, torment; *(mil)* to harass ‖ *refl & pass* to be troubled

afflict·or -ōris *m* (adf-) subverter

afflict·us -a -um *adj* (adf-) damaged, shattered; downhearted; vile

afflī·gō -gĕre -xī -ctus *tr* (adf-) to knock down; to batter; to injure, damage; to distress, afflict; *(fig)* to crush

affl·ō -āre -āvī -ātus *tr* (adf-) to blast *(w. heat, lightning); (w. dat)* 1 to breathe on, blow on; 2 to impart to ‖ *intr (of winds)* to blow; *(of smells)* to be wafted; to blow favorably ‖ *pass (of sounds or smells)* to carry toward

afflu·ens -entis *adj* (adf-) flowing; affluent; abounding, numerous

affluenter *adv* (adf-) lavishly, abundantly

affluenti·a -ae *f* (adf-) flow; abundance; extravagance

afflu·ō -ĕre -xī -xum *intr* (adf-) *(w. dat or ad)* 1 to flow to *or* towards, glide by; 2 to flock to; *(w. abl)* to abound in

af·for -fārī -fātus sum *tr* (adf-) to address, accost ‖ *pass* to be destined

affore = adfutur·us -a -um esse

afforem = adessem

afformīd·ō -āre *intr* (adf-) to be afraid

afful·geō -gēre -sī *intr* (adf-) to shine, beam; to dawn; to appear; *(w. dat)* to shine on

af·fundō -fundĕre -fūdī -fūsus *tr* (adf-) *(w. dat)* 1 to pour, sprinkle *(s.th.)* on; 2 to send *or* dispatch *(s.o.)* to ‖ *refl & pass (w. dat)* to prostrate oneself before

aflu·ō -ĕre -xī *intr* (abf-) to flow away; to be abundant; *(w. abl)* to abound in; *(w. ex)* to issue from, come from

Afrāni·us -a -um *adj* Roman clan name *(nomen), esp.* Lucius Afranius *(comic poet)* ‖ Lucius Afranius *(one of Pompey's generals)*

Āfric·a -ae *f* originally the district of Carthage, made a Roman province after the 3rd Punic War in 146 B.C.; continent of Africa; *(fig)* inhabitants of Africa

Āfricān·us -a -um *adj* African ‖ *m* Roman

honorary name *(agnomen)* conferred upon the two Scipios

Āfric·us -a -um *adj* African ‖ *m* S.W. wind

Agamemn·ō(n) -onis *m* king of Mycenae, son of Atreus and Aërope, brother of Menelaus, murdered by his wife Clytemnestra

Agamemnonid·ēs -ae *m* son of Agamemnon *(i.e., Orestes)*

Agamemnoni·us -a -um *adj* of Agamemnon, descended from Aga-memnon

Aganipp·ē -ēs *f* fountain on Mt. Helicon sacred to the Muses

agās·ō -ōnis *m* stable boy; driver; lackey

Agathocl·ēs -is *m* king of Sicily, son of a potter, famous for his war with Carthage over the possession of Sicily *(361–287 B.C.)*

Agāv·ē -ēs *f* wife of Echion, king of Thebes, and mother of Pentheus

agedum *interj* come on!; well!

agell·us -ī *m* little field, plot

agēm·a -atis *n (mil)* honor guard

Agēn·or -oris *m* son of Belus, king of Phoenicia, father of Cadmus and Europa, and ancestor of Dido

Agēnorid·ēs -ae *m* descendant of Agenor; Cadmus; Perseus

a·ger -grī *m* (arable) land, (tilled) field *(opp:* campus = untilled, open land); ground; soil; farm, estate; territory, land, district; country *(opp:* urbs); ager publicus state-owned land; in agrum in depth *(opp:* in fronte in frontage) ‖ *mpl* countryside

agg·er -eris *m* rubble; soil; rampart; breakwater; dike, dam; fortification; ramp; pile, heap, collection; ridge, mound, hill; funeral pyre; agger ripae bank *(of river);* agger (viae) causeway

agger·ō -āre -āvī -ātus *tr* to pile up, fill up; to amass; to increase; *(fig)* to stimulate, intensify

ag·gerō -gerĕre -gessī -gestus *tr* (adg-) to bring forward; to pile up; *(w. dat)* to heap *(accusations, benefits)* on

aggest·us -ūs *m* (adg-) accumulation; terrace

agglomer·ō -āre -āvī -ātus *tr* (adg-) to gather together ‖ *refl & intr* to gather

agglūtin·ō -āre -āvī -ātus *tr* (adg-) to glue, paste; to solder ‖ *refl (w. ad)* to stick close to

aggravesc·ō -ĕre *intr* (adg-) to grow heavy; *(of diseases)* to get worse

aggrav·ō -āre -āvī -ātus *tr* (adg-) to weigh down; to make *(conditions)* worse, aggravate; to increase the force of *(a blow); (fig)* to burden, oppress

ag·gredior -gredī -gressus sum *tr* (adg-) to approach; to address; to attack; *(w. inf)* to undertake to ‖ *intr (w. ad) (fig)* to tackle

aggreg·ō -āre -āvī -ātus *tr* (adg-) to assemble; *(w.* in *acc)* include (in); to implicate; *(leg) (w. dat)* to lump together with **‖** *refl & pass* to flock together; *(w. dat or* **ad)** to join

aggressi·ō -ōnis *f* (adg-) attack; *(rhet)* introduction

aggressus *pp of* **aggredior (adg-)**

agil·is -is -e *adj* agile, nimble, quick; busy, active

agilit·ās -ātis *f* agility, nimbleness, quickness; activity

agitābil·is -is -e *adj* mobile

agitāti·ō -ōnis *f* motion, movement, agitation; activity; waving *(of arms)*

agitāt·or -ōris *m* driver; charioteer

agit·ō -āre -āvī -ātus *tr* to set in motion; to drive on, impel; to hunt; to scour *(for game);* to brandish, wave *(weapon);* to pursue *(an objective);* to shake *(reins);* to drive *(vehicle);* to ride *(horse);* to tend *(flocks);* to urge, support, insist on; to practice *(justice, a trade);* to exercise *(the body);* to engage in *(conversation);* to enjoy *(peace, fame);* to observe, celebrate; to obey, carry out; to spend, pass *(time);* to toss, disturb; to distress; to stimulate, arouse *(mind, emotions);* to deride, insult; to criticize; to discuss; to cherish *(hope);* **secum** *(or* **animo** *or* **mente)** to think about, consider, ponder; *(w. indirect question)* to debate *(in one's mind)* **‖** *intr* to live, spend one's life

Aglaur·ōs -ī *f* daughter of Cecrops

agm·en -inis *n* herd, flock, troop, crowd; body, mass; army column; procession; retinue, escort; course, flow *(of a stream);* movement *(of oars);* **agmen claudere** *(or* **cogere)** to bring up the rear; **agmen ducere** to form the van; **agmen primum** the van; **agmine** *(or* **uno agmine** *or* **agmine facto)** in marching formation; in a body

agn·a -ae *f* lamb *(female)*

ag·nascor -nascī -nātus sum *intr* to be born subsequently *(after the father has made his will);* **testamentum agnascendo rumpitur** a will is broken by the subsequent birth (of a son)

agnāti·ō -ōnis *f* blood relationship *(on the father's side)*

agnāt·us -ī *m* relative *(on the father's side)*

agnell·us -ī *m* little lamb

agnīn·a -ae *f* mutton, lamb

agniti·ō -ōnis *f* recognition, acknowledgement, admission; knowledge

ag·noscō -noscěre -nōvī -nitus *tr* to recognize, identify; to acknowledge; to own up to, admit to

agn·us -ī *m* lamb

-āg·ō -inis *fem suf* mostly formed from verbs in **-āre: imago** image; also from other sources: **cartilago** cartilage

ag·ō agěre ēgī actus *tr* to drive, lead, conduct; to chase, hunt; to drive away, steal; to spend *(time);* to do; to manage, administer, carry on; to transact; to discuss; to play, act the part of; to plead *(a case);* to exercise, practice; to hold *(an office);* to celebrate *(triumph);* to work at, be busy on; to have in mind, plan; to push *(siege works)* forward; to emit *(smoke, flames);* to trace *(one's descent);* *(fig)* to dispel *(fear, hunger, etc.);* to spend, pass *(time, life); (of plants)* to put forth *(roots, sprouts);* to drive *(chariot);* to sail *(ship);* to construct *(anything linear: rampart, tunnel);* **agere furti** to accuse of theft; **agere reum** to indict a defendant; **aliud** *(or* **aliam rem) agere** not to attend to one's business; **animam agere** to breathe one's last; **gratias agere** to thank; **in crucem agere** to crucify; **iter** *(or* **cursum) agere** to make one's way; **nugas agere** to act foolishly; **praedam** *(or* **boves) agere** to rustle cattle; **primas partes agere** to play the lead role; **proelium agere** to do battle; **quid agis?** how do you do? **quo agis?** what's your point?; **satis agere** to have more than enough to do; **spumas agere** to foam *(at the mouth)* **‖** *refl* to go, come; to grow; to behave, comport oneself **‖** *pass* to be done, happen, occur, come to pass; to be involved, be at stake; **bene agitur** things turn out well; **quid agitur?** what's going on? **‖** *intr* to take action, act; to be busy; to bargain; to live, dwell; *(theat)* to act; **age!** come on! *(in assent)* O.K., very well; **bene (male) agere cum aliquo** to treat s.o. well (badly); **cum populo** *(or* **ad populum) agere** to address the people; **quo tu agis?** where are you off to?

ag·ōn -ōnis *m* contest

agrāri·us -a -um *adj* agrarian **‖** *mpl* land-reform party

agrest·is -is -e *adj* rustic, country; boorish; wild; savage

agricol·a -ae *m* farmer, peasant

Agricol·a -ae *m* Gnaeus Julius Agricola *(father-in-law of Tacitus)*

agricultūr·a -ae *f* agriculture

Agrigent·um -ī *n* city on S. coast of Sicily *(modern Agrigento)*

agripet·a -ae *m* colonist, settler

Agripp·a -ae *m* Marcus Vipsanius Agrippa *(son-in-law of Augustus, husband of Julia, and father of Agrippina)*

Agrippīn·a -ae *f* Vipsania Agrippina, daughter of Agrippa, wife of Tiberius and mother of Drusus *(d. 20 A.D.)* **‖** Vipsania Agrippina Major, wife of Germanicus and mother of Caligula *(d. 33 A.D.)* **‖** Julia Agrippina Minor, daughter of the previous Agrippina and

Germanicus, and mother of Nero *(murdered by Nero in 59 A.D.)*
āh *interj* ah!, ha!, oh!
aha *interj* aha!
ai *interj (denoting grief)* ah!
āin = aisne *(see* aio*)*
aiō *tr & intr (used mainly in pres and imperf indic)* I say; I say yes, I say so; I assert, tell relate; **ain (=aisne) tandem?** *(or* **ain tu?** *or* **ain tute** *or* **ain vero?)** *(coll) (expressing surprise)* do you really mean it?, you don't say!, really?
Āj·ax -ācis *m* son of Telamon, king of Salamis **‖** son of Oïleus, king of the Locri
-al -ālis *neut suf* forms neuter nouns: **animal** animal; **cubital** elbow cushion
āl·a -ae *f* wing; armpit; squadron *(of cavalry);* flank *(of battle line)*
alabas·ter -trī *m,* **alabastr·um -ī** *n* perfume box
ala·cer *or* **ala·cris -cris -cre** *adj* lively, brisk; quick; eager; active; cheerful
alacrit·ās -ātis *f* liveliness, briskness; quickness; eagerness; cheerfulness
alap·a -ae *f* slap
ālār·is -is -e *adj (mil)* consisting of auxiliary cavalry
ālāri·us -a -um *adj* consisting of auxiliary troops **‖** *mpl* auxiliaries, allies
ālāt·us -a -um *adj* winged
alaud·a -ae *f* lark
Alb·a -ae *f* town *(also called Alba Longa)* founded by Ascanius
Albān·ī -ōrum *mpl* inhabitants of Alba Longa
Albān·um -ī *n* Alban estate; Alban wine
albāt·us -a -um *adj* dressed in white
alb·eō -ēre -uī *intr* to be white
albesc·ō -ĕre *intr* to become white, whiten; to dawn; *(of hair)* to turn gray
albic·ō -āre -āvī -ātum *or* **albic·or -ārī -ātus sum** *intr* to be white, be whitish
albid·us -a -um *adj* white, whitish
Albi·ōn -ōnis *f* Britain
albitūd·ō -inis *f* whiteness
Albul·a -ae *f* earlier name of the Tiber River
albul·us -a -um *adj* whitish
alb·um -ī *n* white; white tablet, record, list, register
Albune·a -ae *f* fountain at Tibur; nymph of that fountain
alb·us -a -um *adj* flat white; bright, shining, clear *(sky, light, sun, etc.);* favorable; clad in white; light-skinned, fair; whitened, made white; favorable, auspicious; gray *(hair);* pale *(from fear, sickness);* **album opus** stucco work; **albus aterne sit nescire** not to know a person from Adam *(literally, not to know whether he is white or black)* **‖** *m* white man

Alcae·us -ī *m* Greek lyric poet from the Island of Lesbos *(fl. 610 B.C.)*
alcēd·ō -inis *f* kingfisher, halcyon
alcēdoni·a -ōrum *npl* halcyon days; *(fig)* deep calm, tranquillity
alc·ēs -is *f* elk
Alcest·is -is *f* loyal wife of Admetus
Alcibiad·ēs -ae *or* **-is** *or* **-ī** *m* Athenian politician, disciple of Socrates *(450?– 404 B.C.)*
Alcīd·ēs -ae *m* descendant of Alceus, *esp.* Hercules
Alcimed·ē -ēs *f* wife of Aeson and mother of Jason
Alcino·üs -ī *m* king of the Phaeacians, who entertained Ulysses
Alc(u)mēn·a -ae *or* **Alcmēn·ē -ēs** *f* wife of Amphitryon and mother of Hercules by Jupiter
alcy·ōn -onis *f* **(hal-)** halcyon *(bird believed to build its nest on the sea)*
Alcyon·ē -ēs *or* **Alcyon·a -ae** *f* **(Hal-)** daughter of Aeolus and wife of Cyex *(both of whom were changed into halcyons)* **‖** wife of Meleager **‖** one of the Pleiades
āle·a -ae *f* dice game; gambling; die; risk, gamble; **aleā ludere** to gamble; **jacta alea est** the die is cast
āleāri·us -a -um *adj* gambling
āleāt·or -ōris *m* gambler
āleātōri·us -a -um *adj* gambling
Ālect·ō -ūs *f* **(Āll-)** one of the three Furies
āle·ō -ōnis *m* gambler
āl·es -itis *adj* winged **‖** *mf* winged creature, bird **‖** *m* poet; Cupid **‖** *f* augury, omen
alesc·ō -ĕre *intr* to grow up
Alexan·der -drī *m* Paris, son of Priam and Hecuba **‖** Alexander the Great, king of Macedon *(356–323 B.C.)*
Alexandrē·a -ae *f* **(-drī·a)** Greek city of N. Egypt, founded by Alexander the Great
Alexandrīn·us -a -um *adj* Alexandrine; characteristic of Alexandria
alg·a -ae *f* seaweed
alg·ens -entis *adj* cold; **algens toga** thin toga
al·geō -gēre -sī *intr* to be cold; to feel cold; to endure cold; *(fig)* to be left out in the cold
al·gescō -gescĕre -sī *intr* to catch a cold
algid·us -a -um *adj* cold
Algid·us -a -um *adj* of Mt. Algidus **‖** *m* mountain in Latium, S. of Tusculum
alg·or -ōris *m* cold; fit of shivering
alg·us -ūs *m* the cold
aliā *adv* by another way
aliās *adv* at another time, at other times; previously; subsequently; in other circumstances, otherwise; apart from this, in any case, besides; all the same, never-

theless; **alias**...**alias** at one time...at another, sometimes...sometimes
āliāt·um -ī *n* food flavored with garlic
alibī *adv* elsewhere; otherwise, in other respects; in another passage *(in a book, speech)*; **alibi**...**alibi** in one place...in another, here...there; **alibi aliter** differently in different places; **alius alibi** one in one place, another in another
alic·a -ae *f* emmer *(type of wheat)*
alicāri·us -a -um *adj* of emmer **‖** *f* prostitute
alicubi *adv* somewhere; anywhere; occasionally
alicul·a -ae *f* light cape
alicunde *adv* from somewhere; from someone else
aliēnāti·ō -ōnis *f* transfer *(of property);* alienation; aversion; **alienatio mentis** insanity
aliēnigen·a -ae *m* foreigner, stranger *(born in another country)*
aliēn·ō -āre -āvī -ātus *tr* to transfer, sell; to give up *(children)* for adoption; to alienate, set at variance; to treat as an enemy; to remove, separate; to drive mad; **a sensu alienare** to deprive of feeling; **paene alienatā mente** almost driven mad **‖** *pass* to fall into s.o. else's hands; *(mil)* to fall into the enemy's hands; *(w. ab)* to recoil from
aliēn·us -a -um *adj* another's; foreign; contrary; hostile; strange; unsuitable; incongruous, inconsistent; inconvenient; **alienum est** it is out-of-place **‖** *m* stranger, foreigner **‖** *n* another's property; foreign soil **‖** *npl* another's affairs
ālif·er *or* **alig·er -era -erum** *adj* winged, wearing wings
alimentāri·us -a -um *adj* (alum-) relating to welfare
aliment·um -ī *n* (alum-) nourishment, food, provisions; fuel **‖** *npl* means of livelihood; alms
alimōni·a -ae *f or* **alimōn·ium -(i)ī** *n* nourishment, food; support; cost of living
aliō *adv* to another place, elsewhere; to another topic; to another policy; for another purpose; **alio**...**alio** in one direction...in another; **alius alio** one in one direction, another in another
aliōquī(n) *adv* otherwise, in other respects, for the rest; apart from these considerations; besides; in general; in any case
aliorsum *or* **aliōvorsum** *adv* (-sus) in another direction; in a different manner; in a different sense
ālip·ēs -edis *adj* wing-footed, swift-footed
alipt·ēs *or* **alipt·a -ae** *m* wrestling trainer, rubdown man
aliquā *adv* somehow; to some extent
aliquam *adv* to some degree; **aliquam multi** fairly many

aliquamdiū *adv* (-quan-) for some time; for a considerable distance
aliquandō *adv* sometime or other, once; at any time, ever; now and then; for once, now; finally, now at last; someday *(in the future)*
aliquantill·um -ī *n* a bit
aliquantisper *adv* for a while
aliquantō *adv* somewhat, to some extent, a little, rather
aliquantulum *adv* somewhat
aliquantul·us -a -um *adj* little **‖** *n* a small amount
aliquantum *adv* somewhat, a little, rather
aliquant·us -a -um *adj* considerable **‖** *n* a certain amount *(of);* a certain degree *(of);* a bit, a part
aliquātenus *adv* for some distance; to a certain extent; in some respects, partly; up to a point
ali·quī -qua -quod *adj* some; *(after a negative,* si, *etc.)* any at all
aliquid *adv* to some extent
ali·quid -cūjus *pron* something, anything; something important; **ad aliquid esse** *(of a term)* to be relative; **aliud aliquid** something else; **aliquid vini** some wine; **est aliquid** *(w. inf)* it is something to **‖** *adv* to some degree
ali·quis -cūjus *pron* someone, somebody, anyone; someone important
aliquō *adv* to some place, somewhere
aliquot *indecl adj* some, several
aliquotiens *adv* several times
aliquōvorsum *adv* in one direction or another
aliter *adv* otherwise, else; **aliter**...**aliter** in one way...in another; **aliter atque** now in one way, now in another; **aliter esse** *or* **aliter se habere** to be different; **non** *(or* **haud) aliter quam** *(or* **ac) si** just as if
aliubī *adv* elsewhere; **aliubi**...**aliubi** here...there
āl·ium -(i)ī *n* (all-) garlic
aliunde *adv* from another place; **aliunde**...**aliunde** from one place...from another; **alius aliunde** one from one place, another from another
ali·us -a -ud *adj (gen singl is generally* **alterius;** *dat:* **alteri)** another, other, different; *(w.* ac, atque, et, nisi, quam) other than **‖** *pron* another; **alii**...**alii** some...others; **alius**...**alius** one...another, the one...the other; **alius atque alius** first one person, then another; **alius ex alio** one after another
al·lābor -lābī -lapsus sum *intr* (adl-) to glide, slide, slip; to flow
allabōr·ō -āre *intr* (adl-) to work hard
allacrim·ō -āre *intr* (adl-) to weep
allaps·us -ūs *m* (adl-) slithering
allātr·ō -āre -āvī -ātus *tr* (adl-) to bark

at; *(fig)* to revile; *(of sea)* to break against

allāt·us -a -um *pp of* **affero**

allaudābil·is -is -e *adj* praiseworthy

allaud·ō -āre *tr* **(adl-)** to praise highly

all·ēc -ēcis *n* **(hall-)** fish sauce

Allect·ō -ūs *f* **(ālec-)** Alecto *(one of the three Furies)*

allect·ō -āre *tr* **(adl-)** to allure, entice

allēgāti·ō -ōnis *f* **(adl-)** intercession; allegation

allēgāt·us -ūs *m* **(adl-)** prompting, instigation

allēg·ō -āre -āvī -ātus *tr* **(adl-)** to commission; to deputize; to put up; to dispatch; to allege; to instigate; *(w. dat)* to lay *(prayers)* before

al·lĕgō -legĕre -lēgī -lectus *tr* **(adl-)** to select; to appoint *(to an office)*

allēgori·a -ae *f* allegory

allevāment·um -ī *n* **(adl-)** alleviation

allevāti·ō -ōnis *f* lifting; alleviating, easing

allev·ō -āre -āvī -ātus *tr* **(adl-)** to lift up, raise; to alleviate; to comfort; to lighten

Alli·a -ae *f* tributary of the Tiber where the Gauls defeated the Romans in 390 B.C.

allice·faciō -facĕre -fēcī -factus *tr* to entire, allure

al·liciō -licĕre -lexī -lectus *tr* **(adl-)** to attract; to bring on *(sleep);* to attract the attention of; to win over

allī·dō -dĕre -sī -sus *tr* **(adl-)** *(w. dat or ad or in + acc)* to dash *(s.th.)* against ‖ *pass* to be shipwrecked

Alliens·is -is -e *adj* of the Allia River; of the battle at the Allia River

allig·ō -āre -āvī -ātus *tr* **(adl-)** to bind; to bandage *(wounds);* to tie up; to grip firmly; to hold together; to freeze solid; to curdle *(milk);* to curb, restrict; to fetter; to hinder, detain; to involve, implicate; *(w. ad)* to bind *(s.th.)* to; *(of laws)* to be binding on

al·linō -linĕre -lēvī -litus *tr* **(adl-)** to smudge; *(w. dat)* to smear *(s.th.)* on

all·ium -(i)ī *n* garlic

Allobrog·ēs -um *mpl* Gallic tribe in Gallia Narbonensis

allocūti·ō -ōnis *f* **(adl-)** address; pep talk

alloqu·ium -(i)ī *n* **(adl-)** address; conversation; reassuring words

allo·quor -quī -cūtus sum *tr* **(adl-)** to speak to, address; to invoke *(gods);* to console, comfort

allubesc·ō -ĕre *intr* to be lovely

alluc·eō -ēre -xī *intr* *(w. dat)* be a light for

allūdi·ō -āre *intr* **(adl-)** to play, frolic

allū·dō -dĕre -sī -sus *tr* **(adl-)** to play with ‖ *intr* to play, joke; *(of waves) (w. dat)* to lap; *(w. dat or ad)* to allude playfully to

allu·ō -ĕre -ī *tr* **(adl-)** *(of rivers, the sea)* to

flow past, lap, touch; *(of water)* to touch, wet *(a part of the body)*

alluvi·ēs -ēī *f* **(adl-)** pool *(left by flood waters);* silt

alluvi·ō -ōnis *f* **(adl-)** flood; alluvial land

alm·us -a -um *adj* nourishing; kind, gracious

aln·us -ī *f* alder tree; *(fig)* ship

al·ō -ĕre -uī -tus *or* **-itus** *tr* to nurse, breast-feed; to feed, nourish; to promote the growth of; to raise *(children, animals);* to support *(family, etc.); (of places, employment)* to provide a livelihood for; to foment *(discord);* to encourage; to promote the interests of; to increase; to strengthen

alo·ē -ēs *f* **(bot)** aloe *(whose bitter juice was used as a purgative);* bitterness

Alōeus *m* a son of Poseidon and Canace

alogi·a -ae *f* folly, nonsense

Alōïd·ae -ārum *mpl* the giants Otus and Ephialtes, sons of Poseidon and Iphimedeia, the wife of Aloeus

Alp·ēs -ium *fpl* Alps

alpha *indecl n* alpha *(first letter of the Greek alphabet)*

Alphē·us *or* **Alphī·us** *or* **Alphē·os -ī** *m* Alpheus *(chief river of the Peloponnesus)*

Alpic·us -a -um *adj* Alpine

Alpīn·us -a -um *adj* Alpine

alsī *perf of* **algeo** *and* **algesco**

als(i)·us -a -um *adj* chilly, cold

altār·ia -ium *npl* altar; burnt-offerings

altē *adv* high, on high, highly; from a great height; deeply, far, remotely; intensely, profoundly

alt·er -era -erum *adj* one *(of two);* a second, the second, the next ‖ *pron* one *(of two),* the one, the other; a second one, the second one, the next one; anyone else; another *(one's fellow man);* **alter...alter** the one...the other, the former...the latter; **unus et** *(or* **aut) alter** one or two

alterās *adv* at another time

altercāti·ō -ōnis *f* altercation, dispute; *(phil)* debate

altercāt·or -ōris *m* disputant

alterc·ō -āre *or* **alterc·or -ārī -ātus sum** *intr* to argue, wrangle; to argue back and forth *(in court)*

alternīs *adv* by turns, alternately

altern·ō -āre -āvī -ātus *tr* to do by turns; to alternate, arrange in alternating order; to exchange ‖ *intr* to alternate

altern·us -a -um *adj* one after another, alternate; mutual; every other; **alternā vice** *(or* **alternis vicibus)** alternately; in turn, successively; **in alternum** for one another, reciprocally; **ire per alternas vices** to go back and forth

alteru·ter -tra -trum *(fem also* **altera utra;** *neut also* **alterum utrum)** *adj* one

(of two), either, one or the other **II** *pron* one, either one, one or the other
Althae·a -ae *f* mother of Meleager
alticinct·us -a -um *adj* energetic
altil·is -is -e *adj* fattened, fat; *(fig)* rich **II** *f* fattened fowl
altison·us -a -um *adj* sounding from on high; sublime
altiton·ans -antis *adj* thundering on high
altitūd·ō -inis *f* height; depth; *(fig)* profundity *(of mind)*; loftiness *(of style)*; ad *or* in altitudinem vertically
altiusculē *adv* rather high
altiuscul·us -a -um *adj* rather high
altivol·ans -antis, altivol·us -a -um *adj* high-flying
alt·or -ōris *m* foster father
altrim secus *adv* on the other side
altrinsecus *adv* (**alter-**) on the other side
altr·ix -īcis *f* foster mother; wet nurse; *(of the earth)* nourisher; motherland
altrōvorsum *adv* (**-sus**) on the other hand
alt·us -a -um *adj* high; deep; profound *(wisdom)*; deep, loud *(sound)*; intense *(heat, cold)*; thick *(fog)*; high-born, ancient *(lineage)* **II** *n* high seas, the deep; heaven; **ab alto** from on high, from heaven; **ex alto** far-fetched; **ex alto petere** (*or* **repetere**) to go far afield for
ālūcin·or -ārī -ātus sum *intr* (**hāl-, alluc-**) to ramble on; to rave
alumn·a -ae *f* foster daughter
alumn·us -ī *m* foster son
alūt·a -ae *f* soft leather; shoe; purse
alv(e)ār·ium -(i)ī *n* beehive
alveol·us -ī *m* bowl, basin; bathtub; river bed; game board
alve·us -ī *m* hollow; tub; bathtub; riverbed; hull of boat; game board; beehive
alv·us -ī *f (m)* belly, bowels, stomach; womb; rectum; boat; beehive; **alvum purgare** (*or* **solvere**) to move the bowels; **alvus fusa** (*or* **cita**) diarrhea
am- *pref see* **ambi-**
amābil·is -is -e *adj* lovable, lovely, attractive; delightful
amābilit·ās -ātis *f* attractiveness
amābiliter *adv* lovingly, delightfully
Amalthē·a -ae *f* nymph who fed infant Jupiter with goat's milk **II** Cumaean sibyl
āmandāti·ō -ōnis *f* sending away
āmand·ō -āre -āvī -ātus *tr* (**amend-**) to send away
am·ans -antis *adj* loving, affectionate; **amans patriae** patriotic **II** *mf* lover
amanter *adv* lovingly, affectionately
āmanuens·is -is *m* secretary
amārac·us -ī *mf* marjoram *(aromatic plants whose leaves are used as seasoning)*
amarant·us -ī *m* amaranth *(imaginary flower that never fades)*
amārē *adv* bitterly
amāriti·ēs -ēī *f* bitterness

amāritūd·ō -inis *f* bitterness; tang; sadness
amār·or -ōris *m* bitterness
amār·us -a -um *adj* bitter, pungent, tangy; shrill; brackish; **nux amara** almond
Amaryll·is -idis *f* conventional name for a shepherdess
amāsi·ō -ōnis *m* lover
amāsiuncul·a -ae *f* darling
amāsiuncul·us -ī *m* lover
amās·ius -(i)ī *m* lover
amāt·a -ae *f* loved one
Amāt·a -ae *f* mother of Lavinia
Amath·ūs -untis *f* town in Cyprus
Amathūsiac·us -a -um *adj* of Amathus
Amathūsi·us -a -um *adj* of Amathus **II** *f* Venus
amāti·ō -ōnis *f* love affair
amāt·or -ōris *m* lover; friend; **amator patriae** patriot
amātorcul·us -ī *m* poor little lover
amātōriē *adv* lovingly
amātōri·us -a -um *adj* erotic, love **II** *n* love charm
amātr·ix -īcis *f* mistress, girl friend
Amaz·ōn -onis *or* **Amazon·is -idis** *f* Amazon
Amazonic·us -a -um *adj* Amazonian
amb- *pref see* **ambi-**
ambact·us -ī *m* vassal
ambāg·ēs -is *f* winding, labyrinth; doubletalk; digression; ambiguity, obscurity; **per ambages** enigmatically
amb·edō -esse -ēdī -ēsus *tr* to eat up; to waste, squander; *(of fire)* to char
ambestr·ix -īcis *f* gluttonous woman
ambi- *pref (before vowels usually* **amb-**; *before consonants* **ambi-, am-, an-**) around
ambig·ō -ěre *tr* to go around, avoid; to call into question, debate **II** *intr* to waver, hesitate, be undecided; to argue, debate, wrangle **II** *v impers* **ambigitur** it is uncertain
ambiguē *adv* indecisively; ambiguously; in an untrustworthy manner
ambiguit·ās -ātis *f* ambiguity
ambigu·us -a -um *adj* wavering, changeable; uncertain; disputed; unreliable, untrustworthy; ambiguous, dark, obscure **II** *n* doubt, uncertainty; paradox
amb·iō -īre -īvī *or* **-iī -itus** *tr* to go the round of; to go around, encircle; to throng; to go round, go past; to embrace; to include; *(pol)* to campaign for **II** *intr* to move in an orbit; to rotate
ambiti·ō -ōnis *f* ambition *(in good and bad sense)*; popularity; flattery; partiality, favoritism; pomp, ostentation; *(pol)* campaigning *(by lawful means)*
ambitiōsē *adv* ambitiously; ostentatiously; from a desire to please
ambitiōs·us -a -um *adj* winding; public-

ity-conscious; ambitious; ostentatious; eager for popularity
ambit·us -ūs *m* winding, revolution; circuit, circumference, border; orbit; ostentation; circumlocution; *(pol)* illegal campaign practices, bribery; **ambitus verborum** *(or* **orationis)** phrase; *(rhet)* rounded and balanced sentence, period
ambiv·ium -(i)ī *n* road junction
amb·ō -ae -ō *adj* both, two **ll** *pron* both, the two
Ambraci·a -ae *f* district of Epirus
Ambraciens·is -is -e *adj* of Ambracia
Ambraciōt·ēs -ae *m* an Ambracian
Ambraci·us -a -um *adj* of Ambracia
ambrosi·a -ae *f* food for the gods; imaginary healing plant
ambrosi·us -a -um *adj* **(-e·us)** ambrosial, divine
ambūbāi·a -ae *f* Syrian singer and courtesan **ll** *(bot)* wild endive
ambulācr·um -ī *n* walk, avenue
ambulāti·ō -ōnis *f (act; place)* walk
ambulātiuncul·a -ae *f* short walk; small promenade
ambulāt·or -ōris *m* stroller *(person);* peddler
ambulātōri·us -a -um *adj* movable
ambul·ō -āre -āvī -ātus *tr* to traverse, travel **ll** *intr* to walk, take a walk; to march; to travel; to strut; *(of things)* to extend, run; **bene ambula!** bon voyage!
amb·ūrō -ūrĕre -ussī -ustus *tr* to burn up; to scorch; to scald; to cremate; *(of cold)* to numb, nip
ambustulāt·us -a -um *adj* half-roasted
amell·us -ī *m (bot)* wild aster *(plant having daisylike flowers of various colors)*
ām·ens -entis *adj* insane; foolish
āmenti·a -ae *f* insanity; folly
āment·ō -āre -āvī -ātus *tr* **(amm-)** to fit *(a javelin)* with a strap
āment·um -ī *n* **(amm-)** strap
Ameri·a -ae *f* town in Umbria
Amerīn·us -a -um *adj* of Ameria; produced in Ameria **ll** *m* Amerian
am·es -itis *m* pole for fowler's net; fence rail
amethystināt·us -a -um *adj* dressed in violet-blue
amethystin·us -a -um *adj* violet-blue; set with amethysts **ll** *npl* violet-blue garments
amethyst·us -ī *f* amethyst
amīc·a -ae *f* girlfriend, lady friend; mistress
amīcē *adv* in a friendly way
ami·ciō -cīre -cuī *or* **-xī -tus** *tr* to wrap around; to cover, clothe, wrap
amīciter *adv* in a friendly way
amīciti·a -ae *f* friendship
amictori·um -ī *n* wrap

amict·us -ūs *m* wrap, cloak; clothing; fashion *(in dress)*
amīcul·a -ae *f* girl friend
amicul·um -ī *n* wrap, mantle **ll** *npl* clothing
amīcul·us -ī *m* pal, buddy
amīc·us -a -um *adj* friendly; supportive; favorable, congenial; helpful; dear, welcome; **amicus reipublicae** patriotic **ll** *m* friend; lover; partisan, supporter; disciple **ll** *f see* **amica**
āmigr·ō -āre *intr* to move (away)
Amilcar *see* **Hamilcar**
āmissi·ō -ōnis *f* loss
amit·a -ae *f* aunt *(father's sister)*
Amitern·um -ī *n* town in the Sabine district, birthplace of Sallust
ā·mittō -mittĕre -mīsī -missus *tr* to lose; to let slip, miss; to let go, release; to let fall, drop; **animam** *(or* **spiritum) amittere** to lose one's life; **fidem amittere** to break one's word; **spe amissā** having given up hope
amm- = **adm-**
amment·ō -āre *see* **amento**
amment·um -ī *n* **(āmen-)** strap
amnicol·a -ae *mf* riverside plant
amnicul·us -ī *m* brook
amn·is -is *m (f)* river; **secundo amni** downstream
am·ō -āre -āvī -ātus *tr* to love, like, be fond of; to fall in love with; **amabo (te)** *(coll)* please **ll** *intr* to be in love
amoenē *adv* charmingly, pleasantly
amoenit·ās -ātis *f* charm
amoen·us -a -um *adj* charming, pleasant
āmōl·ior -īrī *tr* to remove; to put aside, put away; to get rid of, put out of the way, dispose of *(a person);* to refute **ll** *refl* to remove oneself, clear out
amōm·um -ī *n (bot)* spice plant; spice obtained from this plant
am·or -ōris *m* love; affection; object of affection, love; liking, fondness, attachment; strong desire, yearning; love song; Cupid; **amor patriae** patriotism **ll** *mpl* love affair
āmōti·ō -ōnis *f* removal
ā·moveō -movēre -mōvī -mōtus *tr* to remove; to withdraw, put away; to lay aside *(suspicion, etc.);* to get rid of; to banish; to deprive of rights; to dispel *(fear);* to steal; **ex animo amovere** to put out of one's mind **ll** *refl* to retire, withdraw
Amphiarā·üs -ī *m* famous Greek seer, son of Oecle(u)s *(or* Apollo) and Hypermestra, one of the Seven against Thebes
Amphiarēïad·ēs -ae *m* descendant of Amphiaraus, his son Alcmaeon
amphiboli·a -ae *f* ambiguity
Amphilochi·a -ae *f* small district at the E. end of the Ambracian Gulf

Amphiloch·us -ī *m* son of Amphiaraus, and founder of Argos Amphilochium the chief town of Amphilocia

Amphī·ō(n) -onis *m* son of Zeus and Antiope, twin brother of Zethus, and husband of Niobe

Amphīoni·us -a -um *adj* of Amphion

Amphipol·is -is *f* town in Macedonia, near the mouth of the Strymon

amphitheātr·um -ī *n* amphitheater

Amphitrīt·ē -ēs *f* wife of Neptune; *(fig)* the sea

Amphitry·ō(n) *or* **Amphitru·ō -ōnis** *m* husband of Alcmena

Amphitryōniad·ēs -ae *m* Hercules

amphor·a -ae *f* amphora; liquid measure *(c. 7 gallons)*

ampl·a -ae *f* opportunity

amplē *adv* amply; grandly, splendidly

am·plector -plectī -plexus sum *tr* to embrace, hug; to cling to; to accept gladly, welcome; to comprise, extend over, cover, include; to encircle *(enemy forces);* to grasp, grip; to understand; *(of serpent)* to coil itself around; *(mil)* to comprehend

amplex·ō -āre *or* **amplex·or -ārī -ātus sum** *tr* to embrace; to welcome; to cling to, grasp; to espouse, cherish

amplex·us -ūs *m* circuit; embrace, caress; coil *(of snake)*

amplificātiō -ōnis *f* extension, enlargement; *(rhet)* amplification

amplificāt·or -ōris *m* enhancer

amplificē *adv* splendidly

amplific·ō -āre -āvī -ātus *tr* to enlarge, extend, widen; to increase; to extol; *(rhet)* to enlarge upon, develop

ampli·ō -āre -āvī -ātus *tr* to widen, enlarge; to enhance; to postpone *(judgment);* adjourn *(court in order to gather more evidence);* to magnify, glorify; *(leg)* to postpone *(trial)*

ampliter *adv* splendidly; fully, very

amplitūd·ō -inis *f* width, size, bulk, extent; greatness, dignity, importance; high rank; *(rhet)* amplification, development

amplius *adv* any further, any more, any longer; besides; further, more, longer; **amplius hoc** what is more, in addition; **amplius uno die** one day longer; **nec amplius** no longer; **nemo amplius** no one else; **nihil amplius** nothing else; **quid amplius (quam)** what else (than) ‖ *n* more, a larger amount; **amplius negoti** more trouble

ampliusculē *adv* rather more freely

ampl·us -a -um *adj* ample, large, wide, spacious; strong, great, powerful; grand, imposing; eminent, prominent, illustrious

Ampsanct·us -ī *m* valley and lake in Samnium with toxic exhalations, regarded as an entrance to the lower world

ampull·a -ae *f* bottle; bombast

ampullār·ius -(i)ī *m* bottle-maker

ampull·or -ārī -ātus sum *intr* to be bombastic

amputāti·ō -ōnis *f* pruning

amput·ō -āre -āvī -ātus *tr* to lop off, prune; to curtail, shorten; **amputata loqui** to speak disconnectedly

Amūl·ius -(i)ī *m* king of Alba Longa, brother of Numitor, and granduncle of Romulus and Remus

amurc·a -ae *f* dregs of oil

Amycl·ae -ārum *fpl* town in Laconia, the birthplace of Castor and Pollux

Amyclae·us -a -um *adj* of Amyclae

Amyclīd·ēs -ae *m* Hyacinthus *(worshiped at Amyclae)*

amygdal·a -ae *f* almond tree

amygdal·um -ī *n* almond

amyst·is -idis *f* drinking bottoms up

an *conj (introducing the second or further part of a multiple question, direct or indirect)* or, or whether; **haud scio an I** am inclined to think, probably

anabathr·a -ōrum *npl* bleachers

Anacre·ōn -ontis *m* lyric poet of Teos *(fl 540 B.C.)*

anadēm·a -atis *n* headband

anaglypt·a -ōrum *npl* work in bas-relief

anagnost·ēs -ae *m* reader, reciter

analect·a -ae *m* slave who cleaned up the crumbs

analectr·is -idis *f* shoulder pad *(to improve the figure)*

analogi·a -ae *f* ratio; *(gram)* analogy *(similarity in inflection and derivatives of words); (phil)* method of reasoning from similar cases

anancaec·um -ī *n* large cup that must be emptied "bottoms up"

anapaest·us -a -um *adj (pros)* anapestic ‖ *m* anapest (∪ ∪ —) ‖ *n* poem in anapestic meter; anapestic line *or* passage

Anāp·us -ī *m* river in Sicily

an·as -atis *f* duck

anaticul·a -ae *f* (anet-) *(sometimes as term of endearment)* duckling

anatīn·us -a -um *adj* (anet-) duck's

anatocism·us -ī *m* compound interest

Anaxagor·ās -ae *m* Greek philosopher, teacher of Pericles and Euripides *(500?–428 B.C.)*

Anaximan·der -drī *m* Greek philosopher of Miletus *(610–547 B.C.)*

Anaximen·ēs -is *m* Greek philosopher of Miletus *(fl 544 B.C.)*

an·ceps *or* **ancip·es -cipitis** *adj* two-headed; facing in two directions; exposed on both sides; two-edged; twin-peaked; amphibious; of doubtful allegiance, untrustworthy; unreliable, unpredictable; *(of a person)* undecided, wavering; *(of a battle)* fought on two fronts; *(of enemies)* attacking on both sides; *(of dangers, evils)* arising from two sources, double, twofold; *(of roads)* leading in two directions; *(of battles)* undecided, hanging in the balance; *(of words)* ambiguous; *(of situations)* hazardous, critical ‖ *n* danger, peril

Anchīs·ēs -ae *m* son of Capys, lover of Venus, and, by her, father of Aeneas

Anchīsē·us -a -um *adj* of Anchises

Anchīsiad·ēs -ae *m* son of Anchises, Aeneas

ancīl·e -is *n* small figure-eight shield *(esp. one of twelve such kept by the Salii in the shrine of Mars and carried in religious processions)*

ancill·a -ae *f* slave girl

ancillār·is -is -e *adj* having the status of a slave girl

ancillul·a -ae *f* little slave girl

Ancōn·a -ae *f* seaport in N. Picenum

ancor·a -ae *f* (**anch-**) anchor

ancorāl·e -is *n* anchor cable

ancorāri·us -a -um *adj* of an anchor

Anc·us Marti·us -ī *m* the fourth king of Rome

Ancӯr·a -ae *f* Ankara, capital of Galatia

andabat·a -ae *m* blindfolded gladiator

And·ēs -ium *fpl* village near Mantua, birthplace of Vergil

Andri·us -a -um *adj* of the Greek island of Andros ‖ *mpl* people of Andros ‖ *f* woman from Andros

Androge·ōs -ō *or* **Androge·ōn -ōnos** *or* **Androge·us -ī** *m* Androgeüs *(son of Minos and Pasiphaë, whose death Minos avenged by attacking Athens)*

androgyn·us -ī *m or* **androgynē -ēs** *f* hermaphrodite

Andromach·a -ae *or* **Andromach·ē -ēs** *f* Hector's wife

Andromed·a -ae *or* **Andromed·ē -ēs** *f* daughter of Cepheus and Cassiope, rescued from a sea monster by Perseus

andr·ōn -ōnis *m* corridor

Andronīc·us -ī *m* Livius Andronicus *(fl 241 B.C., first epic and dramatic poet of Latin literature)*

Andr·os *or* **Andr·us -ī** *f* Aegean island

ānell·us -ī *m* little ring

anēt(h)·um -ī *n (bot)* dill *(aromatic herb whose seeds and leaves are used as seasoning)*

-āne·us -a -um *adjl suf* chiefly from nouns denoting a place: **circumforāneus** connected with (the business) of the forum

anfract·us -ūs *m* curve *(of road, seashore);* spiral, coil; *(astr)* orbit; *(rhet)* circumlocution

angell·us -ī *m* small angle

angin·a -ae *f* tonsillitis; throat infection

angiport·us -ūs *m or* **angiport·um -ī** *n* alley

ang·ō -ĕre *tr* to choke, strangle; to distress; to tease; to trouble

ang·or -ōris *m* strangling, suffocation; anguish

anguicom·us -a -um *adj* snake-haired

anguicul·us -ī *m* small snake

anguif·er -era -erum *adj* snaky, having snakes in place of hair, snake-haired; *(of places)* snake-infested

anguigen·a -ae *m* offspring of a dragon; Theban

anguill·a -ae *f* eel

anguine·us -a -um *adj* snaky; serpent-like

anguīn·us -a -um *adj* snaky

anguip·ēs -edis *adj* serpent-footed

angu·is -is *mf* snake, serpent ‖ **Anguis** *m* Dragon, Serpent, Hydra *(constellations)*

Anguiten·ens -entis *m* Ophiuchus *(constellation)*

angulār·is -is -e *adj* angular

angulāt·us -a -um *adj* (**angl-**) angular

angul·us -ī *m* angle, corner; nook, recess; **ad pares angulos** *(or* **rectis angulis)** at right angles

angustē *adv* within narrow limits; closely; hardly, scarcely; briefly, concisely

angusti·ae -ārum *fpl* narrow place; defile; narrow passage, strait; shortage, scarcity, want, deficiency; difficulty, tight spot; limitations; distress, straits; narrow-mindedness; poverty of vocabulary; **angustiae spiritūs** shortness of breath

angusticlāvi·us -a -um *adj* wearing a tunic with a narrow purple stripe *(a sign of equestrian rank)*

angust·ō -āre -āvī -ātus *tr* to narrow down; to reduce in size *or* amount; to choke

angust·us -a -um *adj* narrow, close; short, brief *(time);* scanty *(means);* tight *(reins);* difficult, critical; narrow-minded; base, mean ‖ *n* a confined space; narrowness; critical condition, danger; **in angustum adducere** *(or* **cogere, concludere, deducere)** to narrow down, compress, reduce

anhēlāti·ō -ōnis *f* panting

anhēlit·us -ūs *m* panting, difficulty in breathing, puffing; breath, breathing; vapor

anhēl·ō -āre -āvī -ātus *tr* to breathe out, to pant after ‖ *intr* to pant, puff; to exhale; *(of fire, sea)* to roar

anhēl·us -a -um *adj* panting

anicul·a -ae *f* little old lady

Aniē(n)s·is -is -e *or* **Aniēn·us -a -um** *adj* of the Anio *(Tiber tributary)*

anīl·is -is -e *adj* of an old woman; **aniles fabulae** old wives' tales

anīlit·ās -ātis *f* old age *(of women)*

anīliter *adv* like an old woman

anim·a -ae *f* air, wind, breeze; breath; breath of life, life; soul *(as principle of life, opposed to* **animus** *as principle of*

thought and feelings); spirit, ghost; **animam agere** to gasp for breath; **animam ducere** to draw a breath; **animam edere** *(or* **efflare** *or* **emittere** *or* **exspirare)** to breathe one's last; **animam trahere** to struggle to breathe
animadversi·ō -ōnis *f* attention, observation; mention; remark; criticism; punishment
animadvers·or -ōris *m* observer
animadver·tō -tĕre -tī -sus *tr* (**-vort-**) to pay attention to, attend to; to notice, observe, realize; to criticize; to punish
anim·al -ālis *n* animal; living creature
animāl·is -is -e *adj* consisting of air; animate, living **‖** *mfn* living creature, animal
anim·ans -antis *adj* living, animate **‖** *mfn* living thing; animal
animāti·ō -ōnis *f* living being
animāt·us -a -um *adj* courageous; inclined, disposed; *(w.* **erga** *or* **in +** *acc)* disposed toward
anim·ō -āre -āvī -ātus *tr* to make alive, animate; to encourage
animōsē *adv* courageously; eagerly
animōs·us -a -um *adj* courageous; energetic; violent *(wind, fire);* proud; spunky *(horse)*
animul·a -ae *f* little soul, little life
animul·us -ī *m* darling
anim·us -ī *m (cf* **anima)** intellect, understanding; mind; thought, reason; memory; knowledge; sense, consciousness; judgment, opinion; imagination; heart, feelings, passions; spirit, courage, morale; disposition, character; pride, haughtiness; will, purpose, desire, inclination; pleasure, delight; confident hope; **aequo animo** patiently, calmly; **animo causā** for amusement; **animo libenti** gladly; **bono animo esse** to take heart; **ex animo** from the bottom of the heart, sincerely; **ex animo effluere** to slip one's mind; **in animo habere** *(w.* **inf)** to have in mind to, intend to
Ani·ō -ōnis *m* tributary of the Tiber
Ani·us -ī *m* king and priest on Delos
ann- = **adn-**
Ann·a -ae *f* sister of Dido **‖** **Anna Perenna** goddess of the returning year
annāl·is -is -e *adj* lasting a year, annual; **lex annalis** law fixing the minimum age for holding public offices **‖** *mpl* annals, chronicle
annat·ō -āre -āvī -ātum *intr* (**adn-**) *(w. dat or* **ad)** to swim to
anne *conj (alternate form of* **an)** or, or whether
anne·ctō -ctere -xuī -xus *tr* (**adn-**) *(w.* **dat** *or* **ad)** to tie, connect, annex *(s.th.)* to; *(w. dat)* to apply *(s.th.)* to
annex·us -ūs *m* connection

annicul·us -a -um *adj* (**-ucul-**) one year old; lasting only one year
annī·tor -tī -sus *or* **-xus sum** *intr* (**adn-**) try one's hardest; to give support; *(w. dat or w.* **ad)** to lean on; *(w.* **ut** *or inf)* to strive to
anniversāri·us -a -um *adj* employed annually, renewed annually; occurring every year, growing every year; *(of games, festivals, sacrifices)* celebrated annually, annual
ann·ō -āre -āvī -ātum *intr* (**adn-**) *(w. dat, w.* **ad,** *w.* **acc** *of limit of motion)* to swim to *or* towards; *(w. dat)* to swim along with
annōn *conj* or not; **suntne di annon?** are there gods or not?
annōn·a -ae *f* year's crop; grain; price of grain; cost of living; high price
annōs·us -a -um *adj* aged, old
annotāti·ō -ōnis *f* (**adn-**) notation, remark
annōtin·us -a -um *adj* last year's
annot·ō -āre -āvī -ātus *tr* (**adn-**) to note *(in writing),* put on record; to observe, notice; to register, designate
annumer·ō -āre -āvī -ātus *tr* (**adn-**) *(w. dat)* to count out *(money)* to; *(w. dat or* **in +** *acc)* to add *(s.th.)* to, include *(s.o.)* among
annunti·ō -āre -āvī -ātus *tr* (**adn-**) to announce, make known, proclaim
an·nuō -nuĕre -nuī -nūtus *tr* (**adn-**) to designate by a nod; to indicate, declare; *(w. dat)* to promise, grant *(s.th.)* to **‖** *intr* to nod assent; *(w. dat)* to nod assent to, be favorable to, smile on
ann·us -ī *m* year; season; age, time of life; year of office; year's produce, crops; **ad annum** for the coming year, a year from now; **anno** last year; **anno exeunte** *(or* **anno pleno)** at the end of the year; **annum** *(or* **in annum)** for a year; **annus meus (tuus,** *etc.)* my (your, *etc.)* year of office; **annus solidus** a full year
annu·us -a -um *adj* lasting a year; annual, yearly **‖** *npl* yearly pay, pension
an·quīrō -quīrĕre -quīsivī -quīsītus *tr* to search carefully; to examine, inquire into; *(w. gen or abl of the charge)* to accuse *(s.o.)* of **‖** *intr* to hold an inquest
ans·a -ae *f* handle; *(fig)* opportunity
ansāt·us -a -um *adj* having handles; **homo ansatus** man with arms akimbo
ans·er -eris *m* goose *(male),* gander
Antae·us -ī *m* Libyan giant, son of Earth, killed by Hercules **‖** name of a Carthaginian general
ante *adv* before, previously, in the past; in front; forwards; **ante...quam** before; **anno ante** a year ago; **multis annis ante** many years before that
ante *prep (w.* **acc) 1** before, in front of: **ante urbis portas** before the city gates;

2 before *(in time):* **ante diem** before the due date, too early; *(in dates):* **ante diem quartum Idus Martias** *(instead of* quarto die ante Idus Martias) *or abbr* **a.d. IV Id. Mart.** three days before the Ides of March; **ante tempus** before time, prematurely; **3** *(in preference, choice)* more than, above; **ante omnia** first of all; above all

ante- *pref (used in the senses of the adv)*

anteā *adv* before, previously, formerly; **jam antea** already in the past

anteact·us -a -um *adj (of time)* that has passed

anteambul·ō -ōnis *m* one who runs before *(to clear the way),* blocker

ante·capiō -capĕre -cēpī -ceptus *tr* to receive beforehand; to take possession of beforehand, preoccupy; to anticipate

ante·cēdō -cēdĕre -cessī -cessus *tr* precede; to outdo, surpass ‖ *intr (w. dat)* **1** to have precedence over; **2** to excel, surpass

antecell·ō -ĕre *tr* to surpass ‖ *intr (w. dat)* *(w. abl of respect or* **in** *+ abl)* to surpass *(s.o.)* in

antecessi·ō -ōnis *f* antecedent cause

antecess·or -ōris *m (mil)* scout ‖ *mpl* advance guard

antecurs·or -ōris *m (mil)* scout ‖ *mpl* vanguard

ante·eō -īre -īvī *or* **-iī** *tr* to precede; to surpass; to anticipate, prevent ‖ *intr* to precede; to take the lead; *(w. dat)* **1** to go before; **2** to surpass

ante·ferō -ferre -tulī -lātus *tr* to prefer; to anticipate

antefix·um -ī *n* antefix *(image, statue, etc., affixed to roofs and gutters of temples or homes)*

ante·gredior -gredī -gressus sum *tr* to precede

antehab·eō -ēre -uī *tr* to prefer

antehāc *adv* before now, formerly

antelātus *pp of* **antefero**

antelogi·um -ī *n* preamble, introduction

antelūcān·us -a -um *adj* pre-dawn

antemerīdiān·us -a -um *adj* before noon

ante·mittō -mittĕre -mīsī -missus *tr* to send out ahead

Antemn·ae -ārum *fpl* ancient town in Latium

Antemnāt·ēs -ium *mpl* the people of Antemnae

antenn·a *or* **antemn·a -ae** *f* yardarm, sail yard, sail

Antēn·or -oris *m* Trojan founder of Patavium *(Padua)*

Antēnorid·ēs -ae *m* descendant of Antenor; native of Patavium *(Padua)*

anteoccupāti·ō -ōnis *f (rhet)* anticipation of an opponent's arguments

antepart·um -ī *n* (-pert-) thing *or* property acquired in the past

ante·pēs -pedis *m* forefoot

antepīlān·ī -ōrum *mpl* front ranks *(soldiers drawn up in the first two lines of a battle formation)*

antepoll·eō -ēre *tr* to surpass in strength ‖ *intr (w. dat)* to be superior to *(s.o.)* in strength

ante·pōnō -pōnĕre -posuī -positus *tr* to place *or* station in front of; to place before *(in time);* to prefer, esteem more highly; *(w. dat)* to give *(a person)* preference over *(another)* to serve *(food);* to put *(a word, prefix, or letter)* before *(a word)*

antepot·ens -entis *adj* very wealthy

antequam *or* **ante...quam** *conj* before; sooner...than

Anter·ōs -ōtis *m* avenger of unrequited love *(son of Venus and Mars)*

ant·ēs -ium *mpl* rows *(of vines, soldiers, etc.)*

antesignān·us -ī *m* soldier fighting in front of the standards to defend them; leader, protagonist

ante·stō *or* **anti·stō -stāre -stitī** *intr* to excel; *(w. dat)* to be superior to

antest·or -ārī -ātus sum *tr* to call as witness

ante·veniō -venīre -vēnī -ventus *tr* to come before, arrive ahead of; to anticipate, thwart; to surpass ‖ *intr* to arrive first; to become more distinguished; *(w. dat)* **1** to anticipate; **2** to get ahead of; **3** to be better than, surpass

antever·tō -tĕre -tī -sus *tr* (-vort-) to go *or* come before; to anticipate; to prefer ‖ *intr* to act first; to go out first, set out first; *(w. dat)* to outweigh

antevol·ō -āre *intr* to dash out ahead

Antiān·us -a -um *adj* of Antium

Antiās -ātis *adj* of Antium ‖ *mpl* people of Antium

Antiātīn·us -a -um *adj* of Antium

Anticat·ō -ōnis *m* title of the books which Caesar wrote in answer to Cicero's panegyric *Cato*

anticipāti·ō -ōnis *f* preconception

anticip·ō -āre -āvī -ātus *tr* to anticipate; to have a preconceived idea of; **viam anticipare** to take the lead *(in a race)*

antīc·us -a -um *adj* front, foremost

Anticyr·a -ae *f* name of several Greek towns famous for their hellbore *(used to cure insanity)*

antideā, antideō, antidhāc *adv* old forms for **anteā, anteō, antehāc**

antidot·um -ī *n or* **antidot·os** *or* **antidot·us -ī** *f* antidote

Antigon·ē -ēs *or* **Antigon·a -ae** *f* Antigone *(daughter of Oedipus ‖ daughter of Laomedon)*

Antigon·us -ī *m* Greek name, *esp.* one of

the generals of Alexander the Great **ǁ** Antigonus Doson

Antiloch·us -ī *m* son of Nestor

Antiochī·a -ae *f* (**-chē·a**) Antioch, chief city of Syria

Antioch·us -ī *m* name of seven kings of Syria **ǁ** Academic philosopher, teacher of Cicero and Brutus

Antiop·a -ae *or* **Antiop·ē -ēs** *f* Antiopa *(mother, by Jupiter, of Amphion and Zethus)*

Antiphat·ēs -ae *m* king of the Laestrygonians **ǁ** son of Sarpedon, killed by Turnus

antiquāri·us -a -um *adj & m* antiquarian

antīquē *adv* in former times; in the good old style

antīquit·ās -ātis *f* antiquity; the ancients; the good old days

antīquitus *adv* in former times, of old; from ancient times; in the old style

antīqu·ō -āre -āvī -ātus *tr* to reject *(law, bill)*

antīqu·us -a -um *adj* (**-tic-**) old, ancient; old-fashioned, venerable; long-standing *(friendship);* located *or* lying in front **ǁ** *mpl* ancients, ancient authors **ǁ** *n* antiquity; old custom

antisophist·ēs -ae *m (rhet)* opponent in argument

antist·es -itis *m* high-priest *(of temple or deity);* authority *(of an art, philosophical school)* **ǁ** *f* high-priestess

Antisthen·ēs -is *or* **-ae** *m* pupil of Socrates and founder of Cynic philosophy *(455?– 360 B.C.)*

antistit·a -ae *f* high-priestess

antithet·on -ī *n (rhet)* antithesis

Ant·ium -(i)ī *n* coastal town in Latium *(modern Anzio)*

antli·a -ae *f* pump; treadmill

Antōni·us -a -um *adj* Roman clan name *(nomen), esp.* Marcus Antonius *(orator, consul in 99 B.C.)* **ǁ** Marcus Antonius *(triumvir, consul in 44 B.C.)*

antr·um -ī *n* cave, cavern

Anūb·is -is *or* **-idis** *m* jackal-headed Egyptian god

ānulār·ius -(i)ī *m* ring maker

ānul·us -a -um *adj* wearing a ring

ānul·us -ī *m* ring, signet ring

ān·us -ī *m* anus, rectum; ring

ăn·us -ūs *f* old woman; hag

-ān·us -a -um *adjl suf* **1** from common nouns: **urbanus** of the cit; **2** from place names: **Romanus** from *or* of Rome, Roman; **3** from personal names: **Claudi-anus** of Claudius, Claudian

anxiē *adv* uneasily

anxiet·ās -ātis *f* anxiety, worry; meticulousness

anxif·er -era -erum *adj* disquieting

anxitūd·ō -inis *f* anxiety, worry

anxi·us -a -um *adj* worried, anxious, uneasy; meticulous

Anx·ur -uris *m & n* coastal town of Latium *(modern Terracina)*

Anyt·us -ī *m* one of Socrates' three accusers

Āonid·ēs -um *fpl* Muses *(named after the section of Boeotia, called Aonia, where Mt. Helicon is located)*

Āoni·us -a -um *adj* Boeotian; Theban; of the Muses; of Helicon; poetic **ǁ** *f* Boeotia

Aorn·os -ī *adj (masc only)* having no birds, birdless

apage *interj* go!; scram!

Apamē·a -ae *f* name of several towns in Asia Minor, *esp.* that in Syria and that in Phrygia

apēliōt·ēs -ae *m* east wind

Apell·ēs -is *m* Greek painter *(fl 4th cent. B.C.)*

Āpennīnicol·a -ae *m* (**App-**) inhabitant of the Apennines

Āpennīnigen·a -ae *adj (masc only)* born on the Apennines

Āpennīn·us -a -um *adj* (**App-**) Apennine **ǁ** *m* Apennine Mountains

a·per -prī *m* wild boar; meat of wild boar as food

aper·iō -īre -uī -tus *tr* to open, uncover, lay bare, disclose, reveal; to prove, demonstrate; to explain; to recount; to cut open, split; to usher in *(a new year);* to introduce *(a subject); (mil)* to spread out *(forces); (topog)* to bring into view; **locum aperire** *(w. dat)* to open the way to, afford an opportunity for **ǁ** *refl (of flowers)* to open; to come into view

apertē *adv* openly, frankly, candidly

apert·ō -āre *tr* to bare

apert·us -a -um *pp of* **aperio ǁ** *adj* bare, uncovered, exposed; without decks; clear *(style);* frank, candid; plain, evident; accessible, unobstructed **ǁ** *n* open space; **in aperto** in the open; **in aperto esse** to be clear, evident, well known, notorious

ap·ex -icis *m* point, tip; top, summit; conical flamen's hat; cap, crown; crowning glory; long mark over a vowel, macron

ap(h)eliōt·ēs -ae *m* the E. wind

aphract·us -ī *f or* **aphract·um -ī** *n* cargo ship without a deck

Aphrodīsi·a -ōrum *npl* festival in honor of Aphrodite

aphronit·um -ī *n* washing soda, sodium carbonate

apiār·ius -iī *m* beekeeper

apiastr·um -ī *n* a variety of balm

Apīc·ius -iī *m* gourmet of the lst cent. A.D.

apicul·a -ae *f* little bee

apin·ae -ārum *fpl* trifles, nonsense

ap·is -is *f (gen pl:* **-um** *&* **-ium**) bee

Āp·is -is *or* **-idis** *m* Egyptian sacred bull

ap·iscor -iscī -tus sum *tr* to pursue; to get,

reach, gain; to get, obtain; *(lit & fig)* to grasp; to get hold of; **litem apisci** to win a lawsuit

ap·ium -iī *n* celery; parsley

aplustr·e -is *or* **aplustr·um -ī** *n (naut)* curved ornamental stern

Apoclēt·ī -ōrum *mpl* select committee *(of Aetolian League)*

apodytēr·ium -(i)ī *n* dressing room *(of a bath)*

apolactiz·ō -āre *tr* to kick aside

Apollinār·is -is -e *adj* of Apollo; **ludi Apollinares** games in honor of Apollo, instituted after the victory at Cannae **‖** *n* place sacred to Apollo

Apoll·ō -inis *m* son of Jupiter and Latona, twin brother of Diana, god of the sun, divination, archery, healing, poetry, and music

Apollodōr·us -ī *m* rhetorician, teacher of Augustus

Apollōni·a -ae *f* name of several cities: on the S. coast of Illyricum; on the S. coast of the Black Sea; in Crete

apolog·us -ī *m* story, fable

Apon·us -ī *m* warm spring near Padua

apophorēt·a -ōrum *npl* presents for departing house guests

apoproēgmen·a -ōrum *npl* things that have been rejected

aposphrāgism·a -atis *n* device on signet ring, seal

apothēc·a -ae *f* warehouse, storeroom

apparātē *adv* **(adp-)** sumptuously

apparāti·ō -ōnis *f* **(adp-)** preparation

apparāt·us -a -um *adj* **(adp-)** getting *or* making ready, preparing; providing

apparāt·us -ūs *m* equipment, apparatus, gear; equipping, organization; armaments; stock, store; rhetorical devices; pomp, magnificence

appār·ens -entis *adj* **(adp-)** visible

appāreō -ēre -uī -itum *intr* **(adp-)** to appear, become visible, be visible; to be seen, show oneself, show up; to materialize, take shape; to appear, look *(e.g., unhappy);* to be perceptible *(to the senses);* to be clearly..., be seen to be; *(of facts)* to be clear, be evident, be obvious; *(w. dat)* **1** to wait on, serve; **2** to obey *(laws);* **nec caput nec pes apparet mihi** I can make neither head nor tail of it; **nusquam apparere** to have disappeared **‖** *v impers* it is evident, it is clear; **ut apparet** apparently

appāriti·ō -ōnis *f* **(adp-)** attendance, service; provision **‖** *fpl* household servants

appārit·or -ōris *m* servant; attendant of public official *(e.g., aide, lictor, secretary)*

appar·ō -āre -āvī -ātus *tr* **(adp-)** to prepare; to provide; to organize *(weddings, public games, war);* *(w. inf or* **ut)** to get

ready to **‖** *refl (w.* in + *acc)* to prepare oneself for, equip oneself for

appellāti·ō -ōnis *f* **(adp-)** addressing; *(w. ad)* appeal to *(in general; to higher authority);* naming, calling by name; designation, name, title; pronunciation; *(gram)* common noun

appellāt·or -ōris *m (leg)* one who appeals, appellant

appell·ō -āre -āvī -ātus *tr* **(adp-)** to speak to, address, accost; to appeal to, call on, beseech; to make overtures to, approach; to invoke *(god as witness);* to demand payment of; to call up *(to pay a debt or obligation);* to recognize (as), style officially; to name, call; to mention by name, use the name of, mention; to pronounce; to designate, term, call; to demand payment of; *(leg)* to sue; **imperatorem appellare** to hail as "Imperator" **‖** *intr* to appeal

ap·pellō -pellĕre -pulī -pulsus *tr* **(adp-)** *(w. dat or* **ad) 1** to drive *(s.th.)* to; **2** to move *(military equipment, personnel)* to; **3** to steer *(ship)* to **‖** *pass (w.* **ad)** *(of a ship)* to put in at **‖** *intr (of a ship)* to land

appendicul·a -ae *f* small addition

append·ix -icis *f* addition; related topic; hanger-on

appen·dō -děre -dī -sus *tr* **(adp-)** to hang; to weigh; to pay out; *(fig)* to weigh, consider

Appenn- = **āpenn-**

appet·ens -entis *adj* **(adp-)** greedy; *(w. gen)* eager for, craving

appetenter *adv* **(adp-)** greedily, avidly

appetenti·a -ae *f* **(adp-)** *(w. gen)* the craving for, desire for; **cibi appetentia** appetite (for food)

appetīti·ō -ōnis *f* **(adp-)** grasping; desire, appetite; *(w. gen)* **1** the craving for; **2** the reaching out for; **appetitio naturalis** *(or* **ex natura** *or* **animi)** instinctive desire, appetite *(for),* impulse *(towards)*

appetīt·us -ūs *m* **(adp-)** desire, appetite *(esp. natural or instinctive)*

appet·ō -ĕre -īvī *or* **-iī -ītus** *tr* **(adp-)** to try to reach; to lay hold of; to strive after, aim for; to seek the friendship of; to court; to make for, head for; to attack, assault; to have an appetite for *(food);* to tackle *(a job)* **‖** *intr (of events)* to approach, draw near

Appiān·us -a -um *adj* of Appia, a town in Phrygia **‖** of Appius Claudius the decemvir **‖** *m* Appian of Alexandria *(historian of the 2nd cent. A.D.)*

Appi·as -adis *f* a nymph of the Appian fountain, near the temple of Venus Genetrix **‖** title of Venus

Appiet·ās -ātis *f* the rank *or* status of an Appius

apping·ō -ĕre *tr* (adp-) to paint; to write (*s.th.*) in addition (*to a verbal picture*)

Appi·us -a -um *adj* Appian; **aqua Appia** Appian Aqueduct (*built by Appius Claudius Caecus*); **via Appia** Appian Way (*road between Rome and Capua, built by the same man*) ‖ *m* Roman first name, *esp.* of the Claudian clan: Appius Claudius Crassus (*consul and decemvir in 451 B.C.*) ‖ Appius Claudius Caecus (*censor in 312 B.C.*) ‖ Appius Claudius Caudex (*consul in 264 B.C.*) ‖ Appius Claudius Pulcher (*consul in 54 B.C., censor in 50 B.C.*) ‖ **Appi Forum** town in Latium on the Appian Way

applau·dō -děre -sī -sus *tr* (adp-) to strike, slap; **terrae applaudere** to dash to the ground ‖ *intr* to applaud

applicāti·ō -ōnis *f* (adp-) application

applicāt·us -a -um *adj* (adp-) (*w. ad*) inclined to; (*w. dat*) lying close to, attached to

applicit·us -a -um *adj* (adp-) (*w. dat*) adjacent to

applic·ō -āre -āvī *or* **-uī -ātus** *or* **-itus** *tr* (adp-) to bring into close contact; (*w. dat or ad*) **1** to apply, attach, add, join (*s.th.*) to; **2** to steer (*ship*) toward; **3** to apply (*mind, attention*) to; (*w. ad*) to place (*geographically*) near to ‖ *refl* to lean (against); to sit down (on); (*w. ad*) to devote oneself to, apply oneself to ‖ *intr* (*of ships*) to put in (*at*), land

applōdō *see* **applaudo**

applōr·ō -āre -āvī *intr* (adpl-) to lament

ap·pōnō -pōněre -posuī -positus *tr* (adp-) to serve (*food*); (*w. dat or ad*) to put or lay (*s.th.*) near, at, *or* beside; (*w. dat*) **1** to set (*food*) before; **2** to appoint, assign (*s.o.*) to; **3** to reckon (*s.th.*) as; **modum apponere** (*dat*) set a limit to

apporrect·us -a -um *adj* (adp-) stretched out near *or* beside

apport·ō -āre -āvī -ātus *tr* (adp-) to carry, bring (to); to bring along, bring with one; to import; to present (*a play*); to bring in its train, cause; (*w. dat*) to carry (*s.th.*) to

apposc·ō -ěre *tr* to demand in addition

appositē *adv* (adp-) appropriately

apposit·us -a -um *pp of* **appono** ‖ *adj* (*w. ad*) suited to; (*w. dat*) situated near, bordering on

appōt·us -a -um *adj* (adp-) drunk

apprec·or -ārī -ātus sum *tr* (adp-) to pray to, worship

apprehen·dō *or* **appren·dō -děre -dī -sus** *tr* (adp-) to seize, take hold of; to arrest; to take up (*topic*); (*mil*) to occupy

apprīmē *adv* (adp-) chiefly; very

ap·primō -prĭměre -pressī -pressus *tr* (adp-) (*w. dat*) to press (*s.th.*) close to

approbāti·ō -ōnis *f* (adp-) approbation, approval; proof; decision

approbāt·or -ōris *m* (adp-) one who seconds *or* approves

approbē *adv* (adp-) very well

approb·ō -āre -āvī -ātus *tr* (adp-) to approve; to prove; to prove (*statement*) true

appromitt·ō -ěre *tr* (adp-) to promise in addition

apprōn·ō -āre -āvī -ātus *refl* (adp-) to lean forward

approper·ō -āre -āvī -ātus *tr* (adp-) to hasten, speed up ‖ *intr* to hurry

appropinquāti·ō -ōnis *f* (adp-) approach

appropinqu·ō -āre -āvī *intr* (adp-) to approach; (*w. dat or ad*) to come near, approach

appugn·ō -āre -āvī -ātus *tr* (adp-) to fight, attack

appuls·us -ūs *m* (adp-) landing; approach; influence, impact

aprīcāti·ō -ōnis *f* sunbathing

aprīc·or -ārī -ātus sum *intr* to sunbathe

aprīc·us -a -um *adj* sunny ‖ *n* sunny spot; sunshine, light of day

Aprīl·is -is -e *adj* of April; **mensis Aprilis** April ‖ *m* April (*second month of the old calendar until 153 B.C.*)

aprugn·us -a -um *adj* of a wild boar

aps- = **abs-**

apsinth·ium -(i)ī *n* (abs-) (*bot*) wormwood (*yielding a bitter abstract used in flavoring wine*)

apsūmēd·ō -inis *f* a devouring

aptē *adv* closely; suitably

apt·ō -āre -āvī -ātus *tr* to fasten, fit, adjust; to make ready, equip

apt·us -a -um *adj* tied, bound, fastened; fitted together; suitable, adapted; neat, orderly, in good order, in good condition; handy, convenient; (*w. abl*) provided with; (*w. ex or adv*) following from, dependent on; (*w. ad or in acc*) **1** equipped for, ready for; **2** efficient at, good at; **3** convenient for; **4** useful for; **5** favorable for; **causae inter se aptae** connected causes

apud *prep* (*w. acc*) at, by, near, among; at the house of; in (*a building, town*); in the care of, in the hands of, in possession of; before, in the presence of; in the writings of; (*with influence*) over; **apud gentes** (*or* **homines**) in the whole world; **apud me (te)** in my (your) care; at my (your) house; **apud mensam** at table; **apud principia** on parade; **apud se esse** to be in one's right mind

Āpūli·a -ae *f* district in S.W. Italy

Āpulic·us -a -um *adj* Apulian

Āpul·us -a -um *adj* Apulian

aqu·a -ae *f* water; rain, rainfall; aqueduct; **aquā et igni interdicere** to outlaw (*lit-*

erally, to forbid from water and fire);
aquam praebere *(w. dat)* to entertain
(guests) ‖ *fpl* spa, baths
aquaeduct·us -ūs *m* aqueduct
aquāliculus -ī *m* potbelly
aquāl·is -is -e *adj* water- ‖ *m* washbasin
aquāri·us -a -um *adj* of water ‖ *m* water-
conduit inspector ‖ *n* water supply
Aquār·ius -(i)ī *m (astr)* Aquarius *(constellation and sign of the zodiac)*
aquātic·us -a -um *adj* growing in water;
watery, moist, humid ‖ *npl* well-watered places; marshes
aquātil·is -is -e *adj* living or growing in
water, aquatic; watery
aquāti·ō -ōnis *f* fetching water; water hole
aquāt·or -ōris *m* water carrier
aquil·a -ae *f* eagle *(bird; Roman legionary
standard); (fig)* legion; gable *(of house)*
Aquilēi·a -ae *f* town in Venetia at head of
the Adriatic
aquil·ex -egis *m* water finder, dowser;
water conduit inspector
aquilif·er -erī *m* standardbearer
aquilīn·us -a -um *adj* eagle's
aquil·ō -ōnis *m* north wind; North
aquilōni·us -a -um *adj* northerly
aquil·us -a -um *adj* swarthy
Aquīn·ās -ātis *adj* of Aquinum ‖ *m* citizen
of Aquinum
Aquīn·um -ī *n* town of the Volsci, birthplace of Juvenal
aquol·a *or* **acul·a -ae** *f* **(aquu-)** brook;
small amount of water
aqu·or -ārī -ātus sum *intr* to fetch water
aquōs·us -a -um *adj* well-watered; rainy;
humid; *(med)* dropsical
aquul·a -ae *f* brook
ār·a -ae *f* altar ‖ **Ara** *(astr)* Altar *(constellation)*
arabarch·ēs -ae *m* customs officer in Egypt
Arabi·a -ae *f* Arabia
Arabic·us *or* **Arabi·us** *or* **Arab·us -a -um**
adj Arabian
Arab·s -is *m* Arab
Arachn·ē -ēs *f* Lydian girl whom Minerva
changed into a spider
arāne·a -ae *f* spider; cobweb
arāneol·a -ae *f* small spider
arāneol·us -ī *m* small spider
arāneōs·us -a -um *adj* full of cobwebs;
resembling cobwebs
arāne·us -a -um *adj* spider's ‖ *m* spider ‖
n spider web
Ar·ar -aris *(acc:* **Arrarim)** *m* Rhone tributary *(modern Saône)*
arāti·ō -ōnis *f* cultivation, tilling; agriculture; arable land
arātiuncul·a -ae *f* small plot; small farm
arāt·or -ōris *m* farmer ‖ *adj* plow-
arātr·um -ī *n* plow
Arāt·us -ī *m* Greek author, from Soli in

Cilicia, of poem on astronomy *(fl 270
B.C.)*
Arax·ēs -is *m* river in Armenia ‖ river in S.
Persia
arbi·ter -trī *m* eyewitness, spectator;
judge; *(leg)* arbitrator *(with wider discretionary power than a* **judex)**; ruler,
director, controller
arbitr·a -ae *f* eyewitness
arbitrāriō *adv* uncertainly
arbitrāri·us -a -um *adj* discretionary; arbitrary
arbitrāt·us -ūs *m* decision; inclination,
pleasure; **arbitratu** *(w. gen)* at the discretion of; *(leg)* according to the decision of *(an official arbitrator);* **arbitratu
meo, tuo** *(coll)* to my (your) heart's
content
arbitr·ium -(i)ī *n* (process of) arbitration
(before an arbitrator); independent judgment; settlement *(of a matter);* mastery,
power, control; wishes, desires; whim,
caprice; **ad arbitrium nostrum** as much
as we please; **mei arbitrii est** it is in my
power; **sui arbitrii esse** to be one's own
master; **suo arbitrio** on one's own initiative
arbitr·ō -āre -āvī -ātus *tr* to think, judge;
(w. a predicate) to consider ‖ *pass (of a
dispute)* to be settled
arbitr·or -ārī -ātus sum *tr & intr* to decide or judge *(as an arbitrator);* to consider, judge, think; to reckon, suppose,
imagine; *(w. inf)* to think it proper
arb·or *or* **arb·ōs -oris** *f* tree; mast, oar,
ship; gallows
arborēt·um -ī *n* plantation of trees
arbore·us -a -um *adj* of a tree; tree-like
arbuscul·a -ae *f* small tree, sapling
Arbuscul·a -ae *f* actress in the time of
Cicero
arbust·us -a -um *adj* wooded, planted
with trees ‖ *n* orchard; vineyard planted
with trees ‖ *npl* trees
arbute·us -a -um *adj* of arbutus
arbut·um -ī *n* wild strawberry *(fruit of
arbutus)*
arbut·us -ī *f* arbutus, strawberry tree
arc·a -ae *f* chest, box, safe; coffin; prison
cell
Arcādi·a -ae *f* district in central Peloponnesus, famed for its pastoral beauty
Arcādic·us *or* **Arcādi·us -a -um** *adj*
Arcadian
arcānō *adv* in secret; in confidence
arcān·us -a -um *adj* secret, concealed;
private; trustworthy *(friend)* ‖ *n* secret;
sacred mystery
Arc·as -ados *m* inhabitant of Arcadia,
Arcadian ‖ **Arcas**, son of Callisto by
Jupiter, eponymous hero of Arcadia ‖
Mercury, who was born on Mt. Cyllene
in Arcadia

arc·eō -ēre -uī *tr* to shut up, enclose; to keep out *(rain, cold)*; to keep at a distance, keep off; to hinder, prevent; to control, govern; to prevent, stop; *(w. abl)* to protect from, rescue from

Arcesil·ās -ae *or* **Arcesilā·üs -ī** *m* philosopher of the 3rd cent. B.C., founder of the Middle Academy

arcessīt·us -a -um *pp of* **arcesso (accers-) ‖** *adj* foreign; far-fetched; self-inflicted *(death)*

arcessīt·us -ūs *m* call, summons

arcess·ō *or* **accers·ō -ĕre -īvī** *or* **-iī -ītus** *tr* to send for, summon; to raise *(money)*; to drag in *(gratuitously)*; to induce *(sleep, tears)*; to bring upon oneself *(troubles)*; to derive; to import; *(leg)* to arraign

archetyp·us -a -um *adj* original, autograph **‖** *n* original

Archiloch·us -ī *m* Greek iambic and elegaic poet of Paros *(c. 714–676 B.C.)*

archimagīr·us -ī *m* chef

Archimēd·ēs -is *or* **-ī** *m* Greek scientist of Syracuse *(287?–212 B.C.)*

archipīrāt·a -ae *m* pirate captain

architect·ō -āre -āvī -ātus *tr* to design

architect·ōn -onis *m* architect

architect·or -ārī -ātus sum *tr* to design; to build; *(fig)* to devise

architectūr·a -ae *f* architecture

architect·us -ī *m* architect; designer, deviser

arch·ōn -ontis *m* archon *(a chief magistrate of Athens)*

Archȳt·as -ae *m* Pythagorean philosopher of the 4th cent. B.C.

arcisell·ium -(i)ī *n* chair *(with rounded back)*

arciten·ens -entis *adj* holding a bow; **dea arcitenens** Diana **‖ Arcitenens** *m* Apollo; *(astr)* Sagittarius *(constellation and sign of the zodiac)*

Arctophyl·ax -ācis *m (astr)* Boötes *(constellation)*

arct·os -ī *m* North Pole; North; north wind; night **‖ Arctos** *m* the Great and Little Bear *(double constellation)*

arctūr·us -ī *m* brightest star in Boötes

arcuāt·us -a -um *adj* bow-shaped; covered *(carriage)*

arcul·a -ae *f* small box

arculār·ius -iī *m* maker of small jewel boxes

arcu·ō -āre -āvī -ātus *tr* to curve

arc·us -ūs *m* bow; rainbow; curve; arch; triumphal arch; one of the five zones of the sky

ardali·ō -ōnis *m* busybody

arde·a -ae *f* heron **‖ Ardea** town in Latium

Arde·ās -ātis *adj* of Ardea **‖** *mpl* the people of Ardea

Ardeātīn·us -a -um *adj* of Ardea

ard·ens -entis *adj* blazing, burning, hot, fiery; gleaming; intense *(emotions)*; zealous, eager; high *(fever)*; bright *(colors, stars)*

ardenter *adv* ardently, passionately; eagerly

ardeō ardēre arsī arsūrus *tr* to be in love with **‖** *intr* to be on fire, burn, blaze; to flash, glow; to smart, burn; *(of countries)* to be in turmoil; *(of corpses)* to be cremated; *(of seas)* to be rough

ardesc·ō -ĕre *intr* to catch fire; to gleam, glitter; *(of passions)* to become more intense

ard·or -ōris *m* heat, flame; flashing, brightness; heat *(of passions)*; loved one, flame

Arduenn·a -ae *f* forest in the N. of Gaul *(modern Ardennes)*

ardu·us -a -um *adj* steep, high; uphill; erect; difficult; *(of hopes)* difficult to realize **‖** *n* height; difficulty; **in arduum** *(or* **per arduum)** upwards, uphill; high into the air

āre·a -ae *f* open space; forecourt *(of temple)*; park, playground; building site; threshing floor; bald spot

āre·faciō -facĕre -fēcī -factus *tr* to dry up

Arelāte *indecl n* town in S. Gaul *(Arles)*

arēna *see* **harena**

ār·ens -entis *adj* dry, parched; parching *(thirst)*

ār·eō -ēre *intr* to be dry; to be thirsty

Arēopagīt·ēs -ae *m* member of the Areopagus

Arēopag·us -ī *m* criminal court in Athens; hill where this court met

Ar·ēs -is *m* Greek god of war *(counterpart of Mars)*

ār·escō -escĕre -uī *intr* to become dry; to wither; *(of streams)* to run dry

aretālog·us -ī *m* teller of tall tales

Arethūs·a -ae *f* nymph pursued by river god Alpheus in the Peloponnesus and changed into a fountain **‖** fountain at Syracuse

Arē·us -a -um *adj* of Ares; **Areus pagus** court of the Areopagus

Argē·ī -ōrum *mpl* figures of men made of straw and thrown annually into the Tiber

argentāri·us -a -um *adj* silver; silvery; financial; banker's **‖** *m* banker **‖** *f* banking; bank; silver mine

argentāt·us -a -um *adj* silver-plated; *(hum)* concerned with money

argenteol·us -a -um *adj* (-tiol-) silver

argente·us -a -um *adj* silver, silvery; *(hum)* of money **‖** *m* silver coin

argent·um -ī *n* silver; silver plate; money, cash; **argentum bigatum** silver coin stamped with a two-horse chariot; **argentum signatum** silver coin; **argentum vivum** mercury, quicksilver

Argē·us *or* **Argei·us** *or* **Argī·us -a -um** *adj* Argive; Greek

Arg·ī -ōrum *mpl or* **Argos** *n (only nom & acc)* Argos *(town in N.E. Peloponnesus)*

Argīlēt·um -ī *n (also* **Argī lētum)** district in Rome between the Quirinal and Capitoline HIlls

argill·a -ae *f* potter's clay

Arginūs(s)·ae -ārum *fpl* group of three islands off the coast of Asia Minor, the scene of an Athenian naval victory in 406 B.C.

argīt·is -idis *f* vine with white grapes

Argīv·us -a -um *adj* Argive; Greek

Arg·ō -ūs *(acc & abl:* **Argō)** *f* Jason's ship

Argolic·us -a -um *adj* Argive; Greek

Argol·is -idis *adj (fem only)* Argive ‖ Argive woman ‖ the Argolid *(district around Argos)*

Argonaut·a -ae *m* Argonaut

Argos *n (only nom & acc)* Argos *(see* **Argi)**

Argō·us -a -um *adj* of the Argo

argūmentāti·ō -ōnis *f* argumentation; proof

argūment·or -ārī -ātus sum *tr* to adduce as proof; to support by arguments; *(w.* **de** + *abl)* to conclude from ‖ *intr* to adduce arguments, argue

argūment·um -ī *n* evidence, proof; argument; theme, plot; topic, subject; motif *(of artistic representation);* **ex argumento** from the facts of the case

arg·uō -uĕre -uī -ūtus *tr* to prove; to reveal, betray; to accuse, charge, impeach *(person);* to find fault with *(thing);* to prove guilty, convict

Arg·us -ī *m* many-eyed monster set over Io and killed by Mercury

argūtāti·ō -ōnis *f* creaking

argūtē *adv* shrewdly

argūti·ae -ārum *fpl* subtlety; sophistry; wit

argūt·ō -āre -āvī *tr* to say childishly

argūt·or -ārī -ātus sum *intr* to chatter

argūtul·us -a -um *adj* somewhat subtle

argūt·us -a -um *adj* clearcut, bright, distinct; piercing; bright, smart, witty *(person);* clear-voiced, melodious; rustling *(leaves);* babbling *(brook);* chirping *(birds, crickets);* pungent *(smell);* expressive *(eyes, gestures)*

argyrasp·is -idis *adj* wearing a silver shield

-āri·a -ae *fem suf* forms nouns **1** denoting a place: **argentaria** a bank; **2** a female agent: **libraria** female secretary

Ariadn·a -ae *or* **Ariadn·ē -ēs** *f* Ariadna *(daughter of King Minos; she extricated Theseus from the Labyrinth)*

Arīci·a -ae *f* town in Latium on the Via Appia

āridul·us -a -um *adj* somewhat dry

ārid·us -a -um *adj* dry, parched; withered; meager; dry *(style)*

ari·ēs -etis *m* ram; battering ram; bulwark *(used as breakwater);* **ariete crebro** with constant ramming ‖ **Aries** Aries *(sign of Zodiac)*

ariet·ō -āre -āvī -ātus *tr* to batter, ram; **inter se arietari** to collide ‖ *intr* to collide; to trip; *(w.* **in** + *acc)* to ram against

Ariobarzān·ēs -is *m* king of Cappadocia

Arī·ōn -onis *m* early Greek poet and musician, rescued from drowning by a dolphin

Ariovist·us -ī *m* king of Germanic tribe

-ār·is -is -e *adj suf* collateral with **-ālis** but used when the stem contains an **l: consularis** consular

arist·a -ae *f* ear of grain

Aristae·us ī *m* son of Apollo and Cyrene *(said to have taught man beekeeping and to have been the first to plant olive trees)*

Aristarch·us -ī *m* Alexandrine critic and scholar *(fl 156 B.C.);* stern critic

Aristīd·ēs -ae *m* Athenian politician and general in thetime of Persian Wars, famous for his honesty ‖ author from Miletus

aristolochi·a -ae *f (bot)* birthwort *(plant believed to aid in childbirth)*

Aristophan·ēs -is *m* Greek comic playwright *(c. 450?–385? B.C.)*

Aristotel·ēs -is *or* **-ī** Aristotle *(384–322 B.C.)*

arithmētic·us -a -um *adj* of numbers ‖ *f or npl* arithmetic

āritūd·ō -inis *f* dryness

-ar·ium -(i)ī *n suf* denoting a place, *e.g.,* **armāmentārium** place for keeping arms, arsenal

-ār·ius -(i)ī *m suf* denoting "dealer in", *e.g.,* **librārius** bookseller

arm·a -ōrum *npl* armor, defensive arms *(opp* **tela** weapons to throw or thrust); war, warfare; camp life; armed men, troops; equipment, tools; utensils; nature's arms *(teeth, claws, etc.);* **ad arma adire** *(or* **venire)** to resort to military force; **arma conferre cum** to clash with; **arma ferre contra** *or* **in** *(w. acc)* to fight against; **arma inferre** *(dat)* to make war on; **arma ponere** *(or* **deponere)** to lay down one's arms; **arma venatoria** hunting gear; **levia arma** light-armed troops

armāment·a -ōrum *npl* ship's gear; equipment

armāmentār·ium -(i)ī *n* arsenal

armāriol·um -ī *n* cabinet, chest, closet

armār·ium -(i)ī *n* cupboard, chest; bookcase

armātūr·a -ae *f* outfit, equipment; armor; light-armed troops

armāt·us -a -um *adj* armed; equipped **‖** *m* armed man, soldier

armāt·us -ūs *m* amor; **gravis armatus** heavy-armed troops

Armeni·a -ae *f* (-min-) country in N.E. Asia Minor

armeniāc·um -ī *n* apricot

armeniāc·us -ī *f* apricot tree

Armeni·us -a -um *adj* Armenian; **prunum Armenium** apricot **‖** *m* an Armenian

armentāl·is -is -e *adj* of the herd

armentār·ius -(i)ī *m* herdsman

arment·um -ī *n* herd

armif·er -era -erum *adj* arms-bearing, armed, warlike; **deus armifer** Mars; **dea armifera** Minerva

armig·er -era -erum *adj* armed; producing warriors; *(of a field sown with dragon's teeth)* producing armed men **‖** *m* armed man; bodyguard; armor-bearer **‖** *f* armor-bearer *(female);* **Jovis armigera** Jove's armor-bearer *(i.e., the eagle)*

armill·a -ae *f* armlet, bracelet

armillātus -a -um *adj* wearing a bracelet

Armilustr·um -ī *n* ceremony of purifying arms

armipot·ens -entis *adj* powerful in arms, valiant

armison·us -a -um *adj* reverberating with arms

arm·ō -āre -āvī -ātus *tr* to arm; to rouse to arms

arm·us -ī *m* shoulder, shoulder blade, upper arm; flank *(of animal)*

Arniens·is -is -e *adj* name of one of the tribes at Rome

ar·ō -āre -āvī -ātus *tr* to plow, till

Arpīnās -ātis *adj* of Arpinum

Arpīn·um -ī *n* town in Latium, birthplace of Marius and Cicero

arq- = arc-

arquāt·us -a -um *adj* jaundiced

arr- = adr-

arrab·ō -ōnis *m* earnest money, token payment, deposit; **arrabo amoris** token of love

arrect·us -a -um *pp of* **arrigo ‖** *adj* upright; steep

arrēp·ō -ĕre -sī *intr* (adr-) *(w. dat or* ad) to creep towards, steal up on

Arrēt·ium -(i)ī *n* town in Etruria, known for its pottery

arrexī *perf of* **arrigo**

arrī·deō -dēre -sī -sus *tr* (adr-) to smile at **‖** *intr (w. dat)* **1** to smile at, smile on; **2** to laugh with; **3** to be favorable to; **4** to please

ar·rigō -rigĕre -rexī -rectus *tr* (adr-) to erect; to arouse, excite; to prick up *(ears);* **animum arrigere** to arouse courage; **in digitos arrectus** on tiptoe; **oculi arrecti** staring eyes

ar·ripiō -ripĕre -ripuī -reptus *tr* (adr-) to snatch, seize eagerly; to get hold of; to obtain, acquire; to head eagerly for *(destination);* to jump at *(a chance, excuse); (of disease)* to attack; to assail, attack suddenly; *(fig)* to grasp quickly; *(leg)* to arrest, arraign

arrīsī *perf of* **arrideo**

arrō·dō -dĕre -sī -sus *tr* (adr-) to gnaw at, nibble away part of

arrog·ans -antis *adj* (adr-) arrogant

arroganter *adv* (adr-) arrogantly

arroganti·a -ae *f* (adr-) arrogance; presumption

ar·rogō -āre -āvī -ātus *tr* (adr-) to question; to lay claim to, arrogate; to claim to possess; to assign, attribute

arrōsī *perf of* **arrodo**

arrōsus *pp of* **arrodo**

Arrun·s -tis *m* Etruscan proper name, tradionally given to the younger sons

ars artis f skill; craft, trade; craftsmanship; work of art; invention, device; trick, stratagem; *(mil)* tactic; profession, occupation; method, way, manner, means; artificial means, artificiality; science, theory; manual, textbook; **arte** cunningly; **bonae** *(or* **liberales) artes** liberal arts; **ex arte** systematically; **istae artes** evil practices, bad habits

Arsac·ēs -is *m* first king of the Parthians; title of his successors

arsī *perf of* **ardeo**

Artaban·us -ī *m* name of several Parthian kings

artē *or* **arctē** *adv* closely, tightly; *(to love)* deeply, dearly; *(to sleep)* soundly

Artem·is -idis *f* Greek counterpart of Diana

artēri·a -ae *f* windpipe; artery

arthrītic·us -a -um *adj* arthritic

articulātim *adv* piecemeal; *(to speak)* articulately, distinctly

articul·ō -āre *tr* to articulate

articul·us -ī *m* joint, knuckle; finger; toe; limb; point of time, juncture; *(gram)* single word *(of a sentence); (gram)* clause; *(gram)* (definite, indefinite) article; *(gram)* pronoun, pronominal adjective; **in articulo temporis** in the nick of time

artif·ex -icis *adj* (-tuf-) skilled, ingenious, professional; creative, productive; cunning; skillfully made, cunningly wrought; *(w. gen,* **ad** *or* **in** + *acc)* skilled in, expert in; broken, trained *(horse)*

artif·ex -icis *m* craftsman, artist, master, professional; performer, actor, musician; author *(of book);* originator, contriver; *(w. gen or* **ad** *or* **in** + *abl)* expert in

artificiōsē *adv* skillfully; systematically

artificiōs·us -a -um *adj* skillful, ingenious, accomplished; artificial

artific·ium -(i)ī *n* skill, talent; work of art;

trade, profession; cleverness, cunning; theory

arti·us -a -um *adj* sound in mind and body

art·ō -āre -āvī -ātus *tr* (**arct-**) to pack closely; to compress, contract; to limit; to tighten

artolagan·us -ī *m* cake

artopt·a -ae *m* bread pan; baker

artu·a -ōrum *npl* limbs

art·us -a -um *adj* close, tight; confined, restricted; narrow; dense; firm; scanty, small; needy; parsimonious, stingy; strict; sound *(sleep)* ‖ *n* narrow space; tight spot, difficulty; **in artum colligere** to summarize

art·us -ūs *m* joint; limb

ārul·a -ae *f* small altar

arund·ō -inis *f* reed; shaft, arrow; pipe, flute; pen; fishing rod; hobby-horse; *(in weaving)* comb

arvīn·a -ae *f* grease

arv·us -a -um *adj* arable, plowed ‖ *n* arable land, soil, land; plain; region; grain

arx arcis *f* citadel; fortress, stronghold; place of refuge; hilltop, peak; *(fig)* mainstay, protection; summit, pinnacle; **arcem facere e cloaca** *(prov)* to make mountains out of molehills; **arx caeli** height of heaven; **arx corporis** head; **Romae septem arces** seven hills of Rome

-ās *adv suf:* **alias** elsewhere

-ās -ātis *adjl suf* **1** originally used in ethnic adjectives from the names of Italian towns: **Arpinas** of *or* connected with Arpinum; **2** extended to other stems to form adjectives and substantives: **optimas** aristocratic; **optimates** aristocrats

ās assis *m* pound *(divisible into 12 ounces);* bronze coin, penny; jugerum *(c. 3/5 of an acre);* undivided estate; **heres ex asse** sole heir; **non assis facere** not to give a hoot about

Ascān·ius -(i)ī *m* son of Aeneas and Creusa and founder of Alba Longa

ascen·dō -děre -dī -sus *tr* (**ads-**) to climb; to mount *(horse);* to board *(ship)* ‖ *intr* to climb up, ascend; *(of voice, river)* to rise; *(w.* **ad** *or* **in** + *acc)* to climb, climb up to; *(w.* **super** *or* **supra** + *acc)* to rise above, surpass; **per gradūs ascendere** to climb the stairs

ascensi·ō -ōnis *f* climbing up, ascent

ascens·us -ūs *m* (**ads-**) ascent; means of ascending, approach; step, degree; flight of stairs; *(fig)* climb, rise

ascia -ae *f* ax, hatchet; mason's trowel; **sub asciā** while still under construction

asc·iō -īre *tr* (**ads-**) to associate with oneself

asc·iscō -iscěre -īvī -ītus *tr* (**ads-**) to adopt; to approve *(a bill);* to assume, arrogate; to receive, admit *(as ally, citizen, etc.);*

to hire; *(w.* **in** + *acc)* to admit *(to citizenship, the senate);* **inter patricios asciscere** to admit to the patrician order

ascīt·us -a -um *adj* acquired *(as opposed to innate)*

Asclēpiad·ēs -is *m* famous doctor of Prusa in Bithynia, who practised in Rome *(d. 40 B.C.)*

ascop·a -ae *f* small leather pouch

Ascr·a -ae *f* birthplace of Hesiod in Boeotia, near Mt. Helicon

Ascrae·us -a -um *adj* of Ascra; **Ascraeus poeta** *or* **senex** Hesiod

ascrī·bō -běre -psī -ptus *tr* (**ads-**) to add *(by writing);* to impute, ascribe; to enroll, register; to reckon, number, class

ascriptīci·us -a -um *adj* (**ads-**) enrolled, registered

ascripti·ō -ōnis *f* (**ads-**) addition *(in writing)*

ascriptīv·us -ī *m* (**ads-**) *(mil)* reserve

ascript·or -ōris *m* (**ads-**) supporter

Asculān·us -ī *m* inhabitant of Asculum

Asc(u)l·um -ī *n* chief town of Picenum in N. Italy

asell·a -ae *f* ass *(female)*

asell·us -ī *m* ass, donkey

Asi·a -ae *f* Asia; Asia Minor *(modern Turkey);* kingdom of Troy

Asiān·us -a -um *adj* & *m* Asian

Asiātic·us -a -um *adj* connected with Asia or the East *(esp. Asia Minor and the Roman province of Asia);* **mare Asiaticum** Carpathian Sea

asīl·us -ī *m* horsefly

asināri·us -a -um *adj* connected with asses; **via asinaria** a road S.E. of Rome ‖ *m* ass-driver

asin·us -ī *m* ass; fool

Ās·is -idis *f* Asia; Asia Minor

Āsi·us -a -um *f* of Asia, of Asia Minor

Āsōp·us *or* **Āsōp·os -ī** *m* a river in Boeotia, personified as the father of Aegina

asōt·us -ī *m* playboy, rake

asparag·us -ī *m* asparagus

aspargō *see* **aspergo**

aspectābil·is -is -e *adj* visible

aspect·ō -āre -āvī -ātus *tr* (**ads-**) to look at, gaze at; to look with respect at; *(of a place)* to face; to obey *(orders)*

aspectus *pp* of **aspicio**

aspect·us -ūs *m* (**ads-**) look, sight, glance; sense of sight; eyes, expression in the eyes, look; range of vision, view; appearance, aspect; sight, vision; **primo aspectu** at first sight; **sub oculorum aspectum cadere** to come into view; **uno aspectu** at a glance

aspell·ō -ěre *tr* to drive away

asp·er -era -erum (**asprīs** = **asperīs**) *adj* rough, uneven; harsh, severe, stormy *(climate);* grating, hoarse *(sound);* pungent, strong *(odor);* rough, hard; unkind, cruel, bitter, rude *(character);* austere, rigid *(person);* wild, fierce *(animal);* rough, annoying, adverse *(circumstances);* embossed *(cup, etc.);* craggy; rugged *(style)*

asperē *adv* roughly; harshly, sternly, severely

asper·gō -gĕre -sī -sus *tr* (ads-) (-spar-) to sprinkle, scatter; to taint; *(w. dat)* to sprinkle *(s.th.)* on

asperg·ō -inis *f* (ads-) (-spar-) sprinkling; spray

asperit·ās -ātis *f* uneveness, roughness; severity, fierceness; difficulty, trouble

aspernāti·ō -ōnis *f* disdain

aspernor -ārī -ātus sum *tr* to disdain, spurn, reject

asper·ō -āre -āvī -ātus *tr* to make rough *or* uneven, roughen; to exasperate; to make worse

aspersi·ō -ōnis *f* sprinkling

aspiciō aspicĕre aspexī aspectus *tr* (ads-) to catch sight of, spot; to look at; to inspect, look over; to look *(a person)* in the eye; to visit; to consider; to picture

aspīrāti·ō -ōnis *f* (ads-) breathing; exhalation; *(gram)* aspiration *(making an h sound)*

aspīr·ō -āre -āvī -ātum *intr* to breathe, blow; *(w. dat or ad or in + acc)* to aspire to, desire to reach *or* obtain, come near to obtaining; *(w. dat)* to favor

asp·is -idis *f* asp *(poisonous snake of N. Africa)*

asportātiō -ōnis *f* removal

asport·ō -āre -āvī -ātus *tr* to carry away, remove; *(of vehicles)* to haul away

asprēt·a -ōrum *npl* rough terrain

Assarac·us -ī *m* king of Troy, son of Tros, and grandfather of Aeneas

assecl·a -ae *m* (ads-) hanger-on

assectāti·ō -ōnis *f* (ads-) (political) support

assectāt·or -ōris *m* (ads-) attendant, companion; disciple; devotee; *(pol)* supporter

assect·or -ārī -ātus sum *tr* (ads-) to follow closely; to escort; to be an adherent of, follow

assecul·a -ae *m* (ads-) hanger-on

assensi·ō -ōnis *f* (ads-) approval, applause; agreement, belief II *fpl* expressions of approval

assens·or -ōris *m* (ads-) backer, supporter

assens·us -ūs *m* (ads-) assent, approval; agreement; belief

assentāti·ō -ōnis *f* (ads-) assent, agreement; flattery

assentātiuncul·a -ae *f* (ads-) bit of flattery

assentāt·or -ōris *m* (ads-) yes-man

assentātōriē *adv* (ads-) flatteringly

assentātr·ix -īcis *f* (ads-) flatterer *(female)*

assen·tiō -tīre -sī -sum *or* **assen·tior -tīrī**

-sus sum *intr* (ads-) to agree; *(w. dat)* assent to, agree with, approve

assent·or -ārī -ātus sum *intr* (ads-) to agree always; *(w. dat)* 1 to agree always with; 2 to humor

asse·quor -quī -cūtus sum *tr* (ads-) to pursue, go after; to catch up to, reach; to gain, obtain, procure; to achieve, attain, win *(wisdom, citizenship, etc.);* to come up to, equal, match; to comprehend, understand

ass·er -eris *m* pole; joist, rafter; pole on which a litter was carried

asser·ō -ĕre -uī -tus *tr* (ads-) to set free, liberate *(slave);* to protect, defend; to claim, appropriate; **in servitutem asserere** to claim *(s.o.)* as one's slave

as·serō -serĕre -sēvī -sītus *tr* *(w. dat)* to plant *(s.th.)* close to

asserti·ō -ōnis *f* (ads-) declaration of civil status

assert·or -ōris *m* (ads-) defender, protector, champion; *(leg)* claimant *(who claims a person as his slave)*

asserv·iō -īre -īvī *or* **-iī** *intr* (ads-) *(w. dat)* to apply oneself to

asserv·ō -āre -āvī -ātus *tr* (ads-) to preserve; keep *(records);* to watch; to keep in custody; *(mil)* to guard

assessi·ō -ōnis *f* (ads-) company, (legal) support, standing by

assess·or -ōris *m* (ads-) adviser; *(leg)* counselor

assess·us -ūs *m* (ads-) legal assistance

assevēranter *adv* (ads-) emphatically

assevērāti·ō -ōnis *f* (ads-) assertion; emphasis; earnestness; *(rhet)* emphasizing particle *(e.g., eheu)*

assevēr·ō -āre -āvī -ātus *tr* (ads-) to assert emphatically; *(of things)* to give clear evidence of; to be serious about II *intr* to be serious

as·sideō -sidēre -sēdī -sessus *tr* (ads-) to sit near; *(mil)* to besiege II *intr* to sit nearby; *(w. dat)* 1 to sit near, stand by, take care of, keep *(s.o.)* company; 2 to be busily engaged in; 3 *(of places)* to be situated close to; 4 to attend to, mind; 5 to resemble; 6 *(mil)* to encamp near; 7 *(mil)* to set up a blockade against

as·sīdō -sīdĕre -sēdī *intr* (ads-) to sit down; *(of birds)* to land, alight

assiduē *adv* (ads-) assiduously, continually

assiduit·ās -ātis *f* (ads-) constant presence; persistence, frequent recurrence

assiduō *adv* (ads-) continually

assidu·us -a -um *adj* (ads-) constantly present; persistent, incessant; tireless, busy; restless *(sea)* II *m* taxpayer; rich man

assignāti·ō -ōnis *f* (ads-) allotment *(of land)*

assign·ō -āre -āvī -ātus *tr* (ads-) to mark out, allot, assign *(land); (w. dat)* **1** to confer *(honors)* on; **2** to ascribe to, impute to; **3** to attribute to; **4** to entrust to the care of

as·siliō -silīre -siluī -sultum *intr* (ads-) to jump; *(w. dat)* **1** to jump upon, leap at; **2** *(mil)* to make a sudden assault on; *(w. ad)* **1** to jump to; **2** to have recourse to

assimil·is -is -e *adj* (ads-) *(w. gen or dat)* similar to, like

assimiliter *adv* (ads-) in like manner

assimulāti·ō -ōnis *f* (ads-) similarity; comparison; pretense

assimulāt·us -a -um *adj* (ads-) similar; counterfeit

assimul·ō -āre -āvī -ātus *tr* (ads-) (-mil-) to pretend; to resemble, imitate; *(w. dat)* to compare to

as·sistō -sistĕre -titī *intr* (ads-) to stop; to stand nearby; *(w. ad)* to stand at *or* near; *(w. dat)* to assist, defend; *(mil) (w. in + acc)* to take up a position against; *(leg)* to assist in court; *(leg) (w. dat)* to assist, defend

assitus *pp of* **assero**

assol·eō -ēre *intr* (ads-) to be usual

asson·ō -āre *intr* (ads-) *(w. dat)* to echo

assuctus *pp of* **assugo**

assūdesc·ō -ĕre *intr* (ads-) (-asc-) to break out into a sweat

assue·faciō -facĕre -fēcī -factus *tr* (ads-) to train; *(w. dat or ad or inf)* to accustom *(s.o.)* to

assu·escō -escĕre -ēvī -ētus *tr* (ads-) *(w. dat)* to accustom *(s.o.)* to, make *(s.o.)* familiar with **‖** *intr (w. dat,* **ad,** *or w. inf)* to become used to; *(w. dat)* to become intimate with

assuētūd·ō -inis *f* (ads-) habit, custom; intimacy

assuēt·us -a -um *pp of* **assuesco ‖** *adj* accustomed, customary, usual; *(w. abl)* trained in; *(w. dat,* **ad** *or* **in** *+ acc or inf)* accustomed to, used to; *(w. dat)* intimate with

assū·gō -gĕre -xī -ctus *tr* (ads-) to suck in

assul·a -ae *f* splinter, chip, shaving

assulātim *adv* into splinters

assult·ō -āre -āvī -ātus *tr* (ads-) to assault **‖** *intr (w. dat)* to jump at, jump to

assult·us -ūs *m* (ads-) assault

assūm·ō -ĕre -psī -ptus *tr* (ads-) to take in addition, add; to adopt; to usurp; to claim, assume; to employ, hire; to derive, borrow; to gain, acquire *(qualities);* to take *(food, drink, bait);* to take along *(as companion);* **sibi assumere** to lay claim to

assumpti·ō -ōnis *f* (ads-) assumption; adoption; acquisition; claim; *(in logic)* minor premise; *(rhet)* taking up *(of a point)*

assumptīv·us -a -um *adj* (ads-) resting on external evidence, extrinsic

assū·ō -ĕre *tr* (ads-) *(w. dat)* to sew *(e.g. patch)* on

assur·gō -gĕre -rexī -rectum *intr* (ads-) to stand up; to rise; to increase, swell; *(of hair)* to stand on end; *(w. dat)* to rise out of respect for

ass·us -a -um *adj* roasted; dry *(sunbathing without anointing)* **‖** *n* roast

assuxī *perf of* **assugo**

Assyri·a -ae *f* Assyria

Assyri·us -a -um *adj* Assyrian **‖** *mpl* Assyrians

ast *conj (old form of* **at)** but

Astart·ē -ēs *f* Syro-Phoenician goddess, counterpart of Venus

Asteri·a -ae *f* sister of Leto, who was metamorphosed into a quail at Delos

astern·ō -ĕre *tr* (ads-) to strew **‖** *pass* to prostrate oneself

astic·us -a -um *adj* city, urban

astipulāt·or -ōris *m* (ads-) legal assistant; supporter, adherent

astipul·or -ārī -ātus sum *intr* (ads-) *(w. dat)* to side with

astit·uō -uĕre -uī -ūtus *tr* to place near; *(w. ad)* to make *(s.o.)* stand near

ast·ō -āre -itī *intr* (ads-) to stand erect, stand up, stand nearby; *(w. dat)* to assist

Astrae·a -ae *f* goddess of justice

astrep·ō -ĕre -uī *tr* (ads-) to assail *(with shouts)* **‖** *intr* to shout in support

astrictē *adv* (ads-) concisely; strictly

astrict·us -a -um *pp of* **astringo ‖** *adj* drawn together, tight; stingy; concise

astrif·er -era -erum *adj* starry

astri·ngō -ngĕre -nxī -ctus *tr* (ads-) to tighten, bind fast; to obligate; to restrain; to freeze; to pledge; *(fig)* to numb; *(fig)* to compress, abridge; to occupy *(attention);* to embarrass; to implicate *(in a crime);* **fidem astringere** to give one's word; **inter se astringere** to fasten together

astrologi·a -ae *f* astronomy; astrology

astrolog·us -ī *m* astronomer; astrologer

astr·um -ī *n* star; constellation **‖** *npl* stars; sky, heaven

astr·uō -ĕre -ī -ctus *tr* (ads) to build as an additional structure; **nobilitatem alicui astruere** to add nobility to s.o.

astū *indecl n* (**asty**) the city *(i.e.,* Athens)

astup·eō -ēre -uī *intr (w. dat)* to be amazed at, be enthralled by

ast·us -ūs *m* cunning; trick

astūtē *adv* slyly

astūti·a -ae *f* cunning; astuteness; trick

astūt·us -a -um *adj* cunning, clever

Astyag·ēs -is *m* king of Media and grandfather of Cyrus

Astyan·ax -actis *m* son of Hector and Andromache

asȳl·um -ī *n* refuge, asylum

at *conj* but; *(in a transition)* but on the other hand; *(in anticipation of an opponent's objection)* but, it may be objected; *(in an ironical objection)* but really, but after all; *(after a negative clause, to introduce a qualification)* but at least; **at contra** but on the contrary; **at tamen** but at least

Atābul·us -ī *m* sirocco, S.E. wind

Atalant·a -ae *or* **Atlant·ē -ēs** *f* daughter of King Schoeneus, defeated by Hippomenes in a footrace ‖ daughter of Iasius and participant in the Calydonian boar hunt

atat *(or* **attat)** *interj (expressing surprise or fear)* aha!, oh!

atav·us -ī *m* great-great-great-grandfather; ancestor

ātell·a -ae *f* Campanian town

ātellān·a -ae *f* comic farce *(originated in Atella)*

ā·ter -tra -trum *adj* flat black *(different from* **niger** glossy black); dark; gloomy; malicious; poisonous; unlucky, illomened

Atham·ān -ānis *m* inhabitant of Athamia

Athamāni·a -ae *f* district in Epirus

Athamantē·us -a -um *adj* of Athamas *(referring to Phrixus or Palaemon)*

Atham·ās -antis *m* king of Thessaly, father of Helle and Phrixus by Nephele, and of Learchus and Melecertes by Ino

Athēn·ae -ārum *fpl* Athens

Athēniens·is -is -e *adj* Athenian

Athēnodōr·us -ī *m* Stoic philosopher, teacher of Augustus

athe·os -ī *m* atheist

āthlēt·a -ae *m* athlete; boxer; wrestler

āthlēticē *adv* athletically

āthlētic·us -a -um *adj* athletic ‖ *f* athletics

Ath·os *or* **Atho -ōnis** *m* mountain on the peninsula of Acte in Chalcidice

ātīn·a -ae *f* town in Latium ‖ town in Lucania

ātīn·ās -ātis *m* of Atina ‖ *mpl* the people of Atina

Atl·ā(n)s -antis *m* Atlas *(giant supporting the sky, son of Iapetus and Clymene)* ‖ Mt. Atlas *(on N.W. coast of Africa)*

Atlantē·us -a -um *adj* Atlantic

Atlantiad·ēs -ae *m* grandson of Atlas, Mercury ‖ great-grandson of Atlas, Hermaphroditus

Atlantic·us -a -um *adj* Atlantic

Atlant·is -idis *or* **-idos** *f* daughter *or* female descendant of Atlas

atom·os -ī *f* atom

atque *conj* and *(used before vowels and "h") see* **ac**

atquī *conj* but yet, and yet; however, rather, and yet

ātrāment·um -ī *n* ink; **atramentum sutorium** black shoe polish

ātrāt·us -a -um *adj* dressed in black *(for mourning)*

Atr·eūs -eī *m* son of Pelops, brother of Thyestes, father of Agamemnon and Menelaus

ātricol·or -ōris *adj* black

Atrīd·ēs -ae *m* descendant of Atreus

ātriens·is -is *m* butler

ātriol·um -ī *n* small hall, anteroom

ātrit·ās -ātis *f* blackness

ātrīt·us -a -um *adj* blackened

ātr·ium -(i)ī *n* atrium *(first main room of Roman house)*; hall *(of temple or public building)* ‖ *npl* house; palace

atrōcit·ās -ātis *f* hideousness; fierceness, brutality, cruelty; severity, rigor

artōciter *adv* horribly, fiercely, cruelly, grimly

Atrop·os -ī *f* one of the three Fates

atrōt·us -a -um *adj* invulnerable

atr·ox -ōcis *adj* atrocious, horrible; hideous; frightful; cruel, fierce; harsh, stern, unyielding, grim

attactus *pp of* **attingo**

attact·us -ūs *m* **(adt-)** touch, contact

attag·ēn -ēnis *m* woodcock *(game bird)*

attagēn·a -ae *f* woodcock *(game bird)*

Attalic·us -a -um *adj* of Attalus; Pergamean; rich, splendid; covered with gold brocade ‖ *npl* gold brocade

Attal·us -ī *m* king of Pergamum

attamen *conj* but still, but yet

attat *or* **attatae** *interj see* **atat**

attegi·a -ae *f* hut, cottage

attemperātē *adv* **(adt-)** on time, at the right time

attempt·ō -āre -āvī -ātus *tr* **(adt-)** to attempt; to test; to tempt, try to seduce; to call into question; to attack

atten·dō -dĕre -dī -tus *tr* **(adt-)** to notice, mark; to pay attention to, mind, consider; **animo attendere** to listen to; **animum attendere** to pay attention; **aures attendere** to listen closely ‖ *intr* to pay attention, listen

attentē *adv* **(adt-)** attentively

attenti·ō -ōnis *f* attention

attentō *see* **attemptō**

attent·us -a -um *pp of* **attendo** ‖ *adj* attentive; careful; frugal; industrious

attenuātē *adv* plainly, in a plain style

attenuāt·us -a -um *adj* weak, weakened; shortened, brief; over-refined, affected; plain, bald *(style)*

attenu·ō -āre -āvī -ātus *tr* **(adt-)** to weaken; to thin; to lessen, diminish; to impoverish ‖ *pass* to become thinner, shrink

at·terō -terĕre -trīvī -trītus *tr* **(adt-)** to rub (against), wear away, wear out; to reduce in dimensions, diminish; to impair *(faculties, qualities);* to reduce *(military forces);* to weaken, exhaust; to waste, fritter away; destroy

attest·or -ārī -ātus sum *tr* (adt-) to attest
attex·ō -ĕre -uī -tus *tr* (adt-) to add *(by weaving);* to add on
Atth·is -idis *f* Attica
Attic·a -ae *f* district of Greece, with Athens as its capital
Atticē *adv* in the Athenian style
Atticiss·ō -āre *tr & intr* to speak in the Athenian (Attic) manner
Attic·us -a -um *adj* Attic, Athenian ‖ *m* Titus Pomponius Atticus *(friend of Cicero, 109–32 B.C.)* ‖ *f* daughter of Atticus
attigō *see* attingo
at·tineō -tinēre -tinuī -tentus *tr* (adt-) to hold tight, hold on to, hold back; to reach for ‖ *intr (w.* ad) to pertain to, relate to, refer to, concern; quod ad me attinet as far as I am concerned
at·tingō -tingĕre -tigī -tactus *tr* (adt-) to touch, come in contact with; to reach, arrive at; to touch *(food),* taste; to touch, lie near, border; to touch upon, mention lightly; to touch, strike, attack; to touch, affect; to undertake, engage in; to take in hand, manage; to resemble; to concern, belong to
Att·is -idis *m* priest of Cybele
attoll·ō -ĕre *tr* (adt-) to lift up, raise; to erect; to stir up *(dust, sea);* to cause *(river)* to rise; to hold aloft, carry; to exalt; to uplift; iras atollere to rouse anger ‖ *refl & pass* to rise; to appear; to grow
atton·deō -dēre -dī -sus *tr* (adt-) to clip, shave, shear; to prune; to crop; *(fig)* to fleece, cheat, clip
attonit·us -a -um *adj* (adt-) thunderstruck, stunned, dazed, astonished; inspired; frantic, frenzied
atton·ō -āre -uī -itus *tr* (adt-) to strike with lightning; to drive crazy
attorqu·eō -ēre *tr* (adt-) to wind up *(before hurling)*
attra·hō -hĕre -xī -ctus *tr* (adt-) to attract; to drag in; to cause to happen, bring on; to draw toward oneself; to bend *(a bow);* to draw up *(the feet);* to contract, draw together
attrect·ō -āre -āvī -ātus *tr* (adt-) to touch, handle; to appropriate to oneself
attrepid·ō -āre *intr* (adt-) to hobble along
attrib·uō -uĕre -uī -ūtus *tr* (adt-) to allot, assign; to appoint *(to a post);* to put under the command of; to attribute; to bestow, give; to impose *(taxes)*
attribūti·ō -ōnis *f* (adt-) *(gram)* predicate; *(leg)* transference of a debt *(to another person, obligating him)*
attribūt·um -ī *n* (adt-) *(gram)* predicate
attrīt·us -a -um *pp of* attero ‖ *adj* worn away, wasted; thin; hardened
au *interj* ouch!

au·ceps -cupis *m* fowler, bird trapper; poulterer; spy, eavesdropper
auctār·ium -(i)ī *n* addition, overweight *(in a purchase)*
auctific·us -a -um *adj* increasing
aucti·ō -ōnis *f* increase; auction
auctiōnāri·us -a -um *adj* auction-
auctiōn·or -ārī -ātus sum *intr* to hold an auction
auctit·ō -āre *tr* to keep increasing
auct·ō -āre *tr* to increase; *(w. abl)* to bless with
auctor -ōris *m* originator, author; writer, historian; reporter, harbinger *(of news);* acknowledged expert, authority *(for statment or theory);* proposer *(of a law);* supporter, backer; vendor, seller; progenitor *(of a clan, family, race);* founder *(of city);* model, example; adviser, counselor; teacher; guarantor, security; leader, statesman; source, thrower, dealer *(of missile, wound, death);* auctor esse *(w.* ut, ne + *subj)* to advocate, advise; to move that, propose that; faenoris auctor lender; me auctore on my initiative; pecuniae auctor person responsible for or owing a sum of money; rerum omnium auctor parensque the Creator *(literally, the author and parent of all things);* sine auctore anonymous
auctōrāment·um -ī *n* contract; pay
auctōrit·ās -ātis *f* origination, source, cause; view, opinion, judgment; advice, encouragement; power, authority, weight, influence, prestige; leadership; importance, significance, worth, consequence; example, model, precedent; authority *(for establishing a fact);* document, record; decree *(of senate);* right of ownership, title
auctōr·ō -āre -āvī -ātus or auctōr·or ārī *tr* to hire out, sell ‖ *refl & pass* to hire oneself out
auct·us -a -um *pp of* augeo ‖ *adj* blessed *(with children, good omens)*
auct·us -ūs *m* increase, growth; abundance, prosperity
aucup·ium -(i)ī *n* fowling; trap; eavesdropping; aucupia verborum quibbling
aucup·ō -āre -āvī -ātus or aucup·or -ārī -ātus sum *tr* to lie in wait for, watch for; to chase, strive after, catch ‖ *intr* to trap birds
audāci·a -ae *f* boldness, courage, daring; recklessness, effrontery, audacity; bold deed ‖ *fpl* adventures
audāc(i)ter *adv* boldly
aud·ax -ācis *adj* bold, daring; reckless
aud·ens -entis *adj* bold, daring
audenti·a -ae *f* boldness, daring
audeō audēre ausus sum *tr* to dare, risk; vix ausim *(old perf subj active)* credere

I could scarcely dare to believe **ll** *intr* to dare, be bold

audi·ens -entis *m* hearer, listener **ll** *mpl* audience

audienti·a -ae *f* hearing, attention; **audientiam facere** to command attention, command silence

aud·iō -īre -īvī *or* **-iī -ītus** *tr* to hear, listen to; to be taught by, learn from; to grant; to accept, agree with, yield to; to obey; to be called, be named; to be reported, be regarded

audīti·ō -ōnis *f* hearsay, rumor

audīt·ō -āre -āvī *tr* to hear

audīt·or -ōris *m* hearer; student

audītōr·ium -(i)ī *n* lecture hall; the audience

audīt·us -ūs *m* hearing, sense of hearing; hearsay

auferō auferre abstulī ablātus *tr* to take away, bear off; to remove, withdraw; to steal; to sweep away, kill, destroy; to gain, obtain; to learn, understand; to mislead; to lead into a digression; to abduct; to captivate; **pedes auferre** to go away **ll** *pass* **e conspectu auferri** to disappear from sight **ll** *refl* to go away

Aufid·us -ī *m* river in Apulia

au·fugiō -fugĕre -fūgī *tr* to shun, flee from **ll** *intr* to run away, escape

Aug·ē -ēs *f* mother of Telephus by Hercules

Augē·ās -ae *m* king of Elis, whose stables were cleaned by Hercules

au·geō -gēre -xī -ctus *tr* to increase, enlarge, augment, spread; to magnify; to exalt; to exaggerate; to emphasize; to enrich; to honor, advance, promote; to reinforce; to feed *(flame);* to raise *(voice);* to endow

augesc·ō -ĕre *intr* to begin to grow; to become larger, increase; to prosper; *(of river)* to rise

aug·ur -uris *mf* augur *(priest who foretold future by observing birds);* seer

augurācul·um -ī *n* place of augury *(later known as the* **arx***)*

augurāl·is -is -e *adj* augural, augur's **ll** *n* area in a Roman camp where the general took the auguries

augurāti·ō -ōnis *f* prophesying

augurātō *adv* after taking the auguries

augurāt·us -ūs *m* office of augur

augurāt·us -a -um *adj* consecrated after taking the auspices

augur·ium -(i)ī *n* observation of omens, interpretation of omens, augury; sign, omen; prophecy; foreboding

auguri·us -a -um *adj* of augurs; **ius augurium** the right to take auguries

augur·ō -āre -āvī -ātus *or* **augur·or -ārī -ātus sum** *tr* to consult by augury; to consecrate by augury; to predict, proph-

esy; to conjecture, imagine **ll** *intr* to act as augur; to take auspices

August·a -ae *f* title of wife, mother, grandmother, daughter, or sister of the emperor

Augustāl·is -is -e *adj* of Augustus; **sodales Augustales** priests of deified Augustus **ll** *npl* games in honor of Augustus

Augustān·us -a -um *adj* Augustan

augustē *adv* reverently, solemnly

Augustiān·ī -ōrum *mpl* Nero's claque in the theater

Augustīn·us -a -um *adj* of Augustus

august·us -a -um *adj* august, sacred, venerable; majestic

August·us -a -um *adj* Augustan, imperial; **mensis Augustus** August **ll** *m* honorary cognomen of Octavius Caesar after 27 B.C. and of subsequent emperors

aul·a -ae *f* inner court, hall *(of house);* palace; royal court; people of the royal court, the court

aulae·um -ī *n* curtain **ll** *npl* curtain, tapestries

aulic·us -a -um *adj* courtly, princely **ll** *m* courtier

Aul·is -is *or* **-idis** *f* port in Boeotia from which Greeks sailed for Troy

auloed·us -ī *m* singer accompanied by reed pipe

aur·a -ae *f* breeze; breath of air, wind; air, atmosphere; heights, heaven; upper world; odor, exhalation; daylight, publicity; **ad auras ferre** to make known, publicize; **ad auras venire** to come to the upper world; **aura auri** the gleam of gold; **auram captare** to sniff the air; **aura popularis** popular favor; **auras fugere** to hide; **aura spei** breath of hope; **sub auras** to light, into the air; into the open air

aurāri·us -a -um *adj* gold, golden **ll** *f* gold mine

aurāt·us -a -um *adj* made of gold; gold-plated; golden; glittering; **aurata pellis** the Golden Fleece

Aureli·us -a -um *adj* Roman clan name *(nomen), esp.* Marcus Aurelius *(Roman Emperor* A.D. *161–180)* **ll** named after an Aurelius, *esp.* Via Aurelia *(running along the Etruscan coast to the Maritime Alps)*

aureol·us -a -um *adj* gold; splendid

aure·us -a -um *adj* gold, golden; gilded; gilt; beautiful, magnificent; brilliant **ll** *m* gold coin

auricom·us -a -um *adj* golden-haired; with golden foliage

auricul·a -ae *f* (**ōr-**) ear; *(leg)* **auriculam tangere** to agree to be a witness

aurif·er -era -erum *adj* producing or containing gold; *(of trees)* bearing golden apples

aurif·ex -icis *m* (**auru-**) goldsmith

aurīg·a -ae *mf (ōr-)* charioteer; *(fig)* pilot **‖ Auriga** *m* Auriga *(constellation)*

aurīgāti·ō -ōnis *f* chariot-driving

aurigen·a -ae *m* offspring of gold *(i.e., Perseus)*

aurig·er -era -erum *adj* gold-bearing; gilded

aurīg·ō -āre -āvī -ātum *intr* to drive a chariot; to compete in a chariot race

aur·is -is *f* ear; **aurem admovere** to listen; **auribus servire** to flatter; **aures adhibere** to pay attention; **in aurem dextram** *(or* **in aurem utramvis) dormire** to sleep soundly, be unconcerned

auriscalp·ium -(i)ī *n (med)* earpick, probe

aurītul·us -ī *m (long-eared)* ass

aurīt·us -a -um *adj* long-eared; attentive; nosey; **testis aurītus** witness by hearsay only **‖** *m* rabbit, hare

aurōr·a -ae *f* dawn, daybreak; the East **‖ Aurora** goddess of dawn

aur·um -ī *n* gold; color of gold, golden luster; gold cup; gold necklace; gold jewelry; gold plate; golden fleece; gold money; Golden Age

Aurunc·a -ae *f* town in Campania, birthplace of the poet Lucilius

Aurunc·us -a -um *adj* of Arunca **‖** *mpl* people of Arunca

auscultāti·ō -ōnis *f* obedience

auscultāt·or -ōris *m* listener

auscult·ō -āre -āvī -ātus *tr* to listen to; to overhear **‖** *intr* (w. dat) to obey, listen to

ausim *see* **audeo**

Auson·ēs -um *mpl* Ausonians *(ancient inhabitants of central Italy)*

Ausoni·a -ae *f (poet)* Italy

Ausonid·ae -ārum *mpl (poet)* Italians

Ausoni·us -a -um *adj (poet)* Ausonian, Italian **‖** *mpl (poet)* Ausonians, Italians

ausp·ex -icis *mf* augur, soothsayer; *(fig)* guide, director, protector **‖** *mpl* witnesses *(at a marriage ceremony)*

auspicātō *adv* after taking the auspices; auspiciously

auspicāt·us -a -um *adj* consecrated *(by auguries);* auspicious, lucky

auspic·ium -(i)ī *n (often used in the plural)* auspices *(from behavior of birds or chickens);* right to take the auspices; sign, omen; command, leadership, authority; inauguration; **auspicia incerta** ambiguous auspices; **auspicium habere** to have the right to take auspices; **auspicium facere** *(of birds)* to give a sign; **pullarium in auspicium mittere** to send the keeper of chickens to take the auspices; **tuis auspiciis** under your command *(or* leadership)

auspic·ō -āre -āvī *intr* to take the auspices

auspic·or -ārī -ātus sum *tr* to inaugurate, make a ceremonial beginning of; to enter upon **‖** *intr* to take auspices; to make a start

aus·ter -trī *m* south wind; the South

austērē *adv* austerely, severely

austērit·ās -ātis *f* austerity

austēr·us -a -um *adj* austere, stern, harsh *(person);* pungent *(odor);* harsh *(taste);* drab, dark *(color);* serious *(talk);* gloomy, hard *(circumstances);* dry *(wine)*

austrāl·is -is -e *adj* southern; **cingulus** *(or* **regio** *or* **ora) australis** torrid zone

austrīn·us -a -um *adj* southerly, from the south; southern

aus·us -a -um *pp of* **audeo ‖** *n* daring attempt, enterprise, venture; outrage

aut *conj* or; *(correcting what precedes)* or rather, or else; *(adding emphatic alternative)* or at least; **aut...aut** *(introducing two or more logically exclusive alternatives)* either...or; **unus aut alter** one or two

autem *conj (regularly follows an emphatic word)* but, on the other hand, however; *(in transitions)* now

autheps·a -ae *f* cooker *(utensil)*

autograph·us -a -um *adj* written with one's own hand, autograph

Autolyc·us -ī *m* father of Anticlea, maternal grandfather of Ulysses

automat·on *or* **automat·um -ī** *n* automaton

automat·us -a -um *adj* automatic, spontaneous, voluntary

Automed·ōn -ontis *m* charioteer of Achilles **‖** *n* automaton

Autono·ē -ēs *f* daughter of Cadmus, wife of Aristaeus, and mother of Actaeon

autumnāl·is -is -e *adj* autumn-, fall-

autumn·us -a -um *adj & m* autumn

autum·ō -āre -āvī -ātus *tr* to assert, say

auxiliār·is -is -e *adj* auxiliary **‖** *mpl* auxiliary troops, auxiliaries

auxiliāri·us -a -um *adj* auxiliary

auxiliāt·or -ōris *m* helper

auxiliāt·us -ūs *m* help, aid

auxili·or -ārī -ātus sum *intr (w. dat)* **1** to give help to; **2** *(of things)* to be helpful to, be of use to; **3** *(med)* to relieve, heal, cure

auxil·ium -(i)ī *n* help; *(med)* relief, remedy; **auxilio esse** *(w. dat)* to be of assistance to **‖** *npl* auxiliary troops; reinforcements

avārē *adv* greedily

avāriter *adv* greedily

avāriti·a -ae *f* avarice, greed; gluttony

avār·us -a -um *adj* greedy, avaricious; *(w. gen)* eagerly desirous of, greedy for

avē! *see* **aveo**

āve·hō -here -xi -ctus *tr* to haul away **‖** *pass* to ride away, sail away

ā·vellō -vellĕre -vellī *(or* **-vulsī** *or* **-volsī) -vulsus** *(or* **-volsus)** *tr* to pull *or* pluck

away; to tear off; to separate, remove **ll**
refl & pass (w. **ab)** to tear oneself away
from, withdraw from
avēn·a -ae *f* oats; reed, stalk, a straw;
shepherd's pipe
Aventīn·us -a -um *adj* Aventine **ll** *m & n*
Aventine Hill *(one of the Seven Hills of
Rome)* **ll** son of Hercules
av·eō -ēre *tr* to desire, long for, crave; *(w.
inf)* to long to **ll** *intr* to say good-bye;
ave!, avete! hello!, farewell!, good-bye!;
avere jubeo I send greetings
Avernāl·is -is -e *adj* of Lake Avernus
Avern·us -a -um *adj* birdless; of Lake
Avernus **ll** *m* Lake Avernus *(near Cumae,
reputed entrance to the underworld)*
āverr·ō -ēre -ī *tr* to sweep away
āverrunc·ō -āre *tr* to avert
āversābil·is -is -e *adj* abominable
āvers·or -ārī -ātus sum *tr* (**-vor-**) to repulse, reject, refuse; to shun, avoid; to
send away **ll** *intr* to turn away *(in displeasure, shame, contempt)*
āvers·or -ōris *m* embezzler
āvers·us -a -um *pp of* **averto ll** *adj* turned
back, reversed; rear, in the rear; *(of blows)*
coming from the rear; distant, remote;
out-of-the-way; disinclined, alienated,
unfavorable, hostile; *(w. dat or* **ab)** averse
to, hostile to, opposed to, estranged from
ll *n* the back part, the back; **in aversum**
backwards **ll** *npl* the back; hinterland
ā·vertō -vertĕre -vertī -versus *tr* (**-vor-**)
to turn away, avert; to embezzle, misappropriate; to divert, distract; to alienate
ll *refl* to retire **ll** *intr* to withdraw, retire
avi·a -ae *f* grandmother; old wives' tale
āvi·a -ōrum *npl* wasteland
aviāri·us -a -um *adj* of birds, bird **ll** *n*
aviary; haunt of wild birds
avidē *adv* eagerly, greedily
avidit·ās -ātis *f* eagerness, longing; avarice
avid·us -a -um *adj* eager, earnest; greedy;
voracious, gluttonous; *(w. gen or dat or*
in *acc)* eager for
av·is -is *f* bird; sign, omen; **avis alba** *(or
rara)* rarity
avīt·us -a -um *adj* grandfather's; ancestral; old
āvi·us -a -um *adj* pathless; out-of-the-
way, lonely; untrodden; wandering,
straying; going astray
āvocāment·um -ī *n* diversion, recreation
āvocāti·ō -ōnis *f* distraction
āvoc·ō -āre -āvī -ātus *tr* to call away; to
divert, remove, withdraw; to amuse; to
distract *(attention);* to interrupt *(work)*
āvol·ō -āre -āvī -ātum *intr* to fly away; to
dash off
āvulsus *pp of* **avello**
avuncul·us -ī *m* (maternal) uncle; **avun-
culus magnus** granduncle

av·us -ī *m* grandfather; forefather
-ax -ācis *suf* implying tendency, ability:
capax ability to hold, **dicax** tendency to
talk, **pertinax** tendency to hold on
Axen·us -ī *m* Black Sea
āxill·a -ae *f* armpit
ax·is -is *m* axle; wagon, chariot; the earth's
axis; north pole; vault of heaven; region,
climate, country; board, plank

B

babae *interj* great!, wonderful!
Babyl·ō -ōnis *m* Babylonian; rich man
Babyl·ōn -ōnis *f* city on the Euphrates
River
Babylōni·a -ae *f* country between Tigris
and Euphrates
Babylōnic·a -ōrum *npl* Babylonian tapestry
Babylōniēns·is -is -e *adj* Babylonian
Babylōni·us -a -um *adj* Babylonian **ll** *mpl*
Babylonians
bāc·a -ae *f* berry; olive; fruit; pearl
bācāt·us -a -um *adj* adorned with pearls;
monile bacatum pearl necklace
bacc·ar -aris *n* cyclamen *(plant with showy
white, pink, or red flowers)*
Bacch·a -ae *f* Bacchante *(female member
of the orgiastic cult of Bacchus)*
bacchābund·us -a -um *adj* raving
Bacchān·āl -ālis *n* site sacred to Bacchus
ll *npl* Bacchanalian orgies
bacchant·ēs -(i)um *fpl* Bacchantes
bacchāti·ō -ōnis *f* orgy, revelry
**Bacchē(i)·us, Bacchic·us, Bacchi·us -a
-um** *adj* Bacchic
bacch·or -ārī -ātus sum *intr* to celebrate
the rites of Bacchus; to revel, rage, run
wildly about; *(of a place)* to be the scene
of Bacchanalian orgies; *(of a rumor)* to
run wild
Bacch·us -ī *m* god of wine; *(fig)* vine, wine
baceol·us -a -um *adj (coll)* nutty
bācif·er -era -erum *adj* bearing berries;
bearing olives
bacill·um -ī *n* small staff, wand; lictor's
staff
Bactr·a -ōrum *npl* Bactra *(capital of
Bactria, a province of Parthia)*
Bactriān·us -a -um *adj* Bactrian **ll** *mpl*
Bactrians
Bactri·us -a -um *adj* Bactrian
bacul·um -ī *n or* **bacul·us -ī** *m* a cane;
(lictor's) staff; scepter
badiz·ō -āre *intr* to go, walk
Baeticāt·us -a -um *adj* dressed in clothes
of Baetican wool
Baetic·us -a -um *adj* of the Baetis river **ll**
mpl the people of Baetica **ll** *f* Baetica
(Roman province in S. Spain)

Baet·is -is m river in Spain (modern Guadalquivir)

Baeturi·a -ae f part of the province of Baetica

Bagō·ās -ae m eunuch (used to guard women's quarters)

Bagrad·a -ae m river in N. Africa

Bāi·ae -ārum fpl resort town at N. end of Bay of Naples ‖ villa at Baiae

Bāi·ānus -a -um adj of Baiae

bājul·ō -āre tr to carry, bear

bājul·us -ī m porter

bālaen·a or **ballaen·a -ae** f(balēn-) whale

balanāt·us -a -um adj anointed with balsam; embalmed

balan·us -ī mf acorn; date; balsam; type of shell-fish

balatr·ō -ōnis m jester, buffoon

bālāt·us -ūs m bleating

balb·us -a -um adj stammering, lisping ‖ **Balbus** m Roman family name, cognomen, esp. Lucius Cornelius Balbus, a supporter of Caesar, defended by Cicero in 56 B.C.

balbūt·iō or **balbutt·iō -īre** tr & intr to stammer, stutter; to babble

Baliāric·us -a -um adj Balearic

Baliār·is -is -e adj (Bale-) Balearic; **Baliares insulae** Balearic Islands (Majorca and Minorca)

baline·um -ī n bath

ballēna see **balaena**

Balli·ō -ōnis m actor playing the worthless fellow; worthless fellow

ballist·a -ae f (bālis-) artillery piece (for hurling stones and other missiles)

ballistār·ium -iī n artillery emplacement

balne·ae -ārum fpl (balin-) baths

balneāri·us -a -um adj (balin-) of a bath ‖ npl baths

balneāt·or -ōris m (balin-) bath superintendent

balneol·ae -ārum fpl baths

balneol·um -ī n small bath

balne·um -ī n (balin-) (pl also: **balne·ae -ārum**) bathroom; public baths; bathing, taking a bath

bāl·ō -āre -āvī -ātum intr to bleat

balsam·um -ī n balsam tree ‖ npl balsam (used as perfume)

balte·us -ī m or **balte·um -ī** n belt; shoulder-strap; woman's belt

bal·ux -ūcis f gold dust

Bandusi·a -ae f pleasant fountain on Horace's Sabine farm

Bantīn·us -a -um adj of the town of Bantia in Apulia

baptistēr·ium -iī n bath

barāthr·um -ī n abyss, chasm, pit; lower world

barb·a -ae f beard (of man or animals); **barbam demittere** to grow a beard; **barbam vellere** to tuck on the beard (as a sign of insult)

barbar·a -ae f foreign woman

barbarē adv in a foreign langue; savagely; (of diction, etc.) rudely

barbari·a -ae or **barbari·ēs -ēī** f foreign country; strange land; rudeness, lack of culture; barbarity, brutality

barbaric·us -a -um adj barbarian; barbaric; foreign, outlandish

barbariēs see **barbaria**

barbarism·us -ī m barbarism (error in pronunciation or expression)

barbar·us -a -um adj foreign; barbarous ‖ mf foreigner; barbarian ‖ n barbarism

barbātul·us -a -um adj wearing a short beard

barbāt·us -a -um adj bearded; adult; old-time ‖ m old-timer

barbig·er -era -erum adj bearded

barbit·os -ī m (f) lyre

barbul·a -ae f short beard

Barc·a -ae m name of Carthaginian family to which Hamilcar, Hannibal, and Hasdrubal belonged

Barcae·ī -ōrum mpl the people of Barce (city of Cyrenaica)

barcal·a -ae m simpleton

Barcīn·us -a -um adj of the Barca family, Barcan

bard·us -a -um adj stupid, dull

bār·is -idos f flat-bottomed boat

Bār·ium -(i)ī n coastal town in Apulia (modern Bari)

bār·ō -ōnis m dunce, blockhead

barrīt·us -ūs m trumpeting (of elephants); war cry

barr·us -ī m elephant

bascaud·a -ae f basin (of British origin)

bāsiāti·ō -ōnis f kissing; kiss

bāsiāt·or -ōris m one who kisses

basilic·a -ae f basilica, courthouse

basilicē adv royally

basilic·us -a -um adj royal; splendid

bāsi·ō -āre -āvī -ātus tr to kiss

bāsiol·um -ī n little kiss, peck

bas·is -is f base, support; pedestal; base (of a triangle)

bās·ium -(i)ī n kiss

Bassar·eūs -eī m Bacchus

Bassaric·us -a -um adj of Bacchus

Bassar·is -idos f Bacchante

Bastarn·ae -ārum mpl (Bat-) Germanic tribe close to the mouth of the Danube

Batāv·us -a -um adj of the Batavi, Batavian ‖ mpl people of Lower Germany

batioc·a -ae f drinking cup

Bat·ō -ōnis m Illyrian rebel leader

bā(t)tu·ō -āre tr to beat, pound; (vulg) to screw ‖ intr to fence

Batt·us -ī m legendary founder of Cyrene

Battiad·ēs -ae m inhabitant of Cyrene

Bauc·is -idis f wife of Philemon

Baul·ī -ōrum *mpl* town between Baiae and Misenum

baxe·a -ae *f* kind of sandal

beātē *adv* happily ‖ *interj* great!; bravo!

beātit·ās -ātis *f* happiness

beātitūd·ō -inis *f* happiness

beātul·us -a -um *adj (of a deceased person)* of blessed memory

beāt·us -a -um *adj* happy; prosperous; fertile; abundant; wealthy, rich; sumptuous ‖ *n* happiness

Bebryci·a -ae *f* territory of the Bebryces in Asia Minor

Bebryci·us -a -um *adj* of Bebrycia *or* of the Bebryces

Bedriac·um -ī *n* **(Betr-)** village between Mantua and Cremona

Belg·ae -ārum *mpl* inhabitants of N. Gaul

Belgic·us -a -um *adj* of the Belgae; **Gallia Belgica** N. part of the province of Gallia Comata, occupied by the Belgae

Belg·ium -iī *n* country of the Belgae

Bēlīd·ēs -ae *m* descendant of Belus

Bēlīd·ēs -um *fpl* Danaids *(descendants of Belus)*

bellāri·a -ōrum *npl* sweets, dessert

bellāt·or -ōris *adj (masc only)* warlike; **bellator equus** war horse ‖ *m* warrior, fighter

bellātōri·us -a -um *adj* warlike

bellātr·ix -īcis *f* warrior *(female)*

bellē *adv* prettily, nicely, well; **belle esse** to have a nice time; **belle est** all is well *(of health);* **se belle habere** to be in good health

Belleroph·ōn -ontis *or* **Bellerophont·ēs -ae** *m* slayer of Chimera and rider of Pegasus

Bellerophontē·us -a -um *adj* of Bellerophon

belliātul·us -a -um *adj* pretty little

belliāt·us -a -um *adj* pretty

bellicōs·us -a -um *adj* warlike

bellic·us -a -um *adj* war-, military; warlike, fierce ‖ *n* bugle; bugle call

bellig·er -era -erum *adj* warring; war-

belliger·ō -āre -āvī -ātum *or* **belliger·or -ārī -ātus sum** *intr* to fight a war, be at war, fight

bellipot·ens -entis *adj* mighty *or* valiant in war ‖ *m* Mars

bell·ō -āre -āvī -ātum *or* **bell·or -ārī -ātus sum** *intr* to wage war, be at war; to fight

Bellōn·a -ae *f* **(Duell-)** goddess of war

bellul·us -a -um *adj* pretty, cute

bell·um -ī *n* **(duell-)** war; warfare

bell·us -a -um *adj* pretty; fine, nice

bēlu·a -ae *f* beast, brute, monster

bēluāt·us -a -um *adj* embroidered with figures of beasts

bēluōs·us -a -um *adj* full of monsters

Bēl·us -ī *m* Baal ‖ king of Tyre and father of Dido ‖ king of Egypt, father of Danaüs and Aegyptus

Bēnāc·us -ī *m* lake near Verona *(modern Lago di Garda)*

bene *adv* well; thoroughly, very, quite; elegantly; **bene ambula!** bon voyage!; **bene audire** to be well spoken of; **bene dicite!** hush!; **bene emere** to buy at a bargain; **bene esse** *(w. dat)* to be well with, to be doing all right; **bene est** it's O.K.; **bene ferre** to put up with in good spirits; **bene sum** *or* **mihi bene est** I am content; **se bene habere** to be happy, be content; to do well; **bene sentire de** (+ *abl*) to have sound views about; **bene sperare** to be optimistic; **bene vendere** to sell at a good price ‖ *interj (w. acc or dat) (in drinking to health)* here's to you!

benedicē *adv* with friendly words

benedī·cō -cĕre -xī -ctus *intr (w. dat)* to speak well of, praise; *(eccl)* to bless

bene·faciō -facĕre -fēcī -factus *tr* to do *(s.o.)* a service, confer a benefit on; **multa erga** (+ *acc*) **benefacere** to do many kindnesses to

beneficenti·a -ae *f* beneficence, kindness

beneficiāri·ī -ōrum *mpl* soldiers exempt from menial tasks

benefic·ium -(i)ī *n* **(benif-)** kindness, favor, benefit, service; help, support; promotion; right, privilege; **beneficio** *(w. gen)* thanks to; **beneficium accipere et reddere** to receive and return a favor

benefic·us -a -um *adj* generous, liberal, obliging

Benevent·um -ī *n* town in Samnium in S. Italy *(modern Benevento)*

benevolē *adv* **(beniv-)** kindly

benevol·ens -entis *adj* **(beniv-)** kindhearted, benevolent, obliging

benevolenti·a -ae *f* **(beniv-)** benevolence, kindness, goodwill; favor

benevol·us -a -um *adj* **(beniv-)** kind, benevolent ‖ *m* well-wisher

benignē *adv* kindly, courteously; mildly; generously, liberally

benignit·ās -ātis *f* kindness, friendliness, courtesy; generosity

benign·us -a -um *adj* kind-hearted; mild; liberal; favorable; bounteous

be·ō -āre -āvī -ātus *tr* to make happy; to bless; to enrich; to refresh

Berecynt(h)i·us -a -um *adj* Berecyntian; epithet of Cybele

Berecynt·us -ī *m* mountain in Phrygia sacred to Cybele

Berenīc·ē -ēs *f* female name, *esp.* the daughter of the Jewish King Agrippa I; **crinis Berenices** "hair of Berenice" *(constellation, named after the wife of Ptolemy Euergetes)*

bēryll·us -ī *m* beryl *(precious stone)*

bēs be(s)sis *m* two thirds; **bes alter** one and two thirds; **faenus bessibus** interest at ⅔% per month *or* 8% per year
bēsāl·is -is -e *adj* comprising two-thirds
Bess·ī -ōrum *mpl* a people of Thrace
Bessic·us -a -um *adj* of the Bessi
besti·a -ae *f* beast, wild beast
bestiāri·us -a -um *adj* of wild beasts **‖** *m* wild-beast fighter
bestiol·a -ae *f* insect
bēt·a -ae *f* beet
bēta *indecl n* beta *(second letter of the Greek alphabet)*
bētāce·us -a -um *adj* of a beet
bētiz·ō -āre *intr* to be languid
bi- *pref* consisting of, having, measuring two of the things named, *e.g.:* **bimar·is -is -e** of *or* connected with two seas
bibliopōl·a -ae *m* bookseller
bibliothēc·a -ae *f* library
bibliothēcār·ius -iī *m* librarian
bib·ō -ēre -ī *tr* to drink; to visit, live near *(river); (fig)* to take in, absorb **‖** *intr* to drink; to guzzle
bibul·us -a -um *adj* fond of drinking; absorbent; thirsty; *(of ears)* eager to hear
bi·ceps -cipitis *adj* two-headed; twin-peaked
biclīn·ium -(i)ī *n* table for two
bicol·or -ōris *adj* two-colored, of two colors
bicorn·is -is -e *adj* two-horned; two-pronged
bicorp·or -oris *adj* double-bodied
bid·ens -entis *adj* with two teeth; with two points; two-pronged **‖** *m* hoe, mattock; sacrificial animal; sheep
bident·al -ālis *n* place struck by lightning
Bidīn·us -a -um *adj* of Bidis *(town in Sicily)*
bīdu·um -ī *n* two-day period; two days
bienn·ium -(i)ī *n* two-year period; two years; in *(or* per*)* biennium for two years
bifāriam *adv* on both sides, twofold; in two parts; in two ways; in two directions
bifāri·us -a -um *adj* double, twofold
bif·er -era -erum *adj* bearing (fruit *or* flowers) twice (a year)
bifid·us -a -um *adj* split in two, forked, cloven
bifor·is -is -e *adj* having two doors; having two holes *or* openings; *(of sound)* double, coming from double pipes
biformāt·us -a -um *adj* double, having two forms
beform·is -is -e *adj* double, having two forms
bifr·ons -ontis *adj* two-faced
bifurc·us -a -um *adj* two-pronged **‖** *n* crotch
bīg·ae -ārum *fpl* two-horse chariot; team of horses

bīgāt·us -a -um *adj (of a coin)* stamped with the image of a two-horse chariot
bijug·is -is -e *or* **bijug·us -a -um** *adj* two-horse
Bilbil·is -is *f* town in Hispania Tarraconensis, birthplace of Martial
bilībr·is -is -e *adj* two-pound
bilingu·is -is -e *adj* two-tongued; bilingual; deceitful, two-faced
bīl·is -is *f* bile; wrath; **bilis atra** melancholy; insanity; **bilem movere** *(w. dat)* to get *(s.o.)* angry
-bil·is -is -e *adjl suf* denoting ability, *e.g.:* **terribilis** able to frighten
bil·ix -īcis *adj* with a double thread
bilustr·is -is -e *adj* lasting for two lustra *(i.e., ten years)*
bimar·is -is -e *adj* situated between two seas
bimarīt·us -ī *m* bigamist
bimāt·er -ris *adj* having two mothers, twice-born *(Bacchus)*
bimembr·is -is -e *adj* half-man, half-beast **‖** *m* centaur
bime(n)str·is -is -e *adj* two-month-old; lasting two months
bīmul·us -a -um *adj* two-year-old
bīm·us -a -um *adj* two-year-old; lasting two years
bīn·ī -ae -a *adj* two by two, two each; two at a time; two *(per day, year, etc.); a* set of, a pair of; double, twofold; **inter bina castra** between the two camps
binoct·ium -(i)ī *n* period of two nights
binōmin·is -is -e *adj* having two names
Bi·ōn -ōnis *f* Greek philosopher, noted for his sharp sayings
Biōnē·us -a -um *adj* typical of Bion, satirical
bipalm·is -is -e *adj* two palms long *or* broad
bipartītō *adv see* **bipertito**
bipat·ens -entis *adj* opening in two directions
bipedāl·is -is -e *adj* two-foot (long, broad, *or* high)
bipennif·er -era -erum *adj* wielding a two-edged ax
bipenn·is -is -e *adj* two-edged **‖** *f* two-edged ax
bipertītō *adv* **(-part-)** in two parts; **bipertito esse** to be divided
bipertīt·us -a -um *adj* **(-part-)** divided into two parts, bipartite
bip·ēs -edis *adj* two-footed, biped
birēm·is -is -e *adj* two-oared; with two banks of oars **‖** *f* ship with two banks of oars
bis *adv* twice; doubly
Bīsalt·ae -ārum *mpl* a people of Macedonia
Bīsalt·is -is *f* Theophane, daughter of Bisaltes

Biston·es -um *mpl* fierce tribesmen in Thessaly

bisulc·us -a -um *adj* split; forked

Bīthȳni·a -ae *f* a district, later a Roman province, on the N.W. coast of Asia Minor

Bīthȳnic·us -a -um *or* Bīthȳn·us -a -um *adj* Bithynian

bīt·ō -ĕre *intr* to go

bitūm·en -inis *n* asphalt, pitch

bivi·us -a -um *adj* two-way ‖ *n* crossroads, intersection

blaes·us -a -um *adj* lisping; slurring

blandē *adv* flatteringly; coaxingly, seductively, charmingly

blandidic·us -a -um *adj* smooth-spoken, using flattering words

blandiloquentul·us -a -um *or* blandiloqu·us -a -um *adj* smooth, smooth-tongued

blandīment·um -ī *n* flattery, compliment; charm

blandi·or -īrī -ītus sum *intr* (w. dat) 1 to flatter; 2 to coax; 3 to allure; 4 to charm, please; 5 (of dogs) to fawn on; (w. ut + subj) to coax, persuade with blandishments to ‖ refl (w. dat) to delude oneself

blanditer *adv* flatteringly

blanditi·a -ae *or* blanditi·ēs -ēī *f* flattery, compliment; charm

bland·us -a -um *adj* smooth; flattering; fawning; alluring, charming, winsome, pleasant

blater·ō -āre -āvī -ātus *tr* to utter (in a babbling way) ‖ intr to babble

blatt·a -ae *f* cockroach; (insect) bookworm; clothes-moth

blenn·us -ī *m* (coll) idiot, blockhead

blite·us -a -um *adj* silly; tasteless ‖ *n* worthless stuff, trash

blit·um -ī *n* tasteless vegetable (kind of spinach)

boāri·us -a -um *adj* (bov-) cattle-

Boc(c)h·us -ī *m* king of Mauretania, who betrayed Jugurtha to the Romans ‖ king of Mauretania in the time of Julius Caesar

Boeb·ē -ēs *f* lake in Thessaly

Boeōti·a -ae *f* district N. of Attica

Boeōti·us -a -um *or* Boeōt·us -a -um *adj* Boeotian ‖ mpl Boeotians

Boi·ī -ōrum *mpl* Celtic people who migrated from Gaul into N. Italy

bōj·a -ae *f* collar worn by criminals

bōlēt·us -ī *m* mushroom

bol·us -ī *m* throw (of the dice); cast (of the net); (fig) haul, piece of good luck, gain; choice morsel

bombax *interj* strange!; indeed!

bomb·us -ī *m* booming; buzzing, humming

bombȳcin·us -a -um *adj* silk, silken

bomb·ȳx -ȳcis *m* silkworm; silk; silk garment

Bon·a De·a -ae *f* Roman goddess of chastity and fertility, worshipped by women

bonit·ās -ātis *f* goodness, integrity, good behavior; excellence, high quality (of things)

Bonn·a -ae *f* city in Lower Germany (modern Bonn)

Bonōni·a -ae *f* city of Cisalpline Gaul (modern Bologna)

Bonōniens·is -is -e *adj* of Bologna

bon·us -a -um *adj* good; (morally) good; cheerful (face); sound, valid, well-founded (arguments); pretty, shapely; (w. dat) good for; (w. ad) good at; (w. dat or ad) good, kind towards; bona aetas prime of life; bonae artes liberal arts, liberal education; bonae rei esse to be wealthy; bonae res good things, desirable things; wealth; bonae vires full strength; bona forma good appearance; bone vir! sir!; my good fellow!; bono animo esse (or bonum animum habere) to be of good cheer, be in a good mood; to be well-disposed; bono modo in moderation; bono periculo with little risk; bonum est (w. inf) it is good to; bonus a tempestatibus free from storms, fine; bonus stomachus good humor; cum bona pace (w. gen) with the full consent of; (cum) bonā veniā tuā with your kind permission; viri boni decent citizens; (pol) conservatives ‖ mpl decent people; brave men; (pol) conservatives ‖ *n* good thing, good; bono esse alicui to be good for s.o., be profitable to s.o.; cui bono? for whose benefit? ‖ npl goods, property

bo·ō -āre *or* -ĕre *intr* to bawl; to bellow, roar

Boōt·ēs -ae *m* Boötes (constellation)

bore·ās -ae *m* north wind; the North ‖ Boreās god of the north wind

borē·us -a -um *adj* north, northern

Borysthen·ēs -is *m* Scythian river (modern Dnieper)

bōs bovis *m* (gen pl: boum *or* bovum; dat & abl pl: bōbus *or* būbus) ox, bull ‖ mpl cattle ‖ *f* cow

Bosp(h)or·us *or* Bosp(h)or·os -ī *m* strait between Thrace and Asia Minor, connecting Propontis and Black Sea

botell·us -ī *m* small sausage

botul·us -ī *m* a black pudding

bovīl·e -is *n* ox stall, cow stable

Bovill·ae -ārum *fpl* town in Latium on the Appian Way, about 12 miles S. of Rome

bovill·us -a -um *adj* cattle-

brabeut·a -ae *m* umpire

brāc·ae -ārum *fpl* pants, trousers

brācāt·us -a -um *adj* wearing trousers; foreign, barbarian; effeminate

brā(c)chiāl·is -is -e *adj* of the arm

brā(c)chiol·um -ī *n* dainty arm
brā(c)ch·ium -(i)ī *n* arm, lower arm; claw; branch; tendril; arm of the sea; *(naut)* yardarm
brācil·is -is -e *adj (esp. of a tunic)* to be worn with trousers
bracte·a -ae *f* (bratt-) gold leaf; gold foil
bracteol·a -ae *f* (bratt-) very thin gold leaf
brassic·a -ae *f* cabbage
bratt- = bract-
Brenn·us -ī *m* Celtic chieftain who captured Rome about 390 B.C. **‖** Galatian chieftain who invaded Greece in 279 B.C.
brevī *adv* briefly, in a few words; shortly, in a short time; **brevi ante (post)** shortly before (afterwards)
breviār·ium -(i)ī *n* abridgment, summary
brevicul·us -a -um *adj* rather short
breviloqu·ens -entis *adj* concise, of few words
breviloquenti·a -ae *f* conciseness
brevi·ō -āre -āvī -ātus *tr* to shorten; to abbreviate; to pronounce *(a syllable)* short
brev·is -is -e *adj* short, little; low; stunted *(trees); (of depth)* shallow; brief; transient; short-lived; compressed, concise *(style); small (amounts, weights);* modest, simple; small, narrow, confined *(space);* **ad** *(or* **in) breve tempus** for (only) a short time **‖** *f (gram)* short syllable **‖** *n* a short space of time; **ad** *(or* **in) breve** for (only) a short time; **brevi** in a few words, briefly; in a short time, soon; for (only) a short time; after a lapse of a short space of time; **brevi ante** shortly before; **brevi post** shortly after; **in brevi** in a few words, briefly **‖** *npl* shallow water, shallows
brevit·ās -ātis *f* brevity; smallness; shortness; stunted size *(of trees);* short period of time; shortness of life; *(pros)* short quantity; *(rhet)* conciseness, terseness
breviter *adv* for (only) a short time; within a short space of time, quickly; in (only) a few words, briefly; to (only) a short distance; *(pros)* short
Brigant·es -um *mpl* a people of N. Britannia
Brīsē·is -idos *f (acc:* **Brīsēida)** slave and concubine of Achilles
Britann·ī -ōrum *mpl* Britons
Britanni·a -ae *f* (Britt-) Britain
Britannic·us -a -um *adj* British **‖** *m* name taken by Germanicus, son of Claudius and Messalina
Britann·us -a -um *adj* British
Brit(t)·ō -ōnis *m* Briton
Brixi·a -ae *f* town in Cisalpine Gaul *(modern Brescia)*

brocch·us -a -um *adj* buck-toothed
Brom·ius -(i)ī *m* Bacchus
Bront·ēs -ae *m* Brontes *(a Cyclops)*
brūm·a -ae *f* winter solstice, shortest day; (dead of) winter; winter's cold
brūmāl·is -is -e *adj* wintry
Brundis·ium -(i)ī *n* port in S.E. Italy on the Adriatic Sea *(modern Brindisi)*
Bruti·ī -ōrum *mpl* inhabitants of the toe of Italy
Brūt·us -ī *m* Roman family name, cognomen, *esp.* Lucius Junius Brutus *(drove out Tarquinius Superbus)* **‖** Marcus Junius Brutus *(one of the murderers of Julius Caesar)*
brūt·us -a -um *adj* heavy, unwieldy; dull, stupid
būbīl·e -is *n* cow stable
būb·ō -ōnis *mf* owl
būbul·a -ae *f* beef
bubulcit·or -ārī *intr* to tend cattle, be a herdsman; to ride herd
bubulc·us -ī *m* herdsman
būb(u)l·us -a -um *adj* ox-, bull's, cow's; **corius bubulus** oxhide, oxhide whip; **oculus bublus** bull's-eye
būcaed·a -ae *m (coll)* flogged slave
bucc·a -ae *f* cheek; loudmouth; trumpeter; parasite; mouthful; **dicere quidquid in buccam venerit** to say whatever came into his head
buccell·a -ae *f* small mouthful; morsel
bucc·ō -ōnis *f (coll)* fathead
buc(c)ul·a -ae *f* little cheek; visor
bucculent·us -a -um *adj* having fat cheeks; loud-mouthed
būcer(i)·us -a -um *adj* horned
būcin·a -ae *f (curved)* trumpet; war trumpet; shepherd's horn
būcināt·or -ōris *m* trumpeter
būcin·us -ī *m* trumpeter
būcolic·us -a -um *adj* pastoral, bucolic
būcul·a -ae *f* heifer
būf·ō -ōnis *m* toad
-bul·a -ae *fem suf* forms feminine nouns denoting instrument or agent, *e.g.:* **fibula** safety pin
bulb·us -ī *m* bulb; onion
būl·ē -ēs *f (Greek)* council, senate
būleut·a -ae *m* councilor
būleutēr·ium -(i)ī *n* meeting place of a Greek council
bull·a -ae *f* bubble; boss, stud, knob; amulet; locket *(hung around neck of children)*
bullāt·us -a -um *adj* inflated, bombastic; studded; wearing a bulla *(i.e., still a child)*
bull·iō -īre *intr* to bubble, boil
bullul·a -ae *f* little bubble
-bulum -ī *neut suf* denoting instrument or place, *e.g.:* **venabulum** hunting instrument, spear; **stabulum** place for cattle to stand, stable

būmast·us -a -um *adj* having large grapes
būr·a -ae *or* **būr·is -is** *f* curved handle of plow
Būsīr·is -idos *or* **-idis** *m* king of Egypt who sacrificed strangers and was killed by Hercules
bustirap·us -ī *m* grave robber
bustuāri·us -a -um *adj* of a tomb, of a pyre; **gladiator bustiarius** gladiator who fought at a tomb in honor of the dead
bust·um -ī *n* pyre; grave mound, tomb; *(pej) (applied to a person)* ruination
būte·ō -ōnis *m* buzzard
Būt(h)rōt·um (·on) -ī *n or* **Būt(h)rōt·os -ī** *f* town on the coast of Epirus
buxēt·um -ī *n* plantation of boxwood trees
buxif·er -era -erum *adj* producing boxwood trees
bux·um -ī *n (bot)* boxwood tree; *(object made of the hard wood of the boxwood tree):* (spinning) top, comb, writing tablet, flute
bux·us -ī *f* boxwood tree
Byrs·a -ae *f* (Bur-) citadel of Carthage
Byzant·ium -(i)ī *n* city on the Bosporus, later named Constantinople

C

C *abbr* **centum** (one hundred)
C. *abbr* **Gaius** *(Roman first name, praenomen)*
caballīn·us -a -um *adj* horse's; **fons caballinus** *(pej)* "nag's spring" *(i.e., Hippocrene)*
caball·us -ī *m* horse, nag; packhorse; riding horse; **Gorgoneus caballus** Pegasus *(sprung from the blood of the Gorgon Medusa)*
Cabīr·us -ī *m* deity worshiped on Lemnos and Samothrace *(e.g., Bacchus)*
cacātur·iō -īre -iī *intr (vulg)* to want to shit
cachinnāti·ō -ōnis *f* horselaugh
cachinn·ō -āre -āvī -ātum *intr* to laugh loud, roar *(with laughter)*
cachinn·us -ī *m* loud laugh; *(fig)* rippling *(of waves)*
cac·ō -āre -āvī -ātus *tr & intr (vulg)* to shit
cacoëth·es -is *n* malignant tumor; **ca-coethes scribendi** an itch to write
cacozēli·a -ae *f* bad taste *(in style)*
cacozēl·os -on *adj (of style)* in bad taste
cacul·a -ae *m (sl)* soldier's slave
cacūm·en -inis *n* point, tip, top, peak; young shoot; **extremum cacumen** outer limit
cacūmin·ō -āre -āvī -ātus *tr* to make pointed
Cāc·us -ī *m* giant son of Vulcan, living on the Aventine Hill and slain by Hercules

cadāv·er -eris *n* corpse, carcass
cadāverōs·us -a -um *adj* cadaverous, ghastly
Cadmē·is -idos *adj (fem only)* of Cadmus **‖** *f* daughter of Cadmus
Cadmē·us -a -um *adj* Cadmean, Theban; **Tyros Cadmea** Tyre, home city of Cadmus **‖** *f* citadel of Thebes
Cadm·us -ī *m* son of Phoenician king Agenor, brother of Europa, and founder of the citadel of Thebes; **Cadmi terra** Phoenicia
cadō cadĕre cecidī cāsum *intr* to fall, sink, drop; to be slain, die, be sacrificed; to happen, occur, turn out, come to pass; to belong, refer, be suitable, apply; to flag, decline, decay; to vanish, fail, cease; to derive *(from a source); (of parts of the body)* to fall out, be shed; *(of heavenly bodies)* to sink, set; *(of wind, sea, noise)* to die down; *(of words)* to fall from one's lips; *(of efforts)* to come to nothing; *(w. in + acc)* **1** to come upon, arrive at by chance; **2** to fall upon *(the enemy);* **3** to coincide with *(a time, period);* **4** to fall due on *(a date);* **5** to be consistent or compatible with, fit; **6** *(of words, clauses)* to end, terminate in *(e.g., a long syllable);* **7** to fall into *(a category); (w.* **ad** *or* **in** *+ acc)* to lapse into, degenerate into; **apte cadere ad** to be exactly adapted to; **causā cadere** *(leg)* to lose one's case, be convicted; *(fig)* to be in the wrong; **formulā cadere** to lose one's case on a technicality; **huc cadere** to fall so low; **numerose cadere** to sound rhythmical
cādūceāt·or -ōris *m* herald
cādūce·us -ī *m* herald's staff, caduceus
cādūcif·er -era -erum *adj* with herald's staff
cādūc·us -a -um *adj* falling; fallen; inclined to fall, tottery, unsteady, frail, perishable, transitory; *(of hopes, words)* futile; *(of persons)* destined to die, doomed; *(of fire)* likely to go out; *(of streams)* likely to dry up; *(of vines)* drooping; *(leg)* lapsed, without heir; *(mil)* fallen in battle
cadurc·um -ī *n* coverlet; *(fig)* marriage bed
cad·us -ī *m* (large) jar
Cadūsi·ī -ōrum *mpl* the people of Cadusia *(near the Caspian Sea)*
caecigen·us -a -um *adj* born blind
Caecili·us -a -um *adj* Roman clan name, nomen
caecit·ās -ātis *f* blindness; **caecitas animi** moral blindness; **caecitas mentis** mental blindness, lack of discernment
caec·ō -āre -āvī -ātus *tr* to blind; to obscure the judgment of; **astu caecare** *(fig)* to pull the wool over *(s.o.'s)* eyes

Caecub·um -ī *n* Caecuban wine *(from Caecubum in S. Latium)*

Caecul·us -ī *m* son of Vulcan and founder of Praeneste

caec·us -a -um *adj* blind; invisible; vague, random, aimless; uncertain, unknown; unsubstantiated; blinding; obscure, mysterious; dark, gloomy; concealed, disguised; unforeseeable *(dangers);* **die caeco emere** to buy on credit *(i.e., to buy with no definite date of payment)*

caed·ēs -is *f* murder, slaughter, massacre; bloodshed, gore; the slain

caedō caedĕre cecīdī caesus *tr* to hack at; to chop; to strike, beat; to fell; to cut off, cut to pieces; to cut through, sever; to kill, murder; to crack, smash, break; to use up, consume; *(hum)* to devour; **sermones caedere** to exchange chitchat

caedu·us -a -um *adj* ready for felling

caelām·en -inis *n* engraving

caelāt·or -ōris *m* engraver

caelāt·um -ī *n* engraved work

caelātūr·a -ae *f* engraving

cael·ebs -ibis *adj* (**-eps**) unmarried, single *(whether bachelor or widower); (of trees)* not supporting vines

cael·es -itis *adj* heavenly **ll** *mpl* gods

caelest·is -is -e *adj* heavenly, celestial; supernatural, divine **ll** *mf* deity; godlike person **ll** *npl* heavenly bodies

caelibāt·us -ūs *m* celibacy

caelicol·a -ae *mf* inhabitant of heaven *(god or goddess)*

caelif·er -era -erum *adj* supporting the sky

Caelimontān·us -a -um *adj* located on the Caelian Hill

caelipot·ens -entis *adj* powerful in heaven

caelit·ēs -um *mpl* gods in heaven

Caeli·us -a -um *adj* Roman clan name *(nomen)*

Caeli·us Mons *(gen:* **Caeliī Montis)** *m* Caelian Hill *(in Rome)*

cael·ō -āre -āvī -ātus *tr* to engrave in relief, emboss; to carve; to cast; to fashion, compose; to adorn

cael·um -ī *n* engraver's chisel

cael·um -ī *n* sky, heaven(s); air, climate, weather; universe, world; **caelum apertum** *(or* **patens)** the open air; **in caelo esse** to be in seventh heaven; **positio caeli** *(geog)* latitude

caement·um -ī *n* (**cēm-**) *(also used in pl)* crushed stone

Caen·eŭs -eī *or* **-eos** *m* child of Elatus, born a girl, but changed into a boy

Caenīn·a -ae *f* ancient city of Latium *(defeated by Romulus)*

Caen·is -idis *f* child of Elatus, born a girl, but changed into a boy

caenōs·us -a -um *adj* filthy, muddy

caen·um -ī *n* (**cēn-**) filth, mud, slime; *(applied to persons) (sl)* scum

caep·a *or* **cēp·a -ae** *f or* **caep·e** *or* **cēp·e** *(nom, acc, and abl) n* onion

Caepi·ō -ōnis *m* Roman family name *(cognomen), esp.* in the *gens Servilia*

Caer·e -itis *or* **-ētis** *n* city in Etruria *(modern Cerveteri)*

Caer·es -itis *or* **-etis** *adj* of Caere **ll** *mpl* the people of Caere

Caerētān·us -a -um *adj* of Caere

caerimōni·a -ae *f* rite, ceremony; sanctity; awe, reverence **ll** *fpl* rites, ceremonies; practices

caerul·a -ōrum *npl* blue expanse *(of the sky);* blue waters *(of the sea)*

caerul(e)·us -a -um *adj* blue; blue-eyed; dark-blue; greenish-blue; dark

Caes·ar -aris *m* Gaius Julius Caesar *(102?– 44 B.C.)* **ll** honorary title of Octavian and succeeding emperors **ll** cognomen of various members of the imperial family

Caesarē·a -ae *f* name of several towns, *esp.* two in Palestine, one in Cappadocia, and one in Mauretania

Caesare·us -a -um *or* **Caesariān·us -a -um** *adj* connected with Julius Caesar; connected with Augustus; imperial

Caesariān·us -i *m* soldier *or* supporter of Julius Caesar; supporter *or* servant of the Roman emperor

caesariāt·us -a -um *adj* long-haired

caesari·ēs -ēī *f* long, flowing hair

caesim *adv* by chopping, by cutting; with a slashing blow; *(rhet)* in short clauses, in a clipped style

caesi·us -a -um *adj* bluish-gray; blue-eyed; gray-eyed; cat-eyed **ll Caesius** Roman clan name *(nomen)*

Caes·ō -ōnis *m* (**Kaes-**) Roman first name *(praenomen)*

caesp·es -itis *m* sod, turf; grass; altar of sod; rampart made of turf; mound of earth *(esp. as the covering of a grave)*

caest·us -ūs *m* (**cest-**) boxing glove

caes·us -a -um *pp* of **caedo ll** *npl*— **inter caesa et porrecta** *(fig)* at the eleventh hour *(literally, between the victim being slain and offered)*

caetr·a -ae *f* (**cēt-**) short Spanish shield

caetrāt·us -a -um *adj* armed with a shield **ll** *mpl* soldiers armed with a shield; Greek peltasts

Caīc·us -ī *m* (**Cay-**) river in Mysia

Caiēt·a -ae *f* nurse of Aeneas **ll** town on the coast of Latium

cai·ō -āre *tr* to beat, thrash

Caïus *see* **Gaius**

Cala·ber -bra -brum *adj* Calabrian

Calabri·a -ae *f* region of S.E. Italy

Cala·ïs -ïs *m (winged)* son of Boreas and Orithyia, and brother of Zetes

calamāri·us -a -um *adj* for holding pens

Calam·is -idis m Greek sculptor of the 5th cent. B.C.

calamis·ter -tri m curling iron

calamistrāt·us -a -um adj curled (with a curling iron)

calamistr·um -ī n curling iron

calamit·ās -ātis f calamity, disaster; (mil) defeat

calamitōsē adv disastrously

calamitōs·us -a -um adj disastrous; liable to disaster; blighted (fields); hit by disaster, ill-starred ‖ m victim of a disaster

calam·us -ī m reed;, stalk, shoot (of a plant); pen (for writing on paper, as opposed to stilus of metal or bone for writing on wax); arrow; fishing rod; lime rod (smeared at top with lime to catch birds); vine prop; (mus) reed pipe; (collectively or pl) Panpipes

calathisc·us -ī m small wicker basket

calath·us -ī m wicker basket; vessel for holding cheese or curdled milk; wine cup

Cālāti·a -ae f town in Campania

calāt·or -ōris m (kal-) servant; priest's attendant

calautic·a -ae f type of woman's head-dress

calc·ar -āris n spur; (fig) stimulus

calceāment·um -ī n footwear, shoe

calceār·ium -(i)ī n show allowance

calceāt·or -ōris m shoemaker

calceāt·us -ūs m footwear, shoes

calce·ō -āre -āvī -ātus tr to put shoes on; to shoe (animals)

calceolār·ius -(i)ī m shoemaker

calceol·us -ī m small shoe, half-boot; slipper

calce·us -ī m shoe; **calcei mullei** (or **patricii**) red shoes worn by senators who had held curule office; **calceos mutare** (fig) to become a senator (from the shoes that senators wore); **calceos poscere** to leave the table (literally, to call for one's shoes)

Calc(h)·ās -antis m Calchas (Greek seer at Troy)

calci- see **calce-**

calcitr·ō -āre -āvī -ātum intr to kick; to be recalcitrant, kick up one's heels

Calc(h)ēd·ōn -onis f Calchedon (town on the Asiatic side of the Bosphorus, opposite Byzantium)

calcitr·ō -āre -āvī -ātum intr to kick

calcitr·ō -ōnis m kicker; blusterer

calc·ō -āre -āvī -ātus tr to trample; to trample on; to tread (grapes); to set foot on; to tread on accidentally, trip upon; (fig) to spurn; **viam calcare** to tread a path

calculāt·or -ōris m arithmetic teacher; accountant, bookkeeper

calcul·us -ī m pebble, stone; kidney stone;

counter of an abacus; piece (used in games); **calculus albus** white pebble (of acquittal); **calculos** (or **calculum**) **ponere** (or **subducere**) to make a calculation (esp. gains or losses); **calculus ater** black pebble (of condemnation); vote, decision, sentence; **parem calculum ponere cum** to return an equivalent gift to

calda, caldārius, caldus see **calid-**

Calēdoni·a -ae f Caledonia, Scotland

cal(e)·faciō -facĕre -fēcī -factus tr to warm, heat; to rouse, excite

calefact·ō -āre -āvī -ātus tr to warm, heat

Calend- see **Kalend-**

Calēn·us -a -um adj of Cales ‖ n wine from Cales (in Campania)

cal·eō -ēre -uī intr to be warm, be hot; to feel warm; to glow; to be flushed (with wine); to be hot (with lust); to be busy, have one's hands full

Cal·ēs -ium fpl Campanian town famous for its wine

cal·escō -escĕre -uī intr to get warm, get hot; to become excited, get hot

caliandrum see **caliendrum**

calidē adv promptly, quickly

calid·us -a -um adj (cald-) warm, hot; eager, rash; hot-headed; hasty; intoxicating (wine); high (fever) ‖ f warm water ‖ n hot drink; heat

caliendr·um -ī n (-lian-) wig (for women)

calig·a -ae f army boot; (fig) military service

caligāt·us or **caligāri·us -a -um** adj wearing army boots ‖ m (mil) private

cālīginōs·us -a -um adj misty, foggy

cālīg·ō -inis f darkness; mist, fog; dark smoke; gloom; obscurity; mental blindness; dizziness

cālīg·ō -āre tr to veil in darkness, obscure; to make dizzy ‖ intr to be dark, be gloomy; to steam, reek; to be wrapped in mist or darkness; to be blind, grope

caligul·a -ae f small army boot ‖ **Caligula** m nickname given by soldiers to Emperor Gaius when he was a small boy

cal·ix -icis m cup; (fig) wine

Callaec·ī -ōrum mpl a people in the N.W. corner of Spain

callaïn·us -a -um adj turquoise

call·eō -ēre -uī tr to know by experience; to have skill in; (w. inf) to know how to, be able to ‖ intr to grow hard, be callused; (fig) to be thick-skinned, be callous; (w. abl) to be experienced in, be skilled in

callidē adv skillfuly; well; cunningly

callidit·ās -ātis f skill; shrewdness; cunning ‖ fpl clever tricks

callid·us -a -um adj expert, adroit, skillful; ingenious, clever; cunning, wily;

(w. gen, dat, or **in** + *abl)* experienced in; *(w. inf)* skilled at

Callimach·us -ī *m* Alexandrine poet and grammarian *(fl c. 270 B.C.)*

Calliop·ē -ēs *or* **Calliop(ē)·a -ae** *f* Calliope *(Muse of epic poetry)*

call·is -is *mf* rough footpath **‖** *mpl* mountain pasturage; cattle trails

Callistō *indecl f* daughter of Lycaon *(king of Arcadia),* changed into a she-bear and then into the constellation Ursa Major

callōs·us -a -um *adj* thick-skinned, callused; solid, hard

call·um -ī *n or* **call·us -ī** *m* hard skin; *(lit & fig)* callousness; **callum obducere** to produce insensitivity

cal·ō -āre -āvī -ātus *tr* **(kal-)** to announce; to convoke

cāl·ō -ōnis *m* soldier's slave; drudge

cal·or -ōris *m* warmth, heat; glow; passion, love; fire, zeal; fever

Calp·ē -ēs *f* Gibraltar

Calpurni·a -a -um *adj* name of a plebeian clan **‖** *f* Calpurnia *(wife of Julius Caesar)*

calt(h)·a -ae *f (bot)* marigold

caltul·a -ae *f (woman's)* yellow slip *(tied below the breasts)*

calumni·a -ae *f* **(kal-)** false accusation, malicious charge; frameup; conviction for malicious prosecution; false statement, misrepresentation; trickery; sham

calumniāt·or -ōris *m* malicious accuser; shyster

calumni·or -ārī -ātus sum *tr* to accuse fasely; to misinterpret, misrepresent; to blame unjustly; to find fault with **‖** *intr* to bring false accusation; to practice legal chicanery

calv·a -ae *f* bald head, scalp; skull

calvit·ium -(i)ī *n* baldness

calv·us -a -um *adj* bald

cal·x -cis *f* heel; (back of the) hoof; *(fig)* foot, kick; **calcibus caedere** to kick

cal·x -cis *f* lime, limestone; pebble *(used in games);* finish line, goal; **ad calcem pervenire** to reach the goal

Calyd·ōn -ōnis *or* **-ōnos** *f* town in Aetolia, site of the boar hunt led by Meleager

Calydōn·is -idos *adj (fem only)* Calydonian **‖** *f* Calydonian woman *(Dejanira)*

Calydōni·us -a -um *adj* Calydonian

Calyps·ō -ūs *f* nymph *(daughter of Atlas)* who entertained Ulysses on the island of Ogygia

camara *see* **camera**

camell·a -ae *f* drinking cup

camēl·us -ī *m* camel

Camēn·a -ae *f* Muse; poem; poetry

camer·a -ae *f* **(-mar-)** vault, arched roof, arch; flat boat with arched covering

Camerīn·um -ī *n* town in Umbria

Camill·a -ae *f* Volscian female warrior, ally of Turnus against Aeneas

Camill·us -ī *m* Marcus Furius Camillus, who liberated Rome from the Gauls in 390 B.C.

camīn·us -ī *m* fireplace; furnace, forge; vent of subterranean fires; **oleum addere camino** *(prov)* to pour oil on the fire

cammar·us -ī *m* lobster

Campānia -ae *f* district on E. coast of central Italy below Latium

Campān·us -a -um *adj* Campanian

campes·ter *or* **campes·tris -tris -tre** *adj* flat, level; overland *(march); (of city)* situated in a plain; *(of army)* fighting in a plain; *(of sports, elections)* held in the Campus Martius **‖** *n* loincloth **‖** *npl* flat lands

camp·us -ī *m* open field *(opp:* **ager** tilled field); flat space, plain; level surface; *(fig)* field of action, subject of debate; **Campus Martius** Field of Mars *(near the Tiber, used for sports, elections, military exercises)*

cam·ur *or* **cam·urus -ura -urum** *adj* crooked; concave

Canac·ē -ēs *f* daughter of Aeolus, who committed incest with her brother Macareus

canāl·is -is *mf* pipe, conduit; gutter, open drain; channel *(of a river; of the sea);* flow *(of language)*

cancell·ī -ōrum *mpl* railing, grating; barrier *(at sports, public events);* boundaries, limits; **intra cancellos** in a confined space

can·cer -crī *m* crab; the South; tropical heat; *(med)* cancer **‖ Cancer** *(astr)* Cancer, the Crab *(sign of the zodiac)*

cande·faciō -facĕre -fēcī -factus *tr* to make white; to make white-hot

candēl·a -ae *f* candle, taper; waxed cord

candēlābr·um -ī *n* candlestick, candelabrum; lampstand

cand·ens -entis *adj* white, shining, glistening; white-hot *(iron)*

cand·eō -ēre -uī *intr* to be shining white, glitter, shine; to be white-hot

cand·escō -escĕre *intr* to become white, begin to glisten; to get white-hot

candidātōri·us -a -um *adj* of a candidate, candidate's

candidāt·us -a -um *adj* clothed in white **‖** *m* candidate

candidē *adv* in dazzling white; clearly, simply, sincerely

candidul·us -a -um *adj* white, gleaming

candid·us -a -um *adj (cf* **albus** flat white) shiny white, white, bright, dazzling, gleaming, sparkling; lucky, favorable, happy; fair *(complexion);* candid, frank *(person);* bright, cheerful *(mood, circumstances);* clear, bright *(day); (of*

winds) bringing clear weather; white, silvery *(poplar, hair);* clear, unaffected *(style);* **candidus limes** Milky Way; **candida sententia** vote of acquittal
cand·or -ōris *m* brightness, radiance; fair complexion; candor, sincerity, kindness; clarity *(of style)*
cān·ens -entis *adj* gray, white
cān·eō -ēre -uī *intr* to be gray
cānesc·ō -ēre *intr* to become gray; to grow old; *(of discourse)* to become dull, lose force
cān·ī -ōrum *mpl* gray hair(s)
Canicul·a -ae *f (astr)* Canicula, Sirius, Dog Star
canīn·us -a -um *adj* canine; snarling, spiteful; **canina littera** letter R
can·is -is *mf* dog; worst throw *(in dice)* ‖ **Canis** *m (astr)* Canis Major *or* Sirius
canistr·um -ī *n* wicker basket *(for bread, flowers, etc.)*
cāniti·ēs -ēī *f* grayness; *(fig)* gray hair; *(fig)* old age
cann·a -ae *f* reed; reed pipe, flute
cannab·is -ae *f or* **cannab·um -ī** *n* hemp, marijuana; hempen rope
Cann·ae -ārum *fpl* town in Apulia where Hannibal defeated the Romans in 216 B.C.
Cannens·is -is -e *adj* of Cannae
canō canĕre cecinī cantus *tr* to sing; to play *(musical instrument);* to speak in a singsong tone; to sing of; to prophesy, predict; *(mil)* to blow, sound; **signa** *(or* **classicum) canere** to sound the signal for battle ‖ *intr* to sing; to play *(on musical instrument); (of birds)* to sing; *(of roosters)* to crow; *(of frogs)* to croak; **receptui canere** to sound the retreat; **tibiā canere** to play the flute
Canōp·us -ī *m* town on W. mouth of the Nile
can·or -ōris *m* tune, sound, melody, song; tone *(of instruments)*
canōr·us -a -um *adj* melodious, musical; singsong, jingling ‖ *n* melody
Cantabr·ī -ōrum *mpl* tribe in N. Spain
Cantabri·a -ae *f* district in N. Spain
cantām·en -inis *n* incantation, spell
cantāt·or -ōris *m* singer
canthar·is -idis *f* beetle; Spanish fly
canthar·us -ī *m* wide-bellied drinking vessel with handles, tankard
cant(h)ērīn·us -a -um *adj* of a horse
cant(h)ēr·ius -(i)ī *m* gelding; eunuch
canth·us -ī *m* iron rim; wheel
cantic·um -ī *n* song; aria in Roman comedy
cantilēn·a -ae *f* old song, gossip; **cantilenam eandem canere** *(fig)* to harp on the same theme
canti·ō -ōnis *f* singing; incantation, spell, charm

cantit·ō -āre -āvī -ātus *tr* to keep on singing *or* playing
Cant·ium -(i)ī *n* district of Britain *(modern Kent)*
cantiuncul·a -ae *f* catchy tune
cant·ō -āre -āvī -ātus *tr* to sing; to play; to sing of, celebrate; to harp on, keep repeating; to drawl out; to predict; *(of birds)* to sing, crow, warble; *(of actor)* to play the part of ‖ *intr* to sing; to play; *(of instruments)* to sound; to drawl; *(of rooster)* to crow; **ad surdas aures cantare** *(fig)* to preach to deaf ears
cant·or -ōris *m* singer; poet; eulogist; actor, player; musician
cantr·ix -īcis *f* singer, player *(female)*
cant·us -ūs *m* song, tune, melody; incantation; magic spell; prediction; poetry
cān·us -a -um *adj* gray; white; gray-haired; old; age-old *(things);* whitened, foam-capped *(sea); (of trees, plants)* covered with silvery foliage
Canusīn·a -ae *f* garment made of Canusian wool
Canus·ium -(i)ī *n* town in Apulia *(modern Canosa)*
capācit·ās -ātis *f* capacity
Capan·eüs -ēī *m* one of the "Seven against Thebes", killed by lightning
cap·ax -ācis *adj* capacious, spacious, wide, roomy; *(of mind)* able to grasp, receptive; *(w. gen, dat or inf)* big enough for; *(w. gen)* 1 capable of, capable of holding; 2 susceptible of; 3 capable of understanding; **capax navium** navigable
capēd·ō -inis *f* cup, bowl *(used in sacrifices)*
capēduncul·a -ae *f* small cup *or* bowl *(used in sacrifices)*
capell·a -ae *f* she-goat, nanny goat ‖ **Capella** *(star in the constellation Auriga)*
Capēn·a -ae *f* Porta Capena *(gate in the Servian Wall marking the start of the Via Appia)*
ca·per -prī *m* he-goat, billy goat
caperr·ō -āre -āvī -ātus *tr & intr* to wrinkle
capess·ō -ĕre -īvī *or* **-iī -ītus** *tr* (-iss-) to try to reach, make for; to seize, get hold of, snatch at; to take up, engage in; **arma capessere** to take up arms, go to war; **cursum** *(or* **viam) capessere** to take the road (to); **flammam capessere** to catch fire; **poenas capessere** to exact punishment; **rem publicam capessere** to engage in politics ‖ *refl & intr* to go
Caphēr·eüs -ei *m* (-phār-) rocky promontory at the S.E. end of Euboea
capillāment·um -ī *n* wig, toupeé
capillār·e -is *n* hair oil
capillāt·us -a -um *adj* long-haired
capill·us -ī *m* hair *(of the head);* *(single)*

hair; *(of plants)* fibers; hair, fur *(of animals)*

capiō capĕre cēpī captus *(archaic fut:* **capsō)** *tr* to take hold of, grasp; to occupy; to take up *(arms);* assume *(office);* to put on *(clothes, armor);* to catch, capture; to catch *(fish);* to bag *(game);* to captivate, charm; to cheat, mislead, seduce, delude; to trap; to defeat, overcome; to keep under control; to be able to hold, have room for; to convince; to reach, arrive at, land at; to exact *(tribute, penalty);* to extort, accept as a bribe; to take, obtain, enjoy, reap *(profit, advantage);* to cherish, cultivate, adopt *(habits, etc.);* to form, come to, reach *(conclusions, plans, thoughts, resolutions, purposes);* to take, derive, draw, obtain *(examples, proofs, instances);* to receive, experience *(impressions, feelings); (of feeling)* to come over; to suffer, be subjected to *(injury);* to hold, contain, be large enough for; to comprehend, grasp; **animo capere** to grasp, get, understand; **consilium capere** to form a plan; **fidem capere** to be credible; **finem capere** to come to an end; **radicem capere** to take root; **quietem capere** to get some rest, go to sleep; **usu capere** to acquire, inherit ‖ *refl* **se non capere** not to contain oneself, not to control oneself

capi·ō -ōnis *f* taking; **usus capio** acquiring ownership by continuous possession

cap·is -idis *f* bowl *(with one handle, used in sacrifices)*

capistr·ō -āre -āvī -ātus *tr* to halter, muzzle

capistr·um -ī *n* halter, muzzle

capit·al *or* **capit·āle -ālis** *n* capital offense; crime punishable by death

capitāl·is -is -e *adj* relating to the head *or* life; *(leg)* affecting a person's life *or* civil status; *(of crime)* punishable by death, punishable by loss of civil rights; dangerous, deadly, fatal; mortal *(enemy);* first-class, fine

capitāliter *adv* with bitter hostility

capit·ō -ōnis *m (coll)* bighead

Capitōlīn·us -a -um *adj* Capitoline ‖ *m* Capitoline Hill ‖ *mpl* persons in charge of the Capitoline games ‖ *n see* **Capitolium**

Capitōl·ium -(i)ī *n* the Capitol *(temple of Jupiter on the summit of Mons Tarpeius);* the Capitoline Hill *(including temple and citadel);* citadel *(of any city)*

capitulātim *adv* briefly, summarily

capitul·um -ī *n* small head; *(as term of endearment)* dear fellow; end, point *(of an instrument, pole, etc.)*

Cappadoci·a -ae *f* country in E. Asia Minor between Cilicia and Pontus

Cappadoc·us -a -um *adj* Cappadocian

Cappad·ox -ocis *m* inhabitant of Cappadocia; *(pej)* Asiatic

cappar·is -is *f* pickled flower bud of the caper plant *(prickly shrub)*

capr·a -ae *f* she-goat ‖ **Capra** *(astr)* star in the constellation Auriga

capre·a -ae *f* wild she-goat; **Capr(e)ae Palus** Goat's Pool *(in Campus Martius, site of Circus Flaminius)*

Capre·ae -ārum *fpl* Isle of Capri

capreol·us -ī *m* chamois, roebuck; rafter

Capricorn·us -ī *m (astr)* Capricorn

caprifīc·us -ī *f* wild fig tree

caprigen·us -a -um *adj* of goats; **caprigenum pecus** herd of goats

caprimulg·us -ī *m* country bumpkin *(literally, goat milker)*

caprīn·us -a -um *adj* goat-; **de lanā caprinā rixari** *(fig)* to fight over nothing

caprip·ēs -edis *adj* goat-footed

caps·a -ae *f* container, holder, box, case *(esp. for scrolls)*

capsō *see* **capio**

capsul·a -ae *f* small box

capt·a -ae *f* captive *(female)*

captāti·ō -ōnis *f* hunt, quest; **captatio verborum** verbalism

captāt·or -ōris *m* seeker; legacy hunter; **aurae popularis captator** publicity hound

capti·ō -ōnis *f* trick, fraud; loss, disadvantage; verbal quibble

captiōsē *adv* slyly, trickily

captiōs·us -a -um *adj* tricky, captious; harmful, disadvantageous

captiuncul·a -ae *f* quibble, sophism

captīv·ās -ātis *f* captivity; capture

captīv·us -a -um *adj* captured; captive; prisoner's; caught *(in hunting, fishing)* ‖ *mf* prisoner-of-war

capt·ō -āre -āvī -ātus *tr* to try to catch; to keep reaching for; to chase after; to strive after, long for, desire earnestly; to try to find; to try to trap, lure; to try to get the better of *(in an argument);* to adopt *(plan);* to try to cause *(laughter, response in others);* to watch for *(an opportunity);* to begin *(conversation);* **aure** *(or* **auribus) captare** to try to hear, listen in on, eavesdrop on; **cenam captare** to sponge a meal

captūr·a -ae *f* capture; quarry, kill; catch *(in fishing)*

capt·us -a -um *pp of* **capio** ‖ *adj* captive; **oculis et auribus captus** blind and deaf; **mente captus** crazy

capt·us -ūs *m* grasping, taking; capacity, potentiality

Capu·a -ae *f* chief city of Campania

capūd·ō -inis *f* primitive sacrificial vessel

capulār·is -is -e *adj (sl)* ready for the grave

capul·us -ī *m* coffin; hilt, handle
cap·ut -itis *n* head; top, summit; point; principal point, main item; essential thing, matter of prime importance; end *(of anything, esp. when rounded or resembling a head, e.g., of a pole);* source *(of river);* root *(of plant);* top *(of tree);* head, leader; capital *(of country);* main point *(of discourse);* chapter, heading; substance, summary; beginning, first part *(of a speech, action; initial letter, beginnning of a word or sentence);* main course; *(com)* capital; *(leg)* life, civil status; **capitis accusare** to accuse of a capital crime; **capitis damnare** to condemn to death; **capitis res** matter of life and death; **caput demittere** to hang one's head; **diminutio capitis** loss of civil rights; **diminutio capitis maxima** condemnation to death *or* slavery; **diminutio capitis media** loss of citizenship; **diminutio capitis minima** change of status *(as by adoption, marriage)*
Cap·ys -yis *or* **-is** *m* son of Assaracus and father of Anchises **‖** companion of Aeneas **‖** eighth king of Alba Longa
carbase·us -a -um *adj* linen, canvas
carbas·us -a -um *adj* linen **‖** *f* sail, canvas; awning; linen cloth **‖** *npl* linen clothing
carb·ō -ōnis *m* charcoal
carbōnār·ius -(i)ī *m* charcoal burner *(person),* collier
carbuncul·us -ī *m* (live) coal, ember; garnet; *(med)* carbuncle, tumor
carc·er -eris *m* prison; prisoners; *(coll)* jailbird **‖** *mpl* starting gate *(at racetrack);* **ad carceres a calce revocari** to start over from scratch *(literally, to be called back from the chalk line, i.e., finish line, to the starting gate)*
carcerāri·us -a -um *adj* prison-
carchēs·ium -(i)ī *n* drinking cup; masthead *(of ship)*
cardiac·us -a -um *adj* suffering from heartburn **‖** *m* dyspeptic
card·ō -inis *m* (kar-) pivot and socket; hinge; turning point; axis, pole; boundary; region, district *(of a country);* the earth *(as pivot of the universe);* **cardo extremus** old age; **cardo rerum** critical juncture; **cardo summus** zenith *(of the sky)*
cardu·us -ī *m* thistle
cārē *adv* at a high price, dearly
cārect·um -ī *n* a bed of sedge *(reed grass, having solid rather than hollow stems)*
car·eō -ēre -uī *intr (w. abl or gen)* 1 to be without; 2 to miss; 3 to be free from *(trouble, pain, blame);* 4 to keep away from, be absent from; 5 to abstain from; 6 to fail to achieve, be denied; 7 to go without

cār·ex -icis *f* sedge, reed grass *(having solid rather than hollow stems)*
Cāri·a -ae *f* district in S.W. Asia Minor
cari·ēs -ēī *f* decaying; decay, rot; shriveling up
carīn·a -ae *f* keel; ship **‖ Carinae** *fpl* the Keels *(district in Rome between the Esquiline and Caelian Hills)*
cārīnār·ius -(i)ī *m* dyer of yellow
cariōs·us -a -um *adj* rotten, decayed; crumbly; wrinkled *(old age)*
cār·is -idis *f* shrimp
cārit·ās -ātis *f* dearness, costliness, high price, high cost of living; affection
carm·en -inis *n* song, tune; poem; poetry; lyric poetry; incantation; oracular utterance; ritual formula; legal formula; adage
Carment·a -ae *or* **Carment·is -is** *f* Roman goddess, mother of Evander
Carmentāl·is -is -e *adj* of Carmenta; **Porta Carmentalis** gate at Rome in the Servian Wall
Carment·is -is *or* **Carment·a -ae** *f* Roman goddess, the mother of Evander
carnār·ium -(i)ī *n* meat hook
carnār·ius -(i)ī *m* butcher, dealer in meat
Carnead·ēs -is *m* Greek Academic philosopher of the 2nd cent. B.C.
Carneadē·us -a -um *adj* characteristic of Carneades
carnif·ex -icis *m* (carnu-) executioner; murderer, butcher; scoundrel
carnificīn·a -ae *f* (carnu-) execution; torture
carnific·ō -āre -āvī -ātus *tr* to execute, butcher
car·ō -nis *or* **carn·is -is** *f* meat; **caro bubula** beef; **caro ferina** venison; **caro putida** carrion; *(fig)* rotten egg
Carpathi·us -a -um *adj* of the island of Carpathus *(between Crete and Rhodes);* **Carpathius senex (vates)** Proteus
carpatīn·a -ae *f* rough-leather shoe
carpent·um -ī *n* two-wheeled covered carriage *(used esp. by women)*
carp·ō -ēre -sī -tus *tr* to pluck, pick; to carp at; to enjoy, make use of; to crop *(grass); (mil)* to harass; to cut to pieces; to card *(wool); (of wild animals)* to tear at; **auras vitales carpere** to breathe the breath of life; **diem carpere** to make the most of the present; **gyrum carpere** to go in a circle; **iter (or viam) carpere** to make one's way, travel; **pensum (or vellera) carpere** to spin
carptim *adv* piecemeal, separately; selectively; at different times; at various points; gradually
carpt·or -ōris *m* carver *(at table)*
carrūc·a -ae *f* four-wheeled carriage
carr·us -ī *m,* **carr·um -ī** *n* Gallic type of wagon

Carthae·us -a um *adj* of Carthaea *(town on the Greek island of Ceos)*

Carthāginiens·is -is -e *adj* (Kar-) Carthaginian

Carthāg·ō -inis *f* (Kar-) Carthage *(city in N. Africa, founded in 9th cent. B.C.)*

Carthēi·us -a -um *adj see* **Carthaeus**

caruncul·a -ae *f* scrap of meat

cār·us -a -um *adj* dear, expensive; dear, loving, affectionate

Cār·us -ī *m* Roman family name *(cognomen)*

cas·a -ae *f* cottage, cabin, hut

Casc·a -ae *m* Roman family name *(cognomen), esp.* Gaius and Publius Servilius Casca Longus *(two of Caesar's assassins)*

casc·us -a -um *adj* old-time, primitive

cāseol·us -ī *m* small piece of cheese

cāse·us -ī *m or* **cāse·um -ī** *n* cheese

casi·a -ae *f* wild cinnamon tree; fragrant shrub

Caspi·us -a -um *adj* Caspian; **mare Caspium** Caspian Sea; **sinus Caspius** Caspian Sea; **Caspiae pylae** *(or* **portae)** name of passes in the Caucasus mountains S. of the Caspian Sea

Cassandr·a -ae *f* prophetic daughter of Priam and Hecuba, believed by no one

cassid·a -ae *f* metal helmet

Cassiop·ē -ēs *or* **Cassiopē·a -ae** *f* wife of Cepheus and mother of Andromeda, afterwards changed into a constellation

cass·is -idis *f* metal helmet

cass·is -is *m (often pl)* hunting net, snare; spider web; **casses alicui tendere** to set a trap for s.o.

cassiter·um -ī *n* tin

Cass·ius -(i)ī *m* Gaius Cassius Longinus *(of one Caesar's murderers)*

cass·ō -āre *intr* to totter

cass·us -a -um *adj* empty, hollow; *(fig)* empty, groundless, pointless; *(w. abl)* deprived of, devoid of, without; **cassus lumine** without life; **in cassum** to no purpose, pointlessly

Castali·a -ae *f* spring at Delphi, associated with Apollo and Muses

Castal·is -idis *adj (fem only)* Castalian; **sorores Castalides** Muses **‖** *f* Muse

Castali·us -a -um *adj* of Castalia, of Apollo, of the Muses, of the Delphic oracle, Castalian

castane·a -ae *f* chestnut tree; chestnut

castē *adv* chastely, purely, spotlessly; virtuously; devoutly

castellān·us -a -um *adj* of a fort(ress) **‖** *mpl* occupants of a fort(ress)

castellātim *adv* one fort(ress) after another; **castellatim dissipati** (troops) stationed in various fortresses

castell·um -ī *n* fort, fortress; *(fig)* stronghold, refuge; small reservoir *or* center of distribution on an aqueduct

castēri·a -ae *f* rower's quarters

castīgābil·is -is -e *adj* punishable

castīgāt·ō -ōnis *f* correction, punishment; censure, reproof

castīgāt·or -ōris *m* castigator

castīgātōri·us -a -um *adj* reproving

castīgāt·us -a -um *adj* firm *(breast)*

castīg·ō -āre -āvī -ātus *tr* to correct, make right; to reprove, find fault with

castimōni·a -ae *f* purity, morality; chastity; ceremonial purification

castit·ās -ātis *f* chastity, purity

cast·or -oris *m* beaver **‖** **Castor** Castor, son of Tyndareus, twin brother of Pollux, brother of Helen and Clytemnestra, and patron of sailors; **aedes** *(or* **templum)** **Castoris** temple of Castor (and Pollux)

castore·um -ī *n* strong-smelling secretion of beavers, used in medicine

castr·a -ōrum *npl* camp; day's march; the service, army life; *(pol)* party; *(phil)* school; **bina castra** two camps; **castra facere** *(or* **munire** *or* **ponere)** to construct a camp; **castra habere** to be encamped; **castra movere** to break camp; **castra una** one camp

castrens·is -is -e *adj* camp-, military; characteristic of soldiers; **corona castrensis** crown conferred on first soldier to enter an enemy's camp

castr·ō -āre -āvī -ātus *tr* to castrate

castr·um -ī *n* fort, fortress **‖** *npl see* **castra**

cast·us -a -um *adj* chaste, pure, guiltless; *(of places)* free from crime; holy, religious, pious, sacred

casul·a -ae *f* little hut, little cottage

cās·us -ūs *m* falling; fall, downfall, overthrow, end; chance, event, occurrence; occasion, opportunity; emergency; misfortune, accident; plight; eventuality, possible situation, contingency; death; fate; *(gram)* case; **non consulto sed casu** not on purpose but accidentally

cataclysm·os -ī *m* deluge

catafract- *see* **cataphract-**

catagraph·us -a -um *adj* print *(dress)*

catamīt·us -ī *m* catamite **‖** **Catamītus** Ganymede

cataphag·ās -ae *m* glutton

cataphract·ēs -ae *m* coat of mail

cataphract·us -a -um *adj* clad in mail

cataplūs *m (nom only)* putting into port, ship's arrival

catapult·a -ae *f* catapult

catapultāri·us -a -um *adj* catapulted, shot *(from a catapult)*

cataract·a *or* **catarract·a -ae** *or* **catar(r)(h)act·ēs -ae** *f* rapids, cataract; sluice; portcullis

cataractri·a -ae *f (fictitious)* spice

catast·a -ae *f* platform on which slaves were displayed for sale

catē *adv* skillfully, wisely

catēj·a -ae *f* javelin

catell·a -ae *f* puppy *(female)*; small chain *(worn by women)*

catell·us -ī *m* puppy; small chain

catēn·a -ae *f* chain; series; curb, restraint **‖** *fpl* chains, fetters

catēnāt·us -a -um *adj* chained

caterv·a -ae *f* crowd, throng, band, mob; troop *(of actors)*; *(mil)* troop

catervārius -a -um *adj* in a crowd

catervātim *adv* in groups; in herds, in flocks; in crowds

cathedr·a -ae *f* armchair, cushioned seat; sedan chair; teacher's chair

Catilīn·a -ae *m* Lucius Sergius Catiline *(leader of conspiracy in 63 B.C.)*

catill·ō -āre -āvī -ātum *intr* to lick the plate

catill·us -ī *m or* **catill·um -ī** *n* plate

catīn·us -ī *m* plate, bowl, dish

Cat·ō -ōnis *m* Marcus Porcius Cato *(model of Roman aristocratic conservatism, 239–149 B.C.)* **‖** Marcus Porcius Cato Uticensis *(grandson of the former, archenemy of Julius Caesar, 95–45 B.C.)*

Catull·us -ī *m* Gaius Valerius Catullus *(lyric and elegiac poet of Verona, 86–54 B.C.)* **‖** a mime writer

catul·us -ī *m* puppy; whelp, cub **‖**

Catulus Roman family name *(cognomen)*, esp. Quintus Lutatius Catulus *(consul in 78 B.C.)*

cat·us -a -um *adj* clever; sly

Caucasi·us -a -um *adj* of the Caucasus; **portae Caucasiae** pass through the Caucusus Mountains

Caucas·us -ī *m* Caucasus Mountains

caud·a -ae *f* tail **(cōd-)** *(of an animal)*; tailend; *(vulg)* penis; **caudam jactare** *(w. dat)* to flatter; **caudam movere** to wag the tail; **caudam trahere** to be mocked

caude·us -a -um *adj* wooden

caud·ex -icis *m* **(cōd-)** trunk *(of tree)*; block *(of wood to which one was tied for punishment)*; book, tablet; ledger; *(coll)* blockhead

caudicāl·is -is -e *adj* wood-splitting

Caudīn·us -a -um *adj* of Caudium, Caudine; **Furculae Caudinae** Caudine Forks *(where Romans suffered a great defeat at the hands of Samnites)*

Caud·ium -(i)ī *n* town in Samnium

caul·ae -ārum *fpl* fence; sheepfold; *(anat)* pores

caulicul·us -ī *m* small stalk; small cabbage

caul·is -is *f* stalk, stem; cabbage

caup·ō -ōnis *m* innkeeper

caupōn·a -ae *f* inn, tavern; innkeeper *(female)*; retail shop

caupōni·us -a -um *adj* of an inn *or* shop

caupōn·or -ārī -ātus sum *tr* to trade in, traffic in

caupōnul·a -ae *f* small inn; small shop

caus·a *or* **causs·a -ae** *f* cause, grounds, motive, reason; good reason, just cause; pretext, pretense; inducement, occasion; side, party, faction; condition, situation, position; responsibility, blame; *(leg)* case, trial, plea; *(med)* case, symptoms; *(rhet)* matter of discussion, subject matter; matter, business, concern; **causā** *(postpositive) (w. gen)* for the sake of, because of; **animi causā** for the sake of amusement; **causae amicitiae** ties of friendship; **causae necessitudinis** friendly relations; **causam agere** *(or* **dicere** *or* **orare)** to plead a case; **causam cognoscere** *(of a judge)* to examine a case; **in causā esse** to be responsible; **meā causā** for my sake; as far as I am concerned, for all I care; **non sine causā** with good reason; **ob hanc causam** because of this; **per causam** *(w. gen)* under the pretense of; **valetudinis causā** for reasons of (poor) health; **vestrā causā** in your interests

causāri·us -a -um *adj* sick; **missio causaria** *(mil)* medical discharge **‖** *m* soldier with medical discharge

causi·a -ae *or* **cause·a -ae** *f* wide-brimmed Macedonian hat

causidic·us -ī *m* lawyer; shyster

causific·or -ārī -ātus sum *intr* to make excuses

caus·or -ārī -ātus sum *tr* to give as an excuse, pretend

caussa *see* **causa**

causul·a -ae *f* poor reason; *(leg)* petty lawsuit

cautē *adv* cautiously, carefully; without risk

cautēl·a -ae *f* precaution, caution

caut·ēs -is *f* **(cōt-)** *(usu. pl)* rock, crag, cliff; *(fig)* hard-heartedness

cautim *adv* warily, cautiously

cauti·ō -ōnis *f* caution, wariness; guarantee, provision; *(leg)* bond, bail; **mea (or mihi) cautio est** I must see to it, I must take care

caut·or -ōris *m* wary person; *(leg)* bondsman

caut·us -a -um *pp of* **caveo ‖** *adj* cautious, careful; safe, secure

cavaed·ium -(i)ī *n* inner court of a Roman house

cave·a -ae *f* cavity; enclosure for animals: cage, den, hole, stall, beehive; auditorium, theater; **prima cavea** section of auditorium for nobility; **ultima cavea** section for lower classes

caveō cavēre cāvī cautus *tr* to guard against, beware of; to keep clear of; to stipulate, decree, order; to guarantee; **cave canem!** beware of the dog! **‖** *intr* to be careful, look out, be on one's guard;

(w. abl or **ab)** to be on one's guard against; *(w.* **ab)** to get a guarantee from; *(w. dat)* **1** to guarantee, give a guarantee to; **2** to provide for, take care of; **cave tangere** (= **noli tangere)** do not touch!

cavern·a -ae *f* hollow; cavity *(in tooth);* cavern; hole; den, lair; hold *(of ship)* **ǁ** *fpl* vault *(of sky)*

cavill·a -ae *f* jeering, scoffing

cavillāti·ō -ōnis *f* banter, scoffing; quibbling

cavillāt·or -ōris *m* scoffer; quibbler

cavill·or -ārī -ātus sum *tr* to scoff at, mock, criticize, satirize **ǁ** *intr* to scoff, jeer; to quibble

cav·ō -āre -āvī -ātus *tr* to hollow out, excavate, dig a hole in; to pierce, run through

cav·us -a -um *adj* hollow, hollowed; concave, vaulted; deep-channeled *(river)* **ǁ** *m & n* depression; cave, cavern; burrow, hole *(of an animal);* hole, cavity, hollow; aperture, perforation; **cavum aedium** inner court of a house

-ce demonstrative enclitic appended to pronouns and adverbs (like colloquial English *here, there,* with *this* or *that);* **hice** *(for* **hicce)** this *(here);* **hujusce** of this *(here);* (when followed by the enclytic **-ne,** the form becomes **-ci: hicine, sicine)**

Cē·a *or* **Cī·a -ae** *or* **Cē·os -ī** *f* Ceos *(Greek island in the Cyclades)*

Cecropi·a -ae *f* Athens

Cecropid·ēs -ae *m* descendant of King Cecrops; **Cecropidae** Athenians

Cecrop·is -idis *or* **idos** *f* female descendant of Cecrops; Aglauros; Procne; Philomela; Athenian woman

Cecropi·us -a -um *adj* of Cecrops; Athenian

Cecr·ops -opis *m* first king of Athens

cēd·ens -entis *adj* unresisting

cēdō cēdĕre cessī cessus *tr* to grant, concede, yield, give up **ǁ** *intr* to go, move, walk, walk along; to go away, depart, withdraw; *(usu. w.* **vitā)** to pass away, die; *(of time)* to pass; *(of events)* turn out; *(w. dat)* **1** to befall, fall to the lot of; **2** to yield to, submit to, give in to; **3** to be inferior to; **4** to comply with, conform to, obey; *(w.* **in** + *acc)* **1** to result in; **2** to be changed into, become; *(w.* **pro** + *abl)* **1** to pass for; **2** to be the equivalent of; **3** to be the price of; **bonis** *(or* **possessionibus) alicui cedere** to give up *or* cede one's property to s.o.; **foro cedere** to go bankrupt

cedo *(pl:* **cette)** *(old impv)* give here, hand over, bring here; let's hear, tell, out with; look at; **cedo dum!** all right! **cedo ut inspiciam** let me have a look

cedr·us -ī *f* cedar; cedarwood; cedar-wood oil

Celaen·ō -ūs *f* daughter of Atlas and one of the Pleiades **ǁ** one of the Harpies **ǁ** greedy woman

cēlāt·um -ī *n* secret

cele·ber -bris -bre *adj* crowded, populous, frequented; well-attended; famous; well-known, common, usual; solemn, festive; numerous, repeated, frequent

celebrāti·ō -ōnis *f* large assembly; festival, celebration; widespread use **ǁ** *fpl* throngs

celebrāt·us -a -um *adj* crowded, populous; much-frequented; celebrated, famous; solemn, festive; common, current

celebrit·ās -ātis *f* crowd; large assembly; publicity; frequency; fame

celebr·ō -āre -āvī -ātus *tr* to frequent; to crowd, fill; to inhabit; to celebrate, observe; to honor, worship; to escort, attend; to practice, exercise; to announce, publicize; **sermone celebrare** to discuss

cel·er -eris -ere *adj* fast; agile, quick; hurried; rash, hasty; passing quickly

celere *adv* quickly

Celer·ēs -um *mpl* mounted bodyguards of Roman kings

celerip·ēs -edis *adj* swift-footed **ǁ** *m* race horse

celerit·ās -ātis *f* speed; quickness; excessive speed

celeriter *adv* quickly; soon, early

celer·ō -āre -āvī *tr* to quicken, speed up **ǁ** *intr* to be quick, rush, hurry

celeum·a -atis *n* boatswain's call *(giving time to the rowers)*

Cele·us -ī *m* king of Eleusis and father of Triptolemus

cell·a -ae *f* storeroom; silo; small room; *(coll)* hole-in-the-wall, poor man's apartment; sanctuary *(of temple where statue stood);* cell *(of beehive);* cubicle *(in a bathing establishment or in a brothel);* porter's room

cellāri·us -a -um *adj* of a storeroom **ǁ** *m* one in charge of the storeroom

cellul·a -ae *f* (-ola) small storeroom; small room; porter's lodge; slave's room

cēl·ō -āre -āvī -ātus *tr* to hide, conceal; to keep secret, keep quiet about; to conceal the identity of; *(w. acc of thing and acc of person from whom one conceals)* to keep *(s.o.)* in the dark about *(s.th.),* hide *(s.th.)* from *(s.o.)* **ǁ** *refl & pass* to pass out of view; **celari de** *(w. abl)* to be kept in ignorance of

cel·ox -ōcis *adj* swift, quick **ǁ** *f* light, fast boat

cels·us -a -um *adj* high, lofty, towering, prominent; erect; lofty *(thoughts);* high *(rank);* proud; *(of head)* held high; tall *(animals, person, trees, buildings)*

Celt·ae -ārum *mpl* Celts
Celtib·ēr -ērī *mpl* a Celtiberian **‖** *mpl* Celtiberians *(early people of central Spain)*
cēn·a -ae *f* dinner; dish, course
cēnācul·um -ī *n* dining room *(usually on the upper floor);* upper floor, attic; attic apartment
cēnātic·us -a -um *adj* dinner
cēnāti·ō -ōnis *f* dining room
cēnātōri·a -ōrum *npl* formal wear; dinner apparel
cēnāt·us -a -um *adj* having dined; stuffed from feasting
cēnit·ō -āre *intr* to dine often
cēn·ō -āre -āvī -ātus *tr* to dine on, eat **‖** *intr* to dine, eat dinner
cens·eō -ēre -uī -us *tr* to think, believe, suppose, imagine, expect; to esteem, appreciate, value; *(of senator)* to propose, move, vote; to recommend; to suggest, advise; *(of the Senate and other bodies and supreme magistrates)* to decide, resolve; *(of the censor)* to estimate, rate, assess, tax; to register *(possessions); (w. abl)* to measure by; **censeo** *(in replies)* I think so; **quid censes?** what is your opinion? *(formula used by the presiding magistrate to invite a senator to express his opinion)* **‖** *pass (w. abl)* to be valued for, have one's reputation based on; *(as deponent)* to reckon, count (as)
censi·ō -ōnis *f* tax assessment; punishment *(imposed by the censor)*
cens·or -ōris *m* censor *(one of two magistrates who took the census and exercised general control over morals);* severe judge of morals; critic
censōri·us -a -um *adj* of the censors; subject to censure; rigid, stern; **funus censorium** public funeral; **homo censorius** ex-censor; **lex censoria** contract *(drawn up by censors)* for leasing buildings
censūr·a -ae *f* office of censor, censorship; censure
cens·us -ūs *m* census; register of the census; income bracket; wealth, property; rich presents; **censum agere** *(or* **habere)** to hold a census; **censu prohibere** to exclude from citizenship
centaurē·um -ī *n* **(-i·um, -i·on)** centaury *(herb)*
Centaurē·us -a -um *adj* of Centaurs
Centaur·us -ī *m* Centaur *(half-man, half-horse); (astr)* Centaurus *(a constellation)*
centēn·ī -ae -a *adj* one hundred each; **deciens centena milia passuum** ten hundred thousand (one million) paces, one thousand miles
centēsim·us -a -um *adj* hundredth **‖** *f* hundredth part, one percent; *(com)* 1% monthly, 12% annually

centi·ceps -cipitis *adj* hundred-headed
centiēs *adv* **(-iens)** a hundred times; *(fig)* a good many times
centiman·us -a -um *adj* hundred-handed
cent·ō -ōnis *f* patchwork, quilt
centr·um -ī *n* center
centum *indecl adj* hundred
centumgemin·us -a -um *adj* hundredfold
centumpl·ex -icis *adj* hundredfold
centumpond·ium -(i)ī *n* hundred pounds, hundred-pound weight
centumvirāl·is -is -e *adj* of the centumvirs
centumvir·ī -ōrum *mpl* panel of one hundred *(jurors chosen annually to try civil suits under a quaestor, esp. concerning inheritances)*
centuncul·us -ī *m* piece of patchwork, blanket *(made of patchwork)*
centuri·a -ae *f (mil)* company, century *(nominally 100 soldiers); (pol)* century, voting division; unit of land *(100 heredia, 200 jugera, i.e., c. 133 acres)*
centuriātim *adv (mil, pol)* by companies *or* centuries
centuriāt·us -a -um *adj (mil, pol)* divided into companies *or* centuries; **comitia centuriata** centuriate assembly *(legislative body that met in the Campus Martius to elect high magistrates, decree war, etc.)*
centuriāt·us -ūs *m* rank of centurion; division into centuries
centuri·ō -ōnis *m* centurion *(commander of an infantry company)*
centuri·ō -āre -āvī -ātus *tr* to divide into centuries or companies
centuriōnāt·us -ūs *m* rank of centurion; revision of the list of centurions
centuss·is -is *m* a hundred *asses (coins, i.e., about $1)*
cēnul·a -ae *f* light dinner
cēnum *see* **caenum**
Ceōs *see* **Cea**
cēpa *or* **cepe** *see* **caepa**
Cephallāni·a -ae *f* Greek island in the Ionian Sea
Cephal·us -ī *m* husband of Procris, whom he accidentally killed
Cēphē·is -idos *f* daughter of Cepheus, Andromeda
Cephēi·us -a -um *adj* descended from Cepheus
Cēphēnes -um *mpl* a people of Ethiopia
Cēphēn·us -a -um *adj* of the Cephenes, Ethiopian
Cēph·eūs -ĕī *m* king of the Cephenes, father of Andromeda
Cēphīs·os -ī *m* Cephissus *(river in Attica; river in Phocis)*
cēr·a -ae *f* wax; writing tablet *(covered with wax);* wax seal; wax bust of an ancestor; cell *(of beehive)*
Ceramīc·us -ī *m* cemetery of Athens

cērār·ium -(i)ī *n* fee for affixing a seal
cerast·ēs -ae *m* horned serpent
ceras·um -ī *n* cherry
ceras·us -ī *f* cherry tree; cherry
cērāt·us -a -um *adj* waxed ‖ *n* wax-salve *(made of wax and oil)*
Cerber·us -ī *m* three-headed dog guarding entrance to lower world
cercopithēc·us -ī *m* long-tailed monkey
cercūr·us -ī *m* swift-sailing ship
cerd·ō -ōnis *m* (common) laborer
Cereāl·is -is -e *adj* of Ceres; of grain; arma Cerealia utensils for grinding and baking ‖ *npl* festival of Ceres *(April 10)*
cerebrōs·us -a -um *adj* hot-headed
cerebr·um -ī *n* brain; head, skull; hot temper; *(fig)* brains
Cer·ēs -eris *f* goddess of grain and fruits and mother of Proserpina; grain, wheat; bread; food
cēre·us -a -um *adj* of wax, waxen; wax-colored; soft, pliant ‖ *m* candle
cērinth·a -ae *f* wax flower
cērin·us -a -um *adj* wax-colored
Cermal·us -ī *m* (Germ-) part of the Palatine Hill in Rome
cernō cernĕre crēvī crētus *tr* to sift; to distinguish, make out, see; to understand, see; to decide, decree, determine; hereditatem cernere to accept an inheritance formally; vitam cernere to decide a question of life or death
cernu·us -a -um *adj* leaning forward; headfirst
cērōm·a -atis *n* wrestler's oil; *(fig)* wrestler
cērōmatic·us -a -um *adj* smeared with oil, oily, greasy
cerrīt·us -a -um *adj* possessed by Ceres, crazy, frenzied
certām·en -inis *n* contest, match; rivalry; *(mil)* battle, combat
certātim *adv* with a struggle, in rivalry
certāti·ō -ōnis *f* contest; rivalry, discussion, debate
certē *adv* surely, certainly; of course; *(in answers)* certainly; *(to restrict an assertion)* at least
certō *adv* for sure; in fact, really
cert·ō -āre -āvī -ātus *tr* to contest ‖ *pass* to be fought over ‖ *intr (w.* de + *abl)* to fight over, struggle for; *(w.* cum) to fight with, struggle with, compete with; *(w. inf)* to strive to; *(leg)* to debate
cert·us -a -um *adj* certain; fixed; regular; specific, particular, definite; faithful, trusty; unerring; unwavering; certiorem facere to inform; certum est mihi *(w. inf)* I am determined ‖ *n* certainty; certum habere to regard as certain; pro certo for sure; pro certo habere to be assured

cērul·a -ae *f* piece of wax; cerula miniata red pencil *(of a critic)*
cēruss·a -ae *f* ceruse, white paint
cērussāt·us -a -um *adj* painted white
cerv·a -ae *f* doe
cervīc·al -ālis *n* pillow, cushion
cervīcul·a -ae *f* slender neck
cervīn·us -a -um *adj* of a stag
cerv·ix -īcis *f (often in plural with same meaning as singular)* neck; in cervicibus nostris esse *(fig)* to be on our necks; a cervicibus nostris avertere *(fig)* to get *(s.o.)* off our necks; cervicibus sustinere to shoulder *(responsibility)*
cerv·us -ī *m* stag, deer; *(mil)* palisade
cessāti·ō -ōnis *f* cessation; letup; delay; idleness, inactivity
cessāt·or -ōris *m* loafer
cessāt·us -a -um *adj* having been in abeyance; *(of land)* having been left fallow; spent in idleness
cessi·ō -ōnis *f (leg)* surrendering
cess·ō -āre -āvī -ātum *intr* to cease; to let up, slack off, become remiss; to be idle, do nothing; to lie fallow; to fail, not function; *(w. inf)* to hesitate to, be slow to; *(of things)* to stop, give out; *(of things)* to be at rest, be motionless; *(of things)* to be neglected, remain unused; *(w. abl or* ab) to be free of, be clear of, be wanting in; *(leg)* to fail to take action, default; *(leg)* to fail to appear in court
cessus *pp of* cedo
cest·os *or* cest·us -ī *m* brassière
cestrosphendon·ē -ēs *f* artillery piece for hurling stones
cētār·ium -(i)ī *n* fish pond
cētār·ius -(i)ī *m* fishmonger; fisherman
cētē *see* cetus
cētera *adv* otherwise, in all other respects, for the rest
cēterōquī(n) *adv* otherwise, in all other respects, for the rest
cēterum *adv* but, still; for the rest, otherwise; however that may be
cēter·us -a -um *adj* the other, the remaining, the rest of ‖ *pron masc pl & fem pl* the others, all the rest, everybody else ‖ *n* the rest; de cetero for the rest; otherwise; for the future; in ceterum in the future
Cethēg·us -ī *m* Gaius Cornelius Cethegus *(fellow conspirator of Catiline)*
cette *see* cedo
cēt·us *or* cēt·os -ī *(nom & acc npl:* cētē) *m* large sea animal: whale, shark, dolphin, seal; sea-monster
ceu *conj (in comparisons)* as, just as; *(in comparative conditions)* as if, just as if; ceu cum as when
cēv·eō -ēre *intr (cf.* criso) *(of a male) (sl)* to move the hips, shake it up

Cē·yx -ȳcis *m* king of Trachis, changed into a kingfisher *(bird)*

Chaerōnē·a -ae *f* town in Boeotia where Philip of Macedon defeated the Greeks in 338 B.C.

Chalcidic·us -a -um *adj* of Chalchis *(in Euboea);* of Cumae *(in Italy)*

Chaldae·us -a -um *adj* Chaldean **‖** *m* astrologer, fortuneteller

chalybēi·us -a -um *adj* steel-

Chalyb·es -um *mpl* people of Pontus in Asia Minor noted as steel-workers and iron-workers

chal·ybs -ybis *m* steel; iron

Chāon·es -um *mpl* tribe in Epirus

Chāoni·us -a -um *adj* Chaonian; of Epirus **‖** *f* Chaonia *(in Epirus)*

Cha·os -ī *n* chaos, the unformed world; a Chao from the beginning of the world

char·a -ae *f* wild cabbage (?)

Charit·ēs -um *fpl* the Graces

Char·ōn -onis *m* ferryman of the lower world

chart·a -ae *f* sheet of papyrus; thin sheet of metal **‖** *fpl (fig)* writings

chartul·a -ae *f* sheet of papyrus; note

Charybd·is -is *f* whirlpool between Italy and Sicily *(regarded as a female monster); (fig)* cruel person

Chatt·ī -ōrum *mpl* Germanic tribe

Chauc·ī -ōrum *mpl* Germanic tribe

Chēl·ae -ārum *fpl (astr)* the Claws *(of the constellation Scorpio); (astr)* Libra

chelydr·us -ī *m* poisonous water snake

chelys *(gen not in use; acc:* **chelyn)** *f* tortoise; lyre

cheragr·a -ae *f* arthritis in the hand

chīliarch·ēs -ae *or* **chīliarch·us -ī** *m* commander of 1,000 men; Persian chancellor *(highest office next to the king)*

Chimaer·a -ae *f* fire-breathing female monster, with lion's head, goat's body, and dragon's tail

Chimaerifer·a -ae *adj (fem only) (of Lycia)* that produced the Chimaera

Chi·os *or* **Chi·us -ī** *f* Chios *(Greek island off the coast of Ionia)*

chīrograph·um -ī *n* (-graf-) one's handwriting; manuscript; written promise; **falsum chirographum** forgery

Chīr·ō(n) -ōnis *m* Chiron *(Centaur, tutor of Hercules, Achilles, etc.); (astr)* Chiron *(constellation)*

chīronom·ōn -untos *adj* gesticulating

chīronom·os -ī *m* pantomimist

chīrurgi·a -ae *f* surgery

chīrurgic·us -ī *m* surgeon

chīrurg·us -ī *m* surgeon

Chi·us -a -um *adj & mf* Chian **‖** *n* Chian wine **‖** *npl* Chian cloth

chlamydāt·us -a -um *adj* wearing a military cape

c(h)lam·ys -ydis *or* **-ydos** *f* military cape; gold-brocaded cape

Choeril·us -ī *m* incompetent panegyrist of Alexander the Great

chorāg·ium -(i)ī *n* stage properties

chorāg·us -ī *m* theatrical producer

choraul·ēs -ae *m* flute player *(who accompanied the choral dance)*

chord·a -ae *f* string *(of musical instrument);* cord, rope

chorē·a -ae *f* dance

chorē·us -ī *m* trochee (— ◡)

chorocitharist·ēs -ae *m* one who accompanied a chorus on the lyre

chor·us -ī *m* chorus; choir

Chrem·ēs -ētis *m* miserly old character in plays of Terence

Christiān·us -ī *m* Christian

Christ·us -ī *m* Christ

Chrȳsē·ïs -idis *or* **-idos** *f* Agamemnon's slave girl, daughter of Chryses

Chrȳs·ēs -ae *m* priest of Apollo

Chrȳsipp·us -ī *m* famous Stoic philosopher *(290–210 B.C.)*

chrȳsolith·os -ī *m* chrysolite, topaz

chrȳs·os -ī *m* gold

cibāri·us -a -um *adj* of food; common, coarse *(food for slaves)* **‖** *npl* rations, provisions, food allowance

cibāt·us -ūs *m* food; feed, fodder

cib·ō -āre -āvī -ātus *tr* to feed

cibōr·ium -(i)ī *n* chalice

cib·us -ī *m* food; feed; meal; nutriment; fuel; **cibum capere** to take food, eat food, eat a meal

cicād·a -ae *f* cicada; harvest fly

cicātrīcōs·us -a -um *adj* scarred, covered with scars

cicātr·ix -īcis *f* scar

cicc·us -ī *m* core of pomegranate; *(sl)* junk

cic·er -eris *m* chickpea; testicle

Cicer·ō -ōnis *m* Cicero *(Marcus Tullius Cicero, orator and politician, 106–43 B.C.)* **‖** Quintus Tullius Cicero *(his brother, 102–43 B.C.)* **‖** Marcus Tullius Cicero *(his son, consul in 30 B.C.)*

cichorē·um *or* **cichōri·um -ī** *n* endive

cicima(li)ndr·um -ī *n* comic name for an imaginary seasoning

Cicon·es -um *mpl* Thracian tribe

cicōni·a -ae *f* stork

cic·ur -uris *adj* tame

cicūt·a -ae *f* hemlock tree; hemlock poison; pipe, flute *(carved from hemlock wood)*

-cīd·a -ae *m suf* denoting one who cuts *or* kills *(e.g.,* **lapicida** stonecutter; **matricida** murderer of one's mother)

cidar·is -is *f* tiara *(of Persian king)*

cieō ciēre cīvī citus *tr* to set in motion, move; to stir up, rouse up, muster; to call for, send for; to summon for help; to invoke, appeal to; to bring about; to cause, make; **lacrimas ciere** to shed tears; **stragem ciere** to wreak havoc

Cilici·a -ae *f* country and Roman province in S.E. Asia Minor

cilic·ium -(i)ī *n* rug *or* blanket of goat's hair

Cilici·us -a -um *adj* Cilician **ll** *n* garment made of goat's hair

Ciliss·a -ae *f* Cilician woman

Cil·ix -icis *adj & m* Cilician

-cill·um -i *neut suf* forms diminutives: **corcillum** heart

-cill·us -ī *masc suf* forms diminutives from diminutives: **penicillus** (small) painter's brush

Cim·ber -brī *m* Cimbrian **ll** Roman family name *(cognomen)*

Cimbr·ī -ōrum *mpl* Germanic tribe that invaded Gaul and Italy at the end of the 2nd cent. B.C. and was defeated by Marius

Cimbric·us -a -um *adj* Cimbrian

cīm·ex -icis *m* bedbug

Cimmeri·ī -ōrum *mpl* people in the Crimea **ll** people living in perpetual darkness in caves at Cumae

cinaedic·us -a -um *adj* lewd

cinaed·us -ī *m* catamite; homosexual

cincinnāt·us -a -um *adj* curly-haired **ll** **Cicinnatus** *m* Lucius Quinctius Cincinnatus *(Roman war hero, appointed dictator in 458 B.C.)*

cincinn·us -ī *m* lock of curled hair; *(rhet)* artificial expression

cincticul·us -ī *m* small belt *or* sash

cinctūr·a -ae *f* belt, sash

cinctus *pp of* cingo

cinct·us -ūs *m* tucking up; belt, sash; **cinctus Gabinius** Gabinian style of wearing toga *(usually employed at religious festivals)*

cinctūt·us -a -um *adj* wearing a belt *or* sash; old-fashioned

cinefact·us -a -um *adj* reduced to ashes

cinerār·ius -(i)ī *m* hairdresser

cin·gō -gĕre -xī -ctus *tr* to surround, encircle; to enclose *(a space);* to wreathe *(head);* to tuck up *(garment)* **ll** *pass* to get dressed; to form a circle; **cingi in proelia** to gear up for battle; **ferrum cingi** to put on one's sword

cingul·a -ae *f* belt; sash; girth; sword belt; chastity belt

cingul·um -ī *n* belt; sword belt; sash; girdle; chastity belt

cingul·us -ī *m* zone *(of the earth)*

cinifl·ō -ōnis *m* hairdresser

cin·is -eris *m (f)* ashes; ruin, death

-cin·ium -(i)ī *neut suf* denoting activity or profession *(e.g.,* **latrocinium** robbing, robbery)

Cinn·a -ae *m* Lucius Cornelius Cinna *(notorious consul 87–84 B.C.)*

cinnamōm·um *or* **cinnam·um -ī** *n* cinnamon **ll** *npl* cinnamon sticks

cinxī *perf of* cingo

Cinyr·ās -ae *m* father of Myrrha, and, by her, also father of Adonis

cip(p)·us -ī *m* stake, post, pillar; gravestone; *(mil)* palisade

Circa *see* Circe

circā *adv* around, round about; all around, in the vicinity **ll** *prep (w. acc)* around, surrounding, about, in the neighborhood of, near; through; attending, escorting; concerning, in respect to; *(of time)* around, about, towards; *(w. numbers)* about, nearly, almost

Circae·us -a -um *adj* of Circe

circāmoer·ium -(i)ī *n* area on both sides of a city wall

Circ·ē -ēs *or* **Circ·a -ae** *f* Circe *(famous witch, daughter of Sol and Perse)*

circens·is -is -e *adj* of the racetrack **ll** *mpl* races

circin·ō -āre -āvī -ātus *tr* to make round; to circle

circin·us -ī *m (geometer's)* compass

circiter *adv* about, nearly, approximately **ll** *prep (w. acc)* about, near

circlus *see* circulus

circueō *see* circumeo

circuitiō *see* circumitio

circuit·us -ūs *m* circuit; going around, revolution; detour; circumference; beating around the bush; *(rhet)* period

circulātim *adv* in groups

circulāt·or -ōris *m* peddler; itinerant performer

circulātr·ix -īcis *f* peddler *(female);* itinerant performer *(female)*

circul·or -ārī -ātus sum *intr* to gather a crowd around oneself

circ(u)l·us -ī *m* circle, circuit; ring, hoop; social circle; *(astr)* orbit

circum *adv* about, all around **ll** *prep (w. acc)* around, about; in the neighborhood of

circum- *suf* around, about: **circumstare** to stand around

circum·agō -agĕre -ēgī -actus *tr* to turn around; to turn *(e.g., a wheel);* to sway **ll** *refl & pass* to turn around; *(of feelings)* to change; to change *(in form);* to go out of one's way; *(of time)* to pass, roll around

circumar·ō -āre -āvī *tr* to plow around

circumcaesūr·a -ae *f* contour, outline

circumcī·dō -dĕre -dī -sus *tr* to cut around, trim; to cut short, cut down on; to abridge, shorten; to circumcise

circumcircā *adv* all around

circumcīs·us -a -um *pp of* circumcido **ll** *adj* steep, inaccessible; abridged

circumclū·dō -dĕre -sī -sus *tr* to shut in, enclose; *(mil)* to surround; *(fig)* circumvent

circumcol·ō -ĕre *tr* to live near

circumcurs·ō -āre -āvī *tr* & *intr* to run around

circum·dō -dăre -dedī -datus *tr* to surround, enclose, encircle; *(w. dat)* to place *or* put *(s.th.)* around

circumdŭ·cō -cĕre -xī -ctus *tr* lead around, draw around; *(w. double acc)* to lead *(s.o.)* around to; **aliquem omnia praesidia circumducere** to lead s.o. around to all the garrisons

circumducti·ō -ōnis *f* perimeter; *(w. gen)* cheating out of; *(rhet)* period

circum·eō -īre -īvī *or* -iī -itus *tr* to go around, go around to, visit, make the rounds of; to surround, encircle, encompass; to circumvent, deceive, cheat ‖ *intr* to go around, make a circuit

circumequit·ō -āre *tr* to ride around *(on horseback)*

circumerr·ō -āre -āvi *tr* & *intr* to wander around, prowl around

circum·ferō -ferre -tūlī -lātus *tr* to carry around, hand around; to publicize, spread around; to purify; **oculos circumferre** to glance about ‖ *pass* to revolve

circumfle·ctō -ctĕre -xī -xus *tr* to turn around, wheel about

circumfl·ō -āre *tr* to blow around; *(fig)* to buffet

circumflu·ō -ĕre -xī *tr* to flow around; to surround; to overflow ‖ *intr* to be overflowing, abound

circumflu·us -a -um *adj* flowing around; surrounded *(by water)*

circumforāne·us -a -um *adj* strolling about from market to market, itinerant; around the forum

circumfrem·ō -ĕre -uī *intr* to groan all around

circum·fundō -fundĕre -fūdī -fūsus *tr* to pour around; to surround, cover, envelop ‖ *refl* & *pass* to crowd around; *(w. dat)* to cling to

circumgem·ō -ĕre *tr* to growl around *(e.g., a sheepfold)*

circumgest·ō -āre *tr* to carry around

circum·gredior -gredī -gressus sum *tr* to surround *(esp. to attack)*

circu(m)iti·ō -ōnis *f* going around; patrolling; beating around the bush

circumitus see circuitus

circumjac·eō -ēre *intr (w. dat)* to lie near, border on, be adjacent to

circumject·us -ūs *m* an encompassing

circum·jiciō -jicĕre -jēcī -jectus *tr* to throw *or* place around; to surround; *(w. dat)* to throw *(s.th.)* around *(s.o. or s.th.)*; **fossam circumjicere** to dig a trench all around

circumject·us -a -um *adj* surrounding, encompassing, taking in

circumlāt·us -a -um *pp* of circumfero

circumlav·ō -āre *or* -ĕre *tr* to wash around, wash the sides of

circumlīg·ō -āre -āvī -ātus *tr* to bind; *(w. dat)* to tie *(s.th.)* to

circum·linō -linĕre -lēvī -litus *tr* to smear all over, to anoint; to cover; *(fig)* to clothe

circumlu·ō -ĕre *tr* to flow around

circumluvi·ō -ōnis *f* island *(formed by a river flowing in a new channel)*

circum·mittō -mittĕre -mīsī -missus *tr* to send around

circummūg·iō -īre *intr* to moo around

circummūn·iō -īre -īvī -ītus *tr* (-moen-) to fortify *(with wall, moat, etc.)*

circummūnīti·ō -ōnis *f* investment *(of town)*; circumvallation

circumpadān·us -a -um *adj* situated along the Po River

circumpend·eō -ēre *intr* to hang around

circumplaud·ō -ĕre *tr* to applaud from every direction

circumple·ctor -ctī -xus sum *tr* to embrace; to surround

circumplic·ō -āre -āvī -ātus *tr* to wind up; to coil around; *(w. dat)* to wind *(s.th.)* around

circum·pōnō -pōnĕre -posuī positus *tr (w. dat)* to place *or* set *(s.th.)* around

circumpōtāti·ō -ōnis *f* round of drinks

circumrēt·iō -īre *tr* to snare

circumrō·dō -dĕre -sī -sus *tr* to nibble all around; to hesitate to say; to slander

circumsaep·iō -īre -sī -tus *tr* (-sēp-) to fence in, enclose

circumscind·ō -ĕre *tr* to strip off

circumscrī·bō -bĕre -psī -ptus *tr* to draw a line around, mark the boundaries of; to limit, circumscribe; to set aside; to defeat the purpose of; to trap, defraud

circumscriptē *adv* concisely; *(rhet)* in periodic style

circumscripti·ō -ōnis *f* encircling; circle; limits, boundary; outline, definition; cheating; *(rhet)* periodic sentence

circumscript·or -ōris *m* cheat

circumscript·us -a -um *pp* of circumscribo ‖ *adj* restricted; concise; *(rhet)* periodic, rounded-off

circumsec·ō -āre -uī -tus *tr* to cut around; to circumcize

circum·sedeō -sedēre -sēdī -sessus *tr* to beset, besiege, blockade

circumsēpiō see circumsaepio

circumsessi·ō -ōnis *f* blockading

circum·sīdō -sīdĕre -sēdī -sessus *tr* to besiege, surround, invest

circumsil·iō -īre *tr* & *intr* to hop around

circum·sistō -sistĕre -stetī *tr* to stand around, surround

circumson·ō -āre -uī -ātus *tr* to make resound, cause to re-echo ‖ *intr* to resound everywhere; *(w. dat)* to resound to

circumson·us -a -um *adj* noisy
circumspectātr·ix -īcis *f* spy *(female)*
circumspecti·ō -ōnis *f* looking around; circumspection, caution
circumspect·ō -āre *tr* to watch for, search carefully for; to catch sight of ‖ *intr* to keep looking around, look around anxiously
circumspect·us -a -um *pp of* circumspicio ‖ *adj* well-considered, guarded *(words)*; circumspect, cautious
circumspect·us -ūs *m* consideration; commanding view; contemplation
circum·spiciō -spicĕre -spexī -spectus *tr* to look around at, survey; to catch sight of; to consider, examine ‖ *refl* to think highly of oneself ‖ *intr* to be circumspect, be cautious, be on the watch
circumstant·ēs -ium *mpl* bystanders
circum·stō -stāre -stetī *tr* to surround, envelop; *(of terror, etc.)* to grip ‖ *intr* to stand around
circumstrep·ō -ĕre -uī -itus *tr* to shout at on all sides, surround with noise *or* shouts
circumsurg·ens -entis *adj (of mountains)* rising all around
circumtent·us -a -um *adj* tightly covered
circumter·ō -ĕre *tr* to rub shoulders with, crowd around
circumtext·us -a -um *adj* with embroidered border
circumton·ō -āre -uī *tr* to crash around, thunder around
circumtons·us -a -um *adj* clipped *or* trimmed all around
circumvā·dō -dĕre -sī *tr* to attack on every side; *(of terror)* to grip
circumvag·us -a -um *adj* flowing around, encircling
circumvall·ō -āre -āvī -ātus *tr* to blockade ‖ *refl* to form a blockade
circumvecti·ō -ōnis *f* carting around *(of merchandise)*; circular course, revolution *(of sun)*
circumvect·ō -āre -āvī -ātus *tr* to carry around ‖ *pass* to travel around, sail around
circumve·hor -hī -ctus sum *tr* to ride around (to), sail around (to), travel around (to); to travel past
circumvēl·ō -āre *tr* to envelop, cover
circum·veniō -venīre -vēnī -ventus *tr* to enclose, surround; to go around to; to distress, beset; to circumvent, cheat; to prosecute *or* convict unjustly
circumver·tō -tĕre -tī -sus *tr* (-vor-) to turn *(s.th.)* around ‖ *pass* to turn around; **rota circumvertitur axem** the wheel revolves around its axle
circumvest·iō -īre *tr* to clothe
circumvinc·iō -īre *tr* to tie up
circumvīs·ō -ĕre *tr* to look around, glare around at

circumvolit·ō -āre -āvī *tr & intr* to fly around, dash about, rove around; to hover around
circumvol·ō -āre -āvī *tr* to fly around, dart around ‖ *intr* to hover about, hover over, flit about
circumvol·vō -vĕre -vī -ūtus *tr* to wind, roll around ‖ *refl & pass (w. dat or acc)* to revolve around, wind oneself around
circ·us -ī *m* circle; racetrack; *(astr)* orbit
Circ·us Falamini·us -ī *m* racetrack built by Gaius Flaminius Nepos in the Campus Martius in 220 B.C.
Circ·us Maxim·us -ī *m* oldest racetrack in Rome, between the Palatine and Aventine Hills
cirrāt·us -a -um *adj* curly-haired
Cirrh·a -ae *f* (Cyrr-) town near Delphi, sacred to Apollo
Cirrhae·us -a -um *adj* of Cirrha; of Apollo
cirr·us -ī *m* lock, curl; forelock
Cirt·a -ae *f* town in Numidia
Cirtens·ēs -ium *mpl* inhabitants of Cirta
cis *prep (w. acc)* on this side of *(on the Roman side of)*; *(of time)* within
cis- *pref* used in the sense of the preposition
Cisalpīn·us -a -um *adj* Cisalpine *(on the Roman side of the Alps)*
cis·ium -(i)ī *n* gig *(light, two-wheeled carriage)*
Cisp·ius -(i)ī *m* (Cesp-) one of the summits of the Esquiline Hill
Cisrhenān·us -a -um *adj* dwelling on the W. side of the Rhine
Cissē·is -idis *f* daughter of Cisseus *(i.e., Hecuba)*
Ciss·eŭs -eī *m* king of Thrace and father of Hecuba
cist·a -ae *f* box, chest *(esp. of wicker)*; ballot box
cistell·a -ae *f* small box
cistellātr·ix -īcis *f* female slave in charge of the money box
cistellul·a -ae *f* small box
cistern·a -ae *f* cistern, reservoir
cistophor·us -ī *m* Asiatic coin *(with a representation of a bearer of the cista of Dionysus on it)*
cistul·a -ae *f* small box
citātim *adv* quickly, hurriedly
citāt·us -a -um *adj (of animals)* speeded up; *(of limbs)* moved quickly; *(of pace, actions)* quick, speedy; *(of bowels)* loose; **citato equo** at full gallop
citāt·us -ūs *m* impulse
citeri·or -or -us *adj* on this side, near *(to Rome)*; earlier; *(nearer to the present)* later, more recent; more down-to-earth, nearer home; *(w. abl)* earlier than
citerius *adv* short of
Cithaer·ōn -ōnis *m* Greek mountain range dividing Attica from Boeotia

cithar·a -ae *f* lyre
citharist·a -ae *m* lyre player
citharistri·a -ae *f* lyre player *(female)*
cithariz·ō -āre *intr* to play the lyre
citharoed·us -ī *m* singer *(playing the lyre)*
citim·us -a -um *adj* (lying) nearest
citius *adv* sooner, rather; **dicto citius** no sooner said than done; **serius aut citius** sooner or later
cito *adv* quickly; soon
cit·ō -āre -āvī -ātus *tr* to excite, rouse; to call, summon; to call to witness, appeal to; to arouse, produce; to cite *(as an authority)*
citrā *adv* on this side, on the near side; **citra cadere** to fall short ‖ *prep (w. acc)* 1 on this side of, on the near side of: **citra mare** on this side of the sea, in Italy; 2 *(of time)* since, before: **citra Trojana tempora** before the Trojan period; 3 just short of, less than, except: **peccavi citra scelus** I committed a fault just short of a crime; 4 regardless of *(e.g., a person's wishes):* **citra senatūs populique auctoritatem** regardless of *or* without regard for the authority of the senate and the people
citre·us -a -um *adj* of citrus wood
citrō *adv* to this side, this way; **ultro (et) citro** *(or* **citro ultroque)** to and fro, up and down; mutually
citr·um -ī *n* wood of the citron tree; table *(made of citron wood)*
citr·us -ī *f* citron tree
cit·us -a -um *pp of* **cieo** ‖ *adj* quick
cīvic·us -a -um *adj* civil; civilian; suitable for one as a civilian; **corona civica** civic crown *(given to war hero for saving s.o.'s life)*
cīvīl·is -is -e *adj* civil, civic; civilian; forensic, legal; political; unassuming; **jus civile** private *or* civil law; civil rights; **ratio civilis** political science; **res civilis** *(or* **civiles)** politics; **vir civilis** statesman
cīvīlit·ās -ātis *f* politics; courtesy
cīvīliter *adv* like a citizen; as an ordinary citizen should; politely
cīv·is -is *mf* citizen; fellow citizen; private citizen
cīvit·ās -ātis *f* state; community; city; citizenship
clād·ēs -is *f* disaster; loss; *(mil)* defeat, carnage; destruction; ruins; *(of person)* scourge, destroyer
clam *adv* secretly, privately; stealthily; **clam habere aliquem** to keep s.o. in the dark ‖ *prep (w. abl or acc)* without the knowledge of; **neque clam me est** nor is it unknown to me; **clam patre** without the father's knowledge
clāmāt·or -ōris *m* loudmouth
clāmitāti·ō -ōnis *f* bawling, racket

clāmit·ō -āre -āvī -ātus *tr & intr* to cry out, yell
clām·ō -āre -āvī -ātus *tr* to shout, yell; to proclaim; to call upon ‖ *intr* to shout
clām·or -ōris *m* shout; acclamation; applause; battle cry; noise; wailing
clāmōsē *adv* with a shout, loudly
clāmōs·us -a -um *adj* yelling, noisy; loud-barking *(dog)*
clanculum *adv* secretly; privately ‖ *prep (w. acc)* unknown to
clandestīnō *adv* secretly
clandestīn·us -a -um *adj* clandestine
clang·ō -ĕre *intr (of eagle)* to scream
clang·or -ōris *m* clang, noise; blast *(of trumpet);* cry, scream *(of bird);* baying *(of dog)*
clārē *adv* clearly; out loud; brightly; with distinction, honorably; **clare legere** to read aloud
clār·eō -ēre *intr* to be clear, be distinct, be bright; to be evident; to be famous
clār·esco -escĕre -uī *intr* to become clear, become distinct; to become bright; to become famous; *(of sound)* to get loud
clārigāti·ō -ōnis *f* reparation; fine
clārig·ō -āre -āvī -ātum *intr* to demand satisfaction, demand reparation
clārison·us -a -um *adj* clear-sounding
clārit·ās -ātis *f* loudness; clarity; brightness; distinction, renown
clāritūd·ō -inis *f* brightness; fame
Clari·us -a -um *adj* of the island of Claros, *esp.* as epithet of Apollo
clār·ō -āre -āvī -ātus *tr* to clarify, explain; to light up, illuminate; to make famous
Clar·os -ī *f* town in Asia Minor famous for a temple and oracle of Apollo
clār·us -a -um *adj* loud; clear, bright; plain, manifest; famous; notorious; **clara lux** broad daylight; **clarior luce** clearer than daylight; **vir clarissimus** gentleman of the Senate
classiāri·us -a -um *adj* naval ‖ *mpl* marines
classicul·a -ae *f* flotilla
classic·us -a -um *adj* first-class, belonging to the highest class of citizens; naval ‖ *m* trumpeter who summoned the *comitia centuriata* ‖ *mpl* marines, sailors ‖ *n* battle signal; bugle call; **classicum canere** to sound the bugle *(to begin battle; to announce a capital trial or an execution)*
class·is -is *f* fleet; *(social)* class; grade, class *(of pupils);* band, group; **classi** with a fleet, at sea; in a naval battle
clāt(h)rāt·us -a -um *adj* barred
clāt(h)r·ī -ōrum *mpl* bars; railings
claud·eō -ēre *or* **claud·ō -ĕre** *intr* to be lame, to limp; to falter; to be imperfect
Claudiān·us -a -um *adj* connected with

members of the Claudian clan, *esp.* the Emperor Claudius

claudicāti·ō -ōnis *f* limping

claudic·ō -āre *intr* to be lame, to limp; to incline to one side; to be halting, be defective; to be deficient, fall short

Claud·ius -(i)ī *m* Appius Claudius Caecus *(censor in 312 B.C. and builder of the Appian Way and Appian aqueduct)* ‖ the Roman Emperor Claudius *(Tiberius Claudius Nero Germanicus, reigned 41–54 A.D.)*

clau·dō -děre -sī -sus *tr* to shut, close; to bring to a close, conclude; to shut up; to lock up, imprison; *(mil)* to blockade, hem in; to limit; to cut off, block; to keep secret, suppress *(feelings, thoughts);* **agmen claudere** to bring up the rear; **numeris** *(or* **pedibus) claudere** to put into verse; **transitum claudere** to block traffic

claud·us -a -um *adj* **(clōd-)** lame, limping; crippled, imperfect, defective; wavering; untrustworthy

claustell·um -ī *n* **(clos-)** keyhole

claustr·a -ōrum *npl* lock, bolt, bar; gate; dam, dike; barrier, barricade; cage, den; fortress; defenses

clausul·a -ae *f* close, conclusion *(of a letter, speech, argument; of a transaction);* clause *(in a law or document);* end *(of a word, of a line of verse);* *(rhet)* close of a periodic sentence with particular regard to its rhythm

claus·us -a -um *pp of* **claudo** ‖ *adj* closed, inaccessible *(place);* *(of a person)* impervious to feelings; shut, locked up; enclosed *(in a container)* ‖ *n* enclosure

Claus·us -ī *m* a Sabine chief, reputed ancestor of the *gens Claudia* ‖ *mpl* members of the *gens Claudia*

clāv·a -ae *f* cudgel, club

clāvār·ium -iī *n* soldier's allowance for shoe nails

clāvāt·or -ōris *m* club-bearer

clāvīcul·a -ae *f* tendril; key; pivot

clāvig·er -era -erum *adj* carrying a club; carrying keys ‖ *m* club bearer *(Hercules);* key bearer *(Janus)*

clāv·is -is *f* key; hook *(for rolling a hoop);* **clavīs adimere uxori** to take the keys away from a wife, get a divorce

clāv·us -ī *m* nail; rivet; rudder, helm; purple stripe *(worn on the tunic, broad for senators and their sons, narrow for equites);* **clavo** *(or* **clavo trabali) figere** to nail; *(fig)* to nail down, clinch; **clavum rectum tenere** to keep a steady course; **clavus anni** beginning of the year; **clavus trabalis** spike *(large nail)*

clēm·ens -entis *adj* gentle, mild, kind, compassionate; mild, calm *(weather)*

clēmenter *adv* gently, mildly, kindly, compassionately; at an easy pace; **colles clementer adsurgentes** gently rising hills

clēmenti·a -ae *f* mildness, clemency, compassion

Cleopatra -ae *f* daughter of Ptolemy Auletes and queen of Egypt *(d. 31 B.C.)*

clep·ō -ěre -sī -tus *tr* to steal

clepsydr·a -ae *f* water clock; *(fig)* time *(allotted to speakers);* **clepsydram dare** *(w. dat)* to give *(s.o.)* the floor; **clepsydram petere** to ask to have the floor

clept·ēs -ae *m* thief

cli·ens -entis *m* client *(e.g., ex-slave protected by a former owner acting as patron);* follower, retainer; vassal ‖ *mpl* clients *(the citizens of an Italian or other city in their relationship to their Roman patronus)*

client·a -ae *f* client *(female)*

clientēl·a -ae *f* clientele; patronage, protection; clientship *(the relationship of a provincial city or a foreign people to their Roman patronus);* vassalage ‖ *fpl* allies, dependants

clientul·us -ī *m (as term of contempt)* just a poor client

clīnām·en -inis *n* swerve

clīnāt·us -a -um *adj* bent, inclined

clīnic·us -ī *m* clinical physician *(who tends patients at their bedside)*

Clī·ō -ūs *f* Muse of history

clipeāt·us -a -um *adj* armed with a *(round)* shield

clipe·um -ī *n* *or* **clipe·us -ī** *m* round bronze shield; medallion; disc *(of sun)*

clītell·ae -ārum *fpl* packsaddle

clītellāri·us -a -um *adj* carrying a packsaddle

clīvōs·us -a -um *adj* hilly; steep

clīv·us -ī *m* sloping ground, incline, hill; slope, pitch; *(fig)* uphill struggle; **adversus clivum** uphill; **primi clivi** foothills

Clīv·us Sac·er *(gen:* **Clīv·i Sac·ri)** *m* Sacred Incline *(part of the Via Sacra ascending the Capitoline Hill, also called* **Clivus Capitolinus)**

cloāc·a -ae *f* sewer, drain; **cloaca maxima** main sewer *(draining the area of the Roman Forum)*

Cloācīn·a -ae *f* Venus *(the "purifier")*

Clōdi·a -ae *f* sister of the notorious tribune Clodius

Clōdiān·us -a -um *adj* Clodian, of the Clodian faction

Clōd·ius -(i)ī *m* Publius Clodius Pulcher *(notorious tribune of the plebs, enemy of Cicero, killed in 52 B.C.)*

Cloeli·a -ae *f* Roman girl who was given as hostage to Porsenna and escaped by swimming the Tiber back to Rome

Clōthō *(gen not in use; acc:* **Clōthō)** *f* one of the three Fates

clu·eō -ēre *or* clu·eor -ērī *intr* to be spoken of as, be known for; **ut nomen cluet** as the word implies

clūn·is -is *mf* buttock ‖ *mpl & fpl* buttocks; hind quarters *(of an animal)*

clūr·a -ae *f* ape

clūrīn·us -a -um *adj* of apes

Clūs·ium -(i)ī *n* chief Etruscan town

Clūs·ius -(i)ī *m* Janus

Clymen·ē -ēs *f* mother of Phaëthon

clyst·ēr -ēris *m* an injection; *(fig)* syringe

Clyt(a)em(n)estr·a -ae *f* Clytemnestra *(wife of Agamemnon, sister of Helen, Castor, and Pollux, and mother of Electra, Iphigenia, and Orestes)*

Cn. *abbr* **Gnaeus** *(Roman first name, praenomen)*

Cnid·os *or* Cnid·us -ī *f* town in Caria, famous for the worship of Venus

coacervāti·ō -ōnis *f* accumulation

coacerv·ō -āre -āvī -ātus *tr* to gather into a heap; to accumulate; to make *(by heaping up)*

coac·escō -escĕre -uī *intr* to become sour

coacti·ō -ōnis *f* collection *(of money);* abridgment

coact·ō -āre *tr* to force

coact·or -ōris *m* collector *(of money, taxes);* **agminis coactores** rearguard elements

coact·us -a -um *pp of* **cogo** ‖ *adj* forced, unnatural, hypocritical ‖ *n* felt cloth ‖ *npl* felt cloak

coact·us -ūs *m* coercion, compulsion

coaedific·ō -āre -āvī -ātus *tr* to build *(a town);* to build up *(an area),* fill with buildings

coaequ·ō -āre -āvī -ātus *tr* to level off; to treat as equal, equate

coagmentāti·ō -ōnis *f* union; joint

coagment·ō -āre -āvī -ātus *tr* to join together; to construct; to fit *(words)* together

coagment·um -ī *n* joint

coāgul·um -ī *n* rennet *(curdled milk taken from the stomach of young mammals);* curds

coal·escō -escĕre -uī -itum *intr* (cŏl-) to grow together, coalesce; *(of wounds)* to close; to become unified; to grow firm, take root; to become established, thrive

coangust·ō -āre -āvī -ātus *tr* (conang-) to contract, compress; to limit, restrict

coarct- *see* coart-

coargu·ō -ĕre -ī *tr* to bring out into the open *(usu. s.th. undesirable);* to prove conclusively, demonstrate; to refute, prove wrong *or* guilty; *(w. gen of the charge)* to prove *(s.o.)* guilty of

coartāti·ō -ōnis *f* crowding together; tightening

coart·ō -āre -āvī -ātus *tr* to narrow, make narrower; to crowd together, confine; to

pack *(e.g., the Forum);* to shorten; to abridge

coax·ō -āre *intr (of frogs)* to croak

Cōcal·us -ī *m* mythical king of Sicily who protected Daedalus

Coccēï·us -a -um *adj* Roman clan name *(nomen), esp.* Marcus Cocceius Nerva, emperor A.D. 96–98

coccināt·us -a -um *adj* dressed in scarlet

coccin(e)·us -a -um *adj* scarlet ‖ *npl* scarlet clothes; scarlet coverlets

cocc·um -ī *n* scarlet

coc(h)le·a -ae *f* snail

coc(h)leār·(e) -is *n* spoon

cocilendr·um -ī *n* an imaginary magical seasoning

cocl·es -itis *m* person blind in one eye ‖ **Cocles** Horatius Cocles *(commonly called Horatio and famous for defending the Pons Sublicius against Porsenna's army)*

coctil·is -is -e *adj* baked; brick-

coct·or -ōris *m* cook

coct·us -a -um *pp of* **coquo** ‖ *adj* cooked; roasted; baked *(bricks);* ripe; *(fig)* mild ‖ *n* cooked food

Cōcȳt·us -ī *m* river of the lower world

Cōdēt·a -ae *f* piece of ground in the Campus Martius

cōdex *see* caudex

cōdicill·ī -ōrum *mpl* (-cell-) fire logs; set of writing tablets; note; petition to the emperor; rescript from the emperor; supplement to a will, codicil

Codr·us -ī *m* last king of Athens

coēgī *perf of* **cogo**

coel- *see* cael-

Coel·ē -ēs *adj (fem only)* **Coele Syria** "Hollow Syria" *(the S. part of Syria, esp. the region between Lebanon and Antilebanon);* **Coele Thessalia** the plain of Thessaly

co·emō -emĕre -ēmī -emptus *tr* to buy up

coēmpti·ō -ōnis *f* fictitious sale of an estate; marriage *(contracted by fictitious sale of contracting parties)*

coēmptiōnāl·is -is -e *adj* of a marriage by fictitious sale

coen- *see* caen-

co·eō -īre -iī -itus *tr* **societatem coire** to form an alliance ‖ *intr* to come together; to meet, assemble; to be united, combine; to mate, copulate; to have sexual intercourse; to congeal, curdle; to agree; to conspire; to clash *(in combat); (of wounds)* to close

cŏep·ī -isse -tus *(v. defect) tr & intr* to begin

cŏept·ō -āre -āvī -ātus *tr* to begin eagerly; *(w. inf)* to try to ‖ *intr* to make a beginning

cŏept·um -ī *n (usu. pl)* undertaking, enterprise, attempt

coept·us -ūs *m* beginning; undertaking
coëpulōn·us -ī *m* dinner guest
coërc·eō -ēre -uī -itus *tr* to enclose, confine, hem in; to limit; to restrain, check, control
coërciti·ō -ōnis *f* physical restraint, coercion; inflicting of summary punishment by a magistrate; right to inflict summary punishment
coēt·us -ūs *m* coming together, meeting; crowd, company; gang; combination
Coē·us -ī *m* Titan, father of Latona
cōgitātē *adv* deliberately, carefully
cōgitāti·ō -ōnis *f* thinking, deliberating; reflection; thought, plan, idea; reasoning power, imagination
cōgitāt·us -a -um *adj* well-considered, deliberate ‖ *npl* thoughts, ideas
cōgit·ō -āre -āvī -ātus *tr* to consider, ponder, reflect on; to imagine; *(w. inf)* to intend to ‖ *intr* to think
cognāti·ō -ōnis *f* relationship by birth; agreement, resemblance, affinity; relatives, family
cognāt·us -a -um *adj* related by birth; related, similar, akin ‖ *mf* relative
cogniti·ō -ōnis *f* learning, acquiring knowledge; knowledge; notion, idea; recognition; *(w. gen)* knowledge of, acquaintance with; *(leg)* inquiry, hearing, trial
cognit·or -ōris *m* attorney; defender, protector; witness
cognitūr·a -ae *f* the duty of an attorney
cognit·us *pp of* cognosco ‖ *adj* acknowledged, known; familiar
cognit·us -ūs *m* act of getting to know; dignus cognitu worth knowing; jucundus cognitu pleasant to know
cognōm·en -inis *n* surname, family name *(e.g.,* Caesar; *a second* cognomen, *called* agnomen *by later grammarians, was given as an honorary name to a person for some achievement, e.g.,* Africanus); additional title of a god *(e.g.,* Jupiter Feretrus); nickname; derived name *(esp. of places);* a duce Tarpeiā mons est cognomen adeptus the hill took its name from Tarpeia *(the enemy's)* guide
cognōment·um -ī *n* family name; name
cognōmināt·us -a -um *adj* synonymous
cognōmin·is -is -e *adj* like-named, with the same name
cognōmin·ō -āre -āvī -ātus *tr* to give *(s.o.)* a surname *or* nickname
cogn·oscō -oscĕre -ōvī -itus *tr* to become acquainted with, get to know, learn; to recognize, identify; to inquire into, investigate; *(mil)* to reconnoiter; cognovisse to know
cōgō cōgĕre coēgī coactus *tr* to gather together, collect; to assemble; to round up; to gather *(crops);* to collect, raise

(money, taxes); to force, compel; to pressure; to exact, extort; to infer, conclude; to prove conclusively; to compress *(into a mass);* to abridge; to shorten, restrict in time; to form *(e.g., wrinkles by contraction);* to thicken, condense, curdle; agmen cogere to bring up the rear; in ordinem cogere to bring to order, bring back into line
cohaer·ens -entis *adj* adjoining, continuous; consistent; harmonious
cohaerenti·a -ae *f* organic structure
cohae·reō -rēre -sī -sum *intr* to stick *or* cling together, cohere; to be consistent, be in agreement; *(w.* cum) 1 to be closely connected with; 2 to be in harmony with; 3 to be consistent with; inter se cohaerere to be consistent
cohae·rescō -rescĕre -sī *intr* to stick together, cohere; to adhere
cohēr·ēs -ēdis *mf* joint-heir
cohib·eō -ēre -uī -itus *tr* to hold together, hold close; to confine; to clothe; to keep *(information, etc.)* secret, suppress; to check the growth of *(e.g., power);* to withold *(assent);* to hold back, repress *(emotions);* to check, stop *(an action, etc.);* *(w. acc & inf)* to prevent ‖ refl to remain, stay *(in a place);* to exercise self-restraint
cohonest·ō -āre *tr* to honor, pay respect to; to make respectable
cohorr·escō -escĕre -uī *intr* to shiver all over
cohor·s -tis *f* barnyard; retinue, escort; *(mil)* cohort *(comprising 3 maniples or 6 centuries and forming one-tenth of a legion, or 600 men)*
cohortāti·ō -ōnis *f* encouragement
cohorticul·a -ae *f* little cohort
cohort·or -ārī -ātus sum *tr* to encourage, cheer up, urge on
coïti·ō -ōnis *f* meeting; encounter; conspiracy; coalition
coït·us -ūs *m* meeting; junction, meeting place; sexual intercourse
col- *pref see* con-
-col·a -ae *masc suf* denotes a person who inhabits, tills, or worships: amnicola one who dwells by the river; agricola one who tills the field; Junonicola one who worships Juno
colaph·us -ī *m* punch
Colch·is -idis *f* country on E. end of the Black Sea ‖ Colchian woman, Medea
Colchic·us, Colch·us -a - um *adj* Colchian, of Colchis
cōle·ī -ōrum *mpl (vulg)* balls; si coleos haberemus if we had the balls *(i.e., if we dared assert ourselves)*
cōl·is -is *m* stalk; cabbage
collabasc·ō -ĕre *intr* (conl-) to waver, totter

collabefact·ō -āre *tr* **(conl-)** to shake hard
collabe·fīō -fierī -factus sum *intr* **(conl-)** to collapse, be ruined; to sink down
collā·bor -bī -psus sum *intr* **(conl-)** to fall down, collapse; to sink
collacrimāti·ō -ōnis *f* **(conl-)** weeping
collacrim·ō -āre -āvī -ātus *tr* **(conl-)** to cry bitterly over ‖ *intr* to cry together
collacte·a -ae *f* **(-ti·a)** foster sister
collār·e -is *n or* **collār·is -is** *m* collar
Collāti·a -ae *f* old town in Latium
Collātīn·us -ī *m* husband of Lucretia
collāti·ō -ōnis *f* **(conl-)** bringing together; contribution of money, collection, fund; comparison; *(gram)* comparison; **collatio prima** comparative; **collatio secunda** superlative
collāt·or -ōris *m* **(conl-)** contributor
collātus *pp of* **confero**
collaudāti·ō -ōnis *f* **(conl-)** warm praise
collaud·ō -āre -āvī -ātus *tr* **(conl-)** to praise highly
collax·ō -āre *tr* to loosen
collect·a -ae *f* contribution of money
collectāne·us -a -um *adj* collected from various sources
collectīci·us -a -um *adj* hastily gathered
collecti·ō -ōnis *f* **(conl-)** gathering; recapitulation; inference; *(phil)* syllogism
collectus *pp of* **colligo** (to collect)
collect·us -ūs *m* collection
collēg·a -ae *m* **(conl-)** colleague *(in office);* associate; fellow member
collēg·ium -(i)ī *n* **(conl-)** association in office; official body, board, college; guild, corporation; club, society
collībert·us -ī *m* **(conl-)** fellow ex-slave
collib·uit *or* **collub·uit -uisse -itum** *v impers* **(conl-)** it pleases
collī·dō -děre -sī -sus *tr* **(conl-)** to smash to pieces, crush; to strike together; to cause to clash, set at variance ‖ *pass* to be at variance, conflict; *(of teeth)* to chatter
colligāti·ō -ōnis *f* **(conl-)** binding together, connection
collig·ō -āre -āvī -ātus *tr* **(conl-)** to tie together, connect; to unite, combine; to unite *(by social, political ties);* to fasten, chain; to hinder, stop; **vasa colligare** to gather up one's gear ‖ *refl (w. dat)* to join up with
col·ligō -ligěre -lēgī -lectus *tr* **(conl-)** to pick up; to gather together, collect; to attain, acquire *(esp. by natural processes);* to compile *(in a book);* to build (up) *(a reputation);* to hitch up, tuck up *(clothing);* to furl *(sails);* to gather in *(the reins);* to harvest *(fruit, crops);* to summarize, sum up; to contract, compress, concentrate; to acquire gradually, amass; to infer, conclude, gather; *(of numbers, totals)* to amount

to; to enumerate; **animum** *(or* **mentem)** **colligere** to compose oneself; **ignes colligere** to catch fire; **vasa colligere** *(mil)* to gather up one's gear, break camp ‖ *refl & pass* to pull oneself together; to amount to; *(of winds, clouds, dust)* to gather; *(of anger)* to build up
collīne·ō -āre -āvī -ātus *tr* **(-ni·ō) (conl-)** to aim, direct ‖ *intr* to hit the mark
col·linō -liněre -lēvī -litus *tr* **(conl-)** to smear; to defile
Collīn·us -a -um *adj* of the Quirinal Hill; **Collina Porta** Colline Gate *(near the Quirinal Hill)*
colliquefact·us -a -um *adj* **(conl-)** melted, dissolved
coll·is -is *m* hill
collocāti·ō -ōnis *f* **(conl)** arrangement; giving in marriage
collocāt·us -a -um *adj* **(conl-)** *(geog)* located, lying
colloc·ō -āre -āvī -ātus *tr* **(conl-)** to place *(in a particular place);* to put in order, arrange; to station, deploy *(troops);* to give in marriage; to lodge, quarter; to occupy, employ; to spend, invest *(money);* to bestow; *(w.* **in** + *acc or abl)* to devote *(time, energy)* to; **in tuto** *(or* **in tutum)** **collocare** to make safe ‖ *pass* to occur, be found
collocuplēt·ō -āre -āvī -ātus *tr* **(conl-)** to enrich
collocūti·ō -ōnis *f* **(conl-)** conversation; debate, discussion; conference
colloqu·ium -(i)ī *n* **(conl-)** conversation; discussion, conference; interview
collo·quor -quī -cūtus sum *tr* **(conl-)** to talk to ‖ *intr* to talk (with), converse; *(w. acc & inf)* to say in conversation (that)
collubet *see* **collibet**
collūc·eō -ēre *intr* **(conl-)** to shine brightly, be entirely illuminated; *(fig)* to glitter
colluctāti·ō -ōnis *f* **(conl-)** struggling
colluct·or -ārī -ātus sum *intr* **(conl-)** *(w.* **cum)** to wrestle *(with)*
collū·dō -děre -sī -sum *intr* **(conl-)** to play together; to be in collusion; *(w. dat)* to play with
coll·um -ī *n or* **coll·us -ī** *m* neck; bottleneck
col·luō -luěre -luī -lūtus *tr* **(conl-)** to wash out, rinse; to wash away
collūsi·ō -ōnis *f* **(conl-)** collusion
collūs·or -ōris *m* **(conl-)** playmate; fellow gambler
collustr·ō -āre -āvī -ātus *tr* **(conl-)** to light up; to survey, inspect; *(in painting)* to represent in bright colors
collutulent·ō -āre *tr* **(conl-)** to soil, defile
colluvi·ō -ōnis *or* **colluvi·ēs -ēī** *f* **(conl-)** sewage; dregs; impurities; impure mixture; turmoil; rabble

collyb·us -ī *m* **(collu-)** conversion of currency; rate of exchange

collȳr·a -ae *f* pasta, noodles, macaroni

collȳric·us -a -um *adj* **jus collyricum** noodle soup

colō colĕre coluī cultus *tr* to till, cultivate, work; to live in; to guard, protect; to honor, revere, worship; to adorn, dress; to practice, follow; to experience, live through, spend

colocāsi·a -ae *f* lotus, water lily

colōn·a -ae *f* peasant woman

colōni·a -āe *f* colony; *(coll)* town; settlers, colonists; **coloniam deducere** *(or* **mittere)** to send out settlers

colōnic·us -a -um *adj* colonial

colōn·us -ī *m* farmer; colonist, settler

Coloph·ōn -ōnis *m* city in Ionia, one of the "birthplaces" of Homer

col·or *or* **col·os -ōris** *m* color, tint; external condition; complexion; tone, style; luster; grace; colorful pretext

colōrāt·us -a -um *adj* colored, tinted; tanned; swarthy; trumped up

colōr·ō -āre -āvī -ātus *tr* to color; to tan; *(fig)* to give a certain tone to

colossē·us -a -um *adj* colossal

coloss·us *or* **coloss·os -ī** *m* colossus *(any large statue of a Roman emperor, made to rival the orginal Colossus)* **ǁ Colossus Rhodi** the Colossus of Rhodes

colostr·a -ae *f or* **colostr·ūm -ī** *n* **(-lust-)** first milk after childbirth, colostrum

colu·ber -brī *m* snake, adder

colubr·a -ae *f* snake, adder *(female)*

colubrif·er -era -erum *adj* snaky

colubrīn·us -a -um *adj* cunning

cōl·um -ī *n* strainer, colander

columb·a -ae *f* pigeon, dove *(female)*

columb·ar -āris *n* pigeonhole

columbār·ium -(i)ī *n* pigeonhole; niche in a sepulcher

columbīn·us -a -um *adj* of a dove *or* pigeon **ǁ** *m* little dove

columb·us -ī *m* pigeon, dove

columell·a -ae *f* small column

colum·en -inis *n* height, summit, peak; roof; ridgepole; head, leader; *(fig)* "crown", "jewel"; *(fig)* cornerstone *(of an argument); (fig)* very embodiment *(of a quality);* **summum columen** highest point *(of an orbit)*

column·a -ae *f* column, pillar; support; waterspout; *(vulg)* penis; **columnae Herculis** *(or* **Hesperiae)** the Pillars of Hercules; **columna Maenia** whipping post *(in the Forum for thieves and slaves and to which debtors were summoned for trial);* **Protei columnae** the Pillars of Proteus, the "borders of Eygpt" **ǁ** *fpl* portico; bookshop

columnār·ium -(i)ī *n* tax on house pillars

columnār·ius -(i)ī *m* debtor *(convicted at the* **Columna Maeniga)**

columnāt·us -a -um *adj* supported by pillars; **os columnatum** *(fig)* the head supported by one's arms

colurn·us -a -um *adj* of hazelwood

col·us -ī *or* **-ūs** *mf* distaff

colūte·a -ae *f* pod-like kind of fruit

cōlȳphi·a -ōrum *npl* choice cuts of meat, loin cuts

com- *pref see* **con-**

com·a -ae *f* hair *(of head);* mane; fleece; foliage; grass; *(poet)* rays

com·ans -antis *adj* hairy, long-haired; plumed *(helmet);* leafy; **comans stella** comet

cōmarch·us -ī *m* village chief

comāt·us -a -um *adj* long-haired; leafy; **Gallia Comata** Gaul other than the province existing after the conquest by Caesar

combib·ō -ĕre -ī *tr* **(conb-)** to drink up; to absorb; to swallow, engulf; to repress, conceal *(tears);* to absorb *(knowledge)*

combib·ō -ōnis *m* **(conb-)** drinking partner

comb·urō -ūrere -ussī -ustus *tr* **(conb-)** to burn up, consume; *(fig)* to ruin

com·edō -edĕre *(or* **-esse) -ēdī -ēsus** *(or* **estus)** *tr* to eat up, consume; to squander **ǁ** *refl* to pine away; *(fig)* feast one's eyes on

com·es -itis *mf* companion; fellow traveler; associate, partner; attendant; staff member; concomitant

comesse *see* **comedo**

comestus *pp of* **comedo**

comēsus *pp of* **comedo**

comēt·ēs -ae *m* comet

cōmicē *adv* like a comedy

cōmic·us -a -um *adj* of comedy, comic; **comicum aurum** stage money **ǁ** *m* actor, playwright *(of comedy)*

cōminus *see* **comminus**

cōm·is -is -e *adj* polite; *(w. dat or* **erga** *or* **in** *+ acc)* kind toward

cōmī(s)sābund·us -a -um *adj* riotous; drunken; boozing

cōmī(s)sāti·ō -ōnis *f* drinking party

cōmī(s)sāt·or -ōris *m* reveler

cōmī(s)s·or -ārī -ātus sum *intr* to carouse, make merry

cōmit·ās -ātis *f* politeness, kindness

comitāt·us -a -um *adj* **(by)** accompanied *(w. abl);* **comitatior** accompanied by a larger following, better attended

comitāt·us -ūs *m* escort, retinue; court *(of emperor, king);* company *(traveling together),* caravan

cōmiter *adv* politely; kindly

comitiāl·is -is -e *adj* of the assembly; **dies comitialis** day on which the comitia could transact business; **morbus comi-**

tialis epilepsy *(so called because its occurrence could cause an assembly to be adjourned)*
comitiāt·us -ūs *m (pol)* assembly
comit·ium -iī *n* comitium, assembly place, voting place **‖** *npl* popular assembly; elections; **comitia habere** to hold elections
comit·ō -āre -āvī -ātus *or* **comit·or -ārī -ātus sum** *tr* to accompany; to escort; to share *(a fate);* to attend *(a funeral); (of ancestral busts)* to be carried at *(a funeral)* **‖** *intr (w. dat)* to be present with, attend
comm·a -atis *n (gram)* phrase, part of a line
commacul·ō -āre -āvī -ātus *tr* to spot; to defile
commanip(u)lār·is -is *m* army buddy
commarīt·us -ī *m* fellow husband
commeāt·us -ūs *m* passage; traffic; convoy; *(mil)* furlough; *(mil)* lines of communication; *(mil)* supplies; **in commeatu esse** to be on furlough
commedit·or -ārī *tr* to practice hard; to imitate
com·mēiō -mēiĕre -mi(n)xī mi(n)ctus *tr (sl)* to wet, pee
commemin·ī -isse *(v. defect) tr & intr* to remember well
commemorābil·is -is -e *adj* memorable
commemorāti·ō -ōnis *f* **(conm-)** reminder; recollection, remembrance
commemor·ō -āre -āvī -ātus *tr* **(conm-)** to remember; to bring up, mention, relate
commendābil·is -is -e *adj* commendable
commendātīci·us -a -um *adj* of recommendation, of introduction
commendāti·ō -ōnis *f* recommendation; commendation, praise; approval, esteem; excellence
commendāt·or -ōris *m* backer
commendātr·ix -īcis *f* backer *(female)*
commendāt·us -a -um *adj* recommended; acceptable, suitable
commend·ō -āre -āvī -ātus *tr* to entrust; to recommend; to commit *(to writing, posterity);* to commend **‖** *refl (w. dat)* to devote oneself to
commentāriol·um -ī *n* notebook; essay
commentār·ium -(i)ī *n or* **commentār·ius -(i)ī** *m* **(conm-)** notebook, diary, journal; record, register; textbook; (collection of) notes; **a commentariis** official in charge of records
commentāti·ō -ōnis *f* careful study; treatise, commentary, textbook; *(rhet)* argument
commentīci·us -a -um *adj* thought-out; imaginary, fictitious
comment·or -ārī -ātus sum *tr* to think over, consider; to contrive, make up; to

write, compose; to discuss; to practice, prepare *(a speech)*
comment·or -ōris *m* inventor, deviser
comment·us -a -um *pp of* **comminiscor ‖** *adj* fictitious, invented, pretended **‖** *n* invention; fabrication; intention
comme·ō -āre -āvī -ātum *intr* to come and go; to back and forth; to travel repeatedly; *(of water)* to pass, flow; to travel around; to commute; to pass *(from one state to another)*
commerc·ium -(i)ī *n* trade, commerce; dealing, business; communication, correspondence; exchange *(of goods),* trafficking; goods, merchandise; sexual intercourse; *(leg)* right to engage in trade, commercial rights; *(w. gen)* right to buy and sell *(a commodity), e.g.:* **commercium agri** right to buy and sell land; **commercium linguae** common language *(shared by various tribes);* **jus commercii** trading rights
commerc·or -ārī -ātus sum *tr* **(conm-)** to purchase
commer·eō -ēre -uī -itus *or* **commer·eor -ērī -itus sum** *tr* **(conm-)** to deserve fully, merit; to be guilty of
com·mētior -mētīrī -mensus sum *tr* **(conm-)** to measure; *(w. cum)* to measure *(s.th.)* in terms of
commēt·ō -āre -āvī *intr* to go often, come and go
commigr·ō -āre -āvī -ātum *intr* to move, migrate
commīlit·ium -(i)ī *n* military comradeship
commīlit·ō -ōnis *m* army buddy
commināti·ō -ōnis *f* violent threat
com·mingō -mingĕre -minxī -mictus *tr (sl)* to pee on; to wet *(bed);* **commictum caenum** *(sl)* dirty skunk
com·miniscor -minisci -mentus sum *tr* to think up, contrive; to fabricate *(lie);* to state falsely, pretend, allege
commin·or -ārī -ātus sum *tr* to threaten, make a threat of
commin·uō -uĕre -uī -ūtus *tr* to lessen considerably; to smash, shatter; *(fig)* to crush, humiliate
comminus *adv* hand to hand; near at hand; **comminus conferre signa** to engage in hand-to-hand fighting
commi·sceō -scēre -scuī -xtus *tr* to mix together; to confuse; to unite, bring together; *(w. cum)* to discuss with
commiserāti·ō -ōnis *f (rhet)* appeal for compassion *or* pity
commiseresc·ō -ĕre *intr (w. gen)* to feel pity for **‖** *v impers* **me commiserescit ejus** I pity him
commiser·or -ārī -ātus sum *tr* to feel sympathy for **‖** *intr (rhet)* to try to evoke sympathy

commīsī *perf of* **committo**

commissi·ō -ōnis *f* commencement

commissūr·a -ae *f* connection; joint

commiss·us -a -um *pp of* **committo** ‖ *n* offense, crime; secret, trust; undertaking; thing confiscated

commītig·ō -āre *tr* (conm-) to soften up

com·mittō -mittĕre -mīsī -missus *tr* (conm-) to bring together; to join together, make continuous, connect, combine; to cause to compete, match *(for a fight, etc.);* to begin, commence *(games);* to undertake; to commit *(crime),* do *(s.th. wrong);* to incur *(penalty);* to bring about, effect; to give up, forfeit, hand over; to engage in *(battle, war); (w. dat)* 1 to take *(a person or matter)* before *(s.o.)* for a verdict, decision, *or* approval; 2 to entrust *(a person or thing)* to *(s.o.); hostes pugnae (or proelio)* **committere** to engage the enemy; **memoriae committere** to commit to memory; **omnes inter se committere** to set all at variance with one another; **proelium** *(or* **pugnam) committere** to go into action, engage the enemy ‖ *refl (w.* **in** + *acc)* to venture into ‖ *intr* to commit an offense, break the law

commodē *adv* properly, appropriately; neatly; adequately, satisfactorily; at the right moment; conveniently, readily; helpfully, obligingly; tastefully; comfortably

commodit·ās -ātis *f* timeliness, right time; proportion, symmetry; convenience, comfort; pleasantness, kindness; *(rhet)* aptness of expression

commodō *adv* suitably, conveniently

commod·ō -āre -āvī -ātus *tr* to adjust, adapt; to bestow, supply, lend, give; **aurem** *(or* **aures) commodare** to lend an ear; **manum commodare** to lend a helping hand ‖ *refl* **mihi te commodare** to put yourself at my disposal ‖ *intr* to be obliging; *(w. dat)* to be accommodating to, help

commodulē *or* **commodulum** *adv* nicely, conveniently

commodum *adv* at a good time; in the nick of time; **commodum cum** just at the time when

commod·um -ī *n* convenience; opportunity; profit, advantage; privilege; loan; pay, reward; **commodo tuo** at your convenience; **ex commodo** *(or* **per commodum)** *(w. gen)* at the convenience of

commod·us -a -um *adj* convenient, suitable, fit; timely; opportune *(time);* comfortable; advantageous; agreeable, obliging, pleasant *(person);* good *(health);* **quod commodum est** just as you please

Commod·us -ī *m* Roman Emperor *(son of Marcus Aurelius, reigned A.D. 180–192)*

commōl·ior -īrī -ītus sum *tr* to set in motion, move with effort

commone·faciō -facĕre -fēcī -factus *tr* to call to mind; *(w. acc of person and gen of thing)* to remind *(s.o.)* of

common·eō -ēre -uī -itus *tr* to remind, warn; *(w. gen or* **de** + *abl)* to remind *(s.o.)* of

commoniti·ō -ōnis *f* reminder

commo(n)str·ō -āre -āvī -ātus *tr* to point out; to show where *(a person, thing, place)* is

commorāti·ō -ōnis *f* stay; delay *(rhet)* dwelling on a point

com·morior -morī -mortuus sum *intr (w. dat or* **cum)** to die with

commor·or -ārī -ātus sum *tr* to stop, detain ‖ *intr* to linger, stay, stop off; **in sententiā commorari** to stick to an opinion

commōti·ō -ōnis *f* motion; commotion; **animi commotio** excitement

commōtiuncul·a -ae *f* slight agitation

commōt·us -a -um *adj* excited, nervous; deranged *(mind);* angry; impassioned; *(rhet)* lively *(style)*

com·moveō -movēre -mōvī -mōtus *tr* to stir up, shake; to disturb, upset; to excite, shake up; to arouse, provoke; to generate, produce; *(fig)* to touch, move; to influence; to impress; to cause, start *(a war, battle);* to dislodge *(an enemy);* to call in *(a debt)*

commūn·e -is *n* common property; community; **in commune** 1 publicly; 2 for the good of all; 3 jointly; 4 in general terms

commūnicāti·ō -ōnis *f* sharing; *(rhet)* deliberating with the audience

commūnic·ō -āre -āvī -ātus *or* **commūnic·or -ārī -ātus sum** *tr* to share; to unite, link; to impart, communicate; to discuss together; to plan together

commūni·ō -ōnis *f* sharing; kinship, association

commūn·iō -īre -īvī *or* **-iī -ītus** *tr* (-moen-) to fortify; to build and fortify; *(fig)* to strengthen, fortify

commūn·is -is -e *adj* (conm-) common, joint; common, ordinary; public; universal, general; familiar; courteous; democratic; *(of arguments)* applicable to either side; **communis est conjectura** it is open to conjecture; **communis est aestimatio** it is a matter of opinion; **loca communia** public places; **loci communes** general topics; **sensus communis** civic *or* public spirit ‖ *n see* **commune** ‖ *npl* the common good; *(poet)* common lot

commūnit·ās -ātis *f* sharing, partnership; joint possession; social ties, fellowship, togetherness; affability

commūniter *adv* in common

commūnīti·ō -ōnis *f* road building; *(fig)* preparation, introduction

commurmur·ō -āre *or* **commurmur·or -ārī -ātus sum** *intr* to murmur, grumble

commūtābil·is -is -e *adj* changeable, subject to change; interchangeable

commūtāti·ō -ōnis *f* change, alteration; shift; exchange; reversal

commūtāt·us -ūs *m* change

commūt·ō -āre -āvī -ātus *tr* to change, alter; to interchange, exchange; to barter; to give in exchange; *(w. abl or* cum) to exchange *(s.th.)* for; **verba commutare** to exchange words, talk

cōm·ō -ěre -psī -ptus *tr* to set, do, braid *(the hair);* to adorn, deck out

cōmoedi·a -ae *f* comedy

cōmoedicē *adv* as in comedy

cōmoed·us -a -um *adj* of comic actors **ǁ** *m* comic actor

comōs·us -a -um *adj* with long hair; hairy; leafy

compaciscor *see* **compeciscor**

compacti·ō -ōnis *f* framework

compact·us -a -um *pp of* **compingo ǁ** *adj* compact, well-built **ǁ** *n* compact

compāg·ēs -is *f* construction; joint, seam; structure, framework; *(anat)* joint

compāg·ō -inis *f* (conp-) (act of) fastening; connection; framework, structure

comp·ar -aris *adj* (conp-) similar, alike; equal; *(w. dat)* matching, resembling **ǁ** *mf* buddy; playmate; perfect match; spouse

comparābil·is -is -e *adj* (conp-) comparable, similar

comparātē *adv* (conp-) comparatively

comparāti·ō -ōnis *f (from* con- + parō) preparation; acquisition, procuring, obtaining, provision *(by purchasing or otherwise);* arrangement, settlment

comparāti·ō -ōnis *f (from* compar- + ō) comparison; relative position *(of planets); (gram)* comparative degree; *(rhet)* argument based on the law of probability; **ex comparatione** *(w. gen)* in comparison with; **comparatio pro portione** proportion

comparātīv·us -a -um *adj* (conp-) comparative; *(gram)* that is in the comparative degree

compār·eō -ēre -uī *intr* (conp-) to be visible, be plain, be evident; to appear; to be at hand, be present

compar·ō -āre -āvī -ātus *tr (from* con- + parō) to prepare, make preparations for; to purchase; to plan, devise; to put together, get together, provide; to match; to set up *(courts, a body of laws);* to procure, get, collect; to appoint; to establish, institute; to raise *(troops);* to compose *(writings);*

comparare inter se *(esp. of consuls)* to arrange, settle

compar·ō -āre -āvī -ātus *tr (from* compar- + ō) to unite; to match, pit; to align; to estimate; to compare *(with or to);* to point out by way of comparison

compas·cō -cěre — -tus *tr & intr* (conp-) to feed together

compascu·us -a -um *adj* (conp-) of public grazing; **compascuus ager** public pasture land

compec·iscor -iscī -tus sum *intr* (-pac-) to make a compact, reach an agreement

compect·us -a -um *adj* in agreement **ǁ** *n* agreement, compact; **(de) compecto** by previous agreement

comped·iō -īre — -ītus *tr* (conp-) to shackle

compedīt·us -a -um *pp of* **compedio ǁ** *adj* shackled **ǁ** *m* shackled slave

compēgī *perf of* **compingo**

compellāti·ō -ōnis *f* (conp-) rebuke; *(rhet)* addressing, apostrophizing

compell·ō -āre -āvī -ātus *tr* (conp-) to address, speak to; to call upon, appeal to; to challenge; *(w. predicate adj)* to call *(s.o., e.g., disloyal, etc.);* to rebuke, call to account; *(leg)* to arraign

com·pellō -pellěre -pulī -pulsus *tr* (conp-) to drive together, round up; to crowd together; to compel, drive; *(of wind, waves)* to drive, push, force; *(w.* **in** + *acc)* to drive *(s.o.)* into; *(w.inf or* **ut** + *subj)* to compel *(s.o.)* to *(do s.th.);* to coerce, constrain; to reduce by force *(to some state or condition);* to clench *(teeth);* to localize, concentrate *(fighting)*

compendiāri·us -a -um *adj* (conp-) short, abridged; **via compendiaria** shortcut

compend·ium -(i)ī *n* (conp-) careful weighing; saving *(of money);* profit; shortening, abridging; shortcut; **compendium facere** *(w. gen)* to save oneself the trouble of; **compendi fieri** to be brief; **compendio servire** to serve one's own private interests

compensāti·ō -ōnis *f* compensation

compens·ō -āre -āvī -ātus *tr* (conp-) to compensate for, make up for; to balance mentally

comper·cō -cěre -sī *tr* (conp-) to save up, hoard up

comperendināti·ō -ōnis *f or* **comperendināt·us -ūs** *m* (conp-) *(leg)* two-day adjournment

comperendin·ō -āre -āvī -ātus *tr* (conp-) to adjourn *(court)* for two days; to put off *(defendant)* for two days

comper·iō -īre -ī -tus *or* **comper·ior -īrī -tus sum** *tr* (conp-) to find out, discover, learn; **compertum habeo** *or* **compertum mihi est** I know for certain

compern·is -is -e *adj* **(conp-)** having thighs close together

compert·us -a -um *adj* ascertained; well authenticated; *(w. gen)* convicted of; **compertum habeo** I have verified; **nihil comperti** no certainty; **pro comperto** *(to regard)* as certain; **res comperta** *(or* **compertae)** reliable information

comp·ēs -edis *f* **(conp-)** *(usu. pl)* shackles *(for the feet)*, fetters; bond *(of love)*

compesc·ō -ĕre -uī *tr* **(conp-)** to confine, restrain; to imprison; to close, block *(entrances)*; to check the movement of, steady; to stop, restrain *(activity of any kind)*; to calm *(a storm)*; to control *(a person)*; to subdue, quell, crush *(an enemy, a mutiny)*; to curb *(one's tongue, one's words)*; to stifle *(feelings, fears, laughter)*; to quench *(thirst)*; to allay *(hunger)*; **compesce dicere injuste!** stop speaking unfairly!; **compesce digito labellum!** put your finger to your lip! *(to indicate silence)*

competīt·or -ōris *m* **(conp-)** competitor; rival claimant *(to the throne)*; rival bidder *(at an auction)*; *(pol)* fellow candidate

competītr·ix -īcis *f* **(conp-)** competitor *(female)*

compet·ō -ĕre -īvī *or* **-iī -ītum** *intr* **(conp-)** to come together, meet; *(of events)* to coincide; to be adequate, be suitable; *(w. ad)* to be capable of ‖ *v impers* **si competit** if it is convenient; *(w. ut)* if it happens that

compīlāti·ō -ōnis *f* **(conp-)** burglary

compīl·ō -āre -āvī -ātus *tr* **(conp-)** to pillage; to plagiarize

com·pingō -pingĕre -pēgī -pactus *tr* **(conp-)** to put together, construct; to compose; to lock up, put *(in jail)*

Compitāl·ia -ium *npl* **(Conp-)** festival of the Lares at crossroads, celebrated twice annually at the crossroads with flowers

Compitālici·us -a -um *adj* **(Conp-)** of the crossroads

Compitāl·is -is -e *adj* **(Conp-, Compet-)** associated with the festival at the crossroads

compit·um -ī *n* **(conp-)** crossroads; *(fig)* crucial decision

complac·eō -ēre -uī *or* **-itum** *intr* **(conp-)** *(w. dat)* to suit just fine

complān·ō -āre -āvī -ātus *tr* **(conp-)** to level; to raze

comple·ctor -ctī -xus sum *tr* **(conp-)** to embrace, hug; to display affection for, display esteem for; to clasp *(the right hand)*; *(of sleep)* to hold in its embrace; *(fig)* to embrace, take up *(a cause, a course of action)*; to grip, grasp, cling to; to encircle, surround, enclose; to comprise; to take in, include within its limits

(an area); *(of power, reputation, knowledge)* to extend over, embrace; to involve, associate, include *(in a relationship, class, activity)*; to include, cover *(in a book or speech)*; to state in a concise manner, sum up; to grasp, understand; **animo** *(or* **mente) complecti** to comprehend, take in; **memoriā complecti** to keep in mind

complēment·um -ī *n* **(conp-)** complement, completion

compl·eō -ēre -ēvī -ētus *tr* **(conp-)** to fill, fill up; to fill with sound, make resound; to supply, furnish; to complete; to impregnate; to bring *(a legion)* to full strength; *(mil)* to man

complēt·us -a -um *adj* **(conp-)** complete, perfect

complexi·ō -ōnis *f* **(conp-)** combination, collection, group; *(rhet)* summary

complex·us -ūs *m* **(conp-)** embrace; *(fig)* love, affection; close combat; mental grasp; grouping *(of words)*; envelopment

complicāt·us -a -um *adj* **(conp-)** complicated

complic·ō -āre -āvī *(or* **-uī) -ātus** *(or* **-itus)** *tr* **(conp-)** to fold up

complō·dō -dĕre -sī -sus *tr* **(conp-)** to clap *(the hands)* together

complōrāti·ō -ōnis *f or* **complōrāt·us -ūs** *m* **(conp-)** wailing, lamentation

complōr·ō -āre -āvī -ātus *tr* **(conp-)** to mourn for

complūr·ēs -ēs -a *or* **-ia** *adj* **(conp-)** several, a fair number of

complūriens *adv* **(-iēs) (conp-)** several times, a good many times

compluscul·ī -ae -a *adj* **(conp-)** several

compluv·ium -(i)ī *n* **(conp-)** compluvium *(quadrangular, inward-sloping central part of the roof of a Roman house to direct rain to a pool below, called* **impluvium)**

com·pōnō -pōnĕre -posuī -positus *tr* **(conp-)** to put together, join; to place *(things together)*; to store up, hoard; to lay aside, put away; to build; to compose, write; to arrange, settle, agree upon; to match; to match up *(pairs)*; to compare; to treat as comparable; to balance *(e.g., deeds with words)*; to lay out *(the dead)*; to put in an urn; to bury; to arrange in order, lay out; to arrange systematically; to arrange properly, adjust; to deploy *(troops)*; to arrange, plan, organize *(a plan of action)*; to make up, fabricate *(a false report, story)*; to reconcile; to concoct, contrive; to quell *(a revolt)*; to subdue *(rebels)*; to calm, soothe, appease *(a person)*; to reconcile *(estranged friends)*; to settle *(disputes, problems, affairs)*; **bellum componere**

to end a war *(by coming to terms);* in **maestitiam compositus** putting on the appearance of sadness; **vultum componere** to put on a false front
comport·ō -āre -āvī -ātus *tr* **(conp-)** to bring together, bring in, collect, accumulate
comp·os -otis *adj* **(conp-)** *(w. gen or abl)* in possession of, master of, having control over; **compos animi** *(or* **mentis)** sane; **compos sui** self-controlled; **compos voti** having one's prayer answered
compositē *adv* **(conp-)** in an orderly manner; *(of actions)* deliberately; **composite dicere** to speak logically
compositi·ō -ōnis *f* **(conp-)** putting together, fitting together, connecting, arranging, composition; matching *(of gladiators, etc.);* reconciliation *(of friends);* orderly arrangement *(of words)*
compositō *adv* **(conp-)** by prearrangement
composit·or -ōris *m* **(conp-)** writer
compos(i)tūr·a -ae *f* **(conp-)** structure
composit·us -a -um *pp of* **compono** ‖ *adj* compound *(words, etc.);* composite, blended; orderly, tidy; calm *(sea);* composed, calm ‖ *n* compound medication; **de** *(or* **ex) composito** by agreement, as agreed ‖ *npl* law and order, settled situation
compotāti·ō -ōnis *f* **(conp-)** drinking party
compot·iō -īre -īvī -ītus *tr* **(conp-)** *(w. acc of person and abl of thing)* to make *(s.o.)* master of ‖ *pass (w. abl)* to attain
compōt·or -ōris *m,* **compōtr·ix -īcis** *f* **(conp-)** drinking partner
comprans·or -ōris *m* **(conp-)** dinner companion, fellow guest
comprecāti·ō -ōnis *f* **(conp-)** public supplication
comprec·or -ārī -ātus sum *tr* **(conp-)** to pray earnestly to, implore, invoke; *(w. acc of thing)* to pray for; *(w.* **ut** + *subj)* to pray that
comprehen·dō -děre -dī -sus *or* **compren·dō -děre -dī -sus** *tr* **(conp-)** to bind together, unite; to hold together *(e.g., w. ropes);* to take hold of, grasp; to catch; to attack; to arrest; to capture; to occupy; to detect; to comprehend; to express; to describe, recount; **animo** *(or* **mente) comprehendere** to apprehend, appreciate; **ignem comprehendere** to catch fire; **memoriā comprehendere** to remember; **numero comprehendere** to count, enumerate
comprehensibil·is -is -e *adj* **(conp-)** **(-dibilis)** comprehensible, intelligible
comprehensi·ō *or* **comprensi·ō -ōnis** *f* **(conp-)** seizing; arrest; comprehension, perception; combining; *(rhet)* period
comprendō *see* **comprehendo**

compressi·ō -ōnis *f* **(conp-)** pressing closely; embrace; *(rhet)* compression
compress·or -ōris *m* rapist
compress·us -ūs *m* **(conp-)** compression; embrace; rape
com·primō -priměre -pressī -pressus *tr* **(conp-)** to press together, compress; to close; to embrace; to check, curb; to keep back, suppress, withhold, conceal; to rape; to hold *(one's breath);* **compressis manibus sedere** to sit on folded hands, not lift a finger; **ordines comprimere** to close ranks
comprobāti·ō -ōnis *f* **(conp-)** full approval
comprobāt·or -ōris *m* **(conp-)** enthusiastic approver
comprob·ō -āre -āvī -ātus *tr* **(conp-)** to approve, sanction, acknowledge; to prove, establish, verify; to cofirm; to justify
comprōmiss·um -ī *n* **(conp-)** *(leg)* compromise *(agreement between the parties to abide by the arbitrator's decision)*
comprō·mittō -mittěre -mīsī -missum *intr* **(conp-)** *(leg)* to compromise *(to agree to abide by the arbitrator's decision)*
comptiōnāl·is -is -e *adj* *(of worn-out goods)* suitable to be sold in batches
compt·us -a -um *pp of* **como** ‖ *adj* *(of hair)* set, neatly arranged; *(of person)* dressed up; *(of speech, writing)* polished
compt·us -ūs *m* hairdo
compulī *perf of* **compello**
compulsus *pp of* **compello**
compun·gō -gěre -xī -ctus *tr* **(conp-)** to puncture, prick; to tatoo; to prod
comput·ō -āre -āvī -ātus *tr* **(conp-)** to compute, count
computresc·ō -ěre *intr* **(conp-)** to rot
Cōm·um -ī *n* Como *(town N. of Po River, modern Como)*
con- *pref (also:* **co-, col-, com-, cor-) 1** together; **conjungere** to join together; **2** up, completely, fully: **consumere** to use up; **concredere** to trust completely; **3** with: **conspirare** to plot with *(s.o.);* **4** hard: **conjicere** to throw hard, fling
cōnām·en -inis *n* effort, struggle; support; *(often pl)* endeavor, attempt
cōnāt·um -ī *n* effort; venture
cōnāt·us -ūs *m* effort; endeavor; thrust *(with weapon)*
concac·ō -āre -āvī -ātus *tr* *(vulg)* to soil, shit
concaed·ēs -ium *fpl* log barricade
concale·faciō -facěre -fēcī -factus *tr* to warm up, heat
concal·esc·ō -escěre -uī *intr* to grow quite warm; to glow *(e.g., with love)*
concall·escō -escěre -uī *intr* to grow hard; *(fig)* to become insensitive
concamerāt·us -a -um *adj* vaulted

Concān·us -ī m one of a Spanish tribe that drank horse's blood

concastīg·ō -āre -āvī -ātus tr to dress down; to chastise, punish

concav·ō -āre tr to curve, bend

concav·us -a -um adj concave, hollow; deep-sunken (eyes); deep (valley)

con·cēdō -cēděre -cessī -cessus tr to give up; to pardon, overlook; to grant ‖ intr to go away; to withdraw, retire; to pass away, die; (w. dat) 1 to yield to, succumb to; 2 to submit to, comply with; 3 to make allowances for, pardon; 4 to be inferior to; (w. in + acc) to pass over to, be merged into; fato (or naturae or vitā) concedere to die

concelebr·ō -āre -āvī -ātus tr to frequent; to fill; to pursue (studies); to enliven; to celebrate; to publish, proclaim

concēnāti·ō -ōnis f dinner party

concenti·ō -ōnis f singing together

concenturi·ō -āre tr to assemble by centuries (groups of hundreds); (fig) to marshal

concent·us -ūs m concert; harmony; shouting in unison; blending

concepti·ō -ōnis f conception; (leg) formula

concept·us -a -um pp of concipio ‖ adj concepta verba formula

concept·us -ūs m conception; embryo, fetus

concerp·ō -ěre -sī -tus tr to tear up, tear to shreds; (fig) to cut up, revile

concertāti·ō -ōnis f wrangling

concertāt·or -ōris m rival

concertātōri·us -a -um adj controversial

concert·ō -āre -āvī -ātus tr to quarrel over; to rival ‖ intr to fight, quarrel

concessi·ō -ōnis f concession; admission (of guilt with a plea for mercy)

concess·ō -āre -āvī intr (w. inf) to cease to, stop (doing s.th.)

concess·us -ā -um pp of concedo ‖ adj allowable, lawful ‖ n concession

concess·us -ūs m permission; concessu Caesaris with Caesar's permission

conch·a -ae f clam, oyster, mussel, murex; clamshell, oyster shell; pearl; purple dye; trumpet (of Triton); vessel (for ointments, etc.); vulva

conch·is -is f bean

conchīt·a -ae m clam digger

conchul·a -ae f a small shellfish

conchȳliāt·us -a -um adj purple

conchȳl·ium -(i)ī n shellfish, clam, oyster; murex; purple dye, purple ‖ npl purple garments

concīd·ō -ěre -ī intr to collapse; to fall (in battle); (fig) to decline, fall, fail, decay, perish; (of winds) die down

concī·dō -děre -dī -sus tr to cut up, cut to pieces, kill; to beat severely; (fig) to

demolish (w. arguments); (rhet) to chop up (sentences)

con·cieō -ciēre -cīvī -cītus or con·ciō -cīre -cīvī -cītus tr to assemble; to shake; (fig) to stir up

conciliābul·um -ī n public meeting place

conciliāti·ō -ōnis f union, bond; conciliating; inclination, bent

conciliāt·or -ōris m mediator; agent

conciliātrīcul·a -ae f madame (of a brothel); dear matchmaker

conciliātr·ix -īcis f match-maker; promoter (of relationships)

conciliāt·us -a -um adj (w. ad) endeared to, disposed toward

conciliāt·us -ūs m union, joining

concili·ō -āre -āvī -ātus tr to bring together, unite; to win over; to bring about (by mediation); to acquire, win

concil·ium -(i)ī n popular assembly (esp. that of the plebs in Rome); private meeting; council; union; association; a hearing in council; deliberation, debate; (pol) a league of states; in uno concilio together

concin·ens -entis adj harmonious

concinnē adv nicely, daintily

concinnit·ās -ātis or concinnitūd·ō -inis f elegance; excessive refinement

concinn·ō -āre -āvī -ātus tr to prepare for use, make ready; to repair; to touch up; to make up, concoct; to give rise to; to make, drive (e.g., insane); lacrumentem concinnas tuam uxorem you are making your wife cry

concinn·us -a -um adj symmetrical; elegant; courteous, nice; polished

concin·ō -ěre -uī tr to sing of; to prophesy ‖ intr to sing or play together; (fig) to agree

conciō see concieo

conciō see contio

concipil·ō -āre -āvī tr to seize, carry off

con·cipiō -cipěre -cēpī -ceptus tr to take in, absorb; to imagine, think; to understand, perceive; to conceive; to produce, form; (of things) to contain, hold; to contract (disease); to catch (fire); to entertain (hope); to frame (in formal language); to announce (in formal language); (w. abl, adv, ab, ex) to draw, derive from (a source); to utter solemnly; verba concepta solemn utterance

concīsē adv concisely

concīsi·ō -ōnis f (rhet) dividing a sentence into short phrases

concīs·us -a -um pp of concīdo ‖ adj cut up, cut short, terse; minute, very small

concitātē adv vigorously, vividly

concitāti·ō -ōnis f rapid movement; excitement; disturbance, riot

concitāt·or or concit·or -ōris m instigator, ring-leader; rabble-rouser

concitāt·us -a -um *adj* excited; rapid

concit·ō -āre -āvī -ātus *tr* to stir up, rouse, urge; to spur on *(horses, etc.)*; to agitate, stir up, disturb; to awaken; to summon, assemble; to galvanize into action; to infuriate; to bring about, cause, occasion

concitor *see* **concitator**

conclāmāti·ō -ōnis *f* loud shouting, yell; acclamation

conclāmit·ō -āre *intr* to keep on shouting, keep on yelling

conclām·ō -āre -āvī -ātus *tr* to shout, yell; to call to *(for help)*; to call repeatedly by name, bewail *(the dead)*; to exclaim; **jam conclamatum est** *(coll)* all's lost; **vasa conclamare** *(mil)* to give the signal to pack up; **ad arma conclamare** to sound the call to arms

conclāv·e -is *n* room; public toilet

conclū·dō -děre -sī -sus *tr* to shut up, enclose; to include, comprise; to round off, conclude *(speech, letter)*; to end rhythmically; to deduce, conclude

conclūsē *adv (rhet)* in a rhythmical cadence

conclūsi·ō -ōnis *f* conclusion; *(mil)* blockade; *(rhet)* summation

conclūsiuncul·a -ae *f* false conclusion

conclūs·us -a -um *pp of* **concludo** ‖ *adj* confined, restricted

concol·or -ōris *adj* of the same color

concomitāt·us -a -um *adj* escorted

conco·quō -quěre -xī -ctus *tr* to cook thoroughly; to boil down; to digest; to stomach, put up with; to cook up, concoct *(ideas)*; to weigh seriously; to ripen ‖ *intr* to digest one's food

concordi·a -ae *f* harmony, concord

concorditer *adv* harmoniously

concord·ō -āre -āvī -ātum *intr* to be of one mind; to be in harmony, agree

concor·s -dis *adj* of the same mind, agreeing, harmonious

concoxī *perf of* **concoquo**

concrēbr·escō -escěre -uī *intr* to grow strong

concrēd·ō -ěre -idī -itus *tr* to entrust; to confide *(a secret)*

concrem·ō -āre -āvī -ātus *tr* to burn to ashes, burn down

concrep·ō -āre -uī *intr* to rattle, creak, grate, clash, sound, make noise; **digitis concrepare** to snap the fingers ‖ *tr* to cause to sound *or* to rattle

con·crescō -crescěre -crēvī -crētum *intr* to grow together; to congeal; to curdle; to clot; to stiffen; to take shape, grow, increase

concrēti·ō -ōnis *f* condensing, congealing; matter, substance

concrēt·us -a -um *pp of* **concresco** ‖ *adj* grown together, compounded; solid,

hard; frozen; matted; condensed, dense; curdled; inveterate, ingrained; dim *(light)* ‖ *n* hardness; solid matter

concrēvī *perf of* **concresco**

concrīmin·or -ārī -ātus sum *intr* to make bitter charges

concruci·ō -āre *tr* to torture

concubīn·a -ae *f* concubine

concubīnāt·us -ūs *m* free love

concubīn·us -ī *m* catamite, homosexual

concubit·us -ūs *m* reclining together; sexual intercourse

concubi·us -a -um *adj* **concubiā nocte** at bedtime ‖ *n* intercourse

conculc·ō -āre -āvī -ātus *tr* trample under foot, despise, treat with contempt

concumbō concumběre concubuī concubitum *intr* to sleep together; *(w.* **cum)** to sleep with, have intercourse with

concup·iscō -iscěre -īvī *or* **-iī -ītus** *tr* to long for; to strive for

concūr·ō -āre *tr* to take good care of

concur·rō -rěre -rī -sum *intr* to run together, flock together; to unite; to strike one another, crash; to happen at the same time, coincide; *(mil)* to clash; *(w.* **ad)** to have recourse to; *(of jaws)* to snap together; *(of facts, statements)* to agree

concursāti·ō -ōnis *f* running together, assembly; rushing about; *(mil)* skirmish

concursāt·or -ōris *m* skirmisher

concursi·ō -ōnis *f* concourse; *(gram)* collocation *(of vowels)*; *(rhet)* repetition for emphasis

concurs·ō -āre -āvī -ātus *tr* to run around to; **domos concursare** to run from house to house ‖ *intr* to rush around excitedly, dash up and down; *(mil)* to skirmish

concurs·us -ūs *m* a running together, concourse, assembly; combination; collision *(of atoms)*; *(astr)* conjunction; *(gram)* juxtaposition *(of letters)*; *(leg)* joint right; *(mil)* charge, clash

concussi·ō -ōnis *f* shaking; earthquake

concuss·us -ūs *m* shaking, shock

concu·tiō -těre -ssī -ssus *tr* to bang together; to convulse; to shake; to shatter; to harass, upset, shock; to stir up; to wave *(weapon, hand)*; to weaken, shake *(authority, confidence)*

condal·ium -(i)ī *n* (slave's) ring

condec·et -ēre *v impers* it befits

condecor·ō -āre -āvī -ātus *tr* to adorn; to grace

condemnāt·or -ōris *m* accuser; *(leg)* prosecutor

condemn·ō -āre -āvī -ātus *tr* to condemn, doom; to blame; *(leg)* to prosecute successfully, convict, sentence

condens·ō -āre -āvī -ātus *tr* to pack together

condens·us -a -um *adj* crowded, packed

condici·ō -ōnis *f* contract, arrangement;

stipulation, terms, condition; state, situation, circumstances; state of health; legal status; rank, place; marriage contract, marriage; prospective marriage partner, good match; nature, character; choice, option; **eā condicione ut** on the condition that; **in condicione manere** to stick to an agreement; **nullā condicione** by no means; **sub condicione** conditionally; **vitae condicio** living conditions

condī·cō -cĕre -xī -ctus *tr* to talk over, arrange together; **(ad) cenam condicere** *(w. dat)* to make a dinner engagement with

condignē *adv* very worthily

condign·us -a -um *adj (w. abl)* fully deserving of, fully worthy of

condīment·um -ī *n* seasoning, spice

cond·iō -īre -īvī *or* **-iī -ītus** *tr* to season; to pickle, preserve; to embalm; *(fig)* to give zest to

condiscipul·a -ae *f* schoolmate *(female)*

condiscipulāt·us -ūs *m* companionship at school

condiscipul·us -ī *m* schoolmate

condi·scō -scĕre -dicī *tr* to learn by heart

condīti·ō -ōnis *f* seasoning; method of preserving *(food)*

condit·or -ōris *m* founder, builder; originator *(of a practice; of a product);* organizer; creator; *(as honorary title)* preserver; author, writer

condit·or -ōris *m* seasoner

conditōr·ium -(i)ī *n* coffin; tomb

condīt·us -a -um *pp of* **condio** ‖ *adj* seasoned, spicy; elegant *(style)*

condit·us -a -um *pp of* **condo** ‖ *adj* concealed, secret; sunken *(eyes)*

condixī *perf of* **condico**

con·dō -dĕre -didī -ditus *tr* to build, found; to write, compose; to establish *(a practice, institution);* to store up, hoard; to preserve; to keep safe; to plunge *(a weapon);* to drown out *(a sound);* to put *(in prison, chains)*

condoce·faciō -facĕre -fēcī -factus *tr* to train well

condoc·eō -ēre -uī -tus *tr* to teach thoroughly

condol·escō -escĕre -uī *intr* to begin to ache, get very sore; *(fig)* to feel grief

condōnāti·ō -ōnis *f* donation

condōn·ō -āre -āvī -ātus *tr* to give, present; to permit; to deliver over *(to enemy, for punishment);* to adjudge; *(w. double acc)* to make *(s.o.)* a present of *(s.th.); (w. acc of thing and dat of person)* to forgive, pardon *(s.o. an offense)*

condorm·iō -īre *intr* to sleep soundly

condorm·iscō -iscĕre -īvī *or* **-iī** *intr* to fall soundly asleep

condūcibil·is -is -e *adj* advantageous, profitable; *(w. ad or in + acc)* just right for

condu·cō -cĕre -xī -ctus *tr* to bring together, collect, assemble; to connect, unite; to rent; to borrow; to induce, bribe; to employ, hire; to contract for, undertake a contract in connection with *(buildings, etc.)* ‖ *intr* to be of use; *(w. dat)* **1** to be useful to, be of use to; **2** to be profitable to; **3** to be fitting for; **4** to be conducive to; *(w. ad or in + acc)* to be conducive to

conductīci·us -a -um *adj* mercenary; rented *(house)*

conducti·ō -ōnis *f* bringing together; recapitulation; the taking of a lease, renting

conduct·or -ōris *m* contractor; lessee, tenant

conduct·us -a -um *pp of* **conduco** ‖ *mpl* hired men; mercenaries ‖ *n* rented apartment, rented house; lease, contract

conduplicāti·ō -ōnis *f* doubling; *(hum)* embrace

conduplic·ō -āre -āvī -ātus *tr* to double; **corpora conduplicare** to embrace

condūr·ō -āre -āvī -ātus *tr* to harden

cond·us -ī *m* storeroom manager

cōne·ctō -ctĕre -xuī -xus *tr* **(conn-)** to tie; to connect, join, link; to state as a conclusion; **nodum conectere** to tie a knot; **per affinitatem conexus** *(w. dat)* related by marriage to

cōnexi·ō -ōnis *f* logical conclusion

cōnexuī *perf of* **conecto**

cōnex·us -a -um *pp of* **conecto** ‖ *adj* linked; related, associated; interdependent ‖ *n* logical connection, necessary consequence

cōnex·us -ūs *m* connection

confābul·or -ārī -ātus sum *tr* to discuss ‖ *intr* to have a talk

confarreāti·ō -ōnis *f* solemn marriage ceremony before the Pontifex Maximus and ten witnesses

confarre·ō -āre -āvī -ātus *tr* to marry with solemn rites; to contract *(marriage)*

confātāl·is -is -e *adj* bound by the same fate

confecti·ō -ōnis *f* preparation; completion; conclusion, end; compiling; mastication

confect·or -ōris *m* finisher, executor; destroyer

confer·ciō -cīre — -tus *tr* to stuff, cram, pack together; to stuff full

con·ferō -ferre -tulī -lātus *or* **collātus** *tr* to bring together; to contribute *(money, etc.);* to condense, compress; to assemble *(ideas, plans, etc.);* to discuss, talk over; to bear, convey, direct; to devote, apply; to confer, bestow, give, lend, grant; to ascribe, impute, assign; to postpone; *(w. in + acc)* to change *(s.o. or s.th.)* into; to compare, contrast; **capita conferre** to put heads together, confer; **gradum conferre cum** to walk together with;

lites conferre to quarrel; **pedem cum pede conferre** to fight toe to toe; **sermones conferre cum** to engage in conversation with; **signa conferre** to begin fighting ‖ *refl (w.* in + *acc)* 1 to go to, head for; 2 to have recourse to; 3 to join *(a group, etc.)*

confertim *adv (mil)* shoulder to shoulder **confert·us -a -um** *pp of* **confercio** ‖ *adj* crowded, packed, thick, dense; *(mil)* shoulder to shoulder

confervēfac·iō -ĕre *tr* to make glow, make melt

confer·vescō -vescĕre -buī *or* **-vuī** *intr* to begin to boil

confessi·ō -ōnis *f* confession, acknowledgment; admission of guilt; token, proof

confess·us -a -um *pp of* **confiteor** ‖ *adj* acknowledged, incontrovertible ‖ *m* confessed criminal ‖ *n* admission; **ex confesso** admittedly, beyond doubt; **in confessum venire** to be generally admitted

confestim *adv* immediately, suddenly

confici·ens -entis *adj* productive, efficient; *(w. gen)* 1 productive of; 2 efficient in ‖ *npl (w. gen)* sources of

con·ficiō -ficĕre -fēcī -fectus *tr* to make, manufacture, process, refine; to do, perform, accomplish; to carry out, discharge; to celebrate *(a rite, festival);* to make ready, prepare; to complete, execute, fulfill; to bring about, cause; to bring together, collect; to secure, obtain; to use up, wear out, exhaust; to finish off, destroy, kill; to run through, waste *(money, inheritance);* to chew *(food);* to disgest *(food);* to spend, pass *(time);* to compose, write; to set down in writing, record; to demonstrate; to cover *(a distance); (of grief, worry)* to overwhelm

conficti·ō -ōnis *f* fabrication

confictus *pp of* **confingo**

confīd·ens -entis *adj* trustful; self-confident; presumptuous, smug

confīdenter *adv* confidently; smugly

confīdenti·a -ae *f* confidence; self-confidence, smugness

confīdentiloqu·us -a -um *adj* speaking confidently

confī·dō -dĕre -sus sum *intr* to have confidence, be confident; *(w. dat)* to confide in, rely on, trust, believe

confī·gō -gĕre -xī -xus *tr* to fasten, join together; to pierce, transfix; *(fig)* to paralyze

con·fingō -fingĕre -finxī -fictus *tr* to make up, fabricate

confīn·is -is -e *adj* having common boundaries, adjoining; *(fig)* akin

confīn·ium -(i)ī *n* common boundary, frontier; border; *(fig)* borderline ‖ *npl* limits, confines

confinxī *perf of* **confingo**

con·fiō -fierī *intr* to be accomplished; to occur, happen; *(w.* ex) to be made from

confirmāti·ō -ōnis *f* confirmation, encouragement; verification; *(rhet)* presentation of evidence

confirmāt·or -ōris *m* guarantor

confirmāt·us -a -um *adj* resolute, confident, courageous; established, well-attested

confirmit·ās -ātis *f* firmness; stubbornness

confirm·ō -āre -āvī -ātus *tr* to strengthen; to establish on a firm basis; to develop *(mind, character);* to reinforce; to sanction, ratify; to encourage; to corroborate; to assert positively; *(w. acc & inf)* to prove that; to prove the existence of; to give assurances of, affirm; *(mil)* to strengthen *(a position)* ‖ *refl* to recover, gain strength ‖ *pass* to become mature

confisc·ō -āre -āvī -ātus *tr* to deposit in a treasury; to confiscate *(for the public treasury)*

confīsi·ō -ōnis *f* confidence

con·fiteor -fitērī -fessus sum *tr* to confess, acknowledge, admit; to reveal ‖ *intr* to confess; *(poet)* to admit defeat

confixī *perf of* **configo**

confixus *pp of* **configo**

conflagrāti·ō -ōnis *f* conflagration; eruption *(of a volcano)*

conflagr·ō -āre -āvī -ātum *intr* to burn, be on fire; to be burnt down; *(fig)* to be utterly destroyed

conflicti·ō -ōnis *f* conflict

conflict·ō -āre -āvī -ātus *tr (usu. used in the passive)* to strike down; to ruin; to afflict, torment; to buffet

conflict·or -ārī -ātus sum *intr* to struggle, wrestle

conflict·us -ūs *m* clash, collision

conflī·gō -gĕre -xī -ctus *tr* to knock together, beat, clap ‖ *intr* to clash, fight, battle; *(w.* cum) to come into conflict with, clash with; *(w.* adversus + *acc or* contra + *acc)* to fight against; **inter se confligere** to collide with one another

confl·ō -āre -āvī -ātus *tr* to kindle, ignite; to inflame *(passions);* to melt down *(metals);* to raise *(army, money, etc.);* to concoct *(a lie);* to run up *(debt);* to bring about, cause, to hatch *(plot);* to organize *(riot)*

conflu·ens -entis *m (often pl)* confluence

conflu·ō -ĕre -xī *intr* to flow together; *(fig)* to flock together, come in crowds; *(of things)* to gather

con·fodiō -fodĕre -fōdī -fossus *tr* to dig up *(soil);* to stab; *(fig)* to harm

confore = **confutūrum esse** to be about to happen

conformāti·ō -ōnis *f* shape, form; fashion;

idea, notion; arrangement *(of words)*; expression *(in voice)*; *(rhet)* figure of speech

conform·ō -āre -āvī -ātus *tr* to shape, fashion, put together; to describe, delineate; to train, educate; to bring into harmony

confoss·us -a -um *pp of* **confodio ‖** *adj* full of holes, punctured

confractus *pp of* **confringo**

confragōs·us -a -um *adj* rough, rugged **‖** *npl* rugged terrain

confrem·ō -ĕre -uī *intr* to grumble; to resound, ring

confric·ō -āre — -ātus *tr* to rub vigorously; to massage

con·fringō -fringĕre -frēgī -fractus *tr* to smash, crush; to ruin, undo **‖** *pass (of ships)* to be wrecked

con·fugiō -fugĕre -fūgī *intr* to flee, take refuge, run for help; *(w. ad)* 1 to have recourse to; 2 to appeal to

confug·ium -(i)ī *n* place of refuge, sanctuary, shelter

confulg·eō -ēre -sī *intr* to glitter, sparkle

con·fundō -fundĕre -fūdī -fūsus *tr* to pour together, blend, mingle; to mix up, jumble together, confuse, bewilder; to spread, diffuse

confūsē *adv* in confusion

confūsi·ō -ōnis *f* mixing, blending; confusion, mixup; **confusio oris** blush

confūs·us -a -um *pp of* **confundo ‖** *adj* confused; troubled *(look)*

confūt·ō -āre -āvī -ātus *tr* to keep from boiling over; to repress, stop; to confute

confu·tuō -tuĕre -tuī -tūtus *tr (vulg)* to screw; **quidquid puellarum confutuere** to screw any and every girl

congel·ō -āre -āvī -ātus *tr* to cause to freeze up, harden; to curdle; *(fig)* to chill; **in lapidem congelare** to petrify **‖** *intr* to freeze, freeze up; to become hard; to become inactive

congemināti·ō -ōnis *f* doubling

congemin·ō -āre -āvī -ātus *tr* to double

congem·ō -ĕre -uī -itus *tr* to deplore deeply **‖** *intr* to gasp, sigh, groan

con·ger -grī *m* eel

congeri·ēs -ēī *f* heap, pile

con·gerō -gerĕre -gessī -gestus *tr* to bring together; to heap up, build up; to build, erect; to keep up, multiply; to repeat *(arguments)*; *(w. in + acc)* 1 to shower *(weapons)* on; 2 to heap *(curses, favors)* upon

congerr·ō -ōnis *m* playmate

congestīci·us -a -um *adj* piled up

congestus *pp of* **congero**

congest·us -ūs *m* heap, mass

congiāl·is -is -e *adj* holding a gallon

congiāri·us -a -um *adj* holding a gallon **‖** *n* gift of one gallon *(e.g., of olive oil*

apiece to the people); bonus *(to the army)*; gift of money *(to the people)*; gift, donation

cong·ius -(i)ī *m* liquid measure *(about 6 pints)*

conglaci·ō -āre -āvī *intr* to freeze up

conglisc·ō -ĕre *intr* to blaze up

conglobāti·ō -ōnis *f* massing together

conglob·ō -āre -āvī -ātus *tr* to make round, form into a ball; to mass together

comglomer·ō -āre -āvī -ātus *tr* to roll up; to group together, crowd together **‖** *refl (w. in + acc)* to crowd into

conglūtināti·ō -ōnis *f* gluing together; *(fig)* combining *(of words)*

conglūtin·ō -āre -āvī -ātus *tr* to glue, cement; *(fig)* to cement

congraec·ō -āre -āvī -ātus *tr* to squander like a Greek

congrātulāti·ō -ōnis *f* congratulations

congrātul·or -ārī -ātus sum *intr* to offer congratulations; *(of several persons)* to express their joy

con·gredior -gredī -gressus sum *tr* to meet, accost, address; to engage **‖** *intr* to come together, meet; *(w. cum)* 1 to meet with; 2 to associate with; 3 to fight against

congregābil·is -is -e *adj* gregarious

congregāti·ō -ōnis *f* flocking together, congregation, union, association

congreg·ō -āre -āvī -ātus *tr* to herd together; to assemble; to group together **‖** *pass* to flock together; **pares cum paribus facillime congregantur** *(prov)* birds of a feather flock together

congressi·ō -ōnis *f* meeting, conference

congressus *pp of* **congredior**

congress·us -ūs *m* meeting, association, society; union, combination; hostile encounter; fight; sexual intercourse

congru·ens -entis *adj* coinciding, corresponding; suitable; consistent; self-consistent, uniform

congruenter *adv* consistently; *(w. dat or* **ad)** in conformity with; **congruenter naturae vivere** to live in conformity with nature

congruenti·a -ae *f* consistency; similarity; good proportion

congru·ō -ĕre -ī *intr* to coincide; to correspond, agree, be consistent; *(w. ad or* **cum)** to correspond to, agree with, be consistent with; *(w. dat or* **in + acc)** to agree with

congru·us -a -um *adj* agreeing

cōniciō *or* **cōiciō** *see* **conjicio**

cōnif·er *or* **cōnig·er -era -erum** *adj* coniferous

cōnī·tor -tī -xus sum *or* **-sus sum** *intr* to make a great effort, struggle, exert oneself; *(w. in + acc)* to struggle toward, try to reach

cōn·īveō -īvēre -īvī *or* **-ixī** *intr* **(conn-)** to close the eyes; to blink; *(of sun, moon)* to be eclipsed; to be drowsy; *(w.* in + *acc)* to connive at, overlook

conjecti·ō -ōnis *f* throwing, barrage *(of missiles);* conjecture; guesswork; interpretation *(of dreams, etc.);* prophecy; **conjectionem facere** to draw a conclusion

conject·ō -āre -āvī -ātus *tr* (coject-) to conjecture, infer

conject·or -ōris *m* interpreter of dreams, seer

conjectr·ix -īcis *f* interpreter of dreams, seeress

conjectūr·a -ae *f* (coject-) conjecture, guess; inference; interpretation

conjectūrāl·is -is -e *adj* conjectural

conject·us -ūs *m* throwing together; crowding together; connecting; heap, crowd, pile; throwing, hurling; turning, directing *(eyes);* casting *(a glance);* barrage *(of stones, missiles);* **ad** *(or* **intra) teli conjectum venire** to come within range of a weapon

con·jiciō -jicĕre -jēcī -jectus *tr* to hurl, cast; pile together; to conclude, infer; to conjecture; to interpret **‖ refl se in fugam** *(or* **in pedes) conjicere** to take to one's heels

conjugāl·is -is -e *adj* conjugal

conjugāti·ō -ōnis *f (gram)* etymological relationship *(of words)*

conjugāt·or -ōris *m* uniter *(said of Hymen, god of marriage)*

conjugiāl·is -is -e *adj* marriage-

conjug·ium -(i)ī *n* union *(e.g., of body and soul);* marriage, wedlock; mating *(of animals); (fig)* spouse

conjug·ō -āre -āvī -ātus *tr* to join in marriage; to form *(a friendship);* **verba conjugata** *(gram)* cognates

conjunctē *adv* conjointly; at the same time; hypothetically; in intimacy

conjunctim *adv* jointly

conjuncti·ō -ōnis *f* combination, union; association, connection; friendship, intimacy; marriage; relationship *(by blood or marriage);* sympathy, affinity; *(gram)* conjunction

conjunct·us -a -um *adj (w.* dat *or* abl*)* bordering on, near; *(w.* dat *or* abl *or* cum*)* **1** connected with; **2** agreeing with, conforming with **‖** *n* connection

conjun·gō -gĕre -xī -ctus *tr* to join together; to unite in making *(war);* to join in marriage; to unite *(by bonds of friendship); (w.* dat*)* to add *(e.g., words)* to *(e.g., a letter)*

con·junx -jugis *m* (-jux) spouse, husband **‖** *mpl* married couple **‖** *f* spouse, wife; fiancée; bride; the female *(of animals)*

conjūrāti·ō -ōnis *f* plot, conspiracy; alliance

conjūrāt·us -a -um *adj* bound together by an oath, allied, associated; *(mil)* sworn in **‖** *mpl* conspirators

conjūr·ō -āre -āvī -ātum *intr* to take an oath together; to plot, conspire

conjux *see* **conjunx**

conl- = **coll-**

conm- = **comm-**

Con·ōn -ōnis *(acc:* -ōna) famous Athenian admiral *(fl c. 400 B.C.)* **‖** famous mathematician and astronomer of Samos *(fl c. 230 B.C.)*

cōnōpī·um -ī *n* (-pē·um) mosquito net; bed with net, canopy bed

cōn·or -ārī -ātus sum *tr* to try

conquassāti·ō -ōnis *f* severe shaking, disturbance

conquass·ō -āre -āvī -ātus *tr* to shake hard; *(fig)* shatter, upset, disturb

conque·ror -rī -stus sum *tr* to complain bitterly about, deplore **‖** *intr* to complain bitterly

conquesti·ō -ōnis *f* complaining, complaint; *(rhet)* appeal for sympathy; *(w.* gen, w. de + abl *or* adversus + acc*)* complaint about

conquest·us -ūs *m* loud complaint

conqui·escō -escĕre -ēvī -ētum *intr* to rest, take a rest; to go to sleep; to find rest, find recreation; to keep quiet, remain inactive; to slacken; to lie dormant; to stop, pause

con·quiniscō -quiniscĕre -quexī *intr* to crouch down, squat

conquī·rō -rĕre -sīvī *or* **-siī -sītus** *tr* to search for, look for; to procure, bring together, collect; *(fig)* to go after *(e.g., pleasures)*

conquīsīti·ō -ōnis *f* search, procuring, collection; *(mil)* recruitment, draft

conquīsīt·or -ōris *m* (-quist-) recruiting officer

conquīsīt·us -a -um *pp of* **conquiro ‖** *adj* select, choice

conr- = **corr-**

consaep·iō -īre -sī -tus *tr* (-sēp-) to fence in, enclose

consaept·um -ī *n* (-sēp-) enclosure

consalūtāti·ō -ōnis *f* exchange of greetings

consalūt·ō -āre -āvī -ātus *tr* to greet *(as a group),* greet cordially **‖** *intr* **inter se consalutare** to greet one another, exchange greetings

consān·escō -escĕre -uī *intr* to heal up; to recover

consanguine·us -a -um *adj* related by blood **‖** *m* brother **‖** *mpl* relatives **‖** *f* sister

consanguinit·ās -ātis *f* blood relationship; **consanguinitate propinquus** closely related

consauci·ō -āre -āvī -ātus *tr* to wound severely

conscelerāt·us -a -um *adj* wicked, depraved, criminal; *(fig)* rotten to the core
consceler·ō -āre -āvī -ātus *tr* to stain with guilt, dishonor, disgrace
conscen·dō -děre -dī -sus *tr* to climb up, ascend; to climb *(tree);* to mount *(horse, chariot);* to board *(ship);* **aequor navibus conscendere** to go to sea **‖** *intr* to climb up; to climb aboard
conscensi·ō -ōnis *f* embarkation; **in naves conscensio** boarding the ships
conscienti·a -ae *f* joint knowledge; consciousness, knowledge; conscience; scruples; remorse
con·scindō -scinděre -scidī -scissus *tr* to tear up, tear to pieces; *(fig)* to tear apart, abuse
consc·iō -īre -īvī *tr* to have on one's conscience
consc·iscō -iscěre -īvī *or* **-iī -ītus** *tr* to decree, decide on; *(w.* sibi) to inflict on oneself; **sibi mortem consciscere** to decide on suicide
consci·us -a -um *adj* cognizant, conscious, aware; *(w. gen or dat)* having knowledge of, privy to **‖** *mf* partner; accomplice; confidant(e), confederate
conscre·or -ārī -ātus sum *intr* to clear the throat
conscrī·bō -běre -psī -ptus *tr* to enlist, enroll; to write up, compose; to prescribe
conscripti·ō -ōnis *f* record
conscript·us -a -um *pp of* **conscribo ‖** *m* senator; **patres conscripti** gentlemen of the Senate **‖** *n (leg)* deposition
consec·ō -āre -uī -tus *tr* to cut up into small pieces, dismember
consecrāti·ō -ōnis *f* consecration; deification *(of emperors)*
consecr·ō -āre -āvī -ātus *tr* to consecrate; to dedicate to the gods below, doom to destruction, execrate; to immortalize; to hallow; to deify
consectāri·us -a -um *adj* conclusive
consectāti·ō -ōnis *f* eager pursuit
consectātr·ix -īcis *f* eager pursuer
consecti·ō -ōnis *f* cutting up
consect·or -ārī -ātus sum *tr* to follow eagerly, go after; to chase, hunt; to overtake; to imitate, follow
consecūti·ō -ōnis *f* effect, consequences; *(rhet)* order, sequence
consen·escō -escěre -uī *intr* to grow old, grow old together; to become gray; to become obsolete; to waste away, fade, decline; to degenerate
consensi·ō -ōnis *f* agreement, unanimity; harmony; plot
consens·us -ūs *m* agreement, unanimity; harmony; plot; **consensu** with one accord; **in consensum vertere** to become a general custom

consentāne·us -a -um *adj (w. dat or* cum) **1** agreeing with; **2** according to, in accord with; **3** proper for; **consentaneum est** it is reasonable **‖** *npl* concurrent circumstances
consenti·ens -entis *adj* unanimous
consen·tiō -tīre -sī -sus *tr* to agree on; to consent to; **bellum consentire** to agree on war, vote for war **‖** *intr* to agree; *(w. inf)* to agree to, plot to; *(w.* cum) to fit in with, be consistent with
consēp- = consaep-
consequ·ens -entis *adj* reasonable; corresponding; logical; suitable **‖** *n* consequence, conclusion
consequenter *adv* consequently
consequenti·a -ae *f* consequence; natural sequence; **per consequentias** consequently
conse·quor -quī -cūtus sum *tr* to follow, follow up, pursue, go after; to catch up with, catch; to reach, attain to; to arrive at; *(fig)* to follow, copy, imitate; to obtain, get, acquire; to understand; *(of speech)* to do justice to; *(of time)* to come after, follow; to result from
con·serō -serěre -sēvī -situs *tr* to sow, plant
conser·ō -ěre -uī -tus *tr* entwine, tie, join, string together; **manum** *(or* **manūs) conserere** to fight hand-to-hand; **proelium** *(or* **pugnam) conserere** to begin to fight
consertē *adv* in close connection
conserv·a -ae *f* fellow slave *(female)*
conservāti·ō -ōnis *f* preservation
conservāt·or -ōris *m* preserver, defender
conservātr·ix -īcis *f* protectress
conservit·ium -(i)ī *n* fellowship in slavery
conserv·ō -āre -āvī -ātus *tr* to keep safe, preserve, maintain; to act in accordance with, observe; *(fig)* to keep intact
conserv·us -ī *m* fellow slave
consess·or -ōris *m* one who sits next to another *(at a feast, assembly, court of justice, public games)*
consess·us -ūs *m* a sitting together, an assembly, a court, an audience
consīderātē *adv* deliberately, with caution
consīderāti·ō -ōnis *f* consideration, examination
consīderāt·us -a -um *adj* cautious; well-considered, deliberate
consīder·ō -āre -āvī -ātus *tr* to inspect, examine; to consider, reflect on
consid·ium -(i)ī *n* court of justice
con·sīdō -sīděre -sēdī *or* **-sīdī -sessum** *intr* to sit down, be seated; to hold sessions, be in session; to settle, stay *(in residence);* to settle, sink; *(fig)* to sink; to subside, calm down; *(mil)* to encamp, take up a position

consign·ō -āre -āvī -ātus *tr* to seal, sign; to certify, vouch for; to record *(in a sealed document)*; to put on record

consil·escō -escĕre -uī *intr* to fall silent; to become still, calm down

consiliāri·us -a -um *adj* counseling **||** *m* counselor, consultant; cabinet member *(of an emperor)*

consiliāt·or -ōris *m* counselor

consiliō *adv* intentionally

consili·or -ārī -ātus sum *intr* to deliberate; to give advice

consil·ium -(i)ī *n* consultation, deliberation; advice; council; council of war; plan, stratagem; measure; decision; purpose, intention; policy; judgment, wisdom, discretion, sense; *(emperor's)* cabinet; consilio *(or* consiliis*)* alicujus on s.o.'s instructions; consilium capere *(or* inire *or* suscipere*)* to form a plan, come to a decision; consilium mihi est *(w. inf)* I intend to; in consilio esse to be available for consultation; non est consilium mihi *(w. inf)* I don't mean to; privato consilio for one's own purpose

consiluī *perf of* consilesco

consimil·is -is -e *adj* quite similar; *(w. gen or dat)* just like

consip·iō -ĕre *intr* to be sane

con·sistō -sistĕre -stitī *intr* to come to a stop, stop, pause, halt; *(w. cum)* to talk with; to take a stand; to stand still; to grow hard, become solid, set; *(of ships)* to come to anchorage, to ground; *(of travelers)* to halt on a journey; to be firm, be steadfast, endure; to be, exist; to come into existence; to continue in existence, remain; to occur, take place; *(mil)* to take up a position, be posted, make a stand; *(w. abl or in + abl)* 1 to consist of; 2 to depend on; 3 to be based on; 4 to base one's case on; *(w. abl, w. in + abl, w. de or ex + abl)* comprised of

consiti·ō -ōnis *f* sowing, planting

consit·or -ōris *m* sower, planter

consitūr·a -ae *f* sowing, planting

consōbrīn·a -ae *f* first cousin *(female)*

consōbrīn·us -ī *m* first cousin

consoc·er -erī *m* father-in-law

consociāti·ō -ōnis *f* association

consociāt·us -a -um *adj* shared

consoci·ō -āre -āvī -ātus *tr* to join in *(plans, activities);* to share **||** *intr* to enter into a partnership

consōlābil·is -is -e *adj* consolable

consōlāti·ō -ōnis *f* consolation, comfort; encouragement; allaying

consōlāt·or -ōris *m* comforter

consōlātōri·us -a -um *adj* comforting; litterae consolatoriae letter of condolence

consōlor -ārī -ātus sum *tr* to console,

comfort; to reassure, soothe, encourage; to relieve

consomni·ō -āre -āvī *tr* to dream about

conson·ō -āre -uī *intr* to sound together, ring, resound, reecho; *(w. dat or* cum*)* to harmonize with, agree with; inter se consonare to agree, be in accord

conson·us -a -um *adj* harmonious

consōp·iō -īre -īvī *or* -ītus *tr* to put to sleep

consor·s -tis *adj* having a common lot; common; shared in common **||** *mf* partner **||** *m* brother **||** *f* sister

consorti·ō -ōnis *f* partnership; association; fellowship

consort·ium -(i)ī *n* community of goods; partnership; participation; *(w. gen)* partnership in

conspect·us -a -um *pp of* conspicio **||** *adj* visible; in full sight; conspicuous, striking

conspect·us -ūs *m* look, sight, view; (sense of) sight; mental view; appearance on the scene; conspectu in medio before all eyes

consper·gō -gĕre -sī -sus *tr* to sprinkle; to splatter

conspiciend·us -a -um *adj* worth seeing; distinguished

conspicill·um -ī *n* lookout (post)

con·spiciō -spicĕre -spexī -spectus *tr* to look at attentively, observe, fix the eyes upon; to catch sight of, spot; to look at with admiration; to face *(e.g., the Forum)* **||** *pass* to be conspicuous, be noticed, be admired; to attract attention

conspic·or -ārī -ātus sum *tr* to catch sight of, spot, see; *(in a passive sense)* to be conspicuous

conspicu·us -a -um *adj* visible, in sight; conspicuous, striking, remarkable, distinguished

conspīrāti·ō -ōnis *f* agreement, unanimity, harmony; plot

conspīrāt·us -a -um *adj* conspiring, conspiratorial

conspīr·ō -āre -āvī -ātum *intr* to act in harmony; to agree; to conspire

conspons·or -ōris *m* co-guarantor

con·spuō -spuĕre -spuī -spūtus *tr* to spit on

conspurc·ō -āre -āvī -ātus *tr* to defile, mess up; to defile sexually

conspūt·ō -āre -āvī -ātus *tr* to spit on

constabil·iō -īre -īvī *or* -iī -ītus *tr* to stabilize, put on a firm basis

const·ans -antis *adj* constant, uniform, steady, fixed, stable, regular, invariable, persistent; consistent; *(fig)* faithful, trustworthy

constanter *adv* constantly, steadily, uniformly, invariably; consistently

constanti·a -ae *f* constancy, steadiness, firmness, perseverance; consistency,

harmony; steadfastness; self-posses-
sion

consternāti·ō -ōnis f consternation, dismay, alarm; disorder, disturbance; mutiny; wild rush, stampede

constern·ō -āre -āvī -ātus tr to shock; to
startle; to stampede; to derange; (w. ad
or in + acc) to drive (by fear, etc.) to
(some action)

con·sternō -sternĕre -strāvī -strātus tr to
spread, cover; to pave; to thatch;
constrata navis ship with deck

constīp·ō -āre -āvī -ātus tr to pack together

constit·uō -uĕre uī -ūtus tr to set up,
erect; settle (e.g., people in a place); to
establish; to settle on, fix (date, price,
penalty); to arrange, organize; to designate, appoint, assign; to decide, arbitrate, decree, judge; (mil) to station, post,
deploy; (w. inf) to decide to

constitūti·ō -ōnis f constitution, nature;
disposition; regulation, ordinance; definition; (rhet) issue, point of discussion

constitūt·us -a -um pp of **constituo** ‖ adj
ordered, arranged; **bene constitutum
corpus** good constitution ‖ n agreement,
arrangement

con·stō -stāre -stĭtī intr to stand together;
to agree, correspond; to stand firm, be
constant; to stand still, stand firm; to be
in existence; (com) to tally, be correct;
(w. abl of price) to cost; **ratio constat**
the account tallies, is correct ‖ v impers
it is a fact, it is known; **non mihi satis
constat** I have not quite made up my
mind; **satis constat** it is an established
fact, all agree

constrāt·us -a -um adj paved ‖ n platform; deck (of ship); flooring

con·stringō -stringĕre -strinxī -strictus
tr to tie together, tie up; to chain; (fig) to
restrain, inhibit, control; to bound, limit,
confine; to limit in time; to knit (the
brow); to tone up (the body); (rhet) to
condense

constructi·ō -ōnis f building, construction; arrangement (of words)

constru·ō -ĕre -xī -ctus tr to heap up; to
construct; to arrange in a group; (gram)
to construct

constuprāt·or -ōris m rapist

constupr·ō -āre -āvī -ātus tr to rape

consuā·deō -dēre -sī -sus ‖r to advocate ‖
intr (w. dat) to try to persuade

Consuāl·ia -ium npl feast of Consus (ancient Italic god of fertility, celebrated on
August 21 and December 15)

consuās·or -ōris m adviser

consūcid·us -a -um adj very juicy

consūd·ō -āre -āvī intr to sweat profusely

consuē·faciō -facĕre -fēcī -factus tr to
accustom, inure

consu·escō -escĕre -ēvī -ētus tr to accustom, inure ‖ intr to become accustomed;
(w. inf) to become accustomed to, get
used to; (w. cum) to cohabit with

consuēti·ō -ōnis f sexual intercourse

consuētūd·ō -inis f custom, habit; usage,
idiom; social ties; sexual intercourse; **ad
consuetudinem** (w. gen) according to
the custom of; (ex) **consuetudine** from
habit; **pro mea consuetudine** as is my
habit; **ut fert consuetudo** as is usual

consuēt·us -a -um pp of **consuesco** ‖ adj
customary

con·sul -sulis m consul (one of the two
highest magistrates of the Roman Republic); **consul designatus** consul-elect;
consulem creare (or **dicere,** or **facere**)
to elect a consul; **consul ordinarius** regular consul (who entered office in January 1); **consul suffectus** substitute consul (chosen in the course of the year to
fill a vacancy)

consulār·is -is -e adj consular; **aetas
consularis** minimum legal age to be consul (42 years); **comitia consularia** consular elections; **vir consularis** a man of
consular rank ‖ m ex-consul

consulāriter adv like a consul, in a manner worthy of a consul

consulāt·us -ūs m consulship; **consulatum
gerere** to hold the consulship; **consulatum petere** to run for the consulship;
se consulatu abdicare to resign from
the consulship

consul·ō -ĕre -uī -tus tr to consult; to
consider; to advise (s.th.), offer as advice; **boni** (**optimi**) **consulere** to think
well (very highly) of ‖ intr to deliberate,
reflect; (w. dat) to look after; (w. ad or in
+ acc) to reflect on, take into consideration; (w. in + acc) to take measures
against; (w. de + abl) to pass sentence on

consultāti·ō -ōnis f mature deliberation,
consideration; consulting; inquiry; subject of consultation

consultē adv deliberately, with due deliberation, prudently

consultō adv on purpose

consult·ō -āre -āvī -ātus tr to reflect on,
consider maturely; to ask (s.o.) for advice, consult ‖ intr to deliberate; (w. dat)
to look after, take care of; **in medium**
(or **in commune**) **consultare** to look
after the common good

consult·or -ōris m counselor, consultant;
advisee, client

consultr·ix -īcis f protectress

consult·us -a -um pp of **consulo** ‖ adj
skilled, experienced ‖ m expert; **juris
consultus** legal expert, attorney ‖ n deliberation, consideration; decree, decision; response (from an oracle); **bene
consultum** a good measure; **male**

consultum an ill-advised measure; **senatūs consultum** decree of the Senate
consummāt·us -a -um *adj* consummate, perfect
consumm·ō -āre -āvī -ātus *tr* to sum up; *(of numbers)* to add up to; to finish, accomplish, perfect; to complete *(public works)*
consūm·ō -ĕre -psī -ptus *tr* to consume, use up, exhaust; to devour; to wear out; to waste
consumpti·ō -ōnis *f* consumption; wasting
consumpt·or -ōris *m* spend-thrift
con·suō -suĕre -suī -sūtus *tr* to sew up
consur·gō -gĕre -rexī -rectum *intr* to stand up; to rise in a body; *(w.* ad *or in + acc)* to aspire to
consurrecti·ō -ōnis *f* rising up, standing up in a body
Cons·us -ī *m* ancient Italic deity of agriculture and fertility
consusurr·ō -āre -āvī *intr* to whisper to one another
contābē·faciō -facĕre -fēcī -factus *tr (fig)* to run *(s.o.)* down
contāb·escō -escĕre -uī *intr* to waste away
contabulāti·ō -ōnis *f* flooring; story
contabul·ō -āre -āvī -ātus *tr* to cover with boards; to construct with multiple stories; to bridge, span
contact·us -ūs *m* touch, contact; contagion; *(fig)* infection
contāg·ēs -is *f* touch, contact
contāgi·ō -ōnis *f* touching; touch, contact; contagion, infection
contāg·ium -(i)ī *n* touch, contact; contagion; moral contamination
contāmināt·us -a -um *adj* contaminated, polluted; vile
contāmin·ō -āre -āvī -ātus *tr* to contaminate, pollute; to adulterate; to defile, desecrate; to ruin, spoil
contechn·or -ārī -ātus sum *intr* to devise plots; to think up tricks
conte·gō -gĕre -xī -ctus *tr* to cover up; to hide; to protect; to put a roof on; to bury
contemer·ō -āre -āvī -ātus *tr* to defile
contem·nō -nĕre -psī -ptus *tr* to regard with contempt, look down on, despise; to treat with contempt; to pay no attention to, disregard; to have nothing to do with
contemplāti·ō -ōnis *f* viewing, surveying; contemplation, consideration
contemplāt·or -ōris *m* contemplator, observer
contemplāt·us -ūs *m* contemplation
contempl·ō -āre -āvī -ātus *or* **contempl·or -ārī -ātus sum** *tr* to observe, survey, gaze on, contemplate
contemptim *adv* contemptuously; fearlessly

contempti·ō -ōnis *f* scorn; contempt; disregarding, belittling
contempt·or -ōris *m* despiser
contemptr·ix -īcis *f* despiser *(female)*
contempt·us -a -um *pp of* **contemno** ‖ *adj* contemptible
contempt·us -ūs *m* contempt; **contemptui esse** to be an object of contempt
conten·dō -dĕre -dī -tus *tr* to stretch, draw tight; to tune *(instrument);* to aim, shoot, hurl; to strain, exert; to assert, hold, allege; to compare, contrast; **cursum** *(or* **iter) contendere** to make one's way ‖ *intr* to exert oneself; to contend, compete, fight; to dispute, argue; to travel, march; to match, contrast; *(w.* de + abl) to demand from; *(w. inf)* to be in a hurry to; *(w.* in + acc) to rush to, head for; *(w.* ad) to strive for, aspire to; *(w.* cum) 1 to contend with, argue with; 2 to fight with
contentē *adv (from* **contendo)** vehemently, vigorously
contentē *adv (from* **contineo)** in a restricted way, sparingly
contenti·ō -ōnis *f* stretching, tension; exertion, effort; competition; quarrel; contrast, comparison, antithesis; *(gram)* comparison of adjectives; *(rhet)* crescendo; **in contentionem venire** *or* **vocari** *(or* **in contentione poni)** to become the subject of a dispute
content·us -a -um *pp of* **contendo** ‖ *adj* tense, strained; energetic
content·us -a -um *pp of* **contineo** ‖ *adj* content, satisfied
contermin·us -a -um *adj* neighboring; *(w. dat)* adjacent to
con·terō -terĕre -trīvī -trītus *tr* to grind to powder, pulverize, crush; to wear out; *(fig)* to wear down; *(fig)* to trample on; to expunge, wipe out; to waste *(time, effort);* to exhaust *(topic)*
conterr·eō -ēre -uī -itus *tr* to scare the life out of
contest·or -ārī -ātus sum *tr* to call to witness; *(fig)* to prove, attest; **litem contestari** to open a lawsuit by calling witnesses
contex·ō -ĕre -uī -tus *tr* to weave together; to make by joining, devise, build; to link, join *(words);* to compose *(writings);* to dream up
contextē *adv* in a coherent manner
context·us -a -um *pp of* **contexo** ‖ *adj* interwoven; coherent; continuous, uninterrupted
context·us -ūs *m* joining together; coherence; continuity, connection; structure; plan, course
contic·escō -escĕre *or* **contic·iscō -iscĕre -uī** *intr* to become quite still, fall completely silent; to keep silence; *(fig)* to abate, cease

conticin·ium -(i)ī *n* silence of the night

contignāti·ō -ōnis *f* floor, story

contign·ō -āre -āvī -ātus *tr* to lay a floor on

contigu·us -a -um *adj* contiguous, touching, adjoining, within reach; *(w. dat)* bordering on, near

contin·ens -entis *adj* continuous, unbroken; homogeneous; adjacent, close; next, immediately following; self-controlled, moderate; restrained; *(w. dat)* contiguous with **‖** *f* interior *(of a country);* mainland **‖** *n* main point *(of argument);* **ex continenti** *(or* **in continenti)** without delay

continenter *adv* in unbroken succession; without interruption; *(sitting)* close together; moderately

continenti·a -ae *f* repression; self-control

con·tineō -tinēre -tinuī -tentus *tr* to hold *or* keep together; to keep within bounds, confine; to contain, comprise, include; to control, repress

con·tingō -tingĕre -tigī -tactus *tr* to come into contact with; to touch, border on; to reach, attain; to infect; to contaminate; *(fig)* to touch, affect **‖** *intr* to happen, turn out, come to pass; *(w. dat)* to touch, border on **‖** *v impers* it happens, turns out; *(w. dat)* it befalls one

continuāti·ō -ōnis *f* unbroken series, succession; *(rhet)* period

continu·ō -āre -āvī -ātus *tr* to make continuous, join together, connect; to extend *(in time or space);* to continue, carry on, draw out, prolong; to pass, occupy *(time)* **‖** *pass (w. dat)* **1** to be contiguous with, adjacent to; **2** to follow closely upon **‖** *intr* to continue, last

continuō *adv* immediately; right from the first; without more ado; continuously; necessarily

continu·us -a -um *adj* continuous, unbroken; successive; **dies continuos quinque** (for) five days in a row

conti·ō -ōnis *f* meeting, rally; public meeting *(of the people or soldiers);* speech, pep talk; **contionem habere** to give a speech; to give a pep talk

contiōnābund·us -a -um *adj* haranguing, holding forth

contiōnāl·is -is -e *adj* like in assembly; demogogic

contiōnāri·us -a -um *adj* mob-like

contiōnāt·or -ōris *m* demogogue

contiōn·or -ārī -ātus sum *intr* to hold forth at a rally, to harangue; to come to a rally **‖** *tr (w. acc & inf)* to say at a rally (that)

contiuncul·a -ae *f* small rally

contoll·ō -ĕre *tr* **gradum contollere** to step up *(to a person)*

conton·at -āre *v impers* it is thundering loud

contor·qeō -quēre -sī -tus *tr* to twist, whirl; to throw hard; to twist *(words)* around

contortē *adv* intricately

contortiōn·ēs -um *fpl* intricacies *(of language)*

contort·or -ōris *m* perverter; **contortor legum** shyster

contortul·us -a -um *adj* terribly complicated

contortuplicāt·us -a -um *adj* all tangled up

contort·us -a -um *pp of* **contorqueo ‖** *adj* involved, intricate

contrā *adv* in opposition, opposite, in front, face to face; in turn, in return; on the other hand; on the other side; reversely, in the opposite way, the other way; on the contrary, conversely; **contra atque** *(or* **ac)** contrary to, otherwise than; **contra dicere** to reply; to raise objections; **contra dicitur** the objection is raised; **contra ferire** to make a counterattack; **contra qua fas est** contrary to divine law; **contra quam senatus consuluisset** contrary to what the Senate would have decided; **quin contra** nay on the contrary

contrā *prep (w. acc)* **1** opposite, opposite to, facing, towards: **contra septentriones** facing north; **2** *(in a hostile sense)* against, with, in opposition to: **contra patriam exercitum ducere** to lead an army against one's country; **3** injurious to, unfavorable to: **quod contra se ipsum sit dicere** to say what is against one's own interests; **4** in defiance of: **contra senatum proficisci** to depart in defiance of the Senate; **5** in violation of: **contra jus gentium** in violation of international law; **6** contrary to, the reverse of **contra exspectationem omnium** contrary to universal expectation; **contra spem** contrary to hope, unexpectedly; **7** in comparison with: **nunc contra istum librum faveo orationi quam nuper dedi** now in comparison with that book I prefer the speech which I recently gave *(you)*

contracti·ō -ōnis *f* contraction; shortening *(of syllable);* **contractio animi** depression; **contractio nervorum** cramp

contractiuncul·a -ae *f* slight mental depression

contract·us -a -um *pp of* **contraho ‖** *adj* contracted; narrow, limited *(place);* brief; pinching *(poverty);* limited in scope; parsimonious; terse *(style)*

contract·us -ūs *m* contraction

contrā·dīcō -dīcĕre -dixī -dictum *tr* to contradict **‖** *intr (w. dat)* **1** to contradict; **2** to speak against

contrādicti·ō -ōnis *f* objection, refutation

contra·hō -hĕre -xī -ctus *tr* to draw together; to contract; to collect, assemble; to shorten, narrow, abridge; to lessen; to wrinkle; to bring about, accomplish, cause, produce, incur; to conclude *(a bargain);* to transact *(business);* to settle *(an account);* to complete *(business arrangements)*

contrāposit·um -ī *n* antithesis

contrārie *adv* in opposite directions; in a different way

contrāri·us -a -um *adj* opposite; contrary, conflicting; hostile, antagonistic; from the opposite direction; reciprocal, mutual; *(w. dat)* opposed to, contrary to **ǁ** *n* the opposite, the contrary, the reverse; antithesis; **contrario** on the contrary; **e(x) contrario** on the contrary; on the opposite side; **in contraria** *(or* **contrarium)** in the opposite direction; **in contaria versus** changed into its opposite

contrectābiliter *adv* **(-tract-)** appreciably, tangibly

contrectāti·ō -ōnis *f* **(-tract-)** handling, touching; fondling, caressing

contrect·ō -āre -āvī -ātus *tr* **(-tract-)** to touch, handle; *(sl)* to fondle; *(sl)* to have sexual intercouse with; to deal with *(a subject)*

contrem·iscō -iscěre *tr* to shudder at **ǁ** *intr* to tremble all over; to waver

contrem·ō -ěre -uī *intr* to tremble all over; to quake

contrib·uō -uěre -uī -ūtus *tr* to bring together, enroll together; to associate, unite incorporate; to contribute, add

contrist·ō -āre -āvī -ātus *tr* to sadden; to cast gloom over, darken, cloud

contrīt·us -a -um *pp of* **contero ǁ** *adj* worn out, common, trite

contrōversi·a -ae *f* controversy, quarrel, dispute; debate; civil lawsuit, litigation; subject of litigation; contradiction; question

contrōversiōs·us -a -um *adj* controversial

contrōvers·us -a -um *adj* disputed, controversial; questionable, undecided

contrucīd·ō -āre -āvī -ātus *tr* to cut down, massacre; *(sl)* to make a mess of

contrū·dō -děre -sī -sus *tr* to push hard; to crowd together

contrunc·ō -āre -āvī -ātus *tr* to hack to pieces

contuberⅰal·is -is *m* army buddy; junior staff officer; *(coll)* husband *(of slave);* personal attendant; companion, colleague **ǁ** *f* wife *(of slave)*

contubern·ium -(i)ī *n* sharing the same tent; wartime friendship; army tent; serving as a junior staff officer; concubinage; marriage *(among slaves);* hovel *(of slave couple)*

contudī *perf of* **contundo**

contu·eor -ērī -itus sum *tr* to look intently at; to catch sight of; to be within sight of *(a place)*

contuit·us *or* **contūt·us -ūs** *m* sight, observation

contumāci·a -ae *f* insubordination, defiance; *(leg)* contempt

contumāciter *adv* defiantly

contum·ax -ācis *adj* insubordinate, defiant

contumēli·a -ae *f* mistreatment; outrage; abuse; insult, affront

contumēliōsē *adv* abusively; outrageously

contumēliōs·us -a -um *adj* insulting, outrageous, humiliating; abusive, rude

contumul·ō -āre -āvī -ātus *tr* to bury

con·tundō -tunděre -tudī -tūsus *tr* to crush, grind, pound; to bruise; *(fig)* to crush, subdue; to baffle; to outdo *(performance)*

conturbāti·ō -ōnis *f* disorder; dismay, consternation

conturbāt·or -ōris *m* bankrupt

conturbāt·us -a -um *adj* confused, distracted, in confusion

conturb·ō -āre -āvī -ātus *tr* to confuse, throw into confusion; to disturb; to upset *(plans);* **rationes** *(or* **rationem) conturbare** to be bankrupt **ǁ** *intr* to go bankrupt

cont·us -ī *m* pole

contūsus *pp of* **contundo**

cōnūbiāl·is -is -e *adj* conjugal

cōnūb·ium -(i)ī *n* intermarriage; right to intermarry; marriage; sexual intercourse; **jus conubi** right to intermarry

cōn·us -ī *m* cone; apex *(of helmet)*

convad·or -ārī -ātus sum *tr* to subpoena

conval·escō -escěre -uī *intr* to grow strong, thrive; to convalesce; *(fig)* to improve; *(leg)* become valid

convall·is -is *f* valley

convās·ō -āre -āvī -ātus *tr* to pack, pack up

convect·ō -āre -āvī -ātus *tr* to gather

convect·or -ōris *m* fellow passenger

conve·hō -hěre -xī -ctus *tr* gather, bring in *(esp. the harvest);* to convey, ship *(to one place)*

con·vellō -vellěre -vellī -vulsus *tr* **(-vols-)** to tear away, pull off, pluck, wrest; to tear to pieces, dismember; to break, shatter; *(fig)* to turn upside down, subvert, overthrow; **convellere signa** to break camp

conven·ae -ārum *mpl or fpl* strangers; refugees, vagabonds, the homeless

conveni·ens -entis *adj* agreeing, harmonious, consistent; appropriate; *(w. dat or* **cum)** consistent with, appropriate to; *(w. ad)* appropriate for, suitable for

convenienter *adv* consistently; suitably; *(w. cum or ad)* in conformity with

convenienti·a -ae *f* agreement, accord, harmony; conformity

con·veniō -venīre -vēnī -ventus *tr* to meet, go to meet; to interview; *(leg)* to sue; **Regulus convenit me in praetoris officio** Regulus met me at the installation of a praetor **‖** *intr* to come together, meet, gather; to make an agreement; to coincide; to converge; to unite, combine; to come to an agreement, agree; to fit; *(w.* **ad)** to fit *(as a shoe fits the foot); (w.* **dat** *or* **cum** *or* **ad** *or* **in** + *acc)* to be applicable to, appropriate to; **bene convenire** to be on good terms; to fit well; **in matrmonium cum viro convenire** *(of a bride)* to get married; **viro in manum convenire** *(of a bride)* to come under the control of her husband **‖** *v impers* it is befitting; it is agreed; **bene convenit nobis** we get along well; **convenit inter se** *(w. dat)* there is harmony among

conventīci·us -a -um *adj* coming together, met by chance **‖** *n* fee paid for attending the assembly

conventicul·um -ī *n* small gathering; smal meeting place

conventi·ō -ōnis *f* assembly; agreement contract

convent·um -ī *n* contract, agreement

convent·us -ūs *m* gathering, assembly; congress; district court; company, corporation; agreement; **ex conventu** by agreement; of one accord; **conventum agere** to hold court

converber·ō -āre -āvī -ātus *tr* to beat soundly, bash

conver·rō -rĕre -rī -sus *tr* (**-vorr-**) to sweep out; to brush thoroughly; *(fig)* to scoop up *(e.g., an inheritance)*

conversāti·ō -ōnis *f* familiarity, close association *(with people);* **conversatio parit contemptum** *(prov)* familiarity breeds contempt

conversi·ō -ōnis *f* rotation; cycle; transposition, inversion; alteration; political change, upheaval; *(rhet)* repetition of word at end of clause; *(rhet)* balancing of phrases; *(rhet)* period

convers·ō -āre -āvī -ātus *tr* to turn around **‖** *refl* to revolve

conver·tō -tĕre -tī -sus *tr* (**-vor-**) to rotate; to turn back, reverse; *(fig)* to turn, direct *(attention, laughter);* to convert, transform; to translate; to turn upside down; to convulse, shake; to turn *(e.g., horse)* around; to shift, transfer; to transpose, invert *(an arrangement);* to turn aside, divert; to distract *(the mind);* to repulse *(attackers);* **ad se** *(or* **in se) convertere** to attract *(e.g., attention);* **in fugam convertere** to put to flight; **signa convertere** to face about; **terga con-**

vertere to turn tail **‖** *refl* to turn around; *(mil)* to retreat **‖** *intr* to return; to change, turn; *(w.* **in** + *acc)* to be changed into, turn into

convest·iō -īre *tr* to clothe, cover

convex·us -a -um *adj* rounded off; arched, convex; concave; sloping down **‖** *n* vault, arch, dome

convīciāt·or -ōris *m* heckler

convīci·or -ārī -ātus sum *intr* to jeer; *(w. dat)* to heckle, jeer at

convīc·ium -(i)ī *n* noise, chatter; wrangling; jeers, heckling, abuse; cry of protest; reprimand; **aliquem conviciis consectari** to heckle s.o.

convicti·ō -ōnis *f* socializing, association, companionship; companions

convict·or -ōris *m* bosom pal

convict·us -ūs *m* socializing, association

con·vincō -vincĕre -vīcī -victus *tr* to refute, prove wrong; *(leg)* to convict; to prove, demonstrate clearly; **devotionem convincere** *(of a god)* to grant a request

convīs·ō -ĕre -ī -us *tr* to examine, search; to go to visit

convīv·a -ae *m* (*f*) guest; dinner guest

convīvāl·is -is -e *adj* convivial, festive

convīvāt·or -ōris *m* host; master of ceremonies

convīv·ium -(i)ī *n* banquet, dinner party; party; **convivium agitare** *(coll)* to throw a party **‖** *npl* dinner guests

convī·vō -vĕre -xī -ctum *intr* to live together; to live at the same time; *(w.* **cum)** to dine with

convīv·or -ārī -ātus sum *intr* to feast together, have a party

convocāti·ō -ōnis *f* calling together

convoc·ō -āre -āvī -ātus *tr* to convoke

convol·ō -āre -āvī -ātum *intr* to flock together

convol·vō -vĕre -vī -ūtus *tr* to roll together; to roll up *(scroll);* to fasten together, interweave; to wrap; **terga convolvere** *(of snakes)* to writhe **‖** *refl* to roll along; to go in a circle

convom·ō -ĕre -uī -itus *tr* to vomit all over

convortō *see* **converto**

convulner·ō -āre -āvī -ātus *tr* (**-vol-**) to wound seriously

convulsus *pp of* **convello**

coöper·iō *or* **cōperi·ō -īre -uī -tus** *tr* (**cōp-**) to cover; to overwhelm

coöptāti·ō -ōnis *f* (**cōp-**) coöptation *(election of a colleague by incumbents)*

coöpt·ō -āre -āvī -ātus *tr* (**cōp-**) to coöpt

coör·ior -īrī -tus sum *intr* to rise; to be born; to originate; to appear suddenly; *(of war)* to break out; *(mil)* to go on the attack

coört·us -ūs *m* rising, originating

Cō·os *or* **Co·us -ī** *f* small island in the Aegean, famous for its wine and fine linen

cōp·a -ae *f* barmaid

cophin·us -ī *m* basket

cōpi·a -ae *f* abundance, supply, store; plenty; multitude, large number; wealth, prosperity; opportunity, means; command of language, fluency; *(w. gen)* power over; *(w. dat)* access to; **copia dicendi** *(or* **verborum)** command of language, wide vocabulary, richness of expression; **pro copiā** as one's circumstances allow **‖** *fpl* troops, armed forces; provisions, supplies

cōpiol·ae -ārum *fpl* small contingent of troops

cōpiōsē *adv* abundantly; *(rhet)* fully, at length, eloquently

cōpiōs·us -a -um *adj* plentiful; well-supplied, rich; eloquent, fluent; *(w. abl)* abounding in, rich in

cop·is -idis *f* small, curved sword

cōpō *see* **caupo**

cōp·s -is *adj* rich, well-supplied; *(of the chest)* swelling *(with pride)*

copt·a -ae *f* crisp cake

cōpul·a -ae *f* cord, string, rope, leash; *(fig)* tie, bond

cōpulāti·ō -ōnis *f* coupling, joining, union; combining *(of words)*

cōpulāt·us -a -um *adj* closely connected; compound, complex; close, intimate *(relationship)*

cōpul·ō -āre -āvī -ātus *tr* to couple, join; *(fig)* to unite; *(w. dat or* **cum)** to couple with, join to, combine with **‖** *refl & pass* to unite *(for practical purposes)*

cōpul·or -ārī -ātus sum *tr* to join, clasp; **dextras copulari** to shake hands

coqu·a -ae *f* cook *(female)*

coquīn·ō -āre -āvī -ātum *intr* to be a cook

coquīn·us -a -um *adj* of cooked and baked food

co·quō -quĕre -xī -ctus *tr* to cook; to fry, roast, boil, bake; to brew; to bake *(bricks, bread);* to fire *(pottery);* to smelt *(ore);* to season *(lumber);* to burn, parch; to ripen; to digest *(food);* to disturb, worry; to concoct, dream up; to hatch *(plots)*

coqu·us *or* **coc·us -ī** *m* cook

cor cordis *n* heart; mind, judgment; dear friend; **aliquid cordi habere** to take s.th. to heart; **cordi esse** *(w. dat)* to please, be dear to, be agreeable to; **cor habere** to have common sense; **si vobis non fuit cordi** *(w. acc & inf)* if it was not to your liking that **‖** *npl* friends, souls

coracīn·us -ī *m* dark-colored species of fish

corall·ium -(i)ī *n* **(cūrali-)** coral

cōram *adv* in person, personally; publicly, openly; in someone's presence, face to face **‖** *prep (coming before or after abl)* before, in the presence of, face to face with

corb·is -is *m (f)* wicker basket

corbīt·a -ae *f* slow-sailing merchant ship

corbul·a -ae *f* small basket

corcōta *see* **crocota**

corcōtāri·us -a -um *adj* concerned with saffron-colored clothes

corcul·um -ī *n* little heart; sweetheart; poor fellow; the Wise *(name given to Publius Scipio Nasica)*

Corcŷr·a -ae *f* island off coast of Epirus, sometimes identified with Scheria, the island of Alcinoüs

cordātē *adv* wisely, prudently

cord·ax -ācis *m* trochaic meter; indecent dance

cordol·ium -(i)ī *n* heartache

Cordub·a -ae *f* Cordova *(in S. Spain)*

cordŷl·a -ae *f* baby tuna

Corfīn·ium -(i)ī *n* town in central Italy, center of the Social War

coriandr·um -ī *n (bot)* coriander *(aromatic herb, used as seasoning)*

Corinn·a -ae *f* Greek lyric poetess *(fl c. 500 B.C.)*

Corinthiac·us -a -um *or* **Corinthiens·is -is -e** *adj* Corinthian

Corinthi·us -a -um *adj* Corinthian; **aes Corinthium** alloy of gold, silver, and copper used in expensive jewelry **‖** *mpl* Corinthians **‖** *npl* costly Corinthian products

Corinth·us *or* **Corinth·os -ī** *f* Corinth

Coriolān·us -ī *m* Gnaeus Marcius Coriolanus *(notorious Roman general who led the Volsci against Rome)*

cor·ium -(i)ī *n or* **cor·ius -(i)ī** *m* skin, hide; leather; bark; peel, rind; *(sl)* one's hide; **corio suo ludere** *(sl)* to risk one's own hide; **corium alicujus petere** *(sl)* to be after s.o.'s hide

Cornēli·us -a -um *adj* Roman clan name *(nomen)* and tribal name; **lex Cornelia** a law proposed by any member of the Cornelian clan *(esp. Sulla)*

corneol·us -a -um *adj* made of horn; *(fig)* hard, tough

corne·us -a -um *adj* of horn; of cornel wood; of the cornel tree

cornic·en -inis *m* horn blower

cornīc·or -ārī -ātus sum *tr (sl)* to croak, say in a croaking voice **‖** *intr* to caw

cornīcul·a -ae *f* poor little crow

corniculār·ius -(i)ī *m* soldier decorated with horn-shaped medal for bravery; adjutant to a centurion

cornicul·um -ī *n* **(cornu-)** little horn; *(mil)* horn-shaped decoration

cornig·er -era -erum *adj* horned

cornip·ēs -edis *adj* hoofed

corn·ix -īcis *f* crow; *(pej)* old crow

corn·ū -ūs *or* **corn·um -ī** *n* horn *(of animals, insects);* drinking vessel *(made from a horn);* funnel *(made from a horn);*

horn, trumpet; lantern; funnel; oil cruet; hoof; bill *(of bird)*; horn *(of moon)*; tip *(of a bow)*; branch *(of river)*; arm *(of lake)*; tongue *(of land)*; crest socket *(of helmet)*; roller end *(of scroll)*; *(mil)* wing, flank; **cornua addere** *(w. dat)* to give courage to, add strength to; **cornua sumere** to gain strength; **cornu Copiae** cornucopia; **cornu Indicum** ivory

corn·um -ī *n* cornel cherry; spear
corn·us -ī *f* cornel cherry tree; dogwood tree; spear, shaft, javelin
coroll·a -ae *f* small garland
corollār·ium -(i)ī *n* garland; gilt wreath *(given as reward to actors)*; gift, tip
corōn·a -ae *f* crown, garland; circle of bystanders; *(mil)* cordon of besiegers; *(mil)* ring of defense; **corona civica** decoration for a saving a life; **corona muralis** decoration for being the first to scale an enemy wall; **corona navalis** decoration for naval victory; **corona obsidialis** decoration for breaking a blockade; **sub corona vendere** to sell *(captives)* as slaves; **sub corona venire** *(of captives)* to be sold at auction **ǁ Corona** *(astr)* Ariadne's crown, Corona Borealis
corōnāri·us -a -um *adj* for a crown; **aurum coronarium** gold collected in the provinces for a victorious general's crown
Corōnē·a -ae *f* town in Boeotia
Corōn·eūs -eī *m* king of Phocis, whose daughter was changed into a crow
Corōnīd·ēs -ae *m* Aesculapius, son of Coronis
corōn·is -idis *f* symbol for showing the end of a book, colophon
Corōn·is -idis *f* mother, by Apollo, of Aesculapius
corōn·ō -āre -āvī -ātus *tr* to crown, wreathe; to enclose, encircle, shut in
corporāt·us -a - um *adj* incorporated; having a tangible body
corpore·us -a -um *adj* physical, of the body, bodily; corporeal, substantial; of flesh
corpulent·us -a -um *adj* corpulent
corp·us -oris *n* body; matter, substance; flesh; plumpness; trunk *(of tree)*; corpse; person, individual; frame, structure, framework; community; corporation; society, union, guild; particle, grain; sum *(of money)*; *(literary)* corpus; *(in geometry)* a solid; **corporis** *(w. noun)* body, bodily, physical; **corporis custos** bodyguard; **corpus reipublicae** the body politic; **toto corpore** with all one's strengh
corpuscul·um -ī *n* puny body; particle, atom; *(coll)* little fellow
corrā·dō -děre -sī -sus *tr* **(conr-)** to scrape together, rake up; *(coll)* to scrape *(money)* together

correcti·ō -ōnis *f* **(conr-)** correction, improvement, amendment; rhetorical restatement
correct·or -ōris *m* **(conr-)** corrector, reformer
correct·us -a -um *pp of* **corrigo ǁ** *adj* improved, correct
correp·ō -ěre -sī -tum *intr* **(conr-)** to creep, slink; **in dumeta correpere** *(coll)* to beat around the bush, indulge in jargon
correptē *adv* **(conr-)** with a short vowel *or* syllable
correptius *adv* **(conr-)** more briefly; **correptius exire** to end in a short vowel
correptus *pp of* **corripio (conr-) ǁ** *adj* short *(syllable, vowel)*
correxī *perf of* **corrigo**
corrīd·eō -ēre *intr* **(conr-)** to laugh out loud
corrigi·a -ae *f* shoelace
cor·rigō -rigěre -rexī -rectus *tr* **(conr-)** to straighten out; to smooth out; to correct, improve, reform; to make up for *(delay)*; to make the best of
cor·ripiō -ripěre -ripuī -reptus *tr* **(conr-)** to take hold of, snatch up; to seize *(a person)*; to seize unlawfully; *(of a current)* to carry off; to steal, carry off; to enrapture, sweep off one's feet; to attack suddenly; to speed up, rush; to shorten, contract; to abridge *(a literary work)*; to reproach; to cut short *(period of time)*; *(gram)* to pronounce *(a word)* with a short syllable, pronounce *(a syllable)* short; **arma corripere** to go to war; **gradum corripere** to pick up the pace; **igne** *(or* **flammā) corripere** to ignite, set on fire; **in se corripere** to absorb **ǁ** *refl* to bestir oneself, jump up, hurry off
corrōbor·ō -āre -āvī -ātus *tr* **(conr-)** to strengthen, invigorate; *(fig)* to fortify, encourage; *(mil)* to reinforce **ǁ** *refl &* *pass* to become mature
cor·rōdō -rōděre -rōsī -rōsus *tr* **(conr-)** to gnaw, chew up
corrog·ō -āre -āvī -ātus *tr* **(conr-)** to go asking for, collect, drum up, solicit; to invite, summon
corrōsus *pp of* **corrodo**
corrūg·ō -āre -āvī -ātus *tr* **(conr-)** to wrinkle; **nares corrugare** *(w. dat)* to make s.o. turn up his nose
cor·rumpō -rumpěre -rūpī -ruptus *tr* **(conr-)** to burst, to break to pieces, smash; to destroy completely, ruin, waste; to mar; to corrupt; to adulterate; to falsify, tamper with; to bribe; to seduce
corru·ō -ěre -ī *tr* **(conr-)** to shatter, wreck, ruin **ǁ** *intr* to fall down, tumble, sink; *(fig)* to fall, fail, sink
corruptē *adv* **(conr-)** corruptly, perversely; in a lax manner

corruptēl·a -ae *f* (conr-) corruption, seduction; bribery; corrupting influence
corrupti·ō -ōnis *f* (conr-) corruption, ruining, breaking up; corrupt condition
corrupt·or -ōris *m or* **corruptr·ix -īcis** *f* (conr-) corrupter, seducer, briber
corrupt·us -a -um *pp of* **corrumpo (conr-)** ‖ *adj* corrupt, spoiled, bad, ruined
Corsic·a -ae *f* Corsica
cort·ex -icis *m (f)* bark, shell, hull, rind; cork; **nare sine cortice** to swim without a cork life preserver; *(fig)* to be on one's own
cortīn·a -ae *f* kettle, caldron; tripod; *(fig)* vault of heaven
corulus *see* **corylus**
cōrus *see* **caurus**
corusc·ō -āre -āvī *tr* to shake, wave, brandish ‖ *intr* to flit, flutter; to oscillate; to tremble; to flash, gleam
corusc·us -a -um *adj* oscillating, vibrating, tremulous; flashing, gleaming, glittering
corv·us -ī *m* raven; *(mil)* grapnel
Coryb·ās -antis *m* priest of Cybele
Corybant·ēs -um *mpl* the Corybantes *(priests of goddess Cybele)*
Corybanti·us -a -um *adj* of the Corbyantes
Cōryci·us -a -um *adj* of the Corycian mountain-caves on Mt. Parnasus
Cōrycid·es -um *fpl* **nymphae Corycides** the Muses
cōryc·us -ī *m* punching bag
corylēt·um -ī *n* cluster of hazel trees
coryl·us -ī *f* (-rul-) hazel tree
corymbif·er -era -erum *adj* wearing *or* carrying clusters of ivy berries ‖ *m* Bacchus
corymb·us -ī *m* cluster *(esp. of ivy berries)*
coryphae·us -ī *m* leader, head
cōrȳt·os *or* **cōrȳt·us -ī** *m* quiver
cōs- = **cons-**
cōs cōtis *f* whetstone
cosmēt·a -ae *f* slave girl in charge of the wardrobe
cosmic·os -ē -on *adj* worldly, fashionable
cosm·os -ī *m* the universe, cosmos ‖ a chief magistrate of Crete
cost·a -ae *f* rib; *(fig)* side, wall
cost·um -ī *n* perfume
cothurnāt·us -a -um *adj* wearing buskins; suitable to tragedy, tragic
cothurn·us -ī *m* high boot; hunting boot; buskin *(worn by tragic actors);* subject of tragedy; tragedy; lofty style of Greek tragedy
cōtīd- = **cottid-**
cottab·us -ī *m* game which consisted of flicking drops of wine on a bronze vessel
cottan·a -ōrum *npl* (-on·a) Syrian figs
cottīdiānō *adv* (cōt-, quōt-) daily
cottīdiān·us -a -um *adj* (cōt-, quōt-) daily; everyday, ordinary

cottīdiē *adv* (cōt-, quōt-) daily
coturn·ix -īcis *f* quail
Cot·ys -yis *m* name of several Thracian kings
Cotȳt·ō -ūs *f* Thracian goddess of orgiastic rites
Cotytti·a -ōrum *npl* festival of Cotytto
Coüs *see* **Coos**
Cō·us -a -um *adj* Coan, of Cos ‖ *n* Coan wine ‖ *npl* Coan garments
covinnār·ius -(i)ī *m* soldier who fought from a chariot
covinn·us -ī *m* war chariot *(of Britons and Belgae, with scythes attached to the axles),* coach *(for travel)*
cox·a -ae *f* hip; haunch *(of an animal)*
coxend·ix -īcis *f* hip; hipbone
crābr·ō -ōnis *m* hornet; **irritare crabrones** *(fig)* to stir up a hornet's nest
cramb·ē -ēs *f* cabbage; **crambe repetita** warmed-over cabbage; *(fig)* same old story, hackneyed writing
Crant·or -ōris *m* Greek Academic philosopher *(fl 300 B.C.)*
crāpul·a -ae *f* drunkenness; hangover; **crapulam obdormire** to sleep off a hangover
crāpulāri·us -a -um *adj* for getting rid of a hangover
crās *adv* tomorrow
crassē *adv* thickly; rudely, confusedly; dimly
crassitūd·ō -inis *f* thickness, density; dregs
crass·us -a -um *adj* thick, dense; stout, plump; *(fig)* dense, dull
Crass·us -ī *m* Lucius Licinius Crassus *(famous orator, d. 90 B.C.)* ‖ Marcus Licinius Crassus Dives *(triumvir) (112?–53 B.C.)*
crastin·us -a -um *adj* tomorrow's; **die crastini** *(old abl form)* tomorrow ‖ *n* tomorrow; **in crastinum differre** to put off till tomorrow
crāt·ēr -ēris *m or* **crātēr·a -ae** *f* mixing bowl; bowl; crater of a volcano ‖ **Crater** *m (astr)* Bowl *(a constellation)*
crāt·is -is *f* wickerwork; lattice work; harrow; ribs of shield; crisscross structure; cage; *(anat)* rib cage; *(mil)* faggots *(for filling trenches)*
creāti·ō -ōnis *f* election, appointment; procreation *(of children)*
creāt·or -ōris *m* creator; procreator, father; founder; one who appoints
creātr·ix -īcis *f* creatress; mother
crē·ber -bra -brum *adj* numerous, crowded; repeated; frequent; luxuriant, prolific *(growth)*
crēbr·ēscō -ēscēre -uī *intr* to increase; to become frequent; to become widespread; to gain strength
crēbrit·ās -ātis *f* frequency; density
crēbrō *adv* repeatedly, frequently, again and again; thickly, densely

crēdibil·is -is -e *adj* credible, trustworthy; convincing, plausible; likely; **credibile est** *(w. acc & inf)* it is probable that

crēdibiliter *adv* credibly

crēdit·or -ōris *m* creditor, lender

crēd·ō -ĕre -idī -itus *tr* to lend, loan; to entrust; to believe, accept as true; to believe in; to think, suppose, imagine; *(w. predicate adj)* to believe to be, regard as ‖ *intr (w. dat)* to believe, put faith in, have trust *or* confidence in; **credas** one would imagine, you can imagine; **credo** *(in replies)* I think so; *(parenthetical)* I suppose ‖ **refl** *(w. dat)* to entrust oneself to ‖ *v impers* **satis creditum est** it is believed on good evidence

crēdulit·ās -ātis *f* credulity, trustfulness

crēdul·us -a -um *adj* credulous, trustful; gullible; *(w. dat or in + acc)* trusting in

crem·ō -āre -āvī -ātus *tr* to burn; to burn alive; *(of fire)* to consume; to cremate; *(w. dat)* to offer as a burnt offering to

Cremōn·a -ae *f* town in N. Italy

Cremōnens·is -is -e *adj* of Cremona

crem·or -ōris *m* thick broth; gravy; thickened juice

cre·ō -āre -āvī -ātus *tr* to create; to produce; to elect *or* appoint *(to office);* to cause, occasion; to beget, bear

Cre·ōn -ontis *or* **Cre·ō -onis** *or* **-ōnis** *m* Creon *(brother of Jocasta and brother-in-law of Oedipus)* ‖ Creon *(king of Corinth who gave his daughter in marriage to Jason)*

crep·er -era -erum *adj* dark; *(fig)* obscure, uncertain, doubtful

crepid·a -ae *f* slipper, sandal

crepidāt·us -a -um *adj* wearing sandals *or* slippers

crepid·ō -inis *f* base, pedestal; pier; dike; curb, sidewalk

crepidul·a -ae *f* small sandal *or* slipper

crepitācill·um -ī *n* small rattle

crepit·ō -āre -āvī -ātum *intr* to make noise, rattle, creak, chatter, rumble, rustle; *(of flames)* to crackle

crepit·us -ūs *m* noise, rattle, creak, chatter, rumble, rustle, crackle; *(vulg)* fart; **crepitum ventris emittere in convivio** *(vulg)* to let a fart at a dinner party; **crepitus digitorum** snap(ping) of the fingers

crep·ō -āre -uī *tr* to rattle; to talk noisily about, rattle on about ‖ *intr* to make noise, rattle, crackle, creak, chatter, rustle; *(of the stomach)* to rumble; *(of doors)* to creak; *(of flames)* to crackle; *(vulg)* to fart

crepundi·a -ōrum *fpl* toy rattle; **in crepundiis** in earliest childhood

crepuscul·um -ī *n* twilight; dimness, obscurity ‖ *npl* darkness

Crē·s -ētis *m* a Cretan; Cretan dog

crescō crescĕre crēvī crētum *intr* to come into being, arise; to grow, grow up; to increase *(in size, amount, numbers, length, quantity, dimensions);* to swell; to expand; *(of rivers)* to rise; *(of period of time)* to advance, progress; to prosper, thrive; to become great; to swell with pride; **crescunt nobis animi** our spirits rise; **die crescente** as the day progressed

Crēsi·us -a -um *adj* Cretan

Cress·a -ae *adj (fem only)* Cretan; of chalk ‖ *f* Cretan woman; Ariadne

crēt·a -ae *f* whitish clay; clayey soil; chalk; finish line *(in a chariot race);* **creta figularis** *(or* **figlina)** potter's clay; **creta fullonia** fuller's earth; **creta sutoria** shoe polish

Crēt·a -ae *or* **Crēt·ē -ēs** *f* Crete; *(fig)* the Cretans

Crētae·us -a -um *adj* Cretan

Crētān·ī -ōrum *mpl* Cretans

crētāt·us -a -um *adj* whitened with chalk *(feet of slaves about to be auctioned off);* dressed in white *(as candidate)*

crēte·us -a -um *adj* of chalk, of clay, clayey

Crētic·us -a -um *adj* Cretan ‖ *m (pros)* Cretic (foot) (— ∪ —)

crēti·ō -ōnis *f (leg)* formal acceptance of an inheritance; *(leg)* terms laid down for making the declaration of acceptance

Crēt·is -idis *adj (fem only)* Cretan

crētōs·us -a -um *adj* clayey

crētul·a -ae *f* white clay

crēt·us -a -um *pp of* **cerno** *and of* **cresco** ‖ *adj (w. abl or* **ab** *or* **de)** sprung from

Creūs·a -ae *f* daughter of Priam and wife of Aeneas ‖ daughter of Creon (king of Corinth), and wife of Jason ‖ mother of Ion

crībr·um -ī *n* sieve; **imbrem in cribrum gerere** *(fig)* to swim against the tide *(literally, to carry rain water in a sieve)*

crīm·en -inis *n* indictment; reproach; guilt; crime; **esse in crimine** to be arraigned; **in crimen adduci** *(or* **poni** *or* **venire** *or* **vocari)** to be indicted; *(of actions)* to be called into question

crīmināl·is -is -e *adj (leg) (opp.* **civilis)** criminal

crīmināti·ō -ōnis *f* indictment; accusation; slander

crīmināt·or -ōris *m* accuser

crīmin·ō -āre *or* **crīmin·or -āri -ātus sum** *tr* to indict, accuse; to slander; to complain of; to denounce

crīminōsē *adv* by way of accusation, accusingly; slanderously

crīminōs·us -a -um *adj* accusatory, reproachful; shameful

crīnāl·is -is -e *adj* for the hair; **acus crinalis** hairpin ‖ *n* hairpin

crīn·is -is *m (f)* hair *(of the head);* lock of hair; tail of a comet

crīnīt·us -a -um *adj* long-haired; **crinita draconibus ora** *(Medusa's)* snake-haired head; **crinitae angue sorores** snake-haired sisters; **stella crinita** *(or* **sidus crinitum)** comet

crīs·ō -āre -āvī -ātum *intr (sl) (of a woman)* to wiggle the buttocks, shake it up *(cf.* **ceveo)**

crisp·ans -antis *adj* curly; wrinkled

crisp·ō -āre -āvī -ātus *tr* to curl, wave *(hair);* to wave, brandish *(weapons)*

crispul·us -a -um *adj* having short curly hair

crisp·us -a -um *adj* curled, waved; curly-headed; wrinkled; tremulous, quivering

crist·a -ae *f* cockscomb; crest, plume; **mons veneris**

cristāt·us -a -um *adj* crested, plumed

critic·a -ōrum *npl* literary criticism

critic·us -ī *m* critic

croce·us -a -um *adj* of saffron; yellow, golden

crocin·um -ī *n* saffron oil *(used as perfume)*

crōc·iō *or* **groc·iō -īre** *intr* to croak

crocodīl·us -ī *m* (-dill-) crocodile

crocōt·a -ae *f* saffron-colored dress *(worn by women and transvestites)*

crocōtāri·us -a -um *adj* of saffron-colored clothes

crocōtul·a -ae *f* saffron-colored dress

croc·us -ī *m or* **croc·um -ī** *n* saffron; saffron color; saffron oil

Croes·us -ī *m* king of Lydia, famous for his wealth *(590?–546 B.C.)*

crotalistri·a -ae *f* castinet dancer

crotal·um -ī *n* castanet

Crotō(n) -ōnis *or* **Crotōn·a -ae** *f* Crotona *(town in S. Italy)*

cruciābilitāt·ēs -um *fpl* torments

cruciābiliter *adv* with torture

cruciāment·um -ī *n* torture

cruciāt·us -ūs *m* torture; mental torment; instrument of torture

cruci·ō -āre -āvī -ātus *tr* to put on the rack, torture; *(fig)* to torment ‖ *refl or pass* to suffer mental anguish

crūdēl·is -is -e *adj* cruel, hardhearted; *(w. in + acc)* cruel toward

crūdēlit·ās -ātis *f* cruelty

crūdēliter *adv* cruelly

crūd·escō -escĕre -uī *intr* to become fierce; *(of battle, disease)* to get rough

crūdit·ās -ātis *f* indigestion

crūd·us -a -um *adj* bloody, bleeding; uncooked *(food);* raw *(meat; wound);* unripe, green *(fruit);* untanned *(hide);* undigested *(food);* suffering from indiges-

tion; hoarse; hardy, vigorous *(old age);* coarse, rude; fierce, wild, savage

cruent·ō -āre -āvī -ātus *tr* to bloody, stain with blood; *(fig)* to wound

cruent·us -a -um *adj* gory, blood-stained; bloodthirsty; blood-red

-cr·um -ī *neut suf* denoting place or instrument: **sepulcretum** cemetery; **involucrum** wrapper, envelope

crumēn·a -ae *f* (-mīn-) purse, pouch; *(fig)* money supply

crumill·a -ae *f* small purse

cru·or -ōris *m* blood, gore ‖ *mpl* bloodshed, murder

cruppellāri·ī -ōrum *mpl* warriors in full armor

crūrāl·is -is -e *adj* of the shin; **fasciae crurales** puttees

crūricrepid·a -ae *m (hum) (of one who has chains rattling around his legs)* "rattle-legs"

Crūrifrag·ius -(i)ī *m (comic slave name)* "Broken-shins"

crūs crūris *n* leg; shin; upper support of a bridge

cruscul·um -ī *n* little leg

crusm·a -atis *n* tune

crust·a -ae *f* crust, shell; peel, rind; inlaid work

crustul·um -ī *n* cookie

crust·um -ī *n* pastry

Crustumīn·us -a -um *adj* of Crustumerium *or* Crustumium *(town in the Sabine district)*

crux crucis *f* cross; crucifixion; torment; tormentor; **ī in malam crucem!** *(coll)* go hang yourself!

crypt·a -ae *f* (cru-) underground passage, covered gallery; tunnel; crypt

cryptoportic·us -ūs *f* covered walk

crystallin·us -a -um *adj* (crus-) made of crystal ‖ *npl* crystal vases

crystall·us -ī *f or* **crystall·um -ī** *n* (crus-) crystal

cub·ans -antis *adj* lying down; low-lying

cubiculāri·us -a -um *adj* bedroom- ‖ *m* chamberlain

cubicul·um -ī *n* bedroom; emperor's box in the theater *or* circus; **a cubiculo** (imperial) chamberlain

cubīl·e -is *n* bed, couch; marriage bed; lair, nest, hole; kennel

cubit·al -ālis *n* elbow cushion

cubitāl·is -is -e *adj* of the elbow; one cubit long *(i.e., 17 to 21 inches)*

cubit·ō -āre -āvī -ātum *intr* to lie down, be in the habit of lying down; *(w. cum)* to go to bed with, have intercourse with

cubit·um -ī *n* elbow; forearm; cubit; **cubitum ponere** *(fig)* to sit down to dinner

cubitūr·a -ae *f* reclining, lying down

cubit·us -ūs *m* lying down; sexual intercourse

cub·ō -āre -uī *or* **-āvī -itum** *intr* to lie, lie down; to recline at table; to lie in bed; to take one's rest, sleep; to be confined to bed; *(of bones)* to rest; *(of roof)* to slope; *(of towns)* to lie on a slope; *(w.* **cum)** to have intercourse with

cub·us -ī *m* cube; lump

cucull·us -ī *m* cowl, hood

cucūl·us -ī *m* cuckoo; *(pej)* ninny

cucum·is -is *or* **-eris** *m* cucumber

cucum·a -ae *f* large kettle *(for cooking)*

cucurbit·a -ae *f* gourd; *(sl)* dolt, dummy; *(med)* cupping glass

cūd·ō -ĕre *tr* to strike, beat, pound; to thresh; to forge; to coin, stamp

cuicuimodī *or* **quoiquoimodī** *adj* of any kind

cūj·ās *or* **cūj·ātis -ātis** *interrog pron* from what country?; **Scipio eum percontatus est quis et cujas esset** Scipio asked who he was and from what country he came

cūjus *(gen of* **quī, quae, quod, quis, quid)** *pron (interrog)* whose, of whom **‖** *(interrog)* whose?

cūjusnam *(gen of* **quisnam, quidnam)** *pron (interrog)* just whose, exactly whose?

-cul·a -ae *fem suf* forms diminutives: **uxorcula** dear wife

culcit·a -ae *f* mattress, feather tick; cushion, pillow

culcitell·a *or* **culcitul·a -ae** *f* small cushion

cūleus *see* **culleus**

cul·ex *or* **cul·ix -icis** *mf* gnat

culīn·a -ae *f* kitchen; cuisine

culle·us -ī *m* (**cūle-**) leather bag *(for holding liquids);* leather sack *(in which criminals were sewn and drowned); (sl)* scrotum

culm·en -inis *n* peak; summit; stalk; *(fig)* pinnacle, height; **fabae culmen** bean stalk

culm·us -ī *m* stalk, stem; straw, thatch; hay

culp·a -ae *f* fault, blame; sense of guilt; imperfection, fault, defect; *(poet)* cause of blame; **in culpā esse** *(or* **versari)** to be at fault

culpit·ō -āre *tr* to blame

culp·ō -āre -āvī -ātus *tr* to blame, reproach; to find fault with, complain of

cult·a -ōrum *npl* standing crops; grain fields

cultē *adv* elegantly, sophisticatedly

cultell·us -ī *m* small knife

cul·ter -trī *m* knife; razor; plowshare

culti·ō -ōnis *f* cultivation, tilling

cult·or -ōris *m* tiller, cultivator, planter, farmer; inhabitant; supporter; worshiper

cultrār·ius -(i)ī *m* one who slew the victim

cultr·ix -īcis *f* cultivator *(female);* worshiper *(female);* inhabitant *(female)*

cultūr·a -ae *f* tilling, cultivating; agriculture; cultivation *(e.g., of the mind, important friendships)*

cult·us -a -um *pp of* **colo ‖** *adj* tilled, cultivated; neat, prim; refined, civilized, cultured

cult·us -ūs *m* tilling, cultivation; care, tending *(of flocks);* training, education; culture, refinement, civilization; high style of living; luxury; style of dress, fancy clothes; fancy outfit; worship, reverence; cult; management *(of a household);* **cultus corporis** personal care, personal grooming; **cultus vitae** standard of living

culull·us -ī *m* drinking cup

-cul·um -ī *neut suf* **1** denoting places: **cubiculum** place for sleeping; **2** denoting instruments: **curriculum** small chariot

cūl·us -ī *m (sl)* ass, anus

-cul·us -ī *masc suf* **1** forming diminutives: **pisciculus** little fish; **2** nouns ending in **-o, -onis** and **-o -inis** take the form **-un-** before the suffix **-culus: sermunculus** small talk; **homunculus** little man, puny person

cum *prep (w. abl)* **1** *(accompaniment)* with, together with; **2** *(time)* at the same time with, at the time of, at, with; **3** *(circumstance, manner, etc.)* with, under, in, in the midst of, among, in connection with; **cum eo quod** *or* **cum eo ut** on the condition that; **cum pace** peacefully; **cum prima luce** at dawn; **cum primis** especially, particularly; **mecum** at my house; with me

cum, quum, *or* **quom** *conj* when, at the time when; whenever; while; as; since, now that, because; although; **cum maxime** just when; especially when, just while; just then; **cum primum** as soon as; **cum…tum** both…and, not only…but also, while…so too; **praesertim cum** *or* **cum praesertim** especially since; **quippe cum** since of course; **utpote cum** seeing that

Cūm·ae -ārum *fpl* town on the coast of Campania, residence of its famous Sibyl

Cūmae·us -a -um *adj* Cumaean

Cūmān·us -a -um *adj* Cumaean **‖** *n* Cicero's estate near Cumae

cūmātil·is -is -e *adj* sea-colored

cumb·a *or* **cymb·a -ae** *f* boat, skiff

cumer·a -ae *f* bin

cumīn·um -ī *n* cumin *(medicinal plant, said to produce paleness)*

cummi *indecl n or* **cumm·is -is** *f* **(gumm-)** gum

cumque, cunque, *or* **quomque** *adv* at any time

cumulātē *adv* fully, completely, abundantly

cumulāt·us -a -um *adj* heaped; abundant, vast, great; *(w. gen or abl)* abounding in

cumul·ō -āre -āvī -ātus *tr* to heap up, pile up; accumulate; to fill up, overload; to increase, augment; *(fig)* to crown

cumul·us -ī *m* heap, pile; increase; *(fig)* finishing touch, crown; *(fig)* peak, pinnacle; **summus cumulus** highest point

cūnābul·a -ōrum *npl* cradle

cūn·ae -ārum *fpl* cradle; *(poet)* nest

cunctābund·us -a -um *adj* hesitant

cunct·ans -antis *adj* hesitant, slow to act; clinging

cunctanter *adv* hesitantly, slowly

cunctāti·ō -ōnis *f* hesitation, reluctance, delay

conctāt·or -ōris *m* dawdler, slow-poke, procrastinator ‖ **Cunctātor** Quintus Fabius Maximus Cunctator *(cautious general who constantly avoided battles with Hannibal, d. 203 B.C.)*

cunct·or -ārī -ātus sum *intr* to hesitate, delay, linger; to be in doubt; **cunctatu brevi** after a moment's hesitation

cunct·us -a -um *adj* all together, the whole, all, entire

-cund·us -a -um *adjl suf* denoting a tendency: **iracundus** inclined toward anger, irascible

cuneātim *adv* in the form of a wedge, in tight formation

cuneāt·us -a -um *adj* wedge-shaped

cune·ō -āre -āvī -ātus *tr* to fasten with a wedge; *(fig)* to wedge in, squeeze in

cuneol·us -ī *m* small wedge; pin

cune·us -ī *m* wedge; wedge-form section of seats in the theater; *(mil)* troops formed in shape of wedge

cunīculōsus -a -um *adj* full of rabbits

cunīcul·us -ī *m* rabbit; burrow, hole; tunnel; water conduit, channel; *(mil)* mine

cunil·a -ae *f (bot)* savory *(aromatic plant used as seasoning)*

cunniling·us -a -um *adj (vulg)* cunt-sucking

cunnu·s -ī *m (vulg)* cunt

cunque *see* **cumque**

cūp·a -ae *f* vat

cuped- = **cupped-**

cupidē *adv* eagerly

Cupīdine·us -a -um *adj* Cupid's, charming, alluring

cupidit·ās -ātis *f* eagerness, longing, desire; passion, lust; ambition; greed; object of one's desire

cupīd·ō -inis *mf* eagerness, desire; carnal desire, lust; greed ‖ **Cupido** *m* Cupid, son of Venus

cupid·us -a -um *adj* eager; lecherous; ambitious; *(w. gen)* desirous of, longing for, fond of, enthusiastic about

cupi·ens -entis *adj* eager, enthusiastic; *(w. gen)* desirous of, longing for, fond of, enthusiastic about

cupienter *adv* eagerly

cup·iō -ere -īvī *or* **-iī -ītus** *tr* to wish, be eager for, long for, desire

cupīt·or -ōris *m* daydreamer

cuppēdenār·ius -(i)ī *m* pastry baker

cuppēdi·a -ōrum *npl* or **cūpēdi·a -ae** *f* sweets; delicacies; sweet tooth

cuppēdinār·ius -(i)ī *m* **(cūpēd-)** confectioner

cuppēd·ō -inis *f see* **cupido**

cupp·ēs -edis *adj* gluttonous

cupressēt·um -ī *n* cypress grove

cupresse·us -a -um *adj* cypress-

cupressif·er -era -erum *adj* cypress-bearing

cupress·us -ī *or* **-ūs** *f* cypress tree

cūr *or* **qūr** *or* **cuūr** *or* **quor** *adv* why

cūr·a -ae *f* care, concern, worry; carefulness, attention, pains; (a person's) attention; heartache; object of concern; sweetheart; task, reponsibility, post; administration, management, charge; trusteeship, care; guardian, keeper; study, reflection; literary effort, study, literary work; *(w. gen)* eagerness for, anxiety about, zeal for; *(med)* treatment; *(med)* cure; **in curā esse** *(w. dat)* to be a matter of concern to, be dear to; **in curā habere** to hold dear, care dearly about; **curā** purposely; **curae esse** *(w. dat)* to be of concern to; to be dear to; **curae habere** to hold dear

cūrābil·is -is -e *adj* troublesome; needing medical treatment

cūral·ium *or* **corall·ium -(i)ī** *n* coral

cūrāti·ō -ōnis *f* management, administration; office; *(med)* treatment

cūratius *adv* more carefully

cūrāt·or -ōris *m* superintendent, manager; *(leg)* guardian

cūrātūr·a -ae *f* care, attention; superintendence

cūrāt·us -a -um *adj* well cared-for; anxious, sollicitous, earnest

curculi·ō -ōnis *m* **(gurg-)** weevil; *(vulg)* penis

curculiuncul·us -ī *m* little weevil; *(fig)* trifle

Cur·ēs -ium *mpl* ancient Sabine town

Cūrēt·es -um *mpl* people of Crete who attended Jupiter at his birth

cūri·a -ae *f* Senate Building; meeting of the Senate; curia, ward *(one of the 30 wards into which Romulus had divided the people)*

cūriāl·is -is -e *adj* belonging to a ward ‖ *m* ward member

cūriātim *adv* by wards

cūriāt·us -a -um *adj* composed of wards; passed by the assembly of wards; **comitia**

curiata assembly of wards, curiate assembly

cūri·ō -ōnis m ward boss; **curio maximus** chief ward boss

cūriōsē adv carefully; curiously

cūriōsit·ās -ātis f curiosity, inquisitiveness

cūriōs·us -a -um careful, diligent; curious, inquisitive; careworn

cur·is or quir·is -ītis f spear

cūr·ō -āre -āvī -ātus tr to take care of, look after, attend to, trouble oneself about; to worry about; to take charge of, see to; to procure; to provide for the payment of, settle up; to attend to *(the body with food, washing, etc.); (med)* to treat; *(med)* to cure; **cura ut** see to it that; *(at end of letter)* **cura ut valeas** take care of yourself; **cutem curare** to look after one's appearance

curriculō adv at full speed, on the double

curricul·um -ī n race; lap; racetrack; racing chariot; *(fig)* career

curr·ō currĕre cucurrī cursus tr to run over, skim over, traverse ‖ intr to run, dash; to sail; to move quickly, flow along; to fly; *(of night, day)* to pass

curr·us -ūs m chariot, car; war chariot; triumphal car; triumph; racing chariot; *(poet)* plow wheel; *(poet)* ship

cursim adv on the double, quickly

cursit·ō -āre -āvī intr to keep running around, run up and down; to vibrate

curs·ō -āre -āvī intr to run around, run up and down

curs·or -ōris m runner, racer; courier; errand boy

cursūr·a -ae f running; haste, speed

curs·us -ūs m running, speeding, speed; trip; course, direction; suitable time or weather for travel; rapid movement, flow; progress; **magno cursu** at top speed; **cursus honorum** political career

Curt·ius -a -um adj Roman clan name *(nomen), esp.* Quintus Curtius Rufus *(who wrote a history of Alexander the Great's campaigns)* ‖ **Lacus Curtius** area of the Roman Forum that was once a pond

curt·ō -āre -āvī -ātus tr to shorten; *(hum)* to circumcise

curt·us -a -um adj shortened; gelded, castrated; *(hum)* circumcised; broken; defective

curūl·is -is -e adj official, curule; **aedilis curulis** patrician aedile; **sella curulis** curule chair, official chair *(inlaid with ivory, used by consuls, praetors, and patrician aediles)*

curvām·en -inis n curve, bend

curvātūr·a -ae f curvature; **curvatura rotae** rim of a wheel

curv·ō -āre -āvī -ātus tr to curve, bend, arch; *(fig)* to affect, move, stir

curv·us -a -um adj curved, bent; crooked; concave, arched; hollow, winding *(stream, shore); (fig)* crooked ‖ n wrong, crookedness

-c·us -a -um adjl suffix formed from nouns: **bellicus** warlike

cusp·is -idis f point; bayonet; spearhead; spear, javelin; trident; scepter; sting *(of a scorpion)*

custōdēl·a -ae f charge, custody *(of a person or thing)*

custōdi·a -ae f protection, safekeeping, defense; preservation *(of a practice, etc.);* place for safekeeping; watch, care; sentry, guard; sentry post; custody, confinement, prison; prisoner, *(collectively)* prisoners; **custodiam agitare** to be on guard; **in liberā custodiā** under surveillance, under house arrest

custōd·iō -īre -īvī or -iī -ītus tr to guard, watch over, protect, defend; to hold in custody; to keep an eye on; to keep carefully, preserve; **memoriā custodire** to keep in mind

cust·ōs -ōdis m guard; guardian; watchman; protector; jailer; *(mil)* sentinel; **custos corporis** bodyguard ‖ mpl garrison ‖ f guardian; protectress; container

cutīcul·a -ae f skin

cut·is -is f skin; **cutem curare** to look after one's appearance; *(fig)* to look after one's own skin

Cyan·ē -ēs f spring in Syracuse; nymph who was changed into that spring

cyathiss·ō -āre -āvī intr to ladle out wine

cyath·us -ī m ladle; liquid measure *(half pint)*

cybae·a -ae f merchant ship

Cybel·ē -ēs f (-bēbē) Phrygian goddess of fertility, worshipped in Rome as Ops or Magna Mater ‖ mountain of Phrygia

Cybelēi·us -a -um adj of Cybele

Cybel·us -ī m mountain in Phrygia

cyb·ium -(i)ī n young tuna fish

Cyclad·ēs -um fpl Cyclades *(group of islands, roughly forming a circle, in the Aegean Sea)*

cycl·as -adis f woman's formal gown ‖ **Cyclas** one of the Cyclades Islands

cyclic·us -a -um adj cyclic; **poeta cyclicus** cyclic poet *(one of a group of poets treating epic sagas revolving around the Trojan War)*

Cyclopi·us -a -um adj Cyclopian

Cycl·ops -ōpis m one-eyed giant of Sicily, *esp.* Polyphemus

cycladāt·us -a -um adj wearing a formal gown

cycn·us -ī m (cyg-) swan; *(fig)* poet ‖ **Cycnus** king of the Ligurians, changed into a swan, and placed among the stars as a constellation ‖ son of Neptune

Cyd·ōn -ōnis adj Cydonian, of Cydonea

(a city on the N. coast of Crete) ‖ *m* inhabitant of Cydonea
Cydōnae·us -a -um *adj* (-ē·us) Cydonian; *(esp. as poetic epithet for arrows)* Cretan
Cydōne·a -ae *f* city on the N. coast of Crete
Cydōni·us -a -um *adj* Cretan ‖ *n* quince
cygnus *see* **cycnus**
cylindr·us -ī *m* cylinder; roller *(for rolling the ground);* cylindrical jewel
Cyllēn·ē -ēs *or* **-ae** *f* mountain in Arcadia where Mercury was said to have been born
Cyllēnē·us *or* **Cyllēni·us -a -um** *adj* of Mt. Cyllene ‖ *m* Mercury
cymb·a -ae *f* (cum-) boat, skiff
cymbal·um *or* **cymbal·on -ī** *n* (*usu. pl, esp. as used in the worship of Cybele)* cymbal; *(fig)* tedious speaker
cymb·ium -(i)ī *n* small cup
Cynicē *adv* like the Cynics
Cynic·us -a -um *adj* Cynic, relating to the Cynic philosophy ‖ *m* Cynic philosopher, *esp.* Diogenes, its founder *(412– 323 B.C.)*
cynocephal·us -ī *m* dog-headed ape
Cynosūr·a -ae *f (astr)* Cynosure *(the constellation Ursa Minor)*
Cynthi·us -a -um *adj* of Mt. Cynthus; Cynthian ‖ *m* Apollo ‖ *f* Diana
Cynth·us -ī *m* low mountain on Delos, where Latona is said to have given birth to Apollo and Diana
cypariss·us -ī *f* cypress tree
cypress·us -ī *or* **-ūs** *f* cypress tree; box made of cypress
Cypri·us -a -um *adj* Cypriote; **aes Cyprium** copper ‖ *f* Venus
Cypr·us *or* **Cyp·ros -ī** *f* Cyprus *(island off S. coast of Asia Minor)*
Cypsel·us -ī *m* despot of Corinth *(reigned 655–625 B.C.)*
Cȳrēn·ē -ēs *for* **Cyrēn·ae -ārum** *fpl* chief city of Greek settlement in N.E. Africa
Cȳrēnae·us *or* **Cȳrēnaic·us -a -um** *or* **Cȳrēnens·is -is -e** *adj* of Cyrene
Cȳrē·us -a -um *adj* of Cyprus
Cyrnē·us -a -um *adj* Corsican
Cyrn·os -ī *f* Greek name for Corsica
Cȳr·us -ī *m* father of Cambyses and founder of the Persian monarchy in 559 B.C. *(d. 529 B.C.)* ‖ Cyrus the Younger, son of Darius Nothus, whose famous march against his brother Artaxerxes is recorded by Xenophon *(d. 401 B.C.)*
Cyt·ae -ārum *fpl* town in Colchis, reputed birthplace of Medea
Cytae·is -idis *f* Medea
Cythēr·a -ōrum *npl* island off the S. coast of the Peloponnesus, famous for the worship of Venus
Cytherē·is -idis *f* Venus
Cytherēī·us -a -um *adj* Cytherean; **heros Cytherēïus** Aeneas ‖ *f* Venus

Cytherē·us -a -um *adj* Cytherean ‖ *f* Venus
cytis·us -ī *mf or* **cytis·um -ī** *n* clover
Cytōriāc·us -a -um *adj* of Cytorus, Cytorian; **pecten Cytoriacus** comb made of boxwood
Cytōr·us *or* **Cytōr·os -ī** *m* mountain in Paphlagonia, famous for its boxwood
Cȳzicēn·us -a -um *adj* of Cyzicus
Cyzic·um -ī *n or* **Cyzic·us** *or* **Cyzic·os -ī** *f* town on S. coast of Propontis

D

D *abbr* **quingenti** five hundred
D. *abbr* **Decimus** *(Roman first name, praenomen)*
Dāc·ī -ōrum *mpl* Dacians
Dāci·a -ae *f* Roman province on the lower Danube *(roughly modern Rumania)*
Dācic·us -a -um *adj* Dacian ‖ *m* gold coin struck under Domitian, conqueror of Dacia
dactylic·us -a -um *adj (pros)* dactylic
dactyliothēc·a -ae *f* ring case
dactyl·us -ī *m (pros)* dactyl (— ∪ ∪)
daedal·us -a -um *adj* skillful, artistic; intricately constructed ‖ **Daedal·us -ī** *m* builder of the Labyrinth in Crete and the first person to construct wings and fly
Damascēn·us -a -um *adj* of Damascus ‖ *npl* plums from Damascus
Damasc·us *or* **Damasc·os -ī** *f* city in Syria
damm·a *or* **dām·a -ae** *f* deer; venison
damnāti·ō -ōnis *f* condemnation; *(w. gen of the crime)* conviction on the charge of; **damnatio ambitūs** conviction on illegal campaign practices; **condemnatio pecuniae** a fine
damnātōri·us -a -um *adj (leg)* guilty *(verdict)*
damnāt·us -a -um *adj (leg)* found guilty; hateful, damn
damnific·us -a -um *adj* harmful
damnigerul·us -a -um *adj* injurious
damn·ō -āre -āvī -ātus *tr (leg)* to find guilty, convict; to sentence, condemn; to secure the condemnation of; to offer as a sacrifice, doom to the gods below; to pass judgment on *(a case); (w. dat of the aggrieved person)* to deliver by judicial sentence to, award *(s.o. s.th.); (w. abl)* to fine *(s.o.)* in the amount of; *(w. gen or abl)* to find fault with for; *(w. gen or abl of the charge)* to find *(s.o.)* guilty of; **aliquem voti damnare** to condemn s.o. to the amount he has vowed; **capite** *(or* **capitis) damnare** to condemn to death; **de majestate damnare** to find guilty of treason; **exilio damnari** to be sentenced to ex-

ile; **voti damnare** to oblige *(s.o.)* to fulfill a vow

damnōsē *adv* ruinously

damnōs·us -a -um *adj* damaging, destructive; prodigal; **canes damnosi** crap *(worst throw of dice)*

damn·um -ī *n* loss, damage, harm; fine; defect; *(w. gen)* forfeiture of; *(mil)* losses; **damnum explere** *(or* **sarcire)** to make good a loss; **damnum facere** to incur a loss; to cause loss *(to another)*; **naturae damnum** a natural defect

Dana·ē -ēs *f* daughter of Acrisius and mother, by Zeus, of Perseus

Danaïd·es -um *fpl* fifty daughters of Danaüs

Dana·üs -ī *m* Danaüs *(son of Belus and brother of Aegyptus and king of Argos)* **ǁ** *mpl* Greeks

danist·a -ae *m* moneylender, banker

danistic·us -a -um *adj* moneylending, banking

danō *see* **do**

Dānuv·ius -(i)ī *m* Upper Danube *(opp:* **Hister** = Lower Danube)

Daphn·ē -ēs *f* nymph pursued by Apollo and changed into a laurel tree

Daphn·is -idis *(acc:* **-im** *or* **-in)** *m* handsome young Sicilian shepherd, inventor of pastoral poetry

dapin·ō -āre *tr* to serve *(food)*

dap·s -is *f* ceremonial feast; feast; banquet; feed *(for animals)*

dapsil·is -is -e *adj* sumptuous, costly

Dardanid·ēs -ae *m* descendant of Dardanus; Trojan; Roman

Dardan·is -idis *or* **-idos** *adj (fem only)* Trojan

Dardan·us -a -um *adj* Dardanian, Trojan; Roman *(descendant of Aeneas)* **ǁ** *m* son of Jupiter and ancestor of the Trojan race **ǁ** *mpl* Illyrian tribe; a people of Asia Minor

Dārē·us *or* **Dārī·us -ī** *m* Darius *(521–485 B.C., Persian king whose generals were defeated by the Greeks at Marathon in 490 B.C.)* **ǁ** Darius Nothus *(424–405 B.C., son of Artaxerxes I)* **ǁ** Darius Codomanus *(last king of Persia, reigned 336–331 B.C.)*

datāri·us -a -um *adj* to be handed out, to be given away

datātim *adv* giving *or* tossing from hand to hand *(in games)*

dati·ō -ōnis *f* giving, allotting; transfer *(e.g., of property)*

datīv·us -a -um *adj & m (gram)* dative

dat·ō -āre -āvī -ātus *tr* to keep giving

dat·or -ōris *m* giver

dat·us -ūs *m* giving

Daul·is -idis *f* town in Phocis, famous for the fable of Procne and Philomela

Daun·us -ī *m* mythical king of Apulia, the father of Turnus

dē *prep (w. abl)* **1** *(of space)* down from, from, away from, out of; **2** *(of origin)* from, of, descended from: **Priami de stirpe Diores** Diores of Priam's lineage; **3** *(of separation)* from among, out of: **noctem de die facere** to make night out of day; **4** *(in partitive sense)* of, out of: **dimidium de praedā dare** to give half of the booty; **5** *(of time)* immediately after; **diem de die** day after day; **6** *(of reference)* about, on, concerning, of, in respect to: **oratio de domo sua** a speech concerning his own home; **7** according to, in imitation of: **castae de more puellae** like a chaste girl *(literally, according to the manner of a chaste girl)*; **8** *(of cause)* for, on account of, because of: **quā de causā** for that reason, wherefore; **9** *(of which s.th. is made)* **templum de marmore** a marble temple, a temple (made) of marble; **10** *(indicating persons over whom victory is gained)* over: **de Samnitibus triumphavit** he held a triumph for his victory over the Samnites; **11** *(indicating change)* from, out of: **de templo carcerem facere** to make a prison out of a temple; **de improviso** unexpectedly; **de industriā** on purpose; **de integro** afresh, all over again; **de nocte** *(or* **de vigiliā)** at night; **de novo** anew

dē- **(dĕ** before vowels and **h)** *pref* indicating: **1** motion down from or away: **dependere** to hang down; **2** removal, deprivation: **despolire** to despoil; **3** left behind: **derelinquere** to leave behind; **4** reversal of process: **deonerare** to unload; **5** completely, to the end: **depugnare** to fight it out, fight to the finish; **6** down, from the right path or state or norm: **deformis** ugly; **7** intensity: **deamare** to love passionately

de·a -ae *(dat & abl pl:* **deābus)** *f* goddess

dealb·ō -āre -āvī -ātus *tr* to whiten, whitewash

deambulāti·ō -ōnis *f* strolling, walking about, walk, stroll

deambul·ō -āre -āvī -ātum *intr* to go for a walk

deam·ō -āre -āvī -ātus *tr* to love passionately

dearm·ō -āre -āvī -ātus *tr* to disarm

deartu·ō -āre -āvī -ātus *tr* to tear limb from limb, dismember

deasci·ō -āre -āvī -ātus *tr* to smooth with an ax; *(fig)* to cheat, con

dēbacch·or -ārī -ātus sum *intr* to rant and rave

dēbellāt·or -ōris *m* conqueror

dēbell·ō -āre -āvī -ātus *tr* to fight it out

with, wear down, subdue **II** *intr* to fight it out to the end; to bring a war to an end

dēb·eō -ēre -uī -itus *tr* to owe; to be responsible for; *(w. inf)* 1 to have to, be obliged to; 2 to be destined to; **debeo abire I** ought to leave **II** *pass (w. dat)* to be due to

dēbil·is -is -e *adj* crippled, frail, feeble; ineffective

dēbilit·ās -ātis *f* lameness; debility, weakness, feebleness

dēbilitāti·ō -ōnis *f* disabling, enfeebling

dēbilit·ō -āre -āvī -ātus *tr* to disable; to debilitate, weaken; to unnerve; *(fig)* to paralyze

dēbiti·ō -ōnis *f* debt

dēbit·or -ōris *m* debtor; person under obligation

dēbit·um -ī *n* debt; obligation

dēblater·ō -āre -āvī -ātus *tr* & *intr* to blurt out

dēcant·ō -āre -āvī -ātus *tr* to repeat monotonously; to reel off **II** *intr* to sing on to the end; to stop singing

dē·cēdō -cēdĕre -cessī -cessum *intr* to withdraw, depart, clear out; to retreat; to make way, make room, yield; to disappear; to die; to abate, subside, cease; to go wrong; *(w. dat)* to give in to; *(w. de + abl)* to give up, abandon, relinquish

decem *indecl adj* ten

Decem·ber -bris -bre *adj* December, of December; **mensis December** (month of) December *(tenth month of the Roman calendar until 153 b.c.)* **II Decem·ber -bris** *m* December

decemjug·is -is *m* ten-horse chariot

decemped·a -ae *f* ten-foot measuring rod, ten-foot rule

decempedāt·or -ōris *m* surveyor

decempl·ex -icis *adj* tenfold

decemprīm·ī *or* **decem prīm·ī -ōrum** *mpl* ten-man council *(governing Italic towns)*

decemscalm·us -a -um *adj* ten-oared

decem·vir -virī *m* decemvir *(member of a board of ten)*

decemvirāl·is -is -e *adj* decemviral; **leges decemvirales** laws passed by the decemviri

decemvirāt·us -ūs *m* decemvirate

decemvir·ī -ōrum *mpl* board of ten *(appointed in Rome at different times and for various purposes: maintaining Sibylline books, distribution of land; codifying the XII Tables; deciding whether a person was free or slave);* **decemviri sacris faciundis** commission for attending to religious matters

decenn·is -is -e *adj* ten-year, lasting ten years

dec·ens -entis *adj* decent, proper, becoming; handsome, pretty

decenter *adv* decently, properly

decenti·a -ae *f* decency, propriety

dē·cernō -cernĕre -crēvī -crētus *tr* to sift, separate; to decide, determine, settle; to resolve, decree, vote; to decide by combat; to fight, combat **II** *intr* to contend, compete, struggle; to put forward a proposal; *(w. de or pro + abl)* to fight over, fight for *(in court)*

dēcerp·ō -ĕre -sī -tus *tr* to pluck off, tear off, break off; to gather *(fruit, grapes);* to pick *(flowers);* to derive *(e.g., benefits, satisfaction);* **aliquid de gravitate decerpere** to detract somewhat from dignity

dēcertāti·ō -ōnis *f* decisive struggle

dēcert·ō -āre -āvī -ātum *intr* to fight it out, decide the issue

dēcessi·ō -ōnis *f* withdrawing; retirement, departure *(from a province);* decrease; disappearance

dēcess·or -ōris *m* retiring official; predecessor *(opp: successor)*

dēcess·us -ūs *m* withdrawal; retirement *(of an official from a province);* decease, death

dec·et -ēre -uit *(used only in inf and 3rd sing & pl) tr* to befit; to lend grace to; to adorn **II** *v impers (w. inf)* it is proper for *(s.o.)* to; *(w. dat & inf)* it is proper *or* right for *(s.o.)*

dēcī·dō -dĕre -dī *intr* to fall down; to die; to drop; to sink; *(of things)* to fail, go wrong; to end up, land; *(of plants)* to wilt

dēcī·dō -dĕre -dī -sus *tr* to cut off, cut away; to cut down; to cut short, terminate; to settle *(a matter);* **pennas decidere** *(w. dat) (fig)* to clip *(s.o.'s)* wings **II** *intr (w. cum)* to come to terms with

deciens *adv* (**-iēs**) ten times; **deciens centena milia** *(or simply* **deciens**) a million; **bis deciens** two million

decimānus *see* **decumanus**

decimum *adv* for the tenth time

decim·us -a -um *adj* (**-cum-**) the tenth; **cum decimo** tenfold; **cum decimo effecit ager** the field produced a tenfold return

dē·cipiō -cipĕre -cēpī -ceptus *tr* to deceive, cheat; to dupe, mislead; to frustrate, disappoint; to escape the notice of; **aliquem laborum decipere** to make s.o. forget his troubles

dēcīsi·ō -ōnis *f* settlement

dēcīsum *pp of* **dēcīdō**

Dec·ius -(i)ī *m* Publius Decius Mus *(father and son, who gave their lives to save the Roman army)*

dēclāmāti·ō -ōnis *f* practice in public speaking; practice speech; theme *(in a practice speech)*

dēclāmāt·or -ōris *m* student of public speaking, declaimer

dēclāmātōri·us -a -um *adj* rhetorical

dēclāmit·ō -āre -āvī -ātus *tr* to plead *(cases)* ‖ *intr* to practice public speaking

dēclām·ō -āre -āvī -ātus *tr* to recite ‖ *intr* to practice public speaking, declaim

dēclārāti·ō -ōnis *f* declaration, disclosure, announcement; **declaratio amoris** an expression of affection

dēclār·ō -āre -āvī -ātus *tr* to make clear, make evident, disclose; to proclaim, announce officially; to show, prove, demonstrate; to mean, express, signify; to declare *(e.g., s.o. consul)*

dēclīnāti·ō -ōnis *f* deviation, swerve; inclination; avoidance; digression; *(gram)* declension

dēclīn·ō -āre -āvī -ātus *tr* to deflect; to parry, avoid; *(gram)* to decline, conjugate ‖ *intr* to deviate; to digress

dēclīvē -is *n* slope; **per declive** downwards

dēclīv·is -is -e *adj* sloping, steep, down-hill

dēclīvit·ās -ātis *f* sloping terrain

dēcoct·or -ōris *m* bankrupt

dēcoct·us -a -um *pp of* **decoquo** ‖ *adj* luscious; ripe; over-ripe; mellow *(style)* ‖ *f* cold drink

dēcoll·ō -āre -āvī -ātus *tr* to behead

dēcōl·ō -āre -āvī *intr* to drain away, come to naught, fail

dēcol·or -ōris *adj* off-color, faded; dark-skinned; degenerate, depraved

dēcolōr·ō -āre -āvī -ātus *tr* to discolor, stain, deface; to disgrace

dēco·quō -quĕre -xī -ctus *tr* to boil down, boil thoroughly; to bring to ruin; to digest *(food)* ‖ *intr* to go bankrupt

dec·or -ōris *m* beauty, grace, elegance, charm; ornament

decōrē *adv* beautifully, gracefully; suitably, properly

decor·ō -āre -āvī -ātus *tr* to beautify, adorn, embellish; to decorate, honor

decōr·us -a -um *adj* beautiful, graceful; glorious, noble; suitable, proper, decorous ‖ *n* grace; propriety

dēcoxī *perf of* **decoquo**

dēcrepit·us -a -um *adj* decrepit, broken down, worn out

dē·crescō -crescĕre -crēvī -crētum *intr* to grow less, become fewer, diminish, fade; *(of time)* to grow shorter; *(of water)* to subside, go down

dēcrēt·us -a -um *pp of* **decerno** ‖ *n* decree, decision; principle

decum·a -ae *f* **(-cim-)** one-tenth; tithe, land tax; largess to the people

decumān·us -a -um *adj* **(-cim-)** paying tithes; of the tenth legion, of the tenth cohort; subject to the 10% tax; **porta decumana** main gate of Roman camp on the side turned away from the enemy ‖ *m* tax collector ‖ *mpl* men of the tenth legion ‖ *f* tax collector's wife

decumāt·ēs -ium *adj* subject to tithes

dē·cumbō -cumbĕre -cubuī *intr* to lie down; to recline at table; to fall *(in battle)*

decuri·a -ae *f* decury *(unit in Roman government consisting of ten families)*; group of ten *(organized for work, recreation, etc.)*; panel *(from which jury members were selected)*; social club, society

decuriāti·ō -ōnis *f or* **decuriāt·us -ūs** *m* dividing into decuries

decuri·ō -āre -āvī -ātus *tr (fig)* to divide into groups; *(pol)* to divide into groups of ten

decuri·ō -ōnis *m* squad leader *(in the cavalry or navy in charge of ten men)*; councilman *(of a municipality or colony)*; chief chamberlain

dē·currō -currĕre -(cu)currī -cursus *tr* to run down, hurry down *(e.g., a path)*; to travel over *(a course)*, to cover *(a distance)*; to make straight for; to turn to *(s.o.)* for help; to pass through *(life)*; to run through *(mentally, in a speech)*, discuss, treat ‖ *intr* to run down; to run for exercise, jog; *(of liquids)* to run down, flow down; *(of terrain)* to slope down; *(of rivers, ships)* to run down to the sea; *(of ships, travelers)* to come to land; to travel downstream; *(mil)* to run through a drill, carry out maneuvers, parade ‖ *v impers* **eo decursum est ut** it got to the point where

dēcursi·ō -ōnis *f* raid; *(mil)* drill, maneuvers, dress parade

dēcurs·us -ūs *m* running down; downward course; *(mil)* maneuvers; *(mil)* dress parade; *(mil)* attack from higher ground; *(rhet)* the flow *(of a sentence, verse)*; **decursio honorum** completion of a political career

dēcurtāt·us -a -um *adj* cut down, cut off short, mutilated; clipped *(style)*

dec·us -oris *n* beauty, glory, honor, dignity; virtue, worth; source of glory ‖ *npl* achievements

dēcuss·ō -āre -āvī -ātus *tr* to divide crosswise *(in the form of an X)*

dēcu·tiō -tĕre -ssī -ssus *tr* to shake off, beat off, strike down; to chop off *(head)*; to break down *(wall with battering ram)*

dēdec·et -ēre -uit *v impers* it ill befits; *(w. inf)* it is a disgrace to

dēdecor·ō -āre -āvī -ātus *tr* to disgrace, dishonor, bring shame to; to make a sham of

dēdecōr·us -a -um *adj* disgraceful, dishonorable, unbecoming

dēdec·us -oris *n* disgrace, dishonor, shame; vice, crime, outrage; *(mil)* disgraceful defeat; **dedecori esse** *(w. dat)* to be a source of disgrace to; **dedecus admittere** to incur disgrace; **per dedecus** disgracefully

dēdicāti·ō -ōnis f dedication, consecration
dēdic·ō -āre -āvī -ātus tr to dedicate, consecrate, set aside; to declare *(property in a census return)*
dēdign·or -ārī -ātus sum tr to disdain, look down on; *(w. double acc)* to scorn *(s.o.)* as; **aliquem maritum dedignari** to regard s.o. as an unworthy husband
dē·discō -discĕre -didicī tr to unlearn, forget
dēditic·ius -(i)ī m prisoner-of-war
dēditi·ō -ōnis f surrender
dēdit·us -a -um pp of dedo **ll** adj *(w. dat)* given to, devoted to; addicted to; *(w.* **in** + *acc)* absorbed in **ll** mpl prisoners-of-war
dēd·ō -ĕre -idī -itus tr to give up, surrender; to devote; to apply; to abandon; **deditā operā** on purpose; **neci** *(or* **ad necem) dedere** to put to death
dēdoc·eō -ēre -uī -tus tr to cause to forget; *(w. inf)* to teach *(s.o.)* not to
dēdol·eō -ēre -uī intr to feel pain no more
dēdol·ō -āre -āvī -ātus tr to hew into shape
dēdū·cō -cĕre -xī -ctus tr to lead *or* draw down; to launch *(ship)*; to accompany, escort; to lead out *(colonists to new colony)*; to conduct *(bride to husband)*, give *(bride)* away; to evict; to subtract, deduct; to summon *(as witness)*; to divert; to mislead; to derive *(name)*; to compose *(poetry)*; to comb out *(hair)*; to draw out *(thread in spinning)*; to lure *(into a trap)*; *(leg)* to arraign; *(pol)* to install *(in a position of authority)*; **rem huc** *(or* **eo) deducere ut** to bring things to the point that
dēducti·ō -ōnis f draining *(of water)*; settling of colonists; subtraction, deduction; inference; *(leg)* eviction; **rationis deductio** line of reasoning; **sine ulla reductione** in full
dēduct·or -ōris m escort
dēduct·us -a -um pp of deduco **ll** adj drawn down; bent inwards, concave; lowered, modest; subtle, well-wrought *(poem)*; **nasus deductus** pug nose
deërr·ō -āre -āvī -ātum intr to go astray, wander away, get lost; to stray; to go wrong
dēfaec·ō -āre -āvī -ātus tr to remove the dregs of, strain; *(fig)* to clear up
dēfatīgāti·ō -ōnis f (-fet-) exhaustion
dēfatīg·ō -āre -āvī -ātus tr (-fet-) to exhaust
dēfatiscor *see* defetiscor
dēfecti·ō -ōnis f failure; defection, desertion; weakening, exhaustion; *(astr)* eclipse; *(gram)* ellipsis; **defectio animi** mental breakdown; **in defectione esse** to be in revolt
dēfect·or -ōris m defector, deserter

dēfect·us -a -um pp of deficio **ll** adj weak, worn out
dēfect·us -ūs m failing, failure; desertion, defection; *(astr)* eclipse
dēfen·dō -dĕre -dī -sus tr to defend, protect, guard; to repel, beat off, avert; to keep off *(the cold, heat);* to answer *(a charge);* to support, uphold *(argument);* to play the part of *(a character); (leg)* to defend; *(w. dat)* to ward off *(s.th. harmful)* from; **solstitium pecori defendere** to ward off the noonday heat from the flock, protect the flock from the noonday heat
dēfensi·ō -ōnis f defense
dēfensit·ō -āre -āvī -ātus tr to defend *(often);* **causas defensitare** to be a lawyer
dēfens·ō -āre -āvī -ātus tr to defend, protect
dēfens·or -ōris m defender, protector; champion *(leg)* defense lawyer; *(leg)* defendant; *(leg)* guardian
dēfensus pp of defendo
dē·ferō -ferre -tulī -lātus tr to bring *or* carry down; to bear off, carry away; to drive *(ship)* off course; to offer, confer, grant; to inform against, indict; to give an account of; to announce, report; to recommend; to register; **aliquem ad aerarium deferre** to recommend s.o. for a monetary reward; **ad consilium deferre** to take into consideration
dēfer·vescō -vescĕre -v(u)ī *or* -buī intr to stop boiling, cool off; *(fig)* to calm down
dēfess·us -a -um adj weary, tired
dēfetigō *see* defatigo
dē·fetiscor -fetiscī -fessus sum intr (-fat-) to get tired; *(w. inf)* to tire of
dē·ficiō -ficĕre -fēcī -fectus tr to fail, disappoint; to desert, abandon **ll** intr to fail, be a failure; *(of supplies, etc.)* to run short, run out; *(of strength, morale)* to fail, sink; *(of sun, moon)* to be eclipsed; *(of a family line, race)* to become extinct; *(of fire)* to die out; *(w. dat or* **ad**) to be insufficient for; *(com)* to be bankrupt; *(mil, pol)* to defect; *(pol)* to secede
dēfī·gō -gĕre -xī -xus tr to fix, fasten down; to drive down; to fix, concentrate *(eyes, attention);* to root to the spot, astound; to bewitch; **in terra defigere** to stick *or* plant *or* set *(s.th.)* up in the ground; to stick *(weapon into s.o.)*
dēfin·gō -gĕre -xī tr to form, mold; to disfigure
dēfīn·iō -īre -īvī *or* -iī -ītus tr to mark out the limits of *(a place);* to limit, restrict; to define; to fix, determine, appoint; to bring to a finish, put an end to; to assign, prescribe
dēfīnītē *adv* precisely

dēfīnīti·ō -ōnis f boundary; *(fig)* marking out, prescribing; definition

dēfīnītīv·us -a -um *adj* finite, limited; definite, precise

dēfīnxī *perf of* **dēfingō**

dē·fīō -fīerī *intr* to fail, be lacking, be in short supply

dēflagrāti·ō -ōnis f conflagration

dēflagr·ō -āre -āvī -ātus *tr* to burn down **ǁ** *intr* to burn down; to perish, be destroyed; *(of passions)* to cool off

dē·flectō -flectĕre -flexī -flexus *tr* to deflect, bend aside, turn away, divert; *(fig)* to modify, twist; to bend *(a bow);* to lead astray **ǁ** *intr* to digress, deviate

dēfl·eō -ēre -ēvī -etus *tr* to cry bitterly for; to lament; to mourn as lost **ǁ** *intr* to cry bitterly

dēflocc·ō -āre -āvī -ātus *tr* to rub the nap off *(cloth); (fig)* to fleece

dēfloccāt·us -a -um *adj (hum)* bald

dēflōr·escō -escĕre -uī *intr* to shed blossoms; *(fig)* to fade, droop

dēflu·ō -ĕre -xī -xum *intr* to flow *or* float down; to glide down; to slide, fall; to drain off, run dry; to vanish, pass away, cease; to go out of style; *(w.* ab) to be descended from

dē·fodiō -fodĕre -fōdī -fossus *tr* to dig down; to hollow out; to bury, hide, conceal

dēfore = **dēfutūrum esse**

dēformāti·ō -ōnis f configuration; disfigurement

dēform·is -is -e *adj* shapeless; misshapen, disfigured, ugly; degrading; degraded; humiliating; unbecoming

dēformit·ās -ātis f deformity, ugliness, hideousness; vileness; lack of good taste *(in writing)*

dēformiter *adv* without grace; shamefully

dēform·ō -āre -āvī -ātus *tr* to form from a pattern; to sketch, delineate; to deform, disfigure, mar

dēfossus *pp of* **dēfodiō**

dēfraud·ō *or* **dēfrūd·ō -āre -āvī -ātus** *tr* to defraud, rob; to cheat; **animum** *(or* se *or* **genium suum) dēfraudāre** to deny oneself some pleasure

dēfrēm·ō -ĕre -uī *intr* to quiet down

dēfrēnāt·us -a -um *adj* unbridled

dēfric·ō -āre -uī -tus *or* **-ātus** *tr* to rub down; to brush *(teeth); (fig)* to satirize

dē·fringō -fringĕre -frēgī -fractus *tr* to break off, break to pieces

dēfrūdō *see* **dēfraudō**

dēfrut·um -ī *n* new wine

dē·fugiō -fugĕre -fūgī *tr* to run away from, avoid, shirk; to evade *(e.g., authority, law)* **ǁ** *intr* to run off

dēfunct·us -a -um *pp of* **dēfungor ǁ** *adj* finished; dead

dē·fundō -fundĕre -fūdī -fūsus *tr* to pour out; to empty

dēfun·gor -gī -ctus sum *intr (w.* abl) 1 to perform, carry out; 2 to finish, be done with; 3 to have done with, get rid of; **dēfunctus honoribus** having ended a public career; **dēfunctus jam sum** I'm safe now; **dēfungi (vitā)** to die; **quasi dēfunctus regis imperio** as if carrying out the king's order; **suā morte dēfunctus est** he died a natural death

dēfūsus *pp of* **dēfundō**

dēfutūt·us -a -um *adj (vulg)* worn out from excessive sex

dēgen·er -eris *adj* degenerate; unworthy; ignoble

dēgener·ō -āre -āvī -ātus *tr* to disgrace, dishonor; to fall short of **ǁ** *intr* to degenerate; *(w.* ad *or* in + *acc)* to sink to

dēger·ō -ĕre *tr* to carry off

dēg·ō -ĕre *tr* to spend, pass *(time);* to spend one's time in **ǁ** *intr* to spend one's time, live

dēgrandin·at -āre *v impers* it is hailing hard

dēgrav·ō -āre — -ātus *tr* to weigh down; *(fig)* to burden, distress, inconvenience, overpower

dē·gredior -gredī -gressus sum *intr* to march down, go down, walk down, descend; *(from a standard)* to depart; **ad pedes dēgredī** to dismount

dēgrunn·iō -īre *intr* to grunt loud

dēgust·ō -āre -āvī -ātus *tr* to taste; *(fig)* to taste, sample, try, experience; *(of weapon)* to graze

dehinc *adv* from here, from now on, after this; then, next; hereafter

dehisc·ō -ĕre *intr* to part, divide, gape, yawn; to develop a crack; *(w.* in + *acc)* to split open and reveal

dehonestāment·um -ī *n* blemish, disfigurement, dishonor, disgrace

dehonest·ō -āre -āvī -ātus *tr* to dishonor, disgrace

dehort·or -ārī -ātus sum *tr* to dissuade, discourage; **multa mē dehortantur ā vobis** many things tell me to keep my distance from you

dein *see* **deinde**

deinceps *adv* one after another, in succession, in order; without interruption; *(of time)* from now on, from then on, after that, after this, next; *(of space)* beyond that; **et deinceps** and so on

deinde *or* **dein** *adv (of place)* from that place, from there; *(of time)* then, thereafter, thereupon, afterwards; *(in enumerating facts, presenting arguments)* secondly, in the next place

Dēïphob·us -ī *m* son of Priam and Hecuba, and husband of Helen after Paris' death

Dējanīr·a -ae *f* daughter of Oeneus and wife of Hercules

dējecti·ō -ōnis *f (leg)* eviction

dēject·us -a -um *pp of* **dejicio ‖** *adj* low, depressed, sunken *(place);* downhearted, depressed, despondent

dējer·ō -āre -āvī -tum *tr & intr* (**-jūr-**) to swear solemnly

dē·jiciō -jicĕre -jēcī -jectus *tr* to throw down, fling down; to fell, kill *(sacrificial victim); (of winds)* to drive off course; to depose, fire *(from office);* to lower *(eyes);* to banish *(feelings); (leg)* to evict; *(mil)* to dislodge; *(w. abl or de + abl)* to deprive *(s.o.)* of, prevent *(s.o.)* from obtaining, rob *(s.o.)* of; **a re publica oculos dejicere** to take one's eyes off the government; **de gradu** *(or* **de loco** *or* **de statu) dejicere** to throw off balance; **mente sua dejectus** driven out of one's mind; **sortem dejicere** to cast a lot *(into an urn)*

dējun·gō -gĕre -xī -ctus *tr* to unyoke; to sever

dējūrō *see* **dejero**

dējuv·ō -āre *tr* to refuse to help

dēlā·bor -bī -psus sum *intr* to slip down, fall down, sink; to glide down, float down; *(of water)* to flow down; *(fig)* to stoop, condescend; *(w.* ad) to be inclined toward, be partial to; *(w.* in + acc) to sneak in among

dēlacer·ō -āre -āvī -ātus *tr* to tear to pieces

dēlāment·or -ārī -ātus sum *tr* to grieve deeply for

delass·ō -āre -āvī -ātus *tr* to tire out, weary

dēlāti·ō -ōnis *f* reporting; informing, denouncing; **nominis delatio** indicting a person

dēlāt·or -ōris *m* reporter; *(leg)* informer

dēlātus *pp of* **defero**

dēlēbil·is -is -e *adj* able to be obliterated

dēlectābil·is -is -e *adj* delightful; delicious

dēlectāment·um -ī *n* delight; amusement, pastime

dēlectāti·ō -ōnis *f* delight, pleasure, amusement; satisfaction

dēlect·ō -āre -āvī -ātus *tr* to delight; to amuse, charm; to attract, allure; **delectari** *(w. abl)* to delight in **‖** *v impers* **me ire delectat** I like to go, I enjoy going

dēlect·us -ūs *m* choosing, choice; *(mil)* recuitment; *(mil)* recruits

dēlēgāti·ō -ōnis *f (leg)* assignment to a third party of a creditor's interest in a debt

dēlēg·ō -āre -āvī -ātus *tr* to assign, appoint *(s.o. to a task);* to ascribe *(credit, blame);* to transfer *(ownership of property)*

dēlēnific·us -a -um *adj* soothing, ingratiating

dēlēniment·um -ī *n* allurement, bait; solace, comfort

dēlēn·iō -īre -iī -ītus *tr* (**-līn-**) to soothe, calm down, console, appease; to allure, win over

dēlēnīt·or -ōris *m* charmer

dēl·eō -ēre -ēvī -ētus *tr* to destroy; to annihilate; to overthrow; to extinguish; to raze; to blot out, erase; to put an end to, abolish

dēlētr·ix -īcis *f* destroyer *(female)*

Dēliac·us -a -um *adj* Delian, of Delos

dēlīberābund·us -a -um *adj* deep in thought

dēlīberāti·ō -ōnis *f* considering, weighing; deliberation, consultation; **habet res deliberationem** the matter requires thought

dēlīberātīv·us -a -um *adj* deliberative; requiring deliberation

dēlīberāt·or -ōris *m* thoughtful person

dēlīberāt·us -a -um *adj* resolved upon, determined

dēlīber·ō -āre -āvī -ātus *tr* to weigh, think over; to resolve; to consult *(an oracle)* **‖** *intr* to deliberate; *(w.* de + abl) to think over; *(w.* cum) to consult

dēlīb·ō -āre -āvī -ātus *tr* to sip, take a sip of; to taste, take a taste of, nibble at; to take away, subtract, remove; to touch on *(subject)*

dēlibr·ō -āre -āvī -ātus *tr* to strip the bark off

dēlibūt·us -a -um *adj* anointed; defiled, smeared, stained; steeped

dēlicātē *adv* delicately; luxuriously

dēlicāt·us -a -um *adj* delicate, dainty, tender; pampered; frivolous; fastidious, squeamish; self-indulgent; luxurious **‖** *mf* favorite

dēlici·ae -ārum *fpl* delight, pleasures; sweetheart, darling; pet, favorite; comforts, luxuries; ornaments; mannerisms, airs; **delicias facere** to enjoy oneself; to have fun *(at s.o. else's expense);* **delicias facere** *(w. dat) (sl)* to play around with *(a girl);* **esse in deliciis** *(w. dat)* to be the pet *or* favorite of; **habere in deliciis** to have as a pet *or* favorite

dēliciol·ae -ārum *fpl* darling

dēlic·ium -(i)ī *n* darling; pet

dēlic·ō -āre *tr* (**-qu·ō**) to make clear

dēlict·um -ī *n* fault, offense, wrong; defect *(in a thing)*

dēlicu·us -a -um *adj* (**-liqu-**)lacking, missing

dēlig·ō -āre -āvī -ātus *tr* (**-leg-**) to tie up, fasten; *(med)* to bandage

dē·ligō -ligĕre -lēgī -lectus *tr* to pick off; to pick out, choose, select; to gather *(mil)* to draft; *(mil)* to hold a draft in *(a place)* dēlin·g(u)ō -g(u)ĕre -xī *tr* to lick off; to have a lick of

dēlīni- = deleni-

dēlin·ō -ĕre — -itus *tr* to smudge

dē·linquō -linquĕre -līquī -lictus *tr (w. neut pron)* to commit *(an offense);* majora delinquere to commit greater wrongs; si quid deliquero if I commit some offense ‖ *intr* to be missing; to be wanting, fall short; to do wrong, commit an offense

dē·liquescō -liquescĕre -licuī *intr* to melt, dissolve; to pine away

dēliqui·ō -ōnis *f* failure; *(w. gen)* failure to get; *(astr)* eclipse

dēliqu·ium -(i)ī *n* failure

dēliquō *see* delico

dēlīrāment·um -ī *n* nonsense, delusion, absurdity

dēlīrāti·ō -ōnis *f* silliness, folly, madness; infatuation; dotage

dēlīr·ō -āre *intr* to be off the beam, be crazy; to rave

dēlīr·us -a -um *adj* crazy, silly; senseless; in dotage

dēlit·escō -escĕre -uī *intr* (-tisc-) to conceal oneself, lie hidden, lurk

dēlītig·ō -āre *intr* to rant, have it out

Dēli·us -a -um *adj* Delian, of Delos, of Apollo ‖ *m* Apollo

Dēl·os -ī *f* sacred island in the Cyclades, where Apollo and Diana were born

Delph·ī -ōrum *mpl* town in Phocis, in Central Greece, famous for the shrine and oracle of Apollo ‖ people of Delphi

Delphic·us -a -um *adj* of Delphi; of Apollo ‖ *f* three-legged table

delphīn·us -ī *or* delph·īn -īnis *m* dolphin ‖ Delphinus *(astr)* Dolphin *(constellation)*

Delph·is -idis *f* Delphic priestess of Apollo

delta *indecl n* delta *(letter of the Greek alphabet)* ‖ Delta the Delta *(of the Nile River)*

Deltōt·on -ī *n (astr)* Triangle *(constellation)*

dēlūbr·um -ī *n* shrine, sanctuary

dēluct·ō -āre -āvī *or* dēluct·or -ārī -ātus sum *intr* to wrestle

dēlūdific·ō -āre -āvī -ātus *tr* to make fun of

dēlū·dō -dĕre -sī -sus *tr* to fool, con

dēlumb·is -is -e *adj* lame

dēlumb·ō -āre *tr* to lame in the loins; *(fig)* to weaken

dēmad·escō -escĕre *intr* to become drenched, become wet; to be moistened

dēmand·ō -āre -āvī -ātus *tr* to hand over, entrust

dēmān·ō -āre -āvī *intr* to run down

dēmarch·us -ī *m* demarch *(chief of a village in Attica); (fig)* tribune of the people

dēm·ens -entis *adj* demented, out of one's mind; senseless, reckless

dēmens·us -a -um *pp of* dēmetior ‖ *n* ration, allowance

dēmenter *adv* insanely

dēmenti·a -ae *f* insanity; folly

dēment·iō -īre *intr* to be insane

dēmer·eō -ēre -uī -itus *or* dēmer·eor -ērī -itus sum *tr* to earn, merit, deserve; to serve well, do a service to, win the favor of

dēmer·gō -gĕre -sī -sus *tr* to sink; to plunge, dip; to bury ‖ *pass (of heavenly bodies)* to set

dēmessus *pp of* demeto

dēmet·ior -īrī -mensus sum *tr* to measure out

dē·metō -metĕre -messuī -messus *tr* to mow, reap, harvest; to pick *(flowers, fruit);* to cut off

Dēmētr·ius -(i)ī *m* Demetrius Poliorcetes, son of Antigonus, and king of Macedonia ‖ Demetrius of Phaleron, famous orator and politician at Athens

dēmigrāti·ō -ōnis *f* emigration

dēmigr·ō -āre -āvī -ātum *intr* to migrate, emigrate, move, depart; *(fig)* to pass on, die

dēmin·uō -uĕre -uī -ūtus *tr* to make smaller, lessen, diminish; to deduct; *(w. abl)* to deprive of; *(w.* de + *abl)* to deduct from; capite deminuere to deprive of civil rights

dēminūti·ō -ōnis *f* lessening, diminution, abridging; *(leg)* right of disposing of property; capitis diminutio loss of civil rights; provinicae diminutio shortening of term of office

dēmīr·or -ārī -ātus sum *tr* to be surprised at, be amazed at

dēmissē *adv* low; humbly, modestly; abjectly

dēmissīci·us -a -um *adj* allowed to hang down, flowing; *(of clothes)* ankle-length

dēmissi·ō -ōnis *f* letting down, sinking, lowering; demissio animi low morale

dēmiss·us -a -um *pp of* demitto ‖ *adj* low, low-lying *(place);* drooping *(lips, etc.);* bent *(head);* flowing, long *(hair); (of clothes)* hanging down, full-length; *(fig)* downhearted, dejected; *(fig)* poor, humble; *(w. abl)* descended from

dēmītig·ō -āre *tr* to calm down

dē·mittō -mittĕre -mīsī -missus *tr* to drop, let drop, let sink; to lower; to dip; to sink *(a well);* to bring downstream; to shed *(blood);* to land *(ship);* to let down *(hair);* to grow *(beard);* to move down *(troops from a higher place);* animum *(or* mentem) demittere to become discouraged; demittere aures ad to deign to listen to ‖ *refl* to descend, go down; to stoop, bend down; *(fig)* to plunge into;

(geog) to slope downwards ‖ *pass* to descend, go down

dēmiurg·us -ī *m* **(dami-)** magistrate in a Greek state

dēm·ō -ĕre -psī -ptus *tr* to take away, remove, withdraw; *(w. dat or abl or ab or de + abl)* to take away from, remove from, subtract from, withhold from; **vincla pedibus demere** to remove the fetters

Dēmocrit·us -ī *m* philosopher from Abdera in Thrace and founder of the atomic theory *(born c. 460 B.C.)*

dēmōl·ior -īrī -ītus sum *tr* to demolish, pull down

dēmōlīti·ō -ōnis *f* demolishing

dēmonstrāti·ō -ōnis *f* pointing out; explanation; description

dēmonstrātīv·us -a -um *adj* showy

dēmonstrāt·or -ōris *m* one who points out, indicator

dēmonstr·ō -āre -āvī -ātus *tr* to point out clearly; to state precisely, explain, describe; to mention, speak of; to demonstrate, prove, establish

Dēmoph(o)·ōn -ontis *m* son of Theseus and Phaedra

dēmor·ior -ī -tuus sum *tr* to be dying for ‖ *intr* to die; to die off; to become extinct

dēmor·or -ārī -ātus sum *tr* to delay, detain; to hinder, block ‖ *intr* to wait

Dēmosthen·ēs -is *or* **-ī** *m* greatest Greek orator *(384–322 B.C.)*

dē·moveō -movēre -mōvī -mōtus *tr* to remove, move away; to dispossess, expel; to oust

demptus *pp of* **demo**

dēmūgīt·us -a -um *adj* bellowing, lowing

dēmul·ceō -cēre -sī *tr* to stroke lovingly, pet

dēmum *adv* at last, finally; not till then; *(to give emphasis)* precisely, exactly, just; *(to give assurance)* in fact, certainly, to be sure, as a matter of fact; **decimo demum anno** not till the tenth year; **modo demum** only now, not until now; **nunc demum** now at last, not until now; **post demum** not until afterwards; **tum demum** then finally, not until then

dēmurmur·ō -āre *tr* to grumble through *(e.g., a performance)*

dēmūtāti·ō -ōnis *f* transformation

dēmūt·ō -āre -āvī -ātus *tr* to change; to make worse ‖ *intr* to fail; to change one's mind

dēnār·ius -iī *m* denarius *(about $1); money*

dēnarr·ō -āre -āvī -ātus *tr* to recount in detail

dēnās·ō -āre *tr* to bite the nose off *(s.o.'s face)*

dēnat·ō -āre *intr* to swim downstream

dēneg·ō -āre -āvī -ātus *tr* to deny, refuse, turn down ‖ *intr* to say no

dēn·ī -ae -a *adj* in sets of ten, ten each, in tens; tenth

dēnicāl·is -is -e *adj* purifying from death; **feriae denicales** purification service *(after death in the household)*

dēnique *adv* finally, at last; in short, in a word; *(for emphasis)* just, precisely; *(ironical)* of course; **octavo denique mense** not till after the eighth month; **tum denique** then at last, only then, not till then

dēnōmin·ō -āre -āvī -ātus *tr (w. ab or ex)* to name after

dēnorm·ō -āre *tr* to make crooked *or* irregular; to disfigure, spoil

dēnot·ō -āre -āvī -ātus *tr* to mark down, specify; to take careful note of; to observe closely

dens dentis *m* tooth; ivory; point, prong; fluke; *(of an elephant)* tusk; **albis dentibus deridere aliquem** *(prov)* to laugh heartily at s.o.; **dens Indus** elephant's tusk

densē *adv* closely, thickly, in quick succession, repeatedly

denseō *see* **denso**

densit·ās -ātis *f* closeness; thickness

dens·ō -āre -āvī -ātus *or* **dens·eō -ēre** *tr* to thicken; to press close together; to close *(ranks);* to condense

dens·us -a -um *adj* dense, close, thick, crowded; frequent, repeated; intense *(love, cold);* concise *(style)*

dentāl·ia -ium *npl* plow beam

dentāt·us -a -um *adj* toothed; serrated; *(of paper)* polished smooth

dentifrangibul·us -a -um *adj (hum)* tooth-breaking ‖ *m* thug ‖ *n* fist

dentifric·ium -(i)ī *n* tooth powder

dentileg·us -ī *m (hum)* toothpicker *(one who picks up teeth after they have been knocked out)*

dentiscalp·ium -(i)i *n* toothpick

dent·iō -īre *intr* to teethe

dēnū·bō -bĕre -psī -ptum *intr (of a woman)* to marry beneath her rank; to go through a mock marriage

dēnūd·ō -āre -āvī -ātus *tr* to strip naked, strip bare; to expose, leave unprotected; *(fig)* to lay bare

dēnumer·ō -āre -āvī -ātus *tr* to pay *(money)* in full, pay down

dēnuntiāti·ō -ōnis *f* intimation; warning, threat; announcement, proclamation; **senatūs denuntiatio** senate ordinance; **testimoni denuntiatio** summons to testify

dēnunti·ō -āre -āvī -ātus *tr* to intimate; to give notice of; to announce officially; to give official warning to; to warn, threaten; *(mil)* to report to; **denuntiare testimonium** *(w. dat)* to give *(s.o.)* a summons to testify

dēnuō adv anew, once more, all over again; **denuo alius** yet another

deoner·ō -āre tr to unload

deopt·ō -āre tr to choose

deorsum adv (-sus) downwards, down; (of position) down below, underneath

deoscul·or -ārī -ātus sum tr to shower with kisses

dēpasciscor see **depeciscor**

dēpact·us -a -um adj fastened down

dēparc·us -a -um adj very stingy

dē·pascō -pascĕre -pāvī -pastus or **dē·pascor -pascī -pastus sum** tr to eat up; to feed on; to graze on; to feed the cattle on (grass, etc.); to consume, to destroy, waste; (fig) to prune off (excesses in style)

dēpec·iscor -iscī -tus sum tr (-pac-) to agree on, come to terms on; to bargain for

dēpe·ctō -ctĕre — -xus tr to comb out; (fig) to flog

dēpeculāt·or -ōris m embezzler, crook

dēpecūl·or -ārī -ātus sum tr to embezzle; to steal

dē·pellō -pellĕre -pulī -pulsus tr to drive off, drive away; to drive out; to avert; (mil) to dislodge; (w. quin or w. ab or de + abl) to deter from, dissuade from, wean from ‖ intr to deviate

dēpend·eō -ēre -ī intr to hang down; (w. abl) to be derived from; (w. ab or de + abl) to depend on; (w. ex) to hang down from

dēpen·dō -dĕre -dī -sus tr to pay up; to pay (penalty)

dēper·dō -dĕre -didī -ditus tr to lose completely; to ruin, destroy

dēper·eō -īre -iī tr to be hopelessly in love with ‖ intr to go to ruin, perish; to be lost, be finished

dēpexus pp of **depecto**

dēpilāt·us -a -um adj plucked; (fig) swindled, gypped

dē·pingō -pingĕre -pinxī -pictus tr to paint, portray; to embroider; (fig) to portray, describe, represent

dēplan·gō -gĕre -xī tr to beat one's breast in mourning over; to grieve over, cry one's heart out over

dēplex·us -a -um adj grasping

dēplōrābund·us -a -um adj complaining bitterly; sobbing

dēplōr·ō -āre -āvī -ātus tr to cry over, mourn; to despair of ‖ intr to cry bitterly, take it hard

dēplu·it -ĕre -it v impers it is raining hard, is pouring down

dē·pōnō -pōnĕre -posuī (posīvī) -pos(i)tus tr to put down, put aside; to get rid of; to bet; to deposit; (w. apud + acc) to entrust to, commit to the care of; **bellum deponere** to give up war; **imperium deponere** to relinquish power

dēpopulāti·ō -ōnis f ravaging, pillaging

dēpopulāt·or -ōris m marauder

dēpopul·ō -āre -āvī -ātus or **dēpopul·or -ārī -ātus sum** tr to ravage, pillage, lay waste; (of diseases) to ravage; (fig) to wreck, destroy

dēport·ō -āre -āvī -ātus tr to carry down; to carry away; to bring home, win (victory); to transport; to banish

dē·poscō -poscĕre -poposcī tr to demand; to require, call for; to request earnestly; to challenge

dēposit·us -a -um pp of **depono** ‖ adj despaired of ‖ n deposit (as down-payment; for safekeeping); **depositi agere** to sue for breach of trust; **depositi damnare** to convict of breach of trust

dēprāvātē adv perversely

dēprāvāti·ō -ōnis f distorting; (fig) distortion; perversity, perversion

dēprāv·ō -āre -āvī -ātus tr to make crooked, distort; to pervert, corrupt, seduce; to misrepresent

dēprecābund·us -a -um adj imploring

dēprecāti·ō -ōnis f supplication, averting by prayer; invocation, earnest entreaty; (w. gen) intercession against (danger, etc.)

dēprecāt·or -ōris m intercessor; (w. gen) champion of

dēprec·or -ārī -ātus sum tr to pray against, avert by prayer; to pray for, beg for; to intercede on behalf of; to plead in excuse ‖ intr to pray; to make an entreaty

dēprehen·dō -dĕre -dī -sus or **dēpren·dō -dĕre -dī -sus** tr to get hold of; to arrest; to catch, intercept; to surprise, catch in the act; to detect, discover; to perceive, understand; to embarrass

dēprehensi·ō -ōnis f detection

dēpress·us -a -um pp of **deprimo** ‖ adj low (voice); low-lying (land)

dē·primō -primĕre -pressī -pressus tr to depress, weigh down; to plant deep; to dig (e.g., trench); to sink (ship) ‖ pass to sink

dēproeli·or -ārī intr to fight it out, battle fiercely

dēprōm·ō -ĕre -psī -ptus tr to take down; to bring out, produce; **pecuniam ex arca depromere** to get the money out of the safe

dēproper·ō -āre tr to make in a hurry ‖ intr to hurry

deps·ō -ĕre -uī -tus tr to knead; (vulg) to feel up

dēpud·et -ēre -uit v impers **eum depudet** he is ashamed

dēpūg·is -is adj (-pȳg-) (masc & fem only) with thin buttocks

dēpugn·ō -āre -āvī -ātum intr to fight hard; to fight it out ‖ v impers (pass) **depugnatum est** they fought hard

dēpulsī *perf of* depello
dēpulsi·ō -ōnis *f* averting; *(rhet)* defense
dēpuls·ō -āre *tr* to push aside; de via depulsare to push out of the way
dēpuls·or -ōris *m* averter
dēpulsus *pp of* depello
dēpung·ō -ĕre *tr* to mark off *(in an account by punching holes)*
dēpurg·ō -āre -āvī -ātus *tr* to clean (out) thoroughly
dēput·ō -āre -āvī -ātus *tr* to prune; to reckon, consider
dēpȳgis *see* depugis
dēque *adv* down, downwards
dērād·ō -ĕre -rāsī -rāsus *tr* to shave off; to scrape off
dērect·us -a -um *pp of* derigo; *see* directus
dērelicti·ō -ōnis *f* neglect
dēre·linquō -linquĕre -līquī -lictus *tr* to leave behind, abandon
dērepente *adv* suddenly
dērēp·ō -ĕre -sī *intr* to creep down
dēreptus *pp of* deripio
dērī·deō -dēre -sī -sus *tr* to deride ‖ *intr* to laugh it off *(i.e., get off scot-free)*
dērīdicul·us -a -um *adj* quite ridiculous, absurd ‖ *n* derision; absurdity; deridiculo esse to be the butt of ridicule
dērig·escō -escĕre -uī *intr* to grow stiff, grow rigid; to curdle
dērigō *see* dirigo
dē·ripiō -ripĕre -ripuī -reptus *tr* to tear off; to remove; to seize; to tear down, pull down
dērīs·or -ōris *m* scoffer
dērīs·us -ūs *m* derision
dērīvāti·ō -ōnis *f* diverting *(of streams);* divergence of sense; derivation *(of words)*
dērīv·ō -āre -āvī -ātus *tr* to draw off, divert; to derive
dērō·dō -dĕre — -sus *tr* to nibble away at
dēróg·ō -āre -āvī -ātus *tr* to propose to repeal *(a law)* in part; to restrict, modify; to take away
dērōs·us -a -um *adj* gnawed away, nibbled
dēruncin·ō -āre -āvī -ātus *tr* to plane off; *(fig)* to rip off
dēru·ō -ĕre -ī *tr* to throw down, demolish; *(w. de + abl)* to detract from
dērupt·us -a -um *adj* rough, steep ‖ *npl* crevasses, crags
dēsaev·iō -īre -(i)ī -ītum *intr* to rage furiously, vent one's rage; to run wild
dēsalt·ō -āre -āvī -ātus *tr* to dance; canticum desaltare to dance a number
descen·dō -dĕre -dī -sum *intr* to climb down, descend, come down; to dismount; to fall, sink; to sink in, penetrate; *(fig)* to go down, sink down, penetrate; *(fig)* to lower oneself, stoop, yield; *(mil)* to march down
descensi·ō -ōnis *f* descent; sailing down;

descensio Tiberina sailing down the Tiber
descens·us -ūs *m* climbing down, descent; slope
desc·iscō -iscĕre -īvī *or* -iī -ītum *intr* to revolt, defect; *(fig)* to depart, deviate; *(w. ab)* to deviate from, break allegiance with, revolt from; a me descii I abandoned my own principles; in monstrum desciscere to degenerate into a monster
descrī·bō -bĕre -psī -ptus *tr* to write out, transcribe, copy; to describe, portray, design, sketch
descriptē *see* discripte
descripti·ō -ōnis *f* diagram, plan; transcript; description; descriptio criminis indictment
descriptus *pp of* describo
dēsec·ō -āre -uī -tus *tr* (-sic-) to cut off
dēser·ō -ĕre -uī -tus *tr* to desert, abandon, forsake; *(leg)* forfeit
dēsert·or -ōris *m* deserter
dēsert·us -a -um *pp of* desero ‖ *adj* deserted; uninhabited ‖ *npl* wilderness, desert
dēserv·iō -īre *intr (w. dat)* to be a slave to, serve devotedly
dēs·es -idis *adj* sitting down, sitting at ease; lazy, idle; apathetic, listless
dēsicc·ō -āre *tr* to dry up; to drain
dē·sideō -sidēre -sēdī *intr* to sit idle, remain inactive
dēsīderābil·is -is -e *adj* desirable
dēsīderāti·ō -ōnis *f* missing, feeling the absence, yearing; desideratio voluptatum yearning for pleasures
dēsīder·ium -(i)ī *n* longing, missing, feeling of loss; want, need, desire; request, petition; ex desiderio laborare to be homesick; me desiderium tenet *(w. gen)* I miss, am homesick for
dēsīder·ō -āre -āvī -ātus *tr* to miss, long for; to call for, require; *(mil)* to lose *(men)* in combat ‖ *pass* to be lost, be missing, be a casualty
dēsidi·a -ae *f* idleness, inactivity; laziness; apathy
dēsidiābul·um -ī *n (coll)* place to lounge, hangout
dēsidiōsē *adv* idly
dēsidiōs·us -a -um *adj* idle, lazy; causing idleness *or* laziness; spent in idleness
dē·sīdō -sīdĕre -sēdī *or* -sīdī *intr* to sink; to subside; to settle down; in imo desidere to settle at the bottom
dēsignāti·ō -ōnis *f* specification; layout; appointment; election
dēsignātor *see* dissignator
dēsign·ō -āre -āvī -ātus *tr* to mark out, point out, designate; to outline; to define, trace; *(of words)* to denote, indicate; to earmark; to appoint, elect; consul designatus consul-elect

dē·siliō -silīre -siluī or -silīvī or -siliī -sultum intr to jump down; to dismount
dē·sinō -sinĕre -sīvī or -s(i)ī -situs tr to give up, abandon, finish with; (w. inf) to stop (doing s.th.); furere desinere to stop raging || intr to stop, come to a stop, end; to stop speaking; (w. gen) to cease from; (w. in + acc) to end in; similiter desinere to have similar endings
dēsipi·ens -entis adj foolish, silly
dēsipienti·a -ae f foolishness
dēsip·iō -ĕre intr to be silly, fool around
dē·sistō -sistĕre -stitī intr to stop, desist; to get stuck, stick; (w. abl or w. ab or de + abl) to desist from, abandon, give up (an action begun); desistere a defensione to give up the defense
dēsitus pp of desino
dēsōl·ō -āre -āvī -ātus tr to leave desolate, leave empty; to leave alone, forsake, abandon; desolatus (w. abl) deprived of
despect·ō -āre tr to look down on, overlook, command a view of; (fig) to look down on, despise
despect·us -a -um pp of despicio || adj contemptible
despect·us -ūs m commanding view, view; contempt, scorn
despēranter adv hopelessly
despērāti·ō -ōnis f desperation, despair
despērāt·us -a -um adj desperate, hopeless; despaired of
despēr·ō -āre -āvī -ātus tr to despair of || intr to despair, give up hope; (w. de + abl) to despair of
despicāti·ō -ōnis f contempt || fpl feelings of contempt
despicāt·us -a -um adj despicable; aliquem despicatum habere to hold s.o. in contempt
despicāt·us -ūs m contempt
despici·ens -entis adj contemptuous; (w. gen) contemptuous of
despicienti·a -ae f contempt
de·spiciō -spicĕre -spexī -spectus tr to despise, look down on || intr to look down; (w. in + acc) to look down on, have a view of
despic·or -ārī -ātus sum tr to despise, disdain
despoliāt·or -ōris m robber
dēspoli·ō -āre -āvī -ātus tr to strip, rob, plunder
despon·deō -dēre -dī -sus tr to pledge, promise solemnly; to promise in marriage; animum (or animos) despondere to lose heart, despair
dēspons·ō -āre tr to betroth
despūm·ō -āre -āvī -ātus tr to skim (off); to work off (i.e., digest) || intr to stop foaming
despu·ō -ĕre tr to spit out, spit down; to

avert by spitting; (fig) to reject || intr to spit on the ground (to avert evil, etc.)
desquām·ō -āre -āvī -ātus tr to scale (fish); (fig) to peel off
destill·ō -āre -āvī -ātus tr to drip, distill || intr to drip, trickle down
destimul·ō -āre tr to goad on
destināti·ō -ōnis f designation; nomination; purpose, intention; locus destinationis destination
destināt·us -a -um adj obstinate; fixed, determined; animus morti destinatus a mind set on death; destinatum est mihi (w. inf) I have made up my mind to || n design, intention; mark (aimed at); ex destinato according to plan
destin·ō -āre -āvī -ātus tr to lash down, secure; to fix, determine, resolve; to earmark; to appoint, designate; to arrange the purchase of; to aim at || intr to make up one's mind || v impers destinatum mihi est I have made up my mind
destit·uō -uĕre -uī -ūtus tr to set apart; to set down, place; to forsake; to leave high and dry, betray, desert; (w. ab) to rob of, leave destitute of
destitūti·ō -ōnis f forsaking, abandonment; disappointment
destrict·us -a -um adj severe, rigid
de·stringō -stringĕre -strinxī -strictus tr to strip; to unsheathe; to give (s.o.) a rubdown; to brush gently against, skim; (of weapon) to graze; (fig) to criticize, satirize
destructi·ō -ōnis f pulling down (e.g., of walls); destruction, demolition; refutation
destru·ō -ĕre -xī -ctus tr to pull down, demolish; (fig) to ruin
dēsubitō or dē subitō adv suddenly
dēsūdasc·ō -ĕre intr to begin to sweat all over
dēsūd·ō -āre -āvī -ātum intr to sweat; (w. dat) (fig) to sweat over
dēsuē·fīō -fierī -factus sum intr (w. ab) to become unused to, get away from
dēsu·escō -escĕre -ēvī -ētum intr (w. inf) to become unaccustomed to, get away from
dēsuētūd·ō -inis f disuse, lack of use
dēsuēt·us -a -um pp of desuesco || adj unused, out of use, obsolete; out of practice; (w. dat) unused to, unfamiliar with
dēsult·or -ōris m circus rider (who leaps from one horse to another); amoris desultor fickle lover, "butterfly"
dēsultōri·us -a -um adj of a circus rider; equus desultorius show horse
dēsultūr·a -ae f jumping down
dē·sum -esse -fuī -futurus intr to fall short, fail; to fail in one's duty; to be absent, be missing; (w. dat) 1 to be absent from, be missing from; 2 to fail to

support; **sibi deësse** to sell oneself short; **tempori deësse** *(or* **occasioni temporis)** **deësse** to pass up the opportunity

dēsūm·ō -ĕre -psī -ptus *tr* to pick out, choose; to undertake; **sibi hostem desumere** to take on an enemy

dēsuper *adv* from above

dēsur·gō -gĕre -rexī -rectum *intr* to rise; **cenā desurgere** to get up from the table; *(euphem)* to go to the toilet

dēte·gō -gĕre -xī -ctus *tr* to detect, uncover, expose, lay bare; to reveal, disclose, betray

dēten·dō -dĕre — -sus *tr* to loosen; to strike *(a tent)*

dētentus *pp of* **detineo**

dēter·geō -gĕre -sī -sus *or* **dēter·gō -gĕre** to wipe off, wipe away; *(fig)* to wipe clean

dēteri·or -or -us *adj* inferior, worse, poorer; lower in value; weaker

dēterius *adv* worse

dētermināti·ō -ōnis *f* boundary; conclusion, end

dētermin·ō -āre -āvī -ātus *tr* to bound, limit; *(rhet)* to conclude *(sentence, period)*

dē·terō -terĕre -trīvī -trītus *tr* to rub away, wear away; to wear out; to lessen, weaken, detract from; **calces alicujus deterere** to tread on s.o.'s heels

dēterr·eō -ēre -uī -itus *tr* to deter, frighten away, discourage; *(w. abl or* **ab** *or* **de +** *abl, or w.* **ne, quin,** *or* **quominus)** to deter *(s.o.)* from, discourage *(s.o.)* from

dētersus *pp of* **detergeo**

dētestābil·is -is -e *adj* detestable

dētestāti·ō -ōnis *f* detestation; curse; *(leg)* formal renunciation

dētest·or -ārī -ātus sum *tr* to curse; to invoke *(the gods)* to avert; to plead against; to detest; *(w.* **in** *+ acc)* to call *(e.g., vengeance)* upon; **invidiam detestari** to avert jealousy, avoid unpopularity

dētex·ō -ĕre -uī -tus *tr* to weave, finish weaving; *(fig)* to finish (off)

dē·tineō -tinĕre -tinuī -tentus *tr* to hold back, keep back; to hold up, detain; to occupy, keep busy; *(w.* **abl** *or* **in** *+ abl)* to keep back from; *(w.* **abl** *or* **in** *+ abl)* to occupy *(day, mind)* with, keep *(s.o.)* busy with

dēton·deō -dēre -dī -sus *tr* to cut off, shear off; *(fig)* to strip off

dēton·ō -āre -uī *intr* to stop thundering; *(of Jupiter)* to thunder down

dētonsus *pp of* **detondeo**

dētor·queō -quēre -sī -tus *tr* to twist *or* bend aside; to twist out of shape; to turn aside; to turn, direct; to avert *(eyes);* to divert, pervert; to distort, misrepresent *(words)*

dētracti·ō -ōnis *f* (**-trect-**) taking away, wresting; removal; *(rhet)* ellipsis

dētractō *see* **detrecto**

dētract·or -ōris *m* detractor

dētra·hō -hĕre -xī -ctus *tr* to drag down, drag away, pull down, pull away; to remove, withdraw; to deprive, rob, strip; to induce to come down *(e.g., an enemy from a strong position);* to disparage, detract, slander; *(w. dat or* **de +** *abl)* to rob *(s.o.)* of

dētrectāti·ō -ōnis *f* drawing back, avoidance; **militiae detrectatio** draft dodging

dētrectāt·or -ōris *m* detractor; shirker

dētrect·ō -āre -āvī -ātus *tr* (**-trac-**) to draw back from, shirk, decline, reject; to disparage; to demean; **militiam detrectare** to dodge the draft

dētrīmentōs·us -a -um *adj* detrimental

dētrīment·um -ī *n* detriment, loss, harm; **detrimentum accipere** *(or* **capere)** to incur a loss; **detrimentum inferre** *(or* **afferre)** to cause harm *or* loss

dētrītus *pp of* **detero**

dētrīvī *perf of* **detero**

dētrū·dō -dĕre -sī -sus *tr* to push down, push away, push off; to postpone; *(mil)* to dislodge; *(leg)* to evict; **aliquem de sua sententia detrudere** to force s.o. to change his mind

dētrunc·ō -āre -āvī -ātus *tr* to cut off, lop off; to mutilate; to behead

dētulī *perf of* **deferro**

dēturb·ō -āre *tr* to beat down, tear down, strike down; to eject, expel, dispossess; *(mil)* to dislodge; **aliquem de sanitate deturbare** to drive a person mad

dēturp·ō -āre *tr* to disfigure

Deucali·ōn -ōnis *m* son of Prometheus who, together with his wife Pyrrha, survived the Deluge

deün·x -cis *m* eleven-twelfths; **heres ex deünce** heir to eleven-twelfths

de·ūrō -ūrĕre -ussī -ustus *tr* to burn up, destroy; *(of frost)* to nip

de·us -ī *(nom pl:* **deī** *or* **dī(i);** *gen pl:* **deōrum** *or* **deum;** *dat and abl pl:* **deīs, dīs** *or* **diīs;** *vocative sg:* **deus)** *m* god, deity ‖ *mpl (of people in high places)* the powers that be; **di boni!** good heavens!; **di hominesque** all the world; **di meliora!** Heaven forbid!; **dis volentibus** with the help of the gods; **di te ament!** bless your little heart!

deustus *pp of* **deuro**

dē·ūtor -ūtī *intr (w. abl)* to mistreat

dēvast·ō -āre -āvī -ātus *tr* to devastate

dēve·hō -hĕre -xī -ctus *tr* to carry down, carry away, carry off, ship off ‖ *pass* to ride down; to sail down

dēvellō dēvellĕre dēvellī *or* **dēvolsī dēvulsus** *or* **dēvolsus** *tr* to pluck

dēvēl·ō -āre *tr* to unveil

dēvener·or -ārī -ātus sum *tr* to worship; to avert by prayer

dē·veniō -venīre -vēnī -ventum *intr* to come down, arrive; *(w. acc of extent of motion or w.* ad *or* in + *acc)* to arrive at, reach; *(w.* ad) to happen to, befall

dēverber·ō -āre -āvī -ātus *tr* to thrash soundly

dēverb·ium -(i)ī *n* spoken parts of a play, unaccompanied by music

dēvers·or -ārī -ātus sum *intr* to stay as a guest; *(w.* apud + *acc)* to stay at the house of

dēvers·or -ōris *m* (-vor-) guest

dēversōriol·um -ī *n* small inn

dēversōri·us -a -um *adj* (-vor-) of an inn, fit to stay at; taberna deversoria inn **||** *n* inn

dēverticul·um -ī *n* (-vort-) side road; detour; digression; refuge; inn, tavern; *(coll)* dive; *(fig)* loophole

dēver·tō -tēre -tī -sum *or* dēver·tor -tī -sus sum *intr* (-vort-) to turn aside, turn away; to stay as guest, spend the night; *(w.* ad *or* apud + *acc)* to stay with, stay at the house of; *(w.* ad) to have recourse to

dēvex·us -a -um *adj* inclining, sloping, steep; *(w.* ad) prone to, inclined to

dēvin·ciō -cīre -xī -ctus *tr* to tie up, clamp; *(fig)* to obligate, unite closely **||** *refl* se vino devincire *(coll)* to get tight on wine

dē·vincō -vincĕre -vīcī -victus *tr* to beat decisively, trounce

dēvinctus *pp of* devincio **||** *adj (w. dat)* strongly attached to

dēvītāti·ō -ōnis *f* avoidance

dēvīt·ō -āre -āvī -ātus *tr* to avoid

dēvi·us -a -um *adj* out of the way; off the beaten track; living apart, solitary, sequestered; inconsistent **||** *npl* wilderness

dēvoc·ō -āre -āvī -ātus *tr* to call down; to call off; to recall; to call away; to allure; deos ad auxilium devocare to invoke the gods for help

dēvol·ō -āre -āvī -ātum *intr* to fly down; to fly away; to hasten down, hasten away

dēvol·vō -vĕre -vī -ūtus *tr* to roll down; *(w.* de) to roll down from **||** *pass* to roll down, go tumbling down; *(w.* ad) to fall back on

dēvor·ō -āre -āvī -ātus *tr* to devour, gulp down; to consume, waste; *(of sea)* to engulf, swallow up; to swallow, mumble *(words);* to repress *(tears);* to bear with patience

dēvor- = dever-

dēvorti·a -ōrum *npl* side roads, detour

dēvōti·ō -ōnis *f* self-sacrifice; cursing; outlawing; incantation, spell; capitis *(or* vitae) devotio sacrifice of one's life

dēvōt·ō -āre -āvī -ātus *tr* to bewitch, jinx

dēvōt·us -a -um *pp of* devoveo **||** *adj*

devoted, faithful; accursed; *(w. dat)* 1 devoted to; 2 addicted to

dē·voveō -vovēre -vōvī -vōtus *tr* to devote, vow, sacrifice, dedicate; to mark out, doom, destine; to curse; to bewitch

dēvulsus *pp of* develo

dext·ans -antis *m* five-sixths

dextell·a -ae *f* little right hand; right-hand man

dex·ter -tera -terum *or* -tra -trum *adj* right, on the right side; handy, dexterous; lucky, propitious, favorable; opportune, right **||** *f* right hand, right side, the right; a dextrā laevāque to the right and left, right and left, everywhere; dextrā with the right hand; *(fig)* with valor; dextrā *(w. gen or acc)* to the right of; dextrae jungere dextram to shake hands; dextram dare *(or* tendere) to give a pledge of friendship

dexterē *or* dextrē *adv* dexterously, skillfully; dextre fortunā uti *(fig)* to play the cards right

dexterit·ās -ātis *f* dexterity; readiness to help

dextrorsum *or* dextrorsus *or* dextrōversum *adv* (-vor-) to the right, towards the right side

dī *see* deus

Dī·a -ae *f* ancient name of the island of Naxos **||** mother of Mercury

diabathrār·ius -(i)ī *m* shoemaker

diadēm·a -ātis *n* diadem

diadēmāt·us -a -um *adj* wearing a diadem, wearing a crown

diaet·a -ae *f* room; cabin *(of ship);* annex *(to the main building); (med)* regimen *(proper exercise, etc.)*

dialecticē *adv* logically

dialectic·us -a -um *adj* dialectical, logical **||** *m* dialectician, logician **||** *f* logic, dialectics **||** *npl* dialectics

dialect·os -ī *f* dialect

Diāl·is -is -e *adj* of Jupiter; of Jupiter's high priest; apex Dialis high priest's miter; flamen Dialis high priest of Jupiter

dialog·us -ī *m* dialogue, conversation; literary composition in the form of a dialogue

Diān·a *or* Dīān·a -ae *f* Diana *(Roman goddess, identified with Artemis); (fig)* Diana's temple; *(fig)* moon; iracunda Diana lunacy

Diāni·us -a -um *adj* Diana's **||** *n* enclosure sacred to Diana

diāri·a -ōrum *npl* daily ration

dibaph·us -ī *f* crimson robe; official robe *(of a magistrate or augur)*

dic·a -ae *f (leg)* lawsuit, case, judicial proceedings; dicam scribere *(w. dat)* to sue s.o.; dicas sortiri to select a jury

dicācit·ās -ātis *f* sarcasm

dicācul·us -a -um *adj* sarcastic

dicāti·ō -ōnis *f* declaration of intent of becoming a citizen

dic·ax -ācis *adj* witty, sharp; sarcastic

dichorē·us -ī *m (pros)* double trochee (— ᴗ — ᴗ)

dici·ō -ōnis *f* jurisdiction; sway, authority, control, rule, dominion, sovereignty; **in** *(or* **sub) dicione esse** *(w. gen)* to be under the control of, be subject to, be under the jurisdiction of; **in dicionem redigere** *(w. gen)* or **dicioni subjicere** *(w. gen)* to bring *(s.o.)* under the control of

dicis causā *or* **grātiā** *adv* for show, for the sake of appearances

dic·ō -āre -āvī -ātus *tr* to dedicate, consecrate; to deify; to inaugurate; to set apart, devote; *(w. dat)* to devote *(e.g., time, energy, self)* to

dīcō dīcěre dixī dictus *tr* to say; to tell, relate; to indicate, mention, specify, point out; to nominate, appoint; to fix, set *(day, date);* to speak, deliver, recite; to pronounce, utter, articulate; to call, name; to assert, state; to describe; to predict; *(w. double acc)* to appoint *(s.o.)* as; **causam dicere** to plead *or* defend a case; **diem dicere** *(w. dat)* to set a date for; **facete dictum!** well put!; **sententiam dicere** to express an opinion; **testimonium dicere** to give evidence

dicrot·a -ae *f* bireme

dicrot·um -ī *n* bireme

Dictae·us -a -um *adj* of Mt. Dicte, Dictaean, Cretan

dictamn·us *or* **dictamn·os -ī** *f (bot)* dittany *(aromatic plant, believed to have magical powers)*

dictāt·a -ōrum *npl* lessons, rules; dictation

dictāt·or -ōris *m* dictator *(emergency magistrate in Rome, legally appointed for a maximum six-month term);* chief magistrate *(of Italic town)*

dictātōri·us -a -um *adj* of a dictator

dictātr·ix -īcis *f* mistress of ceremonies

dictātūr·a -ae *f* dictatorship

Dict·ē -ēs *f* mountain in Crete, the alleged birthplace of Jupiter

dicti·ō -ōnis *f* saying, speaking, uttering; diction, style; conversation; oracular response, prediction; **dictio causae** pleading of a case; **dictio testimoni** right to give testimony; **juris dictio** administration of justice; jurisdiction

dictit·ō -āre -āvī -ātus *tr* to keep saying, to state emphatically; **causas dictitare** to practice law

dict·ō -āre -āvī -ātus *tr* to reiterate, say repeatedly; to dictate; to compose; to suggest, remind

dict·us -a -um *pp of* **dico** ‖ *n* saying, word,

statement; witticism; maxim, proverb; prediction; order, instruction; promise, assurance; derisive remark; **dicta dicere** to make (witty *or* cutting) remarks; **dictis manere** to stick to one's promises

Dictynn·a -ae *f* Cretan goddess Britomartis, identified with Diana

-dicus -a -um *adjl suf;* **-dic·us -ī** *masc suf* denotes one who speaks: **veridicus** saying the truth; **causidicus** one who pleads cases, lawyer

dī·dō *or* **dis·dō -děre -didī -ditus** *tr* to publicize, disseminate; to distribute, hand out

Dīd·ō -ūs *or* **-ōnis** *(acc:* **Dīdō** *or* **Didōn)** *f* daughter of Tyrian king Belus, and foundress and queen of Carthage

dīdū·cō -cěre -xī -ctus *tr* to draw apart, open; to part, sever, separate, split; to undo, untie; to divide, distribute; to scatter, disperse; to untie *(knot);* to break up *(friendships);* to deploy *(forces);* to digest *(food);* to open wide *(mouth); (in mathematics)* to divide; **animus diductus** *(w. abl)* the mind torn between *(alternatives)*

dīducti·ō -ōnis *f* separation into parts, distribution

diēcul·a -ae *f* little while

diērect·us -a -um *adj (coll)* finished, done for; **abi** *(or* **i) dierectus!** *(sl)* go straight to blazes!

di·ēs -ēī *m (but occasionally feminine when referring to a fixed day or time in general)* day; time, period, space of time, interval; daylight; light of day; anniversary; daybreak; season; **diem dicere** *(w. dat)* to impeach, bring an accusation against; **diem ex die** from day to day, day after day; **diem noctemque** day and night; **dies meus** my birthday; **in diem** for the moment; for a future day; **in dies** (more and more) every day; **multo denique die** not till late in the day; **postridie ejus diei** the day after that; **post tertium ejus diei** two days after that

Diespi·ter -tris *m* Jupiter

diffām·ō -āre -āvī -ātus *tr* to spread the news of; to defame, slander

differenti·a -ae *f* difference, diversity; distinguishing characteristic; specific difference, species

differit·ās -ātis *f* difference

differō differre distulī dīlātus *tr* to carry in different directions; to scatter, disperse; to publicize; to postone; to put *(a person)* off; to humor; to get rid of; to bewilder; to disquiet ‖ *intr* to differ, be different; *(w. ab)* to differ from ‖ *v impers* there is a difference; **multum differt** there is a great difference

differt·us -a -um *adj* stuffed; crowded, overcrowded

difficil·is -is -e adj difficult, hard; surly; hard to manage, hard to please

difficiliter adv (-**culter**) with difficulty, barely

difficult·ās -ātis f difficulty, hardship, trouble, distress; surliness; poverty, financial embarrassment

difficulter adv with difficulty, barely

diffīd·ens -entis adj diffident, lacking in confidence; anxious, nervous

diffīdenter adv without confidence, distrustfully

diffīdenti·a -ae f diffidence, mistrust, distrust

diffī·dō -děre -sus sum intr (w. dat) to distrust; to despair of; (w. acc & inf) to have no confidence that; (w. inf) to expect not to

dif·findō -finděre -fīdī -fissus tr to split, divide; **diem diffindere** (fig) to put off the day of the trial

diffing·ō -ěre tr to form differently, remodel; to alter

diffissus pp of **diffindo**

diffit·eor -ērī tr to disavow, disown

diffl·ō -āre -āvī -ātus intr to blow away; to disperse

difflu·ō -ěre -xī -ctum intr to flow in different directions, flow away; to dissolve, melt away, disappear; (w. abl) to wallow in (e.g., luxury)

dif·fringō -fringěre -frēgī -fractus tr to shatter, break apart, smash

dif·fugiō -fugěre -fūgī intr to flee in different directions; to disperse; to disappear

diffug·ium -(i)ī n dispersion

diffundit·ō -āre tr to pour out, scatter; to waste

dif·fundō -funděre -fūdī -fūsus tr to pour out; to scatter, diffuse, spread, extend; to bottle (wine); to give vent to; to cheer up, gladden

diffūsē adv diffusely; fully

diffūsil·is -is -e adj diffusive

diffūs·us -a -um pp of **diffundo** ‖ adj extending over a wide area; extensive (writings); diffuse, expansive (speech)

diffutūt·us -a -um adj (vulg) exhausted by too much sex

dī·gerō -gerěre -gessī -gestus tr to distribute in all directions; to spread about, disperse, divide; to arrange; to interpret

dīgesti·ō -ōnis f arrangement; (rhet) enumeration

dīgestus pp of **digero**

digitul·us -ī m little finger

digit·us -ī m finger; inch (one sixteenth of a Roman foot); toe; **digitis concrepare** to snap the fingers; **digito uno attingere** to touch lightly, touch tenderly; **digitum intendere ad** to point the finger at; **digitum tollere** to make a bid; **digitus**

index index finger; **digitus medius** or **summus** middle finger; **digitus minimus** little finger; **digitus pollex** thumb; **digitus quartus** ring finger; **in digitos arrectus** on tiptoe; **primus** (or **prior**) **digitus** fingertip

dīgladi·or -ārī -ātus sum intr to fight in a gladiatorial contest

dignāti·ō -ōnis f esteem, respect; dignity, honor; rank, status

dignē adv worthily

dignit·ās -ātis f worth, worthiness; dignity; authority, rank, reputation, distinction, majesty; self-respect; dignitary; political office

dign·ō -āre -āvī -ātus or **dign·or -ārī -ātus sum** tr (w. abl) to think worthy of; (w. inf) to think fit to; (w. double acc) to think (s.o.) worthy of being (e.g., a son)

dignōsc·ō or **dīnōsc·ō -ěre** tr to distinguish; (w. abl) to distinguish (s.o.) from; **dominum ac servum dignoscere** to know the difference between master and slave

dign·us -a -um adj worthy, deserving; fit, adequate, suitable, deserved, proper; (w. abl) worthy of

dīgre·dior -dī -ssus sum intr to move apart, separate; to deviate; to digress

dīgressi·ō -ōnis f parting, separation; deviation; digression

dīgressus pp of **digredior**

dīgress·us -ūs m departure; digression

dījūdicāti·ō -ōnis f decision

dījūdic·ō -āre -āvī -ātus tr to decide, settle; **vera et falsa** (or **vera a falsis**) **dijudicare**) to distinguish between truth and falsehood

dījun- = **disjun-**

dī·lābor -lābī -lapsus sum intr to fall apart, break up; (of ice) to melt; to disperse; to decay; (of time) to slip by; (of water) to flow in different directions

dīlacer·ō -āre -āvī -ātus tr to tear to pieces

dīlāmin·ō -āre tr to split in two; to crack (nuts)

dīlani·ō -āre -āvī -ātus tr to tear to pieces

dīlapid·ō -āre -āvī -ātus tr to demolish (a structure of stone); (coll) to squander

dīlapsus pp of **dilabor**

dīlarg·ior -īrī -ītus sum tr to hand out generously, lavish

dīlāti·ō -ōnis f postponement, delay; (leg) adjournment

dīlāt·ō -āre -āvī -ātus tr to dilate, stretch, broaden, extend, enlarge; (fig) to amplify, spread, extend; to drawl out

dīlāt·or -ōris m procrastinator, slowpoke

dīlātus pp of **differo**

dīlaud·ō -āre tr to praise enthusiastically

dīlect·us -a -um pp of **diligo** ‖ adj beloved, dear

dīlect·us -ūs m selection; (mil) selective

service, draft; draftees; recruitment; **dilectum habere** to conduct a draft; **legiones ex novo dilectu conficere** to bring the legions to full strength with new draftees

dīlid·ō -ĕre *tr* to smash to pieces

dīlig·ens -entis *adj* careful, accurate; exacting, strict; thrifty; industrious; *(w. gen)* **1** observant of; **2** devoted to, fond of; *(w. ad or in + acc)* **1** careful in, careful to; **2** conscientious about

dīligenter *adv* carefully, diligently; thoroughly, well

dīligenti·a -ae *f* care, diligence, industry, attentiveness; economy, frugality; *(w. gen)* regard for

dī·ligō -ligĕre -lexī -lectus *tr* to love, esteem; to like; to value, appreciate

dīlōrīc·ō -āre -āvī -ātus *tr* to tear open

dīlūc·eō -ēre *intr* to be clear, be evident; *(w. dat)* to be obvious to

dī·lūcescō -lūcescĕre -luxī *intr* to get light, dawn

dīlūcidē *adv* clearly, distinctly

dīlūcid·us -a -um *adj* clear, distinct, plain, evident

dīlūcul·um -ī *n* daybreak, dawn

dīlūd·ium -(i)ī *n* intermission

dīl·uō -uĕre -uī -ūtus *tr* to wash away; to break up, separate; to dilute; to get rid of *(worries, annoyances);* to atone for; to explain

dīluvi·ēs -ēī *f* flood, deluge

dīluvi·ō -āre *tr* to flood, inundate

dīluv·ium -(i)ī *n* flood, deluge

dimach·ae -ārum *mpl* soldiers who fight either on foot or on horseback

dīmān·ō -āre *intr* to flow in different directions; *(fig)* to spread around

dīmensi·ō -ōnis *f* measurement, dimensions

dī·mētior -mētīrī -mensus sum *tr* to measure off; to count off

dīmēt·or -ārī -ātus sum *tr* to measure *or* mark off

dīmicāti·ō -ōnis *f* fight, combat, struggle; contest, rivalry

dīmic·ō -āre -āvī -ātus *intr* to contend, fight, struggle; **de capite** *(or* **de vitā) dimicare** to fight for one's life

dīmidi·a -ae *f* half

dīmidiāt·us -a -um *adj* half, in half

dīmidi·us -a -um *adj* half; broken (in two); **dimidius patrum, dimidius plebis** half patrician, half plebeian; **parte dimidiā auctus** twice as large **‖** *n* half; **dimidio longior** twice as long; **dimidium militum quam** half as many soldiers as

dīmi·nuō -nuĕre -nuī -nūtus *tr* to shatter

dīmissi·ō -ōnis *f* dismissal; sending out; *(mil)* discharge

dī·mittō -mittĕre -mīsī -missus *tr* to send away, let go; to dismiss *(an assembly);*

to spread; to set free, release; to let off; to scatter, distribute; to let go of, let loose; to let go, let slip, forgo *(a chance, an opportunity);* to divorce *(a wife); (fin)* to settle *(a debt); (fin)* to pay off *(a creditor); (mil)* to discharge *(a soldier),* disband *(an army)*

dimminuō *see* **dīminu·ō**

dī·moveō -movēre -mōvī -mōtus *tr* to move apart, part, separate; to disperse, scatter; to dismiss; to lure away

Dindymēn·ē -ēs *f* Cybele *(named after Dindymus, a mountain in Phrygia sacred to Cybele)*

Dindym·us *or* **Dindym·os -ī** *m* Mt. Dindymus

dīnoscō *see* **dignosco**

dīnumerāti·ō -ōnis *f* enumeration, counting up

dīnumer·ō -āre -āvī -ātus *tr* to enumerate, count up; to count out, pay

diōbolār·is -is -e *adj* costing two obols *(about 2¢)*

Diodot·us -ī *m* Stoic philosopher and tutor of Cicero *(d. 59 b.c.)*

dioecēs·is -is *or* **-eōs** *f* district; governor's jurisdiction

dioecēt·ēs -ae *m* treasurer; secretary of revenue

Diogen·ēs -is *m* Ionic philosopher *(5th cent. b.c.)* **‖** Cynic philosopher from Sinope, in Pontus *(412?–323 b.c.)*

Diomēd·ēs -is *m* son of Tydeus and king of Argos, and hero at Troy

Diō(n) -ōnis *m* Dion *(brother-in-law of the elder Dionysius, the tyrant of Syracuse, and a pupil and friend of Plato's)*

Diōn·ē -ēs *or* **Diōn·a -ae** *f* mother of Venus

Dionȳsi·a -ōrum *npl* festival of Dionysus

Dionȳs·ius -(i)ī *m* tyrant of Syracuse *(430–367 b.c.)* **‖** Dionysius the Younger *(397–330? b.c.)*

Dionȳs·us *or* **Dionȳs·os -ī** *m* Greek god of wine and fertility, equated with Bacchus

diōt·a -ae *f* two-handled wine jar

Dīphil·us -ī *m* Greek comic writer of Sinope, used by Plautus

diplōm·a -atis *n* travel pass *(to travel free on the Imperial post);* certificate

dips·as -adis *f* poisonous snake whose bite provokes thirst

Dipyl·on -ī *n* N.W. gate at Athens

dipyr·us -a -um *adj* twice burned

Dīr·a -ae *f* Fury *(goddess of revenge)*

dīr·ae -ārum *fpl* bad omens; curses

Dircae·us -a -um *adj* Dircean, Boeotian; **cycnus Dircaeus** Boeotian swan *(Pindar, lyric poet from Boeotia)*

Dirc·ē -ēs *f* famous spring in Boeotia

dīrectē *adv* (der-) in a straight line

dīrectō *adv* (dēr-) in a straight line; directly, without intervening procedures

dīrect·us *or* **dērect·us -a -um** *pp of* **dirigo**

II *adj* straight, direct; level; upright, vertical, perpendicular; *(fig)* direct, straightforward, simple; **in directum** *(or* **per directum)** in a straight line; **in directo** on a straight stretch *(of road)*

diremptus *pp of* **dirimo**

dirempt·us -ūs *m* separation

dīreptī·ō -ōnis *f* plundering, pillaging **II** *fpl* acts of pillage; a scramble for a share

dīrept·or -ōris *m* plunderer

dīreptus *pp of* **diripio**

dirib·eō -ēre -uī -itus *tr* to sort *(votes taken out of the ballot box)*

diribiti·ō -ōnis *f* sorting *(of votes)*

diribit·or -ōris *m* sorter (of ballots)

diribitōr·ium -iī *n* sorting room

dīrigō dīrigĕre dīrexī dīrectus *tr* (dē-) to direct; to put in order, arrange, line up, straighten out; to level *(a surface);* to construct *(roads, tunnels, along a given line);* (mil) to deploy

dir·imō -imĕre -ēmī -emptus *tr* to take apart; to part, separate, divide; to break off, disturb, interrupt; to separate, dissolve; to put off, delay; to break off, end, bring to an end; to nullify, bring to naught

dī·ripiō -ripĕre -ripuī -reptus *tr* to tear apart, tear to pieces; to lay waste, pillage; to loot, rob; to steal; to snatch away; to whip out *(sword);* to run after, compete for the company of *(person)*

dīrit·ās -ātis *f* frightfulness; dire event

dī·rumpō -rumpĕre -rūpī -ruptus *tr* to break to pieces, smash, shatter; to break off *(friendship);* to sever *(ties)* **II** *pass* to burst *(w. laughter, envy, etc.)*

dīru·ō -ĕre -ī -tus *tr* to pull apart, demolish, destroy, overthrow; to scatter; to bankrupt; *(mil)* to break up *(enemy formation)*

dīr·us -a -um *adj* dire, awful, fearful; ominous, ill-omened; dreadful; cruel, relentless, fierce; **temporibus diris** in the reign of terror; **venena dira** deadly poisons

dīs dītis *adj* rich; fertile; generous; expensive; *(w. abl)* abounding in **II Dis** *m* Pluto *(king of the lower world)*

dis- *pref* (unchanged before initial **c p t s;** **dī-** before **b d g l m n r,** consonantal **u** and sometimes **i; dif-** before **f; dir-** *(by rotacism)* before vowels and **h** *(with rare exceptions);* it commonly signifies **1** separation or dispersion or both: **diffugere** to flee away; **discedere** to draw apart; **2** the reversal of a previous process: **disjungere** to disunite, separate; **3** a negative sense: **displicere** to displease, not please

dis·cēdo -cēdĕre -cessī -cessum *intr* to go away, depart; to separate, be severed; to disperse, be dissipated, disappear; to split open, come apart; *(of wife)* to separate

(from husband); to deviate, swerve; to pass away, cease; *(mil)* to march off, break camp; *(mil)* to come off *(victorious, etc.);* (w. abl) **1** to forsake *(e.g., friends);* **2** to deviate from, swerve from; *(w.* **ex** *or* **de** *+ abl)* to depart from; *(w.* **ad)** to depart for; *(w.* **in** *+ acc)* to vote for; **discedere in Catonis sententiam** to vote for Cato's proposal; **ut discedatur ab** apart from

disc·ens -entis *m* learner, apprentice, trainee

disceptāti·ō -ōnis *f* dispute, difference of opinion; discussion, debate

disceptāt·or -ōris *m,* **disceptātr·ix -īcis** *f* arbitrator

discept·ō -āre -āvī -ātus *tr* to debate, dispute, discuss, treat; to decide, settle **II** *intr* to act as judge, arbitrate; to argue; to be at stake

dis·cernō -cernĕre -crēvī -crētus *tr* to separate, mark off, divide; to keep apart; to distinguish between; to discern, make out

discerp·ō -ĕre -sī -tus *tr* to mangle, mutilate; *(fig)* to tear apart *(with words, arguments)*

discessi·ō -ōnis *f* separation, division; divorce; *(in the Senate)* division, formal vote; **discessio sine ulla varietate** unanimous vote

discess·us -ūs *m* separation, parting; departure; banishment; marching off

discid·ium -(i)ī *n* parting; discord, disagreement; divorce

discīd·ō -ĕre -ī *tr* to cut up

discinct·us -a -um *pp of* **discingo II** *adj* without a belt; dissolute, loose; effeminate, voluptuous

di·scindō -scindĕre -scĭdī -scissus *tr* to tear apart, tear open, rend; **amicitias discindere** to break off the ties of friendship

discin·gō -gĕre -xī -ctus *tr* to take off; to loosen; to disarm

disciplīn·a -ae *f* instruction, training, teaching, education; learning, knowledge, science; discipline, branch of study; custom, habit; system; **militaris disciplina** basic training; **reipublicae disciplina** statesmanship

discipul·a -ae *f* pupil *(female)*

discipul·us -ī *m* pupil; disciple, follower

discissus *pp of* **discindo**

disclū·dō -dĕre -sī -sus *tr* to keep apart, shut off; to seal up, seal off; to assign

discō discĕre didĭcī *tr* to learn; to get to know, become acquainted with; to be told *(e.g., the truth);* (w. inf) to learn how to

discobol·us -ī *m* discus-thrower

discol·or -ōris *adj* of a different color; of different colors; *(w. dat)* different from

discondūc·ō -ĕre *intr* to be unprofitable, be prejudicial

disconven·iō -īre *intr* to disagree; to be inconsistent ‖ *v impers* there is disagreement

discordābil·is -is -e *adj* discordant, disagreeing

discordi·a -ae *f* discord, dissension, disagreement; mutiny

discordiōs·us -a -um *adj* prone to discord, mutinous

discord·ō -āre *intr* to quarrel, disagree; *(w. dat or ab)* 1 to be be out of harmony with; 2 to be opposed to

discor·s -dis *adj* discordant; at variance; contradictory, inconsistent; warring *(winds, etc.); (w. abl)* inconsistent with, different from

discrepanti·a -ae *f* discrepancy, dissimilarity, difference

discrepāti·ō -ōnis *f* disagreement, dispute

discrepit·ō -āre *intr* to be completely different

discrep·ō -āre -āvī *or* **-uī** *intr* to be different in sound, sound different; to be out of tune; to disagree; to be different, vary; to be inconsistent; to be disputed; *(w. dat or abl or ab or cum)* 1 to disagree with; 2 to be different from; 3 to be inconsistent with ‖ *v impers* there is a difference of opinion, it is a matter of dispute, it is undecided

discrī·bō -bĕre -psī -ptus *tr* to distribute, divide; to classify; to assign, apportion; *(w. in + acc)* to distribute among, divide among

discrīm·en -inis *n* dividing line; interval, intervening space, division, distance, separation; discrimination, difference, distinction; critical moment, turning point; crisis, jeopardy, peril, danger, risk; decision, determination; decisive battle; difference in pitch; **res in discrimine est** the situation is at a critical stage; **parvum discrimen leti** narrow escape from death

discrīmin·ō -āre -āvī -ātus *tr* to divide, separate; to apportion

discriptē *adv* in an orderly way, lucidly, distinctly

discripti·ō -ōnis *f* distribution, classification

discript·us -a -um *pp of* **discribo** ‖ *adj* well-arranged, sorted, classified

discruci·ō -āre -āvī -ātus *tr* to torture; to distress, torment

discumbō discumbĕre discubuī discubitum *intr (of several)* to take their places at the table; *(of several)* to go to bed

discup·iō -ĕre *tr (coll)* to want badly; *(w. inf) (coll)* to be dying to

dis·currō -currĕre -cucurrī *or* **-currī -cursum** *intr* to run in different directions, scamper about, run up and down, dash around

discurs·us -ūs *m* running up and down, running about; *(mil)* pincer movement

disc·us -ī *m* discus

discu·tiō -tĕre -ssī -ssus *tr* to knock apart; to smash to pieces, shatter; to shake off; to break up, disperse *(an assembly, gathering);* to dispel *(danger, sleep);* to frustrate, bring to naught; to suppress, destroy

disertē *adv* eloquently, clearly

disertim *adv* clearly, distinctly

disert·us -a -um *adj* fluent, eloquent; clear, articulate

disject·ō -āre -āvī -ātus *tr* to toss about

disject·us -a -um *pp of* **disjicio** ‖ *adj* scattered; dilapidated

disject·us -ūs *m* scattering

dis·jiciō -jicĕre -jēcī -jectus *tr* to drive apart, scatter; to tear to pieces; to ruin; to frustrate, wreck; *(mil)* to break up *(enemy formation)*

di(s)junctē *adv* in separate words, separately

di(s)juncti·ō -ōnis *f* separation, alienation; divination; variation; dilemma; *(rhet)* asyndeton *(succession of phrases or clauses without conjunction)*

di(s)junct·us -a -um *adj* separate, distinct; distant, remote; disjointed, disconnected, incoherent; logically opposed ‖ *npl* opposites

di(s)jun·gō -gĕre -xī -ctus *tr* to unyoke; to sever, divide, part, remove; to separate; to alienate

dispālesc·ō -ĕre *intr* to be spread abroad, get around

dispāl·or -ārī -ātus sum *intr* to wander around; to straggle, stray off

dis·pandō -pandĕre — -pansus *tr* (-pen-) to stretch out, extend; to expand

dis·pār -paris *adj* different, unlike; unequal; ill-matched

disparāt·us -a -um *adj* separate, distinct; negatively opposite *(e.g.,* **sapere et non sapere** to be wise and not to be wise)

disparil·is -is -e *adj* dissimilar

dispariliter *adv* differently

dispar·ō -āre -āvī -ātus *tr* to separate; to make different ‖ *intr* to be different

dispartiō, dispartior *see* **dispertio**

dispectus *pp of* **dispicio**

dis·pellō -pellĕre -pulī -pulsus *tr* to dispel, drive away; to disperse

dispend·ium -(i)ī *n* expense, cost; loss *(as result of a transaction)*

dispendō *see* **dispando**

dis·pennō -pennĕre — -pessus *tr* to stretch out, extend; to expand

dispensāti·ō -ōnis *f* weighing out, doling out; management, superintendence, administration; office of treasurer

dispensāt·or -ōris *m* household manager, chief butler; cashier; treasurer

dispens·ō -āre -āvī -ātus *tr* to weigh out, pay out; to distribute, manage *(household stores);* to regulate, manage

dispercut·iō -ĕre *tr* to knock out; **cerebrum dispercutere** *(w. dat)* to knock *(s.o.'s)* brains out

disper·dō -dĕre -didī -ditus *tr* to spoil, ruin; to squander

disper·eō -īre -iī *intr* to go to ruin; to go to waste; to be undone, perish; **disperii!** *(coll)* I'm finished!; **dispeream si** *(coll)* I'll be darned if

disper·gō -gĕre -sī -sus *tr* (-sparg-) to scatter about, disperse; to splatter; to distribute, scatter *(e.g., men)* without organization; to spread, extend *(war, rumor, etc.)*

dispersē *adv* here and there; occasionally

dispersus *pp of* **dispergo**

dispers·us -ūs *m* dispersal

dispert·iō -īre -īvī *or* **-iī -ītus** *or* **dispert·ior -īrī -ītus sum** *tr* to distribute, divide; to assign *(e.g., gates, areas)* as posts to be guarded

dispertīti·ō -ōnis *f* distribution, sharing

dispessus *pp of* **dispando**

di·spiciō -spicĕre -spexī -spectus *tr* to see clearly, make out, distinguish, detect; to consider carefully, perceive, discover; to reflect on **ǁ** *intr* to see clearly

displic·eō -ēre -uī -itum *intr* to be unpleasant, be displeasing; *(w. dat)* to displease; **sibi displicere** to be dissatisfied with oneself; to be in a bad mood

dis·plōdō -plōdĕre — -plōsus *tr & intr* to burst apart

dis·pōnō -pōnĕre -posuī -positus *tr* to place here and there; to distribute; to arrange, set in order; to station, post, assign; to adjust; to dispose; **diem disponere** to arrange the day's schedule

dispositē *adv* orderly, methodically

dispositi·ō -ōnis *f* orderly arrangement, development *(of a theme)*

dispositūr·a -ae *f* order, arrangement

disposit·us -a -um *pp of* **dispono ǁ** *adj* well-arranged; methodical, orderly

disposit·us -ūs *m* order, arrangement

dispud·et -ēre -uit *v impers (w. inf)* it's a great shame to

dispulsus *pp of* **dispello**

dispun·gō -gĕre -xī -ctus *tr* to check, balance, audit *(accounts)*

disputāti·ō -ōnis *f* argument, discussion, debate

disputāt·or -ōris *m* disputant

disput·ō -āre -āvī -ātus *tr* to dispute, discuss; *(com)* to estimate; to examine, treat, explain **ǁ** *intr* to argue, argue one's case

disquīr·ō -ĕre *tr* to examine closely

disquīsīti·ō -ōnis *f* inquiry, investigation

disrumpō *see* **dirumpo**

dissaep·iō -īre -sī -tus *tr* to separate, wall off, fence off

dissaept·um -ī *n* partition, barrier

dissāvi·or *or* **dissuāvi·or -ārī** *tr* to kiss passionately

dissec·ō -āre -uī -tus *tr* to cut up, dissect

dissēmin·ō -āre -āvī -ātus *tr* to disseminate

dissensi·ō -ōnis *f* difference of opinion, disagreement; dissension; conflict, incompatibility

dissens·us -ūs *m* dissension, discord

dissentāne·us -a -um *adj* disagreeing, dissenting; conflicting; contrary

dissen·tiō -tīre -sī -sum *intr* to dissent, disagree; to differ, be in conflict, be inconsistent; *(w. dat or ab or cum)* to differ with; *(w. ab)* to differ from, be opposed to

disserēn·at -āre -āvit *v impers* it is clearing up

dis·serō -serĕre -sēvī -situs *tr* to scatter; to sow here and there; to stick in the ground at intervals

disser·ō -ĕre -uī -tus *tr* to discuss; to examine; to arrange **ǁ** *intr (w. de + abl)* to discuss

disserp·ō -ĕre *intr* to creep around; to spread gradually

disserti·ō -ōnis *f* severance, a disconnecting

dissert·ō -āre -āvī -ātus *tr* to discuss

dissertus *pp of* **dissero** *(to discuss)*

dis·sideō -sidēre -sēdī *intr* to be distant, be remote; to live far apart; to disagree; to differ, be unlike; *(of garment)* to be on crooked; *(w. ab or cum)* to disagree with

dissignāti·ō -ōnis *f* arrangement

dissignāt·or -ōris *m* **(dēsig-)** master of ceremonies; usher *(at theater);* undertaker, mortician

dissign·ō -āre -āvī -ātus *tr* to regulate; to arrange; to contrive

dissil·iō -īre -uī *intr* to fly apart, burst, split, break up; to be dissolved

dissimil·is -is -e *adj* dissimilar, different; *(w. gen or dat or w. atque or ac)* different from

dissimiliter *adv* differently

dissimilitūd·ō -inis *f* difference

dissimulābiliter *adv* furtively

dissimulanter *adv* secretly, slyly

dissimulanti·a -ae *f* faking, hiding

dissimulāti·ō -ōnis *f* dissimulation; Socratic irony; pretended ignorance

dissimulāt·or -ōris *m* dissembler, faker

dissimul·ō -āre -āvī -ātus *tr* to conceal, disguise; to keep secret; to pretend not to see, ignore

dissipābil·is -is -e *adj* **(dissu-)** that may be dissipated

dissipāti·ō -ōnis f (dissu-) dispersal, dissipation; distribution
dissip·ō or **dissup·ō -āre -āvī -ātus** tr to scatter, disperse; to demolish, overthrow; to squander, dissipate; to circulate, spread; to drive away (worries); (mil) to break up (enemy formation)
dissitus pp of **dissero** (to scatter)
dissociābil·is -is -e adj incompatible; irreconcilable
dissociāti·ō -ōnis f separation
dissoci·ō -āre -āvī -ātus tr to dissociate, separate; to ostracize; to set at variance; to divide into factions; to detach
dissolūbil·is -is -e adj dissoluble, separable
dissolūtē adv disconnectedly, loosely; carelessly
dissolūti·ō -ōnis f dissolution, breakup; abolition; destruction; refutation; looseness, dissoluteness; (rhet) asyndeton
dissolūt·us -a -um adj disconnected, loose; careless, negligent, remiss; loose, dissolute ‖ n (rhet) asyndeton
dissol·vō -věre -vī -ūtus tr to dissolve, melt; to dismantle; to disband; to make to disappear; to free, release; to loosen, undo; to solve (problem); to break up; to pay (debt); to refute; to weaken, wear out; to put an end to, do away with; to refute (argument); **animam dissolvere** to die; **legem dissolvere** to rescind a law; **poenam dissolvere** to pay the penalty
disson·us -a -um adj dissonant, discordant, jarring, confused (sounds); (w. abl) differing from, different from
dissor·s -tis adj having a different fate; (w. ab) unshared by
dissuā·deō -dēre -sī -sus tr to advise against; to dissuade ‖ intr to argue against an idea
dissuāsi·ō -ōnis f dissuasion; (w. gen) opposition to, objection to
dissuās·or -ōris m opponent
dissuāvior see **dissavior**
dissult·ō -āre intr to fly apart, burst
dissu·ō -ěre -uī -tus tr to take the stitches out of, undo
dissupō see **dissipo**
distaed·et -ēre v impers (w. gen) it makes (one) tired of; **me distaedet loqui** I'm sick and tired of talking
distanti·a -ae f distance, remoteness; difference, diversity
disten·dō or **disten·nō -děre -dī -tus** tr to stretch apart, stretch out; to distend; to cause to swell or bulge; to fill to capacity; to distract; to perplex ‖ pass to swell; to bulge
distent·us -a -um pp of **distendo** ‖ adj distended ‖ pp of **distineo** ‖ adj busy, occupied, distracted

distermin·ō -āre -āvī -ātus tr to serve as a boundary between, separate by a boundary, divide, limit
distich·on -ī n (pros) couplet
distinctē adv distinctly, clearly
distincti·ō -ōnis f distinction, differentiation, discrimination; distinctive quality (of a thing); difference; punctuation mark; division, paragraphing
distinct·us -a -um pp of **distinguo** ‖ adj distinct, separate; studded, adorned; varied, diversified; lucid (speaker); eminent
distinct·us -ūs m distinction, difference
dis·tineō -tinēre -tinuī -tentus tr to keep apart, separate; to detain, hold back, hinder; to employ, engage; to divert; to put off, delay; to keep divided; to stand in the way of; to distract
distin·guō -guěre -xī -ctus tr to mark off; to distinguish; to specify; to set off (w. colors, gold, etc.); to punctuate
dist·ō -āre intr to stand apart, be separate, be distant; to differ; (w. dat or ab) to differ from; (w. abl) to be separated by (a period of time) ‖ v impers there is a difference, it makes a difference
distor·queō -quēre -sī -tus tr to twist, distort; to curl (lips); to roll (eyes); **cogitationem distorquere** to rack one's brains
distorti·ō -ōnis f twisting; contortion
distort·us -a -um pp of **distorqueo** ‖ adj distorted, misshapen, deformed; perverse
distracti·ō -ōnis f pulling apart; dividing; discord, dissension
distract·us -a -um adj severed; rarefied; distracted, perplexed
distra·hō -hěre -xī -ctus tr to pull or drag apart, separate forcibly; to tear away, drag away, remove; to distract; to sever; to alienate; to prevent, frustrate; to end, settle (e.g., disputes); to sell retail; to sell (land) in lots
distrib·uō -uěre -uī -ūtus tr to distribute
distribūtē adv methodically
distribūti·ō -ōnis f distribution, apportionment, division
district·us -a -um adj drawn in opposite directions; distracted; busy, engaged
di·stringō -stringěre -strinxī -strictus tr to draw apart; to distract, draw attention to
distrunc·ō -āre -āvī -ātus tr to cut in two, hack apart
distulī perf of **differo**
disturbāti·ō -ōnis f demolition
disturb·ō -āre tr to throw into confusion; to demolish; to break up (a marriage); to frustrate
dītesc·ō -ěre intr to get rich
dīthyrambic·us -a -um adj (pros) dithyrambic

dithyramb·us -ī *m* dithyramb *(song in honor of Bacchus)*

dīti·ae -ārum *fpl* riches

dīt·ō -āre -āvī -ātus *tr* to enrich, make rich **‖** *pass* to get rich

diū *adv* by day, in the daytime; long, for a long time; in a long time; **diu noctuque** by day and by night; **jam diu** this long; **satis diu** long enough

diurn·us -a -um *adj* of the day, by day, day-, daytime; daily, of each day; day's, of one day; **merum diurnum** daytime drinking **‖** *n* account book **‖** *npl* record, journal, diary

dī·us *or* **dīv·us -a -um** *adj* godlike, divine; divinely inspired; having the brightness of day

diūtīnē *adv* for a long time

diūtīn·us -a -um *adj* long, lasting, long-lasting

diūtissimē *adv* for a very long time; longest; **jam diutissime** long long ago

diūtius *adv* longer, still longer; **paulum diutius** a little too long

diūturnit·ās -ātis *f* length of time, long duration; durability

diūturn·us -a -um *adj* long, long-lasting; chronic

dīv·a -ae *f* goddess

dīvāric·ō -āre -āvī -ātus *tr* to stretch out, spread **‖** *pass* to stand *or* sit with legs apart

dī·vellō -vellĕre -vellī -vulsus *or* **-volsus** *tr* to tear apart; to tear away; to untie; to wrest, remove, separate; to estrange

dīvend·ō -ĕre -idī -itus *tr* to sell retail

dīverber·ō -āre -āvī -ātus *tr* to split; to batter; to zip through, fly through

diverb·ium -(i)ī *n (theat)* dialogue

dīversē *adv* (-vor-) in different directions, differently

dīversit·ās -ātis *f* distance; diversity; difference; difference of opinion; difference of method; direct opposite; inconsistency; *(w. gen or* **inter** *+ acc)* difference between

dīvers·us -a -um *adj* (-vor-) in different directions; *(of roads)* running *or* leading in different directions; moving from opposite directions, converging; facing *or* turned in two *(or more)* directions; *(w.* **ab**) leading away from; situated at a distance from each other, apart, separate; distant, remote; opposite; of the opposing side *(in war)*, hostile; unsettled, irresolute; dissimilar, distinct, inconsistent; different *(from one another in quality, quantity, purpose, degree, effect, etc.)*; *(w. dat or gen or* **ab** *or* **quam**) different from, the reverse of **‖** *mpl* individuals **‖** *n* opposite direction, different quarter, opposite side, opposite view; **ex diverso** from a different direction; on

opposite sides; from *or* on the opposing side; in contrast, on the other hand; on the contrary; from a different point of view, in turn; in reverse, vice versa; **in diversum** in a different direction; for a different reason; to a different effect; vice versa; **per diversum** crosswise **‖** *npl* different parts; **in diversa** in different directions; **per diversa** for different reasons

dīver·tō -tĕre -tī -sum *intr* (-vor-) to go different ways; to turn off; to stop off, stay

dīv·es -itis *adj* rich; costly; precious, sumptuous; plentiful; *(w. gen or abl)* rich in, abounding in

dīvex·ō -āre -āvī -ātus *tr* to ravage; to harass

dīvidi·a -ae *f* worry, trouble; nuisance; dissension, antagonism

dī·vidō -vidĕre -vīsī -vīsus *tr* to divide; to distribute, share; to break up, destroy; to arrange, apportion; to separate, distinguish; to segregate, keep apart; to accompany *(songs with music)*; **dimidium dividere** to go halves *(w. s.o.)*; **sententiam dividere** to break down a proposal *(so as to vote on each part separately)*

dīvidu·us -a -um *adj* divisible; divided, separated; forked

dīvīnāti·ō -ōnis *f* clairvoyance; forecasting, predicting, divination; *(leg)* selection of the most suitable prosecutor

dīvīnē *adv* through divine power; prophetically; divinely, gorgeously

dīvīnit·ās -ātis *f* divinity, godhead; prophetic power, clairvoyance; excellence

dīvīnitus *adv* from heaven, from god; providentially; prophetically; divinely, in a godlike manner; excellently

dīvīn·ō -āre -āvī -ātus *tr* to divine, predict; to guess

dīvīn·us -a -um *adj* divine, heavenly; divinely inspired, prophetic; godlike; gorgeous, excellent; **divinum jus** natural law; **divinum jus et humanum** natural and positive law; **divinum scelus** sacrilege; **rem divinam facere** to worship; to sacrifice; **res divina** rite; **res divinae** religious affairs, religion; celestial matters **‖** *m* prophet **‖** *npl* divine matters; religious duties; **divina humanaque** things divine and human, the whole world; **divina humanaque agere** to perform religious and secular duties

dīvīsi·ō -ōnis *f* division, distribution

dīvīs·or -ōris *m* distributor; agent hired by a candidate to give out bribes

dīvīs·us -a -um *pp of* **divido ‖** *adj* separate, distinct

dīvīs·us -ūs *m* division, distribution; **facilis divisui** easily divided dīviti·ae -ārum *fpl* riches; richness *(of soil);* costly things

dīvolg- = divulg-

dīvor- = diver-

dīvort·ium -(i)ī *n* divorce; fork *(of road or river);* divortium facere cum to divorce *(a woman)*

dīvulgāt·us -a -um *adj* common, widespread

dīvulg·ō -āre -āvī -ātus *tr* to divulge, spread among the people; to publish *(book);* to publicize, advertise

dīvulsus *pp of* divello

dīv·us *or* dī·us -a -um *adj* divine, deified ‖ *m* god, deity; title applied to dead emperors ‖ *n* sky; the open; sub divo out in the open; sub divum rapere to bring out into the open

dō dare dědī datus (danit = dat; danunt = dant; dane = dasne; duim, duis, duit = dem, dēs det; *(in Plautus:* dan = dasne; datin = datisne; dabin = dabisne; duas = des) *tr* to give; to offer, dedicate; to pay out *(money);* to confer; to permit, grant; to give up, hand over; to communicate, tell; to ascribe, impute, assign; to cause, make; to furnish, afford, present; to admit; to administer *(medicine);* to utter, give expression to, announce; amplexus dare to embrace; comoediam dare to present a comedy; concilium *(or* contionem) dare to allow a private person to address the assembly; conspectum dare to make visible; damnum dare to cause damage; fabulam dare to present a play; jus *(or* jura) dare to give laws, give a constitution, administer justice; leto *(or* morti) dare to send *(s.o.)* to *(his)* death; legem dare to enact a law; litteras dare to mail a letter; locum dare *(w. dat)* to make way for; manūs dare to surrender; nomen dare to enlist; operam dare *(w. dat)* to pay attention to, devote attention to, look out for; palam dare to make clear; poenam *(or* poenas *or* supplicium) dare to pay the penalty; satis dare *(w. dat)* to give satisfaction to, satisfy; Senatum dare to allow a private person to address the Senate; spatium dare to make room; terga dare to take to one's heels; velum dare to set sail; veniam dare to grant pardon; venum dare to put up for sale ‖ refl to present oneself; to plunge, rush; se dare militem *(or* militiae) to enlist in the service

doc·eō -ēre -uī -tus *tr* to teach, instruct; to give instructions to; to tell, inform *(s.o. of a fact);* (w. double acc) to teach *(s.o. s.th.);* fabulam docere to produce a play, put on a play

dochm·ius -iī *m (pros)* dochmiac foot *(consisting of iamb and cretic)* (∪ ˉ ˉ ∪ ˉ)

docil·is -is -e *adj* easily taught, teachable; ready to listen

docilit·ās -ātis *f* aptitude for learning

doctē *adv* skillfully; cleverly

doct·or -ōris *m* teacher

doctrīn·a -ae *f* teaching, instruction, education, training; lesson; erudition, learning; science

doct·us -a -um *pp of* doceo ‖ *adj* learned, skilled, experienced, trained; clever, shrewd; *(w. abl or ad or* in + *abl)* skilled in, clever at

document·um -ī *or* docum·en -inis *n* (doci-) example, model, pattern; object lesson, warning; proof, evidence

Dōdōn·a -ae *f* town in Epirus, famous for the oracular oak tree sacred to Jupiter

Dōdōnae·us -a -um *adj* of Dodona

Dōdōn·is -idis *adj (fem only)* of Dodona

dodr·ans -antis *m* three-fourths; heres ex dodrante heir to three-fourths of an estate

dōdrantāri·us -a -um *adj* tabulae dondrantariae account books connected with the Valerian Law of 86 B.C., which reduced debts by three-fourths

dogm·a -atis *n* doctrine, tenet

Dolabell·a -ae *m* Roman family name *(cognomen)* in the *gens Cornelia, esp.* Publius Cornelius Dolabella, Cicero's son-in-law *(d. 43 B.C.)*

dolābr·a -ae *f* pickax, mattock

dol·ens -entis *adj* painful, smarting, distressing; grieving

dolenter *adv* painfully; with sorrow

dol·eō -ēre -uī -itus *tr* to give pain to, hurt ‖ *intr* to feel pain; to hurt, be sore, ache, smart; to grieve, be sorry, be hurt; take offense; *(w. dat)* to give pain to, afflict; caput mihi dolet I have a headache

dōliār·is -is -e *adj (coll)* fat, tubby

dōliol·um -ī *n* small barrel

dōl·ium -iī *n* large earthenware barrel

dol·ō -āre -āvī -ātus *tr* to chop; to beat up, drub; *(fig)* to hack out *(e.g., a poem)*

dol·ō -ōnis *m* pike *(having a wooden shaft and a short iron point);* topsail

Dol·ōn -ōnis *m* Dolon *(Trojan spy)*

Dolop·es -um *mpl* tribe of Thessaly

dol·or -ōris *m* pain, ache; grief, distress; indignation, resentment, chagrin; pathos; object of grief; capitis dolor headache; dentium dolor toothache; esse dolori *(w. dat)* to be a cause of grief *or* resentment to

dolōsē *adv* shrewdly, slyly

dolōs·us -a -um *adj* wily, cunning

dol·us -ī *m* trick; deceit; cunning; dolus malus *(leg)* malice aforethought, fraud

domābil·is -is -e *adj* able to be tamed

domesticātim *adv* at home, by use of one's domestics

domestic·us -a -um *adj* of the house *or*

home; domestic, household; familiar, private, personal; native, of one's own country; **bellum domesticum** civil war ‖ *mpl* members of the household, one's staff
domī *see* **domus**
domicēn·ium -(i)ī *n* a meal at home
domicil·ium -(i)ī *n* residence, home
domin·a -ae *or* **domn·a** -ae *f* lady of the house; mistress, owner; lady; sweetheart; wife; *(as a title of courtesy)* Ma'am
domin·ans -antis *adj* ruling, dominant; **nomen dominans** word in its literal sense, normal word ‖ *m* ruler
domināti·ō -ōnis *f* mastery; tyranny, despotism; dominion, kingdom ‖ *fpl* control; supremacy; rulers
domināt·or -ōris *m* arbitrary ruler, lord
dominātr·ix -īcis *f* ruler, mistress
domināt·us -ūs *m* absolute rule, sovereignty; ownership; mastery
dominic·us -a -um *adj* master's; mistress's; owner's; belonging to the emperor ‖ **Dominic·a** -ae *f (eccl)* the Lord's day, Sunday
domin·ium -(i)ī *n* rule, dominion; ownership; banquet, feast
domin·or -ārī -ātus sum *intr* to be master, be lord, have dominion; to domineer; *(w. in + acc or abl)* to lord it over, dominate
domin·us -ī *m* owner, proprietor; master, ruler, lord; tyrant; commander; lover; manager *(of a troupe); (as a courtesy title)* Sir; *(as imperial title)* His Imperial Highness; **convivii dominus** host ‖ **Dominus** *(eccl)* the Lord
domiport·a -ae *f* house-carrier *(snail)*
Domitiān·us -ī *m* Domitian *(Titus Flavius Domitianus, son of Vespasian and Roman emperor, 81–96 A.D.)*
domit·ō -āre -āvī *tr* to train, break in
domit·or -ōris *m* tamer; conqueror
domitr·ix -īcis *f* tamer *(female)*
domit·us -ūs *m* taming
domīt·us -a -um *adj* house-bound, kept at home
dom·ō -āre -uī -itus *tr* to tame, break in; to domesticate; to master, subdue, vanquish, conquer
dom·us -ūs *or* -ī *(dat:* **domō** *or* **domuī;** *abl* **domō** *or* **domū;** *loc:* **domī,** *rarely* **domō** *or* **domuī;** *gen pl:* **domōrum** *or* **domuum)** *f* house, home; mansion, palace; family, household; school *(of philosophers);* building *(of any sort);* seat *(an an activity);* **domi** at home; by one's own resources; **domi militiaeque** at home and in the field; in peace and in war; **domi tuae** at your home; **domo** from home; from the house; from one's own resources; **domum** *(to one's)* home; *(coll)* into one's pocket
dōnābil·is -is -e *adj* worthy of a gift

dōnār·ium -(i)ī *n* gift repository of a temple; sanctuary; altar; votive offering
dōnāti·ō -ōnis *f* donation
dōnātīv·um -ī *n (mil)* bonus
dōnec *(also* **dōnicum)** *conj* while; as long as; until
dōn·ō -āre -āvī -ātus *tr* to present, grant; to condone, excuse; to forgive, let off; to give up, sacrifice; **aliquem civitate donare** to present s.o. with citizenship; **civitatem alicui donare** to bestow citizenship on s.o.
dōn·um -ī *n* gift, present; votive offering, sacrifice; **ultima dona** funeral rites, obsequies
dorc·as -adis *f* gazelle
Dōr·ēs *or* **Dōr·is** -um *mpl* Dorians *(one of the four Hellenic tribes, inhabiting the Peloponnese in the classical period; also, the inhabitants of Doris in N. Greece)*
Dōricē *adv* in the Dorian dialect
Dōric·us -a -um *adj* Doric ‖ *mpl* the Dorians
Dōr·is -idis *or* -idos *adj (fem only)* Dorian, Doric ‖ *f* district in N. Greece ‖ the S.W. tip of Caria with its offshore islands ‖ a sea-goddess, wife of Nereus and mother of fifty sea nymphs
Dōri·us -a -um *adj* Dorian
dorm·iō -īre -īvī *or* -iī -ītum *intr* to sleep; to fall asleep; to be idle, be unconcerned
dormītāt·or -ōris *m* night-prowler
dormīt·ō -āre -āvī *intr* to be sleepy, be drowsy; to nod, fall asleep
dormīt·or -ōris *m* sleeper
dormītōri·us -a -um *adj* for sleeping; **cubiculum dormitorium** bedroom
dors·um -ī *n* back; ridge; reef
doryphor·os *or* **doryphor·us** -ī *m* spearman
dōs dōtis *f* dowry; endowment
Dossenn·us -ī *m* hunchback, clown *(well-known character in early Italic comedy)*
dōtāl·is -is -e *adj* of a dowry, given as a dowry, dotal
dōtāt·us -a -um *adj* endowed; **dotatissimus** richly endowed
dōt·ō -āre -āvī -ātus *tr* to endow
drachm·a *or* **drachum·a** -ae *f* drachma *(Greek coin approximately the value of a denarius, c. $1)*
drachumiss·ō -āre *intr* to work for a drachma a day
drac·ō -ōnis *m* dragon; huge serpent ‖ **Draco** Draco *(Athenian lawgiver, notorious for his severity, c. 621 B.C.); (astr)* Dragon *(constellation)*
dracōnigen·us -a -um *adj* sprung from a dragon; **urbs draconigena** Thebes
drāpet·a -ae *m* runaway slave
drauc·us -ī *m* athlete
drom·as -adis *m* dromedary, camel
drom·os -ī *m* parade ground

drop·ax -acis *m* hair-remover

Druid·ēs -um *or* **Druid·ae -ārum** *mpl* Druids *(priests and sages of the Gauls and Britons)*

Drūsill·a -ae *f* Livia Drusilla *(second wife of Augustus and mother of Tiberius, 58 B.C.–A.D. 29)* ‖ sister of Caligula ‖ daughter of Caligula, murdered in infancy

Drūs·us -ī *m* Livius Drusus *(tribune of the people with Gaius Gracchus in 122 B.C.)* ‖ Marcus Livius Drusus *(former's son, famous orator and tribune of the people in 91 B.C.)* ‖ Nero Claudius Drusus *(son of Livia, brother of Tiberius, 38 B.C.–A.D. 9)*

dry·as -adis *f* dryad *(wood nymph)*

Dryop·ē -ēs *f* mother of Amphissus

Dryop·es -um *mpl* a people of Epirus

dubiē *adv* doubtfully; **haud dubie** undoubtedly, indubitably

dubitābil·is -is -e *adj* doubtful

dubitanter *adv* doubtingly, hesitantly

dubitāti·ō -ōnis *f* doubt, uncertainty; wavering, hesitancy; hesitation, delay; *(rhet)* pretended embarrassment *(to win over sympathy)*

dubit·ō -āre -āvī -ātus *tr* to doubt; to consider, ponder, wonder ‖ *intr* to be doubtful, be in doubt, be uncertain, be perplexed; to deliberate; to waver, hesitate, delay

dubi·us -a -um *adj* wavering, doubtful, dubious, uncertain; precarious, critical; adverse, difficult; dim *(light)*; overcast *(sky)*; indecisive *(battle)*; **haud pro dubio habere** to regard as beyond doubt; **in dubium venire** to come into question; **in dubium vocare** to call into question; **procul dubio** undoubtedly

ducāt·us -ūs *m* military leadership, command

ducēnāri·us -a -um *adj* receiving an annual salary of 200,000 sesterces *(c. $50,000)*

ducēn·ī -ae -a *adj* two hundred each

ducentēsim·a -ae *f* half-percent tax

ducent·ī -ae -a *adj* two hundred

ducentiens *adv* (**-iēs**) two hundred times

dūc·ō dūcěre duxī ductus *tr* to lead, guide, direct, conduct; to command; to march; to draw, pull; to draw out, prolong; to stall *(s.o.)*; to pull at *(oars)*; to mislead, take in, fool; to draw, attract; to draw *(lots)*; to draw in, breathe in; to sip, drink; to trace; to construct, form, fashion, shape; to run, build *(a wall from one point to another)*; to drive *(vehicles)*; to assume, get *(a name)*; *(of a man)* to marry; to calculate, compute; to regard, consider, hold, account; to derive, trace *(lineage)*; to spin *(wool)*; *(of a road)* to lead, take *(s.o.)*; **ducere triumphum** to hold a triumph; **id parvi ducere** to consider it of little importance; **initium** *(or* **rationem) ducere** to take account *(of)*, pay attention *(to)*; **principium ducere** *(w. ab)* to start from, originate from, trace to, e.g.: **belli initium a fame ducere** to trace the beginning of the war to hunger; **uxorem ducere** *(of the groom)* to get married, take a wife

ductil·is -is -e *adj (of a river)* that is led along a course

ductim *adv* in a continuous stream

ductit·ō -āre -āvī -ātus *tr* to take home, marry *(a woman)*; to lead on, trick

duct·ō -āre -āvī -ātus *tr* to lead; to draw; to accompany, escort

duct·or -ōris *m* leader, commander, general; guide; pilot

duct·us -ūs *m* drawing, conducting; line, row; leadership, command; **aquae ductus** aqueduct; **oris ductus** facial expression

dūdum *adv* a short time ago; just now; once, formerly; **cum dudum** just as; **haud dudum** not long ago, just now; **jam dudum** for some time; **jam dudum eum exspecto** I have been waiting for him a long time; **quam dudum** how long; **ut dudum** just as

Duill·ius *or* **Duīl·ius -(i)ī** *m* Duilius *(Roman consul who won Rome's first naval victory, off Sicily, in 260 B.C.)*

duim, duis duit *see* **do**

dulcēd·ō -inis *f* sweetness; pleasantness, charm, delightfulness

dulc·escō -escěre *intr* to become sweet

dulciāri·us -a -um *adj* **pistor dulciarius** confectioner, pastry baker

dulcicul·us -a -um *adj* rather sweet

dulcif·er -era -erum *adj* full of sweetness, sweet

dulc·is -is -e *adj* sweet; pleasant, delightful; dear, affectionate, kind

dulciter *adv* sweetly; pleasantly

dulcitūd·ō -inis *f* sweetness

dūlicē *adv* like a slave

Dūlich·ium -iī *n or* **Dūlichi·a -ae** *f* Dulichium *(island in the Ionian Sea)*

Dūlich·ius -(i)ī *m* Ulysses

dum *adv* up to now, yet, as yet; now; **age dum!** *(pl:* **agite dum!)** come now!; all right!; **nemo dum** no one (as) yet; **non dum** not yet

dum *conj* while; as long as; until; provided that, if only; **dum modo** *or* **dummodo** provided that, if only; **exspectabam dum rediret** I was waiting for him to return

dūmēt·um -ī *n* thicket, underbrush

dummodo *conj* provided that

dūmōs·us -a -um *adj* overgrown with bushes, bushy

dumtaxat *adv (with numbers)* up to, at most, not exceeding; *(with small numbers)* only, just; not less than, at least;

(limiting a statement) at any rate, at least, strictly speaking; up to a point **‖** *conj* provided that, as long as; **non dumtaxat**...**sed** not just...**but** also

dūm·us -ī *m* bush, bramble

du·o -ae -o *(dat & abl pl:* **duōbus, duābus, duōbus)** *adj* two

duodeciens *adv* (**-ciēs**) twelve times

duodecim *indecl adj* twelve

duodecim·us -a -um *adj* (**-cum-**) twelfth

duodēn·ī -ae -a *adj* twelve each, twelve, apiece; a dozen; **duodenis assibus** at 12%

duodēquadrāgēsim·us -a -um *adj* thirty-eighth

duodēquadrāgintā *indecl adj* forty-eight

duodēquinquāgēsim·us -a -um *adj* forty-eighth

duodētrīciens *adv* (**-ciēs**) twenty-eight times

duodētrīgintā *indecl adj* twenty-eight

duodēvīcēn·ī -ae -a *adj* eighteen each

duodēvīgintī *indecl adj* eighteen

duoetvīcēsimān·ī -ōrum *mpl* soldiers of the twenty-second legion

duoetvīcēsim·us -a -um *adj* (**-cens-**) twenty-second

duovirī *see* **duumviri**

dupl·a -ae *f* a double amount of money; double the price

dupl·ex -icis *adj* twofold, double; divided into two; in double rows; double, twice as big; twice as long; complex, compound; two-faced, double-dealing, false

duplicār·ius -iī *m* soldier receiving double pay

dupliciter *adv* doubly; in two ways; into two categories

duplic·ō -āre -āvī -ātus *tr* to double up, bend over; to double *(in size, length, quantity)*

dupl·us -a -um *adj* double, twice as much, twice as large **‖** *f see* **dupla ‖** *n* double the price; **in duplum** twice the amount; **in duplum ire** to pay twice as much

dupond·ius -(i)ī *m or* **dupond·ium -(i)ī** *n* two-ass coin *(worth c. 2¢)*

dūrābil·is -is -e *adj* durable, lasting

dūracin·us -a -um *adj* having a hard berry

dūrām·en -inis *n* hardness

dūrate·us -a -um *adj* wooden

dūrē *or* **dūriter** *adv* hard, sternly, rigorously, roughly; stiffly, awkwardly

dūr·escō -escĕre -uī *intr* to grow hard, harden; to become solid

dūrit·ās -ātis *f* hardness, toughness; harshness

dūriter *see* **dure**

dūriti·a -ae *or* **dūriti·ēs -ēī** *f* hardness; austerity; strictness, harshness, rigor; oppressiveness; insensibility, callousness

dūriuscul·us -a -um *adj* somewhat hard, rather harsh

dūr·ō -āre -āvī -ātus *tr* to harden, solidify; *(fig)* to harden, inure, toughen up; to make insensible; to dull, blunt **‖** *intr* to be tough, be inured; to become hard; *(of liquids)* to become solid; to endure, last, hold out; to continue unchanged, remain; *(of food)* to keep; *(of hills)* to continue unbroken, extend

dūr·us -a -um *adj* hard; lasting; rough *(to the senses);* tough, hardy; rough, rude, uncouth; shameless, brazen; harsh, cruel; callous, insensitive; severe, oppressive; parsimonious

duum·vir *or* **duo·vir** *or* **II·vir -virī** *m* duumvir *(member of a board of two) (see* **duumvirī)**

duumvirāt·us -ūs *m* duumvirate, office of duumvir

duumvir·ī -ōrum *or* **duovir·ī** *or* **II·virī -ōrum** *mpl* two-man board; **duumviri ad aedem faciendam** two-man board for the construction of a temple; **duumviri juri dicundo** two-man board of colonial magistrates; pair of judges; **duumviri navales** two-man board to equip the navy; **duumviri perduellionis** criminal court *(to try cases of treason);* **duumviri sacrorum** two-man board in charge of the Sibylline books

dux ducis *m* (*f*) general; guide; leader, head, ringleader; driver *(of chariot);* captain *(of ship),* commander *(of naval force);* **dux gregis** shepherd

Dymant·is -idos *f* daughter of Dymas, Hecuba

Dym·ās -antis *m* father of Hecuba

dynam·is -is *f* store, plenty

dynast·ēs -ae *m* ruler, (Eastern) prince

Dyrr(h)ach·ium -(i)ī *n* Adriatic port in Illyria, serving as landing place for those sailing from Italy to Greece *(modern Durazzo)*

dysenteri·a -ae *f* dysentery

dyspepsi·a -ae *f* indigestion

ē *prep see* **ex**

ē- *pref see* **ex-**

-ē *advl suf* forms adverbs from o-stem adjectives: **clare** clearly; but in prosody, **benĕ, malĕ**

eā *adv* there; that way

ea ejus *pron* she

eādem *adv* the same way, by the same route; at the same time; likewise, by the same token

eāpropter *adv* therefore

eapse = **ipsa** *(old feminine emphatic form of* **ipse***)*

eātenus *adv* to such a degree, so far

ebenus *see* **hebenus**

ebes *see* **hebes**

ēbib·ō -ĕre -ī -itus *tr* to drink up, drain; *(of things)* to absorb, swallow up; to spend on drinks

ebiscum *see* **hibiscum**

ēbīt·ō -ĕre *intr* to go out

ēbland·ior -īrī -ītus sum *tr* to coax out, obtain by flattery

Eborāc·um -ī *n* (**Ebur-**) town in Britain *(modern York)*

eborāt·us -a -um *adj* (**ebur-**) adorned with ivory

ēbriet·ās -ātis *f* drunkenness

ēbriol·us -a -um *adj* tipsy

ēbriōsit·ās -ātis *f* habitual drunkenness, heavy drinking

ēbriōs·us -a -um *adj* addicted to drinking; *(of grapes)* addictive

ēbri·us -a -um *adj* drunk; drunken *(acts, words),* of a drunk; *(fig)* intoxicated *(e.g., w. love, power)*

ēbull·iō -īre -iī *or* **īvī** *tr* to babble about; **animam ebullire** *(coll)* to give up the ghost ‖ *intr* to bubble up

ebul·um -ī *n or* **ebul·us -ī** *f (bot)* dwarf elder *(small tree having clusters of white flowers and red or blackish berry-like fruit)*

eb·ur -oris *n* ivory; ivory object *(e.g., statue, flute, scabbard);* elephant's tusk; elephant; curule chair *(of a magistrate, ornamented with ivory)*

eburāt·us -a -um *adj* inlaid with ivory

eburneol·us -a -um *adj* made of ivory

eburne·us *or* **eburn·us -a -um** *adj* ivory; white as ivory; **dentes eburnei** tusks; **ensis eburneus** sword with ivory hilt

ec- *pref (prefixed to interrogatives with intensive or indefinite force, e.g.,* **ecquis** is there anyone who?)

ēcastor *interj (used mainly by women)* by Castor!

ecca, eccam, eccās *see* **ecce**

ecce *interj* see!, look!, look here! here!; *(followed by accusative in early literature; also followed by nominative from time of Cicero on)* **ecce me** here I am!; **ecce nos** here we are!; *(colloquially combined with the pronouns* **is, ille, iste: ecca** *(i.e.,* **ecce + ea***) (fem sing)* here she is!; *(neut pl)* here they are!; **eccam** *(i.e.,* **ecce + eam***)* here she is!; **eccilla** *or* **eccistam** there she is!; **eccillum** *or* **eccum** here he is!; **eccos** here they are!; *(calling attention to something non-visual)* mark this!; *(in vivid narrative, introducing a surprising event)* lo and behold!

eccerē *interj* there!

eccheum·a -atis *n* pouring out

eccill- *see* **ecce**

eccist- *see* **ecce**

ecclēsi·a -ae *f* Greek assembly of the people; *(eccl)* church, congregation

eccōs *interj see* **ecce**

eccum *interj see* **ecce**

ecdic·us -ī *m* public prosecutor; public defender

ecf- = **eff-**

echidn·a -ae *f* viper ‖ **Echidna** Hydra; **Echidna Lernaea** Lernaean Hydra ‖ monstrous mother of Cerberus, half woman and half serpent

Echidnē·us -a -um *adj* of Echidna; **canis Echidneus** Cerberus

Echīnad·es -um *fpl* cluster of small islands off Acarnania

echīn·us -ī *m* sea urchin; dishpan

Echī·ōn -onis *m* hero who sprang from the dragon's teeth sown by Cadmus, married Agave, and became father of Pentheus ‖ an argonaut

Echīonid·ēs -ae *m* Pentheus, son of Echion

Echīoni·us -a -um *adj* Cadmean, Theban

ēch·ō -ūs *(acc: -ō or* **-ōn***) f* nymph who was changed by Hera into an echo

eclog·a -ae *f* literary selection; eclogue

eclogāri·ī -ōrum *mpl* excerpted literary passages

ecquandō *adv* ever, at any time; *(in indirect questions)* whether ever

ecquī *conj (in indirect questions)* whether

ecqu·ī -ae *(or* **-a***)* **-od** *interrog adj* any at all, really any

ec·quid -cūjus *pron* anything at all; *(in questions)* whether, if at all

ec·quis -cūjus *pron* any at all, anyone at all; *(in indirect questions)* whether anyone

ecquō *adv* anywhere

ecule·us -ī *m* foal, colt; small equestrian statue; torture rack; hobbyhorse

edācit·ās -ātis *f* gluttony

ed·ax -ācis *adj* gluttonous; *(fig)* devouring, destructive

ēdent·ō -āre -āvī -ātus *tr (sl)* to knock the teeth out of

ēdentul·us -a -us *adj* toothless, old

edepol *interj* by Pollux!, gad!

eder·a *or* **heder·a -ae** *f* ivy

ēdī·cō -cĕre -xī -ctus *tr* to proclaim; to decree; to appoint

ēdicti·ō -ōnis *f* edict, decree

ēdict·ō -āre -āvī -ātus *tr* to proclaim, publish

ēdict·um -ī *n* edict, proclamation; edict of a praetor listing rules he would follow in his capacity as judge

ē·discō -discĕre -didicī *tr* to learn by heart, learn thoroughly

ēdisser·ō -ĕre -uī -tus *tr* to explain in detail, analyze fully

ēdissert·ō -āre -āvī -ātus *tr* to explain fully, explain in detail

ēditīci·us -a -um *adj* set forth, proposed; **judices editicii** panel of jurors *(subject to challenge by defendant)*

ēditi·ō -ōnis *f* statement, account; publication; edition *(of book); (leg)* declaration *(of the form of judicial procedure to be followed)*

ēdit·us -a -um *adj* high; raised, rising; *(fig)* exalted; **locus editus** height, hill **‖** *n* height; ordinance; **ex edito** from a height; **in edito** on a hill; *(fig)* on a pedestal

ēd·ō -ēre -idī -itus *tr* to give out, put forth, bring forth, emit; to give birth to, bear; to publish; to tell, announce, disclose; to show, display, produce, perform; to bring about, cause; to bring forward *(witnesses); (leg)* to give the defendant notice of; **animam edere** to give up the ghost

edō edĕre *(or* **esse) ēdī ēsus** *tr* to eat; *(fig)* to devour, consume, destroy; **pugnos edere** *(sl)* to eat fists, eat a knuckle sandwich

ēdoc·eō -ēre -uī -tus *tr* to teach thoroughly; to instruct clearly; to inform; to show clearly; *(w. double acc)* to te꞉ ꞉l *(s.o. s.th.)* well

ēdol·ō -āre -āvī -ātus *tr* to hew out: *(fig)* tₒ hew into shape

ēdom·ō -āre -uī -itus *tr* to conquer thoroughly; to overcome *(vices, difficulties)*

Ēdōn·ī -ōrum *or* **Ēdōn·es -um** *mpl* Thracian tribe noted for its heavy drinking

Ēdōn·is -idis *adj (fem only)* Edonian **‖** *f* Bacchante

Ēdōn·us -a -um *adj* Edonian

ēdorm·iō -īre -īvī *or* **-iī ītus** *tr* to sleep off; to sleep through *(e.g., a lecture);* **crapulam edormire** to sleep off a hangover **‖** *intr* to sleep soundly

ēdormisc·ō -ĕre *tr* to sleep off

ēducāti·ō -ōnis *f* raising *(of children, animals)*

ēducāt·or -ōris *m* fosterer; foster father

ēducātr·ix -īcis *f* foster mother; nurse

ēduc·ō -āre -āvī -ātus *tr* to bring up, raise *(children, animals);* to produce *(fruit, grain)*

ēdū·cō -cĕre -xī -ctus *tr* to draw out, to take away; to build high; to drain off *(liquids);* to draw *(sword);* to spend *(time);* to lead out *(army);* to raise *(children, animals);* **in jus educere** to take to court

edūl·ia -ium *npl* eatables

edūl·is -is -e *adj* edible, eatable

ēdūr·ō -āre *intr* to last, endure

ēdūr·us -a -um *adj* hard, tough; *(fig)* tough

Ēëti·ōn -ōnis *m* father of Andromache and king of Thebe in Cilicia

effarciō *see* **effercio**

effāt·us -a -um *pp of* **effor ‖** *adj* solemnly pronounced **‖** *n* pronouncement; axiom, proposition

effectē *adv* consummately

effecti·ō -ōnis *f* accomplishment, performance; efficient cause

effectīv·us -a -um *adj* effective; practical

effect·or -ōris *m,* **effectr·ix -īcis** *f* producer, author

effect·us -a -um *pp of* **efficio ‖** *adj* finished, complete **‖** *n* effect

effect·us -ūs *m* effecting; completion; effect, result; **ad effectum adducere** to bring to completion; **cum effectu** in fact, actually; **effectu** in effect, to all intents and purposes; **sine effectu** without a decisive result

effēminātē *adv* effeminately

effēmināt·us -a -um *adj* (ecf-) effeminate

effēmin·ō -āre -āvī -ātus *tr* (ecf-) to make a woman of; to represent as a woman, regard as female; to emasculate **‖** *pass* to become unmanly

efferāt·us -a -um *adj* wild, savage

effercio *or* **effarciō -cīre -sī -tus** *tr* (ecfer-, ecfar-) to stuff; to fill in *(e.g., a ditch)*

efferit·ās -ātis *f* wildness, barbarism

effer·ō -āre -āvī -ātus *tr* (ecf-) to make wild, brutalize; to exasperate

efferō efferre extulī ēlātus *tr* (ecf-) to carry out, bring out, bring forth; to utter, express, to publish, spread *(news);* to carry out for burial, bury; to produce, bear; to name, designate; to lift up, raise; to promote, advance; to bring out, expose; to praise, extol; to sweep off one's feet; *(w. ex)* copy out *(of some text);* **in lucem efferre** *(of fields)* to produce *(crops);* **gressum** *(or* **pedem) efferre** to go forth **‖** *refl* to arise; to be haughty, be conceited **‖** *pass (fig)* to be carried away

effert·us -a -um *pp of* **effercio ‖** *adj* chockfull, crammed, bulging

efferv·eō -ēre *or* **efferv·ō -ĕre** *intr* to boil over; *(of bees, etc.)* to come pouring out; *(of volcano)* to erupt

efferv·escō -escĕre -ī *intr* to boil, boil over; to burst forth; to get all worked up; to seethe; to rage; *(of words) (fig)* to become heated

effer·us -a -um *adj* very wild, savage

effēt·us -a -um *adj* worn out, spent; vain, delusive; *(w. gen)* incapable of

efficācit·ās -ātis *f* efficiency

efficāciter *adv* efficiently, effectively

effic·ax -ācis *adj* efficient, effective, efficacious

effici·ens -entis *adj* efficient, effective; **res efficientes** *(phil)* efficient causes

efficienter *adv* efficiently

efficienti·a -ae *f* efficiency, efficacy, influence

ef·ficiō -ficĕre -fēcī -fectus *tr* **(ecf-)** to bring about, bring to pass, effect, cause, produce; to make, form; to construct; to finish, complete, accomplish; to show, prove; *(w.* **ut)** to bring it about that; to carry out *(an order); (of component parts)* to constitute; to cover *(a distance in travel); (of numbers)* to amount to, add up to; *(of a field)* to produce, yield; to compose *(a speech, an essay); (w. double acc)* to elect *(s.o., e.g., consul)* **‖** *pass* to follow; **ita efficitur ut** thus it follows that

effictus *pp of* **effingo**

effigi·ēs -ēī *or* **effigi·a -ae** *f* effigy, likeness, semblance; opposite number; copy, imitation; image; statue, figure, portrait; ghost, phantom

ef·fingō -fingĕre -finxī -fictus *tr* **(ecf-)** to mold, form, fashion; to imitate; to wipe out, wipe clean; to represent, portray; to imagine

effiō *pass of* **efficio**

efflāgitāti·ō -ōnis *f* urgent demand

efflāgitāt·us -ūs *m* insistence

efflāgit·ō -āre *tr* to demand, insist on; to pester *(s.o. with requests)*

efflictim *adv* **(ecf-)** passionately

efflict·ō -āre *tr* **(ecf-)** to strike dead

efflī·gō -gĕre -xī -ctus *tr* **(ecf-)** to strike dead, exterminate

effl·ō -āre -āvī -ātus *tr* **(ecf-)** to breathe out; **animam efflare** to expire

efflōr·escō -escĕre -uī *intr* **(ecf-)** to bloom; *(fig)* to flourish

efflu·ō -ĕre -xī *intr* **(ecf-)** to flow out, flow forth, run out; to slip away, drop out, disappear; *(of rumor)* to get out, circulate; *(of secret)* to leak out; **ex animo** *(or* **memoriā) effluere** to slip one's mind

effluv·ium -(i)ī *n* outlet

effo·diō -dĕre -dī -ssus *tr* **(ecf-, exf-)** to dig up; to gouge out *(eyes);* to hollow out; to root out; to make *(by digging),* to erase; **humum** *(or* **terram) effodere** to dig a hole in the ground

(ef·for) -fārī -fātus sum *tr* **(ecf-)** to say out loud, tell; *(in augury)* to mark off, consecrate *(an area)* **‖** *intr* to speak out

effossus *pp of* **effodio**

effrēnātē *adv* **(ecf-)** without restraint, out of control

effrēnāti·ō -ōnis *f* impetuosity

effrēnāt·us -a -um *adj* **(ecf-)** unbridled; *(fig)* unbridled, unrestrained

effrēn·us -a -um *adj* unbridled; *(fig)* uncontrolled

ef·fringō -fringĕre -frēgī -fractus *tr* **(ecf-)** to break open, smash, break off; to break down *(door)*

ef·fugiō -fugĕre -fūgī *tr* **(ecf-, exf-)** to escape; to keep away from *(a person or place);* to avoid; to escape the grasp of, slip out of *(the hands);* to escape the notice of **‖** *intr* to escape, slip away; *(w. abl or w.* **ab** *or* **ex)** to escape from

effug·ium -(i)ī *n* escape, flight; means of escape; avoidance

efful·geō -gēre -sī *or* **effulg·ō -ĕre** *intr* to shine forth, gleam, flash, glitter; *(fig)* to shine forth

effult·us -a -um *adj* propped up

ef·fundō -fundĕre -fūdī -fūsus *tr* **(ecf-)** to pour out, pour away; to emit; to utter *(sounds);* to allow *(rain water)* to run off; to shed *(tears);* to hurl, shower *(weapons); (w.* **in** + *acc)* to shower *(praises)* on; *(of the stomach)* to throw up; to give up, let go, abandon, resign; to knock down, overturn *(walls, buildings);* to produce in abundance; to lavish, waste *(money, energy); (of tree)* to spread out *(branches);* to empty out *(bags, etc.);* to give vent to, pour out **‖** *refl & pass* to come pouring out; *(of rain)* to pour down; *(of a river) (w.* **ab)** to begin to flow from, have its source at; **super ripam effundi** to overflow its banks

effūsē *adv* far and wide; at random, in disorder; lavishly; immoderately

effūsi·ō -ōnis *f* **(ecf-)** outpouring, rushing out; shedding; effusion; profusion, lavishness, extravagance **‖** *fpl* excesses

effūs·us -a -um *pp of* **effundo** **‖** *adj* spread out, extensive; *(of troops)* thinly spread out *(over a large area);* straggly, disorderly; relaxed, loose; disheveled; lavish; unrestrained; immoderate; *(w.* **in** + *acc)* very prone to *(some weakness),* passionately devoted to *(some cause);* **effusissimis habenis** at full speed

effūt·iō -īre -īvī *or* **-iī -ītus** *tr & intr* to blab, babble

effut·uō -uĕre -uī -ūtus *tr* **(ecf-)** *(vulg)* to wear out through excessive sex

ēgelid·us -a -um *adj* tepid; cool

eg·ens -entis *adj* needy, poor; *(w.* **gen)** in need of, needing

egēn·us -a -um *adj* needy, destitute; *(w.* **gen)** in need of, needing

eg·eō -ēre -uī *intr* to be needy, suffer want; *(w.* **gen)** **1** to be in need of; **2** to lack, be without; **3** to want, desire, miss

Ēgeri·a -ae *f* nymph whom King Numa visited at night for advice

ē·gerō -gerĕre -gessī -gestus *tr* to carry out, take away, remove; to discharge, vomit, emit

egest·ās -ātis *f* need, want, poverty; *(w.* **gen)** lack of

ēgesti·ō -ōnis *f* squandering

ēgestus *pp of* **egero**

ego *pron* I

egomet *pron* I personally, I and nobody else

ē·gredior -gredī -gressus sum *tr* to go beyond, pass; to quit; *(fig)* to surpass **‖** *intr* to go out, come out; to march out; to set sail; to disembark, land; to go up, climb; *(fig)* to digress

ēgregiē *adv* exceptionally, singularly, uncommonly, splendidly

ēgregi·us -a -um *adj* exceptional, uncommon; distinguished, illustrious; **vir egregius** *(title given under the Empire to officials of equestrian rank)* the honorable...

ēgressus *pp of* **egredior**

ēgress·us -ūs *m* way out, exit; departure; disembarking, landing; mouth *(of river);* digression **‖** *mpl* comings and goings

ēgurgit·ō -āre *tr* to pour out, lavish

ehem *interj (expressing pleasant surprise)* ha!, aha!

ēheu *interj (expressing pain)* oh!

eho *interj (often expressing rebuke)* look here!, see here!; **eho dum!** look here now!

ei *interj* **hei** *(expressing fear or dismay)* ah!

ēia *or* **hēia** *interj (expressing joy or surpise)* ah!; ah ha!; good!; *(expressing haste)* quick!, come on!; **eia age** come on!, up then!

ējacul·or -ārī -ātus sum *tr* to squirt **‖** *refl (of water, etc.)* to squirt

ējectāment·a -ōrum *npl* refuse; jetsam

ējecti·ō -ōnis *f* ejection; banishment, exile

ēject·ō -āre -āvī -ātus *tr* to spout forth; to keep throwing up *(e.g., blood)*

eject·us -ūs *m* emission

ējer·ō -āre -āvī -ātus *tr* (**ējūr-**) to refuse under oath, abjure, forswear; to deny under oath; to resign, abdicate; to disown, abandon

ē·jiciō -jicĕre -jēcī -jectus *tr* to throw out, drive out, put out, eject, expel; to banish; to utter; to run aground; to reject, disapprove; to boo *(s.o.)* off the stage **‖** *refl (of passions)* to come to the fore, break out **‖** *pass* to be stranded

ējulāti·ō -ōnis *f* lamenting

ējulāt·us -a - um *adj* wailing

ējul·ō -āre *intr* (**hēj-**) to wail, lament

ējūrō *see* **ejero**

ējusdemmodī *see* **modus**

-ēl·a, -ell·a -ae *fem suf* forms diminutives chiefly from verbs: **querela** complaint *(from* **queri** to complain)

ēlā·bor -bī -psus sum *intr* to glide off; to slip away, escape; to pass away, disappear; *(w. abl or super + acc)* to glance off

ēlabōrāt·us -a -um *adj* studied, overdone; elaborate, finished

ēlabōr·ō -āre -āvī -ātus *tr* to work out,

elaborate; to produce **‖** *intr* to make a great effort, take great pains; *(w. inf)* to strive to

ēlāmentābil·is -is -e *adj* pathetic

ēlangu·escō -escĕre -ī *intr* to slow down, slacken, let up

ēlapsus *pp of* **elabor**

ēlātē *adv* proudly

ēlāti·ō -ōnis *f* elation, ecstasy

ēlātr·ō -āre *tr* to bark out

ēlāt·us -a -um *pp of* **effero ‖** *adj* high, elevated; exalted; haughty, proud

ē·lavō -lavāre -lāvī -lautus *or* **-lōtus** *tr* to wash out; *(coll)* to clean out, rob **‖** *intr* to be cleaned out, be wrecked; **elavare bonis** *(coll)* to be broke

Ele·a -ae *f* town in Lucania in S. Italy, modern Velia, birthplace of Eleatic philosophy

Eleāt·ēs -ae *m* inhabitant of Elea *(i.e., Zeno)*

Eleātic·ī -ōrum *mpl* Eleatics, Eleatic philosophers *(Parmenides and Zeno)*

ēlecebr·a -ae *f* (**exl-**) snare; seductress

ēlectē *adv* tastefully

ēlectil·is -is -e *adj* choice, dainty

ēlecti·ō -ōnis *f* choice, selection

ēlect·ō -āre *tr* to select, choose; to wheedle out, coax out *(a secret)*

Ēlectr·a -ae *f* daughter of Agamemnon and Clytemnestra **‖** Pleiad, daughter of Atlas and mother of Dardanus

ēlectr·um -ī *n* amber; gold-silver alloy **‖** *npl* amber beads

ēlect·us -a -um *pp of* **eligo ‖** *adj* select, choice; *(mil)* elite

ēlect·us -ūs *m* choice

ēleg·ans -antis *adj* elegant; choosy; fine, choice, select

ēleganter *adv* elegantly, tastefully

ēleganti·a -ae *f* elegance, refinement, taste, propriety

elegē·um -ī *n* (**gīum**) elegiac poem

eleg·ī -ōrum *mpl* elegiac verses

elegī·a -ae *f* (**-gē·a**) elegy

Elel·eus -eī *m (epithet of)* Bacchus

elementāri·us -a -um *adj* engaged in learning the rudiments; **senex elementarius** old schoolteacher

element·um -ī *n* first principle, element; atom, particle; letter of the alphabet **‖** *npl* rudiments, elements; beginnings; ABC's

elench·us -ī *m (pear-shaped)* pearl **‖** *mpl* criticisms

elephantomach·a -ae *m* fighter mounted on an elephant

elephant·us -ī *or* **eleph·ās -antis** *m* elephant; *(fig)* ivory

Ēlē·us -a -um *adj* of Elis *(in the Peloponnese)*

Eleus·īn -īnis *f* Eleusis *(town in Attica, sacred to Demeter, the Roman Ceres)*

Eleusīn·us -a -um *adj* Eleusinian; **Eleusina Mater** Demeter *or* the Roman Ceres
eleutheri·a -ae *f* freedom
ēlev·ō -āre -āvī -ātus *tr* to lift up, raise; to alleviate; to lessen; to make light of
Ēli·as -adis *adj (fem only)* Elian, Olympic
ēlic·iō -ēre -uī -itus *tr* to elicit, draw out; to lure out, entice; to conjure up
ēlicitus *pp of* **elicio**
Ēlic·ius -(i)ī *m (epithet of)* Jupiter
ēlī·dō -děre -sī -sus *tr* to knock out, strike out, tear out, force out; to shatter, smash to pieces, crush; to force out, stamp out
ē·ligō -ligěre -lēgī -lectus *tr* (-leg-) to pluck out; to pick out, choose
ēlīmin·ō -āre *tr* to carry outside; to spread abroad
ēlīm·ō -āre -āvī -ātus *tr* to file; to finish off, perfect
ēlingu·is -is -e *adj* speechless; *(fig)* inarticulate
ēlingu·ō -āre *tr* to tear out *(s.o.'s)* tongue
Ēl·is -idis *f* (**Āl-**) town and district on the W. coast of the Peloponnesus in which Olympia is located
-ēl·is -is -e *adjl suf* formed from nouns and adjectives: **crudelis** cruel
Eliss·a *or* **Elīs·a -ae** *f* Dido
ēlīsus *pp of* **elido**
ēl·ix -icis *m* drainage ditch
ēlix·us -a -um *adj* boiled; *(sl)* soused
-ell·a -ae *fem suf* forms diminutives: **cistella** a little box
ellam = **ecce + illam** there she is!
elleborōs·us -a -um *adj* crazy
ellebor·us -ī *m or* **ellebor·um -ī** *n* (**hell-**) helleborus *(plant used to cure mental illness)*
ellips·is -is *f* ellipsis
ellum = **ecce + illum** there he is!
-ell·us -ī *masc suf* forms diminutives: **agellus** small plot
ēloc·ō -āre -āvī -ātus *tr* to lease out, rent out
ēlocūti·ō -ōnis *f* style of speaking, delivery
ēlog·ium -(i)ī *n* saying, maxim; inscription, epitaph; codicil *(in a will)*; criminal record
ēloqu·ens -entis *adj* eloquent
ēloquenter *adv (used in comp & supl degree)* eloquently
ēloquenti·a -ae *f* eloquence
ēloqu·ium -(i)ī *n* eloquence
ēlo·quor -quī -cūtus sum *tr* to speak out, declare; to divulge, tell ‖ *intr* to speak, give a speech
ēlōtus *pp of* **elavo**
ēlū·ceō -cēre -xī *intr* to shine forth; to glitter
ēluct·or -ārī -ātus sum *tr* to struggle out of, struggle through *(e.g., deep snow)*; to

surmount *(difficulties)* ‖ *intr* to force a way out
ēlūcubr·ō -āre -āvī -ātus *or* **ēlūcubr·or -ārī -ātus sum** *tr* to compose by lamplight
ēlū·dō -děre -sī -sus *tr* to elude, parry, avoid; to escape, shun; to delude, deceive; to make fun of; to get the better of, outmaneuver ‖ *intr* to end the game; to behave outrageously with impunity, have free play *(for outrageous conduct)*
ēlū·geō -gēre -xī *tr* to mourn for ‖ *intr* to cease to mourn
ēlumb·is -is -e *adj* (-bus -a -um) having a dislocated hip; bland *(style)*
ē·luō -luěre -luī -lūtus *tr* to wash off, wash clean; to wash away; to rinse out; *(fig)* to wash away, get rid of ‖ *intr (coll)* to loose one's property, be cleaned out
ēlūsus *pp of* **eludo**
ēlūt·us -a -um *pp of* **eluo** ‖ *adj* watery, insipid; weak
ēluvi·ēs -ēī *f* inundation, overflow; sewage; ravine
ēluvi·ō -ōnis *f* deluge
Elvīn·a -ae *f* (**Hel-**) epithet of Ceres
Elysi·us -a -um *adj* Elysian
Ēlys·ium -iī *n* realm of the blessed in the lower world
em *interj* (**hem**) *(in offering some object or fact to s.o., often followed by a dat)* here (there) you are!
emācit·ās -ātis *f* fondness for shopping, mania for buying
ēmad·escō -escěre -uī *intr* to become soaked
ēmancipāti·ō -ōnis *f* (-cup-) emancipation; transfer of property
ēmancipāt·us -a -um *adj* transferred; sold
ēmancip·ō -āre -āvī -ātus *tr* (-cup-) to transfer; to declare *(a son)* free and independent, emancipate; to surrender, abandon
ēmān·ō -āre -āvī -ātum *intr* to flow down; to trickle out, leak out; to become known ‖ *v impers* **emanabat** *(w. acc & inf)* word got out that
Ēmathi·a -ae *f* Macedonia; Thessaly, Pharsalus
Ēmath·is -idis *adj (fem only)* Macedonian ‖ *fpl* the Pierides
Ēmathi·us -a -um *adj* Macedonian, Thessalian, Pharsalian
ēmātūr·escō -escěre -uī *intr* to begin to ripen; to soften; *(fig)* to mellow
em·ax -ācis *adj* fond of shopping; *(fig) (of a prayer)* bargaining with the gods, haggling
emblēm·a -atis *n* mosaic; inlay
embol·ium -(i)ī *n* interlude; insertion *(in literary work)*
ēmendābil·is -is -e *adj* capable of correction
ēmendātē *adv* faultlessly

ēmendāti·ō -ōnis f emendation
ēmendāt·or -ōris m, ēmendātr·ix -īcis f corrector, reformer
ēmendāt·us -a -um adj faultless
ēmendīc·ō -āre -āvī -ātus tr to get by begging
ēmend·ō -āre -āvī -ātus tr to emend, correct; to reform, improve, revise; to atone for
ēmensus pp of emetior
ēment·ior -īrī -ītus sum tr to falsify, fabricate, feign ‖ intr to tell a lie
ēmerc·or -ārī -ātus sum tr to buy up; to obtain through bribery
ēmer·eō -ēre -uī -itus or ēmer·eor -ērī -itus sum tr to earn; to lay under obligation, do (s.o.) a favor; (mil) to serve out (term of service) ‖ intr to serve out one's time in the army
ēmer·gō -gĕre -sī tr to raise (from the water) ‖ refl & pass to raise oneself up, rise ‖ intr to emerge; to rise (in power); to extricate oneself; (w. ex) to get clear of
ēmerit·us -a -um pp of emereo ‖ adj (mil) discharged; (fig) ready to be let out to pasture ‖ m veteran
ēmersus pp of emergo
emetic·a -ae f an emetic
ē·mētior -mētīrī -mensus sum tr to measure out; to traverse, travel over; to live through; to impart
ēmet·ō -ĕre tr to mow down
ēmi- = hemi-
ēmic·ō -āre -uī -ātum intr to dart out, dash out; (of liquids) to spurt out; (of flame) to shoot out; (fig) to stand out, be conspicuous
ēmigr·ō -āre -āvī -ātum intr to move out, depart; e vita emigrare to pass on
ēmināti·ō -ōnis f threatening, blustering
ēmin·ens -entis adj projecting, prominent, high; eminent
ēminenti·a -ae f projection, prominence; (in painting) highlights, foreground
ēmin·eō -ēre -uī intr to stand out, project; to be conspicious; (in paintings) to be highlighted, stand out against a background
ēmin·or -ārī tr to threaten
ēminus adv at long range, at a distance; from afar
ēmīr·or -ārī -ātus sum tr to be greatly surpised at, stand aghast at
ēmissār·ium -(i)ī n drain, outlet
ēmissār·ius -(i)ī m scout, spy
ēmissīci·us -a -um adj spying; oculi emissicii prying eyes
ēmissi·ō -ōnis f discharge, hurling, shooting; releasing, letting off
ēmissus pp of emitto
ēmiss·us -ūs m emission, sending forth; hurling, shooting

ē·mittō -mittĕre -mīsī -missus tr to send out; to hurl, shoot; to let go, let slip, let loose, drop, release, let out; to publish; to allow to escape; to emancipate, set at liberty; to utter; to pass up (opportunity); animam emittere to give up the ghost ‖ refl & pass (w. ex) to break out of
emō emĕre ēmī emptus tr to buy; (w. gen or abl of price) to buy (s.th.) at; to pay for; to gain, obtain; to bribe; bene emere to buy at a bargain; in diem emere to buy on credit; male emere to pay dearly for
ēmoder·or -ārī tr to moderate
ēmodul·or -ārī tr to sing the praises of, celebrate in song
ēmōl·ior -īrī -ītus sum tr to accomplish with great effort
ēmoll·iō -īre -īvī or -iī -ītus tr to soften; to make mild; to enervate
ēmol·ō -ĕre — tr to grind up
ēmolument·um -ī n profit; advantage
ēmon·eō -ēre tr to admonish earnestly
ēmor·ior -ī -tuus sum intr to die; to die off; (of a fire) to die down; (of river) to peter out; (fig) to die out
ēmortuāl·is -is -e adj of death
ēmortuus pp of emorior
ē·moveō -movēre -mōvī -mōtus tr (exm-) to move out, remove, expel; to dislodge; to shake (e.g., foundations of a wall)
Empedocl·ēs -is or -ī m philosopher of Sicily who is said to have jumped into crater of Mt. Etna (fl 444 B.C.)
emphas·is (-is) f emphasis, stress
empīric·us -ī m empiricist (physician who relies on experience rather than on scientific theory)
empor·ium -(i)ī n market town; trade mart, market
empti·ō -ōnis f buying, purchase; thing purchased, purchase
emptit·ō -āre -āvī -ātus tr to be in the habit of buying, buy (regularly)
empt·or -ōris m buyer, customer
empt·um -ī n a purchase
emptus pp of emo
ēmūg·iō -īre tr to bellow out
ēmul·geō -gēre — -sus tr to drain off (milk); to drain (a swamp)
ēmunct·us -a -um adj refined; snobbish; naris emunctae esse to have discriminating tastes
ēmun·gō -gĕre -xī -ctus tr to blow the nose of; to swindle; (w. abl) to cheat (s.o.) of ‖ refl & pass to blow one's nose
ēmūn·iō -īre -īvī or -iī -ītus tr to build up; to fortify; to make a road through (woods)
ēn interj (in questions) really?; (in commands) come on!; (to call attention) hey!
ēnarrābil·is -is -e adj describable, intelligible

ēnarrāti·ō -ōnis *f* description; analysis
ēnarr·ō -āre -āvī -ātus *tr* to explain in
detail; to describe; to interpret
ēnascor ēnascī ēnātus sum *intr* to grow
out, sprout, arise; to be born
ēnat·ō -āre -āvī -ātum *intr* to swim away,
escape by swimming; *(fig)* to get away
with it
ēnātus *pp of* enascor
ēnāvig·ō -āre -āvī -ātus *tr* to sail across,
traverse **ll** *intr* to sail away; *(fig)* to
escape
encaust·us -a -um *adj* burnt in, painted in
encaustic *(i.e., with molten wax as paint)*
Encelad·us *or* **Encelad·os -ī** *m* one of the
giants whom Jupiter buried under Mount
Etna
endrom·is -idis *f* athlete's bathrobe
Endymi·ōn -ōnis *m* handsome young man
with whom Luna fell in love and who
was doomed to everlasting sleep on Mt.
Patmos; any handsome young man
ēnec·ō *(or* ēnicō) **-āre -uī** *(or* -āvī) **-tus** *(or*
-ātus) *tr* to kill, kill off; to exhaust, wear
out; *(coll)* to kill, pester to death
ēnervāt·us -a -um *adj* without sinews,
without muscles; without energy
ēnerv·is -is -e *or* **enerv·us -a -um** *adj*
weak, feeble
ēnerv·ō -āre -āvī -ātus *tr* to weaken, enervate, render impotent
ēnicō *see* eneco
enim *conj* namely, for instance; yes, indeed, certainly; in fact, to be sure; *(in
replies)* of course, no doubt; for, because
enimvērō *adv* yes indeed, to be sure, certainly; *(ironically)* of course
Enīp·eūs -eī *m* tributary of the River Peneus
in Thessaly
ēnīsus *pp of* enitor
ēnit·eō -ēre -uī *intr* to shine out, sparkle;
to be conspicuous
ēnit·escō -escēre *intr* to begin to shine,
begin to brighten; to become conspicuous
ēnī·tor -tī -sus *or* **-xus sum** *tr* to work
one's way up, climb; to give birth to **ll**
intr to exert oneself, make an effort; *(w.
inf)* to struggle to, strive to
ēnixē *adv* strenuously, earnestly
ēnix·us -a -um *pp of* enitor **ll** *adj* strenuous, earnest
Enni·us -(i)ī *m* father of Latin literature,
writer of tragedy, comedy, epic, and satire *(239–169 B.C.)*
Ennosigae·us -ī *m (epithet of Neptune)*
Earthshaker
ēn·ō -āre -āvī -ātum *intr* to swim out,
swim away, escape by swimming
ēnōdātē *adv* without knots; clearly
ēnōdāti·ō -ōnis *f* solution, explanation
ēnōd·is -is -e *adj* without knots; clear

ēnōd·ō -āre -āvī -ātus *tr* to explain, clarify
ēnorm·is -is -e *adj* enormous; shapeless,
irregular; ill-fitting *(clothes);* extravagant *(style)*
ēnormit·ās -ātis *f* enormity; irregular shape
ēnōt·escō -escēre -uī *intr* to become known
ēnot·ō -āre -āvī -ātus *tr* to take notes of,
note down
ensicul·us -ī *m* little sword
ensif·er *or* **ensig·er -era -erum** *adj* with a
sword, wearing a sword
ens·is -is *m* sword
-ens·is -is -e *adjl suf* forms adjectives
mainly from words denoting places:
Atheniensis Athenian, from Athens
enterocēl·ē -ēs *f* hernia of the intestines
enterocēlic·us -a -um *adj* suffering from
an intestinal hernia
entheāt·us -a -um *adj* filled with divine
frenzy
enthe·us -a -um *adj* inspired; inspiring,
that fills with divine frenzy
enthymēm·a -atis *n* thought, reflection;
(phil) condensed syllogism
ēnū·bō -bēre -psī *intr (of a woman)* to
marry outside her rank
ēnucleātē *adv* precisely
ēnucleāt·us -a -um *adj* precise, to the
point; straightforward, simple *(style);*
fine-drawn *(agruments)*
ēnucle·ō -āre -āvī -ātus *tr (fig)* to examine
carefully; to weigh *(one's decision)*
ēnumerāti·ō -ōnis *f* enumeration
ēnumer·ō -āre -āvī -ātus *tr* to count up; to
count out, pay out; to recount, detail,
enumerate
ēnuntiāti·ō -ōnis *f* announcement; *(in
logic)* assertion; proposition *(gram)* pronunciation *(of a word or syllable)*
ēnunti·ō -āre -āvī -ātus *tr* to disclose,
reveal, betray; to say, assert, express; to
proclaim publicly; *(gram)* to pronounce
(a word or syllable)
ēnupti·ō -ōnis *f* right of a woman to marry
outside her clan
ēnutr·iō -īre -īvī *or* **-iī -ītus** *tr* to nourish,
raise, bring up
Enȳ·ō (-us) *f* Greek goddess of war
eō īre īvī *or* **iī itum** *intr* to go; to walk, sail,
ride; *(of time)* to pass; *(of events)* to go
on, happen, turn out; *(of things)* to give
way; *(mil)* to march; *(w. abl)* to stem
from; **in sententiam ire** *(pol)* to vote for
a bill
eō *adv* there, to that place; to that end, to
that purpose; so far, to such an extent, to
such a pitch; on that account, for that
reason, with that in view; **eo ero brevior**
I will be all the briefer; **eo magis** all the
more; **eo maxime quod** especially because; **eo quo** to the place to which;
quo…eo the…the…; **quo plus potestis,
eo moderatius imperio uti debetis** the

more power you have, the more moderately you ought to use that power; **eo quod** because; **eo...ut** to such an extent...that

eōdem *adv* to the same place, purpose, *or* person

Ēōs *(nom only) f* Dawn *(the Latin Aurora, daughter of Hyperion and Theia or Euryphaëssa)*

Ēō·us -ī *m* morning star **‖** inhabitant of the East **‖** one of the horses of the sun **‖** dawn

Ēō·us -a -um *adj* of the dawn; Eastern, oriental **‖** *m* morning star; dawn; an oriental

Epamīnond·ās -ae *m* famous Theban general who defeated the Spartans in two great battles *(c. 371 B.C.)*

epaphaeres·is -is *f* a second close clip *(of the hair)*

Epaph·us -ī *m* son of Jupiter and Io

ēpast·us -a -um *adj* eaten up

Epē·us *or* **Epī·us -ī** *m* builder of the Trojan horse

ephēb·us -ī *m (Greek)* young man

ephēmer·is -idis *or* **-idos** *f* diary; journal

Ephes·us *or* **Ephes·os -ī** *f* city on the coast of Asia Minor with famous temple of Diana

ephippiāt·us -a -um *adj* riding a saddled horse

ephipp·ium -iī *n* saddle

ephor·us -ī *m* ephor *(Spartan magistrate)*

Ephyr·a -ae *or* **Ephyr·ē -ēs** *f* ancient name of Corinth

Epicharm·us -ī *m* Sicilian Greek writer of early comedy *(530?–440 B.C.)*

epichys·is -is *f* wine ladle

epicōp·us -a -um *adj* phaselus epicopus rowboat

epicroc·us -a -um *adj* thin yellow *(garment)* **‖** *n* thin yellow garment

Epicūr·us -ī *m* Greek philosopher, born on Samos *(342–270 B.C.)*

epic·us -a -um *adj* epic **‖** **Epic·ī -orum** *mpl* Epic poets

epidictic·us -a -um *adj* showy

epidīpn·is -idis *f* dessert

epigramm·a -atis *or* **-atos** *n* inscription, epitaph; short poem, epigram

epilog·us -ī *m* epilogue, peroration

epimēni·a -ōrum *npl* month's rations

Epimēth·eûs -eī *m* son of Iapetus and brother of Prometheus

epinīc·ion -iī *n* victory song

epiraed·ium -iī *n* horse-drawn carriage

Ēpīrōt·ēs -ae *m* native of Epirus

Ēpīr·us *or* **Ēpīr·os -ī** *f* district of N.W. Greece

epistol·ium -iī *n* note

epistul·a -ae *f* (**-tol-**) letter

epistulār·is -is -e *adj* (**-tol-**) concerned

with letters; **chartae epistulares** writing paper

epitaph·ium -(i)ī *n* eulogy

epithalam·ium -(i)ī *n* wedding song

epithēc·a -ae *f* addition, increase

epitom·a -ae *or* **epitom·ē -ēs** *f* epitome, abridgment

epitȳr·um -ī *n* olive salad

epoch·ē -ēs *f* suspension of judgment

ep·ops -opis *m* hoopoe *(an Old World bird having a fanlike crest and a slender downward-curving bill)*

epos *(nom & acc only) n* epic

ēpōt·us -a -um *adj* (**exp-**) drunk dry, drained to the dregs

epul·ae -ārum *fpl* courses, dishes; sumptuous meal; **epulae regum** dinner fit for a king

epulār·is -is -e *adj* at dinner, of a dinner; **sermo epularis** talk at dinner, table talk

epulāti·ō -ōnis *f* banqueting

epul·ō -ōnis *m* dinner guest; **Tresviri** *(or* **Septemviri) Epulones** college of priests who superintended the state dinner to the gods

epul·or -ārī -ātus sum *tr* to feast on **‖** *intr* to attend a dinner; *(w. abl)* to feast on

epul·um -ī *n* banquet, feast

equ·a -ae *f* mare

equ·es -itis *m* rider; trooper, cavalryman; cavalry **‖** *mpl* cavalry

Equ·es -itis *m* knight; capitalist *(member of Roman middle class);* equestrian order, bourgeoisie

eques·ter *or* **equest·ris -tris -tre** *adj* equestrian; cavalry; middle-class

equidem *adv* truly, indeed, in any event; of course, to be sure; *(w. first person)* for my part, as far as I am concerned

equīn·us -a -um *adj* horse's

equīri·a -ōrum *npl* (**equirr-**) horse race

equitāt·us -ūs *m* cavalry

equit·ō -āre -āvī -ātum *intr* to ride, ride a horse

equule·us -ī *m* foal, colt; small equestrian statue; torture rack

equ·us -ī (**equos** *and* **equom** *in pre-Augustan period,* **ecus** *and* **ecum** *from Aug. period to end of 1st cent. A.D.,* **equus** *and* **equum** *after that) m* horse; **equis virisque** *(or* **equis viris)** *(fig)* with might and main; **equo merere** to serve in the cavalry; **equo vehi** to ride a horse; **equus bipes** sea horse; in **equo** mounted **‖** *mpl* chariot

er·a *or* **her·a -ae** *f* lady of the house

ērādīc·ō -āre -āvī -ātus *tr* (**exr-**) to uproot; to destroy utterly

ērā·dō -děre -sī -sus *tr* to scratch out, erase, obliterate

eran·us -ī *m* mutual insurance society *(in Greece)*

Erāt·ō *(nom and voc only) f* Muse of erotic poetry; Muse

Eratosthen·ēs -is *m* Alexandrine geographer, poet, and philosopher *(276–196 B.C.)*
erc- *see* **herc-**
Ereb·us -ī *m* god of darkness, son of Chaos and brother of Night; lower world
Erechth·éūs -eī *m* king of Athens, son of Hephaestus **ǁ** grandson of former and son of Pandion
Erechthē·us -a -um *adj* of Erechtheus; *(poet)* Athenian
Erechthīd·ae -ārum *mpl* descendants of Erechtheus; *(poet)* Athenians
ērect·us -a -um *pp of* **erigo ǁ** *adj* erect, upright; noble, elevated, lofty; haughty; attentive, alert, tense; resolute, courageous
ērēp·ō -ĕre -sī *tr* to crawl through *(a field);* to crawl up *(a mountain)* **ǁ** *intr* to crawl out
ērepti·ō -ōnis *f* robbery
ērept·or -ōris *m* robber
ēreptus *pp of* **eripio**
Eretri·a -ae *f* city on the island of Euboea, birthplace of the philosopher Menedemus
Eretriac·ī -ōrum *mpl* philosophers of the school of Menedemus
ergā *(prep) (w. acc)* to, towards; against; next to
ergastul·um -ī *n* prison *(on a large estate where unruly slaves were kept);* chain gang
ergō *adv* therefore, consequently; *(resumptive)* well then, I say, as I was saying; *(w. imperatives)* then, now
ergō *prep (w. preceding gen)* for the sake of, in consequence of; **illius ergo** for his sake
Erichthon·ius -iī *m* king of Athens **ǁ** son of Dardanus, father of Tros, and king of Troy
ēric·ius -(i)ī *m* hedgehog; *(mil)* beam with iron spikes
Ēridan·us -ī *m* Po river *(so called by the Greeks); (astr)* constellation
erifug·a -ae *m* runaway slave
ē·rigō -rigĕre -rexī -rectus *tr* to set up straight, straighten out *(e.g., tree);* to set up, erect; to cheer up, encourage; to arouse, excite; *(mil)* to deploy troops on a slope **ǁ** *refl & pass* to raise oneself, get up
Ērigon·ē -ēs *f (astr)* Virgo *(constellation)*
eríl·is -is -e *or* **heríl·is -is -e** *adj* master's, mistress's
Erīn·ys -yos *f* Fury; *(fig)* frenzy
Eriphȳl·a -ae *or* **Eriphȳl·ē -ēs** *f* wife of the seer Amphiaraus; a treacherous wife
ē·ripiō -ripĕre -ripuī -reptus *tr* to snatch away, pull out, tear out; to deliver, rescue; to rob; *(w. dat or w. ab or ex)* to take away from, rescue from **ǁ** *refl* to escape
-ern·us -a -um *adj1 suf* forms adjectives denoting times: **hestiernus** yesterday's

ērogāti·ō -ōnis *f* expenditure, outlay, payment
ērogit·ō -āre *tr* to try hard to find out
ērog·ō -āre -āvī -ātus *tr* to allocate, expend; to bequeath; *(w. in + acc)* **1** to allocate to, spend on; **2** to bequeath to
Er·ōs -ōtis *m* Love, Cupid, Eros
errābund·us -a -um *adj* wandering, straggling
errātic·us -a -um *adj* erratic, wandering; **stella erratica** planet
errāti·ō -ōnis *f* wandering
errāt·um -ī *n* error, mistake
errāt·us -ūs *m* roving, wandering about
err·ō -āre -āvī -ātum *intr* to wander, roam; to lose one's way, stray; to waver; to err, make a mistake, be mistaken; *(w. in + abl)* to be mistaken about
err·ō -ōnis *m* vagrant, vagabond
err·or -ōris *m* wandering; wavering, uncertainty; error; cause of error, deception; maze, winding, intricacy
ērubescendus -a -um *adj* enough to make one blush, shameful
ērub·escō -escĕre -uī *tr* to blush at; to be ashamed of; to respect **ǁ** *intr* to grow red, redden; to blush
ērūc·a -ae *f (bot)* cole *(type of cabbage)*
ēruct·ō -āre -āvī -ātus *tr* to belch, vomit
ērud·iō -īre -iī *or* **-īvī -ītus** *tr* to educate, teach, instruct; *(w. double acc)* to teach *(s.o. s.th.)*
ērudītē *adv* learnedly
ērudīti·ō -ōnis *f* instructing, instruction; erudition, learning
ērudītul·us -a -um *adj* somewhat experienced, somewhat skilled
ērudīt·us -a -um *adj* educated, learned, accomplished
ēruī *perf of* **eruo**
ē·rumpō -rumpĕre -rūpī -ruptus *tr* to cause to break out; to give vent to; **iram in hostes erumpere** to vent one's wrath on the enemy **ǁ** *intr* to burst out, break out
ēru·ō -ĕre -ī -tus *tr* to uproot, dig out; to tear out *(eyes);* to undermine, demolish, destroy; to draw out, elicit; to churn up *(sea);* to blow up
ērupti·ō -ōnis *f* eruption; *(mil)* sortie, sally
ēruptus *pp of* **erumpo**
er·us *or* **her·us -ī** *m* master of the house, head of the family; lord, owner
ērutus *pp of* **eruo**
erv·um -ī *n (bot)* vetch *(cultivated for its edible seeds)*
Erycīn·us -a -um *adj* of Mt. Eryx *(in N.W. Sicily);* of Venus; Sicilian **ǁ** *f* Venus
Erymanth·is -idos *f* Callisto *(changed first into a bear and then into a constellation)*
Erymanth·us -ī *m* mountain range in Arcadia, where Hercules killed a boar

Erythē·a -ae *f* small island in the Bay of Gades, home of the giant Geryon
erythīn·us -ī *m* red mullet *(fish)*
Er·yx -ycis *or* **Eryc·us -ī** *m* Eryx *(mountain on N.W. coast of Sicily, famous for its temple to Venus)* ‖ son of Venus and Butes, half-brother of Aeneas
esc·a -ae *f* dish; food; bait
escāri·us -a -um *adj* of food; of bait ‖ *npl* dishes, courses
escen·dō -děre -dī -sus *tr & intr* to climb, climb up; to sail up
escensi·ō -ōnis *f* climbing up; hostile raid *(from the coast)*
escens·us -ūs *m* ascent
-esc·ō -ěre *vbl suf* formed from nouns and adjectives, with inchoative force: **senescere** to begin to be old, get old
esculent·us -a -um *adj* edible ‖ *npl* edibles, foodstuffs
esculētum *see* **aesculetum**
esculus *see* **aesculus**
-ēsim·us *or* **-ensim·us -a -um** *suf* used to form ordinal numbers from 20 to 1000
ēsit·ō -āre -āvī -ātus *tr* (essi-) to be used to eating
Esquili·ae -ārum *fpl* Esquiline Hill
Esquilīn·us -a -um *adj* Esquiline ‖ *f* Esquiline gate
esse *inf of* **sum** to be; *inf of* **ēdō** to eat
essedār·ius -(i)ī *m* soldier *or* gladiator fighting from a chariot
essed·um -ī *m* Gallic war chariot; light traveling carriage
essenti·a -ae *f* essence
essitō *see* **esito**
-ess·ō -ěre -īvī *or* **-iī -ītus** *vbl suf* with conative force: **capessere** to try to catch, snatch at, catch at eagerly, strive for
estr·ix -īcis *f* glutton *(female)*
ēsuriāl·is -is -e *adj* (ess-) of hunger
ēsur·iō -īre — -ītus *tr* (ess-) to be hungry for ‖ *intr* to be hungry
essuri·ō -ōnis *m* a hungry man
ēsurīti·ō -ōnis *f* hunger
ēsus *pp of* **edo**
ēs·us -ūs *m* eating
et *adv* besides, also; even, I mean
et *conj* and; *(for emphasis)* and even, yes and; *(antithetical)* however, but; **et...et** both...and, not only...but also
etenim *conj* for, and as a matter of fact
etēsi·ae -ārum *mpl (fpl)* periodic winds *(on the Aegean Sea)*
ēthic·ē -ēs *f* ethics
ēthologi·a -ae *f* portrayal of character
ētholog·us -ī *m* impersonator
etiam *adv & conj* also, and also, besides, likewise; *(of time)* yet, as yet, still, even now; *(in affirmation)* yes, yes indeed, certainly, by all means; *(emphatic)* even, rather; *(w. emphatic imperatives)* but just; **etiam atque etiam** again and again

etiamnunc *or* **etiamnum** *adv* even now, even at the present time, still
etiamsī *conj* even if, although
etiamtum *or* **etiamtunc** *adv* even then, till then, still
Etrūri·a -ae *f* district N. of Rome
Etrusc·us -a -um *adj* Etruscan, of Etruria
etsī *conj* even if, although
-ēt·um -ī *neut suf* formed mainly from names of plants to denote the place where they grow: **rosetum** rose bed
etymologi·a -ae *f* etymology
eu *interj (sometimes ironic)* fine!, great!
Euān *or* **Euhān** *m* cult title of Bacchus, cult cry
eu·ans *or* **euh·ans -antis** *adj* crying Eu(h)an *(Bacchic cry)*
euax *interj* hurray!
Euboe·a -ae *f* Greek island off E. coast of Attica and Boeotia
Euēn·us -ī *m* a king of Aetolia, father of Marpessa ‖ river in Aetolia
euge *or* **eugepae** *interj* terrific!
euhans *see* **euans**
Euhēmer·us -ī *m* Greek writer who attempted to prove that all ancient myths were basically historical events *(fl 316 B.C.)*
Euh·ius -iī *m* Bacchus
Euhoe *or* **Euoe** *interj* ecstatic cry of revelers at festival of Bacchus
Euius *see* **Euhius**
Eumenid·ēs -um *fpl* Eumenides *or* Erinyes *or* Furies *(goddesses of vengeance)*
eunūch·us -ī *m* eunuch
Euoe *see* **Euhoe**
Euphorb·us -ī *m* brave Trojan warrior whose soul Pythagoras asserted had transmigrated to himself
Euphrāt·ēs -is *or* **-ae** *or* **-ī** *m* Euphrates River
Eupol·is -idis *or* **-is** *m* Athenian comic playwright *(446?–411 B.C.)*
Eurīpid·ēs -is *m* Athenian tragic playwright *(485–405 B.C.)*
eurīp·us -ī *m* channel; trench running between the arena and the seats in the Circus Maximus ‖ **Euripus** strait between Boeotia and Euboea
Eurōp·a -ae *or* **Eurōp·ē -ēs** *f* Europe ‖ Europa, daughter of Agenor and mother of Sarpedon, Rhadamantus, and Minos by Jupiter, who, in the shape of a bull, carried her off to Crete
Eurōt·ās -ae *m* chief river of Laconia in S. Greece, on which Sparta stood
Eur·us -ī *m* S.E. wind; east wind; wind
Eurydic·ē -ēs *f* wife of Orpheus
Eurysth·eūs -eī *m* king of Argos who imposed the Twleve Labors on Hercules
Euryt·is -idos *f* daughter of Eurytus, king of Oechalia *(i.e., Iole)*
-e·us -a -um *adjl suf* formed from nouns,

usually to denote material: **ligneus** (made) of wood, wooden

euschēmē *adv* gracefully

Euterp·ē -ēs *f* Muse *(later associated with the reed pipe)*

Euxīn·us Pont·us -ī *m* Black Sea

ēvā·dō -děre -sī -sus *tr* to pass, pass by; to pass through, escape **ǁ** *intr* to go out; to turn out to be, become, prove to be; to get away; to climb

ēvag·or -ārī -ātus sum *tr* to stray beyond, transgress **ǁ** *intr (fig)* to spread; *(mil)* to maneuver

ēval·escō -escěre -uī *intr* to grow strong; to increase; *(of a word or expression)* to gain currency; *(w. inf)* to be able to; *(w. in + acc)* to develop into

ēvalid·us -a -um *adj* very strong

Evan·der *or* **Evan·drus -drī** *m* Evander *(Arcadian who founded Pallanteum at the foot of the Palatine Hill)*

ēvān·escō -escěre -uī *intr* to vanish, pass away, die away; to be forgotten; *(of liquids)* to evaporate

ēvānid·us -a -um *adj* vanishing

ēvast·ō -āre -āvī -ātus *tr* to devastate, wreck completely

ēvāsus *pp of* **evado**

ēve·hō -hěre -xī -ctus *tr* to carry out; to spread abroad; to lift up, raise **ǁ** *pass* to ride, sail, drift

ē·vellō -vellěre -vellī *or* **-vulsī -vulsus** *tr* to pluck out; to eradicate; to extract *(teeth)*

ē·veniō -venīre -vēnī -ventum *intr* to come out, come forth; to come to pass, happen; to turn out, result, end **ǁ** *v impers* it happens

ēvent·um -ī *n* event, occurrence; result, effect, consequence; fortune; experience

ēvent·us -ūs *m* event, accident, fortune, lot, fate; good fortune, success; issue, consequence, result

Evēn·us -ī *m* river in Aetolia

ēverber·ō -āre -āvī -ātus *tr* to hit hard; to beat up

ēverricul·um -ī *n* broom; dragnet

ēver·rō -rěre -rī -sus *tr* to sweep out; *(fig)* to clean out, strip

ēversi·ō -ōnis *f* overthrow, subversion, destruction

ēvers·or -ōris *m* destroyer

ēversus *pp of* **everro** *and of* **everto**

ēver·tō -těre -tī -sus *tr* (-vor-) to overturn, turn upside down; to overthrow; to turn out, expel; to subvert, destroy, ruin

ēvestīgāt·us -a -um *adj* tracked down

ēvictus *pp of* **evinco**

ēvid·ens -entis *adj* evident, visible, plain, clear, obvious

ēvidenter *adv* plainly, obviously

ēvidenti·a -ae *f* obviousness; evidence; *(rhet)* vividness

ēvigil·ō -āre -āvī -ātus *tr* to watch through *(the night);* to work through the night writing *(e.g., books)* **ǁ** *intr* to be wide-awake; *(fig)* to be on one's toes

ēvīl·escō -escěre -uī *intr* to depreciate, become worthless

ēvin·ciō -cīre -xī -ctus *tr* to tie up; to crown, wreathe

ē·vincō -vincěre -vīcī -victus *tr* to conquer completely, trounce; to prevail over

ēvinctus *pp of* **evincio**

ēvirāt·us -a -um *adj* effeminate

ēvir·ō -āre -āvī -ātus *tr* to castrate, emasculate

ēviscer·ō -āre -āvī -ātus *tr* to disembowel, gut, eviscerate; to mangle

ēvītābil·is -is -e *adj* avoidable

ēvītāti·ō -ōnis *f* avoidance

ēvīt·ō -āre -āvī -ātus *tr* to avoid, escape

ēvocāt·ī -ōrum *mpl* veterans called up again, reenlisted veterans

ēvocāt·or -ōris *m* recruiter

ēvoc·ō -āre -āvī -ātus *tr* to call out, summon; to challenge; to evoke, excite, stir; *(mil)* to call up *(for service)*

ēvolgō *see* **evulgo**

ēvol·ō -āre -āvī -ātum *intr* to fly out, fly away; to rush out; *(fig)* to soar

ēvolūti·ō -ōnis *f* unrolling a scroll; *(fig)* reading

ēvolsi·ō -ōnis *f* extraction

ēvol·vō -věre -vī -ūtus *tr* to roll out, unroll, unfold; to spread; to read, study; to disclose; to free, extricate; to repel; to evolve, develop

ēvom·ō -ěre -uī -itus *tr* to vomit, spew out, disgorge

ēvulg·ō -āre -āvī -ātus *tr* (-vol-) to divulge, make public

ēvulsi·ō -ōnis *f* extraction

ēvulsus *pp of* **evello**

ex *or* **ē** *prep (w. abl)* **1** *(of space)* out of, from: **ex concilio ire** to come out of the assembly; **2** *(of space)* down from: **se ex altissimo praecipitare** to jump down from a great height; **3** *(of space)* up from: **e lecto surgere** to get up from his bed; **4** *(of time)* from, from…onward, following, since: **ex eo** *(or* **ex illo** *or* **ex quo)** from that time on, ever since then; **5** *(of time)* right after: **ex imbre** right after the rain; **6** *(of material of which s.th. consists)* of: **statua ex auro** a statue of gold; **7** *(of parentage, racial origin)* by, from; **tres filios ex ea generavit** he had three children by her; **8** *(of cause or origin)* from, through, by, on account of, by reason of: **ex aere alieno commotus** upset because of his debts; **9** *(derivation of a word)* from, after: **appellata est ex viro virtus** "manliness" is derived from "man"; **10** *(in partitive sense)* of, out of, from among: **paucos ex suis deperdidit**

he lost few of his own men; **11** *(indicating extent):* **copiae ex parte deletae, ex parte captae** troops partly destroyed, partly captured; **12** *(indicating repetition)* after: **bella ex bellis serere** to sow the seeds of war after war; **dies ex die** day after day; **13** *(indicating recovery)* **ex vulnere refectus** recovered from a wound; **14** *(indicating point from which action is performed)* from: **ex equo pugnare** to fight from a horse *(i.e., on horseback);* **ex itinere pugnare** to fight en route; **15** *(indicating conformity)* after, according to, in conformity with: **ex consuetudine cotidianā** according to their daily habit; **17** *(w. verbs of learning)* from: **ex litteris tuis intellexi** I understood from your letter

ex- or **ē-** *pref* (ex- normally before vowels, **c, q, p, s, t;** s is sometimes absorbed, e.g., **expectare; ex** is dropped in **escendere, epotare; e-** before **g, b, d, r, l, m, n, i, u;** with **f, ff-** is commonly formed, also **ecf-**) **1** out: **exire** to go out; **2** away: **ēfugere** to run away; **3** well, thoroughly: **ēdiscere** to learn thoroughly, learn by heart; **4** hard, up: **ēverberare** to beat hard, beat up; **5** *(negative, deprivation)* -less, un-: **exsanguis** unbloody; **exos** boneless; **6** up: **exaggerare** to pile up

exacerb·ō -āre -āvī -ātus *tr* to exasperate, enrage; to exacerbate, make worse

exacti·ō -ōnis *f* driving out, expulsion; demanding; exaction, collection; supervision *(of public works)*

exact·or -ōris *m* expeller; collector; supervisor

exact·us -a -um *pp of* **exigo** ‖ *adj* exact, precise

exac·uō -uĕre -uī -ūtus *tr* to sharpen; to stimulate, spur, inflame

exadversum *or* **exadversus** *adv* (-vor-) on the opposite side ‖ *prep (w. dat or acc)* across from, right opposite

exaedificāti·ō -ōnis *f* construction

exaedific·ō -āre -āvī -ātus *tr* to finish building, build, construct; *(fig)* to complete

exaequāti·ō -ōnis *f* leveling; uniformity

exaequ·ō -āre -āvī -ātus *tr* to level, make level; *(fig)* to equal, regard as equal ‖ *pass (w. dat)* to be put on the same level with

exaestu·ō -āre -āvī -ātum *intr* to seethe, boil; to ferment

exaggerāti·ō -ōnis *f* exaltation; *(rhet)* intensification *(by repetition or piling up);* **animi exaggeratio** broadening of the mind

exagger·ō -āre -āvī -ātus *tr* to pile up; to enlarge; to enhance

exagitāt·or -ōris *m* critic

exagit·ō -āre -āvī -ātus *tr* to stir up, keep on the move; to scare away; to criticize, satirize; to irritate; to arouse *(feelings)*

exagōg·a -ae *or* **exagoge -ēs** *f* exportation

exalb·escō -escĕre -uī *intr* to turn pale

exām·en -inis *n* swarm; crowd; tongue of a scale; weighing, consideration

examussim *adv* exactly

exānim·ō -āre -āvī -ātus *tr* to weigh, balance; to examine, consider critically

exancl·ō -āre -āvī -ātus *tr* to draw off, drain; to go through *(e.g., a war)*

exanimāl·is -is -e *adj* dead, lifeless; deadly

exanimāti·ō -ōnis *f* breathlessness; terror, panic

exanim·is -is -e *or* **exanim·us -a -um** *adj* breathless, terrified; lifeless; fainting

exanim·ō -āre -āvī -ātus *tr* to knock the breath out of; to wind, tire, weaken; to deprive of life, kill; to scare out of one's wits; to dishearten; to agitate

exanimus *see* **exanimis**

exar·descō -descĕre -sī -sum *intr* to catch fire; *(lit & fig)* to flare up

exār·escō -escĕre -uī *intr* to become quite dry, dry up

exarm·ō -āre -āvī -ātus *tr* to disarm

exar·ō -āre -āvī -ātus *tr* to plow up; to raise, produce; to write *(on wax with a stylus),* write down, note; to furrow, wrinkle; **frontem rugis exarare** to knit one's brows

exasper·ō -āre -āvī -ātus *tr* to make rough, roughen; to exasperate; to make worse

exauctōr·ō -āre -āvī -ātus *tr (mil)* to discharge; *(mil)* to give a dishonorable discharge to

exaud·iō -īre -īvī *or* **-iī -ītus** *tr* to hear clearly; to discern; to perceive, understand; to listen to; to grant

exaug·eō -ēre *tr* to increase greatly

exaugurāti·ō -ōnis *f* deconsecration

exaugur·ō -āre -āvī -ātus *tr* to deconsecrate

exauspic·ō -āre -āvī *intr (w. ex) (hum)* to come out of *(e.g., chains)* with good auspices

exb- = **eb-**

exballist·ō -āre *tr* to finish off, batter down the defenses of

exbibō *see* **ebibo**

exc- = **exsc-**

excaec·ō -āre -āvī -ātus *tr* to blind; to block up *(a river, pipe);* to dim, darken

excalceāt·us -a -um *adj* unshod; *(of an actor)* not wearing the buskin, acting in comedy ‖ *mpl* comic actors

excalce·ō -āre *tr* **excalceare pedes** take off the shoes

excandescenti·a -ae *f* mounting anger, outburst of anger

excand·escō -escĕre -uī *intr* to grow white

hot; to burst into a rage, flare up, reach a pitch *(of emotion)*

excant·ō -āre -āvī -ātus *tr* to charm away

excarnific·ō -āre -āvī -ātus *tr* (-nu-) to tear to pieces, torture to death; to torment *(mentally)*

excav·ō -āre -āvī -ātus *tr* to hollow out

ex·cēdō -cēdĕre -cessī -cessus *tr* to exceed, pass, surpass **II** *intr* to go out, go away, withdraw, depart, disappear; to die; **e medio** *(or* **e vita) excedere** to depart this life

excell·ens -entis *adj* excellent, superior

excellenter *adv* excellently

excellenti·a -ae *f* excellence, superiority; **per excellentiam** par excellence

excell·ō -ĕre -uī *intr* to excel; *(w. dat or* **super** + *acc)* to be superior to, surpass; *(w. abl or* **in** + *abl)* to be superior in, excel in

excelsē *adv* high, loftily

excelsit·ās -ātis *f* loftiness

excels·us -a -um *adj* high, lofty; tall; eminent **II** *n* height, high ground; high social status; **in excelso aetatem** *(or* **vitam) agere** to be in the limelight

excepti·ō -ōnis *f* exception, restriction, limitation; *(leg)* objection raised by a defendant against an accuser's statement; *(leg)* a limiting clause

except·ō -āre -āvī -ātus *tr* to catch; to pick up

exceptus *pp of* **excipio**

ex·cernō -cernĕre -crēvī -crētus *tr* to sift out, separate

excerp·ō -ĕre -sī -tus *tr* to pick out, extract, to choose; to gather; to leave out, omit

excerpt·um -ī *n* excerpt

excess·us -ūs *m* departure; death; digression

excetr·a -ae *f* water-snake; spiteful woman

excidi·ō -ōnis *f* destruction

excid·ium -iī *n* destruction, overthrow; cause of destruction

excīd·ō -ĕre -ī *intr* to fall out; *(of an utterance)* to slip out; to pass away, perish; to degenerate; to disappear; to be forgotten; *(w. in* + *acc)* to degenerate into; *(w. abl or* ex) 1 to be deprived of, lose; 2 to forget, miss; *(w. dat or* de + *abl)* 1 to fall from; 2 to escape from *(lips);* **e memoriā excidere** to slip one's mind

excī·dō -dĕre -dī -sus *tr* to cut out, cut off, cut down; to raze, demolish; *(fig)* to banish, eliminate

excieō *see* **excio**

exc·iō -īre -īvī *or* **-iī -ītus** *or* **-ĭtus** *or* **exci·eō -ēre** *tr* to call *(s.o.)* out, summon; to awaken; to disturb; to frighten; to stir up, excite; to produce, occasion

ex·cipiō -cipĕre -cēpī -ceptus *tr* to take out, remove; to rescue; to exempt; to

take, receive, catch, capture; to follow, succeed to; to intercept; to be exposed to; to incur; to welcome; to take up eagerly; to listen to, overhear; to except, make an exception of; to reach *(a place);* to mention in particular; to take on, withstand

excīsi·ō -ōnis *f* destruction

excīsus *pp of* **excīdo**

excitāt·us -a -um *adj* excited, lively, vigorous; loud

excit·ō -āre -āvī -ātus *tr* to wake up, rouse; to raise, stir up; to erect, construct, produce; to cause, occasion; *(fig)* to arouse, awaken, inspire, stimulate, enliven, encourage; to startle

excītus *or* **excĭtus** *pp of* **excio**

excīvī *pp of* **excio**

exclāmāti·ō -ōnis *f* exclamation

exclām·ō -āre -āvī -ātus *tr & intr* to exclaim, shout, yell

exclū·dō -dĕre -sī -sus *tr* to exclude, shut out, shut off; to remove, separate; to hatch; *(coll)* to knock out *(an eye);* to prevent

exclūsi·ō -ōnis *f* exclusion

exclūsus *pp of* **excludo**

excoctus *pp of* **excoquo**

excōgitāti·ō -ōnis *f* thinking up, inventing, contriving

excōgitāt·us -a -um *adj* carefully thought up; choice

excōgit·ō -āre -āvī -ātus *tr* to think up, devise, contrive

ex·colō -colĕre -coluī -cultus *tr* to tend, cultivate, work carefully; to refine, ennoble, perfect, improve; to adorn; to worship

ex·coquō -coquĕre -coxī -coctus *tr* to cook out, boil away; to dry up; to bake thoroughly; to temper *(steel)*

excor·s -dis *adj* senseless, silly

excrēment·um -ī *n* excretion *(spittle, urine, etc.);* excrement

excreō *see* **ex(s)creo**

ex·crescō -crescĕre -crēvī -crētum *intr* to grow out; to grow up, rise up

excruciābil·is -is -e *adj* deserving torture

excruci·ō -āre -āvī -ātus *tr* to torture, torment

excubi·ae -ārum *fpl* standing guard; sentry; watchfire

excubit·or -ōris *m* sentry

excub·ō -ĕre -uī -itum *intr* to sleep out of doors, to be attentive, be on the alert; *(mil)* to stand guard

excū·dō -dĕre -dī -sus *tr* to beat out, strike out; to hammer out; to forge; to hatch *(eggs); (fig)* to hammer into shape, write up

exculc·ō -āre -āvī -ātus *tr* to kick out; to tread down on; to stomp

excultus *pp of* **excolo**

excūrāt·us -a -um *adj* carefully attended to

ex·currō -currĕre -cucurrī *or* **-currī -cursum** *intr* to run out, dash out; *(mil)* to sally forth, make an incursion; to project, extend; *(fig)* to fan out, expand

excursi·ō -ōnis *f* sally, sortie; excursion; short trip *(away from a place)*; journey, expedition; digression; outset, opening *(of a speech)*

excurs·or -ōris *m* skirmisher; emissary; courier

excurs·us -ūs *m* sally, sortie, raid, charge; expedition, short trip *(away from a place)*; journey; digression; *(geog)* projection

excūsābil·is -is -e *adj* excusable

excūsātē *adv* excusably, without blame

excūsāti·ō -ōnis *f* excuse

excūsāt·us -a -um *adj* free from blame, exempt

excūs·ō -āre -āvī -ātus *tr* to free from blame, excuse; to except; to make excuses for, apologize for; to allege in excuse, plead as an excuse

excussus *pp of* **excutio**

excūsus *pp of* **excudo**

excu·tiō -tĕre -ssī -ssus *tr* to shake out, shake off, shake loose; to knock out *(e.g., teeth)*; *(of a horse)* to throw; to shake out *(a garment)*; to jilt, give the cold shoulder to; to toss, throw, shoot; to search; to examine, investigate; to discover; *(fig)* to shake off

exd- = ed-

exdorsu·ō -āre *tr* to fillet

exec- *see* **exsec-**

ex·edō -esse *or* **-edĕre -ēdī -ēsus** *tr* to eat up, consume; to destroy; to prey on; to make hollow; to wear away, corrode; to emaciate

exedr·a -ae *f (semi-circular recess in a wall for sitting, often used for lectures)* sitting room; lecture hall

exedr·ium -(i)ī *n* small sitting room

exempl·ar *or* **exempl·āre -āris** *n* copy; transcript; likeness; pattern, model, ideal

exemplār·is -is -e *adj* following a model ‖ *m* copy; transcript

exempl·um -ī *n* sample, example, typical instance; precedent; pattern, make, character; model, pattern *(of conduct)*; object lesson; warning; copy; transcript; portrait

exemptus *pp of* **eximo**

exenter·ō -āre -āvī -ātus *tr* (-int-) to disembowel, gut; *(fig)* to empty *(purse)*

ex·eō -īre -īvī *or* **-iī -itus** *tr* to pass beyond, cross; to ward off, avoid; *(fig)* to exceed ‖ *intr* to go out, go forth; to go away, withdraw, depart, retire; to march out; to disembark; to pour out, gush out, flow out; to escape, be freed; to pass away, perish; *(of time)* to run out; to get out, become public; to burgeon forth; *(of hills)* to rise

exeq- = exseq-

exerc·eō -ēre -uī -itus *tr* to exercise, train; to keep *(s.o.)* busy, keep *(s.o.)* going; to supervise; to cultivate, work *(the soil)*; to occupy *(the mind)*; to practice *(medicine, patience, skills, etc.)*; to carry into effect; to annoy, bother; to worry; to last through *(e.g., winter)*; to levy, collect *(taxes)*; to use *(instruments, materials)*; to wield *(power, authority)*; to run *(a business)*; to carry on *(investigation)*; *(mil)* to drill, train; **aleam exercere** to gamble; **causidicos exercere** to keep the lawyers busy; **faenus exercere** to lend money at interest; **imperium exercere** to wield power; **justitiam exercere** to administer justice; **legem exercere** to enforce a law; **quaestionem de sicariis exercere** to conduct prosecutions for murder; **vectigalia exercere** to levy taxes, collect taxes ‖ *refl* to exercise, do exercises

exercitāti·ō -ōnis *f* exercise, practice, experience, training; cultivation; *(w. gen)* practice in

exercitāt·us -a -um *adj* experienced, trained, disciplined; troubled

exercit·ium -(i)ī *n* exercise, training, practice; written exercise; proficiency

exercit·ō -āre -āvī -ātus *tr* to keep in training, train, exercise; to habituate; to trouble

exercit·or -ōris *m* trainer

exercit·us -a -um *pp of* **exerceo** ‖ *adj* disciplined; experienced; trying, tough; troubled, harassed

exercit·us -ūs *m* army; infantry; army of followers; swarm, flock, multitude; *(pol)* assembly of the people

exerō *see* **exsero**

exēs·or -ōris *m* corrosive factor, underminer

exēsus *pp of* **exedo**

exf- *see* **eff-**

exhalāti·ō -ōnis *f* exhalation, vapor

exhāl·ō -āre -āvī -ātus *tr* to exhale, give off; **animam** *(or* **vitam)** **exhalare** to breathe one's last ‖ *intr* to exhale; to steam

exhau·riō -rīre -sī -stus *tr* to draw out, empty; to drain, exhaust; to deplete; to take away, remove; to drain dry; to bring to an end; to undergo, endure; to carry out *(task)*; to discuss fully

exhērēd·ō -āre -āvī -ātus *tr* to disinherit

exhēr·ēs -ēdis *adj* disinherited

exhib·eō -ēre -uī -itus *tr* to hold out; to present, produce; to display, exhibit; to cause, occasion; to render, make

exhilar·ō -āre -āvī -ātus *tr* to cheer up

exhorr·escō -escĕre -uī *tr* to shudder at **ǁ** *intr* to be terrified

exhortāti·ō -ōnis *f* encouragement **ǁ** *fpl* words of encouragement

exhort·or -ārī -ātus sum *tr* to encourage, exhort

ex·igō -igĕre -ēgī -actus *tr* to drive out, push out, thrust out, expel; to demand, exact, collect; to require; to pass, spend, complete *(life, time);* to finish, conclude; to ascertain; to weigh, consider, estimate; to examine; to test; to dispose of

exiguē *adv* slightly, sparingly, barely; briefly

exiguit·ās -ātis *f* shortness, smallness; meagerness, scantiness, scarcity

exigu·us -a -um *adj* slight, short, small, meager, scanty, poor, paltry, inadequate; a little, a bit of **ǁ** *n* a bit, a small amount

exiliō *see* **exsilio**

exīl·is -is -e *adj* thin, small, meager, feeble, poor; dreary; depleted *(ranks);* worthless; insincere; *(rhet)* dry, flat, jejune *(style)*

exīlit·ās -ātis *f* thinness; meagerness; dreariness

exīliter *adv* concisely; drearily; parsimoniously; jejunely

exilium *see* **exsilium**

exim *see* **exinde**

eximiē *adv* exceptionally

eximi·us -a -um *adj* excepted; exempt; choice, select; special, exceptional

ex·imō -imĕre -ēmī -emptus *tr* to take out, take away, remove; to exempt; to free, release, let off; to make an exception of; to waste, lose *(time);* to banish *(worries)*

exin *see* **exinde**

exinān·iō -īre -īvī *or* **-iī -ītus** *tr* to empty; to drain, dry up; to weaken; to strip; *(fig)* to clean out, fleece

exinde *or* **exim** *or* **exin** *adv* from that place, from that point; *(in enumerating)* after that, next, then, furthermore; *(of time)* from that point, after that, then; accordingly

existimāti·ō -ōnis *f* (**-tum-**) opinion, view, judgment, favorable opinion; appraisal; decision, verdict; reputation, good name; *(com)* credit; **vulgi existimatio** public opinion; **existimatio tibi est** it is for you to judge

existimāt·or -ōris *m* critic, judge

existim·ō -āre -āvī -ātus *tr* (**-tum-**) to form an opinon of, judge, consider, regard; to think, suppose; **in hostium numero existimare** to regard as an enemy

existō *see* **exsisto**

exitiābil·is -is -e *adj* deadly, fatal

exitiāl·is -is -e *adj* deadly, fatal

exiti·ō -ōnis *f* going out, exit

exitiōs·us -a -um *adj* deadly, destructive

exit·ium -(i)ī *n* destruction, ruin; cause of destruction; death

exit·us -ūs *m* going out, exit, departure; way out, outlet; end, close, conclusion; **ad exitum adducere** to bring to a close

exl- = el-

exlecebra *see* **elecebra**

ex·lex -lēgis *adj* without law, exempt from the law; lawless

exm- = em-

exo- = exso-

exobsecr·ō -āre -āvī -ātus *tr* (**exops-**) to beg earnestly, entreat

exocul·ō -āre -āvī -ātus *tr* to knock the eyes out of

exod·ium -(i)ī *n* finale; farce *(presented after the main feature)*

exol·escō -escĕre -ēvī -ētum *intr* (**exs-**) to decay, fade; to become obsolete; to grow up, become an adult

exolēt·us -a -um *adj* full-grown **ǁ** *m (fig)* male prostitute

exoner·ō -āre -āvī -ātus *tr* to unload; to empty; *(fig)* to relieve, free

exoptābil·is -is -e *adj* highly desirable, long-awaited

exoptāt·us -a -um *adj* longed-for, welcome, desired

exopt·ō -āre -āvī -ātus *tr* to long for, wish earnestly for, desire greatly

exōrābil·is -is -e *adj* accessible, sympathetic

exōrābul·a -ōrum *npl* enticements, bait, entreaties

exōrāt·or -ōris *m* successful petitioner

exor·dior -dīrī -sus sum *tr & intr* to begin, start, commence

exord·ium -(i)ī *n* beginning, start, commencement; origin; introduction

exor·ior -īrī -tus sum *intr* to come out, come forth, rise, appear; to begin, arise, be caused, be produced

exornāti·ō -ōnis *f* embellishment

exornāt·or -ōris *m* embellisher

exorn·ō -āre -āvī -ātus *tr* to fit out, furnish, equip, provide, supply; to adorn, embellish, decorate, set off

exōr·ō -āre -āvī -ātus *tr* to prevail upon, win over; to gain *or* obtain by entreaty; to appease

exors·us -a -um *pp of* **exordior ǁ** *npl* beginning, commencement; introduction, preamble

exors·us -ūs *m* beginning, commencement; introduction

exortus *pp of* **exorior**

exort·us -ūs *m* rising; the East

ex·os -ossis *or* **exoss·is -is -e** *adj* boneless

exoscul·or -ārī -ātus sum *tr* to kiss lovingly, kiss tenderly

exoss·ō -āre -āvī -ātus *tr* to bone, take the bones out of

exostr·a -ae f movable stage; **in exostra** in public

exōs·us -a -um adj hating, detesting

exōtic·us -a -um adj foreign, exotic; **Graeca exoctica** Magna Graecia (S. Italy)

exp- = exsp-

expall·escō -escĕre -uī tr to turn pale at, dread || intr to turn pale

expalliāt·us -a -um adj robbed of one's cloak

expalp·ō -āre -āvī -ātus tr to coax out

ex·pan·dō -dĕre -dī -sus or **-passus** tr to spread out, unfold, expand

expassus pp of **expando**

expatr·ō -āre -āvī -ātus tr to squander

expav·escō -escĕre -ī tr to panic at || intr to panic

expect- = exspect-

expecūliāt·us -a -um adj stripped of one's savings

exped·iō -īre -īvī or **-iī -ītus** tr to untie, unwrap; to unfetter; to extricate (a person from a confined position); to disentangle; to get ready; to clear for action; to clear (roads of obstacles); to solve, clear up (problems); to settle (a debt); to get (s.o.) out of (troubles); to put in order, arrange, settle, adjust, set right; to explain, clear up; to disclose; to recount, relate; to supply, provide; to accomplish, achieve || refl to prepare oneself, get ready || intr to be useful, be profitable; to set out (on a military expedition); to turn out (in a certain manner); (w. dat) to be useful to || v impers (w. inf) it is useful to, is advantageous to

expedītē adv freely, nimbly; quickly, expeditiously; unambiguously

expedīti·ō -ōnis f (military or naval) expedition, campaign; special mission; (rhet) proof by elimination

expedīt·us -a -um adj unencumbered, unhampered, unobstructed; ready, prompt; ready at hand, convenient; agile; (of roads) easy to travel, fast; quick (mind); (mil) light-armed; **in expedito** in readiness, at hand; without hindrance

ex·pellō -pellĕre -pulī -pulsus tr to drive out, expel; to disown

expen·dō -dĕre -dī -sus tr to weigh out; to pay out, pay down, lay out, expend; to rate, estimate; to ponder, consider; to pay (penalty)

expens·us -a -um adj paid out, spent || n payment, expenditure

expergē·faciō -facĕre -fēcī -factus tr to awaken, wake up; to arouse

exper·giscor -gisci -rectus sum intr to wake up; to be alert

experg·ō -ĕre -ī -itus tr to wake up

experi·ens -entis adj enterprising, active; (w. gen) ready to undergo

experienti·a -ae f test, trial, experiment; experience, practice; effort

experīment·um -ī n test, experiment, proof; experience; person serving as a test, test-case

exper·ior -īrī -tus sum tr to test, try, prove; to experience, endure, find out; to try to do, attempt; to measure strength with || intr to go to court

experrectus pp of **expergiscor**

exper·s -tis adj (w. gen) 1 having no share in, having no part in; 2 devoid of, free from, without

expert·us -a -um pp of **experior** || adj tried, tested, proved; (w. gen) experienced in

expetess·ō -ĕre tr to desire, long for

expet·ō -ĕre -īvī or **-iī -ītus** tr to ask for, demand; to exact (penalty); to ask about; to aim at, head for; to desire, long for || intr (w. in + acc) to befall; to fall upon, assail

expiāti·ō -ōnis f expiation, atonement; satisfaction; purification

expictus pp of **expingo**

expīlāti·ō -ōnis f pillaging, ransacking, looting

expīlāt·or -ōris m plunderer, looter, robber

expīl·ō -āre -āvī -ātus tr to plunder, rob, ransack; to plagiarize

ex·pingō -pingĕre -pinxī -pictus tr to paint; to depict

expi·ō -āre -āvī -ātus tr to purify; to atone for, expiate; to avenge; to appease; to avert (a curse, bad omen)

expīrō see **exspiro**

expisc·or -ārī -ātus sum tr to go fishing for (information)

explānātē adv plainly, clearly

explānāti·ō -ōnis f explanation; clear pronunciation

explānāt·or -ōris m interpreter

explānāt·us -a -um adj plain

explān·ō -āre -āvī -ātus tr to explain, make clear; to flatten out; to pronounce distinctly

explaudō see **explodo**

explēment·um -ī n filling, stuffing

expl·eō -ēre -ēvī -ētus tr to fill up; to complete; to satisfy (desires); to make good (losses); to fulfill, perform, accomplish, discharge

explēti·ō -ōnis f satisfying, fulfillment

explēt·us -a -um adj full, complete, perfect

explicātē adv clearly, plainly

explicāti·ō -ōnis f unfolding, uncoiling; analysis; interpretation

explicāt·or -ōris m, **explicātr·ix -īcis** f explainer, interpreter

explicāt·us -a -um adj plain, clear-cut, straightforward explicāt·us -ūs *m* unfolding; explanation, interpretation

explicit·us -a -um *adj* disentangled; simple, easy

explic·ō -āre -āvī *(or* -uī) -ātus *(or* -itus) *tr* to unfold, unroll; to spread out; to loosen, undo; to set free; to arrange, adjust, settle; to exhibit; to explain; to display

ex·plōdō -plōdĕre -plōsī -plōsus *tr* (-plaud-) to drive off the stage *(by clapping)*; to boo; to disapprove of, discredit

explōrātē *adv* after careful examination; for sure, for certain

explōrāti·ō -ōnis *f* exploration, examination

explōrāt·or -ōris *m* scout, spy

explōrāt·us -a -um *adj* sure, certain; safe, secure; *(w. abl)* clear of; **exploratum** *(or* **pro explorato) habere** to know for sure

explōr·ō -āre -āvī -ātus *tr* to explore, investigate; to probe, search; to test, try, try out; *(w. acc & inf)* to ascertain that; *(w. ut, ne)* to insure (that; that not); *(mil)* to reconnoiter

explōsi·ō -ōnis *f* driving off the stage, booing

expol·iō -īre -īvī *or* -iī -ītus *tr* to polish; to finish off *(a building e.g., with plaster); (fig)* to embellish, adorn, refine

expolīti·ō -ōnis *f* polishing, finishing off, embellishing

expolīt·us -a -um *adj* polished, lustrous; refined

ex·pōnō -pōnĕre -posuī -positus *or* -postus *tr* to put out, bring out (into the open); to expose *(children to die)*; to leave in an exposed position; to display, put on show; to make available; to reveal; to publish; to exhibit; to relate; to explain; to offer, tender; to set on shore, land; to send *(s.o.)* sprawling; *(w. dat or* **ad** *or* **adversus** *+ acc)* to expose to

expor·rigō *or* expor·gō -rigĕre -rexī -rectus *tr* to stretch out, spread (out); **exporge frontem!** *(coll)* quit frowning! ‖ *refl (geog)* to extend, reach

exportāti·ō -ōnis *f* exportation

export·ō -āre -āvī -ātus *tr* to carry out; to export

ex·poscō -poscĕre -poposcī *tr* to demand, beg, insist upon; to demand the surrender of; *(w. double acc)* to ask *(s.o.)* for *(s.th.)*

expositīci·us -a -um *adj* foundling

expositi·ō -ōnis *f* exposing; *(rhet)* statement, description, explanation

exposit·us -a -um *pp of* expono ‖ *adj* frank; affable; plain, trite

expostulāti·ō -ōnis *f* insistent demand; complaint

expostul·ō -āre -āvī -ātus *tr* to demand, insist on; to complain of; *(w.* **cum** *of person)* to complain about *(s.th.)* to *(s.o.)* ‖ *intr (w.* **cum)** to lodge a complaint with

expostus *pp of* expono

expōtus *see* epōtus

express·us -a -um *adj* distinct, clear, express; *(w. ad)* closely modeled on

ex·primō -primĕre -pressī -pressus *tr* to press out, squeeze out; to extort; to press upwards, raise; to model, form, portray; to stamp *(a design on a surface);* to represent; to imitate, copy; *(w. ad)* to model on *(a pattern);* to describe; to express; to translate; to pronounce, articulate; **exprimere in melius** to improve on

exprobrāti·ō -ōnis *f (w. gen)* reproach arising from

exprobr·ō -āre -āvī -ātus *tr* to reproach, find fault with; *(w. dat)* to cast *(s.th.)* up to, put the blame for *(s.th.)* on ‖ *intr (w. dat)* to complain to

exprōm·ō -ĕre -psī -ptus *tr* to bring out, fetch out *(from storage);* to give vent to; to disclose, display, exhibit; to utter, express, state; to bring into play, put to use

expugnābil·is -is -e *adj* vulnerable to attack

expugnāci·or -or -us *adj* more potent

expugnāti·ō -ōnis *f* assault; *(w. gen)* assault on; ruin

expugnāt·or -ōris *m* attacker; **expugnator pudicitiae** rapist

expugn·ō -āre -āvī -ātus *tr* to assault, storm; to break into, plunder *(a home);* to defeat; *(fig)* to overcome, sweep aside *(conditions, purposes); (fig)* to achieve, accomplish; *(fig)* to extort, wrest, gain; to persuade, overcome the resistance of

expulsi·ō -ōnis *f* expulsion

expuls·ō -āre -āvī -ātus *tr* to drive out, expel

expuls·or -ōris *m* expeller

expulsus *pp of* expello

expultr·ix -īcis *f* expeller *(female)*

expun·gō -gĕre -xī -ctus *tr* to expunge; *(fin)* to cancel *(a debt)*, check off the list as paid; *(vulg)* to prick thoroughly

expurgāti·ō -ōnis *f* (-pūrig-) justification, excuse; cleansing

expurg·ō -āre -āvī -ātus *tr* (-pūrig-) to cleanse, purify; to cure; to vindicate; to excuse, justify

expūtesc·ō -ĕre *intr* to rot away

exput·ō -āre -āvī -ātus *tr* to prune, lop off; to consider; to figure out

exquīrō exquīrĕre exquīsīvī exquīsītus *tr* (-quaer-) to look into, ask about; to look for; to search, examine; to find out; **pretium exquirire** to work out a price

exquīsītē *adv* carefully, accurately; exquisitely

exquīsīt·us -a -um *pp of* exquiro ‖ *adj* carefully considered; meticulous; choice, exquisite

exr- = er-

exrādīcitus *adv* (ērād-) utterly

exsaev·iō -īre *intr* to lose its fury

e(x)sangu·is -is -e *adj* bloodless; pale; feeble; causing paleness

ex(s)ar·ciō -cīre -sī -tus *tr* (ex(s)er-) to patch up, mend

ex(s)ati·ō -āre -āvī -ātus *tr* to satisfy fully

exsaturābil·is -is -e *adj* appeasable

exsatur·ō -āre -āvī -ātus *tr* to satisfy completely, glut

exsce- = esce-

ex(s)cindō ex(s)cindĕre ex(s)cidī ex(s)cissus *tr* to annihilate, demolish; to exterminate *(a people)*

ex(s)cre·ō -āre -āvī -ātus *tr* to cough up, spit out

exscrī·bō -bĕre -psī -ptus *tr* to write down; to write out in full; to copy; *(fig)* to take after, resemble

ex(s)culp·ō -ĕre -sī -tus *tr* to carve out; to scratch out, erase; *(fig)* to extort

ex(s)ec·ō *or* **ex(s)ic·ō -āre -uī -tus** *tr* to cut out, cut away, cut off; to castrate; to deduct

ex(s)ecrābil·is -is -e *adj* accursed; bitter, merciless, deadly; amounting to execration

ex(s)ecrāti·ō -ōnis *f* curse, execration; solemn oath

ex(s)ecrāt·us -a -um *adj* accursed, detestable

ex(s)ecr·or -ārī -ātus sum *tr* to curse ‖ *intr* to take a solemn oath

ex(s)ecti·ō -ōnis *f* cutting out

ex(s)ecūti·ō -ōnis *f* execution, performance; administration *(of a province); development (of a subject)*

ex(s)ecūtus *pp of* **ex(s)equor**

ex(s)equi·ae -ārum *fpl* funeral procession; funeral service; **ex(s)equias ire** to attend a funeral

ex(s)equiāl·is -is -e *adj* funeral; **carmina exsequialia** dirges

ex(s)e·quor -quī -cūtus sum *tr* to follow out; to accompany to the grave; to perform, execute, carry out; to follow up, investigate; to pursue, go after; to avenge, punish; to say, tell, relate; to describe; to enumerate, go through; *(rhet)* to develop *(a topic);* **verbis exsequi** to enumerate

ex(s)er·ō -ĕre -uī -tus *tr* to untie, disconnect; to stretch out *(one's arms);* to stick out *(one's tongue);* to bare, uncover

ex(s)ert·ō -āre -āvī -ātus *tr* to keep on stretching *or* sticking out

ex(s)ertus *pp of* **ex(s)ero** ‖ *adj* uncovered, bare; protruding

ex(s)ībil·ō -āre -āvī -ātus *tr* to hiss off the stage

ex(s)iccāt·us -a -um *adj* dry, uninteresting

ex(s)icc·ō -āre -āvī -ātus *tr* to dry up; to drain dry

ex(s)icō *see* **ex(s)eco**

exsign·ō -āre -āvī -ātus *tr* to mark down exactly, write down in detail

ex(s)il·iō -īre -uī *intr* to jump out; to be startled; **ex(s)ilire gaudio** to jump for joy

ex(s)il·ium -(i)ī *n* exile; place of exile

ex·(s)istō -(s)istĕre -(s)titī -(s)titum *intr* to come out, come forth; to appear, emerge; to exist, be; to arise, proceed; to turn into; to be visible ‖ *v impers* it follows as a consequence

ex(s)ol·vō -vĕre -vī -ūtus *tr* to loosen, untie; to release, set free; to discharge, pay; to keep, fufill; to satisfy *(hunger);* to break open, wound; to solve; to explain; to throw off, get rid of; to repay, requite; to give out *(awards, punishment)*

ex(s)omn·is -is -e *adj* sleepless

ex(s)or·beō -bēre -psī *tr* to absorb; to suck up, drain; to gulp down; to exhaust; *(fig)* to gobble up *(wealth, etc.)*

ex(s)or·s -tis *adj* without lots; chosen specially; *(w. gen)* having no share in, free from

ex(s)pati·or -ārī -ātus sum *intr* to go off course; to flow away from its course; to digress; to expatiate

ex(s)pectābil·is -is -e *adj* expected, anticipated

ex(s)pectāti·ō -ōnis *f* expectation, anticipation, suspense; **exspectationem facere** to cause suspense

ex(s)pectāt·us -a -um *adj* expected, awaited, desired

exspect·ō -āre -āvī -ātus *tr* to await, wait for, look out for; to hope for, anticipate, long for ‖ *intr* to wait with anticipation

exsper·gō -gĕre — -sus *tr* to sprinkle, scatter

ex(s)pēs *adj (only in nom sing)* hopeless, without hope

ex(s)pīrāti·ō -ōnis *f* breathing out, exhalation

ex(s)pīr·ō -āre *tr* to breathe out, exhale, emit ‖ *intr* to be exhaled; to expire, breathe one's last; *(fig)* to come to an end, cease

ex(s)plend·escō -escĕre -uī *intr* to glitter, shine; to become conspicuous

ex(s)poli·ō -āre -āvī -ātus *tr* to strip; to pillage

ex(s)p·uō -uĕre -uī -ūtus *tr* to spit out; *(fig)* to banish *(e.g., cares)*

ex(s)tern·ō -āre -āvī -ātus *tr* to startle, scare; to terrify; to stampede

ex(s)till·ō -āre -āvī *intr* to drip, trickle out; to melt
ex(s)timulāt·or -ōris *m* instigator
ex(s)timul·ō -āre -āvī -ātus *tr* to goad; *(fig)* to stir up
ex(s)tincti·ō -ōnis *f* extinction
ex(s)tinct·or -ōris *m* extinguisher; suppressor; destroyer
ex(s)tin·guō -guĕre -xī -ctus *tr* to extinguish, put out; to destroy, kill; to abolish, annul **ǁ** *pass* to die, die out; to be forgotten
ex(s)tirp·ō -āre -āvī -ātus *tr* to pull up by the roots, extirpate, root out, eradicate
ex(s)t·ō -āre ex(s)titī *intr* to stand out, protrude, project; to stand out, be prominent, be conspicuous; to be visible; to appear; to exist, be extant
ex(s)tructi·ō -ōnis *f* erection, construction
exstruct·um -ī *n* platform
ex(s)tru·ō -ĕre -xī -ctus *tr* to pile up; to build, erect, construct
ex(s)uct·us -a -um *pp of* **ex(s)ugo ǁ** *adj* dried up
ex(s)ūd·ō·ō -āre -āvī -ātus *tr* to sweat over; to exude **ǁ** *intr* to ooze out
ex(s)ū·gō -gĕre -xī -ctus *tr* to suck out; *(fig)* to draw out *(moisture)*
ex(s)·ul -ulis *mf* exile, refugee
ex(s)ul·ō -āre -āvī *intr* to be an exile, be a refugee
ex(s)ultāti·ō -ōnis *f* exultation, jumping for joy
ex(s)ultim *adv* friskily
ex(s)ult·ō -āre -āvī *intr* to jump up; to frisk about; *(of horses)* to rear, prance; *(of heart)* to throb; to exult, rejoice, jump for joy; to revel, run riot; to boast; *(of speech)* to jump around
ex(s)uperābil·is -is -e *adj* conquerable
ex(s)uperanti·a -ae *f* superiority
ex(s)uper·ō -āre -āvī -ātus *tr* to surmount; to tower above; to exceed; to be too strong for, overpower; to outdo; to outlive **ǁ** *intr* to rise; to be superior, excel, to be conspicuous; to gain the upper hand; *(of flames)* to shoot up
ex(s)urd·ō -āre -āvī -ātus *tr* to deafen; to dull *(the senses)*
ex(s)ur·gō -gĕre -rexī *intr* to get up, rise, stand up; to swell; *(fig)* to recover strength; **foras ex(s)urgere** to get up and go out
exsuscit·ō -āre -āvī -ātus *tr* to rouse from sleep; to fan *(fire);* to excite, stir up
ext·a -ōrum *npl* vital organs
extāb·escō -escĕre -uī *intr* to waste away; to pine away; to disappear
extār·is -is -e *adj* used for cooking the sacrificial victim; sacrificial
extemp(u)lō *adv* immediately, right away; on the spur of the moment
exten·dō -dĕre -dī -tus *or* **-sus** *tr* to stretch

out, spread out, extend; to enlarge, increase; to widen; to prolong, continue; to pass, spend; to exert, strain; **labellum extendere** to pout *(literally, to extend the lip);* **vires omnes imperii extendere** to do everything in one's power **ǁ** *refl* to exert oneself **ǁ** *pass* to stretch out, extend; to be stretched out at full length
extent·ō -āre -āvī -ātus *tr* to exert, strain
extent·us -a -um *pp of* **extendo ǁ** *adj* extensive, wide; level; **per funem extentum ire** to walk a tightrope
extenuāti·ō -ōnis *f* belittlement
extenuāt·us -a -um *adj* thinned, reduced; trifling; weak, faint
extenu·ō -āre -āvī -ātus *tr* to thin out; to lessen; to detract from
exter *or* **exter·us -a -um** *adj* exterior, outward; foreign, strange; **mare exterum** the ocean *(as opposed to the Mediterranean Sea)* **ǁ** *m* foreigner
exterebr·ō -āre -āvī -ātus *tr* to bore out; to extort
exter·geō -gēre -sī -sus *or* **exter·gō -gĕre** *tr* to wipe out, wipe away; to wipe clean; *(fig)* to clean out
exteri·or -or -us *adj* exterior, outer
exterius *adv* on the outside
extermin·ō -āre -āvī -ātus *tr* to drive out, banish; to put aside, put away; to dismiss *(from the mind)*
extern·us -a -um *adj* external, outward; foreign, strange **ǁ** *m* foreigner, stranger, foreign enemy **ǁ** *npl* foreign goods
ex·terō -terĕre -trīvī -trītus *tr* to rub out, wear away; *(fig)* to crush
exterr·eō -ēre -uī -itus *tr* to terrify; *(w. abl)* to frighten out of
extersī *perf of* **extergeo**
extersus *pp of* **extergeo**
exters·us -ūs *m* the wiping
exterus *see* **exter**
extex·ō -ĕre -uī -tus *tr* to unweave; *(fig)* to cheat
extim·escō -escĕre -uī *tr* to become terribly afraid of, dread **ǁ** *intr* to become afraid
extim·us -a -um *adj* outermost, farthest, most remote
extisp·ex -icis *m* soothsayer *(who makes predictions by inspecting the entrails of animals)*
extispic·ium -(i)ī *n* the examination of entrails as a means of divination
extoll·ō -ĕre *tr* to lift up; to erect; to postpone; to extol, praise; to raise, exalt; to keep raised, hold up; to beautify; **animos extollere** to raise the morale **ǁ** *refl & pass (of heavenly bodies)* to rise
extor·queō -quēre -sī -tus *tr* to wrench, wrest; to dislocate; to extort
extorr·is -is -e *adj* driven out of one's country, banished, exiled

extorsī *perf of* extorqueo
extort·or -ōris *m* extortionist
extort·us -a -um *pp of* extorqueo ‖ *adj* deformed
extrā *adv* outside, on the outside; from the outside; extra quam except in the case that; extra quam si unless ‖ *prep (w. acc)* **1** outside, outside of: extra nostrum ordinem outside our class; extra ordinem outside the usual order, extraordinarily, exceptionally; extra sortem by direct appointment *(literally, outside the casting of lots);* **2** beyond (the limits of): extra meum fundum beyond (the limits of) my farm; extra teli jactum beyond the range of the weapon, out of range; **3** beyond the scope of, not subject to: extra leges beyond the scope of the laws, not subject to the laws; **4** free from, without: extra modum immoderately, abnormally *(literally, without measure);* extra numerum not in meter; off-key; extra numerum es mihi *(fig)* you don't count in my eyes; **5** apart from, except: omnes extra me everyone except me; **6** aside from: extra jocum all joking aside
extra·hō -here -xī -ctus *tr* to pull out, drag out; to draw *(water)* out; to pull up *(to higher ground);* to prolong; to waste *(time);* to extricate, rescue; to remove; to tow *(a ship)* out
extrāne·us -a -um *adj* extraneous, external, irrelevant; foreign ‖ *mf* stranger; foreigner
extraordināri·us -a -um *adj* extraordinary
extrāri·us -a -um *adj* outward, external; unrelated *(by family ties)*
extrēm·a -ōrum *npl* extremities, last measures, last resort; end *(e.g., of life, of strip of land);* (mil) rear elements
extrēmit·ās -ātis *f* extremity, end
extrēmō *adv* finally, at last
extrēmum *adv* finally, at last; for the last time
extrēm·us -a -um *adj* extreme, outermost, on the end; latest, last, hindmost; the last part of, end of; the tip of, the edge of; *(of degree)* utmost, extreme; lowest; extrema aetas advanced old age; extrema cauda tip of the tail; extremā lineā amare to love at a distance; extrema manus final touches; extremis digitis attingere to touch lightly; to hold tenderly; to touch lighly on; extremo tempore finally; extremus ignis flickering flame; in extremo libro secundo at the end of the second book ‖ *n* end; limit; edge; tip; bottom; extremity; conclusion; ad extremum at last; at the end; utterly; in extremo in mortal danger, in a crisis

extrīc·ō -āre -āvī -ātus *or* extrīc·or -ārī -ātus sum *tr* to extricate; to clear up; to obtain with difficulty
extrinsecus *adv* from the outside, from abroad; outside, on the outside
extrītus *pp of* extero
extrīvī *perf of* extero
extrū·dō -dere -sī -sus *tr* to push out; to eject, expel, drive out; to keep out *(e.g., the sea with dikes)*
ex·tumeō -ēre -uī *intr* to swell up
ex·tundō -tundere -tudī -tūsus *tr* to beat out, hammer out; to fashion; to devise; to extort, get *(a promise, concession)* out of
exturb·ō -āre -āvī -ātus *tr* to drive out, chase out, drive away; to divorce; to knock out; to disturb, upset; matrimonio exturbare to divorce *(a woman)*
exūber·ō -āre -āvī -ātum *intr* to grow luxuriantly; to abound
exul *see* exsul
exulō *see* exsulo
exulcer·ō -āre -āvī -ātus *tr* to make sore; to aggravate; to exasperate; to wound the feelings of
exulul·ō -āre -āvī -ātus *tr* to invoke with cries ‖ *intr* to howl, ululate
exunctus *pp of* exungo
exund·ō -āre -āvī *intr* to gush up, well up; to overflow; in litora exundare to wash ashore
exun·g(u)ō -g(u)ere -xī -ctus *tr* to rub down with oil
ex·uō -uere -uī -ūtus *tr* to take off, pull off; to shake off; to undress; to strip; to deprive *(of possessions);* to release; to cast aside, cast off; to bare
exurg·eō -ēre *tr* to squeeze out
ex·ūrō -ūrere -ussī -ustus *tr* to burn out; to burn up; to burn down; to dry up; to consume, destroy; to purge away; *(fig)* to inflame; vivum *(or* vivam) exurere to burn alive
exusti·ō -ōnis *f* conflagration
exust·us -a -um *pp of* exuro
exūtus *pp of* exuo ‖ *adj* bare; unum pedem exutus with one foot bare
exuvi·ae -ārum *fpl* spoils; souvenir; hide, skin; slough *(of snake);* clothing; symbols of the gods *(e.g., lightning bolt, scepter, etc., carried in procession)*
exuv·ium -(i)ī *n* spoils

F

fab·a -ae *f* bean
fabāl·is -is -e *adj* bean-; stipulae fabales bean stalks
fabell·a -ae *f* short story; fable; play
fa·ber -bra -brum *adj* skilled ‖ *m* crafts-

man; smith; carpenter; builder; **faber aerarius** coppersmith; **faber ferrarius** blacksmith; **faber marmoris** marble worker; **faber navalis** ship builder; **faber sandapilarum** bier maker; **faber tignarius** carpenter

Fab·ius -(i)ī *m* Quintus Fabius Maximus Cunctator *(see* **cunctātor)**

fabrē *adv* skillfully

fabrēfact·us -a -um *adj* constructed by craftsmen

fabric·a -ae *f* craft, trade, industry; workshop; workmanship; process of building, construction, production; **fabricam fingere** *(w.* **ad)** *(coll)* to pull a trick on

fabricāti·ō -ōnis *f* construction; structure

fabricāt·or -ōris *m* builder, producer, creator, architect

fabric·or -ārī -ātus sum *or* **fabric·ō -āre -āvī -ātus** *tr* to make, build, construct, produce; to forge; to prepare, form; to coin *(words)*

fabrīl·is -is -e *adj* craftsman's, carpenter's, smith's, builder's, sculptor's; skilled ‖ *npl* tools

fābul·a -ae *f* story, tale; talk, conversation; conversation piece; small talk; gossip; affair, matter; myth, legend; drama, play; dramatic poem; **fabula est** *(w. acc & inf)* legend has it that, the story goes that; **fabulae!** *(coll)* baloney!; **fabulam dare** *(or* **docere)** to present a play; **lupus in fabula!** *(coll)* speak of the devil!; **quae haec est fabula?** *(coll)* what's that you are saying?

fābulār·is -is -e *adj* legendary; **historia fabularis** mythology

fābulāt·or -ōris *m* story-teller; writer of fables

fābul·or -ārī -ātus sum *tr* to say, invent ‖ *intr* to talk, chat, gossip

fābulōs·us -a -um *adj* legendary; incredible; fictitious, mythical ‖ *n* myth, legend

fabul·us -ī *m* bean

facess·ō -ěre -īvī *or* **-iī -ītus** *tr* to do eagerly, perform, accomplish; to bring on, cause, create; **negotium alicui facessere** to cause s.o. trouble; *(leg)* to bring a case against s.o.; **rem facessere** *(leg)* to sue ‖ *intr* to go away, depart, take off; *(lit & fig)* to retire; **cubitum facessere** to go to sleep

facētē *adv* facetiously, humorously, wittily, amusingly, brilliantly

facēti·ae -ārum *fpl* clever thing; clever talk, witticism, humor

facēt·us -a -um *adj* witty, humorous; fine, elegant; brilliant

faci·ēs -ēī *f* face; look, facial expression; appearance; make, form, shape, outline; nature, character; pretense, pretext; **a facie** in the face, in front; **in facie** *(w.*

gen) in the presence of; **in faciem** *(w. gen)* so as to give the appearance of; into the presence of; **primā facie** at first sight

facilě *adv* easily, without trouble; unquestionably, far, by far; generally; quite, fully; promptly, readily, willingly; pleasantly, well; **non facile** hardly

facil·is -is -e *adj* easy; nimble; convenient, suitable; ready, quick; easygoing, goodnatured; favorable; prosperous; gentle *(breeze);* easily borne, slight *(loss);* tame, obedient *(animals);* **ex** *(or* **e) facili** easily; **facile est** *(w. inf)* it is easy to; **facile est de** *(+ abl)* it does not matter about; **facilis victu** well-to-do, well-off; **facilius est ut** it is more likely that; **in facili esse** to be easy

facilit·ās -ātis *f* facility, ease, easiness; readiness; fluency; aptitude; good nature; courteousness; levity

faciliter *adv (pedantic for* **facile)**

facinorōs·us -a -um *adj & m* **(-ner-)** criminal; wicked

facin·us -oris *n* deed, act; event; crime, outrage; criminal

faci·ō facěre fēcī factus (faxim = fēcerim; faxō = fēcerō) *tr* to make; to do, perform; to fashion, frame, create; to build, erect; to produce, compose; to produce *(young);* to bring about, cause, occasion; to acquire, get, gain; to incur, suffer; to render, grant, give, confer; to assert, say, represent, depict; to choose, appoint; to follow, practice; to regard, prize, value; **aliquem certiorem facere de** *(+ abl)* to inform s.o. about; **copiam facere** *(w. dat)* to afford *(s.o.)* the opportunity; **dies facere** to spend days; **fac ita esse** suppose it were so, granted that it is so; **fidem facere** to give one's word; **gratiam facere** to grant pardon, excuse; **gratum (pergratum) facere** *(w. dat)* to do s.o. a (great) favor; **pecuniam** *(or* **stipendium) facere** to make money, earn money; **pretium facere** to name the price; **promissum facere** to fulfill a promise; **sacra facere** to sacrifice, offer sacrifice; **verba facere** to speak; **viam facere** *(w. dat)* to make way for ‖ *intr* to do, act; to take part, take sides; *(w. dat or* **ad)** to be satisfactory for, be fit for, do for; *(of medicines)* to work; *(w. ad)* to be effective in dealing with; **suā causā** *(or* **suā re) facere** to act in one's own interests; *(euph. for relieving oneself)* to do one's duty

facteon = faciendum

facti·ō -ōnis *f* doing; making; party, faction; partisanship; band, group; troupe *(of actors);* social set, association; **quae haec factio est?** *(coll)* what's this all about?

factiōs·us -a -um *adj* busy; well-connected; belonging to a faction; factious, subversive, revolutionary

factit·ō -āre -āvī -ātus *tr* to keep doing, keep making; to practice *(e.g., trade);* *(w. double acc)* to declare *(s.o.)* to be *(e.g., heir)*

fact·or -ōris *m* maker; perpetrator *(of crime);* **factores et datores** pitchers and catchers *(in ballgame)*

fact·us -a -um *pp of* **facio ‖** *n* deed, act; accomplishment, exploit; misdeed; **dictum factum** no sooner said than done

facul·a -ae *f* little torch

facult·ās -ātis *f* opportunity; feasibility; ability, capacity, skill; material resources; *(of things)* power, potency; supply *(of money, ships, men);* convenience; *(w. gen)* **1** power over; **2** skill in; **facultas ingenii** expertise **‖** *fpl* talents; resources

fācundē *adv* eloquently

fācundi·a -ae *f* eloquence

facundit·ās -ātis *f* eloquence

fācund·us -a -um *adj* eloquent

faece·us -a -um *adj* foul

faecul·a -ae *f* (fēc-) wine lees *(when dried, used as medicine or spice)*

faenebr·is -is -e *adj* (fēn-) of interest; lent at interest

faenerāti·ō -ōnis *f* (fēn-) lending at interest, investment

faenerātō *adv* with *or* at interest

faenerāt·or -ōris *m* (fēn-) money lender, investor

faener·or -ārī -ātus sum *or* **faener·ō -āre -āvī -ātus** *tr* (fēn-) to lend at interest; to invest *(money);* to finance; to ruin *(e.g., a province)* through high interest rates **‖** *intr* to yield interest, bring profit

faene·us -a -um *adj* made of hay

faenicul·um -ī *n* fennel *(used as seasoning or medicine)*

faenīl·ia -ium *npl* (fēn-) hayloft

faenisec·a -ae *m* (fēn-) reaper, farmer

faen·um -ī *n* (fēn-) hay; **faenum habet in cornu** *(sl)* he's crazy *(literally, he has hay on his horns)*

faen·us -oris *n* (fēn-) interest; debt *(as result of heavy interest);* capital; *(fig)* profit, gain, advantage; **faenore** at interest; **in faenore** on loan

faenuscul·um -ī *n* (fēn-) a little interest

fae·x -cis *or* **fex fēcis** *f* wine lees, dregs; sediment; slag; impure mixture; *(fig)* scum

fāgine·us *or* **fāgin·us** *or* **fāge·us -a -um** *adj* beech

fāg·us -ī *f* beech tree

fal·a *or* **phal·a -ae** *f* movable wooden siege tower; scaffold

falāric·a -ae *f* (phal-) incendiary missile

falcār·ius -(i)ī *m* sickle maker

falcāt·us -a -um *adj* fitted with scythes; sickle-shaped, curved

falcif·er -era -erum *adj* scythe-bearing

falc·ō -ōnis *m* pigeon-toed person

Faleri·ī -ōrum *mpl* city of Etruria

Falern·us -a -um *adj* Falernian; **ager Falernus** district in N. Campania, famous for its wine **‖** *n* Falernian wine

Falisc·us -a -um *mpl* Faliscan **‖** *mpl* a people of S. E. Etruria

fallāci·a -ae *f* deception, deceit, trick

fallācit·ās -ātis *f* deceptiveness

fallāciter *adv* deceptively; falsely

fall·ax -ācis *adj* deceptive, deceitful; spurious, false

fall·ens -entis *adj* deceptive

fallō fallĕre fefellī falsus *tr* to cause to fall, trip; to lead into error, mislead; to deceive, trick, dupe, cheat; to fail to live up to, disappoint; to while away *(time);* to escape the clutches of; to escape the notice of, slip by; to disguise; **faciem alicujus fallere** to impersonate s.o.; **fidem fallere** to break one's word; **oculos fallere** to be invisible; **opinionem fallere** *(w. gen)* to fail to live up to the expectations of **‖** *pass* **nisi** *(or* **ni) fallor** unless I'm mistaken **‖** *intr* to go unnoticed **‖** *v impers* **me fallit** I am wrong

falsār·ius -(i)ī *m* forger

falsē *adv* falsely

falsidic·us -a -um *adj* speaking falsely, lying

falsific·us -a -um *adj* acting dishonestly

falsijūri·us -a -um *adj* swearing falsely

falsiloqu·us -a -um *adj* lying

falsimōni·a -ae *f* trick, deception

falsipar·ens -entis *adj* bastard

falsō *adv* mistakenly, wrongly, erroneously; falsely, deceitfully

fals·us -a -um *adj* false, untrue; mistaken, wrong, erroneous; lying, deceitful; vain, groundless, empty; spurious, sham, fictitious **‖** *n* error; lying; lie, falsehood; perjury

fal·x -cis *f* sickle; pruning hook, pruning knife; *(mil)* hook for pulling down walls

fām·a -ae *f* talk, rumor, report, news; saying, tradition; *(w. gen)* reputation *(for);* fame, renown, name; infamy, notoriety; public opinion

fāmēlic·us -a -um *adj* famished

fam·ēs -is *f* hunger; starvation; famine; fasting; *(fig)* craving; *(rhet)* bald style, poverty of expression

fāmigerāti·ō -ōnis *f* rumor

fāmigerāt·or -ōris *m* gossip, rumor-monger

famili·a -ae *or* **-ās** *f* household slaves, domestics; gang of slaves; retinue of servants; household; house, family; family estate; sect, school; **familia gladiatorum** stable of gladiators; **familiam**

ducere to head a sect; **pater familias** head of the family

familiār·is -is -e *adj* domestic, family-, household-; familiar, intimate; private, personal *(as opposed to public); (in augury)* one's own *(part of the sacrificial animal);* **res familiaris** one's private property, estate, patrimony ‖ *m* servant, slave; acquaintance; close friend

familiārit·ās -ātis *f* close friendship, intimacy; familiarity; *(of things)* close relationship

familiāriter *adv* in the manner of a close friend; thoroughly; as if at home, in a familiar manner; familiarly

fāmōs·us -a -um *adj* much talked of; famous, renowned; infamous; slanderous, libelous; **carmen famosum** lampoon

famul·a -ae *f* maid, slave-girl

famulār·is -is -e *adj* of slaves, servile

famulāt·us -ūs *m* slavery, servitude

famul·or -ārī -ātus sum *intr* to be a slave; *(w. dat)* to serve

famul·us -a -um *adj* servile ‖ *m* servant, attendant; slave ‖ *f see* **famula**

fānātic·us -a -um *adj* belonging to a temple; fanatic, enthusiastic, inspired; frantic ‖ *mf* temple attendant

fand·us -a -um *adj* that may be spoken

fān·um -ī *n* shrine, sanctuary; temple

fār farris *n* spelt *(type of wheat);* coarse meal, grits; sacrificial meal; bread; dog biscuit ‖ *npl* grain

far·ciō -cīre -sī -tus *tr* to stuff; to fatten *(birds for table); (w.* **in** + *acc)* to cram into ‖ *refl* to gorge oneself

farfar·us *or* **farfer·us -ī** *m* coltsfoot *(plant w. heart-shaped leaves)*

farīn·a -ae *f* flour; powder; *(fig)* character, quality

-fāriam *advl suf* forms multiplicative adverbs denoting -sided: **multifariam** many-sided

farrāg·ō -inis *f* mash *(for cattle); (fig)* medley, hodgepodge

farrāt·us -a -um *adj* filled with grain, made with grain

fart·is -is *f* stuffing, filling; mincemeat; **fartim facere ex hostibus** to make mincemeat of the enemy

fart·or -ōris *m* fattener of poultry

far·tus -us -a -um *pp of* **farcio** ‖ *adj* well-fed; crammed, gorged

fās *indecl n* divine law; sacred duty, divine will, fate; right; natural law; **fas est** it is right, it is lawful; it is permissible; **fas tibi est** you have the right; **omne fas est fidere** there is every reason to trust

fasci·a -ae *f* bandage; bra(ssière); diaper; headband, fillet; wisp of cloud

fasciātim *adv* in bundles

fascicul·us -ī *m* small bundle

fascin·ō -āre -āvī -ātus *tr* to cast an evil eye on, bewitch, jinx; to envy

fascin·um -ī *n or* **fascin·us -ī** *m* evil eye; jinx; witchcraft; charm, amulet; *(vulg)* penis

fasciol·a -ae *f* ribbon; headband

fasc·is -is *m* bundle, pack, parcel; fagot; load, burden; baggage ‖ *mpl* fasces *(bundle of rods and ax, carried before high magistrates by lictors as symbols of authority);* high office, supreme power, consulship

fassus *pp of* **fateor**

fast·ī -ōrum *mpl* calendar, almanac; annals; register of higher magistrates ‖ **Fasti** poem by Ovid

fastīd·iō -īre -īvī *or* **-iī -ītus** *tr* to despise, snub, turn up the nose at ‖ *intr* to feel disgust, feel squeamish; to be snobbish, be haughty

fastīdiōsē *adv* fastidiously, squeamishly; disdainfully, snobbishly

fastīdiōs·us -a -um *adj* fastidious, squeamish; disdainful, snobbish; refined, delicate; nauseating

fastīd·ium -(i)ī *n* fastidiousness, distaste, squeamishness, disgust, loathing; snobbishness, haughtiness; **(in) fastidio esse** to be repugnant; **in fastidium ire** to become repugnant

fastīgātē *adv* sloped, at an angle

fastīgāt·us -a -um *adj* rising to a point; sloping down

fastīg·ium -(i)ī *n* gable; pediment; roof; ceiling; slope; height, elevation; top, edge; depth, depression; completion; rank, dignity; main point, heading; highlight *(of a story, etc.)*

fastīg·ō -āre -āvī -ātus *tr* to make pointed; to taper; to cause to slope, incline ‖ *refl* & *pass* to taper; to narrow

fastōs·us -a -um *adj* disdainful

fast·us -a -um *adj (of day)* lawful *(for transaction of business);* **dies fastus** court day ‖ *mpl see* **fasti**

fast·us -ūs *m* contempt; arrogance

fātāl·is -is -e *adj* fateful, destined, preordained; fatal, deadly; **deae fatales** Fates

fātāliter *adv* by fate, by destiny

fateor fatērī fassus sum *tr* to admit, acknowledge, confess; to profess, declare; **fatendi modus** *(gram)* the indicative mood ‖ *intr* to admit guilt, confess; to say yes; *(w. inf)* to agree to

fātican·us -a -um *adj* (-cin-) prophetic

fātidic·us -a -um *adj* prophetic

fātif·er -era -erum *adj* fatal, deadly

fatīgāti·ō -ōnis *f* fatigue

fatīg·ō -āre -āvī -ātus *tr* to fatigue, weary, tire out; to wear down; to worry, torment, bother; to pray to constantly

fātiloqu·a -ae *f* prophetess

fatisc·ō -ĕre or **fatisc·or -ī** intr to split, crack, give way; (fig) to become exhausted, wear out

fatuē adv foolishly

fatuit·ās -ātis f silliness

fāt·um -ī n divine utterance, oracle; fate, destiny, doom; calamity; ruin; death; (fig) cause of death, cause of ruin; **ad fata novissima** to the last; **fato functus** dead; **fato obire** to meet death; **fatum est** it is fated; **fatum proferre** to put off fate, prolong life ‖ npl what fate has in store, the future

fātus pp of **for**

fatu·us -a -um adj silly, foolish; clumsy; tasteless (food) ‖ m fool

fauc·ēs -ium (poet: abl singl: **fauce**) fpl throat; gullet; neck; strait, channel; pass, gorge; mouth (of river); entrance (to harbor, home, building, cave, lower world); jaws, maw (of wild animals); crater (of volcano); neck (of vase, jar); **fauces premere** (w. gen) to throttle s.o.

Faun·us -ī m king of Latium, father of Latinus and worshiped as the Italian Pan ‖ mpl Fauns, woodland spirits

faustē adv favorably, auspiciously

faustit·ās -ātis f fertility; good fortune, happiness

Faustul·us -ī m shepherd who rescued and raised Romulus and Remus

faust·us -a -um adj auspicious, favorable; lucky ‖ **Faustus** personal name (agnomen) of the son of the dictator Sulla

faut·or or **favit·or -ōris** m, **fautr·ix -īcis** f patron, supporter, fan

fave·a -ae f favorite girl, pet slave girl

faveō favēre fāvī fautum intr (w. dat) to be favorable to, favor, support, side with; (w. inf) to be eager to; **favere linguis** (or **ore**) to observe a reverential silence

favill·a -ae f ashes, embers; (fig) spark, beginnings

favitor see **fautor**

Favōn·ius -(i)ī m West Wind (also called Zephyrus)

fav·or -ōris m favor, support; applause; appreciation (shown by applause)

favōrābil·is -is -e adj popular

favōrābiliter adv in order to win popularity

fav·us -ī m honeycomb ‖ mpl honey

fax facis f torch; wedding torch, wedding; funeral torch, funeral; meteor, shooting star, comet; firebrand; fire, flame; guiding light; instigator; flame of love; stimulus, incitement; cause of ruin or destruction; **dicendi faces** fiery eloquence; **dolorum faces** pangs of grief

faxim, faxō see **facio**

febrīcul·a -ae f slight fever

febrīculōs·us -a -um adj fever-ridden; prone to fevers

febr·is -is f fever

Febru·a -ōrum npl Roman festival of purification and expiation, celebrated on February 15

Februāri·us -a -um adj & m February (twelfth month of the Roman calendar until the reform of 153 b.c.)

febru·um -ī n purification

fēcundit·ās -ātis f fertility, fruitfulness; (rhet) overstatement

fēcund·ō -āre -āvī -ātus tr to fertilize

fēcund·us -a -um adj fertile, fruitful; abundant, rich; fertilizing; (w. gen or abl) rich in, abounding in

fel fellis n gallbladder; gall, bile; bitterness, animosity; poison

fēl·ēs or **fēl·is -is** f cat

fēlīcit·ās -ātis f fertility; luck, piece of luck; felicity, happiness

fēlīciter adv fruitfully, abundantly; luckily; happily; sucessfully; favorably

fēlis see **feles**

fēl·ix -īcis adj fruit-bearing; fruitful, fertile; favorable, auspicious; lucky; happy; successful; well-aimed

fellāt·or -ōris m one who practices oral sex

fell·ō -āre -āvī -ātus tr to practice oral sex with ‖ intr to practice oral sex

fēmell·a -ae f girl, young lady

fēmin·a -ae f female; woman

femināl·ia -ium npl stockings (to cover the thighs)

fēmine·us -a -um adj woman's; effeminate, unmanly

fēminīn·us -a -um adj female; (gram) feminine

fem·ur -oris or **-inis** n thigh

fēn- = **faen-**

fenestr·a -ae f window; hole (for earrings); (fig) opening, opportunity; (mil) breach (in a wall)

-f·er -era -erum adjl suf denotes bearing, carrying, or bringing: **conifer** bearing cones

fer·a -ae f wild beast, wild animal

ferāciter adv fruitfully

ferācius adv more fruitfully

Fērāl·ia -ium npl (**Fĕr-**) festival of the dead, celebrated on February 17th or 21st

ferāl·is -is -e adj associated with death or the dead; funeral-; deadly, fatal, gloomy, dismal; **papilio feralis** funerary butterly (symbolizing the soul)

fer·ax -ācis adj fertile, fruitful; (w. gen) productive of

fercul·um -ī n food tray; dish; course; litter (for carrying spoils in a victory parade or cult images in a religious procession)

fercul·us -ī m litter bearer

ferē or **fermē** adv approximately, nearly, almost, about, just about; generally, as a

rule, usually; *(w. negatives)* practically; **haud fere** *(or* **non fere)** hardly ever; **nemo fere** practically no one
ferentār·ius -(i)ī *m* light-armed soldier; eager helper
Feretr·ius -(i)ī *m* epithet of Jupiter on the Capitoline Hill
feretr·um -ī *n* litter, bier
fēri·ae -ārum *fpl* holidays, vacation; *(fig)* leisure
fēriāt·us -a -um *adj* vacationing, taking it easy; dressed for the holiday; unemployed; **dies feriatus** holiday
fericulum = **ferculum**
ferīn·us -a -um *adj* of wild animals; brutish; **caro ferina** venison; **vita ferina** life in the wild **ǁ** *f* venison
fer·iō -īre *tr* to strike, hit, shoot, knock; to kill; to slaughter, sacrifice *(an animal);* to coin; *(fig)* to strike, reach, affect; *(fig)* to cheat, trick; **cornu ferire** to butt; **foedus ferire** to conclude a treaty; *(fig)* to strike a bargain; **securi ferire** to behead; **verba ferire** to coin words
ferit·ās -ātis *f* wildness, fierceness
fermē *see* **ferē**
ferment·um -ī *n* ferment; yeast
ferō ferre tulī *or* **tetulī lātus** *tr* to bear, carry; to bear, produce; to bear, endure; to lead, drive, conduct, direct; to bring, offer; to receive, acquire, obtain, win; to carry off, plunder, ravage; to manifest, display; to make known, report, say, tell; to call; to propose, bring forward; to allow, permit; to cause, create; to set in motion; to call, name; *(of circumstances, etc.)* to suggest; *(in accounting)* to enter; to carry *(e.g., a ward in an election);* **aditum ferre** to approach; **aegre ferre** to be annoyed at; to take it hard; **caelo supinas manus ferre** to raise the hands heavenward in prayer; **crimina ferre in** *(w. acc)* to bring charges against; **cursum** *(or* **iter) ferre** to go, proceed, pursue a course; **hunc inventorem artium ferunt** they call him the inventor of the arts; **in oculis ferre** *(fig)* to have before one's eyes, have on one's mind; **judicem ferre** to propose as judge; **judicem ferre** *(w. dat)* to propose a judge to *(i.e., to go to court with);* **laudibus ferre** to extol; **legem ferre** to propose a bill; **moleste ferre** to be annoyed at; **ore ferre** to show *(by one's looks);* **osculum ferre** *(w. dat)* to give *(s.o.)* a kiss; **pedem** *(or* **pedes) ferre** to come, go, move, get going; **prae se ferre** to display, manifest; **repulsam ferre** to experience defeat *(at polls);* **responsum ferre** to get an answer; **sententiam ferre** to pass judgment; to cast a vote; **signa ferre** *(mil)* to begin marching; **suffragium ferre** to cast a vote, cast a ballot; **ventrem ferre** to be

pregnant **ǁ** *refl* to go, proceed; to rush, flee; *(of rivers)* to flow; **se ferre obviam** *(w. dat)* to rush to meet **ǁ** *pass (of things)* to be carried along; to extend; *(of sounds)* to carry **ǁ** *intr* to say *(e.g., ut* **ferunt** as people say, as they say); to allow, permit *(e.g., si* **occasio tulerit** if the occasion permit); to lead *(e.g., iter ad oppidum* **ferebat** the road led to the town)
ferōci·a -ae *f* fierceness, ferocity; fighting spirit; pride, presumption
ferōc·iō -īre *intr* to rampage
ferōcit·ās -ātis *f* fierceness, ferocity; aggressiveness; presumption
ferōciter *adv* ferociously, aggressively; defiantly, arrogantly
Fērōni·a -ae *f* early Italic goddess of groves and springs, and patroness of ex-slaves
fer·ox -ōcis *adj* fierce, ferocious; warlike; defiant; arrogant
ferrāment·um -ī *n* tool, implement
ferrāri·us -a -um *adj* iron, of iron; **faber ferrarius** blacksmith; **officina** *(or* **taberna) ferraria** blacksmith shop **ǁ** *fpl* iron mines; iron works
ferrātil·is -is -e *adj* fit to be chained
ferrāt·us -a -um *adj* iron-plated; iron-tipped; in chains; in armor; **calx ferrata** spur **ǁ** *mpl* soldiers in armor
ferre·us -a -um *adj* iron, of iron; cruel, hardhearted; firm, unyielding; armored; inexorable, inflexible *(fate, laws);* **ferreus somnus** death
ferricrepin·us -a -um *adj (coll)* clanking with chains
ferriter·ium -(i)ī *n (coll)* brig *(jail)*
ferriter·us -ī *m (coll)* glutton for punishment
ferritrīb·ax -ācis *adj (coll)* chainsore *(from dragging chains)*
ferrūgine·us -a -um *adj* rust-colored, dark, dusky
ferrūg·ō -inis *f* rust, verdigris; dark-red; dark color; gloom
ferr·um -ī *n* iron; tool, implement; iron object: sword, dart, arrowhead, ax, plowshare, crowbar, spade, scissors, stylus, curling iron, *(surgical)* knife; gladiatorial fight; **ferro atque igni** with fire and sword; **ferro decernere** to decide by force of arms; **ferrum sumere** to resort to arms
ferrūm·en -inis *n* adhesive, cement
fertil·is -is -e *adj* fertile, fruitful, productive; fertilizing; life-giving; profitable, lucrative; *(w. gen, dat, or abl)* productive of
fertilit·ās -ātis *f* fertility
ferul·a -ae *f* reed, stalk; rod, whip
fer·us -a -um *adj* wild; uncultivated, untamed; savage, uncivilized; rude, cruel, fierce; wild, bleak *(place)* **ǁ** *m* wild beast;

wild horse; lion; stag II *f* wild beast, wild animal

ferve·faciō -facĕre -fēcī -factus *tr* to heat, boil

ferv·ens -entis *adj* seething, burning, hot; red-hot *(iron); (of mind)* in turmoil; *(fig)* hot, heated, violent, impetuous, ardent; **fervens ira oculis** anger sparkling in the eyes

ferventer *adv (fig)* heatedly, impetuously

ferv·eō -ēre *or* **ferv·ō -ĕre -ī** *intr* to boil, seethe, steam; to foam; to swarm; to be busy, bustle about; *(fig)* to burn, glow, rage, rave; **fervet opus** the work goes on at a feverish pace

fervesc·ō -ĕre *intr* to become boiling hot, grow hot, begin to boil

fervid·us -a -um *adj* boiling, seething, hot; fermenting *(grapes);* hot, highly spiced; *(fig)* hot, fiery, violent, impetuous, hot-blooded

fervō *see* **ferveo**

ferv·or -ōris *m* heat; boiling; fermenting; fever; raging *(of the sea); (fig)* heat, vehemence, ardor, passion

Fescenni·a -ae *f* town in Etruria

Fescennīn·us -a -um *adj* Fescennine II *mpl* Fescennine verses *(coarse, boisterous form of dramatic dialogue)*

fess·us -a -um *adj* tired out, worn out; weakened *(by wounds, disease, etc.); (fig)* demoralized, depressed; *(w. abl)* weary of, sick of

festīnanter *adv* quickly

festīnāti·ō -ōnis *f* hurry, haste

festīnātō *adv* hurriedly

festīn·ō -āre -āvī -ātus *tr* to perform, *(or* make *or* do) without delay; to move *(s.th.)* quickly; to accelerate; **jussa festinare** to carry out orders promptly II *intr* to rush, hurry; to bustle; to be in a hurry; *(w. inf)* to be anxious to, lose no time in

festīn·us -a -um *adj* hasty, speedy

festīvē *adv* gaily; *(coll)* humorously; *(coll)* delightfully, neatly, nicely

festīvit·ās -ātis *f* festivity, gaiety, fun; *(rhet)* humor, liveliness *(of speaker, speech)*

festūc·a -ae *f* (**fis-**) stalk; rod *(with which slaves were tapped when freed)*

fest·us -a -um *adj* festive, joyous, in holiday mood; **dies festus** holiday II *n (often plural in singular sense)* holiday, festival; **festum agere** to observe a holiday

fētiāl·is -is -e *adj* negotiating, diplomatic; fetial, of the fetial priests II *m* fetial *(member of a college of priests who performed the ritual in connection with declaring war and making peace)*

fētid·us -a -um *adj* (**foet-**) fetid, stinking

fētūr·a -ae *f* breeding, bearing; offspring, young

fēt·us -a -um *adj* pregnant, breeding; fruitful, teeming, productive

fēt·us -ūs *m* childbirth; laying *(of eggs); (of plants)* producing, bearing; offspring, young; fruit, produce; *(fig)* product *(of mind or imagination)*

fī *interj (at a bad smell)* phew!

fī·ber -brī *m* beaver

fibr·a -ae *f* fiber, filament; lobe *(of liver, lungs)* II *fpl* entrails

fībul·a -ae *f* clasp, safety pin, brooch; barrette; clamp; bolt, peg; chastity clamp *(worn through the prepuce to prevent sexual intercourse)*

fīcĕdul·a -ae *f*(**-cēd-**) beccafico, fig-pecker *(small bird)*

fictē *adv* falsely, fictitiously

fictil·is -is -e *adj* clay-, earthen II *n* jar; clay statue II *npl* earthenware

ficti·ō -ōnis *f* forming, formation; disguising; supposition; fiction

fict·or -ōris *m* shaper, sculptor, molder; attendant of priest who kneaded the sacrificial cake

fictr·ix -īcis *f* maker, molder *(female)*

fictūr·a -ae *f* shaping, fashioning

fict·us -a -um *pp of* **fingo** II *adj* false, fictitious; insincere *(person, character, emotions);* false *(witness);* **vox ficta** falsehood II *n* falsehood; pretense; fiction

fīcul·a -ae *f* little fig

fīculn(e)·us -ā -um *adj* of a fig tree

fīc·us -ī *or* **-ūs** *f* fig; fig tree; **prima ficus** early autumn II *fpl* hemorrhoids

fideicommiss·um -ī *n* trust fund

fidēli·a -ae *f* earthen pot, bucket; **duo parietes de eādem fediliā dealbare** *(prov)* to kill two birds with one stone *(literally, to whitewash two walls with one bucket)*

fidēl·is -is -e *adj* faithful, loyal; trustworthy, true, sure; safe *(ship, port, advice, etc.); (w. dat or* ad) faithful to II *m* confidant

fidēlit·ās -ātis *f* fidelity, loyalty

fidēliter *adv* faithfully, loyally; securely, certainly

Fidēn·ae -ārum *fpl* ancient town near Rome *(once the rival of Rome)*

fīd·ens -entis *adj* self-confident; bold; *(w. gen)* confident in

fīdenter *adv* confidently; boldly

fīdenti·a -ae *f* self-confidence; assurance; boldness

fid·ēs -ēī *f* trust, faith, reliance, confidence; credence, belief; trustworthiness, conscientiousness, honesty; promise, assurance; word, word of honor; protection, guarantee; safe conduct; confirmation, proof; *(com)* credit; **bonae fidei** in good faith; **bonā fide** *(or* ex bonā fide) in good faith; really, genuinely; **de fide**

malā in bad faith; **Di vostram fidem!**
for heaven's sake!; **fide decedere** to
cease to be loyal; **fidei causā** as proof of
(one's) trustworthiness; **fidem dare** to
give one's word; **fidem alicujus decipere** to deceive s.o. through (misplaced)
trust, betray s.o.'s trust; **fidem facere**
(w. dat) 1 to convince; 2 to place trust in;
fidem fallere to break one's word; **fidem
firmare** to make good one's word, back
up one's promise; **fidem habere** to be
credible, be believed, have credibility;
fidem habere *(w. dat)* to have confidence in, give credence to; **fidem
obsecrare** to beg for support *or* protection; **fidem obligare** to pledge one's
word, make a solemn promise, guarantee one's loyalty; **fidem obstringere** *(w.
dat)* to pledge one's word to; **fidem
praestare** *(or* **servare** *or* **tenere** *or*
retinere) to keep one's word; **fides
publica** promise of immunity; safe conduct; **in fide manere** to remain loyal;
meā (tuā) fide on my *(your)* word;
optimā fide with the utmost honesty;
pro fidem deum! for heaven's sake!;
res fidesque capital and credit
fid·ēs -is *f* string *(of musical instrument)* **ll**
fpl stringed instrument, lyre; *(fig)* lyric
poetry; **fidibus canere** to play the lyre;
fidibus discere to learn to play the lyre;
fidibus scire to know how to play the
lyre
fidī *perf of* **findo**
fidic·en -inis *m* lyre player; *(fig)* lyric
poet
fidicin·a -ae *f* lyre player *(female)*
fidicul·a -ae *f* small lyre **ll** *fpl* torture rack
Fid·us -(i)ī *m* epithet of Jupiter; **medius
fidius!** honest to goodness!, so help me
God!
fīdō fīděre fīsus sum *intr (w. dat or abl)* to
trust, put confidence in
fīdūci·a -ae *f* trust, confidence, reliance;
self-confidence; trustworthiness; guarantee; *(w. gen)* confident hope of; *(leg)*
deposit, pledge, security; **fiduciā** *(w. gen)*
with reliance on
fīdūciāri·us -a -um *adj* held in trust, fidu-
ciary; of a trustee
fīd·us -a -um *adj* trusty, dependable; certain, sure, safe
figlīn·us -a -um *adj* **(figul-)** potter's
figment·um -ī *n* figment; unreality
fī·gō -gěre -xī -xus *or* **-ctus** *tr* to fix,
fasten, affix, attach, nail; to drive in; to
pierce; to erect, set up; to build; to put
up, hang up, post; **cruci** *(or* **in cruce)**
figere *(or simply* **figere)** to crucify; **dicta
animo figere** to let the words sink in;
lumine figere *(poet)* to stare at
figulār·is -is -e *adj* potter's
figul·us -ī *m* potter; bricklayer

figūr·a -ae *f* figure, shape, form; phantom,
host; nature, kind; figure of speech
figūrāti·ō -ōnis *f* forming; form, shape;
description, sketch
figūrāt·us -a -um *adj* figurative
figūr·ō -āre -āvī -ātus *tr* to shape, form,
mold, fashion; to train; *(w. in + acc)* to
transform into; *(rhet)* to embellish *(a
speech)* with rhetorical figures
fīlātim *adv* thread by thread
fīli·a -ae *f (dat & abl pl:* **fīliābus)** daughter
filicāt·us -a -um *adj* engraved with fern
patterns
fīliol·a -ae *f* little daughter, dear daughter
fīliol·us -ī *m* little son, dear son
fīl·ius -(i)ī *m* son; **terrae filius** a nobody
fil·ix -icis *f* fern
fīl·um -ī *n* thread; fillet; string, cord; wick;
figure, shape *(of a woman);* build *(of a
person);* texture, quality, style *(of
speech);* *(fig)* character; **filo pendere** to
hang by a thread, be in a precarious
situation
fimbri·ae -ārum *fpl* fringe, border
fim·us -ī *m* dung, manure; mire
findō fiṅděre fidī fissus *tr* to split **ll** *refl &
pass* to fork, split
fingō fingěre finxī fictus *tr* to shape, form;
to mold, model *(in clay, wax);* to arrange
(esp. the hair), trim; to imagine, suppose, think; to contrive, invent; to pretend, feign; to train, influence *(s.o.)* to
be; to compose *(poetry);* to disguise
(looks); to trump up *(charges);* *(w.
double acc)* to represent as, depict as;
ars fingendi sculpture; **linguā fingere**
to lick **ll** *refl* to pretend to be; *(w. ad)* 1
to adapt oneself to; 2 to be subservient to
fīni·ens -entis *m* horizon
fīn·iō -īre -īvī *or* **-iī -ītus** *tr* to limit; *(fig)*
to set bounds to, limit, restrain; to mark
out, fix, determine; to put an end to,
finish, complete **ll** *pass & intr* to come to
an end
fīn·is -is *m (f)* boundary, border, limit;
end; purpose, aim; extreme limit, summit, highest degree; starting point; goal;
death; **eādem fini** within the same period; **fine** *(w. gen)* up to, as far as; **finem
facere** *(w. gen or dat)* to put an end to; **in
fine** in conclusion; **quā fine** *(or* **quā
fini)** up to the point where; up to what
point?; **quem ad finem** how long, to
what extent **ll** *mpl* boundaries, country,
territory, land
fīnītē *adv* to a limited degree; specifically
fīnitim·us -a -um *adj* **(-tum-)** neighboring, bordering; *(w. dat)* 1 bordering on;
2 *(fig)* bordering on, akin to **ll** *mpl* neighbors
fīnīt·or -ōris *m* surveyor
fīnīt·us -a -um *pp of* **finio** **ll** *adj* limited;
(rhet) rhythmical

fīō fierī factus sum *intr* to come into being, arise; to be made; to be done; to become, get; to happen, occur; *(of events, festivals, etc.)* to take place, be held; *(of physical phenomena)* to arise, develop; *(w. gen of price)* to be valued at; *(in arithmetic)* to equal; **fiat** so be it; **fieri non potest quin** it is inevitable that; **fieri potest ut** it is possible that; **ita fit ut** *(or* **quo fit ut)** thus it happens that; **plurimi fieri** to valued highly; **quid fiet?** *(w. dat)* what's going to happen to?; **quoad fiat** as far as is possible ‖ *v impers* a sacrifice is being offered
firmām·en -inis *n* prop, support
firmāment·um -ī *n* prop, support; mainstay; main point
firmāt·or -ōris *m* promoter
firmē *adv* firmly, steadily
firmit·ās -ātis *f* firmness, stability; strength
firmiter *adv* firmly, tight, ; securely, safely; resolutely
firmitūd·ō -inis *f* firmness, strength, durability; vigor; stability; **memoriae firmitudo** unfaltering memory
firm·ō -āre -āvī -ātus *tr* to strengthen, support, reinforce; to encourage; to assure; to fortify; to put *(laws, institutions)* on a firm footing, establish; to guarantee; to assert, affirm; to substantiate, vouch for *(a statement or its veracity);* **aliquem in se** *(or* **sibi) firmare** to make sure of the loyalty of; **animum firmare** to get up one's courage; **fidem firmare** to make good one's word, back up one's promise; **gradum firmare** to walk resolutely; **oculos** *(or* **vultum) firmare** to look determined ‖ *refl* to brace oneself
firm·us -a -um *adj* firm, strong; stable; hardy, sound *(health);* solid, substantial *(food);* steadfast, trusty; lasting
fiscāl·is -is -e *adj* fiscal, of the imperial treasury
fiscell·a -ae *f* small basket
fiscin·a -ae *f* wicker basket, wickerwork; **cum porcis cum fiscina** *(fig)* lock, stock, and barrel *(literally, with pigs and with wicker basket)*
fisc·us -ī *m* basket; money box; imperial treasury *(distinct from state treasury:* **aerarium)** state revenues
fissil·is -is -e *adj* easily split; split
fissi·ō -ōnis *f* dividing, splitting
fiss·us -a -um *pp of* **findo** ‖ *adj* cloven, divided ‖ *n* split
fistūca *see* **festuca**
fistul·a -ae *f* pipe, tube; water pipe; hollow reed; flute; *(med)* fistula
fistulāt·or -ōris *m* who who plays a shepherd's pipe
fistulāt us -a -um *adj* provided with pipes
fīsus *pp of* **fido**

fix·us -a -um *pp of* **figo** ‖ *adj* fixed, immovable; irrevocable; *(w. abl)* fitted with
flābellifer·a -ae *f* female slave who waved a fan
flābellul·um -ī *n* small fan
flābell·um -ī *n* fan
flābil·is -is -e *adj* of air
flābr·a -ōrum *npl* gusts of wind; breezes, winds
flacc·eō -ēre *intr* to be flabby; to lose heart; *(of a speech)* to get dull
flacc·escō -escĕre -uī *intr* to become flabby; to wither, droop
flaccid·us -a -um *adj* flaccid, flabby; weak, feeble
flacc·us -a -um *adj* flabby; flap-eared
flagell·ō -āre -āvī -ātus *tr* to whip
flagell·um -ī *n* whip; scourge; riding crop; young shoot, sucker; tentacle *(of polyp);* pang *(of conscience)*
flāgitāti·ō -ōnis *f* demand
flāgitāt·or -ōris *m* persistent demander
flāgitiōsē *adv* shamefully, disgracefully
flāgitiōs·us -a -um *adj* shameful, disgraceful, scandalous
flāgit·ium -(i)ī *n* shame, disgrace, scandal; good-for-nothing
flāgit·ō -āre -āvī -ātus *tr* to demand; *(w. double acc, or w. ab)* to demand *(s.th.)* of *(s.o.)*
flagr·ans -antis *adj* blazing, flaming, hot; shining, glowing, glittering; ardent, hot, vehement, eager
flagranter *adv* vehemently, ardently
flagranti·a -ae *f* blaze, glow; passionate love; **flagiti flagrantia** utter disgrace
flagritrib·a -ae *m (coll) (said of a slave)* victim of constant whipping, whipping boy
flagr·ō -āre -āvī *tr* to burn with love for ‖ *intr* **(fragl·ō)** to blaze, be on fire; *(w. abl)* **1** to glow with, flare up in; **2** to be the victim of *(e.g., envy)*
flagr·um -ī n whip; whipping
flām·en -inis *m* flamen *(priest of a specific deity);* **flamen Dialis** priest of Jupiter
flām·en -inis *n* gust, gale; breeze
flāminic·a -ae *f* wife of a flamen; priestess
Flāminīn·us -ī *m* Titus Quintus Flamininus *(consul of 198 B.C, and conqueror of Philip V of Macedon at Cynoscephalae in 197 B.C.)*
flāmin·ium -(i)ī *n* office of flamen, priesthood
Flāmini·us -a -um *adj* Flaminian; **via Flaminia** road leading N. from Rome to Ariminum ‖ *m* Gaius Flaminius *(conqueror of Insubrian Gauls in 223 B.C., and builder of the Circus Flaminius and Flaminian road)*
flamm·a -ae *f* flame, fire, blaze; star; torch; burning fever; glow, passion; sweetheart; danger; flare-up *(of violence);* **flammam**

adjicere (*or* **suggerere**) (*w. dat*) to fan the flames of; **flammam concipere** to catch fire; **in flamma** in flames, ablaze

flammār·ius -(i)ī *m* maker of bridal veils

flammeol·um -ī *n* (*flame-colored*) bridal veil

flammesc·ō -ĕre *intr* to become inflamed, become fiery

flamme·us -a -um *adj* flaming, fiery; flashing (*eyes*); flame-colored ‖ *n* (*flame-colored*) bridal veil

flammif·er -era -erum *adj* fiery

flamm·ō -āre -āvī -ātus *tr* to set on fire; (*fig*) to get (*s.o.*) all excited ‖ *pass* to glow, flame

flammul·a -ae *f* little flame

flāt·us -ūs *m* blowing, breathing, breath; breeze, wind; snorting; arrogance; **flatum emittere** (*sl*) to break wind

flāv·ens -entis *adj* yellow, golden

flāv·eō -ēre *intr* to be yellow, be blond(e)

flāvesc·ō -ĕre *intr* to become yellow, become golden-yellow

Flāvi·us -a -um *adj* Flavian; **gens Flavia** Flavian clan (*to which the emperors Vespasian, Titus, and Domitian belonged*)

flāv·us -a -um *adj* yellow; blond; reddish-yellow, golden ‖ *m* gold coin

flēbil·is -is -e *adj* pitiful, pathetic, deplorable; tearful

flēbiliter *adv* tearfully, mournfully

fle·ctō -ctĕre -xī -xus *tr* to bend, curve; to turn, wheel about, turn around; to wind, twist; to curl (*hair*); to direct, avert, turn away (*eyes, mind, etc.*); to double, sail around (*a cape*); to inflect (*voice*); to change (*mind*); to persuade, move, appease; to handle (*reins, tiller*); to guide, steer; **animum** (*or* **mentem**) **flectere** to give way, bend; **viam** (*or* **iter**) **flectere** (*w.* **ad**) to make one's way toward, head toward; **vultum flectere** to change one's expression ‖ *refl & pass* (*geog*) to wind, curve ‖ *intr* to turn; to go

flēmin·a -um *npl* swollen ankles

fl·eō -ēre -ēvī -ētus *tr* to cry for, mourn (for) ‖ *intr* to cry

flēt·us -ūs *m* crying ‖ *mpl* tears

flexanim·us -a -um *adj* moving, touching, persuasive

flexī *perf of* **flecto**

flexibil·is -is -e *adj* flexible; shifty

flexil·is -is -e *adj* flexible, pliant

flexiloqu·us -a -um *adj* ambiguous

flexi·ō -ōnis *f* bending, turning; winding (*path*); inflection (*of voice*)

flexip·ēs -edis *adj* creeping (*ivy*)

flexuōs·us -a -um *adj* winding

flexūr·a -ae *f* bending, winding

flex·us -a -um *pp of* **flecto** ‖ *adj* curved, twisting; involved, obscure (*language*);

modulated (*voice*); (*of a syllable*) having a circumflex

flex·us -ūs *m* bending, curving, turning, winding; bend, curve; shift, change, transition; curling (*of hair*); inflection (*of voice*)

flict·us -ūs *m* clashing, banging together, collision

flō flāre flāvī flātus *tr* to blow; to breathe, exhale; to coin (*money*); to play (*flute, songs*) ‖ *intr* to blow; to breathe

flocc·us -ī *m* tuft of wool; down; **flocci facere** (*or* **pendere**) to think little of, not give a hoot about

Flōr·a -ae *f* goddess of flowers (*honored on April 28-May 3*)

Flōrāl·ia -ium *npl* festival of Flora (*on April 28*)

Flōrālici·us -a -um *adj* of the Floralia

Flōrāl·is -is -e *adj* connected with Flora *or* her festival

flōr·ens -entis *adj* blooming; prosperous; flourishing; illustrious; strong, powerful; vivid (*speaker*); (*w. abl*) in the prime of, at the height of

flōr·eō -ēre -uī *intr* to blossom, bloom; (*of wine*) to foam, froth, ferment; (*of arts*) to flourish; to be prosperous, be eminent; (*w. abl*) **1** to abound in; **2** to swarm with, be filled with; **aetate florere** to be in one's prime

flōr·escō -escĕre -uī *intr* to begin to bloom; to increase in renown

flōre·us -a -um *adj* flowery; made of flowers

flōridul·us -a -um *adj* flowery; pretty; in the bloom of youth

flōrid·us -a -um *adj* flowery; covered with flowers; fresh, pretty; florid (*style*)

flōrif·er -era -erum *adj* flowery

flōrileg·us -a -um *adj* (*of bees*) going from flower to flower

flōs flōris *m* flower; bud, blossom; best (*of anything*); prime (*of life*); youthful beauty; innocence, chastity; crown, glory; aroma (*of wine*); best period, heyday, zenith; (*rhet*) literary ornament

floscul·us -ī *m* little flower; flower, pride, glory; (*rhet*) literary ornament

fluctifrag·us -a -um *adj* surging, wave-breaking (*shore*)

fluctig·er -era -erum *adj* wave-borne

fluctuāti·ō -ōnis *f* wavering, vacillation

fluctu·ō -āre -āvī -ātus *or* **fluctu·or -ārī -ātus sum** *intr* to fluctuate, undulate, wave; to be restless; to waver, vacillate

fluctuōs·us -a -um *adj* rough (*sea*)

fluct·us -ūs *m* wave; flowing, undulating; turbulence, commotion; disorder, unrest; **fluctus in simpulo** (*prov*) tempest in a teacup

flu·ens -entis *adj* loose, flowing; (*mor-*

ally) loose; smooth, fluent *(speech, composition)*

fluent·a -ōrum *npl* flow, stream, river

fluenter *adv* like a wave

fluid·us -a -um *or* **flūvid·us** -a -um *adj* flowing, fluid; soft; relaxing

fluit·ō -āre *intr* to float, swim; to sail; to toss about; to hang loose, flap; to be uncertain, waver; to stagger; *(of fluids)* to flow

flūm·en -inis *n* flowing, stream; river; *(fig)* flood *(e.g., of tears, words);* **flumine adverso** upstream; **secundo flumine** downstream

flūmine·us -a -um *adj* river-

flu·ō -ĕre -xī -xum *intr* to flow; to run down, drip; to overflow; to fall gradually, sink, drop, slip; to droop; to pass away, vanish, perish; *(of time)* to slip by; *(of plans)* to proceed, develop; to melt; to be fluent; to be monotonous; *(w.* **ab** *or* **ex) 1** to spring from, arise from, proceed from; **2** *(of words)* to be derived from; *(of crowds)* to stream, flock; *(of branches)* to spread; *(of clothes, hair)* to hang loosely, flow; *(phil)* to be in a state of transition *or* flux

fluviāl·is -is -e *adj* river-, of a river

flūvidus *see* **fluidus**

fluviātil·is -is -e *adj* river-, found in rivers; **equus fluviatilis** hippopotamus; **fluviatiles naves** river boats

fluv·ius -(i)ī *m* river; running water; stream

fluxī *perf of* **fluo**

flux·us -a -um *adj* flowing, loose; careless; loose, dissolute; frail, weak; transient, perishable

fōcāl·e -is *n* scarf

fōcil·ō -āre -āvī -ātus *tr* to warm, revive; *(fig)* to foster, cherish

fōcul·um -ī *n* stove

focul·us -ī *m* brazier; *(fig)* fire

foc·us -ī *m* hearth, fireplace; brazier; funeral pile; altar; *(fig)* home, family

fodic·ō -āre -āvī -ātus *tr* to poke, nudge

fodiō fodĕre fōdī fossus *tr* to dig, dig out; *(fig)* to prod

foecund- = **fecund-**

foedē *adv* foully, cruelly, shamefully

foederāt·us -a -um *adj* federated, allied

foedifrag·us -a -um *adj* treaty-breaking, treacherous

foedit·ās -ātis *f* foulness, hideousness

foed·ō -āre -āvī -ātus *tr* to make filthy, foul up; to make hideous, disfigure; to mutilate, mangle; to ravage savagely *(land);* to darken, dim *(light);* to pollute, defile; to disgrace

foed·us -eris *n* treaty, charter; league; compact, agreement; law; **aequo foedere** on equal terms, mutually; **foedere certo** by fixed law; **foedere pacto** by fixed agree-

ment; **foedus icere** to conclude a treaty; **foedus rumpere** to break a treaty

foed·us -a -um *adj* foul, filthy, disgusting; horrible, shocking

foen- = **faen-**

foet·eō -ēre *intr* **(faet-, fēt-)** to stink

foetid·us -a -um *adj* **(faet-, fēt-)** fetid, stinking

foet·or -ōris *m* **(faet-, fēt-)** stink, stench

foetu- = **fētu-**

foliāt·us -a -um *adj* leafy **ll** *n* perfume *(made from aromatic leaves)*

fol·ium -(i)ī *n* leaf; petal; **folium recitare Sibyllae** *(coll)* to tell the gospel truth *(literally, to read aloud the leaf of the Sibyl)*

follicul·us -ī *m* small bag, sack; shell, skin; eggshell; large inflated ball

foll·is -is *m* bag, sack; punching bag; inflated ball; bellows; moneybag; puffed-out cheeks

follīt·us -a -um *adj* enclosed in a sack

fōment·um -ī *n* compress, dressing; *(fig)* remedy, solace, alleviation

fōm·es -itis *m* tinder

fon·s -tis *m* spring, fountain; spring water, water; stream; headwaters, source *(of river);* *(fig)* source, origin

fontān·us -a -um *adj* spring-

fonticul·us -ī *m* little spring, little fountain

for fārī fātus sum *tr & intr* to say, speak

forābil·is -is -e *adj* vulnerable; *(w. abl)* vulnerable to

forām·en -inis *n* hole, opening; socket; pore; stop *(in musical pipe)*

forās *adv* *(w. verbs implying motion)* out, outside, out of doors; *(w. verbs of selling, lending)* into the hands of outsiders; *(w. verbs of publishing)* into the light of day; **vocatus ad cenam foras** invited out to dinner; **foras cenare** to eat out

forc·eps -ipis *f* tongs; tweezers; pliers; clippers; claw *(of a crab)*

ford·a -ae *f* pregnant cow

fore = **futur·us** -a -um **esse** to be about to be

forem = **essem**

forens·is -is -e *adj* of the Forum, in the Forum; public *(as opp. to domestic);* forensic, of the lawcourts *(because the lawcourts were located in the Forum)* **ll** *npl* street clothes

forf·ex -icis *f* scissors; tongs, forceps

forficul·ae -ārum *fpl* scissors

foric·a -ae *f* public toilet

for·is -is *f* door; entrance, opening **ll** *fpl* double doors; **in foribus** in the doorway

forīs *adv* outside, out of doors; outside the Senate; among the people; among strangers, in public life; abroad, in foreign countries; from outside, from abroad; **a foris** from outside; **foris cenare** to eat out; **foris esse** to be bankrupt

form·a -ae f form, shape, figure; beauty, good looks; image; mold, stamp; shoemaker's last; vision, apparition, phantom; species, form, nature, sort, kind; outline, design, sketch, plan; map

formāl·is -is -e adj formal

formāment·um -ī n shape

formāt·or -ōris m shaper, creator

formātūr·a -ae f fashioning, shaping

Formi·ae -ārum fpl town on S. coast of Latium

formīc·a -ae f ant

formīcīn·us -a -um adj ant-like

formīdābil·is -is -e adj terrifying, formidable

formīd·ō -āre -āvī -ātus tr to dread ‖ intr to be afraid

formīd·ō -inis f fear, terror; (religious) dread, awe; bogy; threats

formīdolōsē adv (-dul-) dreadfully, terribly

formīdolōs·us -a -um adj (-dul-) formidable, alarming; fearful, frightened

form·ō -āre -āvī -ātus tr to form, shape, mold, build; (w. in + acc) to transform into, make into; to make, produce, invent; to imagine; to shape, direct; to instruct; to depict, represent; (gram) to inflect

formōsē adv beautifully, gracefully

formōsit·ās -ātis f beauty, good looks

formōs·us -a -um adj shapely, beautiful, handsome, good-looking

formul·a -ae f nice shape, beauty; list, register; legal position; formula; contract, agreement; rule, regulation; pattern, type; charter (of a government); (leg) regular form of judicial procedure; (leg) provisions (of a law); (phil) principle; **formula quaestionis** the rule of evidence; **formulam accipere** to be sued; **formulam edere** (or **intendere** or **scribere**) to bring an action, bring suit

fornācāl·is -is -e adj of an oven

fornācul·a -ae f small oven

forn·ax -ācis f oven, furnace; kiln; forge

fornicāti·ō -ōnis f arch, vaulting

fornicāt·us -a -um adj arched

forn·ix -icis m arch, vault; arcade; brothel

fornus see **furnus**

for·ō -āre -āvī -ātus tr to bore, pierce

fors adv perhaps, chances are

for·s -tis f chance, luck, accident; **forte** by chance, accidentally, by accident; perhaps; **vidistine forte eum?** did you happen to see him?

forsan or **forsit** or **forsitan** adv perhaps

fortasse or **fortassis** adv perhaps

forte see **fors**

forticul·us -a -um adj quite bold, rather brave

fort·is -is -e adj brave, courageous; strong, mighty, powerful; resolute, steadfast, firm; loud, noisy (sounds); (of cities) rich in resources or manpower; decent, honorable (conduct); drastic (remedies); vigorous (speakers); strong, potent (medicine, wine)

fortiter adv bravely, boldly; strongly, vigorously, firmly; justifiably

fortitūd·ō -inis f fortitude, bravery, courage; strength; resolution

fortuītō adv fortuitously, by chance, accidentally; haphazardly

fortuīt·us -a -um adj fortuitous, accidental; random, haphazard

fortūn·a -ae f chance, luck, fate, fortune; good luck, prosperity; bad luck, misfortune; lot; opportunity; circumstances; state, rank, position; property, goods, fortune; **fortunae mandare** to leave to chance; **fortunam alicujus sequi** to follow s.o.'s leadership; **fortunam suam sequi** to follow one's star; **fortunam temptare** (or **periclitari**) to tempt fate; **in fortuna positus esse** (or **fortunae subjectus esse**) to be left to chance, be dependent on luck; **per fortunas!** (in earnest entreaties) for heaven's sake! ‖ fpl riches, fortune

fortūnātē adv happily; prosperously; successfully

fortūnāt·us -a -um adj fortunate, lucky, prosperous; happy; rich

fortūn·ō -āre -āvī -ātus tr to make happy, make prosperous; to bless

forul·ī -ōrum mpl bookshelves

for·um -ī n forum, civic center; shopping center, marketplace; market town; trade, commerce; public life, public affairs; jurisdiction; popular assembly; the bar, the courts; game board; **ad forum deducere** to escort (a young man) to the Forum to assume the toga of manhood; **cedere foro** to go bankrupt; **extra suum forum** beyond his jurisdiction; **Forum Boarium** cattle market; **Forum Olitorium** produce market; **Forum Piscatorium** fish market; **Forum Romanum** Roman Forum; **in foro** outside one's home, in public; **forum agere** to hold court; **forum attingere** to enter public life; **in foro versari** to be engaged in business

For·um Appiī (gen: **Fori Appiī**) n town in Latium on the Via Appia

for·us -ī m gangway; tier of seats; tier of a beehive

foss·a -ae f ditch, trench; moat; canal; **fossam deprimere** to dig a ditch

fossi·ō -ōnis f digging

foss·or -ōris m digger; (fig) lout

fossūr·a -ae f digging

fossus pp of **fodio**

fōtus pp of **foveo**

fove·a -ae f small pit; (lit & fig) pitfall

foveō fovēre fōvī fōtus *tr* to warm, keep warm; to refresh, soothe; to bathe; to massage; to freshen *(breath);* to nurse *(wounds);* to fondle, caress; to cherish *(hope);* to foster, nurture; to take the side of; to support, encourage; to pamper

fract·us -a -um *pp of* **frango ‖** *adj* interrupted, irregular; weak, feeble

frāg·a -ōrum *npl* strawberries

fragil·is -is -e *adj* fragile, brittle; crackling; frail, flimsy; unstable; impermanent, uncertain

fragilit·ās -ātis *f* fragility; frailty

fraglō *see* **flagro**

fragment·um -ī *n* fragment, remnant

frag·or -ōris *m* crash, noise, uproar, din; applause; clap of thunder

fragōs·us -a -um *adj* broken, uneven, rough; crashing, roaring

frāgr·ō *or* **frāgl·ō -āre -āvī** *intr* to smell sweet, be fragrant; to reek

frame·a -ae *f* German spear

frangō frangĕre frēgī fractus *tr* to break to pieces, smash to pieces, shatter; to grind, crush *(grain);* to curl *(hair);* to make *(waters)* choppy; to violate, break *(treaty, law, promise); (fig)* to break down, overcome, crush, dishearten, humble; to repress *(feelings);* to weaken, soften; to inflict a crushing blow on *(a nation); (esp. of old age)* to exhaust, wear out; to break the force of; to move, touch; **diem mero frangere** to break up the day with wine; **iter frangere** to force a way; **navem frangere** to wreck a ship **‖** *pass* to suffer shipwreck; to relent

frātell·us -ī *m* little brother

frā·ter ·tris *m* brother; cousin; *(euphem)* (homosexual) sex partner; **frater germanus** full brother; **frater patruelis** first cousin *(on father's side)*

frātercul·us -i *m* little brother

frāternē *adv* like a brother

frāternit·ās -ātis *f* brotherhood

frātern·us -a -um *adj* fraternal; brotherly; brother's

frātricīd·a -ae *m* murderer of a brother, fratricide

fraudāti·ō -ōnis *f* swindling

fraudāt·or -ōris *m* swindler, cheat

fraud·ō -āre -āvī -ātus *tr* to swindle, cheat, defraud; to embezzle; *(w. abl)* to cheat *(s.o.)* out of

fraudulenti·a -ae *f* dishonesty

fraudulent·us -a -um *adj* fraudulent, dishonest; deceitful, treacherous

frau·s -dis *f* fraud, deception, trickery; error, delusion; offense, crime; harm, damage; *(person)* fraud, cheat; **sine fraude** without harm to oneself, unscathed; without risk of punishment, with impunity; **fraudem legi facere** to violate the law

fraxine·us -a -um *adj* made of ash wood

fraxin·us -ī *f* ash tree; spear *(made of ash wood)*

fraxinus -a -um *adj* of ash wood

frēgī *perf of* **frango**

fremibund·us -a -um *adj* (-meb-) roaring

fremid·us -a -um *adj* growling

fremit·us -ūs *m* roar, growl, rumble, hum; din, noise; grumbling, muttering; loud buzz of approval

frem·ō -ĕre -uī -itus *tr* to grumble at, complain loudly about; to demand angrily, clamor for; to declare noisily **‖** *intr* to roar, growl, snort, howl; to grumble; to resound

frem·or -ōris *m* roaring, grumbling; murmuring

frend·ō -ĕre -uī *intr* to gnash the teeth; **dentibus frendere** to gnash the teeth

frēnī *see* **frenum**

frēn·ō -āre -āvī -ātus *tr* to bridle, curb; *(fig)* to curb

frēn·um -ī *n or* **frēn·a -ōrum** *npl or* **frēn·ī -ōrum** *mpl* reins; bridle, bit; *(fig)* curb, control, restraint; *(poet)* riding *(on horseback);* **frena** *(or* **frenos** *or* **frenum) accipere** *(or* **pati)** to take the bit, learn obedience; **frena** *(or* **frenos) dare** *(or* **effundere** *or* **immittere** *or* **laxare** *or* **remittere)** to loosen the reins; **frena (ab)rumpere** to snap the reins, bolt; **frena** *(or* **frenos) tenere** *(or* **moderari)** *(w. gen)* to hold the reins of, be in control of; **in frenis** *(or* **sub freno)** under control

frequ·ens -entis *adj* crowded, packed, filled; in crowds, numerous; frequent, repeated, usual, common; full, plenary *(Senate session); (of persons)* constant, regular; *(may be rendered adverbially)* often, frequently, *e.g.:* **frequens et audivi et adfui** I was often at your side and heard you speak; *(w. abl)* **1** crowded with; **2** densely covered with; **frequens emporium** well-stocked market; **frequens est** *(w. inf)* it is a common practice to

frequentāti·ō -ōnis *f* piling up, concentration

frequenter *adv* in crowds, in large numbers; frequently, in quick succession; commonly, widely; **frequenter habitari** *(or* **coli)** to be densely populated

frequenti·a -ae *f* crowd; crowded assembly, large attendance; dense mass; populousness; populous district; crowdedness; abundance; multitude; population; frequency; conscientious performance *(of duties)*

frequent·ō -āre -āvī -ātus *tr* to crowd, people, populate; *(w. abl)* to pack with, stock with, crowd with; to assemble in a crowd; to crowd around *(a person);* to attend *(e.g., games)* in large numbers; to sue frequently; to say over and over again; to do often, repeat; to use frequently; to frequent, resort to; to visit often; to celebrate, observe *(festival, ceremony);* to attend *(a meeting, school, lecture);* to appear on *(the stage);* to inhabit *(a place)* **ll** *pass* to become common

fretens·is -is -e *adj* **mare fretense** Strait of Messina

fret·um -ī *n* strait, channel; sea, the deep; waters; *(fig)* seething flood

frēt·us -a -um *adj (w. dat or abl)* relying on, confident of, depending on; *(w. acc & inf)* confident that

fret·us -ūs *m* strait

fric·ō -āre -uī -tus *or* **-ātus** *tr* to rub; to chafe; to rub down, massage

frictus *pp of* **frigo**

frīgefact·ō -āre *tr* to cool

frīg·eō -ēre *intr* to be cold, be chilly; to freeze; *(fig)* to be numbed, be lifeless, be dull; *(fig)* to get a cool reception, get the cold shoulder; *(of words)* to fall flat; *(of an old man)* to lack vigor; to have nothing to do, be idle

frīgesc·ō -ĕre frixī *intr* to become cold, become chilled; to become lifeless; *(of a speech)* to fall flat

frīgid·a -ae *f* cold water

frīgidāri·us -a -um *adj* cooling

frīgidē *adv* feebly; coolly

frīgidul·us -a -um *adj* rather cold; rather faint

frīgid·us -a -um *adj* cold, cool; numbed, dull, lifeless; indifferent, unimpassioned; flat, insipid, trivial **ll** *f* cold water

frīg·ō frīgĕre frixī frictus *tr* to roast, fry

frīg·us -oris *n* cold, coldness, chill, coolness; frost; cold of winter, winter; coldness of death, death; chill, fever; shudder, chill; cold region; cold reception; coolness, indifference; slowness, inactivity **ll** *npl* cold spell

frigutt·iō -īre *intr* to stutter

fringill·a -ae *f* a songbird

fri·ō -āre -āvī -ātus *tr* & *refl* & *pass* to crumble

fritill·us -ī *m* dice box

frīvol·us -a -um *adj* frivolous, trifling, worthless, sorry, pitiful **ll** *npl* trifles

frixī *perf of* **frigesco** *and* **frigo** *and* **frigeo**

frondāt·or -ōris *m* pruner

frond·eō -ēre *intr* to have leaves; *(of places)* to be green with trees

·**frondesc·ō -ĕre** *intr* to get leaves

fronde·us -a -um *adj* leafy

frondif·er -era -erum *adj* leafy

frondōs·us -a -um *adj* full of leaves, leafy

fron·s -dis *f* foliage; leafy bough, green bough; chaplet, garland

fron·s -tis *f* forehead, brow; front end,

front; face, look; façade; vanguard; exterior, appearance; outer end of a scroll; sense of shame; **a fronte** in front; **frons firma** *(fig)* a bold front; **frons prima** front line; **frontem contrahere** *(or* **adducere** *or* **constringere** *or* **obducere)** to frown; **frontem ferire** to tap oneself on the forehead *(in annoyance);* **frontem remittere** *(or* **exporrigere)** to smooth the brow, cheer up, relax; **frontis tenerae videri** to seem to blush *(literally, to seem to be of sensitive brow);* **in fronte** *(in measuring land)* in breadth, in frontage; **salvā fronte** without shame; **tenuis frons** low forehead

frontāl·ia -ium *npl* frontlet *(ornament for forehead of horse)*

front·ō -ōnis *m* person with bulging forehead

fructuāri·us -a -um *adj* productive; subject to land tax

fructuōs·us -a -um *adj* fruitful, productive

fructus *pp of* **fruor**

fruct·us -ūs *m* fruit, produce; proceeds, profit, income, return, revenue; enjoyment, satisfaction; benefit, reward, results, consequence

frūgāl·is -is -e *adj* thrifty, frugal

frūgālit·ās -ātis *f* frugality, economy; temperance; honesty; worth

frūgāliter *adv* frugally, economically; temperately

frūgēs *see* **frux**

frūgī *indecl adj* frugal; temperate; honest; worthy; useful; proper; **frugi esse** to do the right thing

frūgif·er -era -erum *adj* fruitful, productive, fertile; profitable

frūgifer·ens -entis *adj* fruitful

frūgileg·us -a -um *adj (of ants)* food-gathering

frūgipar·us -a -um *adj* fruitful

fruitus *pp of* **fruor**

frūmentāri·us -a -um *adj* of grain, grain-; grain-producing; of provisions; **res frumentaria** *(mil)* supplies, quartermaster **ll** *m* grain dealer; *(mil)* forager

frūmentāti·ō -ōnis *f (mil)* foraging

frūmentāt·or -ōris *m* grain merchant; *(mil)* forager

frūment·or -ārī -ātus sum *intr (mil)* to forage

frūment·um -ī *n* grain; wheat **ll** *npl* grain fields; crops

frūn·iscor -iscī -ītus sum *tr* to enjoy

fruor fruī fructus sum *or* **fruitus sum** *tr* to enjoy; **ll** *intr (w. abl)* **1** to enjoy, delight in; **2** to enjoy the company of; **3** *(law)* to have the use and enjoyment of

frustillātim *adv* in bits

frustrā *adv* in vain, uselessly, for nothing; without reason, groundlessly; **frustra**

discedere to go away disappointed; **frustra esse** to be mistaken; **frustra habere** to have *(s.o.)* confused
frustrām·en -inis *n* deception, error
frustrāti·ō -ōnis *f* deception; frustration
frustrāt·us -ūs *m* deception; **frustratui habere** *(coll)* to take for a sucker
frustr·or -ārī -ātus sum *or* **frustr·ō -āre** *tr* to deceive, trick; to disappoint; to frustrate
frustulent·us -a -um *adj* full of crumbs
frust·um -ī *n* crumb, bit, scrap; **frustum pueri** *(coll)* whippersnapper
frutect·um *or* **fruticēt·um -ī** *n* thicket, shrubbery **‖** *npl* bushes
frut·ex -icis *m* shrub, bush; stem, trunk; *(coll)* blockhead
fruticētum *see* **frutectum**
frutic·ō -āre -āvī *or* **frutic·or -ārī** *intr* to sprout; to become bushy; *(fig) (of hair)* to become bushy
fruticōs·us -a -um *adj* bushy, overgrown with bushes
frux frūgis *f or* **frūg·ēs -um** *fpl* produce; crops; grain; vegetables; bread, meal; barley meal *(for sacrifice);* fruits, benefit; *(singl)* morality, honesty; **ad frugem bonam se recipere** to turn over a new leaf; **bonae frugi esse** to be honest, be thrifty; **expers frugis** worthless; **frugem facere** to do the decent thing
fūcāt·us -a -um *adj* artificial *(color);* dyed, colored, painted; phony
fūc·ō -āre -āvī -ātus *tr* to dye, tint; to apply makeup to; to disguise, falsify
fūcōs·us -a -um *adj* painted, colored; artificial, spurious
fūc·us -ī *m* (red) paint; rouge; drone; beeglue; disguise; pretense, deceit
fūdī *perf of* **fundo**
fue *or* **fu** *interj* phui!
fug·a -ae *f* flight, escape; avoidance; exile; speed, swift passage; disappearance; *(w. gen)* avoidance of, escape from; **fugae sese mandare** *(or* **fugam capere** *or* **fugam capessere** *or* **fugam facere** *or* **se in fugam conferre** *or* **se in fugam conjicere** *or* **sese in fugam dare)** to flee; **in fugam conferre** *(or* **in fugam conjicere** *or* **in fugam dare** *or* **in fugam impellere)** to put to flight; **fugam petere** to look for a means of escape
fugācius *adv* more cautiously, with one eye on flight
fug·ax -ācis *adj* apt to flee, fleeing; shy, timid; swift; transitory; *(w. gen)* shy of, shunning, avoiding, steering clear of, averse to
fugi·ens -entis *adj* fleeing, retreating; *(w. gen)* avoiding, averse to
fugiō fugĕre fūgī fugitus *tr* to escape, escape from, get away from; to run away from, shun, avoid; to succeed in avoid-ing; to vanish from; to be repelled by; to leave *(esp. one's country);* to be averse to, dislike; to escape the notice of, be unknown to; **fuge** *(w. inf)* do not...!; **fugere conspectum** *(w. gen)* to keep out of sight of; **fūgit me ratio** I made a mistake; **fūgit me scribere** it slipped my mind to write **‖** *intr* to flee, escape, run away; to go into exile; to vanish; to pass away, perish; to begin to decay; *(w. ab)* to keep away from, shrink from; *(of things)* to slip out of one's grasp or control
fugit·ans -antis *adj* fleeing; *(w. gen)* averse to
fugit·ō -āre *tr* to run away from, shun **‖** *intr* to run away
fugitīv·us -a -um *adj* & *m* runaway, fugitive
fug·ō -āre -āvī -ātus *tr* to put to flight, rout, drive away, chase away; to exile, banish; to avert
fulcīm·en -inis *n* support, prop
ful·ciō -cīre -sī -tus *tr* to prop up, support; to sustain, strengthen; **pedibus fulcire** to tread
fulcr·um -ī *n* bedpost; couch leg; *(fig)* bed, couch
ful·geō -gēre -sī *or* **fulg·ō -ĕre** *intr* to gleam, flash, blaze, shine, glare; to be conspicuous, be illustrious
fulgid·us -a -um *adj* flashing, shining
fulgō *see* **fulgeo**
fulg·or -ōris *m* flash; flash of lightning, lightning; brightness; splendor, glory; *(astr)* meteor; *(astr)* bright star
fulg·ur -uris *m* flash of lightning; place struck by lightning
fulgurāl·is -is -e *adj* of lightning; *(books)* on lightning
fulgurāt·or -ōris *m* interpreter of lightning
fulgurīt·us -a -um *adj* struck by lightning
fulgur·ō -āre -āvī -ātum *intr* to lighten, send lightning **‖** *v impers* it is lightning
fulic·a -ae *or* **ful·ix -icis** *f* waterfowl *(perhaps the coot)*
fūlīg·ō -inis *f* soot *(used as a cosmetic, in paint, in medications, in ink)*
fulix *see* **fulica**
full·ō -ōnis *m* fuller *(person who shrank, beat, pressed, cleaned, and whitened cloth with chalk)*
fullōni·a -ae *f* fuller's craft, fulling
fullōnic·a -ae *f* fuller's craft, fulling; fuller's shop
fullōni·us -a -um *adj* fuller's
fulm·en -inis *n* thunderbolt, lightning bolt; *(fig)* bolt out of the blue
fulment·a -ae *f* heel
fulmine·us -a -um *adj* of lightning, lightning-; shine, sparkling, flashing
fulmin·ō -āre -āvī -ātum *intr* to lighten; *(fig)* to flash

fulsī *perf of* **fulcio** *and* **fulgeo**
fultūr·a -ae *f* support, prop
fultus *pp of* **fulcio**
fulv·us -a -um *adj* yellow, yellowish brown, reddish yellow, tawny; strawberry-blond
fūme·us -a -um *adj* smoky, murky
fūmid·us -a -um *adj* smoky, full of smoke; smoking; steaming
fūmif·er -era -erum *adj* smoking
fūmific·ō -āre -āvī *intr* to smoke; to burn incense
fūmific·us -a -um *adj* smoking, steaming
fūm·ō -āre -āvī *intr* to smoke, fume; to steam; to reek
fūmōs·us -a -um *adj* smoky; grimy from smoke; smoked *(food)*
fūm·us -ī *m* smoke; fume; steam, vapor **‖** *mpl* clouds of smoke
fūnāl·e -is *n* taper of wax-soaked rope; chandelier, candelabrum
fūnambul·us -ī *m* tightrope walker
functi·ō -ōnis *f* performance
funct·us -a -um *pp of* **fungor ‖** *adj* dead **‖** *mpl* the dead
fund·a -ae *f* sling; pebble *(used in a sling);* dragnet
fundām·en -inis *n* foundation; **fundamina ponere** to lay the foundations
fundāment·um -ī *n* foundation; *(fig)* basis, ground, beginning; **a fundamentis** utterly; **fundamenta agere** *(or* **jacĕre** *or* **locare)** to lay the foundation(s)
fundāt·or -ōris *m* founder
fundāt·us -a -um *adj* well-founded, established
Fund·ī -ōrum *mpl* town in Latium
fundit·ō -āre -āvī -ātus *tr* to sling, hurl with a sling; *(fig)* to sling *(e.g., words)* around
fundit·or -ōris *m* slinger
funditus *adv* from the bottom, utterly, entirely
fund·ō -āre -āvī -ātus *tr* to found; to put on a firm basis, establish; to secure, make fast **‖** *pass (w. abl)* to be based on
fundō fundĕre fūdī fūsus *tr* to pour, pour out; to smelt *(metals);* to cast *(in metal);* to pour in streams, shower, hurl; to pour out, empty; to spread, extend, diffuse; to bring forth, bear, yield in abundance; to throw to the ground, bring down; to give up, lose, waste; to pour out *(words); (mil)* to pour in *(troops); (mil)* to rout
fund·us -ī *m* bottom; farm, estate; *(leg)* sanctioner, authority
fūnebr·is -is -e *adj* funeral-, funerary; deadly, murderous
fūnerāt·us -a -um *adj* done in, killed; **prope funeratus** almost sent to *(one's)* grave
fūnere·us -a -um *adj* funerary, mourning; deadly, fatal

fūner·ō -āre -āvī -ātus *tr* to bury; to bring *(s.o.)* to his grave, kill
fūnest·ō -āre -āvī -ātus *tr* to defile with murder, desecrate
fūnest·us -a -um *adj* funereal, mourning; lamentable; polluted *(through contact with a corpse);* deadly, fatal, calamitous; sad, dismal, mournful
fungīn·us -a -um *adj* of a mushroom
fun·gor -gī -ctus sum *tr* to perform, execute; **diem** *(or* **vitam) fungi** to die **‖** *intr (w. abl)* **1** to perform, execute, discharge, do; **2** to busy oneself with, be engaged in; **3** to finish complete; *(w.* **pro** *+ abl)* to act as; **fato** *(or* **morte** *or* **vitā** *or* **officio) fungi** to die
fung·us -ī *m* mushroom, fungus; candle snuffer; *(fig)* clown
fūnicul·us -ī *m* cord
fūn·is -is *m* rope, cable, cord; rigging; **funem reducere** *(fig)* to change one's mind; **per extentum funem ire** *(lit & fig)* to walk a tightrope; **sequi potius quam ducere funem tortum** to follow the lead rather than to lead
fūn·us -eris *n* funeral, funeral rites; burial; corpse; death; murder; havoc, ruin, destruction; **sub funus** on the brink of the grave **‖** *npl* shades of the dead
fūr fūris *mf* thief; *(fig)* rogue
fūrācissimē *adv* just like a thief
fūr·ax -ācis *adj* thievish
furc·a -ae *f* fork; fork-shaped prop *(for supporting vines, bleachers, etc.);* pillory *(used to punish slaves); (topog)* defile, pass
furcifer·a -ae *f* rascal *(female)*
furcif·er -erī *m* rogue, rascal
furcill·a -ae *f* pitchfork; **furcillā extrudi** *(coll)* to be given the bum's rush
furcill·ō -āre -āvī -ātus *tr* to support, prop up
furcul·a -ae *f* fork-shaped prop **‖** *fpl* narrow pass, defile; **Furculae Caudinae** Caudine Forks *(mountain pass in Samnium where Roman army was trapped in 321 b.c. and made to pass under the yoke)*
furenter *adv* furiously
furf·ur -uris *m* chaff; bran
furi·a -ae *f* frenzy, madness, rage; remorse; madman **‖ Furia** Fury *(one of the three goddesses of vengeance: Megaera, Tisiphone, and Alecto)*
furiāl·is -is -e *adj* frenzied, frantic, furious; infuriated; of the Furies
furiāliter *adv* frantically
furibund·us -a -um *adj* frenzied, frantic, mad; inspired
fūrīn·us -a -um *adj* of thieves
furi·ō -āre -āvī -ātus *tr* to drive mad, infuriate
furiōsē *adv* in a rage, in a frenzy

furiōs·us -a -um *adj* frenzied, frantic, mad, furious; maddening

furn·us -ī *m* (**for-**) oven; bakery

fur·ō -ĕre *intr* to be out of one's mind; to rush furiously around; to rage, rave

fūr·or -ārī -ātus sum *tr* to steal, pilfer; to pillage; to plagiarize; to obtain by fraud **‖** *refl* to steal away

fur·ŏr -ōris *m* madness, rage, fury, passion; furor, excitement; prophetic frenzy, inspiration; passionate love

furtific·us -a -um *adj* thievish

furtim *adv* secretly; imperceptibly

furtīvē *adv* secretly, stealthily

furtīv·us -a -um *adj* stolen; secret, hidden, furtive

furt·um -ī *n* theft, robbery; trick; secret action, intrigue; secret love **‖** *npl* intrigues; secret love affair; stolen goods

fūruncul·us -ī *m* petty thief

furv·us -a -um *adj* black, dark, gloomy, eerie; **dies furvus** unlucky day

fuscin·a -ae *f* trident

fusc·ō -āre -āvī -ātus *tr* to darken, blacken

fusc·us -a -um *adj* dark; dim, ill-lit *(room);* hoarse *(voice);* dark-skinned, swarthy; low, muffled *(sound)*

fūsē *adv* widely, extensively; in great detail; loosely, roughly

fūsil·is -is -e *adj* molten, liquid-

fūsi·ō -ōnis *f* outpouring, effusion

fust·is -is *m* club; stick; beating to death *(as military punishment)*

fustitudin·us -a -um *adj (hum)* whip-happy

fustuār·ium -(i)ī *n* beating to death *(as military punishment)*

fūs·us -a -um *pp of* **fundo ‖** *adj* spread out; broad, wide; diffuse *(style)*

fūs·us -ī *m* spindle

futtile *adv* uselessly, in vain

futtil·is -is -e *adj* (**fūtil-**) brittle; futile, worthless; trifling

futtilit·ās -ātis *f* (**fūtil-**) futility, uselessness

fut·uō -uĕre -uī -ūtus *tr (vulg)* to have intercourse with, screw *(a woman)*

futūr·us -a -um *adj* coming, future; impending, imminent; **tempus futurum** *(gram)* future tense **‖** *n* the future; **in futurum** for the future **‖** *npl* future events, the future

futūti·ō -ōnis *f (vulg)* sex, screwing

futūt·or -ōris *m (vulg)* sex partner

futūtr·ix -īcis *adj (fem only) (vulg)* lecherous **‖** *f* sex partner *(female)*

G

gabat·a -ae *f* plate, dish

Gabi·ī -ōrum *mpl* ancient town just outside Rome

Gabīni·us -a -um *adj* of the Gabinian clan

Gabīn·us -a -um *adj* of Gabii **‖** *mpl* the people of Gabii

Gād·ēs -um *fpl or* **Gād·is -is** *f* Cadiz *(in S. Spain)*

Gādītān·us -a -um *adj* of Gades **‖** *mpl* the people of Gades **‖** *fpl* dancing girls from Gades **‖** *n* dance by Gades dancing girls

gaes·um -ī *n* (**gēs-**) Gallic spear

Gaetūl·us -a -um *adj* Gaetulian, African **‖** *mpl* a people in N.W. Africa along the Sahara Desert

Gāï·a -ae *f* Gaia *(archaic feminine form of Gaius, surviving in ritual and legal language as a name for any woman)*

Gā·ius -iī Gaius *(Roman praenomen; the names of Gaius and Gaia were formally given to the bridegroom and bride respectively at the wedding ceremony)*

Galat·ae -ārum *mpl* Galatians *(a people of central Asia Minor)*

Galatē·a -ae *f* sea nymph loved by Acis and Polyphemus

Galati·a -ae *f* Galatia *(Roman province in Asia Minor)*

Galb·a -ae *m* Roman emperor *(A.D. 68–69)*

galban·us -a -um *adj* of galbanum

galban·um -ī *n* galbanum *(resinous sap of a Syrian plant)*

galbe·us -ī *m* armband *(worn as ornament or for medical purposes)*

galbināt·us -a -um *adj* dressed in chartreuse

galbin·us -a -um *adj* chartreuse; yellowish; *(fig)* effeminate **‖** *npl* chartreuse clothes

gale·a -ae *f* helmet *(usu. of leather)*

galeāt·us -a -um *adj* helmeted

gale·ō -āre *tr* to equip with a helmet

galēricul·um -ī *n* leather cap

galērīt·us -a -um *adj* wearing a leather cap

galēr·um -ī *n or* **galēr·us -ī** *m* leather cap; ceremonial cap *(worn by pontifices, flamines, etc.);* wig

gall·a -ae *f* gallnut *(nutlike growth on a plant)* **‖** *f* Gallic woman

Gall·ī -ōrum *mpl* Gauls *(inhabitants of modern France, Belgium, and N. Italy)*

Galli·a -ae *f* Gaul

Gallicān·us -a -um *adj* Gallic

gallicin·ium -(i)ī *n* cockcrow, daybreak

Gallic·us -a -um *adj* Gallic; belonging to the priests of Cybele; **canis Gallicus** a breed of hunting dog **‖** *f* Gallic shoe

gallīn·a -ae *f* chicken, hen; *(as term of endearment)* chick

gallīnāce·us -a -um *adj* of domestic fowl; **gallus gallinaceus** rooster; **lac gallinaceum** *(hum)* hen's milk *(i.e., an impossible thing)*

gallīnār·ius -(i)ī *m* poultry farmer; one who looks after the poultry used in augury

Gallograec·ī -ōrum *mpl* Galatians *(Celts*

who migrated from Gaul to Asia Minor in 3rd cent. B.C.)
Gall·us -a -um *adj* Gallic ‖ *m* a Gaul; priest of Cyblele; Galatian
gall·us -ī *m* rooster
gāne·a -ae *f or* **gāne·um -ī** *n* low-class restaurant, dive; gluttonous eating
gāne·ō -ōnis *m* glutton
gāneum *see* **ganea**
Gangarid·ae -ārum *mpl* an Indian people near the Ganges
Gang·ēs -is *m* Ganges River
Gangētic·us -a -um *adj* Indian
gann·iō -īre *intr* to snarl
gannīt·us -ūs *m* snarling
Ganymēd·ēs -is *m* Ganymede *(handsome boy carried off to Olympus by an eagle to become the cupbearer of the gods and catamite of Zeus)*.
Ganymēdē·us -a -um *adj* of Ganymede
Garamant·ēs -um *mpl* tribe in N. Africa
Garamant·is -idos *adj (fem only) (poet)* African
Gargān·us -ī mountain in S.E. Italy
Gargar·a -ōrum *npl* a peak in the Ida mountain range; town in that region
garr·iō -īre -īvī *tr* to chatter, prattle; **nugas garrire** to talk nonsense ‖ *intr* to chatter, chat; *(of frogs)* to croak
garrulit·ās -ātis *f* talkativeness; chattering
garrul·us -a -um *adj* garrulous, talkative; blabbing; *(of birds)* chattering; *(time)* for chattering
gar·um -ī *n* fish sauce
gaud·ens -entis *adj* cheerful
gaudeō gaudēre gavīsus sum *tr* to rejoice at; **gaudium gaudere** to feel joy ‖ *intr* to rejoice; *(w. abl)* to be glad about, feel pleased at, delight in; **in se gaudere** *(or* **in sinu) gaudere** to be secretly glad
gaud·ium -(i)ī *n* joy, gladness, delight; cause of joy, source of delight; **gaudium nuntiare** to announce good news; **mala mentis gaudia** gloating
gaul·us -ī *m* bucket
gausap·a -ae *f or* **gausap·e -is** *or* **gausap·um -ī** *n* coarse woolen cloth; felt; shaggy beard
gāvīsus *pp of* **gaudeo**
gaz·a -ae *f* royal treasure; treasure, riches
gelasīn·us -ī *m* dimple
gelidē *adv* coldly; indifferently
gelid·us -a -um *adj* cold, icy, frosty; ice-cold, stiff, numbed ‖ *f* ice-cold water
gel·ō -āre -āvī -ātus *tr & intr* to freeze
Gelōn·ī -ōrum *mpl* Scythian tribe
gel·u -ūs *n or* **gel·um -ī** *n* cold; frost; ice; chill, coldness *(of death, old age, fear)*
gemebund·us -a -um *adj* groaning
gemellipar·a -ae *f* mother of twins
gemell·us -a -um *adj & m* twin
gemināti·ō -ōnis *f* doubling; repetition

gemin·ō -āre -āvī -ātus *tr* to double; to join, unite; to pair; to do repeatedly ‖ *intr* to become double
gemin·us -a -um *adj* twin; paired, double, twofold, two, both; similar ‖ *m* twin
gemit·us -ūs *m* sigh, groan
gemm·a -ae *f* bud; gem, jewel; jeweled goblet; signet ring, signet; eye *(of a peacock's tail);* literary gem; pebble *(for marking days);* a piece in a game-board
gemm·ans -antis *adj* adorned with gems; decorated
gemmāt·us -a -um *adj* set with gems, jeweled
gemme·us -a -um *adj* set with jewels, jeweled; brilliant, glittering, sparkling
gemmi·fer -fera -ferum *adj* containing gems; gem-producing
gemm·ō -āre -āvī -ātum *intr* to sprout, bud; to sparkle
gem·ō -ĕre -uī -itus *tr* to sigh over, lament ‖ *intr* to sigh, groan, moan; to creak
Gemōni·ae -ārum *fpl* steps on the Aventine slope from which the corpses of criminals were thrown into the Tiber River
gen·a -ae *f* cheek; eyelid ‖ *fpl* cheeks; region about the eyes, eyes
geneālog·us -ī *m* genealogist
gen·er -erī *m* son-in-law; daughter's fiancé; brother-in-law
generāl·is -is -e *adj* general, universal
generāliter *adv* in general, generally
generasc·ō -ĕre *intr* to be generated
generātim *adv* by species, by classes; in general, generally
generāt·or -ōris *m* producer, father
gener·ō -āre -āvī -ātus *tr* to beget, procreate, father; *(of places, of the body)* produce; to engender, arouse *(emotions)*
generōsē *adv* with dignity, nobly
generōsit·ās -ātis *f* good breeding, nobility of stock
generōs·us -a -um *adj* of good stock, highborn, noble; noble-minded; high-spirited
genes·is -is *f* birth; horoscope
genesta *see* **genista**
genetīv·us -a -um *adj* inborn, innate; *(gram)* genitive ‖ *m (gram)* genitive case
genetr·ix -īcis *f* (-nit-) mother, ancestress
geniāl·is -is -e *adj* nuptial, bridal; genial; joyous, merry, festive
geniāliter *ad* merrily
geniculāt·us -a -um *adj* knotted, having knots, jointed
genist·a -ae *f* (-nest-) broom plant
genitābil·is -is -e *adj* productive
genitāl·is -is -e *adj* generative, productive; of birth; **dies genitalis** birthday ‖ *n* genital organ
genitāliter *adv* fruitfully
genit- = **genet-**

genit·or -ōris *m* father; creator; source, cause
genitrix *see* **genetrix**
genitūr·a -ae *f* horoscope
genitus *pp of* **gigno**
gen·ius -iī *m* guardian spirit *(of person, place, or thing); (hum)* personfication of all natural appetites, natural inclination; talent
gen·ō -ěre *see* **gigno**
gen·s -tis *f (Roman)* clan *(sharing the same nomen and, theoretically, the same ancestor);* stock; tribe; nation, people; country; class, set, race; species, breed; descendant, offspring; *(poet)* herd, flock, hive **ǁ** *fpl* the peoples of the world; rest of the world *(apart from the Romans),* foreign nations; **longe gentium abire** to be far, far away; **minime gentium** by no means; **ubi gentium** where in the world
gentic·us -a -um *adj* tribal; national
gentīlici·us -a -um *adj* of a Roman clan, of the extended family
gentīl·is -is -e *adj* family, hereditary; tribal; national **ǁ** *m* clansman, kinsman
gentīlit·ās -ātis *f* clan relationship
gen·ū -ūs *n* knee; **genibus minor** kneeling; **genibus nixus** on one's knees; **genuum junctura** knee joint
genuāl·ia -ium *npl* garters
genuī *perf of* **gigno**
genuīn·us -a -um *adj* innate, natural
genuīn·us -a -um *adj* of the cheek; jaw, of the jaw **ǁ** *mpl* back teeth
-gen·us -a -um *adjl suf* forms adjectives meaning "born of": **caeligenus** heavenborn
gen·us -eris *n* race, descent, lineage, breed, stock, family; noble birth; tribe; nation, people; descendant, offspring, posterity; kind, sort, species, class; rank, order, division; fashion, style, way; matter, respect; genus; sex; *(gram)* gender; **aliquid id genus** *(acc of respect instead of gen of quality)* something of that sort; **genus humanum** *(or* **genus hominum)** the human race, mankind; **in omni genere** in every respect; **sui generis** in a class of its *(her, his, their)* own, unique
geōgraphi·a -ae *f* geography
geōmetr·ēs -ae *m* geometer, mathematician
geōmetri·a -ae *f* geometry
geōmetric·us -a -um *adj* geometrical **ǁ** *f* geometry **ǁ** *npl* geometry
georgic·us -a -um *adj* agricultural **ǁ** *npl* Georgics *(poems on farming by Vergil)*
ger·ens -entis *adj (w. gen)* managing *(e.g., a business)*
germānē *adv* sincerely
Germān·ī -ōrum *mpl* Germans
Germāni·a -ae *f* Germany
Germānic·us -a -um *adj* Germanic **ǁ** *m*

cognomen of Tiberius's nephew and adoptive son *(15 B.C.–A.D. 19)*
germānit·ās -ātis *f* brotherhood, sisterhood *(relationship between brothers and sisters of the same parents; relationship between colonies of the same mothercity)*
germān·us -a -um *adj* having the same parents; brotherly, sisterly; genuine, real, true **ǁ** *m* full brother **ǁ** *f see* **germana**
germ·en -inis *n* sprout, shoot; bud; embryo
germin·ō -āre -āvī -ātus *tr* to put forth, grow *(hair, wings, etc.)* **ǁ** *intr* to sprout
gerō gerěre gessī gestus *tr* to bear, carry *(in one's hands); (of things)* to have in it, contain; to bear *(fruit);* to bear, carry *(in the womb);* to wear *(clothing);* to have; to hold *(consulship, etc.);* to spend, pass *(time);* to bring; to display, exhibit; to entertain *(feelings);* to assume; to carry on, manage; to govern, regulate, administer; to carry out, transact, do, accomplish; **bellum gerere** to fight a war, carry on a war; **dum ea geruntur** while that was going on; **gerere morem** *(w. dat)* to gratify; **personam gerere** *(w. gen)* to play the part of; **rem gerere** to run a business, conduct an affair **ǁ** *refl* to behave; *(w.* pro + *abl)* to claim to be for; **se medium gerere** to remain neutral
ger·ō -ōnis *m* porter
gerr·ae -ārum *interj* nonsense!
gerulifigul·us -ī *m* accomplice; *(w. gen)* accomplice in
gerul·us -ī *m* porter
Gēry·ōn -onis *or* **Gēryon·ēs -ae** *m* Geryon *(three-headed monster of Spain that was slain by Hercules)*
gessī *perf of* **gero**
gestām·en -inis *n* load; article(s) worn; load, pack, burden; vehicle, litter **ǁ** *npl* ornaments; accouterments; arms
gestāti·ō -ōnis *f* ride *(on horseback, in litter, in vehicle);* drive *(place),* walk *(place)*
gestāt·or -ōris *m* bearer, carrier
gesti·ō -ōnis *f* performance
gesti·ō -īre -īvī *or* **-iī** *intr* to be delighted, be thrilled; to be eager; *(w. inf)* to be itching to, long to
gestit·ō -āre -āvī *tr* to be in the habit of carrying *or* wearing
gest·ō -āre -āvī -ātus *tr* to bear, wear, carry; to take for a ride *(in a litter, in a vehicle, on horseback);* to spread, blab, tell; to cherish, harbor *(thoughts)* **ǁ** *pass* to ride, drive, sail *(esp. for pleasure)*
gest·or -ōris *m* tattler
gestuōs·us -a -um *adj* gesturing; suggestive
gest·us -a -um *pp of* **gero ǁ** *adj* **res gestae** deeds, accomplishments **ǁ** *n* business; deed

gest·us -ūs *m* gesture; gesticulation; posture, bearing, attitude

Get·ae -ārum *mpl* Thracian tribe on the Lower Danube

Geticē *adv* in Getic, in the Getic language

Getic·us -a -um *adj* of the Getae; Thracian

gibb·us -ī *m or* **gibb·a -ae** *f* hump

Gigant·ēs -um *mpl* Giants *(race of gigantic size that tried to storm heaven and were placed under various volcanoes)*

gignō gignĕre genuī genitus *or* **gen·ō -ĕre** *tr* to beget, bear, produce; to cause, occasion; to give rise to, bring about; to create, begin ‖ *pass* to be born; *(of faculties, parts of the body)* to be produced; *(w. abl)* to be born of, spring from; *(phil)* to come into being

gilv·us -a -um *adj* pale-yellow; **equus gilvus** palomino

gingīv·a -ae *f* gum *(of mouth)*

-gintā *indecl suf* forms numerals from 30 to 90

glabell·us -a -um *adj* bald, smooth

gla·ber -bra -brum *adj* bald, smooth ‖ *m* young slave, favorite slave

glaciāl·is -is -e *adj* icy, frozen

glaci·ēs -ēī *f* ice

glaci·ō -āre -āvī -ātus *tr* to turn into ice, freeze ‖ *intr* to congeal, harden

gladiāt·or -ōris *m* gladiator; ruffian; assassin ‖ *mpl* gladiatorial combat, gladiatorial show; **gladiatores dare** *(or* **edere)** to stage a gladiatorial show

gladiātōri·us -a -um *adj* gladiatorial; **munus gladiatorium** gladiatorial show ‖ *n* gladiator's pay

gladiātūr·a -ae *f* gladiatorial profession

glad·ius -(i)ī *m* sword; murder, death; **gladium educere** *(or* **stringere)** to draw the sword; **gladium recondere** to sheathe the sword; **jus** *(or* **potestas) gladii** right to try and punish a capital crime *(granted by emperor to provincial governors)*

glaeb·a -ae *f* (**glēb-**) lump of earth, clod; soil, land; lump, piece

glaebul·a -ae *f* (**glēb-**) small lump; bit of land, small farm

glaesum *see* **glesum**

glandif·er -era -erum *adj* acorn-bearing

gland·ium -(i)ī *n* candy

glan·s -dis *f* acorn, beechnut, chestnut; pellet *(for a sling); (anat)* head of the penis

glāre·a -ae *f* gravel

glāreōs·us -a -um *adj* full of gravel, gravelly

glaucōm·a -atis *(acc fem singl:* **glaucumam)** *n* cataract; **glaucumam ob oculos objicere** *(w. dat)* to throw dust into *(s.o.'s)* eyes

glau·cus -a -um *adj* gray-green, grayish; bright, sparkling ‖ **Glauc·us -ī** *m* leader of the Lycians in the Trojan War ‖ fish-

erman of Euboea who was changed into a sea deity ‖ son of Sisyphus

glēb- = **glaeb-**

glēs·um *or* **glaes·um -ī** *n* amber

glī·s -ris *m* dormouse *(small, furry-tailed Old World rodent resembling a small squirrel in appearance and habits)*

glisc·ō -ĕre *intr* to grow, swell up, spread, blaze up; to grow, increase

globōs·us -a -um *adj* spherical, round

glob·us -ī *m* ball, sphere, globe; crowd, throng, gathering; clique

glomerām·en -inis *n* ball, globe

glomer·ō -āre -āvī -ātus *tr* to form into a ball; to gather up, roll up; to collect, gather together, assemble ‖ *refl & pass* to gather, assemble

glom·us -eris *n* ball of yarn

glōri·a -ae *f* glory, fame; pride; feeling of pride; source of pride, pride and joy; false pride, vanity, boasting; glorious deed; thirst for glory, ambition

glōriāti·ō -ōnis *f* boasting, pride

glōriol·a -ae *f* bit of glory

glōri·or -ārī -ātus sum *tr (only w. neuter pron as object)* to boast about; **haec gloriari** to boast about this, be proud of this; **idem gloriari** to make the same boast, be proud of the same thing ‖ *intr* to be proud; to boast; *(w. abl or w.* **de** *or* **in** + *abl)* to take pride in, boast about; *(w.* **ad versus** + *acc)* to boast *or* brag to *(s.o.)*

glōriōsē *adv* gloriously, proudly; boastfully, pompously

glōriōs·us -a -um *adj* glorious, illustrious; eager for glory, ambitious; boastful; proud

glossēm·a -atis *n* word to be glossed

glūb·ō -ĕre *tr* to peel, skin

glūt·en -inis *n* glue

glūtināt·or -ōris *m* bookbinder

glūtin·ō -āre -āvī -ātus *tr* to glue together; *(med)* to close *(wounds)*

glutt·iō -īre -īvī *or* **-iī -ītus** *tr* (**glūt-**) to gulp down

glutt·ō -ōnis *m* glutton

Gnae·us *or* **Gnē·us -ī** *m* Roman first name *(praenomen, abbreviated Cn.)*

gnār·us -a -um *adj* skilled, expert; known, familiar; *(w. gen)* having knowledge of, familiar with, expert in, experienced in

gnāta *see* **nata**

gnātus *see* **natus**

gnōbilis *see* **nobilis**

gnoscō *see* **nosco**

Gnōsi·a -ae *or* **Gnōsi·as -adis** *or* **Gnōs·is -idis** *f* Ariadne *(daughter of King Minos of Cnossos)*

Gnō(s)s·us -ī *f* Cnossos *(ancient capital of Crete and residence of King Minos)*

gnōtus *see* **notus**

gōb·ius -(i)ī *m* (**cōb-**) goby *(small fish)*

Gorgi·as -ae *m* famous orator and sophist from Sicily *(480–c.390 B.C.)*

Gorg·ō -ōnis *f* Gorgon *(one of three daughters of Phorcys and Ceto: Stheno, Medusa, and Euryale)*

Gorgone·us -a -um *adj* Gorgonian; **Gorgoneus equus** Pegasus; **Gorgoneus lacus** the spring Hippocrene *(on Mt. Helicon)*

grabāt·us -ī *m* cot; army cot

Gracch·us -ī *m* Roman family name *(cognomen);* Tiberius Sempronius Gracchus *(social reformer, and tribune in 133 B.C.)* ‖ Gaius Sempronius Gracchus *(younger brother of Tiberius and tribune in 123 B.C.)*

gracil·is -is -e *adj* slim, slender; thin, skinny; poor; slight, insignificant; plain, simple *(style)*

gracilit·ās -ātis *f* slenderness; thinness, leanness, meagerness

grācul·us -ī *m* **(gracc-)** jackdaw *(glossy, black European bird resembling the crow)*

gradātim *adv* step by step, gradually, little by little

gradāti·ō -ōnis *f* flight of steps; tiers of seats *(in theater); (rhet)* series of propositions of ascending emphasis

gradior gradī gressus sum *intr* to go, walk, step

Grādīv·us *or* **Gradīv·os -ī** *m* epithet of Mars

grad·us -ūs *m* step, pace, walk, gait; step, degree, grade, stage; approach, advance, progress; status, rank; station, position; step, rung, stair; footing, stance; **concito gradu** on the double; **de gradu dejicere** *(fig)* to throw off balance; **gradum celerare** *(or* **corripere)** to pick up the pace; **gradum conferre** *(mil)* to come to close quarters; **gradūs ferre** *(mil)* to charge; **pleno gradu** on the double; **per gradūs** by degrees; **per gradūs ascendere** to climb the stairs; **suspenso gradu** on tiptoe

Graecē *adv* Greek, in Greek; **Graece discere (legere, loqui, scire)** to learn (read, speak, know) Greek

Graeci·a -ae *f* Greece; **Magna Graecia** Greek cities along the coast of S. Italy

graeciss·ō -āre *intr* to ape the Greeks; to speak Greek

graec·or -ārī *intr* to go Greek, act like a Greek

Graecul·us -a -um *adj (pej)* Greek through and through, hundred-percent Greek ‖ *mf (pej)* Greekling, dirty little Greek

Graec·us -a -um *adj & mf* Greek ‖ *n* Greek, Greek language

Grājugen·a -ae *m* Greek *(by birth)*

Grāj·us -a -um *adj* Greek ‖ *mpl* Greeks

grall·ae -ārum *fpl* stilts

grallāt·or -ōris *m* stilt walker

grām·en -inis *n* grass; meadow, pasture; plant, herb

grāmine·us -a -um *adj* grassy, of grass

grammatic·us -a -um *adj* grammatical, of grammar ‖ *m* teacher of literature and language; philologist ‖ *f & npl* grammar; philology

grammatist·a -ae *f* elementary school teacher

grānāri·a -ōrum *npl* granary

grandaev·us -a -um *adj* old, aged

grandesc·ō -ĕre *intr* to grow, grow big

grandicul·us -a -um *adj* rather large; pretty tall

grandif·er -era -erum *adj* productive, producing large crops

grandiloqu·us -ī *m* big talker

grandin·at -āre *v impers* it is hailing

grand·iō -īre *tr* to enlarge, increase

grand·is -is -e *adj* full-grown, grown up, tall; large, great; aged; important; powerful, strong; lengthy *(book, speech);* intense *(emotions);* proud, noble *(words, sentiments);* grand, lofty *(style);* dignified *(person);* loud, strong *(voice);* heavy *(debt);* dignified *(speaker);* **aevo** *(or* **aetate) grandis** advanced in years, elderly

grandit·ās -ātis *f* grandeur

grand·ō -inis *f (m)* hail

grānif·er -era -erum *adj (of an ant)* grain-carrying

grān·um -ī *n* small particle, grain; seed; kernel; stone *(in fruit);* **granum piperis** peppercorn

graphiār·ium -(i)ī *n* case for holding a stylus, "pencil box"

graphicē *adv* in the manner of a painter; vividly, graphically; *(coll)* perfectly, properly, thoroughly

graphic·us -a -um *adj* artistic; *(coll)* exquisite, first-class

graph·ium -(i)ī *n* stylus

grassāt·or -ōris *m* tramp; bully, hoodlum; mugger, prowler

grassātūra -ae *f* holliganism

grass·or -ārī -ātus sum *intr* to advance, press on; to prowl; to run riot, rage; *(w. adversus or in + acc)* to attack, waylay, mug

grātē *adv* willingly, with pleasure; gratefully

grātēs *(gen not in use)* *fpl* thanks, gratitude; **grates agere** *(w. dat)* to thank; **grates habere** *(w. dat)* to feel grateful toward

grāti·a -ae *f* grace, charm, pleasantness, loveliness; influence, prestige; popularity; love, friendship; service; favor, kindness; thanks, gratitude; cause, reason, motive; **cum gratiā** *(w. gen)* to the satisfaction of; with the approval of; **eā gratiā**

ut for the reason that; **exempli gratiā** for example; **gratiā** *(w. gen) (postpositive)* for the sake of, on account of; **gratiam facere** *(w. dat of person and gen of thing)* pardon *(s.o.)* for *(a fault)*; **gratias agere** *(w. dat)* to thank; **gratias habere** *(w. dat)* to be grateful to; **in gratiam** *(w. gen)* in order to win the favor of, in order to please; **in gratiam habere** to regard *(s.th.)* as a favor; **meā gratiā** for my sake; **quā gratiā?** why?

Grāti·ae -ārum *fpl* Graces *(Aglaia, Euphrosyne, and Thalia)*

grātificāti·ō -ōnis *f* kindness, favor

grātific·or -ārī -ātus sum *tr* to give up, surrender, sacrifice ‖ *intr (w. dat)* 1 to do *(s.o.)* a favor; 2 to gratify, please *(s.o.)*; 3 to humor *(s.o.)*

grātiōs·us -a -um *adj* popular, influential; obliging

grātīs *adv* gratis, free, for nothing

grāt·or -ārī -ātus sum *intr* to rejoice; to express gratitude; *(w. dat)* to congratulate; **invicem inter se gratari** to congratulate one another

grātuītō *adv* gratuitously, gratis, for nothing; for no particular reason

grātuīt·us -a -um *adj* done for mere thanks, gratuitous, free, spontaneous; voluntary; unprovoked

grātulābund·us -a -um *adj* congratulating

grātulāti·ō -ōnis *f* congratulation; rejoicing, joy; public thanksgiving

grātulāt·or -ōris *m* well-wisher

grātul·or -ārī -ātus sum *intr* to be glad, rejoice; *(w. dat)* 1 to congratulate; 2 to render thanks to

grāt·us -a -um *adj* pleasing, pleasant, agreeable, welcome; thankful, grateful; deserving thanks, earning gratitude; popular ‖ *n* favor; **gratum facere** *(w. dat)* to do *(s.o.)* a favor

gravanter *adv* reluctantly

grāvātē *adv* with difficulty; unwillingly, grudgingly

gravātim *adv* with difficulty; unwillingly

gravēdinōs·us -a -um *adj* prone to catch colds, susceptible to colds

gravēd·ō -inis *f* cold, head cold

graveol·ens -entis *adj* stinking

gravesc·ō -ĕre *intr* to grow heavy; *(fig)* to get worse

graviditās -ātis *f* pregnancy

gravid·ō -āre -āvī -ātus *tr* to impregnate

gravid·us -a -um *adj* loaded, filled, full; pregnant; *(w. abl)* teeming with

grav·is -is -e *adj* heavy, weighty; burdensome; grave, serious; troublesome, oppressive, painful, harsh, hard, severe, unpleasant; indigestible *(food)*; important, influential; venerable, dignified; grave, serious; pregnant; hostile; relentless; obnoxious *(person)*; exorbitant *(prices)*; low, deep *(voice)*; flat *(note)*; harsh, bitter, offensive *(smell, taste)*; impressive *(speech)*; stormy *(weather)*; labored *(breathing)*; oppressive *(heat)*; unhealthy *(climate, place, season)*; dangerous *(animal, person)*; *(mil)* heavy-armed

gravit·ās -ātis *f* weight; severity, harshness; seriousness; importance; dignity, influence, authority; pregnancy; violence, vehemence; offensiveness *(of smell)*; unhealthfulness *(of climate, place, season)*

graviter *adv* heavily, ponderously; hard, violently, vehemently; severely, harshly; unpleasantly; sadly, sorrowfully; with dignity, with propriety, with authority; *(to feel)* deeply; *(to smell)* offensive; *(to speak)* impressively; **graviter ferre** to take *(s.th.)* hard

grav·ō -āre -āvī -ātus *tr* to weigh down, load (down); to be burdensome to, be oppressive to; to aggravate; to increase

grav·or -ārī -ātus sum *tr* to feel annoyed at, object to; to refuse, decline; to bear with reluctance, regard as a burden ‖ *intr* to feel annoyed

gregāl·is -is -e *adj* of the herd *or* flock; common; **miles gregalis** a private; **sagulum gregale** a private's uniform ‖ *mpl* comrades, companions

gregāri·us -a -um *adj* of the flock *or* herd; common, ordinary; **miles gregarius** a private ‖ *m (mil)* a private

gregātim *adv* in flocks, in herds, in crowds

grem·ium -(i)ī *n* lap, bosom; womb

gressus *pp of* **gradior**

gress·us -ūs *m* step; course, way

gre·x -gis *m* flock, herd; swarm; company, group, crowd, troop, set, clique, gang; theatrical cast, troupe

gruis *see* **grus**

grunn·iō -īre -īvī *or* **-iī -ītum** *intr* **(grund-)** to grunt

grunnīt·us -ūs *m* grunt, grunting

gru·ō -ĕre *intr (of a crane)* to honk

grū·s *or* **gru·is -is** *mf* crane

gryps grȳpis *m* griffin *(fabled monster having the head and wings of an eagle and the body of a lion)*

gubernāc(u)l·um -ī *n* rudder, tiller, helm ‖ *npl (fig)* helm

gubernāti·ō -ōnis *f* navigation

gubernāt·or -ōris *m* navigator, pilot, helmsman; ruler, governor, director

gubernātr·ix -īcis *f* directress

gubern·ō -āre -āvī -ātus *tr* to navigate, pilot; to direct, govern

gul·a -ae *f* gullet, throat; palate, appetite; gluttony

gulōs·us -a -um *adj* appetizing, dainty; fond of fine foods

gurg·es -itis *m* abyss, gulf, whirlpool; waters, flood, depths, sea; spendthrift
gurgul·ō -ōnis *m* gullet; windpipe
gurgust·ium -(i)ī *n* dark hovel; *(fig)* hole in the wall
gustātōr·ium -(i)ī *n* appetizer
gustāt·us -ūs *m* sense of taste; flavor, taste
gust·ō -āre -āvī -ātus *tr* to taste; *(fig)* to enjoy; to overhear ‖ *intr* to have a snack
gust·us -ūs *m* tasting; flavor, taste; appetizer; small portion, taste
gutt·a -ae *f* drop; spot, speck
guttātim *adv* drop by drop
guttāt·us -a -um *adj* spotted
guttul·a -ae *f* tiny drop
gutt·ur -uris *n (m)* gullet, throat, neck ‖ *npl* throat, neck
gūt·us -ī *m* (**gutt-**) cruet, flask
Gy·ās -ae *m* hundred-armed giant
Gȳg·ēs -is *or* **-ae** *m* king of Lydia *(reigned 716–678 B.C.)*
gymnasiarch·us -ī *m* manager of a gymnasium
gymnas·ium -(i)ī *n* gymnasium
gymnastic·us -a -um *adj* gymnastic
gymnic·us -a -um *adj* gymnastic
gymnosophist·ae -ārum *mpl* Hindu Stoics
gynaecē·um -ī *or* **gynaec·īum -(i)ī** *n* women's apartment in a Greek house
gypsāt·us -a -um *adj* covered with gypsum, white with gypsum
gyps·ō -āre -āvī -ātus *tr* to whiten with gypsum *(the feet of slaves put up for auction);* to plaster up
gyps·um -ī *n* gypsum; plaster of Paris
gȳr·us -ī *m* circle, cycle, ring; *(astr)* orbit, course; **in gypros ire** to go in circles; **in gyrum** in a circle; all around

H

ha *interj* expression of joy, satisfaction, *or* laughter
habēn·a -ae *f* strap ‖ *fpl* reins; *(fig)* reins of government; **habenae rerum** reins of state; **habenas adducere** *(or* **dare** *or* **effundere** *or* **immittere)** *(w. dat)* to give free rein to; **habenas premere** to tighten the reins; **immissis habenis** at full speed
hab·eō -ēre -uī -itus *tr* to have; to hold; to possess; to own; to keep, retain, detain; to have at one's disposal, have available; to have on one's side, have in one's favor; to control, have under one's control; to involve, entail; to have knowledge of *(facts, information);* to afford, give *(e.g., pleasure);* to have on, wear *(clothes);* to treat, handle, use; *(of a vessel)* to hold, contain; to be made up of, consist of; *(of*

feelings) to beset, come over, grip; to hold, conduct *(meeting, inquiry, census);* to deliver, give *(speech),* give *(a talk);* to keep, observe *(a law, edict, practice); (of owner, inhabitant)* to occupy, inhabit; to pronounce, utter *(words);* to spend, live *(life, youth);* to hold, manage, govern, wield; to hold, think, consider, believe; to occupy, engage, busy; to occasion, produce, render; to know, be informed of, be acquainted with; to take, accept, endure, bear; **animo habere** *(w. inf)* to have in mind to, intend to; **certum habere** to regard as certain; **comitia habere** to hold an assembly; to hold elections; **contionem habere** to hold a meeting *or* rally; **gratiam habere** to be grateful; **in animo habere** to have on one's mind, have in mind; **justum habere** *(w. inf)* to have a duty to; **locum priorem habere** to have the lead *(in a race);* **melius habere** *(w. inf)* to think it better to; **necesse habere** *(w. inf)* to have an obligation to; **parum habere** *(w. inf)* to think it a minor matter to; **parum habere violasse** to think nothing of having violated; **pro certo habere** to regard it as certain; **pro explorato habere** to regard it as an established fact; **rus me nunc habet** I am now in the country; **secum habere** to have with one *or* in one's possession, have in one's company; **secum** *(or* **sibi) habere** to keep *(s.th.)* to oneself, keep secret ‖ *refl (w. adv)* to be, feel *(well, etc.);* **bene vos habetis** you are doing fine; **me male habeo** I'm doing lousy; **quo pacto te habes?** how are you doing?; **sic res se habet** that's the situation, that's the way things are; **singulos ut sese haberet rogitans** asking each and every one how he was doing ‖ *intr (w. adv or abl)* to be, live, dwell *(in a place);* **habet!** *(said of gladiator receiving fatal wound)* he's had it!; **hic ego habeo** I live here ‖ *v impers* **bene habet** (that's) fine!, O.K. then!; **sic habet** that's how it is
habil·is -is -e *adj* handy; easy to handle; suitable, convenient; active; *(of vehicles)* easy to control
habilit·ās -ātis *f* aptitude
habitābil·is -is -e *adj* fit to live in
habitāti·ō -ōnis *f* residence; (cost of) rent
habitāt·or -ōris *m* inhabitant; occupant, tenant *(of house, apartment)*
habit·ō -āre -āvī -ātus *tr* to live in, inhabit ‖ *intr* to dwell, live
habitūd·ō -inis *f* condition, appearance; bearing
habitur·iō -īre *tr* to like to have
habit·us -a -um *pp of* **habeo** ‖ *adj* in good

physical condition; **corpulentior et habitior videri** to look stouter and in better physical condition
habit·us -ūs m condition *(of the body);* physical make-up, build, looks, form, shape; circumstances; style, style of dress; character, quality; disposition, state of feeling; posture
hāc *adv* this way, in this way
hactenus *adv* to this place, thus far; until now, hitherto, so far; to this extent, so much; *(in writing)* to this point; **haec hactenus** enough of this
Hadri·a -ae f **(Adr-)** Adriatic Sea
Hadriac·us -a -um *adj* Adriatic
Hadriān·us -a -um *adj* **(Adr-)** Adriatic ‖ m Hadrian *(Roman emperor, A.D. 117-138)*
Hadriātic·us -a -um *adj* Adriatic
haec hōrum *(neut pl of* **hoc)** *adj & pron* these
haec hūjus *(older form:* **haece; gen: hujusce)** *(fem of* **hic)** *adj* this; the present, the actual; the latter; *(occasionally)* the former; **haec...haec** one...another ‖ *pron* this one, she; the latter; *(occasionally)* the former; **haec...haec** one...another one; **haecine (haec** *w. interrog enclitic* **-ne)** is this...?
haece *see* **haec**
haecine *see* **haec**
Haed·ī -ōrum *mpl (astr)* the Kids *(pair of stars in the constellation Auriga)*
haedili·a -ae f little goat
haedill·us -ī m *(term of endearment)* little goat
haedīn·us -a -um *adj* kid's, goat's
haedul·us -ī m little kid, little goat
haed·us -ī m young goat, kid
Haemōni·a -ae f Thessaly
Haem·us *or* **Haem·os -ī** m mountain range in N. Thrace
hae·reō -rēre -sī -sum *intr* to cling, stick; to hang around, linger, stay, remain fixed, remain in place; to be rooted to the spot; to come to a standstill, stop; to be embarrassed, be at a loss, hesitate, be in doubt; *(w. dat or abl or w.* **in** + *abl)* **1** to cling to, stick to, be attached to; **2** to loiter in, hang around in, waste time in *(a place) or at (an activity);* **3** to adhere to, stick by *(an opinion, purpose);* **4** to gaze upon; **5** to keep close to; **in terga** *(or* **tergis** *or in* **tergis) hostium haerere** to keep on the enemy's tail
haeresc·ō -ĕre *intr* to stick together
haeres·is -is f philosophical school
haesitābund·us -a -um *adj* hesitating, faltering
haesitanti·a -ae f hesitancy
haesitāti·ō -ōnis f hesitation, indecision
haesitāt·or -ōris m hesitator
haesit·ō -āre -āvī -ātum *intr* to get stuck;

to hesitate; to stammer; to be undecided, be at a loss
hahae, hahahahae *interj* expression of joy, satisfaction, *or* laughter
halagor·a -ae f salt market
hāl·ans -antis *adj* fragrant
hāl·ēc *or* **(h)all·ēc -ēcis** n *(·ex)* fish sauce; fish soup
haliaeët·os -ī m osprey *(large hawk that preys on fish, also called fish hawk)*
hālit·us -ūs m breath; steam, vapor
hal(l)ūcin·ō -āre *or* **hālūcin·or -ārī -ātus sum** *tr* to say in a distracted state ‖ *intr* to have hallucinations; to ramble
hāl·ō -āre *tr* to exhale ‖ *intr* to be fragrant
halopant·a -ae m scoundrel
halōs·is -is *(acc:* **-in)** f capture
halt·ēr -ēris m weight held in the hand by an athlete
hālūcinor *see* **hal(l)ucino**
ham·a *or* **am·a -ae** f bucket
Hamādry·as -adis *(dat pl:* **Hamādryasin)** f wood nymph
hāmātil·is -is -e *adj* with hooks
hāmāt·us -a -um *adj* hooked
Hamilc·ar -aris m Carthaginian general in the First Punic War, surnamed Barca, and father of Hannibal *(d. 228 B.C.)*
hāmiōt·a -ae f fisher(man)
Hamm·ō(n) *or* **Amm·ōn -ōnis** m Ammon *(Egyptian god, represented as a ram, who had a famous oracle in Libya and was identified with Jupiter Ammon);* **ultimus Ammon Afrorum** deepest Africa
hāmul·us -ī m small hook
hām·us -ī m hook, fishhook; barb
Hannib·al -alis m son of Hamilcar Barca and famous general in the Second Punic War *(240-182 B.C.)*
har·a -ae f pen, coop, stye
(h)arēn·a -ae f sand; seashore, beach; arena ‖ *fpl* desert
(h)arēnāri·a -ae f sandpit
(h)arēnōs·us -a -um *adj* sandy
hariol·a -ae f fortuneteller *(female)*
hariol·or -ārī -ātus sum *intr* to foretell the future; to talk gibberish
hariol·us -ī m fortuneteller
harmoni·a -ae f harmony ‖ **Harmonia** wife of Cadmus, founder and first king of Thebes
harpag·ō -āre -āvī -ātus *tr (coll)* to hook *(to steal)*
harpag·ō -ōnis m hook; harpoon; grappling hook; greedy person
Harpalyc·ē -ēs f Thracian princess, raised as a warrior
harpast·um -ī n handball
harp·ē -ēs f sickle; scimitar
Harpȳj·a -ae f harpy *(creature with head of a woman and body of a bird)*
(h)arundif·er -era -erum *adj* reed-bearing

(h)arundine·us -a -um *adj* of reeds
(h)arund·ō -inis *f* reed, cane, fishing rod; pen; shepherd's pipe; shaft, arrow; fowler's rod; weaver's comb; **(h)arundo Indica** bamboo
(h)arusp·ex -icis *m* soothsayer *(interpreter of internal organs, prodigies, and lightning)*
(h)aruspic·a -ae *f* soothsayer *(female)*
(h)aruspicīn·us -a -um *adj* of divination **ǀǀ** *f* the art of divination
(h)aruspic·ium -(i)ī *n* divination
(H)asdrub·al -alis *m* brother of Hannibal *(d. 207 B.C.)* **ǀǀ** son-in-law of Hamilcar Barca *(d. 221 B.C.)*
hast·a -ae *f* spear *(weapon; spear stuck into ground at public auction; symbol of the centumviral court, which dealt with cases of property and inheritance);* **sub hastā vendere** to sell at auction
hastāt·us -a -um *adj* armed with a spear **ǀǀ** *mpl* soldiers in the first line of a Roman battle formation
hastīl·e -is *n* shaft; spear; rod
(h)au *interj* oh!, ow!, ouch!
haud *or* **haut** *or* **hau** *adv* hardly; not, not at all, by no means
hau(d)quāquam *adv* by no means whatsoever, not at all
hau·riō -rīre -sī -stus *tr* to draw, draw up, draw out; to drain, drink up; to spill, shed *(blood); (of water)* to swallow up, engulf; *(of flames)* to devour; to consume, use up *(resources);* to scoop up; to hollow out; to derive; *(fig)* to have one's fill of; *(fig)* drink in
haustr·um -ī *n* scoop *(on a water-wheel)*
haustus *pp of* **haurio**
haust·us -ūs *m* drawing *(of water);* drinking, swallowing; drink, draft; handful; stream *(of blood)*
haut *see* **haud**
haveō *see* **aveo**
hebdom·as -ados *f* week; a group of seven; fever occurring at seven-day intervals
Hēb·ē -ēs *f* goddess of youth, daughter of Juno, and cupbearer of the gods
(h)eben·us -ī *m* ebony
heb·eō -ēre *intr* to be blunt, be dull; *(of light)* to grow dim; *(of anger)* to die down; *(fig)* to be sluggish, be inactive
heb·es -etis *adj* blunt, dull; faint, dim; dull, obtuse, stupid
hebesc·ō -ĕre *intr* to grow blunt, grow dull; to become faint *or* dim; to lose vigor
hebet·ō -āre -āvī -ātus *tr* to blunt, dull, dim
Hebr·us -ī *m* principal river in Thrace
Hecat·ē -ēs *f* goddess of magic and witchcraft, identified with Diana
hecatomb·ē -ēs *f* hecatomb *(public sacrifice of 100 oxen to the gods)*

Hect·or -oris *m* son of Priam and Hecuba, husband of Andromache
Hecub·a -ae *or* **Hecub·ē -ēs** *f* (-cab-) wife of Priam *(was metamorphosed into a dog)*
(h)eder·a -ae *f* ivy
(h)ederig·er -era -erum *adj* wearing ivy
(h)ederōs·us -a -um *adj* overgrown with ivy
hēdycr·um -ī *n* perfume
hei, hēia *see* **ei, ēia**
Helen·a -ae *or* **Helen·ē -ēs** *f* Helen of Troy *(wife of Menelaus, sister of Clytemnestra, Castor, and Pollux)*
Helen·us -ī *m* prophetic son of Priam and Hecuba
Hēliad·es -um *fpl* daughters of Helios and sisters of Phaëthon, who were changed into poplar trees and whose tears were changed into amber
helic·a -ae *f* spiral
Helicā·ōn -onis *m* the son of Antenor and founder of Patavium
Helicāoni·us -a -um *adj* of Helicaon *(i.e., of Patavium)*
Helic·ē -ēs *f* *(astr)* Big Bear *(constellation Ursa Major); (poet)* N. regions
Helic·ōn -ōnis *m* mountain in Boeotia sacred to Muses and Apollo
Helicōniad·es *or* **Helicōnid·es -um** *fpl* Muses
Helicōni·us -a -um *adj* of Helicon
hēliocamīn·us -ī *m* sun-room
Hell·as -adis *or* **-ados** *f* (mainland of) Greece
Hell·ē -ēs *f* daughter of Athamas and Nephele who, while riding the golden-fleeced ram, fell into the Hellespont *(= Helle's Sea)* and drowned
hellebor- = **ellebor-**
Hellespont·us -ī *m* Hellespont *(modern Dardanelles)*
hellu·ō -ōnis *m* glutton; squanderer
hellu·or -ārī -ātus sum *intr* to be a glutton
(h)el·ops *or* **ell·ops -opis** *m* highly-prized fish *(perhaps the sturgeon)*
helvell·a -ae *f* delicious herb
Helvēti·us -a -um *adj* Helvetian **ǀǀ** *mpl* Helvetians *(a people of ancient Switzerland)*
helv·us -a -um *adj* pale-yellow
hem *interj (expression of surprise)* well!
hēmerodrom·us -ī *m* courier
hēmicill·us -ī *m (pej)* mule
hēmicycl·ium -(i)ī *n* semicircle of seats
hēmīn·a -ae *f* half a sextarius *(half a pint)*
hendecasyllab·ī -ōrum *mpl (pros)* hendecasyllabics *(verses with eleven syllables)*
hēpatiāri·us -a -um *adj* of the liver
heptēr·is -is *f* galley *(perhaps)* with seven banks of oars
hera *see* **era**

Hēr·a -ae f Greek goddess, identified with Juno

Hēraclē·a -ae f name of numerous towns (esp. a part of Lucania on the Siris River and, in Sicily, a town between Lilybaeum and Agrigentum) ‖ epic poem on the subject of Hercules

Hēraclīt·us -ī m early Greek philosopher of Ephesus who believed fire to be the primary element (Ē 513 B.C.)

Hērae·a -ōrum npl festival in honor of the Greek goddess Hera

herb·a -ae f blade; stalk; herb; plant; grass, lawn; **adhuc tua messis in herba est** (prov) don't count your chickens before they are hatched (literally, your harvest is still on the stalk); **herba mala** weed

herbesc·ō -ěre intr to sprout

herbe·us -a -um adj grass-green

herbid·us -a -um adj grassy; full of weeds

herbif·er -era -erum adj grassy, grass-producing; made of herbs; bearing magical herbs

herbigrad·us -a -um adj (of a snail) that crawls on the grass

herbōs·us -a -um adj grassy; made with herbs; resembling vegetation

herbul·a -ae f small plant

(h)ercisc·ō -ěre intr to divide an inheritance

hercle or **hercule** or **ercle** interj (used for emphasis or to express strong feeling, normally used by the male sex only) by Hercules!

(h)erct·um -ī n inheritance

Herculānens·is -is -e adj of Herculaneum ‖ m district of Herculaneum ‖ mpl inhabitants of Herculaneum

Herculāne·um -ī n town on the Bay of Naples, destroyed by the volcano of Mt. Vesuvius in A.D. 79

Hercul·ēs -is or **-ī** or **-eī** m son of Jupiter and Alcmena, husband of Deianira

Herculēs or **Herc(u)le** interj by Hercules! (see hercle)

Herculē·us -a -um adj of Hercules

Hercyni·us -a -um adj Hercynian, of Hercynia (a region of the forest-covered mountains extending from the Rhine to the Carpathians)

here see **heri**

hērēdipet·a -ae m legacy hunter

hērēditāri·us -a -um adj of an inheritance; inherited, hereditary

hērēdit·ās -ātis f inheritance; hereditary succession; **hereditas sine sacris** an inheritance without encumbrances

hērēd·ium -(i)ī n inherited estate

hēr·ēs -ēdis m heir (to an estate, throne); **heres ex dodrante** heir to three-quarters of an estate; (w. ordinal numbers, indicating order of succession): **heres Pelopis tertius** Pelop's heir third in or-

der of succession (i.e., Agamemnon) ‖ f heiress

herī or **heri** or **here** adv yesterday

herif-, herīl- = **erif-, eril-**

Hermaphrodīt·us -ī m son of Hermes and Aphrodite who combined with the nymph Salmacis to become one bisexual person

Hermathēn·a -ae f a herm (i.e., a quadrangular pillar) with a bust of Athena

Herm·ēs -ae m Greek god identified with Mercury; herm (quadrangular pillar with the bust of Hermes, or later, of other gods)

Hermion·ē -ēs or **Hermion·a -ae** f Hermione (daughter of Helen and Menelaus and wife of Orestes)

Herm·us -ī m gold-rich river in the Greek district of Aeolis

Hērodot·us -ī m father of Greek history, born at Halicarnassus on coast of Asia Minor (484–425 B.C.)

hērōïc·us -a -um adj heroic, epic

hērōïn·a -ae f demigoddess, heroine

hērō·is -idis f demigoddess, heroine

hēr·ōs -ōōs m hero (mythological figure; a man with heroic qualities)

hērō·us -a -um adj heroic, epic ‖ m dactylic hexameter; a dactyl

Hersili·a -ae f wife of Romulus

herus see **erus**

Hēsiod·us -ī m Hesiod (early Greek poet from Boeotia, 8th cent. B.C.)

Hēsion·ē -ēs or **Hēsion·a -ae** f Hesione (daughter of Laomedon, king of Troy, whom Hercules rescued from a sea monster)

Hesperi·a -ae f the land of the evening star (i.e., Italy and Spain)

Hesperid·es -um fpl daughters of Hesperus who guarded the golden apples beyond Mount Atlas

Hesper·us or **Hesper·os -ī** m evening star

hestern·us -a -um adj yesterday's

hetairi·a -ae f secret society

hetairic·ē -ēs f Macedonian mounted guard

heu! interj (expression of pain or dismay) oh!, ah!

heus! interj (to draw attention) say there!, hey!

hexame·ter -tra -trum adj (pros) hexameter, having six metrical feet (applied esp. to dactylic hexamter) ‖ mpl verse in this meter

hexaphor·um -ī n litter carried by six men

hexēr·is -is f ship (perhaps) with 6 banks of oars

hiāt·us -ūs m opening; open mouth; mouthing, bluster; basin (of a fountain); (w. gen) greedy desire for; chasm; (pros) hiatus

Hibēr·ēs -um mpl Spaniards ‖ tribe south of the Caucasas

Hibēri·a -ae f Iberian peninsula (Greek name for Spain)

Hibēric·us -a -um *adj* Spanish

hībern·a -ōrum *npl (mil)* winter quarters; winter-quartering

hībernācul·a -ōrum *npl* winter bivouac; winter residence

Hiberni·a -ae *f* Ireland

hībern·ō -āre -āvī -ātum *or* **hībern·or -ārī -ātus sum** *intr* to spend the winter; to stay in winter quarters; *(fig)* to hibernate

hībern·us -a -um *adj* winter-, in winter, wintry; designed for winter use

Hibēr·us -ī *m* river in Spain *(modern Ebro)*

hibisc·um -ī *n (bot)* hibiscus *(plant w. large, showy flowers)*

hibrid·a -ae *mf* **(hyb-)** hybrid, mongrel, half-breed

hīc *(or* **hic) hūjus** *(older form:* **hīce hūjusce)** *adj* this; the present, the actual; the latter; *(occasionally)* the former; **hic**...**hic** one...another **‖** *pron* this one, he; this man; myself, yours truly *(i.e., the speaker or writer);* the latter; *(occasionally)* the former; *(in court)* the defendant, my defendant; **hic**...**hic** one...another; **hicine (hic +** *interrog* enclitic **-ne)** is this...?

hīc *adv* here, in this place; at this point; in this affair, in this particular

hīce *see* **hic**

hīcine *see* **hic**

hiemāl·is -is -e *adj* winter, wintry; stormy

hiem·ō -āre -āvī -ātum *intr* to spend the winter; to be wintry, be cold, be stormy

hiem·s *or* **hiem·ps -is** *f* winter; cold; storm

Hiemps·ala -alis *m* name of several N. African kings, *esp.* a grandson of Massinissa and cousin of Jugurtha, by whom he was killed

Hier·ō(n) -ōnis *m* Hieron *(ruler of Syracuse and patron of philosophers and poets, d. 466 B.C.)* **‖** Hieron *(ruler of Syracuse and friend of the Romans in First Punic War, 306?–215 B.C.)*

Hierosolym·a -ae *f or* **Hierosolym·a -ōrum** *npl* Jerusalem

hiet·ō -āre *intr* to keep yawning

hilarē *adv* cheerfully, merrily

hilar·is -is -e *adj* cheerful, merry

hilarit·ās -ātis *f* cheerfulness

hilaritūd·ō -inis *f* cheerfulness

hilar·ō -āre -āvī -ātus *tr* to cheer up

hilarul·us -a -um *adj* cheerful little

hilar·us -a -um *adj* cheerful, merry

hill·ae -ārum *fpl* smoked sausage

(H)īlōt·ae -ārum *mpl* Helots *(serfs of the Spartans)*

hīl·um -ī *n (usu. after a neg.)* the least bit

hinc *adv* from here, from this place; on this side, here; for this reason; from this source; after this, from now on, henceforth; *(partitive)* of this, of these; **hinc illinc** from one side to the other

hinn·iō -īre -iī *intr* to whinny, neigh

hinnīt·us -ūs *m* neighing

hinnule·us -ī *m* fawn, young deer

hi·ō -āre -āvī *tr* to mouth, sing with mouth wide open **‖** *intr* to open, be open; to gape; to yawn; to make eyes *(in surprise or greedy anticipation); (rhet)* to be disjointed

hippagōg·os -ī *f* ship for transporting horses

Hipparch·us -ī *m* son of Pisistratus, tyrant of Athens, slain in 514 B.C.

Hippi·ās -ae *m* son of Pisistratus (tyrant of Athens), and tyrant of Athens himself *(527–510 B.C.)*

hippocentaur·us -ī *m* centaur

Hippocrat·ēs -is *m* founder of scientific medicine *(c. 460–380 B.C.)*

Hippocrēn·ē -ēs *f* spring on Mt. Helicon, sacred to the Muses and produced when the hoof of Pegasus hit the ground there

Hippodam·ē -ēs *or* **Hippodamē·a** *or* **Hippodamī·a -ae** *f* Hippodamia *(daughter of Oenamaüs, king of Elis, and wife of Pelops)* **‖** Hippodamia *(daughter of Adrastus and wife of Pirithoüs)*

hippodrom·os -ī *m* racetrack

Hippolyt·ē -ēs *or* **Hippolyt·a -ae** *f* Hippolyte *(Amazonian wife of Thesesus)* **‖** wife of Acastus, king of Magnesia

Hippolyt·us -ī *m* **(Ipp-)** son of Theseus and Hippolyte

hippoman·es -is *n* discharge of a mare in heat; membrane of the head of a newborn foal

Hippomen·ēs -is *m* young man who competed with Atalanta in a race and won her as his bride

Hippōn·ax -actis *m* Greek satirist *(Ē 540 B.C.)*

hippotoxot·ae -ārum *mpl* mounted archers

hippūr·us -ī *m* goldfish

hīr·a -ae *f* empty gut

hircīn·us -a -um *adj* **(-quīn-)** goat-, of a goat

hircōs·us -a -um *adj* smelling like a goat

hirc·us -ī *m* **(-qu·us)** goat

hirne·a *or* **hirni·a -ae** *f* jug

hirsūt·us -a -um *adj* hairy, hirsute, shaggy; bristly; prickly; rude

Hirt·ius -(i)ī *m* Aulus Hirtius *(consul in 43 B.C. and author of the eighth book of Caesar's Memoirs on the Gallic War)*

hirt·us -a -um *adj* hairy, shaggy; uncouth

hirūd·ō -inis *f* leech, bloodsucker

hirundinīn·us -a -um *adj* swallow's

hirund·ō -inis *f* swallow *(bird)*

hisc·ō -ěre *tr* to murmur, utter **‖** *intr* to (begin to) open, gape, yawn; to open the mouth; to split open

Hispān·ī -ōrum *mpl* Spaniards

Hispāni·a -ae *f* Spain

Hispāniens·is -is -e *adj* Spanish

hispid·us -a -um *adj* hairy, shaggy; rough, rugged *(terrain)*
(H)is·ter -trī *m* Lower Danube *(also applied to the whole river)*
histori·a -ae *f* history; account, story; theme *(of a story)*
historic·us -a -um *adj* historical ‖ *m* historian
histric·us -a -um *adj* theatrical
histri·ō -ōnis *m* actor
histriōnāl·is -is -e *adj* theatrical; histrionic
histriōni·a -ae *f* dramatics, art of acting
hiulcē *adv* with frequent hiatus
hiulc·ō -āre *tr* to split open
hiulc·us -a-um *adj* split, split open; open, gaping; with hiatus
hōc hūjus *(old form:* **hōce;** *gen:* **hūjusce)** *(neut of* **hic)** *adj* this; the present, the actual; the latter; *(occasionally)* the former ‖ *pron* this one, it; the latter; *(occasionally)* the former; *(w. gen)* this amount of, this degree of, so much; **hoc erat quod** this was the reason why; **hoc est** that is, I mean, namely; **hocine (hoc + *interrog enclitic* -ne)** is this…?; **hoc facilius** all the more easily
hōce *see* **hoc**
hōcine *see* **hoc**
hodiē *adv* today; nowadays; still, to the present; at once, immediately; **hodie mane** this morning; **numquam hodie** *(coll)* never at all
hodiern·us -a -um *adj* today's; **hodiernus dies** this day, today
holit·or -ōris *m* grocer
holitōri·us -a -um *adj* vegetable
hol·us -eris *n* vegetable; *(collectively)* vegetables; **holus atrum** cabbage-like plant growing on the seashore
holuscul·um -ī *n (pej)* vegetables
Homērē·us -a -um *or* **Homērī·us -a -um** *adj* Homeric
Homēric·us -a -um *adj* Homeric
Homēr·us -ī *m* Homer
homicīd·a -ae *m* murderer
homicīd·ium -(i)ī *n* homicide, murder, manslaughter
hom·ō -inis *mf* human being, man, person, mortal; mankind, human race; fellow; fellow creature; member of a military force; **mi homo!** my good man! ‖ *mpl* people; **inter homines esse** to be alive; to see the world
homull·us -ī *or* **homunci·ō -ōnis** *or* **homuncul·us -ī** *m* poor guy
honest·a -ae *f* lady
honestāment·um -ī *n* ornament
honest·ās -ātis *f* good reputation, respectability; sense of honor, respect; beauty, grace; integrity; decency ‖ *fpl* respectable persons, decent people
honestē *adv* honorably, respectably, de-

cently; honestly, fairly; **honeste genitus** *(or* **natus)** high-born
honest·ō -āre -āvī -ātus *tr* to honor, dignify; to grace, adorn; to put a good face on
honest·us -a -um *adj* honored, respected; honorable, decent, respectable; handsome; well-born, of high rank ‖ *n* a virtue, a good
hon·or *or* **hon·ōs -ōris** *m* honor, esteem; position, office, post; mark of honor, reward, prize, acknowledgment; recompense, fee; offering, sacrifice, rites *(to the gods or the dead);* grace, beauty, charm; glory, fame, reputation; **honor mortis** *(or* **sepulturae)** funeral rites; **honoris causā** out of respect, with all respect; **in honore esse** to meet general approval; **praefari honorem** to begin with an apology; **pugnae honor** military glory; **tempus honoris** term of office
honōrābil·is -is -e *adj* honorable, respectable
honōrār·ium -(i)ī *n* honorarium
honōrāri·us -a -um *adj* complimentary, honorary; **summa (pecunia) honoraria** sum of money contributed by a magistrate to the treasury on entering office
honōrātē *adv* with honor, honorably
honōrāt·us -a-um *adj* honored, respected; in high office; honorable, respectable; **honoratum habere** to hold in honor
honōrificē *adv* honorably, respectfully
honōrific·us -a -um *adj* conferring honor, complimentary
honōr·ō -āre -āvī -ātus *tr* to honor, respect; to embellish, decorate
honōr·us -a -um *adj* conferring honor, complimentary; deserving honor
honōs *see* **honor**
hoplomach·us -ī *m* heavy-armed gladiator
hōr·a -ae *f* hour; time; season; **ad horam** on time, punctually; **horas quaerere** to ask what time it is; **in diem et horam** continually; **in horam vivere** to live from hand to mouth; **quota hora est?** what time is it? ‖ *fpl* hours; time; clock; **horas inspicere** to look at the clock; **horas quaerere ab aliquo** to ask s.o. the time; **omnibus horis** at all hours, at all times; **omnium horarum** suited to all occasions; **quotas horas nuntiare** to say what time it is, tell the time
Hor·a -ae *f* wife of Quirinus *(i.e., of deified Romulus),* called Hersilia before her death
Hōr·ae -ārum *fpl* Hours *(daughters of Jupiter and Themis, who kept watch at the gates of heaven)*
hōrae·us -a -um *adj* pickled; seasoned; in season
Horāt·ius -(i)ī *m* Horace *(Quintus Horatius Flaccus, poet, 65–8 B.C.)* ‖ Horatio

(*Horatius Cocles, defender of the bridge across the Tiber in the war with Porsenna*)
horde·um -ī *n* (ord-) barley
hōri·a -ae *f* fishing boat
hōriol·a -ae *f* small fishing boat
horiz·ōn -ontos *m* horizon
hornō *adv* this year, during this year
hornōtin·us -a -um *adj* this year's
horn·us -a -um *adj* this year's
hōrolog·ium -iī *n* clock, water clock, sundial
hōroscop·us or **hōroscop·os -ī** *m* horoscope; eastern horizon
horrend·us -a -um *adj* horrendous, horrible; awesome
horr·ens -entis *adj* dreadful, awful
horr·eō -ēre -uī *tr* to dread; to shudder at, shrink from; to be amazed at; to regard (*gods, etc.*) with awe ‖ *intr* to stand on end, stand up straight; to get gooseflesh; to shiver, tremble; to bristle; to look frightful, look unkempt; to have a gloomy character
horr·escō -escĕre -uī *tr* to dread, become terrified at ‖ *intr* to stand on end; (*of the sea*) to become rough; to begin to shake or shiver; to start, be startled
horre·um -ī *n* barn, shed; silo, granary; wine cellar; storehouse (*of bees*), beehive
horribil·is -is -e *adj* horrible, terrifying; amazing; rough, uncouth
horridē *adv* roughly, rudely; harshly
horridul·us -a -um *adj* rather shaggy; somewhat shabby; (*rhet*) somewhat unsophisticated (*style*)
horrid·us -a -um *adj* shaggy, prickly; bristly (*pig*); choppy (*sea*); disheveled (*appearance*); rugged, wild (*terrain*); rude, uncouth (*manner*); horrible; shivering (*from cold*)
horrif·er -era -erum *adj* causing shudders; freezing, chilling; terrifying
horrificē *adv* awfully, in a frightening way
horrific·ō -āre -āvī *tr* to make rough, ruffle; to terrify, frighten
horrific·us -a -um *adj* frightful, terrifying
horrison·us -a -um *adj* frightening (*sound*), frightening to hear
horr·or -ōris *m* bristling; shivering, shuddering; horror, dread; awe, reverence; chill; thrill
horsum *adv* this way
hortām·en -inis *n* injunction; encouragement; incentive
hortāment·um -ī *n* encouragement
hortāti·ō -ōnis *f* exhortation, encouragement
hortāt·or -ōris *m* backer, supporter, rooter; instigator

hortāt·us -ūs *m* encouragement, cheering, cheer
Hortens·ius -(i)ī *m* Quintus Hortensius (*lawyer and friendly competitor of Cicero, 114–50 B.C.*)
hort·or -ārī -ātus sum *tr* to encourage, cheer, incite, instigate; to give a pep talk to (*soldiers*)
hortul·us -ī *m* little garden
hort·us -ī *m* garden; garden used by Epicurus as a place of teaching; (*fig*) philosophical system ‖ *mpl* park
hosp·es -itis *m* host, entertainer; guest, visitor; friend; stranger, foreigner
hospit·a -ae *f* hostess; guest, visitor; friend; stranger, foreigner
hospitāl·is -is -e *adj* host's; guest's; hospitable ‖ *npl* guest room
hospitālit·ās -ātis *f* hospitality
hospitāliter *adv* hospitably, as a guest
hospit·ium -(i)ī *n* hospitality; ties of hospitality, friendship; welcome; guest room; lodging; inn
hospit·or -ārī -ātus sum *intr* to be put up (*as a guest*)
hosti·a -ae *f* victim, sacrificial animal; **hostia major** full-grown victim
hostiāt·us -a -um *adj* bringing sacrificial victims
hostic·us -a -um *adj* hostile, of the enemy; foreign ‖ *n* enemy territory
hostific·us -a -um *adj* hostile, bitter
hostīl·is -is -e *adj* enemy-, hostile
hostīliter *adv* like an enemy, in a hostile manner
Hostīl·ius -(i)ī *m* Tullus Hostilius (*third king of Rome*)
hostīment·um -ī *n* compensation
host·iō -īre *tr* to get even with ‖ *intr* to get even
host·is -is *mf* (public) enemy; stranger
hūc *adv* here, to this place; to this point, so far; to such a pitch; for this purpose; **huc atque illuc** here and there, in different directions; **hucine?** (**huc** + *interrog enclitic*) so far?
hui! *interj* wow!
hūjus(ce)modī *adj* (*indecl*) of this sort, this kind of
hūmānē *adv* like a human being; politely, gently, with compassion
hūmānit·ās -ātis *f* human nature; humanity; kindness, compassion, human feeling; courtesy; culture, refinement, civilization
hūmāniter *adv* like a human being; reasonably; gently, with compassion
hūmānitus *adv* humanly; humanely, kindly, compassionately
hūmān·us -a -um *adj* of a human being; human; humane, kind, compassionate; courteous; cultured, refined, civilized
humāti·ō -ōnis *f* burial

hūme- = **ume-**
hūmid- = **umid-**
humil·is -is -e *adj* low, low-lying, low-growing; short *(in stature)*; humble; lowly, poor, obscure; insignificant; petty, unimportant; small-minded, cheap; humiliated, humbled
humilit·ās -ātis *f* lowness, lack of stature; lowliness, insignificance; small-mindedness; humiliation; humility, subservience
humiliter *adv* low, deeply; abjectly
hum·ō -āre -āvī -ātus *tr* to bury
hum·us -ī *f* ground, earth, soil; land, region, country; **humi** on *(or* in) the ground
hyacinthin·us -a -um *adj* of the hyacinth; crimson
hyacinth·us *or* **hyacinth·os** -ī *m* hyacinth ‖ **Hyacinth·us** *or* **Hyacinth·os** -ī *m* Hyacinth *(Spartan youth who was accidentally killed by Apollo and from whose blood hyacinths sprang)*
Hyad·es -um *fpl* Hyades *(group of 7 stars in the head of the constellation Taurus whose rising indicated rain)*
hyaen·a -ae *f* hyena
hyal·us -ī *m* glass
Hyantē·us -a -um *adj* Boeotian
Hy·ās -antis *m* son of Atlas; **sidus Hyantis** the Hyades
Hybl·a -ae *or* **Hybl·ē** -ēs *f* Sicilian town on the slopes of Mt. Aetna, famous for its honey
Hyblae·us -a -um *adj* of Hybla; **Hyblaeus liquor** honey
hybrid·a -ae *mf* hybrid, mongrel, half-breed
Hydasp·ēs -is *m* tributary of the Indus River
Hȳdr·a -ae *f* Hydra *(seven-headed water snake killed by Hercules)* ‖ monster guarding the gate to the lower world *(mother of Cerberus)* ‖ *(astr)* Hydra *or* Anguis *(constellation)*
hydraulic·us -a -um *adj* hydraulic
hydraul·us -ī *m* water organ
hydri·a -ae *f* water jug, urn
Hydrocho·us -ī *m (astr)* Aquarius
hydrōpic·us -a -um *adj* dropsical
hydr·ops -ōpis *m* dropsy
hydr·us *or* **hydr·os** -ī *m* water snake; snake; dragon
Hygi·a -ae *f* goddess of health
Hȳlae·us -ī *m* centaur who wounded Milanion, the lover of Atalanta
Hyl·ās -ae *m* favorite of Hercules who was carried off by the nymphs
Hyll·us -ī *m* son of Hercules and husband of Iole
Hym·ēn -enis *or* **Hymenae·us** *or* **Hymenae·os** -ī *m* Hymen *(god of marriage)*; wedding ceremony; wedding; wedding song
Hymett·us *or* **Hymett·os** -ī *m* mountain in

E. Attica, famous for its honey and marble
Hypan·is -is *m* river in Sarmatia *(modern Yuzhnyy Bug)*
hyperpat·on -ī *n (rhet)* transposition of words *or* clauses
hyperbol·ē -ēs *f* hyperbole
Hyperbore·ī -ōrum *mpl* people in the land of the midnight sun
Hyperī·ōn -onis *or* -onos *m* son of Titan and Earth, father of the Sun
Hypermestr·a -ae *or* **Hypermestr·ē** -ēs *f* only one of the 50 daughters of Danaüs who did not kill her husband on her wedding night
hypocaust·um *or* **hypocaust·on** -ī *n* subfloor heating chamber
hypodidascal·us -ī *m* assitant teacher
hypomnēm·a -atis *n* note, reminder
hypothec·a -ae *f (fin)* collateral
Hypsipyl·ē -ēs *f* queen of Lemnos at the time of the Argonauts
Hyrcāni·a -ae *f* country on S.E. side of the Caspian Sea
Hyrcān·us -a -um *adj* of Hyrcania; **mare Hyrcanum** Caspian Sea
hysteric·us -a -um *adj* having a gynecological ailment

ia- = **ja-**
-i·a -ae *fem suf* forms abstract nouns from adjectives: **audacia** boldness *(from audax bold)*
Iacch·us -ī *m* Bacchus; wine
iambē·us -a -um *adj (pros)* iambic
iambic·us -a -um *adj (pros)* iambic
iamb·us -ī *m (pros)* iamb (⏑ —); iambic trimeter *(consists of three double feet, i.e., of six iambic feet)*; iambic poem; iambic poetry
ianthin·us -a -um *adj* violet-colored ‖ *npl* violet clothes
Īapet·us -ī *m* a Titan, father of Prometheus, Epimetheus, and Atlas
Īapyd·es -um *mpl* (-pud-) an Illyrian tribe
Īāp·yx -ygis *adj* Iapygian ‖ *m* son of Daedalus who ruled in S. Italy ‖ wind that blew from Apulia to Greece
Īas·ius -(i)ī *m* son of Jupiter and Electra and brother of Dardanus
Īās·ō(n) -onis *m* Jason *(son of Aeson and leader of the Argonauts)*
iasp·is -idis *f* spear
Ībēr- = **Hiber-**
ibi *or* **ibī** *adv* there, in that place; then, on that occasion; therein
ibidem *or* **ibīdem** *adv* in the same place, just there; in the place already mentioned, therein, thereon; at that very

moment, there and then; at the same time; in the same matter

īb·is *is or* **-idis** *f* ibis *(bird sacred to the Egyptians)*

Īcariōt·is -idis *adj* of Penelope **‖** *f* Penelope *(daughter of Icarius)*

Īcari·us -a -um *adj* of Icarus, Icarian; of the Icarian Sea; **Canis Icarius** *(astr)* Dog Star **‖** *m* father of Penelope **‖** *n* Icarian Sea

Īcar·us -ī *m* son of Daedalus, who, on his flight from Crete with his father, fell into the sea

ichneum·ōn -onis *m* ichneumon *(Egyptian rat that eats crocodile eggs)*

īcī *perf of* **ico**

-īci·us -a -um *adjl suf* **1** used to form adjectives from nouns denoting officers, relationships, etc.: **tribunicius** tribunician; **patricius** patrician; **2** denoting the time of birth, of a birthday: **nātālicius** of the time of birth, belonging to a birthday; **3** used to form adjectives from past participles: **expositicius** exposed, foundling; **4** used to form adjectives from nouns denoting materials: **latericius** brick-, of brick *(from* **later** brick)*

-icō *vbl suf* **1** used to form verbs from adjectives: **claudicare** to be lame, to limp *(from* **claudus** lame, limping); **2** used to form verbs from other verbs: **fodicare** to stab *(from* **fodere** to stab, dig)*

īc·ō -ĕre -ī -tus *tr* to hit, strike, shoot; to sting, bite; **foedus icere** to conclude a treaty

īc·ōn -onis *f* image

īconic·us -a -um *adj* giving an exact image

icteric·us -a -um *adj* jaundiced

ict·is -idis *f* weasel

ictus *pp of* **ico**

ict·us -ūs *m* stroke, blow, hit; cut; sting, bite; wound; range; *(musical or metrical)* beat; *(fig)* shock, blow; **sub ictum** within range

id *adv* for that reason, therefore

id ejus *(neut of* is) *adj* this, that, the aforesaid **‖** *pron* it; a thing, the thing; **ad id** for that purpose; **aliquid id genus** s.th. of that sort, s.th. like that; **cum eo ut** on condition that, with the stipulation that; **eo plus** the more; **ex eo** from that time on; as a result of that, consequently; **id consili** some sort of plan, some plan; **id temporis** at that time; of that age; **in id** to that end; **in eo esse** to depend on it; **in eo esse ut** to be so far gone that, to get to the point where

Īd·a -ae *or* **Īd·ē -ēs** *f* mountain range near Troy **‖** mountain in Crete where Jupiter was brought up

Īdae·us -a -um *adj* Idaean, of Mt. Ida *(in Crete or near Troy)*

Īdal·ium -(i)ī *n* city in Cyprus dear to Venus

idcircō *adv* on that account, for that reason, therefore

īdem eadem īdem *adj* the same, the very same, exactly this; *(often equivalent to a mere connective)* also, likewise **‖** *pron* the same one

identidem *adv* again and again, continually; now and then, at intervals

ideō *adv* therefore

idiōt·a -ae *m* layman, amateur; private individual

īdōl·on -ī *n* apparition, ghost

idōneē *adv* suitably

idōne·us -a -um *adj* suitable, fit, proper; *(w. dat or w.* **ad** *or* **in** + *acc)* fit for, capable of, suited for, convenient for, sufficient for

Īd·ūs -uum *fpl* Ides *(15th day of March, May, July, and October, and 13th day of the other months; interest, debts, and tuition were often paid on the Ides)*

ie- = je-

-iens *or* **-iēs** *advl suf* forming numerals and adjectives to denote a number of times: **centiens** a hundred times; **totiens** so many times

iens euntis *pres p of* **eo**

-iens·is -is -e *adjl suf* used to form ethnic adjectives from place names: **Carthaginiensis** Carthaginian

igitur *adv* then, therefore, accordingly; *(resumptive after parenthetical matter)* as I was saying; *(in summing up)* so then, in short

ignār·us -a -um *adj* ignorant, unaware, inexperienced; unsuspecting; senseless; unknown, strange, unfamiliar; *(w. gen)* unaware of, unfamiliar with, ignorant of

ignāvē *adv* listlessly, lazily

ignāvi·a -ae *f* listlessness, laziness; cowardice

ignāviter *adv* listlessly, lazily

ignāv·us -a -um *adj* listless, lazy, idle, inactive; relaxing; cowardly; unproductive, useless

ignesc·ō -ĕre *intr* (-nis-) to catch fire, become inflamed, burn; *(fig)* to flare up

igne·us -a -um *adj* of fire, on fire, fiery; red-hot; fiery, ardent *(person)*

ignicul·us -ī *m* small fire, little flame; sparkle; *(lit & fig)* spark

ignif·er -era -erum *adj* fiery

ignigen·a -ae *m* son of fire *(epithet of Bacchus)*

ignip·ēs -edis *adj* fiery-footed

ignipot·ens -entis *adj* lord of fire *(epithet of Vulcan)*

ign·is -is *m* fire; watch fire, fire signal; torch; lightning, bolt of lightning; funeral pyre; star; brightness, glow, splendor; *(fig)* fire, rage, fury, love, passion; flame, sweetheart; agent of destruction, fanatic **‖** *mpl* love poems

ignōbil·is -is -e *adj* unknown, obscure, insignificant, undistinguished; low-born, ignoble

ignōbilit·ās -ātis *f* obscurity; humble birth

ignōmini·a -ae *f* ignominy, dishonor, disgrace; *(mil)* dishonorable discharge; **ignominiā afficere** to dishonor, disgrace; **ignominia senātūs** public censure imposed by the Senate

ignōminiōs·us -a -um *adj* disgraced; ignominious, disgraceful, shameful **‖** *m (person)* disgrace

ignōrābil·is -is -e *adj* unknown

ignōranti·a -ae *f* ignorance

ignōrāti·ō -ōnis *f* ignorance

ignōr·ō -āre -āvī -ātus *tr* to not know, be ignorant of, be unfamiliar with; to be unaware of, know nothing about; to fail to recognize; to mistake, misunderstand; to ignore, disregard, take no notice of

ignōsc·ens -entis *adj* forgiving, indulgent

ig·nōscō -nōscĕre -nōvī -nōtum *intr (w. dat)* to pardon, forgive, excuse; *(w. dat of person and acc of the offense)* to pardon, forgive, excuse *(s.o. a fault)*

ignōt·us -a -um *adj* unknown, unfamiliar, strange; inglorious; unnoticed; low-born, ignoble; vulgar; ignorant

īl·ex -icis *f* holm oak *(European evergreen oak with foliage resembling that of a holly)*

Īli·a -ae *f* Rhea Silvia *(daughter of Numitor and mother of Romulus and Remus)*

Īl·ia -ium *npl* flank, side *(of the body extending from the hips down to the groin)* guts, intestines; belly, groin, private parts

Īliac·us -a -um *adj* Trojan

Īli·as -adis *f Iliad;* Trojan woman

īlicet *adv (ancient form for adjourning an assembly)* you may go; *(expressing dismay)* it's all over!, finished!; at once, immediately

īlicō *adv* on the spot, right then and there, immediately

īlign(e)·us -a -um *adj* of holm oak

Īl·ios -iī *f* Ilium, Troy

Īlĭthȳi·a -ae *f* goddess who aided women in childbirth

Īl·ium -iī *n or* **Īl·ion -iī** *n or* **Īl·ios -iī** *f* Ilium, Troy

Īli·us -a -um *adj* of Ilium, Trojan

illā *adv* that way

ill·a -īus *adj fem* that; that famous **‖** *pron* that one, she

illabefact·us -a -um *adj* (inl-) unbroken, uninterrupted; unimpaired

illā·bor -bī -psus sum *intr* (inl-) to flow; to sink, fall; to fall in, cave in; to slip; *(w.*

dat or w. **ad** *or in* + *acc)* to flow into, enter into, penetrate

illabōr·ō -āre *intr* (inl-) *(w. dat)* to work at, work on

illāc *adv* that way

illacessīt·us -a -um *adj* (inl-) unprovoked

illacrimābil·is -is -e *adj* (inl-) unlamented, unwept; inexorable

illacrim·ō -āre -āvī *or* **illacrim·or -ārī -ātus sum** *intr* (inl-) *(w. dat)* to cry over

ill·aec *(acc:* **-anc;** *abl:* **-āc)** *adj fem* that **‖** *pron* she

illaes·us -a -um *adj* (inl-) unharmed

illaetābil·is -is -e *adj* (inl-) sad, melancholy

illapsus (inl-) *pp of* **illabor**

illaque·ō -āre -āvī -ātus *tr* (inl-) to trap, entangle

illātus (inl-) *pp of* **infero**

illaudāt·us -a -um *adj* (inl-) unworthy of praise, unpraised

ill·e -īus *adj masc* that; that famous; the former; **ille aut ille** this or that, such and such **‖** *pron* that one; he; the former one

illecebr·a -ae *f* (inl-) attraction, allurement

illecebrōs·us -a -um *adj* (inl-) alluring, seductive

illectus (inl-) *pp of* **illicio**

illect·us -a -um *adj* (inl-) unread

illect·us -ūs *m* (inl-) allurement

illepidē *adv* (inl-) inelegantly, rudely

illepid·us -a -um *adj* (inl-) inelegant, lacking refinement

illēvī *perf of* **illino**

ill·ex -icis *mf* (inl-) lure, decoy

ill·ex -ēgis *adj* (inl-) lawless

illexī *perf of* **illicio**

illibāt·us -a -um *adj* (inl-) undiminished, unimpaired, intact

illīberāl·is -is -e *adj* (inl-) stingy

illīberālit·ās -ātis *f* (inl-) stinginess

illīberāliter *adv* (inl-) stingily

ill·ic *(acc:* **-unc;** *abl:* **-ōc)** *adj masc* that **‖** *pron* he

illic *adv* there, in that place; in that matter, therein

il·liciō -licĕre -lexī -lectus *tr* (inl-) to allure, attract; to seduce, mislead

illicitāt·or -ōris *m* (inl-) hired bidder *(one who bids at an auction to make others bid higher)*

illicit·us -a -um *adj* (inl-) unlawful

illī·dō -dĕre -sī -sus *tr* (inl-) to smash to pieces, crush; *(w. dat or w.* **ad** *or in* + *acc)* to smash *(s.th.)* against

illig·ō -āre -āvī -ātus *tr* (inl-) to attach, connect; to tie, bind; to oblige, obligate; to impede; to involve, tie up

illim *adv* from there

illīm·is -is -e *adj* unmuddied, clear

illinc *adv* from there; on that side

il·linō -linĕre -lēvī -litus *tr* (inl-) to cover;

to smear; *(w. dat)* to smear *or* spread *(s.th.)* on, cake *(s.th.)* on

illiquefact·us -a -um *adj* (inl-) melted

illīsī *perf of* **illido**

illīsus *pp of* **illido**

illi(t)terāt·us -a -um *adj* (inl-) uneducated, illiterate

illitus *pp of* **illino**

illō(c) *adv* there, at that place; at that point

illōt·us *or* **illaut·us -a -um** *adj* (inl-) unwashed, dirty

illūc *adv* to that place, in that direction; to that person, to him, to her; to that matter; to that point

ill·ūc *(acc; -ūc; abl -ōc) adj neut* that **ǁ** *pron* it

illūc·eō -ēre *intr* (inl-) *(w. dat)* to shine on

illū·cescō -cescĕre -xī *intr* (inl-) to grow light, dawn; to begin to shine

ill·ud -īus *adj neut* that; the former **ǁ** *pron* it

illū·dō -dĕre -sī -sus *tr* (inl-) to make fun of, ridicule; to waste, fritter away *(time, life)* **ǁ** *intr (w. dat) (coll)* to play around with *(sexually)*

illūminātē *adv* (inl-) clearly

illūmin·ō -āre -āvī -ātus *tr* (inl-) to illuminate, light up, make bright; to illustrate

illūsī *perf of* **illudo**

illūsi·ō -ōnis *f* (inl-) irony

illustr·is -is -e *adj* (inl-) bright, clear, brilliant; plain, distinct, evident; distinguished, famous, illustrious, noble

illustr·ō -āre -āvī -ātus *tr* (inl-) to light up, illuminate; to make clear, clear up, explain; to make famous; to embellish

illūsus *pp of* **illudo**

illuvi·ēs -ēī *f* (inl-) filth, dirtiness; mud; inundation; *(of a person) (pej)* scum

illuxī *perf of* **illucesco**

Illyric·us -a -um *adj* Illyrian **ǁ** *n* Illyria

Illyri·us -a -um *adj & m* Illyrian **ǁ** *f* Illyria *(on the E. coast of the Adriatic Sea)*

Īl·us -ī *m* son of Tros, father of Laomedon, and founder of Ilium **ǁ** Ascanius

-im *advl suf*

imāgināri·us -a -um *adj* imaginary

imāginātiōn·ēs -um *fpl* imaginings

imāgin·or -ārī -ātus sum *tr* to imagine

imāg·ō -inis *f* image, likeness, picture, bust; bust of ancestor; ghost, vision; echo; appearance, semblance, shadow; mental picture, concept, thought, idea; figure of speech, simile, metaphor

imbēcillit·ās -ātis *f* (inb-) weakness, feebleness; helplessness

imbēcill·us -a -um *adj* (inb-) weak, feeble; helpless; *(of medicine)* ineffective

imbell·is -is -e *adj* (inb-) anti-war; unwarlike; peaceful, quiet; ineffective *(weapon); (pej)* unfit for war, soft

im·ber -bris *m* rain, rainstorm; *(lit & fig)* shower; rain cloud; rainwater; water *(in general);* snowstorm; hail-storm; flood of tears

imberb·is -is -e *or* **imberb·us -a -um** *adj* (inb-) beardless

imbib·ō -ĕre -ī *tr* (inb-) to imbibe, drink in; (animo) imbibere to absorb, form *(e.g., an opinion)*

imbit·ō -ĕre *tr* (inb-) to enter

imbr·ex -icis *f* tile

imbric·us -a -um *adj* rainy

imbrif·er -era -erum *adj* rainy

im·buō -buĕre -buī -būtus *tr* to wet, soak; to dip; to moisten; to stain, taint, infect; to imbue, fill, steep; to instruct; *(w. ad)* to introduce to

imitābil·is -is -e *adj* imitable, capable of being imitated

imitām·en -inis *n* imitation, copy; image, likeness

imitāment·um -ī *n* imitation **ǁ** *npl* pretense

imitāti·ō -ōnis *f* imitation; mimicking, copying; copy, counterfeit

imitāt·or -ōris *m,* **imitātr·ix -īcis** *f* imitator

imitāt·us -a -um *adj* fictitious, copied

imit·or -ārī -ātus sum *tr* to imitate, copy; to portray; to ape

immad·escō -escĕre -uī *intr* (inm-) to become wet

immāne *adv* (inm-) savagely

immān·is -is -e *adj* (inm-) huge, enormous, monstrous; inhuman, savage

immānit·ās -ātis *f* (inm-) vastness, enormity; savageness, cruelty

immansuēt·us -a -um *adj* (inm-) untamed, savage, wild

immātūrit·ās -ātis *f* (inm-) immaturity; prematureness; overanxiousness

immātūr·us -a -um *adj* (inm-) immature; unripe; premature

immedicābil·is -is -e *adj* (inm-) incurable

immem·or -oris *adj* (inm-) forgetful, forgetting; negligent, heedless; **immemor patriae** forgetting (one's) country

immemorābil·is -is -e *adj* (inm-) not worth mentioning; untold

immemorāt·a -ōrum *npl* (inm-) novelties, things hitherto untold

immensit·ās -ātis *f* (inm-) immensity **ǁ** *fpl* immense stretches

immens·us -a -um *adj* (inm-) immense, unending, immeasurable, huge **ǁ** *n* infinity, infinite space

immer·ens -entis *adj* (inm-) undeserving, innocent

immer·gō -gĕre -sī -sus *tr* (inm-) to immerse, dip, plunge; to overwhelm, drown; *(w. in + acc)* to dip *(s.th.)* into **ǁ** *refl (w. in + acc)* 1 to plunge into; 2 to insinuate oneself into

immeritō *adv* (inm-) undeservedly, innocently

immerit·us -a -um *adj* (inm-) undeserving, innocent; undeserved; **immerito meo** through no fault of mine
immersābil·is -is -e *adj* (inm-) unsinkable
immersī *perf of* immergo
immersus *pp of* immergo
immētāt·us -a -um *adj* (inm-) unmeasured, undivided
immigr·ō -āre -āvī -ātum *intr* (inm-) to immigrate; *(w.* in + *acc)* **1** to move into; **2** to invade
immin·eō -ēre *intr* (inm-) to project, stick out; to be near, be imminent; to threaten, menace; *(w. dat)* **1** to look out over, overlook *(a view);* **2** to hover over, loom over, threaten; *(w. dat or* in + *acc)* to be intent on, be eager for
immin·uō -uĕre -uī -ūtus *tr* (inm-) to lessen, curtail; to weaken, impair; to infringe upon, encroach upon, violate, subvert, destroy
imminūti·ō -ōnis *f* (inm-) lessening; mutilation; *(rhet)* understatement
im·misceō -miscēre -miscuī -mixtus *tr* (inm-) to mix in, intermix, blend; *(fig)* to mix up, confuse; **manūs manibus immiscere** *(of boxers)* to mix it up **ll** *refl & pass (w. dat)* **1** to join, join in with, mingle with, get lost in *(e.g., a crowd);* **2** to blend with, disappear in *(e.g., the night, a cloud)*
immiserābil·is -is -e *adj* (inm-) unpitied
immisericorditer *adv* (inm-) unmercifully
immisericor·s -dis *adj* (inm-) merciless
immīsī *perf of* immitto
immissi·ō -ōnis *f* (inm-) letting *(e.g., saplings)* grow
immissus *pp of* immitto
immīt·is -is -e *adj* (inm-) unripe, sour, green *(fruit);* sour *(wine);* harsh; rude; cruel, ruthless, pitiless
im·mittō -mittĕre -mīsī -missus *tr* (inm-) to send *(to or into);* to steer *(a ship);* to guide *(a horse);* to insert; to let in, let go in, admit; to let go of, let drop; to let fly, throw; to let *(death, ills)* loose *(on);* to direct the flow of *(water, air, etc., into or against);* **habenas immittere** to slacken the reins **ll** *refl & pass* to go *(into);* to leap *(into);* *(geog)* to extend *(to, into)*
immixtus (inm-) *pp of* immisceo
immō *adv (in contradiction or correction of preceding words)* nay, on the contrary, or rather, more precisely; *(in confirmation of preceding words)* quite so, yes indeed; **immo vero** yes and in fact
immōbil·is -is -e *adj* (inm-) motionless, unshaken; immovable; fixed, unalterable; clumsy, unwieldy
immoderātē *adv* (inm-) immoderately
immoderāti·ō -ōnis *f* (inm-) lack of moderation, excess

immoderāt·us -a -um *adj* (inm-) unmeasured, limitless; immoderate, uncontrolled, excessive
immodestē *adv* (inm-) immoderately, shamelessly
immodesti·a -ae *f* (inm-) lack of self-control; excesses; insubordination
immodest·us -a -um *adj* (inm-) immoderate, uncontrolled
immodicē *adv* (inm-) excessively
immodic·us -a -um *adj* (inm-) huge, enormous; immoderate, excessive; *(w. gen or abl)* given to, excessive in
immodulāt·us -a -um *adj* (inm-) unrhythmical
immolāti·ō -ōnis *f* (inm-) sacrifice
immolāt·or -ōris *m* (inm-) sacrificer
immōlīt·us -a -um *adj* (inm-) constructed, erected **ll** *npl* buildings
immol·ō *or* inmol·ō -āre -āvī -ātus *tr* (inm-) to sprinkle the feet of *(the victim)* with coarse flour in preparation for sacrifice; to immolate, sacrifice
immor·deō -dēre — -sus *tr* to bite into; *(fig)* stimulate
immor·ior -ī -tuus sum *intr* (inm-) *(w. dat)* to die in, die upon; *(fig)* to get sick over
immor·or -ārī -ātus sum *intr* (inm-) *(w. dat)* to dwell upon
immors·us -a -um *adj* bitten into; excited, stimulated
immortāl·is -is -e *adj* (inm-) immortal
immortālit·ās -ātis *f* (inm-) immortality
immortāliter *adv (coll)* (inm-) infinitely, eternally
immortuus (inm-) *pp of* immorior
immōt·us -a -um *adj* (inm-) unmoved, immovable; unshaken, undisturbed, steadfast
immūg·iō -īre -īvī *or* -iī -ītum *intr* (inm-) to bellow; to roar
immulg·eō -ēre *tr* (inm-) to milk
immunditi·a -ae *f* (inm-) dirtiness, filth
immund·us -a -um *adj* (inm-) dirty, filthy
immūn·iō -īre -īvī *or* -iī *tr* (inm-) to reinforce, fortify
immūn·is -is -e *adj* (inm-) without duty *or* office; tax-exempt; free, exempt; pure, innocent; *(w. abl or* ab) free from, exempt from; *(w. gen)* **1** free of, free from; **2** devoid of, without; **3** having no share in
immūnit·ās -ātis *f* (inm-) immunity, exemption; exemption from tribute
immūnīt·us -a -um *adj* (inm-) unfortified; unpaved *(road)*
immurmur·ō -āre *intr* (inm-) to grumble; *(w. dat) (of the wind)* to whisper among
immūtābil·is -is -e *adj* (inm-) immutable, unchangeable; changed
immūtābilit·ās -ātis *f* (inm-) immutability

immūtāti·ō -ōnis *f* **(inm-)** exchange, substitution; *(rhet)* metonymy

immūtāt·us -a -um *adj* **(inm-)** unchanged

immūt·ō -āre -āvī -ātus *tr* **(inm-)** to change, alter; to substitute

inm- = imm-

impācāt·us -a -um *adj* **(inp-)** unsubdued

impactus *pp of* **impingo**

impall·escō -escĕre -uī *intr* **(inp-)** *(w. abl)* to turn pale at

imp·ār -aris *adj* **(inp-)** uneven, odd *(numbers);* uneven *(in size or length);* unlike *(in color or appearance);* unequal; unfair; ill-matched; crooked; *(w. dat)* **1** not a match for, inferior to; **2** unable to cope with

imparāt·us -a -um *adj* **(inp-)** unprepared

impariter *adv* **(inp-)** unequally

impast·us -a -um *adj* **(inp-)** unfed, hungry

impati·ens -entis *adj* **(inp-)** impatient; *(w. gen)* **1** impatient with; **2** unable to endure, unable to take *(e.g., the heat);* **impatiens irae** unable to restrain one's anger

impatienter *adv* **(inp-)** impatiently; intolerably

impatienti·a -ae *f* **(inp-)** *(w. gen)* inability *or* unwillingness to endure

impavidē *adv* **(inp-)** fearlessly

impavid·us -a -um *adj* **(inp-)** fearless, undismayed

impedīment·um -ī *n* **(inp-)** impediment, hindrance; difficulty **‖** *npl* baggage; mule train

imped·iō -īre -īvī *or* **-iī -ītus** *tr* **(inp-)** to entangle; to hamper, hinder; to entwine, encircle; to clasp, embrace; to block *(road);* to hinder, prevent; to embarrass; *(w. ne, quin, or quominus)* to prevent *(s.o.)* from

impedīti·ō -ōnis *f* **(inp-)** hindrance **‖** *npl* cases of obstruction

impedīt·us -a -um *adj* **(inp-)** hampered; obstructed, blocked; difficult, intricate; impassable; busy, occupied

impēgī (inp-) *perf of* **impingo**

im·pellō -pellĕre -(pe)pulī -pulsus *tr* **(inp-)** to strike against, strike; to reach *(the ears);* to push, drive, drive forward, impel, propel; to urge, persuade; to stimulate, induce; to force, compel; to put to rout; to swell *(sails)*

impend·eō -ēre *intr* **(inp-)** to be near, be at hand, be imminent, threaten; *(w. dat)* to hang over; *(w. dat or* **in** *+ acc)* to hover over, loom over

impendiōs·us -a -um *adj* **(inp-)** extravagant, free-spending

impend·ium -(i)ī *n* **(inp-)** expense, cost, outlay; interest *(paid out);* loss

impen·dō -dĕre -dī -sus *tr* **(inp-)** to weigh out, pay out; to expend, devote, apply, employ; *(w.* **in** *+ acc)* **1** to spend *(money)*

on; **2** to expend *(effort)* on; **3** to pay *(attention)* to

impenetrābil·is -is -e *adj* **(inp-)** impenetrable

impens·a -ae *f* **(inp-)** expense, cost, outlay; waste; contribution; **impensam facere** to incur an expense; **meis impensis** at my expense

impensē *adv* **(inp-)** at a high cost, expensively; with great effort

impens·us -a -um *pp of* **impendo ‖** *adj* high, costly, expensive; strong, vehement; earnest **‖** *n* high price

imper·ans -antis *m* **(inp-)** master, ruler

imperāt·or -ōris *m* **(inp-)** commander, general; commander in chief; emperor; director; master, ruler

imperātōri·us -a -um *adj* **(inp-)** of a general, general's; imperial

imperātr·ix -īcis *f* **(inp-)** controller, mistress

imperāt·um -ī *n* **(inp-)** command, order

impercept·us -a -um *adj* **(inp-)** unperceived, unknown

imperc·ō -ĕre *intr* **(w. dat) (inp-)** to spare, take it easy on

impercuss·us -a -um *adj* **(inp-)** noiseless

imperdit·us -a -um *adj* **(inp-)** not killed, unscathed

imperfect·us -a -um *adj* **(inp-)** unfinished; imperfect; undigested *(food)*

imperfoss·us -a -um *adj* **(inp-)** unpierced, not stabbed

imperiōs·us -a -um *adj* **(inp-)** masterful, commanding; imperial; magisterial; tyrannical, overbearing, domineering, imperious

imperītē *adv* **(inp-)** unskillfully, clumsily; in an ignorant manner

imperīti·a -ae *f* **(inp-)** inexperience, awkwardness, ignorance

imperit·ō -āre -āvī -ātus *tr & intr* **(inp-)** to command, rule, govern

imperīt·us -a -um *adj* **(inp-)** inexperienced, unfamiliar, ignorant, unskilled; *(w. gen)* inexperienced in, unacquainted with, ignorant of

imper·ium -(i)ī *n* **(inp-)** supreme administrative power *(exercised by the kings, subsequently by certain magistrates and provincial governors, and later by Roman emperors);* absolute authority *(in any sphere);* dominion, sway, government; empire; command, order; right to command; authority; exercise of authority; military commission, military command; mastery; sovereignty; realm, dominion; public office, magistracy; term of office

imperjūrāt·us -a -um *adj* **(inp-)** sacrosanct

impermiss·us -a -um *adj* **(inp-)** forbidden

imper·ō -āre -āvī -ātus *tr* **(inp-)** to requisition, give orders for, order, demand; *(w. acc of thing and dat of source demanded from)* to demand *(e.g., hostages)* from **ll** *intr* to be in command, rule, be master; *(w. dat)* to give orders to, order, command, govern, master, exercise control over; *(gram)* to express a command

imperterrit·us -a -um *adj* (inp-) undaunted, fearless

impert·iō -īre *tr* (inp-) *(w. dat)* to impart, communicate, bestow, assign, direct *(s.th.)* to, share *(s.th.)* with; *(w. acc of person and abl of thing)* to present *(s.o.)* with

imperturbāt·us -a -um *adj* (inp-) unperturbed, unruffled

impervi·us -a -um *adj* (inp-) impassable; *(w. dat)* impervious to

impete *(abl singl)* m with an assault, with a charge

impetibil·is -is -e *adj* (inp-) intolerable

impet·ō -ĕre *tr* (inp-) to make for; to attack

impetrābil·is -is -e *adj* (inp-) obtainable; successful

impetrāti·ō -ōnis *f* (inp-) obtaining one's request

impetr·iō -īre *tr* (inp-) to try to obtain through favorable omens

impetr·ō -āre -āvī -ātus *tr* (inp-) to obtain, procure *(by asking)*; to achieve, accomplish, bring to pass

impet·us -ūs *m* (inp-) attack, assault; rush; impetus; impetuosity, vehemence, vigor; violence, fury, force; wide expanse *(of sea, sky)*; *(w. gen)* sudden burst of; *(w. inf or ad)* impulse to *(do s.th.)*; **animi impetus** impulse, urge; **omni impetu** with all one's might

impex·us -a -um *adj* (inp-) uncombed, unkempt, tangled

impiē *adv* (inp-) wickedly

impiet·ās -ātis *f* (inp-) impiety, irreverence, lack of respect; disloyalty

impi·ger -gra -grum *adj* (inp-) diligent, active, energetic

impigrē *adv* (inp-) energetically, actively

impigrit·ās -ātis *f* (inp-) energy, activity

im·pingō -pingĕre -pēgī -pactus *tr* (inp-) *(w. dat or in + acc)* **1** to fasten to; **2** to pin against, force against, dash against; **3** to press *or* force *(s.th.)* on; **4** to fling at

impi·ō -āre -āvī -ātus *tr* (inp-) to desecrate; to make disrespectful

impi·us -a -um *adj* (inp-) impious, godless, irreverent, disrespectful; disobedient; disloyal; wicked, unscrupulous; **Tartara impia** Tartarus, the abode of the impious

implācāt·us -a -um *adj* (inp-) implacable, inexorable, insatiable

implacid·us -a -um *adj* (inp-) restless; rough, wild

impl·eō -ēre -ēvī -ētus *tr* (inp-) to fill up; to satisfy; to fatten; to make pregnant; to enrich; to cover with writing, fill up *(a book)*; to discharge, execute, implement; to complete, end; to occupy, take up *(time)*; to make up, amount to; to fulfill, satisfy *(wishes, hopes, prophecies, appetites)*

implex·us -a -um *adj* (inp-) entwined; involved

implicāti·ō -ōnis *f* (inp-) interweaving; network; **implicatio rei familiaris** financial embarrassment

implicāt·us -a -um *adj* (inp-) involved, intricate

implicisc·or -ī *intr* (inp-) to become confused

implicitē *adv* (inp-) intricately

implicitus *pp of* implico **ll** *adj* confused; **implicitus morbo** disabled by sickness

implic·ō -āre -āvī -ātus *or* -āre -uī -itus *tr* (inp-) to entwine, wrap; to intertwine; to involve; to envelop; to embrace, clasp, grasp; to connect, join, unite; to implicate; to kindle *(a fire)* **ll** *refl* **se dextrae implicare** to clasp *(s.o.'s)* right hand **ll** *pass* to be intimately associated; to be embroiled

implōrāti·ō -ōnis *f* (inp-) imploring

implōr·ō -āre -āvī -ātus *tr* (inpl-) to implore, appeal to; *(w. double acc)* to beg *(s.o.)* for; *(w. ab)* to ask for *(s.th.)* from

impl·uit -uĕre -uit *or* -ūvit -ūtum *intr* (inp-) *(w. dat)* to rain on

implūm·is -is -e *adj* (inp-) featherless, unfledged; without wings

impluviāt·us -a -um *adj* (inpl-) square, shaped like an impluvium

impluv·ium -(i)ī *n* (inp-) impluvium, rain basin *(square basin built into the floor of the atrium to hold rain water; (rarely = **compluvium:** square opening in the roof of the atrium of a Roman house to get rid of smoke and let in light and air)*

impolītē *adv* (inp-) simply, without fancy words

impolīt·us -a -um *adj* (inp-) unpolished, rough; lacking culture; *(of materials)* in the crude state

impollūt·us -a -um *adj* (inp-) unsullied

im·pōnō -pōnĕre -posuī -positus *or* -postus *tr* (inp-) to impose; *(w. dat or in + acc)* to place on, lay on, set on; *(w. dat or super + acc)* to build *(house, bridge, city)* on; *(w. dat or ad)* to station *(soldiers)* in *or* at; *(w. dat or ad or in + acc)* to apply *(remedies)* to; *(w. dat)* **1** to place *(s.o.)* in command *or* control of, put *(s.o.)* in charge of; **2** to put *(garments)* on *(s.o.)*; **3** to impose *(taxes, terms, laws, responsibilites, limits, etc.)* on; **4** to inflict *(wounds, blows, punishment)* on; *(w. dat, w. in + acc, in + abl, or supra +*

acc) to place, put, set, lay *(s.th. or s.o.)* on **ll** *intr (w. dat)* **1** to impose upon; **2** to trick, cheat

import·ō -āre -āvī -ātus *tr* **(inp-)** to bring in, import; to introduce; to bring about, cause; *(w. dat)* to inflict *(damage, trouble)* on

importūnit·ās -ātis *f* **(inp-)** importunity, rudeness, insolence; unfitness

importūn·us -a -um *adj* **(inp-)** inconvenient; unsuitable, out of place; troublesome, annoying; lacking consideration for others, rude, ruthless; stormy *(weather);* grim *(looks);* ill-omened

importuōs·us -a -um *adj* **(inp-)** without a harbor

imp·os -otis *adj* **(inp-)** out of control; *(w. gen)* not having control of; **impos animi** *(or* **mentis** *or* **sui)** out of one's mind

impositus (inp-) *pp of* **impono** **ll** *adj* situated, located

impossibil·is -is -e *adj* **(inp-)** impossible

impostus *pp of* **impono**

imposuī *perf of* **impono**

impot·ens -entis *adj* **(inp-)** impotent, powerless; lacking self-control, uncontrollable, wild, violent; *(w. gen)* having no control over; **impotens sui** *(or* **animi)** out of one's mind

impotenter *adv* **(inp-)** impotently, weakly; without self-control, lawlessly, intemperately

impotenti·a -ae *f* **(inp-)** weakness, helplessness; lack of self-control, violence, fury, lawlessness

impraesentiārum *adv* **(inp-)** for the present, under present circumstances

imprans·us -a -um *adj* **(inp-)** without breakfast *or* lunch, fasting

imprecāti·ō -ōnis *f* **(inp-)** the calling down of curses, imprecation

imprec·or -ārī -ātus sum *tr* **(inp-)** to call down *(a curse);* to invoke

impressī *perf of* **imprimo**

impressi·ō -ōnis *f* **(inp-)** pressure; attack, charge; rhythmical beat; emphasis; impression *(on the mind)*

impressus *pp of* **imprimo**

imprīmīs *or* **in prīmīs** *adv* **(inp-)** in the first place; chiefly, especially

im·primō -primere -pressī -pressus *tr* **(inp-)** to press down; to impress, imprint, stamp *(a seal, marks, patterns);* to thrust, drive in *(esp. weapons);* to plant *(the feet, kisses);* *(fig)* to impress; **animum quasi ceram imprimere** to impress the mind like wax

improbāti·ō -ōnis *f* **(inp-)** disapproval; *(leg)* discrediting *(of a witness)*

improbē *adv* **(inp-)** badly, wickedly, wrongfully; recklessly; persistently

improbit·ās -ātis *f* **(inp-)** wickedness, depravity; roguishness

improb·ō -āre -āvī -ātus *tr* **(inp-)** to disapprove of, condemn, blame, reject

improbul·us -a -um *adj* **(inp-)** somewhat impudent, naughty

improb·us -a -um *adj* below standard, inferior; bad, shameless; rebellious, unruly; restless, indomitable, self-willed; cruel, merciless; persistent; disloyal, ill-disposed; *(of language)* offensively rude

imprōcēr·us -a -um *adj* **(inp-)** undersized

imprōdict·us -a -um *adj* **(inp-)** not postponed

imprompt·us -a -um *adj* **(inp-)** slow

improperāt·us -a -um *adj* **(inp-)** unhurried

impropri·us -a -um *adj* **(inp-)** *(gram)* improper, incorrect

improsp·er -era -erum *adj* **(inp-)** unfortunate

improsperē *adv* **(inp-)** unfortunately

imprōvidē *adv* **(inp-)** without foresight, thoughtlessly

imprōvid·us -a -um *adj* **(inp-)** not foreseeing, not anticipating; *(w. gen)* indifferent to

imprōvis·us -a -um *adj* **(inp-)** unexpected; **de improviso** *(or* **ex improviso** *or* **improviso)** unexpectedly **ll** *npl* emergencies

imprūd·ens -entis *adj* **(inp-)** not foreseeing, unsuspecting; off one's guard; inconsiderate; foolish, imprudent; *(w. gen)* **1** unaware of, ignorant of; **2** heedless of; **3** not experienced in

imprūdenter *adv* **(inp-)** without foresight, thoughtlessly, unintenionally; foolishly, imprudently

imprūdenti·a -ae *f* **(inp-)** thoughtlessness; ignorance, imprudence

impūb·ēs -eris *or* **impūb·is -is -e** *adj* **(inp-)** youthful, young, underage; beardless *(cheeks);* innocent, chaste, celibate, virgin; **anni impubes** childhood years

impud·ens -entis *adj* **(inp-)** shameless

impudenter *adv* **(inp-)** shamelessly, impudently; immodestly

impudenti·a -ae *f* **(inp-)** shamelessness, impudence; immodesty

impudīciti·a -ae *f* immodesty, lewdness, shamelessness

impudīc·us -a -um *adj* **(inp-)** immodest, lewd, shameless

impugnāti·ō -ōnis *f* **(inp-)** assault, attack

impugn·ō -āre -āvī -ātus *tr* **(inp-)** to assault, attack; *(fig)* to impugn; *(w. acc & inf)* to assert in opposition *(that)*

impulsi·ō -ōnis *f* **(inp-)** pressure; impulse

impuls·or -ōris *m* **(inp-)** instigator

impulsus *pp of* **impello**

impuls·us -ūs *m* **(inp-)** blow, impact, shock; impulse; instigation, incitement

impūne *adv* **(inp-)** with impunity, unpunished, scot-free; safely, unscathed

impūnit·ās -ātis *f* (inp-) impunity
impūnītē *adv* (inp-) with impunity
impūnīt·us -a -um *adj* (inp-) unpunished; unrestrained; safe
impurāt·us -a -um *adj* (inp-) filthy
impūrē *adv* (inp-) impurely
impūrit·ās -ātis *f* (inp-) impurity
impūriti·ae -ārum *fpl* (inp-) filth
impūr·us -a -um *adj* (inp-) impure; unclean, filthy
imputāt·us -a -um *adj* (inp-) unpruned, untrimmed
imput·ō -āre -āvī -ātus *tr* (inp-) to charge to someone's account, enter in an account; *(w. dat)* 1 to charge to; 2 to ascribe to; 3 to give credit for *(s.th.)* to; 4 to put the blame for *(s.th.)* on
īmul·us -a -um *adj* cute little
īm·us -a -um *adj* deepest, lowest; last; the bottom of, the foot of, the tip of **ll** *n* bottom, depth; **ab imo** utterly; **ab immo ad summum** from top to bottom; **ex imo** utterly, completely **ll** *npl* lower world
in *prep (w. abl)* 1 in, on, upon; 2 among; 3 at; 4 before; 5 under; 6 *(of time)* during, within, in, at, in the course of, on the point of; 7 in case of; 8 in relation to; 9 subject to; 10 affected by; 11 engaged in, involved in **ll** *(w. acc)* 1 into; 2 up to, as far as *(a point of space or time);* 3 *(indicating person towards whom feelings are directed)* towards, to, for; 4 until; 5 about, respecting; 6 *(w. verbs of opposition or hostility)* against; 7 for, with a view to; 8 according to, after; *(w. verbs of sending, traveling)* to *(a country, city);* 9 *(w. verbs of spending)* on; 10 *(w. verbs of distributing)* among
in- *pref* (n *is assimilated to following* l, m, *and* r; *becomes* m *before* b *and* p; *disappears before* gn) 1 *combines, usu. with verbs, in the local or figurative senses of the preposition, e.g.,* inaedificare to build in *(a place); also with intensive force, e.g.,* increpare to make a loud noise; 2 *inchoative:* insudare to begin to sweat, break out in a sweat; 3 *negative or privative pref, e.g.:* incognitus unknown
inaccess·us -a -um *adj* inaccessible
inac·escō -escĕre -uī *intr* to turn sour
Īnachid·ēs -ae *m* descendant of Inachus *(esp.* Perseus and Epaphus)
Īnach·us *or* Īnach·os -ī *m* first king of Argos and father of Io
inacuī *perf of* inacesco
inadsc- = inasc-
inadt- = inatt-
inadust·us -a -um *adj* unburned
inaedific·ō -āre -āvī -ātus *tr* to build on, build as an addition, erect, construct; to wall up, barricade; *(w. in + abl)* to build *(s.th.)* on top of
inaequābil·is -is -e *adj* uneven

inaequābiliter *adv* unevenly, unequally
inaequāl·is -is -e *adj* uneven, unequal; unlike; changeable, inconstant
inaequālit·ās -ātis *f* unevenness
inaequāliter *adv* unevenly
inaequāt·us -a -um *adj* unequal
inaequ·ō -āre -āvī -ātus *tr* to level off
inaestimābil·is -is -e *adj* inestimable; invaluable; valueless
inaestu·ō -āre *intr* to seethe; to flare up
inaffectāt·us -a -um *adj* unaffected, natural
inamābil·is -is -e *adj* hateful, revolting
inamāresc·ō -ĕre *intr* to become bitter
inambitiōs·us -a -um *adj* unambitious
inambulāti·ō -ōnis *f* walking about, strutting about
inambul·ō -āre -āvī *intr* to walk up and down; to stroll about
inamoen·us -a -um *adj* unpleasant
ināni·ae -ārum *fpl* emptiness
inānilogist·a -ae *m* chatterbox
inānīment·um -ī *n* empty space
inanim·us -a -um *adj* inanimate
inān·is -is -e *adj* empty, void; deserted, abandoned, unoccupied; hollow; worthless, idle; lifeless, unsubstantial; penniless; unprofitable; groundless **ll** *n* empty space, vacuum; emptiness; worthlessness
inānit·ās -ātis *f* empty space, emptiness; uselessness, worthlessness
ināniter *adv* uselessly, vainly
inarāt·us -a -um *adj* untilled, unplowed
inar·descō -descĕre -sī *intr* to catch fire, burn, glow
ināresc·ō -ĕre *intr* to become dry, dry up
inarsī *perf of* inardesco
inascens·us -a -um *adj* not climbed
inassuēt·us -a -um *adj* unaccustomed
inattenuāt·us -a -um *adj* undiminished; unappeased
inaud·ax -ācis *adj* timid
inaud·iō - īre -īvī *or* -iī -ītus *tr* (indau-) to hear, learn, get wind of
inaudīt·us -a -um *adj* unheard-of, unprecedented; unusual; without a court hearing
inaugurātō *adv* after taking the auspices
inaugur·ō -āre -āvī -ātus *tr* to inaugurate, consecrate, install **ll** *intr* to take the auspices
inaurāt·us -a -um *adj* gilded, gilt
inaur·es -ium *fpl* earrings
inaur·ō -āre -āvī -ātus *tr* to goldplate, gild; to line the pockets of *(s.o.)* with gold
inauspicātō *adv* without consulting the auspices
inauspicāt·us -a -um *adj* undertaken without auspices; unlucky
inaus·us -a -um *adj* unattempted
inb- = imb-

incaedu·us -a -um *adj* uncut, unfelled
incal·escō -escĕre -uī *intr* to get warm, get hot; to get excited
incalfac·iō -ĕre *tr* to warm, heat
incallidē *adv* unskillfully
incallid·us -a -um *adj* unskillful; stupid, simple, clumsy
incand·escō -ĕscere -uī *intr* to become white; to get white-hot
incantāt·us -a -um *adj* enchanted
incān·us -a -um *adj* grown gray
incassum *adv* in vain
incastīgāt·us -a -um *adj* unscolded, unpunished
incautē *adv* incautiously, recklessly
incaut·us -a -um *adj* incautious, inconsiderate, thoughtless, reckless; unforeseen, unexpected; unguarded
in·cēdō -cēdĕre -cessī -cessum *intr* to go, walk, move; to step, stride, strut; to proceed; to come along, happen, occur, appear, arrive; to advance, go on; (*of troops*) to march, advance
incelebrāt·us -a -um *adj* unheralded
incēnāt·us -a -um *adj* supperless
incendiārius -(i)ī *m* agitator; arsonist
incend·ium -(i)ī *n* fire; heat
incen·dō -dĕre -dī -sus *tr* to light, set on fire, burn; to light up, make bright; (*fig*) to inflame, fire up, excite, enrage
incēn·is -is -e *adj* dinnerless
incensi·ō -ōnis *f* burning
incensus *pp of* **incendo**
incens·us -a -um *adj* not registered (*w. the censor*)
incepti·ō -ōnis *f* inception, beginning; undertaking
incept·ō -āre -āvī -ātus *tr* to begin; to undertake
incept·or -ōris *m* beginner, originator
incept·us -a -um *pp of* **incipio** ‖ *n* beginning; undertaking, attempt, enterprise; subject, theme
in·cernō -cernĕre -crēvī -crētus *tr* to sift
incēr·ō -āre -āvī -ātus *tr* to wax, cover with wax, coat with wax
incertē *adv* uncertainly
incertō *adv* uncertainly
incert·ō -āre -āvī -ātus *tr* to render doubtful, make uncertain
incert·us -a -um *adj* uncertain; vague, obscure; doubtful; unsure, hesitant ‖ *n* uncertainty, insecurity; contingency; **in incertum** for an indefinite time
incessī *perf of* **incedo**
incess·ō -ĕre -ī *or* **-īvī** *or* **-uī** *tr* to fall upon, assault; to reproach, accuse, attack
incess·us -ūs *m* walk, gait, pace; trampling; invasion, attack; advance; procession
incestē *adv* impurely, sinfully; indecently
in·cīdō -cidĕre -cidī -cāsum *intr* to happen, occur; (*w.* **ad** *or* **in** + *acc*) to fall

into, fall upon; (*w.* **in** + *acc*) 1 to come upon unexpectedly, fall in with; 2 to attack; (*w.* **dat** *or* **in** + *acc*) 1 to occur to attack; (*mentally*); 2 to fall on (*a certain day*); 3 to befall, happen to; 4 to agree with
incī·dō -dĕre -dī -sus *tr* to carve, engrave, inscribe; to cut, sever; (*fig*) to cut into, cut short, put an end to, break off, interrupt
incīl·e -is *n* ditch, trench
incin·gō -gĕre -xī -ctus *tr* to drape; to wreathe; to invest, surround
incin·ō -ĕre *tr* to sing; to play
incipessō *see* **incipisso**
in·cipiō -cipĕre -cēpī -ceptus *tr & intr* to begin, start
incipiss·ō -ĕre *tr* to begin
incīsē *or* **incīsim** *adv* in short phrases
incīsi·ō -ōnis *f* incision; (*rhet*) short phrase
incīsus *pp of* **incīdo**
incitāment·um -ī *n* incentive
incitāti·ō -ōnis *f* inciting, rousing; speed
incitāt·us -a -um *adj* rapid, speedy; **equo incitato** at full gallop
incit·ō -āre -āvī -ātus *tr* to incite, urge on, spur on, drive on; to stimulate; to inspire; to stir up, arouse; to increase; **currentem incitare** (*fig*) to spur a willing horse ‖ *refl* to rush
incit·us -a -um *adj* rapid, swift; immovable; **ad incita** (*or* **ad incitas**) **adigere** to bring to a standstill
inclāmit·ō -āre -āvī -ātus *tr* to cry out against, revile, abuse
inclām·ō -āre -āvī -ātus *tr* to call out to; to invoke; to shout at, scold, revile ‖ *intr* to yell
inclār·escō -escĕre -uī *intr* to become famous
inclēm·ens -entis *adj* harsh, unmerciful; violent (*movement*)
inclēmenter *adv* harshly; rudely
inclēmenti·a -ae *f* harshness, cruelty
inclīnāti·ō -ōnis *f* leaning; inclination, tendency, bias; change; (*gram*) inflection
inclīnāt·us -a -um *adj* inclined, prone; sinking; low, deep; (*gram*) inflected
inclīn·ō -āre -āvī -ātus *tr* to bend, turn; to turn back, drive back, repulse; to shift (*e.g., blame*); to change; (*gram*) to inflect (*nouns or verbs*) ‖ *refl & pass* to lean, bend, turn; to change (*esp. for the worse*) ‖ *pass* (*mil*) to fall back ‖ *intr* to bend, turn, lean, dip, sink; to change, deteriorate; to change for the better
inclit·us -a -um *adj* famous
inclū·dō -dĕre -sī -sus *tr* to shut in, confine, lock up; to include; to insert; to block, shut off, obstruct; to restrain, control; to close, end (*e.g., a day*)
inclūsi·ō -ōnis *f* locking up, confinement
inclut·us -a -um *adj* famous

incoct·us -a -um pp of **incoquo** ‖ adj uncooked, raw; undigested

incōgitābil·is -is -e adj thoughtless, inconsiderate

incōgit·ans -antis adj unthinking, thoughtless

incōgitanti·a -ae f thoughtlessness

incōgitāt·us -a -um adj thoughtless, inconsiderate

incōgit·ō -āre -āvī -ātus tr to think up

incognit·us -a -um adj not investigated; unknown, unrecognized, unidentified, incognito; unparalleled

incohāt·us or **inchoāt·us -a -um** adj only begun, unfinished, imperfect; temporary (structure)

incoh·ō -āre -āvī -ātus tr to begin

incol·a -ae mf inhabitant; resident alien

incol·ō -ěre -uī tr to live in, inhabit, occupy ‖ intr to live, reside

incolum·is -is -e adj unharmed, safe and sound, unscathed, alive; (w. abl) safe from

incolumit·ās -ātis f safety

incomitāt·us -a -um adj unaccompanied

incommendāt·us -a -um adj unprotected

incommodē adv at the wrong time; inconveniently; annoyingly; improperly; unfortunately

incommodestic·us -a -um adj (coll) illtimed, inconvenient

incommodit·ās -ātis f inconvenience; unsuitableness; disadvantage

incommod·ō -āre -āvī -ātum intr (w. dat) to inconvenience, be inconvenient for, be annoying to

incommod·us -a -um adj inconvenient; troublesome, tiresome, annoying; disadvantageous, unfavorable; unpleasant, disagreeable ‖ n inconvenience, discomfort; disadvantage; misfortune, trouble; (med) ailment; (mil) setback, disaster

incommūtābil·is -is -e adj unchangeable

incomparābil·is -is -e adj unequaled, incomparable

incompert·us -a -um adj unknown, undetermined; forgotten

incompositē adv in disorder

incomposit·us -a -um adj disordered, poorly arranged, poorly written; clumsy, awkward (movements); disorganized (troops)

incomprehensibil·is -is -e adj incomprehensible

incompt·us -a -um adj unkempt, messy; untidy; simple, unstudied; unpolished (writing, speech)

inconcess·us -a -um adj forbidden, unlawful

inconcili·ō -āre -āvī -ātus tr to deceive, trick; to rob, fleece

inconcinn·us -a -um adj clumsy, awkward; absurd

inconcuss·us -a -um adj unshaken

inconditē adv confusedly

incondit·us -a -um adj unorganized, disorderly, confused; irregular; rough, undeveloped (style); raw (jokes)

inconsīderātē adv thoughtlessly

inconsīderāt·us -a um adj thoughtless

inconsōlābil·is -is -e adj inconsolable; (fig) incurable

inconst·ans -antis adj inconsistent, fickle, shifty

inconstanter adv inconsistently

inconstanti·a -ae f inconsistency, fickleness

inconsultē adv indiscreetly

inconsult·us -a -um adj indiscreet, illadvised; not consulted

inconsult·us -ūs m lack of consultation; **inconsultu meo** without consulting me

inconsumpt·us -a -um adj unconsumed

incontāmināt·us -a -um adj untainted

incontent·us -a -um adj loose, untuned (string)

incontin·ens -entis adj intemperate

incontinenter adv without self-control, intemperately

incontinenti·a -ae f lack of self-control

inconveni·ens -entis adj unsuitable, dissimilar

inco·quō -quěre -xī -ctus tr to boil (in or with); to dye

incorrect·us -a -um adj uncorrected

incorruptē adv honestly, fairly

incorrupt·us -a -um adj intact, unspoiled, untainted; uncorrupted; not open to bribes, incorruptible; chaste; genuine, authentic

incoxī perf of **incoquo**

incrēb(r)·escō -escěre -uī intr to grow; to rise; to increase; to spread

incrēdibil·is -is -e adj incredible

incrēdibiliter adv incredibly

incrēdul·us -a -um adj incredulous

incrēment·um -ī n growth, increase; increment, addition; addition to the family, offspring

increpit·ō -āre -āvī -ātus tr to scold, rebuke

increp·ō -āre -uī or **-āvī -itus** or **-atus** tr to cause to make noise, cause to ring; to rattle; (of Jupiter) to thunder at; to scold, rebuke; to protest against; (of sounds) to strike (the ears); (w. acc & inf) to say reproachfully that, to remark indignantly that ‖ intr to make noise; to snap, rustle, rattle, clash; to speak angrily; (of a bow) to twang; (of flying object) to whiz, whir; **suspicio tumultūs increpat** the suspicion of a riot sounds the alarm

incr·escō -escěre -ēvī intr to grow, increase; (w. dat or abl) to grow in or upon

incrētus pp of **incerno**

incrēvī perf of **incerno** and **incresco**

incruentāt·us -a -um *adj* unbloodied
incruent·us -a -um *adj* bloodless, without bloodshed
incrust·ō -āre -āvī -ātus *tr* to coat, cover with a coat, encrust
incub·ō -āre -uī -itum *intr (w. dat)* 1 to lie in *or* upon; 2 to lean on; 3 to brood over; 4 to watch jealously over
incū·dō -děre -dī -sus *or* -ssus *tr* to indent by hammering; to emboss
inculc·ō -āre -āvī -ātus *tr* to impress, inculcate; *(w. dat)* to force *(s.th.)* upon
inculpāt·us -a -um *adj* blameless
incultē *adv* uncouthly, roughly
incult·us -a -um *adj* untilled, uncultivated; neglected, slovenly; rough, uneducated, uncivilized **ll** *npl* desert, wilderness, the wilds
incult·us -ūs *m* neglect; dirt, squalor
in·cumbō -cumběre -cubuī -cubitum *intr (w. dat or in + acc)* 1 to lean on *or* against; 2 to lie down on *(bed, couch);* 3 to bend to *(the oars);* 4 to light on, fall on; 5 *(fig)* to press upon, burden, oppress, weigh down; 6 to apply oneself to, take pains with; 7 to pay attention to; *(w. ad or in + acc)* to be inclined towards, lean towards
incūnābul·a -ōrum *npl* baby clothes; *(fig)* cradle, infancy; birthplace; origin, source
incūrāt·us -a -um *adj* neglected; uncured
incūri·a -ae *f* carelessness, negligence
incūriōsē *adv* carelessly
incūriōs·us -a -um *adj* careless, unconcerned, indifferent; neglected
in·currō -currěre -currī *or* -cucurrī -cursus *tr* to attack **ll** *intr (w. dat or in + acc)* 1 to run into, rush at, charge, attack; 2 to invade; 3 to extend to; 4 to meet, run into; 4 to fall on, coincide with
incursi·ō -ōnis *f* incursion, invasion, raid; attack; collision
incurs·ō -āre -āvī -ātus *tr* to attack; to invade **ll** *intr (w. dat or in + acc)* 1 to attack; 2 to run into, bump against; 3 to strike, meet *(e.g., the eyes);* 4 to affect, touch, move
incurs·us -ūs *m* attack; invasion, inroad, raid; collision, impact
incurv·ō -āre -āvī -ātus *tr* to bend, curve
incurv·us -a -um *adj* bent, crooked
inc·ūs -ūdis *f* anvil
incūsāti·ō -ōnis *f* accusation
incūs·ō -āre -āvī -ātus *tr* to blame, find fault with, accuse
incussī *perf of* incutio
incussus *pp of* incutio
incuss·us -ūs *m* shock
incustōdīt·us -a -um *adj* unguarded; unconcealed; imprudent
incūs·us -a -um *pp of* incudo **ll** *adj* forged; embossed; lapis incusus indented millstone

incu·tiō -těre -ssī -ssus *tr* to throw; to produce; *(w. dat or in + acc)* to strike *(s.th.)* on *or* against; *(w. dat)* 1 to strike into, instill in; 2 to throw at, to fling upon; metum incutere *(w. dat)* to strike fear into; scipione in caput alicujus incutere to beat s.o. over the head with a stick
indāgāti·ō -ōnis *f* investigation, search
indāgāt·or -ōris *m,* indāgātr·ix -īcis *f* investigator
indāg·ō -āre -āvī -ātus *tr* to track down, hunt; to investigate, explore
indāg·ō -inis *f* dragnet; indagine agere to ferret out
indaudiō *see* inaudio
inde *adv* from there; from that source, therefrom; from that time on, after that, thereafter; then; from that cause
indēbit·us -a -um *adj* that is not owed, not due
indec·ens -entis *adj* unbecoming, improper, indecent
indecenter *adv* improperly, indecently
indec·eō -ēre *tr* to be improper for **ll** *intr (w. dat)* to be inappropriate to
indēclīnāt·us -a -um *adj* unchanged, constant
indec·or -oris *or* indecor·is -is -e *adj* disgraceful, dishonorable, cowardly
indecōrē *adv* indecently, improperly
indecor·us -a -um *adj* unsightly
indecor·ō -āre -āvī -ātus *tr* to disgrace
indēfens·us -a -um *adj* undefended
indēfess·us -a -um *adj* tireless; not tired
indēflēt·us -a -um *adj* unwept
indēject·us -a -um *adj* undemolished
indēlēbil·is -is -e *adj* indestructible, indelible
indēlībāt·us -a -um *adj* undiminished
indemnāt·us -a -um *adj* unconvicted
indēplōrāt·us -a -um *adj* unwept
indēprens·us -a -um *adj* undetected
indeptus *pp of* indipiscor
indēsert·us -a -um *adj* unforsaken
indēspect·us -a -um *adj* unfathomable
indēstrict·us -a -um *adj* unscathed
indētons·us -a -um *adj* unshorn
indēvītāt·us -a -um *adj* unavoidable, unerring *(e.g., arrow)*
ind·ex -icis *m* index, sign, mark; indication, proof; title *(of book);* informer, spy; index finger
Indi·a -ae *f* India
indicāti·ō -ōnis *f* setting the price; statement, declaration
indīc·ens -entis *adj* not speaking; me indicente without a word from me
indic·ium -(i)ī *n* information, disclosure, evidence; indication, proof; permission to give evidence; reward for giving evidence; indicio esse to give evidence; to be an indication *or* proof; indicium

afferre *(or* deferre*)* to adduce evidence; indicium facere to give away a secret; to give an indication *or* warning

indic·ō -āre -āvī -ātus *tr* to point out; to reveal, disclose; to betray, inform against; to put a price on **‖** *intr* to give evidence

in·dīcō -dīcĕre -dixī -dictus *tr* to proclaim, announce, publish; to summon, convoke; to impose *(a fine);* bellum indicere to declare war; diem indicere to set a date

indict·us -a -um *adj* unsaid; causā indictā without a hearing

Indic·us -a -um *adj* Indian **‖** *m* Indian **‖** *n* indigo

indidem *adv* from the same place; from the same source, from the same thing

indiffer·ens -entis *adj* (morally) indifferent; unconcerned, indifferent

indigen·a -ae *adj masc & fem* native

indig·ens -entis *adj* indigent; *(w. gen)* in need of

indigenti·a -ae *f* indigence, need; craving

indig·eō -ēre -uī *intr (w. gen or abl)* 1 to need, be in need of; 2 to require; *(w. gen)* to crave, desire

indig·es -etis *adj* indigenous, native **‖** *m* native god; national hero

indīgest·us -a -um *adj* unarranged, disorderly, confused, in confusion

indignābund·us -a -um *adj* highly indignant

indign·ans -antis *adj* indignant; *(w. gen)* resentful of

indignāti·ō -ōnis *f* indignation, displeasure; provocation, occasion for indignation **‖** *fpl* expressions of indignation

indignē *adv* unworthily; undeservedly; shamefully, outrageously; indigne ferre *(or* pati*)* to be indignant at

indignit·ās -ātis *f* unworthiness; indignation; indignity, shameful treatment; enormity, shamelessness

indign·or -ārī -ātus sum *tr* to be indignant at, displeased at, angry at, offended by

indign·us -a -um *adj* unworthy, undeserving; undeserved; shameful, scandalous; *(w. abl)* 1 unworthy of; 2 not deserving; 3 not worth; *(w. gen)* unworthy of, undeserving of; indignum! shame!

indig·us -a -um *adj* needy, indigent; *(w. gen or abl)* in need of

indīlig·ens -entis *adj* careless

indīligenter *adv* carelessly

indīligenti·a -ae *f* carelessness

ind·ipiscor -ipiscī -eptus sum *or* indipisc·ō -ĕre *tr* to obtain, get; to win, acquire **‖** *intr (w.* de + *abl)* to gain one's point about

indirept·us -a -um *adj* unplundered

indiscrēt·us -a -um *adj* closely connected, inseparable; used indiscriminately; in-

distinguishable; indiscretum est it makes no difference

indisert·us -a -um *adj* without eloquence

indisposit·us -a -um *adj* confused, disordered

indissolūbil·is -is -e *adj* imperishable, indestructible

indistinct·us -a -um *adj* indistinct; applied without distinction

inditus *pp of* indo

indīvidu·us -a -um *adj* indivisible; inseparable; equal, impartial **‖** *n* atom, indivisible particle

in·dō -dĕre -didī -ditus *tr* to put, place; to introduce; to impart, give; *(w.* in + *acc)* to put *or* place *(s. th.)* into *or* on, insert into

indocil·is -is -e *adj* slow to learn; impossible to teach; untrained, ignorant

indoctē *adv* unskillfully

indoct·us -a -um *adj* untaught, untrained; ignorant, uninformed

indolenti·a -ae *f* freedom from pain; insensibility to pain

indol·ēs -is *f* inborn quality, natural quality; nature, character; natural ability, talent; *(w. gen)* natural capacity for, natural tendency toward

indol·escō -escĕre -uī *intr* to feel sorry; to feel resentment

indomābil·is -is -e *adj* untamable

indomit·us -a -um *adj* untamed, wild; indomitable; unrestrained; unmanageable

indorm·iō -īre -īvī *or* -iī -ītum *intr* to fall asleep; to grow careless; *(w. dat or abl or* in + *abl)* 1 to fall asleep at *or* on; 2 to fall asleep over; 3 to become careless about

indōtāt·us -a -um *adj* without dowry; poor; without funeral rites; ars indotata *(rhet)* unadorned style

indubitābil·is -is -e *adj* indubitable

indubitāt·us -a -um *adj* undoubted

indubit·ō -āre *intr (w. dat)* to begin to distrust, begin to doubt

indubi·us -a -um *adj* undoubted, certain

indūci·ae *or* indūti·ae -ārum *fpl* armistice, truce

indū·cō -cĕre -xī -ctus *tr* to lead in, bring in; to introduce; to induce; to seduce; to overlay, drape, wrap, cover; to put on, clothe; to strike out, erase; to repeal, cancel; to present, exhibit; to mislead, delude; *(w.* in + *acc)* 1 to lead to, lead into, lead against; 2 to bring into, introduce into; 3 to enter into *(account books);* *(w. dat or* super + *acc)* to put *(item of apparel, esp. shoes)* on, spread *(s.th.)* over, wrap *(s.th.)* around, draw *(s.th.)* over; animum *(or* in animum*)* inducere to make up one's mind, convince oneself, be convinced, conclude, suppose, imagine

inducti·ō -ōnis *f* bringing in, introduction, admission; resolution, determination; intention; induction, generalization; **animi inductio** inclination; **erroris inductio** deception

induct·or -ōris *m (hum) (referring to a whip)* persuader

induct·us -a -um *pp of* **induco ‖** *adj* alien, adventitious

induct·us -ūs *m* inducement

indūcul·a -ae *f* slip, petticoat

indulg·ens -entis *adj* indulgent, lenient; *(w. dat or* in + *acc)* lenient toward, kind toward

indulgenter *adv* indulgently, leniently, kindly

indulgenti·a -ae *f* indulgence, leniency, kindness

indul·geō -gēre -sī -sus *tr (w. dat)* to grant, concede *(s.th.)* to; **veniam indulgere** *(w. dat)* to make allowances for **‖** *refl* **sibi indulgere** to be self-indulgent, take liberties **‖** *intr (w. dat)* 1 to be lenient toward, be kind to, be tender to; 2 to yield to, give way to; 3 to indulge in, be addicted to; 4 to make allowance for; 5 *(of deities, fate, etc.)* to look favorably on, show kindness to; 6 to take pleasure in; 7 to devote oneself to *(an activity)*

ind·uō -uěre -uī -ūtus *tr* to put on *(e.g., a tunic)*; to cover, wrap, clothe, array; to envelop; to engage in; to assume, put on; to assume the part of; to involve; *(w. dat)* to put *(e.g., a tunic)* on *(s.o.)*

indup- = **imp-**

indūr·escō -escěre -uī *intr* to become hard, harden

indūr·ō -āre -āvī -ātus *tr* to harden

indūruī *perf of* **induresco**

Ind·us -a -um *adj* Indian **‖** *m* Indian; Ethiopian; mahout

industri·a -ae *f* industry, diligence; **de** *(or* **ex) industria** diligently; **industriā** *(or* **de** *or* **ex industria)** *(or* **ob industriam)** on purpose, deliberately

industriē *adv* industriously, diligently

industri·us -a -um *adj* industrious, diligent, painstaking

indūti·ae *or* **indūci·ae -ārum** *fpl* armistice, truce

indūt·us -ūs *m* wearing; clothing

induvi·ae -ārum *fpl* clothes

inebri·ō -āre -āvī -ātus *tr* to make drunk; *(fig)* to fill *(e.g., the ear with gossip)*

inedi·a -ae *f* fasting; starvation

inēdit·us -a -um *adj* not made known, unknown, unpublished

inēleg·ans -antis *adj* inelegant, undistinguished

inēleganter *adv* without style, poorly; without clear thought

inēluctābil·is -is -e *adj* inescapable

inēmor·ior -ī *intr (w. dat)* to die *(of starvation)* in the sight of *(a feast)*

inempt·us -a -um *adj* unpurchased; without ransom

inēnarrābil·is -is -e *adj* indescribable

inēnarrābiliter *adv* indescribably

inēnōdābil·is -is -e *adj* inexplicable

in·eō -īre -īvī -iī -itus *tr* to enter; to enter upon, undertake, form; to begin, engage in; **ab ineunte pueritiā** from earliest boyhood; **consilium inire** to form a plan; **in consilium inire ut** *(or* **qua** *or* **quemadmodum)** to plan how to *(do s.th.)*; **ineunte vere** at the beginning of spring; **inire numerum** *(w. gen)* to go into an enumeration of, enumerate; **inire rationem** *(w. gen)* to form an estimate of; **inire rationem ut** *(or* **qua** *or* **quemadmodum)** to consider, find out, or figure out how to *(do s.th.)*; **viam inire** to begin a trip; to find a way, devise a means

ineptē *adv* foolishly, absurdly, inappropriately, pointlessly

inepti·a -ae *f* foolishness **‖** *fpl* nonsense; trifles

inept·iō -īre *intr* to be absurd, make a fool of oneself

inept·us -a -um *adj* foolish, silly; inept, awkward, absurd; unsuitable, out of place; tactless, tasteless

inerm·is -is -e *or* **inerm·us -a -um** *adj* unarmed, defenseless; undefended; toothless *(gums)*; harmless; peaceful

inerr·ans -antis *adj* not wandering, fixed

inerr·ō -āre -āvī *intr* to wander about

iner·s -tis *adj* unskilled, incompetent; inactive, sluggish; weak, soft, helpless; stagnant, motionless; ineffective; dull, insipid; numbing *(cold)*; expressionless *(eyes)*; uneventful, leisurely *(time)*

inerti·a -ae *f* lack of skill, ignorance, rudeness; inactivity; laziness

inērudīt·us -a -um *adj* uneducated; crude, inconsiderate

inesc·ō -āre -āvī -ātus *tr* to bait; *(fig)* to bait, trap; to gorge

inēvect·us -a -um *adj* mounted

inēvītābil·is -is -e *adj* inevitable, inescapable

inexcīt·us -a -um *adj* unexcited, calm

inexcūsābil·is -is -e *adj* without excuse; admitting no excuse

inexercitāt·us -a -um *adj* untrained

inexhaust·us -a -um *adj* unexhausted, not wasted; inexhaustible

inexōrābil·is -is -e *adj* inexorable, relentless; unswerving, strict

inexperrect·us -a -um *adj* unawakened

inexpert·us -a -um *adj* untried, untested; novel; *(w. abl or* **adversus** *or* **in** + *acc)* inexperienced in, unaccustomed to

inexpiābil·is -is -e *adj* inexpiable, not to

be atoned for; irreconcilable, implacable

inexplēbil·is -is -e *adj* insatiable

inexplēt·us -a -um *adj* unsatisfied, unfilled

inexplicābil·is -is -e *adj* inextricable; inexplicable, baffling; impassable *(road);* involved, unending *(war);* incurable *(disease)*

inexplōrātō *adv* without reconnoitering

inexplōrāt·us -a -um *adj* unexplored; unfamiliar; not investigated

inexpugnābil·is -is -e *adj* impregnable, unassailable; invincible

inexspectāt·us -a -um *adj* unexpected, unforeseen

inextinct·us -a -um *adj* unextinguished; insatiable

inexsuperābil·is -is -e *adj* insuperable, insurmountable

inextrīcābil·is -is -e *adj* inextricable

infabrē *adv* unskillfully

infabricāt·us -a -um *adj* unshaped, untrimmed, unwrought

infacētē *adv* boorishly

infacēti·ae -ārum *fpl* crudities

infacēt·us -a -um *adj* not witty, not funny, dull, stupid

infācund·us -a -um *adj* ineloquent

infāmi·a -ae *f* bad reputation; disrepute, disgrace; scandal; *(w. gen)* stigma of; *(pol)* public disgrace *(involving loss of some civil rights)*

infām·is -is -e *adj* infamous, notorious, disreputable, disgraceful; disgraced; *(w. in + acc or abl)* suspected of misconduct with; **infamis digitus** middle finger *(used in obscene gestures)*

infām·ō -āre -āvī -ātus *tr* to defame, dishonor, disgrace; to smear *(esp. groundlessly)* **‖** *pass (w. in + acc)* to be suspected of misconduct with

infand·us -a -um *adj* unspeakable, shocking

inf·ans· -antis *adj* speechless, unable to speak; baby-, infant-, young; childish, silly; *(fig)* tongue-tied **‖** *mf* infant

infanti·a -ae *f* infancy; childishness; inability to speak; lack of eloquence; young children

infar- = infer-

infatu·ō -āre -āvī -ātus *tr* to make a fool of

infaust·us -a -um *adj* ill-omened, unpropitious; unfortunate

infect·or -ōris *m* dyer

infect·us -a -um *pp of* **inficio ‖** *adj* not made, not done, undone, unfinished; unwrought *(metals);* unachieved; infeasible; **foedere infecto** without concluding a treaty; **re infectā** without achieving the objective

infēcundit·ās -ātis *f* unfruitfulness

infēcund·us -a -um *adj* unfruitful

infēlicit·ās -ātis *f* bad luck, misfortune

infēlīciter *adv* unhappily; unluckily, unsuccessfully

infēlīc·ō -āre *tr* to make unhappy

infēl·ix -īcis *adj* unfruitful; unhappy; unfortunate, unlucky; causing misfortune, ruinous; ill-omened; pessimistic

infensē *adv* with hostility, aggressively

infens·ō -āre -āvī -ātus *tr* to antagonize; to make dangerous **‖** *intr* to be hostile

infens·us -a -um *adj* hostile, antagonistic; dangerous; *(w. dat or in + acc)* 1 hostile to; 2 dangerous to

infer- = infar-

infer·ciō -cīre -sī -ctus *tr* (-far-) to stuff, cram

infer·a -ōrum *npl* lower world

infer·ī -ōrum *mpl* the dead; the world below

inferi·ae -ārum *fpl* rites and offerings to the dead

inferi·or -or -us *adj* lower, farther down; *(fig)* inferior; subsequent; later, more recent *(period);* (w. abl or in + abl) inferior, worse in *(some respect)*

inferius *adv* lower, at a lower level; too low; at a later stage

infernē *adv* below, beneath

infern·us -a -um *adj* lower; infernal, of the lower world

inferō inferre intulī illātus *tr* to bring in, carry in; to import; to introduce; to bring forward, adduce, produce; *(w. dat)* to cause *(injury, death, delay)* to; to bury, inter; *(w. in + acc)* to reduce to; *(w. dat)* to pay *(money)* to *(e.g., the treasury);* **arma** *(or* **bellum) inferre** *(w. dat)* to make war on; **gradum** *(or* **pedem** *or* **signa) inferre** to advance *(usually to attack);* **conversa signa inferre** *(w. dat)* to turn around and attack; **faces** *(or* **ignem) inferre** *(w. dat)* to set fire to; **honores inferre** to offer a sacrifice; **manūs inferre** *(w. dat)* to lay hands on; **nomen in tabulas inferre** to enter one's name in the records **‖** *refl & pass* to enter; to rush in *or* on; to go, march, charge, plunge; **se in periculum inferre** to expose oneself to danger **‖** *intr* to infer, conclude

inferv·eō -ēre *intr* to come to a boil

infervesc·ō -ēre *intr* to simmer, come to a boil, start to boil

infestē *adv* hostilely, violently

infest·ō -āre -āvī -ātus *tr* to annoy, harass, bother; to attack; to damage; *(of diseases, pests)* to infest

infest·us -a -um *adj* hostile, antagonistic; aggressive, warlike; troubled *(times, conditions);* *(of weapons)* poised to strike; *(of armies)* taking the offensive; *(of things)* harmful, troublesome; *(of*

places) threatened, exposed to danger, insecure; *(w. abl)* **1** dangerous *or* unsafe because of; **2** infested with
inficēt- = infacēt-
in·ficiō -ficĕre -fēcī -fectus *tr* to dip, dye, tint; to infect; to stain; to corrupt, spoil; to imbue, instruct; *(fig)* to poison, infect
infidēl·is -is -e *adj* unfaithful, untrue, disloyal
infidēlit·ās -ātis *f* infidelity, disloyalty
infidēliter *adv* disloyally
infidī *perf of* **infindo**
infid·us -a -um *adj* untrustworthy, treacherous
in·fīgō -fīgĕre -fixī -fixus *tr* to drive in, nail, thrust; to imprint, fix, impress; *(w. dat)* **1** to drive into, thrust into; **2** to impale on; **3** to imprint on *or* in; **4** to fasten to, attach to
infīmātis *see* **infumatis**
infim·us -a -um *(superl of* **inferus)** *adj* (**-fum-**) lowest, last; worst; humblest; **ab infimo colle** at the foot of the hill; **infimum mare** the bottom of the sea **‖** *n* bottom
in·findō -findĕre -fidī -fissus *tr (w. dat)* to cut *(e.g., furrows)* into
infīnit·ās -ātis *f* endlessness, infinity; *(phil)* the Infinite
infīnitē *adv* without bounds, without end, infinitely; without exception
infīniti·ō -ōnis *f* boundlessness, infinity
infīnit·us -a -um *adj* unlimited, boundless; without end, endless, infinite; countless; indefinite
infīrmāti·ō -ōnis *f* invalidation; refutation
infīrmē *adv* weakly, faintly, feebly
infīrmit·ās -ātis *f* weakness, feebleness; infirmity; inconstancy
infīrm·ō -āre -āvī -ātus *tr* to weaken, enfeeble; to refute, disprove; to annul
infīrm·us -a -um *adj* weak, faint, feeble; infirm, sick; trivial; inconstant
infissus *pp of* **infindo**
infit *v defect* he, she, it begins
infiti·ae -ārum *fpl* denial; **infitias ire** *(w. acc)* to deny, refuse to acknowledge as true; to disown, repudiate
infitiāl·is -is -e *adj* negative
infitiāti·ō -ōnis *f* denial
infitiāt·or -ōris *m* repudiator
infiti·ōr -ārī -ātus sum *tr* to deny, repudiate, disown; to contradict
infixī *perf of* **infigo**
infixus *pp of* **infigo**
inflammāti·ō -ōnis *f* setting on fire; *(med)* inflammation; **animi inflammatio** inspiration; **inflammationem inferre** *(w. dat)* to set on fire
inflamm·ō -āre -āvī -ātus *tr* to set on fire, kindle, light up; *(med)* to inflame; *(fig)* to excite

inflāti·ō -ōnis *f* swelling up; flatulence; **habet inflationem faba** beans cause gas
inflātius *adv* rather pompously
inflāt·us -a -um *adj* blown up, inflated; swollen; haughty; turgid *(style)*
inflāt·us -ūs *m* puff, blast; inspiration
infle·ctō -ctĕre -xī -xus *tr* to bend, curve, bow; to tilt, slant; to turn aside; to change *(course);* to influence; to inflect, modulate *(voice)* **‖** *refl & pass* to curve; to change course; to turn around; *(of a person)* to change
inflēt·us -a -um *adj* unwept
inflexī *perf of* **inflecto**
inflexibil·is -is -e *adj* inflexible
inflexi·ō -ōnis *f* bending; modification, adaptation
inflexus *pp of* **inflecto**
inflex·us -ūs *m* curve, bend, winding
inflī·gō -gĕre -xī -ctus *tr (w. dat)* **1** to strike *(s.th.)* against, smash *(s.th.)* against; **2** to inflict *(wound)* on; **3** to bring *(e.g., disgrace)* to
infl·ō -āre -āvī -ātus *tr (of wind)* to blow on; to blow *(horn),* play *(flute); (of a deity)* to inspire; to inflate, fill with conceit; to puff up *(cheeks);* to fill *(sails);* to distend, bloat; to amplify *(sound);* to inflate *(price)*
influ·ō -ĕre -xī *intr (w. in + acc)* **1** to flow into; **2** *(fig)* to spill over into, stream into, pour into; **3** *(of words, ideas)* to sink into, penetrate
in·fodiō -fodĕre -fōdī -fossus *tr* to dig; to bury
informāti·ō -ōnis *f* formation *(of an idea);* sketch; idea
inform·is -is -e *adj* unformed, shapeless; ugly, hideous
inform·ō -āre -āvī -ātus *tr* to form, shape; to sketch *(in words),* give an idea of; to instruct, educate
infor·ō -āre -āvī -ātus *tr* to bring into court
infortūnāt·us -a -um *adj* unfortunate
infortūn·ium -(i)ī *n* misfortune; *(euphem. for punishment)* trouble
infossus *pp of* **infodio**
infrā *adv* below, underneath; down south; down the coast; downstream; lower down *(on the page or in the work);* below the surface; later **‖** *prep (w. acc)* **1** below, beneath, under; **2** inferior *(in quality, rank, etc.)* to; **3** smaller than; **4** lower *(in number)* than; **5** beneath the dignity of, degrading to; **6** submissive to; **7** south of; **infra et supra Ephesum** south and north of Ephesus; **8** after, later than; **9** falling short of *(a target)*
infracti·ō -ōnis *f* breaking; **animi infractio** discouragement
infract·us -a -um *pp of* **infringo ‖** *adj* broken; disjointed *(words);* weakened;

humble, subdued *(tone);* **infractos animos gerere** to feel down and out
infragil·is -is -e *adj* unbreakable, indestructible; vigorous *(voice)*
infrēgī *perf of* **infringo**
infrem·ō -ĕre -uī *intr* to growl, bellow, roar; to rage
infrēnāt·us -a -um *adj* unbridled
infrend·eō -ēre *or* **infrend·ō -ĕre** *intr* to grit the teeth; **dentibus infrendere** to grit the teeth
infrēn·is -is -e *or* **infrēn·us -a -um** *adj* unbridled
infrēn·ō -āre -āvī -ātus *tr* to bridle; to harness; *(fig)* to curb
infrēnus *see* **infrenis**
infrequ·ens -entis *adj* uncrowded, not numerous; poorly attended; thinly populated; unusual, infrequent *(words);* inconstant; irregular; *(mil)* undermanned, below strength; *(mil)* absent without leave
infrequenti·a -ae *f* small number, scantiness; poor attendance; emptiness; depopulated condition *(of a place)*
in·fringō -fringĕre -frēgī -fractus *tr* to break; to break in; to bend; to break up *(sentences);* to impair, affect adversely; to subdue; to weaken, break down; to cause to relent; to foil *(an action);* to render null and void
infr·ons -ondis *adj* leafless
infructuōs·us -a -um *adj* unfruitful; pointless
infūcāt·us -a -um *adj* painted over
infūdī *perf of* **infundo**
inful·a -ae *f* bandage; fillet *(worn by priests, by sacrificial victims; displayed as a sign of submission);* festoon *(hung on doorposts at a wedding)*
infumāt·is -is *m* (**infim-**) one of the lowest *(in rank)*
infumus *see* **infimus**
in·fundō -fundĕre -fūdī -fūsus *tr* to pour in, pour on, pour out; *(w. dat or* **in** + *acc)* **1** to pour into, pour upon; **2** to administer to; **3** to shower *(gifts)* upon; **4** to rain *(missiles)* upon; **5** to stretch out *(the body)* upon; **6** to instil *(ideas, feelings)* in **ll refl** & *pass (w. dat)* to spread out on, relax on
infusc·ō -āre -āvī -ātus *tr* to darken, obscure; to stain, corrupt, sully
infūs·us -a -um *pp of* **infundo ll** *adj* diffused; permeating; fallen *(snow);* crowded; **conjugis infusus gremio** relaxing on the lap of his spouse; **infusis humero capillis** with his hair streaming over his shoulders
ingemin·ō -āre -āvī -ātus *tr* to redouble; to repeat; **ingeminare voces** to call repeatedly; **ignes ingeminare** to flash repeatedly **ll** *intr* to increase in intensity, get worse

ingem·iscō -iscĕre -uī *intr* (**-esc-**) to groan, heave a sigh; *(w. dat or* **in** + *abl)* to groan over, sigh over
ingem·ō -ĕre -uī *tr* to groan over, sigh over **ll** *intr* to groan, moan; *(w. dat)* to sigh over
ingener·ō -āre -āvī -ātus *tr* to engender, generate, produce; *(fig)* to implant
ingeniāt·us -a -um *adj* naturally endowed, talented
ingeniōsē *adv* ingeniously
ingeniōs·us -a -um *adj* ingenious, clever, talented; *(w. dat or* **ad**) naturally suited to
ingenit·us -a -um *adj* inborn, natural
ingen·ium -(i)ī *n* innate quality; nature, temperament, character; bent, inclination; mood; natural ability, talent, intellect; bright person; gifted writer; skill, ingenuity; clever device
ing·ens -entis *adj* huge, vast; great, mighty, powerful; a great amount of, a great number of; very important, momentous; proud, haughty, heroic *(character); (w. abl)* outstanding in; **ingens pecunia a** lot of money
ingenuē *adv* liberally; frankly
ingenuī *perf of* **ingigno**
ingenuit·ās -ātis *f* noble birth; noble character; frankness
ingenu·us -a -um *adj* native, indigenous; natural; free-born; like a freeman, noble; ingenuous, frank
in·gerō -gerĕre -gessī -gestus *tr* to carry in, throw in, heap; to ingest *(food, drink, esp. in large amounts);* to hurl, shoot *(missiles);* to pour out *(angry words);* to heap *(abuse);* to rain *(blows); (w. dat)* to force *(unwelcome things)* on *(s.o.);* to say repeatedly
in·gignō -gignĕre -genuī -genitus *tr* to cause *(plants)* to grow; *(fig)* to implant *(qualities, etc.)*
inglōri·us -a -um *adj* inglorious, without glory, inconspicuous
ingluvi·ēs -eī *f* crop, maw; gluttony
ingrātē *adv* unpleasantly; unwillingly; ungratefully
ingrātific·us -a -um *adj* ungrateful
ingrātiīs *or* **ingrātīs** *f abl pl* unwillingly, against one's will; against another's will; *(w. gen or poss adj)* against the wishes of
ingrāt·us -a -um *adj* unpleasant, unwelcome; ungrateful; receiving no thanks, unappreciated; thankless
ingravesc·ō -ĕre *intr* to get heavier; to become pregnant; *(of troubles)* to grow worse; to become more serious; to become weary; to become dearer *(in price); (of prices)* to become inflated; to become more important
ingre·dior -dī -ssus sum *tr* to enter; to undertake; to begin; to walk in, follow

(footsteps) ‖ *intr* to go in, enter; to go, walk, walk along; to begin, commence; to begin to speak; *(mil)* to go to the attack; *(w.* in + *acc)* 1 to go into, enter; 2 to enter upon, begin, take up, undertake; *(w. dat)* to walk on; **in rem publicam ingredi** to enter politics
ingressi·ō -ōnis *f* entering; walking; gait, pace; beginning
ingress·us -ūs *m* entry; walking; gait; beginning; *(mil)* inroad
ingru·ō -ĕre -ī *intr* to come, come on, rush on; *(of war)* to break out; *(of rain)* to pour down; *(w. dat or* in + *acc)* to fall upon, attack
ingu·en -inis *n* groin; swelling, tumor ‖ *npl* private parts
ingurgit·ō -āre -āvī -ātus *tr* to pour in; to gorge, stuff ‖ *refl* to stuff oneself; *(w.* in + *acc)* 1 to steep oneself in; 2 to devote oneself to
ingustāt·us -a -um *adj* untasted
inhabil·is -is -e *adj* clumsy, unhandy, unwieldy; *(w. dat or* ad) unfit for
inhabitābil·is -is -e *adj* uninhabitable
inhabit·ō -āre -āvī -ātus *tr* to inhabit ‖ *intr (w. dat or* in + *abl)* to live in
inhae·reō -rēre -sī -sum *intr* to stick, cling, adhere; to be inherent; *(w. dat, w.* ad *or* in + *acc)* 1 to cling to; 2 to be closely connected with; 3 to gaze upon
inhae·rescō -rescĕre -sī *intr* to begin to stick, become attached; to become stuck; to become fixed *(in the mind)*
inhal·ō -āre -āvī -ātus *tr (w. dat)* to breathe *(e.g., bad breath)* on *(s.o.)*
inhib·eō -ēre -uī -itus *tr* to hold back, curb, check, control; to use, employ, apply; to inflict *(punishment);* **retro navem** *(or* **navem remis) inhibere** to back up the ship ‖ *intr* to row backwards, backwater; **remis inhibere** to backwater
inhibiti·ō -ōnis *f* backing up
inhi·ō -āre -āvī -ātus *tr* to gape at; to pore over; to cast longing eyes at ‖ *intr* to stand open-mouthed, be amazed; *(w. dat)* to be eager for
inhonestē *adv* dishonorably, disgracefully; dishonestly
inhonest·ō -āre -āvī -ātus *tr* to dishonor, disgrace
inhonest·us -a -um *adj* dishonorable, disgraceful, shameful; indecent; ugly, degrading
inhonōr·us -a -um *adj* defaced
inhorr·eō -ēre -uī *intr* to stand on end, bristle
inhorr·escō -escĕre -uī *intr* to stand on end, bristle; to vibrate; to shiver, tremble, shudder
inhospitāl·is -is -e *adj* inhospitable, unfriendly

inhospitālit·ās -ātis *f* inhospitality
inhospit·us -a -um *adj* inhospitable
inhūmānē *adv* inhumanly; rudely; heartlessly
inhūmānit·ās -ātis *f* inhumanity; churlishness; stinginess; heartlessness
inhūmāniter *adv* impolitely; heartlessly
inhūmān·us -a -um *adj* uncivilized; illbred, discourteous; heartless, brutal
inhumāt·us -a -um *adj* unburied
inibi *or* **inibī** *adv* there, in that place; near at hand
inimīc·a -ae *f (personal)* enemy *(female)*
inimīcē *adv* with hostility, in an unfriendly way
inimīciti·a -ae *f* unfriendliness, enmity ‖ *fpl* feuds
inimīc·ō -āre -āvī -ātus *tr* to make into enemies, set at odds
inimīc·us -a -um *adj* unfriendly, hostile; harmful ‖ *m (personal)* enemy; **inimicissimus suus** his bitterest *(personal)* enemy ‖ *f (personal)* enemy *(female)*
inīque *adv* unequally, unevenly; unfairly
inīquit·ās -ātis *f* unevenness; inequality; disadvantage; unfairness
inīqu·us -a -um *adj* uneven, unequal; not level, sloping; unfair; adverse, harmful; dangerous, unfavorable; prejudiced; excessive; impatient, discontented; **iniquo animo** impatiently, unwillingly ‖ *m* enemy, foe
initi·ō -āre -āvī -ātus *tr* to initiate, begin; to initiate *(into mysteries)*
init·ium -(i)ī *n* entrance; beginning ‖ *npl* elements; first principles; sacred rites, sacred mysteries
initus *pp of* ineo
init·us -ūs *m* entrance; beginning
in·jiciō -jicĕre -jēcī -jectus *tr* to throw, inject; to hurl, discharge *(missiles);* to impose, apply; to inspire, infuse; to cause, occasion; to furnish *(a cause);* to bring up, mention *(a name); (w. dat)* to put *(e.g., a cloak)* on *(s.o.);* **manicas alicui injicere** to put handcuffs on s.o.; **manum injicere** *(w. dat)* 1 to lay hands on; 2 take possession of ‖ *refl (w. dat or* in + *acc)* 1 to throw oneself into, rush into, expose oneself to; 2 to fling oneself down on; 3 *(of the mind)* to turn itself to, concentrate on, reflect on
injūcundit·ās -ātis *f* unpleasantness
injūcundius *adv* rather unpleasantly
injūcund·us -a -um *adj* unpleasant
injūdicāt·us -a -um *adj* undecided
injun·gō -gĕre -xī -ctus *tr* to join, attach, fasten, *(w. dat)* 1 to join to, attach to, fasten to; 2 to inflict on; 3 to impose *(e.g., taxes)* on
injūrāt·us -a -um *adj* not under oath
injūri·a -ae *f* injustice, wrong, outrage; insult, affront; harshness, severity; re-

venge; injury, damage, harm; ill-gotten goods; **injuriā** unjustly, undeservedly, innocently; **per injuriam** unjustly; outrageously
injūriōsē *adv* unjustly, wrongfully
injūriōs·us -a -um *adj* unjust, wrongful; insulting; harmful
injūri·us -a -um *adj* unjust, wrong
injūr·us -a -um *adj* unjust
injussū *(abl only) m* without orders; **injussu meo** without my orders
injuss·us -a -um *adj* unasked, unbidden, voluntary
injustē *adv* unjustly
injustiti·a -ae *f* injustice
injust·us -a -um *adj* unjust
inl- = **ill-**
inm- = **imm-**
innābil·is -is -e *adj* unswimmable
in·nascor -nascī -nātus sum *intr (w. dat)* 1 to be born in; 2 *(of plant life)* grow in *or* on; *(w. in + abl)* 1 to originate in; 2 *(of plant life)* to grow in; 3 *(of minerals)* to occur in, be native to
innat·ō -āre -āvī *tr* to swim ‖ *intr (w. dat)* to swim around in, float on; *(w. in + acc)* to swim into
innāt·us -a -um *pp of* **innascor** ‖ *adj* innate, inborn, natural
innāvigābil·is -is -e *adj* unnavigable
in·nectō -nectĕre -nexuī -nexus *tr* to entwine; to tie, fasten together; to join, attach, connect; *(fig)* to devise, invent, plan
innī·tor -tī -xus sum *or* **-sus sum** *intr (w. abl)* to lean on, rest on, be supported by
inn·ō -āre *tr* to swim; to sail, sail over ‖ *intr (w. abl)* 1 to swim in, float on; 2 to sail on; 3 *(of the sea)* to wash against *(a shore)*
innoc·ens -entis *adj* harmless; innocent; upright; unselfish; *(w. gen)* innocent of
innocenter *adv* innocently, blamelessly; harmlessly
innocenti·a -ae *f* innocence; integrity; unselfishness
innocuē *adv* harmlessly; innocently
innocu·us -a -um *adj* harmless, innocuous; innocent; unharmed
innōt·escō -escĕre -uī *intr* to become known; to become notorious
innov·ō -āre -āvī -ātus *tr* to renew, restore ‖ *refl (w. ad + acc)* to return to
innoxi·us -a -um *adj* harmless; safe; innocent; unhurt; *(w. gen)* innocent of
innub·a -ae *adj (fem only)* unmarried
innūbil·us -a -um *adj* cloudless
innū·bō -bĕre -psī *intr (of a girl) (w. dat)* to marry into *(a family)*
innumerābil·is -is -e *adj* innumerable
innumerābilit·ās -atis *f* countless number
innumerābiliter *adv* in countless ways; countless times

innumerāl·is -is -e *adj* innumerable
innumer·us -a -um *adj* countless
in·nuō -nuĕre -nuī -nūtum *intr* to give a nod; *(w. dat)* to nod to
innupt·a -ae *adj (fem only)* unmarried ‖ *f* unmarried girl, maiden
innutr·iō -īre -īvī *or* **-iī -ītus** *tr (w. abl)* to bring up in
Īn·ō -ūs *f* daughter of Cadmus and Harmonia, wife of Athamas and mother of Learchus and Melicertes
inoblīt·us -a -um *adj* unforgetful
inobrut·us -a -um *adj* not overwhelmed
inobservābil·is -is -e *adj* unnoticed
inobservanti·a -ae *f* inattention
inobservāt·us -a -um *adj* unobserved
inoccidu·us -a -um *adj* never setting
inodōr·us -a -um *adj* odorless
inoffens·us -a -um *adj* unobstructed, uninterrupted, unhindered; unimpaired; smooth *(path)*
inofficiōs·us -a -um *adj* irresponsible; unobliging; **testamentum inofficiosum** a will passing over the relatives
inol·ens -entis *adj* odorless
inol·escō -escĕre -ēvī *tr* to implant ‖ *intr* to become inveterate; *(w. dat)* to grow in, develop in
inōmināt·us -a -um *adj* ill-starred, inauspicious
inopi·a -ae *f* lack, want, need, poverty; scarcity; helplessness; *(rhet)* barrenness *(of style); (rhet)* lack of subject matter
inopīn·ans -antis *adj* unsuspecting, taken by surprise, off one's guard
inopīnanter *adv* unexpectedly
inopīnātō *adv* unexpectedly, by surprise
inopīnāt·us -a -um *adj* unexpected, unsuspected, surprising ‖ *n* surprise; *ex* **inopinato** by surprise, unexpectedly
inōpīn·us -a -um *adj* unexpected
inopiōs·us -a -um *adj (hum) (w. gen)* in need of
in·ops -opis *adj* without means *or* resources; poor, needy, destitute; helpless, weak, forlorn; *(rhet)* bald *(style);* poor *(expression);* deficient in vocabulary; pitiful, contemptible; *(w. gen)* destitute of, stripped of, without; *(w. abl)* lacking in, deficient in, poor in
inōrāt·us -a -um *adj* not presented; **re inoratā** without presenting one's case
inordināt·us -a -um *adj* disordered
inornāt·us -a -um *adj* unadorned; unheralded; *(rhet)* plain *(style)*
inp- = **imp-**
inquam *v defect (the following forms are found: pres:* **inquam, inquis, inquit, inquimus, inquiunt;** *imperfect:* **inquiebat;** *fut:* **inquies, inquiet;** *perfect:* **inquii, inquisti;** *persent subj:* **inquiat;** *impv:* **inque** *or* **inquito**) to say; *(after one or more words of direction quotation, e.g.,*

Desilite, inquit, milites et..."Jump down, fellow soldiers", he says, ." and..."); *(in emphatic repetition, e.g., tuas, tuas inquam suspiciones*...your suspicions, yes I say yours...); **inquit** it is said, one says, they say

inqui·ēs -ētis *adj* restless

inquiēt·ō -āre -āvī -ātus *tr* to disquiet, disturb

inquiēt·us -a -um *adj* restless, unsettled

inquilīn·us -ī *m* tenant, lodger

inquinātē *adv* filthily

inquināt·us -a -um *adj* filthy, foul

inquin·ō -āre -āvī -ātus *tr* to mess up, defile, contaminate

inquī·rō -rĕre -sīvī *or* **-siī -sītus** *tr* to search for, inquire into, examine, pry into **II** *intr* to hold an investigation; to hold a preliminary hearing

inquīsīti·ō -ōnis *f* search, inquiry, investigation; preliminary hearing; *(w. gen)* search for, inquiry into, investigation of

inquīsīt·or -ōris *m* inspector, examiner; spy; *(leg)* investigator

inquīsīt·us -a -um *pp of* **inquiro II** *adj* not investigated, unexamined

inquisīvī *perf of* **inquiro**

inquit *see* **inquam**

inquiunt *see* **inquam**

inr- = irr-

insalūbr·is -is -e *adj* unhealthy, unhealthful

insalūtāt·us -a -um *adj* ungreeted

insānābil·is -is -e *adj* incurable

insānē *adv* insanely, madly

insāni·a -ae *f* insanity, madness, frequency; rapture; mania; excess; **ad insaniam** to the point of madness

insān·iō -īre -īvī *or* **-iī -ītum** *intr* to be insane; to be absurd; to be wild, rave; *(w. in + acc)* to be crazy about

insānit·ās -ātis *f* insanity

insānum *adv (coll)* exceedingly, very

insān·us -a -um *adj* insane, crazy; absurd, foolish; excessive, extravagant; monstrous, outrageous; inspired; maddening

insatiābil·is -is -e *adj* insatiable; voracious; that cannot cloy

insatiābiliter *adv* insatiably

insatiet·ās -ātis *f* insatiable desire

insaturābil·is -is -e *adj* insatiable

insaturābiliter *adv* insatiably

inscen·dō -dĕre -dī -sus *tr* to climb up; to get up on *(horse, chariot)* **II** *intr* to climb up; **in arborem inscendere** to climb a tree; **in currum inscendere** to climb into a chariot; **in navem inscendere** to board a ship

inscensi·ō -ōnis *f* mounting; **in navem inscensio** embarkation

inscensus *pp of* **inscendo**

insci·ens -entis *adj* unaware; silly, ignorant, stupid

inscienter *adv* ignorantly; inadvertently

inscītē *adv* ignorantly, unskillfully

inscīti·a -ae *f* ignorance; inexperience; lack of skill; neglect

inscīt·us -a -um *adj* ignorant; stupid

insci·us -a -um *adj* unaware; ignorant, silly, stupid

inscri·bō -bĕre -psī -ptus *tr* to inscribe; to ascribe; to title *(a book); (w. dat)* **1** to assign, attribute to; **2** to apply to; **3** to address *(a letter)* to; *(w. dat or in + abl)* to write *(s.th.)* on *or* in; **aedes venales** *(or* **mercede) inscribere** to advertise a house for sale

inscripti·ō -ōnis *f* inscribing; branding *(of slaves);* inscription; title *(of book)*

inscript·us -a -um *pp of* **inscribo II** *adj* unwritten; *(of a book)* entitled **II** *n* inscription; brand (mark); title *(of a book)*

insculp·ō -ĕre -sī -tus *tr* to cut, carve, engrave; *(w. dat or abl or in + abl)* to cut, carve, *or* engrave on; **in animo** *(or* **in mente) insculpere** to imprint on the mind

insēdī *perf of* **insideo** *and* **insido**

insectāti·ō -ōnis *f* hot pursuit

insectāt·or -ōris *m* persecutor

insect·or -ārī -ātus sum *or* **insect·ō -āre** *tr* to pursue, chase, attack; to heckle, harrass

insect·us -a -um *adj* indented, notched; **animalia insecta** insects **II** *n* insect

insecūtus *pp of* **insequor**

insēdābiliter *adv* unquenchably

insen·escō -escĕre -uī *intr (w. dat)* to grow old amidst, grow old over; *(of the moon)* to wane

insensil·is -is -e *adj* imperceptible

insepult·us -a -um *adj* unburied

insequ·ens -entis *adj* next, following, succeeding

inse·quor -quī -cūtus sum *tr* to follow (immediately behind); to succeed, follow up; to attack, go for; to persecute; to catch up with; to reproach; to strive after **II** *intr* to follow, come next; to pursue the point; *(w. inf)* to proceed to

in·serō -serĕre -sēvī -situs *tr* to sow, plant; to graft on *(a cutting);* to graft a cutting on *(a tree); (lit & fig)* to implant; **singulos hortos cujusque generis surculis serere** to plant each garden with one kind of cutting

inser·ō -ĕre -uī -tus *tr* to insert; to introduce; to include *(in a book, speech);* to involve; to join, enroll, associate; to mingle, blend; **manūs inserere** *(w. dat)* to lay hands on, seize; **oculos inserere** *(w. in + abl)* to look into *(e.g., s.o.'s heart)*

insert·ō -āre -āvī -ātus *tr* to insert

inserv·iō -īre -īvī *or* **-iī -ītus** *tr* to serve, obey **II** *intr* to be a slave, be a subject; *(w. dat)* **1** to serve, be subservient to; **2** to be subject to; **3** to be devoted to; **4** to pay attention to

insessus *pp of* **insideo** *and* **insido**
insēvī *perf of* **insero** (to plant)
insībil·ō -āre -āvī -ātum *intr (of the wind)* to whistle
in·sideō -sidēre -sēdī -sessus *tr* to hold, occupy **‖** *intr* to sit down; to settle down; to be deep-seated; *(w. abl or in + abl)* **1** to sit on; **2** to settle down on *or* in; **3** *(fig)* to be fixed in, be stamped in
insidi·ae -ārum *fpl* ambush; plot, trap; **insidias dare** *(or* **collocare** *or* **parare** *or* **struere)** *(w. dat)* to lay a trap for
insidiāt·or -ōris *m* soldier in ambush; *(fig)* plotter, subversive
insidi·or -ārī -ātus sum *intr (w. dat)* **1** to lie in wait for; **2** to plot against; **3** to watch for, be on the lookout for *(e.g., opportunity)*
insidiōsē *adv* insidiously, by underhand means
in·sīdō -sīdĕre -sēdī -sessus *tr* to occupy, keep possession of, possess **‖** *intr* to sink in, penetrate; *(of diseases)* to become deep-seated; *(w. dat)* to settle in *or* on; *(w. in + abl)* to become fixed in, become imbedded in
insign·e -is *n (s.th. worn or carried as an indication of rank or status)* insignia, mark; coat of arms; signal; honor, distinction; brilliant passage, gem; *(mil)* decoration, medal **‖** *npl* insignia, regalia, uniform; outer trappings
insign·iō -īre -īvī *or* **-iī -ītus** *tr* to make conspicuous, distinguish, mark
insign·is -is -e *adj* conspicuous, distinguished; prominent, eminent, extraordinary, singular
insignītē *adv* notably, extraordinarily
insigniter *adv* remarkably
insignīt·us -a -um *adj* marked, conspicuous, clear, glaring; distinguished, striking, notable
insil·ia -ium *npl* treadle *(of a loom)*
insil·iō -īre -uī *or* **-īvī** *tr* to jump up on, mount **‖** *intr (w. dat)* to jump on; *(w. in + acc)* **1** to jump into *or* on(to); **2** to mount; **3** to climb aboard
insimulāti·ō -ōnis *f* allegation *(of a crime)*; charge, accusation
insimul·ō -āre -āvī -ātus *tr* to allege; to charge, accuse
insincēr·us -a -um *adj* adulterated; not genuine, insincere
insinuāti·ō -ōnis *f (rhet)* winning sympathy *(in a speech)*
insinu·ō -āre -āvī -ātus *tr* to bring in secretly, sneak in **‖** *refl (w. inter + acc)* to wriggle in between, work one's way between *or* among; **se insinuare in familiaritatem** *(w. gen)* to ingratiate oneself with

insipi·ens -entis *adj* foolish
insipienter *adv* foolishly
insipienti·a -ae *f* foolishness
in·sistō -sistĕre -stitī *tr* to stand on, trample on; to set about, keep at *(a task, etc.)*; to follow, chase after; **iter** *(or* **viam)** **insistere** to pursue a course **‖** *intr* to stand, stop, come to a stop; to pause; *(w. dat)* **1** to tread on the heels of, pursue closely; **2** to press on with; **3** to dwell upon; *(w. dat or in + abl)* to persist in; *(w. ad or in + acc)* **1** to keep at, keep after, keep the pressure on; **2** pursue vigorously
insiti·ō -ōnis *f* grafting; grafting time
insitīv·us -a -um *adj* grafted; *(fig)* spurious
insit·or -ōris *m* grafter *(of trees)*
insit·us -a -um *pp of* **insero ‖** *adj* inborn, innate; incorporated
insociābil·is -is -e *adj* incompatible
insōlābiliter *adv* unconsolably
insol·ens -entis *adj* unaccustomed, unusual; immoderate, excessive; extravagant; insolent; *(w. gen or in + abl)* **1** unaccustomed to; **2** inexperienced in; **in aliena re insolens** free with someone else's money
insolenter *adv* unusually; excessively; insolently
insolenti·a -ae *f* unusualness, novelty, strangeness, inexperience; affectation; insolence, arrogance
insolesc·ō -ĕre *intr* to become proud, become insolent; to become elated
insolid·us -a -um *adj* soft
insolit·us -a -um *adj* unaccustomed; inexperienced; unusual, strange, uncommon **‖** *n* the unusual
insomni·a -ae *f* insomnia
insomn·is -is -e *adj* sleepless
insomn·ium -(i)ī *n* sleeplessness; dream; vision in a dream *or* trance
inson·ō -āre -uī *intr* to make noise; to sound, resound, roar; **calamis insonare** to play the reed pipe; **flagello insonare** to crack the whip; **pennis insonare** to flap the wings
ins·ons -ontis *adj* innocent; harmless
insōpīt·us -a -um *adj* sleepless
insop·or -ōris *adj* sleepless
inspeciōs·us -a -um *adj* homely
inspecti·ō -ōnis *f* inspection
inspect·ō -āre -āvī -ātus *tr* to look at, view, observe, examine **‖** *intr* to look on; **inspectante Roscio** with Roscius looking on, under the eyes of Roscius
inspectus *pp of* **inspicio**
inspēr·ans -antis *adj* not hoping, not expecting
insperāt·us -a -um *adj* unhoped for, unexpected, unforeseen; unwelcome; **(ex) insperato** unexpectedly

insper·gō -gĕre -sī -sus *tr* to sprinkle on

in·spiciō -spicĕre -spexī -spectus *tr* to inspect, look into, examine; to look at, watch; to consider; to comprehend, grasp; to investigate; to look at, consult *(books);* to look into *(the mirror)* **‖** *intr (w.* **in** + *acc)* to look into

inspīc·ō -āre -āvī -ātus *tr* to make pointed

inspīr·ō -āre -āvī -ātus *tr* to inspire, infuse, enkindle **‖** *intr (w.* **dat)** to blow on, breathe on

inspoliāt·us -a -um *adj* undespoiled

insp·uō -uĕre -uī -ūtus *tr* to spit on **‖** *intr (w.* **dat)** to spit on

inspūt·ō -āre -āvī -ātus *tr* to spit on

instābil·is -is -e *adj* unstable, unsteady; not remaining still; *(fig)* changeable

inst·ans -antis *adj* present; immediate, threatening, urgent

instanter *adv* vehemently, insistently

instanti·a -ae *f* presence; earnestness, insistence; concentration

instar *indecl n* image, likeness, appearance, resemblance; *(w.* **gen)** like, equal to, as large as, worth, as good as; **ad instar** *(w.* **gen)** according to the standard of

instaurāti·ō -ōnis *f* renewal, repetition

instaurātīv·us -a -um *adj* begun anew, repeated

instaur·ō -āre -āvī -ātus *tr* to set up; to renew, repeat, start all over again *(esp. games and celebrations because of alleged bad omens in the initial event);* to repay, requite

in·sternō -sternĕre -strāvī -strātus *tr* to cover; to lay *(a floor, deck)*

instīgāt·or -ōris *m,* **instīgātr·ix -īcis** *f* instigator, ringleader

instīg·ō -āre -āvī -ātus *tr* to instigate, goad on, stimulate, incite

instill·ō -āre -āvī -ātus *tr (w.* **dat)** to pour *(s.th.)* on, instill *(s.th.)* in

instimulāt·or -ōris *m* instigator

instimul·ō -āre -āvī -ātus *tr* to stimulate, urge on, goad on

instinct·or -ōris *m* instigator

instinct·us -a -um *adj* aroused, fired up; infuriated; inspired

instipul·or -ārī -ātus sum *intr* to bargain

instit·a -ae *f* border, flounce; band, ribbon; *(fig)* lady

institī *perf of* **insisto** *and* **insto**

institi·ō -ōnis *f* standing still

instit·or -ōris *m* salesman, huckster

instit·uō -uĕre -uī -ūtus *tr* to set, fix, plant; to set up, erect, establish; to arrange; to build, make, construct; to prepare; to provide, furnish; to institute, organize, set up; to appoint, designate; to undertake, begin; to control, direct, govern; to teach, train, instruct, educate; *(w.* **inf)** to decide to

institūti·ō -ōnis *f* arrangement; custom; instruction, education; **morum institutio** established custom **‖** *fpl* principles of education

institūt·um -ī *n* plan, program; practice, custom, usage; precedent; principle; decree, regulation, stipulation, terms; purpose, intention; **ex instituto** according to custom, by convention **‖** *npl* teachings, precepts, principles of education

in·stō -stāre -stitī *tr* to follow, pursue; to work hard at; to menace, threaten **‖** *intr* to be at hand, approach, be impending; to insist; *(w.* **dat** *or* **in** + *abl)* to stand on *or* in; *(w.* **dat)** **1** to be close to; **2** to be on the heels of, pursue closely; **3** to harass

instrātus *pp of* **insterno**

instrāvī *perf of* **insterno**

instrēnu·us -a -um *adj* lethargic

instrēp·ō -āre -uī -itum *intr* to creak, rattle

instructi·ō -ōnis *f* construction; array, formation; instruction

instructius *adv* with better preparation

instruct·or -ōris *m* supervisor; preparer

instruct·us -a -um *pp of* **instruo** **‖** *adj* equipped, furnished; prepared, arranged; instructed, versed

instruct·us -ūs *m* equipment; *(rhet)* stock-in-trade *(of an orator)*

instrūment·um -ī *n* instrument, tool, utensil; equipment; dress, outfit; repertory, stock-in-trade; means, supply, provisions; *(leg)* document, deed, instrument

instru·ō -ĕre -xī -ctus *tr* to build up, construct; to furnish, prepare, provide, fit out; to instruct; *(mil)* to deploy

insuās·um -ī *n* dark-orange color

insuāv·is -is -e *adj* unpleasant, disagreeable

insūd·ō -āre -āvī *intr* to sweat, break a sweat; *(w.* **dat)** to drip sweat on

insuēfact·us -a -um *adj* accustomed

insu·escō -escĕre -ēvī -ētus *tr* to accustom, familiarize **‖** *intr (w.* **dat,** *w.* **ad** *or w.* **inf)** to get used to

insuēt·us -a -um *adj* unusual; *(w.* **gen** *or* **dat,** *w.* **ad** *or w.* **inf)** unused to

insuēvī *perf of* **insuesco**

insul·a -ae *f* island; apartment building

insulān·us -ī *m* islander

insulār·ius -(i)ī *m* superintendent *(of an apartment building)*

insulsē *adv* in poor taste; insipidly, absurdly

insulsit·ās -ātis *f* lack of taste; silliness, absurdity

insuls·us -a -um *adj* unsalted, without taste; coarse, tasteless, insipid; silly, absurd; bungling **‖** *fpl* silly creatures *(i.e., women)*

insult·ō -āre -āvī -ātus *tr* to insult, scoff at, taunt; *(of votaries)* to dance about in

ǁ *intr* to jump, gambol, prance; to gloat; *(w. abl)* **1** to jump in, cavort in, gambol on, jump upon; **2** to gloat over; *(w. dat or* **in** + *acc)* **1** to scoff at; **2** to gloat over
insultūr·a -ae *f* jumping on *or* in
in·sum -esse -fuī *intr* to be there, exist; *(w. dat or* **in** + *acc)* **1** to be in, be on; **2** to be implied in, be contained in, belong to
insūm·ō -ěre -psī -ptus *tr* to spend, devote, waste; *(w. dat or* **in** + *acc)* to devote to, apply to; *(w. abl or* **in** + *abl)* to expend on; **operam insumere** *(w. dat)* to devote effort to, waste effort on
in·suō -suěre -suī -sūtus *tr* to sew up; *(w. dat)* **1** to sew up in; **2** to embroider *(s.th.)* on
insuper *adv* above, overhead, on top; from above; moreover, besides, in addition **ǁ** *prep (w. acc)* above, over, over and above; *(w. abl)* in addition to, besides
insuperābil·is -is -e *adj* insurmountable; unconquerable
insur·gō -gěre -rexī -rectum *intr* to rise, stand up, stand high, tower; to rise, increase, grow, grow intense; to rise to power; *(of language)* to soar; *(w. dat)* **1** to rise up against; **2** to strain at *(e.g., oars)*
insusurr·ō -āre -āvī -ātus *tr (w. dat)* to whisper *(s.th.)* to; **insusurrare in aurem** *(w. gen)* to whisper in *(s.o.'s)* ear; **sibi cantilenam insusurrare** to hum a tune to oneself **ǁ** *intr* to whisper; *(of wind)* to blow gently
intāb·escō -escěre -uī *intr* to melt away gradually, dissolve gradually; *(fig)* to waste away, pine away
intactil·is -is -e *adj* intangible
intact·us -a -um *adj* untouched; uninjured, intact; unpolluted; untried; unmarried, virgin, chaste
intact·us -ūs *m* intangibility
intāmināt·us -a -um *adj* unsullied
intect·us -a -um *pp of* **intego ǁ** *adj* uncovered; naked; open, frank
integell·us -a -um *adj* fairly pure *or* chaste; in fair condition
inte·ger -gra -grum *adj* whole, complete, intact; unhurt, unwounded; healthy, sound; new; fresh; pure, chaste; untouched, unaffected; unbiased; unattempted; unconquered; unbroken *(horse);* not worn, unused; inexperienced; virtuous, honest, blameless; healthy, sane; *(mil)* having suffered no losses; **ab** *(or* **de** *or* **ex) integro** anew, all over again; **in integrum restituere** to restore to a former condition; to pardon; **integrum alicui esse** *(w. inf)* to be in someone's power to
inte·gō -gěre -xī -ctus *tr* to cover up; to protect
integrasc·ō -ěre *intr* to start all over again

integrāti·ō -ōnis *f* renewal, new beginning
integrē *adv* wholly, entirely; honestly; correctly
integrit·ās -ātis *f* soundness; integrity; innocence; purity, chastity
integr·ō -āre -āvī -ātus *tr* to make whole; to heal, repair; to renew, begin again; to refresh, reinvigorate
integument·um -ī *n* covering; lid; wrapping; protection
intellectus *pp of* **intellego**
intellect·us -ūs *m* intellect; perception; comprehension, understanding
intelleg·ens -entis *adj* intelligent; *(w. gen)* appreciative of; *(w.* **in** + *abl)* versed in
intellegenter *adv* intelligently
intellegenti·a -ae *f* intelligence; understanding, knowledge; perception, judgment, discrimination, taste; skill; concept, notion; *(w. gen)* knowledge of, understanding of; *(w.* **in** + *abl)* judgment in
intelle·gō -gěre -xī -ctus *tr* to understand, perceive, comprehend; to realize, recognize; to have an accurate knowledge of, be an expert in **ǁ** *intr (in answers)* **I** understand, I get it
intemerāt·us -a -um *adj* undefiled, pure, chaste; pure, undiluted
intemper·ans -antis *adj* intemperate, without restraint; lewd
intemperanter *adv* intemperately
intemperanti·a -ae *f* intemperance, lack of self-control; extravagance; *(w. gen)* unrestrained use of
intemperāri·ae -ārum *fpl* wild outbursts; wildness
intemperātē *adv* intemperately
intemperāt·us -a -um *adj* excessive
intemperi·ēs -ēī *f* wildness, excess; outrageous conduct, excesses; **intemperies aquarum** heavy rain; **intemperies caeli** stormy weather
intempestīvē *adv* at a bad time, at the wrong time
intempestīv·us -a -um *adj* untimely; unseasonable *(weather);* poorly timed
intempest·us -a -um *adj* unseasonable; dark, dismal; unhealthy; **nox intempesta** dead of night
intemptāt·us -a -um *adj* (-tent-) unattempted, untried
inten·dō -děre -dī -tus *or* **-sus** *tr* to stretch, stretch out, extend, spread out; to stretch, bend *(e.g., a bow);* to aim, shoot *(weapon);* to spread *(sails);* *(of winds)* to fill *(sails);* to cover *(e.g., with festoons);* to increase, magnify, intensify; to intend; to urge, incite; to aim at, intend; to assert, maintain; to raise *(voice);* to stretch *(truth);* to direct, turn, focus *(mind, attention);* to pitch *(tent);* **cursum** *(or* **iter) intendere** to direct one's course

‖ *intr* (*w.* in + *acc*) **1** to direct one's effort to, apply oneself to; **2** to turn to
intentātus *see* **intemptatus**
intentē *adv* intently, attentively
intenti·ō -ōnis *f* stretching, straining; tension, tautness; attention; effort, exertion; aim, intention; accusation; *(leg)* statement of the charge
intent·ō -āre -āvī -ātus *tr* to stretch out; to aim, direct; to threaten; to brandish threateningly; **manūs intentare** to shake hands; **oculos intentare** to fix one's gaze *(on)*
intent·us -a -um *pp of* **intendo** ‖ *adj* tense, taut; intent, attentive; eager; tense, nervous; strict *(discipline);* vigorous *(speech)*
intent·us -ūs *m* stretching out, extending *(of the palms)*
intep·eō -ēre -uī *intr* to be lukewarm
intep·escō -escĕre -uī *intr* to get warm, be warmed
inter *prep* (*w.* acc) **1** between, among, amidst; **2** during, within, in the course of; **inter cenam** during dinner; **inter haec** during these events, in the meantime; **inter talia opera** during such frenetic activites; **3** *(in classifying)* among, in, with; **inter se** each other, one another, mutually
inter- *pref* with one of the senses of the preposition
interaestu·ō -āre *intr* to retch
interāment·a -ōrum *npl* framework of a ship
Interamn·a -ae *f* town in Latium on the Liris River ‖ town in Umbria, birthplace of Tacitus
interāresc·ō -ĕre *intr* to dry up
interātim *adv* meanwhile
interbib·ō -ĕre *tr* to drink up
interbīt·ō -ĕre *intr* to come to nothing
intercalār·is -is -e *adj* intercalary, added *(to the calendar)*
intercal·ō -āre -āvī -ātus *tr* to intercalate, add *(to the calendar)*
intercapēd·ō -inis *f* interruption, break, pause
inter·cēdō -cēdĕre -cessī -cessum *intr* to come *or* go in between; *(of time)* to intervene, pass, occur; to act as an intermediary; to intercede; *(of tribunes)* to exercise the veto; *(w. dat)* **1** to veto, protest against; **2** to interfere with, obstruct, hinder
intercepti·ō -ōnis *f* interception
intercept·or -ōris *m* embezzler
interceptus *pp of* **intercipio**
intercessi·ō -ōnis *f* intercession, mediation; *(tribune's)* veto
inter·cīdō -cidĕre -cǐdī *intr* to fall short, miss the mark; to happen in the meantime; to drop out, be lost

inter·cīdō -cīdĕre -cīdī -cīsus *tr* to cut through, sever; to cut off, cut short; to cut the seals of, tamper with *(documents)*
intercin·ō -ĕre *tr* to interrupt with song *or* music
inter·cipiō -cipĕre -cēpī -ceptus *tr* to intercept; to trap *(animals);* to draw *(water illegally from the aqueduct);* to steal, usurp *(rights, honors);* to interrupt, cut off, cut short *(a conversation);* to appropriate; to misappropriate; to receive by mistake *(e.g., poison); (mil)* to cut off *(the enemy); (mil)* to capture; *(mil)* to be struck by *(e.g., spear intended for another)*
intercīsē *adv* piecemeal
intercīsus *pp of* **intercido**
interclū·dō -dĕre -sī -sus *tr* to shut off, shut out, cut off; to stop, block up; to hinder, prevent; to blockade, shut in; to cut off, intercept; to separate, divide
interclūsi·ō -ōnis *f* stopping; parenthetical matter; **animae interclusio** short-windedness
interclūsus *pp of* **intercludo**
intercolumn·ium -(i)ī *n* space between columns, intercolumniation
inter·currō -currĕre -cucurrī -cursum *intr* to intervene, mediate; to mingle; to rush in
intercurs·ō -āre -āvī -ātum *intr* to crisscross; **inter se intercursare** to crisscross each other
intercurs·us -ūs *m* intervention
interc·us -utis *adj* between the skin and flesh; **aqua intercus** dropsy
inter·dīcō -dīcĕre -dixī -dictus *tr* to forbid, prohibit ‖ *intr* to issue a prohibition, issue an injunction; **aquā et igni interdicere** (*w. dat*) to outlaw *(s.o.),* banish *(s.o.)* (*literally, to prohibit s.o. from receiving water and fire)*
interdicti·ō -ōnis *f* prohibiting; **aquae et igni interdictio** banishment
interdict·um -ī *n* prohibition; contraband; injunction *(by praetor or promagistrate)*
interdictus *pp of* **interdico**
interdiū *or* **interdiūs** *adv* by day, in the daytime
interdixī *perf of* **interdico**
inter·dō -dăre -dedī -datus *tr* (·**duō**) to place between, place at intervals, interpose; **ciccum** (*or* **floccum** *or* **nihil**) **interduim** *(sl)* I don't give a hoot
interduct·us -ūs *m* punctuation
interdum *adv* sometimes, now and then, occasionally; meanwhile
interdu·ō *see* **interdo**
intereā *adv* meanwhile, in the interim; anyhow, nevertheless
interemptus *pp of* **interimo**
inter·eō -īre -iī -itum *intr* to die; to be

done for, be finished, perish, be lost; to become extinct

interequit·ō -āre -āvī -ātus *tr* to ride between *(e.g., the ranks or columns)* ‖ *intr* to ride *(on horseback)* in between

interfāti·ō -ōnis *f* interruption

interfecti·ō -ōnis *f* killing

interfect·or -ōris *m*, **interfectr·ix -īcis** *f* killer, murderer

inter·ficiō -ficĕre -fēcī -fectus *tr* to kill; to destroy

inter·fīō -fierī *intr* to be destroyed

inter·fluō -fluĕre -flūxī *tr* to flow between ‖ *intr* to flow in between

inter·fodiō -fodĕre -fōdī -fossus *tr* to pierce, penetrate

interf·or -ārī -ātus sum *tr & intr* to interrupt

interfug·iō -ĕre *intr* to slip in between

interfulg·eō -ēre *intr (w. abl)* to shine amid *or* among

interfūs·us -a -um *adj* spread here and there; *(w. acc)* flowing between

interibi *adv* in the meantime

interim *adv* meanwhile; for the moment; sometimes; however, anyhow

inter·imō -imĕre -ēmī -emptus *tr* to do away with, abolish; to kill

interi·or -or -us *adj* inner, interior; internal; inner side of; more remote *(places, peoples, esp. far from the seacoast)*; secret, private; deeper, more profound; more intimate, more personal, more confidential

interiti·ō -ōnis *f* ruin, destruction; *(violent or untimely)* death

interit·us -ūs *m* ruin; *(violent or untimely)* death; dissolution *(of institutions, society, material things)*; extinction

interius *adv* on the inside; inwardly; in the middle; too short; *(to listen)* closely; more deeply

interjac·eō -ēre *intr (w. dat)* to lie between

interjaciō *see* **interjicio**

interjecti·ō -ōnis *f (gram)* interjection; *(rhet)* parenthetical remark *or* phrase

interject·us -a -um *pp of* **interjicio** ‖ *adj (w. dat or* inter + *acc)* set *or* lying between

interject·us -ūs *m* interposition; interval

inter·jiciō -jicĕre -jēcī -jectus *tr* to interpose; *(w. dat or* inter + *acc)* **1** to throw *or* set *(s.th.)* between; **2** to intermingle *(s.th.)* with, intermix *(s.th.)* with

interjun·gō -gĕre -xī -ctus *tr* to join together; to clasp

inter·lābor -lābī -lapsus sum *intr* to glide in between, flow in between

inter·legō -legĕre -lēgī -lectus *tr* to pick *or* pluck here and there

inter·linō -linĕre -lēvī -litus *tr* to smear; to daub in the gaps *(of a structure)*; to tamper with *(a document to falsify it)*

interlo·quor -quī -cūtus sum *intr* to interrupt

interlū·ceō -ēre -xī *intr* to shine through; to be lightning now and then; to be transparent; to be plainly visible

interlūni·a -ōrum *npl* new moon

interlu·ō -ĕre *tr* to flow between; to wash

intermenstru·us -a -um *adj* of the new moon ‖ *n* new moon

intermināt·us -a -um *adj* endless

intermin·or -ārī -ātus sum *tr (w. dat)* to threaten *(s.o.)* with *(s.th.)* ‖ *intr* to threaten

inter·misceō -miscēre -miscuī -mixtus *tr* to intermingle

intermissi·ō -ōnis *f* intermission, pause, interruption; interval of time; *(leg)* adjournment

inter·mittō -mittĕre -mīsī -missus *tr* to interrupt, break off, suspend; to omit, neglect; to leave gaps in, leave unoccupied, leave undefended; to allow *(time)* to pass ‖ *intr* to pause, stop

intermixtus *pp of* **intermisceo**

inter·morior -morī -mortuus sum *intr* to die suddenly; to faint

intermortu·us -a -um *adj* dead; unconscious; *(fig)* half-dead

intermundi·a -ōrum *npl* outer space

intermūrāl·is -is -e *adj* intermural, between two walls

internāt·us -a -um *adj (w. dat)* growing among *or* between

internecīn·us -a -um *adj* internecine, exterminating, of extermination

interneci·ō -ōnis *f* massacre

internecīv·us -a -um *adj* exterminating; **bellum internecivum** war of extermination

internec·ō -āre -āvī -ātus *tr* to exterminate

internect·ō -ĕre *tr* to intertwine

internit·eō -ēre *intr* to shine out

internōd·ium -(i)ī *n (anat)* space between two joints

inter·noscō -noscĕre -nōvī -nōtus *tr* to distinguish, pick out; *(w. ab)* to distinguish *(one thing)* from *(another)*

internunti·ō -āre *intr* to exchange messages

internunt·ius -(i)ī *m*, **internunti·a -ae** *f* messenger, courier; mediator, go-between

intern·us -a -um *adj* internal; civil, domestic

in·terō -terĕre -trīvī -trītus *tr* to rub in; to crumble up

interpellāti·ō -ōnis *f* interruption

interpellāt·or -ōris *m* interrupter; petitioner

interpell·ō -āre -āvī -ātus *tr* to interrupt, break in on; to disturb, obstruct; to raise an objection; to accost with a request

interpol·is -is -e *adj* patched up, touched up, made like new

interpol·ō -āre -āvī -ātus *tr* to refurbish, touch up; to make like new

inter·pōnō -pōněre -posuī -positus *tr* to insert, interpose, intersperse; to add as an ingredient; to include *(in a speeech or book)*; to introduce, bring into play; to introduce as witness *or* participant; to admit *(a person)*; to let *(time)* pass; to alter, falsify *(writings)*; to allege, use as a pretext; *(w. inter + acc)* to place between; **auctoritatem interponere** to assert one's authority, exert one's influence; **fidem interponere** to give one's one's word; **fidem suam in eam rem interponere** to give his word in that matter; **operam** *(or* **studium) interponere** to apply effort **‖** *refl* to interfere; to intervene in order to veto; *(w. dat or in + acc)* to interfere with, meddle with, get mixed up with **‖** *pass (of time)* to elapse in the meantime, intervene; to lie between; *(of writing)* to contain insertions

interpositi·ō -ōnis *f* insertion; introduction; inclusion; parenthetical statement

interpositus *pp of* **interpono**

interposit·us -ūs *m* interposition

interpr·es -etis *mf* mediator, negotiator; middleman, broker; interpreter; expounder; translator

interpretāti·ō -ōnis *f* interpretation, explanation; meaning; translation

interpret·or -ārī -ātus sum *tr* to interpret, construe; to infer, conclude; to decide; to translate

inter·primō -prīměre -pressī -pressus *tr* to squeeze; **fauces interprimere** to choke

interpuncti·ō -ōnis *f* punctuation

interpunct·um -ī *n* pause *(between words and sentences)*; punctuation mark

interpunct·us -a -um *adj* well-divided; *(w. abl)* interspersed with

interpun·gō -gěre -xī -ctus *tr* to divide *(words)* with punctuation, punctuate; to intersperse

interqui·escō -escěre -ēvī *intr* to rest awhile; to pause awhile

interregn·um -ī *n* interregnum *(time between the death of one king and election of another or similar interval between consuls)*

inter·rex -rēgis *m* interrex, regent

interrit·us -a -um *adj* undaunted

interrogāti·ō -ōnis *f* question; interrogation, cross-examination; argument developed by question and answer

interrogāt·um -ī *n* question; **ad interrogatum respondere** to answer the question

interrog·ō -āre -āvī -ātus *tr* to ask, question; to interrogate, cross-examine; to

sue; to seek information from; **casus interrogandi** *(gram)* genitive case; **sententiam interrogare** to ask *(a senator's)* opinion; **lege** *(or* **legibus) interrogare** *(leg)* to arraign, indict **‖** *intr* to ask a question, ask questions; to argue, reason

interrumpō interrumpěre interrūpī interruptus *tr* to break apart, break in half; to break up, smash; to divide, scatter; to interrupt, break off

interruptē *adv* with interruptions

interruptus *pp of* **interrumpo**

intersaep·iō -īre -sī -tus *tr* to fence off, enclose; to stop up, close, cut off

inter·scindō -scinděre -scidī -scissus *tr* to tear apart, tear down; to cut off, separate

interscrī·bō -běre -psī -ptus *tr* to write *(s.th.)* in between

interser·ō -ěre -uī *tr* to interpose; to allege as an excuse

interspīrāti·ō -ōnis *f (rhet)* breathing pause, correct breathing *(in delivering a speech)*

interstinct·us -a -um *adj* blotchy

interstin·guō -guěre -xī -ctus *tr* to spot, blotch; to extinguish

interstring·ō -ěre *tr* to strangle

inter·sum -esse -fuī *intr* to be present, assist, take part; to differ; to be of interest; *(w. dat)* 1 to be present at, attend; 2 take part in; *(w. in + acc)* to be present at **‖** *v impers* there is a difference; it makes a difference; it is of importance; it is of interest; *(w. inter + acc or in + abl)* there is a difference between; *(w. gen or with fem of poss pronouns* **meā, tuā, nostrā,** *etc.)* it makes a difference to, it is of importance to, it concerns (me, you, us, etc.); *(w. gen of value, e.g.,* **magni, permagni, tanti,** *or w. adv* **multum, plurimum, maxime)** it makes a (great, very great, such a great) difference, it is of (great, very great, such great) concern; **ne minimum quidem interest** there is not the slightest difference; **nihil omnino interest** there is no difference whatever

intertext·us -a -um *adj* interwoven

intertra·hō -hěre -xī -ctus *tr (w. dat)* to take *(s.th.)* away from

intertrīment·um -ī *n* wear and tear; loss, wastage

interturbāti·ō -ōnis *f* confusion, turmoil

interturb·ō -āre -āvī *tr* to confuse

intervall·um -ī *n* interval, space, distance; gap, opening; interval of time, spell; pause; break, intermission; contrast, difference *(in degree, quality, etc.)*; **ex intervallo** at *or* from a distance; after a while; at intervals; **ex intervallis** at intervals; **longo intervallo** after a long while, much later;

per intervallum *(or* intervalla) at intervals

inter·vellō -vellĕre -vulsī -vulsus *tr* to pluck here and there

inter·veniō -venīre -vēnī -ventus *tr* to interfere with **ǁ** *intr* to happen along, come on the scene; to intervene, intrude; to happen, crop up; *(w. dat)* to interfere with, interrupt, put a stop to, come in the way of, oppose, prevent

intervent·or -ōris *m* intruder, untimely visitor

intervent·us -ūs *m* intervention; intrusion; mediation

interver·tō -tĕre -tī -sus *tr* (-vort-) to divert, embezzle

intervīs·ō -ĕre -ī -us *tr* to drop in on; to visit from time to time

intervolit·ō -āre -āvī *intr* to flit about

intervom·ō -ĕre -uī -itus *tr (w.* inter + *acc)* to throw up amongst

intervulsus *pp of* intervello

intestābil·is -is -e *adj* infamous, notorious; detestable, shameful

intestātō *adv* intestate

intestāt·us -a -um *adj* intestate; unconvicted by witnesses

intestīn·us -a -um *adj* internal **ǁ** *n* alimentary canal; intestine; **intestinum tenue** small intestine

intexī *perf of* intego

intex·ō -ĕre -uī -tus *tr* to interweave, interlace; to weave; to embroider; to surround, envelop

intib·um -ī *n* (inty-) endive

intimē *adv* intimately, cordially

intim·us -a -um *adj* (-tum-) innermost; deepest, most abstruse, most profound; most secret, most intimate **ǁ** *m* close friend

intin·gō -gĕre -xī -ctus *tr* to dip, soak; to color *(w. cosmetics)*

intolerābil·is -is -e *adj* intolerable; irresistible

intolerand·us -a -um *adj* intolerable

intoler·ans -antis *adj* intolerable; *(w. gen)* unable to stand, unable to put up with

intoleranter *adv* intolerably, immoderately, excessively

intoleranti·a -ae *f* impatience

inton·ō -āre -uī -itus *tr* to thunder forth **ǁ** *intr* to thunder

intons·us -a -um *adj* unshorn, untrimmed; long-haired; rude

intor·queō -quēre -sī -tus *tr* to twist, turn, roll; *(w.* circum + *acc)* to wrap *(s.th.)* around; *(w. dat or* in + *acc)* to hurl *(e.g., spear)* at

intort·us -a -um *adj* twisted; tangled; *(fig)* crooked

intrā *adv* on the inside, inside, within; inward

intrā *prep (w. acc)* 1 inside, within; **intra**

parietes within the walls, at home, privately; **intra se** to oneself, privately; by oneself, alone; in one's own country, at home; 2 inside *(a period of time),* within, during, in the course of, in less than; **intra hos dies** within these (last few) days; 3 within the limits of, without passing beyond, on this side of, short of *(a certain point);* **modice hoc facere aut etiam intra modum** to do this with moderation and even keep on the safe side of moderation; **intra teli jactum progredi** to come within range; **intra (et) extra** inside and out, on both sides

intrābil·is -is -e *adj* approachable

intractābil·is -is -e *adj* intractable, unmanageable; formidable

intractāt·us -a -um *adj* untamed; unbroken *(horse);* unattempted

intrem·iscō -iscĕre -uī *intr* to begin to tremble

intrem·ō -ĕre -uī *intr* to shake, tremble, shiver

intrepidē *adv* calmly, intrepidly

intrepid·us -a -um *adj* calm, intrepid, not nervous; untroubled

intrīc·ō -āre -āvī -ātus *tr* to entangle, involve

intrinsecus *adv (opp:* extrinsecus) on the inside; to the inside, inwards

intrīt·us -a -um *adj* not worn away; *(fig)* not worn out

intrō *adv* inwards, inside, in

intr·ō -āre -āvī -ātus *tr & intr* to enter; to penetrate

introdū·cō -cĕre -xī -ctus *tr* to bring in, lead in; to introduce; to raise *(a subject, point)*

introducti·ō -ōnis *f* introduction

intrō·eō -īre -īvī *or* -iī -itum *tr & intr* to enter

intrō·ferō -ferre -tulī -lātus *tr (w.* in + *acc)* to carry into; **pedem introferre** *(w.* in + *acc)* to set foot in

intrō·gredior -gredī -gressus sum *intr* to step inside

introit·us -ūs *m* entrance; hostile entry; invasion; beginning, prelude

intrōlātus *pp of* introfero

intrō·mittō -mittĕre -mīsī -missus *tr* to let in, admit; to send in; to introduce

introrsum *adv* (-sus) inwards, towards the inside; *(fig)* inwardly

intrō·rumpō -rumpĕre -rūpī -ruptus *tr* to break in, enter by force

introspect·ō -āre *tr* to look in on

intrō·spiciō -spicĕre -spexī -spectus *tr* to look into; to look at, regard; *(fig)* to look into, examine **ǁ** *intr (w.* in + *acc) (lit & fig)* to look into, inspect

intub·um -ī *n* endive

intu·eor -ērī -itus sum *or* intu·or -ī *tr* to look at, gaze at; to consider, take into consideration; to look up to, have regard for; to keep an eye on; to examine visually, inspect **terram intueri** to look down at the ground

intum·escō -escĕre -uī *intr* to swell up, rise; *(of voice)* to grow louder; *(of river)* to rise, become swollen; to become angry; to get a big head, swell with pride

intumulāt·us -a -um *adj* unburied

intuor *see* **intueor**

inturbid·us -a -um *adj* undisturbed, quiet

intus *adv* inside, within; at home, in; to the inside; from within

intūt·us -a -um *adj* unsafe; unprotected unguarded, defenseless

inul·a -ae *f* elecampane *(tall, coarse plant with yellow flowers)*

inult·us -a -um *adj* unavenged; unpunished

inumbr·ō -āre -āvī -ātus *tr* to shade; to cover

inundāti·ō -ōnis *f* inundation, flood

inund·ō -āre -āvī -ātus *tr* to inundate, flood **ǁ** *intr* to overflow; **sanguine inundare** to run red with blood

inun·g(u)ō -g(u)ĕre -xī -ctus *tr* to anoint

inurbānē *adv* impolitely, rudely

inurbān·us -a -um *adj* impolite; unsophisticated, rude, rustic

inur·geō -gēre -sī *intr* to butt

in·ūrō -ūrĕre -ussī -ustus *tr* to burn in, brand, imprint; *(w. dat)* 1 to brand upon, imprint upon, affix to; 2 to inflict upon

inūsitātē *adv* unusually, strangely

inusitāt·us -a -um *adj* unusual, strange, uncommon, extraordinary

inustus *pp of* **inuro**

inūtil·is -is -e *adj* useless; unprofitable; impractical; injurious, harmful

inūtilit·ās -ātis *f* uselessness; harmfulness

inūtiliter *adv* uselessly; harmfully

invā·dō -dĕre -sī -sus *tr* to come *or* go into, enter; to enter upon, undertake, attempt; to invade, attack, rush upon; *(fig)* to seize, take possession of **ǁ** *intr* to come *or* go in; to invade; *(w. in + acc)* 1 to invade; to assail; 2 to seize; 3 to get possession of; 4 to rush to embrace

inval·escō -escĕre -uī *intr* to grow stronger; *(fig)* to increase in power; to grow in frequency; to predominate

invalid·us -a -um *adj* weak; feeble; dim *(light, fire)*; inadequate; ineffectual

invāsī *perf of* **invado**

invāsus *pp of* **invado**

invecti·ō -ōnis *f* importation, importing; arrival by boat

inve·hō -hĕre -xī -ctus *tr* to carry in, bring in, ship in *(by cart, horse, boat, etc.)*; *(w. dat)* to bring *(e.g., evils)* upon **ǁ** *refl (w. acc or* in + *acc)* to rush against, attack **ǁ** *pass* to ride, drive, sail; *(w. acc or* in +

acc) 1 to ride into, sail into; 2 to attack; 3 to inveigh against, attack *(w. words)*; **invehi equo** to ride a horse; **invehi nave** to sail

invendibil·is -is -e *adj* unsaleable

in·veniō -venīre -vēnī -ventus *tr* to come upon, find, come across, discover; to find out; to invent, devise; to learn, ascertain; to get, reach, earn

inventi·ō -ōnis *f* inventiveness; inventing, invention

invent·or -ōris *m,* **inventr·ix -īcis** *f* inventor, author, discoverer

invent·us -a -um *pp of* **invenio ǁ** *n* invention, discovery

invenust·us -a -um *adj* having no sex appeal; homely, unattractive; unlucky in love

inverēcund·us -a -um *adj* disrespectful, immodest, shameless

inverg·ō -ĕre *tr (w. dat or* in + *acc)* to pour upon

inversi·ō -ōnis *f* inversion *(of words)*; irony; allegory

invers·us -a -um *pp of* **inverto ǁ** *adj* turned upside down; turned inside out; **manus inversa** back of the hand

inver·tō -tĕre -tī -sus *tr* to invert, turn upside down, upset, reverse, turn inside out; to transpose, reverse; to pervert, abuse, misrepresent; to use ironically

invesperasc·it -ĕre *v impers* evening is approaching, twilight is falling

investīgāti·ō -ōnis *f* investigation; search

investīgāt·or -ōris *m* investigator

investīg·ō -āre -āvī -ātus *tr* to track, trace, search after; to investigate, search into, search after

inveter·ascō -ascĕre -āvī *intr* to begin to grow old, get old; to become fixed, become established; to become rooted, grow inveterate; to become obsolete

inveterāti·ō -ōnis *f* chronic illness

inveterāt·us -a -um *adj* inveterate, long-standing

invexī *perf of* **inveho**

invicem *or* **in vicem** *adv* in turn, taking turns, one after another, alternately; mutually, each other; **defatigatis invicem integri succedunt** fresh troops take turns in relieving the exhausted troops

invict·us -a -um *adj* unconquered; invincible

invid·ens -entis *adj* envious, jealous

invidenti·a -ae *f* envy, jealousy

invideō -vidēre -vīdī -vīsus *tr* to envy, be jealous of **ǁ** *intr (w. dat)* to envy, begrudge; *(w. dat of person and abl of cause or* in + *abl)* to begrudge *(s.o. s.th.)*, to envy *(s.o.)* because of *(s.th.)*

invidi·a -ae *f* envy, jealousy; unpopularity; **invidiae esse** *(w. dat)* to be the cause of envy to; **invidiam habere** to be unpopular

invidiōsē *adv* spitefully; so as to bring unpopularity on an opponent

invidiōs·us -a -um *adj* envious; spiteful; envied; enviable, causing envy

invid·us -a -um *adj* envious, jealous; *(w. dat)* hostile to, unfavorable to

invigil·ō -āre -āvī -ātum *intr* to be alert, be on one's toes; *(w. dat)* to be on the lookout for, keep an eye on, pay attention to, watch over; *(w. pro + abl)* to watch over

inviolābil·is -is -e *adj* inviolable; invulnerable, indestructible

inviolātē *adv* inviolately

inviolāt·us -a -um *adj* inviolate, unhurt; inviolable

invisitāt·us -a -um *adj* unusual, strange; not seen before, unknown

invīs·ō -ěre -ī -us *tr* to visit, go to see; to look into, inspect; to look after; to catch sight of

invīs·us -a -um *pp of* **invideo** ‖ *adj* unseen; hated, detested; hostile

invītāment·um -ī *n* attraction, allurement, inducement

invītāti·ō -ōnis *f* invitation; challenge

invītāt·us -ūs *m* invitation

invītē *adv* unwillingly, against one's wishes

invīt·ō -āre -āvī -ātus *tr* to invite; to entertain; to summon, challenge; to ask, request; to allure, attract; to encourage, court

invīt·us -a -um *adj* reluctant, unwilling, against one's will; **invitā Minervā** against one's better judgment, against the grain

invi·us -a -um *adj* without roads, trackless, impassable ‖ *npl* rough terrain

invocāti·ō -ōnis *f* invocation

invocāt·us -a -um *adj* unbidden

invoc·ō -āre -āvī -ātus *tr* to invoke, call upon; to call out *(name of one's girlfriend in rolling dice);* to pray for; to address *(with an honorific title)*

involāt·us -ūs *m* flight

involgō *see* **involgo**

involit·ō -āre -āvī *intr (w. dat)* (of long hair) to trail over

invol·ō -āre -āvī -ātus *tr* to swoop down on, pounce on ‖ *intr* to swoop down; *(w. in + acc)* to swoop down on

involūcr·um -ī *n* wrapper; cover; envelope; *(fig)* cover-up, front

involūt·us -a -um *adj* complicated

invol·vō -věre -vī -ūtus *tr* to wrap up; to involve, envelop; to cover completely, overwhelm; *(w. dat or in + acc)* to pile *(s.th.)* on ‖ *refl (w. dat) (fig)* to get all wrapped up in

involvol·us -ī *m* caterpillar *(which rolls up the leaves it infests)*

invulg·ō -āre -āvī -ātus *tr* (-vol-) to reveal, publicize ‖ *intr* to give public evidence

iō *interj* ho!

Ī·ō -ūs *or* **-ōnis** *f (acc & abl:* **Īō)** **Io** *(daughter of Argive King Inachus, changed into a heifer and driven by Juno over the world)*

Iocast·a -ae *or* **Iocast·ē -ēs** *f* Jocasta *(wife of Laius, and mother as well as wife of Oedipus)*

Iōlā·us -ī *m* son of Iphicles and companion of Hercules

Iōl·ē -ēs *f* daughter of Eurytus, who fell in love with Hercules

Iōn·es -um *mpl* Ionians *(Greek inhabitants of the W. coast of Asia Minor)*

Iōnic·us -a -um *adj* Ionic ‖ *m* Ionic dancer ‖ *npl* Ionic dance

Ioni·us -a -um *adj* Ionian ‖ *f* Ionia *(coastal district of Asia Minor)* ‖ *n* Ionian Sea *(off W. coast of Greece)*

iōta *indecl n* iota *(ninth letter of the Greek alphabet)*

Iphianass·a -ae *f* Iphigenia

Iphigenī·a -ae *f* daughter of Agamemnon and Clytemnestra, who was to have been sacrificed at Aulis but was saved by Artemis

Iphit·us -ī *m* Argonaut, son of Eurytus and Antiope

ips·a -īus *or* **-ius** *adj* self, very, just, mere, precisely; in person; by herself, alone; of her own accord ‖ *pron* she herself; lady of the house

ips·e *or* **ips·us -īus** *or* **-ius** *adj* self, very, just, mere, precisely; in person; by himself, alone; of his own accord ‖ *pron* he himself; master; host

ipsim·a -ae *f (coll)* boss

ipsim·us -ī *m (coll)* boss

ips·um -īus *or* **-ius** *adj* self, very, just, mere, precisely; by itself, alone; of itself, spontaneously; **nunc ipsum** just then ‖ *pron* it itself, that itself; **ipsum quod**...the very fact that

ipsus *see* **ipse**

īr·a -ae *f* wrath, resentment

īrācundē *adv* angrily; passionately

īrācundi·a -ae *f* quick temper; anger, wrath, passion, violence; resentment

īrācund·us -a -um *adj* hot-tempered, irritable; angry; resentful

īrasc·or -ārī *intr* to get angry, fly into a rage; *(w. dat)* to get angry with

īrātē *adv* angrily

īrāt·us -a -um *adj* irate, angry, enraged; *(w. dat)* angry at

Īr·is -idis *f* goddess of the rainbow and messenger of the gods

īrōnī·a -ae *f* irony

irrās·us -a -um *adj* unshaven

irratiōnāl·is -is -e *adj* (inr-) irrational

irrau·cescō -cescĕre -sī *intr* **(inr-)** to become hoarse

irrediviv·us -a -um *adj* irreparable

irred·ux -ucis *adj* one-way *(road)*

irreligāt·us -a -um *adj* **(inr-)** not tied

irreligiōsē *adv* **(inr-)** impiously, blasphemously

irreligiōs·us -a -um *adj* **(inr-)** irreligious, impious

irremeābil·is -is -e *adj* **(inr-)** from which there is no return, one-way

irreparābil·is -is -e *adj* **(inr-)** irretrievable; irreparable *(damage)*

irrepert·us -a -um *adj* **(inr-)** undiscovered, not found

irrēp·ō -ĕre -sī -tum *intr* **(inr-)** to creep in; *(fig)* to sneak in; *(w.* ad *or* in + *acc)* to creep toward *or* into; *(fig)* to sneak up on

irreprehens·us -a -um *adj* **(inr-)** blameless

irrequiēt·us -a -um *adj* **(inr-)** restless

irresect·us -a -um *adj* **(inr-)** untrimmed

irresolūt·us -a -um *adj* **(inr-)** not loosened, still tied, unrelaxed

irrēt·iō -īre -īvī *or* **-iī -ītus** *tr* **(inr-)** to net, trap in a net

irretort·us -a -um *adj* **(inr-)** not turned back; **oculo irretorto** without one backward glance

irrever·ens -entis *adj* **(inr-)** irreverent, disrespectful

irreverenter *adv* **(inr-)** irreverently, disrespectfully

irreverenti·a -ae *f* **(inr-)** irreverence, disrespect

irrevocābil·is -is -e *adj* **(inr-)** irrevocable; implacable, relentless

irrevocāt·us -a -um *adj* **(inr-)** not called back, not asked back

irrī·deō -dēre -sī -sus *tr* **(inr-)** to ridicule, laugh at **‖** *intr* to laugh, joke; *(w.* dat) to laugh at

irrīdiculē *adv* **(inr-)** with no sense of humor

irrīdicul·um -ī *n* **(inr-)** laughing stock

irrigāti·ō -ōnis *f* **(inr-)** irrigation

irrig·ō -āre -āvī -ātus *tr* **(inr-)** to irrigate, water; to inundate; *(fig)* to diffuse; *(fig)* to flood, steep, soak

irrigu·us -a -um *adj* **(inr-)** wet, soaked, well-watered; refreshing

irrīsī (inr-) *perf of* **irrideo**

irrīsi·ō -ōnis *f* **(inr-)** ridicule, mockery

irrīs·or -ōris *m* **(inr-)** reviler, mocker

irrīsus (inr-) *pp of* **irrideo**

irrīs·us -ūs *m* **(inr-)** mockery, derision; laughing stock, object of derision

irrītābil·is -is -e *adj* **(inr-)** easily excited; easily enraged, irritable; sensitive

irrītām·en -inis *n* **(inr-)** incentive; provocation

irrītāment·um -ī *n* **(inr-)** incentive; provocation

irrītāti·ō -ōnis *f* **(inr-)** incitement; irritation, provocation; stimulant

irrīt·ō -āre -āvī -ātus *tr* **(inr-)** to provoke, annoy; to incite; to excite, stimulate; to bring on *(a calamity, etc.)*

irrit·us -a -um *adj* **(inr-)** not valid, null and void; futile, pointless, useless; unsuccessful *(person)*

irrogāti·ō -ōnis *f* **(inr-)** imposition *(e.g., of a fine)*

irrog·ō -āre -āvī -ātus *tr* **(inr-)** to impose, inflict; to object to *(proposals)*

irrōr·ō -āre -āvī -ātus *tr* **(inr-)** to moisten with dew; to sprinkle, water; **aquam capiti irrorare** to sprinkle water on (s.o.'s) head

irruct·ō -āre *intr* **(inr-)** to belch

ir·rumpō -rumpĕre -rūpī -ruptus *tr* **(inr-)** to rush into, break down **‖** *intr* to rush in; *(w.* dat *or* in + *acc)* 1 to rush into, rush through; 2 *(fig)* to intrude upon

irru·ō -ĕre -ī *intr* **(inr-)** to rush in, force one's way in; *(w.* dat *or* in + *acc)* 1 to rush into; 2 to rush on; 3 to invade, attack; **irruere in odium** *(w. gen)* to incur the anger of

irrūpī (inr-) *perf of* **irrumpo**

irrupti·ō -ōnis *f* **(inr-)** bursting in; forcible entry; *(mil)* incursion; assault

irrupt·us -a -um (inr-) *pp of* **irrumpo ‖** *adj* unbroken

Ī·rus -ī *m* beggar in the palace of Ulysses in Ithaca

is ejus *adj* this, that, the said, the aforesaid **‖** *pron* he; **is qui** he who, the person who, the one who

Īs·is -is *or* **-idis** *f* Egyptian goddess

Ismari·us -a -um *adj* of Mt. Ismarus in Thrace; Thracian

Īsocrat·ēs -is *m* orator and teacher of rhetoric at Athens *(436–338 B.C.)*

ista *see* **iste**

istāc *adv* that way

istactenus *adv* thus far

istaec *see* **istic**

ist·e -a -ud *adj* that of yours; this, that, the very, that particular; such, of such a kind; that terrible, that despicable **‖** *pron* that one; *(in court)* your client

Isthm·us *or* **Isthm·os -ī** *m (f)* Isthmus of Corinth

ist·ic -aec -oc *or* **-uc** *adj* that, that of yours **‖** *pron* the one, that one

istīc *adv* there, in that place; herein; on this occasion

istinc *adv* from there; from your side; from what you have

istiusmodī *or* **istīmodī** *or* **istīus modī** *or* **istī modī** *adj* that kind of; **istiusmodi scelus** that kind of crime

istō *adv* where you are; therefore; in that matter

istōc *adv* there, to where you are

istorsum *adv* in that direction, that way

istūc *adv* there, to that place, to where you are, that way; **istuc veniam** I'll come to that matter

istūcine *see* istic

istud *see* iste

ita *adv* thus, so, in this manner, in that way; *(of natural consequence)* thus, accordingly, therefore, under these circumstances; *(in affirmation)* yes, true, exactly; *(in questions)* really?, truly?; **ita...ut** *(in comparisons)* just as...so; *(introducing contrast)* whereas...at the same time; *(as adversative)* although...nevertheless; *(introducing result clauses)* so *or* in such a way that; *(as correlatives)* both...and, both...as well as; *(in restriction)* on the condition that, insofar as, on the assumption that; *(of degree)* to such a degree...that, so much...that, so...that; **non ita** not very, not especially; **quid ita?** how so?, what do you mean?

Ītali·a -ae *f* Italy

Ītalic·us -a -um *adj* Italic

Ītal·is -idis *adj* Italian **ll** *fpl* Italian women

Ītali·us -a -um *adj* Italian **ll** *f see* Italia

Ītal·us -a -um *adj* Italian

itaque *adv* and so, and thus, accordingly, therefore, consequently

item *adv* likewise, besides, moreover

it·er -ineris *n* journey, trip; walk; march; day's march; day's journey; route; right of way; duct, passage; method, course, way, road; **ex** *(or* **in) itinere** en route, on the way; **iter facere** to take a trip; to travel; to make way; *(mil)* to march; **iter flectere** to change course; **iter patefacere** to clear a way; **iter terrestre** overland route; **itinere** en route; **maximis itineribus** by marching at top speed

iterāti·ō -ōnis *f* repetition

iter·ō -āre -āvī -ātus *tr* to repeat, renew; to plow again

iterum *adv* again, a second time; **iterum atque iterum** repeatedly, again and again

Ithac·a -ae *or* Ithac·ē -ēs *f* Ithaca *(island off W. coast of Greece in the Ionian Sea and home of Odysseus)*

itidem *adv* in the same way

iti·ō -ōnis *f* going

it·ō -āre -āvī *intr* to go

it·us -ūs *m* going; departure

It·ys -yos *m* son of Tereus and Procne, who was killed by Procne and served up as food to Tereus

iu- = ju-

Ixī·ōn -onis *or* -onos *m* Ixion *(king of the Lapiths, who was tied to a wheel by Jupiter for trying to seduce Juno and sent flying into Tartarus)*

Ixīonid·ēs -ae *m* son of Ixion *(esp. Pirithous)*

Ixīoni·us -a -um *adj* of Ixion

J

jac·eō -ēre -uī -itum *intr* to lie, lie down; to recline *(at table);* to lie ill, be sick; to rest; to lie dead, to have fallen *(in battle);* *(of structures, cities)* to lie in ruins; to linger, stay *(in a place);* *(of places)* to lie, be stituated; *(of places)* to be lowlying, lie low; *(of fields)* to lie idle; *(of prices)* to be low; *(of persons)* to feel low, be despondent; *(of the eyes, face)* to be downcast; *(of hair)* to hang loose; *(of the sea)* to be calm; *(of duties, responsibilities)* to be neglected; to lie prostrate, be powerless; *(of arguments)* to fail, be refuted; to be low in s.o.'s opinion; **amici jacentem animum incitare** to cheer up a friend's despondent mood; **animi militum jacent** the morale of the soldiers is low; **Brundisi jacere** to linger in Brundisi; **in orbem jacere** *(of a group of islands)* to lie in a circle, form a circle; **jacere cum** to have sexual intercourse with; **mihi ad pedes jacere** to lie prostrate at my feet

jaci·ō jacĕre jēcī jactus *tr* to throw, cast, fling; to toss *(head, limbs);* to hurl *(charges, insults);* to lay *(foundations);* to build, establish, set, found, construct; to emit, produce *(heat, light, sparks);* to sow, scatter *(seed);* to throw down; to throw away; to mention, utter, declare, intimate; **contumeliam in aliquem jacere** to hurl the charge of defiance at s.o., charge s.o. with defiance; **fundamenta jacere** to lay the foundations; **voces jaciuntur** words are uttered **ll** *refl* to leap; to rush, burst

jact·ans -antis *adj* boastful, showing off; proud

jactanter *adv* boastfully; ostentatiously; arrogantly

jactanti·a -ae *f* bragging; ostentation

jactāti·ō -ōnis *f* tossing to and fro; swaying; shaking; writhing; bragging, showing off; **jactatio animi** agitation; **jactatio corporis** gesticulation; **jactatio maritima** seasickness

jactāt·us -ūs *m* tossing, waving

jactit·ō -āre *tr* to display, show off

jact·ō -āre -āvī -ātus *tr* to throw, hurl; to toss about, shake; to wave, brandish; to throw away, throw out; to throw overboard; to throw aside, reject; to disturb, disquiet, stir up; to make restless, cause to toss; to consider, discuss; to throw out, mention; to brag about, show off **ll** *refl* to boast, show off, throw one's weight around **ll** *pass* to toss, rock

jactūr·a -ae *f* throwing away, throwing overboard; loss, sacrifice

jactus *pp of* **jacio**
jact·us -ūs *m* toss, throw, cast
jaculābil·is -is -e *adj* missile
jaculāti·ō -ōnis *f* hurling
jaculāt·or -ōris *m* thrower, hurler; light-armed soldier; spearman; hunter
jaculātr·ix -īcis *f* huntress
jacul·or -ārī -ātus sum *tr* to throw; to shoot at; *(fig)* to aim at, strive after
jacul·us -a -um *adj* throwing, casting ‖ *n* dart, javelin; casting net
jājūn- = jejun-
Jālysi·us -a -um *adj* of Jalysos, a town on the island of Rhodes
Jālys·us -ī *m* son of the god Helios, and eponym of the town Jalysos ‖ famous portrait of Jalysus by Protogenes
jam *adv (in the present)* now, already; *(in the past)* already, by then, by that time; *(in the future)* very soon, right away; *(in transition)* now, next, moreover; *(for emphasis)* actually, precisely, quite; *(in conclusion)* then surely; **jam ante(a)** even before that; **jam dudum** long ago, long since; **jam inde** immediately; **jam inde ab** all the while from, continuously from; **jam jam** *(for emphasis or emotive effect)* at last, now finally **jam...jam** at one time...at another; **first...then; jamjamque** at any time now, now all but...; **jam nunc** even now; **jam pridem** long since; **jam primum** to begin with, first of all; **jam tum** even then, even at that time; **quid jam?** *(coll)* what (is the matter) now?
Jānicul·um -ī *n* Roman hill on right bank of the Tiber
Jānigen·a *adj (masc & fem only)* born of Janus
jānit·or -ōris *m* doorman, porter
jānitr·ix -īcis *f* portress
janthin·us -a -um *adj* violet ‖ *n* the color violet ‖ *npl* violet clothes
jānu·a -ae *f* door; doorway, entrance; *(fig)* entrance, approach, gateway; **janua leti** gateway of death, gateway to the lower world
Jānuāri·us -a -um *adj* of Janus; **mensis Januarius** January *(first month, after 153 B.C., of the Roman year)* ‖ *m* January
jān·us -ī *m* covered passage, arcade; **janus imus, janus medius, janus summus** bottom archway, middle archway, top archway *(three archways on the east side of the Forum, where money changers and merchants conducted their business)* ‖ **Jānus** Janus *(old Italic deity, represented as having two faces)* ‖ temple of Janus *(at the bottom of the Argiletum in the Forum)* ‖ **Janus Geminus** *(or* **Janus Quirinus** *or* **Janus Quirini)** shrine of Janus in the Forum consisting of an archway, with doors at the ends that were closed in times of peace

Jāpyd·es -um *mpl* the people of Japydia
Jāpydi·a -ae *f* country in the N. part of Illyria
Jāpygi·a -ae *f* Greek name for part of S.E. Italy, including some or all of Calabria and Apulia
Jāp·yx -ygis *or* **-ygos** *adj* Japygian ‖ *m* son of Daedalus, who gave his name to Japygia ‖ river in Apulia ‖ the N.W.N. wind, which favors the crossing from Italy to Greece
Jarb·a(s) -ae *m* Jarbas *(king of the Gaetulians in N. Africa, whom Dido rejected as a suitor)*
Jarbīt·a -ae *m* Mauretanian, Moor
Jardan·is -idis *f* daughter of Jardanus, king of Lydia *(i.e., Omphale)*
Jās·ō(n) -onis *m* Jason *(son of Aeson, leader of the Argonauts, and husband of Medea)*
Jāsoni·us -a -um *adj* Jason's
Jasp·is -idis *or* **-idos** *f* jasper
Jās·us -ī *f* town on the coast of Caria
jātralipt·ēs -ae *m* masseur
Jāz·yx -ygis *m* member of a people dwelling near the Danube
jec·ur -oris *or* **-ineris** *or* **-inoris** *n* liver; *(as the seat of emotions)* anger, lust
jecuscul·um -ī *n* little liver
jējūnē *adv (fig)* dryly
jējūniōs·us -a -um *adj* **(jājūn-)** *(hum)* abounding in hunger, hungry
jējūnit·ās -ātis *f* **(jājūn-)** fasting; dryness *(of style)*
jējūn·ium -(i)ī *n* fasting, fast; hunger, leanness
jējūn·us -a -um *adj* **(jājūn-)** fasting; hungry; thin; insignificant, paltry; poor *(land);* jejune *(style)*
jentācul·um -ī *n* **(jājen-)** breakfast
jent·ō -āre -āvī *intr* to eat breakfast
Jocast·a -ae *f* wife of Laïus and mother and wife of Oedipus
jocāti·ō -ōnis *f* jesting, humor
jocineris *gen of* **jecur**
joc·or -ārī -ātus sum *or* **joc·ō -āre** *tr* to say in jest ‖ *intr* to joke, crack a joke, be joking
jocōsē *adv* humorously, as a joke, jokingly
jocōs·us -a -um *adj* humorous, funny; fond of jokes
joculār·is -is -e *adj* humorous, funny
joculāri·us -a -um *adj* ludicrous
joculāt·or -ōris *m* joker
jocul·or -ārī -ātus sum *intr* to joke
joc·us -ī *m* (pl: **joc·ī -ōrum** *mpl,* **joc·a -ōrum** *npl)* joke; laughing stock; child's play; **joco remoto** all joking aside; **per jocum** as a joke
jub·a -ae *f* mane; crest

jub·ar -aris *n* radiance, brightness; sunshine

jubāt·us -a -um *adj* crested

ju·beō -bēre -ssī -ssus *tr* to order; to prescribe *(a task);* to designate, appoint; *(med)* prescribe; *(pol)* to order, decree, ratify; **jube fratrem tuum salvere** *(in letters)* best regards to your brother; say good- bye to your brother

jūcundē *adv* pleasantly, delightfully

jūcundit·ās -ātis *f* pleasantness, delight, enjoyment **‖** *fpl* favors

jūcund·us -a -um *adj* pleasant, delightful, agreeable

Jūdae·us -a -um *adj* Jewish **‖** *mf* Jew **‖** *f* Judea, Palestine

Jūdaïc·us -a -um *adj* Jewish; of Judea; *(mil)* stationed in Judea

jūd·ex -icis *m* judge; juror; arbitrator; umpire; critic, scholar; **judex morum** censor; **me judice** in my judgment

jūdicāti·ō -ōnis *f* judicial investigation; *(fig)* judgment, opinion

jūdicāt·us -a -um *adj* decided, determined **‖** *m* condemned person **‖** *n* judicial decision, judgment; precedent; fine; **judicatum facere** to carry out a decision; **judicatum solvere** to pay a fine

jūdicāt·us -ūs *m* judgeship

jūdiciāl·is -is -e *adj* judicial, forensic

jūdiciāri·us -a -um *adj* judiciary

jūdic·ium -(i)ī *n* trial, court; sentence; jurisdiction; opinion, decision; faculty of judging, judgment, good judgment, taste, tact, discretion; criterion; **ad judicium ire** to go to court; **in judicio esse** to be under investigation; **in judicium deducere** *(or* **vocare)** to take to court; **in judicium venire** to come before the court; **judicium agere** to conduct a trial; **judicium dare** *(or* **reddere)** *(of a praetor)* to grant an action; **judicium facere (in + acc)** to pass judgment against; **judicium tenere** *(or* **vincire)** to win a case; **judicium privatum** civil suit; **judicium publicum** criminal trial; **meo judicio** in my judgment; **suo judicio** intentionally; **suprema judicia** last will and testament

jūdic·ō -āre -āvī -ātus *tr* to judge; to examine; to sentence, condemn; to form an opinion of; to conclude; to declare, proclaim; *(w. dat of person and acc of the offense)* to convict *(s.o.)* of; *(w. gen)* to find *(s.o.)* guilty of; *(w. dat of person and gen of the offense)* to convict *(s.o.)* of

jugāl·is -is -e *adj* yoked together; nuptial

jugāti·ō -ōnis *f* tying up

jūger·um -ī *n* jugerum *(land measure, about ⅔ of an acre)*

jūg·is -is -e *adj* continuous, perennial, inexhaustible

jūgl·ans -andis *f* walnut tree; walnut

jugōs·us -a -um *adj* hilly

Jugul·ae -ārum *fpl (astr)* Orion's Belt *(3 stars in the constellation Orion)*

jugul·ō -āre -āvī -ātus *tr* cut the throat of, kill, murder; to destroy; to silence

jugul·um -ī *n,* **jugul·us -ī** *m* throat

jug·um -ī *n* yoke, collar; pair, team; crossbar *(of loom);* thwart *(of boat);* common bond, union; wedlock; pair, couple; mountain ridge; *(mil)* yoke *(consisting of a spear laid crosswise on two upright spears, under which the conquered had to pass)* **‖** *npl* heights

Jugurth·a -ae *m* king of Numidia *(160– 104 B.C.)*

Jūli·a -ae *f* aunt of Julius Caesar and wife of Marius **‖** daughter of Julius Caesar and wife of Pompey *(d. 54 B.C.)* **‖** daughter of Augustus by Scribonia *(39 B.C.– A.D. 14)*

Jūli·us -a -um *adj* Julian; of July; **mensis Julius** July **‖** *m* Roman first name *(praenomen);* July

Jūl·us -ī *m* son of Aeneas *(also called Ascanius)*

jūment·um -ī *n* beast of burden, horse, mule

junce·us -a -um *adj* of reeds; slim, slender

juncōs·us -a -um *adj* overgrown with reeds

junctim *adv* side by side; in succession

juncti·ō -ōnis *f* joining, combination, union

junctūr·a -ae *f* joining, uniting, joint, juncture; connection, relationship; combination

junct·us -a -um *pp of* **jungo ‖** *adj* connected, associated, united, attached

junc·us -ī *m* reed

jun·gō -gĕre -xī -ctus *tr* to join, join together, unite, connect; to yoke, harness; to couple, pair, mate; to bridge *(a river);* to bring together, associate, ally; to add; to compose *(poems);* to combine *(words)*

jūni·or -ōris *adj (mas & fem only)* younger **‖** *mpl* younger men *(esp. of military age, between 17 and 46 years)*

jūniper·us -ī *f* juniper

Jūni·us -a -um *adj* June, of June; **mensis Junius** June **‖** *m* Roman first name *(praenomen);* June

jūn·ix -īcis *f* heifer

Jūn·ō -ōnis *f* daughter of Saturn and wife and sister of Jupiter *(commonly identified with Hera);* woman's tutelary deity *(corresponding to a male's* **genius); Juno Lucina** goddess of childbirth *(applied to Juno and Diana);* **Juno inferna** name of Proserpina *(queen of the lower world);* **Junonis avis** peacock; **Junonis stella** planet Venus

Juppiter *(or* **Jūpiter** *or* **Diespiter) Jovis** *m* son of Saturn, brother and husband of

Juno, and chief god of the Romans *(commonly identified with Zeus)*
jurāt·or -ōris *m* judge; assistant censor
jūrāt·us -a -um *adj* being under oath; having given one's word
jūre *adv* rightfully; with good reason, deservedly; correctly
jūreconsult·us -ī *m* (**jūris-**) legal expert
jūreperītus *see* **jurisperitus**
jurg·ium -(i)ī *n* quarrel **ǁ** *npl* reproaches, abuse
jurg·ō -āre -āvī -ātus *tr* to scold **ǁ** *intr* to quarrel
jūridiciāl·is -is -e *adj* juridical
jūrisconsult·us -ī *m* (**jūre-**) legal expert, lawyer
jūrisdicti·ō -ōnis *f* administration of justice; jurisdiction
jūrisperīt·us -ī *m* (**jūre-**) legal expert, lawyer
jūr·ō -āre -āvī -ātus *tr* to swear; to swear by, attest, call to witness; to swear to, attest; to promise under oath, vow **ǁ** *intr* to swear, take an oath; *(w.* **in** + *acc)* 1 to swear allegiance to; 2 to swear to observe *(the laws, etc.);* 3 to conspire against; **in haec verba jurare** to swear according to the prescribed form; **in verba alicujus jurare** to swear allegiance to s.o.; **jurare calumniam** to swear that the accusation is not false
jūs jūris *n* juice, broth, gravy
jūs jūris *n* law, the laws *(as established by society and custom rather than statute law);* legal system, right, justice; law court; legal right, authority, permission; prerogative; jurisdiction; **in jus ire** to go to court; **jura dare** to prescribe laws, administer justice; **jure** by right, rightfully; **jus dicere** to sit as judge, hold court; **jus gentium** law available to aliens as well as to citizens; international law; **jus praetorium** principles of law contained in a praetor's edict; **jus publicum** constitutional law; **mei juris** subject to my control; **pro jure suo** without exceeding one's rights, at will, freely; in one's own right; **sui juris** *(or* **suo jure)** legally one's own master; **summum jus** strict letter of the law
jūsjūrandum *or* **jūs jūrandum** *(gen:* **jūr·isjūrand·ī** *or* **jūr·is jūrand·ī)** *n* oath; **aliquem jurejurando adigere** to bind s.o. with an oath, have s.o. take an oath
jussū *(abl only)* *m* by order; **meo jussu** by my order
juss·us -a -um *pp of* **jubeo ǁ** *n* order, command, bidding
justē *adv* justly, rightly
justific·us -a -um *adj* just-dealing
justiti·a -ae *f* justice, fairness
justit·ium -(i)ī *n* suspension of legal business, legal holiday; period of mourning; *(fig)* standstill
just·us -a -um *adj* just, fair; justified, well-founded; formal; in due order, according to protocol, regular **ǁ** *n* justice; due measure; **plus quam justo** more than due measure, too much **ǁ** *npl* rights, one's due; regular tasks, formalities; ceremonies, due ceremony; funeral rites, obsequies
Jūturn·a -ae *f* nymph, sister of Turnus, the king of the Rutuli
jūtus *pp of* **juvo**
juvenāl·is -is -e *adj* youthful; juvenile **ǁ Juvenalis** *m* Juvenal *(Decimus Junius Juvenalis, Roman satirist in the time of Domitian and Trajan, c.* A.D. *62–142)*
juvenc·us -a -um *adj* young **ǁ** *m* bullock; young man **ǁ** *f* heifer; girl
juven·escō -escĕre *intr* to grow up; to become young again
juvenīl·is -is -e *adj* youthful; juvenile; cheerful
juvenīliter *adv* youthfully, boyishly
juven·is -is -e *adj* young **ǁ** *m* young man *(between the ages of 20 and 45);* warrior **ǁ** *f* young lady
juven·or -ārī -ātus sum *intr* to act like a kid
juvent·a -ae *f* youth
juvent·ās -ātis *f or* **juvent·ūs -ūtis** *f* youth, prime of life, manhood; *(collectively)* young people, the young, youth
juv·ō juvāre jūvī jūtus *tr* to help; *(of terrain)* to give *(one)* an advantage; to back up *(an opinion);* to benefit, do good to; to please, delight **ǁ** *v impers (w. inf)* it helps to; **juvat me** it delights me, I am glad, I am relieved
juxtā *adv* nearby, in close proximity; alike, in like manner, equally; *(w.* **ac, atque, et, quam,** *or* **cum)** as well as, just the same as **ǁ** *prep (w. acc)* 1 close to, near to, next to; 2 next to, immediately after; 3 near, bordering on; 4 next door to
juxtim *adv* near; equally

K

K. *abbr* **Kaeso** *(Roman first name, praenomen)*
Kalend·ae -ārum *fpl* (**Cal-**) Kalends *(first day of the Roman month);* **tristes Kalendae** gloomy Kalends *(because interest was due on the Kalends)*
Kalendār·ium -(i)ī *n* account book, ledger
Karthāginiens·is -is -e *adj* (**Carth-**) Carthaginian
Karthāg·ō -inis *f* (**Carth-**) Carthage

L

L *abbr* the number 50

L. *abbr* **Lucius** *(Roman first name, praenomen)*

labasc·ō -ĕre *intr* to break up, dissolve; to waver; to give in, yield

lābēcul·a -ae *f* blemish, stain

labe·faciō -facĕre -fēcī -factus *tr* to cause to totter; to shake, weaken; *(fig)* to cause to waver, shake; *(fig)* to undermine *(authority, power)*

labefactāti·ō -ōnis *f* loosening

labefact·ō -āre -āvī -ātus *tr* to shake, loosen, make unsteady; to undermine the authority of; to undermine *(loyalty, etc.)*

lăbell·um -ī *n* lip

lābell·um -ī *n* small basin

labeōs·us -a -um *adj* thick-lipped

lāb·ēs -is *f* fall, falling down; stroke, blow; disaster; cause of disaster; blot, stain; blemish, defect; disgrace, discredit; *(geol)* subsidence, landslide; **labem dare** to collapse

labi·a -ae *f* (thick) lip

Labīcān·us -a -um *adj* of the town of Labici; **via Labicana** a road entering Rome from the S.E. ‖ *n* territory of the Labici

Labīc·ī -ōrum *mpl* small town about 15 miles S.E. of Rome ‖ *mpl* people of Labici

Labiēn·us -a -um *adj* Roman clan name *(nomen)*, esp. Titus Labienus *(Caesar's officer who defected to Pompey, d. 45 B.C.)*

labiōs·us -a -um *adj* thick-lipped

lab·ium -(i)ī *n* lip; **labiis aliquem ductare** *(prov)* to lead s.o. by the nose

lab·ō -āre -āvī *intr* to totter, wobble; to waver, hesitate, be undecided; to fall to pieces, go to ruin

lābor lābī lapsus sum *intr* to glide, slide, slip; to fall, sink; to slip away, disappear, escape; *(of time)* to slip by, pass; *(of liquids, rivers)* to flow; *(of the sun)* to sink down; *(of day)* to decline; *(of style)* to run smoothly; *(of words)* to slip out; *(of a building)* to collapse; *(fig)* to fade; *(fig)* to fall into error, go wrong; **memoriā labi** to have a lapse of memory; **mente labi** to go out of one's mind

lab·or *or* **lab·os -ōris** *m* effort, exertion; work, labor; trouble, distress, suffering; cause of distress; wear and tear; product of work, production; drudgery; **lunae** *(or* **solis)** **labores** eclipse of the moon *(or* sun)

labōrif·er -era -erum *adj* struggling, hard-working

labōriōs·us -a -um *adj* laborious; full of troubles, troublesome; energetic, industrious, hard-working

labōr·ō -āre -āvī -ātus *tr* to work at; to make by toil; to produce *(grain, etc.)*; *(w. internal acc)* to be worried about, be concerned about, e.g.: **hoc homines timent, hoc laborant** people fear this, they are worried about this; **nihil laboro de iis** I am not concerned about them; **nihil laboro, nisi ut salvus sis** my only concern is that you are O.K. *(literally, I am concerned as to nothing except that you be well)* ‖ *intr* to work, perform physical work; to suffer, be troubled; to exert oneself; *(w. abl of cause or* **ab** *or* **ex)** 1 to suffer *(physical pain)* from, e.g.: **(a) stomacho** *(or* **ex stomacho) laborare** to have stomach trouble; **e dolore laborare** to suffer pain; **e renibus laborare** to have kidney problems; **laborantes utero puellae** pregnant girls, girls in labor *(i.e., in giving birth)*; 2 to be distressed at, be anxious about, be worried about, be in trouble because of: **laborat de aestimatione sua** he is anxious *or* worried about his reputation; **ex aere alieno laborare** to be heavily in debt, be in trouble because of debt; **e dolore laborare** to be afflicted with grief; **ex inscientia laborare** to suffer from ignorance; **cujus manu sit percussus, non laboro** I do not concern myself over by whose hand he was struck; *(w.* **in** + *abl)* 1 to be in trouble over, be in danger because of, e.g.: **in re familiari valde laborare** to be in deep trouble over personal finances, be in deep financial trouble; 2 to take pains with, exert oneself on behalf of, e.g.: **multo plus est in reliqua causa laborandum** much greater pains must be taken with the rest of the case *or* lawsuit; *(w.* **in** + *acc)* to strive for, work for, e.g.: **in divitias luxuriamque laborare** to strive for wealth and luxury; *(w.* **in** *or* **ut** + *subj)* to strive to, try to, take pains to, make an effort to, e.g.: **laborabat ut reliquas civitates adjungeret** he tried to annex the rest of the communities; *(w.* **de** + *abl)* to be anxious about, be worried about; **luna laborat** *(astr)* the moon is in eclipse; **silvae laborantes** the groaning forests; **suis laborantibus succurrere** to help his own people in difficulty

labōs *see* **labor**

lăbr·um -ī *n* lip; edge

lābr·um -ī *n* basin, tub, bathtub

labrusc·a -ae *f* wild vine

labrusc·um -ī *n* wild grape

labyrinthē·us -a -um *adj* labyrinthine

labyrinth·us -ī *m* labyrinth, maze *(esp. that built by Daedalus on Crete)*

lac lactis *n* milk; milky sap of plants
Lacaen·a -ae *f* Spartan woman
Lacedaem·ō(n) -onis *f* Sparta
Lacedaemōni·us -a -um *adj* Spartan
lac·er -era -erum *adj* mangled, lacerated; *(of things)* badly damaged
lacerāti·ō -ōnis *f* laceration, tearing, mangling
lacern·a -ae *f* mantle, cloak
lacernāt·us -a -um *adj* cloaked
lacer·ō -āre -āvī -ātus *tr* to lacerate, tear, mangle; to batter, damage; to rack *(w. pain);* to slander, abuse; to waste *(time);* to wreck *(a ship); (fig)* to murder *(a song, speech)*
lacert·us -a -um *adj* muscular ‖ *m* lizard; upper arm; muscle ‖ *mpl* muscles, brawn ‖ *f* lizard *(female)*
lacess·ō -ēre -īvī *or* **-iī -ītus** *tr* to provoke, exasperate; to challenge; to move, arouse
Laches·is -is *f* one of the three Fates
lacini·a -ae *f* flap *(of a garment)*
Lacīn·ium -(i)ī *n* promontory in Bruttium with a temple to Juno
Lac·ō(n) -ōnis *m* Spartan; Spartan dog
Lacōni·a -ae *f* district of the Peloponnesus of which Sparta was the chief city
Lacōnic·us -a -um *adj* Spartan ‖ *n* sweat bath, sauna
lacrim·a -ae *f* (-rum-) tear(drop); *(bot)* gumdrop *(from plant)* ‖ *fpl* tears; dirge
lacrimābil·is -is -e *adj* worthy of tears, deplorable
lacrimābund·us -a -um *adj* tearful, about to break into tears
lacrim·ō -āre -āvī -ātus *tr* (-rum-) to cry for, shed tears over ‖ *intr* to cry, shed tears
lacrimōs·us -a -um *adj* crying, tearful; causing tears, bringing tears to the eyes
lacrimul·a -ae *f* teardrop, little tear; *(fig)* crocodile tear
lacrum- = lacrim-
lact·ans -antis *adj* milk-giving
lactāri·us -a -um *adj* milky
lact·ens -entis *adj* unweaned, still breastfeeding; milky, juicy, tender; full of milk ‖ *m* suckling
lacteol·us -a -um *adj* milk-white
lact·ēs -ium *fpl* small intestines; *(as a dish)* chitterlings; **laxae lactes** empty stomach
lactesc·ō -ēre *intr* to turn to milk
lacte·us -a -um *adj* milky, full of milk; milk-colored, milk-white
lact·ō -āre -āvī -ātus *tr* to cajole, induce
lactūc·a -ae *f* lettuce
lacūn·a -ae *f* ditch, hole, pit; pond, pool; *(fig)* hole, gap
lacūn·ar -āris *n* paneled ceiling
lacūn·ō -āre -āvī -ātus *tr* to panel
lacūnōs·us -a -um *adj* sunken; pitted

lac·us -ūs *m* vat; tank, pool, reservoir, cistern; lake
lae·dō -dere -sī -sus *tr* to knock, strike; to hurt; to rub open; to wound; to break *(promise, pledge);* to harm *(reputation, interests);* to offend, outrage, violate; *(w. ad)* to smash *(s.th.)* against; *(poet)* to mar
laen·a -ae *f* lined coat
Laërt·ēs -ae *m* father of Odysseus
Laëtiad·ēs -ae *m* son of Laërtes, Odysseus
laesī *perf of* **laedo**
laesi·ō -ōnis *f* attack, provocation
Laestrȳg·ōn -onis *or* **-onos** *m* Laestrygonian *(one of the mythical races of cannibals in Italy, founders of Formiae)*
Laestrȳgoni·us -a -um *adj* Lyaestrygonian, of Formiae
laes·us -a -um *pp of* **laedo** ‖ *adj* harmed; **res laesae** adversity
laetābil·is -is -e *adj* cheerful, glad
laet·ans -antis *adj* joyful, glad
laetāti·ō -ōnis *f* rejoicing, joy
laetē *adv* joyfully, gladly
laetific·ans -antis *adj* joyous
laetific·ō -āre -āvī -ātus *tr* to gladden, cheer up ‖ *pass* to rejoice
laetific·us -a -um *adj* joyful, cheerful
laetiti·a -ae *f* joyfulness, gladness, exuberance
laet·or -ārī -ātus sum *intr* to rejoice, be glad
laet·us -a -um *adj* glad, cheerful, rejoicing; happy; fortunate, auspicious; fertile, rich *(soil);* smiling *(grain);* sleek, fat *(cattle);* bright, cheerful *(appearance);* cheering, welcome *(news)*
laevē *adv* awkwardly
laev·us -a -um *adj* left, on the left side; awkward, stupid; ill-omened; lucky, propitious ‖ *f* left hand, left side ‖ *n* the left ‖ *npl* the area on the left
lagan·um -ī *n,* **lagan·us -ī** *m* pancake
lagēna *see* **lagoena**
lagē·os -ī *f* a Greek variety of vine
Lāgē·us -a -um *adj* of Lagus *(i.e., of the Ptolemies),* Egyptian
lagoen·a *or* **lagōn·a** *or* **lagēn·a** *or* **lagūn·a -ae** *f* bottle
lagō·is -idis *f* grouse
lagūna *see* **lagoena**
laguncul·a -ae *f* flask
Lāg·us -ī *m* Ptolemy I, King of Egypt
Lāïad·ēs -ae *m* son of Laius *(Oedipus)*
Lāï·us -ī *m* Laius *(father of Oedipus)*
lall·ō -āre *intr* to sing a lullaby
lām·a -ae *f* swamp, bog
lamber·ō -āre *tr* to tear to pieces
lamb·ō -ēre -ī *tr* to lick, lap; *(of a river)* to lap, flow by; *(of ivy)* to cling to
lāment·a -ōrum *npl* lamentation
lāmentābil·is -is -e *adj* pitiable; doleful; mournful, sorrowful

lāmentāri·us -a -um *adj* sorrowful, pitiful
lāmentāti·ō -ōnis *f* lamentation
lāment·or -ārī -ātus sum *tr* to lament ‖ *intr* to lament, wail, cry
lami·a -ae *f* witch, sorceress
lāmin·a *or* **lammin·a** *or* **lamn·a -ae** *f* plate, thin sheet *(of metal or wood)*; blade; *(coll)* cash; peel, shell
lamp·as -adis *or* **-ados** *f* torch; brightness; light *(of the sun, moon, stars)*; *(w. numerals)* day; meteor; lamp
Lam·us -ī *m* king of the Laestrygonians ‖ son of Hercules and Omphale
lān·a -ae *f* wool; working in wool, spinning; **lana aurea** golden fleece; **lanam trahere** to card wool; **lanas ducere** to spin wool; **rixari de lanā caprinā** *(prov)* to fight over nothing *(literally, to fight over goat wool)*
lānār·ius -(i)ī *m* wool worker
lānāt·us -a -um *adj* woolly ‖ *fpl* sheep
lance·a -ae *f* lance, spear
lancin·ō -āre -āvī -ātus *tr* to squander
lāne·us -a -um *adj* woolen; soft
langue·faciō -facĕre -fēcī -factus *tr* to make tired
langu·ens -entis *adj* languid, drooping, listless
langu·eō -ēre *intr* to be tired, be weary; to be weak, be feeble *(from disease)*; to be sick; *(fig)* to be languid, listless; to be without energy; *(of water)* to be sluggish; *(of plants)* to droop, wilt
langu·escō -escĕre -uī *intr* to become weak, grow faint; to become listless; to decline, decrease; to relax
languidē *adv* weakly; slugglishly
languidul·us -a -um *adj* languid; wilted, drooping *(plants)*
languid·us -a -um *adj* weak, faint; weary; languid, sluggish; listless; lazy; drooping, wilting *(plants)*
langu·or -ōris *m* weakness, faintness, languor; listlessness, sluggishness; apathy; idleness
laniāt·us -ūs *m* mangling ‖ *mpl* mental anguish
laniēn·a -ae *f* butcher shop
lānific·ium -(i)ī *n* weaving
lānific·us -a -um *adj* spinning, weaving, of spinning, of weaving
lānig·er -era -erum *adj* fleecy ‖ *m* sheep *(ram)* ‖ *f* sheep *(ewe)*
lani·ō -āre -āvī -ātus *tr* to tear to pieces, mangle
lanist·a -ae *m* gladiator trainer, fencing master; *(pej)* ringleader
lānit·ium -(i)ī *n* wool
lan·ius -(i)ī *m* butcher; *(pej)* executioner, butcher
lantern·a -ae *f* (lāt-) lantern
lanternār·ius -(i)ī *m* guide
lānūg·ō -inis *f* down *(of plants, on cheeks)*

Lānuv·ium -(i)ī *n* town in Latium on the Appian Way
lan·x -cis *f* dish, platter; pan *(of a pair of scales)*; **aequā lance** impartially
Lāŏco·ōn -ontis *m* son of Priam and priest of Apollo, who, with his two sons, was killed by sea serpents
Lāŏmedontē·us *or* **Lāŏmedonti·us -a -um** *adj* Trojan
Lāŏmedontiad·ēs -ae *m* son of Laomedon, Priam ‖ *mpl* Trojans
lapath·um -ī *n* *or* **lapath·us -ī** *f* sorrel *(plant)*
lapicīd·a -ae *m* stonecutter, quarry worker
lapicīdīn·ae -ārum *fpl* stone quarry
lapidāri·us -a -um *adj* stone; **latomiae lapidariae** stone quarries ‖ *m* stonecutter
lapidāti·ō -ōnis *f* throwing stones, stoning
lapidāt·or -ōris *m* stone thrower
lapide·us -a -um *adj* of stones, stone, stony; **lapideus imber** shower of meteoric stones; **lapideus sum** *(fig)* I am petrified
lapid·ō -āre -āvī -ātus *tr* to throw stones at, stone ‖ *v impers* it is raining stones
lapidōs·us -a -um *adj* full of stones, stony; hard as stone; gritty *(bread)*
lapill·us -ī *m* small stone, pebble; precious stone, gem; piece, counter *(in a game)*; voting pebble
lap·is -idis *m* stone; milestone; platform; boundary stone, landmark; tombstone; precious stone, gem, pearl; stone statue; marble table; **lapides loqui** to speak harsh words
Lapith·ae -ārum *mpl* mountain tribe in Thessaly that fought the centaurs
lapp·a -ae *f* bur *(prickly head or seed vessel of certain plants)*
lapsi·ō -ōnis *f* sliding, slipping; *(fig)* tendency
laps·us -ūs *m* falling, fall, sliding, slipping, gliding, flow, flight; blunder, slip; fall from favor; lapse *(of time)*; course *(of the stars)*; **lapsus rotarum** rolling wheels
laqueār·ia -ium *npl* paneled ceiling
laqueāt·us -a -um *adj* paneled, having a paneled ceiling
laque·us -ī *m* noose; snare; *(fig)* snare, trap ‖ *mpl* subtleties
Lār Laris *(gen plur:* **Larum** *or* **Larium)** *m* tutelary deity, household god; hearth, home ‖ *mpl* hearth, home, house, household, family
lard·um -ī *n* bacon
Lārenti·a -ae *f* *(also* **Acca Lārentia)** wife of Faustulus who reared Romulus and Remus
largē *adv* liberally, generously; in large numbers, in large quantities; to a great extend *or* degree

largific·us -a -um *adj* bountiful
largiflu·us -a -um *adj* gushing
largiloqu·us -a -um *adj* talkative
larg·ior -īrī -ītus sum *tr* to give generously, bestow freely; to lavish; to confer; to grant, concede; to condone, overlook; *(w. dat)* to overlook in favor of: **rogo ut amori nostro plusculum, quam concedat veritas, largiare** I beg you to overlook a little more than truth would allow, in favor of our affection (for each other) ‖ *intr* to give bribes, engage in bribery; *(of time, conditions)* to allow
largit·ās -ātis *f* generosity, bounty
largiti·ō -ōnis *f* generosity; bribery
largīt·or -ōris *m* generous donor; spendthrift; briber
larg·us -a -um *adj* abundant, plentiful, large, much; generous; bountiful, profuse
lārid·um -ī *n* bacon
Lāriss·a -ae *f* (-rīs-) town in Thessaly on the Peneus River, famous for its beauty
Lārissae·us -a -um *adj* (-rīs-) of Larissa
Lār·ius -(i)ī *m* Lake Como
lar·ix -icis *f* larch tree
Lar·s -tis *m* first name *(praenomen)* of Etruscan origin, *usu.* given to the eldest son
larv·a -ae *f* mask; ghost; demon
larvāt·us -a -um *adj* bewitched
lasan·um -ī *n or* **lasan·us -ī** *m* chamber pot
lāsarpīcif·er -era -erum *adj* producing asafetida *(used as an anti-spasmodic)*
lascīvi·a -ae *f* frisking, playfulness; lewdness, sexual freedom; fun
lascīvibund·us -a -um *adj* frisky
lascīv·iō -īre -iī -ītum *intr* to frolic, be frisky; to run riot, run wild; to be in heat
lascīv·us -a -um *adj* playful, frisky; brash, impudent; licentious, horny; luxuriant *(growth)*
lāserpīc·ium -(i)ī *n* silphium *(plant yielding asafetida, used as an anti-spasmodic)*
lassitūd·ō -inis *f* tiredness, lassitude
lass·ō -āre -āvī -ātus *tr* to tire out, exhaust
lassul·us -a -um *adj* somewhat tired
lass·us -a -um *adj* tired, exhausted
lātē *adv* widely, extensively; profusely; **late longeque** far and wide; **late patere** to cover a wide field, have wide application
latebr·a -ae *f* hiding place, hideaway, hideout; *(fig)* loophole
latebricol·a -ae *mf* person who hangs around dives and brothels
latebrōsē *adv* secretly
latebrōs·us -a -um *adj* full of holes; hidden, secret; porous
lat·ens -entis *adj* hidden, secret
latenter *adv* in secret
lat·eō -ēre -uī *intr* to hide, lie hidden; to lurk; to be out of sight, be invisible; to lie below the surface; to keep out of sight, sulk; to live a retired life, remain in obscurity, remain unknown; to escape notice; to be in safety; to avoid a summons, lie low; to be obscure; to take shelter
lat·er -eris *m* brick, tile; brickwork; **laterem lavare** *(prov)* to waste effort *(literally, to wash sun-dried bricks of clay)*; **lateres ducere** to make bricks
laterām·en -inis *n* earthenware
latercul·us -ī *m* small brick; tile; biscuit
laterici·us -a -um *adj* brick, of brick ‖ *n* brickwork
lātern·a -ae *f* (**lant-**) lantern
latesc·ō -ĕre *intr* to hide
lat·ex -icis *m* liquid, fluid; water; spring; wine; oil
latibul·um -ī *n* hiding place, hideout, lair, den; *(fig)* refuge
lāticlāvi·us -a -um *adj* having a broad crimson stripe *(distinctive mark of senators, military tribunes of the equestrian order, and of sons of distinguished families)* ‖ *m* senator; nobleman
lātifund·ium -(i)ī *n* large estate, ranch
Latīnē *adv* Latin, in Latin; in proper Latin; in plain Latin; **Latine docere** to teach Latin; **Latine loqui** to speak Latin; to speak correct Latin; *(coll)* to talk turkey; **Latine reddere** to translate Latin; **Latine scire** to understand Latin
Latīnit·ās -ātis *f* pure Latin, Latinity; Latin rights and privileges
Latīn·us -a -um *adj* Latin; possessing Latin rights and privileges ‖ *m* Latinus *(king of Latium, who gave his daugher Lavinia in marriage to Aeneas)* ‖ *mpl* the Latins, people of Latium ‖ *f* Latin (language) ‖ *n* Latin (language); in **Latinum convertere** to translate into Latin
lāti·ō -ōnis *f* bringing, rendering; formal proposal *(of a law);* **suffragii latio** the franchise
latitād·ō -ōnis *f* lying in concealment
latit·ō -āre -āvī *intr* to keep hiding oneself; to be concealed, hide, lurk; to lie low *(in order to avoid a summons)*
lātitūd·ō -inis *f* breadth, width; latitude; size, extent; wide area; richness of expression; **latitudo verborum** drawl; **in latitudine** *(or* **per latitudinem)** horizontally; **in latitudinem** in width
lātius *adv* of late
Lati·us -a -um *adj* of Latium, Latin, Roman ‖ *n* Latium *(district in W. central Italy, in which Rome is situated);* **jus Latii** *(or* **jus Latium)** Latin political rights and privileges
Lātō·is -idis *f* daughter of Latona, Diana
lātom- = **lautom-**
Lātōn·a -ae *f* mother of Apollo and Diana *(equated with the Greek goddess Leto)*

Lātōnigen·a -ae *mf* child of Latona, Apollo, Diana

Lātōni·us -a -um *adj* of Latona **‖** *f* Diana

lāt·or -ōris *m* bringer, bearer; proposer *(of a law)*

Lātō·us -ī *m* son of Latona, Apollo

lātrāt·or -ōris *m* barker; dog

lātrāt·us -ūs *m* barking

lātrīn·a -ae *f* washroom, toilet

lātr·ō -āre -āvī -ātus *tr* to bark at, snarl at **‖** *intr* to bark; *(fig)* to rant

latr·ō -ōnis *m* mercenary; robber, bandit, brigand; *(of animal or hunter)* predator; *(in chess)* pawn

latrōcin·ium -(i)ī *n* military service *(as a mercenary);* brigandage, banditry, vandalism, piracy; robbery, highway robbery; villany, outrage; band of robbers

latrōcin·or -ārī -ātus sum *intr* to serve as a mercenary; to be a bandit, be a pirate

latruncul·us -ī *m* small-time bandit; piece *(on a battle-game board)*

lātumi·ae -ārum *fpl* stone quarry; prison

lātus *pp of* fero

lāt·us -a -um *adj* wide, broad; extensive; widespread; drawling *(pronunciation);* **in latum** in width; **latus clavus** broad vertical crimson stripe on the tunic of men of the senatorial class

lat·us -eris *n* side, flank; body, person; lungs; lateral surface; coast; *(mil)* flank; **a latere** *(mil)* on the flank; **a latere** *(w. gen)* **1** at the side of, in the company of; **2** from among the friends of; **aperto latere** *(mil)* on the exposed flank; **in latus cubare** to lie on one's side; **latere tecto** scot-free; **latus dare** to expose oneself; **latus tegere** *(w. gen)* to walk by the side of, to escort

latuscul·um -ī *n* small side

laudābil·is -is -e *adj* laudable

laudābiliter *adv* laudably

laudāti·ō -ōnis *f* commendation; eulogy, panegyric, funeral oration; *(in court)* testimony by a character witness

laudāt·or -ōris *m* praiser; eulogist, panegyrist; *(leg)* character witness

laudāt·us -a -um *adj* praiseworthy, commendable, excellent

laud·ō -āre -āvī -ātus *tr* to praise, commend; to name, quote, cite; to pronounce the funeral oration over, eulogize

laure·a -ae *f* laurel tree; laurel branch; laurel crown, bay wreath; triumph

laureāt·us -a -um *adj* laureate, laureled, crowned with laurel; **litterae laureatae** communiqué announcing victory

Laurent·ēs -um *mpl* Laurentians *(people of Lanuvium)*

Laurentin·us *or* **Laurenti·us -a -um** *adj* Laurentian

laureol·a -ae *f* little laurel crown; triumph

laure·us -a -um *adj* laurel, of laurel **‖** *f see* **laurea**

lauricom·us -a -um *adj* laurel-covered *(mountain)*

laurif·er -era -erum *or* **laurig·er -era -erum** *adj* producing laurels; crowned with laurels

laur·us -ī *or* **-ūs** *f* laurel tree, bay; laurel branch; triumph

lau·s -dis *f* praise, commendation; fame, glory; reputation; approval; praiseworthy deed; merit, worth; **laus est** *(w. infor ut w. subj)* it is praiseworthy to **‖** *fpl* eulogy; praises; **laudibus ferre** *(or* **efferre** *or* **tollere) in** *(or* ad**) caelum** to praise to the skies

Laus·us -ī *m* son of Numitor and brother of Rhea Silvia **‖** son of Mezentius, killed by Aeneas

lautē *adv* sumptuously, splendidly

lauti·a -ōrum *npl* state banquet *(given to foreign ambassadors and state guests)*

lautiti·a -ae *f* luxury, high living

lautumi·ae *or* **lātomi·ae** *or* **lātumi·ae -ārum** *fpl* stone quarry *(esp. used as a prison)*

laut·us -a -um *adj* expensive, elegant, fine; well-heeled; refined, fashionable

lavābr·um -ī *n* bath

lavāti·ō -ōnis *f* washing, bathing, bath; bathing kit

Lāvīni·us -a -um *adj* Lavinian, of Lavinium **‖** *n* town in Latium founded by Aeneas **‖** *f* wife of Aeneas

lav·ō lavāre *(or* **lavĕre) lāvī lautum** *(or* **lavātum** *or* **lōtum)** *tr* to wash, bathe; to wet, drench; to wash away **‖** *refl & pass & intr* to wash, wash oneself, bathe

laxāment·um -ī *n* relaxation, respite, letup, mitigation

laxāt·us -a -um *adj* loose, extended *(e.g., ranks)*

laxē *adv* loosely, widely; freely

laxit·ās -ātis *f* roominess; extent, width; freedom of movement

lax·ō -āre -āvī -ātus *tr* to extend, widen, expand; to spread out, scatter; to open up *(passage, hole);* to undo; to loose *(bonds, bolts, doors);* to untie; to relax *(body, mind);* to slacken; to mitigate; *(fig)* to release, relieve; to unstring *(bow)* **‖** *refl* to increase in size, spread out **‖** *pass* to relax **‖** *intr (of prices)* to go down

lax·us -a -um *adj* roomy, wide; loose, slack; prolonged, extended *(time);* far off, distant *(date);* low *(price);* loose-hanging *(clothes);* wide-open *(door);* gaping *(joints, holes);* *(fig)* relaxed, easygoing

le·a -ae *f* lioness

leaen·a -ae *f* lioness

Lēan·der -drī *m* youth of Abydos who

swam across the Hellespont every night to his girlfriend

Learch·us -ī *m* son of Athamas and Ino, killed by his mad father

leb·ēs -ētis *m* cauldron

lectīc·a -ae *f* litter

lectīcār·ius -(i)ī *m* litter bearer

lectīcul·a -ae *f* small litter; small bier

lecti·ō -ōnis *f* selection; reading, reading aloud; perusal; **lectio senatūs** revision of the Senate roll *(by censors)*

lectisterniāt·or -ōris *m* slave who arranged the seating at table

lectistern·ium -(i)ī *n* ritual feast *(at which images of the gods were placed on couches at the table)*

lectit·ō -āre -āvī -ātus *tr* to read and reread; to like to read

lectiuncul·a -ae *f* light reading

lect·or -ōris *m* reader *(esp. a slave who read aloud to his master)*

lectul·us -ī *m* cot; small bed, small couch, settee; humble bier

lect·us -ī *m* bed; couch; dining couch; bier; **lectus genialis** marriage bed *(placed in the atrium)*

lect·us -a -um *pp of* **lego** ‖ *adj* select, choice, special, elite

Lēd·a -ae *f* mother of Helen, Clytemnestra, Castor, and Pollux

lēgāti·ō -ōnis *f* embassy, mission, legation; members of an embassy; work *or* report of work of a mission; nominal staff appointment; command of a legion; **legatio libera** junket

lēgāt·um -ī *n* bequest, legacy

lēgāt·us -ī *m* deputy, representative; ambassador, envoy; adjutant *(of a consul, proconsul, or praetor);* **legatus Augusti** governor of an imperial province; commander *(of a legion)*

lēgī *perf of* **lĕgo** (to read)

lēgif·er -era -erum *adj* lawgiving

legi·ō -ōnis *f* legion *(divided into 10 cohorts and numbering between 4,200 and 6,000 men);* army, active service

legiōnāri·us -a -um *adj* legionary ‖ *m* legionary soldier

lēgirup·a -ae *or* **lēgirupi·ō -ōnis** *m* lawbreaker

lēgitimē *adv* legitimately, lawfully; properly

lēgitim·us -a -um *adj* legitimate; lawful; regular, right, just, proper; genuine; professional *(boxers, gladiators)* ‖ *npl* legal formalities

legiuncul·a -ae *f* under-manned legion

lēg·ō -āre -āvī -ātus *tr* to commission; to send on a public mission, despatch; to delegate, deputize; to bequeath, will; *(fig)* to entrust

lĕgō lĕgĕre lēgī lectus *tr* to read, peruse; to recite, read aloud; to gather, collect, pick;

to pick out, choose; to pick one's way through, cross; to sail by, coast along; to pick up, steal; to pick up *(news, rumor);* **fila legere** to wind up the thread of life; **senatum legere** to read off the Senate roll

lēgulē·ius -(i)ī *m* pettifogger

legūm·en -inis *n* leguminous plant; vegetable; pulse; bean

lemb·us -ī *m* cutter, yacht *(built for speed),* speedboat

lemm·a -ătis *n* theme, subject matter; epigram

Lemnicol·a -ae *m* inhabitant of Lemnos *(i.e., Vulcan)*

lemniscāt·us -a -um *adj* heavily decorated with combat ribbons

lemnisc·us -ī *m* ribbon which hung down from a victor's wreath

Lemni·us -a -um *adj* Lemnian ‖ *m* Lemnian *(i.e., Vulcan)* ‖ *mpl* the people of Lemnos

Lemn·os *or* **Lemn·us -ī** *f* large island in the N. Aegean Sea

Lemur·ēs -um *mpl* ghosts

Lemūri·a -ōrum *npl* night festival to drive ghosts from the house

lēn·a -ae *f* madame *(of brothel)*

Lēnae·us -a -um *adj* Bacchic; **latices Lenaei** wine ‖ *m* Bacchus

lēnē *adv* gently

lēnīm·en -inis *n* consolation

lēnīment·um -ī *n* alleviation

lēn·iō -īre -īvī *or* **-iī -ītus** *tr* to soothe, alleviate, calm ‖ *intr* to calm down

lēn·is -is -e *adj* mild, gentle, soft, smooth, calm; gentle *(slope);* weak, mild *(medicine);* quiet *(sleep);* mellow *(wine);* tolerable, moderate *(conditions);* kind *(person)*

lēnit·ās -ātis *f* mildness, gentleness, softness, smoothness; tenderness, clemency

lēniter *adv* mildly, gently, softly, smoothly; quietly, calmly; halfheartedly; *(of style)* smoothly

lēnitūd·ō -inis *f* mildness, gentleness, softness, smoothness

lēn·ō -ōnis *m* pimp, brothel keeper

lēnōcin·ium -(i)ī *n* pimping, pandering; allurement; alluring makeup; sexy clothes; flattery

lēnōcin·or -ārī -ātus sum *intr* to be a pimp; *(w. dat)* **1** to play up to, pander to; **2** to stimulate, promote

lēnōni·us -a -um *adj* pimp's

lēn·s -tis *f* lentil

lentē *adv* slowly; indifferently, halfheartedly; calmly, leisurely, deliberately

lentesc·ō -ĕre *intr* to get sticky; *(fig)* to soften, weaken

lentiscif·er -era -erum *adj* *(of a region)* producing mastic trees

lentisc·us -ī *f* mastic tree *(small evergreen*

tree that yields an aromatic resin called mastic); toothpick *(made of mastic wood)*

lentitūd·ō -inis *f* slowness; insensibility, apathy, dullness

lent·ō -āre -āvī -ātus *tr* to bend *(under strain)*

lentul·us -a -um *adj* somewhat slow

lent·us -a -um *adj* sticky, clinging; pliant, limber; slow, sluggish; lingering; irresponsive, reluctant, indifferent, backward; slow-moving; tedious; drawling; at rest, at leisure, lazy; calm, unconcerned

lēnul·us -ī *m* little pimp

lēnuncul·us -ī *m* small boat, skiff

le·ō -ōnis *m* lion ‖ **Leo** *(astr)* Leo *(constellation and sign of the zodiac)*

Leōnid·ās -ae *m* king of Sparta *(who fell at Thermopylae after a gallant stand in 480 B.C.)*

leōnīn·us -a -um *adj* lion's, of a lion

Leontīn·ī -ōrum *mpl* town in E. Sicily

lep·as -adis *f* limpet *(shellfish)*

lepidē *adv* charmingly, pleasantly, neatly; *(as affirmativbe answer)* yes; *(of approval)* great!

lepid·us -a -um *adj* charming, delightful, neat; witty, amusing *(writings, remarks)*

lep·ōs or **lep·or -ōris** *m* pleasantness, charm, attractiveness

lep·us -oris *m* hare ‖ **Lepus** *(astr)* Lepus, the Hare *(constellation)*

lepuscul·us -ī *m* little hare

Lern·a -ae *f* marsh near Argos, where Hercules slew the Hydra

Lernae·us -a -um *adj* Lernaean

Lesbi·us -a -um *adj* of Lesbos, Lesbian ‖ *f* fictitious name given by Catullus to his mistress Clodia ‖ *n* Lesbian wine

Lesb·os or **Lesb·us -ī** *f* large island in the N. Aegean, birthplace of Alcaeus and Sappho

less·us *(gen does not occur; acc:* **lessum**) *m* loud wailing

lētāl·is -is -e *adj* lethal, fatal, mortal

Lēthae·us -a -um *adj* of Lethe; infernal; causing drowsiness

lēthargic·us -ī *m* lazy fellow

lētharg·us -ī *m* lethargy

Lēth·ē -ēs *f* Lethe *(river of forgetfulness in lower world)*

lētif·er -era -erum *adj* deadly, fatal; **locus letifer** mortal spot

lēt·ō -āre -āvī -ātus *tr* to kill

lēt·um -ī *n* death; ruin, destruction; **leto dare** to put to death

Leuc·as -adis *f* "White Island", island off W. Greece

leucasp·is -idis *adj* armed with a white shield

Leucipp·us -ī *m* philosopher, teacher of Democritus, and one of the founders of Atomism *(5th cent. B.C.)*

Leuctr·a -ōrum *npl* small town in Boeotia

where Epaminondas defeated the Spartans in 371 B.C.

levām·en -inis *n* alleviation, comfort, consolation

levāment·um -ī *n* alleviation, comfort, consolation

levāti·ō -ōnis *f* lightening, easing; relief, comfort; lessening, mitigation

levicul·us -a -um *adj* somewhat vain

levidens·is -is -e *adj* poor, inferior

levifīd·us -a -um *adj* untrustworthy

lēv·is -is -e *adj* light, not heavy; light-armed; lightly dressed; easily digested; thin, poor *(soil);* nimble; flitting; slight, small; unimportant, trivial; unfounded *(rumor);* easy, simple; mild; gentle, easygoing; capricious, unreliable, fickle; lacking authority; lacking power; unsubstantial, thin; **in levi habere** to make light of

lēv·is -is -e *adj* smooth; slippery; hairless, beardless; delicate, tender; effeminate; smooth *(style)*

levisomn·us -a -um *adj* light-sleeping

lēvit·ās -ātis *f* lightness; mobility, nimbleness; levity, frivolity; *(fig)* shallowness

lēvit·ās -ātis *f* smoothness; *(fig)* fluency

leviter *adv* lightly; slightly, a little, somewhat; easily, without difficulty; nimbly

lev·ō -āre -āvī -ātus *tr* to lift up, raise; to lighten, relieve, ease; to console, comfort; to lift off, remove; to lessen, weaken; to release, free; to take away; to avert; to restore, refresh

lēv·ō -āre -āvī -ātus *tr* to make smooth, polish; to soothe

lēv·or -ōris *m* smoothness

lex lēgis *f* motion, bill; law, statute; rule, regulation; principle, precept; condition, stipulation; **ad legem** neatly; **eā lege ut** with the stipulation that, on condition that; **lege** *(or* **legibus)** legally; **lege agere** to go to court, take legal action; **legem abrogare** to repeal a law; **legem derogare** to amend a bill *or* law; **legem ferre** to propose a bill; **legem jubere** *(of the assembly)* to sanction a law; **legem perferre** to get a bill *or* law passed **leges** constitution; **leges pacis** terms of peace; **sine legibus** without restraint, without control

lībām·en -inis *n* libation; firstfruits

lībāment·um -ī *n* libation; firstfruits

lībāti·ō -ōnis *f* libation

libell·a -ae *f* small silver coin, one tenth of a denarius *(c. 10¢);* small sum; *(carpenter's)* level; **ad libellam** to a tee, exactly; **heres ex libella** sole heir

libell·us -ī *m* booklet, pamphlet; notebook; journal, diary; program; handbill, advertisement; petition; answer to a petition; letter; written accusation, indictment; libel; satirical verse

lib·ens -entis *adj* (lub-) willing, ready, glad; merry, cheerful; **libenti animo** willingly
libenter *adv* (lub-) willingly, gladly, with pleasure
lĭ·ber -brī *m* book, work, treatise; catalog, list, register; letter, rescript; bark *(of a tree)*
līb·er -era -erum *adj* free; open, unoccupied; unrestricted; unprejudiced; outspoken, frank; uncontrolled, unrestricted; *(of states or municipalities)* independent, autonomous; exempt; free of charge; *(w. abl or ab)* free from, exempt from; *(w. gen)* free of **‖** *mpl see* **liberi**
Līb·er -erī *m* Italian fertility god, later identified with Bacchus; wine
Līber·a -ae *f* Proserpine **‖** Ariadne *(the wife of Bacchus)*
Līberāl·ia -ium *npl* festival of Liber *(held on March 17, at which young men received the toga virilis)*
līberāl·is -is -e *adj* relating to freedom, relating to civil status, of free citizens; worthy of a freeman, honorable, gentleman's; courteous; liberal, generous; handsome
līberālit·ās -ātis *f* courtesy, politeness; liberality, generosity; grant, gift
līberāliter *adv* like a freeman, nobly; liberally *(e.g., educated);* courteously; liberally, generously
līberāti·ō -ōnis *f* liberation, freeing; release *(from debt); (leg)* acquittal
līberāt·or -ōris *m* liberator
līberē *adv* freely; frankly; ungrudgingly; like a freeman, liberally
līber·ī -ōrum *or* **-um** *mpl* children; sons; **jus trium liberorum** a privileged status granted by the *Lex Papia Poppaea* of A.D. 9 to fathers of three or more children *(occasionally extended to others)*
līber·ō -āre -āvī -ātus *tr* to free, set free, release; to acquit; to cancel, get rid of *(e.g., debts);* to pay for, cover *(an expense);* to exempt; to manumit; to cross *(threshold);* to draw *(a sword);* to clear *(positions of hostile forces); (w. abl or w. ab or ex)* to free from, release from, acquit of; **fidem liberare** to keep one's promise; **nomina liberare** to cancel debts; **promissa liberare** to fulfill promises **‖** *refl* to pay up a debt
lībert·a -ae *f* freedwoman, ex-slave
lībert·ās -ātis *f* liberty, freedom; status of a freeman; political freedom; freedom of speech, freedom of thought; frankness
lībertīn·us -a -um *adj* of the status of a freedman **‖** *m* freedman, ex-slave **‖** *f* freedwoman, ex-slave
lībert·us -ī *m* freedman, ex-slave
lĭb·et -ēre -uit *or* **libitum est** *v impers**

(lub-) *(w. dat)* it pleases, it is pleasant for, is agreeable to, is nice for *(s.o.); (w. inf)* it is nice, pleasant to *(do s.th.);* **mihi libet** I feel like, want; **qui libet** any you like to mention; **si lubet** if you please; **ut lubet** as you please
libīdin·or -ārī -ātus sum *intr* to gratify lust
libīdinōsē *adv* willfully; arbitrarily
libīdinōs·us -a -um *adj* (lub-) willful; arbitrary; lustful, lecherous
libīd·ō -inis *f* (lub-) desire, longing, inclination, pleasure; will, willfulness, arbitrariness, caprice, fancy; lust, sexual desire; rut, heat; **ad** *(or* **per) libidinem** *(w. gen)* at the pleasure of; **ex libidine** arbitrarily; **libidinem habere in** *(w. abl)* to be fond of, take pleasure in
libīt·a -ōrum *npl* will, pleasure
Libitīn·a -ae *f* burial goddess; implements for burial; grave; death
līb·ō -āre -āvī -ātus *tr* to taste, sip; to pour as a libation, offer, consecrate; to touch lightly, barely touch, graze; to spill, waste; to extract, collect, compile
lībr·a -ae *f* balance, scales; plummet, level; pound *(of 12 ounces)*
lībrāment·um -ī *n* weight; balance, ballast; level surface, horizontal plane; gravity
lībrāri·a -ae *f* forelady *(who weighed out wool for slaves to spin)*
lībrāriol·us -ī *m* copyist, scribe
lībrāri·us -a -um *adj* book-, of books; **taberna libraria** bookstore **‖** *m* copyist, scribe, secretary; bookseller **‖** *n* bookcase
lībrāri·us -a -um *adj* weighing a pound
lībrāt·or -ōris *m* surveyor
lībrāt·us -a -um *adj* horizontal, level; poised; well-aimed
lībrīl·is -is -e *adj* one-pound
lībrit·or -ōris *m* artilleryman
lībr·ō -āre -āvī -ātus *tr* to balance; to poise, level, hurl, launch; to sway
līb·um -ī *n or* **līb·us -ī** *m* cake *(usu. used in sacrficial offerings);* **libum natale** birthday cake
Liburni·a -ae *f* district of Illyria between Istria and Dalmatia
Liburn·us -a -um *adj* Liburnian **‖** *mf* Liburnian **‖** *f* Liburnian galley
Liby·a -ae *or* **Liby·ē -ēs** *f* Libya *(general term for all of N. Africa)*
Libyc·us -a -um *adj* Libyan, N. African
Lib·ys -yos *adj* of N. Africa, N. African **‖** *m* N. African
Libyss·us -a -um *adj* N. African
Libystīn·us *or* **Liby·us -a -um** *adj* Libyan; N. African
Libyst·is -idis *adj (fem only)* N. African
lic·ens -entis *adj* free, unrestrained; licentious; forward, pushy, bold

licenter *adv* freely, without restraint, licentiously; boldly

licenti·a -ae *f* license, freedom; unruly behavior, lawlessness; outspokenness; licentiousness; free imagination; *(w. gen of gerund)* freedom to *(do s.th.);* **ludendi licentia** (unrestricted) freedom to play

lic·eō -ēre -uī *intr* to be for sale; *(w. abl or gen of price)* to cost, fetch

lic·eor -ērī -itus sum *tr* to bid on, bid for, make an offer for **‖** *intr* to bid

lic·et -ēre -uit *or* **-itum est** *v impers* it is permitted, it is lawful; *(w. dat & inf)* it is all right for *(s.o.)* to; **licet** *(to express assent)* yes, O.K.; **mihi licet I** may, I can *(often w. neut. pron as subject):* **si tibi hoc licitum est** if you are allowed to do this; *(w. the force of a conjunction, w. subj)* although, granting that

Lich·ās -ae *m* companion of Hercules

līch·ēn -ēnos *m* lichen *(resin used to cure skin diseases);* ringworm *(a skin disease)*

licitāti·ō -ōnis *f* bidding *(at auction);* haggling

licitāt·or -ōris *m* bidder

licit·or -ārī -ātus sum *tr* to bid for

licit·us -a -um *adj* permissible, lawful, legitimate **‖** *n* lawful action

lict·or -ōris *m* lictor *(attendant and bodyguard of a magistrate)*

li·ēn -ēnis *m* spleen

liēnōs·us -a -um *adj* splenetic

ligām·en -inis *n* string, tie; bandage

ligāment·um -ī *n* bandage

lignār·ius -(i)ī *m* carpenter

lignāti·ō -ōnis *f* gathering of lumber

lignāt·or -ōris *m* woodcutter, lumberjack

ligneol·us -a -um *adj* wooden

ligne·us -a -um *adj* wooden; woody; tough, wiry *(person)*

lign·or -ārī -ātus sum *intr* to gather wood

lign·um -ī *n* wood; *(also pl)* firewood *(as opp. to* **materia** = lumber for building);* stump; log, plank; writing tablet; tree; stone *(of olive, fruit); (various objects made of wood):* spear-shaft, money box, writing tablet, wooden mask, boat; **in silvam ligna ferre** *(prov)* to carry coals to Newcastle *(literally, to carry logs into the woods);* **mobile lignum** puppet

lig·ō -āre -āvī -ātus *tr* to tie, tie up, bandage; to close *(a deal);* to draw tight, knot; to cement *(an alliance);* to unite in harmony; *(w. dat or* **ad**) to tie to

lig·ō -ōnis *m* mattock, hoe; farming

ligul·a *or* **lingul·a -ae** *f* shoe strap; flap; *(geog)* tongue of land

Lig·ur *or* **Lig·us -uris** *mf* Ligurian

Liguri·a -ae *f* Liguria *(district along the N.W. coast of Italy)*

ligūr(r)·iō -īre -īvī *or* **-iī -ītus** *tr* to lick; to pick at, eat daintily; *(fig)* to be dying for; *(fig)* to sponge on

ligū(r)rīti·ō -ōnis *f* constant hankering for food

Ligus *see* **Ligur**

Ligusc·us *or* **Ligustic·us** *or* **Ligustīn·us -a -um** *adj* Ligurian

ligustr·um -ī *n (bot)* privet *(widely used for hedges)*

līl·ium -(i)ī *n (bot)* lily; *(mil)* trench lined with sharp stakes

līm·a -ae *f* file; *(fig)* revision, polishing; **limae labor** *(fig)* the work of polishing

līmātius *adv* in a more polished style

līmātul·us -a -um *adj* refined, sensitive *(judgment)*

līm·ax -ācis *mf* snail

limbulāri·us -a -um *adj* hem-; **textores limbularii** tassel makers, hemmers

limb·us -ī *m* fringe, hem, tassel

līm·en -inis *n* lintel, threshold; doorway, entrance; outset, beginning; starting gate *(at racetrack);* house, home

līm·es -itis *m* country trail; path; road along a boundary; boundary, frontier; *(fig)* limit; boundary marker; channel *(of river);* course *(of life);* track, trail *(of a shooting star);* line of color, streak

līm·ō -āre -āvī -ātus *tr* to file; *(fig)* to polish, refine; to file down, take away from, lessen; to get down to *(the truth)*

līmōs·us -a -um *adj* muddy; growing in mud

limpid·us -a -um *adj* limpid, clear

līmul·us -a -um *adj* squinting

līm·us -a -um *adj* squinting; sidelong

līm·us -ī *m* mud; dirt, grime

līm·us -ī *m* ceremonial apron *(trimmed with purple and worn by priests at sacrifice)*

līne·a -ae *f* line; string, thread; fishing line; plumb line; outline; boundary line, limit; **ad lineam** *(or* **rectā lineā**) in a straight line; vertically; horizontally; **extremā lineā amare** to love at a distance; **lineas transire** to go out of bounds

līneāment·um -ī *n* line; characteristic, feature; outline **‖** *npl* lineaments, lines *(of the face)*

līne·ō -āre -āvī -ātus *tr* to make straight, make perpendicular

līne·us -a -um *adj* flaxen, linen

lin·gō -gĕre -xī -ctus *tr* to lick; to lap up

lingu·a -ae *f* tongue; speech, language, dialect; eloquence; utterance; style *(of s.o.'s speech); (of animals)* note, song, bark; *(geog)* tongue of land; **favete linguis!** observe a sacred silence!; **linguam comprimere** *(or* **tenere**) to hold one's tongue; **linguā promptus** insolent, cheeky; **utraque lingua** both languages *(Greek and Latin)*

lingul·a -ae *f* shoe strap; flap; *(geog)* tongue of land

lingulāc·a -ae *mf* gossip, chatterbox
līnig·er -era -erum *adj* wearing linen
linō linĕre lēvī *or* **līvī litus** *tr* to smear; to erase; to cover, coat; *(fig)* to mess up
linquō linquĕre līquī *tr* to leave, forsake; to depart from; to leave alone; to leave in a pinch **‖** *pass* to faint; **animo linqui** to faint **‖** *v impers* **relinquitur** *(w. ut)* it remains to *(do s.th.)*
linteātus -a -um *adj* canvas-
linte·ō -ōnis *f* linen-weaver
linteol·um -ī *n* small linen cloth
lin·ter -tris *f* skiff; vat, tank
linte·us -a -um *adj* linen **‖** *n* linen; linen cloth; canvas, sail; kerchief
lintricul·us -ī *m* small boat
līn·um -ī *n* flax; linen; thread; rope, line; fishing line; net; linen dress
Lin·us *or* **Lin·os -ī** *m* son of Apollo and instructor of Orpheus and Hercules
Lipar·a -ae *or* **Lipar·ē -ēs** *f* Lipara *(island off the N. coast of Sicily)* **‖** *fpl* the Aeolian Islands
Liparae·us -a -um *or* **Liparens·is -is -e** *adj* of Lipara
lipp·iō -īre -īvī *or* **-iī -ītum** *intr* to have sore eyes; *(of eyes)* to burn
lippitūd·ō -inis *f* running eyes, inflammation of the eyes
lipp·us -a -um *adj* with sore eyes; burning *(eyes); (fig)* half-blind
lique·faciō -facĕre -fēcī -factus *(pass:* **lique·fīō -fierī -factus sum)** *tr* to melt, dissolve; to decompose; to waste, weaken
liqu·ens -entis *adj* clear, limpid; flowing, gliding
liqueō liquēre liquī *or* **licuī** *intr* to be liquid; to be clear **‖** *v impers* it is clear, is apparent, is evident; **liquet mihi** *(w. inf)* I am free to; **non liquet** *(leg)* it is not clear *(legal formula used by a hung jury)*
liquescō liquescĕre licuī *intr* to melt; to decompose; to grow soft, grow effeminate; to become clear; *(fig)* to melt away
liquidē *adv* clearly
liquidiuscul·us -a -um *adj* gentler
liquidō *adv* clearly, plainly, certainly
liquid·us -a -um *adj* liquid, fluid, flowing; clear, transparent; evident; pure *(pleasure);* clear *(voice);* calm *(mind)* **‖** *n* liquid, water; clearness, certainty
liqu·ō -āre -āvī -ātus *tr* to melt, dissolve; to strain, filter
līqu·or -ī *intr* to flow; to melt; *(fig)* to waste away; **in lacrimas liqui** to dissolve into tears
liqu·or -ōris *m* fluidity; liquid, fluid; sea
Līr·is -is *m* river between Latium and Campania
līs lītis *f (old form:* **stlīs stlītis)** matter of dispute; quarrel, dispute; wrangling; *(leg)* lawsuit, litigation; *(leg)* charge, accusation; **lis capitis** criminal charge;

litem aestimare *(or* **taxare)** to assess damages; **litem intendere** *(or* **litem inferre)** *(w. dat)* to bring a suit against, sue *(s.o.)*
litāti·ō -ōnis *f* successful sacrifice *(i.e., obtaining of favorable omens from a sacrifice)*
litātō *adv* with favorable omens
lītera *see* **littera**
Lītern·um -ī *n* town on the coast of Campania
litic·en -inis *m* trumpeter
lītigāt·or -ōris *m (leg)* litigant
lītigiōs·us -a -um *adj* litigious; quarrelsome; disputed
lītig·ium -(i)ī *n* quarrel, dispute
lītig·ō -āre -āvī -tum *intr* to squabble; *(leg)* to go to court
lit·ō -āre -āvī -ātus *tr* to propitiate; to offer by way of atonement; to atone for; **litandum est** atonement must be made **‖** *intr* to obtain favorable omens from a sacrifice; *(of a sacrifice)* to give favorable omens; *(w. dat)* to appease, propitiate
lītorāl·is -is -e *adj* shore-, of the shore
lītore·us -a -um *adj* at *or* along the seashore
litter·a *or* **līter·a -ae** *f* letter *(of the alphabet);* handwriting; **ad litteram** verbatim; **littera salutaris** *(leg)* *(i.e.,* **A** = **absolvo)** vote of acquittal; **littera tristis** *(leg)* *(i.e.,* **C** = **condemno)** vote of guilty **‖** *fpl* epistle, letter, dispatch; edict, ordinance; literature, books, literary works; book learning, liberal education, scholarship; branch of learning; records, account; inscription; **in litteras digerere** to arrange in alphabetical order; **litteras discere** to learn to read and write; **litteras scire** to know how to read and write, be literate
litterāri·us -a -um *adj* of reading and writing; **ludus litterarius** elementary school
litterātē *adv* legibly, in a clear handwriting; literally; learnedly
litterāt·or -ōris *m* elementary-school teacher, schoolmaster
litterātūr·a -ae *f* writing; alphabet; grammar; writings, literature
litterāt·us -a -um *adj* learned, scholarly; liberally educated; devoted to literature; *(of time)* devoted to studies; marked *or* inscribed with letters **‖** *m* man of culture; teacher of literature; scholar
litterul·a -ae *f* small letter **‖** *fpl* short letter, note; slight literary endeavors; ABC's
litūr·a -ae *f* erasure; erased passage; correction; smudge, smear
litus *pp of* **lino**
līt·us -oris *n* seashore, beach, coast;

riverbank; **litus arare** *(prov)* to waste effort *(literally, to plow the shore)*

litu·us -ī *m* cavalry trumpet, clarion; *(fig)* signal; augur's wand *(a crooked staff carried by an augur);* **lituus meae profectionis** signal for my departure

līv·ens -entis *adj* livid; black-and-blue

līv·eō -ēre *intr* to be black-and-blue, be livid; to be envious; *(w. dat)* to be jealous of

līvesc·ō -ĕre *intr* to turn black-and-blue

Līvi·a -ae *f* second wife of Augustus and mother of Tiberius and Drusus (58 B.C.–A.D. 29)

līvidul·us -a -um *adj* inclined to be jealous, somewhat envious

līvid·us -a -um *adj* leaden *(in color);* blue; black-and-blue; jealous, envious, spiteful

Līv·ius -(i)ī *m* Livy *(Titus Livius Patavinus, historian, 58 B.C.–A.D. 17)* ‖ Livius Andronicus *(a Greek who was the first to write Latin poetry, both tragedies and comedies; his first drama was staged in 240 B.C.; he also translated the Odyssey into Saturnian verse)*

līv·or -ōris *m* leaden color; bluish color; black-and-blue mark; jealousy, envy, spite

lix·a -ae *m* peddler *(around a camp),* camp follower

locār·ius -(i)ī *m* ticket broker, gouger *(one who buys up theater seats as an investment)*

locāti·ō -ōnis *f* arrangement, placement; renting out, contract, lease

locāt·or -ōris *m* lessor

locāt·um -ī *n* lease, contract

locell·us -ī *m* small box

locit·ō -āre *tr* to lease out

loc·ō -āre -āvī -ātus *tr* to place, put, set, lay; to establish, constitute, set; to lay *(foundations);* to station *(troops);* to rent out, lease; to contract for; to invest *(effort);* to lend at interest; to farm out *(taxes);* **locare in matrimonium** *(or* **nuptiis** *or* **nuptum)** *(w. dat)* to give in marriage *(to s.o.)*

locul·us -ī *m* little place, spot; pocket

locupl·ēs -ētis *adj* rich; *(w. abl)* rich in, well supplied with; reliable, responsible; **locuples oratione** *(or* **in dicendo)** **esse** to be a polished speaker

locuplēt·ō -āre -āvī -ātus *tr* to make rich, enrich; to embellish *(a building)*

loc·us -ī *(pl:* **loc·ī -ōrum** *mpl* passages, verses; **loc·a -ōrum** *npl* physical places)* *m* place; site; spot; locality, district; seat; town, village; period *(of time);* opportunity, room, occasion; situation, position; category; rank, degree, birth; office, post; passage *(in a book);* topic, subject, point, division;

(mil) post, station; *(in astrology)* house; **adhuc locorum** until now; **ad id locorum** until then; **ex aequo loco dicere** to speak in the Senate; to hold a conversation; **ex** *(or* **de)** **loco superiore dicere** to speak from the Rostra; **ex loco inferiore dicere** to speak before a judge, speak in court; **inde loci** since then; **in eo loci** in such a condition; **in locum** *(w. gen)* in place of, as a substitute for, instead of; **interea loci** meanwhile; **loca** *(vulg)* female genitals; **loci communes** general topics; public places, parks; **loco** *(w. gen)* in stead of, in place of; **loco** *(or* **in loco)** at the right time; on the spot; **loco cedere** to give way, yield; **loco movere** to dislodge; to dislocate *(a limb);* **locum dare** to make way; **locum habere** to be valid, be applicable, hold good; **locum facere** to clear the way; **locum mutare** to change one's residence, move; **locus publicus** public building, public square; **mentem (meam, tuam, ejus) loco movere** *(or* **pellere)** to drive (me, you, him) out of (my, your, his) mind; **nullo loco** under no circumstances; **postea loci** afterwards; **post id locorum** afterwards; **stare loco** to stand still; **ubicumque loci** whenever

lōcust·a -ae *f* locust

Lōcust·a -ae *f* (**Lūc-**) woman notorious as poisoner in the time of Claudius and Nero

locūti·ō -ōnis *f* speech; way of speaking; expression; word; pronunciation

locūtus *pp of* **loquor**

lōd·ix -īcis *f* blanket

logic·us -a -um *adj* logical ‖ *npl* logic

log·os *or* **log·us -ī** *m* word; witticism ‖ *mpl* mere words, empty talk

lōlīgō *see* **lolligo**

lol·ium -(i)ī *n* darnel *(type of grass)*

lollīg·ō -inis *f* (**lōl-**) squid

lollīguncul·a -ae *f* small squid

lōment·um -ī *n* a face cream *(for cleansing skin)*

Londīn·ium -(i)ī *n* London

longaev·us -a -um *adj* aged

longē *adv* far, far off, a long way off; away, distant; out of reach; long, for a long period; *(to speak)* at greater length; *(w. comparatives)* far, by far, much; **longe lateque** far and wide

longinquit·ās -ātis *f* length, extent; remoteness, distance; length, duration

longinqu·us -a -um *adj* long, extensive; far off, distant, remote; from afar, foreign; long, prolonged, continued, tedious; **e(x) longinquo** from far away; **in longinquo** far away

longitūd·ō -inis *f* length; **in longitudinem 1** lengthwise, in length; **2** to an immod-

erate length, too far; **3** for the distant future; **longitudine** *(or* **per longitudinem)** lengthwise
longiuscul·us -a -um *adj* pretty long
longur·ius -(i)ī *m* long pole
long·us -a -um *adj* long; spacious; protracted; tedious; **longa navis** battleship; **longum est** *(w. inf)* it would take too long to **‖** *n* length; **in** *(or* **per) longum** for a long while; **ne longum faciam** to make a long story short
loquācit·ās -ātis *f* talkativeness
loquāciter *adv* long-windedly; at length, in detail
loquācul·us -a -um *adj* rather talkative
loqu·ax -ācis *adj* loquacious, talkative
loquēl·a -ae *f* **(-quell-)** speech; word, expression
loqu·ens -entis *adj* articulate
loquit·or -ārī -ātus sum *intr* to chatter away
loquor loquī locūtus sum *tr* to say; to talk of, speak about; to tell, tell of, mention; *(fig)* to declare, show, indicate **‖** *intr* to speak; to rustle, murmur; **Latine loqui** to speak Latin; *(coll)* to talk turkey; **male loqui** to speak abusively
lōrār·ius -(i)ī *m* slave driver
lōrāt·us -a -um *adj* tied with thongs
lōre·us -a -um *adj* made of strips of leather; **vostra faciam latera lorea** *(coll)* I'll cut your hide to ribbons
lōrīc·a -ae *f* breastplate; parapet; **libros mutare loricis** to exchange books for arms
lōrīcāt·us -a -um *adj* wearing a breastplate, mail-clad
lōrip·ēs -edis *adj* bowlegged
lōr·um -ī *n* strip of leathter, thong, strap; dog's leash; whip, scourge; leather badge **‖** *npl* reins
Lōt·is -idis *f* a nymph who changed into a lotus tree to escape the advances of Priapus
Lōtophag·ī -ōrum *mpl* Lotus-eaters
lōt·os *or* **lōt·us -ī** *f* lotus *(fabulous plant bringing forgetfulness to those who eat its fruit);* flute *(of lotus wood)*
lōtus *see* **lautus**
Lu·a -ae *f* cult partner of Saturn *(to whom captured arms were dedicated)*
lub- = lib-
lubenti·a -ae *f* pleasure
lūbric·ō -āre -āvī -ātus *tr* to oil, grease, make smooth
lūbric·us -a -um *adj* slippery; smooth; slimy; *(of streams)* gently flowing, gliding; deceitful, tricky; precarious, ticklish *(situations, undertakings)* **‖** *n* precarious situation, critical period; unstable condition; **in lubrico poni** to be placed in a dangerous situation; **in lubrico versari** to be in a precarious situation
Lūc·a bōs *(gen:* **Lūc·ae bovis)** *f* elephant

Lūcāni·a -ae *f* district in S.W. Italy
Lūcān·us -a -um *adj* Lucanian **‖** *m* Lucanian **‖** *m* Lucan *(Marcus Annaeus Lucanus, epic poet, condemned to death by Nero, A.D. 39–65)*
lūc·ar -āris *n* funds allocated for public games *(derived from a forest tax)*
lucell·um -ī *n* slight profit
lū·ceō -cēre -xī *intr* to shine, be light, glow, glitter, be clear; *(fig)* to be clear, be apparent, be conspicuous **‖** *v impers* it is light, day is dawning
Lūcer·ēs -um *mpl* **(Lūc-)** one of the three original Roman tribes
lucern·a -ae *f* oil lamp; *(fig)* midnight oil; **ad lucernam** after dark; **ante lucernas** before nightfall; **vinum et lucernae** wine and lamps *(i.e., evening festivities)*
lūcescō lūcescěre luxī *intr* **(-cisc-)** to begin to shine **‖** *v impers* it is getting light
Lūci·a -ae *f* female name
lūcidē *adv* clearly, distinctly
lūcid·us -a -um *adj* shining, bright, clear; lucid
lūcif·er -era -erum *adj* shiny
Lūcif·er -erī *m (astr)* morning star **‖** *(astr)* planet Venus **‖** son of Aurora and Cephalus
lūcifug·us -a -um *adj* light-shunning; avoiding the public eye, sulking
Lūcil·ius -(i)ī *m* Gaius Lucilius *(first Roman satiric poet, c. 180–102 B.C.)*
Lūcīn·a -ae *f* goddess of childbirth; childbirth
lūciscō *see* **lucesco**
Lūc·ius -(i)ī *m* Roman first name *(praenomen; abbr: L.)*
Lucmo *see* **Lucumo**
Lucrēti·a -ae *f* wife of Collatinus, who, having been raped by Sextus Tarquinius, committed suicide in 509 B.C.
Lucrēt·ius -(i)ī *m* Spurius Lucretius *(father of Lucretia and consul in 509 B.C.)* **‖** Lucretius *(Titus Lucretius Carus, philosophical poet, 94?–55? B.C.)*
lucrificābil·is -is -e *or* **lucrific·us -a -um** *adj* profitable
lucrifug·a -ae *m* person not interested in profit, spendthrift
Lucrīn·us -a -um *adj* Lucrine; **Lacus Lucrinus** Lucrine Lake *(near Baiae, famous for its oysters)*
lucripet·a -ae *m* profiteer
lucr·or -ārī -ātus sum *tr* to gain, win *(as profit)* **‖** *intr (w. ex)* to profit from
lucrōs·us -a -um *adj* profitable
lucr·um -ī *n* profit, gain; wealth; greed, love of gain; **lucri facere** to gain for oneself; to make profit; **lucri fieri** to be gained; **lucro esse** *(w. dat)* to be advantageous to *(s.o.);* **ponere in lucro** *(or* **in lucris)** to regard as gain; **vivere de lucro** to be lucky to be alive

luctām·en -inis *n* wrestling; struggle, effort
luct·ans -antis *adj* reluctant
luctāti·ō -ōnis *f* wrestling; struggle, effort
luctāt·or -ōris *m* wrestler
luctific·us -a -um *adj* causing sorrow, calamitous
luctison·us -a -um *adj* sad-sounding
luct·or -ārī -ātus sum *or* **luct·ō -āre** *intr* to wrestle; (*w.* **cum**) to struggle with, grapple with; (*w. inf*) to struggle to
luctuōsē *adv* so as to cause sadness
luctuōsius *adv* more pitifully
luctuōs·us -a -um *adj* causing sorrow, sorrowful; sad, feeling sad
luct·us -ūs *m* sorrow, mourning, grief, distress; signs of sorrow, mourning clothes; source of grief
lūcubrāti·ō -ōnis *f* working by lamp light; evening gossip
lūcubr·ō -āre -āvī -ātus *tr* to compose at night ‖ *intr* to burn the midnight oil
lūculentē *adv* splendidly, well; (*to beat*) soundly; (*to sell*) at an excellent price
lūculenter *adv* brilliantly, smartly
lūculent·us -a -um *adj* bright, brilliant; excellent, fine; good-looking
Lūcull·us -ī *m* Lucius Licinius Lucullus (*Roman general and politician, 117–56 B.C.*)
Luc(u)m·ō -ōnis *m* Etruscan personal name
lūc·us -ī *m* sacred grove; woods
lūdi·a -ae *f* actress; gladiator (*female*)
lūdibr·ium -(i)ī *n* toy, plaything; derision; object of derision, butt of ridicule; frivolous behavior; sham, pretense; (*fig*) sucker; **ludibrio esse** (*w. dat*) to be made a fool of by (*s.o.*), be taken in by (*s.o.*); **ludibrio habere** to take (*s.o.*) for a sucker ‖ *npl* outrages, insults
lūdibund·us -a -um *adj* playful, playing around, having fun; without effort, without danger; carefree
lūdi·cer -cra -crum *adj* for sport, in sport; (*theat*) of the stage, dramatic, acting; **ludicra ars et scaena tota** dramatic art and the stage in general; **ludicra exercitatio** sports; **ludicra res** drama; **ludicras partes sustinere** (*theat*) to play a dramatic role, act on the stage; **ludicrum praemium** sports award; ‖ *n* sport, game; toy; show, public game; stage play
lūdificābil·is -is -e *adj* used in mockery
lūdificāti·ō -ōnis *f* ridiculing, mocking; fooling, tricking
lūdificāt·or -ōris *m* mocker
lūdificāt·us -ūs *m* mockery
lūdific·ō -āre -āvī -ātus *or* **lūdific·or -ārī -ātus sum** *tr* to make a fool of, take for a sucker; to fool, trick
lūdi·ō -ōnis *m* *or* **lūd·ius -(i)ī** *m* actor
lū·dō -děre -sī -sus *tr* to play; to spend

(*time*) in play; to lose (*money*) in gambling; to amuse oneself with, do for amusement, practice as a pastime; to imitate, mimic, do a takeoff on, ridicule; to tease, tantalize; to deceive, delude; **operam ludere** to waste one's efforts; ‖ *intr* to play; to have fun; to jest, joke; to frolic; (*sl*) to play around, make love; **aleā ludere** to play dice; **pilā ludere** to play ball
lūd·us -ī *m* play, game, sport, pastime, diversion; mere child's play; joke, fun; (*sl*) playing around, fooling around, lovemaking; school; public show, public game; **amoto ludo** all joking aside; **in ludum ire** to go to school; **ludum alicui dare** (*w. dat*) to allow s.o. to enjoy himself; **ludum frequentare** to attend school; **ludus gladiatorius** gladiatorial school; **ludus (litterarius, litterarum)** (elementary) school; **per ludum** as a joke, for fun ‖ *mpl* public games, public exhibition; games, tricks; **ludos facere** (*or* **ludos reddere**) (*w. dat*) **1** to play tricks on; **2** to put on a show for; **3** to make fun of; **ludos sibi facere** to amuse oneself; **ludi circenses** festival of public games, contests, *or* theatrical shows held at the racetrack; **ludi magister** school teacher; **ludi magni** special votive games; **ludi plebeii** games given annually by the plebeian aediles on Nov. 4-17; **ludi Romani** games given annually by the curule aediles on Sept. 4-19; **ludi scaenici** public events held in the theater, plays
luell·a -ae *f* expiation, atonement
lu·ēs -is *f* infection, contagion, plague, pestilence; calamity
Lugdūnens·is -is -e *adj* of Lyons
Lugdūn·um -ī *n* Lyons (*town in E. Gaul*)
lū·geō -gēre -xī -ctus *tr* to mourn, lament, deplore ‖ *intr* to mourn, be in mourning; to be in mourning clothes
lūgubr·ia -ium *npl* mourning clothes
lūgubr·is -is -e *adj* mourning; doleful; disastrous
lumbifrag·ium -(i)ī *n* physical wreck
lumbrīc·us -ī *m* earthworm; (*as a term of reproach*) worm
lumb·us -ī *m* loin ‖ *mpl* loins; genitals
lūm·en -inis *n* light; lamp, torch; brightness, sheen, gleam; daylight; light of the eye, eye; light of life, life; window, window light; luminary, celebrity; glory, pride; (*leg*) (*usu. pl*) the amount of light falling on a building to which the owner is entitled; (*rhet*) strong point (*of an argument*); (*rhet*) brilliant phrase *or* expression; **ad lumina prima** until lamp-lighting time, until dusk; **lumen adferre** (*w. dat*) to shed light on (*a subject*); **lumen vitale** light enjoyed by living creatures,

life; **lumina amittere** to go blind; **luminibus captus** blind; **sub lumina prima** around dusk, just before dusk

lūminōs·us -a -um *adj* luminous, dazzling; *(fig)* bright, conspicuous

lūn·a -ae *f* moon; month; night; crescent *(worn as an ornament by senators on their shoes);* **ad lunam** by moonlight; **luna laborans** moon in eclipse, eclipse of the moon; **luna minor** waning moon

Lūn·a -ae *f* town in N. Etruria near modern Carrara

lūnār·is -is -e *adj* lunar, of the moon

lūnāt·us -a -um *adj* crescent-shaped

lūn·ō -āre -āvī -ātus *tr* to make crescent-shaped, curve

lūnul·a -ae *f* little crescent *(ornament worn by women)*

lu·ō -ĕre -ī *tr* to wash; to cleanse, purge; to set free, let go; to pay *(debt, penalty);* to pay as a fine; to suffer, undergo; to atone for, expiate; to satisfy, appease; to avert by expiation *or* punishment; **poenas luere** to suffer a punishment *(by way of expiation)*

lup·a -ae *f* she-wolf; flirt, prostitute

lupān·ar -āris *n* brothel

lupāt·us -a -um *adj* jagged *(like wolf's teeth)* ‖ *npl* jagged bit *(for spunky horses)*

Luperc·al -ālis *n* shrine on the Palatine Hill sacred to Pan

Lupercāl·ia -ium *npl* Lupercalia *(festival of Lycaean Pan, celebrated in February)*

Luperc·us -ī *m* Pan

lupill·us -ī *m (bot)* small lupine

lupīn·us -a -um *adj* wolf's, lupine ‖ *m & n (bot)* lupine *(plant having clusters of flowers of various colors)*

lup·us -ī *m* wolf; *(fish)* pike; jagged bit *(for horse);* grapnel

lurc(h)·ō -ōnis *m* glutton

lūrid·us -a -um *adj* pale-yellow, wan, ghastly, lurid; causing paleness

lūr·or -ōris *m* sallowness, sickly yellow color

-lus -la -lum *suf* forming diminutives, e.g., **lapillus** pebble, **agellus** little field, plot, **homunculus** little man

luscini·a -ae *f* nightingale

lusciniol·a -ae *f* little nightingale

luscin·ius -(i)ī *m* nightingale

lusciōs·us *or* **luscitiōs·us -a -um** *adj* partly blind

lusc·us -a -um *adj* one-eyed

lūsī *perf of* **ludo**

lūsi·ō -ōnis *f* play, game

Lūsitān·ī -ōrum *mpl* Lusitanian

Lūsitāni·a -ae *f* Lusitania *(modern Portugal and W. part of Spain)*

lūsit·ō -āre *intr* to like to play

lūs·or -ōris *m* player; gambler; humorous writer; joker

lustrāl·is -is -e *adj* lustral, propitiatory; quinquennial

lustrāti·ō -ōnis *f* purification, lustration; wandering, traveling

lustr·ō -āre -āvī -ātus *tr* to purify; to travel over, traverse; to check, examine; to go around, encircle; to light up, make bright, illuminate; to scan *(with the eyes);* to consider, review; to survey; *(mil)* to review *(troops)*

lustr·or -ārī -ātus sum *intr* to frequent brothels

lustr·um -ī *n* haunt, den, lair; wilderness; brothel; sensuality; purificatory sacrifice, lustration; lustrum, period of five years; period of years; **ingens lustrum a** century

lūsus *pp of* **ludo**

lūs·us -ūs *m* play, game, sport, amusement; playing around *(amorously)*

lūteol·us -a -um *adj* yellowish

lute·us -a -um *adj* of mud, of clay; muddy; dirty, grimy; (morally) dirty, filthy

lūte·us -a -um *adj* golden-yellow, yellow, orange

lutit·ō -āre *tr* to splatter with mud; *(fig)* to throw mud at

lut·ō -āre -āvī -ātus *tr* to cover with mud, daub; *(fig)* to smear

lutulent·us -a -um *adj* muddy; dirty; *(fig)* filthy; turbid *(style)*

lut·um *or* **lut·us -ī** *n* mud, mire; clay; **in luto esse** *(or* **haerere)** *(fig)* to be in a pickle; **pro luto esse** to be dirt-cheap

lūt·um -ī *n* yellow pigment, yellow

lux lūcis *f* light; light of day, life; daylight; public view, publicity; the public, the world; light of hope, encouragement; glory; elucidation; **luce** *(or* **luci)** by daylight, in the daytime; **lux aestiva** summer; **lux brumalis** winter; **(cum) primā luce** at daybreak

lux·ō -āre -āvī -ātus *tr* to dislocate *(a limb)*

lux·or -ārī -ātus sum *intr* to live riotously, have a ball

luxuri·a -ae *or* **luxuri·ēs -eī** *f* luxuriance; luxury, extravagance, excess, sumptuousness

luxuri·ō -āre -āvī -ātum *or* **luxur·ior -ārī -ātus sum** *intr* to grow luxuriantly; to luxuriate; *(of the body)* to swell up; *(of animals)* to be frisky; to lead a wild life

luxuriōsē *adv* luxuriously, voluptuously

luxuriōs·us -a -um *adj* luxuriant; exuberant; extravagant; voluptuous; highly fertile *(land)*

lux·us -ūs *m* luxury, extravagance, excess; splendor, pomp, magnificence

Lyae·us -a -um *adj* Bacchic ‖ *m* Bacchus; wine

Lycae·us -a -um *adj* Lycaean *(esp. applied to Pan);* **Mons Lycaeus** Mount

Lycaeus *(mountain in Arcadia where Jupiter and Pan were worshiped)*

Lycā·ōn -onis *m* king of Arcadia, whose daughter Callisto was changed into a she-bear and transferred to the sky as the Great Bear

Lycāōn·is -idis *f* daughter of Lycaon *(i.e., Callisto)*

Lycāoni·us -a -um *adj* descended from Lycaon of Arcadia; **axis Lycaonia** North Pole *(where Callisto as the Great Bear is located)*

lychnūch·us -ī *m* lamp stand; **lychnuchus pensilis** chandelier

lychn·us -ī *m* lamp, chandelier

Lyci·a -ae *f* country in S. Asia Minor

Lycī·um -ī *n* **(Lycē-)** the Lyceum *(gymnasium near Athens where Aristotle taught)* ‖ Lyceum *(name given by Cicero to the gymnasium in his Tusculan villa)*

Lyci·us -a -um *adj* of Lycia, Lycian ‖ *mpl* Lycians

Lycomēd·ēs -is *m* king of the Greek island of Scyros, father of Deidamia

Lycophr·ōn -onis *or* **-onos** *m* Alexandrine poet, noted for his obscure style *(born c. 320 B.C.)*

Lycōr·is -idis *or* **-idos** *f* name under which the poet Gallus wrote about his mistress Cytheris

Lycorm·ās -ae *m* old name for the Aetolian river Evenus

Lycti·us -a -um *adj* Cretan, of Lyctos *(a town in Crete)*

Lycurgē·us -a -um *adj* Lycurgan *(resembling the orator Lycurgus, noted for his relentlessness as prosecutor)*

Lycurgīd·ēs -ae *m* son of the Arcadian king Lycurgus *(i.e., Ancaeus, killed by the Calydonian boar)*

Lycurg·us -ī *m* traditional founder of the Spartan constitution ‖ Athenian orator, contemporary with Demosthenes *(born c. 396 B.C.)* ‖ son of Dryas and king of the Edones, who persecuted Bacchus and his worshipers

Lyc·us -ī *m* king of Thebes and husband of Dirce ‖ name of numerous rivers in Asia Minor, *esp.* a tributary of the Menander

Lȳdi·a -ae *f* country in W. Asia Minor

Lȳdi·us -a -um *adj* Lydian

Lȳd·us -a -um *adj* Lydian ‖ *mf* Lydian; Etruscan

lygd·os -ī *f* marble from Paros

lymph·a -ae *f* water nymph; *(poet)* water

lymphātic·us -a -um *adj* frenzied

lymphāt·us -a -um *adj* frenzied, frantic

lymph·ō -āre *tr* to drive crazy ‖ *pass* to be in a state of frenzy

Lyncest·is -idis *adj (fem only)* of the Lycestae, a people of W. Macedonia

Lync·eūs -ēī *m* Argognaut, famed for his sharp eyesight ‖ son of Aegyptus and husband of Hypermestra

Lyncē·us -a -um *adj* of Lynceus the Argonaut; keen-sighted, Lynceus-like

Lyncīd·ēs -ae *m* descendant of Lynceus, husband of Hypermestra *(esp. his great-grandson Perseus)*

lyn·x -cis *or* **-cos** *mf* lynx

lyr·a -ae *f* lyre; *(fig)* lyric poetry ‖ **Lyra** *(astr)* Lyra *(constellation)*

Lyrcē·us -a -um *adj* of Mt. Lyrceum on the borders of Arcadia and Argolis

lyric·us -a -um *adj* of the lyre; lyric ‖ *m* lyric poet ‖ *npl* lyric poetry

Lyrnēs·is -idis *or* **-idos** *f* Briseis *(Achilles' slave girl from Lyrnesos, a town in Phrygia)*

Lȳsan·der -drī *m* Spartan general and statesman *(d. 395 B.C.)*

Lȳsi·ās -ae *m* Athenian orator *(c. 459–c. 380 B.C.)*

Lȳsimach·us -ī *m* bodyguard of Alexander the Great, who later became King of Thrace

M

M *abbr* **mille** one thousand

M. *abbr* **Marcus** *(Roman first name, praenomen)*

M'. *abrr* **Manius** *(Roman first name, praenomen)*

Macarē·is -idos *f* daughter of Macareus *(i.e., Isse)*

Macar·eūs -eī *or* **-eos** *m* son of Aeolus *(who lived in incest with his sister Canace)*

macc·us -ī *m* clown *(in Atellan farces)*

Maced·ō -onis *m* Macedonian

Macedoni·a -ae *f* Macedonia

Macedonic·us -a -um *adj* Macedonian

Macedoniens·is -is -e *adj* Macedonian

Macedoni·us -a -um *adj* Macedonian

macellār·ius -(i)ī *m* grocer

macell·um -ī *n* grocery store; *(fig)* groceries

mac·eō -ēre *intr* to be lean, be skinny

ma·cer -cra -crum *adj* lean; skinny; poor *(soil);* scraggly *(plants)*

Ma·cer -crī *m* Gaius Licinius Macer *(Roman historian and orator, d. 66 B.C.)* ‖ Gaius Licinius Macer Calvus *(son of the former, and orator and poet, 82–46 B.C.)* ‖ Marcus Aemilius Macer *(poet and friend of Vergil and Ovid)*

māceri·a -ae *f* brick *or* stone wall; garden wall

mācer·ō -āre -āvī -ātus *tr* to soak; to soften, tenderize; to weaken, wear down; to worry, annoy, torment ‖ *refl & pass* to fret, worry

macesc·ō -ĕre *intr* to grow thin; *(of fruit)* to shrivel

machaer·a -ae *f* **(macch-)** (single-edged) sword

machaerophor·us -ī *m* soldier armed with a single-edged sword

Machā-ōn -onos *m* famous physician of the Greek army in the Trojan War and son of Aesculapius

Machāoni·us -a -um *adj* of Machaon; *(fig)* medical

māchin·a -ae *f* large mechanism, machine; crane, derrick; pulley, windlass, winch; revolving stage; siege engine; platform on which slaves were exhibited for sale (= **catasta**); cage, pen; *(fig)* scheme, stratagem

māchināment·um -ī *n* contrivance, device; *(mil)* siege engine;

māchinār·ius -(i)ī *m* crane operator

māchināti·ō -ōnis *f* mechanism; machine; trick; art of making machines; *(mil)* field piece

māchināt·or -ōris *m* engineer, machinist; *(fig)* contriver

māchin·or -ārī -ātus sum *tr* to engineer, design, contrive; to scheme

māchinōs·us -a -um *adj* containing a mechanism

maci·ēs -ēī *f* leanness, thinnness; barrenness; poverty *(of soil; of style)*

macilent·us -a -um *adj* skinny

macresc·ō -ĕre *intr* to grow thin

macritūd·ō -inis *f* leanness

macrocoll·um -ī *n* large-size sheet of papyrus

mactābil·is -is -e *adj* deadly

mactāt·us -ūs *m* sacrifice

mactē *interj* well done!; good luck!; bravo!; *(w. gen, acc, or abl)* hurrah for; **macte virtute esto!** bless you for your excellence!; well done!

mact·ō -āre -āvī -ātus *tr* to glorify, honor; to slay *(sacrificially)*, sacrifice; to kill, slaughter, put to death; to destroy, overthrow, ruin; to trouble; *(w. abl)* to afflict or punish with

mact·us -a -um *adj* glorified; struck, smitten

macul·a -ae *f* spot, stain; mesh *(of net)*; *(fig)* blemish, defect

maculōs·us -a -um *adj* spotted; stained

made·faciō -facĕre -fēcī -factus *(pass:* **made·fīō -fierī -factus sum)** *tr* to wet, moisten, drench, soak

mad·ens -entis *adj* wet, moist; flowing *(hair)*; melting *(snow)*; reeking *(w. blood)*

mad·eō -ēre -uī *intr* to be wet, be moist, be soaked, be drenched; to drip; to flow; *(coll)* to be soused; to be full, overflow

mad·escō -escĕre -uī *intr* to become wet, become moist; *(coll)* to get loaded

madidē *adv* drunkenly

madid·us -a -um *adj* wet, moist, drenched; dyed, steeped; *(coll)* drunk, loaded

mad·or -ōris *m* moisture

maduls·a -ae *m (coll)* souse, drunkard

Maean-der *or* **Maean-dros** *or* **Maean·d-rus -drī** *m* river in Asia Minor, famous for its winding course; winding; winding border; devious course

Maecēn·ās -ātis *m* Gaius Cilnius Maecenas *(adviser to Augustus and friend of Vergil and Horace, d. 8 B.C.)*

maen·a -ae *f* sprat *(fish)*

Maenal·is -idis *adj* of Mt. Maenalus, Arcadian; **Maenalis ursa** Callisto *(who was changed into the Great Bear)*

Maenal·us *or* **Maenal·os -ī** *m or* **Maenal·a -ōrum** *npl* Mt. Maenalus *(in Arcadia, sacred to Pan)*

Maen·as -adis *f* Bacchante; frenzied woman

Maeni·us -a -um *adj (name of a Roman clan)* Maenian; **Maenia Columna** pillar in the Forum at which the **triumviri capitales** held court and at which thieves, slaves, and debtors were tried and flogged

Maeon·es -um *mpl* Maeonians *(ancient name of the Lydians)*

Maeoni·a -ae *f* E. part of Lydia; *(from the alleged ancestry of its people)* Etruria

Maeonid·ēs -ae *m* native of Maeonia; Homer; Etruscan

Maeon·is -idis *adj (fem only)* Lydian **ǁ** *f* Maeonian woman *(esp. Arachne or Omphale)*

Maeoni·us -a -um *adj* Lydian; Homeric; Etruscan **ǁ** *f see* **Maeonia**

Maeōt·ae -ārum *mpl* a Scythian people on Lake Maeotis *(Sea of Azov)*

Maeōt·is -idis *adj* Maeotic; Scythian; **Maeotis lacus** Sea of Azov

Maeōti·us -a -um *adj* Maeotian, of the Maeotae *(a Scythian people)*

maer·eō -ēre *tr* to mourn for, grieve for **ǁ** *intr* to mourn, grieve

maer·or -ōris *m* mourning, grief

maestē *adv* mournfully, sadly

maestiter *adv* mournfully, sadly

maestiti·a -ae *f* sadness, sorrow, grief; gloom; dullness *(of style)*

maestitūd·ō -inis *f* sadness

maest·us -a -um *adj* mourning, sad, gloomy

Maev·ius -(i)ī *m* poetaster often ridiculed by Vergil and Horace

māgāl·ia -ium *npl* huts

mage *see* **magis**

mag·ē -ēs *f* magic

magic·us -a -um *adj* magic; **artes magicae** magic

magis *or* **mage** *adv* more, to a greater extent, in a higher degree, rather; **eo magis** (all) the more; **magis...atque**

rather...than; **magis aut minus** more or less; **magis est ut, quod** it is more the case that; **magis magisque** more and more; **magis...quam** rather...than; **non magis...quam** not so much...as

magis·ter -trī m chief, master, director; teacher; adviser, guardian; ringleader, author; (in apposition with noun in the gen) expert; **navis magister** captain, pilot; **magister morum** censor; **magister sacrorum** chief priest

magister·ium -(i)ī n directorship, presidency, superintendence; control, governance; instruction; **magisterium morum** censorship

magistr·a -ae f directress, mistress; instructress, teacher

magistrāt·us -ūs m magistracy; magistrate, official; military command

magmentār·ium -(i)ī n receptacle for a part of the sacrificial animal

magnanimit·ās -ātis f magnanimity; high ideals; bravery

magnanim·us -a -um adj magnanimous, noble, big-hearted; brave

magnāri·us -a -um adj wholesale; **magnarius negotiator** wholesale dealer

Magn·ēs -ētis adj of Magnesia, Magnesian

magn·ēs -ētis adj magnetic; **magnes lapis** magnet

Magnēsi·a -ae f district in E. Thessaly on the Aegean Sea ‖ city in Caria near the Menander River ‖ city in Lydia near Mt. Sipylus

magnēsi·us -a -um adj magnetic; **saxum magnesium** lodestone

magnidic·us -a -um adj talking big

magnificē adv magnificently, splendidly; pompously

magnificenti·a -ae f magnificence, grandeur, splendor; pompousness

magnific·ō -āre -āvī -ātus tr to make much of

magnific·us -a -um adj magnificent, splendid; sumptuous; proud

magniloquenti·a -ae f pompous language, braggadocio; (rhet) lofty style

magniloqu·us -a -um adj (-loc-) sublime; bragging

magnitūd·ō -inis f magnitude; size; large quantity, large number; vastness, extent; greatness; importance; power, might; high station, dignity, high rank; dignity of character; length (of time); intensity (of storm, etc.); strength, loudness (of voice)

magnopere or **magnō opere** adv greatly, very much; particularly; strongly, earnestly, heartily

magn·us -a -um (comp: **major**; superl: **maximus**) adj big, large; important; great; distinguished; impressive; complete, utter, full, pure; high, powerful (in rank); long (time); high (price); loud (voice); heavy (rain); advanced (age); noble (character); **magna itinera** forced marches; **Magna Mater** Cybele; **magno casu occidere** to happen by pure chance; **mare magnum** the ocean; **vir magno jam natu** a man advanced in years ‖ n great thing; great value; boast, proud claim; **magni (pretii) aestimare** (or **magni habere**) to value highly, have a high regard for; **magno emere (vendere)** to buy (sell) at a high price; **magnum spirare** to be proud

Māg·ō -ōnis m brother of Hannibal

mag·us -a -um adj magic; **artes magae** magic ‖ m magician; learned man (among the Persians)

Māi·us -a -um adj & m May ‖ f daughter of Atlas and Pleione and mother of Mercury by Jupiter

mājāl·is -is m castrated hog; (as term of abuse) swine

mājest·ās -ātis f majesty, dignity, grandeur; sovereign power, sovereignty; authority; (as a crime of diminishing the majesty of the Roman people) high treason; **majestas laesa** (or **imminuta**) high treason

māj·or -or -us (comp of **magnus**) adj bigger, larger; greater; more important; **annos natu major quadraginta** forty years older; **in majus ferre** to exaggerate; **majoris (pretii)** at a higher price; **major natu** older ‖ mpl see **majores** ‖ npl worse things, worse sufferings

mājōr·ēs -um mpl ancestors, forefathers

mājuscul·us -a -um adj somewhat greater; a little older

māl·a -ae f cheekbone, upper jaw ‖ fpl cheeks; (fig) jaws (e.g., of death)

malaci·a -ae f calm at sea, dead calm

malaciss·ō -āre -āvī -ātus tr to soften (up)

malac·us -a -um adj soft; luxurious

male adv (comp: **pējus**; superl: **pessimē**) badly, wrongly; wickedly, cruelly, maliciously; unfortunately, unsuccessfully; awkwardly; excessively, extremely, very much; (w. adjectives having a bad sense) terribly, awfully; **male accipere** to treat roughly; **male audire** to be ill spoken of; **male dicere** (w. dat) to say nasty things to; **male existimare de** (w. abl) to have a bad opinion of; **male emere** to buy at a high price; **male facere** (w. dat) to treat badly, treat cruelly; **male factum!** (coll) too bad!; **male ferre** to take (it) hard; **male fidus** unsafe; **male gratus** ungrateful; **male habere** to harass; **male metuere** to be terribly afraid of; **male perdere** to ruin utterly; **male sanus** insane; **male vendere** to sell at a loss; **male vivere** to be a failure in life

maledic·ax -ācis *adj* abusive, foulmouthed
maledicē *adv* abusively, slanderously
maledīc·ens -entis *adj* abusive, foulmouthed
male·dīcō -dīcĕre -dixī -dictum *intr (w. dat)* 1 to speak ill of, abuse, slander; 2 to say nasty things to
maledicti·ō -ōnis *f* abusive language, abuse
maledictit·ō -āre -āvī *intr (w. dat)* to keep saying nasty things to
maledict·um -ī *n* insult, taunt
maledic·us -a -um *adj* abusive, foulmouthed; slanderous
male·faciō -facĕre -fēcī -factum *intr* to do wrong; *(w. dat)* to injure, do wrong to
malefact·or -ōris *m* malefactor
mal(e)fact·um -ī *n* wrong, injury
maleficē *adv* mischievously
maleficenti·a -ae *f* harm, wrong, mischief
malefic·ium -(i)ī *n* evil deed, crime, offense; harm, injury, wrong, mischief; **maleficium admittere** *(or* **committere)** to commit a crime
malefic·us -a -um *adj* wicked, vicious, criminal ‖ *m* mischief-maker
malesuād·us -a -um *adj* seductive
malevol·ens -entis *adj* malevolent, spiteful, malicious ‖ *mf* spiteful person
malevolenti·a -ae *f* malevolence, spitefulness, ill will
malevol·us -a -um *adj* malevolent, spiteful, nasty
Māliac·us -a -um *adj* Malian, of Malis; **sinus Maliacus** Malian Gulf *(in S. Thessaly, modern Gulf of Zeitouni)*
Māliens·is -is -e *adj* of Malis *(a district of S. Thessaly)*
malignē *adv* spitefully; jealously; grudgingly; scantily, poorly
malignit·ās -ātis *f* spite, malice, jealously; stinginess
malign·us -a -um *adj* spiteful, malicious, jealous; stingy; *(fig)* unproductive *(soil);* scanty *(light)*
maliti·a -ae *f* malice, ill-will, bad behavior ‖ *fpl* devilish tricks
malitiōsē *adv* wickedly; craftily
malitiōs·us -a -um *adj* malicious, crafty, wicked, devilish
malleol·us -ī *m* small hammer, small mallet; fiery arrow
malle·us -ī *m* hammer, mallet; **malleus ferreus** pole-ax *(for slaughtering sacrificial animals)*
mālō *or* **māvolō malle māluī** *tr* to prefer; **pecuniam quam sapientiam malle** to prefer money to wisdom; *(w. inf)* to prefer to *(do s.th.); (w. acc & inf, w. ut)* to prefer that ‖ *intr (w. dat)* to incline toward, be more favorably disposed to
mālobathr·um -ī *n* malobathrum oil *(used as perfume)*

mal·um -ī *n* evil, ill; harm; punishment; disaster; hardship, trouble
māl·um -ī *n* apple; **aureum malum** quince; **felix malum** lemon; **malum Persicum** peach; **malum Punicum** *(or* **malum granatum)** pomegranate; **malum silvestre** crab apple
mal·us -a -um *adj* bad; ill, evil; ugly; unpatriotic; adverse, unfavorable; unsucessful; harmful; inappropriate, misplaced; insulting, abusive *(words);* humble *(birth);* **i in malam rem!** *(sl)* go to hell!; **mala aetas** old age; **res mala** trouble ‖ *n see* **malum**
māl·us -ī *m* mast *(of ship);* pole
māl·us -ī *f* apple tree
malv·a -ae *f* mallow *(used as food or mild laxative)*
Mam. *abbr* **Māmercus** *(Roman first name, praenomen)*
Mām·ers -ertis *m* Mars
Māmertīn·ī -ōrum *mpl* inhabitants of Messana who precipitated the First Punic war
mamill·a -ae *f* breast, teat
mamm·a -ae *f* breast *(of a woman);* dug *(of an animal); (baby talk)* mummy, mamma
mammeāt·us -a -um *adj* large-breasted
mammōs·us -a -um *adj* large-breasted, chesty
mānābil·is -is -e *adj* penetrating *(cold)*
manc·eps -ipis *m* purchaser; contractor
mancip·ium -(i)ī *n* (-cup-) formal purchase; possession, right of ownership; slave; **mancipio accipere** to take possession of; **mancipio dare** to turn over possession of; **res mancipi** possessions *(basic to running a farm e.g., land, slaves, livestock, farm implements);* **res nec mancipi** possessions *(other than those needed to run a farm)*
mancip·ō -āre -āvī -ātus *tr* (-cup-) to sell, transfer
manc·us -a -um *adj* crippled, maimed; *(fig)* defective, weak
mandāt·um -ī *n* command, order, commission ‖ *npl* instructions
mandāt·us -ūs *m* command, order
mand·ō -āre -āvī -ātus *tr* to hand over; to commit, entrust; to command, order, enjoin; to commission; to delegate *(authority);* to send a message about, report; to prescribe, specify; **humo aliquem mandare** to bury s.o.; **memoriae** *(or* **animo) mandare** to commit to memory, record ‖ *refl* **se fugae mandare** to run away
man·dō -dĕre -dī -sus *tr* to chew; to champ; to eat, devour; **humum mandere** to bite the dust
mandr·a -ae *f* stable, stall; column of pack animals *or* cattle; checkerboard
mandūc·us -ī *m* mask representing a glutton

māne *indecl n* morning ‖ *adv* in the morning; on the following morning; **bene mane** early in the morning; **cras mane** tomorrow morning; **heri mane** yesterday morning; **hodie mane** this morning; **postridie ejus diei mane** the following morning

man·eō -ēre -sī -sus *tr* to wait for, await ‖ *intr* to stay, remain; to stop off, pass the night; to last, endure, continue, persist; to be left over; **in condicione manere** to stick to an agreement; **in sententiā manere** to stick to an opinion

mān·ēs -ium *mpl* spirits of the dead; lower world; mortal remains

mang·ō -ōnis *m* slave dealer; pushy salesman

manic·ae -ārum *fpl* handcuffs; grappling hook; long sleeves; gloves

manicāt·us -a -um *adj* long-sleeved

manicul·a -ae *f* little hand

manifestē *adv* plainly, distinctly

manifestō *adv* red-handed; plainly, manifestly, evidently

manifest·ō -āre -āvī -ātus *tr* to reveal; to make known; to clarify

manifest·us -a -um *adj* manifest, plain, clear, distinct; exposed, brought to light, detected, caught; *(w. gen)* caught in, convicted of; *(w. inf)* known to

manipl = manipul-

manipulār·is -is -e *adj (mil)* of a maniple *or* company; **miles manipularis** private

manipulātim *adv (mil)* by companies

manip(u)l·us -ī *m* handful *(esp. of hay); (coll)* gang; *(mil)* maniple, company *(three of which constituted a cohort)*

Manl·ius -(i)ī *m* Marcus Manlius Capitolinus *(consul in 392 B.C., who, in 389 B.C. saved the Capitoline from the invading Gauls)* ‖ Titus Manlius Torquatus *(consul in 340 B.C., famous for his military discipline)*

mannul·us -ī *m* little pony

mann·us -ī *m* pony

mān·ō -āre -āvī -ātus *tr* to pour out; to shed *(tears)* ‖ *intr* to drip, trickle; *(w. abl)* to drip with; to leak; to flow, pour; to stream; *(of rumors)* to spread, circulate; *(of secrets)* to leak out; *(fig)* to be derived, emanate

mansi·ō -ōnis *f* staying; stopover

mansit·ō -āre -āvī intr to stay on

mansuē·faciō -facĕre -fēcī -factus *(pass:* mansuē·fīō -fierī -factus sum) *tr* to tame; to civilize

mansu·ēs -is *or* -ētis *adj* tame, mild

mansu·escō -escĕre -ēvī -ētus *tr* to tame ‖ *intr* to become tame; *(fig)* to become gentle; to relent; to grow less harsh

mansuētē *adv* gently, mildly

mansuētūd·ō -inis *f* mildness, gentleness

mansuēt·us -a -um *adj* tame; mild, gentle

mansus *pp of* mando *and* maneo

mantēl·e -is *n* hand towel; napkin; tablecloth

mantēl·ium -(i)ī *n* hand towel; napkin

mantell·um -ī *n* (-tēl-) mantle

mantic·a -ae *f* knapsack

Mantinē·a -ae *f* town in Arcadia, where the Spartans were defeated by the Thebans in 362 B.C.

mantiscin·or -ārī -ātus sum *intr* to predict, prophesy

mant·ō -āre *tr* to wait for ‖ *intr* to stay, remain, wait

Mant·ō -ūs *f* prophetic daughter of Tiresias

Mantu·a -ae *f* town in N. Italy, birthplace of Vergil

manuāl·e -is *n* wooden case for a book

manuāl·is -is -e *adj* that can be held in hand, hand-sized *(e.g., rocks)*

manubi·ae -ārum *fpl* money derived from the sale of booty; *(coll)* proceeds from robbery, loot

manubiāl·is -is -e *adj* obtained from the sale of booty

manubiāri·us -a -um *adj (coll)* bringing in the loot

manūbr·ium -(i)ī *n* handle; hilt

manufestāri·us -a -um *adj* (mani-) plain, obvious

manule·a -ae *f* long sleeve

manuleār·ius -(i)ī *m* sleeve maker

manuleāt·us -a -um *adj* long-sleeved

manūmissi·ō -ōnis *f* manumission, freeing *(of a slave)*

manū·mittō -mittĕre -mīsī -missus *tr* to manumit, set free *(a slave)*

manupret·ium -(i)ī *n* workman's pay, wages; *(fig)* pay, reward

man·us -ūs *f* hand; band, gang, company; force, violence, close combat; finishing touch; handwriting; work; workmanship; trunk *(of elephant);* twigs *(of a tree); (leg)* power of a husband over his wife and children; *(med)* surgery; **ad manum** close at hand, within easy reach; **ad manum habere** to have at hand, have in readiness; **ad manum venire** to come within reach; **ad manus pervenire** to resort to fighting; **aequā manu** *(or* **aequis manibus)** on even terms; **a manu servus** secretary; **de manu** personally; **e manu** at a distance, from a distance; **in manibus esse** *(gen)* to be in the power of; be under the jurisdiction of; **inter manus** under one's hand, in one's arms; **inter manus habere** to have in hand, be busied with; **manibus pedibusque** *(fig)* with might and main; **manu** by hand, artificially; in deed; by force; *(mil)* by force of arms; **manu (e)mittere** to set *(a slave)* free; **manu factus** man-made; **manum committere** *(or* **conserere** *or* **conferre)** to begin to fight; **manum dare** to lend a hand; **manum injicere** *(w. dat)* to lay hands on, arrest; **manūs dare** *(or* **manūs dedere)** to surrender; **manus extrema** *(or* **summa** *or* **ultima)** finishing touches; **manus (ferrea)** grappling iron; **manu tenere** to know for sure; **media manus** a go-between; **per manūs** by hand; by force; from hand to hand, from mouth to mouth, from father to son; **plenā manu** generously; **prae manibus** *(or* **prae manu)** at hand, in readiness; **sub manu** *(or* **sub manum)** at hand, near; immediately, promptly; **suspensā manu** reluctantly

mapāl·ia -ium *npl* African huts; *(fig)* a mess

mapp·a -ae *f* napkin; flag *(used in starting races at the racetrack)*

Marath·ōn -ōnis *f* site in E. Attica of the victory of Miltiades over the Persians *(490 B.C.)*

Marathōni·us -a -um *adj* of Marathon

Marcell·us -ī *m* Roman family name *(cognomen)* in the gens Claudia; Marcus Claudius Marcellus *(nephew of Augustus, 43–23 B.C.)*

marc·eō -ēre *intr* to wither, droop, shrivel; to be weak, be feeble; be decrepit, be run-down; to slack off

marcesc·ō -ēre *intr* to begin to wither, begin to droop; to become weak, become run-down; to become lazy

marcid·us -a -um *adj* withered, droopy; groggy

Marc·ius -(i)ī *m* Ancus Marcius *(fourth king of Rome)*

marcul·us -ī *m* small hammer

mar·e -is *n* sea; saltwater; **mare caelo miscere** to raise a huge storm; *(fig)* to have all hell break loose; **mare inferum** Tyrrhenian Sea; **mare magnum** the ocean; **mare nostrum** Mediterranean Sea; **mare superum** Adriatic Sea; **trans mare** overseas, abroad

Mareōt·a -ae *f* town and lake near Alexandria in Egypt

Mareōtic·us -a -um *adj* Mareotic; Egyptian

margarīt·a -ae *for* **margarīt·um -ī** *n* pearl

margin·ō -āre -āvī -ātus *tr* to furnish with a border; to curb *(a street)*

marg·ō -inis *f* margin, edge, border; frontier; bank *(of a stream)*

Mariān·ī -ōrum *mpl* partisans of Marius

Marīc·a -ae *f* nymph of Minturnae, mother of Latinus

marīn·us -a -um *adj* sea-, marine; seagoing

marisc·a -ae *f* a fig; **tumidae mariscae** the piles

marīt·a -ae *f* wife

marītāl·is -is -e *adj* marital, nuptial; matronly, of a married woman

maritim·us -a -um *adj* (**-tum-**) sea-, of the sea; seafaring, maritime; *(fig)* changeable *(like the sea); ora* **maritima** seacoast **‖** *npl* seacoast

marīt·ō -āre -āvī -ātus *tr* to provide with a husband *or* wife, marry; to train *(a vine to a tree)* **‖** *pass* to get married

marīt·us -a -um *adj* matrimonial, nuptial **‖** *m* husband **‖** *f* wife

Mar·ius -(i)ī *m* Gaius Marius *(conqueror of Jugurtha and of the Cimbri and Teutons, and seven times consul, 157–86 B.C.)*

marm·or -oris *n* marble; marble statue, marble monument; marble vessel; milestone; smooth surface of the sea **‖** *npl* marble pavement

marmore·us -a -um *adj* marble, made of marble; marble-like

Mar·ō -ōnis *m* cognomen of Vergil

marr·a -ae *f* hoe, weeding hook

Mar·s -tis *m* god of war and father of Romulus and Remus; battle, war; engagement; *(astr)* Mars; **aequo Marte** on an equal footing, in an even battle; **stella** *(or* **sidus) Martis** *(astr)* the planet Mars; **suo Marte** by his own exertions, independently

Mars·ī -ōrum *mpl* Marsians *(a people of S. central Italy, regarded as tough warriors)*

marsupp·ium -(i)ī *n* purse, pouch

Marsy·ās *or* **Marsy·a -ae** *m* satyr who challenged Apollo with the flute and was flayed alive upon his defeat **‖** statue of Marsyas in the Roman Forum

Martiāl·ēs -ium *mpl* college of priests of Mars; troops of the **legio Martia** *(Martian legion)*

Martiāl·is -is *m* Martial *(Marcus Valerius Martialis, famous for his epigrams, c. A.D. 40–120)*

Marticol·a -ae *m* worshiper of Mars

Marti·us -a -um *adj* Martian, of Mars; sacred to Mars; descended from Mars; of March; **mensis Martius** March *(third month of the year after the year 153 B.C., originally the first month)* **‖** *m* March

mās maris *adj* male, masculine; manly, brave **‖** *m* male

masculīn·us -a -um *adj* male, masculine

mascul·us -a -um *adj* male, masculine; manly, vigorous **‖** *m* male

mass·a -ae *f* mass, lump; *(coll)* chunk of money; bulk, size; heavy weight *(used in exercising)*

Massaget·ae -ārum *mpl* a nomadic tribe of Scythia

Massic·us -a -um *adj* Massic **‖** *m* Mt. Massicus *(between Latium and Campania, famous for its wine)* **‖** *n* Massic wine

Massili·a -ae *f* Greek Colony on S. coast of Gaul *(modern Marseilles)*

Massyl·ī -ōrum *mpl* tribe of E. Numidia
mastīgi·a *or* **mastīgi·ās -ae** *m* rascal *(whipneeder)*
mastrūc·a -ae *f* skeepskin; *(pej)* ninny
mastrūcāt·us -a -um *adj* dressed in a sheepskin coat
masturbāt·or -ōris *m* masturbator
masturb·or -ārī -ātus sum *intr* to masturbate
matar·a -ae *or* **matar·is -is** *f* Celtic javelin
matell·a -ae *f* chamber pot
matelli·ō -ōnis *m* small pot
mā·ter -tris *f* mother; matron; foster mother; *(in addressing an old woman)* ma'am; *(of animals)* dam; cause, origin, source; motherland, native land; native city; **Magna mater** Cybele; **mater familias** lady of the house
matercul·a -ae *f* little mother, poor mother
māt·erfamiliās -risfamiliās *f* lady of the house, mistress of the household
māteri·a -ae *or* **māteri·ēs -ēī** *f* matter, stuff, material; lumber *(for building);* fuel; subject, subject matter, theme, topic; cause, source; occasion, opportunity; capacity, natural ability; disposition
māteriār·ius -(i)ī *m* lumber merchant
māteriāt·us -a -um *adj* built with lumber; **male materiatus** built with poor lumber
māteriēs *see* **materia**
māteri·or -ārī -ātus sum *intr* to gather wood
mātern·us -a -um *adj* maternal, mother's, of a mother
māterter·a -ae *f* aunt, mother's sister; **matertera magna** grandaunt, grandmother's sister
mathēmatic·a -ae *or* **mathēmatic·ē -ēs** *f* mathematics; astrology
mathēmatic·us -a -um *adj* mathematical, of arithmetic, of geometry ‖ *m* mathematician; astrologer
Matīn·us -ī *m* mountain in Apulia near Horace's birthplace
mātricīd·a -ae *m* murderer of one's mother
mātricīd·ium -(i)ī *n* murder of one's mother, matricide
mātrimōn·ium -(i)ī *n* matrimony, marriage; **in matrimonium accipere** to marry *(a man);* **in matrimonium dare** *(or* **collocare)** to give in marriage; **in matrimonium ducere** to marry *(a woman)*
mātrim·us -a -um *adj* having a mother still living
mātrōn·a -ae *f* married woman, matron, wife; lady
Mātrōnāl·ia -ium *npl* festival celebrated by married women on March 1 in honor of Mars
mātrōnāl·is -is -e *adj* matronly, wifely, womanly

matt·a -ae *f* straw mat
matul·a -ae *f* pot; chamber pot; *(pej)* blockhead
mātūrātē *adv* promptly
mātūrē *adv* at the right time; in good time, in time; at an early date; at an early age; quickly; prematurely
mātūr·escō -escĕre -uī *intr* to get ripe, ripen, mature
mātūrit·ās -ātis *f* ripeness, maturity; harvest season; the proper time; *(fig)* maturity, height, perfection
mātūr·ō -āre -āvī -ātus *tr* to ripen, bring to maturity; to speed up, hasten; *(w. inf)* to be too quick in doing ‖ *intr* to hurry; **maturato opus est** there is no time to lose
mātūr·us -a -um *adj* ripe, mature, full-grown; opportune, at the right time; *(of winter, etc.)* early, coming early; advanced in years; marriageable; mellow
Mātūt·a -ae *f* goddess of the dawn
mātūtīn·us -a -um *adj* morning, early; **dies matutinus** early part of the day; **tempora matutina** morning hours
Mauritāni·a -ae *f* country of N.W. Africa
Maur·us -a -um *adj* Moorish; African
Maurūsi·us -a -um *adj* Moorish, Mauretanian
Māvor·s -tis *m* Mars; warfare; *(astr)* Mars
Māvorti·us -a -um *adj* Martian, of Mars; warlike, martial ‖ *m* Meleager *(son of Mars)*
maxill·a -ae *f* jaw
maximē *adv* **(-xum-)** very, most, especially, particularly; just, precisely; exactly; *(in sequences)* in the first place, first of all; *(in affirmations)* by all means, certainly, yes; **immo maxime** certainly not; **nuper maxime** just recently; **quam maxime** as much as possible; **tum cum maxime** at the precise moment when; **tum maxime** just then; **ut maxime...ita maxime** the more...so much the more
maximit·ās -ātis *f* magnitude
maxim·us -a -um *(superl of* **magnus)** *adj* **(-xum-)** biggest, largest; tallest; greatest *(in amount, number, value, power, or reputation); (with or without* **natu)** oldest; highest, utmost; most important, leading, chief; **maximā voce** at the top of one's lungs
mazonom·um -ī *n* serving dish
meāmet = **meā,** *abl fem sing of* **meus,** *strengthened by* **-met**
meāpte = **meā,** *abl fem sing of* **meus,** *strengthened by* **-pte**
meāt·us -ūs *m* motion, movement; course, channel
mecastor *interj* by Castor! *(used by women)*
mēcum = **cum me**
mēd = **mē** *(archaic form of acc and abl)*

medd·ix -icis m (**mēd-**) magistrate (among the Oscans); **meddix tuticus** chief magistrate

Mēdē·a -ae f daughter of Aeëtes, the king of Colchis, and wife of Jason

Mēdē·is -idos adj magical

med·ens -entis m doctor

med·eor -ērī tr to heal ‖ intr (w. dat) to heal, cure; (w. adversus or contra + acc) to be good for (e.g., a cold, headache)

Mēd·ī -ōrum mpl Medes; Parthians; Persians

Mēdi·a -ae f country of the Medes S. of the Caspian Sea

mediān·us -a -um adj central ‖ n central part, middle

mediast(r)īn·us -ī m servant (without any specific skill)

mēdic·a -ae f alfalfa

medicābil·is -is -e adj curable

medicām·en -inis n medicine, medication; drug, antidote; remedy; tincture; cosmetic; (fig) remedy

medicāment·um -ī n medicine, medication; potion; (fig) relief, antidote; (rhet) embellishment

medicāt·us -a -um adj healing, having healing powers; imbued with magical substances

medicāt·us -ūs m magic charm

medicīn·a -ae f medicine (medication; science of medicine); remedy; doctor's office; (w. gen) (fig) cure for, remedy for; **medicinam exercere** (or **facere**) to practice medicine

medicīn·us -a -um adj of medicine

medic·ō -āre -āvī -ātus tr to medicate, cure; to dye; to poison

medic·or -ārī -ātus sum tr to cure ‖ intr (w. dat) to heal, cure

medic·us -a -um adj medical; healing ‖ m doctor, surgeon ‖ f physician (female), midwife

Mēdic·us -a -um adj Median, of the Medes

medīdi·ēs -ēī f (early form of **meridiēs**) noon; south

mediē adv moderately

mediet·ās -ātis f mean; middle

medimn·um -ī n or **medimn·us -ī** m bushel (containing six modii or "pecks")

mediocr·is -is -e adj of medium size, medium, average, ordinary; undistinguished; mediocre; narrow, small; intermediate

mediocrit·ās -ātis f moderate size or amount; middle course, mean; moderation; mediocrity ‖ fpl moderate passions

mediocriter adv moderately, fairly; not particularly, not very, not much; calmly; with moderation; (w. neg.) in no slight degree, considerably, extraordinarily

Mediolānens·is -is -e adj of Milan

Mediolān·um -ī n Milan

medioxum·us -a -um adj (coll) in the middle, intermediate

meditāment·um -ī n practice, drill, exercise (in school, in the army)

meditātē adv intentionally

meditāti·ō -ōnis f reflection, contemplation; practice; rehearsal; (w. gen) reflection on

meditāt·us -a -um adj premeditated

mediterrāne·us -a -um adj inland ‖ n interior (of a country)

medit·or -ārī -ātus sum tr to think over, reflect on; to practice, rehearse; to have in mind, intend; to plan, design ‖ refl to practice, train ‖ intr to prepare one's speech, rehearse; (w. de + abl) to reflect on, think about;

meditull·ium -(i)ī n the interior (of a country); middle, center

medi·us -a -um adj middle, central, the middle of, in the middle; intermediate; moderate; intervening (time); middling, ordinary, common; undecided, neutral, ambiguous; **dies medius** (or **lux media, sol medius**) midday; the south; **in mediā viā** in the middle of the road; **media pars** half; **medium mare** the high seas ‖ n the middle part, center; the general public; intervening space; intermediate stage; **de** (or **ē**) **medio** from the scene; **in medio** in mid-course; within reach; **in medio positus** made available to all; **in medio ponere** to disclose; **in medium** on behalf of the general public; for the common good; **in medium proferre** to make public; **in medium** (or **in medio**) **relinquere** to leave undecided; **medio temporis** in the meanwhile

medius fidius interj so help me God!; honest to God!

med·ix -icis see **meddix**

medull·a -ae f marrow; (fig) middle ‖ fpl (fig) heart; **imis medullis** in the innermost heart, deep within one's heart

medullitus adv with all one's heart

medullul·a -ae f anseris medullula goose down

Mēd·us -a -um Mede, of the Medes ‖ m son of Aegeus and Medea, the eponymous hero of the Medes

Medūs·a -ae f one of the three Gorgons, whose look turned people to stone

Medūsae·us -a -um adj Medusan; **equus Medusaeus** Pegasus

Megaer·a -ae f one of the three Furies

Megalens·ia or **Megalēs·ia -ium** npl festival of Cybele, celebrated on the 4th of April

Megalens·is -is -e adj of the Magna Mater or Cybele; **ludi Megalenses** games in honor of Cybele

Megar·a -ae *f* wife of Hercules, whom he killed in a fit of madness

Megar·a -ae *f or* **Megar·a -ōrum** *npl* town near Athens on the Saronic Gulf **ll** Greek town in Sicily

Megarē·us *or* **Megaric·us -a -um** *adj* of Megara, Megarean

megistān·es -um *mpl* grandees

meherc(u)le *or* **mehercules** *interj* by Hercules!

mēj·ō -ĕre mixī *or* **minxī mictum** *or* **minctum** *intr (coll)* to pee

mel mellis *n* honey; **meum mel** *(as term of endearment)* my honey **ll** *npl* drops of honey

melancholic·us -a -um *adj* melancholy

melandry·um -ī *n* piece of salted tuna

Melanipp·a -ae *f or* **Melanipp·ē -ēs** *f* Melanippe *(daughter of Aeolus or Desmon, the mother of two children by Neptune)*

Melanth·ius -(i)ī *m* goatherd of Ulysses

melcul·um -ī *n (term of endearment)* little honey

Melea·ger *or* **Melea·gros -grī** *m* Meleager *(son of King Oeneus of Calydon and participant in the famous Calydonian boar hunt)*

Meleagrid·es -um *fpl* sisters of Meleager who were changed into birds

mēl·ēs -is *f* badger

Melicert·a -ae *or* **Melicert·ēs -ae** *m* Melicertes *(son of Ino and Athamas, who was changed into a sea- god, called Palaemon by the Greeks and Portunus by the Romans)*

melic·us -a -um *adj* musical, melodious; lyric

melilōt·os -ī *m* clover-like plant

melimēl·a -ōrum *npl* honey apples

mēlīn·a -ae *f* **(mell-)** leather pouch

Mēlīn·um -ī *n* pigment; Melian white *(from Melos)*

meli·or -or -us *(comp of* **bonus)** *adj* better; kinder, more gracious; **melius est** *(w. inf, w. acc & inf)* it is (would be) preferable to, that

melisphyll·um -ī *n* balm *(herb of which bees are fond)*

Melit·a -ae *or* **Melit·ē -ēs** *f* Malta; a sea nymph

Melitens·is -is -e *adj* Maltese

melius *(comp of* **bene)** *adv* better

meliusculē *adv* pretty well

meliuscul·us -a -um *adj* a little better

mell·a -ae *f* mead *(mixture of honey and water)*

mellicul·us -a -um *adj* sweet as honey

melli·fer -fera -ferum *adj* producing honey

mellific·ō -āre *intr* to make honey

mellill·a -ae *f (term of endearment)* little honey

mellīn·a -ae *f* sweetness, delight

mellīn·a -ae *f* **(mēlī-)** leather pouch *(made from the skin of a badger)*

mellīt·us -a -um *adj* honeyed; sweet as honey

mel·os -eos *n or* **mel·um -ī** *n or* **mel·os -ī** *m* song, tune

Melpomen·ē -ēs *f* Muse of tragic poetry

membrān·a -ae *f* membrane, skin; slough *(of a snake);* parchment; film

membrānul·a -ae *f* small piece of parchment

membrātim *adv* limb by limb; singly, piecemeal; in short sentences

membr·um -ī *n* member, organ, limb, genital; part, division *(of a thing);* apartment, room; member *(of a group); (gram)* clause; *(rhet)* small section of a speech *or* literary work

mēmet *pron (emphatic form of* **mē)** me

memin·ī -isse *(imperative:* **memento; mementote)** *tr* to remember **ll** *tr (w. gen)* to remember, be mindful of

Memn·ōn -ŏnis *m* son of Tithonus and Aurora, king of the Ethiopians, killed by Achilles **ll** statue in Egypt *(actually of Amenhotep III)*

Memnonid·es -um *fpl* birds that rose from the pyre of Memnon

Memnoni·us -a -um *adj* Memnonian; Oriental; Moorish; black

mem·or -oris *adj* mindful, remembering having a good memory; careful, thoughtful; observant; *(w. gen)* mindful of, remembering

memorābil·is -is -e *adj* memorable, remarkable

memorand·us -a -um *adj* worth mentioning, notable

memorāt·us -ūs *m* mention

memori·a -ae *f* memory; remembrance; period of recollection, time, lifetime; a memory, past event, history; historical account; **in memoriā habere** to bear in mind; **in memoriā redire** *(or* **regredi)** to recollect; **in memoriam** *(w. gen)* in memory of; **in memoriā inducere** *(or* **redigere)** to call to mind; **memoriā** *(w. gen)* in the time of; **memoriā tenere** to keep in mind; to remember; **memoriae causā** as a reminder; **memoriae mandare** *(or* **tradere)** to commit to memory; **memoriae prodere** to hand down to posterity; **paulo supra hanc memoriam** not long ago; **post hominum memoriam** within the memory of man; **superiore memoriā** in earlier times

memoriāl·is -is -e *adj* for memoranda

memoriol·a -ae *f* weak memory

memoriter *adv* from memory, by heart; accurately, correctly

memor·ō -āre -āvī -ātus *tr* to mention, bring up; to name, call **ll** *intr (w.* **de** + *abl)* to speak of

Memph·is -is or **-idos** *f* capital city of Pharaonic Egypt
Memphītic·us -a -um *adj* Egyptian
Menan·der or **Menan·dros -drī** *m* Greek playwright of Attic New Comedy *(342– 291 B.C.)*
Menandrē·us -a -um *adj* of Menander
mend·a -ae *f* fault, blemish; slip of the pen
mendāciloqui·or -or -us *adj* more false
mendāc·ium -(i)ī *n* lie
mendāciuncul·um -ī *n* white lie, fib
mend·ax -ācis *adj* mendacious, lying, false **‖** *m* liar
mendīcābul·um -ī *n* beggar
mendīcit·ās -ātis *f* begging
mendīc·ō -āre -āvī -ātus or **mendīc·or -ārī -ātus sum** *tr* to beg, beg for **‖** *intr* to beg, be a beggar
mendīcul·us -a -um *adj* beggarly
mendīc·us -a -um *adj* needy, poverty-stricken; paltry *(meal)* **‖** *m* beggar
mendōsē *adv* faultily, carelessly
mendōs·us -a -um *adj* full of physical defects; full of faults, faulty, incorrect, erroneous; blundering
mend·um -ī *n* defect, fault; blunder
Menelā·us -ī *m* son of Atreus, brother of Agamemnon, and husband of Helen
Menēn·ius -(i)ī *m* Menenius Agrippa *(told the plebs the fable of the belly and the limbs, 494 B.C.)*
Menoec·eūs -eī or **-eos** *m* son of Theban king Creon, who hurled himself off the city walls to save the city
Menoetiad·ēs -ae *m* son of Menoetius *(i.e., Patroclus)*
Menoet·ius -(i)ī *m* one of the Argonauts and father of Patroclus
men·s -tis *f* mind, intellect; frame of mind, attitude; will, inclination; understanding, reason; thought, opinion, intention, plan; courage, boldness; passion, impulse; **addere mentem** to give courage; **captus mente** crazy; **demittere mentem** to lose heart; **in mentem venire** to come to mind; **mentis suae esse** to be in one's right mind
mens·a -ae *f* table; meal, course, dinner; guests at table; counter; bank; sacrificial table, altar; **mens secunda** dessert
mensār·ius -(i)ī *m* banker; treasury official; **triumviri mensarii** board of three treasury officials
mensi·ō -ōnis *f* measure, measuring; *(pros)* quantity *(of a syllable)*
mens·is -is *(gen pl:* **mensium** or **mensum)** *m* month; **primo mense** at the beginning of the month
mens·or -ōris *m* surveyor
menstruāl·is -is -e *adj* for a month
menstru·us -a -um *adj* monthly; lasting for a month **‖** *n* rations for a month;

month's term of office; monthly payment
mensul·a -ae *f* small table
mensūr·a -ae *f* measuring, measurement; standard of measure; amount, size, proportion, capacity, extent, limit, degree; **mensura duorum digitorum** a pinch *(e.g., of salt)*
mensus *pp of* **metior**
ment·a or **menth·a -ae** *f* mint
menti·ens -entis *m (phil)* sophism, fallacy
menti·ō -ōnis *f* mention; **mentionem facere** *(w. gen* or **de** + *abl)* to make mention of; **mentiones serere** *(w. ad)* to throw hints to
ment·ior -īrī -ītus sum *tr* to invent, fabricate; to feign, imitate, fake **‖** *intr* to lie; to act deceitfully
Ment·ōr -ŏris *m* friend of Ulysses **‖** Greek silversmith of 4th cent. B.C.; *(fig)* a work by Mentor
ment·um -ī *n* chin
me·ō -āre -āvī -ātum *intr* to go, pass
mēopte *pron (emphatic form of* **mē)** me, me myself
mephīt·is -is *f* sulfurous fumes
merāc(u)l·us -a -um *adj* pretty pure
merāc·us -a -um *adj* undiluted, pure
mercābil·is -is -e *adj* buyable
merc·ans -antis *m* merchant
mercāt·or -ōris *m* merchant, dealer
mercātōri·us -a -um *adj* mercantile, trading, business; **navis mercatoria** merchant ship
mercātūr·a -ae *f* commerce, trade, trading; purchase **‖** *fpl* goods, wares
mercāt·us -ūs *m* market, marketplace; fair; trade, traffic
mercēdul·a -ae *f* poor pay; low rent
mercennāri·us or **mercēnāri·us -a -um** *adj* hired, paid, mercenary **‖** *m* common laborer
merc·ēs -ēdis *f* pay, wages; bribe; reward, recompense; cost; price; payment *(esp. for effort, pain, misfortune);* injury, detriment; stipulation, condition; retribution, punishment; rent, income, interest; **unā mercede duas res assequi** *(prov)* to kill two birds with one stone *(literally, to buy two things for the price of one)*
mercimōn·ium -(i)ī *n* merchandise, goods, wares
merc·or -ārī -ātus sum *tr* to purchase **‖** *intr* to trade, buy and sell
Mercuriāl·is -is -e *adj* of Mercury **‖** *mpl* corporation of merchants in Rome
Mercur·ius -(i)ī *m* Mercury *(son of Jupiter and Maia, messenger of the gods, patron of commerce, diplomacy, gambling, etc.); (astr)* Mercury; **sidus** *(or* **stella) Mercurii** the planet Mercury
merd·a -ae *f* droppings, excrement
merend·a -ae *f* lunch, snack

mer·eō -ēre -uī -itus *or* **mer·eor -ērī -itus sum** *tr* to deserve, merit, be entitled to; to win, gain *(glory, fame, reproach);* to earn *(money);* **merere pecuniam ut** to accept money on condition that; **stipendia** *(or* **stipendium) merere** *(mil)* to serve **‖** *intr* to serve; to serve in the army; *(w.* **de** *+ abl)* to serve, render service to, do a favor for; **bene de re publica merere** *(or* **mereri)** to serve one's country well; **de te merui** I have done you a favor, I have treated you well; **equo merere** to serve in the cavalry

meretrīciē *adv* like a prostitute

meretrīci·us -a -um *adj* prostitute's

meretrīcul·a -ae *f* cute little wench; *(pej)* the little wench

meretr·ix -īcis *f* prostitute, hooker

merg·ae -ārum *fpl* pitchfork; device for reaping

merg·es -itis *f* sheaf of wheat

mer·gō -gĕre -sī -sus *tr* to dip, plunge, sink; to flood, inundate, engulf, swallow up; to swamp, overwhelm; to bury; to drown **‖** *refl* to dive **‖** *pass* to sink; *(of heavenly bodies)* to go down; to drown; to go bankrupt

merg·us -ī *m* seagull

merīdiān·us -a -um *adj* midday, noon; southern, southerly

merīdiāti·ō -ōnis *f* siesta

merīdi·ēs -ēī *m* midday, noon; south; **spectare ad meridiem** to face south

merīdi·ō -āre -āvī *or* **merīdi·or -ārī -ātus sum** *intr* to take a siesta

Mērion·ēs -ae *m* charioteer of Idomeneus of Crete in Trojan War

meritō *adv* deservedly, rightly

merit·ō -āre -āvī -ātus *tr* to earn regularly

meritōri·us -a -um *adj* rented, hired **‖** *npl* rented lodgings

merit·us -a -um *adj* deserved, just, right, proper, deserving; guilty **‖** *n* service, favor, kindness; merit, worth; blame, fault, offense

merobib·us -a -um *adj* drinking unmixed wine

Merop·ē -ēs *f* one of the Pleiades, daughter of Atlas and Pleione

Merop·s -is *m* king of Ethiopia, husband of Clymene, and reputed father of Phaëthon

mer·ops -opis *m* bee-eater *(bird)*

mers·ō -āre -āvī -ātus *tr* to keep dipping *or* plunging; to drown; *(fig)* to engulf **‖** *pass (w. dat)* to plunge into

mersus *pp of* **mergo**

merul·a -ae *f* blackbird

mer·us -a -um *adj* pure, unmixed, undiluted; *(fig)* nothing but, mere **‖** *n* (undiluted) wine

mer·x -cis *f* merchandise, wares; **mala merx** *(fig)* bad lot

Messallīn·a -ae *f* Valeria Messallina *(wife of Claudius and mother of Britannicus)* **‖** Statilia Messalina *(wife of Nero)*

Messān·a -ae *f* town in N.E. Sicily

Messāpi·us -a -um *adj* of Messapia, of Calabria **‖** *f* town and district of Messapia in S.E. Italy

mess·is -is *f (acc:* **messem** *or* **messim)** harvest; harvest time; **adhuc tua messis in herbā est** *(prov)* don't count your chickens before they are hatched *(literally, your harvest is still on the stalk, i.e., in early stages of growth)*

mess·or -ōris *m* reaper, mower

messōri·us -a -um *adj* reaper's

messuī *perf of* **meto**

messus *pp of* **meto**

mēt·a -ae *f* marker for measuring a lap at a racetrack; haystack; *(fig)* goal, end; *(fig)* turning point

metall·um -ī *n* metal **‖** *npl* mine

metamorphōs·is -is *f* transformation

metaphor·a -ae *f* metaphor

mētāt·or -ōris *m* planner; **metator urbis** city planner

Metaur·us -ī *m* river in Umbria

Metell·us -ī *m* Roman family name *(cognomen);* Quintus Caecilius Metellus Numidicus *(commander of the Roman forces against Jugurtha, 109–107 B.C.)*

Mēthymn·a -ae *f* town on the Island of Lesbos

metīculōsus *see* **metuculosus**

mētior mētīrī mensus sum *tr* to measure; to traverse, travel; to judge, estimate; *(w. dat)* to measure *(s.th.)* out to, distribute *(s. th.)* among; *(w. abl)* to judge *(s.o.)* by the standard of

metō metĕre messuī messus *tr* to reap, mow, gather, harvest; *(fig)* to mow down *(e.g., with the sword)*

mēt·or -ārī -ātus sum *tr* to measure off; to lay out *(e.g., a camp)*

metrēt·a -ae *f* liquid measure *(about nine gallons)*

metūculōs·us -a -um *adj* **(metīc-)** fearful; scary; awful

metu·ens -entis *adj* afraid, anxious

met·uō -uĕre -uī -ūtus *tr* to fear, be afraid of **‖** *intr* to be afraid, be apprehensive

met·us -ūs *m* fear, anxiety; **in metu esse** to be in a state of alarm; to be an object of concern

me·us -a -um *adj* my **‖** *pron* mine; **meā interest** it is of importance to me; **meum est** *(w. inf)* it is my duty to; **meus est** *(coll)* I've got him, he's mine

Mezent·ius -(i)ī *m* Etruscan ruler of Caere, slain by Aeneas

mī = mihi

mīc·a -ae *f* crumb, morsel

Micips·a -ae *m* son of Masinissa and king of Numidia *(148–118 b.c.)* ‖ *mpl (fig)* Numidians, N. Africans

mic·ō -āre -uī *intr* to vibrate, quiver; to twinkle, sparkle, flash

mictur·iō -īre *intr* to have to urinate

Mid·ās -ae *m* king of Phrygia, at whose touch everything turned to gold *(8th cent. b.c.)*

migrāti·ō -ōnis *f* moving, changing residence; migration; *(fig)* metaphorical use

migrō -āre -āvī -ātus *tr* to move, transport; *(fig)* to violate *(a law)* ‖ *intr* to move, change residence; migrate; *(fig)* to change, turn

mīl·es -itis *m* soldier; infantryman; private; *(fig)* army

Mīlēsi·us -a -um *adj* Milesian, of Miletus

Mīlēt·us -ī *f* town on W. coast of Asia Minor ‖ *m* founder of the town of Miletus

mīl·ia -ium *npl* thousands; *see* **mille**

miliār·ium -(i)ī *n* milestone

mīlitār·is -is -e *adj* military

mīlitāriter *adv* in a military manner, like a soldier

mīlitāri·us -a -um *adj* soldierly, military

mīliti·a -ae *f* army; war; the military; military discipline; **militiae** in war, on the battlefield, in the army; **militiae domique** abroad and at home, on the war front and on the home front

mīlit·ō -āre -āvī -ātum *intr* to be a soldier, do military service

mil·ium -(i)ī *n* millet *(a food grain)*

mille *(indecl) adj* thousand; **mille homines** a thousand people ‖ **mīlia** *npl (declinable noun) (gen:* **mīlium)** thousands; *(w. gen):* **duo milia hominum** two thousand people; **duo milia passuum** two miles *(literally, two thousands of paces)*

millēsim·us *or* **millensim·us -a -um** *adj* thousandth

milliār·ium -(i)ī *n* milestone

milliens *or* **milliēs** *adv* a thousand times; innumerable times

Mil·ō -ōnis *m* Titus Annius Papinianus Milo *(defended by Cicero on a charge of having murdered Clodius in 52 b.c.)*

Miltiad·ēs -is *m* Athenian general victorious at Marathon *(490 b.c.)*

mīlvīn·us *or* **miluīn·us -a -um** *adj* rapacious *(as a kite)*

mīlv·us *or* **milv·os** *or* **mīlu·us -ī** *m* kite *(bird of prey);* flying gurnard *(fish); (astr)* mistakenly taken by Ovid as a constellation

mīm·a -ae *f* actress *(of mimes)*

Mimallon·is -idis *f* a Bacchante

Mim·ās -antis *m* one of the Giants

mīmicē *adv* like a mime actor

mīmic·us -a -um *adj* suitable for the mime, farcical

Mimnerm·us -ī *m* Greek elegaic poet of

Colophon on the W. coast of Asia Minor *(fl 630 b.c.)*

mīmul·a -ae *f* miserable little actress

mīm·us -ī *m* mime, farce; actor *(of a mime); (fig)* farce

min·a -ae *f* Greek unit of weight, equal to 100 drachmas, or 100 Roman denarii; Greek coin *(about 100 denarii, i.e., about $100)*

mināci·ae -ārum *fpl* threats

mināciter *adv* threateningly

min·ae -ārum *fpl* threats; projecting points of a wall

minanter *adv* threateningly

mināti·ō -ōnis *f* threatening

min·ax -ācis *adj* threatening, menacing; projecting, jutting out

min·eō -ēre *intr* to project, jut out

Minerv·a -ae *f* goddess of wisdom and of the arts and sciences, identified with Athena; *(fig)* skill, genius; spinning and weaving; **invitā Minervā** against one's better judgment

mingō mingĕre minxī *or* **mixī minctum** *or* **mictum** *intr (coll)* to pee

miniān·us -a -um *adj* vermilion

miniātul·us -a -um *adj* reddish

minimē *or* **minumē** *adv* least of all, least, very little; by no means, certainly not, not in the least; *(w. numerals)* at least; **minime gentium** *(coll)* by no means

minim·us *or* **minum·us -a -um** *(superl of* **parvus)** *adj* smallest, least, very small; slightest, very insignificant; youngest; shortest *(time);* **minimus natu** youngest ‖ *n* the least, minimum; lowest price; **minimo emere** to buy at a very low price; **minimo provocare** to provoke on the flimsiest pretext

mini·ō -āre -āvī -ātus *tr* to color red, paint red

minis·ter -trī *m* servant, attendant, helper; waiter; agent, subordinate, tool

minister·ium -(i)ī *n* activity of a servant *or* attendant, service, attendance; task, duty; office, ministry; occupation, work; agency, instrumentality ‖ *npl* servants

ministr·a -ae *f* servant, attendant, helper; waitress; handmaid

ministrāt·or -ōris *m or* **ministrātr·ix -īcis** *f* assistant, helper

ministr·ō -āre -āvī -ātus *tr* to serve, wait on; to tend; to execute, carry out *(orders); (w. dat)* to hand out *(s.th.)* to; *(w. abl)* to supply *(s.o. or s.th.)* with

minitābund·us -a -um *adj* threatening, menacing

minit·ō -āre *or* **minit·or -ārī -ātus sum** *tr* to make threats of *(e.g., war); (w. acc of thing and dat of person)* to threaten to bring *(e.g., evil, harm)* upon, hold *(s.th.)* threateningly over *(s.o.)* ‖ *intr* to jut out,

project; to be menacing, make threats;
(w. dat) to threaten
min·or -or -us *(comp of* **parvus)** *adj*
smaller, less; shorter *(time);* inferior,
less important; *(w. abl)* **1** *(of time)* too
short for; **2** inferior to; **3** unworthy of;
(w. inf) unfit to, incapable of; **dimidio
minor quam** half as small as; **minor
capitis** deprived of civil rights; **minores
facere filios quam** to think less of the
sons than of; **minor natu** younger **‖** *mpl*
descendants, posterity **‖** *n* less; **minoris
emere** to buy at a lower price; **minus
praedae** less booty
Mīn·ōs -ōis *or* **-ōnis** *m* son of Zeus and
Europa, king of Crete, husband of
Pasiphaë, and, after his death, judge in
the lower world
Mīnōtaur·us -ī *m* monstrous offspring of
Pasiphaë, half man and half bull, kept in
the Labyrinth
minum- = minim-
min·uō -uĕre -uī -ūtus *tr* to diminish,
lessen, reduce; to weaken, lower; to
modify *(plans);* to settle *(controversies);*
to limit *(authority);* to offend against,
try to cheapen *(e.g., the majesty of the
Roman people)* **‖** *intr* to diminish, abate,
ebb; **minuente aestu** at ebbtide
minus *adv* less; not; by no means, not at all
minuscul·us -a -um *adj* smallish
minūt·al -ālis *n* hash, hamburger
minūtātim *adv* piecemeal; bit by bit
minūtē *adv* in a small-minded way
minūtul·us -a -um *adj* tiny
minūt·us -a -um *adj* small, minute; petty,
narrow-minded
Miny·ae -ārum *mpl* descendants of
Minyas, *esp.* the Argonauts
Miny·ās -ae *m* king of Thessaly
mīrābil·is -is -e *adj* remarkable, extraordinary, amazing, wonderful
mīrābiliter *adv* amazingly
mīrābund·us -a -um *adj* astonished, won-
dering
mīrācul·um -ī *n* wonder, marvel; surprise,
amazement; *(pej)* freak; **septem miracula** the seven wonders *(of the ancient
world)*
mīrand·us -a -um *adj* fantastic
mīrāti·ō -ōnis *f* astonishment, wonder
mīrāt·or -ōris *m,* **mīrātr·ix -īcis** *f* admirer
mīrē *adv* surprisingly, strangely; uncommonly; wonderfully; **mire quam** it is
strange how, strangely
mīrificē *adv* wonderfully
mīrific·us -a -um *adj* causing wonder,
wonderful; fascinating
mīrimodīs *adv* in a strange way
mirmill·ō -ōnis *m* gladiator *(who fought
with Gallic arms)*
mīr·or -ārī -ātus sum *tr* to be amazed at,

be surprised at; to look at with wonder,
admire
mīr·us -a -um *adj* amazing, surprising,
astonishing; wonderful; **mirum est** *(w.
acc & inf)* it is surprising that; **est mirum
quam** *(or* **mirum quantum)** it is amazing how, it is amazing to what extent
miscellāne·a -ōrum *npl* **(miscill-)** hash,
hodgepodge
misceō miscēre miscuī mixtus *tr* to mix,
blend, mingle; to combine, associate,
share; to give and take; to mix up, confuse, turn upside down; to mix, prepare,
brew; to fill *(with confused noise, etc.);*
to unite sexually; **arma** *(or* **manūs** *or*
proelium *or* **proelia) miscere** to join
battle
misell·us -a -um *adj* poor little
Mīsēn·um -ī *n* promontory and town near
the Bay of Naples
mis·er -era -erum *adj* poor, pitiful;
wretched, miserable, unhappy; sorry,
worthless
miserābil·is -is -e *adj* miserable, pitiable;
piteous
miserābiliter *adv* pitiably; piteously
miserand·us -a -um *adj* pitiful; deplorable
miserāti·ō -ōnis *f* pity, compassion, sympathy; appeal for sympathy
miserē *adv* wretchedly, miserably, unhappily; pitifully; desperately
miser·eō -ēre -uī -itum *or* **miser·eor -ērī
-itus sum** *intr (w. gen)* to pity, feel sorry
for, sympathize with **‖** *v impers (w. acc
of person who feels pity and gen of object of pity), e.g.,* **miseret** *(or* **miseretur)
me aliorum** I feel sorry for the others
miseresc·ō -ĕre *intr* to feel pity, feel sympathetic; *(w. gen)* to pity, feel sorry for **‖**
*v impers (w. acc of person who feels pity
and gen of object of pity), e.g.,* **me
miserescit viri** I feel sorry for the man,
I pity the man
miseri·a -ae *f* pitiful condition, misery,
distress, trouble
misericordi·a -ae *f* pity, sympathy, compassion; mercy
misericor·s -dis *adj* sympathetic, merciful
miseriter *adv* sadly
miser·or -ārī -ātus sum *tr* to deplore; to
pity **‖** *intr* to feel pity
missicul·ō -āre -āvī -ātus *tr* to keep sending
missil·is -is -e *adj* missile, flying **‖** *npl*
missiles
missi·ō -ōnis *f* release, liberation; sending
off, dispatching; military discharge; dismissal from office; **missio cum ignominiā** dishonorable discharge; **sine
missione** without letup, to the death
missit·ō -āre -āvī -ātus *tr* to keep sending

missus *pp of* **mitto**
miss·us -ūs *m* letting go, throwing, hurling; sending
mītesc·ō -ĕre *intr* to grow mild; to grow mellow, become ripe; *(fig)* to get soft; *(fig)* to become gentle, become tame; *(of feelings)* to become less intense, abate, cool off
Mithr·ās -ae *m* Mithra(s) *(sun-god of the Persians)*
Mithridāt·ēs -is *m* Mithridates the Great *(king of Pontus from 120 to 63 B.C.)*
Mithridātē·us *or* **Mithridātic·us -a -um** *adj* Mithridatic
mītigāti·ō -ōnis *f* mitigation
mītig·ō -āre -āvī -ātus *tr* to mellow, ripen; to soften; to calm down, appease; to make more tolerable, alleviate; to tone down *(a statement);* to soothe, mollify *(feelings);* to civilize
mīt·is -is -e *adj* mellow, ripe, soft; calm, placid; mild, gentle
mitr·a -ae *f* miter, turban
mittō mittĕre mīsī missus *tr* to send; to let fly, throw, hurl, launch; to emit, shed; to let out, utter; to let go of, drop; to free, release; to discharge, dismiss; to pass over in silence; to send for, invite; to pass up, forego; to dedicate *(a book);* to yield, produce; to export; to forget, dismiss *(from the mind);* **sanguinem mittere** to bleed; **sanguinem provinciae mittere** *(fig)* to bleed a province dry; **sub leges orbem mittere** to subject the world to laws; **voces mittere** to utter words
mītul·us -ī *m* limpet *(kind of mussel)*
mixtim *adv* promiscuously
mixtūr·a -ae *f* mixing, blending
mixtus *pp of* **misceo**
Mnēmosyn·ē -ēs *f* mother of the Muses
mnēmosyn·on -ī *n* souvenir
mōbil·is -is -e *adj* mobile, movable, portable; nimble, active; shifty, changing; impressionable, excitable
mōbilit·ās -ātis *f* mobility; agility, quickness; shiftiness, fickleness
mōbiliter *adv* quickly, rapidly
mōbilit·ō -āre -āvī -ātus *tr* to impart motion to, endow with motion
moderābil·is -is -e *adj* moderate
moderām·en -inis *n* control
moderanter *adv* under control
moderātē *adv* with moderation
moderātim *adv* gradually
moderāti·ō -ōnis *f* controlling, control, regulation; curbing, checking; guidance; moderation, self-control
moderāt·or -ōris *m or* **moderātr·ix -īcis** *f* controller, director, guide
moderāt·us -a -um *adj* controlled, well-regulated, orderly, restrained
moder·ō -āre -āvī -ātus *or* **moder·or -ārī**

-ātus sum *tr* to control, direct, guide ‖ *intr (w. dat)* **1** to moderate, restrain; **2** to allay, mitigate
modestē *adv* with moderation, discreetly; modestly
modesti·a -ae *f* moderation, restraint; discretion; modesty, sense of shame, sense of honor, dignity; propriety; mildness *(of weather)*
modest·us -a -um *adj* moderate, restrained; modest, discreet; orderly, obedient
modiāl·is -is -e *adj* containing a *modius or* peck
modicē *adv* moderately, with restraint; in an orderly manner; only slightly
modic·us -a -um *adj* moderate; small; modest, unassuming; ordinary; puny, trifling
modificāt·us -a -um *adj* regulated *(in length),* measured
mod·ius -(i)ī *m modius,* peck *(one- sixth of a medimnus or bushel);* **pleno modio** in full measure
modo *adv* only, merely, simply; *(of time)* just now, just recently, lately; presently, in a moment; **modo...deinde** *(or* **tum, postea, interdum)** first...then, at one time...next time; **modo...modo** now...now, sometimes...sometimes, at one moment...at another; **non modo...sed etiam** *(or* **verum etiam)** not only...but also ‖ *conj* if only, provided that
modulātē *adv* according to measure, in time; melodiously
modulāt·or -ōris *m* director, musician
modul·or -ārī -ātus sum *tr* to regulate the time of, measure rhythmically; to modulate; to sing; to play
modul·us -ī *m* small measure; small stature; unit of measurement
mod·us -ī *m* measured amount, quantity; standard of measurement, unit of measurement, measure; time, rhythm; size, extent, length; due *or* proper measure, limit, boundary; rule, regulation; way, manner, style, mode; kind, form, type; *(gram)* voice *(of a verb);* *(mus)* measure, beat, note, tone; *(poet)* verse, poetry, meter; *(rhet)* rhythmic pattern; **ad modum** *(or* **in modum)** in time, rythmically; **ad modum** *(w. gen) or* **in modum** *(w. gen)* in the manner of, like; **cujusdam modi** of a certain kind, a certain kind of; **cujusdam modi pugna** a certain kind of fight; **cum modo** with restraint, moderately; **ejus modi homo** that kind of person; **ex Tusco modo** in the Etruscan manner *or* style; **hujus modi homo** this kind of person; **modo** moderately; **modum adhibere** *(or* **constituere** *or* **facere** *or* **imponere** *or* **ponere** *or* **statuere)** to impose a limit, set bounds;

nullo modo in no way, not at all; omni modo in every case; praeter *(or* supra) modum excessively; pro modo *(w. gen)* in proportion to; quem ad modum how; quemnam ad modum just how; quid modi? what limit?; quonam modo just how; sine modo without restraint ‖ *mpl* tune, melody, song; poetry, poems

moech·a -ae *f* adulteress

moechiss·ō -āre *tr* to commit adultery with

moech·or -ārī -ātus sum *intr* to have an affair, commit adultery

moech·us -ī *m* adulterer

moen·ia -ium *npl* town walls, ramparts, fortifications; fortified town; castle, stronghold; defenses

moeniō *see* munio

moerus *see* murus

Moes·ī -ōrum *mpl* people of the Lower Danube basin

Moesi·a -ae *f* Moesia *(Roman province S. of the Danube and extending to the Black Sea)*

mol·a -ae *f* millstone; mill; flour ‖ *fpl* mill

molār·is -is *m* millstone; molar *(tooth)*

mōl·ēs -is *f* mass, bulk, pile; massive structure; dam, mole, pier; mass *(of people, etc.);* burden, effort, trouble; calamity; might, greatness

molestē *adv* with annoyance; with difficulty, with trouble; moleste ferre to be annoyed at, be disgruntled at, barely stand *or* tolerate

molesti·a -ae *f* annoyance, trouble; worry; affectation *(of style)*

molest·us -a -um *adj* annoying, troublesome, distressing; labored, affected *(style)*

mōlīm·en -inis *n* great exertion, great effort; attempt, undertaking

mōlīment·um -ī *n* great exertion, great effort

mōl·ior -īrī -ītus sum *tr* to do with great effort, strain at, exert oneself over; to wield, heave, hurl *(missiles);* to wield *(a weapon, an instrument);* to get *(a ship)* under way; to get *(a vehicle)* moving; to rouse *(bodies of men)* to action; to work hard at; to build, erect *(usu. huge constructions);* to displace, shift from its position; to undertake, attempt, to perform; to cause, occasion ‖ *intr* to exert oneself, struggle, take great pains; to make one's way *(w. effort),* proceed

mōlīti·ō -ōnis *f* building, erection; (the action of) shifting *or* moving; rerum molitio the creation

mōlīt·or -ōris *m* builder; contriver, schemer

mōlītr·ix -īcis *f* contriver *(female)*

molitus *pp of* molo ‖ *adj* ground, milled

molītus *pp of* molior

mollesc·ō -ĕre *intr* to become soft; to become gentle; to become effeminate

mollicul·us -a -um *adj* tender, dainty

moll·iō -īre -īvī *or* -iī -ītus *tr* to make soft, soften; *(fig)* to soften, mitigate; to demoralize

mollip·ēs -edis *adj* tender-footed

moll·is -is -e *adj* soft; springy; flexible; flabby; mild, calm; easy; gentle *(slope);* sensitive, impressionable; tender, touching; weak, effeminate; amatory *(verses);* changeable, untrustworthy

molliter *adv* softly; gently, smoothly; effeminately; voluptuously; patiently, with fortitude

molliti·a -ae *or* molliti·ēs -ēī *f* softness; flexibility; tenderness; sensitivity; weakness, irresolution; effeminacy, voluptuousness

mollitūd·ō -inis *f* softness; flexibility; susceptibiltiy

mol·ō -ĕre -uī -itus *tr* to grind

Moloss·us -a -um *adj* Molossian ‖ *m* Molossian hound ‖ *mpl* Molossians *(a people of Epirus)*

mōl·y -yos *n* magic herb

mōm·en -inis *n* movement, motion; momentum

mōment·um -ī *n* movement, motion; alteration; turn, critical time; moment; impulse; momentum; influence; importance; motive

Mon·a -ae *f* Isle of Anglesey

monēdul·a -ae *f* jackdaw *(bird)*

mon·eō -ēre -uī -itus *tr* to call to mind, remind, advise, point out; to warn; to foretell; to teach; to inform

monēr·is -is *f* galley

Monēt·a -ae *f* Juno Moneta *(in whose temple on the Capitoline Hill money was coined);* mint; coin, money; stamp, die *(for money)*

monētāl·is -is -e *adj* of the mint ‖ *m* superintendent of the mint

monīl·e -is *n* necklace

monim- = monum-

monit·a -ōrum *npl* warnings; prophecies; precepts

moniti·ō -ōnis *f* reminder; warning

monit·or -ōris *m* reminder; counselor; teacher; prompter

monit·us -ūs *m* reminder; warning ‖ *mpl* promptings, warnings

monogramm·us -a -um *adj* sketchy, shadowy; unsubstantial, hollow

monopod·ium -(i)ī *n* table with a single central leg

monotrop·us -a -um *adj* single, alone

mon·s -tis *m* mountain; hill; mountain range; mass, heap; montīs auri polliceri *(prov)* to make wild promises *(literally, to promise mountains of gold);* summus mons mountaintop ‖ *mpl* hill country, the hills

monstrāti·ō -ōnis f pointing out
monstrāt·or -ōris m displayer, demonstrator
monstr·ō -āre -āvī -ātus tr to show, point out; to make known; to demonstrate, teach; to indicate, suggest; to appoint, designate II intr to show the way
monstr·um -ī n sign, portent, wonder; warning; monster, monstrosity; atrocity; monstrous event
monstruōsē adv unnaturally
monstruōs·us -a -um adj unnatural, monstrous, strange
montān·us -a -um adj mountain-, of a mountain; mountainous II mpl hill-dwellers (esp. of the seven hills of Rome) II npl mountainous regions
monticol·a -ae m mountaineer
montivag·us -a -um adj wandering over the mountains
montōs·us or **montuōs·us -a -um** adj mountainous
monument·um -ī n reminder; monument, memorial; literary work, book; history; record (written or oral); token of identification II npl recorded tradition; **annalium monumenta** annals; **litterarum monumenta** literary record, document
Mopsopi·us -a -um adj Athenian II f Athens; (ancient name for) Attica
mor·a -ae f delay; pause; spell, period of time; stop-off; (mil) division (of the Spartan army of from 300 to 700 men); **haud morā** without hesitation; **in morā esse** to be a hindrance; **in morā habere** to allow to be a hindrance; **mora est** it will take too long; **moram afferre** to present difficulties, waste time; **moram facere** to obstruct; to cause delay
mōr·a -ae f fool
mōrāl·is -is -e adj moral
morāt·or -ōris m obstructionist; loiterer; (in court) lawyer who spoke only to gain time
mōrāt·us -a -um adj -mannered, -natured; in character; (of a thing) natured; **bene moratus** well-mannered, civilized; **male moratus** ill-mannered, rude; **mirabiliter moratus** he is a strange creature
morbid·us -a -um adj sickly; causing sickness, unwholesome
morbōs·us -a -um adj sickly; sex-crazy, horny; **morbosus in** (w. acc) mad about
morb·us -ī m sickness, disease, ailment; fault, vice; distress; **in morbum cadere** (or **in morbum incidere**) to fall sick
mordācius adv more bitingly; (fig) more radically
mord·ax -ācis adj biting, snapping; (fig) sharp, stinging, caustic; snarling; pungent, tart
mordeō mordēre momordī morsus tr to bite; to eat, devour; to grip; (of cold) to

nip; (of words) to cut, hurt; (of a river) to bite its way through
mordic·ēs -um mpl bites; incisor teeth
mordicus adv by biting, with the teeth; (fig) tightly, doggedly
mōrē adv foolishly
morēt·um -ī n salad
moribund·us -a -um adj dying, at the point of death; mortal; deadly
mōriger·ō -āre or **mōriger·or -ārī -ātus sum** intr (w. dat) 1 to humor, pamper; 2 to yield to; 3 to comply with
mor·ior -ī -tuus sum intr to die; (fig) to decay, pass away, die out; (of fires) to die out; (of flowers) to wither, die off; **moriar nisi** (coll) hope to die if…not
morm·ȳr -ȳris f Pontic fish
mor·or -ārī -ātus sum tr to delay, detain; to entertain, hold the attention of; to hinder, prevent; **nihil morari** (w. acc) 1 to disregard, care nothing for, not value; 2 to have nothing against, have nothing to say against II intr to delay, linger, loiter; to stay, remain; to wait; **quid moror?** (or **quid multis morer?**) why should I drag out the point?, to make a long story short
mōrōsē adv morosely, crabbily
mōrōsit·ās -ātis f moroseness, crabbiness
mōrōs·us -a -um adj morose, crabby; fastidious, particular; (fig) stubborn (disease)
Morph·eūs -eos (acc: -ea) m god of dreams
mors mortis f death; destruction; corpse; bloodshed; **morte communi** of natural causes; **mortem obire** (or **oppetere**) to meet death; **mortem** (or **morti**) **occumbere** to die; **mortem sibi consciscere** to commit suicide (literally, to decide on death for oneself); **mortis honos** burial; **mortis poena** death penalty
mors·a -ōrum npl bits, little pieces
morsiuncul·a -ae f peck, kiss
morsus pp of **mordeo**
mors·us -ūs m bite; pungency; grip; corrosion; gnawing pain; sting; vicious attack
mortāl·is -is -e adj mortal, subject to death; human; transient; man-made II m mortal, human being
mortālit·ās -ātis f mortality; mortals, mankind
morticīn·us -a -um adj & m carrion
mortif·er or **mortif·erus -era -erum** adj lethal, deadly, fatal
mortiferē adv mortally
mortuāl·ia -ium npl dirges
mortu·us -a -um adj dead, deceased; withered, decayed; scared to death; over and done with; half-hearted, feeble II m dead person II mpl the dead
mōrul·us -a -um adj dark, blackberry-colored

mōr·um -ī *n* black mulberry

mōr·us -ī *f* black mulberry tree

mōr·us -a -um *adj* foolish **‖** *mf* fool

mōs mōris *m* custom, usage, practice; caprice, mood; nature; manner; fashion, style; rule, regulation, law; **de more** *(or* **ex more)** according to custom; **more in** the customary manner; **more** *(or* **in morem** *or* **de more)** *(w. gen)* in the manner of, like; **morem gerere** *(w. dat)* to humor *(s.o.),* to indulge *(s.o.* or one's feelings);* **mos majorum** tradition; **nullo more** *(or* **sine more)** without restraint, wildly; lawlessly; **supra morem** more than is usual **‖** *mpl* morals; character; behavior; customs; laws; **ex meis moribus** according to my wishes

Mōs·ēs *or* **Moys·ēs -is** *m* Moses

mōti·ō -ōnis *f* motion, movement

mōtiuncul·a -ae *f* slight attack of fever

mōt·ō -āre -āvī -ātus *tr* to keep moving

mōtus *pp of* **moveo**

mōt·us -ūs *m* motion, movement; gesture; dancing; change *(e.g., of fortune);* impulse, inspiration; passion; revolt, riot; tactical move; *(rhet)* figure of speech; **in motu** active; **in motu esse** to be in a state of flux; **motus animi** emotion; **motus mentis** thought process; **motus pedum** activity; **motus terrae** earthquake

mov·ens -entis *adj* active; restless, shifting; **res moventes** movable property *(e.g., clothes, furniture)* **‖** *npl* motives

moveō movēre mōvī mōtus *tr* to move; to stir, shake, disturb; to cause, occasion, promote; to begin; to undertake; to trouble, torment; to touch, influence, affect; to throw into political turmoil; to eject, expel *(from office, post);* to degrade; to remove, take away; to dislodge *(the enemy);* to shake, cause to waver; to plow; to strum, play *(a musical instrument);* to dissuade; to exert, exercise; to turn over in the mind, ponder; **aliquem loco movere** to dislodge s.o.; **bellum movere** to bring on a war, begin a war; **senatu movere** to remove from the Senate roll; **signa movere** to begin a march; **ventrem movere** to move the bowels; **vocem movere carmine** to raise the voice in song **‖** *refl* to move; to dance; *(of heavenly bodies)* to rise; *(of riots)* to break out; **se ex loco movere** to budge from the spot **‖** *pass & intr* to move; to shake, quake, throb **‖** *intr* to move off, depart; *(of buds)* to sprout, come out

mox *adv* soon, presently; hereafter; next, then; later on

Moys·ēs -is *m* Moses

mūcid·us -a -um *adj* sniveling, snotty; moldy, musty

Mūc·ius -(i)ī *m* Roman clan name *(nomen);* Gaius Mucius Cordus Scaevola *(tried to*

kill Porsenna and, when caught, deliberately burned his right hand)*

mucr·ō -ōnis *m* sharp point, sharp edge; tip; sword; edge, boundary; keenness

mūc·us -ī *m* **(mucc-)** mucus, snot

mūgient·ēs -ium *mpl* oxen

mūg·il *or* **mūg·ilis -ilis** *m* gray mullet *(a sea fish)*

mūgīn·or -ārī -ātus sum *intr* to dilly-dally

mūg·iō -īre -īvī *or* **-iī -ītum** *intr* to moo, bellow, low; to roar, rumble; *(of a bugle)* to blast, sound

mūgīt·us -ūs *m* mooing, bellowing; roaring, rumbling

mūl·a -ae *f* mule

mul·ceō -cēre -sī -sus *or* **mul(c)tus** *tr* to stroke, pet; to stir gently; to soothe, alleviate; to appease; to gladden, delight

Mulcib·er -erī *or* **-eris** *m* Vulcan; *(fig)* fire

mulc·ō -āre -āvī -ātus *tr* to beat up, cudgel; to mistreat, injure; to worst *(in battle)*

mulctr·a -ae *f* milk pail

mulctrār·ium -(i)ī *or* **mulctr·um -ī** *n* milk pail

mul·geō -gēre -sī -sus *or* **-ctus** *tr* to milk

muliebr·is -is -e *adj* woman's, womanly, feminine; womanish, effeminate; *(of deities)* presiding over the lives of women; *(gram)* feminine; **pars muliebris** *(or* **partes muliebres)** female sexual organs **‖** *npl* female sexual organs; **viri muliebria patiuntur** men play the role of women *(i.e., let themselves be used as catamites)*

muliebriter *adv* like a woman; effeminately

muli·er -eris *f* woman; wife

mulierāri·us -a -um *adj* woman's **‖** *m* womanizer, wolf

muliercul·a -ae *f* little *(or* weak *or* foolish)* woman; sissy

mulierōsit·ās -ātis *f* weakness for women

mulierōs·us -a -um *adj* woman-crazy

mūlīn·us -a -um *adj* mulish

mūli·ō -ōnis *m* mule driver

mūliōni·us -a -um *adj* mule driver's

mullul·us -ī *m* little mullet *(fish)*

mull·us -ī *m* red mullet *(fish)*

mulsī *perf of* **mulceo** *and* **mulgeo**

muls·us -a -um *pp of* **mulceo** *and of* **mulgeo ‖** *adj* honeyed, sweet as honey **‖** *f (term of endearment)* honey **‖** *n* mead *(wine mixed with honey)*

mult·a -ae *f* fine; penalty; loss of money; **multam certare** to contest a fine; **multam committere** to incur a fine; **multam dicere** *(w. dat of person and acc of the fine)* to fine *(s. o. a certain amount);* **multam subire** to incur a fine, be fined

multa *adv* much, very; earnestly

mult·a -ōrum *npl* many things; much; **ne multa** in short

multangul·us -a -um *adj* having many angles, many-angled
multātīci·us -a -um *adj* of a fine; **mul-taticia pecunia** fine
multāti·ō -ōnis *f* fine, penalty
multēsim·us -a -um *adj* trifling, negligible
mult·ī -ōrum *mpl* many men, many; multitude, mass, common people
multibib·us -a -um *adj* fond of drinking, heavy-drinking
multicav·us -a -um *adj* porous
multīci·a -ōrum *npl* diaphanous garments
multifāriam *adv* in many places
multifid·us -a -um *adj* divided into many parts; splintered *(wood); (of a river)* having many tributaries
multiform·is -is -e *adj* multiform, manifold
multifor·us -a -um *adj* many-holed; *(flute)* having many stops
multigen·er -eris *or* **multigen·us -a -um** *adj* of many kinds, various
multijug·is -is -e *or* **multijug·us -a -um** *adj* many yoked together; many tied together; *(fig)* various
multiloqu·ax -ācis *adj* talkative
multiloqu·ium -(i)ī *n* talkativeness
multiloqu·us -a -um *adj* talkative
multimodīs *adv* in many ways
multiplex -icis *adj* with many folds; winding, serpentine; manifold; many; *(in comparisons)* many times as great, far greater; varied, complicated; versatile, changeable, many-sided; sly, cunning ‖ *n* manifold return
multiplicābil·is -is -e *adj* manifold, many
multipliciter *adv* in various ways
multiplic·ō -āre -āvī -ātus *tr* to multiply, increase, enlarge; to have *(or* use *or* practice) on many occasions
multipot·ens -entis *adj* mighty, powerful
multitūd·ō -inis *f* great number, multitude, crowd, throng; rabble, common people; population
multivol·us -a -um *adj* passionate
multō *adv (w. comparatives)* much, far, by far, a great deal; **multo aliter ac** far otherwise than, much different from; **multo ante** long before; **multo post** long after; **non multo secus fieri** to turn out just about the same
mult·ō -āre -āvī -ātus *tr* to punish; to fine
mult·us -a -um *(comp:* **plures;** *superl:* **plurimus)** *adj* many a, much, great; abundant, considerable, extensive; tedious, long-winded; full, numerous, thick, loud, heavy; constant; **ad multum diem** till late in the day; **multā nocte** late at night; **multo die** late in the day; *(with plural nouns)* many ‖ *mpl see* **multi** ‖ *n* much; **multi** of great value, highly; **multi facere** to think highly of, make

much of; **multum est** it is of great importance; **multum temporis** a great deal of time, much time ‖ *npl see* **multa**
multum *adv* much, a lot, greatly, very; often, frequently; *(w. comparatives)* much, far; **multum valere** to have considerable influence
mūl·us -ī *m* mule
Mulvi·us -a -um *adj* Mulvian; **Mulvius pons** Mulvian bridge *(across the Tiber, above Rome on the Via Flaminia)*
Mumm·ius -(i)ī *m* Lucius Mummius Achaicus *(conqueror of Corinth, 146 B.C.)*
mundān·us -a -um *adj* of the world ‖ *m* world citizen
mundē *or* **munditer** *adv* neatly, cleanly
munditi·a -ae *or* **munditi·ēs -ēī** *f* neatness, cleanliness; elegance; politeness; refinement of language
mundul·us -a -um *adj* trim, neat
mund·us -a -um *adj* neat, clean, nice; fine, smart, sharp, elegant; choice *(words)* ‖ *m* neat person; world, earth, universe; heavens; mankind; beauty aids; **in mundo** ready, in store; **mundus caeli** firmament
mūnerār·ius -(i)ī *m* producer of gladiatorial shows
mūnerigerul·us -ī *m* bearer of presents
mūner·ō -āre -āvī -ātus *or* **mūner·or -ārī -ātus sum** *tr* to reward, honor, present; *(w. acc of thing and dat of person)* to present *(s.th.)* to
mūni·a -ōrum *npl* official duties *or* functions
mūnic·eps -ipis *mf* citizen of a municipality; fellow citizen, fellow countryman
mūnicipāl·is -is -e *adj* municipal; *(pej)* provincial
mūnicipātim *adv* by municipalities
mūnicip·ium -(i)ī *n* municipality, town *(whose people were Roman citizens, but otherwise autonomous)*
mūnificē *adv* generously
mūnificenti·a -ae *f* generosity
mūnific·ō -āre -āvī -ātus *tr* to treat generously
mūnific·us -a -um *adj* generous; splendid
mūnīm·en -inis *n* defense
mūnīment·um -ī *n* defense, protection, fortification, rampart; *(fig)* shelter, defense, safeguard
mūn·iō -īre -īvī -ītus *tr* (moen-) to defend with a wall, wall in; to fortify, strengthen, defend, protect, secure; to build *(road);* to provide with a road; *(fig)* to guard, shelter, protect, support
mūn·is -is -e *adj* obliging, ready to be of service
mūnīti·ō -ōnis *f* building, fortifying, defending; fortification, rampart, trenches,

lines; **munitio fluminum** bridging of rivers; **munitio viae** road construction
mūnīt·ō -āre *tr* to open up *(a road)*
mūnīt·or -ōris *m* builder *(of fortifications)*
mūnīt·us -a -um *pp of* **munio ‖** *adj* well-fortified, well-protected; *(fig)* safe, protected
mūn·us -eris *n* **(moen-)**service, function, duty; gift; favor, kindness; tax, duty; public entertainment, gladiatorial show; tribute *(to the dead)*, rite, sacrifice; public office; **in munere** *(or* **munere** *or* **pro munere)** as a gift
mūnuscul·um -ī *n* small gift
mūraen·a -ae *f* moray *(eel-like fish)*
mūrāl·is -is -e *adj* wall-, of a wall; wall-destroying; wall-defending
mūr·ex -icis *m* murex, mollusk *(yielding purple dye)*; purple dye, purple; jagged rock; spiked trap *(as defense against cavalry attack)*
muri·a -ae *or* **muri·ēs -ēī** *f* brine *(used for pickling)*
muriātic·um -ī *n* pickled fish
mūricid·us -ī *m* **(murr-)** mouse killer; *(fig)* coward
murmill·ō -ōnis *m* gladiator *(with Gallic arms, who fought against an opponent who used a net)*
murm·ur -uris *n* murmur, murmuring; buzz, hum; roar, crash; growling, grumbling; rumbling; hubbub
murmurill·um -ī *n* low murmur
murmur·ō -āre -āvī -ātus *tr* to murmur against **‖** *intr* to mutter, grumble; to rumble, roar
murr·a *or* **murrh·a** *or* **myrrh·a -ae** *f* myrrh tree; myrrh
murr·a -ae *f* fluorspar *(mineral from which expensive vases were made)*
murre·us -a -um *adj* **(myrrh-)** myrrh-colored, reddish-brown
murre·us -a -um *adj* made of fluor-spar
murt- = **myrt-**
mūr·us -ī *m* wall; city wall(s); dike; rim *(of dish or pot)*; *(fig)* defender, champion
mūs mūris *m* mouse; rat
Mūs·a -ae *f* Muse *(patron goddess of poetry, song, dance, literature, etc.)*; poem, song; talent; poetic inspiration
Mūsae·us *or* **Mūsē·us -a -um** *adj* of the Muses, musical, poetic **‖** *n* institute of philosophy and research at Alexandria
Mūsae·us -ī *m* pre-Homeric bard in the time of Orpheus
musc·a -ae *f* fly; *(fig)* nosey person
muscār·ium -(i)ī *n* fly swatter
muscipul·a -ae *f* or **muscipul·um -ī** *n* mousetrap
muscōs·us -a -um *adj* mossy
muscul·us -ī *m* little mouse; muscle; *(mil)* mantelet

musc·us -ī *m* moss
mūsic·a -ae *or* **mūsic·ē -ēs** *f* or **mūsic·a -ōrum** *npl* music; art of music *(including poetry)*
mūsicē *adv* pleasantly, elegantly
mūsic·us -a -um *adj* relating to the Muses; musical; melodious, tuneful; poetic; *(of a person)* expert in music **‖** *mf* musician
mussit·ō -āre -āvī -ātus *tr* to bear in silence **‖** *intr* to be silent; to mutter, grumble
muss·ō -āre -āvī -ātus *tr* to bear in silence; to brood over **‖** *intr* to mutter, murmur; to hesitate; *(of bees)* to hum
mustāce·us -ī *m* or **mustāce·um -ī** *n* wedding cake *(baked with must and set on laurel leaves)*
mustēl·a -ae *f* (-tell-) weasel
mustēlīn·us -a -um *adj* (-tell-) of a weasel
muste·us -a -um *adj* fresh; *(of a book)* in the early stages
must·um -ī *n* fresh grape juice, must; vintage
mūtābil·is -is -e *adj* changeable; fickle
mūtābilit·ās -ātis *f* mutability; fickleness
mūtāti·ō -ōnis *f* mutation, change; exchange, interchange; translation; **mutatio animi** change of heart
mutil·ō -āre -āvī -ātus *tr* to chop off, lop off, crop; to mutilate; to reduce; to rob
mutil·us -a -um *adj* mutilated; maimed; having chopped-off horns
Mutin·a -ae *f* town of N. Central Italy, S. of the Po *(modern Modena)*, where Decimus Brutus was besieged by Antony *(44–43 B.C.)*
Mutinens·is -is -e *adj* of Mutina
mūtiō *see* **muttio**
mutītiō *see* **muttitio**
mūt·ō -āre -āvī -ātus *tr* to change, shift; to alter; to exchange, interchange, barter, sell; to modify, transform; to vary; to change for the better; to change for the worse; *(w.* **in** + *acc)* to change *(s.th. or s.o.)* into; *(w.* **abl** *or w.* **cum** *or* **pro** + *abl)* to exchange *or* substitute *(s.th. or s.o.)* for; **mutare fidem** to change allegiance, change sides; **mutare latus** to roll over *(in bed)*; *(of fish)* to flip over **‖** *pass* to change; *(w.* **in** + *acc)* to change into; *(w.* **abl)* to change in respect to: **silvae foliis mutantur** the forests change their leaves **‖** *intr* to change; **mutare in melius** *(or* **peius)** to change for the better *(or* for the worse) **‖** *v impers* **non mutat** it makes no difference
mūt·ō *see* **mutto**
mutt·iō -īre -īvī -ītus *tr* **(mūt-)** to mutter
muttīti·ō *or* **mūtīti·ō -ōnis** *f* **(mūt-)** muttering
mutt·ō *or* **mūt·ō -ōnis** *m (vulg)* penis
mūtuē *adv* mutually; in turn
mūtuit·or -ārī *tr* to wish to borrow

mutūniāt·us -a -um *adj (vulg)* having a large penis
mūtuō *adv* mutually, in return
mūtu·or -ārī -ātus sum *tr* to borrow; to obtain, get; to derive
mūt·us -a -um *adj* mute; dumb speechless; silent, still, noiseless; **muta persona** non-speaking actor **‖** *npl* dumb animals
mūtu·us -a -um *adj* mutual, reciprocal, interchangeable; borrowed, lent **‖** *n* loan; reciprocity; **aliquid mutuum accipere** *(or* **sumere)** to borrow s.th.; **aliquid mutuum dare** *(w.* **cum)** to lend s.th. to *(s.o.);* **mutuas pecunias sumere ab** to borrow money from; **mutuum argentum rogare ab** to ask *(s.o.)* for a loan of cash; **mutuum facere cum aliquo** to reciprocate s.o.'s feelings **‖** *npl (w. advl sense)* mutually, reciprocally; **in mutua** towards each other; **per mutua** with one another
Mycēn·ae -ārum *fpl or* **Mycēn·ē -ēs** *f* Mycenae *(city of King Agamemnon in Argolis)*
Mycēn·is -idis *f* Mycenaean girl *(i.e., Iphigenia)*
Mygdon·es -um *mpl* a people of Thrace, some of whom later migrated to Phrygia
Mygdoni·us -a -um *adj* Phrygian
myopar·ōn -ōnis *m* galley
myrīc·a -ae *or* **myrīc·ē -ēs** *f* tamarisk
Myrmidon·es *or* **Myrmidon·ēs -um** *mpl* Myrmidons *(people of Thessaly whom Achilles led in battle)*
Myr·ōn -ōnis *m* famous Greek sculptor *(5th cent. B.C.)*
myropōl·a -ae *m* perfumer
myropōl·ium -(i)ī *n* perfume shop
myrrh- = **murr-**
myrtēt·um -ī *n* (mur-) myrtle grove
myrte·us -a -um *adj* (mur-) myrtle; crowned with myrtle
Myrtō·um Mar·e *(gen:* **Myrtō·ī Mar·is)** *n* Myrtoan Sea *(between the Peloponnesus and the Cyclades)*
myrt·um -ī *n* myrtle berry
myrt·us -ūs *or* **-ī** *f* myrtle tree
Mȳsi·us -a -um *adj* Mysian **‖** *f* Mysia *(country in N.W. Asia Minor)*
myst·a *or* **myst·ēs -ae** *m* priest of the mysteries of Ceres; an initiate
mystagōg·us -ī *n* initiator; tourist guide
mystēr·ium -(i)ī *n* (mist-) secret religion, secret service, secret rite; divine mystery; secret; **mysteria facere** to hold service; **mysteria Romana** festival of Bona Dea
mystic·us -a -um mystic
Mytilēn·ae -ārum *fpl or* **Mytilēn·ē -ēs** *f* Mytilene *(chief of the island of Lesbos)*
Mytilēnae·us -a -um *or* **Mytilēnens·is -is -e** *adj* of Mytilene

N

N. *abbr* **Numerius** *(Roman first name, praenomen);* **Nonae** the Nones; **Nummus** coin
Nabatae·us -a -um *adj* Nabataean; Eastern **‖** *mpl* Nabataeans *(a people of N. Arabia)*
nabl·ia -ium *npl* Phoenician harp
nactus *pp of* **nanciscor**
Naeviān·us -a -um *adj* of Naevius
Naev·ius -(i)ī *m* Gnaeus Naevius *(early Roman dramatic and epic poet, c. 270–200 B.C.)*
Nāï·as -adis *or* **Nā·is -idis** *or* **-idos** *f* Naiad, water nymph,
nam *conj* for; for in that case; *(affirmative)* yes, to be sure; *(transitional)* now, but now, on the other hand
namque *conj* for in fact, for no doubt, for surely
nan·ciscor -ciscī -ctus sum *or* **nactus sum** *tr* to get, obtain; to come across, find; to arrive at; to experience, meet with; to contract *(a disease)*
nān·us -ī *m* dwarf, midget
Napae·ae -ārum *fpl* dell nymphs
nāp·us -ī *m* turnip
Narb·ō -ōnis *m* Narbonne *(city in S. Gaul, from which the province of Narbonese took its name)*
Narbōnens·is -is -e *adj* Narbonese
narciss·us -ī *m* (bot) narcissus **‖** **Narcissus** son of Cephisus and the nymph Liriope, who was changed into a narcissus **‖** powerful freedman of Claudius
nard·um -ī *n or* **nard·us -ī** *f* nard, spikenard *(fragrant ointment)*
nār·is -is *f* nose; **homo acutae naris** *(or* **emunctae naris)** a man of keen perception; **homo naris obesae** dimwit *(literally, thick-nosed man)* **‖** *fpl* nostrils, nose; **nares corrugare** to cause *(s.o.)* to turn up his nose; **naribus ducere** to smell; **naribus uti** *(w. ad)* to turn up the nose at
Narni·a -ae *f* town in Umbria
Narniens·is -is -e *adj* of Narnia
narrābil·is -is -e *adj* to be told
narrāti·ō -ōnis *f* narrative
narrātiuncul·a -ae *f* anecdote
narrāt·or -ōris *m* narrator
narrāt·um -ī *n* account, narrative
narrāt·us -ūs *m* narrative, tale
narr·ō -āre -āvī -ātus *tr* to tell, relate, narrate, recount; to describe, tell about **‖** *intr* to speak, tell; **bene narrare** *(w. de* + *abl)* to tell good news about *(s.o.);* **male narrare** *(w. de* + *abl)* to tell bad news about *(s.o.);* **tibi narro** *(coll)* I'm telling you, I assure you; **quam tu mihi nunc**

navem narras? *(coll)* now, what's this ship you're talking about?

narthec·ium -(i)ī *n* medicine chest

narus *see* gnarus

Nāryci·us -a -um *adj* of Narycum *(birthplace of Ajax, son of Oileus)*

nascor nascī nātus sum *intr* (gn-) to be born; to begin, orginate, spring forth, proceed; to be produced; *(of plants)* to grow; *(of rocks, minerals)* to be found, occur; *(astr)* to rise

Nāsīc·a -ae *m* Roman honorary name *(agnomen)* Publius Cornelius Scipio Nasica *(consul in 191 b.c.)*

Nās·ō -ōnis *m* Ovid *(Publius Ovidius Naso, Roman poet, 43 b.c.–a.d. 17)*

nass·a -ae *f* wicker trap *(for catching fish); (fig)* trap

nassitern·a -ae *f* large water jug

nasturc·ium -(i)ī *n (bot)* watercress

nās·us -ī *m or* nās·um -ī *n* nose; sense of smell; sagacity; scorn; satirical wit; spout, nozzle

nāsūtē *adv* sarcastically

nāsūt·us -a -um *adj* big-nosed; sarcastic, satirical

nāt·a *or* gnāt·a -ae *f* daughter

nātālici·us -a -um *adj* birthday; natal, congenital; dies natalicius birthday ‖ *f* birthday party

nātāl·is -is -e *adj* of birth, natal, congenital; dies natalis birthday ‖ *m* birthday; foundation day *(of city, temple, etc.)* ‖ *mpl* birth, origin, parentage; natalibus suis restituere *(or* reddere*)* to confer the status of a free-born citizen on *(one born into slavery)*

nat·ans -antis *adj* swimming; swimming in the sea, marine ‖ *mf* fish

natāti·ō -ōnis *f* swimming, swim

natāt·or -ōris *m* swimmer

nat·ēs -ium *fpl see* natis

nāti·ō -ōnis *f* tribe, nation, people; race, stock; *(pej)* breed

nat·is -is *f* buttock, rump ‖ *fpl* buttocks, rear end

nātīv·us -a -um *adj* born; inborn, innate, original; native, local; produced by nature, natural; primitive *(words)*

nat·ō -āre -āvī -ātus *tr* to swim (across) ‖ *intr* to swim, float; to flow; to overflow; *(of eyes)* to be glassy; *(of birds)* to fly, glide; to waver, fluctuate; to hover; to move to and fro

natr·ix -icis *f* water snake

nātūr·a -ae *f* nature, natural constitution; character, temperament; ability; distinctive feature *or* characteristic; naturalness *(in art);* order of the world, course of things; element, substance; sex organs; in naturā *(or* in rerum naturā*)* esse to be the natural choices, to be the alternatives; naturā *(or* per naturam*)*

naturally; natura fluminis the natural course of the river; natura rerum (physical) nature; suā naturā of its own accord

nātūrāl·is -is -e *adj* natural; by birth, one's own *(father, son, etc.);* produced by nature; according to nature

nātūrāliter *adv* naturally, by nature

nāt·us *or* gnāt·us -a -um *pp of* nascor ‖ *adj* born; *(w. dat or ad or in + acc)* born for, made for, naturally suited to, fit for; *(w.* annos*)* at the age of…, …years old, *e.g.,* annos viginti natus at the age of twenty, twenty years old; non amplius novem annos natus no more than nine years old; pro re nata *(or* e re nata*)* under the existing circumstances, as matters stand; res nata the situation, the way things are ‖ *m* son ‖ *mpl* children ‖ *f* daughter

nauarch·us -ī *m* ship's captain, skipper

nauclēric·us -a -um captain's ‖ *m* ship owner, captain

nauclēr·us -ī *m* ship's captain

naucul·or -ārī -ātus sum *intr* to go boating, go sailing

nauc·um -ī *n* trifle; *(mostly in gen of value with a negative)* non nauci esse to be good for nothing; non nauci habere to regard as worthless

naufrag·ium -(i)ī *n* shipwreck; wreck, ruin, destruction; wreckage; *(fig)* shattered remains; naufragium facere to be shipwrecked; *(of things)* to be lost ‖ *npl* remnants, shattered remains; naufragia Caesaris amicorum the remnants of Caesar's friends

naufrag·ō -āre -āvī *intr* to suffer shipwreck

naufrag·us -a -um *adj* shipwrecked, of the shipwrecked; causing shipwreck, dangerous to shipping; *(fig)* ruined ‖ *m* shipwrecked person

naul·um -ī *n* fare

naumachi·a -ae *f* simulated naval engagement *(staged as an exercise or for amusement)*

naumachiār·ius -(i)ī *m* person taking part in a mock sea fight

Naupact·us -ī *f* town on the N. shore of the Gulf of Corinth

Naupliad·ēs -ae *m* son of Nauplius, Palamedes

Naupl·ius -(i)ī *m* king of Euboea who wrecked the Greek fleet to avenge the death of his son Palamedes

nause·a -ae *f* seasickness; vomiting, nausea; nausea fluens vomiting

nause·ō -āre -āvī *tr* to make *(s.o.)* throw up; *(fig)* to belch forth, throw up, utter ‖ *intr* to be seasick; to vomit; to feel squeamish, feel disgust; to cause disgust

nauseol·a -ae *f* slight squeamishness

Nausica·ā -ae *f* daughter of Alcinoüs, king of the Phaeacians

naut·a *or* nāvit·a -ae *m* sailor, seaman, mariner; captain

naute·a -ae *f* nausea; bilge water

nautic·us -a -um *adj* nautical, sailor's **ǁ** *mpl* sailors, seamen

nāvāl·is -is -e *adj* naval, of ships, of a ship; castra navalia camp for the protection of ships; forma navalis shape of a ship **ǁ** *n* tackle, rigging **ǁ** *npl* dock, dockyard, shipyard; rigging

nāvē *adv* industriously

nāvicul·a -ae *f* small ship

nāviculāri·us -a -um *adj* of a small ship **ǁ** *m* skipper; ship owner **ǁ** *f* shipping business

nāvifrag·us -a -um *adj* dangerous, treacherous, causing shipwreck

nāvigābil·is -is -e *adj* navigable

nāvigāti·ō -ōnis *f* sailing, navigation, voyage

nāvig·er -era -erum *adj* navigable

nāvig·ium -(i)ī *n* ship; boat

nāvig·ō -āre -āvī -ātus *tr* to sail across, navigate **ǁ** *intr* to sail, put to sea; *(fig)* to swim

nāv·is -is *f* ship; *(astr)* Argo *(constellation);* navem appellere *(or* navem terrae applicare) to land a ship; navem deducere to launch a ship; navem solvere to set sail; navem subducere to beach a ship; navi *(or* navibus) by ship, by sea; navis aperta ship without a deck; navis longa battleship; navis mercatoria merchant vessel; navis oneraria transport, cargo ship; navis praetoria flagship; navis tecta ship with a deck

nāvit·a *see* nauta

nāvit·ās -ātis *f* energy, zeal

nāviter *adv* energetically, zealously, actively, busily; utterly, completely

nāv·ō -āre *tr* to do *or* perform energetically, conduct *or* carry out with vigor; operam navare to act energetically; operam navare *(w. dat)* to render assistance to

nāv·us -a -um *adj* (gn-) energetic, busy

Nax·os -ī *f* largest island of the Cyclades in the Aegean Sea

nē *interj* (*nearly always with a personal or demonstrative pronoun*) indeed, certainly, surely; ne ego homo infelix fui I was indeed an unhappy man **ǁ** *adv* not; ne...quidem (*to negate emphatically the words placed between*) not even; ne timete! do not fear! **ǁ** *conj* that not, lest; so as to prevent *(s.th. from happening);* much less, let alone; ne dicam not to mention; ne mentiar to tell the truth; ne multa *(or* ne multi)s to make a long story short **ǁ** *conj (after verbs and nouns denoting fear)* that

-ne *enclitic (introducing a question and added to the first important word of a clause; it does not imply anything about the expected answer); (introducing an alternative in a question)* Or...?; *(in indirect questions)* whether; *(introducing a double or multiple indirect question)* whether

nebul·a -ae *f* mist, fog, vapor; cloud; smoke; darkness, obscurity

nebul·ō -ōnis *m* loafer, good-for-nothing

nebulōs·us -a -um *adj* foggy

nec *or* neque *adv* not **ǁ** *conj* nor, and not; nec...et not only...but also; nec...nec *(or* neque...neque) neither...nor; nec non *(introducing an emphatic affirmative)* and certainly, and besides

necdum *or* nequedum *conj* and not yet, nor yet

necessāriē *or* necessāriō *adv* necessarily, of necessity

necessāri·us -a -um *adj* necessary, indispensable, needful, requisite; inevitable; pressing, urgent; connected by blood or friendship, related, closely connected **ǁ** *mf* relative, kinsman; friend **ǁ** *npl* necessities

necesse *indecl adj* necessary; unavoidable, inevitable; requisite; necesse esse to be necessary; necesse habere to regard as necessary, regard as inevitable

necessit·ās -ātis *f* necessity, inevitability; compulsion, urgency; requirement; privation, want; relationship, connection, friendship

necessitūd·ō -inis *f* necessity, need, want, distress; relationship, bond, connection, friendship **ǁ** *fpl* ties of friendship; relatives, friends, personal connections

necessum *indecl adj* necessary, requisite; inevitable

necne *conj* or not

nec·ō -āre -āvī -ātus *tr* to kill, murder

necopīn·ans -antis *adj* unaware

necopīnātō *adv* unexpectedly, by surprise

necopīnāt·us -a -um *adj* unexpected; ex necopinato unexpectedly

necopīn·us -a -um *adj* unexpected; unsuspecting; careless, off-guard

nect·ar -aris *n* nectar *(drink of the gods);* nectar *(term for honey, milk, wine, poetry, sweetness)*

nectare·us -a -um *adj* of nectar, sweet *(or* delicious) as nectar

nect·ō nectĕre nexuī *or* nexī nexus *tr* to tie, connect, fasten together, join; to weave; to clasp; to imprison; to fetter; to devise, contrive; *(fig)* to attach

nēcubi *conj* lest anywhere, so that nowhere

nēcunde *conj* lest from anywhere

nēdum *conj (after an expressed or implied negative)* much less, still less; *(after an affirmative)* not to say, much more

nefand·us -a -um *adj* unspeakable, heinous

nefāriē *adv* wickedly, foully

nefāri·us -a -um *adj* nefarious, heinous, criminal **‖** *n* crime, foul deed

nefās *indecl n* crime, wrong, wickedness; act contrary to divine law, sin; criminal, monster; **fas atque nefas** right and wrong; **nefas est** (*w. inf*) it is a crime to; **per omne fas ac nefas** by hook or by crook **‖** *interj* shocking!, dreadful!

nefast·us -a -um *adj* forbidden, unlawful; impious, irreligious; criminal; **dies nefastus** day unfit for business, legal holiday **‖** *n* outrage

negāti·ō -ōnis *f* denial

negit·ō -āre -āvī *tr* to keep denying; to turn down, refuse repeatedly

neglecti·ō -ōnis *f* (nec-) neglect

neglectus (nec-) *pp of* **neglego ‖** *adj* neglected, despised, slighted

neglect·us -ūs *m* (nec-) neglect

negleg·ens -entis *adj* (nec-) negligent, careless, indifferent

neglegenter *adv* (nec-) carelessly

neglegenti·a -ae *f* (nec-) negligence, carelessness, neglect; **epistularum neglegentia** failure to write

negle·gō -gĕre -xī -ctus *tr* (nec-) to be unconcerned about; to neglect, disregard, overlook; to do without; to slight; to make light of; (*w. inf*) to fail to

neg·ō -āre -āvī -ātus *tr* to deny; (*w. acc + inf*) to say that...not **‖** *refl* to refuse one's services **‖** *intr* to say no; to refuse; (*w. dat*) to say no to, turn down (*regarding marriage or sexual favors, dinner invitation, etc.*)

negōtiāl·is -is -e *adj* business-

negōti·ans -antis *m* business man

negōtiāti·ō -ōnis *f* business, trade; business deal; business establishment

negōtiāt·or -ōris *m* businessman; banker; salesman, dealer

negōtiol·um -ī *n* minor matter

negōti·or -ārī -ātus sum *intr* to conduct business; to do banking; to trade; **homo negotians** businessman

negōtiōs·us -a -um *adj* business; busy; **dies negotiosus** workday

negōt·ium -(i)ī *n* business; occupation, employment; matter, thing, affair; situation; difficulty; trouble; banking, money-lending; trade, commerce; **dare negotium alicui ut** to give s.o. the job of; **in magno negotio habere** (*w. inf*) to make a point of; **negotium gerere** to conduct business; **negotium suum** private affairs; **non negotium est quin** there is nothing to do but; **quid negoti est?** what's the matter?; **quid negoti tibi est?** what business is it of yours?; **suum negotium agere** to mind one's own busi-

ness **‖** *npl* commercial activities, business transactions; lawsuits

Nēl·eūs -eī *or* **-eos** *m* king of Pylos and father of Nestor

Nēlīd·ēs -ae *m* descendant of Neleus

Neme·a -ae *or* **Neme·ē -ēs** *f* Nemea (*town in Argolis, where Hercules slew a lion and founded the Nemean games*)

Neme·a -ōrum *npl* Nemean games (*held every two years at Nemea*)

Nemeae·us -a -um *adj* Nemean

Nemes·is -eōs *f* goddess of vengeance

nēm·ō -inis *mf* no one, nobody; a person of no consequence, a nobody; **nemo alius** no one else; **nemo dum** no one yet; **nemo non** every; **nemo quisquam** nobody at all; **nemo unus** no single person, no one by himself; **non nemo** someone, many a one, a few

nemorāl·is -is -e *adj* sylvan

nemorens·is -is -e *adj* of a grove; of Diana's grove

nemoricultr·ix -īcis *f* denizen (*female*) of the forest

nemorivag·us -a -um *adj* roaming the woods

nemorōs·us -a -um *adj* wooded; covered with foliage

nempe *adv* (*in confirmation or in sarcasm*) of course, naturally; (*in questions*) do you mean?

nem·us -oris *n* cluster of trees; grove; sacred grove

nēni·a -ae *f* (naen-) funeral song; doleful song; incantation; ditty

neō nēre nēvī nētus *tr* to spin; to weave

Neoptolem·us -ī *m* the son of Achilles (*also called Pyrrhus*)

nep·a -ae *f* scorpion; crab

Nephelē·is -idos *f* Helle (*daughter of Nephele and Athamas*)

nep·ōs -ōtis *m* grandson; nephew; descendant; spendthrift, playboy; **seri nepotes** distant descendants **‖** **Nepos** Cornelius Nepos (*Roman biographer and friend of Cicero, c. 100-25 B.C.*)

nepōtul·us -ī *m* little grandson

nept·is -is *f* granddaughter; descendant (*female*)

Neptūni·us -a -um *adj* of Neptune

Neptūn·us -ī *n* Neptune (*god of the sea and brother of Jupiter*)

nēquam (*comp:* **nēquior;** *superl:* **nēquissimus**) *indecl adj* worthless, bad, good for nothing; naughty; **nequam facere** to be naughty

nēquāquam *adv* by no means, not at all

neque *see* **nec**

nequedum *see* **necdum**

nequ·eō -īre -īvī *or* **-iī -ītum** *intr* (*w. inf*) to be unable to, be incapable of; (*w.* **quin**) to be unable to keep oneself from; **nequit** (*w.* **quin**) it is impossible to

nēqui·or -or -us (comp of **nequam**) adj worse, more worthless

nēquīquam or **nēquicquam** adv pointlessly, for nothing, to no purpose; without good reason; with impunity

nēquissim·us -a -um (superl of **nequam**) adj worst, most worthless

nēquiter adv wickedly; wrongly, with poor results; worthlessly; (in playful use) naughtily

nēquiti·a -ae or **nēquiti·ēs -ēī** f worthlessness, vileness, wickedness; naughtiness

Nērē·is -idis f Nereid, sea nymph (one of the fifty daughters of Nereus)

Nēr·eūs -eī or **-eos** m son of Oceanus and Tethys, and husband of Doris, and father of the Nereids; sea

Nērīnē -ēs f daughter of Nereus

Nēriti·us -a -um adj of Neritus; **dux Neritius** Ulysses; **Neritia ratis** ship of Ulysses

Nērit·os or **Nērit·us -ī** m island near Ithaca

Ner·ō -ōnis m Nero Claudius Caesar (A.D. 38–68; reigned A.D. 54–68)

Nerōniān·us -a -um adj Nero's, Neronian

Nerv·a -ae m Marcus Cocceius Nerva (A.D. 30–98; reigned A.D. 96–98)

nervōsē adv strongly, vigorously

nervōs·us -a -um adj sinewy, brawny, muscular

nerv·us or **nerv·os -ī** m sinew, tendon, muscle; string, wire; bowstring; thong; strap; leather covering of a shield; (vulg) penis; prison **||** mpl power, vigor, strength, nerve, force, energy; **nervi belli pecunia** money, the sinews of war; **nervi conjurationis** the force (i.e., the leaders) behind the conspiracy

nesc·iō -īre -īvī or **-iī -ītus** tr not to know, be ignorant of, be unacquainted with; (w. inf) not to know how to, be unable to; **nescio modo** somehow or other; **nescio quando** sometime or other; **nescio quid** something or other; **nescio quis** someone or other

nesci·us -a -um adj unaware, ignorant; unknown; (w. gen or de + abl) ignorant of, unaware of; (w. inf) not knowing how to, unable to, incapable of; (w. acc & inf) unaware that, not knowing that

Ness·us -ī m centaur who was slain by Hercules with a poisoned arrow for trying to molest his wife

Nest·or -oris m son of Neleus, king of Pylos, and wise counselor of the Greeks at Troy

Nestorid·ēs -ae m son of Nestor (i.e., Antilochus)

neu see **neve**

neu·ter -tra -trum adj neither (of two); neuter; of neither sex **||** pron neither one (of two)

neutiquam or **ne utiquam** adv on no account, in no way

neutrāl·is -is -e adj (gram) neuter

neutrō adv to neither side, in neither direction

neutrubi adv in neither the one place nor the other

nēve or **neu** conj or not, and not; **neve...neve** (or **neu...neu**) neither...nor

nex necis f death; violent death, murder, slaughter; **necem (sibi) consciscere** to decide to commit suicide (literally, to decide on death for oneself); **neci** (or ad **necem) dare** (or **mittere**) to put to death

nexil·is -is -e adj plaited, intertwined

nex·um -ī n slavery for debt; voluntary servitude for debt

nex·us -a -um pp of **necto || m** bondman (person who has pledged his person as security for a debt)

nex·us -ūs m bond; tie (of kinship, etc.); legal obligation; grip (in wrestling); embrace; combination **||** mpl coils (of snake); knotty problem

nī adv not; **quid ni?** why not? **|| conj** (in prohibition or negative purpose) that not; (in negative condition) if not, unless

nīcētēr·ium -(i)ī n prize

nict·ō -āre -āvī -ātum or **nict·or -ārī -ātus sum** intr to blink; to wink; (w. dat) to wink at

nīdāment·um -ī n material for a nest

nīd·or -ōris m steam, vapor, smell

nīdul·us -ī m small nest

nīd·us -ī m nest; nestlings, brood; pigeonhole (fig) home **||** mpl nestlings, brood

ni·ger -gra -grum adj black; dark; swarthy; dismal; unlucky, ill-omened; bad (character); malicious

nigr·ans -antis adj black, dusky

nigr·escō -escĕre -uī intr to grow black, grow dark

nigr·ō -āre -āvī -ātus tr to blacken **||** intr to be black

nigr·or -ōris m blackness, darkness

nihil or **nīl** indecl n nothing; (w. partitive gen) no, not a bit of (e.g., **nihil cibi** no food); **nihil agere** to do nothing, sit still; **nihil aliud** nothing else; **nihil boni** no good, not a bit of good; **nil est** (in replies) it is pointless, it's no good; **nihil dum** nothing so far; **nihil est mihi cum** I have nothing to do with; **nihil est** it doesn't matter; **nihil est quod** (or **cur** or **quamobrem**) there is no reason why; **nihil est ubi** (or **quo**) there is no place where (or to which); **nihil quicquam** nothing whatever; **non nihil** a considerable amount, quite a lot; to a considerable extent

nihilōminus adv nevertheless, just the same; no less

nihil·um or **nīl·um -ī** n nothing; **ad nihilum**

venire to come to nothing; **de nihilo** for nothing, for no reason; **nihili facere** *(or* **pendere)** to consider as worthless; **nihil** *(w. comparatives or words expressing difference, e.g.:* **nihil carius** nothing dearer); **nihilo minus** nonetheless, nevertheless; **pro nihilo putare** *(or* **ducere** *or* **habere)** to regard as worthless, disregard

nīl *see* **nihil**

Nīliac·us -a -um *adj* Nile, of the Nile; Egyptian

nīlum *see* **nihilum**

Nīl·us -ī *m* Nile; god of the Nile; a type of conduit

nimbāt·us -a -um *adj* light, frivolous

nimbif·er -era -erum *adj* stormy

nimbōs·us -a -um stormy, rainy

nimb·us -ī *m* rain cloud, storm cloud; cloud; rainstorm, heavy shower; shower, spray; *(fig)* storm; *(fig)* dense crowd

nimiō *adv* far, much; **nimio plus** far more, much more

nīmīrum *adv* no doubt, certainly sure; *(ironically)* of course

nimis *adv* very, very much, too much; **non nimis** not particularly

nimium *adv* too, too much; very much; **nimium quam** *(or* **nimium quantum)** very much indeed, ever so much, very; **nimium quam es barbarus** you are as uncouth as can be; **non nimium** not particularly, not very much

nimi·us -a -um *adj* very much; very great; too great, extraordinary, excessive; extravagant, intemperate; over-eager; over-confident; *(w. gen or abl of respect)* intemperate in, going overboard about; *(w. dat)* too much for, too strong for; **nimio opere** to excess ‖ *n* excess

ning(u)it ningěre ninguit *or* **ninxit** *v impers* it is snowing

ningu·ēs -ium *fpl* snow flakes; snow; snow-drifts

Nin·os *or* **Nin·us -ī** *m* king of Assyria, legendary founder of Nineveh; Nineveh

Niob·a -ae *or* **Niob·ē -ēs** *f* Niobe *(daughter of Tantalus and wife of Amphion; she was turned into a weeping mountain)*

Nīr·eus -eī *or* **-eos** *m* second-handsomest Greek at Troy *(after Achilles)*

Nīsē·is -idis *f* daughter of Nisus, Scylla

nisi *conj* unless, if not; except; **nisi si** unless, if not; **nisi quia** *(or* **quod)** except that

nīsus *pp of* **nitor**

nīs·us *or* **nix·us -ūs** *m* pressure, effort; labor pains; soaring, flight; posture; **nisu immotus eodem** immobile in the same posture

Nīs·us -ī *m* king of Megara and father of Scylla ‖ friend of Euryalus *(in the Aeneid)*

nītēdul·a -ae *f* dormouse *(squirrel-like rodent)*

nit·ens -entis *adj* shining, bright, sparkling; brilliant; beautiful, glamorous; sleek *(cattle)*; prosperous, thriving; illustrious, outstanding

nit·eō -ēre -uī *intr* to shine, gleam, glisten; to be glamorous; to glow with health; *(of animals)* to be sleek; *(of style)* to be brilliant; *(of fields, plants)* to be luxuriant

nit·escō -escěre -uī *intr* to become shiny, become bright; to begin to glow *(with health or beauty)*; to grow sleek; *(of plants)* to begin to thrive

nitidē *adv* brightly

nitidiusculē *adv* somewhat more sprucely

nitidiuscul·us -a -um *adj* a little more shiny

nitid·us -a -um *adj* shining, bright; glowing, radiant, handsome *(with health or beauty)*; spruce, well-groomed; glossy, lustrous *(hair)*; sleek *(animals)*; luxuriant, lush *(plants, fields)*; cultivated, refined; elegant *(style)*

nit·or -ōris *m* brightness, sheen; luster; glamour, beauty, healthy glow; elegance *(of style)*; dignity *(of character)*

nītor nītī nixus sum *(usually in the literal sense)* or **nīsus sum** *(usually in the figurative sense)* *intr* to make an effort, struggle, strain, strive; to be in labor; to push forward, advance, climb, fly; to contend, insist; *(w. abl or in + acc)* to lean on, support oneself on; *(w. abl or in + abl)* to depend on, rely on, trust to; *(w. ad)* to aspire to; *(w. inf)* to try to, endeavor to, struggle to

nitr·um -ī *n* soda, potash; cleanser

nivāl·is -is -e *adj* snowy; covered with snow; cold, wintry; *(fig)* cold, chilly

nive·us -a -um *adj* snowy, covered with snow; snow-white; cooled with snow

nivōs·us -a -um *adj* snowy

nix nivis *f* snow ‖ *fpl (fig)* gray hair

nix·or -ārī -ātus sum *intr* to struggle hard; *(w. abl)* to lean on, rest on

nixus *pp of* **nitor**

nix·us -ūs *see* **nisus**

nō nāre nāvī *intr* to swim, float; to sail; to fly; *(of eyes)* to be glazed

nōbil·is -is -e *adj* known, familiar; noted; notable, remarkable, noteworthy; famous; notorious; noble; thoroughbred; fine, excellent; *(w. abl of cause)* famous for, noted for; **nobile est** *(w. acc & inf)* it is well-known that ‖ *m* notable, nobleman, aristocrat

nōbilit·ās -ātis *f* fame, renown; noble birth; nobility; the nobility, the nobles; excellence

nōbiliter *adv* with distinction

nōbilit·ō -āre -āvī -ātus *tr* to make generally

known, call attention to; to make famous; to make notorious

noc·ens -entis *adj* harmful; *(w. abl)* guilty of **ll** *m* guilty person, criminal

noc·eō -ēre -uī -itum *intr (w. dat)* to harm, injure; haud ignarus nocendi well aware of the mischief

nocīv·us -a -um *adj* harmful, injurious

noctif·er -erī *m* evening star *(nightbringer)*

noctilūc·a -ae *f* moon *(she who shines by night)*

noctivag·us -a -um *adj (esp. of heavenly bodies)* wandering at night

noctū *adv* by night, at night

noctu·a -ae *f* owl *(night bird)*

noctuābund·us -a -um *adj* traveling by night

noctuīn·us -a -um *adj* of owls

nocturn·us -a -um *adj* nocturnal, of night, at night, by night, night-

noctuvigil·us -a -um *adj* awake at night

nocu·us -a -um *adj* harmful

nōd·ō -āre -āvī -ātus *tr* to tie in a knot, knot

nōdōs·us -a -um *adj* knotty

nōd·us -ī *m* knot; knot *(in wood);* node *(in stem of grass or plant);* bond, tie; obligation; knotty point, problem, difficulty; coil *(of serpent);* check, restraint; **igneus nodus** fireball

Nōl·a -ae *f* town of Campania E. of Naples *(where Augustus died)*

nōlō nolle nōluī *tr (w. inf)* to be unwilling to, wish not to, refuse to **ll** *intr* to be unwilling; *(2nd person imperative w. inf to form negative command)* do not...: noli *(pl:* nolite) tangere do not touch!

Nom·as -adis *or* -ados *mf* nomad; Numidian

nōm·en -inis *n* name; clan *(or* middle) name *(e.g., Julius, as distinct from the praenomen, or first name, e.g., Gaius, and the cognomen, or family name, e.g., Caesar);* good name, reputation; title; stock, race; bond, claim, debt; debtor; pretext, pretense, excuse; authority; sake, behalf; reason, cause; responsibility; heading, category; entry *(of a loan, etc., in a ledger);* *(gram)* noun; **aetatis nomine** on the pretext of age; on account of age; **eo nomine** on that account; **nomen alicujus accipere** *(or* **recipere)** *(of a presiding judge)* to consent to hear the case against s.o.; **nomen dare** *(or* **edere** *or* **profiteri)** to enlist *(in the army; as a colonist);* **nomen deferre** *(w. gen)* to bring an accusation against, accuse *(s.o.);* **nomen dissolvere** *(or* **nomen expedire** *or* **nomen solvere)** *(com)* to liquidate an account, pay off a debt; **nomen Latinum** those with Latin rights; **nomen Romanum** the Roman people;

nomina facere *(com)* to enter a business transaction in a ledger; **nomina magna** big shots, celebrities; **nomina sua exigere** to collect one's debt; **nomine** *(w. gen)* by the authority of, in the name of; on the pretext of; in the guise of; **non re sed nomine** not in reality but in name only; **oppidum nomine Nola** a town named Nola; **per nomen** *(w. gen)* on the pretext of; in the guise of; **sub nomine** *(w. gen)* by the authority of, in the name of; **suo nomine** on one's own responsibility; **uno nomine** in a word

nōmenclāt·or -ōris *m* name-caller *(slave who accompanied his master and discreetly identified those whom they met, esp. during a political campaign)*

Nōment·um -ī *n* town in Latium on the Sabine border

nōminātim *adv* by name, expressly

nōmināti·ō -ōnis *f* nomination for office; name, term

nōminātīv·us -a -um *adj & m (gram)* nominative

nōminit·ō -āre -āvī -ātus *tr* to name, call, term

nōmin·ō -āre -āvī -ātus *tr* to name, call by name; to mention by name; to make famous; to nominate for office; to denounce, arraign

nomism·a -atis *n* coin; coinage; voucher, token

nōn *adv* not; no; by no means

Non. *abbr* Nonae

Nōn·ae -ārum *fpl* Nones *(the ninth day before the Ides, and so the fifth day in all months, except March, May, July, and October, in which the Nones occurred on the seventh)*

nōnāgensim·us -a -um *adj* (-gēs-) ninetieth

nōnāgiens *adv* (-giēs) ninety times

nōnāgintā *indecl adj* ninety

nōnān·us -a -um *adj* of the ninth legion **ll** *m* soldier of the ninth legion

nōnāri·a -ae *f* prostitute

nōndum *adv* not yet

nōngent·ī -ae -a *adj* nine hundred

nōnne *adv (interrog particle in questions expecting a positive answer)* is it not?; *(in indirect questions)* whether not; **nonne vides?** you see, don't you?, don't you see?; **quaeritur nonne ire statim velis** the question is whether you do not wish to go at once

nōnnull·us -a -um *adj* some, a certain amount of; many a **ll** *pl* some, not a few

nōnnumquam *adv* (-nunq-) sometimes

nōnnusquam *adv* in some places

nōn·us -a -um *adj* ninth **ll** *f* ninth hour

nōn·us decim·us -a -um *adj* nineteenth

Nōric·us -a -um *adj* of Noricum **ll** *n*

Noricum (*Roman province between the Danube and the Alps*)

norm·a -ae *f* (*carpenter's*) square; (*fig*) standard, norm of behavior

nōs *pron* we; us

noscit·ō -āre -āvī -ātus *tr* to examine closely, observe; to know, recognize

noscō noscĕre nōvī nōtus *tr* (gn-) to get to know, become acquainted with, learn; to recognize; to examine, inquire into; to approve of; **novisse** to have become acquainted with, (*and therefore*) to know

nōsmet *pron* (*emphatic form of* **nōs**) we ourselves; us ourselves

nos·ter -tra -trum *adj* our, our own **ǁ** *pron* ours; **noster** our friend; **nostri** our men, our soldiers, our side, our friends

nostrās -ātis *adj* born *or* produced in our country, native, of our country, indigenous

not·a -ae *f* note; mark; sign; letter, character; punctuation mark; brand (*of wine*); marginal note, critical mark; tattoo marks, brand; distinctive mark, distinctive quality; stamp (*on coin*); stigma; nickname; black mark (*against one's name*); reproach, disgrace; nod, sign, beck; sign of the zodiac; **in notam alicujus** so as to humiliate s.o.; **per notas scribere** to write in code **ǁ** *fpl* letters of the alphabet; shorthand notes; memoranda

notābil·is -is -e *adj* notable, noteworthy, memorable; conspicuous

notābiliter *adv* notably, remarkably; perceptibly

notār·ius -(i)ī *m* stenographer; secretary

notāti·ō -ōnis *f* notation, mark; black mark (*of censor*); choice; observation; etymology

notāt·us -a -um *adj* noted, distinguished

nōt·escō -escĕre -uī *intr* to become known

noth·us -a -um *adj* bastard, illegitimate; mongrel, crossbreed; spurious; (*of the moon's light*) reflected

nōti·ō -ōnis *f* acquaintance; (*fig*) notion, idea; (*leg*) investigation

nōtiti·a -ae *or* **nōtiti·ēs -ēī** *f* acquaintance, knowledge; awareness; fame; notion, conception; familiarity (*w. things*); **notitia ei cum Perseo est** he is familiar with Perseus; **notitiam feminae habere** to have sex with a woman

nōt·ō -āre -āvī -ātus *tr* to mark; to mark out; to note, observe; to write down; to record; to take down in shorthand; to mark critically; to brand; to indicate, denote; to reproach; to indicate by a sign; (*of things*) to be a sign of; to mention (*in a speech or writing*)

nōt·or -ōris *m* guarantor

nōt·us -a -um *pp of* **nosco ǁ** *adj* known, well-known; notorious; familiar, custom-

ary; **notum est** (*w. acc + inf*) it is common knowledge that; **notum facere** (*w. acc & inf*) to make it known that; **notum habere** (*w. acc & inf*) to be informed that **ǁ** *m* an acquaintance; one who knows

novācul·a -ae *f* razor

novāl·is -is *f or* **novāl·e -is** *n* field plowed for the first time, reclaimed land; cultivated field; fallow land; crops

novātr·ix -īcis *f* innovator (*female*)

novē *adv* newly, in an unusual manner

novell·us -a -um *adj* new, fresh, young; newly acquired

novem *indecl adj* nine

Novem·ber *or* **Novem·bris -bris -bre** *adj* November; **mensis November** (*9th month of the Roman calendar until 153 B.C.*) **ǁ** **Novem·ber -bris** *m* November

novemdecim *indecl adj* (**noven-**) nineteen

novendiāl·is -is -e *adj* (**novem-**) nine-day; occurring on the ninth day; **cineres novendiales** (*fig*) ashes not yet cold **ǁ** *n* nine-day festival (*to mark the appearance of an omen*); funeral feast (*held nine days after death*)

novēn·ī -ae -a *adj* in groups of nine, nine each, nine

novensil·ēs -ium *mpl* new gods (*introduced from abroad*)

noverc·a -ae *f* stepmother

novercāl·is -is -e *adj* stepmother's, of a stepmother; like a stepmother

novīci·us -a -um *adj* new, brand new; recently imported (*slaves*); recently discovered (*things*); (*pej*) new-fangled

noviens *or* **noviēs** *adv* nine times

novissimē *adv* of late, very recently

novissim·us -a -um *adj* latest, last, final; most recent; most extreme, utmost; **novissimum agmen** (*mil*) the rear; **novissima verba** parting words **ǁ** *mpl* (*mil*) rear guard **ǁ** *npl* the worst

novit·ās -ātis *f* newness, novelty; innovation; rareness, strangeness, unusualness; unexpectedness; recently acquired rank (*condition of being a* **novus homo**); **novitas rerum** revolution

nov·ō -āre -āvī -ātus *tr* to make new, renew, renovate; to repair; to refresh; to change; to coin (*words*); **res renovare** to bring about a revolution

nov·us -a -um *adj* new; young; fresh; novel; unexpected; strange, unusual, unheard-of; recent, modern; unused; inexperienced; renewed, revived, as good as new; newly recuited (*soldiers*); inexperienced; subversive (*plans, activities*); fallow (*field*); newly arrived (*in a place*); **novae tabernae** new shops (*on N. side of the Forum*); **novus homo** self-made man (*first man of a family to reach a curule office*); **res nova** a new development; **res novae** revolution

nox noctis _f_ night; night activity; sleep; death; darkness, blindness; mental darkness, ignorance; gloom; **ad multam noctem** till late at night; **nocte** _(or_ **de nocte)** at night, by night; **noctem et diem** night and day; **sub noctem** at nightfall ‖ _fpl_ **noctes et dies** night and day, continually

nox·a -ae _f_ harm, injury; offense; fault, guilt, responsibility; **in noxā esse** to be guilty of wrongdoing; **noxae** _(or_ ad _or_ in + acc) **dedere** to hand _(s.o.)_ over for punishment; **noxā** _(or_ **noxis) solutus** _(of a slave in a formula of sale)_ guilty of no prior injurious conduct

noxi·us -a -um _adj_ harmful, noxious; guilty; _(w. gen)_ guilty of ‖ _f_ harm, damage, injury; blame, guilt; fault; offense; **in noxiā esse** to be at fault

nūbēcul·a -ae _f_ little cloud; gloomy expression

nūb·ēs -is _f or_ **nūb·is -is** _m_ cloud; gloom; veil

nūbif·er -era -erum _adj_ cloudy; cloud-capped; cloud-bringing _(wind)_

nūbigen·a -ae _adj (masc only) (of the Centaurs, whom Ixion fathered on a cloud-image of Hera; of Phrixus, son of the cloud-goddess Nephele)_ born of clouds

nūbil·is -is -e _adj_ marriageable

nūbil·us -a -um _adj_ cloudy; cloud-bringing _(wind);_ troubled; gloomy, melancholy

nūbō nūběre nupsī -nuptum _intr_ (of a woman) to marry; _(w. dat)_ to marry _(a man);_ to be married to _(a man)_ ‖ _refl_ to get married

Nūceri·a -ae _f_ town in Campania

Nūcerīn·us -a - um _adj_ of Nuceria

nucifrangibul·um -ī _n (coll)_ nut-cracker _(i.e., teeth)_

nucle·us -ī _m_ nut; kernel, stone _(of fruit)_

nudius _adv_ it is now the...day since, _e.g.,_ **nudius tertius** it is now the third day since _(by Roman reckoning, the day before yesterday);_ **nudius dies dedi ad te epistolam** it is now the third day since I mailed you a letter; ago, _e.g.,_ **nudius tertius decimus** thirteen days ago _(twelve days ago by our reckoning, since the Romans counted both the first and last day)_

nūd·ō -āre -āvī -ātus _tr_ to strip, bare; to lay bare, uncover; to explain; to strip _(a person of office or rank);_ to empty _(a building)_ of all its occupants; _(mil)_ to leave undefended; _(w. abl)_ to divest of; **terga nudare** to expose their backs _(to attack)_

nūd·us -a -um _adj_ nude, naked; lightly clothed; bare, empty; defenseless; poor, needy; mere, simple, sole, only; _(w. gen_

or abl or w. **ab)** bare of, without, stripped of, deprived of

nūg·ae -ārum _fpl_ nonsense, baloney; trivia; trash, junk; good-for-nothing, a nobody; **nugae** _(or_ **nugas)!** nonsense!; baloney!; **nugae sunt** it's no use; **nugas agere** to waste one's effort

nūgāt·or -ōris _m_ joker; fibber; babbler; braggart

nūgātōri·us -a -um _adj_ worthless, useless, nonsensical; frivolous

nūg·ax -ācis _adj_ nonsensical; frivolous

nūgigerul·us -ī _m_ dealer in women's apparel

nūg·or -ārī -ātus sum _intr_ to talk nonsense; _(w. dat)_ to tell tall stories to

null·us -a -um _adj_ no; _(coll)_ not, not at all; non-existent; of no account ‖ _pron_ none

num _adv (of time, used only w._ **etiam)** now, _e.g.,_ **etiam num** now, even, now, still ‖ _adv (interrog particle expecting negative answer)_ surely not, really, actually, _e.g.,_ **num ista est nostra culpa?** is that really our fault?; that isn't our fault, is it? ‖ _conj (in indirect questions)_ whether

Num. _abbr_ **Numerius** _(Roman first name, praenomen)_

Num·a -ae _m_ Numa Pompilius _(second king of Rome)_

numell·a -ae _f_ shackle, restrainer

nūm·en -inis _n_ nod; will, consent; divine will; divine power; divine majesty; divinity, deity, godhead

numerābil·is -is -e _adj_ easily counted, few in number

numerāt·um -ī _n_ cold cash

numerāt·us -a -um _adj_ counted out, paid down; in cold cash

numerō _adv_ at the right time, just now; too soon

numer·ō -āre -āvī -ātus _tr_ to number, count; to pay out, pay down _(money);_ to consider; to enumerate, mention; to relate, recount; to reckon as one's own, possess, own; _(w._ **in** + abl _or_ **inter** + acc) to count among, include in _(a category);_ _(w._ **in** + acc) to allocate to; _(w. pred. adj)_ to treat as, class as; **Senatum numerare** to count the Senate _(to see whether a quorum is present)_

numerōsē _adv_ rhythmically

numerōs·us -a -um _adj_ numerous; rhythmical

numer·us -ī _m_ number; mere cipher; class, category; rank, position; estimation, regard; portion _(of work),_ part, function; _(often w._ **suus)** the proper number, the full number, full complement; _(gram)_ number; _(mil)_ division, troop; _(mus, rhet)_ rhythm, meter, verse; _(mus)_ tune; _(pros)_ quantity, measure; **ad numerum** _(or_ **in numerum)** _(mus, pros, rhet)_ rhythmically, in time; **aliquo (nullo) numero esse** to be of some (no) account; **extra numerum** *(mus)* off beat, out of time; **in numero esse** to be included in a group; **in numero habere** *(w. gen)* to be regarded as, be ranked among; **nullo numero esse** to be of no account; **numero** at the right time, just now; too soon, too early; **numero huc advenis ad prandium** you are arriving here too early for lunch; **suum numerum navium habere** to have one's full complement of ships; **super** *(or* **supra) numerum** not attached to the regular staff **‖** *mpl* mathematics; astronomy; notes of the scale; melody; **ad numeros** *(mus, pros)* rhythmically, in time; **in numeris esse** to be on active duty; **omnibus numeris perfectus** perfect in every detail

Numid·a -ae *m* Numidian

Numidi·a -ae *f* Numidia *(country of N. Africa; Roman province, extending W. and S. of Carthage)*

Numidic·us -a -um *adj* Numidian

Numit·or -ōris *m* king of Alba, brother of Amulius, father of Ilia *(or* Rhea Silvia), and grandfather of Romulus and Remus

nummāri·us -a -um *adj* financial; *(pej)* mercenary, venal

nummāt·us -a -um *adj* rich; **bene nummatus** well-to-do, well-off

nummulār·ius -(i)ī *m* money changer

nummul·ī -ōrum *mpl* petty cash

numm·us -ī *m* coin; cash, money; sesterce *(small silver coin, worth about a dime);* small sum, trifle; **in nummis habere** to have in cash

numquam *adv* **(nun-)** never; **non numquam** sometimes

numquid *adv (to introduce direct question):* **numquid meministi?** do you remember?; *(to introduce an indirect question)* whether

nunc *adv* now; nowadays, today; now, in view of this, but as matters now stand; **nunc ipsum** at this very moment; **nunc...nunc** at one time...at another, once...once

nuncupāti·ō -ōnis *f* name, title; public pronouncing *(of vows);* nomination *(to some position)*

nuncup·ō -āre -āvī -ātus *tr* to name, call; to take *(a vow)* publicly; to appoint *(as heir);* to utter the name of, invoke; to address *(a person)*

nundin·ae -ārum *fpl* market day *(occurring regularly at intervals of eight days, i.e., every ninth day by Roman reckoning);* marketplace; market town; mart

nundināl·is -is -e *adj* market-

nundināti·ō -ōnis *f* marketing, trading

nundin·or -ārī -ātus sum *tr* to traffic in;

to buy **‖** *intr* to hold a market, attend a market; to trade; to gather in crowds

nundin·um -ī *n* market time; **inter nundinum** the time between two market periods; **trinum nundinum** a sequence of three market periods *(i.e., 24 days)*

nunq- = numq-

nunti·a -ae *f* messenger *(female)*

nuntiāti·ō -ōnis *f* announcement *(by an augur)*

nunti·ō -āre -āvī -ātus *tr* to bring word of; to announce, declare; to report *(omens);* to give warning of *(some future event);* **gaudium nuntiare** to bring good news; **salutem nuntiare** to send greetings

nunti·us -a -um *adj* bringing news, announcing **‖** *m* messenger, courier; message, news; order, injunction; **nuntium remittere** *(w. dat)* to send a letter of divorce to, to divorce *(a wife)* **‖** *n* message, communication

nūper *adv* recently, lately; in modern times

nūper·us -a -um *adj* recent

nupt·a -ae *f* bride, wife

nupti·ae -ārum *fpl* marriage, wedding

nuptiāl·is -is -e *adj* nuptial, wedding

nur·us -ūs *f* daughter-in-law; young lady, young married woman

nusquam *adv* nowhere; on no occasion; for nothing, to nothing; **nusquam alibi** nowhere else; **nusquam esse** not to exist; **nusquam gentium** nowhere in the world; **plebs nusquam alio nata, quam ad serviendum** the plebs, born for nothing else than to serve

nūt·ō -āre -āvī -ātus *intr* to keep nodding; to sway to and fro, totter; to waver

nūtrīcāt·us -ūs *m* breast-feeding

nūtrīc·ius -(i)ī *m (child's)* guardian

nūtrīc·ō -āre -āvī -ātus *or* **nūtrīc·or -ārī -ātus sum** *tr* to breast-feed, nurse; to nourish, promote the growth of *(plants, animals);* to rear, bring up, support; to take care of, attend to; to cherish, cultivate

nūtrīcul·a -ae *f* nanny; wet-nurse; *(of persons or things)* fosterer

nūtrīm·en -inis *n* nourishment

nūtrīment·um -ī *n* nourishment **‖** *npl* upbringing *(of a child)*

nūtr·iō -īre -īvī *or* **-iī -ītus** *or* **nūtrior nūtrīrī nūtrītus sum** *tr* to breast-feed, suckle; to support with food, nourish; to feed *(animals, plants, fire);* to build up *(resources);* to take care of, attend to *(the skin, hair);* to bring up *(a child);* to raise *(animals, crops);* to give rise to, foster, promote *(a condition, feeling);* to treat *(a wound, sick person);* to look after *(material things);* to deal gently with *(faults, people at fault)*

nūtrīt·or -ōris *m* one who feeds

nūtr·ix -īcis *f* nurse **‖** *fpl* breasts

nūt·us -ūs *m* nod; hint, intimation; nod of assent; will, pleasure; command; gravitation, gravitational pull; **nutus et renutus** nod of assent and nod of dissent
nux nucis *f* nut; nut tree; almond tree; **nuces relinquere** *(fig)* to put away childish things; **nux abellana** *(or* **avellana)** hazelnut; **nux castanea** chestnut; **nux Graeca** (sweet) almond; **nux juglans** walnut; **nux pinea** pine cone
Nyctē·is -idis *f* Antiope *(daughter of Nycteus, wife of Lycus (king of Thebes) and mother of Amphion and Zethus)*
Nyct·eūs -eī *or* -eos *m* father of Antiope
nymph·a -ae *or* nymph·ē -ēs *f* bride; nymph; *(fig)* water
Nȳs·a -ae *f* legendary mountain on which Bacchus was alleged to have been born *(usually located in India)*
Nȳsae·us *or* Nȳsi·us -a -um *adj* of Nysa, Nysaean
Nȳs·eūs -eī *or* -eos *m* Bacchus
Nȳsigen·a -ae *m* native of Nysa

O

ō *interj* oh!
Ōari·on -ōnis *m* Orion
Ōax·ēs *or* Ōax·is -is *m* river in Crete *(or perhaps on the E. frontier of the Empire)*
ob *prep (w. acc)* **1** before, in front of: **ob oculos** *(or* **ob os)** before one's eyes, right in front of s.o., under s.o.'s very nose; **2** on account of, because of, for: **quam ob rem** for which reason, accordingly, wherefore; **quas ob causas** for what reasons, why; **3** for the sake of, in the interest of: **ob rem publicam** for the sake of the country; **4** as a reward *or* punishment for, in return for: **ob mendacium tuum** in punishment for your lie; **5** *(in connection with bribes)* in payment for: **ob tua edicta pecuniae dabantur** you were given money *(i.e., bribes)* in payment for your edicts; **6** in connection with: **ob rem** to the purpose, usefully, profitably; **ob suam partem** on one's own account
ob- *pref (also* oc-, of-, og-, op-; the b is lost in **omitto** and **operio)** conveying the sense of: **1** movement towards a meeting: **obeo** to go to meet; **2** covering a surface: **oblimo** to cover with mud; **obduco** to cover the surface of; **3** protecting: **obduco** to draw *or* place as a protection *or* obstacle; **4** of overwhelming: **opprimo** to oppress; **5** counterbalancing: **oppono** to set off against by way of balance; **6** confrontation: **obsto** *(w. dat)* to stand in the way, obstruct; **7** surprise or the unexpected: **obvenio** *(w.*

dat) to fall to the lot of; **8** pleasant effect: **oblecto** to delight, entertain; **9** hostility: **obtrecto** to mistreat, disparage; **10** assault: **occido** to kill
obaerāt·us -a -um *adj* deeply in debt ‖ *m* debtor
obambul·ō -āre -āvī -ātus *tr* to prowl all over, prowl about *(e.g., the city)* ‖ *intr* to walk about; to wander; to prowl about; *(w. dat)* to prowl about near; *(w.* **ante +** *acc)* to wander around in front of
obarm·ō -āre -āvī -ātus *tr* to arm
obar·ō -āre -āvī -ātus *tr* to plow up, plow over
obb·a -ae *f* decanter, beaker
obbrūt·escō -escĕre -uī *intr* to grow dull
obc- = occ-
ob·dō -dĕre -didī -ditus *tr* to set before; to fasten *(a bolt);* to close, lock *(a door);* to expose
obdorm·iō -īre -īvī *or* -iī -ītum *intr* to fall asleep
obdorm·iscō -iscĕre *intr* to fall fast asleep
ob·dūcō -dūcĕre -duxī -ductus *tr (w.* **ad)** to lead *(troops)* toward *or* against; to extend in front as a barrier *or* protection; to fasten *(bolt);* to obstruct, block; to screen, protect; to cover the surface of; to draw over as a covering; to veil, envelop; to swallow; to put on *(clothes);* to bring forward as an opposing candidate; to pass *(time);* to dig *(ditch); (w. dat of thing protected)* to draw *or* place *(s.th.)* over; *(w. dat or* **ad)** to pit *(s.o. or s.th.)* against; **tenebras obducere** *(w. dat)* to cast darkness over
obducti·ō -ōnis *f* veiling, covering
obduct·ō -āre *tr* to introduce as a rival
obduct·us -a -um *pp of* **obduco** ‖ *adj* cloudy; gloomy; **obductus cicatrix a** closed scar
obdūr·escō -escĕre -uī *intr* to grow hard, harden; to become insensitive; **Gorgonis vultu obdurescere** to become petrified *(literally, to grow hard at the sight of the Gorgon)*
obdūr·ō -āre -āvī -ātum *intr* to stick it out
ob·eō -īre -īvī *or* -iī -itus *tr* to go to meet; to travel, travel to, travel across; to wander through, traverse, encircle; to visit; to run over, review, enumerate *(in a speech);* to undertake, engage in; **diem edicti** *(or* **diem** *or* **diem suum** *or* **diem extremum** *or* **mortem)** **obire** to meet one's death ‖ *intr* to go; to pass away, die; to fade, disappear; *(of heavenly bodies)* to set
obequit·ō -āre -āvī -ātum *intr* to ride up *(on horseback); (w. dat)* to ride up to
oberr·ō -āre -āvī -ātum *intr* to ramble about, wander around; *(w. abl)* **1** to wander among; **2** to make a mistake on *or* at

obēs·us -a -um *adj* obese; swollen; crude, coarse

ōb·ex -icis *mf* bar, bolt; barrier

obf- = **off-**

obg- = **ogg-**

obhae·rescō -rescĕre -sī *intr* to get stuck

obīr·ascor -ascī -ātus sum *intr (w. dat)* to get angry with

obiter *adv* on the way, as one goes along; *(fig)* in passing, incidentally

obitus *pp of* **obeo**

obit·us -ūs *m* approach, visit; death, passing; ruin, downfall; *(astr)* setting

objac·eō -ēre -uī *intr (w. dat)* to lie before, lie at

objectāti·ō -ōnis *f* reproach

object·ō -āre -āvī -ātus *tr* to oppose; to expose, endanger; to throw in the way; to cause *(delay); (w. dat)* 1 to impute to, throw up *(faults)* to; 2 to bring a charge of *(e.g., madness)* against, fling *(charges, abuse)* at; *(w. dat & acc & inf)* to throw a hint to *(s.o.)* that

object·us -a -um *pp of* **objicio** ‖ *adj* lying in the way, lying in front; *(w. dat)* 1 opposite; 2 exposed to ‖ *npl* charges

object·us -ūs *m* interposition; obstacles, hindrance; protection; *(w. gen)* protection afforded by

ob·jiciō -jicĕre -jēcī -jectus *tr* to hold up as an example; to bring up, cite *(before an opponent as a ground for disapproval or condemnation),* throw up in one's face; to set up as a defense, use as a barrier *or* defense; to bar, shut *(the gates to prevent entry by an enemy);* to throw in, use, deploy *(troops); (w. dat)* 1 to throw *or* set *(e.g., food, fodder)* before; 2 to expose *(people)* to *(the wild beasts);* 3 *(coll)* to toss *or* hand out *(money)* to; 4 to put *(a bandage)* on *(a part of the body);* 5 to turn *(a ship)* so as to face *(e.g., a hostile shore);* to set up as a defense against; 6 to hold out *(false hopes, incentives, temptations)* to; 7 to throw up *(faults, weaknesses, etc.)* to, lay *(faults)* to one's charge; **hi exercitui Caesaris luxuriem objiciebant** they were charging Caesar's army with extravagance; 8 to subject *(s.o.)* to *(danger, misfortune);* 9 to bring up, throw in *(troops)* against; **exceptionem objicere** to raise an objection; **interdum metus animo objicitur** at times fear crosses my mind; **portas objicere** to bar the gates; **religionem objicere** to raise the matter of religious scruples *(as a hindrance to some action);* **signum objicere** to raise an omen as an objection *(to some action)* ‖ *refl (w. dat)* to expose oneself to; **turba oculis meis modo se objecit** a crowd just came into view ‖ *pass (w. dat)* to happen to, befall, occur to; *(geog)*

(w. dat) to be located near *or* opposite *(to)*

objurgāti·ō -ōnis *f* scolding, rebuke

objurgāt·or -ōris *m* critic

objurgātōri·us -a -um *adj* reproachful

objurgit·ō -āre -āvī -ātus *tr* to keep on scolding

objurg·ō -āre -āvī -ātus *tr* to scold, rebuke, reprimand; to correct; to deter

oblangu·escō -escĕre -ī *intr* to taper off

oblātrātr·ix -īcis *f* nagging woman

oblātus *pp of* **offero**

oblectām·en -inis *n* delight

oblectāment·um -ī *n* delight, amusement; pastime

oblectāti·ō -ōnis *f* delight, amusement; attraction; *(w. gen)* diversion from

oblect·ō -āre -āvī -ātus *tr* to delight, amuse, entertain, attract; to spend *(time)* pleasantly ‖ *refl* to amuse oneself, enjoy oneself

oblēvī *perf of* **oblino**

ob·līdō -līdĕre -līsī -līsus *tr* to rush; to squeeze *(the throat),* strangle

obligāti·ō -ōnis *f* binding, pledging; obligation

obligāt·us -a -um *adj* obliged, under obligation; *(w. dat)* owed by right to, due to

oblig·ō -āre -āvī -ātus *tr* to tie up, bandage; to bind, obligate, put under obligation, make liable; to hamper; to earmark; to embarrass; to mortgage *(property); (w dat)* to pledge to, devote to; **fidem obligare** to pledge one's word, make a solemn promise; to guarantee one's loyalty ‖ *refl* to bind oneself, pledge oneself ‖ *pass* to be liable; *(w. abl)* 1 to be guilty of; 2 to be obliged to, compelled to

oblīm·ō -āre -āvī -ātus *tr* to cover with mud; to dissipate, squander

ob·linō -linĕre -lēvī *or* **līvī -itus** *tr* to smear, daub, coat; to seal up *(jar); (fig)* to sully, sully the reputation of; *(fig)* to overload

oblīquē *adv* sideways; zigzag; *(fig)* indirectly

oblīqu·ō -āre -āvī -ātus *tr* to turn aside, twist, shift, slant; to avert *(eyes)*

oblīqu·us -a -um *adj* slanting, crosswise, sideways; zigzag; from the side; indirect *(language);* sly; envious; downhill *(road);* **obliquus oculus** disapproving look; envious look ‖ *n* side; **ab** *(or* **ex)** **obliquo** from the side, at an angle, obliquely; **in obliquum** at an angle, sideways; **per obliquum** diagonally across

oblīsī *perf of* **oblido**

oblīsus *pp of* **oblido**

oblit·escō -escĕre -uī *intr* to hide, disappear

oblitter·ō -āre -āvī -ātus *tr (-līt-)* to erase; to cancel; *(fig)* to blot out; **nomina oblitterare** to cancel debts

oblituī *perf of* **oblitesco**

oblītus *pp of* **oblino**

oblītus *pp of* **obliviscor**

oblīvi·ō -ōnis *f* oblivion; forgetting; forgetfulness

oblīviōs·us -a -um *adj* forgetful, oblivious; *(wine)* causing forgetfulness

oblī·viscor -viscī -tus sum *tr* to forget ‖ *intr* to forget; *(w. gen)* to forget, neglect, disregard, be indifferent to

oblīv·ium -(i)ī *n* forgetfulness, oblivion

oblocūt·or -ōris *m* one who contradicts

oblong·us -a -um *adj* oblong

ob·loquor -loquī -locūtus sum *intr (w. dat)* **1** to interrupt; **2** to rail at; **3** to accompany *(musically)*

obluct·or -ārī -ātus sum *tr (w. dat)* to struggle with, fight against

oblūdi·ō -āre *intr* to make a fool of oneself

oblūd·ō -ĕre *tr* to play jokes on

obmōl·ior -īrī -ītus sum *tr* to make a barricade of; to block up *(a gap)*

obmurmur·ō -āre -āvī -ātum *intr (w. dat)* to roar in answer to

obmūt·escō -escĕre -uī *intr* to become silent, hush up; to cease

obnāt·us -a -um *adj (w. dat)* growing on *(e.g., a river bank)*

ob·nītor -nītī -nixus sum *intr* to strain, struggle, put on the pressure; *(w. dat)* **1** to press against, lean against; **2** to resist, oppose

obnixē *adv* with all one's might; obstinately

obnix·us -a -um *pp of* **obnitor** ‖ *adj* steadfast, firm, obstinate

obnoxiē *adv* guiltily; submissively

obnoxiōsius *adv* more slavishly

obnoxiōs·us -a -um *adj* submissive

obnoxi·us -a -um *adj* submissive, servile, obedient; weak, timid; *(w. dat)* **1** subservient to; **2** at the mercy of; **3** exposed to *(harm, danger, storms, etc.)*; **4** indebted to, under obligation to; **5** legally liable to, answerable to; **obnoxium est** *(w. inf)* it is dangerous to

ob·nūbō -nūbĕre -nupsī -nuptus *tr* to veil, cover *(the head)*

obnuntiāti·ō -ōnis *f* announcement *(of omens)*

obnunti·ō -āre -āvī -ātum *intr* to make an announcement; to make an announcement that the omens are adverse; to announce bad news

oboedi·ens -entis *adj* obedient; *(w. dat or ad)* obedient to; **dicto oboediens** obedient to the command

oboedienter *adv* obediently

oboedienti·a -ae *f* (**-bēd-**) obedience

oboed·iō -īre -īvī *or* **-iī -ītum** *intr (w. dat)* **1** to obey, listen to; **2** *(of things)* to respond to

obol·eō -ēre -uī *tr* to smell of ‖ *intr* to smell, stink

obor·ior -īrī -tus sum *intr* to rise. rise up, appear; *(fig) (of thoughts, sudden events)* occur, spring up

obp- = opp-

obrēp·ō -ĕre -sī -tus *tr* (**opr-**) to creep up on, sneak up on ‖ *intr* to creep up; *(w. dat)* **1** to creep up on, sneak up on, take by surprise; **2** to trick, cheat; *(w. in + acc)* to steal over; **obrepere ad honores** to worm one's way into high positions

obrept·ō -āre -āvī -ātum *intr* (**opr-**) to sneak up

obrēt·iō -īre -īvī *or* **-iī -ītus** *tr* to entangle

obrig·escō -escĕre -uī *intr* to stiffen; to freeze

obrōd·ō -ĕre *tr* to gnaw at

obrog·ō -āre -āvī -ātum *intr (w. dat)* to supersede

obru·ō -ĕre -ī -tus *tr* to cover up, cover, hide, bury; to overwhelm, overthrow; to sink, cover with water, swamp; to overflow; to overpower, surpass, obscure, eclipse ‖ *intr* to fall to ruin

obruss·a -ae *f* test, proof

obsaep·iō -īre -sī -tus *tr* (**-sēp-**) to fence in; to block *(road); (fig)* to block

obsatur·ō -āre -āvī -ātus *tr* to cloy ‖ *pass (w. gen)* to have enough of

obscaen- = obscen-

obscaev·ō -āre -āvī -ātum *intr (w. dat)* to augur well for; to augur ill for

obscēnē *adv* (**-scaen-**) obscenely

obscēnit·ās -ātis *f* (**-scaen-**) obscenity

obscēn·us -a -um *adj* (**-scaen-**) obscene, indecent; dirty, filthy; ominous ‖ *m* sexual pervert; foul-mouthed person ‖ *npl* sexual *or* excretory parts *or* functions, private parts

obscūrāti·ō -ōnis *f* obscuring, darkening; disappearance

obscūrē *adv* indistinctly, dimly; in an underhand manner; cryptically; imperceptibly; **obscure ferre** to conceal, keep secret

obscūrit·ās -ātis *f* obscurity

obscūr·ō -āre -āvī -ātus *tr* (**ops-**) to obscure, darken; to cover, hide; to suppress; to veil *(words); (of love)* to blind

obscūr·us -a -um *adj* (**ops-**) obscure; dark, shady; dim, indistinct, dimly seen, shadowy; barely visible; not openly expressed, unpublicized; obscure, unintelligible; secret; reserved; vague, uncertain; gloomy ‖ *n* the dark, darkness; obscurity; **in obsucro est** it is not clear, it is doubtful

obsecrāti·ō -ōnis *f* (**ops-**) entreaty; public supplication of the gods

obsecr·ō -āre -āvī -ātus *tr* (**ops-**) to entreat, appeal to, implore; **fidem obse-**

crare to beg for protection *or* support; **te obsecro** I beseech you, please
obsecund·ō -āre -āvī -ātum *intr* (ops-) *(w. dat)* to comply with, humor
obsecūtus *pp of* **obsequor**
obsēp- = obsaep-
obsequ·ens -entis *adj* (ops-) compliant, obedient; indulgent, gracious *(gods); (w. dat)* obedient to
obsequenter *adv* (ops-) compliantly
obsequenti·a -ae *f* (ops-) compliance, deference
obsequiōs·us -a -um *adj* (ops-) compliant, deferential
obsequ·ium -(i)ī *n* (ops-) compliance, indulgence; obedience, allegiance
ob·sequor -sequī -secūtus sum *intr* (ops-) *(w. dat)* 1 to comply with, yield to, give in to; 2 to gratify, humor
obser·ō -āre -āvī -ātus *tr* (ops-) to bolt, lock up
ob·serō -serěre -sēvī -situs *tr* (ops-) to sow *or* plant thickly; to fill, cover
observābil·is -is -e *adj* perceptible; capable of being guarded against
observ·ans -antis *adj* attentive; *(w. gen)* 1 respectful of; 2 attentive to; 3 careful about
observanti·a -ae *f* regard, respect; *(w. gen or* in + *acc)* regard for, respect for
observāti·ō -ōnis *f* (ops-) observation; caution, care; observance, usage, practice; remark, observation; safeguarding, protection
observāt·or -ōris *m* observer
observit·ō -āre -āvī -ātus *tr* to watch carefully, note carefully
observ·ō -āre -āvī -ātus *tr* to watch; to watch out for *(dangers, opportunities);* to watch for *(to ensnare);* to take careful note of; to guard; to observe, keep, obey, comply with; to pay attention to, pay respect to; to regard as important *or* authoritative; to keep to *(a date); (w. predicate)* to regard as, accept as; to adopt *(a course of action); (w.* ut*)* to follow *(such a course of action)* that
obs·es -idis *mf* (opses) hostage; guarantee, pledge; bail
obsessi·ō -ōnis *f* blockade
obsess·or -ōris *m* (ops-) frequenter, regular visitor; blockader
ob·sideō -sidēre -sēdī -sessus *tr* (ops-) to sit near *or* at, remain by *or* near; to frequent; to block, choke; to occupy, fill; to look out for, watch closely; to keep guard over; *(mil)* to besiege, blockade
obsidiāl·is -is -e *adj (mil)* for breaking a blockade
obsidi·ō -ōnis *f (mil)* blockade, siege
obsid·ium -(i)ī *n* (ops-) *(mil)* blockade, siege; status of hostage

ob·sīdō -sīděre -sēdī -sessus *tr* to take possession of, occupy *(so as to bar passage); (mil)* to besiege, blockade
obsignāt·or -ōris *m* sealer; witness; **obsignator testamenti** witness to a will
obsign·ō -āre -āvī -ātus *tr* (ops-) to seal, to sign and seal; *(fig)* to stamp
ob·sistō -sistěre -stitī -stitum *intr* (ops-) *(w. dat)* 1 to stand in the way of, block; 2 to resist, oppose; 3 to disapprove of, forbid
obsitus (ops-) *pp of* **obsero** (to sow) ‖ *adj (w. abl)* overgrown with, covered with
obsole·faciō -facěre -fēcī -factus *tr (pass:* **obsole·fīō -fierī -factus sum** *intr)* to degrade, lower the dignity of
obsol·escō -escěre -ēvī -ētum *intr* to go out of style, become obsolete; to fade away; to suffer degradation; *(of reputation)* to become tarnished; *(of persons)* to sink into obscurity
obsolētē *adv* shabbily
obsolēt·us -a -um *adj* out of date, obsolete; worn out; shabby, threadbare; soiled, dirty; low, poor; *(of language)* hackneyed, trite
obsōnāt·or -ōris *m* (ops-) shopper *(for groceries)*
obsōnāt·us -ūs *m* (ops-) shopping *(for groceries)*
obsōn·ium -(i)ī *n* (ops-) shopping; groceries ‖ *npl* groceries; pension
obsōn·ō -āre -āvī -ātus *or* **obsōn·or -ārī -ātus sum** *tr* (ops-) to shop for *(groceries);* **famem obsonare** to work up an appetite ‖ *intr* to go shopping; to provide food; *(w.* de + *abl)* to provide a feast for
obsŏn·ō -āre -āvī -ātum *intr* (w. dat) to drown out
obsorb·eō -ēre -uī *tr* (ops-) to gulp down
obstanti·a -ae *f* obstacle
obstetr·ix -īcis *f* (ops-) midwife
obstinātē *adv* resolutely, with determination; obstinately, stubbornly
obstināti·ō -ōnis *f* determination; obstinacy, stubbornness
obstināt·us -a -um *adj* determined, fixed; obstinate, stubborn
obstin·ō -āre -āvī -ātus *tr* (ops-) to set one's mind on, persist in ‖ *intr (w.* ad*)* to persist in
obstipescō *see* **obstupesco**
obstīp·us -a -um *adj* bent, bent forwards, bowed; **capite obstipo stare** to stand with bowed head
obstit·us -a -um *adj* struck by lightning
ob·stō -stāre -stitī -stātum *intr* (ops-) to stand in the way, raise opposition; *(w. dat)* 1 to stand in the way of, block the path of; 2 to block the view of, stand in front of; 3 to oppose, object to, resist, obstruct; 4 to constitute a boundary to;

(w. ne or quin *or* quominus *or* cur non*)* to prevent *(s.o.)* from

obstrep·ō -ĕre -uī -itus *tr* **(ops-)** to fill with noise, drown out **‖** *intr* to make a racket, make noise; *(w. dat)* **1** to shout at, drown out, interrupt with shouts; **2** *(of the sea)* to resound against

obstrin·gō -gĕre -xī obstrictus *tr* **(ops-)** to tie a rope tightly around *(a neck); (w. ob + acc)* to tie onto; to tie up, shut in, confine; *(fig)* to involve, put under obligation *(by an agreement, oath);* to pledge, promise *(s.th.);* **fidem obstringere** *(w. dat)* to pledge one's word to; **in verba alicujus obstringere** to have *(s.o.)* swear loyalty to s.o. **‖** *refl & pass (w. abl)* **1** to get involved in; **2** to be guilty of

obstructi·ō -ōnis *f* obstruction

obstructus *pp of* **obstruo**

obstrū·do -dĕre -sī -sus *tr* **(obt-)** to gulp down; *(w. dat)* to force *(s.th.)* upon, thrust *(s.th.)* upon

obstru·ō -ĕre -xī -ctus *tr* **(ops-)** to pile up, block up, stop up; *(w. dat)* to block *or* close *(e.g., a road)* against

obstrūsus *pp of* **obstrudo**

obstupe·faciō -facĕre -fēcī -factus *tr* to stun, astonish, strike dumb, daze; *(of drinks)* to stupefy; to paralyze *(emotions, etc.)*

obstup·escō -escĕre -uī *intr* **(-stip-)** to be astounded, be stunned, be paralyzed; to be struck with awe *or* wonder; *(of the body)* to become numb

obstupid·us -a -um *adj* **(ops-)** struck dumb, stunned, dazed, astounded

ob·sum -esse -fui *or* **offuī -futūrus** *intr (w. dat)* **1** to be opposed to, be against; **2** to be prejudicial to; **3** to be harmful to; **nihil obest dicere** there is no harm in saying

ob·suō -suĕre -suī -sūtus *tr* to sew on; to sew up

obsurd·escō -escĕre -uī *intr* to become deaf; *(fig)* to turn a deaf ear

ob·tegō -tegĕre -texī -tectus *tr* **(opt-)** to cover up *(w. clothing);* to protect; to conceal, screen; to keep secret

obtemperāti·ō -ōnis *f (w. dat)* obedience to, submissiveness to

obtemper·ō -āre -āvī -ātum *intr* **(opt-)** *(w. dat)* to comply with, be submissive to, obey

obten·dō -dĕre -dī -tus *tr* **(opt-)** to spread, stretch out; to offer as an excuse; to envelop; to conceal; to allege **‖** *pass (w. dat)* to lie opposite; **obtentā nocte** under cover of darkness

obtent·us -ūs *m* **(opt-)** screen, cover; pretext, pretense

ob·terō -terĕre -trīvī -trītus *tr* to trample on, trample down, crush; *(fig)* to trample on, degrade, destroy, crush

obtestāti·ō -ōnis *f* calling to witness; solemn invocation; solemn appeal

obtest·or -ārī -ātus sum *tr* **(opt-)** to call as witness; to make an appeal to, implore, entreat

obtex·ō -ĕre -uī -tus *tr* to cover, veil

obtic·eō -ēre -uī *intr* **(opt-)** to be silent

obtic·escō -escĕre -uī *intr* **(opt-)** to fall silent; to be dumbstruck

ob·tineō -tinēre -tinuī -tentus *tr* **(opt-)** to hold on to, keep up, persist in; to possess; to maintain, preserve, uphold; to remain in charge of; to retain military control of; to achieve *(a goal),* gain *(one's point);* to secure *(rights);* to win *(one's case);* to secure *(one's rights);* to cover, extend over; to constitute; to comprise; *(of conditions)* to prevail over; to hold *(a rank, position; an opinion);* **auctoritatem obtinere** *(w. gen)* to have the authority of; **locum obtinere** *(w. gen)* to fulfill the function of; **rem obtinere** to be successful, be victorious; **vim obtinere** *(w. gen)* to have the force of **‖** *intr* to carry the day, get one's way, succeed; *(of an opinion, report)* to be generally accepted

ob·tingō -tingĕre -tigī *intr* **(opt-)** to happen, occur; *(w. dat)* to happen to, befall

obtorp·escō -escĕre -uī *intr* **(opt-)** to become numb, become stiff; to become insensible

obtor·queō -quēre -sī -tus *tr* **(opt-)** to twist; to restrain with a noose

obtrectāti·ō -ōnis *f* **(opt-)** detraction, disparagement

obtrectāt·or -ōris *m* **(opt-)** detractor

obtrect·ō -āre -āvī -ātus *tr* **(opt-)** to treat spitefully, mistreat, disparage; to carp at **‖** *intr (w. dat)* to detract from, disparage

obtrītus *pp of* **obtero**

obtrīvī *perf of* **obtero**

obtrūdō *see* **obstrudo**

obtrunc·ō -āre -āvī -ātus *tr* **(opt-)** to cut off, cut down; *(in battle)* to cut down, kill

ob·tueor -tuērī -tuitus sum *or* **optu·or -ī** *tr* **(opt-)** to gaze at, gaze upon; to see clearly

ob·tundō -tundĕre -tudī -tūsus *or* **-unsus** *tr* **(opt-)** to beat, beat on, thump on; to blunt; *(fig)* to pound away at, stun; to deafen; to annoy

obturb·ō -āre -āvī -ātus *tr* **(opt-)** to throw into disorder; *(fig)* to disturb, confuse, distract

obtur·gescō -gescĕre -tursī *intr* to begin to swell

obtūr·ō -āre -āvī -ātus *tr* **(opt-)** to block up, plug up; **aures obturare** to refuse to listen; **os alicujus obturare** to shut s.o. up

obtūs·us *or* **obtuns·us -a -um** *pp of*

obtundo ‖ *adj* dull; blunt; husky, coarse *(voice); (of utterances)* obtuse; *(of actions)* blunt, lacking in refinement
obtūt·us -ūs *m* (opt-) stare, gaze
obumbr·ō -āre -āvī -ātus *tr* to overshadow, shade; to darken, obscure; to cover; screen
obunc·us -a -um *adj* hooked
obust·us -a -um *adj (of a stake)* having an end burned to a point; nipped *(by cold)*
obvāg·iō -īre *intr* to bawl
obvall·ō -āre -āvī -ātus *tr* to fortify *(with a rampart)*
ob·veniō -venīre -vēnī -ventum *intr* to come up, happen, come one's way; *(w. dat)* 1 to fall to *(s.o.'s)* lot; 2 to come to *(s.o.'s)* notice
obvers·or -ārī -ātus sum *intr* to make an appearance, show oneself; *(fig)* to appear *(before one's eyes, mind)*
obvers·us -a -um *adj (w. ad)* 1 turned toward, facing; 2 inclined to; *(w. dat)* engaged in ‖ *m* opponent
ob·vertō -vertĕre -vertī -versus *tr* (-vor-) *(w. dat or ad)* to turn *(s.th.)* towards *or* in the direction of; *(w. in + acc)* to turn *(e.g., soldiers)* to face *(e.g., the enemy)* ‖ *pass (w. ad)* to turn toward
obviam *or* **ob viam** *adv (w. dat)* 1 to meet, in order to meet, in the way of; 2 *(fig)* opposed to; **effundi obviam** *(w. dat)* to pour *or* rush out to meet; **obviam esse** *(w. dat)* 1 to meet; 2 to oppose, resist; 3 to be at hand, be handy; **obviam ire** *(or* **obviam procedere)** *(w. dat)* 1 to go to meet; 2 to face up to *(dangers);* **obviam obsistere** *(w. dat)* to stand in the way of; **obviam prodire** *(or* **proficisci** *or* **progredi)** *(w. dat)* to go to meet; **obviam venire** *(w. dat)* to come *or* go to meet
obvigilāt·um -ī *n* vigilance
obvi·us -a -um *adj* in the way; exposed, open; accessible *(person);* ready, at hand; *(w. dat)* 1 to meet, so as to meet; 2 opposed to; 3 exposed to, open to; **obvius esse** *(w. dat)* to meet, encounter
obvol·vō -vĕre -vī -ūtus *tr* to wrap up, cover up
occaec·ō -āre -āvī -ātus *tr* (obc-) to blind; to darken, obscure; to hide; *(of fear)* to numb
occall·escō -escĕre -uī *intr* (obc-) to become thick-skinned, become callused; *(fig)* to become callous, become insensitive
occan·ō -ĕre -uī *intr (mil)* to sound the charge
occāsi·ō -ōnis *f* opportunity, good time, right moment, chance; pretext; *(mil)* surprise, raid; **ex occasione** at the right time; **occasionem amittere** to lose the opportunity; **occasionem arripere** to

seize the opportunity; **per occasionem** *(or* **occasiones)** at the right time
occāsiuncul·a -ae *f* nice little opportunity
occās·us -ūs *m* setting; sunset; the West; *(fig)* downfall, ruin, death
occāti·ō -ōnis *f* harrowing, breaking up of the soil
occāt·or -ōris *m* harrower
oc·cēdō -cēdĕre -cessī -cessum *intr* to go up; **obviam occedere** *(w. dat)* to go to meet
occent·ō *or* **occant·ō -āre -āvī -ātus** *tr* (obc-) to serenade; to satirize in verse
occept·ō -āre -āvī -ātus *tr* to begin
occid·ens -entis *m* the setting sun; the West
occīdi·ō -ōnis *f* massacre, annihilation; **occidione occidere** to massacre
oc·cīdō -cīdĕre -cīdī -cīsus *tr* to kill; to murder; to knock down; to bring about the ruin of; *(fig)* to be the death of; to pester to death
oc·cĭdō -cidĕre -cĭdī -cāsum *intr* to fall, fall down; *(of the sun)* to set; to fall, be slain; *(of hope, etc.)* to fade; *(of species)* to become extinct, die out; *(fig)* to be ruined, be done for; **occidi!** I'm finished! **vita occidens** the twilight of life
occidu·us -a -um *adj* setting; western; *(fig)* sinking, fading, dying
occill·ō -āre -āvī -ātus *tr* to smash
oc·cinō -cinĕre -cecinī *or* **-cinuī** *or* **occan·ō -ĕre -uī** *intr* to sing inauspiciously, sound ominous
oc·cipiō -cipĕre -cēpī -ceptus *tr & intr* (-cup-) to begin
occipit·ium -(i)ī *or* **occip·ut -itis** *n* back of the head
occīsi·ō -ōnis *f* murder, killing
occīs·or -ōris *m* murderer, killer
occīsus *pp of* **occīdō**
occlāmit·ō -āre -āvī -ātus *tr* to shout at ‖ *intr* to shout, yell
occlū·dō -dĕre -sī -sus *tr* (obc-) to close up, shut up, lock up; to close access to *(buildings);* to restrain
occ·ō -āre -āvī -ātus *tr* to harrow, break up *(the soil)*
occub·ō -āre *intr* to lie; to rest; **crudelibus umbris occubare** to lie dead in the cruel lower world
occulc·ō -āre -āvī -ātus *tr* to trample down
occul·ō -ĕre -uī -tus *tr* to cover; to cover up, hide
occultāti·ō -ōnis *f* concealment, hiding
occultāt·or -ōris *m* one who conceals
occultē *adv* secretly, in secret
occult·ō -āre -āvī -ātus *tr* to hide, conceal; to suppress, keep *(facts, information)* secret ‖ *refl & pass* to hide
occult·us -a -um *pp of* **occulō** ‖ *adj* hidden, secret; clandestine; recondite *(expressions);* invisible *(forces of nature);*

reserved *(person)* ‖ *n* concealment; secret; **ex occulto** from a concealed position; **in occulto** in hiding; **per occultum** without being observed, secretly

oc·cumbō occumbĕre occubuī occubitus *tr* to meet *(death)* ‖ *intr* to fall dying; *(w. dat or abl)* to meet *(death);* **occumbere per** *(w. acc)* to die at the hands of

occupāti·ō -ōnis *f* occupation, employment, business; business engagement, task, job; occupying *(of a town);* preoccupation, concentration, close attention

occupāt·us -a -um *adj* occupied, busy, engaged

occup·ō -āre -āvī -ātus *tr* to occupy; to seize; to grasp, grab; to win, gain; to attack, strike down; to outstrip, overtake; to fill up, occupy *(a space);* to assume *(title, position);* to invest; to loan, lend; to head for, reach; to forestall; to take by surprise; to take the lead over *(competitor); (w. inf)* to be the first to

oc·currō -currĕre -currī *or* **-cucurrī -cursum** *intr* (obc-) to run up; *(w. dat)* **1** to run up to, run to meet, hurry to meet; **2** to rush against, attack; **3** to resist, oppose, counteract; **4** to meet, answer, reply to, object to; **5** to relieve, remedy; **6** to occur to, suggest itself to, present itself to; **7** run into, run up against, get involved in

occursāti·ō -ōnis *f* hustle and bustle; excited welcome; officiousness

occurs·ō -āre -āvī -ātus *tr* (obc-) to run to meet ‖ *intr (w dat)* **1** to run to meet, come to meet, meet; **2** to attack, charge, oppose; **3** *(of thoughts)* to occur to

occurs·us -ūs *m* meeting; *(w. gen)* running into *(s.o. or s.th.)*

Ōceanīt·is -idis *or* **-idos** *f* ocean nymph, daughter of Oceanus

ōcean·us -ī *m* ocean ‖ **Ōceanus** Oceanus *(son of Uranus and Ge and father of the river gods and ocean nymphs)*

ocell·us -ī *m* eye; gem; darling

ōcim·um -ī *n* basil *(seasoning)*

ocin·um -ī *n* fodder *(possibly clover)*

ōci·or -or -us *adj* swifter, quicker

ōcius *adv (superl:* **ōcissimē)** more swiftly, more quickly; sooner; more easily; immediately, on the spot; *(w. abl)* rather than; **ocius serius** sooner or later; **quam ocissime** as quickly as possible

ocre·a -ae *f* greave, shin guard

ocreāt·us -a -um *adj* wearing shin guards

octaphoros *see* **octophoros**

octāv·a -ae *f* one-eighth; eighth hour of the day *(i.e., 2:00 p.m.)*

Octāvi·a -ae *f* sister of Augustus, wife of Gaius Marcellus, and later of Marc Antony *(64–11 B.C.)* ‖ daughter of Claudius and wife of Nero *(murdered in A.D. 62)*

Octāv·ius -(i)ī *m* Gaius Octavius *(Augustus, who, upon adoption by Julius Caesar, became Gaius Julius Caesar Octavianus, 63 B.C.–A.D. 14)*

octāvum *adv* for the eighth time

octāv·us -a -um *adj* eighth; **octava pars** one-eighth ‖ *f see* **octāva** ‖ *n* **cum octavo efficere** to produce an eightfold yield

octāv·us decim·us -a -um *adj* eighteenth

octiens *or* **octiēs** *adv* eight times

octingentēsim·us -a -um *adj* eight hundredth

octingent·ī -ae -a *adj* eight hundred

octip·ēs -edis *adj* eight-footed

octiplicāt·us -a -um *adj* eightfold

octō *indecl adj* eighteen

Octō·ber -bris -bre *adj* October, of October; **mensis October** October *(8th month of the Roman calendar until 153 B.C.)* ‖ **Octo·ber -ris** *m* October

octōdecim *indecl adj* eighteen

octōgēnāri·us -a -um *adj & m* octogenarian

octōgēn·ī -ae -a *adj* eighty each

octōgē(n)sim·us -a -um *adj* eightieth

octōgiē(n)s *adv* eighty times

octōjug·is -is -e *adj* eight-horse

octōn·ī -ae -a *adj* eight at a time, eight each

octōphor·os -os -on *adj* **(octa-)** carried by eight men ‖ *n* litter carried by eight men

octupl·us -a -um *adj* eightfold ‖ *n* eightfold fine

octuss·is -is *m* sum of eight "asses" *(small coins, i.e., 8¢)*

oculāt·us -a -um *adj* having eyes; exposed to view, conspicuous; **oculatus testis** eyewitness

ocule·us -a -um *adj* many-eyed

oculissim·us -a -um *adj (hum)* dearest

oculitus *adv (to love s.o.)* like one's own eyes, dearly

ocul·us -ī *m* eye; eye, bud *(in plants);* sight, vision; mind's eye; **aequis oculis** contentedly; **altero oculo captus** blind in one eye; **ante oculos** in full view; *(fig)* obvious; **ante oculos ponere** to imagine; **ex oculis abire** to go out of sight, disappear; **in oculis** in view, in public, in the limelight; **in oculis ferre** *(or* **gestare)** to hold dear, value; **oculos adjicere** *(w. ad)* to eye; to covet; **oculos dejicere ab** to take one's eyes off; *(fig)* to lose sight of; **oculos pascere** *(w. abl)* to feast one's eyes on; **sub oculis** *(w. gen)* in the presence of, under the very nose of

ōdī odisse ōsus *tr* to have taken a dislike to, dislike, hate, be disgusted with

odiōsē *adv* hatefully; unpleasantly

odiōsic·us -a -um *adj (hum)* odious, unpleasant, annoying

odiōs·us -a -um *adj* odious, unpleasant, annoying
od·ium -(i)ī *n* dislike, aversion, hatred; object of hatred, nuisance; dissatisfaction, disgust; offensive conduct, insolence; **odio esse** *(w. dat)* to be hateful to, be disliked by, be hated by ‖ *npl* feelings of hatred
od·or *or* **od·ōs -ōris** *m* odor, smell, scent; stench; pleasant smell, fragrance; perfume; inkling, suggestion, hint ‖ *mpl* perfume
odōrāti·ō -ōnis *f* smell, smelling
odōrāt·us -a -um *adj* fragrant, scented
odōrāt·us -ūs *m* smell, smelling; sense of smell
odōrif·er -era -erum *adj* fragrant
odōr·ō -āre -āvī -ātus *tr* to make fragrant
odōr·or -ārī -ātus sum *tr* to sniff at, scent; to aspire to, aim at; to be sniffing after, search for, investigate; to get a smattering of
odōr·us -a -um *adj* smelly; fragrant; keen-scented
odōs *see* **odor**
Odrys·ae -ārum *mpl* a people of the Thracian interior
Odrysi·us -a -um *adj & m* Thracian
Odyssē·a *or* **Odyssī·a -ae** *f* the Odyssey
Oea·ger *or* **Oea·grus -grī** *m* Oeager *(king of Thrace and father of Orpheus)*
Oeagri·us -a -um *adj* Thracian
Oea·gus -grī *m* king of Thrace and father of Orpheus
Oebalid·ēs -ae *m* male descendant of Oebalus *(see* **Oebalus)** ‖ *mpl* Castor and Pollux
Oebali·us -a -um *adj* Spartan; Tarentine; Sabine ‖ *f* Tarentum *(Spartan colony in S. Italy)*
Oebal·us -ī *m* king of Sparta, father of Tyndareus, and grandfather of Helen, Clytemnestra, Castor and Pollux
Oedip·ūs -odis *or* **-ī** *m* Oedipus
Oen·eūs -eī *or* **-eos** *m* king of Calydon, husband of Althaea, and father of Meleager and Dejanira
Oenīd·ēs -ae *m* descendant of Oeneus; Meleager; Diomedes
Oenoma·üs -ī *m* king of Pisa in the Peloponnesus and father of Hippodamia
oenophor·um -ī *n* wine-bottle basket
Oenopi·a -ae *f* ancient name of Aegina
oenopōl·ium -(i)ī *n* wine shop
Oenōtri·us -a -um *adj* Oenotrian, Italic ‖ *f* ancient name of S.E. Italy; Italy
oestr·us -ī *m* horsefly, gadfly; fancy, inspiration
oesyp·um -ī *n* (-sop-) lanolin
Oet·a -ae *or* **Oet·ē -ēs** *f* Mt. Oeta *(in S. Thessaly, on which Hercules died)*
Oetae·us -a -um *adj* Oetean ‖ *m* Hercules
ofell·a -ae *f* small chunk of meat

off·a -ae *f* lump; dumpling; lump, swelling
offectus *pp of* **officio**
offen·dō -děre -dī -sus *tr* to bump, bump against, stub, strike, hit; to hit upon, come upon, meet with, bump into, stumble upon, find; to offend, shock; to annoy, disgust; to hurt *(feelings)*; to injure *(reputation)*; **nihil offendere** to suffer no damage, receive no injury ‖ *intr* to blunder, make a mistake; to give offense, be offensive; to fail, take a loss, be defeated, come to grief; to run aground; *(w. dat or* **in** + *abl)* to hit against, bump against; *(w. dat)* to give offense to; *(w.* **in** + *acc)* to take offense at; **terrae offendere** to run aground
offens·a -ae *f* offense, affront; displeasure, resentment, hatred; crime; **offensā** *(w. gen)* out of hatred for
offensi·ō -ōnis *f* stubbing; tripping, stumbling; obstacle; setback, mishap; detriment; affront, outrage ‖ *fpl* offensive acts; feelings of displeasure
offensiuncul·a -ae *f* slight mishap
offens·ō -āre -āvī -ātus *tr & intr* to bump
offens·us -a -um *pp of* **offendo** ‖ *adj* offensive, odious; *(w. dat)* offended at, displeased with
offens·us -ūs *m* bump; shock; offense
offerō offerre obtulī oblātus *tr* to offer, bring forward, present, show; to cause; to confer, bestow; to inflict; to deliver, hand over ‖ *refl (w. adj)* to show oneself to be; *(w. dat)* **1** to meet, encounter; **2** to expose oneself to *(e.g., danger);* **3** to give oneself up to *(an authority);* **4** to offer one's services to, volunteer for ‖ *refl & pass (esp. of an apparition)* to appear; *(of an idea)* to suggest itself
offerūment·a -ae *f (said humorously of a blow or welt)* present
officīn·a *or* **opificīn·a -ae** *f* shop, workshop, factory; office; artist's studio; training school
of·ficiō -ficěre -fēcī -fectum *intr (w. dat)* to get in the way of, interfere with, oppose; to obstruct, hinder; to be detrimental to
officiōsē *adv* obligingly, courteously
officiōs·us -a -um *adj* ready to serve, obliging; dutiful; officious
offic·ium -(i)ī *n* service, favor, kindness, courtesy; obligation, duty; function, part; social obligation, social call, social visit; ceremony; ceremonial observance, attendance; official duty; employment, business, job; sense of duty, conscience; allegiance; **officio togae virilis interesse** to attend the ceremony of the assuming of the manly toga
of·figō -figěre -fixī -fixus *tr* to fasten down, nail down, drive in
offirmāt·us -a -um *adj* determined

offirm·ō -āre -āvī -ātus *refl & intr* to steel oneself, be determined

offlect·ō -ěre *tr* to turn *(s.th.)* around

offrēnāt·us -a -um *adj* curbed

offrēn·ō -āre -āvī -ātus *tr (fig)* to curb

offūci·a -ae *f* cosmetic; *(fig)* trick, deception

offul·geō -gēre -sī *intr (w. dat)* to shine on

of·fundō -funděre -fūdī -fūsus *tr* to pour out; to cover; to fill; to eclipse **‖** *pass (w. dat)* to pour out over, spread over

oggann·iō -īre -īvī *or* **-iī -ītus** *tr or intr* to growl

ogger·ō -ěre *tr* to bring, offer

Ōgyg·ēs -is *or* **Ōgyg·us -ī** *m* mythical king of Thebes, in whose reign the Deluge allegedly occurred

Ōgygi·us -a -um *adj* Theban; **Ōgygius deus** Theban god *(i.e., Bacchus)*

oh *interj* oh!

ōhē *or* **ohē** *interj* whoa!

Oïl·eūs -eī *or* **-eos** *m* king of Locris in N. Greece and father of Ajax the archer

ole·a -ae *f* olive; olive tree

oleāgin·us -a -um *adj* olive, of an olive tree

oleāri·us -a -um *adj* oil, of oil **‖** *m* oil merchant

oleas·ter -trī *m* oleaster, wild olive tree

Ōleni·us -a -um *adj* of Olenus *(town in Achaia and Aetolia)*; Achaian, Aetolian

ol·ens -entis *adj* smelling; fragrant; smelly, stinking; musty

ol·eō -ēre -uī *tr* to smell of, smell like; *(fig)* to betray **‖** *intr* to smell; *(w. abl)* to smell of

ole·um -ī *n* olive oil, oil; *(fig)* palestra; **oleum addere camino** *(prov)* to pour oil on the fire; **oleum et operam perdere** to waste time and effort

ol·faciō -facěre -fēcī -factus *tr* to smell

olfact·ō -āre -āvī -ātus *tr* to sniff at

olid·us -a -um *adj* smelly

ōlim *adv* once, once upon a time; at the time; for a good while; someday *(in the future)*, hereafter; now and then, at times; ever, at any time

olit- = holit-

olīv·a -ae *f* olive; olive tree; olive wreath; olive branch; olive staff

olīvēt·um -ī *n* olive grove

olīvi·fer -fera -ferum *adj* producing olives, olive-growing

olīv·um -ī *n* olive oil; ointment; *(fig)* palestra

oll·a -ae *f* pot, jar

olle *or* **ollus = ille**

ol·or -ōris *m* swan

olōrīn·us -a -um *adj* swan-

olus *see* holus

Olympi·a -ae *f* Olympia *(region in Elis, in the Peloponnesus, where the Olympic games were held)*

Olympi·a -ōrum *npl* Olympic games

Olympiac·us -a -um *adj* Olympic

Olympi·as -adis *or* **-ados** *f* Olympiad *(period of 4 years between Olympic games, starting in 776 B.C., according to which the Greeks reckoned time)* **‖** wife of Philip V of Macedon and mother of Alexander the Great

Olympic·us -a -um *adj* Olympic, of the games held at Olympia

Olympionīc·ēs -ae *m* Olympic victor

Olympi·us -a -um *adj* Olympian *(cult title of Zeus); (of games)* Olympic, held at Olympia; *(of temple)* dedicated to Olympian Zeus

Olymp·us -ī *m* Mt. Olympus *(on the boundary of Macedonia and Thessaly, regarded as the home of the gods)*

omās·um -ī *n* tripe

ōm·en -inis *n* omen *(good or bad)*; foreboding; **omen accipere** to believe an event to be an omen; **prima omina** first marriage; **(procul) omen abesto!** *(or* **quod omen di avertant!)** God forbid!

ōment·um -ī *n* fatty membrane covering the bowels; the bowels

ōmināt·or -ōris *m* diviner

ōmin·or -ārī -ātus sum *tr* to foretell, predict, forebode

ōminōs·us -a -um *adj* ominous

omīsī *perf of* omitto

omiss·us -a -um *pp of* omitto **‖** *adj* remiss, negligent, heedless

omittō omittěre omīsī omissus *tr* to let go; to let go of, let fall, drop; to give up, abandon; to omit, pass over; to overlook, disregard; to release from custody; to allow to escape; to discard

omnigen·us -a -um *adj (also indecl)* every kind of

omnimodīs *or* **omnimodō** *adv* by all means, wholly

omnīnō *adv* altogether, entirely, wholly; *(w. numerals)* in all; *(in generalizations)* in general; *(in concessions)*, no doubt, to be sure, yes, by all means; **haud omnino** *(or* **non omnino)** not quite, not entirely; absolutely not, not at all; not expressly; **omnino nemo** absolutely no one

omnipar·ens -entis *adj* all-producing *(earth)*

omnipot·ens -entis *adj* omnipotent

omn·is -is -e *adj* all, every; every kind of; the whole **‖** *mpl* all, everybody **‖** *n* the universe **‖** *npl* all things, everything; all nature; all the world

omnitu·ens -entis *adj* all-seeing

omnivag·us -a -um *adj* roving everywhere

omnivol·us -a -um *adj* all-craving

Omphal·ē -ēs *f* Lydian queen who bought Hercules as a slave for a year

ona·ger *or* **ona·grus -grī** *m* wild ass

onāg·os -ī *m* ass-driver

Onchesmīt·ēs -ae *m* wind blowing from Onchesmus *(harbor in Epirus)*
onerāri·us -a -um *adj* carrying freight; jumenta oneraria beasts of burden; oneraria *(or* navis oneraria*)* freighter, transport
oner·ō -āre -āvī -ātus *tr* to load, load down, burden; *(fig)* to overload, oppress; *(fig)* to pile on, aggravate
onerōs·us -a -um *adj* onerous, burdensome, oppressive; heavy
on·us -eris *n* burden; load; freight, cargo; trouble; tax burden; fetus, embryo; oneri esse *(w. dat)* to be a burden to
onust·us -a -um *adj* loaded down, burdened; filled, full
on·yx -ychis *mf* onyx; onyx box
opācit·ās -ātis *f* shade, darkness
opāc·ō -āre -āvī -ātus *tr* to shade, make shady
opāc·us -a -um *adj* shady; dark, obscure ‖ *npl* opaca locorum shady places; opaca viarum dark streets
opell·a -ae *f* light work; small effort
oper·a -ae *f* effort, pains, exertion; work; care, attention; service, assistance; leisure, spare time; laborer, workman, artisan; a day's work *(by one person);* operae esse *(or* operae pretium esse*)* to be worthwhile; operam dare to take pains, exert oneself, be busied, pay attention, give attention, apply oneself; operam funeri dare to attend a funeral; operam magistro dare *(or* reddere*)* to attend a teacher's lectures, study under a teacher; operam ludere *(or* perdere*)* to waste one's time and effort; operam sermoni dare to listen to a conversation; operam tonsori dare to go see a barber, get a haircut; operā meā *(tuā, etc.)* through my (your, *etc.)* agency, thanks to me (you, *etc.)*
operāri·us -a -um *adj* working; working for hire ‖ *m* workman ‖ *f* working woman
opercul·um -i *n* lid, cover
operīment·um -ī *n* lid, cover
oper·iō -īre -uī -tus *tr* to cover, cover up; to shut; to hide; to clothe; to bury; to bury with a shower of missiles
oper·or -ārī -ātus sum *intr* to work hard, take pains; *(w. dat)* 1 to work hard at, be busied with, be engaged in; 2 to perform *(religious services);* 3 to attend; 4 to worship
operōsē *adv* with great effort, at great pains
operōs·us -a -um *adj* active, busy, painstaking; troublesome, difficult, elaborate; efficacious, powerful *(drugs)*
opertus *pp of* operio ‖ *adj* closed; hidden; secret ‖ *n* secret; secret place; in operto inside, in secret ‖ *npl* depth; veiled oracles

operuī *perf of* operio
opēs *see* ops
ophīt·ēs -ae *m* serpentine *(type of marble)*
Ophiūsi·us -a -um *adj* Cyprian ‖ *f* old name of Cyprus
ophthalmi·ās -ae *m* a type of fish
ophthalmic·us -ī *m* eye-doctor
Opic·us -a -um *adj* Oscan; boorish; ignorant *(esp. of Latin),* uncultured
opif·er -era -erum *adj* helpful
opif·ex -icis *m* maker, creator; craftsman, mechanic
opifīcīn·a -ae *f* workshop
opific·ium -(i)ī *n* work
ōpili·ō -ōnis *m* shepherd
opīmē *adv* splendidly; richly
opīmit·ās -ātis *f* prosperity
opīm·us -a -um *adj* fat, plump; fertile, fruitful; rich, enriched; abundant, plentiful; sumptuous, splendid; lucrative; noble; spolia opima armor stripped from one general by another on the field of battle
opīnābil·is -is -e *adj* conjectural, imaginary
opīnāti·ō -ōnis *f* mere opinion, conjecture, supposition, hunch
opīnāt·us -a -um *adj* supposed, imagined
opīnāt·us -ūs *m* supposition
ōpini·ō -ōnis *f* opinion; conjecture, guess, supposition; expectation; general impression; estimation; rumor; reputation, bad reputation; amplius opinione beyond expectation, beyond all hopes; celerius opinione sooner than expected; hac opinione ut under the impression that; in opinione esse *(w. acc & inf)* to be of the opinion that; praebere opinionem timoris to convey the impression of fear; praeter opinionem contrary to expectation, sooner than expected; ut opinio mea est as I suppose
opīn·ō -āre *or* opīn·or -ārī -ātus sum *tr* to suppose, imagine, conjecture ‖ *intr (parenthetical)* to suppose, imagine
opiparē *adv* splendidly, sumptuously
opipar·us -a -um *adj* splendid, sumptuous, ritzy
opisthograph·us -a -um *adj* written on the back; in opisthographo on the reverse side of a document
opitul·or -ārī -ātus sum *intr (w. dat)* to bring help to, assist
oport·et -ēre -uit *v impers* it is right, it is proper; me abire oportet I ought to go, I should go
op·pangō -pangĕre -ēgī -pactus *tr* to affix, imprint
oppect·ō -ĕre *tr* to comb off; *(coll)* to pluck, pick at, eat
oppēdō -ĕre *intr* (vulg) *(w. dat)* 1 to fart at; 2 *(fig)* to deride, mock
opper·ior -īrī -tus sum *tr* to wait for; *(w.*

num) to wait and see whether **‖** *intr* to wait

oppet·ō -ĕre -īvī *or* **-iī -ītus** *tr* to meet, encounter *(prematurely)* **‖** *intr* to meet death, die

oppidān·us -a -um *adj* of a town, in a town; *(pej)* provincial **‖** *mpl* townspeople

oppidō *adv* absolutely, quite; *(as affirmative answer)* exactly, extremely; **oppido quam breve intervallum** an extremely short distance

oppidul·um -ī *n* small town

oppid·um -ī *n* town

oppigner·ō -āre -āvī -ātus *tr* to pledge

oppīl·ō -āre -āvī -ātus *tr* to shut up, shut off

oppl·eō -ēre -ēvī -ētus *tr* to fill up, fill completely

op·pōnō -pōnĕre -posuī -positus *tr* to put, place, station; to oppose; to expose, lay bare, open; to wager; to mortgage; to bring forward, adduce, allege; to reply, object; to compare; **currum opponere** to block a rival's chariot

opportūnē *adv* at the right time

opportūnit·ās -ātis *f* opportunity, chance *(to do s.th.);* right time, opportuneness; advantage; suitability, fitness, convenience

opportūn·us -a -um *adj* opportune, suitable, convenient; advantageous, useful; exposed; **tempore opportunissimo** in the nick of time

oppositi·ō -ōnis *f* opposition

opposit·us -a -um *pp of* **oppono ‖** *adj* opposite; *(w. dat)* opposite, across from

oppressi·ō -ōnis *f* force, violence, violent seizure; suppression, overthrow

oppressiuncul·a -ae *f* slight pressure

oppressus *pp of* **opprimo**

oppress·us -ūs *m* pressure

op·primō -primĕre -pressī -pressus *tr* (**obp-**) to press down, weigh down; to pressure, put pressure on; to shut; to overwhelm; to put down, quell; to sink *(ship);* to subvert, overthrow, crush, overpower; to conceal, suppress; to catch

opprobrāment·um -ī *n* disgrace, scandal

opprobr·ium -(i)ī *n* (**obp-**) disgrace, scandal, reproach; cause of disgrace; taunt, abuse, abusive word

opprobr·ō -āre -āvī -ātus *tr* (**obp-**) to throw up *(s.th.)* to *(s.o. as a reproach)*

oppugnāti·ō -ōnis *f* (**opr-**) assault; *(fig)* attack, accusation

oppugnāt·or -ōris *m* (**obp-**) assailant

oppugn·ō -āre -āvī -ātus *tr* to assault, attack, storm; *(fig)* attack, assail

ops opis *f* power, might; help, aid; influence, weight; **non opis est nostrae** it is not in our power; **ope meā** with my help; **opem ferre** *(w. dat)* to bring help to, help **‖** *fpl* wealth, resources, means; military *or* political resources; **(ex) summis opibus** with all one's might **‖ Ops** *(goddess of abundance (sister and wife of Saturn and mother of Jupiter)*

ops- = **obs-**

optābil·is -is -e *adj* desirable

optāti·ō -ōnis *f* wishing, wish

optātō *adv* according to one's wish

optāt·us -a -um *adj* longed-for, desired, welcome **‖** *n* wish, desire

optigō *see* **obtego**

optim·ās -ātis *m* (**-tum-**) aristocrat **‖** *mpl* aristocracy, aristocratic party

optimē *(superl of* **bene**) *adv* (**-tum-**) very well; thoroughly; best; most opportunely, just in time

optim·us -a -um *(superl of* **bonus**) *adj* (**-tum-**) very good, best; excellent; most beneficial, most advantageous; *(of a legal title)* most valid, having the soundest basis; **in optimam partem** most favorably; **optimā fide** with the utmost honesty; **optimum est** *(w. inf)* it is best to; **optimum factu est** *(w. inf)* the best thing to do is to; **ut optimus maximusque** *(leg) (of property)* in its optimum condition *(i.e., free from all encumbrances)*

opti·ō -ōnis *f* option, choice **‖** *m* helper, assistant; *(mil)* adjutant

optīv·us -a -um *adj* chosen

opt·ō -āre -āvī -ātus *tr* to choose, select; to pray for; to wish for, desire

optum- = **optim-**

opul·ens -entis *adj* opulent, rich

opulentē *or* **opulenter** *adv* richly

opulenti·a -ae *f* opulence, wealth; resources; power

opulentit·ās -ātis *f* opulence; power

opulent·ō -āre -āvī -ātus *tr* to make rich, enrich

opulent·us -a -um *adj* opulent, rich; sumptuous; powerful

op·us -eris *n* work; product of work: structure, building; literary work, composition, book; work of art, workmanship; deed, achievement; literary genre; occupation, employment; what a person is expected to do, function, business; *(w. gen) (poet)* a thing the size of; *(mil)* offensive works, siege works; *(mil)* defensive works, fortifications; **dulce opus peragere** to perform one's pleasant business *(i.e., sexual intercourse);* **in opere** at work; **magno opere** greatly, to a great extent; **majore (summo) opere** to a greater (the greatest) extent; **opere** *(w. gen)* through the agency of; **quanto opere** how much, how greatly; **tanto opere** so much, so greatly; **operis alicujus esse** to be s.o.'s doing; **opus est** *(w. dat of person in need and abl of person or thing needed)* to need, e.g.,

opus est mihi duce I need a leader; **sui operis esse** to be part of one's business
opuscul·um -ī *n* little work, minor work
-or -ōris *m suf* forms nouns denoting **1** abstracts, *e.g.:* **candor** whiteness; **amor** love; **2** doer of the action of the verb, *e.g.,* **amator** lover
ōr·a -ae *f* boundary, border, edge; coastline, coast; region, district; cable, hawser; *(fig)* people of the coast, people of the region; division of the world; **ora maritima** seacoast **‖** *fpl* region, land; **orae extremae** the most distant lands, farthest shores; **orae luminis** *(or* **orae superae)** the upper world
ōrāc(u)l·um -ī *n* oracle; prophesy
ōrāri·us -a -um *adj* coasting; **navis oraria** coasting vessel, coaster
ōrāt·a -ōrum *npl* prayer, requests
ōrāti·ō -ōnis *f* faculty of speech; speech, language; style of speech, manner of speaking, style, expression; oration, speech; theme, subject; prose; eloquence; dialect; imperial rescript; **orationem habere** to give a speech; **oratio soluta** *(or* **oratio prorsa)** prose; **orationis pars** part of speech
ōrātiuncul·a -ae *f* short speech, insignificant speech
ōrāt·or -ōris *m* orator, speaker; suppliant; spokesman
ōrātōriē *adv* oratorically
ōrātōri·us -a -um *adj* orator's, oratorical
ōrātr·ix -īcis *f* suppliant *(female)*
ōrāt·us -ūs *m* request
orb·a -ae *f* orphan
orbāt·or -ōris *m* murderer *(of s.o.'s children or parents)*
Orbil·ius -(i)ī *m* Lucius Orbilius Pupillus *(Horace's teacher in Venusia)*
orb·is -is *m* circle; disk, ring; orbit *(of heavenly bodies);* quoit; hoop; wheel; spinning wheel; potter's wheel; round shield; eye socket, eye; globe, earth, world, universe; region, territory, country; circuit, round; rotation; cycle, period; zodiac; *(rhet)* balance; **magnus orbis** a year; **orbis caeli** vault of heaven; **Orbis Lacteus** Milky Way; **orbis luminis** eye; **orbis noster** our section of the world; **orbis oculi** eyeball; **orbis terrae** *(or* **terrarum)** earth, world, universe
orbit·a -ae *f* rut; *(astr)* orbit; *(fig)* routine
orbit·ās -ātis *f* childlessness, widowhood, orphanhood
orbitōs·us -a -um *adj* full of ruts
orb·ō -āre -āvī -ātus *tr* to bereave of parents, father, mother, children, husband, *or* wife; to strip, rob, deprive; to make destitute
orb·us -a -um *adj* bereaved, bereft; destitute; orphaned, fatherless; childless; wid-

owed; *(w. gen or abl or* **ab)** bereft of, without **‖** *mf* orphan
orc·a -ae *f* vat
Orcad·es -um *fpl* islands N. of Scotland *(modern Orkneys)*
orch·as -adis *f* a kind of olive
orchestr·a -ae *f* senatorial seats *(in the theater);* orchestra *(area in front of the Greek stage where the chorus sang and danced)*
Orc·us -ī *m* lower world; Pluto *(king of the lower world);* death
orde- = horde-
ordināri·us -a -um *adj* ordinary, usual, regular; normally elected *(consul)*
ordinātim *adv* in order, in good order; in sucession; regularly
ordināti·ō -ōnis *f* orderly arrangement; orderly government
ordināt·us -a -um *adj* regular; appointed
ordin·ō -āre -āvī -ātus *tr* to set in order, arrange, regulate; to govern, rule; to record chronologically
ordior ordīrī orsus sum *tr* to begin, undertake; to describe **‖** *intr* to begin; to begin to speak
ord·ō -inis *m* line, row; series; row of seats *(in theater);* order, methodical arrangement; order, class; social standing, rank, position; *(mil)* line, file *(of soldiers),* company, century, command of a company *or* century; **amplissimus ordo** senatorial order; **ex ordine** in succession, without a break; **extra ordinem** extraordinarily, especially, uncommonly; **in ordine** *(mil)* in regular order, in battle array; **in ordinem cogere** *(or* **redigere)** to put *(s.o.)* in his place, tell *(s.o.)* off; **ordine** *(or* **in ordine** *or* **per ordinem)** in order, in sequence; in a straight line; in detail; with regularity, regularly **‖** *mpl* officers of a company; promotions
Orē·as -adis *or* **-ados** *f* Oread *(mountain nymph)*
Orest·ae -ārum *mpl* tribe on the borders of Macedonia and Epirus
Orest·ēs -is *or* **-ae** *m* son of Agamemnon and Clytemnestra
orex·is -is *f* craving, appetite
organic·us -ī *m* organist
organ·um -ī *n* instrument, implement; musical instrument; water organ; organ pipe; **organum hydraulicum** water organ
orgi·a -ōrum *npl* Bacchic revels; orgies
orichalc·um -ī *n* copper ore; brass
ōricill·a -ae *f* little ear; lobe
ori·ens -entis *m* rising sun, morning sun; morning; day; land of the rising sun, Orient, the East
orīg·ō -inis *f* origin, source, beginning, start; birth, lineage, descent; race, stock, family; founder, progenitor; derivation *(of a word)*

Ōrī·ōn -ōnis *or* -ōnos *m* giant hunter, killed by Diana and turned into a constellation; *(astr)* Orion

orior orīrī ortus sum *intr* to rise; to get up; to become visible, appear; to be born, originate, be descended; to proceed, begin, start; *(of a spring, river)* to rise; *(of living creatures)* to come into existence, be born; *(of plants)* to come up, sprout; *(of events)* to arise, crop up; **homo a se ortus** a self-made man

Ōrīthȳi·a -ae *f* daughter of Erechtheus, king of Athens

oriund·us -a -um *adj* descended; *(w. abl)* originating from, originally from *(a place)*

ornāment·um -ī *n* equipment, trappings, apparatus; ornament, decoration; trinket, jewel; *(fig)* distinction; pride and joy; *(rhet)* rhetorical device

ornātē *adv* ornately, elegantly

ornātr·ix -īcis *f* hairdresser *(female)*

ornāt·us -ūs *m* equipment; apparel, outfit; furniture; decoration, ornament; preparation; *(rhet)* rhetorical embellishment

orn·ō -āre -āvī -ātus *tr* to equip, fit out, furnish; to outfit, dress; to set off, decorate, adorn; to show *(s.o.)* respect; *(w. abl)* 1 to honor with; 2 *(of things)* to give distinction to, enhance

orn·us -ī *f (bot)* mountain ash

ōr·ō -āre -āvī -ātus *tr* to beg, entreat, implore, plead with; to ask for; *(w. double acc)* to ask *(s.o.)* for; *(leg)* to plead *(a case)* ‖ *intr* to plead, beg, pray; *(w. cum)* to plead with, argue with

Orōd·ēs -is *m* name of several eastern kings, *esp.* Orodes II of Parthia, whose general defeated Crassus at Carrhae *(53 B.C.)*

Oront·ēs -is *or* -ae *m* chief river of Syria ‖ companion of Aeneas

Orontē·us -a -um *adj* from the River Orontes, Syrian

Orph·eūs -eī *or* -eos *m* famous musician and poet, husband of Eurydice

Orphē·us *or* Orphic·us -a -um *adj* Orphic

ors·us -a -um *pp of* ordior ‖ *npl* beginnings; utterance, words; attempt

ors·us -ūs *m* beginning; attempt, undertaking

orthographi·a -ae *f* spelling

ortus *pp of* orior

ort·us -ūs *m* rising; sunrise, daybreak; the East; birth *(of living creatures);* origin; source; **solis ortus** sunrise; the East; beginning, dawning *(of a period)*

Ortygi·a -ae *or* Ortygi·ē -ēs *f* Ortygia *(old name of Delos)* ‖ Ortygia *(island in the port of Syracuse)* ‖ Ortygia *(old name of Ephesus)*

Ortygi·us -a -um *adj* of Ortygia, Delian; Syracusan

or·yx -ygis *m* gazelle

oryz·a -ae *f* rice

os ossis *n* bone; marrow, innermost parts; kernel *(of a nut);* stone *(of fruit)* ‖ *npl* bones; skeleton; **ossa legere** to collect the bones *(from a pyre)*

ōs ōris *n* mouth; beak; voice, speech; expression; lip, face, countenance, look; sight, presence *(of a person);* impudence; mask; opening, orifice, front; **favete ore!** observe a respectful silence!; **habere aliquid in ore** to be talking about s.th. continually; **in ora hominum venire** to become a household name; **in ore omnium esse** to be on the lips of all; **in os aliquem laudare** to praise s.o. to his face; **os amnis** mouth of a river; **os durum** hardened look *or* expression; **os laedere** *(w. dat)* to insult s.o. to his/her face; **os oblinere** *(w. dat)* to hoodwink *(s.o.);* **os ostendere** to show one's face; **os timidum** expression of fear; **os venae** opening in a blood vessel; **per ora ferri** to go from mouth to mouth; **per** *(or* **praeter)** **ora nostra** before our eyes; **summo ore** just with the lips; **tria Dianae ora** the three forms of Diana; **uno ore** unanimously

osc·en -inis *mf* bird of augury *(e.g, crow, raven, owl)*

oscill·um -ī *n* small mask

oscit·ans -antis *adj* yawning; *(fig)* indifferent, bored

oscit·ō -āre -āvī -ātus *or* oscit·or -ārī -ātus sum *intr* to gape; to yawn

osculāti·ō -ōnis *f* kissing

oscul·or -ārī -ātus sum *tr* to kiss; *(fig)* to make a fuss over

oscul·um -ī *n* kiss; mouth, lips *(usually, puckered for a kiss);* **breve osculum** peck

Osc·us -a -um *adj* Oscan ‖ *mpl* Oscans *(ancient people of Campania and Samnium)*

Osīr·is -is *or* -idis *m* Egyptian god, husband of Isis

ōs·or -ōris *m* hater

Oss·a -ae *f* mountain in N.E. Thessaly

osse·us -a -um *adj* bony

osten·dō -děre -dī -tus *or* -sus *tr* to hold out for inspection; to show, exhibit, display, expose; to stretch out, stretch forth; to bring to one's attention; to expose; to reveal, disclose; to declare, make known; to represent in art; **os ostendere** to show one's face ‖ *refl* to show oneself, appear; **se optime ostendere** to appear very friendly

ostentāti·ō -ōnis *f* display, ostentation, showing off; mere show, pretense

ostentāt·or -ōris *m* show-off

ostent·ō -āre -āvī -ātus *tr* to show, exhibit; to show off, display, parade, boast of; to declare, point out, set forth ostent·um -ī n portent, prodigy

ostent·us -ūs m display, show; **ostentui** for appearances

Osti·a -ae f or Osti·a -ōrum npl Ostia (port town at mouth of Tiber)

ostiār·ium -(i)ī n tax on doors

ostiār·ius -(i)ī m doorman

ostiātim adv from door to door

ost·ium -(i)ī n door; entranceway; entrance, mouth

ostre·a -ae f or ostre·um -ī n oyster

ostreāt·us -a -um adj covered with oyster shells; (fig) black-and-blue

ostreōs·us -a -um adj abounding in oysters

ostri·fer -fera -ferum adj producing oysters, oyster-bearing

ostrīn·us -a -um adj purple

ostr·um -ī n purple dye; purple; purple garment, purple coverlet

ōsus pp of odi

-ōs·us -a -um adjl suf (formed chiefly from nouns) abounding in, rich in, full of: **ostreosus** abounding in oysters

Oth·ō -ōnis m Marcus Salvius Otho (Roman emperor in A.D. 69) ‖ Lucius Roscius Otho (author of the law of 67 B.C. reserving 14 rows in theaters for the equestrian order)

Othr·ys -yos m mountain range in S Thessaly

ōtiol·um -ī n bit of leisure

ōti·or -ārī -ātus sum intr to take it easy

ōtiōsē adv at leisure; leisurely, without haste; calmly, fearlessly

ōtiōs·us -a -um adj at leisure, relaxing, having nothing to do; free from official obligations; quiet, calm; undisturbed; unconcerned, indifferent, neutral; passionless; having no practical use, useless; superfluous, unnecessary; leading a peaceful existence; (of land) unoccupied, vacant ‖ m private person (not holding public office); civilian, non-combatant

ōt·ium -(i)ī n leisure, free time, relaxation; freedom from public affairs; retirement; peace, quiet; peaceful relations (with another country); ease, idleness, inactivity; calm weather; respite, lull; (**in**) **otio** (or **per otium**) at leisure, undisturbed

ovāti·ō -ōnis f ovation, minor triumph (in which the victor went on foot rather than driving a chariot)

ovāt·us -a -um adj triumphal, of an ovation

Ovid·ius -(i)ī m Ovid (Publius Ovidius Naso, Latin poet, born at Sulmo, 43 B.C.–A.D. 17)

ovīl·e -is n sheepfold; voting enclosures in the Campus Martius

ovīlis -is -e adj sheep-, of sheep

ovill·us -a -um adj sheep-, of sheep ‖ f mutton, lamb

ov·is -is f sheep; wool; simpleton

ov·ō -āre -āvī -ātum intr to rejoice; to hold a celebration; to celebrate a minor triumph

ōv·um -ī n egg ‖ npl wooden balls used to mark the laps at the racetrack

oxycomin·a -ōrum npl pickled olives

oxygar·um -ī n fish sauce containing vinegar

P

P. abbr **Publius** (Roman first name, praenomen)

pābulāti·ō -ōnis f foraging

pābulāt·or -ōris m forager

pābul·or -ārī -ātus sum intr to forage; to feed, graze; (coll) to make a living

pābul·um -ī n feed, fodder; pasturage, grass; (fig) nourishment, fuel

pācāl·is -is -e adj of peace

pācāt·us -a -um adj peaceful, quiet, calm; (of people) living in peace; of peacetime; **pacatae ramus olivae** the olive branch, symbolic of peace; **vici male pacati** villages not completely pacified ‖ n peaceful countryside

Pachȳn·um -ī n or Pachȳn·os -ī f S.E. point of Sicily

pācif·er -era -erum adj peace-bringing, peaceful; (of olive and laurel) symbolizing peace

pācificāti·ō -ōnis f pacification

pācificāt·or -ōris m peacemaker

pācificātōri·us -a -um adj peace-making

pācific·ō -āre -āvī -ātus tr to pacify, appease ‖ intr to make peace, conclude peace

pācific·us -a -um adj peace-making; peaceable

pac·iscor -iscī -tus sum tr to bargain for, agree upon; to stipulate; to barter; to become engaged to ‖ intr to come to an agreement, strike a bargain, make a contract; (w. inf) to agree to, pledge oneself to

pac·ō -āre -āvī -ātus tr to pacify, soothe; to reclaim (land)

pact·a -ae f fiancée; bride

pacti·ō -ōnis f pact, contract, agreement; treaty, terms; condition, stipulation; collusion; (leg) settlement (in a dispute); **pactio nuptialis** marriage contract

Pactōl·us or Pactol·os -ī m river in Lydia famous for its gold

pact·or -ōris m contractor, party (in a contract); negotiator

pact·us -a -um pp of **paciscor** and **pango** ‖ n pact, contract, agreement; way, man-

ner; **aliquo pacto** somehow; **hoc pacto**
in this way; **in pacto manere** to stick to
an agreement; **quo pacto** how, in what
way

Pācuv·ius -(i)ī m Marcus Pacuvius *(c. 220–
133 B.C., Roman tragic poet, native of
Brundisium and nephew of Ennius)*

Pad·us -ī m Po River *(in N. Italy)*

Padūs·a -ae f one of the mouths of the Po
River

pae·ān -ānis m hymn to Apollo; paean,
hymn of praise, victory song **‖ Paean**
epithet of Apollo as god of healing

paedagōg·ium -iī n (pēd-) training school
for pages

paedagōg·us -ī m (pēd-) slave in charge of
school children; *(fig)* guide, leader

paedīc·ō -ōnis m (pēd-) homosexual,
pederast

paedīc·ō -āre -āvī -ātus tr (pēd-) to have
homosexual relations with *(boys)*

paed·or -ōris m (ped-) filth

pael·ex -icis f (pēl-, pell-) concubine, mistress

paelicāt·us -ūs m (pēl-) concubinage

Paelign·ī -ōrum mpl (Pēl-) a people of
central Italy

paene adv nearly, almost

paeninsul·a -ae f peninsula

paenitend·us -a -um adj regrettable

paenitenti·a -ae f (poen-) repentance, regret

paenit·eō -ēre -uī paenitūrus tr (poen-)
to cause to regret; to displease **‖** intr (w.
gen) to regret **‖** v impers (w. acc of
person), e.g., **me paenitet** I am sorry;
(w. acc of person and gen of thing), e.g.,
me paenitet consili I regret the plan, I
am dissatisfied with the plan; (w. acc of
person and inf or **quod**), e.g., **eos
paenitet animum tuum offendisse** (or
**eos paenitet quod animum tuum
offenderint**) they regret having offended
your feelings

paenul·a -ae f travel coat; raincoat

paenulāt·us -a -um adj wearing a traveling coat or raincoat

pae·ōn -ōnis m (pros) metrical foot containing one long and three short syllables *(first paeonic:* — ∪ ∪ ∪; *second
paeonic:* ∪ — ∪ ∪; *third paeonic:* ∪ ∪
— ∪; *fourth paeonic:* ∪ ∪ ∪ —)

Paeon·es -um mpl a people inhabiting
Paeonia

Paeoni·a -ae f Paeonia *(the country N. of
Macedonia)*

paeōni·us -a -um adj healing, medicinal;
herba paeonia peony

Paestān·us -a -um adj of Paestum

Paest·um -ī n town in Lucania in S. Italy,
famous for its roses

paetul·us -a -um adj slightly squint-eyed

paet·us -a -um adj squinting, squint-eyed;

leering **‖ Paetus** m Roman family name
(cognomen)

pāgān·us -a -um adj of a village, rustic;
ignorant **‖** m villager, peasant; *(pej)* yokel

Pagas·a -ae f or **Pagas·ae -ārum** fpl town
on the E. coast of Thessaly from which
the Argo set sail

Pagasae·us -a -um adj Pagasean **‖** m Jason

pāgātim adv by villages, village by village, in every village

pāgell·a -ae f small page or sheet

pāgin·a -ae f page; *(poet)* piece of writing;
in imā paginā at the bottom of the page

pāginul·a -ae f small page or sheet

pāg·us -ī m village; canton, province; country people, villagers

pāl·a -ae f spade

palaestr·a -ae f palestra, wrestling school,
gymnasium; school of rhetoric; rhetorical training; school; wrestling; exercise;
brothel

palaestricē adv as at the palestra

palaestric·us -a -um adj of the palestra,
gymnastic **‖** f gymnastics

palaestrīt·a -ae m wrestling coach; director of a palestra

palam adv openly, publicly, plainly; **palam
esse** to be public, be well known; **palam
facere** to make public, disclose **‖** prep
(w. abl) before, in the presence of, face
to face with

Palātīn·us -a -um adj Palatine; imperial

Palāt·ium -(i)ī n Palatine Hill; palace; a
temple on the Palatine

palāt·um -ī n or **palāt·us -ī** m *(anat)* palate; *(fig)* taste; *(fig)* literary taste

pale·a -ae f chaff

paleār·ia -ium npl dewlap *(fold of skin
that hangs from the neck of a bovine
animal)*

Pal·ēs -is f Italic goddess of shepherds and
flocks

Palīc·ī -ōrum mpl twins sons of Jupiter
and the nymph Thalia

Palīl·is -is -e adj of Pales **‖** npl feast of
Pales *(celebrated April 21)*

palimpsest·um -ī n palimpsest *(parchment
from which writing has been erased and
new writing put on)*

Palinūr·us -ī m pilot of Aeneas who fell
overboard and drowned **‖** promontory
named after Palinurus

paliūr·us or **paliūr·os -ī** mf *(bot)* Christ's
thorn

pall·a -ae f ladies' long outdoor dress
(counterpart of the male's toga); male
outer garment *(restricted to non-Ro-
mans);* tragic actor's costume

pallac·a -ae f concubine

Pallacīn·a -ae f section of Rome near the
Circus Flaminius

Palladi·us -a -um *adj* of Pallas, associated with Pallas Athene *(Minerva)* ‖ *n* statue of Pallas; Palladium *(Trojan statue of Pallas allegedly stolen by Odysseus and said subsequently to have been brought to Rome, since the safety of the city depended on it)*

Pallantē·um -ī *n* city in Arcadia, the home of Pallas ‖ city founded by Evander in Italy where Rome later stood

Pallantē·us -a -um *adj* of Pallas *(great-grandfather of Evander)*

Pall·ās -antis *m* great-grandfather of Evander ‖ son of Evander ‖ son of Pandion and brother of Aegeus ‖ father of Minerva

Pall·as -adis *or* **-ados** *f* Athene; olive oil, oil; olive tree; Palladium *(Trojan statue of Pallas)*

pall·ens -entis *adj* pale; chartreuse, yellowish; sick-looking; dim *(light)*

pall·eō -ēre -uī *intr* to be pale, look pale; to have a pale *(greenish or yellowish)* color; to fade; to be dim; *(w. dat)* to grow pale over, worry about

pall·escō -escĕre -uī *tr* to turn pale at ‖ *intr* to turn pale; to turn yellow; to fade, grow dim

palliāt·us -a -um *adj* wearing a Greek cloak; **fabula palliata** Latin play with Greek setting and characters

pallidul·us -a -um *adj* somewhat pale

pallid·us -a -um *adj* pallid, pale; gray-green, yellow-green, chartreuse

palliolātim *adv* in a mantle

palliolāt·us -a -um *adj* wearing a pallium

palliol·um -ī *n* short cloak; hood

pall·ium -(i)ī *n* pallium *(rectangular material worn mainly by men, esp. Greek men, as an outer garment);* bed cover, couch cover

pall·or -ōris *m* pallor, pale complexion; **pallorem ducere** to turn pale

pallul·a -ae *f* small outer garment *(see* **palla)**

palm·a -ae *f* palm of the hand, hand; palm tree, date; palm branch; palm wreath; palm of victory, first prize; victory; victor *(carrying a palm);* oar, oar blade

palmār·is -is -e *adj* excellent, deserving of the palm *or* prize ‖ *n* masterpiece

palmāri·us -a -um *adj* prize-winning, excellent ‖ *n* masterpiece

palmāt·us -a -um *adj* embroidered with palm-branch design; **tunica palmata** embroidered tunic *(with palm-branch design, worn by a general)*

palm·es -itis *m* vine shoot, vine branch, vine; branch, twig *(of any tree)*

palmēt·um -ī *n* palm grove

palmi·fer -fera -ferum *adj* producing palms, palm-bearing

palmōs·us -a -um *adj* full of palm trees

palmul·a -ae *f* oar blade; date *(fruit of the palm tree)*

pāl·or -ārī -ātus sum *intr* to roam about, wander aimlessly

palpāti·ō -ōnis *f* stroking ‖ *fpl* flatteries

palpāt·or -ōris *m* flatterer

palpebr·a -ae *f* eyelid

palpit·ō -āre -āvī *intr* to throb, palpitate, quiver

palp·ō -āre -āvī -ātus *or* **palp·or -ārī -ātus sum** *tr* to stroke, pat; to wheedle, coax; to flatter ‖ *intr (w. dat)* **1** to coax; **2** to flatter

palp·us -ī *m* palm of the hand; coaxing, flattery

palūdāment·um -ī *n* general's cloak

palūdāt·us -a -um *adj* wearing a general's cloak

palūdōs·us -a -um *adj* swampy

palumb·ēs -is *mf* pigeon, dove

pāl·us -ī *m* stake, post; wooden sword *(used in practice)*

pal·ūs -ūdis *f* swamp, marsh; sedge

palus·ter *(or* **-tris)** **-tris -tre** *adj* swampy, marshy; growing in a swamp; used, *or* located in a swamp ‖ *npl* swamp, marshland

pampine·us -a -um *adj* of vine tendrils, made of vine leaves; **odor pampineus** bouquet of wines

pampin·us -ī *m (f)* vine shoot, tendril; vine leaf; tendril *(of any kind)*

Pā·n -nos *m* Pan *(Greek god of flocks, shepherds, and woods, often identified with Faunus)*

panacē·a -ae *f or* **panac·ēs -is** *mf or* **panac·ēs -is** *n* panacea, cure-all

Panaetōlic·us -a -um *adj* Pan-Aetolian

pānār·ium -(i)ī *n* breadbox; breadbasket; food basket; picnic basket

Panchāï·a -ae *f* region in Arabia famous for its frankincense

panchrest·os -os -on *adj* good for everything, universally useful; **panchreston medicamentum** *(hum)* bribery *(the cure-all medication)*

pancraticē *adv (coll)* fine, splendidly; **pancratice valere** to get along splendidly

pancrat·ium *or* **pancrat·ion -iī** *n* contest which included the skills of boxing and wrestling

Pandar·us -ī *m* famous Lycian archer in the Trojan army ‖ companion of Aeneas, killed by Turnus

pandicul·or -ārī -ātus sum *intr (of a person while yawning)* to stretch

Pandī·ōn -onis *or* **-onos** *m* king of Athens and father of Procne and Philomela

Pandīoni·us -a -um *adj* of Pandion

pan·dō -dĕre -dī -sus *or* **passus** *tr* to spread out, extend, expand, unfold; to open, lay open, throw open; to open up *(a road);* to make *(a place)* accessible, open *(a building); to* reveal, make known, publish; *(mil)* to deploy

pand·us -a -um *adj* curved

pangō pangĕre panxī *or* **pepegī** *or* **pēgī pactus** *tr* to fasten, fix, drive in; to fix, set *(boundaries);* to settle *(a matter);* to agree upon, determine; to write, compose, celebrate, record; to promise in marriage; to provide; **indutias pangere cum** to conclude an armistice with

pānice·us -a -um *adj* made of bread; **milites panicei** *(coll)* Breadville brigade *(humorous coinage applied to bakers)*

pānicul·a -ae *f* tuft

pānic·um -ī *n* Italian millet *(cereal grass, raised for its seed or small grains to be used as food)*

pān·is -is *m* bread; loaf of bread; **panem coquere** to bake bread; **panis cibarius** coarse bread; **panis secundus** stale bread

Pānisc·us -ī *m* little Pan

pannicul·us -ī *m* rag

pannōs·us -a -um *adj* tattered, threadbare; dressed in rags

Pannoni·us -a -um *adj* Pannonian **ǁ** *f* Pannonia *(country of Lower Danube in the area of modern Austria)*

pannūce·us *or* **pannūci·us -a -um** *adj* ragged; shriveled, wrinkled

pann·us -ī *m* patch; rag

Panop·ē -ēs *or* **Panopē·a -ae** *f* a sea nymph

pans·a -ae *adj (masc & fem only)* flatfooted **ǁ Pansa** *m* Roman family name *(cognomen), esp.* Gaius Vibius Pansa *(cos. 43 B.C.)*

pansus *pp of* **pando**

panthēr·a -ae *f* panther

Panthoid·ēs -ae *m* son of Panthus, *(i.e., Euphorbus, a Trojan warrior)*

Panth·us -ī *m* priest of Apollo at Troy and father of Euphorbus

pantic·ēs -um *mpl* guts; sausages

papae *interj (in delight)* great!, wonderful!; *(in pain)* ouch!; *(in astonishment)* wow!

pāp·as -ae *or* **-atis** *m* papa *(baby-talk for pedagogue)*

papāv·er -eris *n (m)* poppy; poppyseed

papāver·us -a -um *adj* of poppies

Paphi·ē -ēs *f* Paphian goddess, Venus; *(poet)* heterosexual love

Paphi·us -a -um *adj* of Paphos

Paph·os -ī *f* town in S.W. Cyprus sacred to Venus **ǁ** *mf* child of Pygmalion

pāpili·ō -ōnis *m* butterfly; moth

papill·a -ae *f* nipple, teat; breast

papp·ō -āre *tr* to eat *(soft food)*

papp·us -ī *m* hairy seed *(of certain plants)*

papul·a -ae *f* pimple

papȳrif·er -era -erum *adj* papyrus-producing

papȳr·us -ī *f or* **papȳr·um -ī** *n* papyrus

pār paris *adj* equal, like, on a par, equally matched, well-matched; suitable, adequate; of equal size; *(w. dat or* **cum)** equal to, comparable to, similar to, as large as; *(w. limiting abl, w.* **ad** *or in +* **acc)** equal, similar, alike in; **par est** it is right, it is proper; **par proelium** even *or* indecisive battle; **ut par est** *(used parenthetically)* as is only right **ǁ** *m* companion; equal, mate, spouse; **pares cum paribus facillime congregantur** *(prov)* birds of a feather flock together **ǁ** *n* pair, couple, the like; **par pari** tit for tat

parābil·is -is -e *adj* available

parasīt·a -ae *f* parasite *(female)*

parasītas·ter -trī *m* poor parasite

parasītāti·ō -ōnis *f* sponging

parasītic·us -a -um *adj* parasitical

parasīt·or -ārī -ātus sum *intr* to be a parasite, sponge, freeload

parasīt·us -ī *m* parasite, sponger, freeloader

parātē *adv* with perparation; carefully; readily, promptly

parāti·ō -ōnis *f* preparing, procuring, acquisition

paratragoed·ō -āre *intr* to talk in the tragic style, be melodramatic, ham it up

parāt·us -a -um *adj* prepared, ready; ready at hand, available; furnished, equipped; learned, well-versed, skilled; *(w. dat or* **ad) 1** ready for; **2** equipped to; *(w. inf)* prepared to, ready to; *(w. abl or in +* **abl)** versed in, experienced in

parāt·us -ūs *m* preparation; equipment, outfit; clothing, apparel; *(food at dinner table)* spread

Parc·a -ae *f* goddess of Fate, Fate

parcē *adv* sparingly, thriftily; moderately, with restraint; stingily; rarely

parcēprōm·us -ī *m* stingy person

parcō parcĕre pepercī parsūrus *tr* to spare, use sparingly **ǁ** *intr* to be sparing, economize; *(w. dat)* **1** to spare, use carefully; **2** to show mercy to, take it easy on; **3** to show consideration for; **4** to abstain from, refrain from; *(w. inf)* to cease to

parc·us -a -um *adj* thrifty, economical, frugal; stingy; moderate, conservative; slight, little, scanty, paltry *(thing given)*

pard·us -ī *m* leopard

pār·ens -entis *adj* obedient, submissive **ǁ** *mpl* subjects

par·ens -entis *m* parent, father; ancestor; grandparent; founder; inventor; **parens patriae** father of one's country **ǁ** *mpl* ancestors **ǁ** *f* parent, mother; mother country; mother city

parentāl·is -is -e *adj* parental; **dies parentalis** memorial day **ǁ** *npl* festival in honor of dead ancestors and relatives

parent·ō -āre -āvī -ātum *intr* to hold a memorial service in honor of dead parents *or* relatives; *(w. dat)* 1 to offer sacrifice to *(the dead)*; 2 to avenge *(dead person with the death of another person)*; 3 to appease, satisfy

pār·eō -ēre -uī -itum *intr* to appear, be visible, be evident, be at hand; *(w. dat)* 1 to obey, be obedient to; 2 to comply with; 3 to be subject to, be subservient to; 4 to yield to, gratify, satisfy *(pleasures, etc.)*; 5 to fulfill *(promises)*

pari·ēs -etis *m* wall *(inner or outer wall of house or other building)*; intra parietes in private, at home, under one's own roof

parietin·ae -ārum *fpl* tumble-down walls; *(lit & fig)* ruins

Parīl·ia -ium *npl* (Palīl-) festival of Pales *(April 21)*

Parīl·is -is -e *adj* (Palīl-) connected with Pales *or* her festival

paril·is -is -e *adj* equal, like; aetas parilis same age, like age

pariō parĕre peperī partus *tr* to bear, bring forth, give birth to; *(of animals)* to produce, spawn, lay *(eggs)*; *(of countries, of the earth)* to produce, be a source of; *(of things)* to give rise to; *(fig)* to create, devise, cause, accomplish; to acquire

Par·is -idis *m* son of Priam and Hecuba ‖ pantomime actor in the reign of Nero ‖ pantomime actor in the reign of Domitian

pariter *adv* equally, in like manner, as well, alike; at the same time, at one and the same time, together; side by side; evenly, uniformly; in equal quantity *or* degree; at once; pariter ac *(or* atque *or* ut) as well as; pariter ac si just as if; pariter cum together with, at the same time as

parit·ō -āre *tr (w. inf)* to get ready to

Par·ium *or* Par·ion -iī *n* town of the Troad near the entrance to the Propontis *(modern Kemer)*

Pari·us -a -um *adj* Parian, of Paros

parm·a -ae *f* small round shield

parmāt·us -a -um *adj* armed with a small, round shield, light-armed

parmul·a -ae *f* small round shield

Parnās·is -idis *or* Parnāsi·us -a -um *adj* of Parnassus, Parnassian

Parnās·us *or* Parnās·os -ī *m* mountain forming the backdrop to Apollo's shrine at Delphi

par·ō -āre -āvī -ātus *tr* to prepare, make ready, provide, furnish; to get, procure, acquire, gather, purchase ‖ *refl* to get ready ‖ *intr* to get ready, make preparations, make arrangements; *(w. dat or* ad) to get ready for

paroch·a -ae *f* room and board *(which provincials had to provide for traveling Roman officials)*

paroch·us -ī *m* official host *(provided accommodations for traveling Roman dignitaries)*

parops·is -idis *f* dish for serving dessert

Par·os *or* Par·us -ī *f* Greek island of the Cyclades, famous for its white marble

parr·a -ae *f* owl

Parrhas·is -idis *or* -idos *f* Arcadian woman; Callisto *(as Ursa Major)*

Parrhasi·us -a -um *adj* Arcadian; Parrhasia virgo Callisto *(as Ursa Major)* ‖ *f* district in Arcadia

parricīd·a -ae *mf* parricide *(murderer of one's parent or close relative)*; assassin of a high magistrate; murderer; traitor, outlaw

parricīd·ium -(i)ī *n* parricide *(murder of a parent or close relative)*; murder; assassination; high treason

par·s -tis *f* part, portion, share, section; fraction; side, direction, region; part, function, duty; part of body, member *(esp. genital organs)*; ab omni parte in every respect; a parte partly; exiguā parte in a slight degree; ex alterā parte on the other hand; ex parte partly; ex eā parte *(or* in eam partem) quatenus to the extent that; in eam partem in that direction; in that sense; in parte *(of* in partem) partly, in part; in such a manner; in parte alicujus rei esse to form part of s.th., be included in s.th.; in pejorem partem rapere to put a worse construction on; in utramque partem in both directions; magnā ex parte to a great degree; major pars populi the majority; maximam partem for the most part; minor pars populi a minority; pars dimidia (tertia, quarta, *etc.*) one half (one-third, one-fourth, *etc.*); pars...pars, pars...alii some...others; pars orationis *(gram)* part of speech; parte in part, partly; pro meā parte to the best of my ability; pro ratā parte in a fixed proportion; pro parte in part, partially; pro parte semissā half and half; pro suā parte *(or* pro virili parte) to the best of one's ability ‖ *fpl* part, role; task, function; character; political party; pieces, fragments; scraps *(esp. of food)*; omnibus partibus in all respects; partes obscenae privates, private parts; per partes *(or* partibus) (so much) at a time, in stages; tres partes three-fourths; tuae partes sunt the task *(or* decision) devolves on you

parsimōni·a -ae *f* parsimony, thrift

Parthā·ōn -onis *m* king of Calydon, the son of Agenor and Epicaste and father of Oeneus

Parthāoni·us -a -um *adj* of Parthaon; Calydonian

parthenic·ē -ēs *f (bot)* chamomile *(plant*

with white flowers, used medicinally and as tea)
Parthenopae·us -ī *m* one of the Seven against Thebes, the son of Meleager and Atalanta
Parthenop·ē -ēs *f* ancient name of Naples *(named after the Siren Parthenope who was supposedly buried there)*
Parthi·a -ae *f* Parthia *(country located S.E. of the Caspian Sea)*
Parthic·us -a -um *adj* Parthian; honorary title of several Roman Emperors
Parth·us -a -um *adj & m* Parthian
partic·eps -ipis *adj (w. gen)* sharing in, taking part in **ǁ** *m* partner, confederate; *(w. gen)* partner in
particip·ō -āre -āvī -ātus *tr* to make *(s.o.)* a partner; to share *(s.th.)*
particul·a -ae *f* bit, particle, grain
partim *adv* partly, in part, to some extent; for the most part; *(w. gen or* **ex**) some of; **partim...partim** some...others, partly...partly
parti·ō -ōnis *f* bringing forth, producing
part·iō -īre -īvī -ītus *or* **part·ior -īrī -ītus sum** *tr* to share; to distribute, apportion, divide
partītē *adv* with proper divisions
partīti·ō -ōnis *f* division, distribution, sharing; classification; *(rhet)* division of a speech
partitūd·ō -inis *f* bearing *(of young)*
partur·iō -īre -īvī *tr* to teem with; to be ready to produce; to bring forth, yield; *(fig)* to brood over **ǁ** *intr* to be in labor
part·us -a -um *pp of* **pario ǁ** *adj* acquired **ǁ** *n* acquisition; gain; store
part·us -ūs *m* giving birth; birth; young, offspring; embryo; *(fig)* beginnings
parum *adv & indecl n* a little, too little, insufficiently; **parum est** it is not enough; **parum habere** to regard as unsatisfactory; **satis eloquentiae sapientiae parum** enough eloquence but too little wisdom
parumper *adv* for a little while, just for a moment
parvit·ās -ātis *f* smallness
parvul·us -a -um *adj* (**-vol-**) tiny; slight, petty; young **ǁ** *n* childhood, infancy; **ab parvulis** from childhood, from infancy
parv·us -a -um *(comp:* minor; *superl:* minimus) *adj* small, little, puny; short; young; brief, short *(time)*; slight; insignificant, unimportant; low, cheap *(price)* **ǁ** *n* a little, trifle; childhood, infancy; **a parvis** *(or* **a parvo**) from childhood, from infancy; **parvi esse** to be of little importance; **parvi facere** *(or* **aestimare** *or* **habere** *or* **ducere**) to think little of, care little for; **parvi pretii** of little worth; **parvi refert** it makes little difference, it matters little;

parvo at a low price; **parvo animo esse** to be small-minded
pasceol·us -ī *m* moneybag
pascō pascěre pāvī pastus *tr* to feed; to be food for; to pasture, keep, raise *(animals); (of land)* to provide food for; to cultivate, cherish; to feed *(fire; flames of passion);* to pile up *(debts);* to grow *(beard);* to lay waste, ravage *(fields);* to use *(land)* as pasturage; to feast *(the eyes, the mind)* **ǁ** **refl & pass** to support oneself; *(w. abl)* to get rich on, grow fat on **ǁ** *pass (of animals)* to graze; to feed; *(w. abl)* **1** to feast on, thrive on; **2** to gloat over **ǁ** *intr* to feed, graze
pascu·us -a -um *adj* grazing, pasture **ǁ** *n* pasture
Pāsipha·ē -ēs *or* **Pāsipha·a -ae** *f* Pasiphaë *(daughter of Helios, sister of Circe, wife of Minos, and mother of Phaedra, Ariadne, and the Minotaur)*
pass·er -eris *m* sparrow; flounder; **passer marinus** ostrich *(because imported from overseas)*
passercul·us -ī *m* little sparrow
passim *adv* here and there; all over the place; at random, without order, indiscriminately
passit·ō -āre *intr (of a starling)* to sing
passīv·us -a -um *adj (gram)* passive
passus *pp of* **pando** *and of* **patior ǁ** *adj* spread out, extended, open; disheveled; *(of grapes and other fruits spread out in the sun)* dried, dry **ǁ** *f* raisin **ǁ** *n* raisin wine
pass·us -ūs *m* step, pace; footstep, track; **mille passūs** thousand paces, a mile; **tria milia passuum** three miles
pastill·us -ī *m* lozenge
pasti·ō -ōnis *f* pasture, grazing
past·or -ōris *m* shepherd
pastōrāl·is -is -e *adj* pastoral
pastōrici·us -a -um *or* **pastōri·us -a -um** *adj* shepherd's, pastoral
pastus *pp of* **pasco**
past·us -ūs *m* the feeding of animals; pasture; fodder, feed
patagiār·ius -(i)ī *m* fringe maker
patagiāt·us -a -um *adj (tunic)* with fringes
Patar·a -ae *f or* **Patar·a -ōrum** *npl* town in Lycia with an oracle of Apollo
Patar·eūs -eī *or* **-eos** *m* Apollo
Patavīn·us -a -um *adj* of Patavium
Patav·ium -(i)ī *n* city in N. Italy, birthplace of Livy *(modern Padua)*
pate·faciō -facěre -fēcī -factus *(pass:* **pate·fīō -fierī)** *tr* to uncover, reveal; to open *(gates, windows, buildings, containers, etc.);* to throw open; to open up, make accessible; to bring to light; to disclose; *(mil)* to deploy; *(mil) (w. dat)* to expose to *(attack)*
patefacti·ō -ōnis *f* disclosure

patell·a -ae *f* pan, dish, plate
pat·ens -entis *adj* open, accessible; extensive; exposed; evident
patentius *adv* more openly; more clearly
pat·eō -ēre -uī *intr* to stand open, be open; to be accessible; to be exposed; to open, stretch out, extend; to be clear, be plain, be well-known; to be attainable, be free; *(of the mind)* to be open, be receptive; *(of wounds)* to gape; **late patere** to have wide application, cover a wide field
pa·ter -tris *m* father; **pater cenae** host; **pater familias** head of the family; **quartus pater** great-great-grandfather **‖** *mpl* forefathers; patricians; senators; **patres conscripti** gentlemen of the Senate
pater·a -ae *f* flat dish, saucer *(used esp. in making libations)*
paterfamiliās patrisfamiliās *m* head of the family
patern·us -a -um *adj* father's, paternal, fatherly; ancestral; of a native country, native
pat·escō -escěre -uī *intr* to be opened, be open; to stretch out, extend; to be disclosed, be divulged, become evident; *(mil)* to be deployed
pathic·us -a -um *adj* lustful
patibil·is -is -e *adj* tolerable; sensitive
patibulāt·us -a -um *adj* fastened to a yoke *or* gibbet, pilloried
patibul·um -ī *n* pillory *(fork-shaped yoke to which criminals were fastened);* fork-shaped gibbet
pati·ens -entis *adj* hardy, tough; hard; stubborn, unyielding; patient, tolerant; *(w. gen or* ad) able to endure, inured to, able to take; **amnis patiens navium** navigable river
patienter *adv* patiently
patienti·a -ae *f* patience, endurance; resignation; submissiveness; sexual submission
patin·a -ae *f* dish, pan
patināri·us -a -um *adj* of pans; in a pan; **strues patinaria** pile of dishes
patior patī passus sum *tr* to experience, undergo, suffer; to put up with, allow; to submit to *(sexually);* **aegre pati** to resent, be displeased with
patrāt·or -ōris *m* perpetrator
patrāt·us -ī *adj (masc only)* **pater patratus** plenipotentiary senator *(sent on a foreign mission)*
patri·a -ae *f* native land, native city, home
patricē *adv* like a patrician
patriciāt·us -ūs *m* status of patrician
patrici·us -a -um *adj & m* patrician
patrimōn·ium -(i)ī *n* patrimony, inheritance
patrim·us -a -um *adj* having a father still living

patriss·ō -āre *intr* to take after one's father
patrīt·us -a -um *adj* father's, inherited from one's father
patri·us -a -um *adj* father's, of a father, fatherly; ancestral; traditional, hereditary; native **‖** *f see* **patria**
patrō -āre *tr* to bring about, effect, achieve, perform; to finish, conclude; **bellum patrare** to bring a war to an end; **jus jurandum patrare** to take an oath *(confirming a treaty);* **pacem patrare** to conclude a peace; **promissa patrare** to fulfill promises **‖** *intr* to reach a sexual climax
patrōcin·ium -(i)ī *n* patronage, protection; legal defense, legal representation
patrōncin·or -ārī -ātus sum *intr* to be a patron, afford protection; *(w. dat)* to serve *(s.o.)* as patron, protect, defend
Patrōcl·us -ī *m* son of Menoetius and friend of Achilles
patrōn·a -ae *f* legal protectress, patroness; defender; safeguard
patrōn·us -ī *m* legal protector, patron; advocate *(in court);* defender
patruēl·is -is -e *adj* on the father's side, cousin's; **frater patruelis** cousin; **soror patruelis** cousin *(female)* **‖** *m* cousin
patru·us -a -um *adj* of a *(paternal)* uncle **‖** *m* father's brother, paternal uncle; **patruus magnus** great-uncle, granduncle
patul·us -a -um *adj* open, standing open; spreading, spread out, broad
pauciloqu·ium -(i)ī *n* reticence
paucit·ās -ātis *f* paucity, scarcity, small number
paucul·ī -ae -a *adj* just a few, very few **‖** *npl* few words
pauc·i -ae -a *adj* few **‖** *pron masc pl* few, a few; the select, elite; **inter paucos** *(or* **in paucas** *or* **in paucis)** *(in connection with an adj)* among a few, especially, unusually, uncommonly **‖** *pron neut pl* a few things, a few words; **paucis** in a few words, briefly
paul(l)ātim *adv* little by little, gradually, by degrees; a few at a time
paul(l)isper *adv* for a little while
paul(l)ō *adv (as abl of degree of difference in comparisons)* a little, somewhat; **paulo ante** a little earlier; **paulo post** a little later
paul(l)ulō *adv* somewhat, a little; cheaply, at a low price
paul(l)ulum *adv* somewhat, a little
paul(l)ul·us -a -um *adj* very little **‖** *n* very little, a bit; **paullulum pecuniae** a bit of money, very little money
paul(l)um *adv* a little, to some extent
paul(l)·us -a -um *adj* small, little **‖** *n* a bit, trifle; **post paulum** after a bit

Paul(l)·us -ī *m* Lucius Aemilius Paulus Macedonicus *(conqueror of Macedonia at Pydna in 168 B.C.)*

paup·er -eris *adj* poor *(financially)*; scanty, meager; *(w. gen)* poor in **ǁ** *mf* pauper

paupercul·us -a -um *adj* poor little

pauperi·ēs -ēī *f* poverty

pauper·ō -āre -āvī -ātus *tr* to impoverish; *(w. abl)* to rob *(s.o.)* of

paupert·ās -ātis *f* poverty

paus(s)·a -ae *f* pause, intermission, stop, end; **pausam dare** *(or* **facere)** to make a pause, take a break; **pausam facere** *(w. dat)* put an end to

pauxillātim *adv* little by little

pauxillisper *adv* bit by bit

pauxillulum *adv* a little, a bit **ǁ** *n (w. gen)* a bit of

pauxillul·us -a -um *adj* tiny

pauxill·us -a -um *adj* very little, tiny **ǁ** *n* small amount

pavefact·us -a -um *adj* frightened

paveō pavēre pāvī *tr* to be scared of, be terrified at **ǁ** *intr* to be terrified, tremble with fear

pavesc·ō -ěre *tr* to get scared of **ǁ** *intr* to begin to be alarmed

pāvī *perf of* **pasco** *and of* **paveo**

pavidē *adv* in panic

pavid·us -a -um panicky, alarmed, trembling with fear, startled; with beating heart, nervous; causing alarm

pavīment·ō -āre *tr* to pave

pavīment·um -ī *n* pavement; floor

pav·iō -īre -īvī *or* **-iī -ītus** *tr* to strike, beat

pavit·ō -āre *tr* to be panicky over **ǁ** *intr* to quake with fear, be scared to death; to shiver *(w. fever)*

pāv·ō -ōnis *or* **pāv·us -ī** *m* peacock

pav·or -ōris *m* panic, terror, dread; dismay; quaking, shivering; **pavorem injicere** *(w. dat)* to strike terror into

pax pācis *f* peace; peace treaty; reconciliation; compact, agreement; harmony, tranquility; favor, pardon *(from the gods);* **cum bona pace** with full consent; **pace tuā** with your leave, with your permission

pax *interj* quiet, enough!

pecc·ans -antis *m* offender, sinner

peccāt·um -ī *n* fault, mistake, slip; moral offense, sin

pecc·ō -āre -āvī -ātum *intr* to make a mistake, blunder; to make a slip in speaking; to be wrong; to sin

pecorōs·us -a -um *adj* rich in cattle

pect·en -inis *m* comb; plectrum; rake; pubic bone; pubic region; scallop *(as seafood)*

pectō pectěre pex(u)ī pexus *or* **pexitus** *tr* to comb; to card *(wool); (hum)* to thrash

pect·us -oris *n* breast; chest; heart, feeling; soul, conscience; mind, understanding; person, character; **toto pectore** heart and soul

pecū *(gen not in use; pl:* **pecua)** *n* flock, herd **ǁ** *npl* farm animals; cattle; pastures

pecuāri·us -a -um *adj* **(pequ-)** of sheep, of cattle; **res pecuaria** livestock **ǁ** *m* cattleman, cattle breeder, rancher **ǁ** *f* livestock **ǁ** *npl* herds of cattle, herds of sheep

pecūlāt·or -ōris *m* embezzler

pecūlāt·us -ūs *m* **(peq-)** embezzlement

pecūliār·is -is -e one's own, as one's own private property; special; exceptional, singular

pecūliāriter *adv* specially

pecūliāt·us -a -um *adj* well off

pecūli·ō -āre -āvī -ātus *tr* to provide with personal property

pecūl·ium -(i)ī *n* personal property *or* savings *(of a slave or a son under his father's control)*

pecūni·a -ae *f* money; property, possessions

pecūniāri·us -a -um *adj* pecuniary, financial, money

pecūniōs·us -a -um *adj* rich, well-off; profitable

pec·us -oris *n* cattle, herd, flock; sheep; head of cattle; livestock; **pecus equinum** stud; *(pej)* cattle

pec·us -udis *f* head of cattle; beast; sheep; domestic animal; land animal *(as opposed to birds and fish); (pej)* brute, beast, swine

pedāl·is -is -e *adj* one-foot-long

pedār·ius -(i)ī *m* senator of lower standing *(who lets others step all over him)*

pedāt·us -ūs *m* one of the three formal stages in issuing an ultimatum

ped·es -itis *m* infantryman, footsoldier; pedestrian; **equites peditesque** all Roman citizens

pedes·ter *or* **pedes·tris -tris -tre** *adj* infantry; pedestrian; on land, by land; written in prose; prosaic, plain

pedetem(p)tim *adv* by feeling one's way, step by step, slowly, cautiously

pedic·a -ae *f* foot chain, fetter; trap, snare

pedīculōs·us -a -um *adj* lousy

pēd·is -is *mf* louse

pedisequ·a -ae *f* attendant, handmaid

pedisequ·us -ī *m* attendant

peditastell·us -ī *m* poor infantryman

peditāt·us -ūs *m* infantry

pēdit·um -ī *n (vulg)* fart

Pedi·us -a -um *adj* name of a Roman clan *(nomen) (esp. Quintus Pedius, Caesar's nephew);* **lex Pedia** law providing a trial for Caesar's murderers

pēd·ō pēděre pepēdī pēditum *intr (vulg)* to fart

Ped·ō -ōnis *m* Roman family name *(cog-*

nomen), *esp.* Albinovanus Pedo, a poet and friend of Ovid

ped·um -ī *n* shepherd's crook

Pēgas·us *or* **Pēgasēï·us -a -um** *adj* of Pegasus, Pegasean

Pēgas·is -idis *or* **-idos** *adj (fem only)* of Pegasus *(with reference to Hippocrene)* ‖ *f* fountain nymph ‖ *fpl* Muses

Pēgas·us *or* **Pegas·os -ī** *m* winged horse that sprang from the blood of Medusa

pegm·a -atis *n* bookcase; scaffold

pējerātiuncul·a -ae *f* petty oath

pējerāt·us -a -um *adj* (-jūr-) offended by false oaths; **jus pejeratum** false oath

pējer·ō -āre -āvī -ātus *tr* (-jūr-) to swear falsely by ‖ *intr* to swear a false oath; *(coll)* to lie

pējerōs·us -a -um *adj* (-jūr-) perjured

pēj·or -or -us *(comp of* **malus***) adj* worse

pējus *(comp of* **male***) adv* worse

pelagi·us -a -um *adj* of the sea

pelag·us -ī *n* sea, open sea

pēlam·is -idis *or* **pēlam·ys -ydis** *f* young tuna fish

Pelasg·ī -ōrum *mpl* aborigines of Greece; *(poet)* certain early inhabitants of Italy; *(poet)* Greeks *(opp:* Trojans); *(poet)* Argives *(opp:* Thebans)

Pēl·eüs -eī *or* **-eos** *m* king of Thessaly, son of Aeacus, husband of Thetis, and father of Achilles

Pēli·a -adis *adj (fem only)* of Mt. Pelion

Pēli·as -adis *adj (fem only)* of Mt. Pelion, from Mt. Pelion

Peli·ās -ae *m* king of Iolcos in Thessaly and uncle of Jason

Pēlīd·ēs -ae *m* descendant of Peleus; Achilles; Neoptolemus

Pēl·ion -(i)ī *n* mountain in E. Thessaly

Pēli·us *or* **Pēliac·us -a -um** *adj* of Mt. Pelion

Pell·a -ae *or* **Pell·ē -ēs** *f* Pella *(city in Macedonia, birthplace of Alexander the Great)*

pellāci·a -ae *f* charm, allurement

Pellae·us -a -um *adj* of *or* from Pella; **Pellaeus juvenis** Alexander

pell·ax -ācis *adj* seductive, alluring

pellecti·ō -ōnis *f* perusal

pel·liciō -licĕre -lexī *or* **licuī -lectus** *tr* to captivate, allure, entice, coax

pellicul·a -ae *f* small *or* thin hide, skin

pelli·ō -ōnis *m* furrier

pell·is -is *f* skin, hide; leather; felt; tent; shield cover; **detrahere pellem** to expose one's true character *(literally, to take off one's hide);* **ossa ac pellis** mere skin and bones

pellīt·us -a -um *adj* clothed in skins; wearing a leather coat

pellō pellĕre pepulī pulsus *tr* to push, beat, strike, knock; to beat *(drum, chest);* to knock at *(door);* thrust, to drive, im-

pel; to rouse, stimulate; to drive away, eject, expel; to banish; to repel, drive back, rout; to strum *(lyre, etc.);* to affect, impress, strike; to stomp *(the earth)*

pelluc- = perluc-

Pelopēï·as -ados *or* **Pelopē·us -a -um** *adj* Pelopian, of Pelops; Mycenaean; Phrygian

Pelopē·is -idos *f* descendant of Pelops *(female)*

Pelopid·ae -ārum *mpl* descendants of Pelops

Peloponnens·is -is -e *adj* (-nnēs-) Peloponnesian

Peloponnēsiac·us *or* **Peloponnēsi·us -a -um** *adj* Peloponnesian

Peloponnēs·us *or* **Peloponnēs·os -ī** *f* Peloponnesus *(modern Morea)*

Pel·ops -opis *m* son of Tantalus, father of Atreüs and Thyestes, and grandfather of Agamemnon and Menelaüs

pelōr·is -idos *m* large mussel

Pelōr·us *or* **Pelōr·os -ī** *m* N.E. promontory of Sicily

pelt·a -ae *f* small leather shield

peltast·a -ae *m* soldier armed with a small leather shield

peltāt·us -a -um *adj* armed with a small leather shield

Pēlūs·ium -(i)ī *n* city on the E. mouth of the Nile

pelv·is -is *f* basin, shallow bowl

penāri·us -a -um *adj* for storing food; **cella penaria** pantry

Penāt·ēs -ium *mpl* Penates, household gods; Penates of the State; hearth; house; home *(also applied to a nest, a hive, a temple)*

penātig·er -era -erum *adj* carrying the houshold gods

pendeō pendēre pependī *intr* to hang (down), be suspended; to hang loose; to be flabby; to be weak; to be in suspense, be uncertain, hesitate; to hang around, loiter; to hang in the air, hover, float; to overhang; *(of plants)* to droop; *(w. abl or* **ab, de,** *or* **ex** + *abl)* **1** to hang down from, hang by; **2** to depend on, be dependent upon; **3** to be based on, hinge on; **4** to result from; **5** to hang onto; *(w.* **in** + *abl)* to be poised on, hover in, hover over; **animi pendere** to be in suspense, be perplexed; **pendere ab ore** *(w. gen)* to hang on *(s.o.'s)* words, listen with rapt attention to; **pendere ex vultu** *(w. gen)* to gaze intently at *(s.o.'s)* face

pendō pendĕre pependī pensus *tr* to weigh, weigh out; to pay, pay out; to ponder, consider, value, esteem; **flocci pendere** to think little of; **magni (parvi) pendere** to think much (little) of; **poenas pendere** to pay the penalty; **supplicia pendere** to suffer punishment

pendul·us -a -um *adj* hanging, hanging down; doubtful, uncertain

Pēnē·is -idos *or* **Pēnēj·us -a -um** *adj* of the Peneus River *(in Thessaly)*

Pēnelop·a -ae *or* **Pēnelop·ē -ēs** *f* Penelope *(daughter of Icarius and Periboea and wife of Ulysses)*

penes *prep (w. acc of person only)* in the possession of, in the power of, belonging to, resting with; at the house of, with; **penes se esse** to be in one's senses, be in one's right mind

penetrābil·is -is -e *adj* penetrating, piercing; penetrable

penetr·āl·e -is *n see* **penetralis**

penetrāl·is -is -e *adj* penetrating, piercing; inner, internal, interior **ǁ** *n* inner part, inmost recess *(of a building);* inner shrine *(of a temple);* shrine of the Penates; house, home **ǁ** *npl* the interior, center; inner chambers; sanctuary; *(geog)* the interior, hinterlands

penetr·ō -āre -āvī -ātus *tr* to penetrate, enter; to cross *(river);* **pedem penetrare intra** *(w. acc)* to set foot inside **ǁ** *refl* to go; **foras se penetrare** to go outside **ǁ** *intr* to penetrate, enter; *(w. ad)* to go as far as, go all the way to, reach, gain entrance to; *(w. in + acc)* to enter, penetrate

Pēnē·us *or* **Pēnī·os -ī** *m* the Peneüs River *(largest river in Thessaly)* **ǁ** river god, the father of Cyrene and Daphne

pēnicill·us -ī *m or* **pēnicill·um -ī** *n* paint brush; sponge

pēnicul·us -ī *m* brush; sponge

pēn·is -is *m* tail; penis; lechery

penitē *adv* deep down inside

penitus *adv* internally, inside, deep within, deeply; from within; thoroughly, through and through; heartily

penit·us -a -um *adj* inner, inward

penn·a -ae *f* feather; wing; flight

pennāt·us -a -um *adj* feathered

pennig·er -era -erum *adj* winged, feathered

pennipot·ens -entis *adj* able to fly

pennul·a -ae *f* little wing

pensil·is -is -e *adj* hanging; supported on arches; suspended in mid-air

pensi·ō -ōnis *f* payment *(esp. by installments),* installment; rent money; compensation

pensit·ō -āre -āvī -ātus *tr* to pay; to weigh, ponder, consider **ǁ** *intr* to be taxable

pens·ō -āre -āvī -ātus *tr* to weigh out; to weigh, ponder, consider, examine; to compare, contrast; to pay; to atone for; to repay, compensate, requite

pens·um -ī *n* work quota; duty, task; consideration, scruple; **nihil pensi habere** *(or* **ducere)** to have no scruples; **pensi esse** *(w. dat)* to be of value to, be of

importance to; **pensi habere** *(or* **ducere)** to value, consider of importance

pensus *pp of* **pendo**

pentēr·is -is *f* galley, quinquereme

Penthesilē·a -ae *f* Amazon warrior queen, killed by Achilles at Troy

Penth·eūs -eī *or* **-eos** *m* king of Thebes, son of Echion and Agave, grandson of Cadmus

pen·um -ī *n or* **pen·us -ūs** *f (m) or* **pen·us -oris** *n* food, provisions *(in the pantry)*

pēnūri·a -ae *f* want, need, dearth

pen·us -ūs *f (m) see* **penum**

pependī *perf of* **pendeo** *and of* **pendo**

pepercī *perf of* **parco**

peperī *perf of* **pario**

pepl·um -ī *n or* **pepl·us -ī** *m* robe for the statue of Athena

pepulī *perf of* **pello**

per *prep (w. acc) (of space)* through; all over *(an area, space),* throughout; along *(a linear direction); (of time)* through, during, for, in the course of, over a period of; *(of agency)* through, by, by means of, at the hands of; *(of means or manner)* through, by, under pretense of; *(w. refl pron)* for one's *or* its own sake, on its own account, by: **multiplicare VI per IIII fit XXIIII** multiplying 6 by 4 gives 24; **per causam** on the grounds *(that);* **per manūs tradere** to pass from hand to hand; **per me** as far as I am concerned; **per me stat** it is due to me *(that),* it is my fault *(that);* **per omnia** in all respects, throughout; **per speciem** on the pretext *(of);* **per omnes deos jurare** to swear by all the gods; **per se** in itself, by itself *(or* himself, herself, *etc.);* **per tempus** at the right time; **per Tiberim** along the Tiber

per- *pref* conveying the idea of: **1** through: **perfringere** to break through; **2** intensive force: **perfacile** very easy; **3** throughly, to the end: **perficere** to complete; **perlegere** to read through to the end; **perdomare** to tame thoroughly; **4** of going in the wrong direction: **pervertere** to turn the wrong way; **perfidia** treachery *(a trust, gone in the wrong direction)*

-per *advl suf* denoting the duration or the number of times, *e.g.:* **paulisper** for a little while

pēr·a -ae *f* pouch *(bag slung over the shoulder for carrying the day's provisions)*

perabsurd·us -a -um *adj* completely absurd

peraccommodāt·us -a -um *adj* very convenient

perā·cer -cris -cre *adj* very sharp

peracerb·us -a -um *adj* very harsh, very sour

peracesc·ō -ěre *intr* to turn completely sour

peracti·ō -ōnis f conclusion; last act *(of a play)*
peractus pp of **perago**
peracūtē adv very acutely
peracūt·us -a -um adj very sharp; very clear *(voice, intellect)*
peradulesc·ens -entis adj very young
peradulescentul·us -ī m very young man
peraequē adv quite equally, uniformly; in all cases, invariably; **omnes peraeque** all alike
peragit·ō -āre -āvī -ātus tr to harass
per·agō -agĕre -ēgī -actus tr to carry through to the end, complete, accomplish; to pierce; to travel through; to harass, disturb, trouble; to describe, relate, go over; to work, till, cultivate *(the soil);* to fulfill *(hopes, promises);* to live out *(a period of time);* to come to the end of *(of period of time);* to treat *(a subject)* thoroughly; to use up *(resources);* to deliver *(a speech); (leg)* to prosecute to a conviction; **partes peragere** to play the part
peragrāti·ō -ōnis f traveling
peragr·ō -āre -āvī -ātus tr to travel through, travel, traverse **||** intr *(fig)* to spread, penetrate
peram·ans -antis adj *(w. gen)* very fond of
peramanter adv very lovingly
perambul·ō -āre -āvī -ātus tr to walk through; to walk about in; to travel about in, tour
peramīcē adv in a very friendly way
peram·ō -āre -āvī -ātus tr to show a great liking for
peramoen·us -a -um adj very pleasant, very charming
perampl·us -a -um adj very large; very spacious
perangustē adv very narrowly
perangust·us -a -um adj very narrow
perantīqu·us -a -um adj very ancient, very old
perapposit·us -a -um adj very suitable, very appropriate
perardu·us -a -um adj very difficult
perargūt·us -a -um adj very clear; very sharp, very witty
perarmāt·us -a -um adj heavily armed
perar·ō -āre -āvī -ātus tr to plow through; to furrow; to write on *(a wax tablet);* to inscribe
pērātim adv bag by bag
perattentē adv very attentively
peraudiend·us -a -um adj that must be heard to the end
perbacch·or -ārī -ātus sum tr to carouse through *(e.g., the night)*
perbeāt·us -a -um adj very happy
perbellē adv very prettily
perbene adv very well

perbenevol·us -a -um adj very friendly, very well-disposed
perbenignē adv very kindly
perbib·ō -ĕre -ī tr to drink up, drink in, imbibe
perbīt·ō -ĕre intr to perish, die
perbland·us -a -um adj very attractive, very charming
perbon·us -a -um adj very good, excellent
perbrev·is -is -e adj very short, very brief; **perbrevi** *(or* **perbrevi tempore)** in a very short time
perbreviter adv very briefly
perc·a -ae f perch *(fish)*
percalefact·us -a -um adj warmed through and through
percal·escō -escĕre -uī intr to become quite hot
percall·escō -escĕre -uī tr to become thoroughly versed in **||** intr to become very hardened
percār·us -a -um adj very dear; very costly
percaut·us -a -um adj very cautious
percelebr·ō -āre -āvī -ātus tr to make widely known **||** pass to be quite famous
percel·er -eris -ere adj very rapid
perceleriter adv very rapidly
per·cellō -cellĕre -culī -culsus tr to knock down, beat down, overthrow; to scare to death; to ruin; to send scurrying; *(lit & mil)* to hit hard
percens·eō -ēre -uī tr to count up; to review, survey; to travel all through *(a country)*
percepti·ō -ōnis f comprehension; reaping, harvesting **||** fpl concepts
percept·us -a -um pp of **percipio ||** n rule, principle
percī·dō -dĕre -dī -sus tr to smash to pieces
perci·eō -ēre or **perc·iō -īre -īvī** or **-iī -ītus** tr to stir up, set in motion; to excite
per·cipiō -cipĕre -cēpī -ceptus tr to get a good hold of; to catch; to occupy, seize; to gather in, harvest, reap; *(of the senses)* to take in, perceive, feel; *(of feelings)* to get hold of, get the better of, come over *(s.o.);* to learn, know, comprehend, perceive
percit·us -a -um pp of **percieo** and of **percio ||** adj aroused, provoked; impetuous, excitable
percoctus pp of **percoquo**
percol·ō -āre -āvī -ātus tr to strain, filter
percol·ō -colĕre -coluī -cultus tr to reverence, revere, worship; to beautify; to crown, complete
percōm·is -is -e adj very courteous
percommodē adv very conveniently; very well; very suitably
percommod·us -a -um adj very convenient, very comfortable; very suitable
percontāti·ō -ōnis f thorough investigation

percontāt·or -ōris *m* inquisitive fellow; interrogator
percont·or -ārī -ātus sum *tr* to question, investigate, interrogate; *(w. double acc)* to ask *(s.o. s.th.)*
percontum·ax -ācis *adj* very defiant
per·coquō -quĕre -xī -ctus *tr* to cook thoroughly; to heat thoroughly; to ripen; to scorch, blacken
percrēb(r)·escō -escĕre -uī *tr* to become widespread; to get to be widely believed
percrep·ō -āre -uī *intr* to resound, ring
percruci·or -ārī -ātus sum *intr* to be tormented
perculsus *pp of* **percello**
percult·us -a -um *pp of* **percolō** ‖ *adj* decked out; *(coll)* all dolled up
percupid·us -a -um *adj (w. gen)* very fond of
percup·iō -ĕre -īī -ītus *tr* to desire greatly; *(w. inf)* to be very eager to, be dying to
percūriōs·us -a -um *adj* very curious
percūr·ō -āre -āvī -ātus *tr* to treat successfully, heal
percurrō percurrĕre per(cu)currī percursus *tr* to run through, run along, run over, pass over, speed over; *(fig)* to scan briefly, look over; *(in a speech)* to treat in succession, go over, run over; *(of feelings)* to run through, penetrate, pierce ‖ *intr* to run fast, hurry along; *(w. ad)* to dash to; *(w. per + acc)* **1** to run through *or* across, travel through; **2** *(fig)* to run through, mention quickly, treat in succession
percursāti·ō -ōnis *f* traveling; a tour
percursi·ō -ōnis *f* quick survey
percurs·ō -āre -āvī -ātum *tr & intr* to roam about
percussi·ō -ōnis *f* hitting, striking; snapping *(of fingers); (mus)* beat, time
percuss·or -ōris *m* assassin
percussus *pp of* **percutio**
percuss·us -ūs *m* impact; striking
percu·tiō -tĕre -ssī -ssus *tr* to beat *or* hit hard; to strike *(w. lightning, sword, etc.); (of snakes)* to bite; to knock at *(door);* to strum *(lyre, etc.);* to smash; to pierce, stab, run through; to shoot; to kill; to shock, make a deep impression on; to astound; to dig *(ditch);* to coin *(money);* to trick, cheat; **fusti percutere** to beat to death; **securi percutere** to behead
perdecōr·us -a -um *adj* very pretty
perdēlīr·us -a -um *adj* very silly, quite irrational; quite crazy
perdeps·ō -ĕre -uī *tr* to knead thoroughly; *(sl)* to feel up *(sexually)*
Perdiccās -ae *m* founder of the Macedonian monarchy ‖ Perdiccas II, King of Macedonia from 454 to 413 B.C. ‖ Perdiccas III *(d. 359 B.C.)* ‖ distinguished general of Alexander the Great *(d. 321 B.C.)*

perdifficil·is -is -e *adj* very difficult
perdifficiliter *adv* with great difficulty
perdign·us -a -um *adj (w. abl)* quite worthy of
perdīlig·ens -entis *adj* very diligent, very conscientious
perdīligenter *adv* very diligently, very conscientiously
per·discō -discĕre -didicī *tr* to learn thoroughly, learn by heart
perdisertē *adv* very eloquently
perditē *adv* recklessly, desperately
perdit·or -ōris *m* destroyer
perdit·us -a -um *adj* ruined, done-for; degenerate; infamous; reckless, incorrigible, hopeless; lost
perdit·us -ūs *m* ruination
perdiū *adv* for a very long time
perdiūturn·us -a -um *adj* protracted, long-lasting
perdīv·es -itis *adj* very rich
perd·ix -īcis *mf* partridge ‖ **Perdix** Perdix, nephew of Daedalus, who was changed into a partridge
per·dō -dĕre -didī -ditus *tr* to wreck, ruin, destroy; to waste, squander; to lose; **perdere operam** to waste one's efforts
perdoc·eō -ēre -uī -tus *tr* to teach thoroughly
perdoctē *adv* very skillfully
perdoct·us -a -um *pp of* **perdoceo** ‖ *adj* very learned, very skillful
perdol·eō -ēre -uī -itum *intr* to be annoyed; to be a cause of annoyance
perdolesc·ō -ĕre *intr* to become hurt, become annoyed
perdom·ō -āre -uī -itus *tr* to tame completely, subdue, subjugate
perdormisc·ō -ĕre *intr* to sleep on, keep on sleeping
perdū·cō -ĕre -xī -ctus *tr* to lead, guide *(to a destination);* to bring *(to court); (of roads)* to lead *(to); (of a pimp)* to take *(s.o.)* to *(s.o. else's bed);* to cover, spread; to prolong, drag out; to induce; to seduce; *(w. ad)* **1** to lead, guide, escort to; **2** to build, run *(wall, ditch, road, etc.)* to; **3** to prolong, drag out, continue *(s.th.)* to *or* until; **4** to win over to, convince of
perduct·ō -āre -āvī -ātus *tr* to lead, guide
perduct·or -ōris *m* guide; pimp
perdūdum *adv* long long ago
perduelli·ō -ōnis *f* treason
perduell·is -is *m* enemy
perdūr·ō -āre -āvī -ātum *intr* to last, hold out
per·edō -edĕre -ēdī -ēsus *tr* to eat up, devour; *(of things)* to eat away
peregī *perf of* **perago**
peregrē *adv* abroad, away from home; from abroad; **peregre abire** *(or* **peregre exire)** to go abroad
peregrīn·a -ae *f* foreign woman

peregrīnābund·us -a -um *adj* traveling around, touring

peregrīnāti·ō -ōnis *f* living abroad; foreign travel, touring; *(of animals)* roaming, ranging

peregrīnāt·or -ōris *m* traveler *(abroad)*, tourist

peregrīnit·ās -ātis *f* foreign manners, outlandish ways; alien status

peregrīn·or -ārī -ātus sum *intr* to live abroad; to travel abroad; *(fig)* to be a stranger

peregrīn·us -a -um *adj* foreign; strange; alien, exotic; outlandish; *(fig)* strange; *(fig)* inexperienced; **amores peregrini** love affairs with foreign women; **praetor peregrinus** praetor who tried cases involving disputes between foreigners and Roman citizens; **terror peregrinus** fear of a foreign enemy ‖ *mf* foreigner, alien

perēleg·ans -antis *adj* very elegant

perēleganter *adv* very elegantly

perēloqu·ens -entis *adv* very eloquent

peremn·is -is -e *adj* **auspicia peremnia** auspices taken before crossing a river

peremptus *pp of* **perimo**

perendiē *adv* the day after tomorrow

perendin·us -a -um *adj* **dies perendinus** the day after tomorrow

perenn·is -is -e *adj* perennial, continual, everlasting

perenniserv·os -ī *m* slave for life

perennit·ās -ātis *f* continuance, perpetuity

perenn·ō -āre *intr* to last

pērenticīd·a -ae *m (hum)* purse snatcher

per·eō -īre -iī -itum *intr* to pass away, pass on, die; to go to waste, perish, be destroyed; to be lost, be ruined, be undone; to be desperately in love, pine away; *(of snow)* to melt away; *(of iron)* to rust away; **perii!** *(coll)* I'm finished!, I'm washed up!

perequit·ō -āre -āvī -ātus *tr* to ride through *(on horseback)* ‖ *intr* to ride around *(on horseback)*

pererr·ō -āre -āvī -ātus *tr* to roam around, wander through; to survey, look *(s.o.)* over ‖ *intr* to roam all around

perērudīt·us -a -um *adj* very learned, erudite

perēsus *pp of* **peredo**

perexcels·us -a -um *adj* very high up

perexiguē *adv* very sparingly

perexigu·us -a -um *adj* tiny; insignificant; very short *(day)*

perexpedīt·us -a -um *adj* readily available

perfacētē *adv* very wittily

perfacēt·us -a -um *adj* very witty

perfacile *adv* very easily

perfacil·is -is -e *adj* very easy

perfamiliār·is -is -e *adj* very close, intimate ‖ *mf* very close friend

perfectē *adv* completely; perfectly

perfecti·ō -ōnis *f* completion; perfection

perfect·or -ōris *m* perfecter; **dicendi perfector** stylist

perfect·us -a -um *pp of* **perficio** ‖ *adj* complete, finished; perfect; *(gram)* perfect; **praeteritum perfectum** perfect tense

per·ferō -ferre -tulī -lātus *tr* to carry through; to endure to the end, bear with patience, put up with; to drive home *(a weapon)*; to deliver *(message)*, bring news of; to cause *(news)* to reach; to keep up *(an attitude, activity)* to the end; *(of things)* to be capable of accommodating; *(pol)* to get *(a law)* passed

per·ficiō -ficĕre -fēcī -fectus *tr* to complete, finish, bring to an end; to accomplish, carry out, execute; to perfect; to cause; *(w. ut, ne)* to bring it about (that, that not)

perfic·us -a -um *adj* that completes *or* perfects

perfidē *adv* dishonestly

perfidēl·is -is -e *adj* completely trustworthy

perfidi·a -ae *f* treachery, perfidy

perfidiōsē *adv* treacherously

perfidiōs·us -a -um *adj* treacherous, false

perfid·us -a -um *adj* treacherous, false; untrustworthy, dishonest, sneaky ‖ *m* a sneak

perfī·gō -gĕre -xī -xus *tr* to pierce

perflābil·is -is -e *adj* airy; invisible

perflāgitiōs·us -a -um *adj* utterly disgraceful

perflāt·us -ūs *m* draft

perfl·ō -āre -āvī -ātus *tr* to blow across, blow through; to blow throughout *(a period)* ‖ *intr* to blow hard, blow continuously

perfluctu·ō -āre -āvī -ātus *tr* to surge through

perflu·ō -ĕre -xī -xus *intr* to flow along; to leak all over; *(w. per)* to flow through

per·fodiō -fodĕre -fōdī -fossus *tr* to dig through; to pierce, stab

perfor·ō -āre -āvī -ātus *tr* to bore through, pierce; to make by boring

perfortiter *adv* very bravely

perfoss·or -ōris *m* borer; **parietum perfossor** burglar *(literally, one who bores through walls)*

perfossus *pp of* **perfodio**

perfractus *pp of* **perfringo**

perfrem·ō -ĕre *intr* to snort loud

perfrequ·ens -entis *adj* very crowded, overcrowded

perfric·ō -āre -uī -tus *or* **-ātus** *tr* to rub hard, rub all over; **os perfricare** to rub away blushes, put on a bold front

perfrīgefac·iō -ĕre *tr (fig)* to send a chill over, make shudder

per·frīgescō perfrīgescĕre perfrixī perfrictum *intr* to become chilled; to catch a bad cold

perfrīgid·us -a -um *adj* ice-cold

per·fringō -fringĕre -frēgī -fractus *tr* to break through; to break into; to break to pieces, smash; to break down *(a door); (fig)* to break up *(conspiracy); (fig)* to break *(the law); (med)* to fracture

per·fruor -fruī -fructus sum *intr (w. abl)* 1 to enjoy fully; 2 to perform gladly

perfug·a -ae *m* military deserter; political turncoat; refugee

per·fugiō -fugĕre -fūgī *intr (w. ad or in + acc)* 1 to flee to for refuge; 2 to desert to; 3 to have recourse to

perfug·ium -(i)ī *n* place of refuge, shelter, sanctuary; way of escape; *(fig)* an escape; excuse, defense; means of protection *or* safety

perfuncti·ō -ōnis *f* performance, performing, discharge

perfunctus *pp of* **perfungor**

per·fundō -fundĕre -fūdī -fūsus *tr* to drench, bathe; to flood; to sprinkle; to dye; *(of river)* to flow through; *(of sun)* to drench *(w. light, color); (fig)* to fill, steep, inspire ‖ *refl & pass* to bathe, take a bath

perfun·gor -gī -ctus sum *tr* to enjoy ‖ *intr (w. abl)* 1 to perform, discharge, fulfill; 2 to endure, undergo; 3 to get rid of; 4 to be finished with, be done with; 5 to enjoy

perfur·ō -ĕre *intr* to rage wildly, rage on and on

perfūsus *pp of* **perfundo**

Pergam·a -ōrum *npl or* **Pergam·um -ī** *n* Pergamum *(citadel of Troy),* Troy

Pergame·us -a -um *adj* Trojan ‖ *f* Pergamea *(name given by Aeneas to his city on Crete)* ‖ *mpl* Trojans

Pergam·os -ī *f or* **Pergam·um -ī** *n or* **Pergam·on -ī** *n* Pergamum *(city of Mysia famous for its library and temple of Aesculapius)*

pergaud·eō -ēre *intr* to be very glad

pergn·oscō -oscĕre -ōvī *tr* to be well-acquainted with

per·gō -gĕre -rexī -rectus *tr* to go on interruptedly with, continue; *(w. inf)* to continue to; **iter pergere** to go on one's way ‖ *intr* to go straight on, continue, proceed; *(w. ad)* 1 to make one's way toward; 2 to pass on to, proceed to *(esp. a topic);* **perge modo!** go on now!, now get going!

pergraec·or -ārī *intr (coll)* to go completely Greek, have a ball

pergrand·is -is -e *adj* very large, huge; **pergrandis natu** very old

pergraphic·us -a -um *adj* perfectly drawn

pergrāt·us -a -um *adj* very pleasant ‖ *n*

distinct pleasure; **pergratum mihi feceris si** you would be doing me a very great favor if

pergrav·is -is -e *adj* very heavy; very important; very impressive

pergraviter *adv* very seriously

pergul·a -ae *f* open porch *(used for business, as a school, as a brothel)*

perhib·eō -ēre -uī -itus *tr* to present; to assert, regard, maintain; to call, name; to adduce, cite; **testimonium perhibere** to bear witness

perhīlum *adv* very little

perhonōrificē *adv* with all due respect, very respectfully

perhonōrific·us -a -um *adj* very complimentary; very respectful

perhorr·escō -escĕre -uī *tr* to begin to shudder at; to develop a terror of ‖ *intr* to begin to tremble violently

perhūmāniter *adv* very kindly

perhūmān·us -a -um *adj* very kind

Pericl·ēs -is *m* famous Athenian statesman *(495–429 B.C.)*

perīclitāti·ō -ōnis *f* test, experiment

perīclit·or -ārī -ātus sum *tr* to test, put to the test, try; to jeopardize; to risk ‖ *intr* to be in danger, be in jeopardy; to run a risk; *(w. abl)* to be in danger of losing *(life, reputation, etc.);* **capite periclitari** to risk one's life

perīculōsē *adv* dangerously

perīculōs·us -a -um *adj* dangerous, risky, perilous

perīc(u)l·um -ī *n* danger, peril, risk; trial, attempt; experiment, test; literary venture; *(leg)* case, trial, lawsuit, legal record, sentence; **periculum facere** to run the risk; try it out; *(w. gen)* to test, put to the test *(e.g., s.o.'s loyalty);* **periculum facere ex aliis** to learn from the mistakes of others; **periculum intendere** *(w. dat)* to expose *(s.o.)* to danger, endanger *(s.o.);* **volo periculum facere an** I want to see whether

peridōne·us -a -um *adj* very suitable; *(w. dat or* ad) well-adapted to, well-suited to

Perillē·us -a - um *adj* of Perillus

Perill·us -ī *m* Athenian sculptor who made for the tyrant Phalaris a bronze bull in which to roast people alive

perillustr·is -is -e *adj* very clear; very illustrious, very distinguished

perimbēcill·us -a -um *adj* very weak, very feeble

per·imō -imĕre -ēmī -emptus *tr* to take away completely; to destroy; to kill

perimpedīt·us -a -um *adj* rough *(terrain);* full of obstacles

perincommodē *adv* very inconveniently

perincommod·us -a -um *adj* very inconvenient

perinde *adv* in the same manner, equally,

just as, quite as; *(w.* **ac, atque, ut, prout,** *or* **quam)** just as; *(w.* **ac si, quasi, tamquam,** *or* **quamsi)** just as if; **non perinde** not particularly, not as much as one would expect

perindulg·ens -entis *adj* very tender; *(w.* **ad)** very tender toward

perinfirm·us -a -um *adj* very weak

peringeniōs·us -a -um *adj* very gifted

perinīqu·us -a -um *adj* very unfair; very upset, very annoyed; very impatient; very reluctant; **periniquo animo pati** *(or* **ferre)** to be quite upset at, be very reluctant about

perinsign·is -is -e *adj* very remarkable

perinvīt·us -a -um *adj* very unwilling

period·us -ī *f (rhet)* period *(a group of at least two words organically related in grammar and sense, and spoken without pause)*

peripatētic·us -a -um *adj* Peripatetic, Aristotelian ‖ *mpl* Peripatetics, Aristotelians

peripetasmat·a -um *npl* curtains, drapes

Periph·ās -antis *m* king of Attica, changed into an eagle by Zeus

periphras·is -is *f (acc:* **-in)** circumlocution

perīrāt·us -a -um *adj* very angry; *(w. dat)* very angry with

periscel·is -idis *f* anklet

peristrōm·a -atis *n* carpet; bedspread

peristȳl·ium -(i)ī *or* **peristȳl·um** *or* **peristȳl·on -ī** *n* peristyle *(inner court surrounded by a colonnade)*

perītē *adv* skillfully, expertly

perīti·a -ae *f* experience, practical knowledge, skill; *(w.* **gen)** experience in, familiarity with, knowledge of

perīt·us -a -um *adj (w. gen or abl, w.* **in +** **abl** *or* **ad)** experienced in, skillful in, expert in *or* at, familiar with; *(w. inf)* skilled in, expert at, *e.g.,* **peritus cantare** skilled in singing; **juris peritus** expert in the law, legal adviser, lawyer

perjūcundē *adv* very pleasantly

perjūcund·us -a -um *adj* very pleasant

perjūr·ium -(i)ī *n* perjury; false oath; false promise

perjūrō -āre *tr* **(-jer-)** to swear falsely by ‖ *intr* to swear a false oath, commit perjury; *(coll)* to lie

perjūr·us -a -um *adj* **(-jer-)** perjured, oathbreaking; *(coll)* lying

per·lābor -lābī -lapsus sum *intr* to glide along, skim across *or* over; *(w.* **per +** **acc)** **1** to slip through; **2** to slip along, glide along; *(w.* **ad)** to come, move, glide, *or* slip toward; *(w.* **in +** *acc)* to glide into, slip into

perlaet·us -a -um *adj* very glad, most joyful

perlapsus *pp of* **perlabor**

perlātē *adv* very extensively

perlat·eō -ēre -uī *intr* to be completely hidden

perlātus *pp of* **perfero**

perlecti·ō -ōnis *f* thorough perusal

per·legō -legĕre -lēgī -lectus *tr* to scan, survey thoroughly, to read through; to recount *(in a speech)*

perlepidē *adv* very nicely

perlev·is -is -e *adj* very light; very slight

perleviter *adv* very lightly; very slightly

perlib·ens -entis *adj* **(-lub-)** very willing

perlibenter *adv* **(-lub-)** very gladly, very willingly

perlīberāl·is -is -e *adj* very well-bred

perlīberāliter *adv* very generously

perlib·et -ēre *v impers* **(lub-) perlibet me** *(w. inf)* I should very much like to

perliciō *see* **pellicio**

perlit·ō -āre -āvī -ātus *tr* to sacrifice *(in order to get a favorable omen);* ‖ *intr* **bove perlitare** to sacrifice an ox *(to obtain a favorable omen)*

perlongē *adv* a long way off

perlonginqu·us -a -um *adj* very long; very tedious

perlong·us -a -um *adj* very long

perlub- = **perlib-**

per·lūceō -lūcēre *intr* **(pell-)** to shine clearly, be bright; to be clearly visible; to be transparent; to be clear, be intelligible

perlūcidul·us -a -um *adj* transparent

perlūcid·us -a -um *adj* **(pell-)** very bright; transparent

perluctuōs·us -a -um *adj* very sad

per·luō -luĕre -luī -lūtus *tr* to wash thoroughly; to wash off; to bathe

perlustr·ō -āre -āvī -ātus *tr* to traverse; to scan, survey, review

permade·faciō -facĕre -fēcī -factus *tr* to soak through and through, drench

permad·escō -escĕre -uī *intr* to become drenched

permagn·us -a -um *adj* very big; very great; very important ‖ *n* great thing; **permagno** at a very high price, very dearly; **permagnum aestimare** *(w. inf)* to think it quite something to

permānanter *adv* pervasively

permānasc·ō -ĕre *intr (of a report)* to leak out

perman·eō -ēre -sī -sum *intr* to last, continue, hold out, remain, persist; *(of the voice)* to remain steady; **permanere esse** to continue to be

permān·ō -āre -āvī -ātus *tr* to seep through, penetrate ‖ *intr* to penetrate; *(w.* **ad** *or* **in +** *acc)* **1** to seep through to; **2** to seep into, penetrate; **3** *(fig)* to reach, extend, penetrate

permansi·ō -ōnis *f* persistence, continuance

permarīn·us -a -um *adj* seagoing
permātūr·escō -escĕre -uī *intr* to become fully ripe
permediocr·is -is -e *adj* completely normal, very moderate
permeditāt·us -a -um *adj* well-rehearsed, well-trained
permējō -mējĕre -mi(n)xī -i(n)ctus *tr (sl)* to soak with urine, urinate all over
permensus *pp of* **permetior**
perme·ō -āre -āvī -ātus *tr* to go through, cross over, cross **ǁ** *intr (w.* **in** + *acc)* to penetrate; *(w.* **per** + *acc)* to penetrate, permeate
Permess·us -ī *m* river in Boeotia sacred to Apollo and the Muses
per·mētior -mētīrī -mensus sum *tr* to measure exactly; to travel over, traverse; to pass right through *(a period of time);* **permetiri oculis** to take stock of, eye appraisingly
per·mingō -mingĕre -minxī -mi(n)ctus *tr (sl)* to soak with urine, urinate all over
permīr·us -a -um *adj* very surprising, truly amazing
per·misceō -miscēre -miscuī mixtus *tr* to mix together, blend thoroughly, intermingle; to unite *(by marriage); (fig)* to involve, embroil; *(fig)* to mix up, confuse, treat as identical; to throw into confusion **ǁ** *pass (w.* **cum**) to combine with; *(w. abl or* **ex**) to consist of, be made up of
permissi·ō -ōnis *f* permission; unconditional surrender; *(as rhetorical device)* concession
permiss·us -a -um *pp of* **permitto ǁ** *n* permission
permiss·us -ūs *m* permission, leave
permitiāl·is -is -e *adj* destructive
permiti·ēs -ēī *f* wasting away; ruin; *(of persons)* source of ruin, ruination
per·mittō -mittĕre -mīsī -missus *tr* to let through, let go through; to hurl; to give up, surrender; to concede, relinquish; to let loose, let go; to let, permit, allow, grant; *(w. dat)* to surrender *(s.th.)* to, entrust *(s.th.)* to, grant *(s.th.)* to; *(w.* **in** + *acc)* to send flying at, hurl at
permixtē *or* **permixtim** *adv* confusedly; indiscriminately
permixti·ō -ōnis *f* mixture; confusion, bedlam
permixt·us -a -um *pp of* **permisceo ǁ** *adj* confused; promiscuous; composite
permodest·us -a -um *adj* very modest, very moderate
permolestē *adv* with much trouble; **permoleste ferre** to be quite annoyed at
permolest·us -a -um *adj* very troublesome, very annoying
permol·ō -ĕre *tr* to grind up; **alienas uxores permolere** *(sl)* to have sex with other men's wives

permōti·ō -ōnis *f* excitement; **animi permotio** *(or* **mentis permotio)** deep emotion
per·moveō -movēre -mōvī -mōtus *tr* to stir up, churn up *(the sea);* to move deeply, make a deep impression on; to excite, agitate, upset; to influence, induce
permul·ceō -cēre -sī -sus *tr* to stroke, pet; to soothe, calm down, relax; to smooth *(one's hair);* to charm, delight; to appease
permultō *adv* by far, much, far
permultum *adv* very much; **permultum ante** very often before; **permultum interest** it makes a world of difference
permult·us -a -um *adj* very much; *(w. pl nouns)* very many **ǁ** *n* a lot, much
permūn·iō -īre -īvī *or* **-iī -ītus** *tr* to fortify thoroughly; to finish fortifying
permūtāti·ō -ōnis *f* interchange; exchange; bartering; substitution, switch; reversal *(of an arrangment);* turning upside down, revolution; alternation, transformation
permūt·ō -āre -āvī -ātus *tr* to change *or* alter completely, transform; to interchange; to remit by bill of exchange; to reverse *(an order, arrangmement);* to turn topsy-turvy *(w. abl or* **cum** *or* **pro** + *abl)* **1** to exchange for, replace with; **2** to receive in exchange for; **3** to acquire at the price of; **4** to substitute for
pern·a -ae *f* ham
pernecessāri·us -a -um *adj* very necessary; very closely related **ǁ** *m* close friend; close relative
pernecesse *indecl neut adj* very necessary, indispensable
perneg·ō -āre -āvī -ātus *tr* to deny flatly; to turn down flat
per·neō -nēre -nēvī -nētus *tr (of the Fates)* to spin out
perniciābil·is -is -e *adj* ruinous
pernici·ēs -ēī *f* ruin, destruction, disaster; pest, curse
perniciōsē *adv* perniciously, ruinously
perniciōs·us -a -um *adj* pernicious, ruinous
pernīcit·ās -ātis *f* agility, nimbleness, swiftness
pernīciter *adv* nimbly, swiftly
perni·ger -gra -grum *adj* jet black; very dark *(eyes)*
pernimium *adv* much too much
pern·ix -īcis *adj* agile, nimble, swift
pernōbil·is -is -e *adj* very famous
pernoct·ō -āre -āvī -ātum *intr* to spend the night
per·noscō -noscĕre -nōvī -nōtus *tr* to examine thoroughly; to become fully acquainted with, get accurate knowledge of
pernōt·escō -escĕre -uī *intr* to become generally known

per·nox -noctis *adj* all-night; **luna pernox** full moon

pernumer·ō -āre -āvī -ātus *tr* to count up

pēr·ō -ōnis *m* clodhopper *(worn by peasants and soldiers)*

perobscūr·us -a -um *adj* very obscure; very vague

perō·dī -disse -sus *tr* to detest, loathe

perodiōs·us -a -um *adj* very annoying

perofficiōsē *adv* with attention, with great devotion; very politely

pērōnāt·us -a -um *adj* wearing clodhoppers

peropportūnē *adv* very conveniently, most opportunely

peropportūn·us -a -um *adj* most opportune, very convenient, well-timed

peroptātō *adv* very much in accordance with one's wishes

peroptāt·us -a -um *adj* greatly desired, longed-for

peropus *indecl n* great need; **peropus est** *(w. acc & inf)* it is essential that

perōrāti·ō -ōnis *f* peroration, summation

perornāt·us -a -um *adj* very flowery

perorn·ō -āre -āvī -ātus *tr* to enhance the prestige of

perōr·ō -āre -āvī -ātus *tr* to bring *(a case, discussion)* to a close **‖** *intr* to bring a speech to a close; *(leg)* to wind up a case, give the summation

perōs·us -a -um *adj* hating, detesting; hated, hateful

perpāc·ō -āre -āvī -ātus *tr* to silence completely; to pacify thoroughly

perparcē *adv* most stingily

perparvul·us -a -um *adj* tiny

perparv·us -a -um *adj* very small

perpast·us -a -um *adj* well-fed

perpauc·ī -ae -a *adj* very few **‖** *npl* very few words

perpaucul·ī -ae -a *adj* very few

perpaulum *adv* somewhat, slightly

perpaul·um -ī *n* small bit

perpaup·er -eris *adj* very poor

perpauxill·um -ī *n* little bit

perpave·faciō -facĕre -fēcī -factus *tr* to frighten the daylights out of

per·pellō -pellĕre -pulī -pulsus *tr* to push hard; to urge strongly, force; to drive all the way

perpendicul·um -ī *n or* **perpendicul·us -ī** *n* plumb line; **ad perpendiculum** perpendicularly

perpen·dō -dĕre -dī -sus *tr* to weigh carefully, consider; to value, judge

perperam *adv* incorrectly, wrongly; by mistake

Perpern·a *or* **Perpenn·a -ae** *m* Roman family name *(cognomen)*, *esp.* Marcus Perperna Vento, partisan and later murderer of Sertorius

perp·es -etis *adj* continuous, uninterrupted

perpessi·ō -ōnis *f* endurance

per·petior -petī -pessus sum *tr* to endure, put up with, stand; to allow, permit

perpetr·ō -āre -āvī -ātus *tr* to accomplish, go through with, carry out, perform; to perpetrate, commit; to fulfill *(a promise); (w. ut)* to bring it about that

perpetuē *adv* constantly

perpetuit·ās -ātis *f* perpetuity

perpetuō *adv* constantly; forever

perpetu·ō -āre -āvī -ātus *tr* to perpetuate

perpetu·us -a -um *adj* perpetual, continuous; general, universal; whole; **quaestiones perpetuae** standing courts; permanent committees **‖** *n* **in perpetuum** continuously; forever

perplac·eō -ēre *intr (w. dat)* to please immensely

perplexābil·is -is -e *adj* perplexing, puzzling

perplexābiliter *adv* perplexingly

perplexē *or* **perplexim** *adv* confusedly, unintelligibly

perplex·or -ārī *intr* to cause confusion

perplex·us -a -um *adj* intricate, complicated; ambiguous; muddled, mistaken; baffling *(words)*

perplicāt·us -a -um *adj* entangled

perplu·ō -ĕre *intr (of roof, etc.)* to let the rain in; *(of rain)* to come in

perpol·iō -īre -īvī *or* **-iī -ītus** *tr* to bring to a high polish; *(fig)* to polish up, perfect

perpolīt·us -a -um *adj* polished, refined

perpopul·or -ārī -ātus sum *tr* to ravage, devastate

perpōtāti·ō -ōnis *f* heavy drinking; drinking party

perpōt·ō -āre -āvī -ātus *tr* to drink up **‖** *intr* to drink heavily, carouse

per·primō -primĕre -pressī -pressus *tr* to press hard, squeeze hard

perpropinqu·us -a -um *adj* very near **‖** *m* very close relative

perprūrisc·ō -ĕre *intr* to begin to itch all over

perpugn·ax -ācis *adj* very belligerent

perpul·c(h)er -c(h)ra -c(h)rum *adj* very beautiful, very handsome

perpulsus *pp of* **perpello**

perpurg·ō -āre -āvī -ātus *tr* to cleanse thoroughly, clean up; *(fig)* to clear up

perpusill·us -a -um *adj* puny

perput·ō -āre -āvī -ātus *tr* to prune back hard; to explain in detail

perquam *adv* very, extremely

per·quīrō -quīrĕre -quīsīvī *or* **-quīsiī -quīsītus** *tr* to search carefully for; to examine carefully

perquīsītius *adv* more accurately, more critically

perquīsīt·or -ōris *m* enthusiast

perrārō *adv* very rarely

perrār·us -a -um *adj* very rare

perrecondit·us -a -um *adj* recondite
perrectus *pp of* **pergo**
perrēp·ō -ēre -sī *tr* to creep through; to crawl along *(the ground)*
perrept·ō -āre -āvī *tr* to creep through, sneak through ‖ *intr* to creep around
perrexī *perf of* **pergo**
Perrhaeb·us -a -um *adj* of Perrhaebia *(a mountainous region of N. Thessaly)* ‖ *m* inhabitant of Perrhaebia
perrīdiculē *adv* most absurdly
perrīdicul·us -a -um *adj* utterly absurd
perrogāti·ō -ōnis *f* passage *(of a law)*
perrog·ō -āre *tr* to ask for in turn; to question in turn; to poll *(opinions); (pol)* **sententias perrogare** to have roll call *(in the Senate)*
per·rumpō -rumpěre -rūpī -ruptus *tr* to break through, force one's way through; to break in two, shatter, smash; to offend against, violate ‖ *intr* to break through, make a breakthrough
Pers·a *or* **Pers·ēs -ae** *m* Persian
Pers·a -ae *f* a daughter of Oceanus, wife of the sun, and mother of Circe, Perses *(father of Hecate)*, Aeëtes, and Pasiphaë
persaepe *adv* very often
persalsē *adv* very wittily
persals·us -a -um *adj* very witty
persalūtāti·ō -ōnis *f* round of greetings, greeting all in turn
persalūt·ō -āre -āvī -ātus *tr* to salute one after another
persanctē *adv* very solemnly
persapi·ens -entis *adj* very wise
persapienter *adv* very wisely
perscienter *adv* very skillfully
per·scindō -scinděre -scīdī -scissus *tr* to tear to pieces; to split
perscīt·us -a -um *adj* very clever, very smart
per·scrībō -scrīběre -scripsī -scriptus *tr* to write out; to describe fully, give in detail; to finish writing; to record, register; to enter *(into an account book);* to write out in full *(as opposed to abbreviating);* **pecuniam perscribere** to write a check for *(a certain sum of money)*
perscripti·ō -ōnis *f* entry, official record; check, payment by check
perscript·or -ōris *m* bookkeeper, accountant
perscriptus *pp of* **perscribo**
perscrūt·or -ārī -ātus sum *tr* to search or examine thoroughly, scrutinize
persec·ō -āre -uī -tus *tr* to dissect; to cut through; to lance *(a boil)*
persect·or -ārī -ātus sum *tr* to follow eagerly, investigate
persecūti·ō -ōnis *f* pursuit; *(leg)* right to sue; *(leg)* prosecution, suing
persecūtus *pp of* **persequor**

per·sedeō -sedēre -sēdī -sessum *intr* to remain seated
persegn·is -is -e *adj* very slow-moving
Persē·is -idis *or* **-idos** *adj (fem only)* of Persa; of Perseus ‖ *f* daughter of Persa *(Hecate, Circe)* ‖ Persa
persen·tiō -tīre -sī -sus *tr* to perceive clearly, to feel deeply
persentisc·ō -ěre *tr* to become fully conscious of; to begin to feel deeply
Persephon·ē -ēs *f* daughter of Demeter and Zeus and queen of the lower world *(named Proserpina by the Romans)*
persequ·ens -entis *adj* pursuing; *(w. gen)* given to the pursuit *or* practice of
perse·quor -quī -cūtus sum *tr* to follow persistently, follow up; to be in hot pursuit of, be on the heels of; to chase after, catch up to; to follow verbatim; to imitate, copy; to take vengeance on; to follow out, execute; to describe, explain; *(leg)* to prosecute
Pers·ēs *or* **Pers·a -ae** *or* **Pers·eūs -eī** *or* **-eos** *m* Perseus *(last king of Macedonia, conquered by Aemilius Paulus at Pydna in 169 B.C.)*
Pers·eūs -eī *or* **-eos** *m* son of Jupiter and Danaë, and slayer of Medusa ‖ *see* **Perses**
Persē·us *or* **Persē·us -a -um** *adj* of Perseus *(son of Jupiter and Danaë)*
persevēr·ans -antis *adj* persevering, persistent, relentless
persevēranter *adv* persistently
persevēranti·a -ae *f* perseverance
persevēr·ō -āre -āvī -ātus *tr* to persist in ‖ *intr* to persevere
persevēr·us -a -um *adj* very strict
Persi·a -ae *or* **Pers·is -idis** *or* **-idos** *f* Persia
Persic·us -a -um *adj* Persian; *(fig)* luxurious, soft; of Perseus *(king of Macedonia);* **malum Persicum** peach ‖ *mpl* Persians ‖ *f* peach tree ‖ *n* peach ‖ *npl* Persian history
per·sīdō -sīděre -sēdī *intr* to sink down; *(w. ad or in + acc)* to penetrate
persign·ō -āre -āvī -ātus *tr* to record in detail *(articles in an inventory)*
persimil·is -is -e *adj* very similar; *(w. gen or dat)* very similar to
persimpl·ex -icis *adj* very simple
Pers·is -idis *or* **-idos** *adj (fem only)* Persian ‖ *f* Persia; Persian woman
Pers·ius -(i)ī *m* Persius *(Aulus Persius Flaccus, satirist in the reign of Nero, A.D. 34–62)*
persoll·a -ae *f* little mask; *(pej)* you ugly little thing!
persōl·us -a -um *adj* all alone
per·solvō -solvěre solvī -solūtus *tr* to solve; to explain; to pay up, pay in full; to pay *(a penalty);* to fulfill *(a vow);* to carry out *(a duty);* to render *(thanks);* to offer *(sacrifice); (w. gen)* pay the pen-

alty for *(a crime); (w. dat)* to pay *(the penalty)* at the hands of; to solve *(a problem, riddle);* **ab omnibus ei poenae persolutae sunt** punishment was inflicted on him by all; **debitum naturae persolvere** to pay one's debt to nature *(i.e., to die);* **honorem dis persolvere** to offer sacrifices to the gods; **grates dis persolvere** to render thanksgiving to the gods; **gratiam dis persolvere** to render thanks to the gods; **justa persolvere** to pay honors to the dead; **poenas dis hominibusque persolvere** to suffer punishment at the hands of gods and men; **vectigalia persolvere** to pay taxes; **vota persolvere** to fulfill vows

persōn·a -ae *f* mask; part, character; pretense; personality; person; *(gram)* person; *(leg)* the person involved in a case; **ab** *(or* **ex** *or* **in) suā personā** *(acting, speaking)* in one's own name, on one's own behalf; **in personā** *(w. gen)* in the case of, in the instance of; **mea persona** my personality *or* character; **personae fictio** personification; **persona muta** a character with no speaking part

persōnāl·is -is -e *adj* personal

persōnāliter *adv* personally

persōnāt·us -a -um *adj* wearing a mask, masked; *(fig)* under false pretenses, putting on a front; **pater personatus** the father in the play; **personata fabula** a play in which actors wear masks; **personatus histrio** an actor wearing a mask

persōn·ō -āre -uī -ātus *tr* to make *(a place)* resound; to shout out; to sing loudly, belt out *(a song);* **aurem personare** to make the ear ring ‖ *intr* to resound, reecho; *(of a musician w. abl. of instrument)* to play loudly on *(e.g., the lyre); (of a singer)* to sing loudly; **citharā personare** to produce loud music on the lyre

perspargō *see* **perspergo**

perspectē *adv* intelligently

perspect·ō -āre -āvī -ātus *tr* to examine carefully; to watch steadily ‖ *intr* to look all around, have a look around

perspect·us -a -um *pp of* **perspicio** ‖ *adj* well-known, clear, evident; **res penitus perspectae** matters clearly understood

perspecul·or -ārī -ātus sum *tr* to explore thoroughly; *(mil)* to reconnoiter

persper·gō -gĕre -sī -sus *tr* (**-spar-**) to sprinkle; to strew *(w. flowers)*

perspexī *perf of* **perspicio**

perspic·ax -ācis *adj* sharp-sighted; keen, penetrating, perspicacious

perspicienti·a -ae *f* clear perception

per·spiciō -spicĕre -spexī -spectus *tr* to see through; to look through; to look closely at, look over, examine, inspect, observe; to discern, ascertain; to prove

perspicuē *adv* clearly

perspicuit·ās -ātis *f* clarity

perspicu·us -a -um *adj* clear; transparent; clearly visible, conspicuous; plain, evident; lucid *(expression)*

perspīr·ō -āre *intr* to blow steadily

perspissō *adv* very slowly

persternō -sternĕre -strāvī -strātus *tr* to pave *(a road)* along its full length

perstimul·ō -āre -āvī -ātus *tr* to stimulate; to continue to stir up

per·stō stāre -stitī -stātum *intr* to stand firm, hold one's ground; to remain standing; to remain unchanged, last; to be firm, persevere, hold out; *(of soldiers)* to continue under arms; *(of things)* to remain stationary; *(w. inf)* to continue obstinately to *(do s.th.)*

perstrātus *pp of* **persterno**

perstrep·ō -ĕre -uī *intr* to make a loud noise, make a lot of noise

perstringō perstringĕre perstrinxī perstrictum *tr* to tie, tie up; to make unfavorable mention of; *(of sounds)* to grate on; to blunt, deaden *(the senses);* to dazzle *(the eyes);* to deafen *(the ears); (of a weapon)* to graze; to glance over; to touch lightly on; to wound *(s.o. 's)* feelings, offend; **Crassus meis litteris perstrictus est** Crassus was offended by *(or* took offense at*)* my letter; **horror ingens spectantes perstrinxit** a deep shudder came over the onlookers

perstudiōsē *adv* enthusiastically

perstudiōs·us -a -um *adj (w. gen)* very fond of, enthusiastic about

persuā·deō -dēre -sī -sum *intr (w. dat)* to persuade, convince; **sibi persuasum habere** to have oneself convinced

persuāsi·ō -ōnis *f* convincing; conviction, belief

persuāstr·ix -īcis *f* seductress

persuāsum *pp of* **persuadeo**

persuās·us -ūs *m* persuasion

persubtīl·is -is -e *adj* of very fine texture; very subtle, very ingenious

persult·ō -āre -āvī -ātus *tr* to prance about; to scour *(woods)* ‖ *intr* to gambol, prance, run around

per·taedet -taedēre -taesum est *v impers (w. acc of person = subject in English and gen of thing = object in English)* to be weary of, be sick and tired of, be bored with, *e.g.,* **me hujus negotii pertaedet** I am sick and tired of this business

perte·gō -gĕre -xī -ctus *tr* to cover up, cover completely; to roof over

pertempt·ō -āre -āvī -ātus *tr* (**-tent-**) to test thoroughly; to sound *(s.o.)* out; to consider well; *(fig)* to fill, pervade; **gaudia pertemptant pectus** joy fills *(their)* hearts

perten·dō -děre -dī -sus or **-tus** tr to press on with, continue, carry out **‖** intr to press on, continue, persevere, keep going

pertenu·is -is -e adj very thin, very slight, very small, very fine

perterebr·ō -āre -āvī -ātus tr to bore through

perter·geō -ēre -sī -sus tr to wipe off; (of air) to brush lightly against

perterre·faciō -facěre -fēcī -factus tr to scare the life out of

perterr·eō -ēre -uī -itus tr to frighten, terrify; (w. ab) to frighten (s.o.) away from

perterricrep·us -a -um adj terrible-sounding, rattling frightfully

pertex·ō -ěre -uī -tus tr to bring to an end, go through with, accomplish; to complete the composition of (a speech, writing)

pertic·a -ae f pole; rod, staff; ten-foot measuring pole; (fig) measure

pertimefact·us -a -um adj thoroughly frightened

pertim·escō -escěre -uī tr to be alarmed at, become afraid of **‖** intr to become very frightened or alarmed

pertināci·a -ae f stubbornness; perseverance, determination

pertināciter adv stubbornly, tenaciously; through thick and thin

pertin·ax -ācis adj very tenacious; persevering, steadfast; stubborn

pertin·eō -ēre -uī intr to reach, extend; (w. per + acc) 1 to pervade; 2 reach; (w. ad) 1 to extend to, reach; 2 to pertain to, relate to, concern; 3 to apply to, be applicable to, suit, be suitable to; 4 to be conducive to; 5 to belong to; **quod pertinet** (w. ad) as regards

perting·ō -ěre tr to get as far as, reach **‖** intr to extend; **collis in inmensum pertingens** a hill extending a very long distance

pertoler·ō -āre -āvī -ātus tr to put up with, endure to the end

pertorqu·eō -ēre tr to twist, distort

pertractātē adv in a trite manner

pertractāti·ō -ōnis f handling, treatment

pertract·ō -āre -āvī -ātus tr to handle; (fig) to treat systematically; to examine in detail

per·trahō -trahěre -traxī -tractus tr to drag along; to drag by force (to s.th. unpleasant); to lure, lead on (an enemy); to tow

pertrect- = pertract-

pertrist·is -is -e adj very sad; very stern

pertulī perf of **perfero**

pertumultuōsē adv very excitedly, hysterically

per·tundō -tunděre -tudī -tūsus tr to punch a hole through, perforate

perturbātē adv in confusion

perturbāti·ō -ōnis f confusion, disorder; riot; distress, agitation; strong emotion

perturbātr·ix -īcis f disturbing element

perturbāt·us -a -um adj disturbed, troubled; excited, alarmed; embarrassed

perturb·ō -āre -āvī -ātus tr to throw into confusion, confuse; to disturb; to embarrass; to upset; to alarm

perturp·is -is -e adj downright shameful

pertūs·us -a -um pp of **pertundo ‖** adj perforated; tattered (clothes)

pērul·a -ae f small satchel

perun·g(u)ō -g(u)ěre -xī -ctus tr to anoint thoroughly

perurbān·us -a -um adj very polite; very sophisticated **‖** m snob

per·ūrō -ūrěre -ussī -ustus tr to burn up; to consume; to inflame, rub sore; to scorch; (of cold) to nip, bite; (fig) to fire, inflame

Perusi·a -ae f town in Etruria (modern Perugia)

Perusīn·us -a -um adj of Perusia **‖** mpl inhabitants of Perusia **‖** n an estate in Perusia

perussī perf of **peruro**

perustus pp of **peruro**

perūtil·is -is -e adj very useful

per·vādō -vāděre -vāsī -vāsus tr to pass through, go through; to pervade **‖** intr to spread; to penetrate; (w. ad or in + acc) 1 to go as far as, spread to; 2 to reach, arrive at; 3 to penetrate; (w. per + acc) to spread through or over

pervagāt·us -a -um adj widespread, prevalent, well-known; general, common; of widespread application

pervag·or -ārī -ātus sum tr to spread through or over, pervade **‖** intr to wander all over, range about; (w. ad) 1 to spread to, extend to; 2 to be known as far as

pervag·us -a -um adj wandering about

perval·eō -ēre intr (of a magnet) to retain (its) power

pervariē adv in various versions

pervast·ō -āre -āvī -ātus tr to devastate

pervāsus pp of **pervado**

perve·hō -hěre -xī -ctus tr to bring, carry, convey; to bring (e.g, supplies) through **‖** pass to ride, drive, sail; **in portum pervehi** to sail into port, reach port

pervell·ō -ěre -ī tr to pull hard; to pinch hard; to excite, arouse; to cause to twinge; (fig) to disparage; **aurem alicui pervellere** to pull s.o.'s ear (as a reminder)

per·veniō -venīre -vēnī -ventus tr to come to, reach **‖** intr to come up; to arrive; (w. ad or in + acc) 1 to arrive at, reach; 2 (fig) to attain to

pervēn·or -ārī tr to search through, scour (e.g., all the city)

perversē adv (-vors-) wrongly, perversely
perversāriō adv (-vors-) in a wrong-headed way, wrongly
perversit·ās -ātis f perversity, unreasonableness; distortion
pervers·us -a -um adj (-vors-) turned the wrong way, awry, crooked; cross-eyed; (fig) crooked, wrong, perverse; (fig) spiteful, malicious
per·vertō -vertěre -vertī -versus tr (-vort-) to overturn, upset, knock down; to invert the order of; to cause to face in the opposite direction; to bend out of shape, distort; to misrepresent, falsify (statements); to divert to an improper use, misuse, abuse; to undo, destroy; to pervert, spoil
pervesperī adv late in the evening
pervestīgāti·ō -ōnis f thorough search, examining, investigation
pervestīg·ō -āre -āvī -ātus tr to track down; to examine in detail; (fig) to trace, detect
pervet·us -eris adj very old, ancient
pervetust·us -a -um adj very ancient
pervexī perf of **perveho**
perviam adv **perviam facere** to make accessible
pervicāci·a -ae f persistence; (pej) stubbornness; **pervicacia in hostem** obstinate resistance to the enemy
pervicācius adv more stubbornly
pervic·ax -ācis adj persistent, determined; (pej) headstrong, stubborn
pervīcī perf of **pervinco**
pervictus pp of **pervinco**
per·videō -vidēre -vīdī -vīsus tr to look over, survey; to see through; to examine, investigate; to realize, perceive fully
pervig·eō -ēre -uī intr to continue to thrive
pervig·il -ilis adj wide-awake, ever watchful
pervigilāti·ō -ōnis f religious vigil
pervigil·ium -(i)ī n all-night vigil
pervigil·ō -āre -āvī -ātus tr to spend or pass (nights, days) without sleep ‖ intr to stay awake all night, keep an all-night vigil
pervīl·is -is -e adj very cheap
per·vincō -vincěre -vīcī -victus tr to defeat completely, completely get the better of; to outdo; to outbid; to convince; to prove ‖ intr to win, succeed; to carry a point; (w. ut) to succeed in, bring it about that; **non pervicit ut referrent consules** he did not succeed in having the consuls make a formal proposal
pervīsus pp of **pervideo**
pervi·us -a -um adj crossable, passable; open at both ends; perforated; accessible; open to entreaty ‖ n passage
per·vīvō -vīvěre -vixī intr to live on, go on living
pervolgō see **pervulgo**

pervolit·ō -āre -āvī -ātus tr & intr to fly about, flit about
pervol·ō -āre -āvī -ātus tr to fly through, fly about, flit about; to dart through, pass quickly over ‖ intr to fly about, flit about; (w. in + acc) to fly through to, arrive at, reach
per·volō -velle tr to wish very much; **te quam primum pervelim videre** I'd like very much to see you as soon as possible
pervolūt·ō -āre -āvī -ātus tr to turn over often, read through (a book scroll)
per·volvō -volvěre -volvī -volūtus tr to roll (s.o.) over; to keep reading, read through (a scroll) ‖ refl to roll around ‖ pass to be busy
pervor- = **perver-**
pervulgāt·us -a -um adj (-vol-) widely known, very common
pervulg·ō -āre -āvī -ātus tr (-vol-) to make known, make public, publicize; to frequent ‖ refl to prostitute oneself
pēs pedis m foot (of body, of table, of couch; in verse); rope at lower part of a sail, sheet; **ad pedes descendere** to dismount (in order to fight on foot); **ad pedes pugna** an infantry fight; **aequis pedibus labi** to sail on an even keel; **ante pedes** in plain view; **in pedes** feet first; **pede dextro** (or **felice** or **secundo**) auspiciously (the right foot being associated with good omens); **pedem conferre** to come to close quarters; **pedem ferre** to come; to go; **pedem ponere** (w. in + abl) to set foot in; **pedem referre** to step back, retreat; **pedes tollere** to lift the legs (for sexual intercourse); **pedibus** on foot; **pedibus claudere** to set to verse, put in meter; **pedibus ire in sententiam** (w. gen) to vote in favor of the proposal of; **pedibus itur in sententiam** the proposal is put to a vote; **pedibus merere** (or **pedibus mereri**) to serve in the infantry; **pedibus vincere** to win a footrace; **plano pede** on level ground; **pugna ad pedes** infantry battle; **se in pedes conjicere** (or **se in pedes conferre** or **se in pedes dare** or **se pedibus dare**) to take to one's heels; **servus a pedibus** footman; **sub pedibus** under one's sway
pessimē (superl of **male**) adv (-sum-) worst; most wickedly; most unfortunately; by a stroke of bad luck
pessim·us -a -um (superl of **malus**) adj (-sum-) worst; most villainous; most distressing
Pessin·ūs -untis m Galatian town on the borders of Phrygia, famous for its cult of Cybele
pessul·us -ī m bolt (of a door)
pessum adv down, to the ground, to the bottom; **pessum dare** (or **pessumdare**

as one word) to send to the bottom, sink, drown, ruin, destroy; **pessum ire** to go down, sink, go to pot
pestif·er -era -erum *adj* pestilential; destructive, pernicious, disastrous ‖ *m* troublemaker
pestiferē *adv* disastrously
pestil·ens -entis *adj* pestilential, unhealthful; *(fig)* disastrous
pestilenti·a -ae *f* pestilence, plague; unhealthful atmosphere *or* climate
pestilit·ās -ātis *f* pestilence, plague
pest·is -is *f* contagious disease; plague; death, destruction; instrument of death *or* destruction; *(of persons)* troublemaker, anarchist, subversive
petal·ium -(i)ī *n* thin sheet of metal
petasāt·us -a -um *adj* wearing a hat; *(fig)* ready to travel
petas·ō -ōnis *m* ham
petasuncul·us -ī *m* little ham
petas·us -ī *m* broad-rimmed hat
petaur·um -ī *n* springboard
Petēli·a -ae *f* town in Bruttium, besieged by Hannibal
petess·ō -ĕre *tr* (**-tiss-**) to be eager for, pursue; **pugnam petessere** to be spoiling for a fight
petīti·ō -ōnis *f* attack, blow, thrust, aim; petition, request, application; *(leg)* claim, suit, suing, right to sue; *(pol)* candidacy, political campaign; **petitioni se dare** to become a candidate
petīt·or -ōris *m* applicant; *(leg)* plaintiff; *(pol)* political candidate
petītr·ix -īcis *f (leg)* plaintiff *(female)*
petītur·iō -īre *intr (pol)* to be eager for office
petīt·us -a -um *pp of* **peto** ‖ *adj* **longe petitus** far-fetched ‖ *n* request
pet·ō -ĕre -īvī *or* **-iī -ītus** *tr* to make for, head for; to attack; to strive after; to aim at; to demand, require, exact; to ask for; to claim, lay claim to, sue for; to beg, entreat; to look for, go in search of, search for; to run after, chase *(girls);* to go and fetch; to obtain; to draw *(a sigh);* to run for *(office);* to refer to, relate to; *(w. dat or ad or in + acc)* to demand *(s.o. or s.th.) (for a specific purpose),* e.g., **custodem in vincla petere** to demand that the watchdog be chained; **astra petere** to mount to the stars; **terram petere** to fall to the earth
petorrit·um -ī *n* (**-tōri-**) open four-wheeled carriage *(of Celtic origin)*
petr·a -ae *f* rock, crag
Petr·a -ae *f* Petra *(name of several towns, esp. the chief town of Arabia Petraea)*
Petrei·us -ī *m* Roman clan name *(nomen), esp.* Marcus Petreius *(legate of Gaius Antonius against Catiline and later of Pompey in the Civil War)*

Petrīn·um -ī *n* place near Sinuessa on the border between Latium and Campania ‖ estate in this area
petr·ō -ōnis *m* yokel
Petrōn·ius -(i)ī *m* Petronius Arbiter *(author and master of cermonies at the court of Nero)*
petul·ans -antis *adj* petulant, brash, smart-alecky; *(of sexual behavior)* horny
petulanter *adv* brashly, rudely
petulanti·a -ae *f* petulance, brashness; *(of speech)* rudeness; *(of sexual behavior)* horniness
petulc·us -a -um *adj* butting, apt to butt
Peuceti·a -ae *f* Peucetia *(S. section of Apulia)*
Peuceti·us -a -um *adj* of Peucetia
pexī *perf of* **pecto**
pex·us -a -um *pp of* **pecto** ‖ *adj* neatly combed; new, still having the nap on
Phaeāc·es -um *mpl* Phaeacians *(people living on a utopian island, according to the Odyssesy)*
Phaeāci·us -a -um *adj* Phaeacian ‖ *f* Phaeacia *(sometimes identified with Corcyra and ruled by King Alcinoüs)*
Phaeāc·us -a -um *adj* Phaeacian
Phae·ax -ācis *or* **-ācos** *m* Phaeacian ‖ *m* Phaeacian; well-fed man
Phaedr·a -ae *f* daughter of Minos and wife of Theseus
Phaedr·us -ī *m* one of the Socratic circle, who gave his name to a dialogue of Pīato ‖ Epicurean philosopher of Athens, who taught Cicero ‖ writer of fables, freedman of Augustus
Phaesti·as -adis *or* **-ados** *adj (fem only)* a woman of Phestum
Phaesti·us -a -um *adj* of Phestum
Phaest·um -ī *n* town in S. Crete
Phaët(h)·ōn -ontis *or* **-ontos** *m* son of Helios, who was killed by Zeus while driving his father's chariot
Phaëthonte·us -a -um *adj* of Phaëthon
Phaët(h)ontiad·es -um *fpl* sisters of Phaëthon, who were turned into trees
Phaëthont·is -idis *or* **-dos** *adj (fem only)* of Phaëthon ‖ *fpl* sisters of Phaëthon
Phaëthūs·a -ae *f* the eldest sister of Phaëthon
pha·ger -grī *m* fish *(sea-bream?)*
phalang·a -ae *f* wooden roller *(for moving ships and siege engines)*
phalangit·ae -ārum *mpl* soldiers belonging to a Macedonian phalanx
phal·anx -angis *f* phalanx *(compact body of heavy-armed men in battle formation first developed by the Macedonians)*
phalāric·a -ae *f* (**fal-**) firebrand, fiery missile *(shot by a catapult or thrown by hand)*

Phalar·is -idis *m* a tyrant of Agrigentum on S. coast of Sicily, notorious for the bronze bull in which he roasted his victims *(c. 570–554 B.C.)*

phaler·ae -ārum *fpl* military medals; medallions *(worn by horses on the forehead and chest)*

phalerāt·us -a -um *adj* wearing medals, decorated; ornamental

Phalēr·éüs -eī *or* **-eos** *m* Demetrius of Phalerum *(Athenian statesman)*

Phalēric·us -a -um *adj* of Phaleron

Phalēr·um -ī *n* Athenian harbor

phantasm·a -atis *n* phantom, ghost

Pha·ōn -ōnis *f* legendary Lesbian, reputed lover of Sappho

pharetr·a -ae *f* quiver

pharetrāt·us -a -um *adj* carrrying a quiver

Phari·us -a -um *adj* of Pharos, Pharian; *(poet)* Egyptian

pharmaceutri·a -ae *f* witch, sorceress

pharmacopōl·a -ae *m* druggist; *(pej)* quack

Pharnac·ēs -is *m* Pharnaces I *(king of Pontus and grandfather of Mithridates, died c. 169 B.C.)* ‖ Pharnaces II *(son of Mithridates the Great, easily defeated by Caesar at Zela in 47 B.C.)*

Phar·os *or* **Phar·us -ī** *f (m)* Pharos *(island lying off Alexandria);* lighthouse *(built on the E. tip of Pharos by Ptolemy II Philadelphus);* a lighthouse *(in general); (poet)* Egypt

Pharsālic·us -a -um *adj* of Pharsalus

Pharsāli·us -a -um *adj* Pharsalian ‖ *f* Pharsalia *(district of Thessaly)*

Pharsāl·os *or* **Pharsāl·us -ī** *f* town in Thessaly near which Caesar defeated Pompey *(48 B.C.)*

phasēl·us *or* **phasēl·os -ī** *mf* kidney bean; light passenger ship

Phāsiac·us -a -um *adj* of the River Phasis in Colchis; Colchian

phāsiān·a -ae *f* pheasant *(female)*

phāsiān·us -ī *m* pheasant

Phāsi·as -ados *adj (fem only)* Colchian ‖ *f* Medea

Phās·is -idis *or* **-idos** *m* river in Colchis

phasm·a -atis *n* specter, ghost

Phēgē·us -a -um *adj* of Phegeus, king of Psophis in Arcadia, the father of Alphesiboea

Phēm·ius -(i)ī *m* minstrel of Ithaca

Phene·us *or* **Phene·os -ī** *m or* **Phene·on -ī** *n* a town and stream with subterranean channels in Arcadia

Pher·ae -ārum *fpl* city in Thessaly, home of Admetus

Pherae·us -a -um *adj* of Pherae

Phereclē·us -a -um *adj* of Phereclus *(the builder of Paris' ship)*

phial·a -ae *f* saucer

Phīdiac·us -a -um *adj* of Phidias

Phīdi·ās -ae *m* Greek sculptor and friend of Pericles *(fl 440 B.C.)*

Philaen·ī -ōrum *mpl* two Carthaginian brothers who agreed to be buried alive to establish the frontier between Carthage and Cyrene

Philamm·ōn -ōnis *m* legendary musician, son of Apollo

philēm·a -atis *n* kiss

Philēm·ō(n) -onis *m* Philemon *(pious rustic who was changed into an oak tree while his wife Baucis was changed into a linden tree)*

Philippens·is -is -e *adj* of Philippi ‖ *mpl* the people of Philippi

Philippē·us -a -um *adj* of Philip II of Macedon *(esp. as epithet of gold coins minted by Philip)*

Philipp·ī -ōrum *mpl* city in Macedonia where Octavian and Antony defeated Brutus and Cassius *(42 B.C.)*

Philippic·ae -ārum *fpl* Philippics *(series of vitriolic speeches directed at Antony by Cicero)*

Philippopol·is -eōs *f* city in Thessaly

Philipp·us -ī *m* name of several kings of Macedon *(esp. Philip II, father of Alexander, c. 382–336 B.C.)*

Philist·us -ī *m* historian, from Syracuse *(d. 356 B.C.)*

philiti·a *or* **phiditi·a -ōrum** *npl* public meals at Sparta

Phillyrid·ēs -is *m* son of Philyra *(i.e., Chiron)*

Phil·ō(n) -ōnis *m* Philo *(Academic philosopher and teacher of Cicero)*

Philoctēt·ēs -ae *m* Greek warrior who was abandoned by the Greek army on the island of Lemnos

philologi·a -ae *f* love of study; study of literature

philolog·us -a -um *adj* learned, scholarly ‖ *m* scholar

Philomēl·a -ae *f* daughter of Pandion; she and her sister Procne were changed into nightingales

philosoph·a -ae *f* philosopher *(female)*

philosophē *adv* philosophically

philosophi·a -ae *f* philosophy

philosoph·or -ārī -ātus sum *intr* to pursue philosophy; to philosophize, moralize

philosoph·us -a -um *adj* philosophical ‖ *m* philosopher

philtr·um -ī *n* love potion

philyr·a -ae *f* inner bark of the lime tree *(from which bands for chaplets were made)*

Philyr·a -ae *f* nymph, the mother of Chiron by Saturn

Philyrēi·us -a -um *adj* of Philyra; of Chiron; **heros Philyraeius** Chiron

phīm·us -ī *m* dice box

Phīnēi·us -a -um *adj* of Phineus

Phīn·eūs -ēī *or* **-eos** *m* king of Thrace, plagued by the Harpies
Phīnid·ēs -ae *m* descendant of Phineus
Phlegeth·ōn -ontis *m* river of fire in the lower world
Phlegethont·is -idis *adj (fem only)* of Phlegethon
Phlegrae·us -a -um *adj* of Phlegra *(where the Giants were said to have been struck by lightning in battle with the gods)*
Phlegy·ae -ārum *mpl* a people of Thessaly
Phlegy·ās -ae *m* king of the Lapiths, son of Ares, and father of Ixion
Phlī·ūs -untis *f* city of N.E. Peloponnesus
phōc·a -ae *or* **phōc·ē -ēs** *f* seal
Phōcae·a -ae *f* Ionian city on the coast of Asia Minor
Phōcaeens·is -is -e *adj* of Phocaea ‖ *mpl* the people of Phocaea
Phōcae·us -a -um *adj* of Phocaea ‖ *mpl* the people of Phocaea
Phōcaïc·us *or* **Phōci·us -a -um** *adj* Phocian
Phōc·is -idis *or* **-idos** *f* region of central Greece containing the oracle of Delphi
Phoeb·as -ados *f* prophetess, priestess of Apollo
Phoeb·ē -ēs *f* Phoebe *(moon goddess, the sister of Phoebus, identified with Diana);* night
Phoebēi·us -a -um *adj* of Phoebus *(as sun-god and as god of prophecy, music, and healing);* of Aesculapius; **ales Phoebeius** the raven; **anguis Phoebeius** the snake of Aesculapius
Phoebē·us -a -um *adj* of Phoebus
Phoebigen·a -ae *m* son of Phoebus *(i.e., Aesculapius)*
Phoeb·us -ī *m* Apollo as sun-god; sun
Phoenic·a -ae *or* **Phoenīc·ē -ēs** *f* Phoenicia
Phoenīc·es -um *mpl* Phoenicians
phoenīcopter·us -ī *m* flamingo
Phoeniss·a -ae *f* Phoenician woman *(esp. Dido)*
phoen·ix -īcis *or* **-īcos** *m* phoenix *(a bird said to live 500 years and from whose ashes a young phoenix would be born)*
Phoen·ix -īcis *or* **-īcos** *m* Phoenician ‖ son of Amyntor and companion of Achilles ‖ son of Agenor and brother of Cadmus
Phol·us -ī *m* name of a Centaur
phōnasc·us -ī *m* voice teacher
Phorc·is -idos *f* daughter of Phorcus; Medusa ‖ *fpl* the Graeae
Phorc·us -ī *m* son of Neptune and father of Medusa and the other Gorgons and the Graeae
Phorcȳn·is -idis *or* **-idos** *f* Medusa
Phormi·ō -ōnis *m* Athenian admiral *(died c. 428 B.C.)* ‖ Peripatetic philosopher who lectured Hannibal on military science
Phraāt·ēs -ae *m* king of Parthia
phrenēs·is -is *f* frenzy, delirium

phrenētic·us -a -um *adj* frenetic, frantic, delirious
Phrix·us *or* **Phrix·os -ī** *m* son of Athamas and Nephele and brother of Helle
phronēs·is -is *f* wisdom
Phryg·es -um *mpl* Phrygians
Phrygi·a -ae *f* a country comprising part of the central and W. Asia; *(poet)* Troy
phrygi·ō -ōnis *m* **(fryg-)** embroiderer
Phrygi·us -a -um *adj & mf* Phrygian; Trojan
Phrȳn·ē -ēs *f* Athenian courtesan who offered to rebuild Thebes when it was destroyed by Alexander the Great
Phry·x -gis *or* **-gos** *adj* Phrygian *(often w. reference to Troy or the Trojans)*
Phthī·a -ae *f* home of Achilles in Thessaly
Phthī·as -adis *f* woman from Phthia
Phthīōt·a *or* **Phthiot·ēs -ae** *m* native of Phthia
P(h)thīōtic·us -a -um *adj* of Phthia
phthis·is -is *f* tuberculosis
Phthī·us -a -um *adj* of Phthia
phȳ *interj* bah!
phylac·a -ae *f* prison
Phylac·ē -ēs *f* city of Thessaly, where Protesilaus was king
Phylacē·is -idos *adj (fem only)* of Phylace, *or* of Phylacus, the founder of Phylace
Phylacēi·us -a -um *adj* of Phylace *or* Phylacus; **conjunx Phylaceia** Laodamia *(wife of Protesilaus)*
Phylacid·ēs -ae *m* descendant of Phylacus, son of Diomede *(esp. Protesilaus)*
phylarch·us -ī *m* tribal chief
Phyllēi·us -a -um *adj* of the city of Phyllus in Thessaly; **Phylleius juvenis** Caeneus
Phyll·is -idis *or* **-idos** *f* daughter of King Sithon of Thrace, who was changed into an almond tree ‖ stock female name in poetry
physic·a -ae *or* **physic·ē -ēs** *f* natural science
physicē *adv* scientifically
physic·us -a -um *adj* natural, physical, belonging to natural philosophy *or* physics ‖ *m* natural philosopher, physicist ‖ *npl* natural science
physiognōm·ōn -onis *m* physiognomist
physiologi·a -ae *f* natural science
piābil·is -is -e *adj* expiable
piāculār·is -is -e *adj* expiatory; demanding expiatory rites ‖ *npl* expiatory sacrifices
piācul·um -ī *n* propitiatory sacrifice, victim; atonement, expiation; remedy; crime, sacrilege; punishment
piām·en -inis *n* atonement
pīc·a -ae *f* magpie, jay
picāri·a -ae *f* place where pitch is made
pice·a -ae *f* pine tree, spruce
Pīc·ens -entis *adj* Picene, of Picenum

Pīcentīn·us -a -um *adj* of Picenum; of Picentia *(town in S. Campania)*

Pīcēn·um -ī *n* distinct on the Adriatic coast of central Italy

Pīcēn·us -a -um *adj & m* Picene **II** *n see* Picenus

pice·us -a -um *adj* made of pitch; pitch-black

pic·ō -āre -āvī -ātus *tr* to tar, coat with pitch

pict·or -ōris *m* painter **II Pictor** Quintus Fabius Pictor *(earliest Roman historian, who wrote a history of Rome in Greek, fl 225 B.C.)*

pictūr·a -ae *f* painting; (art of) painting; embroidery

pictūrāt·us -a -um *adj* painted; embroidered

pict·us -a -um *pp of* pingo **II** *adj* painted; embroidered *(in color);* tabula picta a painting

pīc·us -ī *m* woodpecker **II Picus** son of Saturn and grandfather of Latinus; Picus was changed by Circe into a woodpecker

piē *adv* dutifully; affectionately

Pīeri·a -ae *f* district of S. E. Macedonia

Pīer·is -idos *f* daughter of Pieros; Muse **II** *fpl* the nine Muses

Pīeri·us -a -um *adj* Pierian; poetic; musical **II** *f see* Pieria **II** *fpl* Muses

Pīer·os *or* **Pīer·us -ī** *m* Pieros *(King of Emathia, or Macedonia, who named his nine daughters after the Muses; they were defeated in a contest with the Muses and were changed into birds)*

piet·ās -ātis *f* sense of responsibility, sense of duty; devotion, piety; *(of gods)* due regard *(for human beings);* kindness, tenderness; loyalty to the gods and country; *(w dat or* adversus *or* erga *or* in + acc) respect for, devotion to, loyalty to

pi·ger -gra -grum *adj* apathetic, slow, lazy; reluctant, unwilling; numbing *(cold);* slow-moving, tedious *(war, etc.);* backward, slow, dull

pig·et -ēre -uit *or* **-itum est** *v impers* it irks, pains, annoys; *(w. gen of cause of feeling), e.g.:* piget stultitiae meae I am irked by my own foolishness; *(w. inf), e.g.:* illa me composuisse piget I regret having written those verses

pigmentār·ius -(i)ī *m* paint dealer

pigment·um -ī *n* pigment, paint, color; coloring *(of style)*

pignerāt·or -ōris *m* mortgagee

pigner·ō -āre -āvī -ātus *tr* to mortgage; to pawn; *(fig)* to pledge

pigner·or -ārī -ātus sum *tr* to take as a pledge, accept in good faith; to lay claim to; to assure

pign·us -eris *or* **-oris** *n* pledge, security, guarantee; hostage; mortgage; income

from mortgages; wager, stake; *(fig)* pledge, assurance **II** *npl* children

pigrē *adv* slowly, sluggishly

pigriti·a -ae *or* **pigriti·ēs -ēī** *f* sluggishness, laziness

pigr·ō -āre -āvī *or* **pigr·or -ārī** *intr* to be slow, be sluggish, be lazy

pīl·a -ae *f (vessel for pounding)* mortar; pillar; pier; funerary monument *(w. cavity for mortal remains)*

pīl·a -ae *f* ball; ball game; globe; ballot *(used by jury);* mea pila est the ball is mine, I've won; pilā ludere to play ball

pīlān·us -ī *m* soldier in the third rank in battle

pīlāt·us -a -um *adj* armed with javelin

Pīlāt·us -ī *m* Pontius Pilate *(prefect of Judea, A.D. 26–36)*

pīlent·um -ī *n* ladies' carriage

pilleāt·us -a -um *adj* (pīl-) wearing a felt skullcap *(as a symbol of freed status)*

pilleol·us -ī *m* (small) skullcap

pille·um -ī *n or* **pille·us -ī** *m or* **pīle·um -ī** *n* felt cap *or* hat *(worn by Romans at festivals, esp. at the Saturnalia, and given to a slave when freed as a symbol of his freedom);* freedom

pilōs·us -a -um *adj* hairy

pīl·um -ī *n* javelin

Pīlumn·us -ī *m* primitive Italic deity

pīl·us -ī *m* maniple *or* company of the triarii; company of veteran reserves; primi pili centurio chief centurion of a legion; primus pilus chief centurion *(of the triarii and therefore of the legion)*

pil·us -ī *n* hair; non pili facere to not care a whit for

Pimpl·a -ae *f* spring in Pieria sacred to the Muses

Pimplē·a -ae *or* **Pi(m)plē·is -idis** *or* idos *f* Muse

Pi(m)plē(i)·us -a -um *adj* of Pimpla **II** *f* the spring at Pimpla

pīn·a -ae *f* a bivalve shellfish

Pīnāri·us -a -um *adj* name of a patrician clan at Rome, concerned with the cult of Hercules

Pindaric·us -a -um *adj* Pindaric

Pindar·us -ī *m* Pindar *(Greek lyric poet from Thebes in Boetoia, 519–438 B.C.)*

Pind·us -ī *m* mountain range separating Thessaly from Macedonia, connected with the Muses

pīnēt·um -ī *n* pine forest

pīne·us -a -um *adj* pine-, of pine

pingō pingěre pinxī pictus *tr* to draw, paint; to embroider; to depict, represent, portray; to stain, color; to decorate; *(rhet)* to embellish

pingu·e -is *n* fat

pinguesc·ō -ěre *intr* to get fat; to become fertile

pingu·is -is -e *adj* fat; fatty, greasy; *(of*

lamps) full of oil; *(of torches)* full of pitch; juicy; full-bodied *(wine)*; rich, full *(sound)*; rich, fertile *(land)*; fat, sleek *(cattle)*; thick *(in dimension)*; strong *(words)*; *(of altars)* caked with fat and blood; dense; stupid, dull; clumsy *(writing)*; quiet, comfortable *(life, home, retreat)*; **crura luto pinguia** legs caked with mud

pīnif·er *or* **pīnig·er -era -erum** *adj* pine-producing, pine-covered

pinn·a -ae *f* feather; wing; flight; fin; feathered arrow; pinnacle, battlement

pinnāt·us -a -um *adj* feathered, winged

pinnig·er -era -erum *adj* winged; feathered; having fins

pinnip·ēs -edis *adj* wing-footed

pinnipot·ens -entis *adj* able to fly

pinnirap·us -ī *m* crest-snatcher *(gladiator who tried to get the crest of his opponent's helmet)*

pinnul·a -ae *f* little wing

pīnotēr·ēs -ae *m* hermit crab

pinsit·ō -āre *tr* to pound (continually)

pī(n)s·ō -ĕre -ī *(or* -**uī)** -**us** *(or* -**itus)** *tr* to pound

pīn·us -ūs *or* -**ī** *f* pine tree, fir tree; pine forest; ship; torch; wreath of pine

pi·ō -āre -āvī -ātus *tr* to appease by sacrifice, propitiate; to honor with religious rites, worship; to purify with religious rites; to atone for, expiate; to avert

pip·er -eris *n* pepper

pipinn·a -ae f childish term for the penis

pīpil·ō -āre *intr* to chirp

pīpi·ō -āre *intr* to chirp

pīpul·um -ī *n* or **pīpul·us -ī** *m* shrieking, yelling

Pīrae·ēus *or* **Pīrae·us -ī** *m* or **Pīrae·a -ōrum** *npl* Piraeus *(principal harbor of Athens)*

Pīrae·us -a -um *adj* of Piraeus **||** *mpl* inhabitants of Piraeus

pīrāt·a -ae *m* pirate

pīrātic·us -a -um *adj* pirate **||** *f* piracy; **piraticam facere** to practice piracy

Pīrēn·ē -ēs *or* **Pīrēn·a -ae** *f* Pirene *(spring on the citadel of Corinth near which Bellerophon caught Pegasus)*

Pīrēn·is -idos *adj (fem only)* of the spring of Pirene

Pīritho·üs -ī *m* son of Ixion and king of the Lapiths

pir·um -ī *n* pear

pir·us -ī *f* pear tree

Pīs·a -ae *f or* **Pīs·ae -ārum** *fpl* Pisa *(capital of Pisatis in Elis on the Alpheus River)*

Pīs·ae -ārum *fpl* Pisa *(ancient city of N. Etruria, alleged to have been founded by the people of Greek Pisa)*

Pīsae·us -a -um *adj* of Pisa **||** *f* Hippodamia

Pīsān·us -a -um *adj* of Pisa *(in Etruria)*

Pisaur·um -ī *n* city in Umbria on the Adriatic coast *(modern Pisaro)*

piscāri·us -a -um *adj* fish; of fishing; **forum piscarium** fish market

piscāt·or -ōris *m* fisherman; fishmonger

piscātōri·us -a -um *adj* fishing; fish

piscāt·us -ūs *m* fishing; fish; *(fig)* good haul

piscicul·us -ī *m (lit & fig)* little fish

piscīn·a -ae *f* fish pond; swimming pool

piscīnār·ius -(i)ī *m* person fond of swimming pools *or* of fish ponds

pisc·is -is *m* fish **||** **Pisces** *mpl (astr)* Pisces *(constellation)*

pisc·or -ārī -ātus sum *intr* to fish

piscōs·us -a -um *adj* full of fish

pisculent·us -a -um *adj* well-stocked with fish

Pisid·a -ae *m* Pisidian *(inhabitant of Pisidia, referred to in contempt for the alleged addiction of the Pisidians to augury)*

Pisidi·a -ae *f* region in S. Asia Minor

Pīsistratid·ae -ārum *mpl* sons of Pisistratus *(Hippias & Hipparchus)*

Pīsistrat·us -ī *m* enlightened tyrant of Athens *(560–527 B.C.)*

pīsō *see* **pinso**

Pīs·ō -ōnis *m* Roman family name *(cognomen)* of the Calpurnian clan **||** Gnaeus Calpurnius Piso *(consul 7 B.C., accused of the murder of Germanicus in A.D. 19)* **||** Gaius Calpurnius Piso *(alleged leader of the conspiracy against Nero in A.D. 65)*

pistill·um -ī *n* or **pistill·us -ī** *m* pestle

pist·or -ōris *m* miller; baker

Pistōriens·is -is -e *adj* of Pistorium *(town in Etruria)*

pistōri·us -a -um *adj* baker's; **opus pistorium** pastry

pistrill·a -ae *f* small mill; small bakery

pistrīn·a -ae *f* flour mill; bakery

pistrīnens·is -is -e *adj* of *or* belonging to a bakery

pistrīn·um -ī *n* flour mill; bakery; drudgery

pistr·is -is *or* **pistr·ix -īcis** *f* sea monster; whale, shark; swift ship; *(astr)* the Whale *(constellation)*

pīstus *pp of* **pi(n)so**

pīs·um -ī *n* pea

Pitan·ē -ēs *f* Aeolian settlement on the coast of Asia Minor near Pergamum

pithēc·ium -(i)ī *n* little monkey

Pitthē·is -idos *f* daughter of Pittheus *(i.e., Aethra)*

Pitth·eüs -ēī *or* -**eos** *m* king of Troezen and father of Aethra, the mother of Theseus

Pitthē·us *or* **Pitthēi·us -a -um** *adj* of Pittheus

pītuīt·a -ae *f* phlegm; rheum; head cold

pītuītōs·us -a -um *adj* full of phlegm, phlegmatic

pity·ōn -ōnos *m* woods of pine trees
pi·us -a -um *adj* conscientious, dutiful; god-fearing, godly, holy; fatherly, motherly, brotherly, sisterly; affectionate; patriotic; good; sacred, holy *(objects connected with religion)*
pix pīcis *f* a sphinx
pix picis *f* pitch **ll** *fpl* chunks of pitch
plācābil·is -is -e *adj* easily appeased; pacifying, appeasing
plācābilit·ās -ātis *f* readiness to forgive, conciliatory disposition
plācām·en -inis *n* means of appeasing, peace-offering
plācāment·um -ī *n* means of appeasing, peace-offering
plācātē *adv* calmly, quietly
plācāti·ō -ōnis *f* pacifying, propitiating
plācāt·us -a -um *adj* calm, quiet; appeased, reconciled
plac·ens -entis *adj* pleasing
placent·a -ae *f* flat cake, pancake
placenti·a -ae *f* agreeableness
Placenti·a -ae *f* town on the river Po *(modern Piacenza)*
plac·eō -ēre -uī -itum *intr (w. dat)* to please, satisfy, give pleasure to, be acceptable to; **sibi placere** to be pleased with oneself **ll** *v impers* it seems right, seems proper; it is settled, is agreed; it is resolved, is decided; **eis placitum est ut considerarent** they decided to consider; **senatui placuit** the senate decided
placidē *adv* calmly, gently, quietly
placid·us -a -um *adj* calm; gentle; quiet, peaceful; tame *(animal)*
placit·ō -āre *intr* to be very pleasing
placit·us -a -um *adj* pleasing, acceptable; agreed upon **ll** *n* principle, belief, tenet; **ultra placitum laudare** to praise excessively
plāc·ō -āre -āvī -ātus *tr* to calm, quiet; to appease; to reconcile
plāg·a -ae *f* blow; wound, gash, welt; *(fig)* blow
plăg·a -ae *f* region, tract, zone; hunting net; mesh of a net; curtain; *(fig)* trap
plagiār·ius -(i)ī *m* plunderer; kidnapper; plagiarist
plăgig·er -era -erum *adj* covered with welts
plăgigerul·us -a -um *adj* covered with welts
plăgipatid·ēs -ae *m* whipping boy
plăgōs·us -a -um *adj* quick to use the rod
plagul·a -ae *f* curtain
plagūsi·a -ae *f* a kind of shellfish
planctus *pp of* **plango**
planct·us -ūs *m* beating
planc·us -a -um *adj* flatfooted
plānē *adv* clearly, distinctly; legibly; completely, quite; certainly, to be sure
plan·gō -gěre -xī -ctus *tr* to strike, beat; to

beat *(head, breast as sign of grief)*; to lament, bewail; *(fig)* to wring the hands **ll** *pass* to beat one's breast; *(of bird)* to flap its wings **ll** *intr* to wail
plang·or -ōris *m* striking, beating; beating of the breast, wailing
plāniloqu·us -a -um *adj* outspoken
plānip·ēs -edis *m* barefooted actor *(in the role of a slave)*
plānit·ās -ātis *f* distinctness
plāniti·ēs -ēī *or* **plāniti·a -ae** *f* flat surface, level ground, plain
plant·a -ae *f* sprout, shoot, young plant, seedling; *(anat)* sole
plantār·ia -ium *npl* cuttings, slips
plantār·ium -(i)ī *n* seedling bed *(for starting seedlings)*
plān·us -a -um *adj* flat, level, even; plain, clear **ll** *n* level ground; plain; **de plano** easily; **e plano** out of court
plan·us -ī *m* tramp; con-man
plasm·a -atis *n* phoney accent
Platae·ae -ārum *fpl* Plataea *(town in Boeotia where the Greeks defeated the Persians in 479 B.C.)*
Plataeens·is -is -e *adj* of Plataea **ll** *mpl* Plataeans
platale·a -ae *f* spoonbill *(waterfowl)*
platan·ōn -ōnis *m* grove of plane trees
platan·us -ī *or* **-ūs** *f* plane tree
plate·a *or* **platē·a -ae** *f* street
Plat·ō(n) -ōnis *m* Plato *(Greek philosopher, 429–348 B.C.)*
Platōnic·us -a -um *adj* Platonic **ll** *mpl* Platonists
plau·dō -děre -sī -sus *tr* (plōd-) to slap, clap, beat **ll** *intr* to clap, beat, flap; *(w. dat)* to applaud, approve of; **alis plaudere** to flap the wings; **manibus plaudere** to clap the hands
plausibil·is -is -e *adj* deserving of applause
plaus·or *or* **plōs·or -oris** *m* applauder
plaustr·um -ī *n* (plos-) wagon, cart; **plaustrum percellere** *(fig)* to upset the applecart **ll Plaustrum** *(astr)* the Great Bear *(constellation)*
plausus *pp of* **plaudo**
plaus·us -ūs *m* clapping, flapping; applause
Plautīn·us -a -um *adj* of Plautus
Plauti·us -a -um *adj* of Plautus
Plaut·us -ī *m* Plautus *(Titus Maccius Plautus, Roman writer of comedies, born in Umbria, c. 254–184 B.C.)*
plēbēcul·a -ae *f* rabble
plēbēi·us *or* **plēbēj·us -a -um** *adj* plebeian, of the common people; common, low, vulgar **ll** *m* plebeian
plēbicol·a -ae *m* democrat; demagogue
plēbis(s)cīt·um -ī *n* decree of the assembly of the plebeians
plebs *or* **pleps plēbis** *or* **plēb·ēs -ēī** *f* the

plebeians, common people; the masses, proletariat

plectil·is -is -e *adj* plaited, braided

plectō plectĕre plexī plexus *tr* to plait, braid

plect·ō -ĕre *tr* to beat; to punish

plectr·um -ī *n* plectrum; *(fig)* lyre

Plēï·as -adis *or* **-ados** Pleiad **‖** *fpl* Pleiades *(seven daughters of Atlas and Pleione, who were placed among the stars)*

Plēïon·ē -ēs *f* daughter of Oceanus and Tethys, wife of Atlas, and mother of the Pleiades

Plēmyr·ium -(i)ī *n* headland at the S. end of the Bay of Syracuse

plēnē *adv* fully, completely

plēn·us -a -um *adj* full; stout, plump; pregnant; filled, satisfied; full, packed; strong, loud *(voice);* full-length, unabridged, uncontracted; plentiful; advanced *(years);* complete

ple·ō -ēre *tr* to fill

plērumque *adv* generally, mostly, for the most part; often, frequently

plēr·usque -aque -umque *adj* a very great part of, the greater part of, most; a good many; **plerique omnes** nearly all **‖** *mpl* most people, the majority **‖** *n* the greatest part

Pleur·ōn -ōnis *f* a city in Aetolia

-pl·ex -icis *adjl suf usu.* formed from numerals, equivalent to the English "-fold", *e.g.:* **centumplex** hundredfold

plex·us -a -um *pp of* **plecto ‖** *adj* plaited

plicātr·ix -īcis *f* woman who folds clothes, folder

plic·ō -āre -āvī *or* **-uī -ātus** *or* **-itus** *tr* to fold, wind, coil up

Plīn·ius -(i)ī *m* Pliny the Elder *(Gaius Plinius Secundus, author of a work on natural history, d. A.D. 79)* **‖** Pliny the Younger *(Gaius Plinius Caecilius Secundus (his nephew), author of Letters and Panegyric to Trajan, A.D. 61–114)*

plīpi·ō -āre *intr (of a hawk)* to caw

plōdō *see* **plaudo**

plōrābil·is -is -e *adj* dismal

plōrātill·us -a -um *adj* tearful

plōrāt·or -ōris *m* mourner

plōrāt·us -ūs *m* wailing, crying

plōr·ō -āre -āvī -ātus *tr* to cry over **‖** *intr* to cry aloud, wail

plostell·um -ī *n* small cart

plostr·um -ī *n* wagon

ploxen·um -ī *n* (-xin-) wagon body

pluit pluĕre pluit *v impers (tr)* it is raining *(stones, blood, etc.)* **‖** *v impers (intr)* it is raining; *(w. abl)* it is raining *(stones, etc.)*

plūm·a -ae *f* down, soft feather; *(collectively)* down, feathers

plūmātil·e -is *n* dress embroidered with feathers

plūmāt·us -a -um *adj* covered with feathers

plumbe·us -a -um *adj* lead-, of lead, leaden; oppressive *(weather);* dull *(blade);* cheap *(wine);* stupid

plumb·um -ī *n* lead; pellet *(for a sling);* pipe; ruler *(for drawing lines);* **plumbum album** *(or* **candidum)** tin

plūme·us -a -um *adj* downy; filled with down; like feathers

plūmip·ēs -edis *adj* with feathered feet

plūm·ō -āre -āvī -ātum *tr* to cause to be covered with feathers

plūmōs·us -a -um *adj* feathered, covered with feathers

plūrāl·is -is -e *adj (gram)* plural

plūrāliter *adv (gram)* in the plural

plūr·ēs -ēs -a *adj* more; several; too many; **pluribus (verbis)** at great length, in greater detail **‖** *mpl* most people, the majority; the dead, "the majority" **‖** *npl* more things

plūrifāriam *adv* extensively, in many places

plūrimum *adv* (-rum-) very much, especially, commonly, generally, mostly; **plurimum valere** to be most powerful, have the greatest influence

plūrim·us -a -um *(superl of* **multus)** *adj* (-rum-) many a; most; very much; very many; very great, very intense; very powerful, very violent; **plurimam salutem dare** to send warmest greetings **‖** *mpl* most people, a very great number of people **‖** *n* a great deal; **plurimi facere** to think very highly of, think a great deal of; **plurimi vendere** to sell at the highest price; **quam plurimo vendere** to sell at the highest possible price; **quam plurimum** as much as possible

plūs *adv* more; **multo plus** much more; **plus minus** more or less; **paulo plus** a little more

plūs plūris *(comp of* **multus)** *adj* more **‖** *n* more, too much; **plus animi** more courage; **plus nimio** much too much; **plus plusque** more and more; **pluris esse** *(gen of value)* to be of more value, be worth more, be higher, be dearer **‖** *npl* more things; **quid plura?** why say more?, in short

plūscul·us -a -um *adj* a little more, somewhat more **‖** *n* a little more

plute·us -ī *m or* **plute·um -ī** *n* barrier, screen; low wall; parapet; headboard *or* footboard of bed *or* couch; *(fig)* couch; *(fig)* dining couch; bier; lectern; bookcase; *(mil)* movable mantlet *or* shed used to protect soldiers in siege works

Plūt·ō(n) -ōnis *m* Pluto *(king of the lower world, husband of Proserpina, and brother of Jupiter and Neptune)*

Plūtōni·us -a -um *adj* of Pluto

pluvi·a -ae *f* rain
pluviāl·is -is -e *adj* rain-, of rain, rainy
pluvi·us -a -um *adj* rain-, of rain, rainy; **pluvia aqua** rain water; **pluvius arcus** rainbow ‖ *f* rain
pōcill·um -ī *n* small drinking cup
pōc(u)l·um -ī *n* drinking cup; drink, draft; **poculum (ducere** *or* **exhaurire)** to drain a cup
poda·ger -gra -grum *adj* suffering from sore feet
podagr·a -ae *f* arthritis
podagrōs·us -a -um *adj* arthritic
Podalīri·us -ī *m* legendary physician, son of Aesculapius
pōd·ex -icis *m (sl)* ass, behind
pod·ium -(i)ī *n* balcony; box seat *(for the emperor)*
Poeantiad·ēs -is *m* son of Poeas, Philoctetes
Poeanti·us -a -um *adj* of Poeas ‖ *m* Philoctetes
Poe·ās *or* **Poe·ans -antis** *m* father of Philoctetes
poēm·a -atis *n (dat & abl pl:* **poematibus** *or* **poematis)** poem; poetry
poēmat·ium -(i)ī *n* short poem
poen·a -ae *f* punishment; penalty, fine; compensation, recompense, retribution, satisfaction; hardship, loss, pain; *(in games)* penalty; **poenam** *(or* **poenas) dare** *(or* **dependere, pendere, persolvere, reddere, solvere, suscipere, sufferre)** to pay the penalty; **poenam** *(or* **poenas) capere** *(or* **exigere, persequi, petere, repetere, reposcere)** to exact a penalty, demand satisfaction; **poena mortis** death penalty
Poenici·us -a -um *adj* Punic, Carthaginian
Poenīn·ī -ōrum *mpl* the Pennine Alps *(from Mont Blanc to Monte Rosa)*
poeniō *see* **punio**
Poenul·us -ī *m* little Phoenician *(i.e., Zeno the Stoic)*
Poen·us -a -um *adj* Phoenician; Carthaginian ‖ *m* Carthaginian *(esp. Hannibal)*
poēs·is -is *f* art of poetry; poetry, poems
poēt·a -ae *m* poet; playwright; *(fig)* person of great skill, artist
poētic·a -ae *or* **poētic·ē -ēs** *f* art of poetry; poetics
poēticē *adv* poetically
poētic·us -a -um *adj* poetic
poētri·a -ae *f* poetess
poētr·is -idis *or* **-idos** *f* poetess
pol *interj* by Pollux!; Gads!; **certo pol** most assuredly
Polem·ōn -ōnis *m* Platonic philosopher, disciple of Xenocrates and teacher of Zeno
Polemōnē·us -a -um *adj* professing the philosophy of Polemon
polent·a -ae *f* pearl barley

polentāri·us -a -um *adj* caused by eating barley
pol·iō -īre -īvī *or* **-iī -ītus** *tr* to polish; to smooth; *(fig)* to polish
polītē *adv* in a polished manner, with taste, smoothly, elegantly
polītic·us -a -um *adj* political
polīt·us -a -um *adj (lit & fig)* polished, smooth
poll·en -inis *n* *or* **poll·is -inis** *mf* flour
poll·ens -entis *adj* strong, powerful
pollenti·a -ae *f* might, power
poll·eō -ēre *intr* to be strong, be powerful; to be capable, be able; to have influence; *(of medicines)* to be efficacious; **in re publica plurimum pollere** to have tremendous influence in politics
poll·ex -icis *m* thumb; big toe; **pollicem premere** to press the thumb *(against the index finger to indicate approval);* **pollicem vertere** to turn the thumb down *(to indicate disapproval)*
pollic·eor -ērī -itus sum *tr* to promise
pollicitāti·ō -ōnis *f* promise
pollicit·or -ārī -ātus sum *tr* to keep promising
pollicit·us -a -um *pp of* **polliceor** ‖ *n* promise
pollinārí·us -a -um *adj* flour
polli(n)ct·or -ōris *m* mortician
pollin·gō -gěre -xī -ctus *tr* to prepare (a corpse), lay out
Polli·ō -ōnis *m* Gaius Asinius Pollio *(orator, poet, historian, and patron of literature, 76 b.c.–a.d. 4)*
poll·is -inis *mf* flour
pol·lūceō -lūcēre -luxī -luctus *tr* to offer up *(as a sacrifice);* to serve *(food, a meal)*
pollūcibiliter *adv* sumptuously
polluctūr·a -ae *f* sumptuous dinner
pol·luō -luěre -luī -lūtus *tr* to pollute; to violate; to dirty, soil
Poll·ux *or* **Poll·ūcēs -ūcis** *m* Pollux *(son of Tyndareus and Leda, twin brother of Castor, and patron of boxers)*
pol·us -ī *m* pole *(either end of the axis on which the heavenly spheres were believed to revolve);* star; sky; heaven; **polus australis** South Pole; **polus superior** North Pole
Polyb·ius -iī *m* Greek historian and friend of Scipio Aemilianus *(c. 203–120 b.c.)*
Polyclīt·us -ī *m* (**-clēt-**) Polycletus *(Greek sculptor of Argos, fl c. 452–412 b.c.)*
Polycrat·ēs -is *m* ruler of Samos in the 6th cent. b.c., patron of the arts and close friend of Anacreon
Polydam·ās -antos *m* (**Pōl-**) Trojan warrior, son of Panthus and friend of Hector
Polydōrē·us -a -um *adj* of Polydorus
Polydōr·us -ī *m* youngest son of Priam and Hecuba

Polyhymni·a -ae *f* one of the Muses; Muse of lyric poetry

Polym(n)est·ōr -oris *m* king of Thracian Chersonese, husband of Ilione (the daughter of Priam), and murderer of Polydorus

Polynīc·ēs -is *m* son of Oedipus and Jocasta, and brother of Eteocles, Antigone, and Ismene, and leader of the Seven against Thebes

Polyphēm·us -ī *m* son of Neptune and one of the Cyclopes

pōlyp·us -ī *m* polyp *(sea animal; tumor)*

Polyxen·a -ae *or* **Polyxen·ē -ēs** *f* Polyxena *(daughter of Priam and Hecuba whom Pyrrhus, son of Achilles, sacrificed at his father's tomb)*

Polyxeni·us -a -um *adj* of Polyxena

pōmāri·us -a -um *adj* fruit, of fruit trees ‖ *m* fruit vendor ‖ *n* orchard

pōmēr·ium -(i)ī *n* (-moer-) space kept free of buildings inside and outside a city wall

pōmif·er -era -erum *adj* fruit-bearing

Pōmōn·a -ae *f* Roman goddess of fruit

pōmōs·us -a -um *adj* loaded with fruit

pomp·a -ae *f* solemn procession; parade; retinue; pomp, ostentation

Pompēï·a *or* **Pompēj·a -ae** *f* Julius Caesar's second wife, the daughter of Quintus Pompeius Rufus *(consul in 88 B.C.)* ‖ a daughter of Pompey, who married Faustus Cornelius Sulla

Pompēïān·us *or* **Pompējān·us -a -um** *adj* Pompeian ‖ *mpl* inhabitants of Pompeii ‖ soldiers or followers of Pompey

Pompēï·us *or* **Pompēj·us -ī** *m* Gnaeus Pompeius Strabo *(father of the the triumvir)* ‖ Pompey the Great *(Gnaeus Pompeius Magnus, Roman general and politician, 106–48 B.C.)* ‖ Sextus Pompeius Magnus *(his younger son, killed in 35 B.C.)*

Pompēj·i -ōrum *mpl* city about 10 miles S. of Naples, destroyed by Vesuvius in A.D. 79

Pompil·ius -(i)ī *m* Numa Pompilius *(second king of Rome and traditional founder of Roman state religion)*

pompil·us -ī *m* pilot-fish

Pompōniān·us -a -um *adj* of a member of the Pomponian clan

Pompōn·ius -(i)ī *m* Lucius Pomponius *(of Bononia, a writer of Atellan farces (c. 109–32 B.C.)* ‖ Titus Pomponius Atticus *(the friend and correspondent of Cicero (109–32 B.C.)* ‖ Publius Pomponius Secundus *(writer of dramatic verse)*

Pomptīn·us -a -um *adj* Pomptine; **Pomptinae paludes** Pomptine Marshes *(in Latium)*

pōm·um -ī *n* fruit; fruit tree

pōm·us -ī *f* fruit tree

ponder·ō -āre -āvī -ātus *tr (lit & fig)* to weigh

ponderōs·us -a -um *adj* weighty, massive; *(fig)* dignified

pondō *indecl* *n* pound, pounds; *(in advl sense)* in weight; *(where specific number of pounds is given, the numeral is usually expressed in the neuter:* **argenti pondo bina selibras in militem praestare** to offer two and a half pounds of silver per soldier); **auri quinque pondo** five pounds of gold; **duo pondo saxum** a two-pound rock; **quot pondo ted esse censes nudum?** how many pounds do you think you weigh nude?

pond·us -eris *n* weight; mass; burden; importance; stability of character ‖ *npl* balance, equilibrium

pōne *adv* behind, after, back ‖ *prep (w. acc)* behind

pōnō pōnĕre posuī pos(i)tus *tr* to put, set, place; to put down, put aside; to pitch *(camp)*; to station, post *(troops)*; to lay *(foundation, keel)*; to build, found *(town, colony, building)*; to plant *(tree)*; *(of trees)* to shed leaves; to serve *(food)*; to stage *(a play)*; to lay down *(arms)*; to take off *(clothes, ornaments)*; to cut *(beard, hair, fingernails)*; to arrange, smooth *(the hair)*; to take *(steps)*; to deposit *(money)*; to bet *(money)*; to lend *(money)* at interest; to set aside, store; to lay out, spend *(time, effort, etc.)*; to file *(legal claim)*; to lay down *(rule, law)*; to stage *(a play)*; to yield up *(life, breath)*; to get rid of, drop; to esteem, value; to classify; to appoint *(to specific position)*; to calm *(sea)*; to lay *(egg)*; to fix *(penalty, price)*; to offer *(award)*; to depict *(in art)*; to assume, suppose; to quote, cite; to state *(in writing or speech)*; to pose, ask *(question)*; to spend *(time, money, energy)*; to give as security; to give *(a name)*; to lay out for burial; *(w. in + abl)* to base or stake *(upon)*; **finem ponere** *(w. dat)* to put an end to; **genu ponere** to kneel down; **in loco** *(or* **loco** *or* **in numero) ponere** to place in a class or category; **in medio ponere** to make accessible to all; **modum ponere** *(w. dat)* to limit, set bounds to ‖ *intr (of snow)* to fall; *(of wind)* to drop, stop; to be neutral

pon·s -tis *m* bridge; gangway; drawbridge; deck

Ponti·ae -ārum *fpl* island in the Tuscan Sea S. of Circeii

ponticul·us -ī *m* small bridge

Pontic·us -a -um *adj* Pontic, of Pontus *(region around the Black Sea)*; **mare Ponticum** Black Sea; **nux Pontica** hazelnut; **radix Pontica** rhubarb

pontif·ex -icis *m* (-tuf-) pontiff, pontifex,

priest (one of a board of 15); **pontifex maximus** chief pontiff
pontificāl·is -is -e adj pontifical
pontificāt·us -ūs m pontificate
pontific·us -a -um adj pontifical
pont·ō -ōnis m ferry
pont·us -ī m sea; sea water
Pont·us -ī m Euxine or Black Sea; region around the Black Sea **‖ Pontus** (kingdom of Mithridates, between Bithynia and Armenia, after 63 B.C. a Roman province)
pop·a -ae m priest's assistant (who slew the victim)
popan·um -ī n sacrificial cake
popell·us -ī m rabble, mob
popīn·a -ae f low-class restaurant, dive; food sold at a low-class restaurant
popīn·ō -ōnis m diner at a low-class restaurant
popl·es -itis m hollow of the knee; knee; **duplicato poplite** on bended knee; **contento poplite** with a stiff knee
Poplicola see **Publicola**
poposcī perf of **posco**
poppysm·a -atis n smacking of the lips (to indicate satisfaction)
populābil·is -is -e adj destructible
populābund·us -a -um adj ravaging
populār·is -is -e adj of the people, people's; approved by the people, popular; favoring the people, democratic; demagogic; of the same country, native; common, coarse **‖** mf fellow countryman; party member; fellow member, associate; (w. gen) partner or associate in **‖** mpl people's party, democrats **‖** npl general-admission seats
populārit·ās -ātis f courting popular favor; fellow citizenship
populāriter adv like the people; like a demagogue, to win popular favor; **populariter loqui** to use slang
populāti·ō -ōnis f ravaging
populāt·or -ōris m, **populātr·ix -īcis** f ravager, destroyer
populāt·us -ūs m devastation
pōpule·us -a -um adj of poplars, poplar-
pōpulif·er -era -erum adj poplar-bearing
pōpuln(e)us -a -um adj of poplar
popul·ō -āre -āvī -ātus or **popul·or -rī -ātus sum** tr to ravage, devastate, lay waste; (fig) to pillage, ruin, spoil
pŏpul·us -ī m the people (as political community); nation; public, crowd; citizens (as opposed to soldiers), civilians; region, district
pōpul·us -ī f poplar tree
por- pref giving the sense of "forth", e.g.: **portendo** to stretch forth
porc·a -ae f sow
porcell·a -ae f little sow, suckling pig

porcell·us -ī m little hog, suckling pig
Porci·a -ae f daughter of Cato Uticensis, married first to Marcus Bibulus, consul in 59 B.C., and afterwards to Marcus Brutus, the assassin of Julius Caesar
porcīnār·ius -(i)ī m pork seller
porcīn·us -a -um adj hog's, pig's **‖** f pork
Porc·ius -(i)ī m Cato (Marcus Porcius Cato the Censor 235–149 B.C.) **‖** Cato Uticensis (Marcus Porcius Cato Uticensis (95–46 B.C.)
porcul·a or **porculēn·a -ae** f little sow
porcul·us -ī m little pig
porc·us -ī m pig, hog
porgō see **porrigo**
porphyrētic·us -a -um adj made of porphyry (a purple-streaked marble)
porphyri·ō -ōnis f type of waterfowl
Porphyri·ōn -ōnis m one of the Giants who fought against the gods
porphyrīt·ēs -ae adj of porphyry **‖** m porphyry
Porphyr·ius -(i)i m Porphyry (Neo-Platonic philosopher, born A.D. 233, who edited the works of Plotinus)
porrecti·ō -ōnis f extending, stretching out
porrect·us -a -um pp of **porrigo** and **porricio ‖** adj stretched out, extended, extensive, long; protracted; laid out, dead; (fig) wide-spread **‖** npl offerings
por·riciō -ricĕre -rexī -rectus tr to offer up; **inter caesa et porrecta** (prov) at the last moment, at the eleventh hour (literally, between the slaughtering and the offering)
por·rigō -rigĕre -rexī -rectus tr to reach out, stretch out, extend; to stretch out (in sleep or death); to offer, present, hand; to lengthen (a syllable) **‖** refl & pass to extend
porrīg·ō -inis f dandruff
Porrim·a -ae f cult name of the birth-goddess Antevorta
porrō adv forwards; farther on, on; far off, at a distance; long ago; in the future, hereafter; again, in turn; next, furthermore, moreover, on the other hand
porr·um -ī n or **porr·us -ī** m leek; chive
Porsenn·a or **Porsēn·a** or **Porsinn·a -ae** m Lars Porsen(n)a (king of Clusium in Etruria who sided with Tarquin in a war against Rome)
port·a -ae f city-gate; gate; entrance; outlet; camp-gate (of which there were always four: praetoria, principalis, decumanus, quaestoria)
portāti·ō -ōnis f carrying
porten·dō -dĕre -dī -tus tr to indicate, foretell, portend, predict
portentific·us -a -um adj abnormal
portentōs·us -a -um adj abnormal, unnatural; monstrous

portent·um -ī *n* portent, omen, sign; monstrosity, monster; fantasy, far-fetched fiction; *(as term of contempt)* monster

portentus *pp of* **portendo**

porthm·eūs -eī *or* **-eōs** *m* ferryman *(i.e., Charon)*

porticul·a -ae *f* small portico

portic·us -ūs *f* portico, colonnade; *(mil)* gallery *(formed by placing vineae end to end);* Stoicism

porti·ō -ōnis *f* portion, share; ratio, proportion; installment, payment; **pro portione** proportionately, relatively

portiscul·us -ī *m* gavel *(used to keeping time for rowers)*

portit·or -ōris *m* customs officer; ferryman, boatman

port·ō -āre -āvī -ātus *tr* to carry; to bring

portōr·ium -(i)ī *n* port-duty, customs duty; tax *(on peddlers)*

portul·a -ae *f* small gate

Portūn·us -ī *m* tutelary deity of harbors

portuōs·us -a -um *adj* having good harbors

port·us -ūs *m* port, harbor; haven, refuge; mouth of a river

posc·a -ae *f* sour drink

poscō poscĕre poposcī *tr (weaker than* **flāgitō**) to ask, request, beg, demand; to ask for in marriage; *(at auction)* to bid for; *(of things)* to require, demand, need, call for, make necessary; *(w.* **ab**) to ask for *(s.th.)* from, demand *(s.th.)* of; *(w. double acc)* to demand *(s.th.)* of *(s.o.),* ask *(s.o.)* for *(s.th.)*

posculent·us -a -um *adj* drinkable

pōsi·a -ae *f* (paus-) unripe olive

Posīd·ēs -ae *m* favorite freedman of the Emperor Claudius

Posīdōn·ius -(i)ī *m* Stoic philosopher at Rhodes, teacher of Cicero *(135–51 b.c.)*

positi·ō -ōnis *f* putting, placing, setting; position, posture; situation

posit·or -ōris *m* builder

positūr·a -ae *f* posture; formation

posit·us -a -um *pp of* **pono** ‖ *adj* situated, located; stretched out, lying down

posit·us -ūs *m* position, site; arrangement; *(gram)* position *(of a syllable)*

possessi·ō -ōnis *f* possession; getting possession, occupation; estate

possessiuncul·a -ae *f* small estate

possess·or -ōris *m* possessor, occupant; *(leg)* defendant

possibil·is -is -e *adj* possible

pos·sideō -sidēre -sēdī -sessus *tr* to possess, occupy; to have, own; to dwell in, live in; *(fig)* to take hold of; *(poet)* to take up *(space)* with one's bulk

pos·sīdō -sīdĕre *tr* to take possession of, occupy, seize

possum posse potuī *intr* to be able; **multum (plus, plurimum) posse** to have

much (more, very great) influence; **non possum quin exclamem I** can't help shouting out; **quantum** *(or* **ut) fieri potest** as far as is possible

post *also* **poste** *adv (of place)* behind, back, backwards; *(of time)* later, afterwards; *(of order)* next; **aliquanto post** somewhat later; **multis post annis** many years later ‖ *prep (w. acc) (of place)* behind; *(of time)* after, since

post- *pref used in the senses of the adverb*

posteā *adv* afterwards, after this, after that, hereafter, thereafter

posteāquam *conj (also as two words)* after; ever since, from the time that

posteri·or -or -us *adj* later, next, following; latter, posterior; inferior; hind *(e.g., legs)*

posterit·ās -ātis *f* the future, afterages, posterity, later generations; offspring *(of animals);* **in posteritatem** in the future

posterius *adv* later, at a later date

poster·us -a -um *adj* following, ensuing, next, subsequent, future ‖ *mpl* future generations, posterity, descendants ‖ *n* future time; next day; consequence; **in posterum** until the next day; for the future

post·ferō -ferre *tr* to treat as less important, esteem less; to sacrifice

postgenit·us -a -um *adj* born later ‖ *mpl* later generations

posthab·eō -ēre -uī -itus *tr* to consider of secondary importance; to slight, neglect; *(w. dat)* to think *(s.th.)* less important than

posthāc *adv* hereafter, in the future

posthinc *or* **post hinc** *adv* from here, next

posthōc *or* **post hōc** *adv* after this, afterwards

postibi *adv* afterwards, then

postīcul·um -ī *n* small building in the rear, outhouse

postīc·us -a -um *adj* rear-, back- ‖ *n* back door

postid *adv* then, afterwards

postideā *adv* afterwards, after that

postilēn·a -ae *f* rump; buttocks

postili·ō -ōnis *f* sacrifice demanded by the gods to make up for a previous omission in sacrifice

postillā(c) *adv* afterwards

post·is -is *m* doorpost; door ‖ *mpl* double doors

postlīmin·ium -(i)ī *n* right to return home and resume one's former rank and privileges after exile or capture; recovery, restoration

pos(t)merīdiān·us -a -um *adj* afternoon

postmerīdiē *adv* in the afternoon

postmodo *or* **postmodum** *adv* after a bit, a little later, afterwards

postpart·or -ōris *m* successor, heir

post·pōnō -pōnĕre -posuī -positus *tr* to consider of secondary importance; to postpone; *(w. dat)* to consider *(s.th.)* of less importance than, set *(s.th.)* aside in favor of; **omnibus rebus postpositis** laying aside everything

postprincip·ium -(i)ī *n (also written as two words)* sequel; **postprincipia** *(mil)* second line of battle

postput·ō -āre -āvī -ātus *tr (also written as two words)* to consider of secondary importance; *(w.* **prae** + *abl)* to consider *(s.th.)* less important than

postquam *conj* after, when

postrēmō *adv* at last; finally

postrēmum *adv* for the last time, last of all

postrēm·us -a -um *(superl of* **posterus)** *adj* last; latest, most recent; last in line, rear; least important; lowest, worst ‖ *n* the end; **ad postremum** in the end, finally; in the last place

postrīdiē *adv* on the day after, on the following day; **postridie mane** the next morning ‖ *prep (w. gen),* e.g., **postridie ejus diei** on the day after that; *(w. acc),* e.g., **postridie ludos** on the day after the games

postrīduō *adv* on the day after

postscaen·ium -(i)ī *n* backstage

post·scrībō -scrībĕre -scripsī -scriptus *tr (w. dat)* to add *(e.g., a name)* to; **Tiberi nomen suo postscribere** to add the name of Tiberius to his own

postulāt·a -ōrum *npl* demands, claims, requests

postulāti·ō -ōnis *f* demand, request, desire; complaint; *(leg)* application for permission to present a claim

postulāt·or -ōris *m* one who makes demands; plaintiff

postulāt·um -ī *n* demand; request

postulāt·us -ūs *m* petition, request

postul·ō -āre -āvī -ātus *tr* to demand, claim; to look for as due, expect; *(of things)* to require; *(leg)* to arraign, prosecute; *(leg)* to apply for *(a writ from the praetor to prosecute)*

Postumi·us -a -um *adj* Roman clan name *(nomen),* esp. Aulus Postumius Tubertus *(father-in-law of Cincinnatus)* ‖ Gaius Postumius *(a soothsayer consulted by Sulla)*

postum·us -a -um *adj* last, latest-born; born after the father's death

Postum·us -ī *m* Roman first name *(praenomen),* subsequently in use as a family name *(cognomen)*

postus *pp of* **pono**

Postvert·a -ae *f* goddess presiding over breech births

posuī *perf of* **pono**

pōtāti·ō -ōnis *f* drinking; drinking party

pōtāt·or -ōris *m* drinker

pot·ens -entis *adj* capable; mighty, powerful, strong; efficacious, potent; influential; *(w. gen)* **1** capable of, equal to, fit for; **2** having power over; **3** presiding over; **4** having obtained *(one's wish);* **5** having carried out *(an order)*

potentāt·us -ūs *m* political power, rule, dominion

potenter *adv* powerfully, mightily, effectually, vigorously; according to one's ability

potenti·a -ae *f* force, pow�ⲣr; political power *(esp. unconstitutional power in contrast to* **potestas)**

potēr·ium -iī *n* goblet

potest·ās -ātis *f* power, ability, capacity; efficacy, force; public authority, rule, power, sway, dominion, sovereignty, empire; magisterial power, magistracy, office; possibility, opportunity *(to choose, decide),* discretion, power of choice; permission; person in office, magistrate, ruler; property, quality

Pothīn·us -i *m* minister of Ptolemy XIII of Egypt, who ordered the assassination of Pompey the Great

potin *or* **potin'** = **potisne** can you?

pot·iō -īre -īvī -ītus *tr (w. acc and gen)* to put *(s.o.)* under the power of

pōti·ō -ōnis *f* drinking; drink, draught; magic potion

pōtiōnāt·us -a -um *adj (w. abl)* having been given a drink of

pot·ior -īrī -ītus sum *tr* to acquire, get possession of ‖ *intr (w. abl)* to acquire, get possession of, become master of, get hold of

poti·or -or -us *(comp of* **potis)** *adj* more powerful; more precious; better, preferable, superior; more important; *(w. gen)* having greater control over

potis *or* **pote** *indecl adj* able, capable; possible

potissimum *adv* chiefly, especially

potissim·us -a -um *adj* chief, principal, most important

pōtit·ō -āre -āvī -ātus *tr* to drink (habitually)

pōtiuncul·a -ae *f* a little drink

potius *adv* rather, more, by preference; **potius quam** more than, rather than

Potni·as -ados *adj (fem only)* of Potniae *(a Boeotian village)*

pōt·ō -āre -āvī -ātus *or* -**us** *tr* to drink; to absorb ‖ *intr* to drink

pōt·or -ōris *m* drinker; a drunk

pōtr·ix -īcis *f* drinker *(female)*

pōtulent·us -a -um *adj* drinkable; tipsy ‖ *npl* drinks

pōt·us -a -um *pp of* **poto** ‖ *adj* drunk

pōt·us -ūs *m* drinking; a drink

prae *adv* before, in front; in preference ‖ *prep (w. abl)* **1** *(in its literal sense, usu.*

w. refl pron, in certain phrases) before, in front of: **prae se** in front of oneself, publicly, openly, plainly; **prae se ferre** to display, manifest, profess; **prae manu** at hand; **2** compared with, in comparison with: **Gallis prae magnitudine corporum suorum brevitas nostra contemptui est** in comparison with the size of their own bodies the Gauls hold our shortness of stature in contempt; **3** by reason of, in consequence of, because of, for: **prae laetitiā lacrimare** to weep for joy; **nec loqui prae maerore potuit** he could not speak because of his grief; **4** in consequence of, out of: **prae pudore** out of shame

prae- *pref* indicating **1** position in front, ahead: **praecedere** to go in front, go ahead; **2** position in the end: **praeurere** to burn at the extremity; **praeacuere** to sharpen to a point; **3** temporal precedence: **praedicere** to tell in advance; **4** with adjectives, pre-eminence in the quality concerned: **praeacutus** very sharp; **5** rank: **praeesse** to be in charge; **praetor** one in charge; **6** protection: **praesidium** defense, protection

praeac·uō -uĕre -uī -ūtus *tr* to sharpen to the point

praeacūt·us -a -um *adj* very sharp; pointed

praealt·us -a -um *adj* very high; very deep

praeb·eō -ēre -uī -itus *tr* to hold out, offer, present; to supply, give; to exhibit, represent, show; to give up, yield, surrender; to cause, occasion; to permit, allow; **praebere aurem** *(or* **aures)** *(w. dat)* to listen to; **praebere exemplum** to set an example; **praebere suspicionem** to cause suspicion **‖** *refl* to show oneself, behave; to offer oneself as

praebib·ō -ĕre -ī -itus *tr (w. dat)* to drink *(e.g., a toast)* to

praebit·or -ōris *m* supplier

praecalid·us -a -um *adj* very hot

praecalv·us -a -um *adj* very bald

praecant·ō -āre -āvī -ātus *tr* (-cen-) to cast a spell over **‖** *intr (w. dat)* to recite a spell over

praecantr·ix -īcis *f* witch, enchantress

praecān·us -a -um *adj* prematurely gray

prae·caveō -cavēre -cāvī -cautus *tr* to take precautions against, guard against, try to avoid **‖** *intr* to take precautions, be on one's guard; *(w. dat)* to look out for, look after; *(w. abl)* to guard against, be on one's guard against

prae·cēdō -cēdĕre -cessī -cessus *tr* to precede, go out before, lead; to surpass **‖** *intr* to excel; *(w. dat)* to excel, be superior to

praecell·ens -entis *adj* excellent, outstanding, preeminent

praecell·ō -ĕre *tr* to surpass, outdo **‖** *intr*

to distinguish oneself, excel; to take precedence; *(w. dat)* **1** to rule over; **2** to surpass

praecels·us -a -um *adj* towering

praecenti·ō -ōnis *f* musical prelude

praecentō *see* **praecanto**

praecentus *pp of* **praecino**

praecēpī *perf of* **praecipio**

praec·eps -ipitis *adj* headfirst; downhill, steep, precipitous; sinking *(sun);* swift, rushing, violent; hasty, rash, inconsiderate; dangerous **‖** *n* edge of a cliff, cliff; *(fig)* brink; danger; **in praeceps** *(or* **per praeceps)** headlong, straight downward; **in praecipiti** on the edge; *(fig)* on the brink of disaster

praeceps *adv* headfirst

praecepti·ō -ōnis *f* preconception; precept, rule; instruction; *(leg)* receiving *(of an inheritance)* in advance *(of the general partition of an estate)*

praecept·or -ōris *m,* **praceptr·ix -īcis** *f* teacher, tutor

praecept·um -ī *n* instruction, bit of advice; rule; maxim; order, direction

praecerp·ō -ĕre -sī -tus *tr* to pick beforetime; *(w. dat) (fig)* to snatch away from

praecī·dō -dĕre -dī sus *tr* to lop off, cut off; to cut short; to cut, cut through; to damage, mutilate; to break off, end suddenly *(a speech, etc.);* to end, destroy *(hopes, etc.);* to refuse, decline

praecin·gō -gĕre -xi -ctus *tr* to gird; to surround, ring; to dress **‖** *pass* to be surrounded, be ringed; **altius praecinctus** with tunic tucked up higher; *(fig)* more energetic(ally); **ense cingi** to wear a sword; **male cinctus** improperly dressed; **recte cinctus** properly dressed

prae·cinō -cinĕre -cinuī -centus *tr* to predict; *(w. dat)* to predict *(s.th.)* to **‖** *intr* to make predictions; *(w. dat)* to sing or play before *or* at *(e.g., sacrifice, dinner, etc.)*

prae·cipiō -cipĕre -cēpī -ceptus *tr* to take in advance, occupy in advance; to receive in advance; to grasp beforehand, anticipate; to teach, instruct, direct, advise, order, bid, warn; to prescribe; **aliquantulum viae** *(or* **temporis)** **praecipere** *(or* **iter praecipere)** to get a headstart; **animo** *(or* **cogitatione)** **praecipere** to imagine beforehand, reckon on, anticipate, expect; **artem nandi praecipere** to give swimming instructions; **gaudium praecipere** to rejoice in advance; **oculis praecipere** to see beforehand, get a preview of; **opinione praecipere** to suspect; **pecuniam mutuam praecipere** to get an advance loan

praecipitanter *adv* at top speed

praecipit·ō -āre -āvī -ātus *tr* to throw down headfirst; to hasten, hurry, precipitate **‖** *refl* to throw oneself down, throw oneself headfirst, jump down, dive; to sink **‖** *intr* to rush headfirst, rush at top speed, rush thoughtlessly; to fall, sink; to be ruined

praecipuē *adv* especially, chiefly

praecipu·us -a -um *adj* special, peculiar, particular; chief, principal; distinguished, excellent, extraordinary **‖** *n* excellence, superiority **‖** *npl* outstanding *or* important elements; **praecipua rerum** highlights

praecīsē *adv* briefly, concisely; absolutely

praecīs·us -a -um *pp of* **praecido ‖** *adj* abrupt, precipitous; rugged, rough; brief, shortened *(speech);* clipped *(words)*

praeclārē *adv* very clearly; excellently; *(to express agreement)* very good, excellent

praeclār·us -a -um *adj* very clear; very nice; splendid, noble, distinguished, excellent; famous; notorious

praeclū·dō -děre -sī -sus *tr* to shut, shut off, obstruct, bar the way of; to hinder, impede, stop; to preclude *(an action, event);* **portas consuli praecludere** to shut the gates in the consul's face; **vocem praecludere alicui** to shut s.o. up, hush s.o. up

praec·ō -ōnis *m* crier, herald; auctioneer; *(fig)* eulogist

praecōgit·ō -āre -āvī -ātus *tr* to premeditate

praecognit·us -a -um *adj* known beforehand, foreseen

prae·colō -colěre -coluī -cultus *tr* to cultivate prematurely; *(fig)* to embrace prematurely

praecomposit·us -a -um *adj* arranged beforehand; studied, self-conscious

praecōni·us -a -um *adj* of a public crier; of an auctioneer **‖** *n* crier's office; proclamation, announcement; praising, praise

praeconsum·ō -ěre -psī -ptus *tr* to spend *or* use up beforehand

praecontract·ō -āre *tr* to consider in advance

praecoqu·is -is -e *adj* premature; precocious

praecordi·a -ōrum *npl* midriff; lower chest; chest; diaphragm; insides, stomach; breast, heart *(as seat of emotions)*

praecor·rumpō -rumpěre -rūpī -ruptus *tr* to bribe in advance

prae·cox -cocis *adj* premature; early, precocious

praecupid·us -a -um *adj (w. gen)* very fond of

praecurrent·ia -ium *npl* antecedents

prae·currō -currěre -(cu)currī cursus *tr* to precede, anticipate; to outdo, surpass **‖** *intr* to run out ahead, take the lead; *(w. ante + acc)* to run out ahead of; *(w. dat)* to outdo

praecursi·ō -ōnis *f* previous occurrence; *(mil)* skirmish; *(rhet)* warmup *(of the audience)*

praecurs·or -ōris *m* forerunner; spy; *(mil)* scout; *(mil)* advance guard

praecursōri·us -a -um *adj* sent in advance

prae·cutiō -cutěre *tr* to wave, brandish in front

praed·a -ae *f* booty, spoils, plunder; prey; *(of fish)* catch; *(in hunting)* the game; prize, profit; **praedae esse** *(w. dat)* to fall prey to; **vocamus in partem praedamque Jovem** we invite Jupiter to share the game

praedābund·us -a -um *adj* pillaging, plundering, marauding

praedamn·ō -āre -āvī -ātus *tr* to condemn beforehand; **spem praedamnare** to give up hope too soon

praedāti·ō -ōnis *f* plundering

praedāt·or -ōris *m* marauder, looter, vandal; hunter; greedy man

praedātōri·us -a -um *adj* marauding, looting; graspy, greedy

praedāt·us -ūs *m* robbery

praedēlass·ō -āre *tr* to tire out, weaken beforehand

praediāt·or -ōris *m* real-estate dealer

praediātōri·us -a -um *adj* concerned with real-estate; **jus praediatorium** *(leg)* mortgage law

praedicābil·is -is -e *adj* praiseworthy, laudable

praedicāti·ō -ōnis *f* announcement, publication; praise, commendation

praedicāt·or -ōris *m* eulogist

praedĭc·ō -āre -āvī -ātus *tr* to announce; to report; to assert; to praise, recommend

prae·dīcō -dīcěre -dixī -dictus *tr* to mention beforehand *or* earlier; to prearrange; to predict; to order beforehand, command beforehand

praedicti·ō -ōnis *f* prediction

praedict·um -ī *n* prediction, prophecy; command, order; **velut ex praedicto** as if by prearrangement

praediol·um -ī *n* small estate, small farm

praedisc·ō -ěre *tr* to learn beforehand, find out in advance

praedisposit·us -a -um *adj* previously arranged

praedit·us -a -um *adj* gifted; *(w. abl)* endowed with, provided with, furnished with

praed·ium -iī *n* estate, farm; collateral *(consisting of land);* **praedium urbanum** *(whether in town or in the country)* building site

praedīv·es -itis *adj* very rich

praedīvīn·ō -āre -āvī -ātus *tr* to know in advance, have a presentiment of

praed·ō -ōnis *m* robber; pirate

praedoct·us -a -um *adj* instructed beforehand

praed·or -ārī -ātus sum *tr* to raid, plunder, loot, rob; *(fig)* to rob, ravish; **amores alicujus praedari** to steal s.o.'s sweetheart away ‖ *intr* to plunder, loot, make a raid; *(w.* **ex)** to prey on, profit by, take advantage of, *e.g.,* **ex alterius inscientiā praedari** to prey on *or* take advantage of another's ignorance

prae·dūcō -dūcĕre -duxī -ductus *tr* to run *or* construct *(trench, wall)* out in front *(as a defense)*

praedulc·is -is -e *adj* very sweet; *(fig)* very satisfying *(honor, reward)*

praedūr·us -a -um *adj* very tough *(skin);* tough, brawny

praeēmin·eō *or* **praemin·eō -ēre** *tr* to surpass, excel ‖ *intr* to project, stick out

prae·eō -īre -īvī *or* **-iī** *tr* to lead, precede; to read out, dictate, lead *(prayers)* ‖ *intr* to go out ahead, take the lead; *(w. dat)* to walk in front of

praefāti·ō -ōnis *f* preface, introduction; formula

praefātus *pp of* **praefor**

praefectūr·a -ae *f* supervision, superintendence; office of prefect, superintendency; government of a district; prefecture *(Italian city governed by a Roman prefect);* territory of a prefecture, district

praefect·us -ī *m* prefect, supervisor, superintendent; command; governor; *(w. gen or dat)* supervisor of, commander of, prefect *or* governor of

prae·ferō -ferre -tulī -lātus *tr* to hold out, carry in front; *(w. dat or* **quam)** to prefer *(one thing)* to *(another);* to anticipate; to display, reveal, betray; to offer, present; to offer as a model ‖ *refl & pass (w. dat)* to surpass ‖ *pass* to ride past, ride by, march past; to outflank

paefer·ox -ōcis *adj* very defiant

praeferrāt·us -a -um *adj* iron-tipped; *(coll)* chained *(slave)*

praefervid·us -a -um *adj (lit & fig)* boiling

praefestīn·ō -āre -āvī -ātus *tr* to hurry past; *(w. inf)* to be in a big hurry to

praefic·a -ae *f* hired mourner *(female)*

prae·ficiō -ficĕre -fēcī -fectus *tr* to put *(s.o.)* in charge; *(w. double acc)* to appoint *(s.o.)* as; *(w. dat)* to put *(s.o.)* in charge of, set *(s.o.)* over, appoint *(s.o.)* to command

praefīd·ens -entis *adj* too trustful; overconfident; *(w. dat)* too trustful of; **homines sibi praefidentes** overconfident people

praefī·gō -gĕre -xī -xus *tr* to fix, fasten, set up in front, fasten on the end; *(w. abl)* to tip with; *(w. in + abl)* to impale on; **capistris praefigere** to muzzle

praefin·iō -īre -īvī *or* **-iī ītus** *tr* to determine in advance; to prescribe, appoint; to limit

praefīnītō *adv* in the prescribed manner

praefiscinē *or* **praefiscinī** *or* **praefascinē** *adv* so as to avoid bad luck; meaning no offense

praefixī *perf of* **praefigo**

praefix·us -a -um *pp of* **praefigo** ‖ *adj* cuspidibus praefixus pointed; **ferro praefixus** iron-tipped

praeflōr·ō -āre -āvī -ātus *tr* to deflower beforehand; *(fig)* to tarnish

praeflu·ō -ĕre *tr & intr* to flow by

praefōc·ō -āre -āvī -ātus *tr* to suffocate; to block *(windpipe, road)* ‖ *pass* to choke

prae·fodiō -fodĕre -fōdī -fossus *tr* to bury beforehand; to dig in front of; **portas praefodere** to dig trenches in front of the gates

prae·for -fārī -fātus sum *tr* to say beforehand, utter in advance, preface; to address in prayer beforehand; to foretell; to invoke ‖ *intr* to pray beforehand; *(w. dat)* to pray before

praefractē *adv* obstinately

praefract·us -a -um *pp of* **praefringo** ‖ *adj* determined; abrupt

praefrīgid·us -a -um *adj* very cold

prae·fringō -fringĕre -frēgī -fractus *tr* to break off at the tip; to break to pieces, smash

praeful·ciō -cīre -sī -tus *tr* to prop up, support in front; *(w. dat)* to use *(s.o.)* as a prop *or* support for

praeful·geō -gēre -sī *intr* to shine forth, glitter, sparkle

praegelid·us -a -um *adj* very cold

praegest·iō -īre *intr* to be very eager

praegn·ans -antis *or* **praegn·ās -ātis** *adj* pregnant; *(w. abl)* full of, swollen with

praegracil·is -is -e *adj* lanky

praegrand·is -is -e *adj* huge; very great; very powerful

praegrav·is -is -e *adj* very heavy; weighed down; very troublesome

praegrav·ō -āre -āvī -ātus *tr* to weigh down; to outweigh; *(fig)* to burden

prae·gredior -gredī -gressus sum *tr* to go in advance of, go ahead of; to go by, go past; *(fig)* to outstrip ‖ *intr* to walk out in front; *(w. dat)* to precede, lead

praegressi·ō -ōnis *f* procession; *(fig)* precedence

praegress·us -ūs *m* prior occurrence

praegustāt·or -ōris *m* taster, sampler

praegust·ō -āre -āvī -ātus *tr* to taste beforehand, sample, get a sample of

praehib·eō -ēre -uī -itus *tr* to offer, furnish, supply; to utter, speak; **operam praehibere** to offer help

praejac·eō -ēre *tr* to lie before, be located in front of **ǁ** *intr (w. dat)* to lie before

praejūdicāt·us -a -um *adj* decided beforehand; prejudiced; **opinio praejudicata** prejudice **ǁ** *n* prejudged matter; prejudice; **id pro praejudicato ferre** to take it as a foregone conclusion

praejūdic·ium -(i)ī *n* preliminary hearing; prejudice; presumption; precedent, example

praejūdic·ō -āre -āvī -ātus *tr* to decide beforehand, prejudge **ǁ** *intr (w. dat of disadvantage)* to be prejudicial to

prae·juvō -juvāre -jūvī *tr* to help in advance

prae·lābor -lābī -lapsus sum *tr & intr* to glide along, glide, by, float by

praelamb·ō -ēre *tr* to lick beforehand

praelarg·us -a -um *adj* very ample

praelātus *pp of* **praefero**

praelaut·us -a -um *adj* plush

praelecti·ō -ōnis *f* lecture

prae·legō -legĕre -lēgī -lectus *tr* to lecture on; to sail past

praelig·ō -āre -āvī -ātus *tr* to tie up; *(w. dat)* to tie *(s.th.)* to

praelong·us -a -um *adj* very long; very tall

prae·loquor -loquī -locūtus sum *tr* to make *(a speech)* before s.o. else; to say by way of preface; *(leg)* to present *(a case)* first; **ǁ** *intr* to speak first

prae·lūceō -lūcēre -lūxī *tr (fig)* to enkindle *(hope)* **ǁ** *intr (w. dat)* **1** to throw light on; **2** to outshine, outdo, surpass; **3** to light the way for

praelūsi·ō -ōnis *f* prelude

praelustr·is -is -e *adj* magnificent

praemandāt·a -ōrum *npl (leg)* warrant for arrest

praemand·ō -āre -āvī -ātus *tr* to recommend beforehand; to order in advance

praemātūrē *adv* too soon, prematurely

praemātūr·us -a -um *adj* premature

praemedicāt·us -a -um *adj* protected by drugs *or* charms

praemeditāti·ō -ōnis *f* premeditation, prior consideration

praemedit·or -ārī -ātus sum *tr* to think over beforehand; to practice; to practice on *(e.g., a lyre);* **mala praemeditata** premeditated crimes

praemerc·or -ārī -ātus sum *tr* to buy in advance

praemetu·ens -entis *adj* apprehensive, anxious

praemetuenter *adv* anxiously; cautiously

praemetu·ō -ĕre *tr* to fear beforehand **ǁ** *intr (w. dat)* to be apprehensive about

praemin·eō -ēre *tr* to surpass, exceed **ǁ** *intr* to stand out prominently

prae·mittō -mittĕre -mīsī -missus *tr* to send out ahead, send in advance **ǁ** *intr* to send word

praem·ium -(i)ī *n* prize, reward, recompense; exploit *(worthy of reward);* gift, bribe

praemolesti·a -ae *f* apprehension, presentiment of trouble

praemōl·ior -īrī *tr* to prepare beforehand, work at in advance

praemon·eō -ēre -uī -itus *tr* to forewarn; to warn of; to foreshadow, presage, predict

praemonit·us -ūs *m* premonition, forewarning

praemonstrāt·or -ōris *m* guide

praemonstr·ō -āre -āvī -ātus *tr* to point out the way to, guide, direct; to predict

praemor·deō -dēre -dī *or* **-sī -sus** *tr* to bite the tip off *(fig)* to crib, pilfer

praemor·ior -ī -tuus sum *intr* to die too soon, die prematurely

praemūn·iō -īre -īvī -ītus *tr* to fortify in front; to protect, secure **ǁ** *intr (fig) (of a lawyer)* to prepare one's defenses

praemūnīti·ō -ōnis *f (rhet)* preparation, conditioning *(of the minds of the hearers)*

praenarr·ō -āre -āvī -ātus *tr* to relate beforehand

praenat·ō -āre -āvī *tr & intr* to float past, flow by

praenāvig·ō -āre -āvī -ātum *tr & intr* to sail by

Praenest·e -is *n (f)* ancient town in Latium *(c. 20 miles S.E. of Rome, modern Palestrina)*

Praenestīn·us -a -um *adj & m* Praenestine

praenit·eō -ēre -uī *intr (w. dat)* **1** to outshine; **2** to appear more attractive to

praenōm·en -inis *n* first name

prae·nōscō -noscĕre -nōvī *tr* to find out beforehand, foreknow

praenōti·ō -ōnis *f* innate idea, preconception

praenūbil·us -a -um *adj* heavily clouded; dark, gloomy

praenunti·a -ae *f* harbinger, omen

praenunti·ō -āre -āvī -ātus *tr* to foretell

praenunti·us -a-um *adj* foreboding **ǁ** *m* forecaster, harbinger, omen

praeoccupāti·ō -ōnis *f* seizing beforehand, advance occupation

praeoccup·ō -āre -āvī -ātus *tr* to occupy before another; to preoccupy; to anticipate, prevent

praeol·et -ēre *or* **praeolit -ĕre** *v impers* a smell is emitted, there is a strong smell; **praeolit mihi quo tu velis** I scent your wishes before you express them

praeopt·ō -āre -āvī -ātus *tr* to prefer

praepand·ō -ĕre *tr* to spread, extend; *(fig)* to reveal

praeparāti·ō -ōnis *f* preparation

praeparāt·us -a -um *adj* prepared, supplied, furnished, ready **‖** *n* stores; *ex ante preparato* from the stores; *(fig)* by previous arrangement

praepar·ō -āre -āvī -ātus *tr* to get ready, prepare, prepare for; to gather together; to furnish beforehand; to plan in advance

praepedīment·um -ī *n* impediment

praeped·iō -īre -īvī *or* **-(i)ī -ītus** *tr* to shackle, chain; to hinder, obstruct, hamper; to embarrass

praepend·eō -ēre *intr* to hang down in front

praep·es -etis *adj (of birds of omen)* flying straight ahead, of good omen; winged, swift of flight **‖** *mf* bird of good omen; bird, large bird

praepilāt·us -a -um *adj* tipped with a ball; *missile praepilatum* blunted missile

praepingu·is -is -e *adj* very fertile

praepoll·eō -ēre -uī *intr* to be very powerful; to be superior; *(w. dat)* to surpass in power

praeponder·ō -āre -āvī -ātus *tr* to outweigh; to regard as superior **‖** *intr* to weigh more

prae·pōnō -pōnĕre -posuī -positus *tr (w. dat)* **1** to place, set, put *(s.th.)* in front of *or* before *(s.o.);* **2** to serve *(s.o. food);* **3** to entrust *(s.o.)* with; **4** to put *(s.o.)* in charge of *or* in command of; **5** to prefer *(s.o. or s.th.)* to, give priority to

praeport·ō -āre -āvī -ātus *tr* to carry before oneself

praepositi·ō -ōnis *f* preference; prefixing; *(gram)* preposition

praeposit·um -ī *n* preferable thing *(i.e., s.th. short of absolute good)*

praeposit·us -a -um *pp of* **praepono ‖** *adj* preferred, preferable **‖** *m* prefect, commander **‖** *n* that which is desirable, a desirable good

praeposterē *adv* out of the proper order

praeposter·us -a -um *adj* inverted, in the wrong order; badly timed; topsy-turvy; preposterous

praeposuī *pref of* **praepono**

praepot·ens -entis *adj* very powerful; *(w. gen)* in full control of

praeproperanter *or* **praeproperē** *adv* very quickly, too fast

praeproper·us -a -um *adj* very quick; overhasty, sudden

praepūt·ium -(i)ī *n* foreskin

praequam *conj* in comparison to; *nihil hoc est, praequam alios sumptūs facit* this is nothing in comparison to the other expenses that he runs up

praequest·us -a -um *adj* complaining beforehand; *multa praequestus* having first voiced many complaints

praeradi·ō -āre *tr* to outshine

praerapid·us -a -um *adj* very swift

praereptus *pp of* **praeripio**

praerig·escō -escĕre -uī *intr* to become very stiff

prae·ripiō -ripĕre -ripuī -reptus *tr* to snatch away, carry off; to anticipate, forestall; to count on too soon, presume upon; *(w. dat)* to snatch from

prae·rōdō -rōdĕre -rōsī -rōsus *tr* to bite the end of, nibble at; *digitos praerodere* to bite the fingernails

praerogātīv·us -a -um *adj* asked before others; *(pol)* voting first, privileged; *omen praerogativum* omen to vote first **‖** *f (pol)* first tribe *or* century to vote; *(pol)* vote of the first tribe *or* century to vote; *(pol)* previous election; sure sign, omen

praerōsī *perf of* **praerodo**

praerōsus *pp of* **praerodo**

prae·rumpō -rumpĕre -rūpī -ruptus *tr* to break off, tear away *(s.th.)* in front

praerupt·us -a -um *adj* broken off, broken up; rough *(terrain);* steep; hasty, impetuous; *(of an utterance)* cut short **‖** *n* precipice, steep place; *(fig)* dangerous undertaking

praes *adv* at hand

prae·s -dis *m* bondsman, surety; collateral

praesaep- = **praesep-**

praesāgāti·ō -ōnis *f* power of knowing the future, presentiment

praesāg·iō -īre -īvī *or* **-iī** *or* **praesāg·ior -īrī** *tr* to have forebodings of, feel beforehand; to forebode, portend

praesāgīti·ō -ōnis *f* presentiment, strange feeling; prophetic power

praesāg·ium -(i)ī *n* presentiment prophetic instinct; portent; prediction

praesāg·ō -āre -āvī *tr* to have a presentiment of

praesāg·us -a -um *adj* prophetic

praesc·iō -īre -īvī -ītus *tr* to know beforehand

praesc·iscō -iscĕre -(i)ī *tr* to find out *or* learn beforehand

praesci·us -a -um *adj* prescient, having foreknowledge; **praescius venturi** foreseeing the future

prae·scrībō -scrībĕre -scripsī -scriptus *tr* to prefix in writing; to describe beforehand; to determine in advance, prescribe, ordain; to dictate; to outline, map out; to put forward as an excuse

praescripti·ō -ōnis *f* heading, title; preface; pretext; limit, law; limit, restriction

praescript·um -ī *n* regulation, rule; boundary line; route

praesec·ō -āre -uī -tus *tr* to cut off; to cut away; to pare *(nails)*

praesegmin·a -um *npl* clippings
praes·ens -entis *adj* present, in person, face to face; at hand; existing, contemporary; prompt, immediate, instant; impending; efficacious, powerful, effective; influential; resolute; *(of a god)* read to help, propitious; *(of payment)* in cash; **in praesens tempus** for the present; **in rem prasentem venire** to come to the very spot; **(in) re praesenti** on the spot; **praesens pecunia** cold cash; **praesenti die** on the day in question; **sermo praesens** a face-to-face talk ‖ *n* present time; **ad** *(or* **in)** **praesens** for the present; **in praesenti** on the spot; in the present case; on the present occasion
praesensī *perf of* **praesentio**
praesensi·ō -ōnis *f* presentiment; preconception
praesensus *pp of* **praesentio**
praesentāne·us -a -um *adj (of a poison)* having an immediate effect
praesentāri·us -a -um *adj* paid in cash on the spot
praesenti·a -ae *f* presence; efficacy, effect; **animi praesentia** presence of mind; resolution; **in praesentiā** at present, in the present state of affairs; **in praesentiā esse** to be present, be available; **in praesentiam** for the present
praesen·tiō -tīre -sī -sensus *tr* to feel beforehand, to realize in advance, have strange feelings about
praesēp·e -is *n or* **praesēp·ēs -is** *f* **(-saep-)** stall, stable; crib, manger; *(coll)* brothel; *(coll)* lodgings, room
praesēp·iō -īre -sī -tus *tr* **(-saep-)** to fence in, barricade
praesertim *adv* especially, particularly; **praesertim cum** especially because
praeserv·iō -īre *intr (w. dat)* to serve *(s.o.)* as a slave
praes·es -idis *m* guard, guardian, protector, defender; president, superintendent; captain, pilot; governor *(of a province)* ‖ *f* guardian, protectress
praesid·ens -entis *m* president, ruler
prae·sideō -sidēre -sēdī *tr* to guard, protect, defend; to command, be in command of ‖ *intr* to be in charge, be in command; *(w. dat)* **1** to watch over, guard, protect; **2** to preside over, direct, manage; **3** to command
praesidiāri·us -a -um *adj* on garrison duty
praesid·ium -(i)ī *n* protection, defense; assistance; *(mil)* guard, garrison; *(mil)* garrison post, defensive position; *(naut)* convoy; **praesidium agitare** to stand guard
praesignific·ō -āre -āvī -ātus *tr* to indicate in advance, foretoken
praesign·is -is -e *adj* outstanding

praeson·ō -āre -uī *tr & intr* to sound beforehand
praesparg·ō -ĕre *tr* to strew, scatter
praestābil·is -is -e *adj* excellent, outstanding; of outstanding importance
praest·ans -antis *adj* outstanding
praestanti·a -ae *f* excellence, preëminence, superiority
praestantissimē *adv* exceptionally well
praestern·ō -ĕre *tr* to strew in front
praest·es -itis *m* guardian, protecting deity
praestīgi·ae -ārum *fpl* sleight of hand; juggling; tricks; illusion
praestīgiāt·or -ōris *m*, **praestīgiātr·ix -īcis** *f* juggler; magician; imposter
praestin·ō -āre -āvī -ātus *tr* to buy, shop for, bargain for
praesti·tuō -tuĕre -tuī -tūtus *tr* to fix *or* set up beforehand; to prescribe
praestitus *pp of* **praesto**
praestō *adv* at hand, ready, present, here; **praesto esse** *(w. dat)* **1** to be on hand for, attend, serve, be helpful to, aid; **2** to be in the way of, resist, oppose
prae·stō -stāre -stitī -stitus *(fut participle:* **praestātūrus)** *tr* to be superior to, outdo; to show, exhibit, give evidence of, display; to answer for, be responsible for, take upon oneself; to perform, discharge, fulfill; to keep, maintain, retain; to present, offer, supply; **fidem praestare** to keep one's word; **impetūs populi praestare** to be responsible for popular outbreaks; **nihil praestare** to be answerable for nothing; **officia praestare** to perform duties; **socios salvos praestare** to keep the allies safe; **terga hosti praestare** to show one's back to the enemy, retreat; **virtutem praestare** to display courage ‖ *refl* to show oneself, behave ‖ *intr* to stand out, be outstanding, be preëminent ‖ *v impers* it is preferable, it is better
praestōl·or -ārī -ātus sum *or* **praestōl·ō -āre** *tr* to wait for, expect ‖ *intr (w. dat)* to wait for, await
prae·stringō -stringĕre -strinxī -strictus *tr* to draw together, constrict, squeeze; to graze; *(fig)* to touch lightly on; to blunt *(an edge);* to blind, dazzle *(the eyes);* to dazzle, baffle; to throw into the shade
praestru·ō -ĕre -xī -ctus *tr* to build up, to block up, stop up; to build up *(e.g., confidence)* beforehand
praes·ul -ulis *or* **praesultāt·or -ōris** *m* dancer *(at the head of a religious procession)*
praesult·ō -āre -āvī -ātum *intr (w. dat)* to dance in front of, jump around in front of
prae·sum -esse -fuī -futūrus *intr* to preside; **in provinciā praeesse** to govern a

province; *(w. dat)* **1** to preside over, be in charge of, be in command of; **2** to be preëminent in

prae·sūmō -sūmĕre -sumpsī -sumptus *tr* to take in advance; to anticipate, presume, take for granted

praesumpti·ō -ōnis *f* anticipation; presumption; *(rhet)* anticipation *(of an opponent's objections)*

praesūt·us -a -um *adj* sewed up; covered

praete·gō -gĕre -xī -ctus *tr* to protect; to shelter

praetempt·ō -āre -āvī -ātus *tr* to try out in advance, test in advance; to grope for

praeten·dō -dĕre -dī -tus *tr* to hold *or* stretch in front of oneself; to present; to offer an an excuse, give as pretext, allege, pretend; *(w. dat)* to hold *(e.g., a toga)* in front of *(e.g., the eyes)* **‖** *pass (of places) (w. dat)* to lie to the front of *or* opposite

praetent·ō -āre *tr* to allege

praetep·escō -escĕre -uī *intr (of love)* to glow, grow warm

praeter *conj* besides, other than **‖** *prep (w. acc)* **1** *(of place)* past, by, along, before, in front of: **praeter castra copias suas ducere** to lead his troops past *or* in front of the camp; **2** beyond in degree, surpassing: **praeter spem** beyond hope, unexpectedly; **3** despite, contrary to: **praeter speciem** despite appearances; **praeter consuetudinem** contrary to normal usage, contrary to custom; **4** in addition to, as well as, besides: **praeter haec** besides this, moreover; **praeter id quod** in addition to the fact that; **5** except, but, other than: **nunc quidem praeter nos nemo est** now there's really no one but us; **6** exclusive of, except for: **praetores quotannis praeter paucos locupletati sunt** the praetors with few exceptions were getting rich every year

praeter *adv* by, past

praeter- *pref* by, past

praeterag·ō -ĕre *tr (w. double acc)* to drive *(e.g., a horse)* past *(a place)*

praeterbīt·ō -ĕre *tr & intr* to go by *or* past

praeter·dūcō -dūcĕre -duxī -ductus *tr* to lead by, conduct past

praetereā *adv (also written as two words)* besides, moreover; hereafter, thereafter

praeter·eō -īre -īvī *or* **-iī -itus** *tr* to go past, pass by; to skip, pass over in silence; to escape the notice of; to go beyond; to surpass **‖** *intr* to go by

praeterequit·ans -antis *adj* riding by *(on horseback)*

praeter·ferō -ferre -tulī -lātus *tr (w. double acc)* to carry *or* take *(s.o.)* past *(s.th.)* **‖** *pass* to move by *(a place)*

praeterflu·ō -ĕre *tr & intr* to flow by

praeter·gredior -gredī -gressus sum *tr* to

march by, go past; to surpass **‖** *intr* to march by, go past

praeterhāc *adv* in addition

praeterit·us -a -um *pp of* **praetereo ‖** *adj* past, bygone, former; *(gram)* **(tempus) praeteritum** past tense

praeter·lābor -lābī -lapsus sum *tr & intr* to glide by, slip past

praeterlātus *pp of* **praeterfero**

praeterme·ō -āre *tr & intr* to go past

praetermissi·ō -ōnis *f* leaving out, omission; passing over, neglecting; *(w. gen)* omission of

praeter·mittō -mittĕre -mīsī -missus *tr* to let pass, let go by; to leave undone; to pass over, omit, disregard, overlook, neglect

praeternāvig·ō -āre *tr* to sail past

prae·terō -terĕre -trīvī *tr* to wear down in front

praeterquam *or* **praeter quam** *conj* except that; **praeterquam qui** apart from a person who; **praeterquam quod** apart from the fact that; *(w. illipsis)* **num quo crimine is esset accusatus praeterquam veneni?** had he ever been charged with any crime except that of poisoning?; **praeterquam bis** except on two occasions

praetertulī *perf of* **praeterfero**

praetervecti·ō -ōnis *f* passing by; sailing past; riding by

praeter·vehor -vehī -vectus sum *tr & intr* to pass by *or* past; to ride by; to sail by; to march *or* go by

praetervol·ō -āre *tr & intr* to fly by; *(of opportunity)* to slip by; to escape

praetex·ō -ĕre -uī -tus *tr* to border, edge, fringe; to adorn in front; *(fig)* to cloak, conceal, disguise; to use as a pretext, allege, pretend

praetext·a -ae *f* crimson-bordered toga *(worn by higher magistrates and by freeborn boys and possibly girls);* tragedy; **praetextas docere** to put on tragedies

praetextāt·us -a -um *adj* wearing the toga praetexta *(crimson-bordered toga);* underage, juvenile; **mores praetextati** loose morals

praetext·um -ī *n* adornment, glory; pretext, cloak

praetext·us -a -um *pp of* **praetexo ‖** *adj* bordered; wearing the crimson-bordered toga; **fabula praetexta** Roman tragic drama **‖** *f see* **praetexta ‖** *n* pretext, pretense, excuse

praetext·us -ūs *m* show, appearance; pretext

praetim·eō -ēre *intr* to be apprehensive

praetinct·us -a -um *adj* previously dipped

praet·or -ōris *m* praetor *(judicial magistrate, accompanied by six lictors);* *(during early days of the Republic)* chief magistrate, chief executive; *(in Italian municipalities)* chief magistrate; **praetor peregrinus** praetor who had jurisdiction over cases involving a Roman and a foreigner; **praetor urbanus** *(or* **urbis)** praetor with jurisdiction over cases involving Roman citizens; **pro praetore** magistrate with extended governorship, or other persons ranked as such

praetōriān·us -a -um *adj* praetorian, belonging to the emperor's bodyguard; **miles praetorianus** a praetorian guard ‖ *mpl* praetorian guard

praetŏrici·us -a -um *adj* received from the praetor *(at public games)*

praetŏri·us -a -um *adj* of the commander in chief, of the commander *or* general; praetor's; propraetor's; **cohors praetoria** general's bodyguard; **comitia praetoria** praetorial elections; **navis praetoria** flagship; **porta praetoria** camp gate nearest the general's tent; **turba praetoria** crowd around the praetor ‖ *n* general's quarters, headquarters; official residence of the governor in a province; council of war; emperor's bodyguard; palace, mansion

praetor·queō -quēre -sī -tus *tr* to twist beforehand; to strangle first

praetract·ō -āre *tr* to consider in advance

praetrepid·ō -āre *intr* to tremble in anticipation

praetrepid·us -a -um *adj* very nervous, trembling

praetrīvī *perf of* **praetero**

praetrunc·ō -āre -āvī -ātus *tr* to cut off; to lop off the tip of

praetulī *perf of* **praefero**

Praetūtiān·us -a -um *adj* of the Praetutii *(a people of Picenum)*

praetūr·a -ae *f* praetorship; propraetorship

praeumbr·ans -antis *adj* casting a shadow; *(fig)* overshadowing

praeust·us -a -um *adj* burnt at the tip, hardened by fire at the point; frostbitten

praeut *conj* as compared with, when compared with

praeval·ens -entis *adj* exceptionally powerful, exceptionally strong

praeval·eō -ēre -uī *intr* to be stronger, have more power; to have greater influence; to have the upper hand

praevalid·us -a -um *adj* unusually strong, unusually powerful, imposing; too strong

praevāricāti·ō -ōnis *f (leg)* collusion

praevāricāt·or -ōris *m (leg)* prosecutor in collusion with the defense

praevaric·or -ārī -ātus sum *intr (leg) (of an attorney)* to act in collusion with his opposite to secure a particular outcome to a trial

praevār·us -a -um *adj* very crooked; very knock-kneed

prae·vehor -vehī -vectus sum *tr (of a river)* to flow by ‖ *intr* to ride in front, ride by; to sail by

prae·veniō -venīre -vēnī -ventus *tr* to come before, precede, get the jump on, anticipate; to prevent ‖ *intr* to come before, precede

praeverb·ium -(i)ī *n (gram)* prefix

praeverr·ō -ĕre *tr* to sweep *(the ground)* before

praever·tō -tĕre -tī -sus *or* **prae·vertor -vertī -versus sum** *tr (-vort-)* to go before, precede, outrun, outstrip; to turn to first, attend to first; to prefer; to come before, anticipate; to prevent; to reoccupy; *(w. dat or* **prae** *+ abl)* to prefer *(s.o. or s.th.)* to ‖ *intr (w. dat or* **ad)** to go first to, turn to first, attend to first

prae·video -vidēre -vīdī -vīsus *tr* to foresee

praeviti·ō -āre -āvī -ātus *tr* to taint *or* pollute beforehand

praevi·us -a -um *adj* going before, leading the way

praevol·ō -āre -āvī *intr* to fly out in front

pragmatic·us -a -um *adj* experienced, worldly-wise ‖ *m* legal adviser

pran·deō -dēre -dī -sus *tr* to eat for breakfast, eat for lunch ‖ *intr* to have breakfast, have lunch

prand·ium -(i)ī *n* breakfast; lunch

pransit·ō -āre *intr* to usually eat breakfast *or* lunch

prans·or -ōris *m* guest at lunch

pransōri·us -a -um *adj* suitable for lunch

prans·us -a -um *pp of* **prandeo** ‖ *adj* having had breakfast *or* lunch, after eating; well-fed; **pransus potus** having been wined and dined

prasināt·us -a -um *adj* wearing a green outfit

prasiniān·us -ī *m* fan of the green faction *(at the racetrack)*

prasin·us -a -um *adj* green; **factio prasina** the Greens *(one of the stables of horses at the racetrack)*

prātens·is -is -e *adj* meadow-, growing in a meadow

prātul·um -ī *n* small meadow

prāt·um -ī *n* meadow; *(fig)* broad expanse of the sea ‖ *npl* meadow grass

prāvē *adv* crookedly; improperly, wrongly, badly, poorly; **prave facti versūs** poorly written verses

prāvit·ās -ātis *f* crookedness, distortion; impropriety, irregularity; perverseness, depravity

prāv·us -a -um *adj* crooked, distorted, deformed; irregular, improper, wrong, bad; perverse, vicious

Praxitel·ēs -ī *or* **-ūs** *or* **-ae** *m* Athenian sculptor *(4th cent. B.C.)*

Praxitelī·us -a -um *adj* of Praxiteles

precāriō *adv* upon request

precāri·us -a -um *adj* obtained by prayer; dependent on another's will, uncertain, precarious

precāti·ō -ōnis *f* prayer; **precationes facere** to say prayers

precāt·or -ōris *m* intercessor, suppliant

precēs = *pl of* prex

preci·ae -ārum *fpl* grapevine

prec·or -ārī -ātus sum *tr* to entreat, supplicate, pray to; to pray for; to wish for; *(w. double acc)* to pray to *(s.o.)* for; *(w. acc of thing and abl of person)* to request *(s.th.)* from; *(w.* **pro** + *abl)* to entreat *(e.g., the gods)* on behalf of; *(w.* **ut, ne)** to pray that, pray that not; **longum Augusto diem precari** to wish Augustus long life ‖ *intr* to pray; *(w.* **ad)** to pray to, *e.g.,* **di ad quos precantur** the gods to whom they pray; **male precari** to curse, utter curses

prehen·dō *or* pren·dō -děre -dī -sus *tr* to take hold of, grasp, seize; to detain; to arrest; to catch, surprise; to reach, arrive at; to grasp, understand; *(w.* **in** + *abl)* to catch a person in the act of; *(mil)* to occupy

prēl·um -ī *n* wine press, oil press; clothes press

premō preměre pressī pressus *tr* to press, squeeze; to lie down on *(the ground); (of things)* to be on top of, rest on; to bury *(in the ground);* to trample on; to get on top of, have sex with *(a woman);* to hug *(the shore);* to suppress, hide; to cover, crown; to press hard, bear down on; to weigh down, burden; to put emphasis on *(a point of argument);* to chase, attack; to weigh down, load; to press together, close; to choke, throttle; to block *(an entranceway);* to keep shut up, prevent from escaping; to curb, stop *(movement, an action, a process);* to depress, lower; to submerge, sink; to drown out *(a noise); (of sleep, death)* to overcome, overpower; *(of darkness)* to cover, hide; to mark, impress; to prune; to pressure, urge, importune; to degrade, humble, disparage; to abridge, condense, compress *(words, thoughts);* to press *(wine, oil);* to subjugate; *(geog)* to hem in, surround; **forum premere** to frequent the forum, walk about in the forum; **oculos premere** to close the eyes *(of a dead person);* **pollicem premere** to give the good luck sign *(by pressing the thumb against the index finger);* **vestigia premere** *(w. gen)* **1** to follow hard upon the tracks of; **2** *(fig)* to follow in *(s.o.'s)* tracks; **vocem premere** to fall silent ‖ *refl & pass* to lower oneself *(in dignity),* stoop ‖ *refl* to huddle together

prensāti·ō -ōnis *f (pol)* campaign

prens·ō *or* prehens·ō -āre -āvī -ātus *tr* to take hold of, clutch at, grab; to buttonhole ‖ *intr (pol)* to campaign

prensus *pp of* prendo

pressē *adv* distinctly, with articulation; concisely; accurately, simply

pressī *perf of* premo

pressi·ō -ōnis *f* pressure *(exerted by the fulcrum of a lever);* fulcrum

press·ō -āre -āvī -ātus *tr* to press, exert pressure on; to weigh down

pressūr·a -ae *f* pressure

press·us -a -um *pp of* premo ‖ *adj* closed, shut tight; compact, dense; low *(sound),* subdued *(voice);* tight *(embrace);* deliberate *(pace);* concise *(style);* **basia pressa** one kiss after another; **copia lactis pressi** a supply of cheese

press·us -ūs *m* pressure; expression *(of the face)*

pretiōsē *adv* at great cost, expensively

pretiōs·us -a -um *adj* precious, valuable· expensive; extravagant

pret·ium -(i)ī *n* price; value, worth; reward, return, recompense; bribe; pay, wages; ransom; **ad pretium redigere** to put a price on; **in pretio esse** to be prized; to be held in high esteem; **in pretio habere** to prize, hold in high esteem; **pretio meo (tuo)** at my (your) expense; **pretium curae esse** to be worth the trouble; **pretium facere** to set a price; **pretium habere** to have value, be worth something; **pretium operae esse** to be worth the effort, be worthwhile

prex precis *f (usu. pl)* prayer; request; intercession; curse, imprecation

Priamē·is -idos *f* daughter of Priam, Cassandra

Priaméi·us -a -um *adj* of Priam

Priāmid·ēs -ae *m* son of Priam

Priam·us -ī *m* Priam *(son of Laomedon, husband of Hecuba, father of Hector, Paris, Cassandra, etc., king of Troy)*

Priāp·us -ī *m* son of Dionysus and Aphrodite, god of gardens and vineyards, and protector of flocks

prīdem *adv* formerly, previously; once *(in the past);* long ago; **haud ita pridem** not so long ago, not long before; **jam pridem** long ago; **quam pridem?** for how long?; how long ago?

prīdiān·us -a -um *adj* of the day before

prīdiē *adv* the day before

Priēn·ē -ēs *f* coastal town in Ionia, opposite Miletus

prīm·a -ōrum *npl* first part, beginning; first principles *or* elements; **cum primis** among the first, especially; chiefly; first of all; **in primis** above all, chiefly, particularly, especially

prīm·ae -ārum *fpl* lead, first rank, highest

place, highest importance; **primas dare**
(w. dat) to attach supreme importance to
prīmaev·us -a -um adj youthful
prīmān·ī -ōrum mpl soldiers of the first
legion
prīmāri·us -a -um adj first in rank; first-
rate
prīmē adv to the highest degree
prīmigeni·us -a -um adj first-born
prīmipīlār·is -is m ranking centurion of a
legion
prīmipīl·us -ī m ranking centurion of a
legion
prīmiti·ae -ārum fpl first fruits; (fig) beginnings; **a primitiis** from the beginning, thoroughly
prīmitus adv originally, at first; for the
first time
prīmō adv first, in the first place; at first,
at the beginning
prīmord·ium -(i)ī n origin, beginning;
commencement; beginning of a new
reign
prīmōr·is -is -e adj first, leading; the front
of, the beginning of; tip of; first, earliest;
front (teeth, battle line); principal; basic; leading (men); **digituli primores**
fingertips; **in labris primoribus** on the
tip of one's tongue ‖ mpl leaders, chiefs;
(mil) front ranks
prīmulum adv for the first time; at first,
first of all
prīmul·us -a -um adj very first
prīmum adv first, in the first place, before
all else; at first; for the first time; **cum
primum** (or **ubi primum** or **ut primum**)
as soon as; **primum dum** in the first
place; **quam primum** as soon as possible
prīmumdum adv in the first place
prīm·us -a -um adj first; foremost; principal; distinguished; nearest; basic, fundamental; first-class; that is in the earliest stages; the front of; front (teeth); the
tip of, end of; **primā fronte** (or **facie**)
outwardly, at first glance; **primas partes
agere** to play the lead role; **primi pedes**
forefeet; **primis digitis** with or at the
fingertips; **primo anno** at the beginning
of the year or season; **primo quoque
tempore** at the very earliest opportunity; **primus in provinciam introiit** he
was the first to enter the province; **primus
quisque** the very first, the first possible;
each in turn ‖ mpl leading citizens ‖ fpl
see **primae** ‖ n beginning; front; **a primo**
from the first; **in primo** in the beginning; (mil) at the head of the column ‖
npl see **prima**
princ·eps -ipis adj first; earliest; original;
leading, in front; foremost, chief ‖ m
leader, chief; emperor; (mil) maniple,
company; (mil) captain, company com-

mander, centurion; (mil) rank of centurion; **princeps primus** a centurion ranking second among the six centurions of a
legion ‖ mpl (mil) soldiers of the second
line (between the **hastati** and the **triarii**),
second line
principāl·is -is -e adj first, foremost; original, primitive; chief, principal; of the
emperor; **via principalis** (mil) main
street (of a camp); **porta principalis**
(mil) main gate (of a camp)
principāt·us -ūs m first place; post of
commander in chief; principate; rule,
sovereignty; origin, beginning; **princi-
patum tenere** to occupy first place, be
in the lead
principi·a -ōrum npl first principles; foundations; (mil) front line, front-line troops;
(mil) headquarters
principiāl·is -is -e adj initial
principiō adv in the beginning, at first
princip·ium -(i)ī n beginning, start; starting point; origin; beginner, originator;
basis; premise; (pol) first to vote; (pol)
right to vote first; **a principio** in the
beginning, at first; **de principio** right
from the start; **principium capere** (or
sumere or **exordiri**) to begin; **principium ducere ab** to originate with ‖ npl
foundations; (mil) headquarters; (mil)
the second line in order of battle; (phil)
rudimentary particles of matter, elements
pri·or -or -us comp; no positive exists) adj
previous, preceding, prior, former; more
fundamental, basic; better, superior, preferable; (of kings, rulers) the elder; **in
priorem partem** in a forward direction;
priores partes agere to play a more
important role ‖ mpl forefathers, ancestors, ancients ‖ fpl (only acc) lead, preference ‖ npl earlier events
priscē adv in the old-fashioned style
prisc·us -a -um adj old, ancient; old-time,
old-fashioned; former, previous
Prisc·us -ī m Roman family name (cognomen), esp. Lucius Tarquinius Priscus
(the fifth king of Rome) ‖ Quintus
Servilius Priscus Fidenas (conqueror of
the Veientes and Fidenates in 435 B.C.) ‖
Helvidius Priscus (prominent Stoic under Nero and Vespasian)
pristin·us -a -um adj former, earlier; pristine, primitive, original; preceding, previous, yesterday's ‖ n in **pristinum
restituere** to restore to its former condition
pristis see **pistrix**
prius adv earlier, before, previously,
sooner, first; sooner, rather
priusquam conj (also written as two
words) before
prīvātim adv privately, in private; as a
private citizen; at home

prīvāti·ō -ōnis *f* removal, negation
prīvāt·us -a -um *adj* private; personal, individual, peculiar; isolated; ordinary *(language)* ‖ *m* private citizen; civilian; subject *(of a ruler)* ‖ *n* privacy, retirement; private property, private land; **ex privato** out of one's own pocket; **in privato** in private; **in privatum** for private use
Prīvern·ās -ātis *adj* of Privernum ‖ *mpl* the people of Privernum
Prīvern·um -ī *n* Latin town founded by the Volscians
prīvigna -ae *f* stepdaughter
prīvign·us -ī *m* stepson ‖ *mpl* stepchildren
prīvilēg·ium -(i)ī *n* privilege, special right; *(pol)* special bill directed against *or* in favor of an individual
prīv·ō -āre *tr (w. abl)* **1** to deprive of, rob of; **2** to release from, relieve of, free from
prīv·us -a -um *adj* every, each, single; own, private; *(w. gen)* deprived of
prō *adv (w. ut)* just as, according as ‖ *prep (w. abl)* before, in front of; in the presence of; for, on behalf of, in favor of, in the service of, on the side of; instead of, for, in lieu of; just as, the same as, for; in proportion to; according to; in comparison with; by virtue of; in name of; **esse pro** (+ *abl*) to be as good as, be the equivalent of; **esse** *(or* **stare pro** + *abl)* to be on the side of *(s.o.);* **pro certo habere** to regard *(s.th.)* as certain; **pro eo** just the same; **pro eo atque** *(or* **ac)** just as, the same as; **pro eo quod** in view of the fact that; **pro eo quantum** in proportion to, according as; **pro eo ut** instead of the case being that; **pro herede** in his capactiy as heir; **pro occiso relictus** left for dead; **pro rostro orationem habere** to speak from the rostrum; **pro se quisque** each one for himself, individually; **pro sententiā dicere** to state as his opinion; **pro testimonio dicere** to state by way of evidence; **pro vallo carros objiciunt** they put their wagons in the way to serve as a barricade; **utrum pro ancilla me habes an filia?** do you regard me as a maid or a daughter? ‖ *interj* oh!; **pro di immortales!** oh, heavens above!
pro- *pref* **1** forward movement: **progredi** to go forward; **2** downward movement: **proclivis** downhill; **3** action in front: **protegere** to cover in front; **4** bringing into the open: **prodere** to bring out, publish; **5** priority in time: **providere** to see beforehand; **6** advantage: **prodesse** *(w. dat)* to be advantageous to, be good for
proāgor·us -ī *m* mayor *(in some Greek provincial towns)*

proauct·or -ōris *mf* early ancestor
proavi·a -ae *f* great-grandmother
proavīt·us -a -um *adj* great-grandfather's, ancestral
proav·us -ī *m* great-grandfather; ancestor, forefather
probābil·is -is -e *adj* worthy of approval, commendable, acceptable; pleasing, agreeable; probable, plausible, likely
probābilit·ās -ātis *f* probability
probābiliter *adv* probably
probāti·ō -ōnis *f* approval, approbation; criterion, test; proof
probāt·or -ōris *m* approver, supporter, backer
probāt·us -a -um *adj* approved, acceptable; tried, tested, good; esteemed
probē *adv* correctly, well, satisfactorily; thoroughly, very, very much; **haud probe** not really, no; **pereo probe** *(coll)* I'm absolutely a goner
probit·ās -ātis *f* probity, uprightness, honesty, goodness; sexual purity; good behavior
problēmat·a -ōrum *npl (rhet)* difficult questions for debate, problems
prob·ō -āre -āvī -ātus *tr* to approve, commend, esteem; to make good, represent as good, make acceptable; to pronounce judgment on; to pronounce approval of; to make credible, prove, show, demonstrate; to test, try, inspect; **probare pro** *(w. abl)* to pass *(s.o.)* off as ‖ *pass* **probari pro** *(w. abl)* to pass for, be taken for
probosc·is -idis *f* snout; trunk *(of an elephant)*
probriperlecebr·ae -ārum *fpl* temptations
probrōs·us -a -um *adj* scandalous, shameful, abusive
probr·um -ī *n* abuse, invective, reproach; shameful act; lewdness, indecency; shame, disgrace; charge of disgraceful conduct
prob·us -a -um *adj* good, honest, upright, virtuous, decent; *(coll)* real, proper, downright
Prob·us -ī *m* Roman family name *(cognomen),* esp. Marcus Valerius Probus *(grammarian of the 1st cent.* A.D.*)*
Proc·a *or* **Proc·ās -ae** *m* Proca *(king of Alba Longa and father of Numitor and Amulius)*
procācit·ās -ātis *f* brashness
procāciter *adv* brashly
proc·ax -ācis *adj* brash
prō·cēdō -cēdĕre -cessī -cessum *intr* to proceed, go forward, advance; to make progress; to come out *(in public),* show oneself, appear; to come forth, arise; *(of time)* to pass, elapse; to turn out, result, succeed; to continue
procell·a -ae *f* violent wind, squall, hurri-

cane, storm; *(fig)* violence, commotion, storm; *(mil)* charge

prōcell·ō -ĕre·*tr* to throw down II *refl se procellere* in mensam to flop down at the table

procellōs·us -a -um *adj* gusty

prōcērē *adv* far

procer·ēs -um *mpl* leading men *(of a society, etc.);* leaders *(of a profession, art)*

prōcērit·ās -ātis *f* height, tallness; length II *fpl* the different heights

prōcērius *adv* farther, to a greater extent, more

prōcēr·us -a -um *adj* tall *(person, tree);* long *(neck, beak);* lofty *(idea); (pros)* long; palmae procerae open palms

prōcessī *perf of* procedo

prōcessi·ō -ōnis *f* advance

prōcess·us -a -um *pp of* procedo II *adj* advanced *(age)*

prōcess·us -ūs *m* advance, progress

Prochyt·a -ae *or* Prochyt·ē -ēs *f* small island off the Campanian coast

proc·ī -ōrum *mpl* class of leading citizens under the Servian constitution

prō·cidō -cidĕre -cidī *intr* to fall forwards, fall over, fall down, fall prostrate

prōcinctū *(abl only) m* in procinctu ready for combat, on red alert

prōclāmāt·or -ōris *m* loudmouth

prōclām·ō -āre -āvī -ātus *tr* to yell out; to exclaim; *(w. acc & inf)* to cry out that II *intr* to yell; to practice public speaking

Procl·ēs -is *m* one of the first pair of kings to reign at Sparta, together with Eurysthenes

prōclīn·ō -āre -āvī -ātus *tr* to bend, bend forward; res proclinata critical situation, crisis

prōclīv·e -is *n* slope, descent; in proclivi esse to be easy

prōclīvī *adv* downhill; effortlessly

prōclīv·is -is -e *or* prōclīv·us -a -um *adj* sloping down; sloping forward; downhill; easy; *(w. ad)* inclined to, disposed to, ready for; *(of years, seasons)* declining; *(fig)* going downhill, insecure; *(w. ad)* inclined to

prōclīvit·ās -ātis *f* proclivity, tendency, predispostion

prōclīviter *adv* readily; easily, effortlessly

prōclīv·us *see* proclivis

Procn·ē -ēs *f* (Prog-) Procne *(daughter of Pandion, sister of Philomela, wife of Tereus, and mother and murderess of Itys; she was changed into a swallow);* swallow

proc·ō -āre *or* proc·or -ārī *tr* to require, demand

prōcons·ul -ulis *m* vice-consul, proconsul; governor of a province; military commander

prōconsulār·is -is -e *adj* proconsular

prōconsulāt·us -ūs *m* proconsulship, proconsulate

prōcrāstināti·ō -ōnis *f* procrastination

prōcrastin·ō -āre -āvī -ātus *tr* to put off till the next day, postpone II *intr* to procrastinate

prōcreāti·ō -ōnis *f* procreation

prōcreāt·or -ōris *m* procreator; creator

prōcreātr·ix -īcis *f* mother

prōcre·ō -āre -āvī -ātus *tr* to procreate, beget; to produce

prōcresc·ō -ĕre *intr* to spring forth, be produced; to continue to grow, grow up

Procr·is -is *or* -idis *f* wife of Cephalus, who mistook her for a wild beast and shot her with bow and arrow

Procrust·ēs -ae *m* notorious robber in Attica who stretched his victims to the length of his bed or mutilated them if they were too tall

prōcub·ō -āre -uī *intr* to lie stretched out

prōcū·dō -děre *tr (lit & fig)* to hammer out, forge

procul *adv* at a distance, in the distance; far away, a great way off; from a distance, from far; haud procul afuit quin legatos violarent they came close to outraging the ambassadors; non procul ab not far from

prōculc·ō -āre -āvī -ātus *tr* to trample upon, trample down

Proculēi·us -ī *m* Roman clan name *(nomen), esp.* Gaius Proculeius *(friend of Augustus and literary patron)*

prōcumbō prōcumbĕre prōcubuī prōcubitum *intr* to fall down, sink down; to lean forward, bend over, be broken down; to lie down; *(fig)* to go to ruin; *(topog)* to extend, spread

prōcūrāti·ō -ōnis *f* attention; *(w. gen)* 1 concern for, care for; 2 responsibility for, charge over; 3 management of, administration of; 4 procuratorship of; 5 expiation of

prōcūrāt·or -ōris *m* procurator, manager, administrator; agent, deputy; governor of a *(minor)* province

prōcūrātr·ix -īcis *f* superintendent *(female)*

prōcūr·ō -āre -āvī -ātus *tr* to look after, attend to; to administer *(as procurator);* to have charge of; to avert by sacrifice; to expiate II *intr* to serve as procurator

prō·currō -currĕre -(cu)currī -cursum *intr* to run out ahead, dash forward; to jut out, project

prōcursāti·ō -ōnis *f* sally, charge

prōcursātōr·ēs -um *mpl* skirmishers

prōcurs·ō -āre *intr* to keep charging out; to continue to skirmish

prōcurs·us -ūs *m* sally, charge

prōcurv·us -a -um *adj* curving forwards; curving, winding *(shore)*

proc·us -ī m suitor; gigolo **‖** mpl class of leading citizens in the Servian constitution; **impudentes proci** shameless candidates

Procyŏn -ōnis m (astr) Lesser Dog Star (the constellation Canis Minor)

prōdactus pp of **prodigo**

prōdeambul·ō -āre intr to go out for a walk

prōd·eō -īre -iī -itum intr to go out, come out, go forth, come forth; (of plants) to come out; to appear in public; to come forward (in the assembly or court); to appear (on stage); to go ahead, advance; **in proelium prodire** to go into battle; **obviam prodire** (w. dat) to out to meet (s.o.); (e.g., of a cliff) to jut out, project

prō·dīcō -dīcĕre -dixī -dictus tr to set (a date) beforehand (for some activity); **praetor reo atque accusatoribus diem prodixit** (leg) the praetor announced the date of the trial to the defendant as well as the plaintiffs

Prodic·us -ī m sophist of Ceos, contemporary with Socrates

prōdigē adv lavishly

prōdigenti·a -ae f extravagance; **prodigentia opum** wasting of resources

prōdigiāl·is -is -e adj marked with prodigies

prōdigiāliter adv to a fantastic degree

prōdigiōs·us -a -um prodigious; freakish

prōdig·ium -(i)ī n prodigy, portent; unnatural crime, monstrous crime; monster, freak

prōd·igō -igĕre -ēgī tr to squander, waste

prōdig·us -a -um adj wasteful; lavish, openhanded; (w. gen) free with; **animae prodigus** free with or careless with one's life; **herbae prodigus locus** spot with luxurious growth of grass

prōditi·ō -ōnis f betrayal, treason; **proditionem agere** (w. dat) to commit treason against, betray

prōdit·or -ōris m betrayer, traitor

prō·dō -dĕre -didī -ditus tr to bring out, bring forth, produce; to reveal, disclose; (of a writer, esp. w. **memoriā** or **memoriae** or **ad memoriam**) to record, relate, report, hand down, transmit; to proclaim; to appoint; to give up, surrender; to forsake, betray; to prolong; (w. dat) **1** to betray to; **2** to reveal to

prōdoc·eō -ēre tr to teach publicly

prodrom·us -ī m forerunner; northerly winds (that precede the Etesian winds)

prō·dūcō -dūcĕre -duxī ductus tr to bring out, bring forth; to produce; to promote, advance; to bring to light; to bring into the world; to raise, bring up; to educate; to drag out, protract; to lengthen (a syllable); to lead on, induce; to put off, adjourn; to put (a slave) up for sale; to

produce, perform (on the stage); (leg) to bring to court

prōduct·a -ōrum npl preferable things, preferences

prōductē adv long; **producte litteram dicere** to pronounce the letter or vowel long

prōducti·ō -ōnis f lengthening

prōduct·ō -āre tr to drag out

prōduct·us -a -um pp of **produco ‖** adj lengthened, prolonged, long

proēgmen·on -ī n preference

proeliār·is -is -e adj battle-, of battle

proeliāt·or -ōris m combatant

proeli·or -ārī -ātus sum intr to battle

proel·ium -(i)ī n battle, combat, fight **‖** npl fighting men, warriors

Proetid·es -um fpl daughters of Proetus, who were driven mad by Hera and imagined that they were cows

Proēt·us -ī m Proëtus, king of Argos or Tiryns, twin-brother of Acrisius

profān·ō -āre -āvī -ātus tr to profane

profān·us -a -um adj unconsecrated, ordinary; impious; ill-omened

profātus pp of **profor**

prōfēcī perf of **proficio**

profecti·ō -ōnis f setting out, departure; source (of money)

profectō adv really, actually

profectus pp of **proficiscor**

prōfectus pp of **proficio**

prōfect·us -ūs m progress, advance; success; profit

prō·ferō -ferre -tulī -lātus tr to bring forward, advance, bring out; to extend, enlarge; to put off, postpone; to produce, discover, invent; to make known, publish; to express; to mention, cite, quote; **in medium** (or **in lucem**) **proferre** to publish, disclose; **pedem proferre** to advance; **res proferre** (leg) to declare a recess; **signa proferre** (mil) to march forward

professi·ō -ōnis f public acknowledgment, profession, declaration; registration (at which property, etc., was declared); profession, business

profess·or -ōris m professor, teacher

professōri·us -a -um adj professorial; professional, expert

professus pp of **profiteor**

profest·us -a -um adj non-holiday, ordinary; **dies profestus** workday

prō·ficiō -ficĕre -fēcī -fectum intr to make progress, make headway, advance; to have success; to be useful, do good, help, be conducive; **nihil proficere** to do no good

pro·ficiscor -ficiscī -fectus sum intr to set out, start, go, depart; to originate, proceed, arise

pro·fiteor -fitērī -fessus sum tr to declare

publicly, acknowledge, confess, profess; to offer freely, promise, volunteer; to follow as a profession, practice *(e.g., law)*; to make a declaration of, register *(property, etc., before a public official)*; **indicium profiteri** to volunteer evidence, testify freely; **nomen profiteri** to put one's name in as a candidate; **se adjutorem profiteri** *(w.* ad*)* to volunteer to help *(s.o.)* ‖ *intr* to make a confession, make an admission; to be a professor, be a teacher

prōflīgāt·or -ōris *m* big spender
prōflīgāt·us -a -um *adj* profligate
prōflīg·ō -āre -āvī -ātus *tr* to knock to the ground, knock down; to defeat; to bring to an end, do away with, finish off; to ruin, crush; to degrade, debase
prōfl·ō -āre -āvī -ātus *tr* to breathe out
prōflu·ens -entis *adj* flowing along; fluent *(speech)* ‖ *f* running water
prōfluenter *adv* easily, effortlessly
prōfluenti·a -ae *f* fluency
prōflu·ō -ere -xī *intr* to flow out; to flow along; *(fig)* to proceed; **gravedo profluit** the head cold results in a runny nose
prōfluv·ium -(i)ī *n* flow
prō·for -fārī -fātus sum *tr* to say, declare ‖ *intr* to speak out
prōfūdī *perf of* profundo
prō·fugiō -fugĕre -fūgī -fugitūrus *tr* to run away from, escape from ‖ *intr* to run away, escape; *(w.* ad*)* to take refuge with, take refuge at the house of
profug·us -a -um *adj* fugitive; banished, exiled; nomadic ‖ *m* refugee
prō·fundō -fundĕre -fūdī -fūsus *tr* to pour, pour out; to shed *(blood, tears)* freely; to utter; to give vent to; to spend freely, squander; **animam** *(or* spiritum*)* **profundere** to breathe one's last; **vitam pro patriā profundere** to give one's life for one's country ‖ *refl & pass* to come pouring out; to sprout
profund·us -a -um *adj* deep; boundless, vast; dense *(forest, cloud)*; high; infernal; *(fig)* bottomless, boundless ‖ *n* depth; the deep, deep sea; abyss
profūsē *adv* in disorder, haphazardly, helter-skelter; extravagantly
profūsi·ō -ōnis *f* profusion
profūs·us -a -um *pp of* profundo ‖ *adj* extravagant, lavish, profuse; excessive, expensive
prōgen·er -erī *m* granddaughter's husband
prōgener·ō -āre -āvī -ātus *tr* to beget, give birth to; to produce
prōgeni·ēs -ēī *f* offspring, progeny; line, family; lineage, descent
prōgenit·or -ōris *m* progenitor
prō·gignō -gignĕre -genuī -genitus *tr* to beget, produce
prōgnāriter *adv* precisely, exactly

prognāt·us -a -um *adj (w.* abl *or* ab *or* ex*)* born of, descended from ‖ *m* child; grandson
Prognē *see* **Procne**
prognostic·on *or* **prognostic·um -ī** *n* sign of the future, prognostic
prō·gredior -gredī -gressus sum *intr* to go forward, march forward; to advance; to go on, make headway, make progress; to go forth, go out
prōgressi·ō -ōnis *f* progress, advancement; increase, growth; *(rhet)* climax
prōgressus *pp of* progredior
prōgress·us -ūs *m* progress, advance; march *(of time or events)*
prōh *interj* oh!; **proh di immortales!** oh, heavens above!
prohib·eō -ēre -uī -itus *tr* to hold back, check, hinder, prevent, avert, keep off; to prohibit; to preclude; to keep away; to defend, protect; *(w.* ne, quominus, *or in negative contexts* quin*)* to keep *(s.o.)* from *(doing s.th.)*
prohibiti·ō -ōnis *f* prohibition
proïnde *or* **proïn** *(or* proin *as monosyllable) adv* so then, consequently, accordingly; equally; likewise; **proinde atque** *(or* ac *or* ut *or* quam*)* just as, exactly as; **proinde atque si** *(or* ac si *or* quasi*)* just as if
prōjēcī *perf of* projicio
prōjectīci·us -a -um *adj* exposed, abandoned *(child)*
prōjecti·ō -ōnis *f* stretching out; **projectio bracchii** stretching out of the arm
prōject·us -a -um *pp of* projicio ‖ *adj* jutting out; prostrate, stretched out; abject, contemptible; downcast; *(w.* ad*)* prone to
prōject·us -ūs *m* projection, extension
prō·jiciō -jicĕre -jēcī -jectus *tr* to throw down; to throw away, abandon, forsake; to fling from oneself as unwanted, discard; to hold out, extend; to banish, exile; to neglect, desert; to blurt out; to give up, sacrifice; to put off, delay; to throw overboard; *(w.* in + acc *or* ad*)* to abandon to *(a fate),* expose to; **projicere in exilium** to drive out, banish ‖ *refl* to throw oneself, plunge; to rush; *(w.* in + acc*)* to give way to *(a feeling, tears, habit);* **se projicere ad pedes** *(w.* gen*)* to throw oneself at the feet of; **se projicere ex nave** to jump overboard; **se projicere in Forum** to rush into the Forum; **se projicere in muliebres fletus** to give way to unmanly weeping ‖ *pass (geog)* to extend; *(of a promontory)* to jut out ‖ *intr* to jut out
prō·lābor -lābī -lapsus sum *intr* to glide forward, slip *or* move forward; to fall forwards, fall on one's face; to slip out; *(of words)* to slip out, escape; to be led

on, led astray *(by fear, greed, etc.); (fig)* to fail, go to ruin, collapse; **prolabi per equi caput** to go flying over the head of the horse

prōlapsi·ō -ōnis *f* slipping

prōlapsus *pp of* **prolabor**

prōlāti·ō -ōnis *f* extension *(of territory);* adducing, mentioning *(of precedents);* delay, postponement

prōlāt·ō -āre *tr* to extend; to put off, delay

prōlātus *pp of* **profero**

prōlect·ō -āre -āvī -ātus *tr* to lure

prōl·ēs -is *f* offspring, progeny, children; descendants; race, stock; child; young man

prōlētār·ius -(i)ī *m* proletarian ‖ *mpl* proletariat

prōli·ciō -cĕre *tr* to entice, bring out, lead on; to incite

prōlixē *adv* freely, wildly, readily, cheerfully

prōlix·us -a -um *adj* long, freely growing, wild *(beard, hair, etc.);* favorable *(circumstances)*

prōlocūtus *pp of* **proloquor**

prōlog·us -ī *m* prologue *(of a play);* actor who gives the prologue

prōloquor -quī -cūtus sum *tr & intr* to speak out

prōlub·ium -(i)ī *n* desire, inclination, yen

prōlū·dō -dĕre -sī -sum *tr* to be a prelude to ‖ *intr* to practice; *(of boxers)* to spar, shadowbox

prō·luō -luĕre -luī -lūtus *tr* to wash out, flush, wash off; *(of water)* to wash away; to wet, drench; to wash clean, wash out

prōlūsi·ō -ōnis *f* practice fight, dry run; sparring

prōlūtus *pp of* **proluo**

prōluvi·ēs -ēī *f* flood; discharge, excrement

prōmercāl·is -is -e *adj* sold in the open market

prōmer·eō -ēre -uī -itus *or* **prōmer·eor -ērī -itus sum** *tr* to deserve, merit, earn ‖ *intr* to be deserving; *(w. de + abl)* to deserve the gratitude of; **bene de multis promerere** *(or* **promereri)** to deserve the full gratitude of many people

prōmerit·um -ī *n* favor; reward, due; merit; guilt; **bene (male) promeritum** a good (bad) turn

Promēth·eūs -eī *or* **-eos** *m* son of Iapetus and Clymene, brother of Epimetheus, and discoverer of use of fire, which he taught to men

Promēthē·us -a -um *adj* Promethean, of Prometheus

Promēthīd·ēs -ae *m* son of Prometheus, Deucalion *(who, with his wife Pyrrha, survived the Deluge)*

prōmin·ens -entis *adj* prominent, projecting ‖ *n* headland

prōmin·eō -ēre -uī *intr* to jut out, stick out, stick up; *(of persons)* to lean out, bend forward; *(w.* **in** *+ acc)* to reach down to, reach out for

prōmiscam *or* **promiscē** *or* **prōmiscuē** *adv* in common; without distinction; all at the same time *or* in the same place

prōmisc(u)·us -a -um *adj* promiscuous, haphazard, indiscriminate; in common, open to all; common

prōmissi·ō -ōnis *f* promise

prōmiss·or -ōris *m* one who promises *or* guarantees

prōmiss·us -a -um *adj* allowed to grow, long ‖ *n* promise; prediction

prō·mittō -mittĕre -mīsī -missus *tr* to send forth; to let *(e.g., hair)* grow; to promise, guarantee; to predict as certain; to give hope of; **ad cenam** *(or* **ad aliquem) promittere** to accept an invitation to dinner *(or* to s.o.'s home); **damni infecti promittere** to guarantee compensation for damage done; **promittere (in matrimoniam)** to promise *(one's daughter)* in marriage ‖ *refl (w.* **ad)** to have expectations of attaining; **sibi promittere** to promise oneself, look forward to, count on

prōm·ō -ĕre -(p)sī -ptus *tr* to bring out, draw out; to produce *(arguments);* to bring to light, reveal; to bring out, express *(ideas, emotions)*

prōmon·eō -ēre *tr* to warn openly

prōmontōr·ium -(i)ī *n* promontory

prōmōt·a -ōrum *npl* second choice

prō·moveō -movēre -mōvī -mōtus *tr* to move *(s.th.)* forward, cause to advance; to enlarge, extend; to effect, accomplish; to encourage, egg on; to promote *(to higher office);* to bring to light, reveal; to postpone; **gradum** *(or* **pedem) promovere** to step forward; **nihil promovere** to accomplish nothing, do no good, make no progress ‖ *intr* to make headway

promptārius *see* **promptuarius**

promptē *adv* readily; willingly; fluently

prompt·ō -āre *tr* to give out, distribute; to be treasurer of

promptuāri·us -a -um *adj* of a storehouse, storage-; **cella promptuaria** *(coll)* jail, cooler ‖ *n* storeroom, cupboard

prompt·us -a -um *pp of* **promo** ‖ *adj* at hand, readily available; easy; glib *(tongue);* brought to light, evident; bold, enterprising; *(w. dat or* **ad** *or* **in** *+ acc)* **1** readily inclined to; **2** ready *or* prepared for; *(w.* **in** *+ abl)* quick at; *(w.* **adversus** *+ acc)* ready for, prepared against; *(w. inf)* ready to, quick to; **promptum est** *(w. inf)* it is an easy matter to

prompt·us -ūs *m* **in promptu 1** within easy reach, at one's disposal *or* command; **2** in full view, in a prominent position; **3** within one's powers *or* capabilities; **4** at one's command; **in promptu esse** to be obvious; **in promptu gerere** (*or* **habere** *or* **ponere**) to display

prōmulgāti·ō -ōnis *f* (*pol*) promulgation, official publication (*of a proposed law*)

prōmulg·ō -āre -āvī -ātus *tr* to promulgate, to publish, publicize

prōmuls·is -idis *f* hors d'oeuvres

prōmuntur·ium *or* **prōmontor·ium -(i)ī** *n* promontory

prōm·us -ī *m* butler

prōmūtu·us -a -um *adj* (*fin*) on credit, advanced as a loan

prōnē *adv* downwards; slantwise

pronep·ōs -ōtis *m* great-grandson

pronept·is -is *f* great-grandaughter

pronoe·a -ae *f* divine providence

prōnōm·en -inis *n* (*gram*) pronoun; (*gram*) demonstrative pronoun

prōnub·a -ae *f* matron of honor (*who conducted the bride to the husband's home*); (*of Juno, Bellona, Tisiphone*) patroness of marriage

prōnuntiāti·ō -ōnis *f* proclamation, declaration; verdict; pronunciation (*of words*); proposition (*in logic*); (*rhet*) delivery

prōnuntiāt·or -ōris *m* narrator

prōnuntiāt·um -ī *n* proposition (*in logic*)

prōnunti·ō -āre -āvī -ātus *tr* to proclaim, announce; to express (*opinion, judgment*); to pronounce (*words*); to hold out, promise (*rewards*) publicly; to recite, deliver; to narrate, relate; **sententiam pronuntiare** (*pol*) to announce a motion (*for discussion in the Senate*), to put a motion to a vote **ǁ** *intr* (*theat*) (*of an actor*) speak one's lines

prōnūper *adv* quite recently

prōnur·us -ūs *f* grandson's wife

prōn·us -a -um *adj* leaning, inclined, bending, stooping, bent over, bent forwards; swift, rushing, dashing, moving swiftly along; sloping, steep (*hill, road*); sinking, setting (*sun, etc.*); downhill; easy; (*w. dat or* **ad** *or* **in** + *acc*) inclined toward, disposed toward, prone to; (*w. dat*) inclined to favor (*e.g., a winner*) **ǁ** *n* downward tendency, gravity **ǁ** *npl* slopes

pro(h)oemi·or -ārī *intr* to make an introduction *or* preface

pro(h)oem·ium *or* **pro(h)ēm·ium -(i)ī** *n* introduction, preface; prelude; (*fig*) prelude (*e.g., to a fight*)

propāgāti·ō -ōnis *f* propagation, reproduction; prolongation; transmission (*to posterity*); **nominis propagatio** perpetuation of the name

propāgāt·or -ōris *m* one who extends (*s.th.*) in time; **propagator provinciae**

grantor of an extended provincial command

propāg·ō -āre -āvī -ātus *tr* to produce (*plants*) from slips; to produce (*offspring*); to propagate (*race, religion*); to extend (*territory*); to prolong (*a period, life*); to cause (*a family name, tradition*) to endure, hand down (*to posterity*)

propāg·ō -inis *f* slip (*from which a plant is propagated*); offspring, progeny; race, line; descendants

prōpalam *adv* openly, publicly

prōpatul·us -a -um *adj* open **ǁ** *n* open space; **in propatulo habere** to display

prope (*comp:* **propius;** *superl:* **proxime**) *adv* near, nearby; (*of time*) near, at hand; (*of degree*) nearly, almost, practically, just about; (*w.* **ab** + *abl*) close by, near to; **prope est cum** the time has come when **ǁ** *prep* (*w. acc*) near, near to; **prope diem** very soon, any day now

propediem *adv* very soon, any day now

prō·pellō -pellĕre -pulī -pulsus *tr* to propel, drive forward; to push over, overturn, upset; to drive away, drive out; to banish, expel

propemodo *or* **propemodum** *adv* nearly, practically, almost

prōpen·deō -dēre -dī -sum *intr* to hang down; (*w.* **in** + *acc*) to be inclined to, be favorably disposed to

prōpensē *adv* readily, willingly

prōpensi·ō -ōnis *f* propensity

prōpens·us -a -um *pp of* **propendeo ǁ** *adj* weighty; approaching; inclined; ready, willing; (*w. dat, w.* **ad** *or* **in** + *acc*) favorably disposed to, partial to; **propenso animo** with ready mind, willingly; **propensus in alteram partem** inclined toward the other point of view

properanter *adv* hastily, quickly

properanti·a -ae *f* haste

properāti·ō -ōnis *f* haste

properātō *adv* hastily, speedily

properāt·us -a -um *adj* hurried, hasty, speedy **ǁ** *n* speed; **properato opus est** speed is required

properē *adv* hastily, in haste, quickly; without hesitation

properip·ēs -edis *adj* quick-moving, quick-footed

proper·ō -āre -āvī -ātus *tr* to speed up; to prepare hastily, do in haste **ǁ** *intr* to be quick; to go *or* move quickly

Propert·ius -(i)ī *m* Sextus Aurelius Propertius (*Latin elegiac poet, native of Umbria, c. 50–15 B.C.*)

proper·us -a -um *adj* quick, speedy

prōpex·us -a -um *adj* combed forward

prophēt·a -ae *m* prophet

propīn *n* (*only nom and acc in use*) apéritif

prōpīnāti·ō -ōnis *f* toast

prōpīn·ō -āre -āvī -ātus *tr* to drink (*e.g., a*

cup of wine) as a toast; to drink a toast to *(s.o.); (w. dat)* **1** to drink *(e.g., a cup of wine as a toast)* to; **2** to pass on *(a cup)* to

propinqu·a -ae *f* relative *(female)*
propinquē *adv* near at hand
propinquit·ās -ātis *f* proximity, nearness, vicinity; relationship, affinity; friendship
propinqu·ō -āre -āvī -ātus *tr* to bring on; to hasten **‖** *intr* to approach; *(w. dat)* to draw near to, approach
propinqu·us -a -um *adj* near, neighboring; *(of time)* near, at hand; closely related; *(w. dat)* akin to; **in spe propinquā missiōnis** in the hope of an early discharge; **nulla propinqua spes** no hope for the near future; **spes propinqui reditūs** hope for an early return **‖** *mf* relative **‖** *n* neighborhood; **in propinquo** in the vicinity; *(of time, events)* near at hand, in the offing
propi·or -or -us *adj* nearer, closer; *(of time)* earlier; later, more recent; more closely related, more like, more nearly resembling; more imminent; more intimate, closer *(tie);* of more importance, of more concern; *(of battle)* fought at close range; shorter *(route); (w. dat)* **1** nearer to, closer to; **2** closer to *(in resemblance),* more like; **3** to be favorably disposed to; *(w. acc or w.* **ab + *abl)*** closer to **‖** *npl* closer side *(e.g., of a river);* more recent events
propiti·ō -āre -āvī -ātus *tr* to propitiate
propiti·us -a -um *adj (w. dat)* **1** propitious towards; **2** favorably disposed towards
propnigē·um or **propnigē·on -ī** *n* sweat room *(of a bath)*
Prōpoētid·es -um *fpl* Cyprian girls who denied the divinity of Venus, becoming the first prostitutes, subsequently turned to stone
propōl·a -ae *f* retailer
prōpollu·ō -ĕre *tr* to further pollute
prō·pōnō -pōnĕre -posuī -positus *tr* to put *or* place forward, expose to view, display; to propose, suggest; to imagine; to offer, propose; to say, report, relate, publish; to threaten; to denounce; to design, determine, intend
Propontiac·us -a -um *adj* of the Propontis
Propont·is -idis *or* **-idos** *f* Propontis, Sea of Marmora
prōporrō *adv* furthermore; wholly
prōporti·ō -ōnis *f* proportion, symmetry; *(gram)* analogy
prōport·ō -āre *tr* to cite
prōpositi·ō -ōnis *f* proposition; intention, purpose; theme; basic assumption *(in logic)*
prōposit·us -a -um *pp of* **propono ‖** *adj* exposed, open; accessible; impending,

at hand **‖** *n* intention, purpose; main point, theme; first premise *(in logic);* **mihi propositum** it is my intention, it is my plan; **propositum habēre** to have as one's object
prōpraet·or -ōris *m* propraetor *(ex-praetor as governor of a province)*
propriē *adv* in the strict sense; properly; strictly for oneself, personally; peculiarly, especially
propriet·ās -ātis *f* property, peculiarity, quality
propritim *adv* specifically, properly
propri·us -a -um *adj* own, very own; special, peculiar, individual, particular, personal; lasting
propter *adv* near, near at hand
propter *prep (w. acc)* near, close, next to; on account of, because of, for the sake of; through, by means of; **propter quod** wherefore
prop, tereā *or* **propter eā** *adv* for that reason, therefore, on that account; **pro-pterea quod** for the very reason that
prōpudiōs·us -a -um *adj* shameful
prōpud·ium -(i)ī *n* shameful act; *(said of a person)* disgrace
prōpugnācul·um -ī *n* rampart, battlement; defense; *(fig)* safeguard
prōpugnāti·ō -ōnis *f* defense, vindication; protection
prōpugnāt·or -ōris *m* defender, champion
prōpugn·ō -āre -āvī -ātus *tr* to defend **‖** *intr* to come out and fight; to fight **a** defensive action, repel an assault; *(fig)* to put up a defense
prōpulsāti·ō -ōnis *f* repulse
prōpuls·ō -āre -āvī -ātus *tr* to drive off, repel; *(fig)* to ward off, repel
prōpulsus *pp of* **propello**
Propylae·a -ōrum *npl* Propylaea *(monumental gateway, esp. the entrance to the Athenian Acropolis)*
prōquaest·or -ōris *m* proquaestor *(magistrate who, after his quaestorship in Rome, was associated as a financial officer with a proconsul in the administration of a province)*
prōquam *or* **prō quam** *conj* just as, according as
prōr·a -ae *f* prow; *(fig)* ship; **mihi prora et puppis est** my intention from first to last is ʾ*(literally, it is prow and stern to me)*
prōrēp·ō -ĕre -sī -ptum *intr* to creep ahead, crawl out
prōrēt·a -ae *m* lookout man at the prow
prōreus *m (nom only)* look-out man at the prow
prō·ripiō -ripĕre -ripuī -reptus *tr* to drag forth, drag out; to rush **‖** *refl* to rush, dash
prōrogāti·ō -ōnis *f* extension *(of a term of office);* putting off

prōrog·ō -āre -āvī -ātus *tr* to extend, prolong; to put off, postpone

prors·a *or* **prōs·a -ae** *f* prose

prorsum *or* **prōsum** *adv* forwards, straight ahead; *(as an intensive)* altogether, absolutely; *(w. negatives)* absolutely, at all, *e.g.,* **prorsum nihil** absolutely nothing, nothing at all

prorsus *or* **prōsus** *adv* forward; straight *(to the destination); (intensifying a word, phrase, etc., which it may either precede or follow)* altogether, absolutely; *(w. a negative)* absolutely, at all; *(emphasizing the second and stronger of two related terms)* more than that, even; *(connecting a clause or sentence with what precedes)* in fact, all in all; *(in summing up)* in short, in a word; *(w. demonstrative pron or adv, emphasizing correspondence)* exactly, just

prō·rumpō -rumpĕre -rūpī -ruptus *tr* to make *(s.th.)* burst forth; to give vent to; to emit ‖ *pass* to rush forth, rush out ‖ *intr* to rush forth; *(of vapors, etc.)* to burst forth; *(of news)* to come out; *(mil)* to make an attack

prōru·ō -ĕre -ī -tus *tr* to overthrow, demolish ‖ *intr* to rush forth; to tumble

prōrupt·us -a -um *pp of* **prorumpo** ‖ *adj* unrestrained

prōs·a -ae *f* prose

prōsāpi·a -ae *f* stock, race, line

proscaen·ium -(i)ī *n* (**-scēn-**) stage

pro·scindō -scindĕre -scidī -scissus *tr* to plow up, break up; *(fig)* to criticize harshly, cut to pieces

proscrī·bō -bĕre -psī -ptus *tr* to publish in writing; to proclaim, announce; to advertise *(for sale, etc.);* to confiscate *(property);* to punish with confiscation; to proscribe, outlaw *(people)*

proscripti·ō -ōnis *f* advertisement; proscription, political purge; notice of confiscation; notice of outlawry

proscriptur·iō -īre *intr* to be eager to hold a proscription *or* purge

proscript·us -a -um *pp of* **proscribo** ‖ *m* outlaw

prōsec·ō -āre -uī -tus *tr* to cut off *(esp. parts of a sacrificial victim)*

prōsecūtus *pp of* **prosequor**

prōsed·a -ae *f* prostitute

prōsēmin·ō -āre -āvī -ātus *tr* to sow, scatter about, plant; to propagate, raise

prōsen·tiō -tīre -sī *tr* to sense *or* realize beforehand, get wind of

prō·sequor -sequī -secūtus sum *tr* to escort, attend; to pursue *(enemy);* to chase, follow; to follow up *(actions, words);* to go on with, continue *(a topic);* to describe in detail; to follow, imitate; to honor, reward *(with);* to send *(s.o.)* on

his *or* her way with gifts; *(of events)* to occur after, succeed

prōser·ō -ĕre *tr* to stick out *(e.g., the tongue)*

Prōserpīn·a -ae *f* daughter of Ceres and wife of Pluto

prōserp·ō -ĕre *intr* to creep *or* crawl forwards, creep along

proseuch·a -ae *f* synagogue

prōsil·iō -īre -uī *or* **-īvī** *or* **-iī** *intr* to jump forward, jump up; to jump to one's feet; *(of blood)* to spurt; *(of sparks)* to shoot out, fly; to dash

prōsoc·er -erī *m* wife's grandfather; husband's grandfather

prosōdi·a -ae *f* the tone *or* accent of a syllable, prosody

prosōpopoei·a -ae *f* impersonation

prospect·ō -āre -āvī -ātus *tr* to view, look out at, gaze upon; *(of places)* to look towards, command a view of, face; to look for, hope for; *(w. indir. ques.)* to look to see *(what, whether)*

prospectus *pp of* **prospicio**

prospect·us -ūs *m* distant view; view; faculty of sight; a sight *(thing seen)*

prospecul·or -ārī -ātus sum *tr* to look out for, watch for ‖ *intr* to look around, reconnoiter

prosper *see* **prosperus**

prosperē *adv* favorably, luckily, as desired, successfully

prosperit·ās -ātis *f* success, good fortune, prosperity; **prosperitas valetudinis** good health

prosper·ō -āre *tr* to cause to succeed, make happy

prosp·erus *or* **prosp·er -era -erum** *adj* successful, fortunate, lucky, favorable, prosperous

prospicienti·a -ae *f* foresight, precaution

pro·spiciō -spicĕre -spexī -spectus *tr* to see in the distance; to spot; to command a view of; to watch for; to look out for, provide for; to foresee ‖ *intr* to look forward; to look into the distance, have a view; to be on the lookout, exercise foresight; *(w. in + acc)* to command a view of, overlook; **ex superioribus in urbem prospicere** to have a view of the city from a vantage point; **parum prospiciunt oculi** the eyes are near-sighted

pro·sternō -sternĕre -strāvī -strātus *tr* to throw to the ground, knock down; *(of sickness)* to strike down; to wreck, ruin, overthrow, subvert; to demean ‖ *refl* to debase oneself; **se prosternere ad pedes** *(w. gen)* to throw oneself at the feet of, fall down before

prostibil·is -is *f* prostitute

prostibul·um -ī *n* prostitute

prostit·uō -uěre -uī -ūtus *tr* to expose for sale; to prostitute

prostitūt·a -ae *f* prostitute

pro·stō -stāre -stitī -stitum *intr* to project, stick out; *(of wares)* to be set up for sale; to prostitute oneself, be a prostitute

prōstrātus *pp of* **prosterno**

prōstrāvī *perf of* **prosterno**

prōsubig·ō -ěre *tr* to dig up in front

prō·sum -desse -fuī -futūrus *intr* to be useful, do good, be profitable; *(w. dat)* to be good for, do *(s.o.)* good; **multum prodesse** to do a lot of good

prōsum *adv see* **prorsum**

Prōtagor·ās -ae *m* Greek sophist, contemporary of Socrates, born at Abdera *(c. 485–415 B.C.)*

prōte·gō -gěre -xī -ctus *tr* to cover in front, cover up; to cover with a roof; to shelter, protect; *(fig)* to cover, defend, protect

prōtēl·ō -āre -āvī -ātus *tr* to chase away

prōtēl·um -ī *n* team of oxen in tandem; row, series

prōten·dō -děre -dī -tus *tr* to stretch forth, stretch out, extend

prōtent·us -a -um *pp of* **protendo** ‖ *adj* extended

prōtenus *see* **protinus**

prō·terō -terěre -trīvī -trītus *tr* to wear down; to rub out; to trample down, trample under foot; *(fig)* to trample upon, rub out, crush

prōterr·eō -ēre -uī -itum *tr* to scare away

protervē *adv* brashly, brazenly

protervit·ās -ātis *f* brashness

proterv·us -a -um *adj* brash, brazen

Prōtesilāě·us -a -um *adj* of Protesilaus

Prōtesilā·us -ī *m* first Greek casualty in the Trojan War, husband of Laodamia

Prōt·eūs -eī *or* **-eos** *m* a god of the sea with power to assume various forms

prothȳmē *adv* willingly, readily

prothȳmi·a -ae *f* willingness, readiness

prōtinam *adv* immediately

prōtinus *or* **prōtenus** *adv* straight on, forward, farther on; continuously, right on, without pause; on the spot

prōtoll·ō -ěre *tr* to stretch out *(hand);* to put off, postpone

prōtopraxi·a -ae *f (fin)* priority *(among creditors receiving payment)*

prō·trahō -trahěre -traxī -tractus *tr* to drag forward, drag out; to produce; to reveal, bring to light

prōtrītus *pp of* **protero**

prōtrīvī *perf of* **protero**

prōtrū·dō -děre -sī -sus *tr* to push forwards, push out; to postpone

prōturb·ō -āre -āvī -ātus *tr* to drive ahead, drive on in confusion; to drive away, repel; to knock down

proūt *(or* **prout,** *scanned as one syllable)*

conj as, just as; in sor far as, in as much as; *(introducing alternatives)* **prout...ita** according to whether...or

prōvect·us -a -um *adj* advanced; **aetate provectus** advanced in years; **nox provecta erat** the night had been far advanced

prōve·hō -hěre -xī -ctus *tr* to carry forwards; to transport, convey; to lead, lead on; to promote, advance, raise ‖ *pass* to ride, drive, move, *or* sail ahead

prō·veniō -venīre -vēnī -ventum *intr* to go on, proceed; to succeed; to come out, appear; *(of plants, seeds)* to come out, come up, grow; to come about, happen

prōvent·us -ūs *m* result, outcome; succcess; yield, produce; harvest

prōverb·ium -iī *n* proverb

prōvexī *perf of* **proveho**

prōvid·ens -entis *adj* prudent

prōvidenter *adv* prudently, with foresight

prōvidenti·a -ae *f* foresight, foreknowledge; precaution; **providentia deorum** divine providence

prō·videō -vidēre -vīdī -vīsus *tr* to see in the distance; to see coming; to foresee; to provide for; to provide against, guard against, avert, avoid; to look after, look out for, care for; to prepare, make ready; *(w. ut)* to see to it that ‖ *intr* to exercise forethought, take precautions; *(w. dat or* **de** *+ abl)* to look after, care for ‖ *v impers* **provisum est** care was taken

prōvid·us -a -um *adj* foreseeing; prudent, cautious; provident; *(w. gen)* providing for

prōvinci·a -ae *f* province; sphere of administration *or* jurisdiction; office, duty, charge; public office, commission, command, administration; sphere of action

prōvinciāl·is -is -e *adj* provincial, of a province; in a province; **bellum provinciale** war in a province; **molestia provincialis** annoyance of administering a province ‖ *m* provincial

prōvinciātim *adv* province by province

prōvīsi·ō -ōnis *f* foresight; precaution; *(w. gen)* precaution against

prōvīsō *adv* with forethought

prōvīs·ō -ěre *tr* to go out to see; to be on the lookout for

prōvīs·or -ōris *m* lookout *(person);* provider

prōvīsū *m (abl only)* by looking forward; *(w. objective gen)* **1** by foreseeing *(e.g., danger);* **2** by providing, providing for

prōvīsus *pp of* **provideo**

prō·vīvō -vīvěre -vixī *intr* to live on, go on living

prōvocāti·ō -ōnis *f* challenge; *(leg)* appeal

prōvocāt·or -ōris *m* challenger; a type of gladiator

prōvoc·ō -āre -āvī -ātus *tr* to challenge *(a*

person, a statement); to provoke; to exasperate; to stir, stimulate; **bellum provocare** to provoke a war; **beneficio provocatus** touched *or* stirred by an act of kindness; **in aleam provocare** to challenge to a game of dice; **provocare maledictis** to provoke *or* exasperate with nasty remarks **ǁ** *intr (leg)* to appeal; *(leg) (w.* ab) to appeal from the decision of *(a magistrate); (leg) (w.* ad) to appeal to *(a higher authority)*

prōvol·ō -āre -āvī *intr* to fly out, rush out, dash out

prōvol·vō -věre -vī -ūtus *tr* to roll forward, roll along; to roll over, overturn; to humble; to ruin **ǁ** *refl* to prostrate oneself, fall down, grovel

prōvom·ō -ěre *tr* to vomit, throw up

prōvorsus *adv* straight ahead

prōvulg·ō -āre -āvī -ātus *tr* to make publicly known

prox *interj (comic representation of a fart):* **dum enitor, prox! jam paene inquinavi pallium** as I struggle to my feet, bang! I darn near soiled my clothes

proxenēt·a -ae *m* business agent

proximē *adv* (-**umē**) *(superl of* **prope**) *(of place)* nearest, next; *(of time)* most recently, just recently; *(w. acc)* 1 close to, next to, at the side of; 2 very much like, resembling; *(w. dat) (of place)* next to; **proxime atque** almost as much as, nearly the same as; **proxime Pompeium sedebam** I was sitting next to Pompey; **quam proxime** *(w. dat or acc)* as close as possible to

proximit·ās -ātis *f* proximity, vicinity; resemblance, similarity; close relationship

proximō *adv* very *(or* just) recently

proxim·us -a -um *adj* (-**xum-**) nearest, next; adjoining; living nearby; readiest at hand; *(of time)* immediately preceding, previous, most recent, following, latest, last; just mentioned; closely related; *(of affections)* closely devoted; *(of cause)* immediate, proximate; *(of an argument)* relevant; very like *(in character, resemblance);* nearest *(in degree);* next *(in rank, worth),* second-best; next in order; most direct *(route);* **proximum est ut** (+ *subj)* it is most likely that; the next point is that; the next thing is to **ǁ** *m* close relative, next of kin; heir next in succession; friend, intimate **ǁ** *n* neighborhood; the house next door; the recent past; **de proximo** aptly, very closely; **ex proximo** from the readiest source; close by; **in proximo** within easy reach; close at hand; **in proximum** for the following day

prūd·ens -entis *adj* foreseeing; conscious, aware; skilled, skillful, experienced; prudent, discreet, sensible, intelligent; *(w. gen or abl or w.* **in** + *abl)* 1 aware of, conscious of; 2 familiar with; 3 skilled in, experienced in, versed in **ǁ** *m* expert; *(leg)* jurist

prūdenter *adv* prudently, cautiously; skillfully

prūdenti·a -ae *f* foreseeing; prudence, discretion, good sense; **prudentia juris publici** *(leg)* knowledge of *or* experience in public law

pruīn·a -ae *f* frost; winter; **pruinae** a covering of frozen snow

pruīnōs·us -a -um *adj* frosty

prūn·a -ae *f* live coal

prūnice·us -a -um *adj* made of plum-tree wood

prūniti·us -a -um *adj* of plum-tree wood

prūn·um -ī *n* plum

prūn·us -ī *f* plum tree

prūrīg·ō -inis *f* itch, tickle; yen

prūr·iō -īre *intr* to itch, tickle; to have an itch; to be sexually aroused; *(w.* **in** + *acc)* to be itching for

Prūsi·ās *or* **Prūsi·a -ae** *m* Prusias *(name of several kings of Bithynia, esp. Prusias Cholus, d. about 182 B.C., with whom Hannibal took refuge after his defeat)*

prytanē·um *or* **prytanī·um -ī** *n* town hall *(in some Greek cities where the Prytanes, or magistrates, held meetings and dined)*

prytan·is -is *m* magistrate in some Greek states

psall·ō -ěre -ī *intr* to play the cithara

psaltēr·ium -(i)ī *n* cithara *(form of harp)*

psalt·ēs -ae *m* cithara-player, citharist

psaltri·a -ae *f* citharist *(female)*

Psamath·ē -ēs *f* a sea nymph, wife of Aeacus and mother of Phocus **ǁ** daughter of the Argive King Crotopus

psec·as -adis *f* female slave who perfumed her lady's hair; typical name of maidservants

psell·us -a -um *adj* faltering in speech

psēphism·a -atis *n (pol)* plebiscite of the Greek assembly

Pseudocat·ō -ōnis *m* a make-believe Cato

Pseudol·us -ī *m* "Little Liar" *(title of a play by Plautus)*

pseudomen·os *or* **pseudomen·us -ī** *m (phil)* fallacious syllogism

Pseudophilipp·us -ī *m* "False Philip" *(i.e., Andriscus, who claimed to be the son of Perseus of Macedon and was defeated by the Romans in 148 B.C.)*

pseudothyr·um -ī *n* hidden door

psīlocithrist·a -ae *m* one who plays the lyre without singing in accompaniment

psithi·us -a -um *adj* the name of a type of vine **ǁ** *fpl* grapes

psittac·us -ī *m* parrot

Psōph·is -idos *f* town in Arcadia to the S. of Mt. Erymanthus

Psȳch·ē -ēs *f* girlfriend of Cupid, made immortal by Jupiter

psychomantī·um *or* **psychomantē·um -ī** *n* place of séance

-pte *enclitic (added to pronouns, usu. w. poss adj and esp. in abl)* self, own; **sonitu suopte titinant aures** the ears are ringing (with their own sound)

ptisanār·ium -(i)ī *n* gruel

Ptolomae·um -ī *n* name of a gymnasium ‖ tomb of the Ptolemies

Ptolemae·us -ī *m* Ptolemy *(name of a series of thirteen Egyptian kings descended from Latus, one of Alexander the Great's generals)*

pūb·ens -entis *adj* full of sap, succulent, vigorous

pūber *see* **pubes**

pūbert·ās -ātis *f* puberty; manhood; sign of maturity, beard; physical signs of puberty

pūb·ēs *or* **pūb·er -eris** *adj* grown up, adult; downy, covered with down ‖ *mpl* grown-ups, men

pūb·ēs -is *f* pubic hair; private parts; puberty; adult population, manpower; throng

pūb·escō -escĕre *intr* to reach the age of puberty, arrive at maturity; *(of plants)* to grow up, ripen; *(of meadows, fields)* to be clothed, covered *(e.g., with flowers)*

pūblic·a -ae *f* prostitute

pūblicān·us -a -um *adj* of public revenues ‖ *m* revenue agent, publican, tax collector ‖ *f* public prostitute

pūblicāti·ō -ōnis *f* confiscation; disclosure

pūblicē *adv* publicly; officially, on behalf of the state, for the state; at public expense; generally, universally; **publice dicere** to speak officially

pūblicitus *adv* at public expense, at the expense of the state; publicly

Pūblici·us -a -um *adj* Publician *(Roman clan name, nomen); Clivus Publicius* Publician Slope *(road leading up to the Aventine Hill)*

pūblic·ō -āre -āvī -ātus *tr* to confiscate; to throw open to the general public; to prostitute

Pūblicol·a -ae *m* **(Popl-)** Publius Valerius Publicola *(regarded as one of the first consuls, fl 509 B.C.)*

pūblic·us -a -um *adj* public, of the people, common; of the state, state, national; ordinary, vulgar; general; **causa publica** affair of national importance; *(leg)* federal case *(i.e., criminal case);* **id bono publico facere** to do it for the public good; **publica acta** the public record, the official gazette; **res publica** state, government, politics, public life, country; **rem publicam inire** to enter politics

‖ *m* public official **‖** *n* public, publicity; public property; national treasury; federal revenue; **de publico** at public expense; **in publico** in public, publicly; **in publicum prodire** to go out in public; **in publicum redigere** to hand over to the national treasury **‖** *f* prostitute

pudend·us -a -um *adj* shameful, scandalous; **pars pudenda** genitals **‖** *npl* genitals

pud·ens -entis *adj* modest, bashful

pudenter *adv* modestly, bashfully

pud·eō -ēre -uī *or* **puditum est** *tr* to make ashamed, put to shame **‖** *intr* to be ashamed **‖** *v impers (w. acc of person and gen or abl of cause of feeling), e.g.,* **me tui pudet** I am ashamed of you

pudibund·us -a -um *adj* modest, bashful

pudīcē *adv* chastely, modestly, decently; in a subdued style

pudīciti·a -ae *f* chastity, purity

pudīc·us -a -um *adj* chaste, pure

pud·or -ōris *m* shame, sense of shame, decency, modesty; sense of honor, propriety; cause for shame, disgrace; blush

puell·a -ae *f* girl; girlfriend, sweetheart; young wife

puellār·is -is -e *adj* young girl's, girlish, youthful

puellāriter *adv* girlishly

puellul·a -ae *f* little girl; little sweetheart

puell·us -ī *m* little boy, lad; catamite

pu·er *also* **pu·erus -erī** *m* boy, lad; servant, slave; page; bachelor; **a pueris** *(or* **a puero)** from childhood on; **ex pueris excedere** to outgrow childhood

puerasc·ō -ĕre *intr* to approach boyhood

puercul·us -ī *m* little son

puerīl·is -is -e *adj* boyish, childish, youthful, puerile

puerīliter *adv* like a child, childishly

puer(i)ti·a -ae *f* childhood; boyhood

puerper·a -ae *f* woman in labor; woman who has given birth

puerper·ium -(i)ī *n* childbirth, delivery, giving birth

puerper·us -a -um *adj* easing labor pains, helping childbirth

puertia *see* **pueritia**

puerul·us -ī *m* little boy; little slave

pūg·a *or* **pȳg·a -ae** *f* rear, buttocks

pug·il -ilis *m* boxer

pugilāti·ō -ōnis *f* boxing

pugilātōri·us -a -um *adj* boxing-; **follis pugilatorius** punching bag

pugilāt·us -ūs *m* boxing match

pugilicē *adv* like a boxer

pugillār·is -is -e *adj* hand-size **‖** *mpl & npl* set of tablets; notebook

pūgi·ō -ōnis *m* dagger

pūgiuncul·us -ī *m* small dagger

pugn·a -ae *f* fistfight, brawl; fight, combat, battle

pugnācit·ās -ātis *f* pugnacity, aggressiveness
pugnāciter *adv* aggressively
pugnācul·um -ī *n* fortress
pugnant·ēs -ium *mpl* fighters, warriors
pugnant·ia -ium *npl* contradictions, inconsistencies
pugnāt·or -ōris *m* fighter, combatant
pugnātōri·us -a -um *adj* used in fighting; **arma pugnatoria** combat weapons
pugn·ax -ācis *adj* pugnacious, scrappy, aggressive; quarrelsome; dogged
pugne·us -a -um *adj* of the fist; **hospitio pugneo accipere** *(hum)* to welcome s.o. with a reception of fists; **merga pugnea** *(hum)* punch reaper
pugn·ō -āre -āvī -ātus *tr* to fight; **clara pugna ad Perusiam pugnata est** a brilliant battle was fought at Perusia; **proelia, bella pugnare** to fight battles, wars ‖ *intr* to fight; to contend, dispute; *(w. dat or* **cum**) **1** to fight, fight against, struggle with, oppose; **2** to contradict
pugn·us -ī *m* fist
pulchell·us -a -um *adj* cute little
pul·c(h)er -c(h)ra -c(h)rum *adj* beautiful, fair, handsome
Pul·cher -chri *m* Roman family name *(cognomen)* in the Claudian clan, *esp.* Publius Clodius Pulcher *(tribune of 58 B.C.)*
pulchrē *adv* beautifully, attractively; thoroughly, perfectly; *(in gloating or irony)* nicely; *(as exclamation)* fine!; **pulchre mihi est** I am fine
pulchritūd·ō -inis *f* beauty; excellence, attractiveness
pūlē·ium -(i)ī *n (bot)* pennyroyal, mint; *(fig)* fragrance, pleasantness
pūl·ex *or* **pūl·ix -icis** *m* flea
pullār·ius -(i)ī *m* keeper of the sacred chickens
pullāt·us -a -um *adj* wearing black, in black, in mourning
pullul·ō -āre -āvī -ātus *intr* to sprout; *(of animals)* to produce young
pull·us -a -um *adj* dark-gray, dark, blackish; mourning-; **toga pulla** mourning toga ‖ *n* dark-gray garment
pull·us -ī *m* young *(of animals)*, foal, offspring, chick; favorite boy, catamite; sprout, shoot ‖ *mpl* chickens *(used in divination)*
pulmentār·ium -(i)ī *n* relish, appetizer
pulment·um -ī *n* relish; appetizer; food
pulm·ō -ōnis *m* lung
pulmōne·us -a -um *adj* of the lungs, pulmonary
pulp·a -ae *f* lean meat; *(pej)* flesh *(man's carnal nature)*
pulpāment·um -ī *n* meat; game
pulpit·um -ī *n* platform; stage
pulp·ō -āre *intr* to make the sound of a vulture

puls pultis *f* pulse, porridge, mush
pulsāti·ō -ōnis *f* knock
puls·ō -āre -āvī -ātus *tr* to batter, keep hitting; to knock at; to strum *(lyre);* to beat on, strike against; *(fig)* to jolt ‖ *intr* to throb
pulsus *pp of* **pello**
puls·us -ūs *m* push, pushing; beat, beating, striking, stamping; blow, stroke; trampling; *(fig)* impression, influence
pultāti·ō -ōnis *f* knocking *(at door)*
Pultiphagōnid·ēs -ae *m (humorous patronymic)* son of Porridge-eater
pultiphag·us -ī *m* porridge eater
pult·ō -āre *tr* to knock at
pulvere·us -a -um *adj* dust-, of dust; dusty; fine as dust; raising dust
pulverulent·us -a -um *adj* dusty; raising dust; covered with dust
pulvill·us -ī *m* small cushion
pulvīn·ar -āris *n* cushioned couch; sacred couch for the images of the gods; seat of honor
pulvīnār·ium -(i)ī *n* cushioned seat of a god; *(naut)* dry dock
pulvīn·us -ī *m* pillow, cushion; seat of honor
pulv·is -eris *m (f)* dust, powder; scene of action, arena, field; effort, work
pulviscul·us -ī *m* fine dust; fine powder
pūm·ex -icis *m (f)* pumice *(esp. used to polish books and also used as a depilatory);* lava
pūmice·us -a -um *adj* pumice-; lava-
pūmic·ō -āre -āvī -ātus *tr* to polish with pumice
pūmili·ō -ōnis *m* midget, dwarf; pygmy
pūmil·ius -(i)ī *m* dwarf, pygmy
pūmil·us -a -um *adj* of short stature, dwarf
punctim *adv* with the point, with the pointed end
punct·um -ī *n* prick, puncture; point; spot, dot; moment; *(gram)* clause, phrase; *(math)* point; *(pol)* vote, ballot *(dot made on wax tablet to indicate vote);* **puncto temporis eodem** at the same instant; **punctum temporis** moment, point in time, instant
pungō pungĕre pupugī *or* **pepugī punctus** *tr* to prick, puncture, dent; to sting, bite; to cause *(a wound);* to stab; *(fig)* to sting, annoy, disturb
Pūnicān·us -a -um *adj* Punic, Carthaginian, in the Carthaginian style
Pūnicē *adv* **(Poen-)** Punic, in the Punic language
pūnice·us -a -um *adj* **(poen-)** reddish, scarlet, crimson ‖ **Puniceus (Poen-)** Punic, Carthaginian
Pūnic·us -a -um *adj* **(Poen-)** Punic, Carthaginian; red, crimson, reddish, pink; **Punicum malum** *(or* **pomum)** pomegranate ‖ *n* pomegranate

pūn·iō -īre -īvī *or* **-iī -ītus** *or* **pūn·ior -īrī -ītus -sum** *tr (older form:* **poen-)** to punish; to avenge **‖** *intr* to inflict punishment

pūnīti·ō -ōnis *f* punishment

pūnit·or -ōris *m* avenger

pūp·a -ae *f* doll, puppet; girl, kid

pūpill·a -ae *f* orphan girl, ward; minor; *(anat)* pupil

pūpillār·is -is -e *adj* of an orphan, belonging to an orphan

pūpill·us -ī *m* orphan boy, ward

Pūpini·us -a -um *adj* **ager Pupinius** a barren district between Rome and Tusculum

Pūpi·us -a -um *adj* Roman clan name *(nomen), esp.* Publius Pupius *(a tragedian)*

pupp·is -is *(acc sing usu.* **puppim)** *f* stern; ship; *(coll)* back; **a puppi** astern

pūpul·a -ae *f* little girl, kid; *(anat)* pupil, eye

pūpul·us -ī *m* little boy, kid

pūp·us -ī *m* boy, child, kid

pūrē *adv* clearly, brightly; plainly, simply; chastely, purely

purgām·en -inis *n* dirt, filth; means of expiation, purification

purgāment·a -ōrum *npl* offscourings, dirt, filth, garbage; *(term of abuse)* trash, garbage

purgāti·ō -ōnis *f* cleansing, cleaning, cleanup; justification

purgāt·us -a -um *adj* cleansed, clean, pure

purg·ō -āre -āvī -ātus *tr* to cleanse, clean; to clear, clear away, remove; to clear of a charge; to excuse, justify; to refute; to purify ritually; to purge *(the body)* **‖** *refl & pass (of water, the sky)* to become clear

pūrific·ō -āre -āvī -ātus *tr* to purify

pūriter *adv* purely, cleanly; **vitam puriter agere** to lead a clean life

purpur·a -ae *f* purple dye *(ranging in shade from blood-red to deep violet);* purple, deep-red, royal purple, crimson; royal-purple cloth; royal-purple robe; royalty; consular diginity; imperial dignity

purpurāri·us -a -um *adj* (royal) purple; relating to the purple dyeing *or* to the selling of purple cloth

purpurasc·ō -ěre *intr* to turn purple

purpurāt·us -a -um *adj* wearing royal purple **‖** *m* courtier

purpure·us -a -um *adj* purple, crimson, royal purple *(and various shades as applied to roses, poppies, grapes, lips, flesh, blood, wine, dawn, sun at sunrise, hair)*

purpurissāt·us -a -um *adj* rouged

purpuriss·um -ī *n* rouge; red dye

pūr·us -a -um *adj* pure, clear, clean; cleared, cleansed; cleansing, purifying;

chaste; plain, naked, unadorned, natural; plain *(toga),* without crimson border; faultless *(style); (leg)* unconditional, absolute; *(leg)* subject to no religious claims **‖** *n* clear sky

pūs pūris *n* pus; *(fig)* venom, malice

pusill·us -a -um *adj* petty, puny **‖** *n* bit, trifle

pūsi·ō -ōnis *m* little boy

pūsul·a *or* **pussul·a** *or* **pustul·a -ae** *f* pimple; blister

pusulāt·us *or* **pustulāt·us -a -um** *adj* refined, purified *(silver)*

putām·en -inis *n* shell *(of nuts, eggs, turtles);* peel *(of fruit)*

putāti·ō -ōnis *f* pruning

putāt·or -ōris *m* pruner

pute·al -ālis *n* low wall *(around a well or sacred spot),* stone enclosure; **puteal Libonis** stone enclosure in Roman Forum near which much business was transacted

puteāl·is -is -e *adj* of a well

pūtē·faciō -facěre -fēcī -factus *tr* to cause to rot; to cause to crumble

pūt·eō -ēre -uī *intr* to stink; to be rotten

Puteolān·us -a -um *adj* of Puteoli

Puteol·ī -ōrum *mpl* Puteoli *(commercial city on the coast of the Bay of Naples, modern Pozzuoli)*

pu·ter *or* **pu·tris -tris -tre** *adj* putrid, rotting; crumbling; flabby

pūt·escō -escěre -uī *intr* to become rotten

pute·us -ī *m* well; pit; dungeon

pūtidē *adv* disgustingly; affectedly

pūtidiuscul·us -a -um *adj* rather tedious

pūtid·us -a -um *adj* stinking, rotten; worn-out *(brain);* rotten *(person);* offensive *(words, actions);* unnatural, disgusting *(style)*

putill·us -a -um *adj* tiny

put·ō -āre -āvī -ātus *tr* to trim, prune; to think, ponder, consider, judge; to suppose, imagine; to reckon, estimate, value; to believe in, recognize *(gods);* to clear up, settle *(accounts);* **magni putare** to think highly of; **pro certo putare** to regard as certain **‖** *intr* to think, imagine, suppose

pūt·or -ōris *m* stench; rottenness

putre·faciō -facěre -fēcī -factus *tr* to rot; to cause to crumble, soften

putresc·ō -ěre *intr* to become rotten, get moldy

putrid·us -a -um *adj* rotten; flabby

putris *see* **puter**

put·us -a -um *adj (ancient word for* **purus** *and usu. used in combination with* **purus)** pure, bright, perfectly pure; splendid; unmixed; unmitigated; **certum pondus argenti puri puti** a certain weight of perfectly pure silver **‖** *m* boy

pyct·a *or* **pyct·ēs -ae** *m* boxer

Pydn·a -ae _f_ Pydna _(city in Macedonia near which Aemilius Paulus defeated Perseus, king of Macedonia, 169 B.C.)_
pyel·us -ī _m_ bathtub
pȳg·a -ae _f_ rear, buttocks
pȳgarg·us -ī _m_ kind of antelope
Pygmae·ī -ōrum _mpl_ Pygmies _(a dwarfish race, esp. in Africa, said to have been constantly at war with cranes, by whom they were always defeated)_
Pygmae·us -a -um _adj_ of the Pygmies; **avis Pygmaeus** a crane
Pygmali·ōn -ōnis _or_ **-ōnos** _m_ son of Belus and brother of Dido **‖** king of Cyprus who fell in love with a statue
Pylad·ēs -ae _or_ **-is** _m_ son of Strophius and friend of Orestes
Pyladē·us -a -um _adj_ worthy of Pylades
Pyl·ae -ārum _fpl_ Thermopylae
Pylaemen·ēs -is _m_ king of the Paphlagonians and ally of Priam
Pylaïc·us -a -um of Thermopylae
Pyli·us -a -um _adj_ of Pylos **‖** _m_ Nestor
Pyl·os -ī _f_ Pylos _(home of Nestor in S.E. Peloponnesus)_
pyr·a -ae _f_ pyre
pȳram·is -idis _or_ **-idos** _f_ pyramid; cone
Pȳram·us -ī _m_ neighbor and boyfriend of Thisbe
Pȳrēnae·us -a -um _adj_ of the Pyrenees
Pȳrēn·ē -ēs _f (geog)_ the Pyrenees
Pyrēn·eūs -eī _m_ king of Thrace who tried to rape the Muses
pyrethr·um -ī _n_ Spanish camomile _(medicinal plant)_
Pygens·is -is -e _adj_ of (the town of) Pyrgi
Pyrg·ī -ōrum _mpl_ town on the coast of Etruria
Pyriphlegeth·on -ontos _m_ one of the rivers of the lower world _(= Phlegethon)_
pyrōp·us -ī _m_ bronze
Pyrrh·a -ae _f_ daughter of Epimetheus, wife of Deucalion, and survivor of the Deluge
Pyrrhi·as -adis _adj (fem only)_ of (the town of) Pyrrha in Lesbos
Pyrrh·ō(n) -ōnis _m_ Pyrrho _(philosopher of Elis, contemporary of Aristotle and founder of the school of Skepticism, c. 360–270 B.C.)_
Pyrrhōnē·us -a -um _adj_ of the school founded by Pyrrho
Pyrrh·us -ī _m_ son of Achilles and founder of Epirus _(also called Neoptolemus)_ **‖** king of Epirus who invaded Italy against the Romans in 280 B.C. _(319–272 B.C.)_
Pȳthagor·ās -ae _m_ Greek philosopher and mathematician _(6th cent. B.C.)_ **‖** a servant of Nero
Pȳthagorē·us _or_ **Pȳthagoric·us -a -um** _adj_ Pythagorean
Pȳthi·as -adis _f_ typical name for a slave girl in comedy

Pȳthic·us -a -um _adj_ Pythian, Delphic
Pȳthi·us -a -um _adj_ Pythian, Delphic **‖** _m_ Apollo **‖** _f_ Pythia _(priestess of Apollo at Delphi)_ **‖** _npl_ Pythian games _(held in honor of Apollo every four years at Delphi)_
Pȳth·ō -ūs _f_ ancient name of Delphi _or_ its oracle
Pȳth·ōn -ōnis _or_ **-ōnos** _m_ dragon slain by Apollo near Delphi
pȳtism·a -atis _n_ mouthful of wine _(spat out after tasting)_
pȳtiss·ō -āre _tr_ to spit out _(wine after tasting it)_
pyx·is -idis _or_ **-idos** _f_ powder box, cosmetic box

Q

Q. _abbr_ **Quīntus** _(first name, praenomen)_
quā _adv (interrog)_ by which road? which way? in which direction? by which route? where? by what means? how? **‖** _(rel)_ where; to the extent that; in so far as; in as much as; in the manner in which, as **‖** _(indef)_ by any route; by any chance, in any way; **qua...qua** partly...partly, both...and
quācumque _adv_ **(-cunq-)** wherever, by whatever way, in whatever way; by whatever means, howsoever
quādamtenus _adv_ to a certain point, only so far and no farther
quadr·a -ae _f_ square table, dining table; square crust; square bit, cube _(of cheese, etc.)_; slice _(of bread, cake)_
quadrāgēn·ī -ae -a _adj_ forty each
quadrāgēsim·us -a -um _adj_ **(-gensi-)** fortieth **‖** _f_ one-fortieth; 2½% tax
quadrāgiēs _adv_ **(-giens)** forty times
quadrāgintā _indecl adj_ forty
quadr·ans -antis _m_ one-fourth, a quarter; penny _(smallest coin, worth one sixth of Roman_ as); quarter of a pound; quarter pint _(quarter of a sextarius)_; **quadrante lavatum ire** to take a bath for a penny _(usual price of a bath)_
quadrant·al -ālis _n_ five-gallon jar
quadrantāri·us -a -um _adj_ quarter; **mulier quadrantaria** two-bit wench _(woman who sells herself for a pittance)_; **tabulae quadrantariae** record of debts reduced to a fourth
quadrāt·us -a -um _adj_ square; stocky _(build)_; 90-degree _(angle)_; compact _(style)_; cube, cubic **‖** _n_ square; square object; cube
quadri- _pref_ consisting of, having four of the things named
quadrīdu·um -ī _n_ four-day period; **in quadriduo** within four days; **quadriduo**

for a period of four days; within the next four days; **quadriduo ante (post)** four days before (after)

quadrienn·ium -(i)ī *n* four-year period, four years

quadrifāriam *adv* in four directions; in four ways; in four places; in fours

quadrifid·us -a -um *adj* split into four parts

quadrīg·a -āe *f or* **quadrīg·ae -ārum** *fpl* four-horse team *(running four abreast)*; four-horse chariot

quadrīgāri·us -a -um *adj* connected with chariot racing

quadrīgār·ius -(i)ī *m* chariot racer

quadrīgāt·us -a -um *adj (of a coin)* stamped with the image of a four-horse chariot

quadrīgul·ae -ārum *fpl (figurine of a)* four-horse chariot

quadrijūg·is -is -e *or* **quadrijug·us -a -um** *adj* drawn by a four-horse team *(yoked abreast); (of horses)* yoked four abreast **ǁ** *mpl* four-horse team

quadrilībr·is -is -e *adj* four-pound

quadrīmul·us -a -um *adj* only four years old

quadrīm·us -a -um *adj* four-year-old

quadringēnāri·us -a -um *adj* consisting of four hundred men each

quadringēn·ī -ae -a *adj* four hundred each

quadringentēsim·us -a -um *adj* four-hundredth

quadringentiē(n)s *adv* four hundred times

quadripertītō *adv* in four parts, in four divisions

quadripertīt·us -a -um *adj* four-fold

quadrirēm·is -is -e *adj* having four banks of oars *(or possibly with four rowers to every bench)* **ǁ** *f* quadrireme

quadriv·ium -(i)ī *n* crossroads

quadr·ō -āre -āvī -ātus *tr* to make square; to complete; *(rhet)* to round out, give rhythmic finish to *(a speech)* **ǁ** *intr* to make a square; to be exact; *(of accounts)* to agree, come out right, tally; *(w. dat or* **in** + *acc)* to suit, fit

quadr·um -ī *n* square; **in quadrum redigere sententiam** *(rhet)* to balance a sentence *(by changing word order)*

quadruped·ans -antis *adj* galloping **ǁ** *mpl* horses

quadruped·us -a -um *adj* galloping

quadrup·ēs -edis *adj* four-footed; on all fours **ǁ** *mf* quadruped

quadruplāt·or -ōris *m* informer *(who received ¼ of the forfeiture);* corrupt judge

quadrupl·ex -icis *adj* quadruple, fourfold

quadruplic·ō -āre -āvī -ātus *tr* to quadruple

quadrupl·or -ārī -ātus sum *intr* to be an informer, be a whistleblower

quadrupl·us -a -um *adj* quadruple, fourfold **ǁ** *n* four times the amount

quaerit·ō -āre -āvī -ātus *tr* to keep looking for; to keep asking

quae·rō -rēre -sīvī *or* **-siī -sītus** *tr* to look for, search for; to try to get; to get, obtain; to try to gain, earn, acquire; to miss, lack; to require, demand, call for; to ask, interrogate; to examine, investigate; to plan, devise, aim at; *(w. inf)* to try to, wish to; *(w.* **ab** *or* **de** *or* **ex** + *abl)* to ask *(s.th.)* of *or* from *(s.o.)* **ǁ** *intr* to hold an examination; *(w.* **de** + *abl)* to ask about; **quid quaeris?** *(introducing a short, clinching remark)* what more can I say?; **si quaeris** *(or* **si quaerimus)** to tell the truth

quaesīti·ō -ōnis *f (leg)* questioning under torture

quaesīt·or -ōris *m (leg)* judge *(praetor or other official who presided over a criminal trial)*

quaesīt·us -a -um *pp of* **quaero ǁ** *adj* select, special; far-fetched; artificial, affected **ǁ** *npl* gains, earnings, acquisitions, store

quaes·ō -ĕre *tr* to try to obtain; to beg, ask for, request **ǁ** *intr* to carry out a search; **quaeso** *(usually parenthetical)* please; *(w. direct questions)* please tell me; *(in exclamations)* just look!; take note!

quaesticul·us -ī *m* slight profit

quaesti·ō -ōnis *f* inquiry, investigation, questioning, examination; *(leg)* judicial investigation, criminal trial, court of inquiry, court; *(leg)* questioning under torture, third degree; *(leg)* question, subject of investigation, case; *(leg)* court record; *(w.* **de** + *abl of the nature of the charge)* court investigating a charge of *(e.g., forgery);* **in quaestione versari** to be under investigation; **quaestio extraordinaria** investigation by a special board; **quaestio inter sicarios** murder trial, court investigating a murder; **quaestio perpetua** standing court; **quaestioni praesse** to preside over a case; **servos in quaestionem dare** *(or* **ferre)** to hand over slaves for questioning under torture

quaestiuncul·a -ae *f* minor *or* trivial question; small problem, puzzle

quaest·or -ōris *m* quaestor *(serving, at various periods as: financial officer; treasury official; public prosecutor of criminal offenses; aide to a provincial governor; army paymaster; personal aide to the emperor);* **pro quaestore** acting quaestor, vice-quaestor

quaestōri·us -a -um *adj* quaestor's, of a quaestor; employed in a quaestor's office; qualified for the rank of quaestor; having quaestorian rank *(i.e., having held* *the office of quaestor);* **ager quaestoria** conquered land sold on behalf of the state treasury; **porta quaestoria** the gate nearest the quaestor's tent *(perhaps* **porta decumana)** ‖ *m* ex-quaestor ‖ *n* quaestor's tent in a camp; quaestor's residence in a province

quaestuōs·us -a -um *adj* profitable, productive; acquiring wealth; eager to make a profit, acquisitive; good at moneymaking; enriched, wealthy

quaestūr·a -ae *f* quaestorship; *(fig)* public funds

quaest·us -ūs *m* gain, profit; acquisition; way of gaining a livelihood, job, occupation, business, trade; income; *(fig)* benefit, advantage; **ad quaestum** for profit, to make a profit; **in quaestu esse** to be profitable; **in quaestu habere** to derive profit from; **pecuniam in quaestu relinquere** to deposit money at interest; **quaestui rem publicam habere** to use public office for personal profit; **quaestum facere** to make money, make a living; **quaestūs facere** to make gains

quālibet *adv* (**-lub-**) anywhere, everywhere; in any way, as you please

quāl·is -is -e *adj* what sort of, what kind of; of such a kind, such as, as; *(w. quotations and citations)* as, as for example; **in hoc bello, quale** in this war, the likes of which; **qualis erat!** what a man he was!

quāl·iscumque -iscumque -ecumque (**-cunque**) *adj* of whatever kind; of any kind whatsoever, any at all; **homines, qualescumque sunt** people, no matter what kind they are; **qualiscumque** *(or* **qualecumque) est** such as it is, for what it is worth

quāl·islibet -islibet -elibet *adj* of whatever kind, of whatever sort

quāl·isnam -isnam -enam *adj* just what kind of

quālit·ās -ātis *f* quality, nature; property, characteristic; high quality; *(gram)* mood *(of a verb)*

quāliter *adv* as, just as

quāl·us -ī *m or* **quāl·um -ī** *n* wicker basket, straw basket

quam *adv (in questions and exclamations)* how, how much; *(in comparisons)* as, than; *(with superlatives)* as…as possible, *e.g.,* **quam celerrime** as fast as possible; **quam plurimo vendere** to sell at the highest price possible; **quam primum** as soon as possible; *(indicating numerical proportion)* **dimidium (duplex,** *etc.)* **quam** half as much as (twice as much as, *etc.); (as the correlative of* **tam)** the…the: **quam magis id reputo, tam magis uror** the more I think it over, the madder I get; *(after verbs of preferring)*

than: **praestat nemini imperare quam alicui servire** it is preferable to rule over no one than to be a slave to someone

quamdiū *or* **quam diū** *interrog & rel adv* how long ‖ *conj* as long as

quamlibet *adv* (**-lub-**) as much as you please

quamobrem *or* **quam ob rem** *adv* for what reason, why; for which reason, wherefore, why

quamquam *conj* although

quamvīs *adv (with adj or adv)* however, no matter how; ever so; **illa quamvīs ridicula essent** no matter how funny they were ‖ *conj* although

quānam *adv* by what route *or* way

quandō *adv (in questions)* when, at what time; *(indefinite, after* **si, ne, num)** ever, at any time ‖ *conj* when, because, since

quandōcumque *adv* (**-cunque**) at some time or other, some day ‖ *conj* whenever; as often as, no matter when

quandōque *adv* at some time, at one time or other, some day ‖ *conj* whenever; as often as; since

quandōquidem *conj* in as much as, whereas, seeing that

quantill·us -a -um *interrog adj* how much?, how little?

quantit·ās -ātis *f* quantity; size

quantō *adv* by how much, how much; **quanto…tanto** the…the: **quanto longior nox est, tanto brevior dies it** the longer night is, the shorter the day becomes

quantopere *or* **quantō opere** *adv* by how much, how much; with how great effort, how carefully

quantulum *adv* how little; **quantulum interest utrum** how little difference it makes whether

quantul·us -a -um *adj* how great, how much, how little, how small, how insignificant

quantuluscumque quantulacumque quantulumcumque *adj* however small, however unimportant

quantum *adv* as much as, so much as, as great an extent; how much, how far, to what extent; *(w. comparatives)* the more, the greater; **quantum in me fuit** as much as I could, to the best of my ability; **quantum maximā voce potuit** at the top of his voice; **quantum potest** as much *(or* fast, quickly, soon, long, *etc.)* as possible

quantumcumque *adv* as much as; however much, however little; to whatever degree, as far as

quantumlibet *adv (also written as two words)* however much

quantusquantus quantaquanta quantumquantum *adj (also written as two* *words)* however big, however great, of whatever degree **‖** *n* however much, whatever

quantumvīs *adv (also written as two words)* however; **quantumvis rusticus** however unsophisticated, although unsophisticated

quant·us -a -um *adj (interrogative or exclamatory)* how great, how much, of what size, of what importance, of what worth **‖** *n* **in quantum** to whatever extent, as far as; **quanti** *(gen of price)* how much, how high, how dearly, at what price; **quanto** *(abl of price)* at what price, for how much; **quantum frumenti** how much grain **‖** *pl* how many

quant·uscumque -acumque -umcumque *adj* however great; of whatever size; however small; however trifling; however important *(or* unimportant); **quanticumque** at whatever price, at whatever cost

quant·uslibet -alibet -umlibet *adj* however great; ever so great

quant·usvīs -avīs -umvīs *adj* of whatever size, amount, degree, *etc.*, you wish; however big, however great, no matter how great

quāpropter *adv* wherefore, why

quāquā *adv* by whatever route, in whatever way

quāquam *adv* in any way; anywhere

quārē *or* **quā rē** *adv* by what means, how; in what way, from what cause, why; whereby; wherefore; **nec quid nec quare** without why or wherefore

quart·a -ae *f* a fourth, one quarter

Quart·a -ae *f* female first name *(praenomen)*

quartadecumān·ī -ōrum *mpl* **(-decim-)** *mpl* soldiers of the 14th legion

quartān·us -a -um *adj* occurring every fourth day **‖** *f* quartan fever **‖** *mpl* soldiers of the 4th legion

quartār·ius -(i)ī *m* quarter pint

quartō *adv* for the fourth time

quartum *adv* for the fourth time; in the fourth place, fourthly

quart·us -a -um *adj* fourth

quart·us decim·us -a -um *adj* fourteenth

quasi *adv* as it were, so to speak; about, nearly, almost; allegedly **‖** *conj* on the charge that; as would be the case if; *(expressing the supposed reason for an action)* on the grounds that; *(introducing a hypothetical situation after verbs of asserting or supposing)* saying that, believing that, to the effect that: **sparsit rumorem, quasi...bellum gerere non possit** he spread a rumor to the effect that he could not fight a war

quasill·um -ī *n or* **quasill·us -ī** *m* small basket

quassāti·ō -ōnis *f* (violent) shaking

quass·ō -are *tr* to keep shaking, keep tossing, keep waving; to batter, shatter, smash to pieces; *(fig)* to shake, weaken **‖** *intr (of the head)* to keep on shaking

quass·us -a -um *pp of* **quatio ‖** *adj* shattered, broken; quavering *(voice)*; chopped *(wood)*

quate·faciō -facěre -fēcī -factus *tr* to shake; *(fig)* to weaken

quātenus *adv* how far, to what point; as far as, till when, how long; to what extent; **est quatenus** there is an extent to which **‖** *conj* as far as; insofar as, in as much as, seeing that, since, as

quater *adv* four times

quater decie(n)s *adv* fourteen times

quatern·ī -ae -a *adj* four together, four in a group, four each

quatiō quatěre — quassus *tr* to shake, cause to tremble, cause to vibrate; to brandish, wave about; to beat, strike, drive; to batter, crush; *(fig)* to touch, move, affect; *(fig)* to plague, harass

quattuor *indecl adj* four

quattuordecim *indecl adj* fourteen

quattuor·vir -virī *m* member of a board of four *(one of the four chief magistrates of a municipium; member of a committee of four at Rome)*

quattuorvirāt·us -ūs *m* membership on the board of four

quāvīs *adv* anyway you like, in any possible way

quax·ō -āre *intr (of frogs)* to croak

-que *enclitic conj* and; **-que...-que** *(mostly poetical)* both...and; **terrā marīque** on land and on sea

-que *suf used in the formation of certain adverbs and conjunctions, e.g.:* **itaque** and so, therefore; *esp. to give indefinite force to relative pronouns and adverbs, e.g.,* **quandoque** at some time or other, someday

quemadmodum *or* **quem ad modum** *adv* in what way, how **‖** *conj* just as, as

qu·eō -īre -īvī *or* **-iī -ītum** *intr* to be able; *(w. inf)* to be able to

quercēt·um -ī *n* oak forest

querce·us -a -um *adj* oak-, of oak

querc·us -ūs *f* oak tree; oak-leaf crown *(awarded to a soldier who saved a citizen in battle);* acorns

querēl·a -ae *f* (**-ell-**) complaint; grievance; protest; difference of opinion

queribund·us -a -um *adj* full of complaints; whining *(voice)*

querimōni·a -ae *f* complaint, grievance; elegy

querit·or -ārī *intr* to keep complaining

quern·us -a -um *adj* oak-, of oak

queror querī questus sum *tr* to complain of, complain about; to lament **‖** *intr* to complain; *(of birds)* to sing, warble, sing sadly, coo mournfully

Querquētulān·us -a -um *adj (as name of various places and deities associated with oaks)* oak-, covered with oak trees; **mons Querquetulanus** Oak Hill *(an old name for the Caelian Hill in Rome;* **Porta Querquetulana** Oak Gate *(probably between the Caelian and the Esquiline Hills)*

querquēt·um -ī *n* oak forest

querul·us -a -um *adj* complaining, full of complaints, querulous; plaintive; warbling, cooing

questi·ō -ōnis *f* complaining

questus *pp of* queror

quest·us -ūs *m* complaint; plaintive note *(of the nightingale)*

quī quae *or* **qua quod** *adj (interrog)* which, what, what kind of; *(indef)* any **II** *pron (rel)* who, that; *(indef, after* **si, nisi, num, ne)** anyone

quī *adv* how; why; at what price; whereby; in some way, somehow

quia *conj* because

quianam *adv (interrog)* why in fact?

quicquam cūjusquam *pron* anything

quicque cūjusque *pron* each (one)

quīcum *(old abl of* **quī** *and* **cum)** *pron* with whom, with which

quīcumque quaecumque quodcumque *(also* **-cunque, -quomque)** *pron & adj (rel & indef)* whoever, whosoever, everyone who, whatever, whatsoever, everything ever

quid *adv* how?; why? **quid agis?** how do you do?; **quid plura?** why say more?

quid cūjus *pron (interrog)* what?; *(w. gen)* what kind of?: **quid mulieris uxorem habes?** what sort of woman do you have as your wife?; *(indef, after* **si, nisi, num, ne)** anything

quīdam quaedam quiddam *pron* a certain one, a certain person, a certain thing

quīdam quaedam quoddam *adj* a certain; *(to soften an expression)* a kind of, what one might call

quidem *adv (emphasizing the word before it)* indeed, in fact; *(qualifying or limiting)* at least, at any rate; *(concessive)* it is true; of course; all right; *(exemplifying)* for example; **ne…quidem** *(emphasizing the intervening word)* not even, *e.g.,* **ne tu quidem** not even you

quidnam cūjusnam *pron (interrog)* just what?

quidnam *adv* why in the world

quidnī *adv* why not?

quidpiam cūjuspiam *pron* anything, something

quidpiam *adv* in some respect

quidquid *or* **quicquid** *(gen and dat not in use; abl:* **quōquō)** *pron* whatever, what-

soever, everything which; **per quidquid deorum** by all the gods

quidquid *adv* to whatever extent, the further

quīdum *adv* how so?

qui·ēs -ētis *f* quiet, rest, peace; calm, lull; neutrality; sleep; dream; sleep of death, death

qui·escō -escĕre -ēvī -ētum *intr* (contracted forms: **quiesse** = **quievisse; quierunt** = **quieverunt; quierem** = **quieveram)** to rest, keep quiet, be inactive; to fall asleep; to sleep, be asleep; to lie still, be still, be undisturbed; to say no more, be quiet; *(of the dead)* to find rest; to pause, make a pause; *(of a person)* to be calm, remain calm, be unruffled; *(of physical forces, of conditions)* to die down, subside, be still; *(of things)* to cease to operate; to be neutral, keep neutral, take no action; to refrain from violence, make no disturbance, remain peaceful; *(of troops)* to make no move; *(w. inf)* to cease to, stop; to take no steps to, omit to; *(w.* **ab** + *abl)* to be free from

quiētē *adv* quietly, calmly

quiēt·us -a -um *adj* at rest, resting, free from exertion, inactive; quiet; peaceful, undisturbed; netural; calm; still, silent; idle **II** *npl* period of peace

quīlibet quaelibet quodlibet (-lubet) *pron* anyone, any you wish, no matter who, anything, anything you wish, no matter what, everything

quīlibet quaelibet quodlibet (-lubet) *adj* any, any at all, any you wish

quīn *adv (interrog)* why not; *(corroborative)* in fact, as a matter of fact **II** *conj* so that not, without; **facere non possum, quin ad te mittam librum** I can't help sending you the book; **nullo modo introire possem, quin viderent me** I just couldn't walk in without their seeing me; *(after verbs of preventing, opposing)* from: **milites aegre sunt retenti quin oppidum oppugnarent** the soldiers could barely be kept from assaulting the town; *(after verbs of hesitation, doubt, suspicion):* **non dubito quin** I do not doubt that; *(esp. representing a nominative of a relative pronoun with a negative)* that…not: **nemo aspicere potest quin dicat** no one can look on without saying; **nemo est quin velit** there is no one who does not prefer

quīnam quaenam quodnam *adj* which, what, just which, just what

quīnavīcēnāri·us -a -um *adj* of twenty-five: **lex annorum quinavicenaria** the law prohibiting those under twenty-five years of age from making contracts

Quincti·us -a -um *adj* Roman clan name *(nomen), esp.* Lucius Quinctius Cincin-

natus *(called on his farm to become dictator in 458 B.C.)* ‖ Titus Quinctius Flamininus *(consul in 198 B.C., who "liberated" Greece from Macedonia)* ‖ Publius Quinctius *(represented by Cicero in his first case, in 81 B.C.)*
quinc·unx -uncis *m* five-twelfths; 5% *(interest);* the figure five *(as arranged on dice or cards)*
quindeciē(n)s *adv* fifteen times
quindecim *indecl adj* fifteen
quindecimprīm·ī -ōrum *mpl* executive board of fifteen *(magistrates of a municipality)*
quindecimvirāl·is -is -e *adj* of the board of fifteen
quindecimvir·ī -ōrum *mpl* board of fifteen; **quindecimviri Sibylini** board of fifteen in charge of the Sibylline Books
quingēnāri·us -a -um *adj* of five hundred each, consisting of five hundred *(men, pounds, etc.)*
quingēn·ī -ae -a *adj* five hundred each
quingentēsim·us -a -um *adj* five-hundredth
quingent·ī -ae -a *adj* five hundred
quingentiē(n)s *adv* five hundred times
quīn·ī -ae -a *adj* five each; **quini deni** fifteen each; **quini viceni** twenty-five each
quinquāgēn·ī -ae -a *adj* fifty each
quinquāgēsim·us -a -um *adj* fiftieth ‖ *f* 2% tax
quinquāgintā *indecl adj* fifty
Quinquātr·ūs -uum *fpl or* **Quinquātr·ia -ium** *npl* festival in honor of Minerva *(celebrated from March 19 to 23 esp. by the trades and professions under her patronage);* **quinquatrūs minores** *(or* **minusculae)** festival of Minerva held on June 13
quinque *indecl adj* five
quinquennāl·is -is -e *adj* quinquennial, occurring every five years; five-year, lasting five years
quinquenn·is -is -e *adj* five-year-old, of five years
quinquenn·ium -(i)ī *n* five-year period, five years
quinqueped·al -ālis *n* five-foot ruler
quinquepertīt·us -a -um *adj* five-fold, divided into five parts
quinqueprīm·ī -ōrum *mpl* five-man board of magistrates
quinquerēm·is -is -e *adj* having five banks of oars ‖ *f* quinquereme
quinque·vir -virī *m* member of a five-man board *(created at various times for various purposes)*
quinquevirāt·us -ūs *m* membership on a board of five
quinquiē(n)s *adv* five times
quinquipl·ex -icis *adj* fivefold; **cera**

quinquiplex tablet consisting of five sheets
quinquiplic·ō -āre -āvī -ātus *tr* to multiply by five
Quint·a -ae *f* woman's name *(praenomen)*
quintadecimān·ī -ōrum *mpl* **(-decum-)** soldiers of the 15th legion
quintān·us -a -um *adj* of the fifth ‖ *mpl* members of the fifth legion ‖ *f* camp street running between the 5th and 6th maniple *(used as a market street of the camp)*
Quintiliān·us -ī *m* Quintilian *(Marcus Fabius Quintilanus, orator and professor of rhetoric, A.D. c. 35–95)*
Quintīl·is *or* **Quinctīl·is -is -e** *adj & m* July *(fifth month of the old Roman calendar until 153 B.C.; renamed* **Julius** *after the Julian reform of the calendar)*
Quint·ius *or* **Quinct·ius -(i)ī** *m* Roman clan name *(nomen)*
quintō *or* **quintum** *adv* for the fifth time
quint·us -a -um *adj* fifth ‖ **Quintus** *m* Roman first name *(praenomen)*
quint·us decim·us -a -um *adj* fifteenth
quippe *adv* of course, naturally, obviously, by all means ‖ *conj* since, for; **quippe qui** since he *(is, was, will be one who),* inasmuch as he; **multa Caesar questus est quippe qui vidisset** Caesar complained a lot since he had seen
quippiam = **quidpiam**
quippinī *adv* why not?; of course, to be sure
Quirīnāl·is -is -e *adj* of Quirinus *(i.e., Romulus);* **collis Quirinalis** Quirinal Hill *(one of the seven hills of Rome)* ‖ *npl* festival in honor of Romulus *(celebrated on February 17)*
Quirīn·us -a -um *adj* of Quirinus ‖ *m* Quirinus *(epithet of Romulus after his deification, of Janus, of Augustus, and of Antony)*
Quir·īs -ītis *m* Roman citizen; inhabitant of Cures *(Sabine town) (after the union of the Sabines and Romans, the Romans called themselves* **Quirites** *in their peace-time capacity. They were styled on all solemn occasions* **Populus Romanus Quirites(que);** *in later times it was distorted into* **Populus Romanus Quirites)**
quirītāti·ō -ōnis *f* shrieking, shriek
quirītāt·us -ūs *m* shriek, scream
Quirītēs -ium *mpl (pl form of* **Quirīs)** *(see* **Quiris)** Roman citizens; **jus Quiritium** legal rights enjoyed by Roman citizens
quirīt·ō -āre *tr & intr* to shriek, scream
quis cūjus *pron (interrog)* who, which one; *(indef)* anyone
quīs = **quibus**
quisnam quaenam *(see* **quidnam)** *pron (interrog)* who, just who

quispiam cūjuspiam *pron* someone
quispiam quaepiam quodpiam *adj* any
quisquam cūjusquam *pron* anyone
quisque cūjusque *pron* each, each one, everybody, everyone; **doctissimus quisque** everyone of great learning, all the most learned; **optimus quisque** all the best ones
quisque quaeque quodque *or* **quidque** *or* **quicque** *adj* each
quisquili·ae -ārum *fpl or* **quisquili·a -ōrum** *npl* refuse, scraps, trash, junk
quisquis *(gen and dat not in use; abl:* **quōquō)** *pron* whoever, whosoever; everyone who; everyone, each
quīvīs quaevīs quidvīs *pron* anyone at all, anyone you please; **quivis unus** any one person
quō *adv (interrog)* where?, to what place?; what for?, to what purpose?; *(after* **si, nisi,** *or* **ne)** to any place, anywhere; **quo...eo** the...the; **quo magis...eo magis** the more...the more ‖ *conj* where, to which place; whereby, wherefore; *(replacing* **ut** *when the clause contains a comparative)* in order that, so that
quoad *adv* how far; to what extent; by what time, how soon; how long; **est modus quoad** there is a limit up to which ‖ *conj* as long as; as far as; until, until such time as
quōcircā *adv* for which reason, wherefore, therefore, that's the reason
quōcumque (-cunque, -quomque) *adv* to whatever place, wherever
quod *conj* because; as for the fact that; the fact that; insofar as; as far as; **quod si** *(or* **quodsi)** but if
quōdammodō *or* **quōdam modo** *adv* in a way
quoi = cui
quoiquoimodī *see* **cuicuimodi**
quoivīsmodī *see* **cuivismodi**
quōjus = cujus
quōlibet *adv* anywhere you please, anywhere at all
quom *see* **cum**
quōminus *conj* that not; *(after verbs of hindering)* from, *e.g.,* **deterrere aliquem quominus aliquid habeat** to keep s.o. from having s.th.
quōmodo *adv (interrog)* how, in what way; *(rel)* just as, as
quōmodocumque *adv* in whatever way, however
quōmodonam *interrog adv* where?, whereto?; to what purpose?, to what end?
quōnam *interrog* where on earth?, just where(to)? **quonam usque** just how much longer? to what possible degree? to what conceivable end?
quondam *adv* once, at one time, formerly;

at times, once in a while; someday, one day *(in the future)*
quōniam *conj* because, seeing that, now that
quōpiam *adv* at any place, anywhere
quōquam *adv* to any place; in any direction, anywhere
quoque *adv (always succeeds the word it emphasizes)* too
quōquō *adv* to whatever place, wherever
quōquōmodo *adv* in whatever way, however
quōquōversum *adv* **(-vorsum, -sus)** in every direction, every way
quorsum *interrog & rel adv* **(-sus)** in what direction, whereto; to what end, why
quot *indecl adj (interrog)* how many; *(correlative)* as many; **quot Kalendis** every first of the month; **quot mensibus** every month
quotannīs *adv* every year
quotcumque *indecl adj* however many
quotēn·ī -ae -a *adj* how many each
quotīdiān·us -a -um *adj* (cōt-, cott-) daily
quotīdiē *adv* (cōt-, cott-) daily
quotiē(n)s *adv (interrog)* how many times; *(correlative)* as often as, whenever
quotiē(n)scumque *or* **quotiē(n)scunque** *adv* however many, no matter how many
quotquot *indecl adj* however many; **quotquot annis** every year; **quotquot mensibus** every month
quotum·us -a -um *adj* which in number, which in order
quot·us -a -um *adj* which, what; what a small, what a trifling; **quota hora est?** what time is it?; **quota pars** *(or* **portio)** what part, what portion; **quotus quisque** how few?; **quotus quisque philosophorum invenitur** how few of the philosophers are found *or* how rarely is one of the philosophers found?
quot·uscumque -acumque -umcumque *adj* just what, just which
quōusque *adv* how far, how long, till when; to what degree
quōvīs *adv* to any place whatsoever, anywhere; **quovis gentium** anywhere in the world
qūr *or* **quūr** *see* **cur**

R

rabidē *adv* rabidly, madly; furiously
rabid·us -a -um *adj* rabid, mad; furious, raving, uncontrolled
rabi·ēs *(gen not in use) f* madness; *(fig)* rage, anger, fury, wild passion; ferocity *(of animals);* rabies
rabiōsē *adv* furiously, madly
rabiōsul·us -a -um *adj* half-mad

rabiōs·us -a -um *adj* rabid *(animal);* mad; frenzied, furious

rabō -ōnis *m (shortened form of* **arrabo)** token payment, earnest money

rabul·a -ae *m* ranting lawyer

racēmif·er -era -erum *adj* clustered; covered with grape clusters

racēm·us -ī *m* cluster, bunch *(esp. of grapes); (fig)* wine

radi·ans -antis *adj* shining, beaming, radiant

radiāt·us -a -um *adj* spoked; having rays, radiant

rādīcitus *adv* by the roots, root and all; *(fig)* completely, utterly

rādīcul·a -ae *f* small root; radish

radi·ō -āre *or* **radi·or -ārī** *intr* to radiate, shine

radiōs·us -a -um *adj* radiant

rad·ius -(i)ī *m* stake, stick; spoke; ray, beam; shuttle; radius; measuring rod; elongated variety of olive

rād·ix -īcis *f* root; radish; foot *(of hill or mountain);* base, foundation; basis, origin

rā·dō -dĕre -sī -sus *tr* to scrape, scratch; to shave; to scratch out, erase; to graze, touch in passing; to strip off; *(of wind)* to lash

raed·a -ae *f* **(rēd-)** four-wheeled carriage, coach

raedār·ius -(i)ī *m* coach driver

Raeti·us -a -um *adj* **(Rhaet-)** Rhaetian ‖ *f* Rhaetia *(Alpine country between Germany and Italy)*

Raetic·us -a -um *adj* **(Rhaet-)** Rhaetian

Raet·us -a -um *adj & m* **(Rhaet-)** Rhaetian

rall·us -a -um *adj* thin, threadbare

rāmāl·ia -ium *npl* brushwood, undergrowth

rāment·a -ae *f or* **rāment·um -ī** *n* chip, shaving

rāmes *see* **ramex**

rāme·us -a -um *adj* of branches, of boughs

rām·ex -icis *m or* **ram·es -itis** *m* rupture; blood vessel of the lung ‖ *mpl* lungs

Ramn·ēs *or* **Ramnens·ēs -ium** *mpl* one of the three original Roman tribes; *(fig)* blue bloods

rāmōs·us -a -um *adj* having many branches, branching; branch-like

rāmul·us -ī *m* twig

rām·us -ī *m* branch, bough; branch *(of an antler);* genealogical branch

rān·a -ae *f* frog; **rana quaxat** the frog croaks

ranc·ens -entis *adj* putrid, stinking

rancidul·us -a -um *adj* stinky, rank; rather disgusting

rancid·us -a -um *adj* rancid, rank, stinking; disgusting

ranc·ō -āre *intr (of a tiger)* roar

rānuncul·us -ī *m* little frog, tadpole

rapācid·a -ae *m (hum patronymic)* son of a thief

rapācit·ās -ātis *f* rapacity, greediness

rap·ax -ācis *adj* rapacious, grasping, greedy for plunder; insatiable

raphan·us -ī *m* radish

rapidē *adv* rapidly; *(to burn)* fiercely

rapidit·ās -ātis *f* rapidity, velocity, swiftness, rush

rapid·us -a -um *adj* tearing away, seizing; fierce, consuming, white-hot *(fire);* rapid, swift, rushing, impetuous

rapīn·a -ae *f* rapine, pillage; prey

rap·iō -ĕre -uī -tus *tr* to seize and carry off; to snatch, tear, pluck; to drag off; to hurry, drive, cause to rush; to carry off by force, ravish; to ravage, lay waste; to lead on hurriedly; **flammam rapere** to catch fire; **in jus rapere** to haul off to court ‖ *refl* to hurry, dash, take off

raptim *adv* hurriedly; suddenly

rapti·ō -ōnis *f* abduction, ravishing

rapt·ō -āre *tr* to seize and carry off; to abduct, kidnap; to drag away; to drag along; to plunder; **in jus raptare** to haul off to court

rapt·or -ōris *m* plunderer, robber; abductor

rapt·us -a -um *pp of* **rapio** ‖ *n* plunder, loot

rapt·us -ūs *m* snatching away; looting, robbery; abduction, kidnapping

rāpul·um -ī *n* little turnip

rāp·um -ī *n* turnip

rārē *adv* rarely; sparsely; loosely

rārē·faciō -facĕre -fēcī -factus *tr* to rarefy, thin out

rārē·fīō -fierī -factus sum *intr* to become less solid, rarefy

rāresc·ō -ĕre *intr* to grow thin, lose density, become rarefied; to grow wider, widen out, open up; to become fewer; to disappear, die away

rārit·ās -ātis *f* looseness of texture; thinness; small number; sparseness; infrequency; rarity

rārō *adv* rarely, seldom

rār·us -a -um *adj* wide apart, of loose texture, thin; scattered, far apart; scarce, sparse; few; uncommon, rare; unusual; *(mil)* in open rank

rāsī *perf of* **rado**

rāsil·is -is -e *adj* shaved smooth, scraped, polished

rāsit·ō -āre -āvī -ātus *tr* to shave (regularly)

rastell·us -ī *m* rake *(usu. of wood)*

rastr·um -ī *(pl:* **rastr·ī -ōrum** *mpl) n* rake; mattock

rāsus *pp of* **rado**

rati·ō -ōnis *f* calculation, computation, reckoning, account; register; matter, affair, business, transaction; consideration, respect; grounds; guiding principle; scheme, system, method; procedure; theory, doctrine; science; relation, connection, reference; fashion, way, style; reasoning, reason, judgment, understanding; reasonableness; order, law, rule; view, opinion; *(w. gen)* a reason for; **(libertus) a rationibus** bookkeeper, accountant; **fugit te ratio** *(coll)* you're off your rocker; **non erat ratio amittere ejusmodi occasionem** there was no reason to pass up that kind of opportunity; **pares rationes facere cum** to square accounts with; **popularis ratio** popular cause; **pro ratione** proportionately; according to the rule, properly; **propter rationem** *(w. gen)* out of regard for; **ratio aeraria** rate of exchange; **ratio atque usus** theory and practice; **ratio constat** the account tallies; **ratione** with good reason; according to the rules, properly; **rationem conferre** *(or* **deferre** *or* **referre)** *(w. gen)* to render *or* give an account of, account for; **rationem (de)ducere** to make a calculation, reckon; **rationem habere cum** to have to do with; **rationem inire** to calculate, make a calculation; to embark on a scheme; **ratio vitae** pattern of life, life style

ratiōcināti·ō -ōnis *f* exercise of the reasoning powers, reasoning; theory, theorizing; deduction, inference

ratiōcinātīv·us -a -um *adj* concerned with reasoning, syllogistic

ratiōcināt·or -ōris *m* accountant

ratiōcin·or -ārī -ātus sum *tr & intr* to calculate, reckon; to reason, argue, conclude, infer

ratiōnāl·is -is -e *adj* rational; theoretical; dialectical

ratiōnār·ium -(i)ī *n* financial survey

rat·is -is *f* raft; *(poet)* ship, craft **‖** *fpl* pontoons

ratiuncul·a -ae *f* small account; trifling reason; petty argumentation

rat·us -a -um *pp of* **reor ‖** *adj* reckoned, calculated; fixed, established, settled, certain, sure; approved; **pro rata parte** *(or* **pro ratā)** in proportion, proportionately; **ratum facere** *(or* **efficere)** to confirm, ratify, approve; **ratum habere** *(or* **ducere)** to consider valid, regard as certain *or* sure

raucison·us -a -um *adj* hoarse-sounding

rauc·us -a -um *adj* raucous, hoarse; screaming, strident; scraping; deep, deep-voiced

raud·us *n* **(rōd-, rūd-)** copper coin; lump

rauduscul·um -ī *n* **(rōd-, rūd-)** bit of money

Ravenn·a -ae *f* Ravenna *(port and naval base)*

rāv·iō -īre *intr* to be hoarse

rāv·is -is *f* hoarseness

rāv·us -a -um *adj* grayish

re- *pref (also* **red-)** *denoting* **1** movement back, in reverse: **revocare** to call back; **2** reversal of an action, un-: **retegere** to uncover; **3** restoration: **revalescere** to recover again; **4** response: **respondere** to respond; **rescribere** to answer *(in writing)*; **5** opposition: **rebellare** to rebel; **6** separation: **removere** to remove; **7** repeated action: **replere** to refill; **reïterare** repeat again and again

re·a -ae *f* defendant; guilty woman

Rēa *see* **Rhea**

rēapse *adv* **(-abs-)** in fact, actually, really

Reāt·e -is *n* Sabine town

Reātīn·us -a -um *adj* of Reate

rebellāti·ō -ōnis *f* rebellion

rebellātr·ix -īcis *adj (fem only)* rebellious; **rebellatrix Germania** rebellious Germany

rebelli·ō -ōnis *f* rebellion

rebell·is -is -e *adj* rebellious **‖** *mpl* rebels

rebell·ium -(i)ī *n* rebellion

rebell·ō -āre -āvī -ātum *intr* to rebel

rebīt·ō -ēre *intr* to go back

rebo·ō -āre *tr* to make reecho **‖** *intr* to reecho, bellow back

recalcitr·ō -āre *intr* to kick back

recal·eō -ēre *intr* to get warm again; *(of a river)* to run warm *(e.g., w. blood)*

recal·escō -escĕre -uī *intr* to grow warm again

recal·faciō -facĕre -fēcī *tr* to warm up again

recalv·us -a -um *adj* bald in front, with receding hairline

recand·escō -escĕre -uī *intr* to grow white; *(w. dat)* to grow hot, glow in response to

recanō *see* **recino**

recant·ō -āre -āvī -ātus *tr* to recant; to charm back, charm away **‖** *intr* to reecho

reccidō *see* **recido**

re·cēdō -cēdĕre -cessī -cessum *intr* to go back; to go away, withdraw, recede; to give ground, fall back; to depart; to vanish; to stand back, be distant

recell·ō -ĕre *intr* to recoil

recens *adv* just, recently, lately

rec·ens -entis *adj* recent, fresh, young; newly arrived, just arrived; modern; fresh; rested; **recentissimus** latest **‖** *npl* recent events

recens·eō -ēre -uī -sus *tr* to count, enumerate, number, survey; to recount, go over again, retell; *(mil)* to review; *(pol) (of a censor)* to revise the roll of, review, enroll

recensi·ō -ōnis *f* revision

recensus *pp of* **recenseo**

recens·us -ūs *m* review; census; valuation *(of property)*

recēpī *perf of* **recipio**

receptācul·um -ī *n* receptacle, container; reservoir; place of refuge, shelter; hiding place

recepti·ō -ōnis *f* reception

recept·ō -āre *tr* to take back; to welcome frequently into the home, entertain; to tug at **‖** *refl* to beat a hasty retreat

recept·or -ōris *m or* **receptr·ix** -īcis *f* shelterer; concealer

recept·us -a -um *pp of* **recipio ‖** *n* obligation

recept·us -ūs *m* taking back, recantation; way of escape; refuge; return; *(mil)* retreat; **(signum) receptui canere** to sound the retreat

recessī *perf of* **recedo**

recessim *adv* backwards

recess·us -ūs *m* retreat, withdrawal; departure; secluded spot, retreat; inner room, central chamber; recess; background

recharmid·ō -āre *ref* to stop being a Charmides *(character in Roman comedy)*

recidīv·us -a -um *adj* recurring, returning; rebuilt

reci·dō -děre -dī -sus *tr* to cut back, cut off, cut away, cut down; to abridge, cut short

re·cǐdō -ciděre -cǐdī -cāsum *or* **reccǐd·ō** -ěre *intr* to fall back; to jump back, recoil; to suffer a relapse; *(fig)* to fall back, sink, relapse; to turn out, result; *(w.* **ad** *or* **in** + *acc)* to pass to, be handed over to

recin·gō -gěre -xī -ctus *tr* to loosen, undo, take off

recin·ō -ěre *tr* to repeat, reecho **‖** *intr* to sound a warning

reciper- = **recuper-**

re·cipiō -cipěre -cēpī -ceptus *tr* to keep back, keep in reserve; to withdraw, bring back, carry back; to retake, recover, regain; to take in, accept, receive, welcome; to gain, collect, take in, make *(money)*; to take up, assume, undertake; to guarantee, pledge; *(mil)* to retake, recapture, seize, take, occupy; **ad se** *(or* **in se) recipere** to take upon oneself, take the responsibility for, promise, guarantee **‖** *refl* to get hold of oneself again, regain composure, recover, come to again; to retreat, escape; **se recipere** *(w.* **ad** *or* **in** + *acc)* to retreat to, escape to, find refuge in

reciproc·ō -āre -āvī -ātus *tr* to move back and forth; to turn back; to back up *(e.g., a ship),* reverse the direction of; to reverse, convert *(a proposition)* **‖** *intr (of the tide)* to ebb and flow, rise and fall

reciproc·us -a -um *adj* ebbing and flowing, going backwards and forwards

recīsus *pp of* **recido**

recitāti·ō -ōnis *f* reading aloud, recitation

recitāt·or -ōris *m* reader, reciter

recit·ō -āre -āvī -ātus *tr* to read out, read aloud, recite; to name in writing, appoint, constitute; **senatum recitare** to have roll call in the Senate

reclāmāti·ō -ōnis *f* cry of disapproval; shout of protest

reclāmit·ō -āre *intr* to voice disapproval; *(w. dat)* to protest against

reclām·ō -āre -āvī -ātus *tr* to protest **‖** *intr* to raise a protest, shout objections; to reverberate; *(w. dat)* to express disapproval to, contradict

reclīn·is -is -e *adj* reclining, leaning back

reclīn·ō -āre -āvī -ātus *tr* to bend back, lean back, rest; *(w.* **ab**) to distract *(s.o.)* from **‖** *refl* to lean

reclū·dō -děre -sī -sus *tr* to open; to lay open, disclose; to draw *(sword);* to break up *(the soil)*

recoctus *pp of* **recoquo**

recōgit·ō -āre -āvī -ātum *tr* to consider, think over **‖** *intr* (w. **de** + *abl*) to think again about, reconsider

recogniti·ō -ōnis *f* formal inspection

reco·gnoscō -gnoscěre -gnōvī -gnitus *tr* to call to mind again, review; to recognize; to look over, examine, inspect, investigate; to certify, authorize

recol·ligō -ligěre -lēgī -lectus *tr* to gather again, gather up, collect; **te recollige!** get hold of yourself! take heart! **‖** *refl* to pull oneself together

re·colō -colěre -coluī -cultus *tr* to till again; to honor again; to call to mind, think over, consider; to cultivate once more; to practice again, resume

recomment·or -ārī -ātus sum *tr* to remember, recall

recomminisc·or -ī *tr* to call to mind again, recall

recomposit·us -a -um *adj* rearranged

reconciliāti·ō -ōnis *f* winning back again, reestablishment, restoration; reconciliation

reconciliāt·or -ōris *m* reconciler; **pacis reconciliator** restorer of peace

reconcili·ō -āre -āvī -ātus *tr* to bring back, regain, recover; to restore, reestablish; to win over again, conciliate; to bring together again, reconcile

reconcinn·ō -āre *tr* to set right again, repair

recondit·us -a -um *adj* hidden, concealed; recondite, abstruse, profound; reserved *(person)*

recon·dō -děre -didī -ditus *tr* to put back again; to put away, hoard; to hide, conceal; to plunge *(sword);* to close *(eyes)* again; to store up *(in the mind)*

reconfl·ō -āre *tr* to rekindle

reco·quō -quĕre -xī -ctus *tr* to cook, boil, *or* bake again; to recast, remold
recordāti·ō -ōnis *f* recollection, remembrance
record·or̄ -ārī -ātus sum *tr & intr* to recall, recollect, remember
recoxī *perf of* recoquo
recre·ō -āre -āvī -ātus *tr* to recreate, restore, renew; *(fig)* to revive, refresh
recrep·ō -āre *intr* to reecho
re·crescō -crescĕre -crēvī *intr* to grow again; to be renewed
recrūd·escō -escĕre -uī *intr (of a wound)* to open up again; *(of a revolt)* to break out again
rectā *adv* by a direct route, straight
rectē *adv* in a straight line; rightly, correctly; suitably, properly, well; quite; *(in answers)* well, right, quite well, fine
recti·ō -ōnis *f* direction, controlling
rect·or -ōris *m* guide, controller; rider, driver *(of an animal);* leader; master; pilot; tutor; *(mil)* commander; *(naut)* helmsman, pilot; *(pol)* ruler, governor
rect·us -a -um *pp of* **rego** ‖ *adj* in a straight line, straight, direct; correct, right, proper, appropriate; just, upright, conscientious, virtuous; standing erect; *(impartial)* judge; straight-forward *(expression);* sheer *(cliff);* **aere recto cantare** to play a reed pipe; **casus rectus** *(gram)* nominative case; **funis rectus** tightrope; **rectis oculis** with eyes not lowered, without flinching ‖ *n* right; uprightness, rectitude, virtue; **in rectum** in a straight line; in a vertical position *or* direction, vertically; straight forward
recub·ō -āre *intr* to lie on one's back, lie down, rest
rēcul·a -ae *f* little thing
recultus *pp of* **recolo**
re·cumbō -cumbĕre -cubuī *intr* to lie down (again); to recline *(esp. at table);* to sink down *(e.g., in a swamp);* to fall; *(of fog)* to settle down
recuperāti·ō -ōnis *f* recovery
recuperāt·or -ōris *m* **(-cip-)** recoverer; *(leg)* arbiter *(member of a bench of from 3 to 5 men who expedited cases needing speedy decisions)*
recuperātōri·us -a -um *adj* **(-cip-)** of the special court for summary civil suits
recuper·ō -āre -āvī -ātus *tr* **(-cip-)** to regain, recover, get back; to win over again
recūr·ō -āre -āvī -ātus *tr* to restore, refresh, restore to health
recur·rō -rĕre -rī -sum *intr* to run back, hurry back; to return *(to the starting point of a cycle);* to recur, come back *(to the mind);* *(of a process)* to run in the oppposite direction; to revert *(to a former condition);* *(w. ad)* to have recourse to

recurs·ō -āre *intr* to keep running back; to keep recurring
recurs·us -ūs *m* return; retreat
recurv·ō -āre -āvī -ātus *tr* to curve, bend back
recurv·us -a -um *adj* curving, curved, bent, crooked
recūsāti·ō -ōnis *f* refusal; *(leg)* objection, protest; *(leg)* counterplea
recūs·ō -āre -āvī -ātus *tr* to raise objections to, reject, refuse; *(w. inf)* to be reluctant to, refuse to ‖ *intr* to raise an objection; to make a rebuttal
recuss·us -a -um *adj* reverberating
recu·tiō -tĕre -ssī -ssus *tr* to strike *(so as to cause to resound)*
recutīt·us -a -um *adj* raw *(skin, from being rubbed);* circumcised
red- *see* **re-**
redactus *pp of* **redigo**
redambul·ō -āre *intr* to walk back
redam·ō -āre *tr* to love in return
redardesc·ō -ĕre *intr* to blaze up again
redargu·ō -ō -ī *tr* to disprove, refute, contradict; to disprove the existence of
redauspic·ō -āre *intr* to take the auspices again
red·dō -dĕre -didī -ditus *tr* to give back, return, restore, replace; to repay; to repeat *(words);* to recite, rehearse *(words);* to produce *(a sound);* to ascribe, attribute; to translate; to utter in response; to render, make; to give as due, pay, grant, deliver; to reflect, reproduce, imitate; **animam a pulmonibus reddere** to exhale *(literally, to give back a breath from the lungs);* **causam reddere** to give a reason *or* explanation; **conubia reddere** to grant intermarriage rights; **judicium reddere** to administer justice; to grant a trial; **jura reddere** to administer justice; **litteras reddere** to deliver a letter; **morbo naturae debitum reddere** to die of disease; **poenas reddere** to suffer punishment; **qui te nomine reddet** who will bear your name; **rationem reddere** to render an account *(financial or other);* **reddere hosti cladem** to pay back the enemy for the massacre; **talia ei reddere** to answer him in words such as this; **veniam reddere** *(w. dat)* to forgive; **verbum pro verbo reddere** to translate word for word; **vitam reddere** to die ‖ *refl* to return
redempti·ō -ōnis *f* ransoming; bribing; revenue collection
redempt·ō -āre *tr* to ransom (repeatedly)
redempt·or -ōris *m* contractor; revenue agent
redemptūr·a -ae *f* undertaking of public contracts
redemptus *pp of* **redimo**

red·eō -īre -iī -itum *intr* to go back, come back, return; *(of a speaker)* to return *(to the theme);* *(w.* ad*)* **1** to return to, revert to; **2** to fall back on, have recourse to; **3** to be reduced to; **4** *(of power, inheritances, etc.)* to revert to, devolve upon; **ad se redire** to come to again, regain consciousness; to control oneself

redhāl·ō -āre *tr* to exhale

redhib·eō -ēre -uī -itus *tr (of a vendor)* to take back *(a defective purchase); (of a purchaser)* to return *(a defective purchase)*

red·igō -igĕre -ēgī -actus *tr* to drive back, lead back, bring back; to call in, collect, raise, make *(money);* to gather in *(crops);* to repel *(the enemy);* to reduce *(in quantity, number, or to a condition);* to force, compel, subdue; *(w. double acc)* to render, make; *(w.* in *or* sub *+ acc)* to bring under the power of; **ad vanum et irritum redigere** to make meaningless; to make null and void; **in memoriam redigere** to remember, recall; **in ordinem redigere** to bring into line; **in provinciam redigere** to reduce to the status of a province; **in potestatem redigere** *(w.* gen*)* to bring under the control of; **in publicum** *(or* **in aerarium***)* **redigere** to turn over *(money)* to the public treasury

redimīcul·um -ī *n* band, chaplet, fillet; chain, fetter

redim·iō -īre -iī -ītus *tr* to crown, wreathe; to surround, encircle

red·imō -imĕre -ēmī -emptus *tr* to buy back; to ransom, redeem; to buy off, ward off, avert; to pay for, compensate for, atone for; *(com)* to get by contract, collect under contract

redintegrāti·ō -ōnis *f* renewal; repetition

redintegr·ō -āre *tr* to make whole again, restore, revive, refresh; *(mil)* to bring to full strength

redipisc·or -ī *tr* to get back

rediti·ō -ōnis *f* return

redit·us -ūs *m* return; *(fig)* restoration; *(astr)* orbit, revolution; *(fin)* revenue, proceeds, return; **(in) reditu esse** to yield a return

redivia *see* **reduvia**

redivīv·us -a -um *adj* second-hand

redol·eō -ēre -uī *tr* to smell of, smell like **‖** *intr* to smell, be redolent

redōn·ō -āre -āvī -ātus *tr* to restore, give back again; to give up, abandon

redorm·iō -īre *intr* to go back to sleep (again)

redū·cō -cĕre -xī -ctus *tr* to lead back, bring back; to draw back; to revive *(a practice);* to escort *(an official, as mark of honor, to his home);* to remarry *(after a separation);* to restore to normal, restore to a previous condition; to withdraw *(troops); (leg)* to make retrospective; **gradum reducere** to draw back; **in gratiam reducere** to restore to favor; **in memoriam reducere** to recall; **rem huc reducere ut** to make it possible that

reducti·ō -ōnis *f* restoration

reduct·or -ōris *m* restorer

reduct·us -a -um *pp of* **reduco ‖** *adj* remote, secluded, aloof

redunc·us -a -um *adj* bent backwards, curved backwards

redundanti·a -ae *f* excess; redundancy

redund·ō -āre -āvī -ātum *tr* to cause to overflow; **aqua redundata** the overflow **‖** *intr* to overflow; to be too numerous, be too large; *(of writers)* to be excessive; to be soaked *(e.g., w. blood); (w. abl)* to abound in; *(w.* ex *or* de *+ abl)* to stream from, overflow with

reduvi·a *or* **redivi·a -ae** *f* hangnail

red·ux -ucis *adj* **(redd-)** guiding back, rescuing; that brings back home *(esp. a soldier on a foreign mission);* brought back, restored

reduxī *perf of* **reduco**

refecti·ō -ōnis *f* restoration, repairing; regaining one's strength; convalescence

refectus *pp of* **reficio**

refell·ō -ĕre -ī *tr* to refute, disprove

refer·ciō -cīre -sī -tus *tr* **(refarc-)** to stuff, cram, choke, crowd

refer·iō -īre *tr* to strike back

referō referre rettulī relātus *tr* to bring back, carry back; to give back, return, restore; to pay back, repay; to (re)echo *(a sound);* to renew, revive, repeat; to direct, focus, turn *(mind, attention);* to present again, represent; to say in turn, reply; to announce, report, relate, tell; to note down, enter, register, record; to consider, regard; to refer, attribute, ascribe; to bring up, spit out, vomit; **gradum referre** to go back, retreat; **gratiam referre** to do a return favor; **gratias referre** to return thanks, show gratitude; **pedem referre** to go back, retreat; **pedes fertque refertque** he walks up and down; **rationes referre ad aerarium** to make an accounting to the treasury; **vestigia referre** to retrace footsteps **‖** *refl* to go back, return **‖** *intr (pol)* to make a motion, make a proposal; **ad senatum referre** *(w.* de *+ abl)* to bring before the Senate the matter of, make a proposal to the Senate about **‖** *v impers* it is of importance, it is of consequence; **meā (tuā, nostrā) refert** it is of importance *or* of advantage to me (you, us); **non refert utrum** it makes no difference whether; **parvi refert** *(w. inf)* it is of little importance, of little advantage to; **quid refert?** what's the difference?

refert·us -a -um *pp of* **refercio** ‖ *adj*
packed, crammed; crowded

referv·eō -ēre *intr* to boil over, bubble over

refervesc·ō -ěre *intr* to begin to boil *or*
bubble

refībul·ō -āre *tr* to unpin

re·ficiō -ficěre -fēcī -fectus *tr* to rebuild,
repair, restore; to revive *(hope, etc.)*; to
refresh, invigorate; to get *(e.g., money)*
back again; to reappoint

refī·gō -gěre -xī -xus *tr* to unfasten, undo;
to take down *(posters, etc.)*; to annul
(laws)

refing·ō -ěre *tr* to refashion

refixus *pp of* **refigo**

reflāgit·ō -āre *tr* to demand again, ask
back

reflāt·us -ūs *m* headwind

re·flectō -flectěre -flexī -flexus *tr* to bend
back *or* backwards, turn around, turn
away; *(fig)* to turn back, bring back,
change

refl·ō -āre -āvī -ātus *tr* to breathe out
again ‖ *intr* to blow in the wrong direction

reflu·ō -ěre *intr* to flow back, run back; to
overflow

reflu·us -a -um *adj* ebbing, receding

refocill·ō -āre -āvī -ātus *tr* to rewarm; to
revive

reformāt·or -ōris *m* reformer

reformīdāti·ō -ōnis *f* dread

reformīd·ō -āre -āvī -ātus *tr* to dread,
stand in awe of; to shrink from, shun

reform·ō -āre -āvī -ātus *tr* to reshape,
remold, transform

re·foveō -fovēre -fōvī -fōtus *tr* to warm
again; to restore, revive, refresh

refractāriol·us -a -um *adj* a bit refractory,
somewhat stubborn

refractus *pp of* **refringo**

refrāg·or -ārī -ātus sum *or* **refrāg·ō -āre**
intr (w. dat) to oppose, resist, thwart

refrēn·ō -āre -āvī -ātus *tr* to curb, restrain, keep down, control

refric·ō -āre -uī -ātus *tr* to rub open,
scratch open; to irritate, reopen *(a
wound)*; *(fig)* to exasperate; *(fig)* to renew ‖ *intr* to break out again

refrīger·ō -āre -āvī -ātus *tr* to cool, cool
off, chill; to refresh; to weary, exhaust ‖
pass to grow cool; to grow weary

re·frīgescō -frīgescěre -frixī *intr* to grow
cool, become cool; *(fig)* to lose force,
flag, abate, fail, grow dull, grow stale;
(fig) to fall flat

re·fringō fringěre -frēgī -fractus *tr* to
break open, break down; to tear off
(clothes); *(fig)* to break, check, destroy,
put an end to

re·fugiō -fugěre -fūgī *tr* to run away from;
to avoid ‖ *intr* to run away, escape; to
disappear

refug·ium -(i)ī *n* place of refuge; recourse

refug·us -a -um *adj* receding, vanishing ‖
m fugitive, refugee

reful·geō -gēre -sī *intr* to gleam, reflect
(light), glitter

re·fundō -funděre -fūdī -fūsus *tr* to pour
back, pour out ‖ *pass* to flow back; to
overflow

refūtāti·ō -ōnis *f* refutation

refūtāt·us -ūs *m* refutation

refūt·ō -āre -āvī -ātus *tr* to repress, suppress; to refute, disprove

rēgāliol·us -ī *m* wren

rēgāl·is -is -e *adj* regal, kingly; royal

rēgāliter *adv* royally; despotically

regel·ō -āre -āvī -ātus *tr* to thaw

re·gerō -gerěre -gessī gestus *tr* to carry
back, throw back; *(fig)* to throw back
(remarks)

rēgi·a -ae *f* palace; cou·ι *(royal or imperial establishment)*; capital; *(in camp)*
king's tent; regia *(originally the house
of King Numa in the Roman Forum and
later the residence of the Pontifex Maximus)*

rēgiē *adv* royally; despotically

Rēgiens·is -is -e *or* **Rēgīn·us -a -um** *adj*
(Rhēg-) of Rhegium ‖ *mpl* inhabitants
of Rhegium *(in Bruttium in S. Italy)*

rēgific·us -a -um *adj* fit for a king

Rēgill·um -ī *n or* **Rēgill·ī -ōrum** *mpl* Sabine
town from which the Fabian clan is said
to have come

Rēgill·us -ī *m* family name *(cognomen)* in
the Aemilian clan ‖ name of a small lake
south of Gabii *(now dri·d up)* where the
Romans defeated the Latins in 496 B.C.

regim·en -inis *n* steering *(of a ship)*; steering oar; control *(of a horse)*; direction,
control *(of public and private affairs)*

rēgīn·a -ae *f* queen

Rēgīn·us -a -um (Rhēg-) of Rhegium *(in
Bruttium)* ‖ *mpl* inhabitants of Rhegium

regi·ō -ōnis *f* straight linv line, direction;
boundary, boundary line; region, area,
quarter, neighborhood; ward *(of Rome)*;
district, province *(of a c juntry)*; department, sphere; geographical position; **ab
recta regione** in a straight line; **de recta
regione deflectere** to veer off the straight
path; **e regione** in a straight line, directly; *(w. gen or dat)* in the opposite
direction to, exactly opposite; **rectā
regione** by a direct route

regiōnātim *adv* by districts

rēgi·us -a -um *adj* king's, royal, regal; like
a king, worthy of a king magnificent ‖
mpl king's troops ‖ *f see* **regia**

reglūtin·ō -āre *tr* to unglue

regnāt·or -ōris *m* ruler, sovereign

regnātr·ix -īcis *adj (fem only)* reigning,
imperial

regn·ō -āre -āvī -ātum *intr* to reign; to be

supreme, hold sway; to dominate; to rule the roost, play (the part of a) king; *(w. gen)* to be king of; *(w.* in + *acc)* to rule over
regn·um -ī *n* monarchy, royal power, kingship; absolute power, despotism; supremacy, control, direction, sovereignty; kingdom, realm; domain, estate
regō regĕre rexī rectus *tr* to keep in a straight line; to keep on a proper course; to guide, conduct; to guide *(morally);* to manage, direct; *(mil)* to command; *(pol)* to rule, govern; **imperium regere** to exercise dominion, rule supreme; **regere finīs** *(leg)* to mark out the limits
re·gredior -gredī -gressus sum *intr* to step *or* go back; to come back, return; *(mil)* to march back, retreat
regressi·ō -ōnis *f (mil)* withdrawl; *(rhet)* repetition
regress·us -ūs *m* return; retreat
rēgul·a -ae *f* ruler *(for drawing straight lines or measuring);* rod, bar; rule, standard, model, principle *(in conduct, language)*
rēgul·us -ī *m* petty king; prince **ǁ Regulus** Marcus Atilius Regulus *(Roman general who refused to let himself be ransomed in the First Punic War)* **ǁ** Marcus Aquilius Regulus *(an informer under Nero, later a successful advocate)*
regust·ō -āre -āvī -ātus *tr* to taste again; *(fig)* to delve again into *(e.g., literature)*
reject·a -ōrum *npl (phil)* things which, while not absolutely bad, should be avoided
rejectāne·us -a -um *adj* to be rejected
rejecti·ō -ōnis *f* rejection; *(leg)* challenging; **rejectio judicum** challenging potential jury members
rejectus *pp of* **rejicio**
re·jiciō -jicĕre -jēcī -jectus *tr* to throw back; to throw over one's shoulders; to beat back, repel; to reject; to refer, direct, assign; to postpone; *(leg)(of judges)* to challenge, overrule; **rem rejicere** *(w. ad)* to refer the matter *(to s.o. for decision);* **potestas rejiciendi** *(leg)* right to challenge
relā·bor -bī -psus sum *intr* to slide *or* glide back; to sink down *(upon a couch); (of rivers)* to flow back; to sail back; *(fig)* to return
relangu·escō -escĕre -ī *intr* to faint; to be relaxed, relax; to weaken
relāti·ō -ōnis *f* report *(made by a magistrate to the Senate or the Emperor);* repetition; **relatio criminis** *(leg)* responding to a charge
relāt·or -ōris *m (pol)* proposer of a motion in the Senate
relātus *pp of* **refero**
relāt·us -ūs *m* official report; narration; recital

relaxāti·ō -ōnis *f* relaxation; easing off, mitigation
relax·ō -āre -āvī -ātus *tr* to stretch out, widen, open; to loosen, open; to release, set free; to relax; to cheer up; to mitigate
relectus *pp of* **relego**
relēgāti·ō -ōnis *f* banishment; sending into retirement
relēg·ō -āre -āvī -ātus *tr* to send away, remove; to send into retirement, retire; to banish; to relegate; to shift *(blame, responsibility);* to give back
re·lĕgō -legĕre -lēgī -lectus *tr* to collect again, gather up; to travel over, sail over again; to go over, review *(in thought, in a speech);* to reread
relentesc·ō -ĕre *intr* to slack off, cool off
relev·ō -āre -āvī -ātus *tr* to lighten; to lift up *or* raise again; *(fig)* to relieve, ease the pain of; to lessen in force; to soothe
relicti·ō -ōnis *f* abandonment
relictus *pp of* **relinquo ǁ** *adj* abandoned, forsaken
relicuus *see* **reliquus**
relīd·ō -ĕre *tr* to dash back *(in the direction from which s.th. came)*
religāti·ō -ōnis *f* tying back *or* up
religi·ō -ōnis *f* religion; religious scruple, sense of right, conscience; misgivings; reverence, awe; *(pej)* superstition; sanctity, holiness; sect, cult; mode of worship; object of veneration, sacred object, sacred place; divine service, worship, ceremonies; religious practice, ritual; religious taboo; manifestation of divine sanction; *(w. gen)* scruple about, scrupulous regard for
religiōsē *adv* religiously, reverently, piously; scrupulously, conscientiously, carefully, exactly
religiōs·us -a -um *adj* religious, reverent, pious, devout; scrupulous, conscientious, exact, precise, accurate; superstitious; sacred, holy, consecrated; subject to religious claims, under religious liability
relig·ō -āre -āvī -ātus *tr* to tie back, tie up; to moor *(ship);* to untie, unfasten; to bind *(with a wreath, ribbon)*
re·linō -linĕre -lēvī *tr* to unseal
re·linquō -linquĕre -līquī -lictus *tr* to leave behind, not take along; to bequeath; to let remain; to leave alive; to forsake, abandon, leave in the lurch; to relinquish, resign; to leave unmentioned; **in medio (or in medium) relinquere** to leave *(a question)* open; **locum integrum relinquere** to leave the place untouched
reliqu·ī -ōrum *mpl* the rest, the others; the survivors; posterity
reliqui·ae -ārum *fpl* remains, remnants
reliqu·us -a -um *adj (also* **-cuus)** remaining, left over, left; subsequent, future *(time);* outstanding *(debt)* **ǁ** *mpl see*

reliqui ‖ *n* remainder, rest, residue; **in reliquum** in the future, for the future; **nihil reliqui facere** to leave nothing undone, leave no stone unturned; **reliquum est** *(w. inf or ut)* it only remains to; **reliquum aliquid facere** *(or* **aliquid reliqui facere)** to leave s.th. behind, neglect s.th.

rellig- = **relig-**

relliqu- = **reliq-**

relū·ceō -cēre -xī *intr* to reflect light, gleam, shine out, blaze

relū·cescō -cescĕre -xī *intr* to grow bright again, clear

reluct·or -ārī -ātus sum *intr* to fight back, put up a struggle, resist; to be reluctant

remacresc·ō -ĕre *intr* to shrink and become thin

remaledīc·ō -ĕre *intr* to return abuse

remand·ō -ĕre *tr* to chew again

reman·eō -ēre -sī -sum *intr* to stay behind; to remain, continue *(in a certain state)*

remān·ō -āre *intr* to flow back

remansi·ō -ōnis *f* staying behind

remed·ium -(i)ī *n* remedy, cure

remensus *pp of* **remetior**

reme·ō -āre -āvī -ātus *tr* to retrace, relive ‖ *intr* to go back, come back, return

re·mētior -mētīrī -mensus sum *tr* to remeasure; to retrace, go back over

rēm·ex -igis *m* rower, crew member

Rēm·ī -ōrum *mpl* a people of Gaul *(near modern Rheims)*

rēmigāti·ō -ōnis *f* rowing

rēmig·ium -(i)ī *n* rowing; oars; oarsmen, rowers; **remigium alarum** flapping of wings

rēmig·ō -āre -āvī *intr* to row

remigr·ō -āre -āvī -ātum *intr* to move back

reminisc·or -ī *tr* to call to mind, remember ‖ *intr* to remember; *(w. gen)* to be mindful of, be conscious of, remember

re·misceō -miscēre — -mixtus *tr* to mix up, intermingle; **veris falsa remiscere** to mix in lies with the truth

remissē *adv* mildly, gently

remissi·ō -ōnis *f* release; easing, letting down, lowering; relaxing *(of muscles)*; relaxation, recreation; mildness, gentleness; submissiveness; abating, diminishing; remission *(of debts)*

remiss·us -a -um *adj* relaxed, loose, slack; mild, gentle; remiss; easy-going, indulgent; gay, merry, light; low, cheap *(price)*; **remissiore uti genere dicendi** to speak in a lighter vein

re·mittō -mittĕre -mīsī -missus *tr* to send back; to release; to slacken, loosen; to emit, produce, let out, give off; to return, restore; to reecho *(a voice)*; to give up, reject, resign, concede; to relax, relieve

(the mind); to pardon; to remit, *(penalty, debt, obligation)*; *(w. inf)* to stop *(doing s.th.)*; **frontem** *(or* **os** *or* **vultum) remittere** to relax the tense expression; **loqui remittere** to stop speaking; **nihil remittere** to spare no effort; **repudium remittere** to send a notice of divorce ‖ *intr (of wind, rain)* to let up, slack off

remixtus *pp of* **remisceo**

remōl·ior -īrī -ītus sum *tr* to push *or* move back *or* away, heave back

remollesc·ō -ĕre *intr* to soften again; to weaken

remoll·iō -īre -īvī -ītus *tr* to soften

remor·a -ae *f* hindrance, delay

remōrāmin·a -um *npl* hindrances, delays

remor·deō -dēre -dī -sus *tr* to bite back; to attack in return; to worry, nag

remor·or -ārī -ātus sum *tr* to hinder, delay, hold back ‖ *intr* to loiter, linger, delay, stay behind

remōtē *adv* at a distance, far away

remōti·ō -ōnis *f* withdrawal; removal, elimination *(of a condition);* **remotio criminis** the shifting of a charge

remōt·us -a -um *adj* removed, out of the way, far off, remote, distant; *(fig)* remote, apart, separate; dead; *(w. ab)* **1** removed from, separate from, apart from; **2** clear of, free from

re·moveō -movēre -mōvī -mōtus *tr* to move back, withdraw; to put away, remove; to shroud, veil; to substract; *(fig)* to put out of sight, set aside, abolish

remūg·iō -īre *intr* to bellow back; *(fig)* to reecho, resound

remul·ceō -cēre -sī -sus *tr* to stroke, smooth back; **caudam remulcere** to put the tail between the legs *(in fear)*

remulc·um -ī *n* towline, towrope

Remul·us -ī *m* a king of Alba Longa

remūnerāti·ō -ōnis *f* remuneration, recompense, reward

remūner·or -ārī -ātus sum *or* **remūner·ō -āre** *tr* to repay, remunerate

Remūri·a -ōrum *npl* **(Le-)** festival held in May to appease the spirits of the dead

remurmur·ō -āre *tr & intr* to murmur in reply

rēm·us -ī *m* oar; **ad remos dare** to assign *(s.o.)* as rower; **remi corporis** *(fig)* hands and feet *(of a swimmer)*; **remis** by rowing; **remis incumbere** to lean to the oars

Rem·us -ī *m* twin brother of Romulus

renarr·ō -āre *tr* retell

re·nascor -nascī -nātus sum *intr* to be born again; to rise again, spring up again, be restored; to reappear; to recur

renāvig·ō -āre *intr* to sail back

ren·eō -ēre *tr* to unravel, undo

rēn·ēs -(i)um *mpl* kidneys

renīd·ens -entis *adj* beaming, glad

renīd·eō -ēre *intr* to reflect (light), glitter,

shine; to smile, grin all over; to beam with joy

renīdesc·ō -ĕre *intr* to grow bright, gleam, begin to glitter

renī·tor -tī *intr* to fight back, put up a struggle, resist

ren·ō -āre -āvī *intr* to swim back, float back

rēn·ō -ōnis *m* (rhē-) reindeer skin *(used for clothing)*

renōd·ō -āre -āvī -ātus *tr* to tie back in a knot; to untie

renovām·en -inis *n* renewal, new form

renovāti·ō -ōnis *f* renovation, renewal; revision; *(fin)* compound interest

renov·ō -āre -āvī -ātus *tr* to make new again; to renovate, repair, restore; to plow up *(a fallow field);* to reopen *(a wound);* to revive *(an old custom, etc.);* to start *(a battle)* all over again; to refresh *(the memory);* to repeat, keep repeating, reaffirm; **faenus renovare in singulos annos** *(fin)* to compound the interest on a yearly basis

renumer·ō -āre -āvī -ātus *tr* to count over again, recount; to pay back, repay

renuntiāti·ō -ōnis *f* formal *or* official report, announcement

renunti·ō -āre -āvī -ātus *tr* to report; to announce; to retract *(a promise, statement);* to renounce *(an alliance, a friendship);* to reject; to call off *(a previous engagement);* (w. double acc) to announce *or* declare *(s.o.)* elected as; *(w. acc & inf)* to bring back word that; **legationem renuntiare** *(of an ambassador)* to give an account of an embassy; **repudium renuntiare** to break off an engagement; **sibi renuntiare** to say to oneself, remind oneself ‖ *intr* to take back a message; *(w. dat)* to withdraw from, renounce, give up

renunt·ius -(i)ī *m* reporter

renu·ō -ĕre -ī *tr* to nod refusal to, turn down, decline, say no to, reject ‖ *intr* to shake the head in refusal; *(w. dat)* to say no to, deny *(a charge)*

renūt·ō -āre -āvī *intr* to refuse emphatically

reor rērī ratus sum *tr* to think, deem; *(w. acc & inf)* to think that; *(w. acc & adj as objective complement)* to regard *(s.th.)* as ‖ *intr* to think, suppose

repāgul·a -ōrum *npl* bolts, bars; *(fig)* restraints, regulations, rules, limits

repand·us -a -um *adj* curved backwards, concave; *(shoes)* with turned-up toes

reparābil·is -is -e *adj* capable of being repaired, reparable, retrievable

reparc·ō -ĕre repersī *intr* (w. dat) to be sparing with, take it easy on

repar·ō -āre -āvī -ātus *tr* to get again, acquire again; to recover, retrieve, make

good; to restore, renew; to repair; to recruit *(a new army);* **vina merce reparare** to get wine in exchange for wares, barter for wine

repastināti·ō -ōnis *f* the act of turning *(the ground)* over again for planting

repastin·ō -āre -āvī -ātus *tr* to turn *(the ground)* over again for planting

re·pectō -pectĕre -pexī -pexus *tr* to comb back; to comb again

repellō repellĕre reppulī repulsus *tr* to drive back, push back, repel; to reject; to remove; to refute

repen·dō -dĕre -pendī -pensus *tr* to repay, pay back; to ransom; *(fig)* to repay in kind, requite, recompense, reward; to compensate for; to balance, balance out; **magna rependere** to pay back in full

rep·ens -entis *adj* sudden, unexpected; completely new

repensus *pp of* rependo

repente *adv* suddenly, all of a sudden; unexpectedly

repentīnō *adv* suddenly; unexpectedly, without warning

repentīn·us -a -um *adj* sudden, unexpected; hasty, impetuous

reperc·ō -ĕre *intr* (w. dat) **1** to be sparing with; **2** to refrain from

repercussī *perf of* repercutio

repercuss·us -a -um *pp of* repercutio ‖ *adj* rebounding; reflected, reflecting; echoed, echoing

repercuss·us -ūs *m* reverberation, echo, repercussion; reflection

reper·cutiō -cutĕre -cussī -cussus *tr* to make *(s.th.)* rebound, make reverberate, make reflect

reperiō reperīre repperī repertus *tr* to find, discover; to find again; to get, procure, win; to find out, ascertain, realize; to invent, devise

repertīci·us -a -um *adj* newly discovered

repert·or -ōris *m* discoverer, inventor, author

repert·us -a -um *pp of* reperio ‖ *npl* discoveries, inventions

repetīti·ō -ōnis *f* repetition; *(w.* **in** *+ acc)* going back to; *(rhet)* anaphora

repetīt·or -ōris *m* claimant

repet·ō -ĕre -īvī *or* -iī -ītus *tr* to head back to, try to reach again, return to; to aim at again; to fetch back; to attack again; to persecute again; to demand anew; to demand back, claim, demand in compensation, retake; to trace back, retrace; to trace in thought, think over, recall, recollect; to repeat, undertake again, resume, renew; **animo** *(or* **memoriā)** **repetere** to recall; **lex de pecuniis** *(or* **rebus) repetundis** law on extortion *(literally, law concerning recovering money or property);* **memoriam repetere** to recall the memory; **pecuniam repetere** to sue for the recovery of money; **poenam** *(or* **poenas)** **repetere** to demand satisfaction; **res repetere** to sue for the recovery of property; **reus pecuniarum repetundarum** guilty of extortion ‖ *intr (w.* **ad)** to head back to

repetund·ae -ārum *fpl* money extorted; extortion; **repetundarum argui** to be charged with extortion; **repetundarum teneri** to be held on an extortion charge

repexus *pp of* **repecto**

repl·eō -ēre -ēvī -ētus *tr* (**reppl-**) to refill, replenish; to fill to the brim; to make up for, replace, compensate for; *(mil)* to recruit, bring *(an army)* to full strength

replēt·us -a -um *pp of* **repleo** ‖ *adj* filled, full; *(of the body)* well-filled out; *(w. abl or gen)* **1** full of; **2** fully endowed with

replicāti·ō -ōnis *f* folding back, rolling back, rolling up; reflex action

replic·ō -āre -āvī -ātus *tr* to fold back, turn back; to unfold

rēp·ō -ěre -sī *intr* to crawl, creep

re·pōnō -pōněre -posuī -positus *or* **-postus** *tr* to put back, set back, lay *(e.g., the head)* back; to replace; to restore; to substitute; to lay out, stretch out *(the body);* to lay aside, store, keep, preserve; to renew, repeat; to place, class; to repay, requite; **in sceptra reponere** to reinstate in power; **membra reponere** *(w. ab or* **in** + *abl)* to stretch out on *(e.g., a bed);* **se in cubitum reponere** to rest on one's elbow; **spem reponere** *(w.* **in** + *abl)* to put one's hopes in *or* on, count on

report·ō -āre -āvī -ātus *tr* to bring back; to report; **victoriam reportare** to win a victory

reposc·ō -ěre *tr* to demand back; to ask for, claim, require, demand

repositiōr·ium -(i)ī *n* large serving dish

repos(i)t·us -a -um *pp of* **repono** ‖ *adj* out-of-the-way, remote

repost·or -ōris *m* restorer

repostus *pp of* **repono**

repōti·a -ōrum *npl* second round of drinks, seconds

repperī *perf of* **reperio**

reppulī *perf of* **repello**

repraesentāti·ō -ōnis *f* vivid presentation; *(fin)* cash payment

repraesent·ō -āre -āvī -ātus *tr* to present again, show, exhibit, display, depict; to do immediately, accomplish instantly; to rush, speed up *(e.g., plans);* to anticipate; to pay in cash; to apply *(medicines)* immediately

reprehen·dō *or* **repren·dō -děre -ī -sus** *tr* to hold back; to restrain, check; to blame, find fault with, criticize; to refute; *(leg)* to prosecute, convict, condemn

repre(he)nsi·ō -ōnis *f* checking, check;

finding fault, blame, criticism, rebuke; *(rhet)* refutation; *(rhet)* self-correction

reprehens·ō -āre *tr* to hold back (continually)

reprehens·or -ōris *m* critic

reprendō *see* **reprehendo**

reprensō *see* **reprehenso**

repress·or -ōris *m* one who represses

re·primō -priměre -pressī -pressus *tr* to hold back, keep back; to restrain, limit, confine, curb, repress, suppress ‖ *refl* to control oneself; *(w.* **ab)** to refrain from

reprōmissi·ō -ōnis *f* counter-promise, promise in return

reprō·mittō -mittěre -mīsī -missus *tr* to promise in return ‖ *intr (leg) (w. dat)* to make a counter-promise to *(s.o.)*

rept·ō -āre -āvī -ātum *intr* to crawl around

repudiāti·ō -ōnis *f* repudiation; refusal, rejection; refusal to approve a policy

repudi·ō -āre -āvī -ātus *tr* to repudiate, scorn; to refuse, reject; to jilt; to divorce

repudiōs·us -a -um *adj* objectionable, offensive

repud·ium -(i)ī *n* repudiation, separation, divorce; **repudium renuntiare** *(or* **remittere)** *(w. dat)* to send a letter of divorce to

repuerasc·ō -ěre *intr* to become a child again; to behave childishly

repugn·ans -antis *adj* contradictory, inconsistent ‖ *npl* contradictions, inconsistencies

repugnanter *adv* reluctantly

repugnanti·a -ae *f* contradiction, inconsistency; conflicting demands; incompatibility

repugn·ō -āre -āvī -ātum *intr* to fight back; *(w. dat)* **1** to oppose, offer opposition to, fight against, be against; **2** to disagree with, be inconsistent with, be incompatible with; *(w.* **contra** + *acc)* to fight against

repuls·a -ae *f* defeat at the polls; rebuff, cold shoulder; **repulsa consulatūs** defeat in running for the consulship; **repulsam ferre** to suffer a defeat, lose an election

repuls·ans -antis *adj* throbbing; reechoing

repuls·us -a -um *pp of* **repello** ‖ *adj* rejected, spurned

repuls·us -ūs *m* reverberation, echo

repung·ō -ěre *tr* to goad again

repurg·ō -āre -āvī -ātus *tr* to clean again; to purge away, remove

reputāti·ō -ōnis *f* rethinking, reconsideration, review; subject of thought, reflection

reput·ō -āre -āvī -ātus *tr* to think over, reflect upon, reconsider; to count back, calculate

requi·ēs -ētis *f* rest, relief; relaxation;

break, pause, intermission; recreation, amusement, hobby; *(w. gen)* rest from
requi·escō -escĕre -ēvī -ētus *tr* to put to rest, quiet down, calm down ‖ *intr* to rest, take a rest; to come to rest, stop, end; to relax; to find peace, be consoled, find relief; to rest, lie quietly, sleep; *(of the dead)* to rest, sleep
requiēt·us -a -um *adj* rested up
requīrit·ō -āre *tr* to keep asking for; to be on a constant lookout for
re·quīrō -quīrĕre -quīsīvī *or* **-quīsiī -quīsītus** *tr* to look for, search for, hunt for; to miss; to ask; to ask for, demand, require; *(w. ab or de + abl)* to ask *or* demand *(s.th.)* from *or* of
requīsītum -ī *n* a need
rēs reī *or* **rēī** *f* thing; matter, affair; object; cirumstance; event, occurrence; deed; condition, case; reality, truth, fact; property, possessions, wealth; estate, effects; benefit, advantage, interest, profit; business affair, transaction; cause, reason, motive, ground; historical event; theme, topic, subject matter; *(leg)* case, suit; *(mil)* operation, campaign, battle; *(pol)* state, government, politics; **ab re** contrary to interests, disadvantageous, useless; **ad rem pertinere** to be relevant to the matter at hand; **ex re** according to circumstances, according to the situation; **ex re istius** for his good; **ex re publica** for the common good, in the public interest; **ex tua re** to your advantage; **in re** *(or* **re ipsā** *or* **reāpse** *or* **re verā)** in fact, in reality; **in re praesenti** on the spot; **in rem** for the good, useful, advantageous; **in rem praesentem** on the spot; **nil ad rem est** *(frequently with ellipsis of* **est)** it is not to the point, it is irrelevant; **ob eam rem** for that reason; **ob rem** to the purpose; **pro re** according to circumstances; **quae res?** what's that? what are you talking about?; **re** in fact, in practice, in reality, actually, really; **rem agere** *(leg)* to conduct a case; **rem gerere** *(mil)* to conduct a military operation; **rem solvere** to settle a matter; **res capitalis** *(or* **res capitis)** *(leg)* a case involving the death penalty *or* loss of civil rights; **res familiaris** private property; **res frumentaria** grain situation; grain supply; foraging; **res judiciaria** administration of justice, department of justice; **res mihi tecum** I have some business with you; **res pecuaria et rustica** livestock; **res rustica** agriculture; **res publica** state, government, politics, public life, commonwealth, country; **res sit mihi cum his** let me handle them; **res soli** real property, real estate *(as contrasted with* **res mobilis);** **res uxoria** marriage; dowry; **res Veneris**

sexual intercourse, love making ‖ *fpl* physical phenomena; property; affairs, public affairs; **rerum** *(w. superl adj)* the best in the world: **rerum facta est pulcherrima Roma** Rome became the most beautiful city in the world; **rerum potiri** to get control of the government; **rerum scriptor** historian, annalist; **res gestae** exploits, accomplishments, military achievements; **res novae** revolution; **res Persicae** Persian history, Parthian history; **res prolatae** business adjourned *(for the holiday);* **res publicas inire** to enter politics; **res secundae** prosperity; **summa rerum** world; universe; **tibi res tuas habe** *(formula for divorce)* take your things and go!
resacr·ō *or* **resecr·ō -āre** *tr* to ask again for; to free from a curse
resaevi·ō -īre *intr* to go wild again
resalūtāti·ō -ōnis *f* a greeting in return
resalūt·ō -āre -āvī -ātus *tr* to greet in return
resān·escō -escĕre -uī *intr* to heal again
resar·ciō -cīre -sī -tus *or* **-sus** *tr* to patch up, repair; to make good *(a loss)*
re·scindō -scindĕre -scīdī -scissus *tr* to tear off; to cut down; to tear open; to rescind, repeal; *(fig)* to expose
re·sciscō -sciscĕre -scīvī *or* **-scii -scītus** *tr* to find out, learn, ascertain
re·scrībō -scrībĕre -scrīpsī -scrīptus *tr* to write back in reply; to rewrite, revise; to enlist, enroll; to pay back, repay ‖ *intr* to write a reply
rescript·um -ī *n* imperial rescript
resec·ō -āre -uī -tus *tr* (-sic-) to cut back, cut short; to reap; *(fig)* to trim, curtail; **ad vivum resecare** to cut to the quick
resecr·ō *see* **resacro**
resectus *pp of* **reseco**
resecūtus *pp of* **resequor**
resēmin·ō -āre *tr* reproduce
re·sequor -sequī -secūtus sum *tr* to reply to, answer
reser·ō -āre -āvī -ātus *tr* to unlock, unbar, open; to disclose; to begin *(a year)*
reserv·ō -āre -āvī -ātus *tr* to reserve, hold back; to spare; to hold on to; to store
res·es -idis *adj* remaining, left; lazy, idle, inactive; slow, sluggish; calm
re·sideō -sidēre -sēdī *intr* to sit down, settle back; to sink down, settle, subside; to calm down
re·sīdō -sīdĕre -sēdī *or* **-sīdī** *intr* to sit down; *(of a person lying down)* to sit up; *(of birds)* to perch; *(after rising or climbing)* to fall back, sink back; *(of things)* to come to rest, lodge; *(of colonists)* to settle; *(of water)* to go down, subside; *(of swellings)* to go down, shrink; *(of natural features)* to dip (down); *(of wind, flame, rain)* to die down; *(of a person)* to

quiet down; *(of activity, condition)* to diminish in intensity, abate; *(mil)* to encamp

residu·us -a -um *adj* remaining, left; in arrears, outstanding *(money)* ‖ *n* the remainder, the rest

resign·ō -āre -āvī -ātus *tr* to unseal, open; to disclose; to give up, resign; to annul, cancel; to destroy *(confidence)*

resil·iō -īre -uī *or* **-iī** *intr* to spring back, jump back; to recoil; to contract

resīm·us -a -um *adj* turned-up, snub

rēsīn·a -ae *f* resin *(secreted by various trees, used to preserve and season wine, used as a depilatory, etc.)*

rēsīnāt·us -a -um *adj* rubbed with resin, resined

resip·iō -ĕre *tr* to taste of, taste like, have the flavor of

resip·iscō -iscĕre -īvī *or* **-iī** *or* **-uī** *intr* to come to one's senses

resist·ens -entis *adj* firm, tough

re·sistō -sistĕre -stitī *intr* to stand still, stop, pause; to stay, stay behind, remain; to resist, put up resistance; to rise again; *(w. dat)* **1** to be opposed to, resist; **2** to reply to

resolūt·us -a -um *adj* loose, limp; effeminate

re·solvō -solvĕre -solvī -solūtus *tr* to untie, unfasten, undo; to open; to dissolve, melt, thaw; to relax *(the body);* to stretch out *(the limbs);* to unravel; to cancel; to dispel; to unnerve, enervate; to release, set free

resonābil·is -is -e *adj* resounding, answering *(echo)*

reson·ans -antis *adj* echoing

reson·ō -āre -āvī *tr* to repeat, reecho, resound with, make ring ‖ *intr* to resound, ring, reecho; *(w. ad)* to resound in answer to

reson·us -a -um *adj* resounding, re- echoing

resorb·eō -ēre *tr* to suck in, swallow again

respargō *see* **respergo**

respect·ō -āre *tr* to look back on; to keep an eye on, care for; to have regard for, respect; to gaze at, look at ‖ *intr* to look back; to look around

respectus *pp of* **respicio**

respect·us -ūs *m* backward glance, looking back; looking around; refuge; respect, regard, consideration; **respec·tum habere** *(w. dat or* **ad)** to have respect for

.resper·gō -gĕre -sī -sus *tr* **(-spar-)** to sprinkle, splash, spray; to defile

respersi·ō -ōnis *f* sprinkling, splashing

respersus *pp of* **respergo**

re·spiciō -spicĕre -spexī -spectus *tr* to look back at, see behind oneself; to look around for; to look back upon *(the past, etc.);* to look at, gaze at; to regard, con-

template, consider; to notice; to look after, take care of, see to; to respect ‖ *intr* to look back; to look around; *(w. ad)* to look at, gaze at

respīrām·en -inis *n* respiration, breathing; exhalation; letup, rest, pause *(to catch one's breath),* breathing space

respīrāti·ō ōnis *f* respiration, breathing; breathing pause; *(fig)* exhalation, emission of vapor

respīrāt·us -ūs *m* respiration

respīr·ō -āre -āvī -ātus *tr* to breathe, breathe out, exhale ‖ *intr* to breathe, take a breath, breathe again; to recover *(from fright, etc.); (of combat, passions, etc.)* to slack off, die down, subside; **a continuis cladibus respirare** to catch one's breath again after continuous fighting; **ab metu respirare** to recover from a shock

resplend·eō -ēre *intr* to glitter

respon·deō -dēre -dī -sus *tr* to answer; to say in reply; to say in refutation; **ficta respondere** to make up answers; **hoc quod rogo responde** answer my question; **multa respondere** to give a lengthy reply; **par pari respondere** to give tit for tat; **verbum verbo respondere** to answer word for word ‖ *intr* to answer, reply; *(of officials, seers, priests)* to give an official *or* formal reply; to echo; to satisfy the claims *(of a creditor); (leg)* to answer a summons to appear in court; *(of lawyers)* to give an opinion, give legal advice; *(of priests)* to give a response *(from a god); (w. dat)* **1** to answer, reply to; **2** to match, balance, correspond to, be equal to; **3** to resemble; **4** to measure up to; **amori amore respondere** to return love for love; **nominibus respondere** to pay off debts

responsi·ō -ōnis *f* response, answer, reply; refutation; *(rhet)* **sibi ipsi responsio** a reply to one's own arguments

responsit·ō -āre -āvī *intr* to give professional legal advice

respons·ō -āre *intr* to answer, reply; to reecho; *(w. dat)* **1** to answer to, agree with; **2** to resist, defy; **3** to talk back to *(in disobedience)*

respons·or -ōris *m* respondent

respons·us -a -um *pp of* **respondeo** ‖ *n* answer, response; oracular response; *(leg)* professional advice; **responsum auferre** *(or* **ferre)** *(w. ab)* to receive an answer from; **responsum referre** to deliver an answer

rēspūblica reīpūblicae *f* state, government, politics, public life, commonwealth, country; **rempublicam inire** to enter politics; *(see also* **res publica)**

respu·ō -ĕre -ī *tr* to spit out; to cast out, eject, expel; to refuse, to reject

restagn·ō -āre *intr* to form pools; to run over, overflow; to be inundated

restaur·ō -āre -āvī -ātus *tr* to restore, rebuild; to renew, take up again

resticul·a -ae *f* thin rope, cord

restincti·ō -ōnis *f* quenching

restin·guō -guĕre -xī -ctus *tr* to quench, extinguish, put out; to snuff out; to exterminate, destroy

resti·ō -ōnis *f* rope dealer; *(hum)* roper *(person who is whipped with ropes)*

restipulāti·ō -ōnis *f* counterclaim

restipul·or -ārī -ātus sum *tr* to stipulate in return ‖ *intr* to make a counterclaim

rest·is -is *f (acc:* **restem** *or* **restim***)* rope

restit·ō -āre *intr* to stay behind, lag, behind; to keep offering resistance

restitr·ix -īcis *f* stay-at-home *(female)*

resti·tuō -tuĕre -tuī -tūtus *tr* to set up again; to restore, rebuild, reconstruct; to renew, reestablish, revive; to bring back, restore, reinstate; to give back, return, replace; to restore, repair, remedy; to reenact *(a law);* to reverse; to revoke, undo, cancel, make void; to make good, compensate for, repair

restitūti·ō -ōnis *f* restoration; reinstatement, pardon; recall *(from exile)*

restitūt·or -ōris *m* restorer, rebuilder

restitūtus *pp of* **restituo**

re·stō -stāre -stitī *intr* to stand firm, stand one's ground, resist; to stay behind, stay in reserve; to be left over ‖ *v impers (w. inf or* **ut***)* it remains to *(do s.th.)*

restrictē *adv* sparingly; exactly, precisely

restrict·us -a -um *pp of* **restringo** ‖ *adj* tied back, tight; stingy; moderate, strict, stern

re·stringō -stringĕre -strinxī -strictus *tr* to tie *(the hands, arms)* behind one; to draw tight, tie; to tighten; to draw back the cover from *(s.th. concealed); (of dogs)* to show *(the teeth) (fig)* restrain; *(fig)* to restrict the activity of

resūd·ō -āre *intr* to sweat, ooze

result·ō -āre *intr* to rebound; to resound, reverberate

resūm·ō -ĕre -psī -ptus *tr* to resume; to recover *(strength)*

resu·ō -ĕre -uī -ūtus *tr* to undo the stitching of

resupīn·ō -āre -āvī -ātus *tr* to throw *(s.o.)* on his back, throw over, throw down; *(coll)* to knock for a loop; to break down *(door)*

resupīn·us -a -um *adj* lying on the back; bent back, thrown back; leaning backward; proud *(gait)*

resur·gō -gĕre -rexī -rectum *intr* to rise again; to appear again

resuscit·ō -āre *tr* to resuscitate

retardāti·ō -ōnis *f* retardation

retard·ō -āre -āvī -ātus *tr* to retard, slow down, hold back, delay; to keep back, check, hinder ‖ *intr* to lag behind

retax·ō -āre *tr* to rebuke

rēt·e -is *n* net; *(fig)* trap

rete·gō -gĕre -xī -ctus *tr* to uncover; to unclothe, expose; to open; to reveal, make visible; to disclose *(secrets)*

retempt·ō -āre -āvī -ātus *tr* to attempt again, try again; to test again

reten·dō -dĕre -dī -tus *or* **-sus** *tr* to release from tension, unbend, relax

retenti·ō -ōnis *f* holding back; slowing down; withholding *(assent)*

retent·ō -āre *tr* to hold back, hold tight; to attempt again; to retain the loyalty of; to keep *(feelings)* in check

retentus *pp of* **retendo** *and* **retineo**

retexī *perf of* **retego**

retex·ō -ĕre -uī -tus *tr* to unravel; to cancel, reverse, annul, undo; to weave anew; to renew, repeat; to correct, revise; to retract *(words)*

rēti·a -ae *f* net

rētiār·ius -(i)ī *m* net-man *(gladiator who tried to entangle his opponent in a net)*

reticenti·a -ae *f* reticence; *(rhet)* abrupt pause; **poena reticentiae** punishment for suppression of truth

retic·eō -ēre -uī *tr* to be silent about, suppress, keep secret ‖ *intr* to be silent, keep silent; *(w. dat)* to make no answer to

rēticulāt·us -a -um *adj* covered with a net; net-shaped, reticulate

rēticul·um -ī *n* small net; hair net; meshwork bag *(for protecting bottles);* racket *(for playing ball)*

retinācul·a -ōrum *npl* cable, rope

retin·ens -entis *adj (w. gen)* clinging to, sticking to

retinenti·a -ae *f* retention

re·tineō -tinēre -tinuī -tentus *tr* to hold back, keep back; to restrain; to keep, retain; to hold in reserve; to preserve, maintain, uphold; to hold, engross *(attention);* to detain, delay

retinn·iō -īre *intr* to ring again, ring out, tinkle in response

reton·ō -āre *intr* to resound

retor·queō -quēre -sī -tus *tr* to twist *or* bend back; to hurl back *(weapons);* **mentem retorquere** to change the mind; **oculos retorquere** *(w. ad)* to look back wistfully at

retorrid·us -a -um *adj* parched, dried out, withered; wily, shrewd

retortus *pp of* **retorqueo**

retractāti·ō -ōnis *f* holding back, hesitation; **sine retractatione** without hesitation

retractāt·us -a -um *adj* revised

retract·ō *or* **retrect·ō -āre** *tr* to rehandle, take in hand again, undertake once more, take up once more; to reexamine, review; to revise || *intr* to refuse, decline; to be reluctant

retract·us -a -um *adj* remote, distant

retra·hō -hĕre -xī -ctus *tr* to draw back, withdraw, pull back; to bring to light again, make known again; *(fig)* to drag away, remove

retrectō *see* **retracto**

retrib·uō -uĕre -uī -ūtus *tr* to hand back; to repay

retrō *adv* backwards, back; to the rear; behind, on the rear; in the past, formerly, back, past; in return; on the contrary, on the other hand; in reverse order *(of words);* counting back to an earlier date, retrospectively; *(w. reference to reasoning)* back to first principles

retro·agō -agĕre -ēgī -actus *tr* to drive backward; to reverse the order of, invert; to repeat backwards

retrō·cēdō -dĕre -cessī -cessum *intr* to move backward; to withdraw, retire

retrorsum *adv* (-**sus**) back, backwards, in reverse; in reverse order

retrū·dō -dĕre — -sus *tr* to push back; to hide, conceal

retundō retundĕre retudī *(or* **rettudī) retunsus** *(or* **retūsus)** *tr* to pound back; to dull, blunt; *(fig)* to deaden, weaken, repress, restrain

retuns·us *or* **retūs·us -a -um** *pp of* **retundo** || *adj* blunt, dull; *(fig)* dull

re·us -ī *m (either of the two parties involved in litigation)* defendant, the accused, plaintiff; convict, criminal, culprit; *(w. gen)* person charged with; **in reos recipere** *(or* **referre)** to list among the accused; **reum agere** to try a defendant; **reum facere** to indict, bring a defendant to trial; **reum postulare** to prosecute, force to face a trial

reval·escō -escĕre -uī *intr* to regain one's strength, recover; to become valid again

re·vehō -vehĕre -vexī -vectus *tr* to carry back, bring back || *pass* to ride back, drive back; to sail back; *(fig)* to go back *(e.g., to an earlier period)*

re·vellō -vellĕre -vellī -vulsus *tr* to pull out, pull back, tear off, tear out; to tear up *(the ground),* dig up; *(fig)* to unmask *(deception)*

revēl·ō -āre -āvī -ātus *tr* to unveil, uncover

re·veniō -venīre -vēnī -ventum *intr* to come again, come back, return

rēvērā *adv* in fact, actually

reverbĕr·ō -āre -āvī -ātus *tr* to beat back

reverend·us -a -um *adj* venerable, awe-inspiring; deserving respect

rever·ens -entis *adj* reverent, respectful

reverenter *adv* respectfully

reverenti·a -ae *f* reverence, respect

rever·eor -ērī -itus sum *tr* to revere, respect, stand in awe of

reversi·ō -ōnis *f* (-**vor-**) turning back *(before reaching one's destination);* recurrence

revert·ō -ĕre -ī *or* **re·vertor -verti -versus sum** *intr* (-**vor-**) to turn back, turn around, come back, return; *(in speaking)* to return, revert

revictus *pp of* **revinco**

revid·eō -ēre *tr* to go back to see

revin·ciō -cīre -xī -ctus *tr* to tie back, tie behind, tie up

re·vincō -vincĕre -vīcī -victus *tr* to conquer in turn; to refute, convict of falsehood; *(w. acc or gen of the charge)* to convict *(s.o.)* of

revinctus *pp of* **revincio**

revir·escō -escĕre -uī *intr* to become green again; to grow young again; to grow again, grow strong again, revive

revīs·ō -ĕre *tr* to revisit; to look back to see || *intr* to come *or* go back; *(w. ad)* **1** to look at again, look back at; **2** to return to, revisit

re·vīviscō -vīviscĕre -vixī *intr* (-**escō**) to come back to life, be restored to life, revive; *(fig)* to recover, gain strength

revocābil·is -is -e *adj* capable of being recalled; **non revocabilis** irrevocable

revocām·en -inis *n* recall

revocāti·ō -ōnis *f* calling back, recall; calling away; retraction

revoc·ō -āre -āvī -ātus *tr* to call back, recall; to call off, withdraw *(troops);* to call back *(a performer)* for an encore; to bring back to life, revive; *(leg)* to arraign again; to regain *(strength, etc.);* to resume *(career, studies);* to revoke, retract; to check, control; to cancel; *(w. ad)* to refer, apply, subject, submit *(s.o. or s.th.)*

revol·ō -āre -āvī *intr* to fly back

revolsus *see* **revulsus**

revolūbil·is -is -e *adj* able to be rolled back; **non revolubilis** irrevocable *(fate)*

revol·vō -vĕre -vī -ūtus *tr* to roll back, unroll, unwind; to retravel; to unroll, read over, read again *(a scroll);* to reexperience; to go over, think over || *pass* to revolve; to come around again, recur, return

revom·ō -ĕre -uī *tr* to throw up again, disgorge

revor- = **rever-**

revorr·ō -ĕre *tr* to sweep back

revulsus *pp of* **revello**

rex rēgis *m* king; patron; queen bee

Rhadamanth·us *or* **Rhadamanth·os -ī** *m* son of Jupiter, brother of Minos, and one of the three judges in the lower world

Rhaet·ī -ōrum *mpl* people of Rhaetia

Rhaeti·a -ae *f* Alpine country between Germany and Italy

Rhamn·ūs -untos *f* Attic deme famous for its statue of Nemesis

Rhamnūsi·us -a -um *adj* of the deme of Rhamnus; **Rhamnusia virgo** the goddess worshiped at Rhamnus *(i.e., Nemesis)*

rhapsōdi·a -ae *f* Homeric lay, selection from Homer; **rhapsodia secunda** second book *(of Homer)*

Rhe·a -ae *f* Cybele

Rhe·a Silvi·a -ae *f* daughter of Numitor and mother of Romulus and Remus by Mars, the god of war

rhēd- = raed-

Rhēg·ium -(i)ī *n (also* **Rēg-)** town on the toe of Italy

Rhēnān·us -a -um *adj* of *or* on the Rhine

rhēn·ō -ōnis *f* reindeer skin *(used as clothing)*

Rhēn·us -ī *m* the Rhine

Rhēs·us -ī *m* Thracian king who fought as an ally of Troy

rhēt·or -oris *m* rhetorician, teacher of rhetoric; orator

rhētoric·a -ae *or* **rhētoric·ē -ēs** *f* rhetoric, public speaking

rhētoric·a -ōrum *npl* treatise on rhetoric

rhētoricē *adv* rhetorically, in an oratorical manner

rhētoric·us -a -um *adj* rhetorician's, rhetorical; **doctores rhetorici** professors of rhetoric; **libri rhetorici** textbooks on rhetoric

rhīnocer·ōs -ōtis *or* **-ōtos** *m* rhinoceros; vessel made of a rhinoceros's tusk; **pueri nasum rhinocerotis habent** the children turn up their noses

rhō *indecl n* rho *(seventeenth letter of the Greek alphabet)*

Rhodan·us -ī *m* the Rhone River

Rhodiens·is -is -e *or* **Rhodi·us -a -um** *adj* Rhodian, of Rhodes **‖** *mpl* Rhodians

Rhodop·ē -ēs *f* mountain range in Thrace

Rhodopēj·us -a -um *adj* Thracian

Rhod·os *or* **Rhod·us -ī** *f* Rhodes *(island off the S.W. coast of Asia Minor)*

Rhoetē·us -a -um *adj* Trojan; of the promontory of Rhoeteum; **Rhoeteus ductor** Aeneas; **Rhoeteum profundum** sea near the promontory of Rhoeteum **‖** *n* promontory on the Dardanelles near Troy

rhomb·us -ī *m* magic wheel; turbot *(fish)*

rhomphae·a -ae *f* long javelin

rhythmic·us -a -um *adj* rhythmical **‖** *m* teacher of prose rhythm

rhythm·os *or* **rhythm·us -ī** *m* rhythm; symmetry

rhyt·ion -iī *n* conical cup *or* urn

rīc·a -ae *f* veil *(worn by Roman women at sacrifice)*

rīcin·ium -(i)ī *n* short mantle with a cowl

rict·um -ī *n* snout; wide-open mouth

rict·us -ūs *m* snout; wide-open mouth; **risu rictum diducere** to break into a broad grin **‖** *mpl* jaws, gaping jaws

rīde·ō rīdēre rīsī rīsus *tr* to laugh at, ridicule; to smile upon **‖** *intr* to laugh; to smile, grin; *(w. dat or* **ad)** to smile at, laugh at

rīdibund·us -a -um *adj* laughing

rīdiculāri·us -a -um *adj* funny, laughable **‖** *npl* jokes

rīdiculē *adv* jokingly, humorously; ridiculously

rīdiculōs·us -a -um *adj* funny, amusing; ridiculous

rīdicul·us -a -um *adj* funny, amusing, laughable; ridiculous, silly **‖** *m* joker, clown **‖** *n* joke

riēn·ēs -ium *mpl* kidneys

rig·ens -entis *adj* rigid, stiff

rig·eō -ēre -uī *intr* to be stiff, be rigid; to be numb; to stand on end, stand erect; to stand stiff; to be unmoved by entreaties

rig·escō -escĕre -uī *intr* to grow stiff, become numbed; to stiffen, harden; to stand on end

rigid·a -ae *f (vulg)* penis in erect state

rigidē *adv* rigorously, severely

rigid·us -a -um *adj* rigid, stiff, hard, inflexible; stern, severe; rough, rude; erect *(penis)*

rig·ō -āre *tr* to wet, moisten, water; to conduct, convey *(water)*

rig·or -ōris *m* stiffness; numbness, cold; hardness; sternness

rigu·us -a -um *adj* constantly flowing, irrigating; well-watered, irrigated; **‖** *npl* irrigated areas, flood plain; irrigation ditches

rīm·a -ae *f* crack; chap *(in the skin)*; **rimas agere** to cause cracks to develop; **rimas ducere** to develop cracks

rīm·or -ārī -ātus sum *tr* to lay open, tear open; to pry into, search, examine; to search for *(facts)*; to rummage about for; to ransack; **naribus rimari** to sniff at; **oculis rimari** to scrutinize

rīmōs·us -a -um *adj* full of cracks; leaky

ringor ringī rictus sum *intr* to open the mouth wide; to show the teeth; to snarl; *(fig)* to be snappy

rīp·a -ae *f* river bank; **aequoris ripa** seashore

Ripae·us -a -um *adj (also* **Rhip-)** of the Rhipean mountains; **mons R(h)ipaeus** legendary mountain range in the extreme north

rīpul·a -ae *f* riverbank

risc·us -ī *m* chest, trunk

rīsion·ēs -um *fpl* laughs

rīs·or -ōris *m* scoffer; teaser

rīs·us -ūs *m* laugh, laughter, smile; laughingstock; **risum continere** to keep from

laughing; **risum movere** *(w. dat)* to make *(s.o.)* laugh; **risūs captare** to try to make people laugh, try to get a laugh
rīte *adv* according to religious usage; duly, justly, rightly, fitly; in the usual way, customarily
rīt·us -ūs *m* rite, ceremony; custom, habit, way, manner, style; **ritū** *(w. gen)* in the manner of, like; **pecudum ritū** like cattle
rīvāl·is -is *m* one who uses the same stream, neighbor; one who uses the same mistress, rival
rīvālit·ās -ātis *f* rivalry
rīvul·us *or* **rīvol·us -ī** *m* brook
rīv·us -ī *m* brook, stream; artificial watercourse, channel; flow *(of water in the aqueducts)*
rix·a -ae *f* brawl, fight; squabble
rix·or -ārī -ātus sum *intr* to brawl, come to blows, fight; to squabble
rōbīginōs·us -a -um *adj* (**rub-**) rusty; envious
rōbīg·ō -inis *f* rust; blight, mildew; film *(on teeth),* tartar
rōbore·us -a -um *adj* (**-bur-**) oak-
rōbor·ō -āre -āvī -ātus *tr* to strengthen
rōb·ur *or* **rob·us -oris** *n* hardwood; oak; prison *(at Rome, also called Tullianum);* objects made of hardwood: lance, club, bench; physical strength, power, toughness; power *(of mind);* best part, flower, choice, cream, élite; stronghold
rōb·us -a -um *adj* red
rōbust·us -a -um *adj* hardwood; oak; robust, strong, tough *(body);* firm, solid *(character)*
rō·dō -děre -sī -sus *tr* to gnaw, gnaw at; to rust, corrode; to say nasty things about, slander, run down
rogāl·is -is -e *adj* of a funeral pyre
rogāti·ō -ōnis *f* proposal, bill *(in the Roman assembly);* request, invitation; *(rhet)* question; **rogationem ferre** to introduce a bill; **rogationem perferre** to pass a bill; **rogationem suadere** to back, push, *or* speak in favor of a bill; **rogationi intercedere** to veto a bill
rogātiuncul·a -ae *f* inconsequential bill; minor question
rogāt·or -ōris *m* proposer *(of a bill to the Roman assembly);* poll clerk *(who collects and counts votes);* beggar
rogāt·us -ūs *m* request
rogitāti·ō -ōnis *f (pol)* bill
rogit·ō -āre -āvī -ātus *tr* to keep asking (for)
rog·ō -āre -āvī -ātus *tr* to ask, ask for, beg, request; to question; to invite; to nominate for election; to bring forward for approval, introduce, propose *(bill); (w. double acc)* to ask *(s.o. for s.th.);* **legem rogare** to introduce a bill; **milites sacramento rogare** to swear in soldiers;

senatorem sententiam rogare to ask a senator for his opinion, ask a senator how he votes; **sententias rogare** to call the roll *(in the Senate);* **populum rogare** to ask the people about a bill, to propose *or* introduce a bill; **primus sententiam rogari** to have the honor of being the first *(senator)* to be asked his view, be the first to vote
rog·us -ī *m or* **rog·um -ī** *n* funeral pyre; *(fig)* grave, destruction
Rōm·a -ae *f* Rome; Roma *(goddess of Rome)*
Rōmān·us -a -um *adj* Roman **‖** *mpl* Romans
Rōmule·us -a -um *adj* of Romulus; Roman
Rōmulid·ae -ārum *mpl* descendants of Romulus, Romans
Rōmul·us -a -um *adj* of Romulus; Roman **‖** *m* Romulus *(son of Rhea Silvia and Mars, twin brother of Remus, and founder as well as first king of Rome)*
rōrāri·ī -ōrum *mpl* skirmishers *(light-armed Roman troops who usually initiate an attack and then withdraw)*
rōrid·us -a -um *adj* dewy
rōrif·er -era -erum *adj* dewy, dew-bringing
rōr·ō -āre -āvī -ātus *tr* to drip, trickle, pour drop by drop; to moisten **‖** *intr* to drop dew, scatter dew
rōs rōris *m* dew; moisture; spray; water; teardrop; **ros Arabus** perfume; **ros marinus** *(or* **maris)** rosemary *(see* **rosmarīnum);** **rores pluvii** drizzle; **rores sanguinei** drops of blood
ros·a -ae *f* rose; rosebush; rose bed; wreath of roses
rosāce·us -a -um *adj (crown)* of roses; **oleum rosaceum** rose oil
rosār·ium -(i)ī *n* rose garden
roscid·us -a -um *adj* wet with dew; consisting of dew; dewy *(conditions; as epithet of the moon, stars, associated with dew);* moistened, sprayed
Rosc·ius -(i)ī *m* Lucius Roscius Otho *(Cicero's friend, whose law in 67 B.C. reserved 14 rows of seats in the theater for members of the equestrian order)* **‖** Quintus Roscius *(famous Roman actor and friend of Cicero, d. 62 B.C.)* **‖** Sextus Roscius *(of Ameria, defended by Cicero in a patricide trial in 80 B.C.)*
Rōse·a -ae *f* low-lying district between Reate and the Veline Lake
rosēt·um -ī *n* rose bed, rose garden
rose·us -a -um *adj* made of roses; rose-colored *(covering a wide range of reds);* rosy, pink *(dawn, sunset, cheeks, skin)*
Rōse·us -a -um *adj* of Rosea
rosmarīn·um -ī *n* rosemary *(shrub used in medicines, in perfumes, and as a seasoning)*

rostell·um -ī n little beak; pointed nose (of a rodent)

rostrāt·us -a -um adj beaked; (ship) having a pointed bow; **columna rostrata** column adorned with the beaks of conquered vessels to commemorate a naval victory; **corona rostrata** navy medal (awarded to the first man to board an enemy ship)

rostr·um -ī n bill, beak; snout, muzzle; curved bow (of ship) ‖ npl rostrum (in the Roman Forum, so called because it was adorned with the beaks of ships taken from the battle of Antium, 338 B.C.); **pro rostris orationem habere** to give a speech from the rostrum

rōsus pp of **rodo**

rot·a -ae f wheel; potter's wheel; torture wheel; mill wheel; magic wheel; child's hoop; disk (of a heavenly body); chariot, car (of sun, moon, time); **aquarum rota** water wheel

rot·ō -āre -āvī -ātus tr to turn, whirl about ‖ pass to roll around; to revolve

rotul·a -ae f little wheel

rotundē adv smoothly, elegantly

rotundit·ās -ātis f roundness

rotund·ō -āre -āvī -ātus tr to make round; (fig) round off (numbers)

rotund·us -a -um adj rolling, revolving; round, circular, spherical; rounded, perfect; well-turned, smooth, polished (style)

rube·faciō -facĕre -fēcī -factus tr to make red, redden

rebell·us -a -um adj reddish

rub·ens -entis adj red; blushing

rub·eō -ēre intr to be red, be ruddy; to be bloody; to blush

ru·ber -bra -brum adj red (including shades of orange); ruddy; **Saxa Rubra** village on the Via Flaminia N. of Rome; **Mare Rubrum** Red Sea

rub·escō -escĕre -uī intr to get red, redden; to blush

rubēt·a -ae f toad

rūbēt·a -ōrum npl bramble bushes, thicket of brambles

rube·us -a -um adj bramble, of brambles

Rubic·ō(n) -ōnis m Rubicon (small stream marking the boundary between Italy and Cisalpine Gaul)

rubicundul·us -a -um adj reddish

rubicund·us -a -um adj red, reddish; ruddy, flushed (complexion)

rubid·us -a -um adj red; ruddy

rūbīg- = robig-

rub·or -ōris m redness; blush; bashfulness, sense of shame; shame, disgrace

rubrīc·a -ae f red clay; red ochre; red chalk; chapter heading (of book of law, painted red)

rub·us -ī m bramble bush; blackberry bush; blackberry

ructātr·ix -īcis adj (fem only) (of foods) that causes belching

ruct·ō -āre -āvī -ātus or **ruct·or -ārī -ātus sum** tr & intr to belch

ruct·us -ūs m belch, belching

rud·ens -entis m rope ‖ mpl rigging

Rudi·ae -ārum fpl town in Calabria in S. Italy (birthplace of Ennius)

rudiār·ius -(i)ī m retired gladiator

rudīment·um -ī n first attempt, beginning; early training; **rudimentum adulescentiae ponere** to pass the beginning of his youth; **rudimentum militare** basic training ‖ npl first lessons; fruits of one's early training

Rudīn·us -ā -um adj of Rudiae

rud·is -is f stick; rod; practice sword; wooden sword (presented to a retiring gladiator)

rud·is -is -e adj in the natural state; raw, undeveloped, rough, wild, unformed; inexperienced, unskilled, ignorant; uncultured, uncivilized; unsophisticated; (of land) not yet cultivated, virgin; (of wool) uncombed; (of artefacts) crude, roughly fashioned; (of movement) awkward, clumsy; (of fruit) unripe; (of animals) unbroken; (of recruits) raw; (of literary works) crude, unpolished, rough; (w. gen or abl, w. ad + acc or in + abl) inexperienced in, ignorant of, awkward at

rud·ō -ĕre -īvī -ītum intr (rūd-) to roar, bellow; (of a donkey) to bray; (of inanimate things) to creak loudly

rud·or -ōris m roar, bellow

rūd·us -eris n crushed stone; rubble; piece of brass

rūful·us -a -um adj reddish

Rūful·ī -ōrum mpl military tribunes appointed by a general (as opposed to military tribunes elected by the people)

rūf·us -a -um adj red; red-haired ‖ **Rufus** m frequent Roman family name

rūg·a -ae f wrinkle; crease, small fold; shallow groove

rūg·iō -īre intr to bellow, roar

rūg·ō -āre intr to become wrinkled, become creased

rūgōs·us -a -um adj wrinkled, shriveled, corrugated

ruīn·a -ae f tumbling down, fall; collapse; debris, ruins; crash; catastrophe, disaster, destruction; defeat; wrecker, destroyer; (fig) downfall, ruin; (fig) source of ruin or destruction; **ruinam dare (or trahere)** to fall with a crash

ruīnōs·us -a -um adj liable to ruin, going to ruin, tumbling; ruined, dilapidated

Rull·us -ī m Roman family name (cognomen) (esp. Publius Servilius Rullus, whose agrarian bill was defeated by Cicero in 63 B.C.)

rum·ex -icis *mf* sorrel *(grown as a vegetable, used in salads)*
rūmific·ō -āre *tr* to report
rūmifer·ō -āre *tr* to carry reports of
Rūmīn·a -ae *f* Roman goddess who was worshiped near the fig tree under which the she-wolf had suckled Romulus and Remus
Rūmīnāl·is -is -e *adj* **ficus Ruminalis** fig tree of Romulus and Remus
rūmināti·ō -ōnis *f* chewing of the cud; *(fig)* rumination, thinking over
rūmin·ō -āre -āvī -ātus *tr* to chew again **‖** *intr* to chew the cud
rūm·or -ōris *m* rumor, hearsay; shouting, cheering, noise; popular opinion, current opinion; reputation, fame; notoriety; calumny; **adverso rumore esse** to be in bad repute, be unpopular
rumpi·a -ae *f* long Thracian javelin
rumpō rumpěre rūpī ruptus *tr* to break, break down, break open; to burst, burst through; to tear, split; to cause to snap; to tear, rend *(hair, clothes);* to cause *(s.th.)* to break; to force, make *(e.g., a path)* by force; to break in on, interrupt, cut short; to break, violate *(a law, treaty);* to break out in, utter *(complaints, etc.);* **amores rumpere** to break off a love affair; **nuptias rumpere** to annul a marriage; **silentium** *(or* **silentia) rumpere** to break silence **‖** *refl & pass* to burst forth, erupt
rūmuscul·ī -ōrum *mpl* gossip
rūn·a -ae *f* dart
runc·ō -āre -āvī -ātus *tr* to weed, weed out
ru·ō -ěre -ī -tus *tr* to throw down, hurl to the ground; to level *(e.g., sand dunes);* to destroy, overthrow, lay waste; to sweep headlong; to upturn, churn up **‖** *intr* to dash, rush, hurry; *(of vehicles)* to go fast; *(of buildings)* to fall down, collapse; *(of fortunes)* to go to ruin; *(of rain)* to come pouring down; *(of the sun)* to set rapidly; *(w.* **in** *+ acc)* **1** to charge, swoop down on; **2** to proceed with haste *or* impatience to *(an action);* **curru in bella ruere** to go into battle on the double
rūp·ēs -is *f* cliff
rupt·or -ōris *m* breaker, violator
ruptus *pp of* **rumpo**
rūricol·a -ae *mf* rustic, peasant **‖** *m* ox
rūrigěn·a -ae *m* one born in the country, farmer
rūr·ō -āre *intr* to live in the country
rursus *or* **rursum** *or* **rūsum** *adv* back, backwards; on the contrary, on the other hand; in turn; again, a second time; *(in the direction from which one has come)* back again; once more; **rursus rursusque** again and again; **rursum prorsum** *(or* **rursus (ac) prorsus)** back and forth, backward and forward

rūs rūris *n* the country, countryside, lands, fields; farm, estate; **rure redire** to return from the country; **ruri** in the country; **ruri** *(or* **rure) vitam agere** to live in the country; **rus ire** to go into the country **‖** *npl* countryside
rusc·um -ī *n or* **rusc·us -ī** *m* broom *(of twigs)*
russāt·us -a -um *adj* red, ruddy; clothed in red
russ·us -a -um *adj* red, russet; red-haired
rustic·a -ae *f* country girl
rusticān·us -a -um *adj* rustic, country, rural
rusticāti·ō -ōnis *f* country life
rusticē *adv* like a farmer; plainly, simply; boorishly
rusticit·ās -ātis *f* simple country ways, rusticity; boorishness, coarseness
rustic·or -ārī -ātus sum *intr* to live in the country
rusticul·us -a -um *adj* of the country, in the country, rural; plain, simple, unspoiled, unsophisticated coarse, boorish **‖** *m* farmer **‖** *f* country girl
rūstic·us -a -um *adj* of the country, rural, rustic, country-; plain, simple, provincial, rough, gross, awkward, prudish **‖** *m* rustic; *(pej)* hick **‖** *f* country girl
rūsum *see* **rursus**
rūt·a -ae *f* rue *(bitter he. b);* bitterness, unpleasantness
rūt·a -ōrum *npl* minerals; **ruta caesa** *(or* **ruta et caesa)** *(leg)* everything mined or cut down on an estate, timber and minerals
rutābul·um -ī *n* spatula; poker *(instrument with flattened end)*
rūtāt·us -a -um *adj* flavored with rue *(a bitter herb);* bitter
rutil·ō -āre -āvī -ātus *tr* to make red, color red, dye red **‖** *intr* to glow red
rutil·us -a -um *adj* red, reddish yellow; strawberry-blond
rutr·um -ī *n* shovel
rūtul·a -ae *f* a bit of rue *(biter herb)*
Rutul·ī -ōrum *mpl* ancient people of Latium whose capital was Ardea
rutus *pp of* **ruo**

S

Sab·a -ae *f* town in Arabia Felix, famous for its incense
Sabae·us -a -um *adj* Sabaean, of the Sabaeans *(people of S.W. Arabia)* **‖** *f* Sabaea *(country of the Sabaeans, modern Yemen)*
Sabāz·ius -(i)ī *m* Bacchus **‖** *npl* festival in honor of Bacchus
sabbat·a -ōrum *npl* Sabbath

sabbatāri·a -ae *f* Sabbath-keeper *(i.e., Jewish woman)*
Sabell·us -a -um *adj* Sabellian, Sabine ‖ *m* Sabine *(i.e., Horace)*
Sabīn·us -a -um *adj* Sabine; **herba Sabina** *(bot)* savin *(a juniper, used to produce a drug)*; **oleum Sabinum** oil derived from savin ‖ *m* Roman family name *(cognomen)* *(e.g.,* Flavius Sabinus, the father of the Emperor Vespasian) ‖ *mpl* an ancient people of central Italy ‖ *f* Sabine woman ‖ *n* Sabine wine; Horace's Sabine farm
sabul·um -ī *n or* **sabul·ō -ōnis** *m* gravel, coarse sand
saburr·a -ae *f* gravel; ballast
saburr·ō -āre -āvī -ātus *tr* to ballast; *(coll)* to gorge with food
Sac·ae -ārum *mpl* (Sag-) Scythian tribe
saccipēr·ium -(i)ī *n* purse
sacc·ō -āre -āvī -ātus *tr* to filter, strain
saccō -ōnis *m (pej) (of a rich person)* moneybags
saccul·us -ī *m* little bag; pouch
sacc·us -ī *m* sack, bag; pouch; bag for straining liquids, strainer
sacell·um -ī *n* chapel, shrine
sa·cer -cra -crum *adj* sacred, holy, consecrated; devoted to a deity for destruction, accursed; detestable; criminal, infamous ‖ *n see* **sacrum**
sacerd·ōs -ōtis *m* priest ‖ *f* priestess
sacerdōtāl·is -is -e *adj* priestly
sacerdōt·ium -(i)ī *n* priesthood
sacrāment·um -ī *n* guarantee, deposit *(sum of money which each of the parties to a lawsuit deposits and which is forfeited by the loser)*; civil lawsuit; dispute; oath; voluntary oath of recruits; military oath; **eum obligare militiae sacramento** to swear him into the army; **justis sacramentis contendere** to argue on equal terms; **omnes sacramento adigere** *(or* **rogare)** *(mil)* to swear them all in; **sacramentum dicere** *(mil)* to sign up; **sacramentum dicere** *(w. dat)* to swear allegiance to
Sacrān·us -a -um *adj* of the Sacrani *(a people from Reate in Italy)*
sacrār·ium -(i)ī *n* shrine, chapel; sacristy
sacrāt·us -a -um *adj* hallowed, consecrated, holy, sacred
sacrif·er -era -erum *adj* carrying sacred objects
sacrificāl·is -is -e *adj* sacrificial
sacrificāti·ō -ōnis *f* sacrificing
sacrific·ium -(i)ī *n* sacrifice; **sacrificium facere** *(or* **perpetrare)** *(w. dat)* to offer a sacrifice to
sacrific·ō -āre -āvī -ātus *tr & intr* to sacrifice
sacrificul·us -ī *m* sacrificing priest
sacrific·us -a -um *adj* sacrificial

sacrileg·ium -(i)ī *n* sacrilege; temple robbing
sacrĭlĕg·us -a -um *adj* sacrilegious; profane, impious, wicked ‖ *m* temple robber; wicked person ‖ *f* impious woman
sacr·ō -āre -āvī -ātus *tr* to consecrate; to dedicate; to set apart, devote, give; to doom, curse; to hallow, declare inviolable; to hold sacred, worship; to immortalize
sacrōsanct·us -a -um *adj* sacred, inviolable, sacrosanct
sacr·um -ī *n* holy object, sacred vessel; holy place, temple, sanctuary; religious rite, act of worship, religious service; festival; sacrifice; victim ‖ *npl* worship, religion; secret, mystery; inviolability; **sacra facere** to sacrifice; **sine sacris hereditatis** *(fig)* godsend, windfall
saeclum *see* **saeculum**
saec(u)lār·is -is -e *adj* (sēc-) centennial
saec(u)l·um -ī *n* (sēc-) generation, lifetime; century; spirit of the age, fashion
saepe *adv* often
saepenumerō *or* **saepe numerō** *adv* oftentimes, on many occasions
saep·ēs -is *f* (sēp-) hedge, fence, enclosure
saepiculā *adv* often
saepīment·um -ī *n* (sēp-) hedge, fence, enclosure
saep·iō -īre -sī -tus *tr* (sēp-) to fence in, hedge in, enclose; to surround, encircle; to guard, fortify, protect, strengthen
saepissim·us -a -um *adj* very frequent
saepsī *perf of* **saepio**
saept·um -ī *n* (sēp-) fence, wall, enclosure; stake; sheepfold; voting booth ‖ *npl* enclosure; voting booths, polls
saeptus *pp of* **saepio**
saet·a -ae *f* (sēt-) bristle, stiff hair
saetig·er -era -erum *adj* (sēt-) bristly ‖ *m* wild boar
saetōs·us -a -um *adj* (sēt-) shaggy, bristly
saevē *adv* savagely, fiercely
saevidic·us -a -um *adj* spoken in anger
saev·iō -īre -iī -ītum *intr* to be fierce, be savage, be furious; *(of persons)* to be brutal, be violent
saeviter *adv* savagely, cruelly
saeviti·a -ae *f* rage, fierceness; brutality, savageness *(of persons)*
saevitūd·ō -inis *f* savageness
saev·us -a -um *adj* raging, fierce, cruel; brutal, savage, barbarous
sāg·a -ae *f* witch; wise woman
sagācit·ās -ātis *f* sagacity, shrewdness; keenness
sagāciter *adv* keenly, with keen scent *or* sight; with insight
Sagan·a -ae *f* name of a witch
Sagar·is -is *m* river flowing from Phyrgia into the Black Sea ‖ fictitous name of a Trojan

Sagarīt·is -idis *f* nymph, daughter of the river Sagaris, loved by Attis

sagāt·us -a -um *adj* wearing a military cloak

sag·ax -ācis *adj* keen-scented; sharp, preceptive *(mind)*

sagīn·a -ae *f* stuffing, fattening up; food, rations; rich food; fattened animal; fatness *(from overeating)*

sagīn·ō -āre -āvī -ātus *tr* to fatten

sāg·iō -īre *tr* to perceive quickly

sagitt·a -ae *f* arrow **‖ Sagitta** *(astr)* Sagitta *(constellation);* an arrow in the constellation Sagittarius

sagittāri·us -a -um *adj* of *or* for an arrow **‖** *m* archer **‖ Sagittārius** *m (astr)* Sagittarius *(constellation)*

sagittāt·us -a -um *adj* barbed

sagittif·er -era -erum *adj* carrying an arrow

Sagittipot·ens -entis *m (astr)* Sagittarius *(constellation)*

sagm·en -inis *n* tuft of sacred herbs *(plucked in the Capitol by the consul or praetor and worn by the Fetiales as a sign of inviolability)*

sagulāt·us -a -um *adj* wearing a military coat **‖** *m* soldier

sagul·um -ī *n* short military coat *(esp. that of general officers)*

sag·um -ī *n* coarse mantle; military uniform; **ad sagum ire** *(or* **sagum sumere)** to get into uniform; **in sagis esse** to be in uniform, to go to war

Saguntīn·us -a -um *adj & m* Saguntine

Sagunt·um -ī *n or* **Sagunt·us** *or* **Sagunt·os -ī** *f* Saguntum *(city on E. coast of Spain (modern Sagunto), which Hannibal attacked thus bringing on the First Punic War)*

sāl salis *m (n)* salt; salt water, sea; seasoning; flavor; good taste, elegance; pungency *(of words);* wit, humor, sarcasm **‖** *mpl* wisecracks

Salaci·a -ae *f* a sea goddess

salac·ō -ōnis *m* show-off, braggart

salamandr·a -ae *f* salamander

Salamīni·us -a -um *adj* of Salamis **‖** *mpl* people of Salamis

Salam·is -īnos *or* **-īnis** *(acc:* **Salamīna;** *(abl:* **Salamīne)** *f* island in the Saronic Gulf near Athens, opposite Eleusis **‖** city in Cyprus

Sal(a)pi·a -ae *f* port in N. Apulia

salapūt·ium -(i)ī *n* midget

Salāri·a -ae *f* Via Salaria *(from Porta Collina to the Sabine district)*

salāri·us -a -um *adj* salt, of salt; **annona salaria** revenue from salt works; **Via Salaria** Salt Road *(from the Porta Collina to the Sabine district)* **‖** *m* saltfish dealer **‖** *n* salary, allowance *(originally the allowance given to soldiers for salt); (fig)* meal

sal·ax -ācis *adj* lustful; salacious, provocative

salebr·a -ae *f* jolting; rut; roughness *(of speech)*

salebrōs·us -a -um *adj* rough, uneven

Sālentīn·ī -ōrum *mpl* **(Sall-)** a people who occupied the S.E. extremity of Italy

Salern·um -ī *n* town on the Campanian coast S.E. of Naples *(modern Salerno)*

Saliār·is -is -e *adj* Salian, of the Salii; sumptuous

Saliāt·us -ūs *m* Salian priesthood

salict·um -ī *n* willow grove

salient·ēs -ium *fpl* springs, fountains

salign·us -a -um *adj* willow

Sali·ī -ōrum *mpl* college of twelve priests dedicated to Mars who went in solemn procession through Rome on the Kalends of March

salill·um -ī *n* small salt shaker

salīn·ae -ārum *fpl* salt pits, salt works; **salinae Romanae** salt works at Ostia *(a state monopoly)*

salīn·um -ī *n* salt shaker

sal·iō -īre -uī *or* **-iī -tum** *tr (of an animal)* to mount **‖** *intr* to jump, leap, hop

Salisubsal(i)·ī -ōrum *mpl* dancing priests of Mars

saliunc·a -ae *f* wild nard *(aromatic plant)*

Sal·ius -(i)ī *m* priest of Mars *(see* **Salii)**

salīv·a -ae *f* saliva; taste, flavor

sal·ix -icis *f* willow tree

Sallentīnī *see* **Salentini**

Sallustiān·us -a -um *adj* of Sallust; **horti Sallustiani** park in the N. part of Rome owned by Sallust **‖** *m* imitator of Sallust's style **‖** *n* a Sallustian expression

Sallust·ius -(i)ī *m* Sallust *(Gaius Sallustius Crispus, Roman historian, 86–34 B.C.)* **‖** Gaius Sallustius Crispus *(his great-nephew and adopted son, an advisor to Agustus and Tiberius, d. A.D. 20)*

Salmac·is -idis *f* fountain at Halicarnassus on the W. coast of Asia Minor, which made all who drank from it soft and effeminate

Salmōn·eus -eī *m* son of Aeolus who imitated lightning and was thrown by Jupiter into Tartarus

Salmōn·is -idis *or* **-idos** *f* Tyro *(daughter of Salmoneus)*

Sal·ō -ōnis *f* tributary of the River Ebro *(modern Jalon)*

Salōn·ae -ārum *fpl* city on the Illyrian coast *(near modern Split)*

salp·a -ae *f* saupe *(type of fish)*

salsāment·um -ī *n (usu. pl)* salted food *(esp. fish)*

salsē *adv* facetiously, humorously

salsipot·ens -entis *adj* ruling the sea

salsūr·a -ae *f* (process of) pickling

sals·us -a -um *adj* salted; briny, salty;

facetious, humorous, witty **II** *npl* salty food; witty remarks, satirical writings

saltāti·ō -ōnis *f* dancing, dance

saltāt·or -ōris *m* dancer

saltātōri·us -a -um *adj* dance-, for dancing

saltātr·ix -īcis *f* dancing girl

saltāt·us -ūs *m* dance

saltem *adv* at least, in any event, anyhow; **non** *(or* **neque) saltem** not even

salt·ō -āre -āvī -ātus *tr & intr* to dance

saltuōs·us -a -um *adj* wooded, covered with forest

salt·us -ūs *m* defile, pass; wooded pasture; opening in the woods, glade; forest; jungle; ravine; *(vulg)* female pudenda

salt·us -ūs *m* jump, leap; *(fig)* step, stage; **saltum dare** to leap

salū·ber *or* **salū·bris -bris -bre** *adj* healthful, healthy, wholesome; *(w. dat or* ad) good for, beneficial to

salūbrit·ās -ātis *f* healthiness, wholesomeness; health, soundness

salūbriter *adv* healthfully; healthily; beneficially; **emere salubriter** to buy cheaply

saluī *pref of* **salio**

sal·um -ī *n* billow; sea in motion; high seas; **aerumnoso navigare salo** *(poet)* to sail a sea of troubles; **tirones salo nauseāque confecti** recruits, hit hard by seasickness

sal·ūs -ūtis *f* health; welfare; prosperity; safety; greeting, best regards; **salutem dicere** *(abbr:* **s.d.)** to send greetings; *(at end of letter)* to say goodbye; **salutem magnam dicere** *(w. dat)* to send warm greetings to, bid fond farewell to, say goodbye to; **salutem plurimam dicere** *(abbr:* **s.p.d)** to send warmest greetings; *(at end of letter)* to give best regards

salūtār·is -is -e *adj* salutary, healthful, wholesome; beneficial, advantageous, useful; *(w.* ad) good for, beneficial for; *(w. dat)* beneficial to; **ars salutaris** art of healing; **salutaris littera** vote of acquittal *(letter* **A** *for* **Absolvo)**

salūtāriter *adv* beneficially

salūtāti·ō -ōnis *f* greeting, salutation; formal morning reception at the house of an important person; callers; **ubi salutatio defluxit** when morning callers have dispersed

salūtāt·or -ōris *m*, **salūtātr·ix -īcis** *f* morning caller

salūtif·er -era -erum *adj* health-giving

salūtigerul·us -a -um *adj* bringing greetings

salūt·ō -āre -āvī -ātus *tr* to greet, wish well; to send greetings to; to pay respects to, pay a morning call on; to pay reverence to *(gods);* to welcome; *(w. double acc)* to hail as

salvē *adv* well; in good health; **saltine** *(or* **satisne) salve?** *(supply* **agis** *or* **agit** *or* **agitur)** *(coll)* everything O.K.?

salv·eō -ēre *intr* to be well, be in good health; to be getting along well; **salve, salvete** *(or* **salveto)!** hello!, good morning!, good day!; goodbye!; **salvebis a meo Cicerone** my son Cicero wishes to be remembered to you; **te salvere jubeo** I bid you good day; **vale, salve** goodbye

salv·us -a -um *adj* well, sound, safe, unharmed; living, alive; *(w. noun or pronoun in an abl absolute)* without violation of, without breaking, *e.g.,* **salvā lege** without breaking the law; **salvos sum** *(coll)* I'm O.K.

Samae·ī -ōrum *mpl* inhabitants of Cephallenia

sambūc·a -ae *f* triangular stringed instrument, small harp

sambūcistri·a -ae *f* harpist *(female)*

Sam·ē -ēs *or (less frequently)* **Sam·os -ī** *f* ancient name of the island of Cephallenia

Samiol·us -a -um *adj* of Samian ware

Sami·us -a -um *adj* of Samos, Samian; **Juno Samia** Juno worshiped at Samos; **testa Samia** Samian potsherd *(noted for its thinness);* **vir Samius** Pythagoras **II** *mpl* Samians **II** *npl* delicate Samian pottery

Samn·īs -ītis *adj* Samnite **II** *m* gladiator armed with Samnite weapons **II** *mpl* the Samnites

Samn·ium -(i)ī *n* country of central Italy, whose inhabitants were the offshoot of the Sabines

Sam·os *or* **Sam·us -ī** *(acc:* **-um** *or* **-on)** *f* an island off the W. coast of Asia Minor, famous as the birthplace of Pythagoras **II** *see* **Same**

Samothrāc·a -ae *f* Samothrace *(island off the Thracian coast)*

Samothrāc·es -um *mpl* Samothracians

Samothrāci·us -a -um *adj* Samothracian **II** *f* Samothrace *(island in N. Aegean Sea)*

sam(p)s·a -ae *f* crushed olive

sānābil·is -is -e *adj* curable

sānāti·ō -ōnis *f* healing, curing

san·ciō -cīre -xi -ctus *tr* to fulfill *(a threat, prophecy);* to ratify *(laws, agreements, treaties);* to enact *(a law);* to sanction *(a policy, practice);* to confirm the possession of *(property);* to condemn; *(w. abl of the penalty)* to make *(an offense, a person)* punishable by law with; **Solon capite sanxit qui in seditione non alterius utrius partis fuisset** Solon condemned to death anyone who did not side with one party or the other in a revolution

sanctē *adv* solemnly, reverently, religiously, conscientiously, purely

sanctimōni·a -ae f sanctity, sacredness; chastity

sancti·ō -ōnis f consecration; sanctioning; penalty clause *(that part of the law that provided for penalties against those breaking that law)*, sanction

sanctit·ās -ātis f sanctity, sacredness, inviolability; integrity; purity

sanctitūd·ō -inis f sanctity

sanct·or -ōris m enactor *(of laws)*

sanct·us -a -um *adj* consecrated, hallowed, sacred, inviolable, holy; venerable, august, divine; chaste

Sanc·us -ī m epithet of Semo *(a god of Sabine origin)*

sandaliāri·us -a -um *adj* sandal-maker's; **Apollo Sandaliarius** Apollo of Shoemakers' Street

sandaligerul·ae -ārum *fpl* maids who brought slippers to their mistress

sandal·ium -iī n sandal *(one in which the toes were covered; cf.* **solea)**

sandapil·a -ae f cheap coffin

sand·yx -ȳcis f vermilion, scarlet

sānē *adv* sanely, reasonably, sensibly; certainly, doubtless, truly, very; *(ironically)* of course, naturally; *(w. negatives)* really, at all; *(in concessions)* to be sure, however; *(in answers)* yes, of course; *(w. imperatives)* then; **haud** *(or* **non)** **sane** not very; **nihil sane** absolutely nothing; **sane quam** extremely

sanesc·ō -ēre *intr* to get well; to heal

Sangari·us -a -um *adj* living near the Sangaris River *(in Phrygia)* ‖ *m* Sangaris River

sanguin·ans -antis *adj* bleeding; bloodthirsty

sanguināri·us -a -um *adj* bloodthirsty

sanguine·us -a -um *adj* bloody, bloodstained; blood-red

sanguinolent·us -a -um *adj* bloody, bloodstained; blood-red; vindictive

sangu·is -inis m blood; descent, parentage, family; descendant; murder, bloodshed; *(fig)* lifeblood, source of vitality, life, strength; forcefulness, life, vigor *(of a speech);* **sanguinem dare** to bleed; **sanguinem effundere** *(or* **profundere)** to bleed heavily; **sanguinem haurire** to shed *(s.o.'s)* blood; **sanguinis missio** *(med)* bloodletting; **sanguinem mittere** *(of a physician)* to let blood, bleed

sani·ēs -ēī f blood *(from a wound);* gore; foam, froth; venom

sānit·ās -ātis f health; sanity; common sense, discretion; solidity, healthy foundation *(for victory, etc.);* soundness, propriety *(of style)*

sann·a -ae f mocking grimace, sneer, face

sanni·ō -ōnis m clown

sān·ō -āre -āvī -ātus *tr* to cure, heal; to correct, repair; to allay, quiet, relieve

Sanquāl·is -is -e *adj* of Sancus *(Sabine deity);* **Sanqualis avis** osprey

Santon·ī -ōrum *mpl* Gallic tribe N. of the Geronne

Santonic·us -a -um *adj* of the Santoni; **herba** *(or* **virga)** **Santona** wormwood *(bitter aromatic herb used as a tonic)*

Santr·a -ae m a grammarian of the time of Varro

sān·us -a -um *adj* sound, hale, healthy; sane, rational, sensible; sober; *(w. ab)* free from *(faults, etc.)*

sanxī *perf of* **sancio**

sap·a -ae f (distilled) new wine

sāperd·a -ae m a fish *(from the Black Sea)*

sapi·ens -entis *adj* wise, sensible, judicious, discreet ‖ *m* sensible person; sage, philosopher; man of discriminating taste, connoisseur; title given to jurisconsults

sapienter *adv* wisely, sensibly

sapienti·a -ae f wisdom; common sense; philosophy; knowledge *(of principles, methods)*, science

sap·iō -ĕre -īvī *or* **-iī** *tr* to have the flavor of, taste of; to smell like; to understand ‖ *intr* to have the sense of taste; to have sense, be sensible, be discreet, be wise

sāp·ō -ōnis m hair dye

sap·or -ōris m taste, flavor; delicacy; refinement, sense of taste

Saphh·ō -ūs f Greek lyric poetess of Lesbos *(born c. 612 B.C.)*

sarcin·a -ae f package, bundle, pack; burden *(of a womb);* sorrow, trouble ‖ *fpl* luggage, gear; movable goods, chattels, belongings

sarcināri·us -a -um *adj* luggage-, of luggage; **jumenta sarcinaria** pack animals

sarcināt·or -ōris m patcher, botcher

sarcināt·us -a -um *adj* loaded down

sarcinul·ae -ārum *fpl* small bundles, little trousseau

sar·ciō -cīre -sī -tus *tr* to patch, fix, repair

sarcophag·us -ī m stone coffin

sarcul·um -ī n garden hoe

Sardanapal(l)·us -ī m last king of Assyria *(c. 9th cent.)* whose decadence was legendary

Sard·ēs *or* **Sard·īs -ium** *fpl* Sardis *(capital of Lydia)*

Sardiān·us -a -um *adj* Sardian ‖ *mpl* inhabitants of Sardis

Sardini·a -ae f Sardinia

Sardiniens·is -is -e *adj* Sardinian

Sardis *see* **Sardes**

sardon·yx -ychis *or* **-ychos** m (f) sardonyx *(precious stone)*

Sardō·us *or* **Sard·us -a -um** *adj & m* Sardinian

sarg·us -ī m sar *(fish)*

sar·iō -īre -uī *intr* **(sarr-)** to hoe

sarīs(s)·a -ae f long Macedonian lance

sarīs(s)ophor·os -ī m Macedonian lancer

Sarmat·ae -ārum *mpl* Sarmatians *(barbarous people of S.E. Russia)*
Sarmati·a -ae *f* Sarmatia
Sarmaticē *adv* Sarmatian, in the Sarmatian language
Sarmatic·us -a -um *adj* Sarmatian
sarment·um -ī *n* brushwood **‖** *npl* twigs, fagots
Sarn·us -ī *n* river in Campania near Paestum *(modern Sarno)*
Sarpēd·ōn -onis *or* **-onos** *m* King of Lycia who was killed by Patroclus at Troy
Sarr·a -ae *f* old name for Tyre
sarrāc·um -ī *n* **(serr-)** wagon
Sarrān·us -a -um *adj* Tyrian, Phoenician; dyed (Tyrian) purple
sarriō *see* **sario**
sarsī *perf of* **sarcio**
sartāg·ō -inis *f* frying pan; hodgepodge
sart·us *or* **sarct·us -a -um** *pp of* **sarcio ‖** *adj (occurring only with* **tectus**) in good repair; **aedem Castoris sartam tectam tradere** to hand over the temple of Castor in good repair **‖** *npl* repairs; **sarta tecta exigere** to complete the repairs
sat *indecl adj* enough, sufficient, adequate **‖** *n* enough; **sat agere** *(w. gen)* to have enough of, have one's hands full with
sat *adv* sufficiently, quite; **sat scio** I am quite sure
sat·a -ōrum *npl* crops
sat·agō -agěre -ēgī *intr* to have trouble enough, have one's hands full
satell·es -itis *mf* bodyguard, attendant, follower; *(pej)* lackey; partisan; *(w. gen)* accomplice in *(crime)*
sati·ās -ātis *f* sufficiency; overabundance, satiety, satisfied desire
Saticul·us -ī *m* inhabitant of Saticula *(Samnite town)*
satiet·ās -ātis *f* sufficiency, adequacy; satiety, weariness, disgust
satin' *or* **satine** *adv* quite, really
sati·ō -āre -āvī -ātus *tr* to satisfy, appease; to avenge; to fill, glut; to saturate; to cloy
sati·ō -ōnis *f* sowing, planting **‖** *fpl* sown fields
satis *or* **sat** *indecl adj* enough, sufficient, adequate **‖** *n* enough; *(leg)* satisfaction, security, guarantee; **satis accipere** to receive a guarantee; **satis dare** *(w. dat)* to give a guarantee to; **satis facere** *(w. dat)* to satisfy; to pay *(a creditor);* to make amends to *(by word or deed)*, apologize to; **satis facere** *(w. dat of person and acc & inf)* to satisfy *(s.o.)* with proof that, demonstrate sufficiently to *(s.o.)* that; **satis superque dictum est** more than enough has been said
satis *adv* enough, sufficiently, adequately; **satis bene** pretty well
satisdati·ō -ōnis *f* putting up bail, giving a guarantee

satis·dō -dare -dedī -datum *intr* (also written as two words) see **satis**
satis·faciō -facěre -fēcī -factus *tr (also written as two words) see* **satis**
satisfacti·ō -ōnis *f* amends, satisfaction; apology, excuse
satius *(comp of* **satis**) *adj (neut only)* **satius est** *(w. inf)* it is better *or* preferable to
sat·or -ōris *m* sower, planter; father; promoter, author
satrapē·a *or* **satrapī·a -ae** *f* satrapy *(office or province of a satrap)*
satrap·ēs *or* **satrap·a -ae** *m* satrap *(provincial governor in the Persian empire)*
sat·ur -ura -urum *adj* full, well-fed, stuffed; plump; fertile; deep *(color)*
satur·a -ae *f* **(satir-)** dish of mixed ingredients; mixture, hodgepodge; medley, variety show; literary medley of prose and poetry; satire, satirical poem; **in** *(or* **per)** **saturam** at random; collectively, en block; **per saturam ferre** to propose as a rider to a bill
saturēi·a -ōrum *npl* savory *(seasoning)*
saturit·ās -ātis *f* satiety; plenty, overabundance
Sāturnāli·a -ium *npl* festival in honor of Saturn, beginning on the 17th of December and lasting several days; **io Saturnalia!** cry of merrymakers at this festival; **non semper Saturnalia erunt** *(fig)* it won't be Christmas forever
Sāturni·a -ae *f* Juno *(daughter of Saturn)*
Sāturnīn·us -ī *m* Lucius Appuleius Saturninus *(demagogic tribune in 103 and 100 b.c.)*
Sāturni·us -a -um *adj* Saturnian; **Saturnius numerus** Saturnian meter *(archaic Latin meter based on stress accent)* **‖** *m* Jupiter; Pluto
Sāturn·us -ī *m* Saturn *(Italic god of agriculture, equated with the Greek god Cronos, ruler of the Golden Age, and father of Jupiter, Neptune, Juno, and Pluto)*
satur·ō -āre -āvī -ātus *tr* to fill, satisfy, glut, cloy, saturate; to satisfy, content
sat·us -a -um *pp of* **sero** (to plant) **‖** *npl* see **sata**
sat·us -ūs *m* sowing, planting; begetting; race, stock; seed *(of knowledge)*
satyrisc·us -ī *m* little satyr
satyr·us -ī *m* satyr; satyr play *(in which chorus consisted of satyrs)*
sauciāti·ō -ōnis *f* wounding
sauci·ō -āre -āvī -ātus *tr* to wound
sauci·us -a -um *adj* wounded; *(fig)* smitten, offended, hurt; melted *(snow)* **‖** *mpl* the wounded
saurocton·os -ī *m (as title of a statue)* lizard killer
Sauromat·ae -ārum *fpl* Sarmatians *(barbaric tribe of S. Russia)*

sāviāti·ō -ōnis *f* (suav-) kissing
sāviol·um -ī *n* (suav-) little kiss, peck
sāvi·or -ārī -ātus sum *tr* (suav-) to kiss
sāv·ium -(i)ī *n* (suav-) puckered lips; kiss
saxātil·is -is -e *adj* rock-, living among rocks **ǁ** *m* saxatile *(fish)*
saxēt·um -ī *n* rocky place; stone quarry
saxe·us -a -um *adj* rocky, stony; **umbra saxea** shade of the rocks
saxific·us -a -um *adj* petrifying, changing objects into stone
saxifrag·us -a -um *adj* rock-breaking
saxōs·us -a -um *adj* rocky, stony
saxul·um -ī *n* small rock *or* crag
sax·um -ī *n* boulder, rock; Tarpeian Cliff *(W. side of the Capitoline Hill)*
scabellum *see* scabillum
sca·ber -bra -brum *adj* itchy; rough, scurfy
scābī *perf of* scabo
scabi·ēs -ēī *f* itch; eczema; *(fig)* itch
scabill·um -ī *n* (-bell-) stool, footstool; castanet tied to the ankle
scabiōs·us -a -um *adj* itchy, mangy; moldy
scabō scabēre scābī *tr* to scratch
Scae·a port·a -ae *f* Scaean gate *(W. gate of Troy)*
scaen·a -ae *f* (scēn-) stage; backdrop, scenery; scene; *(fig)* public view, publicity; melodramatic behavior; pretense; pretext; canopy *(of forest acting like a backdrop);* **tibi scenae serviendum est** you must keep yourself in the limelight
scaenicē *adv* (scēn-) like on the stage
scaenic·us -a -um *adj* (scēn-) of the stage, theatrical, scenic; **ludi scaenici** plays
scaev·a -ae *f* favorable omen
Scaevol·a -ae *m* Gaius Mucius Cordus Scaevola *(Roman hero who infiltrated Porsenna's camp to kill Porsenna, and on being discovered, burned off his own right hand)* **ǁ** Quintus Mucius Scaevola *(consul in 95 B.C. and pontifex maximus)*
scaev·us -a -um *adj* left, on the left; perverse **ǁ** *f* sign *or* omen appearing on the left *(hence, unfavorable)*
scāl·ae -ārum *fpl* ladder; flight of stairs, stairs
scalm·us -ī *m* oarlock; oar; boat
scalpell·um -ī *n* scalpel
scalptōr·ium -(i)ī *n* back-scratcher
scalptūr·a -ae *f* engraving
scalp·ō -ĕre -sī -tus *tr* to carve; to scratch; to tickle, titillate
scalpr·um -ī *n* chisel; knife; penknife
scalpsī *perf of* scalpo
scalpurr·iō -īre *intr* to scratch
Scaman·der -drī *m* river at Troy *(also called Xantus)*
scamb·us -a -um *adj* bowlegged
scammōne·a -ae *f (bot)* scammony *(plant with trumpet-like flowers similar to the morning-glory, used as a laxative)*

scamn·um -ī *n* bench; stool; throne
scan·dō -dĕre -dī *tr* to climb, scale; to climb aboard; to mount **ǁ** *intr* to climb; *(of buildings)* to rise, tower
scandul·a -ae *f* shingle *(of a roof)*
Scantīni·us -a -um *adj* Roman clan name *(nomen);* **lex Scantinia** law against unnatural vice
scaph·a -ae *f* light boat, skiff
scaph·ium -iī *n* (scaf-) boat-shaped drinking cup; chamber pot
scapul·ae -ārum *fpl* shoulder blades; shoulders; back
scāp·us -ī *m* shaft *(of a column)*; stalk *(of a plant)*
scarīf·ō -āre *tr* to scratch open
scar·us -ī *m* scar *(fish)*
scatebr·a -ae *f* bubbling spring
scat·eō -ēre -uī *or* scat·ō -ĕre *intr* to bubble up, gush out; to teem
scatur(r)īgi·ō -inis *f* spring
scaturr·iō -īre *intr* to bubble, gush; to bubble over with enthusiasm
scaur·us -a -um *adj* clubfooted
scaz·ōn -ontis *m* scazon *(iambic trimeter with a spondee in the last foot)*
scelerātē *adv* criminally, wickedly
scelerāt·us -a -um *adj* profaned, desecrated; outlawed; criminal, wicked, infamous; **campus sceleratus** open field near the Colline gate where unchaste Vestals were buried alive; **vicus sceleratus** street on Esquiline Hill where Tullia, daughter of Servius Tullius, drove over her father's corpse **ǁ** *m* criminal; rascal
sceler·ō -āre -āvī -ātus *tr* to defile
scelerōs·us -a -um *adj* steeped in wickedness
scelestē *adv* wickedly, criminally
scelest·us -a -um *adj* wicked, villainous, criminal
scel·us -eris *n* wicked deed, crime, wickedness; calamity; criminal
scēn- = scaen-
sceptrif·er -era -erum *adj* sceptered
sceptr·um -ī *n* scepter **ǁ** *npl* kingship, dominion, authority; kingdom; **sceptra Asiae tenere** to hold sway in Asia
sceptūch·us -ī *m* scepter-bearer *(high officer of state in the East)*
sched·a *or* scid·a -ae *f* sheet, page
sc(h)ēm·a -ae *f,* sc(h)ēm·a -atis *or* -atos *n* figure, form; style; figure of speech
schid·a -ae *f* (scid-) sheet *(of papyrus)*; one of the strips forming a sheet of papyrus
Schoenē·is -idos *f* daughter of Schoeneus, Atalanta
Schoenēi·us -a -um *adj* of Schoeneus **ǁ** *f* Atalanta
Schoen·ēūs -eī *m* king of Boeotia and father of Atalanta

schoenobat·ēs -ae *m* tightrope-walker

schoen·us -ī *m* cheap perfume

schol·a -ae *f* school; lecture hall; lecture; learned debate; sect, followers

scholastic·us -a -um *adj* school, scholastic **‖** *m* rhetoric teacher, rhetorician; grammarian

scida *see* **scheda**

scidī *perf of* **scindo**

sci·ens -entis *adj* aware of a fact, cognizant; having full knowledge, with one's eyes wide open; *(w. gen)* cognizant of, familiar with, expert in; *(w. inf)* knowing how to

scienter *adv* wisely, expertly

scienti·a -ae *f* knowledge, skill, expertise; science; *(w. de or in + abl)* expertise in, skill in

sciī *perf of* **scio**

scīlicet *adv* of course, evidently, certainly; *(ironically)* naturally, of course; *(as an explanatory particle)* namely, that is to say

scill·a -ae *f* **(squi-)** squill *(seaside plant of the lily family)*

scīn = **scisne**, *i.e.*, **scis + ne** do you know?

scindō scindĕre scidī scissus *tr* to cut, split, tear apart, tear open; to divide, separate; to interrupt

scintill·a -ae *f* spark; speck

scintill·ō -āre *intr* to sparkle, flash

scintillul·a -ae *f* little spark

sciō scīre scīvī *or* **sciī scītus** *tr* to know; to realize, understand; to have skill in; *(w. inf)* to know how to

Scīpiad·ēs -ae *m* one of the Scipio family, a Scipio

scīpi·ō -ōnis *m* ceremonial staff *or* baton *(generally made of ivory and carried by persons of rank, such as a seer or a general at his triumph)* **‖ Scīpiō** family name *(cognomen)* in the famous gens Cornelia **‖ Publius Cornelius Scipio Africanus Major** *(victor in the Second Punic War, 236–184 B.C.)* **‖ Publius Cornelius Scipio Aemilianus Africanus Minor** *(victor in Third Punic War, c. 185–132 B.C.)*

Scīr·ōn -ōnis *or* **-ōnos** *m* robber who waylaid travelers on the road near Megara *(killed by Theseus)*

s(c)irpe·us -a -um *adj* wicker-, of wicker **‖** *f* wickerwork

s(c)irpicul·a -ae *f* wicker basket

s(c)irpicul·us -ī *m* wicker basket

s(c)irp·us -ī *m* bulrush

sciscitāt·or -ōris *m* interrogator

sciscit·ō -āre *or* **sciscit·or -ārī -ātus sum** *tr* to ask, question, interrogate; to consult; *(w. acc of thing asked and* **ex** *or* **ab** *of person asked)* to ask *(s.th.)* of *(s.o.),* check on *(s.th.)* with *(s.o.)* **‖** *intr* (w. **de** + *abl)* to ask about

sciscō sciscĕre scīvī scītus *tr (pol)* to approve, adopt, enact, decree; to learn, ascertain

sciss·or -ōris *m* carver *(person cutting meat at the table)*

scissūr·a -ae *f* crack, cleft

sciss·us -a -um *pp of* **scindo ‖** *adj* split, rent; furrowed *(cheeks);* shrill *(voice)*

scītāment·a -ōrum *npl* delicacies, choice tidbits

scītē *adv* expertly

scīt·or -ārī -ātus sum *tr* to ask; to consult *(oracle);* (w. acc of thing and **ab** *or* **ex**) to ask *(s.th.)* of *(s.o.)* **‖** *intr* (w. **de** + *abl)* to ask *or* inquire about

scītul·us -a -um *adj* neat, pretty

scīt·um -ī *n* statute, decree

scīt·us -a -um *adj* experienced, skillful; suitable, proper; judicious, sensible, witty; smart, sharp *(appearance);* (w. gen) skilled in, expert at

scīt·us -ūs *m* decree, enactment

sciūr·us -ī *m* squirrel

scīvī *perf of* **scio** *and of* **scisco**

-sc·ō -ĕre *vbl suf* normally used only in the present system with inchoative force, *e.g.,* **lūcescō** to begin to shine

scob·is -is *f* sawdust, scrapings, filings

scom·ber -brī *m* mackerel

scōp·ae -ārum *fpl* broom

Scop·ās -ae *m* Greek sculptor from the island of Paros *(4th cent. B.C.)*

scopulōs·us -a -um *adj* rocky, craggy

scopul·us -ī *m* rock, cliff, crag; promontory; archery target

scorpi·ō -ōnis *or* **scorp·ius** *or* **scorp·ios -(i)ī** *m* scorpion; *(mil)* catapult **‖ Scorpio** *(astr)* Scorpion *(constellation)*

scortāt·or -ōris *m* a john *(prostitute's customer)*

scorte·us -a -um *adj* leather

scort·or -ārī *intr* to associate with prostitutes

scort·um -ī *n* prostitute; sex fiend *(of either sex)*

screāt·us -ūs *m* clearing of the throat

scre·ō -āre *intr* to clear the throat, hawk, hem

scrīb·a -ae *m* clerk, secretary

scrib(i)līt·a -ae *f* cheese cake

scrībō scrībĕre scripsī scriptus *tr* to write, draw; to write down; to write out, compose; to draw up, draft *(a law, treaty, decree);* to create *(characters, episodes in a play);* to lay down in writing, prescribe; to register *(a person);* to draft *(colonists to a place);* to name *(in a will);* to enlist *(soldiers);* *(w. double acc)* to appoint *(s.o.)* as **‖** *intr* to write

scrīn·ium -(i)ī *n* case for scrolls; letter case; portfolio

scripsī *perf of* **scribo**

scripti·ō -ōnis *f* writing; composition; spelling; wording, text

scriptit·ō -āre -āvī -ātus *tr & intr* to keep writing, write regularly

script·or -ōris *m* writer; scribe, secretary; author; **rerum scriptor** historian

scriptul·a -ōrum *npl* lines on a game board

scriptūr·a -ae *f* writing; composing; written work, composition; tax paid on public pastures; testamentary provision

script·us -a -um *pp of* **scribo ǁ** *n* composition, treatise, work, book; actual text *(of a law, document);* literal meaning, letter *(as opposed to spirit);* **duodecim scripta** a type of game board; **orationem de scripto dicere** to read off a speech; **voluntas legis, non tantum scriptum** the spirit of the law, not only the letter *(of the law)*

scrīpul·um -ī *n* **(script-)** small weight, smallest measure of weight, scruple *(one twenty-fourth of an uncia, or ounce)*

scrob·is -is *mf* ditch, trench; grave

scrōf·a -ae *f* breeding sow

scrōfipasc·us -ī *m* pig breeder

scrūpe·us -a -um *adj* full of sharp rocks, made of jagged rocks, jagged

scrūpōs·us -a -um *adj* full of sharp rocks, jagged, rough

scrūpulōsē *adv* scrupulously, precisely, carefully

scrūpulōs·us -a -um *adj* full of sharp projections of rock, jagged; scrupulous, meticulous, precise

scrūpul·us -ī *m* uneasy feeling, scruple, worry, headache; thorny problem

scrūp·us -ī *m* rough *or* sharp stone; uneasiness

scrūt·a -ōrum *npl* trash, junk

scrūtāt·or -ōris *m* examiner

scrūt·or -ārī -ātus sum *tr* to scrutinize, examine

sculp·ō -ěre -sī -tus *tr* to carve, chisel, engrave

sculpōne·ae -ārum *fpl* clogs, wooden shoes

sculpsī *perf of* **sculpo**

sculptil·is -is -e *adj* carved, engraved

sculpt·or -ōris *m* sculptor

sculptūr·a -ae *f* carving; sculpture

sculptus *pp of* **sculpo**

scurr·a -ae *m* jester, comedian; city slicker

scurrīl·is -is -e *adj* scurrilous, offensive

scurrīlit·ās -ātis *f* offensive humor, scurrility

scurrīliter *adv* with offensive humor, like a buffoon

scurr·or -ārī *intr* to clown around

scūtāl·e -is *n* thong of a sling

scūtār·ius -(i)ī *m* shield-maker

scūtāt·us -a -um *adj* carrying a shield ǁ *mpl* troops armed with shields

scutell·a -ae *f* saucer, shallow bowl

scutic·a -ae *f* whip

scūtigerul·us -a -um *m* shield-bearer

scutr·a -ae *f* pan, flat dish

scutul·a -ae *f* wooden roller

scutulāt·us -a -um *adj* diamond-shaped ǁ *npl* checkered clothing

scūtul·um -ī *n* small shield

scūt·um -ī *n* oblong shield; *(fig)* shield, defense, protection

Scyll·a -ae *f* female monster on Italian side of Straits of Messina, that snatched and devoured sailors from passing ships ǁ daughter of Nisus who betrayed her father by cutting off his purple lock of hair

Scyllae·us -a -um *adj* Scyllan

scymn·us -ī *m* cub, whelp

scyph·us -ī *m* goblet, cup

Scȳr·os *or* **Scȳr·us -ī** *f* island off Euboea

Scyth·a *or* **Scyth·ēs -ae** *m* Scythian *(member of nomadic tribe N. of the Black Sea)*

Scythi·a -ae *f* country N. of the Black Sea

Scythic·us -a -um *adj* Scythian

Scyth·is -idis *f* Scythian woman

s. d. *abbr* **salutem dicere**

sē *or* **sēsē** *(gen:* **suī;** *dat:* **sibi;** *acc & abl:* **sē** *or* **sēsē** *pron (refl)* himself, herself, itself, themselves; one another; **ad se** *(or* **apud se)** at home; **apud se** in one's senses; **inter se** each other, one another, mutually; **in se** associated with each other, one another, together; **per se** by himself *(herself, etc.),* alone

sē- *pref (also* **sēd-,** **sŏ-)** added to verbs, *etc.:* **1** *in the sense of* "apart", "aside", *e.g.:* **seducere** to take aside; **seditio a** going apart, mutiny; **2** *sometimes privative, e.g.:* **socors** lacking in vitality, inactive

sēb·um -ī *n* tallow, grease, suet

sē·cēdō -cēděre -cessī -cessum *intr* to withdraw; to depart; to rebel, go on a sit-down strike, secede; **in otium secedere** to retire

sē·cernō -cerněre -crēvī -crētus *tr* to separate; to dissociate; to distinguish; to reject, set aside

sēcessi·ō -ōnis *f* withdrawal; secession

sēcess·us -ūs *m* retirement, retreat; isolated spot; country retreat

sēclū·dō -děre -sī -sus *tr* to shut off, shut up; to shut out; to seclude, bar; to hide

sec·ō -āre -uī -tus *tr* to cut, cut off; to reap; to carve *(meat);* to split up *(in classification);* to cut through, traverse *(e.g., the sea);* to cut short; to settle, decide; to follow, chase; to castrate; *(med)* to cut out, excise, cut off, amputate; **viam secare** to open up a path

sēcrēti·ō -ōnis *f* dividing, separating *(into constituent parts)*

sēcrētō *or* **sēcrētē** *adv* separately, individually, apart; secretly; in private; away from one's companions

sēcrēt·us -a -um *pp of* **secerno ǁ** *adj* separate; isolated, solitary; secret; *(w. gen or abl)* deprived of, in need of **ll** *n* secret, mystery; mystic rite, mystic emblem; secret nature *(of a business);* abstruseness *(of a subject);* private conversation *or* interview, audience; isolated spot; **a secreto** *(or* **in secreto** *or* **in secretum)** in private; **secreto in occulto cum aliquo agere** to discuss *(s.th.)* with s.o. in a private conversation; **secretum dare (petere)** to grant (ask for) an audience

sect·a -ae *f* path; way, method, course; school of thought; political party; code of behavior; **secta (vitae)** way of life, occupation

sectāri·us -a -um *adj* followed (by the flock)

sectāt·or -ōris *m* follower, adherent

sectil·is -is -e *adj* cut, divided

secti·ō -ōnis *f* cutting; auctioning off of confiscated property; a buying up of confiscated property in lots; right to confiscated property; things so to be sold, lots

sect·or -ōris *m* speculator in confiscated estates *(one who buys up confiscated property with the intention of reselling);* **sector zonarius** purse-snatcher

sect·or -ārī -ātus sum *tr* to keep following, follow eagerly, run after; to hunt *(game);* to go about searching for; to imitate; to run after *(girls);* to avenge; to follow *(an example, practice);* to go regularly to, frequent; to aim continually at *(an objective)*

sectūr·a -ae *f* incision; stone quarry

sectus *pp of* **seco**

sēcubit·us -ūs *m* sleeping alone

sēcub·ō -āre -uī *intr* to sleep by oneself; to live alone

secuī *perf of* **seco**

sēcul- = saecul-

secund·a -ōrum *npl* success

secund·ae -ārum *fpl (theat)* secondary role in a play; *(fig)* second fiddle

secundān·ī -ōrum *mpl* soldiers of the second legion

secundāri·us -a -um *adj* secondary; second-rate, inferior

secundō *adv* secondly

secund·ō -āre -āvī -ātus *tr* to favor, further; to make *(conditions)* favorable for travel; **secundans ventus** favorable wind, tail wind

secundum *adv* after, behind **ll** *prep (w. acc)* **1** *(of space)* beside, by, along, alongside: **ire secundum me** to walk beside me; **legiones secundum flumen duxit** he led the troops along the river; **2** *(of time)* immediately after: **secundum ludos** immediately after the games; **3** *(in rank or quality)* next to, after: **secundum deos homines hominibus utiles esse**

possunt next to the gods, people can be helpful to people; **4** *(of agreement)* according to, in compliance with: **secundum naturam vivere** to live in accordance with nature; **5** *(leg)* in favor of, to the advantage of; **abscentibus secundum praesentes facillime dabat** when a party (to the suit) was absent, he would very readily decide in favor of the party present

secund·us -a -um *adj* following; next, second *(in time; in rank);* backing, favorable, supporting; secondary, subordinate, inferior, second-string; alternate *(heir); (w. dat or* **ab**) second only to; **anno secundo** the next year; **a mensis fine secunda dies** the second-last day of the month; **in secundam aquam** with the current; **res secundae** success, prosperity; **secundae partes** supporting role; **secunda mensa** dessert; **secundo flumine** downstream, with the current; **secundo lumine** on the following day; **secundo mari** with the tide; **secundo populo** with the backing of the people; **secundus panis** stale bread; **secundus ventus** tailwind, fair wind **ll Secundus** *m* Roman first name *(praenomen)* **ll** *fpl see* **secundae ll** *npl see* **secunda**

sēcūrē *adv* securely, safely

sēcūricul·a -ae *f* hatchet

sēcūrif·er -era -erum *adj* carrying an ax, ax-carrying

sēcūrig·er -era -erum *adj* carrying an ax, ax-wielding

sēcūr·is -is *f (acc: usu.* **securim)** ax, hatchet; *(fig)* blow, mortal blow; *(fig) (from the ax in the fasces, usu. pl)* power of life and death, supreme authority, sovereignty; **graviorem rei publicae infligere securim** to inflict a more serious blow on the State

sēcūrit·ās -ātis *f* freedom from care, unconcern, composure; freedom from danger, security, safety; false sense of security; carelessness

sēcūr·us -a -um *adj* carefree; secure, safe; cheerful; careless; offhand

secus *indecl n* sex; **secus muliebre** females; **secus virile** males

secus *adv* otherwise, differently; **haud** *(or* **haut** *or* **non) secus ac** *(or* **non secus quam)** not otherwise than, just as, exactly as; **haud** *(or* **haut** *or* **non) secus si** exactly as if, just as though; **si secus accidet** if it turns out otherwise *(than expected),* if it turns out badly

secūt·or -ōris *m* chaser *(gladiator who fought against the net-man)*

secūtus *pp of* **sequor**

sed *or* **set** *conj* but; but also

sēdātē *adv* sedately, calmly

sēdāti·ō -ōnis *f* calming

sēdāt·us -a -um *adj* calm, composed
sēdecim *indecl adj* sixteen
sēdēcul·a -ae *f* little seat, low stool
sedentāri·us -a -um *adj* sedentary
sedeō sedēre sēdī sessum *intr* to sit, remain seated; *(of magistrates, esp. judge)* to sit, preside, hold court, be a judge; *(of an army)* to remain encamped; to keep the field; to settle down to a blockade; to be idle, be inactive; *(of clothes)* to fit; *(of places)* to be low-lying; to sink, settle; to be firm, be fixed, be established; to stick fast, be stuck; to be determined
sēd·ēs -is *f* seat, chair, throne; residence, home; last home, burial place; base, foundation, bottom
sēdī *perf of* **sedeo**
sedīl·e -is *n* seat, chair **II** *npl* seats in the theater; rowers' benches
sēditi·ō -ōnis *f* sedition, insurrection, mutiny; dissension, quarrel, disagreement; warring *(of elements)*
sēditiōsē *adv* seditiously, in mutiny
sēditiōs·us -a -um *adj* seditious, mutinous; quarrelsome; troubled
sēd·ō -āre -āvī -ātus *tr* to calm, settle, still
sēdū·cō -cēre -xī -ctus *tr* to lead aside, draw aside, lead off, withdraw; to carry off; to lead astray; to put aside; to divide, split
sēducti·ō -ōnis *f* taking aside
sēduct·us -a -um *pp of* **seduco II** *adj* distant, remote
sēdulit·ās -ātis *f* application, earnestness; officiousness
sēdulō *adv* diligently; intentionally
sēdul·us -a -um *adj* diligent, busy; officious
sēduxī *perf of* **seduco**
seg·es -etis *f* grainfield; crop; arable land
Segest·a -ae *f* town in N.W. Sicily
Segestān·us -a -um *adj* of Segesta **II** *mpl* people of Segesta **II** *n* territory of Segesta
segmentāt·us -a -um *adj* trimmed with a flounce *(decorative border)*
segment·um -ī *n* section, segment; trimming, flounce; zone *(of the earth)*
segnip·ēs -edis *adj* slow-footed
segn·is -is -e *adj* slow; inactive; sluggish, lazy
segniter *adv* slowly; lazily
segniti·a -ae *or* **segniti·ēs -ēī** *f* slowness; inactivity; laziness
sēgreg·ō -āre -āvī -ātus *tr* to segregate, separate; to dissociate; **ad sese segregandos a ceteris** for the purpose of dissociating themselves from the rest; **sermonem segregare** to break off a conversation; **suspicionem a se segregare** to ward off suspicion from oneself
Sējāniān·us -a -um *adj* of Sejanus **II** *mpl* partisans of Sejanus
Sējān·us -ī *m* Roman family name *(cogno-*

men) (esp. Lucius Aelius Sejanus, the notorious praetorian prefect under the Emperor Tiberius)
sējugāt·us -a -um *adj* separated, detached
sējug·is -is *m* six-horse chariot
sējug·ō -āre -āvī -ātus *tr (w. ab)* to separate from, detach from
sējunctim *adv* separately
sējuncti·ō -ōnis *f* separation, division
sējun·gō -gěre -xī -ctus *tr* to separate, part, sever; *(fig)* to sever, part, disconnect; to distinguish
sēlecti·ō -ōnis *f* choice, selection
sēlectus *pp of* **seligo**
sēlēgī *perf of* **seligo**
Seleucī·a -ae *f* name of several towns in Asia
Seleuc·us -ī *m* name of a line of six kings of Syria, whose ancestor, Seleucus Nicator, was a general under Alexander the Great and founded the Syrian monarchy *(c. 358–280 B.C.)*
sēlibr·a -ae *f* half pound
sē·ligō -ligěre -lēgī -lectus *tr* to select
Selīn·ūs -untis *f* town on the S.W. coast of Sicily **II** town on the coast of Cilicia
sell·a -ae *f* chair, stool *(normally without back or armrests)*; portable chair, sedan chair; **sella curulis** magistrate's chair
sellāriol·us -a -um *adj (place)* for sitting *or* lounging
sellār·ius -(i)ī *m* lecher
sellistern·ium -(i)ī *n* sacred banquet in honor of goddesses
sellul·a -ae *f* stool; sedan chair
sellulāri·us -a -um *adj* sedentary; **artifex sellularius** craftsman who sits at his job **II** *mpl* sedentary craftsmen
sēmanimis *see* **semianimis**
semel *adv* once, one time; but once, once and for all; the first time; ever, at some time, at any time; **semel aut iterum** once or twice
Semel·ē -ēs *or* **Semel·a -ae** *f* Semele *(daughter of Cadmus and mother of Bacchus by Jupiter)*
Semelēi·us -a -um *adj* of Semele
sēm·en -inis *n* seed; seedling, young plant, shoot: offspring; race, stock; *(in physics)* particle; *(fig)* instigator, root: **semen omnium malorum** root of all evils
sēmenstris *see* **semestris**
sēmentif·er -era -erum *adj* seed-bearing, fruitful
sēment·is -is *f* sowing, planting; young crops; **ut sementem feceris, ita metes** *(prov)* as you sow, so shall you reap
sēmentīv·us -a -um *adj* at seed time, of the sowing season
sēmerm·is -is -e *adj* half-armed
sēmestr·is -is -e *adj* **(-mens-)** for six months, half-yearly, semi-annual
sēmēs·us -a -um *adj* half-eaten

sēmet = *emphatic form of* se
sēmi- *pref before nouns and adjectives with the sense of* "half-" *(sometimes* sēm- *before vowels, e.g.:* semesus half-eaten; sem(i)animus half-alive; *also reduced to* sē- *e.g.:* selibra half pound
sēmiadapert·us -a -um *adj* half-open
sēmianim·is -is -e *or* sēm(i)anim·us -a -um *adj* half-dead
sēmiapert·us -a -um *adj* half-open
sēmib·ōs -ōvis *adj (masc only)* half-ox; semibos vir the Minotaur
sēmica·per -prī *m (masc only)* half-goat *(i.e., Pan or Faunus)*
sēmicrem(āt)·us -a -um *adj* half-burned
sēmicubitāl·is -is -e *adj* half-cubit long *or* wide
sēmide·us -a -um *adj* semidivine ‖ *m* demigod
sēmidoctus -a -um *adj* half-educated
sēm(i)erm·is -is -e *or* sēm(i)erm·us -a -um *adj* half-armed
sēm(i)ēs·us -a -um *adj* half-eaten
sēmifact·us -a -um *adj* half-finished
sēmifer·us -a -um *adj* half-beast; half-savage ‖ *m* centaur
sēmifult·us -a -um *adj* half-propped
sēmigermān·us -a -um *adj* half-German
semigraec·us -a -um *adj* half-Greek
sēmigrav·is -is -e *adj* half-drunk
sēmigr·ō -āre -āvī -ātum *intr* (w. ab) to go away from, move away from
sēmihi·ans -antis *adj* half-open
sēmihom·ō -inis *adj (masc only)* half-man, half-beast; subhuman
sēmihōr·a -ae *f* half hour
sēmi·lacer -lacera -lacerum *adj* half-mangled
sēmilaut·us -a -um *adj* half-washed
sēmilīb·er -era -erum *adj* half-free
sēmilix·a -ae *f (pej) (of a commander)* sad sack, little more than a camp follower
sēmi·marīnus -marīna -marīnum *adj* half-submerged
sēmim·ās -aris *adj* half-male, gelded, castrated ‖ *m* hermaphrodite
sēmimortu·us -a -um *adj* half-dead
sēminār·ium -(i)ī *n* nursery garden; *(fig)* breeding ground
sēmināt·or -ōris *m* originator
sēmin·(ex) -ecis *adj* half-killed, half-dead
sēmin·ium -(i)ī *n* breeding; stock
sēmin·ō -āre *tr* to sow; to beget, procreate; to produce
sēminūd·us -a -um *adj* half-naked
sēmipāgān·us -ī *m* little clown
sēmiplēn·us -a -um *adj (forces)* at half-strength; *(ships)* half-manned
sēmiputāt·us -a -um *adj* half-pruned
Semīram·is -idis *f* famous queen of Assyria, builder of Babylon and consort and successor of King Ninus

Semīrami·us -a -um *adj* of Semiramis; Babylonian
sēmirās·us -a -um *adj* half-shaven
sēmireduct·us -a -um *adj* bent back halfway
sēmi·refectus -refecta -refectum *adj* half-repaired
sēm·is -issis *m* half; half an as *(small coin);* ½% per month *or* 6% per annum; non semissis homo worthless fellow
sēmisen·ex -is *m* elderly gent
sēmisepult·us -a -um *adj* half-buried
sēmisomn·is -is -e *or* sēmisomn·us -a -um *adj* half-asleep
sēmisupīn·us -a -um *adj* half-prone
sēmit·a -ae *f* path, lane, track
sēmitāl·is -is -e *adj* of byways, backroad
sēmitāri·us -a -um *adj* back-alley
sēm(i)ustilāt·us -a -um *adj* (-tul-) half-burned
sēmi·vir -virī *adj* half-man, half-beast; unmanned; unmanly ‖ *m* half-man; eunuch
sēmivīv·us -a -um *adj* half-alive, half-dead
sēmod·ius -iī *m* half a peck
sēmōt·us -a -um *adj* remote, distant; private, intimate ‖ *npl* faraway places
sē·moveō -movēre -mōvī -mōtus *tr* to separate, remove, exclude
semper *adv* always, ever
sempitern·us -a -um *adj* everlasting
Semprōnius *see* Gracchus
sēmunci·a -ae *f* half ounce *(one twenty-fourth of a Roman pound);* trifle
sēmunciāri·us -a -um *adj* half-ounce; faenus semunciarium interest at the rate of one twenty-fourth of the capital *(i.e., about 5% per annum)*
sēmust·us -a -um *adj* half-burned
senācul·um -ī *n* open-air meeting place of the Senate in the Forum
sēnāriol·us -ī *m (pros)* trifling trimeter
sēnāri·us -a -um *adj (pros)* six-foot *(verse)* ‖ *m (pros)* iambic trimeter
senāt·or -ōris *m* senator
senātōri·us -a -um *adj* senatorial; in the Senate; of a senator
senāt·us -ūs *m* Senate; Senate session; senatūs consultum *(also* senatus-consultum*)* decree of the Senate; senatum dare *(or* praebere*)* to grant an audience with the Senate; to give *(s.o.)* the floor
Senec·a -ae *m* Lucius Annaeus Seneca *(Stoic philosopher and instructor of Nero, 4 B.C.–A.D. 65)*
senect·us -a -um *adj* aged, old ‖ *f* old age, senility
senect·ūs -ūtis *f* old age; old person
sen·eō -ēre *intr* to be old
sen·escō -escĕre -uī *intr* to get old; to decline, become feeble, lose strength; to wane, draw to a close

sen·ex -is *adj* aged, old **II** *m* old man
sēn·ī -ae -a *adj* six each, in groups of six, six at a time; *(used in multiplication):* aspice bis senos cycnos! see those twelve swans!; seni deni sixteen each
senīl·is -is -e *adj* of old people, of an old man; aged; senile
sēni·ō -ōnis *m* a six *(on dice)*
seni·or -or (-us) *(comp of* senex*) adj* older, elder; more mature *(years)* **II** *m* elderly person, an elder *(over 45 years of age)*
sen·ium -iī *n* feebleness of age, decline, senility; decay; grief, trouble; gloom; crabbiness; old man
sens·a -ōrum *npl* thoughts, sentiments, ideas
sensī *perf of* sentio
sensicul·us -ī *m* petty aphorism
sensif·er -era -erum *adj* producing a sensation
sensil·is -is -e *adj* capable of sensation, sentient
sensim *adv* gropingly; tentatively; carefully; gradually, gently
sens·us -a -um *pp of* sentio **II** *npl see* sensa
sens·us -ūs *m* capacity for feeling, sensation; sense *(of hearing, etc.);* self-awareness, consciousness; awareness *(of conditions, situations);* feeling, emotion, sentiment; attitude, frame of mind; idea, thought; understanding, judgment, viewpoint; meaning, sense *(of a word);* intent, plan of action; self-contained expression, sentence; **communes sensūs** commonplaces, trite topics; **cum sensu** with taste; **sensus communis** civic pride, concern for the common good
sententi·a -ae *f* opinion, view, judgment; purpose, intention; *(in the Senate)* motion, proposal; meaning, sense; plan of action; sentence; maxim; *(leg)* verdict, sentence; **de sententiā** *(w. gen)* in accordance with the wishes of; **ex animi (mei) sententiā** *(in an oath)* to the best of (my) knowledge; **ex meā sententiā** in my opinion; to my liking; **in sententiam alicujus pedibus ire** to vote in favor of s.o.'s proposal *(literally, to go on foot to s.o.'s proposal);* **sententiam dicere** *(in the Senate)* to express a view; **sententia est** *(w. inf)* I intend to; **sententiam pronuntiare** *(or* dicere*)* to pronounce *or* give the verdict
sententiol·a -ae *f* phrase; maxim
sententiōsē *adv* sententiously, in moralizing style
sententiōs·us -a -um *adj* full of meaning, pregnant, sententious
senticēt·um -ī *n* thorny bush
sentīn·a -ae *f* bilge water; cesspool; bilge; *(fig)* dregs, scum, rabble
sen·tiō -tīre -sī -sus *tr* to perceive with the senses, feel, hear, see, smell; to realize;

to observe, notice; to experience; to think, judge **II** *intr (leg)* to vote, decide
sent·is -is *m* thorny bush, briar
sentisc·ō -ēre *tr* to begin to realize; to begin to observe, perceive
sent·us -a -um *adj* rough, rugged; untidy *(person)*
s(e)orsum *or* s(e)orsus *adv* apart, separately; *(w.* abl *or* ab*)* apart from
sēparābil·is -is -e *adj* separable
sēparātim *adv* apart, separately
sēparāti·ō -ōnis *f* severing, separation
sēparātius *adv* less closely, more widely
sēparāt·us -a -um *adj* separate, distinct, different
sēpar·ō -āre -āvī -ātus *tr* to separate, divide, part; to distinguish
sepelībil·is -is -e *adj* that may be buried
sepeliō sepelīre sepelīvī *or* sepeliī sepultus *tr* to bury; *(fig)* to overwhelm, ruin, destroy, suppress
sēpēs *see* saepes
sēpi·a -ae *f* (saep-) cuttlefish
sēpīment·um *see* saepimentum
sēpio *see* saepio
sēpiol·a -ae *f* little cuttle fish
sē·pōnō -pōnere -posuī -positus *tr* to set aside, drop, discard; to banish; to disregard, forget; to separate, pick out, select; to reserve; to remove, take away, exclude; to distinguish
sēposit·us -a -um *adj* remote, distant; select; distinct; private
seps sēpos *mf* snake
sēpse = *emphatic* sē
septem *indecl adj* seven
Septem·ber -bris -bre *adj* September, of September; **mensis September** September *(seventh month of the old Roman calendar until 153 B.C.)* **II Semptem·ber -bris** *m* September
septemdecim *indecl adj* (-ten-) seventeen
septemflu·us -a -um *adj* seven-mouthed *(Nile)*
septemgemin·us -a -um *adj* sevenfold
septempedāl·is -is -e *adj* seven-foot, seven-foot-high
septempl·ex -icis *adj* sevenfold
septemrēm·is -is -e *adj* having rowers arranged in sevens
septem·vir -virī *m* septemvir *(member of a board of seven, established in 44 B.C. to distribute land to veterans)* **II** *mpl* board of seven officials; **septemviri epulonum** college of priests responsible for sacred feasts
septemvirāl·is -is -e *adv* of the septemvirs, septemviral **II** *mpl* septemvirs
septemvirāt·us -ūs *m* office of the septemvirs
septemvirī *see* septemvir
septentri·ō -ōnis *m* the North; **ad** *or* **in septentrionem** to the north, northward

septentriōnāl·is -is -e *adj* (septem-) northern; Oceanus septentrionalis the North Sea ‖ *npl* northern regions, the North
septentriōn·ēs -um *mpl* (septem-) *(seven stars near the North Pole belonging to the Great Bear)* Great Bear; *(the seven stars of the Little Bear)* Little Bear; northern regions, the North; north wind
septēnār·ius -(i)ī *m (pros)* heptameter *(verse of seven feet)*
septendecim *indecl adj* (septem-) seventeen
septēn·ī -ae -a *adj* seven each, in groups of seven; septeni deni seventeen each, seventeen in a group
septentr- = septemtr-
septiens *or* **septiēs** *adv* seven times
septimān·us -a -um *adj* of *or* on the seventh ‖ *mpl* soldiers of the seventh legion
septimum *adv* for the seventh time
septim·us -a -um *adj* (-tum-) seventh
septim·us decim·us -a -um *adj* seventeenth
septingentēsim·us -a -um *adj* seven hundreth
septingent·ī -ae -a *adj* seven hundred
septuāgēsim·us -a -um *adj* seventieth
septuāgintā *indecl adj* seventy
septuenn·is -is -e *adj* seven-year-old
septum *see* **saeptum**
septun·x -cis *m* seven ounces; seven-twelfths
septus *pp of* sepio *(see* **saepio**)
sepulc(h)rāl·is -is -e *adj* of a tomb, sepulchral, funeral
sepulc(h)rēt·um -ī *n* grave, tomb
sepulc(h)r·um -ī *n* grave, tomb
sepultūr·a -ae *f* burial
sepultus *pp of* sepelio
Sēquan·us -a -um *adj* of the Sequani ‖ *mf* the Seine River ‖ *mpl* the Sequani *(a tribe of E. Gaul)*
sequ·ax -ācis *adj* following, pursuing; penetrating *(fumes);* eager
sequ·ens -entis *adj* next, following
seques·ter -tra -trum *(or* -ter -tris -tre) *adj* intermediate; negotiating; pace sequestrā under the protection of a truce ‖ *m* trustee *(with whom money or property is deposited);* agent, go-between ‖ *n* sequestro dare *(or* **ponere**) to put in trust
sequius *or* **secius** *(comp of* **secus**) *adv* less; worse, more unfavorably; differently, otherwise; nec eo secius nonetheless; nihilo *(or* nilo) sequius nevertheless
sequor sequī secūtus sum *tr* to follow; to escort, accompany, go with; to chase, pursue; to come after *(in time);* to go after, aim at; to head for ‖ *intr* to go after, follow, come next; *(of words)* to come naturally

Ser. *abbr* **Servius** *(Roman first name, praenomen)*
ser·a -ae *f* bolt, bar *(of door)*
Serāp·is -is *or* -**idis** *m* (Sar-) Egyptian god of healing
serēnit·ās -ātis *f* fair weather; serenity; favorableness
serēn·ō -āre -āvī -ātus *tr* to make fair, clear up, brighten
serēn·us -a -um *adj* clear, bright, fair; cloudless; cheerful, serene ‖ *n* clear sky, fair weather
Sēr·es -um *mpl* Chinese
seresc·ō -ēre *intr* to dry off
Sergi·us -(i)ī *m* Roman clan name *(nomen)* esp. Lucius Sergius Catilina *(praetor in 68 B.C. and leader of the conspiracy put down by Cicero in 63 B.C.)*
sēri·a -ae *f* large jar
sēri·a -ōrum *npl* serious matters, serious business
Sēric·us -a -um *adj* Chinese ‖ *npl* silks
seri·ēs -ēī *f* series, row, succession; train, sequence, order, connection; lineage
sēriō *adv* seriously, in all sincerity
sērius *adv* later; too late; serius ocius sooner or later
sēri·us -a -um *adj* serious, earnest ‖ *n* serious matter; seriousness, earnestness ‖ *npl see* **seria**
serm·ō -ōnis *m* conversation, talk; discussion, discourse; common talk, rumor, gossip; language; diction; prose, everyday language
sermōncin·or -ārī -ātus sum *intr* to talk, converse
sermuncul·us -ī *m* small talk
ser·ō -ēre -uī -tus *tr* to join, connect; to entwine, wreathe; to compose, combine, contrive
serō serĕre sēvī satus *tr* to sow, plant; *(fig)* to sow the seed of
sērō *adv (comp:* **sērius;** *superl:* **sērissimē)** late; too late
serp·ens -entis *mf (large)* snake, serpent, dragon ‖ **Serpens** *m (astr)* Draco *(constellation);* Serpens *(constellation, in the hand of Ophiuchus)*
serpentigen·a -ae *m* dragon offspring
serpentip·ēs -ĕdis *adj* dragon-footed
serperastr·um -ī *n* splint *(for straightening the crooked legs of children);* (mil) officer who keeps his soldiers in check
serpillum *see* **serpyllum**
serp·ō -ēre -sī *intr* to creep, crawl; to wind; to move along slowly, spread slowly
serpyll·um -ī *n* (-pill-, -pull-) wild thyme *(used for seasoning)*
serr·a -ae *f* saw
serrāc·um -ī *n* (sarr-) large wagon
serrāt·us -a -um *adj* serrated, toothed *(like a saw);* notched

serrul·a -ae f small saw
sert·a -ae f wreath
sert·a -ōrum npl wreathes; festoons
Sertōriān·ī -ōrum mpl partisans of Sertorius
Sertōr·ius -(i)ī m general of Marius, assassinated in Spain by Perperna (c. 122–72 B.C.)
sert·us -a -um pp of **sero** (to join) **II** f see **serta II** npl see **serta**
seruī perf of **sero** (to join)
ser·um -ī n whey (milk serum, the watery liquid separating from curds)
sēr·us -a -um adj late; too late; occurring at a late hour; advanced, far gone; **anni seri** ripe years; **ulmus sera** slow-growing elm **II** n late hour; **in serum rem trahere** to drag out the matter until late
serv·a -ae f slave (female)
servābil·is -is -e adj retrievable
serv·ans -antis adj keeping; (w. gen) observant of
servāt·or -ōris m, **servātr·ix -īcis** f savior, preserver, deliverer
servīl·is -is -e adj slave, servile
servīliter adv slavishly
serv·iō -īre -īvī or **-iī -ītum** intr to be a servant or slave; to be obedient; (of buildings, land) to be mortgaged; (w. dat) **1** to be a slave to, be subservient to; **2** to serve; **3** to comply with, conform to; **4** to humor; **5** to be devoted to; **6** to work at; **7** to serve, be of use to
servit·ium -(i)ī n slavery; slaves
servitūd·ō -inis f servitude, slavery
servit·ūs -ūtis f slavery; slaves; property liability, easement
Serv·ius Tull·ius -(i)ī m sixth king of Rome (credited with building the Servian Wall of tufa around Rome)
serv·ō -āre -āvī -ātus tr to watch over, preserve, protect; to store, preserve; to keep, retain; to serve; to keep to, continue to dwell in
servol·a -ae f (-ula) young slave girl
servolicol·a -ae f slave of a slave (female)
servol·us -ī m (-ulus) young slave
serv·us or **serv·os -a -um** adj slave, servant **II** mf slave, servant
sescēnār·is -is -e adj (sexc-) a year and a half old
sescēnāri·us -a -um adj six-hundred-man (cohort)
sescēn·ī -ae -a adj six hundred each, in groups of six hundred
sescentiens or **sescentiēs** adv (sexc-) six hundred times
sēsē see **se**
sesqui adv (-que) more by a half, one and a half times
sesqui- pref indicating that a quantity is multiplied by one and a half, e.g., **sesquihora** an hour and a half; with

ordinal numbers, it gives a number consisting of a unit and the fraction indicated by the numeral, e.g., **sesquitertius** one and a third times as big; **sesquioctavus** one and an eighth times as big
sesquialt·er -era -erum adj (sesque-) one and a half times
sesquihōr·a -ae f an hour and a half
sesquilībr·a -ae f one and a half pounds
sesquimod·ius -(i)ī m a peck and a half
sesquioctāv·us -a -um adj (sesque-) one and one-eighth times as big
sequiop·us -eris n (seque-) one and a half days' work
sequipedāl·is -is -e adj one and a half feet long (or high, wide, thick, square, etc.)
sesqui·pēs -pedis m distance or length of one and a half feet
sesquiplāg·a -ae f a stroke and a half
sesquipl·ex -icis adj one and a half times as much
sesquipl·us -a -um adj one and a half times as big **II** n one and a half times as much
sesquiterti·us -a -um adj (sesque-) one and a third times as big
sessibul·um -ī n seat, chair
sessil·is -is -e adj (of the back of a centaur) for sitting on; (of plants) low-growing
sessi·ō -ōnis f sitting; session; loafing
sessit·ō -āre -āvī -ātum intr to sit a lot, keep sitting, rest
sessiuncul·a -ae f small group (sitting down together for a discussion)
sess·or -ōris m spectator; resident
sessōr·ium -iī n sitting room
sestertium -ī n (coll) a mere 100,000 sesterces
sestert·ium -(i)ī n (or declined as gen pl) 100,000 sesterces
sestert·ius -iī (gen pl: **sestertium**) (abbr: HS) m sesterce (small silver coin, equal to about one-fourth of a denarius, i.e., about 25¢, and used as the ordinary Roman unit in accounting; sums below 2000 sesterces are expressed by a cardinal number, e.g., **ducenti sesterii**; sums from 2000 upwards are expressed by **milia sestertium** (or **sestertia**, with the distributives, or group-numbers (**bina, quinquagena**, etc.); sums of 1,000,000 and upwards are expressed by the numeral adverb in **-iens** (**-ies**) with **sestertium** (taken as a gen pl or declined as a neuter singular noun: **deciens** (i.e., **deciens centena milia**) **sestertium** = one million sesterces)
Sest·os or **Sest·us -ī** f city on the Hellespont
sēt- = saet-
Sēti·a -ae f town in Latium famous for its wine (modern Sezza)
Sētīn·us -a -um adj Setine **II** n Setine wine, wine from Setia

sētius *comp adv* (**sēc-**) later, more slowly; to a lesser degree, less readily; otherwise; nihilo setius just the same, nonetheless; **quo setius** *(w. subj)* so as to delay *or* prevent *(s.th. from happening):* **impedimento est Caepio quo setius lex feratur** Caepio is an impediment to having the law passed

seu *conj* or if; or; **seu...seu** whether...or

sevērē *adv* severely, sternly; seriously, in earnest; solemnly; **severe dicere** to speak plainly

sevērit·ās -ātis *f* severity, sternness; self-discipline; seriousness

sevēritūd·ō -inis *f* severity, sternness; seriousness *(of expression)*

sevēr·us -a -um *adj* severe, strict, austere; serious, grave; ruthless, grim; plain, unadorned *(style of writing, architecture)*

sēvī *perf of* **sero** (to plant)

sēvoc·ō -āre -āvī -ātus *tr* to call aside, call away; to remove, withdraw; to separate; to appropriate *(from the common fund)*

sēv·um -ī *n* tallow, grease, suet

Sex. *abbr* **Sextus** *(Roman first name, praenomen)*

sex *indecl adj* six

sexāgēnāri·us -a -um *adj* sixty-year-old

sexāgēn·ī -ae -a *adj* sixty each; sixty at a time; sixty

sexāgē(n)sim·us -a -um *adj* sixtieth

sexāgiens *or* **sexāgiēs** *adv* sixty times

sexāgintā *indecl adj* sixty

sexangul·us -a -um *adj* hexagonal

sexcēn- = sescen-

sexcēnāri·us -a -um *adj* six-hundred-man *(cohort)*

sexenn·is -is -e *adj* six-year-old; **sexenni die** in a six-year period

sexenn·ium -(i)ī *n* six-year period, six years

sexiens *or* **sexiēs** *adv* six times

sexprīm·ī *or* **sex prīm·ī -ōrum** *mpl* six-member council *(in provincial towns)*

sextadecimān·ī -ōrum *mpl* soldiers of the sixteenth legion

sext·ans -antis *m* one-sixth; small coin *(one-sixth of an* **as); one-sixth of a pint

sextār·ius -(i)ī *m* pint

Sextīl·is -is -e *adj* of Sixtilis *(the sixth month of the old Roman year, which began in March; Sextilis was afterwards called August in honor of Augustus)*

sextul·a -ae *f* sixth of an ounce

sextum *adv* for the sixth time

sext·us -a -um *adj* sixth

sext·us decim·us -a -um *adj* sixteenth

sex·us -ūs *m* sex; *(gram)* gender

sī *conj* if; **o sī** *(expressing a wish)* if only!; **si forte** if by any chance, in the hope that; **si maxime** however much; **si minus** if not; **si modo** provided that; **si vero** *(expressing scepticism)* if really

sibī *see* **se**

sībil·a -ōrum *npl* hisses, hissing

sībil·ō -āre -āvī -ātus *tr* to hiss at; to whistle at **‖** *intr* to hiss; to whistle

sībil·us -a -um *adj* hissing; whistling **‖** *m* & *n* hissing; whistling; rustling

Sibyll·a -ae *f* (**Sibu-**) sibyl *(esp. the sibyl at Cumae)*

Sibyllīn·us -a -um *adj* Sibylline

sīc *adv* thus, so, in this way; thus, as follows; in these circumstances; in such a way, to such a degree; *(in assent)* yes

Sicān·ī -ōrum *mpl* ancient people of Italy who migrated to Sicily

Sicāni·a -ae *f* Sicily

Sicān·is -idis *adj* Sicilian

Sicāni·us -a -um *adj* Sicilian **‖** *f* Sicily

Sicān·us -a -um *adj* Sicilian **‖** *mpl see* **Sicani**

sīcār·ius -(i)ī *m* murderer, assassin; **inter sicarios accusare (defendere)** to prosecute (defend) on a murder charge

siccē *adv* firmly; *(rhet)* plainly

siccit·ās -ātis *f* dryness; drought; firmness, solidity; plainness *(of style)*

sicc·ō -āre *tr* to dry, dry up; to drain; **cruores siccare** to stanch the blood

siccocul·us -a -um *adj* dry-eyed

sicc·us -a -um *adj* dry; thirsty; sober; firm, solid *(body);* solid *(argument);* dry, insipid *(style)*

Sicili·a -ae *f* Sicily

sicilicissit·ō -āre *intr* to act like a Sicilian

sīcīlicul·a -ae *f* sickle

Siciliens·is -is -e *adj* Sicilian

sīcine *adv* is this how...?

sīcubi *adv* if anywhere, wheresoever

sīcul·a -ae *f* little dagger; *(vulg)* penis

Sicul·ī -ōrum *mpl* ancient Italic people who migrated to Sicily; Sicilians

sīcunde *conj* if from some place

sīcut *or* **sīcutī** *conj* as, just as; *(in elliptical clauses)* just as, like; *(introducing a comparison)* as it were, so to speak; *(introducing an example)* as for instance; *(of condition)* as, in the same condition as; as if, just as if; **sicut...ita** although...yet

sīcutī *adv (archaic form of* **sicut)**

Sicy·ōn -ōnis *mf* town in the N. Peloponnesus

Sicyōni·us -a -um *adj* Sicyon **‖** *mpl* inhabitants of Sicyon

sīdere·us -a -um *adj* starry; star-spangled; heavenly, divine

sīdō sīdĕre sīdī *intr* to sit down; to settle; *(of birds)* to land; to sink; to settle down, subside; *(of ships)* to be grounded

Sīd·ōn -ōnis *f* city of Phoenicia

Sīdōn·is -idis *adj* Phoenician **‖** *f* Dido; Europa; Anna

Sīdōni·us -a -um *adj* Sidonian, Phoenician; Theban **‖** *mpl* Sidonians

sīd·us -eris *n* constellation; star, heavenly

body; sky, heaven; light, glory, beauty, pride; season; climate, weather; *(in astrology)* star, destiny

Sigambr·ī -ōrum *mpl* German tribe

Sīgē·um *or* **Sīgē·on -ī** *n* promontory near Troy

Sīgē(i)·us -a -um *adj* Sigean; Trojan

sigillār·ia -ium *or* **-iōrum** *npl* small objects of pottery stamped in relief with figures *or* ornamentation **‖** art market in Rome **‖** festival forming the final day of the Saturnalia

sigillāt·us -a -um *adj* adorned with little figures *or* patterns in relief

sigill·um -ī *n* statuette, figurine; stamped *or* embossed figure, a relief; figure woven in tapestry

sigm·a -atis *n* semicircular couch *(for reclining at table)*

signāt·or -ōris *m* sealer, signer; witness

signāt·us -a -um *adj* marked with a stamp, coined

signif·er -era -erum *adj* bearing the constellations, starry **‖** *m* standard-bearer; chief, leader

signific·ans -antis *adj* clear, distinct, expressive; significant, meaningful

significanter *adv* clearly, graphically; meaningfully, significantly

significāti·ō -ōnis *f* signal, indication, sign, mark; meaning, sense, signification; emphasis; expression of approval, applause

signific·ō -āre -āvī -ātus *tr* to show, indicate, express, point out; to intimate; to notify, publish; to portend; to mean, signify **‖** *intr* to make signs, indicate

Signīn·us -a -um *adj* of *or* from Signia *(town in Latium, modern Segni, famous for its astringent variety of wine);* **opus Signinum** waterproof plaster

signipot·ens -entis *adj* ruling over the constellations

sign·ō -āre -āvī -ātus *tr* to mark, stamp, impress, imprint; to seal, seal up; to coin; to signify, indicate, express; to adorn; to distinguish, note

sign·um -ī *n* sign; indication, proof; military standard, banner; password; cohort, maniple; omen; symptom; shop sign; statue; a figure *(in a relief, picture, or embroidery);* device on a seal, seal; heavenly sign, constellation; **ab signis discedere** to break ranks, disband; **signa conferre** to engage in close combat; **signa constituere** to concentrate troops; **signa constituere** to halt; **signa conversa ferre** to wheel around and attack; **signa ferre** to break camp; **signa movere in hostem** to advance against the enemy; **signa proferre** to march forward; **signa servare** to keep the order of battle; **signa sequi** to march in rank; **signa subsequi** to keep the or-

der of battle; **signa transferre** to desert, join the other side; **signis collatis** in regular battle formation

sīlān·us -ī *m* waterspout *(originally designed as a head of Silenus)*

Silar·us -ī *m* **(Siler-)** Sele River *(forming the boundary between Lucania and Campania and flowing by the town of Paestum)*

sil·ens -entis *adj* silent, calm, quiet **‖** *mpl* the dead

silent·ium -(i)ī *n* silence; inactivity; **silentium facere** to obtain silence; to keep silent; **silentium significare** to call for silence

Sīlēn·us -ī *m* teacher and companion of Bacchus, usually drunk; a Silenus *(woodspirit)*

sil·eō -ēre -uī *tr* to leave unmentioned, say nothing about **‖** *intr* to be silent, be still; to keep silent; to be hushed; to rest, cease

sil·er -eris *n* willow

silesc·ō -ĕre *intr* to become silent, fall silent, become hushed

sil·ex -icis *mf* flint stone, lava stone *(used in road paving and other construction);* cliff, crag; *(fig)* hardheartedness

silicern·ium -(i)ī *n* funeral meal; *(coll)* old fossil

silīg·ō -inis *f* winter wheat; wheat flour

siliqu·a -ae *f* pod, husk **‖** *fpl* pulse *(the edible seeds of certain leguminous plants, as lentils, peas)*

sillyb·us -ī *m* label *(giving the title of the scroll)*

sīl·ō -ōnis *m* snub nose

silua *see* **silva**

siluī *perf of* **sileo**

silūr·us -ī *m* European catfish

sīl·us -a -um *adj* snub-nosed

silv·a *or* **silŭ·a -ae** *f* woods, forest; shrubbery, bush, foliage, crop, growth; mass, quantity; material, supply

Silvān·us -ī *m* god of woods **‖** *mpl* woodland gods

silvesc·ō -ĕre *intr (of a vine)* to run wild

silvestr·is -is -e *adj* wooded, overgrown with woods; woodland, living in the woods; wild, growing wild; rural, pastoral **‖** *npl* woodlands

silvicol·a -ae *mf* denizen of the forest

silvicultr·ix -īcis *adj (fem only)* living in the woods

silvifrag·us -a -um *adj (of the wind)* forest-smashing

silvōs·us -a -um *adj* wooded, woody

sīmi·a -ae *f* ape

simil·is -is -e *adj* similar; *(w. gen, mostly of persons, or dat, mostly of things)* similar to, resembling, like; **homines inter se similes** people resembling one another; **veri similis** probable, realistic **‖** *n* comparison, parallel

similiter *adv* similarly; **similiter atque** *(or* ac) just as; **similiter ut si** just as if
similitūd·ō -inis *f* likeness, resemblance; imitation; analogy; comparison, simile; monotony; *(w. gen or dat)* similarity to; **est homini cum deo similitudo** there is a resemblance between man and a god
sīmiol·us -ī *m* little monkey
simītū *adv* at the same time; *(w.* cum + abl) together with
sīm·ius -iī *m* monkey, ape
Simo·īs -entis *m* stream at Troy
Simōnid·ēs -is *m* lyric poet of the Greek island of Ceos *(E 500 b.c.)* ‖ iambic poet of the Greek island of Amorgos *(7th cent. b.c.)*
simpl·ex -icis *adj* single, simple; unmixed; plain, natural; frank; naive; in single file
simplicit·ās -ātis *f* simplicity; candor, frankness
simpliciter *adv* simply, plainly, frankly, candidly
simpul·um -ī *n* small ladle
simpu(v)·ium -(i)ī *n* libation bowl
simul *adv* together, at the same time; likewise; *(w. abl or* cum) together with; **simul atque** *(or* ac *or* et) as soon as; **simul...simul** both...and ‖ *conj* as soon as
simulācr·um -ī *n* image, likeness, representation; form, shape, phantom, ghost; conception; sign, emblem; mere shadow; portraiture, characterization
simulām·en -inis *n* imitation, copy
simul·ans -antis *adj* imitating; *(w. gen)* imitative of, able to imitate
simulātē *adv* insincerely, deceitfully
simulāti·ō -ōnis *f* faking, bluffing, bluff, pretense; **simulatione** *(w. gen)* under the pretense of
simulāt·or -ōris *m* imitator; pretender, phoney
simul·ō -āre -āvī -ātus *tr* (simil-) to imitate, copy; to represent; to put on the appearance of, simulate
simult·ās -ātis *f* enmity, rivalry, feud; jealousy; grudge
sīmul·us -a -um *adj* rather snub-nosed
sīm·us -a -um *adj* snub-nosed
sīn *conj* if however, if on the other hand, but if
sināp·i *or* **sināp·e -is** *n,* **sināp·is -is** *f* (white) mustard
sincērē *adv* sincerely, honestly
sincērit·ās -ātis *f (physical)* soundness; purity; sincerity, integrity
sincēr·us -a -um *adj* sound, whole, clean; untainted; sincere, real, genuine
sincip·ut -itis *or* **sincipitāment·um -ī** *n* half a head *(as food);* cheek, jowl *(of a hog);* brain
sind·ōn -ōnis *f* fine cotton *or* linen fabric, muslin

sine *prep (w. abl)* without
singillātim *or* **singulātim** *adv* singly
singlāriter *see* singulariter
singulār·is -is -e *adj* single, alone, one at a time; specific, peculiar, special; individual; unique ‖ *mpl* crack troops
sing(u)lāriter *adv* singly; particularly
singulāri·us -a -um *adj* single, separate; unique
singulātim *adv* singly, individually
singul·ī -ae -a *adj* single, one at a time, individual; one each, one apiece; **in singulos dies** on each successive day; every day, daily *(w. comp or words denoting increase or decrease):* **crescit in dies singulos hostium numerus** the number of the enemy increases daily; **in singulos homines** per man ‖ *mpl* individuals
singultim *adv* sobbingly, with sobs
singult·iō -īre *intr* to hiccup; to throb
singult·ō -āre -āvī -ātus *tr* to gasp out; to utter with sobs ‖ *intr* to gasp, sob
singult·us -ūs *m* sob, gasp; squirt *(of water, etc.);* death rattle
singul·ī -ae -a *adj* one by one, single; each one, one apiece
sinis·ter -tra -trum *adj* left, on the left; *(because in Roman augury the augur faced south, having the East on the left)* favorable, auspicious, lucky; *(because in Greek augury the augur faced north, having the East on his right)* unfavorable, inauspicious, unlucky; wrong, perverse, improper ‖ *mpl* soldiers on the left flank ‖ *f* left, left hand; left side; **a sinistrā** on the left ‖ *n* left side
sinisterit·ās -ātis *f* awkwardness
sinistrē *adv* badly, wrongly
sinistr(ō)rsum *or* **sinistrō(r)sus** *adv* to the left
sinō sinĕre sīvī *or* **siī situs** *tr* to allow; **sine modo** only let, if only
Sin·ōn -ōnis *m* Greek soldier who talked the Trojans into dragging the wooden horse into Troy
Sinōp·a -ae *or* **Sinōp·ē -ēs** *f* Sinope *(Greek colony on the S. coast of the Euxine or Black Sea)*
Sinuess·a -ae *f* (Sino-) city near the border between Latium and Campania
sīn·um -ī *n* large drinking cup
sinu·ō -āre -āvī -ātus *tr* to wind, curve; to fill out *(sails)*
sinuōs·us -a -um *adj* winding, sinuous, serpentine
sīn·us -ī *m* large drinking cup
sin·us -ūs *m* indentation, curve, fold, hollow; fold of the toga about the breast, pocket, purse; breast, bosom, lap; bay, gulf, lagoon; winding coast; valley, hollow; heart *(e.g., of a city),* interior; intimacy; **in sinu meo est** he/she is dear to me

sīpar·ium -(i)ī n (theat) curtain; **post siparium** behind the scenes

sīp(h)·ō -ōnis m siphon; fire engine

sīphuncul·us -ī m small pipe

Sipyl·us or **Sipyl·os -ī** m mountain in Lydia on which Niobe was changed into a rock

sīquandō or **si quandō** conj if ever

sīquidem conj if in fact

siremps or **sirempse = si rem ipsam** adj the same; **sirempse legem ussit esse Jupiter** Jupiter ordered the law to be the same

Sīr·ēn -ēnis f Siren (sea nymph that had the power of charming sailors to their death with her song)

Sīri·us -a -um adj of Sirius, of the Dog Star ‖ m Sirius, Dog Star (in the constellation Canis Major)

sirp·e -is n (bot) silphium (from which gum was extracted)

sīr·us -ī m underground silo

sīs = sī vīs please, if you please

sistō sistĕre stitī or **stetī** status tr to cause to stand, make stand, put, place, set; to set up (monument); to establish; to stop, check, arrest; to put an end to; to produce in court; **pedem** (or **gradum**) **sistere** to halt, stop; **vadimonium sistere** to answer bail, show up in court ‖ refl to present oneself, appear, come ‖ pass **sisti non potest** the crisis cannot be met, the case is hopeless ‖ intr to stand, rest; to stop, stay; to stand firm, last, endure; to show up in court; (w. dat or contra + acc) to stand firm against

sistrāt·us -a -um adj with a tambourine

sistr·um -ī n tambourine, rattle

Sīsyphid·ēs -ae m descendant of Sisyphus, Ulysses

Sisyphi·us -a -um adj of Sisyphus; **sanguine cretus Sisyphio** born of the stock of Sisyphys (i.e., Ulysses)

Sīsyph·us or **Sīsyph·os -ī** m Sisyphus (son of Aeolus, king of Corinth, whose punishment in Hades was to roll a rock repeatedly up a hill)

sitell·a -ae f lottery urn

Sīth·ōn -onis adj Thracian

Sīthon·is -idis or **-idos** or **Sīthoni·us -a -um** adj Thracian ‖ mpl Thracians

sitīculōs·us -a -um adj thirsty

siti·ens -entis adj thirsting, thirsty; arid, parched; parching; (w. gen) thirsting for, eager for

sitienter adv thirstily, eagerly

sit·iō -īre tr to thirst for ‖ intr to be thirsty

sit·is -is f thirst; (w. gen) thirst for

sitīt·or -ōris m thirsty person; **sititor aquae** thirster for water

sittybus see **sillybus**

situl·a -ae f bucket; basin, urn

sit·us -a -um pp of **sino** ‖ adj situated, located, lying; founded; (w. **in** + abl) resting on, dependent on

sit·us -ūs m position, situation, site; structure; neglect; mustiness; dust, dirt; idleness, inactivity, lack of use

sīve or **seu** conj or if; or; **sive...sive** whether...or

sīvī perf of **sino**

smaragd·us or **smaragd·os -ī** f (m) emerald

smar·is -idis f a small sea fish

smīl·ax -acis adj (bot) smilax (an evergreen climbing plant)

Sminth·eūs -eī m epithet of Apollo

Smyrn·a -ae f town on W. coast of Asia Minor

sobol- = subol-

sōbriē adv soberly, moderately; sensibly

sōbriet·ās -ātis f sobriety

sobrīn·a -ae f cousin (female, on the mother's side)

sobrīn·us -ī m cousin (on the mother's side)

sōbri·us -a -um adj sober; temperate; sensible, reasonable

soccul·us -ī m small slipper

socc·us -ī m slipper; low shoe (worn by actors in comedy); (fig) comedy

soc·er or **soc·erus -erī** m father-in-law

soci·a -ae f associate, companion, ally, partner (female)

sociābil·is -is -e adj compatible, intimate

sociāl·is -is -e adj allied, confederate; nuptial, conjugal; sociable

sociāliter adv sociably

socienn·us -ī m buddy; partner

societ·ās -ātis f companionship, fellowship; association, society; partnership; alliance, confederacy

soci·ō -āre -āvī -ātus tr to unite, associate; to share

sociofraud·us -ī m double-crosser, heel

soci·us -a -um adj joint, allied, confederate; held in common, common ‖ m associate, companion, ally, partner ‖ f see **socia**

socordi·a -ae f silliness, stupidity; apathy, laziness

socordius adv too apathetically

soc·ors -ordis adj silly, stupid; apathetic, lazy, inactive

Sōcrat·es -is m Athenian philosopher (469– 399 B.C.)

Sōcrátic·ī -ōrum mpl Socratics

socr·us -ūs f mother-in-law

sodālici·us -a -um adj of companionship ‖ n companionship, intimacy; society, secret society

sodāl·is -is m companion, fellow, buddy, crony; member (of a society, priestly college, etc.); accomplice; **sodālis Augustalis** member of a fraternity associated with the cult of Augustus

sodālit·ās -ātis f companionship, fellowship; society, club, association; secret society

sodālit- = **sodalic-**

sōdēs = **si audes** if you will, please

sōl sōlis m sun; sunlight, sunshine; day

sōlāciol·um -ī n a bit of comfort

sōlāc·ium -(i)ī n (sōlāt-) comfort, relief

sōlām·en -inis n comfort

sōlār·is -is -e adj sun-; **lumen solare** sunlight, sunshine

sōlār·ium -(i)ī n sundial; clock; sunny spot, balcony

sōlāt- = **solac-**

sōlāt·or -ōris m comforter

solduri·ī -ōrum mpl retainers (of a chieftain)

soldus see **solidus**

sole·a -ae f sole; sandal (with toes exposed; cf. **sandalium**); fetter; sole (flatfish)

soleār·ius -(i)ī m sandal-maker

soleāt·us -a -um adj wearing sandals

soleō solēre solitus sum intr (w. inf) to be in the habit of, be used to; usually: e.g., **solet cenare sero** he usually eats late; (w. cum + abl) to have sex with

solidē adv solidly; thoroughly, downright; firmly

solidit·ās -ātis f solidity

solid·ō -āre -āvī -ātus tr to make firm; to make dense; to strengthen

sol(i)d·us -a -um adj solid, firm, dense; whole, entire; genuine; trustworthy; resolute ‖ n entire sum, total; a solid; mass, substance; solid earth

sōliferre·um -ī n all-iron spear

sōlistim·us -a -um adj (-umus) perfect; **tripudium solistimum** perfectly auspicious omen

sōlitāri·us -a -um adj solitary, lonely

sōlitūd·ō -inis f loneliness; deprivation; solitude; wilderness; (w. gen) state of being forsaken by ‖ fpl desert, wilderness

solit·us -a -um adj usual, customary, characteristic ‖ n the usual, the customary; **formosior solito** more handsome than usual; **magis** (or **plus**) **solito** more than usual

sol·ium -(i)ī n seat, chair; throne; dominion, sway; bathtub; stone coffin

sōlivag·us -a -um adj roaming alone; single, solitary

sollemn·is -is -e adj annual, periodic; solemn, religious; usual ‖ n usage, practice; solemn rite, solemnity, ceremony; feast; sacrifice; festival, games (in honor of Roman holy days)

sollemniter adv solemnly, religiously

soll·ers -ertis adj (sōl-) skilled, skillful, expert, clever

sollerti·a -ae f (sōl-) skill, shrewdness; clever plan; (w. gen) skill in

sollicitāti·ō -ōnis f vexation; anxiety; incitement, instigation

sollicitē adv anxiously, with solicitude; diligently

sollicit·ō -āre -āvī -ātus tr to shake, disturb; to disquiet, annoy, molest; to worry, make anxious; to provoke, tempt; to stir up, incite to revolt

sollicitūd·ō -inis f anxiety, uneasiness; worry; solicitude; (w. gen) anxiety over

sollicit·us -a -um adj stirred up, stormy (sea); tossed (by the waves); troubled, disturbed, restless; solicitous, anxious, worried; incited to revolt

sollif- = **solif-**

sollist- = **solist-**

soloecism·us -ī m mistake in grammar, solecism

Sol·ō(n) -ōnis m Solon (famous Athenian legislator c. 640–560 B.C.)

sōl·or -ārī -ātus sum tr to console; to relieve, mitigate (fear, etc.)

sōlstiāl·is -is -e adj of the summer solstice; midsummer's; solar

sōlstit·ium -(i)ī n summer solstice, midsummer, summer heat

sol·um -ī n bottom, ground, floor; soil, land, country; sole (of foot, shoe)

sōlum adv only, merely, barely; **non solum...sed etiam** not only...but also

sōl·us -a -um adj only, single, sole, alone; lonely, solitary

solūtē adv loosely, freely, without hindrance; negligently; without vigor

solūti·ō -ōnis f loosening; payment

solūt·us -a -um adj loose, untied, unbandaged; negligent; free; fluent; unrhythmical; uncontrolled; exempt, free; unbiased; unbridled

sol·vō -věre -vī -uī -ūtus tr to loosen, untie (a cord); to release; to dissolve, break up; to detach, disengage; to unlock, open; to melt; to relax (the body); to smooth, soothe; to impair, weaken, destroy; to acquit; to accomplish, fulfill; to pay, pay off; to solve, explain; to break (a siege); to break down (a barrier); to undergo (punishment); to get rid of (feelings); to loosen (the bowels); to remove (surgical dressings); to unharness, unyoke (animals); to disperse into the atmosphere, dissipate; to enervate, sap the strength of (a person); **crines solvere** to let down the hair (in mourning); **navem** (or **ratem**) **solvere** to cast off, set sail; **ora solvere** to open the mouth (to speak) ‖ intr to weigh anchor, set sail

Solym·a -ōrum npl Jerusalem

Solym·us -a -um adj of Jerusalem ‖ mpl mountain tribe, supposed to have given its name to Jerusalem

somniculōsē adv sleepily, drowsily

somniculōs·us -a -um *adj* sleepy, drowsy
somnif·er -era -erum *adj* soporific, sleep-inducing; deadly *(poison)*
somni·ō -āre -āvī -ātus *tr* to dream of; to day-dream about, imagine; **somnium somniare** to have a dream **ǁ** *intr* to dream; to daydream
somn·ium -(i)ī *n* dream, vision; day-dreaming
somn·us -ī *m* sleep; night; sleep of death; indolence
sonābil·is -is -e *adj* noisy
sonip·ēs -ĕdis *adj* loud-hoofed **ǁ** *m* steed
sonit·us -ūs *m* sound, noise, clang
sonivi·us -a -um *adj* noisy
son·ō -āre -uī -itus *tr* to utter, say sound, express; to denote, mean; to sound like **ǁ** *intr* to sound; to ring, resound, make a noise; to be spoken of as
son·or -ōris *m* sound, noise, clang
sonōr·us -a -um *adj* sonorous, loud, noisy, clanging
sons sontis *adj* guilty, criminal; *(w. abl of the crime)* guilty of **ǁ** *m* guilty one, criminal
sontic·us -a -um *adj* serious, critical
sonuī *perf of* **sono**
son·us -a -um *adjl suf* denotes *"sounding"*, e.g.: **raucisonus** hoarse-sounding
son·us -ī *m* sound, noise; tone
sophi·a -ae *f* wisdom
sophist·ēs *or* **sophist·a -ae** *m* sophist
Sophocl·ēs -is *or* **-ī** Greek writer of tragedies *(c. 495–406 B.C.)*
Sophoclē·us -a -um *adj* Sophoclean
soph·us -a -um *adj* wise **ǁ** *m* wise man, sage
sōp·iō -īre -īvī *or* **-iī -ītus** *tr* to put to sleep; to stun, knock unconscious; *(fig)* to calm, settle, lull
sop·or -ōris *m* deep sleep; stupor; apathy; sleeping potion
sopōrāt·us -a -um *adj* stupefied; unconscious; buried in sleep; allayed *(grief)*; soporific
sopōrif·er -era -erum *adj* sleep-inducing
sopōr·us -a -um *adj* drowsy
Sōract·e -is *n* mountain in Etruria about 25 miles N.E. of Rome
sōrac·um -ī *n* box, carton
sorb·eō -ēre -uī -itus *tr* to suck in, gulp down; to absorb; *(fig)* to swallow
sorbil(l)·ō -āre -āvī -ātus *tr* to sip
sorbilō *adv* drop by drop, bit by bit
sorbiti·ō -ōnis *f* broth
sorb·um -ī *n* (sorv-) Juneberry
sorb·us -ī *f* (sorv-) Juneberry tree
sord·eō -ēre *intr* to be dirty, be shabby; to appear worthless
sord·ēs -is *f* dirt, filth; shabbiness, squalor; greed, stinginess; moral turpitude; meanness *(of behavior)*; low rank, low condition; rabble, scum; **sordes ver-**

borum vulgarity **ǁ** *fpl* rags, dark clothes *(often worn as a sign of mourning)*
sord·escō -escĕre -uī *intr* to become dirty, become soiled
sordidāt·us -a -um *adj* in shabby clothes *(esp. as sign of mourning)*
sordidē *adv* vilely; greedily
sordidul·us -a -um *adj* rather soiled, rather shabby; *(fig)* low
sordid·us -a -um *adj* dirty, filthy; shabby; soiled, stained; dressed in mourning clothes; low *(rank)*; vulgar
sorditūd·ō -inis *f* dirt, filth
sōr·ex -icis *m* shrewmouse
sōricīn·us -a -um *adj* squealing like mice
sōrīt·ēs -ae *m* sorites *(logical conclusion drawn from cumulative arguments)*
sor·or -ōris *f* sister; cousin; companion, playmate; **sorores doctae** Muses; **sorores tres** three Fates; **sorores tristes** gloomy Fates
sorōricīd·a -ae *m* murderer of a sister
sorōri·us -a -um *adj* sister's, of a sister; sisterly; **stuprum sororium** incest with a sister
sors sortis *f* lot; casting of lots, decision by lot; prophecy; fate, destiny, lot in life; portion, share; sort, kind
sorsum *see* **seorsum**
sortileg·us -a -um *adj* prophetic **ǁ** *m* soothsayer, fortuneteller
sort·iō -īre -īvī *or* **-iī -ītus** *or* **sort·ior -īrī -ītus sum** *tr* to cast lots for; to allot, assign by lot, appoint by lot; to obtain by lot; to choose, select; to share, divide; to receive, get by chance **ǁ** *intr* to cast *or* draw lots
sortīti·ō -ōnis *f* drawing lots, determining by lots
sortītō *adv* by lot; by fate
sortīt·us -ūs *m* lottery
Sosi·ī -ōrum *mpl* the Sosii *(two brothers famous as booksellers in Rome at the time of Horace)*
sosp·es -itis *adj* safe and sound; auspicious, lucky
sospit·a -ae *f* preserver *(epithet of Juno)*
sospitāl·is -is -e *adj* beneficial
sospit·ō -āre *tr* to preserve, protect
Sōt·ēr -ēris *m* savior, protector
Sōtēri·a -ōrum *npl* party for a person recovering from an illness
Sp. *abbr* **Spurius** *(Roman first name, praenomen)*
spād·ix -icis *m* chestnut-brown horse
spad·ō -ōnis *m* eunuch
spar·gō -gĕre -sī -sus *tr* to scatter, sprinkle, strew; to disperse; to disseminate; to spot, dapple
sparsi·ō -ōnis *f* sprinkling
spars·us -a -um *pp of* **spargo ǁ** *adj* freckled, spotty
Spart·a -ae *or* **Spart·ē -ēs** *f* Sparta *(capital of Laconia)*

Spartac·us -ī *m* Thracian gladiator who led a revolt of gladiators against Rome in 73–71 B.C.

Spartān·us -a -um *adj* Spartan

Spartiāt·ēs -ae *m* Spartan

Spartiātic·us *or* **Spartic·us -a -um** *adj* Spartan

spart·um *or* **spart·on -ī** *n* Spanish broom *(fibrous plant used in making ropes, nets, etc.)*

sparul·us -ī *m* bream *(fish)*

spar·us *m or* **spar·um -ī** *n* hunting spear

spath·a -ae *f* broad two-edged sword

spati·or -ārī -ātus sum *intr* to stroll, take a walk; to walk solemnly; to spread out

spatiōsē *adv* extensively; long

spatiōs·us -a -um *adj* extensive; spacious; wide; *(of time)* long, lengthy; *(of vowel)* long; *(w. advl force)* with its *(his, etc.)* great size

spat·ium -(i)ī *n* space, room, extent; open space, public square; distance *(between two points);* walk, promenade *(place);* lap *(of a race);* racetrack; interval, period; time, opportunity; *(pros)* measure, quantity

speci·ēs -ēī *f* sight, view; outward appearance; outline, shape; fine appearance, beauty; deceptive appearance, show, semblance, pretense, pretext; resemblance; display, splendor; apparition; image, statue; idea, notion; reputation; species, sort; *(leg)* specific legal situation *or* case; **ad** *(or* **in) speciem** for show; **in speciem** *(or* **per speciem)** as a pretext, for the sake of appearances; **prīmā specie** at first sight; **specie** outwardly, to all appearances; **specie** *(w. gen)* **1** in the guise of; **2** on the pretext of

specill·um -ī *n* probe *(surgical instrument)*

specim·en -inis *n* mark, sign, proof; example; model, ideal

speciō specĕre spexī spectus *tr* to look at

speciōsē *adv* splendidly

speciōs·us -a -um *adj* handsome, good-looking, beautiful; plausible; specious

spectābil·is -is -e *adj* visible; remarkable

spectāc(u)l·um -ī *n* sight, spectacle; public performance, show; stage play; theater

spectām·en -inis *n* sign, proof

spectāti·ō -ōnis *f* observation, view; examining, testing

spectāt·or -ōris *m* observer; spectator; critic, judge **‖** *mpl* audience

spectātr·ix -īcis *f* onlooker, observer; spectator *(female)*

spectāt·us -a -um *adj* tried, tested, proved; esteemed, distinguished

specti·ō -ōnis *f* observing the auspices; right to take the auspices

spect·ō -āre -āvī -ātus *tr* to observe, watch; to face in the direction of; to consider; to

bear in mind; to aim at, tend towards; to examine, test

spectr·um -ī *n* specter, apparition

specul·a -ae *f* lookout, watchtower; summit; **in speculis** on the lookout

speculābund·us -a -um *adj* on the lookout

speculār·is -is -e *adj* transparent **‖** *n* windowpane *(of mica),* window

speculāt·or -ōris *m* spy; explorer

speculātōri·us -a -um *adj* for spying, for reconnaissance **‖** *f* reconnaissance ship

speculātr·ix -īcis *f* spy *(female)*

specul·or -ārī -ātus sum *tr* to reconnoiter, observe, watch for

specul·um -ī *n* mirror *(made of polished metal)*

spec·us -ūs *m (n)* cave, cavern; *(any artificial excavation)* hole, pit, tunnel, ditch; cavity *(of a wound, etc.)*

spēlae·um -ī *n* (-lē-) den, cave

spēlunc·a -ae *f* cave

spērābil·is -is -e *adj* to be hoped for

spērāt·us -a -um *adj* hoped for, desired **‖** *f* fiancée

Sperchē·is -idos *adj (fem only)* of the Spercheus River

Sperchē·us -ī *m* **(-chi-)** Spercheus *(large river in Thessaly)*

spernō spernĕre sprēvī sprētus *tr* to spurn, scorn, reject; to speak disdainfully of; to separate, dissociate

spēr·ō -āre -āvī -ātus *tr* to hope for, expect, look forward to; to trust, trust in; to anticipate, await in fear; *(w. acc & inf; also w. nom & inf in imitation of the Greek; also w. ut + subj)* I hope that; **id quod nōn sperō** I hope that is not the case, I hope not **‖** *intr* to hope; **bene sperāre** to be optimistic; **nōn sperō** I hope not

spēs speī *f* hope; expectation; anticipation, apprehension *(of evil);* person *or* thing on which hopes are based, *e.g.:* **Gaius Marius spes subsidium patriae** Gaius Marius, the hope and safeguard of our country; *(applied to one's offspring)* one's hopes for the future, *e.g.:* **mea carissima filiola et spes reliqua nostra** my dearest little daughter and our only remaining hope; **in spe** in prospect; **in spe** *(w. gen)* with the prospect of; **in spem** *(w. gen)* so as to give the promise of; **praeter spem** beyond all expectation

sp(h)aer·a -ae *f* sphere, globe; ball; one of the imaginary spheres in which the heavenly bodies were supposed to travel around the earth; working model of the universe

sphaeristēr·ium -iī *n* ball field, ball court

Sphin·x -gis *or* **-gos** *f* sphinx *(esp. the Sphinx of Boeotia whose riddle Oedipus was able to solve);* the Sphinx of Egypt at Giza

spīc·a -ae *f* point; ear *(of grain);* tuft, top, head *(of plants)*
spīce·us -a -um *adj* made of ears of grain
spīcul·um -ī *n* point; sting; dart, arrow
spīc·um -ī *n* ear *(of grain)*
spīn·a -ae *f* thorn; thornbush; prickle *(of animals);* spike *(of asparagus);* backbone, spine; *(fig)* thorny question
spīnēt·um -ī *n* thorn hedge, thorny thicket
spīne·us -a -um *adj* made of thorns
spīnif·er *or* spīnig·er -era -erum *adj* prickly, thorny
spīnōs·us -a -um *adj* thorny, prickly; *(fig)* thorny, difficult; obscure *(style)*
spint·ēr -ēris *m* bracelet
Spinth·ēr -ēris *m* Roman family name *(cognomen)*
spintri·a -ae *m* male prostitute *(given to particularly perverted acts)*
spinturnīc·ium -iī *n* bird of ill omen
spīn·us -ī *or* -ūs *f* thornbush
spīr·a -ae *f* coil *(of serpent);* chin strap
spīrābil·is -is -e *adj* good to breathe, life-giving *(air)*
spīrācul·um -ī *n* pore; vent
spīrāment·um -ī *n* vent; air hole; windpipe; breathing space, pause; **animae spiramenta** lungs
spīrit·us -ūs *m* breathing, breath; breeze, wind; air, air current; wind of the bowels; breath of life, life; inspiration; spirit, soul; character, courage; enthusiasm, vigor; pride, arrogance; morale; *(gram)* aspiration; **extremus** *(or* **ultimus) spiritus** one's last breath; **spiritum ducere** to take a breath
spīr·ō -āre -āvī -ātus *tr* to breathe, blow; to exhale; to give off the odor of, smell of; to aspire to, aim at **‖** *intr* to breathe; to be alive; to breathe after exertion, recover one's breath; *(of the wind)* to blow, blow auspiciously, be favorable; *(of things)* to give off an odor; *(of a quality)* to emanate; to have poetic inspiration
spissāment·um -ī *n* stopper, plug
spissāt·us -a -um *adj* condensed, concentrated
spissē *adv* thickly, closely, tightly; with effort, slowly
spissesc·ō -ēre *intr* to condense, become thick, become more compact
spissigrad·us -a -um *adj* slow-paced
spiss·ō -āre -āvī -ātus *tr* to condense, concentrate; to pack tightly; to intensify *(efforts)*
spiss·us -a -um *adj* thick; tight; dense; solid, compact; slow, sluggish; late; closely-woven, thick; packed, crowded; *(of blows, kisses)* coming thick and fast
splēn splēnis *m* spleen
splend·eō -ēre *intr* to be clear and bright; to shine, gleam; to become glossy; to be

illustrious, be glorious; to be resplendent
splendesc·ō -ēre *intr* to become bright, begin to shine; *(w. abl)* to take on luster from
splendidē *adv* splendidly, brilliantly
splendid·us -a -um *adj* clear and bright, gleaming, glistening, sparkling; spotless, noble *(character);* splendid; sumptuous; showy; illustrious
splend·or -ōris *m* splendor; brightness, brilliance; clearness
splēniāt·us -a -um *adj* wearing a patch
splēn·ium -iī *n* patch
spoliāti·ō -ōnis *f* stripping, plundering; unjust deprivation *(of honor, dignity);* ousting *(from office)*
spoliāt·or -ōris *m*, spoliātr·ix -īcis *f* despoiler, robber
spoliāt·us -a -um *adj* stripped, robbed
spoli·ō -āre -āvī -ātus *tr* to strip; to pillage, plunder, rob; to take away *(possessions)*
spol·ium -iī *n* hide, skin; spoils, booty, loot **‖** *npl* arms, equipment, etc., stripped from an enemy; **spolia opima** the spoils taken by a Roman general from the enemy leader he had killed in single combat; **spolia secunda** lesser spoils
spond·a -ae *f* bedframe, sofa frame; bed, sofa
spondā(u)l·ium -(i)ī *n* ritual hymn accompanied by a flute
spondeō spondēre spopondī sponsus *tr* to promise solemnly, pledge, vow; to promise in marriage; to vouch for, back up **‖** *intr (leg)* to give a guarantee, put up bail; *(w.* **pro** *+ abl)* to vouch for
spondē·us -ī *m (pros)* spondee *(foot consisting of two long syllables)*
spondyl·us -ī *m* a kind of shellfish, mussel
spongi·a -ae *f* (-ge-) sponge; sponge eraser; quilted corslet
spons·a -ae *f* fiancée
sponsāl·ia -ium *npl* engagement; engagement party
sponsi·ō -ōnis *f* solemn promise; guarantee; bet; *(leg)* agreement between two parties that the loser pay a certain sum to the winner
spons·or -ōris *m* guarantor, surety; **Ammonius sponsor promissorum Cleopatrae** Ammon, who backs up the promises of Cleopatra
spons·us -a -um *pp of* spondeo **‖** *m* fiancé, bridegroom **‖** *f see* sponsa **‖** *n* agreement, engagement
spons·us -ūs *m* contract
sponte *(abl only) f (of persons, mostly with poss adj)* of one's own accord, voluntarily, deliberately, purposely; by oneself, unaided; *(of things)* of itself, spontaneously; on its own account, for its own

sake; **meā (suā,** *etc.)* **sponte** of my own *(his own, her own, etc.*) accord; **sponte aetatis** as a consequence of one's years; **sponte naturae (suae)** of its own nature, naturally, spontaneously; **suā sponte** considered in itself, inherently, essentially

spopondī *perf of* **spondeo**

sport·a -ae *f* plaited basket

sportell·a -ae *f* little basket

sportul·a -ae *f* little basket *(in which gifts of food were given by the patron to his clients);* dole, present *(of food or money);* gift

sprēt·or -ōris *m* despiser, scorner

sprētus *pp of* **sperno**

sprēvī *perf of* **sperno**

spūm·a -ae *f* foam, froth; hair dye; **spumas agere ore** to froth at the mouth

spūmāt·us -a -um *adj* covered with foam

spūmesc·ō -ĕre *intr* to grow foamy

spūme·us -a -um *adj* foaming

spūmif·er *or* **spūmig·er -era -erum** *adj* foaming

spūm·ō -āre -āvī -ātum *intr* to foam, froth; *(of places, things)* to be covered with foam; **equi terga spumantia** the back of the horse soaked with sweat

spūmōs·us -a -um *adj* full of foam, foaming; bombastic

spuō spuěre spuī spūtus *tr* to spit, spit out **ǁ** *intr* to spit

spurcāt·us -a -um *adj* foul, filthy

spurcē *adv* filthily; offensively; in filthy language

spurcidic·us -a -um *adj* foul-mouthed, smutty, obscene

spurcific·us -a -um *adj* smutty

spurciti·a -ae *or* **spurciti·ēs -ēī** *f* filth, smut

spurc·ō -āre -āvī -ātus *tr* to make filthy, foul up; to defile

spurc·us -a -um *adj (morally)* filthy

spūtātilic·us -a -um *adj* deserving to be spit on, contemptible, disgusting

spūtāt·or -ōris *m* spitter

spūt·ō -āre -āvī -ātus *tr* to spit, spit out; to avert *(by spitting)*

spūt·um -ī *n* spit, sputum

squāl·eō -ēre -uī *intr* to be rough, be scaly; to be coated, be clotted, be stiff; to be covered with filth, be caked with mud; *(of clouds, shade)* to be dark, be murky; *(of places)* to be covered with weeds, be overgrown; *(of land)* to lie waste *(from neglect, barrenness);* *(of persons)* to wear mourning clothes

squālidē *adv* harshly, roughly

squālid·us -a -um *adj* rough, scaly; stiff, caked with dirt; squalid; in mourning; coarse *(speech);* barren, waste *(land)*

squāl·or -ōris *m* squalor, dirtiness; desolation; uncouthness *(of style);* squalid clothes *(as a sign of mourning)*

squal·us -ī *m* a type of sea fish

squām·a -ae *f* scale; scale armor; scale-like yellow band on the abdomen of a bee

squāme·us -a -um *adj* scaly

squāmif·er *or* **squāmig·er -era -erum** *adj* scaly **ǁ** *mpl* fish

squāmōs·us -a -um *adj* covered with scales, scaly

squill·a -ae *f* (scill-) shrimp, crayfish

st *interj* shhh!, ssst!

stabilīment·um -ī *n* support, prop; *(fig)* mainstay

stabil·iō -īre -īvī -ītus *tr* to stabilize; to establish firmly

stabil·is -is -e *adj* stable, firm, steady; steadfast, unwavering, immutable

stabilit·ās -ātis *f* stability, firmness, steadiness, durability

stabiliter *adv* firmly; steadfastly

stabul·ō -āre -āvī -ātus *tr* to stable *or* house *(animals)* **ǁ** *intr* to have a stall

stabul·um -ī *n* stable, stall; lair; hut; brothel; *(coll)* flea bag, cheap lodgings

stact·a -ae *or* **stact·ē -ēs** *f* myrrh oil

stad·ium -iī *n* furlong; running track, stadium; stade *(= 625 feet)*

Stagīr·a -ōrum *npl* town in Macedonia, birthplace of Aristotle

Stagīrīt·ēs -ae *m* Aristotle

stāgn·ō -āre -āvī -ātus *tr* to overflow, inundate **ǁ** *intr* to form a pool; to be inundated

stāgn·um -ī *n (expanse of water, natural or artificial)* pool, lake, lagoon, swamp, straits; alloy of silver and lead **ǁ** *npl* the depths

stalagm·ium -(i)ī *n* eardrop, earring *(w. pendant)*

stām·en -inis *n* vertical threads of a loom, warp; thread; string *(of an instrument);* fillet *(worn by priests)*

stāmine·us -a -um *adj* consisting of threads; wrapped in threads

Stat·a -ae *f* a goddess who gave protection against fire

statāri·us -a -um *adj* standing, stationary; *(of plays, actors, speakers)* free from violent action, calm, quiet **ǁ** *mpl* actors in a refined type of comedy **ǁ** *f* refined comedy

statēr·a -ae *f* scales; **statera aurificis** goldsmith's scales

staticul·us -ī *m* pose

statim *adv* at once, on the spot

stati·ō -ōnis *f* standing still, stationary position; station, post; position; residence; anchorage; **in statione** at one's post, on guard **ǁ** *fpl* sentries

Stāt·ius -(i)ī *m* Publius Papinius Statius *(poet of the Silver Age of Latin literature, c. A.D. 40–96)*

statīv·us -a -um *adj* stationary **ǁ** *npl* bivouac; halts; **cum die stativorum** with a rest-day *(on the march)*

stat·or -ōris *m* attendant *(of provincial governor, later of the emperor)* ‖ **Stator** *m* cult title of Jupiter

statu·a -ae *f* statue

statūm·en -inis *n* rib *(of a hull)*

stat·uō -uĕre -uī -ūtus *tr* to cause to stand; to bring to a stop; to fix in the ground, plant; to erect, build; to set up *(a statue)*, set up a statue of; to found *(a city)*; to establish *(a practice, precedent, principle, state of affairs)*; to decide, settle *(matters)*; to decree; to strengthen, support; to appoint *(a time, place)*; *(w. double acc)* to appoint *(s.o.)* as; to determine, fix, set *(a price, payment; penalty, punishment)*; to draw up, arrange *(a battle line)*; *(w.* **utrum**) to make up one's mind whether, decide whether; *(w. inf)* to decide to, resolve to; *(w.* **ut** + *subj)* to decide that; *(w. pred. noun or adj)* to judge, deem; **statuere finem** *(w. dat)* set a limit to

statūr·a -ae *f* stature, height; **brevis (longae) staturae homo** a person of short (tall) stature

stat·us -a -um *pp of* **sisto** ‖ *adj* fixed, set *(times, places, seasons)*; regular, average, normal

stat·us -ūs *m* position; posture; social standing, rank, prestige; state of affairs, situation, condition; *(gram)* mood of the verb; *(leg)* legal position *(in regard to rights, obligations)*; *(mil)* position; *(rhet)* point at issue; **status rei publicae** type of government, form of constitution

statūt·us -a -um *adj* upstanding

steg·a -ae *f (naut)* deck

stell·a -ae *f* star; constellation; **stella comans** *(or* **crinita**) comet; **stella diurna** Lucifer; **stella errans** planet; **stella de caelo lapsa** shooting star; **stella marina** starfish; **stellae quinque** the five *(recognized)* planets *(i.e., Mars, Mercury, Venus, Jupiter, Saturn)*

stell·ans -antis *adj* starry; star-shaped, star-like

stellāt·us -a -um *adj* set with stars, starry; made into a star; **stellatus Argo** *(fig)* Argo with bright eyes

stellif·er *or* **stellig·er -era -erum** *adj* star-bearing, starry

stel(l)i·ō -ōnis *m* newt, lizard *(with spotted back)*

stemm·a -atis *n* genealogical tree, family tree, lineage ‖ *npl* antiquity, history

stercore·us -a -um *adj (vulg)* full of shit

stercor·ō -āre -āvī -ātus *tr* to fertilize, manure

sterculīnum *see* **sterquilinium**

sterc·us -oris *n* manure, dung

steril·is -is -e *adj* sterile, barren; causing barrenness, blighting; empty, bare; unprofitable; unrequited; wild *(tree)*

sterilit·ās -ātis *f* sterility

stern·ax -ācis *adj* bucking *(horse)*

sternō sternĕre strāvī strātus *tr* to strew, spread; to cover *(couch, horse)* with a cloth; to pave *(a road, floor)*; to strike down, lay low, slay; to raze; to overwhelm, defeat utterly; to flatten, smooth; to calm, calm down; **triclinium sternere** to set the table; ‖ *pass* to stretch out *(on the ground)*

sternūment·um -ī *n* sneeze

sternu·ō -ĕre -ī *tr* to give *(an omen)* by sneezing ‖ *intr* to sneeze

Sterop·ē -ēs *f* one of the Pleiades

Sterop·ēs -ae *m* a Cyclops working in Vulcan's blacksmith shop

sterquilīn·ium -(i)ī *or* **sterquilīn·um -ī** *or* **sterculīn·um -ī** *n* manure pile

stert·ō -ĕre *intr* to snore

Stēsichor·us -ī *m* Greek lyric poet of Himera in Sicily *(c. 640–555 B.C.)*

stetī *perf of* **sto**

Sthenel·us -ī *m* king of Mycenae, son of Perseus, and father of Eurystheus ‖ king of the Ligurians and father of Cycnus, who was changed into a swan

stibad·ium -iī *n* semicircular seat

stigm·a -atis *n* mark, brand; stigma *(of disgrace)*

stigmati·ās -ae *m* branded runaway slave

stigmōs·us -a -um *adj* branded

still·a -ae *f* drop; mere drop

stillicid·ium -(i)ī *n* drip, dripping

still·ō -āre -āvī -ātus *tr & intr* to drip

stil·us -ī *m* stylus *(pointed instrument for writing)*; composition; style

stimulāti·ō -ōnis *f* stimulation, incitement

stimulātr·ix -īcis *f* a tease *(female)*

stimule·us -a -um *adj* of goads

stimul·ō -āre -āvī -ātus *tr* to goad, torment; to spur on, incite, excite

stimul·us -ī *m* goad, prick; *(fig)* stimulus, incentive, spur; *(mil)* pointed stake concealed below the ground

stingu·ō -ĕre *tr* to extinguish

stīpāti·ō -ōnis *f* crowd, throng

stīpāt·or -ōris *m* attendant, bodyguard ‖ *mpl* retinue

stīpendiāri·us -a -um *adj* liable to taxes, tributary ‖ *mpl* tributary peoples; mercenary troops

stīpend·ium -(i)ī *n* tax, tribute, tariff; *(mil)* pay; military service; year's service; campaign; **emereri stipendia** to have served out one's term; **emeritis stipendiis** at the end of one's military service, at discharge; **merere** *(or* **mereri**) **stipendia** to serve in the army

stīp·es -itis *m* log; trunk; branch, tree; *(pej)* blockhead

stīp·ō -āre -āvī -ātus *tr* to pack, cram,

crowd; to crowd around, accompany in a groups

stips stipis f donation, gift; alms

stipul·a -ae f stalk, blade; stubble; (mus) reed pipe

stipulāti·ō -ōnis f agreement, bargain; (leg) formal promise

stipulātiuncul·a -ae f insignificant promise

stipulāt·us -a -um adj promised

stipul·or -ārī -ātus sum tr (of a buyer) to demand a guarantee from (the seller that the purchase is fair by asking the formal question "spondesne? dabisne?", i.e., "do you promise? will you give?") ‖ intr (leg) to make a solemn promise (by answering "spondeo, dabo", i.e., "I promise, I shall give")

stīri·a -ae f icicle

stirpitus adv by the roots

stirp·s or **stirp·ēs** or **stirp·is -is** f (m) stock, stem, stalk; root; plant, shrub; race, lineage; offspring, descendant; character, nature; source, origin, beginning, foundation

stīv·a -ae f plow handle

stlattāri·us -a -um adj imported

stō stāre stetī statum intr to stand; (of buildings, cities) to stand still, remain standing; to last, endure; to stand firm; to stand upright; (of hair) to stand on end; (of eyes) to remain fixed; (of battle) to continue; (of a ship) to be moored, ride at anchor; to be motionless; to be stuck; (w. ex) to consist of; to take sides; (w. abl or in + abl) to depend on, rest with; (w. per + acc of person) to depend on, be due to, be the fault of, thanks to; **per me stetit quin** (or **ne** or **quominus**) **proelio dimicaretur** it was due to me that there was no battle; thanks to me, there was no battle; **per me stetit ut** it was due to me that ‖ v impers (w. inf) it is a fixed resolve; **mihi stat** (w. inf) it is my fixed resolve to, I have made up my mind to

Stōic·a -ae f Stoic philosophy

Stōicē adv stoically, like a Stoic

Stōic·us -a -um adj & m Stoic

stol·a -ae f dress (female outer garment, counterpart of the male toga); ceremonial gown (worn by musicians)

stolāt·us -a -um adj wearing a stola; (fig) ladylike

stolidē adv stupidly, brutishly

stolid·us -a -um adj dull, stupid, slow, insensitive; (of things) inert

stomach·or -ārī -ātus sum tr to be indignant at ‖ intr to be angry, fume

stomachōsē adv irritably

stomachōsius adv rather angrily

stomachōs·us -a -um adj irritable

stomach·us -ī m stomach; esophagus, gullet; taste; appetite; irritation, annoyance; **stomachum movere** (or **facere**) to cause annoyance; **stomachus bonus** good appetite; good humor, patience

store·a or **stori·a -ae** f straw mat

strab·ō -ōnis m squinter ‖ **Strabo** see **Pompeius**

strāg·ēs -is f devastation; heap; pile of debris; havoc; massacre

strāgul·us -a -um adj covering, serving as a covering ‖ n rug, carpet; bedspread; horse blanket

strām·en -inis n straw

strāment·um -ī n straw; covering; saddlecloth; **stramentum agreste** straw bed

strāmine·us -a -um adj straw-, made of straw

strangul·ō -āre -āvī -ātus tr to strangle; to suffocate; to constrict; to stifle

strangūri·a -ae f strangury (difficulty with urinating)

stratēgēm·a -atis n stratagem; ruse

stratēg·us -ī m commander, general

stratiōtic·us -a -um adj soldierly

strāt·um -ī n quilt, blanket; bed, couch; horse blanket, saddlecloth; pavement; **strata viarum** paved streets

strātūr·a -ae f paving (of roads)

strāt·us -a -um pp of **sterno** ‖ n see **stratum**

strāvī perf of **sterno**

strēn(u)·a -ae f good-luck omen; lucky gift sent at the New Year

strēnuē adv briskly, quickly, actively, strenuously

strēnuit·ās -ātis f briskness, vigor, liveliness

strēnu·us -a -um adj brisk, vigorous, active; fast (ship); restless

strepit·ō -āre intr to be noisy; to clatter; to rustle

strepit·us -ūs m noise, din, racket; crash, bang, clank; rumble; rustle; creak, squeak

strep·ō -ěre -uī -itus tr to shout ‖ intr to make a noise (of any kind); to rattle, clatter, clang; to rumble; to rustle; to creak, squeak; to roar; to hum; to murmur; (of muscial instruments) to sound, blare; (of places) to ring, resound, be filled

stri·a -ae f groove, channel, furrow

striāt·us -a -um adj grooved, fluted, furrowed ‖ f scallop (sea animal)

strictim adv superficially, cursorily

strictūr·a -ae f mass of hardened iron

strict·us -a -um pp of **stringo** ‖ adj close, tight, narrow

strīd·eō -ēre -ī or **strīd·ō -ěre -ī** intr to make a high-pitched noise; to hiss, whistle; to whizz; to shriek, scream; to grate; to buzz; (of a wound) to gurgle; (of wings) to whirr

strīd·or -ōris m shrill sound, hiss; whiz-

zing; shriek, scream; whine; harsh noise, grating; whirring *(of wings)*
strīdul·us -a -um *adj* shrill, strident; hissing, whistling; creaking
strigil·is -is *f* scraper, strigil *(used by athletes to scrape off the mud)*
strig·ō -āre *intr* to stop; to give out
strigōs·us -a -um *adj* lean, shriveled; bald *(style)*
stringō stringĕre strinxī strictus *tr* to strip, clip; to draw *(a sword);* to draw tight, tie tight; to string *(a bow);* to pick *(fruit);* to strip off *(leaves);* to press together, compress; to graze, scratch; to border on; to touch lightly on *(a subject); (of a river)* to erode
string·or -ōris *m* (**strīg-**) twinge, shock
strix strigis *f* owl, screech owl
stroph·a -ae *f* (**strof-**) trick, feat of skill
Strophad·es -um *fpl* island home of the Harpies
strophiār·ius -(i)ī *m* bra-maker
stroph·ium -iī *n* brassiere, bra; head band
Stroph·ius -(i)ī *m* king of Phocis and father of Pylades
structil·is -is -e *adj* for building; **caementum structile** concrete
struct·or -ōris *m* builder, mason, carpenter; carver *(at table)*
structūr·a -ae *f* construction; structure
structus *pp of* **struo**
stru·ēs -is *f* pile, heap; row of sacrificial cakes
stru·ix -īcis *f* heap, pile
strūm·a -ae *f* tumor, swollen gland
strūmōs·us -a -um *adj (med)* scrofulous
stru·ō -ĕre -xī -ctus *tr* to build, erect; to deploy *(troops);* to arrange, regulate; to occasion; to compose; to construct *(words);* to plot, design, aim at; to load with
strūt(h)ē·us -a -um *adj* **malum strutheum** *n (a small variety of)* quince
strūthocamēl·us -ī *m* ostrich
struxī *perf of* **struo**
Strȳm·ōn -onis *or* **-onos** *m* river on the Macedonian-Thracian border
Strȳmon·is -idis *f* Thracian woman
Strȳmoni·us -a -um *adj* of the Strymon, Thracian
stud·eō -ēre -uī *tr* to desire, be eager for; to make *(s.th.)* one's concern ‖ *intr (w. dat)* **1** to be eager for, be keen on, be enthusiastic about; **2** take pains with, busy oneself with, apply oneself to; **3** to pursue; **4** to study; **5** to be a partisan of
studiōsē *adv* eagerly, enthusiastically, diligently
studiōs·us -a -um *adj* eager, keen, enthusiastic; studious; *(w. gen)* partial to *(a person or cause); (w. gen or dat)* eager for, keen on, enthusiastic about, devoted

to, fond of, desirous of; **litterarum studiosus** studious
stud·ium -(i)ī *n* eagerness, keenness, enthusiasm; devotion *(to a person);* support, goodwill *(esp. in a political sense),* party spirit; study; *(w. gen)* eagerness for, enthusiasm for; *(w. ad or in + acc)* enthusiasm for ‖ *npl* studies; **studia contraria** opposite parties
stultē *adv* foolishly
stultiloquenti·a -ae *f or* **stultiloqu·ium -(i)ī** *n* silly talk
stultiloqu·us -a -um *adj* talking foolishly
stultiti·a -ae *f* foolishness, silliness
stultivid·us -a -um *adj (foolishly)* seeing things that are not there
stult·us -a -um *adj* foolish, silly
stūp·a -ae *f* tow, coarse flax, hemp
stupe·faciō -facĕre -fēcī -factus *(pass:* **stupe·fīō -fierī -factus sum)** *tr* to stupefy, stun, shock
stup·eō -ēre -uī *tr* to be amazed at, marvel at ‖ *intr* to be knocked senseless, be stunned, be astounded, be amazed; to be stopped in one's tracks
stup·escō -escĕre -uī *intr* to become amazed, become bewildered
stūpe·us -a -um *adj* of tow, hempen
stupidit·ās -ātis *f* stupidity
stupid·us -a -um *adj* amazed, astounded; stupid
stup·or -ōris *m* numbness; stupor; bewilderment, confusion; dullness, stupidity
stupp·a -ae *f* hemp, coarse flax
stuppe·us -a -um *adj* hempen
stupr·ō -āre -āvī -ātus *tr* to ravish, rape, to defile; **struprum inferre** *(w. dat)* to have sex with; to violate
stupr·um -ī *n* immorality; illicit sex; fornication *(as distinct from adultery);* rape
stupuī *perf of* **stupeo**
sturn·us -ī *m* starling
Stygi·us -a -um *adj* Stygian; hellish; deadly; dismal, melancholy
Stymphāli(c)·us -a -um *adj* Stymphalian
Stymphāl·um -ī *n or* **Stymphāl·us** *or* **Stymphal·os -ī** *m* district in Arcadia famous for its vicious birds of prey which were killed by Hercules as one his Twelve Labors
Sty·x -gis *or* **-gos** *f* chief river in the lower world; river in Arcadia
suādēl·a -ae *f* persuasion
suā·deō -dēre -sī -sus *tr* to recommend, suggest, propose; to urge, impel, induce ‖ *intr (w. dat)* to advise, urge, suggest to, propose to; **sibi suadere** *(w. acc & inf)* to satisfy *or* convince oneself that
suāsi·ō -ōnis *f* recommendation; support, backing *(a proposal);* persuasive eloquence
suās·or -ōris *m* adviser; advocate, supporter

suāsōri·a -ae f rhetorical exercise *(giving of advice based on historical situations)*

suāsōri·us -a -um *adj* concerned with advice

suās·um -ī *n* dirty gray color

suāsus *pp of* suadeo

suās·us -ūs *m* advice

suāveol·ens -entis *adj* sweet-smelling, fragrant

suāviātiō *see* saviatio

suāvidic·us -a -um *adj* smooth *(verses);* smooth-talking

suāviloqu·ens -entis *adj* smooth-talking, charming

suāviloquenti·a -ae f charming way of talking, smooth talk

suāviolum *see* saviolum

suāvior *see* savior

suāv·is -is -e *adj* charming, pleasant, agreeable, attractive, nice

suāvit·ās -ātis f charm, pleasantness, attractiveness

suāviter *adv* charmingly, pleasantly, attractively, sweetly

suāvitūd·ō -inis f *(term of endearment)* honey, sweetie

suāvium *see* savium

sub *(prep) (w. abl)* 1 under, beneath, underneath: sub sole ardente under the blazing sun; sub divo under the sky, in the open; 2 under the surface of *(the earth, water):* sub terrā below the ground; 3 down in *(a depression, valley):* urbs sub vallibus sita est the city is located down in the valley; 4 close behind: sub ipso ecce volat Diores look, Diores comes flying close behind him; 5 close (up) to: ager noster sub urbe our land close to town; 6 close by: sub dextrā (sinistrā) on the right (left); sub manu close at hand; 7 at the foot of, close to, near, right under *(mountain, wall):* sub radicibus montium at the foothills of the mountains; sub muro stare to stand close to the wall; 8 immediately before, at the approach of: sub vespere at the approach of evening; 9 in the reign of, during the term of office of, under: sub Tiberio Caesare in the reign of Tiberius Caesar; 10 at the hands of: majore sub hoste at the hands of a greater enemy; 11 under the name *or* title of: qui Caesareo juvenes sub nomine crescunt these young men are growing up under Caesar's name; 12 on the pretext of: sub excusatione valitudinis on the pretext of poor health **||** *(w. acc)* 1 to a position below, under, beneath: ejus exercitum sub jugum miserat he had sent his army under the yoke; sub lectum repere to crawl under the bed; 2 to a point at the foot of: succedunt sub montem in quo they advance to the foot of the mountain

on which; 3 up *(walls, mountains):* subire sub montem to go up the mountain; 4 just before *(a point of time, event),* on the eve of: sub idem tempus at almost the same time; sub ipsum spectaculum gladiatorium on the eve of the gladiatorial show; sub occasum solis just before sunset; 5 directly after: sub eas litteras statim recitatae sunt tuae your letter was read aloud right after that letter; 6 in response to: sub hanc vocem fremitus multitudinis fuit at this statement a roar went up in the crowd; 7 into a state of subjection: Ninus totam Asiam sub se redegit Ninus subjected all of Asia to his control

sub- *pref* 1 *(before adjectives and verbs, giving the sense of reduced intensity):* subamārus somewhat bitter; subridere to smile; 2 *(compounded with verbs it gives the senses of the preposition):* 2a *(position underneath):* subscribere to write underneath *or* below; 2b *(movement up from below):* subire to go up, climb; 2c *(movement down):* succīdere to cut down; 2d *(movement close to):* subsequi to follow close behind; 2e *(substitution):* sublegere to substitute; 2f *(secret activity and removal):* subnotare to observe secretly; subducere to remove, steal; 3 *(before nouns, indicating lower rank):* subcenturio assistant centurion

subabsurdē *adv* a bit absurdly

subabsurd·us -a -um *adj* a bit absurd

subaccūs·ō -āre *tr* to blame, find some fault with

subacti·ō -ōnis f working *(of the soil);* development *(of the mind)*

subactus *pp of* subigo

subaerāt·us -a -um *adj (of gold)* having an inner layer of bronze

subagrest·is -is -e *adj* rather uncouth

subālār·is -is -e *adj* carried under the arms

subalb·us -a -um *adj* whitish, off-white

subamār·us -a -um *adj* somewhat bitter

subaquil·us -a -um *adj* somewhat dark *(complexion)*

subarroganter *adv* (subadro-) rather arrogantly

subauscult·ō -āre *tr* to eavesdrop on **||** *intr* to eavesdrop

subbasilicān·us -ī *m* loafer *(hanging around the basilicas)*

subbib·ō -ěre -ī *tr* to drink a little

subbland·ior -īrī *intr (w. dat)* to flirt with

subc- = succ-

subdifficil·is -is -e *adj* rather difficult, a bit difficult

subdiffīd·ō -ěre *intr* to be a little distrustful

subdītīci·us -a -um *adj* phoney

subdītīv·us -a -um *adj* substituted, spurious

subditus *pp of* **subdo**
subdiū *adv* by day
sub·dō -děre -didī -ditus *tr* to put under; to subdue; to substitute; to forge, make up; to spread *(a rumor); (w. dat)* **1** to put or apply *(s.th.)* to, add *(s.th.)* to; **2** to subject *(s.o.)* to ‖ *refl* **se aquis subdere** to plunge into the water
subdoc·eō -ēre *tr* to instruct *(as an assistant instructor)*
subdolē *adv* rather cunningly
subdol·us -a -um *adj* underhand, sly, cunning
subdom·ō -āre *tr* to tame somewhat
subdubit·ō -āre *intr* to be rather undecided
sub·dūcō -dūcěre -duxī -ductus *tr* to draw up from below; to pull up, raise; to remove, take away, steal; to haul up, beach *(a ship);* to withdraw *(troops);* to balance *(accounts)*
subducti·ō -ōnis *f* drydocking, beaching; calculation, computation
sub·edō -eděre *or* **-esse -ēdī -ēsus** *tr* to eat away below *or* eat away at the bottom of; **scopulum unda subedit** water wears away the bottom of the cliff
sub·eō -īre -īvī *or* **-iī -itus** *tr* to enter *(a place; the mind);* to approach, attack; to undergo *(danger, punishment, etc.);* to help, support; to climb; to slip under; to dodge *(a blow)* ‖ *intr* to come *or* go up, climb; to follow; to advance, press forward; *(w.* **ad** *or in + acc)* **1** to come up against, attack; **2** to climb *(a mountain);* **3** to approach, enter
sūb·er -eris *n* cork tree, cork
subf- = **suf-**
subg- = **sugg-**
subhorrid·us -a -um *adj* rather coarse, rather uncouth
subigitāti·ō -ōnis *f (sl) (sexually)* fondling, feeling up
subigitātr·ix -īcis *f (sl)* a tease
subigit·ō -āre -āvī -ātus *tr (sl)* to arouse sexually by fondling, feel up
sub·igō -igěre -ēgī -actus *tr* to turn up, till, plow *(the soil);* to knead *(dough);* to grind, reduce to a powder: **farina in pollinem subacta** flour reduced to a fine powder; to work *(wool into a smooth thread);* to rub down, massage *(the body, also in the erotic sense);* to tame, break in *(an animal);* to train, discipline *(the mind);* to conquer, subdue *(a country);* to row, propel *(a boat);* to make smooth *(by rubbing, polishing);* to lubricate; to whet, sharpen: **subigunt in cote securis** they sharpen their axes on a whetstone; to suppress, quell *(hostilities);* to subdue the spirit of, break the spirits of *(people); (w. inf or* **ut** *+ subj)* to force, constrain *(s.o.)* to; *(w.* **ad**) to drive to:

subegit nos ad necessitudinem dedendi res he drove us to the necessity of giving up our property
subimpud·ens -entis *adj* rather shameless
subinān·is -is -e *adj* rather empty, rather pointless
subinde *adv* immediately afterwards; promptly; from then on; from time to time, now and then
subinsuls·us -a -um *adj* rather insipid
subinvid·eō -ēre *intr (w. dat)* to envy *(s.o.)* a little
subinvīs·us -a -um *adj* rather disliked, somewhat unpopular
subinvīt·ō -āre *tr* to invite unenthusiastically
subīr·ascor -ascī -ātus sum *intr* to be annoyed; *(w. dat)* to be peeved at
subitāri·us -a -um *adj* requiring prompt action; *(of troops)* hastily called up *(to meet an emergency); (of buildings)* hastily erected; **res subitaria** emergency
subitō *adv* suddenly, unexpectedly, at once; **subito dicere** to speak ex-tempore
subit·us -a -um *adj* coming on suddenly, sudden, unexpected; rash *(person);* emergency *(troops)* ‖ *n* emergency; **de subito** *(or* **per subitum**) suddenly
subjac·eō -ēre -uī *intr* to lie nearby; *(w. dat)* to lie under, lie close to; **monti subjacere** to lie at the foot of the mountain
subjecti·ō -ōnis *f* subjection; substitution; forgery
subjectissimē *adv* most humbly
subject·ō -āre -āvī -ātus *tr* to toss up *(from below);* **stimulos subjectare** *(w. dat)* to prod s.o. on
subject·or -ōris *m* forger
subject·us -a -um *pp of* **subjicio** ‖ *adj (w. dat)* **1** located near, bordering (on); **2** subject to; **subjecta materia** subject matter ‖ *m* subject, subordinate, underling
sub·jiciō -jiceře -jēcī -jectus *tr* to throw up, fling up; to bring up; to bring up close, expose; to suggest; to add, append; to suborn; to substitute; to forge; *(w. dat or* **sub** *+ acc)* **1** to put, place *(s.th.)* under; **2** to subject *(s.o.)* to; **3** to classify *(s.th.)* under; **4** to submit *(s.th.)* to *(one's judgment)*
subjun·gō -gěre -xī -ctus *tr (w. dat)* **1** to yoke *or* harness to; **2** to join to, connect with, add to; **3** to make subject to
sub·labor -lābī -lapsus sum *intr* to sink, fall down, collapse; to glide imperceptibly; to fall back, fail
sublātē *adv* loftily, in lofty tones
sublāti·ō -ōnis *f* elevation, raising
sublāt·us -a -um *pp of* **suffero** *and of* **tollo** ‖ *adj* elated
sublect·ō -āre *tr* to coax, cajole

sub·legō -legĕre -lēgī -lectus *tr* to gather up, pick up; to steal; to kidnap; to substitute; to overhear, pick up

sublest·us -a -um *adj* weak; trifling

sublevāti·ō -ōnis *f* alleviation

sublev·ō -āre -āvī -ātus *tr* to lift up, raise, support; to assist; to encourage; to promote, further *(an activity);* to lighten, alleviate; to make up for *(a fault)* ‖ *refl* to get up

sublic·a -ae *f* stake, pile *(esp. for a bridge)*

sublici·us -a -um *adj* resting on piles; **pons sublicius** wooden bridge *(across the Tiber, built by Ancus Marcius, third king of Rome)*

subligācul·um -ī *n* loincloth, shorts

sublig·ar -āris *n* loincloth, shorts

sublig·ō -āre -āvī -ātus *tr (w. dat)* to tie *or* fasten *(e.g., a sword)* to *or* below

sublīmē *adv* aloft, on high

sublīmen *adv* upwards, on high

sublīm·is -is -e *adj* high, raised up, lifted high; *(of ideas)* lofty, grand, exalted; borne aloft, through the sky; aspiring; having lofty ideals; exalted in rank, eminent, distinguished; lofty, majestic *(style)* ‖ *npl* the heights

sublīmit·ās -ātis *f* loftiness, sublimity

sublīm·us -a -um *adj* high, lofty

sublingul·ō -ōnis *m (hum)* dish-licker, dishwasher

sub·linō -linĕre -lēvī -litus *tr* to smear over, coat *(a surface);* to smear the underside of; **os sublinere** *(w. dat)* to pull a practical joke on

sublūc·eō -ēre *intr* to shine faintly; *(w. dat)* to shine through

sub·luō -luĕre -luī -lūtus *tr* to wash underneath; to flow at the foot of *(a mountain);* to wash *(the underside of the body);* **quid solium subluto podice perdis?** why do you ruin the bathtub with washing your behind?

sublustr·is -is -e *adj* dimly lighted; throwing some light, glimmering, flickering

subm- = summ-

sub·nascor -nascī -nātus sum *intr (w. dat)* to grow up underneath

sub·nectō -nectĕre -nexuī -nexus *tr* to fasten, tie *(s.th.)* underneath; to confine; *(w. dat)* to fasten *or* tie *(s.th.)* below *(s.th. else)*

subneg·ō -āre -āvī -ātus *tr* to half-refuse

subni·ger -gra -grum *adj* blackish

subnīsus -a -um *adj* (-nix-) propped up; *(w. dat)* **1** propped up on, resting on, leaning on; **2** relying on, confiding in; **3** elated by

subnot·ō -āre -āvī -ātus *tr* to note down, record, register; to observe secretly

subnub·a -ae *f* rival *(female)*

subnūbil·us -a -um *adj* somewhat cloudy, overcast

sub·ō -āre *intr* to be in heat

subobscēn·us -a -um *adj* somewhat obscene, shady, off-color

subobscūr·us -a -um *adj* somewhat obscure

subodiōs·us -a -um *adj* rather tiresome, rather annoying

suboffend·ō -ĕre *intr* to give some offense

subol·et -ēre *v impers* there is a faint smell; **mihi subolet** I have an inkling, I have a sneaking suspicion

subol·ēs -is *f* offspring; children; the young *(of animals);* race, stock

subolesc·ō -ĕre *intr* to grow up

subor·ior -īrī -tus sum *intr* to rise up in succession, arise, proceed

suborn·ō -are *tr* to equip, supply, provide; to employ as a secret agent, induce secretly, suborn; to dress up *(in a costume, disguise);* to prepare, instruct *(for some underhand purpose)*

subp- = supp-

subr- = surr-

sub·scrībō -scrībĕre -scrīpsī -scriptus *tr* to write underneath; to sign; to write down, record, register ‖ *intr (leg)* to sign an accusation, act as prosecutor; *(w. dat)* **1** to add in writing to; **2** to agree to; *(leg) (w. in + acc)* to sign an accusation against, indict

subscripti·ō -ōnis *f* inscription underneath; signature; s.th. written under a heading; recording *(of an offense by the censor);* record, register; *(leg)* specification *(of crimes)* in an indictment, a count, charge

subscript·or -ōris *m (leg)* signer, co-signer *(of an accusation)*

subscriptus *pp of* subscribo

subsc·ūs -ūdis *f* (sups-) tenon of a dovetail

subsecīvus *see* subsicivus

subsec·ō -āre -uī -tus *tr* to clip, trim, cut off; to pare, clip *(nails)*

subsecūtus *pp of* subsequor

subsell·ium -(i)ī *n* seat, bench; stool; seat *or* bench on a lower level; seat in the Senate; *(leg)* seat in the court *(usu. where the judge, prosecution or the defense and their witnesses sat);* *(fig)* the bench, tribunal, court; seat in the theater; **versatus in utrisque subsellis** experienced as lawyer and judge ‖ *npl* the courts; bleachers *(where the poor people sat);* *(fig)* occupants of the bleachers

subsen·tiō -tīre -sī -sus *tr* to have some inkling of

sub·sequor -sequī -secūtus sum *tr* to follow close after; to pursue; to back up, support; to imitate; to adhere to, conform to; to come after, succeed *(in time or order)* ‖ *intr* to ensue

subserv·iō -īre *intr (w. dat)* **1** to be subject to; **2** to accommodate oneself to, humor; **3** to support, aid

subsicīv·us *or* **subsecīv·us -a -um** *adj* (sup-) *(of land)* left over *(after an allotment);* extra, spare *(time);* extra, overtime *(work)*

subsidiāri·us -a -um *adj* in reserve; *(mil)* reserve ‖ *mpl (mil)* reserves

subsid·ium -(i)ī *n* aid, support; mainstay; place of refuge; protection; *(mil)* reserves; military support, relief; **ad** *(or* **in) subsidium** for support; **subsidio esse** *(w. dat)* to be of help to ‖ *npl (mil)* reserves, reinforcements

sub·sidō -sīdĕre -sēdī *tr* to lie in wait for ‖ *intr* to sit down, crouch down, settle down; to sink, subside, settle; to settle down, establish residence

subsignān·us -a -um *adj (mil)* special reserve *(troops)*

subsign·ō -āre -āvī -ātus *tr* to endorse, subscribe to *(an opinion);* to register, enter, record; to guarantee

subsil·iō -īre -uī *intr* (suss-) (sups-) to jump up

sub·sistō -sistĕre -stitī *tr* to hold out against ‖ *intr* to stand up; to make a stand, take a firm stand; to come to a standstill, stop; to stay behind; *(w. dat)* **1** to take a stand against, oppose, fight; **2** to meet *(an expense)*

subsort·ior -īrī -ītus sum *tr* to choose as a substitute by lot ‖ *intr* to choose a substitute by lot; *(in a passive sense)* to be chosen as a substitute

subsortīti·ō -ōnis *f* substitution by lot

substanti·a -ae *f* substance, essence; means, wealth, property

sub·sternō -sternĕre -strāvī -strātus *tr* to spread underneath; to cover; *(w. dat)* to put at the disposal of, make subservient to; **rem publicam libidini suae substernere** to misuse high office to serve one's lust

substit·uō -uĕre -uī -ūtus *tr* to submit, present; to substitute; *(w. dat or* in locum *w. gen)* to substitute for *or* in place of; **animo** *(or* **oculis) substituere** to imagine

subst·ō -āre *intr* to stand firm, hold out; *(w. dat)* to stand up to

substrātus *pp of* substerno

substrāvī *perf of* substerno

substrict·us -a -um *adj* tight, narrow, small

sub·stringō -stringĕre -strinxī -strictus *tr* to tie up, draw up; to restrain, control; *(w. dat)* to press *(s.th.)* close to

substructi·ō -ōnis *f* substructure, foundation

substru·ō -ĕre -xī -ctus *tr* to lay *(a foundation);* **vias glareā substruere** to lay a foundation of gravel on the roads

subsult·ō -āre *intr* to jump up and down

sub·sum -esse *intr* (sup-) to be near, be at hand; *(w. gen) (of feelings, qualities,* underlying cause *or meaning)* to form the foundation for, be at the bottom of; *(w. dat)* **1** to be below *or* underneath, be under; **2** to be at the foot of; **3** to be (located) at the edge of *(the sea);* **4** to be concealed in; **5** to be (worn) under *(e.g., a tunic);* **6** to be attached to *(a document);* **7** to be subject to, be subservient to

subsūt·us -a -um *adj* trimmed at the bottom

subtē(g)m·en -inis *n* weft, woof *(horizontal threads woven in between the warp threads in a loom);* yarn

subter *adv* (sup-) below, underneath ‖ *prep (w. abl)* beneath, below, underneath, under ‖ *(w. acc)* underneath, beneath; up to, close to, close beneath

subter·dūcō -dūcĕre -duxī -ductus *tr* (sup-) to remove secretly ‖ *refl* to steal away, sneak away

subter·fugiō -fugĕre -fūgī *tr* (sup-) to evade, avoid ‖ *intr* to run off secretly

subter·lābor -lābī *tr* to glide *or* flow under ‖ *intr* to slip away

sub·terō -terĕre -trīvī -trītus *tr* (sup-) to wear away underneath

subterrāne·us -a -um *adj* subterranean, underground

subtex·ō -ĕre -uī -tus *tr* to sew on; to veil, cover; *(fig)* to work up, compose; *(w. dat)* **1** to sew onto; **2** to throw *(a covering)* over; **3** to work *(s.th.)* into *(a story or plot)*

subtīl·is -is -e *adj* (sup-) finely woven; delicate; subtle; discriminating, refined; precise, matter-of-fact

subtīlit·ās -ātis *f* (sup-) fineness, minuteness; slenderness; exactness, precision; simplicity *(of style)*

subtīliter *adv* (sup-) finely, delicately; accurately; plainly, simply

subtim·eō -ēre *intr* to be a bit afraid

sub·trahō -trahĕre -traxī -tractus *tr* (sup-) to drag up from beneath, drag out, draw off; to withdraw, remove; to withhold; to misappropriate, steal; to undermine; to avert *(eyes);* *(w. dat)* to drag *(s.th.)* away from; *(w. abl)* to rescue *(s.o.)* from the threat of, snatch *(s.o.)* from *(impending danger, ruin);* **oculis subtrahere** to remove from sight ‖ *refl* *(w. ab)* to withdraw from, dissociate oneself from *(an activity, responsibility)*

subtrist·is -is -e *adj* rather sad

subtrītus *pp of* subtero

subtrīvī *perf of* subtero

subturpicul·us -a -um *adj* somewhat disgraceful

subturp·is -is -e *adj* rather disgraceful, somewhat scandalous

subtus *adv* below, underneath

subtūs·us -a -um *adj* somewhat bruised
subūcul·a -ae *f* undertunic *(worn by both sexes)*
subulc·us -ī *m* swineherd
Subūr·a -ae *f* noisy business and nightlife district in Rome, N.E. of the Forum between the Esquiline and Quirinal Hills
Subūrān·us -a -um *adj* of the Subura
suburbānit·ās -ātis *f* proximity to Rome
suburbān·us -a -um *adj* suburban, near Rome ‖ *m* suburbanite ‖ *n* suburban Rome
suburb·ium -(i)ī *n* suburb
suburg·eō -ēre *tr (w.* **ad)** to keep *or* turn *(a ship)* close to
subvecti·ō -ōnis *f* transportation
subvect·ō -āre -āvī -ātus *tr* to bring up regularly, transport regularly
subvect·us -ūs *m* bringing up, transportation
sub·vehō -vehĕre -vexī -vectus *tr* to carry *or* bring up, transport
sub·veniō -venīre -vēnī -ventum *intr (w. dat)* to come up to aid, reinforce
subvent·ō -āre *intr (w. dat)* to rush to the aid of
subver·eor -ērī *intr* to be a bit apprehensive
subvers·ō -āre *tr* **(-vors-)** to ruin completely
subvers·or -ōris *m* one who overthrows *(a law)*
subver·tō -tĕre -tī -sus *tr* **(-vort-)** to turn upside down, upset, overthrow, subvert
subvex·us -a -um *adj* sloping upward
subvol·ō -āre *intr* to fly up
subvolturi·us -a -um *adj* vulture-like
subvolv·ō -ĕre *tr* to roll up(hill)
subvor- = **subver-**
succav·us -a -um *adj* hollow underneath
succēdāne·us -a -um *adj* **(succī-)** killed as a substitute
suc·cēdō -cēdĕre -cessī -cessus *tr* to climb; to march on *or* against, advance as far as ‖ *intr* to come up, climb; to come next, follow in succession; to turn out well, turn out successfully; *(w.* **ad, in,** *or* **sub** + *acc)* to climb, climb up; *(w. dat)* **1** to succeed, follow; **2** become a successor to; **3** to succeed in *(an undertaking);* **4** to yield, to submit to; **5** to relieve *(e.g., tired troops);* **6** to enter, go below to *(e.g., a shelter, a grave); (w.* **ad** *or* **in** + *acc) (fig)* to attain *(e.g., high honors),* enter upon *(an inheritance);* **bene succedere** to turn out well
succen·dō -dĕre -dī -sus *tr* to set on fire, set fire to; to light *(a fire); (fig)* to inflame, enkindle
succens·eō -ēre -uī *intr* **(susc-)** *(w. dat)* to be enraged at
succensus *pp of* **succendo**

succenturiāt·us -a -um *adj* **(subc-)** in reserve
succenturi·ō -āre -āvī -ātus *tr* **(subc-)** to receive *(s.o.)* as a substitute into a *centuria*
succenturi·ō -ōnis *m* **(subc-)** assistant centurion, substitute for a centurion
successi·ō -ōnis *f* succession
success·or -ōris *m* successor
success·us -ūs *m* approach, advance uphill; outcome; success
succīdāneus *see* **succedaneus**
suc(c)īdi·a -ae *f* leg *or* side of meat; *(fig)* extra income
suc·cīdō -cīdĕre -cīdī -cīsus *tr* **(subc-)** to cut down, cut off, mow down
suc·cīdō -cidĕre -cĭdī *intr* **(subc-)** to sink, give way; to collapse, fail
succid·us -a -um *adj* **(sūci-)** juicy; *(coll)* plump *(girl)*
succidu·us -a -um *adj* sinking, falling, collapsing, giving way
succint·us -a -um *adj (of a person)* with clothes tucked up; *(of a statement)* concise; *(of a book)* compact; *(fig)* in a state of readiness; *(fig) (w. abl)* equipped with *(a means of defense, military strength);* **cultro succinctus** carrying a knife in his belt
succin·gō -gĕre -xī -ctus *tr* to tuck up; to put on *(a sword);* to equip, arm; to surround closely ‖ *refl* & *pass (w. abl)* to gather up one's clothes with
succingul·um -ī *n* belt
succin·ō -ĕre *tr* to recite in a droning voice ‖ *intr* to chime in *(in conversation); (w. dat)* to accompany *(in singing or playing)*
succīsus *pp of* **succīdo**
succlāmāti·ō -ōnis *f* shouting in reply
succlām·ō -āre -āvī -ātus *tr* **(subc-)** to shout out after; to interrupt with shouts, heckle; *(w. dat)* to shout out *(words)* at
subcoll·ō -āre -āvī -ātus *tr* to carry on one's shoulders
succontumēliōsē *adv* **(subc-)** rather insolently
suc·crescō -crescĕre -crēvī *intr* **(subc-)** to grow up; to be replenished; *(w. dat)* to attain to
succrisp·us -a -um *adj* **(subc-)** rather curly
succulent·us -a -um *adj* **(subc-)** succulent
suc·cumbō -cumbĕre -cubuī -cubitum *intr* **(subc-)** to fall back, sink back; to succumb, yield, submit
suc·currō -currĕre -currī -cursum *intr (w. dat)* **1** to run up to; **2** to run to help; **3** to occur to, enter the mind of; **4** *(topog)* to extend to the foot of ‖ *v impers* the thought occurs
succ·us *or* **sūc·us -ī** *m* sap, juice; taste, flavor; *(fig)* vitality
succuss·us -ūs *m* shaking, jolt

succust·ōs -ōdis *m* **(subc-)** assistant guard
suc·cutiō -cutĕre -cussī -cussus *tr* to toss
up; to jolt *(a rider, vehicle)*
sūcidus *see* **succidus**
sūcin·us -a -um *adj* & *n* amber
suctus *pp of* **sugo**
sucul·a -ae *f* winch, windlass
Sūcul·ae -ārum *fpl (astr)* Hyades
sūculent·us -a -um *adj* juicy, succulent
sūc·us -ī *m* juice; *(of the soil)* moisture;
(fig) sap, vitality
sūdār·ium -(i)ī *n* handkerchief; towel
sūdātōri·us -a -um *adj* sweat-, for sweating ‖ *n* sweat room, sauna
sūdātr·ix -īcis *adj* causing sweat
sud·is -is *f* stake, pile; pike *(weapon)*;
sharp projection, spike
sūd·ō -āre -āvī -ātus *tr* to sweat, exude; to
soak with sweat; *(fig)* to sweat at, sweat
over ‖ *intr* to sweat; to drip
sūd·or -ōris *m* sweat; moisture; *(fig)* hard
work
sūducul·um -ī *n (hum)* sweat-maker *(i.e.,
a whipping post)*
sūd·us -a -um *adj* dry; clear, cloudless ‖ *n*
clear weather, bright sky
Suēbi·a -ae *f* district E. of the Elbe
Suēb·ī -ōrum *mpl* **(Suēv-)** generic name
of a group of German tribes
suescō suescĕre suēvī suētus *tr* to accustom, familiarize ‖ *intr (w. dat or inf)* to
become accustomed to
Suētōn·ius -(i)ī *m* Roman clan name
*(nomen) (esp. that of Gaius Suetonius
Tranquillus, biographer, born c.* A.D. *69)*
suēt·us -a -um *pp of* **suesco** ‖ *adj* usual,
familiar
Suēvī *see* **Suebi**
suf·ēs *or* **sūf·es -etis** *m* chief magistrate at
Carthage
suffarcināt·us -a -um *adj* **(subf-)** stuffed,
padded
suffarcin·ō -āre -āvī -ātus *tr* **(subf-)** to
stuff, cram
suffect·us -a -um *pp of* **sufficio** ‖ *adj*
substitute; **consul suffectus** substitute
consul *(appointed to complete an unex-
pired term of another consul)*
sufferō sufferre sustulī sublātus *tr* **(subf-)**
to suffer, bear, endure; to place at s.o.'s
disposal, offer
suf·ficiō -ficĕre -fēcī -fectus *tr* to lay the
foundation for; to dip, tinge, dye; to
appoint to a vacancy; to yield, supply,
afford ‖ *intr* to be sufficient; *(w. dat)* to
suffice for
suf·fīgō -fīgĕre -fīxī -fīxus *tr* to nail up,
fasten
suffīm·en -inis *n* incense
suffīment·um -ī *n* incense
suff·iō -īre -īvī *or* **-(i)ī -ītus** *tr* to fumigate;
to perfume
suffixus *pp of* **suffigo**

sufflām·en -inis *n* brake *(on a vehicle)*
sufflāmin·ō -āre -āvī -ātus *tr* to apply the
brakes to
sufflāt·us -a -um *adj* puffed up, bloated;
(fig) bombastic; *(fig)* fuming *(w. anger)*
suffl·ō -āre -āvī -ātus *tr* to blow up, inflate
‖ *intr* to blow, puff
suffōc·ō -āre -āvī -ātus *tr* to choke, suffocate
suf·fodiō -fodĕre -fōdī -fossus *tr* **(subf-)**
to stab, pierce; to dig under *(walls)*
suffrāgāti·ō -ōnis *f* **(subf-)** voting *(in s.o.'s
favor)*, support
suffrāgāt·or -ōris *m* **(subf-)** voter; supporter *(at the polls)*, partisan
suffrāgātōri·us -a -um *adj* **(subf-)** partisan
suffrāg·ium -(i)ī *n* **(subf-)** ballot, vote;
right to vote, franchise; decision, judgment; applause, approbation; **suffragium
ferre** to cast a ballot; **suffragium ferre**
(w. **de** *or* **in** + *abl)* to vote on
suffrāg·or -ārī -ātus sum *intr* to cast a
favorable vote; *(w. dat)* to vote in favor
of, support, vote for; **fortunā suffra-
gante** with luck on our side
suffring·ō -ĕre *tr* **(subf-)** to break
suffug·ium -(i)ī *n* shelter, cover
sufful·ciō -cīre -sī -tus *tr* to prop up, underpin, support
suf·fundō -fundĕre -fūdī -fūsus *tr* **(subf-)**
to pour in, fill; to suffuse, spread; to
tinge, color; to infuse; **virgineum ore
ruborem suffundere** *(w. dat)* to make
(s.o.) blush like a girl
suffūr·or -ārī *tr* to filch, snitch
suffusc·us -a -um *adj* **(subf-)** darkish
suffūsus *pp of* **suffundo**
Sugambr·ī -ōrum *mpl* a German tribe living to the E. of the Lower Rhine, above
the Ubii
sug·gerō -gerĕre -gessī -gestus *tr* **(subg-)**
to supply, add; to suggest
suggest·um -ī *n* platform; stage
suggestus *pp of* **suggero**
suggest·us -ūs *m* platform; stage
suggrand·is -is -e *adj* **(subg-)** rather huge
sug·gredior -gredī -gressus sum *tr* & *intr*
(subg-) to approach
sūgillāti·ō -ōnis *f* **(suggill-, subgill-)**
bruise; affront
sūgill·ō -āre -āvī -ātus *tr* to beat black-
and-blue; to affront, insult
sūgō sūgĕre suxī suctus *tr* to suck
suī *see* **se**
suī *perf of* **suo**
suill·us -a -um *adj* of swine; **caro suilla**
pork; **grex suillus** herd of swine ‖ *f* pork
sulc·ō -āre -āvī -ātus *tr* to furrow; to plow;
to score, make a line in
sulc·us -ī *m* furrow; ditch, trench *(for
plants)*; track *(of a wheel or meteor)*;
wrinkle; plowing; wake *(of a ship)*

sulf·ur -uris *n* sulfur

Sull·a -ae *m* (Syll-) Sulla *(Cornelius Sulla Felix, Roman general, dictator, and political reformer, 138–78 B.C.)*

Sullān·ī -ōrum *mpl* (Syll-) partisans of Sulla

sullātur·iō -īre *intr* to wish to be a Sulla

Sulm·ō -ōnis *m* town c. 90 miles E. of Rome, and birthplace of Ovid

Sulmōnens·is -is -e *adj* of Sulmo

sulp(h)·ur *or* **sulf·ur -uris** *n* sulfur

sulp(h)urāt·us -a -um *adj* saturated with sulfur

sulp(h)ure·us -a -um *adj* sulfurous

sultis = **si vultis** if you please

sum esse fuī futūrus *intr* to be; to exist; *(w. gen of possession)* to belong to, pertain to, be characteristic of, be the duty of; *(w. gen or abl of quality)* to be of, be possessed of, have; *(w. gen or abl of value)* to be valued at, cost; *(w. dat)* to belong to; *(w. ab)* to belong to; *(w. ad)* to be designed for; *(w. ex)* to consist of; **est** *(w. inf)* it is possible to, it is permissible to; **est** *(w. ut)* it is possible that; **sunt qui** there are those who, there are people who, they are of the type that

sumbolus *see* **symbolus**

sūm·en -inis *n* breast; teat, udder; breeding sow

summ- = **subm-**

summ·a -ae *f* main thing; chief point, gist, summary; sum, amount; contents, substance; sum of money; sum-total *(of hopes, etc.)*; the whole issue, the whole case; *(phil)* totality of matter, the universe; **ad summam** in short; generally, on the whole; as the crowning touch, to complete it all; **in summā** in all; **in summam** taken as a whole; **ad** *(or* **in) summam prodesse** *(or* **proficere)** to be of general good; **summa honoraria** honorarium, voluntary payment to a lawyer; **summa rerum** the world; supreme power; general welfare; **summa summarum** the whole universe

summān·ō -āre *intr* (subm-) to drip a bit

Summān·us -ī *m* Roman god of night lightning

summ·ās -ātis *adj* aristocratic, first-class

summātim *adv* on the surface; generally, summarily

summē *adv* very, extremely, intensely

summer·gō -gĕre -sī -sus *tr* (subm-) to sink, submerge, drown

summers·us -a -um *adj* (subm-) sunken; living underwater; *(sunk)* below the horizon

summer·us -a -um *adj* (subm-) nearly straight, nearly pure

sumministr·ō -āre -āvī -ātus *tr* (subm-) to furnish

summissē *or* **summissim** *adv* (subm-) in a low voice, softly; modestly, humbly

summissi·ō -ōnis *f* lowering, dropping

summiss·us -a -um *adj* lowered, stooping; lowered, soft *(voice)*; humble, unassuming; submissive; too submissive, abject; *(of hair)* worn long, let down

sum·mittō -mittĕre -mīsī -missus *tr* (subm-) to let down, lower, sink, drop; to let *(hair)* grow long; to lower, reduce, moderate, relax, lessen; to humble; to rear, produce, put forth; to send secretly; to send as a reinforcement; to send as a substitute; **animum summittere** *(w. dat)* to yield to **ǁ** *refl* to bend down, stoop over; to condescend; *(w. dat)* to give in to

summolestē *adv* (subm-) with some annoyance

summolest·us -a -um *adj* (subm-) rather annoying

summon·eō -ēre -uī -itus *tr* to give *(s.o.)* a gentle reminder, remind privately; **patres salutavit nominatim nullo summonente** he greeted senators by name, with no one prompting him

summopere *or* **summō opere** *adv* with the greatest diligence, with utmost effort

summōt·us -a -um *adj* secluded, distant

sum·moveō -movēre -mōvī -mōtus *tr* (subm-) to move up, advance; to clear *(e.g., the court)*; to remove; to expel, banish; to deny admission to, keep off; to clear from the path of a magistrate; to dispense with *(a procedure)*; to ward off *(heat, cold)*; *(fig)* to drive away, forget about *(e.g., worries)*; *(mil)* dislodge

summul·a -ae *f* small sum of money

summum *adv* *(w. numbers)* at most; at latest; **uno aut summum altero proelio** in one or at most two battles

summ·us -a -um *adj* highest, uppermost; the top of, the surface of; last, latest, the end of; greatest, best, top, consummate; finest, first-rate; at the height of *(a season)*; perfect *(peace, tranquility)*; closest, best *(friend)*; most distinguished; middle *(finger)*; *(of affairs, concerns)* most important, of highest importance; *(of a diner)* farthest to the left on the couch *(from the viewpoint of those dining)*; *(of a couch)* to the left of the middle couch; **omnia summa facere** to do one's utmost; **res summa** *(or* **res summae)** critical situation; **res summa** *(or* **respublica summa)** the welfare of the state, the general welfare; **summa cena** main course; **summa manus** finishing touches; **summa mensa** main course; **summa rudis** head instructor in a gladiatorial school *(literally, top practice-sword)*; **summo jure** with the full force of the law **ǁ** *m* head of the table; **ǁ** *f see* **summa ǁ** *n* top, surface; highest place, head of the table; **ab summo aut ab imo** at the top or the bottom of the page **‖** *npl* extremities *(of the body or its parts); general purport (of a writing)*

sūmō sūměre sumpsī sumptus *tr* to take up; to put on, dress oneself in, wear; to exact, inflict *(penalty);* to take up, begin, enter upon; to eat, consume; to assume, suppose, take for granted; to cite, adduce, mention; to assume, appropriate *(a title, name);* to embrace *(a practice, way of life);* to borrow *(words, ideas from other people);* to select; to purchase, buy; to adopt *(a child);* **aliquid mutuum sumere** to borrow s.th.; **arma sumere** to take up arms; **in se sumere** to take upon oneself, assume; **mortem** *(or* **exitium)** *(usu. w.* sponte) **sumere** to commit suicide; **supplicium sumere** to exact punishment

sumpti·ō -ōnis *f* assumption, premiss

sumptuāri·us -a -um *adj* expense-, relating to expenses; *(of laws)* sumptuary, against extravagance

sumptuōsē *adv* sumptuously, expensively

sumptuōs·us -a -um *adj* costly, expensive; lavish, wasteful

sumptus *pp of* **sumo**

sumpt·us -ūs *m* cost, expense; **sumptui esse** *(w. dat)* to be expensive for; **sumptum suum exercere** to earn one's keep; **sumptu tuo** at your expense

Sūn·ium *or* **Sun·ion -iī** *n* S.E. promontory of Attica

suō suěre suī sūtus *tr* to sew, stitch, tack together

suōmet = *emphatic form of* **suo**

suopte = *emphatic form of* **suo**

suovetaurīl·ia -ium *npl* (**suovi-**) sacrifice of a pig, sheep, and bull

supell·ex *or* **suppell·ex -ectilis** *f* furniture, household utensils; tableware; outfit, equipment

sup·er -era -erum *adj see* **superus**

super *adv* on the top, on the surface, above; besides, moreover; in addition to what has been said; **satis superque** enough and to spare; **super esse** to be left over **‖** *prep (w. acc)* over, above; upon, on top of; *(w. numbers)* over, more than; besides, over and above; **alius super alium** one on top of another, one after another; **super cenam** *(or* **mensam)** over dinner, at table *(i.e., during the meal);* **super omnia** *(or* **cuncta)** above all, more than anything **‖** *(w. abl)* above, over, upon, on; concerning, about, in the matter of; besides, in addition to; at *(e.g., midnight)*

super·a -ōrum *npl* upper world, sky; heaven; heavenly bodies

superā *adv* above

superābil·is -is -e *adj* surmountable, climbable; conquerable

superad·dō -děre -didī -ditus *tr* to add besides, add to boot

super·ans -antis *adj* predominant; outstanding, remarkable

superāt·or -ōris *m* conqueror

superbē *adv* arrogantly, haughtily, snobbishly

superbi·a -ae *f* arrogance, haughtiness, snobbishness; pride

superbiloquenti·a -ae *f* haughty tone, arrogant speech

superb·iō -īre *intr* to be haughty; to be proud; to be superb, be magnificent; *(w. abl)* to take pride in

superb·us -a -um *adj* arrogant, haughty, snobbish; proud; overbearing, tyrannical; fastidious, disdainful; superb, magnificent; *(of an honor)* that is a source of pride; *(w. abl)* proud of; **ales superba** the phoenix

supercil·ium -(i)ī *n* eyebrow; frown, will *(of Jupiter);* stern looks; summit, brow *(of a hill);* arrogance, superciliousness; artificial eyebrow

superēmin·eō -ēre *tr* to tower over, top

superfici·ēs -ēī *f* top, surface; *(leg)* fixtures, improvements, buildings *(i.e., anything upon the property but not the land itself)*

superfix·us -a -um *adj* stuck *or* impaled on top of; **rumpiis superfixa capita** heads stuck on top of long spears

super·fīō -fierī *intr* to be over and above; to be left over

superfix·us -a -um *adj* superabundant, running over; *(w. abl)* abounding in

superflu·ō -ěre -xī *intr* to overflow; to be superfluous

superfuī *perf of* **supersum**

super·fundō -funděre -fūdī -fūsus *tr (w. abl)* to shower *(s.th.)* with; *(w. dat)* to pour *(s.th.)* upon **‖** *refl & pass* to spread, spread out, extend

super·gredior -gredī -gressus sum *tr* to walk *or* step over; to surpass

super·ī -ōrum *mpl* the gods above; men on earth; mortals; upper world

superimmin·eō -ēre *intr (w. dat)* to stand over *(s.o. in a threatening manner)*

superimpend·ens -entis *adj* overhanging, towering overhead

super·impōnō -impōněre -imposuī -positus *tr* to place on top, place overhead

superimposit·us -a -um *adj* superimposed

superincid·ens -entis *adj* falling from above

superincub·ans -antis *adj* lying above *or* on top

superin·cumbō -cumběre -cubuī *intr* to lean over; *(w. dat)* to lay oneself down on

superindu·ō -ĕre -ī *tr* to put on over one's other clothes

superin·jiciō -jicĕre -jēcī -jectus *tr* to throw on top

superin·sternō -sternĕre -strāvī -strātus *tr (w. abl)* to cover *(w. s.th.)*

superi·or -or -us *(comp of* **superus)** *adj* higher, upper; the upper part of; past, previous, preceding; older, elder, more advanced; superior, stronger; victorious, conquering; greater; **de loco superiore dicere** to speak from the tribunal, handle a case in court; to speak from the rostra; **ex loco superiore pugnare** to fight from a vantage point

superius *adv (e.g., mentioned)* above

super·jaciō -jacĕre -jēcī -jectus *or* **-jactus** *tr* to throw on top; to overshoot *(a target);* **fidem superjacere** to exceed the bounds of credibility; **natare superjecto aequore** to swim in the flood waters

superjūmentār·ius -(i)ī *m* one charged with looking after the beasts of burden

superlāt·us -a -um *adj* exaggerated

superne *adv* above, from above; on top; **de superne** from above

supern·us -a -um *adj* upper; situated high up; supernal, celestial

super·ō -āre -āvī -ātus *tr* to go over, pass over, rise above; to pass, go past, go beyond; to sail past, double; to outdo, surpass; to surmount *(difficulties);* to live past, live beyond; to overcome, vanquish; to arrive before *or* ahead of; **vitā superare** to survive, outlive **‖** *intr* to mount, ascend; to be superior, have the advantage; to be left over, survive; to be superfluous; to be abundant; to remain to be done; *(w. dat)* to pass over, pass above

superobru·ō -ĕre *tr (also written as two words)* to cover completely, smother

superoccup·ō -āre *tr* to pounce on

superpend·ens -entis *adj* towering overhead

super·pōnō -pōnĕre -posuī -positus *tr (w. dat)* to put *(s.th.)* upon; *(w. in + acc)* to put *(s.o.)* in charge of

superquam quod *conj* in addition to the fact that

superscand·ō -ĕre *tr* to step over, climb over

superscrībō -scrībĕre -scripsī -scriptus *tr* to write over *or* on top of

super·sedeō -sedĕre -sēdī -sessum *tr* (-sid-) to sit on top of **‖** *intr* to sit on top; *(w. abl)* to refrain from, give up, steer clear of; *(w. inf)* to stop *(doing s.th.)*

superstagn·ō -āre -āvī *intr (of a river)* to overflow and form swamps

superst·es -itis *adj* standing by as a witness; surviving; posthumous; *(w. gen or dat)* outliving, surviving *(s.o.);* **superstes**

esse to live on; **superstes esse** *(w. gen or dat)* to outlive *(s.o.)*

superstiti·ō -ōnis *f* superstition; blind adherence to rules

superstitiōsē *adv* superstitiously

superstitiōs·us -a -um *adj* superstitious; ecstatic; blindly adhering to rules

superstit·ō -āre *intr* to be left

superst·ō -āre -stetī *tr* to stand over **‖** *intr (w. dat)* to stand on, stand over

superstrāt·us -a -um *adj* spread over *(as a covering)*

superstru·ō -ĕre -xī -ctus *tr* to build on top

super·sum -esse -fuī -futūrus *intr* to be left over, still exist, survive; to abound; to overflow; to be excessive; to be superfluous; to be adequate, suffice; *(w. dat)* to outlive, survive *(s.o.)*

superte·gō -gĕre -xī -ctus *tr* to cover over

superurg·ens -entis *adj* putting on pressure, adding pressure

super·us *or* **super -a -um** *adj* upper; of this world, of this life; northern; **ad auras superas redire** to come back to life; **mare superum** Adriatic Sea **‖** *mpl see* **superi ‖** *npl see* **supera**

supervac(u)āne·us -a -um *adj* superfluous

supervacu·us -a -um *adj* superfluous

supervād·ō -ĕre *tr* to go over, climb over

super·vehor -vehī -vectus sum *tr* to sail, ride, *or* drive by *or* past

super·veniō -venīre -vēnī -ventus *tr* to come upon, come on top of; to overtake; to come over, close over, cover; to surprise **‖** *intr* to arrive suddenly; *(w. dat)* to come upon by surprise

supervent·us -ūs *m* sudden arrival, unexpected arrival

super·vīvō -vīvĕre -vixī *intr (w. dat)* to outlive

supervolit·ō -āre -āvī *tr* to hover over

supervol·ō -āre -āvī *tr* to fly over **‖** *intr* to fly across

supīn·ō -āre -āvī -ātus *tr* to turn over *(by plowing)*

supīn·us -a -um *adj* face-up; lying on one's back; turned upwards; sloping, sloping upwards; *(of streams)* flowing upwards *(to their source);* on one's back; lazy, careless, indifferent

supp- = subp-

suppactus *pp of* **suppingo (subp-)**

suppaenitet -ēre *v impers* **(subp-)** *(w. acc of person and gen of thing regretted),* e.g., **illum furoris suppaenitet** he somewhat regrets the outburst

suppalp·or -ārī *intr* **(subp-)** *(w. dat)* to coax *(s.o.)* a little

supp·ār -aris *adj* nearly equal

supparasīt·or -ārī *intr (w. dat)* to flatter *(s.o.)* a little like a parasite

suppar·um -ī *n or* **suppar·us -ī** *m* linen dress; small sail
suppeditāti·ō -ōnis *f* (subp-) good supply
suppedit·ō -āre -āvī -ātus *tr* (subp-) to supply, furnish ‖ *intr* to stand by; to be on hand, be in stock, be available; *(w. dat)* to be at hand for; *(w. ad or in + acc)* to be adequate for
suppēd·ō -ĕre *intr (vulg)* to fart quietly
suppernāt·us -a -um *adj* hamstrung
suppeti·ae -ārum *fpl* assistance
suppeti·or -ārī -ātus sum *intr* (subp-) *(w. dat)* to help, assist
suppet·ō -ĕre -īvī *or* **-iī -ītum** *intr* to be at hand, be in stock, be available; *(w. dat)* 1 to be at hand for, be available to; 2 to be equal to, suffice for; 3 to correspond to
suppīl·ō -āre -āvī -ātus *tr* (subp-) to filch, snitch
sup·pingō -pingĕre -pēgī -pactus *tr* (subp-) to fasten underneath
supplant·ō -āre -āvī -ātus *tr* (subp-) to trip up, cause to stumble
supplēment·um -ī *n* (subp-) *(mil)* reinforcement(s)
suppl·eō -ēre -ēvī -ētus *tr* (subp-) to fill up; to make good *(losses, damage, etc.); (mil)* to bring to full strength
suppl·ex -icis *adj* kneeling, on one's knees, in entreaty; humble, submissive ‖ *mf* suppliant
supplicāti·ō -ōnis *f* public thanksgiving, day of prayer; thanksgiving for victory; day of humiliation
suppliciter *adv* suppliantly, humbly
supplic·ium -(i)ī *n* (subp-) kneeling down, bowing down, humble entreaty; public prayer, supplication; *(because criminals were beheaded kneeling)* execution, death penalty; punishment, torture; suffering, pain; **supplicium dare** to atone; **supplicium dare** *(or* **pendere,** *or* **expendere,** *or* **luere)** to pay the penalty, suffer punishment; **supplicium sumere** *(or* **exigere)** to exact punishment; to accept reparation; *(w.* **ab, ex, ex** + *abl)* to exact punishment from, put *(s.o.)* to death
supplic·ō -āre -āvī -ātum *intr* (subpl) *(w. dat)* to go on one's knees to, entreat, beg
supplo·dō -dĕre -sī -sus *tr* (subp-) to stamp *(the foot)*
supplōsi·ō -ōnis *f* (subp-) stamping *(one's foot)*
sup·pōnō -pōnĕre -posuī -positus *tr* (subp-) *(w. dat)* 1 to put, place, set *(s.th.)* under; 2 to put *(s.th.)* next to, add *(s.th.)* to; 3 to substitute *(s.th.)* for; **potentiam in gratiae locum supponere** to substitute power for influence
support·ō -āre -āvī -ātus *tr* (subp-) to bring up, transport
supposītīci·us -a -um *adj* (subp-) spurious

suppositi·ō -ōnis *f* substitution
suppositus *pp of* **suppono**
suppostr·ix -īcis *f* unfair substituter *(female)*
suppressi·ō -ōnis *f* holding back *(of money),* embezzlement
suppress·us -a -um *adj* soft *(voice);* softspoken *(person)*
sup·primō -primĕre -pressī -pressus *tr* (subp-) to press down *or* under; to sink; to repress, stop; to suppress, keep secret; to stifle *(an utterance);* to detain in one's private custody; to retain *(another's money)* in one's possession; to suppress *(feelings)*
supprōm·us -ī *m* assistant butler
suppud·et -ēre *v impers* (subp-) to cause *(s.o.)* a slight feeling of shame; *(w. acc of person and gen of cause), e.g.:* **eorum me suppudet** I am a bit ashamed of them
suppūr·ō -āre -āvī -ātum *intr* to fester
supp·us -a -um *adj* lying on one's back, supine; upside down
supput·ō -āre -āvī -ātus *tr* to trim off the lower branches of; to count, compute
suprā *adv* on top, above; up above; earlier; beyond, more; **supra quam** more than ‖ *prep (usu. w. acc; also w. abl) (sometimes following its object or separated from it by intervening words)* on, on top of; over, above; beyond; *(of time)* before, earlier than; north of; to the far side of; *(of amount)* over, beyond; in charge of; *(w. reference to position at the dining table, from the standpoint of those eating)* on the left of; **Atticus supra me, infra Verrius accubebat** Atticus sat to the left of me, Verrius to the right of me; **gallinaceus supra viri umerum deinde in capite astitit** the rooster stood on the man's shoulder and then on his head; **supra caput** *(in a threatening way)* (hanging) over one's head; **supra terram** above ground
suprālāti·ō -ōnis *f* exaggeration
suprālāt·us -a -um *adj* exaggerated
suprascand·ō -ĕre *tr* to climb over
suprāscript·us -a -um *adj* written above *(as a correction)*
suprēmum *adv* for the last time; as a final tribute
suprēm·us -a -um *(superl of* **superus)** *adj* last, latest, final; highest; greatest, supreme, extreme; critical, desperate *(time);* closing, dying, final; **suprema manus** finishing touches; **suprema multa** maximum fine; **supremum judicium** last will and testament; **supremum supplicium** death penalty; **supremus mons** mountain top ‖ *n* last moment ‖ *npl* moment of death; funeral rites
supt- = **subt-**
Sur- = **Syr-**

sūr·a -ae *f (anat)* calf
surcul·us -ī *m* shoot, sprout, twig; slip, graft
surdas·ter -tra -trum *adj* somewhat deaf
surdit·ās -ātis *f* deafness
surd·us -a -um *adj* deaf; silent, noiseless; unheeding; dull, faint
Sūrēn·a -ae *m* grand vizier *(in Parthia)*
surgō surgĕre surrexī surrectum *intr* to get up; to stand up; to rise; to spring up and grow tall
surr- = subr-
surrancid·us -a -um *adj* (subr-) somewhat rancid *or* spoiled
surrauc·us -a -um *adj* (subr-) somewhat hoarse
surrectus *pp of* surgo *and* surrigo
surrēmig·ō -āre *intr* to row along
Surrentīn·us -a -um *adj* of Surrentum *(modern Sorrento)*
sur·rēpō -rēpĕre -repsī -reptum *tr* (subr-) to creep under, crawl under **II** *intr* to creep up; *(w. dat)* to creep up on
surreptīci·us -a -um *adj* (subr-) surreptitious; stolen
surreptus *pp of* surrepo *and of* surripio
sur·rīdeo -rīdēre -rīsī *intr* (subr-) to smile
surrīdiculē *adv* (subr-) rather humorously
sur·rigō -rigēre -rexī -rectus *tr* (subr-) to raise, lift up, erect
surring·or -ī *intr* (subr-) to grimace, make a face; to be somewhat annoyed
sur·ripiō -ripĕre -ripuī -reptus *tr* (subr-) to snatch secretly, pilfer; *(w. dat)* to pilfer *(s.th.)* from
surrīsī *perf of* surrīdēre
surrog·ō -āre -āvī -ātus *tr* (subr-) to propose as a substitute
surrostrān·ī -ōrum *mpl* (subr-) loafers around the Rostra *(in the Forum)*
surrub·eō -ēre *intr* (subr-) to blush slightly
surrūf·us -a -um *adj* (subr-) reddish
sur·ruō -ruĕre -ruī -rutus *tr* (subr-) to dig under; to loosen at the base; to tear down, demolish; *(fig)* to undermine, subvert
surrustic·us -a -um *adj* (subr-) rather unsophisticated
surrutil·us -a -um *adj* (subr-) reddish
surrutus *pp of* surruo
sursum *adv* (sursus, sūsum, sūsus) upwards, high up; sursum desorsum up and down
sūs suis *m* pig, hog; boar **II** *f* sow
Sūs·a -ōrum *npl* capital of Persia
suscenseō *see* succenseo
suscept·um -ī *n* enterprise, undertaking
suscepti·ō -ōnis *f* undertaking
sus·cipiō -cipĕre -cēpī -ceptus *tr* to catch *(s.th. before it falls)*; to support; to pick up, resume *(conversation)*; to bear *(children)*; to accept, receive *(under one's protection)*; to take up, undertake; to

acknowledge, recognize *(a child)* as one's own
suscit·ō -āre -āvī -ātus *tr* to stir up, shake up; to build, erect; to cause *(s.th.)* to rise; to wake *(s.o.)* up; to encourage; to stir up *(rebellion, love, etc.)*; to rouse *(from inactivity)*; to have *(s.o.)* stand up in court *(as witness)*
suspect·ō -āre -āvī -ātus *tr* to gaze up at; to suspect
suspect·us -a -um *pp of* suspicio **II** *adj* suspect, suspected, mistrusted
suspect·us -ūs *m* view from below; respect, esteem
suspend·ium -(i)ī *n* hanging; hanging oneself
suspen·dō -dĕre -dī -sus *tr* to hang up, hang; to prop up, support; to keep in suspense; to check *(temporarily)*; to interrupt **II** *pass (w.* ex) to depend on
suspens·us -a -um *adj* hanging, balanced; raised, poised; in suspense, uncertain, hesitant; marked by uncertainty; vague *(language); (w.* ex) dependent upon; **in suspenso** in suspense, on tenterhooks; undecided
suspic·ax -ācis *adj* suspicious; mistrustful
suspiciō suspicĕre suspexī suspectus *tr* to look up at; to look up to, admire; to mistrust, suspect **II** *intr* to look up; *(w.* in + *acc)* to look up at *or* into
suspici·ō -ōnis *f* suspicion, mistrust; inkling; faint indication, trace, suggestion; *(w. gen)* suspicion *(of); (w. acc & inf or* quasi) suspicion that; **in suspicionem cadere** to fall under suspicion; **in suspicionem venire** to come under suspicion; **Tarentinorum defectio jam diu in suspicione Romanis fuerat** the revolt of the Tarentines long been suspected by the Romans
suspīciōsē *adv* suspiciously
suspīciōs·us -a -um *adj* mistrustful, suspicious; suspicious-looking; *(w.* in + *acc)* suspicious of
suspic·ō -āre *or* suspic·or -ārī -ātus sum *tr* to mistrust, suspect; to suppose, surmise, believe
suspīrāt·us -ūs *m* deep breath, sigh; labored breathing
suspīr·ium -(i)ī *n* deep breath, sigh; **suspirium ducere** *(or* repetere *or* trahere) to take a deep breath, sigh
suspīr·ō -āre -āvī -ātus *tr* to sigh for **II** *intr* to sigh, heave a sigh
susque dēque *adv* up and down; **de Octavio susque deque est** it's all one *(i.e., of no consequence)* as far as Octavian is concerned
suss- = subs-
sustentāti·ō -ōnis *f* delay
sustent·ō -āre -āvī -ātus *tr* to build up; to hold upright; to support; to sustain *(w.*

food); to maintain; to provide *(s.o. w. food, money, etc.)*, support, maintain; to uphold *(the law)*; to endure, hold up against; to hold back, keep in check; to delay, put off
sus·tineō -tinēre -tinuī *tr* to hold up, support; to hold back, hold in check; to uphold *(the law)*; to sustain, support *(w. food, etc.)*; to bear, endure *(trouble)*; to hold up, delay, put off
sustoll·ō -ĕre *tr* to lift up, raise; to kidnap
sustulī *perf of* **tollo**
sūsum *see* **sursum**
susurrāt·or -ōris *m* mutterer, whisperer
susurr·ō -āre *tr & intr* to mutter, murmur, whisper
susurr·us -a -um *adj* whispering
susurr·us -ī *m* low, gentle noise; murmur, whisper, buzz, hum
sūt·a -ōrum *npl* coat of mail
sūtēl·ae -ārum *fpl* patches; tricks
sūtil·is -is -e *adj* sewn together; **cumba sutilis** boat made of skins; **rosae sutiles** a wreath of roses
sūt·or -ōris *m* shoemaker
sūtōri·us -a -um *adj* shoemaker's ‖ *m (hum)* Shoemaker Emeritus
sūtrīn·us -a -um *adj* shoemaker's ‖ *f* shoemaker's shop
Sūtr·ium -(i)ī *n* town in Etruria
sūtūr·a -ae *f* stitch; seam
sūt·us -a -um *pp of* **suo** ‖ *npl* joints
su·us -a -um *or* **su·os -a -om** *adj* his own, her own, its own, their own, one's own; due, proper, peculiar ‖ *pron masc pl* one's own people, one's own family, one's own friends ‖ *pron neut pl* one's own property
Sybar·is -is *f* town in S. Italy noted for its luxurious living ‖ *m* Sybaris *(boy's name, suggestive of decadence)*
Sybarīt·a -ae *m* Sybarite
Sybarītic·us -a -um *adj* Sybarite; *(fig)* erotic
Sȳchae·us -ī *m* husband of Dido
sȳcophant·a -ae *m* swindler; slanderer; cunning parasite
sȳcophanti·a -ae *f* deceptive trickery
sȳcophantiōsē *adv* deceitfully
sȳcophant·or -ārī -ātus sum *intr* to cheat; *(w. dat)* to pull a fast one on
Syēn·e -ēs *f* town in Egypt *(modern Aswan)*
Sylla *see* **Sulla**
syllab·a -ae *f* syllable
syllabātim *adv* syllable by syllable
Symaethē·us -a -um *adj* of the River Symaethus
Symaeth·is -idis *f* daughter of the river-god Symaethus
Symaeth·us -ī *m* River Symaethus in Sicily near Catana
symbol·a -ae *or* **symbol·ē -ēs** *f* contribution *(of money to a feast)*; *(coll)* blows

symbol·us -ī *m* **(sumb-)** symbol, mark, token
symphōni·a -ae *f* harmony; symphony, band *(of singers or musicians)*
symphōniac·us -a -um *adj* concert-, musical; **pueri symphoniaci** choristers ‖ *mpl* musicians
Symplēgad·es -um *fpl* two islands in the Black Sea which floated about and dashed against each other until they were fixed in place a split second after the Argo sailed by them
symplegm·a -atis *n* tangled group *(of persons embracing or wrestling)*
syngraph·a -ae *f* promissory note
syngraph·us -ī *m* written contract; pass *(for safe-conduct)*
synhedr·us -ī *m* senator *(in Macedonia)*
syn(h)od·ūs -ontos *m* bream *(fish)*
Synnad·a -ōrum *npl or* **Synn·as -adis** *f* town in Phrygia, famous for its colored marble
synthesin·a -ae *f* dinner shirt
synthes·is -is *f* a set of matching articles; dinner service; (matching) dinner clothes
Syph·ax -ācis *m* **(Syf-)** king of Numidia at the time of the Second Punic War, siding with Carthage *(d. 203 B.C.)*
Syrācosi·us -a -um *adj* Syracusan
Syrācūs·ae -ārum *fpl* Syracuse *(chief city of Sicily)*
Syrācūsān·us *or* **Syrācūsi·us -a -um** *adj* Syracusan
Syri·a -ae *f* **(Sur-)** Syria *(usu. including Phoenicia and Palestine)*
Syriac·us -a -um *adj* Syrian; from Syria; produced in Syria
Syriātic·us -a -um *adj* Syrian
Sȳr·inx -ingos *f* nymph who was pursued by Pan and changed into a reed
Syri·us -a -um *adj & m* Syrian; of Syros in the Cyclades
syrm·a -atis *n* robe with a train *(worn esp. by actors in tragedies)*; tragedy
Syrophoen·ix -icis *m* Syrophoenician *(Phoenica was regarded as part of Syria)*
syrt·is -is *f* sand bank, sand dune ‖ **Syrtis** *f* Gulf of Sidra in N. Africa ‖ Gulf of Gabes ‖ *fpl* name of an area of sand dunes on the coast between Carthage and Cyrene
Syr·us -a -um *adj* **(Sur-)** Syrian ‖ *mf* Syrian; proper name of a slave

T

T. *abbr* **Titus** *(Roman first name, praenomen)*
tabān·us -ī *m* horse fly
tabell·a -ae *f* small board, panel; plaque; writing tablet; page *(of a bound note-*

book); ballot; picture, painting; votive tablet; game board; placard, notice; door panel **ǁ** *fpl* notebook

tabellāri·us -a -um *adj (leg)* regulating voting by secret ballot **ǁ** *m* mail carrier, courier

tāb·eō -ēre *intr* to waste away; to melt; to decay; to drip; **tabentes genae** sunken cheeks

tabern·a -ae *f* hut; booth, stall, shop; inn; **taberna diversoria** *(or* **meritoria)** inn

tabernācul·um -ī *n* tent; **tabernaculum capere** *(of an augur)* to set up a tent in which to take the auspices

tabernār·ius -(i)ī *m* shopkeeper

tāb·ēs -is *f* melting; wasting, decay; dwindling, shrinking; decaying matter, rot; disease; moral corruption; means of corruption

tāb·escō -escĕre -uī *intr* to begin to decay; to begin to melt; to rot

tābidul·us -a -um *adj* rotting; wasting

tābid·us -a -um *adj* wasting, decaying; melting; corrupting; infectious

tābific·us -a -um *adj* wasting; melting; *(fig)* gnawing

tabul·a -ae *f* plank, board; writing tablet; painting *(on a panel of wood);* game board; votive tablet; door panel; placard, advertisement; auction notice; will; record; counting board **ǁ** *fpl* account books, records, register, lists; **tabulae novae** clean slate *(i.e., cancellation of debts)*

tabulār·ium -(i)ī *n* archives; archives building

tabulār·ius -(i)ī *m* accountant, bookkeeper

tabulāti·ō -ōnis *f* flooring; floor, story

tabulāt·us -a -um *adj* boarded **ǁ** *n* floor, story; layer; deck *(of a ship);* row *(of trees)*

tāb·um -ī *n* rot, putrid matter; infectious disease, plague

tac·eō -ēre -uī -itus *tr* to be silent about, pass over in silence **ǁ** *intr* to be silent, be still

tacitē *adv* silently; secretly, privately; without publicity; tacitly, without express statement; imperceptibly, quietly

taciturnit·ās -ātis *f* taciturnity; silence; failure to communicate

taciturn·us -a -um *adj* taciturn, silent; noiseless, hushed, quiet

tacit·us -a -um *adj* silent; mute; unmentioned; secret; *(leg)* tacit; **per tacitum** in silence

Tacit·us -ī *m* Gaius(?) Cornelius Tacitus *(Roman historian, c.* A.D. *55–115)*

tactil·is -is -e *adj* tangible

tacti·ō -ōnis *f* touch, touching; feeling, sense of touch

tactus *pp of* **tango**

tact·us -ūs *m* touch; handling; *(fig)* contact, influence

taed·a -ae *f* pine wood; pitch; pine board; pine tree; torch; wedding torch; *(fig)* wedding

tae·det -dēre -sum est *v impers* it irks; *(w. acc of person and gen of the cause),* e.g., **me taedet sermonis tui** I am sick of your talk, your talk irks me

taedi·fer -fera -ferum *adj* carrying a torch, torch-bearing

taed·ium -(i)ī *n* tediousness; weariness, boredom; feeling of disgust; object of disgust; nuisance

Taenarid·ēs -ae *m* man from Taenarus, Spartan *(esp. Hyacinthus)*

Taenar·is -idis *adj (fem only)* Spartan **ǁ** *f* Spartan woman

Taenari·us *or* **Taenare·us -a -um** *adj* of Taenarus, Taenarian; *(poet)* Spartan, Laconian

Taenar·um *or* **Taenar·on -ī** *n, or* **Taenar·os** *or* **Taenar·us -ī** *mf* Taenarus *(promontory at the S. tip of the Peloponnesus, near which a cavern was thought to lead to the lower world);* Hades

taeni·a -ae *f* band, ribbon; string

taesum est *see* **taedet**

tae·ter -tra -trum *adj* **(tet-)** offensive, revolting, loathsome; hideous; *(of actions)* monstrous, horrible

taetrē *adv* foully, hideously

taetricus *see* **tetricus**

tag·ax -ācis *adj* light-fingered *(thief)*

Tag·ēs -is *m* Etruscan god, originator of divination and grandson of Jupiter

tālār·is -is -e *adj* ankle-length **ǁ** *npl* ankle-length clothes; sandals; winged sandals; *(fig)* means of getting away

tālāri·us -a -um *adj* of dice; **ludus talarius** game of dice

talāsiō *interj* **(-lass-)** wedding cry

tāle·a -ae *f* rod, bar, stake

talent·um -ī *n* talent *(Greek weight, varying from state to state, but equal to about 50 lbs.; also a unit of currency, consisting of 60 minae, or about 600 denarii, or about $600);* **talentum magnum** Attic talent *(so called to distinguish it from talents from other cities of lower value)*

tāli·ō -ōnis *f (leg)* punishment in kind, exaction of compensation in kind

tāl·is -is -e *adj* such, of that kind; so great, so excellent; **talis…qualis** such…as

tāliter *adv* in such a way

tālitr·um -ī *n* fillip *(flick with the tip of the middle finger and the thumb)*

talp·a -ae *mf* mole *(animal)*

Talthyb·ius -(i)ī *m* herald of Agamemnon

tāl·us -ī *m* ankle; anklebone; foot; knucklebone *(used in playing dice);* **talis ludere** to play dice; **talos jacere** to roll the dice

tam *adv* to such an extent, to such a degree, so, so much; **tam...quam** the...the; **tam magis...quam magis** the more...the more

tamar·ix -īcis *f* tamarisk *(ornamental shrub or short tree)*

tamdiū *or* **tam diū** *adv* so long, how long; **tamdiu quam** *(or* **tamdiu dum)** as long as

tamen *adv* yet, nevertheless, still, just the same

tamendem *adv* all the same

tamenetsī *conj* even though **ll** *adv* all the same, nevertheless

Tames·is -is *m or* **Tames·a -ae** *f* Thames River

tametsī *conj* even if, although

tamquam *conj* (tan-) as, just as, as much as; just as if; **tamquam si** just as if

Tanagr·a -ae *f* town in Boeotia

Tana·is -is *m* river of Sarmatia *(modern River Don)*

Tanaqu·il -ilis *f* wife of the elder Tarquin

tandem *adv* at last, in the end, finally; *(expressing urgency or impatience)* now, tell me, please, just; **quousque tandem** just how long?

tangō tangĕre tetigī tactus *tr* to touch; to handle, meddle with; to taste; to come to, reach; to border on; to hit, beat; to wash; to anoint; to gall; to move to pity; to dupe; to touch upon, mention; to touch, be related to; to undertake; **de caelo** *(or* **fulmine) tangere** to strike with lightning

tanquam *see* **tamquam**

Tantale·us -a -um *adj* of Tantalus

Tantalid·ēs -ae *m* descendant of Tantalus *(e.g., Atreus, Aegisthus, Agamemnon, Menelaus)*

Tantal·is -idos *f* female descendant of Tantalus *(e.g., Niobe, Hermione)*

Tantal·us -ī *m* son of Jupiter and father of Pelops and Niobe; he was punished in Hades with constant hunger and thirst

tantill·us -a -um *adj* so small, so little **ll** *n* a bit; **tantillo minus** a little less

tantisper *adv* just so long *(and no longer);* just for the moment

tantopere *or* **tantō opere** *adv* so much, so greatly, to such a degree, so earnestly, so hard

tantulum *adv* so little, in the least

tantul·us -a -um *adj* so little, so small **ll** *n* so little, such a trifle; **tantulo vendere** to sell for such a trifling amount

tantum *adv (see also the neut of* **tantus)** so much, so greatly, to such a degree, so far, so long, so; only, just, but just; hardly, scarcely; **non tantum** all but, almost; **non tantum omnes opitulari voluerunt** almost all wished to be of assistance; **non tantum...sed etiam** not only...but also; **tantum modo** only

tantummodo *adv* only

tantundem *adv* just as much, just as far, to the same extent

tant·us -a -um *adj* of such size, so big, so great; so much; so little; so important **ll** *pron neut* so much; so little; so small an amount, so small a number; to such an extent *or* degree; **alterum tantum** twice the amount; **in tantum** to such an extent; **tanti** of such value, worth so much, at so high a price; of little account, of such small importance; **tanto** *(as abl of price)* at such a price, for so much; *(w. comparatives)* by so much, so much the; **tanto melior!** so much the better!; **tanto nequior!** so much the worse!; **tanto ante** (post) so much earlier (later); **tantum est** that is all; **tantum abesse ut...ut** to be so far (from being the case) that; **tantum afuit ut periculosum rei publicae putaret exercitum ut** (+ *subj)* so far was he from thinking that the army was a threat to the country that...; **ter (quater) tantum** three (four) times as much

tant·usdem -adem -undem *adj* just as big, just as large, just as great **ll** *n* the same quantity, just as much; *(w. advl force)* to the same degree, just as much; **tantidem** at the same price; **tantundem est** it comes to the same thing

tapēt·a -ae *m or* **tapēt·um -ī** *n* carpet; tapestry; coverlet

tapēt·ia -ium *npl* tapestry

taratantara *n* sound produced by the trumpet; **at tuba taratantara dixit** but the trumpet went "taratantara"

tardē *adv* slowly; with difficulty; late; **cum tardissime** at the latest

tardesc·ō -ĕre *intr* to become slow; to falter

tardip·ēs -edis *adj* limping

tardit·ās -ātis *f* tardiness; slowness; procrastination; dullness, stupidity

tarditūd·ō -inis *f* tardiness; slowness

tardiuscul·us -a -um *adj* rather slow, slowish, dragging

tard·ō -āre -āvī -ātus *tr* to slow down, delay, hinder; to check *(emotions);* to dull *(the senses)* **ll** *intr* to go slow, take it easy; to hold back

tard·us -a -um *adj* tardy, slow; lingering; mentally slow, mentally retarded; deliberate; crippling; *(of events)* long drawn out, making slow progress

Tarentīn·us -a -um *adj* Tarentine **ll** *mpl* Tarentines

Tarent·um -ī *n* Tarentum *(town on S. coast of Italy, modern Taranto)* **ll** *a* section on the west side of the Campus Martius

tarm·es -itis *m* woodworm, borer

Tarpēi·us -a -um *adj* Tarpeian; **mons**

Tarpeius (or **Tarpeia rupes** (or **Tarpeium saxum**) Tarpeian cliff (on the Capitoline Hill from which criminals were thrown) ‖ f Roman girl who treacherously opened the citadel to the Sabine attackers

tarpezīt·a -ae m (trap-) banker, money-changer

Tarquiniān·us -a -um adj of the Tarquins

Tarquiniens·is -is -e adj of the town of Tarquinii ‖ mpl inhabitants of Tarquinii

Tarquini·ī -ōrum mpl Tarquinii (important Etruscan city on the W. coast of Italy, about seventy miles N. of Rome, modern Tarquinia)

Tarquini·us -a -um adj Tarquinian ‖ m Tarquinius Priscus (fifth king of Rome, c. 616–579 B.C.) ‖ Tarquinius Superbus (seventh and last king of Rome, c. 534–510 B.C.)

Tarracīn·a -ae for **Terracīn·ae -ārum** fpl Terracina (town in Latium)

Tartar·a -ōrum npl or **Tartar·us** or **Tartar·os -ī** m Tartarus (lower level of Hades reserved for notorious criminals)

Tartare·us -a -um adj of Tartarus, infernal

tat or **tatae** interj expression of surprise

tat·a -ae m (coll) daddy; grandpa

Tat·ius -(i)ī m Titus Tatius (king of the Sabines who later ruled jointly with Romulus until the latter had him killed)

tau indecl n the Greek letter tau

taure·us -a -um adj bull's, of a bull; **terga taurea** bulls' hides; drums ‖ f rawhide, whip

Taur·ī -ōrum mpl inhabitants of Chersonesus Tauricus (modern Crimea)

Tauric·us -a -um adj Tauric ‖ mpl the Tauri

taurif·er -era -erum adj (of regions) bull-producing

tauriform·is -is -e adj bull-shaped

taurīn·us -a -um adj bull's; made of bull's hide; bull-like ‖ **Taurīn·us -a -um** of the Taurini (a Ligurian tribe) ‖ mpl the Taurini

Tauri·us -a -um adj Roman clan name (nomen); **ludi Taurii** games held in the Circus Flaminius in honor of the gods of the lower world

taur·us -ī m bull; bronze bull made as an instrument of torture ‖ **Taurus** (astr) Taurus (constellation) ‖ **Taurus** the Taurus mountain range in S.E. Asia Minor

taxāti·ō -ōnis f evaluation, assessment; (leg) maximum sum

taxill·us -ī m small die (for playing dice)

tax·ō -āre -āvī -ātus tr to appraise, assess the value of; to reproach

tax·us -ī f yew tree

Tāyget·ē -ēs f (astr) one of the seven

Pleiads forming the constellation of the Pleiades

Tāyget·us -ī m mountain range in Laconia, separating it from Messenia to the W.

tē pron, acc & abl of **tu**

-te = suf for **tu** and **te**

Teān·um -ī n town in Campania (modern Teano) ‖ town in Apulia (modern Civitate)

techn·a or **techin·a -ae** f trick

technyph·ion -iī n a little workroom

Tecmess·a -ae f mistress of Ajax son of Telamon

tectē adv cautiously, guardedly

tect·or -ōris m plasterer

tectōriol·um -ī n bit of plasterwork

tectōri·us -a -um adj plaster-, of plaster; **opus tectorium** plasterwork, stucco ‖ n plaster, stucco; fresco painting; beauty preparation

tect·um -ī n roof; ceiling; canopy; cover, shelter; house

tect·us -a -um pp of **tego** ‖ adj concealed; secret; guarded (words); reserved, secretive (person) ‖ n see **tectum**

tēcum = cum te

tēd- = **taed-**

Tege·a -ae f town in S.E. Arcadia

Tegeae·us -a -um adj Tegean, Arcadian ‖ m Pan ‖ f Arcadian maiden (esp. Atalanta and Callisto)

Tegeāt·ēs -ae m inhabitant of Tegea

teg·es -etis f piece of matting (used for lying on or as a covering)

tegetīcul·a -ae f small piece of matting

tegill·um -ī n hood, cowl

tegim·en or **teg(u)m·en -inis** n (applied to clothing, armor, skin of an animal or of fruit) cover, covering; vault (of heaven)

tegiment·um or **teg(u)ment·um -ī** n (applied to clothing, armor, skins, shells) cover, covering

tegō tegĕre texī tectus tr to cover; to protect, shelter; to hide; to bury; **tegere latus** (w. gen) to escort (s.o.)

tēgul·a -ae f tile ‖ fpl roof tiles, tiled roof; siding for walls

tegumen see **tegimen**

tegumentum see **tegimentum**

tēl·a -ae f web; warp (horizontal threads of a loom); yarn beam; loom; (fig) design, plan

Telam·ōn -ōnis m son of Aeacus, brother of Peleus, king of Salamis, and father of Ajax and Teucer

Telamōniad·ēs -ae m son of Telamon (esp. Ajax)

Telamōn·ius -(i)ī m Ajax (son of Telamon)

Telegon·us -ī m son of Ulysses and Circe

Telemach·us -ī m son of Ulysses and Penelope

Teleph·us -ī m king of Mysia, wounded by

the spear of Achilles and later cured by
its rust
tēlin·um -ī *n* perfume made of fenugreek
tell·ūs -ūris *f* the earth; ground, earth;
land, country; dry land
tēl·um -ī *n* missile, weapon; spear, javelin,
dart; sword, dagger; ax; shaft *(of light);*
cum telis *(or* **telo)** armed
temerāri·us -a -um *adj* casual, accidental;
rash, thoughtless
temere *adv* by chance, without cause; at
random; rashly, thoughtlessly; **non
temere** not lightly; not easily; hardly
ever; **nullus dies temere intercessit quo
non scriberet** hardly a day ever went by
without his writing
temerit·ās -ātis *f* chance, accident; rashness, thoughtlessness **‖** *fpl* foolhardy
acts
temer·ō -āre -āvī -ātus *tr* to darken,
blacken; to violate, disgrace, defile
Temes·ē -ēs *f or* **Temes·a -ae** *f* town in
Bruttium noted for its copper mines
tēmēt·um -ī *n* intoxicating liquor
temn·ō -ěre *tr* to slight
tēm·ō -ōnis *m* pole, tongue *(of a carriage
or plow);* wagon
Tempē *indecl npl* scenic valley between
Mt. Olympus and Mt. Ossa in Thessaly
temperāment·um -ī *n* blend; moderation;
temperate heat; restraint, balance
temper·ans -antis *adj* self-controlled
temperanter *adv* moderately
temperanti·a -ae *f* self-control, moderation
temperātē *adv* moderately
temperāti·ō -ōnis *f* blending; composition; proportion, symmetry; temperament; organization, constitution; control, controlling power
temperāt·or -ōris *m* controller; temperor
of metal
temperāt·us -a -um *adj* tempered; self-
controlled; moderate
temperī *or* **temporī** *adv* in time, on time;
in due time, at the right time
temperi·ēs -ēī *f* blending; climate; mild
climate, moderate temperature
temper·ō -āre -āvī -ātus *tr* to compound,
combine, blend, temper; to regulate,
modify *(in regard to temperature);* to
adjust; to tune; to govern, control, rule;
to control *(by steering)* **‖** *intr* to be moderate, exercise restraint; *(w. dat)* to exercise control over; *(w. abl or* **ab** + *abl, w.*
quin, quominus, ne, *w. inf)* to refrain
from
tempest·ās -ātis *f* time, period, season,
occasion; stormy weather, storm; misfortune, disaster; hail *(of weapons)*
tempestīvē *adv* at the right time
tempestīvit·ās -ātis *f* right time, timeliness

tempestīvō *adv* at the right time
tempestīv·us -a -um *adj* timely, seasonable, fit; ripe, mature; in good time,
early
templ·um -ī *n* space marked off in the sky
or on the earth for the observation of
omens; open space, quarter; site for a
temple; temple, shrine, sanctuary
temporāl·is -is -e *adj* temporary; temporal
temporāri·us -a -um *adj* temporary;
changeable *(character)*
tempore *or* **temporī** *adv* in time, on time;
in due time, at the right time
temptābund·us -a -um *adj* making constant attempts, trying
temptām·en -inis *n* attempt, effort; *(w.
gen)* test of
temptāment·um -ī *n* attempt, effort; temptation, trial
temptāti·ō -ōnis *f* trial; attack *(of sickness,
of an enemy);* *(w. gen)* attack on
temptāt·or -ōris *m* assailant, attacker
tempt·ō -āre -āvī -ātus *tr* **(tent-)** to test,
feel, probe; to attempt; to attack; to try to
influence, tamper with, tempt, try to induce; to urge, incite, sound out; to worry,
distress
temptus *pp of* **temno**
temp·us -oris *n* time; period, season; occasion, opportunity; right time, good
time, proper period; times, condition,
state, position; need, emergency; *(anat)*
temple; *(pros)* measure, quantity, cadence; **ad tempus** *(or* **temporis causā)**
to suit the occasion; **ante tempus** before
time, too soon; **ex tempore** on the spur
of the moment; **idem temporis** at the
same time; **id temporis** at that time; **in
ipso tempore** in the nick of time; **in
tempore** at the right moment; just in
time; as occasion offers; **in tempus** temporarily, for a time; **per tempus** just in
time; **primum tempus** spring; **pro
tempore** as time permits; according to
circumstances; to suit the occasion;
tempore at an opportune time; **tempori
cedere** to yield to circumstances; **tempus
in ultimum** to the last extremity; **tunc
tempus** for the time, at the time
tēmulent·us -a -um *adj* intoxicated
tenācit·ās -ātis *f* tenacity; miserliness
tenāciter *adv* tightly, firmly
ten·ax -ācis *adj* holding tight, gripping,
clinging; sticky; firm; obstinate; stingy;
(w. gen) clinging to
tendicul·ae -ārum *fpl* little snare, little
noose, little trap
tendō tendēre tetendī tentus *or* **tensus** *tr*
to stretch, stretch out, hold out, spread;
to strain; to head for; to aim, shoot *(an
arrow);* to bend *(a bow);* to tune *(an
instrument);* to pitch *(a tent)* **‖** *intr* to
pitch tents, be encamped; to travel, sail,

move, march; to endeavor; to contend, fight; to exert oneself; *(w. inf)* to try to; *(w.* ad) 1 to tend toward, be inclined toward; 2 to move toward, travel to, aim for; *(w.* contra + *acc)* to fight against

tenebr·ae -ārum *fpl* darkness; night; blindness; dark place, haunts; unconsciousness; death; lower world; obscurity, low station; ignorance; gloomy state of affairs

tenebricōs·us -a -um *adj* dark, gloomy; hidden, concealed *(lust)*

tenebric·us -a -um *adj* dark, gloomy

tenebrōs·us -a -um *adj* dark, gloomy

Tened·os *or* Tened·us -ī *f* Tenedos *(island off the coast of Troy)*

tenellul·us -a -um *adj* tender little, dainty little

tenell·us -a -um *adj* dainty

ten·eō -ēre -uī -tus *tr* to hold, hold tight; to keep; to grasp, comprehend; to comprise; to possess, occupy, be master of; to hold back, restrain, repress; to charm, amuse; to have control of, get the better of; to keep, detain; to hold to, stick to, insist on *(an opinion); (w. inf)* to know how to; cursum *(or* iter *or* viam) tenere to continue on a course; ‖ *refl* to remain *(in a place)*, stay put ‖ *intr* to hold out, last, keep on; to continue, persist; to continue on a course; *(w.* quin, quominus, ne *or inf)* to refrain from; *(w.* ut, ne) to make good one's point (that, that not)

ten·er -era -erum *adj* tender, soft, delicate; young, youthful; impressionable; weak; effeminate; voluptuous

tenerasc·ō *or* teneresc·ō -ĕre *intr* to grow weak; to become flabby

tenerē *adv* softly

tenerit·ās -ātis *f* weakness

teneritūd·ō -inis *f* tender age

tēnesm·os -ī *m* straining at stool

ten·or -ōris *m* uninterrupted course; continuity; uno tenore uninterruptedly

Tēn·os -ī *f* island of the Cyclades

tens·a -ae *f* car carrying images of the gods in procession

tens·us -a -um *pp of* tendo ‖ *adj* stretched, drawn tight; stretched out

tentīg·ō -inis *f* lust

tentō *see* tempto

tentōr·ium -iī *n* tent

tent·us -a -um *pp of* tendo *and* teneo ‖ *adj* stretched, drawn tight

Tentyr·a -ōrum *npl* town in Upper Egypt

tenuī *perf of* teneo

tenuicul·us -a -um *adj* poor, paltry

tenu·is -is -e *adj* thin; fine; delicate; precise; shallow *(groove, etc.);* slight, puny, poor, insignificant; plain, simple; small, narrow

tenuit·ās -ātis *f* thinness, fineness; lean-

ness; simplicity; precision; poverty; simpleness *(of style)*

tenuiter *adv* thinly; slightly; poorly, indifferently; exactly, minutely; superficially

tenu·ō -āre -āvī -ātus *tr* to make thin; to contract; to dissolve; to lessen; to weaken; to rarefy; to make *(the voice)* shrill; to emaciate *(the body)*

ten·us -oris *n* trap, snare

tenus *prep (w. abl, always placed after the noun)* as far as, up to, down to; nomine *(or* verbo) tenus as far as the name goes, nominally

Te·os *or* Te·us -ī *f* town on the coast of Asia Minor, the birthplace of Anacreon

tepe·facio -facĕre -fēcī -factus *tr* to warm up

tepefact·ō -āre *tr* to be in the habit of warming

tep·eō -ēre -uī *intr* to get warm; to grow lukewarm; to glow with love; to be cool, be indifferent

tep·escō -escĕre -uī *intr* to grow warm; to grow lukewarm, grow indifferent

tepid·us -a -um *adj* warm, lukewarm, tepid

tep·or -ōris *m* warmth; coolness, lack of heat *(in a bath);* lack of fire *(in a speech)*

tepuī *perf of* tepeo *and* tepesco

ter *adv* three times

-ter *advl suf* of third-declension adjectives: audacter boldly; stems in -nt- drop -t-: prudenter prudently; also of second-declension adjectives: humaniter kindly

-ter -teri *or* -trī *m* -tera -terum *or* -tra -trum *adjl suf* ofen used to forming pairs: magister master, minister servant; noster our, vester your

terdeciens *or* terdeciēs *adv* thirteen times

terebinth·us -ī *f* terebinth, turpentine tree

terebr·a -ae *f* drill

terebr·ō -āre -āvī -ātus *tr* to bore, drill a hole in, pierce

terēd·ō -inis *f* grubworm

Tēreid·ēs -ae *m* Itys *(son of Tereus)*

Terentiān·us -a -um *adj* of the Terentian clan; *esp.* written, portrayed, *etc.*, by the poet Terence

Terent·ius -(i)ī *m* Terence *(Marcus Terentius Afer, Roman comic poet, c. 190–159 B.C.)*

ter·es -etis *adj* smooth, well-rounded; polished, shapely; round, cylindrical; *(fig)* fine, elegant

Tēr·eūs -eī *or* -eos *m* evil king of Thrace, husband of Procne, and father of Itys

tergemin·us -a -um *adj* triplet, triple

ter·geō -gēre -sī -sus *or* terg·ō -ĕre *tr* to wipe off, wipe dry; to scour; to clean, cleanse

tergīn·um -ī *n* rawhide; scourge

tergiversāti·ō -ōnis f refusal; evasion, subterfuge

tergivers·or -ārī -ātus sum intr to turn one's back; to be shifty

tergō see **tergeo**

terg·um -ī n or **terg·us -oris** n back; ridge; hide; leather; leather objects: bag, shield, drum; (mil) rear; **a tergo** in the rear, from behind; **in tergum** backward

terment·um -ī n sore caused by friction

term·es -itis m branch, bough

Termināl·ia -ium or **-iōrum** npl festival in honor of Terminus (god of boundaries, celebrated on February 23)

termināti·ō -ōnis f the marking of the boundaries of a territory (esp. w. boundary stones or posts); boundary; tract of land along a boundary; end, goal (of an activity); decision, determining; (rhet) arrangement, ending (of a sentence)

termin·ō -āre -āvī -ātus tr to mark off with boundaries, bound, limit; to fix, determine, define; to terminate, conclude; to settle (an issue); (rhet) to round out (a sentence)

termin·us -ī m boundary, limit, bound **‖ Terminus** god of boundaries

tern·ī -ae -a adj three apiece, three each, three at a time; three in a row

terō terĕre trīvī trītus tr to rub; to wear down; to wear out (by constant handling); to make (words, expressions) trite (by repetition), run into the ground; to travel (a road) repeatedly; to trample, crush; to spend, waste (time); to smooth, polish; to sharpen; to thresh (grain); to grind (grain); **otium terere** to waste time in idleness

Terpsichor·ē -ēs f Muse of dancing, of lyric poetry; (fig) poetry

terr·a -ae f the earth; land; earth, ground, soil; country, region, territory; **in terrā** (or **terris**) in the world, in existence; (as contrasted with heaven) on earth; (astr) the planet earth; **terrā ortus** sprung from the earth, indigenous; **terrae filius** a nobody; **terrae** (or **terrarum**) **motus** earthquake

terrāneol·a -ae f crested lark

terrēn·us -a -um adj earthly, terrestrial; earthen **‖** n land, ground

terr·eō -ēre -uī -itus tr to frighten, scare, terrify; to deter

terrestr·is -is -e adj of the earth, on the earth; land, earth; terrestrial; **proelium terrestre** land battle

terre·us -a -um adj earth-born

terribil·is -is -e adj terrible, frightful

terricul·a -ae f bogy; scary thing

terrific·ō -āre tr to terrify

terrific·us -a -um adj terrifying, awe-inspiring, alarming

terrigen·a -ae m earth-born creature

terriloqu·us -a -um adj ominous, alarming

terripav·ium -(i)ī n (**-pud·ium, -puv·ium**) (etymologizing forms of **tripudium**) see **tripudium**

territ·ō -āre -āvī tr to keep frightening; to try to scare, intimidate

territōr·ium -(i)ī n land around a town, territory, suburbs

terr·or -ōris m terror, alarm, dread

terruī perf of **terreo**

ter(r)unc·ius -(i)ī m copper coin (weighing three unciae = three-twelfths of an as or one-fortieth of a **denarius**, i.e., less than 1¢); **heres ex teruncio** heir to one fourth an estate

ters·us -a -um pp of **tergeo ‖** adj clean, neat; terse; polished (writing)

tertiadecimān·ī -ōrum mpl soldiers of the thirteenth legion

tertiān·us -a -um adj recurring every three days, (in our system: every other day), tertian (fever) **‖** mpl soldiers of the third legion

tertiō adv in the third place, thirdly; the third time

tertium adv for the third time

terti·us -a -um adj third

terti·us decim·us -a -um adj thirteenth

teruncius see **terrunicus**

tervenēfic·us -ī m (term of abuse) three-time killer, absolute villain

tesqu·a -ōrum npl wilderness, wilds

tessell·a -ae f cubed mosaic stone

tessellāt·us -a -um adj tesselated

tesser·a -ae f cube; die; watchword, countersign; tally, token; ticket

tesserār·ius -(i)ī m (mil) officer of the day

tesserul·a -ae f small cube; ticket

test·a -ae f brick, tile; jug, crock; potsherd; shellfish; shell (of a crustacean, snail, etc.); fragment, splinter (esp. of a broken tooth or bone)

testāmentāri·us -a -um adj pertaining to a will, testamentary **‖** m forger

testāment·um -ī n testament, will

testāti·ō -ōnis f testifying to a fact; (leg) deposition

testāt·or -ōris m testator (one who makes a will)

testāt·us -a -um adj well-attested; witnessed

testicul·us -ī m testicle

testificāti·ō -ōnis f testifying; proof, evidence

testific·or -ārī -ātus sum tr to give as evidence, give proof of; to testify to; to vouch for; to invoke (e.g., a god) as one's witness; (fig) to give proof of

testimōn·ium -(i)ī n testimony

test·is -is mf witness **‖** m testicle

test·or -ārī -ātus sum tr to give as evidence; to show, prove, vouch for; to call

to witness, appeal to **ll** *intr* to be a witness, testify; to make a will
test·ū -ūs *n see* **testum**
testūdine·us -a -um *adj* of a tortoise; made of tortoise shell
testūd·ō -inis *f* tortoise; tortoise shell; lyre, lute; arch, vault; *(mil)* protective shed *(for besiegers)*
testul·a -ae *f* potsherd
test·um -ī *n* earthenware lid; pot with a lid
tēte = *emphatic form of* **te**
tetendī *perf of* **tendo**
Tēth·ys -yos *f* wife of Oceanus and mother of the sea nymphs; ocean, sea
tetigī *perf of* **tango**
tetradrachm·um -ī *n* (-trach-) Greek silver coin *(worth four drachmas or four denarii or $4)*
tetra·ō -ōnis *m* game bird *(black grouse?)*
tetrarch·ēs -ae *m* tetrarch *(ruler of ¼ of a country); petty prince*
tetrarchi·a -ae *f* tetrarchy
tetrastich·on -ī *n* four-line poem
tetric·us -a -um *adj* stern, gloomy, crabby; harsh, rough
tetrissit·ō -āre *intr* to quack
Teu·cer *or* **Teu·crus -crī** *m* son of Telamon and half-brother of Ajax **ll** son of Scamander of Crete, father-in-law of Dardanus, and later king of Troy
Teucri·a -ae *f* Troy, land of the Teucrians
Teucr·us -a -um *adj* Teucrian, Trojan **ll** *mpl* Trojans
Teuthrantē·us -a -um *adj* Mysian
Teuthranti·us -a -um *adj* of Teuthras; **turba Teuthrantia** fifty daughters of Thespius
Teuthr·ās -antis *m* ancient king of Mysia, father of Thespius
Teuton·ēs -um *or* **Teuton·ī -ōrum** *mpl* Teutons
Teutonic·us -a -um *adj* Teutonic
tex·ō -ĕre -uī -tus *tr* to weave; to plait; to build; to compose
textil·is -is -e *adj* woven; brocaded **ll** *n* fabric
text·or -ōris *m* weaver
textrīn·um -ī *n* weaving; weaving room
textr·ix -īcis *f* weaver *(female)*
textūr·a -ae *f* texture; web; fabric
text·us -a -um *pp of* **texo ll** *n* woven cloth, fabric; web
text·us -ūs *m* texture
texuī *perf of* **texo**
Thā·is -idis *or* **-idos** *f* notorious Athenian prostitute
thalam·us -ī *m* woman's room; bedroom; marriage bed; marriage
thalassic·us *or* **thalassin·us -a -um** *adj* sea-green, aquamarine
Thal·ēs -ae *m* Thales *(early Ionian philosopher of Miletus, regarded as one of the Seven Sages, Ē 575 B.C.)*

Thalī·a *or* **Thalē·a -ae** *f* Muse of comedy and light verse **ll** one of the Graces **ll** a Nereid, sea nymph
thall·us -ī *m* green bough; green stem
Thaps·os -ī *f* city of N. Africa where Caesar defeated the Pompeians *(46 B.C.)*
Thasi·us -a -um *adj* of Thasos; **Thasius lapis** Thasian marble
Thas·os -ī *f* island in the Aegean Sea, off the coast of Thrace
Thaumantē·us -a -um *adj* descended from Thaumas *(a Titan)*
Thaumanti·as -adis *or* **Thaumant·is -idis** *f* Iris *(daughter of the Titan Thaumas)*
theātrāl·is -is -e *adj* theatrical
theātr·um -ī *n* theater
Thēb·ae -ārum *fpl* Thebes *(capital of Boeotia, founded by Cadmus)* **ll** Thebes *(city of Upper Egypt)* **ll** place in Mysia, home of Eetion
Thēba·is -idis *or* **-idos** *adj (fem only)* of Boeotian Thebes; of Thebes in Mysia; of Egyptian Thebes; **Thebais nupta** Theban bride *(i.e., Andromachē)* **ll** *f* Theban woman; district around Egyptian Thebes, the Thebaid
Thēbān·us -a -um *adj & mf* Theban *(of Boeotia, Egypt, or Mysia)*
thēc·a -ae *f* case, box
them·a -atis *n* position of the planets *or* stars at one's birth, horoscope; *(rhet)* theme, topic proposed for debate in a school of rhetoric
Them·is -is *f* goddess of justice and of prophecy
Themistocl·ēs -is *m* Themistocles *(Athenian admiral and statesman, c. 528–459 B.C.)*
Themistoclē·us -a -um *adj* Themistoclean
thensaurius *or* **thensaurus** *see* **thesaurus**
Theocrit·us -ī *m* founder of Greek pastoral poetry, born at Syracuse *(3rd cent. B.C.)*
theolog·us -ī *m* theologian
theologūmen·a -ōn *npl* essays on the gods
therm·ae -ārum *fpl* hot baths, public baths *(which included rooms for social activities, lecture halls, theater, restaurants, workout rooms)*
Thermōd·on -ontis *m* river in Pontus, around which the Amazons were said to have lived
Thermōdontiac·us -a -um *adj* of the River Thermodon *(often applied to Amazons, esp. Hippolyta and Penthesilea, or to things connected with them)*
thermopōl·ium -(i)ī *n* hot-drink shop
thermopot·ō -āre *tr* to supply with warm drinks
Thermopyl·ae -ārum *fpl* (-pul-) Thermopylae *(famous pass in Thessaly, defended by Leonidas and his 400 Spartans in 480 B.C.)*

thermul·ae -ārum *fpl* small hot bath
Thersīt·ēs -ae *m* Greek soldier at Troy notorious for his ugliness
thēsaur·us -ī *m* (**thens-**) storehouse; store, treasure, hoard
Thēs·eūs -eī *or* **-eos** *m* king of Athens, son of Aegeus and husband *(or* lover) first of Ariadne and later of Phaedra
Thēsē·us -a -um *adj* of Theseus
Thēsīd·ae -ārum *mpl* Athenians
Thēsīd·ēs -ae *m* Hippolytus *(son of Theseus)* ‖ *mpl* Athenians
thes·is -is *f (rhet)* general question *(opp:* a particular case)
Thespiad·es -um *fpl* descendants of Thespius *(fifty sons of Thespius's fifty daughters)*
Thespi·ae -ārum *fpl* town in Boeotia near Mt. Helicon
Thesp·is -is *m* traditional founder of Greek tragedy *(his first presentation was in 535 B.C.)*
Thespi·us -a -um *adj* Thespian ‖ *m* a king of Mysia who had fifty daughters; *see* **Thespiades** ‖ *fpl* town in Boeotia near Mt. Helicon
Thessali·a -ae *f* Thessaly *(most northerly district of Greece)*
Thessalic·us -a -um *adj* Thessalian
Thessal·is -idis *or* **-idos** *adj (fem only)* Thessalian ‖ *f* Thessalian woman *(esp. a witch)*
Thessal·us -a -um *adj* Thessalian ‖ *mpl* people of Thessaly
Thestorid·ēs -ae *m* Calchas *(famous Greek seer in the Trojan War)*
thēta *indecl n* the Greek letter theta *(written on tablets by jurors voting for the death sentence)*
Thet·is -idis *or* **-idos** *f* sea nymph, daughter of Nereus and Doris, wife of Peleus, and mother of Achilles
thias·us -ī *m* Bacchic dance; troupe of Bacchic dancers
Thisb·ē -ēs *f* girl in Bablyon, loved by Pyramus ‖ small town in Boeotia
Thoantē·us -a -um *adj* of Thoas
Tho·ās -antis *m* king of the Taurians, slain by Orestes ‖ king of Lemnos and father of Hypsipyle
thol·us -ī *m* rotunda
thōr·ax -ācis *m* breastplate
Thrāc·a -ae *or* **Thrāc·ē -ēs** *f* Thrace *(country N. of the Aegean)*
Thrāci·us -a -um *adj* Thracian ‖ *f* Thrace
Thraex *see* **Threx**
Thr·ax -ācis *m* Thracian
Thre(i)ss·a -ae *f* Thracian woman
Thr·ex -ēcis *or* **Thr·aex -aecis** *m* Thracian gladiator *(i.e., armed like a Thracian with saber and small shield)*
thron·us -ī *m* throne
Thūcydīd·ēs -is *or* **-ī** *m* Thucydides *(Greek*

historian of the Peloponnesian War, c. 456–400 B.C.)
Thūl·ē *or* **T(h)ȳl·ē -ēs** *f* island located in the far north, perhaps Iceland or part of Scandinavia
thunn·us -ī *m* tuna fish
thūr- = **tur-**
Thūri·ī -ōrum *mpl* Thurii *(Greek city on the Tarentine Gulf in S. Italy)*
Thūrīn·us -a -um *adj* & *m* Thurian
thū·s -ris *n* incense, frankincense
Thybris *see* **Tiberis**
Thyēn·ē -ēs *f* nymph who nursed Bacchus
Thyest·ēs -ae *or* **-is** *m* son of Pelops, brother of Atreus, and father of Aegisthus
thymbr·a -ae *f (bot)* savory *(used as a spice in cooking)*
thym·um -ī *n (bot)* thyme *(common garden herb used as seasoning)*
Thyni·a -ae *f* Bithynia *(country of Asia Minor on the S. coast of the Black Sea)*
Thȳniac·us -a -um *adj* Bithynian
Thȳn·us -a -um *adj* & *m* Bithynian
thynn·us -ī *m* tuna fish
Thyōn·eūs -eī *m* Bacchus
thyrs·us -ī *m* Bacchic wand twined with vine leaves and ivy, and crowned with a pine cone
Ti. *abbr* **Tiberius** *(Roman first name, praenomen)*
tiār·a -ae *f or* **tiār·ās -ae** *m* tiara
Tiberīn·is -idis *or* **-idos** *adj (fem only)* of the Tiber
Tiberīn·us -a -um *adj* of the Tiber River ‖ *m* eponymous hero of the Tiber River
Tiber·is *or* **Tibr·is** *or* **Thybr·is -is** *m* Tiber River
Tiber·ius -(i)ī *m* Tiberius *(Roman first name, praenomen); esp.* Tiberius Claudius Nero Caesar *(successor of Augustus, 42 B.C.–A.D. 37, ruling from A.D. 14–37)* ‖ Tiberius Sempronius Gracchus *(socialist reformer, killed in 133 B.C.)*
tībi·a -ae *f* shinbone, tibia; flute
tībiāl·e -is *n* stocking
tībīc·en -inis *m* flutist; prop; pillar
tībīcin·a -ae *f* flutist *(female)*
Tibull·us -ī *m* Albius Tibullus *(Roman elegiac poet, c. 54–19 B.C.)*
Tīb·ur -uris *n* town of Latium on the Anio *(modern Tivoli)*
Tīburn·us -a -um *adj* of Tibur ‖ *m* legendary founder of Tibur
Tībur·s -tis *adj* of Tibur ‖ *mpl* inhabitants of Tibur ‖ *n* estate at Tibur
Tīburtīn·us -a -um *adj* of Tibur; travertine *(stone)* ‖ *n* estate at Tibur
Tībur·us -ī *m* legendary founder of Tibur *(see* **Tiburnus)**
Tīcīn·us -ī *m* tributary of the Po
Tigellīn·us -ī *m* notorious favorite of Nero
tigill·um -ī *n* beam; log
tignāri·us -a -um *adj* carpenter's; **faber**

tignarius carpenter; **officina tignaria** carpenter's shop

tign·um -ī n beam, plank; lumber

tigr·is -is mf tiger

tigr·is -is or **-idis** f tigress

Tigr·is -is or **-idis** m Tigris River

tīli·a -ae f lime tree

Tīmae·us -ī m Greek historian of Sicily (c. 346–250 B.C.) ‖ Pythagorean philosopher of Locri in S. Italy (after whom Plato names one of his dialogues, 5th cent. B.C.)

Timāv·us -ī m river which flows into the gulf of Trieste

Timāgen·ēs -is m brilliant rhetorician in the time of Augustus

timefact·us -a -um adj frightened

tim·eō -ēre -uī tr to fear, be afraid of ‖ intr to be afraid; (w. dat or de or pro + abl) to fear for; (w. ab + abl of source of fear) to fear harm from

timidē adv timidly, fearfully

timidit·ās -ātis f timidity, fearfulness, cowardice

timid·us -a -um adj timid, fearful, cowardly; (w. gen) afraid of

tim·or -ōris m fear; alarm, dread

tinctil·is -is -e adj obtained by dipping

tinctus pp of **tingo**

tine·a -ae f moth (destructive of clothes, books), bookworm

tin·g(u)ō -g(u)ĕre -xī -ctus tr to dip, soak; to dye, color; to tinge; to imbue

tinnīment·um -ī n ringing

tinn·iō -īre -īvī or **-iī -ītus** tr & intr to ring

tinnīt·us -ūs m ring, ringing; tinkling, jingling

tinnul·us -a -um adj ringing, tinkling; shrill

tintin(n)ābul·um -ī n bell; doorbell; cowbell

tintinnācul·us -a -um adj jingling ‖ mpl chain gang

tintin(n)·ō -āre or **tintin(n)·iō -īre** intr to ring

tīn·us -ī f laurustinus (evergreen shrub having white or pinkish flowers)

-tin·us -a -um adjl suf forms adjectives from adverbs denoting time, e.g.: **crastinus** tommorrow's; **pristinus** antique, ancient

-ti·ō -ōnis fem suf forms verbal nouns to denote the action of the verb, e.g.: **actio** act, action; appears as **-sio** from verbs which form the supine in **-sum**, e.g.: **cursio** running

Tīph·ys -yos m pilot of the Argo

tippūl·a -ae f water spider

Tīresi·ās -ae m famous blind seer at Thebes at the time of Oedipus

Tīridāt·ēs -ae m name of three kings of Parthia

tīr·ō -ōnis m novice, beginner; young man

who has just come of age; (mil) recruit ‖ **Tiro** Marcus Tullius Tiro (Cicero's secretary)

tīrōcin·ium -(i)ī n apprenticeship; beginning, first try; (mil) first campaign; (mil) military inexperience; (mil) body of raw recruits

tīruncul·us -ī m beginner, recruit

Tīryn·s -thos f town in the Argolid where Hercules was raised

Tīrynthi·us -a -um adj Tirynthian ‖ m Hercules ‖ mpl the people of Tiryns ‖ f Alcmena

Tīsamen·us -ī m son of Orestes and king of Argos

tisan·a -ae f pearl barley

tisanār·ium -(i)ī n gruel; **tisanarium oryzae** rice gruel

Tīsiphon·ē -ēs f one of the three Furies who haunted murderers

Tīsiphonē·us -a -um adj belonging to Tisiphone; (fig) deserving of punishment by the Furies, guilty

Tīt·ān -ānos or **Tītān·us -ī** m Titan; sun; Prometheus ‖ mpl Titans (giant sons of Uranus and Ge who rebelled against Uranus and put Cronus on the throne)

Tītāni·us -a -um adj of the Titans, Titanic (esp. of the sun, moon, or Prometheus) ‖ m sun-god ‖ f Latona (mother of Apollo and Diana) ‖ Diana ‖ Pyrrha (as descendant of Prometheus) ‖ Circe (as daughter of Sol or Helios)

Tīthōni·us -a -um adj Tithonian ‖ f Aurora (wife of Tithonus)

Tīthōn·us -ī m son of Laomedon and husband of Aurora from whom he received the gift of immortality without eternal youth

Tītiens·is -is -e adj of the Tities tribe

Tīt·iēs -ium mpl one of the three original Roman tribes

tītillāti·ō -ōnis f tickling, titillation;

tītill·ō -āre tr tickle, titillate

Titi·us -a -um adj Roman clan name (nomen)

tittibilīc·ium -(i)ī n trifle

titubanter adv falteringly

titubanti·a -ae f stumbling (in speech)

titubāti·ō -ōnis f (lit & fig) stumbling

titub·ō -āre -āvī -ātum intr to stagger, reel, totter; to falter, waver; to stumble, slip up (in speech)

titul·us -ī m inscription; label; title, heading (of a book, chapter); chapter (of a book); personal title; identification tag; notice, advertisement; pretext, ostensible motive; claim to fame; title of honor; renown; (w. gen) **1** honor or distinction arising from; **2** reputation for

Tit·us -ī m Roman first name (praenomen); esp. Titus Tatius (a Sabine king who is said to have ruled with Romulus until the *latter had him killed)* ‖ the Emperor Titus *(Titus Flavius Vespasianus, son of Vespasian; ruled* A.D. *79–81)*

Tity·os *or* **Tity·us -ī** *m* Tityus *(giant slain by Apollo for attempting to rape Latona and thrown into Tartarus)*

Tītyr·us *or* **Tity·os -ī** *m* shepherd in Vergil's pastorals, sometimes identified with Vergil himself

Tlēpolem·us -ī *m* son of Hercules

Tmar·os -ī *m* mountain in Epirus

Tmōlīt·ēs -is *adj (masc only)* of Mt. Tmolus ‖ *m* wine from Mt. Tmolus

Tmōli·us -a -um *adj* of Mt. Tmolus

Tmōl·us -ī *m* **(Tim-)** Tmolus *(mountain in Lydia famous for its wines)*

toculli·ō -ōnis *m* loan shark

todill·us -ī *m* type of small bird

tōfīn·us -a -um *adj* made of tufa

tōf·us -ī *m* **(toph-)** tufa *(sandstone, used extensively in Republican Rome as building stone)*

tog·a -ae *f* toga *(outer garment of a Roman citizen);* **toga atra** dark toga *(unwhitened toga worn as sign of mourning);* **toga candida** white toga *(fulled with chalk and worn by candidates for office);* **toga picta** brocaded toga *(worn by triumphant generals);* **toga praetexta** crimson-bordered toga *(worn by magistrates and freeborn children);* **toga pulla** dark-gray toga *(worn by mourners);* **toga pura** *(or* **virilis** *or* **libera)** toga of manhood *(worn by young men from about the age of sixteen)*

togāt·a -ae *f* Latin comedy *(on Roman themes and in Roman dress)*

togātār·ius -(i)ī *m* actor in a *fabula togata*

togātul·us -ī *m (pej)* miserable Roman *(of clients paying duty calls)*

togāt·us -a -um *adj* wearing a toga, true Roman; having a civilian occupation *or* status, civilian; peacetime-; **fabula togata** *(theat)* Latin comedy *(written on a native theme and presented in Roman dress);* **Gallia Togata** Cisalpine Gaul *(between the Alps and the Po River)* ‖ *m* Roman citizen; civilian; humble client ‖ *f* prostitute; *see* **togata**

togul·a -ae *f (pej)* little toga

tolerābil·is -is -e *adj* tolerable; patient

tolerābiliter *adv* without stress

toler·ans -antis *adj* tolerant; *(w. gen)* tolerant of, enduring

toleranter *adv* patiently

toleranti·a -ae *f* toleration, endurance

tolerāti·ō -ōnis *f* toleration, endurance

tolerāt·us -a -um *adj* tolerable, endurable

toler·ō -āre -āvī -ātus *tr* to tolerate, endure; to support, maintain, sustain

tollēn·ō -ōnis *m* crane, lift, derrick

tollō tollĕre sustulī sublātus *tr* to lift, raise; to raise *(the voice);* to draw *(lots);*

to have *(a child);* to acknowledge *(a child);* to raise, educate; to weigh *(anchor); (of a ship)* to take on board; *(of a ship)* to have the capacity of; *(of a vehicle)* to pick up, take as a passenger; to win, carry off *(a prize);* to reap *(a profit);* to remove; to do away with, destroy; to cancel, abolish, abrogate; to lift, steal; to uplift, cheer up, excite; to erect, build up; to waste *(time);* **amicum tollere** to cheer up a friend; **animos tollere** to boost morale; **deos tollere** to deny the existence of the gods; **de medio tollere** to kill; **diem tollere** to take a day off *(from work);* **in crucem** *(or* **in furcam) tollere** to crucify ‖ *refl (of plants)* to grow high; **in caelum se tollere** to ascend *or* climb into the sky ‖ *pass* to climb up, rise

Tolōs·a -ae *f* city in Narbonese Gaul *(modern Toulouse)*

Tolōsān·us -a -um *adj* **(Toloss-)** of Tolosa ‖ *mpl* people of Tolosa

Tolōs·as -ātis *adj* produced in Tolosa ‖ *mpl* people of Tolosa

tolūtim *adv* at a trot, jogging

tomāc(u)l·um -ī *n* sausage

tōment·um -ī *n* pillow stuffing

Tom-ī -ōrum *mpl* or **Tom·is -is** *f* Tomi *(town on the Black Sea in modern Romania, where Ovid spent his years in exile)*

Tomīt·ae -ārum *mpl* people of Tomi

Tomītān·us -a -um *adj* of Tomi

tom·us -ī *m* a length of papyrus, sheet

Ton·ans -antis *m* Thunderer *(epithet of several gods, esp. Jupiter)*

tondeō tondēre totondī tonsus *tr* to clip, shear, shave; to prune; to reap, mow; to crop, browse on; *(fig)* to fleece, rob; **usque ad cutem tondere** *(fig)* to swindle, fleece *(literally, the clip right down to the skin)*

tonitrāl·is -is -e *adj* thunderous

tonitr·us -ūs *m* or **tonitr·um -ī** *n* thunder ‖ *mpl or npl* claps of thunder

ton·ō -āre -uī -itūrus *tr* to thunder forth *(words)* ‖ *intr* to thunder

tons·a -ae *f* oar

tonsil·is -is -e *adj* clipped

tonsill·a -ae *f* **(tōs-)** tonsil

tonsit·ō -āre *tr* to shear regularly

tons·or -ōris *m* **(tōs-)** shearer; barber

tonsōri·us -a -um *adj* shaving; barber's

tonstrīcul·a -ae *f* little hairdresser, little barber *(female)*

to(n)strīn·a -ae *f* barber shop

tonstrīn·um -ī *n* trade of a barber, barbering

tonstr·ix -īcis *f* hairdresser, barber *(female)*

tonsūr·a -ae *f* clipping, shearing; **capillorum tonsura** haircut

tons·us -a -um *pp of* **tondeo** ‖ *f see* **tonsa**

tons·us -ūs *m* haircut; hairdo

tonuī *perf of* **tono**

tōph·us -ī *m* (tŏf-) tufa *(sandstone used as building material esp. in the Republican period)*

topiāri·us -a -um *adj* garden, landscape ‖ *m* gardener, landscaper ‖ *f* landscaping

topic·a -ōrum *npl* "commonplaces" *(title of work by Aristotle on which Cicero based his work on this topic)*

topic·ē -ēs *f (rhet)* resourcefulness in finding topics for speeches

-t·or -ōris *masc suf, formed from verbs to denote the doer of the action of the verb, e.g.:* amator lover; *becomes* **-sor** *from verbs which form the past participle in* **-sus**, *e.g.:* **tonsor** shearer, barber

tor·al -ālis *n* valance; coverlet

torcul·ar -āris *or* **torcul·um -ī** *n* wine press, oil press

toreum·a -atis *n* embossed work, relief

-tōr·ium -(i)ī *neut suf often denoting places, e.g.,* **praetorium** headquarters of the praetor *or* commander

torment·um -ī *n* windlass; catapult, artillery piece; shot; torture rack; *(lit & fig)* torture ‖ *npl* artillery

tormin·a -um *npl* colic, bowel trouble

torminōs·us -a -um *adj* suffering from colic, colicky

torn·ō -āre -āvī -ātus *tr* to turn on a lathe

torn·us -ī *m* lathe

torōs·us -a -um *adj* brawny, muscular

torpēd·ō -inis *f* numbness, lethargy, listlessness; stingray *(fish)*

torp·eō -ēre -uī *intr* to numb; to be stiff; to be stupefied; to be groggy

torp·escō -escĕre -uī *intr* to grow numb; to grow listless

torpid·us -a -um *adj* numbed, paralyzed; groggy

torp·or -ōris *m* torpor, numbness; grogginess

torpuī *perf of* **torpeo** *and* **torpesco**

torquāt·us -a -um *adj* wearing a collar *or* necklace ‖ **Torquatus** *m* Titus Manlius Torquatus *(legendary Roman hero who wore a necklace taken from a gigantic Gaul he had slain)*

tor·queō -quēre -sī -tus *tr* to twist, turn, wind; to bend out of shape; to hurl; to wind up *(catapult)*; to turn *(so as to face in the opposite direction)*; to roll *(eyes)*; to crane *(neck)*; to divert the course of; to spin; to curl *(hair)*; to wreathe *(the head)*; *(fig)* to torment; **aliquem torquere** *(w.* **in** *or* **adversus, contra** *+ acc)* to torture s.o. to give evidence against *(s.o.)*

torqu·ēs *or* **torqu·is -is** *m(f)* necklace; collar *(of twisted metal, as military decoration)*

torr·ens -entis *adj* burning, seething; rushing, roaring *(stream)*; fiery *(speech)* ‖ *m* torrent; current

torr·eō -ēre -uī tostus *tr* to roast, bake; to burn, scorch; to parch

torr·escō -escĕre -uī *intr* to become burned; to become parched

torrid·us -a -um *adj* baked, parched; dried up; frostbitten

torr·is -is *or* **torr·us -ī** *m* firebrand

torruī *perf of* **torreo**

torsī *perf of* **torqueo**

tortē *adv* crookedly

tortil·is -is -e *adj* twisted, winding, spiral, coiled

tort·ō -āre *tr* to twist, coil ‖ *pass* to writhe

tort·or -ōris *m* torturer

tortuōs·us -a -um *adj* tortuous, winding; *(fig)* complicated

tort·us -a -um *adj* bent, crooked, curved; coiled, twisted; curly *(hair)*; winding *(road, labyrinth)*

tort·us -ūs *m* twist, coil; **tortūs dare** *(of a serpent)* to form loops

torul·us -ī *m* headband; tuft *(of hair)*

tor·us -ī *m* knot; bulge; muscle, brawn; bed, couch; mattress; cushion; mound; boss; flowery expression; **torus genialis** conjugal bed

torvit·ās -ātis *f* grimness

torv·us -a -um *adj* grim

tostus *pp of* **torreo**

tot *indecl adj* so many, as many; **tot...quot** as many ... as

totiens *or* **totiēs** *adv* so often, so many times

totondī *perf of* **tondeo**

tōt·us -a -um *adj* the whole, all, entire; **totus in illis** totally absorbed in those matters ‖ *n* the whole matter, all; **ex toto** totally; **in toto** on the whole, in general; **in totum** totally

toxic·um -ī *n* poison *(originally, a poison in which arrowheads were dipped)*

trabāl·is -is -e *adj* of *or* for beams; **clavus trabalis** spike; **telum trabale** beam-like shaft

trabe·a -ae *f* ceremonial robe *(with purple stripes and worn by magistrates, augurs, and as dress uniform of the equites)*

trabeāt·us -a -um *adj* wearing a *trabea*

trab·s -is *f* beam, plank; timber; tree; object made of beams: roof, shaft, table, battering ram

Trāch·īn -īnis *or* **Trāch·ȳn -ȳnos** *f* Trachis *(town in Thessaly on Mount Oeta, where Hercules had himself cremated)*

Trāchīni·us -a -um *adj* of Trachin (Trachis) ‖ *m* Ceyx *(king of Trachin)* ‖ *fpl* "Women of Trachis" *(title of a play by Sophocles)*

tractābil·is -is -e *adj* manageable; *(of weather)* fit for navigation

tractāti·ō -ōnis *f* handling, management; discussion, treatment *(of a subject)*

tractātr·ix -īcis *f* masseuse

tractāt·us -ūs *m* touching, handling; management

tractim *adv* little by little, slowly; in a drawn-out manner

tract·ō -āre -āvī -ātus *tr* to drag around, haul, pull; to touch, handle; to deal with, treat; to manage, control; to wield; to conduct, carry on, transact; to practice; to discuss; *(of an actor)* to play the role of; to examine, consider; **male tractare** to mistreat **‖** *refl* to behave, conduct oneself **‖** *intr* to carry on a discussion

tract·us -a -um *pp of* **traho ‖** *adj* fluent; lengthy, continuous *(discourse)*

tract·us -ūs *m* dragging; dragging out, extension *(e.g., of a war);* track, trail; tract, expanse, extent, distance; region, district

tradidī *perf of* **trado**

trāditi·ō -ōnis *f* handing over, surrender; transmission; item of traditional belief, custom, tradition

trādit·or -ōris *m* betrayer, traitor

trā·dō -děre -didī -ditus *tr* to hand over, surrender, deliver; to betray; to hand down, bequeath, transmit, pass on; to relate, recount; to teach **‖** *refl (w. dat)* **1** to surrender to; **2** to devote oneself to

trā·dūcō -dūcěre -duxī -ductus *tr* to bring across *or* over, transfer; to convert, bring over; *(w. ad or in + acc)* to cause *(s.o.)* to change *(from one attitude, habit, etc.)* to *(another);* to exhibit, display; to disgrace; to pass, spend; *(gram)* to derive; **traducere equum** *(of a member of the equestrian order who passed the censor's inspection)* to lead one's horse in the parade

trāducti·ō -ōnis *f* transference; passage *(of time);* metonymy; use of homonyms *or* homophones

trāduct·or -ōris *m* conveyor

trāductus *pp of* **traduco**

trād·ux -ucis *mf* vine branch *(trained across the space between trees in a vineyard)*

trāduxī *perf of* **traduco**

tragicē *adv* as in tragedy

tragicocōmoedi·a -ae *f* melodrama

tragic·us -a -um *adj* of tragedy, tragic; in the tragic style, grand, solemn; of a tragic nature, tragic **‖** *m* writer of tragedies

tragoedi·a -ae *f* tragedy

tragoed·us -ī *m* tragic actor

trāgul·a -ae *f* javelin

trag·us *or* **trag·os -ī** *m* body odor of the armpits; a fish *(of unknown type)*

trah·ax -ācis *adj* greedy

trahe·a -ae *f* sledge, drag *(used as a threshing device)*

tra·hō -hěre -xī -ctus *tr* to draw, drag, trail; *(in a temporal sense)* to bring in its wake; to draw out, pull out, extract; to drag out, protract; to lead, to come leading *(an animal); (of a river)* to carry along; to carry off *(as plunder);* to rob *(persons);* to take along *(on a trip);* to contract, wrinkle *(the brow);* to pull toward one; *(of physical forces)* to attract; to attract, lure, fascinate *(persons);* to draw *(water);* to draw *(conclusions);* to take on, assume; to acquire, get; to spin, manufacture; to win over *(to the other side);* to refer, ascribe; to distract; to keep on considering, ponder; **animam** *(or* **spiritum)** **trahere** to draw in breath; **pedem trahere** *(of a lame person)* to drag one foot

Trājān·us -ī *m* Trajan *(Marcus Ulpius Trajanus, Roman emperor, A.D. 98–117)*

trājecti·ō -ōnis *f* crossing, passage; transposition *(of words);* shift of meaning; exaggeration

trājectus *pp of* **trajicio**

trāject·us -ūs *m* crossing over, passage

trā·jiciō -jicěre -jēcī -jectus *tr* to throw *(a weapon)* across; *(of a weapon)* to pierce, pass through; to place *(a bridge, a bar)* across; to pass through, break through; to move, shift *(s.th. from one place to another); (w. double acc)* to bring *(e.g., troops)* across *(e.g., a river, mountain); (w. trans + acc)* to lead across; *(w. in + acc)* to lead over into; to shift *(words from one part of the sentence to another)* **‖** *intr* to cross over

trālāt- = **translat-**

Trall·ēs -ium *fpl* Tralles *(town in Lydia on the Menander River, variously set in Caria and Lydia)*

Tralliān·us -a -um *adj* of Tralles

trāloqu·or -ī *tr* to talk over, enumerate, recount

trālūceō *see* **transluceo**

trām·a -ae *f* woof, warp *(in some form of weaving)*

trām·es -itis *m* path, track, trail

trāmi- = **transmi-**

trānatō = **transnato**

trān·ō *or* **transn·ō -āre -āvī -ātus** *tr* to swim across; to pass through, permeate **‖** *intr* to swim across; to pass through

tranquillē *adv* quietly, calmly

tranquillit·ās -ātis *f* tranquillity, stillness, calmness

tranquill·ō -āre -āvī -ātus *tr* to calm, quiet, compose

tranquill·us -a -um *adj* tranquil, calm, quiet **‖** *n* calm, quiet, tranquillity; calm sea

Tranquill·us -ī *m* Gaius Suetonius Tranquillus *(biographer of the Emperors, born c. A.D. 69)*

trans *prep (w. acc)* across, over, beyond
trans- *pref (used with verbs or verbal derivatives in the sense of the preposition)*
transab·eō -īre -īvī *or* **-iī** *tr* to pierce, pass right through *(and go some distance beyond)*
transacti·ō -ōnis *f* business transaction, business deal
transact·or -ōris *m* manager, negotiator
transactus *pp of* **transigo**
transad·igō -igĕre -ēgī -āctus *tr* to pierce; to run *(s.o.)* through; *(w. double acc)* to run *(e.g., a sword)* through *(s.o.)*
Transalpīn·us -a -um *adj* Transalpine
transbīt·ō -ĕre *intr* to come *or* go across
transcen·dō -dĕre -dī -sus *tr* to climb *or* step over, surmount; to overstep, transgress ‖ *intr* to climb *or* step across
trans·cīdō -cīdĕre -cīdī -cīsus *tr* to flog thoroughly
trans·scrībō -scrībĕre -scripsī -scriptus *tr* to transcribe, copy off; *(leg)* to transfer, convey
trans·currō -currĕre -(cu)currī -cursum *tr & intr* to hurry, run *or* dash over; to run through; to run past; *(in writing)* to pass over quickly; to skim *(in reading)*
transcurs·us -ūs *m* running through, passage; cursory mention, cursory treatment *(of a subject)*
transd- = trad-
transenn·a -ae *f* (**trās-**) lattice work; lattice window; fowler's net
trans·eō -īre -īvī *or* **-iī -itus** *tr* to cross; to desert; to pass *(in a race);* to pass over, make no mention of; to treat cursorily; to overstep; to surpass ‖ *intr* to go over, go across, pass over; to pass by, go by; to shift *(to another opinion, topic, etc.); (of time)* to pass by; to pass away; *(w. ad + acc)* **1** to cross over to *(a place);* **2** to desert to; *(w. in + acc)* to change into; *(w. per + acc)* to penetrate, permeate
trans·ferō -ferre -tulī -lātus *(or* **trālātus)** *tr* (**trāf-**) to carry *or* bring across; to transfer *(by writing);* to copy; to shift; to transform; to postpone; to translate; to use figuratively
trans·fīgō -fīgĕre -fīxī -fīxus *tr* to pierce; to run *(s.o.)* through
transfigūr·ō -āre -āvī -ātus *tr* to transform
transfīxus *pp of* **transfīgo**
trans·fodiō -fodĕre -fōdī -fossus *tr* to stab, pierce, run through
transform·is -is -e *adj* transformed
transform·ō -āre -āvī -ātus *tr* to transform
transfossus *pp of* **transfodio**
transfret·ō -āre -āvī -ātum *intr* to cross the sea
transfug·a -ae *m* deserter, turncoat

trans·fugiō -fugĕre -fūgī *intr* to go over to the enemy, desert
transfug·ium -(i)ī *n* desertion
trans·fundō -fundĕre -fūdī -fūsus *tr* to transfuse; to pour; *(w. in + acc)* to pour *(a liquid)* into; *(w. ad + acc) (fig)* to shift *(affection, allegiance)* to
transfūsi·ō -ōnis *f* pouring from one vessel into another; *(fig)* intermarriage
transfūsus *pp of* **transfundo**
trans·gredior -gredī -gressus sum *tr* to cross, pass over; to exceed ‖ *intr* to go across; to cross over *(to another party)*
transgressi·ō -ōnis *f* crossing; transition; transposition *(of words)*
transgressus *pp of* **transgredior**
transgress·us -ūs *m* crossing
transiciō *see* **transjicio**
transiect- = transject-
trans·igō -igĕre -ēgī -actus *tr* to pierce, run through; to finish; to settle, transact; to accomplish, perform, conclude; to pass, spend ‖ *intr* to come to an agreement, reach an understanding
transil·iō *or* **transsil·iō -īre -uī** *tr* to jump over, jump across; to overstep; to skip, omit ‖ *intr* to jump across
transit·ans -antis *adj* passing through
transiti·ō -ōnis *f* crossing, passage; switching *(to another party);* contagion, infection; passageway
transitōri·us -a -um *adj* affording a passage *(from one place to another)*
transitus *pp of* **transeo**
transit·us -ūs *m* crossing, passage; passing; traffic; crossing over, desertion; change, period of change, transition; transference of possession *(of);* fading *(of colors);* **in transitu** in passing; **per transitum** by way of transition
translātīci·us -a -um *adj* (**trāl-**) transmitted, traditional, customary; usual, common
translāti·ō -ōnis *f* (**trāl-**) transfer, shift; transporting; translation; metaphor, figure
translātīv·us -a -um *adj* (**trāl-**) transferable
translāt·or -ōris *m* middleman *(in a transfer)*
translātus *pp of* **transferro**
transleg·ō -ĕre *tr (w. dat)* to read out to *(s.o.)*
transloqu·or -ī *tr* (**trāl-**) to recount from the beginning
transluc·eō -ēre *intr* (**trāl-**) to shine through; to be reflected
transmarīn·us -a -um *adj* from beyond the seas, foreign, overseas
transme·ō -āre *tr & intr* (**trām-**) to cross, pass through
transmigr·ō -āre -āvī -ātum *intr* (**trām-**) to move, change residence; to migrate, emigrate

transmin·eō -ēre *intr* to stick out on the other side

transmissi·ō -ōnis *f* crossing, passage

transmissus *pp of* **transmitto**

transmiss·us -ūs *m* passing over, crossing, passage

trans·mittō -mittĕre -mīsī -missus *tr* (**trām-**) to send across; to transmit; to let pass; to hand over, entrust; to pass over, leave unmentioned; to endure; *(w.* in + *acc)* to send *(s.o.)* across to *or* into; *(w.* per + *acc)* to let *(s.o.)* pass through ‖ *intr* to cross over, cross, pass *(from one place to another)*

transmontān·ī -ōrum *mpl* people living across the mountains

trans·moveō -movēre -mōvī -mōtus *tr* to move, transfer

transmūt·ō -āre -āvī -ātus *tr* to change, shift

transnat·ō -āre -āvī -ātus *tr* (**trān-**) to swim (across) ‖ *intr* to swim across

transnō *see* **trano**

transnōmin·ō -āre -āvī -ātus *tr (w. double acc)* to rename as

Transpadān·us -a -um *adj* beyond *or* N. of the Po River

transpect·us -ūs *m* view, prospect

trans(s)pic·iō -ĕre *tr* to look through

trans·pōnō -pōnĕre -posuī -positus *tr* to transfer, move across

transport·ō -āre -āvī -ātus *tr* to transport

transpositus *pp of* **transpono**

transrhenān·us -a -um *adj* beyond the Rhine, E. of the Rhine

transs- = **trans-**

transtiberīn·us -a -um *adj* across the Tiber

transtin·eō -ēre *intr* to provide a link *(from one side to the other)*

transtr·um -ī *n* crossbeam; rower's seat, thwart

transult·ō -āre *intr* to jump across

transūt·us -a -um *adj* pierced through *(w. a pointed object)*

transvecti·ō -ōnis *f* (**trāv-**) transportation; riding past *(in review)*

trans·vehō -vehĕre -vexī -vectus *tr* (**trāv-**) to transport; to carry past *(in a parade)* ‖ *pass* to ride by *(in a parade); (of time)* to elapse

transverber·ō -āre *tr* to pierce through and through, transfix

transversāri·us -a -um *adj* lying crosswise ‖ *n* crosspiece

transversē *adv* crosswise; across one's course

transvers·us *or* **transvors·us -a -um** *adj* (**trāv-**) lying across, lying crosswise; inopportune; astray; in the wrong direction ‖ *n* wrong direction; **de transverso** unexpectedly; **ex transverso** unexpectedly; sideways

transvolit·ō -āre *tr* to flit through, fly through

transvol·ō -āre -āvī -ātus *tr & intr* (**trāv-**) to fly over, fly across, fly by

transvorsus *see* **transversus**

trapēt·um -ī *n or* **trapēt·us -ī** *m* oil press

trapezīt·a -ae *m* banker, money-changer

trapezophor·um -ī *n* ornate table

Trapez·os -untis *or* **-untos** *f* city in Pontus on the Black Sea

Trasumēn·us -ī *m* (**-menn-**) Lake Trasimene *(lake in Etruria, modern Trasimeno, where Hannibal defeated the Romans in 217 B.C.)*

trāv- = **transv-**

traxī *perf of* **traho**

Trebi·a -ae *f* river which flows into the Po near Placentia *(modern Trebbia River, near which Hannibal defeated the Romans in 218 B.C.)*

Trebulān·us -a -um *adj* of Trebula *(town in central Campania);* **ager Trebulanus** district of Trebula

trecēn·ī -ae -a *adj* three hundred each; three hundred each time ‖ *mpl* lots of three hundred *(men)*

trecentēsim·us -a -um *adj* three-hundredth

trecentiē(n)s *adv* three hundred times

trechedipn·um -ī *n* light garment worn to dinner

tredecim *indecl adj* thirteen

tremebund·us -a -um *adj* trembling, shivering

treme·faciō -facĕre -fēcī -factus *tr* to shake, cause to shake

tremend·us -a -um *adj* awe-inspiring, terrible

trem·escō -escĕre -uī *tr* to tremble at ‖ *intr* to tremble

trem·ō -ĕre -uī *tr* to tremble at ‖ *intr* to tremble, shiver, quake

trem·or -ōris *m* trembling, shivering; dread; cause of fright, terror

tremuī *perf of* **tremo** *and* **tremesco**

tremul·us -a -um *adj* trembling, quivering, tremulous, shivering

trepidanter *adv* tremblingly, nervously

trepidāti·ō -ōnis *f* nervousness, alarm; trembling

trepidē *adv* nervously, in alarm

trepid·ō -āre -āvī -ātus *tr* to start at, be startled by ‖ *intr* to be nervous, be jumpy, be alarmed; *(of a flame)* to flicker; *(of streams)* to rush along

trepid·us -a -um *adj* nervous, jumpy; restless; bubbling; perilous, critical, alarming; **in re trepida** in a ticklish situation

trēs trēs tria *adj* three; *(denoting a small number)* a couple of

tress·is -is *m* sum of three *"pennies";* mere trifle

tresvirī *(gen:* **triumvirōrum)** *mpl* triumvirs

Trēver·ī or **Trēvir·ī -ōrum** mpl people E. of Gaul

tri- pref consisting of three of the things named, e.g., **tricornis** having three horns

triangul·us -a -um adj triangular ‖ n triangle

triāri·ī -ōrum mpl soldiers of the third rank in a battle line, reserves

trib·as -adis f female sexual pervert

Triboc·ī -ōrum mpl tribe which settled on the Rhine in the region of modern Alsace

tribuāri·us -a -um adj tribal

tribuī perf of **tribuo**

tribūl·is -is m fellow tribesman

trībul·um -ī n threshing sledge (wooden platform with iron teeth underneath)

tribul·us -ī m caltrop (thistle)

tribūn·al -ālis n platform; tribunal, judgment seat; (in camp) general's platform; cenotaph; **pro tribunali** (or **in** or **e tribunali**) officially

tribūnāt·us -ūs m tribuneship

tribūnici·us -a -um adj tribunician, tribune's ‖ m ex-tribune

tribūn·us -ī m tribune; **tribunus aerarius** paymaster; **tribunus militaris** (or **militum**) military tribune (six in each legion, serving under the legatus, and elected by the people or at times appointed by the commander); **tribunus plebis** tribune of the people (initially two, eventually ten in number, serving in the interests of the plebeians)

trib·uō -uěre -uī -ūtus tr to divide; to distribute, bestow, confer, assign; to give, present; to concede, grant, allow; to ascribe, impute; to devote, spend

trib·us -ūs f tribe (orginally three in number and eventually increased to thirty-five)

tribūtāri·us -a -um adj tributary, subject to tribute; **tributariae tabellae** letters of credit

tribūtim adv by tribes, tribe by tribe

tribūti·ō -ōnis f distribution

tribūt·um -ī n or **tribūt·us -ī** m tribute, tax; contribution

tribūt·us -a -um pp of **tribuo** ‖ adj arranged by tribes

trīc·ae -ārum fpl tricks; nonsense

trīcēn·ī -ae -a adj thirty each; thirty at a time, in groups of thirty

tric·eps -ipitis adj three-headed

trīcēsim·us -a -um adj (-cens-) thirtieth

trichil·a or **tricli·a** or **tricle·a -ae** f bower, arbor; summer house

trīciens or **trīciēs** adv thirty times

triclea see **trichila**

triclia see **trichila**

trīclīn·ium -(i)ī n dining couch (running around three sides of a table); dining room

trīc·ō -ōnis m schemer

trīc·or -ārī intr to cause trouble; to pull tricks

tricorp·or -oris adj triple-bodied

tricusp·is -idis adj three-pronged

trid·ens -entis adj three-pronged ‖ m trident

Tridentif·er or **Tridentig·er -erī** m Trident Bearer (epithet of Neptune)

tridu·um -ī n three-day period, three days

trienn·ia -ium npl triennial festival (celebrated every three years)

trienn·ium -(i)ī n three-year period, three years

tri·ens -entis m one third; coin (one third of a "penny"); third of a pint

trientābul·um -ī n land given by the State to those from whom the State had borrowed, equivalent to one third of the sum which the state owed

trienti·us -a -um adj sold for a third

triērarch·us -ī m captain of a trireme

triēr·is -is -e adj having oars or rowers arranged in threes ‖ f trireme

trietēric·us -a -um adj triennial, recurring every three years ‖ npl festival of Bacchus

trietēr·is -idis or **-idos** f three-year period; triennial festival in honor of Bacchus

trifāriam adv in three places, on three sides; under three headings

trifauc·is -is -e adj triple-throated

trifid·us -a -um adj three-forked; split into three parts

trifil·is -is -e adj having three threads or strands of hair

Trifolīn·us -a -um adj belonging to the district of Trifolium near Naples

trifol·ium -(i)ī n clover

triform·is -is -e adj triple-form (of the goddess having the three aspects of Luna, Diana, and Hecate; of three-headed Geryon; of the Chimera as composed of a lion, snake, and goat)

tri·fūr -fūris m archthief

trifurcif·er -erī m archvillain, hardened criminal

trigemin·us -a -um adj (terg-) threefold, triple ‖ mpl triplets

trīgintā indecl adj thirty

trig·ō(n) -ōnis or **-ōnos** game of catch (played with three players standing to form a triangle); ball (used in this game)

trigōnāl·is -is -e adj **pila trigonalis** ball used in the game of catch

trilībr·is -is -e adj three-pound

trilingu·is -is -e adj three-tongued

tril·ix -īcis adj three-ply, triple-stranded

trime(n)str·is -is -e adj of three months

trimetr·us -ī m (pros) trimeter (metric line consisting of three double feet, e.g., *iambic trimeter, or a line consisting of six iambic feet)*

trimod·ius -iī *m* measure of three pecks

trīmul·us -a -um *adj* three-year-old

trīm·us -a -um *adj* three-year-old

-trīn·a -ae *f suf* denoting the place where an activity is conducted: **tonstrīna** barbershop *(from* **tondere** to cut, shear, clip)

Trīnacr·is -idis *adj* Sicilian

Trīnacri·us -a -um *adj* Sicilian ‖ *m* Empedocles ‖ *f* Sicily

trīn-ī -ae -a *adj* threefold, triple; three each, three at a time; *(w. nouns occurring only in pl)* three: **trinae litterae** three letters, three epistles

Trinobant·ēs -ium *mpl* a British tribe near Essex

trinoctiāl·is -is -e *adj* occurring on three successive nights

trinōd·is -is -e *adj* triple-knotted

trinumm·us -ī *m* popular name for a newly introduced coin of high value ‖ **Trinummus** title of a play by Plautus

triōbol·um -ī *n* three-obol coin, half-dramcha *or* half-denarius piece *(c. 50¢)*

triōn·ēs -um *mpl* team of three oxen used in plowing ‖ **Triōnēs** Great and Little Bear *(constellations)*

Triop·ās -ae *adj (masc & fem only)* of Erysichthon

Triopē·is -idos *f* Mestra *(daughter of Erysichthon and granddaughter of Triopas, king of Thessaly)*

Triopē·ius -(i)ī *m* Erysichthon *(son of Triopas, king of Thessaly)*

triparc·us -a -um *adj* extremely stingy, triply stingy

tripartītō *adv* in three parts, into three parts

tripartīt·us -a -um *adj* **(-pert-)** divided into three parts, threefold

tripector·us -a -um *adj* triple-bodied, triple-chested

tripedāl·is -is -e *adj* three-foot

tripertītus *see* **tripartitus**

trip·ēs -edis *adj* three-legged, three-footed

tripl·ex -icis *adj* threefold, triple ‖ *n* three times as much, triple portion

tripl·us -a -um *adj* triple, threefold

Triptolem·us -ī *m* son of Celeus the king of Eleusis, favorite of Ceres, inventor of agriculture and one of the judges in the lower world

tripudi·ō -āre -āvī -ātum *intr* to perform a ritual dance *(tripudium)*

tripud·ium -(i)ī *n* war dance *(ritual dance in triple time, originally performed by priests in honor of Mars);* favorable omen *(when the sacred chickens ate hungrily, letting some grains fall to the ground in the process)*

trip·ūs -odis *or* **-odos** *m* tripod *(three-footed caldron);* oracle, Delphic oracle

triquetr·us -a -um *adj* triangular; Sicilian

trirēm·is -is -e *adj* having three banks of oars ‖ *f* trireme

trīs *see* **tres**

triscel·um -ī *n* triangle

triscurri·a -ōrum *npl* fantastic nonsense

tristicul·us -a -um *adj* somewhat sad

tristific·us -a -um *adj* saddening

tristimōni·a -ae *f or* **tristimōn·ium -(i)ī** *n* sadness

trist·is -is -e *adj* sad, sorrowful; bringing sorrow, saddening; gloomy, sullen; stern, harsh; disagreeable, offensive *(odor);* bitter, sour *(taste);* unpleasant *(sound)*

tristiter *adv (to cry)* bitterly; distressingly

tristiti·a -ae *or* **tristiti·ēs -ēī** *f* sadness, gloom, gloominess, depression; severity, sternness

trisulc·us -a -um *adj* three-forked

tritavi·a -ae *f* great-great-great-great-grandmother

tritav·us -ī *m* great-great-great-great-grandfather

trīticei·a -ae *f* facetious name of a fish invented to make a pun with *hordeia*

trītice·us -a -um *adj* wheat-

trītic·um -ī *n* wheat

Trīt·ōn -ōnis *m* son of Neptune who blows through a shell to calm the seas ‖ river flowing through Lake Tritonis in N. Africa where Minerva was said to be born

Trītōniac·us -a -um *adj* Tritonian, associated with Minerva

Trītōn·is -idis *or* **-idos** *f* Minerva

Trītōni·us -a -um *adj* Tritonian ‖ *f* Tritonia *(i.e., Minerva)*

trīt·or -ōris *m* grinder

trītūr·a -ae *f* threshing; kneading

trīt·us -a -um *pp of* **tero** ‖ *adj* worn, well-worn; beaten *(path);* experienced, expert; common, trite

trīt·us -ūs *m* rubbing, friction

triumphāl·is -is -e *adj* triumphal; having had a triumph ‖ *npl* triumphal insignia *(without the actual triumph)*

triump(h)e *interj* a cheer shouted in the parade of triumphing generals *or* in the procession of the Arval Brothers

triumph·ō -āre -āvī -ātus *tr* to triumph over, vanquish ‖ *intr (w.* **de** *or* **ex** + *abl)* to celebrate a triumph *(over a people)*

triumph·us -ī *m* triumph, victory parade; victory; **triumphum agere** *(w.* **de** *or* **ex** + *abl)* to celebrate a triumph over *(a conquered people)*

triumv·ir -irī *m* triumvir, commissioner; mayor *(of a provincial town)* ‖ *mpl* triumvirs; **triumviri capitales** superintendents of prisons and executions

triumvirāl·is -is -e *adj* triumviral, of the triumvirs

triumvirāt·us -ūs *m* triumvirate *(appointed at various times to serve various purposes)*

trivenēfic·a -ae *f* nasty old witch

trivī *perf of* **tero**

Trivi·a -ae *f* epithet of Diana

triviāl·is -is -e *adj* appropriate for the street corners, common, vulgar

triv·ium -(i)ī *n* crossroads, intersection; public street; the "gutter"

trivi·us -a -um *adj* of *or* at the crossroads; worshiped at the crossroads **‖** *f see* **Trivia**

-tr·ix -īcis *fem suf corresponding to the masc suf* **-tor** *and denoting female agents, e.g.,* **tonstrix** hairdresser, barber

Trō·as *or* **Trō·jas -adis** *or* **-ados** *adj (fem only)* Trojan **‖** *f* Troad, district of Troy; Trojan woman

trochae·us -ī *m (pros)* trochee *(metrical foot)* (— ◡), tribrach *(metrical foot)* (◡ ◡ ◡)

trochle·a *or* **trochli-ae** *f* block and tackle

troch·us *or* **troch·os -ī** *m* hoop

Troez·ēn -ēnis *or* **-ēnos** *f* town in the Argolid on the E. shore of the Peloponnesus

Troezēni·us -a -um *adj* of Troezen

Trōi·a *or* **Trōj·a -ae** *f* Troy

Trōic·us -a -um *adj* Trojan

Trōil·us -ī *m* son of Priam, killed by Achilles

Trōi·us *or* **Trōj·us -a -um** *adj* Trojan **‖** *f see* **Troia**

Trōjān·us -a -um *adj & m* Trojan

Trōjugen·a *adj (masc & fem only)* Trojan-born, born at Troy, of Trojan descent, Trojan **‖** *m* Trojan

Tromentīn·us -a -um *adj* name of one of the rustic tribes of early Rome

tropae·um -ī *n* trophy, war memorial *(originally armor taken from the enemy and hung on a stake, but later a permanent war monument, set up to mark the defeat of an enemy)*

Trophōn·ius -(i)ī *m* Boeotian oracular god with a shrine at Lebadea

Trōs Trōis *m* Tros *(son of Erichthonius and grandson of Dardanus and king of Phrygia after whom Troy was named)* **‖** a Trojan

trucīdāti·ō -ōnis *f* slaughter, massacre, butchery

trucid·ō -āre *tr* to slaughter, massacre, cut down

trucil·ō -āre *intr (of a thrush)* to chirp

truculentē *or* **truculenter** *adv* grimly, fiercely

truculenti·a -ae *f* ferocity, savagery; harshness; **truculentia caeli** harsh weather

truculent·us -a -um *adj* grim, fierce

trud·is -is *f* pointed pole, pike

trū·dō -děre -sī -sus *tr* to push, shove; to thrust; to force, drive; to put forth *(buds)*

trull·a -ae *f* dipper, ladle, scoop; brazier; wash basin

-tr·um -ī *neut suf denoting instrument, e.g.:* **aratrum** plow

trunc·ō -āre -āvī -ātus *tr* to lop off, maim; to amputate

trunc·us -a -um *adj* lopped; stripped *(of branches and leaves)*, trimmed; maimed, mutilated; imperfect, undeveloped **‖** *m* tree trunk; trunk, body *(of a human being)*; chunk of meat; blockhead

trūsī *perf of* **trudo**

trūs·ō -āre *intr (w. dat)* to keep ramming *(s.o.) (i.e., have sexual intercourse with a girl)*

trūsus *pp of* **trudo**

trutin·a -ae *f* pair of scales; criterion

trutin·or -ārī -ātus sum *tr* to weigh, balance

tru·x -cis *adj* savage, grim, fierce

trybl·ium -(i)ī *n* a kind of bowl

trȳgōn·us ī *m* stingray

tū *pron* you *(singl)*

tuātim *adv* in your manner, as is typical of you

tub·a -ae *f* trumpet *(with a stright tube, as opposed to the cornu) used in war, at religious ceremonies, at the start of public shows, at weddings, funerals, etc.)*

tūb·er -eris *n* lump, hump, swelling; **tuber terrae** *(bot)* truffle *(underground fungus used as food)*

tub·er -eris *f* exotic type of fruit tree **‖** *m* exotic kind of fruit

Tūbert·us -ī *m* Roman family name *(cognomen), esp.* Aulus Postumius Tubertus *(dictator in 431 B.C. and conqueror of the Aequi at Algidus)*

tubic·en -inis *m* trumpeter

tubilustr·ium -(i)ī *n* festival of trumpets *(celebrated on March 23 and May 23 and including a ritual cleaning of the trumpets)*

tuburcin·or -ārī -ātus sum *tr (coll)* to gobble up

tub·us -ī *m* tube, pipe

tuccēt·um *or* **tūcēt·um -ī** *n* sausage

Tucci·a -a -um *adj* Roman clan name *(nomen), esp.* Tuccia *(a Vestal Virgin who vindicated her chastity by carrying water in a sieve)*

tudit·ō -āre *tr* to keep hitting

-tūd·ō -inis *fem suf forms abstract nouns, chiefly from adjectives, e.g.:* **fortitudo** bravery, *from* **fortis** brave

tueor *or* **tuor tuērī tuitus sum** *or* **tūtus sum** *tr* to look at, gaze at, watch, observe; to took after, take care of; to guard, defend, protect; to keep in good order, maintain; to keep up *(practice)*; to preserve the memory of

tugur·ium -(i)ī *n* hut, hovel

tuiti·ō -ōnis *f* protection, support; upkeep, maintenance; **tuitio sui** self-defense

tulī *perf of* **ferro**

Tulli·a -ae *f* Roman female name

Tulliān·um -ī *n* state dungeon at the foot of the Capitoline Hill, said to have been added by Servius Tullius to the *Carcer Mamertinus*

Tulliol·a -ae *f* little Tullia

Tull·ius -(i)ī *m* Roman clan name *(nomen)*, *esp.* Marcus Tullius Cicero *(Roman orator and politician, 106-43 B.C.)* ‖ Servius Tullius *(6th king of Rome)*

Tull·us -ī *m* early first name *(praenomen)*, *esp.* Tullus Hostilius, the third king of Rome

tum *adv* then, at that time; at that moment; in those days; next; moreover, besides; **cum...tum** both...and especially, not only...but also, if...then surely; **tum cum** at the point when, at the time when, just then when; **tum...tum** first...then, at one time...at another, now...now, both...and, partly...partly

tume·faciō -facĕre -fēcī -factus *tr* to cause to swell; *(fig)* to puff up *(with pride)*

tum·eō -ēre -uī *intr* to be swollen, swell up; to be inflated; *(of language or speaker)* to be bombastic; *(of a person)* to be excited, be in a dither, be in a rage; to be proud

tum·escō -escĕre -uī *intr* to begin to swell (up); *(of wars)* to brew; to grow excited; to become enraged; to become inflated

tumid·us -a -um *adj* swollen, swelling; bloated; rising high; proud, puffed up; arrogant; incensed, enraged, exasperated; bombastic

tum·or -ōris *m* tumor, swelling; protuberance, bulging; elevation *(of the ground)*; commotion, excitement; anger, rage; vanity, pride

tumuī *perf of* **tumeo** *and* **tumesco**

tumul·ō -āre -āvī -ātus *tr* to bury

tumulōs·us -a -um *adj* hilly, rolling

tumultuāri·us -a -um *adj* confused, disorderly; makeshift; *(mil)* emergency-, drafted hurriedly to meet an emergency; **exercitus tumultuarius** emergency army; **pugna tumultuaria** irregular battle *(i.e., not fought in regular battle formation)*

tumultuāti·ō -ōnis *f* commotion

tumultu·ō -āre *or* **tumultu·or -ārī -ātus sum** *intr* to make a disturbance; to be in an uproar; *(mil)* to fight in a disorganized way

tumultuōsē *adv* disorderly, in confusion; in panic

tumultuōs·us -a -um *adj* boisterous, turbulent; panicky; **somnia tumultuosa** nightmares

tumult·us -ūs *m* commotion, uproar; insurrection, rebellion, civil war; confusion *(of the mind)*; outbreak *(of crime)*; *(mil)* sudden attack

tumul·us -ī *m* mound; rising; ground swell; burial mound; **tumulus inanis** cenotaph

tūn = tūne (tū + ne) do you?

tunc *adv (of time past)* then, at that time; *(of future time)* then, in that event; *(of succession in time)* thereupon; *(in conclusion)* consequently, in that case; **tunc cum** then when, just when; only when; **tunc demum** not until then; **tunc maxime** just then; **tunc primum** then for the first time; **tunc quando** whenever; **tunc quoque** then too; **tunc vero** then to be sure, exactly then

tundō tundĕre tutudī tunsus *or* **tūsus** *tr* to beat, pound, hammer, thump; to buffet; to thresh; *(fig)* to harp on

tunic·a -ae *f* tunic *(ordinary half-sleeved knee-length garment worn by both sexes)*; military tunic *(made of mail or hides as armor)*; skin, peel, husk, coating; *(anat, bot)* tunic; **tunica molesta** tunic with inflammable material, in which criminals were burned alive; **tunica recta** *(woven on a warp-weighted loom)* bridal tunic; **tunica palmata** tunic embroidered with palm-leaf design, worn by triumphing generals and by magistrates presiding over games

tunicāt·us -a -um *adj* wearing a tunic; in shirt sleeves; coated; covered with (hard) skin, tunicate

tunic(u)l·a -ae *f* short tunic; thin skin; thin coating

tunsus *pp of* **tundo**

tuor *see* **tueor**

turb·a -ae *f* turmoil, disorder, uproar; commotion; brawl; crowd, mob, gang; multitude; common crowd, masses; a large number; *(coll)* rumpus, to-do

turbāment·a -ōrum *npl* means of disturbance

turbātē *adv* in confusion

turbāti·ō -ōnis *f* confusion, disorder

turbāt·or -ōris *m* ringleader, rabble-rouser, demagogue

turbāt·us -a -um *adj* confused, disorderly; disturbed, annoyed

turbell·ae -ārum *fpl* stir, row; **turbellas facere** to cause quite a row

turben *see* **turbo** *m*

turbidē *adv* confusedly, in disorder

turbid·us -a -um *adj* confused, wild, boisterous; muddy, turbid; troubled, perplexed; vehement; disheveled *(hair)*; stormy *(weather, sky)*

turbine·us -a -um *adj* cone-shaped; gyrating like a spinning-top

turb·ō -inis *m or* **turb·en -inis** *n* whirl, twirl; eddy; spinning, revolution; coil; spinning top; reel; spindle; wheel; tornado, whirlwind; wheel of fortune; *(fig)* whirlwind, storm

turb·ō -āre -āvī -ātus *tr* to throw into confusion, disturb, agitate; to break, disorganize *(ranks in battle)*, cause to break ranks; to confuse; to alarm; to muddy; to stir *(a liquid in order to thicken it)*; to stir up *(ingredients; emotions)*; to jumble up *(sounds)*; to wipe out *(tracks, clues)*; to tamper with *(documents)*; to squander *(a fortune)* ‖ *intr* to behave in a disorderly manner, go wild; to be in a state of commotion; to riot, revolt

turbulentē *or* **turbulenter** *adv* boisterously, tumultuously, confusedly

turbulent·us -a -um *adj* turbulent, wild, stormy; disturbed, confused; seditious, trouble-making

turd·a -ae *f or* **turd·us -ī** *m* thrush

tūre·us -a -um *adj* of frankincense

tur·geō -gēre -sī *intr* to be swollen, be puffed up; to be bombastic

turgesc·ō -ĕre *intr* to begin to swell (up); to begin to blow up *(in anger)*

turgidul·us -a -um *adj* poor swollen *(eyes)*

turgid·us -a -um *adj* swollen, puffed up; inflated; turgid, bombastic

tūribul·um -ī *n* censer

tūricrem·us -a -um *adj* incense-burning

tūrif·er -era -erum *adj* producing incense

tūrileg·us -a -um *adj* incense-gathering

turm·a -ae *f* troop, squadron *(of cavalry, originally consisting of 30 men)*; crowd, group

turmāl·is -is -e *adj* of a squadron; equestrian ‖ *mpl* troopers

turmātim *adv* by troops, by squadrons, squadron by squadron

Turn·us -ī *m* king of the Rutuli, killed by Aeneas

turpicul·us -a -um *adj* ugly little; somewhat indecent

turpificāt·us -a -um *adj* corrupted, degenerate

turpilucricupid·us -a -um *adj (coll)* eager to make a fast buck

turp·is -is -e *adj* ugly, deformed; foul, filthy, nasty; disgraceful, shameless, dirty, obscene, indecent

turpiter *adv* repulsively; disgracefully, scandalously, shamelessly

turpitūd·ō -inis *f* ugliness, deformity; foulness; disgrace; moral turpitude

turp·ō -āre -āvī -ātus *tr* to disfigure; to soil, defile, pollute; to disgrace

turrif·er -era -erum *adj see* **turriger**

turrig·er -era -erum *adj* turreted; *(of Cybele)* wearing a turreted crown *(representing earth with its cities)*

turr·is -is *f* turret, tower; howdah *(on an elephant)*; *(fig)* castle, mansion

turrīt·us -a -um *adj* turreted; fortified with turrets; crowned with turrets, adorned with a turret crown

turt·ur -uris *m* turtledove

tūs tūris *m* incense, frankincense

Tusculānens·is -is -e *adj* Tusculan

Tusculān·us -a -um *adj* Tusculan ‖ *n* Tusculan estate *(esp. Cicero's)*

tuscul·um -ī *n* a little incense

Tuscul·us -a -um *adj* Tusculan ‖ *n* Tusculum *(town in Latium near Alba Longa, about 12 miles S. of Rome)*

Tusc·us -a -um *adj* Etruscan

tussicul·a -ae *f* slight cough

tuss·iō -īre *intr* to cough, have a cough

tuss·is -is *(acc:* **tussim;** *abl singl:* **tussi)** *f* cough

tūsus *pp of* **tundo**

tūtām·en -inis *or* **tūtāment·um -ī** *n* means of protection; protector

tūtĕ = tū + te *emphatic form of* **tū**

tūtē *adv* safely

tūtēl·a -ae *f* care, charge, protection, defense; guardianship; charge, thing protected; support, maintenance *(of persons)*; upkeep *(of buildings)*; guardian, keeper; **in suam tutelam (per)venire** *(or* **tutelam accipere** *or* **suae tutelae fieri)** *(of a minor)* to become capable of managing one's own affairs

tūtemet = tū + te + met *emphatic form of* **tū**

tūtō *adv* safely, securely, without risk of harm; **tuto esse** to exist safely

tūt·ō -āre *or* **tūt·or -ārī -ātus sum** *tr* to guard, protect, defend; to keep safe, watch, preserve; to ward off, avert; *(w.* **ab** + *abl or w.* **ad** *or* **adversus** + *acc)* to protect *(s.o.)* from, guard *(s.o.)* against

tūt·or -ōris *m* protector; *(leg)* guardian *(of minors, of women of any age, etc.)*

tutudī *perf of* **tundo**

tūt·us -a -um *pp of* **tueor** ‖ *adj* safe, secure; cautious, prudent ‖ *n* safe place, shelter, security; **ex tuto** from a safe place, in safety

tu·us -a -um *(also* **tu·os -a -om)** *adj* your; your dear *(friend, etc.),* dear to you; typical of you; devoted to you; *(of circumstances)* favorable to you ‖ *pron* yours; **de tuo** at your expense; **in tuo** on your land; **quid tua?** what business is it of yours?; **tua** your girlfriend, your sweetheart; **tuā interest** *(or* **tuā refert** it is of importance to you; **tui** your friends, your people, your family,.your soldiers; **tuum est** *(w. inf)* it is your

duty to, it's up to you to; **tuum est quod**
it is thanks to you that
tuxtax adv *(a word meant to imitate the
sound of blows)* whack, wham; **tuxtax
meo tergo erit** *(coll)* it's going to be
wham, whack all over my back
Tȳd·eūs -eī or **-eos** m Tydeus *(son of
Oeneus, one of the Seven against Thebes,
and father of Diomedes)*
Tȳdīd·ēs -ae m Diomedes *(son of Tydeus)*
tympaniz·ō -āre *intr* to play the drum
tympanotrīb·a -ae m timbrel player,
drummer
tympan·um or **typan·um -ī** n drum, revolving cylinder; solid circular wheel
*(used on carts and wagons); dentated
wheel (used as a waterwheel); (mus)*
drum, timbrel *(esp. used in the worship
of Cybele or Bacchus)*
Tyndar·eūs -eī or **Tyndar·us -ī** m king of
Sparta, husband of Leda, father of Castor and Clytemnestra, and reputed father of Pollux and Helen
Tyndarid·ēs -ae m descendant of Tyndareus *(esp. Castor and Pollux)*
Tyndar·is -idis f descendant of Tyndareus
(esp. Helen and Clytemnestra)
Typhō·eūs -eī or **-eos** or **Tȳph·ōn -ōnis**
m giant who was struck by Jupiter
with lightning and buried under Mt.
Etna
Tȳphōe·us -a -um adj of the monster
Typhoeus
Tȳph·ōn -ōnis m see **Typhoeus**
typ·us -ī m figure, image, bas-relief *(on
the wall)*
tyrannicē adv tyrannically
tyrannicīd·a -ae m assassin of a tyrant
tyrannic·us -a -um adj tyrannical
tyrann·is -idis or **-idos** f tyranny, despotism
tyrannocton·us -ī m tyrannicide, assassin of a tyrant
tyrann·us -ī m monarch, sovereign; *(in a
Greek city-state)* unconstituional (absolute) ruler
Tyrianthin·a -ōrum npl clothes of a violet color
Tyri·us -a -um adj Tyrian, Phoenician;
Carthaginian; Theban; crimson *(because
of the famous dye produced at Tyre)* ‖
mpl Tyrians; Carthaginians
Tȳr·ō -ūs or **-ōnis** f daughter of Salmoneus
and mother of Pelias and Neleus by
Poseidon
Tyr·os or **Tyr·us -ī** f Tyre *(commercial
city of Phoenicia, famous for its crimson dye, or "Tyrian purple"; its dye
works were active until destroyed by the
Crusaders)*
tȳrotarīch·os -ī m dish of salted fish and
cheese *(as an example of a plain diet)*
Tyrrhēni·a -ae f Etruria

Tyrr(h)ēnic·us -a -um adj Etrurian,
Etruscan
Tyrr(h)ēn·us -a -um adj Etrurian, Etrus-
can; **mare Tyrrhenum** Tyrrhenian Sea
*(lying between the W. coast of Italy,
Sardinia, and Sicily);* **Tyrrhenae vo-
lucres** the Sirens ‖ mpl Etruscans
*(Pelasgian people who migrated to
Italy, perhaps from Lydia in Asia Mi-
nor)*
Tyrtae·us -ī m Spartan poet *(7th cent.
B.C.)*
Tyrus see **Tyros**

U

ūb·er -eris adj rich, fertile; fruitful, productive; plentiful; plenty of; valuable;
copious *(tears); (of things)* rich in content; imaginative *(writer, style); (fig)*
productive ‖ n (woman's) breast, nipple;
udder; bosom *(of the earth);* fertility;
fertile soil, fruitful field
ūberius adv more fully, in greater abundance; more fruitfully; with greater exuberance
ūbert·ās -ātis f richness; fertility; pro-
ductiveness; abundance; richness of
content
ūbertim adv copiously; **urbertim flere**
to cry bitterly
ubī or **ubĭ** adv *(interrog)* where; **ubi
gentium** *(or* **terrarum)** *(coll)* where in
the world ‖ conj where, in which;
whereby; with whom, by whom; when,
whenever
ubīcumque conj wherever, wheresoever
‖ adv anywhere, everywhere
Ubi·ī -ōrum mpl German tribe on the
Lower Rhine
ubīnam adv just where?, wherever?;
ubinam gentium where in the world
ubiquāque adv everywhere
ubīque adv everywhere, anywhere
ubiubī conj wherever
ubivīs adv anywhere, everywhere, wherever you please; **ubivis gentium** *(coll)*
anywhere in the world
ūd·ō -ōnis m felt slipper
ūd·us -a -um adj wet, moist; humid
Ūf·ens -entis m river in Latium
-ūg·ō -inis fem suf formed from names of
materials to denote a superficial film,
e.g.: **ferrugo** (iron) rust; formed from
nouns, e.g.: **versperugo** the Evening
Star
-ul·a -ae fem suf forms diminutives, e.g.:
arcula small box or chest
-ulent·us -a -um adj‖ suf forms adjectives
meaning "abounding in", "full of", e.g.:
vīnulentus full of wine, intoxicated

ulcer·ō -āre -āvī -ātus *tr* to cause to fester; *(fig)* to wound
ulcerōs·us -a -um *adj* ulcerous
ulciscor ulciscī ultus sum *tr* to avenge oneself on, take revenge on, punish; to avenge, requite
ulc·us -eris *n* ulcer, sore
ūlīg·ō -inis *f* moisture, dampness
Ulix·ēs -is *or* **-eī** *or* **-ī** *m* Ulysses *(king of Ithaca, son of Laertes, husband of Penelope, and father of Telemachus and Telegonus)*
ull·us -a -um *adj* any
ulme·us -a -um *adj* elm, made of elm; *(hum)* elm-whipped
ulmitrib·a -ae *m (coll)* slaphappy *(from being flogged with elm whips)*
ulm·us -ī *f* elm tree **‖** *fpl* elm whips
uln·a -ae *f* elbow; arm; *(as measure of length, span of the outstretched arms, c. 45 inches)* ell
ulpic·um -ī *n* type of garlic
ulteri·or -or -us *adj* farther, on the farther side, more remote; further, additional, more; longer; in a higher degree; worse; **Gallia Ulterior** Transalpine Gaul; **Hispania Ulterior** the western of the two provinces of the Iberian peninsula **‖** *mpl* more remote people, those beyond **‖** *npl* things beyond
ulterius *adv* to a more distant place, farther away; to a further extent, further, more than that; **ulterius quam** further than
ulterius *prep (w. acc)* beyond
ultimō *adv* finally, last of all
ultimum *adv* finally; for the last time
ultim·us -a -um *adj* **(-tum-)** farthest, most distant, extreme; earliest; latest, final, last; greatest; lowest; meanest **‖** *n* last thing, end; **ad ultimum** to the end; to the extreme; in the highest degree; to the last degree, utterly; *(in an enumeration)* finally; **in ultimo** finally **‖** *npl* extremes; the worst
ulti·ō -ōnis *f* vengeance, revenge
ult·or -ōris *m* avenger, punisher
ultrā *adv* beyond, farther, besides **‖** *prep* **1** *(w. acc) (in a physical sense)* on the farther side of, beyond, past: **nihil est ultra altitudinem montium quo pertimendum est** there is nothing beyond *(i.e., except)* the heights of the mountains that needs to be feared; **2** *(in the temporal sense)* to a point later than, at a later time than, after, past; to a time further back than, earlier than: **ultra mediam noctem** till past midnight; **3** *(of number, measure, degree)* over, beyond, more than, over and above: **non ultra tres versus** not more than three verses; **4** *(in negative sentences, indicating the limit of an activity)* **nihil**

ultra nervos atque cutem morti concederat atrae he had conceded to dark death nothing but sinews and skin *(i.e., his body)*
ultr·ix -īcis *adj (fem only)* avenging *(esp. of the Furies and other agents of retribution)* **‖** *f* avenger
ultrō *adv* to the farther side, beyond; on the other side; on both sides, in both directions; at the opposite end of the scale, conversely; besides, moreover, too; into the bargain, to boot; of one's own accord, without being asked; without being spoken to; unprovoked; **bella inferre ultro** to go to war (although) unprovoked; **ultro et citro** back and forth; **ultro tributa** expenditure incurred by the government for public works
ultus *pp of* **ulciscor**
ulul·a -ae *f* owl
ululāt·us -ūs *m* howling *(esp. of dogs and wolves)*; ulutation, wailing *(esp. of mourners)*; war cry
ulul·ō -āre -āvī -ātus *tr* to howl out, howl at **‖** *intr* to howl; to ululate, wail; *(of places)* to resound
ulv·a -ae *f (bot)* sedge, rush
-ul·um -ī *neut suf forming diminutive neuter nouns:* **speculum** mirror
-ul·us *m and* **-ul·a** *f suf* **1** *forming diminutives:* **calculus** little stone; **2** *adjectives denoting repeated action:* **credulus** regularly believing, credulous; **3** *adjectives denoting diminished intensity:* **ūmidulus** dampish; **4** *nouns denoting instruments:* **furculus** pitchfork; **5** *nouns denoting endearment:* **uxorcula** dear wife
umbell·a -ae *f* umbrella, parasol
Um·ber -bra -brum *adj* Umbrian, of Umbria **‖** *m* Umbrian
umbilīc·us -ī *m* navel, bellybutton; midriff; middle, center; projecting end of dowels *or* cylinders on which scrolls were rolled; cockle, sea snail; **ad umbilicum** *(or* **ad umbilicos)** to the end of the scroll *or* book
umb·ō -ōnis *m* boss *(of a shield)*; shield; elbow
umbr·a -ae *f* shade; shadow; phantom, ghost; mere shadow *(of one's former self)*; semblance; darkness, gloom; shelter, cover; privacy, retirement; umber *(fish)*; **rhetorica umbra** rhetorician's school **‖** *fpl* darkness of night; lower world
umbrāc(u)l·um -ī *n* shade; bower, arbor; school; umbrella, parasol
umbrāticol·a -ae *mf* lounger *(in the shade)*
umbrātic·us -a -um *adj* too fond of the shade, lazy, inactive; secluded; private; **umbraticus doctor** private tutor; pedant

umbrātil·is -is -e *adj* carried out in the shade, private, retired; academic
Umbri·a -ae *f* Umbria *(district in central Italy)*
umbrif·er -era -erum *adj* shady
umbr·ō -āre -āvī -ātus *tr* to shade, cast a shadow on; to overshadow
umbrōs·us -a -um *adj* shady
ūmect·ō -āre -āvī -ātus *tr* (hūm-) to wet, moisten
ūmect·us -a -um *adj* (hūm-) moist, damp
ūm·eō -ēre *intr* to be moist, be damp, be wet
umer·us -ī *m* (hum-) shoulder
ūmesc·ō -ĕre *intr* to become moist, become wet
ūmidul·us -a -um *adj* dampish
ūmid·us -a -um *adj* (hūm-) moist, damp, wet; green *(lumber)* ‖ *n* wet place
ūmif·er -era -erum *adj* laden with moisture
ūm·or -ōris *m* (hūm-) moisture; liquid, fluid
umquam *or* unquam *adv* ever, at any time
ūnā *adv* together; ūnā cum together with; ūnā venire to come along
ūnanim·ans -antis *adj* of one mind, of one accord
ūnanimit·ās -ātis *f* unanimity
ūnanim·us -a -um *adj* (ūnian-) unanimous; of one mind, of one heart
unci·a -ae *f* one-twelfth; ounce *(one-twelfth of a pound or* libra); *(of interest rate)* 1% a year; *(in length)* inch *(25 mm, one twelfth of a foot or* pes)
unciāri·us -a -um *adj* containing one-twelfth; one-ounce; one-inch
unciātim *adv* ounce by ounce, little by little
uncīnāt·us -a -um *adj* hooked, barbed
uncīn·us -ī *m* hook
unciol·a -ae *f* a mere twelfth
unc·ō -āre *intr (of a bear)* to grunt
uncti·ō -ōnis *f* rubdown with oil; *(fig)* wrestling
unctit·ō -āre *tr* to keep rubbing with oil, keep oiling
unctiuscul·us -a -um *adj* somewhat too oily; unctuous
unct·or -ōris *m* anointer, rubdown man, masseur
unct·um -ī *n* sumptuous dinner
unctūr·a -ae *f* anointing
unct·us -a -um *pp of* ung(u)o ‖ *adj* greasy; resinous; sumptuous
uncul·us -a -um *adj* any at all
unc·us -a -um *adj* hooked, barbed; crooked ‖ *m* hook, clamp; grappling iron
und·a -ae *f* water; stream, river; wave; sea, seawater; current *(of air); (fig)* stream, tide, agitated mass

unde *adv* from where, whence; from whom; unde unde *(or* undeunde) by hook or by crook
ūndeciens *or* ūndeciēs *adv* eleven times
ūndecim *indecl adj* eleven
ūndecim·us -a -um *adj* (-decum-) eleventh
undecumque *adv* (-cun-) from whatever place, from whatever source
ūndēn·ī -ae -a *adj* eleven in a group, eleven each, eleven
ūndēnōnāgintā *indecl adj* eighty-nine
ūndēoctōgintā *indecl adj* seventy-nine
ūndēquadrāgēsim·us -a -um *adj* thirty-ninth
ūndēquadrāgintā *indecl adj* thirty-nine
ūndēquinquāgēsim·us -a -um *adj* forty-ninth
ūndēquinquāgintā *indecl adj* forty-nine
ūndēsexāgintā *indecl adj* fifty-nine
undētrīcēsim·us -a -um *adj* twenty-ninth
ūndētrīgintā *indecl adj* twenty-nine
ūndēvīcēsimān·ī -ōrum *mpl* soldiers of the nineteenth legion
ūndēvicēsim·us -a -um *adj* nineteenth
ūndēvīgintī *indecl adj* nineteen
undique *adv* from all directions, on all sides, everywhere; in all respects, completely
undison·us -a -um *adj* of roaring waves; undisoni dei gods of the roaring waves
und·ō -āre -āvī -ātum *intr* to move in waves, undulate; to billow; to overflow
undōs·us -a -um *adj* full of waves, billowy; wave-washed *(shore)*
ūnetvīcē(n)sim·us -a -um *adj* twenty-first
ūnetvīcēsimān·ī -ōrum *mpl* soldiers of the twenty-first legion
ungō *or* unguō ung(u)ĕre unxī unctus *tr* to oil, grease, anoint
ungu·en -inis *n* fat, grease; ointment
unguentāri·us -(i)ī *m* perfumer
unguentāt·us -a -um *adj* anointed; perfumed, wearing perfume
unguent·um -ī *n* ointment; perfume
unguicul·us -ī *m* fingernail; toenail; a teneris unguiculis from earliest childhood
ungu·is -is *m* fingernail; toenail; claw, talon; hoof; ad unguem to a tee, complete, perfect; de tenero ungui from earliest childhood
ungul·a -ae *f* hoof; claw, talon; *(fig)* horse
unguō *see* ungo
ūnicē *adv* singularly; particularly; unice unus one and only
ūnicol·or -ōris *adj* of one and the same color, monochrome
ūnicorn·is -is -e *adj* one-horned
ūnic·us -a -um *adj* one and only, sole; singular, unique; uncommon
ūniform·is -is -e *adj* uniform, having only one shape

ūnigen·a -ae *adj (masc & fem only)* only-begotten, only; of the same parentage
ūniman·us -a -um *adj* one-handed
ūni·ō -ōnis *f* single large pearl
ūnisubsell·ium -(i)ī *n* seat for one
ūniter *adv* jointly
ūniversāl·is -is -e *adj* universal
ūniversē *adv* generally, in general
ūniversit·ās -ātis *f* aggregate, whole; whole world, universe
ūnivers·us -a -um *adj* (-vors-) all, all together; all taken collectively; whole, entire **ll** *n* the whole; whole world, universe; **in universum** on the whole, in general
ūnocul·us -ī *m* one-eyed person
ūnomammi·a -ae *adj (fem)* single-breasted *(Amazon)*
unquam *or* **umquam** *adv* ever, at any time
ūnumquicquid *pron* every little thing
ūn·us -a -um *adj* one, single, only, sole; one and the same; *(indefinite)* one, some; **unus et alter** one or two; **unus quisque** each one, every single one **ll** *pron* someone, a mere individual; **ad unum** to a man
unxī *perf of* **ung(u)o**
ūpili·ō -ōnis *m* shepherd
upup·a -ae *f* hoopoe *(bird with fan-like crest and downward-curving bill);* hoe, mattock
-ūr·a -ae *fem suf forms nouns form nouns ending in* **-tor** *to denote office:* **praetura** praetorship *(from* **paetor**); *forms nouns mainly from verbal derivatives in* **-tus:** **natura** nature *(from* **natus)**
Ūrani·a -ae *or* **Ūrani·ē -ēs** *f* Muse of astronomy
urbānē *adv* politely, courteously; with sophistication; wittily
urbānit·ās -ātis *f* living in the city, city life; refinement; politeness; sophistication; wit; raillery
urbān·us -a -um *adj* of the city, city; courteous; sophisticated; witty; brash, forward **ll** *m* city dweller; *(pej)* city slicker
urbicap·us -ī *m* conqueror of cities
urbic·us -a -um *adj* city-, of the city
urbi·us -a -um *adj* **urbius clivus** slope on the Esquiline Hill
ur·bs *or* **ur·ps -bis** *f* city; the city of Rome
urceol·us -ī *m* little pitcher, little pot
urce·us -ī *m* pitcher, water pot
urc·ō -āre *intr (of a lynx)* to snarl
ūrēd·ō -inis *f* blight *(on plants)*
urgeō urgēre ursī *tr* to prod on, urge forward; to pressure, put pressure on *(s.o.);* to crowd, hem in; to follow up, keep at, stick by **ll** *intr* to be urgent; to be insistent
ūrīn·a -ae *f* urine

ūrīnāt·or -ōris *m* diver
ūrīn·ō -āre *or* **ūrin·or -ārī** *intr* to dive
-ur·iō -īre -īvī *or* **-iī** *suf forming desideratives* (**cenaturire** to wish to eat)
Ūrī·ōn -ōnis *m* Orion
Ūr·ios -iī *m* cult title of Zeus, as the sender of favorable winds
urn·a -ae *f* pot, jar; water pot; voting urn; urn of fate; cinerary urn; money jar; liquid measure *(= one half of an amphora)*
urnul·a -ae *f* small urn
ūrō ūrēre ussī ustus *tr* to burn; to burn up, reduce to ashes, consume; to scorch, parch, dry up; to sting, pain; to nip, frostbite; to rub sore; to corrode; to annoy, gall, burn up, make angry; to inflame *(w. love)*
urps *see* **urbs**
urs·a -ae *f* she-bear **ll Ursa Major** *(astr)* Great Bear *(constellation);* **Ursa Minor** *(astr)* Little Bear *(constellation)*
ursī *perf of* **urgeo**
ursīn·us -a -um *adj* bear-, bear's
urs·us -ī *m* bear
urtīc·a -ae *f (bot)* stinging nettle *(causing a burning rash upon contact);* desire, itch
ūrūc·a *or* **ūrīc·a -ae** *f* caterpillar
ūr·us -ī *m* wild ox
Ūsīpet·ēs -um *mpl* German tribe on the Rhine
ūsitātē *adv* in the usual way, as usual
ūsitāt·us -a -um *adj* usual, customary, familiar; **usitatum est** *(w. inf)* it is customary to
uspiam *adv* anywhere, somewhere, in some place or other
usquam *adv* anywhere *(in any place or to any place)*
usque *adv* all the way, right on; all the time, continuously; even, as much as; *(without addition of an adv or prep)* to the fullest extent, completely; **usque ab** *(w. abl)* all the way from; ever since; **usque ad** *(w. acc)* all the way to; all the way back in time to; **usque adeo** *(or* **usque eo) ut** to such an extent that; **usque quaque** every moment, continually; on all occasions, in everything **ll** *prep (w. acc)* up to, as far as, right until
usquequāque *or* **usque quāque** *adv* everywhere, as far as one can go in either direction; *(fig)* in every conceivable situation; in every possible respect, wholly
ussī *perf of* **uro**
usti·ō -ōnis *f* burning
ust·or -ōris *m* cremator
ustul·ō -āre -āvī -ātus *tr* to scorch, singe
ustus *pp of* **uro**
ūsū·capiō -capĕre -cēpī -captus *tr (leg)* to acquire ownership of *(by long use)*

ūsūcapi·ō -ōnis *f (leg)* acquisition of ownership *(through long use)*

ūsūr·a -ae *f* use, enjoyment; interest *(on capital)*

ūsūrāri·us -a -um *adj* for use and enjoyment; paying interest, interest-bearing

ūsurpāti·ō -ōnis *f* use; *(w. gen)* making use of, use of

ūsurp·ō -āre -āvī -ātus *tr* to use, make *(constant)* use of, employ; to exercise *(a right);* to put into practice *(a custom, operation);* to take possession of, acquire; to usurp; to name, call, speak of; to assume *(a title, honor, esp. arbitrarily);* to take up *(an inheritance);* to perceive *(with the senses),* observe, experience; **memoriam usurpare** *(w. gen)* to invoke the memory of

ūsus *pp of* utor

ūs·us -ūs *m* use, enjoyment; practice, employment; experience, skill; usage, custom; familiarity; usefulness, advantage, benefit; occasion, need, necessity; **ex usu esse** *(or* **usui esse)** *(w. dat)* to be useful to, be a good thing for; **in usu in** one's everyday experience; **in usu esse** to be in use; to be customary; **in usu (meo, tuo,** *etc.***) est** it is to (my, your, *etc.*) advantage; **in usu habere** *(or* **continere)** to keep in use; **quis usus est?** *(w. gen)* what useful purpose is served by?; **scientia et usus** theory and practice; **si usus veniat** if the need should arise, if the opportunity should present itself; **usus adest** a good opportunity comes along; **usus est** *(w. abl)* there is a need of; **usus et fructus** use and enjoyment; **usu venit** it happens, it occurs; **usus venit** *(w. dat)* the need arises for

ūsusfructus *(gen:* ūsūsfructūs) *m* use and enjoyment, usufruct

ut *(or* utī, *an older form, increasingly rare after Cicero, but affected by archaizing authors) adv (in direct and indirect questions; in exclamations)* how; **ut miser est qui!** how pitiful is the man who! **ǁ** *conj (comparative)* as; *(adversative)* although; *(temporal)* when, while; *(purpose)* in order that; *(result, after* **adeo, eo, sic, talis, tam, tantus)** (to such a degree, so, such, so great) that; *(concessive)* granted that; *(introducing examples)* as, as for example; *(after verbs of fearing)* lest, that not; *(introducing an explanation or reason)* as, as being, inasmuch as; *(introducing indirect commands)* that; **ut maxime** at most; **ut perinde** *(or* **proinde)** according to the degree to which; **ut qui** (= **quippe qui)** as is natural for one who; **ut puta** *(indicating an example)* as say, as for example

utcumque *or* utcunque *or* utquomque *adv* however; whenever; one way or another

ūt·ens -entis *adj* having money to spend

ūtensil·is -is -e *adj* useful **ǁ** *npl* utensils, materials, provisions, similar things

ū·ter -tris *m (n)* bag, skin, bottle; inflated bag to keep swimmers afloat

u·ter -tra -trum *adj* which *(of the two)* **ǁ** *pron* which one *(of the two);* one or the other

utercumque utracumque utrumcumque *adj* whichever *(of the two)* **ǁ** *pron* whichever one *(of the two)*

uterlibet utralibet utrumlibet *adj* whichever *(of the two)* you please **ǁ** *pron* whichever one *(of the two)* you please, either one *(of the two)*

uterque utraque utrumque *adj* each *(of the two),* both; **sermones utriusque linguae** conversations in both languages *(i.e., Greek and Latin)* **ǁ** *pron* each one *(of the two),* both; **uterque insaniunt** both are insane

uter·us -ī *m or* uter·um -ī *n* belly, abdomen; womb; potbelly *(of a man);* **uterum gerere** to be pregnant

utervīs utravīs utrumvīs *adj* whichever *(of the two)* you please, either **ǁ** *pron* whichever one *(of the two)* you please, either one

utī *see* ut

ūtibil·is -is -e *adj* useful, practical

Utic·a -ae *f* city in Africa, N.W. of Carthage, where the younger Cato committed suicide in 46 B.C.

Uticens·is -is -e *adj* of Utica **ǁ** *m* posthumous title of Cato

ūtil·is -is -e *adj* useful, profitable, practical; *(w. dat or* ad + *acc)* fit for, useful for, practical in

ūtilit·ās -ātis *f* usefulness, advantage

ūtiliter *adv* usefully, profitably

utinam *conj (introducing a wish)* if only, would that

utīque *adv* anyhow, at least, at any rate; in particular, especially; without condition, absolutely; *(after negatives)* on any account; *(in obeying instructions)* without fail; **cur utique** exactly why

ūtor ūtī ūsus sum *intr (w. abl)* 1 to use, make use of: **coqui his condimentis utuntur** cooks use these seasonings; 2 to enjoy: **valetudine prosperā uti** to enjoy good health; 3 to practice, experience: **portis patefactis eo die pace primum usi sunt** as the gates were thrown open they experienced peace for the first time on that day; 4 to enjoy the friendship *or* companionship of: **multos jam annos te usi sumus** for many years now we have enjoyed your friendship; 5 *(w. adv or abl of manner)* to treat: omnibus sociis clementiā uti to treat all our allies with kindness; **familiariter utebar Caesare I** was on familiar terms with Caesar; **6** to hold *(office, military command):* **honore uti** to hold office; **tribuni milites et imperio et insignibus consularibus usi sunt** the military tribunes held military commands and wore the consular insignia; **7** to handle, manage, control: **bene armis, optime equis usus est** he managed arms well and horses very well; **8** to consume *(food or drink):* **qui vetere vino utuntur** who drink old wine; **9** to wear *(clothes):* **solutis vestibus utuntur Gratiae** the Graces wear loose dresses; **10** to live *or* spend one's time *(in a place):* **eo mari uti consuerunt** they were used to living on (the coast of) that sea; **11** to play *(a musical instrument):* **qui fidibus aut tibiis uti volunt** those who want to play the lyre or the flute

utpote *adv (reinforcing explanatory phrases or clauses)* as one might expect, as is natural, naturally, inasmuch as; **utpote cum** as you might expect since; **utpote qui** inasmuch as *(he is one)* who, inasmuch as he, because he

utrār·ius -(i)ī *m* water carrier, water boy

utric(u)lār·ius -(i)ī *m* bagpipe player

utrimque *or* **utrinque** *adv* from *or* on both sides, on either side; **utrimque constitit fides** on both sides their word of honor held good

utrō *adv* to which of the two sides, in which direction

utrobīque *adv* on both sides, on either hand

utrōlibet *adv* to either side

utrōque *adv* to both sides, in both directions

utrōqueversum *adv* **(-vors-)** in both directions

utrubi *adv* at *or* on which of the two sides

utrubīque *adv* on both sides, on either hand

utrum *conj* whether

utut *adv* in whatever way, however

ūv·a -ae *f* grape; grapes; bunch of grapes; vine; swarm of bees; *(anat)* uvula; **uva passa** raisin *(literally, grape spread out to dry)*

ūvesc·ō -ĕre *intr* to become moist; *(fig)* to get drunk

ūvidul·us -a -um *adj* a little moist, dampish

ūvid·us -a -um *adj* wet, moist, damp; humid; drunk

ux·or -ōris *f* wife; mate *(of animals)*

uxorcul·a -ae *f* dear (little) wife

uxorcul·ō -āre -āvī *intr* to play the role of a wife

uxōri·us -a -um *adj* of a wife, wifely; very fond of a wife; henpecked

V

V, v is used in this dictionary to represent consonantal *u*

vac·ans -antis *adj* vacant, unoccupied; at leisure; unemployed; unattached, single; *(w. abl)* lacking, without; **puella vacans** a single girl **ǁ** *npl* unoccupied estates

vacāti·ō -ōnis *f* freedom, exemption *(from duty, service, etc.);* exemption from military service; payment for being exempted from military service; vacation, holiday, day off

vacc·a -ae *f* cow

vaccīn·ium -(i)ī *n (bot)* hyacinth

vaccul·a -ae *f* heifer

vacē·fīō -fierī *intr* to become empty, be emptied, be vacated

vacerr·a -ae *f* fence post

vacerrōs·us -a -um *adj (pej)* cracked, crazy

vacillāti·ō -ōnis *f* tottering

vacill·ō -āre -āvī -ātum *intr* **(vacc-)** to stagger, reel; to vacillate, waver; to be untrustworthy

vacīvē *adv* at leisure

vacīvit·ās -ātis *f* want, lack

vacīv·us -a -um *adj* **(voc-)** *(of a place)* unoccupied, vacant; *(w. gen)* free of, devoid of, free from

vac·ō -āre -āvī -ātum *intr* **(voc-)** to be empty, be vacant; to be unoccupied; to be ownerless; to be without, not to contain; to be free, be carefree; to be at leisure, have free time; *(of things)* to lie idle; to be *(romantically)* unattached; *(w. abl or ab)* **1** to be free from; **2** to be devoid of; **3** to abstain from; **4** to be exempt from *(duty, responsibility); (w. dat or w.* **ad** *or in + acc)* to be free for, have time for, have spare time for; *(w. inf)* to have leisure to, have time to; **populo vacare** to remain aloof from the people; **res publica et milite et pecuniā vacat** the country is relieved from furnishing an army and money; **semper philosophiae vaco** I always have time for philosophy **ǁ** *v impers (w. dat)* there is time for, there is room for; *(w. inf)* there is time to *or* for

vacuāt·us -a -um *adj* empty

vacuē·faciō -facĕre -fēcī -factus *tr* to empty, clear, free

vacuit·ās -ātis *f* freedom, exemption; emptiness; empty space; vacancy *(in an office); (w. gen or w. ab)* freedom from *(s.th. undesirable)*

Vacūn·a -ae *f* Sabine goddess, later identified with Victory

Vacūnāl·is -is -e *adj* of the goddess Vacuna

vacu·ō -āre -āvī -ātus *tr* to empty, clear, free; to strip *(a place of defenders, inhabitants)*

vacu·us -a -um *adj* empty, clear, free; vacant; worthless, useless; single, umarried; widowed; at leisure; carefree; *(w. gen or abl or w. ab)* free from, devoid of, without; *(w. dat)* free for

vadimōn·ium -(i)ī *n (leg)* promise *(to appear in court)*, bail *(given as a guarantee of one's appearance in court);* **vadimonium deserere** to default, jump bail; **vadimonium differre** to postpone appearance in court, grant a continuance; **vadimonium facere** to put up bail; **vadimonium sistere** to appear in court

vadis *see* **vas**

vādō vādĕre vāsī *intr* to go, make one's way, advance

vad·or -ārī -ātus sum *tr (of a plaintiff)* to demand that *(s.o.)* put up bail; to sue

vadōs·us -a -um *adj* shallow

vad·um -ī *n or* **vad·us -ī** *m* shallow place, shallow, ford; shallow part of the sea, shoal; bottom *(of the sea)*, depths; sea, waters

vae *interj* woe!; *(w. acc or dat)* woe to

va·fer -fra -frum *adj* sly, cunning; subtle; ingenious

vafrē *adv* slyly, cunningly

vagē *adv* far and wide

vāgīn·a -ae *f* sheath, scabbard; hull *(of ear of grain)*

vāg·iō -īre -īvī *or* **-iī** *intr (esp. of an infant)* to cry, bawl; *(of hares)* to squeal

vāgīt·us -ūs *m* cry

vāg·or -ōris *m* cry *(of a baby)*

vag·or -ārī -ātus sum *or* **vag·ō -āre** *intr* to wander, range, roam

vag·us -a -um *adj* wandering, roaming; shifting, inconstant; rambling *(speech);* roundabout *(explanation);* haphazard, erratic; fickle; *(of lovers)* changing from one partner to another; **stella vaga** planet

vāh *interj (expressing dismay, pain, annoyance, contempt, or surpise)* ah!, oh!

vaha *interj (expressing pleasant surprise)* aha!

valdē *adv* greatly, intensely; *(w. adj or adv)* very; *(as affirmative reply)* yes, certainly, to be sure

valē *interj* goodbye!

val·ens -entis *adj* strong, powerful; healthy, well; coarse *(fabrics);* strong *(medicine);* vigorous *(plants);* potent, effective *(remedies; arguments)*

valenter *adv* strongly; energetically

valentul·us -a -um *adj* sturdy, robust

val·eō -ēre -uī valitūrus *intr* to be strong; to be vigorous; to be powerful; to be effective; to prevail, succeed; to be influential; to be valid; to be strong

enough, be adequate, be capable, be able; to be of value, be of worth; to mean, signify; **te valere jubeo I** bid you farewell, goodbye to you; **vale** *(pl: valete)* goodbye; **vale dicere** to say goodbye, take leave

Valeriān·us -a -um *adj* belonging to Valerius

Valeri·us -a -um *adj* Roman clan name *(nomen), esp.* Publius Valerius Publicola, recorded as one of the first two consuls in 509 B.C.

valesc·ō -ĕre *intr* to grow strong, thrive; to grow powerful

valētūdinār·ium -(i)ī *n* hospital

valētūd·ō -īnis *f* state of health; good health; ill health, illness; **bona** *(or* **commoda** *or* **firma** *or* **prospera** *or* **secunda) valetudo** good health; **adversa** *(or* **infirma** *or* **mala)** poor health; **valetudinis causā** for reasons of (poor) health

Valgi·us -a -um *adj* Roman clan name *(nomen), esp.* Gaius Valgius Rufus *(an Augustan poet and grammarian)*

valg·us -a -um *adj* knock-kneed

validē *adv* strongly, vehemently; *(in replies)* of course, certainly, definitely

valid·us -a -um *adj* strong, powerful, able; healthy; robust; fortified; influential; efficacious

vallār·is -is -e *adj* of a rampart; **corona vallaris** crown awarded to the first soldier to scale the enemy's rampart

vall·ēs *or* **vall·is -is** *f* valley

vall·ō -āre -āvī -ātus *tr* to fortify with a rampart, wall in; to protect, defend

vall·um -ī *n* palisade of stakes on top of an embankment; rampart

vall·us -ī *m* stake, pale; rampart with palisades, stockade; tooth *(of a comb)*

valv·ae -ārum *fpl* folding doors, double doors

vānesc·ō -ĕre *intr* to vanish, fade

vānidic·us -a -um *adj* lying; boasting **ll** *m* liar; boaster

vāniloquenti·a -ae *f* empty talk, mere talk

vāniloquidōr·us -ī *m* liar, windbag

vāniloqu·us -a -um *adj* talking nonsense; lying; bragging

vānit·ās -ātis *f* falsity, unreality, deception, untruth; bragging; lying; vanity; worthlessness; frivolity

vānitūd·ō -inis *f* falsehood

vann·us -ī *f* winnowing fan

vān·us -a -um *adj* empty, vacant; groundless; pointless; hollow, unreal; lying, false; boastful; conceited, vain **ll** *n* emptiness; uselessness; deceptive appearance

vapidē *adv* poorly, badly

vapid·us -a -um *adj* flat, vapid, spoiled, bad; morally corrupt

vap·or -ōris *m* vapor, steam; warmth *(of the sun)*

vapōrār·ium -(i)ī *n* steam room

vapōr·ō -āre -āvī -ātus *tr* to steam up; to warm, heat ‖ *intr* to steam

vapp·a -ae *f* sour wine; *(pej)* brat, good-for-nothing

vāpulār·is -is -e *adj* in for a flogging

vāpul·ō -āre *intr* to get a beating; *(of savings, etc.)* to take a beating

vārē *adv* in a straddling manner

varianti·a -ae *f* diversity, variety

Vāriān·us -a -um *adj* of Varus *(i.e., Publius Quintilius Varus, whose legions were cut to pieces in Germany)*

variāti·ō -ōnis *f* diversification; variation; divergence

vāric·ō -āre -āvī -ātus *intr* to spread the legs, stand with legs spread apart

varicōs·us -a -um *adj* vericose

vāric·us -a -um *adj* with legs wide apart

variē *adv* variously; in different degrees; differently; severally, respectively; in a varied style; with changing colors

variet·ās -ātis *f* variety, difference, diversity; vicissitudes; inconstancy

vari·ō -āre -āvī -ātus *tr* to vary, diversify, change, make different; to give variety to; to variegate ‖ *intr* to change color; to vary, differ, change; to be diversified; to differ in opinion; to waver; **bellum variante fortunā** a war with varying success, a war with ups and downs ‖ *v impers* **si variaret** if there were a difference of opinion

vari·us -a -um *adj* variegated, of different colors; varied; composed of different elements, motley; many-sided *(personality)*; conflicting *(opinions, reports)*; changing, fluctuating *(conditions, fortunes)*; versatile; inconstant, unsteady; untrustworthy, fickle *(character)*

Var·ius -(i)ī *m* Lucius Varius Rufus *(epic and tragic poet and friend of Virgil and Horace, died c. 12 B.C.)*

var·ix -icis *mf* varicose vein

Varr·ō -ōnis *m* Roman family name, *(cognomen, esp.* Gaius Terentius Varro *(consul in 216 B.C. and joint commander at Cannae)* ‖ Marcus Terentius Varro *(antiquarian, philologist, and librarian, 116–27 B.C.)* ‖ Publius Terentius Varro Atacinus *(born 82 B.C., poet, translator of Apollonius Rhodius' "Argonautica")*

vār·us -a -um *adj* knock-kneed; bent, crooked; opposed, contrary

vas vadis *m (leg)* bondsman *(person who provides surety or bail)*

vās vāsis *or* **vās·um -ī** *(pl:* **vās·a -ōrum)** *n* vessel, dish; utensil, implement ‖ *npl* equipment, gear; **vasa colligere** *(mil)* to

pack up one's gear; **vasa conclamare** *(mil)* to give the signal to pack the gear; **vasa coquitatoria** pots and pans

vāsār·ium -(i)ī *n* allowance for furnishings *(given to a provincial governor)*

vasculār·ius -(i)ī *m* metal worker; seller of housewear items

vascul·um -ī *n* small vessel

vastāti·ō -ōnis *f* devastation

vastāt·or -ōris *m* devastator

vastē *adv* vastly, widely; coarsely, harshly; violently

vastific·us -a -um *adj* devastating

vastit·ās -ātis *f* wasteland, desert; state of desolation, emptiness; devastation, destruction; vastness, immensity; great open spaces

vastiti·ēs -ēī *f* ruin, destruction

vast·ō -āre -āvī -ātus *tr* to leave desolate; to lay waste; to cut *(troops)* to pieces

vast·us -a -um *adj* desolate; devastated; vast, enormous; uncouth; clumsy; unrefined *(pronunciation)*

vāt·ēs *or* **vat·is -is** *m* seer, prophet; bard, poet ‖ *f* prophetess; poetess

Vātican·us -a -um *adj* Vatican; **mons** *(or* **collis) Vaticanus** hill in Rome on the right bank of the Tiber

vāticināti·ō -ōnis *f* prophesying, soothsaying, prophecy

vāticināt·or -ōris *m* prophet, seer

vāticin·ium -(i)ī *n* prophecy

vāticin·or -ārī -ātus sum *tr* to foretell, prophesy; to keep harping on ‖ *intr* to prophesy; to rant and rave, talk wildly

vāticin·us -a -um *adj* prophetic

vatill·um -ī *n* brazier

vātis *see* **vates**

vati·us -a -um *adj* knock-kneed

-ve *conj (enclitic)* or; **-ve…-ve** either…or

vēcordi·a -ae *f* **(vae-)** senselessness; madness

vēc·ors -ordis *adj* **(vae-)** senseless; insane

vectāti·ō -ōnis *f* riding *(on horseback or in a carriage)*

vectīg·al -ālis *n* tax; revenue; duty; tariff; private income; produce providing personal income; payment given to a magistrate *or* provincial governor; private income *or* revenue; **vectigal aedilicium** payment exacted by an aedile to finance games

vectīgāl·is -is -e *adj (of persons, cities, etc.)* subject to taxation, taxed, taxable; *(of land, etc.)* yielding taxes; **pecunia vectigalis** money raised by taxes

vecti·ō -ōnis *f* conveyance, transporting

vect·is -is *m* crowbar, lever; bar, bolt *(on a door or gate)*

Vect·is -is *f* Isle of Wight

vect·ō -āre -āvī -ātus *tr* to carry, transport *(by an habitual agent or means of* *conveyance)* || *pass* to ride, drive, travel; **equo vectari** to ride a horse; **nave vectari** to sail

vect·or -ōris *m* bearer, carrier; rider; passenger

vectōri·us -a -um *adj* of transportation; **navigia vectoria** cargo ships

vectūr·a -ae *f* transportation, conveyance; freight costs; fare

vectus *pp of* **veho**

Vēdiov·is *or* **Vējov·is -is** *m* Anti-Jove *(Etruscan divinity of the lower world, identified with the Jupiter of the lower world)* || Little Jove *(identified with the infant Jupiter)*

veget·ō -āre *tr* to invigorate

veget·us -a -um *adj* vigorous; lively *(rhythm, time, mind, thoughts)* vivacious, energetic; invigorating; vivid *(colors);* **intervallum temporis vegetissimum agricolis** a space of time extremely busy for the farmers

vēgrand·is -is -e *adj* not huge, puny

vehem·ens -entis *adj* (**vēm-**) vehement; intense *(heat, cold);* strong, powerful *(force);* strong *(taste, flavor);* potent *(drink, medicine);* severe *(pain);* serious *(illness);* drastic *(actions);* forceful, strongly expressive, tremendous *(writing, speech);* imperious, overmastering; forceful *(arguments);* violent *(men, animals, natural phenomena);* vigorous, active *(person);* ardent, great *(love)*

vehementer *adv* (**vēm-**) vehemently, impetuously; with great force, violently; firmly, strongly; energetically; in an impassioned manner; *(w. reference to feelings)* strongly, overpoweringly; *(modifying adjectives)* immensely, tremendously

vehic(u)l·um -ī *n* vehicle, wagon, cart; means of transportation; **praefectus vehiculorum** director of the imperial post

veh·is -is *m* (*f*) wagonload

vehō vehĕre vexī vectus *tr* to carry, convey, transport || *pass* to travel, ride, sail, be borne along

Vei·ens -entis *or* **Veientān·us -a -um** *adj* of Veii

Vei·ī *or* **Vē·ī -ōrum** *mpl* old Etrurian city about 12 miles from Rome, captured by Camillus *(396 b.c.)*

Vējov·is -is *or* **Vēdjovis -is** *m* ancient deity worshiped on the Capitol at Rome, considered to be the lower-world counterpart of Jupiter

vel *adv* even, actually; perhaps; for instance; **vel...vel** either...or

Vēlābrens·is -is -e *adj* of the Velabrum

Vēlābr·um -ī *n* low ground between the Capitoline and Palatine where a market was located

vēlām·en -inis *n* drape, covering, veil; clothing, robe; olive branch wrapped in woll *(symbol carried by a suppliant)*

vēlāment·um -ī *n* covering, wrapping; a wrap; olive branch wrapped in wool *(symbol carried by a suppliant); (fig)* screen, cover-up

vēlār·ium -(i)ī *n* awning *(over the open-air theater)*

vēlāt·ī -ōrum *mpl (mil)* reserves

vēl·es -itis *m* light-armed soldier, skirmisher

Veli·a -ae *f* the Velia *(ridge connecting the Palatine and Oppian hills at Rome)* || town and port in Lucania

Veliens·is -is -e *adj* of the Velia in Rome || of Velia *(Lucanian town)*

vēlif·er -era -erum *adj* sail-, sailing; **carina velifera** sailboat, sailing ship

vēlificāti·ō -ōnis *f* sailing

vēlific·ō -āre -āvī -ātus *or* **vēlific·or -ārī -ātus sum** *tr* to sail through || *intr* to sail; *(w. dat)* **1** to be under full sail toward, set one's course for; **2** to be hell-bent on *(e.g., high office)*

Velīn·us -a -um *adj* of Velia *(Lucanian town and port);* of the River Velinus; **lacus Valinus** Valine Lake *(fed by the Veline river);* **tribus Velina** one of the 35 Roman tribes, belonging to that region

Velīn·us -ī *m* river and lake in the Sabine territory

vēlitār·is -is -e *adj* of light-armed troops

vēlitāti·ō -ōnis *f* skirmishing

Velitern·us -a -um *adj* of Velitrae

vēlitēs = *pl of* **veles**

vēlit·or -ārī -ātus sum *or* **vēlit·ō -āre** *intr* to make an irregular attack, skirmish; *(fig)* to indulge in a verbal skirmish

Velitr·ae -ārum *fpl* Volscian town in Latium on the S. side of the Alban Hills

vēlivol·us -a -um *adj* speeding along under sail; sail-covered *(sea)*

Vēli·us -a -um *adj* Roman clan name, *(nomen),* esp. Velius Longus *(a grammarian of the age of Trajan)*

velle *inf of* **volo**

vellic·ō -are *tr* to pluck, pinch, nip; to carp at, rail at

vellō vellĕre vellī *or* **vulsī** *or* **volsī vulsus** *or* **volsus** *tr* to pluck, pull, tear at, tear away, tear out; to tear up, tear down, destroy

vell·us -eris *n* fleece, skin, pelt; wool || *npl* fleecy clouds

vēl·ō -āre -āvī -ātus *tr* to veil, wrap, envelop; to cover, clothe; to encircle, crown; to cover up, hide; to adorn *(temples, etc., ritually);* **velatus** sail-clad, fitted with sails

vēlōcit·ās -ātis *f* velocity, speed

vēlōciter *adv* speedily, swiftly

vēl·ox -ōcis *adj* speedy, swift

vēl·um -ī *n* sail; veil; curtain, awning, covering; **plenis velis** full speed ahead; **remis velisque** *(fig)* with might and main; **(ventis) vela dare** to set sail; **vela facere** to spread one's sails

velut *or* velutī *adv* as, just as, even as; as for example; *(to introduce a simile)* as, as it were; *(in elliptical clauses)* like; **velut** *(or* **velut si)** just as if, just as though, as if, as though

vēmens *see* vehemens

vēn·a -ae *f* blood vessel *(whether vein or artery); (contrasted with* **arteria)** vein; artery *(believed to conduct air or food and drink to the body);* duct *(in the body);* penis; vein, streak *(in wood, stone, minerals);* vein *(of ore);* channel, trench; watercourse; store of talent *or* ability; natural disposition; strength; **vena aquae** streamlet **‖** *fpl (fig)* heart, core

vēnābul·um -ī *n* hunting spear

Venā·fer -fra -frum *or* Venāfrān·us -a -um *adj* of Venafrum

Venāfr·um -ī *n* Samnite town in S. central Italy

vēnālici·us -a -um *adj* for sale **‖** *m* slave dealer **‖** *npl* merchandise, imports and exports

vēnāl·is -is -e *adj* for sale; open to bribe **‖** *mf* slave offered for sale

vēnātic·us -a -um *adj* hunting

vēnāti·ō -ōnis *f* hunt, hunting; wild-beast show; game

vēnāt·or -ōris *m* hunter

vēnātōri·us -a -um *adj* hunter's

vēnātr·ix -īcis *f* huntress

vēnātūr·a -ae *f* hunting

vēnāt·us -ūs *m* hunting

vendibil·is -is -e *adj* marketable; on sale; attractive, popular, acceptable

venditāti·ō -ōnis *f* advertising; showing off

venditāt·or -ōris *m* hawker, self-advertiser

venditi·ō -ōnis *f* sale

vendit·ō -āre -āvī -ātus *tr* to try to sell; to advertise; to give as a bribe **‖** *refl (w. dat)* to ingratiate oneself with

vendit·or -ōris *m* vendor, seller; recipient of a bribe

vend·ō -ěre -idī -itus *tr* to put up for sale; to sell, vend; to sell *(s.o.)* out, betray; to advertise; to praise, recommend

venēfic·a -ae *f* poisoner; sorceress, witch; *(term of abuse)* hag, witch

venēfic·ium -(i)ī *n* poisoning; poison; magical herb; magic, supernatural influence; dye; *(fig)* pernicious moral influence; malicious speech

venēfic·us -a -um *adj* poisoning, poisonous; magic **‖** *m* poisoner; sorcerer, magician

venēnāt·us -a -um *adj* poisonous, venomous; filled with poison; magic; bewitched, enchanted; *(fig)* venomous, bitter

venēnif·er -era -erum *adj* poisonous, venomous

venēn·ō -āre -āvī -ātus *tr (lit & fig)* to poison

venēn·um -ī *n* poison; drug, potion; magic charm; sorcery; ruin; dye; virulence *(of speech)*

vēn·eō -īre -iī -itūrus *intr* to go up for sale, be sold

venerābil·is -is -e *adj* venerable, revered

venerābund·us -a -um *adj* reverend; reverential, worshiping

venerand·us -a -um *adj* venerable, august

venerāti·ō -ōnis *f* veneration, reverence, deep respect

venerāt·or -ōris *m* respecter, adorer; admirer

Vener·us *or* Veneri·us -a -um *adj* of Venus; of sexual love, erotic; **res Veneriae** sexual intercourse **‖** *m* Venus throw *(best throw of the dice, when each of the four dice turns up a different number)* **‖** *mpl* attendants in Venus' temple

vener·or -ārī -ātus sum *or* vener·ō -āre *tr* to venerate, revere, worship, pray to; to implore, beg; to pray for

Venet·ī -ōrum *mpl* a people in N.E. Italy in the region of modern Venice **‖** a tribe in Gallia Lugdunensis

Veneti·a -ae *f* district of the Veneti in W. Gaul

Venetic·us -a -um *adj* of the Veneti *(of Gallia Lugdunensis)*

Venet·us -a -um *adj* Venetian; bluish **‖** *m* Venetian; a Blue *(i.e., a member of one of the racing factions in Rome)*

veni·a -ae *f* kindness, favor, goodwill; permission; pardon, forgiveness; **veniam dare** *(w. dat)* 1 to grant forgiveness to; 2 to do a favor to; 3 to grant permission to; **veniam petere** to ask permission; **veniā vestrā** with your leave

Venīli·a -ae *f* Italian nymph *(wife of Faunus or of Janus)*

veni·ō venīre vēnī ventum *intr* to come; to be coming, be on the way; to appear in court; to come to dinner; *(of plants)* to come up; *(w. in + acc)* 1 to come into; 2 to enter into *(an agreement, friendship, etc.);* 3 to fall into *(e.g., trouble, disgrace, etc.);* **in buccam venire** to be on the tip of the tongue; **in mentem venire** to come to mind

vēn·or -ārī -ātus sum *tr & intr* to hunt

vent·er -ris *m* stomach, belly; womb; embryo, unborn child; belly, protuberance;

appetite, gluttony

ventil·ō -āre -āvī -ātus *tr* to fan, wave; to display, show off

venti·ō -ōnis *f* coming

ventit·ō -āre -āvī -ātum *intr* to keep coming, come regularly

ventōs·us -a -um *adj* windy, full of wind; of the wind; wind-like, swift as the wind; conceited; fickle

ventricul·us -ī *m* belly; ventricle *(of the heart)*

ventriōs·us -a -um *adj* pot-bellied

ventul·us -ī *m* breeze

vent·us -ī *m* wind; intestinal wind; *(fig)* storm; **ventum emittere** to break wind

vēnūcul·a -ae *f* grape *(of the type well suited for preserving)*

vēn·um *(gen not in use; dat:* **vēnō)** *n* sale, that which is for sale; for sale; **venum** *(or* **veno) dare** to put up for sale, sell; to sell as a slave; **venum** *(or* **veno) dari** to be sold; **venum** *(or* **veno) ire** to go up for sale, be sold

vēnum·dō -dare -dedī -datus *tr* (**-und-**) to put up for sale, sell

ven·us -eris *f* beauty, charm; sexual intercourse, sex; mating; beloved, love ‖ **Venus** Venus *(goddess of love and beauty; planet);* Venus-throw *(see* **Venereus)**

Venusi·a -ae *f* town in Apulia *(birthplace of Horace, modern Venosa)*

Venusīn·us -a -um *adj* of Venusia

venust·ās -ātis *f* beauty, charm, attraction

venustē *adv* prettily, charmingly

venustul·us -a -um *adj* cute, pretty

venust·us -a -um *adj* charming, attractive; interesting *(writing, writer)*

vēpallid·us -a -um *adj* very pale

veprēcul·a -ae *f* little brier bush

vepr·ēs -is *m* (*f*) brier, bramble bush

vēr vēris *n* spring, springtime; youth

vērātr·um -ī *n* *(bot)* helebore *(used as a drug to treat insanity)*

vēr·ax -ācis *adj* truthful

verbēn·a -ae *f* *(bot)* verbena *(plant with clusters of flowers of various colors)* ‖ *fpl* sacred branches worn by heralds and priests

verb·er -eris *n* scourge, rod, whip; flogging, scourging; thong *(of a sling and similar weapon)* ‖ *npl* strokes, flogging

verberābilissum·us -a -um *adj* altogether deserving of a flogging

verberābund·us -a -um *adj* flogging all the way

verberāti·ō -ōnis *f* flogging

verberetill·us -a -um *adj* deserving of a flogging

verbere·us -a -um *adj* deserving of a flogging

verber·ō -āre -āvī -ātus *tr* to flog, scourge,

whip; to batter, beat

verber·ō -ōnis *m* rascal *(deserving of flogging)*

verbivēlitāti·ō -ōnis *f* verbal skirmish

verbōsē *adv* verbosely

verbōs·us -a -um *adj* verbose

verb·um -ī *n* word; verb; saying, expression; proverb; mere talk, mere words; formula; **ad verbum** word for word, verbatim; **verba dare** *(w. dat)* to cheat *(s.o.);* **verba facere** to speak, make a speech; **verbi causā** *(or* **verbi gratiā)** for instance; **verbo** orally; in a word, briefly; nominally, in name only; in theory; **verbo de verbo** *(or* **verbum pro verbo** *or* **verbum verbo)** word for word

Vercell·ae-ārum *fpl* town in N.W. Gaul *(modern Vercelli)*

Vercingetor·ix -igis *m* famous leader of the Arverni in the Gallic War

vercul·um -ī *n* *(term of endearment)* sweet springtime

vērē *adv* really, truly

verēcundē *adv* bashfully, modestly

verēcundi·a -ae *f* bashfulness, shyness, modesty; respect, awe, reverence; sense of shame; feeling of disgrace, disgrace, shame

verēcund·or -ārī *intr* to be bashful, be shy, feel ashamed

verēcund·us -a -um *adj* bashful, shy, modest, reserved

verēd·us -ī *m* fast hunting horse

verend·us -a -um *adj* awesome ‖ *npl* sexual organs

ver·eor -ērī -itus sum *tr* to revere, have respect for; to fear ‖ *intr* to feel uneasy, be anxious, be afraid; *(w. gen)* to stand in awe of, be afraid of; *(w. dat)* to be afraid for; *(w.* **de** + *abl)* to be apprehensive about; *(w.* **ut)** to be afraid that not; *(w.* **ne)** to be afraid that

veretr·um -ī *n* male sexual organ

Vergili·ae -ārum *fpl* *(astr)* Pleiades *(constellation)*

Vergil·ius *or* **Virgil·ius -(i)ī** *m* Roman clan name *(nomen),* esp. Vergil *(Publius Vergilius Maro, epic poet of the Augustan Age, 70–19 B.C.)*

Vergīni·us -a -um *adj* Roman clan name *(nomen),* esp. Lucius Verginius *(said to have killed his daughter to save her from the lust of Appius Claudius and thus to have brought about the overthrow of the decemvirs in 449 B.C.)* ‖ *f* his daughter

verg·ō -ĕre *tr* to cause to move in a downward direction, incline; to tilt down ‖ *intr* to turn, incline; to slope back *or* away; to decline; to lie, be situated; *(w.* **ad)** **1** to verge toward; **2** to face (toward); **3** to incline toward, tend toward *(usu. a worse condition);* **3** *(w.* **in** + *acc)* to sink into, lapse into *(lethargy, old age)*

vēridic·us -a -um *adj* truthful, speaking the truth; truly spoken

vēriloqu·ium -(i)ī *n* argument based on the true meaning of a word

vērīsimil·is -is -e *adj* probable, likely; realistic

vērīsimilitūd·ō -inis *f* probability, likelihood

vērit·ās -ātis *f* truth, truthfulness; real life, reality; honesty, integrity; correctness *(in eytmology and grammar);* **ex veritate** in accordance with the truth

vēriverb·ium -(i)ī *n* truthfulness

vermiculāt·us -a -um *adj* inlaid with wavy lines, vermiculated

vermicul·us -ī *m* grubworm, maggot; **in vermiculo** in the larval state

vermin·a -um *npl* stomach cramps

verm·is -is *m* worm

vern·a -ae *mf* home-born slave *(born in the master's house);* native

vernācul·us -a -um *adj* of home-born slaves; home-grown, native, domestic; of the neighborhood; indigenous; proletarian; *(of troops)* levied locally; *(w. gen)* native to *(a place)* **‖** *mf* home-born slave

vernīl·is -is -e *adj* servile; obsequious

vernīlit·ās -ātis *f* slavishness; rude behavior, impudence

vernīliter *adv* slavishly

vern·ō -āre *intr* to show signs of spring; to burgeon, break into bloom; to be young

vernul·a -ae *mf* young slave *(born in the master's house);* native

vern·us -a -um *adj* spring, of spring; **tempus vernum** springtime

vērō *adv* in truth, in fact; certainly, to be sure; even; however

Vērōn·a -ae *f* city in N. Italy, birthplace of Catullus

Vērōn(i)ens·is -is -e *adj* Veronese

verp·a -ae *f* penis *(as protruded from the foreskin)*

verp·us -a -um *adj* circumsized; having the foreskin drawn back

verr·ēs -is *m* pig, boar **‖ Verres** Gaius Cornelius Verres *(notorious governor of Sicily in 73–70 B.C.)*

verrīn·us -a -um *adj* of a boar, of a pig, pork

ver·rō -rĕre -rī -sus *tr* (vor-) to pull, drag, drag away, carry off; to sweep, scour, brush; *(of the wind)* to whip across, sweep *(the land)*

verrūc·a -ae *f* wart *(on the body);* small failing, minor blemish

verrūcōs·us -a -um *adj* full of warts; *(fig)* full of blemishes

verrunc·ō -āre *intr* to turn out well

versābil·is -is -e *adj* shifting, movable

versābund·us -a -um *adj* revolving

versātil·is -is -e *adj* capable of turning, revolving, movable; versatile

versicapill·us -a -um *adj* having hair that has turned gray, graying

versicol·or -ōris *adj* changing colors, of various colors

versicul·us -ī *m* short line, single line *(of verse or prose),* versicle **‖** *mpl* poor little verses

versificāti·ō -ōnis *f* versification

versificāt·or -ōris *m* versifier

versific·ō -āre *tr* to put into verse **‖** *intr* to write verse

versipell·is -is *m* one can change appearance at will; werewolf

vers·ō -āre -āvī -ātus *tr* (vor-) to keep turning, spin, whirl; to twist, bend, wind *(material in order to change its shape);* to turn *(the eyes)* this way and that *(in uncertainty);* to keep shifting *(the limbs in restlessness);* to keep turning, maneuver *(a vehicle, a horse);* to swing *(a weapon)* in all directions; to stir *(the contents of a vessel, esp. the lots in an urn);* to keep turning over *(the ground, as in plowing); (fig)* to influence, sway *(a person in one direction or another); (pej)* to manipulate *(a person); (fig)* to turn over in the mind, ponder, consider; *(w.* **in** + *acc)* to focus *(the mind)* on; *(rhet)* to vary the expression *(of an idea)* **‖** *refl* to keep going around, keep on revolving; to spin around *(so as to face in the opposite direction)*

vers·or -ārī -ātus sum *intr* (vor-) to come and go frequently; to live, stay; to be, be in operation, obtain; *(w. adverbs)* to behave *(in a certain way);* to revolve; to spin around *(so as to face in the opposite direction);* to toss, writhe; *(w.* **in** + *abl)* **1** to be involved in, be engaged in, be busy with; **2** to stay in, live in, pass one's time in *(a place, among persons, or in surroundings);* **3** *(of things)* to be concerned with, have to do with; **4** to be subject to; **5** *(of an idea, mental image)* to be constantly present in *(the mind);* **6** *(of a speaker)* to dwell on; **in ore vulgi versari** to be constantly on people's lips

versōri·a -ae *f (naut)* rope used to set sail at an angle in order to tack

versum *adv* (vor-) *(usu. after another adv of direction)* back; **rusum vorsum** backward; **sursum vorsum** up and down

versūr·a -ae *f* (vor-) rotation; loan *(of money to pay another debt);* **versuram facere** *(w.* ab) to get a loan from *(s.o. to pay another);* **versurā solvere** to pay off *(another debt)* with borrowed money

versus *pp of* **verro** *and* **verto**

vers·us -ūs *m* (vor-) turning; furrow; line, row; turn, step *(in a dance); (poet)* line, verse

versus *or* **versum** *adv* (vor-) *(w.* ad*)* towards, in the direction of; *(w.* in + *acc)* into, in towards; **si in urbem versus venturi erunt** if they intend to come into the city; **sursum versus** upwards

versūtē *adv* (vor-) cunningly

versūti·ae -ārum *fpl* cunning, tricks

versūtiloqu·us -a -um *adj* smooth-talking, sly

versūt·us -a -um *adj* (vors-) clever, shrewd, ingenious; sly, cunning, deceitful

vert·ex -icis *m* (vor-) whirlpool, eddy, strong current; whirlwind, tornado; crown *or* top of the head; head; top, summit *(of mountain);* pole *(of the heavens);* **ex vertice** from above

verticōs·us -a -um *adj* swirling, full of whirlpools

vertīg·ō -inis *f* turning, whirling; dizziness

vert·ō -ĕre -ī versus *tr* (vor-) to turn, turn around, spin; to reverse; to invert, tilt; to change, alter, transform; to turn over, plow; to overturn, knock down; to destroy; to subvert, ruin; to ascribe, impute; to translate; *(w.* ab*)* to deflect from **‖** *refl (w.* in + *acc)* to change into **‖** *pass (w.* in + *acc)* to turn into; *(w.* in + *abl)* **1** to be in *(a place or condition);* **2** to be engaged in, be involved in **‖** *intr* to turn; to change; to turn out; *(w.* in + *abl)* to center on, depend upon

vertrag·us -ī *m* Gallic greyhound

Vertumn·us -ī *m* (Vor-) god of the changing seasons

ver·ū -ūs *n* spit *(for roasting);* javelin, dart

veruīn·a -ae *f* spit; small javelin

vērum *adv* truly; yes; *(in responses)* true but, yes but; but in fact; but yet, but even; yet, still; **non solum** *(or* modo *or* tantum)...**verum** *(usu. followed by* et, etiam *or* quoque) not only...but also

vērumtamen *adv* nevertheless

vēr·us -a -um *adj* true, actual, genuine, real; fair, reasonable **‖** *n* truth, reality; honor, duty, right; **veri similis** probable; realistic; **veri similitudo** probability

verūt·um -ī *n* dart, javelin

verūt·us -a -um *adj* armed with a javelin *or* dart

verv·ex -ēcis *m* wether, castrated hog; *(term of abuse)* muttonhead

vēsāni·a -ae *f* (vae-) insanity, madness

vēsāni·ens -entis *adj* raging

vēsān·us -a -um *adj* (vae-) insane; furious, savage, raging

vesc·or -ī *intr (w. abl)* to feed on, eat, to feast on, enjoy

vesc·us -a -um *adj* nibbled off; little, feeble; corroding, consuming

Veser·is -is *m* stream in Campania where Publius Decius Mus and Titus Manius Torquatus defeated the Latins in 340 B.C.

vēsīc·a -ae *f* bladder; bombast; objects made of bladder: purse, cap, football, lantern

vēsīcul·a -ae *f* little bladder; little bag

vesp·a -ae *f* wasp

Vespāsiān·us -ī *m* Vespasian *(Titus Flavius Vespasianus Sabinus, Roman Emperor, A.D. 70–79)*

Vespāsi·us -a -um *adj* Roman clan name *(nomen), esp.* Vespasia Polla *(mother of the Emperor Vespasian)*

vesp·er -erī *or* **-eris** *m* evening; supper; the West; **ad vesperum** toward evening; **primo vespere** early in the evening; **sub vespere** towards evening; **tam vesperi** so late in the evening; **vespere** *or* **vesperi** in the evening

vesper·a -ae *f* evening

vesper·ascō -ascĕre -āvī *intr* to grow towards evening; **vesperascente die** as the day was getting late **‖** *v impers* evening is coming

vespertili·ō -ōnis *m* bat

vespertīn·us -a -um *adj* evening-, in the evening; western

vesperūg·ō -inis *f* evening star

vespill·ō -ōnis *m* mortician

Vest·a -ae *f* Roman goddess of the hearth

Vestāl·is -is -e *adj* Vestal, of Vesta; **virgo Vestalis** Vestal virgin

ves·ter -tra -trum *adj* (vos-) your *(pl);* **‖** *pron* yours; **vestri** your friends, your relatives, your soldiers, your school, your party; **vestrum est** *(w. inf)* it is up to you to; **voster** your master

vestibul·um -ī *n* entrance, forecourt; beginning

vestīg·ium -(i)ī *n* footstep, step; footprint, track; trace, vestige; moment, instant

vestīg·ō -āre *tr* to track, trace; to check, find out

vestīment·um -ī *n* clothing; garment; blanket

Vestīn·us -a -um *adj* of the Vestini **‖** *mpl* the Vestini *(Oscan-speaking tribe of the central Apennines)*

vest·iō -īre -īvī *or* **-iī -ītus** *tr* to dress, clothe; to adorn, array, attire; *(fig)* to dress, clothe

vestiplic·a -ae *f* laundress, folder *(employed in ironing and folding clothes)*

vest·is -is *f* garment, dress; clothing; coverlet; tapestry; blanket; slough, skin *(of a snake);* **vestem mutare** to change one's clothes; to put on mourning clothes; **vestis longa** full dress including the full-length stola

vestispic·a -ae *f* female servant in charge of clothes

vestīt·us -ūs *m* clothing, clothes, dress, apparel; ornament *(of speech);* **mutare vestitum** to put on mourning clothes; **redire ad suum vestitum** to end the mourning period

Vesuvi·us -a -um *adj* of Mt. Vesuvius; **mons Vesuvius** Mt. Vesuvius

veter·a -um *npl* tradition, antiquity

veterāmentāri·us -a -um *adj* dealing in second-hand clothes

veterān·us -a -um *adj* & *m* veteran

veter·ascō -ascĕre -āvī *intr* to grow old

veterāt·or -ōris *m* old hand, expert; sly old fox

veterātōriē *adv* cunningly, slyly

veterātōri·us -a -um *adj* cunning

veter·ēs -um *mpl* the ancients; ancient authors

veterīn·us -a -um *adj* of burden ǁ *fpl* & *npl* beasts of burden

veternōs·us -a -um *adj* lethargic; sleepy, drowsy

vetern·us -ī *m* lethargy; old age; drowsiness; listlessness *(of old age)*

vetit·um -ī *n* prohibition

vet·ō -āre -uī -itus *tr* (vot-) to forbid, prohibit, oppose; to veto; *(w. inf, w.* **ne, quominus)** to prevent from; *(w. inf, w.* **acc & inf, w. ne, w. quin)** to forbid *(s.o. to do s.th.)*

vetul·us -a -um *adj* poor old

vet·us -eris *adj* old, aged; long-standing ǁ *mpl see* **veteres** ǁ *npl see* **vetera**

vetust·ās -ātis *f* age; ancient times, antiquity; long duration, great age

vetust·us -a -um *adj* old, ancient; old-time, old-fashioned, good old *(days, etc.);* antiquated

vexām·en -inis *n* shaking, quaking

vexāti·ō -ōnis *f* shaking, jolting, tossing; distress

vexāt·or -ōris *m* jostler; harasser; troublemaker

vexī *perf of* **veho**

vexillār·ius -(i)ī *m* standard-bearer ǁ *mpl* special reserves

vexillāti·ō -ōnis *f (mil)* detachment

vexill·um -ī *n* standard, flag, banner *(esp. the red flag hoisted above the general's tent as the signal for battle);* replica of the military banner, awarded for distinguished service; detachment of troops; **vexillum praeponere** to hoist the red flag *(as the signal for battle)*

vex·ō -āre *tr* to shake, toss; to vex, annoy; to harass *(troops)*

vi·a -ae *f* way, road, street, highway; march, journey; method; right way, right method; **inter vias** on the road; **in via**

(frontage) on the road; **viam munire** to build a road; *(fig)* to pave the way; isle *(in the theater);* **via recta** a direct route; **via vitae** pathway of life

viāl·is -is -e *adj* of the highway

viāri·us -a -um *adj* for highway maintenance

viāticāt·us -a -um *adj* provided with traveling money

viātic·us -a -um *adj* for the trip, for traveling, travel ǁ *n* travel allowance, provisions for the journey; *(mil)* soldier's saving fund

viāt·or -ōris *m* traveler; passenger; *(leg)* bailiff

vīb·ex -īcis *f* welt *(from a blow)*

vibr·ō -āre *tr* to brandish, wave around; to hurl ǁ *intr* to vibrate, quiver; *(of the tongue)* to flick

vīburn·um -ī *n (bot)* viburnum *(ornamental shrub, the bark of which was used in medicine)*

vīcān·us -a -um *adj* village- ǁ *mpl* villagers

Vic·a Pot·a *(gen:* **Vic·ae Pot·ae)** *f* a goddess of victory

vicāri·us -a -um *adj* substitute ǁ *m* substitute, deputy, proxy; under-slave *(kept by another slave)*

vīcātim *adv* from street to street; from village to village; in hamlets

vice *prep (w. gen)* on account of; like, after the manner of

vicem *adv* in turn ǁ *prep (w. gen)* instead of, in place of; on account of; like, after the manner of

vīcēnāri·us -a -um *adj* of the number twenty

vīcēn·ī -ae -a *adj* twenty each, twenty apiece, twenty at a time, twenty in a group

vīcēsimān·ī -ōrum *mpl* soldiers of the twentieth legion

vīcēsimāri·us -a -um *adj* derived from the 5% tax

vīcēsim·us -a -um *adj* (vīcens-) twentieth ǁ *f* 5% tax

vīcess·is -is *m* coins worth 20 "asses" *(i.e., c. 20¢)*

vici·a -ae *f* vetch *(grown for its edible seeds and used as fodder for animals)*

vīciē(n)s *adv* twenty times

vīcināl·is -is -e *adj* neighboring, nearby

vīcīni·a -ae *f* neighborhood; nearness, proximity

vīcīnit·ās -ātis *f* neighborhood, proximity; the neighborhood *(i. e., the neighbors)*

vīcīn·us -a -um *adj* neighboring, nearby; near; imminent ǁ *mf* neighbor ǁ *n* neighborhood; **ex vicino** of a similar nature; **in vicino** in close proximity

vicis *(gen; the nom singl and gen pl do not*

occur; acc singl: **vicem;** *abl singl:* **vice)** *f* change, interchange, alternation; succession; exchange; interaction; return, recompense, retaliation; fortune, misfortune, condition, fate; plight, lot; changes of fate; duty, office, position; function, capacity, office; **ad vicem** (*w. gen*) after the manner of; **in vicem** (*or* **in vices** *or* **per vices**) in turn, alternately; **in vicem** (*or* **invicem**) (*w. gen*) instead of, in place of; vice in return; **vice** (*w. gen*) *or* **vicem** (*w. gen*) in place of, as a substitute for; **vice versā** (*or* **vicibus versis**) vice-versa, conversely; **vicibus** in return

vicissim *or* **vicissātim** *adv* in turn, again

vicissitūd·ō -inis *f* change, interchange; regular succession, alternation; reversal, vicissitude; reciprocation

victim·a -ae *f* (**-tum-**) victim; sacrifice

victimār·ius -(i)ī *m* (**-tum-**) assistant at sacrifices

victit·ō -āre -āvī -ātum *intr* to live, subsist; (*w. abl*) to live on, subsist on

vict·or -ōris *m* victor; (*in apposition*) **victor exercitus** victorious army

victōri·a -ae *f* victory

victōriāt·us -ī *m* victory coin (*of silver, stamped with the image of victory*)

Victōriol·a -ae *f* figurine of Victory

victr·ix -īcis *adj* (*fem & neut only*) victorious, triumphant

victus *pp of* **vinco**

vict·us -ūs *or* **-ī** *m* living, means of livelihood; way of life; food, sustenance

vīcul·us -ī *m* hamlet

vīc·us -ī *m* village, hamlet; ward, quarter (*in a city*); street, block

vidēlicet *adv* clearly, evidently; (*in irony*) of course, naturally; (*in explanations*) namely

viden = **vidēsne?** do you see?, do you get it?

videō vidēre vīdī vīsus *tr* to see, look at; to know; to consider; to understand, realize; (*w. ut*) to see to it that, take care that ‖ *pass* to seem, appear ‖ *v impers pass* it seems right, it seems good; **dis visum est** the gods decided (*literally, it seemed* (*right*) *to the gods*

vidu·a -ae *f* widow; spinster

viduit·ās -ātis *f* bereavement; want, lack; widowhood

vīdul·us -ī *m* leather travel bag, suitcase, knapsack

vidu·ō -āre -āvī -ātus *tr* to deprive, bereave; (*w. gen or abl*) to deprive of; **viduata** left a widow

vidu·us -a -um *adj* bereft, destitute; unmarried; (*w. abl or* **ab**) bereft of, destitute of, without ‖ *f see* **vidua**

Vienn·a -ae *f* chief city of the Allobroges in Gallia Narbonensis (*modern Vienne*)

viēt·or -ōris *m* cooper

viēt·us -a -um *adj* shriveled

vig·eō -ēre -uī *intr* to thrive, be vigorous, flourish

vig·escō -escĕre -uī *intr* to become vigorous, gain strength, become lively

vīgēsim·us -a -um *adj* twentieth

vig·il -ilis *adj* awake, wakeful; alert, one one's toes ‖ *m* watchman, guard, sentinel; fireman, policeman

vigil·ans -antis *adj* watchful, alert; disquieting (*worries*)

vigilanter *adv* vigilantly, alertly

vigilanti·a -ae *f* wakefulness; vigilance, alertness

vigil·ax -ācis *adj* alert; disquieting, sleep-disturbing (*worries*)

vigili·a -ae *f* wakefulness, sleeplessness, insomnia; vigil; vigilance, alertness; watch (*one of the four divisions of the night for keeping watch*); (*mil*) standing guard; (*mil*) guards, sentinels; **vigilias agere** (*or* **agitare** *or* **servare**) to keep watch

vigil·ō -āre -āvī -ātus *tr* to spend (*the night*) awake; to make, do, perform, write (*s.th.*) while awake at night ‖ *intr* to stay awake; to be watchful; to be alert; (*w. dat*) to be attentive to

vīgintī *indecl adj* twenty

vīgintī·vir -virī *m* member of a board of twenty (*appointed by Caesar in 59 B.C. to distribute parcels of land in Campania*) ‖ member of a board of twenty in municipal administration

vīgintīvirāt·us -ūs *m* membership on the board of twenty

vig·or -ōris *m* vigor, liveliness

vīlic·a -ae *f* (**vill-**) foreman's wife, manager's wife

vīlic·ō -āre -āvī -ātum *intr* (**vill-**) to be a foreman, be a manager (*of an estate*)

vīlic·us -ī *m* (**vill-**) foreman, manager (*of an estate*)

vīl·is -is -e *adj* cheap, inexpensive; common, worthless, contemptible

vīlit·ās -ātis *f* lowness of price, cheapness, low price; worthlessness

vīliter *adv* cheaply, at a low price

vill·a -ae *f* country home; farmhouse; **villa rustica** farmhouse, homestead; **villa urbana** (*also in the country, with no farm attached*) country villa

villic- = **vilic-**

villōs·us -a -um *adj* hairy, shaggy, bushy

villul·a -ae *f* small farmhouse; small villa

vill·um -ī *n* drop of wine

vill·us -ī *m* hair; fleece; nap (*of cloth*)

vīm·en -inis *n* osier; basket

vīment·um -ī *n* osier

Vīmināl·is -is -e *adj* Viminal; **Viminalis collis** Viminal Hill (*one of the seven hills of Rome*)

vīmine·us -a -um *adj* made of osiers

vīn *or* **vīn'** = **visne?** do you wish?, ya' wanna?

vīnāce·us -a -um *adj* grape, of grape ‖ *n* grape seed

Vīnāl·ia -ium *npl* wine festival; **Vinalia priora** earlier wine festival *(celebrated on April 23, when libations of wine from the previous year were poured to Jupiter);* **Vinalia rustica** country wine festival *(celebrated on August 19 and 20 in honor of Jupiter in thanksgiving for the successful harvest)*

vīnāri·us -a -um *adj* wine- ‖ *m* wine dealer; vintner ‖ *npl* wine flasks

vincibil·is -is -e *adj* easily won

vin·ciō -cīre -xī -ctus *tr* to bind, tie; to wrap; to encircle, surround; to restrain; *(med)* to bandage; *(med)* to ligature; *(rhet)* to link together, arrange rhythmically

vincō vincĕre vīcī victus *tr* to conquer; to get the better of, beat, defeat; to outdo; to convince, refute, persuade; to prove, demonstrate; to outlast, outlive ‖ *intr* to win, be victorious; to prevail; to succeed

vinct·us -a -um *pp of* **vincio** ‖ *adj* fettered, in bonds

vincul·um *or* **vincl·um -ī** *n* chain; fetter, cord, band; sandal strap; thong, rope; mooring cable; tether ‖ *npl* bonds, fetter; imprisonment; prison; **vincula publica** chains worn by a state prisoner; **aliquem in vincula conjicere** to put s.o. into chains

Vindelic·us -a -um *adj* of the Vindelici ‖ *mpl* people living between the Raetian Alps and the Danube

vindēmi·a -ae *f* vintage

vindēmiāt·or -ōris *m* grape picker

vindēmiol·a -ae *f* small vintage; minor sources of income

Vindēmit·or -ōris *m (astr)* a star in Virgo

vind·ex -icis *adj* avenging ‖ *m (leg)* claimant; defender, protector, champion; liberator; avenger, punisher

Vind·ex -icis *m* Roman family name *(cognomen)*, esp. Gaius Julius Vindex *(leader of a rebellion in Gaul against Nero in* A.D. *69)*

vindicāti·ō -ōnis *f* avenging, punishment; *(leg)* claim

vindici·ae -ārum *fpl* legal claim; things *or* persons claimed; championship, protection; **vindicias dare** *(or* **dicere** *or* **decernere)** to hand over the things *or* persons claimed

vindic·ō -āre -āvī -ātus *tr* to lay legal claim to; to protect, defend; to appropriate; to demand; to demand unfairly; to claim as one's own; to avenge, punish; **in libertatem vindicare** to set free, liberate *(literally, to claim for freedom)*

vindict·a -ae *f* rod used in the ceremony of setting slaves free; defense, protection; vengeance, revenge, satisfaction

vīne·a *or* **vīni·a -ae** *f* vineyard; vine; *(mil)* shed *(used to defend besiegers against enemy missiles)*

vīnēt·um -ī *n* vineyard

vīnipoll·ens -entis *adj* powerful through wine

vīnit·or -ōris *m* vine dresser

vinnul·us -a -um *adj* charming

vīnolenti·a -ae *f* (vīnul-) wine drinking, intoxication

vīnolent·us -a -um *adj* (vīnul-) drunk

vīnōs·us -a -um *adj* addicted to wine; tasting *or* smelling of wine

vīn·um -ī *n* wine

viol·a -ae *f* violet *(flower; color; dye)*

violābil·is -is -e *adj* vulnerable

violār·ium -(i)ī *n* bed of violets

violār·ius -(i)ī *m* dyer of violet

violāti·ō -ōnis *f* violation, profanation

violāt·or -ōris *m* violator, profaner

viol·ens -entis *adj* violent, raging

violenter *adv* violently, vehemently

violenti·a -ae *f* violence

violent·us -a -um *adj* violent

viol·ō -āre -āvī -ātus *tr* to violate; to outrage, harm by violence

vīper·a -ae *f* viper; *(poisonous)* snake

vīpere·us -a -um *adj* viper's; snake's

vīperīn·us -a -um *adj* viper's, snake's

Vipsāni·us -a -um *adj* Roman clan name *(nomen);* **porticus Vipsania** Vipsanian portico *(forming part of the Pantheon built by Agrippa in the Campus Martius)* ‖ Agrippa *(Marcus Vipsanius Agrippa, Augustus' friend and sucessful admiral)* ‖ *f* Vipsania *(esp. Vipsania Agrippina, daughter of Agrippa and the first wife of Emperor Tiberius)*

vir virī *m* man; he-man, hero; husband; lover; manhood, virility; *(mil)* infantryman

virāg·ō -inis *f* female warrior; heroine

Virb·ius -(i)ī *m* local deity, the reincarnation of Hipppolytus, worshipped with Diana at Aricia ‖ son of Hippolytus

virect·um -ī stretch of green

vir·eō -ēre -uī *intr* to be green; to be fresh, be vigorous, flourish

virēs = *pl of* **vis**

vir·escō -escĕre -uī *intr* to turn green

virg·a -ae *f* twig, sprout; graft; rod, switch *(for flogging);* wand; walking stick, cane; colored stripe in a garment; branch of a family tree

virgāt·or -ōris *m* flogger

virgāt·us -a -um *adj* made of twigs *or* osiers; striped

virgēt·um -ī *n* osier thicket

virge·us -a -um *adj* of twigs, of kindling wood

virgi(n)dēmi·a -ae f (hum) harvest of birch rods (i.e., a sound flogging)
virgināl·is -is -e adj maiden's, girl's, girlish **ll** n female organ
virgināri·us -a -um adj girl's
virgine·us or virgini·us -a -um adj virgin, of or for a virgin; proper to a virgin; of virgins
virginit·ās -ātis f girlhood; virginity
virg·ō -inis f (marriageable) girl, maiden; virgin **ll Virgo** Virgo (constellation; aqueduct constructed by Marcus Vipsanius Agrippa)
virgul·a -ae f little twig; wand; **virgula divina** divining rod
virgult·um -ī n thicket; shrub **ll** npl brushwood; firewood; slips (of trees)
virgult·us -a -um adj covered with brushwood
virguncul·a -ae f lass, young girl
Viriāt(h)·us -ī m Lusitanian who led a guerilla war against Rome (147–140 B.C.)
virid·ans -antis adj green
virid(i)ār·ium -(i)ī n garden
virid·is -is -e adj green; fresh, young **ll** npl greenery
viridit·ās -ātis f greenness; freshness
virid·ō -āre tr to make green **ll** intr to turn green
Vir(i)domar·us -ī m Insubrian leader killed in battle by Marcus Claudius Marcellus, 222 B.C., who thereby won the spolia opima
virīl·is -is -e adj male, masculine; adult; manly; (gram) masculine; **pars virilis** male sexual organ; **pro virili parte** (or **portione**) to the best of one's ability **ll** npl manly or heroic deeds; male sexual organs
virīlit·ās -ātis f manhood, virility
virīliter adv manfully, like a man
virīpot·ens -entis adj almighty
virītim adv man by man; per man; individually
virōs·us -a -um adj slimy; strong-smelling, fetid, stinking
virt·ūs -ūtis f manliness, manhood, virility; strength; valor, gallantry; excellence, worth; special property; moral excellence, goodness, virtue; good quality, high quality (of persons, animals, things); potency, effectiveness (of drugs, medications); **virtute** (w. gen) through the good services of, thanks to **ll** fpl achievements; gallant deeds
vir·us -ī n venom; slime; stench, pungency; saltiness
vīs (gen not in use; dat & abl: vi; acc: vim; pl: vīr·ēs -ium) f power, strength, force; influence, energy; hostile force, violence, attack; amount, quantity; meaning, force (of words); binding force

(of a law); value, amount; **magna vis** (w. gen) a large number of, a large amount of; **omnis vis** (w. gen) the whole range of, the sum total of; **per vim** forcibly; **suā vi** in itself, intrinsically; **summā vi** with utmost energy; **vi** by force; **vim adferre** (w. dat) 1 to do violence to; 2 to rape; 3 to kill; **vim adferre sibi** (or **vitae suae**) to take one's own life; **vim facere** to make an assault; **vim habere** (w. gen) to be equivalent (in amount) to **ll vires** fpl strength; resources; potency, power (of herbs, drugs); (mil) military strength, fighting power; control, influence; financial resources, assets; powers of intellect, capability; meaning (of words); value, amount; **pro viribus** with all one's might
viscāt·us -a -um adj smeared with birdlime
viscer·a -um npl fleshy parts of the body (as distinct from skin and bones); viscera, internal organs; womb; heart, vitals, bowels; (fig) innermost part, bowels, heart; center (esp. of the earth); (fig) bosom friend, favorite; (fig) person's flesh and blood (family, offspring)
viscerāti·ō -ōnis f public distribution of meat
visc·ō -āre -āvī -ātus tr to catch in birdlime
visc·um -ī n or visc·us -ī m mistletoe; birdlime
visc·us -eris n (anat) organ; entrails **ll** npl see viscera
vīsend·us -a -um adj worth going to see, worth visiting
vīsī perf of viso
vīsi·ō -ōnis f appearance, apparition; notion, idea
vīsit·ō -āre -āvī -ātus tr to keep seeing; to visit, go to visit
vīs·ō -ěre -ī tr to look at with attention, view; to come or go to look at; to find out; to go and see, visit; to look in on (the sick) **ll** intr to go and look; (w. ad) to go to visit, call on (esp. an invalid)
vispillō see vespillo
viss·iō -īre intr (sl) to fart softly
vīs·um -ī n sight, appearance
Visurg·is -is m river in N. Germany (modern Weser)
vīsus pp of video
vīs·us -ūs m (faculty of) sight; thing seen, sight, vision
vīt·a -ae f life; way of life; means of living, livelihood; manner of life; course of life, career; biography
vītābil·is -is -e adj undesirable, deserving to be shunned
vītābund·us -a -um adj taking evasive action

vītāl·is -is -e *adj* of life, vital; life-giving; likely to live, staying alive; able to survive; living, alive ‖ *npl (anat)* vital parts

vītāliter *adv* vitally

vītāti·ō -ōnis *f* avoidance

Vitell·ius -(i)ī *m* Vitellius *(Aulus Vitellius, Roman Emperor, from January 2 to December 22, A.D. 69)*

vitell·us -ī *m* little calf; yolk *(of egg)*

vīte·us -a -um *adj* of the vine

vīticul·a -ae *f* little vine

vītif·er -era -erum *adj* producing vines, vine-producing

vītigen·us -a -um *adj* produced from the vine

viti·ō -āre -āvī -ātus *tr* to spoil, corrupt, violate, mar; to falsify

vitiōsē *adv* faultily, badly, corruptly; **vitiose se habere** to be defective

vitiōsit·ās -ātis *f* corrupt *or* bad condition

vitiōs·us -a -um *adj* faulty, defective; (morally) corrupt, bad, depraved

vīt·is -is *f* vine; vine branch; centurion's staff; centurionship

vītisāt·or -ōris *m* vine planter

vit·ium -(i)ī *n* fault, flaw; defect, disorder; sin, offense, vice; flaw in the auspices; injurious quality, disadvantage; augural impediment, unfavorable augury; **in vitio esse** to be in a defective state, be defective; *(leg)* legal defect, technicality; **meo vitio pereo** I am ruined through my own fault; **vitio** *(w. gen)* through the fault of; **vitio dare** *(or* **vertere)** to regard as a fault; **vitium capere** *(or* **facere)** to develop a defect; **vitium dicere** *(w. dat)* to insult s.o.

vīt·ō -āre -āvī -ātus *tr* to avoid, evade

vīt·or -ōris *m* basket-maker

vitre·us -a -um *adj* glass, of glass; glassy ‖ *npl* glassware

vītric·us -ī *m* stepfather

vitr·um -ī *n* glass; blue dye

vitt·a -ae *f* headband, fillet

vittāt·us -a -um *adj* wearing a fillet

vitul·a -ae *f* heifer

vitulīn·us -a -um *adj & f* veal

vītul·or -ārī *intr* to shout for joy

vitul·us -ī *m* calf, young bull; foal; seal

vituperābil·is -is -e *adj* blameworthy

vituperāti·ō -ōnis *f* blaming, censuring; blame; scandalous conduct, blameworthiness

vituperāt·or -ōris *m* censurer

vituper·ō -āre -āvī -ātus *tr* to criticize, find fault with; to declare *(an omen)* invalid

vīvācit·ās -ātis *f* will to live; life-force; vitality

vīvār·ium -(i)ī *n* game preserve, zoo; fish pond

vīvāt·us -a -um *adj* animated, lively

vīv·ax -ācis *adj* long-lived; long-lasting, enduring; quick to learn

vīvē *adv* in a lively manner

vīverād·ix -īcis *f* rooted cutting *(i.e., having roots)*

vīvescō *or* **vīviscō vīviscĕre** *intr* to become alive, come to life; to grow lively, get full of life

vīvid·us -a -um *adj* teeming with life, full of life; true to life, vivid, realistic; quick, lively *(mind);* vivid *(expression)*

vīvirād·ix -īcis *f see* **viveradix**

vīviscō *see* **vivesco**

vīv·ō vīvĕre vixī victum *intr* to be alive, live; to be still alive, survive; to reside; *(w. abl or* **de** *+ abl)* to live on, subsist on

vīv·us -a -um *adj* alive, living; lively; fresh; natural *(rock);* speaking *(voice);* **argentum vivum** quicksilver; **calx viva** lime ‖ *n (com)* capital; **ad vivum resecare** to cut to the quick

vix *adv* scarcely; hardly, with difficulty, barely

vixdum *adv* hardly then, scarcely yet

vocābul·um -ī *n* word, term; name, designation; noun; common noun

vōcāl·is -is -e *adj* having a voice, gifted with speech, speaking; gifted with song, singing; tuneful ‖ *f (gram)* vowel

vocām·en -inis *f* name, designation

vocāti·ō -ōnis *f* invitation *(to dinner);* *(leg)* summons

vocāt·or -ōris *m* inviter, host

vocāt·us -ūs *m* summons, call

vōciferāti·ō -ōnis *f* loud cry, yell

vōcifer·ō -āre *or* **vōcifer·or -ārī -ātus sum** *tr & intr* to shout, yell

vocit·ō -āre -āvī -ātus *tr* to call habitually, usually call, name; to shout out again and again

voc·ō -āre -āvī -ātus *tr* to call, name; to summon; to call upon, invoke *(the gods);* to invite *(to dinner);* *(w. double acc)* to call *(s.o. s.th.);* to call for, require; *(w.* **de** *+ abl)* to name *(s.o., s.th.)* after; *(mil)* to challenge; **ad se vocare** to summon; **aliquem ex jure manum consertum vocare** *(leg)* to call out of court to settle the issue by physical combat; **in arma vocare** to call to arms; **in dubium vocare** to call into question; **in jus vocare** to summon to court; **in odium vocare** to bring into disfavor; **in periculum vocare** to lead into danger

vōcul·a -ae *f* weak voice; soft note, soft tone; whisper, gossip

volaem·um -ī *n* (volē-) type of large pear

Volāterr·ae -ārum *fpl* old Etruscan hill town *(modern Volterra)*

Volāterrān·us -a -um *adj* of Volaterrae

volātic·us -a -um *adj* flying, winged; transitory, passing; inconstant volātil·is -is -e *adj* able to fly; rapid; transitory

volāt·us -ūs *m* flight

Volcānāl·ia -ium *npl* (Vulc-) festival of Vulcan *(August 23)*

Volcāni·us -a -um *adj* (Vulc-) of Vulcan; acies Vulcania Vulcan's battleline *(i.e., fire spreading in a line);* arma Vulcania arms made by Vulcan *(for Achilles)*

Volcān·us -ī *m* (Vul-) Vulcan *(god of fire, son of Jupiter)*

vol·ens -entis *adj* willing; permitting; ready; favorable ‖ *m* well-wisher

Voles·us -ī *m* Roman family name *(nomen), esp.* the father of Publius Valerius Publicola

volg- = vulg-

volit·ans -antis *m* winged insect

volit·ō -āre -āvī -ātum *intr* to flit about, fly about, flutter; to move quickly; to hover, soar

vol·ō -āre -āvī -ātum *intr* to fly

volō velle voluī *tr* to wish, want; to propose, determine; to hold, maintain; to mean; to prefer ‖ *intr* to be willing

Vologēs·us -ī *m* name of several Arsacid kings of Parthia

volōn·ēs -um *mpl* volunteers *(slaves who enlisted after the battle of Cannae, 216 B.C.)*

volpēs *see* vulpes

Volsc·us -a -um *adj* Vulscan ‖ *mpl* Volscians *(ancient people in S. Latium, subjugated by the Romans in 5th & 4th cent. B.C.)*

volsell·a -ae *f* tweezers

Volsini·ī -ōrum *mpl* Etruscan city

volsus *pp of* vello

volt = *older form of* vult he *(or* she *or* it) wishes

voltis = *older form of* vultis you wish

Voltumn·a -ae *f* Etruscan goddess in whose temple the twelve Etruscan states met

Volt·ur -uris *m* (Vul-) mountain of Apulia near the border of Samnium

Volturn·um -ī *n* town at the mouth of the Volturnus river ‖ old name of Capua

Volturn·us -ī *m* river flowing from the Apennines to the coast of Campania ‖ name for a S.E. wind

voltus *see* vultus

volūbil·is -is -e *adj* turning, spinning, revolving, swirling; voluble, rapid, fluent; changeable

volūbilit·ās -ātis *f* whirling motion; roundness; volubility; fluency; mutability

volūbiliter *adv* rapidly; fluently

volu·cer -cris -cre *adj* flying, winged; rapid, speedy

volu·cer -cris *m* bird

volucr·is -is *f* bird; fly; volucris Junonis the bird of Juno *(i.e., a peacock)*

voluī *perf of* volo

volūm·en -inis *n* roll, book; chapter; whirl, eddy; coil; fold

Volumni·us -a -um *adj* Roman clan name *(nomen)*

voluntāri·us -a -um *adj* voluntary ‖ *mpl* volunteers

volunt·ās -ātis *f* will, wish, desire, purpose, aim, intention; inclination; goodwill, sympathy; willingness, approval; choice, option; last will and testament; attitude *(good or bad);* meaning *(of words);* ad voluntatem *(w. gen)* according to the wishes of; de *(or* ex) voluntate *(w. gen)* at the desire of; voluntate *(w. gen)* with the consent of

volup *adv* to one's satisfaction, with pleasure; volup esse to be a source of pleasure; volup facere *(w. dat)* to cause *(s.o.)* pleasure

voluptābil·is -is -e *adj* agreeable, pleasant

voluptāri·us -a -um *adj* pleasant, agreeable; voluptuous ‖ *m* voluptuary

volupt·ās -ātis *f* pleasure, enjoyment, delight ‖ *fpl* sensual pleasures; games, sports, public performances

voluptuōs·us -a -um *adj* pleasant, agreeable; giving pleasure

Volusi·us -a -um *adj* Roman clan name *(nomen), esp.* name of a Roman epic poet, mocked by Catullus

volūtābr·um -ī *n* wallow *(for swine)*

volūtābund·us -a -um *adj* wallowing about

volūtāti·ō -ōnis *f* rolling about, tossing about; wallowing; restlessness

volūt·ō -āre -āvī -ātus *tr* to roll about, turn over; to engross; to think over ‖ *pass* to wallow, luxuriate

volūtus *pp of* volvo

volva *see* vulva

vol·vō -věre -vī -ūtus *tr* to roll, turn about, wind; *(of a river)* to roll *(e.g., rocks)* along; to breathe; to unroll, read *(books, scrolls);* to pour out, utter fluently; to consider, weigh; *(of time)* to bring on, bring around; to form *(a circle);* to undergo *(troubles)* ‖ *pass* to roll, tumble; to revolve ‖ *intr* to revolve; to roll on, elapse

vōm·er *or* vōm·is -eris *m* plowshare; *(vulg)* penis

vomic·a -ae *f* sore, boil, abscess, ulcer; annoyance

vōmis *see* vomer

vomit·ō -āre *intr* to vomit *(frequently)*

vomiti·ō -ōnis *f* vomiting

vomit·us -ūs *m* vomiting; vomit

vom·ō -ěre -uī -itus *tr & intr* to vomit, throw up

vorāg·ō -inis *f* deep hole, abyss, chasm, depth

vor·ax -ācis *adj* swallowing, devouring; greedy, ravenous

vor·ō -āre -āvī -ātus *tr* to swallow, devour; *(fig)* to devour *(by reading)*

vors- = **vers-**

vort- = **vert-**

vōs *pron* you *(pl); (refl)* yourselves

vōsmet *pron (emphatic form of* **vōs***)* you yourselves

voster *see* **vester**

vōtīv·us -a -um *adj* votive, promised in a vow

votō *see* **veto**

vōt·um -ī *n* solemn vow *(made to a deity);* votive offering *(made for a prayer answered);* prayer, wish; thing wished for, wish; **compos voti** *(or* **voto***)* **esse** to have had one's prayer answered; **in voto est** *(w. inf)* it is *(my)* wish to; **in voto est** *(w.* **ut** + *subj or w.* **acc** & *inf)* it is *(my)* wish that; **voti reus** obligated to fulfill a vow; **voto major** surpassing one's fondest hopes; **votum est** *(w. inf)* it is *(my)* hope to; **votum est** *(w.* **ut** + *subj or w. acc* & *inf)* it is *(my)* hope that

voveō vovēre vōvī vōtus *tr* to vow, promise solemnly, pledge, devote *(to a deity);* to wish, wish for

vox vōcis *f* voice; sound, tone, cry, call; word *(written or spoken);* utterance, saying, expression; proverb; language; accent

Vulcānus *see* **Volcanus**

vulgār·is -is -e *adj* (vol-) common, general, usual, everyday; low-class; unimportant, routine *(business);* well-known, often repeated *(story)*

vulgāriter *adv* (vol-) in the usual way; commonly

vulgāt·or -ōris *m* (vol-) divulger

vulgāt·us -a -um *adj* (vol-) common, general; well-known; notorious

vulgivag·us -a -um *adj* roving; promiscuous

vulg·ō -āre -āvī -ātus *tr* (vol-) to spread, publish, broadcast; to divulge; to prostitute; to level, make common

vulgō *adv* (vol-) generally, publicly, everywhere

vulg·us -ī *n* (vol-) masses, public, people; crowd; herd, flock; rabble, populace; **in vulgus** *(or* **in vulgum***)* to the general public, publicly

vulnerāti·ō -ōnis *f* (vol-) wounding, wound

vulner·ō -āre -āvī -ātus *tr* (vol-) to wound; to damage

vulnific·us -a -um *adj* inflicting wounds

vuln·us -eris *n* (vol-) wound; blow, stroke; blow, disaster

vulpēcul·a -ae *f* (vol-) little fox, sly little fox

vulp·ēs -is *f* (vol-) fox; craftiness, cunning

vuls·us *or* **vols·us -a -um** *pp of* **vello** ‖ *adj* plucked, beardless, effeminate

vulticul·us -ī *m* (vol-) mere look

vult·um *see* **vultus**

vultuōs·us -a -um *adj* (vol-) full of airs, affected, stuck-up

vult·ur -uris *m* (vol-) vulture ‖ **Vultur** *m* mountain in Apulia

vulturīn·us -a -um *adj* (vol-) vulture-like, of a vulture

vultur·ius -(i)ī *m* (vol-) vulture

Vulturn·us -ī *m* (Vol-) principal river of Campania *(modern Volturno)*

vult·us -ūs *m* (vol-) face; looks, expression, features; look, appearance

vulv·a -ae *f* (vol-) wrapper, cover; womb; female genitalia, vulva; sow's womb *(as a delicacy)*

X

X = **decem** ten

Xanthipp·e -ēs *f* wife of Socrates

Xanthipp·us -ī *m* father of Pericles ‖ Spartan commander of the Carthaginians in the First Punic War

Xanth·us -ī *m* river at Troy, identified with the Scamander River ‖ river and town of the same name in Lycia ‖ name applied by Vergil to a river in Epirus

xen·ium -iī *n* gift, present *(given by a guest to a host or by a host to a guest)*

Xenocrat·ēs -is *m* Greek philosopher, a disciple of Plato

Xenophan·ēs -is *m* early Greek philosopher *(c. 565–470 B.C.)*

Xenoph·ōn -ontis *m* Greek historian and pupil of Socrates *(c. 430–354 B.C.)*

xērampelin·ae -ārum *fpl* reddish-purple clothes

Xerx·ēs -is *m* Persian king, defeated at Salamis *(c. 519–465 B.C.)*

xiphi·ās -ae *m* swordfish

xyst·us -ī *m or* **xyst·um -ī** *n* open colonnade *or* portico, walk

Y

Y, y letter adopted from Greek into the Roman alphabet for the transliteration of words containing an upsilon *(for which u was used earlier),* and pronounced approximate as German ü. It appears to have been in use by the time of Cicero; but its use was restricted to foreign words

Z

Zacynth·us *or* **Zacynth·os -ī** *f* island off W. Greece ‖ name for Saguntum, supposed to have been colonized by people from Zacynthus

Zaleuc·us -ī *m* traditional lawgiver of the Locrians

Zam·a -ae *f* town in Numidia where Scipio defeated Hannibal and brought the Second Punic War to an end *(202 B.C.)*

zāmi·a -ae *f* harm, damage, loss

Zanclae·us -a -um *adj* of Zancle

Zancl·ē -ēs *f* old name of Messana in N. Sicily

Zanclēi·us -a -um *adj* of Zancle

zēlotypi·a -ae jealousy

zēlotyp·us -a -um *f* jealous

Zēn·ō(n) -ōnis *m* Zeno the Stoic *(founder of Stoic philosophy and native of Citium in Cyprus, 335–263 B.C.)* ‖ Zeno *(Epicurean philosopher, the* teacher of Cicero and Atticus, born c. 150 B.C.)

Zephyr·us *or* **Zephyr·os -ī** *m* zephr; west wind; wind

Zēt·ēs -ae *m* one of the two sons of Boreas *(Aquilo)*

Zēth·us *or* **Zēt·os -ī** *m* son of Jupiter and Antiope and brother of Amphion

Zeux·is -idis *m* Greek painter of Heraclea in Lucania *(fl c. 400 B.C.)*

zinzi·ō -āre *intr (of a blackbird)* to sing

zmaragd·us -ī *mf* emerald

zōdiac·us -a -um *adj* of the zodiac; **zodiacus circulus** *(or* **orbis)** the zodiac ‖ *m* zodiac

Zōil·us -ī *m* a native of Amphipolis, proverbially stern critic of Homer, Plato, and others

zōn·a -ae *f* belt, sash; money belt; zone

zōnāri·us -a -um *adj* of a belt ‖ *m* belt maker

zōnul·a -ae *f* little belt

zōthēc·a -ae *f* niche; bay, recess

zōthēcul·a -ae *f* little alcove

A

a *indef article (when modifying a substantive, is unexpressed in Latin);* **— little carelessly** parum attente; **— little later** paulo post; **ten denarii — pound** decem denarii per libras; **twice — year** bis in anno

aback *adv* **taken —** attonit·us -a -um

abandon *tr* (de)relinquĕre

abandonment *s* derelicti·o -onis *f*

abashed *adj* erubesc·ens -entis

abate *tr (to lower)* imminuĕre; *(to slacken)* laxare; *(price)* remittĕre ‖ *intr (to lessen)* imminuĕre; *(to decline)* decedĕre; *(of passion)* defervescĕre

abbey *s* abbati·a ae *f*

abbot *s* abb·as -atis *m*

abbreviate *tr* breviare

abbreviation *s* not·a -ae *f*

ABC's *spl* primae litter·ae -arum *fpl;* **to know one's —** litteras scire

abdicate *tr* abdicare ‖ *intr* se abdicare

abdication *s* abdicati·o -onis *f*

abdomen *s* abdom·en -inis *n*

abduct *tr* abducĕre; *(a girl)* rapĕre

abduction *s* rapt·us -ūs *m*

aberration *s (departure from right)* err·or -oris *m; (deviation from straight line)* declinati·o -onis *f*

abet *tr* adjuvare; **to — a crime** minister in maleficio esse

abeyance *s* **to be in —** jacēre

abhor *tr* abhorrēre ab *(w. abl)*

abhorrence *s* detestati·o -onis *f*

abhorrent *adj* (to) alien·us -a -um *(abl or* ab + *abl)*

abide *tr* tolerare ‖ *intr* manēre; **— by** stare in *(w. abl)*

abiding *adj* mansur·us -a -um

ability *s (power)* potest·as -atis *f; (mental capacity)* ingen·ium -(i)i *n;* **to the best of one's —** pro sua parte

abject *adj* abject·us -a -um

abjectly *adv* abjecte, humiliter

ablative *s* ablativ·us -i *m*

able *adj (having the power)* pot·ens -entis; *(having mental ability)* ingenios·us -a -um; **not — to fight** non pugnae potens; **not to be — to** nequire *(w. inf);* **to be — to** posse *(w. inf)*

able-bodied *adj* valid·us -a -um

ablution *s* abluti·o -onis *f*

ably *adv* ingeniose

abnormal *adj* enorm·is -is -e

aboard *adv* in nave: **to go — a ship** navem conscendĕre

abode *s* domicil·ium -(i)i *n*

abolish *tr* tollĕre, abolēre

abolition *s* aboliti·o -onis *f*

abominable *adj* detestabil·is -is -e

abominably *adv* execrabiliter, odiose

abominate *tr* abominari, detestari

abomination *s* detestati·o -onis *f; (terrible crime)* flagit·ium -(i)i *n*

aborigines *spl* aborigin·es -um *mf*

abortion *s* abort·us -ūs *m;* **to perform an —** partum abigĕre

abortive *adj* abortiv·us -a -um; *(unsuccessful)* irrit·us -a -um

abound *intr* abundare, superesse; **to — in** abundare *(w. abl)*

abounding *adj* **— in** abund·ans -antis *(w. dat or abl)*

about *adv (almost)* fere, ferme; *(approximately)* circa, circiter; **in — ten days** decem circiter diebus

about *prep (of place)* circa, circum *(w. acc); (of number)* circa, ad *(w. acc); (of time)* circa, sub *(w. acc); (concerning)* de *(w. abl)*

above *adv* supra, insuper; **from —** desuper, superne

above *prep* supra, super *(w. acc);* **— all** ante omnia; **— all others** praeter omnes ceteros; **to be — —** *(e.g., bribery)* indignari *(w. acc)*

abrasion *s* attrit·us -ūs *m*

abreast *adv* pariter; **to walk — of s.o.** latus alicui tegĕre

abridge *tr* breviare, contrahĕre; **to — a book** in compendium redigĕre

abridgment *s* epitom·e -es *f*

abroad *adv (in a foreign land)* peregre; *(of motion, out of doors)* foras; *(of rest, out of doors)* foris; **from —** extrinsec·us -a -um ; *(w. verbs)* peregre; **to be** *or* **go abroad** peregrinari; **to get —** *(of news)* divulgari

abrogate *tr* abrogare, rescindĕre

abrupt *adj (sudden)* subit·us -a -um; *(rugged)* praerupt·us -a -um

abruptly *adv* subito, repente

abruptness *s* rapidit·as -atis *f*

abscess *s* vomic·a -ae *f*

absence *s* absenti·a -ae *f;* **in my —** me absente

absent *adj* abs·ens -entis; **— without leave** *(mil)* infrequ·ens -entis

absent *tr* **to — oneself** se removēre; *(not show up)* non comparēre

absentee *s* abs·ens -entis *mf*

absolute *adj* absolut·us -a -um, summ·us -a -um; *(unlimited)* infinit·us -a -um; **— power** dominat·us -ūs *m*, tyrann·is -idis *f;* **— ruler** domin·us -i *m*, tyrann·us -i *m*

absolutely *adv (unconditionally)* praecise; *(completely)* utique, prorsus; **— nothing** nihil prorsus; **to rule — over** dominari *(w. dat)*

absolution *s* absoluti·o -onis *f*

absolve *tr* veniam dare *(w. dat);* **to — from** absolvĕre ab *(w. abl)*

absorb *tr* absorbēre, (com)bibĕre; *(fig)* tenēre

absorbent *adj* bibul·us -a -um

abstain *intr* (**from**) se abstinēre *(w. abl)*

abstemious *adj* abstemi·us -a -um

abstinence *s* abstinenti·a -ae *f; (from food)* inedi·a -ae *f*

abstract *tr* (**from**) abstrahĕre (ab + *abl); (an idea)* separare

abstract *s* compend·ium -(i)i *n; in the —* in abstracto

abstract *adj (idea)* mente percept·us -a -um; *(quantity)* abstract·us -a -um

abstraction *s* separati·o -onis *f; (idea)* noti·o -onis *f*

abstruse *adj* abstrus·us -a -um

absurd *adj* absurd·us -a -um

absurdity *s* inepti·a -ae *f*

abundance *s* abundanti·a -ae *f,* copi·a -ae *f*

abundant *adj* abund·ans -antis, larg·us -a -um; **to be —** abundare

abundantly *adv* abundanter, copiose

abuse *s (wrong use)* abus·us -ūs *m; (insult)* injuri·a -ae *f,* convic·ium -(i)i *n;* **to heap — on** contumeliosissime maledicĕre *(w. dat)*

abuse *tr (to misuse)* abuti *(w. abl); (sexually)* stuprare; *(w. words)* maledicĕre *(w. dat)*

abusive *adj (toward)* contumelios·us -a -um (in + *acc); (person)* maledic·us -a -um; **to be — to** abuti *(w. abl)*

abusively *adv* contumeliose

abyss *s* profund·um -i *n; (fig)* barathr·um -i *n*

academic *adj* academic·us -a -um

academy *s* academi·a -ae *f*

accede *intr* **to — to** assentire *(w. dat)*

accelerate *tr & intr* accelerare

acceleration *s* accelerati·o -onis *f*

accent *s* accent·us -ūs *m,* vo·x -cis *f; (peculiar tone of a people)* son·us -i *m;* **a Greek —** son·us -i *m* linguae Graecae; **to place an acute (grave, circumflex) — on a word** acutam (gravem, circumflexam) vocem in verbo ponĕre

accent *tr (in speaking)* acuĕre; *(in writing)* fastigare

accent mark *s* fastig·ium -(i)i *n*

accentuation *s (in speaking)* accent·us -ūs *m; (in writing, expr. by gerundive):* **careful in the — of syllables** in syllabis acuendis diligens

accept *tr* accipĕre, recipĕre; *(to approve of)* probare

acceptable *adj* (**to**) accept·us -a -um, probabil·is -is -e *(w. dat);* **to be — to** placēre *(w. dat)*

acceptably *adv* apte

acceptance *s* accepti·o -onis *f; (approval)* probati·o -onis *f*

access *s* adit·us -ūs *m,* access·us -ūs *m; — to books** copi·a -ae *f* librorum; **to gain**

— to penetrare ad *(w. acc);* **to have — to** admitti *(w. dat)*

accessible *adj (of places)* pat·ens -entis; *(of persons)* facil·is -is -e; **to be — to** patēre *(w. dat)*

accession *s (addition)* accessi·o -onis *f; — to the throne** regni princip·ium -(i)i *n*

accessory *adj* adjunct·us -a -um; *(to a crime)* consci·us -a -um

accessory *s* affin·is -is *mf; — to this crime** affinis *mf* huic facinori

accident *s* cas·us -ūs *m;* **by —** casu

accidental *adj* fortuit·us -a -um; *(nonessential)* adventici·us -a -um

accidentally *adv* casu, forte

acclamation *s (shouts of applause)* clam·or -oris *m,* acclamati·o -onis *f; (oral vote)* conclamati·o -onis *f*

accommodate *tr (adapt)* (**to**) accommodare *(w. dat); (w. lodgings)* hospitium parare *(w. dat); (of an auditorium, etc.)* tenēre

accommodation *s* accommodati·o -onis *f; (convenience)* commodit·as -atis *f; —s* deversor·ium -(i)i *n*

accompaniment *s* concinenti·a -ae *f;* **to sing to the — of the flute** ad tibiam concinĕre

accompany *tr* comitari; *(mus)* concinĕre *(w. dat)*

accomplice *s* (**in**) partic·eps -itis *m (w. gen or* in + *abl)*

accomplish *tr* efficĕre, perficĕre

accomplished *adj (skilled)* erudit·us -a -um; *(of a speaker)* disert·us -a -um

accomplishment *s (completion)* peracti·o -onis *f; —s* re·s -rum *fpl* gestae

accord *s* consens·us -ūs *m;* **of one's own —** sua sponte, ultro; **to be in — with** convenire *(w. dat);* **with one —** unanimiter

accordance *s* **in — with** secundum *(w. acc),* pro *(w. abl),* ex *(w. abl)*

accordingly *adv* proinde, itaque

according to *prep* secundum *(w. acc)*

accost *tr* appellare, compellare; *(sexually)* lenare

account *s (financial)* rati·o -onis *f; (statement)* memori·a -ae *f; (story)* narrati·o -onis *f; (esteem)* reputati·o -onis *f;* **of little —** parvi pretii; **of no —** nullius pretii; **on — of** ob, propter *(w. acc);* **on that —** propterea; **to be entered into an — ** rationibus inferri; **to call to — ** rationem poscere; **to give an —** rationem reddere; **to take — of** rationem habēre *(w. gen)*

account *tr (to consider)* ducĕre; *(to esteem)* aestimare; **to — for** rationem reddere *(w. gen);* **to — for his absence** rationem adferre cur absit

accountable *adj* (**for**) re·us -a -um *(w. gen)*

accountant s ratiocinat·or -oris m
accredited adj aestimat·us -a -um
accretion s accessi·o -onis f
accrue intr accrescĕre; **to —** to accedĕre (w. dat), redundare in (w. acc)
accumulate tr accumulare II intr crescĕre, augēri
accumulation s congest·us -ūs m; (pile) cumul·us -i m
accuracy s (pains bestowed) cur·a -ae f; (exactness) subtilit·as -atis f
accurate adj exact·us -a -um; (of a definition, observation) subtil·is -is -e
accurately adv exacte; subtiliter
accursed adj exsecrat·us -a -um
accusation s accusati·o -onis f; (charge) crim·en -inis n; **to bring an — against** accusare
accusative s accusativ·us -i m
accusatory adj accusatori·us -a -um
accuse tr (of) accusare (w. gen or de + abl); **to — falsely** calumniari
accused s re·us -i m, re·a -ae f
accuser s accusat·or -oris m, accusatr·ix -icis f
accusingly adv accusatorie
accustom tr (to) assuefacere (w. abl, dat or ad + acc, or inf); **to — oneself or become —ed to** assuescĕre (w. dat), ad, in (w. acc); **to be —ed to** solēre (w. inf)
ache s dol·or -oris m
ache intr dolēre; **my head —s** caput mihi dolet
achieve tr conficere; (to win) consequi
achievement s res, rei f gesta
acid s acid·um -i n
acid adj acid·us -a -um
acknowledge tr agnoscĕre; (a child) tollĕre
acknowledgement s confessi·o -onis f; (money receipt) apoch·a -ae f
acme s fastig·ium -(i)i n
acorn s glan·s -dis f
acoustics spl acustic·a -orum npl
acquaint tr (with) certiorem facĕre (de + abl); **to — oneself with** cognoscĕre
acquaintance s familiarit·as -atis f; (person) familiar·is -is mf
acquainted adj not·us -a -um; **— with** gnar·us -a -um (w. gen); **to become — with** cognoscĕre
acquiesce intr (in) acquiescĕre (in + abl), stare (w. abl or in + abl)
acquiescence s assens·us -ūs m
acquire tr adipisci, nancisci
acquisition s quaest·us -ūs m; (thing acquired) quaesit·um -i n
acquisitive adj quaestuos·us -a -um
acquit tr (of) absolvere (de + abl); **to — oneself** se gerĕre
acquittal s absoluti·o -onis f
acre s juger·um -i n (actually .625 of an acre)
acrid adj a·cer -cris -cre

acrimonious adj acerb·us -a -um
acrimony s acerbit·as -atis f
acrobat s funambul·us -i m
across adv in transversum
across prep trans (w. acc)
act s (deed, action) fact·um -i n; (decree) decret·um -i n; (theat) act·us -ūs m; **caught in the —** manifestari·us -a -um; **in the very —** in flagranti; **public —s** act·a -orum npl
act tr (role) agĕre II intr agĕre; **to — as a friend** amicum agĕre; **to — as a servant** servile officium tueri
acting s acti·o -onis f
action s acti·o -onis f; act·us -ūs m; (deed) fact·um -i n; (leg) acti·o -onis f; (mil) pugn·a -ae f; (of speaker) gest·us -ūs m; **to bring an — against** actionem intendere in (w. acc)
actionable adj (leg) obnoxi·us -a -um
active adj (life) actuos·us -a -um; (mind) veget·us -a -um; (busy) impi·ger -gra -grum; (gram) activ·us -a -um; **verb in the — voice** verbum agendi modi
actively adv impigre; (energetically) gnaviter
activity s agitati·o -onis f; (energy) industri·a -ae f, gnavit·as -atis f
actor s histri·o -onis m, act·or -oris m; (in comedy) comoed·us -i m; (in tragedy) tragoed·us -i m
actress s mim·a -ae f [Note: females did not normally act in regular Roman dramas]
actual adj ver·us -a -um
actuality s verit·as -atis f
actually adv re verā
acumen s acum·en -inis n
acute adj (angle, pain) acut·us -a -um; (vision, intellect) a·cer -cris -cre
acutely adv acute, acriter
acuteness s (of senses, intellect) aci·es -ei f
adage s proverb·ium -(i)i n
adamant adj obstinat·us -a -um
adamant s adam·as -antis n
adapt tr accommodare, aptare
adaptation s accommodati·o -onis f
adapted adj apt·us -a -um
add tr (to) addĕre, adjicĕre (w. dat or ad + acc); (in speaking) superdicĕre; (in writing) subscribĕre; **to — up** computare; **to be —ed to** accedĕre (w. dat or ad + acc)
adder s colub·er -ri m; (female) colubr·a -ae f
addict tr **to be —ed to** se tradere (w. dat)
addicted adj **— to** dedit·us -a -um (w. dat)
addition s accessi·o -onis f, adjecti·o -onis f; **in —** praeterea, insuper; **in — to** praeter (w. acc), super (w. acc)
additional adj additici·us -a -um
address s alloqu·ium -(i)i n; (on letter) inscripti·o -onis f; (speech) conti·o -onis

f, orati·o -onis *f; (adroitness)* dexterit·as -atis *f*

address *tr (to speak to)* alloqui, compellare; *(a letter)* inscribĕre

adduce *tr (witness, evidence)* producĕre; *(arguments)* afferre

adept *adj* (in) perit·us -a -um (+ *gen or abl* or in + *abl)*

adequacy *s* sufficienti·a -ae *f*

adequate *adj* suffici·ens -entis; **to be —** sufficĕre

adequately *adv* satis, apte

adhere *intr* (to) haerēre, cohaerēre *(w. dat, abl, or* in + *acc);* **to — to** *(fig)* stare in *(w. abl)*

adherence *s* adhaes·us -ūs *m*

adherent *s* assectat·or -oris *m*

adhesion *s* adhaesi·o -onis *f*

adhesive *adj* ten·ax -acis

adieu *interj* vale, valete; **to bid —** valēre jubēre

adjacent *adj* confin·is -is -e; **to be — to** adjacēre *(w. acc, dat,* ad + *acc)*

adjective *s* adjectiv·um -i *n*

adjectively *adv* pro apposito; **the word is used —** vocabulum pro apposito ponitur

adjoin *tr* adjacēre *(w. dat)*

adjoining *adj* conjunct·us -a -um

adjourn *tr* differre; *(leg)* ampliare ‖ *intr* diferri

adjournment *s* dilati·o -onis *f; (leg)* amplificati·o -onis *f*

adjudge *tr* adjudicare

adjudicate *tr* addicĕre

adjunct *s* adjunct·um -i *n*

adjure *tr* obtestari

adjust *tr* (to) aptare, accommodare *(w. dat or* ad + *acc); (to put in order)* componĕre ‖ *intr* (to) se accommodare (+ *dat or* ad + *acc)*

adjustment *s* accommodati·o -onis *f; (of a robe)* structur·a -ae *f*

adjutant *s* opti·o -onis *m*

administer *tr (to manage)* administrare; *(medicines)* adhibēre; *(oath)* adigĕre; **to — justice** jus dicĕre

administration *s* administrati·o -onis *f;* **— of justice** jurisdicti·o -onis *f;* **— of public affairs** procurati·o -onis *f* rei-publicae

administrative *adj* ad administrationem pertin·ens -entis

administrator *s* administrat·or -oris *m,* procurat·or -oris *m*

admirable *adj* admirabil·is -is -e

admiral *s* classis praefect·us -i *m*

admiration *s* admirati·o -onis *f*

admire *tr* admirari

admirer *s* admirat·or -oris *m; (lover)* am·ans -antis *mf*

admiringly *adv use participle:* admir·ans -antis

admissible *adj* accipiend·us -a -um

admission *s* confessi·o -onis *f; (being let in)* adit·us -ūs *m,* access·us -ūs *m;* **by his own —** confessione sua

admit *tr (to allow to enter)* admittĕre; *(e.g., into the senate)* asciscĕre; *(to grant as valid)* dare; *(to acknowledge)* agnoscĕre; **it is —ed** constat; **to — flatly** profiteri palam

admittedly *adv* sane

admonish *tr* admonēre

admonition *s (act)* admoniti·o -onis *f; (words used)* monit·um -i *n*

adolescence *s* adulescenti·a -ae *f*

adolescent *adj* adulesc·ens -entis

adolescent *s* adulescentul·us -i *m*

adopt *tr (a child)* adoptare; *(an adult)* arrogare; *(customs, laws)* asciscĕre; *(a plan)* capĕre, inire

adoption *s* adopti·o -onis *f; (of an adult)* arrogati·o -onis *f; (of a custom)* assumpti·o -onis *f*

adoptive *adj* adoptiv·us -a -um

adorable *adj* adorand·us -a -um

adoration *s* adorati·o -onis *f*

adore *tr* adorare; *(fig)* demirari

adorn *tr* decorare, ornare

adornment *s (act)* exornati·o -onis *f; (object)* ornament·um -i *n*

Adriatic *adj* Adriatic·us -a -um

adrift *adv* **to be —** fluctuare; **to set —** aperto mari committĕre

adroit *adj* callid·us -a -um; *(dexterous)* dex·ter -tra -trum

adroitness *s* callidit·as -atis *f;* dexterit·as -atis *f*

adulation *s* adulati·o -onis *f*

adult *adj* adult·us -a -um; **— population** pub·es -is *f*

adult *s* adult·us -i *m;* **—s** pub·es -is *f*

adulterate *tr* adulterare

adulteration *s* adulterati·o -onis *f*

adulterer *s* adult·er -eri *m*

adulteress *s* adulter·a -ae *f*

adulterous *adj* adulterin·us -a -um

adultery *s* adulter·ium -(i)i *n;* **to commit —** adulterare

advance *tr (to more forward)* promovēre; *(money)* in antecessum solvĕre; *(a cause)* fovēre; *(to promote)* provehĕre; *(an opinion)* praeferre ‖ *intr (to go forward)* procedĕre; *(of steady movement on foot)* incedĕre; *(in riding or sailing)* provehi; *(to progress)* proficĕre; *(mil)* gradum *(or* pedem) inferre; **as the day —ed** die procedente

advance *s* progress·us -ūs *m;* **in —** ante; **to pay in —** pecuniam nondum debitam solvĕre

advanced *adj* provect·us -a -um; **at an — age** provectā aetate; **—ed in years** grand·is -is -e natu *(or* aevo)

advance guard *s* primum agm·en -inis *n*

advance man *s* praecurs·or -oris *m*

advancement *s* promoti·o -onis *f*
advantage *s (benefit)* commod·um -i *n; (a real good)* bon·um -i *n; (profit)* emolument·um -i *n; (usefulness)* utilit·as -atis *f;* **to be of —** prodesse; **to have an — over** praestare *(w. dat); to take — of* uti *(w. abl); (pej)* sibi quaestui habēre; **to take — of an opportunity** occasionem nancisci
advantageous *adj* util·is -is -e, fructuos·us -a -um
advantageously *adv* utiliter
advent *s* advent·us -ūs *m*
adventure *s* cas·us -ūs *m*
adventurer *s* periclitat·or -oris *m*
adventurous *adj* aud·ax -acis
adverb *s* adverb·ium -(i)i *n*
adverbial *adj* adverbial·is -is -e
adverbially *adv* adverbialiter
adversary *s* adversar·ius -(i)i *m,* adversatr·ix -icis *f*
adversative *adj* adversativ·us -a -um
adverse *adj (mostly winds)* advers·us -a -um; *(times)* asp·er -era -erum; **— circumstances** re·s -rum *fpl* asperae
adversely *adv* male, infeliciter
adversity *s* re·s -rum *fpl* adversae; *(fig)* re·s -rum *fpl* asperae
advertise *tr* proscribĕre
advertisement *s (poster)* proscripti·o -onis *f*
advice *s* consil·ium -(i)i *n;* **to ask s.o. for —** aliquem consulĕre, aliquem consilium rogare; **to give —** suadēre *(w. dat)*
advisable *adj* it is **— to** expedit *(w. inf)*
advise *tr* suadēre *(w. dat)*
advisedly *adv* consulto
adviser *s* consult·or -oris *m*
advocate *s (leg)* advocat·us -i *m; (fig)* patron·us -i *m*
advocate *tr* suadēre
aedile *s* aedil·is -is *m*
aedileship *s* aedilit·as -atis *f*
aegis *s* aeg·is -idis *f; (fig)* tutel·a -ae *f*
aerial *adj* aëri·us -a -um
affability *s* affabilit·as -atis *f*
affable *adj* affabil·is -is -e
affably *adv* affabiliter
affair *s* negot·ium -i(i) *n,* res, rei *f; (love)* amor·es -um *mpl*
affect *tr (to influence)* afficĕre; *(to move)* movēre; *(to pretend)* simulare
affectation *s* affectati·o -onis *f*
affected *adj* simulat·us -a -um; *(style)* putid·us -a -um
affection *s* am·or -oris *m,* affecti·o -onis *f*
affectionate *adj* am·ans -antis
affectionately *adv* amanter
affidavit *s* per tabulas testimon·ium -(i)i *n*
affiliated *adj* **to be — with a college** in collegio cooptari
affinity *s* affinit·as -atis *f;* **to have no — with** longe remot·us -a -um ab *(w. abl)*

affirm *tr* affirmare
affirmation *s* affirmati·o -onis *f*
affirmative *adj* affirm·ans -antis; **I reply in the —** aio; **to give an — answer** fateri ita se rem habere
affix *tr* affigĕre
afflict *tr* affligĕre; **to be —ed with** conflictari *(w. abl)*
affliction *s (cause of distress)* mal·um -i *n; (state of distress)* miseri·a -ae *f*
affluence *s* diviti·ae -arum *fpl*
affluent *adj* div·es -itis
afford *tr (opportunity, etc.)* praebēre; **I cannot —** res mihi non suppetit ad *(w. acc)*
affray *s* rix·a -ae *f*
affront *tr* contumeliā affligĕre
affront *s* contumeli·a -ae *f*
afield *adv* in agro; *(astray)* vag·us -a -um, err·ans -antis
afloat *adj* nat·ans -antis; **to get a ship —** navem deducĕre
afoot *adv* pedibus; **to be —** *(fig)* geri; **what is —?** quid geritur?
aforementioned *adj* supra dict·us -a -um
afraid *adj* timid·us -a -um; **to be — (of)** timēre; **to make — terrēre**
afresh *adv* de integro, de novo
Africa *s* Afric·a -ae *f*
African *adj* African·us -a -um
African *s* Af·er -ri *m*
after *prep* post *(w. acc),* ab, ex *(w. abl); (in rank or degree)* secundum *(w. acc);* **(and) — all** (et) re verā; **— an interval** interposito deinde spatio; **— that** subinde; **a little —** paulo post; **named — his father** a patre nominat·us -a -um: **right —** sub *(w. acc);* **the day —** postridie
after *conj* postquam
afternoon *s* postmeridian·um -i *n;* **in the — post** meridiem, postmeridie
afternoon *adj* postmeridian·us -a -um
afterthought *s* posterior cogitati·o -onis *f*
afterwards *adv* postea
again *adv* iterum, rursus; *(hereafter)* posthac; *(in turn)* invicem; *(further)* porro; **— and —** identidem; **once — denuo; over — denuo**
against *prep* contra *(w. acc); (in a hostile manner)* adversus *(w. acc),* in *(w. acc);* **— the current** adverso flumine; **to lean — a tree** se ad arborem applicare; **to be — adversari**
age *s (time of life)* aet·as -atis *f; (era)* saecul·um -i *n,* aet·as -atis *f;* **don't ask me my —** noli me percontari meum aevum; **of the same — aequaev·us -a -um; old — senect·us -utis *f;* to be of — sui juris esse; **twelve years of —** duodecim annos nat·us -a -um; **under — inpub·is -is -e**
age *tr* aetate conficĕre ‖ *intr* maturescĕre; *(to grow old)* senescĕre

aged *adj* aetate provect·us -a -um; **a man — forty** vi·r -i *m* annos quadraginta natus

agency *s* acti·o -onis *f; (means)* oper·a -ae *f; (office)* procurati·o -onis *f;* **through the — of** per *(w. acc)*

agent *s (doer)* act·or -oris *m; (com)* procurat·or -oris *m,* negotiorum curat·or -oris *m;* **man is a free —** homo sui juris est

agglomeration *s* congeri·es -ei *f*

aggrandize *tr* amplificare

aggrandizement *s* amplicati·o -onis *f*

aggravate *tr (to make worse)* aggravare; *(a wound)* ulcerare; *(to annoy)* vexare; **to become —d** ingravescĕre

aggravating *adj* molest·us -a -um

aggravation *s (annoyance)* vexati·o -onis *f*

aggregate *adj* tot·us -a -um; **in the —** in toto

aggression *s* incursi·o -onis *f;* **to commit — against** incursionem hostiliter facere in *(w. acc)*

aggressive *adj* hostil·is -is -e

aggressor *s* qui bellum ultro infert

aggrieve *tr* dolore afficĕre

aggrieved *adj* qui injuriam accepit

aghast *adj* stupefact·us -a -um; **to stand — obstupescĕre**

agile *adj* agil·is -is -e

agility *s* agilit·as -atis *f*

agitate *tr (to move rapidly to and fro)* agitare; *(to excite)* agitare; *(to disturb)* perturbare

agitated *adj (sea)* tumultuos·us -a -um; *(fig)* turbulent·us -a -um

agitation *s (violent movement)* agitati·o -onis *f; (mental or political disturbance)* commoti·o -onis *f*

agitator *s* vulgi turbat·or -oris *m*

ago *adv* abhinc; **a short time —** haud ita pridem; **long —** jamdudum, multo ante; **some time —** pridem; **three years —** abhinc tres annos

agonize *intr* (ex)cruciari

agonizing *adj* cruci·abil·is -is -e

agony *s* acerbissimus dol·or -oris *m;* **to be in —** dolore angi

agrarian *adj* agrari·us -a -um

agree *intr* consentire; *(to make a bargain)* pascisci; *(of facts)* constare, convenire; **it had been —ed** convenerat; **it is generally —ed** fere convenit; **to — with s.o. about** assentire alicui de *(w. abl)*

agreeable *adj (pleasing)* grat·us -a -um; *(of persons)* commod·us -a -um; *(acceptable)* accept·us -a -um

agreeably *adv* grate, accommode

agreement *s* consens·us -ūs *m; (pact)* pacti·o -onis *f,* pact·um -i *n; (proportion)* symmetri·a -ae *f; according to the* **— ex pacto: there is general —** fere convenit

agricultural *adj* rustic·us -a -um; **the Latins were an — people** Latini agriculturae studebant

agriculture *s* agricultur·a -ae *f*

ah *interj* ah!; *(of grief, indignation)* vah!; *(of admiration)* eja!; **— me** eheu!

ahead *adv* use verb with prefix prae- or pro-; **— of time** ante tempus; **to get — of s.o.** aliquem praevenire; **go —, tell mihi!** agedum, dic mihi!; **to walk — of s.o.** aliquem praecedĕre

aid *s* auxil·ium -(i)i *n*

aid *tr* adjuvare

aide-de-camp *s* opti·o -onis *m*

ail *tr* dolēre *(w. dat)*

ailment *s* mal·um -i *n*

aim *s (mark)* scop·us -i *m; (fig)* fin·is -is *m,* proposit·um -i *n*

aim *tr* (in)tendĕre **‖** *intr* **to — at** *(a target)* destinare; *(to try to hit)* petĕre; *(to try to attain)* affectare; *(virtue, renown)* spectare

aimless *adj* van·us -a -um

aimlessly *adv* sine ratione

air *s* a·ër -eris *(acc:* aëra) *m; (upper air)* aeth·er -eris *m; (air in motion)* aur·a -ae *f; (attitude)* habit·us -ūs *m;* **— shaft** aestuar·ium -(i)i *n;* **in the open —** sub divo; **to let in fresh —** auras admittĕre; **to put on —s** se jactare; **up in the —** *(fig)* in medio relict·us -a -um

air *tr* ventilare; *(to disclose)* patefacĕre

airhead *s (coll)* cucurbit·a -ae *f*

airily *adv* hilare

airing *s* ventilati·o -onis *f; (of an idea)* praedicati·o -onis *f*

airy *adj* perflabil·is -is -e

aisle *s* al·a -ae *f*

ajar *adj* semiapert·us -a -um

akimbo *adv* **to stand with arms —** ansat·us -a -um stare

akin *adj (to)* finitim·us -a -um *(w. dat)*

alabaster *s* alabas·ter -tri *m*

alacrity *s* alacrit·as -atis *f*

alarm *s (loud notice of danger)* clam·or -oris *m; (sudden fright)* pav·or -oris *m;* **to sound the —** signum monitorium dare; *(mil)* classicum canĕre

alarm *tr* perturbare; **to become —ed** expavescĕre

alas *interj* eheu!

albumen *s* album·en -inis *n*

alchemist *s* alchemist·a -ae *m*

alchemy *s* alchimi·a -ae *f*

alcohol *s* spirit·us -ūs *m* vini

alcoholic *adj* alcoholic·us -a -um

alcoholic *s* bibos·us -i *m*

alcove *s* zothec·a -ae *f*

ale *s* cerevisi·a -ae *f*

alert *adj* intent·us -a -um; **— mind** erecta men·s -tis *f*

alert *s* monitorium sign·um -i *n;* **on the —** intent·us -a -um; **to sound the —** signum monitorium dare

alert *tr (to warn)* praemonēre; *(to rouse)* excitare
alertness *s* alacrit·as -atis *f*
alias *s* nom·en -inis *n* mentitum
alibi *s (excuse)* speci·es -ei *f;* **to have an** —dicĕre se alibi fuisse; *(fig)* se excusare
alien *adj* peregrin·us -a -um
alien *s* alienigen·a -ae *mf*
alienate *tr* alienare
alienation *s* alienati·o -onis *f*
alight *intr* descendĕre; *(from a horse)* desilire; *(of birds)* **(on)** insidĕre *(w. dat)*
alight *adj* illustr·is -is -e
alike *adj* simil·is -is -e
alike *adv* pariter
alimony *s* alimon·ium -(i)i *n*
alive *adj* viv·us -a -um; *(fig)* ala·cer -cris -cre
all *adj* omn·is -is -e; *(denoting a unity of parts in a body)* univers·us -a -um; — **the most learned** doctissimus quisque
all *pron* omn·es -ium *mpl & fpl,* omn·ia -ium *npl;* **in** — in summā; **not at** — haudquaquam; **nothing at** — nihil omnino; **one's** — propr·ium -(i)i *n*
all *adv* — **over** undique; — **along** usque ab initio; — **but** tantum non; — **the better** tanto melius; — **the more** eo magis; — **too late** immo jam sero
allay *tr* sedare; **to be** —**ed** temperari
allegation *s* affirmati·o -onis *f*
allege *tr* arguĕre; —**ing that** tamquam *(w. subj)*
allegiance *s* fid·es -ei *f;* **to swear** — sacramentum dicĕre
allegorical *adj* allegoric·us -a -um
allegorize *intr* allegorice scribĕre, allegorizare
allegory *s* allegori·a -ae *f*
allergic *adj* **(to)** obnoxi·us -a -um (+ *dat)*
allergy *s* allergi·a -ae *f*
alleviate *tr* levare
alleviation *s* levati·o -onis *f*
alley *s* angiport·us -ūs *m*
alliance *s (by marriage)* affinit·as -atis *f; (of states)* foed·us -eris *n*
allied *adj (pol)* foederat·us -a -um, soci·us -a -um; *(related)* finitim·us -a -um
alligator *s* crocodil·us -i *m*
alliteration *s* alliterati·o -onis *f*
allocate *tr (funds)* attribuĕre; *(to assign)* distribuĕre
allocation *s (of funds)* attributi·o -onis *f; (money)* attribut·um -i *n*
allot *tr* assignare
allotment *s* assignati·o -onis *f;* **an** — **of land** ag·er -ri *m* assignatus
allow *tr* concedĕre *(w. dat),* sinĕre; **it is** —**ed** licet; **it is** — **by Caesar** licet per Caesarem; **to** — **for** indulgēre *(w. dat);* **to** — **of** admittĕre
allowable *adj* licit·us -a -um; **it is** —**fas est**
allowance *s (permission)* permissi·o -onis

f; (concession) veni·a -ae *f; (portion)* porti·o -onis *f; (money)* stipend·ium -(i)i *n; (food)* diari·a -orum *npl*
alloy *s* mixtur·a -ae *f; (of metals)* temperati·o -onis *f*
alloy *tr* miscēre et temperare
all-seeing *adj* omnitu·ens -entis
all-time *adj* post hominum memoriam
allude *intr* **to** — **to** attingĕre
allure *tr* allicĕre
allurement *s* blandiment·um -i *n*
alluring *adj* bland·us -a -um
allusion *s* significati·o -onis *f*
allusive *adj* obliqu·us -a -um
allusively *adv* oblique
alluvial *adj* alluvi·us -a -um; —**soil** alluvi·o -onis *f*
alluvium *s* alluvi·o -onis *f*
ally *s* soc·ius -(i)i *m,* soci·a -ae *f*
ally *tr* sociare
almanac *s* fast·i -orum *mpl*
almighty *adj* omnipot·ens -entis
almond *s* amygdal·a -ae *f*
almond tree *s* amygdal·us -i *f*
almost *adv* paene, fere
alms *spl* stip·s -is *f*
aloft *adv (motion & rest)* sublime
alone *adj* sol·us -a -um; *(only)* un·us -a -um; **all** — persol·us -a -um; **to leave** — deserĕre; **to let** — mittĕre
alone *adv* solum
along *adv* porro, protinus; **all** — jamdudum; — **with** unā cum *(w. abl);* **to bring** — afferre; **to get** — **with** consentire cum *(w. abl)*
along *prep* per *(w. acc),* praeter *(w. acc)* secundum *(w. acc)*
aloof *adv* procul; **to keep** — **from the senate** curiā abstinēre; **to stand** — abstare
aloud *adv* clare
alphabet *s* element·a -orum *npl*
alphabetical *adj* litterarum ordine
alphabetically *adv* **to arrange** — **in** litteram digĕre
Alpine *adj* Alpin·us -a -um
Alps *spl* Alp·es -ium *fpl*
already *adv* jam
also *adv* etiam, et, necnon
altar *s* ar·a -ae *f*
alter *tr* mutare, commutare
alterable *adj* mutabil·is -is -e
alteration *s* mutati·o -onis *f*
altercation *s* altercati·o -onis *f*
alternate *adj* altern·us -a -um
alternate *tr & intr* alternare
alternately *adv* invicem, per vices
alternation *s* vicissitud·o -inis *f*
alternative *adj* alt·er -era -erum, alternat·us -a -um
alternative *s* alternata condici·o -onis *f,* opti·o -onis *f*
although *conj* quamquam

altitude *s* altitud·o -inis *f*
altogether *adv* omnino
altruism *s* beneficenti·a -ae *f*
always *adv* semper
amalgamate *tr* miscēre
amalgamation *s* mixti·o -onis *f*
amass *tr* cumulare
amateur *s* idiot·a -ae *m*
amatory *adj* amatori·us -a -um
amaze *tr* obstupefacěre
amazed *adj* **(at)** stupefact·us -a -um (cum + *abl*)
amazement *s* stup·or -oris *m*
amazing *adj* mir·us -a -um
amazingly *adv* mirabiliter
Amazon *s* Amaz·on -onis *f*
Amazonian *adj* Amazoni·us -a -um
ambassador *s* legat·us -i *m*
amber *s* electr·um -i *n*
ambidextrous *adj* aequiman·us -a -um
ambiguity *s* ambiguit·as -atis *f*
ambiguous *adj* ambigu·us -a -um
ambition *s* ambiti·o -onis *f*
ambitious *adj* laudis (*or* gloriae) studios·us -a -um; *(worker)* assidu·us -a -um; *(self-seeking)* ambitios·us -a -um
amble *intr* ambulare
ambrosia *s* ambrosi·a -ae *f*
ambush *s* insidi·ae -arum *fpl*
ambush *tr* insidiari (*w. dat*)
ameliorate *tr* corrigěre, meliorem *or* melius facěre ‖ *intr* melior *or* melius fieri
amenable *adj* tractabil·is -is -e
amend *tr* emendare ‖ *intr* proficěre
amendment *s* emendati·o -onis *f*
amends *spl* satisfacti·o -onis *f*; **to make —** satisfacěre
amenity *s* amoenit·as -atis *f*; *(comfort)* commod·um -i *n*
America *s* Americ·a -ae *f*; **Central —** America Media; **North —** America Septentrionalis; **South —** America Australis
American *adj* American·us -a -um
American *s* American·us -i *m*, American·a -ae *f*
amethyst *s* amethyst·us -i *f*
amiable *adj* amabil·is -is -e
amiably *adv* suaviter
amicable *adj* amic·us -a -um
amicably *adv* amice
amid *prep* inter (*w. acc*)
amiss *adv* perperam; **to take —** aegre ferre
amity *s* amiciti·a -ae *f*
ammonia *s* ammoniac·a -ae *f*
ammonium *s* ammon·ium -(i)i *n*
ammunition *s* missilium copi·a -ae *f*
amnesty *s* veni·a -ae *f*
among *prep* inter (*w. acc*), apud (*w. acc*); **from —** ex (*w. abl*)
amorous *adj* amatori·us -a -um; *(sexual)* libidinos·us -a -um

amorphous *adj* inform·is -is -e
amount *s* summ·a -ae *f*
amount *intr* **to —** to efficěre ad *(w. acc)*, esse ad *(w. acc)*; **it —s to the same thing** tantundem est; **to — to something** bonum exitum umquam factur·us -a -um esse; **what does it — to?** quid istuc valet?
amphitheater *s* amphitheatr·um -i *n*
ample *adj* ampl·us -a -um
amplification *s* amplificati·o -onis *f*
amplify *tr* amplificare
amply *adv* ample
amputate *tr* amputare
amputation *s* amputati·o -onis *f*
amuck *adv* **to run —** delirare
amulet *s* amulet·um -i *n*
amuse *tr* oblectare; **to — oneself** se oblectare
amusement *s* oblectati·o -onis *f*; *(that which amuses)* oblectament·um -i *n*
amusing *adj* festiv·us -a -um
an *indef article, unexpressed in Latin*
anachronism *s* temporum inversi·o -onis *f*
analogous *adj* analog·us -a -um
analogy *s* analogi·a -ae *f*
analysis *s* analys·is -is -eos *f*; **to make an — of a compound substance** compositum in principia redigěre
analytical *adj* analytic·us -a -um
analytically *adv* per analysin
analyze *tr* in principia redigěre; *(words)* subtiliter enodare
anapest *s* anapaestus pe·s -dis *m*
anapestic *adj* anapaestic·us -a -um
anarchist *s* civ·is -is *m* seditiosus
anarchy *s* effrenata licenti·a -ae *f*; **to cause —** turbare omnia et permiscēre; **to have — ** nullum omnino imperium habēre
anathema *s* anathem·a -atis *n*
anatomical *adj* anatomic·us -a -um
anatomy *s* anatomi·a -ae *f*
ancestor *s* proav·us -i *m*; **—s** major·es -um *mpl*
ancestry *s* gen·us -eris *n*
anchor *s* ancor·a -ae *f*; **to lie at —** in ancoris stare; **to weigh —** ancoram tollěre
anchor *tr* ad ancoras deligare ‖ *intr* in ancoris stare
anchorage *s* stati·o -onis *f*
ancient *adj* antiqu·us -a -um, vetust·us -a -um; **in — times** antiquitus; **the —s** veter·es -um *mpl*; *(authors)* antiqu·i -orum *mpl*
and *conj* et, ac, atque, -que; **— so forth** et perinde; **— then** deincepsque
anecdote *s* fabell·a -ae *f*
anemic *adj* exsangu·is -is -e
anew *adv* denuo
angel *s* angel·us -i *m*
angelic *adj* angelic·us -a -um
anger *s* ir·a -ae *f*
anger *tr* irritare
angle *s* angul·us -i *m*

angler s piscat·or -oris m
angrily adv irate
angry adj irat·us -a -um; **to be — (with)** irasci (w. dat); **to make —** irritare
anguish s ang·or -oris m
angular adj angular·is -is -e
animal s anim·al -alis n; (wild beast) besti·a -ae f, fer·a -ae f; (domestic) pec·us -oris n
animate adj animal·is -is -e
animate tr animare; (fig) excitare
animated adj veget·us -a -um
animation s (bestowal of life) animati·o -onis f; (liveliness) vig·or -oris m
animosity s acerbit·as -atis f
ankle s tal·us -i m
ankle-length adj talar·is -is -e
anklet s periscel·is -idis f
annalist s annalium script·or -oris m
annals spl annal·es -ium mpl
annex s diaet·a -ae f
annex tr (nations) adjicĕre, adungĕre
annexation s adjecti·o -onis f
annihilate tr delēre, ex(s)tinguĕre
annihilation s exstincti·o -onis f
anniversary adj anniversari·us -a -um
anniversary s festus di·es -ei m anniversarius
annotate tr annotare
annotation s annotati·o -onis f
announce tr nuntiare, indicĕre; (to report) renuntiare; (officially) denuntiare; (laws, etc.) proscribĕre
announcement s denuntiati·o -onis f; (report) renuntiati·o -onis f
announcer s nunt·ius -(i)i m
annoy tr vexare, male habēre; **to be —ed at** stomachari ob (w. acc)
annoyance s molesti·a -ae f
annoying adj molest·us -a -um
annual adj annu·us -a -um
annually adv quotannis
annuity s annua pecuni·a -ae f
annul tr (contract, law) infirmare; (a law) abrogare; **to — a marriage** dirimĕre nuptias
annulment s infirmati·o -onis f; abrogati·o -onis f
anoint tr ung(u)ĕre
anointing s uncti·o -onis f
anomalous adj enorm·is -is -e; (gram) anomal·us -a -um
anomaly s enormit·as -atis f; (gram) anomali·a -ae f
anonymous adj sine nomine
anonymously adv sine nomine
another adj ali·us -a -ud; —'s alien·us -a -um; **at — time** alias; **in — place** alibi; **one after —** alius ex alio; **one — inter** se; **one…— ** ali·us -a -ud…ali·us -a -ud; **to — place** alio
answer tr respondēre (w. dat); (by letter) rescribĕre (w. dat); (to correspond to) congruĕre cum (w. abl) ‖ intr **to — for** rationem reddere (w. gen); **to — to the name of** vocari
answer s respons·um -i n; (solution) explicati·o -onis f
answerable adj re·us -a -um; **to be — for** praestare (acc)
ant s formic·a -ae f
antagonism s adversit·as -atis f
antagonist s adversar·ius -(i)i m, adversatr·ix -icis f
antarctic adj antarctic·us -a -um
antecedent adj anteced·ens -entis
antecedent s anteced·ens -entis n; (gram) nom·en -inis n antecedens
antechamber s atriol·um -i n
antedate tr diem vero antiquiorem ascribĕre (w. dat); (to precede in time) aetate antecedĕre (w. dat or acc)
antelope s antilop·e -es f
antenna s antenn·a -ae f
antepenult s syllab·a -ae f antepaenultima
anterior adj anter·ior -ior -ius
anteroom s atriol·um -i n
anthem s hymn·us -i m elatior; **national —** patrium carm·en -inis n
anthology s anthologi·a -ae f
anticipate tr anticipare; (to expect) spectare; (mentally) praesumĕre
anticipation s anticipati·o -onis f, praesumpti·o -onis f
anticlimax s clim·ax -acis f inversa
antics spl mot·us -uum mpl ridiculi
antidote s antidot·ium -(i)i n
antipathy s antipathi·a -ae f
antiquarian adj antiquari·us -a -um
antiquarian s antiquar·ius -(i)i m
antiquated adj antiquat·us -a -um
antique adj prisc·us -a -um ; **— statues** sign·a -orum npl operis antiqui
antique s antiqui artificis op·us -eris n
antiquity s antiquit·as -atis f
anti-Semitic adj Judaeis avers·us -a -um
anti-Semitism s Judaeorum od·ium -(i) n
antithesis s contrar·ium -(i)i n
antler s corn·u -us n
antonym s verb·um -i n contrarium
anus s an·us -i m
anvil s inc·us -dis f
anxiety s anxiet·as -atis f
anxious adj anxi·us -a -um; (eager) (for) studios·us -a -um (w. gen)
anxiously adv anxie; (eagerly) avide
any adj ull·us -a -um; (after si, ne, nisi, num) quis, quid; **at — time** aliquando
any adv — **longer** diutius; — **more** amplius
anybody pron aliquis; (after si, nisi, ne, num) quis; (interrog) ecquis, numquis; (after negative) quisquam; **— you wish** quisvis, quislibet
anyhow adv quoquomodo; (in any event) utique
anyone see **anybody**

anything *pron* aliquid, quicquam; *(after si,* nisi, ne, num) quid; *(interrog)* ecquid, numquid; *(after negative)* quisquam; — **you wish** quidlibet; **hardly** — nihil fere

anyway *adv* quoquomodo; *(at least, in any event)* utique

anywhere *adv (in any place)* alicubi; *(frequently after* si) uspiam; *(usu. w. negative)* usquam; *(anywhere you please)* ubivis; *(to any place, usu. w.* si, ne, num) quo

aorta *s* grandis ven·a -ae *f* cordis

apart *adv* seorsum, separatim; — **from** praeter *(w. acc);* **to be** — distare; **to fall** — dilabi; **to set** — seponěre; **to stand** — distare

apartment *s* cenacul·um -i *n*

apartment building *s* insul·a -ae *f*

apathetic *adj* lent·us -a -um

apathy *s* apathi·a -ae *f*

ape *s* sim·ius -(i)i *m,* simi·a -ae *f*

ape *tr* imitari

aperture *s* foram·en -inis *n*

apex *s* cacum·en -inis *n*

aphorism *s* sententi·a -ae *f*

aphrodisiac *s* sature·um -i *n*

apiary *s* alvear·ium -(i)i *n*

apiece *adv no exact Latin equivalent, but its sense is expressed by distributive numerals, e.g.:* **they went out with two garments** — cum binis vestimentis exierunt; **he stationed one legion** — **at Brindisium and Tarentum** legiones singulas posuit Brindisi, Tarenti

aplomb *s* confidenti·a -ae *f*

apocalypse *s* apocalyps·is -is *f*

apocryphal *adj* apocryph·us -a -um

apogee *s* apogae·um -i *n*

apologetic *adj* se excus·ans -antis

apologize *intr* satis facěre; **to** — **for s.o.** aliquem excusare

apology *s* excusati·o -onis *f;* **to make an** — **for** excusare

apoplectic *adj* apoplectic·us -a -um

apoplexy *s* apoplexi·a -ae *f*

apostasy *s* apostasi·a -ae *f*

apostate *s* apostat·a -ae *m*

apostle *s* apostol·us -i *m*

apostolic *adj* apostolic·us -a -um

apostrophe *s* apostroph·e -es *f; (gram)* apostroph·us -i *f*

apothecary *s (drugstore)* tabern·a -ae *f* medicina; *(druggist)* medicamentar·ius -(i)i *m*

apotheosis *s* apotheosis -is *f*

appall *tr* exterrēre

apparatus *s* apparat·us -ūs *m*

apparel *s* vestit·us -ūs *m*

apparel *tr* vestire

apparent *adj* manifest·us -a -um; *(seeming)* fict·us -a -um

apparently *adv* specie, per speciem

apparition *s* speci·es -ei *f*

appeal *intr (leg) (to a magistrate)* appellare *(acc); (to the people)* provocare **(ad +** *acc);* **to** — **to** *(to be attractive to)* allicěre; *(to the gods)* obtestari

appeal *s (leg)* appellati·o -onis *f; (to the people)* provocati·o -onis *f; (entreaty)* obtestati·o -onis *f; (attractiveness)* suavit·as -atis *f*

appealing *adj* suav·is -is -e; *(imploring)* suppl·ex -icis

appear *intr (to be visible)* apparēre; *(to show up)* comparēre; *(to arise suddenly)* oriri; *(to seem)* vidēri; *(in public, on the stage)* prodire; **to begin to** — patescěre

appearance *s (becoming visible)* aspect·us -ūs *m; (outward show)* speci·es -ei *f; (likelihood)* similitud·o -inis *f; (vision)* vis·um -i *n;* **for the sake of** —**s** ad speciem; **to all** —**s** ut videtur; **to keep up** —**s** speciem gerěre; **to make one's** — **in public** in publicum prodire; **to make one's appearance on the stage** in proscaenium prodire

appease *tr* placare

appeasement *s* placati·o -onis *f*

appellation *s* appellati·o -onis *f*

append *tr* subscriběre

appendage *s* append·ix -icis *f*

appendix *s* append·ix -icis *f; (anat)* append·ix -icis *f* coli

appetite *s* appetit·us -ūs *m; (for food)* cibi appetenti·a -ae *f;* **lack of** — inedi·a -ae *f;* **to control the** —**s** appetitūs regěre

appetizer *s* gustati·o -onis *f*

applaud *tr* applauděre *(w. acc or dat); (to praise)* approbare **‖** *intr* plauděre

applause *s* plaus·us -ūs *m;* **to look for** — plausūs captare

apple *s* mal·um -i *n;* — **of my eye** meus ocell·us -i *m*

apple peel *s* malicor·ium -(i)i *n*

apple tree *s* mal·us -i *f*

appliance *s* instrument·um -i *n*

applicable *adj* (to) commod·us -a -um *(w. dat)*

applicant *s* petit·or -oris *m*

application *s (act of requesting)* petiti·o -onis *f; (act of applying)* adhibiti·o -onis *f; (industry)* sedulit·as -atis *f; (med)* foment·um -i *n*

apply *tr (to put on or to) (to)* adhibēre *(w. dat or* ad + *acc); (to wounds)* inponěre *(w. dat or* in + *acc);* **to** — **oneself** to se conferre ad *(w. acc);* **to** — **the mind to** animum adhibēre ad *(w. acc)* **‖** *intr* **to** — **to** pertinēre ad *(w. acc),* caděre in *(w. acc);* **to** — **for** petěre

appoint *tr* designare, creare, dicěre

appointment *s* creati·o -onis *f; (agreement to meet)* constitut·um -i *n; (order)* mandat·um -i *n;* **I have an** — **with you** constitutum tecum habeo; **to keep an** — ad constitutum venire

apportion *tr* dividĕre
apportionment *s* divisi·o -onis *f*
apposition *s* appositi·o -onis *f;* **a noun in** — **with** vocabulum appositum *(w. dat)*
appraisal *s* aestimati·o -onis *f; (com, fin)* taxati·o -onis *f*
appraise *tr* aestimare; *(com, fin)* taxare
appraiser *s* aestimat·or -oris *m; (com, fin)* taxat·or -oris *m*
appreciable *adj* aestimabil·is -is -e, haud exigu·us -a -um
appreciate *tr (to esteem)* magni aestimare; *(to discern)* cognoscĕre
appreciation *s* aestimati·o -onis *f; (gratitude)* grati·a -ae *f;* **to show** — **to s.o. for** gratiam alicui referre ob *(+ acc)*
apprehend *tr (to arrest; to grasp)* apprehendĕre
apprehension *s (arrest; understanding)* apprehensi·o -onis *f; (fear)* tim·or -oris *m,* sollicitud·o -inis *f*
apprehensive *adj* sollicit·us -a -um
apprentice *s* tir·o -onis *m*
apprenticeship *s* tirocin·ium -(i)i *n*
apprize *tr* **(of)** certiorem facere (de + *abl)*
approach *tr* appropinquare *(w. dat); (to approximate)* accedĕre *(w. dat or* ad + *acc)* ‖ *intr* appropinquare, accedĕre; *(of an event)* appetĕre
approach *s* access·us -ūs *m; (of time)* appropinquati·o -onis *f; (by sea)* appuls·us -ūs *m*
approachable *adj (person)* facil·is -is -e; *(place)* pat·ens -entis
approbation *s* approbati·o -onis *f*
appropriate *adj* conveni·ens -entis, apt·us -a -um, idone·us -a -um; **it is** — **to** convenit *(w. inf or acc & inf)*
appropriate *tr (to claim)* vindicare; *(to claim presumptuously)* arrogare; *(money)* **(to)** dicĕre *(w. dat)*
appropriately *adv* apte, congruenter
appropriateness *s* convenienti·a -ae *f,* congruenti·a -ae *f*
appropriation *s* vindicati·o -onis *f; (of money)* **(for)** destinati·o -onis *f* (in + *acc)*
approval *s* approbati·o -onis *f*
approve *tr* approbare; *(a law)* sciscĕre ‖ *intr* **to** — **of** probare
approved *adj* probat·us -a - um
approximate *adj* proxim·us -a -um
approximate *tr* accedĕre ad *(w. acc)*
approximately *adv* prope, propemodum; *(w. numbers)* ad *(w. acc)*
approximation *s* **the nearest** — quod proximum est
apricot *s* armeniac·um -i *n*
apricot tree *s* armeniac·a -ae *f*
April *s* April·is -is *m or* mens·is -is *m* Aprilis; **on the first of** — Kalendis Aprilibus
apron *s* sublig·ar -aris *n*

apt *adj* apt·us -a -um; **to be** — **to** *(w. inf)* solēre *(w. inf)*
aptitude *s* **(for)** ingen·ium -(i)i *n* (ad + *acc)*
aptly *adv* apte
aptness *s (fitness)* convenienti·a -ae *f; (talent)* ingen·ium -(i)i *n; (tendency)* proclivit·as -atis *f*
aquatic *adj* aquatic·us -a -um
aqueduct *s* aquaeduct·us -ūs *m*
aquiline *adj (nose)* adunc·us -a -um
arable *adj* arabil·is -is -e; — **land** arv·um -i *n*
arbiter *s* arbit·er -ri *m*
arbitrarily *adv* ad arbitrium
arbitrary *s* libidinos·us -a -um; *(imperious)* imperios·us -a -um
arbitrate *tr & intr* disceptare
arbitration *s* arbitr·ium -(i)i *n*
arbitrator *s* arbi·ter -tri *m*
arbor *s* umbracul·um -i *n*
arc *s* arc·us -ūs *m*
arcade *s* portic·us -ūs *f*
arch *s* arc·us -ūs *m,* forn·ix -icis *f*
arch *tr* arcuare, fornicare
arch *adj (chief)* summ·us -a -um; — **enemy** summus adversar·ius -(i)i *m*
archaeological *adj* archaeologic·us -a -um
archaeologist *s* vi·r -ri *m* monumentorum antiquitatis peritissimus
archaeology *s* archaeologi·a -ae *f*
archaic *adj* prisc·us -a -um
archaism *s* locuti·o -onis *f* obsoleta
archbishop *s* archiepiscop·us -i *m*
archer *s* sagittar·ius -(i)i *m; (astr)* Arciten·ens -entis *m*
archery *s* ar·s -tis *f* sagittandi
archetype *s* archetyp·um -i *n*
archipelago *s* mar·e -is *n* insulis crebrum
architect *s* architect·us -i *m*
architectural *adj* architectonic·us -a -um
architecture *s* architectur·a -ae *f*
archives *spl* tabul·ae -arum *fpl; (place)* tabular·ium -(i)i *n*
arctic *adj* arctic·us -a -um
ardent *adj* ard·ens -entis
ardently *adv* ardenter
ardor *s* ard·or -oris *m*
arduous *adj* ardu·us -a -um
area *s (open space; in geometry)* are·a -ae *f; (region)* regi·o -onis *f*
arena *s* (h)aren·a -ae *f*
Argonaut *s* argonaut·a -ae *m*
argue *tr (to reason)* arguĕre; *(to discuss)* disceptare de *(w. abl);* **to** — **a case** causam agĕre ‖ *intr* disputare; *(to wrangle)* altercari
argument *s (discussion)* disputati·o -onis *f; (heated)* altercati·o -onis *f; (reason in support of a position)* argument·um -i *n;* **the force of his** — vis *f* argumenti ejus; **to get into an** — in litem ambiguam descendĕre; **to put up an** — recusare

argumentation s argumentati·o -onis f,
rati·o -onis f
argumentative adj litigios·us -a -um
aria s cantic·um -i n
arid adj arid·us -a -um; (fig) jejun·us -a
-um
aridity s aridit·as -atis f
aright adv recte
arise intr surgĕre; (of a group) consurgĕre;
(of a storm, etc.) oriri, cooriri; (suddenly) exoriri; (to come into existence)
exsistĕre; (to orginate) (**from**) nasci (ex
+ abl)
aristocracy s (class) optimat·es -ium
mpl; (government) optimatium domi-
nat·us -ūs m
aristocrat s optim·as -atis m
aristocratic adj patrici·us -a -um
arithmetic s arithmetic·a -ae f
ark s arc·a -ae f
arm tr armare
arm s bracch·ium -(i)i n; (upper arm)
lacert·us -i m; (of the sea) sin·us -ūs m;
(of a chair) anc·on -onis m; **at —'s
length** eminus (adv); **to carry in
one's —s** in manibus gestare; **to carry
under one's —s** sub ala portare; **with
—s akimbo** ansat·us -a -um; **with
folded —s** compressis manibus; **with
open —s** sinu complexuque ‖ spl arm·a
-orum npl; **by force of —** vi et armis; **to
be under —** in armis esse; **to lay down
—** ab armis discedĕre; **to take up —**
arma sumĕre
armada s class·is -is f magna
armament s apparat·us -ūs m belli
armchair s anconibus fabrefacta sell·a
-ae f
armed adj armat·us -a -um
armistice s induti·ae -arum fpl; **to break
off an —** indutias tollĕre
armlet s bracchiol·um -i n; (bracelet)
armill·a -ae f
armor s arm·a -orum npl
armorbearer s armig·er -eri m
armory s armamentar·ium -(i)i n
armpit s al·a -ae f
army s exercit·us -ūs m; (in battle) aci·es
-ei f; (on the march) agm·en -inis n; **to
join the —** ad militiam ire
aroma s arom·a -atis n; (of wine) flo·s
-ris m
aromatic adj aromatic·us -a -um
around adv circum, circa; **all —** undique
around prep circum (w. acc); (approximately) circa, ad (w. acc)
arouse tr suscitare; (to wake up) e somno
excitare; (fig) excitare; **to — suspicion**
suspicionem movēre
arraign tr accusare
arraignment s accusati·o -onis f
arrange tr (to set in order) ordinare; (the
hair) componĕre, comĕre; (a plan, meet-

ing) constituĕre; (matters, a cloak to
hang properly) collocare; (to agree)
pacisci; (to put each thing separately in
its place) digerĕre; **—ed in a circle** in
orbe disposit·us -a -um
arrangement s ord·o -inis m; (of the year,
of elections) ordinati·o -onis f; (of matters, of a garment) collocati·o -onis f; (of
a speech, of books) context·us -ūs m; **the
— was that** convenit ut
array s vestit·us -ūs m; (mil) aci·es -ei f
array tr vestire; (mil) instituĕre
arrears s reliqu·a -orum npl, residuae
pecuni·ae -arum fpl; **to be in —** relinqui
arrest s prehensi·o -onis f
arrest tr (ap)prehendĕre; (movement)
tardare; **to — the attention of all** omnes
in se convertĕre
arrival s advent·us -ūs m; (by sea)
appuls·us -ūs m
arrive intr advenire; (by ship or on horseback) advehi; (of a ship) appelli; **to — at**
pervenire ad (w. acc); **to — before the
messengers** nuntios praevenire; **to — in**
(a place, country) pervenire in (w. acc)
arrogance s arroganti·a -ae f
arrogant adj arrog·ans -antis
arrogantly adv arroganter
arrow s sagitt·a -ae f
arrowhead s spicul·um -i n
arsenal s armamentar·ium -(i)i n; (naval)
naval·ia -ium npl
arsenic s arsenic·um -i n
arson s incend·ium -(i)i n malo dolo
arsonist s incendiar·ius -(i)i m
art s ar·s -tis f; (practice of some craft)
artific·ium -(i)i n; **fine —s** art·es -ium
fpl elegantes; **to study —** arti studēre
artery s arteri·a -ae f
artful adj callid·us -a -um
artfully adv callide
art gallery s pinacothec·a -ae f
article s (object) res rei f; (ware) mer·x
-cis f; (term) condici·o -onis f; (clause in
a law) cap·ut -itis n; (gram) articul·us -i
m; **— of faith** decret·um -i n fidei
articulate tr articulatim dicĕre
articulate adj dilucid·us -a -um
articulately adv articulate
articulation s (distinct utterance) expla-
nati·o -onis f; (anat) commissur·a -ae f
artifice s artific·ium -(i)i n
artificial adj (produced by human hands)
artificios·us -a -um; (not genuine)
factici·us -a -um
artificially adv arte; (by human hands)
manu
artillery s torment·a -orum npl
artisan s opif·ex -icis m; (usu. in hard
material) fa·ber -bri m
artist s (of any of the fine arts) artif·ex
-icis m; (painter) pict·or -oris m
artistic adj artif·ex -icis

artistically *adv* artificiose
as *conj & adv* ut; *(while)* ut, dum, cum; *(as article of comparison, denoting equality)* atque, ac; *(for example)* velut, ut, sicut; *(because)* cum; —...— *(degree)* tam...quam, aeque...atque; — **far** — quoad; — **good** — aeque bonus atque; — **great**—tantus...quantus; — if quasi; — is ut est; — it were tamquam; — **long** — tamdiu, tantisper dum, quam diu; — **many** — totidem; — **much** tantum; — **often** — toties...quoties; — **soon** — cum primum: — **though** quasi; — **well** as ac, atque; — yet adhuc; **just** — **if** perinde ac si; **not** — yet nondum
ascend *tr & intr* ascendĕre
ascendency *s (superior influence)* potenti·a -ae *f;* **to gain the** — superior fieri
ascension *s* ascensi·o -onis *f*
ascent *s* ascensi·o -onis *f,* ascens·us -ūs *m;* **during the** — **to the summit** dum in summum ascenditur
ascertain *tr* comperire
ascetic *adj* ascetic·us -a -um
ascetic *s* ascet·a -ae *m*
asceticism *s* duriti·a -ae *f*
ascribe *tr* ascribĕre
ash *s* cin·is -is -eris *m; (tree)* fraxin·us -i *f;* —es cin·is -is -eris *m; (esp. ashes of the dead)* ciner·es -um *mpl*
ashamed *adj* pudibund·us -a -um; **I am** — **ed of** pudet me *(w. gen);* **I am** — **to tell** pudet me referre; **there is nothing to be** —**ed of** non est quod pudeatur
ashen *adj* pallid·us -a -um
ashore *adv (motion)* in terram; *(rest)* in litore; **to go** — in terram egredi
Asia *s* Asi·a -ae *f*
Asian *adj* Asian·us -a -um
Asiatic *adj* Asiatic·us -a -um
aside *adv* seorsum; **to call** — evocare; **to set** *or* **put** — seponĕre; **to take** — seducĕre; **to turn** — deflectĕre
aside from *prep* praeter *(w. acc)*
asinine *adj* asinin·us -a -um
ask *tr* rogare; *(to beg, petition for, esp. of a request made to a superior)* petĕre; *(to demand)* poscĕre, postulare; **to ask s.o. for s.th.** aliquem aliquid rogare; **to** — **that (that not)** rogare *(w. ut or ne +* *subj);* **I** — **you this question** hoc te rogo; **to** — **further questions** quaerĕre ultra; **to** — **many questions** multa quaerĕre *or* rogare; **to** — **one question after another** aliud ex alio quaerĕre; **to** — **questions** interrogare; **to** — **why** requirĕre quamobrem **ǁ** *intr* **to**—**about** percontari; **to** — **for** petĕre
askance *adv* **to look** — **(at)** limis oculis aspicĕre
asleep *adj* dormi·ens -entis; **half** — semisomn·us -a -um; **to be (sound)** — *(arte)* dormire; **to fall** — obdormiscĕre

asp *s* asp·is -idis *f*
asparagus *s* asparag·us -i *m*
aspect *s* aspect·us -ūs *m*
aspen *s* popul·us -i *f* tremula
asperity *s* acerbit·as -atis *f*
aspersion *s* opprobr·ium -(i)i *n;* **to cast** — **on** calumniari
asphalt *s* bitum·en -inis *n*
asphyxiation *s* asphyxi·a -ae *f*
aspirant *s* **(to)** appetit·or -oris *m (w. gen)*
aspiration *s* affectati·o -onis *f;* **to have lofty** —**s** magna spectare
aspire *intr* **to** — **to** appetĕre, affectare
aspiring *adj* **(after)** appet·ens -entis *(w. gen)*
ass *s* asin·us -i *m,* asin·a -a -ae *f; (fool)* asin·us -i *m; (anat)* clun·es -ium *mpl*
assail *tr* appetĕre; *(mil)* oppugnare
assailable *adj* expugnabil·is -is -e
assailant *s* oppugnat·or -oris *m*
assassin *s* percuss·or -oris *m*
assassinate *tr* per insidias interficĕre
assassination *s* caed·es -is *f* per insidias
assault *s* oppugnati·o -onis *f;* **aggravated** — *(leg)* vis *f;* — **and battery** vis *f* inlata; **sexual** — stuprati·o -onis *f;* **to take by** — expugnare
assault *tr (a person)* manus inferre *(w. dat); (sexually)* stuprum inferre *(w. dat); (in speech)* invehi in *(w. acc); (mil)* oppugnare
assay *tr (metals)* spectare
assay *s (of metals)* obruss·a -ae *f*
assemblage *s* congregati·o -onis *f*
assemble *tr* cogĕre; *(to call together)* convocare **ǁ** *intr* convenire
assembly *s* coet·us -ūs *m; (mil, pol)* conti·o -onis *f; (electoral)* comiti·a -orum *npl;* **in the** — pro contione; **to hold an** — comitia *(or* contionem) habēre
assent *s* assens·us -ūs *m*
assent *intr* **(to)** assentiri *(w. dat);* **to** — **to a request** petenti annuēre
assert *tr* affirmare, confirmare; *(to maintain, claim)* asserĕre
assertion *s* affirmati·o -onis *f; (claim)* asserti·o -onis *f*
assess *tr* taxare; *(for tax purposes)* censēre
assessment *s* taxati·o -onis *f; (for tax purposes)* cens·us -ūs *m*
assessor *s* cens·or -oris *m*
assets *spl* bon·a -orum *npl*
assiduous *adj* assidu·us -a -um
assiduously *adv* assidue
assign *tr* attribuĕre; *(land, duties)* assignare; *(time)* praestituĕre; *(task)* delegare; *(to allege)* afferre; *(in writing)* praescri-bĕre
assignment *s* attributi·o -onis *f; (of land, duties)* assignati·o -onis *f; (in school)* pens·um -i *n*
assimilate *tr* assimulare; *(food)* digerĕre; *(knowledge)* concipĕre

assimilation *s* digesti·o -onis *f*
assist *tr* adesse *(w. dat)*, adjuvare
assistance *s* auxil·ium -(i)i *n;* **to be of —** **to** auxilio esse *(w. dat)*
assistant *s* adjut·or -oris *m*, adjutr·ix -icis *f*
associate *s* soc·ius -(i)i *m*
associate *adj* soci·us -a -um
associate *tr* consociare, adjungĕre **‖** *intr* **to — with** familiariter uti *(w. dat)*
association *s* societ·as -atis *f; —* **with s.o** consociati·o -onis *f (w. gen)*
assort *tr* digerĕre
assortment *s (arrangement)* digesti·o -onis *f;* **a large — of jewelry** gemm·ae -arum *fpl* plurimae et cujuve generis
assuage *tr* allevare
assume *tr* assumĕre; *(a task)* suscipĕre; *(improperly)* arrogare; *(to take for granted in argument)* ponĕre; *(a role)* induĕre
assumption *s* assumpti·o -onis *f; (improper)* arroganti·a -ae *f; (hypothesis)* sumpti·o -onis *f*
assurance *s* fiduci·a -ae *f; (confidence)* confidenti·a -ae *f; (guarantee)* fid·es -ei *f*
assure *tr (to promise)* confirmare, affirmare; **to be** *or* **feel —ed** confidĕre
assured *adj (e.g, victory)* explorat·us -a -um
assuredly *adv* profecto
asterisk *s* asterisc·us -i *m*
asthma *s* asthm·a -atis *n;* **to have —** suspirio laborare
asthmatic *adj* asthmatic·us -a -um
astonish *tr* stupefacĕre
astonished *adj* attonit·us -a -um; **to be — at** obstupescĕre *(w. dat)*
astonishing *adj* mir·us -a -um
astonishingly *adv* admirabiliter
astonishment *s* admirati·o -onis *f; (speechlessness)* stup·or -oris *m*
astound *tr* (ob)stupefacĕre; **to be —d** stupēre
astray *adv* vag·us -a -um; **to go —** errare; **to lead s.o. —** aliquem transversum agĕre
astride *adv* equitantium modo posit·us -a -um
astrologer *s* astrolog·us -i *m*, mathematic·us -i *m*
astrology *s* astrologi·a -ae *f*
astronomer *s* astrolog·us -i *m*
astronomical *adj* astronomic·us -a -um
astronomy *s* astronomi·a -ae *f*
astute *adj* astut·us -a -um
asunder *adv* seorsum; *use verb with prefix* dis- *or* se-; **to tear —** discerpĕre
asylum *s* asyl·um -i *n*
at *prep (of place)* ad *(w. acc); (strictly, near)* apud *(w. acc); (usu. with names of towns, harbors, villas)* in *(w. abl)*, or *locative case; (at the house of)* apud *(w. acc); (of time) use abl case; —* **all** omnino, prorsum; **—first** primo, initio;

— home domi; **— least** duxtaxat, utique; **— once** momento, continuo; **— present** in praesentiā; **— the right time** in tempore
atheism *s* deos esse negare *(used as a neuter noun)*
atheist *s* athe·os -i *m*
Athenian *adj* Athenae·us -a -um
Athenian *s* Atheniens·is -is *m*
Athens *s* Athen·ae -arum *fpl*
athlete *s* athlet·a -ae *mf*
athletic *adj* athletic·us -a -um
athletics *spl* ar·s -tis *f* athletica
atlas *s* orbis terrarum descripti·o -onis *f*
atmosphere *s* cael·um -i *n*
atmospheric *adj* caeli *(gen)*
atom *s* atom·us -i *f*
atomic *adj* atomic·us -a -um; **— bomb** pyrobol·um -i *n* atomicum; **— energy** vis *f* atomica; **— theory** atomorum doctrin·a -ae *f*
atone *intr* **to — for** (ex)piare
atonement *s* expiati·o -onis *f*
atrocious *adj* atro·x -ocis
atrocity *s (atrociousness)* atrocit·as -atis *f; (deed)* atrox facin·us -eris *n*
atrophy *s* atrophi·a -ae *f*
atrophy *intr* tabescĕre
attach *tr (to fasten to)* annectĕre, adjungĕre; *(e.g., meaning)* subjicĕre; **to — importance to s.th.** aliquid magni aestimare; **to — oneself to s.o.** se alicui adjungĕre; **to be —ed to** adhaerēre *(w. dat)*
attachment *s (contact)* junctur·a -ae *f; (devotion)* stud·ium -(i)i *n;* **my — to the Roman people** studium meum in populum Romanum
attack *s* impet·us -ūs *m; (usu. on a town)* oppugnati·o -onis *f; (by cavalry)* incurs·us -ūs *m; (of a disease)* tentati·o -onis *f; (verbal)* petiti·o -onis *f*
attack *tr* aggredi; *(esp. w. physical force)* adoriri, vim inferre *(w. dat); (towns)* oppugnare; *(of a disease)* tentare, invadĕre; *(verbally)* petĕre; **—ed by a sudden illness** corrept·us -a -um subitā valetudine
attacker *s* aggress·or -oris *m; (mil)* oppugnat·or -oris *m*
attain *tr* adipisci, consequi; **to — to** pervenire ad *(w. acc)*
attainable *adj (by request)* impetrabil·is -is -e; **to be — patēre**
attempt *s* conat·us -ūs *m*
attempt *tr* conari, temptare, moliri
attend *tr (to accompany)* comitari; *(to escort)* prosequi; *(school, wedding, senate session)* frequentare; *(to be present at, e.g., a meeting)* adesse *(w. dat); (of a doctor)* assidēre *(w. dat);* **to — to** procurare, animadvertĕre
attendance *s (in great numbers)* frequenti·a -ae *f; (of a doctor)* assiduit·as -atis *f*

attendant *adj* adjunct·us -a -um; — **circumstances** adjunct·a -orum *npl*
attendant *s (to officials)* apparit·or -oris *m; (servant)* minist·er -ri *m*, ministr·a -ae *f; (of a temple)* aeditu·us -i *m*
attention *s* attentus anim·us -i *m*, animi attenti·o -onis *f;* **to attract** — animos hominum ad se convertere; **to call** — **to** indicare; **to call for** — animadverti jubēre; **to hold our** — animos nostros tenēre; **to pay** — **to** operam dare *(w. dat)*
attentive *adj* attent·us -a -um
attentively *adv* attente
attenuate *tr* attenuare, extenuare
attenuation *s* extenuati·o -onis *f*
attest *tr* testificare
attestation *s* testificati·o -onis *f*
attic *s* cenacul·um -i *n*
Attic *adj* Attic·us -a -um
Attica *s* Attic·a -ae *f*
attire *tr* vestire
attire *s* vestit·us -ūs *m*
attitude *s* habit·us -ūs *m; (of the body)* stat·us -ūs *m*
attorney *s* cognit·or -oris *m*
attorney general *s* advocat·us -i *m* fisci
attract *tr (lit & fig)* trahěre; **to** — **a buyer** emptorem adducěre; **to** — **the attention of all** oculos omnium in se convertěre
attraction *s* vis *f* attractionis; *(fig)* illecebr·a -ae *f*
attractive *adj* illecebros·us -a -um
attractively *adv* blande
attractiveness *s* lep·os -oris *m*
attributable *adj* ascribend·us -a -um
attribute *s* propr·ium -(i)i *n*, qualit·as -atis *f*
attribute *tr* (at)tribuěre; *(to attribute wrongly)* affingěre
attrition *s* attrit·us -ūs *m*
attune *tr* modulari
auburn *adj* fulv·us -a -um
auction *s* aucti·o -onis *f; (by the state)* hast·a -ae *f;* **to hold an** — auctionem habēre
auction *tr* **to** —**off** auctione venděre; *(by the state)* sub hasta venděre
auctioneer *s* praec·o -onis *m*
audacious *adj* aud·ax -acis
audaciously *adv* audacter
audacity *s* audaci·a -ae *f*
audible *adj* clar·us -a -um
audibly *adv* clarā voce
audience *s* auditor·es -um *mpl*, spectator·es -um *mpl; (bystanders)* coron·a -ae *f;* **to ask for a private** — secretum petěre
audit *s* rationum inspecti·o -onis *f*
audit *tr* inspicěre
auditory *adj* auditori·us -a -um
Augean *adj* Augiae *(gen)*
auger *s* terebr·a -ae *f*
augment *tr* augēre, ampliare ‖ *intr* augēri
augmentation *s* increment·um -i *n*

augur *s* aug·ur -uris *m;* —**'s staff** litu·us -i *m*
augur *intr* augurari
augury *s* augur·ium -(i)i *n*
August *s* August·us -i *m or* mens·is -is *m* Augustus; **on the first of** — Kalendis Augustis
Augustan *adj* Augustal·is -is -e
aunt *s (pateral)* amit·a -ae *f; (maternal)* materter·a -ae *f*
auricle *s* auricul·a -ae *f*
auspices *spl* auspic·ium -(i)i *n;* **to take the** — auspicari; **under the** —**s of** sub clientela *(w. gen);* **without taking the** —**s** inauspicato
auspicious *adj* fel·ix -icis
auspiciously *adv* feliciter
austere *adj* auster·us -a -um
austerely *adv* austere
austerity *s* austerit·as -atis *f*
authentic *adj* genuin·us -a -um
authenticate *tr* recognoscěre
authenticity *s* auctorit·as -atis *f*
author *s (originator)* auct·or -oris *mf; (writer)* script·or -oris *m; (inventor)* condit·or -oris *m*
authoritative *adj* grav·is -is -e; *(reliable)* cert·us -a -um; *(imperious)* imperios·us -a -um
authority *s* auctorit·as -atis *f; (leave)* licenti·a -ae *f; (power of a magistrate)* imper·ium -(i)i *n; (expert)* auct·or -oris *m;* **on good** — gravi auctore; **the authorities** magistrat·us -uum *mpl*
authorization *s* auctorit·as -atis *f*
authorize *tr* **to** — **s.o. to** auct·or -oris *m* esse alicui *(w. gerundive)*
authorship *s (origin)* auct·or -oris *m*
autobiography *s* lib·er -ri *m* de vita sua
autocracy *s* dominati·o -onis *f*
autocrat *s* domin·us -i *m*
autocratic *adj* tyrannic·us -a -um
autograph *s* chirograph·um -i *n*
autograph *tr* manu suā scriběre
automatic *adj* automatari·us -a -um
automaton *s* automat·on -i *n*
autumn *s* autumn·us -i *m*
autumn(al) *adj* autumnal·is -is -e
auxiliaries *spl* auxili·a -orum *npl*
auxiliary *adj* auxiliar·is -is -e
avail *tr* prodesse *(w. dat);* **to** — **oneself of** uti *(w. abl);* **what do laws** —**?** quid leges faciunt? ‖ *intr* valēre
avail *s* **but to no** — sed frustra; **to be of no** — usui non esse
available *adj* in promptu
avalanche *s* nivis ruin·a -ae *f*
avarice *s* avariti·a -ae *f*
avaricious *adj* avar·us -a -um
avariciously *adv* avare
avenge *tr* ulcisci, vindicare
avenger *s* ult·or -oris *m*, vind·ex -icis *mf*
avenging *adj* ultr·ix -icis
avenue *s* vi·a -ae *f*

average *s* med·ium -(i)i *n;* **on the —** peraeque
average *adj* peraeque duct·us -a -um
average *tr (to calculate)* peraeque ducĕre; *(to amount to)* peraequare
aversion *s* fastid·ium -(i)i *n;* **to have an — for** fastidire
avert *tr* avertĕre
aviary *s* aviar·ium -(i)i *n*
avid *adj* avid·us -a -um
avidly *adv* avide
avocation *s* stud·ium -(i)i *n*
avoid *tr* evitare; *(a blow)* declinare
avoidable *adj* evitabil·is -is -e
avoidance *s* vitati·o -onis *f*
avow *tr* fateri
avowal *s* confessi·o -onis *f*
avowedly *adv* ex professo
await *tr* exspectare, manēre
awake *adj* vigil·ans -antis, desomn·is -is -e; **to be —** vigilare
awaken *tr* somno excitare ‖ *intr* expergisci
award *s* praem·ium -(i)i *n*
award *tr* tribuĕre; *(leg)* addicĕre
aware *adj* gnar·us -a -um; **to be — of** scire
awareness *s* conscienti·a -ae *f*
away *adv use verbs with prefix* ab-; **— with you!** abi hinc!; **far —** procul; **to be —** abesse; **to fly —** avolare; **to go —** abire
awe *s* reverenti·a -ae *f;* **to stand in — of** verēri
aweful *adj* terribil·is -is -e
awefully *adv* terribiliter
awesome *adj* verend·us -a -um
awhile *adv* paulisper, aliquamdiu
awkward *adj* inept·us -a -um; *(unwieldly)* inhabil·is -is -e
awkwardly *adv* inepte
awkwardness *s* inepti·a -ae *f*
awl *s* subul·a -ae *f*
awning *s* velar·ium -(i)i *n*
awry *adv* oblique; **to go —** perquam evenire
ax *s* secur·is -is *f*
axiom *s* proloqu·ium -(i)i *n*
axis *s* ax·is -is *m*
axle *s* ax·is -is *m*
azure *adj* caerule·us -a -um

B

baa *s* balat·us -ūs *m*
baa *intr* balare
babble *s* garrulit·as -atis *f*
babble *intr* blatire; **to — on about** effutire
babbler *s* blater·o -onis *m*
babbling *adj* garrul·us -a -um
babe *s* inf·ans -antis *mf*
baboon *s* cynocephal·us -i *m*
baby *s* inf·ans -antis *mf*
baby *tr* indulgēre *(w. dat)*
babyish *adj* infantil·is -is -e

bacchanal *s* bacch·ans -antis *m,* bacch·a -ae *f*
Bacchanalia *spl* bacchanal·ia -ium *npl*
bacchanalian *adj* bacchanal·is -is -e
Bacchic *adj* bacchic·us -a -um
Bacchus *s* Bacch·us -i *m*
bachelor *s* caeleb·s -is *m; (degree)* bacchelaure·us -i *m*
bachelorhood *s* caelibat·us -ūs *m*
back *s* terg·um -i *n,* dors·um -i *n;* **at one's —** a tergo; **— of the classroom** posterior par·s -tis *f* scholae; **lying on one's —** resupin·us -a -um; **to climb on his —** super dorsum ejus ascendĕre; **to turn one's —** on contemnĕre
back *adv* retro, retrorsum; *or use verbs with prefix* re- *or* retro-
back *tr* favēre *(w. dat)* ‖ *intr* **to — away from** refugĕre; **to — down** recedĕre; **to — out** se recipĕre; **to — up** retrogradi; *(of water)* refluĕre
backbite *tr* **— a friend** amicum absentem rodĕre
backbiting *s* mors·us -ūs *m*
backbiter *s* maledic·us -i *m*
backboard *s* plute·us -i *m*
backbone *s* spin·a -ae *f*
back door *s* postic·um -i *n*
backer *s* faut·or -oris *m; (pol)* suffragat·or -oris *m*
background *s (in paintings)* abscedent·ia -ium *npl; (causes)* ort·ūs -ūs *m; (of a person)* prior aet·as -atis *f*
backside *s (anat)* clun·es -ium *mpl*
backstairs *spl* posticae scal·ae -arum *fpl*
backward *adv* retro, retrorsum
backward *adj (reversed)* supin·us -a -um; *(slow)* tard·us -a -um; **to be —** cunctari
backwardness *s* tardit·as -atis *f*
bacon *s* lard·us -i *m;* **to bring home the —** habēre panem
bad *adj* mal·us -a -um; *(usu. morally bad)* improb·us -a -um; *(health, weather)* advers·us -a -um; *(harmful)* noxi·us -a -um; *(road)* iniqu·us -a -um; *(rotten)* putid·us -a -um; **— news** acerbum nunt·ium -(i)i *n;* **it is — to** *(w. inf)* alienum est *(w. inf);* **to go —** corrumpi; **wine is — for you** alienum tibi vinum est
badge *s* insign·e -is *n*
badger *s* mel·es -is *f*
badger *tr* vexare
badly *adv* male; improbe; **to want —** valde cupĕre
badness *s* maliti·a -ae *f; (moral)* improbit·as -atis *f*
baffle *tr* eludĕre
bag *s* sacc·us -i *m; (dim.)* saccul·us -i *m*
baggage *s* sarcin·ae -arum *fpl; (mil)* impediment·a -orum *npl*
bail *s* vadimon·ium -(i)i *n;* **to be out on —** vadari; **to put up — for** spondēre pro *(w. abl)*

bail *tr* **to — s.o. out** *(leg)* aliquem vadari; *(fig)* aliquem e periculo servare; **to — out the boat** sentinam e navicula egerĕre; **to — out water** sentinam egerĕre

bailiff *s (in a courtroom)* viat·or -oris *m; (manager of an estate)* villic·us -i *m*

bailiwick *s* jurisdicti·o -onis *f*

bait *s* esc·a -ae *f; (fig)* incitament·um -i *n;* **to put the — on the hook** escam hamo imponĕre

bait *tr* inescare; *(to tease)* lacessĕre

bake *tr* coquĕre

baker *s* pist·or -oris *m,* pistr·ix -icis *f*

bakery *s* pistrin·a -ae *f*

balance *s (pair of scales)* trutin·a -ae *f; (equilibrium)* aequilibr·ium -(i)i *n; (in bookkeeping)* reliqu·a -orum *npl; (fig)* compensati·o -onis *f*

balance *tr* librare; **to — accounts** rationes dispungĕre; **to — joy with grief** laetitiam cum doloribus compensare **‖** *intr* constare; **the account —s** ratio constat

balance sheet *s* rati·o -onis *f* accepti et expensi

balancing *s* — **of accounts** dispuncti·o -onis *f*

balcony *s* maenian·um -i *n*

bald *adj* calv·us -a -um; *(style)* arid·us -a -um; **to be —** calvēre

baldness *s* calvit·ium -(i)i *n; (of style)* aridit·as -atis *f*

bale *s* fasc·is -is *m*

bale *tr (hay)* in fasces colligĕre

baleful *adj* pernicios·us -a -um

balk *s (of wood)* tign·um -i *n*

balk *tr* frustrari

ball *s* globul·us -i *m; (for playing)* pil·a -ae *f;* —**s** *(anat) (sl) (lit & fig)* cole·i -orum *mpl;* **to play —** pilā ludĕre

ballad *s* carm·en -inis *n*

ballast *s* saburr·a -ae *f*

ballast *tr* saburrare

ballet *s* pantomim·us -i *m*

ballet dancer *s* pantomim·us -i *m,* pantomim·a -ae *f*

ballot *s* suffrag·ium -(i)i *n;* **to cast a —** suffragium ferre

ballot box *s* cist·a -ae *f*

balm *s* balsam·um -i *n*

bamboo *s* arund·o -inis *f* Indica

ban *s* interdict·um -i *n*

ban *tr* interdicĕre

banana *s* arien·a -ae *f*

band *s (group)* man·us -ūs *f; (gang)* caterv·a -ae *f; (for the head)* inful·a -ae *f; (of musicians)* symphoni·a -ae *f*

band *intr* **to — together** conjungi; *(pej)* conjurare

bandage *s* fasci·a -ae *f*

bandage *tr (a wound)* astringĕre; *(an arm, etc.)* deligare

bandit *s* latr·o -onis *m*

banditry *s* latrocin·ium -(i)i *n*

bandy *tr* **to — words with s.o.** sermonem serĕre *(w. dat)*

bane *s (fig)* pest·is -is *f*

baneful *adj* pestifer·us -a -um

bang *s* sonit·us -ūs *m*

bang *tr* verberare; **to — together** concrepare **‖** *intr* sonitum facĕre; **to — on the door** fores pulsare

bangle *s* circul·us -i *m*

banish *tr (from the confines of a state)* exterminare; *(usual formula in time of Cicero)* aquā et igni interdicĕre; *(temporarily)* relegare; *(to some island)* deportare; *(cares, etc.)* pellĕre

banishment *s (act)* relegati·o -onis *f,* interdicti·o -onis *f* aquā et igni; *(state)* exil·ium -(i)i *n*

banister *s* epimed·ion -(i)i *n*

bank *intr* **to — on** niti *(w. abl)*

bank *s (of river)* rip·a -ae *f; (of earth)* agg·er -eris *m; (com)* argentari·a -ae *f*

banker *s* argentar·ius -(i)i *m*

banking *s* argentaria negotiati·o -onis *f;* **to be engaged in —** argentariam facĕre

bankrupt *s (person)* decoct·or -oris *m;* **to be —** decoquĕre; **to go —** foro cedĕre, conturbare

bankruptcy *s* decocti·o -onis *f*

banner *s* vexill·um -i *n*

banquet *s* conviv·ium -(i)i *n; (religious)* epul·ae -arum *fpl;* **to go to** *or* **attend a —** convivium inire

banter *s* cavillati·o -onis *f*

banter *intr* cavillari

bantering *s* cavillati·o -onis *f*

baptism *s* baptism·a -atis *n*

baptize *tr* baptizare

bar *s* vect·is -is *f; (of door)* ser·a -ae *f; (of gate)* ob·ex -icis *m; (ingot)* lat·er -eris *m; (legal profession)* for·um -i *n;* —**s** *(of a cage)* clathr·i -orum *mpl;* **of the —** forens·is -is -e; **to practice at the —** causas agĕre

bar *tr (the door)* obserare; *(to keep away)* prohibēre; **to — s.o. from campaigning** submovēre aliquem petitione; **to — s.o.'s way** obstare alicui

barb *s* ham·us -i *m; (sting)* acule·us -i *m*

barbarian *adj* barbar·us -a -um

barbarian *s* barbar·us -i *m,* barbar·a -ae *f*

barbaric *adj* barbaric·us -a -um

barbarism *s* barbari·a -ae *f; (in speech)* barbarism·us -i *m*

barbarity *s* ferocit·as -atis *f*

barbarous *adj* barbar·us -a -um

barbed *adj* hamat·us -a -um

barber *s* tons·or -oris *m,* tonstr·ix -icis *f*

barbershop *s* tonstrin·a -ae *f*

bard *s* vat·es -is *m*

bare *adj* nud·us -a -um; *(style)* press·us -a -um

bare *tr* nudare

barefaced *adj (shameless)* impud·ens

-entis; *(unconcealed)* evidentissim·us -a -um

barefoot *adj & adv* nudis pedibus

bareheaded *adj* nudo capite

barely *adv* vix, aegre

bargain *s* pact·um -i *n;* **a good —** empti·o -onis *f* secunda; **to buy at a —** bene eměre; **to strike a —** pacisci

bargain *intr* pascisci; **to — for** depacisci

barge *s* lint·er -ris *f*

barge *intr* **to — in** *(coll)* intervenire

bark *s (of tree)* cort·ex -icis *m; (of dog)* latrat·us -ūs *m; (ship)* rat·is -is *f*

bark *intr* latrare; **to — at** allatrare

barking *s* latrat·us -ūs *m*

barley *s* horde·um -i *n*

barley *adj* hordeac·us -a -um; **— flour** hordeaca farin·a -ae *f*

barmaid *s* cauponae ministr·a -ae *f*

barn *s* horre·um -i *n*

barnyard *s* cohor·s -tis *f*

barometer *s* barometr·um -i *n*

barometric *adj* barometric·us -a -um

baron *s* bar·o -onis *m*

baroness *s* baroniss·a -ae *f*

barracks *spl* castr·a -orum *npl* stativa

barrel *s* cup·a -ae *f*

barrel hoop *s* circul·us -i *m* de cupa

barren *adj* steril·is -is -e

barrenness *s* sterilit·as -atis *f*

barricade *s* claustr·a -orum *npl,* agg·er -eris *m; (of logs)* concaed·es -ium *fpl*

barricade *tr* obsaepire

barrier *s* sept·um -i *n; (fig)* claustr·a -orum *npl*

barrister *s* causidic·us -i *m*

barter *s* permutati·o -onis *f* mercium

barter *tr* mutare *(w. acc of thing given and abl of thing received);* **to — booty for wine** praedam vino mutare ‖ *intr* **(with)** merces mutare (cum + *abl)*

base *adj* humil·is -is -e; *(morally)* turp·is -is -e; *(coinage)* adulterin·us -a -um

base *s (groundwork; of a column)* bas·is -is *f; (mil)* castr·a -orum *npl*

base *tr* fundare; **to — the country on laws** civitatem legibus fundare

baseless *adj* van·us -a -um

basement *s* cell·a -ae *f*

baseness *s* turpitud·o -inis *f*

bash *tr (coll)* percutěre; **to — in** perfringěre; **to — in a man's head** alicui caput perfringěre

bashful *adj* verecund·us -a -um

bashfully *adv* verecunde

bashfulness *s* verecundi·a -ae *f*

basic *adj* prim·us -a -um

basilica *s* basilic·a -ae *f*

basin *s* pelv·is -is *f; (reservoir)* labr·um -i *n*

basis *s* bas·is -is *f*

bask *intr* **to — in the sun** apricari

basket *s* corb·is -is *f; (money basket)* fisc·us -i *m; (for flowers, fruit)* calath·us -i *m;*

(small food basket) sportell·a -ae *f*

bas-relief *s* anaglypt·a -orum *npl; (on plates, vessels)* toreum·a -atis *n*

bass *s (fish)* perc·a -ae *f* fluvialis; *(mus)* son·us -i *m* gravissimus; **to sing —** voce imā cantare

bassinet *s* cun·ae -arum *fpl*

bastard *adj* spuri·us -a -um

bastard *s* noth·us -i *m*

baste *tr* lardo perfunděre; *(in sewing)* suturam *(w. gen)* solute suěre

bastion *s* propugnacul·um -i *n*

bat *s (bird)* vespertili·o -onis *m; (club)* clav·a -ae *f*

batch *s* mass·a -ae *f; (pile)* cumul·us -i *m*

bath *s* balne·um -i *n; (public)* balne·a -orum *npl; (bath and community center)* therm·ae -arum *fpl;* **to take a cold (hot) —** frigidā (calidā) aquā lavari

bathe *tr* lavare; *(face, sore limb)* fověre ‖ *intr* lavari

bather *s* qui lavat; *(swimmer)* natat·or -oris *m;* **—s** lavant·es -ium *mpl*

bathing *s* lavati·o -onis *f; (swimming)* natati·o -onis *f*

bathroom *s* balneol·um -i *n; (toilet)* latrin·a -ae *f*

bathtub *s* sol·ium -(i)i *n*

baton *s* virg·a -ae *f*

battalion *s* cohor·s -tis *f*

batter *s* farin·a -ae *f* lacte ovisque mixta

batter *tr* verberare; *(to shake by battering)* percutěre; **to — down** ariete dejicěre

battering ram *s* ari·es -etis *m*

battle *s (general & mil)* pugn·a -ae *f; (mil)* proel·ium -(i)i *n*

battle *tr* certare ‖ *intr* proeliari

battle-ax *s* bipenn·is -is *f*

battle-cry *s* clam·or -oris *m* militum; *(of barbarians)* barit·us -ūs *m*

battlefield *s* loc·us -i *m* pugnae, aci·es -ei *f*

battle formation *s* aci·es -ei *f*

battlement *s* pinn·a -ae *f*

baubles *spl* tric·ae -arum *fpl*

bawd *s* len·a -ae *f*

bawdy *adj* obscen·us -a -um

bawl *intr* clamitare; *(to cry)* flēre; *(of babies)* vagire

bawling *s* vociferati·o -onis *f; (crying)* flet·us -ūs *m; (by a baby)* vagit·us -ūs *m*

bay *s (of the sea)* sin·us -ūs *m; (tree)* laur·us -i *f;* **at —** obsess·us -a -um; **to keep at —** arcēre

bay *adj (light-colored)* helv·us -a -um; *(horse)* spad·ix -icis; *(of bay tree)* laure·us -a -um

bay *intr* ululare

bayonet *s* pugi·o -onis *m*

bayonet *tr* pugione foděre

bazaar *s* for·um -i *n* rerum venalium

be *intr* esse; *(of a situation)* se habēre, versari; **— gone!** apage!; **that is the situation** sic res se habent; **to — absent**

abesse; **to — against** adversari; **to — among** interesse *(w. dat)*; **to — for** favēre *(w. dat)*, stare cum *(w. abl)*; **to — present** adesse, interesse

beach *s* act·a -ae *f*, lit·us -oris *n*

beach *tr (a ship)* subducĕre

beacon *s* ign·is -is *m* in specula; *(lighthouse)* phar·us -i *f*

bead *s* bac·a -ae *f*

beagle *s* parvus can·is -is *m* venaticus

beak *s* rostr·um -i *n*

beaked *adj* rostrat·us -a -um

beaker *s (cup)* pocul·um -i *n; (decanter)* obb·a -ae *f*

beam *s (of wood)* trab·s -is *f; (of light)* jub·ar -aris *n; (ray)* rad·ius -(i)i *m*

beaming *adj* nit·ens -entis

bean *s* fab·a -ae *f; (kidney bean)* phasel·us -i *mf*

bear *tr (to carry)* portare, ferre; *(to endure)* ferre, pati; *(to produce)* ferre; *(to beget)* parĕre; **to — away** auferre; **to — in mind** recordari; **to — out** *(to confirm)* arguĕre; **to — witness** testari ‖ *intr* **to — down on** *(to approach)* appropinquare *(w. dat); (to press)* inniti in *(w. acc); (to oppress)* opprimĕre; **to — with** indulgēre *(w. dat)*

bear *s* urs·us -i *m*, urs·a -ae *f*

bearable *adj* tolerabil·is -is -e

beard *s* barb·a -ae *f; (of grain)* arist·a -ae *f;* **to cut his first —** barbatorium facĕre; **to grow a —** barbam summittĕre

bearded *adj* barbat·us -a -um

beardless *adj* inberb·is -is -e

bearer *s (porter)* bajul·us -i *m; (of litter)* lecticar·ius -(i)i *m; (of letter)* tabellar·ius -(i)i *m; (of news)* nunt·ius -(i)i *m*

bearing *s (posture)* gest·us -ūs *m; (direction)* regi·o -onis *f;* **to get one's —s** regionem reperire; **to have a — on** pertinēre ad *(w. acc)*

beast *s* besti·a -ae *f*, belu·a -ae *f; (brutish person)* belu·a -ae *f*

beastly *adj* beluin·us -a -um

beast of burden *s* jument·um -i *n*

beat *tr (to punish)* verberare; *(to knock on)* pulsare; *(to conquer)* vincĕre; *(the breast, drum)* plangĕre; **to — back** repellĕre; **to — down** demoliri; **to — in** perfringĕre; **to — the daylights out of** pulchre percopolare ‖ *intr* palpitare; **to — upon** *(of rain)* impluĕre in *(w. acc); (of waves)* illidĕre; **to — around the bush** circuitu uti, schemas loqui

beat *s (blow)* plag·a -ae *f*, ict·us -ūs *m; (of the heart)* palpitati·o -onis *f; (mus)* ict·us -ūs *m; (patrol area)* circuiti·o -onis *f*

beaten *adj (defeated)* vict·us -a -um; *(worn)* trit·us -a -um

beating *s* verberati·o -onis *f; (defeat)* repuls·a -ae *f; (of the heart)* palpitati·o -onis *f;* **to get a —** vapulare

beautiful *adj* pul·cher -chra -chrum; *(shapely)* formos·us -a -um

beautifully *adv* pulchre

beautify *tr* ornare

beauty *s* pulchritud·o -inis *f*

beaver *s* fi·ber -bri *m*

beaver skin *s* pell·is -is *f* fibrina

because *conj* quod, quia, quoniam

because of *prep* ob, propter *(w. acc)*

beck *s* nut·us -ūs *m;* **at the — and call** ad arbitrium

beckon *tr* nutu vocare

become *tr* decēre ‖ *intr* fieri; **to — friends with me once again** in gratiam mecum redire

becoming *adj* dec·ens -entis

becomingly *adv* decenter

bed *s* lect·us -i *m; (in the garden)* areol·a -ae *f; (of a river)* alve·us -i *m;* **to go to —** cubitum ire; **to make the —** lectum sternĕre

bedaub *tr* oblinĕre

bedbug *s* sciniph·is -is *m*

bedding *s* stragul·um -i *n*

bedeck *tr* ornare

bedevil *tr (to enchant)* fascinare

bedfellow *s* soc·ius -(i)i *m* lecti

bedlam *s* tumult·us -ūs *m*

bedpost *s* fulcr·um -i *n*

bedraggled *adj* sordid·us -a -um

bedridden *adj* valetudinari·us -a -um; **to be —** lecto tenēri

bedroom *s* cubicul·um -i *n*

bedstead *s* spond·a -ae *f*

bedtime *s* hor·a -ae *f* somni

bee *s* ap·is -is *f*

beech tree *s* fag·us -i *f*

beef *s* bubul·a *f*

beefsteak *s* frust·um -i *n* bubulum

beehive *s* alve·us -i *m*

beekeeper *s* apiar·ius -(i)i *m*

beeline *s* **to make a — for** directā viā contendĕre ad *(w. acc)*

beer *s* cerevisi·a -ae *f*

beet *s* bet·a -ae *f*

beetle *s* scarabae·us -i *m*

befall *tr* contingĕre *(w. dat)* ‖ *intr* accidĕre, contingĕre

befit *tr* decēre

befitting *adj* dec·ens -entis; **it is —** decet

before *prep (in front of)* ante *(w. acc)*, pro *(w. abl); (in time)* ante *(w. acc); (in the presence of)* coram *(w. abl); (leg)* apud *(w. acc);* **— all things** imprimis; **— long** jamdudum; **— now** antehac

before *conj* antequam, priusquam

beforehand *adv* antea

befoul *tr* inquinare

befriend *tr* in amicitiam recipĕre

beg *tr* petĕre, orare ‖ *intr* mendicare; **to — for** deprecari; *(alms)* mendicare; **to — s.o. to** aliquem deprecari ut *(w. subj);* **to — from door to door** ostiatim mendicare

beget *tr* gignĕre

beggar *s* mendic·us -i *m*

begging *s* mendicit·as -atis *f;* **to go —** mendicare

begin *tr & intr* incipĕre; *(without finishing)* inchoare; *(to initiate)* instituĕre; **to — with** primum (omnium)

beginner *s* tir·o -onis *m*

beginning *s (the act of starting)* incepti·o -onis *f; (the start itself)* init·ium -(i)i *n; (origin)* orig·o -inis *f;* **at the — of winter** ineunte *or* primā hieme; **in the —** inter initia; **—s** principi·a -orum *npl*

begrudge *tr* **to — my enemy his victory** amici victoriae invidēre

beguile *tr* fraudare

behalf *s* **on — of** pro *(w. abl)*

behave *intr* se gerĕre; **to — toward** uti *(w. abl);* **well-behaved** bene morat·us -a -um

behavior *s* mor·es -um *mpl;* **your — towards me was unfriendly** inimice te in me gessisti

behead *tr* decollare

beheading *s* decollati·o -onis *f*

behest *s* juss·um -i *n*

behind *adv* pone, a tergo; **to be left —** relinqui

behind *prep* post *(w. acc); (esp. w. verbs of motion)* pone *(w. acc); (in support)* pro *(w. abl);* **from —** a tergo; **to talk about a friend — his back** absentem amicum rodĕre

behind *s (coll)* clun·es -ium *mpl*

behold *tr* conspicĕre

behold *interj* ecce!, en!

behoove *tr* **it behooves you to** *(w. inf)* oportet te *(w. inf)*

beige *adj* rav·us -a -um

being *s* en·s -tis *n;* **human —** hom·o -inis *m*

bejewelled *adj* gemmat·us -a -um

belabor *tr (to thrash)* verberare; *(to harp on)* cantare

belch *s* ruct·us -ūs *m*

belch *tr* **to — forth** eructare **‖** *intr* ructare

beleaguer *tr* obsidēre

belfry *s* turr·is -is *f* campanis instructa

belie *tr (to prove false)* refellĕre; *(to disappoint)* frustrari; *(to disguise)* dissimulare

belief *s* fid·es -ei *f; (conviction) (in)* opini·o -onis *f (w. gen or de + abl)*

believe *tr (thing)* credĕre; *(person)* credĕre *(w. dat); (to suppose)* existimare; **to make —** simulare

believer *s* cred·ens -entis *mf*

bell *s (large)* campan·a -ae *f; (small)* tintinnabul·um -i *n*

belle *s* bella puell·a -ae *f*

belles-lettres *spl* litter·ae -arum *fpl* exquisitiores

belligerent *adj (at war)* belliger·ans -antis; *(scrappy)* pugn·ax -acis

bellow *intr* mugire

bellow *s* mugit·us -ūs *m*

bellows *spl* foll·is -is *m*

bell pepper *s* pip·er -eris *n* rotundum

bell tower *s* turr·is -is *f* campanis instructa

belly *s* ven·ter -tris *m; (womb)* uter·us -i *m*

bellyache *s* tormin·a -um *npl;* **to have a —** dolēre a torminibus

belong *intr* **to — to** esse *(w. dat); (to be related)* pertinēre ad *(w. acc); (to be a member of)* in numero *(w. gen)* esse

belongings *spl* bon·a -orum *npl*

below *adj* infer·us -a -um

below *adv* infra

below *prep* infra *(w. acc)*

belt *s* cingul·um -i *n; (of women's clothes)* zon·a -ae *f; (sword belt)* balte·us -i *m; (area)* zon·a -ae *f;* **to tighten one's —** sumptui parcĕre

bemoan *tr* deplorare

bench *s* scamn·um -i *n; (esp. for senators and judges)* subsell·ium -(i)i *n; (for rowers)* transtr·um -i *n*

bend *tr* flectĕre, curvare; *(to cause to lean)* inclinare; *(the bow)* intendĕre, flectĕre; *(to persuade)* inflectĕre; **to — back** reflectĕre; **to — down** deflectĕre **‖** *intr (e.g., of iron)* se inflectĕre; *(to give in)* cedĕre; **to — down** *or* **over** *(to stoop)* se inclinare, se demittĕre

bend *s* curvam·en -inis *n;* **— in the road** flex·us -ūs *m* viae

bending *s* inclinati·o -onis *f*

beneath *adv* subter

beneath *prep* sub *(w. acc or abl);* **he thinks these matters are — him** arbitratur has res infra se positas

benediction *s* benedicti·o -onis *f*

benefaction *s* benefic·ium -(i)i *n*

benefactor *s* largit·or -oris *m,* patron·us -i *m*

benefactress *s* patron·a -ae *f*

beneficence *s* beneficenti·a -ae *f*

beneficent *adj* benefi·cus -a -um

beneficial *adj* util·is -is -e, commod·us -a -um; **to be —** prodesse

benefit *s (deed)* benefic·ium -(i)i *n; (advantage)* commod·um -i *n;* **to have the — of** frui *(w. abl);* **to whose — is it?** cui bono est?

benefit *tr* prodesse *(w. dat),* juvare **‖** *intr* proficĕre; *(financially)* lucrari; **to — from** utilitatem capĕre ex *(w. abl)*

benevolence *s* benevolenti·a -ae *f*

benevolent *adj* benevol·us -a -um

benevolently *adv* benevole

benign *adj* benign·us -a -um

benignly *adv* benigne

bent *adj* flex·us -a -um, curv·us -a -um; **— backwards** recurv·us -a -um; **— forwards** pron·us -a -um; **— inwards** camur·us -a -um; **— on** *(fig)* attent·us -a -um ad *(w. acc)*

bent *s* curvatur·a -ae *f; (inclination)* inclinati·o -onis *f*

benumb *tr* torpore afficĕre
bequeath *tr* legare
bequest *s* legat·um -i *n*
bereave *tr* orbare
bereavement *s* orbit·as -atis *f*
bereft *adj* — **of** orbat·us -a -um *(w. abl or gen)*
berry *s* bac·a -ae *f*
berth *s (cabin)* diaet·a -ae *f; (space for ship at anchor)* stati·o -onis *f;* **to give wide** — **to** devitare
beseech *tr* obsecrare
beset *tr* urgēre; *(mil)* obsidēre
beside *prep* ad *(w. acc)*, juxta *(w. acc);* — **the point** nihil ad rem; **to be** — **oneself** delirare; **to sit** — **s.o.** assidēre alicui; **to walk** — **s.o.** alicui latus tegĕre
besides *adv* praeterea, ultro
besides *prep* praeter *(w. acc)*
besiege *tr* obsidēre; *(fig)* circumsedēre
besmirch *tr* inquinare
best *adj* optim·us -a -um; *(most advantageous)* commodissim·us -a -um; **it is** — **to** optimum est *(w. inf)*, maxime prodest *(w. inf)*
best *s* flo·s -ris *f;* **to do one's** — pro virili parte agĕre; **to have the** — **of it** praevalēre; **to make the** — **of it** aequo animo ferre; **to the** — **of one's ability** pro viribus
best *tr* exsuperare
bestial *adj* bestial·is -is -e
bestir *tr (to move)* ciēre; **to** — **oneself** *(to wake up)* expergisci
best man *s* pronub·us -i *m*
bestow *tr (on)* tribuĕre, deferre *(w. dat)*
bestowal *s* largiti·o -onis *f*
bestower *s* largit·or -oris *m*
bet *s* sponsi·o -onis *f;* **to lose a** — sponsionis condemnari; **to win a** — sponsione vincĕre
bet *tr* ponĕre; **to** — **that…** sponsionem facĕre *(& acc + inf)*
betide *intr* evenire
betoken *tr* portendĕre
betray *tr* prodĕre; *(feelings)* arguĕre
betrayer *s* prodit·or -oris *m*
betroth *tr* despondēre
betrothal *s* sponsal·ia -ium *npl*
betrothed *adj* spons·us -a -um
better *adj* mel·ior -ior -ius; *(preferable)* praestant·ior -ior -ius; — **half** *(fig)* alter·a -ae *f;* **for the** — in melius; **it is** — **to** *(w. inf)* commodius est *(w. inf);* **to be** — *(in health)* melius esse; **to get** — convalescĕre; **to get the** — **of** praevalēre *(w. abl)*
better *adv* melius, potius
better *tr* meliorem *(or* melius*)* facĕre, corrigĕre; **to** — **oneself** proficĕre
betterment *s* correcti·o -onis *f*
betters *spl* melior·es -um *mpl*
between *prep* inter *(w. acc)*

betwixt *prep* inter *(w. acc)*
bevel *tr* obliquare
beverage *s* pot·us -ūs *m*
bevy *s* gre·x -gis *m*
bewail *tr* deplorare
beware *intr* cavēre; **to** — **of** cavēre
bewilder *tr* confundĕre
bewildered *adj* confus·us -a -um
bewilderment *s* confusi·o -onis *f*
bewitch *tr* fascinare; *(to charm)* demulcēre
beyond *adv* ultra
beyond *prep* ultra *(w. acc)*, extra *(w. acc); (motion)* trans *(w. acc);* **to go** — **the limits** egredi extra terminos
bias *s (prejudice)* inclinati·o -onis *f; (line)* line·a -ae *f* obliqua
bias *tr* inclinare
Bible *s* Bibli·a -orum *npl*
Biblical *adj* Biblic·us -a -um
bibliography *s* bibliographi·a -ae *f*
bicker *intr* altercari
bickering *s* altercati·o -onis *f*
bid *tr (to order)* jubēre; *(to invite)* invitare; *(at auction)* licitari; **to** — **farewell** valedicĕre
bid *s* licitati·o -onis *f;* **to make a** — licitationem facĕre
bidder *s* licitat·or -oris *m*
bidding *s (command)* juss·um -i *n; (at auction)* licitati·o -onis *f;* **at his** — jussu ejus; **to do s.o.'s** — jussum alicujus exsequi
bide *tr* **to** — **one's time** tempus idoneum opperiri
biennial *adj* biennial·is -is -e
bier *s* feretr·um -i *n; (euphem)* vitalis lect·us -i *m*
big *adj* magn·us -a -um, ing·ens -entis; — **with child** gravida; — **with young** praegn·ans -antis
bigamist *s* bimarit·us -i *m*
bigamy *s* bigami·a -ae *f*
big mouth *s* **to be a** — *(coll)* durae buccae esse
bigot *s* qui suae opinioni nimium fidit
bigoted *adj* obstinate suae opinioni de partibus *(or* de religione *or* de genere*)* dedit·us -a -um
bigotry *s* nimia suae de partibus *(or* de religione *or* de genere*)* opinioni fiduci·a -ae *f*
bile *s* bil·is -is *f*
bilge water *s* sentin·a -ae *f*
bilious *adj* bilios·us -a -um
bilk *tr* fraudare
bill *s (of bird)* rostr·um -i *n; (proposed law)* rogati·o -onis *f; (com)* rati·o -onis *f* debiti; — **of indictment** subscripti·o -onis *f;* **to introduce a** — legem ferre; **to pass a** — legem perferre; **to turn down a** — legem *or* rogationem antiquare
billet *s* hospit·ium -(i)i *n*
billion *s* billi·o -onis *f*

billow s fluct·us -ūs m
billowy adj fluctuos·us -a -um
bin s (in wine cellar) locul·us -i m; (for grain) lac·us -ūs m
bind tr ligare; (wounds) stringĕre; (to obligate) obligare; (books) conglutinare; **to — fast** devincĕre; **to — together** colligare; **to — up** alligare; (med) astringĕre
binding adj obligatori·us -a -um; (law) rat·us -a -um
binding s religati·o -onis f
binoculars spl binocular·es -um mpl
biographer s vitae script·or -oris m
biography s vit·a -ae f
biology s biologi·a -ae f
biologist s biologic·us -i m
biped s bip·es -edis m
birch adj betulin·us -a -um
birch tree s betul·a -ae f
bird s av·is -is f; **—s of a feather flock together** pares cum paribus facillime congregantur
birdcage s cave·a -ae f
birdcall s fistul·a -ae f aucupatoria
birdlime s visc·um -i n
bird's nest s nid·us -i m
birth s part·us -ūs m; (lineage) gen·us -eris n
birthday s di·es -ei m natalis
birthday cake s lib·um -i n
birthday party s natalici·a -ae f
birthplace s patri·a -ae f
birthright s ju·s -ris n e genere ortum
biscuit s crustul·um -i n
bisect tr in duas partes aequales secare
bishop s episcop·us -i m
bison s bis·on -ontis m
bit s (for horse) fren·um -i n; (small amount) aliquantul·um -i n; (of food) off·a -ae f; **a — of peace** aliquid quietis; **— by —** minutatim; **to cut to —s** minutatim secare
bitch s can·is -is f
bite s mors·us -ūs m; (by an insect) ict·us -ūs m
bite tr mordēre; (of pepper, frost) urĕre; (of an insect) icĕre
biting adj (apt to bite) mord·ax -acis; (cutting) asp·er -era -erum
bitter adj (lit & fig) amar·us -a -um; (hatred) asp·er -era -erum (painful, sharp) acerb·us -a -um; **— taste in the mouth** amarum o·s -ris n
bitterly adv (denoting wounded feeling) amare; (implying anger or harshness) aspere; (implying hostility) infense
bitterness s amarit·as -atis f; (fig) acerbit·as -atis f; (wounded feeling) amaritud·o -inis f
bitters spl absinth·ium -(i)i n
bivouac s excubi·ae -arum fpl
bivouac intr excubare

blab tr blaterare; **to — out** effutire ‖ intr deblaterare
black adj (shiny black) ni·ger -gra -grum; (dull black) a·ter -tra -trum; (looks) tru·x -cis
black s (color) nigr·um -i n; (person) Aethi·ops -opis m; **dressed in —** pullat·us -a -um
black-and-blue adj livid·us -a -um; **— mark** liv·or -oris m
blackberry s mor·um -i n
blackbird s merul·a -ae f
blacken tr nigrare
black eye s ocul·us -i m sugillatus
blacklist s proscripti·o -onis f
blacklist tr proscribĕre
black magic s magicae art·es -ium fpl
blackness s nigriti·a -ae f
blacksmith s ferrarius fa·ber -bri m
bladder s vesic·a -ae f
blade s (edge) lamin·a -ae f; (of grass) herb·a -ae f; (of oar) palm·a -ae f
blamable adj culpabil·is -is -e
blame tr improperare (w. dat), culpare; **you are to —** in culpā es
blame s culp·a -ae f
blameless adj inte·ger -gra -grum
blame-worthy adj vituperabil·is -is -e
blanch tr candefacĕre ‖ intr exalbescĕre, pallescĕre
bland adj bland·us -a -um; (food) len·is -is -e
blandishment s blanditi·a -ae f
blank adj inan·is -is -e; (expression) stolid·us -a -um
blanket s lod·ix -icis f; (dim.) lodicul·a -ae f
blare s strepit·us -ūs m
blare intr strepere
blaspheme tr blasphemare
blasphemous adj blasphem·us -a -um
blasphemy s blasphemi·a -ae f
blast s (of wind) flam·en -inis n; (of musical instrument) flat·us -ūs m; **— of wind** flat·us -ūs m
blast tr discutĕre
blaze s (glare) fulg·or -oris m; (fire) incend·ium -(i)i n; **go to —s** (coll) i in malam crucem!
blaze tr **to — a trail** semitam notare ‖ intr ardēre; **fires were —ing** ignes flagrabant; **to — up** exardescĕre
bleach tr dealbare
bleachers spl sedil·ia -ium npl lignea
bleak adj immit·is -is -e; (outlook, hope) incommod·us -a -um
bleary-eyed adj lipp·us -a -um; **to be —** lippire
bleat intr balare
bleating s balat·us -ūs m
bleed intr sanguinem fundĕre
bleeding adj crud·us -a -um
bleeding s sanguinis profusi·o -onis f; (bloodletting) sanguinis missi·o -onis f

blemish *s (flaw)* vit·ium -(i)i *n; (on the body)* mend·um -i *n; (moral)* macul·a -ae *f*
blemish *tr* maculare
blend *tr* commiscēre; **to — in** immiscēre **ll** *intr* **to — in with** se immiscēre *(w. dat)*
blend *s* mixtur·a -ae *f; (proportionate)* temperi·es -ei *f*
bless *tr* beare; *(consecrate)* consecrare; *(w. success)* secundare; *(eccl)* benedicēre; **— your little heart!** di te ament!
blessed *adj* beat·us -a -um; *(of dead emperors)* div·us -a -um
blessing *s (thing)* bon·um -i *n; (eccl)* benedicti·o -onis *f*
blight *s* robig·o -inis *f; (fig)* tab·es -is *f*
blight *tr* robigine afficĕre; *(fig)* nocēre *(w. dat)*
blind *adj (lit & fig)* caec·us -a -um
blind *tr (lit & fig)* occaecare
blindfold *tr* oculos obligare *(w. dat)*
blindfolded *adj* oculis obligatis
blindly *adv* temere
blindness *s* caecit·as -atis *f*
blinds *spl (on window)* transenn·a -ae *f*
blink *intr* connivēre
bliss *s* beatitud·o -inis *f*
blissful *adj* beat·us -a -um
blissfully *adv* beate
blister *s* pustul·a -ae *f*
blister *intr* pustulare
bloated *adj* sufflat·us -a -um
block *s (of wood)* stip·es -itis *f; (of marble, stone)* mass·a -ae *f; (in a city)* vic·us -i *m; (obstruction)* impediment·um -i *n;* **— by —** vicatim
block *tr (e.g., the road)* obstruĕre; *(to choke up)* opplēre; **to — s.o.'s way** obstare alicui; **to — up** *(e.g. a window)* obstruĕre
blockade *s* obsidi·o -onis *f;* **to lift a —** obsidionem solvĕre; **to undergo a —** in obsidione teneri
blockade *tr* obsidēre
block and tackle *spl* trochle·a -ae *f*
blockhead *s* caud·ex -icis *m*
blood *s* sangu·is -inis *m; (outside the body)* cru·or -oris *m; (lineage)* gen·us -eris *n;* **to let —** sanguinem mittĕre; **there was bad — between him and Caesar** huic simultas cum Caesari intercedebat; **to stain with —** cruentare
bloodless *adj* exsangu·is -is -e; *(without bloodshed)* incruent·us -a -um
blood pressure *s* pressur·a -ae *f* sanguinis
blood-red *adj* sanguine·us -a -um
blood relative *s* consanguine·us -i *m*
bloodshed *s* caed·es -is *f*
bloodshot *adj* **— eyes** cruore suffusi ocul·i -orum *mpl*
bloodstained *adj* cruent·us -a -um
bloodsucker *s* sanguisug·a -ae *f*
bloodthirsty *adj* sanguinari·us -a -um
blood vessel *s* ven·a -ae *f*

bloody *adj* sanguine·us -a -um
bloom *s* flo·s -ris *m;* **to be in —** florid·us -a -um esse
bloom *intr* florēre; **to begin to —** florescĕre
blooming *adj* flor·ens -entis
blossom *s* flo·s -ris *m;* **to shed its —s** deflorēre
blossom *intr* florēre
blot *s* macul·a -ae *f*
blot *tr* maculare; **to — out** delēre; *(to erase)* oblit(t)erare
blotch *s (stain)* macul·a -ae *f; (on the skin)* var·us -i *m*
blotchy *adj* maculos·us -a -um
blow *s (stroke)* plag·a -ae *f; (blow which wounds)* ict·us -ūs *m; (w. the fist)* colaph·us -i *m; (fig)* plag·a -ae *f*
blow *tr* flare; *(a horn)* inflare; **to — out** *(candle)* ex(s)tinguĕre; **to — the nose** se emungĕre; **to — up** pulvere nitrato destruĕre **ll** *intr* flare; **to — over** *(of a storm)* cadĕre; **to — up** *(to get angry)* irasci
blowing *s* sufflati·o -onis *f*
blowup *s* scandal·um -i *n; (anger)* ir·a -ae *f*
blubber *s* ad·eps -ipis *m* balaenarum
blubber *intr (coll)* plorare
blue *adj* caerule·us -a -um; *(dark blue)* cyane·us -a -um; *(pale blue)* subcaerule·us -a -um; *(melancholy)* melancholic·us -a -um
blue *s* caeruleus col·or -oris *m; (concrete)* caerule·um -i *n;* **—s** melancholi·a -ae *f;* **to have the —s** melancholic·us -a -um esse
blue-grey *adj (eyes)* caesi·us -a -um
blueprint *s* form·a -ae *f*
bluff *s* rup·es -is *f; (false threat)* simulata audaci·a -ae *f*
bluff *tr* decipĕre **ll** *intr* simulatā audaciā uti
blunder *s* err·or -oris *m; (in writing)* mend·um -i *n*
blunder *intr* errare
blunderer *s* hom·o -inis *m* ineptus
blunt *adj (dull)* heb·es -itis; *(person)* inurban·us -a -um; *(speech)* impolit·us -a -um
blunt *tr* hebetare
bluntly *adv* liberius
bluntness *s* hebetud·o -inis *f; (fig)* rusticit·as -atis *f*
blur *s* macul·a -ae *f*
blur *tr* obscurare
blurred *adj* **the eyes are —** oculi caligant; **to have — vision** quasi per caliginem vidēre
blurt *tr* **to — out** effutire
blush *s* rub·or -oris *m*
blush *intr* erubescĕre
bluster *intr (to swagger)* declamare, se jactare; *(of the wind)* saevire

bluster s *(boasting)* jactati·o -onis f; *(din)* strepit·us -ūs m
blustery adj ventos·us -a -um
boar s a·per -pri m
board s *(of wood)* tabul·a -ae f; *(food)* vict·us -ūs m; *(council)* colleg·ium -(i)i n; *(judicial)* quaesti·o -onis f; *(for games)* alve·us -i m
board tr **to — a ship** navem conscendĕre; **to — up** contabulare ‖ intr *(to be a boarder)* victitare; **to — with** devertĕre apud *(w. acc)*
boarder s deversit·or -oris m
boarding house s deversor·ium -(i)i n
boardwalk s ambulacr·um -i n in litore
boast intr gloriari, se jactare
boast s jactanti·a -ae f
boastful adj glorios·us -a -um
boasting s gloriati·o -onis f
boat s navig·ium -(i)i n
boatman s naut·a -ae m
bode tr portendĕre
bodiless adj incorporal·is -is -e
bodily adj corporis *(gen)*
body s corp·us -oris n; *(corpse)* cadav·er -eris n; *(person)* hom·o -inis m; *(of troops)* man·us -ūs f; *(of cavalry)* turm·a -ae f; *(frame)* compag·es -ium fpl; **to come in a —** agmine facto occurrĕre
bodyguard s satellit·es -um mpl; *(of the emperor)* cohor·s -tis f praetoria
bog s pal·us -udis f
bog tr **to — down** mergĕre; **to get —ed down** in luto haesitare; *(fig)* haesitare
bogus adj *(counterfeit)* adulterin·us -a -um; *(sham)* simulat·us -a -um; *(fictitious)* commentici·us -a -um
boil tr *(to cause to boil)* fervefacĕre; *(to cook)* coquĕre; **to — down** *(food)* decoquĕre; *(facts)* coartare ‖ intr fervēre; *(fig)* bullire; **to — over** effervescĕre; **to — with indignation** indignatione bullire
boil s *(med)* furuncul·us -i m
boiler s ahen·um -i n
boisterous adj *(noisy)* turbid·us -a -um; *(stormy)* procellos·us -a -um
bold adj aud·ax -acis
bold-faced adj impud·ens -entis
boldly adv audacter
boldness s audaci·a -ae f
bolster s cervic·al -alis n
bolster tr fulcire
bolt s *(of a door)* pessul·us -i m, ser·a -ae f; *(of lightning)* ful·men -inis n; *(pin)* clav·us -i m; *(screw)* cochle·a -ae f
bolt tr obserare; **—ed doors** oppessulatae for·es -ium fpl; **to — down** *(food)* devorare ‖ intr *(of a horse)* se proripĕre; *(pol)* a factione deficĕre
bomb s missil·e -is n dirumpens
bomb tr missilibus dirumpentibus concutĕre

bombard tr tormentis verberare; *(fig)* lacessĕre
bombardment s tormentis verberati·o -onis f
bombast s ampull·ae -arum fpl
bombastic adj tumid·us -a -um; **to be —** ampullari
bond s vincul·um -i n; *(legal document)* syngraph·a -ae f; *(of love)* copul·a -ae f
bondage s servit·us -utis f; *(captivity)* captivit·as -atis f
bondsman s *(slave)* famul·us -i m; *(leg)* spons·or -oris m
bone s os, ossis n; *(of fish)* spin·a -ae f
bone adj *(of bone)* osse·us -a -um
bone tr *(to remove bones from)* exossare
boneless adj ex·os -ossis
bonfire s ign·es -ium mpl festi
bonnet s redimicul·um -i n
bonus s praem·ium -(i)i n
bony adj osse·us -a -um
boogieman s larv·a -ae m
book s li·ber -bri m; **by the —** *(fig)* pro modo; **to write a —** librum componĕre
bookbinder s glutinat·or -oris m
bookcase s forul·i -orum mpl
bookish adj libris dedit·us -a -um
bookkeeper s tabular·ius -(i)i m, dispensat·or -oris m
bookshelf s plute·us -i m
bookstore s librari·a -ae f
bookworm s tine·a -ae f; *(fig)* librorum hellu·o -onis m
boom s *(of ship)* longur·ius -(i)i m; *(of harbor)* repagul·um -i n; *(sound)* sonit·us -ūs m; *(of waves)* frag·or -oris m
boon s benefic·ium -(i)i n
boor s rustic·us -i m
boorish adj rustic·us -a -um
boorishness s rusticit·as -atis f
boost tr efferre
boot s calce·us -i m; *(soldier's)* calig·a -ae f; *(peasant's)* per·o -onis m; *(tragic)* cothurn·us -i m
boot tr *(coll)* calce petĕre ‖ intr prodesse; **to —** insuper
booth s tabern·a -ae f
border s *(edge)* marg·o -inis mf; *(seam)* fimbri·a -ae f; *(boundary)* fin·is -is m; *(frontier)* lim·es -tis m; **to mark the —** finem discernĕre
border tr attingĕre ‖ intr **to — on** attingĕre
bordering adj finitim·us -a -um
bore tr terebrare; *(a person)* obtundĕre; **to — a hole in** excavare; **to — a hole through s.th.** aliquid perforare; **to — out** exterebrare
bore s *(tool)* terebr·a -ae f; *(fig)* molest·us -i m
borer s terebr·a -ae f
born adj nat·us -a -um; **to be —** nasci; *(fig)* oriri
borough s municip·ium -(i)i n

borrow *tr* mutuari; *(fig)* imitari
borrowed *adj* mutu·us -a -um
bosom *s* sin·us -ūs *m; (of female)* mammill·ae -arum *fpl*
bosom friend *s* intimus familiar·is -is *m*
boss *s (owner)* domin·us -i *m; (coll)* ipsim·us -i *m; (ornamental fixture)* bull·a -ae *f; (on a shield)* umb·o -onis *m*
boss *tr* dominari in *(w. acc)*
botanical *adj* herbari·us -a -um
botanist *s* herbar·ius -(i)i *m*
botany *s* ar·s -tis *f* herbaria
botch *tr* male gerĕre
both *adj* amb·o -ae -o; *(of pairs)* gemin·us -a -um; *(each of two)* ut·erque, -raque, -rumque; — **parents** uterque par·ens -entis *m;* **in** — **directions** utroque; **on** — **sides** utrimque
both *pron* amb·o -ae -o; *(w. singular verb)* ut·erque, -raque, -rumque
both *conj* —...**and** et...et
bother *tr* vexare ‖ *intr* **to** — **about** operam dare *(w. dat)*
bother *s* negot·ium -(i)i *n*
bothersome *adj* molest·us -a -um
bottle *s* ampull·a -ae *f; (large)* lagoen·a -ae *f*
bottle *tr* in ampullas infundĕre
bottom *s* fund·us -i *m; (of a ship)* carin·a -ae *f; (of a mountain)* rad·ix -icis *m;* **the** — **of the sea** imum mar·e -is *n*
bottom *adj* im·us -a -um
bottomless *adj* profund·us -a -um
bough *s* ram·us -i *m*
boulder *s* sax·um -i *n*
bounce *tr* repercutĕre; *(coll)* ejicĕre ‖ *intr* resilire
bounce *s (leap)* salt·us -ūs *m; (energy)* vig·or -oris *m*
bound *adj* alligat·us -a -um; **it is** — **to happen** necesse est accidat; **to be** — **for** tendĕre ad *or* in *(w. acc)*
bound *s (leap)* salt·us -ūs *m;* **to set** —**s** modum facĕre
bound *tr* terminare, continēre; **they are** — **ed on one side by the Rhine** unā ex parte flumine Rheno continentur ‖ *intr (to leap)* salire
boundary *s* fin·is -is *m; (esp. fortified)* lim·es -itis *m*
boundless *adj* infinit·us -a -um
bountiful *adj* larg·us -a -um
bounty *s* largit·as -atis *f*
bouquet *s* corollar·ium -(i)i *n; (of wine)* flo·s -ris *m*
bout *s* certam·en -inis *n*
bow *s* arc·us -ūs *m; (in a ribbon)* plex·us -ūs *m*
bow *s (of ship)* pror·a -ae *f; (bending)* capitis summissi·o -onis *f;* **to take a** — caput summittĕre
bow *tr* flectĕre; *(one's head)* demittĕre ‖

intr se demittĕre; **to** — **to** *(to accede to)* obtemperare *(w. dat)*
bowels *spl* alv·us -i *f*
bower *s* umbracul·um -i *n*
bowl *s* crater·a -ae *f; (for libations)* pater·a -ae *f*
bowlegged *adj* valg·us -a -um
bowman *s* sagittar·ius -(i)i *m*
bowstring *s* nerv·us -i *m*
box *s (chest)* arc·a -ae *f; (for books)* caps·a -ae *f; (for clothes, etc.)* cist·a -ae *f; (for perfume, medicine)* pyx·is -idis *f*
box *tr (to enclose in a box)* includĕre; *(an opponent)* pugillare cum *(w. abl);* **to** — **s.o. on the ear** alicui alapam adhibēre ‖ *intr* pugillare
boxer *s* pug·il -ilis *m*
boxing *s* pugillat·us -ūs *m*
boxing glove *s* caest·us -ūs *m*
boxing match *s* pugillat·us -ūs *m*
boy *s* pu·er -eri *m; (dim.)* puerul·us -i *m*
boyhood *s* pueriti·a -ae *f;* **from** — **a puero**
boyish *adj* pueril·is -is -e
bra *s* stroph·ium -(i)i *n*
brace *s (strap)* fasci·a -ae *f; (pair)* pa·r -ris *n; (prop)* fulment·um -i *n*
brace *tr (to bind)* ligare; *(to strengthen)* firmare; *(to prop)* fulcire; **to** — **oneself for** se comparare ad *(w. acc)*
bracelet *s* armill·a -ae *f*
bracket *s* mutul·us -i *m;* —**s** *(in writing)* unc·i -orum *mpl*
brag *intr* se jactare
braggart *s* jactat·or -oris *m*
bragging *s* jactanti·a -ae *f*
braid *s* limb·us -i *m; (of hair)* spir·a -ae *f*
braid *tr* plectĕre
brain *s* cerebr·um -i *n;* —**s** *(talent)* ingen·ium -(i)i *n;* **to have (no)** —**s cor** (non) habēre
brain *tr (sl)* caput elidĕre *(w. dat)*
brainless *adj* soc·ors -ordis
brainstorm *s* inflat·us -ūs *m* spiritūs
brain trust *s* consil·ium -(i)i *n* sapientium
brake *s (on wagon)* sufflam·en -inis *n; (thicket)* dumet·um -i *n;* **to apply the** —**s** rotam sufflaminare
bramble *s* dum·us -i *m; (thorny bush)* sent·is -is *m*
branch *s (of tree)* ram·us -i *m; (of pedigree)* stemm·a -atis *n; (of knowledge)* disciplin·a -ae *f*
branch *intr* **to** — **out** ramos porrigĕre; *(fig)* scindi, diffundi
branch office *s* officin·a -ae *f* auxiliaria
brand *s (mark)* stigm·a -atis *n; (com)* not·a -ae *f; (type)* gen·us -eris *n; (of fire)* fa·x -cis *f*
branding iron *s* caut·er -eris *m*
brandish *tr* vibrare
brandy *s* vini spirit·us -ūs *m*
brash *adj* temerari·us -a -um
brass *s* orichalc·um -i *n*

brassiere *s* stroph·ium -(i)i *n*
brat *s* procax pusi·o -onis *m*
brave *adj* fort·is -is -e
brave *tr* sustinēre
bravely *adv* fortiter
bravery *s* fortitud·o -inis *f*
bravo *interj* macte!
brawl *s* rix·a -ae *f*
brawl *intr* rixari
brawler *s* rixat·or -oris *m*
brawling *adj* jurg·ans -antis
brawn *s* lacert·us -i *m*
brawny *adj* lacertos·us -a -um
bray *intr* rudĕre
braying *s* rudit·us -ūs *m*
brazen *adj* aëne·us -a -um; *(fig)* impud·ens -entis
brazier *s* focul·us -i *m*
breach *s* ruin·a -ae *f; (of treaty)* dissid·ium -(i)i *n;* — **in the wall** ruin·a -ae *f* muri; **to commit a** — **of promise** fidem frangĕre; **to make a small** — **in the wall** aliquantulum muri discutĕre
bread *s* pan·is -is *m; (fig)* vict·us -ūs *m;* **loaf of** — panis *m;* **to earn one's** — sibi victum quaerĕre
bread basket *s* panar·ium -(i)i *n*
breadcrumb *s* mic·a -ae *f* panis
breadth *s* latitud·o -inis *f;* **in** — **in** latitudinem
break *tr (arm, dish, treaty, one's word)* frangĕre; *(the law)* violare; *(leg, ankle)* suffringĕre; *(silence)* rumpĕre; *(camp)* movēre; *(in several places)* diffringĕre; **to** — **a fall** casum mitigare; **to** — **apart** diffringĕre; **to** — **a treaty** foedus frangĕre; **to** — **down** *(to demolish)* demoliri; **to** — **down into** *(categories)* deducĕre in *(w. acc);* **to** — **formation** ordinem solvĕre; **to** — **in** *(a horse)* domare; **to** — **in pieces** confringĕre; **to** — **off** *(e.g., a branch)* praefringĕre; *(friendship or action)* dirumpĕre; *(a meeting, conversation)* interrumpĕre; **to** — **one's word** fidem frangĕre; **to** — **open** effringĕre; **to** — **up** dissolvĕre **‖** *intr* frangi, rumpi; *(of day)* illuscescĕre; *(of strength)* deficĕre; **to** — **forth** erumpĕre; **to** —**into** *(e.g., a house)* irrumpĕre *(w. acc or intra + acc); (e.g., a city)* invadĕre *(w. acc or in + acc);* **to** — **loose from** se eripĕre ex *(w. abl);* **to** — **off** *(to stop short)* repente desinĕre; **to** — **out** erumpĕre; *(of trouble)* exardescĕre; *(of war)* exoriri; *(of fire)* grassari; **to** — **up** dissolvi, dilabi; *(of a meeting)* dimitti; **to** — **with** dissidēre ab *(w. abl)*
break *s (of a limb)* ruptur·a -ae *f;* (interruption) intercaped·o -inis *f;* (for rest) intervall·um -i *n,* vacati·o -onis *f;* (escape) effug·ium -(i)i *n;* — **of day** prima lu·x -cis *f*

breakage *s* fractur·a -ae *f*
breakdown *s (of health)* debilit·as -atis *f;* (mechanical) defect·us -ūs *m;* (division) deducti·o -onis *f*
breaker *s* fluct·us -ūs *m* a saxo fractus
breakfast *s* jentacul·um -i *n;* **for** — **in** jentaculum; **to eat** — jentare
breakfast *intr* jentare
breakneck *adj* praec·eps -ipitis
breakup *s* dissoluti·o -onis *f*
breakwater *s* mol·es -is *f* lapidum in mari structa
breast *s* pect·us -oris *n; (of a woman)* mamm·a -ae *f; (when filled with milk)* ub·er -eris *n; (fig)* praecord·ia -ium *npl;* **to make a clean** — **of it** confiteri omnia
breastbone *s* stern·um -i *n*
breast-feed *tr* uberibus alēre
breastplate *s* loric·a -ae *f*
breath *s* spirit·us -ūs *m,* anim·a -ae *f;* — **of air** aur·a -ae *f;* **deep** — anhelit·us -ūs *m;* **out of** — anhel·us -a -um; **to catch one's** — obstipescĕre; **to draw a** — spiritum trahĕre; **to hold one's** — animam continēre; **to take a** — animam *or* spiritum ducĕre; **to take one's** — **away** exanimare; **to waste one's** — operam perdĕre
breathe *tr* ducĕre, spirare; *(to whisper)* susurrare; **to** — **fire** flammas exspirare; **to** — **one's last** animam exspirare **‖** *intr* spirare, respirare; **to** — **upon** inspirare *(w. dat)*
breather *s (breathing space)* spat·ium -(i)i *n*
breathing *s* respirati·o -onis *f*
breathless *adj* exanim·is -is -e
breeches *spl* brac·ae -arum *fpl*
breed *s* gen·us -eris *n*
breed *tr* parĕre, gignĕre; *(to cause)* producĕre; *(to raise)* educare, alĕre; **familiarity** —**s contempt** conversatio parit contemptum
breeder *s (man)* generat·or -oris *m; (animal)* matr·ix icis *f; (fig)* nutr·ix -icis *f*
breeding *s* fetur·a -ae *f;* **good** — humanit·as -atis *f*
breeze *s* aur·a -ae *f*
breezy *adj* ventos·us -a -um
brethren *spl* fratr·es -um *mpl*
brevity *s* brevit·as -atis *f*
brew *s* cerevisiae ferment·um -i *n*
brew *tr* concoquĕre **‖** *intr* excitari
brewer *s* cerevisiae coct·or -oris *m*
brewery *s* officin·a -ae *f* ad cerevisiam concoquendam
bribe *s* pret·ium -(i)i *n,* praem·ium -(i)i *n,* pecuni·a -ae *f*
bribe *tr* (pecuniā) corrumpĕre
briber *s* corrupt·or -oris *m*
bribery *s* corrupti·o -onis *f; (pol)* ambit·us -ūs *m*
brick *s* lat·er -eris *m*

brick *adj* laterici·us -a -um
bricklayer *s* laterum struct·or -oris *m*
bridal *adj* nuptial·is -is -e; **— bed** genialis tor·us -i *m;* **— suite** thalam·us -i *m;* **— veil** flamme·um -i *n*
bride *s* nupt·a -ae *f*
bridegroom *s* marit·us -i *m*
bridesmaid *s* pronub·a -ae *f*
bridge *s* pon·s -tis *m*
bridge *tr* pontem imponĕre *(w. dat)*
brief *adj* brev·is -is -e
brief *tr* edocēre
brief *s (leg)* commentar·ius -(i)i *m*
briefing *s* mandat·a -orum *npl*
briefly *adv* breviter, paucis (verbis)
brigade *s (infantry)* legi·o -onis *f; (cavalry)* turm·a -ae *f*
brigadier *s* tribun·us -i *m* militum
brigand *s* latr·o -onis *m*
brigandage *s* latrocin·ium -(i)i *n*
bright *adj* clar·us -a -um; *(stars, gems)* lucid·us -a -um; *(beaming)* nitid·us -a -um; *(smart)* a·cer -cris -cre; *(eyes)* veget·us -a -um
brighten *tr* illuminare ‖ *intr* lucescĕre, clarescĕre; **his face —ed up** vultus ejus in hilaritatem solutus est
brightly *adv* clare, lucide
brightness *s* nit·or -oris *m,* cand·or -oris *m; (of sky)* serenit·as -atis *f*
brilliance *s* splend·or -oris *m; (ability)* lu·x -cis *f;* **— of style** nit·or -oris *m* orationis
brilliant *adj* splendid·us -a -um; *(esp. fig: achievement, speech, battle, etc.)* luculent·us -a -um
brilliantly *adv* splendide, luculente
brim *s (rim)* or·a -ae *f; (border)* marg·o -inis *mf;* **to fill to the —** ad summam oram implēre
brimful *adj* ad summum plen·us -a -um
brimstone *s* sulf·ur -uris *n*
brine *s* salsament·um -i *n; (the sea)* sal·um -i *n*
bring *tr* **(to)** afferre (ad + *acc); (by carriage, etc.)* advehĕre; *(letters, report, news)* perferre; **to — about** efficĕre, perficĕre; **to — along** afferre; **to — (s.o.) around** circumagĕre (aliquem); **to — back** referre, reducĕre; *(to recall)* revocare; *(by force, authority)* redigĕre; **to — before a court of law** producĕre in judicium; **to —** *(a matter)* **before the senate** ad senatum referre de *(w. abl);* **to — credit to** fidem ferre *(w. dat);* **to — down** deferre; *(e.g., a tower)* dejicĕre; **to — forth** prodĕre, depromĕre; *(to yield)* ferre; **to — forward** proferre; **to — in** inferre; *(on a vehicle)* invehĕre; *(money, profit)* efficĕre; **to — it about that** efficĕre ut; **to — on** afferre; *(illness, fever)* adducĕre; *(fig)* objicĕre; **to — oneself to** animum inducĕre ut *(w. subj);*

to — out *(to reveal)* proferre; *(to elicit)* elicĕre; *(the wine)* (ex)promĕre; *(a book)* prodĕre; **to — over** perducĕre; *(fig)* perducĕre, conciliare; **to — to** adducĕre; **to — together** conferre; *(to assemble)* cogĕre, contrahĕre; *(esp. forces)* comparare; *(estranged persons)* conciliare; **to — to pass** efficĕre; **to — under one's control** subigĕre; **to — up** subducĕre; *(children)* educare; *(to vomit)* evomĕre; *(a topic)* mentionem facĕre de *(w. abl)*
brink *s* marg·o -inis *mf;* **on the — of death** morti vicin·us -a -um; **to be on the — of disaster** in summo discrimine versari
brisk *adj (lively)* ala·cer -cris -cre; *(wind)* vehement·ior -ior -ius; *(weather)* frigid·us -a -um; **to be —** vigēre
briskly *adv* alacriter
briskness *s* alacrit·as -atis *f,* vig·or -oris *m*
bristle *s* saet·a -ae *f*
bristle *intr* horrēre
bristly *adj* saetos·us -a -um
Britain *s* Britanni·a -ae *f*
British *adj* Britannic·us -a -um
brittle *adj* fragil·is -is -e
broach *tr* in medium proferre
broad *adj* lat·us -a -um; *(grin)* solut·us -a -um; *(general)* commun·is -is -e; **in — daylight** *(fig)* propalam; **to sleep till — daylight** ad multum diem dormire
broadcast *tr* divulgare
broaden *tr (to widen)* dilatare; *(to enlarge)* ampliare ‖ *intr* in latitudinem crescĕre, latescĕre
broadsword *s* glad·ius -(i)i *m*
brocade *s* seric·um -i *n* aureo *(or* argento) filo intertextum
broccoli *s* brassic·a -ae *f* oleracea Botyrtis
brochure *s* libell·us -i *m*
broil *s* rix·a -ae *f*
broil *tr* torrēre ‖ *intr* torrēri
broken *adj* fract·us -a -um; *(by age, hard times)* confect·us -a -um; *(faltering)* infract·us -a -um; **— in** domit·us -a -um
broken-hearted *adj* deject·us -a -um
broker *s* arillat·or -oris *m*
bronze *s* ae·s -ris *n*
bronze *adj* aëne·us -a -um
brooch *s* fibul·a -ae *f*
brood *s* prol·es -is *f; (of birds, etc. hatched together)* fetur·a -ae *f*
brood *intr* **to — over** *(lit & fig)* incubare *(w. dat),* parturire
brook *s* rivul·us -i *m*
brook *tr* tolerare, pati
broom *s* scop·ae -arum *fpl*
broth *s* ju·s -ris *n*
brothel *s* lupan·ar -aris *n*
brother *s* fra·ter -tris *m*
brotherhood *s* fraternit·as -atis *f; (organization)* sodalit·as -atis *f*
brother-in-law *s* lev·ir -iri *m*
brotherly *adj* fratern·us -a -um

brow *s* fron·s -tis *f; (of a hill)* dors·um -i *n;*
  to knit the — frontem contrahĕre
browbeat *tr* minis et terrore commovēre
brown *adj (w. a dash of yellow)* fulv·us -a
  -um; *(chestnut color)* spad·ix -icis; *(of
  skin)* adust·us -a -um
browse *intr* depasci
bruise *tr* contundĕre; *(to make black-and-
  blue)* sugillare
bruise *s* contusi·o -onis *f; (black-and- blue)*
  suggillati·o -onis *f*
bruise mark *s* liv·or -oris *m*
brunette *s* puell·a -ae *f* subfusca
brunt *s* tota vis *f*
brush *s (scrub brush)* penicul·us -i *m;
  (painter's)* penicill·us -i *m; (skirmish)*
  aggressi·o -onis *f; (bushes)* vigult·a
  -orum *npl*
brush *tr (lightly)* verrĕre; *(teeth)* purgare;
  (shoes) detergēre; **to — aside** spernĕre;
  to — away or **out** detergēre ‖ *intr* **to —
  past s.o.** aliquem praetereundo leviter
  terĕre
brutal *adj* imman·is -is -e
brutality *s* immanit·as -atis *f*
brutally *adv* immaniter
brute *adj* brut·us -a -um
brute *s* belu·a -ae *f*
brutish *adj* imman·is -is -e
bubble *s* bull·a -ae *f*
bubble *intr* bullire, bullare; *(of a spring)*
  scatēre
bubbling *s* bullit·us -ūs *m; (of a spring)*
  scatebr·a -ae *f*
bubbly *adj (person)* argutiis scat·ens
  -entis
buccaneer *s* pirat·a -ae *m*
buck *s* cerv·us -i *m; (he-goat)* hirc·us -i *m*
bucket *s* situl·a -ae *f;* **to kick the —** *(coll)*
  animam ebullire
buckle *s* fibul·a -ae *f*
buckle *tr* fibulā nectĕre ‖ *intr (to bend)*
  flecti; *(to collapse)* collabi; **to — down**
  se applicare; **to — up** se fibulā nectĕre
buckler *s* parm·a -ae *f*
bucolic *adj* bucolic·us -a -um
bud *s* gemm·a -ae *f; (of a flower)* cal·yx
  -ycis *m;* **to nip s.th. in the —** aliquid
  maturum occupare
bud *intr* gemmare
budge *tr* ciēre, movēre ‖ *intr* se movēre,
  loco cedĕre
budget *s* pecuniae rati·o -onis *f*
buffalo *s* ur·us -i *m*
buffet *s (sideboard)* abac·us -i *m; (slap)*
  alap·a -ae *f*
buffet *tr* jactare
buffoon *s* scurr·a -ae *f;* **to play the —**
  scurrari
bug *s* cim·ex -icis *mf*
buggy *s (two-wheeled)* carpent·um -i *n;
  (four-wheeled)* pertorrit·um -i *n*
bugle *s* bucin·a -ae *f,* corn·u -us *n*

bugle call *s* classic·um -i *n*
bugler *s* bucinat·or -oris *m*
build *tr (house, ship)* aedificare; *(house,
  walls)* (ex)struĕre; *(bridge)* fabricare;
  (wall, rampart)* ducĕre; *(road)* munire;
  (hopes)* ponĕre; **to — up** exstruĕre
builder *s* aedificat·or -oris *m,* struct·or
  -oris *m*
building *s (act)* aedificati·o -onis *f,*
  exstructi·o -onis *f; (structure)* aedi-
  fic·ium -(i)i *n*
building site *s* are·a -ae *f*
bulb *s* bulb·us -i *m*
bulge *intr (swell)* tumēre; *(to stand out)*
  prominēre
bulge *s* tub·er -eris *n*
bulk *s* amplitud·o -inis *f; (mass)* mol·es -is
  f; (greater part) major par·s -tis *f*
bulkiness *s* magnitud·o -inis *f*
bulky *adj (huge)* ing·ens -entis; *(difficulty
  to handle)* inhabil·is -is -e
bull *s* taur·us -i *m*
bulldog *s* can·is -is *m* Moloss·us
bulldozer *s* machin·a -ae *f* aggerandi
bullet *s* glan·s -dis *f* plumbea
bulletin *s* libell·us -i *m; (news)* nunt·ius
  -(i)i *m*
bulletin board *s* tabul·a -ae *f* publica
bullfrog *s* ran·a -ae *f* ocellata
bullion *s (gold)* aur·um -i *n* infectum;
  (silver) argent·um -i *n* infectum
bullock *s* juvenc·us -i *m*
bull's eye *s* scop·us -i *m* medius; **hit the —**
  scopum medium ferire
bully *s* scordal·us -i *m*
bully *tr* procaciter lacessĕre
bulwark *s (wall)* moen·ia -ium *npl; (any
  means of defense)* propugnacul·um -i *n;
  (fig)* ar·x -cis *f*
bump *s (swelling)* tub·er -eris *n; (thump)*
  plag·a -ae *f,* sonit·us -ūs *m*
bump *tr* pulsare, pellĕre ‖ *intr* **to — against**
  offendĕre
bumpy *adj* tuberos·us -a -um; *(road,
  ground)* iniqu·us -a -um
bun *s (roll)* lib·um -i *n,* collyr·is -idis *f*
bunch *s* fascicul·us -i *m; (of grapes)*
  racem·us -i *m; (group)* glob·us -i *m*
bunch *intr* **to — together** glomerari
bundle *s* fasc·is -is *m; (of straw)* manipul·us
  -i *m*
bundle *tr* **to — up** *(with clothes)* coöperire
bungle *tr (a job)* inscite gerĕre, inscite
  agĕre ‖ *intr* errare
bungler *s* imperit·us -i *m*
buoy *tr* **to — up** sublevare
buoyancy *s* levit·as -atis *f; (fig)* hilarit·as
  -atis *f*
buoyant *adj* lev·is -is -e; *(fig)* hilar·is -is -e
burden *s* on·us -eris *n*
burden *tr* onerare
burdensome *adj* oneros·us -a -um
bureau *s* minister·ium -(i)i *n; (chest)*

armar·ium -(i)i *n; (for clothes)* vestiar·ium -(i)i *n*
burglar *s* effractar·ius -(i)i *m*
burglary *s* (domūs) effractur·a -ae *f*
burial *s (act)* sepultur·a -ae *f; (ceremony)* fun·us -eris *n*
burial place *s* sepulchr·um -i *n*
burlesque *s* ridicula imitati·o -onis *f*
burly *adj* corpulent·us -a -um
burn *tr* urěre, cremare; **to — down** deurěre; **to — out** exurěre; **to — up** comburěre **‖** *intr* flagrare, ardēre; **to — down** deflagrare; **to — out** exstingui; **to — up** conflagrare
burn *s* adusti·o -onis *f; (injury)* ambust·um -i *n*
burning *adj* ard·ens -entis
burn-out *s* defecti·o -onis *f* virium
burrow *s* cunicul·us -i *m*
burrow *intr* defoděre
bursar *s* dispensat·or -oris *m*
burst *s (spurt)* impet·us -ūs *m; (noise)* frag·or -oris *m; —* **of anger** iracundiae impet·us -ūs *m; —* **of applause** clamor·es -um *mpl*
burst *tr* rumpěre; *(with noise)* disploděre; **to — asunder** dirumpěre; **to — open** effrangěre **‖** *intr* rumpi; **to — forth** prorumpěre; **to — in** irrumpěre; **to — out** erumpěre; **to — out laughing** risum effunděre
bury *tr* sepelire; *(to hide)* abděre; **to — the sword in his side** lateri abděre ensem
bush *s* frut·ex -icis *m; (thorny bush)* dum·us -i *m;* **to beat around the —** circuitione uti
bushel *s* medimn·us -i *m*
bushy *adj (full of bushes)* dumos·us -a -um; *(full of branches)* ramos·us -a -um; *(tail)* villos·us -a -um
busily *adv* impigre, sedulo
business *s* negot·ium -(i)i *n; (trade, calling)* ar·s -tis *f; (matter)* res, rei *f; (establishment)* officin·a -ae *f;* **I always made it my — to be present** ego id semper egi ut adessem; **to mind one's own —** negotium suum agěre; **what — do you have here?** quid negotii tibi hic est?; **what — is it of his?** quid illius interest?
business agent *s* negotiorum curat·or -oris *m*
businessman *s* negotiat·or -oris *m*
buskin *s* cothurn·us -i *m*
bust *s* imag·o -inis *f; (bosom)* pectus -oris *n; (woman's)* mammill·ae -arum *fpl*
bustle *s (hurry)* festinati·o -onis *f; (running to and fro)* discurs·us -ūs *m*
bustle *intr* festinare; **to — about** discurrěre
busy *adj* occupat·us -a -um; *(time)* operos·us -a -um; *(w. business matters)* negotios·us -a -um
busy *tr* **to — oneself** versari
busybody *s* ardali·o -onis *m*

but *prep* praeter *(w. acc)*
but *adv* modo, tantum
but *conj* sed; *(stronger)* at; **— if** quodsi; sin; **— if not** sin aliter
butcher *s* lan·ius -(i)i *m; (fig)* carnif·ex -icis *m*
butcher *tr (animals)* caeděre; *(people)* contrucidare
butcher shop *s* lanien·a -ae *f*
butchery *s* trucidati·o -onis *f*
butler *s* prom·us -i *m*
butt *s (mark)* met·a -ae *f; (backside)* clun·es -ium *mpl; —* **of ridicule** ludibr·ium -(i)i *n*
butt *tr* arietare **‖** *intr* **to — in** interpellare
butter *s* butyr·um -i *n*
butter *tr (bread)* (panem) butyro inducěre; **to — s.o. up** blandiri *(w. dat)*
buttercup *s* ranuncul·us -i *m* tuberosus
butterfly *s* papili·o -onis *m*
buttermilk *s* lactis ser·um -i *n*
buttock *s* clun·is -is *mf*
button *s* globul·us -i *m* vestiarius
button *tr* globulo nectěre
buttress *s* anter·is -idis *f*
buttress *tr* suffulcire
buxom *adj* ampl·us -a -um
buy *tr* eměre, mercari; **to — back** *or* **off** rediměre; **to — up** coěměre
buyer *s* empt·or -oris *m*
buying *s* empti·o -onis *f*
buzz *s* bomb·us -i *m*
buzz *intr* bombilare
buzzard *s* bute·o -onis *m*
by *prep (agency)* a, ab *(w. abl); (of place) (near)* apud *(w. acc); (along)* secundum *(w. acc); (past)* praeter *(w. acc); (in oaths)* per *(w. acc); —* **and —** mox; **means of** per *(w. acc); —* **oneself** per se; *(alone)* sol·us -a -um
bygone *adj* praeterit·us -a -um; *(olden)* prisc·us -a -um
bylaw *s* praescript·um -i *n*
bypass *s* circuit·us -ūs *m*
bypass *tr* ambire
bystander *s* spectat·or -oris *m*
byway *s* deverticul·um -i *n*
byword *s* proverb·ium -(i)i *n*

C

cab *s (for hire)* cis·ium -(i)i *n* meritorium
cabbage *s* brassic·a -ae *f; (head of cabbage)* caul·is -is *m*
cabin *s (cottage)* cas·a -ae *f; (on a ship)* daiet·a -ae *f*
cabin boy *s* pu·er -eri *m* nauticus
cabinet *s* armar·ium -(i)i *n; (pol)* consil·ium -(i)i *n* principis
cabinet member *s* consiliat·or -oris *m*
cable *s* rud·ens -entis *m; (for anchor)* ancoral·e -is *n*

cackle *intr (of hens)* gracillare; *(of geese)* gingrire
cackle *s* gingrit·us -ūs *m*
cacophony *s* dissonae voc·es -ium *fpl*
cactus *s* cact·us -i *f*
cadaver *s* cadav·er -eris *n*
cadaverous *adj* cadaveros·us -a -um
cadence *s* numer·us -i *m*
cadet *s* discipul·us -i *m* militaris
cage *s* cave·a -ae *f; (for large animals)* sept·um -i *n*
cage *tr* in cavea *or* septo includĕre
caged *adj* caveat·us -a -um
cahoots *spl* **be in — with** colludĕre cum *(w. abl)*
cajole *tr* lactare
cake *s* placent·a -ae *f; (birthday cake)* lib·um -ī *n*
calamitous *adj* calamitos·us -a -um
calamity *s* calamit·as -atis *f;* **to suffer —** calamitatem perferre
calculate *tr* computare; *(fig)* existimare
calculated *adj* subduct·us -a -um
calculation *s* computati·o -onis *f; (fig)* ratiocinati·o -onis *f*
calculator *s* computat·or -oris *m*
caldron *s* cortin·a -ae *f; (of copper)* ahen·um -i *n*
calendar *s* fast·i -orum *mpl*
calends *spl* Kalend·ae -arum *fpl*
calf *s* vitul·us -i *m,* vitul·a -ae *f; (anat)* sur·a -ae *f*
caliber *s (fig)* ingen·ium -(i)i *n*
call *s* vocati·o -onis *f; (shout)* clam·or -oris *m; (visit)* salutati·o -onis *f; (summons)* accit·us -ūs *m;* **social** — offic·ium -(i)i *n;* **to make** *or* **pay a social —** officium peragĕre
call *tr (to summon)* ad se vocare; *(to name)* appellare, vocare; **to — aside** sevocare; **to — away** avocare; **to — back** revocare; **to — down** devocare; **to — forth** evocare; *(to cause)* provocare; *(fig)* elicĕre; **to — in** *(money)* cogĕre; *(for advice)* advocare; *(a doctor)* arcessĕre; **to — off** *(to cancel)* revocare, tollĕre; *(to read)* citare; **to — out** *(to call forth)* evocare; *(to shout)* exclamare; **to — to account** *(to upraid)* compellĕre; **to — together** convocare; **to — to mind** recordari; **to — to witness** testari; **to — up** *(mil)* evocare ǁ *intr* **to — for** *(to demand)* poscĕre; *(to require)* requirĕre; **to — on** *(to invoke)* invocare; *(for help)* implorare; *(to visit)* visĕre
caller *s* salutat·or -oris *m*
calling *s (profession)* ar·s -tis *f; (station)* stat·us -ūs *m*
callous *adj* callos·us -a -um; *(fig)* exper·s -tis sensūs; **to become —** occallescĕre *(fig)* obduriscĕre
callus *s* call·us -i *m*

calm *adj (unruffled)* tranquill·us -a -um; *(sleep, sea, speech, old age)* placid·us -a -um; *(mentally)* aequ·us -a -um
calm *tr* sedare, tranquillare
calming *s* sedati·o -onis *f*
calmly *adv* tranquille, placide; *(of a person)* aequo animo
calmness *s (lit & fig)* tranquillit·as -atis *f;* **with —** aequo animo
calumny *s (abuse)* maledict·um -i *n; (slander)* calumni·a -ae *f*
camel *s* camel·us -i *m*
cameo *s* imag·o -inis *f* ectypa
camouflage *s* dissimulati·o -onis *f*
camouflage *tr* dissimulare
camp *s* castr·a -orum *npl;* **summer —** aestiv·a -orum; *npl* **winter —** hibern·a -orum *npl*
camp *adj* castrens·is -is -e
camp *intr* castra ponĕre
campaign *s (mil)* expediti·o -onis *f,* stipend·ium -(i)i *n; (pol)* (for) petiti·o -onis *f (w. gen)*
campaign *intr (mil)* stipendium merēre; *(pol)* ambire
campaigning *s (pol)* ambiti·o -onis *f*
camp follower *s* cal·o -onis *m*
camphor *s* camphor·a -ae *f*
can *s* pyx·is -idis *f* stannea
can *intr* posse; *(to have the power)* pollēre; **I — not** nequeo, non possum
canal *s* foss·a -ae *f* navigabilis
canary *s* fringill·a -ae *f* Canaria
cancel *tr* tollĕre; *(to cross out)* cancellare, delēre
cancellation *s* deleti·o -onis *f; (fig)* aboliti·o -onis *f*
cancer *s* can·cer -cri *m,* carcinom·a -atis *n*
cancerous *adj* concros·us -a -um
candid *adj* apert·us -a -um
candidate *s (for)* candidat·us -i *m (w. gen);* **to announce oneself as —** profiteri
candidly *adv* aperte, libere
candied *adj* succharo condit·us -a -um
candle *s* candel·a -ae *f*
candlestick *s* candelabr·um -i *n*
candor *s* cand·or -oris *m*
candy *s* sacchar·um -i *n* crystallinum
cane *s (walking stick)* bacul·us -i *m; (reed)* harund·o -inis *f*
cane *tr* baculo verberare
canine *adj* canin·us -a -um
canister *s* pyx·is -idis *f*
canker *s* rubig·o -inis *f*
cannibal *s* anthropophag·us -i *m*
cannon *s* torment·um -i *n*
cannonball *s* glob·us -i *m* missilis
canoe *s* scaph·a -ae *f*
canon *s* can·on -onis *m*
canonical *adj* canonic·us -a -um
canopy *s* canope·um -i *n*
cantata *s* carm·en -inis *n* ad musicam accommodatum

canteen s *(flask)* laguncul·a -ae f; *(mil)* caupon·a -ae f castrensis

canter s lenis quadrupedans grad·us -ūs m

canter intr leniter currĕre

canticle s cantic·um -i n

canto s li·ber -bri m

canton s pag·us -i m

canvas s linte·um -i n crassum; *(for painting)* textil·e -is n

cap s pille·us -i m; *(worn by certain priests)* galer·us -i m

capability s facult·as -atis f

capable adj *(skilled)* soller·s -tis, perit·us -a -um; *(of)* cap·ax -acis *(w. gen)*; — **of enduring** *(cold, hunger, etc.)* pati·ens -entis *(w. gen)*; — **of holding 500 spectators** cap·ax -acis quingentorum spectatorum

capably adv scite

capacious adj cap·ax -acis

capacity s *(extent of space)* capacit·as -atis f; *(extent of mental power)* mensur·a -ae f; *(ability)* ingen·ium -(i)i n

cape s promontor·ium -(i)i n; *(garment)* humeral·e -is n

caper s *(leap)* exsultati·o -onis f; *(prank)* ludibr·ium -(i)i n; *(bold criminal act)* scel·us -eris n; **to pull a** — scelus patrare

capital adj *(chief)* praecipu·us -a -um; *(offense, punishment)* capital·is -is -e; *(letters)* uncial·is -is -e

capital s *(chief city)* cap·ut -itis n; *(archit)* capitul·um -i n; *(com)* cap·ut -itis n, sor·s -tis f

capitalist s fenerat·or -oris m

capitol s capitol·ium -(i)i n

capitulate intr se dedĕre

capitulation s dediti·o -onis f

capon s cap·o -onis m

caprice s libid·o -inis f

capricious adj inconst·ans -antis

capriciously adv inconstanter

Capricorn s Capricorn·us -i m

capsize tr evertĕre ‖ intr everti

capsule s capsul·a -ae f; *(bot)* vascul·um -i n

captain s *(in infantry)* centuri·o -onis m; *(in cavalry)* praefect·us -i m; *(in navy)* navarch·us -i m; *(of merchant ship)* navis magis·ter -tri m

caption s capitul·um -i n; *(leg)* praescripti·o -onis f

captious adj *(tricky)* captios·us -a -um; *(carping)* moros·us -a -um

captivate tr capĕre

captive adj captiv·us -a -um

captive s captiv·us -i m, captiv·a -ae f

captor s capt·or -oris m; *(of a city)* expugnat·or -oris m

capture s comprehensi·o -onis f; *(of a city)* expugnati·o -onis f; *(of animals)* captur·a -ae f

capture tr capĕre, excipĕre; *(city)* expugnare; *(by surprise)* opprimĕre

car s *(chariot)* curr·us -ūs m; *(carriage)* raed·a -ae f; *(modern)* automobil·e -is n

caravan s commeat·us -ūs m

carbon s carbon·ium -(i)i n

carbuncle s carbuncul·us -i m

carcass s cadav·er -eris n

card s chart·a -ae f

cardboard s chart·a -ae f crassior

cardinal adj principal·is -is -e; *(color)* ru·ber -bra -brum; *(numbers)* cardinal·is -is -e

cardinal s *(eccl)* cardinal·is -is m

care s *(anxiety, oversight, attention)* cur·a -ae f; *(diligence)* diligenti·a -ae f; *(charge)* tutel·a -ae f; *(watching over)* custodi·a -ae f; — **was taken by the senate to** *(w.inf)* opera a senatu data est ut; **to take** — **of** curare

care intr curare; **to** — **for** *(to look after)* curare; *(to be fond of, with negatives)* morari; **I don't** — **for wine** ego vinum nihil moror

career s curricul·um -i n; *(pol)* curs·us -ūs m honorum

carefree adj secur·us -a -um

careful adj *(attentive)* dilig·ens -entis; *(cautious)* caut·us -a -um; *(of work)* accurat·us -a -um

carefully adv diligenter; caute

careless adj negleg·ens -entis

carelessly adv neglegenter

carelessness s incuri·a -ae f; *(stronger)* neglegenti·a -ae f

caress s amplex·us -ūs m

caress tr fovēre

cargo s on·us -eris n; **to put a ship's** — **aboard** navem onerare

caricature s gryll·us -i m

caricature tr in pejus fingĕre

carnage s strag·es -is f

carnal adj carnal·is -is -e

carnival s feri·ae -arum fpl ante quadragesimam

carnivorous adj carnivor·us -a -um

carol s cant·us -ūs m

carouse intr comissari

carp s cyprin·us -i m

carp intr **to** — **at** carpĕre

carpenter s fa·ber -bri m tignarius

carpentry s materiatur·a -ae f fabrilis

carpet s tapet·e -is n

carriage s vehicul·um -i n, raed·a -ae f; *(esp. women's)* carpent·um -i n

carrier s bajul·us -i m

carrion s car·o -nis f morticina

carrot s carot·a -ae f

carry tr ferre; *(of heavier things)* portare; *(by vehicle)* vehĕre; *(a law)* perferre; **to** — **away** auferre; evehĕre; **to** — **in** importare; invehĕre; **to** — **off** auferre; *(by force)* rapĕre; **to** — **on** *(to conduct)* exercēre; *(war)* gerĕre; **to** — **out** efferre; evehĕre; *(to perform)* exsequi; **to** —

through perferre; **to — weight** auctoritatem habēre **‖** *intr* (*of sound*) audiri; **to — on** pergĕre; (*to behave*) se gerĕre

cart *s* plaustr•um -i *n;* (*dim.*) plostell•um -i *n;* (*two-wheeled, drawn by oxen*) carr•us -i *m;* **putting the — before the horse** praeposteris consiliis

cart *tr* plaustro vehĕre; **to — off** plaustro evehĕre

carve *tr* sculpĕre; (*to engrave*) caelare; (*at table*) secare

carver *s* (*engraver*) caelat•or -oris *m;* (*at table*) sciss•or -oris *m*

carving *s* caelatur•a -ae *f*

carving knife *s* cultell•us -i *m*

cascade *s* praeceps aquae laps•us -ūs *m*

case *s* (*leg*) caus•a -ae *f;* (*matter, circumstances, condition*) res, rei *f;* (*instance*) exempl•um -i *n;* (*container*) involucr•um -i *n;* (*patient*) aeg•er -ri *m,* aegr•a -ae *f;* (*gram*) cas•us -ūs *m;* **if that's the —** si res sic habet; **in any —** utcumque; **in no — nequaquam; in the — of Priam** in Priamo; **since that's the —** quae cum ita sint

casement *s* biforis fenestr•a -ae *f*

cash *s* numm•i -orum *mpl;* numerat•um -i *n;* **in hard — in nummis: to pay —** praesenti pecuniā solvĕre

cash box *s* arc•a -ae *f*

cashier *s* dispensat•or -oris *m*

cash payment *s* repraesentati•o -onis *f*

cask *s* cad•us -i *m*

casket *s* capul•us -i *m*

cast *s* (*throw*) jact•us -ūs *m;* (*mold*) typ•us -i *m;* **— of characters** distributi•o -onis *f* partium in singulos actores

cast *tr* jacĕre; (*metal*) fundĕre; (*a vote*) ferre; **to — aside** abjicĕre; **to — down** dejicĕre; **to — in** injicĕre; **to — off** (*skin*) exuĕre; (*fig*) ponĕre; **to — out** ejicĕre, expellĕre; **to — upon** superinjicĕre; (*fig*) aspergĕre **‖** *intr* **to — off** navem solvĕre

castanet *s* crotal•um -i *n*

castaway *s* perdit•us -i *m*

caste *s* ord•o -inis *m*

castigate *intr* castigare

castle *s* castell•um -i *n*

castor oil *n* cicinum ole•um -i *n*

castrate *tr* castrare

castration *s* castrati•o -onis *f*

casual *adj* fortuit•us -a -um; (*person*) negleg•ens -entis

casually *adv* fortuito, casu

casualty *s* cas•us -ūs *m*

cat *s* fel•es -is *f*

cataclysm *s* cataclysm•os -i *m*

catacombs *spl* catacumb•ae -arum *fpl*

catalogue *s* catalog•us -i *m*

cataract *s* cataract•a -ae *f;* (*of the eyes*) glaucom•a -atis *n*

catastrophe *s* calamit•as -atis *f*

catcall *s* irrisi•o -onis *f*

catch *s* (*of fish*) praed•a -ae *f;* (*fastening*) fibul•a -ae *f;* **to think s.o. a great — aliquem magni facĕre; what's the — ?** quid est captatio?

catch *tr* capĕre; (*unawares*) excipĕre; (*to surprise*) deprehendĕre; (*falling object*) excipĕre, suscipĕre; (*in a net*) illaquēre; (*fish*) captare; (*birds*) excipĕre; **to — a cold** gravedine affligi; **to — fire** ignem *or* flammam concipĕre; **to — hell** convicium habēre; **to — his eye** experimentum oculorum ejus capĕre; **to — red-handed** deprehendĕre; **to — sight of** conspicĕre **‖** *intr* **to — at** arripĕre; **to — on** comprehendĕre; **to — up to** consequi

catching *adj* (*contagious*) contagios•us -a -um; (*fig*) grat•us -a -um

categorical *adj* categoric•us -a -um

categorically *adv* categorice

category *s* categori•a -ae *f*

cater *intr* cibum suppeditare; **to — to** indulgēre (*w. dat*)

caterer *s* obsonat•or -oris *m*

caterpillar *s* eruc•a -ae *f*

cathedral *s* ecclesi•a -ae *f* cathedralis

catholic *adj* catholic•us -a -um

cattle *s* pec•us -oris *n*

cauliflower *s* brassic•a -ae *f* oleracea botryitis

causal *adj* causal•is -is -e

cause *s* caus•a -ae *f;* (*motive*) rati•o -onis *f*

cause *tr* facĕre, efficĕre; (*to stir up*) movēre; **to — a quarrel** litem facĕre; **to — him to leave** facĕre ut abeat

causeless *adj* sine causa

causeway *s* agg•er -eris *m*

caustic *adj* caustic•us -a -um; (*fig*) mord•ax -acis

cauterize *tr* adurĕre

caution *s* cauti•o -onis *f;* **to use great — diligenter** circumspicĕre; **with — pedetemptim**

caution *tr* (ad)monēre

cautious *adj* caut•us -a -um

cautiously *adv* caute

cavalcade *s* pomp•a -ae *f*

cavalier *s* equ•es -itis *m*

cavalry *s* equitāt•us -ūs *m*

cave *s* spec•us -ūs *m*

cavern *s* cavern•a -ae *f*

cavernous *adj* cavernos•us -a -um

caviar *s* ov•a -orum *npl* acipenseris

cavity *s* cav•um -i *n;* (*anat*) lacun•a -ae *f*

caw *intr* crocire, crocitare

cease *intr* desinĕre; (*temporarily*) intermittĕre

ceaseless *adj* perpetu•us -a -um

ceaselessly *adv* perpetuo

cedar *s* cedr•us -ūs *f*

cedar *adj* cedre•us -a -um

cede *tr* cedĕre (*w. abl*)

ceiling s camer·a -ae f; (panelled) lacun·ar -aris n
celebrate tr celebrare; (in song) canĕre
celebrated adj cele·ber -bris -bre
celebration s celebrati·o -onis f; (of rites) sollemn·e -is n
celebrity s celebrit·as -atis f; (person) vi·r -ri m illustris
celery s heleoselin·um -i n
celestial adj caelest·is -is -e
celibacy s caelibat·us -ūs m
celibate adj caeleb·s -is
cell s cell·a -ae f
cellar s hypoge·um -i n
cement s ferrum·en -inis n
cement tr ferruminare; (to glue) conglutinare **‖** intr coalescĕre
cemetery s sepulcret·um -i n
cenotaph s cenotaph·ium -(i)i n
censer s turibul·um -i n
censor s cens·or -oris m
censorship s censur·a -ae f; (of literature) literarum censur·a -ae f
censure s vituperati·o -onis f
censure tr animadvertĕre; (officially) notare
census s civium enumerati·o -onis f; (in the Roman sense) cens·us -ūs m; **to conduct a —** recensum populi agĕre
cent s centesim·a -ae f; **I don't owe anyone a red —** assem aerarium nemini debeo
centaur s centaur·us -i m
centenary adj centenari·us -a -um
centenary s centesimus ann·us -i m
center s med·ium -(i)i n; (math) centr·um -i n; **in the — of the town** in medio oppido
center tr in centrum ponĕre **‖** intr **to — on** niti (w. abl)
central adj medi·us -a -um
centralize tr (authority) ad unum deferre
centurion s centuri·o -onis m
century s saecul·um -i n; (mil, pol) centuri·a -ae f
ceramic adj fictil·is -is -e
ceramics s ar·s -tis f figlina; (objects) fictil·ia -ium npl
cereal s cereal·e-is n
cerebellum s cerebell·um -i n
cerebrum s cerebr·um -i n
ceremonial adj sollemn·is -is -e
ceremonial s sollemn·e -is n; (religious) rit·us -ūs m
ceremonious adj solemn·is -is -e; (person) officios·us -a -um
ceremoniously adv rite
ceremony s caerimoni·a -ae f; (pomp) apparat·us -ūs m; **religious ceremonies** religion·es -um fpl
certain adj (sure) cert·us -a -um; (indefinite) quidam quaedam quoddam; **for —** pro certo; **it is certain that** constat (w. acc & inf)

certainly adv profecto
certainty s cert·um -i n; (belief) fid·es -ei f
certificate s testimon·ium -(i)i n
certify tr confirmare
cessation s cessati·o -onis f; (temporary) intermissi·o -onis f; **— of hostilities** induti·ae -arum fpl
chafe tr urĕre; (w. the hand) fricare; (to excoriate) atterĕre; (to vex) irritare **‖** intr stomachari
chaff s pale·a -ae f; (fig) quisquili·ae -arum fpl
chagrin s stomach·us -i m
chagrined adj **to be —** stomachari
chain s caten·a -ae f; (necklace) torqu·es -is mf; (fig) seri·es -ei f; **dog on a —** can·is -is m catenis vinctus
chain tr catenas injicĕre (w. dat)
chaingang s compedit·i -orum mpl
chair s sell·a -ae f; (w. rounded back) arcisell·ium -(i)i n; (of a teacher) cathedr·a -ae f; (of a magistrate) sella f curulis
chair tr (a meeting) praesidēre (w. dat), praeesse (w. dat)
chairperson s praes·es -idis mf
chalice s cal·ix -icis m
chalk s cret·a -ae f
chalk tr cretā notare; (cover with chalk) cretā illinĕre; **to — up** notare
chalky adj (chalk-like) cretace·us -a -um; (full of chalk) cretos·us -a -um
challenge s provocati·o -onis f; (leg) rejecti·o -onis f
challenge tr provocare; (a claim) vindicare; (validity) recusare; (leg) rejicĕre
challenger s provocat·or -oris m
challenging adj provoc·ans -antis
chamber s (room) conclav·e -is n; (bedroom) cubicul·um -i n; (pol) curi·a -ae f
chambermaid s ancill·a -ae f cubicularia
chamber pot s lasan·um -i n
champ tr & intr mandĕre; **to — on the bit** frena dente premĕre
champagne s vin·um -i n effervescens
champion s propugnat·or -oris m
championship s titul·us -i m victoriae
chance s (accident) cas·us -ūs m; (opportunity) potest·as -atis f; (prospect) sp·es -ei f; (fig) ale·a -ae f; **by —** casu, forte; **by some — or other** nescio quo casu; **game of —** ale·a -ae f; **to give s.o. a —** to potestatem alicui facĕre (w. inf); **to stand a —** potestatem habēre; **to take a —** periculum adire
chance tr periclitari **‖** intr accidĕre; often expressed by the adverb forte: **I —ed to see the aedile** aedilem forte conspexi; **to — on** occurrĕre (w. dat)
chance adj fortuit·us -a -um
chancel s cancell·us -i m
chancellor s cancellar·ius -(i)i m

chandelier *s* candelabr·um -i *n*

change *s* mutati·o -onis *f; (complete)* commutati·o -onis *f*, permutati·o -onis *f; (variety)* variet·as -atis *f; (of fortune)* vicissitud·o -inis *f; (coins)* numm·i -orum *mpl* minores; — **of clothes** mutati·o -onis *f* vestis; — **of heart** animi mutati·o -onis *f;* **for a** — varietatis causā

change *tr* mutare; *(completely)* commutare; **to** — **into** convertěre in *(w. acc)* ‖ *intr* mutari, variare; *(of the moon)* renovari; **to** — **for the better (worse)** in meliorem (pejorem) partem mutari; **to** — **into** verti in *(w. acc)*

changeable *adj* mutabil·is -is -e; *(fickle)* inconst·ans -antis

changeless *adj* immutabil·is -is -e

changeling *s* supposit·us -i *m*

channel *s* canal·is -is *m; (of rivers)* alve·us -i *m; (arm of the sea)* fret·um -i *n; (groove)* stri·a -ae *f*

channel *tr* sulcare, excavare; *(to guide)* ducěre

chant *s* cant·us -ūs *m*

chant *tr* cantare

chaos *s* cha·os -i *n; (confusion)* perturbati·o -onis *f*

chaotic *adj* confus·us -a -um

chap *s* fissur·a -ae *f; (person)* hom·o -inis *m; (boy)* pu·er -eri *m*

chap *tr* diffinděre; —**ed lips** fissur·ae -arum *fpl* labrorum ‖ *intr* scindi

chapel *s* sacell·um -i *n*

chapter *s* cap·ut -itis *n*

char *tr* amburěre

character *s* mor·es -um *mpl; (inborn)* indol·es -is *f*, ingen·ium -(i)i *n; (repute)* existimati·o -onis *f; (type)* gen·us -eris *n; (letter)* litter·a -ae *f; (theat)* person·a -ae *f;* **to assume the** — **of a plaintiff** petitoris personam capěre

characteristic *s* propr·ium -(i)i *n*

characteristic *adj* propri·us -a -um; **it is** — **of a father to protect his family** patris est familiam suam tegěre

characteristically *adv* proprie

characterize *tr* describěre, pingěre

charade *s* mim·us -i *m;* —**s** aenigm·a -atis *n* syllabicum

charcoal *s* carb·o -onis *m*

charge *s* accusati·o -onis *f; (leg)* crim·en -inis *n; (mil)* impet·us -ūs *m; (into enemy territory)* incurs·us -ūs *m; (command)* mandat·um -i *n; (trust)* cur·a -ae *f*, custodi·a -ae *f; (office)* mun·us -eris *n; (cost)* impens·a -ae *f;* **free of** — gratis; **to be in** — praeesse *(w. dat);* **to bring** —**s against** litem intenděre *(w. dat);* **to put in** — **of** praeficěre *(w. dat);* **to take** — **of** curare

charge *tr (to attack)* incurrěre *(w. dat or acc); (to enjoin upon)* mandare *(w. dat of person and* ut *w. subj);* **to** — **a certain**

price for goods pretium statuěre merci; **to** — **an expense to the citizens** sumptum civibus inferre; **to** — **a fixed price** pretium certum constituěre; **to** — **s.o. with** *(a crime)* arguěre aliquem *(w. gen or abl of the charge)* ‖ *intr (to make a charge)* irruěre

charger *s* bellat·or -oris *m*

chariot *s* curr·us -ūs *m; (for racing)* curricul·um -i *n; (for war)* essed·um -i *n*

charioteer *s* aurig·a -ae *m; (combatant in a chariot)* essedar·ius -(i)i *m*

charitable *adj* benign·us -a -um; *(lenient in judgment)* mit·is -is -e

charitably *adv* benigne

charity *s* liberalit·as -atis *f; (Christian love)* carit·as -atis *f*

charlatan *s* ostentat·or -oris *m; (quack doctor)* pharmacopol·a -ae *m*

charm *s (attractiveness)* venust·as -atis *f*, lep·os -oris *m; (spell)* carm·en -inis *n; (amulet)* amulet·um -i *n*

charm *tr (to bewitch)* incantare; *(to delight)* capěre; **to lead a** —**ed life** vitam divinitus munitam gerěre

charmer *s* fascinat·or -oris *m; (fig)* delici·ae -arum *fpl*

charming *adj* lepid·us -a -um; *(beautiful)* venust·us -a -um

chart *s* tabul·a -ae *f; (nautical)* nautica tabul·a -ae *f*

chart *tr* designare

charter *tr (to hire)* conducěre; *(to grant a charter to)* diploma donare *(w. dat)*

charter *s (instrument conferring privileges)* diplom·a -atis *n*

chase *s (hunt)* venati·o -onis *f; (pursuit)* insectati·o -onis *f*

chase *tr (to hunt)* venari; *(to engrave)* caelare; *(romantically)* petěre; **to** — **away** abigěre ‖ *intr* **to** — **after** petěre

chasing *s* caelatur·a -ae *f*

chasm *s* hiat·us -ūs *m*

chaste *adj* cast·us -a -um

chastely *adv* caste

chasten *tr (to chastise)* castigare; *(to moderate)* moderare

chastise *tr* castigare

chastisement *s* castigati·o -onis *f*

chastiser *s* castigat·or -oris *m*

chastity *s* castit·as -atis *f*

chat *s* familiaris serm·o -onis *m;* **to have a** — fabulari

chat *intr* fabulari

chattel *s* res, rei *f* mancipi; —**s** bon·a -orum *npl*

chatter *s* clang·or -oris *m; (idle talk)* garrulit·as -atis *f; (of teeth)* crepit·us -ūs *m*

chatter *intr* balbutire; *(of birds)* caněre; **my teeth** — dentibus crepito

cheap *adj* vil·is -is -e; **to be** — **as dirt** pro luto esse; **to sell** —**er** minoris venděre

cheaply *adv* bene, vili (pretio); **to live —** parvo sumptu vivĕre

cheapen *tr* pretium minuĕre *(w. gen)*

cheapness *s* vilit·as -atis *f*

cheat *tr* decipĕre; **to — s.o. out of his money** aliquem pecuniā fraudare

cheat *s* plan·us -i *m*

cheater *s* fraudat·or -oris *m*

check *tr (to restrain, e.g., an onset, flow of blood, eager horses)* inhibēre; *(to slow down)* retardare; *(accounts)* dispungĕre; *(to verify)* comprobare; **to — off** notare

check *s (bill)* rati·o -onis *f; (restraint)* coërciti·o -onis *f; (reprimand)* reprehensi·o -onis *f; (disadvantage)* detriment·um -i *n;* **to hold in —** supprimĕre; **to write a — for** argentum perscribĕre *(w. dat)*

checkered *adj* vari·us -a -um

cheek *s* gen·a -ae *f; (when puffed out by eating, blowing)* bucc·a -ae *f*

cheekbone *s* maxill·a -ae *f*

cheer *s* clam·or -oris *m;* **to be of good —** bono animo esse

cheer *tr* hortari; **to — up** exhilare; **— up!** bono animo es!

cheerful *adj* hilar·is -is -e

cheerfully *adv* hilariter

cheerfulness *s* hilarit·as -atis *f*

cheerless *adj* illaetabil·is -is -e

cheese *s* case·us -i *m*

chef *s* coqu·us -i *m* peritus

chemical *adj* chemic·us -a -um

chemical *s* chemic·um -i *n*

chemist *s* chemiae perit·us -i *m*

chemistry *s* chemi·a -ae *f*

cherish *tr* fovēre; *(fig)* colĕre

cherry *s* ceras·um -i *n*

cherry-red *adj* cerasin·us -a -um

cherry tree *s* ceras·us -i *f*

chess *s* latruncul·i -orum *mpl*

chest *s (anat)* pect·us -oris *n; (box)* arc·a -ae *f,* armar·ium -(i)i *n; (for clothes)* vestiar·ium -(i)i *n*

chestnut *s* castane·a -ae *f*

chestnut tree *s* castane·a -ae *f*

chew *tr* manducare; **to — the cud** ruminare; **to — out** *(coll)* objurgare

chicanery *s* praevaricati·o -onis *f*

chick *s* pull·us -i *m; (term of endearment)* pull·a -ae *f*

chicken *s* pull·us -i *m* gallinaceus, gallin·a -ae *f*

chicken-hearted *adj* ignav·us -a -um

chicory *s* cichore·um -i *n*

chide *tr* increpitare

chief *adj* princ·eps -ipis; *(first in rank)* primari·us -a -um; **— justice** summus jud·ex -icis *m*

chief *s* princ·eps -ipis *m; (ringleader)* cap·ut -itis *n*

chiefly *adv* praecipue, inprimis

chieftain *s* du·x -cis *m*

child *s* inf·ans -antis *mf,* fil·ius -(i)i *m;* **children** liber·i -orum *mpl;* **to bear a —** parturire; **with — gravida**

childbearing *s* part·us -ūs *m*

childbirth *s* part·us -ūs *m*

childhood *s* infanti·a -ae *f,* pueriti·a -ae *f;* **from —** a puero *or* a pueris

childish *adj* pueril·is -is -e

childishly *adv* pueriliter

childless *adj* orb·us -a -um

childlike *adj* pueril·is -is -e

chill *s* frig·us -oris *n; (of the body)* horr·or -oris *m*

chill *tr* refrigerare

chilly *adj* frigidul·us -a -um; *(susceptible to cold)* alsios·us -a -um

chime *s* son·us -i *m*

chime *intr* concinĕre; **to — in** succinĕre; *(to interrupt)* interpellare

chimera *s* chimaer·a -ae *f*

chimney *s* camin·us -i *m*

chin *s* ment·um -i *n;* **to drop the —** labrum demittĕre

China *s* Ser·es -um *mpl*

china *s* murrhin·a -orum *npl*

Chinese *adj* Seric·us -a -um

chink *s* rim·a -ae *f; (sound)* tinnit·us -ūs *m*

chink *intr* tinnire

chip *s* assul·a -ae *f; (of pottery)* frag-ment·um -i *n*

chip *tr (wood)* ascio dedolare; *(to break off a piece of)* praecidĕre; **to — in** *(money)* conferre

chipper *adj* ala·cer -cris -cre

chirp *s (of birds)* pipat·us -ūs *m; (of crickets)* strid·or -oris *m*

chirp *intr (of birds)* pipilare; *(of crickets)* stridĕre

chisel *s* scalpr·um -i *n*

chisel *tr* scalpro caedĕre; *(to cheat)* emungĕre; *(to borrow)* mutuare

chivalrous *adj* magnanim·us -a -um

chivalry *s (knighthood)* equestris dignit·as -atis *f; (spirit)* magnanimit·as -atis *f*

chococlate *s* chocolat·um -i *n*

choice *s* electi·o -onis *f; (power of choosing)* opti·o -onis *f; (diversity)* variet·as -atis *f*

choice *adj* elect·us -a -um

choir *s* chor·us -i *m*

choke *tr* strangulare ‖ *intr* strangulari

choking *s* strangulati·o -onis *f*

choose *tr* eligĕre; **to — to** *(to prefer to)* malle *(w. inf)*

chop *s* ofell·a -ae *f; pork —* ofella *f* porcina

chop *tr (wood)* dolabrā caedĕre; **to — off** praecidĕre; **to — up** minutatim concidĕre

choral *adj* symphoniac·us -a -um

chord *s* nerv·us -i *m*

chorus *s* chor·us -i *m*

chorus girl *s* ambubai·a -ae *f*

Christ *s* Christ·us -i *m*

christen *tr* baptizare

Christendom s cuncti Christian·i -orum *mpl*
Christian adj Christian·us -a -um
Christian s Christian·us -i *m*
Christianity s Christianism·us -i *m*
Christmas s fest·um -i n nativitatis Christi; **it won't be — forever** *(fig)* non semper Saturnalia erunt; **Merry —** ! festum natalem Christi!; **to celebrate — all year long** *(fig)* semper Saturnalia agĕre
Christmas carol s cantic·um -i n de Christi natali
Christmas day s Christi di·es -ei *m* natalis
Christmas eve s di·es -ei *m* proximus ante festum nativitatis Christi
chronic adj long·us -a - um
chronicle s annal·es -ium *mpl*
chronological adj **in — order** conservatis notisque temporibus
chronology s temporum ord·o -inis *m*
chubby adj crass·us -a -um
chuckle intr pressā voce cachinnare
chum s convict·or -oris *m*
church s ecclesi·a -ae *f*
churl s rustic·us -i *m*
churlish adj importun·us -a -um
churlishly adv importune
cider s hydromel·um -i n
cinder s favill·a -ae *f*
cinnamon s cinnamom·um -i n
cipher s *(code)* not·a -ae *f; (a nobody)* numer·us -i *m; (zero)* nihil n; **to write in —** per notas scribĕre
circle s circul·us -i *m; (anything round)* orb·is -is *m;* **family —** coron·a -ae *f* domi; **to form a —** *(to stand in a circle)* in orbem consistĕre; **to ride in a —** in orbem equitare
circle tr circumdare, cingĕre ‖ intr circulum ducĕre
circuit s circuit·us -ūs *m;* **to make a —** circumire, circumagi
circuitous adj flexuos·us -a -um; **by a — route** circuitu; **to take a — route** circumagi
circular adj rotund·us -a -um
circulate tr *(to spread)* in vulgum spargĕre ‖ intr *(of money)* in usum venire; *(to flow)* circumfluĕre; *(of news)* percrebescĕre
circulation s circulati·o -onis *f*
circumcise tr circumcidĕre
circumcised adj recutit·us -a -um
circumcision s circumcisi·o -onis *f*
circumference s ambit·us -ūs *m; (geom)* peripheri·a -ae *f*
circumflex s circumflex·us -ūs *m*
circumlocution s circumlocuti·o -onis *f,* **by —** per ambitum verborum
circumscribe tr circumscribĕre
circumspect adj circumspect·us -a -um
circumspection s circumspecti·o -onis *f*
circumstance s res, rei *f; (circumstances*

collectively) temp·us -oris n; **according to —s** pro re, pro tempore; **in humble —s** tenui re; **to yield to —** tempori cedĕre
circumstantial adj *(incidental)* adventici·us -a -um; **to rest on — evidence** conjecturā contineri
circumvent tr circumscribĕre
circumvention s circumscripti·o -onis *f*
circus s circ·us -i *m; (performance)* circens·es -ium *mpl*
cistern s cistern·a -ae *f*
citadel s ar·x -cis *f*
citation s *(summons)* vocati·o -onis *f; (quotation)* loc·us -i *m* allatus; *(act of quoting)* prolati·o -onis *f*
cite tr *(leg)* evocare, citare; *(to quote)* proferre; *(in writing)* ponĕre
citizen s civ·is -is *mf; (of a municipality)* munic·eps -ipis *mf*
citizenship s civit·as -atis *f*
city adj urban·us -a -um
city s urb·s -is *f*
city council s decurion·es -um *mpl*
civic adj civil·is -is-e
civil adj civil·is -is -e; *(polite)* urban·us -a -um; **— rights** civile ju·s -ris n
civilian s togat·us -i *m*
civilian adj togat·us -a -um, privat·us -a -um
civility s comit·as -atis *f*
civilization s cult·us -ūs *m*
civilize tr excolĕre
clad adj indut·us -a -um
claim s *(demand)* postulati·o -onis *f; (leg)* vindici·ae -arum *fpl; (land)* a·ger -gri *m* assignatus; *(assertion)* affirmati·o -onis *f;* **to lay —** to vindicare
claim tr *(to demand)* postulare; *(esp. leg)* vindicare; *(to assert)* affirmare; **to — the thing as ours** rem nostram vindicare
claimant s petit·or -oris *m*
clam s my·ax -acis *m*
clamber intr scandĕre; **to — down** descendĕre; **to — up** *(e.g., a mountain)* scandĕre
clammy adj umid·us -a -um
clamor s clam·or -oris *m*
clamor intr vociferari; **to — for** flagitare
clamp s confibul·a -ae *f*
clamp tr constringĕre
clan s gen·s -tis *f*
clandestine adj clandestin·us -a -um
clandestinely adv clam, furtim
clang s clang·or -oris *m*
clang intr clangĕre
clank s crepit·us -ūs *m*
clank intr crepare
clap s *(of hands)* plaus·us -ūs *m; (of thunder)* frag·or -oris *m;* **a loud — of thunder** gravis fragor *m*
clap tr **to — the hands** manūs complodĕre; **to — a man in prison** aliquem in vincula conjicĕre ‖ intr plaudĕre

claptrap *s* apparat·us -ūs *m*
clarification *s* explicati·o -onis *f*
clarify *tr* deliquare
clarion *s* litu·us -i *m*
clarity *s* clarit·as -atis *f*
clash *s* concurs·us -ūs *m; (sound)* crepit·us -ūs *m; (fig)* dissonanti·a -ae *f; (of colors)* repugnanti·a -ae *f*
clash *intr* concurrēre; *(to make a noise by striking)* concrepare; *(fig)* collidi
clasp *s* fibul·a -ae *f; (embrace)* amplex·us -ūs *m*
clasp *tr (to embrace)* amplecti; *(to grasp)* comprehendēre
class *s (pol)* class·is -is *f*, ord·o -inis *m; (of pupils)* class·is -is *f; (kind)* gen·us -eris *n*
class *tr (e.g., according to wealth)* describēre; **to — as** in numero *(w. gen)* habēre
classical *adj* classic·us -a -um
classics *spl* scriptor·es -um *mpl* classici
classification *s* descripti·o -onis *f*
classify *tr* describēre
clatter *s* strepit·us -ūs *m*
clatter *intr* strepare, crepitare
clause *s (gram)* articul·us -i *m*, membr·um -i *n; (leg)* cap·ut -itis *n*
claw *s (of birds)* ungul·a -ae *f; (of a crab)* bracch·ium -(i)i *n*
claw *tr* lacerare
clay *s* lut·um -i *n; (white potter's clay)* argill·a -ae *f;* **made of —** fictil·is -is -e
clayey *adj* argillace·us -a -um
clean *adj* mund·us -a -um; *(lit & fig)* pur·us -a -um
clean *tr* mundare, purgare; **to — s.o. out** *(of money)* aliquem excatarissare
cleanliness *s* munditi·a -ae *f*
cleanly *adv* omnino, penitus
cleanse *tr* purgare; *(by washing)* abluēre; *(by rubbing)* detergēre
clear *adj* clar·us -a -um; *(unclouded)* seren·us -a -um; *(liquids)* limpid·us -a -um; *(transparent)* pellucid·us -a -um; *(voice)* liquid·us -a -um; *(style)* lucid·us -a -um; *(explanation)* illustr·is -is -e; *(manifest)* conspicu·us -a -um; *(conscience)* rect·us -a -um; *(mind)* sag·ax -acis; **— of** exper·s -tis *(w. gen);* **it is — manifestum est;** *(leg)* liquet; **to keep — of** evitare
clear *tr* purgare; *(to make open)* expedire; *(to acquit)* absolvēre; *(land)* exstirpare; *(the table)* mundare; *(profit)* lucrari; **to — away** detergēre, amovēre; *(by force)* amoliri; **to — out** emundare; **to — up** enodare **‖** *intr (of weather)* disserenascēre; **— out!** apage!
clearance *s* purgati·o -onis *f; (space)* intervall·um -i *n*
clearly *adv* clare; *(obviously)* aperte
clearness *s* clarit·as -atis *f; (of sky)*

serenit·as -atis *f; (of style)* perspicuit·as -atis *f*
clear-sighted *adj* **to be —** clare decernēre
cleavage *s* discid·ium -(i)i *n*
cleave *tr* findēre **‖** *intr* **to — to** adhaerēre *(w. dat)*
cleaver *s* dolabr·a -ae *f*
cleft *s* rim·a -ae *f,* fissur·a -ae *f*
clemency *s* clementi·a -ae *f*
clement *adj* clem·ens -entis
clench *tr* comprimēre; **to — the fist** manum comprimēre
clergy *s* cler·us -i *m*
cleric *s* cleric·us -i *m*
clerk *s* scrib·a -ae *m*
clever *adj* callid·us -a -um
cleverly *adv* callide
cleverness *s* callidit·as -atis *f*
click *s* crepit·us -ūs *m*
click *intr* crepitare
client *s* cli·ens -entis *mf*
cliff *s* rup·es -is *f*
climate *s* cael·um -i *n*
climax *s* gradati·o -onis *f*
climb *tr* ascendēre; *(to the top)* conscendēre; **to — (up) a tree** in arborem inscendēre, arborem conscendēre **‖** *intr* ascendēre
climb *s* ascens·us -ūs *m*
clinch *vt* confirmare
cling *intr (to)* adhaerēre *(w. abl or dat or* ab + *abl);* **to — together** cohaerēre
clink *s* tinnit·us -ūs *m*
clink *intr* tinnire
clip *s* fibul·a -ae *f*
clip *tr (to cut)* tondēre; *(words, tail)* mutilare
clipping *s* tonsur·a -ae *f;* **—s** resegmin·a -um *npl*
cloak *s* pall·ium -(i)i *n; (cape with hood for travel)* paenul·a -ae *f; (mil)* sag·um -i *n; (general's)* paludament·um -i *n;* **wearing a —** palliat·us -a -um
cloak *tr* dissimulare, tegēre
clock *s* horolog·ium -(i)i *n*
clod *s* glaeb·a -ae *f; (pej)* caud·ex -icis *m*
clog *s* sole·a -ae *f* lignea
clog *tr (to hinder, fetter)* impedire; *(to block up)* obstruēre
cloister *s* portic·us -ūs *f; (eccl)* monaster·ium -(i)i *n*
close *adj (near)* propinqu·us -a -um; *(dense)* dens·us -a -um; *(tight)* art·us -a -um; *(imtimate)* intim·us -a -um; *(shut)* occlus·us -a -um; *(atmosphere)* crass·us -a -um; **at — quarters** comminus *(adv);* **— attention** anim·us -i *m* attentissimus; **to be on the —est possible terms with s.o.** aliquo familiarissime uti; **to be — at hand** adesse, instare; **to keep — to** adhaerēre *(w. dat)*
close *tr* claudēre; *(eyes, lips)* premēre; *(to end)* finire; **in —ing** denique; **to — down**

claudĕre; **to — a bargain** pascisci; **to —
up** praecludĕre **ǁ** *intr* coire, claudi; **to —
in on the enemy** undique fauces hostium
premĕre
close *s* fin·is -is *m;* **at the — of the year**
exeunte anno; **to bring to a —** finire; **to
draw to a —** terminari
close *adv* prope, juxta; **— to** *(near)* prope
(w. acc), juxta *(w. acc); (almost)* paene
closely *adv* prope; *(attentively)* attente
closet *s* armar·ium -(i)i *n; (for clothes)*
vestiar·ium -(i)i *n*
closing *adj* ultim·us -a -um
closing *s* conclusi·o -onis *f*
clot *s* concretus cru·or -oris *m*
clot *intr* concrescĕre
cloth *s* pann·us -i *m; (linen)* linte·um -i *n*
clothe *tr* vestire, induĕre
clothes *spl* vestiment·a -orum *npl*
clothier *s* vestiar·ius -(i)i *m*
clothing *s* vestit·us -ūs *m;* **an article of —**
vestiment·um -i *n*
cloud *s* nub·es -is *f; (dark storm cloud)*
nimb·us -i *m;* **small —** nebecul·a -ae *f*
cloud *tr* nubibus velare; *(fig)* obscurare **ǁ**
intr **to — up** nubescĕre
cloudburst *s* maximus im·ber -bris *m;* **I
arrived in Capua in a —** maximo imbri
Capuam veni
cloud-capped *adj* nubif·er -era -erum
cloudless *adj* seren·us -a -um
cloudy *adj* nubil·us -a -um; **somewhat —**
subnubil·us -a -um; **to get —** nubilare
clout *s* ict·us -ūs *m;* **to have —** *(coll)*
plurimum posse
clove *s (of garlic)* nucle·us -i *m*
cloven *adj* bisulc·us -a -um; **— hoofs**
ungul·ae -arum *fpl* spissae
clover *s* trifol·ium -(i)i *n*
clown *s* scurr·a -ae *m*
clown *intr* **to — around** scurrari
clownish *adj* scurril·is -is -e
cloy *tr* satiare
cloying *adj* putid·us -a -um
club *s (cudgel)* clav·a -ae *f; (society)*
sodalit·as -atis *f,* colleg·ium -(i)i *n*
club *tr* clavā dolare
cluck *intr* glocidare, singultire
cluck *s* singult·us -ūs *m*
clue *s* indic·ium -(i)i *n*
clump *s* mass·a -ae *f;* **— of trees**
arbust·um -i *n*
clumsily *adv* inscite, rustice
clumsiness *s* insciti·a -ae *f,* rusticit·as -atis *f*
clumsy *adj* inscit·us -a -um, rustic·us -a
-um; *(of things)* inhabil·is -is -e
cluster *s (of fruit, flowers, berries)*
corymb·us -i *m; (of people)* coron·a -ae *f*
cluster *intr* congregari; **to — around**
stipare
clutch *s* ungul·a -ae *f;* **from one's —es** e
manibus; **in one's —es** in sua potestate
clutch *tr* arrigĕre

clutter *s* congeri·es -ei *f*
clutter *tr* **to — up** conturbare
coach *s (four-wheeled)* raed·a -ae *f; (two-
wheeled, closed in, with arched top, for
women)* carpent·um -i *n; (trainer)*
exercit·or -oris *m; (of gladiators)*
lanist·a -ae *m*
coach *tr* exercēre
coagulate *intr* coïre
coagulation *s* coagulati·o -onis *f*
coal *s* carb·o -onis *m;* lapis gagas *(gen:*
lapidis gagatis)
coalesce *intr* coalescĕre
coalition *s* conjuncti·o -onis *f*
coal mine *s* fodin·a -ae *f* carbonaria
coarse *adj (materials)* crass·us -a -um;
(unfinished) rud·is -is -e; *(manners)*
incult·us -a -um
coarseness *s* crassitud·o -inis *f; (of manners)* rusticit·as -atis *f*
coast *s* or·a -ae *f;* **the — is clear** nihil
obstat
coast *intr* **to — along the shore** oram
praetervehi
coastal *adj* maritim·us -a -um
coastline *s* or·a -ae *f* maritima
coat *s* paenul·a -ae *f; (of animals)* pell·is
-is *f; (of paint, plaster)* inducti·o -onis *f*
coat *tr* illinĕre, obducĕre; **—ed tongue**
lingu·a -ae *f* fungosa
coating *s* inducti·o -onis *f*
coat of arms *s* insign·ia -ium *npl*
coat of mail *s* loric·a -ae *f*
coax *tr* blandiri
coaxing *s* blandiment·a -orum *npl*
coaxing *adj* bland·us -a -um
coaxingly *adv* blande
cobbler *s* sut·or -oris *m*
cobweb *s* arane·um -i *n*
cock *s* gall·us -i *m*
cock-a-doodle-do *interj* cocococo
cockeyed *adj* **— person** strab·o -onis *m*
cock fight *s* rix·a -ae *f* gallorum
cockroach *s* blatt·a -ae *f*
cocky *adj* jact·ans -antis
cocoa *s* fab·a -ae *f* Cacao
cocoanut *s* nu·x -cis *f* palmae Indicae
cocoon *s* globul·us -i *m*
coddle *tr* indulgēre *(w. dat)*
code *s (laws)* leg·es -um *fpl; (rules)*
praecept·a -orum *npl; (system of symbols)* not·ae -arum *fpl;* **in —** per notas;
Justinian — cod·ex -icis *m* Justinianeus
co-ed *s (coll)* condiscipul·a -ae *f*
codicil *s* codicill·i -orum *mpl*
codify *tr* digerĕre
coerce *tr* coercēre, cogĕre
coercion *s* coerciti·o -onis *f*
coeval *adj (with)* aequal·is -is -e *(w. dat)*
coexist *intr* simul existĕre
coffee *s* coffe·um -i *n;* **cup of —** pocill·um
-i *n* caffei
coffeepot *s* oll·a -ae *f* caffei

coffer *s* arc·a -ae *f*

coffin *s* capul·us -i *m*

cog *s* den·s -tis *m*

cogent *adj* grav·is -is -e

cognate *adj* cognat·us -a -um

cognition *s* cogniti·o -onis *f*

cognizance *s* cogniti·o -onis *f;* **to take —
of** cognitionem tractare de *(w. abl)*

cognizant *adj* **(of)** consci·us -a -um *(w.
gen)*

cohabit *intr* consuescĕre

cohabitation *s* consuetud·o -inis *f*

coheir *s* coher·es -edis *mf*

cohere *intr* cohaerēre

coherence *s* context·us -ūs *m*

coherent *adj* cohaer·ens -entis

coherently *adv* constanter

cohesion *s* cohaerenti·a -ae *f*

cohesive *adj* ten·ax -acis

cohort *s* cohor·s -tis *f*

coil *s* spir·a -ae *f*

coil *tr* glomerare ‖ *intr* glomerari

coin *s* numm·us -i *m*

coin *tr (to mint)* cudĕre; *(to stamp)* signare;
(words) fingĕre

coinage *s* monet·a -ae *f*

coincide *intr* **(with)** congruĕre (cum + *abl*)

coincidence *s* concursati·o -onis *f*

coincidental *adj* fortuit·us -a -um

coined *adj* monetal·is -is -e

cold *adj* frigid·us -a -um, gelid·us -a -um;
to be — frigēre; **to become —** frigescĕre

cold *s* frig·us -oris *n; (med)* graved·o -inis
f; **to catch a —** gravedinem contrahĕre;
to have a — gravedine dolēre

coldly *adv (fig)* frigide

coldness *s* frig·us -oris *n*

colic *s* tormin·a -um *npl*

colicky *adj* colic·us -a -um

collapse *s* ruin·a -ae *f*

collapse *intr* collabi

collar *s* collar·e -is *n*

collar *tr* collo comprehendĕre

collar bone *s* jugul·um -i *n*

collate *tr* conferre

collateral *adj (lines of descent)* trans-
vers·us -a -um; *(effect)* adjunct·us -a -um

collateral *s (com)* sponsi·o -onis *f*

colleague *s* colleg·a -ae *m*

collect *tr* conferre, colligĕre; *(to assemble)*
convocare; *(money)* exigĕre; **to — oneself** mentem *or* animum colligĕre; **to —
paintings and statues** tabulas signaque
comparare ‖ *intr (restore)* colligi

collected *adj* **to be —** praesentis animi esse

collection *s (act)* collecti·o -onis *f; (pile or
group collected)* congeri·es -ei *f; (literary)* corp·us -oris *n*

collective *adj* commun·is -is -e

collectively *adv* communiter, unā

college *s* colleg·ium -(i)i *n*

collegiate *adj* collegial·is -is -e

collide *intr* confligĕre

collision *s* conflicti·o -onis *f;* **a — of ships**

with one another concurs·us -ūs *m*
navium inter se

colloquial *adj* cotidian·us -a -um; **— language** serm·o -onis *m* cotidianus

collusion *s* collusi·o -onis *f;* **to be in —
with** colludĕre cum *(w. abl)*

colon *s (anat)* col·um -i *n; (gram)* col·on
-i *n*

colonel *s* tribun·us -i *m* militum

colonial *adj* colonic·us -a -um

colonist *s* colon·us -i *m*

colonize *tr* coloniam deducĕre in *(w. acc)*

colonnade *s* portic·us -ūs *f*

colony *s* coloni·a -ae *f*

color *s* col·or -oris *m;* **—s** vexill·um -i *n;*
with flying —s magnā cum gloriā

color *tr* colorare; *(to dye)* tingĕre

colossal *adj* imman·is -is -e

colossus *s* coloss·us -i *m*

colt *s* equul·us -i *m*

column *s* column·a -ae *f; (line)* agm·en
-inis *n*

comb *tr* pectĕre

comb *s* pect·en -inis *m*

combat *s* pugn·a -ae *f;* **— with wild beasts**
venati·o -onis *f*

combat *tr* pugnare cum *(w. abl)*

combatant *s* pugnat·or -oris *m*

combative *adj* pugn·ax -acis

combination *s (act)* conjuncti·o -onis *f;
(result)* junctur·a -ae *f; (of various ingredients)* compositi·o -onis *f;* **— of syllables** coït·us -ūs *m* syllabarum

combine *tr* conjungĕre, miscēre; *(in due
proportion)* temperare ‖ *intr* coïre; *(of
persons)* conspirare

combustible *adj* igni obnoxi·us -a -um

combustion *s* combusti·o -onis *f;* **during
—** dum comburitur

come *intr* venire; *(to arrive)* pervenire; *(to
happen)* fieri; *(of sleep)* accedĕre; **—
here!** istoc accede!; **to — about** evenire,
fieri; **to — across** occurrĕre *(w. dat);* **to
— after** (sub)sequi; **to — again** revenire;
to — along procedĕre; *(to accompany)*
comitari; **to — apart** solvi; **to — at** *(in
a hostile manner)* petĕre; **to — away**
abscedĕre; **to — back** revenire; **to —
before** praevenire; **to — between**
intervenire; **to — by** praeterire; *(to get)*
acquirĕre; **to — down** *(to descend)*
descendĕre; *(e.g., to the sea)* devenire;
to — down from antiquity ex antiquitate
tradi; **to — down with an illness** morbo
corripi; **to — first** antevenire; **to —
forth** exire; *(fig)* exoriri; **to — forward**
prodire; **to — in** introire; **to — into play**
accedĕre; **to — near** appropinquare,
accedĕre; **to — off** *(e.g., stem comes off
the apple)* recedĕre ab *(w. abl);* **to — off
victorious** victor discedĕre; **to — off
without a loss** sine detrimento discedĕre;
to — on pergĕre; *(to progress)* proficĕre;

to — on top of *(s.th. else)* supervenire *(w. dat)*; to — out (of) exire (ex + *abl)*; *(to be published)* edi, emitti; *(of teeth)* cadĕre; *(of evidence)* emergĕre; *(to end)* evenire; to — over supervenire; *(to a different part)* transgredi; *(of feelings, conditions)* obire, occupare; to — round *(fig)* transgredi; to — to advenire ad *or* in *(w. acc); (to cost)* vēnire *(w. gen of price); (after fainting)* resipiscĕre; to — to a head concoqui; to — to one's senses ad se redire; to — to pass evenire, fieri; to — to the assistance of subvenire*(w. dat);* to — together convenire; to — up subvenire; *(to occur)* provenire; to — up to *(to approach)* accedĕre ad *(w. acc);* to — upon *(to find)* invenire; *(to attack, as diseases)* ingruĕre *(w. dat);* whatever —s into s.o.'s head quae cuique libuissent

comedian *s* scurr·a -ae *m; (theat)* comoed·us -i *m*

comedy *s* comoedi·a -ae *f*

comely *adj* venust·us -a -um

comet *s* comet·es -ae *m*

comfort *s* solat·ium -(i)i *n;* —s commod·a -orum *npl*

comfort *tr* consolari

comfortable *adj* commod·us -a -um; **make yourselves** — rogo ut vobis suaviter sit

comfortably *adv* commode

comforter *s* consolat·or -oris *m*

comforting *adj* consol·ans -antis

comic *adj* comic·us -a -um

comic *s* scurr·a -ae *m*

comical *adj* ridicul·us -a -um

coming *adj* ventur·us -a -um

coming *s* advent·us -ūs *m*

comma *s* comm·a -atis *n*

command *s (order)* juss·um -i *n; (mil)* imper·ium -(i)i *n; (jurisdiction)* provinci·a -ae *f;* — of language copi·a -ae *f* verborum; to be in — of praesse *(w. dat);* to give a — to imperare *(w. dat);* to hold supreme military — summam imperii tenēre; to put s.o. in — of aliquem praeficĕre *(w. dat)*

commander *s* du·x -cis *m,* praefect·us -i *m*

commander-in-chief *s* imperat·or -oris *m*

commandment *s* mandat·um -i *n*

commemerate *tr* celebrare

commemoration *s* celebrati·o -onis *f*

commence *tr & intr* incipĕre

commencement *s* init·ium -(i)i *n*

commend *tr* approbare; *(to recommend; to commit)* commendare

commendable *adj* probabil·is -is -e

commendation *s* commendati·o -onis *f,* lau·s -dis *f*

comment *intr* commentari; to — on annotare, commentari

comment *s* sententi·a -ae *f; (note)* annotati·o -onis *f*

commentary *s* commentar·ium -(i)i *n;* —s commentari·i -orum *mpl*

commentator *s* interpr·es -etis *m*

commerce *s* commerc·ium -(i)i; to engage in — negotiari

commercial *adj* mercatori·us -a -um

commiserate *intr* to — with misereri *(w. gen)*

commiseration *s* misericordi·a -ae *f*

commission *s* mandat·um -i *n; (group)* consil·ium -(i)i *n;* out of — ex usu; to do business on — ex mandato negotiari

commission *tr* delegare, mandare

commissioner *s* curat·or -oris *m;* highway — viarum curator *m;* police — praefect·us -i *m* vigilum; water — aquarum curator *m*

commit *tr (crime)* admittĕre; *(to entrust)* committĕre; to — to memory ediscĕre; to — an error errare; to — a sin peccare; to — to prison in carcerem conjicĕre; to — to writing litteris mandare

commitment *s* pign·us -oris *n*

committee *s* consil·ium -(i)i *n*

commodity *s* mer·x -cis *f*

common *adj (shared)* commun·is -is -e, public·us -a -um; *(ordinary)* cotidian·us -a -um, vulgar·is -is -e; *(well-known)* vulgat·us -a -um; *(gram)* commun·is -is -e; — people vulg·us -i *n;* to have — sense cor habēre

commoner *s* plebe·us -i *m;* —s pleb·s -is *f*

commonly *adv* vulgo, fere

commonplace *adj* vulgar·is -is -e

commonwealth *s* res, rei *f* publica

commotion *s* tumult·us -ūs *m*

commune *intr* confabulari

communicate *tr* communicare; *(information)* impertire **||** *intr* to — with communicare *(w. dat)*

communicative *adj* affabil·is -is -e

communion *s* communi·o -onis *f*

community *s* civit·as -atis *f*

commutation *s* mutati·o -onis *f; (reduction)* remissi·o -onis *f*

commute *tr* commutare; his death sentence was —ed to exile capitis damnato exilium ei permissum est **||** *intr (travel)* ultro citroque commeare

commuter *s* commeat·or -oris *m*

compact *adj* spiss·us -a -um

compact *s* pact·um -i *n; (esp. public)* foed·us -eris *n;* to abide by the — in pacto manēre; to make a — *(of two parties)* foedus inter se facĕre

compact *tr* densare

compactly *adv* spisse, confertim

companion *s* com·es -itis *m; (mil)* contubernal·is -is *m*

companionship *s* sodalit·as -atis *f;* to enjoy s.o.'s — aliquo familiariter uti

company *s (com)* societ·as -atis *f; (guests)*

conviv·ium -(i)i *n;* *(mil)* centuri·o -onis *f;* *(theat)* gre·x -gis *m*
comparable *adj* comparabil·is -is -e
comparative *adj* aliorum ratione habitā; *(gram)* comparativ·us -a -um
comparative *s (gram)* comparativ·um -i *n,* grad·us -ūs *m* comparativus
comparatively *adv* comparative
compare *tr* comparare, conferre; —ed with adversus *(w. acc)*
comparison *s* comparati·o -onis *f;* in — with adversus *(w. acc)*
compartment *s* locul·us -i *m*
compass *s (instrument)* circin·us -i *m; (magnetic)* ac·us -ūs *f* magnetica; *(limits)* fin·es -ium *mpl*
compass *tr* circumdare
compassion *s* misericordi·a -ae *f*
compassionate *adj* misericor·s -dis
compassionately *adv* misericorditer
compatibility *s* congruenti·a -ae *f*
compatible *adj* congru·us -a -um
compatriot *s* civ·is -is *m*
compeer *s* aequal·is -is *mf*
compel *tr* compellĕre, cogĕre
compendium *s* summar·ium -(i)i *n*
compensate *tr* compensare ‖ *intr* to — for repensare, rependĕre
compensation *s (act)* compensati·o -onis *f; (pay)* merc·es -edis *f; (for damages)* poen·a -ae *f*
compete *intr* certare
competence *s* facult·as -atis *f; (legal capacity)* ju·s -ris *n*
competent *adj* perit·us -a -um; *(leg)* locupl·es -etis
competently *adv* satis idoneë
competition *s* certam·en -inis *n*
competitor *s* petit·or -oris *m*
compilation *s (act)* collecti·o -onis *f; (result)* collectane·a -orum *npl*
compile *tr* componĕre
compiler *s* composit·or -oris *m*
complacency *s* am·or -oris *m* sui
complacent *adj* qui sibi placet
complain *tr (about)* queri (super + *abl)*
complaint *s* querel·a -ae *f; (leg)* crim·en -inis *n; (med)* vit·ium -(i)i *n;* **to raise —s** querelas facĕre
complement *s* complement·um -i *n; (mil)* numer·us -i *m;* **to give the legions their full — of men** complēre legiones
complete *adj (entire)* plen·us -a -um; *(untouched)* integ·er -ra -rum; *(finished)* perfect·us -a -um; *(set)* just·us -a -um
complete *tr (years)* complēre; *(public works)* consummare; *(to accomplish)* perficĕre, peragĕre
completely *adv* plane, prorsus
completion *s* completi·o -onis *f; (accomplishment)* perfecti·o -onis *f,* confecti·o -onis *f*
complex *adj* multipl·ex -icis

complexion *s* col·or -oris *m*
complexity *s* multiplex natur·a -ae *f*
compliance *s* obtemperati·o -onis *f;* in — with an agreement ex pacto et convento
compliant *adj* obsequ·ens -entis
complicate *tr* impedire
complicated *adj* implicat·us -a -um
complication *s* implicati·o -onis *f*
complicity *s* conscienti·a -ae *f*
compliment *s* blandiment·um -i *n;* **as a —** honoris gratiā; **to pay s.o. a —** gratulari *(w. dat)*
compliment *tr* gratulari *(w. dat)*
complimentary *adj* honorific·us -a -um
comply *intr* **to — with** obsequi *(w. dat)*
component *s* element·um -i *n*
compose *tr* componĕre; *(verses)* condĕre; *(to calm)* sedare; **to — oneself** tranquillari
composed *adj* tranquill·us -a -um
composer *s* script·or -oris *m; (mus)* musicorum modorum script·or -oris *m*
composite *adj* composit·us -a -um
composition *s (act)* compositi·o -onis *f; (in literature)* scripti·o -onis *f; (work composed)* script·um -i *m*
composure *s* tranquillit·as -atis *f;* **to bear with —** aequo animo ferre; **to lose one's —** perturbari
compound *adj* composit·us -a -um
compound *s* compositi·o -onis *f; (noun)* compositum verb·um -i *n*
compound *tr* componĕre, duplicare
compound interest *s* anatocism·us -i *m*
comprehend *tr* continēre; *(to understand)* comprehendĕre
comprehensible *adj* perspicu·us -a -um
comprehension *s (act of grasping)* comprehensi·o -onis *f; (power of understanding)* intellect·us -ūs *m*
comprehensive *adj* ampl·us -a -um
compress *tr* comprimĕre; *(to abridge)* coartare
compress *s (med)* foment·um -i *n*
compression *s* compressi·o -onis *f*
comprise *tr* continēre; **to be —ed of** constare ex *(w. abl)*
compromise *s (bilateral)* compromiss·um -i *n; (unilateral)* accommodati·o -onis *f*
compromise *tr* compromittĕre; *(to imperil)* in periculum ac discrimen vocare ‖ *intr* pacisci
compulsion *s* necessit·as -atis *f;* **by —** per vim
compulsory *adj* necessari·us -a -um
compunction *s* compuncti·o -onis *f;* **I feel —** me paenitet
computation *s* computati·o -onis *f*
compute *tr* computare
computer *s* computat·or -oris *m*
comrade *s* sodal·is -is *m; (mil)* contubernal·is -is *m*
comradeship *s* societ·as -atis *f*

con *tr (coll)* defraudare; **to — s.o out of his money** aliquem pecuniā defraudare
concave *adj* concav·us -a -um
conceal *tr* celare, occultare, abděre
concealed *adj* celat·us -a -um
concealment *s (act)* occultati·o -onis *f; (place)* latebr·ae -arum *fpl;* **to be in —** latebras agěre
concede *tr* conceděre
conceit *s* superbi·a -ae *f*
conceited *adj* superbiā tum·ens -entis
conceivable *adj* quod fingi potest
conceive *tr* concipěre **‖** *intr* **to — of** fingěre
concentrate *tr* in unum locum contrahěre **‖** *intr* **to — on** animum intenděre in *(w. acc)*
concentration *s* in unum locum contracti·o -onis *f; (fig)* animi intenti·o -onis *f*
concept *s* sententi·a -ae *f*
conception *s (in womb)* concept·us -ūs *m; (idea)* informati·o -onis *f*
concern *s (affair)* res, rei *f,* negot·ium -(i)i *n; (worry)* cur·a -ae *f; (importance)* moment·um -i *n;* **it is of — to me** mihi curae est
concern *tr* pertiněre ad *(w. acc); (to worry)* sollicitare; **as far as I'm —ed** per me; **it —s me** meā refert
concerned *adj* sollicit·us -a -um
concerning *prep* de *(w. abl)*
concert *s (mus)* concent·us -ūs *m,* symphoni·a -ae *f;* **in — ex** composito
concert *tr* **— a plan** consilium inire
concession *s* concessi·o -onis *f; (thing)* concess·um -i *n; (com)* conducti·o -onis *f;* **to make a —** conceděre
conch *s* conch·a -ae *f*
conciliate *tr* conciliare
conciliation *s* conciliati·o -onis *f*
conciliatory *adj* pacific·us -a -um
concise *adj* press·us -a -um
concisely *adv* presse
conciseness *s* brevit·as -atis *f*
conclave *s* conclav·e -is *n*
conclude *tr (to end)* terminare; *(to infer)* colligěre; **I must — my speech** mihi perorandum est; **to — a treaty** foedus icěre
conclusion *s (end)* fin·is -is *m,* conclusi·o -onis *f; (of speech)* perorati·o -onis *f; (inference)* conclusi·o -onis *f;* **in — ad** ultimum; **they came to the — that** eis placuit ut; **to draw the —** colligěre
conclusive *adj* firm·us -a -um
concoct *tr* concoquěre; *(to contrive)* fingěre, conflare
concoction *s* pot·us -ūs *m; (fig)* machinati·o -onis *f*
concomitant *adj* adjunct·us -a -um
concord *s* concordi·a -ae *f*
concordat *s* pact·um -i *n*
concourse *s* concurs·us -ūs *m*
concrete *adj* concret·us -a -um; **in the —, not in the abstract** re, non cogitatione

concrete *s* concret·um -i *n*
concubinage *s* concubinat·us -ūs *m*
concubine *s* concubin·a -ae *f*
concupiscence *s* libid·o -inis *f*
concur *intr* consentire
concurrence *s* consensi·o -onis *f*
concussion *s (med)* quassatur·a -ae *f*
condemn *tr* damnare; **to — to death** capitis damnare
condemnation *s* damnati·o -onis *f*
condensation *s* densati·o -onis *f*
condense *tr* (cond)densare **‖** *intr* densari
condescend *intr* se summittěre
condescending *adj* fastidios·us -a -um
condescendingly *adv* fastidiose
condescension *s* comit·as -atis *f*
condition *s (state)* stat·us -ūs *m,* condici·o -onis *f; (stipulation)* condici·o -onis *f,* le·x -gis *f;* **in excellent — habitissim·us -a -um; in bad (good) — male (bene)** habit·us -a -um; **on — that** eā lege ut; **physical — corporis** habit·us -ūs *m*
condition *tr* informare
conditional *adj* condicional·is -is -e
conditionally *adv* condicionaliter
condole *intr* **to — with** dolēre cum *(w. abl)*
condolence *s* consolati·o -onis *f;* **I gave him my —** doloris ejus particeps factus sum; **letter of —** litter·ae -arum *fpl* consolatoriae
condone *tr* condonare
conducive *adj* util·is -is -e ad *(w. acc)*
conduct *s (behavior)* mor·es -um *mpl; (management)* administrati·o -onis *f*
conduct *tr (to lead)* adducěre; *(to manage)* administrare
conductor *s* duct·or -oris *m*
conduit *s* canal·is -is *m*
cone *s* con·us -i *m*
confection *s* cupped·o -inis *f*
confectioner *s* cuppedinar·ius -(i)i *m*
confectionery *s* cuppedi·a -orum *npl*
confederacy *s (treaty)* foed·us -eris *n; (allied states)* civitat·es -um *fpl* foederatae
confederate *adj* foederat·us -a -um
confederate *s* soc·ius -(i)i *m*
confederation *s* civitat·es -um *fpl* foederatae
confer *tr* deferre, tribuěre **‖** *intr* colloqui, conferre
conference *s* colloqu·ium -(i)i *n*
confess *tr* confiteri, fateri
confessedly *adv* ex confesso
confession *s* confessi·o -onis *f*
confidant *s* consci·us -(i)i *m,* consci·a -ae *f*
confide *tr* committěre **‖** *intr* **to — in** confiděre *(w. dat)*
confidence *s* fid·es -ei *f; (assurance)* fiduci·a -ae *f; (esp. self-confidence)* confidenti·a -ae *f;* **to have — in** fidem

habēre *(w. dat);* **to inspire —** in fidem
facĕre *(w. dat)*
confident *adj* fid·ens -entis
confidential *adj (worthy of confidence)*
fid·us -a -um; *(secret)* secret·us -a -um
confidently *adv* fidenter
configuration *s* figur·a -ae *f*
confine *tr* includĕre; *(to restrain)* cohibēre;
(to limit) circumscribĕre
confined *adj* art·us -a -um, angust·us -a
-um; **to be — to bed** lecto teneri
confines *spl* confin·ium -(i)i *n; (boundary)* fin·es -ium *mpl;* **on the —** of
finitim·us -a -um *(w. dat);* **within the —**
of in confinio *(w. gen)*
confirm *tr* confirmare; *(to prove)* comprobare; *(to ratify)* sancire
confirmation *s* confirmati·o -onis *f*
confirmed *adj* (con)firmat·us -a -um; *(habitual)* inveterat·us -a -um; *(proved)*
comprobat·us -a -um
confiscate *tr* publicare
confiscation *s* publicati·o -onis *f*
conflagration *s* incend·ium -(i)i *n*
conflict *s* pugn·a -ae *f;* **to be in —** *(fig)*
inter se repugnare
conflict *intr* inter se repugnare
conflicting *adj* repugn·ans -antis
confluence *s* conflu·ens -entis *m*
conform *intr (to)* obtemperare *(w. dat),* se
accommodare ad *(w. acc)*
conformation *s* conformati·o -onis *f*
conformity *s* convenienti·a -ae *f;* **in —**
with secundum *(w. acc)*
confound *tr (to confuse)* confundĕre; *(to
disconcert)* exanimare
confounded *adj* nefand·us -a -um
confront *tr* obviam ire *(w. dat),* se opponĕre
(w. dat)
confrontation *s* obstanti·a -ae *f*
confuse *tr* confundĕre, turbare
confused *adj* confus·us -a -um, turbat·us
-a -um
confusedly *adv* confuse
confusion *s* confusi·o -onis *f*
confutation *s* refutati·o -onis *f*
confute *tr* confutare
congeal *tr* congelare **||** *intr* concrescĕre, se
congelare
congenial *adj* consentane·us -a -um
congenital *adj* nativ·us -a -um
congested *adj* refert·us -a -um
congestion *s (traffic)* frequenti·a -ae *f,*
concurs·us -ūs *m;* **nasal —** stillati·o
-onis *f*
congratulate *tr* gratulari *(w. dat)*
congratulations *spl* gratulati·o -onis *f;*
— ! macte virtute esto *(pl:* estote)!
congratulatory *adj* gratulabund·us -a -um
congregate *tr* congregare **||** *intr* congregari
congregation *s* coët·us -ūs *m*
conical *adj* conic·us -a -um
conifer *s* arb·or -oris *f* conifera

conjectural *adj* conjectural·is -is -e
conjecturally *adv* ex conjectura
conjecture *s* conjectur·a -ae *f*
conjecture *tr* conjectare
conjugal *adj* conjugal·is -is -e
conjugate *tr* declinare
conjugation *s* declinati·o -onis *f*
conjunction *s* concurs·us -ūs *m; (gram)*
conjuncti·o -onis *f*
conjure *tr (to beseech solemnly)* obtestari;
to — up *(ghosts)* eliciēre; *(fig)* excogitare,
effingĕre
conjurer *s* mag·us -i *m*
con-man *s* plan·us -i *m*
connect *tr* connectĕre; *(in a series)* serĕre
connected *adj* conjunct·us -a -um; *(by
marriage)* affin·is -is -e; *(of buildings)*
(to) adfict·us -a -um *(w. dat);* **to be
closely — with** inhaerēre *(w. dat);* **to be
— with s.o. by blood and race** aliquem
sanguine ac genere contingĕre
connection *s* conjuncti·o -onis *f,* nex·us
-ūs *m; (kin)* necessitud·o -inis *f; (by
marriage)* affinit·as -atis *f*
connivance *s* indulgenti·a -ae *f*
connive *intr* connivēre
connoisser *s* doctus existimat·or -oris *m*
connotation *s* significati·o -onis *f* latens
connubial *adj* connubial·is -is -e
conquer *tr* vincĕre
conqueror *s* vict·or -oris *m,* victr·ix -icis *f*
conquest *s* victor·ia -ae *f*
consanguinity *s* consanguinit·as -atis *f*
conscience *s* conscienti·a -ae *f;* **guilty —**
mala conscientia *f;* **to have no —** nullam
religionem habēre
conscientious *adj* pi·us -a -um, religios·us
-a -um
conscientiously *adv* diligenter
conscious *adj* consci·us -a -um
consciously *adv* scienter
consciousness *s (awareness)* conscienti·a
-ae *f;* **to lose —** animum relinquĕre; **to
regain —** resipiscĕre
conscript *s* tir·o -onis *m*
conscript *tr* conscribĕre
conscription *s* delect·us -ūs *m*
consecrate *tr* consecrare
consecration *s* consecrati·o -onis *f*
consecutive *adj* continu·us -a -um
consecutively *adv* continenter
consent *intr* consentire
consent *s* consens·us -ūs *m;* **to give one's
—** permittĕre; **with the — of the people**
secundo populo; **without my —** me
invito
consequence *s* consecuti·o -onis *f,*
event·us -ūs *m;* **a man of —** hom·o
-inis *m* auctoritate praeditus; **as a —** ex
eo; **it is of great —** magni interest; **it is
of no —** nihil refert; **thing of no —**
parva res, rei *f*
consequent *adj* consequ·ens -entis

consequently *adv* igitur, itaque

consequential *adj* consentane·us -a -um

conservation *s* conservati·o -onis *f*

conservative *adj* a rebus novandis abhorr·ens -entis; *(pol)* reipublicae statūs conservandi studios·us -a -um; — **party** optimat·es -um *mpl*

conserve *tr* conservare

consider *tr* considerare; *(to deem)* aestimare, ducĕre; *(to respect)* respicĕre

considerable *adj* aliquantul·us -a -um; *(of persons)* illustr·is -is -e; *(of size)* ampl·us -a -um

considerably *adv* aliquantum; *(w. comp)* multo, aliquanto

considerate *adj* human·us -a -um

consideration *s* considerati·o -onis *f*; *(regard)* respect·us -ūs *m*; *(ground, motive)* rati·o -onis *f*; *(payment)* pret·ium -(i)i *n*; **out of** — **for** ob *(w. acc)*; **to have** — **for the wounded;** sauciorum rationem habēre; **to show** — **for s.th.** alicujus rei respectum habēre

considering *prep* pro *(w. abl)*

consign *tr* mandare

consignment *s* **goods given** (*or* **sent**) **on** — merc·es -ium *fpl* ex perscriptione traditae (*or* missae)

consist *intr* **to** — **of** constare ex *(w. abl)*, consistĕre ex *(w. abl)*

consistency *s* constanti·a -ae *f*; *(viscosity)* crassitud·o -inis *f*

consistent *adj* const·ans -antis

consistently *adv* constanter

consolable *adj* consolabil·is -is -e

consolation *s* consolati·o -onis *f*; *(thing)* solac·ium -(i)i *n*

console *tr* consolari

consolidate *tr* solidare, stabilire

consonant *adj* conson·us -a -um

consonant *s* conson·ans -antis *f*

consort *s* conju·x -gis *mf*

consort *intr* **to** — **with** familiariter uti *(w. abl)*, se associare cum *(w. abl)*

conspicuous *adj* conspicu·us -a -um

conspicuously *adv* insigniter

conspiracy *s* conjurati·o -onis *f*

conspirator *s* conjurat·us -i *m*

conspire *intr* conjurare

constable *s* viat·or -oris *m*

constancy *s* constanti·a -ae *f*

constant *adj* *(fixed)* const·ans -antis; *(loyal)* fid·us -a -um; *(incessant)* perpetu·us -a -um

constantly *adv* assidue, perpetuo

constellation *s* sid·us -eris *n*

consternation *s* consternati·o -onis *f*; **to be in** — trepidare; **to throw into** — perterrēre

constipated *adj* **he is** — venter ejus est astrictus

constipation *s* alv·us -i *f* astricta

constituent *s* *(part)* element·um -i *n*; —**s** *(pol)* suffragator·es -um *mpl*

constitute *tr* constituĕre

constitution *s* *(physical)* habit·us -ūs *m*; *(pol)* reipublicae leg·es -um *fpl*

constitutional *adj* legitim·us -a -um

constitutionally *adv* legitime

constrain *tr* cogĕre

constraint *s* vis *f*; **by** — per vim

construct *tr* construĕre; *(esp. things of mechanical kind)* fabricare

construction *s* constructi·o -onis *f*, fabricati·o -onis *f*; *(of a road)* muniti·o -onis *f*; *(interpretation)* interpretati·o -onis *f*

construe *tr* interpretari; *(gram)* construĕre

consul *s* cons·ul -ulis *m*; — **elect** consul *m* designatus

consular *adj* consular·is -is -e; **a man of** — **rank** consular·is -is *m*

consulship *s* consulat·us -ūs *m*; **during my** — me consule; **in the** — **of Caesar and Bibulus** Caesare et Bibulo consulibus; **to hold the** — consulatum gerĕre; **to run for the** — consulatum petĕre

consult *tr* consultare ‖ *intr* deliberare

consultation *s* consultati·o -onis *f*

consume *tr* consumĕre

consumer *s* empt·or -oris *m*

consuming *adj* ed·ax -acis

consummate *adj* summ·us -a -um

consummate *tr* consummare

consummation *s* consummati·o -onis *f*; *(end)* exit·us -ūs *m*

consumption *s* consumpti·o -onis *f*; *(disease)* tab·es -is *f*

consumptive *adj* **to be** — tabe laborare

contact *s* contact·us -ūs *m*; *(connection)* necessitud·o -inis *f*; **to come in** — **with** contingĕre

contagion *s* contag·ium -(i)i *n*; *(esp. fig)* contagi·o -onis *f*

contagious *adj* contagios·us -a -um

contain *tr* continēre; *(to hold, as a vessel)* capĕre

container *s* receptacul·um -i *n*, va·s -sis *n*

contaminate *tr* contaminare

contamination *s* contaminati·o -onis *f*

contemplate *tr* contemplari; *(some action)* considerare

contemplation *s* contemplati·o -onis *f*; *(of an action)* considerati·o -onis *f*

contemplative *adj* contemplativ·us -a -um

contemporaneous *adj* aequal·is -is -e

contemporaneously *adv* simul

contemporary *s* aequaev·us -i *m*

contempt *s* contempt·us -ūs *m*

contemptible *adj* contempt·us -a -um

contemptibly *adv* abjecte

contemptuous *adj* fastidios·us -a -um

contend *tr* *(to aver)* affirmare ‖ *intr* contendĕre; *(to dispute)* verbis certare; **to** — **against** adversari

contending *adj* avers·us -a -um

content *adj* (with) content·us -a -um *(w. abl)*

content *tr* satisfacĕre *(w. dat)*

contented *adj* content·us -a -um

contentedly *adv* aequo animo

contention *s* contenti·o -onis *f*

contentious *adj* pugn·ax -acis; *(litigious)* litigios·us -a -um

contentment *s* aequus anim·us -i *m*

contents *spl* quod inest, quae insunt; *(of a book)* argument·um -i *n; (see* **table of contents**)

contest *s* certam·en -inis *n*

contest *tr (to dispute)* resistĕre *(w. dat); (leg)* lege agĕre de *(w. abl)*

contestant *s* petit·or -oris *m*

context *s* context·us -ūs *m*

contiguous *adj* contigu·us -a -um

continence *s* continenti·a -ae *f*

continent *adj* contin·ens -entis

continent *s* par·s -tis *f* terrae

contingent *s* man·us -ūs *f*

continual *adj* continu·us -a -um; *(lasting)* perpetu·us -a -um

continually *adv* assidue, continenter

continuance *s* continuati·o -onis *f; (leg)* prolati·o -onis *f*

continuation *s* continuati·o -onis *f*

continue *tr* continuare; *(leg)* proferre ‖ *intr* pergĕre; *(to last)* persistĕre

continuity *s* continuit·as -atis *f*

continuous *adj* continu·us -a -um, perpetu·us -a -um

continuously *adv* continenter

contortion *s* contorti·o -onis *f*

contour *s* lineament·um -i *n*

contraband *s* interdict·a -orum *npl*

contraception *s* conceptionis inhibiti·o -onis *f*

contraceptive *adj* conceptionis inhibit·ens -entis

contraceptive *s* atoc·ium -(i)i *n*

contract *tr* contrahĕre ‖ *intr* contrahi; **to — for** pacisci, locare; *(of the party undertaking the work)* conducĕre; **to — for the making of a statue** statuam faciendam locare

contract *s* pact·um -i *n; (on the part of the hirer)* locati·o -onis *f; (on the part of the one hired)* redempti·o -onis *f*

contraction *s* contracti·o -onis *f; (of a word)* compend·ium -(i)i *n*

contractor *s* conduct·or -oris *m*

contradict *tr* contradicĕre; **to — oneself** secum pugnare, pugnantia loqui

contradiction *s* contradicti·o -onis *f; (inconsistency)* repugnanti·a -ae *f*

contradictory *adj* contradictori·us -a -um, repugn·ans -antis

contraption *s* machin·a -ae *f*

contrary *adj (opposite)* contrari·us -a -um; *(fig)* repugn·ans -antis; **— to** contra *(w. acc)*

contrary *s* contrar·ium -(i)i *n;* **on the —** contra

contrast *s* comparati·o -onis *f,* oppositi·o -onis *f*

contrast *tr* comparare, opponĕre ‖ *intr* discrepare

contribute *tr* contribuĕre, conferre ‖ *intr* **to — towards** conferre ad *or* in *(w. acc)*

contribution *s* contributi·o -onis *f; (money)* stip·s -is *f; (gift)* don·um -i *n*

contributor *s* collat·or -oris *m,* donat·or -oris *m*

contributory *adj* contribu·ens -entis

contrite *adj* paenit·ens -entis

contrition *s* paenitenti·a -ae *f; (eccl)* contriti·o -onis *f*

contrivance *s (act)* machinati·o -onis *f; (thing)* machin·a -ae *f*

contrive *tr* excogitare, machinari

control *s (restraint)* continenti·a -ae *f; (power)* moderati·o -onis *f,* potest·as -atis *f*

control *tr* continēre; *(to govern)* imperare *(w. dat)*

controller *s* moderat·or -oris *m*

controversial *adj* controvers·us -a -um

controversy *s* controversi·a -ae *f*

contusion *s* contusi·o -onis *f*

conundrum *s* aenigm·a -atis *n*

convalesce *intr* convalescĕre

convalescent *adj* convalesc·ens -entis

convene *tr* convocare ‖ *intr* coïre

convenience *s* commodit·as -atis *f; (thing)* commod·um -i *n;* **at your —** commodo tuo, ex commodo

convenient *adj* commod·us -a -um; *(time, occasion)* opportun·us -a -um

conveniently *adv* commode, opportune

convention *s* convent·us -ūs *m; (custom)* consuetud·o -inis *f*

conventional *adj* vulgat·us -a -um

converge *intr* vergĕre, coïre

conversant *adj* perit·us -a -um; **to be — with** versari in *(w. abl)*

conversation *s* colloqu·ium -(i)i *n*

conversational *adj* in colloquio usitat·us -a -um

converse *intr* colloqui

converse *s* convers·us -ūs *m*

conversely *adv* e converso

conversion *s* conversi·o -onis *f*

convert *tr* convertĕre

convert *s* neophyt·us -i *m*

convertible *adj* commutabil·is -is -e

convex *adj* convex·us -a -um

convey *tr* convehĕre, advehĕre; *(to impart)* significare; *(leg)* abalienare

conveyance *s (act)* advecti·o -onis *f; (vehicle)* vehicul·um -i *n; (leg)* abalienati·o -onis *f*

convict *s* qui ad poenam damnatus est

convict *tr* (of) convincĕre *(w. gen of the offense);* **—ed of a lie** mendacii manifest·us -a -um

conviction *s (leg)* damnati•o -onis *f; (belief)* persuasi•o -onis *f;* **it is my firm —** mihi persuasissimum est

convince *tr* persuadēre *(w. dat)*

convinced *adj* **I am firmly — that** plenus persuasionis sum *(w. acc & inf)*

convincing *adj* ad persuadendum apt•us -a -um; **there is — proof that** magno argumento est *(w. acc & inf)*

convivial *adj* hilar•is -is -e

conviviality *s* hilarit•as -atis *f*

convocation *s* convocati•o -onis *f*

convoke *tr* convocare

convoy *s (naut)* praesidiaria class•is -is *f*

convulse *tr* convellēre

convulsions *spl* spasm•us -i *m;* **to have —** spasmo vexari

convulsive *adj* spastic•us -a -um

coo *intr* canēre

cooing *s* cant•us -ūs *m*

cook *s* coqu•us -i *m,* coqu•a -ae *f*

cook *tr* coquēre; **to — up** *(fig)* excogitare **ǁ** *intr* coquēre

cooked *adj* elix•us -a -um

cookie *s* crustul•um -i *n*

cool *adj* frigidul•us -a -um; *(fearless)* impavid•us -a -um; *(indifferent)* frigid•us -a -um

cool *s* **to keep one's —** mentem compescere

cool *tr* refrigerare **ǁ** *intr* refrigerari; *(fig)* defervescēre; **to — off** intepescēre

cooling *adj* frigoric•us -a -um

coolness *s* frig•us -oris *n; (indifference)* lentitud•o -inis *f; (calmness)* aequus anim•us -i *m*

coop *s (for chickens)* cave•a -ae *f*

coop *tr* **to — up** includēre

cooperate *intr* unā agēre

cooperation *s* adjument•um -i *n*

cope *intr* **to — with** certare cum *(w. abl);* **to be able to — with** par *(w. dat)* esse; **to be unable to — with** impar *(w. dat)* esse

copious *adj* copios•us -a -um

copiously *adv* copiose

copper *s* cupr•um -i *n,* ae•s -ris *n*

copper *adj* cuprin•us -a -um

coppersmith *s* aerar•ius -(i)i *m*

copulate *intr* coïre

copulation *s* coït•us -ūs *m*

copulative *s (gram)* copulativ•us -a -um

copy *s* exempl•ar -aris *n*

copy *tr (to imitate)* imitari; *(in writing)* **(from)** exscribēre (ex + *abl*)

coquette *s* lup•a -ae *f*

coquettish *adj* lasciv•us -a -um

coral *adj* coralin•us -a -um

coral *s* coral•ium -(i)i *n*

cord *s* funicul•us -i *m*

cordial *adj* benign•us -a -um; *(sincere)* sincer•us -a -um; **to give s.o. a — welcome** aliquem benigne excipēre

cordiality *s* comit•as -atis *f*

cordially *adv* benigne, ex animo

cordon *s* coron•a -ae *f*

cordon *tr* **to — off** saepire

corduroy *s* textil•e -is *n* crassum et striatum

core *s (of fruit)* volv•a -ae *f; (fig)* nucle•us -i *m*

Corinth *s* Corinth•us -i *f*

Corinthian *adj* Corinthiac•us -a -um

cork *s* cort•ex -icis *m; (stopper)* obturament•um -i *n*

corn *s* ze•a -ae *f; (on toe)* call•us -i *m*

corned beef *s* bubul•a -ae *f* muriatica

corner *s* angul•us -i *m; (of street)* compit•um -i *n; (tight spot)* angusti•ae -arum *fpl*

corner *tr* impedire; *(com)* coëmēre ad quaestum

cornice *s* coron•a -ae *f*

cornucopia *s* corn•u -ūs *n* copiae

corollary *s* corollar•ium -(i)i *n*

coronation *s* coronati•o -onis *f*

coronet *s* diadem•a -atis *n*

corporal *adj* corporal•is -is -e, corporis *(gen);* **— punishment** veber•a -orum *npl*

corporal *s* decuri•o -onis *m*

corporate *adj* corporat•us -a -um

corporation *s* colleg•ium -(i)i *n*

corporeal *adj* corporeal•is -is -e

corps *s* legi•o -onis *f*

corpse *s* cadav•er -eris *n*

corpulent *adj* corpulent•us -a -um

corpuscle *s* corpuscul•um -i *n*

correct *adj* correct•us -a -um

correct *tr* corrigēre; *(to remove faults)* emendare; *(to chastise)* castigare

correction *s* correcti•o -onis *f;* emendati•o -onis *f;* castigati•o -onis *f*

corrective *adj* ad corrigendum apt•us -a -um

corrective *s* remed•ium -(i)i *n*

correctly *adv* probe, integre

correlation *s* mutua rati•o -onis *f*

correspond *intr* congruēre; *(to each other)* inter se congruēre; *(by letter)* epistularum commercium habēre

correspondence *s* congruenti•a -ae *f; (exchange of letters)* epistularum commerc•ium -(i)i *n*

correspondent *s* epistularum script•or -oris *m*

corridor *s* andr•on -onis *m*

corroborate *tr* confirmare

corrode *tr* erodēre

corrosion *s* rosi•o -onis *f*

corrosive *adj* corrosiv•us -a -um; *(fig)* mord•ax -acis

corrupt *tr* corrumpēre

corrupt *adj* corrupt•us -a -um, putrid•us -a -um; *(accessible to bribery)* venal•is -is -e; *(text)* depravat•us -a -um

corrupter *s* corrupt•or -oris *m,* corruptr•ix -icis *f*

corruption *s* corrupti•o -onis *f*

corsage *s* fascicul•us -i *m* florum

corselet *s (mil)* loric·a -ae *f*
cortege *s* comitat·us -ūs *m*
cosily *adv* commode
cosmetic *s* medicam·en -inis *n; (rouge-like)* fuc·us -i *m*
cost *s (price)* pret·ium -(i)i *n; (expense)* impens·a -ae *f;* — **of living** anon·a -ae *f*
cost *intr* constare *(usu. w. abl of definite price);* **how much does it** —? quanti constat?; **it** —**s nothing** gratis constat; **the victory** — **the lives of many** victoria morte multorum constitit; **to** — **200 denarii** ducentis denariis constare
costliness *s* carit·as -atis *f*
costly *adj* pretios·us -a -um; *(extravagant)* sumptuos·us -a -um
costume *s* habit·us -ūs *m*
cosy *adj* commod·us -a -um
cot *s* grabat·us -i *m*
cottage *s* cas·a -ae *f*
cotton *s* gossyp·ium -(i)i *n*
cotton *adj* gossypin·us -a -um
couch *s* cubil·e -is *n; (esp. for dining)* lect·us -i *m*
cough *s* tuss·is -is *(acc:* tussim) *f;* **to have a bad** — male tussire
cough *tr* **to** — **up** extussire ‖ *intr* tussire
council *s* concil·ium -(i)i *n*
councilor *s* consiliar·ius -(i)i *m*
counsel *tr* consulĕre
counselor *s* consiliat·or -oris *m*
count *s* com·es -itis *m*
count *s* computati·o -onis *f; (total)* summ·a -ae *f; (of indictment)* cap·ut -itis *n*
count *tr* numerare, computare; *(to regard)* habēre, ducĕre; **to** — **out** *or* **up** enumerare; **to** — **out to** annumerare *(w. dat)* ‖ *intr* aestimari, habēri; **to** — **upon** confidĕre *(w. dat); you can* — **on it that** erit tibi perspectum *(w. acc & inf)*
countenance *s* vult·us -ūs *m*
countenance *tr* indulgēre *(w. dat)*
counter *s (of shop, kitchen)* abac·us -i *m; (in games)* calcul·us -i *m*
counteract *intr* obsistĕre *(w. dat); (a sickness)* medēri *(w. dat)*
counterattack *s* impet·us -ūs *m* contra hostium impetum
counterattack *intr* impetum contra hostium impetum facĕre
counterfeit *tr (to pretend)* simulare; *(money)* adulterare
counterfeit *s* monet·a -ae *f* adulterina
counterfeit *adj* simulat·us -a -um; *(money)* adulterin·us -a -um
counterfeiter *s* falsar·ius -(i)i *m*
countermand *tr* irritum facĕre
counterpart *s (person)* pa·r -ris *n; (thing)* res, rei *f* gemella
countersign *tr* contrascribĕre
countless *adj* innumerabil·is -is -e
country *s* terr·a -ae *f; (territory)* fin·es -ium *mpl; (not city)* ru·s -ris *n; (native)* patri·a -ae *f; of what* — cuj·as -atis; **of what** — **are you?** cujates estis?
country *adj* rustic·us -a -um
country estate *s* suburban·um -i *n*
country-fresh *adj* agrest·is -is -e
country house *s* vill·a -ae *f* urbana
countryman *s* civ·is -is *m*
countryside *s* agr·i -orum *mpl*
couple *s* pa·r -ris *n; (married couple)* marit·i -orum *mpl;* **a couple of** aliquantul·i -ae -a
couple *tr* copulare ‖ *intr (of animals)* coïre
courage *s* virt·us -utis *f,* anim·us -i *m;* **to lose** — animum demittĕre; **to take** — bono animo esse
courageous *adj* fort·is -is -e
courageously *adv* fortiter
courier *s* curs·or -oris *m,* nunt·ius -(i)i *m; (letter carrier)* tabellar·ius -(i)i *m*
course *s (movement, of ship, of river, of stars, etc.)* curs·us -ūs *m; (of life)* rati·o -onis *f; (of water)* duct·us -ūs *m; (route)* it·er -ineris *n; (at table)* fercul·um -i *n; (order)* seri·es -ei *f; (for racing)* circ·us -i *m,* stad·ium -(i)i *n;* **in due** — mox; **in the** — **of** inter *(w. acc); of* — de more, profecto; *(sarcastically)* scilicet; **to be driven off** — cursu excuti; **to change** — iter flectĕre
court *s (leg)* for·um -i *n,* judic·ium -(i)i *n; (open area)* are·a -ae *f; (inner court of a house)* atr·ium -(i)i *n; (palace)* aul·a -ae *f; (retinue)* comitat·us -ūs *m;* **to take to** — in judicium vocare
court *tr* colĕre, ambire; *(a woman)* petĕre; *(danger)* se offerre *(w. dat)*
court costs *spl* litis impens·ae -arum *fpl*
courteous *adj* com·is -is -e
courteously *adv* comiter
courtesan *s* meretr·ix -cis *f*
courtesy *s* comit·as -atis *f;* — **of** beneficio *(w. gen)*
courtesy call *s* offic·ium -(i)i *n*
courthouse *s* basilic·a -ae *f*
courtier *s* aulic·us -i *m*
courtly *adj* aulic·us -a -um
court-martial *s* judic·ium -(i)i *n* castrense
courtship *s* procati·o -onis *f*
courtyard *s* are·a -ae *f*
cousin *s (on mother's side; used also for cousin in general)* consobrin·us -i *m,* consobrin·a -ae *f; (on father's side)* patruel·is -is *mf*
cove *s* sin·us -ūs *m*
covenant *s* pact·um -i *n*
covenant *s* pacisci
cover *s (for concealment and shelter)* tegment·um -i *n; (lid)* opercul·um -i *n; (mil)* praesid·ium -(i)i *n; (pretense)* speci·es -ei *f;* **under** — **of the artillery** tormentis munit·us -a -um; **under** — **of darkness** nocte adjuvante
cover *tr* tegĕre, operire; *(to hide)* celare; **to**

— **up** obtegĕre; *(against the cold)* bene operire
coverlet *s* stragul·um -i *n; (for bed or couch)* toral·e -is *n*
covet *tr* concupiscĕre
covetous *adj* appet·ens -entis
covey *s* gre·x -gis *m*
cow *tr* domare
coward *s* hom·o -inis *m* ignavus
cowardice *s* ignavi·a -ae *f*
cowardly *adj* ignav·us -a -um
cower *intr* subsidĕre
coy *adj* verecund·us -a -um
coyly *adv* verecunde
coyness *s* verecundi·a -ae *f*
cozily *adv* commode
cozy *adj* commod·us -a -um
crab *s* can·cer -cri *m*
crabby *adj* moros·us -a -um
crack *s* rim·a -ae *f; (noise)* crepit·us -ūs *m;* **at the — of dawn** primā luce
crack *tr* findĕre; *(nuts, etc.)* perfringĕre; *(a code)* enodare; **to — jokes** joca dicĕre ‖ *intr* rimas agĕre; *(to sound)* crepitare; *(of the voice)* irraucescĕre; **to — down on** castigare
cracked *adj* rimos·us -a -um; *(crazy)* delir·us -a -um
cracker *s* crustul·um -i *n*
crackle *intr* crepitare
crackling *s* crepit·us -ūs *m*
cradle *s* cunabul·a -orum *npl*
cradle *tr* fovēre
craft *s (trade)* artific·ium -(i)i *n; (skill)* ar·s -tis *f; (cunning)* dol·us -i *m; (naut)* navig·ium -(i)i *n*
craftily *adv* callide
craftsman *s* artif·ex -icis *m*
craftsmanship *s* artific·ium -(i)i *n*
crafty *adj* callid·us -a -um
cram *tr* farcire; **to — together** constipare ‖ *intr (for an examination)* cuncta confertim menti inculcare
cramp *s* spasm·us -i *m*
cramp *tr* comprimĕre; **to be —ed for space** in angusto sedēre
crane *s (bird)* gru·s -is *mf; (machine)* tollen·o -onis *f*
crank *s (machine)* unc·us -i *m; (person)* moros·us -i *m*
crank *tr* volvĕre
crash *s* frag·or -oris *m*
crash *intr* fragorem dare; **to come —ing down** corruĕre
crass *adj* crass·us -a -um
crate *s* cist·a -ae *f*
crater *s* crat·er -eris *m*
crave *tr* concupiscĕre
craven *adj* ignav·us atque abject·us -a -um
craving *s* desider·ium -(i)i *n*
crawfish *s* astac·us -i *m*
crawl *intr* repĕre
crawl *s (of babies)* reptati·o -onis *f*

crayon *s* cret·a -ae *f*
craze *s* fur·or -oris *m*
craziness *s* dementi·a -ae *f*
crazy *adj (person)* dem·ens -entis; *(idea)* insuls·us -a -um; **— about birds** moros·us -a -um in aves; **to drive s.o. —** mentem *(w. gen)* alienare
creak *s* strid·or -oris *m*
creak *intr* stridēre
creaking *s* strid·or -oris *m*
creaking *adj* stridul·us -a -um
cream *s* crem·or -oris *m* lactis; *(fig)* flo·s -ris *m*
crease *s* plic·a -ae *f*
crease *tr* duplicare ‖ *intr* plicari
create *tr* creare; *(in the mind)* fingĕre
creation *s (act)* creati·ŏ -onis *f; (world)* summ·a -ae *f* rerum, mund·us -i *m; (fig)* op·us -eris *n*
creative *adj* creatr·ix -icis; *(able)* ingenios·us -a -um
creator *s* creat·or -oris *m; (originator)* auct·or -oris *m,* opif·ex -icis *m*
creature *s (living)* anim·al -alis *n; (tool)* minis·ter -tri *m*
credence *s* fid·es -ei *f;* **to gain —** fidem habēre; **to give — to** credĕre *(w. dat)*
credentials *spl* testimoni·a -orum *npl*
credibility *s* fid·es -ei *f*
credible *adj* credibil·is -is -e; *(of persons)* locupl·es -etis
credit *s (faith)* fid·es -ei *f; (authority)* auctorit·as -atis *f; (reputation)* existimati·o -onis *f; (com)* fid·es -ei *f; (recognition)* lau·s -dis *f;* **to buy on —** in diem emĕre; **to have —** fide stare
credit *tr* credĕre *(w. dat); (com)* acceptum referre *(w. dat);* **to — my teacher with my success** successum meum magistro ascribo
creditable *adj* honest·us -a -um
credit card *s* tabell·a -ae *f* tributaria
creditor *s* credit·or -oris *m*
credulity *s* credulit·as -atis *f*
credulous *adj* credul·us -a -um
creed *s* fid·es -ei *f*
creek *s* riv·us -i *m*
creep *intr* repĕre; **it makes my skin —** facit ut horream
crescent *s* lun·a -ae *f* crescens
crescent-shaped *adj* lunat·us -a -um
crest *s* crist·a -ae *f*
crested *adj* cristat·us -a -um
crew *s* gre·x -gis *m; (naut)* naut·ae -arum *mpl; (rowers)* remig·es -um *mpl*
crib *s (manger)* praesep·e -is *n; (for a baby)* lectul·us -i *m*
cricket *s* gryll·us -i *m*
crier *s* praec·o -onis *m*
crime *s* scel·us -eris *n*
criminal *adj* scelest·us -a -um
criminal *s* scelest·us -i *m*
criminally *adv* nefarie

crimp *tr* crispare
crimson *adj* coccine·us -a -um
crimson *s* cocc·um -i *n*
cringe *intr* abhorrēre; *(to behave servilely)* se demittĕre, adulari
cripple *s* claud·us -i *m*
cripple *tr* debilitare; *(fig)* frangĕre
crippled *adj (in the hands)* manc·us -a -um; *(lame)* claud·us -a -um
crisis *s* discrim·en -inis *n*
criterion *s* norm·a -ae *f*
critic *s* reprehens·or -oris *m; (literary)* cens·or -oris *m*
critical *adj (relating to criticism; crucial)* critic·us -a -um; *(blaming)* censori·us -a -um
criticism *s* reprehensi·o -onis *f; (literary)* judic·ium -(i)i *n,* ar·s -tis *f* critica
criticize *tr* reprehendĕre; *(literature)* judicare
croak *intr* coaxare; *(of ravens)* crocitare; *(to complain)* queritari; *(to die) (coll)* animam ebullire
croaking *s (of frogs)* clam·or -oris *m; (of ravens)* crocitati·o -onis *f; (complaining)* querimoni·a -ae *f*
crock *s* oll·a -ae *f*
crocodile *s* crocodil·us -i *m*
crook *s (shepherd's)* ped·um -i *n; (thief)* fu·r -ris *m*
crook *tr* curvare
crooked *adj* curvat·us -a -um; *(fig)* dolos·us -a -um
crop *s (of grain)* seg·es -itis *f; (of a bird)* ingluvi·es -ei *f*
crop *tr* tondēre; *(to harvest)* metĕre; *(to browse)* carpĕre
cross *s (structure)* cru·x -cis *f; (figure)* decuss·is -is *m; (fig)* cruciat·us -ūs *m*
cross *adj (across)* transvers·us -a -um; *(contrary)* contrari·us -a -um; *(peevish)* acerb·us -a -um; *(hybrid)* mixt·us -a -um
cross *tr* transire; *(a river)* trajicĕre; *(a mountain)* transcendĕre; *(to thwart)* frustrari, adversari; *(hybrids)* miscēre; **to — the legs** poplites alternis genibus imponĕre; **to — out** expungĕre
crossbar *s* tign·um -i *n* transversum; *(line)* line·a -ae *f* transversa
crossbow *s* arcuballist·a -ae *f*
crossbreed *s* hibrid·a -ae *mf*
crossbreed *tr* miscēre
crosscut *s* secti·o -onis *f* in transversum
cross-examination *f* interrogati·o -onis *f*
cross-examine *tr* interrogare
cross-eyed *adj* strab·us -a -um; **he is —** strabo est
crossing *s* transit·us -ūs *m; (of a river)* traject·us -ūs *m; (of roads)* biv·ium -(i)i *n; (of three roads)* triv·ium -(i)i *n; (of four roads)* quadriv·ium -(i)i *n*
crossroads *spl* quadriv·ium -(i)i *n; (esp. in the country)* compit·a -orum *npl*

crosswise *adv* decussatim
crotch *s (anat)* bifurc·um -i *n*
crouch *intr* subsidĕre; **in a — subsid·ens -entis**
crow *s (bird)* corn·ix -icis *f; (of rooster)* gallicin·ium -(i)i *n*
crow *intr (of roosters)* cucurire; *(to boast)* gloriari
crowbar *s* vect·is -is *m*
crowd *s* frequenti·a -ae *f; (mob)* turb·a -ae *f; (of people flocking together)* concurs·us -ūs *m; (common people)* vulg·us -i *n*
crowd *tr* frequentare **‖** *intr* **to — around** stipare, circumfundi *(w. dat);* **to — together** congregari
crowded *adj* frequ·ens -entis; **— together** confert·us -a -um
crowing *s* cant·us -ūs *m*
crown *s (of king)* insign·e -is *n* regium; *(wreath)* coron·a -ae *f; (power)* regn·um -i *n; (top)* vert·ex -icis *m; (fig)* ap·ex -icis *m*
crown *tr* insigne regium capiti *(w. gen)* imponĕre; **to — the temples with flowers** tempora floribus cingĕre
crucifix *s* imag·o -inis *f* Christi crucifixi
crucifixion *s* crucis supplic·ium -(i)i *n*
crucify *tr* crucifigĕre
crude *adj* rud·is -is -e, incult·us -a -um
crudely *adv* inculte
cruel *adj* crudel·is -is -e
cruelly *adv* crudeliter
cruelty *s* crudelit·as -atis *f*
cruet *s* gutt·us -i *m*
cruise *intr* circumvectari, navigare
cruise *s* navigati·o -onis *f*
crumb *s* mic·a -ae *f*
crumble *tr* friare **‖** *intr* friari; *(to fall down)* corruĕre
crumbling *adj* friabil·is -is -e
crumple *tr* corrugare
crumpled *adj* corrugat·us -a -um
crunch *tr* dentibus frangĕre
crush *tr* contundĕre; *(fig)* opprimĕre
crush *s* contusi·o -onis *f; (crowd)* frequenti·a -ae *f* densissima
crust *s* crust·um -i *n*
crusty *adj* crustos·us -a -um; *(fig)* cerebros·us -a -um
crutch *s* bacul·um -i *n*
cry *s (shout)* clam·or -oris *m; (of a baby)* vagit·us -ūs *m*
cry *tr* clamare; **to — out** exclamare **‖** *intr (to shout)* clamare; *(to shout repeatedly)* clamitare; *(to weep)* lacrimare, flēre; *(of infants)* vagire
crying *s* flet·us -ūs *m; (of a baby)* vagit·us -ūs *m*
crypt *s* crypt·a -ae *f*
cryptic *adj* occult·us -a -um
crystal *adj* cyrstallin·us -a -um
crystal *s* crystall·um -i *n*
crystal-clear *adj* pellucid·us -a -um

cub *s* catul·us -i *m*
cube *s* cub·us -i *m*
cubic *adj* cubic·us -a -um
cubit *s* cubit·um -i *n*
cuckoo *s* cucul·us -i *m*
cucumber *s* cucum·is -eris *m*
cud *s* rum·en -inis *n;* **to chew the —** ruminare
cudgel *s* fust·is -is *m*
cue *s (hint)* nut·us -ūs *m,* indic·ium -(i)i *n; (theat)* verb·um -i *n* monitorium
cuff *s (of sleeve)* extrema manic·a -ae *f; (blow)* colaph·us -i *m*
cull *tr* decerpĕre
culminate *intr* ad summum venire
culmination *s* fastig·ium -(i)i *n*
culpable *adj* culpand·us -a -um
culprit *s* re·us -i *m,* re·a -ae *f*
cultivate *tr (land, mind, friendship)* colĕre
cultivation *s* cultur·a -ae *f*
cultivator *s* cult·or -oris *m*
culture *s* cultur·a -ae *f*
culvert *s* cloac·a -ae *f*
cumbersome *adj* inhabil·is -is -e
cunning *adj (clever)* callid·us -a -um; *(sly)* astut·us -a -um
cup *s* pocul·um -i *n*
cupbearer *s* pocillat·or -oris *m*
cupboard *s* armar·ium -(i)i *n*
Cupid *s* Cupid·o -inis *m*
cupidity *s* cupidit·as -atis *f*
cupola *s* thol·us -i *m*
cur *s (coll)* can·is -is *m* nothus; *(fig)* scelest·us -i *m*
curable *adj* sanabil·is -is -e
curative *adj* medicabil·is -is -e
curator *s* curat·or -oris *m*
curb *s (& fig)* fren·um -i *n; (of the road)* crepid·o -inis *f*
curb *tr* frenare; *(fig)* refrenare
curbstone *s* crepid·o -inis *m*
curdle *tr* coagulare **ǁ** *intr* coïre
cure *s (remedy)* remd·ium -(i)i *n; (process)* sanati·o -onis *f*
cure *tr* sanare; *(to pickle)* salire
curiosity *s* curiosit·as -atis *f; (thing)* miracul·um -i *n*
curious *adj* curios·us -a -um; *(strange)* mirabil·is -is -e
curiously *adv* curiose
curl *s (natural)* cirr·us -i *m; (artificial)* cincinn·us -i *m*
curl *tr* crispare **ǁ** *intr* crispari; *(of smoke)* volvi
curler, curling iron *s* calamistr·um -i *n*
curly *adj* crisp·us -a -um
currency *s* monet·a -ae *f; (use)* us·us -ūs *m;* **to gain —** percrebrescĕre
current *adj (opinion)* vulgar·is -is -e; *(in general use)* usitat·us -a -um
current *s* vis *f* fluminis *n; (of air)* afflat·us -ūs *m;* **against the —** adverso flumine; **with the —** secundo flumine

curse *s* maledict·um -i *n; (fig)* pest·is -is *f*
curse *tr* maledicĕre *(w. dat)* **ǁ** *intr* maledicĕre
cursed *adj* exsecrabil·is -is -e
cursing *s* convic·ium -(i)i *n*
cursorily *adv* strictim
cursory *adj* lev·is -is -e, brev·is -is -e
curt *adj* abrupt·us -a -um
curtail *tr (to cut off a part of)* praecidĕre; *(to diminish)* minuĕre
curtain *s* aulae·um -i *n*
curvature *s* curvatur·a -ae *f*
curve *s (of road, river)* flex·us -ūs *m*
curve *tr* incurvare, flectĕre **ǁ** *intr* incurvari
curved *adj* curv·us -a -um; *(as a sickle)* falcat·us -a -um
cushion *s* pulvin·us -i *m; (for sitting on)* sedular·ium -(i)i *n; (fig)* levam·en -inis *n*
custard *s* artolagan·us -i *m*
custodian *s* cust·os -odis *m,* curat·or -oris *m*
custody *s* tutel·a -ae *f,* custodi·a -ae *f;* **to keep in —** custodire; **to take into —** in vincula conjicĕre
custom *s* mo·s -ris *m,* consuetud·o -inis *f;* **according to the — of the Roman people** more populi Romani
customary *adj* consuet·us -a -um; *(regularly occurring)* sollemn·is -is -e
customer *s* cli·ens -entis *m; (buyer)* empt·or -oris *m*
customs *spl (tax)* portor·ium -(i)i *n*
customs officer *s* portit·or -oris *m*
cut *tr* secare; *(to fell)* caedĕre; *(to mow)* succidĕre; **to — apart** dissecare; **to — away** recidĕre, abscindĕre; **to — down** caedĕre; *(to kill)* occidĕre; **to — in pieces** concidĕre; **to — off** praecidĕre; *(to intercept)* intercludĕre; **to — open** incidĕre; **to — out** exsecare; *(out of a rock, etc.)* excidĕre; **to — short** intercidĕre; *(to abridge)* praecidĕre; *(to interrupt)* interpellare; **to — short the school day** ludum artare; **to — to pieces** concidĕre; **to — up** minutatim concidĕre; *(the enemy)* trucidare
cuticle *s* cuticul·a -ae *f*
cutlass *s* ens·is -is *m*
cutlery *s* cultr·i -orum *mpl*
cutlet *s* frust·um -i *n*
cutthroat *s* sicar·ius -(i)i *m*
cutting *adj (sharp)* acut·us -a -um; *(fig)* acerb·us -a -um
cutting *s (act)* secti·o -onis *f; (thing)* segm·en -inis *n; (for planting)* taleol·a -ae *f*
cuttlefish *s* sepi·a -ae *f*
cycle *s* orb·is -is *m; (of events)* ord·o -inis *m*
cylinder *s* cylindr·us -i *m*
cylindrical *adj* cylindrat·us -a -um
cymbal *s* cymbal·um -i *n*
cynic *adj* cynic·us -a -um

cynic *s* cynic·us -i *m*
cynical *adj* acerb·us -a -um
cynicism *s* acerbit·as -atis *f*
cypress *s* cypress·us -i *f*

D

dab *s* massul·a -ae *f*
dab *tr* to — on illinĕre
dabble *intr* to — in leviter attingĕre
dad, daddy *s* tat·a -ae *m*
dactyl *s* dactyl·us -i *m*
dactylic *adj* dactylic·us -a -um
daffodil *s* asphodel·us -i *m*
daffy *adj (coll)* delir·us -a -um
dagger *s* pugi·o -onis *m*
daily *adj* co(t)tidian·us -a -um
daily *adv* co(t)tidie
dainties *spl* cuppedi·a -orum *npl*
dainty *adj* delicat·us -a -um
dairy *s* cell·a -ae *f* lactaria
dairy farm *s* fund·us -i *m* lactarius
daisy *s* bell·is -idis *f*
dale *s* vall·is -is *f*
dally *intr (to linger)* morari; *(to trifle)* nugari; *(amorously)* blandiri
dam *s* mol·es -is *f; (of animals)* mat·er -ris *f*
dam *tr* to — up (operibus) obstruĕre
damage *s (loss)* damn·um -i *n; (injury)* nox·a -ae *f*
damage *tr* laedĕre; *(a person)* fraudi esse *(w. dat);* to — s.o.'s reputation aestimationem alicujus violare
dame *s* domin·a -ae *f; (girl)* puell·a -ae *f*
damn *tr* damnare, exsecrari
damnable *adj* damnabil·is -is -e
damnably *adv* damnabiliter
damnation *s* damnati·o -onis *f*
damp *adj* (h)umid·us -a -um
dampen *tr* humectare; *(fig)* restringĕre
dampness *s* ulig·o -inis *f*
damsel *s* puell·a -ae *f*
dance *s* saltat·us -ūs *m*
dance *tr* to—a number canticum desaltare ‖ *intr* saltare
dancing *s* saltati·o -onis *f*
dandelion *s* taraxac·um -i *n*
dandruff *s* porrig·o -inis *f*
dandy *adj* bell·us -a -um
dandy *s* hom·o -inis *m* bellus
danger *s* pericul·um -i *n;* to be in — of periclitari *(w. abl);* to be in grave — in praecipite esse
dangerous *adj* periculos·us -a -um
dangerously *adv* periculose; *(seriously)* graviter
dangle *tr* suspendĕre ‖ *intr* pendĕre
dank *adj* (h)umid·us et frigid·us -a -um
dappled *adj* maculos·us -a -um; *(horse)* guttat·us -a -um

dare *tr* provocare ‖ *intr* audēre
daring *adj* aud·ax -acis
daring *s* audaci·a -ae *f*
dark *adj* obscur·us -a -um; *(in color)* fusc·us -a -um; *(gloomy)* a·ter -tra -trum; *(stern)* atr·ox -ocis; —est night spississima no·x -ctis *f;* — eyes nigri ocul·i -orum *mpl;* to grow — nigrescĕre
dark *s* tenebr·ae -arum *fpl;* after — de nocte; in the — *(i.e., secretly)* clam et occulte; to be in the — *(i.e., ignorant)* caligare; to keep in the — celare
darken *tr* obscurare; *(colors)* fuscare
darling *adj* suavissim·us -a -um
darling *s* delici·ae -arum *fpl*
darn *tr* resarcire
darn *interj* hercule!
dart *s* spicul·um -i *n*
dart *intr (to move quickly)* provolare; *(of snake's tongue)* vibrare; to — out emicare
dash *tr (to splash)* aspergĕre; *(hopes)* frustrari; to — against allidĕre ad *(w. acc);* to — off *(letter)* scriptitare; to — to pieces discutĕre; to — to the ground affligĕre ‖ *intr* ruĕre
dash *s* impet·us -ūs *m; (animation)* alacrit·as -atis *f; (small amount)* mensur·a -ae *f* duorum digitorum
dashing *adj* ala·cer -cris -cre; *(showy)* nitid·us -a -um
data *spl* fact·a -orum *npl*
date *s* di·es -ei *m,* temp·us -oris *n; (fruit)* palmul·a -ae *f;* out of — obsolet·us -a -um; to — adhuc; up to — rec·ens -entis
date *tr* diem ascribĕre *(w. dat)* ‖ *intr* to — from originem trahĕre ab *(w. abl)*
date palm *s* palm·a -ae *f*
dative *s* dativ·us -i *m*
daub *tr* oblinĕre
daughter *s* fili·a -ae *f*
daughter-in-law *s* nur·us -i *f*
daunt *tr* perterrēre
dauntless *adj* impavid·us -a -um
dauntlessly *adv* impavide
dawdle *intr* cessare
dawn *s* auror·a -ae *f;* at — primā luce
dawn *intr* dilucescĕre; to — on *(fig)* occurrĕre *(w. dat)*
day *s* di·es -ei *m;* by — interdiu; — by — in dies; — and night diem noctemque; every — co(t)tidie; from — to — in dies; next — postridie; one — *(in the past)* quodam die; some — olim; the — after postridie; the — after that postridie ejus diei; the — after tomorrow perendie; the — before pridie
day *adj* diurn·us -a -um
daybreak *s* at — primā luce; before — antelucio
daydream *s* somn·ium -(i)i *n*
daydream *intr* vigilans somniare
daylight *s* lu·x -cis *f*

daystar *s* Lucif·er -eri *m*
daytime *s* temp·us -oris *n* diurnum; **in the — interdiu
daze *s* stup·or -oris *m*
daze *tr* obstupefacĕre
dazzle *tr* praestringĕre
dazzling *adj* fulgid·us -a -um
deacon *s* diacon·us -i *m*
dead *adj* mortu·us -a -um
dead *s* — **of night** media no·x -ctis *f;* **dead of winter** brum·a -ae *f;* **the — man·es -ium, mortu·i -orum *mpl*
dead *adv* omnino, prorsus
deaden *tr* obtundĕre
dead end *s* fundul·a -ae *f; (fig)* cessati·o -onis *f*
deadly *adj* mortif·er -era -erum; *(hatred)* capital·is -is -e
deaf *adj* surd·us -a -um; **to be — to** non audire; **to go —** obsurdescĕre; **to turn a — ear** obsurdescĕre
deafen *tr* exsurdare
deaf-mute *adj* surd·us idemque mut·us -a -um
deafness *s* surdit·as -atis *f*
deal *s (quantity)* copi·a -ae *f,* vis *f; (com)* negot·ium -(i)i *n;* **a good — longer** multo diutius; **a good — of** aliquantum *(w. gen)*
deal *tr* partiri; **to — him a blow in the stomach** pugnos in ventrem ingerĕre ‖ *intr (com)* negotiari; **easy to — with** tractabil·is -is -e; **to — with** *(a thing)* agĕre *(w. abl); (a person)* uti *(w. abl)*
dealer *s* negotiat·or -oris *f; (in a small shop)* coci·o -onis *f*
dealing *s* negotiati·o -onis *f;* **to have —s with** commercium habēre cum *(w. abl)*
dean *s* decan·us -i *m*
dear *adj (highly valued; high-priced)* car·us -a -um; **my — friend!** mi amice!
dear *interj* O —! *(in dismay)* hei!; *(in embarrassment)* au au!
dearly *adv (intensely)* valde; *(at high cost)* magni
dearness *s* carit·as -atis *f*
dearth *s* inopi·a -ae *f*
death *s* mor·s -tis *f; (in violent form)* ne·x -cis *f;* **to meet one's — mortem obire; **to put to —** ad mortem dare
deathbed *s* tor·us -i *m* extremus
deathless *adj* immortal·is -is -e
deathlike *adj* mortuos·us -a -um
deathly *adj* pallid·us -a -um
debase *tr* depravare; *(coinage)* adulterare; **to — oneself** se demittĕre
debasement *s* adulterati·o -onis *f*
debatable *adj* controversios·us -a -um, ambigu·us -a -um
debate *s* disceptati·o -onis *f*
debate *tr* disceptare de *(w. abl)* ‖ *intr* disserĕre
debater *s* disputat·or -oris *m*

debauchery *s* licenti·a -ae *f*
debilitate *tr* debilitare
debit *s* expens·um -i *n*
debit *tr* in expensum referre
debt *s* ae·s -ris *n* alienum; *(fig)* debit·um -i *n;* **to pay off a —** aes alienum persolvĕre; **to run up a —** aes alienum conflare
debtor *s* debit·or -oris *m*
decade *s* dec·as -adis *f*
decadence *s* occas·us -ūs *m*
decadent *adj* degen·er -era -erum
decalogue *s* decalog·us -i *m*
decamp *intr* castra movēre
decant *tr* diffundĕre
decanter *s* lagoen·a -ae *f*
decapitate *tr* detruncare
decay *s* tab·es -is *f; (fig)* defecti·o -onis *f*
decay *intr* putrescĕre, tabescĕre
decease *s* decess·us -i *m*
deceased *adj* defunct·us -a -um
deceit *s* frau·s -dis *f,* dol·us -i *m*
deceitful *adj* fall·ax -acis
deceitfully *adv* fallaciter
deceive *tr* decipĕre, fallĕre
December *s* Decem·ber -bris *m or* mens·is -is *m* December; **on the first of —** Kalendis Decembribus
decency *s* decor·um -i *n*
decent *adj* dec·ens -entis
decently *adv* decenter
deception *s* fallaci·a -ae *f*
deceptive *adj* fall·ax -acis
decide *tr & intr* decernĕre; **the Senate decided** senatui placuit; **to — to** *(w. inf)* constituĕre *(w. inf)*
decided *adj* cert·us -a -um
deciduous *adj* caduc·us -a -um
decimate *tr* decimare; *(fig)* depopulari
decipher *tr* enodare
decision *s* sententi·a -ae *f; (of deliberative body)* decret·um -i *n; (of Senate)* auctorit·as -atis *f; (leg)* judic·ium -(i)i *n*
decisive *adj* cert·us -a -um; **— battle** decretoria pugn·a -ae *f*
deck *s* pon·s -tis *m;* **ship with a —** nav·is -is *f* constrata
deck *tr* ornare; *(tables)* sternĕre; **—ed out in** subornat·us -a -um *(w. abl)*
declaim *intr* declamare
declamation *s* declamati·o -onis *f*
declamatory *adj* declamatori·us -a -um
declaration *s* declarati·o -onis *f; (of war)* denuniati·o -onis *f*
declarative *adj* declarativ·us -a -um
declare *tr* declarare; *(to say out plainly)* edicĕre; *(war)* indicĕre ‖ *intr* **to — for** favēre *(w. dat)*
declension *s* declinati·o -onis *f*
declinable *adj* declinabil·is -is -e
decline *s (slope)* decliv·e -is *n; (of strength, etc.)* deminuti·o -onis *f;* **to cause a — in prices** pretia levare
decline *tr (to refuse)* recusare; *(gram)*

declinare, flectĕre; **to — battle** pugnam
detrectare **‖** *intr* inclinare; *(to decay,
fail)* deficĕre, decrescĕre; *(of prices)*
laxare
decode *tr* enodare
decompose *tr* resolvĕre **‖** *intr* putrescĕre,
dissolvi
decomposition *s* dissoluti·o -onis *f*
decorate *tr* ornare
decoration *s (act)* ornati·o -onis *f; (ornament)* ornament·um -i *n; (distinction)*
dec·us -oris *n*
decorator *s* exornat·or -oris *m*
decorous *adj* decor·us -a -um
decorously *adv* decore
decorum *s* decor·um -i *n*
decoy *s* ill·ex -icis *mf*
decoy *tr* allicĕre
decrease *s* imminuti·o -onis *f*
decrease *tr* imminuĕre **‖** *intr* decrescĕre;
(of prices) retro abire
decreasingly *adv* in minus
decree *s* decret·um -i *n; (of the Senate)*
consult·um -i *n; (of the assembly)*
scit·um -i *n*
decree *tr* decernĕre; **the people —ed**
populus jussit
decrepit *adj* decrepit·us -a -um
decry *tr* vituperare
dedicate *tr* dedicare; *(a book)* dicare; **to —
oneself to** se dedĕre *(w. dat)*
dedication *s* dedicati·o -onis *f; (of a book)*
nuncupati·o -onis *f*
deduce *tr* deducĕre; *(to infer)* colligĕre
deduct *tr* deducĕre; **to — from the capital
what has been paid in interest** de capite
deducĕre quod usuris pernumeratum est
deduction *s* deducti·o -onis *f; (inference)*
conclusi·o -onis *f*
deed *s* fact·um -i *n; (pej)* facin·us -oris *n;
(leg)* syngraph·a -ae *f;* **good —** bene-
fic·ium -(i)i *n*
deem *tr* ducĕre, habēre
deep *adj* alt·us -a -um; *(very deep)*
profund·us -a -um; *(of sounds)* grav·is
-is -e; *(of color)* satur; *(sleep)* art·us -a
-um; *(recondite)* recondit·us -a -um; **—
silence fell** ingens silentium factum est;
in — thought cogitabund·us -a -um
deep *s* alt·um -i *n*
deepen *tr* defodĕre; *(e.g., affection)* augēre
‖ *intr* alt·ior -ior -ius fieri
deeply *adv* alte; *(inwardly)* penitus; *(fig)*
graviter, valde; **to be — grieved** graviter
dolēre; **to be — in love** graviter amare
deep-sunk *adj (eyes)* concav·us -a -um
deer *s* cerv·us -i *m,* cerv·a -ae *f*
deface *tr* deformare
defaced *adj* deform·is -is -e
defacement *s* deformit·as -atis *f*
defamation *s* obtrectati·o -onis *f*
defamatory *adj* probros·us -a -um
defame *tr* diffamare, infamare

default *s* delict·um -i *n*
defeat *s* repuls·a -ae *f; (mil)* clad·es -is *f*
defeat *tr* vincĕre, superare; *(to baffle)*
frustrari; **to — a bill** rogationem
antiquare
defect *s* vit·ium -(i)i *n*
defect *intr (to desert)* deficĕre
defection *s* defecti·o -onis *f; (to the enemy)* transfug·ium -(i)i *n*
defective *adj* vitios·us -a -um; *(gram)*
defectiv·us -a -um
defend *tr* defendĕre; *(leg)* patrocinari *(w.
dat)*
defendant *s* re·us -i *m,* re·a -ae *f*
defender *s* defens·or -oris *m; (leg)*
patron·us -i *m*
defense *s (act)* defensi·o -onis *f;* prae-
sid·ium -(i)i *n; (leg)* patrocin·ium -(i)i *n;
(speech)* defensi·o -onis *f*
defenseless *adj* infens·us -a -um; *(unarmed)* inerm·is -is -e
defensible *adj* defensibil·is -is -e
defensive *adj* **— and offensive alliance**
societ·as -atis *f* ad bellum defendendum
atque inferendum facta; **—and offensive weapons** tela ad tegendum et
adnocendum; **to put s.o. on the —**
aliquem ad sua defendenda cogĕre
defer *tr* differre **‖** *intr* **to — to** obsequi
(w. dat)
deference *s* observanti·a -ae *f;* **out of —**
reverenter
deferential *adj* (**to**) observ·ans -antis *(w.
gen)*
defiance *s* contempti·o -onis *f;* **in — of the
law** invitis legibus
defiant *adj* insol·ens -entis
deficiency *s* defect·us -ūs *m; (of supplies,
water, money)* penuri·a -ae *f*
deficient *adj* (**in**) in·ops -opis *(w. gen);* **to
be —** deesse
deficit *s* lacun·a -ae *f;* **there is a —** deficit;
to make up the — lacunam explēre
defile *s* fauc·es -ium *fpl*
defile *tr* inquinare; *(usu. fig)* contaminare
defilement *s* contaminati·o -onis *f*
define *tr* definire
definite *adj* definit·us -a -um
definitely *adv* definite, certe
definition *s* definiti·o -onis *f*
definitive *adj* definitiv·us -a -um
definitively *adv* definite
deflect *tr* deflectĕre
deflection *s* deflecti·o -onis *f*
deflower *tr* devirginare
deform *tr* deformare
deformed *adj* deform·is -is -e
deformity *s* deformit·as -atis *f*
defraud *tr* fraudare
defray *tr* suppeditare; **to — the costs**
sumptūs suppeditare
deft *adj* agil·is -is -e, habil·is -is -e
deftly *adv* scite

defunct *adj* defunct·us -a -um
defy *tr* contemnĕre
degeneracy *s* mor·es -um *mpl* deteriores
degenerate *adj* degen·er -eris
degradation *s* ignomini·a -ae *f*
degrade *tr (to lower rank)* in ordinem redigĕre; *(fig)* dehonestare
degrading *adj* indign·us -a -um
degree *s* grad·us -ūs *m;* **to such a — that** adeo ut
deification *s* consecrati·o -onis *f*
deify *tr* inter deos referre
deign *tr* dignari
deism *s* deism·us -i *m*
deity *s* num·en -inis *n*
dejected *adj* demiss·us -a -um
dejection *s* animi abjecti·o -onis *f*
delay *s* mor·a -ae *f*
delay *tr* demorari ‖ *intr* morari
delectable *adj* delectabil·is -is -e
delegate *s* legat·us -i *m*
delegate *tr (to depute)* delegare; *(to entrust)* demandare
delegation *s (act)* mandat·us -ūs *m; (group)* legati·o -onis *f*
delete *tr* delēre
deleterious *adj* noxi·us -a -um
deliberate *adj* deliberat·us -a -um
deliberate *intr* deliberare, consulĕre
deliberately *adv* de industria
deliberation *s* deliberati·o -onis *f*
delicacy *s* subtilit·as -atis *f; (food)* cuppedi·a -ae *f*, matte·a -ae *f*
delicate *adj (of fine texture)* subtil·is -is -e; *(e.g., girl)* delicat·us -a -um; *(taste, work of art)* eleg·ans -antis; *(health)* infirm·us -a -um; *(matter)* lubric·us -a -um
delicious *adj* sapid·us -a -um
delight *s* delectati·o -onis *f; (cause of delight)* delici·ae -arum *fpl*
delight *tr* delectare ‖ *intr* **to — in** delectari *(w. abl)*
delighted *adj* (with) delectat·us -a -um *(w. abl)*
delightful *adj* suav·is -is -e
delightfully *adv* suaviter
delineate *tr* delineare, describĕre
delineation *s* descripti·o -onis *f*
delinquency *s* delict·um -i *n*
delinquent *adj* noxi·us -a -um
delinquent *s* nox·ius -(i)i *m*, noxi·a -ae *f*
delirious *adj* delir·us -a -um
delirium *s* delir·ium -(i)i *n*
deliver *tr (to hand over)* tradĕre; *(to free)* liberare; *(to surrender)* prodĕre; *(a speech)* habēre, dicĕre; *(sentence)* dicĕre; *(message)* referre; *(blow)* intendĕre; *(child)* obstetricari; *(a letter)* reddĕre
deliverance *s* liberati·o -onis *f*
deliverer *s* liberat·or -oris *m*
delivery *s (freedom)* liberati·o -onis *f; (of goods)* traditi·o -onis *f; (of a speech)* dicti·o -onis *f; (childbirth)* part·us -ūs *m*

delude *tr* deludĕre
deluge *s* diluv·ium -(i)i *n*
deluge *tr* obruĕre, inundare
delusion *s* delusi·o -onis *f*
demagogue *s* publicol·a -ae *m*
demand *s* postulati·o -onis *f*
demand *tr* postulare, flagitare
demarcation *s* confin·ium -(i)i *n*
demean *tr* **to — oneself** se demittĕre
demeanor *s* gest·us -ūs *m*
demerit *s* vit·ium -(i)i *n; (mark)* vitii not·a -ae *f*
demigod *s* her·os -oïs *m*
demise *s* decess·us -ūs *m*
democracy *s* civit·as -atis *f* popularis
democrat *s* civ·is -is *m* popularis
democratic *adj* popular·is -is -e; **— party** part·es -ium *fpl* populares
democratically *adv* populi voluntate
demolish *tr* demoliri
demolition *s* demoliti·o -onis *f*
demon *s* daem·on -onis *m*
demonstrable *adj* demonstrabil·is -is -e
demonstrably *adv* manifeste
demonstrate *tr (to show)* monstrare; *(to prove)* demonstrare
demonstration *s (proof)* demonstrati·o -onis *f; (display)* ostent·us -ūs *m*
demonstrative *adj* demonstrativ·us -a -um
demoralization *s* depravati·o -onis *f*
demoralize *tr (to corrupt)* depravare; *(to discourage)* percellĕre
demote *tr* loco movēre
demotion *s* a gradu moti·o -onis *f*
demure *adj* modest·us -a -um
demurely *adv* modeste
den *s* latibul·um -i *n; (in a home)* tablin·um -i *n*
deniable *adj* infitiand·us -a -um
denial *s* negati·o -onis *f; (refusal)* repudiati·o -onis *f;* **to give s.o. a flat —** praecise alicui negare
denomination *s (name)* denominati·o -onis *f; (sect)* sect·a -ae *f*
denominator *s* numer·us -i *m* dividens
denotation *s* denotati·o -onis *f*
denote *tr* declarare
denounce *tr (to inform against)* deferre; *(to condemn)* reprehendĕre
dense *adj* dens·us -a -um; *(crowded)* spiss·us -a -um; *(stupid)* crass·us -a -um
densely *adv* dense, crebro
density *s* densit·as -atis *f*
dent *s* not·a -ae *f*
dent *tr* imprimĕre, cavare
dented *adj* collis·us -a -um
dentist *s* dentium medic·us -i *m*
dentistry *s* dentium medicin·a -ae *f*
denude *tr* nudare
denunciation *s (by informer)* delati·o -onis *f; (condemnation)* reprehensi·o -onis *f*
deny *tr* negare

depart *intr* abire; *(to die)* obire; **to — for his province** abire in provinciam
departed *adj* defunct·us -a -um
department *s (of administration)* provinci·a -ae *f*, administrati·o -onis *f; (branch)* gen·us -eris *n*
departure *s* abit·us -ūs *m; (death)* obit·us -ūs *m*
depend *tr* **to — on** dependēre de *(w. abl)*, niti *(w. abl);* **it —s on you** in te positum est; **it — a lot on whether** plurimum refert num
dependable *adj* fid·us -a -um
dependant *s* cli·ens -entis *mf*
dependence *s* fiduci·a -ae *f*
dependency *s* provinci·a -ae *f*
dependent *adj* obnoxi·us -a -um
depict *tr (to paint)* pingĕre; *(in words)* describĕre, depingĕre
deplete *tr* deminuĕre
depletion *s* deminuti·o -onis *f*
deplorable *adj* miserabil·is -is -e
deplore *tr* deplorare
deploy *tr (mil)* expedire
deponent *adj (gram)* depon·ens -entis
depopulate *tr* vacuefacĕre
deportment *s* gest·us -ūs *m*
depose *tr* summovēre; *(leg)* testificari
deposit *s* deposit·um -i *n; (earnest money)* arrhab·o -onis *m; (of fluids)* sedim·en -inis *n;* **to put down 10 denarii as a —** decem denarios arrhaboni dare
deposit *tr (for safekeeping)* **(with)** deponĕre (apud + *acc)*
deposition *s (leg)* testimon·ium -(i)i *n*
depositor *s* deposit·or -oris *m*
depot *s (com)* empor·ium -(i)i *n; (mil)* armamentar·ium -(i)i *n*
depraved *adj* prav·us -a -um
depravity *s* pravit·as -atis *f*
deprecate *tr* deprecari
deprecation *s* deprecati·o -onis *f*
depreciate *tr* detrectare
depreciation *s* detrectati·o -onis *f; (of price)* vilit·as -atis *f*
depredation *s* spoliati·o -onis *f*
depress *tr* deprimĕre; *(fig)* infringĕre
depressed *adj (low-lying)* depress·us -a -um; *(despondent)* demiss·us -a -um; *(flat)* plan·us -a -um; *(hollow)* cav·us -a -um
depressing *adj* trist·is -is -e
depression *s* depressi·o -onis *f; (emotional)* anim·us -i *m* fractus
deprivation *s (act)* privati·o -onis *f; (state)* inopi·a -ae *f*
deprive *tr* privare
depth *s* altitud·o -inis *f;* **a hundred feet in —** *(as opposed to frontage)* centum pedes in agrum; **the —s** profund·um -i *n*
deputation *s* legati·o -onis *f*
deputy *s* legat·us -i *m*
derange *tr* conturbare
deranged *adj* mente capt·us -a -um

derangement *s (of mind)* mentis alientati·o -onis *f*
dereliction *s* derelicti·o -onis *f*
deride *tr* irridēre
derision *s* irrisi·o -onis *f*
derisive *adj* irrid·ens -entis
derivation *s* derivati·o -onis *f*
derivative *adj* derivativ·us -a -um
derive *tr* (de)ducĕre; *(words)* derivare **‖** *intr* procedĕre
derogatory *adj* indign·us -a -um
descend *intr* descendĕre; **to — on** *(to attack)* irrumpĕre in *(w. acc)*
descendant *s* progeni·es -ei *f;* **the —s** poster·i -orum *mpl*
descent *s* descens·us -ūs *m; (slope)* cliv·us -i *m; (lineage)* gen·us -eris *n*
describe *tr* describĕre
description *s* descripti·o -onis *f*
desecrate *tr* profanare
desecration *f* violati·o -onis *f*
desert *s* desert·a -orum *npl*
desert *tr* deserĕre, relinquĕre **‖** *intr* deserĕre; *(esp. mil)* transfugĕre
deserter *s* desert·or -oris *m; (mil)* transfug·a -ae *m*
desertion *s* deserti·o -onis *f; (esp. mil)* transfug·ium -(i)i *n*
deserts *spl* merit·a -orum *npl;* **he got his —** habet quod sibi debebatur
deserve *tr* merēre, merēri
deservedly *adv* merito, jure
deserving *adj* **(of)** dign·us -a -um *(w. abl)*
design *s (of a building, etc.)* descripti·o -onis *f; (drawing)* adumbrati·o -onis *f; (plan)* form·a -ae *f*
design *tr* designare; *(to draw in lines)* delineare; *(to sketch)* adumbrare; *(fig)* machinari
designate *tr* designare
designation *s (appointment)* designati·o -onis *f; (name)* nom·en -inis *n*
designer *s (of s.th. new)* invent·or -oris *m; (one who designs as an architect)* designat·or -oris *m; (of a stratagem)* fabricat·or -oris *m*
designing *adj* callid·us -a -um
desirable *adj* desiderabil·is -is -e
desire *s* cupidit·as -atis *f; (longing)* desider·ium -(i)i *n; (sexual)* libid·o -inis *f*
desire *tr* cupĕre, optare; *(to long for what is lacking)* desiderare
desirous *adj* **(of)** cupid·us -a -um *(gen)*
desist *intr* **(from)** desistĕre *(w. abl or* de + *abl)*
desk *s* mens·a -ae *f* scriptoria
desolate *adj* desolat·us -a -um; *(of persons)* afflict·us -a -um
desolate *tr* desolare
desolation *s* solitud·o -inis *f*
despair *s* desperati·o -onis *f*
desperado *s* sicar·ius -(i)i *m*

desperate *adj (hopeless)* desperat·us -a -um; *(dangerous)* periculos·us -a -um; **in their — situation** in extremis rebus suis; **to take — measures** ad extrema descendĕre
desperately *adv* vehementer; **to be — in love** perdite amare
desperation *s* desperati·o -onis *f*
despicable *adj* despicabil·is -is -e
despise *tr* despicĕre, spernĕre
despite *prep* contra *(w. acc)*
despoil *tr* spoliare
despondency *s* animi abjecti·o -onis *f*, tristiti·a -ae *f*
despondent *adj* abject·us -a -um; **to be —** animo demisso esse
despondently *adv* animo demisso
despot *s* tyrann·us -i *m*
despotic *adj* tyrannic·us -a -um
despotically *adv* tyrannice
despotism *s* dominati·o -onis *f*
dessert *s* secunda mens·a -ae *f*
destination *s* loc·us -i *m* destinationis
destine *tr* destinare
destiny *s* fat·um -i *n*, sor·s -tis *f*
destitute *adj (of)* inop·is -is *(w. gen or abl)*, eg·ens -entis *(w. gen)*
destitution *s* inopi·a -ae *f*
destroy *tr* destruĕre, delēre; **to be —ed** interire
destroyer *s* delet·or -oris *m*, deletr·ix -icis *f*
destruction *s* exit·ium -(i)i *n*
destructive *adj* exitial·is -is -e
desultory *adj* inconst·ans -antis
detach *tr* sejungĕre; *(by breaking)* abscindĕre; *(by pulling)* avellĕre
detached *adj* sejunct·us -a -um
detachment *s (act)* sejuncti·o -onis *f; (mil)* man·us -ūs *f; (aloofness)* secess·us -ūs *m*
detail *s* **—s** singul·a -orum *npl;* **in —** singulatim; **to go into —** per singula ire
detail *tr* exsequi, enarrare
detain *tr* tenēre, retinēre
detect *tr* detegĕre, deprehendĕre
detection *s* deprehensi·o -onis *f*
detective *s* inquisit·or -oris *m*
detention *s* retenti·o -onis *f*
deter *tr* deterrēre
detergent *s* smagm·a -atis *n*
deteriorate *tr* deteri·orem -orem -us facĕre **‖** *intr* deteri·or -or -us fieri
determination *s (resolution)* constanti·a -ae *f; (decision)* consil·ium -(i)i *n*
determine *tr (to fix)* determinare; *(to decide)* constituĕre
determined *adj (resolute)* firm·us -a -um; *(fixed)* cert·us -a -um
detest *tr* detestari
detestable *adj* detestabil·is -is -e
detestation *s* detestati·o -onis *f*
dethrone *tr* regno depellĕre
detonate *intr* crepare
detonation *s* frag·or -oris *m*

detour *s* flex·us -ūs *m;* **to take a —** flectĕre viam
detract *tr* detrahĕre **‖** *intr* **to — from** obtrectare
detraction *s* obtrectati·o -onis *f*
detractor *s* obtrectat·or -oris *m*
detriment *s* detriment·um -i *n*
detrimental *adj* damnos·us -a -um; **to be — to** detrimento esse *(w. dat)*
devastate *tr* vastare
devastating *adj* damnos·us -a -um
devastation *s (act)* vastati·o -onis *f; (state)* vastit·as -atis *f*
develop *tr (to evolve)* evolvĕre; *(to unfold)* explicare; *(to improve)* excolĕre; *(a person)* alĕre **‖** *intr* crescĕre; *(to advance)* progredi; **to — into** evadĕre in *(w. acc)*
development *s (unfolding)* explicati·o -onis *f; (advance)* progress·us -ūs *m;* **— of events** event·us -ūs *m;* **to attain full —** adolescĕre
deviate *intr* **(from)** se declinare (de + *abl*); *(to act in violation of)* **(from)** discedĕre (ab + *abl*); **not to — from the course** cursum tenēre
deviation *s* declinati·o -onis *f*
device *s* artific·ium -(i)i *n*, machin·a -ae *f; (plan)* consil·ium -(i)i *n; (emblem)* sign·um -i *n*
devil *s* diabol·us -i *m;* **go to the —!** abi in malam crucem!; **those —s!** istae larvae!
devilish *adj* diabolic·us -a -um; *(fig)* nefand·us -a -um
devious *adj* devi·us -a -um; *(person)* astut·us -a -um
devise *tr* excogitare
devoid *adj* exper·s -tis *(w. gen or abl);* **to be — of** carēre *(w. abl)*
devolve *intr* **to — upon** cedĕre in *(w. acc); (by inheritance)* pervenire ad *(w. acc)*
devote *tr* devovēre, consecrare; **to — oneself to** se dedĕre *(w. dat)*
devoted *adj* **(to)** dedit·us -a -um *(w. dat)*, studios·us -a -um *(w. dat)*
devotee *s* cult·or -oris *m*
devotion *s* devoti·o -onis *f;* **—s** prec·es -um *fpl*
devour *tr* vorare; *(fig)* haurire
devout *adj* pi·us -a -um
devoutly *adv* pie
dew *s* ro·s -ris *m*
dewdrop *s* gutt·a roscida *f*
dewy *adj* roscid·us -a -um
dexterity *s* callidit·as -atis *f*
dexterous *adj* callid·us -a -um
dexterously *adv* callide
diabolical *adj* diabolic·us -a -um
diadem *s* diadem·a -atis *n*
diagnose *tr* discernĕre
diagnosis *s* diagnos·is -is *f*
diagonal *adj* diagonal·is -is -e
diagonally *adv* in transversum
diagram *s* form·a -ae *f*

dial *s (of clock)* hor·ae -arum *fpl*
dialect *s* dialect·us -i *f*
dialectic *adj* dialectic·us -a -um
dialectics *s* dialectic·a -ae *f*
dialogue *s* serm·o -onis *m; (written discussion)* dialog·us -i *m*
diameter *s* diametr·os -i *f*
diamond *s* adam·as -antis *m*
diaper *s* fasci·ae -arum *fpl*
diaphragm *s* sept·um -i *n* transversum
diarrhea *s* alvi defusi·o -onis *f*
diary *s* diar·ium -(i)i *n*
diatribe *s* convic·ium -(i)i *n*
dice *spl* ale·ae -arum *fpl; (the game)* ale·a -ae *f;* to roll the — aleas jactare; to play — aleā ludĕre
dictate *tr* dictare; *(to prescribe)* praescribĕre
dictate *s* praescript·um -i *n*
dictation *s* dictati·o -onis *f;* to take — dictata exscribĕre
dictator *s* dictat·or -oris *m*
dictatorial *adj* dictatori·us -a -um
dictatorship *s* dictatur·a -ae *f*
diction *s* dicti·o -onis *f*
dictionary *s* glossiar·ium -(i)i *n*
didactic *adj* didascalic·us -a -um
die *s* ale·a -ae *f;* the — is cast alea jacta est
die *intr* mori; to — laughing risu emori; to — off demori; to — out emori
diet *s (food)* victūs rati·o -onis *f; (dietary regime)* diaet·a -ae *f*
diet *intr* victūs rationem inire
dietary *adj* diatetic·us -a -um
differ *intr* differre; *(in opinion)* dissentire; *(to disagree)* discrepare
difference *s* differenti·a -ae *f; (wide difference)* distanti·a -ae *f; (disagreement)* discrepanti·a -ae *f;* — of opinion dissensi·o -onis *f;* it makes no — nihil interest; there is no — between god and god nihil inter deum et deum interest; there isn't the slightest — between them ne minimum quidem inter eos interest; what — does it make whether...? quid refert utrum...?
differentiate *tr* discernĕre
differently *adv* aliter; *(variously)* varie, diverse
differing *adj* disson·us -a -um
difficult *adj* difficil·is -is -e; *(blocked up, e.g., a road)* impedit·us -a -um; it is a — thing to magnum est *(w. inf)*
difficulty *s* difficult·as -atis *f;* with — aegre
diffidence *s (distrust)* diffidenti·a -ae *f; (modesty)* verecundi·a -ae *f*
diffident *adj* diffid·ens -entis; *(modest)* verecund·us -a -um
diffuse *adj* diffus·us -a -um; *(verbally)* verbos·us -a -um
diffuse *tr* diffundĕre
diffusely *adv* effuse

diffusion *s* diffusi·o -onis *f*
dig *tr* fodĕre; to — a hole in the ground terram excavare; to — a hole in the wall *(wood)* parietem (lignum) perfodĕre; to — up *(e.g., the garden, the earth)* confodĕre
digest *s* summar·ium -(i)i *n*
digest *tr* concoquĕre
digestion *s* concocti·o -onis *f*
digestive *adj* peptic·us -a -um
digging *s* fossi·o -onis *f*
digit *s* numer·us -i *m*
dignified *adj* grav·is -is -e
dignify *tr* honestare
dignitary *s* vir -i *m* amplissimus
dignity *s* dignit·as -atis *f*
digress *intr* digredi
digression *s* digressi·o -onis *f*
dike *s* agg·er -eris *m*
dilapidated *adj* ruinos·us -a -um
dilate *tr* dilatare ‖ *intr* dilatari
dilatory *adj* cunctabund·us -a -um
dilemma *s (difficulty)* angusti·ae -arum *fpl; (logical)* dilemm·ā -atis *n;* to be in a — haerēre in salebra
diligence *s* diligenti·a -ae *f*
diligent *adj* dilig·ens -entis
diligently *adv* diligenter
dilute *tr* diluĕre
dilution *s* mixtur·a -ae *f*
dim *adj* heb·es -etis, obscur·us -a -um; to be — hebēre; to become — hebescĕre
dim *tr* hebetare ‖ *intr* hebescĕre
dimension *s* mensur·a -ae *f;* to take the —s of mensuram *(w. gen)* agĕre
diminish *tr* minuĕre; *(weight, value, authority)* levare ‖ *intr* minui
diminutive *adj* exigu·us -a -um; *(gram)* deminutiv·us -a -um
diminutive *s* deminutiv·um -i *n*
dimness *s* hebetud·o -inis *f*
dimple *s* gelasin·us -i *m*
din *s* strepit·us -ūs *m;* to make a — strepere
dine *intr* cenare; to — out foris cenare
diner *s* conviv·a -ae *mf*
dingy *adj* squalid·us -a -um
dining couch *s* tor·us -i *m*
dining room *s* cenati·o -onis *f*, triclin·ium -(i)i *n*
dinner *s* cen·a -ae *f;* to eat — cenare, cenam sumĕre; what did you have for — quid in cenā habuisti?
dinner clothes *spl* cenatori·a -orum *npl*
dinner guest *s* conviv·a -ae *mf*
dinner party *s* conviv·ium -(i)i *n*
dint *s* by — of per *(w. acc)*
dip *tr* immergĕre; *(to wet by dipping)* ting(u)ĕre ‖ *intr* mergi; to — into *(fig)* attingĕre
dip *s (decrease)* deminuti·o -onis *f; (slope)* declivit·as -atis *f;* to take a — natare
diphthong *s* diphthong·us -i *f*
diploma *s* diplom·a -atis *n*

diplomatic *adj (fig)* sag·ax -acis
dipper *s* trull·a -ae *f;* **Big Dipper** Urs·a -ae
f Major; **Little Dipper** Urs·a -ae *f* Minor
dire *adj* dir·us -a -um
direct *adj* (di)rect·us -a -um
direct *vt* dirigĕre; *(to manage)* administrare; *(to order)* jubēre; *(a weapon)* intendĕre; *(a letter)* inscribĕre; **to** — **attention to** animum attendĕre ad *(w. acc)*
direction *s (act)* directi·o -onis *f; (quarter)* par·s -tis *f; (management)* administrati·o -onis *f; (instruction)* mandat·um -i *n; (order)* praecept·um -i *n;* **in all** —**s** in omnes partes; **in a sourtherly** — in meridiem versus; **in both** — utroque; **in every** — quoquoversus; **in the** — **of Gaul** in Galliam versus; **in the** — **of Rome** Romam versus
directive *s* mandat·um -i *n*
directly *adv* directe, rectā; *(immediately)* statim; **to go** — ire rectā
director *s* rect·or -oris *m*
directory *s (office of director)* magister·ium -(i)i *n; (list, catalog)* ind·ex -icis *m*
dirge *s* neni·a -ae *f*
dirt *s* sord·es -is *f (usu. pl); (mud)* lut·um -i *n*
dirt-cheap *adj* pro luto
dirtiness *s* spurciti·a -ae *f*
dirty *adj* sordid·us -a -um, spurc·us -a -um; *(fig)* obscen·us -a -um; — **old man** salax sen·ex -is *m;* — **talk** serm·o -onis *m* obscenus
dirty *tr* spurcare, foedare
disability *s* imbecillit·as -atis *f*
disable *tr (to weaken)* debilitare; *(to cripple)* mutilare; *(a ship)* afflictare
disabled *adj* invalid·us -a -um; *(maimed)* manc·us -a -um; **totally** — omnibus membris capt·us -a -um
disabuse *tr* errorem eripĕre *(w. dat)*
disadvantage *s* incommod·um -i *n*
disadvantaged *adj* incommodat·us -a -um
disadvantageous *adj* incommod·us -a -um, iniqu·us -a -um
disagree *intr* (**with**) dissentire (ab + *abl*); **the food** —**d with me** cibus stomachum offendit
disagreeable *adj* injucund·us -a -um; *(smell)* graveol·ens -entis; *(person)* importun·us -a -um
disagreement *s* dissensi·o -onis *f*
disallow *tr* vetare
disappear *intr* evanescĕre; **to** — **from sight** e conspectu fugĕre
disappearance *s* exit·us -ūs *m*
disappoint *tr* fallĕre, frustrari
disappointment *s (act)* frustrati·o -onis *f; (result)* incommod·um -i *n*
disapproval *s* improbati·o -onis *f*

disapprove *tr* improbare ‖ *intr* **to** — **of** improbare
disarm *tr* exarmare
disarrange *tr* turbare
disarray *s* perturbati·o -onis *f*
disaster *s* calamit·as -atis *f; (mil)* clad·es -is *f*
disastrous *adj* calamitos·us -a -um
disastrously *adv* calamitose
disavow *tr* diffiteri, infiteri
disavowal *s* infitiati·o -onis *f*
disband *tr* dimittĕre ‖ *intr* dimitti
disbelief *s* incredulit·as -atis *f*
disbeliever *s* incredul·us -i *m*
disburse *tr* expendĕre, erogare
disbursement *s* erogati·o -onis *f,* impens·a -ae *f*
disc *s* orb·is -is *m*
discard *tr* abjicĕre
discern *tr (to distinguish)* discernĕre; *(to see clearly)* perspicĕre
discernible *adj* dignoscend·us -a -um
discerning *adj* perspic·ax -acis
discernment *s (faculty)* discrim·en -inis *n; (act)* perspicienti·a -ae *f*
discharge *s (release)* liberati·o -onis *f; (mil)* missi·o -onis *f; (of missiles)* conject·us -ūs *m,* emissi·o -onis *f; (of duty)* perfuncti·o -onis *f; (bodily)* defluxi·o -onis *f;* **dishonorable** — missio *f* cum ignominiā
discharge *tr (to perform)* perfungi *(w. abl); (mil)* dimittĕre; *(debt)* exsolvĕre; *(defendant)* absolvĕre; *(missiles)* immittĕre, conjicĕre
disciple *s* discipul·us -i *m*
discipline *s* disciplin·a -ae *f; (punishment)* castigati·o -onis *f*
discipline *tr* disciplinā instituĕre; *(to punish)* castigare
disclaim *tr* infitiari
disclaimer *s* infitiati·o -onis *f*
disclose *tr (to reveal)* patefacĕre, detegĕre; *(to tell)* promĕre; *(to divulge)* enuntiare
disclosure *s* patefacti·o -onis *f*
discolor *tr* decolorare ‖ *intr* decolorari; *(to fade)* pallescĕre
discomfit *tr* profligare
discomfort *s* incommod·um -i *n*
discomfort *tr* incommodare
disconcerting *adj* molest·us -a -um
disconnect *tr* disjungĕre
disconsolate *adj* maest·us -a -um
discontent *s* offensi·o -onis *f*
discontent *tr* offendĕre
discontented *adj* parum content·us -a -um
discontentedly *adv* animo iniquo
discontinue *tr* intermittĕre ‖ *intr* desinĕre
discord *s* discordi·a -ae *f; (mus)* dissonanti·a -ae *f*
discordant *adj* discor·s -dis; *(mus)* disson·us -a -um

discount *tr* deducĕre; *(to disregard)* praetermittĕre

discount *s (com)* decessi·o -onis *f*

discourage *tr* animum (animos) *(w. gen)* infringĕre; *(to dissuade)* dehortari; **to be —d** animo (animis) deficĕre, animum (animos) demittĕre

discouragement *s* animi infracti·o -onis *f*

discouraging *adj* advers·us -a -um

discourse *s* serm·o -onis *m; (written)* libell·us -i *m*

discourse *intr* (on) disserĕre de *(w. abl)*

discourteous *adj* inurban·us -a -um

discourteously *adv* inurbane

discourtesy *s* inurbanit·as -atis *f*

discover *tr* invenire; *(to explore)* explorare

discoverable *adj* indagabil·is -is -e

discoverer *s* invent·or -oris *m*

discovery *s* inventi·o -onis *f; (thing discovered)* invent·um -i *n*

discredit *s* dedec·us -oris *n;* macul·a -ae *f;* **to be a — to one's family** familiae suae dedecori esse; **to bring — upon oneself** maculam suscipĕre *(w. abl of cause)*

discredit *tr (to disbelieve)* non credĕre *(w. dat); (to disgrace)* labem inferre *(w. dat)*

discreet *adj* caut·us -a -um, prud·ens -entis

discrepancy *s* discrepanti·a -ae *f*

discretion *s (tact)* judic·ium -(i)i *n; (entire control)* arbitr·ium -(i)i *n;* **at one's —** ad arbitrium suum

discretionary *adj* lib·er -era -erum; **to give s.o. — power** liberum arbitrium alicui permittĕre

discriminate *tr* distinguĕre

discriminating *adj* discern·ens -entis

discrimination *s (act of distinguishing)* distincti·o -onis *f; (discernment)* discrim·en -inis *n; (prejudice)* opini·o -onis *f* praejudicata

discuss *tr* disputare

discussion *s* disputati·o -onis *f;* **there was a long — about** diu disputatum est de *(w. abl)*

disdain *tr* fastidire

disdain *s* fastid·ium -(i)i *n;* **to treat with —** dedignari

disdainful *adj* fastidios·us -a -um

disdainfully *adv* fastidiose

disease *s* morb·us -i *m*

diseased *adj* aegrot·us -a -um

disembark *tr* e nave exponĕre ‖ *intr* e nave exire

disenchant *tr* errorem demĕre *(w. dat)*

disengage *tr* expedire, eximĕre

disentangle *tr* explicare

disfavor *s* invidi·a -ae *f,* offens·a -ae *f;* **to be in great — with s.o.** magnā in offensā esse apud aliquem; **to fall into — with s.o.** suscipere invidiam apud aliquem

disfigure *tr* deformare

disfranchise *tr* civitatem adimĕre *(w. dat)*

disgorge *tr* evomĕre

disgrace *s* dedec·us -oris *n,* ignomini·a -ae *f; (thing)* flagit·ium -(i)i *n; (public disgrace)* ignomin·ia -ae *f;* **to become a source of — to** dedecori esse *(w. dat)*

disgrace *tr* dedecorare

disgraceful *adj* dedecor·us -a -um

disgracefully *adv* turpiter

disguise *s* vestit·us -ūs *m* alienus; *(fig)* person·a -ae *f;* **in —** mutatā veste

disguise *tr* dissimulare

disgust *s* taed·ium -(i)i *n*

disgust *tr* stomachum movēre *(w. dat);* **I am —ed with** me taedet *(w. gen),* me piget *(w. gen)*

disgusting *adj* foed·us -a -um

disgustingly *adv* foede

dish *s (flat)* patin·a -e *f; (large)* lan·x -cis *f; (course)* fercul·um -i *n;* **to wash the —es** vasa coquinatoria eluĕre

dishearten *tr* animum (animos) *(w. gen)* infringĕre; **to be —ed** animum (animos) demittĕre

disheveled *adj (hair)* pass·us -a -um

dishonest *adj* fraudulent·us -a -um; *(lying)* mend·ax -acis

dishonestly *adv* dolo malo

dishonesty *s* frau·s -dis *f*

dishonor *s* dedec·us -oris *n*

dishonor *tr* dedecorare

dishonorable *adj* inhonest·us -a -um

dishonorably *adv* inhoneste

dishpan *s* labr·um -i *n* (ad vasa coquinatoria eluenda)

disillusion *tr* errorem adimĕre *(w. dat)*

disinclination *s* declinati·o -onis *f*

disinfect *tr* contagia depellĕre de *(w. abl)*

disinfectant *s* remed·ium -(i)i *n* ad contagia depellenda aptum

disinherit *tr* exheredare

disintegrate *intr* dilabi

disinter *tr* effodĕre

disinterested *adj* inte·ger -gra -grum

disinterestedly *adv* integre

disjoin *tr* disjungĕre

disjointed *adj* incomposit·us -a -um

disjointedly *adv* incomposite

disk *s* orb·is -is *m*

dislike *s* od·ium -(i)i *n*

dislike *tr* aversari

dislocate *tr* luxare

dislocation *s* luxatur·a -ae *f*

dislodge *tr* depellĕre

disloyal *adj* perfid·us -a -um

disloyally *adv* perfide

disloyalty *s* perfidi·a -ae *f*

dismal *adj* maest·us -a -um

dismally *adv* maeste

dismantle *tr* diruĕre

dismay *s* consternati·o -onis *f*

dismay *tr* percellĕre

dismember *tr* membratim dividĕre

dismemberment *s* mutilati·o -onis *f*
dismiss *tr* dimittĕre; *(fear)* mittĕre
dismissal *s* dimissi·o -onis *f*
dismount *intr* ex equo desilire
disobedience *s* inobedienti·a -ae *f*
disobedient *adj* parum obedi·ens -entis
disobey *tr* non obedire *(w. dat)*
disorder *s* confusi·o -onis *f; (of mind)* perturbati·o -onis *f; (med)* mal·um -i *n; (pol)* tumult·us -ūs *m*
disordered *adj* turbat·us -a -um; *(of mind or body)* aegrot·us -a -um
disorderly *adj* inordinat·us -a -um; *(of troops)* effus·us -a -um; *(unruly)* turbulent·us -a -um
disorganization *s* dissoluti·o -onis *f*
disorganize *tr* conturbare
disorganized *adj* dissolut·us -a -um
disown *tr (statement)* infitiari; *(heir)* abdicare; *(thing)* repudiare
disparage *tr* obtrectare
disparagement *s* obtrectati·o -onis *f*
disparaging *adj* obtrect·ans -antis
disparate *adj* dispa·r -ris
disparity *s* discrepanti·a -ae *f*
dispassionate *adj* frigid·us -a -um
dispassionately *adv* frigide
dispatch *tr* mittĕre; *(to finish)* perficĕre; *(to kill)* interficĕre
dispel *tr* dispellĕre, depellĕre
dispensary *s* medicamentaria tabern·a -ae *f*
dispensation *s* distributi·o -onis *f; (exemption)* immunit·as -atis *f*
dispense *tr* distribuĕre; *(to release)* solvĕre ‖ *intr* **to — with** remittĕre
dispenser *s* dispensat·or -oris *m*
disperse *tr* dispergĕre, dissipare ‖ *intr* diffugĕre; *(gradually)* dilabi
dispersion *s* dispersi·o -onis *f*
dispirited *adj* animo fract·us -a -um
displace *tr* summovĕre; **—ed person** profug·us -i *m*, profug·a -ae *f*
displacement *s* amoti·o -onis *f*
display *s (exhibit)* ostent·us -ūs *m; (ostentation)* ostentati·o -onis *f*
display *tr* ostendĕre; *(to show off)* ostentare
displease *tr* displicĕre *(w. dat)*
displeased *adj* offens·us -a -um; **to be — at** aegre ferre
displeasing *adj* ingrat·us -a -um
displeasure *s* offens·a -ae *f*
disposable *adj* in promptu
disposal *s* dispositi·o -onis *f;* **at your —** penes te
dispose *tr* disponĕre, ordinare; *(to incline)* inclinare ‖ *intr* **to — of** *(to settle)* componĕre; *(to sell)* abalienare; *(to get rid of)* tollĕre
disposed *adj* inclinat·us -a -um; *(pej)* pron·us -a -um
disposition *s (arrangement)* dispositi·o -onis *f; (character)* indol·es -is *f*
dispossess *tr (of)* pellĕre *(w. abl)*

disproportion *s* inconcinnit·as -atis *f*
disproportionate *adj* inaequal·is -is -e
disproportionately *adv* inaequaliter
disprove *tr* refellĕre, redarguĕre
disputable *adj* disputabil·is -is -e
dispute *s (debate)* disputati·o -onis *f; (argument)* altercati·o -onis *f;* **beyond —** indisputabil·is -is -e; **that is a matter of — id disputari potest**
dispute *tr & intr* disputare
disputed *adj* controvers·us -a -um
disqualification *s* impediment·um -i *n*
disqualify *tr* excipĕre; **to — s.o. from** aliquem excipĕre ex *(w. abl) or* ne *or* quominus
disquiet *tr* inquietare
disquieted *adj* inquiet·us -a -um
disquisition *s* disputati·o -onis *f*
disregard *s* **(for)** incuri·a -ae *f (w. gen)*, neglegenti·a -ae *f (w. gen)*
disregard *tr* neglegĕre, omittĕre
disreputable *adj* infam·is -is -e
disrepute *s* infami·a -ae *f*
disrespect *s* neglegenti·a -ae *f*
disrespectul *adj (toward)* negleg·ens -entis (in + *acc*)
disrespectfully *adv* parum honorifice
disrupt *tr* disturbare
disruption *s* discid·ium -(i)i *n*
dissatisfaction *s* displicenti·a -ae *f*
dissatisfied *adj* parum content·us -a -um
dissatisfy *tr* male satisfacĕre *(w. dat)*
dissect *tr* insecare
dissection *s* incisi·o -onis *f*
dissemble *tr & intr* dissimulare
disseminate *tr* disseminare
dissension *s* dissensi·o -onis *f*
dissent *s* dissensi·o -onis *f*
dissent *intr* dissentire
dissertation *s* dissertati·o -onis *f*
dissimilar *adj* dissimil·is -is -e
dissimiliarity *s* dissimilitud·o -inis *f*
dissipate *tr* dissipare ‖ *intr* dissipari
dissipation *s* dissipati·o -onis *f*
dissolute *adj* dissolut·us -a -um
dissolution *s* dissoluti·o -onis *f*
dissolve *tr* dissolvĕre; *(to melt)* liquefacĕre; *(meeting)* dimittĕre ‖ *intr* liquescĕre; *(to break up)* dissolvi
dissonance *s* dissonanti·a -ae *f*
dissonant *adj* disson·us -a -um
dissuade *tr* dissuadĕre *(w. dat)*
dissuasion *s* dissuasi·o -onis *f*
distaff *s* col·us -i *m*
distance *s* distanti·a -ae *f,* spat·ium -(i)i *n; (long way)* longinquit·as -atis *f;* **at a —** procul, longe
distant *adj* dist·ans -antis; *(remote)* longinqu·us -a -um; *(fig)* parum familiar·is -is -e; **to be —** abesse, distare
distaste *s* **(for)** fastid·ium -(i)i *n (w. gen)*
distasteful *adj (of food)* tet·er -ra -rum; *(fig)* odios·us -a -um

distemper s morb·us -i m
distend tr distendĕre; (sails) tendĕre
distil tr & intr stillare, destillare
distinct adj (different) divers·us -a -um; (clear) distinct·us -a -um
distinction s (act of distinguishing) distincti·o -onis f; (the thing distinguished) discrim·en -inis n; (mark, badge) insign·e -is n; (honor) hon·or -oris m; (status) amplitud·o -inis f; (decoration) praem·ium -(i)i n; **a man of —** vir -i m illustris; **without —** promiscue
distinctive adj propri·us -a -um
distinguish tr distinguĕre, discernĕre; **to — oneself** enitēre
distinguishable adj spectand·us -a -um
distinguished adj insign·is -is -e
distort tr distorquēre; (words) detorquēre; (to misinterpret) male interpretari
distortion s distorti·o -onis f; (fig) depravati·o -onis f
distract tr distrahĕre, vocare
distracted adj distract·us -a -um; (distraught) vecor·s -dis
distraction s (cause) avocament·um -i n; (state) distracti·o -onis f animi; (w. verbs of loving, etc.) **to —** efflictim
distraught adj vecor·s -dis
distress s miseri·a -ae f, dol·or -oris m; (straits) angusti·ae -arum fpl
distress tr angĕre, afflictare
distressed adj sollicit·us -a -um
distressing adj importun·us -a -um
distribute tr distribuĕre
distributer s distribut·or -oris m
distribution s distributi·o -onis f
district s regi·o -onis f
distrust s diffidenti·a -ae f
distrust tr diffidĕre (w. dat)
distrustful adj (of) diffid·ens -entis (w. dat)
distrustfully adv diffidenter
disturb tr perturbare; (to render anxious) sollicitare; (to upset) commovēre; (s.o.'s sleep) inquietare
disturbance s perturbati·o -onis f; (pol) tumult·us -ūs m
disturber s **— of the peace** turbat·or -oris m otii
disuse s desuetud·o -inis f
ditch s foss·a -ae f
ditty s cantilen·a -ae f
divan s lectul·us -i m
dive s salt·us -ūs m; (coll) popin·a -ae f
dive intr mergi; (of a submarine) urinari
diver s urinat·or -oris m
diverge intr deflectĕre, declinare; (of view) discrepare
diverse adj divers·us -a -um
diversification s variati·o -onis f
diversify tr variare
diversion s (recreation) oblectament·um -i n; (of a river) derivati·o -onis f; (pastime) avocati·o -onis f

diversity s diversit·as -atis f
divert tr (rivers) avertĕre, divertĕre; (attention) avocare; **to — s.o.'s anger and turn it on oneself** iram alicujus in se derivare
divest tr exuĕre, nudare; **to — oneself of** exuĕre, ponĕre
divide tr dividĕre; (to distribute) partiri; **to — the year into 12 months** annum in duodecim menses describĕre ‖ intr se scindĕre; **to — by ten** (math) decem partes dicĕre
divination s divinati·o -onis f
divine adj divin·us -a -um
divine tr divinare; (to guess) conjicĕre
divinely adv divinitus
diviner s aug·ur -uris m, harusp·ex -icis m
divinity s divinit·as -atis f; (god) num·en -inis n
divisible adj dividu·us -a -um
division s divisi·o -onis f; (part) par·s -tis f; (mil) legi·o -onis f; **— of opinion** dissensi·o -onis f
divorce s divort·ium -(i)i n
divorce tr divortium facĕre cum (w. abl)
divulge tr vulgare, divulgare
dizziness s vertig·o -inis f
dizzy adj vertiginos·us -a -um
do tr agĕre, facĕre; (to carry out, succeed in doing) efficĕre; **to — a hitch in the army** stipendia facĕre; **to — a kindness** beneficium facĕre; **to — s.o. in** aliquem pessum dare; **what have I to — with you?** quid mihi et tibi est? ‖ intr agĕre; (for emphatic auxiliary, use vero: **I — wish to go** cupio vero ire); (when **I —!** is used to answer a question, repeat the verb in the question: **— you believe? I —**. credisne? credo.); **how — you —?** quid agis?; **it will — you good** proderit tibi; **it won't — to** non satis est (w. inf); **that'll —!** satis est!; **to — away with** tollĕre, perdĕre; **to — well** (to make out well) recte facĕre; (to have good health) bene valēre; **to — without** carēre (w. abl); **to have enough to —** satagĕre; **what's doing?** quid agitur?
docile adj docil·is -is -e, tractabil·is -is -e
dock s naval·e -is n; (leg) cancell·i -orum mpl
docket s memnisc·us -i m
dockyard s naval·ia -ium npl
doctor s medic·us -i m; (teacher) doct·or -oris m
doctorate s doctoris grad·us -ūs m
doctrine s doctrin·a -ae f, dogm·a -atis n
document s instrument·um -i n
dodge s dol·us -i m
dodge tr eludĕre; (to shift aside and so avoid) declinare; **to — the draft** sacramentum detrectare
doe s cerv·a -ae f

dog *s* can·is -is *mf;* **to go to the —s** *(coll)* pessum ire
dogged *adj* pervic·ax -acis
doggedness *s* pervicaci·a -ae *f*
doggerel *s* inepti versicul·i -orum *mpl*
dog house, dog kennel *s* canis cubil·e -is *n*
dogma *s* dogm·a -atis *n*
dogmatic *adj* dogmatic·us -a -um; *(pej)* arrog·ans -antis
dogmatism *s* arroganti·a -ae *f*
dog star *s* canicul·a -ae *f*
doing *s* facin·us -eris *n*
dole *s* sportul·a -ae *f*
dole *tr* **to — out** parce dare
doleful *adj* lugubr·is -is -e
dolefully *adv* maeste
doll *s* pup·a -ae *f*
dollar *s* thaler·us -i *m*
dolphin *s* delphin·us -i *m*
dolt *s* caud·ex -icis *m*
domain *s (kingdom)* regn·um -i *n;* **public — ag·er -ri *m* publicus
dome *s* thol·us -i *m*
domestic *adj* domestic·us -a -um
domestic *s* famul·us -i *m,* famul·a -ae *f*
domesticate *tr* domare
domicile *s* domicil·ium -(i)i *n*
dominant *adj* praeval·ens -entis; **to be — auctoritate pollēre; **to become — potent·ior -ior -ius fieri
dominate *intr* **(over)** dominari (in *acc*)
domination *s* domin·ium -(i)i *n*
domineer *intr* dominari
domineering *adj* imperios·us -a -um
dominion *s* imper·ium -(i)i *n*
don *tr* induēre
donation *s* donati·o -onis *f*
done *adj* **have — with fear!** omitte timorem!; **no sooner said than — dictum factum; **well done!** macte virtute!
donkey *s* asell·us -i *m*
donor *s* donat·or -oris *m,* donatr·ix -icis *f*
doom *s* fat·um -i *n*
doom *tr* damnare
door *s* janu·a -ae *f,* ost·ium -(i)i *n;* for·es -ium *fpl; (folding doors)* valv·ae -arum *fpl;* **out of doors** *(position)* foris; *(direction)* foras
doorkeeper *s* ostiar·ius -(i)i *m*
doorpost *s* post·is -is *m*
doorstep *s* lim·en -inis *n*
doorway *s* ost·ium -(i)i *n*
Doric *adj* Doric·us -a -um
dormant *adj* res·es -idis; *(hidden)* lat·ens -entis; **to lie —** jacēre
dormitory *s* dormitor·ium -(i)i *n*
dorsal *adj* dorsal·is -is -e
dose *s* mensur·a -ae *f*
dot *s* punct·um -i *n*
dot *tr* punctum imponēre *(w. dat)*
dotage *s* sen·ium -(i)i *n*
dotard *s* sen·ex -is *m* delirus
dote *tr* **to — on** deamare

doting *adj* deam·ans -antis
double *adj* dupl·ex -icis; *(of pairs)* gemin·us -a -um; *(as much again)* dupl·us -a -um; *(meaning)* ambigu·us -a -um
double *s* dupl·um -i *n;* **on the — curriculo, concitu gradu
double *tr* duplicare; *(a cape)* praetervehi **ll** *intr* duplicari
double-dealing *s* frau·s -dis *f*
double-dealing *adj* versut·us -a -um
double-edged *adj* bipenn·is -is -e
double-talk *s* simulati·o -onis *f* et fallaci·a -ae *f*
doubly *adv* dupliciter
doubt *s* dub·ium -(i)i *n; (distrust)* suspici·o -onis *f;* **there is no — that** non dubium est quin *(w. subj)*
doubt *tr* dubitare *(w. acc of neuter pronoun only; otherwise use* de + *abl);* **I do not — that** non dubito quin *(w. subj)*
doubtful *adj (of persons)* dubi·us -a -um; *(of things)* incert·us -a - um, anc·eps -ipitis
doubtfully *adv* dubie; *(hesitatingly)* dubitanter
doubtless *adv* haud dubie, sine dubio
dough *s* fari·na -ae *f* ex aqua subacta
doughty *adj* fort·is -is -e
douse *tr (to put out)* exstinguēre; *(to drench)* madefacēre
dove *s* columb·a -ae *f*
dowdy *adj* inconcinn·us -a -um
down *s* plum·a -ae *f; (of hair)* lanug·o -inis *f; (of plants)* papp·us -i *m*
down *adv* deorsum; *(often expressed by the prefix* de-: **to flow —** defluēre); **to pay money —** repraesentare pecuniam; **to run —** decurrēre; **—from** de *(w. abl);* **— to** usque ad *(w. acc)*
down *prep* de *(w. abl)*
down *adj* decliv·is -is -e; *(depressed)* demiss·us -a -um; *(financially)* ad inopiam redact·us -a -um; **to feel — and out** infractos animos gerēre **to hit a man when he is —** jacentem ferire
downcast *adj (in low spirits)* demiss·us -a -um; **with — eyes** dejectis in terram oculis
downfall *s* occas·us -ūs *m*
downhearted *adj* animo fract·us -a -um
downhill *adj* decliv·is -is -e, pron·us -a -um; **it was all — proclivia omnia erant; **the last part of the road is —** ultima via est prona
downhill *adv* per declive; **as his business went —** inclinatis rebus suis
downpour *s* im·ber -bris *m* maximus
downright *adv* prorsus, plane
downright *adj* direct·us -a -um; *(unmixed)* mer·us -a -um
downstream *adv* secundo flumine
downward *adj* decliv·us -a -um, pron·us -a -um

downwards *adv* deorsum
downy *adj* plume·us -a -um
dowry *s* do·s -tis *f*
doze *intr* dormitare
dozen *adj & pron* duodecim *(indecl)*
drab *adj* cinere·us -a -um
draft *s (drink)* haust·us -ūs *m; (mil)* dilect·us -ūs *m; (breeze)* aur·a -ae *f; (first copy)* exempl·ar -aris *n; (money)* syngraph·a -ae *f; (of net)* jact·us -ūs *m; (of ship)* immersi·o -onis *f*
draft *tr (mil)* conscribĕre
drag *s (fig)* impediment·um -i *n;* **to be a — on** *s. o.* aliquem retardare
drag *tr* trahĕre; *(w. suddenness or violence)* rapĕre; **to — away** abstrahĕre; **to — down** detrahĕre; **to — out** protrahĕre **ǁ** *intr* trahi; **to — on** protrahi
dragnet *s* tragul·a -ae *f*
dragon *s* drac·o -onis *m*
drain *s* cloac·a -ae *f*
drain *tr (marshland)* siccare; *(a cup, the treasury, strength)* exhaurire
drainage *s* exsiccati·o-onis *f*
drainage ditch *s* incil·e -is *n*
drake *s* an·as -atis *m*
drama *s (single play)* fabul·a -ae *f; (genre)* dram·a -atis *n*
dramatic *adj* scenic·us -a -um; *(fig)* animum mov·ens -entis
dramatics *s* histrioni·a -ae *f*
dramatist *s* poet·a -ae *m* scaenicus
dramatize *tr* ad scaenam componĕre
drape *s* aulae·um -i *n*
drape *tr (to wrap)* amicire; *(to cover)* velare
drapery *s* aulae·a -orum *npl*
drastic *adj* severissim·us -a -um
draw *tr (to pull)* trahĕre; *(a picture)* delineare; *(inference)* colligĕre; *(bow)* adducĕre; *(sword)* educĕre; *(water)* haurire; *(breath)* ducĕre; *(geometrical figures)* describĕre; **to — aside** seducĕre; **to — apart** diducĕre; **to — away** avertĕre; **to — back** retrahĕre; **to — blood** cruorem ducĕre; **to — off** detrahĕre, abducĕre; *(wine)* depromĕre; **to — out** extrahĕre; *(fig)* elicĕre; **to — the conclusion** colligĕre; **to — together** contrahĕre; **to — up** subducĕre; *(to write)* componĕre; *(mil)* instituĕre **ǁ** *intr* **to — back** pedem referre; *(fig)* recedĕre; **to — near** appropinquare; **to — up to** *(of ships)* appetĕre
drawback *s* impediment·um -i *n*
drawbridge *s* pon·s -tis *m* versatilis
drawer *s* locul·us -i *m*
drawing *s* pictur·a -ae *f* linearis
drawl *s* lentior pronuntiati·o -onis *f*
drawl *intr* voces lentius pronuntiando trahĕre
dread *s* formid·o -inis *f*
dread *adj* dir·us -a -um

dreadful *adj* terribil·is -is -e
dreadfully *adv* horrendum in modum
dream *s* somn·ium -(i)i *n;* **in a — in** somno
dream *tr & intr* somniare; **to — about** somniare de *(w. abl)*
dreamer *s (fig)* nugat·or -oris *m*
dreamy *adj* somniculos·us -a -um
drearily *adv* triste
dreariness *s* solitud·o -inis *f*
dreary *adj (place)* vast·us -a -um; *(person)* trist·is -is -e
dredge *tr* machinā alveum *(w. gen)* perfodĕre
dregs *spl* fae·x -cis *f; (fig)* sentin·a -ae *f*
drench *tr* madefacĕre
dress *s* cult·us -ūs *m*
dress *tr* vestire, induĕre; *(to deck out)* exornare; *(wounds)* curare; *(the hair)* comĕre; **—ed in a (fancy) coat** subornat·us -a -um aliculā; **—ed in white** amict·us -a -um veste alba; **to — down** *(to chew out)* pilare; **to get —ed** amiciri; *(in fancy clothes)* se exornare **ǁ** *intr* se induĕre **ǁ** *s* (woman's garment) tunic·a -ae *f; (full-length)* vest·is -is *f* longa
dresser *s* vestiar·ium -(i)i *n*
dressing *s* ornati·o -onis *f; (sauce)* ju·s -ris *n; (stuffing)* fart·um -i *n; (med)* foment·um -i *n*
dressing room *s (at a bath)* apodyter·ium -(i)i *n*
dribble *intr* stillare
drift *s (intent)* proposit·um -i *n*
drift *intr* fluitare
drifter *s* larifug·a -ae *m*
drill *s (tool)* terebr·a -ae *f; (mil)* exercitati·o -onis *f*
drill *tr (to bore)* terebrare; *(mil)* exercēre; *(students)* instituĕre
drink *tr* bibĕre, potare; **to — in** *(fig)* haurire; **to — up** epotare **ǁ** *intr* bibĕre; **to — to** propinare *(w. dat)*
drink *s* pot·us -ūs *m,* poti·o -onis *f*
drinkable *adj* potabil·is -is -e
drinker *s* pot·or -oris *m; (habitual)* potat·or -oris *m*
drinking *s* poti·o -onis *f*
drinking *adj* bibos·us -a -um
drinking cup *s* scyph·us -i *m*
drinking straw *s* siph·o -onis *m*
drip *s* stillicid·ium -(i)i *n*
drip *intr* destillare
drive *tr* agĕre, pellĕre; *(to force)* compellĕre; *(to steer)* gubernare; *(a vehicle)* agitare; *(to convey)* vehĕre; **to — away** abigĕre; *(fig)* depellĕre; *(in confusion)* deturbare; **to — back** repellĕre; **to — home** *(fig)* animo infigĕre; **to — in** *(sheep, etc.)* cogĕre; *(nails)* infigĕre; **to — off** abigĕre; **to — on** impellĕre; **to — out** expellĕre; **to — out of one's mind** infuriare; **to — up** subigĕre **ǁ** *intr (in a*

carriage) vehi; **to — off** *(in a carriage)* avehi; **to — on** *or* **past** praetervehi

drive *s (in carriage)* vectur·a -ae *f; (energy)* vis *f,* impigrit·as -atis *f*

drivel *s* saliv·a -ae *f; (fig)* inepti·ae -arum *fpl*

drivel *intr (fig)* delirare

driver *s* agitat·or -oris *m; (of a chariot)* aurig·a -ae *m*

drizzle *s* levis pluvi·a -ae *f*

drizzle *intr* leniter pluĕre

dromedary *s* drom·as -adis *m*

drone *s (bee)* fuc·us -i *m; (buzz)* bomb·us -i *m; (person)* cessat·or -oris *m*

drone *intr* murmurrare

droop *tr* demittĕre **‖** *intr* languēre

drooping *adj* languid·us -a -um

drop *s* gutt·a -ae *f; (a drop as falling)* still·a -ae *f; (fall)* cas·us -ūs *m,* laps·us -ūs *m; (decrease)* deminuti·o -onis *f; (a little bit)* paulul·um -i *n;* **— by —** stillatim

drop *tr (purposely)* demittĕre, dejicĕre; *(to let slip)* omittĕre; *(to lay low)* sternĕre; *(a hint)* emittĕre; *(anchor)* jacĕre; *(work)* desistĕre ab *(w. abl)* **‖** *intr (to lessen)* cadĕre, concidĕre; *(to trickle)* (de)stillare; *(to fall)* decidĕre; *(esp. from the sky)* delabi, decidĕre; **to — behind** cessare; **to — down** decidĕre; **to — in on** visĕre; **to — off** to sleep obdormire; **to — out of** excidĕre de *(w. abl)*

drop-out *s* destit·or -oris *m* de schola

droppings *spl* merd·ae -arum *fpl*

drought *s* siccit·as -atis *f*

drove *s* gre·x -gis *m*

drown *tr* demergĕre; *(fig)* opprimĕre; **to — out** obscurare **‖** *intr* submergi

drowsily *adv* somniculose

drowsy *adj* somniculos·us -a -um

drub *tr* pulsare, verberare

drudge *s (slave)* mediastin·us -i *m*

drudgery *s* oper·a -ae *f* servilis

drug *s* medicament·um -i *n*

druggist *s* medicamentar·ius -(i)i *m*

drugstore *s* apothec·a -ae *f*

Druids *spl* Druid·ae -arum *mpl*

drum *s* tympan·um -i *n*

drum *tr* **to — up** exquirĕre **‖** *intr* tympanum pulsare; **to — on the table** mensam digitis pulsare

drummer *s* tympanist·a -ae *m*

drunk *adj* ebri·us -a -um; *(habitually)* ebrios·us -a -um

drunk, drunkard *s* ebrios·us -i *m,* ebrios·a -ae *f*

drunken *adj* ebri·us -a -um

drunkenness *s* ebriet·as -atis *f*

dry *adj* arid·us -a -um, sicc·us -a -um; *(thirsty)* sicc·us -a -um; *(wine)* auster·us -a -um; *(boring)* jejun·us -a -um

dry *tr* siccare; **to — out** exsiccare; **to — up** arefacĕre **‖** *intr* arescĕre

dryad *s* dry·as -adis *f*

drydock *s* siccum naval·e -is *n*

dry land *s* arid·um -i *n*

dryness *s* siccit·as -atis *f*

dry run *s* simulacr·um -i *n*

dual *adj* dual·is -is -e

dub *tr* appellare

dubious *adj* dubi·us -a -um; *(shady)* anc·eps -ipitis

duck *s* an·as -atis *f*

duck *tr (in the water)* deprimĕre; *(an issue)* evitare **‖** *intr* se inclinare

duckling *s* anaticul·a -ae *f*

duct *s* tub·us -i *m*

due *adj (owed)* debit·us -a -um; *(merited)* merit·us -a -um, just·us -a -um; **— honors** meriti honor·es -um *mpl;* **— to** propter *(w. acc),* causā *(w. gen);* **to be — to** fieri ab *(w. abl);* **to fall — on the fifth day** in quintum diem cadĕre

due *s* debit·um -i *n;* **—s** stipendi·a -orum *npl;* **to give everyone his —** suum cuique tribuĕre

due *adv* rectā; **— east** rectā ad orientem

duel *s* singulare certam·en -inis *n*

duel *intr* viritim pugnare

duet *s* bicin·ium -(i)i *n*

duffel bag *s* sarcinul·a -ae *f*

duke *s* du·x -cis *m*

dull *adj* heb·es -itis; *(mind)* tard·us -a -um

dull *tr* hebetare

dullness *s* tardit·as -atis *f*

duly *adv* rite, recte

dumb *adj* mut·us -a -um; *(fig)* stupid·us -a -um

dumbfounded *adj* obstupefact·us -a -um; *(speechless)* elingu·is -is -e

dummy *s* effigi·es -ei *f; (stupid person)* bar·o -onis *m*

dumpling *s* farinae subactae globul·us -i *m*

dumpy *adj* brev·is -is -e et obes·us -a -um

dunce *s* bar·o -onis *m*

dung *s* sterc·us -oris *n; (of birds)* merd·ae -arum *fpl*

dungeon *s* rob·ur -oris *n*

dupe *s* credul·us -i *m*

dupe *tr* decipĕre

duplicate *adj* dupl·ex -icis

duplicate *s* exempl·ar -aris *n*

duplicate *tr* duplicare

duplicity *s* duplicit·as -atis *f*

durability *s* firmit·as -atis *f*

durable *adj* durabil·is -is -e

duration *s (period of time itself)* spat·ium -(i)i *n; (lastingness)* diurnit·as -atis *f;* **of long —** diuturn·us -a -um; **of short —** brev·is -is -e

during *prep* inter *(w. acc),* per *(w. acc)*

dusk *s* crepuscul·um -i *n*

dusky *adj* fusc·us -a -um

dust *s* pulv·is -is -eris *m*

dust *tr* detergĕre

dusty *adj* pulverulent·us -a -um

dutiful *adj* pi·us -a -um, officios·us -a -um
duty *s (social or moral)* offic·ium -(i)i *n;*
(task) mun·us -eris *n; (tax)* portor·ium
-(i)i *n;* **to be on** — *(mil)* stationem agĕre;
when I do my — *(coll)* cum mea facio
dwarf *s* pumili·o -onis *m*
dwarfish *adj* pumil·us -a -um
dwell *intr* habitare; **to** — **upon** commorari
in *(w. abl)*
dweller *s* incol·a -ae *mf*
dwelling place *s* sed·es -is *f*
dwindle *intr* imminui, decrescĕre
dye *s* tinctur·a -ae *f*
dye *tr* ting(u)ĕre, inficĕre
dying *adj* moribund·us -a -um
dynamic *adj (fig)* vehem·ens -entis
dynamics *spl* dynamic·a -ae *f*
dynasty *s* dom·us -ūs *f* regnatrix; **under
the Flavian** — potiente rerum Flaviā
domu
dysentery *s* dysenteri·a -ae *f*
dyspepsia *s* dyspepsi·a -ae *f*

E

each *adj & pron* quisque, quidque; *(of
two)* uterque, utraque utrumque; *(individually)* singul·i -ae -a; — **and every**
unusquisque, unaquaeque, unumquod-
que; — **day** cot(t)idie; — **other** inter se,
invicem; **he stationed one legion** — **in
Brundisium, Tarentum, and Sepon-
tum** legiones singulas posuit Brindisi,
Tarenti, Seponti
eager *adj* **(for)** cupid·us -a -um *(w. gen)*,
avid·us -a -um *(w. gen)*
eagerly *adv* cupide, avide
eagerness *s* avidit·as -atis *f*
eagle *s* aquil·a -ae *f*
ear *s* aur·is -is *f; (outer ear)* auricul·a -ae *f;
(of corn)* spic·a -ae *f;* **to give** — **to** aurem
praebēre *(w. dat)*
earache *s* auris dol·or -oris *m;* **to have an**
— ab aure laborare
earl *s* com·es -itis *m*
early *adj (in the morning)* matutin·us -a
-um; *(coming naturally early)* matur·us
-a -um; *(before its time)* praematur·us -a
-um, praec·ox -ocis; *(of early date)*
antiqu·us -a -um; *(beginning)* prim·us -a
-um; **from** — **youth** a prima adolescen-
tia; **in** — **spring** primo vere; **in** — **times**
antiquitus
early *adv (in the morning)* mane; *(too
soon)* praemature; *(in good time)* mature; — **enough** satis temperi; — **in the
morning** bene mane; **his father died** —
pater ejus decessit mature
earmark *tr* destinare
earn *tr* merēre, merēri; **to** — **a living**
quaestum facĕre

earnest *adj (eager)* intent·us -a -um; *(serious)* seri·us -a -um; — **money** arrab·o
-onis *m*
earnest *s* **in** — ex bona fide, serio
earnestly *adv* intente, valde
earnestness *s* gravit·as -atis *f*
earnings *spl* quaest·us -ūs *m*
earrings *spl* inaur·es -ium *fpl; (of several
pearls)* crotali·a -orum *npl*
earth *s* terr·a -ae *f; (globe)* orb·is -is *m*
terrarum; **of** —, **made of** — terren·us -a
-um, terre·us -a -um
earthen *adj* terren·us -a -um; *(pottery)*
fictil·is -is -e
earthenware *s* fictil·ia -ium *npl*
earthly *adj (made of earth)* terren·us -a
-um; *(opposed to heavenly)* terrestr·is -is
-e; **for what** — **reason** quare tandem
earthquake *s* terrae mot·us -ūs *m*
earthwork *s* op·us -eris *n* terrenum
earthy *adj (humor)* terren·us -a -um
ease *s (leisure)* ot·ium -(i)i *n; (easiness)*
facilit·as -atis *f;* **at one's** — otios·us -a
-um; **to live in** — in otio vivēre; **to set
s.o.'s mind at** — alicujus animum
tranquillum reddere; **to speak with** —
solute loqui
ease *tr* levare; *(to assuage)* mitigare; **to** —
oneself alvum exonerare
easily *adv* facile
east *adj* oriental·is -is -e
east *s* ori·ens -entis *m; from* — **to west** ab
oriente ad occidentem; **on the** — ab
oriente; **to sail** — ad *or* in orientem
navigare
Easter *s* pasch·a -ae *f*
Easter *adj* paschal·is -is -e
easterly *adj* oriental·is -is -e
eastern *adj* oriental·is -is -e
Eastertime *s* temp·us -oris *n* paschale
eastward *adv* ad orientem
east wind *s* Eur·us -i *m*
easy *adj* facil·is -is -e; *(graceful)* lepid·us -a
-um; *(without obstacles, e.g., a road)*
expedit·us -a -um; *(life)* otios·us -a -um; —
to understand intellectu facil·is -is -e
easygoing *adj* secur·us -a -um
eat *tr* esse; *(to live on)* vesci *(w. abl);* **to** —
away corrodĕre; **to** — **breakfast** jentare;
to — **dinner** cenare; **to** — **lunch**
prandēre; **to** — **up** comesse ‖ *intr* esse,
cenare; **to** — **and drink** cibum et
potionem adsumĕre; **to** — **out** foris
cenare
eatable *adj* esculent·us -a -um
eating *s* es·us -ūs *m*
eaves *spl* suggrund·ae -arum *fpl*
eavesdrop *intr* subauscultare; — **on**
subauscultare
eavesdropper *s* auc·eps -ipis *m*
ebb *s* recess·us -ūs *m;* — **and flow** aestūs
recessus *m* et access·us -ūs *m;* **to be at a
low** — *(fig)* jacēre

ebb *intr* recedĕre; *(fig)* decrescĕre
ebony *s* eben·um -i *n*
eccentric *adj* abnorm·is -is -e
ecclesiastic *adj* ecclesiastic·us -a -um
echo *s* ech·o -us *f*, imag·o -inis *f*
echo *tr* repercutĕre; *(to repeat what s.o. has said)* subsequi; **to — a sound** sonum referre **ll** *vi* resonare
echoing *adj* reson·us -a -um
eclectic *adj* eclectic·us -a -um
eclipse *s* defecti·o -onis *f*
eclipse *tr* obscurare
eclogue *s* eclog·a -ae *f*
economic *adj* economic·us -a -um, ad opes publicas pertin·ens -entis
economical *adj* frugi *(indecl)*, parc·us -a -um
economically *adv* parce
economics *s* publicarum opum scienti·a -ae *f*
economist *s* qui rei publicae opes exponit
economize *intr* (on) parcĕre *(w. dat); (of the state)* publicos sumptūs minuĕre
economy *s* frugalit·as -atis *f*; **public —** publicarum opum administrati·o -onis *f*
ecstasy *s (trance)* ecstas·is -is *f*; *(rapture)* elati·o -onis *f* voluptaria; **to be in —** laetitiā gestire
eddy *s* vort·ex -icis *m*
eddy *intr* in se volutari
edge *s (very often expressed by* extrem·us -a -um *modifying the substantive); (margin)* marg·o -inis *mf; (of knife, etc.)* aci·es -ei *f; (of forest)* or·a -ae *f*; **on —** anxi·us -a -um; **on the —** in praecipiti
edge *tr (garment)* praetexĕre; *(to sharpen)* acuĕre **ll** *intr* **to — away** sensim abscedĕre; **to — closer** sensim appropinquare
edgewise *adv* **to get in a word —** vocem in sermonem insinuare
edging *s* limb·us -i *m*
edible *adj* edul·is -is -e
edict *s* edict·um -i *n*
edification *s* humanit·as -atis *f*
edifice *s* aedific·ium -(i)i *n*
edify *tr* ad humanitatem excolĕre
edit *tr* edĕre; *(to correct)* emendare
edition *s* editi·o -onis *f*
editor *s* edit·or -oris *m*
educate *tr* erudire, instituere
educated *adj* erudit·us -a -um
education *s* eruditi·o -onis *f*
educational *adj* scholastic·us -a -um
educator *s* praecept·or -oris *m*
eel *s* anguill·a -ae *f*
eerie *adj* prodigios·us -a -um
efface *tr* delēre
effect *s* effect·um -i *n; (show)* jactati·o -onis *f*; **cause and —** caus·a -ae *f* et consecuti·o -onis *f*; **—s** bon·a -orum *npl;* **for mere —** ad jactationem; **in —** reapse; **to go into —** valēre; **to have an —** valēre; *(med)* pollēre; **to have a benefi-**

cial — on prodesse *(w. dat); **to have a harmful** *or* **negative — on** obesse *(w. dat);* **to put into —** efficacem reddĕre; **to take —** operari; **to the same —** in eandem sententiam; **to this —** hujusmodi; **without —** frustra
effect *tr* conficĕre
effective *adj* profici·ens -entis, effic·ax -acis
effectively *adv* efficienter; **to speak —** plurimum in dicendo valēre
effectual *adj* effic·ax -acis
effeminancy *s* molliti·es -ei *f*
effeminate *adj* effeminat·us -a -um
effeminately *adv* effeminate
effete *adj* effet·us -a -um
efficacious *adj* effic·ax -acis
efficaciously *adv* efficaciter
efficacy *s* virt·us -utis *f*
efficiency *s* efficienti·a -ae *f*
efficient *adj* effici·ens -entis
efficiently *adv* efficienter
effigy *s* effigi·es -ei *f*
effort *s* nis·us -ūs *m;* **to be worth the —** pretium operae esse; **to make an —** eniti; **with great —** enixe
effortless *adj* facil·is -is -e
effortlessly *adv* sine labore
effrontery *s* os oris *n;* **you have the — to** *(w. inf)* os tibi inest ut *(w. subj)*
effusion *s* effusi·o -onis *f*
effusive *adj* effus·us -a -um
effusively *adv* effuse
egg *s* ov·um -i *n;* **fried —s** ova *npl* fricta; **hard-boiled —** ovum *n* durum excoctum; **scrambled —** ova *npl* permixta; **soft-boiled —** apali·um -i *n;* **to lay an —** ovum parĕre
egg *tr* **to — on** concitare
egghead *s* hom·o -inis *m* ingeniosus
egg-shaped *adj* oval·is -is -e
eggshell *s* putam·en -inis *n*
egg white *s* ovi alb·um -i *n*
egotism *s* am·or -oris *m* sui
egotist *s* sui amat·or -oris *m*
egotistical *adj* sibi soli consul·ens -entis
egress *s* egress·us -ūs *m*
egress *intr* egredi
eight *adj* octo *(indecl);* **— times** octies
eighteen *adj* duodeviginti *(indecl)*
eighteenth *adj* duodevicesim·us -a -um
eighth *adj* octav·us -a -um
eighth *s* octava par·s -tis *f*
eightieth *adj* octogesim·us -a -um
eighty *adj* octoginta *(indecl)*
either *adj & pron* u·ter -tra -trum
either *conj* **—...or** vel...vel; *(where the alternatives are mutually exclusive)* aut...aut
eject *tr* ejicĕre
ejection *s* ejecti·o -onis *f*
eke *tr* **to — out a livelihood** victum aegre parare

elaborate *adj* elaborat·us -a -um
elaborate *tr* elaborare **ll** *intr* (on) singullatim loqui (de + *abl*)
elaboration *s* lim·a -ae *f*
elapse *intr* praeterire
elastic *adj* elastic·us -a -um
elasticity *s* elasticit·as -atis *f*
elated *adj* to be — efferri
elation *s* anim·us -i *m* elatus
elbow *s* cubit·um -i *n;* resting on one's — in cubitum erect·us -a -um; to lean one one's — cubito inniti; to rub —s with conversari cum (*w. abl*)
elbow *tr* cubitis pulsare; to — one's way through the crowd cubitis turbam depulsare de via
elder *adj* maj·or -or -us natu
elderberry *s* (*bush*) sambuc·us -i *f;* (*berry*) sambuc·um -i *n;* — wine vin·um -i *n* sambuceum
elderly *adj* aetate provect·ior -ior -ius
eldest *adj* maxim·us -a -um natu
elect *adj* designat·us -a -um; (*elite*) lect·us -a -um
elect *tr* creare, eligĕre
election *s* (*act of choosing*) electi·o -onis *f;* —s (*pol*) comiti·a -orum *npl;* to hold —s comitia habēre
election day *s* di·es -ei *m* comitialis
electioneering *s* ambiti·o -onis *f*
elective *adj* (*pol*) suffragiis creat·us -a -um; (*of choice*) elegend·us -a -um
elective *s* disciplin·a -ae *f* electa
electric(al) *adj* electric·us -a -um
electric chair *s* sell·a -ae *f* electrica
electricity *s* vis *f* electrica
electrify *tr* electricā vi afficĕre; (*to thrill*) vehementer excitare
electrocute *tr* vi electricā interficĕre
elegance *s* eleganti·a -ae *f*
elegant *adj* eleg·ans -antis
elegantly *adv* eleganter
elegiac *adj* elegiac·us -a -um; — verse eleg·i -orum *mpl*
elegy *s* elegi·a -ae *f*
element *s* element·um -i *n;* —s principi·a -orum *npl* rerum; (*fig*) rudiment·a -orum *npl;* to be out of one's — peregrinus et hospes esse
elemental *adj* primordi·us -a -um
elementary *adj* simpl·ex -icis; — instruction element·a -orum *npl*
elementary school *s* lud·us -i *m* litterarius
elementary school teacher *s* litterar·ius -(i)i *m*, litterari·a -ae *f*
elephant *s* elephant·us -i *m*
elevate *tr* levare, (at)tollĕre; (*fig*) efferre
elevated *adj* edit·us -a -um
elevation *s* elati·o -onis *f;* (*height*) altitud·o -inis *f;* (*hill*) loc·us -i *m* editus
eleven *adj* undecim (*indecl*)
eleventh *adj* undecim·us -a -um
elf *s* num·en -inis *n* pumilum

elicit *tr* elicĕre
eligible *adj* (*pol*) qui per leges deligi potest; (*bachelor*) optabil·is -is -e
eliminate *tr* amovēre, tollĕre
elimination *s* use a verbal paraphrase
elision *s* elisi·o -onis *f*
elite *adj* elect·us -a -um
elite *s* flo·s -ris *m*
elk *s* alc·es -is *f*
ellipsis *s* ellips·is -is *f*
elliptical *adj* elliptic·us -a -um
elm *s* ulm·us -i *f*
elocution *s* pronuntiati·o -onis *f*
elongate *tr* producĕre
elongated *adj* praelong·us -a -um
elope *intr* insciis atque invitis parentibus cum amatore (*or* amatrice) domo fugĕre
elopement *s* clandestina fug·a -ae *f* et nupti·ae -arum *fpl*
eloquence *s* eloquenti·a -ae *f;* (*natural*) facundi·a -ae *f*
eloquent *adj* disert·us -a -um
eloquently *adv* diserte
else *adj* anyone — quivis alius; anything —? aliquid amplius?; no one — nem·o -inis *m* alius; nothing — nihil aliud; who — ? quis alius?
else *adv* (*besides*) praeterea; (*otherwise*) aliter; or — alioquin; somewhere — (*position*) alibi; (*direction*) alio
elsewhere *adv* (*position*) alibi; (*direction*) alio
elucidate *tr* illustrare, explicare
elucidation *s* explicati·o -onis *f*
elude *tr* eludĕre
elusive *adj* (*difficult to grasp*) fug·ax -acis; (*difficult to describe*) recondit·us -a -um
Elysian *adj* Elysi·us -a -um; — Fields Camp·i -orum *mpl* Elysii
emaciate *tr* macerare
emaciated *adj* ma·cer -cra -crum; to become — emacrescĕre
emaciation *s* maci·es -ei *f*
emanate *intr* emanare
emanation *s* exspirati·o -onis *f*
emancipate *tr* (*a son*) emancipare; (*a slave*) manumittĕre
emancipation *s* (*of a son*) emancipati·o -onis *f;* (*of a slave*) manumissi·o -onis *f*
emasculate *tr* emasculare
emasculated *adj* (*lit & fig*) effeminat·us -a -um
embalm *tr* condire
embalmment *s* different modes of — corporum condiendorum mod·i -orum *mpl* diversi
embankment *s* agg·er -eris *m*
embargo *s* to lay an — on ships naves ab exitu prohibēre; to lift the — on ships naves dimittĕre
embark *tr* imponĕre **ll** *intr* (in navem) conscendĕre; to — upon (*fig*) ingredi
embarkation *s* conscensi·o -onis *f;* (*usu.*

expressed by the verb: **after the — of the army** exercitu in naves imposito)
embarrass *tr* perturbare; **to be —ed** erubescĕre; **to be —ed by a deformity** deformitatem iniquissime ferre
embarrassing *adj* erubescund·us -a -um
embarrassment *s* conturbati·o -onis *f;* (*financial*) angusti·ae -arum *fpl*
embassy *s* legati·o -onis *f*
embellish *tr* exornare; **to — facts rather than report them accurately** res gestas magis exornare quam fideliter narrare
embellishment *s* (*act*) exornati·o -onis *f;* (*result*) ornament·um -i *n*
ember *s* favill·a -ae *f*
embezzle *tr* peculari
embezzlement *s* peculat·us -ūs *m*
embezzler *s* peculat·or -oris *m*
embitter *tr* exacerbare
embittered *adj* exacerbat·us -a -um
emblazon *tr* insignire
emblem *s* indic·ium -(i)i *n;* (*badge*) insign·e -is *n*
emblematic *adj* symbolic·us -a -um
embodiment *s* effigi·es -ei *f*
embody *tr* includĕre, informare
emboss *tr* caelare
embrace *s* amplex·us -ūs *m*
embrace *tr* amplecti
embroider *tr* acu pingĕre
embroidery *s* (*art*) ar·s -tis *f* acu pingendi; (*product*) pictur·a -ae *f* in textili (facta); picta vest·is -is *f*
embroil *tr* implicare
embroilment *s* implicati·o -onis *f*
embryo *s* part·us -ūs *m* inchoatus
emend *tr* emendare
emendation *s* emendati·o -onis *f*
emerald *s* smaragd·us -i *f*
emerge *intr* emergĕre; (*to arise*) existĕre
emergency *s* discrim·en -inis *n*
emigrant *s* emigr·ans -antis *mf*
emigrate *intr* (**to**) emigrare (in + *acc*)
emigration *s* emigrati·o -onis *f*
eminence *s* praestanti·a -ae *f;* (*rise in the ground*) loc·us -i *m* editus
eminent *adj* emin·ens -entis, egregi·us -a -um, ornatissim·us -a -um
eminently *adv* insigniter
emissary *s* legat·us -i *m*
emission *s* emissi·o -onis *f*
emit *tr* emittĕre
emotion *s* animi mot·us -ūs *m;* **strong —** permoti·o -onis *f*
emotional *adj* affectūs animi mov·ens -entis
emperor *s* imperat·or -oris *m;* (*title chosen by Augustus*) princ·eps -ipis *m*
emphasis *s* vis *f,* impressi·o -onis *f*
emphasize *tr* (*a word*) premĕre; (*idea*) exprimĕre
emphatic *adj* grav·is -is -e
emphatically *adv* graviter

empire *s* imper·ium -(i)i *n*
empirical *adj* empiric·us -a -um
empirically *adv* ex experimentis
empiricism *s* empiric·e -es *f*
employ *tr* (*to use*) uti (*w. abl*); (*to hire*) adhibēre; **to — precaution** uti observatione
employer *s* conduct·or -oris *m*
employment *s* (*act*) us·us -ūs *m;* (*occupation*) quaest·us -ūs *m;* (*hiring*) conducti·o -onis *f*
empower *tr* potestatem (*w. dat*) facĕre
empress *s* imperatr·ix -icis *f*
emptiness *s* inanit·as -atis *f;* (*fig*) vanit·as -atis *f*
empty *adj* vacu·us -a -um, inan·is -is -e; (*street*) desert·us -a -um; (*fig*) van·us -a -um; (*stomach*) jejun·us -a -um
empty *tr* (*contents*) vacue facĕre; (*bottle, stomach*) exhaurire; (*to strip bare*) exinanire **ǁ** *intr* (*of river*) se effundĕre
empty-handed *adj* inan·is -is -e; (*without a gift*) immun·is -is -e
empty-headed *adj* frivol·us -a -um
emulate *tr* (*to rival*) aemulari; (*to imitate*) imitari
emulation *s* aemulati·o -onis *f*
emulous *adj* (**of**) aemul·us -a -um (*w. gen*)
enable *tr* facultatem (*w. dat*) facĕre
enact *tr* sancire; (*of the plebs*) sciscĕre; (*of the Roman people*) jubēre; (*of a absolute ruler*) imponĕre
enactment *s* sancti·o -onis *f*
enamel *s* smalt·um -i *n*
enamel *adj* smaltin·us -a -um
enamored *adj* **to be — of** deamare
encamp *intr* castra ponĕre
encampment *s* castr·a -orum *npl*
encase *tr* includĕre
encaustic *adj* encaustic·us -a -um
enchant *tr* fascinare; (*fig*) capĕre
enchanted *adj* incantat·us -a -um, capt·us -a -um
enchanting *adj* (*fig*) venust·us -a -um
enchantment *s* incantament·um -i *n;* (*fig*) illecebr·ae -arum *fpl*
enchantress *s* mag·a -ae *f*
encircle *tr* circumdare
enclose *tr* includĕre; (*with a fence*) saepire; **to — a document in a letter** libellum litteris subjicĕre
enclosure *s* saept·um -i *n*
encompass *tr* complecti
encore *s* revocati·o -onis *f;* **he received an — revocatus est**
encounter *s* (*meeting*) congress·us -ūs *m;* (*fight*) pugn·a -ae *f*
encounter *tr* (*unexpectedly*) occurrĕre (*w. dat*), offendĕre; (*the enemy*) obviam ire (*w. dat*); **to — death** mortem oppetĕre
encourage *tr* cohortari; (*of one cast down*) animum *or* animos (*w. gen*) confirmare

encouragement s hortat·us -ūs m; confirmati·o -onis f
encroach intr invadĕre; **to — upon** occupare; (rights) imminuĕre; **to—upon a neighbor's land** terminos agri proferre
encroachment s usurpati·o -onis f; (on rights) imminuti·o -onis f
encumber tr impedire
encumbrance s impediment·um -i n
encyclical s litter·ae -arum fpl publicae pontificales
encyclopedia s encyclopaedi·a -ae f
end s fin·is -is m, termin·us -i m; (termination of life) exit·um -i n; (aim) proposit·um -i n; (of a speech) perorati·o -onis f; **at the — of the letter** in extremis litteris; **at the — of the year** exeunte anno; **in the —** denique; **to come to an — finem** capĕre; **to put an — to** finem imponĕre (w. dat); **to the — of spring** ad ultimum ver; **toward the — of his life** tempore extremo; **to what —?** quo?, quorsum?
end tr finire, terminare ‖ intr desinĕre, finem capĕre; (of time) exire
endanger tr in periculum vocare
endear tr carum reddĕre
endearing adj car·us -a -um
endearment s blanditi·ae -arum fpl
endeavor s conat·us -ūs m
endeavor intr conari, niti
ending s fin·is -is m, exit·us -ūs m
endless adj infinit·us -a -um
endlessly adv sine fine
endorse tr comprobare; (a check) chirographum a tergo (w. gen) inscribĕre
endow tr donare
endowed adj (with) praedit·us -a -um (w. abl)
endowment s (of body or mind) do·s tis f; (financial) dotati·o -onis f
endurable adj tolerabil·is -is -e
endurance s patienti·a -ae f; (duration) durati·o -onis f
endure tr tolerare ‖ intr durare
enduring adj toler·ans -antis; (lasting) durabil·is -is -e
enemy s (public) host·is -is m; (private) inimic·us -i m, inimic·a -ae f
enemy adj hostic·us -a -um, infest·us -a -um; inimic·us -a -um
energetic adj impi·ger -gra -grum
energy s vis f
enervate tr enervare
enforce tr **to — the law** legem exercēre
enfranchise tr civitate donare; (a slave) manumittĕre
enfranchisment s civitatis donati·o -onis f; (of a slave) manumissi·o -onis f
engage tr (to employ) adhibēre; (attention) occupare; (to involve) implicare; (enemy) proelium facĕre cum (w. abl), dimicare cum (w. abl) ‖ intr **to — in**

suscipĕre, ingredi; **to — in battle** proeliari
engaged adj (to marry) spons·us -a -um; **to be — in** versari in (w. abl)
engagement s (to marry) pacti·o -onis f nuptialis; (business) occupati·o -onis f; (mil) proel·ium -(i)i n; **to break off the — sponsum** repudiare
engaging adj suav·is -is -e
engender tr gignĕre
engine s machin·a -ae f
engineer s machinat·or -oris m; (mil) fa·ber -bri m
engineering s machinalis scienti·a -ae f
English adj Anglic·us -a -um
English s **to know —** Anglice scire; **to speak —** Anglice loqui; **to teach —** Anglice docēre
engrave tr caelare
engraver s caelat·or -oris m
engraving s caelatur·a -ae f
engross tr (in) animum occupare in (w. abl); **to be —ed in** tot·us -a -um esse in (w. abl)
engulf tr devorare, mergĕre
enhance tr amplificare
enhancement s amplificati·o -onis f
enigma s aenigm·a -atis n
enigmatic adj ambigu·us -a -um
enigmatically adv per aenigmata
enjoin tr jubēre
enjoy tr frui (w. abl); (to have the benefit of, e.g., good health, friendship) uti (w. abl)
enjoyment s fruct·us -ūs m; (the sense of pleasure itself) delectati·o -onis f
enlarge tr amplificare
enlargement s amplificati·o -onis f
enlighten tr (physically) illustrare; (mentally) illuminare; (to instruct) erudire
enlightened adj erudit·us -a -um
enlightenment s humanit·as -atis f
enlist tr (support) conciliare; (mil) conscribĕre; (to swear in) sacramento adigĕre ‖ intr sacramentum dicĕre
enlistment s conscripti·o -onis f
enliven tr excitare
enmity s simult·as -atis f; **to be at — with** in simultate esse cum (w. abl); **to feel — toward** simultatem habēre cum (w. abl)
ennoble tr honestare, nobilitare
ennui s taed·ium -(i)i n
enormity s immanit·as -atis f
enormous adj imman·is -is -e
enormously adv praeter modum
enough adj satis (indecl); **— trouble** satis laboris; **time —** satis temporis
enough adv satis; **more than —** satis superque
enrage tr infuriare
enrapture tr rapĕre; **to be —d** gaudio efferri
enrich tr locupletare, ditare

enroll *tr* adscribĕre; **to — s.o. in the patrician order** aliquem inter patricios asciscĕre

enshrine *tr* consecrare

ensign *s (banner)* sign·um -i *n; (officer)* signif·er -eri *m*

enslave *tr* in servitutem redigĕre

enslavement *s* servit·us -utis *f*

ensnare *tr* illaquēre; *(fig)* illicĕre

ensue *intr* insequi

ensuing *adj* insequ·ens -entis

entail *tr* adferre

entangle *tr* implicare

entanglement *s* implicati·o -onis *f*

enter *tr* intrare, ingredi, inire; *(office)* inire; *(to pierce)* penetrare in *(w. acc);* **to — in a memorandum** in libellum referre; **to — in an account book** in rationem inducĕre; **to — politics** rem publicam inire **‖** *intr* intrare, ingredi, inire; **to — into an alliance with s.o.** societatem cum aliquo facĕre; **to — upon** *(to undertake)* suscipĕre; *(a magistracy)* inire

enterprise *s (undertaking)* incept·um -i *n; (project)* op·us -eris *n; (venture)* aus·um -i *n; (pej)* facin·us -oris *n; (enterprising disposition)* alacer ac promptus anim·us -i *m*

enterprising *adj* ala·cer -cris -cre et prompt·us -a -um

entertain *tr (a guest)* excipĕre; *(idea)* admittĕre; *(to amuse)* oblectare

entertainer *s* ludi·o -onis *m; (host)* hosp·es -itis *m*

entertaining *adj* festiv·us -a -um

entertainment *s (amusement)* oblectati·o -onis *f; (cultural, esp. at a dinner party)* acroam·a -atis *n; (by the host)* hospit·ium -(i)i *n;* **public —s** spectacul·a -orum *npl*

enthrall *tr* captare

enthusiasm *s* stud·ium -(i)i *n*

enthusiastic *adj* studios·us -a -um

enthusiastically *adv* studiose

entice *tr* allicĕre

enticement *s* illecebr·a -ae *f*

enticing *adj* illecebros·us -a -um

entire *adj* tot·us -a -um, univers·us -a -um

entirely *adv* omnino

entirety *s expressed by* univers·us -a -um: **to look at the matter in its —** rem universam contemplari

entitle *tr (a book, essay)* inscribĕre; *(to name)* appellare; *(to give title to)* potestatem dare *(w. dat);* **to be —d to do anything** jus aliquid faciendi habēre; dignus esse qui aliquid faciat

entity *s* en·s -tis *n*

entomb *tr* sepulchro condĕre

entomologist *s* entomologic·us -i *m*

entomology *s* entomologi·a -ae *f*

entourage *s* comitat·us -ūs *m*

entrails *spl* ext·a -orum *npl*

entrance *s* adit·us -ūs *m*, introit·us -ūs *m;*

(act) ingressi·o -onis *f;* **at the — to the theater** in aditu theatri

entrance hall *s* vestibul·um -i *n*

entrance way *s* ost·ium -(i)i *n*

entrap *tr* illaquēre

entreat *tr* obsecrare

entreaty *s* obsecrati·o -onis *f*

entree *s* cen·a -ae *f* altera

entrench *tr (lit & fig)* vallare; **to — oneself** subsidĕre

entrenchment *s* muniment·um -i *n*

entrepreneur *s* negotiat·or -oris *m*

entrust *tr* committĕre

entry *s (act)* ingressi·o -onis *f,* introït·us -ūs *m; (of house)* ost·ium -(i)i *n; (in accounts)* nom·en -inis *n*

entwine *tr* implicare, implectĕre

enumerate *tr* enumerare

enumeration *s* enumerati·o -onis *f*

enunciate *tr (words)* exprimĕre; *(to predicate)* enuntiare

enunciation *s (of sounds)* explanati·o -onis *f; (setting forth)* enuntiati·o -onis *f*

envelop *tr* involvĕre

envelope *s* involucr·um -i *n*

enviable *adj* invidios·us -a -um

envious *adj* invid·us -a -um

environment *s* circumject·a -orum *npl*

environs *spl* vicinit·as -atis *f*

envision *tr* fingĕre

envoy *s* legat·us -i *m*

envy *s* invidi·a -ae *f*

envy *tr* invidēre *(w. dat)*

enzyme *s* enzym·a -ae *f*

eons *spl* plurima saecul·a -orum *npl*

ephemeral *adj (brief)* brev·is -is -e; *(perishable)* caduc·us -a -um

epic *adj* epic·us -a -um

epic *s* epos *n (only in nom & acc),* poem·a -atis *n* epicum

epicure *s* hellu·o -onis *m*

Epicurean *adj (of Epicurus)* Epicure·us -a -um; *(fig)* voluptari·us -a -um

Epicurean *s* Epicure·us -i *m; (hedonist)* voluptar·ius -(i)i *m*

epidemic *adj* epidem·us -a -um

epidemic *s* pestilenti·a -ae *f*

epidermis *s* epiderm·is -is *f*

epiglottis *s* epiglott·is -idis *f*

epigram *s* epigramm·a -atis *n*

epilepsy *s* comitalis morb·us -i *m*

epilogue *s* epilog·us -i *m*

epiphany *s* epiphani·a -ae *f*

episcopal *adj* episcopal·is -is -e

episode *s* embol·ium -(i)i *n*

epistle *s* epistol·a -ae *f*

epitaph *s* titul·us -i *m* (sepulcri)

epithet *s* epithet·on -i *n*

epoch *s* saecul·um -i *n*

equal *adj* aequ·us -a -um; *(matching)* pa·r -ris; **to be — to the task** muneri par esse

equal *s* pa·r -ris *mf & n;* to be on an — with the gods in aequo diis stare
equal *tr* aequare
equality *s* aequalit·as -atis *f;* to be on — with in aequo *(w. dat)* stare
equalization *s (act)* exaequati·o -onis *f; (state)* aequalit·as -atis *f*
equally *adv* aeque
equanimity *s* aequus anim·us -i *m*
equation *s* aequati·o -onis *f*
equator *s* aequat·or -oris *m*
equatorial *adj* aequinoctial·is -is -e
equestrian *adj* equestr·is -is -e
equestrian *s* equ·es -itis *m*
equidistant *adj* to be — aequo intervallo inter se distare
equilibrium *s* aequilibr·ium -(i)i *n*
equinox *s* aequinoct·ium -(i)i *n*
equip *tr* ornare; *(with arms)* armare
equipment *s* instrument·um -i *n,* apparat·us -ūs *m*
equitable *adj* aequ·us -a -um
equitably *adv* aeque
equity *s* aequ·um -i *n*
equivalence *s* aequalit·as -atis *f*
equivalent *adj* pa·r -ris, aequ·us -a -um; one gold coin is — to ten silver ones pro argenteis decem aureus unus valet
equivalent *s* quod idem valet
equivocal *adj* ambigu·us -a -um
equivocate *intr* tergiversari
era *s* temp·us -oris *n*
eradicate *tr* eradicare, exstirpare
eradication *s* exstirpati·o -onis *f*
erase *tr* eradĕre, delēre
erasure *s* litur·a -ae *f*
ere *conj* priusquam
ere *prep* ante *(w. acc);* — long mox; — now ante hoc tempus
erect *adj* erect·us -a -um
erect *tr (to raise)* errigĕre; *(to build)* exstruĕre; *(statue)* ponĕre, statuĕre
erection *s (building)* extructi·o -onis *f; (setting up)* erecti·o -onis *f*
erotic *adj* erotic·us -a -um
err *intr* errare, peccare
errand *s* mandat·um -i *n*
erratic *adj* inconst·ans -antis
erroneous *adj* fals·us -a -um; to be — in erratis esse
erroneously *adv* perperam
error *s* err·or -oris *m; (in writing)* mend·um -i *n*
erudite *adj* erudit·us -a -um
erudition *s* eruditi·o -onis *f*
erupt *intr* erumpĕre
eruption *s* erupti·o -onis *f*
escalade *tr (to increase)* augĕre; *(to intensify)* intendĕre ‖ *intr* (in)crescĕre, ingravescĕre
escapade *s* facin·us -oris *n* temerarium
escape *s* effug·ium -(i)i *n*
escape *tr* fugĕre; *(in a quiet way)* subter-

fugĕre; to — the notice of fallĕre ‖ *intr* effugĕre
escort *s* comitat·us -ūs *m; (protection)* praesid·ium -(i)i *n*
escort *tr* prosequi
especially *adv* praecipue, maxime
essay *s* experiment·um -i *n; (treatise)* libell·us -i *m*
essay *tr* conari
essence *s* essenti·a -ae *f*
essential *adj* necessari·us -a -um
essentially *adv* necessario
establish *tr* constituĕre; *(to settle firmly)* stabilare; *(to prove)* probare
establishment *s (act)* constituti·o -onis *f; (com)* negot·ium -(i)i *n*
estate *s (landed property)* fund·us -i *m,* a·ger -gri *m; (state)* stat·us -ūs *m*
esteem *s* aestimati·o -onis *f;* to hold in high (highest) — magni (maximi) facĕre
esteem *tr* aestimare; to — highly (more, very highly) magni (pluris, maximi) facĕre
estimable *adj* aestimand·us -a -um
estimate *s (valuation)* aestimati·o -onis *f; (judgment)* judic·ium -(i)i *n;* to form an — judicium facĕre; to give an — modum impensarum explicare
estimation *s* aestimati·o -onis *f*
estimator *s* aestimat·or -oris *m*
estrange *tr* alienare
estrangement *s* alienati·o -onis *f*
estuary *s* aestuar·ium -(i)i *n*
eternal *adj* aetern·us -a -um
eternally *adv* in aeternum
eternity *s* aeternit·as -atis *f*
ether *s* aeth·er -eris *m*
ethereal *adj* aethere·us -a -um
ethical *adj* moral·is -is -e
ethics *spl* ethic·e -es *f; (of an individual)* mor·es -ium *mpl*
etymology *s* etymologi·a -ae *f*
eulogize *tr* laudare
eulogy *s* laudati·o -onis *f*
eunuch *s* eunuch·us -i *m; (pej)* spad·o -onis *m*
euphemism *s* euphemism·us -i *m*
euphemistic *adj* — expression vo·x -cis *f* per euphemismum usurpata
euphony *s* vocalit·as -atis *f*
Europe *s* Europ·a -ae *f*
European *adj* Europae·us -a -um
evacuate *tr* vacuefacĕre; *(people)* deducĕre; *(bowels)* exonerare
evacuation *s (mil)* deducti·o -onis *f;* — of the bowels alvi purgati·o -onis *f*
evade *tr* eludĕre
evaluate *tr* aestimare
evaluation *s* aestimati·o -onis *f*
evangelical *adj* evangelic·us -a -um
evangelist *s* evangelist·a -ae *m*
evangelize *tr* evangelizare
evaporate *tr* exhalare ‖ *intr* exhalari

evaporation *s* exhalati·o -onis *f*
evasion *s* *(avoidance)* fug·a -ae *f; (dodging)* tergiversati·o -onis *f; (round-about speech)* ambag·es -um *fpl;* **to practice** — tergiversari
evasive *adj* ambigu·us -a -um
evasively *adv* ambigue
eve *s* vesp·er -eri *m; (of a feastday)* vigili·ae -arum *fpl;* **on the** — **of** sub *(w. acc)*
even *adj* aequal·is -is -e; *(level)* plan·us -a -um; *(of numbers)* pa·r -ris; **to get** — **with** ulcisci
even *adv* etiam; *(esp. to emphasize single words)* vel; — **if,** — **though** etsi, etiamsi; — **so** nihilominus; **not** — ne...quidem
evening *s* vesp·er -eri *m;* **all** — totā vesperā; **in the** — vespere, vesperi; — **falls** vesperascit; **good** —! salve!, *(pl:* salvete!); **toward** — sub vesperum; **in the early** — primo vespere; **yesterday** — heri vesperi; **very late in the** — pervespere
evening *adj* vespertin·us -a -um
evening star *s* Hesper·us -i *m*
evenness *s* aequalit·as -atis *f*
event *s* res, rei *f; (adverse)* cas·us -ūs *m; (outcome)* event·us -ūs *m;* **in all** —**s** saltem; **in any** — utique; **in the** — **of** si
eventful *adj* memorabil·is -is -e
eventual *adj* ultim·us -a -um
eventually *adv* aliquando
ever *adv (always)* semper; *(at any time)* umquam; *(after* si, nisi, num, ne) quando; — **since** ex quo (tempore); **for** — in aeternum; **greater than** — major quam umquam; **more than** — magis quam umquam
evergreen *adj* semperviv·us -a -um
everlasting *adj* sempitern·us -a -um
evermore *adv* **for** — in aeternum
every *adj* omn·is -is -e, quisque, quaeque, quodque; — **day** co(t)tidie, in dies; — **now and then** interdum; — **other day** alternis diebus
everybody *pron (each one)* quisque; *(all)* omn·es -ium *mpl; (stronger)* nem·o -inis *m* non; — **for himself** pro se quisque
everyday *adj* co(t)tidian·us -a -um; *(ordinary)* usitat·us -a -um
everyone *pron see* **everybody**
everything *pron* omn·ia -ium *npl*
everywhere *adv* ubique
evict *tr* expellĕre, detrudĕre
eviction *s* expulsi·o -onis *f*
evidence *s* testimon·ium -(i)i *n; (information given)* indic·ium -(i)i *n;* **to give** — testari; **to give** — **against s.o.** testimonium dare in aliquem; **to turn state's** — indicium profiteri; **on what** — **will you convict me?** quo me teste convinces?
evidence *tr* testari
evident *adj* manifest·us -a -um; **it is** — apparet, manifestum est, constat

evidently *adv* manifeste
evil *adj* mal·us -a -um
evil *s* mal·um -i *n*
evildoer *s* malefact·or -oris *m*
evil-minded *adj* malevol·us -a -um
evince *tr* praestare
evoke *tr* evocare, excitare
evolution *s* progress·us -ūs *m*
evolve *tr* evolvĕre per gradus **‖** *intr* evolvi per gradus
exact *adj* exact·us -a -um; *(persons)* dilig·ens -entis; **at the** — **time** ipso tempore
exact *tr* exigĕre
exaction *s* exacti·o -onis *f*
exactly *adv* accurate; — **as** sic ut
exactness *s* accurati·o -onis *f*
exaggerate *tr* in majus extollĕre; *(numbers)* augēre; **to** — **the facts** egredi veritatem, excedĕre actae rei modum
exaggeration *s* superjecti·o -onis *f* veri; **falsehoods and** —**s** falsa et majora vero; **he is given to** — omnia in majus extollĕre solet
exalt *tr* amplificare, efferre
exaltation *s* elati·o -onis *f*
examination *s* investigati·o -onis *f; (leg)* examinati·o -onis *f; (in school)* probati·o -onis *f;* **to fail an** — probatione cadĕre; **to pass an** — probatione feliciter evadĕre
examine *tr* investigare, scrutari; *(witnesses)* interrogare; *(students)* probare
examiner *s* investigat·or -oris *m;* probat·or -oris *m*
example *s* *(illustration)* exempl·um -i *n; (lesson)* document·um -i *n;* **for** — exempli gratiā; **to set an** — exemplum praebēre
exasperate *tr* exasperare
exasperation *s* ir·a -ae *f*
excavate *tr* excavare
excavation *s* excavati·o -onis *f*
exceed *tr* excedĕre, superare
exceedingly *adv* magnopere, valde
excel *tr* superare **‖** *intr* excellĕre
excellence *s* excellenti·a -ae *f*
Excellency *s* illustrissim·us -i *m*
excellent *adj* praest·ans -antis
excellently *adv* egregie, optime
except *tr* excipĕre
except *prep* praeter *(w. acc);* — **that** nisi quod
exception *s* excepti·o -onis *f;* **with the** — **of** praeter *(w. acc);* **with this** — hoc excepto; **without a single** — ne uno quidem excepto; **without** — ad un·um -am -um
exceptional *adj* praest·ans -antis
exceptionally *adv* praeter modum
excess *s* nim·ium -(i)i *n;* **to be in** — superesse; **to** — nimis; **to go to** — **in anything** nimium esse in aliqua re
excess *adj* nimi·us -a -um

excessive *adj* immodic·us -a -um
excessively *adv* immodice, nimis
exchange *s (of goods)* permutati·o -onis *f;*
(of money) collyb·us -i *m*
exchange *tr (for)* permutare *(w. abl)*
excise *tr* excidĕre
excision *s* exsecti·o -onis *f*
excitable *adj* mobil·is -is -e; *(irritable)*
irritabil·is -is -e
excite *tr* excitare; *(to inflame)* incendĕre
excitement *s* commoti·o -onis *f; (that which
excites)* incitament·um -i *n;* **to feel** —
excitari
exclaim *tr* exclamare; *(as a group)*
conclamare; *(in reply)* succlamare
exclamation *s* exclamati·o -onis *f*
exclude *tr* excludĕre
exclusion *s* exclusi·o -onis *f*
exclusive *adj* propri·us -a -um; — of praeter
(w. acc)
exclusively *adv* solum
excommunicate *tr* excommunicare
excommunication *s* excommunicati·o
-onis *f*
excrement *s* excrement·um -i *n*
excrete *tr* excernĕre
excretion *s (act)* excreti·o -onis *f; (result)*
excrement·um -i *n*
excruciating *adj* cruci·ans -antis, acer-
bissim·us -a -um
exculpate *tr* (ex)purgare
excursion *s* it·er -ineris *n* voluptatis causā
susceptum
excusable *adj* excusabil·is -is -e
excuse *s* excusati·o -onis *f; (pretext)*
praetext·um -i *n*
excuse *tr* ignoscĕre *(w. dat);* **to — oneself**
se excusare
execute *tr (a criminal)* supplicio capitis
afficĕre; *(to perform)* exsequi, efficĕre
execution *s* exsecuti·o -onis *f; (capital
punishment)* supplic·ium -(i)i *n* capitis
executioner *s* carnif·ex -icis *m*
executive *adj* ad administrationem per-
tin·ens -entis
executive *s* administrat·or -oris *m*
executor *s* curat·or -oris *m* testamenti
exemplary *adj* eximi·us -a -um
exemplification *s* exempl·um -i *n*
exemplify *tr* exemplum *(w. gen)* exponĕre
exempt *tr* eximĕre
exempt *adj (from)* vacu·us -a -um (ab +
abl); (from tribute) immun·is -is -e, lib·er
-era -erum
exemption *s* immunit·as -atis *f; (from military service)* vacati·o -onis *f* militiae
exercise *s* exercitati·o -onis *f; (athletic)*
palaestr·a -ae *f; (mil)* exercit·ium -(i)i *n;*
(literary) them·a -atis *n*
exercise *tr* exercēre **ǁ** *intr* se exercēre
exert *tr* adhibēre; **to — oneself** viribus
eniti
exertion *s* contenti·o -onis *f*

exhalation *s* exhalati·o -onis *f*
exhale *tr* exhalare **ǁ** *intr* exspirare
exhaust *tr* exhaurire; *(to tire)* defatigare,
conficĕre
exhausted *adj* fatigat·us -a -um; **to be** *or*
become — a viribus deficĕre
exhaustion *s* defecti·o -onis *f* virium
exhibit *tr* exhibēre; *(games)* edĕre
exhibition *s* exhibiti·o -onis *f; (display)*
ostentati·o -onis *f; (public performance)*
lud·i -orum *mpl; (gladiatorial show)*
mun·us -eris *n*
exhilarate *tr* exhilare
exhilarating *adj* animum exhilar·ans
-antis; **the morning air is** — exhilarant
animos aurae matutinae
exhilaration *s* hilarit·as -atis *f*
exhort *tr* hortari
exhortation *s* hortam·en -inis *f; (act)*
hortati·o -onis *f*
exhume *tr* exhumare
exigency *s* necessit·as -atis *f*
exile *s (temporary)* ex(s)il·ium -(i)i *n; (for
life)* deportati·o -onis *f; (person)* exs·ul
-ulis *mf*
exile *tr* exterminare; *(for a time)* relegare;
(for life) deportare
exist *intr* esse, ex(s)istĕre; *(to be extant)*
exstare; *(of human beings)* vivĕre
existence *s* existenti·a -ae *f; (of human
beings)* vit·a -ae *f*
exit *s* exit·us -ūs *m*
exonerate *tr* absolvĕre
exorbitant *adj* immodic·us -a -um; **to make
— demands** immodice postulare
exotic *adj* exotic·us -a -um
expand *tr* expandĕre, extendĕre **ǁ** *intr*
expandi, se extendĕre
expanse *s* spat·ium -(i)i *n*
expansion *s* expansi·o -onis *f*
expatriate *tr* exterminare
expatriate *s* exs·ul -ulis *mf*
expect *tr* exspectare; **not —ing** necopin·ans
-antis; **sooner than —ed** opinione
celerius
expectancy *s* spe·s -i *f*
expectation *s* exspectati·o -onis *f;* **contrary to —** praeter opinionem
expectorate *tr & intr* exspuĕre
expediency *s* utilit·as -atis *f*
expedient *adj* util·is -is -e; **it is — that**
expedit *(w. acc & inf)*
expedient *s* mod·us -i *m*
expedite *tr* expedire, maturare
expedition *s (mil)* expediti·o -onis *f;
(speed)* celerit·as -atis *f;* **to lead troops
on an —** copias educĕre in expeditionem
expeditious *adj* cel·er -eris -ere
expeditiously *adv* celeriter; **as — as possible** quam celerrime
expel *tr* expellĕre
expend *tr* impendĕre
expenditure *s* impens·a -ae *f*

expense s impens·a -ae f, sumpt·us -ūs m;
at great — magno sumptu
expensive adj car·us -a -um, pretios·us -a
-um, sumptuos·us -a -um
expensively adv sumptuose
experience s us·us -ūs m, experienti·a -ae
f; **military —** usus m in re militari;
political — usus m in republica; **a man
of long —** vi·r -ri m longā experientiā
experience tr experiri, cognoscĕre; **to —
in daily life** in usu habēre
experienced adj (in) perit·us -a -um (w.
gen)
experiment s experiment·um -i n
experimental adj usu comparat·us -a -um
expert adj (in) perit·us -a -um (w. gen)
expertly adv scienter, callide
expertness s callidit·as -atis f
expiate tr expiare, luĕre
expiation s expiati·o -onis f
expiration s exit·us -ūs m; **at the — of the
fifth year** quinto anno exeunte
expire intr exspirare; (of time) exire
explain tr explanare, explicare
explanation s explanati·o -onis f
expletive s explement·um -i n
explicit adj explicat·us -a -um
explicitly adv aperte, plane
explode tr displodĕre; (fig) explodĕre **ǁ**
intr displodi
exploit s facin·us -oris n; **—s** re·s -rum fpl
gestae
exploit tr uti (w. abl); (pej) abuti (w. abl)
exploration s indagati·o -onis f
explore tr explorare, indagare
explorer s explorat·or -oris m
explosion s frag·or -oris m
exponent s interpr·es -itis m
export tr exportare, evehĕre
exporter s exportat·or -oris m
exports spl merc·es -ium fpl quae ex-
portantur
expose tr exponĕre; (to bare) nudare; (to
uncover) detegĕre; (to danger) objicĕre;
to be —ed to patēre (w. dat)
exposition s expositi·o -onis f
exposure s (to cold) expositi·o -onis f; (of
guilt) deprehensi·o -onis f
expound tr exponĕre, interpretari
express adj express·us -a -um
express tr exprimĕre; **to — oneself** loqui,
dicĕre
expression s verb·um -i n; (of the face)
vult·us -ūs m; **joy beyond —** gaudia
majora quam quae verbis exprimi
possint
expressive adj signific·ans -antis; (fig)
loqu·ax -acis; **— of ind·ex** -icis (w. gen)
expressly adv plane
expulsion s exacti·o -onis f
expunge tr oblitterare
expurgate tr expurgare
exquisite adj exquisit·us -a -um

exquisitely adv exquisite
extant adj superst·es -itis; **to be —** exstare
extempore adv ex tempore
extemporaneous adj extemporal·is -is -e
extemporaneously adv ex tempore
extemporize intr subita dicĕre
extend tr extendĕre; **to — the empire**
ampliare imperium; **to — the governor's
term** prorogare imperium **ǁ** intr extendi;
to — to tendĕre ad (w. acc)
extension s extenti·o -onis f; (lengthening) producti·o -onis f; (e.g., of the fingers) porrigi·o -onis f; (of size) prolati·o
-onis f
extensive adj lat·us -a -um
extensively adv late
extent s spat·ium -(i)i n; (of a country)
fin·es -ium mpl; **to a great —** magnā ex
parte; **to some —** aliquā ex parte; **to this
—** hactenus
extenuating adj **— circumstances** eae res
quibus culpa minuitur
exterior adj exter·ior -ior -ius
exterior s speci·es -ei f
exterminate tr ad internecionem delēre
extermination s interneci·o -onis f
external adj extern·us -a -um
externally adv extrinsecus
extinct adj exstinct·us -a -um; **to become
—** obolescĕre
extinction s exstincti·o -onis f
extinguish tr exstinguĕre
extol tr laudibus efferre
extort tr extorquēre
extortion s pecuni·ae -arum fpl repetundae
extortionist s extort·or -oris m
extra adj addit·us -a -um
extra adv insuper, praeterea
extract s (chemical) expressi·o -onis f;
(literary) excerpt·um -i n; (synopsis)
compend·ium -(i)i n
extract tr extrahĕre; (to squeeze out)
exprimĕre; (teeth) evellĕre; (from a literary source) excerpĕre
extraction s (act) evulsi·o -onis f; (descent) stirp·s -is f; **of German —**
oriund·us -a -um a Germanis
extraneous adj alien·us -a -um
extraordinarily adv praeter modum
extraordinary adj extraordinari·us -a -um,
insolit·us -a -um; (outstanding) eximi·us
-a -um
extravagance s sumpt·us -ūs m
extravagant adj (exceeding bounds)
immodic·us -a -um; (in expenditure)
sumptuos·us -a -um; (spending) pro-
dig·us -a -um
extravagantly adv immodice; (expensively) sumptuose; (lavishly) profuse,
prodige
extreme adj extrem·us -a -um
extreme s extrem·um -i n; **from one — to
another** ab imo ad summum; **in the —**

ad extremum; **to go to —s** descendĕre ad extrema

extremely *adv* summe, perquam

extremist *s* assectat·or -oris *m* rerum novarum

extremity *s* extremit·as -atis *f*, extrem·um -i *n*; **extremities of the body** eminentes part·es -ium *fpl* corporis; **we have been reduced to extremities** ad extrema perventum est

extricate *tr* expedire, extrahĕre

extrinsic *adj* extrane·us -a -um

extrude *tr* extrudĕre ‖ *intr* extrudi

exuberance *s* (*of growth*) luxuri·es -ei *f*; (*of spirit*) redundanti·a -ae *f*

exuberant *adj* luxurios·us -a -um; (*unrestrained*) effus·us -a -um; **to be —** (*of style*) redundare

exude *tr* exudare ‖ *intr* emanare

exult *intr* exsultare, gestire

exultant *adj* laetabund·us -a -um

exultantly *adv* laete

exultation *s* exsultati·o -onis *f*

eye *s* ocul·us -i *m*; (*of needle*) foram·en -inis *n*; (*of plant*) gemm·a -ae *f*; **blind in one —** lusc·us -a -um; **keep your —s open!** cave circumspicias!; **to be in the public —** scaenae servire; **to keep an — on** cavēre, in oculis habēre; **to shut one's —s to** conivēre

eye *tr* aspicĕre

eyeball *s* oculi orb·is -is *m*

eyebrow *s* supercil·ium -(i)i *n*

eyeglasses *spl* perspicill·a -orum *npl*

eyelash *s* palpebrarum pil·us -i *m*

eyelid *s* palpebr·a -ae *f*

eyesight *s* aci·es -ei *f*; **to lose one's —** oculos perdĕre

eyesore *s* (*fig*) res, rei *f* taetra

eyewitness *s* oculatus test·is -is *m*

F

fable *s* fabul·a -ae *f*

fabled *adj* fabulos·us -a -um

fabric *s* textil·e -is *n*, text·um -i *n*; (*framework*) fabric·a -ae *f*

fabricate *tr* fabricare; (*fig*) fingĕre

fabrication *s* fabricati·o -onis *f*; (*fig*) mendac·ium -(i)i *n*

fabulous *adj* mirabil·is -is -e

fabulously *adv* perquam

face *s* faci·es -ei *f*, o·s -ris *n*; (*forward part of anything*) fron·s -tis *f*; **— to —** coram; **— to — with** coram (*w. abl*); **on the — of it** primā facie; **to lose —** honestatem amittĕre; **to make a —** os ducĕre; **to one's —** coram

face *tr* (*to look towards*) aspicĕre; (*to withstand, e.g., danger*) obviam ire (*w. dat*); (*to confront*) se opponĕre (*w. dat*) ‖ *intr*

spectare; **to — about** (*mil*) signa convertĕre; **to — north** (**south,** *etc.*) ad *or* in septentrionem (meridiem, *etc.*) spectare

face powder *s* fuc·us -i *m*

facet *s* gemmae superfici·es -ei *f*; (*fig*) aspect·us -ūs *m*

facetious *adj* facet·us -a -um

facetiously *adv* facete

facilitate *tr* facilius reddĕre

facility *s* (*skill*) facult·as -atis *f*; (*ease*) facilit·as -atis *f*; **—s** commod·a -orum *npl*

facing *s* (*archit*) tector·ium -(i)i *n*

facing *adj* adversus (*w. acc*)

facsimile *s* imag·o -inis *f*

fact *s* fact·um -i *n*, res, rei *f*; **as a matter of —** enimvero; **in —** vero, quidem; **the — that** quod

faction *s* facti·o -onis *f*; (*party*) part·es -ium *fpl*

factory *s* officin·a -ae *f*

faculty *s* facult·as -atis *f*; (*educ*) ord·o -inis *m*

fade *intr* (*of colors*) pallēre; (*of strength, etc.*) marcescĕre

fag, fagot *s* (*sl*) cinaed·us -i *m*

fail *tr* (*to disappoint*) deficĕre; (*to desert*) deserĕre, destituĕre; **time, voice, lungs — me** me dies, vox, latera deficiunt; **to — a test** probatione cadĕre; **words — me** quid dicam non invenio ‖ *intr* deficĕre; (*educ*) cadĕre; (*com*) decoquĕre

fail *s* **without —** certo, omnino

failing *s* (*deficiency*) defect·us -ūs *m*; (*fault*) vit·ium -(i)i *n*; (*ceasing*) remissi·o -onis *f*

failure *s* (*of strength, breath, supplies*) defecti·o -onis *f*; (*lack of success*) offensi·o -onis *f*; (*com*) ruin·a -ae *f* fortunarum; (*person*) hom·o -inis *m* perditus; (*fault*) vit·ium -(i)i *n*

faint *adj* (*weary*) fess·us -a -um; (*drooping*) languid·us -a -um; (*sight, etc.*) heb·es -itis; (*sound*) surd·us -a -um; (*colors*) pallid·us -a -um; (*courage*) timid·us -a -um

faint *intr* collabi, animo linqui

faint-hearted *adj* ignav·us -a -um

faintness *s* (*of impression*) levit·as -atis *f*; (*of body*) langu·or -oris *m*

fair *adj* (*handsome*) pul·cher -chra -chrum; (*complexion*) candid·us -a -um; (*hair*) flav·us -a -um; (*weather*) seren·us -a -um; (*wind*) secund·us -a -um; (*impartial*) aequ·us -a -um; (*ability*) mediocr·is -is -e; **— and square** sine fuco ac fallaciis

fair *s* nundin·ae -arum *fpl*

fairly *adv* aeque; (*somewhat*) aliquantulum; (*moderately*) mediocriter

fairness *s* (*justice*) aequit·as -atis *f*; (*of complexion*) cand·or -oris *m*

fairy *s* (*water fairy*) nymph·a -ae *f*; (*wood fairy*) dry·as -adis *f*

faith *s* fid·es -ei *f;* **in good —** ex bona fide; **to have — in** credĕre *(w. dat)*

faithful *adj* fid·us -a -um, fidel·is -is -e

faithfully *adv* fideliter

faithfulness *s* fidelit·as -atis *f*

faithless *adj* infidel·is -is -e

faithlessly *adv* perfide

falcon *s* falc·o -onis *m*

fall *s* *(drop)* cas·us -ūs *m; (by slipping)* laps·us -ūs *m; (autumn)* autumn·us -i *m; (e.g., of a tower)* ruin·a -ae *f; (of a town)* excid·ium -(i)i *n; (decrease)* deminuti·o -onis *f; (moral)* laps·us -ūs *m;* **the —s** desiliens aqu·a -ae *f*

fall *intr* cadĕre; *(several together)* concidĕre; *(to die)* occidĕre; *(to abate)* decrescĕre; *(violently)* corruĕre; *(to occur)* accidĕre, incidĕre; *(by lot)* contingĕre; **to — apart** dilabi; **to — at the feet of** procubare ad pedes *(w. gen);* **to — asleep** in somnum decidĕre; **to — away** desciscĕre; **to — back** recidĕre; *(to retreat)* pedem referre; **to — back on** recurrĕre ad *(w. acc);* **to — down on** *(e.g., the bed)* decidĕre in *(w. acc);* **to — due** cadĕre; **to — for** *(a person)* amore perdi in *(w. acc); (a trick)* falli *(w. abl);* **to — forwards** procidĕre, prolabi; **to — in love with** amare, coepisse amare; **to — into** incidĕre in *(w. acc);* **to — in with** *(to meet)* incidĕre in *(w. acc); (to agree)* congruĕre cum *(w. abl);* **to — into a trap** in plagas incidĕre; **to — into the hands of** in manus *(w. gen)* incidĕre, in potestatem *(w. gen)* devenire; **to — off** *(e.g., a wagon)* decidĕre de *or* ex *(w. abl); (fig)* in deterius mutari; **to — on** *(a certain day)* incidĕre in *(w. acc);* **to fall on the ground** in terram incidĕre; **to — on one's sword** in gladium incumbĕre; **to — on top of** incidĕre super *(w. acc);* **to — out** *(mil)* ordine egredi; **to — out of** excidĕre de *(w. abl); (fig)* in deterius mutari; **to — out with** *(in disagreement)* dissentire ab *(w. abl);* **to — short of** non contingĕre; **to — over** *(to topple over)* cadĕre; *(to stumble over)* pedem offendĕre ad *(w. acc);* **to — short** deficĕre; **to — short of the goal** metam non contingĕre; **to — sick** in morbum incidĕre; **to — to** *(of inheritances, etc.)* obvenire *(w. dat);* **to — to the ground** in terram decidĕre; **to — under** *(to be listed under)* cadĕre sub *(w. acc);* **to — under s.o.'s sway** in ditionem alicujus venire, in potestatem alicujus cadĕre; **to — upon** incidĕre ad *(w. acc); (to assail)* incidĕre in *(w. acc);* **to let —** demittĕre

fallacious *adj* fall·ax -acis

fallacy *s* capti·o -onis *f*

fallible *adj* errori obnoxi·us -a -um

fallow *adj (land)* noval·is -is -e; **to lie —** cessare

false *adj* fals·us -a -um; *(counterfeit)* adulterin·us -a -um

falsehood *s* comment·um -i *n*

falsely *adv* falso

falsify *tr (documents)* corrumpĕre; *(to tamper with)* vitiare

falsity *s* fals·um -i *n*

falter *intr (to stammer)* haesitare; *(to totter)* titubare

falteringly *adv* titubanter

fame *s* fam·a -ae *f,* clarit·as -atis *f*

famed *adj* clar·us -a -um

familiar *adj* **(with)** familiar·is -is -e *(w. dat); (well known)* not·us -a -um; **to be on — terms with** familiariter uti *(w. abl)*

familiarity *s* familiarit·as -atis *f;* **to be on terms of — with** familiariter uti *(w. abl)*

familiarize *tr* **(with)** assuefacĕre *(w. dat)*

family *s* famili·a -ae *f;* **— on the father's (mother's) side** paternum (maternum) gen·us -eris *n;* **to come from a good —** honesto loco nat·us -a -um esse

family *adj* familiar·is -is -e; **— inheritance** heredit·as -atis *f* gentilica; **— name** gentile nom·en -inis *n;* **— secrets** arcan·a -orum *npl* domūs; **— tree** gen·us -eris *n*

famine *s* fam·es -is *f*

famished *adj* famelic·us -a -um

famous *adj* clar·us -a -um

famously *adv* insigniter

fan *s* flabell·um -i *n; (admirer)* faut·or -oris *m; (winnowing)* vann·us -i *m*

fan *tr* ventilare; *(fire)* accendĕre; *(fig)* excitare

fanatic *adj* fanatic·us -a -um

fanaticism *s* fur·or -oris *m* religiosus

fancied *adj* fict·us -a -um

fanciful *adj* commentici·us -a -um

fancy *s* imaginati·o -onis *f; (caprice)* libid·o -inis *f; (liking)* prolub·ium -(i)i *n*

fancy *tr* imaginari

fang *s* den·s -tis *m*

fantastic *adj (unreal)* van·us -a -um; *(wonderful)* mir·us -a -um

far *adj* longinqu·us -a -um; **on the — side of the Po** ultra Padum

far *adv* procul; *(of degree)* longe; **as — as** quantum, quatenus; *(up to)* tenus *(always after the governed word) (w. abl or gen);* **as — as the neck** cervicibus tenus; **by —** longe, multo; **by — the wealthiest state** longe opulentissima civit·as -atis *f;* **— away** procul; **— and near** longe lateque; **— be it from me to say** equidem dicĕre nolim; **— from it!** minime!; **— off** procul; **— otherwise** longe aliter; **how — ** quoad, quousque; **so — ** hactenus; **thus — ** hactenus; **to be — away (from)** longe abesse (ab + *abl);* **to be very — from the truth** longissime abesse a vero

farce s *(lit & fig)* mim·us -i m
farcical adj mimic·us -a -um
farcically adv mimice
fare s *(food)* vict·us -ūs m; *(money)* vectur·a -ae f; *(for sea travel)* nav·ium -(i)i n; *(passenger)* vect·or -oris m
fare intr agĕre, se habēre
farewell interj vale! *(pl:* valete!)
far-fetched adj conquisit·us -a -um
far-flung adj late pat·ens -entis
farm s fund·us -i m
farm tr *(to till)* arare, colĕre; *(taxes)* redimĕre; **to — out** locare
farmer s agricol·a -ae m
farm house s vill·a -ae f *(rustica)*
farming s agricultur·a -ae f
farm worker s colon·us -i m
farsighted adj provid·us -a -um
farther adj ulter·ior -ior -ius
farther adv longius, ulterius; **no — than** non ultra quam; **to advance —** procedĕre ulterius
farthermost adj ultim·us -a -um
farthest adj ultim·us -a -um
fasces spl fasc·es -ium fpl
fascinate tr capĕre
fascinating adj mirific·us -a -um
fascination s blanditi·a -ae f
fashion s mod·us -i m, mo·s -ris m; **to be in —** more fieri; **to go out of —** obsolescĕre
fashion tr fabricare; *(to form a figure of)* effingĕre
fashionable adj eleg·ans -antis; **it is —** moris est
fashionably adv ad morem
fast adj *(swift)* cel·er -eris -ere; *(firm)* firm·us -a -um; *(tight)* astrict·us -a -um; *(shut)* occlus·us -a -um; *(color)* stabil·is -is -e; *(talk)* expedit·us -a -um
fast adv *(swiftly)* celeriter; *(firmly)* firmiter; **to be — asleep** arte dormire
fast s jejun·ium -(i)i n; **to break the —** jejunium solvĕre; **to keep the —** jejunium servare
fast intr jejunare, cibo abstinēre
fasten tr affigĕre, astringĕre; *(to tie)* ligare; **to — down** defigĕre; **to — to** *(w. nails, rivets)* affigĕre *(w. dat or ad + acc)*; *(by tying)* annectĕre, illigare *(w. dat or ad + acc)*; **to — together** *(w. nails, etc.)* configĕre; *(by tying)* connectĕre, colligare ‖ intr **to — upon** arripĕre
fastener s *(clip)* fibul·a -ae f
fastening s vincul·um -i n
fastidious adj fastidios·us -a -um
fastidiously adv fastidiose
fasting s jejun·ium -(i)i n
fasting adj abstin·ax -acis
fat adj pingu·is -is -e; **to get —** pinguescĕre
fat s ad·eps -ipis mf
fatal adj fatal·is -is -e, letal·is -is -e
fatality s cas·us -ūs m fatalis
fatally adv fataliter

fate s fat·um -i n, sor·s -tis f
fated adj fatal·is -is -e
fateful adj fatal·is -is -e
Fates spl Parc·ae -arum fpl
father s pa·ter -tris m; **— of the family** paterfamilias *(gen:* patrisfamilias) m; **on the —'s side** patri·us -a -um
fatherhood s paternit·as -atis f
father-in-law s soc·er -eri m
fatherless adj orb·us -a -um
fatherly adj patern·us -a -um
fathom s uln·a -ae f
fathom tr penitus cognosĕre
fathomless adj profund·us -a -um
fatigue s (de)fatigati·o -onis f
fatigue tr (de)fatigare
fatigued adj (de)fatigat·us -a -um
fatten tr saginare ‖ intr **to — up** pinguescĕre
fatty adj pingu·is -is -e; **all — substances** omnia quae adipis naturam habent
fatuous adj fatu·us -a -um
fault s culp·a -ae f, delict·um -i n; **I am at — in** culpā sum, penes me culpa est; **to be at —** *(leg)* in noxā esse; **to find — with** vituperare
faultless adj inte·ger -gra -grum; *(without blemish)* emendat·us -a -um
faultlessly adv emendate
faulty adj vitios·us -a -um; *(having errors)* mendos·us -a -um
faun s faun·us -i m
favor s fav·or -oris m; *(good will of a party or nation)* grati·a -ae f; *(good turn)* benefic·ium -(i)i n; *(a favor done)* grati·a -ae f; **to ask s.o. a —** gratiam ab aliquo petĕre; **to be in — of** favēre *(w. dat);* **to be in — with s.o.** cum aliquo in gratiā esse; **to do s.o a —** gratum alicui facĕre; **to do s.o. a bigger —** gratius alicui facĕre; **to return s.o. a —** gratiam alicui referre; **to restore s.o. to —** aliquem in gratiam restituĕre
favor tr favēre *(w. dat),* secundare; **to — severer measures** asperiora suadēre
favorable adj prosper·us -a -um; *(wind, circumstances, auspices, gods)* secund·us -a -um; *(suitable)* idone·us -a -um
favorably adv benigne; **to be — disposed toward s.o.** bono animo esse in aliquem; **to hear —** benigne audire
favored adj grat·us -a -um
favorite adj dilect·us -a -um
favorite s delici·ae -arum fpl
favoritism s iniquit·as -atis f
fawn s hinnule·us -i m
fawn intr **to — on** adulari
fawning adj bland·us -a -um
fear s met·us -ūs m; *(timidity, as a variety of* metus) tim·or -oris m; **to be in — in** metu esse; **to be inspired with —** metum capĕre
fear tr & intr metuĕre, timēre

fearful *adj* (**of**) timid·us -a -um *(w. gen or ad + acc); (terrible)* terribil·is -is -e, dir·us -a -um

fearless *adj* impavidu·s -a -um

fearlessly *adv* impavide, intrepide

feasibility *s* possibilit·as -atis *f*

feasible *adj* possibil·is -is -e

feast *s* epul·ae -arum *fpl; (religious)* di·es -ei *m* festus

feast *tr* pascĕre; **to — one's eyes on** oculos pascĕre *(w. abl)* ‖ *intr* epulari

feat *s* facin·us -oris *n;* **— of arms** facinus *n* militare; **—s** re·s -rum *fpl* gestae

feather *s* penn·a -ae *f; (downy)* plum·a -ae *f*

feather *tr* **to — one's nest** opes accumulare

feathered *adj* pennat·us -a -um

feathery *adj* plumos·us -a -um

feature *s* lineament·um -i *n; (fig)* propriet·as -atis *f*

February *s* Februar·ius -(i)i *m or* mens·is -is *m* Februarius; **on the first of —** Kalendis Februariis

federal *adj* foederat·us -a -um

federalize *tr* confoederare

federation *s* consociati·o -onis *f*

fee *s* merc·es -edis *f; (for tuition)* Minerv·al -alis *n; (for membership)* honorar·ium -(i)i *n*

feeble *adj* infirm·us -a -um; *(senses, impression made)* heb·es -etis

feebly *adv* infirme

feed *tr* pascĕre; *(to nourish)* alĕre; *(of streams, etc.)* servire *(w. dat)* ‖ *intr* (**on**) pasci *(w. abl)*

feed *s* pabul·um -i *n*

feeding *s* pasti·o -onis *f*

feel *tr (hunger, pain, heat, cold, etc.)* sentire; *(with hands)* tentare; **to — compassion for** misereri *(w. gen);* **to — grief** dolēre; **to — one's way** viam tentare; *(fig)* caute et cogitate rem tractare; **to — pain** dolore affici; **to — pity for** misereri *(w. gen);* **to — the pulse** *(med)* pulsum venarum attingĕre, venas tentare ‖ *intr* **to — good** se bene habēre; **to — happy** gaudēre; **to — sad** maest·us -a -um esse

feel *s* tact·us -ūs *m*

feeler *s* experiment·um -i *n;* **to send out a — to** tentare

feeling *s (touch, sensation)* tact·us -ūs *m; (sensibility)* sens·us -ūs *m; (emotion)* affect·us -ūs *m; (taste)* judic·ium -(i)i *n; (compassion)* misericordi·a -ae *f;* **to hurt s.o.'s —s** aliquem offendĕre

feign *tr* fingĕre, dissimulare

feint *s* simulati·o -onis *f*

felicitous *adj* fel·ix -icis

felicity *s* felicit·as -atis *f*

feline *adj* felin·us -a -um

fell *adj* dir·us -a -um

fell *tr (trees)* caedĕre; *(person)* sternĕre

fellow *s (companion)* soc·ius -(i)i *m; (coll)* hom·o -inis *m;* **my good —, what have you there?** mi homo, quid istuc est?; **young —** adulescentul·us -i *m*

fellow citizen *s* civ·is -is *mf*

fellow countryman *s* civ·is -is *m*

fellow creature *s* hom·o -inis *m*

fellow man *s* alt·er -erius *m*

fellow member *s* sodal·is -is *mf*

fellow passenger *s* convect·or -oris *m*

fellow soldier *s* commilit·o -onis *m*

fellow student *s* condiscipul·us -i *m,* condiscipul·a -ae *f*

fellowship *s* sodalit·as -atis *f; (award)* stipend·ium -(i)i *n* in sumptūs studiosorum

fellow townsman *s* munic·eps -ipis *m*

felon *s* scelest·us -i *m*

felonious *adj* scelest·us -a -um

felony *s* scel·us -eris *n*

felt *adj* coact·us -a -um

felt *s* coact·a -orum *npl*

female *adj* muliebr·is -is -e

female *s* muli·er -eris *f*

feminine *adj* muliebr·is -is -e, femin·eus -a -um; *(gram)* feminin·us -a -um

fence *s* saep·es -is *f*

fence *tr* saepire; **to — off** saepire ‖ *intr* batuĕre

fencing *s* gladii ar·s -tis *f*

fend *tr* **to — off** arcēre ‖ *intr* **to — for oneself** sibi consulĕre

ferment *s* ferment·um -i *n; (fig)* aest·us -ūs *m*

ferment *tr* fermentare; *(fig)* excitare ‖ *intr* fermentari; *(fig)* fervēre

fermentation *s* fermentati·o -onis *f*

fern *s* fil·ix -icis *f*

ferocious *adj* truculent·us -a -um

ferociously *adv* truculente

ferocity *s* saeviti·a -ae *f*

ferret *tr* **to — out** eruĕre

ferry *s* traject·us -ūs *m*

ferry *tr* trajicĕre

ferryboat *s* cymb·a -ae *f*

ferryman *s* portit·or -oris *m*

fertile *adj* fertil·is -is -e

fertility *s* fertilit·as -atis *f*

fertilize *tr* laetificare

fertilizer *s* laetam·en -inis *n*

fervent *adj* ard·ens -entis

fervently *adv* ardenter

fervid *adj* fervid·us -a -um

fervidly *adv* fervide

fervor *s* ferv·or -oris *m*

fester *intr* suppurare

festival *s* fest·um -i *n*

festive *adj* festiv·us -a -um

festivity *s (celebration)* solemn·ia -ium *npl; (gaiety)* festivit·as -atis *f*

festoon *s* sert·um -i *n*

fetch *tr (to summon)* arcessĕre; *(to go to get)* petĕre

fetid *adj* foetid·us -a -um
fetter *s* comp·es -edis *m*
fetter *tr* compedes imjicĕre *(w. dat); (fig)* impedire
feud *s* simult·as -atis *f*
fever *s* febr·is -is *f;* **high —** ardens febris *f;* **slight —** febricul·a -ae *f;* **to have** *(or* **to run) a —** febricitare
feverish *adj* febriculos·us -a -um
few *adj* pauc·i -ae -a; **a —** aliquot *(indecl);* **in a — words** paucis
fiasco *s* calamit·as -atis *f*
fiber *s* fibr·a -ae *f*
fibrous *adj* fibrat·us -a -um
fickle *adj* mobil·is -is -e
fickleness *s* mobilit·as -atis *f*
fiction *s* ficti·o -onis *f*
fictitious *adj* fict·us -a -um
fictitiously *adv* ficte
fiddle *s* fid·es -ium *fpl*
fiddle *intr* fidibus canĕre
fiddler *s* fidic·en -inis *m*
fidelity *s* fidelit·as -atis *f*
fidget *intr* trepidare
fidgety *adj* inquiet·us -a -um
field *s* a·ger -gri *m; (plowed)* arv·um -i *n; (undeveloped)* camp·us -i *m; (sports)* are·a -ae *f; (mil)* aci·es -ei *f; (of studies)* disciplin·a -ae *f*
fieldpiece *s* torment·um -i *n*
fiend *s* diabol·us -i *m*
fiendish *adj* diabolic·us -a -um
fierce *adj* atr·ox -ocis; *(intensive)* fer·ox -ocis
fiercely *adv* atrociter; ferociter
fierceness *s* atrocit·as -atis *f;* ferocit·as -atis *f*
fiery *adj* igne·us -a -um; *(fig)* ard·ens -entis
fife *s* tibi·a -ae *f*
fifteen *adj* quindecim *(indecl);* **— times** quindecies
fifteenth *adj* quint·us decim·us -a -um
fifth *adj* quint·us -a -um; **for the — time** quinto
fifth *s* quinta par·s -tis *f*
fiftieth *adj* quinquagesim·us -a -um
fifty *adj* quinquaginta *(indecl)*
fig *s* fic·us -i *f*
fight *s* pugn·a -ae *f; (battle)* proel·ium -(i)i *n; (brawl)* rix·a -ae *f; (boxing)* pugilati·o -onis *f*
fight *tr* pugnare cum *(w. abl)* **‖** *intr* pugnare; *(to brawl)* rixari; *(to box)* pugilari; *(w. sword)* digladiari; **to — it out** depugnare; **to — hand to hand** cominus pugnare
figment *s* **— of the imagination** figment·um -i *n*
figurative *adj* translat·us -a -um
figuratively *adv* per translationem
figure *s* figur·a -ae *f; (any form)* form·a -ae *f; (in a painting)* imag·o -inis *f;* **to cut a —** *(to play a part)* partes agĕre

figure *tr (to think)* putare; **to — out** excogitare **‖** *intr* **to — on** niti *(w. abl)*
figured *adj (adorned w. figures)* sigillat·us -a -um
figure of speech *s* figur·a -ae *f* orationis
filament *s* fil·um -i *n*
filbert *s* nu·x -cis *f* avellana
file *s (for iron)* lim·a -ae *f; (for woodwork)* scobin·a -ae *f; (for papers)* scap·us -i *m; (cabinet)* scrin·ium -(i)i *n; (row)* ord·o -inis *m;* **in single —** singul·i -ae -a per ordinem
filial *adj* pi·us -a -um
filigree *s* diatret·a -orum *npl*
filings *spl* scob·is -is *f*
fill *s* **to have one's —** se replēre
fill *tr* implēre; *(office)* fungi *(w. abl);* **to — up** complēre, explēre **‖** *intr* **to — up on** se implēre *(w. abl)*
fillip *s* talitr·um -i *n*
filly *s* equul·a -ae *f*
film *s* membranul·a -ae *f*
filmy *adj* membranace·us -a -um; *(fig)* caliginos·us -a -um
filter *s* col·um -i *n*
filter *tr* percolare **‖** *intr* percolari
filtering *s* percolati·o -onis *f*
filth *s* sord·es -ium *fpl*
filthiness *s* squal·or -oris *m; (fig)* obscenit·as -atis *f*
filthy *adj* sordid·us -a -um; *(fig)* obscen·us -a -um
filtration *s* percolati·o -onis *f*
fin *s* pinn·a -ae *f*
final *adj* ultim·us -a -um
finally *adv* denique, postremo
finance *s (private)* res, rei *f* familiaris; *(public)* rati·o -onis *f* aeraria
finance *tr* faenerare
financial *adj* pecuniari·us -a -um
find *tr* invenire, reperire; *(to hit upon)* offendĕre; **to — out** cognoscĕre
finder *s* repert·or -oris *m*
findings *spl* compert·a -orum *npl*
fine *adj (thin)* tenu·is -is -e; *(opp. of coarse)* subtil·is -is -e; *(superior)* perbon·us -a -um; *(nice)* bell·us -a -um; *(weather)* seren·us -a -um; **— arts** art·es -ium *fpl* elegantiores *(or* ingenuae); **to feel —** se bene habēre
fine *s* mul(c)t·a -ae *f*
fine *tr* mul(c)tare
finery *s* munditi·ae -arum *fpl*
finesse *s* arguti·ae -arum *fpl*
finger *s* digit·us -i *m; (of glove)* digital·e -is *n;* **index —** index digitus *m;* **little — minimus** digitus *m;* **middle — medius** digitus *m; (as an obscene gesture)* digitus *m* inpudicus *or* infamis; **ring — minimo** proximus digitus *m;* **to point the — at** digitum intendĕre ad *(w. acc);* **to snap the —s** digitis concrepare

finger *tr* tractare; *(to inform on)* deferre; *(mus)* pulsare
fingernail *s* ungu·is -is *m*
fingertip *s* summus digit·us -i *m*
finicky *adj* fastidios·us -a -um; — **appetite** fastid·ium -(i)i *n*
finish *s* fin·is -is *m; (in art)* perfecti·o -onis *f; (polish)* politur·a -ae *f*
finish *tr* conficěre; *(to put an end to)* terminare; to — **off** conficěre; *(to use up)* consuměre; *(to destroy)* perděre; *(to kill)* occiděre; **to— speaking** sermonem finire **‖** *intr* desiněre; **to add the —ing touch to** ultimam manum adferre *(w. dat)*
finite *adj* finit·us -a -um
fire *s* ign·is -is *m; (conflagration)* incend·ium -(i)i *n; (of artillery)* conject·us -ūs *m; (fig)* ard·or -oris *m;* **by — and sword** ferro ignique; **on —** flagr·ans -antis; **to be on —** arděre; **to catch —** ignem conciněre; **to set on —** incenděre
fire *tr* accenděre; *(missile)* conjicěre
fire alarm *s* sign·um -i *n* monitorium incendii
firebrand *s* fa·x -cis *f*
fire chief *s* praefect·us -i *m* vigilum
fire engine *s* siph·o -onis *m*
fireman *s* vig·il -is *m*
fireplace *s* foc·us -i *m*
fireproof *adj* ignibus impervi·us -a -um
fireside *s* foc·us -i *m*
firewood *s* lign·um -i *n*
firm *adj* firm·us -a -um; *(foundation)* stabil·is -is -e; **to stand —** perstare
firm *s (com)* societ·as -atis *f*
firmament *s* cael·um -i *n*
firmly *adv* firme, firmiter; *(w. firm hold)* tenaciter
firmness *s* firmit·as -atis *f*
first *adj* prim·us -a -um; *(of two)* pri·or -or -us; **among the —** in primis
first *adv* primum; **at —** primo; **— of all** imprimis
first aid *s* prima curati·o -onis *f*
firstborn *adj* primogenit·us -a -um
first fruits *spl* primiti·ae -arum *fpl*
fiscal *adj* aerari·us -a -um; *(belonging to the emperor's finances)* fiscal·is -is -e
fish *s* pisc·is -is *m;* **little —** *(lit & fig)* piscicul·us -i *m*
fish *tr* piscari; **to — for** *(fig)* expiscari
fisherman *s* piscat·or -oris *m*
fishhook *s* ham·us -i *m*
fishing *s* piscat·us -ūs *m*
fishing line *s* lin·um -i *n*
fishing rod *s* arund·o -inis *f*
fish market *s* for·um -i *n* piscarium
fish pond *s* piscin·a -ae *f*
fishy *adj* piscient·us -a -um; *(fig)* suspicios·us -a -um
fissure *s* fissur·a -ae *f*

fist *s* pugn·us -i *m;* **to make a —** pugnum facěre
fistfight *s* **to have a —** pugnis certare
fit *s (of anger, etc.)* impet·us -ūs *m;* **a good —** vestiment·um -i *n* bene factum; **by — and starts** carptim; **fainting —** defecti·o -onis *f;* **—s** morb·us -i *m* comitialis; **to have the —s** *(fig)* delirare; *(in anger)* furěre
fit *adj (for)* apt·us -a -um, idone·us -a -um *(w. dat); (healthy)* san·us -a -um
fit *tr* accommodare; *(to apply)* applicare; **to — out** instruěre, ornare **‖** *intr* convenire; **to — in with** congruěre cum *(w. abl);* **to—together** inter se cohaerēre
fitful *adj (sleep)* inquiet·us -a -um
fitly *adv* apte
fitness *s* convenienti·a -ae *f; (of persons)* habilit·as -atis *f*
fitting *adj* dec·ens -entis; **it is —** convenit, decet
five *adj* quinque *(indecl); (distributives)* quin·i -ae -a, *modifying nouns which have no singular, e.g.,* **five camps** quina castr·a -orum *npl;* **— times** quinquies; **— years** quinquenn·ium -(i)i *n*
fix *s* **a quick —** praesens remed·ium -(i)i *n;* **to be in a —** *(coll)* in angustiis versari
fix *tr (to repair)* reficěre, corrigěre; *(to patch)* resarcire; *(arrange)* disponěre; *(to adjust)* accommodare; *(meals)* parare; *(to fasten)* figěre; *(the eyes)* intenděre; *(time)* dicěre; *(to avenge)* ulcisci **‖** *intr* **to — upon** inhaerēre *(w. dat)*
fixed *adj (day, boundaries)* cert·us -a -um; **— resolve** men·s -tis *f* solida; **— stars** stell·ae -arum *fpl* inerrantes; **— upon** *(intent upon)* intent·us -a -um *(w. dat)*
fixture *s* affix·um -i *n*
fizz *intr* sibilare
flabbiness *s* molliti·a -ae *f*
flabby *adj* flacc·us -a -um
flaccid *adj* flaccid·us -a -um
flag *s* vexill·um -i *n*
flag *tr* signo indicare **‖** *intr* languescěre; *(to lose interest)* refrigescěre
flagrant *adj* nefari·us -a -um
flagship *s* nav·is -is *f* praetoria
flail *s* pertic·a -ae *f*
flail *tr* fustibus cuděre
flake *s* squam·a -ae *f;* **snow —s** plumeae niv·es -ium *fpl*
flaky *adj (sl)* delir·us -a -um
flame *s* flamm·a -ae *f*
flame *intr* flammare; **to — up** scintillare; *(fig)* exardescěre
flank *s (of animal)* il·ia -ium *npl; (mil)* lat·us -eris *n;* **on the —** a latere
flank *tr* tegěre latus *(w. gen)*
flap *s (of dress)* lacini·a -ae *f*
flap *tr* plauděre *(w. abl)* **‖** *intr (to hang loosely)* fluitare

flare *s* fulg·or -oris *m; (torch)* fa·x -cis *f*
flare *intr (to blaze)* coruscare; **to — up** *(of diseases)* urgēre; *(of anger, passions)* exardescĕre
flash *s* fulg·or -oris *m; — of lightning* ict·us -ūs *m* fulminis
flash *intr* fulgēre, coruscare
flashy *adj* fucat·us -a -um
flask *s* laguncul·a -ae *f*
flat *adj (level)* plan·us -a -um; *(not mountainous)* campes·ter -tris -tre; *(on one's back)* supin·us -a -um; *(on one's face)* pron·us -a -um; *(insipid)* vapid·us -a -um; **to fall —** *(e.g., of a play, speech)* frigēre
flatfooted *adj* plaut·us -a -um
flatly *adv* palam
flatness *s* planiti·es -ei *f*
flatten *tr* complanare; *(to prostrate)* prosternĕre
flatter *tr* blandiri
flatterer *s* adulat·or -oris *m*
flattering *adj* bland·us -a -um
flatulence *s* inflati·o -onis *f*
flaunt *tr* jactare
flaunting *adj* glorios·us -a -um
flaunting *s* jactati·o -onis *f*
flavor *s* sap·or -oris *m; (substance)* condiment·um -i *n*
flavor *intr* condire
flaw *s (defect)* vit·ium -(i)i *n; (chink)* rimul·a -ae *f*
flawless *adj* sine vitio
flax *s* lin·um -i *n*
flaxen *adj* line·us -a -um
flay *tr* deglubare
flea *s* pul·ex -icis *m*
flea market *s* for·um -i *n* rerum venalium
fleck *s* macul·a -ae *f*
fledgling *s* pull·us -i *m*
flee *tr* effugĕre ‖ *intr* fugĕre; **to — to** confugĕre ad *or* in *(w. acc)*
fleece *s* vell·us -eris *n*
fleece *tr (fig)* spoliare
fleecy *adj* lanig·er -era -erum
fleet *s* class·is -is *f*
fleet *adj* cel·er -eris -ere
fleet-footed *adj* celerip·es -edis
fleeting *adj* fug·ax -acis
flesh *s* car·o -nis *f;* **in the —** viv·us -a -um
flesh wound *s* car·o -nis *f* vulnerata
fleshy *adj* corpore·us -a -um; *(fat)* corpulent·us -a -um
flexibility *s* flexibilit·as -atis *f; (fig)* molliti·es -ei *f*
flexible *adj (lit & fig)* flexibil·is -is -e
flick *s* crepit·us -ūs *m; (of the finger)* talitr·um -i *n*
flick *tr* **to — away** excutĕre
flicker *intr (of a flame)* trepidare
flickering *adj* tremul·us -a -um; **— lamps** occidentes lucern·ae -arum *fpl*
flier *s* libell·us -i *m*
flight *s (flying)* volat·us -ūs *m; (escape)*

effug·ium -(i)i *n; (covey)* gre·x -gis *m; — of steps* gradati·o -onis *f;* **to put to —** fugare; **to take to —** terga vertĕre
flighty *adj* lev·is -is -e
flimsy *adj* praetenu·is -is -e; *(trivial)* frivol·us -a -um
flinch *intr* tergiversari; *(to start)* absilire
fling *s* jact·us -ūs *m*
fling *tr* conjicĕre; **to — away** abjicĕre; **to — down** dejicĕre; **to — open** rejicĕre, patefacĕre
flint *s* sil·ex -icis *mf*
flinty *adj* silice·us -a -um
flippancy *s* protervit·as -atis *f*
flippant *adj* prompt·us -a -um atque lev·is -is -e
flippantly *adv* temere ac leviter
flirt *s* lup·us -i *m,* lup·a -ae *f*
flirt *intr* **to — with** *(a person)* subblandiri *(w. dat); (an idea)* ludĕre cum *(w. abl)*
flirtation *s* leves amor·es -um *mpl*
flit *intr* volitare
float *s (raft)* rat·es -is *f; (on fishing line)* cort·ex -icis *m*
float *tr (to launch)* deducĕre ‖ *intr* fluitare; *(in the air)* volitare
flock *s* gre·x -gis *m;* **in —s** gregatim
flock *intr* **to — around** circumfluĕre *(w. acc);* **to — to** affluĕre ad *(w. acc);* **to — together** congregari
floe *s* fragment·um -i *n* glaciei
flog *tr* verberare
flogging *s* verberati·o -onis *f;* **to get a —** vapulare
flood *s (deluge)* diluv·ium -(i)i *n; (of tears, words)* flum·en -inis *n;* **the Flood** inundanti·a -ae *f* terrarum
flood *tr (lit & fig)* inundare ‖ *intr* inundare
floodgates *spl* cataract·ae -arum *fpl;* **to open the — of** *(fig)* effundĕre habenas *(w. gen)*
floodtide *s* access·us -ūs *m*
floor *s (ground)* sol·um -i *n; (paved)* paviment·um -i *n; (story)* tabulat·um -i *n;* **to lay the —** pavimentum facĕre; *(on an upper story)* contabulare; **to throw on the —** in pavimentum projicĕre
floor *tr (to knock down)* sternĕre
flooring *s* contabulati·o -onis *f*
floral *adj* flore·us -a -um
flotilla *s* classicul·a -ae *f*
flounce *s* instit·a -ae *f*
flounder *s (fish)* pass·er -eris *m*
flounder *intr* volutari; *(in speech)* haesitare
flour *s* farin·a -ae *f; (finest)* poll·en -inis *m*
flourish *s (mus)* taratantara *n (indecl)*
flourish *tr* vibrare; *(to sound)* canĕre ‖ *intr* florēre; *(mus)* praeludĕre
flour mill *s* pistrin·a -ae *f*
flout *tr (to scorn)* spernĕre; *(to mock)* deridēre
flow *s* fluxi·o -onis *f; (of the tide)* access·us -ūs *m; (of words)* flum·en -inis *n*

flow *intr* fluĕre; **to — into** influĕre in *(w. acc)*; **to — past** praeterfluĕre
flower *s (lit & fig)* flo·s -ris *m*
flower *intr* florescĕre
flower bed *s* are·a -ae *f*
flowery *adj* florid·us -a -um
fluctuate *intr* jactari, se jactare
fluctuation *s* mutati·o -onis *f*
flue *s* cunicul·us -i *m* fornacis
fluency *s* volubilit·as -atis *f*
fluent *adj* volubil·is -is -e
fluently *adv* volubiliter
fluid *adj* fluid·us -a -um
fluid *s* um·or -oris *m*
fluke *s (of anchor)* den·s -tis *m; (luck)* fortuit·um -i *n*
flurry *s* commoti·o -onis *f; —* **of activity** festinati·o -onis *f*
flush *s (blush)* rub·or -oris *m; (onrush)* impet·us -ūs *m*
flush *tr (to purge)* proluĕre; **to — out** *(game)* excitare ‖ *intr* erubescĕre
fluster *tr* turbare, inquietare
flute *s* tibi·a -ae *f; (archit)* stri·a -ae *f*
fluting *s (archit)* striatur·a -ae *f*
flutist *s* tibic·en -inis *m*
flutter *s (of wings)* plaus·us -ūs *m; (bustle)* festinati·o -onis *f; (vibration)* trem·or -oris *m; (of the heart)* palpitati·o -onis *f*
flutter *intr (of a heart)* palpitare; *(of a bird)* volitare; *(w. alarm)* trepidare
flux *s* flux·us -ūs *m; to be in a state of —* fluĕre
fly *s* musc·a -ae *f*
fly *intr* volare; *(to flee)* fugĕre; **to — apart** dissilire; **to — away** *or* **off** avolare; **to — in the face of** lacessĕre; **to — open** dissilire, patēre; **to — out** evolare, provolare; **to — under** subtervolare; **to — up** subvolare
flying *adj* volatil·is -is -e
flying *s* volat·us -ūs *m*
foal *s* pull·us -i *m; (of horse)* equul·us -i *m; (of asses)* asell·us -i *m*
foal *tr & intr* parĕre
foam *s* spum·a -ae *f*
foam *intr* spumare; *(of sea)* aestuare
foaming *adj* spum·ans -antis
foamy *adj* spume·us -a -um
focus *tr* **to — attention** *(or* **mind) on** animum attendĕre ad *(w. acc)*
fodder *s* pabul·um -i *n*
foe *s (public)* host·is -is *m; (private)* inimic·us -i *m,* inimic·a -ae *f*
fog *s* nebul·a -ae *f*
foggy *adj* nebulos·us -a -um
foible *s* vit·ium -(i)i *n*
foil *s (for fencing)* rud·is -is *f; (leaf of metal)* lamin·a -ae *f; (very thin)* bracte·a -ae *f; (fig)* umbr·a -ae *f*
foil *tr* eludĕre, frustrari
fold *s* sin·us -ūs *m; (wrinkle)* rug·a -ae *f; (for sheep; the Church)* ovil·e -is *n*

fold *tr* plicare; **to — up** complicare
foliage *s* fron·s -dis *f*
folio *s* li·ber -bri *m* maximae formae
folk *s* homin·es -um *mpl;* **common —** vulg·us -i *n,* pleb·s -is *f*
folk music *s* music·a -ae *f* vulgaris
folk song *s* carm·en -inis *n* vulgare
follow *tr* sequi; *(closely)* instare *(w. dat),* assequi; *(immediately after)* subsequi; *(instructions)* parēre *(w. dat); (to understand)* intellegĕre; **to — the calling of a merchant, banker, soothsayer** mercaturam, argentariam, haruspicinam facĕre; **to — up** *(to the end)* persequi ‖ *intr* insequi; **it —s that** sequitur ut; **to — up on** persequi; **to — upon** supervenire *(w. dat)*
follower *s* sectat·or -oris *m; (hanger-on)* assec(u)l·a -ae *mf*
following *s (attendants)* comitat·us -ūs *m; (pol)* facti·o -onis *f*
following *adj* sequ·ens -entis, proxim·us -a -um, poster·us -a -um
folly *s* stultiti·a -ae *f*
foment *tr* fovēre
fond *adj* **(of)** am·ans -antis *(w. gen),* studios·us -a -um *(w. gen);* **to be — of** amare
fondle *tr* mulcēre, fovēre
fondly *adv* amanter
fondness *s* **(for)** *(persons, country)* carit·as -atis *f* (erga *w. acc);* **(for)** *(things)* stud·ium -(i)i *n (w. gen)*
food *s* cib·us -i *m*
fool *s* stult·us -i *m,* fatu·us -i *m; to make a — of** ludificare; **to make a — of oneself** fatuari, ineptire
fool *tr* fallĕre
foolhardily *adv* temere
foolhardy *adj* temerari·us -a -um
foolish *adj* stult·us -a -um
foolishly *adv* stulte
foot *s (of men, animals, tables, chairs)* pe·s -dis *m; (of mountain)* rad·ix -icis *m; (of pillar)* bas·is -is *f;* **on —** pedibus; **to set — in** pedem ponĕre in *(w. abl);* **to tread under —** calcare
foot *tr* **to — a bill** impensam sumĕre
football *s* pil·a -ae *f* pedalis
foothold *s* grad·us -ūs *m* stabilis
footing *s* grad·us -ūs *m;* **on an equal —** ex aequo; **to be on an equal — with** in aequo stare *(w. dat);* **to get one's —** locum capĕre; **to lose one's —** de gradu labi
footpath *s* semit·a -ae *f*
footprint *s* vestig·ium -(i)i *n*
footrace *s* curs·us -ūs *m*
foot soldier *s* ped·es -itis *m*
footstool *s* scabell·um -i *n*
footwear *s* calceament·um -i *n*
fop *s* hom·o -inis *m* delicatus
foppish *adj* delicat·us -a -um

for *prep (extent of time or space) render by*
acc; *(price) render by gen or abl; (on
behalf of; in place of; instead of; in
proportion to, consideration of)* pro *(w.
abl); (purpose)* ad *(w. acc); (cause)* causā
*(w. gen)(always after the governed
word)*, ob *(w. acc); (after negatives)*
prae *(w. abl); (toward)* erga *(w. acc);
(out of, for, e.g., joy, fear)* prae *(w. abl);
(to denote the appointment of a definite
time)* in *(w. acc);* as **for** quod attinet ad
(w. acc); — all that nec eo selius; —
nothing gratis, gratuito; *(in vain)* frustra;
for the last three months in ternos
novissimos menses; — **the rest of the
year** in reliquum anni tempus; — **these
reasons** his de causis; **good** — **nothing**
ad nullam rem util·is -is -e; **to be** — *(to
be in favor of)* studēre *(w. dat)*, favēre
(w. dat); **to live** — **the day** in diem
vivēre; **what** —? quare?

for *conj (generally first in a clause)* nam,
siquidem, *(never first)* enim

forage *s* pabul·um -i *n*
forage *intr* pabulari
foray *s* incursi·o -onis *f*
forbear *intr* desistēre
forbearance *s* patienti·a -ae *f*
forbid *tr* vetare, prohibēre
forbidding *adj* odios·us -a -um
force *s* vis *(acc:* vim; *abl:* vi; *pl:* vires)
f; —**s** *(mil)* vir·es -ium *fpl,* copi·ae -arum
fpl; **in** — valid·us -a -um
force *tr* cogēre, impellēre; *(a door)*
rumpēre; **to** — **down** detrudēre; **to** —
out extrudēre, extorquēre; **to** — **s.o. to
surrender** redigēre aliquem in dicionem
forced *adj (unnatural)* quaesit·us -a -um;
— **march** magnum *or* maximum it·er
-ineris *n*
forceps *spl* forc·eps -ipis *mf*
forcible *adj* per vim fact·us -a -um
forcibly *adv* per vim, vi
ford *s* vad·um -i *n*
ford *tr* vado transire
fore *adj* pr·ior -ior -ius
forearm *s* bracch·ium -(i)i *n*
forearm *tr* praemunire; **to be** —**ed**
praecavēre
forebears *spl* major·es -um *mpl*
forebode *tr* portendēre
foreboding *s* portent·um -i *n; (feeling)*
praesensi·o -onis *f*
foreboding *adj* presag·us -a -um
forecast *s* praedicti·o -onis *f*, conjectur·a
-ae *f*
forecast *tr* praedicēre
forecastle *s* pror·a -ae *f*
foredoom *tr* praedestinare
forefather *s* atav·us -i *m;* —**s** major·es
-um *mpl*
forefinger *s* index digit·us -i *m*

forego *tr* dimittēre
foregone conclusion *s* praejudicat·um -ī
n; **to take it as** — id pro praejudicato
ferre
foregoing *adj* pr·ior -ior -ius
forehead *s* fron·s -tis *f*
foreign *adj (of another country)* extern·us
-a -um; *(opposite of home-produced)*
adventici·us -a -um; *(that has come from
abroad)* peregrin·us -a -um; *(not pertaining to)* alien·us -a -um; **to live (travel)
in a** — **country** peregrinari
foreigner *s* peregrin·us -i *m,* peregrin·a -ae *f*
foreknowledge *s* providenti·a -ae *f*
foreman *s* procurat·or -oris *m; (on an
estate)* villic·us -i *m*
foremost *adj* prim·us -a -um; *(of chief
importance)* princ·eps -ipis
forenoon *s* antemeridianum temp·us -oris
n; **in the** — ante meridiem
forensic *adj* forens·is -is -e
foreground *s* prior par·s -tis *f*
forerunner *s* praenunt·ius -(i)i *m,* prae-
curs·or -oris *m*
foresee *tr* providēre
foreseeing *adj* provid·us -a -um
foresight *s* providenti·a -ae *f; (precaution)*
provisi·o -onis *f*
forest *adj* silvestr·is -is -e
forest *s* silv·a -ae *f*
forestall *tr* praeoccupare
foretell *tr* praedicēre
forethought *s* providenti·a -ae *f*
forewarn *tr* praemonēre
forewarning *s* praemonit·us -ūs *m*
forfeit *s* mult·a -ae *f*
forfeit *tr* multari *(w. abl)*
forfeiture *s* amissi·o -onis *f*
forge *s* forn·ax -acis *f* ferraria
forge *tr* excudēre; *(a document) (strictly:
to substitute)* subjicēre, supponēre; **to**
— **a signature on** *(a document)* signo
adulterino obsignare
forged *adj* fals·us -a -um
forger *s (of wills)* subject·or -oris *m; (of
any document)* falsar·ius -(i)i *m*
forgery *s* fals·um -i *n*
forget *tr* oblivisci *(w. gen)*
forgetful *adj* oblivios·us -a -um
forgetfulness *s* oblivi·o -onis *f*
forgive *tr* ignoscēre *(w. dat)*
forgiveness *s* veni·a -ae *f*
forgiving *adj* ignosc·ens -entis
fork *s* furc·a -ae *f; (small fork)* furcul·a -ae
f; (in the road) biv·ium -(i)i *n*
forked *adj* bifurc·us -a -um .
forlorn *adj* destitut·us -a -um
form *s* form·a -ae *f; (document)* formul·a
-ae *f;* **in due** — rite
form *tr* formare; *(to produce)* efficēre; *(a
plan, partnership, alliance)* inire; **to** —
a long line agmen longum facēre; **to** —
an opinion judicium facēre; **to** — **such**

bitter enmities tam graves simultates excipĕre **‖** *intr* nasci, fieri

formal *adj* just·us -a -um; *(stiff)* composit·us -a -um

formality *s* rit·us -ūs *m;* **formalities** just·a -orum *npl;* **with due —** rite

formation *s* conformati·o -onis *f;* **in —** instruct·us -a -um

former *adj* pr·ior-ior -ius; *(immediately preceding)* super·ior -ior -ius; *(original, olden)* pristin·us -a -um; **the —…the latter** ille…hic

formerly *adv* antehac, antea

formidable *adj* formidabil·is -is -e

formless *adj* inform·is -is -e

formula *s* formul·a -ae *f;* *(leg)* acti·o -onis *f*

forsake *tr* deserĕre

forswear *tr* adjurare

fort *s* castell·um -i *n*

forth *adv (often expressed in Latin by a prefix, e.g.,* **to go —** exire); **and so —** et cetera; **from that day —** inde, ex eo (die)

forthcoming *adj* futur·us -a -um; **to be —** praesto esse

forthright *adj* apert·us -a -um

forthwith *adv* protinus, extemplo

fortieth *adj* quadragesim·us -a -um

fortification *s* muniment·um -i *n*

fortify *tr* munire

fortitude *s* fortitud·o -inis *f*

fortress *s* castell·um -i *n*

fortuitous *adj* fortuit·us -a -um

fortuitously *adv* fortuito

fortunate *adj* fortunat·us -a -um

fortunately *adv* feliciter

fortune *s* fortun·a -ae *f;* *(estate)* op·es -ium *fpl,* res, rei *f;* **bad —** fortuna *f* adversa; **good —** fortuna *f* prospera; **to make a —** rem facĕre; **to squander one's —** rem dissipare; **to tell —s** hariolari

fortuneteller *s* hariol·us *m,* hariol·a -ae *f;* *(pej)* sortileg·us -i *m*

fortunetelling *s* hariolati·o -onis *f*

forty *adj* quadraginta *(indecl)*

forum *s* for·um -i *n*

forward *adv* prorsus, prorsum; *(often expressed by the prefix* pro-, *e.g.,* **to move —** promovēre)

forward *adj (cocky)* proterv·us -a -um; **— motion** progress·us -ūs *m*

foster *tr* alĕre, fovēre

foster brother *s* collacte·us -i *m*

foster child *s* alumn·us -i *m,* alumn·a -ae *f*

foster father *s* alt·or -oris *m*

foster mother *s* altr·ix -icis *f*

foster sister *s* collacte·a -ae *f*

foul *adj (dirty)* foed·us -a -um; *(language)* obscen·us -a -um; *(weather)* turbid·us -a -um; *(deed)* foed·us -a -um; *(smell)* te·ter -tra -trum; **— play** dol·us -i *m* malus; **to run — of** inruĕre in *(w. acc)*

foul *tr* inquinare; *(morally)* contaminare; **to — up** *(coll)* conturbare

foully *adv* foede

foul-mouthed *adj* maledic·us -a -um

found *tr* fundare, condĕre

foundation *s* fundament·um -i *n;* **to lay the — for** *(lit & fig)* fundamenta jacĕre *(w. gen)*

founder *s* condit·or -oris *m*

founder *intr (lit & fig)* pessum ire

foundling *s* expositic·ius -(i)i *m;* expositici·a -ae *f*

fountain *s* fon·s -tis *m*

fountainhead *s* cap·ut -itis *n* fontis

four *adj* quattuor *(indecl);* **— each** quatern·i -ae -a; **— times** quater; **— years** quadrenn·ium -(i)i *n;* **on all —s** rep·ens -entis

fourfold *adj* quadrupl·us -a -um

four-footed *adj* quadrup·es -edis

fourscore *adj* octoginta *(indecl)*

fourteen *adj* quattuordecim *(indecl)*

fourteenth *adj* quart·us decim·us -a -um

fourth *adj* quart·us -a -um; **for the — time** quartum

fourth *s* quarta par·s -tis *f;* **three —s** tres part·es -ium *fpl*

fourthly *adv* quarto

fowl *s* av·is -is *f;* *(domestic)* gallin·a -ae *f*

fox *s* vulp·es -is *f;* **an old —** *(coll)* veterat·or -oris *m*

foyer *s* vestibul·um -i *n*

fracas *s (brawl)* rix·a -ae *f;* *(quarrel)* iurg·ium -(i)i *n*

fraction *s* par·s -tis *f* exigua; *(math)* fracti·o -onis *f*

fracture *s* fractur·a -ae *f*

fracture *tr* frangĕre

fragile *adj* fragil·is -is -e

fragility *s* fragilit·as -atis *f*

fragment *s* fragment·um -i *n*

fragrance *s* suavis od·or -oris *m*

fragrant *adj* suaveol·ens -entis

frail *adj* infirm·us -a -um

frailty *s* infirmit·as -atis *f*

frame *s (of a picture)* form·a -ae *f;* *(of the body* figur·a -ae *f;* *(of buildings, etc.)* compag·es -is *f;* *(of bed)* spond·a -ae *f;* **— of mind** habit·us -ūs *m* animi

frame *tr* fabricari; *(to contrive)* moliri; *(a picture)* in forma includĕre; *(a person)* falso insimulare; *(to draw up a form of words)* concipĕre

framework *s* compag·es -is *f;* *(of wood)* contignati·o -onis *f*

France *s* Galli·a -ae *f*

franchise *s* ju·s -ris *n* suffragii

frank *adj* lib·er -era -erum

frankincense *s* tu·s -ris *n*

frankly *adv* libere

frankness *s* libert·as -atis *f*

frantic *adj* fur·ens -entis

frantically *adv* furenter

fraternal *adj* fratern·us -a -um
fraternally *adv* fraterne
fraternity *s* sodalit·as -atis *f*
fraternize *intr* conversari
fratricide *s (doer)* fratricid·a -ae *m; (deed)* fratris parricid·ium -(i)i *n*
fraud *s* frau·s -dis *f; (leg)* dol·us -i *m* malus
fraudulent *adj* fraudulent·us -a -um
fraudulently *adv* fraudulenter
fraught *adj (with)* plen·us -a -um *(w. abl)*
fray *s* rix·a -ae *f; (contest)* certam·en -inis *n*
freak *s* monstr·um -i *n; (whim)* libid·o -inis *f: —* **of nature** lus·us -ūs *m* naturae
freakish *adj* monstruos·us -a -um
freckle *s* lentig·o -inis *f*
freckled *adj* lentiginos·us -a -um
free *adj* lib·er -era -erum; *(disengaged) (from)* vacu·us -a -um *(w. abl); (generous)* liberal·is -is -e; *(from duty, taxes)* immun·is -is -e; *(unencumbered)* exped·it·us -a -um; **for —** gratis; **to be — from** vacare *(w. abl)*
free *tr* liberare; *(slave)* manumittĕre; *(son)* emancipare
freebooter *s* praed·o -onis *m*
freeborn *adj* ingenu·us -a -um
freely *adv* libere; *(of one's own accord)* sponte, ultro; *(frankly)* aperte; *(generously)* large
freedman *s* libert·us -i *m*
freedom *s* libert·as -atis *f*
freedwoman *s* libert·a -ae *f*
free will *s* volunt·as -atis *f;* **of one own —** suā sponte
freeze *tr & intr* gelare; **to — up** congelare
freezing *adj* gelid·us -a -um
freight *s (cargo)* on·us -eris *n; (cost)* vectur·a -ae *f*
freighter *s* nav·is -is *f* oneraria
French *adj* Gallic·us -a -um; **in —** Gallice; **to speak —** Gallice loqui
frenzied *adj* fur·ens -entis
frenzy *s* fur·or -oris *m*
frequency *s* frequenti·a -ae *f*
frequent *adj* frequ·ens -entis
frequent *tr* frequentare
frequenter *s* frequentat·or -oris *m*
frequently *adv* frequenter
fresco *s* op·us -eris *n* tectorium
fresh *adj (food, etc.)* rec·ens -entis; *(cool)* frigidul·us -a -um; *(not tired)* inte·ger -gra -grum; *(forward)* proterv·us -a -um; *(green)* virid·is -is -e; *(water)* dulc·is -is -e
freshen *tr* recreare, renovare ‖ *intr (of wind)* increbrescĕre; **to — up** se recreare
freshly *adv* recenter
freshman *s* tir·o -onis *m*
freshness *s* viridit·as -atis *f*
fret *intr* angi, stomachari
fretful *adj* stomachos·us -a -um

fretting *s* sollicitud·o -inis *f*
friction *s* fricti·o -onis *f*
fried *adj* frict·us -a -um; **— eggs** ov·a -orum *npl* in oleo fricta
friend *s* amic·us -i *m*, amic·a -ae *f*, familiar·is -is *mf; (of a thing)* amat·or -oris *m*
friendless *adj* amicorum in·ops -opis
friendliness *s* humanit·as -atis *f*
friendly *adj* amic·us -a -um; **in a — manner** amice
friendship *s* amiciti·a -ae *f*
frieze *s* zoöphor·us -i *m*
fright *s* terr·or -oris *m*
frighten *tr* terrēre; **to — away** absterrēre
frightening *adj* terrific·us -a -um
frightful *adj* terribil·is -is -e
frightfully *adv* foede
frigid *adj* frigid·us -a -um
frigidity *s* frigidit·as -atis *f*
frigidly *adv* frigide
frill *s (plaited border)* instit·a -ae *f; —s (fig)* tric·ae -arum *fpl*
fringe *s (trim)* fimbri·ae -arum *fpl; (border)* marg·o -inis *m*
fringe *adj (outer)* ultimus -a -um; *(secondary)* secundari·us -a -um
frisk *tr* scrutari ‖ *intr* lascivire
fritter *s* lagan·um -i *n*
fritter *tr* **to — away** terĕre
frivolity *s* levit·as -atis *f*
frivolous *adj* frivol·us -a -um
frivolously *adv* nugatorie
frizzle *tr* crispare
frizzled *adj* calamistrat·us -a -um
fro *adv* **to and —** huc illuc
frock *s* stol·a -ae *f*
frog *s* ran·a -ae *f*
frolic *intr* lascivire
from *prep* a(b) *(w. abl); (denoting strictly descent from above, but used in other senses; subtraction; source)* de *(w. abl); (from within, out of)* e(x) *(w. abl); (cause)* ob *(w. acc);* **— above** desuper; **— day to day** diem de die; **— within** intrinsecus; **— without** extrinsecus
front *s* fron·s -tis *f; (on the march)* primum agm·en -inis *n; (appearance)* speci·es -ei *f;* **in —** a fronte, adversus; **in — of** *(in the presence of)* coram *(w. abl); (position)* pro *(w. abl);* **the — of the house** frons *f* aedium
front *adj* pr·ior -ior -ius; *(teeth, feet)* prim·us -a -um; **— door** antic·um -i *n*
frontage *s* fron·s -tis *f;* **a hundred feet of —** centum pedes in fronte
frontal *adj* advers·us -a -um; **— attack** impet·us -ūs *m* ex adverso
frontier *s* lim·es -itis *m*
frontline *s (mil)* principi·a -orum *npl*
frost *s* pruin·a -ae *f*
frostbitten *adj* torrid·us -a -um
frosty *adj* gelid·us -a -um

froth *s* spum·a -ae *f*
froth *intr* spumare
frothy *adj* spume·us -a -um
frown *s* contracti·o -onis *f* frontis
frown *intr* frontem contrahĕre
frozen *adj* frigore concret·us -a -um
frugal *adj* frugi *(indecl)*
frugality *s* frugalit·as -atis *f*
frugally *adv* frugaliter
fruit *s* fruct·us -ūs *m; (esp. orchard fruit)* pom·um -i *n; (of tree)* mal·a -orum *npl;* —s of the earth frug·es -ium *fpl*
fruitful *adj* fecund·us -a -um; *(actually yielding fruit)* frugif·er -era -erum
fruitfully *adv* fecunde
fruitfulness *s* fecundit·as -atis *f*
fruitless *adj* steril·is -is -e; *(fig)* irrit·us -a -um
fruitlessly *adv* frustra
fruit tree *s* pom·us -i *f*
frustrate *tr (to break off, e.g., an undertaking)* dirimĕre, ad irritum redigĕre; *(to baffle)* frustrari
frustrating *adj* incommod·us -a -um
frustration *s* frustrati·o -onis *f*
fry *s (dish of things fried)* frix·a -ae *f*
fry *tr* frigĕre
frying pan *s* sartag·o -inis *f*
fuel *s* aliment·um -i *n;* to add — to the flames *(fig)* oleum addĕre camino
fugitive *s (from country or home)* profug·a -ae *mf; (pej)* fugitiv·us -i *m,* fugitiv·a -ae *f*
fugitive *adj* fugitiv·us -a -um
fulcrum *s (of lever)* pressi·o -onis *f*
fulfill *tr (a duty)* explēre, praestare; *(prophecy)* implēre; to — a promise promissum exsolvĕre
fulfilled *adj (prayer, hope)* rat·us -a -um
fulfillment *s (carrying out)* exsecuti·o -onis *f; (of a prophecy, etc.)* perfecti·o -onis *f*
full *adj (of)* plen·us -a -um *(w. gen or abl); (filled up)* explet·us -a -um; *(entire)* solid·us -a -um; *(satisfied)* sat·ur -ura -urum; *(dress)* fus·us -a -um
full-blown *adj (flowers)* apert·us -a -um; *(mature)* adult·us -a -um
full-grown *adj* adult·us -a -um
fully *adv (completely)* plene; *(quite)* penitus, prorsus
full moon *s* plenilun·ium -(i)i *n*
fumble *tr (the ball)* demittĕre ‖ *intr* haesitare; to — for explorare
fume *s* halit·us -ūs *m*
fume *intr* exaestuare
fumigate *tr* fumigare, suffire
fumigation *s* suffit·us -ūs *m*
fun *s* joc·us -i *m;* pure — mera hilar·ia -ium *npl;* to have — se oblectare; to make — of eludĕre
function *s* mun·us -eris *n,* offic·ium -(i)i *n*
function *intr* fungi, munus implēre
functionary *s* magistrat·us -ūs *m*

fund *s* pecuni·a -ae *f* collecta; *(store of anything)* copi·a -ae *f;* —s pecunia *f,* op·es -um *fpl*
fundamental *adj* prim·us -a -um
fundamentally *adv* funditus, penitus
funeral *s* fun·us -eris *n; (funeral procession and obsequies)* exsequi·ae -arum *fpl;* to attend a — (con)venire in funus
funeral *adj* funere·us -a -um; to perform the — rites parentare
funereal *adj* funebr·is -is -e
fungus *s* fung·us -i *m*
funnel *s* infundibul·um -i *n*
funny *adj* ridicul·us -a -um
fur *s* vill·i -orum *mpl*
furious *adj* furios·us -a -um
furiously *adv* furiose
furl *tr* complicare; *(sail)* legĕre
furlough *s* commeat·us -ūs *m;* on — in commeatu; to grant a — commeatum dare; to obtain a — commeatum sumĕre
furnace *s* forn·ax -acis *f*
furnish *tr* suppeditare; *(to fit out)* ornare, instruĕre
furnished *adj* instruct·us -a -um
furniture *s* suppel·ex -ectilis *f*
furrow *s* sulc·us -i *m*
furry *adj* villos·us -a -um
further *adj* ulter·ior ior -ius
further *adv* ultra, longius
further *tr (to serve)* servire *(w. dat); (to promote)* promovēre; *(to aid)* adjuvare; to — our own interests nostris commodis servire
furtherance *s* progress·us -ūs *m*
furthermore *adv* porro, praeterea
furthest *adj* ultim·us -a -um
furthest *adv* longissime
furtive *adj* furtiv·us -a -um
furtively *adv* furtim, furtive
fury *s* fur·or -oris *m*
fuse *tr* fundĕre ‖ *intr* coalescĕre
fusion *s* fusur·a -ae *f*
fuss *s* perturbati·o -onis *f;* to make a great — over nothing laborare in angusto, tumultuari
fuss *intr* satagĕre, tumultuari
fussy *adj* fastidios·us -a -um
futile *adj* futil·is -is -e
futility *s* futilit·as -atis *f*
future *adj* futur·us -a -um; for all — time in posterum
future *s* futur·a -orum *npl,* posterum temp·us -oris *n;* in the — posthac, in posterum
futurity *s* posterit·as -atis *f*

G

gab *s* garrulit·as -atis *f*
gab *intr* garrire

gable *s* fastig·ium -(i)i *n*
gadfly *s* taban·us -i *m*
gag *s* joc·us -i *m*
gag *tr* os obstruĕre *(w. dat)*
gaiety *s* hilarit·as -atis *f*
gaily *adv* hilare
gain *s* lucr·um -i *n*
gain *tr* consequi, acquirĕre; *(victory)* consequi, adipisci; *(by asking)* impetrare; *(office, military command)* capĕre; **to — access to a person** penetrare ad aliquem; **to — ground** *(fig)* increbrescĕre; **to — possession of** potiri *(w. abl)*
gainful *adj* lucros·us -a -um
gainsay *tr* contradicĕre *(w. dat)*
gait *s* incess·us -ūs *m*
gala *adj* festiv·us -a -um
gala *s* festivit·as -atis *f*
galaxy *s* orb·is -is *m* lacteus
gale *s* procell·a -ae *f*
gall *s* bil·is -is *f*
gall *tr* urĕre
gallant *adj* fort·is -is -e; *(polite)* officios·us -a -um
gallant *s* amat·or -oris *m*
gallantly *adv* fortiter
gallantry *s* fortitud·o -inis *f*
gall bladder *s* fe·l -llis *n*
galleon *s* nav·is -is *f* oneraria
gallery *s* portic·us -ūs *f; (open)* peristyl·ium -(i)i *n; (for paintings)* pinacothec·a -ae *f*
galley *s* nav·is -is *f* longa; *(two banks of oars)* birem·is -is *f; (three banks of oars)* trirem·is -is *f; (kitchen)* culin·a -ae *f*
Gallic *adj* Gallic·us -a -um
galling *adj* mord·ax -acis
gallon *s* cong·ius -(i)i *n*
gallop *s* citissimus curs·us -ūs *m;* **at a — ** citato equo
gallop *intr (of a horse)* quadrupedare; *(of the rider)* citato equo contendĕre
gallows *s* patibul·um -i *n*
gallstone *s* calcul·us -i *m*
galore *adv* satis superque
galvanize *tr* incitare
gamble *tr* **to — away** in aleā perdĕre ‖ *intr* aleā ludĕre
gambler *s* aleat·or -oris *m*
gambling *s* ale·a -ae *f*
gambol *s* salt·us -ūs *m*
gambol *intr* lascivire
game *s* lud·us -i *m; (w. dice)* ale·a -ae *f; (venison)* praed·a -ae *f;* **to make — of** ludificari
gamecock *s* gall·us -i *m* rixosus
gander *s* ans·er -eris *m*
gang *s* gre·x -gis *m,* man·us -ūs *f*
gang *intr* **to — together** conjurare; **to — up on** conspirare in *(w. acc)*
gangrene *s* gangren·a -a *f*
gangster *s* grassat·or -oris *m*
gangway *s* for·us -i *m*
gap *s* hiat·us -ūs *m*

gape *intr* hiare; **to — at** attonito animo inhiare *(w. dat)*
gaping *adj* hi·ans -antis; *(fig)* stupid·us -a -um
garb *s* vestit·us -ūs *m*
garbage *s* quisquili·ae -arum *fpl*
garble *tr* corrumpĕre
garden *s* hort·us -i *m*
gardener *s* hortulan·us -i *m; (ornamental)* topiar·ius -(i)i *m*
gardening *s* hortorum cult·us -ūs *m; (ornamental)* topiaria ar·s -tis *f*
gargle *intr* gargarizare
gargling *s* gargarizati·o -onis *f*
garland *s* coron·a -ae *f*
garlic *s* al·ium -(i)i *n*
garment *s* vestiment·um -i *n*
garner *tr* colligĕre
garnish *tr* ornare
garret *s* cenacul·um -i *n*
garrison *s* praesid·ium -(i)i *n*
garrison *tr (a post w. troops)* praesidium collocare in *(w. abl)*
garrulity *s* garrulit·as -atis *f*
garrulous *adj* garrul·us -a -um
garter *s* periscel·is -idis *f*
gas *s (anat)* inflati·o -onis *f; (gasoline)* ole·um -i *n* bituminosum
gash *s* patens plag·a -ae *f*
gash *tr* caesim ferire
gasp *s* anhelit·us -ūs *m*
gasp *intr* anhelare; **to — for breath** singultare animam
gas station *s* stati·o -onis *f* olei bituminosi
gastric *adj* stomachi *(gen)*
gastronomy *s* gul·a -ae *f*
gate *s* port·a -ae *f*
gateway *s* adit·us -ūs *m*
gather *tr (to assemble)* colligĕre; *(fruit, nuts, flowers)* legĕre; *(to infer)* colligĕre, conjicĕre; *(to suspect)* suspicari; **to — up** colligĕre ‖ *intr* convenire
gathering *s* convent·us -ūs *m; (collecting)* collecti·o -onis *f*
gaudily *adv* laute
gaudiness *s* lautiti·a -ae *f*
gaudy *adj* laut·us -a -um
gauge *s* modul·us -i *m*
gauge *tr* metiri
gaunt *adj* ma·cer -cra -crum
gauntlet *s* digital·ia -ium *npl;* **to throw down the — ** provocare
gauze *s* co·a -orum *npl*
gawky *adj* inept·us -a -um
gay *adj* hilar·is -is -e; *(homosexual)* cinaed·us -a -um
gay *s* cinaed·us -i *m*
gaze *s* conspect·us -ūs *m; (fixed look)* obtut·us -ūs *m*
gaze *intr* tueri; **to — at** intueri
gazelle *s* dorc·as -adis *f*
gazette *s* act·a -orum *npl* diurna
gazetteer *s* itinerar·ium -(i)i *n*

gear s apparat·us -ūs m
gelatin s glutin·um -i n
gelding s canter·ius -(i)i m
gem s gemm·a -ae f
gender s gen·us -eris n
genealogy s propagin·es -um fpl
general adj (as opposed to specific)
general·is -is -e; (wide-spread) vulgar·is
-is -e; (shared by all) commun·is -is -e,
public·us -a -um; **in** — ad summum, in
universum
general s du·x -cis m, imperat·or -oris m
generalize intr in summam loqui
generally adv (opp: specifically: membratim) generatim; (for the most part)
plerumque, fere
generalship s duct·us -ūs m
generate tr generare
generation s (act of producing) generati·o
-onis f; (age) aet·as -atis f
generic adj general·is -is -e
generosity s liberalit·as -atis f
generous adj liberal·is -is -e
generously adv liberaliter
genesis s orig·o -inis f
genial adj com·is -is -e
geniality s comit·as -atis f
genially adv comiter
genitals spl genital·ia -ium npl
genitive s genitiv·us -i m
genius s vi·r -ri m ingeniosus
genteel adj urban·us -a -um
gentile adj gentil·is -is -e
gentile s gentil·is -is mf
gentility s nobilit·as -atis f
gentle adj mit·is -is -e; (gradual) moll·is
-is -e; (wind, etc.) len·is -is -e; (tame)
mansuet·us -a -um
gentleman s vi·r -ri m honestus
gentleness s clementi·a -ae f; (gradual-
ness) lenit·as -atis f; (tameness) man-
suetud·o -inis f
gently adv leniter, clementer; (gradually)
sensim
gentry s optimat·es -um mpl
genuine adj sincer·us -a -um
genuinely adv sincere
genus s gen·us -eris n
geographer s geograph·us -i m
geographical adj geographic·us -a -um
geography s geographi·a -ae f
geological adj geologic·us -a -um
geologist s geolog·us -i m
geology s geologi·a -ae f
geometric(al) adj geometric·us -a -um
geometry s geometri·a -ae f
germ s germ·en -inis n
German adj Germanus -a -um
germane adj affin·is -is -e
Germany s Germani·a -ae f
germinate intr germinare
germination s germinat·us -ūs m
gerund s gerund·ium -(i)i n

gesticulate intr gesticulari
gesture s gest·us -ūs m
gesture intr gestu indicare
get tr (to acquire) nancisci; (to receive)
accipĕre; (by entreaty) impetrare; (to
fetch) afferre; (to understand) comprehendĕre; (a cold) incidĕre in(w. acc);
to — back recuperare; **to — down**
depromĕre; **to — hold of** prehendĕre; **to
— in** (crops) condĕre; **to get** (a defendant) **off** expedire, servare; **to — out** (a
spot) oblitterare; (to extort) extorquēre;
to — ready parare; **to — rid of** tollĕre;
(a person) amoliri; **to — the better of**
superare; **to — together** cogĕre ‖ intr
(to become) fieri; **to — abroad** palam
fieri; **to — along well** bene se habēre; **to
— away** aufugĕre, evadĕre; **to — at**
ulcisci; **to — back** reverti; **to — down**
descendĕre; **to — dressed** amiciri; **to —
even with** malum vicissim dare (w. dat);
to — in pervenire; **to — off** aufugĕre; **to
— on** procedĕre; (a horse) conscendĕre;
to — on well bene se habēre; (to succeed) bene succedĕre; **to — out** exire; (e
curru) descendĕre; **to — out of being
led away** evadĕre ne seducatur; **to —
over** (a wall) transcendĕre; (difficulty)
superare; (a sickness) convalescĕre ex
(w. abl); **to — ready** sese parare; **to —
through** (to complete) conficĕre; **to —
together** congregari, convenire; **to —
under the table** mensam subire; **to —
up** surgĕre; (as a group) consurgĕre;
(from sleep) expergisci; (out of respect
to s.o.) assurgĕre
ghastly adj (deadly pale) lurid·us -a -um;
(shocking) foed·us -a -um
ghost s umbr·a -ae f; (haunting spirit)
larv·a -ae f; **to give up the** — animam
ebullire
ghostly adj spirital·is -is -e
giant s gig·as -antis m
gibberish s nug·ae -arum fpl
gibbet s patibul·um -i n
gibe s irrisi·o -onis f
gibe tr & intr irridēre
giblets spl gingeri·a -orum npl
giddiness s vertig·o -inis f
giddy adj vertiginos·us -a -um; (light-
minded) lev·is -is -e
gift s don·um -i n, mun·us -eris n; (e.g., of
beauty) do·s -tis f
gifted adj ingenios·us -a -um; (endowed)
praedit·us -a -um
gig s (carriage) cis·ium -(i)i n
gigantic adj praegrand·is -is -e
giggle intr summissim cachinnare
gild tr inaurare
gilded adj inaurat·us -a -um
gilding s (art) auratur·a -ae f; (gilded work)
aur·um -i n inductum
gill s branchi·a -ae f

gilt *adj* inaurat·us -a -um
gin *s* junipero infectus spirit·us -ūs *m*
ginger *s* zinziberi *n (indecl)*
gingerly *adv* pedetemptim
giraffe *s* camelopardal·is -is *f*
gird *tr* cingĕre; **to — oneself** cingi
girder *s* tign·um -i *n*
girdle *s* cingul·um -i *n*
girdle *tr* cingĕre
girl *s* puell·a -ae *f; (unmarried girl)* virg·o -inis *f*
girlhood *s* puellaris aet·as -atis *f*
girlish *adj* puellar·is -is -e
girth *s (measure around)* ambit·us -ūs *m; (of a horse)* cingul·a -ae *f*
gist *s* summ·a -ae *f*
give *tr* dare; *(as a gift)* donare; *(to deliver)* tradĕre; **— it to "em"!** adhibete!; **not — a hoot about s.o.** aliquem dupundii non facĕre; **to — in marriage** in matrimonium dare; **to — away** donare; *(to betray)* prodĕre; **to — back** reddĕre; **to — forth** emittĕre; **to — oneself up to se** addicĕre *(w. dat)*; **to — off** emittĕre; **to — out** edĕre; **to — s.o. a dirty look** respicĕre aliquem minus familiari vultu; **to — s.o. the slip** alicui subterfugĕre; **to — up** *(hope, power)* deponĕre; *(to abandon)* dimittĕre; **to — up the ghost** animam ebullire; **to — way** *(to yield)* cedĕre; *(to comply)* obsequi; *(mil)* pedem referre ‖ *intr* **to — in** cedĕre
giver *s* dat·or -oris *m*
giving *s* dati·o -onis *f*
glacial *adj* glacial·is -is -e
glacier *s* mol·es -is *f* conglaciata
glad *adj* laet·us -a -um; **to be —** gaudēre
gladden *tr* laetificare
glade *s* nem·us -oris *n*
gladiator *s* gladiat·or -oris *m*
gladiatorial *adj* gladiatori·us -a -um; **— show** mun·us -eris *n*
gladiola *s* gladiol·us -i *m*
gladly *adv* libenter
gladness *s* gaud·ium -(i)i *n*
glamor *s* nit·or -oris *m*
glamorous *adj* nitid·us -a -um; **to be —** nitēre
glance *s* aspect·us -ūs *m;* **at a —** primō aspectu; **to cast a — at** strictim aspicĕre
glance *intr* **to — at** strictim aspicĕre; *(in reading)* strictim legĕre; **to — off** stringĕre
gland *s* glandul·a -ae *f*
glare *s* fulg·or -oris *m*
glare *intr* fulgēre; **to — at** torvis oculis tueri
glaring *adj* fulg·ens -entis; *(striking)* manifest·us -a -um
glass *s* vitr·um -i *n; (for drinking)* cal·ix -icis *m* vitreus
glass *adj* vitre·us -a -um
glassmaker *s* vitrar·ius -(i)i *m*

glassware *s* vitre·a -orum *npl*
glaze *tr* vitrum illinĕre *(w. dat)*
gleam *s* fulg·or -oris *m; (fig)* aur·a -ae *f;* **slight — of hope** levis aur·a -ae *f* spei
gleam *intr* coruscare
gleaming *adj* corusc·us -a -um
glean *tr* colligĕre
gleaning *s* spicileg·ium -(i)i *n*
glee *s* laetiti·a -ae *f*
gleeful *adj* laet·us -a -um
gleefully *adv* laete
glen *s* vall·is -is *f*
glib *adj* volubil·is -is -e
glibly *adv* volubiliter
glide *intr* labi
glimmer *s* lu·x -cis *f* dubia; **— of hope** specul·a -ae *f*
glimmer *intr* sublucēre
glimpse *s* aspect·us -ūs *m* brevis; **to have a — of** dispicĕre
glisten *tr* nitēre
glistening *adj* nitid·us -a -um
glitter *s* fulg·or -oris *m*
glitter *intr* fulgēre
gloat *intr* oculos pascĕre; **to — over** oculos pascĕre *(w. abl),* insultare (in + *acc*)
globe *s* glob·us -i *m; (earth)* orb·is -is *m* terrarum
globular *adj* globos·us -a -um
globule *s* globul·us -i *m*
gloom *s* tenebr·ae -arum *fpl; (fig)* tristiti·a -ae *f*
gloomily *adv* maeste
gloomy *adj* tenebros·us -a -um; *(fig)* maest·us -a -um
glorification *s* glorificati·o -onis *f*
glorify *tr* glorificare
glorious *adj* glorios·us -a -um
gloriously *adv* gloriose
glory *s* glori·a -ae *f*
glory *intr* **(in)** gloriari (in + *abl*)
gloss *s (on a word)* interpretati·o -onis *f; (sheen)* nit·or -oris *m*
gloss *tr* annotare; **to — over** colorare
glossary *s* glossar·ium -(i)i *n*
glossy *adj* nitid·us -a -um
glove *s* chirothec·a -ae *f*
glow *s* ard·or -oris *m*
glow *intr* ardēre
glowing *adj* ard·ens -entis; *(w. heat)* cand·ens -entis; **to speak in — terms about** ornatissime loqui de *(w. abl)*
glowingly *adv* ferventer
glue *s* glut·en -inis *n*
glue *tr* glutinare; **to — together** conglutinare
glum *adj* maest·us -a -um
glut *tr* satiare
glutton *s* hellu·o -onis *m*
gluttonous *adj* gulos·us -a -um
gnarled *adj* nodos·us -a -um
gnash *tr* **to — the teeth** dentibus frendĕre

gnat *s* cul·ex -icis *m*
gnaw *tr & intr* rodĕre
gnawing *adj* mord·ax -acis
go *s (try)* conat·us -ūs *m;* **to have a — at** tentare; **to make a — of it** rem bene gerĕre; **on the —** nav·us -a -um
go *intr* ire; **to — about** *(work)* aggredi; **to — abroad** peregre exire; **to — after** petĕre; **to — against** obstare, adversari *(w. dat);* **to — along with** assentire *(w. dat);* **to — around** circumire; **to — aside** discedĕre; **to — astray** errare; **to — back** reverti; **to — back on one's word** fidem fallĕre; **to — before** praeire *(w. dat);* **to — between** intervenire; **to — beyond** egredi; *(fig)* excedĕre; **to — by** *(to pass)* praeterire; *(the rules)* servare; *(promises)* stare *(w. abl);* **to — down** descendĕre; *(of sun)* occidĕre; *(of ship)* mergi; *(of price)* laxari; *(of swelling)* se summittĕre; **to — for** petĕre; *(to fetch a person)* adducĕre; *(a thing)* adferre; *(the bait)* appetĕre; **to — forth** exire; **to — in** introire; **to — into** inire; **to — off** abire; *(as gun)* displodĕre; **to — on** *(to continue)* pergĕre; *(to happen)* fieri, agi; **to — out** exire; *(of fire)* exstingui; **to — out ahead** antecedĕre; **to — out of doors** prodire; **to — over** *(to cross)* transire; *(a subject)* percurrĕre; *(to examine)* perscrutari; *(to repeat)* repetĕre; **to — straight** rectum iter vitae insistĕre; **to — through** *(to travel through)* obire; *(to suffer)* perferre; **to — through with** pertendĕre; **to — to** adire, accedĕre; **to — to and fro** commeare; **to — towards** petĕre; **to — under** submergi; **to — up** subire *(w. acc); (of prices)* ingravescĕre; **to — with** comitari
goad *s* stimul·us -i *m*
goad *tr* instigare; *(fig)* stimulare; *(to exasperate)* exasperare
goal *s* fin·is -is *m; (at the racetrack)* cal·x -cis *f*
goat *s* ca·per -pri *m,* capr·a -ae *f*
gobble *tr* devorare
gobbler *s* hellu·o -onis *m*
go-between *s* internunt·ius -(i)i *m,* internunti·a -ae *f*
goblet *s* pocul·um -i *n*
goblin *s* larv·a -ae *f*
god *s* de·us -i *m;* **God** De·us -i *m;* **— forbid!** Deus averruncet!; **— willing** Deo volente; **thank —** Deo gratias!; **ye —s di** superi!
god-awful *adj* taeterrim·us -a -um
goddess *s* de·a -ae *f*
godhead *s* deit·as -atis *f*
godless *adj* impi·us -a -um
godlike *adj* divin·us -a -um
godliness *s* piet·as -atis *f*
gold *adj* aure·us -a -um
gold *s* aur·um -i *n*

golden *adj* aure·us -a -um
goldfinch *s* cardel·is -is *f*
goldfish *s* hippur·us -i *m*
gold leaf *s* auri bracte·a -ae *f*
gold mine *s* aurifodin·a -ae *f*
goldsmith *s* aurif·ex -icis *m*
good *adj* bon·us -a -um; *(morally)* prob·us -a -um; *(useful)* util·is -is -e; *(beneficial)* salutar·is -is -e; *(kindhearted)* benevol·us -a -um; *(fit)* idone·us -a -um; **— for you!** macte virtute esto! *(pl:* estote!); **I am having a — time** mihi pulchre est; **it is — to** *(w. inf)* commodum est *(w. inf);* **it is not — to** *(w. inf)* non convenit *(w. inf);* **to be — for** prodesse *(w. dat);* **to do s.o. — alicui** prodesse; **to have a — time** *(to celebrate)* genio indulgĕre; **to make — compensare**; **to seem —** videri
good *n* bon·um -i *n; (profit)* lucr·um -i *n;* **for — in** perpetuum; **—s** bon·a -orum *npl; (for sale)* merc·es -cium *fpl*
good *interj* bene!; **very — bone sane!**
goodbye *interj* vale! *(pl:* valete!); **to say — vale jubĕre**
good-for-nothing *s* **to be a — nihil hominis esse**
good-for-nothing *adj* nequam *(indecl)*
goodly *adj (amount)* ampl·us a -um; **a — number of** nonnull·i -ae -a
good-natured *adj* facil·is -is -e
goodness *s* bonit·as -atis *f; (moral)* probit·as -atis *f; (generosity)* benignit·as -atis *f*
goose *s* anser -eris *m*
gooseberry *s* acin·us -i *m* grossulae
gore *s* cru·or -oris *m*
gore *tr* cornibus confodĕre
gorge *s* angusti·ae -arum *fpl*
gorge *tr* **to — oneself** se ingurgitare
gorgeous *adj* magnific·us -a -um
gorgeously *adv* laute
Gorgon *s* Gorg·o -onis *f*
gory *adj* cruent·us -a -um
gospel *s* evangel·ium -(i)i *n*
gossamer *s* arane·a -ae *f*
gossip *s (talk)* gerr·ae -arum *fpl; (person)* garrul·us -i *m,* gerrul·a -ae *f*
gossip *intr* garrire
gouge *tr* **to — out s.o.'s eye** oculum alicui eruĕre
gourd *s* cucurbit·a -ae *f*
gourmand *s* hellu·o -onis *m*
gout *s* arthrit·is -idis *f; (in the feet)* podagr·a -ae *f; (in the hands)* chiragr·a -ae *f*
govern *tr* imperare *(w. dat),* gubernare
governess *s* magistr·a -ae *f*
government *s* res, rei *f* publica
governor *s (of a province)* praes·es -idis *m; (of an imperial province)* legat·us -i *m; (of a Roman province)* procons·ul -ulis *m; (of a smaller province)* procurat·or -oris *m*
governorship *s* praefectur·a -ae *f*

gown *s (of Roman citizen)* tog·a -·ae *f; (of women)* stol·a -ae *f*

grab *tr* rapĕre; **to — hold of** invadĕre; **to — with both hands** injicĕre utramque manum *(w. dat)*

grace *s* grati·a -ae *f; (pardon)* veni·a -ae *f;* to say **—** *(before meals)* consecrationem recitare; *(after meals)* gratias agĕre

grace *tr (to adorn)* decorare; *(to add honor and distinction)* honestare

graceful *adj* decor·us -a -um

gracefully *adv* decore

gracefulness *s* venust·as -atis *f*

graceless *adj* illepid·us -a -um

Graces *spl* Grati·ae -arum *fpl*

gracious *adj* benign·us -a -um

graciously *adv* benigne

gradation *s* grad·us -ūs *m; (rhet)* gradati·o -onis *f*

grade *s* grad·us -ūs *m; (test)* not·a -ae *f*

gradient *s* proclivit·as -atis *f*

gradual *adj* per gradus

gradually *adv* gradatim, sensim

graduate *tr* ad gradum admittĕre ‖ *intr* gradum suscipĕre

graduate *s* qui gradum academicum adeptus est

graft *s* surcul·us -i *m; (pol)* ambit·us -ūs *m*

graft *tr* inserĕre

grain *s (single)* gran·um -i *n;* frument·um -i *n; (in wood)* fibr·a -ae *f;* **against the —** transversis fibris; *(fig)* invitā Minervā; **with a — of salt** cum grano salis

grammar *s* grammatic·a -ae *f*

grammarian *s* grammatic·us -i *m*

grammatical *adj* grammatic·us -a -um

granary *s* horre·um -i *n*

grand *adj* grand·is -is -e; **— old style of oratory** grandis orati·o -onis *f*

grandchild *s* nep·os -otis *m,* nept·is -is *f*

granddaughter *s* nept·is -is *f*

grandeur *s* majest·as -atis *f*

grandfather *s* av·us -i *m*

grandiloquent *adj* grandiloqu·us -a -um

grandmother *s* avi·a -ae *f*

grandson *s* nep·os -otis *m*

grant *tr (to bestow)* concedĕre; *(usu. s.th. that is due)* tribuĕre; *(to acknowledge)* fatēri; *(in geometry)* dare; **—ed, he himself is nothing** esto, ipse nihil est; **— that** sit quidem ut; **to take for —ed** sumĕre

grant *s* concessi·o -onis *f;* **to make anyone a — of anything** aliquid alicui concedĕre

granular *adj* granos·us -a -um

grape *s* uv·a -ae *f,* acin·us -i *m*

grape picker *s* vindemit·or -oris *m*

grapevine *s* vit·is -is *f*

graphic *adj* express·us -a -um

graphically *adv* expresse, graphice

grapnel *s* unc·us -i *m*

grapple *intr* luctari

grappling iron *s* man·us -ūs *f* ferrea

grasp *s (act of grasping; comprehension)* comprehensi·o -onis *f;* **he escaped my —** manus meas effugit; **to wrest from one's —** de manibus extorquēre; **within one's —** inter manūs

grasp *tr* prehendĕre; *(mentally)* comprehendĕre ‖ *intr* **to — at** *(lit & fig)* captare

grasping *adj* avar·us -a -um

grass *s* gram·en -inis *n,* herb·a -ae *f*

grasshopper *s* grill·us -i *m*

grassy *adj* graminos·us -a -um

grate *s* clathr·i -orum *mpl; (hearth)* camin·us -i *m*

grate *tr* conterĕre ‖ *intr* stridĕre; **to — upon s.o.** alicujus animum offendĕre

grateful *adj* grat·us -a -um

gratefully *adv* grate

gratification *s* gratificati·o -onis *f; (pleasure, delight)* volupt·as -atis *f,* delectati·o -onis *f;* **— of natural desires** expleti·o -onis *f* naturae

gratify *tr* gratificari *(w. dat)*

gratifying *adj* grat·us -a -um

grating *s* cancell·i -orum *mpl; (sound)* strid·or -oris *m*

gratis *adv* gratis

gratitude *s* grati·a -ae *f;* **to feel —** gratiam habēre; **to show —** gratiam referre

gratuitous *adj* gratuit·us -a -um

gratuitously *adv* gratuito

gratuity *s* stip·s -is *f*

grave *adj* grav·is -is -e; *(stern)* sever·us -a -um

grave *s* sepulcr·um -i *n*

gravedigger *s* tumulorum foss·or -oris *m*

gravel *s* glare·a -ae *f*

gravelly *adj* glareos·us -a -um

gravely *adv* graviter

gravestone *s* monument·um -i *n*

graveyard *s* sepulcret·um -i *n*

gravitate *intr* vergĕre

gravitation *s* ponderati·o -onis *f*

gravity *s (importance; gravitational pull)* gravit·as -atis *f; (personal)* severit·as -atis *f*

gravy *s* ju·s -ris *n*

gray *adj* can·us -a -um; **to become —** canescĕre

gray-eyed *adj* caesi·us -a -um

gray-headed *adj* can·us -a -um

grayish *adj* canesc·ens -entis

grayness *s* caniti·es -ei *f*

graze *tr (cattle)* pascĕre; *(to touch lightly)* perstingĕre ‖ *intr* pasci

grease *s* ad·eps -ipis *m*

greasy *adj* unct·us -a -um

great *adj* magn·us -a -um; *(thirst)* ing·ens -entis; **as — as** tant·us...quant·us -a -um; **— amount of money** ingens pecuni·a -ae *f;* **— big** grand·is -is -e; **it**

was really —! bene fuit merhercule; **how —** quant·us -a -um; **so —** tant·us -a -um; **very —** permagn·us -a -um, maxim·us -a -um
great-granddaughter s pronept·is -is f
great-grandfather s prova·us -i m
great-grandmother s proavi·a -ae f
great-grandson s pronep·os -otis m
greatness s magnitud·o -inis f
great-uncle s avuncul·us -i m major
greaves spl ocre·ae -arum fpl
Grecian adj Graec·us -a -um
greed s avariti·a -ae f
greedily adv avide
greediness s avariti·a -ae f
greedy adj avid·us -a -um
Greek adj Graec·us -a -um
Greek s Graec·us -i m; **to know (read, speak) —** Graece scire (legěre, loqui)
green adj virid·is -is -e; *(dark-green)* prasin·us -a -um; *(fresh)* crud·us -a -um; *(unripe, e.g., apples)* crud·us -a -um; **to become —** virescěre
green s col·or -oris m viridis; *(lawn)* loc·us -i m herbidus; **—s** holer·a -um npl
greenhouse s viridar·ium -(i)i n hibernum
greenish adj subvirid·is -is -e
greenness s viridit·as -atis f; *(fig)* crudit·as -atis f
greet tr salutare, salutem dicěre *(w. dat)*
greeting s salutati·o -onis f; **to return a —** resalutare
gregarious adj gregal·is -is -e; *(person)* social·is -is -e
grenade s pyrobol·us -i m
grey see **gray**
greyhound s vertag·us -i m, vertag·a -ae f
gridiron s craticul·a -ae f
grief s maer·or -oris m; **good —!** mehercules!; **to come to —** perire
grievance s querell·a -ae f
grieve tr dolore afficěre ‖ intr maerēre, dolēre
grievous adj grav·is -is -e
grievously adv graviter
griffin s gry·ps -pis m
grill tr assare; *(w. questions)* interrogare
grill s craticul·a -ae f
grim adj torv·us -a -um; *(e.g., winter)* deform·is -is -e
grimace s rict·us -ūs m
grimly adv torve
grin s subris·us -ūs m distortus
grin intr distorto vultu subridēre
grind tr *(grain)* molěre; *(in mortar)* contunděre; *(on whetstone)* exacuěre; **to — out a song** canticum extorquěre; **to — the teeth** dentibus frenděre
grindstone s co·s -tis f
grip s comprehensi·o -onis f
grip tr comprehenděre
grisly adj horrend·us -a -um
grist s farin·a -ae f

gristle s cartilag·o -inis f
gristly adj cartilaginos·us -a -um
grit s haren·a -ae f
gritty adj harenos·us -a -um
grizzly adj can·us -a -um
groan s gemit·us -ūs m
groan intr geměre
grocer s olitar·ius -(i)i m
groceries spl obsoni·a -orum npl
grocery store s tabern·a -ae f cibaria
groggy adj titub·ans -antis
groin s ingu·en -inis n
groom s novus marit·us -i m
groom tr curare
groove s stri·a -ae f
groove tr striare
grope intr praetentare
gropingly adv pedetentim
gross adj *(corpulent)* crass·us -a -um; *(indelicate)* indecor·us -a -um; *(coarse)* rud·is -is -e; *(inordinate)* nimi·us -a -um; *(ignorance, folly)* ing·ens -entis
grossly adv nimium
grotesque adj distort·us -a -um
grotto s antr·um -i n
ground s sol·um -i n, terr·a -ae f; *(level ground)* sol·um -i n; *(reason)* rati·o -onis f; *(place)* loc·us -i m; **on the —** humi; **to be burnt to the —** ad solum exuri; **to fall to the —** ad terram deciděre; **to gain —** proficěre; **to level with the —** solo adaequare; **to lose —** receděre; *(mil)* pedem referre
ground tr fundare; *(to teach)* imbuěre; *(a ship)* subducěre ‖ intr *(naut)* haerēre
ground floor s sol·um -i n
groundless adj van·us -a -um; *(false)* fals·us -a -um
groundwork s fundament·um -i n
group s *(band)* man·us -ūs f; *(class)* gen·us -eris n; *(crowd)* glob·us -i m
group tr disponěre ‖ intr **to — around** circulari, stipari
grouping s dispositi·o -onis f
grouse s *(bird)* tetra·o -onis m
grove s nem·us -oris n; *(sacred grove)* luc·us -i m
grovel intr repěre, se prosterněre
grow tr colěre, serěre ‖ intr crescěre; *(to become)* fieri; *(of vegetables)* nasci; *(to shoot up)* se promittěre; **to let the hair, beard — long** capillam, barbam promittěre; **to — back** renasci; **to — out** excrescěre; **to — out of** *(e.g., a wall)* innasci *(w. dat or in + abl)* *(fig)* oriri ex *(w. abl)*; **to — over** *(e.g., of a skin over a wound)* induci *(w. dat)*; **to — up** adolescěre; *(to arrive at puberty)* pubescěre
grower s cult·or -oris m
growl s fremit·us -ūs m
growl intr freměre; **to — at** ogganire
grown-up adj adult·us -a -um

growth *s* increment·um -i *n;* **full —** maturit·as -atis *f*

grub *s* vermicul·us -i *m; (food)* vict·us -ūs *m*

grub *intr* effodĕre

grudge *s* invidi·a -ae *f;* **to hold a — against** succensēre *(w. dat)*

grudgingly *adv* invit·us -a -um *(adj in agreement with the subject)*

gruelling *adj* (de)fatig·ans -antis

gruesome *adj* tae·ter -tra -trum

gruff *adj* asp·er -era -erum

gruffly *adv* aspere

gruffness *s* asperit·as -atis *f*

grumble *intr* murmurare; **to — about** queri de *(w. abl)*

grumpy *adj* stomachos·us -a -um

grunt *s* grunnit·us -ūs *m*

grunt *intr* grunnire

guarantee *s* fid·es -ei *f; (money)* sponsi·o -onis *f; (person who guarantees)* va·s -dis *m; (in legal contracts)* satisdati·o -onis *f;* **to give, recieve a —** fidem dare, accipĕre

guarantee *tr* fidem dare *(w. dat),* spondēre

guaranteed *adj* spons·us -a -um

guarantor *s* spons·or -oris *m*

guard *s* custodi·a -ae *f; (mil)* praesid·ium -(i)i *n; (person)* cust·os -odis *mf;* **to be on one's — against** praecavēre; **to mount —** custodiam agĕre

guard *tr* custodire **‖** *intr* **to — against** cavēre

guarded *adj* caut·us -a -um

guardedly *adv* caute

guardhouse *s* carc·er -eris *m* militaris

guardian *s* cust·os -odis *mf; (of minor or orphan)* tut·or -oris *m*

guardianship *s* custodi·a -ae *f; (of minor or woman)* tutel·a -ae *f*

guess *s* conjecti·o -onis *f*

guess *tr & intr* conjicĕre, divinare

guest *s* hosp·es -itis *mf; (at dinner)* conviv·a -ae *mf*

guidance *s* duct·us -ūs *m; (advice)* consil·ium -(i)i *n;* **under the — of the deity** deo ducente

guide *s* duct·or -oris *m*

guide *tr (as a local guide)* ducĕre; *(to manage, control)* regĕre

guidebook *s* itinerar·ium -(i)i *n*

guild *s* colleg·ium -(i)i *n*

guile *s* dol·us -i *m*

guileful *adj* dolos·us -a -um

guileless *adj* simpl·ex -icis

guilt *s* culp·a -ae *f*

guilty *adj* son·s -tis; **— of** noc·ens *(w. gen or abl);* **to punish the —** sontes punire

guinea hen *s* meleagr·is -idis *f*

guise *s* speci·es -ei *f; (features, dress)* habit·us -ūs *m;* **under the — of** sub specie *(w. gen)*

guitar *s* cithar·a -ae *f* Hispanica

gulf *s* sin·us -ūs *m*

gull *s* merg·us -i *m*

gullet *s* gul·a -ae *f*

gullibility *s* credulit·as -atis *f*

gullible *adj* credul·us -a -um

gulp *s* singult·us -ūs *m*

gulp *tr* **to — down** obsorbēre **‖** *intr* singultare

gum *s* gummi *n (indecl); (anat)* gingiv·a -ae *f*

gumption *s* alacrit·as -atis *f*

gun *s* sclopet·um -i *n;* **to jump the —** signum praevertĕre; **to stick to one's —s** in sententiā stare

gurgle *intr* singultare; *(of a stream)* murmurare

gurgling *s* singult·us -ūs *m; (of a stream)* murmurati·o -onis *f*

gush *s* effusi·o -onis *f,* erupti·o -onis *f; (of water)* scatebr·a -ae *f;* **w. a — of tears** profusis lacrimis

gush *intr* scaturire; **to — out** prorumpĕre; *(of blood from a wound)* emicare

gust *s* flam·en -inis *n*

gusto *s* stud·ium -(i)i *n*

gusty *adj* procellos·us -a -um

gut *s* intestin·um -i *n*

gut *tr* extenterare; *(a building)* amburĕre

gutted *adj (by fire)* ambust·us -a -um

gutter *s* canal·is -is *m,* riv·us -i *m;* **to clean out the —** rivos deducĕre

guttural *adj* guttural·is -is -e

guy *s* **poor —** homuncul·us -i *m;* **that —** iste

guzzle *tr & intr* potare

guzzler *s* pot·or -oris *m*

gymnasium *s* gymnas·ium -(i)i *n*

gymnastic *adj* gymnastic·us -a -um

gymnastics *spl* palaestric·a -ae *f*

gynecology *s* gynaecologi·a -ae *f*

gypsum *s* gyps·um -i *n*

gyrate *intr* in gyrum verti

H

haberdasher *s* linte·o -onis *m*

haberdashery *s* tabern·a -ae *f* vestiaria

habit *s* consuetud·o -inis *f; (dress)* habit·us -ūs *m;* **to be in the — of** consuescĕre *(w. inf);* **to break the —** abscedĕre ab usu; **to get into the — of** se assuefacĕre *(w. inf)*

habitation *s* habitati·o -onis *f*

habitual *adj* usitat·us -a -um

habitually *adv* de more, ex more

habituate *tr* assuefacĕre

hack *s (cut)* plag·a -ae *f; (coach) (coll)* raed·a -ae *f* meritoria

hack *tr* caedĕre; **to — to pieces** concidĕre

hackneyed *adj* trit·us -a -um

haddock *s* gad·us -i *m*

hag *s* an·us -ūs *f*
haggard *adj* ma·cer -cra -crum
haggle *intr* licitari
haggler *s* licitat·or -oris *m*
hail *s* grand·o -inis *f (m)*
hail *intr* it is —ing grandinat
hail *tr* appellare
hail *interj* salve! *(pl: salvēte!)*
hailstone *s* grandinis gran·um -i *n*
hair *s (of head or beard)* capill·us -i *m*, *(or* capill·i -orum *mpl); (in locks or dressed)* crin·is -is *m; (hair as an orament, of men or women)* com·a -ae *f; (single)* pil·us -i *m; (of a animals)* saet·a -ae *f;* **he was within a — 's breadth of** nil propius est factum quam ut; **to split —s** cavillari
haircut *s* tons·us -ūs *m*
hairdresser *s* tonstri·x -icis *f*
hairless *adj (of head)* calv·us -a -um; *(of body)* gla·ber -bra -brum
hairnet *s* reticul·um -i *n*
hair oil *s* capillar·e -is *n*
hairpin *s* crinal·e -is *n*
hairy *adj* pilos·us -a -um; *(chest)* saetos·us -a -um, hirsut·us -a -um
hale *adj* **— and hardy** san·us et robust·us -a -um
half *s* dimidia par·s -tis *f*
half *adv* dimidio; *(partly)* partim; **— and —** pro parte semissā
half *adj* dimidiat·us -a -um, dimidi·us -a -um; **— the drinks** dimidiae potion·es -um *fpl*
half alive *adj* semiviv·us -a -um
half asleep *adj* semisomn·us -a -um
halfbreed *s* hybrid·a -ae *mf*
half brother *s (on mother's side)* fra·ter -tris *m* uterin·us; *(on father's side)* fra·ter -tris *m* consanguineus
half-burnt *adj* semiust·us -a -um
half-cooked *adj* semicoct·us -a -um
half-dead *adj* semianim·us -a -um
half-eaten *adj* semes·us -a -um
half-finished *adj* semiperfect·us -a -um
half-full *adj* semiplen·us -a -um
half-hour *s* semihor·a -ae *f*
half-moon *s* lun·a -ae *f* dimidiata; *(shape)* lunul·a -ae *f*
half-open *adj* semiapert·us -a -um
half pint *s (sl)* homuncul·us -i *m*
half pound *s* selibr·a -ae *f*
half sister *s (on mother's side)* sor·or -oris *f* uterina; *(on father's side)* sor·or -oris *f* consanguinea
halfway *adj* medi·us -a -um
half-year *adj* semestr·is -is -e
hall *s* atr·ium -(i)i *n*
hallo *interj* heus!
hallucinate *intr* alucinari
hallucination *s* alucinati·o -onis *f*
hallway *s* andr·on -onis *m; (at front of house)* vestibul·um -i *n*

halo *s* coron·a -ae *f*
halt *s* paus·a -ae *f,* mor·a -ae *f;* **to come to a —** consistĕre
halt *tr* sistĕre ‖ *intr* consistĕre; *(to limp)* claudicare
halter *s* capistr·um -i *n*
halting *adj* claud·us -a -um; *(fig)* haesitabund·us -a -um
halve *tr* ex aequo dividĕre
ham *s* pern·a -ae *f; (back of the knee)* popl·es -itis *m*
hamlet *s* vic·us -i *m*
hammer *s* malle·us -i *m*
hammer *tr* malleo tundĕre
hamper *s* corb·is -is *m*
hamstring *s* poplitis nerv·us -i *m*
hamstring *tr* poplitem succidĕre *(w. dat); (fig)* impedire
hand *s* man·us -ūs *f; (handwriting)* chirograph·um -i *n; (of dial)* gnom·on -onis *m; (worker)* operar·ius -(i)i *m;* **at —** praesto, ad manum; **by —** manu; **from — to —** de manu in manum; **— in —** junctis manibus; **— off!** noli(te) tangĕre; **—s up!** tolli(te) manus!; **left —** laev·a -ae *f,* sinistr·a -ae *f;* **old —** veterat·or -oris *m;* **on the one —, on the other** unā ex parte…alterā ex parte; *or use* hic…ille; **on the other —** contra; **right —** dext(e)r·a -ae *f;* **these things are not in our —s** haec non sunt in nostra manu; **to be near at —** subesse; **to have a — in** s.th. interesse alicui rei; **to have clean —s** manūs pecuniae abstinentes habēre; **to have in —** in manibus habēre; **to have one's —s full** satis agĕre; **to lay —s on** manum injicĕre *(w. dat);* **to live from — to mouth** in horam vivĕre; **to pass a thing from — to —** aliquid de manu in manum tradĕre; **shake —s** dextram dextrae jungĕre; **to take in —** suscipĕre
hand *tr* tradĕre, porrigĕre; **to be —ed over to** *(by a judge)* adjudicari *(w. dat);* **to — around** circumferre; **to —down** tradĕre; **to — in** reddĕre; **to — over** tradĕre; *(to betray)* prodĕre
handbill *s* libell·us -i *m*
handbook *s* enchirid·ion -(i)i *n*
handcuffs *spl* manic·ae -arum *fpl*
handful *s* manipul·us -i *m*
handicraft *s* artific·ium -(i)i *n*
handiwork *s* opific·ium -(i)i *n*
handkerchief *s* sudar·ium -(i)i *n*
handle *s* manubr·ium -(i)i *n; (of a cup)* ansul·a -ae *f*
handle *tr* tractare
handling *s* tractati·o -onis *f*
handsome *adj* pul·cher -chra -chrum
handsomely *adv* pulchre; *(liberally)* liberaliter
handsomeness *s* pulchritud·o -inis *f*
handwriting *s* chirograph·um -i *n*

handy *adj (of things)* habil·is -is -e; *(of persons)* soller·s -tis; *(at hand)* praesto
hang *tr* suspendēre; *(by a line)* appendēre; *(the head)* demittĕre ‖ *intr* pendēre; **—ing down** demiss·us -a -um; **to — down** dependēre; **to — on to** haerēre *(w. dat)*; **to — over** imminēre *(w. dat)*
hanger-on *s* assecl·a -ae *m*
hanging *adj* pensil·is -is -e
hanging *s (execution)* suspend·ium -(i)i *n;* **—s** aulae·a -orum *npl*
hangman *s* carnif·ex -icis *m*
hangout *s* latebr·ae -arum *fpl*
hangover *s* crapul·a -ae *f;* **to sleep off a —** crapulam obdormire
hanker *intr* **— for** desiderare
haphazard *adj* fortuit·us -a -um
happen *intr* accidĕre, fieri, contingĕre; **I happened to see** forte vidi; **it happens that** contingit ut; **to — upon** incidĕre in *(w. acc)*
happily *adv* feliciter, beate
happiness *s* felicit·as -atis *f*
happy *adj* beat·us -a -um
harangue *s* conti·o -onis *f;* **to give a —** contionem habēre
harangue *tr & intr* contionari
harass *tr* vexare
harassment *s* vexati·o -onis *f*
harbinger *s* praenunt·ius -(i)i *m,* prae-nunti·a -ae *f*
harbor *s* port·us -ūs *m*
harbor *tr* excipĕre; **to — hopes, thoughts** portare spes, cogitationes
hard *adj* dur·us -a -um; *(difficult)* difficil·is -is -e; *(severe)* a·cer -cris -cre; **to become —** durescĕre
hard *adv* valde, sedulo, summā vi
harden *tr* durare; *(fig)* indurare ‖ *intr* durescĕre; *(fig)* obdurescĕre
hardhearted *adj* dur·us -a -um
hardiness *s* rob·ur -oris *n*
hardly *adv* vix, aegre; **— any** null·us -a -um fere
hardness *s* duriti·a -ae *f; (fig)* acerbit·as -atis *f*
hardship *s* lab·or -oris *m*
hardware *s* ferrament·a -orum *npl*
hardware store *s* tabern·a -ae *f* ferraria
hardy *adj* robust·us -a -um
hare *s* lep·us -oris *m*
harem *s* gynaece·um -i *n*
hark *interj* heus!
harken *intr* audire; **to — to** auscultare *(w. dat)*
harlot *s* meretr·ix -icis *f*
harm *s* injuri·a -ae *f;* **to come to —** detrimentum accipĕre
harm *intr* nocēre *(w. dat),* laedĕre
harmful *adj* noxi·us -a -um
harmless *adj* innocu·us -a -um
harmonious *adj* canor·us -a -um; *(fig)* concor·s -dis

harmoniously *adv* consonanter; *(fig)* concorditer
harmonize *tr* componĕre ‖ *intr* concinĕre; *(fig)* consentire
harmony *s* harmoni·a -ae *f; (fig)* concordi·a -ae *f*
harness *s* equi ornament·a -orum *npl*
harp *s* lyr·a -ae *f*
harpist *s* psalt·es -ae *m*
harpoon *s* jacul·um -i *n* hamatum
harpoon *tr* jaculo hamato transfigĕre
Harpy *s* Harpyi·a -ae *f*
harrow *s* irp·ex -icis *m*
harrow *tr* occare
harsh *adj* asp·er -era -erum; *(sound)* rauc·us -a -um; *(fig)* dur·us -a -um, inclem·ens -entis, sever·us -a -um
harshly *adv* aspere, severe
harshness *s* asperit·as -atis *f*
harvest *s* mess·is -is *f*
harvest *tr* metĕre
hash *s* minut·al -alis *n*
hash *tr* comminuĕre
haste *s* festinati·o -onis *f;* **in —** propere; **to make —** properare
hasten *tr & intr* properare
hastily *adv* propere, raptim; *(without reflection)* temere
hastiness *s* celerit·as -atis *f; (without reflection)* temerit·as -atis *f*
hasty *adj* temerari·us -a -um
hat *s* petas·us -i *m*
hatch *s (naut)* foram·en -inis *n*
hatch *tr (fig)* coquĕre; *(of chickens)* ex ovis excludĕre
hatchet *s* asci·a -ae *f*
hate *s* od·ium -(i)i *n*
hate *tr* odisse
hateful *adj* odios·us -a -um, invis·us -a -um; **to be — to** odio esse *(w. dat)*
hatefully *adv* odiose
hatred *s* od·ium -(i)i *n*
haughtily *adv* superbe
haughtiness *s* superbi·a -ae *f*
haughty *adj* superb·us -a -um
haul *s (catch)* captur·a -ae *f; (transport)* vectur·a -ae *f*
haul *tr* trahĕre; **to — up** subducĕre
haunch *s* clun·is -is *f*
haunt *s* loc·us -i *m* frequentatus; *(of animals)* lateb·rae -arum *fpl*
haunt *tr* frequentare; *(to disturb)* inquietare
haunted *adj* ab larvis frequentat·us -a -um
have *tr* habēre; *(to be obliged)* debēre; **I — confidence** fiducia est mihi
haven *s* port·us -ūs *m*
have-not *s* paup·er -eris *mf*
havoc *s* strag·es -is *f;* **to wreak —** stragem dare
hawk *s* accipi·ter -tris *mf*
hawk *tr* venditare; **to — up phlegm** pituitam exsecrare per tussim
hawker *s* circulat·or -oris *m*

hawk-eyed *adj* lynce·us -a -um
hawser *s* retinacul·um -i *n*
hay *s* faen·um -i *n*
hayloft *s* faenil·ia -ium *npl*
haystack *s* faeni met·a -ae *f*
hazard *s* pericul·um -i *n*
hazardous *adj* periculos·us -a -um
haze *s* nebul·a -ae *f*
hazelnut *s* nu·x -cis *f* avellana
hazy *adj* nebulos·us -a -um; *(fig)* obscur·us -a -um
he *pron* hic, is; *(male)* ma·s -ris *m*
head *s* cap·ut -itis *n;* *(mental faculty)* ingen·ium -(i)i *n;* *(fig)* princ·eps -ipis *m;* **back of the** — occipit·um -i *n;* **from** — **to foot** ab imis unguibus usque ad verticem summum; — **first** praec·eps -itis; — **over heels in love** tot·us -a -um in amore; **it all came to a head** in discrimen summa rerum adducta est; **to come into s.o's** — alicui in mentem venire; **to come to a** — *(of a boil)* caput facěre; **to put** —**s together** capita conferre; **use your** — ! cogita *(pl:* cogitate)! **wine goes to my** — vinum in cerebrum mihi abit
head *adj* prim·us -a -um
head *tr* praesse *(w. dat),* ducěre ‖ *intr* **to** — **for** tenděre ad *(w. acc)*
headache *s* capitis dol·or -oris *m*
heading *s* titul·us -i *m*
headland *s* promuntor·ium -(i)i *n*
headless *adj* trunc·us -a -um
headlong *adv* praec·eps -itis
headquarters *spl* praetor·ium -(i)i *n*
head start *s* **to get a** — iter praecipěre; *(fig)* aliquantum temporis praecipěre
headstrong *adj* contum·ax -acis
headway *s* **to make** — proficěre
headwind *s* vent·us -i *m* adversus
heady *adj* *(of wine)* fervid·us -a -um
heal *tr* mederi *(w. dat),* sanare ‖ *intr* sanescěre; *(of wounds)* coalescěre
healer *s* medic·us -i *m*
healing *adj* salutar·is -is -e
healing *s* sanati·o -onis *f*
health *s* *(good or bad)* valetud·o -inis *f;* **bad (delicate, good, ill)** — adversa (infirma, secunda, incommoda) valetud·o -inis *f;* **to be in good** — bene valēre; **to drink to the** — **of** propinare *(w. dat);* **to enjoy excellent** — optima valitudine uti
healthful *adj* salubr·is -is -e
healthily *adv* salubriter
healthy *adj* san·us -a -um; *(places)* salubr·is -is -e
heap *s* cumul·us -i *m,* acerv·us -i *m*
heap *tr* acervare; **to** — **up** accumulare, exstruěre; **to** — *(blows, favors, abuse)* **upon** congerěre (plagas, beneficia, maledicta) *(w. dat or* in + *acc)*
hear *tr* audire; *(to learn)* cognoscěre, accipěre

hearing *s* *(act)* auditi·o -onis *f;* *(sense)* audit·us -ūs *m;* *(leg)* cogniti·o -onis *f;* **hard of** — surdas·ter -tra -trum
hearken *intr* auscultare; **to** — **to** auscultare *(dat)*
hearsay *s* auditi·o -onis *f*
heart *s* cor cordis *n;* *(fig)* anim·us -i *m;* **from the** — animo; **my** — **was in my mouth** anima mihi in naso erat; **to learn by** — ediscěre; **to love with all one's** — toto pectore amare
heartache *s* *(fig)* cur·a -ae *f*
heartbreak *s* ang·or -oris *m*
heartbroken *adj* ae·ger -gra -grum animi
heartburn *s* praecordium dol·or -oris *m*
heart-felt *adj* haud simulat·us -a -um
hearth *s* foc·us -i *m*
heartily *adv* cum summo studio
heartiness *s* alacrit·as -atis *f*
heartless *adj* inhuman·us -a -um
heartlessly *adv* inhumane
hearty *adj* sincer·us -a -um; *(meal)* laut·us -a -um
heat *s* cal·or -oris *m,* ard·or -oris *m;* *(fig)* ferv·or -oris *m;* — **of the day** aest·us -ūs *m*
heat *tr* calfacěre ‖ *intr* calescěre
heathen *adj* pagan·us -a -um
heathen *s* pagan·us -i *m*
heating *s* calefacti·o -onis *f*
heave *tr* attollěre; **to** — **a sigh** gemitum ducěre ‖ *intr (to swell)* fluctuare; *(of the chest)* anhelare
heaven *s* cael·um -i *n;* — **forbid!** dii meliora! **good** —**s** ! pro divum fidem!; **thank** — dis gratia; **to move** — **and earth** caelum ac terras miscēre
heavenly *adj* caelest·is -is -e
heavily *adv* graviter; *(slowly)* tarde
heaviness *s* gravit·as -atis *f*
heavy *adj* grav·is -is -e; *(sad)* maest·us -a -um; *(rain)* magn·us -a -um
Hebraic *adj* Hebraic·us -a -um
Hebrew *adj* Hebrae·us -a -um
Hebrew *s* Hebrae·us -i *m;* *(language)* lingu·a -ae *f* Hebraea; **to know (read, speak)** — Hebraice scire (legěre, loqui)
hecatomb *s* hecatomb·e -es *f*
heckle *tr* interpellěre
heckler *s* conviciat·or -oris *m*
hectic *adj* febriculos·us -a -um
hedge *s* saep·es -is *f*
hedge *tr* **to** — **in** saepire; **to** — **off** intersaepire ‖ *intr* tergiversari
hedgehog *s* eric·ius -(i)i *m*
heed *s* cur·a -ae *f;* **to take** — curare
heed *tr* curare, observare; *(to obey)* parēre *(w. dat)*
heedless *adj* incaut·us -a -um; — **of** immem·or -oris *(w. gen)*
heedlessness *s* neglegenti·a -ae *f*
heel *s* cal·x -cis *mf;* **to take to one's** —**s** se in pedes conjicěre

hefty *adj* robust·us -a -um; *(thing)* ing·ens -entis
heifer *s* juvenc·a -ae *f*
height *s* altitud·o -inis *f; (of person)* procerit·as -atis *f; (top)* culm·en -inis *n; (fig)* fastig·ium -(i)i *n*
heighten *tr* amplificare, augēre
heinous *adj* atr·ox -ocis
heir *s* her·es -edis *m;* **sole** *or* **universal** — her·es -edis *m* ex asse
heir apparent *s* her·es -edis *m* legitimus
heiress *s* her·es -edis *f*
heirloom *s* res, rei *f* hereditaria
hell *s* infer·i -orum *mpl;* **to catch** — convicium habēre
Hellenic *adj* Hellenic·us -a -um
Hellenism *s* Hellenism·us -i *m*
hellish *adj* infern·us -a -um
hello *interj* salve *(pl:* salvete)
helm *s* gubernacul·um -i *n*
helmet *s (of leather)* gale·a -ae *f; (of metal)* cass·is -idis *f*
helmsman *s* gubernat·or -oris *m*
help *s* auxil·ium -(i)i *n*
help *tr* adjuvare, opem ferre *(w. dat)*
helper *s* adjut·or -oris *m,* adjutr·ix -icis *f*
helpful *adj* util·is -is -e
helpless *adj* inop·s -is
helplessness *s* inopi·a -ae *f*
hem *interj* hem!, ahem!
hem *s* lacini·a -ae *f*
hem *tr* circumsuēre; **to** — **in** circumsidēre; *(by entrenchments)* circumvallare
hemisphere *s* hemisphaer·ium -(i)i *n*
hemlock *s* cicut·a -ae *f*
hemorrhage *s* sanguinis profluv·ium -(i)i *n*
hemorrhoids *spl* haemorrhoid·a -ae *f*
hemp *s* cannab·is -is *f*
hempen *adj* cannabin·us -a -um
hen *s* gallin·a -ae *f*
hence *adv* hinc; *(consequently)* igitur
henceforth *adv* posthac, dehinc
henchman *s* adjut·or -oris *m*
henpecked *adj* uxori·us -a -um
her *pron* eam, illam, hanc
her *adj* ejus, illius, hujus; — **own** su·us -a -um
herald *s* fetial·is -is *m; (crier)* praec·o -onis *m*
herald *tr* (prae)nuntiare
herb *s* herb·a -ae *f*
herd *s* gre·x -gis *m; (pej)* vulg·us -i *n*
herd *tr* **to** — **together** congregare ‖ *intr* **to** — **together** congregari
herdsman *s* armentar·ius -(i)i *m*
here *adv* hic; — **and now** depraesentiarium; — **and there** passim
hereafter *adv* posthac
hereby *adv* ex hoc, hinc
hereditary *adj* hereditari·us -a -um
heredity *s* gen·us -eris *n;* **by** — jure hereditario, per successiones
herein *adv* in hoc, in hac re, hic

heresy *s* haeres·is -is *f*
heretical *adj* haeretic·us -a -um
hereupon *adv* hic
herewith *adv* unā cum hac re
heritage *s* heredit·as -atis *f*
hermaphrodite *s* androgyn·us -i *m*
hermit *s* eremit·a -ae *m*
hermitage *s* eremitae cell·a -ae *f*
hernia *s* herni·a -ae *f*
hero *s* vi·r -ri *m; (demigod)* her·os -oïs *m*
heroic *adj (age)* heroïc·us -a -um; fortissim·us -a -um
heroically *adv* fortissime
heroine *s* virag·o -inis *f; (myth)* heroïn·a -ae *f*
heroism *s* virt·us -utis *f*
heron *s* arde·a -ae *f*
herring *s* hareng·a -ae *f*
hers *pron* ejus, illius
herself *pron (refl)* se; *(intensive)* ipsa; **to** — sibi; **with** — secum
hesitant *adj* dubi·us -a -um
hesitantly *adv* cunctanter
hesitation *s* dubitati·o -onis *f; (in speaking)* haesitati·o -onis *f*
heterogeneous *adj* divers·us -a -um
hew *tr* dolare, caedēre
hey *interj* ohe!; — **you!** heus tū!
hiatus *s* hiat·us -ūs *m*
hiccup *s* singult·us -ūs *m*
hiccup *intr* singultire
hidden *adj* occult·us -a -um; **to lie** — latēre
hide *s* cor·ium -(i)i *n; (pelt)* pell·is -is *f*
hide *tr* abdēre, celare ‖ *intr* latēre
hide and seek *s* **to play** — per lusum latitare
hideous *adj* foed·us -a -um
hideously *adv* foede
hideousness *s* foedit·as -atis *f*
hiding *s* occultati·o -onis *f; (whipping)* verberati·o -onis *f*
hiding place *s* latebr·a -ae *f*
hierarchy *s* hierarchi·a -ae *f*
high *adj* alt·us -a -um; *(rank)* ampl·us -a -um; *(price)* magn·us -a -um; *(wind)* vehem·ens -entis; *(fever)* ard·ens -entis; *(note)* acut·us -a -um; *(expensive)* car·us -a -um; *(ground)* edit·us -a -um; *(virtue, good, etc.)* summ·us -a -um; **at a** — **price** magni (pretii) *or* magno pretio; — **opinion** magna opini·o -onis *f;* — **sea** alt·um -i *n;* — **tide** maximus aest·us -ūs *m*
high *adv* alte; **to aim** — magnas res appetēre; **from on** — desuper; **on** — sursum versum
highborn *adj* generos·us -a -um
high-flown *adj* inflat·us -a -um
highhanded *adj* insol·ens -entis
highhandedly *adv* insolenter
highlander *s* montan·us -i *m*
highlands *spl* regi·o -onis *f* montuosa
highlights *spl* praecipu·a -orum *npl* rerum

highly *adv (value)* magni; *(intensity)* vehementer, valde

high-minded *adj (noble)* magnanim·us -a -um; *(arrogant)* imperios·us -a -um

high priest *s* pontif·ex -icis *m*, sacerd·os -otis *m* maximus

high treason *s* majest·as -atis *f* (laesa); **convicted of** — de majestate damnat·us -a -um

highway *s* vi·a -ae *f*

hijacker *s* latr·o -onis *m*

hike *s* ambulati·o -onis *f*

hilarious *adj* hilar·is -is -e

hilariously *adv* hilare

hilarity *s* hilarit·as -atis *f*

hill *s* coll·is -is *m*

hillock *s* tumul·us -i *m*

hillside *s* cliv·us -i *m*

hilly *adj* clivos·us -a -um

hilt *s* capul·us -i *m*

him *pron* eum, illum, hunc; **of** — ejus, illius hujus

himself *pron (refl)* se; *(intensive)* ipse; **to** — sibi; **with** — secum

hind *s* cerv·a -ae *f*

hind *adj* poster·ior -ior -ius; — **end** *(coll)* sed·es -is *f*

hinder *tr* impedire, prohibēre; *(to block)* obstare *(w. dat)*

hindmost *adj* postrem·us -a -um

hindrance *s* impediment·um -i *n*

hinge *s* card·o -inis *m*

hinge *intr* **to** — **on** *(fig)* niti *(w. abl)*

hint *s* significati·o -onis *f*; **to throw clear** —**s** nec dubias significationes jacēre

hint *tr* suggerēre

hip *s* cox·a -ae *f*

hippodrome *s* hippodrom·os -i *m*

hippopotamus *s* hippopotam·us -i *m*

hire *s* conducti·o -onis *f*

hire *tr* conducēre; **to** — **oneself out** auctorari; **to** — **out** locare

hired *adj* conduct·us -a -um, mercenari·us -a -um

hireling *s* mercenar·ius -(i)i *m*

his *adj* ejus, illius, hujus; — **own** su·us -a -um, propri·us -a -um

hiss *s* sibil·us -i *m*

hiss *tr & intr* sibilare

historian *s* historic·us -i *m*

historical *adj* historic·us -a -um

history *s* histori·a -ae *f*; **ancient**— antiqua historia *f*; **modern** — recentioris aetatis historia *f*; **to write a** — **of the Roman people** res gestas populi Romani perscribēre

histrionic *adj* histrional·is -is -e

hit *s* plag·a -ae *f*, ict·us -ūs *m*; *(success)* success·us -ūs *m*

hit *tr* icēre, ferire; *(of an illness)* affligēre, occupare; **to** — **it off** with convenire cum *(w. abl)*; **you've** — **the nail on the head** acu rem tetigisti ‖ *intr* **to** — **upon** offendēre

hitch *s* nod·us -i *m;* **there is a** — haeret res (in salebrā)

hitch *tr* conjungēre

hither *adv* huc

hither *adj* citer·ior -ior -ius

hitherto *adv (of time)* adhuc; *(of place)* huc usque

hive *s* alve·us -i *m*

hoard *s* acerv·us -i *m*

hoard *tr* coacervare, recondēre

hoarder *s* accumulat·or -oris *m*

hoarse *adj* rauc·us -a -um; **to get** — irraucescēre

hoarsely *adv* raucā voce

hoary *adj* can·us -a -um

hoax *s* frau·s -dis *f*

hobble *intr* claudicare

hobby *s* avocament·um -i *n*

hobnob *intr* conversari

hock *s* popl·es -itis *m*

hoe *s* sarcul·um -i *n*

hoe *tr* sarculare

hog *s* porc·us -i *m*

hogwash *s* quisquili·ae -arum *fpl*

hoist *tr* sublevare

hold *s (of ship)* cavern·a -ae *f;* **to get** *or* **take** — **of** prehendēre; *(with both hands)* comprehendēre

hold *tr* tenēre; *(to contain)* capēre; *(to think)* habēre; *(elections, meeting, discussions)* habēre; *(office, consulship, etc.)* gerēre; **able to** — *(e.g., of a theater)* cap·ax -acis *(w. gen);* **to** — **back** retinēre; *(laughter, tears)* tenēre; **to** — **court** *(leg)* quaerēre; **to** — **forth** *(e.g., hands)* porrigēre; *(to offer)* praebēre; **to** — **in** inhibēre, cohibēre; **to** — **in honor** in honore habēre; **to** — **off** arcēre; **to** — **one's breath** animam comprimēre; **to** — **one's tongue** tacēre; **to** — **out** *(e.g., hands)* protendēre; **to** — *(e.g., a compress)* **to** *(e.g., one's cheek)* admovēre (fomentum) ad (malam); **to** — **up** attollēre; **to** — **up one's head** mentum tollēre ‖ *intr* **to** — **back** cunctari; **to** — **forth** *(to speak)* contionari; **to** — **on to** tenēre; **to** — **out** *(to last)* durare, permanēre

holder *s* possess·or -oris *m; (instrument)* receptacul·um -i *n*

holding *s* possessi·o -onis *f*

hole *s* foram·en -inis *n; (of mice, etc.)* cav·um -i *n;* **to dig a** — **in the ground** locum in terra excavare; **to dig a** — **in the wall** parietem perfodēre

hole-in-the-wall *s (cheap lodgings)* stabul·um -i *n*

holiday *s* di·es -ei *m* festus; —**s** feri·ae -arum *fpl;* **public** — di·es -ei *m* sollemnis

holiness *s* sanctit·as -atis *f*

hollow *adj* cav·us -a -um; *(fig)* inan·is -is -e

hollow *s* cav•um -i *n; (depression)* lacun•a -ae *f;* — **of the hand** cava man•us -ūs *f*
hollow *tr* **to** — **out** excavare
holly *s* il•ex -icis *n* aquifolium
holocaust *s* holocaust•um -i *n*
holy *adj* sanct•us -a -um
homage *s* cult•us -ūs *m;* **to pay** — **to** colĕre
home *s* aed•es -ium *fpl,* dom•us -ūs *f;* **at** — domi; **from** — domo
home *adv (motion)* domum; *(place where)* domi
home *adj* domestic•us -a -um
homeless *adj* tecto car•ens -entis
homeliness *s* rusticit•as -atis *f*
homely *adj* rustic•us -a -um
homemade *adj* domestic•us -a -um
homemaker *s* materfamilias *(gen:* matrisfamilias) *f*
homesick *adj* appet•ens -entis tecti sui; **to be** — ex desiderio tecti sui laborare
homesickness *s* tecti sui desider•ium -(i)i *n*
homestead *s* fund•us -i *m*
homeward *adv* domum
homicidal *adj* cruent•us -a -um
homicide *s (person)* homicid•a -ae *m; (deed)* homicid•ium -(i)i *n*
homily *s* tractat•us -ūs *m* moralis
homogeneous *adj* pari naturā praedit•us -a -um
homosexual *adj* cinaed•us -a -um; — **partner** *(euphem)* fra•ter -tris *m*
homosexual *s* cinaed•us -i *m*
hone *tr* acuĕre
honest *adj* prob•us -a -um; *(truthful)* ver•ax -acis; — **to God,** — **to goodness** mediusfidius
honesty *s* probit•as -atis *f*
honey *s* mel mellis *n; (term of endearment)* melill•a -ae *f*
honeycomb *s* fav•us -i *m*
honeysuckle *s* clymen•us -i *m*
honor *s* hon•or -oris *m; (mark of distinction)* dignit•as -atis *f;* **on your** — per fidem; **sense of** — pud•or -oris *m;* **word of** — fid•es -ei *f*
honor *tr* honorare; *(to respect)* colĕre
honorable *adj* honest•us -a -um
honorably *adv* honeste
honorary *adj* honorari•us -a -um
hood *s* cucull•us -i *m*
hoof *s* ungul•a -ae *f*
hook *s* unc•us -i *m; (esp. for fishing)* ham•us -i *m;* **by** — **or by crook** quocumque modo
hook *tr (to catch w. a hook)* inuncare; *(fig)* capĕre
hooked *adj* hamat•us -a -um; *(crooked)* adunc•us -a -um
hoop *s* circul•us -i *m; (toy)* troch•us -i *m; (shout)* clam•or -oris *m*
hoot *s* cant•us -ūs *m;* **not give a** — **about** pili facĕre *(w. acc)*

hoot *tr* explodĕre ‖ *intr* obstrepĕre; *(of owls)* canĕre
hop *s* salt•us -ūs *m*
hop *intr* salire, subsaltare
hope *s* spe•s -i *f*
hope *intr* sperare; **to** — **for** exspectare
hopeful *adj* bonae spei
hopefully *adv* magnā cum spe
hopefuls *spl (persons)* spe•s -rum *fpl*
hopeless *adj* desperat•us -a -um
hopelessly *adv* desperanter
hopelessness *s* desperati•o -onis *f*
horde *s* turb•a -ae *f; (wandering)* vaga multitud•o -inis *f*
horizon *s* fini•ens -entis *m*
horizontal *adj* librat•us -a -um
horizontally *adv* per libram
horn *s* corn•u -us *n*
horned *adj* cornig•er -era -erum
hornet *s* crab•o -onis *m*
horny *adj* sal•ax -acis
horoscope *s* horoscop•us -i *m;* **to have the same** — uno astro esse
horrible *adj* horribil•is -is -e
horribly *adv* horribili modo
horrid *adj* horrid•us -a -um
horrify *tr* horrificare
horror *s* horr•or -oris *m; (strong aversion)* od•ium -(i)i *n*
hors d'oevres *spl* promuls•is -idis *f*
horse *s* equ•us -i *m,* equ•a -ae *f*
horseback *s* **on** — **in equo; to fight on** — ex equo pugnare; **to ride on** — in equo vehi
horsehair *s* pil•us -i *m* equinus
horsefly *s* taban•us -i *m*
horseman *s* equ•es -itis *m*
horse race *s* curricul•um -i *n* equorum
horseradish *s* armoraci•a -ae *f*
horseshoe *s* sole•a -ae *f* (equi)
horsewhip *s* scutic•a -ae *f*
horsewhip *tr* scuticā verberare
horticultural *adj* ad hortorum cultum pertin•ens -entis
horticulture *s* hortorum cult•us -ūs *m*
hose *s (tube)* tubul•us -i *m; (stocking)* tibial•e -is *n*
hosiery *s* feminal•ia -ium *npl*
hospitable *adj* hospital•is -is -e
hospitably *adv* hospitaliter
hospital *s* valetudinar•ium -(i)i *n*
hospitality *s* hospitalit•as -atis *f*
host *s (entertainer)* hosp•es -itis *m; (army)* copi•ae -arum *fpl; (immense number)* multitud•o -inis *f; (wafer)* hosti•a -ae *f*
hostage *s* obs•es -idis *mf*
hostess *s* hospit•a -ae *f; (at an inn)* caupon•a -ae *f*
hostile *adj* infens•us -a -um; *(forces, soil)* hostil•is -is -e; **in a** — **manner** hostiliter, infense
hot *adj* calid•us -a -um; *(boiling)* ferv•ens

-entis; *(seething)* aestuos·us -a -um; *(of spices)* a·cer -cris -cre; *(fig)* ard·ens -entis; **to be** — calēre; **to become** — calescĕre; **to be in** — **water** *(coll)* in angustiis versari

hotel *s* hospit·ium -(i)i *n*

hot-headed *adj* cerebros·us -a -um

hot-tempered *adj* stomachos·us -a -um

hound *s* catul·us -i *m*

hound *tr* instare *(w. dat)*

hour *s* hor·a -ae *f;* **at all** —s omnibus horis; **from** — **to** — in horas

hourly *adv* in horas

house *s* dom·us -ūs *m,* aed·es -ium *fpl; (family)* dom·us -ūs *m,* gen·s -tis *f;* **at the** — **of** apud *(w. acc)*

house *tr* domo excipĕre; *(things)* condĕre

housebreaker *s* effractar·ius -(i)i *m*

household *adj* familiar·is -is -e

household *s* famili·a -ae *f*

householder *s* paterfamilias *(gen:* patris- familias) *m*

household gods *spl* Lar·es et Penat·es -um *mpl*

housekeeper *s* prom·us -i *m*

housekeeping *s* rei familiaris cur·a -ae *f*

housemaid *s* ancill·a -ae *f*

housewife *s* materfamilias *(gen:* matris- familias) *f*

hovel *s* tugur·ium -(i)i *n*

hover *intr* pendēre; **to** — **over** impendēre *(w. dat)*

how *adv* quomodo, quo pacto; *(to what degree)* quam; — **far is Rome from Veii?** quantum distat Roma a Veiis?; — **long ago** quam pridem, quam dudum; — **many** quot; — **much** quantum; — **often** quotiens; — **soon** quam dudum

however *adv (nevertheless)* tamen, autem; *(in whatever way)* quoquomodo; *(to whatever degree)* quamvis *(esp. w. adj or adv; followed by subj);* — **great** quant·uscumque -acumque -umcumque; — **many** quotquot; — **often** quoties- cumque

howl *s* ululat·us -ūs *m*

howl *intr (lit & fig)* ululare

hub *s* ax·is -is *m*

hubbub *s* tumult·us -ūs *m; (noise of brawl- ing)* convic·ium -(i)i *n*

huckster *s* instit·or -oris *m*

huddle *intr* coacervari; —**ed together** confert·i -ae -a

huddle *s* coron·a -ae *f*

hue *s* col·or -oris *m;* **to raise a** — **and a cry** conclamare; *(to complain)* conqueri

huff *s* offensi·o -onis *f;* **to be in a** — stomachari

huff *intr* stomachari

hug *s* complex·us -ūs *m*

hug *tr* complecti, amplecti

huge *adj* ing·ens -entis; *(of monstrous size)* imman·is -is -e; — **sum of money** ingens

pecuni·a -ae *f*

hugeness *s* immanit·as -atis *f*

hulk *s (hull of unseaworthy ship)* alve·us -i *m* desertus; *(heavy ship)* nav·is -is *f* oneraria

hulking, hulky *adj* grav·is -is -e

hull *s* alve·us -i *m*

hum *s* murm·ur -uris *m; (of bees)* bomb·us -i *m*

hum *intr* murmurare; *(of bees)* bombilare

human *adj* human·us -a -um; — **feelings** humanit·as -atis *f*

human being *s* hom·o -inis *m*

humane *adj* human·us -a -um

humanely *adv* humane

humanity *s* humanit·as -atis *f; (people)* homin·es -um *mpl*

humanize *tr* excolĕre

humble *adj (modest)* summiss·us -a -um; *(obscure)* humil·is -is -e

humble *tr* deprimĕre; **to** — **oneself before s.o.** se summittĕre alicui

humbly *adv* summisse

humdrum *adj (dull)* molest·us -a -um; *(banal)* trit·us -a -um

humid *adj* humid·us -a -um

humidity *s* hum·or -oris *m*

humiliate *tr* deprimĕre

humiliating *adj* humil·is -is -e

humiliation *s* humilati·o -onis *f*

humility *s* humilit·as -atis *f*

humor *s* festivit·as -atis *f; (mood)* anim·us -i *m;* **he is in bad** — tristis est; **he is in good** — festivus est; **sense of** — festivit·as -atis *f*

humor *tr* indulgēre *(w. dat)*

humorous *adj* facet·us -a -um

humorously *adv* festive

hump *s* gibb·er -eris *m*

humpbacked *adj* gibb·er -era -erum

hunch *s* opini·o -onis *f;* **to have a** — opinari

hundred *adj* centum *(indecl);* — **times** centie(n)s

hundredfold *adj* centupl·ex -icis

hundredfold *s* centupl·um -i *n*

hundredth *adj* centesim·us -a -um

hunger *s* fam·es -is *f; (voluntary)* inedi·a -ae *f*

hunger *intr* esurire; **to** — **for** cupĕre

hungrily *adv* avide, voraciter

hungry *adj* esuri·ens -entis; **to be** —esurire

hunt *s* venati·o -onis *f*

hunt *tr* venari ‖ *intr* **to** — **for** quaerĕre

hunter *s* venat·or -oris *m; (horse)* equ·us -i *m* venaticus

hunting *s* venat·us -ūs *m;* **to go** — venari

hunting *adj* venatic·us -a -um; — **gear** venationis apparat·us -ūs *m* — **spear** venabul·um -i *n*

huntress *s* venatr·ix -icis *f*

hurdle *s* crat·es -is *f; (obstacle)* ob·ex -icis *mf*

hurl *tr* conjicĕre
hurray *interj* evax!
hurricane *s* procell·a -ae *f*
hurried *adj* praeproper·us -a -um; *(too hasty)* praec·eps -ipitis
hurriedly *adv* raptim; *(carelessly)* negligenter
hurry *tr* rapĕre; **to — away** abripĕre **‖** *intr* properare, festinare; *(to rush hurriedly)* ruĕre; **to — along** se agĕre
hurry *s* festinati·o -onis *f;* **in a —** festinanter; **to be in a —** festinare
hurt *s* injuri·a -ae *f*
hurt *adj* sauci·us -a -um; *(emotionally)* sauci·us -a -um, offens·us -a -um
hurt *tr* nocēre *(w. dat)*, laedĕre; *(fig)* offendĕre **‖** *intr* dolēre
husband *s* marit·us -i *m*
husbandry *s* agricultur·a -ae *f*
hush *s* silent·ium -(i)i *n*
hush *tr* comprimĕre; *(a secret)* celare **‖** *intr* tacēre
hush *interj* st!
husk *s* follicul·us -i *m; (of beans, etc.)* siliqu·a -ae *f; (of grain)* glum·a -ae *f*
husky *adj* robust·us -a -um; *(of voice)* rauc·us -a -um
hustle *tr* trudĕre **‖** *intr* inter se trudĕre
hustler *s* hom·o -inis *m* strenuus
hut *s* tugur·ium -(i)i *n*
hyacinth *s* hyacinth·us -i *m*
hybrid *s* hybrid·a -ae *f*
Hydra *s* Hydr·a -ae *f*
hydraulic *adj* hydraulic·us -a -um
hydrophobia *s* hydrophobi·a -ae *f*
hyena *s* hyaen·a -ae *f*
hymn *s* hymn·us -i *m*
hyperbole *s* hyperbol·e -es *f*
hypercritical *adj* nimis sever·us -a -um
hyphen *s* hyphen *(indecl) n*
hypochondriac *s* melancholic·us -i *m*
hypocrisy *s* simulati·o -onis *f*
hypocrite *s* simulat·or -oris *m*
hypocritical *adj* simulat·us -a -um
hypothesis *s* hypothes·is -is *m*
hypothetical *adj* hypothetic·us -a -um
hysteria *s* delirati·o -onis *f*
hysterical *adj* delir·us -a -um

I

I *pron* ego; **— myself** egomet
iamb *s (pros)* iamb·us -i *m*
iambic *adj (pros)* iambe·us -a -um
ice *s* glaci·es -ei *f*
iceberg *s* glaciei niviumque concreta stru·es -is *f*
ice water *s* nivata aqu·a -ae *f*
icicle *s* stiri·a -ae *f*
icy *adj* glacial·is -is -e
idea *s (notion)* noti·o -onis *f; (thought)*

sententi·a -ae *f;* **it's a good — to expedit** *(w. inf)*
ideal *adj* perfect·us -a -um
ideal *s* exempl·ar -aris *n*
idealist *s* hom·o -inis *m* summae virtutis
idealistic *adj* omnibus virtutibus ornat·us -i *m*
identical *adj* idem eadem idem
identify *tr* agnoscĕre
idiocy *s* fatuit·as -atis *f*
idiosyncrasy *s* propr·ium -(i)i *n*
idiot *s* fatu·us -i *m*
idiotic *adj* fatu·us -a -um
idle *adj* vacu·us -a -um; *(pointless)* van·us -a -um; *(lazy)* ignav·us -a -um; **to be —** cessare
idle *tr* **to — away** terĕre **‖** *intr* cessare, vacare
idleness *s* cessati·o -onis *f*
idler *s* cessat·or -oris *m*
idle talk *s* nug·ae -arum *fpl*
idly *adv* segniter
idol *s* simulacr·um -i *n; (eccl)* idol·um -i *n; (fig)* delici·ae -arum *fpl*
idolater *s* idololatr·es -ae *m*
idolatrous *adj* idololatric·us -a -um
idolatry *s* idololatri·a -ae *f*
idolize *tr* venerari
idyl *s* idyll·ium -(i)i *n*
if *conj* si; **as —** quasi, tamquam; **and —,** **but —** quodsi; **even —** etiamsi; **— not** ni, nisi; **— only** si modo
iffy *adj (coll)* dubi·us -a -um
igneous *adj* igne·us -a -um
ignite *tr* accendĕre **‖** *intr* flammam concipĕre, exardescĕre
ignoble *adj* ignobil·is -is -e; *(base)* turp·is -is -e
ignobly *adv* turpiter
ignominious *adj* ignominios·us -a -um
ignominiously *adv* ignominiose
ignominy *s* ignomini·a -ae *f*
ignoramus *s* nesap·ius -(i)i *m,* nesapi·a -ae *f*
ignorance *s* ignoranti·a -ae *f*
ignorant *adj* ignar·us -a -um; *(unlearned)* indoct·us -a -um; **to be — of** ignorare
ignorantly *adv* inscienter
ignore *tr* praeterire; *(to omit)* neglegĕre
Iliad *s* Ili·as -adis *f*
ill *adj* aegrot·us -a -um; *(evil)* mal·us -a -um; **to be —** aegrotare; **to fall —** in morbum incidĕre
ill *adv* male
ill *s* mal·um -i *n*
ill-advised *adj* inconsult·us -a -um
ill-boding *adj* infaust·us -a -um
ill-bred *adj* inhuman·us -a -um
ill-disposed *adj (toward)* malevol·us -a -um *(w. dat)*
illegal *adj* illicit·us -a -um
illegitimate *adj* haud legitim·us -a -um; *(of birth)* noth·us -a -um

illegitimately *adv* contra legem
ill-fated *adj* infel·ix -icis
ill-gotten *adj* male part·us -a -um
ill health *s* valetud·o -inis *f*; adversa
illiberal *adj* illiberal·is -is -e
illicit *adj* illicit·us -a -um
illicitly *adv* illicite
illiteracy *s* ignorati·o -onis *f* legendi scribendique
illiterate *adj* illiterat·us -a -um
illness *s* morb·us -i *m*
illogical *adj* absurd·us -a -um
illogically *adv* absurde
ill-omened *adj* infel·ix -icis
ill-starred *adj* infel·ix -icis
ill-tempered *adj* iracund·us -a -um
illuminate *tr* illuminare
illumination *s* illuminati·o -onis *f*
illusion *s* err·or -oris *m*
illusive *adj* van·us -a -um
illusory *adj* fall·ax -acis
illustrate *tr (to shed light on)* illustrare; *(to exemplify)* exempla *(w. gen)* adducĕre; *(to draw)* delineare; *(to picture)* in tabulis depingĕre
illustration *s (example)* exempl·um -i *n; (picture)* tabul·a -ae *f*
illustrious *adj* illustr·is -is -e
ill will *s* malevolenti·a -ae *f*
image *s* sign·um -i *n; (esp. a portrait or bust)* imag·o -inis *f; (esp. a figure of a god)* simulacr·um -i *n*
imagery *s* imagin·es -um *fpl*
imaginary *adj* commentici·us -a -um
imagination *s* cogitati·o -onis *f*
imaginative *adj* ingenios·us -a -um
imagine *tr* fingĕre
imbecile *s* fatu·us -i *m*
imbedded *adj* (in) infix·us -a -um (in + *abl*)
imbibe *tr* imbibĕre
imbue *tr* imbuĕre
imitate *tr* imitari
imitation *s (act)* imitati·o -onis *f; (thing)* imag·o -inis *f*
imitator *s* imitat·or -oris *m,* imitatr·ix -icis *f*
immaculate *adj* immaculat·us -a -um
immaterial *adj* incorporal·is -is -e; *(unimportant)* nullius momenti
immeasurable *adj* immens·us -a -um
immeasurably *adv* longe longeque
immediate *adj* proxim·us -a -um
immediately *adv* statim, confestim; — after sub *(w. acc)*
immemorial *adj* antiquissim·us -a -um; from time — ex omni memoria aetatum
immense *adj* immens·us -a -um
immensely *adv* vehementer
immensity *s* immensit·as -atis *f*
immerse *tr* (im)mergĕre
immersion *s* immersi·o -onis *f*
imminent *adj* immin·ens -entis; to be — instare

immobile *adj* immobil·is -is -e
immobility *s* immobilit·as -atis *f*
immoderate *adj* immodic·us -a -um
immoderately *adv* immodicᵉ
immodesty *s* immodesti·a -ae *f*
immolate *tr* immolare
immolation *s* immolati·o -onis *f*
immoral *adj* prav·us -a -um
immorality *s* perditi mor·es -um *mpl*
immortal *adj* immortal·is -is -e
immortality *s* immortalit·as -atis *f*
immortalize *tr* immortalitati tradĕre
immovable *adj (lit & fig)* immobil·is -is -e
immunity *s* immunit·as -atis *f;* promise of — fid·es -ei *f* publica
immutability *s* immutabilit·as -atis *f*
immutable *adj* immutabil·is -is -e
imp *s* pu·er -eri *m* protervus
impact *s* impuls·us -ūs *m*
impair *tr* imminuĕre
impale *tr* palo infigĕre; — oneself on a pointed stake se acuto vallo induĕre
impart *tr* impertire, communicare
impartial *adj* aequ·us -a -um
impartiality *s* aequit·as -atis *f*
impartially *adv* aequabiliter, to judge — aequo (animo) judicare
impassable *adj* impervi·us -a -um
impassioned *adj* vehem·ens -entis; with — gestures ardenti motu gestuque
impassive *adj* sensu car·ens -entis
impatience *s* impatienti·a -ae *f*
impatient *adj* iniquo animo; to be — with iniquo animo ferre
impatiently *adv* iniquo animo
impeach *tr* nomen *(w. gen)* deferre
impeachment *s* delati·o -onis *f* nominis
impede *tr* impedire
impediment *s* impediment·um -i *n; (in speech)* haesitati·o -onis *f*
impel *tr* impellĕre
impending *adj* immin·ens -entis
impenetrable *adj* impenetrabil·is -is -e; *(fig)* occult·us -a -um
impenitence *s* impaenitenti·a -ae *f*
imperative *adj* inst·ans -antis; *(gram)* imperativ·us -a -um
imperceptible *adj* tenuissim·us -a -um
imperceptibly *adv* sensim
imperfect *adj* imperfect·us -a -um
imperfection *s* vit·ium -(i)i *n*
imperfectly *adv* imperfecte
imperial *adj (of an emperor)* principal·is -is -e; *(becoming an emperor)* august·us -a - um
imperil *tr* in discrimen adducĕre
imperious *adj* imperios·us -a -um
imperiously *adv* imperiose
imperishable *adj* incorrupt·us -a -um
impermeable *adj* impervi·us -a -um
impersonal *adj (detached)* incurios·us -a -um; *(gram)* impersonal·is -is -e
impersonally *adv* impersonaliter

impersonate *tr* sustinēre partes *(w. gen)*
impertinence *s* protervit·as -atis *f*
impertinent *adj* proterv·us -a -um; *(not to the point)* nihil ad rem
impertinently *adv* proterve
impervious *adj* impervi·us -a -um
impetuosity *s* impet·us -ūs *m*
impetuous *adj* violent·us -a -um
impetus *s* impet·us -ūs *m*
impiety *s* impiet·as -atis *f*
impinge *intr* — on incidĕre *(w. dat)*
impious *adj* impi·us -a -um; *(stronger)* nefari·us -a -um
impiously *adv* impie; *(stronger)* nefarie
impish *adj* proterv·us -a -um
implacable *adj* implacabil·is -is -e
implacably *adv* implacabiliter
implant *tr* inserĕre, ingenerare
implement *s* instrument·um -i *n; (iron tool)* ferrament·um -i *n*
implement *tr* exsequi
implicate *tr* implicare
implication *s* indic·ium -(i)i *n;* **by** — tacite
implicit *adj* tacit·us -a -um; *(absolute)* summ·us -a -um
implicitly *adv* tacite
implied *adj* tacit·us -a -um; **to be — in** inesse in *(w. abl)*
implore *tr* implorare
imply *tr* significare
impolite *adj* inurban·us -a -um
impolitely *adv* inurbane
impoliteness *s* inurbanit·as -atis *f*
impolitic *adj* inconsult·us -a -um
import *tr* importare, invehĕre
import *s (meaning)* significati·o -onis *f;* **—s** importatici·a -orum *npl*
importance *s* moment·um -i *n;* **of** — grav·is -is -e; **to be a person of great —** plurimum pollēre; **to be of great —** magni esse
important *adj* magn·us -a -um; *(weighty)* grav·is -is -e; **an — and wealthy city** gravis atque opulenta civit·as -atis *f;* **to be —** magni (momenti *or* negotii) esse; **to be very —** maximi (momenti *or* negotii) esse
importunate *adj* importun·us -a -um
importune *tr* flagitare, sollicitare
impose *tr* imponĕre; *(to enjoin)* injungĕre ‖ *intr* **to — upon** abuti *(w. abl)*
imposition *s (excessive burden)* importunit·as -atis *f; (act)* use imponĕre
impossibility *s* impossibilit·as -atis *f*
impossible *adj* impossibil·is -is -e; **it is —** non fieri potest
imposter *s* fraudat·or -oris *m*
imposture *s* frau·s -dis *f*
impotence *s* infirmit·as -atis *f; (sexual)* sterilit·as -atis *f*
impotent *adj* infirm·us -a -um; *(sexually)* steril·is -is -e
impound *tr* publicare; *(animals)* includĕre

impoverish *tr* in egestatem redigĕre
impoverished *adj* eg·ens -entis
impractical *adj* inutil·is -is -e
imprecate *tr* imprecari, exsecrari
imprecation *s* exsecrati·o -onis *f*
impregnable *adj* inexpugnabil·is -is -e
impregnate *tr* gravidam facĕre
impregnation *s* fecundati·o -onis *f*
impress *tr* imprimĕre; *(a person)* movēre; **to — s.th. on s.o.** alicui inculcare aliquid *(w. dat)*
impression *s* impressi·o -onis *f; (copy)* exempl·ar -aris *n;* **to make an — on** (com)movēre
impressive *adj* grav·is -is -e
impressively *adv* graviter
imprint *s* impressi·o -onis *f*
imprint *tr* imprimĕre; **to be —ed on the mind** in animum imprimi
imprison *tr* in vincula conjicĕre
imprisonment *s* custodi·a -ae *f*
improbable *adj* haud credibil·is -is -e
impromptu *adj* subit(ari)·us -a -um
impromptu *adv* ex tempore
improper *adj* indecor·us -a -um
improperly *adv* indecore
improve *tr* mel·iorem -iorem -ius facĕre; *(where a fault exists)* emendare; *(soil)* laetificare ‖ *intr* mel·ior -ior -ius fieri
improvement *s* emendati·o -onis *f; (progress made)* profect·us -ūs *m;* **to make —** proficĕre
improvident *adj* improvid·us -a -um
improvise *tr* ex tempore dicĕre *or* componĕre
imprudence *s* imprudenti·a -ae *f*
imprudent *adj* imprud·ens -entis
imprudently *adv* imprudenter
impugn *tr* inpugnare, in dubium vocare
impulse *s* impet·us -ūs *m* animi
impulsive *adj* temerari·us -a -um
impulsively *adv* impetu quodam animi
impunity *s* impunit·as -atis *f;* **with —** impune
impure *adj* impur·us -a -um
impurely *adv* impure
impurity *s* impurit·as -atis *f*
in *prep* in *(w. abl); (in the writings of)* apud *(w. acc); (of time)* render by *abl; (denoting rule, standard or manner)* in *(w. acc),* e.g., **— the manner of slaves** servilem in modum; **— that** quod; **— the course of the night** de nocte; **— the course of the third watch** de tertia vigilia; **— the likeness of** ad similitudinem *(w. gen);* **— the month of September** (de) mense Septembri; **— the same manner** ad eundem modum, eodem modo
in *adv (motion)* intro; *(rest)* intra, intus
inability *s* impotenti·a -ae *f*
inaccessible *adj* inacess·us -a -um; **to be — (of a person)** rari aditūs esse
inaccuracy *s* indiligenti·a -ae *f*

inaccurate *adj* parum accurat·us -a -um
inaccurately *adv* parum accurate
inactive *adj* iner·s -tis
inactivity *s* inerti·a -ae *f*
inadequate *adj* im·par -paris
inadequately *adv* parum, haud satis
inadmissible *adj* illicit·us -a -um
inadvertent *adj* imprud·ens -entis
inadvertently *adv* imprudenter; *more frequently expressed by the adjective* imprud·ens -entis
inalienable *adj* quod alienari non potest
inane *adj* inan·is -is -e
inanimate *adj* inanim·us -a -um
inapplicable *adj* to be — non valēre
inappropriate *adj* haud apt·us -a -um
inappropriately *adv* parum apte
inarticulate *adj* indistinct·us -a -um
inartistic *adj* dur·us -a -um
inasmuch as *conj* quandoquidem
inattentive *adj* haud attent·us -a -um
inattentively *adv* neglegenter
inaudible *adj* to be — audiri non posse
inaugurate *tr* inaugurare
inauguration *s* inaugurati·o -onis *f*
inauspicious *adj* infaust·us -a -um
inauspiciously *adv* malo omine
inborn *adj* innat·us -a -um
incalculable *adj* inaestimabil·is -is -e; *(fig)* immens·us -a -um
incantation *s* incantament·um -i *n*
incapable *adj* incap·ax -acis; to be — of non posse *(w. inf)*
incapacitate *tr* debilitare
incarcerate *tr* in carcerem conjicĕre
incarnate *adj* incarnat·us -a -um
incarnation *s* incarnati·o -onis *f*
incautious *adj* incaut·us -a -um
incautiously *adv* incaute
incendiary *adj* incendiari·us -a -um
incense *s* tu·s -ris *n*
incense *tr* ture fumigare; *(to anger)* incendĕre
incentive *s* incitament·um -i *n*
incessant *adj* assidu·us -a -um
incessantly *adv* assidue
incest *s* incest·us -ūs *m*
incestuous *adj* incest·us -a -um
inch *s* unci·a -ae *f;* — by — unciatim
incident *s* cas·us -ūs *m*
incidental *adj* fortuit·us -a -um
incidentally *adv* casu, inter alias res
incision *s* incisur·a -ae *f*
incisive *adj* a·cer -cris -cre
incite *tr* incitare
incitement *s* incitament·um -i *n*
incivility *s* rusticit·as -atis *f*
inclemency *s* inclementi·a -ae *f; (of weather)* asperit·as -atis *f*
inclement *adj* asp·er -era -erum
inclination *s (act, propensity)* inclinati·o -onis *f; (slope)* proclivit·as -atis *f*
incline *s* acclivit·as -atis *f*

incline *tr & intr* inclinare
inclined *adj* propens·us -a -um; I am — to believe crediderim
include *tr (to enclose)* includĕre; *(to comprise)* comprehendĕre; —ing me me haud excepto; —ing your brother in his frater tuus
inclusive *adj expressed by* adnumerare: from the 1st to the 10th — a primo die ad decimum adnumeratum *(or* ipso decimo adnumerato)*
incognito *adv* alienā indutā personā
incoherent *adj* perturbat·us -a -um; to be — non cohaerēre
incoherently *adv* to speak — male cohaerentia loqui
income *s* quaest·us -ūs *m*
incomparable *adj* incomparabil·is -is -e
incomparably *adv* unice
incompatibility *s* repugnanti·a -ae *f*
incompatible *adj* repugn·ans -antis
incompetence *s* insciti·a -ae *f*
incompetent *adj* inscit·us -a -um
incomplete *adj* imperfect·us -a -um
incomprehensible *adj* quod mente non comprehendi potest
inconceivable *adj* incredibil·is -is -e
inconclusive *adj* anc·eps -ipitis
incongruous *adj* male congru·ens -entis, inconveni·ens -entis
inconsiderable *adj* exigu·us -a -um
inconsiderate *adj* inconsiderat·us -a -um
inconsistency *s* discrepanti·a -ae *f*
inconsistent *adj* inconst·ans -antis; to be — with abhorrēre ab *(w. abl)*
inconsistently *adv* inconstanter
inconsolable *adj* inconsolabil·is -is -e
inconstancy *s* inconstanti·a -ae *f*
inconstant *adj* inconst·ans -antis
incontestible *adj* non contentend·us -a -um
incontinence *s* incontinenti·a -ae *f*
incontinent *adj* incontin·ens -entis
incontrovertible *adj* quod refutari non potest
inconvenience *s* incommod·um -i *n*
inconvenience *tr* incommodare
inconvenient *adj* incommod·us -a -um
inconveniently *adv* incommode
incorporate *tr* adjicĕre; *(to unite, esp. politically)* contribuĕre; *(to form into a corporation)* constituĕre
incorporeal *adj* incorporal·is -is -e
incorrect *adj* mendos·us -a -um
incorrectly *adv* perperam
incorrigible *adj* perdit·us -a -um
incorrigibly *adv* perdite
incorrupt *adj* incorrupt·us -a -um
incorruptibility *s* incorruptibilit·as -atis *f*
incorruptible *adj* incorruptibil·is -is -e; *(upright)* inte·ger -gra -grum
increase *s* increment·um -i *n; (act)* accreti·o -onis *f*
increase *tr* augēre, ampliare ‖ *intr* augeri,

crescĕre
incredible *adj* incredibil·is -is -e
incredibly *adv* incredibiliter
incredulity *s* incredulit·as -atis *f*
incredulous *adj* incredul·us -a -um
increment *s* increment·um -i *n*
incriminate *tr* criminari
incubate *tr* incubare
incubation *s* incubati·o -onis *f*
inculcate *tr* inculcare
inculcation *s* inculcati·o -onis *f*
incumbent *adj* it is — on oportet *(w. acc)*
incumbent *s* qui honorem gerit
incur *tr* subire; *(guilt)* admittĕre
incurable *adj* insanabil·is -is -e
incursion *s* incursi·o -onis *f*
indebted *adj* obaerat·us -a -um; *(obliged)* obnoxi·us -a -um; to be — to s.o. for a sum of money pecuniam alicui debēre
indecency *s* impudicit·as -atis *f*
indecent *adj* impudic·us -a -um
indecently *adv* impudice
indecision *s* haesitati·o -onis *f*
indecisive *adj* anc·eps -ipitis
indeclinable *adj* indeclinabil·is -is -e
indeed *adv* vere, profecto; *(concessive)* quidem; *(reply)* certe, vero; *(interrog)* itane?
indefatigable *adj* indefatigabil·is -is -e
indefensible *adj* *(an action)* non excusand·us -a -um; *(mil)* parum firm·us -a -um; to be — defendi non posse
indefinite *adj* incert·us -a -um; *(vague)* anc·eps -ipitis; *(gram)* infinit·us -a -um
indelible *adj* indelibil·is -is -e
indelicate *adj* putid·us -a -um
indemnify *tr* damnum restitutĕre *(w. dat)*
indemnity *s* indemnit·as -atis *f*
indent *tr* incisuris signare
indentation *s* incisur·a -ae *f*
indented *adj* incis·us -a -um; *(serrated)* serrat·us -a -um
independence *s* libert·as -atis *f*
independent *adj* lib·er -era -erum; *(one's own master)* sui pot·ens -entis; *(leg)* sui juris
independently *adv* libere, suo arbitrio
indescribable *adj* inenarrabil·is -is -e
indescribably *adv* inenarrabiliter
indestructible *adj* perenn·is -is -e, indelebil·is -is -e
indeterminate *adj* indefinit·us -a -um
index *s* ind·ex -icis *m*
Indian *adj* Indic·us -a -um
Indian *s* Ind·us -i *m*
indicate *tr* indicare, significare; to — that docēre *(w. acc & inf)*
indication *s* indic·ium -(i)i *n*
indicative *s* *(gram)* indicativus mod·us -i *m*
indict *tr* nomen *(w. gen)* deferre
indictment *s* nominis delati·o -onis *f*; bill

of — libell·us -i *m*
indifference *s* aequus anim·us -i *m;* *(apathy)* lentitud·o -inis *f*
indifferent *adj* *(apathetic)* indiffer·ens -entis; *(mediocre)* mediocr·is -is -e; to be — to s.th. aliquid nil morari
indifferently *adv* indifferenter
indigenous *adj* *(home-grown)* vernacul·us -a -um; *(of people)* indigen·a -ae; the — Latins indigenae Latini
indigent *adj* eg·ens -entis
indigestible *adj* crud·us -a -um
indigestion *s* crudit·as -atis *f*
indignant *adj* indignabund·us -a -um; — at indign·ans -antis *(w. gen);* to be — indignari
indignantly *adv* indignanter
indignation *s* indignati·o -onis *f*
indignity *s* indignit·as -atis *f*
indirect *adj* indirect·us -a -um; — discourse obliqua orati·o -onis *f*
indirectly *adv* indirecte
indiscreet *adj* inconsult·us -a -um
indiscreetly *adv* inconsulte
indiscretion *s* imprudenti·a -ae *f;* driven by youthful — licentiā juvenali impuls·us -a -um
indiscriminate *adj* promiscu·us -a -um
indiscriminately *adv* sine discrimine
indispensable *adj* omnino necessari·us -a -um
indisposed *adj* (to) avers·us -a -um (ab + *abl);* *(sick)* aegrot·us -a -um
indisputable *adj* cert·us -a -um
indissoluble *adj* indissolubil·is -is -e
indistinct *adj* parum clar·us -a -um
indistinctly *adv* parum clare
individual *adj* *(of one only)* singular·is -is -e; *(of more than one)* singul·i -ae -a; *(particular)* quidam quaedam, quoddam; *(peculiar)* propri·us -a -um
individual *s* hom·o -inis *mf;* —s singul·i -ae -a; to benefit the country or —s civitatem aut singulis civibus prodesse
individually *adv* singulatim
individuality *s* proprium ingen·ium -(i)i *n*
indivisible *adj* indivisibil·is -is -e
indolence *s* inerti·a -ae *f*
indolent *adj* in·ers -ertis
indomitable *adj* indomit·us -a -um
indorse *tr* ratum facĕre
indubitable *adj* indubitabil·is -is -e
indubitably *adv* sine dubio
induce *tr* inducĕre, adducĕre
inducement *s* incitament·um -i *n*
indulge *tr* indulgēre *(w. dat)*
indulgent *adj* indulg·ens -entis
indulgently *adv* indulgenter
industrial *adj* ad artes quaestuosas pertin·ens -entis
industrialist *s* magis·ter -tri *m* officinarum
industrious *adj* industri·us -a -um
industriously *adv* industrie

industry s *(effort)* industri•a -ae f; *(com)* art•es -ium fpl quaestuosae
inebriated adj ebri•us -a -um
ineffable adj ineffabil•is -is -e
ineffective adj irrit•us -a -um; **to be —** effectu carēre
ineffectual adj ineffic•ax -acis
ineffectually adv frustra
inefficiency s segniti•a -ae f
inefficient adj segn•is -is -e
inelegant adj ineleg•ans -antis
ineligible adj non eligend•us -a -um
inept adj inept•us -a -um
ineptitude s inepti•ae -arum fpl
inequality s inaequalit•as -atis f *(social)* iniquit•as -atis f
inequitable adj iniqu•us -a -um
inert adj in•ers -ertis
inertia s inerti•a -ae f
inevitable adj inevitabil•is -is -e
inevitably adv necessario
inexact adj haud accurat•us -a -um; *(of persons)* indilig•ens -entis
inexcusable adj inexcusabil•is -is -e
inexhaustible adj inexhaust•us -a -um
inexorable adj inexorabil•is is -e
inexperience s imperiti•a -ae f
inexperienced adj imperit•us -a -um
inexplicable adj inexplicabil•is -is -e
inexpressible adj inenarrabil•is -is -e
inextricable adj inextricabil•is -is -e
infallibility s erroris immunit•as -atis f
infallible adj qui errare non potest
infamous adj infam•is -is -e
infamously adv cum infamia
infancy s infanti•a -ae f
infant s inf•ans -antis mf
infanticide s *(deed)* infanticid•ium -(i)i n; *(person)* infanticid•a -ae m
infantile adj infantil•is -is -e
infantry s peditat•us -ūs m
infatuate tr infatuare; *(w. love)* urēre
infatuated adj mente capt•us -a -um
infatuation s dementi•a -ae f
infect tr inficĕre; *(fig)* contaminare
infection s contagi•o -onis f
infectious adj contagios•us -a -um
infer tr colligĕre, conjicĕre
inference s conjectur•a -ae f
inferior adj deter•ior -ior -ius
infernal adj infern•us -a -um
infertile adj steril•is -is -e
infertility s sterilit•as -atis f
infest tr infestare
infidel s infidel•is -is mf
infidelity s infidelit•as -atis f
infiltrate tr se insinuare in *(w. acc)*
infinite adj infinit•us -a -um
infinitely adv infinite; *(coll)* infinito
infinitive s infinitiv•um -i n
infinity s infinit•as -atis f
infirm adj infirm•us -a -um
infirmary s valetudinar•ium -(i)i n

infirmity s infirmit•as -atis f
inflame tr *(lit & fig)* inflammare; *(fig)* incendĕre
inflammable adj ad exardescendum facil•is -is -e
inflammation s inflammati•o -onis f
inflammatory adj turbulent•us -a -um
inflate tr inflare
inflated adj inflat•us -a -um
inflation s inflati•o -onis f
inflect tr *(gram)* declinare
inflection s declinati•o -onis f
inflexible adj inflexibil•is -is -e; *(fig)* obstinat•us -a -um
inflexibly adv obstinate
inflict tr infligĕre, inferre; **to — a deadly blow** mortiferam plagam infligĕre; **to — punishment on s.o.** aliquem supplicio afficĕre; **to — wounds on** vulnera inferre *(w. dat)*
influence s grati•a -ae f; **to have — on** valēre apud *(w. acc);* **to have (great, more, very great) influence on** magnum (plus, plurimum) posse apud *(w. acc)*
influence tr movēre
influential adj auctoritate grav•is -is -e
influenza s catarrh•us -i m
influx s influxi•o -onis f
inform tr certiorem facĕre, docēre; **having been —ed about this** his rebus cognitis ‖ intr **to — against** deferre de *(w. abl)*
informant s ind•ex -icis m
information s re•s -rum fpl, nunt•ius -(i)i m; **having received this —** his rebus cognitis
informer s delat•or -oris m
infraction s infracti•o -onis f
infrequency s rarit•as -atis f
infrequent adj rar•us -a -um
infrequently adv raro
infringe tr infringĕre ‖ intr **to — upon** usurpare
infringement s immunuti•o -onis f
infuriate tr efferare
infuse tr infundĕre; *(fig)* injicĕre
infusion s infusi•o -onis f
ingenious adj ingenios•us -a -um, soll•ers -ertis
ingeniously adv sollerter
ingenuity s sollerti•a -ae f
ingenuous adj ingenu•us -a -um
ingest tr ingerĕre
inglorious adj inglori•us -a -um
ingloriously adv sine gloriā
ingrained adj insit•us -a -um
ingratiate tr **to — oneself with** gratiam inire ab *(w. abl)*
ingratitude s ingratus anim•us -i m
ingredient s *(generally not expressed by a noun)* element•um -i n; **a composition, the —s of which** compositio quae habet;

the medication consists of the following —s medicamentum constat ex his
inhabit *tr* incolĕre
inhabitable *adj* habitabil·is -is -**e**
inhabitant *s* incol·a -ae *mf*
inhale *tr* haurire, ducĕre **‖** *intr* spiritum
ducĕre
inharmonious *adj* disson·us -a -um
inherent *adj* inhaer·ens -entis; **to be — in**
inhaerēre in *(w. abl),* inesse in *(w. abl)*
inherit *tr* excipĕre
inheritance *s* heredit·as -atis *f;* **to come
into an —** hereditatem adire
inhospitable *adj* inhospital·is -is -e
inhuman *adj* inhuman·us -a -um
inhumanly *adv* inhumane
inhumanity *s* inhumanit·as -atis *f*
inimical *adj* inimic·us -a -um
inimitable *adj* inimitabil·is -is -e
iniquitous *adj* improb·us -a -um
iniquity *s* improbit·as -atis *f*
initial *adj* prim·us -a -um
initial *s* prima nominis litter·a -ae *f*
initiate *tr* initiare
initiation *s* initiati·o -onis *f*
initiative *s* vis *f*
inject *tr* injicĕre, immittĕre
injection *s* injecti·o -onis *f*
injudicious *adj* inconsult·us -a -um
injudiciously *adv* inconsulte
injunction *s* mandat·um -i *n;* **to get an —**
ad interdictum venire
injure *tr* nocēre *(w. dat),* laedĕre
injurious *adj* noxi·us -a -um
injury *s* detriment·um -i *n;* **to do great —**
magnum detrimentum adferre
injustice *s* injustiti·a -ae *f; (act of injustice)* injuri·a -ae *f*
ink *s* atrament·um -i *n*
inkling *s* obscura significati·o -onis *f;* **to
have an —** suspicari
inland *adj* mediterrane·us -a -um
in-law *s* affin·is -is *mf*
inlay *tr* inserĕre; *(with mosaic)* tessellare
inlet *s* aestuar·ium -(i)i *n*
inmate *s* inquilin·us -i *m*
inmost *adj* intim·us -a -um
inn *s* deversor·ium -(i)i *n, (esp. of an inferior type)* caupon·a -ae *f*
innate *adj* innat·us -a -um
inner *adj* inter·ior -ior -ius
innermost *adj* intim·us -a -um
innkeeper *s* caup·o -onis *m; (female)*
caupon·a -ae *f*
innocence *s* innocenti·a -ae *f*
innocent *adj* innoc·ens -entis
innocently *adv* innocenter
innocuous *adj* innocu·us -a -um
innocuously *adv* innocue
innovate *tr* novare
innovation *s* novit·as -atis *f*
innovative *adj* multa nov·ans -antis
innovator *s* qui multa novat

innumerable *adj* innumerabil·is -is -e
inoculate *tr* serum inserĕre *(w. dat)*
inoffensive *adj* innoxi·us -a -um
inopportune *adj* inopportun·us -a -um
inopportunely *adv* parum in tempore
inordinate *adj* immoderat·us -a -um
inordinately *adv* immoderate
inquest *s* inquisiti·o -onis *f; (leg)* quaesti·o
-onis *f;* **an — was held on the cause of
death** quaesitum est quae mortis causa
fuisset
inquire *intr* **(into)** inquirĕre
inquiry *s* quaesti·o -onis *f*
inquisition *s* inquisiti·o -onis *f*
inquisitive *adj* curios·us -a -um
inquisitor *s* quaesit·or -oris *m*
inroad *s* incursi·o -onis *f;* **to make —s
into territory** incursiones in fines facĕre
insane *adj* insan·us -a -um
insanely *adv* insane
insanity *s* insanit·as -atis *f*
insatiable *adj* insatiabil·is -is -e
inscribe *tr* inscribĕre
inscription *s* inscripti·o -onis *f*
inscrutable *adj* occult·us -a -um
insect *s* insect·um -i *n*
insecure *adj* haud tut·us -a -um
insecurity *s* **feeling of —** sollicitud·o
-inis *f*
insensible *adj* insensil·is -is -e; *(fig)* dur·us
-a -um
inseparable *adj* inseparabil·is -is -e
insert *tr* inserĕre, interponĕre; *(in writing)*
ascribĕre
insertion *s* interpositi·o -onis *f*
inside *adj* inter·ior -ior -ius
inside *adv* intus
inside *prep* intro *(w. acc)*
inside *s* interior par·s -tis *f*
inside of *prep* intra *(w. acc)*
insidious *adj* insidios·us -a -um
insidiously *adv* insidiose
insight *s* cogniti·o -onis *f;* **to have a profound — into human character** mores
hominum atque ingenia penitus perspecta
habēre
insignia *spl* insign·ia -ium *npl*
insignificance *s* exiguit·as -atis *f*
insignificant *adj* exigu·us -a -um, nullius
momenti
insincere *adj* insincer·us -a -um
insincerely *adv* haud sincere
insincerity *s* ingen·ium -(i)i *n* haud
sincerum
insinuate *tr* insinuare; *(to hint)* operte
significare
insinuation *s* significati·o -onis *f*
insipid *adj* insuls·us -a -um
insipidly *adv* insulse
insist *intr* instare; **to — on** urgēre
insistence *s* pertinaci·a -ae *f*
insolence *s* insolenti·a -ae *f*
insolent *adj* insol·ens -entis

insoluble *adj* insolubil·is -is -e; *(fig)* inexplicabil·is -is -e

insolvent *adj* decoct·us -a -um; **I am in-solvent** solvendo non sum

inspect *tr* inspicĕre; *(mil)* recensēre

inspection *s* inspecti·o -onis *f; (mil)* recensi·o -onis *f*

inspector *s* curat·or -oris *m*

inspiration *s (divine)* afflat·us -ūs *m; (prophetic)* fur·or -oris *m; (idea)* noti·o -onis *f*

inspire *tr* inspirare; **divinely —ed** divino spiritu instinct·us -a -um; **to — s.o. with courage** animos alicui addĕre; **to — s.o. with fear** alicui formidinem injicĕre

instability *s* instabilit·as -atis *f*

install *tr (mechanically)* instruĕre; *(w. augural solemnity)* inaugurare

installation *s* inaugurati·o -onis *f; (mechanical)* constructi·o -onis *f; (mil)* castr·a -orum *npl* stativa

installment *s (com)* pensi·o -onis *f*

instance *s* exempl·um -i *n;* **at my — me** auctore; **for —** exempli gratiā; **for — when** ut enim cum; **in this —** in hac re

instance *tr* memorare

instant *adj* praes·ens -entis; **this —** statim

instantaneous *adj* praes·ens -entis

instantaneously *adv* continuo

instead *adv* potius, magis

instead of *prep* pro *(w. abl)*

instigate *tr* instigare, concitare

instigation *s* instigati·o -onis *f;* **at your —** te auctore

instigator *s* instigat·or -oris *m*

instill *tr* instillare

instinct *s* natur·a -ae *f*

instinctive *adj* natural·is -is -e

instinctively *adv* naturā

institute *tr* instituĕre

institute *s* institut·um -i *n*

institution *s (act)* instituti·o -onis *f; (thing instituted)* institut·um -i *n*

instruct *tr (to teach)* instituĕre; *(to order)* mandare *(w. dat or* ut, ne)

instruction *s* instituti·o -onis *f,* doctrin·a -ae *f;* **—s** mandat·a -orum *npl;* **to give —s to** mandare *(w. dat)*

instructive *adj* ad docendum apt·us -a -um

instructor *s* doc·ens -entis *mf*

instrument *s* instrument·um -i *n; (mus)* organ·um -i *n; (leg)* syngraph·a -ae *f*

instrumental *s* util·is -is -e; **you were — in bringing s.th. to pass** tuā operā factum est; *(in negative sentences)* **you were instrumental in not...**per te stetit quominus

instrumentality *s* oper·a -ae *f*

insubordinate *adj (mutinous)* seditios·us -a -um; *(disobedient)* male par·ens -entis

insubordination *s (mutiny)* sediti·o -onis *f;* **to be guilty of —** per licentiam ducibus non parēre

insufferable *adj* intolerand·us -a -um

insufficiency *s* inop·ia -ae *f*

insufficient *adj* haud suffici·ens -entis

insufficiently *adv* haud satis

insular *adj* insulan·us -a -um

insulate *tr* segregare

insult *s* contumeli·a -ae *f*

insult *tr* contumeliā afficĕre

insulting *adj* contumelios·us -a -um

insultingly *adv* contumeliose

insuperable *adj* insuperabil·is -is -e

insurance *s* cauti·o -onis *f* indemnitatis

insurance company *s* eran·us -i *m*

insurance policy *s* cauti·o -onis *f* indemnitatis

insure *tr* praecavēre de damnis

insurgent *adj* rebell·is -is -e

insurgent *s* rebell·is -is *m*

insurmountable *adj* inexsuperabil·is -is -e

insurrection *s* rebelli·o -onis *f; (civil strife)* sediti·o -onis *f*

intact *adj* incolum·is -is -e

intangible *adj* intactil·is -is -e

integral *adj* necessari·us -a -um

integrity *s* integrit·as -atis *f*

intellect *s* intellect·us -ūs *m*

intellectual *adj* intelleg·ens -entis

intelligence *s* intellegenti·a -ae *f; (information)* nunti·us -(i)i *m*

intelligent *adj* intelleg·ens -entis

intelligently *adv* intellegenter

intelligible *adj* intelligibil·is -is -e

intelligibly *adv* intellegibiliter

intemperance *s* intemperanti·a -ae *f*

intemperately *adv* intemperanter

intend *tr* in animo habēre

intended *adj* destinat·us -a -um; *(of future spouse)* spons·us -a

intense *adj* a·cer -cris -cre; *(heat, cold)* magn·us -a -um; *(excessive)* nimi·us -a -um

intensively *adv* vehementer

intensify *tr* intendĕre

intensity *s* vehementi·a -ae *f,* vis *f*

intent *adj* intent·us -a -um; **to be — on** animum intendĕre in *(w. acc)*

intently *adv* intente

intention *s* consil·ium -(i)i *n; (meaning)* significati·o -onis *f*

intentionally *adv* de industriā

inter *tr* inhumare

intercede *intr (on behalf of)* deprecari (pro + *abl)*

intercept *tr* excipĕre

intercession *s* deprecati·o -onis *f; (of a tribune)* intercessi·o -onis *f*

intercessor *s* deprecat·or -oris *m*

interchange *s* permutati·o -onis *f*

interchange *tr* permutare

intercourse *s (sexual)* coït·us -ūs *m; (social)* consuetud·o -inis *f*

interdict *tr* interdicĕre *(w. acc of person*

and abl of thing; dat of person and acc of thing)
interdiction *s* interdicti·o -onis *f*
interest *s (attention)* stud·ium -(i)i *n; (advantage)* us·us -ūs *m; (fin)* faen·us -oris *n;* **it is in my —** meā interest
interest *tr (to affect the mind)* tenēre; *(to delight)* delectare; **children are —ed in games** liberi ludis tenentur
interested *adj* **— in** studios·us -a -um *(w. gen),* attent·us -a -um *(w. dat)*
interesting *adj* jucund·us -a -um
interfere *intr* se interponĕre *(w. dat); (to prevent s.th.)* intercedĕre; **the tribunes will not — with the praetor's making a motion** tribuni non praetori intercessuri sunt, quominus referat
interference *s* intercessi·o -onis *f*
interim *s* intervall·um -i *n;* **in the —** interim
interior *adj* inter·ior -ior -ius
interior *s* interior par·s -tis *f*
interjection *s* interjecti·o -onis *f*
interlinear *adj* interscript·us -a -um
interlude *s* embol·ium -(i)i *n*
intermarriage *s* connub·ium -(i)i *n*
intermarry *intr* matrimonio inter se conjungi
intermediary *s* internunti·us -(i)i *m*
intermediate *adj* medi·us -a -um
interment *s* sepultur·a -ae *f*
interminable *adj* infinit·us -a -um
intermission *s* intercaped·o -inis *f*
intermittent *adj* intermitt·ens -entis
intermittently *adv* interdum
internal *adj* intestin·us -a -um
internally *adv* intus, interne
international *adj* inter gentes
interpolate *tr* interpolare
interpolation *s* interpolati·o -onis *f*
interpret *tr* interpretari
interpretation *s* interpretati·o -onis *f*
interpreter *s* interpr·es -etis *mf*
interrogate *tr* interrogare
interrogation *s* interrogati·o -onis *f*
interrogative *adj* interrogativ·us -a -um
interrupt *tr* interrumpĕre; *(speech)* interpellĕre
interruption *s* interrupti·o -onis *f; (of a speaker)* interpellati·o -onis
intersect *tr* intersecare
intersection *s* intersecti·o -onis *f; (of roads)* quadriv·ium -(i)i *n*
intersperse *tr* inmiscēre
intertwine *tr* intertexĕre
interval *s* intervall·um -i *n*
intervene *intr (to be between)* interjacēre; *(to come between)* intercedĕre, intervenire
intervening *adj* medi·us -a -um
intervention *s* intervent·us -ūs *m*
interview *s* colloqu·ium -(i)i *n*
interview *tr* percontari

interweave *tr* intertexĕre
intestinal *adj* ad intestina pertin·ens -entis
intestine *adj* intestin·us -a -um
intestine *s* intestin·um -i *n;* **the small —** intestin·um -i *n* tenue
intimacy *s* consuetud·o -inis *f*
intimate *adj* familiar·is -is -e; *(stronger than preced.)* intim·us -a -um
intimately *adv* familiariter, intime
intimate *tr* indicare
intimation *s* indic·ium -(i)i *n*
intimidate *tr* absterrēre
intimidation *s* min·ae -arum *fpl*
into *prep* in *(w. acc)*
intolerable *adj* intolerabil·is -is -e
intolerably *adv* intoleranter
intolerance *s* intoleranti·a -ae *f*
intolerant *adj* intoler·ans -antis
intonation *s* accent·us -ūs *m*
intone *tr* cantare
intoxicate *tr* ebrium *(or* ebriam) reddĕre
intoxicated *adj* ebri·us -a -um
intoxication *s* ebriet·as -atis *f*
intractable *adj* intractabil·is -is -e
intrepid *adj* intrepid·us -a -um
intrepidly *adv* intrepide
intricate *adj* contort·us -a -um
intricately *adv* contorte
intrigue *s* artifici·a -orum *npl*
intrigue *tr* tenēre, capĕre
intriguing *adj* illecebros·us -a -um
intrinsic *adj* ver·us -a -um; **it has no — worth** res ipsa per se nullius pretii est
intrinsically *adv* vere
introduce *tr* inducĕre; *(a person)* tradĕre
introduction *s (preamble)* praefati·o -onis *f; (of a speech)* exord·ium -(i)i *n; (to a person)* introducti·o -onis *f*
instrospection *s* sui contemplati·o -onis *f*
introspective *adj* se ipsum inspici·ens -entis
introvert *s* hom·o -inis *m* umbraticus
intrude *intr* se interponĕre; **to — on** se imponĕre *(w. dat)*
intruder *s* intervent·or -oris *m; (into a home)* effract·or -oris *m*
intrusion *s* irrupti·o -onis *f*
intuition *s* intuit·us -ūs *m*
intuitive *adj* intuitiv·us -a -um
intuitively *adv* mentis propriā vi ac naturā
inundate *tr* inundare
inundation *s* inundati·o -onis *f*
invade *tr* invadĕre in *(w. acc)*
invader *s* invas·or -oris *m*
invalid *adj* irrit·us -a -um
invalid *s* aegrot·us -i *m,* aegrot·a -ae *f*
invalidate *tr* irrit·um -am -um facĕre
invaluable *adj* inaestimabil·is -is -e
invariable *adj* immutabil·is -is -e
invariably *adv* semper
invasion *s* incursi·o -onis *f*
invective *s* convic·ium -(i)i *n*

inveigh *intr* **to — against** invehi in *(w. acc),* insectari

invent *tr* invenire; *(to contrive)* excogitare, fingĕre

inventive *adj* ingenios·us -a -um

invention *s (act)* inventi·o -onis *f; (thing invented)* invent·um -i *n*

inventor *s* invent·or -oris *m,* inventr·ix -icis *f*

inventory *s* bonorum ind·ex -icis *m*

inverse *adj* invers·us -a -um

inversely *adv* inverso ordine

inversion *s* inversi·o -onis *f*

invert *tr* invertĕre

invest *tr (money)* collocare; *(to besiege)* obsidēre

investigate *tr* investigare; *(leg)* quaerĕre, cognoscĕre

investigation *s* investigati·o -onis *f; (leg)* cogniti·o -onis *f*

investigator *s* investigat·or -oris *m; (leg)* quaesit·or -oris *m*

investment *s (of money)* collocati·o -onis *f; (money invested)* locata pecuni·a -ae *f; (mil)* obsessi·o -onis *f*

inveterate *adj* inveterat·us -a -um

invigorate *tr* corroborare

invigorating *adj* apt·us -a -um ad corpus firmandum

invincible *adj* insuperabil·is -is -e, invict·us -a - um

inviolable *adj* sacrosanct·us -a -um

inviolate *adj* inviolat·us -a -um

invisible *adj* invisibil·is -is -e

invitation *s* invitati·o -onis *f*

invite *tr* invitare; **to — to dinner** ad cenam vocare

inviting *adj* suav·is -is -e

invitingly *adv* suaviter

invocation *s* invocati·o -onis *f*

invoice *s* libell·us -i *m*

invoke *tr* invocare

involuntarily *adv* sine voluntate

involuntary *adj* haud voluntari·us -a -um; **— bodily action** naturalis acti·o -onis *f* corporis

involve *tr* involvĕre; *(to comprise)* continēre

involved *adj (intricate)* involut·us -a -um; *(occupied)* implicat·us -a -um; **to be — in debt** aere alieno laborare; **to be — in many errors** multis erroribus implicari; **to be — in war** illigari bello

invulnerable *adj* invulnerabil·is -is -e

inward *adj* inter·ior -ior -ius

inwardly *adv* intus, intrinsecus

inwards *adv* introrsus

Ionian *adj* Ionic·us -a -um

irascible *adj* iracund·us -a -um

Ireland *s* Hiberni·a -ae *f*

iris *s* ir·is -idis *f*

Irish *adj* Hibernic·us -a -um

irk *tr* incommodare; **I am —ed, it irks me** me taedet

irksome *adj* molest·us -a -um

iron *s* ferr·um -i *n*

iron *adj* ferre·us -a -um

ironical *adj* ironic·us -a -um

ironically *adv* per ironiam

irony *s* ironi·a -ae *f*

irradiate *tr* illustrare **‖** *intr* effulgēre

irrational *adj* irrational·is -is -e

irrationally *adv* absurde

irreconcilable *adj* implacabil·is -is -e; *(incompatible)* omnino inter se contrari·i -ae -a

irrecoverable *adj* irreparabil·is -is -e

irrefutable *adj* certissim·us -a -um

irregular *adj (having no regular form)* enorm·is -is -e; *(not uniform)* inaequal·is -is -e; *(fever)* incert·us -a -um; *(gram)* anomal·us -a -um; **— army** exercit·us -ūs *m* tumultuarius

irregularity *s* enormit·as -atis *f; (gram)* anomali·a -ae *f;* **to be guilty of some —** peccare aliquid

irrelevant *adj* alien·us -a -um; **it is —** nil ad rem pertinet

irreligious *adj* impi·us -a -um erga deos; *(actions)* irreligios·us -a -um

irremediable *adj* insanabil·is -is -e

irreparable *adj* irreparabil·is -is -e

irreproachable *adj* inte·ger -gra -grum

irresistible *adj* invict·us -a -um

irresolute *adj* incert·us -a -um (sententiae); *(permanent characteristic)* parum firm·us -a -um

irresolutely *adv* dubitanter

irresolution *s* dubitati·o -onis *f,* anim·us -i *m* parum firmus

irresponsibility *s* incuri·a -ae *f*

irresponsible *adj* incurios·us -a -um

irretrievable *adj* irreparabil·is -is -e

irreverence *s* impiet·as -atis *f*

irreverent *adj* irrever·ens -entis (deorum)

irrevocable *adj* irrevocabil·is -is -e

irrigate *tr* irrigare

irrigation *s* irrigati·o -onis *f*

irritability *s* iracundi·a -ae *f*

irritable *adj* iracund·us -a -um

irritate *tr* irritare; *(a wound)* inflammare

irritation *s* irritati·o -onis *f*

island *s* insul·a -ae *f*

islander *s* insulan·us -i *m*

islet *s* parva insul·a -ae *f*

isolate *tr* secernĕre

issue *s (result)* event·us -ūs *m; (question)* res, rei *f; (offspring)* prol·es -is *f; (of a book)* editi·o -onis *f; (of money)* emissi·o -onis *f*

issue *tr (to distribute)* distribuĕre; *(orders)* edĕre, promulgare; *(money)* erogare; *(book)* edĕre **‖** *intr* emanare, egredi; *(to turn out, result)* evenire

isthmus *s* isthm·us -i *m*

it *pron* id

itch *s* prurig·o -inis *f*

itch *intr* prurire; *(fig)* gestire
item *s* res, rei *f*
itinerant *adj* circumforane‧us -a -um
itinerary *s* itinerar‧ium -(i)i *n*
its *pron* ejus; — **own** su‧us -a -um
itself *pron (refl)* se, sese; *(intensive)* ipsum
ivory *s* eb‧ur -oris *n*
ivory *adj* eburne‧us -a -um
ivy *s* heder‧a -ae *f*

J

jab *s* puls‧us -ūs *m*
jab *tr* fodicare
jabber *intr* blaterare
jabbering *s* garrulit‧as -atis *f*
jackass *s* asin‧us -i *m*
jacket *s* tunic‧a -ae *f*
jack-of-all-trades *s* hom‧o -inis *m* omnis Minervae
jackpot *s* **to hit the —** Venerem jacĕre
jaded *adj* defess‧us -a -um
jagged *adj* serrat‧us -a -um; *(of rocks)* praerupt‧us -a -um
jail *s* carc‧er -eris *m*
jail *tr* in carcere includĕre
jailbird *s* furcif‧er -eri *m*
jailer *s* carcerar‧ius -(i)i *m*
jam *s* baccarum conditur‧a -ae *f*; **to be in a —** in angustiis versari
jam *tr* frequentare; *(to obstruct)* obstruĕre
jamb *s* post‧is -is *m*
jangle *tr & intr* crepitare
janitor *s* janit‧or -oris *m*
January *s* Januar‧ius -(i)i *m or* mens‧is -is *m* Januarius; **on the first of —** Kalendis Januariis
jar *s* oll‧a -ae *f*; *(large, with 2 handles)* amphor‧a -ae *f*
jar *tr (to shock)* offendĕre; *(of sound)* strepĕre ‖ *intr* discrepare
jargon *s* confusae voc‧es -ium *fpl*
jarring *adj* disson‧us -a -um
jaundice *s* morb‧us -i *m* regius
jaundiced *adj* icterici‧us -a -um; **to see things with — eyes** omnia in deteriorem partem interpretari
jaunt *s* excursi‧o -onis *f*; **to take a —** excurrĕre
jaunty *adj* veget‧us -a -um
javelin *s* jacul‧um -i *n*; **to hurl a —** jaculari
jaw *s* mal‧ae -arum *fpl*; **—s** fauc‧es -ium *fpl*
jawbone *s* maxill‧a -ae *f*
jay *s* gracul‧us -i *m*
jealous *adj* zelotyp‧us -a -um
jealousy *s* zel‧us -i *m*
jeer *s* irris‧us -ūs *m*
jeer *tr* deridēre ‖ *intr* deridēre; **to —at** irridēre
jelly *s* cyl‧on -i *n*

jellyfish *s* pulm‧o -onis *m*
jeopardize *tr* periclitari
jeopardy *s* pericul‧um -i *n*
jerk *s* mot‧us -ūs *m* subitus; *(person)* vapp‧a -ae *m*
jerk *tr (to push)* subito trudĕre; *(to pull)* subito revellĕre
jerky *adj* salebros‧us -a -um
jest *s* joc‧us -i *m;* **in —** jocose
jest *intr* jocari
jester *s* joculat‧or -oris *m; (buffoon)* scurr‧a -ae *m*
jestingly *adv* per jocum
Jesus *s* Jes‧us -u *(dat, abl, voc:* Jesu; *acc:* Jesum) *m*
jet *s* scatebr‧a -ae *f*
jet-black *adj* nigerrim‧us -a -um
jetty *s* mol‧es -is *f*
Jew *s* Judae‧us -i *m*
jewel *s* gemm‧a -ae *f*
jeweler *s* gemmar‧ius -(i)i *m*
jewelry *s* gemm‧ae -arum *fpl*
Jewess *s* Judae‧a -ae *f*
Jewish *adj* Judae‧us -a -um
jilt *tr* repudiare
jingle *s* tinnit‧us -ūs *m*
jingle *intr* tinnire
jitters *spl* scrupul‧um -i *n;* **to give s.o. the —** scrupulum alicui injicĕre
job *s* negot‧ium -(i)i *n*
jobless *adj* quaestūs exper‧s -tis
jockey *s* agas‧o -onis *m*
jocular *adj* jocular‧is -is -e
jog *intr* tolutim currĕre
join *tr (to connect)* conjungĕre, connectĕre; *(to come into the company of)* se jungĕre *(w. dat); (to join as a companion)* supervenire *(w. dat); (to go over to)* transire; **—ing hands** manibus nex‧i -ae -a ‖ *intr* conjungi; **to — in** particeps esse *(w. gen);* **to — together** inter se conjungi
joint *adj* commun‧is -is -e
joint *s (anat)* articul‧us -i *m; (of a plant)* genicul‧um -i *n*, nod‧us -i *m; (of a structure)* compag‧es -inis *f*
jointed *adj* geniculat‧us -a -um
jointly *adv* unā, communiter
joist *s* tign‧um -i *n*
joke *s* joc‧us -i *m;* **as a —** per jocum; **to make a — of** jocum risumque facĕre
joke *intr* jocari; **to be —ing** jocari
joker *s* joculat‧or -oris *m*
joking *s* jocati‧o -onis *f;* **all — aside** joco remoto
jokingly *adv* per jocum
jolly *adj* hilar‧is -is -e
jolt *s (im)*puls‧us -ūs *m*
jolt *tr* jactare; *(fig)* percellĕre ‖ *intr* jactari
jolting *s* jactati‧o -onis *f*
jostle *tr* pulsare
jot *s* hil‧um -i *n;* **not a —** minime; **to care not a — for** non flocci facĕre
journal *s* ephemer‧is -idis *f*

journalist *s* script·or -oris *m* actorum
journey *s* it·er -ineris *n*
journey *intr* iter facĕre; **to — abroad** peregrinari
journeyman *s* opif·ex -icis *m*
Jove *s* Jupiter Jovis *m*
jovial *adj* hilar·is -is -e
jowl *s* bucc·a -ae *f*
joy *s* gaud·ium -(i)i *n*
joyful *adj* laet·us -a -um
joyfully *adv* laete
joyless *adj* illaetabil·is -is -e
jubilant *adj* laetitiā exsult·ans -antis
jubilation *s* exsultati·o -onis *f*
jubilee *s* ann·us -i *m* anniversarius
Judaic *adj* Judaïc·us -a -um
Judaism *s* Judaïsm·us -i *m*
judge *s* jud·ex -icis *m;* *(in criminal cases)* quaesit·or -oris *m*
judge *tr* judicare; *(to think)* existimare; *(to value)* aestimare; *(to decide between)* dijudicare
judgment *s* judic·ium -(i)i *n,* sententi·a -ae *f;* **in my —** sententiā meā; **to pronounce —** jus dicĕre; **to sit in — over** jus dicĕre inter *(w. acc)*
judgment seat *s* tribun·al -alis *n*
judicial *adj* judicial·is -is -e; **— proceedings** judici·a -orum *npl*
judicially *adv* jure
judicious *adj* sapi·ens -entis
judiciously *adv* sapienter
jug *s* urce·us -i *m*
juggle *intr* praestigias agĕre
juggler *s* praestigiat·or -oris *m*
juice *s* suc·us -i *m*
juicy *adj* sucos·us -a -um
July *s* Jul·ius -(i)i *or* mens·is -is *m* Julius; **on the first of —** Kalendis Juliis
jumble *s* congeri·es -ei *f*
jumble *tr* permiscēre
jump *s* salt·us -ūs *m*
jump *tr* transalire ‖ *intr* salire; **to —at** *(opportunity)* captare; **to — for joy** dissilire gaudimonio; **to — up** exsurrigĕre
junction *s* conjuncti·o -onis *f;* *(roads)* compit·um -i *n*
juncture *s* temp·us -oris *n;* **at this —** hic
June *s* Jun·ius -(i)i *m or* mens·is -is *m* Junius; **on the first of —** Kalendis Juniis
jungle *s* silv·ae -arum *fpl*
junior *adj* min·or -or -us natu
juniper *s* juniper·us -i *f*
junk *s* scrut·a -orum *npl*
jurisdiction *s* jurisdicti·o -onis *f*
jurisprudence *s* jurisprudenti·a -ae *f*
jurist *s* jurisconsult·us -i *m*
juror *s* jud·ex -icis *m*
jury *s* judic·es -um *mpl*
just *adj* just·us -a -um; *(fair)* aequ·us -a -um; *(deserved)* merit·us -a -um
just *adv* *(only)* modo; *(exactly)* prorsus;

(w. adv) demum, denique; **— after** sub *(w. acc);* **— as** perinde ac, sic ut; **— before** sub *(w. acc);* **— now** modo; **— so** ita prorsus; **— then** tunc maxime; **— what?** quidnam?; **— who?** quisnam?
justice *s* justiti·a -ae *f; (just treatment)* jus juris *n; (person)* praet·or -oris *m*
justifiable *adj* excusat·us -a -um
justifiably *adv* jure
justification *s* excusati·o -onis *f*
justify *tr* excusare, expurgare
jut *intr* prominēre; **to — out** procurrĕre; **to — out into the sea** in aequor procurrĕre
juvenile *adj* juvenil·is -is -e; **— delinquent** adulesc·ens -entis *m* noxius
juvenile *s* adulesc·ens -entis *mf*
juxtaposition *s* propinquit·as -atis *f;* **to put in —** apponĕre

K

kale *s* cramb·e -es *f*
keel *s* carin·a -ae *f*
keel *intr* **to — over** collabi
keen *adj* a·cer -cris -cre
keenly *adv* acriter
keenness *s* *(of scent)* sagacit·as -atis *f; (of sight)* aci·es -ei *f; (of pain)* acerbit·as -atis *f; (enthusiasm)* stud·ium -(i)i *n*
keep *tr* tenēre; *(to preserve)* servare; *(to celebrate)* agĕre; *(to guard)* custodire; *(to obey)* observare; *(to support)* alĕre; *(animals)* alĕre, pascĕre; *(to store)* condĕre; **to — annoying** subinde molestare; **to — apart** distinēre; **to — at bay** sustinēre; **to — away** arcēre; **to — back** retinēre, cohibēre; *(to conceal)* celare; **to — back nothing** nihil reticēre; **to — back tears** lacrimas tenēre; **to — company** comitari; **to — down** reprimĕre; **to — from** prohibēre; **to — in** cohibēre; **to — in custody** asservare; **to — in line the wavering Senate** confirmare labantem ordinem; **to — in mind** in memoria habēre; **to — off** arcēre, defendĕre; **to — to oneself** secum habēre; **to — pace with** pariter ire cum *(w. abl);* **to — secret** celare; **to — together** continēre; **to — under control** compescĕre; **to — under lock and key** clavi servare; **to — up** sustinēre; **to — up one's courage** animo erecto esse; **to — up with** subsequi; **to — your eyes on** oculos intentare in *(w. acc)* ‖ *intr (to last)* durare; **to — away from** abstinēre ab *(w. abl)*
keep *s* custodi·a -ae *f*
keeper *s* cust·os -odis *m*
keeping *s* tutel·a -ae *f;* **in — with** pro *(w. abl)*
keepsake *s* monument·m -i *n*
keg *s* cad·us -i *m*

kennel *s* stabul·um -i *n* caninum
kerchief *s* sudar·ium -(i)i *n*
kernel *s* nucle·us -i *m;* (*fig*) medull·um -i *n*
kettle *s* leb·es -etis *f*
kettledrum *s* tympan·um -i *n* aeneum
key *s* clav·is -is *f;* (*pitch*) voculati·o -onis *f;* (*clue*) ans·a -ae *f*
keyhole *s* claustell·um -i *n*
kick *s* cal·x -cis *mf*
kick *tr* calce ferire; **to — the bucket** (*coll*) animam ebullire ‖ *intr* calcitrare
kid *s* haed·us -i *m;* (*boy*) parvul·us -i *m*
kid *tr & intr* ludificari
kidnap *tr* surripēre
kidnapper *s* plagiar·ius -(i)i *m,* plagiari·a -ae *f*
kidnapping *s* plag·ium -(i)i *n*
kidney *s* ren renis *m*
kidney bean *s* phasel·us -i *m*
kill *s* nex necis *f;* (*prey*) praed·a -ae *f*
kill *tr* interficĕre; (*by cruel means*) necare; (*by wounds or blows*) caedĕre; **to — time** tempus perdĕre
killer *s* interfect·or -oris *m*
kiln *s* forn·ax -acis *f*
kin *s* cognat·i -orum *mpl;* **next of —** proxim·i -orum *mpl*
kind *adj* benign·us -a -um
kind *s* gen·us -eris *n;* **that — of war** ejus modi bell·um -i *n;* **what — of** qual·is -is -e, qui quae quod
kindhearted *adj* benign·us -a -um
kindle *tr* incendēre, accendĕre
kindly *adj* human·us -a -um
kindly *adv* benigne
kindness *s* benignit·as -atis *f;* (*deed*) benefic·ium -(i)i *n;* **to bestow a — on s.o.** beneficium apud aliquem collocare; **to do (return) an act of —** beneficium dare (reddĕre)
kindred *adj* consanguine·us -a -um
kindred *s* consanguinit·as -atis *f;* (*relatives*) consanguine·i -orum *mpl,* consanguine·ae -arum *fpl*
king *s* re·x -gis *m*
kingdom *s* regn·um -i *n*
kingfisher *s* alced·o -inis *f*
kingly *adj* regi·us -a -um; (*worthy of a king*) regal·is -is -e
kinsman *s* necessar·ius -(i)i *m*
kinswoman *s* necessari·a -ae *f*
kiss *s* oscul·um -i *n*
kiss *tr* osculari
kissing *s* osculati·o -onis *f*
kit *s* apparat·us -ūs *m*
kitchen *s* culin·a -ae *f*
kite *s* (*bird*) milv·us -i *m*
kith and kin *spl* propinqu·i -orum et adfin·es -ium *mpl*
kitten *s* catul·us -i *m* felinus
knack *s* sollerti·a -ae *f*
knapsack *s* per·a -ae *f*
knave *s* scelest·us -i *m*

knead *tr* subigĕre
knee *s* gen·u -us *n;* **on bended —** duplicato poplite; **to fall at s.o.'s —s** (*in entreaty*) se ad genua alicujus projicĕre; **to fall on one's —s** to genua ponĕre (*w. dat of person so honored*)
kneecap *s* patell·a -ae *f*
knee-deep *adj* genibus tenus alt·us -a -um
kneel *intr* genibus niti; **to — down** ad genua procumbĕre
knell *s* campan·a -ae *f* funebris
knife *s* cul·ter -tri *m;* (*for surgery*) scalpr·um -i *n*
knight *s* equ·es -itis *m*
knighthood *s* equestris dignit·as -atis *f*
knightly *adj* eques·ter -tris -tre
knit *tr* texĕre; **to — the brow** frontem contrahĕre
knob *s* tub·er -eris *n;* (*on door*) bull·a -ae *f*
knock *s* puls·us -ūs *m*
knock *tr* **to — down** dejicĕre, sternĕre; (*fig*) (*at auction*) addicĕre; **to — in** impellĕre; **to — one's head against the wall** caput ad parietem offendĕre; **to — out** excutĕre; **to — out s.o.'s brains** cerebrum alicui excutĕre ‖ *intr* **to — about** (*to ramble*) vagari; **to — at** pulsare, percutĕre
knocking *s* pulsati·ō- onis *f*
knock-kneed *adj* var·us -a -um
knoll *s* tumul·us -i *m*
knot *s* nod·us -i *m;* (*of people*) turbul·a -ae *f;* **to tie a —** nodum facĕre; **to untie a —** nodum expedire
knot *tr* nodare
knotty *adj* nodos·us -a -um; (*fig*) spinos·us -a -um
know *tr* scire; (*a person*) novisse; **not to — ignorare, nescire; to — how to** scire (*w. inf*)
knowing *adj* callid·us -a -um
knowingly *adv* scienter
knowledge *s* scienti·a -ae *f;* (*of s.th.*) cogniti·o -onis *f;* **without the — of** clam (*w. abl*); **without your —** clam vobis
known *adj* not·us -a -um; **— to me by sight** familiar·is -is -e oculis meis; **to become —** enotescĕre; **to make —** divulgare
knuckle *s* digiti articul·us -i *m*
knuckle *intr* **to — under** to cedĕre (*w. dat*)
kowtow *intr* (**to**) adulari (*w. dat*)

L

label *s* pittac·ium -(i)i *n*
labor *s* lab·or -oris *m;* (*manual*) oper·a -ae *f;* (*work done*) op·us -eris *n;* **to be in —** laborare in utero; **woman in —** puerper·a -ae *f*

labor *intr* laborare, eniti; **to — under** laborare *(w. abl)*

laboratory *s* officin·a -ae *f*

labored *adj* affectat·us -a -um

laborer *s* operar·ius -(i)i *m*

labyrinth *s* labyrinth·us -i *m*

labyrinthine *adj* labyrinthic·us -a -um; *(fig)* inextricabil·is -is -e

lace *s* op·us -eris *n* reticulatum

lace *tr (to tie)* nectĕre; *(to tighten)* astringĕre

lacerate *tr* lacerare

laceration *s* lacerati·o -onis *f*

lack *s* inopi·a -ae *f*

lack *tr* carēre *(w. abl)*

lackey *s* pedisequ·us -i *m*

laconic *adj* brev·is -is -e

lad *s* pu·er -eri *m*

ladder *s* scal·ae -arum *fpl;* **one — unae** scalae

laden *adj* onust·us -a -um

ladle *s* ligul·a -ae *f,* trull·a -ae *f*

ladle *tr* ligulā fundĕre

lady *s* domin·a -ae *f*

lag *intr* cessare

lagoon *s* lacun·a -ae *f*

lair *s* cubil·e -is *n*

laity *spl* laïc·i -orum *mpl*

lake *s* lac·us -ūs *m*

lamb *s* agn·us -i *m,* agn·a -ae *f; (meat)* agnīn·a -ae *f*

lame *adj* claud·us -a -um; **— in one leg** claud·us -a -um altero pede; **to be —** claudicare

lamely *adv (fig)* inconcinne

lameness *s* claudit·as -atis *f*

lament *s* lament·um -i *n*

lament *tr* lamentari ‖ *intr* deplorare

lamentable *adj* lamentabil·is -is -e

lamentation *s* lamentati·o -onis *f*

lamp *s* lucern·a -ae *f*

lampoon *s* libell·us -i *m*

lance *s* lance·a -ae *f*

lance *tr* incidĕre

land *s* terr·a -ae *f; (soil)* sol·um -i *n; (as a possession)* a·ger -gri *m;* **public —** ager publicus *(or* agri publici);* **on — and sea** terrā marique

land *tr* in terram exponĕre ‖ *intr* egredi, appellĕre

land *adj (animals, route)* terren·us -a -um; *(animals, route, troops)* terrestr·is -is -e; *(battle)* pedes·ter -tris -tre

landing *s* egress·us -ūs *m*

landing place *s* appuls·us -ūs *m*

landlady *s* domin·a -ae *f*

landlord *s* (insulae) domin·us -i *m*

landmark *s* lap·is -idis *m*

landscape *s* regionis sit·us -ūs *m*

landslide *s* terrae laps·us -ūs *m*

land tax *s* vectig·al -alis *n*

lane *s* semit·a -ae *f*

language *s* lingu·a -ae *f; (diction)* orati·o

-onis *f;* **abusive and insulting — against s.o.** maledice contumelioseque dict·a -orum *npl* in aliquem

languid *adj* languid·us -a -um

languish *intr* languēre

languishing *adj* languid·us -a -um

languor *s* langu·or -oris *m*

lanky *adj* prolix·us -a -um

lantern *s* la(n)tern·a -ae *f*

lap *s* sin·us -ūs *m; (fig)* grem·ium -(i)i *n*

lap *tr* lambĕre

lapse *s* laps·us -ūs *m; (error)* peccat·um -i *n;* **after a — of one year** interjecto anno

lapse *intr* labi; **to — into** recidĕre in *(w. acc)*

larceny *s* furt·um -i *n*

lard *s* ad·eps -ipis *mf*

large *adj* magn·us -a um; **to a — extent** magnā ex parte

largely *adv* plerumque

largess *s* largiti·o -onis *f;* **to give a —** largiri

lark *s* alaud·a -ae *f*

larynx *s* gutt·ur -uris *n.*

lascivious *adj* lasciv·us -a -um

lasciviously *adv* lascivē

lash *s (blow)* verb·er -eris *n; (whip)* flagell·um -i *n*

lash *tr* verberare flagellare; *(to censure severely)* castigare; *(to fasten)* annectĕre, alligare

lashing *s* verberati·o -onis *f*

lass *s* puell·a -ae *f*

lassitude *s* lassitud·o -inis *f*

last *adj* postrem·us -a -um, ultim·us -a -um; *(immediately preceding)* proxim·us -a -um; *(in line)* novissim·us -a -um; **at — demum;** **for the — time** postremo; **— but one** paenultim·us -a -um; **— night** proximā nocte; **the night before —** superiore noctē

last *intr* durare; **to — for some time** aliquod tempus habēre, **to — long** *(of a fever, etc.)* diu permanēre

lasting *adj* diuturn·us -a -um

lastly *adv* denique, postremo

latch *s* pessul·us -i *m*

latch *tr* oppessulare

late *adj* ser·us -a -um; *(loitering behind time)* tard·us -a -um; *(far advanced)* mult·us -a -um; *(recent in date)* rec·ens -entis; *(deceased)* demortu·us -a -um; *(of an emperor)* divus; **Homer was not —er than Lycurgus** Homerus non infra Lycurgum fuit; **it was — in the day** serum erat diei; **till — at night** ad multam noctem

late *adv* sero; **all too — immo jam sero, — at night** multā nocte; **— in life** seri anni; **too — serius**

lately *adv* modo, nuper, recens

latent *adj* occult·us a -um

lateral *adj* lateral·is -is -e

Latin *adj* Latin·us -a -um ‖ *s* **to learn** — Latine discěre; **to speak** — Latine loqui; **to teach** — Latine docěre; **to translate into** — Latine redděre; **to understand** — Latine scire

Latinity *s* Latinit·as -atis *f*

latitude *s* latitud·o -inis *f; (fig)* libert·as -atis *f*

latter *adj* poster·ior -ior -ius; **the** — hic

lattice *s* cancell·i -orum *mpl*

laudable *adj* laudabil·is -is -e

laudably *adv* laudabiliter

laudatory *adj* laudativ·us -a -um

laugh *s* ris·us -ūs *m*

laugh *intr* ridēre; **to** — **at** ridēre; *(to mock)* irridēre

laughable *adj* ridicul·us -a -um

laughingstock *s* ludibr·ium -(i)i *n*

laughter *s* ris·us -ūs *m; (loud, indecorous)* cachinnati·o -onis *f*

launch *tr* deducěre; *(to hurl)* jaculari ‖ *intr* **to** — **out** proficisci

laundress *s* lotr·ix -icis *f*

laundry *s* lavator·ium -(i)i *n*

laureate *adj* laureat·us -a -um

laurel *adj* laure·us -a -um

laurel tree *s* laur·us -i *f*

lava *s* liquefacta mass·a -ae *f*

lavish *adj* prodig·us -a -um

lavish *tr* prodigěre, profunděre

lavishly *adv* prodige

law *s* lex legis *f; (right)* jus juris *n; (divine)* fas *n (indecl);* **to break the** — leges violare; **to introduce a** — legem ferre; **to pass a** — legem perferre

law-abiding *adj* bene morat·us -a -um

law court *s* judic·ium -(i)i *n; (building)* basilic·a -ae *f*

lawful *adj* legitim·us -a -um; **it is** — fas est

lawfully *adv* legitime

lawless *adj* exl·ex -egis

lawlessness *s* licenti·a -ae *f*

lawn *s* pratul·um -i *n*

lawsuit *s* caus·a -ae *f*

lawyer *s* jurisconsult·us -i *m*

lax *adj* lax·us -a -um

laxity *s* remissi·o -onis *f*

lay *tr (to put)* poněre; *(eggs)* parěre; *(foundations)* jacěre; *(hands)* injicěre; **to** — **an ambush** insidiari; **to be laid up** cubare; **to** — **aside** poněre; *(cares, fear)* amovēre; **to** — **before** proponěre; **to** — **claim to** arrogare, vindicare; **to** — **down** *(office)* resignare; *(rules)* statuěre; **to** — **down arms** ab armis disceděre; **to** — **hands on s.th.** aliquid invaděre; **to** — **hold of** prehenděre; **to** — **it on the line** *(coll)* directum loqui; **to** — **out** *(money)* expenděre; *(plans)* designare; **to** — **siege to** obsidēre; **to** — **the blame on** culpam conferre in *(w. acc);* **to** — **up** conděre; **to** — **waste** vastare

lay *s (mus)* cantilen·a -ae *f*

layer *s* lamin·a -ae *f; (stratum)* cor·ium -(i)i *n; (of a plant)* propag·o -inis *f*

lazily *adv* ignave, pigre

laziness *s* pigriti·a -ae *f*

lazy *adj* ignav·us -a -um

lead *s* plumb·um -i *n*

lead *adj* plumbe·us -a -um

lead *tr (life)* agěre; **to** — **about** circumducěre; **to** — **away** abducěre; **to** — **off** divertěre; **to** — **on** conducěre ‖ *intr (of a road)* **to** — **to** ducěre ad; **to** — **up to** tenděre ad *(w. acc)*

leaden *adj* plumbe·us -a -um

leader *s* du·x -cis *m*, duct·or -oris *m*

leadership *s* duct·us -ūs *m*

leading *adj* princ·eps -cipis

leaf *s* fol·ium -(i)i *n; (of vine)* pampin·us -i *m; (of paper)* sched·a -ae *f; (of metal)* bracte·a -ae *f;* **to turn over a new** — ad bonam frugem se recipere

leafless *adj* fronde nudat·us -a -um

leafy *adj* frondos·us -a -um

league *s* foed·us -eris *n*

leak *s* rim·a -ae *f*

leak *intr* rimas agěre, perfluěre

leaky *adj* rimos·us -a -um

lean *adj* ma·cer -cra -crum

lean *tr* inclinare ‖ *intr* inclinare, niti; — **ing forward** inclinat·us -a -um; **to** — **against** se applicare *(w. dat);* **to** — **back** se inclinare; **to** — **on** inniti in *(w. abl)*

leap *s* salt·us -ūs *m*

leap *intr* salire; **to** — **for joy** exsultare

leap year *s* bisextilis ann·us -i *m*

learn *tr* discěre; *(from elders)* accipěre; **to** — **by heart** ediscěre ‖ *intr* **to** — **about** cognoscěre; *(to be informed about)* certior fieri de *(w. abl)*

learned *adj* doct·us -a -um

learnedly *adv* docte

learning *s* doctrin·a -ae *f*, eruditi·o -onis *f*

lease *s* conducti·o -onis *f; (act on part of proprietor)* locati·o -onis *f*

lease *tr* conducěre; **to** — **out** locare

leash *s* lor·um -i *n*, cingul·um -i *n*

leash *tr* cingulo alligare

least *adj* minim·us -a -um

least *adv* minime; **at** — utique; *(emphasizing a particular word)* saltem

least *n* minim·um -ī *n;* **not in the** — ne minimum quidem

leather *s (tanned or untanned)* cor·ium -(i)i *n; (tanned)* alut·a -ae *f*

leather *adj* scorte·us -a -um

leathery *adj* lent·us -a -um

leave *tr* relinquěre; *(to entrust)* mandare, traděre; *(legacy)* legare; **to** — **behind** relinquěre; **to** — **out** omittěre ‖ *intr (to depart)* disceděre, abire; **to** — **off** desiněre

leave *s* permissi·o -onis *f;* — **of absence** commeat·us -ūs *m;* **to ask** — veniam petěre; **to obtain** — impetrare; **to take**

— of valēre jubēre; **with your —** pace tuā (vestrā)
leaven *s* ferment·um -i *n*
leaven *tr* fermentare
lecherous *adj* libidinos·us -a -um
lector *s* lect·or -oris *m*
lecture *s* lecti·o -onis *f*, acroas·is -is *f*; **to give a —** acroasin facĕre
lecture *tr* *(to reprove)* objurgare ‖ *intr* acroases facĕre, scholas habēre
lecturer *s* lect·or -oris *m*
ledge *s* projectur·a -ae *f*; *(of a cliff)* dors·um -i *n*
ledger *s* cod·ex -icis *m* (accepti et expensi)
leech *s* sanguisug·a -ae *f*
leer *intr* limis oculis spectare
leering *adj* lim·us -a -um
left *adj* laev·us -a -um, sinis·ter -tra -trum; **on the —** a sinistrā; **to the —** sinistrorsum, ad sinistram
left-handed *adj* laev·us -a -um
leftover *adj* reliqu·us -a -um
leftovers *spl* reliqui·ae -arum *fpl*
leg *s* cru·s -ris *n*; *(of table, etc.)* pes pedis *m*
legacy *s* legat·um -i *n*
legacy hunter *s* captat·or -oris *m*
legal *adj* legitim·us -a -um
legally *adv* legitime, lege
legalize *tr* sancire
legate *s* legat·us -i *m*
legation *s* legati·o -onis *f*
legend *s* fabul·a -ae *f*; *(inscription)* titul·us -i *m*
legendary *adj* commentici·us -a -um, fabulos·us -a -um
legging *s* ocre·a -ae *f*
legible *adj* legibil·is -is -e
legion *s* legi·o -onis *f*
legislate *intr* leges dare
legislation *s* leg·es -um *fpl*, legum dati·o -onis *f*
legislator *s* legum lat·or -oris *m*
legitimate *adj* legitim·us -a -um
legitimately *adv* legitime
leisure *s* ot·ium -(i)i *n*; **at —** otios·us -a -um
leisure *adj* otios·us -a -um, vacu·us -a -um; **— activity** op·us -eris *n* subsicivum
leisure time *s* temp·us -oris *n* vacuum
leisurely *adj* lent·us -a -um
lemon *s* pom·um -i *n* citreum
lemonade *s* aqu·a -ae *f* limonata
lend *tr* commodare; **to — money** pecuniam mutuam dare; *(at interest)* pecuniam faenerare; **to — one's ear to** aures praebēre *(w. dat)*
length *s* longitud·o -inis *f*; *(of time)* longinquit·as -atis *f*; **at —** tandem
lengthen *tr* producĕre, protrahĕre
lengthwise *adv* in longitudinem
lengthy *adj* long·us -a -um
leniency *s* lenit·as -atis *f*

lenient *adj* len·is -is -e
leniently *adv* leniter
lentil *s* len·s -tis *f*
leopard *s* leopard·us -i *m*
leper *s* lepros·us -i *m*
leprosy *s* lepr·ae -arum *fpl*
less *adj* min·or -or -us
less *adv* minus
lessee *s* conduct·or -oris *m*
lessen *tr* minuĕre ‖ *intr* decrescĕre
lesson *s* document·um -i *n*; *(a portion for reading)* lecti·o -onis *f*; **let him learn a — from me** habeat me ipsum sibi documento; **to give —s in** docēre; **to give —s in grammar** grammaticam docēre
lessor *s* locat·or -oris *m*
lest *conj* ne
let *tr* *(to allow)* sinĕre, permittĕre; *(to lease)* locare; **to — alone** omittĕre; **to — down** *(to disappoint)* deësse *(w. dat)*; **to — fall** a manibus mittĕre; **to — fly** emittĕre; **to — go** (di)mittĕre; **to — in** admittĕre; **to — off** absolvĕre; **to — out** emittĕre; **to — pass** omittĕre; **to — slip an opportunity** occasionem amittĕre ‖ *intr* **to — up** residēre; **the rain is letting up** imber detumescit
lethargic *adj* lethargic·us -a -um
lethargy *s* letharg·us -i *m*
letter *s* *(of alphabet)* litter·a -ae *f*; *(epistle)* litter·ae -arum *fpl*, epistul·a -ae *f*; **by — per litteras; to the —** ad verbum
letter carrier *s* tabellar·ius -(i)i *m*
lettered *adj* litterat·us -a -um
lettering *s* titul·us -i *m*
lettuce *s* lactuc·a -ae *f*
level *adj* plan·us -a -um
level *s* planiti·es -ei *f*; *(tool)* libr·a -ae *f*; **to be on a — with** par esse *(w. dat)*
level *tr* (ad)aequare; *(to destroy)* diruĕre; **to — to the ground** solo aequare
lever *s* vect·is -is *m*
levity *s* levit·as -atis *f*
levy *s* delect·us -ūs *m*
levy *tr* *(troops)* conscribĕre; *(tax)* exigĕre
lewd *adj* incest·us -a -um
lewdly *adv* inceste
lewdness *s* impudiciti·a -ae *f*
liable *adj* obnoxi·us -a -um
liar *s* mend·ax -acis *mf*
libation *s* libati·o -onis *f*; **to pour a —** libare
libel *s* calumni·a -ae *f*
libel *tr* calumniari
libelous *adj* famos·us -a -um
liberal *adj* liberal·is -is -e; *(free)* lib·er -era -erum; **— arts** art·es -ium *fpl* liberales
liberality *s* liberalit·as -atis *f*
liberally *adv* liberaliter
liberate *tr* liberare; *(a slave)* manumittĕre
liberation *s* liberati·o -onis *f*

liberator s liberat·or -oris m
libertine s hom·o -inis m dissolutus
liberty s libert·as -atis f; **at** — lib·er -era -erum; **to be at** — licet (w. dat of English subject); **to take liberties with s.o.** liberius se in aliquem gerĕre
librarian s librar·ius -(i)i m
library s bibliothec·a -ae f
license s (permission) copi·a -ae f, potest·as -atis f; (freedom) licenti·a -ae f
license tr potestatem dare (w. dat)
licentious adj dissolut·us -a -um
licentiously adv dissolute
lick tr lambĕre; (daintily) ligurrire; **to** — **the plate** catillare; **to** — **out** elingĕre; **to** — **up** delingĕre
lictor s lict·or -oris m
lid s operiment·um -i n
lie s mendac·ium -(i)i n; **to give the** — **to** redarguĕre; **to tell a** — mentiri
lie intr (to tell a lie or lies) mentiri; (to be lying down) jacēre, cubare; (to be situated) sit·us -a -um esse; **to** — **down** jacēre; **to** — **in wait for** insidiari (w. dat); **to** — **on or upon** incubare (w. dat); **to** — **on one's back** resupinus jacēre; **to** — **on one's left (right) side** in latus sinistrum (dextrum) cubare; **to** — **on one's stomach** pronus jacēre
lieu s **in** — **of** loco (w. gen)
lieutenant s legat·us -i m; (mil) centuri·o -onis m
life s vit·a -ae f; (age) aet·as -atis f; (fig) alacrit·as -atis f; **to lose one's** — animam amittĕre; **spark of** — animul·a -ae f; **to lead the** — **of Riley** vitam Chiam gerĕre
life blood s suc·us -i m et sangu·is -inis m
life-giving adj alm·us -a -um
lifeless adj inanim·us -a -um; (fig) exsangu·is -is -e, frigid·us -a -um
lifelessly adv frigide
life style s vitae proposit·um -i n
lifetime s aet·as -atis f
lift tr tollĕre; **to** — **her hand to her face** manum ad faciem suam admovēre; **to** — **up** attollĕre
ligament s ligament·um -i n
ligature s ligatur·a -ae f
light s lu·x -cis f, lum·en -inis n; (lamp) lucern·a -ae f; — **and shade** (in painting) lum·en -inis n et umbr·ae -arum fpl; **to bring to** — in lucem proferre; **to throw** — **on** lumen adhibēre (w. dat)
light adj (in weight) lev·is -is -e; (bright) lucid·us -a -um; (of colors) candid·us -a -um; (easy) facil·is -is -e; (nimble) agil·is -is -e; (wine) tenu·is -is -e, len·is -is -e; (food) lev·is -is -e; **to grow** — lucescĕre
light tr accendĕre; (to illuminate) illuminare ‖ intr flammam concipĕre; **to** — **upon** offendĕre; **to** — **up** (fig) hilar·is -is -e fieri
lighten tr (to illumintate) illustrare;

(weight) allevare, exonerare ‖ intr (in the sky) fulgurare
light-hearted adj hilar·is -is -e
lighthouse s phar·us -i f
lightness s levit·as -atis f
lightning s fulg·ur -uris n; (in its destructive effects) fulm·en -inis n; **struck by** — de caelo tact·us -a -um
like adj simil·is -is -e (w. dat); (equal) par (w. dat), aequ·us -a -um (w. dat)
like prep instar (w. gen); tamquam, ut
like tr amare; **he** — **s to paint** libentissime pingit; **I** — **this** hoc mihi placet; **I** — **to do this** me juvat hoc facĕre
likelihood s verisimilitud·o -inis f
likely adj verisimil·is -is -e, probabil·is -is -e; **it is most** — **that** proximum est ut
likely adv probabiliter
liken tr comparare
likeness s similitud·o -inis f; (portrait) effigi·es -ei f
likewise adv pariter, similiter, item
liking s am·or -oris m; (fancy) libid·o -inis f; **according to one's** — ex libidine
lilac s syring·a -ae f vulgaris
lily s lil·ium -(i)i n
lily of the valley s convallaria majal·is -is f
limb s art·us -ūs m, membr·um -i n; (of tree) ram·us -i m
limber adj flexil·is -is -e
lime s cal·x -cis f
limestone s cal·x -cis f
lime tree s tili·a -ae f
limit s fin·is -is m, mod·us -i m; **to set** —**s to** finire
limit tr finire, terminare; (to restrict) circumscribĕre
limitation s circumscripti·o -onis f
limited adj finit·us -a -um; (time) brev·is -is -e; (resources) exigu·us -a -um
limp s claudicati·o -onis f
limp intr claudicare
limp adj flaccid·us -a -um
limpid adj limpid·us -a -um
linden tree s tili·a -ae f
line s (drawn) line·a -ae f; (row) seri·es -ei f; (lineage) stirp·s -is m, gen·us -eris n; (mil) aci·es -ei f; (of poetry) vers·us -ūs m; (cord) fun·is -is m; **in a straight** — rectā lineā; **I will write a few** —**s in answer to your letter** pauca ad tuas litteras rescribam; **the front** — (mil) principi·a -orum npl; **to draw a** — lineam ducĕre; **to keep s.o. in** — imperare (w. dat)
line tr (the streets) saepire; **to** — **a garment with wool** vestem introrsum lanā obducĕre
lineage s gen·us -eris n
lineal adj linear·is -is -e
lineally adv rectā lineā
lineament s lineament·um -i n

linear *adj* linear·is -is -e
linen *s* linte·um -i *n*, lin·um -i *n*
linen *adj* linte·us -a -um; — **cloth** linteol·um -i *n*
linger *intr* morari, cunctari
lingering *adj* cunctabund·us -a -um
lingering *s* cunctati·o -onis *f*
linguist *s* linguarum perit·us -i *m*
linguistics *s* linguistic·a -ae *f*
liniment *s* linit·us -ūs *m*
link *s* (*of chain*) anul·us -i *m*; (*bond*) vincul·um -i *n*
link *tr* connectĕre, conjungĕre
linseed *s* lini sem·en -inis *n*
lint *s* linament·um -i *n*
lintel *s* lim·en -inis *n* superum
lion *s* le·o -onis *m*
lioness *s* leaen·a -ae *f*
lip *s* labr·um -i *n*; (*edge*) or·a -ae *f*; **to be on everyone's** —**s** in ore esse omni populo
liquefy *tr* liquefacĕre
liquid *adj* liquid·us -a -um
liquid *s* um·or -oris *m*
liquidate *tr* persolvĕre
liquor *s* temet·um -i *n*
lisp *s* balbutire
lisping *adj* blaes·us -a -um
list *s* numer·us -i *m*; (*naut*) inclinati·o -onis *f*; — **of charges** subscripti·o -onis *f*
list *tr* enumerare ‖ *intr* (*naut*) inclinare
listen *intr* auscultare; **to** — **to** auscultare (*w. dat*); — **to me!** ausculta mihi!
listless *adj* languid·us -a -um
listlessly *adv* languide
litany *s* litani·a -ae *f*
literal *adj* litteral·is -is -e
literally *adv* ad verbum
literary *adj* (*person*) litterat·us -a -um; — **pursuits** studi·a -orum *npl* litterarum; — **style** scribendi gen·us -eris *n*
literature *s* litter·ae -arum *fpl*
litigant *s* litig·ans -antis *mf*
litigate *intr* litigare
litigation *s* li·s -tis *f*
litter *s* (*vehicle*) lectic·a -ae *f*; (*of straw, etc.*) strament·um -i *n*; (*brood*) fet·us -ūs *m*; (*refuse*) reject·a -orum *npl*
litter *tr* spargĕre; **to** — **the streets** scruta viis spargĕre ‖ *intr* rejecta dispergĕre
little *adj* parv·us -a -um
little *adv* parum, paulum; **a** — paulum, pusillum; — **by** — paulatim
little *s* aliquantul·um -i *n*
little people *spl* (*coll*) popul·us -i *m* minutus
live *tr* **to** — **it up** ferias agĕre ‖ *intr* vivĕre, vitam agĕre; (*to reside*) habitare; **to** — **on** vesci (*w. abl*); **to** — **up to** aequiparare
live *adj* viv·us -a -um
livelihood *s* vict·us -ūs *m*; **to gain a** — victum quaeritare

lively *adj* veget·us -a -um
liver *s* jec·ur -oris *n*
livid *adj* livid·us -a -um; **to be** — livēre
living *adj* viv·us -a -um
living *s* (*livelihood*) vict·us -ūs *m*
lizard *s* lacert·a -ae *f*
load *s* on·us -eris *n*
load *tr* onerare
loaded *adj* (*rich*) saplut·us -a -um; (*drunk*) uvid·us -a -um
loaf *s* pan·is -is *m*
loaf *intr* cessare
loafer *s* cessat·or -oris *m*, cessatr·ix -icis *f*
loafing *s* cessati·ō -ōnis *f*
loam *s* lut·um -i *n*
loan *s* mutu·um -i *n*
loan *tr* faenerari
loathe *tr* fastidire
loathing *s* fastid·ium -(i)i *n*
loathsome *adj* tae·ter -tra -trum
lobby *s* vestibul·um -i *n*
lobe *s* lob·us -i *m*
lobster *s* astac·us -i *m*
local *adj* loci (*gen*), regionis (*gen*)
locality *s* loc·us -i *m*
lock *s* (*of door*) ser·a -ae *f*; (*of hair*) crin·is -is *m*; —, **stock, and barrel** cum porcis, cum fiscinā; **to be kept under** — **and key** esse sub clavi
lock *tr* obserare, oppessulare; **to** — **in** includĕre; **to** — **out** excludĕre; **to** — **up** concludĕre
locker *s* loculament·um -i *n*
locket *s* capsell·a -a *f*
locust *s* locust·a -ae *f*
lodge *tr* **to** — **a complaint against s.o.** nomen alicujus deferre ‖ *intr* (*with*) deversari (apud + *acc*); (*to stick*) inhaerēre
lodger *s* hosp·es -itis *m*; (*in a tenement*) insular·ius -(i)i *m*
lodging *s* hospit·ium -(i)i *n*; **to take up** — hospitium accipĕre
loft *s* tabulat·um -i *n*
lofty *adj* (ex)cels·us -a -um; (*fig*) sublim·is -is -e
log *s* stip·es -itis *m*
logic *s* dialectic·a -orum *npl*
logical *adj* logic·us -a -um; (*reasonable*) rational·is -is -e
logically *adv* ex ratione
loin *s* lumb·us -i *m*
loiter *intr* cessare
loiterer *s* cessat·or -oris *m*
loll *intr* recumbĕre
lone *adj* sol·us -a -um
loneliness *s* solitud·o -inis *f*
lonely *adj* solitari·us -a -um
lonesome *adj* solitari·us -a -um
long *adj* long·us -a -um; (*of time*) diuturn·us -a -um; (*lengthened; syllable*) product·us -a -um; **a** — **way off** longinqu·us -a -um; **for a** — **time** jam diu

long *adv* diu; **a little** —**er** paulo longius; — **how long?** quamdiu? — **after** multo post; — **ago** jamdudum, jampridem; — **before** multo ante; **too** — nimis diu
long *intr* avēre; **to** — **for** desiderare
longed-for *adj* expectat·us -a -um
longevity *s* longaevit·as -atis *f*
longing *s* desider·ium -(i)i *n*
longing *adj* avid·us -a -um
longingly *adv* avide
longitude *s* longitud·o -inis *f*
long-lasting *adj* diutin·us -a -um
long-lived *adj* viv·ax -acis
long-standing *adj* vetustissim·us -a -um
long-suffering *adj* pati·ens -entis
long-winded *adj* long·us -a -um
look *s* (*act of looking*) aspect·us -ūs *m;* (*facial expression*) vult·us -ūs *m;* (*appearance*) speci·es -ei *f;* —**s** (*general appearance*) habit·us -ūs *m*
look *intr* aspicěre; (*to seem*) videri; **he** —**s stern** severitas inest in vultu ejus; — **!** aspice!; **to** — **about** circumspicěre; **to** — **after** curare; **to** — **after oneself** sibi consulěre; **to** — **around** respicěre, circumspicěre; **to** — **around for** prospicěre; **to** — **at** intuēri, aspicěre; (*to study*) considerare; **to** — **back** respicěre; **to** — **down** despicěre; **to** — **down upon** despicěre (*w. acc*)*;* **to** — **for** quaerěre; **to** — **forward to** exspectare; **to** — **glad** laetitiam vultu aperte ferre; **to look into** (*lit & fig*) inspicěre; (*to examine*) perscrutari; **to** — **into one's own mind** introspicěre in mentem suam; **to** — **on** intueri, observare; **to** — **out** prospicěre; **to** — **out for** quaerěre; **to** — **out of the window** ex fenestra prospicěre; **to** — **s.o. in the face** rectis oculis aliquem adspicěre; **to** — **towards** spectare; **to** — **up** suspicěre, oculos erigěre; **to** — **up to** (*implying respect*) suspicěre; **to** — **up to heaven** in caelum suspicěre; **to** — **upon** habēre
looker-on *s* spectat·or -oris *m*
look-out *s* (*person*) speculat·or -oris *m;* **to keep a careful** — omnia circumspectare
loom *s* tel·a -ae *f*
loom *intr* in conspectum prodire
loop *s* sin·us -ūs *m*
loophole *s* (*fig*) effug·ium -(i)i *n*
loose *adj* lax·us -a -um; (*flowing, slack*) flux·us -a -um; (*not chaste*) dissolut·us -a -um; — **bowels** fusa alv·us -i *f*
loosely *adv* laxe; (*dissolutely*) dissolute
loosen *tr* solvěre, laxare ‖ *intr* solvi
lop *tr* **to** — **off** praeciděre; (*in pruning*) amputare
lop-sided *adj* inaequal·is -is -e
loquacious *adj* loqu·ax -acis
lord *s* domin·us -i *m*
Lord *s* Domin·us -i *m*
lord *intr* **to** — **it over** dominari in (*w. acc*)

lordly *adj* imperios·us -a -um
lordship *s* dominati·o -onis *f*
lore *s* doctrin·a -ae *f*
lose *tr* amittěre, perděre; **to** — **one eye** altero oculo capi; **to** — **heart** deficěre; **to** — **one's way** (ab)errare
loss *s* (*act*) amissi·o -onis *f;* damn·um -i *n;* (*mil, pol*) repuls·a -ae *f;* **to incur some** — aliquid damni contrahěre; **to suffer a** — damnum (*or* jacturam) facěre
lost *adj* perdit·us -a -um; — **in admiration** satur·us -a -um admiratione; **to be** — perire; **to get** — aberrare
lot *s* sor·s -tis *f;* (*destiny*) fat·um -i *n;* (*piece of land*) agell·us -i *m;* **a** — (*coll*) multum; **a** — **better** (*coll*) multo melior; **casting of** —**s** sortiti·o -onis *f;* —**s of people** mult·i -orum *mpl;* **to draw** —**s for** sortiri
lotion *s* liniment·um -i *n*
lottery *s* sortiti·o -onis *f*
loud *adj* magn·us -a -um ‖ *adv* magnā voce
lounge *s* (*room*) exedr·ium -(i)i *n;* (*couch*) lectul·us -i *m*
lounge *intr* otiari
louse *s* pedicul·us -i *m*
lousy *adj* pediculos·us -a -um; (*coll*) foed·us -a -um
lout *s* rustic·us -i *m*
loutish *adj* rustic·us -a -um
love *s* am·or -oris *m;* **to fall in** — **with** in amorem (*w. gen*) inciděre
love *tr* amare, diligěre
love affair *s* am·or -oris *m*
loveliness *s* venust·as -atis *f*
lovely *adj* venust·us -a -um
love potion *s* philtr·um -i *n*
lover *s* am·ans -antis *mf;* (*homosexual partner*) fra·ter -tris *m*
lovesick *adj* amore ae·ger -gra -grum
loving *adj* am·ans -antis
low *adj* (*close to the ground; in status*) humil·is -is -e; (*of price*) vil·is -is -e; (*of birth*) obscur·us -a -um; (*low-pitched*) grav·is -is -e; (*not loud*) summiss·us -a -um; (*depressed*) trist·is -is -e; (*vile*) turp·is -is -e; **at** — **tide** ubi aestus recessit
low *adv* humiliter; summissā voce
low *intr* mugire
lowborn *adj* degen·er -eris
lower *tr* demittěre, depriměre; (*price*) imminuěre
lower *adj* infer·ior -ior -ius; **of the** — **world** infer·us -a -um; **the** — **world** infer·i -orum *mpl*
lowermost *adj* infim·us -a -um
lowing *s* mugit·us -ūs *m*
lowlands *spl* campestr·ia -ium *npl*
lowly *adj* humil·is -is -e
loyal *adj* fidel·is -is -e, fid·us -a -um
loyally *adv* fideliter
loyalty *s* fidelit·as -atis *f*

lubricate *tr* unguĕre
lucid *adj* lucid·us -a -um; **if a madman has a — interval** si furiosus intermissionem habet
Lucifer *s* Lucif·er -eri *m*
luck *s* fortun·a -ae *f;* **bad —** fortun·a -ae *f,* infortun·ium -(i)i *n;* **good —** fortun·a -ae *f*
luckily *adv* feliciter
luckless *adj* infel·ix -icis
lucky *adj* fel·ix -icis; **— stiff** Fortunae fil·ius -(i)i *m*
lucrative *adj* lucrativ·us -a -um
lucre *s* lucr·um -i *n*
ludicrous *adj* ridicul·us -a -um
ludicrously *adv* ridicule
luggage *s* sarcin·ae -arum *fpl*
lukewarm *adj* tepid·us -a -um; *(fig)* segn·is -is -e, frigid·us -a -um
lukewarmly *adv* segniter
lull *s* qui·es -etis *f*
lull *tr* sopire; *(to calm, as a storm)* sedare; *(fig)* demulcēre
lullaby *s* lall·um -i *n*
lumber *s* materi·a -ae *f*
luminary *s* lum·en -inis *n*
luminous *adj* lucid·us -a -um; *(fig)* dilucid·us -a -um
lump *s* glaeb·a -ae *f,* mass·a -ae *f; (on the body)* tub·er -eris *n*
lump *tr* **to — together** coacervare
lumpy *adj* glaebos·us -a -um
lunacy *s* alienati·o -onis *f* mentis
lunar *adj* lunar·is -is -e
lunatic *s* insan·us -i *n*
lunch *s* prand·ium -(i)i *n;* **to have for —** in prandium habēre
lunch *intr* prandēre
luncheon *s* prand·ium -(i)i *n*
lung *s* pulm·o -onis *m*
lunge *s* ict·us -ūs *m*
lunge *intr* prosalire
lurch *s* propuls·us -ūs *m;* **to leave in a —** derelinquĕre
lurch *intr* titubare
lure *s* illecebr·a -ae *f,* esc·a -ae *f*
lure *tr* allicĕre; *(an animal)* inescare
lurk *intr* latēre
luscious *adj* praedulc·is -is -e
lush *adj* luxurios·us -a -um
lust *s* libid·o -inis *f; (for power, etc.)* cupidit·as -atis *f*
lust *intr* concupiscĕre
luster *s* splend·or -oris *m*
lustful *adj* libidinos·us -a -um
lustfully *adv* libidinose, lascive
lustily *adv* valide
lusty *adj* valid·us -a -um
luxuriance *s* luxuri·es -ei *f*
luxuriant *adj* luxurios·us -a -um
luxuriate *intr* luxuriare
luxurious *adj* sumptuos·us -a -um
luxuriously *adv* sumptuose

luxury *s* luxuri·a -ae *f*
lye *s* lixivi·a -ae *f*
lying *adj* mend·ax -acis
lying *s* mendacit·as -atis *f*
lymph *s* lymph·a -ae *f*
lynx *s* lyn·x -cis *mf*
lyre *s* lyr·a -ae *f*
lyric *adj* lyric·us -a -um
lyric *s* (lyricum) carm·en -inis *n*

M

macaroni *s* collyr·a -ae *f*
mace *s* virg·a -ae *f*
machination *s* dol·us -i *m*
machine *s* machin·a -ae *f*
machinery *s* machinament·um -i *n*
mackerel *s* scom·ber -bri *m*
mad *adj* furios·us -a -um; **to be —** furĕre
madam *s* domin·a -ae *f*
madden *tr* mentem alienare *(w. dat); (fig)* furiare
madly *adv* furiose; **to be — in love** insane amare
madman *s* hom·o -inis *m* furiosus
madness *s* fur·or -oris *m*
magazine *s (journal)* ephemer·is -idis *f; (storehouse)* horre·um -i *n*
maggot *s* verm·is -is *m*
magic *adj* magic·us -a -um
magic *s* magica ar·s -tis *f*
magically *adv* velut magicā quadam arte et vi
magician *s* mag·us -i *m*
magisterial *adj* ad magistratum pertin·ens -entis
magistracy *s* magistrat·us ūs *m*
magistrate *s* magistrat·us ūs *m*
magnanimity *s* magnanimit·as -atis *f*
magnanimous *adj* magnanim·us -a -um
magnet *s* magn·es -etis *m*
magnetic *adj* magnetic·us -a -um
magnetism *s* vis *f* magnetica
magnetize *tr* megneticā vi afficĕre
magnificence *s* magnificenti·a -ae *f*
magnificent *adj* magnific·us -a -um
magnificently *adv* magnifice
magnify *tr* amplificare
magnitude *s* magnitud·o -inis *f*
maid *s* ancill·a -ae *f*
maiden *s* virg·o -inis *f*
maidenhood *s* virginit·as -atis *f*
maidenly *adj* virginal·is -is -e
mail *s (letters)* epistol·ae -arum *fpl; (armor)* loric·a -ae *f*
mail *tr* dare
mailman *s* tabellar·ius -(i)i *m*
maim *tr* mutilare
maimed *adj* manc·us -a -um
main *adj* praecipu·us -a -um; **the — point** cap·ut -itis *n;* **in the —** magnā ex parte

main *s* pelag·us -i *m*
mainland *s* contin·ens -entis *f*
mainly *adv* praecipue
maintain *tr (to keep)* tenēre; *(to keep alive)* alĕre; *(to defend)* sustinēre; *(to argue)* affirmare
maintenance *s (support)* sustentati·o -onis *f; (means of living)* vict·us -ūs *m*
majestic *adj* august·us -a -um; **how — was his address!** quanta fuit in oratione majestas!
majesty *s* majest·as -atis *f*
major *adj* ma·jor -jor -jus
major *s (mil)* tribun·us -i *m* militaris; *(in logic)* major praemiss·a -ae *f*
majority *s* major par·s -tis *f*
make *s* form·a -ae *f*, figur·a -ae *f*
make *tr* facĕre; *(by molding, shaping)* fingĕre; *(to render)* reddĕre; *(to appoint)* creare; *(to force)* cogĕre; **to — amends for** corrigĕre; **to — haste** festinare; **— light of** parvi facĕre; **to — money** pecuniam facĕre; **to — much of** magni facĕre; **to — over** transferre; **to — peace** pacem parēre; **to — public** publicare; **to — the bed** lectum sternĕre; **to — up** *(story)* fingĕre; **to — up with (s.o)** reverti in gratiam cum *(w. abl);* **to — use of** uti *(w. abl);* **to — way for** cedĕre *(w. dat),* viam dare *(dat)* ‖ *intr* **to — away with** amovēre; **to — for** petĕre
make-believe *adj* fict·us -a -um
maker *s* fabricat·or -oris *m*
make-up *s* compositi·o -onis *f; (disposition)* indol·es -is *f; (cosmetics)* fuc·us -i *m*
maladministration *s* mala administrati·o -onis *f*
malady *s* morb·us -i *m*
malcontent *adj* dissid·ens -entis
male *adj* masculin·us -a -um
male *s* ma·s -ris *m*
malefactor *s* hom·o -inis *m* maleficus
malevolence *s* malevolenti·a -ae *f*
malevolent *adj* malevol·us -a -um
malice *s* malevolenti·a -ae *f*
malicious *adj* malevol·us -a -um
maliciously *adv* malevolo animo
malign *tr* obtrectare
malignant *adj* malevol·us -a -um; *(med)* malign·us -a -um
malleable *adj* ductil·is -is -e
mallet *s* malle·us -i *m*
malpractice *s* delict·a -orum *npl*
maltreat *tr* vexare; *(w. blows, etc.)* mulcare
mama *s* mamm·a -ae *f*
man *s (human being)* hom·o -inis *m; (male)* vir viri *m*
man *tr (ships)* complēre; *(the walls)* praesidio firmare
manacle *s* manic·a -ae *f*
manacle *tr* manicas injicĕre *(w. dat)*
manage *tr* curare; *(esp. on large scale)* administrare, gerĕre

manageable *adj* tractabil·is -is -e
management *s* cur·a -ae *f*, administrati·o -onis *f*
manager *s* curat·or -oris *m; (steward)* procurat·or -oris *m; (of an estate)* villic·us -i *m*
mandate *s* mandat·um -i *n*
mane *s* jub·a -ae *f*
maneuver *s (mil)* decurs·us -ūs *m; (trick)* dol·us -i *m*
maneuver *intr (mil)* decurrĕre; *(fig)* machinari, tractare
mange *s* scabi·es -ei *f*
manger *s* praesep·e -is *n*
mangle *tr* lacerare, dilaniare
mangy *adj* sca·ber -bra -brum
manhood *s* virilit·as -atis *f; (period of puberty)* pubert·as -atis *f*
mania *s* insani·a -ae *f*
maniac *s* furios·us -i *m*
manifest *adj* manifest·us -a -um
manifest *tr* manifestare, declarare
manifestation *s* patefacti·o -onis *f*
manifestly *adv* manifeste
manifesto *s* edict·um -i *n*
manifold *adj* vari·us -a -um
manipulate *intr* tractare
manipulation *s* tractati·o -onis *f*
mankind *s* gen·us -eris *n* humanum
manliness *s* virt·us -utis *f;* **to act with —** viriliter agĕre
manly *adj* viril·is -is e
manner *s* mod·us -i *m; (custom)* consuetud·o -inis *f;* **after the — of** ritu *(w. gen),* more *(w. gen);* **bad —s** rusticit·as -atis *f;* **good —s** urbanit·as -atis *f*
mannerism *s* mala affectati·o -onis *f*
mannerly *adj* urban·us -a -um
mannikin *s* homuncul·us -i *m*
man-of-war *s* nav·is -is *f* longa
manor *s* praed·ium -(i)i *n*
man servant *s* serv·us -i *m*
mansion *s* dom·us ūs *f*
manslaughter *s* homicid·ium -(i)i *n*
mantel *s* plute·us -i *m* fornacis
mantle *s (women's outdoor wear)* pall·a -ae *f; (fig)* velament·um -i *n*
mantle *tr* tegĕre, dissimulare
manual *adj* manual·is -is -e; **— labor** oper·a -ae *f* quae manibus exercetur
manual *s* enchiridi·on -onis *n*
manufacture *s* fabric·a -ae *f*
manufacture *tr* fabrefacĕre
manufacturer *s* fabricat·or -oris *m*
manure *s* sterc·us -oris *n*
manure *tr* stercorare
manuscript *s* cod·ex -icis *m*
many *adj* mult·i -ae -a; **a good —** nonnull·i -ae -a; **as —…as** quot…tot; **how —** quot *(indecl);* **in — ways** multifariam; **so —** tot *(indecl)*
many-colored *adj* multicol·or -oris
map *s* tabul·a -ae *f* geographica

map 572 **maternal**

map *tr* **to — out** designare
maple *adj* acern·us -a -um
maple tree *s* ac·er -eris *n*
mar *tr* foedare; *(esp. fig)* deformare
marauder *s* praedat·or -oris *m*
marauding *s* praedati·o -onis *f*
marble *adj* marmore·us -a -um
marble *s* marm·or -oris *n*
March *s* Mart·ius -(i)i *m or* mens·is -is *m* Martius; **on the first of —** Kalendis Martiis
march *s* it·er -ineris *n*
march *tr* ducěre **‖** *intr* iter facěre, inceděre; **to — on** signa proferre; **to — on a town** oppidum aggredi
mare *s* equ·a -ae *f*
margin *s* marg·o -inis *mf*
marginal *adj* margini ascript·us -a -um
marigold *s* calth·a -ae *f*
marine *adj* marin·us -a -um
marine *s* mil·es -itis *m* classicus
mariner *s* naut·a -ae *m*
maritime *adj* maritim·us -a -um
mark *s* not·a -ae *f*; *(sign, token)* indic·ium -(i)i *n*; *(brand)* stigm·a -atis *n*; *(target)* scop·us -i *m*; *(of wound)* cicatr·ix -icis *f*; *(characteristic) expressed with gen after verb* esse, *e.g.,* **it is the — of a small mind** pusilli animi est
mark *tr* notare; *(to observe)* animadvertěre; *(with pencil, etc.)* designare; **to — out** metari
marker *s* ind·ex -icis *mf*
market *s* macell·um -i *n*
marketable *adj* venal·is -is -e
market day *s* nundin·ae -arum *fpl*
marketing *s* empti·o -onis *f*
marketplace *s* for·um -i *n*
market town *s* empor·ium -(i)i *n*
marmalade *s* quil·on -onis *n* ex aurantiis confectum
marquee *s* tabernacul·um -i *n*
marriage *s* matrimon·ium -(i)i *n*; **to give a daughter in —** filiam in matrimonio collocare
marriageable *adj (girl)* nubil·is -is -e
marriage alliance *s* affinit·as -atis *f*
marriage contract *s* pacti·o -onis *f* nuptialis
married *adj (of a woman)* nupta; *(of a man)* maritus; **to get —** matrimonio conjungi
marrow *s* medull·a -ae *f*
marry *tr (said of a man)* in matrimonium ducěre, uxorem ducěre; *(said of a woman)* nuběre *(w. dat)*
marsh *s* pal·us -udis *f*
marshal *s* du·x -cis *m*
marshal *tr* disponěre
marshy *adj* palus·ter -tris -tre
mart *s* empor·ium -(i)i *n*
martial *adj* bellicos·us -a -um
martyr *s* mart·yr -yris *mf*

martyrdom *s* martyr·ium -(i)i *n*
marvel *s* miracul·um -i *n*
marvel *intr* **to — at** mirari
marvelous *adj* mir·us -a -um
marvelously *adv* mire
masculine *adj* mascul·us -a -um; *(gram)* masculin·us -a -um
mash *s* mixtur·a -ae *f*; *(for cattle)* forag·o -inis *f*
mash *tr* commiscěre; *(to bruise)* contunděre
mask *s* person·a -ae *f*
mask *tr (fig)* dissimulare
mason *s* lapidar·ius -(i)i *m*
masonry *s* op·us -eris *n* caementicium
mass *adj* tot·us -a -um; *(large-scale)* magnari·us -a -um
mass *s* mol·es -is *f*; *(large amount)* copi·a -ae *f*; *(of people)* turb·a -ae *f*; *(eccl)* miss·a -ae *f*; **the —es** vulg·us -i *n*
mass *tr* congerěre, coacervare **‖** *intr* congeri, coacervari
massacre *s* trucidati·o -onis *f*
massacre *tr* trucidare
massage *s* iatraliptic·e -es *f*
massage *tr* fricare
masseur *s* iatralipt·es -ae *m*
massive *adj* solid·us -a -um
mast *s (of ship)* mal·us -i *m*; *(for cattle)* glan·s -dis *f*
master *s* domin·us -i *m*; *(teacher)* magis·ter -tri *m*; *(controller)* arbi·ter -tri *m*; **to be — of** potens esse *(w. gen)*, compos esse *(w. gen)*; **not be — of** impotens esse *(w. gen)*
master *tr* superare; *(to learn)* perdiscěre; *(passion)* continěre
masterful *adj* pot·ens -entis, imperios·us -a -um
masterly *adj* perit·us -a -um
masterpiece *s* magnum op·us -eris *n*
mastery *s* dominati·o -onis *f*; **having — of** pot·ens -entis *(w. gen)*
masticate *tr* manděre
mastiff *s* Moloss·us -i *m*
mat *s* teg·es -etis *f*
match *s (marriage)* nupti·ae -arum *fpl*; *(contest)* certam·en -inis *n*; *(an equal)* par paris *mf*; **a — for** par *(w. dat)*; **not a — for** impar *(w. dat)*
match *tr* adaequare **‖** *intr* quadrare
matchless *adj* incomparabil·is -is -e
matchmaker *s* nuptiarum conciliat·or -oris *m*, conciliatr·ix -icis *f*
mate *s* soc·ius -(i)i *m*, soci·a -ae *f*; *(spouse)* conju·(n)x -gis *mf*
mate *intr* coïre
material *adj* corpore·us -a -um; *(significant)* haud lev·is -is -e
material *s* materi·a -ae *f*
materially *adv* magnopere
maternal *adj* matern·us -a -um; **— aunt** materter·a -ae *f*; **— uncle** avuncul·us -i *m*

maternity *s* condici·o -onis *f* matris
mathematical *adj* mathematic·us -a -um
mathematician *s* mathematic·us -i *m*
mathematics *s* mathematic·a -ae *f*
matrimony *s* matrimon·ium -(i)i *n*
matrix *s* form·a -ae *f*
matron *s* matron·a -ae *f*
matronly *adj* matronal·is -is -e
matter *s (substance)* materi·a -ae *f; (affair)* res, rei *f; (med)* pus puris *n;* no —
nihil interest; **what's the** — **with you?**
quid tibi est?
matter *intr impers* refert; **it does not** —
nihil interest, nihil refert; **it** —**s a lot**
multum *or* magnopere refert; **what does
that** — **to me (to you)?** quid refert meā
(tuā)?
matting *s* teget·es -um *fpl*
mattress *s* culcit·a -ae *f*
mature *adj* matur·us -a -um
mature *intr* maturare
maturely *adv* mature
maturity *s* maturit·as -atis *f*
maul *tr* mulcare
mausoleum *s* mausole·um -i *n*
maw *s* ingluvi·es -ei *f*
mawkish *adj* putid·us -a -um
mawkishly *adv* putide
maxim *s* axiom·a -atis *n*
maximum *adj* quam maxim·us -a -um
May *s* Mai·us -i *m or* mens·is -is *m* Maius;
on the first of — Kalendis Maiis
may *intr* posse; **I may go** *(denoting law-
fulness, permission)* licet mihi ire; *(possibility, expressed by subj):* eam; **perhaps s.o. may say** fortasse quispiam
dixerit
maybe *adv* forsitan, fortasse
mayor *s* praet·or -oris *m*
maze *s* labyrinth·us -i *m*
me *pron* **by** — a me; **to** — mihi; **with** —
mecum
mead *s (drink)* muls·um -i *n*
meadow *s* prat·um -i *n*
meager *adj* exil·is -is -e; *(insufficient)*
exigu·us -a -um
meagerly *adv* exiliter
meagerness *s* exilit·as -atis *f*
meal *s* cib·us -i *m; (flour)* farin·a -ae *f;* **to
eat a** — cibum sumĕre
mean *adj (middle)* medi·us -a -um; *(low)*
humil·is -is -e; *(cruel)* vil·is -is -e
mean *s* med·ium -(i)i *n*
mean *tr* significare; *(after s.th. has been
mentioned)* dicĕre, *e.g.,* **of course, you**
— **Plato** Platonem videlicet dicis; *(to
intend)* velle, in animo habēre; **quid
sibi vult pater?** what does my father
mean?
meander *intr* sinuoso cursu labi
meaning *s* sens·us -ūs *m*, significati·o
-onis *f*
meaningful *adj* signific·ans -antis

meanness *s (lowliness)* humilit·as -atis *f;
(cruelty)* crudelit·as -atis *f*
means *spl (way, method)* rati·o -onis *f,*
mod·us -i *m;* **by all** — maxime, omnino;
by fair — recte; **by** — **of** *render by abl
or per (w. acc);* **by no** — haudquaquam
meanwhile *adv* interea, interim
measles *spl* morbill·i -orum *mpl*
measurable *adj* mensurabil·is -is -e
measure *s* mensur·a -ae *f; (proper measure)* mod·us -i *m; (course of action)*
rati·o -onis *f; (leg)* rogati·o -onis *f;* **beyond** — supra modum; **in some** — aliquā
ex parte; **to take** —**s** consulĕre *(w. dat of
that on behalf of which;* in + *acc of
person against whom)*
measure *tr* metiri; **to** — **off** metari
measurement *s* mensur·a -ae *f*
meat *s* car·o -nis *f*
meat tray *s* carnar·ium -(i)i *n*
mechanic *s* opif·ex -icis *m*
mechanical *adj* mechanic·us -a -um
mechanically *adv* mechanicā quādam arte
mechanics *s* mechanica ar·s -tis *f*
mechanism *s* mechanati·o -onis *f*
medal *s* insign·e -is *n*
medallion *s* numism·a -atis *n* sollemne
meddle *intr* (in) se interponĕre (in + *acc*)
meddler *s* ardali·o -onis *m*
meddlesome *adj* curios·us -a -um
medial *adj* medi·us -a -um
median *adj* dimidi·us -a -um
median *s* mediocrit·as -atis *f*
mediate *tr* conciliare ‖ *intr* se interponĕre
ad componendam litem; **to** — **between
estranged friends** aversos amicos
componĕre
mediation *s* intercessi·o -onis *f*
mediator *s* intercess·or -oris *m*
medical *adj* medic·us -a -um; — **practice**
medicin·a -ae *f*
medicate *tr* medicare
medication *s* medicament·um -i *n*
medicinal *adj* medic·us -a -um
medicine *s (science)* medicin·a -ae *f; (remedy)* medicament·um -i *n;* **to practice** —
medicinam exercēre
medieval *adj* medii aevi *(gen used as adj)*
mediocre *adj* mediocr·is -is -e
mediocrity *s* mediocrit·as -atis *f*
meditate *intr* cogitare
meditation *s* cogitati·o -onis *f*
meditative *adj* cogitabund·us -a -um
Mediterranean *s* mar·e -is *n* internum,
mar·e -is *n* nostrum
medium *s (middle)* med·ium -(i)i *n; (expedient)* mod·us -i *m; (agency)* conciliat·or
-oris *m*
medium *adj* mediocr·is -is -e
medley *s* farrag·o -inis *f*
meek *adj* mit·is -is -e; *(unassuming)*
summiss·us -a -um
meekly *adv* summisse

meekness *s* anim·us -i *m* summissus
meet *adj* apt·us -a -um; **it is —** convenit
meet *tr* convenire, obviam ire *(w. dat);*
(danger, death, etc.) obire ‖ *intr*
convenire; **to —** with offendĕre
meet *s* *(contest)* certam·en -inis *n*
meeting *s* *(of two or many individuals)*
congressi·o -onis *f; (assembly)* con-
vent·us -ūs *m; (for consultation)* con-
sil·ium -(i)i *n;* **to hold a —** conventum
habēre, consilium habēre
melancholy *s* maestiti·a -ae *f*
melancholy *adj* maest·us -a -um
melee *s* tumult·us -ūs *m*
mellow *adj* matur·us -a -um; *(from drink-*
ing) temulent·us -a -um
melodious *adj* canor·us -a -um
melodiously *adv* canore, modulate
melodramatic *adj* **to be —** paratra-
goedare
melody *s* mel·os -eos *n*
melt *tr* liquefacĕre; **to — down** conflare ‖
intr liquescĕre
melting *s* liquati·o -onis *f*
melting pot *s* fictil·e -is *n*
member *s* membr·um -i *n; (fig)* sodal·is -is *m*
membrane *s* membran·a -ae *f*
memento *s* monument·um -i *n*
memoirs *spl* commentari·i -orum *mpl*
memorable *adj* memorabil·is -is -e
memorandum *s* not·a -ae *f*
memorial *adj* monument·um -i *n*
memory *s* memori·a -ae *f; from —* ex
memoriā, memoriter; **in — of** in memoriam *(w. gen);* **in the — of man** post
hominum memoriam; **to commit to —**
ediscĕre; **to have a good —** esse memoriā
bonā
menace *s* min·ae -arum *fpl*
menace *tr* minari, minitari; *(of things)*
imminēre *(w. dat)*
menacing *adj* min·ax -acis; *(only of per-*
sons) minitabund·us -a -um
mend *tr* emendare; *(clothes)* sarcire ‖ *intr*
(to improve in health) mel·ior -ior -ius
fieri
mendicant *s* mendic·us -i *m,* mendic·a -ae *f*
menial *adj* servil·is -is -e
menial *s* serv·us -i *m,* serv·a -ae *f*
menses *spl* menstru·a -orum *npl*
mental *adj* mente concept·us -a -um
mentally *adv* mente, animo
mention *s* menti·o -onis *f;* **to make — of**
mentionem facĕre *(w. gen)*
mention *tr* commemorare; *(by name)*
nominare; **not to —** silentio praeterire;
not to — the others ne de alteris referam
mercantile *adj* mercatori·us -a -um
mercenary *adj* mercenari·us -a -um
mercenary *s* mil·es -itis *m* mercenarius
merchandise *s* merc·es -ium *fpl*
merchant *s* mercat·or -oris *m; (in a mar-*
ket) macellar·ius -(i)i *m*

merchant ship *s* nav·is -is *f* mercatoria
merciful *adj* misericor·s -dis
mercifully *adv* misericorditer
merciless *adj* immisericor·s -dis
mercilessly *adv* immisericorditer
mercurial *adj* a·cer -cris -cre
Mercury *s* Mercur·ius -(i)i *m*
mercury *s* argent·um -i *n* vivum
mercy *s* misericordi·a -ae *f*
mere *adj* mer·us -a -um
merely *adv* tantummodo, solum
meretricious *adj* meretrici·us -a -um
merge *tr* confundĕre ‖ *intr* confundi
meridian *s* meridianus circul·us -i *m*
merit *s* merit·um -i *n*
merit *tr* merēre, merēri
meritorious *adj* laudabil·is -is -e
mermaid *s* nymph·a -ae *f*
merrily *adv* festive, hilare
merry *adj* festiv·us -a -um, fest·us -a -um;
Merry Christmas fausta festa Christi
Nataliti·a -ae *f*
merrymaking *s* festivit·as -atis *f*
mesh *s* *(of net)* macul·a -ae *f*
mess *s* *(dirt)* squal·or -oris *m; (confusion)*
rerum perturbati·o -onis *f*
message *s* nunt·ius -(i)i *m,* nunt·ium -(i)i *n*
messenger *s* nunt·ius -(i)i *m*
metal *adj* metallic·us -a -um
metal *s* metall·um -i *n*
metallurgy *s* metallurgi·a -ae *f*
metamorphosis *s* transfigurati·o -onis *f*
metaphor *s* translati·o -onis *f*
metaphorical *adj* translat·us -a -um
metaphorically *adv* per translationem
metaphysical *adj* metaphysic·us -a -um
metaphysics *s* metaphysic·a -ae *f; (as a*
title) metaphysic·a -orum *npl*
meteor *s* fa·x -cis *f* caelestis
meteorology *s* meteorologi·a -ae *f*
mete out *tr* emetiri
meter *s* metr·um -i *n*
method *s* rati·o -onis *f*
methodical *adj* *(of things)* ratione et viā
fact·us -a -um; *(of a person)* dilig·ens
-entis
methodically *adv* ratione et viā
meticulous *adj* accurat·us -a -um
meticulously *adv* accurate
metonymy *s* metonymi·a -ae *f*
metrical *adj* metric·us -a -um
metropolis *s* cap·ut -itis *n*
mettle *s* anim·us -i *m*
miasma *s* halit·us -ūs *m*
microscope *s* microscop·ium -(i)i *n*
mid *adj* medi·us -a -um
midday *adj* meridian·us -a -um
midday *s* meridi·es -ei *f*
middle *adj* medi·us -a -um; **— age** aet·as
-atis *f* media
middle *s* med·ium -(i)i *n;* **in the middle of**
the road in mediā viā
midget *s* pumili·o -onis *mf*

midnight s media no·x -ctis f; **around —** mediā circiter nocte
midriff s diaphragm·a -atis n
midst s med·ium -(i)i n; **in the midst of** inter (w. acc)
midsummer s summa aest·as -atis f
midway adv medi·us -a -um; **he stood — between the lines** stabat medius inter acies
midwife s obstetr·ix -icis f
midwinter s brum·a -ae f
midwinter adj brumal·is -is -e
mien s habit·us -ūs m; (facial expression) vult·us -ūs m
might s vis f; **with all one's —** summā ope
might intr render by imperfect subjunctive
mightily adv valde
mighty adj validissim·us -a -um; **— Homer** ingens Homer·us -i m
migrate intr migrare
migration s peregrinati·o -onis f
migratory adj migr·ans -antis; **— birds** volucr·es -um fpl advenae
mild adj mit·is -is -e; (esp. of weather) clem·ens -entis; **to grow —** mitescěre
mildew s muc·or -oris m
mildewed adj **to become —** mucorem contrahěre
mildness s lenit·as -atis f; (of weather) clementi·a -ae f
mile s mille n passūs; **three —s** tria milia passuum
milestone s milliar·ium -i(i) n
militant adj milit·ans -antis
military adj militar·is -is -e; **— command** imper·ium -(i)i n; **— service** militi·a -ae f
military s militi·a -ae f
militia s militi·a -ae f domestica
milk s lac lactis n
milk tr mulgēre
milky adj lacte·us -a -um
Milky Way s Vi·a -ae f Lactea
mill s mol·a -ae f
millenium s mille ann·i -orum mpl
miller s pist·or -oris m
million adj decies centena milia (w. gen)
millionaire s hom·o -inis m praedives
millstone s mol·a -ae f
mime s mim·us -i m
mimic s imitat·or -oris m
mimic tr imitari
mimicry s imitati·o -onis f
mince tr concidēre; **not to — words** Latine loqui
mind s men·s -tis f; **to be in one's right —** compo·s -tis mentis suae esse; **to call to — recordari**; **to change one's —** mentem mutare; **to come to —** in mentem venire, (coll) in buccam venire; **to make up one's — constituěre**; **to show presence of —** schemas non loqui

mind tr (to look after) curare; (to regard) respicěre; (to object to) aegre ferre; **to — one's own business** suum negotium agěre
mindful adj mem·or -oris
mine s fodin·a -ae f, metall·um -i n; (fig) thesaur·us -i m
mine tr effoděre
mine adj me·us -a -um
miner s metallic·us -i m
mineral s metall·um -i n
mineral adj metallic·us -a -um
mineralogist s metallorum perit·us -i m
mineralogy s metallorum scienti·a -ae f
mingle tr commiscēre ‖ intr se immiscēre
miniature s minuta tabul·a -ae f
minimum adj quam minim·us -a -um
minimum s minim·um -i n
minion s clien·s -tis mf
minister s adminis·ter -tri m
minister intr ministrare
ministry s ministrati·o -onis f
minor s pupill·us -i m, pupill·a -ae f
minor adj min·or -or -us
minority s minor par·s -tis f
minstrel s fidic·en -enis m
mint s (for making money) monet·a -ae f; (bot) menth·a -ae f
mint tr cuděre
minute s temporis moment·um -i n; **to keep —s** acta diurna conficěre
minute adj (small) minut·us -a -um; (exact) accurat·us -a -um
minutely adv minute, subtiliter
miracle s miracul·um -i n
miraculous adj miraculos·us -a -um
miraculously adv miraculose
mirage s imag·o -inis f ficta
mire s lut·um -i n
mirror s specul·um -i n
mirth s hilarit·as -atis f
mirthful adj hilar·is -is -e
misadventure s infortun·ium -i(i) n
misapply tr abuti (w. abl)
misapprehend tr male intellegěre
misapprehension s falsa concepti·o -onis f
misbehave intr indecore se gerěre
misbehavior s morum pravit·as -atis f
miscalculate intr errare
miscalculation s err·or -oris m
miscarriage s abort·us -ūs m; (fig) malus success·us -ūs m
miscarry intr abortum facěre; (fig) male succeděre
miscellaneous adj miscellane·us -a -um
mischance s infortun·ium -(i)i n
mischief s malefic·ium -(i)i n; (of children) lascivi·a -ae f; **to refrain from doing any —** ab injuria et maleficio temperare
mischievous adj malefic·us -a -um; (playful) lasciv·us -a -um
misconceive tr male intellegěre

misconception *s* falsa opini·o -onis *f*
misconduct *s* delict·um -i *n;* **to be guilty of** — delictum in se admittĕre
misconstrue *tr* male interpretari
misdeed *s* delict·um -i *n*
misdemeanor *s* levius delict·um -i *n*
misdirect *tr* fallĕre
miser *s* avar·us -i *m*
miserable *adj* mis·er -era -erum
miserably *adv* misere
miserly *adj* avar·us -a -um
misery *s* miseri·a -ae *f*
misfortune *s* infortun·ium -(i)i *n*
misgiving *s* sollicitud·o -inis *f;* **to have —s about** diffidĕre *(w. dat)*
misgovern *tr* male administrare
misguide *tr* seducĕre
misguided *adj (fig)* dem·ens -entis
mishap *s* incommod·um -i *n*
misinform *tr* falsa docēre *(w. acc)*
misinterpret *tr* male interpretari
misinterpretation *s* prava interpretati·o -onis *f*
misjudge *tr* male judicare
mislay *tr* amittĕre
mislead *tr* seducĕre, decipĕre
mismanage *tr* male gerĕre
mismanagement *s* mala administrati·o -onis *f*
misnomer *s* falsum nom·en -inis *n*
misplace *tr* alieno loco ponĕre; **confidence in such persons is —ed** iis male creditur
misprint *s* errat·um -i *n* typographicum, mend·um -i *n*
misquote *tr* aliis verbis ponĕre
misquotation *s* falsa prolati·o -onis *f*
misrepresent *tr* detorquēre
misrepresentation *s* sinistra interpretati·o -onis *f*
misrule *s* prava administrati·o -onis *f*
miss *s* err·or -oris *m; (term of respect)* domin·a -ae *f*
miss *tr (to overlook)* omittĕre; *(one's aim)* non attingĕre; *(to feel the want of)* desiderare ‖ *intr (to fall short)* errare
misshapen *adj* deform·is -is -e
missile *s* missil·e -is *n*
missing *adj* abs·ens -entis; **to be —** deësse
mission *s (delegation, sending)* missi·o -onis *f; (goal)* fin·is -is *m*
misspell *tr* perperam scribĕre
misspend *tr* prodigĕre
misstate *tr* parum accurate memorare
misstatement *s* fals·um -i *n*
mist *s* nebul·a -ae *f*
mistake *s* err·or -oris *m; (written)* mend·um -i *n;* **to make a —** errare
mistake *tr* **to — *(s.o. or s.th.)* for** habēre pro *(w. abl)*
mistaken *adj* fals·us -a -um; **to be —** falli; **unless I am —** ni fallor
mistletoe *s* visc·um -i *n*
mistress *s* domin·a -ae *f,* her·a -ae *f; (par-*

amour) concubin·a -ae *f; (teacher)* magistr·a -ae *f*
mistrust *s* diffidenti·a -ae *f*
mistrust *tr* diffidēre *(w. dat)*
mistrustful *adj* diffid·ens -entis
mistrustfully *adv* diffidenter
misty *adj* nebulos·us -a -um
misunderstand *tr* perperam intellegĕre
misunderstanding *s* falsa opini·o -onis *f; (among friends)* offensi·o -onis *f*
misuse *s* abus·us -ūs *m;* **that is a — of the term** id est verbum alieno loco adhibēre
misuse *tr* abuti *(w. abl); (to 'revile)* conviciari
mite *s (bit)* parvul·us -i *m; (coin)* sext·ans -antis *m*
miter *s* mitr·a -ae *f*
mitigate *tr* mitigare
mitigation *s* mitigati·o -onis *f*
mix *tr* miscēre; **to — in** admiscēre; **to — up** commiscēre; *(fig)* confundĕre
mixed *adj* promiscu·us -a -um
mixture *s* mixtur·a -ae *f*
moan *s* gemit·us -ūs *m*
moan *intr* gemĕre
moat *s* foss·a -ae *f*
mob *s* turb·a -ae *f,* vulg·us -i *n*
mob *tr* stipare
mobile *adj* mobil·is -is -e
mobility *s* mobilit·as -atis *f*
mock *tr* irridēre
mock *adj* mimic·us -a -um; **— death** mimica mor·s -tis *f;* **— sea battle show** naumachiae spectacul·um -i *n*
mockery *s* irrisi·o -onis *f*
mode *s* mod·us -i *m; (fashion)* us·us -ūs *m;* **— of life** vitae praeposit·um -i *n*
model *s* exempl·ar -aris *n;* **on the — of** ad simulacrum *(w. gen)*
model *tr* formare; *(e.g., a statue)* fingĕre; **to — oneself after** imitari
moderate *adj* moderat·us -a -um
moderate *tr* moderari, temperare
moderately *adv* moderate
moderation *s* moderati·o -onis *f*
moderator *s* praes·es -idis *mf*
modern *adj* rec·ens -entis
modest *adj (restricted)* modest·us -a -um; *(slight)* modic·us -a -um
modestly *adv* verecunde
modesty *s* modesti·a -ae *f*
modification *s* mutati·o -onis *f*
modify *tr* (im)mutare
modulate *tr* flectĕre
modulation *s* flexi·o -onis *f*
moist *adj* (h)umid·us -a -um
moisten *tr* (h)umectare
moisture *s* hum·or -oris *m*
molar *s* den·s -tis *m* genuinus
molasses *s* sacchari fae·x -cis *f*
mold *s* form·a -ae *f; (mustiness)* muc·or -oris *m*
mold *tr* formare, fingĕre ‖ *intr* mucescĕre

molder *intr* putrescĕre
moldiness *s* muc·or -oris *m*
moldy *adj* mucid·us -a -um
mole *s (animal)* talp·a -ae *f; (sea wall)* mol·es -is *f; (on skin)* naev·us -i *m*
molecule *s* particul·a -ae *f*
molehill *s* **to make mountains out of —s** e rivo flumina magna facĕre
molest *tr* vexare
molt *tr* plumas ponĕre
molten *adj* liquefact·us -a -um
moment *s* temporis moment·um -i *n;* **at any —** omnibus momentis; **at the very —** ipso tempore; **for a —** paulisper; **in a —** momento temporis
momentarily *adv* statim
momentary *adj* brev·is -is -e
momentous *adj* magni momenti *(gen, used adjectively)*
monarch *s* re·x -gis *m*
monarchical *adj* regi·us -a -um
monarchy *s* regn·um -i *n*
monastery *s* monaster·ium -(i)i *n*
monetary *adj* pecuniari·us -a -um
money *s* pecuni·a -ae *f*
moneychanger *s* numular·ius -(i)i *m*
moneylender *s* faenerat·or -oris *m*
mongrel *s* hybrid·a -ae *m*
monitor *m* admonit·or -oris *m*
monk *s* monach·us -i *m*
monkey *s* sim·ius -(i)i *m*, simi·a -ae *f*
monogram *s* monogramm·a -atis *n*
monologue *s* monologi·a -ae *f*
monopolize *tr* monopolium exercēre in *(w. acc)*
monopoly *s* monopol·ium -(i)i *n*
monosyllabic *adj* monosyllab·us -a -um
monosyllable *s* monosyllab·um -i *n*
monotonous *adj* semper idem (eadem, idem); *(sing-song)* canor·us-a -um
monotony *s* taed·ium -(i)i *n*
monster *s* monstr·um -i *n*
monstrosity *s* monstr·um -i *n*
monstrous *adj* monstros·us -a -um
monstrously *adv* monstrose
month *s* mens·is -is *m;* **on the first of the —** Kalendis
monthly *adj* menstru·us -a -um
monthly *adv* singulis mensibus
monument *s* monument·um -i *n*
monumental *adj (huge)* ing·ens -entis; *(important)* grav·is -is -e
mood *s* animi habit·us -i *m; (gram)* mod·us -i *m*
moodiness *s* morosit·as -atis *f*
moody *adj* moros·us -a -um
moon *s* lun·a -ae *f;* **the — is shining** luna nitescit
moonlight *s* lunae lum·en -inis *n;* **by —** per lunam
moonstruck *adj* lunatic·us -a -um
Moor *s* Maur·us -i *m*
moor *tr* religare, ancoris retinēre

moor *s* tesc·a -orum *npl*
mop *s* penicul·us -i *m*
mop *tr* detergēre
mope *intr* maerēre
moral *adj (relating to morals)* moral·is -is -e; *(morally proper)* honest·us -a -um
moral *s (of story)* document·um -i *n*
morale *s* anim·us -i *m; (of several)* anim·i -orum *mpl;* **— is low** animi deficiunt
morality *s* boni mor·es -um *mpl*
moralize *intr* de moribus disserĕre
morals *spl* mor·es -um *mpl*
morass *s* pal·us -udis *f*
morbid *adj* morbid·us -a -um
more *adj* plus *(w. gen); (pl)* plur·es -es -ia; *(denoting greater extent of space or time)* amplius: **for — than four hours** amplius quattuor horis; **— and —** magis magisque; **— or less** plus minus; **— than** plus quam; **— than enough** ultra quam satis; **no — than** non diutius; **and what's —, he even comes into the senate** immo vero etiam in senatum venit
moreover *adv* praeterea
morning *s* mane *n (indecl)*, temp·us -oris *n* matutinum; **early in the —** bene mane; **from — till evening** a mane usque ad vesperam; **good —!** salve!; **in the —** mane; **this —** hodie mane
morning *adj* matutin·us -a -um
morning star *s* Lucif·er -eri *m*
morose *adj* moros·us -a -um
morosely *adv* morose
moroseness *s* morosit·as -atis *f*
morsel *s* off·a -ae *f*
mortal *adj* mortal·is -is -e; *(deadly)* mortif·er -era -erum
mortal *s* mortal·is -is *mf*
mortality *s* mortalit·as -atis *f*
mortally *adv* mortifere; **to be — wounded** mortiferum vulnus accipĕre
mortar *s* mortar·ium -(i)i *n*
mortgage *s* hypothec·a -ae *f*
mortgage *tr* obligare
mortify *tr (to vex)* offendĕre
mosaic *s* tessellatum op·us -eris *n*
mosaic floor *s* tesselatum et sectile paviment·um -i *n*
mosquito *s* cul·ex -icis *m*
moss *s* musc·us -i *m*
mossy *adj* muscos·us -a -um
most *adj* plurim·us -a -um, plerusque, -aque, -umque; **for the — part** maximam partem; **— people** plerique
most *adv (w. verbs)* maxime; *(w. adjectives and adverbs, expressed by superl., or w. adjectives ending in -ius, expressed w.* maxime *w. positive);* **— enthusiastically** animosissime
mostly *adv* plerumque
moth *s* blatt·a -ae *f*
moth-eaten *adj* blattis peres·us -a -um
mother *s* ma·ter -tris *f*

motherhood *s* matris condici•o -onis *f*
mother-in-law *s* socr•us -ūs *f*
motherless *adj* matre orb•us -a -um
motherly *adj* matern•us -a -um
motion *s* moti•o -onis *f; (proposal of a bill)* rogati•o -onis *f;* **to make a** — ferre; **to set in** — ciēre
motionless *adj* immot•us -a -um
motive *s* caus•a -ae *f,* rati•o -onis *f*
motive *adj* mov•ens -entis
motley *adj* vari•us -a -um
mottled *adj* maculos•us -a -um
motto *s* sententi•a -ae *f*
mound *s (round)* tumul•us -i *m; (reaching lengthwise)* agg•er -eris *m*
mount *s* mon•s -tis *m*
mount *tr* conscendĕre **‖** *intr* ascendĕre
mountain *s* mon•s -tis *m*
mountaineer *s* montan•us -i *m*
mountainous *adj* montan•us -a -um
mountain top *s* culm•en -inis *n* summi montis
mounted *adj* inscens•us -a -um; *(on horse)* equistr•is -is -e
mourn *tr & intr* lugēre
mourner *s* plorat•or -oris *m*
mournful *adj* lugubr•is -is -e
mournfully *adv* maeste
mourning *s* luct•us -ūs *m; (dress)* vest•is -is *f* lugubris; **in** — pullat•us -a -um; **to go into** — vestitum mutare
mouse *s* mu•s -ris *m*
mousetrap *s* muscipul•um -i *n*
mouth *s* os, oris *n; (of beast)* fau•x -cis *f; (of river)* ost•ium -(i)i *n; (of bottle)* lur•a -ae *f*
mouthful *s* buccell•a -ae *f*
mouthpiece *s* interpr•es -etis *m*
movable *adj* mobil•is -is -e
movables *spl* mobil•ia -ium *npl*
move *tr* movēre; *(emotionally)* com-movēre; *(to propose)* ferre **‖** *intr* movēri, se movēre; *(to change residence)* migrare; **to** — **on** progredi
movement *s* mot•us -ūs *m*
moving *adj* flebil•is -is -e
mow *tr* secare
mower *s* faenis•ex -icis *mf*
mowing *s* faenisic•ium -(i)i *n*
much *adj* mult•us -a -um; **as** —...**as** tantus...quantus; **how** — quant•us -a -um; **how** — **does this cost?** quanti hoc constat?; — **less** nedum; **so** — tant•us -a -um; **too** — nimi•us -a -um; **very** — plurim•us -a -um
much *adv* multum; *(w. comparatives)* multo; **very** — plurimum
muck *s* sterc•us -oris *n*
mucous *adj* mucos•us -a -um
mucus *s* muc•us -i *m*
mud *s* lut•um -i *n,* lim•us -i *m*
muddle *tr* turbare; *(fig)* perturbare
muddle *s* turb•a -ae *f*

muddy *adj* lutulent•us -a -um; *(troubled)* turbid•us -a -um
muffle *tr* involvĕre; **to** — **up** obvolvĕre
muffled *adj* surd•us -a -um
mug *s* pocul•um -i *n*
mug *tr* mulcare
mugger *s* percuss•or -oris *m*
muggy *adj* humid•us -a -um
mulberry *s* mor•um -i *n*
mulberry tree *s* mor•us -i *f*
mule *s* mul•us -i *m*
muleteer *s* muli•o -onis *m*
mulish *adj* obstinat•us -a -um
multifarious *adj* vari•us -a -um
multiplication *s* multiplicati•o -onis *f*
multiply *tr* multiplicare **‖** *intr* augēri
multitude *s* multitud•o -inis *f; (crowd)* turb•a -ae *f*
mumble *tr & intr* murmurare
munch *tr* manducare
mundane *adj* mundan•us -a -um
municipal *adj* municipal•is -is -e
municipality *s* municip•ium -(i)i *n*
munificence *s* munificenti•a -ae *f*
munificent *adj* munific•us -a -um
munificently *adv* munifice
munitions *spl* belli apparat•us -ūs *m*
mural *adj* mural•is -is -e
murder *s* caed•es -is *f,* nex, necis *f*
murder *tr* necare; **to** — **a song** lacerare canticum
murderer *s* homicid•a -ae *mf*
murderous *adj* cruent•us -a -um
murky *adj* caliginos•us -a -um
murmur *s* murm•ur -uris *n*
murmur *tr & intr* murmurare
murmuring *s* admurmurati•o -onis *f*
muscle *s* muscul•us -i *m*
muscular *adj* musculos•us -a -um
Muse *s* Mus•a -ae *f*
muse *intr* secum agitare
mushroom *s* bolet•us -i *m*
music *s* music•a -ae *f; (of instruments and voices)* cant•us ūs *m*
musical *adj (of persons)* music•us -a -um; *(of sound)* canor•us -a -um
musician *s* music•us -i *m,* music•a *f; (of stringed instrument)* fidic•en -inis *m; (of wind instruments)* tibic•en -inis *m*
must *s* must•um -i *n*
must *intr* **I** — **go** mihi eundum est, me oportet ire, debeo ire, necesse est (ut) eam
mustard *s* sinap•i -is *n*
muster *tr* lustrare; *(fig)* cogĕre; **to** — **up courage** animum sumĕre **‖** *intr* coïre
muster *s* copiarum lustrati•o -onis *f*
musty *adj* mucid•us -a -um
mutable *adj* mutabil•is -is -e
mute *adj* mut•us -a -um
mutilate *tr* mutilare, truncare
mutilated *adj* mutil•us -a -um
mutilation *s* mutilati•o -onis *f*
mutineer *s* seditios•us -i *m*

mutinous *adj* seditios·us -a -um
mutiny *s* sediti·o -onis *f*
mutiny *intr* seditionem facĕre
mutter *s* murmurati·o -onis *f*
mutter *tr & intr* mussare
mutton *s* ovillin·a -ae *f*
mutual *adj* mutu·us -a -um
mutually *adv* mutuo, inter se
muzzle *s* capistr·um -i *n*
muzzle *tr* capistrare
my *adj* me·us -a -um; — **own** propri·us
-a -um
myriad *adj (innumerable)* sescent·i -ae -a
myrrh *s* myrrh·a -ae *f*
myrtle *s* myrt·us -i *f*
myself *pron (refl)* me; *(intensive)* ipse,
egomet; **to** — mihi
mysterious *adj* arcan·us -a -um
mysteriously *adv* arcane
mystery *s* myster·ium -(i)i *n; (fig)* res, rei
f occultissima
mystical *adj* mystic·us -a -um
mystically *adv* mystice
mystify *tr* confundĕre
myth *s* myth·os -i *m*
mythical *adj* fabulos·us -a -um
mythology *s* histori·a -ae *f* fabularum

N

nab *tr* prehendĕre
nadir *s* fund·us -i *m*
nag *s* caball·us -i *m*
nag *tr* objurgitare
naiad *s* naï·as -adis *f*
nail *s* clav·us -i *m; (of finger, of toe)*
ungu·is -is *m*
nail *tr* clavīs (con)figĕre *(w. dat of that to
which);* **to** — **to the cross** cruci figĕre
naive *adj* simpl·ex -icis
naively *adv* simpliciter
naked *adj* nud·us -a -um
nakedly *adv (fig)* aperte
name *s* nom·en -inis *n; (a significant designation)* appellati·o -onis *f; (good name,
reputation)* fam·a -ae *f; (term)* voca-
bul·um -i *n;* by — nominatim; **her** — **is
Fortunata** Fortunata appellatur *or* illi
nomen est Fortunata *or* illi nomen est
Fortunatae
name *tr (to call by a name; to mention by
name)* nominare; *(to appoint)* dicĕre; **to
be** —**ed after one's father** nominari a
patre
nameless *adj* nominis exper·s -tis
namely *adv* scilicet
nap *s* brevis somn·us -i *n; (of cloth)* vill·us
-i *m;* **to take a** — brevi somno uti
nape *s* — **of the neck** cerv·ix -icis *f*
napkin *s* mapp·a -ae *f*
narcotic *adj* somnific·us -a -um

narcotic *s* medicament·um -i *n* somni-
ficum
nard *s* nard·um -i *n*
narrate *tr* narrare
narration *s* narrati·o -onis *f*
narrative *s* narrati·o *f*
narrator *s* narrat·or -oris *m*
narrow *adj* angust·us -a -um; *(fig)* arct·us
-a -um
narrow *tr* coarctare **‖** *intr* coarctari
narrowly *adv* vix, aegre
narrow-minded *adj* animi angusti *or* parvi
(gen used adjectively)
narrowness *s* angusti·ae -arum *fpl*
nasty *adj (foul)* foed·us -a -um; *(mean)*
turp·is -is -e
natal *adj* natal·is -is -e
nation *s* gen·s -tis *f,* nati·o -onis *f; (organized political community)* popul·us -i *m*
national *adj (expr. by gen of* gens *or* natio
or populus): — **customs** gentis mor·es
-um *mpl;* — **assembly** concil·ium -(i)i *n*
populi
nationality *s* civit·as -atis *f*
nationalize *tr* confiscare
native *adj* indigen·a -ae *mf;* — **land** patri·a
-ae *f;* — **language** patrius serm·o -onis *m*
native *s* indigen·a -ae *mf*
nativity *s* ort·us -ūs *m*
natural *adj (history, law, daughter, death)*
natural·is -is -e; *(not man-made)* nativ·us
-a -um; *(innate; opp: traditus)* innat·us
-a -um
natural disposition *s* indol·es -is *f*
naturalization *s* civitatis donati·o -onis *f*
naturalize *tr* civitate donare
naturally *adv* naturā, naturaliter; *(unaf-
fectedly)* simpliciter; *(of its own accord)*
sponte
natural science *s* physic·a -ae *f*
nature *s (of a specific thing)* natur·a -ae *f;
(universal nature)* rerum natur·a -ae *f;
(mostly of persons)* ingen·ium -(i)i *n;*
second — altera natur·a -ae *f;* **beauties
of** — amoenitat·es -um *fpl* locorum
naught *s* nihil; **to set at** — nihili facĕre
naughty *adj* improbul·us -a -um
nausea *s* nause·a -ae *f; (fig)* fastid·ium
-(i)i *n*
nauseate *tr (fig)* fastidium movēre *(w.
dat);* **to be** —**ed** fastidire
nautical *adj* nautic·us -a -um
naval *adj* naval·is -is -e
nave *s (archit)* nav·is -is *f*
navel *s* umbilic·us -i *m*
navigable *adj* navigabil·is -is -e
navigate *tr* gubernare **‖** *intr* navigare
navigation *s* navigati·o -onis *f; (as a field)*
re·s -rum *fpl* nauticae
navigator *s* gubernat·or -oris *m*
navy *s* class·is -is *f*
nay *adv* non ita
near *prep* prope *(w. acc); (esp. to denote a*

battle site) ad *(w. acc),* apud *(w. acc); (in the vicinity, e.g., of a city)* apud *(w. acc)*
near *adj* propinqu•us -a -um; *(of relation)* proxim•us -a -um; — **at hand** in promptu, praesto
near *adv* prope, juxta
near *tr* appropinquare *(w. dat)*
nearly *adv* prope, fere, ferme
nearness *s* propinquit•as -atis *f*
nearsighted *adj* myop•s -is
neat *adj* mund•us -a -um; *(properly groomed)* compt•us -a -um; *(in good taste)* concinn•us -a -um
neatly *adv* munde; concinne
neatness *s* munditi•a -ae *f*
necessarily *adv* necessario
necessary *adj* necessari•us -a -um; **it is —** opus est; **consultation is —** consulto opus est
necessitate *tr* cogĕre
necessity *s* necessit•as -atis *f; (want)* egest•as -atis *f; (thing)* res necessaria *f;* **— is the mother of invention** ingeniosa est rerum egestas
neck *s (of body or bottle)* cerv•ix -icis *f (often pl. without change of meaning); (of animal)* coll•um -i *n*
necklace *s* monil•e -is *n*
necktie *s* collar•e -is *n*
nectar *s* nect•ar -aris *n*
need *s (necessity)* necessit•as -atis *f; (want)* inopi•a -ae *f;* **there is — of** opus est *(w. abl)*
need *tr* egēre *(w. abl),* indigēre *(w. abl); (to require)* requirēre
needle *s* ac•us -ūs *f*
needless *adj* minime necessari•us -a -um; **— to say** sine dubio
needlessly *adv* sine causā
needy *adj* egen•s -tis
nefarious *adj* nefari•us -a -um
negation *s* negati•o -onis *f*
negative *adj* negativ•us -a -um
negative *s* negati•o -onis *f;* **to answer in the —** negare
neglect *tr* neglegĕre
neglect *s* neglect•us -ūs *m*
neglectful *adj* neglegen•s -tis
negligible *adj* tenu•is -is -e
negotiable *adj* mercabil•is -is -e
negotiate *tr* agĕre de *(w. abl);* **to — a peace** de pacis condicionibus agĕre ‖ *intr* negotiari
negotiation *s* transacti•o -onis *f;* **to settle disputes by —** controversias per colloquia componĕre
negotiator *s* conciliat•or -oris *m; (spokesman)* orat•or -oris *m*
Negro *s* Aethiop•s -is *m*
neigh *intr* hinnire
neigh *s* hinnit•us -ūs *m*
neighbor *s* vicin•us -i *m*
neighborhood *s* vicini•a -ae *f*

neighboring *adj* vicin•us -a -um
neighborly *adj* benign•us -a -um
neither *pron* neu•ter -tra -trum
neither *conj* nec, neque; **—...nor** neque...neque
neophyte *s* tir•o -onis *m*
nephew *s* fratris *(or* sororis*)* fil•ius -(i)i *m*
nepotism *s* nimius in necessarios fav•or -oris *m*
Nereid *s* Nere•is -idos *f*
nerve *s (fig)* audaci•a -ae *f*
nervous *adj* trepid•us -a -um
nervously *adv* trepide
nervousness *s* trepidati•o -onis *f*
nest *s* nid•us -i *m*
nest *intr* nidificare
nestle *intr* recubare
net *s* ret•e -is *n*
net *tr* irritire
netting *s* reticul•um -i *n*
nettle *s* urtic•a -ae *f*
nettle *tr* vexare
network *s* op•us -eris *n* reticulatum
neuter *adj (gram)* neu•ter -tra -trum
neutral *adj* medi•us -a -um
neutrality *s* nullam in partem propensi•o -onis *f*
neutralize *tr* aequare
never *adv* numquam
nevermore *adv* numquam posthac
nevertheless *adv* nihilominus
new *adj* nov•us -a -um
newly *adv* nuper, modo
newcomer *s* adven•a -ae *mf*
news *s (no single Latin counterpart exists) (message)* nunt•ium -(i)i *n,* nunt•ius -(i)i *m;* **any — ?** num quidnam novi?; **good —** boni nuntii *mpl;* **to bring good —** gaudium nuntiare; — **came** nuntiatum est; **when he heard this —** his auditis
newspaper *s* act•a -orum *npl* diurna
next *adj* proxim•us -a -um; *(of time)* insequen•s -tis; **— day** postridie
nibble *tr* arrodĕre; *(fig)* carpĕre ‖ *intr* rodĕre
nice *adj (dainty)* delicat•us -a -um; *(cute)* bell•us -a -um; *(exact)* accurat•us -a -um; *(weather)* seren•us -a -um
nicely *adv (well)* bene; *(exactly)* subtiliter; *(prettily)* belle
nicety *s* subtilit•as -atis *f*
niche *s* aedicul•a -ae *f*
nick *s* incisur•a -ae *f;* **in the very — of** time in ipso articulo temporis
nick *tr* incidĕre
nickname *s* agnom•en -inis *n*
niece *s* fratris *(or* sororis*)* fili•a -ae *f*
niggardly *adj* parc•us -a -um
nigh *adj* propinqu•us -a -um
night *s* no•x -ctis *f;* **at —, by —** nocte, noctu; **good —!** bene valeas et quiescas!; **— after —** per singulas noctes; **to spend the —** pernoctare

nightcap *s (drink)* embasiocoet·as -ae *f*
nightfall *s* at — sub noctem
nightingale *s* luscini·a -ae *f*
nightly *adj* nocturn·us -a -um
nightly *adv* de nocte
nightmare *s* tumultuosum somn·ium -(i)i *n;* **to have —s** per somnium exterrēri
night watch *s* vigili·a -ae *f; (guard)* vig·il -ilis *m*
nimble *adj* agil·is -is -e
nine *adj* novem *(indecl);* — **times** noviens
nineteen *adj* undeviginti *(indecl)*
nineteenth *adj* undevicesim·us -a -um
ninetieth *adj* nonagesim·us -a -um
ninety *adj* nonaginta *(indecl)*
ninth *adj* non·us -a -um
nip *tr* vellicare; *(of frost)* urĕre; — **the thing in the bud!** principiis obsta!; **to — off** desecare
nippers *spl* for·ceps -cipitis *m*
nipple *s* papill·a -ae *f*
no *adj* null·us -a -um; **he has — more money** non plus pecuniae habet; — **more than three times** ter nec amplius; **there is — news** nihil novi est
no *adv* non; — **indeed** minime vero; **to say — negare**
nobility *s* nobilit·as -atis *f; (the nobles as a group)* nobil·es -ium *mpl*
noble *adj* nobil·is -is -e; *(morally)* honest·us -a -um
noble *s* hom·o -inis *m* nobilis
nobleman *s* vir· -i *m* nobilis
nobly *adv* praeclare
nobody *pron* nem·o -inis *m;* **some — or other** nescio qui terrae filius
nocturnal *adj* nocturn·us -a -um
nod *s* nut·us -ūs *m*
nod *intr* nutare; *(to doze)* dormitare; *(in assent)* annuĕre
noise *s* strepit·us -ūs *m; (high-pitched)* strid·or -oris *m; (crash)* frag·or -oris *m; (crackling, rattling)* crepit·us -ūs *m; (esp. of people talking loud)* convic·ium -(i)i *n;* **to make —** strepĕre, crepitare
noise *tr* **to — abroad** evulgare
noiseless *adj* tacit·us -a -um
noiselessly *adv* tacite
noisily *adv* cum strepitu
noisy *adj* clamos·us -a -um
nomad *s* nom·as -adis *mf*
nomadic *adj* vag·us -a -um
nominal *adj* nominal·is -is -e
nominally *adv* nomine, verbo
nominate *tr* nominare
nomination *s* nominati·o -onis *f*
nominative *adj* nominativ·us -a -um
nominee *s* hom·o -inis *m* destinatus
none *pron* nem·o -inis *m*
nonentity *s* nihil·um -i *n*
nones *spl* Non·ae -arum *fpl*
nonplus *tr (to puzzle)* ad incitas redigĕre

nonsense *s* nug·ae -arum *fpl;* —! nugas!; **to talk —** garrire
nonsensical *adj* inept·us -a -um
nook *s* angul·us -i *m*
noon *s* meridi·es -ei *m;* **at —** meridie; **before —** ante meridiem
noonday *adj* meridian·us -a -um
no one *pron* nem·o -inis *m*
noose *s* laque·us -i *m*
nor *conj* nec, neque
norm *s* norm·a -ae *f*
normal *adj* solit·us -a -um
normally *adv* plerumque
north *s* septentrion·es -um *mpl;* **to face —** in septentriones spectare
north *adj* septentrional·is -is -e; — **of** supra + *acc)*
northern *adj* septentrional·is -is -e
northern lights *spl* auror·a -ae *f* Borealis
north pole *s* arct·os -i *f*
northwards *adv* (ad) septentriones versus
north wind *s* aquil·o -onis *m*
nose *s (as a feature of the face)* nas·us -ūs *m; (as a function of smell)* nar·es -ium *mpl;* **having a large —** nasut·us -a -um; **to blow the —** emungĕre
nostril *s* nar·is -is *f*
not *adv* non; *(more emphatic)* haud; — **at all** nullo modo, haudquaquam; — **even** ne...quidem
notable *adj* notabil·is -is -e
notably *adv* insigniter
notary *s* scrib·a -ae *m*
notation *s* notati·o -onis *f*
notch *s* incisur·a -ae *f*
notch *tr* incidĕre
note *s (mark)* not·a -ae *f; (comment)* adnotati·o -onis *f; (mus)* son·us -i *m,* vo·x -cis *f; (com)* chirograph·um -i *n;* **a brief —** scriptur·a -ae *f* brevis
note *tr* notare; *(to notice)* animadvertĕre
notebook *s* libell·us -i *m,* pugillar·es -ium *mpl*
noted *adj* not·us -a -um
noteworthy *adj* notabil·is -is -e
nothing *pron* nihil, nil; **for —** *(free)* gratis, gratuito; *(in vain)* frustra; **good for —** nequam; — **but** nihil nisi; **to think — of** nihili facĕre
notice *s (act of noticing)* notati·o -onis *f; (announcement)* denuntiati·o -onis *f; (sign)* proscripti·o -onis *f,* titul·us -i *m;* **to escape —** latēre; **to escape the — of** fallĕre; **to give — of** denuntiare
notice *tr* animadvertĕre
noticeable *adj* insign·is -is -e
noticeably *adv* insigniter
notification *s* denuntiati·o -onis *f*
notify *tr* certiorem facĕre
notion *s* noti·o -onis *f*
notoriety *s* infami·a -ae *f*
notorious *adj* infam·is -is -e
notwithstanding *adv* nihilominus

notwithstanding *prep expr. by various participles, e.g.,* **notwithstanding the auspices** neglectis auspiciis
nought *pron* nihil; **to set at —** nihili facĕre
noun *s* nom·en -inis *n;* **proper and common —s** nomina propria et appellativa
nourish *tr* alĕre, nutrire
nourishment *s* aliment·um -i *n*
novel *adj* novici·us -a -um, inaudit·us -a -um
novel *s* histori·a -ae *f* commenticia
novelty *s* novit·as -atis *f*
November *s* Novem·ber -bris *m or* mens·is -is *m* November; **on the first of November** Kalendis Novembribus
novice *s* tir·o -onis *m*
now *adv* nunc; *(denoting urgency and emphasis)* jam; *(transitional, esp. in argumentation; never the first word in the sentence)* autem; **— and then** iterdum; **—...— modo...**modo
nowhere *adv* nusquam
noxious *adj* noxi·us -a -um
nozzle *s* ans·a -ae *f*
nude *adj* nud·us -a -um
nudge *tr* fodicare
nudity *s* nudati·o -onis *f*
nugget *s* mass·a -ae *f*
nuisance *s* molesti·a -ae *f;* **what a — it is!** quam molestum est
null *adj* **— and void** irrit·us -a -um; **to be — and void** cessare; **to render —** infringĕre
nullify *tr* irritum facĕre
numb *adj* torpid·us -a -um; **to become —** torpescĕre; **to be —** torpēre
number *s (gram & math)* numer·us -i *m;* **a — of** aliquot; **relying on their superior —s** multitudine freti; **to assemble in large —** frequentissimi convenire; **without —** innumerabil·is -is -e
number *tr* numerare; **a fleet —ing 1000 ships** classis mille numero navium; **to be —ed among** adnumerat·us -a -um *(w. dat)*
numberless *adj* innumer·us -a -um
numbness *s* torp·or -oris *m; (fig)* stup·or -oris *m*
numerical *adj* numeral·is -is -e
numerically *adv* numero
numerous *adj* cre·ber -bra -brum
numismatics *s* doctrin·a -ae *f* nummorum
nuptial *adj* nuptial·is -is -e
nuptials *spl* nupti·ae -arum *fpl*
nurse *s* nutr·ix -icis *f*
nurse *tr (a baby)* nutrire; *(the sick)* curare; *(fig)* fovēre
nursery *s (for children)* infantium diaet·a -ae *f; (for plants)* seminar·ium -(i)i *n*
nurture *tr* nutrire
nut *s* nu·x -cis *f;* **a hard — to crack** *(fig)* quaesti·o -onis *f* nodosa; **he is a —** *(pej)* nuga iste est

nutriment *s* nutriment·um -i *n*
nutrition *s* nutriti·o -onis *f*
nutritious *adj* alibil·is -is -e
nutshell *s* putam·en -inis *n;* **in a —** *(fig)* paucis verbis
nutty *adj* vecor·s -dis
nymph *s* nymph·a -ae *f*

O

oaf *s* stult·us -i *m*
oak *adj* querce·us -a -um
oak *s* querc·us -ūs *f; (esp. timber)* rob·ur -uris *n*
oar *s* rem·us -i *m;* **to pull the —s** remos ducĕre
oarsman *s* rem·ex -igis *m*
oath *s* jusurandum *(gen:* jurisjurandi) *n; (mil)* sacrament·um -i *n;* **false —** perjur·ium -(i)i *n;* **to take an —** jurare; *(mil)* sacramentum dicĕre
oats *spl* aven·a -ae *f*
obdurate *adj* obstinat·us -a -um
obdurately *adv* obstinate
obedience *s* obedienti·a -ae *f*
obedient *adj* obedien·s -tis
obediently *adv* obedienter
obeisance *s* **to make — to** adorare
obelisk *s* obelisc·us -i *m*
obese *adj* obes·us -a -um
obesity *s* obesit·as -atis *f*
obey *tr* parēre *(w. dat)*
obituary *s* Libitinae ind·ex -icis *m*
object *s* object·um -i *n,* res, rei *f; (aim)* proposit·um -i *n*
object *intr (to feel annoyance)* gravari; *(to make objections)* recusare; **to — to** aegre ferre; **I do not —, provided that...**non repugno dummodo...; **I do not — to your leaving** non recuso quominus abeas
objection *s* oppositi·o -onis *f;* **to raise many —s** multa in contrariam partem afferre
objectionable *adj* improbabil·is -is -e
objective *s* proposit·um -i *n*
obligation *s* offic·ium -(i)i *n;* **under —** noxi·us -a -um
obligatory *adj* necessari·us -a -um
oblige *tr (to force)* cogĕre; *(to put under obligation)* obligare; *(to do a favor for)* morigerari *(w. dat);* **to be —ed to** debēre *(w. inf); (to feel gratitude toward)* gratiam habēre *(w. dat)*
obliging *adj* officios·us -a -um
obligingly *adv* officiose
oblique *adj* obliqu·us -a -um
obliquely *adv* oblique
oblong *adj* oblong·us -a -um
obnoxious *adj* invis·us -a -um
obscene *adj* obscen·us -a -um

obscenely *adv* obscene
obscenity *s* obscenit·as -atis *f*
obscure *adj* obscur·us -a -um
obscure *tr* obscurare
obscurely *adv* obscure
obscurity *s* obscurit·as -atis *f; (of birth)* humilit·as -atis *f*
obsequies *spl* exsequi·ae -arum *fpl*
obsequious *adj* nimis obsequen·s -tis
obsequiousness *s* obsequ·ium -(i)i *n*
observable *adj* notabil·is -is -e
observance *s* observanti·a -ae *f; (rite)* rit·us -ūs *m*
observant *adj* attent·us -a -um; — **of** diligen·s -tis *(w. gen)*
observation *s* observati·o -onis *f; (remark)* notati·o -onis *f*
observe *tr (to watch, keep)* observare; *(to remark)* dicĕre
observer *s* spectat·or -oris *m*
obsess *tr* occupare
obsession *s* mentis prehensi·o -onis *f*
obsolescent *adj* **to be** — obsolescĕre
obsolete *adj* obsolet·us -a -um; **to become** — exsolescĕre
obstacle *s* impediment·um -i *n; (barrier)* ob·ex -icis *m*
obstinacy *s* obstinati·o -onis *f*
obstinate *adj* obstinat·us -a -um
obstinately *adv* obstinate
obstreperous *adj* tumultuos·us -a -um
obstruct *tr* obstare *(w. dat)*
obstruction *s* impediment·um -i *n*
obtain *tr* adipisci; *(by asking)* impetrare; **to — pardon** veniam impetrare
obtainable *adj* impetrabil·is -is -e
obtrusive *adj* molest·us -a -um
obtuse *adj* obtus·us -a -um
obviate *tr* praevertĕre
obvious *adj* apert·us -a -um; **it was — that** apparebat *(w. acc & inf)*
obviously *adv* aperte, manifesto
occasion *s* occasi·o -onis *f; (reason)* caus·a -ae *f; (time)* temp·us -oris *n; for the — (temporary)* ad tempus
occasion *tr* locum dare *(w. dat)*
occasional *adj* rar·us -a -um
occasionally *adv* interdum
occidental *adj* occidental·is -is -e
occult *adj* occult·us -a -um
occupant *s* possess·or -oris *m*
occupation *s* possessi·o -onis *f; (employment)* quaest·us -ūs *m*
occupy *tr* occupare; *(to possess)* possidēre; *(space)* complēre
occur *intr* accidĕre; *(to show up, appear)* nasci; *(to the mind)* in mentem venire; **it —ed to me** mihi in mentem venit; **to — at the right time** competĕre
occurrence *s* cas·us -ūs *m*
ocean *s* ocean·us -i *m*
oceanic *adj* oceanens·is -is -e
October *s* Octo·ber -bris *m or* mens·is -is

m October; **on the first of** — Kalendis Octobribus
ocular *adj* ocular·is -is -e
oculist *s* ocularius medic·us -i *m*
odd *adj (of number)* im·par -paris; *(quaint)* insolit·us -a -um; *(remaining)* reliqu·us -a -um
oddity *s* rarit·as -atis *f; (thing)* mir·um -i *n*
oddly *adv* mirum in modum
odds *spl* — **and ends** quisquili·ae -arum *fpl;* **the — are against us** impares sumus; **to be at — with** disidēre ab *(w. abl); to lay — that not* pignore certare ne *(w. subj)*
odious *adj* odios·us -a -um
odium *s* invidi·a -ae *f*
odor *s* od·or -oris *m*
odorous *adj* odorat·us -a -um
Odyssey *s* Odysse·a -ae *f*
of *prep (possession) rendered by gen; (origin)* de *(w. abl),* ex *(w. abl); (concerning)* de *(w. abl); (denoting description or quality) expr. by gen or abl:* **a man — of highest talents** vir summi ingenii *(or* summo ingenio); **one — them** unus de illis *(or* ex illis); **statue of bronze** statua ex aere facta
off *adv* procul, longe; **far —** procul; **to be a long way —** longe abesse; **— with you!** aufer te modo!; **well —** bene nummerat·us -a -um
off *prep* de *(w. abl)*
offend *tr* offendĕre ‖ *intr* **to — against** violare
offender *s* re·us -i *m*
offense *s (fault)* offens·a -ae *f,* delict·um -i *n; (insult)* injuri·a -ae *f; (displeasure)* offensi·o -onis *f;* **to give —** to offendĕre
offensive *adj* injurios·us -a -um; *(odors, etc.)* odios·us -a -um, foed·us -a -um; *(language)* malign·us -a -um; *(aggressive)* bellum inferens; **to go on the —** bellum inferre
offer *tr* offerre, praebēre; **to — help to** opem ferre *(w. dat); to — violence to* vim afferre *(w. dat)*
offer *s* condici·o -onis *f*
offering *s* don·um -i *n*
offhand *adj* incurios·us -a -um
offhand *adv* confestim, illico
office *s (place of work)* officin·a -ae *f; (pol)* hon·or -oris *m; (duty)* offic·ium -(i)i *n;* **through the good —s of** per *(w. acc);* **to reach high —** ad honorem pervenire
officer *s* magistrat·us -ūs *m; (mil)* sagat·us -i *m; (police)* vig·il -ilis *m*
official *adj* public·us -a -um; **— residence** dom·us -ūs *f* publica
official *s* magistrat·us -ūs *m*
officiate *intr* officio *(or* munere) fungi; *(of a clergyman)* rem divinam facĕre
officious *adj* officios·us -a -um

officiously *adv* officiose
offing *s* **in the —** in promptu
offset *tr* compensare
offspring *s* prol·es -is *f*
often *adv* saepe; **very —** persaepe
ogre *s* larv·a -ae *f*
oh *interj* oh!, ohe!
oil *s* ole·um -i *n*
oil *tr* ung(u)ĕre
oil press *s* torcul·ar -aris *n*
oily *adj* oleos·us -a -um; *(like oil)* oleace·us -a -um; **to have an — taste** oleum sapĕre
ointment *s* unguent·um -i *n*
old *adj (aged)* sen·ex -is; *(out of use)* obsolet·us -a -um; *(worn)* trit·us -a -um; *(ancient)* antiqu·us -a -um; **good — days** prisca tempor·a -um *npl;* **of —** olim, quondam; **—er** ma·jor -jor -jus (natu); *(among old people)* sen·ior -ior -ius; **—est** maxim·us -a -um (natu); **to be no more than ten years —** non plus quam decem annos habēre; **to be ten years —** decem annos nat·us -a -um esse; **to grow —** senescĕre
old age *s* senect·us -utis *f*
old-fashioned *adj* prisc·us -a -um
old maid *s* an·us -us *f* innupta
old lady *s* an·us -ūs *f;* **little —** anicul·a -ae *f*
old man *s* sen·ex -is *m*
oligarchy *s* paucorum administrati·o -onis *f* civitatis; *(members of the oligarchy)* optimat·es -um *mpl*
olive *s* ole·a -ae *f,* oliv·a -ae *f*
olive oil *s* ole·um -i *n*
olive grove *s* olivet·um -i *n*
olive tree *s* oliv·a -ae *f*
Olympia *s* Olympi·a -ae *f*
Olympiad *s* Olympi·as -adis *f*
Olympic *adj* Olympic·us -a -um
omelet *s* lagan·um -i *n* de ovis confectum
omen *s* om·en -inis *n;* **to announce unfavorable —s** obnuntiare; **to get favorable —s** litare
ominous *adj* ominos·us -a -um
omission *s* praetermissi·o -onis *f*
omit *tr* (o)mittĕre
omnipotence *s* omnipotenti·a -ae *f*
omnipotent *adj* omnipoten·s -tis
omnivorous *adj* omnivor·us -a -um
on *prep (place)* in *(w. abl); (about, concerning)* de *(w. abl); (ranged with)* ab *(w. abl); (depending, hanging on)* de *(w. abl); (close to, e.g., a river)* juxta *(w. acc),* ad *(w. acc); (on the side of, in the direction of)* ab *(w. abl):* **— the east** ab oriente; **— the west** ab occidente
on *adv* porro; *(continually)* usque; **and so —** et cetera; **from then —** ex eo (tempore); **to drink — till daylight** potare usque ad primam lucem; **to go —** pergĕre; **to move—** procedĕre
once *adv (one time)* semel; *(formerly)* olim, quondam; **at —** statim, illico, continuo;

for — demum; **—...twice...a third time** semel...iterum...tertio; **— and for all** semel (et) in perpetuum; **—more** iterum; **— or twice** semel iterumque; **— upon a time** olim
one *adj* un·us -a -um; **— day** *(in the past)* quodam die; *(in the future)* aliquando; **at — time** simul; **— ladder** unae scal·ae -arum *fpl;* **to have — and the same wish** idem velle
one *pron* un·us -a -um; *(a certain person)* quidam, quaedam, quoddam; **it is all —** perinde est; **— after another** ali·us -a -um ex alio; **— another** inter se, alius alium; **— by —** singulatim; **— or the other** alterut·er alterut·ra alterut·rum; **— or two** un·us -a -um et alt·er -era -erum *(w. pl verb);* **— would think that** time stood still putes stare tempus; **only —** unic·us -a -um
one-eyed *adj* lusc·us -a -um
onerous *adj* oneros·us -a -um
oneself *pron (refl)* se; **by —** per se; **to —** sibi; **with —** secum; *(intensive)* ips·e -a -um
one-sided *adj* inaequal·is -is -e
onion *s* caep·a -ae *f*
only *adj* sol·us -a -um, unic·us -a -um, un·us -a -um
only *adv* solum, tantum; **not —...but also** non solum...sed etiam
only-begotten *adj* unigenit·us -a -um
onset *s* impet·us -ūs *m*
onslaught *s* incurs·us -ūs *m*
onward *adv* porro; **—, soldiers!** porro, milites!
ooze *intr* manare
opaque *adj* opac·us -a -um
open *adj (not shut)* apert·us -a -um, paten·s -tis; *(evident)* manifest·us -a -um; *(sincere)* candid·us -a -um; *(public)* public·us -a -um; *(of a question, undecided)* inte·ger -gra -grum; **in the — (air)** sub divo; **to be —** to *(e.g, bribery, disease)* patēre *(w. dat);* **to lie —** patēre
open *tr* aperire; *(to uncover)* retegĕre; *(letter)* resignare; *(book)* evolvĕre; *(conversation)* exordiri; *(w. ceremony)* inaugurare; *(mouth)* diducĕre; *(door)* recludĕre; **to — up a hole** foramen laxare ‖ *intr* patescĕre, se pandĕre; *(gape)* dehiscĕre; *(of a wound)* recrudescĕre
open-handed *adj* larg·us -a -um
open-hearted *adj* ingenu·us -a -um
opening *s (act)* aperti·o -onis *f; (aperture)* foram·en -inis *n; (e.g., of a cave)* os, oris *n; (opportunity)* loc·us -i *m*
openly *adv* (pro)palam
open-minded *adj* docil·is -is -e
operate *tr* agĕre; *(to manage, e.g., a business)* exercēre ‖ *intr* operari; **to — on** *(surgically)* secare
operation *s (act of doing or working)*

effecti·o -onis *f; (surgical)* secti·o -onis *f; (business)* negot·ium -(i)i *n*
operative *adj* effica·x -cis
operator *s* opif·ex -icis *m*
opinion *s* opini·o -onis *f,* sententi·a -ae *f; good —* of aestimati·o -onis *f* de *(w. abl);* **in my —** meā sententiā; **public —** fam·a -ae *f;* **to be of the —** opinari; **to hold the — that** opinionem habēre *(w. acc & inf)*
opium *s* op·ium -(i)i *n*
opponent *s* adversar·ius -(i)i *m; (pol)* competit·or -oris *m*
opportune *adj* opportun·us -a -um
opportunity *s* occasi·o -onis *f;* **as — offered** ex occasione; **— for revenge** occasio vindictae; **to give s.o. the —** to alicui potestatem dare *(w. gen of gerundive);* **to take** *or* **get the —** occasionem nancisci
oppose *tr* adversari *(w. dat); (w. words)* contra dicĕre *(w. dat);* **to — the idea that** adversari ne *(w. subj)*
opposite *adj* advers·us -a -um
opposite *prep* contra *(w. acc)*
opposition *s* oppositi·o -onis *f; (obstacle)* impediment·um -i *n;* **— party** par·s -tis *f* diversa
oppress *tr* opprimĕre, gravare
oppression *s* injuri·a -ae *f*
oppressive *adj* praegrav·is -is -e; **to become —** ingravescĕre
oppressor *s* tyrann·us -i *m*
opprobrium *s* ignomini·a -ae *f*
optical *adj* opticus -a -um
optician *s* hom·o -inis *m* optices peritus
option *s* opti·o -onis *f;* **you have the — either to...or to** tibi optio datur utrum...an
or *conj* vel, aut, —ve; *(in questions)* an; **either...or** *(mutually exclusive)* aut...aut; *(optional)* vel...vel; **— else** alioquin; **— not** annnon; *(in indirect questions)* necne
oracle *s* oracul·um -i *n*
oracular *adj* fatidic·us -a -um
oral *adj* verbal·is -is -e, verbo tradit·us -a -um
orally *adv* voce, verbis
orange *s* mal·um -i *n* aureum
oration *s* orati·o -onis *f;* **to deliver an —** orationem habēre
orator *s* orat·or -oris *m*
oratorical *adj* oratori·us -a -um
oratory *s* oratoria ar·s -tis *f*
orb *s* orb·is -is *m*
orbit *tr* **to — the earth** orbem terrae circumagĕre
orbit *s (astr)* gyr·us -i *m*
orchard *s* pomar·ium -(i)i *n*
orchestra *s* symphoni·a -ae *f; (part of theater)* orchestr·a -ae *f*
orchid *s* orch·is -is *f*
ordain *tr* edicĕre; *(eccl)* ordinare
ordeal *s* discrim·en -inis *n*

order *s (class, arrangement, sequence)* ord·o -inis *m; (command)* juss·um -i *n; (mil)* imperat·um -i *n;* **to call to —** convocare; **in — to** ut *(w. subj);* **in — not to** ne *(w. subj);* **in short —** brevi; **out of —** ex usu; **out of the regular —** extra ordinem; **to arrange in —** ordinare; **to draw up an army in — of battle** aciem ordinare
order *tr (to command)* jubēre, imperare *(w. dat); (to arrange)* disponĕre, ordinare; *(to ask for)* postulare, poscĕre
orderly *adj* composit·us -i -um; *(well behaved)* modest·us -a -um
orderly *s* accens·us -ūs *m; (mil)* tessarari·us -(i)i *m*
ordinal *adj* ordinal·is -is -e
ordinance *s* edict·um -i *n*
ordinarily *adv* plerumque, fere
ordinary *adj* usitat·us -a -um, solit·us -a -um; *(everyday)* cotidian·us -a -um; *(traditional, not novel)* tralatici·us -a -um
ordnance *s* torment·a -orum *npl*
ore *s* ae·s -ris *n*
organ *s (anat)* par·s *f* corporis, visc·us -eris *n; (mus)* organ·um -i *n;* **the —s** viscer·a -um *npl*
organic *adj* pertinen·s -tis ad partem corporis
organism *s* compag·es -is *f*
organization *s* structur·a -ae *f; (society)* sodalit·as -atis *f*
orgy *s* comissati·o -onis *f*
Orient *s* orien·s -tis *m*
oriental *adj* Asiatic·us -a -um
origin *s* orig·o -inis *f; (birth)* gen·us -eris *n; (source)* fon·s -tis *m*
original *adj* primitiv·us -a -um; *(one's own)* propri·us -a -um; *(new)* inaudit·us -a -um
original *s* archetyp·um -i *n,* exempl·ar -aris *n; (writing)* autograph·um -i *n*
originality *s* propriet·as -atis *f* ingenii
originally *adv* initio, principio
originate *tr* instituĕre **||** *intr* oriri
originator *s* auct·or -oris *m*
ornament *s* ornament·um -i *n*
ornamental *adj* decor·us -a -um
ornate *adj* ornat·us -a -um
ornately *adv* ornate
orphan *s* orb·us -i *m,* orb·a -ae *f*
orphaned *adj* orbat·us -a -um
orphanage *s* orphanotroph·ium -(i)i *n*
orthodox *adj* orthodox·us -a -um
orthography *s* orthographi·a -ae *f*
oscillate *intr* ultro citroque se inclinare; *(fig)* dubitare
oscillation *s* ultro citroque inclinati·o -onis *f; (fig)* dubitati·o -onis *f*
ostensible *adj* simulat·us -a -um
ostensibly *adv* per speciem
ostentation *s* ostentati·o -onis *f*
ostentatious *adj* specios·us -a -um

ostracism *s* relegati·o -onis *f;* *(Athenian custom)* testarum suffragi·a -orum *npl*
ostrich *s* struthiocamel·us -i *m*
other *adj (different)* ali·us -a -ud; *(remaining)* ceter·us -a -um; **every — day** tertio quoque die; **on the — hand** contra; **the — alt·er -era -erum; the — day** nuper; **to attend to — people's affairs** aliena curare
otherwise *adv* aliter; *(in the contrary supposition)* alioquin; **to think —** aliter sentire; **you didn't do it yet; — you would have told me** nondum id fecisti; alioquin mihi narasses
otter *s* lutr·a -ae *f*
ought *intr* **I —** debeo, oportet me
ounce *s* unci·a -ae *f*
our *adj* nos·ter -tra -trum; **— men** nostr·i -orum *mpl*
ours *pron* nos·ter -tra -trum
ourselves *pron refl* nos(met); **by —** per nos; **to —** nobis; *(intensive)* nosmet ips·i -ae
oust *tr* ejicĕre
out *adv (outside)* foris; *(motion)* foras; **— of** de *(w. abl),* ex *(w. abl); (on account of)* ob *(w. acc);* **— of doors** extra ostium, foris; **— of the way** devi·us -a -um; **to dine —** foris cenare; **to flee — of the temple** extra templum profugĕre
outbreak *s* erupti·o -onis *f; (disturbance)* sediti·o -onis *f*
outburst *s* erupti·o -onis *f;* **in an — of anger** impoten·s -tis irae
outcast *s* ex·sul -sulis *m*
outcome *s* event·us -ūs *m*
outcry *s* clam·or -oris *m; (noisy shouting)* convic·ium -(i)i *n*
outdo *tr* superare
outdoors *adv* foris; *(motion)* foras
outer *adj* exter·ior -ior -ius; **— space** intermundi·a -orum *npl*
outermost *adj* extrem·us -a -um
outfit *s* apparat·us -ūs *m; (costume)* habit·us -ūs *m*
outfit *tr* ornare
outflank *tr* circumire
outgrow *tr* excedĕre ex *(w. abl),* staturā superare
outing *s* excursi·o -onis *f*
outlandish *adj* absurd·us -a -um
outlast *tr* diutius durare *(w. abl)*
outlaw *s* proscript·us -i *m*
outlaw *tr* aquā et igni interdicĕre *(w. dat),* proscribĕre
outlay *s* impens·a -ae *f*
outlet *s* exit·us -ūs *m; (for water)* emissar·ium -(i)i *n*
outline *s* adumbrati·o -onis *f;* **to draw the — of a thing** primas modo lineas alicujus rei ducĕre
outline *tr* delineare, adumbrare
outlive *tr* supervivĕre *(w. dat)*

outlook *s* occasi·o -onis *f,* prospect·us -ūs *m*
outlying *adj* extern·us -a -um
outnumber *tr* multitudine superare
outpost *s* stati·o -onis *f*
outpouring *s* effusi·o -onis *f*
output *s* fruct·us -ūs *m*
outrage *s* injuri·a -ae *f*
outrage *tr* injuriā afficĕre
outrageous *adj* flagitios·us -a -um
outrageously *adv* flagitiose
outrank *tr* et aetate et dignitate antecedĕre *(w. dat)*
outright *adj* manifest·us -a -um
outright *adv* prorsus; *(at once)* statim
outrun *tr* cursu superare
outset *s* init·ium -(i)i *n*
outshine *tr* praelucĕre *(w. dat)*
outside *s* par·s -tis *f* exterior; *(appearance)* speci·es -ei *f;* **on the —** extrinsecus
outside *prep* extra *(acc)*
outside *adv* foris, extra; *(motion)* foras; **from —** extrinsecus
outside *adj* extern·us -a -um
outskirts *spl* suburb·ium -(i)i *n;* **just on the — of the province** fere ad extremum provinciae finem
outspoken *adj* liberius dic·ax -acis
outspread *adj* patul·us -a -um
outstanding *adj* praestan·s -tis; *(of debts)* residu·us -a -um
outstretched *adj* porrect·us -a -um
outstrip *tr* cursu superare
outward *adj* extern·us -a -um
outwardly *adv* extrinsecus
outweigh *tr* praeponderare; *(fig)* praevertĕre *(w. dat)*
outwit *tr* deludĕre, dolis vincĕre
oval *adj* ovat·us -a -um
oval *s* ovata form·a -ae *f*
ovation *s* plaus·us -ūs *m; (second-class triumph)* ovati·o -onis *f*
oven *s* furn·us -i *m*
over *prep (across)* super *(w. acc),* trans *(w. acc); (w. verbs of motion, denoting space traversed)* per *(w. acc); (motion over)* super *(w. acc); (position above)* supra *(w. acc); (w. numbers)* plus quam; **— and above** super *(w. acc);* **the water was — a man's head** humanā magnitudine major erat fluminis altitudo
over *adv* supra; *(excess)* nimis; **all —** ubique; **— and above** insuper; **— and —** identidem
overall *adj* tot·us -a -um
overawe *tr* (de)terrēre
overbalance *tr* praeponderare
overbearing *adj* superb·us -a -um
overboard *adv* ex nave
overburden *tr* nimis onerare
overcast *adj* nubil·us -a -um
overcharge *tr* plus aequo exigĕre ab *(w. abl)*

overcoat *s* paenul·a -ae *f*
overdo *tr* exaggerare, in majus extollĕre;
  to — it se supra vires extendĕre
overdue *adj (money)* residu·us -a -um
overestimate *tr* majoris aestimare
overflow *s* inundati·o -onis *f*
overflow *tr* inundare **‖** *intr* abundare
overgrown *adj* obsit·us -a -um; *(too big)*
  praegrand·is -is -e
overhang *tr* impendēre *(w. dat)*
overhanging *adj* impenden·s -tis
overhasty *adj* praeproper·us -a -um
overhaul *tr* reficĕre; *(to pass)* consequi
overhead *adv* desuper
overhear *tr* auscultare
overjoyed *adj* **I am —!** *(coll)* immortaliter
  gaudeo!; **to be — at the sight of a son** ad
  conspectum filii laetitiā exsultare
overladen *adj* praegravat·us -a -um
overland *adj* per terram
overlay *tr* inducĕre, illinĕre
overload *tr* nimis onerare
overlook *tr (not to notice)* praetermittĕre;
  (to pardon) ignoscĕre *(w. dat)*; *(a view)*
  prospicĕre, spectare
overlord *s* domin·us -i *m*
overpower *tr* opprimĕre
overrate *tr* nimis magni aestimare; **to be**
  an —ed man famā minor esse
overreach *tr* circumvenire
overriding *adj* praecipu·us -a -um
overripe *adj* permatur·us -a -um
overrun *tr* occupare
overseas *adj* transmarin·us -a -um
oversee *tr* praeesse *(w. dat)*
overseer *s* curat·or -oris *m*
overshadow *tr* obumbrare; *(fig)* obscurare
overshoot *tr* excedĕre; **to — the mark** ex
  orbita ire; **don't — the mark** ne ultra
  quam est opus contendas
oversight *s (superintendence)* cur·a -ae *f;*
  (carelessness) incuri·a -ae *f*
oversleep *intr* diutius dormire
overspread *tr* obducĕre
overstate *tr* in majus extollĕre
overstep *tr* transgredi
overstock *tr* **to — a shop** tabernam super
  quam est opus rebus venalibus instruĕre
overt *adj* apert·us -a -um
overtime *adj* **— work** oper·a -ae *f* subsiciva
overtly *adv* palam
overtake *tr* consequi
overtax *tr (fig)* abuti *(w. abl)*
overthrow *s* eversi·o -onis *f*
overthrow *tr* evertĕre, dejicĕre
overture *s (proposal)* condici·o -onis *f;*
  (mus) exord·ium -(i)i *n;* **to make —s to**
  agĕre cum *(w. abl)*
overturn *tr* evertĕre; **—ed tables** eversae
  mens·ae -arum *fpl* **‖** *intr* everti
overwhelm *tr* obruĕre, opprimĕre
overwork *tr* immodico labore onerare; **to**
  — oneself plus aequo laborare

owe *tr* debēre
owing to *prep* propter *(w. acc)*
owl *s* bub·o -onis *m*
own *adj* propri·us -a -um; **one's — su·us -a**
  -um, propri·us -a -um
own *tr* tenēre, possidēre; *(to acknowledge)*
  confitēri
owner *s* domin·us -i *m*
ownership *s* domin·ium -(i)i *n*
ox *s* bo·s -vis *m*
oyster *s* ostre·a -ae *f*
oyster shell *s* ostreae test·a -ae *f*

P

pace *s (step)* pass·us -ūs *m,* grad·us -ūs *m;*
  (measure of length; five Roman feet)
  pass·us -ūs *m; (speed)* velocit·as -atis *f;*
  to keep — with pariter ire cum *(w. abl)*
pace *tr* **to — off** passibus emetiri **‖** *intr*
  gradi; **to — up and down** inambulare
pacific *adj* pacific·us -a -um
pacification *s* pacificati·o -onis *f*
pacify *tr* placare
pack *s (bundle)* sarcin·a -ae *f; (of animals,*
  of people) gre·x -gis *m*
pack *tr (items of luggage)* colligĕre; *(to fill*
  completely) frequentare, complēre; *(to*
  compress) stipare **‖** *intr* **to — up** vasa
  colligĕre
package *s* sarcin·a -ae *f*
packet *s* fascicul·us -i *m*
pack horse *s* equ·us -i *m* clitellarius
packsaddle *s* clitell·ae -arum *fpl*
pact *s* pact·um -i *n;* **to make a — pacisci**
pad *s* pulvill·us -i *m*
pad *tr* suffarcinare
padding *s* fartur·a -ae *f*
paddle *s* rem·us -i *m*
paddle *intr* remigare
paddock *s* saept·um -i *n*
pagan *adj* pagan·us -a -um
pagan *s* pagan·us -i *m*
paganism *s* paganit·as -atis *f*
page *s (of book)* pagin·a -ae *f; (boy)* pu·er
  -eri *m;* **at the top (bottom) of the —** ab
  summā (imā) paginā
page *tr* arcessĕre
pageant *s* pomp·a -ae *f*
pail *s* situl·a -ae *f*
pain *s* dol·or -oris *m; (fig)* ang·or -oris *m;*
  — in the neck *(coll)* molest·us -i *m;* **to**
  be in — dolēre; **to take —s** operam dare;
  to take great —s to in magno negotio
  habēre *(w. inf)*
pain *tr* dolore afficĕre **‖** *intr* dolēre
painful *adj* molest·us -a -um; *(bitter, dis-*
  tressful) acerb·us -a -um; **to be extremely**
  — dolores magnos movēre
painfully *adv* magno cum dolore
painkiller *s* medicament·um -i *n* anodynum

painless *adj* doloris exper·s -tis
painstaking *adj* operos·us -a -um
paint *s* pigment·um -i *n*
paint *tr* pingĕre
paintbrush *s* penicill·us -i *m*
painter *s* pict·or -oris *m*
pair *s* par, paris *n; (of oxen)* jug·um -i *n*
pair *tr* conjungĕre ‖ *intr* coïre
palace *s* regi·a -ae *f,* aul·a -ae *f*
palatable *adj* sapid·us -a -um
palate *s* palat·um -i *n; (sense of taste)* gustat·us -ūs *m*
palatial *adj* regi·us -a -um
pale *adj* pallid·us -a -um; **to be** — pallēre; **to grow** — pallescĕre
pale *s* pal·us -i *m; (enclosure)* saept·um -i *n*
paleography *s* palaeographi·a -ae *f*
palette *s* pictoris tabul·a -ae *f*
palisade *s* vall·um -i *n*
pall *s* pall·ium -(i)i *n*
pall *tr* satiare ‖ *intr* vapescĕre
pallet *s* grabat·us -i *m*
palliative *s* leniment·um -i *n*
pallid *adj* pallid·us -a -um
pallor *s* pall·or -oris *m*
palm *s (of the hand; palm tree; palm branch, as token of victory)* palm·a -ae *f;* **to grease s.o.'s** — aliquem pecuniā corrumpĕre; **to win the** — palmam ferre
palmist *s* chiromant·is -idos *mf*
palm off *tr* (**on**) imponĕre *(w. dat)*
palpable *adj* tractabil·is -is -e; *(fig)* manifest·us -a -um
palpitate *tr* palpitare
palsied *adj* paralytic·us -a -um
palsy *s* paralys·is -is *f*
paltry *adj* vil·is -is -e
pamper *tr* indulgēre *(w. dat)*
pamphlet *s* libell·us -i *m*
pan *s* patin·a -ae *f; (for frying)* sartag·o -inis *f*
pan *intr* **to** — **out** *(coll)* evenire
panacea *s* panace·a -ae *f*
pancake *s* lagan·um -i *n*
pandemic *adj* evagat·us -a -um
pandemonium *s* tumult·us -ūs *m*
pander *intr* lenocinari; **to** — **to** indulgēre *(w. dat)*
panderer *s* len·o -onis *m*
pandering *s* lenocin·ium -(i)i *n*
panegyric *s* laudati·o -onis *f*
panel *s (of wall)* abac·us -i *m; (of ceiling)* lacun·ar -aris *n; (of door)* tympan·um -i *n; (of jury)* judic·es -um *mpl; (discussion group)* colleg·ium -(i)i *n*
paneled *adj* laqueat·us -a -um
pang *s* dol·or -oris *m*
panic *s* pav·or -oris *m*
panicky, panic-stricken *adj* pavid·us -a -um
panoply *s* arm·a -orum *npl*
panorama *s* prospect·us -ūs *m*

pant *intr* anhelare; **to** — **after** *(fig)* gestire
pantheism *s* pantheism·us -i *m*
pantheist *s* pantheist·a -ae *m*
Pantheon *s* Panthe·um -i *n*
panther *s* panther·a -ae *f*
panting *adj* anhel·us -a -um
panting *s* anhelit·us -ūs *m*
pantomime *s (play; actor)* mim·us -i *m; (actress)* mima -ae *f*
pantry *s* cell·a -ae *f* penaria
pap *s* papill·a -ae *f*
papa *s* tat·a -ae *m*
paper *s (stationery)* chart·a -ae *f; (newspaper)* act·a -orum *npl* diurna; **—s** script·a -orum *npl*
paper *adj* chartace·us -a -um
papyrus *s* papyr·us -i *f*
par *s* **to be on a** — **with** par esse *(w. dat)*
parable *s* parabol·e -es *f*
parade *s* pomp·a -ae *f; (mil)* decurs·us -ūs *m*
parade *tr* ostentare ‖ *intr (mil)* decurrĕre
paradise *s* paradis·us -i *m*
paradox *s* paradox·um -i *n*
paragon *s* specim·en -inis *n*
paragraph *s* cap·ut -itis *n*
parallel *adj* parallel·us -a -um; *(fig)* consimil·is -is -e
parallel *tr* exaequare
paralysis *s* paralys·is -is *f*
paralytic *adj* paralytic·us -a -um
paralyze *tr* enervare; *(fig)* percellĕre
paralyzed *adj* per omnia membra resolut·us -a -um
paramount *adj* suprem·us -a -um
paramour *s (male)* moech·us -i *m; (female)* meretr·ix -icis *f*
parapet *s* plute·us -i *m*
paraphernalia *s* apparat·us -ūs *m*
paraphrase *s* paraphras·is -is *f*
paraphrase *tr* laxius liberiusque interpretari
parasite *s* parasit·us -i *m*
parasol *s* umbell·a -ae *f*
parcel *s* fascicul·us -i *m; (plot of land)* agell·us -i *m*
parcel *tr* **to** — **out** dispertire
parch *tr* torrēre
parched *adj* torrid·us -a -um
parchment *s* membran·a -ae *f*
pardon *s* veni·a -ae *f;* **to obtain a** — veniam impetrare; **to grant a** — **to** *(leg)* absolvĕre
pardon *tr* ignoscĕre *(dat);* condonare *(w. acc of thing & dat of person); (leg)* absolvĕre; **after being —ed** post impetratam veniam
pardonable *adj* ignoscend·us -a -um
pare *tr (vegetables)* deglubĕre; *(the nails)* resecare
parent *s* paren·s -tis *mf*
parentage *s* gen·us -eris *n*
parental *adj* parental·is -is -e

parenthesis *s* interclusi·o -onis *f*
pariah *s* sentin·a -ae *f* reipublicae
parity *s* parit·as -atis *f*
park *s* hort·i -orum *mpl*
parlance *s* serm·o -onis *m*
parley *s* colloqu·ium -(i)i *n*
parley *intr* colloqui
parliament *s* parlament·um -i *n*
parlor *s* exedr·ium -(i)i *n*
parody *s* parodi·a -ae *f*
parole *s* fid·es -ei *f;* **on —** custodiae immun·is -is -e
parole *tr* fide interositā demittĕre
paroxysm *s* access·us -ūs *m*
parricide *s (murder)* parricid·ium -(i)i *n; (murderer)* parricid·a -ae *mf*
parrot *s* psittac·us -i *m*
parry *tr* avertĕre
parse *tr* notare proprietatesque describĕre
parsimonious *adj* parc·us -a -um
parsimoniously *adv* parce
parsing *s* partium orationis flexi·o -onis *f*
parsley *s* selin·um -i *n*
part *s* par·s -tis *f; (role)* part·es -ium *fpl; (duty)* offic·ium -(i)i *n;* **for the most —** maximā ex parte; **in —** partim; **on the — of** ab (*w. abl*); **to act the — of** sustinēre partes (*w. gen*); **to take — in** interesse (*w. dat*)
part *tr* separare, dividĕre; **to — company** discedĕre ‖ *intr* discedĕre, abire; *(to go open)* dehiscĕre; **to — with** dimittĕre
partial *adj (unfair)* iniqu·us -a -um; *(incomplete)* manc·us -a -um, per partes
partiality *s* iniquit·as -atis *f*
partially *adv* aliquā ex parte
participant *s* parti·ceps -cipis *mf*
participate *intr* **to — in** interesse (*w. dat*), particeps esse (*w. gen*)
participation *s* participati·o -onis *f*
participle *s* particip·ium -(i)i *n*
particle *s* particul·a -ae *f*
particular *adj (special)* praecipu·us -a -um; *(fussy)* fastidios·us -a -um; **in —** potissimum
particularly *adv* praecipue, praesertim
particularize *tr* exsequi
particulars *spl* singul·a -orum *npl*
parting *s* discess·us -ūs *m*
partisan *s* faut·or -oris *m; (guerilla)* factiosus armig·er -eri *m*
partition *s* partiti·o -onis *f; (between rooms)* pari·es -etis *m; (compartment)* loculament·um -i *n*
partition *tr* dividĕre
partitive *adj (gram)* partitiv·us -a -um
partly *adv* partim, ex parte
partner *s* soc·ius -(i)i *m,* soci·a -ae *f,* partic·eps -ipis *mf; (in office)* colleg·a -ae *m; (in marriage)* con·ju(n)x -jugis *mf*
partnership *s* societ·as -atis *f;* **to dissolve a —** dissociari; **to form a —** societatem inire

partridge *s* perd·ix -icis *mf*
party *s (for entertainment)* conviv·ium -(i)i *n; (pol)* part·es -ium *fpl; (detachment)* man·us -ūs *f;* **opposite —** partes diversae; **to join a —** partes sequi
pass *s (defile)* angusti·ae -arum *fpl; (free ticket)* tesser·a -ae *f* gratuita; **things have come to such a — that** eo rerum ventum erat ut
pass *tr (to go by)* praeterire; *(exceed)* excedĕre; *(to approve)* probare; *(time)* degĕre; *(a law)* perferre; *(by the assembly)* jubēre; **he tried to — himself off for Philip** se Philippum ferebat; **pass me the vegetables!** porrige mihi holera!; **to — around** circumferre; **to — down** tradĕre; **to — sentence** jus dicĕre; **to — the test** approbari; **to — up** praetermittĕre ‖ *intr (of time)* transire; *(to walk by)* praeterire; *(to ride by)* praetervehi; **to come to —** fieri, evenire; **to let — praetermittĕre; to let an army — through the country** exercitum per fines transmittĕre; **to — away** *(to die)* perire; *(to come to an end)* transire; **to — by** *(e.g., a park)* praeterire (hortos); *(in a carriage or ship)* praetervehi; **to — for** haberi; **to — on** *(to go forward)* pergĕre; *(to another subject)* transire; *(to die)* perire; **to — out** collabi, intermori; **to — over** *(e.g., of a storm)* transire; *(to make no mention of)* praeterire; **to — over the fact that** mittĕre quod (*w. subj*); **to — through** *(e.g., a town)* transire; *(of an arrow, spear)* ire per (*w. acc*); **to — through enemy lines** per hostes vadĕre
passable *adj (of road)* pervi·us -a -um; *(tolerable)* tolerabil·is -is -e
passably *adv* tolerabiliter
passage *s (act)* transit·us -ūs *m; (by water)* trajecti·o -onis *f; (road)* it·er -ineris *n; (in a book)* loc·us -i *m (pl:* loc·i -orum); **to allow anyone a passage through the province** alicui transitum dare per provinciam
passenger *s* viat·or -oris *m; (in a carriage, aboard ship)* vect·or -oris *m*
passer-by *s* praeter·iens -euntis *mf*
passing *s* obit·us -ūs *m*
passion *s (strong desire of any kind, esp. lust)* cupidit·as -atis *f; (strong emotion)* animi permoti·o -onis *f; (lust)* libid·o -inis *f; (violent anger)* iracundi·a -ae *f;* **to fly into a —** exardescĕre iracundiā et stomacho
passionate *adj* arden·s -tis; *(given to bursts of anger)* iracund·us -a -um
passionately *adv* ardenter; iracunde
passive *adj* passiv·us -a -um
passively *adv* passive
passport *s* diplom·a -atis *n*
password *s* tesser·a -ae *f*
past *adj* praeterit·us -a -um; *(immediately*

preceding) proxim·us -a -um, super·ior -ior -ius
past *s* praeterit·um -i *n; (past tense)* praeteritum temp·us -oris *n*
past *prep* praeter *(w. acc)*
paste *s* farin·a -ae *f* chartaria
paste *tr* glutinare
pasteboard *s* chart·a -ae *f* crassa
pastime *s* oblectament·um -i *n;* **by way of** — oblectamenti causā
pastoral *adj (poetry)* bucolic·us -a -um; *(of shepherds)* pastoral·is -is -e
pastoral *s* bucolic·um -i *n*
pastry *s* crustul·a -orum *npl*
pasture *s* past·us -ūs *m*
pasture *tr* pascĕre **‖** *intr* pasci
pat *tr* permulcēre
patch *s* pann·us -i *m*
patch *tr* resarcire; **to — up** *(fig)* refovēre
patchwork *s* cent·o -onis *m*
patent *adj* manifest·us -a -um
patently *adv* manifesto
paternal *adj* patern·us -a -um; *(like a father)* patri·us -a -um
paternity *s* paternit·as -atis *f*
path *s* semit·a -ae *f*
pathetic *adj* flebil·is -is -e
pathless *adj* invi·us -a -um
pathos *s* vis *f* ad misericordiam movendam
pathway *s* semit·a -ae *f*
patience *s* patienti·a -ae *f*
patient *adj* patien·s -tis
patient *s* ae·ger -gri *m,* aegr·a -ae *f*
patiently *adv* aequo animo
patriarch *s* patriarch·a -ae *m*
patriarchal *adj* patriarchic·us -a -um
patrician *adj* patrici·us -a -um
patrician *s* patric·ius -(i)i *m*
patrimony *s* patrimon·ium -(i)i *n*
patriot *s* aman·s -tis *mf* patriae
patriotic *adj* aman·s -tis patriae
patriotism *s* am·or -oris *m* patriae
patrol *s* circuitor·es -um *mpl*
patrol *tr & intr* circumire
patron *s* patron·us -i *m*
patronage *s* patrocin·ium -(i)i *n*
patroness *s* patron·a -ae *f*
patronize *tr* favēre *(w. dat); (a shop)* frequentare
pattern *s* exempl·ar -aris *n*
paucity *s* paucit·as -atis *f*
paunch *s* ingluvi·es -ei *f*
pauper *s* egen·s -tis *mf*
pause *s* paus·a -ae *f; (break)* intercaped·o -inis *f; (mus)* intermissi·o -onis *f*
pause *intr* subsistĕre; *(to halt)* insistĕre; **to — in speaking** in dicendo subsistĕre
pave *tr* sternĕre; **to — the way to** *(fig)* viam facĕre ad *(w. acc)*
pavement *s* paviment·um -i *n*
pavilion *s* tentor·ium -(i)i *n*
paving stone *s* sax·um -i *n* quadratum
paw *s* pe·s -dis *m*

paw *tr* pedibus pulsare
pawn *s* pign·us -oris *n*
pawn *tr* pignerare
pawnbroker *s* pignernat·or -oris *m*
pay *s* merc·es -edis *f; (mil)* stipend·ium -(i)i *n*
pay *tr (money)* solvĕre; *(in full)* persolvĕre, pendĕre; *(a person)* pecuniam (mercedem) solvĕre *(dat); (mil)* stipendium numerare *(w. dat);* **to — back** restituĕre; *(to avenge)* vindicare; **to — in cash** numerare; **to — off a debt** nomen exsolvĕre, aes alienum persolvĕre; **to — out** numerare; **to — s.o. a compliment** laudare; **to — (s.o.) for** solvĕre *(w. acc of thing and dat of person);* **to — respects to** salutare; **to — the penalty** poenam dare, poenam luĕre **‖** *intr* **it —s** operae pretium est; **to — for** *(merchandise)* emĕre *(w. acc); (a misdeed)* poenas dare ob *(w. acc)*
payable *adj* solvend·us -a -um
payday *s* di·es -ei *f* pecuniae
paymaster *s* dispensat·or -oris *m*
payment *s (act)* soluti·o -onis *f; (sum of money)* pensi·o -onis *f*
pea *s* pis·um -i *n*
peace *s* pa·x -cis *f;* **in a state of —** pacat·us -a -um; **to hold one's —** tacēre; **to live in —** pacem agitare
peaceably *adv* cum bona pace
peaceful *adj* tranquill·us -a -um
peacefully *adv* tranquille
peace-loving *adj* pacis aman·s -tis
peacemaker *s* pacificat·or -oris *m*
peace offering *s* placam·en -inis *n*
peacetime *s* ot·ium -(i)i *n*
peach *s* Persic·um -i *n*
peacock *s* pav·o -onis *mf*
peak *s* vert·ex -icis *m; (of a mountain)* cacum·en -inis *n*
peal *s (of thunder)* frag·or -oris *m; (of bells)* concent·us -ūs *m*
peal *intr* resonare
pear *s* pir·um -i *n*
pearl *s* margarit·a -ae *f*
pearly *adj* gemme·us -a -um
peasant *s* rustic·us -i *m*
peasantry *s* agrest·es -ium *mpl*
pebble *s* calcul·us -i *m*
peck *s* mod·ius -(i)i *m; (perfunctory kiss)* basiol·um -i *n*
peck *tr* vellicare
peculiar *adj* peculiar·is -is -e; *(belonging to one person or thing only)* propri·us -a -um; *(odd)* inusitat·us -a -um, absurd·us -a -um
peculiarity *s* propriet·as -atis *f*
pedagogue *s* paedagog·us -i *m*
pedant *s* scholastic·us -i *m*
pedantic *adj* umbratic·us -a -um
pedantry *s* morosit·as -atis *f*
peddle *tr* venditare

peddler *s* instit·or -oris *m;* **door-to-door** — qui merces suas ostiatim venditat

pedestal *s* bas·is -is *f*

pedestrian *adj* pedes·ter -tris -tre

pedestrian *s* ped·es -itis *m*

pedigree *s* stemm·a -atis *n*

pediment *s* fastig·ium -(i)i *n*

pedophile *s* pedicat·or -oris *m*

pee *intr* (aquam) facĕre

peel *s* cut·is -is *f*

peel *tr* resecare cutem *(w. gen)*

peep *s* conspect·us -ūs *m* fugax

peep *intr* furtim conspicĕre

peephole *s* conspicill·um -i *n*

peer *s* par paris *m*

peer *intr* **to — at** intuēri

peerless *adj* incomparabil·is -is -e

peevish *adj* stomachos·us -a -um

peevishly *adv* stomachose

peg *s* paxill·us -i *m*

pelican *s* pelican·us -i *m*

pellet *s* globul·us -i *m*

pelt *s* pell·is -is *f*

pelt *tr (to hurl)* conjicĕre; **to — s.o. with stones** aliquem lapidare

pen *s* calam·us -i *m; (enclosure)* saept·um -i *n; (for pigs)* suil·e -is *n; (for sheep)* ovil·e -is *n*

pen *tr* scribĕre; **to — in** includĕre

penal *adj* poenal·is -is -e

penalize *tr* mul(c)tare

penalty *s* mul(c)t·a -ae *f*

penance *s* satisfacti·o -onis *f*

pencil *s* graph·is -idis *f*

pencil box *s* graphiar·ium -(i)i *n*

pending *adj* suspens·us -a -um; *(leg)* sub judice

pending *prep* inter *(acc)*

pendulum *s* librament·um -i *n*

penetrate *tr* penetrare ad *(w. acc)* ‖ *intr* penetrare

penetrating *adj (cold)* acut·us -a -um *(keen-sighted)* perspic·ax -acis

penetration *s* aci·es -ei *f* mentis

peninsula *s* paeninsul·a -ae *f*

penitence *s* paenitenti·a -ae *f*

penitent *adj* paenit·ens -entis

penitentiary *s* ergastul·um -i *n*

penknife *s* cultell·us -i *m*

penmanship *s* man·us -ūs *f*

pennant *s* vexill·um -i *n*

penniless *adj* in·ops -opis

penny *s* quadr·ans -antis *m*

pension *s* annu·a -orum *npl*

pensive *adj* meditabund·us -a -um

penultimate *adj* paenultim·us -a -um

people *s* homin·es -um *mpl; (as political entity)* popul·us -i *m; (of a country)* gen·s -tis *f;* **common —** vulg·us -i *n;* **— say** dicunt; **— who say** qui dicunt

people *tr* frequentare

pep *s* alacrit·as -atis *f*

pep talk *s* conti·o -onis *f;* **to give a —** contionem habēre

pepper *s* pip·er -eris *n*

pepper *tr* pipere condire; *(w. blows)* verberare

peppermint *s* menth·a -ae *f*

perceive *tr* percipĕre

percent *s* per centum

percentage *s* porti·o -onis *f*

perceptible *adj* percipiend·us -a -um

perceptibly *adv* sensim

perch *s (for birds)* pertic·a -ae *f; (fish)* perc·a -ae *f*

perch *intr* insidēre

perchance *adv* forte

percolate *tr* percolare ‖ *intr* permanare

percussion *s* percuss·us -ūs *m*

percussion instrument *s* percussionale instrument·um -i *n* musicum

perdition *s* interit·us -ūs *m*

peremptory *adj* arrogan·s -tis

perennial *adj* perenn·is -is -e

perfect *adj* perfect·us -a -um; **to enjoy almost — health** inlaesā prope valetudine uti

perfect *s (gram)* (tempus) praeterit·um perfect·um -i *n*

perfect *tr* perficĕre

perfectly *adv* perfecte

perfidious *adj* perfid·us -a -um

perfidy *s* perfidi·a -ae *f*

perforate *tr* perforare

perforation *s* foram·en -inis *n*

perform *tr* perficĕre, peragĕre; *(duty)* fungi *(w. abl); (theat)* agĕre

performance *s* perfuncti·o -onis *f; (work)* op·us -eris *n; (of a play)* acti·o -onis *f; (play)* fabul·a -ae *f*

performer *s* act·or -oris *m; (theat)* histri·o -onis *f*

perfume *s* od·or -oris *m*

perfume *tr* odoribus imbuĕre

perfunctorily *adv* perfunctorie

perfunctory *adj* perfunctori·us -a -um

perhaps *adv* fortasse, forsitan

peril *s* pericul·um -i *n*

perilous *adj* periculos·us -a -um

perilously *adv* periculose

period *s (of time)* spat·ium -(i)i *n; (chronological)* temp·us -oris *n; (punctuation mark)* punct·um -i *n; (complete phrase or sentence)* period·us -i *m;* **— of life** aet·as -atis *f;* **over a long — of time** in diuturno spatio

periodic *adj* recurr·ens -entis

periodical *s* libell·us -i *m* diurnus

periodically *adv* temporibus statis

periphery *s* peripheri·a -ae *f*

periphrastic *adj* periphrastic·us -a -um

perish *intr* interire, perire

perishable *adj* quae cito corrumpuntur

peristyle *s* peristyl·ium -(i)i *n*

perjure *tr* **to — oneself** perjurare

perjured *adj* perjur·us -a -um

perjury *s* perjur·ium -(i)i *n;* **to commit —** perjurare

perk *intr* **to — up** reviviscĕre

permanence *s* stabilit·as -atis *f*

permanent *adj* perpetu·us -a -um

permanently *adv* perpetuo

permeable *adj* pervi·us -a -um

permeate *tr* permanare, permeare

permissible *adj* **it is — for me to** licet mihi ire *(or* licet eam)

permission *s* potest·as -atis *f;* **to grant — to** permittĕre *(w. dat);* **with your —** bonā tuā veniā

permit *tr* permittĕre *(w. dat)*

permutation *s* permutati·o -onis *f*

pernicious *adj* pernicios·us -a -um

perniciously *adv* perniciose

peroration *s* perorati·o -onis *f*

perpendicular *adj* perpendicular·is -is -e

perpendicular *s* line·a -ae *f* perpendicularis

perpetrate *tr* perficĕre

perpetrator *s* auct·or -oris *m*

perpetual *adj* perpetu·us -a -um

perpetually *adv* perpetuo

perpetuate *tr* perpetuare

perpetuity *s* perpetuit·as -atis *f*

perplex *tr* distrahĕre

perplexing *adj* perplex·us -a -um

perplexity *s* dubitati·o -onis *f*

persecute *tr* insectari

persecution *s* insectati·o -onis *f*

persecutor *s* insectat·or -oris *m*

perseverance *s* perseveranti·a -ae *f*

persevere *intr* perseverare, perstare

persevering *adj* persever·ans -antis

persist *intr* perseverare, perstare

persistence *s* perseveranti·a -ae *f*

persistent *adj* pertin·ax -acis

persistently *adv* pertinaciter

person *s* hom·o -inis *m,* person·a -ae *f;* *(gram)* persona *f;* **in —** ips·e -a

personage *s* person·a -ae *f*

personal *adj* privat·us -a -um; *(gram, leg)* personal·is -is -e; **— appearance** form·a -ae *f* et habit·us -ūs *m*

personality *s* indol·es -is *f*

personally *adv rendered by* ips·e -a

personification *s* prosopopei·a -ae *f*

personify *tr (inanimate objects)* vitam sensumque tribuĕre *(dat);* **to — evil** malum in personam suam constituĕre

personnel *s* soci·i -orum *mpl*

perspective *s (viewpoint)* conspect·us -ūs *m* animi; *(in drawing)* scaenographi·a -ae *f*

perspicacious *adj* perspic·ax -acis

perspicacity *s* perspicacit·as -atis *f*

perspiration *s (sweating)* sudati·o -onis *f;* *(sweat)* sud·or -oris *m*

perspire *intr* sudare

persuade *tr* persuadēre *(w. dat)*

persuasion *s* persuasi·o -onis *f*

persuasive *adj* suasori·us -a -um

persuasively *adv* persuabiliter

pert *adj* proc·ax -acis

pertain *intr* **(to)** pertinēre (ad + *acc*)

pertinence *s* congruenti·a -ae *f*

pertinent *adj* apposit·us -a -um; **to be —** ad rem pertinēre

perturb *tr* perturbare

perturbation *s* perturbati·o -onis *f*

perusal *s* perlecti·o -onis *f*

peruse *tr* perlegĕre

pervade *tr* permanare per (+ *acc*)

perverse *adj* pervers·us -a -um

perversely *adv* perverse

perversion *s* perversit·as -atis *f*

perversity *s* perversit·as -atis *f*

pervert *s* hom·o -inis *m* perversus

pervert *tr* depravare; *(words)* detorquēre

pest *s* pest·is -is *f*

pester *tr* vexare

pestilence *s* pestilenti·a -ae *f*

pestle *s* pistill·um -i *n*

pet *s* delici·ae -arum *fpl;* **to have a dog as a —** canem in deliciis habēre

pet *tr* permulcēre

petal *s* floris fol·ium -(i)i *n*

petition *s* petiti·o -onis *f;* *(pol)* libell·us -i *m*

petition *tr* supplicare

petitioner *s* suppl·ex -icis *m*

petrify *tr* in lapidem convertĕre ‖ *intr* lapidescĕre

petticoat *s* inducul·a -ae *f*

pettiness *s* anim·us -i *m* angustus

petty *adj* minut·us et angust·us -a -um

petulance *s* petulanti·a -ae *f*

petulant *adj* petul·ans -antis

pew *s* subsell·ium -(i)i *n*

phantasy *s* phantasi·a -ae *f*

phantom *s* larv·a -ae *f*

pharmacy *s* tabern·a -ae *f* medicamentaria

phase *s* lunae faci·es -ei *f;* *(fig)* vic·es -ium *fpl*

pheasant *s* phasian·us -i *m,* phasian·a -ae *f*

phenomenal *adj* singular·is -is -e

phenomenon *s* res, rei *f;* *(s.th. remarkable)* miracul·um -i *n*

philanthropic *adj* human·us -a -um

philanthropy *s* humanit·as -atis *f*

philologist *s* philolog·us -i *m*

philology *s* philologi·a -ae *f*

philosopher *s* philosoph·us -i *m*

philosophical *adj* philosophic·us -a -um

philosophically *adv* philosophice; *(calmly)* aequo animo

philosophize *intr* philosophari

philosophy *s* philosophi·a -ae *f;* *(theory)* rati·o -onis *f*

phlegm *s* phlegm·a -atis *n*

phlegmatic *adj* lent·us -a -um

phone *s* telephon·um -i *n*

phone *tr* per telephonum loqui cum *(w, abl,)*

phosphorus *s* phosphor·us -i *m*

phrase *s* locuti·o -onis *f*

phrase *tr* verbis exprimĕre
phraseology *s* loquendi rati·o -onis *f*
physical *adj (relating to nature)* physic·us -a -um; — **strength** corporis vir·es -ium *fpl*
physician *s* medic·us -i *m*
physicist *s* physic·us -i *m*
physics *s* physic·a -orum *npl*
physiognomy *s* physiognomi·a -ae *f*
physiological *adj* physiologic·us -a -um
physiologist *s* physiolog·us -i *m*
physiology *s* physiologi·a -ae *f*
physique *s* corporis habit·us -ūs *m*
pick *tr (to choose)* eligĕre; *(fruit)* carpĕre, legĕre; **to — a quarrel** jurgii causam inferre; **to — out** eligĕre; **to — pockets** manticulari; **to — the teeth** dentes perfodĕre; **to — up** tollĕre
pick *s (tool)* dolabr·a -ae *f; (the best)* flo·s -ris *m*
pickax *s* dolabr·a -ae *f*
picked *adj* elect·us -a -um
picket *s (mil)* stati·o -onis *f*
pickle *s (brine)* muri·a -ae *f; (vegetable)* oxycucum·er -eris *m*
pickled *adj* muria condit·us -a -um; *(drunk)* ebri·us -a -um; — **olives** oxycomin·a -orum *npl*
pickpocket *s* saccular·ius -(i)i *m*
picnic *s* conviv·ium -(i)i *n* sub divo
pictorial *adj* pictori·us -a -um
picture *s* pictur·a -ae *f*
picture gallery *s* pinacothec·a -ae *f*
picturesque *adj* amoen·us -a -um
pie *s* crust·um -i *n;* **apple —** mal·a -orum *npl* in crusto cocta
piece *s* par·s -tis *f; (of food)* frust·um -i *n; (broken off)* fragment·um -i *n; (drama)* fabul·a -ae *f; (very often not expressed by a separate word, e.g.,* **a — of cheese** case·us -i *m;* **a — of ground** agell·us -i *m;* **a — of meat** car·o -nis *f;* **a — of paper** chart·a -ae *f);* **to cut in —s** minute concidĕre; **to fall to —s** dilabi; **to tear to —s** dilaniare; *(e.g., paper)* conscindĕre
piece *tr* **to — together** fabricari
piecemeal *adv* frustatim, separatim
pier *s* mol·es -is *f*
pierce *tr* perforare; *(w. a sword)* perfodĕre; *(fig)* pungĕre
piercing *adj* acut·us -a -um
piety *s* piet·as -atis *f*
pig *s* porc·us -i *m*
pigeon *s* columb·a -ae *f*
pigheaded *adj* obstinat·us -a -um
pigment *s* pigment·um -i *n*
pigsty *s* suil·e -is *n*
pike *s* hast·a -ae *f; (fish)* lup·us -i *m*
pilaster *s* parastatic·a -ae *f*
pile *s* acerv·us -i *m; (nap of cloth)* vill·us -i *m; (for cremation)* rog·us -i *m*
pile *tr* **(on)** congerĕre *(w. dat);* **to — up** exstruĕre ‖ *intr* crescĕre

pilgrim *s* peregrinat·or -oris *m* religionis causā
pilgrimage *s* peregrinati·o -onis *f* religionis causā
pill *s* pilul·a -ae *f*
pillage *s* rapin·a -ae *f*
pillage *tr* diripĕre ‖ *intr* praedari
pillar *s* pil·a -ae *f*
pillow *s* cervic·al ·alis *n*
pillowcase *s* cervicalis tegim·en -inis *n*
pilot *s* gubernat·or -oris *m*
pilot *tr* gubernare
pimp *s* len·o -onis *m*
pimp *tr & intr* lenocinari
pimple *s* pustul·a -ae *f*
pin *s* ac·us -ūs *f; (peg)* clav·us -i *m*
pin *tr* acu figĕre; **to — down** defigĕre; *(fig)* devincire
pin cushion *s* pulvill·us -i *m* acubus servandis
pincers *spl* forc·eps -ipis *mf*
pinch *tr* vellicare; *(of cold; of shoe)* (ad)urĕre
pinch *s (e.g., of salt)* mensur·a -ae *f* duorum *(or* trium) digitorum
pine *s* pin·us -i *f*
pine *intr* **to — away** tabescĕre; **to — for** desiderare
pineapple *s* nu·x -cis *f* pinea
pink *adj* punice·us -a -um; **to be in the — of health** optimā valetudine uti
pinnacle *s* fastig·ium -(i)i *n*
pint *s* sextar·ius -(i)i *m*
pioneer *s* praecurs·or -oris *m*
pious *adj* pi·us -a -um, prob·us -a -um; *(spotless)* sanct·us -a -um
piously *adv* pie, religiose, sancte
pipe *s* tub·us -i *m; (conduit)* canal·is -is *m; (mus)* fistul·a -ae *f*
pipe *tr & intr (mus)* fistulā canĕre
piper *s* fistulat·or -oris *m*
piquant *adj* a·cer -cris -cre; *(fig)* sals·us -a -um
pique *s* offensi·o -onis *f*
pique *tr* offendĕre
piracy *s* latrocin·ium -(i)i *n*
pirate *s* pirat·a -ae *m*
piratical *adj* piratic·us -a -um
pistachio *s* pistac·ium -(i)i *n*
pit *s* fove·a -ae *f; (quarry)* fodin·a -ae *f; (theat)* cave·a -ae *f*
pit *tr* **to — one against another** alium cum alio committĕre
pitch *s* pi·x -cis *f; (sound)* son·us -i *m; (degree)* grad·us -ūs *m; (slope)* fastig·ium -(i)i *n;* **to such a — of** eo *(w. gen)*
pitch *tr (to fling)* conjicĕre; *(camp)* ponĕre; *(tent)* tendĕre
pitcher *s* urce·us -i *m*
pitchfork *s* furc·a -ae *f*
piteous *adj* miserabil·is -is -e
piteously *adv* miserabiliter
pitfall *s* fove·a -ae *f*

pith *s* medull·a -ae *f*
pithy *adj* sententios·us -a -um
pitiable *adj* miserand·us -a -um
pitiful *adj* misericor·s -dis; *(pitiable)* miserand·us -a -um
pitifully *adv* misere
pitiless *adj* immisericor·s -dis
pitilessly *adv* immisericorditer
pittance *s* mercedul·a -ae *f*
pity *s* misericordi·a -ae *f*
pity *tr* misereri *(w. gen);* **I — him** miseret me ejus
pivot *s* cnod·ax -acis *m; (fig)* card·o -inis *m*
placard *s* titul·us -i *m*
place *s* loc·us -i *m (pl:* loc·a -orum *npl);* **in — of** in locum *(w. gen);* **in the first —** primum; **in the last —** postremo; **in the same —** ibidem; **out of —** alien·us -a -um; **to take —** fieri
place *tr* ponĕre; *(pointing to the placing of an object in connection with other objects)* (col)locare
placid *adj* placid·us -a -um
placidly *adv* placide
plagiarism *s* furt·um -i *n* litterarium
plagiarist *s* fu·r -ris *m* litterarius
plagiarize *tr* furari
plague *s* pestilenti·a -ae *f; (fig)* pest·is -is *f*
plague *tr* vexare
plain *s* camp·us -i *m*
plain *adj (clear)* manifest·us -a -um; *(unadorned)* simpl·ex -icis; *(of one color)* unicol·or -oris; *(frank)* sincer·us -a -um; *(homely)* invenust·us -a -um
plainly *adv* plane; simpliciter
plaintiff *s* petit·or -oris *m*
plaintive *adj* flebil·is -is -e
plaintively *adv* flebiliter
plan *s* consil·ium -(i)i *n; (for a building)* form·a -ae *f;* **to form a —** consilium inire
plan *tr* destinare, in animo habēre; *(to scheme)* meditari ‖ *intr* **to — on** in animo habēre
plane *s (tool)* runcin·a -ae *f; (level surface)* planiti·es -ei *f*
plane *tr* runcinare
planet *s* planet·a -ae *f*
plank *s* ax·is -is *m*
plant *s* plant·a -ae *f*
plant *tr* serĕre; **his feet are —ed on** pedes stipantur in *(w. abl);* **to — one's feet on the ground** pedes in terram deferre
plantation *s* plantar·ium -(i)i *n*
planter *s* sat·or -oris *m*
planting *s* sat·us -ūs *m*
plaster *s* tector·ium -(i)i *n*
plaster *tr* tectorium inducĕre *(w. dat)*
plasterer *s* tect·or -oris *m*
plaster of Paris *s* gyps·um -i *n*
plastic *adj* plastic·us -a -um
plastic *s* materi·a -ae *f* plastica
plate *s (dish)* patell·a -ae *f; (of metal)*

lamin·a -ae *f; (dish of silver or gold)* argent·um -i *n*
plateau *s* aequ·um -i *n*
platform *s* suggest·us -ūs *m*
platitude *s* trita sententi·a -ae *f*
Platonic *adj* Platonic·us -a -um
platoon *s* manipul·us -i *m*
platter *s* lan·x -cis *f*
plaudits *spl* plaus·us -ūs *m*
plausible *adj* verisimil·is -is -e
play *s* lud·us -i *m; (theat)* fabul·a -ae *f;* **to be at —** ludĕre
play *tr* ludĕre; *(instrument)* canĕre *(w. abl);* **to — ball** pilā ludĕre; **to — a trick on** ludificari; **to — Latin songs** Latine ludĕre; **to — the lead role** primas partes agĕre; **to — the role of a parasite** parasitum agĕre; **to — with** *(sexually)* ludĕre cum *(w. abl)*
player *s* lus·or -oris *m; (theat)* histri·o -onis *m; (on wind instrument)* tibic·en -inis *m; (on stringed instrument)* fidic·en -inis *m*
playful *adj* ludibund·us -a -um; *(frolicsome)* lasciv·us -a -um
playfully *adv* per ludum
playfulness *s* lascivi·a -ae *f*
playground *s* are·a -ae *f* lusoria
playmate *s* collus·or -oris *m*
plaything *s* ludibr·ium -(i)i *n*
playwright *s* fabularum script·or -oris *m*
plea *s* supplicati·o -onis *f; (one of the grounds for defense as stated in the praetor's edict)* excepti·o -onis *f;* **to enter a — against s.o.** exceptionem objicĕre alicui; **well-founded —** justa exceptio *f*
plead *tr (ignorance)* causari; **to — a case** causam agĕre ‖ *intr* **to — for** petĕre; **to — with s.o.** aliquem supplicare
pleasant *adj* amoen·us -a -um, jucund·us -a -um
pleasantly *adv* jucunde
pleasantry *s* jocosa dicacit·as -atis *f*
please *tr* placēre *(w. dat);* **anyone you —** quilibet, quaelibet; **anything you —** quidlibet; **if you —** si placet; si videtur; **—!** sis (= si vis); amabo te *(coll);* **— God!** Deo volente
pleasing *adj* grat·us -a -um
pleasurable *adj* jucund·us -a -um
pleasure *s* volupt·as -atis *f;* **it is my —** libet; **to derive — from** voluptatem capĕre de *(w. abl)*
plebeian *adj* plebei·us -a -um
plebeians *spl* pleb·s -is *f*
plebiscite *s* plebiscit·um -i *n*
pledge *s* pign·us -oris *n; (proof)* testimon·ium -(i)i *n*
pledge *tr* (op)pignerare, obligare; **to — one's word** fidem obligare
Pleiads *spl* Pleiad·es -um *fpl*
plenary *adj* plen·us -a -um

plenipotentiary s legat·us -i m praepotens
plentiful adj larg·us -a -um
plenty s copi·a -ae f
plethora s redundanti·a -ae f
pleurisy s pleurit·is -idis f
pliable adj tractabil·is -is -e
pliant adj lent·us -a -um
plight s discrim·en -inis n; **in a sorry —** male perdit·us -a -um
plod intr assidue laborare
plodder s sedulus hom·o -inis m
plodding adj sedul·us -a -um
plot s (conspiracy) conjurati·o -onis f; (of ground) agell·us -i m; (of a play) argument·um -i n
plot intr conjurare, moliri
plow s aratr·um -i n
plow tr arare; **to — under** inarare; **to — up** exarare
plowing s arati·o -onis f
plowman s arat·or -oris m
plowshare s vom·er -eris m
pluck s anim·us -i m
pluck tr (flowers, fruit) carpĕre; (feathers) vellĕre; **to — off** decerpĕre; **to — out** evellĕre; **to — up one's courage** animo esse
plug s obturament·um -i n
plug tr obturare
plum s prun·um -i n
plumage s plum·ae -arum fpl
plumber s plumbar·ius -(i)i m
plume s crist·a -ae f
plummet s perpendicul·um -i n
plummet intr praecipitare
plump adj pingu·is -is -e
plum tree s prun·us -i f
plunder s (act) rapin·a -ae f; (booty) praed·a -ae f
plunder tr praedari
plunderer s praedat·or -oris m
plundering s rapin·a -ae f
plundering adj praedatori·us -a -um
plunge tr mergĕre; (sword, etc.) condĕre ‖ intr se mergĕre; **to — into the midst of the enemy** inter mucrones hostium se immergĕre
pluperfect s plus quam perfectum temp·us -oris n
plural adj plural·is -is -e
plural s numer·us -i m multitudinis; **in the — pluraliter**
plurality s multitud·o -inis f; (majority) major par·s -tis f
plush adj laut·us -a -um
ply tr exercēre, urgēre
poach tr (eggs) frigĕre ‖ intr illicita venatione uti
poacher s venat·or -oris m illicitus
pocket s sin·us -ūs m, saccul·us -i m
pocket tr in sacculis condĕre
pocketbook s (small book) pugillar·ia -ium npl; (purse) marsup·ium -(i)i n

pockmark s cicatr·ix -icis f
pod s siliqu·a -ae f
poem s poëm·a -atis n
poet s poët·a -ae m
poetess s poëtri·a -ae f
poetic adj poëtic·us -a -um
poetically adv poëtice
poetics s ar·s -tis f poëtica
poetry s (art) poëtic·e -es f; (poems) poës·is -is f, carm·en -inis n
poignancy s acerbit·as -atis f
poignant adj acerb·us -a -um
point s punct·um -i n; (pointed end) acum·en -inis n; (of sword, etc.) mucr·o -onis m; (point in dispute) quaesti·o -onis f; (in time) articul·a -ae f temporis; **at this very —** hoc ipso in loco; **beside the —** ab re; **from this — on** posthac, hinc; **main —** cap·ut -itis n; **— of view** sententi·a -ae f, opini·o -onis f; **to come to a —** acui; **to be on the — of** in eo esse ut, e.g., he was on the point of being arrested in eo erat (or haud abfuit) ut comprehenderetur; **to such a — that** eo ut; **to the —** ad rem; **up to this —** hactenus
point tr (to sharpen) acuēre; **to — out** monstrare, indicare; **to — the finger at** digitum intendĕre ad (w. acc) ‖ intr **to — at** digito monstrare
pointed adj acut·us -a -um; (fig) (stinging) aculeat·us -a -um
pointer s ind·ex -icis mf
pointless adj supervacu·us -a -um
poise s urbanit·as -atis f
poise tr librare
poison s venen·um -i n
poison tr venenare; (fig) vitiare
poisoning s venefic·ium -(i)i n
poke tr (to jab) fodicare, pungĕre; (w. the elbow) cubito pulsare; (fire) fodĕre; **to — fun at** eludĕre
poker s rutabul·um -i n
polar adj arctic·us -a -um
polarity s polarit·as -atis f
pole s ass·er -eris m; (short pole) asserul·us -i m; (long pole) longur·ius -(i)i m; (of the earth) pol·us -i m; **North (South) Pole** ax·is -is m septentrionalis (meridianus)
police s vigil·es -um mpl
policeman s vig·il -ilis m
policy s rati·o -onis f; (document) chirograph·um -i n
polish s (shine) nit·or -oris m; (refined manners) urbanit·as -atis f
polish tr polire; **to — up** expolire
polite adj urban·us -a -um
politely adv urbane
politeness s urbanit·as -atis f
politic adj pruden·s -tis
political adj civil·is -is -e; **from — motives** per ambitionem; **— supporter** suffragat·or -oris m

politician *s* vir viri *m* civilium rerum peritus

politics *s* respublica *(gen:* reipublicae) *f;* **to enter** — rempublicam inire; **to talk** — **at table** ad mensam res publicas crepare

poll *s* diribitorium -(i)i *n; (survey)* rogati·o -onis *f* sententiarum; **the** —**s** comiti·a -orum *npl*

polling booth *s* saept·um -i *n*

poll tax *s* capitum exacti·o -onis *f*

pollute *tr* polluěre, contaminare

pollution *s* polluti·o -onis *f*

polygamy *s* polygami·a -ae *f*

polysyllabic *adj* polysyllab·us -a -um

polytheism *s* multorum deorum cult·us -ūs *m*

pomegranate *s* mal·um -i *n* Punicum

pommel *tr* pulsare, verberare

pomp *s* apparat·us -ūs *m*

pompous *adj* magnific·us -a -um

pompously *adv* magnifice

pond *s* stagn·um -i *n*

ponder *tr* animo volutare

ponderous *adj* ponderos·us -a -um

pontiff *s* pontif·ex -icis *m*

pontifical *adj* pontifical·is -is -e

pontificate *s* pontificat·us -ūs *m*

pontoon *s* pont·o -onis *m*

pony *s* mannul·us -i *m*

pool *s* lacun·a -ae *f*

pool *tr* conferre

poor *adj* paup·er -eris: *(soil)* ma·cer -cra -crum; *(pitiable)* mis·er -era -erum; *(meager)* exil·is -is -e

poorly *adv* parum, mediocriter

pop *s* crepit·us -ūs *m; (father)* pap·a -ae *m*

pop *intr* crepare; **to** — **out** exsilire

pope *s* pap·a -ae *m*

poplar *s* popul·us -i *f*

poppy, poppyseed *s* papav·er -eris *n*

populace *s* vulg·us -i *n*

popular *adj* popular·is -is -e; — **feeling** sens·us -ūs *m* populi

popularity *s* fav·or -oris *m*, grati·a -ae *f;* **to enjoy** — gratiam habēre

populate *tr* frequentare

population *s* multitud·o -inis *f*

populous *adj* frequ·ens -entis

porcelain *s* fictil·ia -ium *npl* elegantia

porch *s* pergul·a -ae *f*

porcupine *s* hystr·ix -icis *f*

pore *s* foram·en -inis *n*

pore *intr* **to** — **over** scrutari

pork *s* porcin·a -ae *f*

pork chop *s* off·a -ae *f* porcina

porpoise *s* porcul·us -i *m* marinus

porridge *s* pul·s -tis *f*

port *s* port·us -ūs *m*

portal *s* port·a -ae *f*

portend *tr* portenděre

portent *s* portent·um -i *n*

portentous *adj* prodigios·us -a -um

porter *s* atriens·is is *m; (carrier)* bajul·us -i *m*

portfolio *s* scrin·ium -(i)i *n*

portico *s* portic·us -ūs *f*

portion *s* porti·o -onis *f*

portion *tr* partire; **to** — **out** dispertire

portly *adj* **to be** — opimo corporis habitu esse

portrait *s* imag·o -inis *f*

portray *tr* depingěre, exprimēre

pose *s* stat·us -ūs *m*

pose *intr* statum suměre

position *s* positi·o -onis *f; (of the body)* gest·us -ūs *m; (office)* hon·or -oris *m; (rank)* dignit·as -atis *f; (state)* conditi·o -onis *f*

positive *adj* cert·us -a -um; *(opp: negative)* affirmativ·us -a -um; *(gram)* positiv·us -a -um

positively *adv* certo, praecise

possess *tr* possidēre

possession *s* possessi·o -onis *f;* **in the** — **of** penes *(w. acc);* **to gain** — **of** potiri *(w. abl)*

possessive *adj* quaestuos·us -a -um; *(gram)* possessiv·us -a -um

possessor *s* possess·or -oris *m*

possibility *s* facult·as -atis *f*

possible *adj* **as quickly as** — quam celerrime; **it is** — fieri potest; **it is** — **for me to** possum *(w. inf)*

possibly *adv (perhaps)* fortasse; **as carefully as I** — **can** quam diligentissime possum; **I may** — **go to Sicily** fieri potest ut in Siciliam proficiscar

post *s (stake)* post·is -is *m; (station)* stati·o -onis *f; (in a race)* met·a -ae *f*

post *tr (a notice)* in publicum proponěre; *(to station)* collocare: **to** — **a letter** litteras dare

postage *s* vectur·a -ae *f* litterarum

postdate *tr* diem seriorem scriběre *(w. dat)*

poster *s* libell·us -i *m;* **to put up a** — libellum proponěre

posterior *adj* poster·ior -ior -ius

posterity *s* posterit·as -atis *f; (descendants)* poster·i -orum *mpl*

posthaste *adv* quam celerrime

postumous *adj* postum·us -a -um

postman *s* tabellar·ius -(i)i *m*

postpone *tr* differre

postscript *s* adjecti·o -onis *f* litterarum

posture *s* stat·us -ūs *m*

pot *s (of clay)* oll·a -ae *f; (of bronze)* ahen·um -i *n; (chamber pot)* matell·a -ae *f;* **to go to** — pessum ire

pot-bellied *adj* ventrios·us -a -um

potato *s* solan·um -i *n* tuberosum

potentate *s* tyrann·us -i *m*

potential *adj* futur·us -a -um

potion *s* poti·o -onis *f*

potter *s* figul·us -i *m*

pottery *s* fictil·ia -ium *npl*

pouch *s* saccul·us -i *m*

poultry *s* av·es -ium *fpl* cohortales

pounce *intr* **to — on** insilire *(w. dat or in + acc)*

pound *s* libr·a -ae *f (w.* pondo *sometimes added);* **a half —** selibr·a -ae *f;* **a — and a half** sesquilibr·a -ae *f;* **a —** *(or* **per —**) in libras; **a quarter —** quadran·s -tis *f* pondo; **per —** in libras

pound *tr* contundĕre

pour *tr* fundĕre; **to — into** infundĕre *(in + acc);* **to — out** effundĕre; **to — water on his hands** aquam in ejus manūs infundĕre; **to — water on his head** caput illi aquā perfundĕre ‖ *intr* fundi, fluĕre; **to come —ing out** *(of people)* se effundĕre; **to — down** *(of rain)* ruĕre; **to — into** *(of people)* se infundĕre in *(w. acc)*

pouring *adj (rain)* effus·us -a -um

pout *intr* labellum extendĕre

poverty *s* paupert·as -atis *f; (inadequacy)* egest·as -atis *f*

poverty-stricken *adj* inop·s -is

powder *s* pulv·is -eris *m*

powder *tr* pulvere conspergĕre

power *s (strength)* vis *f; (control, dominium)* potest·as -atis *f; (excessive; non-constitutional)* potenti·a -ae *f; (mil, pol)* imper·ium -(i)i *n;* **as far as is in our —** quantum in nobis est; **— of the mind** vir·es -ium *fpl* ingenii; **to have great —** multum posse

powerful *adj (physically)* valid·us -a -um; *(kings, etc.)* poten·s -tis

powerfully *adv* valde

powerless *adj* invalid·us -a -um; **to be —** nil valēre

practical *adj* util·is -is -e; *(sensible)* pruden·s -tis; *(philosophy)* effectiv·us -a -um

practically *adv* usu; *(almost)* fere

practice *s (actual employment or experience)* us·us -ūs *m; (rehearsal)* meditati·o -onis *f; (custom)* consuetud·o -inis *f;* **to have a large — as a doctor** medicus praecipuae celebritatis esse

practice *tr (medicine, patience)* exercēre; *(to rehearse)* meditari

practitioner *s* exercitat·or -oris *m; (medical)* medic·us -i *m*

pragmatic *adj* pragmatic·us -a -um

prairie *s* camp·us -i *m* latissime patens herbisque obsitus

praise *s* lau·s -dis *f*

praise *tr* laudare

praiseworthy *adj* laudabil·is -is -e

prance *intr* exsilire

prank *s* lud·us -i *m*

pray *intr* precari, orare; **to — for** petĕre, precari; **to — to** adorare; **to — to the gods for peace** deos pacem precari

prayer *s* pre·x -cis *f*

preach *tr & intr* praedicare

preacher *s* praedicat·or -oris *m*

preamble *s* exord·ium -(i)i *n*

precarious *adj* precari·us -a -um; **in a most — position** in summo discrimine

precariously *adv* precario

precaution *s* cauti·o -onis *f;* **to take —s** praecavēre

precede *tr* antecedĕre *(w. acc or dat)*

precedence *s* prior loc·us -i *m;* **to take — over** antecedĕre

precedent *s* exempl·um -i *n*

preceding *adj* pr·ior -ior -ius

precept *s* praecept·um -i *n*

preceptor *s* praecept·or -oris *m*

precinct *s* termin·i -orum *mpl; (pol)* regi·o -onis *f*

precious *adj* pretios·us -a -um; **— stone** gemm·a -ae *f*

precipice *s* praec·eps -ipitis *n;* **down a —** in praeceps; **over the —** per praecipitia

precipitate *tr* praecipitare

precipitious *adj* praec·eps -ipitis

precise *adj (exact)* exact·us -a -um; *(particular)* accurat·us -a -um

precisely *adv* subtiliter

precision *s* accurati·o -onis *f*

preclude *tr* praecludĕre

precocious *adj* praec·ox -ocis

preconceive *tr* praecipĕre; **—d idea** praejudic·ium -(i)i *n*

preconception *s* praejudicata opini·o -onis *f*

precursor *s* praenunt·ius -(i)i *m*

predatory *adj* praedatori·us -a -um

predecessor *s* decess·or -oris *m*

predestine *tr* praedestinare

predicament *s* discrim·en -inis *n*

predicate *tr* praedicare

predicate *s* praedicat·um -i *n*

predict *tr* praedicĕre

prediction *s* praedicti·o -onis *f*

predilection *s* **(for)** stud·ium -(i)i *n (w. gen)*

predispose *tr* inclinare

predisposed *adj* **(to)** obnoxi·us -a -um *(w. dat)*

predispostion *s* inclinati·o -onis *f*

predominant *adj* praevalen·s -tis

predominate *intr* praevalēre

preeminent *adj* praecipu·us -a -um

preempt *tr* praeoccupare

preexist *intr* antea exstare *or* esse

preface *s* praefati·o -onis *f*

prefatory *adj* **to make a few — remarks** pauca praefari

prefect *s* praefect·us -i *m*

prefecture *s* praefectur·a -ae *f*

prefer *tr* praeponĕre, praeferre; *(charges)* deferre; **to — to** *(would rather)* malle *(w. inf)*

preferable *adj* pot·ior -ior-ius, praestan-

t·ior -ior -ius; *(when more than two are compared)* potissim·us -a -um
preference *s* fav·or -oris *m;* **in — to** potius quam; **to give — to s.o. over** aliquem anteponĕre *(w. dat)*
prefix *s* praepositi·o -onis *f*
prefix *tr* (**to**) praeponĕre *(dat)*
pregnancy *s* gravidit·as -atis *f*
pregnant *adj* gravid·us -a -um; *(of language)* press·us -a -um
prejudge *tr* praejudicare
prejudice *s* praejudicata opini·o -onis *f*
prejudice *tr* **to be —d against** praejudicatam opinionem habēre in *(w. acc);* **to — the people against** studia hominum inclinare in *(w. acc)*
prejudicial *adj* noxi·us -a -um
preliminary *adj* pr·ior -ior -ius; **to make a few — remarks** pauca praefari
prelude *s* *(mus)* prooēm·ium -(i)i *n;* *(fig)* praelusi·o -onis *f*
premature *adj* praematur·us -a -um
prematurely *adv* ante tempus
premeditate *tr* praemeditari
premier *s* princ·eps -ipitis *m*
premise *s* *(major)* propositi·o -onis *f; (minor)* assumpti·o -onis *f;* **—s** praed·ium -(i)i *n*
premium *s* praem·ium -(i)i *n;* **at a —** car·us -a -um
premonition *s* monit·um -i *n*
preoccupation *s* nescio qua de re sollicitati·o -onis *f*
preoccupied *adj* nescio qua de re sollicit·us -a -um
preoccupy *tr* distringĕre
preparation *s* praeparati·o -onis *f;* **to make careful —s** diligentem praeparationem adhibēre
prepare *tr* parare; *(a medicine)* componĕre; *(a speech, case)* meditari; **to — to** parare *(w. inf)*
preponderance *s* praestanti·a -ae *f*
preposition *s* praepositi·o -onis *f*
preposterous *adj* praeposter·us -a -um
preposterously *adv* praepostere
prerogative *s* ju·s -ris *n*
presage *tr* praesagire
prescribe *tr* mandare; *(a medicine)* praescribĕre
prescription *s* *(med)* compositi·o -onis *f;* **to write a —** medicinam praescribĕre
presence *s* praesenti·a -ae *f;* **in my —** me praesente; **in the — of** coram *(w. abl);* **— of mind** praesenti·a -ae *f* animi
present *adj* praesen·s -tis; **for the — in** praesens tempus; **to be —** adesse; *(of fever, infection)* inesse
present *s* don·um -i *n*
present *tr* *(to give)* donare; *(to introduce)* introducĕre; *(in court)* sistĕre; *(to bring forward)* praebēre, offerre; **an opportunity —s itself** occasio obvenit

presentation *s* *(of gifts)* donati·o -onis *f; (show)* spectacul·um -i *n; (introduction)* introducti·o -onis *f*
presentiment *s* praesag·ium -(i)i *n*
presently *adv* mox, statim
preservation *s* conservati·o -onis *f*
preserve *tr* conservare; *(fruit)* condire
preserver *s* conservat·or -oris *m*
preside *intr* (**over**) praesidēre *(w. dat)*
presidency *s* praefectur·a -ae *f; (term of office)* magister·ium -(i)i *n*
president *s* praes·es -idis *m*
press *s* *(for wine; for printing)* prel·um -i *n;* **hot off the —** modo ex prelo typographico; **to send to the —** prelo subjicĕre
press *tr* primĕre; *(fig)* urgēre; **to — down** deprimĕre; **to — together** comprimĕre ‖ *intr* **to — forward** anniti; **to — on** pergĕre
pressing *adj* urg·ens -entis
pressure *s* pressur·a -ae *f*
pressure *vt* urgēre
prestige *s* auctorit·as -atis *f*
presumably *adv* sane
presume *tr* sumĕre, conjicĕre; *(to take liberties)* sibi arrogare
presumption *s* praesumpti·o -onis *f*
presumptuous *adj* praesumptios·us -a -um
presuppose *tr* praesumĕre
pretend *tr* simulare, fingĕre; **to — to be shocked** fingĕre se inhorrescĕre
pretender *s* simulat·or -oris *m*
pretense *s* simulati·o -onis *f;* **under the — of** per speciem *(w. gen);* **without —** sine fuco
pretension *s* *(claim)* postulati·o -onis *f; (display)* ostentati·o -onis *f;* **to make —s to** affectare
preterite *s* temp·us -oris *n* praeteritum
preternatural *adj* praeter naturam
pretext *s* speci·es -ei *f;* **under the — of** (sub) specie *(w. gen)*
pretor *s* praet·or -oris *m*
pretorian *adj* praetorian·us -a -um
pretorship *s* praetur·a -ae *f*
prettily *adv* belle
pretty *adj* bell·us -a -um
pretty *adv* satis, admodum; **a — considerable quantity** aliquantul·um -i *n;* **— well** mediocriter
prevail *intr* *(to be prevalent)* esse, obtinēre; *(to win)* vincĕre; **to — upon** persuadēre *(w. dat)*
prevalent *adj* (per)vulgat·us -a -um; **to become —** increbrescĕre
prevaricate *intr* praevaricari
prevarication *s* praevaricati·o -onis *f*
prevaricator *s* praevaricat·or -oris *m*
prevent *tr* prohibēre; **to — s.th. from happening** prohibēre ne *(or* quominus) quid fiat
prevention *s* impediti·o -onis *f*

preventive *adj* to adopt all — measures omnia providēre et curare
previous *adj* super·ior -ior -ius
previously *adv* antehac
prey *s* praed·a -ae *f*
prey *intr* to — on praedari
price *s* pret·ium -(i)i *n;* at a high — magni; at a low — parvi; to purchase at an enormous — immenso pretio comparare
priceless *adj* inaestimabil·is -is -e
price tag *s* titul·us -i *m*
prick *tr* pungĕre; *(fig)* stimulare; to — up the ears aures arrigĕre
prickle *s* acule·us -i *m*
prickly *adj* spinos·us -a -um
pride *s* superbi·a -ae *f; (source of pride)* dec·us -oris *n*
pride *tr* to — oneself on jactare
priest *s* sacerd·os -otis *m; (of a particular god)* flam·en -inis *m*
priestess *s* sacerd·os -otis *f*
priesthood *s (office)* sacerdot·ium -(i)i *n*
priestly *adj* sacerdotal·is -is -e
prig *s* hom·o -inis *m* fastidiosus
prim *adj* (nimis) dilig·ens -entis
primarily *adv* praecipue
primary *adj* principal·is -is -e; *(chief)* praecipu·us -a -um
prime *s* flo·s -ris *m;* to be in one's — aetate florēre
prime *adj* prim·us -a -um, optim·us -a -um
primeval *adj* pristin·us -a -um
primitive *adj* primitiv·us -a -um
primordial *adj* primordi·us -a -um
primrose *s* primul·a -ae *f* vulgaris
prince *s* regis fil·ius -(i)i *m*
princely *adj* regi·us -a -um
princess *s* regis fili·a -ae *f*
principal *adj* principal·is -is -e, praecipu·us -a -um
principal *s (of a school)* rect·or -oris *m; (fin)* cap·ut -itis *n*
principality *s* principat·us -ūs *m*
principally *adv* praecipue
principle *s* princip·ium -(i)i *n; (rule of conduct)* praecept·um -i *n;* a man of — vi·r -ri *m* gravis et severus
print *s* not·a -ae *f* impressa; *(cloth)* pann·us -i *m* imaginibus impressus
print *tr* imprimĕre
printer *s* typograph·us -i *m*
printing *s* typographi·a -ae *f*
printing press *s* prel·um -i *n* typographicum
prior *adj* pr·ior -ior -ius
priority *s* primat·us -ūs *m*
prism *s* prism·a -atis *n*
prison *s* carc·er -eris *m;* to throw into — in carcerem conjicĕre
prisoner *s* captiv·us -i *m,* captiv·a -ae *f; (for debt)* nex·us -i *m*
pristine *adj* pristin·us -a -um
privacy *s* secret·um -i *n*

private *adj (secluded)* secret·us -a -um; *(person)* privat·us -a -um; *(tutor)* domestic·us -a -um; *(one's own)* propri·us -a -um; *(mil)* gregari·us -a -um
private *s* mil·es -itis *m* gregarius
privately *adv* clam, secreto; *(in a private capacity)* privatim
privation *s* egest·as -atis *f*
privilege *s* privileg·ium -(i)i *n*
privy *adj* privat·us -a -um; — to consci·us -a -um *(w. gen)*
prize *s (reward)* praem·ium -(i)i *n; (prey)* praed·a -ae *f*
prize *tr* magni aestimare
prize fighter *s* pug·il -ilis *m*
probability *s* veri similitud·o -inis *f*
probable *adj* veri simil·is -is -e
probably *adv* probabiliter
probation *s* probati·o -onis *f*
probe *s (med)* specill·um -i *n*
probe *tr* scrutari
problem *s* quaesti·o -onis *f,* aerumn·a -ae *f; (math)* problem·a -atis *n*
problematical *adj* anc·eps -ipitis
procedure *s* mod·us -i *m* operandi
proceed *intr* procedĕre; *(to go on)* pergĕre; to — against persequi; to — from oriri ex *(w. abl)*
proceedings *spl* act·a -orum *npl; (leg)* acti·o -onis *f*
proceeds *spl* redit·us -ūs *m*
process *s* rati·o -onis *f; (leg)* acti·o -onis *f*
proclaim *tr* pronuntiare
proclamation *s* pronunt·ium -(i)i *n*
proclivity *s* proclivit·as -atis *f*
proconsul *s* procons·ul -ulis *m*
proconsular *adj* proconsular·is -is -e
proconsulship *s* pronconsulat·us -ūs *m*
procrastinate *intr* procrastinare
procrastination *s* procrastinati·o -onis *f*
procreate *tr* procreare
procreation *s* procreati·o -onis *f*
proctor *s* procurat·or -oris *m*
procurable *adj* comparand·us -a -um
procure *tr* comparare
procurement *s* comparati·o -onis *f*
prodigal *adj* prodig·us -a -um
prodigality *s* dissipati·o -onis *f*
prodigious *adj* imman·is -is -e
prodigy *s* prodig·ium -(i)i *n; (fig)* miracul·um -i *n*
produce *s* fruct·us -ūs *m*
produce *tr (to bring forward)* producĕre, proferre; *(to bring into existence)* parĕre; gignĕre; *(to cause)* efficĕre, movēre; *(a play)* docēre; *(public games)* edĕre; *(crops)* ferre
product *s* op·us -eris *n*
production *s (act)* fabricati·o -onis *f*
productive *adj* efficien·s -tis; *(fertile)* fer·ax -acis
productivity *s* feracit·as -atis *f*
profanation *s* violati·o -onis *f*

profane *adj* profan·us -a -um
profanity *s* verb·a -orum *npl* profana
profess *tr* profiteri
professed *adj* manifest·us -a -um
profession *s* professi·o -onis *f*
professional *adj* ad professionem pertinen·s -tis; *(expert)* perit·us -a -um
professor *s* profess·or -oris *m*
proffer *tr* promittĕre
proficiency *s* progress·us -ūs *m*
proficient (in) *adj* perit·us -a -um *(w. gen)*
profile *s* faci·es -ei *f* obliqua; *(portrait)* imag·o -inis *f* obliqua; *(description)* descripti·o -onis *f*
profit *s (financial)* lucr·um -i *n; (benefit)* emolument·um -i *n* bonum
profit *tr* prodesse *(w. dat)* ‖ *intr* **to — by** uti *(w. abl); to — from** proficĕre *(w. abl)*
profitable *adj* fructuos·us -a -um; *(fin)* quaestuos·us -a -um; **to be — for s.o.** prodesse alicui
profitably *adv* utiliter
profitless *adj* inutil·is -is -e
profligacy *s* nequiti·a -ae *f*
profligate *adj* nequam *(indecl)*
profligate *s* nep·os -otis *m*
profound *adj* alt·us -a -um; *(recondite)* abstrus·us -a -um
profoundly *adv* funditus
profundity *s* altitud·o -inis *f*
profuse *adj* profus·us -a -um
profusely *adv* profuse
profusion *s* profusi·o -onis *f*
progeny *s* progeni·es -ei *f*
prognosticate *tr* praedicĕre
prognostication *s* praedicti·o -onis *f*
program *s* institut·um -i *n*, rati·o -onis *f; (booklet)* libell·us -i *m*
progress *s* progress·us -ūs *m;* **to make —** proficĕre
progress *intr* progredi
progression *s* progress·us -ūs *m*
progressive *adj* profici·ens -entis
progressively *adv* gradatim
prohibit *tr* vetare
prohibition *s* interdicti·o -onis *f*
project *s* proposit·um -i *n*
project *tr* projicĕre ‖ *intr* prominēre, exstare; *(of land)* excurrĕre
projectile *s* missil·e -is *n*
projecting *adj* emin·ens -entis
projection *s* projectur·a -ae *f*
proletarian *adj* proletari·us -a -um
proletariat *s* pleb·s -is *f*
prolific *adj* fecund·us -a -um
prologue *s* prolog·us -i *m*
prolong *tr* producĕre; *(term of office)* prorogare
prolongation *s* dilati·o -onis *f; (of term of office)* prorogati·o -onis *f*
promenade *s (walk)* ambulati·o -onis *f; (place)* ambulacr·um -i *n*

promenade *intr* spatiari
prominence *s* eminenti·a -ae *f*
prominent *adj* promin·ens -entis
promiscuous *adj* promiscu·us -a -um
promiscuously *adv* promiscue
promise *s* promiss·um -i *n;* **— of immunity** fid·es -ei *f* publica; **to break a —** fidem fallĕre; **to keep a —** promissum tenēre; **to make a —** fidem dare; **to make many —s** multa promittĕre
promise *tr* promittĕre, polliceri; *(in marriage)* despondēre
promising *adj* bonā spe *(abl used adjectively);* **less —** min·or -or -us opinione
promissory note *s* chirograph·um -i *n*
promontory *s* promontor·ium -(i)i *n*
promote *tr (in rank)* promovēre; *(a cause, etc.)* favēre *(w. dat);* **to — to a higher rank** in ampliorem gradum promovēre
promoter *s* faut·or -oris *m*
promotion *s* amplior grad·us -ūs *m*
prompt *adj* prompt·us -a -um
prompt *tr* subjicĕre, suggerĕre; *(incite)* commovēre
promptly *adv* statim, extemplo
promulgate *tr* promulgare
promulgation *s* promulgati·o -onis *f*
prone *adj* (to) pron·us -a -um (ad *or* in + *acc)*
prong *s* den·s -tis *m*
pronominal *adj* pronominal·is -is -e
pronoun *s* pronom·en -inis *n*
pronounce *tr (to declare)* pronuntiare; *(a word, judicial sentence)* dicĕre
pronunciation *s* pronuntiati·o -onis *f*
proof *s* document·um -i *n; (indication)* indic·ium -(i)i *n*
proof *adj* **— against** impervi·us -a -um *(w. dat)*
proofs *spl (from the press)* plagul·ae -arum *fpl;* **to correct —s** plagulas corrigĕre
prop *s* fulcr·um -i *n*
prop *tr* fulcire; **to — oneself up on** se fulcire *(w. dat)*
propaganda *s* re·s -rum *fpl* ad animos hominum movendos
propagate *tr* propagare; *(information)* disseminare
propagation *s* propagati·o -onis *f;* disseminati·o -onis *f*
propel *tr* propellĕre
propeller *s* propuls·or -oris *m*
propensity *s* propensi·o -onis *f*
proper *adj (becoming)* decor·us -a -um; *(suitable)* idone·us -a -um; **it is — for an orator to speak** decet oratorem loqui
properly *adv (in the strict sense)* proprie; *(fitly)* apte, commode
property *s* bon·a -orum *npl; (characteristic)* virt·us -utis *f*, propriet·as -atis *f;* **private —** res, rei *f* familiaris
prophecy *s* vaticinati·o -onis *f*
prophesy *tr* vaticinari

prophet s vat·es -is mf; (Biblical) prophet·a -ae m

prophetess s vat·es -is f

propitiate tr propitiare

propitiation s propitiati·o -onis f

propitious adj propiti·us -a -um

proportion s proporti·o -onis f; **in —** pro rata parte; **in — to** pro (w. abl)

proportionately adv pro portione

proposal s propositi·o -onis f, condici·o -onis f; **to accept a —** condicionem accipĕre; **to make a — that** condicionem ferre ut

propose tr (esp. a law) ferre; **to — a toast to** propinare (w. dat)

proposition s (offer) condici·o -onis f; (logic) propositi·o -onis f

propound tr proponĕre, exponĕre

proprietor s domin·us -i m

propriety s decor·um -i n

propulsion s propulsi·o -onis f

prosaic adj jejun·us -a -um

proscribe tr proscribĕre

proscription s proscripti·o -onis f

prose s pros·a -ae f

prosecute tr (to carry out) exsequi; (leg) litem intendĕre (w. dat); **to — offenses** delicta exsequi

prosecution s exsecuti·o -onis f; (leg) accusati·o -onis f

prosecutor s accusat·or -oris m

prospect s prospect·us -ūs m; (hope) spes, spei f; **his —s are good** is in bonā spe est

prospective adj futur·us -a -um

prosper intr vigēre

prosperity s re·s -rum fpl secundae

prosperous adj prosper·us -a -um

prosperously adv prospere

prostitute s meretr·ix -icis f

prostitute tr prostituĕre

prostrate tr sternĕre; **to — oneself at the feet of** se projicĕre ad pedes (w. gen)

prostrate adj prostrat·us -a -um; (fig) fract·us -a -um; **to fall —** se projicĕre

prostration s (act) prostrati·o -onis f; (state) anim·us -i m fractus

protect tr (pro)tegĕre

protection s praesid·ium -(i)i n; (protecting power) tutel·a -ae f

protective adj protegen·s -tis

protector s tut·or -oris m

protest s obtestati·o -onis f

protest tr (to assert positively) asseverare; (to object to) obtestari ‖ intr contra dicĕre; **to — against** contra dicĕre (w. dat)

prototype s exempl·ar -aris n

protract tr producĕre

protracted adj product·us -a -um

protrude tr protrudĕre ‖ intr prominēre, eminēre

protuberance s tub·er -eris n; (small lump) tubercul·um -i n

proud adj superb·us -a -um; **to be — of** superbire (w. abl)

proudly adv superbe

prove tr probare ‖ intr (of persons) se praebēre, se praestare; (of a thing, event) evadĕre, fieri, exire

proverb s proverb·ium -(i)i n

proverbial adj proverbial·is -is -e

provide tr (to get ready) parare; (to furnish) suppeditare; (to equip) ornare; **to — by law that** sancire ut ‖ intr **to — for** providēre (w. dat); (of laws) jubēre

provided adj instruct·us -a -um; **well —** refert·us -a -um

provided (that) conj dummodo (w. subj)

providence s providenti·a -ae f

provident adj provid·us -a -um

providential adj divin·us -a -um

providentially adv divinitus

provider s provis·or -oris m

province s provinci·a -ae f

provincial adj provincial·is -is -e; (pej) rustic·us -a -um

provision s (stipulation) condici·o -onis f; **—s** vict·us -ūs m; (mil) commeat·us -ūs m; **with the added —** exceptione adjectā

provisional adj temporari·us -a -um

provisionally adv ad tempus

proviso s condici·o -onis f; **with the — that** eā condicione ut

provocation s provocati·o -onis f

provoke tr (to cause) (com)movēre; (to irritate) irritare, movēre

provoking adj molest·us -a -um

prow s pror·a -ae f

prowess s vir·es -ium fpl

prowl intr vagari, grassari

prowler s praedat·or -oris m

proximity s propinquit·as -atis f

proxy s vicar·ius -(i)i m

prude s tetric·a -ae f

prudence s prudenti·a -ae f

prudent adj prud·ens -entis

prudently adv prudenter

prudish adj tetric·us -a -um

prune s prun·um -i n passum

prune tr (am)putare, resecare

pruning s putati·o -onis f

pruning shears spl fal·x -cis f

pry intr perscrutari; **to — into** investigare

prying adj curios·us -a -um

pseudonym s falsum nom·en -inis n

puberty s pubert·as -atis f

public adj public·us -a -um; (known) vulgat·us -a -um; **in a — capacity** publice; **— affairs** respublica (gen: reipublicae) f

public s public·um -i n, vulg·us -i n; **in —** propalam; (outdoors) foris; **to appear in —** prodire in publicum; **to open** (e.g., a road) **to the —** publicare

publican s publican·us -i m

publication *s* publicati·o -onis *f; (of a book)* editi·o -onis *f; (book)* li·ber -bri *m*
publicity *s* celebrit·as -atis *f*
publicly *adv* propalam
publish *tr* publicare, patefacĕre; *(book)* edĕre
publisher *s* edit·or -oris *m*
pucker *intr* **to — up the lips** osculari
puddle *s* lacun·a -ae *f*
puerile *adj* pueril·is -is -e
puff *s* flat·us -ūs *m*
puff *tr* inflare; **to be —ed up** tumēre ‖ *intr (to pant)* anhelare; **to — up** intumescĕre
puffy *adj* sufflat·us -a -um; *(swollen)* tum·ens -entis
pugilist *s* pug·il -ilis *m*
pugnacious *adj* pugn·ax -acis
pull *tr (to drag)* trahĕre, tractare; **to — apart** distrahĕre; **to — away** avellĕre; **to — down** detrahĕre; *(buildings)* demoliri, destruĕre; **to — out** extrahĕre; *(hair)* evellĕre; *(e.g., a weapon, tooth)* eximĕre; **to — out by the roots** exstirpare; *(weeds)* eruncare ‖ *intr* **to — at** vellicare; **to — through** pervincĕre; *(an illness)* convalescĕre
pull *s (act)* tract·us -ūs *m; (influence)* grati·a -ae *f*
pulley *s* trochle·a -ae *f*
pulmonary *adj* pulmone·us -a -um; *(disease)* pulmonari·us -a -um
pulp *s* pulp·a -ae *f*
pulpit *s (eccl)* cathedr·a -ae *f*
pulsate *intr* palpitare
pulse *s* puls·us -ūs (venarum) *m;* **to feel the —** venas temptare
pulverize *tr* pulverare, contundĕre
pumice *s* pum·ex -icis *m*
pump *s* antli·a -ae *f*
pump *tr* haurire; **to — out, — dry** exhaurire; **to — with questions** percontari
pumpkin *s* pep·o-onis *m*
pun *s* verborum lus·us -ūs *m*
punch *s (tool)* verucul·um -i *n; (blow)* pugn·us -i *m; (drink)* poti·o -onis *f* ex fructuum suco; **to give s.o. a —** pugnum alicui ducĕre
punch *tr* pugnum ducĕre *(w. dat);* **to — a hole in** pungĕre
punch-drunk *adj* stupefact·us -a -um
punching bag *s* coryc·us -i *m*
punctilious *adj* scrupulos·us -a -um
punctual *adj* **to be —** ad tempus venire
punctually *adv* ad tempus
punctuate *tr* interpungĕre
punctuation *s* interpuncti·o -onis *f*
punctuation mark *s* interpunct·um -i *n*
puncture *s* puncti·o -onis *f*
puncture *tr* pungĕre
pungent *adj* acut·us -a -um
Punic *adj* Punic·us -a -um
punish *tr* punire, animadvertĕre in *(w.*

acc), supplicium sumĕre de *(w. abl);* **to — with loss of one half of one's property** multare dimidiā parte; **to — with loss of the priesthood and dowry** multare sacerdotio et uxoris dote
punishable *adj* puniend·us -a -um
punishment *s (act)* puniti·o -onis *f; (penalty)* poen·a -ae *f,* supplic·ium -(i)i *n;* **to inflict — on s.o.** aliquem poenā afficĕre; **without —** impune
puny *adj* pusill·us -a -um
pup *s* catul·us -i *m,* catell·a -ae *f;* **to have —s** catulos parĕre
pupil *s* discipul·us -i *m,* discipul·a -ae *f; (of the eye)* pupill·a -ae *f*
puppet *s* pup·a -ae *f*
puppy *s* catul·us -i *m,* catell·a -ae *f*
purchase *s (act)* empti·o -onis *f; (merchandise)* mer·x -cis *f*
purchase *tr* emĕre, comparare
purchase price *s* pret·ium -(i)i *n; (of grain)* annon·a -ae *f*
purchaser *s* empt·or -oris *m*
pure *adj* pur·us -a -um; *(unmixed)* mer·us -a -um; *(morally)* cast·us -a -um
purely *adv* pure; *(quite)* omnino; *(solely)* solum
purge *tr* purgare, mundare
purge *s* purgati·o -onis *f; (pol)* proscripti·o -onis *f*
purification *s* purificati·o -onis *f*
purify *tr* purificare; *(fig)* expiare
purity *s* purit·as -atis *f; (moral)* castit·as -atis *f*
purple *s* purpur·a -ae *f;* **dressed in —** purpurat·us -a -um
purple *adj* purpure·us -a -um
purport *s* sigificati·o -onis *f,* sententi·a -ae *f;* **a communication to the same —** tabell·ae -arum *fpl* in eandem fere sententiam
purport *tr* significare
purpose *s (aim, end)* proposit·um -i *n,* fin·is -is *m; (wish)* men·s -tis *f;* **on —** consulto; **to no —** frustra, nequaquam; **to what —** quorsum
purpose *tr* in animo habēre
purposely *adv* consulto, de industriā
purr *s* murm·ur -uris *n*
purr *intr* murmurare
purring *s* murmurati·o -onis *f*
purse *s* marsup·ium -(i)i *n*
purse *tr (to pucker up)* astringĕre
pursuance *s* exsecuti·o -onis *f;* **in — of** secundum *(w. acc),* ex *(w. abl)*
pursuant to *prep* secundum *(w. acc)*
pursue *tr (an enemy)* insequi; *(a course, plan)* insistĕre *(w. acc or dat);* **I will not — this subject further** quod non prosequar longius; **to — one's studies** studiis insistĕre; **to — an advantage** utilitatem sequi; **to — wealth and power** opes et potentiam consectari

pursuit *s* insectati·o -onis *f; (striving after)* consectati·o -onis *f; (eager desire for and aiming at; occupation)* stud·ium -(i)i *n*

pus *s* pu·s -ris *n*

push *tr* trudĕre, impellĕre; **to — away** *or* **back** repellĕre **‖** *intr* **to — on** contendĕre, iter facĕre

push *s* puls·us -ūs *m; (strong effort)* nis·us -ūs *m; (mil)* impet·us -ūs *m*

pushy *adj* aud·ax -acis, molest·us -a -um

put *tr* ponĕre, collocare; **to — an end to** finem facĕre *(w. dat);* **to — aside** ponĕre; **to — away** seponĕre, abdĕre; *(in safety)* recondĕre; **to — back** reponĕre; **to — down** deponĕre; *(to suppress)* supponĕre, sedare; *(in writing)* scribĕre; **to — his hand to his mouth** manum ad os apponĕre; **to — in** inserĕre; **to — in order** ordinare; **to — off** *(to postpone)* differre; **to — on** imponĕre *(w. dat); (to add)* addĕre; *(clothes)* se induĕre *(w. abl); (a ring)* (anulum) digito aptare; *(a cap)* (pilleum) capiti suo imponĕre; *(a sword)* cingĕre latus (gladio); **to — on the table** ponĕre super mensam; **to — out** *(the hand)* proferre; *(to remove, e.g., from office)* submovēre; *(a fire)* exstinguĕre; **to — out of one's mind** ex animo delēre; **to — out of the way** demovēre; *(to murder)* de medio tollĕre; **to — together** componĕre, conferre; **to — up** *(to erect)* statuĕre; *(to raise, e.g., hands)* erigĕre; **to — up for sale** venum dare; **‖** *intr* **to — in** *(of ships)* appellĕre; **to — in to port** portum petĕre; **to — out to sea** solvĕre; **to — up with** tolerare

putrefy *intr* putrescĕre

putrid *adj* putrid·us -a -um

putty *s* glut·en -inis *n* vitrariorum

puzzle *s* aenigm·a -atis *n*

puzzle *tr* confundĕre

puzzled *adj* confus·us -a -um

puzzling *adj* perplex·us -a -um

pygmy *s* pygmae·us -i *m*

pylon *s* colum·en -inis *n*

pyramid *s* pyram·is -idis *f*

pyre *s* rog·us -i *m*

Pythagorean *adj* Pythagorae·us -a -um

Pythian *adj* Pythi·us -a -um

Q

quack *s (phoney)* circulat·or -oris *m; (bad physician)* pharmacopol·a -ae *m; (of a duck)* tetrissitat·us -ūs *m*

quack *intr* tetrissitare

quadrangle *s* are·a -ae *f*

quadruped *s* quadrup·es -edis *mf*

quadruple *tr* quadruplicare

quaestor *s* quaest·or -oris *m*

quaestorship *s* quaestur·a -ae *f;* **to hold the —** quaesturam gerĕre

quaff *tr* ducĕre, haurire

quagmire *s* pal·us -udis *f*

quail *s* coturn·ix -icis *f*

quaint *adj* insolit·us -a -um

quake *intr* tremĕre

qualification *s (endowment)* indol·es -is *f; (limitation)* excepti·o -onis *f*

qualified *adj (competent)* perit·us -a -um; *(limited)* modic·us -a -um; **— for** apt·us -a -um ad *(w. acc),* habil·is -is -e ad *(w. acc)*

qualify *tr* aptum *or* idoneum reddĕre; *(to limit)* temperare

quality *s* qualit·as -atis *f; (excellence)* virt·us -utis *f*

qualm *s* fastid·ium -(i)i *n;* **— of conscience** scrupul·us -i *m*

quantity *s* numer·us -i *m,* quantit·as -atis *f;* **a large —** frequenti·a -ae *f*

quarrel *s* jurg·ium -(i)i *n*

quarrel *intr* jurgare, altercari

quarrelsome *adj* jurgios·us -a -um

quarry *s* lapicidin·ae -arum *fpl; (prey)* praed·a -ae *f*

quart *s* duo sextari·i -orum *mpl*

quarter *s (fourth part)* quarta par·s -tis *f,* quadran·s -tis *m; (side, direction)* par·s -tis *f; (district)* regi·o -onis *f;* **at close —s** comminus *(adv);* **—s** *(dwelling)* tect·um -i *n; (temporary abode)* hospit·ium -(i)i *n;* **neither giving nor asking for —** sine missione

quarter *tr* in quattuor partes dividĕre; *(to give lodgings to)* hospitium praebēre *(w. dat)*

quarterly *adj* trimestr·is -is -e

quarterly *adv* tertio quoque mense

quartermaster *s* castrorum praefect·us -i *m*

quash *tr (rebellion)* opprimĕre; *(a law)* rescindĕre

quatrain *s* tetrastich·on -i *n*

quavering *adj* tremul·us -a -um

queasy *adj* nauseabund·us -a -um; **to feel —** nauseare

queen *s* regin·a -ae *f*

queen bee *s* re·x -gis *m* apium

queer *adj* insolit·us -a -um; *(strange)* inept·us -a -um

quell *tr* sedare

quench *tr* exstinguĕre; **to — a thirst** sitim sedare

querulous *adj* querul·us -a -um

query *s* quaesti·o -onis *f*

query *tr & intr* quaerĕre

quest *s* inquisiti·o -onis *f;* **to be in — of** requirĕre; **to go in — of** investigare

question *s* quaesti·o -onis *f,* interrogati·o -onis *f;* **I ask you this —** hoc te rogo; **there is no — that** non dubium est quin; **to ask a —** interrogare, quaerere; **to ask many —s** multa interrogare; **to answer**

a — ad rogatum respondēre; **to call into** — in dubium vocare; **to keep asking** —**s** rogitare; **without** — sine dubio

question *tr* interrogare, percontari; *(to doubt)* dubitare, in dubium vocare; *(to examine)* scrutari

questionable *adj* dubi·us -a -um

questioning *s* interrogati·o -onis *f*

questor *s* quaest·or -oris *m*

questorship *s* quaestur·a -ae *f;* **to hold the** — quaesturam gerĕre

quibble *s* capti·o -onis *f*

quibble *intr* cavillari

quibbler *s* cavillat·or -oris *m*

quibbling *s* cavillati·o -onis *f*

quick *adj* cel·er -eris -ere; *(agile)* agil·is -is -e; *(mentally)* astut·us -a -um; *(w. hands)* facil·is -is -e; *(w. wits)* argut·us -a -um

quicken *tr* accelerare

quickly *adv* cito

quickness *s* celerit·as -atis *f; (of mind)* acum·en -inis *n; (agility)* agilit·as -atis *f*

quicksand *s* syrt·is -is *f*

quicksilver *s* argent·um -i *n* vivum

quiet *adj* quiet·us -a -um; *(silent)* tacit·us -a -um; **to keep** — quiescĕre; *(to refrain from talking)* silēre

quiet *s* qui·es -etis *f; (leisure)* ot·ium -(i)i *n; (silence)* silent·ium -(i)i *n*

quiet *tr* tranquillare, sedare

quill *s* penn·a -ae *f*

quilt *s* culcit·a -ae *f*

quince *s* cydon·ium -(i)i *n*

quintessence *s* medull·a -ae *f*

quip *s* faceti·ae -arum *fpl*

quip *tr* & *intr* per jocum dicĕre

quirk *s* propr·ium -(i)i *n*

quit *tr (to leave)* relinquĕre; *(to stop)* cessare, desinĕre; — **laughing!** noli *(pl:* nolite) ridēre!

quite *adv* omnino, admodum; **not** — parum; *(not yet)* nondum

quiver *s* pharetr·a -ae *f;* **wearing a** — pharetrat·us -a -um

quiver *intr* tremĕre

quivering *s* trem·or -oris *m*

Quixotic *adj* ridicul·us -a -um

quoit *s* disc·us -i *m;* **to play** —**s** disco ludĕre

quota *s* rata par·s -tis *f*

quotation *s (act)* prolati·o -onis *f; (words quoted)* loc·us -i *m* allatus

quote *tr* ponĕre

R

rabbi *s* rabbi *indecl m*

rabbit *s* cunicul·us -i *m*

rabble *s* turb·a -ae *f*

rabid *adj* rabid·us -a -um

race *s (lineage)* gen·us -eris *n; (foot race)* certam·en -inis *n* cursūs; *(horse race)* curs·us -ūs *m* equorum; *(of chariots)* curricul·um -i *n*

race *intr* certare; *(running)* pedibus certare; *(on horseback)* cursu equestri certare

racecourse *s* stad·ium -(i)i *n*

racehorse *s* cel·es -etis *m*

racer *s* curs·or -oris *m*

racetrack *s* curricul·um -i *n*

rack *s (shelf)* plute·us -i *m; (for punishment)* equule·us -i *m;* **to put to the** — equuleo torquēre

rack *tr* **to be** —**ed with pain** dolore distineri; **to** — **one's brain about s.th.** aliquā re scrutandā fatigari

racket *s (noise)* strepit·us -ūs *m; (for tennis)* reticul·um -i *n*

racketeer *s* circulat·or -oris *m*

radiance *s* fulg·or -oris *m*

radiant *adj* fulgid·us -a -um

radiate *tr* emittĕre ‖ *intr* radiare

radiation *s* radiati·o -onis *f*

radical *adj* innat·us -a -um; *(thorough)* tot·us - a -um

radical *s* rerum novarum cupid·us -i *m*

radically *adv* penitus

radish *s* radicul·a -ae *f*

radius *s* rad·ius -(i)i *m*

raffle *s* ale·a -ae *f*

raffle *tr* **to** — **off** aleā vendĕre

raft *s* rat·is -is *f*

rafter *s* trab·s -is *f*

rag *s* pannicul·us -i *m*

rage *s* fur·or -oris *m*

rage *intr* furĕre, saevire

ragged *adj* pannos·us -a -um

ragman *s* centonar·ius -(i)i *m*

raid *s* incursi·o -onis *f*

raid *tr* praedari

raider *s* praedat·or -oris *m*

rail *s* longur·ius -(i)i *m*

rail *tr* **to** — **off** consaepire ‖ *intr* **to** — **at** insectari

railing *s (fence)* saepiment·um -i *n; (abuse)* convic·ium -(i)i *n*

railroad *s* ferrata vi·a -ae *f*

railroad car *s* viae ferratae curr·us -ūs *m*

railroad station *s* viae ferratae stati·o -onis *f*

raiment *s* vestit·us -ūs *m*

rain *s* pluvi·a -ae *f,* imb·er -ris *m*

rain *intr* pluĕre; **it is** —**ing** pluit

rainbow *s* pluvius arc·us -ūs *m*

rain cloud *s* imb·er -ris *m*

rainy *adj* pluvi·us -a -um

raise *tr* tollĕre; *(finger, ladder, eyes)* erigĕre; *(to build)* exstruĕre; *(money)* expedire; *(an army)* (con)scribĕre, comparare; *(siege)* solvĕre; *(children)* educare; *(to stir up)* excitare; *(to promote)* provehĕre; *(price)* augēre; *(crops)* colĕre; *(beard)* demittĕre; **to** — **the cur-**

tain aulaea premĕre; **to — the head**
(eyes) caput (oculos) attollĕre
raisin s (uva) pass•a -ae f
rake s rastell•us -i m; (person) nep•os
-otis m
rake tr radĕre; **to — up** corradĕre
rally s conti•o -onis f
rally tr (mil) in ordines revocare ‖ intr se
colligĕre; (after a retreat) se ex fuga
colligĕre; (from sickness) convalescĕre
ram s ari•es -etis m
ram tr fistucare; (to cram) infercire
ramble s vagati•o -onis f
ramble intr vagari, errare; **to — on** (in
speech) garrire
rambling adj erran•s -tis; (fig) vag•us -a
-um
ramification s ramificati•o -onis f
ramp s agg•er -eris m
rampage s **to go on a —** ferocire
rampage intr furĕre
rampant adj effrenat•us -a -um; (widespread) divulgat•us -a -um
rampart s vall•um -i n
ranch s latifund•ium -(i)i n
rancher s pecuar•ius -(i)i m
rancid adj rancid•us -a -um
rancor s iracundi•a -ae f
random adj fortuit•us -a -um; **at —** temere
range s (row) ord•o -inis m; (of mountain)
jug•um -i n; (reach) jact•us -ūs m; (extent) fin•es -ium mpl; **to be in —** esse
intra teli jactum; **to be out of —** extra
teli jactum abesse; **the enemy were just
within —** non longius hostes aberant
quam quo telum adjici posset
range tr ordinare, disponĕre ‖ intr (to rove
at large) pervagari; (to vary) discrepare
rank s ord•o -inis m, grad•us -ūs m; (high
rank) dignit•as -atis f; **in close —** (mil)
firmis ordinibus; **the — and file** (i.e.,
ordinary soldiers) manipular•es -ium mpl
rank tr in numero habēre ‖ intr in numero
haberi; **to — first** primum locum obtinēre
rank adj luxurios•us -a -um; (extreme)
summ•us -a -um; (of smell) fŏetid•us -a
-um
rankle intr (fig) suppurare
ransack tr diripĕre; (to search thoroughly)
exquirĕre
ransom s (act) redempti•o -onis f; (money)
pret•ium -(i)i n
ransom tr redimĕre
rant intr ampullari; **to — and rave**
debacchari
rap s (slap) alap•a -ae f; (blow) ict•us -ūs
m; (at door) pulsati•o -onis f; (w. knuck-
les) talitr•um -i n; **not to give a —** non
flocci facĕre
rap tr (to criticize) exagitare ‖ intr **to — at**
pulsare
rapacious adj rap•ax -acis
rape s stupr•um -i n per vim

rape tr per vim stuprare
rapid adj rapid•us -a -um
rapidity s rapidit•as -atis f
rapidly adv rapide
rapine s rapin•a -ae f
rapture s exsultati•o -onis f; **to be in —s
of delight** gaudio efferi
rapturous adj exsult•ans -antis
rare adj rar•us -a -um; (meat) semicoct•us
-a -um
rarefy tr rarefacĕre
rarely adv raro
rarity s rarit•as -atis f, paucit•as -atis f;
(thing) res, rei f rara
rascal s scelest•us -i m
rascally adj scelest•us -a -um
rash adj temerari•us -a -um
rash s erupti•o -onis f pustulae
rashly adv temere
rashness s temerit•as -atis f
raspberry s mor•um -i n Idaeum
raspberry bush s mor•a -ae f Idaea
rat s mu•s -ris m; (person) transfug•a -ae
m; **like drowned —s** tamquam mures
udi
rate s proporti•o -onis f; (price) pret•ium
-(i)i n; (scale) norm•a -ae f; **at any —**
utique; **— of exchange** collyb•us -i m;
— of interest faen•us -oris n
rate tr aestimare, taxare; **to — s.o. highly**
aliquem magni facĕre
rather adv potius, prius; (somewhat)
aliquantum, paulo, or render by comparative of adjective or adverb
ratification s sancti•o -onis f
ratify tr sancire, comprobare
rating s aestimati•o -onis f
ratio s proporti•o -onis f
ration s (portion) demens•um -1 n; **—s**
(mil) cibari•a -orum npl
ration tr demetiri
rational adj ratione praedit•us -a -um
rationalize intr ratiocinari
rationally adv ratione, sapienter
rattle s crepit•us -ūs m; (toy) crepitacul•um
-i n
rattle tr crepitare (w. abl) ‖ intr crepare,
crepitare; **to — on** garrire
raucous adj rauc•us -a -um
ravage tr vastare, populari
ravages s vastati•o -onis f
rave intr furĕre, saevire
ravel tr involvĕre
raven s corv•us -i m, corn•ix -icis f
ravenous adj vor•ax -acis
ravenously adv voraciter
ravine s fauc•es -ium fpl
raving adj furios•us -a -um; **to be — mad**
plane furĕre
ravish tr stuprare
raw adj crud•us -a -um; (weather) asp•er
-era -erum; (jokes) incondit•us -a -um
rawboned adj strigos•us -a -um

ray *s* rad·ius -(i)i *m*
raze *tr* solo aequare
razor *s* novacul·a -ae *f*
reach *s (grasp, capacity)* capt·us -ūs *m;* *(of weapon)* jact·us -ūs *m;* **out of my —** extra ictum meum
reach *tr (e.g., a high branch)* contingĕre, attingĕre; *(of space)* pertinēre ad *(w. acc),* extendi ad *(w. acc); (to come up to)* assequi; *(to arrive at)* pervenire ad *or* in *(w. acc); (to hand)* porrigĕre; *(to attain to, e.g., old age)* adipisci
react *intr* affici; **to — to** referre
reaction *s* affect·us -ūs *m*
reactionary *s* qui pristinum rerum statum revocare vult
read *tr & intr* legĕre; **to — aloud** recitare; **to — over** translegĕre; **to — through** perlegĕre; **to — well** commode legĕre
readable *adj* lectu facil·is -is -e
reader *s* lect·or -oris *m*
readily *adv (willingly)* libenter; *(easily)* facile
readiness *s* facilit·as -atis *f;* **in —** in promptu
ready *adj (for)* parat·us -a -um, prompt·us -a -um (ad + *acc*)
real *adj* ver·us -a -um
real estate *s* re·s -rum *fpl* soli *(opp:* re·s -rum *fpl* mobiles); **piece of —** praed·ium -(i)i *n*
real estate broker *s* praediat·or -oris *m*
realistic *adj* verisimil·is -is -e
reality *s* res, rei *f,* verit·as -atis *f;* **in —** re verā
realization *s (e.g., of plans)* effect·us -ūs *m; (of ideas)* comprehensi·o -onis *f*
realize *tr* sentire; *(to effect)* efficĕre, ad exitum perducĕre; **to — great profits from** magnas pecunias facĕre ex *(w. abl)*
really *adv* vero, profecto, re verā; *(surely)* sane, certe
realm *s* regn·um -i *n*
reap *tr* metĕre; *(fig)* percipĕre; **to — the reward for** fructum percipĕre ex *(w. abl)*
reaper *s* mess·or -oris *m*
reappear *intr* redire, revenire; *(from below)* resurgĕre
rear *tr* educare ‖ *intr (of horses)* arrectum se tollĕre
rear *s* terg·um -i *n; (mil)* novissimum agm·en -inis *n;* **on the —** a tergo; **to bring up the —** agmen cogĕre
rearing *s* educati·o -onis *f*
reascend *tr & intr* denuo ascendĕre
reason *s (faculty; reasonable ground)* rati·o -onis *f; (cause)* caus·a -ae *f; (moderation)* mod·us -i *m;* **for good —s** justis de causis; **for that —** ideo, idcirco; **for this —** hāc de causā, itaque, quamobrem; **for —s of poor health** valetudinis causā; **there is no — why** nihil causae est, cur;

to give a — why adferre rationem, quamobrem; **what is the — why** quid est, cur; **with — cum** causā
reasonable *adj (fair)* aequ·us -a -um; *(moderate)* modic·us -a -um; *(judicious)* prud·ens -entis
reasonably *adv* ratione, juste; modice
reasoning *s* ratiocinati·o -onis *f; (discussing)* disceptati·o -onis *f*
reassemble *tr* recolligĕre, cogĕre
reassert *tr* iterare
reassure *tr* confirmare, redintegrare
rebate *s* deminuti·o -onis *f*
rebel *s* rebell·is -is *m*
rebel *intr* rebellare, desciscĕre
rebellion *s* rebelli·o -onis *f*
rebellious *adj* rebell·is -is -e; *(disobedient)* contum·ax -acis
rebirth *s* novus ort·us -ūs *m*
rebound *s* result·us -ūs *m*
rebound *intr* resultare, resilire
rebuff *s* repuls·a -ae *f*
rebuff *tr* repellĕre, rejicĕre
rebuild *tr* reficĕre
rebuke *s* reprehensi·o -onis *f*
rebuke *tr* reprehendĕre, vituperare
rebuttal *s* refutati·o -onis *f*
recall *s* revocati·o -onis *f*
recall *tr* revocare; **to — to mind** in memoriam redigĕre
recant *tr* recantare, retractare
recapitulate *tr* summatim colligĕre
recapitulation *s* repetiti·o -onis *f*
recapture *s* recuperati·o -onis *f*
recapture *tr* recuperare
recede *intr* recedĕre
receipt *s (act)* accepti·o -onis *f; (document)* apoch·a -ae *f;* **—s and expenditures** accept·a -orum *npl* et dat·a -orum *npl*
receive *tr* accipĕre
receiver *s* recept·or -oris *m*
recent *adj* rec·ens -entis
recently *adv* nuper
receptacle *s* receptacul·um -i *n*
reception *s (act)* accepti·o -onis *f; (social event)* hospit·ium -(i)i *n*
receptive *adj* docil·is -is -e; **to be — to treatment** recipĕre curationem
recess *s (place)* recess·us -ūs *m; (in a wall)* adyt·um -n; *(intermission)* intermissi·o -onis *f; (vacation)* feri·ae -arum *fpl; (leg)* justit·ium -(i)i *n*
recipe *s* praescript·um -i *n*
recipient *s* accept·or -oris *m*
reciprocal *adj* mutu·us -a -um
reciprocally *adv* mutuo, invicem
reciprocate *tr* reddĕre ‖ *intr* reciprocare
reciprocity *s* reciprocati·o -onis *f*
recital *s* recitati·o -onis *f*
recitation *s* recitati·o -onis *f*
reckless *adj* temerari·us -a -um
recklessly *adv* temere

reckon *tr* aestimare ‖ *intr* **to — on** confīdĕre *(w. dat)*

reckoning *s* numerati·o -onis *f; (account to be given)* rati·o -onis *f;* **— of time** ratio *f* temporis

reclaim *tr* reposcĕre, repetĕre

recline *intr* recubare; *(at table)* accumbĕre, recumbĕre; *(said of several guests)* discumbĕre

recluse *s* solitarius hom·o -inis *m*

recognition *s* agniti·o -onis *f*

recognizance *s* vadimon·ium -(i)i *n*

recognize *tr* agnoscĕre; *(to acknowledge)* noscĕre; *(to admit)* accipĕre

recoil *intr* resilire; *(in horror)* **(from)** refugĕre (ab + *acc)*

recoil *s* recessi·o -onis *f*

recollect *tr* recordari

recollection *s* recordati·o -onis *f*

recommence *tr* redintegrare ‖ *intr* redire

recommend *tr* commendare

recommendation *s* commendati·o -onis *f;* **letter of —** litter·ae -arum *fpl* commendaticiae

recompense *s* remunerati·o -onis *f*

recompense *tr* remunerare; *(to indemnify)* compensare

reconcilable *adj* placabil·is -is -e; *(of things)* conveni·ens -entis

reconcile *tr* reconciliare, componĕre; **to be —ed** in gratiam restitui

reconciliation *s* reconciliati·o -onis *f*

reconnoiter *tr* perspeculari

reconquer *tr* revincĕre

reconsider *tr* retractare

reconstruct *tr* restituĕre, renovare

reconstruction *s* renovati·o -onis *f*

record *s* monument·um -i *n; (top performance)* palm·a -ae *f;* **—s** act·a -orum *npl,* annal·es -ium *mpl; (in bookkeeping)* tabul·ae -arum *fpl*

record *tr* referre (in tabulas)

recorder *s* procurat·or -oris *m* ab actis

recount *tr* enarrare

recoup *tr* recuperare

recourse *s* refug·ium -(i)i *n;* **to have — to** fugĕre ad; *(to resort to)* descendĕre ad

recover *tr* recuperare ‖ *intr (from an illness)* convalescĕre; *(to come to one's senses)* ad se redire

recoverable *adj* reparabil·is -is -e; *(of persons)* şanabil·is -is -e

recovery *s* recuperati·o -onis *f; (from illness)* recreati·o -onis *f*

recreate *tr* recreare

recreation *s* oblectati·o -onis *f*

recriminate *tr* invicem accusare

recrimination *s* mutua accusati·o -onis *f*

recruit *s* tir·o -onis *m*

recruit *tr (mil)* conscribĕre; *(one's strength)* reficĕre

recruiting *s* delect·us -ūs *m*

recruiting officer *s* conquisit·or -oris *m*

rectify *tr* corrigĕre, emendare

rectitude *s* probit·as -atis *f*

rector *s* rect·or -oris *m*

recumbent *adj* resupin·us -a -um

recur *intr* redire

recurrence *s* redit·us -ūs *m*

recurrent *adj* assidu·us -a -um

red *adj* ru·ber -bra -brum; *(ruddy)* rubicund·us -a -um; **to be —** rubēre; **to grow —** rubescĕre

redden *tr* rubefacĕre, rutilare ‖ *intr* rubescĕre; *(to blush)* erubescĕre

reddish *adj* subru·ber -bra -brum; *(hair)* subruf·us -a -um

redeem *tr* redimĕre

redeemer *s* liberat·or -oris *m; (eccl)* Redempt·or -oris *m*

redemption *s* redempti·o -onis *f*

redhead *s* ruf·us -i *m,* ruf·a -ae *f*

red-hot *adj* cand·ens -entis

redness *s* rub·or -oris *m*

redolent *adj* redol·ens -entis

redouble *tr* ingeminare

redoubt *s* propugnacul·um -i *n*

redound *intr* redundare

redress *s* satisfacti·o -onis *f;* **to demand —** res repetĕre

redress *tr* restituĕre

reduce *tr* minuĕre; *(to a condition)* redigĕre; *(mil)* expugnare

reduction *s* deminuti·o -onis *f; (mil)* expugnati·o -onis *f*

redundancy *s* redundanti·a -ae *f*

redundant *adj* supervacu·us -a -um

reed *s* harund·o -inis *f*

reef *s* scopul·us -i *m*

reek *intr* fumare; **to — of** olēre

reel *s* fus·us -i *m*

reel *intr (to stagger)* titubare

reestablish *tr* restituĕre

reestablishment *s* restituti·o -onis *f*

refer *tr* referre, remittĕre ‖ *intr* **to — to** attingĕre, alludĕre

referee *s* arbi·ter -tri *m*

reference *s* rati·o -onis *f; (place in a book)* loc·us -i *m; (as to character)* commendati·o -onis *f;* **in — to s.th.** ex relatione ad aliquid; **with — to our annals** ad nostrorum annalium rationem

refine *tr* expolire; *(metals)* excoquĕre; *(manners)* excolĕre

refinement *s (of liquids)* purgati·o -onis *f; (fig)* humanit·as -atis *f*

reflect *tr* repercutĕre ‖ *intr* **to — on** considerare, reputare

reflection *s* repercussi·o -onis *f; (thing reflected)* imag·o -inis *f; (thinking over)* considerati·o -onis *f;* **without —** inconsulte

reflective *adj* cogitabund·us -a -um

reflexive *adj* reciproc·us -a -um

reform *tr* reficĕre; *(to amend)* corrigĕre ‖ *intr* se corrigĕre

reform s correcti·o -onis f
reformation s correcti·o -onis f
Reformation s Reformati·o -onis f
reformer s correct·or -oris m
refract tr refringĕre
refraction s refracti·o -onis f
refractory adj contum·ax -acis
refrain s vers·us -ūs m intercularis
refrain intr to — from abstinēre ab (w. abl); I — from speaking abstineo quin dicam; he will not — from boasting non temperabit quin jactet
refresh tr recreare, reficĕre; (the memory) redintegrare
refreshing adj jucund·us -a -um
refreshment s (food) cib·us -i m; (drink) pot·us -ūs m
refuge s refug·ium -(i)i n; to take — with confugĕre in (w. acc)
refugee s profug·us -i m, ex(s)·ul -ulis mf
refulgent adj fulgid·us -a -um
refund tr restituĕre
refund s pecuni·a -ae f restituta
refusal s recusati·o -onis f
refuse tr recusare, negare
refutation s refutati·o -onis f
refute tr refutare, redarguĕre
regain tr recuperare
regal adj regal·is -is -e
regally adv regaliter
regard s rati·o -onis f; (concern) cur·a -ae f; (esteem) grati·a -ae f; give my —s to your brother! fratrem tuum jube salvēre! to have — for rationem (w. gen) habēre; to send best — to salutem plurimam ascribĕre (w. dat)
regard tr (to look at) respicĕre, intueri; (to concern) spectare ad (w. acc); (to esteem) aestimare; (to consider) habēre; to — his word as law pro legibus habēre quae dicat
regarding prep de (w. abl)
regardless adj — of neglegen·s -tis (w. acc); — of order of preference omisso ordine
regency s interregn·um -i n
regenerate tr regenerare
regeneration s regenerati·o -onis f
regent s inter·rex -regis m
regicide s (murderer) regis occis·or -oris m; (deed) caed·es -is f regis
regime s administrati·o -onis f
regimen s vict·us -ūs m
region s regi·o -onis f; in the — of circa (w. acc)
register s (list) tabul·ae -arum fpl
register tr perscribĕre, in tabulas referre; (emotions) ostendĕre ‖ intr nomen dare
registrar s tabular·ius -(i)i m
registration s in tabulas relati·o -onis f, perscripti·o -onis f
registry s tabular·ium -(i)i n
regret s paenitenti·a -ae f

regret tr I — me paenitet (w. gen)
regretful adj paenit·ens -entis
regular adj (common) usitat·us -a -um; (proper) just·us -a -um; (consistent) const·ans -antis; (arranged, coming in order) ordinari·us -a -um
regularity s (orderly arrangement) ord·o -inis m; (evenness, unbroken succession) constanti·a -ae f
regularly adv ordine, constanter
regulate tr ordinare, disponĕre; (to control) moderari
regulation s (act) ordinati·o -onis f; (rule) praecept·um -i n, juss·um -i n
rehabilitate tr restituĕre
rehearsal s meditati·o -onis f
rehearse tr meditari
reign s regn·um -i n
reign intr regnare; to — over regnare in (w. abl), dominari (w. dat)
reimburse tr rependĕre
reimbursement s pecuniae restituti·o -onis f
rein s haben·a -ae f; to give full — to habenas immittĕre (w. dat); to loosen the —s frenos dare; to tighten the —s habenas adducĕre
reindeer s ren·o -onis f
reinforce tr firmare, supplēre
reinforcement s subsid·ium -(i)i n; —s (mil) supplement·um -i n; (fresh troops) novae copi·ae -arum fpl
reinstate tr restituĕre
reinstatement s restituti·o -onis f
reinvest tr iterum locare
reiterate tr iterare
reiteration s iterati·o -onis f
reject tr rejicĕre
rejection s rejecti·o -onis f
rejoice intr gaudēre
rejoin tr redire ad (w. acc) ‖ intr respondēre
rejoinder s respons·um -i n
rekindle tr resuscitare
relapse s to have a — recidĕre
relapse intr recidĕre
relate tr referre, narrare ‖ intr to — to pertinēre ad
related adj propinqu·us -a -um; (by birth) (to) cognat·us -a -um (w. dat); (by marriage) (to) affin·is -is -e (w. dat)
relation s narrati·o -onis f; (reference) rati·o -onis f; (relative) cognat·us -i m, cognat·a -ae f; (relationship) cognati·o -onis f
relationship s (by blood) consanguinit·as -atis f, cognati·o -onis f; (by marriage; connection) affinit·as -atis f
relative adj cum ceteris comparat·us -a -um; (gram) relativ·us -a -um; — to de (w. abl)
relative s cognat·us -i m, cognat·a -ae f
relatively adv comparate; not absolutely but — non simpliciter sed comparatione

relax *tr* remittĕre, relaxare ‖ *intr* se remittĕre
relaxation *s* relaxati·o -onis *f*
relaxing *adj* remissiv·us -a -um
release *s* liberati·o -onis *f*
release *tr* solvĕre; *(a prisoner)* liberare
relegate *tr* relegare
relent *intr* mitescĕre
relentless *adj* inexorabil·is -is -e
relentlessly *adv* sine missione
relevant *adj* to be — ad rem attinēre
reliable *adj* cert·us -a -um; *(person)* fid·us -a -um
reliance *s* fiduci·a -ae *f*
reliant *adj* (on) fret·us -a -um *(w. abl)*
relic *s* reliqui·ae -arum *fpl*
relief *s (alleviation)* levati·o -onis *f; (comfort)* lenim·en -inis *n; (help)* auxil·ium -(i)i *n; (in sculpture)* toreum·a -atis *n; (of sentries)* mutati·o -onis *f*
relieve *tr* levare, mitigare; *(to aid)* succurrĕre *(w. dat); (a guard)* succedĕre *(w. dat)*, excipĕre; **to — oneself** vesicam exonerare; *(coll)* facĕre
religion *s* religi·o -onis *f;* **regard for —** religi·o -onis *f*
religious *adj* religios·us -a -um; **— ceremonies, — rites** religion·es -um *fpl*
relinquish *tr* relinquĕre; *(office)* se abdicare ab *(w. abl)*
relish *s (flavor)* sap·or -oris *m; (enthusiasm)* stud·ium -(i)i *n; (seasoning)* condiment·um -i *n*
relish *tr* gustare, non male appetĕre
reluctance *s* aversati·o -onis *f;* **with —** invite
reluctant *adj* invit·us -a -um
reluctantly *adv* invite
rely *intr* **to — on** confidĕre *(w. dat)*, niti *(w. abl)*
remain *intr* manēre, permanēre; *(of things)* restare; *(to be left over)* superesse; **to — in that condition** subsistĕre in eo habitu
remainder *s* reliqu·um -i *n*
remaining *adj* reliqu·us -a -um
remains *spl* reliqui·ae -arum *fpl*
remark *tr* dicĕre
remark *s* dict·um -i *n*
remarkable *adj* notabil·is -is -e
remarkably *adv* mire, egregie
remedial *adj* remedial·is -is -e; *(med)* medicabil·is -is -e
remedy *s* (for) remed·ium -(i)i *n* (contra + *acc); (a healing drug)* medicament·um -i *n*
remedy *tr* corrigĕre; *(med)* mederi *(w. dat)*
remember *tr* meminisse *(w. gen)*, recordari; **if I — right** si bene memini
remembrance *s* recordati·o -onis *f*
remind *tr* (ad)monēre
reminder *s* admoniti·o -onis *f*
reminisce *intr* meditari; **to — about** recordari

reminiscence *s* recordati·o -onis *f*
remiss *adj* negleg·ens -entis
remission *s* remissi·o -onis *f*
remit *tr* remittĕre
remittance *s* remissi·o -onis *f,* pecuni·a -ae *f*
remnant *s* reliqu·um -i *n; —s* reliqui·ae -arum *fpl*
remodel *intr* reformare, transfigurare
remonstrate *intr* **to — with** objurgare
remorse *s* paenitenti·a -ae *f*
remorseless *adj* immisericor·s -dis
remote *adj* remot·us -a -um
remotely *adv* procul
remoteness *s* longinquit·as -atis *f*
removable *adj* mobil·is -is -e
removal *s* amoti·o -onis *f; (of fear, pain)* depulsi·o -onis *f*
remove *tr* amovēre, tollĕre
remunerate *tr* remunerari
remuneration *s* remunerati·o -onis *f*
rend *tr* lacerare, scindĕre; *(to split)* findĕre
render *tr* reddĕre; *(to translate)* vertĕre; **to — thanks** gratias reddĕre
rendezvous *s* constitut·um -i *n*
renegade *s* transfug·a -ae *f*
renew *tr* renovare, redintegrare; **to — one's strength** recipere ex integro vires
renewal *s* renovati·o -onis *f*
renown *s* fam·a -ae *f*
renowned *adj* praeclar·us -a -um
rent *s* merc·es -edis *f; (tear)* scissur·a -ae *f;* **to pay the — for the room** mercedem cellae dare; **year's —** annua habitati·o -onis *f*
rent *tr (to let out)* locare; *(to hire)* conducĕre; **to — out** locare
renunciation *s* repudiati·o -onis *f*
reopen *tr* iterum aperire; **the discussion was —ed** res retractata est
reorganize *tr* ordinare, constituĕre
repair *tr* reparare, reficĕre; *(clothes)* resarcire
repair *s* refecti·o -onis *f;* **in bad —** ruinos·us -a -um
reparation *s* satisfacti·o -onis *f;* **to make —s** satisfacĕre
repartee *s* sal·es -ium *mpl*
repast *s* cib·us -i *m*
repay *tr* remunerari; *(money)* reponĕre, retribuĕre
repayment *s* remunerati·o -onis *f*
repeal *tr* abrogare, tollĕre
repeal *s* abrogati·o -onis *f*
repeat *tr* iterare, repetĕre; *(a ritual)* instaurare
repeatedly *adv* identidem
repel *tr* repellĕre; *(fig)* aspernari
repent *tr* **I — me** paenitet *(w. gen)* ‖ *intr* **I — paenitet me**
repentance *s* paenitenti·a -ae *f*
repentant *adj* paenit·ens -entis
repercussion *s* repercuss·us -ūs *m*

repetition *s* iterati•o -onis *f*
replace *tr* reponĕre
replant *tr* reserĕre
replenish *tr* replēre
replete *adj* replet•us -a -um
reply *s* respons•um -i *n*
reply *tr & intr* respondēre
report *s (rumor)* fam•a -ae *f; (official)* renuntiati•o -onis *f; (noise)* frag•or -oris *m;* **the — spread** fama percrebuit
report *tr* **(to)** referre, nuntiare, *(officially)* renuntiare *(w. dat)*
reporter *s* relat•or -oris
repose *s* qui•es -etis *f*
repose *intr* quiescĕre
repository *s* receptacul•um -i *n*
reprehend *tr* reprehendĕre
reprehensible *adj* vituperabil•is -is -e
represent *tr (to portray)* repraesentare; *(to stand in the place of another)* personam *(w. gen)* gerĕre; *(a character)* partes *(w. gen)* agĕre
representation *s (act)* repraesentati•o -onis *f; (likness)* imag•o -inis *f*
representative *s* vicar•ius -(i)i *m*
repress *tr* reprimĕre, cohibēre
repression *s* cohibiti•o -onis *f*
reprieve *s* supplicii dilati•o -onis *f;* **to grant a —** supplicium differre
reprimand *s* reprehensi•o -onis *f*
reprimand *tr* reprehendĕre
reprint *tr* denuo imprimĕre
reprisal *s* ulti•o -onis *f;* **to make —s** retaliare
reproach *s* exprobrati•o -onis *f; (disgrace)* opprobr•ium -(i)i *n*
reproach *tr* opprobrare, vituperare
reproachful *adj* objurgatori•us -a -um, contumelios•us -a -um
reprobate *s* perdit•us -i *m*
reproduce *tr* regenerare, propagare; **to — a play** iterum fabulam referre
reproduction *s* regenerati•o -onis *f; (likeness)* effigi•es -ei *f*
reproductive *adj* genital•is -is -e; **— organs** genital•ia -ium *npl*
reproof *s* objurgati•o -onis *f*
reprove *tr* objurgare
reptile *s* besti•a -ae *f* serpens
republic *s* respublica *(gen: reipublicae) f; (modern form)* civit•as -atis *f* popularis
republican *adj* optimatibus addict•us -a -um
repudiate *tr* repudiare
repudiation *s* repudiati•o -onis *f*
repugnance *s* aversati•o -onis *f*
repugnant *adj* avers•us -a -um
repulse *s* depulsi•o -onis *f; (political defeat)* repuls•a -ae *f*
repulse *tr* repellĕre
repulsive *adj* odios•us -a -um
reputable *adj* honest•us -a -um
reputation *s* fam•a -ae *f*

repute *s* fam•a -ae *f*
request *s* petiti•o -onis *f;* **to deny a —** negare roganti; **to grant a —** satisfacĕre petenti
request *tr* petĕre, rogare
require *tr* poscĕre, postulare; *(to need)* egēre *(w. gen); (to call for)* requirĕre, desiderare
requirement *s* necessar•ium -(i)i *n*
requisite *adj* necessari•us -a -um
requisition *s* postulati•o -onis *f*
requital *s* retributi•o -onis *f*
requite *tr* compensare, retribuĕre; *(for a favor)* remunerari
rescind *tr* rescindĕre
rescue *s* liberati•o -onis *f;* **to come to s.o.'s —** subvenire alicui
rescue *tr (to snatch away)* **(from)** eripĕre *(dat or* ab, de, ex *+ abl); (to free)* liberare
research *s* investigati•o -onis *f*
resemblance *s* similitud•o -inis *f*
resemble *tr* simil•is -is -e esse *(w. gen, esp. of persons, or w. dat)*
resembling *adj* simil•is -is -e *(w. gen, esp. of persons, or w. dat)*
resent *tr* aegre ferre
resentful *adj* iracund•us -a -um
resentment *s* indignati•o -onis *f*
reservation *s* retenti•o -onis *f;* **mental —s** exception•es -um *fpl* animo conceptae
reserve *s (restraint)* pud•or -oris *m; (stock)* copi•a -ae *f; (mil)* subsid•ium -(i)i *n;* **—s** *(mil)* subsidiari•i -orum *mpl*
reserve *adj (mil)* subsidiari•us -a -um
reserve *tr* reservare
reserved *adj (of seat)* assignat•us -a -um; *(of disposition)* taciturn•us -a -um
reservoir *s* lac•us -ūs *m; (of an aqueduct)* castell•um -i *n*
reset *tr* reponĕre
reside *intr* habitare; **to — in** inhabitare
residence *s* sed•es -is *f*
resident *s* incol•a -ae *mf*
residue *s* residu•um -i *n*
resign *tr (an office)* se abdicare ab *(w. abl);* **to — oneself to** animum summittĕre *(w. dat)* ‖ *intr* se abdicare
resignation *s* abdicati•o -onis *f; (fig)* aequus anim•us -i *m*
resigned *adj* summiss•us -a -um; **to be —** aequo animo esse; **to be — to** aequo animo ferre
resilience *s* molliti•a -ae *f*
resilient *adj* resili•ens -entis
resin *s* resin•a -ae *f*
resist *tr* resistĕre *(w. dat),* obstare *(w. dat),* repugnare *(w. dat)*
resistance *s* repugnanti•a -ae *f;* **to offer — to** obsistĕre *(w. dat)*
resolute *adj* const•ans -antis
resolutely *adv* constanter
resolution *s (determination)* constanti•a

-ae *f; (decision, decree)* decret·um -i *n;
(of Senate)* consult·um -i *n*
resolve *s* constanti·a -ae *f*
resolve *tr* constituĕre; *(to reduce, convert)*
resolvĕre, dissolvĕre
resonance *s* resonanti·a -ae *f*
resonant *adj* reson·us -a -um
resort *s* loc·us -i *m* celeber
resort *intr* **to —** *to* *(to frequent)* frequentare; *(to have recourse to)* confugĕre ad
(+ acc.); (to lower oneself) descendĕre
ad *(+ acc.)*
resource *s* subsid·ium -(i)i *n;* **—s** op·es
-ium *fpl*
respect *s (high esteem)* observanti·a -ae *f,*
hon·or -oris *m; (regard)* respect·us -ūs
m; (religious awe) religi·o -onis *f, e.g,*
respect for an oath religio juris jurandi;
in every — ex omni parte; **in other —s**
ceterum; **in — to knowledge** scientiā; **to
mention s.o. out of —** aliquem honoris
causā nominare
respect *tr (to esteem highly)* observare; *(to
esteem with fear)* vereri
respectability *s* honest·as -atis *f*
respectable *adj* honest·us -a -um
respectably *adv* honeste
respectful *adj* rever·ens -entis
respectfully *adv* reverenter
respecting *prep* de *(w. abl)*
respective *adj* propri·us -a -um
respectively *adv* proprie
respiration *s* respirati·o -onis *f*
respite *s* intermissi·o -onis *f*
resplendent *adj* splendid·us -a -um
respond *tr & intr* respondēre
respondent *s (leg)* re·us -i *m*
response *s* respons·um -i *n*
responsibility *s* cur·a -ae *f;* **it is my —** est
mihi curae; **it is the — of a father to say
this** patris est haec dicĕre; **sense of —**
piet·as -atis *f*
responsible *adj* obnoxi·us -a -um; *(reliable)* fid·us -a -um; **to be — for** praestare
(w. acc); **to hold anyone —** rationem
reposcĕre ab aliquo
rest *s* qui·es -etis *f; (support)* fulcr·um -i *n;
(remainder)* reliqu·um -i *n;* **the — of the
men** ceter·i -orum *mpl*
rest *tr (to lean)* reclinare ‖ *intr* (re)-
quiescĕre; *(to pause)* cessare; **to — on**
inniti in *(w. abl),* niti *(w. abl);* **—ing on
his elbow** reclinatus in cubitum
restitution *s* restituti·o -onis *f*
restive *adj* contum·ax -acis
restless *adj* inquiet·us -a -um
restlessly *adv* inquiete
restoration *s* restaurati·o -onis *f*
restore *tr* restituĕre, reddĕre; *(to rebuild)*
restaurare, reficĕre; **to — to health** recurare;
to — to order in integrum reducĕre
restrain *tr* coercēre; *(tears, laughter)*
tenēre; *(emotions)* cohibēre

restraint *s* moderati·o -onis *f*
restrict *tr* restringĕre; *(to limit)* **(to)**
definire *(w. dat)*
restriction *s* restricti·o -onis *f*
restrictive *adj (gram)* restringen·s -tis
result *s* exit·us -ūs *m,* event·us -ūs *m;*
without — nequiquam
resume *tr* resumĕre
resumption *s* resumpti·o -onis *f*
resurrection *s* resurrecti·o -onis *f*
resuscitate *tr* resuscitare
retail *tr* divendĕre
retailer *s* caup·o -onis *m*
retail shop *s* caupon·a -ae *f*
retain *tr* retinēre
retainer *s (adherent)* assectat·or -oris *m,
(fee)* arrab·o -onis *m*
retake *tr* recuperare
retaliate *intr* ulcisci
retaliation *s* ulti·o -onis *f*
retard *tr* retardare
retch *intr* sine vomitu nauseare
retention *s* retenti·o -onis *f*
retentive *adj* ten·ax -acis
reticence *s* taciturnit·as -atis *f*
reticent *adj* taciturn·us -a -um
retinue *s* comitat·us -ūs *m*
retire *intr* recedĕre; *(from work)* secedĕre;
(from office) abire; *(for the night)*
dormitum ire
retired *adj* emerit·us -a -um
retirement *s (act)* recess·us -ūs *m; (state)*
ot·ium -(i)i *n*
retiring *adj* modest·us -a -um
retort *s* respons·um -i *n*
retort *tr* respondĕre
retrace *tr* repetĕre
retract *tr (words)* retractare; *(a promise)*
revocare
retraction *s* retractati·o -onis *f*
retreat *s (act; place)* recess·us -ūs *m;
(mil)* recept·us -ūs *m;* **to sound the —**
(mil) receptui canĕre
retreat *intr* recedĕre, se recipĕre
retrench *intr* sumptūs recidĕre
retrenchment *s* recisi·o -onis *f*
retribution *s* retributi·o -onis *f*
retrieve *tr* recuperare, recipĕre
retrievable *adj (loss)* pensabil·is -is -e
retrogression *s* retrogress·us -ūs *m*
retrospect *s* **in —** respicienti
retrospective *adj* respicien·s -tis
return *s (coming back)* redit·us -ūs *m; (gain)*
quaest·us -ūs *m; (profit)* fruct·us -ūs *m*
return *tr (to give back)* reddĕre; *(to send
back)* remittĕre; **to — a favor** gratiam
referre ‖ *intr (to go back)* redire; *(to
come back)* reverti
reunion *s* readunati·o -onis *f*
reunite *tr* iterum conjungĕre; *(to reconcile)*
reconciliare ‖ *intr* reconciliari
reveal *tr* retegĕre, recludĕre; *(to unveil)*
revelare

revel *s* comissati·o -onis *f*
revel *intr* comissari, debacchari
revelation *s* revelati·o -onis *f*
reveler *s* comissat·or -oris *m*
revelry *s* comissati·o -onis *f*
revenge *tr* ulcisci
revenge *s* ulti·o -onis *f*, vindict·a -ae *f*; **to seek —** ultionem petĕre; **to take —** for s.th. small vindictam parvae rei quaerĕre; **to take — on** se vindicare in *(w. acc)*
revengeful *adj* ulciscendi cupid·us -a -um
revenue *s* vectig·al -alis *n*
reverberate *intr* resonare
reverberation *s* resonanti·a -ae *f*
revere *tr* revereri, venerari
reverence *s* reverenti·a -ae *f*; **— due to the gods** deorum caerimoni·a -ae *f*
reverend *adj* reverend·us -a -um
reverent *adj* reveren·s -tis
reverential *adj* venerabund·us -a -um
reverently *adv* reverenter
reverie *s* meditati·o -onis *f*
reversal *s* reversi·o -onis *f*
reverse *s* contrar·ium -(i)i *n; (change)* conversi·o -onis *f; (defeat)* clad·es -is *f;* **to suffer a —** *(mil)* cladem accipĕre; *(pol)* repulsam ferre
reverse *tr* invertĕre, (com)mutare; *(decision)* rescindĕre, abrogare
revert *intr* reverti
review *s* recogniti·o -onis *f; (of a book)* censur·a -ae *f; (mil)* recensi·o -onis *f)*
review *tr* recensēre
reviewer *s* cens·or -oris *m*
revile *tr* maledicĕre *(w. dat)*
revise *tr* corrigĕre; *(laws)* retractare
revision *s* emendati·o -onis *f; (literary);* recensi·o -onis *f*
revisit *tr* revisĕre, revisitare
revival *s* redanimati·o -onis *f; (fig)* renovati·o -onis *f*
revive *tr* resuscitare; *(to renew)* renovare; *(strength)* refovēre ‖ *intr* reviviscĕre
revocation *s* revocati·o -onis *f*
revoke *tr* revocare; *(a law)* rescindĕre, abrogare
revolt *s* rebelli·o -onis *f; (civil discord)* sediti·o -onis *f;* **to rise in — against s.o.** cooriri in aliquem
revolt *tr* offendĕre ‖ *intr* deficĕre
revolting *adj* tae·ter -tra -trum
revolution *s (e.g., of a wheel)* conversi·o -onis *f; (change)* commutati·o -onis *f; (of planets)* ambit·us -ūs *m; (pol)* res novae *fpl*
revolutionary *adj* seditios·us -a -um
revolutionary *s* hom·o -inis *m* rerum novarum cupidus
revolutionize *tr* novare
revolve *tr (in mind)* volutare ‖ *intr* revolvi
revulsion *s* revulsi·o -onis *f*
reward *s* praem·ium -(i)i *n*
reward *tr* praemio afficĕre

rewrite *tr* rescribĕre
rhapsody *s* rhapsodi·a -ae *f*
rhetoric *s* rhetoric·a -ae *f;* **to practice —** declamare
rhetorical *adj* rhetoric·us -a -um
rhetorician *s* rhet·or -oris *m*
rheumatism *s* dol·or -oris *m* artuum
rhinoceros *s* rhinocer·os -i *m*
rhubarb *s* rad·ix -cis *f* Pontica
rhyme *s* homŏeoteleut·on -i *n*
rhythm *s* numer·us -i *m*
rhythmical *adj* numeros·us -a -um
rib *s* cost·a -ae *f*
ribbed *adj* costat·us -a -um
ribbon *s* taeni·a -ae *f; (as badge of honor)* inful·a -ae *f*
rice *s* oryz·a -ae *f*
rich *adj* div·es -itis; *(of soil)* opim·us -a -um; *(food)* pingu·is -is -e; *(costly)* laut·us -a -um
richly *adv* copiose, laute
riches *spl* diviti·ae -arum *fpl*
rickety *adj* instabil·is -is -e
rid *tr* liberare; **to get — of** dimittĕre
riddle *s* aenigm·a -atis *n*
ride *tr* **to — a horse** equo vehi ‖ *intr* equitare, equo vehi; **to — off** avehi
rider *s (on horse)* rect·or -oris *m; (in carriage)* vect·or -oris *m; (attached to documents)* adjecti·o -onis *f*
ridge *s* jug·um -i *n,* dors·um -i *n*
ridicule *s* ridicul·um -i *n*
ridicule *tr* irridēre
ridiculous *adj* ridicul·us -a -um
ridiculously *adv* ridicule
riding *s* equitati·o -onis *f; (in a carriage)* vectati·o -ōnis *f*
rife *adj (with)* frequ·ens -entis *(w. abl)*
riffraff *s* fae·x -cis *f* populi
rifle *tr* expilare
rifle *s* scoplet·um -i *n* striatum
rig *tr* adornare; *(ship)* ornare
rigging *s* fun·es -ium *mpl*
right *adj (correct)* rect·us -a -um; *(opp. of left)* dex·ter -tra -trum; *(just)* just·us -a -um; *(suitable)* idone·us -a -um, apt·us -a -um; *(true, reasonable)* ver·us -a -um; **on the — hand** dextrā; **to do the — thing** frugem facĕre
right *s (hand)* dextr·a -ae *f; (leg)* ju·s -ris *n; (what is permitted by God or conscience)* fas *n (indecl); by what — quo jure; on the — as you come in* dextrā introeunti; **the —** *(of knights and senators)* **to wear the gold ring** jus anuli
right *tr* emendare, corrigĕre; *(a fallen statue)* restituĕre; *(to avenge)* vindicare
righteous *adj* just·us -a -um
righteousness *s* justiti·a -ae *f*
rightful *adj* legitim·us -a -um
rightfully *adv* juste
right-hand *adj* dex·ter -tra -trum; **— man** dextell·a -ae *f*

rigid *adj* rigid·us -a -um
rigidly *adv* rigide
rigidity *s* rigidit·as -atis *f*
rigor *s* rig·or -oris *m*
rigorous *adj* dur·us -a -um
rill *s* rivul·us -i *m*
rim *s* or·a -ae *f*, marg·o -inis *f*; *(of a jar)* labr·um -i *n*; *(of a wheel)* canth·us -i *m*
rind *s* crust·a -ae *f*
ring *s* anul·us -i *m*; *(of people)* coron·a -ae *f*; *(for fighting)* aren·a -ae *f*; *(sound)* sonit·us -ūs *m*; *(of bells)* tinnit·us -ūs *m*
ring *tr* **to — a bell** tintinnabulum tractare ‖ *intr* tinnire, resonare; **to — with laughter** exsonare omni risu
ringing *s* tinnit·us -ūs *m*
ringleader *s* instigat·or -oris *m*, instigatr·ix -icis *f*
rinse *tr* colluĕre; **to — out** eluĕre
rinsing *s* colluvi·es -ei *f*
riot *s* tumult·us -ūs *m*; **to run —** luxuriari
riot *intr* tumultuari, seditionem movēre
rioter *s* seditios·us -i *m*
riotous *adj* seditios·us -a -um; **— living** luxuri·a -ae *f*
rip *tr* scindĕre; **to — apart** discindĕre; *(fig)* discerpĕre
ripe *adj* matur·us -a -um
ripen *tr* maturare ‖ *intr* maturescĕre
ripple *intr* trepidare
ripple *s* flucticul·us -i *m*
rise *intr* oriri; *(from a seat, from sleep; of the sun)* surgĕre; *(in a body)* consurgĕre; *(out of respect)* assurgĕre; *(of the voice)* crescĕre; **to — again** resurgĕre; **to — up against** adoriri
rise *s* ort·us -ūs *m*; *(to higher office)* ascens·us -ūs *m*; *(slope)* cliv·us -i *m*; **— in the ground** loc·us -i *m* editus; **to give — to** parĕre, gignĕre, excitare
riser *s* **early — ** tempestiv·us -i *m*
rising *s* ort·us -ūs *m*
rising *adj* orien·s -tis; **gently — ground** loc·us -i *m* paulatim ab imo acclivis; **— star** *(fig)* adolescen·s -tis *m* summā spe et animi et ingenii praeditus
risk *s* pericul·um -i *n*; **to be at —** periclitari; **to run a —** periculum subire
risk *tr* in periculum vocare
rite *s* rit·us -ūs *m*, caeremoni·a -ae *f*
ritual *adj* ritual·is -is -e
ritual *s* rit·us -ūs *m*
rival *s* rival·is -is *mf*; *(pol)* competit·or -oris *m*
rival *adj* aemul·us -a -um
rival *tr* aemulari
rivalry *s* aemulati·o -onis *f*; *(among lovers)* rivalit·as -atis *f*
river *s* flum·en -inis *n*, amn·is -is *m*
rivet *s* clav·us -i *m*
rivet *tr* *(eyes, attention)* defigĕre
rivulet *s* rivul·us -i *m*
road *s* vi·a -ae *f*; *(route)* it·er -ineris *n*; **on**

the — in itinere; **paved —** strat·a -ae *f*; **to build a —** viam munire
roadside *s* **by the —** secundum viam
roam *intr* errare, vagari
roar *s* fremit·us -ūs *m*
roar *intr* fremĕre, rugire
roast *adj* ass·us -a -um
roast *s* ass·um -i *n*
roast *tr* torrēre; *(esp. meat)* assare
rob *tr* rapĕre; **to — s.o. of** spoliare aliquem *(w. abl)* ‖ *intr* latrocinari
robber *s* latr·o -onis *f*
robbery *s* latrocin·ium -(i)i *n*
robe *s* vest·is -is *m*; *(of kings, augurs, knights)* trabe·a -ae *f*; *(of tragic actors)* pall·a -ae *f*
robe *tr* vestire
robin *s* rubecul·a -ae *f*
robust *adj* robust·us -a -um
rock *s* sax·um -i *n*; *(cliff)* rup·es -is *f*; **between a — and a hard place** inter sacrum saxumque
rock *tr* movēre; **to — the cradle** cunas agitare ‖ *intr* vibrare; **to — from side to side** in utramque partem toto corpore vacillare
rocket *s* missil·e -is *n*
rocky *adj* saxos·us -a -um
rod *s* virg·a -ae *f*, ferul·a -ae *f*
roe *s* capre·a -ae *f*; *(of fish)* ov·a -orum *npl*
roebuck *s* capreol·us -i *m*
rogue *s* furcif·er -eri *m*
roguish *adj* nequam *(indecl)*
role *s* part·es -ium *fpl*; **to take the lead —** primas partes suscipĕre
roll *tr* volvĕre; **to — back** revolvĕre; **to — over** evolvĕre; **to — over and over** pervolvĕre; **to — the dice** mittĕre talos; **to — together** *(to twist)* convolvĕre; **to — up** convolvĕre; *(from below)* subvolvĕre ‖ *intr* volvi
roll *s* *(book)* volum·en -inis *f*; *(of names)* alb·um -i *n*; *(bun)* collyr·a -ae *f*; *(sweet roll)* pastill·us -i *m*
rollcall *s* catalogi recitat·o -onis *f*
roller *s* cylindr·us -i *m*
Roman *adj* Roman·us -a -um
Roman *s* Roman·us -i *m*
romance *s* fabul·a -ae *f* amatoria; *(affair)* amor·es -um *mpl*
romantic *adj* amatori·us -a -um
Romeo *s* agag·a -ae *m*
roof *s* tect·um -i *n*; **— of the mouth** palat·um -i *n*
roof *tr* contegĕre, integĕre
room *s* *(of house)* conclav·e -is *n*; *(small room)* cell·a -ae *f*; *(tiny room)* cellul·a -ae *f*; *(space)* loc·us -i *m*, spat·ium -(i)i *n*
room *intr* manēre
roomer *s* hosp·es -itis *m*, deversit·or -oris *m*
roominess *s* laxit·as -atis *f*
roommate *s* contubernal·is -is *mf*
roomy *adj* lax·us -a -um

roost *s* pertic·a -ae *f*
roost *intr* cubitare, insistĕre
rooster *s* gall·us -i *m* gallinaceus
root *s* rad·ix -icis *f;* *(fig)* fon·s -tis *m;* **to take** — coalescĕre
root *tr* **to become** —**ed** *(lit & fig)* radices agĕre; **to be** —**ed** inhaerēre; **to** — **out** eradicare ‖ *intr* **to** — **for** acclamare
rope *s* fun·is -is *m,* rest·is -is *f*
rosary *s* rosar·ium -(i)i *n*
rose *s* ros·a -ae *f*
rosebed *s* rosar·ium -(i)i *n*
rosebud *s* rosae cal·yx -ycis *m*
rosebush *s* frut·ex -icis *f* rosae
rose garden *s* roset·um -ī *n*
rosemary *s* ro·s -ris *m* marinus
rosin *s* resin·a -ae *f*
rostrum *s* rostr·a -orum *npl;* **to speak from the** — pro rostris loqui
rosy *adj* rose·us -a -um; *(fig)* festiv·us -a -um
rot *intr* putrescĕre, tabescĕre
rot *s* putred·o -inis *f,* tab·es -is *f*
rotate *intr* volvi
rotation *s* rotati·o -onis *f;* **in** — per *or* in orbem; — **of command** vicissitud·o -inis *f* imperitandi
rote *s* **by** — memoriter
rotten *adj* putrid·us -a -um
rotunda *s* thol·us -i *m*
rouge *s* fuc·us -i *m*
rough *adj* asp·er -era -erum; *(of character)* dur·us -a -um; *(weather)* inclem·ens -entis; *(shaggy)* hirsut·us -a -um; *(masonry)* impolit·us -a -um
rough-and-ready *adj* prompt·us -a -um
roughen *tr* asperare
roughly *adv* aspere, duriter; *(approximately)* fere
roughneck *s* rup·ex -icis *m*
roughness *s* asperit·as -atis *f;* *(brutality)* ferit·as -atis *f*
round *adj* rotund·us -a -um
round *s* *(in boxing)* congress·us -ūs *m;* **to give a** — **of applause** plausum dare; — **of beef** fem·ur -oris *n* bubulum transverse sectum; —**s of applause** plaus·us -ūs *m* multiplex; **to go the** —**s** *(of a policeman)* vigilias circumire; **to go the** —**s of** circumire *(w. acc)*
round *tr* *(a corner)* circumire; *(a cape)* superare; **to** — **off** concludĕre; **to** — **out** complēre; **to** — **up** cogĕre
roundabout *adj* **in a** — **way** per ambages, circuitu; — **route** circuit·us -ūs *m;* **to tell a** — **story to** ambages narrare *(w. dat)*
rouse *tr* excitare; **a** —**ing harangue** incitata et vehemens conti·o -onis *f*
rout *s* fug·a -ae *f;* *(defeat)* clad·es -is *f;* *(rabble)* vulg·us -i *n;* **to put to** — **in** fugam convertĕre
rout *tr* fugare, fundĕre

route *s* it·er -ineris *n,* vi·a -ae *f*
routine *s* ord·o -inis *m;* **daily** — cotidianus ordo *m*
rove *intr* errare, vagari
rover *s* err·o -onis *m*
row *s* ord·o -inis *m,* seri·es -ei *f;* **in a row** continu·us -a -um; **for seven days in a** — per septem continuos dies; — **of seats** grad·us -ūs *m;* — **of trees** ordo arborum; **three days in a** — triennio continuo
row *tr* remis propellĕre ‖ *intr* remigare; **to** — **hard** remis contendĕre
rower *s* rem·ex -igis *m*
rowing *s* remig·ium -(i)i *n*
royal *adj* regi·us -a -um; *(worthy of a king)* regal·is -is -e; — **power** regn·um -i *n*
royally *adv* regie, regaliter
royalty *s* regn·um -i *n*
rub *tr* fricare; **to** — **away** detergēre; **to** — **down** defricare; **to** — **in** infricare
rub *s* fricat·us -ūs *m;* **and that's the** — hoc opus, hic labor est
rubbing *s* fricti·o -onis *f*
rubbish *s* *(lit & fig)* quisquili·ae -arum *fpl*
rubble *s* rud·us -eris *n*
rubric *s* rubric·a -ae *f*
ruby *s* carbuncul·us -i *m*
rudder *s* gubernacul·um -i *n*
ruddy *adj* rubicund·us -a -um
rude *adj* rud·is -is -e; *(impolite)* inurban·us -a -um, rustic·us -a -um
rudeness *s* inhumanit·as -atis *f*
rudiment *s* element·um -i *n*
rudimentary *adj* elementari·us -a -um
rue *tr* **I rue** me paenitet *(w. gen)*
rueful *adj* maest·us -a -um
ruffian *s* grassat·or -oris *m*
ruffle *s* limb·us -i *m*
rug *s* stragul·um -i *n*
rugged *adj* dur·us -a -um; *(terrain)* praerupt·us -a -um
ruin *s* exit·ium -(i)i *n;* —**s** rud·us -eris *n;* **to go to** — ruĕre, pessum ire, perire
ruin *tr* perdĕre, corrumpĕre; *(morally)* depravare
ruinous *adj* exitios·us -a -um
rule *s* *(instrument; regulation)* regul·a -ae *f;* *(government)* regim·en -inis *n;* **absolute** — dominati·o -onis *f*
rule *tr* regĕre, imperare ‖ *intr* regnare, dominari; **to** — **out** excludĕre; **to** — **over** imperare *(w. dat),* dominari in *(w. acc)*
ruler *s* rect·or -oris *m;* *(instrument)* regul·a -ae *f*
ruling *s* sententi·a -ae *f*
rum *s* sicer·a -ae *f*
rumble *s* murm·ur -uris *n*
rumble *intr* murmurare; **my stomach is** —**ing** sonat mihi circum stomachum
rumbling *s* murm·ur -uris *n*
ruminate *intr* ruminare
rummage *intr* **to** — **through** perscrutari

rummage sale *s* venditi·o -onis *f* scrutaria
rumor *s* rum·or -oris *m*
rump *s* clun·is -is *f*
rumple *s (in garment)* rug·a -ae *f*
rumple *tr* corrugare
run *tr (to manage)* exercēre; **to — a fever**
febricitare; **to — down** *(to disparage)*
detrectare; *(w. vehicle)* obterēre; **to —
her hand over my hair** ducēre capillos
meos lentā manu; **to — up** *(increase)*
augēre; **to — up bills** aes alienum
conflare **‖** *intr* currēre; *(to flow)* fluēre;
to — about discurrēre; **to — after** petēre;
to — around discurrēre; **to — around
the table** discurrēre circa mensam; **to —
away** aufugēre; **to — aground** offendēre;
to — down decurrēre; *(of water)*
defluēre; **to — for office** honorem petēre;
to — foul of impingēre; **to — high** *(of a
river, sea)* tumēre; **to — into** *(to meet)*
occurrēre *(w. dat),* incidēre in *(w. acc);*
to — low deficēre; **to — off** aufugēre;
(of water) defluēre; **to — on** percurrēre,
continuare; **to — out** excurrēre; *(of time)*
exire; *(of supplies)* deficēre; **to — over**
(of fluids) superfluēre; *(details)* percurrēre; **to — short** deficēre; **to —
through** *(to dissipate)* dissipare; **to —
through a list of** exsequi; **to — together**
concurrēre; **to — up to s.o.** accurrēre ad
aliquem
run *s* curs·us -ūs *m;* **in the long —** in exitu;
on the — cursim; **to have the —s** citā
alvo laborare
runaway *s* transfug·a -ae *mf*
rundown *s* compend·ium -(i)i *n*
run-down *adj* defatigat·us -a -um; *(dilapidated)* ruinos·us -a -um
rung *s (of ladder)* grad·us -ūs *m*
run-in *s* altercati·o -onis *f*
runner *s* curs·or -oris *m*
running *s* curs·us -ūs *m;* **— for office**
petiti·o -onis *f* honoris; **— of the government** administrati·o -onis *f* rei
publicae
runny nose *s* distillation·es -um *fpl*
rupture *s (of relations)* discid·ium -(i)i *n;*
(med) herni·a -ae *f*
rupture *tr* rumpēre **‖** *intr* rumpi
rural *adj* rural·is -is -e
ruse *s* dol·us -i *m*
rush *s (plant)* junc·us -i *m; (charge)*
impet·us -ūs *m; (of people)* **(on)** con-
curs·us -ūs *m* (ad + *acc.*)
rush *tr (to attack)* oppugnare; *(to do in a
hurry)* festinare; *(to cause to hurry)*
urgēre **‖** *intr* festinare, ruēre; **to — away**
avolare; **to — forth** se proripēre; **to —
in** irruēre; **to — into** irruēre in *(w. acc);*
to — out evolare, erumpēre
russet *adj* russ·us -a -um
rust *s* rubig·o -inis *f; (of iron)* ferrug·o
-inis *f*

rust *intr* rubiginem trahēre
rustic *adj* rustic·us -a -um
rustic *s* rustic·us -i *m*
rustle *intr* crepitare
rustle *s* crepit·us -ūs *m*
rusty *adj* rubiginos·us -a -um; **to become
—** rubigine obduci; *(fig)* desuescēre
rut *s* orbit·a -ae *f*
ruthless *adj* immisericor·s -dis
ruthlessly *adv* immisericorditer
rye *s* secal·e -is *n*

S

Sabbath *s* sabbat·a -orum *npl;* **to keep the
—** sabbatizare
saber *s* acinac·es -is *m*
sable *s* pell·is -is *f* zibellina
sabotage *s* vastati·o -onis *f* occulta
sabotage *tr* occulte evertēre
saccharin *s* sacchar·on -i *n*
sack *s* sacc·us -i *m; (of leather)* cule·us -i
m; (mil) direpti·o -onis *f*
sack *tr* in saccos condēre; *(mil)* diripēre
sackcloth *s* cilic·ium -(i)i *n;* **in — and
ashes** sordidat·us -a -um
sacrament *s (eccl)* sacrament·um -i *n*
sacred *adj* sa·cer -cra -crum
sacrifice *s (act)* sacrific·ium -(i)i *n; (victim)* hosti·a -ae *f; (fig)* jactur·a -ae *f;* **to
offer (perform) a —** sacrificium agēre
(facēre), rem divinam facēre
sacrifice *tr* sacrificare, immolare; **to — an
eye for** oculum impendēre pro *(w. abl);*
to — one's life for another vitam pro
aliquo profundēre
sacrilege *s* sacrileg·ium -(i)i *n*
sacrilegious *adj* sacrileg·us -a -um
sad *adj* trist·is -is -e, maest·us -a -um
sadden *tr* contristare
saddle *s* ephipp·ium -(i)i *n*
saddle *tr (fig)* imponēre *(w. acc of thing
and dat of person);* **to — a horse** equum
sternēre
saddlebags *spl* clitell·ae -arum *fpl*
sadly *adv* maeste
safe *adj* tut·us -a -um; *(unharmed)*
incolum·is -is -e; *(harmless)* innocu·us
-a -um; *(sure)* cert·us -a -um **— and
sound** salv·us -a -um
safe *s* arc·a -ae *f*
safe-conduct *s* **under —** publicā fide
interpositā
safeguard *tr* tueri
safeguard *s* cauti·o -onis *f;* **there is but
one — against these troubles** horum
incommodorum cautio una est *(followed
by* ut *or* ne)
safekeeping *s* **for —** in fidem
safely *adv* tute
safety *s* sal·us -utis *f;* **in —** tuto

safety pin s fibul·a -ae f
safety valve s spirament·um -i n
saffron s croc·us -i m
saffron adj croce·us -a -um
sagacious adj sag·ax -acis
sagacity s sagacit·as -atis f
sage s *(wise man)* vi·r -ri m sapi·ens -entis
sage adj sapi·ens -entis
sail s vel·um -i n; **to set —** vela dare
sail intr nave vehi, navigare; **to — down to** devehi ad or in *(w. acc)*; **to — up to** subvehi ad or in *(w. acc)*
sailing s navigati·o -onis f
sailor s naut·a -ae m
saint s vi·r -ri m sanctus; femin·a -ae f sancta
saintly adj sanct·us -a -um
sake s **for heaven's —!** pro deum fidem! **for the — of** causā or gratiā *(w. gen);* **for the — of glory** gloriae causā *(or* gratiā)
salable adj vendibil·is -is -e
salacious adj sal·ax -acis
salad s acetari·a -orum npl
salamander s salamandr·a -ae f
salary s salar·ium -(i)i n
sale s venditi·o -onis f; **for —** venal·is -is -e; **to advertise a house for —** aedes venales inscribĕre; **to go up for —** venum ire; **to put up for —** venum dare, prostare
salesman s instit·or -oris m
saline adj sals·us -a -um
saliva s saliv·a -ae f
sallow adj pallid·us -a -um
sally intr eruptionem facĕre
sally s erupti·o -onis f
salmon s salm·o -onis m
saloon s caupon·a -ae f
salt s sa·l -lis m
salt tr salire, sale condire
salting s salsur·a -ae f
saltless adj insals·us -a -um
salt mine s salifodin·a -ae f
salt shaker s salin·um -i n
salty adj sals·us -a -um
salt water s aqu·a -ae f marina
salubrious adj salu·ber -bris -bre
salutary adj salutar·is -is -e
salutation s salutati·o -onis f
salute s sal·us -utis f
salute tr salutare
salvage tr eripĕre, servare
salvage s id quod e nave fracta servatur
salvation s sal·us -utis f
salve s unguent·um -i n
same adj idem, eadem, idem; **at the — time** simul, eodem tempore; **the very —** ipsissim·us -a -um
sameness s identit·as -atis f
sample s exempl·um -i n
sample tr libare
sanctify tr sanctificare

sanctimonious adj sanctitatem affect·ans -antis
sanction s auctorit·as -atis f; **with the —** of the people jussu populi; **without the — of the people** injussu populi
sanction tr ratum facĕre
sanctity s sanctit·as -atis f
sanctuary s sanctuar·ium -(i)i n; *(refuge)* asyl·um -i n
sand s (h)aren·a -ae f
sandal s sole·a -ae f
sandstone s tof·us -i m
sandy adj (h)arenos·us -a -um
sandy-haired adj ruf·us -a -um
sane adj san·us -a -um
sanitary adj salubr·is -is -e
sanity s sanit·as -atis f
sap s suc·us -i m
sap tr haurire
sapling s surcul·us -i m
Sapphic adj Sapphic·us -a -um
sapphire s sapphir·us -i f
sarcasm s asperae faceti·ae -arum fpl
sarcastic adj acerb·us -a -um
sarcastically adv acerbe
sarcophagus s sarcophag·us -i m
sardine s sard·a -ae f
sardonic adj amar·us -a -um
sash s zon·a -ae f
Satan s Satan m *(indecl)*
Satanic adj Satanic·us -a -um
satchel s per·a -ae f
satellite s satell·es -itis mf
satiate tr satiare
satire s satur·a -ae f
satirical adj satiric·us -a -um; *(biting)* mord·ax -acis
satirist s script·or -oris m saturarum
satirize tr arripĕre, notare
satisfaction s volupt·as -atis f; *(of a creditor)* satisfacti·o -onis f; **to derive the greatest — from** incredibilem voluptatem capĕre ex *(w. abl);* **my house gives me great —** domus mea mihi valde placet
satisfactorily adv satis bene
satisfactory adj idone·us -a -um
satisfied adj content·us -a -um
satisfy tr satis facĕre *(w. dat); (thirst, hunger, expectation)* explēre; *(creditors)* satisfacĕre *(w. dat);* **to — your rage** satiare iracundiam tuam
saturate tr saturare
Saturday s di·es -ei m Saturni
Saturn s Saturn·us -i m; **feast of —** Saturnal·ia -ium npl
satyr s satyr·us -i m
sauce s condiment·um -i n; *(of meat)* liquam·en -inis n
saucepan s cacub·us -i m
saucer s patell·a -ae f
saucily adv petulanter
saucy adj petul·ans -antis

saunter *intr* vagari
sausage *s* farcim·en -inis *n*
savage *adj (wild, untamed)* fer·us -a -um; *(cruel)* saev·us -a -um
savagely *adv* atrociter
save *tr* **(from)** servare (ex + *abl);* **to —** **up** reservare
save *prep* praeter *(w. acc)*
saving *s* conservati·o -onis *f;* **—s** pecul·ium -(i)i *n*
savior *s* servat·or -oris *m*
Savior *s* Salvat·or -oris *m*
savor *s* sap·or -oris *m*
savor *tr* sapěre
savory *adj* sapid·us -a -um
saw *s (tool)* serr·a -ae *f; (saying)* proverb·ium -(i)i *n*
saw *tr* serrā secare ‖ *intr* serram ducěre
sawdust *s* scob·is -is *f*
say *tr* dicěre; **no sooner said than done** dictum (ac) factum; **that is to —** scilicet; **to — that...not** negare *(w. acc & inf)*
saying *s* dict·um -i *n; as the* **— goes** ut aiunt
scab *s* crust·a -ae *f*
scabbard *s* vagin·a -ae *f*
scaffold *s* machin·a -ae *f* aedificationis
scald *tr* urěre
scale *s (for weighing)* trutin·a -ae *f; (of fish)* squam·a -ae *f; (gradation)* grad·us -ūs *m; (mus)* diagramm·a -atis *f;* **pair of —s** stater·a -ae *f*
scale *tr (fish)* desquamare; **to — a wall** murum per scalas ascenděre
scallop *s (shellfish)* pect·en -inis *m; (curve)* sin·us -ūs *m*
scalp *s* pericran·ium -(i)i *n*
scaly *adj* squamos·us -a -um
scam *s* frau·s -dis *f*
scam artist *s* plan·us -i *m*
scamp *s* furcif·er -eri *m*
scamper *intr* cursare; **to — about** cursitare, discurrěre; **to — away** aufugěre
scan *tr* examinare; *(verse)* scanděre
scandal *s* opprobr·ium -(i)i *n;* **to be a — to the community** opprobrio esse civitati
scandalize *tr* offenděre
scandalous *adj* probros·us -a -um
scantily *adv* exigue
scanty *adj* exigu·us -a -um
scapegoat *s* piacul·um -i *n*
scar *s* cicatr·ix -icis *f*
scar *tr* cicatricibus foedare
scarce *adj* rar·us -a -um
scarcely *adv* vix; *(with effort)* aegre
scarcity *s* inopi·a -ae *f*
scare *tr* terrěre; **to — off** absterrēre
scarecrow *s* terricul·um -i *n*
scared *adj* territ·us -a -um
scarf *s* amictor·ium -(i)i *n*
scarlet *adj* coccin·us -a -um
scathing *adj* aculeat·us -a -um

scatter *tr* spargěre, dispergěre ‖ *intr* dilabi, diffugěre
scavenger *s* colacar·ius -(i)i *m*
scene *s (vista)* prospect·us -ūs *m; (picture)* pictur·a -ae *f; (theat)* scaen·a -ae *f;* **behind the —s** post siparium; **Italy, the — of the civil war** Italia, arena belli civilis; **on the —** in re praesenti; **to make a —** convicium facěre
scenery *s (theat)* scenae apparat·us -ūs *m; (of nature)* speci·es -ei *f* regionis
scent *s (sense)* odorat·us -ūs *m; (of dogs)* sagacit·as -atis *f; (fragrance)* od·or -oris *m*
scent *tr* odorari
scented *adj* odorat·us -a -um
scepter *s* sceptr·um -i *n*
sceptic *s* sceptic·us -i *m*
sceptical *adj* **to be —** dubitare
schedule *s* schedul·a -ae *f*
scheme *s* consil·ium -(i)i *n; (pej)* dol·us -i *m*
scheme *intr* moliri
scholar *s* philolog·us -i *m*
scholarly *adj* doct·us -a -um
scholarship *s* litter·ae -arum *fpl; (grant)* pecuni·ae -arum *fpl* quae scholari alendo praebentur
scholastic *adj* scholastic·us -a -um
scholiast *s* scholiast·es -ae *m*
school *s* lud·us -i *m; (an advanced school)* schol·a -ae *f;* **elementary —** lud·us -i *m* litterarius; *(group holding like opinions)* sect·a -ae *f*
schoolboy *s* discipul·us -i *m*
schoolgirl *s* discipul·a -ae *f*
schoolmaster *s* ludi magis·ter -tri *m*
schoolroom *s* schol·a -ae *f*
science *s* disciplin·a -ae *f;* **natural —** rati·o -onis *f* physica
scientific *adj* physic·us -a -um
scientifically *adv* ratione
scientist *s* physic·us -i *m*
scimitar *s* acinac·es -is *m*
scion *s* edit·us -i *m*
scissors *spl* forficul·ae -arum *fpl*
scoff *s* cavillati·o -onis *f*
scoff *intr* cavillari; **to — at** irridēre
scoffer *s* irris·or -oris *m*
scold *tr* objurgare
scolding *s* objurgati·o -onis *f*
scoop *s* trull·a -ae *f*
scoop *tr* **to — out** excavare
scoot *intr* provolare
scope *s (extent)* spat·ium -(i)i *n; (range)* aspect·us -ūs *m*
scorch *tr* adurěre
score *s (total)* summ·a -ae *f; (twenty)* viginti *(indecl); (reckoning)* rati·o -onis *f;* **to even the — with** *(fig)* ulcisci; **to keep —** rationem notare; **to know the —** scire quid agatur
score *tr* notare

scorn *s* contempti·o -onis *f*
scorn *tr* contemnĕre
scornful *adj* fastidios·us -a -um
scornfully *adv* contemptim
scorpion *s* scorpi·o -onis *m*
Scot *adj* Scotic·us -a -um
Scotchman *s* Scot·us -i *m*
Scotland *s* Scoti·a -ae *f*
scoundrel *s* furci·fer -feri *m*
scour *tr (to rub clean)* tergēre; *(to roam over)* pervagari
scourge *s* flagell·um -i *n; (fig)* pest·is -is *f*
scourge *tr* flagellare
scourging *s* flagellati·o -onis *f*
scout *s* explorat·or -oris *m*
scout *tr* explorare
scowl *intr* frontem contrahĕre
scowlingly *adv* fronte contractā
scramble *intr* **to — for** diripĕre; **to — up** scandĕre
scrap *s (small piece)* frust·um -i *n; (junk)* metall·um -i *n* scrutarium
scrap *tr* rejicĕre
scrape *s* difficult·as -atis *f; (quarrel)* rix·a -ae *f*
scrape *tr* radĕre; **to — together** *(money, etc.)* corradĕre
scraping *s* rasur·a -ae *f*
scratch *tr* radĕre; *(the head)* scabĕre; **to — up** *(e.g., the earth)* scalpĕre
scratch *s* levis incisur·a -ae *f*
scrawl *s* mala scriptur·a -ae *f*
scrawl *tr & intr* male scribĕre
scream *s* ululat·us -ūs *m*, clam·or -oris *m; (of child)* vagit·us -ūs *m*
scream *intr* ululare; *(of child)* vagire
screech *s* strid·or -oris *m*
screech *intr* stridēre
screen *s* umbracul·um -i *n*
screen *tr* tegĕre
screw *s* cochle·a -ae *f*
screw *tr* torquēre; *(sl)* debattuĕre
scribble *tr & intr* conscribillare
scribe *s* scrib·a -ae *m*
script *s* script·um -i *n; (hand)* man·us -ūs *f*
scroll *s* volum·en -inis *n*
scrub *tr* tergēre
scruple *s* scrupul·us -i *m*
scrupulous *adj* scrupulos·us -a -um
scrupulously *adv* diligenter
scrutinize *tr* scrutari
scrutiny *s* scrutati·o -onis *f*
scuffle *s* rix·a -ae *f*
scuffle *intr* rixari
sculptor *s* sculpt·or -oris *m*
sculpture *s (art)* sculptur·a -ae *f; (work)* sign·um -i *n* (marmoreum)
sculpture *tr* sculpĕre
scum *s* spum·a -ae *f; (fig)* sentin·a -ae *f* reipublicae
scurrilous *adj* scurril·is -is -e

scurry *intr* volitare, properare
scuttle *tr* pertundĕre ac deprimĕre
scythe *s* fal·x -cis *f*
sea *s* mar·e -is *n; by* — mari, nave
sea captain *s* navarch·us -i *m*
seacoast *s* or·a -ae *f* maritima
seafaring *adj* maritim·us -a -um
sea gull *s* lar·us -i *m*
seal *s* sigill·um -i *n; (animal)* phoc·a -ae *f*
seal *tr* signare; **to — up** obsignare
seam *s* sutur·a -ae *f*
seaman *s* naut·a -ae *m*
seamanship *s* nauticarum rerum us·us -ūs *m*
seamstress *s* sarcinatr·ix -icis *f*
sear *tr* adurĕre
search *s* investigati·o -onis *f*, indagati·o -onis *f*
search *tr* investigare; *(to shake down a person)* excutĕre ‖ *intr* quaerĕre; **to — for** quaerĕre; **to — out** exquirĕre
seasick *adj* nauseabund·us -a -um; **to be — nauseare**
seasickness *s* nause·a -ae *f*
season *s* anni temp·us -oris *n; (proper time)* opportunit·as -atis *f*, tempus *n; in due —* (in) tempore; **in —** tempestiv·us -a -um
season *tr* condire; *(fig)* assuefacĕre
seasonable *adj* temptestiv·us -a -um
seasoning *s* condiment·um -i *n*
seat *s* sed·es -is *f*, sell·a -ae *f; (fixed abode)* domicil·ium -(i)i *n; — of honor (in dining room)* loc·us -i *m* praetorius; **to take one's — considĕre**
seat *tr* sede locare; **to — oneself** considĕre
seaweed *s* alg·a -ae *f*
secede *intr* secedĕre
secession *s* secessi·o -onis *f*
seclude *tr* secludĕre
secluded *adj* secret·us -a -um
seclusion *s* solitud·o -inis *f*
second *adj* secund·us -a -um; **a —** alt·er -era -erum; **a — time** iterum; **in the — place** deinde; **ranking — to s.o.** alter ab aliquo; **— to Achilles** ab Achille secundus; **to play — fiddle** secundas partes agĕre
second *s (handler)* adjut·or -oris *m; (of time)* moment·um -i *n* temporis
second *tr* adesse *(w. dat)*, favēre *(w. dat); **to — a motion** in sententiam alicujus dicĕre
secondary *adj* secundari·us -a -um
secondhand *adj* trit·us -a -um
second-rate *adj* infer·ior -ior -ius
secrecy *s* secret·um -i *n; (keeping secret)* silent·ium -(i)i *n*
secret *adj* secret·us -a -um; **to keep — celare**
secret *s* secret·um -i *n; he makes no — of it* neque id occulte fert; **in —** clam; **keep this a —!** haec tu tecum habeto!

to keep a — commissum celare; **to reveal a —** commissum enuntiare

secretary *s* a manu serv·us -i *m*

secrete *tr (to hide)* abdĕre; *(med)* secernĕre

secretion *s* secreti·o -onis *f*

sect *s* sect·a -ae *f*

section *s* secti·o -onis *f*

sector *s* sect·or -oris *m*

secular *adj* profan·us -a -um

secure *adj* tut·us -a -um

secure *tr (to make safe)* munire; *(to obtain)* comparare; *(to fasten)* religare; **to — oneself against fraud** muniri contra fraudes

securely *adv* tuto

security *s* securit·as -atis *f; (pledge)* satisdati·o -onis *f,* pign·us -oris *n*

sedate *adj* sedat·us -a -um

sedate *tr* sedare

sedentary *adj* sedentari·us -a -um

sedge *s* ul·va -ae *f*

sediment *s* sediment·um -i *n*

sedition *s* sediti·o -onis *f*

seditious *adj* seditios·us -a -um

seduce *tr* corrumpĕre, stuprum inferre *(w. dat)*

seducer *s* corrupt·or -oris *m*

seduction *s* corruptel·a -ae *f*

seductive *adj* illecebros·us -a -um

see *tr* vidēre; *(to distinguish w. the eyes)* cernĕre; **to go to —** visĕre; **to — to it that** curare ut **‖** *intr* vidēre; **to — to s.o.'s safety** prospicĕre alicujus saluti

seed *s* sem·en -inis *n; (offspring)* progeni·es -ei *f; (in fruit)* acin·um -i *n*

seedling *s* surcul·us -i *m*

seed-time *s* sement·is -is *f*

seek *tr* quaerĕre, petĕre; *(to strive after)* consectari; **to — to** conari *(w. inf)*

seem *intr* videri

seeming *adj* specios·us -a -um

seemingly *adv* ut videtur, in speciem

seemly *adj* decor·us -a -um

seep *intr* manare

seer *s* vat·es -is *m*

seethe *intr* aestuare

segment *s* segment·um -i *n*

segregate *tr* segregare

segregation *s* separati·o -onis *f*

seismograph *s* apparat·us -ūs *m* ad terrae motum observandum

seize *tr* prehendĕre, arripĕre; *(mil)* occupare; *(fig)* afficĕre

seizure *s* comprehensi·o -onis *f; (med)* accessi·o -onis *f*

seldom *adv* raro; **very —** perraro

select *tr* seligĕre, eligĕre

selection *s (act)* selecti·o -onis *f; (things chosen)* elect·a -orum *npl*

self *pron* ips·e -a -um; **he was never again his old —** coloris sui numquam fuit

self-appointed *adj* sibi arrogan·s -tis

self-assurance *s* confidenti·a -ae *f*

self-centered *adj* sibi dedit·us -a -um

self-confidence *s* fiduci·a -ae *f*

self-confident *adj* sibi fiden·s -tis

self-conscious *adj* pudibund·us -a -um

self-control *s* continenti·a -ae *f*

self-denial *s* abstinenti·a -ae *f*

self-evident *adj* manifest·us -a -um

self-indulgent *adj* intemperan·s -tis

selfish *adj* avar·us -a -um

selfishness *s* avariti·a -ae *f*

self-made *adj* **he is a — man** de nihilo crevit

self-respect *s* pud·or -oris *m*

sell *tr* vendĕre; *(as a practice)* venditare, **to — for 3000 sesterces per pound** vendĕre ternis milibus nummum in libras **‖** *intr* venire, venum ire

seller *s* vendit·or -oris *m*

semblance *s* speci·es -ei *f,* umbr·a -ae *f;* **under the — of a just treaty** sub umbrā foederis aequi

semicircle *s* semicircul·us -i *m*

semicircular *adj* semicircul·us -a -um

Senate *s* senat·us -ūs *m; (building)* curi·a -ae *f;* **— session** senatus *m;* **a — session was held on that very day** senatus eo ipso die agebatur

senatorial *adj* senatori·us -a -um

send *tr* mittĕre; *(on public business)* legare; **to — away** dimittĕre; **to — back** remittĕre; **to — flying into s.o.'s face** immittĕre in alicujus faciem; **to — forward** praemittĕre; **to — into** intromittĕre in *(w. acc)* **‖** *intr* **to — for** arcessĕre

sender *s* script·or -oris *m;* qui mittit

senile *adj* senil·is -is -e

senior *adj* natu maj·or -or -us

seniority *s* aetatis praerogativ·a -ae *f*

seniors *spl* senior·es -um *mpl*

sensation *s* sens·us -ūs *m; (fig)* mir·um -i *n;* **a painful —** doloris sensus; **to make a —** conspici

sensational *adj* mirabil·is -is -e

sense *s (faculty; meaning)* sens·us -ūs *m; (understanding)* prudenti·a -ae *f; (meaning)* vis *f,* significati·o -onis *f*

sense *tr* sentire

senseless *adj* absurd·us -a -um; *(unconscious)* omni sensu caren·s -tis

sensible *adj* prud·ens -entis

sensibly *adv* prudenter

sensitive *adj* sensil·is -is -e; *(touchy)* moll·is -is -e

sensual *adj* voluptari·us -a -um; **— pleasure** corporis volupt·as -atis *f*

sensuality *s* libid·o -inis *f*

sentence *s (gram, leg)* sententi·a -ae *f; (decision of an arbiter)* arbitr·ium (i)i *n;* **to pass — on s.o.** arbitrium de aliquo agĕre; **to pronounce the —** sententiam dicĕre

sentence *tr* damnare, condemnare
sententious *adj* sententios·us -a -um
sentiment *s (opinion)* sententi·a -e *f,* opini·o -onis *f; (feeling)* sens·us -ūs *m*
sentimental *adj* moll·is -is -e
sentimentality *s* animi molliti·es -ei *f*
sentinel, sentry *s* cust·os -odis *m,* vig·il -is *m; (collectively)* stati·o -onis *f;* **to be on sentry duty** in statione esse
separable *adj* separabil·is -is -e
separate *tr* separare, disjungĕre ‖ *intr* separari, disjungi
separate *adj* separat·us -a -um
separately *adv* separatim
separation *s* separati·o -onis *f*
September *s* Septem·ber -bris *m or* mens·is -is *m* Septmber; **on the first of** — Kalendis Septembribus
sepulcher *s* sepulcr·um -i *n*
sepulchral *adj* sepulcral·is -is -e
sequel *s* postprincip·ium -(i)i *n*
sequence *s* ord·o -inis *m*
serenade *tr* occentare
serene *adj* seren·us -a -um
serenely *adv* serene
serenity *s* serenit·as -atis *f*
serf *s* serv·us -i *m*
serfdom *s* servit·ium -(i)i *n*
sergeant *s* opti·o -onis *m*
series *s* seri·es -ei *f*
serious *adj* seri·us -a -um, grav·is -is -e
seriously *adv* serio, graviter; **to take** — in serium convertĕre
seriousness *s* gravit·as -atis *f*
sermon *s* orati·o -onis *f* sacra
serpent *s* serp·ens -entis *m*
servant *s* famul·us -i *m,* famul·a -ae *f,* serv·us -i *m,* serv·a -ae *f*
serve *tr (to be a servant to)* servire *(w. dat); (food)* apponĕre; *(to be useful)* prodesse *(w. dat);* **to — a sentence** poenam subire ‖ *intr (mil)* (stipendia) merēre; *(to suffice)* sufficĕre; **the trunk — the elephant as a hand** proboscis elephanto pro manu est
service *s (favor)* offic·ium -(i)i *n; (mil)* militi·a -ae *f,* stipendi·a -orum *npl; (work)* minister·ium -(i)i *n;* **to be of** — to prodesse *(w. dat)*
serviceable *adj* util·is -is -e
servile *adj* servil·is -is -e
servitude *s* servit·us -utis *f*
sesame *s* sesam·um -i *n*
session *s* sessi·o -onis *f*
sesterce *s* sestert·ius -(i)i *m (used in smaller sums; large sums are expressed by the collective form* sestertium = mille sestertii, *usually with the distributive numeral, e.g.,* **hundred thousand sesterces** centena sestertia, *but also with the cardinal, as,* septem sestertia **seven hundred thousand sesterces)**
set *tr (to place)* ponĕre; *(to make to stand)*

sistĕre, statuĕre; *(diamonds, etc.)* includĕre; *(a broken limb)* collocare; *(course)* dirigĕre; *(example)* praebēre; *(limit)* imponĕre; *(table)* instruĕre; *(plants)* serĕre; *(the clock)* constituĕre; **to — apart** seponĕre; **to — aside** ponĕre; *(to rescind)* rescindĕre; **to — a trap** insidias tendĕre; **to — bounds to** modum *(w. gen)* habēre; **to — down** deponĕre; *(in writing)* perscribĕre; **to — foot in** attingĕre; **to — forth** exponĕre, proponĕre; **to — free** liberare; **to — in motion** ciēre; **to — in order** componĕre; **to — off** *(to adorn)* adornare; **to — on fire** incendĕre; **to —** **one's hopes on** spem collocare in *(w. abl);* **to — s.o. over** aliquem praeficĕre *(w. dat);* **to — up** statuĕre ‖ *intr (of stars, sun)* occidĕre; **to — about waging wars** bella incipĕre; **to — in** *(to begin)* incipĕre; **to — out** proficisci
set *adj (fixed)* cert·us -a -um; *(prescribed, e.g., day, sacrifice)* stat·us -a -um; *(prepared)* parat·us -a -um; **in — terms** composite; **— speech** declamati·o -onis *f*
set *s (a set of two)* pa·r -ris *n; (gear, set of tools)* instrument·um -i *n; (number of persons customarily associated)* glob·us -i *m;* **a — of tools for one's trade** artis instrumentum *n*
setback *s* **to suffer a —** *(mil)* adversum casum experiri; *(pol)* repulsam ferre
setting *s (of sun)* occas·us -ūs *m; (situation)* res, rerum *fpl*
settle *tr* statuĕre; *(business)* transigĕre; *(colony)* deducĕre; *(people, e.g., on public lands)* constituĕre; *(argument)* componĕre; *(debt)* expedire; **to — accounts with** rationes putare cum *(w. abl)* ‖ *intr (to the bottom)* subsidĕre; *(to alight, land)* (on) insidĕre *(w. dat); (to fix one's home)* (in) considĕre *or* insidĕre (in + *abl);* **we —ed among ourselves to** constituimus inter nos ut
settled *adj (sure, certain)* cert·us -a -um
settlement *s (of a colony)* deducti·o -onis *f; (the colony itself)* coloni·a -ae *f; (of an affair)* compositi·o -onis *f; (terms)* pact·um - *n*
settler *s* colon·us -i *m*
seven *adj* septem *(indecl);* **— times** septies
sevenfold *adj* septempl·ex -icis
seventeen *adj* septendecim *(indecl)*
seventeenth *adj* septim·us decim·us -a -um
seventh *adj* septim·us -a -um
seventieth *adj* septuagesim·us -a -um
seventy *adj* septuaginta *(indecl)*
sever *tr* separare ‖ *intr* disjungi
several *adj* aliquot *(indecl)*
severally *adv* singulatim

severe *adj* (*rigorous, strict*) sever·us -a -um; (*wound, punishment*) grav·is -is -e; (*winter*) a·cer -cris -cre; (*cold, pain*) dur·us -a -um

severely *adv* severe, graviter

severity *s* severit·as -atis *f*, gravit·as -atis *f*

sew *tr* suĕre; **to — up** consuĕre

sewer *s* cloac·a -ae *f*

sewing *s* sutur·a -ae *f*

sex *s* (*gender*) sex·us -ūs *m*; (*intercourse*) Ven·us -eris *f*, coït·us -ūs *m*; **to have illicit — with** stuprum inferre (*w. dat*)

sextant *s* sext·ans -antis *m*

sexton *s* aditu·us -i *m*

sexual *adj* sexual·is -is -e; **— desire** libid·o -inis *f*; **— intercourse** Ven·us -eris *f*, coït·us -ūs *m*

shabbily *adv* sordide

shabbiness *s* sord·es -ium *fpl*

shabby *adj* sordid·us -a -um; (*worn out, torn*) obsolet·us -a -um

shackle *tr* compedibus constringĕre

shackles *spl* vincul·a -orum *npl*; (*on the legs*) comped·es -ium *fpl*

shade *s* umbr·a -ae *f*; **—s** (*of the dead*) man·es -ium *mpl*

shade *tr* opacare, adumbrare

shadow *s* umbr·a -ae *f*

shadowy *adj* umbros·us -a -um; (*fig*) inan·is -is -e, exil·is -is -e

shady *adj* opac·us -a -um

shaft *s* (*arrow*) sagitt·a -ae *f*; (*of spear*) hastil·e -is *n*; (*of a mine*) pute·us -i *m*

shaggy *adj* villos·us -a -um

shake *tr* quatĕre, concutĕre; (*head*) nutare; **to — hands with** dextram jungĕre cum (*w. abl*); **to — off a bad reputation** infamiam discutĕre ‖ *intr* tremĕre; (*to totter*) vacillare; **her sides shook with laughter** ejus latera commoverunt risu; **to begin to —** intremescĕre

shaking *s* quassati·o -onis *f*; (*w. cold, fear*) trem·or -oris *m*

shaky *adj* instabil·is -is -e

shallow *adj* (*river, sea*) vados·us -a -um; (*trench*) humil·is -is -e; (*well*) brev·is -is -e; (*fig*) lev·is -is -e; **quite —** minime alt·us -a -um

shallows *spl* vad·a -orum *npl*

sham *s* dol·us -i *m*

sham *adj* simulat·us -a -um

shambles *spl* turb·a -ae *f*

shame *s* pud·or -oris *m*; (*disgrace*) dedec·us -oris *n*; **— on our Senate and morals!** pro senatu et moribus! **— on you!** sit pudor! **to have lost all sense of —** omnem pudorem exuisse; **to put s.o. to —** ruborem alicui incutĕre

shame *tr* rubrem incutĕre (*w. dat*)

shamefaced *adj* verecund·us -a -um

shameful *adj* probros·us -a -um

shamefully *adv* probrose, turpiter

shamless *adj* impud·ens -entis

shamelessly *adv* impudenter

shamrock *s* trifol·ium -(i)i *n*

shank *s* cru·s -ris *n*

shanty *s* tugur·ium -(i)i *n*

shape *s* form·a -ae *f*, figur·a -ae *f*; **to be in good (bad) —** boni (mali) habitūs esse

shape *tr* figurare, formare

shapeless *adj* inform·is -is -e

shapely *adj* formos·us -a -um; (*limbs*) ter·es -etis

shard *s* test·a -ae *f*

share *s* par·s -tis *f*, porti·o -onis *f*

share *tr* partire; (*to enjoy with, have in common with, others*) (**with**) communicare (cum + *abl*) ‖ *intr* **to — in** particeps esse (*w. gen*)

shark *s* p(r)istr·ix -icis *m*

sharp *adj* acut·us -a -um; (*mind*) ac·er -ris -re, sag·ax -acis; (*taste*) acerb·is -is -e

sharpen *tr* acuĕre

sharply *adv* acriter

shatter *tr* quassare, confringĕre; (*to knock apart*) discutĕre

shave *tr* radĕre; **to — off** deradĕre ‖ *intr* barbam radĕre

shaven *adj* adras·us -a -um

shavings *spl* rament·a -orum *npl*

shawl *s* amicul·um -i *n*

she *pron* ea, illa, haec

sheaf *s* fasc·is -is *m*

shear *tr* tondēre

shearing *s* tonsur·a -ae *f*

shears *spl* forfic·es -um *fpl*

sheath *s* vagin·a -ae *f*

sheathe *tr* in vaginam recondĕre

shed *tr* (*tears, blood, etc.*) fundĕre, effundĕre; (*feathers, leaves*) ponĕre; **to — light on a subject** lumen alicui rei adhibēre

shed *s* tugur·ium -(i)i *n*; (*mil*) vine·a -ae *f*

sheep *s* ov·is -is *f*

sheepfold *s* ovil·e -is *n*

sheepish *adj* pudibund·us -a -um

sheepishly *adv* pudenter

sheepskin *s* pell·is -is *f* ovilla

sheer *adj* (*pure, utter*) mer·us -a -um; (*steep*) praerupt·us -a -um

sheet *s* linte·um -i *n*; (*of paper*) sched·a -ae *f*; (*of metal*) lamin·a -ae *f*; **— of papyrus** *s* chart·a -ae *f*

shelf *s* plute·us -i *m*

shell *s* conch·a -ae *f*; (*of nuts*) putam·en -inis *n*

shellfish *s* conch·a -ae *f*

shelter *s* tegm·en -inis *n*; (*refuge*) refug·ium -(i)i *n*; (*lodgings*) hospit·ium -(i)i *n*

shelter *tr* tegēre; (*refugees*) excipĕre

shepherd *s* past·or -oris *m*

shield *s* (*round*) parm·a-ae *f*; (*oblong*) scut·um -i *n*

shift *tr* (*to change*) mutare; (*transfer*)

transferre ‖ *intr* mutari; **to — for one-self** sibi providēre

shift *s (change)* mutati·o -onis *f*

shifty *adj* mobil·is -is -e

shin *s* tibi·a -ae *f*

shine *s* nit·or -oris *n*

shine *intr* lucēre; *(with a bright light)* fulgēre; *(to excel)* praestare; **to — forth** elucēre, enitēre; **to — on** affulgēre *(w. dat)*

shingle *s* tegul·a -ae *f*

shiny *adj* fulgid·us -a -um

ship *s* nav·is -is *f*

ship *tr* navi invehēre; *(to send)* mittĕre

shipbuilder *s* naupeg·us -i *m*

ship owner *s* navicular·ius -(i)i *m*

shipwreck *s* naufrag·ium -(i)i *n;* **to suffer —** naufrag·ium facĕre

shipwrecked *adj* naufract·us -a -um

shirk *tr* abhorrēre ab *(w. abl)*

shirt *s* subucul·a -ae *f*

shiver *intr* horrēre

shiver *s* horr·or -oris *m*

shoal *s (of fish)* exam·en -inis *n; (shallow)* vad·um -i *n*

shock *s* offensi·o -onis *f*

shock *tr* percutĕre; **to be —** inhorrescĕre

shocked *adj* attonit·us -a -um

shocking *adj* tae·ter -tra -trum

shoe *s* calce·us -i *m*

shoemaker *s* sut·or -oris *m*

shook up *adj* consternat·us -a -um, conterrit·us -a -um

shoot *tr (missile)* conjicĕre; *(person)* transfigĕre ‖ *intr* volare; **to — up** crescĕre

shoot *s* surcul·us -i *m*

shooting star *s* fae·x -cis *f* caelestis

shop *s* tabern·a -ae *f*

shop *intr* obsonare, mercari; **to — for** mercari; *(groceries)* obsonare

shopkeeper *s* tabernar·ius -(i)i *m*

shopper *s* obsonat·or -oris *m*

shopping *s* obsonat·us -ūs *m*

shore *s* lit·us -oris *n,* or·a -ae *f*

shore *tr* **to — up** fulcire

short *adj* brev·is -is -e; **in a — time** brevi; **in — ad** summam; **to run —** deficĕre

shortage *s* inopi·a -ae *f*

shortcoming *s* defect·us -ūs *m*

shortcut *s* compendari·a -ae *f*

shorten *tr* contrahĕre; *(to limit)* coarctare; *(a syllable)* corripĕre ‖ *intr* contrahi, minui

shorthand *s* not·ae -arum *fpl;* **to take down in —** notis excipĕre

short-lived *adj* brev·is -is -e

shortly *adv* brevi, mox

shortness *s* brevit·as -atis *f;* **— of breath** asthm·a -atis *n*

shortsighted *adj* my·ops -opis *(fig)* improvid·us -a -um

short-winded *adj* anhel·us -a -um

shot *s* ict·us -ūs *m;* **long —** dubia ale·a -ae *f;* **within —** intra teli jactum

should *intr (ought)* debēre; **I — go** mihi eundum est; **if I — say no** si negem

shoulder *s* umer·us -i *m; (of animals)* arm·us -i *m*

shoulder *tr* suscipĕre

shoulder blade *s* scapul·a -ae *f*

shout *s* clam·or -oris *m; (of approval)* acclamati·o -onis *f*

shout *tr & intr* clamare, acclamare

shove *tr* trudĕre, pulsare; **to — the book under the bed** mittĕre librum subter lectum

shove *s* impulsi·o -onis *f*

shovel *s* rutr·um -i *n*

shovel *tr* rutro tollĕre; **to — out** rutro ejicĕre

show *tr* monstrare; *(to display)* exhibēre; *(to explain)* docēre; **to — off** ostendĕre ‖ *intr* manifest·us -a -um esse; **to — off** se jactare; **to — up** apparēre

show *s (appearance)* speci·es -ei *f; (display)* ostentati·o -onis *f; (pretense)* simulati·o -onis *f; (public entertainment)* spectacul·um -i *n;* **for —** ad speciem; **to put on a public —** spectaculum edĕre

shower *s (rain)* im·ber -bris *m; (of stones, darts)* vis *f,* multitud·o -onis *f; (for bathing)* balne·um -i *n* pensile; **to take a —** balneo pensili uti

shower *tr* fundĕre; **to — down arrows on** infundĕre sagittas *(w. dat)*

showy *adj* specios·us -a -um

shred *s* segment·um -i *n* panni; **not a — of evidence** nihil omnino testimonii; **to tear to —s** discindĕre

shrew *s* muli·er -eris *f* jurgiosa

shrewd *adj* callid·us -a -um

shrewdly *adv* callide

shrewdness *s* callidit·as -atis *f*

shriek *s* ululat·us -ūs *m*

shriek *intr* ululare, ejulare

shrill *adj* peracut·us -a -um

shrimp *s* can·cer -cri *m* pagurus; *(person)* homul·us -i *m*

shrine *s* delubr·um -i *n,* fan·um -i *n*

shrink *tr* contrahēre ‖ *intr* contrahi; *(to withdraw)* refugĕre; **to — from** abhorrēre *or* refugĕre ab *(w. abl)*

shrivel *tr* corrugare ‖ *intr* corrugari

shriveled *adj* rugos·us -a -um

shroud *s* integument·um -i *n*

shroud *tr* involvĕre

shrub *s* frut·ex -icis *m*

shrubbery *s* frutect·um -i *n*

shrug *tr* **to — the shoulders** umeros allevare

shrug *s* umerorum allevati·o -onis *f*

shudder *intr* horrēre; **to — at the sight** horrēre visu

shudder *s* horr•or -oris *m*
shuffle *tr* miscēre **‖** *intr* claudicare
shun *tr* vitare, devitare
shut *tr* claudĕre; **to — in** includĕre; **to — off** occludĕre; **to — out** excludĕre; **to — up** concludĕre **‖** *intr* conticescĕre
shutter *s* foricul•a -ae *f*
shy *adj* timid•us -a -um
shy *intr (of horses)* consternari; **to — away from** abhorrēre ab *(w. abl)*
shyly *adv* timide
shyness *s* verecundi•a -ae *f*
sibyl *s* sibyll•a -ae *f*
sic *tr* **to — the dog on** instigare canem in *(w. acc)*
sick *adj (mentally or physically)* ae•ger -gra -grum; *(physically)* aegrot•us -a -um; **I am — and tired of** me taedet *(w. gen);* **to be —** aegrotare
sicken *tr* fastidium movēre *(w. dat)* **‖** *intr* in morbum incidĕre
sickening *adj* tae•ter -tra -trum
sickle *s* fal•x -cis *f*
sickly *adj* morbos•us -a -um
sickness *s* morb•us -i *m*
side *s (of a body, hill, camp, ship, etc.)* lat•us -eris *n; (direction)* par•s -tis *f; (faction)* part•es -ium *fpl; (kinship)* gen•us -eris *n;* **at the — of** a latere *(w. gen);* **from all —s** undique; **having heard only one —, he condemned her** alterā tantum parte auditā condemnavit eam; **on all —s** undique; **on both —s** utrimque; **one — of the island** unum latus insulae; **on one —** unā ex parte; **on that —** illinc; **on the one —…on the other** hinc…illinc; **on their —** pro illa parte; **on the mother's —** materno genere; **on this —** hinc; **on this — of** cis *(w. acc),* citra *(w. acc);* **to be on the — of** stare ab *(w. abl),* sentire cum *(w. abl);* **to leave s.o.'s —** a latere alicujus discedĕre; **to lie on his —** in latus cubare; **to walk at s.o.'s —** tegĕre latus alicui
side *adj* lateral•is -is -e
side *intr* **to — with** partes sequi *(w. gen),* stare ab *(w. abl),* sentire cum *(w. abl)*
sideboard *s* abac•us -i *m*
sided *adj* **many-sided** multilater•us -a -um; **one-sided** unilter•us -a -um
sidelong *adj* obliqu•us -a -um
sideways *adv* in obliquum, oblique
siege *s* obsidi•o -onis *f;* **to lay — to** obsidēre
siesta *s* meridiati•o -onis *f;* **to take a —** meridiare
sieve *s* cribr•um -i *n; (little sieve)* cribell•um -i *n*
sift *tr* cribrare; *(fig)* scrutari
sigh *s* suspir•ium -(i)i *n*
sigh *intr* suspirare; **to — for** desiderare
sight *s (sense)* vis•us -ūs *m; (act of see-*

ing) aspect•us -ūs *m; (range)* conspect•us -ūs *m; (appearance)* speci•es -ei *f; (show)* spectacul•um -i *n;* **at first — *(on the first appearance of a person or thing)*** primā specie; *(looking at it subjectively)* primo aspectu; **to catch — of** conspicĕre; **to lose — of** e conspectu amittĕre
sight *tr* conspicari
sign *s* sign•um -i *n,* indic•ium -(i)i *n; (mark)* not•a -ae *f; (distinction)* insign•e -is *n; (omen)* portent•um -i *n*
sign *tr (document)* subscribĕre; *(to ratify by signature and seal)* signare; **to — one's name to a letter** nomen epistolae notare
signal *intr* signum dare; *(by a nod)* annuĕre
signal *s* sign•um -i *n; (mil)* classic•um -i *n*
signal *adj* insign•is -is -e
signature *s* nom•en -inis *n*
signer *s* signat•or -oris *m*
signet *s* sigill•um -i *n*
significance *s (meaning)* significati•o -onis *f; (importance)* moment•um -i *n*
significant *adj* signific•ans -antis, magni momenti
signify *tr* significare
silence *s* silent•ium -(i)i *n;* **—!** tace! *(pl:* tacite); **to call for —** silentium facĕre; **to pass over in —** silentio praeterire
silence *tr* comprimĕre; *(by argument)* refutare
silent *adj* tacit•us -a -um; **to become —** conticescĕre; **to be —** tacēre; **to keep s.th. —** aliquid tacēre; **to keep — about s.th.** de aliquo silēre
silently *adv* tacite
silk *s* seric•um -i *n*
silk *adj* seric•us -a -um
silkworm *s* bomb•yx -ycis *mf*
sill *s* lim•en -inis *n* inferum
silly *adj* stult•us -a -um
silver *s* argent•um -i *n*
silversmith *s* fa•ber -bri *m* argentarius
silvery *adj* argente•us -a -um; *(of hair)* can•us -a -um
similar *adj* simil•is -is -e
similarity *s* similitud•o -inis *f*
similarly *adv* similiter, pariter
simile *s* translat•um -i *n*
simmer *intr* lente fervēre
simple *adj* simpl•ex -icis; *(easy)* facil•is -is -e; *(weak-minded)* inept•us -a -um; *(frank)* sincer•us -a -um
simpleton *s* inept•us -i *m*
simplicity *s* simplicit•as -atis *f*
simplify *tr* facil•iorem -iorem -ius reddĕre
simply *adv (in a simple manner)* simpliciter; *(only)* tantummodo
simulate *tr* simulare
simulation *s* simulati•o -onis *f*
simultaneous *adj* eodem tempore

simultaneously *adv* simul, unā

sin *s* peccat·um -i *n*

sin *intr* peccare

since *prep* ex *(w. abl)*, ab *(w. abl)*, post *(w. acc);* **ever** — usque ab *(w. abl)*

since *adv* abhinc; **long** — jamdudum

since *conj (temporal)* ex quo tempore, postquam, cum; *(causal)* quod, quia, quoniam, cum

sincere *adj* sincer·us -a -um

sincerely *adv* sincere

sincerity *s* sincerit·as -atis *f*

sinew *s* nerv·us -i *m*

sinewy *adj* nervos·us -a -um

sinful *adj* prav·us -a -um

sing *tr & intr* canĕre, cantare

singe *tr* adurĕre, amburĕre

singer *s* cantat·or -oris *m,* cantatr·ix -icis *f*

singing *s* cant·us -ūs *m*

single *adj* sol·us -a -um, unic·us -a -um; *(unmarried)* caeleb·s -is; **in — combat** vir unus cum viro congrediendo; **not a — one** ne unus quidem

single *tr* **to — out** eligĕre

singly *adv* singulatim

singsong *s* cantic·um -i *n*

singsong *adj* canor·us -a -um

singular *adj (only one; outstanding; gram)* singular·is -is -e; **in the —** singulariter

singularly *adv* singulariter, unice

sinister *adj* malevol·us -a -um

sink *tr* submergĕre; *(as a hostile act)* deprimĕre; *(money)* collocare ‖ *intr (to settle at the bottom)* (de)sidĕre; *(of ships)* mergi; *(of morale)* cadĕre; **to — in the mud** limo se immergĕre

sink *s* fusor·ium -(i)i *n*

sinless *adj* peccati exper·s -tis

sinner *s* peccat·or -oris *m*

sinuous *adj* sinuos·us -a -um

sip *tr* sorbillare

siphon *s* siph·o -onis *m*

sir *interj (to a master)* ere! *(to an equal)* bone vir! *(to a superior)* vir clarissime!

sire *s* genit·or -oris *m*

siren *s* sir·en -enis *f; (alarm)* classic·um -i *n*

sister *s* sor·or -oris *f*

sisterhood *s* sororum societ·as -atis *f*

sister-in-law *s* glo·s -ris *f*

sisterly *adj* sorori·us -a -um

sit *intr* sedĕre; **to — as judge** jus dicĕre; **to — beside** assidĕre *(w. dat);* **to — down (on)** considĕre (super + *acc);* **to — on** insidĕre *(w. dat);* **to — up** residĕre; *(to stay awake)* vigilare; **to — up all night** pervigilare

site *s* sit·us -ūs *m*

sitting room *s* sessor·ium -(i)i *n*

situated *adj* sit·us -a -um

situation *s* sit·us -ūs *m; (circumstances)* res, rei *f;* **that's the —** res sic se habet

six *adj* sex *(indecl);* — **times** sexies

sixfold *adj* sextupl·us -a -um

sixteen *adj* sedecim *(indecl)*

sixteenth *adj* sext·us decim·us -a -um

sixth *adj* sext·us -a -um

sixth *s* sexta par·s -tis *f*

sixtieth *adj* sexagesim·us -a -um

sixty *adj* sexaginta *(indecl)*

size *s* magnitud·o -inis *f;* **of huge —** ingen·s -tis

skein *s* glom·us -i *m*

skeleton *s* oss·a -ium *npl* corporis

sketch *s* adumbrati·o -onis *f*

sketch *tr* adumbrare, delineare; *(in words)* describĕre

skiff *s* scaph·a -ae *f*

skill *s* sollerti·a -ae *f; (derived from experience)* periti·a -ae *f*

skilled *adj* perit·us -a -um

skillful *adj* scit·us -a -um; *(w. hands)* habil·is -is -e

skillfully *adv* sollerter, scite

skillet *s* cucumell·a -ae *f*

skim *tr* despumare; *(fig)* percurrĕre

skin *s (of man)* cut·is -is *f; (of animals)* pell·is -is *f*

skin *tr* pellem detrahĕre *(w. dat)*

skinny *adj* macilent·us -a -um

skip *tr* praeterire ‖ *intr* subsultare; **to — over** transilire

skirmish *s* leve certam·en -inis *n*

skirmish *intr* levia proelia conserĕre

skirt *s* inducul·a -ae *f*

skirt *tr* tangĕre

skittish *adj* timid·us -a -um

skull *s* cran·ium -(i)i *n;* **fractured —** cap·ut -itis *n* fractum

sky *s* cael·um -i *n;* **under the open —** sub divo

sky-blue *adj* caerule·us -a -um

skylark *s* alaud·a -ae *f*

slab *s* tabul·a -ae *f*

slack *adj* lax·us -a -um

slacken *tr* remittĕre, laxare ‖ *intr* remitti, minui

slag *s* scori·a -ae *f*

slain *adj* occis·us -a -um

slake *tr* exstinguĕre

slander *s* calumni·a -ae *f*

slander *tr* calumniari

slanderer *s* obtrectat·or -oris *m*

slanderous *adj* calumnios·us -a -um

slang *s* vulgaria verb·a -orum *npl*

slant *tr* acclinare; *(fig)* detorquĕre ‖ *intr* proclinari

slanted *adj* transvers·us -a -um

slanting *adj* obliqu·us -a -um

slap *s* alap·a -ae *f*

slap *tr* alapam dare *(w. dat);* **to — s.o. in the face** os alicujus palmā pulsare

slash *s (cut)* caesur·a -ae *f; (blow)* ict·us -ūs *m; (wound)* vuln·us -eris *n*

slash *tr* caedĕre

slaughter *s* trucidati·o -onis *f*
slaughter *tr* trucidare, mactare
slaughterhouse *s* carnar·ium -(i)i *n*
slave *s* serv·us -i *m,* serv·a -ae *f*
slave *intr* sudare
slave dealer *s* mang·o -onis *m*
slavery *s* servitud·o -inis *f*
slave trade *s* venalic·ium -(i)i *n*
slavish *adj* servil·is -is -e
slavishly *adv* serviliter
slay *tr* interficĕre
slayer *s* interfect·or -oris *m*
sledge *s* trahe·a -ae *f*
sleek *adj* nitid·us -a -um
sleep *s* somn·us -i *m*
sleep *tr* **to — off a hangover** crapulam
edormire ‖ *intr* dormire
sleepless *adj* insomn·is -is -e,
sleepy *adj* somniculos·us -a -um
sleet *s* nivosa grand·o -inis *f*
sleeve *s* manic·a -ae *f*
slender *adj* gracil·is -is -e
slice *s* lamin·a -ae *f*
slice *tr* secare
slide *intr* labi
slight *adj* exigu·us -a -um; *(of small account)* lev·is -is -e
slight *s* neglegenti·a -ae *f*
slightly *adv* parum
slily *adv* astute, callide
slim *adj* gracil·is -is -e; **— hope** angusta
spe·s -ei *f*
slime *s* lēv·e -is *n*
slimy *adj* lēv·is -is -e
sling *s* fund·a -ae *f; (med)* fasci·a -ae *f*
sling *tr* jaculari
slink *intr* **to — away** furtim se subducĕre
slip *s* laps·us -ūs *m; (of paper)* schedul·a
f; (error) peccat·um -i *n; (in grafting)*
surcul·us -i *m; (underdress)* subucul·a
-ae *f;* **— of the tongue** lapsus -us *m*
linguae; **— of the pen** mend·um -i *n;* **to**
give s.o. the — aliquem fallĕre
slip *tr (to give furtively)* furtim dare ‖
intr labi; **to let — amittĕre, praetermittĕre; to — away** elabi; *(to leave
furtively)* se subducĕre; **to — out of**
elabi ex *(w. abl); (to escape from)*
excidĕre ex *(w. abl)*
slipper *s* sole·a -ae *f;* **wearing —s**
soleat·us -a -um
slippery *adj* lubric·us -a -um; *(deceitful)*
subdol·us -a -um
slipshot *adj* neglig·ens -entis
slit *s* incisur·a -ae *f*
slit *tr* incidĕre
sliver *s* schidi·a -ae *f*
slobber *intr* **to — on** conspuĕre
slop *s* quisquili·ae -arum *fpl*
slope *s* cliv·us -i *m*
slope *intr* proclinari, vergĕre
sloping *adj* decliv·is -is -e; *(upwards)*
accliv·is -is -e

sloppy *adj (roads)* lutulent·us -a -um;
(work) neglig·ens -entis
slot *s* rim·a -ae *f*
sloth *s* pigriti·a -ae *f*
slothful *adj* pi·ger -gra -grum
slothfully *adv* pigre
slouch *intr* languide incedĕre; **to — down**
(in a chair) parum erecte sedēre
slough *s (of snake)* exuvi·ae -arum *fpl*
slovenly *adj* incompt·us -a -um
slow *adj* tard·us -a -um
slowly *adv* tarde, lente
sluggish *adj* pi·ger -gra -grum
sluggishly *adv* pigre
sluice *s* cataract·a -ae *f*
slumber *s* sop·or -oris *m*
slumber *intr* dormitare
slur *s* macul·a -ae *f*
slur *tr* inquinare; **to — over** mussitare
slut *s* meretr·ix -icis *f*
sly *adj* astut·us -a -um; **on the — clam**
slyness *s* astuti·a -ae *f*
smack *s (flavor)* sap·or -oris *m; (blow)*
alap·a -ae *f; (kiss)* bas·ium -(i)i *n*
smack *tr* ferire; *(to kiss)* basiare ‖ *intr* **to**
— of sapĕre *(w. acc)*
small *adj* parv·us -a -um; *(comp:* min·or
-or -us; *superl:* minim·us -a -um)
smart *adj (clever)* callid·us -a -um; *(elegant)* elegan·s -tis; *(impertinent)*
insolen·s -tis; *(of pace)* vel·ox -ocis
smart *s* dol·or -oris *m*
smart *intr* dolēre
smartly *adv* callide; eleganter
smash *s* concussi·o -onis *f*
smash *tr (also — up)* confringĕre
smashup *s* collisi·o -onis *f*
smattering *s* cogniti·o -onis *f* manca
smear *tr* oblinĕre, illinĕre
smell *s (sense)* odorat·us -ūs *m; (odor)*
od·or -oris *m;* **to have a keen sense of**
— bene olēre
smell *tr* olfacĕre ‖ *intr* olēre; **to —**
bad male olēre; **to — good** bene
olēre, jucunde olēre; **to — like** *or*
of olēre *(w. acc)*
smelly *adj* olid·us -a -um
smelt *tr* coquĕre, fundĕre
smile *s* subris·us -ūs *m;* **with a —**
subrid·ens -entis
smile *intr* subridēre; **to — at** arridēre *(w. dat)*
smirk *s* molestus subris·us -ūs *m*
smirk *intr* moleste subridēre
smite *tr* ferire, percutĕre
smith *s* fab·er -bri *m*
smithy *s* officin·a -ae *f* ferraria
smock *s* tunic·a -ae *f*
smoke *s* fum·us -i *m;* **where there's —**
there's fire flamm·a -ae *f* fumo est
proxima
smoke *tr (meat)* infumare ‖ *intr* fumare
smoky *adj* fumos·us -a -um

smooth *adj* lēv·is -is -e; *(hairless)* gla·ber -bra -brum; *(polished)* ter·es -itis; *(calm)* placid·us -a -um; *(of talk)* bland·us -a -um

smoothly *adv* lēviter; blande

smooth *tr* lēvare; *(to file)* limare; **to — the path to** viam facĕre ad *(w. acc)*

smoothness *s* lev·or -oris *m*

smother *tr (flames, tears, anger)* opprimĕre; *(to choke)* suffocare

smudge *s* lab·es -is *f,* macul·a -ae *f; (smear)* litur·a -ae *f*

smudge *tr* inquinare, maculare

smug *adj* sui content·us -a -um

smuggle *tr* sine portorio exportare *or* importare

smut *s (soot)* fulig·o -inis *f; (foul language, writing)* obscenit·as -atis *f*

smutty *adj* fumos·us -a -um; *(obscene)* obscen·us -a -um

snack *s* merend·a -ae *f*

snack *intr* adedĕre

snail *s* cochle·a -ae *f; (without shell)* lim·ax -acis *f*

snake *s* angu·is -is *m; (large snake)* drac·o -onis *m*

snap *s* crepit·us -ūs *m*

snap *tr (to break off suddenly)* praefrangĕre; **to — the fingers** digitis concrepare; **to — up** corripĕre **ǁ** *intr (to break with a sharp noise)* dissilire; *(to make a sharp sound)* crepare; **to — at** *(w. teeth)* morsu petĕre; *(in speaking)* increpare

snare *s* laque·us -i *m;* **to lay —s for a rival** rivali laqueos disponĕre

snare *tr* illaquēre

snarl *intr* hirrire

snarl *s* hirrit·us -ūs *m*

snatch *tr* rapĕre, corripĕre; **to — away** eripĕre; **to — up** surripĕre

sneak *s* lucifug·a -ae *m*

sneak *intr* repĕre; **to — into** corripĕre in *(w. acc);* **to — out of** repĕre ex *(w. abl);* **to — up on** obrepĕre *(w. dat)*

sneer *s* rhonch·us -i *m*

sneer *intr* irridĕre; **to — at** irridēre

sneeze *s* sternument·um -i *n*

sneeze *intr* sternuĕre

sniff *s* **to get a — of** olfacĕre

sniff *tr* naribus captare; *(cocaine)* naribus ducĕre **ǁ** *intr* odorari

snip *tr* **to — off** praecidĕre

snivel *s* muc·us -i *m*

snivel *intr* mucum resorbēre

snob *s* hom·o -inis *m* fastidiosus

snobbish *adj* fastidios·us -a -um

snore *s* rhonch·us -i *m*

snore *intr* stertĕre

snort *s* fremit·us -ūs *m*

snort *intr* fremĕre

snout *s* rostr·um -i *n*

snow *s* nix, nivis *f*

snow *tr* **to — in** nive obruĕre **ǁ** *v impers* ningĕre; **it is —ing** ningit

snowball *s* glebul·a -ae *f* nivis

snowbound *adj* nivibus obrut·us -a -um

snowdrift *s* niveus agg·er -eris *m*

snowfall *s* nivis cas·us -ūs *m*

snowflakes *spl* ningu·es -um *fpl*

snowstorm *s* ning·or -oris *m*

snow-white *adj* nive·us -a -um

snowy *adj* nival·is -is -e

snub *tr* neglegĕre

snub *s* repuls·a -ae *f*

snuff *tr* **to — out** exstinguĕre

snug *adj* commod·us -a -um

snugly *adv* commode

so *adv* sic, ita, *(before adjectives)* tam; **and — forth** et cetera; **— far** eatenus, adhuc; **— help me** mehercules; **— many** tot; **— much** tant·us -a -um; *(so greatly)* tantopere; **— often** totiens; **— slight a** *(e.g., fever)* tantul·us -a -um; **— so** sic tenuiter; **— that** ut; **— that not** ne; **— then** quapropter; **— what?** quid ergo?

so *pron* **— and —** ille et ille

soak *tr* madefacĕre; *(to soften while soaking)* macerare **ǁ** *intr* madēre

soap *s* sap·o -onis *m*

soar *intr* in sublime ferri; *(of birds)* subvolare

sob *s* singult·us -ūs *m*

sob *intr* singultare

sober *adj* sobri·us -a -um; *(fig)* moderat·us -a -um

soberly *adv* sobrie; moderate

sobriety *s* sobriet·as -atis *f*

sociable *adj* sociabil·is -is -e; *(pleasant in society)* facil·is -is -e

social *adj (companionable)* social·is -is -e; *(life)* commun·is -is -e; *(institutions, laws, customs, duties)* civil·is -is -e; **— call** offic·ium -(i)i *n*

society *s* societ·as -atis *f;* **high —** optimat·es -ium *mpl;* **secret —** sodalit·as -atis *f;* **— as a whole** omnes homin·es -um *mpl*

sock *s* pedal·e -is *n*

socket *s (anat)* cav·um -i *n*

sod *s* caesp·es -itis *m*

soda *s (in natural state)* nitr·um -i *n*

sofa *s* lectul·us -i *m*

soft *adj* moll·is -is -e; *(fruit)* mit·is -is -e; *(fig)* delicat·us -a -um

soften *tr* mollire; *(fig)* lenire **ǁ** *intr* mollescĕre; *(of fruit)* mitescĕre; *(fig)* mitescĕre

softhearted *adj* miseric·ors -ordis

softly *adv* molliter; *(noiselessly)* leniter; *(opp. of loudly)* summissā voce

soil *s* sol·um -i *n,* hum·us -i *f*

soil *tr* inquinare, spurcare

sojourn *s* commorati·o -onis *f*

sojourn *intr* commorari

solace *s* solat·ium -(ı)i *n*

solace *tr* consolari
solar *adj* solar·is -is -e
solder *tr* ferruminare
soldier *s* mil·es -itis *m*
soldierly *adj* militar·is -is -e
soldiery *s* mil·es -itis *m*
sole *adj* sol·us -a -um, unic·us -a -um
sole *s (of shoe)* sol·um -i *n; (anat)* plant·a -ae *f; (fish)* sole·a -ae *f*
solely *adv* solum, tantummodo
solemn *adj* sollemn·is -is -e
solemnity *s* sollemnit·as -atis *f*
solemnly *adv* sollemniter; **to swear —** religiosissimis verbis jurare
solemnize *tr* celebrare
solicit *tr* flagitare; **to — sex from s.o.** aliquem stuprum rogare
solicitation *s* flagiti·o -onis *f*
solicitor *s* flagitat·or -oris *m; (leg)* jurisperit·us -i *m*
solicitous *adj* anxi·us -a -um
solicitude *s* sollicitud·o -inis *f*
solid *adj* solid·us -a -um; *(food)* plen·ior -ior -ius; *(real, true)* firm·us -a -um; **men of — character** homin·es -um *mpl* probati; **— gold** totum aur·um -i *n*
solidly *adv* solide, firme
soliloquize *intr* secum loqui
soliloquy *s* soliloqu·ium -(i)i *n*
solitary *adj* solitari·us -a -um
solitude *s* solitud·o -inis *f*
solstice *s* solstit·ium -(i)i *n*
soluble *adj* dissolubil·is -is -e
solution *s* dilut·um -i *n; (fig)* soluti·o -onis *f*, explicati·o -onis *f*
solve *tr* (dis)solvĕre
solvency *s* facult·as -atis *f* solvendi
some *adj* ali·qui -qua -quod; *(a certain)* quidam quaedam quoddam; *(several)* nonnull·i -ae -a; *(a few)* aliquot *(indecl);* **— twenty days later** aliquos viginti dies post; **— war or other** aliquod bellum, nescio quod bellum; **to drink — wine** aliquid vini bibĕre
some *pron* aliqu·i -ae -a; *(several)* nonnull·i -ae -a; *(certain people)* quidam, quaedam, quaedam; **—...others** alii...alii
somebody *pron* aliquis; **— or other** nescio quis
someday *adv* olim, aliquando
somehow *adv* aliquā (viā); **— or other** nescio quomodo
someone *pron* aliquis; **— else** ali·us -a
something *pron* aliquid; **— else** aliud ultra; **— or other** nescio quid
sometime *adv* aliquando
sometimes *adv* interdum, nonnumquam; **—...—** modo...modo
somewhat *adv* aliquantum; *(w. comparatives)* aliquanto, paulo
somewhere *adv* alicubi; *(w. motion)* aliquo; **— else** alibi; *(w. motion)* alio
somnolence *s* somnolenti·a -ae *f*

somnolent *adj* somnolent·us -a -um
son *s* fil·ius -(i)i *m*
song *s* cant·us -ūs *m*
son-in-law *s* gen·er -eri *m*
sonorous *adj* sonor·us -a -um
soon *adv* mox, brevi (tempore); **as —as** simulatque; **as — as possible** quam primum
sooner *adv* prius; *(preference)* potius; **— or later** serius ocius
soot *s* fulig·o -inis *f*
soothe *tr* mulcēre, lenire
soothsayer *s* vat·es -is *m*
soothsaying *s* vaticinati·o -onis *f*
sooty *adj* fuliginos·us -a -um
sop *s* offul·a -ae *f*
sophism *s* sophism·a -atis *n*
sophist *s* sophist·es -ae *m*
sophisticated *adj* urban·us -a -um
sophistry *s* capti·o -onis *f*
soporific *adj* soporif·er -era -erum
sorcerer *s* mag·us -i *m*
sorceress *s* mag·a -ae *f*
sorcery *s* magae art·es -ium *fpl*
sordid *adj* sordid·us -a -um
sordidly *adv* sordide
sore *adj (aching)* dol·ens -entis; *(angry)* irat·us -a -um
sore *s* ulc·us -eris *n*
sorely *adv* vehementer
sorrow *s* dol·or -oris *m*
sorrow *intr* dolēre
sorrowful *adj* maest·us -a -um
sorrowfully *adv* maeste
sorry *adj* mis·er -era -erum; **I am — about** me paenitet *(w. gen);* **I feel — for** me miseret *(w. gen)*
sort *s* gen·us -eris *n;* **that — of man** ejus generis *(or* modi) vi·r -ri *m*
sort *tr* digerĕre; *(ballots)* diribēre
sot *s* fatu·us -i *m; (drunkard)* potat·or -oris *m*
soul *s (principle of life)* anim·a -ae *f; (principle of intellection and sensation)* anim·us -i *m;* **not a —** nem·o -inis *m; (human being)* mortal·is -is *m*
sound *adj (healthy)* san·us -a -um; *(strong)* valid·us -a -um; *(e.g., apple)* inte·ger -gra -grum; *(true, genuine)* ver·us -a -um; *(sleep)* art·us -a -um; *(stomach)* firm·us -a -um; **to be of — mind** comp·os -otis mentis esse
sound *s* son·us -i *m; (noise)* strepit·us -ūs *m; (of trumpet)* clang·or -oris *m; (strait)* fret·um -i *n;* **loud —** frag·or -oris *m*
sound *tr* **to — the alarm** classicum canĕre; **to — the signal for battle** bellicum canēre; **to — the retreat** receptui canēre; **to — the trumpet** bucinam inflare ‖ *intr* sonare; *(to seem)* videri; **to — off** clamitare
soundly *adv (of beating)* egregie; *(of sleeping)* arte

soundness s sanit·as -atis f; (firmness) firmit·as -atis f; (correctness) integrit·as -atis f

soup s ju·s -ris n; **noodle** — jus collyricum

sour adj acid·us -a -um, acerb·us -a -um; (fig) amar·us -a -um, moros·us -a -um; **I have a** — **stomach** cibus mihi acescit; **to turn** — acescĕre

source s fon·s -tis m

souse s (sl) potat·or -oris m

soused adj (sl) uvid·us -a -um

south s meridi·es -ei m; **to face** — in meridiem spectare

south adj meridian·us -a -um; — **of** infra (w. acc)

southeast adv inter meridiem et solis ortum

southern adj austral·is -is -e, meridional·is -is -e

southward adv in meridiem

southwest adv inter solis occasum et meridiem

south wind s aus·ter -tri m

souvenir s monument·um -i n

sovereign adj suprem·us -a -um

sovereign s princ·eps -ipis m

sovereignty s principat·us -ūs m

sow s scrof·a -ae f

sow tr serĕre; (a field) conserĕre

sower s sat·or -oris m

space s spat·ium -(i)i n; (of time) intervall·um -i n

spacious adj ampl·us -a -um

spaciousness s amplitud·o -inis f

spade s pal·a -ae f; **to call a** — **a** — quamque rem suo nomine appellare

span s (exent) spat·ium -(i)i n; (measure) palm·us -i m; **brief** — **of life** exigua brevit·as -atis f vitae

spangle s bracte·a -ae f

Spaniard s Hispan·us -a -um

Spanish adj (esp. people) Hispan·us -a -um; (esp. things) Hispanic·us -a -um; (esp. foreign things connected with Spain) Hispaniens·is -is -e; **to speak** — Hispanice loqui

spank tr ferire palmā

spanking s **to get a** — vapulare

spar s tign·um -i n

spar intr dimicare; (fig) digladiari

spare tr parcĕre (w. dat)

spare time s tempor·a -rum npl subsciva

sparing adj parc·us -a -um

sparingly adv parce

spark s scintill·a -ae f; (fig) igniçul·us -i m

sparkle intr scintillare

sparkling adj corusc·us -a -um

sparrow s pass·er -eris m

sparse adj rar·us -a -um

Spartan adj Laconic·us -a -um

spasm s distenti·o -onis f nervorum

spasmodically adv interdum

spatter tr aspergĕre; —**ed with rain and mud** imbre lutoque aspers·us -a -um

spatula s spath·a -ae f

spawn s ov·a -orum npl

spawn intr ova parĕre

speak tr loqui, dicĕre; **to** — **Latin** Latine loqui ‖ intr loqui; **to** — **of** dicĕre de (w. abl); **to** — **to** alloqui (w. acc); **to** — **with** colloqui (w. abl)

speaker s dic·ens -entis mf; (speech maker) orat·or -oris m

spear s hast·a -ae f

spear tr hastā transfigĕre

special adj praecipu·us -a -um

speciality s propriet·as -atis f

specially adv praecipue

species s speci·es -ei f

specific adj cert·us -a -um

specify tr subtiliter enumerare

specimen s exempl·um -i n

specious adj specios·us -a -um

speck s macul·a -ae f

speckled adj maculos·us -a -um

spectacle s spectacul·um -i n

spectator s spectat·or -oris m

specter s larv·a -ae f

spectral adj larval·is -is -e

spectrum s spectr·um -i n

speculate intr conjecturam facĕre; (com) foro uti

speculation s (guess) conjectur·a -ae f; (com) ale·a -ae f

speculative adj conjectural·is -is -e

speculator s contemplat·or -oris m; (com) dardanar·ius -(i)i m

speech s (faculty of speech; address) orati·o -onis f; **to make a** — verba facĕre, orationem habēre

speechless adj elingu·is -is -e; **he was struck** — mutus erat ilico

speed s celerit·as -atis f

speed tr **to** — **up** accelerare ‖ intr properare

speedily adv celeriter

speedy adj cit·us -a -um

spell tr scribĕre

spell s incantament·um -i n

spellbound adj fascinat·us -a -um

spelling s orthographi·a -ae f

spend tr (money, time, effort) impendĕre; (time) agĕre, consumĕre; (w. the idea of waste) terĕre; **to** — **effort, money** (on) operam, pecuniam impendĕre (in + acc or w. dat)

spendthrift s prodig·us -i m

spew tr vomĕre

sphere s sphaer·a -ae f; (fig) provinci·a -ae f

spherical adj sphaeric·us -a -um

sphinx s sphin·x -gis f

spice s condiment·um -i n

spice tr condire

spicy adj a·cer -cris -cre

spider *s* aren·a -ae *f*
spider web *s* arane·um -i *n*
spigot *s* epistom·ium -(i)i *n*
spike *s* clav·us -i *m* tabular·is
spill *tr* effundĕre; **to — blood** sanguinem fundĕre
spin *tr* versare; *(thread)* nēre; **to — a top** turbinem versare; **to — a web** telam texĕre ‖ *intr* versari
spinach *s* spinace·a -ae *f* oleracea
spinal *adj* spinae *(gen)*
spine *s* spin·a -ae *f*
spinster *s* innupt·a -ae *f*
spiral *adj* spiral·is -is -e
spiral *s* spir·a -ae *f*
spirit *s* spirit·us -ūs *m;* anim·us -i *m; (temper, disposition)* ingen·ium -(i)i *n;* **full of —** animos·us -a -um; **—s of the dead** man·es -ium *fpl;* **to be in high —s** hilar·is -is -e esse; **to defend with such —** tam enixe defendĕre
spirited *adj* animos·us -a -um
spiritless *adj* ignav·us -a -um
spiritual *adj* animi *(gen)*
spit *s* ver·u -us *n; (spittle)* sput·um -i *n*
spit *tr* spuĕre; **to — out** exspuĕre ‖ *intr* spuĕre; **to — in s.o.'s face** in faciem *(w. gen)* inspuĕre
spite *tr* offendĕre
spite *s* malevolenti·a -ae *f;* **for —** consulto; **in — of** *(no exact Latin equivalent, sometimes expressed by an abl. absolute, e.g.,* **in — of all the arguments of his opponent, he stuck to this guns** contemptis omnibus adversarii rationibus, in sententia sua perseveravit
spiteful *adj* malevol·us -a -um
splash *tr* aspergĕre; **to — the face with warm water** faciem aquā tepidā fovēre
splash *s* sonit·us -ūs *m* undae; *(display)* ostentati·o -onis *f*
splendid *adj* splendid·us -a -um
splendidly *adv* splendide
splendor *s* splend·or -oris *m*
splint *s* ferul·a -ae *f*
splinter *s* assul·a -ae *f;* **bone —** fragment·um -i *n* ossis
splinter *tr* assulatim findĕre
split *s* fissur·a -ae *f*
split *tr* findĕre; **to — one's sides laughing** ilia sua risu dissolvĕre ‖ *intr* findi
spoil *tr (to make faulty)* vitiare; *(a child)* depravare; *(food)* corrumpĕre ‖ *intr (of food)* corrumpi
spoils *spl* spoli·a -orum *npl*
spoke *s* rad·ius -(i)i *m*
spokesman *s* interpr·es -etis *m*
spondee *s* sponde·us -i *m*
sponge *s* spongi·a -ae *f*
sponge *tr* **to — a meal** cenam captare
sponsor *s* spons·or -oris *m*

sponsor *tr* favēre *(w. dat);* **to — games** ludos edĕre
spontaneity *s* alacrit·as -atis *f*
spontaneous *adj* automat·us -a -um
spontaneously *adv* sponte, ultro
spool *s* fus·us -i *m*
spoon *s* cochle·ar -aris *n*
spoonful *s* cochlearis mensur·a -ae *f*
sporadic *adj* rar·us -a -um
sporadically *adv* dispersim
sport *s* lud·us -i *m*
sport *tr* ostentare
sportive *adj* jocos·us -a -um
sportsman *s* venat·or -oris *m; (fig)* aequus lus·or -oris *m*
spot *s* macul·a -ae *f; (stain)* lab·es -is *f; (place)* loc·us -i *m;* **on the — *(immediately)*** ilico; *(in trouble)* in angustiis; **to the same —** eodem
spot *tr* conspicĕre
spotless *adj* immaculat·us -a -um
spotted *adj* maculos·us -a -um
spouse *s* conju(n)·x -gis *mf*
spout *s (rain spout)* o·s -ris *n* canalis; *(of jug)* o·s -ris *n*
spout *tr* ejaculare; *(speeches)* declamare ‖ *intr* emicare
sprain *tr* intorquēre; **to — an ankle** talum intorquēre
sprawl *intr* se fundĕre
spray *s* asperg·o -inis *f*
spray *tr* aspergĕre
spread *tr* pandĕre; *(to make known)* divulgare; **to — a blanket on the floor** extendĕre lodiculam in pavimento ‖ *intr* patēre; *(of rumor)* percrebrescĕre; *(of disease)* serpĕre
spread *s (ranch)* latifund·ium -(i)i *n*
sprig *s* ramul·us -i *m*
sprightly *adj* veget·us -a -um
spring *s (season)* ve·r -ris *n; (leap)* salt·us -ūs *m; (of water)* scaturg·o -inis *f,* fon·s -tis *m*
spring *adj* vern·us -a -um
spring *tr* **to — a leak** rimas agĕre ‖ *intr (to come from)* oriri, enasci; *(of rivers, etc.)* exoriri; *(to leap)* salire; **to — down** desilire; **to suddenly — open** subito se pandĕre
springboard *s* petaur·us -i *m*
springtime *s* vernum temp·us -oris *n*
sprinkle *tr* spargĕre; **to — s.th. on** inspergĕre aliquid *(w. dat or super + acc)* ‖ *intr* rorare
sprout *s* pull·us -i *m*
sprout *intr* pullulare
spruce *adj* laut·us -a -um
spruce *tr* **to — up** mundare ‖ *intr* **to — up** se mundare
spur *s* calc·ar -aris *n; (fig)* incitament·um -i *n;* **on the — of the moment** de improviso
spur *tr (a horse)* calcaribus concitare; *(fig)* urgēre, stimulare

spurious *adj* spuri·us -a -um
spurn *tr* spernĕre
spurt *intr* emicare
sputter *intr* balbutire
spy *s* speculat·or -oris *m*
spy *intr* speculari
squabble *s* rix·a -ae *f*
squabble *intr* rixari
squad *s* manipul·us -i *m*
squadron *s* (*of cavalry*) turm·a -ae *f*; (*of ships*) class·is -is *f*
squalid *adj* squalid·us -a -um
squall *s* procell·a -ae *f*
squalor *s* squal·or -oris *m*
squander *tr* dissipare
squanderer *s* prodig·us -i *m*
square *adj* quadrat·us -a -um; (*fig*) honest·us -a -um; — **foot** quadratus pe·s pedis *m*; — **meal** largior cib·us -i *m*
square *s* quadrat·um -i *n*; (*tool*) norm·a -ae *f*
square *tr* (*math*) quadrare ‖ *intr* convenire, congruĕre; **to — off** pugnis minitari
squash *tr* conterĕre
squash *s* cucurbit·a -ae *f*
squat *intr* subsidĕre
squat *adj* parv·us atque obes·us -a -um
squeak *intr* stridēre
squeak *s* strid·or -oris *m*
squeamish *adj* fastidios·us -a -um; **to feel —** fastidire
squeeze *tr* comprimĕre; **to — out** exprimĕre
squint *intr* strabo esse
squint-eyed *adj* paet·us -a -um
squire *s* armig·er -eri *m*
squirrel *s* sciur·us -i *m*
squirt *tr* projicĕre ‖ *intr* emicare
stab *s* punct·a -ae *f*
stab *tr* fodĕre, perforare
stability *s* stabilit·as -atis *f*
stabilize *tr* stabilire, firmare
stable *adj* stabil·is -is -e
stable *s* stabul·um -i *n*; (*for horses*) equil·e -is *n*; (*for cows, oxen*) bubil·e -is *n*; (*of boxers, gladiators*) famili·a -ae *f*
stack *s* acerv·us -i *m*, stru·es -is *f*
stack *tr* coacervare
staff *s* scipi·o -onis *m*; (*of a magistrate*) contubern·ium -(i)i *n*
staff member, staff officer *s* contubernal·is -is *m*
stag *s* cerv·us -i *m*
stag party *s* conviv·ium -(i)i *n* sine feminis
stage *s* (*theat*) scaen·a -ae *f*; (*degree*) grad·us -ūs *m*; **during the early —s of** inter initia (*w. gen*); — **of life** par·s -tis *f* aetatis
stage play *s* lud·us -i *m* scaenicus
stagger *tr* obstupefacĕre ‖ *intr* titubare

stagnant *adj* stagn·ans -antis; (*fig*) in·ers -ertis
stagnate *intr* stagnare
stagnation *s* cessati·o -onis *f*
stain *s* lab·es -is *f*, macul·a -ae *f*
stain *tr* maculare; (*to dye*) tingĕre
stainless *adj* immaculat·us -a -um
stair *s* grad·us -ūs *m*; — **s** scal·ae -arum *fpl*, grad·ūs -uum *mpl*; **to climb the —** per gradūs ascendĕre
staircase *s* scal·ae -arum *fpl*
stake *s* pal·us -i *m*; (*wager*) deposit·um -i *n*; **to be at —** agi
stake *tr* deponĕre; **to burn at the —** ad palum igni interficĕre
stale *adj* vet·us -eris; (*bread*) secund·us -a -um, hestern·us -a -um
stalk *s* (*of plant*) caul·is -is *m*; (*of grain*) calam·us -i *m*; — **of asparagus** stirp·s -itis *m* asparagi
stalk *tr* (*game*) venari; (*a person*) insidiis persequi
stall *s* stabul·um -i *n*; (*small shop*) tabern·a -ae *f*
stall *tr* sistĕre ‖ *intr* consistĕre
stallion *s* admissar·ius -(i)i *m*
stamina *s* patienti·a -ae *f*
stammer *tr* & *intr* balbutire
stammering *adj* balb·us -a -um
stammering *s* balbuti·es -ei *f*
stamp *s* (*mark*) not·a -ae *f*; (*impression made*) impressi·o -onis *f*; — **of the foot** subplosi·o -onis *f* pedis; (*on a letter*) imag·o -inis *f*
stamp *tr* imprimĕre, notare; (*money*) cudĕre; (*feet*) supplodĕre
stance *s* stat·us -ūs *m*; **to take the — of a fighter** statum proeliantis componĕre
stand *s* (*board with three legs*) tripes mens·a -ae *f*; (*platform*) suggest·us -ūs *m*; (*halt*) mor·a -ae *f*; **to make a — against** restare adversus (*w. acc*)
stand *tr* (*to set upright*) statuĕre; (*to tolerate*) tolerare; **to — one's ground** perstare; **to — one's ground against** subsistĕre (*w. dat*) ‖ *intr* stare; **to keep —ing** perstare; **to — aloof** abstare; **to — at the door** adsistĕre ad fores; **to — by** adesse (*w. dat*); **to — by one's promises** promissis manēre; **to — by one's word** in fide stare; **to — close to** adsistĕre ad (*w. acc*); **to — fast** consistĕre; **to — for office** honorem petĕre; **to — in awe of** in metu habēre; **to — in the way of** obstare (*w. dat*); **to — in need of** indigēre (*w. abl*); **to — on end** (*of hair*) inhorrescĕre; **to — out** exstare, eminēre; **to — still** consistĕre; **to — up** surgĕre; **to — up for s.o.** alicui adesse; **to — up to anyone** coram alicui resistĕre
standard *adj* solit·us -a -um

standard s norm·a -ae f, mensur·a -ae f; (mil) vexill·um -i n

standard-bearer s vexillar·ius -(i)i m

standard of living s consuetud·o -inis f victūs

stand-in s vicar·ius -(i)i m

standing s stat·us -ūs m; **of long —** vet·us -eris

standing adj perpetu·us -a -um

standstill s **to be at a —** haerēre; **to come to a —** consistĕre

stanza s vers·us -ūs m; (of four lines) tetrastich·on -i n

staple adj necessari·us -a -um; (chief) praecipu·us -a -um; **—s** vict·us -ūs m

star s stell·a -ae f, sid·us -eris n; (fig) lum·en -inis n

star intr (theat) primas partes agĕre

starch s amyl·um -i n

starch tr amylare

stare s obtut·us -ūs m

stare intr stupēre; **to — at** intueri

stark adj rigid·us -a -um

stark adv omnino, penitus

starlight s siderum lum·en -inis n

starling s sturn·us -i m

starry adj sidere·us -a -um

start s init·ium -(i)i n; (sudden movement) salt·us -ūs m; (of journey) profecti·o -onis f; **to get a — on s.o.** occupare aliquem; **to get off to a bad —** initia male ponĕre; **to have a two-day — on s.o.** biduo antecessĕre aliquem

start tr incipĕre, instituĕre ‖ intr incipĕre, (ex)oridiri; (to take fright) resilire; **to — out** proficisci

starting gate s carcer·es -um mpl

startle tr territare

starvation s fam·es -is f; **to go on a — diet** abstin·ax -acis esse

starve tr fame interficĕre ‖ intr fame confici

state s stat·us -ūs m; (pol) civit·as -atis f, respublica (gen: reipublicae) f; **— of affairs** re·s -rum fpl; **to be in a better —** in meliore loco esse; **to be in a worse —** deteriore statu esse; **to restore s.th. to its former —** in pristinum statum aliquid restituĕre

state tr affirmare; (of writers) auctor esse; (in writing) scribĕre

statement s dict·um -i n, affirmati·o -onis f; (of a witness in court) testimon·ium -(i)i n; **to make a —** profiteri

statesman s vir m reipublicae administrandae peritus

statesmanship s ar·s -tis f reipublicae administrandae

station s stati·o -onis f

station tr locare, disponĕre

stationary adj stabil·is -is -e, immot·us -a -um

stationery s re·s -rum fpl scriptoriae

stationery store s tabern·a -ae f chartaria

statistics spl cens·us -ūs m

statue s statu·a -ae f, sign·um -i n

stature s statur·a -ae f

status quo s praesens stat·us -ūs m

statute s constitut·um -i n

staunch adj fid·us -a -um, firm·us -a -um

staunch tr **to — the flow of blood** sanguinem cohibēre

stave tr **to — off** arcēre

stay tr detinēre; (to curb) coercēre ‖ intr manēre, commorari; **to — at home** se continēre; **to — away from** abstinēre (w. abl)

stay s (sojourn) mansi·o -onis f; (delay) mor·a -ae f; (prop) fulcr·um -i n; **— of execution** prolati·o -onis f supplicii extremi

steadfast adj const·ans -antis

steadfastly adv constanter

steadily adv firme, constanter

steadiness s constanti·a -ae f

steady adj stabil·is -is -e, firm·us -a -um; (fig) const·ans -antis; **— weather** aequales tempestat·es -um fpl

steak s off·a -ae f bubula

steal tr furari ‖ intr furari; **to — away** se subducĕre

stealth s furt·um -i n; **by —** furtim

stealthily adv furtim

stealthy adj furtiv·us -a -um

steam s vap·or -oris m, fum·us -i m

steam intr vaporare, fumare

steam bath s sudator·ium -(i)i n

steam pipe s vaporar·ium -(i)i n

steed s equ·us -i m bellator

steel s chalyb·s -is m

steel tr **to — oneself against** obdurescĕre contra (w. acc)

steep adj ardu·us -a -um

steep tr madefacĕre; **—ed in crime** inquinat·us -a -um sceleribus

steeple s turr·is -is f

steepness s arduit·as -atis f

steer s juvenc·us -i m

steer tr gubernare, dirigĕre

steering s gubernati·o -onis f

stem s stirp·s -is f; (of a ship) pror·a -ae f

stem tr obsistĕre (w. dat)

stench s foet·or -oris m

step s pass·us -ūs m, grad·us ūs m; (measure) rati·o -onis f, **flight of —s** scal·ae -arum fpl; **— by —** gradatim

step intr gradi

stepbrother s (on father's side) vitrici fil·ius -(i)i m; (on mother's side) novercae fil·ius -(i)i m

stepdaughter *s* privign·a -ae *f*
stepfather *s* vitric·us -i *m*
stepmother *s* noverc·a -ae *f*
stepson *s* privign·us -i *m*
sterile *adj* steril·is -is -e
sterility *s* sterilit·as -atis *f*
sterling *adj* ver·us -a -um
stern *adj* sever·us -a -um
sternly *adv* severe
sternness *s* severit·as -atis *f*
stew *s* carn·es -ium *fpl* cum condimentis elixae; **to be in a —** turbid·us -a -um animi esse
stew *tr* lento igne coquĕre
steward *s* procurat·or -oris *m; (of country estate)* villic·us -i *m*
stewardship *s* procurati·o -onis *f*
stick *s* fust·is -is *m; (cane)* bacul·um -i *n*
stick *tr* figĕre; **to — out a foot on s.o.** *(in order to trip)* pedem alicui opponĕre; **to —one's neck in the noose** cervices nodo condĕre **‖** *intr* haerēre, haesitare; **to — to the usual order** ordinem conservare; **to — to the truth** in veritate manēre; **to — out** eminēre
sticky *adj* viscos·us -a -um
stiff *adj* rigid·us -a -um; *(formal)* frigid·us -a -um
stiffly *adv* rigide; frigide
stiffen *tr* rigid·um -am -um facĕre; *(w. starch)* amylare **‖** *intr* obdurescĕre
stifle *tr* suffocare; *(fig)* opprimĕre
stigma *s* stigm·a -atis *n,* not·a -ae *f*
stigmatize *tr* notare
still *adj* quiet·us -a -um
still *adv (adversative)* tamen; *(as yet)* adhuc, etiamnum; *(w. comparatives)* etiam, etiamnum
still *tr* pacare, sedare
stillborn *adj* abortiv·us -a -um
stillness *s (silence)* silent·ium -(i)i *n; (quiet)* qui·es -etis *f*
stilts *spl* grall·ae -arum *fpl*
stimulant *s* irritament·um -i *n*
stimulate *tr* stimulare
stimulus *s* stimul·us -i *m*
sting *s (on an insect)* acule·us -i *m; (bite)* ict·us -ūs *m; (of conscience)* ang·or -oris *m*
sting *tr (of a bee)* icĕre; *(fig)* mordēre **‖** *intr (to hurt)* dolēre
stinginess *s* sord·es -ium *fpl*
stingy *adj* sordid·us -a -um
stink *s* foet·or -oris *m*
stink *intr* foetēre; **to — of garlic** obolēre allium
stinky *adj* foetid·us -a -um
stint *s* **without — or measure** sine modo aut mensurā
stint *tr* coercēre
stipend *s* salar·ium -(i)i *n*

stipulate *tr* stipulari
stipulation *s* stipulati·o -onis *f;* **with the — that** eā condicione ut
stir *s* tumult·us -ūs *m*
stir *tr* excitare **‖** *intr* se movēre
stirring *adj* ad movendos animos apt·us -a -um
stitch *tr* suĕre
stitch *s* tract·us -ūs *m* acūs; **— in the side** subitus lateris dol·or -oris *m*
stock *s (supply)* copi·a -ae *f; (race)* gen·us -eris *n; (handle)* lign·um -i *n;* **to take — of** permetiri
stock *tr (to provide with)* instruĕre; *(to store)* condĕre; **to —a fishpond** piscinam frequentare
stockade *s* vall·um *n*
stocking *s* tibial·e -is *n*
Stoic *adj* Stoic·us -a -um
Stoic *s* Stoic·us -i *m*
stoical *adj* dur·us -a -um
Stoicism *s* Stoica disciplin·a -ae *f*
stole *s* amict·us -ūs *m*
stolen *adj* furtiv·us -a -um; **— goods** furt·a -orum *npl*
stomach *s* stomach·us -i *m;* **to have — trouble** a stomacho laborare
stomach *tr* tolerare
stone *s* lap·is -idis *m,* sax·um -i *n*
stone *tr* lapidare
stonecutter *s* lapicid·a -ae *m*
stone quarry *s* lapidicin·a -ae *f*
stony *adj (full of stones)* lapidos·us -a -um; *(fig)* dur·us -a -um
stool *s (bench)* scabell·um -i *n; (feces)* alv·us -i *f;* **when the — is not passed** ubi alvus non descendit
stoop *intr* proclinare; *(fig)* se summittĕre
stop *tr* sistĕre **‖** *intr* consistĕre; *(to cease)* desistĕre; **to — off at Rome** Romae subsistĕre
stop *s* mor·a -ae *f;* **to come to a —** consistĕre; **to put a —** **to** comprimĕre
stopgap *s* tibic·en -inis *m*
stoppage *s* obstructi·o -onis *f*
stopper *s* obturament·um -i *n*
store *s (supply)* copi·a -ae *f; (shop)* tabern·a -ae *f*
store *tr* condĕre, reponĕre
storehouse *s* promptuar·ium -(i)i *n; (for grain)* horre·um -i *n; (fig)* thesaur·us -i *m*
stork *s* ciconi·a -ae *f*
storm *s* tempest·as -atis *f*
storm *tr* expugnare **‖** *intr* desaevire; **to come —ing** in se infundĕre
stormy *adj* turbid·us -a -um; *(fig)* tumultuos·us -a -um
story *s* fabul·a -ae *f; (of a building)* tabulat·um -i *n*
storyteller *s* narrat·or -oris *m*
stout *adj* corpulent·us -a -um, plen·us

-a -um; *(brave)* fort·is -is -e; *(strong)* valid·us -a -um

stoutly *adv* fortiter

stove *s* foc·us -i *m*

stow *tr* condĕre ‖ *intr* **to — away** in navi delitescĕre

straddle *tr* cruribus varicatis insistĕre super *(w. acc)*

straggle *intr* palari; **to — over the countryside** palari per agros

straggler *s* palat·us -i *m*

straggly *adj* **— beard** horrida barb·a -ae *f*

straight *adj* rect·us -a -um, direct·us -a -um; **— as a line** lineae modo rect·us -a -um

straight *adv* directo, rectā

straighten *tr* rect·um -am -um facĕre; **to — out** corrigĕre

straightforward *adj* apert·us -a -um

straightway *adv* statim

strain *tr* contendĕre; *(muscle)* luxare; *(to filter)* percolare ‖ *intr* eniti

strain *s* contenti·o -onis *f; (effort)* lab·or -oris *m; (mus)* mod·us -i *m*

strained *adj (style)* arcessit·us -a -um

strainer *s* col·um -i *n*

strait *s* fret·um -i *n;* **to be in dire —s** in angustiis esse

strand *s (of hair)* flocc·us -i *m*

strand *tr* vadis illidĕre

strange *adj* nov·us -a -um, insolit·us -a -um; *(foreign)* peregrin·us -a -um; **— to say** mirabile dictu

strangely *adv* mirum in modum

strangeness *s* novit·as -atis *f*

stranger *s* peregrin·us -i *m;* **a perfect — ** omnino ignot·us -i *m*

strangle *tr* strangulare

strap *s* lor·um -i *n*

stratagem *s* stratagem·a -atis *n*

strategic *adj* bellic·us -a -um

strategy *s* consil·ium -(i)i *n*

straw *adj* stramentici·us -a -um

straw *s* strament·um -i *n; (a single stalk)* culm·us -i *m; (for drinking)* fistul·a -ae *f;* **cottages thatched with — ** cas·ae -arum *fpl* stramento tectae

strawberry *s* frag·um -i *n*

strawberry-blond *adj* fulv·us -a -um

stray *intr* errare, aberrare

stray *adj* err·ans -antis

streak *s* line·a -ae *f; (of character)* ven·a -ae *f*

streak *tr* line·is distinguĕre

stream *s* flum·en -inis *n;* **—s of sweat** riv·i -orum *mpl* sudoris

stream *intr* se effundĕre

streamer *s* vexill·um -i *n*

street *s* vi·a -ae *f; (in city)* vic·us -i *m; (very narrow)* tram·es -itis *m*

street clothes *spl* forens·ia -ium *npl*

street walker *s* muli·er -eris *f* secutuleia

strength *s* vir·es -ium *fpl*

strengthen *tr* confirmare

strenuous *adj* strenu·us -a -um

strenuously *adv* strenue

stress *s (accent)* ict·us -ūs *m; (emphasis)* vis *f; (tension)* tensi·o -onis *f; (importance)* pond·us -eris *n;* **not to lay much — upon a matter** aliquid levi momento aestimare; **to lay — on trifles** addĕre pondus nugis

stress *tr* exprimĕre

stretch *tr* tendĕre; *(to tighten what is already stretched)* contendĕre; *(in different directions)* distendĕre; *(to elongate, e.g., the skin)* producĕre; **to — or relax the muscles** nervos intendĕre aut remittĕre; **to — out the hand to** *(to help s.o.)* manum intendĕre *(w. dat);* **to — the legs** crura in longitudinem extendĕre ‖ *intr* extendi, distendi; *(geog)* tendĕre *(of a person while yawning)* pandiculari; **to — out on the couch** se extendĕre super torum

stretch *s* tract·us -ūs *m*

stretcher *s* lecticul·a -ae *f*

strew *tr* spargĕre, sternĕre

stricken *adj* afflict·us -a -um

strict *adj (severe)* sever·us -a -um; *(accurate)* dilig·ens -entis; **according to the — letter of the law** summo jure; **— meaning of the word** verbi sens·us -ūs *m* proprius; **— truth** verit·as -atis *f* ipsa

strictly *adv* severe; *(carefully)* diligenter; **— speaking** proprie

stricture *s* vituperati·o -onis *f*

stride *s* pass·us -ūs *m* grandis

stride *intr* procedĕre passibus grandibus

strife *s* jurg·ium -(i)i *n*

strike *tr* ferire, percutĕre, icĕre; **I was struck by his boldness** miratus sum audaciam ejus; **struck blind** oculis capt·us -a -um; **struck by lightning** de caelo percuss·us -a -um; **to — a bargain, deal** pacisci; **to — fear into s.o.** incutere timorem in *(w. acc)* ‖ *intr (of workers)* opere faciendo cessare

strike *s* cessati·o -onis *f* operis; *(blow)* ict·us -ūs *m*

striking *adj* insign·is -is -e

strikingly *adv* mirum in modum

string *s* fil·um -i *n; (for bow)* nerv·us -i *m; (mus)* chord·a -ae *f; (fig)* seri·es -ei *f;* **— of pearls** line·a -ae *f* margaritarum

string *tr (a bow)* intendĕre; **to — together** colligare

stringent *adj* sever·us -a -um

stringy *adj* fibrat·us -a -um

strip *tr* (de)nudare, spoliare; **to — off**

(clothes) exuĕre; *(e.g., a tribune of power)* privare; *(of rights)* nudare ‖ *intr* se exuĕre vestibus
strip *s (of cloth; of land)* lacini·a -ae *f; (of paper)* sched·a -ae *f*
stripe *s (streak)* lim·es -itis *m; (welt)* vib·ex -icis *m; (blow)* ict·us -ūs *m; (on toga)* clav·us -i *m*
stripped *adj (e.g., for flogging)* despoliat·us -a -um
strive *intr (after, for)* niti (ad *or* in + *acc*)
striving *s* contenti·o -onis *f*
stroke *s* ict·us -ūs *m,* plag·a -ae *f; (of oar)* puls·us -ūs *m;* — **of luck** lus·us -ūs *m* fortunae mirabilis; — **of the pen** pennae duct·us -ūs *m*
stroke *tr* (per)mulcēre
stroll *s* ambulati·o -onis *f;* **to take a —** spatiari
stroll *intr* spatiari
strong *adj (body, remedy)* valid·us -a -um; *(smell)* grav·is -is -e; *(powerful)* pot·ens -entis; *(feeling)* a·cer -cris -cre; *(language)* vehem·ens -entis
strongly *adv* valide, vehementer
stronghold *s* castell·um -i *n*
structure *s* structur·a -ae *f; (building)* aedific·ium -(i)i *n*
struggle *s* certam·en -inis *f,* pugn·a -ae *f; (fig)* luctati·o -onis *f*
struggle *intr* contendĕre, luctari
strum *tr* pulsare
strumpet *s* scort·um -i *n*
strut *s* incess·us -ūs *m* magnificus
strut *intr* magnifice incedĕre
stubble *s* stipul·a -ae *f*
stubborn *adj* obstinat·us -a -um
stubbornly *adv* obstinate
stubbornness *s* obstinati·o -onis *f*
stuck-up *adj* vultuos·us -a -um
stud *s* clav·us -i *m; (horse)* admissar·ius -(i)i *m*
student *s* discipul·us -i *m,* discipul·a -ae *f; (at university)* scholastic·us -i *m*
studied *adj* meditat·us -a -um
studious *adj* studios·us -a -um discendi
study *s* stud·ium -(i)i *n; (room)* tablin·um -i *n*
study *tr* studēre *(w. dat); (to scrutinize)* perscrutari ‖ *intr* studēre; *(at night)* lucubrare; **to — under a teacher of rhetoric** operam dare dicendi magistro
stuff *s* materi·a -ae *f*
stuff *tr* farcire; *(w. food)* saginare; **to — it down s.o.'s throat** saginare aliquem recusantem
stuffing *s (in cooking)* fart·um -i *n; (in pillow, uphostery)* toment·um -i *n*
stultify *tr* ad irritum redigĕre
stumble *intr* offendĕre· **to — upon** incidĕre in *(w. acc)*

stumbling block *s* offensi·o -onis *f*
stump *s* caud·ex -icis *m*
stun *tr* stupefacĕre; *(fig)* obstupefacĕre
stunted *adj* curt·us -a -um
stupefy *tr* obstupefacĕre
stupendous *adj* permir·us -a -um
stupid *adj* stupid·us -a -um
stupidity *s* stupidit·as -atis *f*
stupidly *adv* stupide
stupor *s* stup·or -oris *m*
sturdiness *s* firmit·as -atis *f*
sturdy *adj* firm·us -a -um
sturgeon *s* acipens·er -eris *m*
stutter *intr* balbutire
stutterer *s* balb·us -i *m*
stye *s* suil·e -is *n*
style *s (kind, manner)* gen·us -eris *n; (literary)* scribendi genus *n; (rhetorical)* dicendi genus *n; (architectural)* structurae genus *n; (of dress)* habit·us -ūs *m;* **in the new —** novo more
style *tr* vocare, nominare
stylish *adj* specios·us -a -um
suave *adj* suav·is -is -e
subdivide *tr* iterum dividĕre
subdivision *s* par·s -tis *f*
subdue *tr* subjicĕre
subject *adj* subject·us -a -um; — **to** subjectus *(w. dat); (disease)* obnoxi·us -a -um *(w. dat)*
subject *tr* subjicĕre, subigĕre
subject *s* subject·us -i *m,* civ·is -is *m; (topic)* res, rei *f,* argument·um -i *n; (gram)* subject·um -i *n*
subjection *s* servit·us -utis *f*
subjective *adj* propri·us -a -um
subjugate *tr* subigĕre
subjunctive *s* subjunctivus mod·us -i *m*
sublime *adj* sublim·is -is -e
sublimely *adv* excelse
submerge *tr* demergĕre, inundare ‖ *intr* se demergĕre
submission *s* obsequ·ium -(i)i *n*
submissive *adj* summiss·us -a -um
submissively *adv* summisse
submit *tr (e.g., a proposal)* referre ‖ *intr* se submittĕre; **to — to** obtemperare *(w. dat)*
subordinate *tr* subjicĕre, supponĕre
subordinate *adj* subject·us -a -um
suborn *tr* subornare
subscribe *intr* **to — to** *(to agree with)* assentiri *(w. dat); (a magazine)* nomine subscripto profiteri se empturum esse *(w. acc)*
subscriber *s* subscript·or -oris *m*
subscription *s* collati·o -onis *f*
subsequent *adj* sequ·ens -entis
subsequently *adv* deinde, postea
subservient *adj* obsequios·us -a -um
subside *intr (of panic, the sea, wind)* desidĕre; *(of passion)* defervescĕre

subsidiary *adj* subsidiari·us -a -um
subsidy *s* subsid·ium -(i)i *n*
subsist *intr* subsistĕre
subsistence *s* vict·us -ūs *m*
substance *s* substanti·a -ae *f; (wealth)* res, rei *f; (gist)* summ·a -ae *f*
substantial *adj* solid·us -a -um; *(real)* ver·us -a -um; *(rich)* opulent·us -a -um; *(important)* magn·us -a -um; *(meal)* plen·us -a -um
substantially *adv* magnā ex parte
substantiate *tr* confirmare
substantive *s* substantiv·um -i *n*
substitute *s* vicar·ius -(i)i *m; as a —* in vicem; **I will go as a — for you** ibo pro te
substitute *tr* **(for)** substituĕre (pro + *abl*), supponĕre (pro + *abl*)
substitution *s* substituti·o -onis *f*
subterfuge *s* perfug·ium -(i)i *n*
subterranean *adj* subterrane·us -a -um
subtle *adj* subtil·is -is -e
subtlety *s* subtilit·as -atis *f*
subtract *tr* deducĕre; **to — the interest paid from the capital** de capite deducĕre quod usuris pernumeratum est
subtraction *s* deducti·o -onis *f*
suburb *s* suburb·ium -(i)i *n*
suburban *adj* suburban·us -a -um
subversion *s* eversi·o -onis *f*
subversive *adj* seditios·us -a -um
subvert *tr* evertĕre
succeed *tr* succedĕre *(w. dat),* insequi **‖** *intr (of persons)* rem bene gerĕre; *(of activities)* prospere evenire
success *s* success·us -ūs *m*
successful *adj (of persons)* fel·ix -icis; *(of things)* prosp·er -era -erum
successfully *adv* prospere, fortunate
succession *s* successi·o -onis *f; (series)* seri·es -ei *f*
successive *adj* continu·us -a -um; **on five — nights** quinque continuis noctibus
successor *s* success·or -oris *m*
succinct *adj* press·us -a -um
succinctly *adv* presse
succor *s* subsid·ium -(i)i *n*
succor *tr* succurrĕre *(w. dat)*
succulence *s* suc·us -i *m*
succulent *adj* suculent·us -a -um
succumb *intr* succumbĕre
such *adj* tal·is -is -e; **—...as** tal·is...qualis
suck *tr* sugĕre; **to — dry** ebibĕre; **to — in** sorbēre; **to — up** exsorbēre
sucker *s (fool)* barcal·a -ae *mf; (bot)* surcul·us -i *m*
suckle *tr* alĕre, mammam dare *(w. dat)*
suction *s* suct·us -ūs *m*
suction cup *s* cucurbitul·a -ae *f*
sudden *adj* subit·us -a -um
suddenly *adv* subito

suds *spl* aqu·a -ae *f* sapone infecta
sue *tr* litem intendĕre *(dat)* **‖** *intr* petĕre
suffer *tr* pati, tolerare; **to — the punishment** poenam dare **‖** *intr* pati; **to — from** laborare *(w. abl);* **—ing from** oppress·us -a -um *(w. abl)*
sufferable *adj* tolerabil·is -is -e
suffering *s* dol·or -oris *m*
suffice *intr* sufficĕre, satis esse
sufficient *adj* satis *(w. gen)*
sufficiently *adv* satis
suffocate *tr* suffocare **‖** *intr* suffocari
suffocation *s* suffocati·o -onis *f*
sugar *s* sacchar·um -i *n*
sugar *tr* saccharo condire
sugar cane *s* arund·o -inis *f* sacchari
suggest *tr* suggerĕre
suggestion *s* suggesti·o -onis *f*
suicide *s* mor·s -tis *f* voluntaria; **to commit —** sibi mortem consciscĕre
suit *s* li·s -tis *f;* **— of clothes** synthes·is -is *f*
suit *tr* accommodare, convenire *(w. dat);* **not —** displicēre *(w. dat)*
suitable *adj* apt·us -a -um
suitcase *s* vidul·us -i *m*
suite *s (apartment)* diaet·a -ae *f; (retinue)* comitat·us -ūs *m*
suitor *s* proc·us -i *m*
sulfur *s* sulf·ur -uris *n*
sulk *intr* aegre ferre
sulky *adj* moros·us -a -um
sullen *adj* contum·ax -acis
sullenly *adv* best expressed by the adjective
sully *tr* inquinare
sultry *adj* aestuos·us -a -um
sum *s* summ·a -ae *f;* **for a large —** magni *or* magno; **for a small —** parvi *or* parvo; **— and substance of a letter** cap·ut -itis *n* litterarum; **— total** summ·a -ae *f* summarum
sum *tr* **to — up** computare; *(to summarize)* summatim describĕre
summarily *adv* summatim
summarize *tr* summatim describĕre
summary *s* summar·ium -(i)i *n*
summer *s* aest·as -atis *f*
summer *adj* aestiv·us -a -um
summit *s* culm·en -inis *n; (fig)* fastig·ium -(i)i *n*
summon *tr* arcessĕre; *(meeting)* convocare; **—ed as a witness** citat·us -a -um testis; **to — to an inquiry** vocare ad disquisitionem; **to — up courage** animum erigĕre
summons *s (leg)* vocati·o -onis *f*
sumptuary *adj* sumptuari·us -a -um
sumptuous *adj* sumptuos·us -a -um
sumptuously *adv* sumptuose
sun *s* sol, solis *m*
sun *tr* **to — oneself** apricari
sunbeam *s* rad·ius -(i)i *m* solis

sunburnt *adj* adust·us -a -um
Sunday *s* di·es -ei *m* solis; *(eccl)* Dominic·a -ae *f*
sunder *tr* separare
sundial *s* solar·ium -(i)i *n*
sundry *adj* divers·i -ae -a
sunflower *s* helianth·us -i *m*
sunken *adj* depress·us -a -um
sunlight *s* sol, solis *m*
sunny *adj* apric·us -a -um
sunrise *s* solis ort·us -ūs *m*
sunset *s* solis occas·us -ūs *m*
sunshine *s* sol, solis *m*
superabundant *adj* nimi·us -a -um
superabundantly *adv* satis superque
superb *adj* magnific·us -a -um
superbly *adv* magnifice
supercilious *adj* superb·us -a -um
superficial *adj* *(fig)* lěv·is -is -e; — **wound** vuln·us -eris *n* quod in summa parte est
superfluity *s* redundanti·a -ae *f*
superfluous *adj* supervacane·us -a -um; **to be regarded as** — pro supervacuo haberi
superhuman *adj* divin·us -a -um; *(fig)* incredibil·is -is -e; — **form** form·a -ae *f* major humanā
superintend *tr* praeesse *(w. dat)*
superintendence *s* cur·a -ae *f*
superintendent *s* curat·or -oris *m; (of an apt.bldg)* procurat·or -oris *m* insulae
superior *adj* super·ior -ior -ius; **to be — in cavalry** plus valēre equitatu
superior *s* praeposit·us -i *m*, qui praeest
superiority *s* praestanti·a -ae *f*
superlative *adj* eximi·us -a -um; *(gram)* superlativ·us -a -um
supernatural *adj* divin·us -a -um; supra naturam
supersede *tr* succeděre *(w. dat)*
superstition *s* superstiti·o -onis *f*
superstitious *adj* superstitios·us -a -um
supervise *tr* procurare
supervision *s* cur·a -ae *f*
supine *adj* supin·us -a -um
supine *s* supin·um -i *n*
supper *s* cen·a -ae *f; after* — cenat·us -a -um; **to eat** — cenare
supple *adj* flexibil·is -is -e
supplement *s* supplement·um -i *n*
supplement *tr* amplificare
suppliant *s* suppl·ex -icis *mf*
supplicate *tr* supplicare
supplication *s* supplicati·o -onis *f*
supplied *adj* **well — with** copios·us -a -um *(w. abl)*
supply *s* copi·a -ae *f;* **supplies** *(mil)* commeat·us -ūs *m*
supply *tr* *(to furnish)* praebēre, suppeditare; *(to fill up)* supplēre; **to be supplied with** suppeditare *(w. abl)*

support *s* *(prop)* fulcr·um -i *n; (help)* subsid·ium -(i)i *n; (maintenance)* aliment·um -i *n; (backing)* stud·ium -(i)i *n*
support *tr* *(to hold up)* fulcire, sustinēre; *(to maintain)* alěre; *(children)* *(leg)* exhibēre; *(to help)* adjuvare
supportable *adj* tolerabil·is -is -e
supporter *s* faut·or -oris *m; (pol)* suffragat·or -oris *m*
suppose *tr* & *intr* opinari, putare
supposition *s* opini·o -onis *f*
suppress *tr* compriměre; *(for a time)* repriměre; *(information)* oppriměre
suppression *s* suppressi·o -onis *f*
supremacy *s* dominat·us -ūs *m; (supreme power)* imper·ium -(i)i *n;* **to exercise** — dominari
supreme *adj* suprem·us -a -um, summ·us -a -um
supremely *adv* unice, maxime
sure *adj* cert·us -a -um; *(faithful)* fid·us -a -um; **I am** — mihi persuadeo
surely *adv* certe, profecto
surf *s* aest·us -ūs *m*
surface *s* superfici·es -ei *f;* — **of the sea** summum mar·e -is *n*
surfeit *s* satiet·as -atis *f*
surfeit *tr* saturare; *(fig)* satiare
surge *s* aest·us -ūs *m*
surge *intr* surgěre, tumescěre; **to — forward** proruěre
surgeon *s* chirург·us -i *m*
surgery *s* chirugi·a -ae *f*
surgical *adj* chirurgic·us -a -um
surly *adj* moros·us -a -um et difficıl·is -is -e
surmise *s* conjectur·a -ae *f;* **to make** — *s* opinari
surmise *tr* conjicěre
surmount *tr* superare
surmountable *adj* superabil·is -is -e
surname *s* cognom·en -inis *n*
surpass *tr* superare, exceděre
surplus *s* residu·um -i *n*
surprise *s* *(feeling)* mirati·o -onis *f; (thing)* mir·um -i *n;* **to catch by** — deprehenděre; **to feel** — mirari; **to the** — **of all, he says**...cunctis improvisis ait; **to take s.o. by** — excipěre aliquem incaut·um -am
surprise *tr* admirationem movēre *(w. dat); (mil)* oppriměre; **to be —d at** mirari, admirari
surprise attack *s* subita incursi·o -onis *f*
surprising *adj* mir·us -a -um
surprisingly *adv* mire, mirabiliter
surrender *s* traditi·o -onis *f; (leg)* cessi·o -onis *f; (mil)* dediti·o -onis *f*
surrender *tr* traděre, deděre ‖ *intr* se deděre, se traděre
surreptitious *adj* furtiv·us -a -um

surreptitiously *adv* furtim
surround *tr* circumdare
surroundings *spl* vicini·a -ae *f*
survey *s* inspecti·o -onis *f; (of land)* mensur·a -ae *f*
survey *tr* oculis lustrare; *(land)* permetiri
surveyor *s* agrimens·or -oris *m*
survival *s* sal·us -utis *f*
survive *tr* supervivĕre *(w. dat)* ‖ *intr* superst·es -itis esse
surviving *adj* superst·es -itis
survivor *s* superst·es -itis *mf*
susceptible *adj* moll·is -is -e; — **to** obnoxi·us -a -um *(w. dat)*
suspect *tr* suspicari, suspectare; **to be —ed of** in suspicionem venire quasi *(w. verb in subjunctive)*
suspend *tr* suspendĕre, differre; **to be — ed from office** summoveri administratione rei publicae
suspense *s* exspectati·o -onis *f;* **in —** suspens·us -a -um; **to end the —** exspectationem discutĕre
suspicion *s* suspici·o -onis *f;* **to come under —** in suspicionem venire; **to throw — on** suspicionem adjungĕre ad *(w. acc)*
suspicious *adj* suspic·ax -acis; *(suspected)* suspect·us -a -um
suspiciously *adv* suspiciose
sustain *tr* sustinēre; *(hardships, loss, injury, etc.)* ferre
sustenance *s* vict·us -ūs *m*
swab *s* penicul·us -i *m*
swab *tr* detergēre
swaddling clothes *spl* incunabul·a -orum *npl*
swagger *intr* se inferre
swallow *s (bird)* hirund·o -inis *f*
swallow *tr* vorare; *(liquids)* sorbēre; **to — up** devorare, absorbēre
swamp *s* pal·us -udis *f*
swamp *tr* demergĕre
swampy *adj* paludos·us -a -um
swan *s* cygn·us -i *m*
swank *adj* laut·us -a -um
swap *tr* permutare
swap *s* permutati·o -onis *f*
swarm *s* exam·en -inis *n*
swarm *intr (of bees)* examinare; *(of people)* congregari
swarthy *adj* fusc·us -a -um
swathe *s* fasci·a -ae *f*
sway *s* dici·o -onis *f,* imper·ium -(i)i *n;* **to hold —** regnare
sway *tr (to influence)* suadēre *(w. dat)* ‖ *intr* vacillare
swear *tr* jurare; **to — in** sacramento adigĕre ‖ *intr* jurare; **to — off** ejurare
sweat *s* sud·or -oris *m;* **to break a —** insudare
sweat *intr* sudare

sweep *tr* verrĕre; **to — out** everrĕre ‖ *intr* **to — by** *(to dash by)* praetervolare
sweet *adj* dulc·is -is -e; *(fig)* bland·us -a -um
sweeten *tr* dulcem facĕre; *(fig)* lenire
sweetheart *s* delici·ae -arum *fpl*
sweetly *adv* dulce; *(fig)* suaviter
sweetness *s* dulced·o -inis *f*
sweets *spl* cuppedi·a -orum *npl*
swell *s* aest·us -ūs *m*
swell *tr* tumefacĕre ‖ *intr* tumēre
swelling *s* tum·or -oris *m*
swelter *intr* aestu laborare
swerve *intr* aberrare
swift *adj* cel·er -eris -ere
swiftness *s* celerit·as -atis *f*
swim *intr* natare; **to — across** tranare; **the floor was swimming in wine** pavimentum natabat vino
swimmer *s* natat·or -oris *m*
swimming *s* natati·o -onis *f; (of the head)* vertig·o -inis *f*
swimming pool *s* piscin·a -ae *f*
swindle *s* frau·s -dis *f*
swindle *tr* fraudare
swindler *s* fraudat·or -oris *m*
swine *s* sus, suis *mf*
swineherd *s* suar·ius -(i)i *m*
swing *s* oscillati·o -onis *f*
swing *tr* librare ‖ *intr* oscillare
swipe *tr (to steal)* subducĕre
switch *s (stick)* virgul·a -ae *f; (change)* transit·us -ūs *m*
switch *tr* commutare ‖ *intr* transire; **to — from wine to water** transire a vino ad aquam; **to — over to the plebs** transire ad plebem
swollen *adj* tumid·us -a -um
swoon *intr* intermori
swoop *s* impet·us -ūs *m*
swoop *intr* **to — down on** involare in *(w. acc);* **to — upon** petĕre
sword *s* glad·ius -(i)i *m;* **with fire and — ** ferro ignique
sycamore *s* sycamor·us -i *f*
sycophant *s* sychophant·a -ae *m*
syllable *s* syllab·a -ae *f*
syllogism *s* syllogism·us -i *m*
symbol *s* symbol·us -i *m*
symbolic *adj* **to be — of s.th.** signum esse alicujus
symbolically *adv* symbolice
symbolize *tr* repraesentare
symmetrical *adj* congru·ens -entis
symmetry *s* symmetri·a -ae *f*
sympathetic *adj* misericor·s -dis
sympathy *s* misericordi·a -ae *f*
symphony *s* symphoni·a -ae *f*
symptom *s* sign·um -i *n*
synagogue *s* synagog·a -ae *f*
syndicate *s* societ·as -atis *f*
synonym *s* verb·um -i *n* idem declarans

synoymous *adj* idem declaran·s -tis; **a Latin word — with the Greek verb·um -i** *n* Latinum quod idem Graeco valet
synopsis *s* synops·is -is *f*
syntax *s* syntax·is -is *f*
system *s* rati·o -onis *f*
systematic *adj* ordinat·us -a -um
systematically *adv* certā ratione
systematize *tr* in ordinem redigĕre

T

tab *s* pittac·ium -(i)i *n; (coll)* rati·o -onis *f* (debiti)
tab *tr* designare, notare
tabernacle *s* tabernacul·um -i *n*
table *s* mens·a -ae *f; (list)* ind·ex -icis *m*, tabul·a -ae *f; (of bronze)* ae·s -ris *n;* **at — apud mensam; to clear the —** mensam auferre; **— of contents:** Earthquakes; Chasms, etc. continenter in hoc libro: De Terrae Motibus; De Terrae Hiatibus, etc.; **to set the — mensam ponĕre; to wait on** —s ad mensas ministrare
tablecloth *s* mantil·e -is *n*
tableland *s* planiti·es -ei *f*
tablespoon *s* ligul·a -ae *f*
tablet *s* tabul·a -ae *f; (pill)* catapot·ium -(i)i *n*
tacit *adj* tacit·us -a -um
tacitly *adv* tacite
taciturn *adj* taciturn·us -a -um
tack *s* clavul·us -i *m*
tack *tr* **to — on** *(in sewing)* assuĕre; *(to add on)* subjicĕre **||** *intr (of ships)* reciprocari
tackle *tr* obsistĕre *(w. dat); (to deal with)* tractare
tackle *s (gear)* apparat·us -ūs *m*
tact *s* urbanit·as -atis *f*
tactful *adj* urban·us -a -um
tactician *s* rei militaris perit·us -i *m*
tactics *spl* belli rati·o -onis *f; (methods)* rati·o -onis *f* rei gerendae
tadpole *s* ranuncul·us -i *m*
tag *s* appendicul·a -ae *f*
tail *s* caud·a -ae *f;* **to turn — tergum** vertĕre
tail *tr* insequi
tailor *s* vestit·or -oris *m*
taint *s* contagi·o -onis *f; (blemish)* vit·ium -(i)i *n*
taint *tr* inficĕre; *(fig)* corrumpĕre
take *tr (in nearly all senses of the English word)* capĕre; *(w. eagerness or haste)* arripĕre; *(what is offered)* accipĕre; *(to require)* requirĕre; *(to grasp, take hold of)* comprehendĕre; *(food, drink, poi-*

son) sumĕre; *(to suppose)* opinari; *(to regard, consider)* accipĕre, habĕre, ducĕre;* **to — a bath** balneo uti; **to — a dislike to** capĕre odium *(w. gen);* **to — as a certainty** sumĕre pro certo; **to — aside** seducĕre; **to — a trip** iter facĕre; **to — a walk** spatiari; **to — away (from)** adimĕre *(w. dat),* auferre *(w. abl);* **to — back** recipĕre, repetĕre; **to — by the hand** manu prehendĕre; **to — captive** capĕre; **to — charge of** curare; **to — credit for** capĕre gratiam *(w. gen);* **to — down** *(words of a speaker)* excipĕre; *(posters, signs)* refigĕre; **to — flight** capĕre fugam; **to — for granted** praesumĕre; **to — from** adimĕre *(w. dat or abl);* **to — great pains to** in magno negotio habĕre *(w. inf);* **to — hold of** *(to grasp)* (com)prehendĕre; *(of a disease)* capĕre; **to — in** *(as guest)* recipĕre; *(to deceive)* decipĕre, fallĕre; **to — in hand** suscipĕre; **to — into consideration** respicĕre; **to — its name from** nomen capĕre ex *(w. abl);* **to — leave of your senses** a te exire; **to — notice of** observare; **to — off** *(clothes, shoes, ring, locket)* detrahĕre; **to — part in** capessĕre partem *(w. gen);* **to — place** fieri; **to — pleasure in** capĕre laetitiam ex *(w. abl);* **to — out** *(to produce)* proferre; *(from storage)* promĕre; **to — out a loan** pecuniam mutuam sumĕre; **to — out of his pocket** de sinu proferre; **to — pity on** capĕre misericordiam *(w. gen);* **to — possession of** occupare; **to — the opportunity** capĕre occasionem; **to — the place of** occupare locum *(w. gen);* **to — to task** exprobrare; **to — up** *(a day)* consumĕre; *(a task)* suscipĕre; *(space)* occupare; *(to snatch up)* corripĕre; *(arms)* capĕre; **to — (it) upon oneself** sibi sumĕre, in se conferre; **to — vengeance on** vindicare **||** *intr* **I'm —ing off** apoculo *(coll);* **it would — too long to** longum esset *(w. inf);* **to — after** similis esse *(w. gen, esp. of persons; w. dat, esp. of things);* **to — off** abire, proficisci; **to — off from** *(e.g., work)* absistĕre *(w. abl);* **to — over completely** plane tenēre
take *s* praed·a -ae *f; (earnings, profits)* captur·a -ae *f*
tale *s* fabul·a -ae *f; (short tale)* fabell·a -ae *f*
talent *s* talent·um -i *n; (fig)* ingen·ium -(i)i *n*
talented *adj* ingenios·us -a -um
talk *s* serm·o -onis *m;* **idle — nug·ae**

-arum *fpl;* **small —** sermuncul·us -i *m*

talk *intr* loqui; **to — tough** durae buccae esse; **to — with** colloqui cum *(w. abl)*

talkative *adj* loqu·ax -acis

talker *s (idle)* blater·o -onis *m*

tall *adj* alt·us -a -um, cels·us -a -um; *(person)* procer·us -a -um; **to be —** excelsā staturā esse

tallow *s* seb·um -i *n*

tally *s* tesser·a -a *f*

tally *intr* convenire

talon *s* ungu·is -is *m*

tambourine *s* tympan·um -i *n*

tame *adj* mansuet·us -a -um

tame *tr* mansuefacěre, domare

tamely *adv* mansuete; *(fig)* ignave

tamer *s* domit·or -oris *m*

taming *s* domit·us -ūs *m*

tamper *intr* **to — with** *(e.g., the jury)* sollicitare; *(writings)* depravare

tan *tr (hides)* perficěre; *(by sun)* adurěre

tan *s* adustus col·or -oris *m;* **to get a —** colorare

tangible *adj* tractabil·is -is -e

tangle *s* implicati·o -onis *f*

tangle *tr* implicare ‖ *intr* **to — with** se implicare in *(w. abl)*

tank *s* lac·us -ūs *m*

tankard *s* canthar·us -i *m*

tanned *adj* adust·us -a -um

tantalize *tr* vexare

tantamount *adj* pa·r -ris

tap *s* levis ict·us -ūs *m*

tap *tr* leviter ferire; *(wine, etc.)* reliněre

tape *s* taeni·a -ae *f*

taper *s* cere·us -i *m*

taper *tr* fastigare ‖ *intr* fastigari

tapestry *s* tapet·e -is *n*

taproom *s* tabern·a -ae *f*

tar *s* pix, picis *f*

tardily *adv* tarde, lente

tardiness *s* tardit·as -atis *f*

tardy *adj* tard·us -a -um

target *s* scop·us -i *m*

tariff *s* portor·ium -(i)i *n*

tarnish *tr* infuscare ‖ *intr* infuscari

tarry *intr* commorari

tart *adj* acerb·us -a -um

tart *s* scriblit·a -ae *f*

task *s* pens·um -i *n;* **to take to —** exprobrare

taste *s (sense)* gustat·us -ūs *m; (flavor)* sap·or -oris *m; (fig)* judic·ium -(i)i *n*

taste *tr* gustare ‖ *intr* sapěre; **to — bad, good** male, bene sapěre; **to — like** redděre saporem *(w. gen),* sapěre

tasteful *adj* eleg·ans -antis; *(neat in arrangement)* concinn·us -a -um

tastefully *adv* eleganter

tasteless *adj* insipid·us -a -um; *(fig)* insuls·us -a -um

tastelessly *adv* insulse

tasty *adj* sapid·us -a -um

tattered *adj* pannos·us -a -um

tatters *spl* pann·i -orum *mpl*

taunt *s* convic·ium -(i)i *n*

taunt *tr* conviciari; **to — s.o. with his low birth** ignobilitatem alicui objicěre

taut *adj* intent·us -a -um

tavern *s* caupon·a -ae *f*

tavern keeper *s* caup·o -onis *m*

tawdry *adj* vil·is -is -e

tax *s* vectig·al -alis *n;* **to pay a — on water** vectigal pro aqua penděre

tax *tr* vectigal imponěre *(w. dat);* **to — oneself to the utmost** contenděre omnes nervos

taxable *adj* vectigal·is -is -e

tax collector *s* exact·or -oris *m*

teach *tr* docěre, instituěre

teachable *adj* docil·is -is -e

teacher *s* docen·s -tis *mf,* magist·er -ri *m,* magistr·a -ae *f; (of elementary school)* litterat·or -oris *m; (of secondary school)* grammatic·us -i *m*

teaching *s* doctrin·a -ae *f*

team *s* jugal·es -ium *mpl; (of animals)* protel·um -i *n*

tear *s* lacrim·a -ae *f; (a rent)* scissur·a -ae *f*

tear *tr* scinděre; **to — apart** discinděre; **to — down** revellěre; *(a building)* diruěre; **to — off** abscinděre; **to — open** rescinděre; **to — out** evellěre; **to — to pieces** (di)laniare, discerpěre; **to — up** *(trees, shrubs)* convellěre; *(paper)* discinděre ‖ *intr (to rush)* volare, ruěre

tease *tr* vexare, luděre

teat *s* mamm·a -ae *f*

technical *adj* propri·us -a -um

technique *s* ar·s -tis *f*

technology *s* officinarum art·es -ium *fpl*

tedious *adj* lent·us -a -um; **it would be — to** longum est *(w. inf)*

tedium *s* taed·ium -(i)i *n*

teem *intr* scatěre, redundare

teethe *intr* dentire

teething *s* dentiti·o -onis *f*

tell *tr* narrare, referre; *(to show, indicate)* docěre; **— me the truth!** dic mihi verum! **to — s.o. to** *(w. inf)* imperare alicui ut *(w. subj)*

teller *s* numerat·or -oris *m*

temerity *s* temerit·as -atis *f*

temper *s* temperati·o -onis *f; (anger)* iracundi·a -ae *f*

temper *tr* temperare

temperament *s* indol·es -is

temperance *s* temperanti·a -ae *f*

temperate *adj* temperat·us -a -um

temperature *s* temperati·o -onis *f*

tempest *s* tempest·as -atis *f*
tempestuous *adj* procellos·us -a -um
temple *s* templ·um -i *n; (anat)* temp·us -oris *n*
temporal *adj* profan·us -a -um
temporarily *adv* ad tempus
temporary *adj* temporari·us -a -um; — **stadium** stadi·um -i *n* ad tempus exstructum
temporize *intr* tempori servire
tempt *tr* temptare; **to — fate** experiri casūs
temptation *s* tentati·o -onis *f*
ten *adj* decem *(indecl);* — **times** decies
tenable *adj* defensibil·is -is -e
tenacious *adj* ten·ax -acis
tenaciously *adv* tenaciter
tenacity *s* tenacit·as -atis *f*
tenancy *s* conducti·o -onis *f*
tenant *s* conduct·or -oris *m; (of an apartment)* insular·ius -(i)i *m*
tenant farmer *s* colon·us -i *m*
tend *tr* curare ‖ *intr (to be wont)* solēre; **I tend to believe** crediderim
tendency *s* inclinati·o -onis *f*
tender *adj* ten·er -eris -ere
tenderly *adv* tenere
tender *tr* deferre
tenderness *s (softness)* tenerit·as -atis *f; (affection)* indulgenti·a -ae *f*
tendon *s* nerv·us -i *m*
tendril *s (of vine)* pampin·us -i *m; (of plants)* clavicul·us -i *m*
tenement *s* conduct·um -i *n*
tenet *s* dogm·a -atis *n*
tenfold *adj* decempl·ex -icis
tennis *s* **to play — pilā** ludĕre
tennis court *s* sphaerister·ium -(i)i *n*
tenor *s (purport)* sens·us -ūs *m; (mus)* vo·x -cis *f* tertia
tense *adj* tent·us -a -um
tense *s (gram)* temp·us -oris *n*
tension *s* intenti·o -onis *f*
tent *s* tentor·ium -(i)i *n*
tentative *adj* tent·ans -antis
tenth *adj* decim·us -a -um
tenuous *adj* tenu·is -is -e
tenure *s (fixed period)* spat·ium -(i)i *n; (possession)* possessi·o -onis *f; (pol)* imperii temp·us -oris *n*
tepid *adj* tepid·us -a -um
term *s (word)* appellati·o -onis *f; (limit)* termin·us -i *m; (condition)* condici·o -onis *f; (length of time)* spat·ium -(i)i *n; (math)* termin·us -i *m*
terminal *adj* extrem·us -a -um
terminal *s* stati·o -onis *f* ultima
terminate *tr* terminare ‖ *intr* terminari; *(of words)* cadĕre
termination *s* terminati·o -onis *f*
terrace *s* agg·er -eris *m; (patio)* solar·ium -(i)i *n*
terrain *s* locorum sit·us -ūs *m*

terrestrial *adj* terrestr·is -is -e
terrible *adj* terribil·is -is -e
terribly *adv* horrendum in modum
terrific *adj* terrific·us -a -um; *(great)* festiv·us -a -um
terrify *tr* terrēre
territory *s* a·ger -gri *m*, territor·ium -(i)i *n*
terror *s* terr·or -oris *m*
terse *adj* press·us -a -um
tersely *adv* presse
test *s* probati·o -onis *f*
test *tr* probare, experiri
testament *s* testament·um -i *n*
testamentary *adj* testamentari·us -a -um
testator *s* testat·or -oris *m*
testicle *s* testicul·us -i *m*
testify *tr* testificari
testimonial *s* laudati·o -onis *f*
testimony *s* testimon·ium -(i)i *n*
testy *adj* stomachos·us -a -um
tether *s* retinacul·um -i *n*
tether *tr* religare
text *s* verb·a -orum *npl* scriptoris
textbook *s* enchirid·ion -(i)i *n*
textile *adj* textil·is -is -e
textile *s* textil·e -is *n*
texture *s* text·us -ūs *m*
than *adv* quam
thank *tr* **to — s.o. for** gratias alicui agĕre ob *(w. acc)*
thankful *adj* grat·us -a -um
thankfully *adv* grate
thankless *adj* ingrat·us -a -um
thanks *spl* grati·ae -arum *fpl;* — **to Caesar, I am free** beneficio Caesaris liber sum; **to give** — gratias agĕre
thanks *interj* gratias!
thanksgiving *s* gratulati·o -onis *f; (public act)* supplicati·o -onis *f*
that *adj* ill·e -a -ud; is, ea id; *(sometimes contemptuous)* ist·e -a -ud
that *pron demonstrative* ill·e -a -ud; is, ea, id; ist·e -a -ud; **that is, if Aquila will allow me** si tamen per Aquila licerit; — **is to say** videlicet; — **was the life!** illud erat vivĕre!
that *conj (purpose, result, command)* ut; *(after verbs of fearing)* ne
thatch *s* strament·um -i *n*
thatch *tr* stramento tegĕre
thaw *tr* (dis)solvĕre ‖ *intr* tabescĕre
the *article not expressed in Latin; however to express celebrity, use* ill·e -a -ud: **the Hercules of Xenophon** Hercules Xenophontius ille
the *adv* —...— quo...eo; — **less he pursued glory,** — **more it followed him** quo minus gloriam petebat eo magis eum sequebatur
theater *s* theatr·um -i *n*
theatrical *adj* theatral·is -is -e

thee *pron* te; **of —** de te; **to —** tibi; **with —** tecum

theft *s* furt·um -i *n*

their *adj* illorum, illarum, illorum; eorum, earum, eorum; **— own** su·us -a -um

them *pron* eos, eas, ea; ill·os -as -a; ist·os -ae -a; **to —** eis, illis, istis

theme *s* argument·um -i *n*

themselves *pron refl* se; **to —** sibi

themselves *pron intensive* ips·i -ae -a

then *adv (at that time)* tum, tunc; *(after that)* deinde; *(therefore)* igitur, ergo; **now and —** interdum; **— and there** e vestigio, ilico

thence *adv* inde, illinc

thenceforth *adv* dehinc

theologian *s* theolog·us -i *m*

theological *adj* theologic·us -a -um

theology *s* theologi·a -ae *f*

theoretical *adj* rational·is -is -e

theorizing *s* ratiocinati·o -onis *f*

theory *s* rati·o -onis *f; the* **— and practice** of war ratio et usus belli

there *adv* ibi; *(thither)* illuc; **— are** sunt; **— is** est

thereabouts *adv* circa, circiter, fere

thereafter *adv* deinde

thereby *adv* eā re, eo

therefore *adv* itaque, igitur, ergo

therefrom *adv* exinde, ex eo

thereupon *adv* subinde

thesis *s* thes·is -is *f*

they *pron* ei eae ea; illi illae illa; isti istae ista

thick *adj* crass·us -a -um; *(closely packed)* dens·us -a -um, spiss·us -a -um

thicken *tr* densare, spissare **‖** *intr* crassescĕre

thicket *s* frutect·um -i *n*

thickly *adv* dense

thickness *s* crassitud·o -inis *f*

thick-headed *adj* bard·us -a -um

thick-skinned *adj* callos·us -a -um

thief *s* fur, furis *m;* **an out and out —** tri·fur -furis *m*

thievery *s* furt·um -i *n*

thigh *s* fem·ur -oris *n;* **to slap the —** femur percutĕre

thin *adj* tenu·is -is -e, exil·is -is -e; *(lean)* ma·cer -cra -crum; **to become —** macrescĕre

thin *tr* attenuare; **to — out** rarefacĕre

thine *adj* tu·us -a -um

thing *s* res, rei *f*

think *tr* cogitare; *(to believe, imagine, etc.)* putare, credĕre; *(to surmise)* suspicari; **to — over** in mente agitare; **‖** *intr* cogitare, putare; **to — highly of** magni habēre; **to — ill of Crassus** male opinari de Crasso

thinker *s* philosph·us -i *m*

thinking *s* cogitati·o -onis *f*

thinness *s* tenuit·as -atis *f*

third *adj* terti·us -a -um

third *s* tertia par·s -tis *f*

thirdly *adv* tertio

thirst *s* sit·is -is *f*

thirst *intr* sitire; **to — for** sitire

thirstily *adv* sitienter

thirsty *adj* siti·ens -entis

thirteen *adj* tredecim *(indecl)*

thirteenth *adj* terti·us decim·us -a -um

thirtieth *adj* tricesim·us -a -um

thirty *adj* triginta *(indecl)*

this *adj* hic, haec, hoc

thistle *s* cardu·us -i *m*

thither *adv* illuc, eo

thong *s* lor·um -i *n*

thorn *s* spin·a -ae *f*

thorn bush *s* vepr·es -is *m*

thorny *adj* spinos·us -a -um; *(fig)* nodos·us -a -um

thorough *adj* perfect·us -a -um

thoroughly *adv* penitus

thoroughbred *adj* generos·us -a -um

thoroughfare *s* perv·ium -(i)i *n*

those *adj see* **that**

thou *pron* tu

though *conj* quamquam, quamvis

though *adv* tamen

thought *s (act, faculty)* cogitati·o -onis *f; (product of thinking)* cogitat·um -i *n*

thoughtful *adj (reflecting)* cogitabund·us -a -um; *(careful)* provid·us -a -um; *(kind)* human·us -a -um

thoughtless *adj* inconsult·us -a -um

thoughtlessly *adv* inconsulte, temere

thousand *adj* mille *(indecl);* **a — times** millies

thousandth *adj* millesim·us -a -um

thrash *tr* verberare

thrashing *s* verber·a -orum *npl*

thread *s* fil·um -i *n*

thread *tr* inserĕre

threadbare *adj* obsolet·us -a -um

threat *s (act)* minati·o -onis *f;* **—s** min·ae -arum *fpl*

threaten *tr* minari *(w. acc of thing and dat of person);* **to — s.o. with death** comminari necem alicui **‖** *intr* imminēre, impendēre

three *adj* tres, tres, tria; **— times** ter

threefold *adj* tripl·ex -icis

three-legged *adj* trip·es -edis

thresh *tr* terĕre

thresher *s* tribul·um -i *n*

threshing *s* tritur·a -ae *f*

threshing floor *s* are·a -ae *f*

threshold *s* lim·en -inis *n*

thrice *adv* ter

thrift *s* parsimoni·a -ae *f*

thriftily *adv* frugaliter

thriftiness *s* frugalit·as -atis *f*

thrifty *adj* parc·us -a -um
thrill *s (delight)* delectati·o -onis *f*
thrill *tr* commovēre
thrilling *adj* mir·us -a -um
thrive *intr* vigēre, virēre
thriving *adj* veget·us -a -um
throat *s* fauc·es -ium *fpl*
throb *s* palpitati·o -onis *f*
throb *intr* palpitare; *(of a vein)* agitare
throes *spl* dol·or -oris *m*
throne *s* sol·ium -(i)i *n; (fig) (regal power)* regn·um -i *n;* **to restore to the —** restituĕre in regnum; **to succeed to the —** recipĕre regnum; *(of emperors)* recipĕre imperium
throng *s* frequenti·a -ae *f*
throng *intr* **to — around** stipare
throttle *tr* strangulare
through *prep* per *(w. acc); (on account of)* ob *(w. acc)*
through *adv* render by compound verb with trans- or per-, *e.g.,* **to read —** perlegĕre; **— and —** omnino
throughout *adv* prorsus
throughout *prep* per *(w. acc)*
throw *tr* jacĕre; *(freq)* jactare; *(to hurl)* conjicĕre; *(esp. missiles)* mittĕre; **to — an apple at s.o.** aliquem malo petĕre; **to — a stone at s.o.** impingĕre lapidem alicui; **to — at** conjicĕre ad, in *(w. acc);* **to — away** abjicĕre; **to — back** rejicĕre; **to — down** dejicĕre; **to — food to the dogs** cibum canibus objicĕre; **to — in the way of** objicĕre *(w. dat);* **to — into the fire** projicĕre in ignem; **to — off** *(a rider)* ejicĕre, excutĕre; *(clothes, bonds)* exuĕre; **to — oneself at the feet of s.o.** ad pedes alicujus se projicĕre; **to — oneself down** *(from a height)* se praecipitare; **to — open** patefacĕre; **to — out** ejicĕre; **to —** *(e.g., a cloak)* **over s.o.** injicĕre (pallium) alicui; **to — together** conjicĕre in unum
throw *s* jact·us -ūs *m*
thrush *s* turd·us -i *m*
thrust *s* impet·us -ūs *m,* ict·us -ūs *m*
thrust *tr* trudĕre, impellĕre; **to — back** retrudĕre; **to — off** detrudĕre; **to — out** extrudĕre; **to — together** contrudĕre
thumb *s* poll·ex -icis *m*
thump *s* percussi·o -onis *f*
thump *tr* tundĕre
thunder *s* tonitr·us -ūs *m*
thunder *intr* tonare
thunderstruck *adj* attonit·us -a -um
thus *adv* ita, sic; **and —** itaque
thwart *tr* obstare *(w. dat)*
thy *adj* tu·us -a -um
tiara *s* diadem·a -atis *n*
tick *s (insect)* ricin·us -i *m; (clicking)*
¹**ĕvis** ict·us -ūs *m*

ticket *s* tesser·a -ae *f; (label)* pittac·ium -(i)i *n*
tickle *tr & intr* titillare
tickling *s* titillati·o -onis *f*
tickish *adj* periculos·us -a -um
tide *s* aest·us -ūs *m*
tidiness *s* munditi·a -ae *f*
tidings *spl* nunt·ius -(i)i *m;* **to bring — of joy** gaudium nuntiare
tie *s* vincul·um -i *n; (of blood, kinship)* necessitud·o -inis *f*
tie *tr* *(al)*ligare; *(in a knot)* nodare, nectĕre; **to — one's hair in a knot** colligĕre capillos in nodum; **to — up** alligare; *(a wound)* deligare
tier *s* ord·o -inis *m*
tiger *s* tigr·is -is *m*
tight *adj* strict·us -a -um, art·us -a -um; *(tense)* intent·us -a -um; **to get — on wine** se vino devincire; **in a — spot** in angustiis
tighten *tr* adstringĕre
tightly *adv* arte; **too — banaaged** nimis adstrict·us -a -um
tile *s* tegul·a -ae *f*
till *conj* dum, donec
till *prep* usque ad *(w. acc)*
till *tr* colĕre
tillage *s* agricultur·a -ae *f*
tiller *s (person)* agricol·a -ae *f; (helm)* gubernacul·um -i *n*
tilt *tr* proclinare
timber *s* materi·a -ae *f*
time *s* temp·us -oris *n; (age, period)* aet·as -atis *f; (leisure)* ot·ium -(i)i *n; (opportunity)* occasi·o -onis *f; (interval)* intervall·um -i *n; (of day)* hor·a -ae *f;* **after so long a —** tanto intervallo; **another —** alias; **around the — of the battle** sub tempus proelii; **at about the same —** sub idem tempus; **at that —** *(at that hour)* ad id temporis; *(in the past)* tum; **at the right —** ad tempus, tempestive; **at the same —** simul; **at the wrong —** intempestive; **for all future —** in posterum; **for a short —** brevi tempore, paulisper; **for a long —** diu; **for a —** parumper; **for some —** aliquamdiu; **for the first —** primum; **for the — being** in tempus; **from that — on** ex eo (tempore); **from — to —** interdum; **I have no —** non est mihi tempus; **in a short —** brevi; **in — ad** tempus, temperi; **it is high — to** tempus maxime est *(w. inf);* **many —s** saepius; **on time** tempestive, ad horam; **there is no — to** cry non vacat flēre; **there is no — to lose** maturato opus est; **there was a — when** tempus erat quum; **to ask what — it is** horas quaerĕre; **to say what — it is** quotas horas nuntiare;

to see what — it is horas inspicĕre; **what — is it?** quota hora est? **you couldn't have come at a better —** non potuisti magis per tempus advenire
time *tr* clepsydrā metiri
timeliness *s* tempestivit·as -atis *f*
timely *adj* tempestiv·us -a -um
timepiece *s* horolog·ium -(i)i *n*
timid *adj* timid·us -a -um
timidity *s* timidit·as -atis *f*
timorous *adj* pavid·us -a -um
tin *s* stann·um -i *n*
tin *adj* stanne·us -a -um
tincture *s* col·or -oris *m*
tinder *s* fom·es -itis *m*
tingle *intr* formicare
tinkle *intr* tinnire
tinsel *s* bracteol·a -ae *f*
tint *tr* tingĕre
tip *s* ap·ex -icis *m; (of sword, horn)* mucr·o -onis *m; (hint)* indic·ium -(i)i *n; (money)* stip·s -is *f;* **on the — of the tongue** in labris primoribus; **— of the nose** imus nas·us -i *m*
tip *tr (to make pointy)* praefigĕre; **to — over** vergĕre
tipple *intr* potare
tippler *s* pot·or -oris *m*
tipsy *adj* ebriol·us -a -um
tiptoe *adv* in digitos errect·us -a -um
tire *tr* fatigare; **to — out** defatigare ‖ *intr* defatigari; **I — of** me taedet *(w. gen)*
tire *s* canth·us -i *m*
tired *adj* fess·us -a -um; **I am sick and — of** me pertaedet *(w. gen);* **— out** defess·us -a -um
tiresome *adj* molest·us -a -um
tissue *s* text·us -ūs *m*
tit *s* **to give s.o. — for tat** alicui par pari respondēre
titanic *adj* ing·ens -entis
tithe *s* decum·a -ae *f*
titillate *tr* titillare
title *s* titul·us -i *m; (of a book)* inscripti·o -onis *f; (of a person)* appellati·o -onis *f; (claim)* ju·s -ris *n*
title *tr* inscribĕre
title page *s* ind·ex -icis *m*
titter *s* ris·us -ūs *m*
to *prep often rendered by the dative; (motion, except with names of towns, small islands)* ad *(w. acc),* in *(w. acc); (reaching to)* tenus *(always placed after the case) (w. gen);* **— and fro** huc illuc; **— my, your, his house** ad me, te, eum; **— the country** rus; **up — usque ad** *(w. acc)*
toad *s* buf·o -onis *m*
toady *s* adulat·or -oris *m*
toast *s (bread)* panis tosti.offul·a -ae *f;*

(health) propinati·o -onis *f;* **to drink a — to** propinare *(w. dat)*
toast *tr* torrēre; *(in drinking)* propinare *(w. dat)*
today *adv* hodie
today *s* hodiernus di·es -ei *m*
toe *s* digit·us -i *m;* **big —** poll·ex -icis *m*
toga *s* tog·a -ae *f*
together *adv* simul, unā
toil *s* lab·or -oris *m*
toil *intr* laborare
token *s* sign·um -i *n*
tolerable *adj* tolerabil·is -is -e
tolerably *adv* mediocriter
tolerance *s* patienti·a -ae *f*
tolerant *adj* toler·ans -antis
tolerate *tr* tolerare
toleration *s* tolerati·o -onis *f*
toll *s* vectig·al -alis *n; (at ports)* portor·ium -(i)i *n*
toll booth *s* tabern·a -ae *f* portorii
toll collector *s* exact·or -oris *m*
tomb *s* sepulcr·um -i *n*
tombstone *s* stel·a -ae *f*
tomorrow *adv* cras; **day after —** perendie; **— morning** cras mane
tomorrow *s* crastinus di·es -ei *m;* **the day after —** perendinus di·es -ei *m*
ton *s* **to have —s of money** nummorum nummos habēre
tone *s* son·us -i *m; (in painting)* col·or -oris *m*
tongs *spl* for·ceps -cipis *mf*
tongue *s* lingu·a -ae *f; (of shoe)* ligul·a -ae *f;* **to hold one's —** linguam continēre; **his name was on the tip of my —** versabatur mihi nomen in primoribus labris
tonsils *spl* tonsill·ae -arum *fpl*
too *adv* nimis, nimium; *(also)* quoque
tool *s* instrument·um -i *n; (dupe)* minis·ter -tri *m*
tooth *s* den·s -tis *m;* **— and nail** totis viribus
toothache *s* dentium dol·or -oris *m*
toothbrush *s* penicul·us -i *m* dentibus purgandis
toothed *adj* dentat·us -a -um
toothless *adj* edentul·us -a -um
toothpick *s* dentiscalp·ium -(i)i *n*
tooth powder *s* dentifric·ium -(i)i *n*
top *adj* summ·us -a -um
top *s* ap·ex -icis *m; (of tree)* cacum·en -inis *n; (of house)* fastig·ium -(i)i *n; (toy)* turb·o -inis *m;* **at the — of the page** ab summā paginā; **on —** supra; **on — of that** insuper; **— of the head** vert·ex -icis *m;* **— of the mountain** summus mon·s -tis *m*
top *tr* superare; **to — it off** in summo
top-heavy *adj* praegrav·is -is -e a superiore parte

topic *s* res, rei *f*, argument·um -i *n*
topmost *adj* summ·us -a -um
topography *s* regionis descripti·o -onis *f*
topple *tr* evertĕre ‖ *intr* titubare
topsy-turvy *adv* **to turn things —** omnia sursum deorsum versare
torch *s* fax, facis *f*
torchlight *s* **by —** ad lumina
torment *s* torment·um -i *n*
torment *tr* cruciare
tormentor *s* carnif·ex -icis *m*
torn *adj* sciss·us -a -um
torpid *adj* torp·ens -entis; **to be —** torpēre
torpor *s* torp·or -oris *m*
torrent *s* torr·ens -entis *m*
torrid *adj* torrid·us -a -um
tortoise, tortoise shell *s* testud·o -inis *f*
torture *s* torment·um -i *n (almost always used in the plural); (pain inflicted by way of punishment or cruelty)* cruciat·us -ūs *m;* **instruments of —** torment·a -orum *npl;* **to question under —** tormentis quaerĕre
torture *tr* torquēre, cruciare
torturer *s* tort·or -oris *m*
toss *s* jact·us -ūs *m*
toss *tr* jactare ‖ *intr* jactari
total *adj* tot·us -a -um, univers·us -a -um
total *s* summ·a -ae *f*
totally *adv* omnino, prorsus
totter *intr* titubare
touch *tr* tangĕre; *(to stir)* movēre; **to — deeply** commovēre ‖ *intr* inter se contingĕre; **to — on** attingĕre
touch *s* tact·us -ūs *m*
touch-and-go *adj* anc·eps -itis
touching *adj* flexanim·us -a -um
touchstone *s (fig)* obruss·a -ae *f*
touchy *adj* stomachos·us -a -um
tough *adj* dur·us -a -um; *(fig)* strenu·us -a -um
tour *s (rounds)* circuit·us -ūs *m; (abroad)* peregrinati·o -onis *f*
tourist *s* peregrinat·or -oris *m*
tournament *s* certam·en -inis *n*
tow *s* stupp·a -ae *f*
tow *tr* remulco trahĕre
toward *prep* versus *(w. acc)*, ad *(w. acc); (of feelings)* erga *(w. acc)*, in *(w. acc); (of time)* sub *(w. acc)*
towel *s* linte·um -i *n*, mantel·e -is *n*
tower *s* turr·is -is *f*
tower *intr* **to — over** imminēre *(w. dat)*
towering *adj* excels·us -a -um
towline *s* remulc·um -i *n*
town *s* oppid·um -i *n*, urb·s -is *f*
town hall *s* curi·a -ae *f*
townsman *s* oppidan·us -i *m*
toy *s* ludibr·ium -(i)i *n*

toy *intr* **to — with** ludĕre cum *(w. abl)*
trace *s* vestig·ium -(i)i *n; (for horses)* helc·ium -(i)i *n;* **no — of a wound** nulla suspici·o -onis *f* vulneris
trace *tr* indagare; *(to outline)* delinēre; **to — back** repetĕre
track *s* vestig·ium -(i)i *n; (path)* semit·a -ae *f*, call·es -is *m*
track *tr* indagare
trackless *adj* avi·us -a -um
tract *s (land; treatise)* tract·us -ūs *m*
trade *s* commerc·ium -(i)i *n; (profession)* artific·ium -(i)i *n;* **to carry on — in** commercium *(w. gen)* facĕre
trade *tr* commutare ‖ *intr* mercaturas facĕre, negotiari; **to — in weapons** commercari tela
trader *s* mercat·or -oris *m*
tradesman *s* opif·ex -icis *m*
tradition *s* traditi·o -onis *f*, mo·s -ris *m* majorum; **there is an old —** ab antiquis traditur
traditional *adj* a majoribus tradit·us -a -um
traffic *s* commerc·ium -(i)i *n; (on street)* transit·us -ūs *m*
tragedian *s (playwright)* tragoed·us -i *m; (actor)* tragicus act·or -oris *m*
tragedy *s* tragoedi·a -ae *f*
tragic *adj (lit & fig)* tragic·us -a -um
tragically *adv* tragice
trail *s* vestig·ium -(i)i *n; (path)* call·es -is *m*
trail *tr* investigare; *(to drag)* trahĕre
train *s (line)* seri·es -ei *f*, ord·o -inis *m; (of robe)* peniculament·um -i *n; (retinue)* comitat·us -ūs *m; (rail)* hamaxostich·us -i *m*
train *tr* instituĕre, exercēre; *(to habituate)* assuefacĕre ‖ *intr* se exercēre
trainer *s* exercit·or -oris *m; (of gladiators)* lanist·a -ae *m*
training *s* instituti·o -onis *f; (practice)* exercitati·o -onis *f*
trait *s* mos, moris *m*
traitor *s* prodit·or -oris *m*
traitorous *adj* perfid·us -a -um
tramp *s* vagabund·us -i *m; (of feet)* puls·us -ūs *m*
tramp *intr* gradi
trample *tr* proterĕre ‖ *intr* **to — on, upon** proterĕre
trance *s* stup·or -oris *m;* **in a — in** excessu mentis; **she fell into a —** cecidit super eam mentis excessus
tranquil *adj* tranquill·us -a -um
tranquility *s* tranquillit·as -atis *f*
tranquilize *tr* tranquillare
transact *tr* transigĕre, agĕre
transaction *s* negot·ium -(i)i *n*
transatlantic *adj* transatlantic·us -a -um
transcend *tr* superare, antecedĕre

transcendental *adj* sublim·is -is -e
transcribe *tr* transcribĕre
transcription *s* transcripti·o -onis *f*
transfer *s* translati·o -onis *f; (of property)* alienati·o -onis *f*
transfer *tr* transferre; *(property)* abalienare
transference *s* translati·o -onis *f*
transfigure *tr* transfigurare
transform *tr* vertĕre, commutare
transformation *s* commutati·o -onis *f*
transgress *tr* violare, perfringĕre
transgression *s* violati·o -onis *f; (deed)* delict·um -i *n*
transgressor *s* violat·or -oris *m*
transient *adj* transitori·us -a -um
transition *s* transit·us -ūs *m*
transitive *adj* transitiv·us -a -um
transitively *adv* transitive
transitory *adj* transitori·us -a -um
translate *tr* convertĕre; **to — into Latin** in sermonem Latinum convertĕre
translation *s* translat·a -orum *npl; generally expressed by the verb:* **to do a good deal of — from** multa convertĕre ex (Graeco, etc.) in patrium sermonem
translator *s* interpr·es -etis *m*
transmission *s* transmissi·o -onis *f*
transmit *tr* transmittĕre
transmutation *s* transmutati·o -onis *f*
transparent *adj* pellucid·us -a -um; *(fig)* perspicu·us -a -um
transpire *intr (to happen)* fieri
transplant *tr* transferre
transport *tr* transportare, transvehĕre
transport *s* vectur·a -ae *f; (ship)* nav·is -is *f* oneraria; *(rapture)* sublimit·as -atis *f*
transportation *s* vectur·a -ae *f*
transpose *tr* transponĕre
trap *s* laque·us -i *m*, pedic·a -ae *f; (fig)* insidi·ae -arum *fpl*
trap *tr* irretire; *(fig)* inlaqueare
trappings *spl* apparat·us -ūs *m; (of horse)* phaler·ae -arum *fpl*
trash *s* scrut·a -orum *npl; (fig)* nug·ae -arum *fpl*
trashy *adj (cheap)* vil·is -is -e; *(obscene)* obscen·us -a -um
travel *tr* **to — a road** viā ire ‖ *intr* iter facĕre; **to — abroad** peregrinari
traveler *s* viat·or -oris *m; (abroad)* peregrinat·or -oris *m*
traverse *tr* peragrare, lustrare
travesty *s* perversa imitati·o -onis *f*
tray *s* fercul·um -i *n*
treacherous *adj* perfid·us -a -um; **to be on — ground** in lubrico versari
treacherously *adv* perfide
treachery *s* perfidi·a -ae *f*
tread *tr* calcare ‖ *intr* incedĕre; **to — upon** insistĕre *(w. dat)*

tread *s* incess·us -ūs *m*
treason *s* perduelli·o -onis *f*
treasonable *adj* perfid·us -a -um
treasure *s* thesaur·us -i *m*
treasure *tr* fovēre, magni aestimare
treasurer *s* aerarii praefect·us -i *m*
treasury *s (of the state)* aerar·ium -(i)i *n; (of the emperor)* fisc·us -i *m*
treat *tr* uti *(w. abl)*, tractare; *(patient)* curare; *(topic)* tractare; *(to entertain)* invitare; **to — gold like mud** habēre aurum pro luto
treatise *s* libell·us -i *m*
treatment *s* tractati·o -onis *f; (med)* curati·o -onis *f*
treaty *s* foed·us -eris *n; ***to make a —** foedus icĕre
treble *adj* tripl·ex -icis; *(of sound)* acut·us -a -um
treble *tr* triplicare
tree *s* arb·or -oris *f*
trellis *s* cancell·i -orum *mpl*
tremble *intr* tremĕre
trembling *adj* tremul·us -a -um
trembling *s* trepidati·o -onis *f*
tremendous *adj* imman·is -is -e
tremendously *adv* valde, vehementer
tremulous *adj* tremul·us -a -um
trench *s* foss·a -ae *f; ***to dig a —** fossam fodĕre
trespass *intr* in alienum fundum ingredi (sine domini permissu)
trespass *n* peccat·um -i *n*
tress *s* crin·is -is *m*
trestle *s* fulciment·um -i *n*
trial *s (attempt)* conat·us -ūs *m; (experiment)* experienti·a -ae *f; (test)* probati·o -onis *f; (suffering)* tribulati·o -onis *f; (leg)* judic·ium -(i)i *n*
trial lawyer *s* act·or -oris *m* causarum
triangle *s* triangul·um -i *n*
triangular *adj* triquetr·us -a -um
tribe *s* trib·us -ūs *f*
tribulation *s* tribulati·o -onis *f*
tribunal *s* tribun·al -alis *n; ***on the —** pro tribunali
tribune *s* tribun·us -i *m*
tribuneship *s* tribunat·us -ūs *m*
tributary *adj* vectigal·is -is -e
tributary *s* amn·is -is *m* in alium influens
tribute *s* tribut·um -i *n; ***to pay a — to s.o.** aliquem laudibus debitis efferre
trick *s* dol·us -i *m; (feat of skill)* stroph·a -ae *f; ***to do some —s** aliqua portenta facĕre
trick *tr* fallĕre
trickle *s* stillicid·ium -(i)i *n*
trickle *intr* stillare
trickster *s* veterat·or -oris *m*
tricky *adj* dolos·us -a-um; *(difficult)* nodos·us -a -um
trident *s* trid·ens -entis *m*

triennial *adj* trienn·is -is -e
trifle *s* res rei *f* parva; —s nug·ae -arum *fpl*
trifle *intr* nugari
trifling *adj* lĕv·is -is -e
trigonometry *s* trigonometri·a -ae *f*
trill *s* son·us -i *m* vibratus
trill *tr* vibrare
trim *adj* compt·us -a -um
trim *tr* adornare; *(to prune)* putare; *(the hair)* tondēre
trim *s* to be in — boni habitūs esse
trimmings *spl* ornat·us -ūs *m*
trinket *s* tric·ae -arum *fpl*
trio *s* trini·o -onis *f*
trip *s* it·er -ineris *n;* to take a — iter facĕre
trip *tr* pedem opponĕre *(w. dat); (fig)* fallĕre **ll** *intr* pedem offendĕre; *(fig)* errare, labi
tripartite *adj* tripartit·us -a -um
tripe *s* omas·um -i *n*
triple *adj* tripl·ex -icis
triple *tr* triplicare
tripod *s* trip·us -odis *m*
trireme *s* trirem·is -is *f*
trisyllabic *adj* trisyllab·us -a -um
trite *adj* trit·us -a -um
triumph *s (victory)* victori·a -ae *f; (entry of victorious general)* triumph·us -i *m;* to hold a — triumphum agĕre
triumph *intr* triumphare; to — over devincĕre; *(of a general)* triumphare de *(w. abl)*
triumphal *adj* triumphal·is -is -e
triumphant *adj (masc)* vict·or -oris; *(fem)* victr·ix -icis
trivial *adj* lev·is -is -e
triviality *s* nug·ae -arum *fpl*
troop *s* caterv·a -ae *f; (of cavalry)* turm·a -ae *f;* —s copi·ae -arum *fpl*
trooper *s (coll)* veteran·us -i *m*
trophy *s* tropae·um -i *n*
tropical *adj* tropic·us -a -um
tropics *spl* zon·a -ae *f* torrida
trot *intr* tolutim ire
trouble *s* lab·or -oris *m,* aerumn·a -ae *f;* to have — with *(e.g., the kidneys)* laborare *(w. abl)*
trouble *tr* vexare, angĕre
troubled *adj* confus·us -a -um; — face vult·us -ūs *m* exercitatus
troublesome *adj* molest·us -a -um; to be — urgēre
trough *s* alve·us -i *m*
trounce *tr (to punish)* castigare; *(to defeat decisively)* devincĕre
troupe *s* gre·x -gis *m*
trousers *spl* brac·ae -arum *fpl*
trout *s* truct·a -ae *f*
trowel *s* trull·a -ae *f*
truant *s* cessat·or -oris *m;* to play — solita ludi munera neglegĕre

truce *s* induti·ae -arum *fpl;* during the — per indutias; to agree to a — indutias cum hostibus pacisci; to break off a — indutias tollĕre
truck *s* carr·us -i *m*
trudge *intr* repĕre; to — over many places calcare plura loca
true *adj* ver·us -a -um; *(genuine)* german·us -a -um; *(faithful)* fid·us -a -um; *(exact)* rect·us -a -um
truffle *s* tub·er -eris *n* terrae
truism *s* ver·um -i *n* tritum
truly *adv* vere, profecto
trump *tr* to — up effingĕre
trumpet *s (mil)* tub·a -ae *f,* aes, aeris *n; (for civilian purposes)* buccin·a -ae *f;* to rouse the men with the — aere viros ciēre
trumpeter *s* tubic·en -inis *m;* buccinat·or -oris *m*
truncheon *s* fust·is -is *m*
trundle *intr* volvēre
trunk *s (of tree)* trunc·us -i *m; (for luggage)* cist·a -ae *f; (of elephant)* probosc·is -is *f,* man·us -ūs *f*
trust *s* fiduci·a -ae *f,* fid·es -ei *f;* to put — in (con)fidĕre *(w. dat)*
trust *tr (persons or acts)* fidĕre *(w. dat); (esp. words spoken)* credĕre *(w. dat); (to entrust)* committĕre; not — his eyes fidem oculorum timēre **ll** *intr* to — in fidĕre *(w. dat)*
trustee *s* fiduciar·ius -(i)i *m*
trusteeship *s* tutel·a -ae *f*
trustful *adj* credul·us -a -um
trusting *adj* fid·ens -entis
trustingly *adv* fidenter
trustworthiness *s* fid·es -ei *f*
trustworthy *adj* fid·us -a -um; *(witness)* locupl·es -etis
trusty *adj* fid·us -a -um
truth *s (abstract)* verit·as -atis *f; (concrete)* ver·um -i *n;* in — vero; this is the — haec sunt vera; to speak the — verum dicĕre
truthful *adj* ver·ax -acis
truthfully *adv* veraciter
try *tr* tentare, temptare; *(to put to the test)* experiri; *(leg)* judicare; *(to hold a judicial inquiry)* cognoscĕre; to — a case causam cognoscĕre; to — one's patience patientiā abuti; to — to obtain affectare
trying *adj* incommod·us -a -um
tub *s* labr·um -i *n*
tube *s* tubul·us -i *m,* fistul·a -ae *f*
tuberculosis *s* tab·es -is *f*
tuck *tr* to — up succingĕre; with tunic —ed up succint·us -a -um
Tuesday *s* di·es -ei *m* Martis
tuft *s* flocc·us -i *m*
tug *s* tract·us -ūs *m; (ship)* nav·is -is *f* tractoria

tug *tr* trahĕre **‖** *intr* **to — at** vellicare
tugboat *s* nav·is -is *f* tractoria
tuition *s* minerv·al -alis *n*
tumble *intr* volvi
tumbler *s* pocul·um -i *n* vitreum
tumor *s* tum·or -oris *m*
tumult *s* tumult·us -ūs *m*
tumultuous *adj* tumultuos·us -a -um
tumultuously *adv* tumultuose
tune *s* cant·us -ūs *m;* **in**   conson·us -a -um; **out of —** abson·us a -um; **to be out of —** discrepare
tuneful *adj* canor·us -a -um
tunic *s* tunic·a -ae *f;* **long-sleeved —** tunica *f* manicata; **small —** tunicul·a -ae *f;* **— reaching to the ankles** tunica *f* talaris; **wearing a tunic** tunicat·us -a -um
tunnel *s* cunicul·us -i *m*
turban *s* mitr·a -ae *f*
turbid *adj* turbid·us -a -um
turbulence *s* agitati·o -onis *f; (air)* flabr·a -orum *npl* violenta
turbulent *adj* turbulent·us -a -um
turf *s* caesp·es -itis *m*
turgid *adj* turgid·us -a -um
turkey *s* meleagris gallopav·o -onis *f;* **to talk —** *(coll)* Latine loqui
turmoil *s* perturbati·o -onis *f;* **mental —** animi commoti·o -onis *f*
turn *s (circuit)* circuit·us -ūs *m; (revolution)* conversi·o -onis *f; (change, course)* vicissitud·o -inis *f; (inclination of the mind)* inclinati·o -onis *f;* **a good —** benefic·ium -(i)i *n;* **in —** invicem; **out of —** extra ordinem; **take a — for the better, worse** melius, pejus ire; **to take —s in fighting** per vices dimicare; **— in the road** flex·us -ūs *m* viae
turn *tr* (con)vertĕre; *(to twist)* torquēre; *(to bend)* flectĕre; **to — around** circumagĕre, volvĕre; **to — aside** deflectĕre; **to — away** avertĕre; **to — back** convertĕre; **to — down** *(to refuse)* recusare, detrectare; **to — into** vertĕre in *(w. acc);* **to — over** *(to hand over)* tradĕre; *(property)* alienare; *(in the mind)* agitare; *(to upset)* evertĕre; **to — over the pages of a book** librum evolvĕre; **to —one's attention to** animadvertĕre; **to — out** ejicĕre; **to — up** *(w. hoe)* invertĕre; **to — up the nose** nares corrugare; **to — upside down** quod sursum est, deorsum facĕre **‖** *intr* verti, versari; **to — against** disciscĕre ab *(w. abl);* **to — around** converti; **to — aside** se declinare; **to — away** aversari; **to — back** reverti; **to — into** mutari in *(w. acc),* vertĕre in *(w. acc);* **to — out** evenire, evadĕre; **to — up** intervenire, adesse

turnip *s* rap·um -i *n*
turpitude *s* turpitud·o -inis *f*
turret *s* turricul·a -ae *f*
turtle *s* testud·o -inis *f*
tusk *s* den·s -tis *m*
tutelage *s* tutel·a -ae *f*
tutor *s* domesticus praecept·or -oris *m*
tweezers *spl* volsell·a -ae *f*
twelfth *adj* duodecim·us -a -um
twelve *adj* duodecim *(indecl);* **— times** duodecies
twentieth *adj* vicesim·us -a -um
twenty *adj* viginti *(indecl);* **— times** vicies
twice *adv* bis
twig *s* ramul·us -i *m*
twilight *s (evening)* crepuscul·um -i *n; (early dawn)* dilucul·um -i *n*
twin *adj* gemin·us -a -um
twin *s* gemin·us -i *m,* gemell·us -i *m*
twine *s* fil·um -i *n*
twine *tr* circumplicare **‖** *intr* **to — around** circumplecti *(w. acc)*
twinge *s* dol·or -oris *m;* **to suffer such —s of conscience that** ita conscientia mentem excitam vexat ut
twinkle *intr* micare
twinkling *s (of eye)* nict·us -ūs *m*
twirl *tr* versare, circumagĕre **‖** *intr* versari
twist *tr* torquēre **‖** *intr* se torquēre
twit *tr* exprobrare, objurgare
twitch *s* vellicati·o -onis *f*
twitch *tr* vellicare **‖** *intr* formicare
twitter *s* pipul·um -i *n*
twitter *tr* minurire
two *adj* duo, duae, duo; **— at a time** bin·i -ae -a; **— camps** bina castr·a -orum *npl;* **— times** bis
two-bit *adj (worthless)* sestertiari·us -a -um
two-edged *adj* anc·eps -ipitis; **— ax** bipenn·is -is *f*
two-faced *adj (pej)* bilingu·is -is -e
twofold *adj* dupl·ex -icis
two-footed *adj* bip·es -edis
two-headed *adj* bic·eps -ipitis
two hundred *adj* ducent·i -ae -a
two-pronged *adj* bid·ens -entis
twosome *s* par, paris *n*
two-time *tr* fraudare
two-timer *s* infidel·is is *mf*
two-way *adj* bivi·us -a -um
type *s* exempl·um -i *n; (class)* gen·us -eris *n; (print)* typ·i -orum *mpl;* **this — of speech** hujus generis orati·o -onis *f*
type *tr* exarare in machinam scriptoriam
typewriter *s* machin·a -ae *f* scriptoria
typhoon *s* turb·o -inis *f*
typical *adj* typic·us -a -um
typically *adv* per typum
typify *tr* imaginem *(w. gen)* fingĕre

typist *s* scrib·a -ae *mf*
tyrannical *adj* tyrannic·us -a -um
tyrannically *adv* tyrannice
tyrannicide *s (act)* tyrannicid·ium -(i)i
  n; (person) tyrannicid·a -ae *m*
tyrannt *s* tyrann·us -i *m*
tyro *s* tir·o -onis *m*

U

ubiquitous *adj* ubique praes·ens -entis
udder *s* ub·er -eris *n*
ugliness *s* deformit·as -atis *f*
ugly *adj* deform·is -is -e; **to make —**
  deformare
ulcer *s* ulc·us -eris *n*
ulcerate *intr* ulcerari
ulcerous *adj* ulceros·us -a -um
ulterior *adj (place)* ulter·ior -ior -ius;
  (time) poster·us -a -um; **— motive**
  rati·o -onis *f* recondita
ultimate *adj* ultim·us -a -um
ultimately *adv* ultimo
umbrage *s* **to take — at** aegre ferre
umbrella *s* umbell·a -ae *f*
umpire *s* arbi·ter -tri *m*
unabashed *adj* intrepid·us -a -um; *(pej)*
  impud·ens -entis
unabated *adj* continu·us -a -um
unable *adj* **(to)** nequi·ens -entis *(w.
  inf);* **— to control his anger** im-
  pot·ens -entis irae; **— to keep up
  with the words of the speaker** male
  subsequ·ens -entis verba dicentis; **to
  be — to** non posse *or* nequire *(w. inf)*
unaccented *adj* accentu caren·s -tis
unacceptable *adj* **(to)** invis·us -a -um
  (w. dat)
unaccompanied *adj* incomitat·us -a
  -um
unaccomplished *adj* infect·us -a -um
unaccountable *adj* inenodabil·is -is -e
unaccountably *adv* praeter opinionem
unaccustomed *adj* insuet·us -a -um
unacquainted *adj* **— with** ignar·us -a
  -um *(w. gen),* exper·s -tis *(w. gen)*
unadorned *adj* inornat·us -a -um
unadulterated *adj* mer·us -a -um
unaffected *adj* simpl·ex -icis
unafraid *adj* impavid·us -a -um
unaided *adj* non adjut·us -a -um
unalterable *adj* immutabil·is -is -e
unaltered *adj* immutat·us -a -um
unanimous *adj* unanim·us -a -um
unanimously *adv* consensu omnium
unanswerable *adj* irrefragabil·is -is -e
unappeased *adj* implacat·us -a -um
unapproachable *adj* inaccess·us -a -um
unarmed *adj* inerm·is -is -e
unasked *adj* injuss·us -a -um
unassailable *adj* inexpugnabil·is -is -e

unassuming *adj* modest·us -a -um
unattached *adj* vacu·us -a -um
unattainable *adj* ardu·us -a -um
unattended *adj (unaccompanied)* sine
  comitatu; *(not cared for)* neglect·us
  -a -um; **— by pain** privat·us -a -um
  dolore
unattractive *adj* invenust·us -a -um
unauthorized *adj* illicit·us -a -um
unavailing *adj* inutil·is -is -e
unavenged *adj* inult·us -a -um
unavoidable *adj* inevitabil·is -is -e
unaware *adj* insci·us -a -um
unbearable *adj* intolerabil·is -is -e
unbeaten *adj* invict·us -a -um
unbecoming *adj* indecor·us -a -um; **it
  is —** dedecet
unbefitting *adj* indecor·us -a -um
unbend *intr* animum remittĕre
unbending *adj* inflexibil·is -is -e
unbiased *adj* sine ira et studio
unbidden *adj* injuss·us -a -um
unbleached *adj* crud·us -a -um
unblemished *adj* intact·us -a -um
unblest *adj* infortunat·us -a -um
unborn *adj* nondum nat·us -a -um
unbridled *adj (lit & fig)* infren·is -is -e
unbroken *adj* irrupt·us -a -um; *(of
  horses)* indomit·us -a -um
unbuckle *tr* refibulare
unburden *tr* exonerare
unbutton *tr* diloricare
uncalled-for *adj* alien·us -a -um
uncanny *adj* mir·us -a -um
uncared-for *adj* neglect·us -a -um
unceasing *adj* assidu·us -a -um
unceasingly *adv* assidue, sine fine
uncertain *adj* incert·us -a -um; **to be
  —** haerēre, vacillare
uncertainty *s* dubitati·o -onis *f*
unchangeable *adj* immutabil·is -is -e
unchanged *adj* immutat·us -a -um
unchanging *adj* immutat·us -a -um
uncharitable *adj* immisericor·s -dis
unchaste *adj* parum cast·us -a -um
uncivil *adj* inurban·us -a -um
uncivilized *adj* incult·us -a -um
unclasp *tr* refibulare
uncle *s (father's brother)* patru·us -i
  m; (mother's brother) avuncul·us -i
  m; **great —** magnus patruus *(or* avun-
  culus) *m*
unclean *adj* immund·us -a -um
uncomfortable *adj* incommod·us -a -um
uncommon *adj* rar·us -a -um; *(outstanding)* egregi·us -a -um
uncommonly *adv* praeter solitum
unconcerned *adj* incurios·us -a -um
unconditional *adj* sine exceptione
unconditionally *adv* nullā condicione
unconnected *adj* disjunct·us -a -um
unconquerable *adj* invict·us -a -um
unconscionable *adj* iniqu·us -a -um

unconcious *adj* omni sensu car·ens -entis; — **of** ignar·us -a -um *(w. gen)*, insci·us -a -um *(w. gen)*
unconstitutional *adj* illicit·us -a -um
uncontrollable *adj* impot·ens -entis
unconventional *adj* insolit·us -a -um
unconvinced *adj* **I am — that** non adductus sum ut credam *(w. acc & inf)*
unconvincing *adj* non verisimil·is -is -e
uncooked *adj* crud·us -a -um
uncorrupted *adj* incorrupt·us -a -um
uncouth *adj* inurban·us -a -um
uncover *tr* detegĕre
uncritical *adj* credul·us -a -um
uncultivated *adj* incult·us -a -um
uncut *adj (hair)* intons·us -a -um, *(wood)* incaedu·us -a -um
undamaged *adj* incolum·is -is -e
undaunted *adj* intrepid·us -a -um
undecided *adj* anc·eps -ipitis; — **whether...or** cunctat·us -a -um utrum...ar
undefended *adj* indefens·us -a -urr
undefiled *adj* incontaminat·us -a -um
undeniable *adj* haud dubi·us -a -um
under *adv* subter, infra
under *prep (position)* sub *(w. abl); (motion)* sub, subter *(w. acc); (less than)* infra *(w. acc);* — **the pretense of** per simulationem *(w. gen)*
underage *adj* impub·es -is
underbid *tr* minoris faciendum conducĕre
underbrush *s* frutect·um -i *n*
undercurrent *s* torr·ens -entis *m* subterfluens; — **of feeling** intimus animi sens·us -ūs *m*
under-done *adj* semicrud·us -a -um
underestimate *tr* minoris aestimare
underfoot *adj* obvi·us -a -um
undergarment *s* subucul·a -ae *f; (worn chiefly by women)* suppar·um -i *n*
undergo *tr* subire; **to — change** se mutare; **to — punishment** poenam dare, poenam sufferre
underground *adj* subterrane·us -a -um
undergrowth *s* virgult·a -orum *npl*
underhanded *adj* clandestin·us -a -um
underhandedly *adv* clam, furtive
underline *tr* subnotare
underling *s* minis·ter -tri *m*
undermine *tr* subruĕre; *(fig)* labefactare
underneath *adv* infra, subter
underneath *prep (position)* infra *(w. acc)*, sub *(w. abl); (motion)* sub *(w. acc)*
underpin *tr* fulcire
underpinnings *spl* fulciment·a -orum *npl*
underrate *tr* minoris aestimare
understand *tr* intellegĕre; *(a language or art)* scire; **to — Latin** Latine scire

understanding *adj* prud·ens -entis
understanding *s* intellect·us -ūs *m; (agreement)* consens·us -ūs *m; (condition)* condici·o -onis *f*
undertake *tr* adire ad *(w. acc)*, suscipĕre; *(to begin)* incipĕre
undertaker *s* libitinar·ius -(i)i *m*
undertaking *s* incept·um -i *n*
undervalue *tr* minoris aestimare
underworld *s* infer·i -orum *mpl*
undeserved *adj* immerit·us -a -um
undeservedly *adv* immerito
undeserving *adj* **(of)** indign·us -a -um *(w. abl)*
undiminished *adj* imminut·us -a -um
undiscernible *adj* impercept·us -a -um
undiscerning *adj* heb·es -etis
undisciplined *adj* immoderat·us -a -um, *(mil)* inexercitat·us -a -um
undisguised *adj* apert·us -a -um
undismayed *adj* interrit·us -a -um
undisputed *adj* cert·us -a -um; **since this is —** quum hoc constet
undistinguished *adj* ignobil·is -is -e
undisturbed *adj* imperturbat·us -a -um; — **peace** immota pa·x -cis *f*
undivided *adj* indivis·us -a -um
undo *tr (knot)* solvĕre; *(fig)* infectum reddĕre, irritum facĕre; *(to ruin)* perdĕre; **you have undone everything** omnia irrita fecisti
undone *adj (no completed)* infect·us -a -um; *(ruined)* perdit·us -a -um; **to be — (to be ruined)** perire
undoubted *adj* haud dubi·us -a -um
undoubtedly *adv* haud dubie
undress *tr* exuĕre ‖ *intr* se exuĕre
undue *adj (excessive)* nimi·us -a -um; *(unfair)* iniqu·us -a -um
undulate *intr* undare, fluctuare
undulating *adj* undulabund·us -a -um
undulation *s* undarum agitati·o -onis *f*
unduly *adv* nimis, plus aequo
undying *adj* aetern·us -a -um
unearth *tr* effodĕre; *(fig)* detegĕre
unearthly *adj* haud mortal·is -is -e
uneasily *adv* turbate; **to sleep —** male dormire
uneasiness *s* sollicitud·o -inis *f*
uneasy *adj* sollicit·us -a -um
uneducated *adj* indoct·us -a -um
unemployed *adj* otios·us -a -um; **to be — cessare**
unemployment *s* cessati·o -onis *f*
unencumbered *adj* expedit·us -a -um
unending *adj* infinit·us -a -um
unendurable *adj* intolerand·us -a -um
unenjoyable *adj* injucund·us -a -um
unenlightened *adj* inerudit·us -a -um
unenviable *adj* non invidend·us -a -um
unequal *adj* inaequal·is -is -e; — **to** im·par -paris *(w. dat)*

unequalled *adj* singular·is -is -e
unequally *adv* impariter
unerring *adj* cert·us -a -um
unerringly *adv* certe
uneven *adj* iniqu·us a -um; *(rough)* asp·era -era -erum
unevenness *s* iniquit·as -atis *f*
unexpected *adj* inopinat·us -a -um; *(unforeseen)* improvis·us -a -um
unexpectedly *adv* de improviso
unexplored *adj* inexplorat·us -a -um
unfading *adj* semper rec·ens -entis
unfailing *adj (friend)* cert·us -a -um; *(waters)* perenn·is -is -e
unfair *adj* iniqu·us -a -um
unfairly *adv* inique
unfaithful *adj* infid·us -a -um
unfamiliar *adj* ignot·us -a -um
unfamiliarity *s* (**with**) imprudenti·a -ae *f (w. gen)*
unfashionable *adj* obsolet·us -a -um
unfasten *tr* resolvĕre, laxare
unfavorable *adj* iniqu·us -a -um; — **and favorable omens** omin·a -um *npl* tristia et laeta
unfavorably *adv* male, inique
unfed *adj* impast·us -a -um
unfeeling *adj* dur·us -a -um
unfetter *tr* vincula demĕre *(w. dat)*
unfinished *adj* imperfect·us -a -um; *(crude)* rud·is -is -e
unfit *adj* inept·us -a -um
unfold *tr* explicare; *(story)* enarrare ‖ *intr* patescĕre
unforeseen *adj* improvis·us -a -um
unforgiving *adj* inexorabil·is -is -e
unfortified *adj* immunit·us -a -um
unfortunate *adj* infel·ix -icis
unfortunately *adv* infeliciter
unfounded *adj* van·us -a -um
unfriendly *adj* parum amic·us -a -um
unfruitful *adj* infecund·us -a -um
unfurl *tr* pandĕre
unfurnished *adj* nud·us -a -um
ungainly *adj* inhabil·is -is -e
ungenerous *adj* illiberal·is -is -e
ungentlemanly *adj* inurban·us -a -um
ungird *tr* discingĕre
ungodly *adj* impi·us -a -um
ungovernable *adj* intractabil·is -is -e
ungraceful *adj* invenust·us -a -um
ungracious *adj* petul·ans -antis
ungrateful *adj* ingrat·us -a -um
ungratefully *adv* ingrate
ungrudging *adj* non invit·us -a -um
ungrudgingly *adv* sine invidia
unguarded *adj* incustodit·us -a -um; *(of words)* inconsult·us -a -um
unhandy *adj* inhabil·is -is -e
unhappily *adv* infeliciter
unhappiness *s* infelicit·as -atis *f*
unhappy *adj* infel·ix -icis
unharness *tr* disjungĕre

unhealthiness *s* mala valetud·o -inis *f; (of a place)* gravit·as -atis *f*
unhealthy *adj* infirm·us -a -um, morbos·us -a -um; *(place, season, wind)* grav·is -is -e
unheard-of *adj* inaudit·us -a -um
unheeded *adj* neglect·us -a -um
unheroic *adj* ignav·us -a -um
unhesitating *adj* prompt·us -a -um
unhindered *adj* expedit·us -a -um
unhinge *tr* de cardine detrahĕre; *(fig)* perturbare
unholy *adj* impi·us -a -um
unhoped-for *adj* insperat·us -a -um
unhurt *adj* incolum·is -is -e
unicorn *s* unicorn·us -i *m*
uniform *adj* aequabil·is -is -e
uniform *s* ornat·us -ūs *m; (mil)* ornat·us -ūs *m* militaris; **in** — subornat·us -a -um
uniformed *adj* subornat·us -a -um
uniformity *s* aequabilit·as -atis *f*
uniformly *adv* aequabiliter
unify *tr* conjungĕre
unilateral *adj* de uno latere tantummodo
unimaginative *adj* heb·es -etis
unimpaired *adj* inte·ger -gra -grum
unimpeachable *adj* probatissim·us -a -um
unimportant *adj* lĕv·is -is -e
uninformed *adj* indoct·us -a -um
uninhabitable *adj* inhabitabil·is -is -e
uninhabited *adj* desert·us -a -um
uninjured *adj* incolum·is -is -e
uninspired *adj* non inspirat·us -a -um
unintelligible *adj* obscur·us -a -um
uninteresting *adj* jejun·us -a -um
uninterrupted *adj* continu·us -a -um
uninviting *adj* injucund·us -a -um
union *s (act)* conjuncti·o -onis *f; (social)* societ·as -atis *f; (agreement)* consens·us -ūs *m; (marriage)* conjug·ium -(i)i *n*
unique *adj* unic·us -a -um
unison *s* concent·us -ūs *m;* **to sing in** — unā voce canĕre
unit *s* unit·as -atis *f,* mon·as -adis *f*
unite *tr* conjungĕre; *(to make into one)* unire ‖ *intr* coïre, coalescĕre
united *adj* consociat·us -a -um; — **opposition** *(pol)* conspirati·o -onis *f*
unity *s* unit·as -atis *f*
universal *adj* universal·is -is -e
universally *adv* universe
universe *s* universit·as -atis *f*
university *s* academi·a -ae *f*
unjust *adj* unjust·us -a -um
unjustly *adv* injuste
unjustifiable *adj* quod nihil excusationis habet
unkempt *adj* incompt·us -a -um

unkind *adj* inhuman·us -a -um
unkindly *adv* inhumane
unknowingly *adv* inscienter
unknown *adj* ignot·us -a -um; — **to his wife** clam uxorem
unlawful *adj* contra jus; *(w. reference to state law)* contra legem; **it is — to** nefas est *(w. inf)*
unlawfully *adv* contra legem
unleavened *adj* non fermentat·us -a -um
unless *conj* nisi
unlike *adj* dissimil·is -is -e; **it is not — going** non est dissimile atque ire
unlimited *adj* infinit·us -a -um
unload *tr* exonerare
unlock *tr* reserare; **with the door unlocked** reseratis foribus
unlooked-for *adj* inopinat·us -a -um
unluckily *adv* infeliciter
unlucky *adj* infel·ix -icis; *(omen)* infaut·us -a -um; — **day** di·es -ei *m* ater
unmanageable *adj* intractabil·is -is -e
unmanly *adj* moll·is -is -e
unmannerly *adj* male morat·us -a -um, inurban·us -a -um
unmarried *adj (man)* cael·ebs -ibis; *(woman)* innupta
unmask *tr* detegĕre
unmatched *adj* singular·is -is -e
unmerciful *adj* immisericor·s -dis
unmercifully *adv* immisericorditer
unmistakable *adj* evid·ens -entis
unmistakably *adv* sine dubio
unmoved *adj* immot·us -a -um
unnatural *adj (event)* monstruos·us -a -um; *(deed)* imman·is -is -e
unnaturally *adv* contra naturam
unnecessarily *adv* ex supervacuo
unnecessary *adj* haud necessari·us -a -um
unnerve *tr* debilitare
unnoticed *adj* praetermiss·us -a -um; **to go — by** latēre inter *(w. acc)*
unobjectionable *adj* culpā exper·s -tis
unoccupied *adj* vacu·us -a -um; *(land)* apert·us -a -um; **to be —** vacare
unofficial *adj* privat·us -a -um
unpack *tr* e cistis eximĕre
unpaid *adj (of money)* debit·us -a -um; *(of service)* gratuit·us -a -um
unpalatable *adj* insuav·is -is -e
unparalleled *adj* singular·is -is -e
unpardonable *adj* cui ignosci non potest
unpatriotic *adj* immem·or -oris patriae
unpleasant *adj* injucund·us -a -um
unpleasantly *adv* injucunde
unpolluted *adj* impollut·us -a -um; *(fig)* intact·us -a -um
unpopular *adj* invis·us -a -um
unpopularity *s* invidi·a -ae *f*
unpracticed *adj* inexpert·us -a -um
unprecedented *adj* inaudit·us -a -um

unprejudiced *adj* candid·us -a -um
unpremeditated *adj* inconsult·us -a -um, subit·us -a -um
unprepared *adj* imparat·us -a -um
unprincipled *adj* improb·us -a -um
unproductive *adj* infecund·us -a -um
unprofitable *adj* inutil·is -is -e
unprofitably *adv* nullis fructibus
unprotected *adj* indefens·us -a -um
unprovoked *adj* ultro
unpunished *adj* inpunit·us -a -um; **to allow a crime to go —** maleficium impune habēre
unqualified *adj* haud idone·us -a -um; *(complete)* consummat·us -a -um
unquenchable *adj* inexstinct·us -a -um
unquestionable *adj* certissim·us -a -um
unquestionably *adv* facile
unquestioning *adj* credul·us -a -um
unravel *tr* retexĕre; *(fig)* enodare
unreasonable *adj* absurd·us -a -um
unreasonably *adv* absurde
unrefined *adj* crud·us -a -um
unrelenting *adj* inplacabil·is -is -e
unremitting *adj* assidu·us -a -um
unrepentant *adj* impaenit·ens -entis
unrestrained *adj* effrenat·us -a -um
unrighteous *adj* injust·us -a -um
unripe *adj* immatur·us -a -um
unrivaled *adj* incomparabil·is -is -e
unroll *tr* evolvĕre
unruffled *adj* immot·us -a -um
unruliness *s* impotenti·a -ae *f*
unruly *adj* impot·ens -entis
unsafe *adj* intut·us -a -um
unsalted *adj* insals·us -a -um
unsatisfied *adj* inexplet·us -a -um
unsatisfactory *adj* non idone·us -a -um
unsavory *adj* insipid·us -a -um; *(disreputable)* foed·us -a -um
unscrew *tr* retorquēre
unseal *tr (letter)* resignare; *(a jar)* relinĕre
unseasonable *adj* intempestiv·us -a -um
unseemly *adj* indecor·us -a -um
unseen *adj* invis·us -a -um
unselfish *adj* suae utilitatis immem·or -oris
unselfishly *adv* liberaliter
unsettle *tr* sollicitare
unsettled *adj* incert·us -a -um; *(of mind)* sollicit·us -a -um
unshaken *adj* immot·us -a -um
unshaved *adj* irras·us -a -um
unsheathe *tr* destringĕre
unsightly *adj* turp·is -is -e
unskilful *adj* imperit·us -a -um
unskilfully *adv* imperite
unskilled *adj* imperit·us -a -um
unsophisticated *adj* simpl·ex -icis
unsound *adj* infirm·us -a -um; *(of mind)* insan·us -a -um; *(ill-founded)* van·us -a -um

unsparing *adj (merciless)* inclem·ens -entis; *(lavish)* larg·us -a -um
unsparingly *adv* inclementer; large
unspeakable *adj* ineffabil·is -is -e
unstable *adj* instabil·is -is -e; *(fig)* lĕv·is -is -e, inconst·ans -antis
unstained *adj* pur·us -a -um; *(honor)* intaminat·us -a -um
unsteadily *adv* inconstanter
unsteady *adj* inconst·ans -antis
unsuccessful *adj* infel·ix -icis
unsuccessfully *adv* infeliciter
unsuitable *adj* incommod·us -a -um
unsuited *adj* haud idone·us -a -um
unsullied *adj* intaminat·us -a -um
unsuspected *adj* non suspect·us -a -um
untamed *adj* indomit·us -a -um
untasted *adj* ingustat·us -a -um
untaught *adj* indoct·us -a -um
unteachable *adj* indocil·is -is -e
untenable *adj* infirm·us -a -um, quod defendi non potest
unthankful *adj* ingrat·us -a -um
untie *tr* solvĕre
until *conj* dum, donec, quoad
until *prep* usque ad *(w. acc),* in *(w. acc);* **to put off — tomorrow** differre in crastinum; **— late at night** in multam noctem; **— now** adhuc
untimely *adj* intempestiv·us -a -um; *(premature)* praematur·us -a -um
untiring *adj* assidu·us -a -um
untold *adj (numberless)* innumer·us -a -um; *(story)* immemorat·us -a -um
untouched *adj* intact·us -a -um; *(fig)* immot·us -a -um
untrained *adj* inexercitat·us -a -um
untried *adj* intemptat·us -a -um
untrodden *adj* non trit·us -a -um
untroubled *adj* tranquill·us -a -um
untrue *adj* fals·us -a -um; *(disloyal)* infid·us -a -um
untrustworthy *adj* infid·us -a -um
unusual *adj* inusitat·us -a -um
unusually *adv* praeter solitum
unutterable *adj* infand·us -a -um
unvarnished *adj (fig)* nud·us -a -um
unveil *tr* detegĕre; *(fig)* patefacĕre
unversed *adj* **— in** imperit·us -a -um *(w. gen)*
unwanted *adj* ingrat·us -a -um; *(superfluous)* supervacane·us -a -um
unwarranted *adj* iniqu·us -a -um
unwary *adj* incaut·us -a -um
unweaned *adj* lacticulos·us -a -um
unwearied *adj* indefess·us -a -um
unwelcome *adj* ingrat·us -a -um
unwieldy *adj* inhabil·is -is -e
unwilling *adj* invit·us -a -um
unwillingly *adv* invite
unwind *tr* revolvĕre; **they unwound their threads** retro sua fila revolverunt

unwise *adj* imprud·ens -entis
unwisely *adv* imprudenter
unworthily *adv* indigne
unworthiness *s* indignit·as -atis *f*
unworthy *adj* **(of)** indign·us -a -um *(w. abl)*
unwrap *tr* explicare, evolvĕre
unwritten *adj* non script·us -a -um
unyielding *adj* inflexibil·is -is -e
unyoke *tr* disjungĕre
up *adv* sursum; (**up** is often expressed in Latin by the prefix con-, com-, cor-, ex-, sub- combined with the verb: **to eat** — comesse; **to finish** — conficĕre; **to snatch** — corripĕre; **to rise** — exsurgĕre; **to lift** — sublevare); **to charge — the hill** erigĕre aciem per adversum collem; **to go — the mountains** ire in adversos montes; **to rise — against us** exsurgĕre adversus *(or* in) nos; **— and down** sursum deorsum; **to run — and down** modo huc modo illuc cursare; **— to** tenus *(w. abl)* *(always placed after its case, e.g.,* **the water come up to the waist** umbilico tenus aqua erat); **—s and downs** modo sic, modo sic
upbraid *tr* castigare verbis
upbringing *s* educati·o -onis *f*
upheaval *s* eversi·o -onis *f*
uphill *adj* accliv·is -is -e; **to have an — struggle** clivo laborare
uphill *adv* adversus clivum, in collen
uphold *tr* servare, sustentare
upkeep *s* impens·a -ae *f*
uplift *tr* sublevare
upon *prep (position)* super *(w. abl),* in *(w. abl); (motion)* super *(w. acc),* in *(w. abl); (directly after)* ex *(w. abl),* sub *(w. abl); (converning)* de *(w. abl);* **— my word** fidem do
upper *adj* super·ior -ior -ius; *(world, air)* super·us -a -um; **an — room** superius cenacul·um -i *n;* **the — classes** superiores *(or* ampliores) ordin·es -um *mpl;* **to get the — hand** superare, vincĕre
uppermost *adj* summ·us -a -um
upright *adj* erect·us -a -um; *(of character)* honest·us -a -um, inte·ger -gra -grum
uproar *s* tumult·us -ūs *m;* **to cause an — tumultuari
uproot *tr* eradicare, erurĕre
upset *tr* evertĕre, subvertĕre; *(to worry)* perturbare
upset *adj* perculs·us -a -um
upside down *adv* **to turn —** sursum deorsum versare
upstairs *adv* sursum
upstart *s* novus hom·o -inis *m; (pej)* terrae fil·ius -(i)i *m*

upstream *adv* adverso flumine
up to *prep* usque ad *(w. acc)*, tenus *(postpositive, w. abl or gen)*
upwards *adv* sursum; **—of** *(of number)* plus quam
urban *adj* urban·us -a -um
urge *tr* urgēre, impellĕre; **to — on** stimulare, incitare; *(horses)* admittĕre
urge *s* impuls·us -ūs *m*
urgency *s* necessit·as -atis *f*
urgent *adj* grav·is -is -e; **whose need was most —** quibus summa necessitudo erat; **to be —** instare
urgently *adv* vehementer
urn *s* urn·a -ae
us *pron* nos; **to —** nobis; **with —** nobiscum
usage *s* us·us -ūs *m*
use *s* us·us -ūs *m;* **no —!** frustra!; **in common —** usitat·us -a -um; **it is no —** n·hil opus est; **to be of —** usui esse; **to be of no —** inutile esse, usum nullum habēre; **to come into —** invalescĕre, in morem venire; **to make — of** uti *(w. abl)*
use *tr* uti *(w. abl); (to take advantage of)* abuti *(w. abl);* **to — s.th. for** aliquid adhibēre *(w. dat);* **to — up** consumĕre, exhaurire ‖ *intr* **I used to** solebam *(w. inf)*
used *adj* usitat·us -a -um; *(second-hand)* trit·us -a -um; **— to** *(accustomed to)* assuet·us -a -um *(w. dat)*
useful *adj* util·is -is -e; **to be —** usui esse
usefully *adv* utiliter, commode
useless *adj* inutil·is -is -e
uselessly *adv* frustra
usual *adj* solit·us -a -um; **as —** ut solet; **more than —** plus solito
usually *adv* plerumque, fere
usurp *tr* invadĕre *(w. acc or in + acc)*, usurpare
usurpation *s* usurpati·o -onis *f*
usurper *s* usurpat·or -oris *m*
usury *s* immodica usur·a -ae *f*
utensils *spl* untensil·ia -ium *npl;* **household —s** instrument·um -i *n;* **kitchen —s** coquinatori·a -orum *npl*
utility *s* utilit·as -atis *f*
utilize *tr* uti *(w. abl)*, adhibēre
utmost *adj* summ·us -a -um
utmost *n* **to do one's —** omnibus viribus contendĕre
utter *adj* tot·us -a -um
utter *tr* emittĕre; *(to reveal what is a secret)* proloqui
utterance *s* dict·um -i *n;* **to give — to one's feelings** exprimĕre dicendo sensa
utterly *adv* omnino, funditus
uttermost *adj* extrem·us -a -um
uvula *s* uvul·a -ae *f*

V

vacancy *s* vacuit·as -atis *f; (in hotel)* cubicul·um -i *n* vacans
vacant *adj* vacu·us -a -um; *(look, stare)* inan·is -is -e; **to be —** vacare
vacate *tr* vacuefacĕre
vacation *s* feri·ae -arum *fpl*
vaccinate *tr* vaccinum inserĕre in *(w. acc)*
vaccination *s* vaccinati·o -onis *f*
vaccine *s* vaccin·um -i *n*
vacillate *intr* vacillare
vacillating *adj* vacill·ans -antis
vacuum *s* inan·e -is *n*
vagabond *s* larifug·a -ae *m*
vagary *s* libid·o -inis *f*
vagina *s* natural·e -is *n*
vagrancy *s* vagati·o -onis *f*
vagrant *adj* vag·us -a -um
vagrant *s* err·o -onis *m*
vague *adj* vag·us -a -um; *(not fixed)* incert·us -a -um; *(ambiguous)* ambigu·us -a -um
vaguely *adv* incerte
vagueness *s* obscurit·as -atis *f*
vain *adj (empty)* van·us -a -um; *(proud)* superb·us -a -um; **in —** frustra
vainly *adv* frustra
vainglorious *adj* glorios·us -a -um
valedictorian *s* valedic·ens -entis *mf*
valedictory *s* orati·o -onis *f* valedicens
valentine *s* chartul·a -ae *f* amatoria
valet *s* cubicular·ius -(i)i *m*
valiant *adj* fort·is -is -e
valid *adj* firm·us -a -um
valley *s* vall·es -is *f*
valor *s* fortitud·o -inis *f*
valuable *adj* pretios·us -a -um
valuables *spl* res, rerum *fpl* pretiosae
valuation *s* aestimati·o -onis *f*
value *s* pret·ium -(i)i *n*
value *tr* aestimare; **to — highly** magni aestimare; **to — s.o. for his prowess** aliquem probare a viribus
valueless *adj* vil·is -is -e
valve *s* epistom·ium -(i)i *n*
vampire *s* vespertili·o -onis *m*
vandal *s* evers·or -oris *m*
vanguard *s (mil)* primum agm·en -inis *n*
vanish *intr* (e)vanescĕre, diffugĕre
vanity *s* vanit·as -atis *f*
vanquish *tr* profligare, devincĕre
vantage *s* commod·um -i *n; —* **point** superior loc·us -i *m*
vapid *adj* vapid·us -a -um
vapor *s* vap·or -oris *m*
variable *adj* vari·ans -antis
variance *s* differenti·a -ae *f;* **at — with** dissid·ens -entis ab *(w. abl);*

to set the state at — serĕre civiles discordias
variation s variet·as -atis f
varicose vein s var·ix -icis f
variety s variet·as -atis f
various adj vari·i -ae -a; **in — ways** varie
variously adv varie
vary tr variare, mutare ‖ intr mutari
vase s vascul·um -i n
vast adj vast·us -a -um
vastly adv valde, maxime
vastness s immensit·as -atis f
vat s cup·a -ae f
vault s (archit) camer·a -ae f; (leap) salt·us -ūs m; (for valuables) thesaur·us -i m
vault intr salire
vaunt tr jactare ‖ intr se jactare
veal s vitulin·a -ae f
veer intr se vertĕre
vegetable s hol·us -eris n
vegetable adj holitari·us -a -um
vehemence s vehementi·a -ae f
vehement adj vehem·ens -entis; (violent) violent·us -a -um
vehemently adv vehementer
vehicle s vehicul·um -i n
veil s velam·en -inis n; (bridal) flamme·um -i n; (fig) integument·um -i n
veil tr velare
vein s ven·a -ae f
velocity s velocit·as -atis f
velvet s velvet·um -i n
vend tr vendĕre
veneer s ligni bracte·a -ae f; (fig) speci·es -ei f
venerable adj venerabil·is -is -e
venerate tr venerari
veneration s venerati·o -onis f
venereal adj venere·us -a -um
vengeance s ulti·o -onis f; **to take — on s.o.** se vindicare ab (w. abl)
venison s ferin·a -ae f
venom s venen·um -i n
venomous adj venenat·us -a -um
vent s spirament·um -i n
vent tr aperire; **to — one's wrath on** iram erumpĕre in (w. acc)
ventilate tr ventilare
ventriloquist s ventriloqu·us -i m
venture s facin·us -eris n; **to risk a —** periculum subire
venture tr periclitari; **to — all** dare summam rerum in aleam
venturesome adj aud·ax -acis
veractiy s veracit·as -atis f
veranda s subdial·e -is n
verb s verb·um -i n
verbal adj verbal·is -is -e
verbally adv verbo
verbatim adv ad verbum
verbose adj verbos·us -a -um

verdict s sententi·a -ae f; **to deliver the —** sententiam pronuntiare
verge s marg·o -inis m; **to be on the —** of non procul abesse ut (w. subj)
verification s affirmati·o -onis f
verify tr probare
vermilion adj minian·us -a -um
vermilion s min·ium -(i)i n
vermin spl bestiol·ae -arum fpl
vernacular s patrius serm·o -onis m
versatile adj versatil·is -is -e
verse s vers·us -ūs m
versed adj (in) versat·us et exercitat·us -a -um (in + abl)
versification s versificati·o -onis f
version s translati·o -onis f; **to give a literal —** of plane vertĕre
vertex s vert·ex -icis m
vertical adj rect·us -a -um; **a — line** perpendicul·um -i n
vertically adv ad perpendiculum
very adj ips·e -a -um; **on the — day on which** ipso die quo
very adv valde, admodum, maxime
vessel s vas, vasis n; (ship) navig·ium -(i)i n
vest s thor·ax -acis m
vestal virgin s virg·o -inis f vestalis
vestibule s vestibul·um -i n
vestige s vestig·ium -(i)i n
vestment s vestiment·um -i n
veteran s veteran·us -i m
veterinarian s veterinar·ius -(i)i m
veterinary adj veterinari·us -a -um
veto s intercessi·o -onis f
veto tr intercedĕre (w. dat)
vex tr vexare
vexation s vexati·o -onis f
via prep per (w. acc)
vial s phial·a -ae f
vibrate intr vibrare
vibration s vibrat·us -ūs m
vicar s vicar·ius -(i)i m
vicarious adj vicari·us -a -um
vice s (shameful deed) flagit·ium -(i)i n; (flaw) vit·ium -(i)i n
vice admiral s classis subpraefect·us -i m
vice chancellor s procancellar·ius -(i)i m
vice president s praesidis vicar·ius -(i)i m
viceroy s subregul·us -i m
vicinity s vicini·a -ae f; **in the — of** circum (w. acc)
vicious adj crudel·is -is -e
viciously adv crudeliter
vicissitude s vicissitud·o -inis f
victim s victim·a -ae f; **to fall — to** obire (w. dat)
victimize tr (to swindle) circumvenire; (to assault, kill) vim inferre (w. dat)
victor s vict·or -oris m, victr·ix -icis f

victorious *adj* vict·or -oris, *(of a female)* victr·ix -icis *(used appositively);* **to be —** vincěre

victory *s* victori·a -ae *f;* **news of —** litter·ae -arum *fpl* victrices; **to win a —** victoriam consequi *or* adipisci; **to gain a — over** s.o. ab aliquo victoriam reportare

vie *intr* certare, contendĕre

view *s* aspect·us -ūs *m,* conspect·us -ūs *m; (from above)* despect·us -ūs *m; (opinion)* sententi·a -ae *f;* **almost in — of the city** paene in conspectu urbis; **in my —** meo judicio; **this is my point of —** hoc sic mihi videtur; **to enjoy a view of** conspectu *(w. gen)* uti; **to get a bird's eye — of the city** omnem urbem sub uno aspectu despicĕre

view *tr* visěre

vigil *s* vigili·ae -arum *fpl; (lasting all night)* pervigil·ium -(i)i *n*

vigilance *s* vigilanti·a -ae *f*

vigilant *adj* vigil·ans -antis

vigilantly *adv* vigilanter

vigor *s* vig·or -oris *m*

vigorous *adj* ala·cer -cris -cre

vigorously *adv* alacriter

vile *adj* vil·is -is -e

vilify *tr* infamare

villa *s* vill·a -ae *f;* **my — at Formiae** meum Formian·um -i *n*

village *s* pag·us -i *m*

villager *s* pagan·us -i *m*

villain *s* scelest·us -i *m*

villany *s* improbit·as -atis *f*

vindicate *tr* vindicare; *(to justify)* probare; *(person)* defendĕre

vindication *s* vindicati·o -onis *f*

vindictive *adj* ultionis cupid·us -a -um

vine *s* vit·is -is *f*

vine arbor *s* pergul·a -ae *f*

vinegar *s* acet·um -i *n*

vinegar bottle *s* acetabul·um -i *n*

vineyard *s* vine·a -ae *f*

vintage *s* vindemi·a -ae *f*

violate *tr* violare

violation *s* violati·o -onis *f*

violator *s* violat·or -oris *m*

violence *s* violenti·a -ae *f*

violent *adj* violent·us -a -um

violently *adv* violenter

virgin *adj* virg·o -inis *f (used appositively);* **— forest** silv·a -ae *f* intacta

virgin *s* virg·o -inis *f*

virile *adj* viril·is -is -e

virility *s* virilit·as -atis *f*

virtually *adv* fere

virtue *s* virt·us -utis *f; (power)* vis *f;* **by — of** per *(w. acc),* ex *(w. abl)*

virtuous *adj* prob·us -a -um, virtute praedit·us -a -um

virtuously *adv* cum virtute, honeste

virulence *s* vis *f*

virulent *adj* virulent·us -a -um

viscera *spl* viscer·a -um *npl*

viscous *adj* viscos·us -a -um

visible *adj* visibil·is -is -e; *(striking, noticeable)* manifest·us -a -um

visibly *adv* manifeste

vision *s (sense)* vis·us -ūs *m; (apparition)* visi·o -onis *f*

visionary *s* somni·ans -antis *mf*

visit *s* salutati·o -onis *f*

visit *tr* visěre, visitare

visitor *s* hosp·es -itis *m*

visor *s* buccul·a -ae *f*

vista *s* prospect·us -ūs *m*

visual *adj* oculorum *(gen)*

vital *adj* vital·is -is -e; *(essential)* necessari·us -a -um

vitally *adv* praecipue

vitality *s* vis *f* vitalis

vitiate *tr* vitiare, corrumpĕre

vituperate *tr* vituperare

vituperation *s* vituperati·o -onis *f*

vivacious *adj* viv·ax -acis

vivaciously *adv* vivaciter

vivid *adj* vivid·us -a -um

vividly *adv* vivide

vivify *tr* vivificare

vocabulary *s* verborum copi·a -ae *f; (list of words)* vocabulorum ind·ex -icis *m*

vocal *adj* vocal·is -is -e

vocation *s* vocati·o -onis *f*

vociferous *adj* clamos·us -a -um

vogue *s* mos, moris *m;* **to be in —** moris esse

voice *s* vox vocis *f*

void *adj* inan·is -is -e; **— of** vacu·us -a -um *(w. abl)*

void *s* inan·e -is *n*

volatile *adj* volatic·us -a -um

volcanic *adj* vulcani·us -a -um

volcano *s* mon·s -tis *m* flammas et vaporem eructans

volition *s* volupt·as -atis *f*

volley *s (fig)* tempest·as -atis *f*

volume *s (book)* volum·en -inis *n; (quantity)* copi·a -ae *f; (of voice)* magnitud·o -inis *f*

voluminous *adj* voluminos·us -a -um; **— writer** script·or -oris *m* per multa diffusus volumina

voluntarily *adv* suā voluntate, ultro

voluntary *adj* voluntari·us -a -um; *(unpaid)* gratuit·us -a -um

volunteer *s* voluntar·ius -(i)i *m; (mil)* mil·es -itis *m* voluntarius

volunteer *intr (mil)* sponte nomen dare; **to — to do** s.th. aliquid ultro facĕre

voluptuous *adj* voluptari·us -a -um

vomit *s* vomiti·o -onis *f*

vomit *tr* voměre

voracious *adj* vor·ax -acis

voraciously *adv* voraciter
vortex *s* vort·ex -icis *m*
vote *s* suffrag·ium -(i)i *n; (fig) (judgment)* sententi·a -ae *f;* **to cast a —** suffragium ferre
vote *intr* suffragium ferre; *(of a judge)* sententiam ferre; *(of a senator)* censēre; **to — for** suffragari *(w. dat)*
voter *s* suffragat·or -oris *m*
votive *adj* votiv·us -a -um
vouch *intr* **to — for** testificari, affirmare
voucher *s* testimon·ium -(i)i *n*
vouchsafe *tr* concedĕre
vow *s* vot·um -i *n*
vow *tr* vovēre ‖ *intr* spondēre
vowel *s* vocal·is -is *f*
voyage *s* navigati·o -onis *f*
voyage *intr* navigare
voyager *s* navigat·or -oris *m*
vulgar *adj* vulgar·is -is -e; *(low)* vil·is -is -e
vulgarity *s* obscenit·as -atis *f*
vulnerable *adj* qui (quae, quod) vulnerari potest; *(of a fortress)* expugnabil·is -is -e
vulture *s* vult·ur -uris *m*

W

wad *s* fascicul·us -i *m*
wade *intr* per vada ire; **to — across** vado transire
wag *tr (the tail)* movēre
wage *tr* **to — war** bellum gerĕre
wager *tr* deponĕre
wager *s* sponsi·o -onis *f*
wages *spl* merc·es -edis *f*
wagon *s* plaustr·um -i *n; (toy)* plostell·um -i *n*
wail *intr* plorare
wailing *s* plorat·us -ūs *m*
waist *s* media par·s -tis *f* corporis
wait *intr* exspectare, opperiri; *(not to depart)* manēre; **to — at tables** ministrare; **to — for** exspectare, opperiri; **to — on** servire *(w. dat)*
wait *s* mor·a -ae *f;* **to lie in — for** insidiari *(w. dat)*
waiter *s* minis·ter -tri *m*
waitress *s* ministr·a -ae *f*
waive *tr* remittĕre
wake *tr* excitare ‖ *intr* **to — up** expergisci
wake *s* tract·us -ūs *m* aquarum a tergo navis; **in the — of** post *(w. acc)*
wakeful *adj* vig·il -is
walk *s (act)* ambulati·o -onis *f; (place)* ambulacr·um -i *n*, xyst·us -i *m; (covered)* portic·us -ūs *f; (gait)* incess·us -ūs *m*

walk *intr* ambulare, incedĕre; **to — out on** *(coll)* deserĕre
wall *s (interior)* pari·es -etis *m; (exterior)* mur·us -i *m; (of town)* moen·ia -ium *npl*, mur·us -i *m*
wall *tr* **to — in** moenibus munire; **to — up** *(w. stones, bricks)* concludĕre (saxis, lateribus)
walled *adj* moenibus munit·us -a -um
wallet *s* per·a -ae *f*
wallop *tr (coll)* percolopare
wallow *intr* volutari
walnut *s* jugl·ans -andis *f*
walrus *s* odoben·us -i *m*
waltz *s* saltati·o -onis *f* in gyrum
waltz *intr* saltare in gyrum
wan *adj* pallid·us -a -um
wander *intr* errare, vagari; **to — about** pervagari; **to — over** pererrare
wanderer *s* err·o -onis *m*
wandering *s* errati·o -onis *f*
wane *intr* decrescĕre
want *s (scarcity)* penuri·a -ae *f; (opp: copia)* inopi·a -ae *f; (extreme want)* egest·as -atis *f;* **to be in —, suffer —** egēre
want *tr* velle; *(to lack)* egēre *(w. abl)*
wanting *adj (defective)* vitios·us -a -um; *(missing)* abs·ens -entis; **to be — deficĕre, deesse
wanton *adj (lewd)* libidinos·us -a -um; *(unwarranted)* iniqu·us -a -um
war *s* bell·um -i *n;* **to declare — on** bellum indicĕre *(w. dat)*
war *intr (against)* bellare adversus *(w. acc)*
warble *intr* canĕre; *(to twitter)* fritinnire
war cry *s* ululat·us -ūs *m*
ward *s (minor)* pupill·us -i *m*, pupill·a -ae *f; (of a city)* regi·o -onis *f;* **— by —** regionatim
ward *tr* **to — off** arcēre, avertĕre
warden *s* carcerar·ius -(i)i *m*
wardrobe *s* vestiar·ium -(i)i *n; (clothes)* vestiment·a -orum *npl*
warehouse *s* horre·um -i *n*
wares *spl* merc·es -ium *fpl*
warfare *s* res, rei *f* bellica
war-horse *s* equ·us -i *m* bellator
warily *adv* caute
warlike *adj* bellig·er -era -erum
warm *adj* callid·us -a -um; *(just warm)* tepid·us -a -um; *(fig)* fervid·us -a -um; **to be — calēre
warm *tr* calefacĕre, tepefacĕre; *(with animal heat)* fovēre; **to — up** *(food)* recoquĕre; *(by exercise)* exercēre
warm-hearted *adj* am·ans -antis
warmly *adv* ardenter; *(kindly)* benigne
warmth *s* cal·or -oris *m; (fig)* ferv·or -oris *m*
warm-up *s* exercitati·o -onis *f*

warn *tr* monēre
warning *s* monit·um -i *n; (lesson)* document·um -i *n*
warp *s* stam·en -inis *n*
warp *tr* torquēre ‖ *intr (of wood)* pandēre
warped *adj* pand·us -a -um
warping *s* pandati·o -onis *f*
warrant *tr (to guarantee)* praestare; *(to justify, call for)* probare
warrant *s* mandat·um -i *n;* — **for arrest** praemandat·a -orum *npl*
warranty *s* satisdati·o -onis *f*
warrior *s* bellat·or -oris *m*
wart *s* verruc·a -ae *f*
wary *adj* caut·us -a -um
wash *tr* lavare; **to — away** abluĕre; **to — out** eluĕre ‖ *intr* lavari
wash *s* linte·a -orum *npl* lavanda; **to send to the —** ad lavandum dare
wash basin *s* aqual·is -is *m*
washing *s* lavati·o -onis *f*
wasp *s* vesp·a -ae *f*
waste *s* detriment·um -i *n; (of time, property)* jactur·a -ae *f*
waste *tr* effundĕre; *(time)* absumĕre, terĕre ‖ *intr* **to — away** tabescĕre
waste *adj* vast·us -a -um; **to lay —** vastare
wasteful *adj* prodig·us -a -um
wastefully *adv* prodige
wasteland *s* solitud·o -inis *f*
watch *s (guard)* vigili·a -ae *f; (sentry)* excubi·ae -arum *fpl;* **to keep —** excubare; **to keep — over** invigilare *(w. dat),* custodire
watch *tr (to observe)* observare, spectare; *(to guard)* custodire
watchful *adj* vigil·ans -antis
watchman *s* vig·il -ilis *m*
watchtower *s* specul·a -ae *f*
watchword *s* tesser·a -ae *f*
water *s* aqu·a -ae *f*
water *tr* irrigare; *(animals)* adaquare
waterboy *s* aquar·ius -(i)i *m*
waterfall *s* deject·us -ūs *m* aquae
waterfront *s* naval·ia -ium *npl*
watering place *s* aquar·ium -(i)i *n*
watermellon *s* cucurbit·a -ae *f* citrulla
watery *adj* aquos·us -a -um
wattle *s* crat·es -is *f*
wave *s* und·a -ae *f,* fluct·us -ūs *m*
wave *tr (hands, arms)* jactare; *(weapon, flag)* quassare ‖ *intr* undare
waver *intr* labare, nutare
wavering *adj* nut·ans -antis
wavy *adj* und·ans -antis; *(hair)* crisp·us -a -um
wax *s* cer·a -ae *f*
wax *adj* cere·us -a -um
wax *tr* incerare ‖ *intr* crescĕre
way *adv (coll)* longe, multo
way *s* vi·a -ae *f; (route)* it·er -ineris *n;*

(manner) mod·us -i *m; (plan, system, method)* rati·o -onis *f; (habit)* mo·s -ris *m;* **all the — from** usque ab *(w. abl);* **all the — to** usque ad *(w. acc);* **a long — off** longinqu·us -a -um; **by the — (incidentally)** obiter; **by — of** viā *(w. gen);* **get out of the —!** abi, apage!; **have it your —!** esto ut lubet!; **in every —** omnibus modis; **in no —** nullo modo; **in the —** obvi·us -a -um; **in this way** ad hunc modum; **to be a long — off** longe distare; **to be in the — of** obesse *(w. dat);* **to be out of the —** devi·us -a -um esse; **to get in the — of** intervenire *(w. dat);* **to get under —** ancoram solvĕre; **to give — (of a structure)** labare; *(to yield)* concedĕre; *(mil)* pedem referre; **to give — to** indulgĕre *(w. dat);* **to have one's own —** res pro arbitrio gerĕre; **to stand in the — of** obstare *(w. dat);* — **in** ingress·us -ūs *m;* — **out** exit·us -ūs *m*
wayfarer *s* viat·or -oris *m*
waylay *tr* insidiari *(w. dat)*
wayward *adj* inconst·ans -antis
we *pron* nos; — **ourselves** *(masc)* nosmet ipsi; *(fem)* nosmet ipsae
weak *adj (in body, mind, resources)* infirm·us -a -um; *(from defects)* debil·is -is -e; *(argument, light, constitution)* tenu·is -is -e; *(senses)* heb·es -etis; *(voice)* exil·is -is -e
weaken *tr* infirmare, debilitare ‖ *intr* hebescĕre, labare
weakly *adv* infirme
weakness *s* infirmit·as -atis *f,* debilit·as -atis *f; (of mind)* imbecillit·as -atis *f; (flaw)* vit·ium -(i)i *n; (of arguments)* levit·as -atis *f*
wealth *s* diviti·ae -arum *fpl; (resources)* op·es -um *fpl; (store, plenty)* copi·a -ae *f*
wealthy *adj* div·es -itis
wean *tr* ab ubere depellĕre; *(fig)* desuefacĕre
weapon *s* tel·um -i *n*
wear *tr (clothes)* gerĕre, gestare; **to — out** terĕre, exedĕre ‖ *intr* durare
wear *s* trit·us -ūs *m;* — **and tear** intertriment·um -i *n*
weariness *s* lassitud·o -inis *f*
wearisome *adj* operos·us -a -um
weary *adj* fess·us -a -um
weather *s* tempest·as -atis *f;* — **conditions** tempestatum habit·us -ūs *m;* **types of —** gener·a -rum *npl* tempestatum
weather *tr* **to — a storm** procellam durare
weatherbeaten *adj* tempestate afflict·us -a -um
weave *tr* texĕre

web s *(spider's)* arane·um -i n; *(on a loom)* tel·a -ae f

wed tr *(a woman)* ducĕre; *(a man)* nubĕre *(w. dat)* ‖ intr *(of bride)* nubĕre; *(of groom)* uxorem ducĕre

wedding s nupti·ae -arum fpl

wedding adj nuptial·is -is -e; **to set the — day** diem nuptiis dicere; **— day** dies -ei m nuptiarum; **— present** nuptiale don·um -i n; **— reception** cen·a -ae f nuptialis

wedge s cune·us -i m

wedlock s matrimon·ium -(i)i n

weed s herb·a -ae f mala

weed tr eruncare

week s hebdom·as -adis f, septiman·a -ae f

weekday s di·es -ei m profestus

weekly adj hebdomadal·is -is -e

weekly adv septimo quoque die

weep intr flēre; **to — for** deplorare

weeping s flet·us -ūs m

weigh tr pendĕre; *(fig)* examinare; **to — down** degravare; *(fig)* opprimĕre; **to — out** expendĕre ‖ intr **to — much** magni ponderis esse

weight s pond·us -eris n; *(heaviness)* gravit·as -atis f; *(influence)* auctorit·as -atis f; *(importance)* moment·um -i n

weighty adj grav·is -is -e

welcome s salutati·o -onis f; **I gave him a warm —** eum amantissime excepi

welcome adj opportunissim·us -a -um

welcome tr benigne excipĕre

welcome interj salve!; pl: salvete!

weld tr (con)ferruminare

welfare s sal·us -utis f; *(charity)* carit·as -atis f

well s pute·us -i m

well adj *(healthy)* san·us -a -um, salv·us -a -um; **it is — to** convenit *(w. inf)*

well adv bene, recte; **he is — off** bene se habet; **I am doing —** mihi bene est; **very —** optime

well interj immo; *(all right)* licet; **— now** age ergo

well-being s sal·us -tis f

well-born adj generos·us -a -um

well-bred adj bene educat·us -a -um

well-deserved adj rite merit·us -a -um

well-done adj optime fact·us -a -um; **— done!** macte virtute esto!

well-known adj nobil·is -is -e

well-read adj litterat·us -a -um

well-spoken adj disert·us -a -um

well-supplied adj copiosissim·us -a -um

well-timed adj opportun·us -a -um

welter s congeri·es -ei f

werewolf s versipell·is -is m

west s occas·us -ūs m (solis); **toward the —** in occasum

western adj occidental·is -is -e

westward adv in occasum

west wind s Zephyr·us -i m

wet adj uvid·us -a -um; *(through and through)* madid·us -a -um; **to get —** madefieri

wet tr madefacĕre

wet-nurse s nutr·ix -icis f

whale s balaen·a -ae f

wharf s naval·e -is n

what adj interrog qui, quae quod; **— sort of** qual·is -is -e

what pron interrog quid, quidnam; **— is this all about?** quid enim?

whatever pron quicquid

whatever adj interrog quicumque, quaecumque, quodcumque

wheat s tritic·um -i n

wheedle tr blandiri; **to — out of s.o.** eblandiri ex aliquo

wheel s rot·a -ae f

wheelbarrow s pab·o -onis m

when adv quando

when conj cum, ubi, ut; **— first** cum primum; **— joking** inter jocos

whence adv unde

whenever adv quandocumque, sicubi

where adv quā, ubi; *(motion)* quo

whereas conj quandoquidem

whereby adv quā viā, quo

wherefore adv quare, quamobrem

wherein adv in quo, in quibus, ubi

whereof adv de quo, de quibus

whereupon adv quo facto; *(then)* deinde

wherever conj quacumque, ubicumque

wherewithal s **to have the — to** unde habēre *(w. inf)*

whet tr acuĕre; **to — the appetite** exacuĕre appetentiam

whether conj *(in single indir. ques.)* num, -ne, an; **—...or** *(in multiple indir. ques.)* utrum...an, -ne...an, or...an; *(in disjunctive conditions)* sive...sive, seu...seu; **—...or not** utrum...necne

whetstone s co·s -tis f

which pron interrog quis quid; *(of two)* ut·er -ra -rum ‖ pron rel qui, quae, quod

which adj interrog qui, quae, quod; *(of two)* u·ter -tra -trum ‖ adj rel qui, quae, quod

whichever pron quicumque, quaecumque, quodcumque; *(of two)* utercumque, utracumque, utrumcumque

whiff s *(slight smell)* od·or -oris m exiguus; **to get a — of** subolēre; **— of air** aur·a -ae f

while s temp·us -oris n, spat·ium -(i)i n; **after a —** paulo post; **a good — after** aliquanto post; **a long —** diu; **for a short —** paulisper; **for a —**

aliquamdiu; **in a little** — in brevi spatio; **once in a** — interdum

while *conj* dum, quoad, donec

while *tr* **to** — **away the time** tempus fallĕre

whim *s* libid·o -inis *f;* **according to their** — **and pleasure** ad eorum arbitrium et nutum

whimper *s* vagit·us -ūs *m*

whimper *intr* vagire

whimsical *adj* mobil·is -is -e

whine *intr* plorare

whinny *s* hinnit·us -ūs *m*

whinny *intr* hinnire

whip *s* flagell·um -i *n*

whip *tr* flagellare; **to** — **out** eripĕre

whippersnapper *s* frust·um -i *n* pueri

whipping *s* **to get a** — vapulare

whirl *tr* torquēre, rotare ‖ *intr* torqueri, rotari

whirl *s* turb·o -inis *m*

whirlpool *s* gurg·es -itis *m*

whirlwind *s* turb·o -inis *m*

whirr *intr* stridēre, increpare

whisk *tr (to brush lightly)* everrĕre; **to** — **away** eripĕre ‖ *intr* **to** — **about** *(to move about quickly)* circumvolitare

whiskbroom *s* scopul·a -ae *f*

whisker *s (of animal)* saet·a -ae *f;* **by a** — vix; —**s** barb·a -ae *f*

whiskey *s* aqu·a -ae *f* vitae

whisper *s* susurr·us -i *m*

whisper *tr & intr* susurrare

whistle *s (sound)* sibil·us -i *m; (pipe)* fistul·a -ae *f; (of wind)* strid·or -oris *m*

whistle *tr* **to** — **some tune** exsibilare nescio quid ‖ *intr* sibilare; *(of the wind)* stridēre

whit *s* **every** — **as good** omnino par; **not a** — **better** nihilo melius

white *adj* alb·us -a -um; *(brilliant)* candid·us -a -um; *(hair)* can·us -a -um; **to be** — albēre, albicare; — **bread** pan·is -is *m* candidus

white *s (the color; of an egg, of the eye)* alb·um -i *n*

whiten *tr* dealbare, candefacĕre ‖ *intr* albescĕre, canescĕre

whitewash *s* albar·ium -(i)i *n; (fig)* fuc·us -i *m*

whitewash *tr* dealbare; *(fig)* fucare

whither *adv* quo, quorsum

whithersoever *adv* quocumque

whitish *adj* subalb·us -a -um

whiz *intr* increpare

who *pron interrog* quis ‖ *pron rel* qui, quae

whoever *pron* quicumque, quaecumque

whole *adj* tot·us -a -um, cunct·us -a -um, univers·us -a -um

whole *s* tot·um -i *n;* **on the** — plerumque, ex toto

wholehearted *adj* sincer·us -a -um

wholesale *adj* magnari·us -a -um; **to carry on** — **business** magnariam mercaturam facĕre

wholesale *adv* acervatim

wholesaler *s* magnarius negotiat·or -oris *m*

wholesome *adj* salutar·is -is -e

wholly *adv* omnino, prorsus

whoop *s* ululat·us -ūs *m*

whoop *intr* ululatum tollĕre

whore *s* scort·um-i *n*

whorehouse *s* lupan·ar -aris *n*

whoremonger *s* scortat·or -oris *m*

whose *pron* cujus; *pl:* quorum, quarum, quorum

why *adv* cur, quamobrem, quare; **just** — cur tandem; **that's** —...quo fit ut; — **not** quidni

wick *s* fil·um -i *n*

wicked *adj* improb·us -a -um

wickedly *adv* improbe, sceleste

wickedness *s* improbit·as -atis *f*

wicker *adj* vimine·us -a -um

wide *adj* lat·us -a -um

widely *adv* late

widen *tr* dilatare ‖ *intr* dilatari

widow *s* vidu·a -ae *f*

widower *s* vidu·us -i *m*

width *s* latitud·o -inis *f;* **ten feet in** — decem pedes in latitudinem

wield *tr (weapon)* tractare, vibrare; **to** — **supreme power** plurimum pollēre

wife *s* ux·or -oris *f; (of a slave)* contubernal·is -is *f*

wifely *adj* uxori·us -a -um

wig *s* capillament·um -i *n*

wiggle *tr* torquēre ‖ *intr* se torquēre; *(of a woman)* crisare

wild *adj* fer·us -a -um; *(desolate)* vast·us -a -um; *(mad)* insan·us -a -um; *(of trees, plants)* silvestr·is -is -e; *(of land)* incult·us -a -um; *(of disposition)* fer·ox -ocis; — **beast** fer·a -ae *f,* fera besti·a -ae *f*

wild *s* **growing in the** — silvestr·is -is -e; **the** —**s** incult·a -orum *npl*

wilderness *s* vastit·as -atis *f*

wildly *adv* saeve, ferociter

wile *s* dol·us -i *m*

wilful *adj* consult·us -a -um

wilfully *adv* consulto

wiliness *s* callidit·as -atis *f*

will *s* volunt·as -atis *f,* anim·us -i *m; (intent)* proposit·um -i *n; (document)* testament·um -i *n; (of gods)* nut·us -ūs *m;* **at** — ad libidinem

will *tr (a legacy)* legare

willing *adj* lib·ens -entis; **to be** — velle

willingly *adv* libenter, libenti animo

willingness *s* volunt·as -atis *f*

wily *adj* va·fer -fra -frum

win *tr* adipisci, consequi; *(victory)* reportare, adipisci; **to** — **a bet** sponsione vincĕre; **to — a court case** judicio vincĕre; **to — friends** amicos acquirĕre; **to — highest honors** amplissimos honores consequi; **to — the hearts of the people** conciliare animos plebis; **to — over** conciliare ‖ *intr* vincĕre

wince *intr* **to — with sudden pain** prae dolore subito horrēre

winch *s* sucul·a -ae *f*

wind *s* vent·us -i *m;* **I got — of it long ago** jam pridem id mihi subolebat

wind *tr* circumvolvĕre; **the plant wound itself around the tree** herba arbori se circumvolvit; **to — up** *(a speech)* concludĕre; *(a clock)* intendĕre; **to — up one's affairs** res domesticas et familiares in ordinem redigĕre

winded *adj* anhel·ans -antis

windfall *s (fig)* lucr·um -i *n* insperatum

winding *adj* flexuos·us -a -um

winding sheet *s* tunic·a -ae *f* funebris

windmill *s* venti mol·a -ae *f*

window *s* fenestr·a -ae *f*

windowpane *s* specular·e -is *n,* fenestrae vitr·um -i *n*

windpipe *s* arteri·a -ae *f* aspera

windy *adj* ventos·us -a -um

wine *s* vin·um -i *n; (undiluted)* mer·um -i *n; (cheap wine)* vapp·a -ae *f;* **dry — austerum vinum** *n*

wined and dined *adj* prans·us et pot·us -a -um

wine cellar *s* cell·a -ae *f* vinaria

wing *s* al·a -ae *f; (mil)* corn·u -ūs *n*

winged *adj* alat·us -a -um

wink *intr* nictare, connivēre

winner *s* vict·or -oris *m*

winning *adj (fig)* amoen·us -a -um

winnings *spl* lucr·um -i *n*

winnow *tr* ventilare

winter *s* hiem·s -is *f;* **in the dead of —** mediā hieme; **to spend the —** hiemare

winter *intr* hiemare, hibernare

winter *adj* hibern·us -a -um, hiemal·is, -is -e; **— clothes** hiberna vestiment·a -orum *npl; —* **time** hiemale temp·us -oris *n*

winter quarters *spl* hibern·a -orum *npl*

wintry *adj* hiemal·is -is -e, brumal·is -is -e

wipe *tr* tergēre; *(lips)* abstergēre; **to be —ed out** *(of a debt)* deperire; **to — away** abstergēre; *(tears)* extergēre; **to — off** *or* **clean** detergēre; **to — out** *(writing)* delēre; **to — the nose** emungĕre

wire *s* fil·um -i *n* ferreum; *(of silver)* fil·um -i *n* argenteum

wisdom *s* sapienti·a -ae *f*

wise *adj* sapi·ens -entis, prud·ens -entis

wise *s (way)* mod·us -i *m;* **in no —** nequaquam

wisely *adv* sapienter, prudenter

wish *s (act of wishing)* optati·o -onis *f; (thing wished)* optat·um -i *n; (prayer)* vot·um -i *n; according to one's —es* de sententiā; **best —es to your brother** salutem plurimam fratri tuo

wish *tr* optare, velle, cupĕre ‖ *intr* **to — for** exoptare, expetĕre

wishing *s* optati·o -onis *f*

wisp *s (of hair, grass, etc.)* manipul·us -i *m*

wistful *adj* desiderii plen·us -a -um

wistfully *adv* oculis intentis

wit *s (intellect)* ingen·ium -(i)i *n; (humor)* faceti·ae -arum *fpl; (person)* hom·o -inis *m* facetus; **to be at one's —s' end** delirare; **to — scilicet**

witch *s* strig·a -ae *f,* mag·a -ae *f*

witchcraft *s* ar·s -tis *f* magica

with *prep* cum *(w. abl); (at the house of)* apud *(w. acc)*

withdraw *tr* seducĕre, avocare; *(words)* revocare ‖ *intr* recedĕre

wither *tr* torrēre ‖ *intr* marcēre

withered *adj* marcid·us -a -um

withhold *tr* retinēre

within *adv* intus, intra; *(on the inside)* intrinsecus; **— and without** intrinsecus et extrinsecus

within *prep (place, time, the law)* intra *(w. acc); (during a definite period)* inter *(w. acc); —* **a few days** paucis diebus

without *adv* extra, exterius; *(out of doors)* foris; **from —** extrinsecus

without *prep* sine *(w. abl),* absque *(w. abl);* **I could in no way enter — their seeing me** nullo modo introire poteram quin me viderent; **to be —** carēre *(w. abl)*

withstand *tr* resistĕre *(w. dat),* obsistĕre *(w. dat)*

witness *s* test·is -is *mf; (to a signature)* obsignat·or -oris *m;* **to bear —** testificari; **to call to —** testari

witness *tr* testificari; *(to see)* interesse *(w. dat),* spectare

witticism *s* dicter·ium -(i)i *n*

wittily *adv* facete, festive

witty *adj* facet·us -a -um

wizard *s* mag·us -i *m*

woe *s* luct·us -ūs *m;* **—s** mal·a -orum *npl*

woeful *adj* luctuos·us -a -um

woefully *adv* misere, flebiliter

wolf *s* lup·us -i *m,* lup·a -ae *f*

woman *s* muli·er -eris *f,* femin·a -ae *f*

womanhood *s* muliebris stat·us -ūs *m*

womanly *adj* muliebr·is -is -e

womb *s* uter·us -i *m*

wonder *s* admirati·o -onis *f; (astonishing object)* miracul·um -i *n;* **to excite —** mirationem facĕre; **seven —s of the world** septem miracula mundi

wonder *intr* mirari; **I — where things are heading** reputo quorsum illa tendant; **to — at** admirari

wonderful *adj* mirabil·is -is -e

wonderfully *adv* mirabiliter

wont *adj* **to be — to** solēre *(w. inf)*

woo *tr* petĕre

wood *s* lign·um -i *n;* **—s** silv·a -ae *f*

wooded *adj* silvos·us -a -um

wooden *adj* ligne·us -a -um

woodland *s* salt·us -ūs *m*

woodman *s* lignat·or -oris *m*

wood nymph *s* Dry·as -adis *f*

woodpecker *s* pic·us -i *m*

woody *adj (full of wood fibers)* lignos·us -a -um; *(covered with woods)* silvos·us -a -um, silvestr·is -is -e

wooer *s* proc·us -i *m*

wool *s* lan·a -ae *f;* **to spin —** lanas ducĕre

woolen *adj* lane·us -a -um

word *s (in context)* verb·um -i *n; (out of context)* vocabul·um -i *n; (spoken)* vox vocis *f,* dict·um -i *n; (promise)* fid·es -ei *f; (news)* nunt·ius -(i)i *m;* **in a —** ad summam; **to break one's —** fidem fallĕre; **to give one's —** fidem dare; **to keep one's —** fidem praestare; **— for —** ad verbum; **—s fail me** quid dicam non invenio

wordy *adj* verbos·us -a -um

work *s (labor, pains)* oper·a -ae *f; (act of working and thing completed)* op·us -eris *n; (labor, trouble)* lab·or -oris *m;* **good —s** recte et honeste fact·a -orum *npl;* **one day's work** una opera *f;* **to throw out of —** de negotio dejicĕre; **you had spent more — and labor** plus operae laborisque consumpseras

work *tr (to exercise)* exercēre; *(to till)* colĕre ‖ *intr* laborare, operari

workman *s (unskilled)* operar·ius -(i)i *m; (skilled)* opif·ex -icis *m; (day laborer)* oper·a -ae *f*

workmanship *s* op·us -eris *n*

workshop *s* officin·a -ae *f*

world *s (universe)* mund·us -i *m,* summ·a -ae *f* rerum; *(earth)* orb·is -is *m* terrarum; *(mankind)* homin·es -um *mpl;* **where in the —** ubi terrarum

worldly *adj* profan·us -a -um

worm *s* verm·is -is *m*

worm *tr* **to — one's way into** se insinuare in *(w. acc)*

worm-eaten, wormy *adj* vermiculos·us -a -um

worry *s* sollicitud·o -inis *f*

worry *tr* sollicitare; **don't — yourself to death** ne te crucia ‖ *intr* sollicitari

worse *adj* pe·jor -jor -jus, deter·ior -ius; **to get —** ingravescĕre; **to turn out for the —** in pejus evenire

worsen *intr* ingravescĕre

worship *s* cult·us -ūs *m,* venerati·o -onis *f*

worship *tr* colĕre, venerari

worshiper *s* cult·or -oris *m*

worst *adj* pessim·us -a -um, deterrim·us -a -um; **— of all** maxime alien·us -a -um

worst *tr* vincĕre

worth *s (value)* pret·ium -(i)i *n; (merit)* dignit·as -atis *f;* **man is of little — worth** hom·o -inis *m* parvi pretii est

worth *adj* dign·us -a -um *(w. abl);* **a slave — any price** serv·us -i *m* quantivis pretii; **he is — a lot of money** divitias maximas habet; **he is — nothing** nihil est; **how much are pigs — here?** quibus hic pretiis porci veneunt?; **it is — knowing** est operae pretium cognoscĕre; **this is — s.th. to me** hoc mihi in lucro est; **to be — a lot** multum valēre

worthless *adj* vil·is -is -e; *(of persons)* nequam *(indecl)*

worthwhile *adj* **to be —** operae pretium esse

worthy *adj (of)* dign·us -a -um *(w. abl)*

wound *s* vuln·us -eris *n*

wound *tr* vulnerare; *(fig)* offendĕre

wounded *adj* sauci·us -a -um

wrangling *s* discordi·a -ae *f*

wrap *tr* involvĕre; **to — the head in his toga** caput obvolvĕre togā; **to — up** complicare; *(against the cold)* involvĕre

wrap *s* amict·us -ūs *m*

wrapper *s* involucr·um -i *n*

wrath *s* ir·a -ae *f,* iracundi·a -ae *f*

wrathful *adj* iracund·us -a -um

wreak *tr* **to — havoc** stragem dare; **to — vengeance on** ulcisci

wreath *s* sert·um -i *n*

wreathe *tr (to twist)* torquēre; *(to adorn with wreathes)* nectĕre

wreck *s (of ship)* naufrag·ium -(i)i *n;* **he is a —** naufragus est

wreck *tr* frangĕre; *(fig)* delēre

wren *s* regul·us -i *m*

wrench *tr* detorquēre, luxare

wrest *s* extorquēre, eripĕre

wrestle *intr* luctari

wretch *s* mis·er -eri *m*

wretched *adj* mis·er -era -erum

wretchedly *adv* misere

wretchedness *s* miseri·a -ae *f*

wring *tr* contorquēre; **to — the neck** gulam frangĕre; **—ing his hands**

manibus inter se constrictis; **to —
out a cloth** linteolum exprimĕre
wrinkle *s* rug·a -ae *f*
wrinkle *tr* corrugare; **to — the forehead** frontem contrahĕre
wrinkled *adj* rugos·us -a -um
wrist *s* primoris man·us -ūs *f*
writ *s* mandat·um -i *n*
write *tr* scribĕre; *(poetry, book)* componĕre; *(history)* perscribĕre
writer *s* script·or -oris *m*
writhe *intr* torqueri
writing *s (act)* scripti·o -onis *f; (result)* script·um -i *n*
wrong *s* nefas *n (indecl)*, injuri·a -ae *f*,
mal·um -i *n;* **to do —** peccare
wrong *adj (opp: erectus)* prav·us -a
-um; *(incorrect, mistaken)* fals·us -a
-um; *(unfair)* iniqu·us -a -um; *(unsuitable)* alien·us -a -um; *(faulty)*
vitios·us -a -um; **if I have done anything —** si quid perperam feci; **to be
—** errare; **what's — with you?** quid
est tecum?
wrong *tr* injuriam inferre *(w. dat)*
wrongdoing *s* probr·um -i *n*
wrongly *adv* perperam, male
wrought *adj* confect·us -a -um
wry *adj* contort·us -a -um; *(of humor)*
mord·ax -acis

Y

yacht *s* priva trirem·is -is -e *f; (smaller
model)* cel·ox -ocis *f*
yank *tr (coll)* vellĕre
yard *s* are·a -ae *f* domūs; *(measure)*
tres pedes *mpl*
yarn *s (of linen)* fil·um -i *n* lini; *(of
wool)* fil·um -i *n* laneum; *(story)*
fabul·a -ae *f*
yawn *s* oscitati·o -onis *f*
yawn *intr* oscitare, hiare; *(to gape open)*
dehiscĕre
year *s* ann·us -i *m;* **at the beginning
(end) of the —** ineunte (exeunte)
anno; **a — from now** ad annum; **every —** quotannis; **five —s** quin-
quenn·ium -(i)i *n;* **four —s** quadren-
n·ium -(i)i *n;* **for a — in** annum; **he is
twenty —s old** viginti annos natus
est; **in his later —s** tempore extremo;
it's ten —s since the law was passed
decem anni sunt quum lata lex est; **I
wish you a happy new —** in annum
laeta opto tibi; **last —** anno superiore;
next — anno proximo; **three —s**
trienn·ium -(i)i *n;* **twice a —** bis (in)
anno; **two —s** bienn·ium -(i)i *n*
yearly *adj* annu·us -a -um
yearly *adv* quotannis

yearn *intr* **to — for** desiderare
yearning *s* desider·ium -(i)i *n*
yeast *s* ferment·um -i *n*
yell *s* ululat·us -ūs *m*
yell *intr* ululare; *(in pain)* ejulare
yellow *adj (hair, gold, sand, grain-
fields, honey)* flav·us -a -us; *(teeth)*
lurid·us -a -um; *(hair, sand)* fulv·us
-a -um
yellowish *adj* subflav·us -a -um
yelp *intr (like a dog)* gannire; **what's
he —ing for?** quid ille gannit?
yes *adv* ita, sic, sane, oppido *(but the
most frequent way in Latin to express
a simple yes is to repeat the word on
which the emphasis rests in the question):* **do you want me? Yes.** visne
me? Te.; **has he sold her? Yes.** eam
vendidit? Vendidit.
yes-man *s* assecl·a -ae *m*
yesterday *adv* heri; **the day before —**
nudiustertius; **— evening** heri vesperi; **— morning** heri mane
yet *adv (contrast, after adversative
clause)* tamen; *(time)* adhuc; *(w. comparatives)* etiam; **as —** adhuc; **not —**
nondum
yew *s* tax·us -i *f*
yield *tr (to produce)* ferre, parĕre; *(to
surrender)* concedĕre ‖ *intr* cedĕre;
to — to cedĕre *(w. dat)*
yield *s* fruct·us -ūs *m; (profit)* quaest·us
-ūs *m*
yoke *s* jug·um -i *n; (fig)* servit·us
-utis *f*
yoke *tr* conjungĕre
yokel *s* rustic·us -i *m*
yolk *s* vitell·us -i *m*
yonder *adv* illic
yonder *adj* ill·e -a -ud
you *pron* tu; *(ye)* vos; **to —** tibi; vobis;
with — tecum; vobiscum
young *adj (children)* parv·us -a -um;
(goat, vine) novell·us -a -um; **—
bride** nova nupt·a -ae *f;* **— lady**
muliercul·a -ae *f;* **— man** juven·is
-is *m*, adulescentul·us -i *m*, adu-
lesc·ens -entis *m*
younger *adj* jun·ior -ior -ius, min·or
-or -us (natu)
youngster *s* adulescentul·us -i *m*
your *adj* tu·us -a -um; *pl:* ves·ter -tra
-trum
yourself *pron refl* te; **by —** per te; **to —**
tibi; **with —** tecum ‖ *pron intensive
you — (masc)* tu ipse; *(fem)* tu ipsa
yourselves *pron refl* vos; **to —** vobis;
with — vobiscum ‖ *pron intensive
you — (masc)* vos ipsi; *(fem)* vos ipsae
youth *s (age)* adulescenti·a -ae *f; (collectively)* juvent·us -utis *f; (young
man)* juven·is -is *m*, adulesc·ens
-entis *m*

youthful *adj* juvenil·is -is -e
youthfully *adv* juveniliter

Z

zeal *s* stud·ium -(i)i *n*
zealot *s* fanatic·us -i *m*
zealous *adj* studios·us -a -um
zealously *adv* studiose, enixe
zenith *s* vert·ex -icis *m*

zephyr *s* Zephyr·us -i *m*
zero *s* nihil *n (indecl)*
zest *s* sap·or -oris *m; (fig)* gustat·us -ūs
   m; — **for true praise** gustatus *m* verae
   laudis
zig-zag *adj* tortuos·us -a -um; — **streets**
   anfract·us -uum *mpl* viarum
zodiac *s* Zodiac·us -i *m*
zone *s* zon·a -ae *f*
zoo *s* vivar·ium -(i)i *n*
zoology *s* zoologi·a -ae *f*

Abbreviations

abbr .... abbreviation	*geog* .... geography	*opp* .... opposite of
abl .... ablative	*geol* .... geology	*p* .... participle
acc .... accusative	*gram* .... grammar	*pass* .... passive
adj .... adjective	*hum* .... humorous	*pej* .... pejorative
adjl .... adjectival	*imperf* ...... imperfect	*perf* .... perfect
adv .... adverb	*impers* ...... impersonal	*phil* .... philosophy
advl .... adverbial	verb	*pl* .... plural
anat .... anatomy	*impv* .... imperative	*poet* .... poetry
archit .... architecture	*indecl* .... indeclinable	*pol* .... politics
astr .... astronomy	*indef* .... indefinite	*pp* .... past
bot .... botany	*indic* .... indicative	participle
c. .... circa, about	*inf* .... infinitive	*pref* .... prefix
cf. .... confer,	*interj* .... interjection	*prep* .... preposition
compare	*interrog* ... interroga-	*pres* .... present
cent. .... century	tive	*pron* .... pronoun
coll .... colloquial	*intr* .... intransitive	*pros* .... prosody
com .... commerce	*leg* .... legal	*prov* .... proverb
comp .... comparative	*lit* .... literal	*refl* .... reflexive
conj .... conjunction	*loc* .... locative	*rel* .... relative
d. .... died	*m* .... masculine	*relig* .... religion
dat .... dative	noun	*rhet* .... rhetoric
defect .... defective	*masc* .... masculine	*s* .... substantive
verb	*math* .... mathemat-	*S.* .... South(ern)
dim. .... diminutive	ics	*singl* .... singular
E. .... East(ern)	*med* .... medicine	*sl* .... slang
eccl .... ecclesiasti-	*mf* .... masculine	*s.o.* .... someone
cal	or	*s.th.* .... something
educ .... education	feminine	*subj* .... subjunctive
euphem .... euphemism	noun	*suf* .... suffix
esp. .... especially	*mil* .... military	*superl* .... superlative
expr. .... expressed	*mpl* .... masculine	*theat* .... theater
f .... feminine	plural	*topog* .... topography
noun	noun	*tr* .... transitive
fem .... feminine	*mus* .... music	verb
fig .... figurative	*n* .... neuter noun	*usu.* .... usually
fin .... finance	*N.* .... North(ern)	*vbl* .... verbal
fl .... floruit,	*naut* .... nautical	*v defect* .... defective
flourished	*neg.* .... negative	verb
fpl .... feminine	*neut* .... neuter	*v impers* ... impersonal
plural	*nom* .... nominative	verb
noun	*npl* .... neuter	*vulg* .... vulgar
fut .... future	plural	*w.* .... with
gen .... genitive	noun	*W.* .... West(ern)

JOHN C. TRAUPMAN, Ph.D. in Classics, Princeton University, was chairman of the Department of Classics, St. Joseph's University (Philadelphia). He is the author of *The New College German & English Dictionary* and *Latin Is Fun, Books I and II*. He has served as President of the Philadelphia Classical Society, the Pennsylvania Classical Association, and the Classical Association of the Atlantic States.

The New College Series

Edwin B. Williams, General Editor

The New College French & English Dictionary
  by Roger J. Steiner
The New College German & English Dictionary
  by John C. Traupman
The New College Italian & English Dictionary
  by Robert C. Melzi
The New College Latin & English Dictionary
  by John C. Traupman
The New College Spanish & English Dictionary
  by Edwin B. Williams

AMSCO SCHOOL PUBLICATIONS, INC.